"No other guide has as much to offer . . . these books are a pleasure to read."   Gene Shalit on the *Today Show*

". . . Excellently organized for the casual traveler who is looking for a mix of recreation and cultural insight."
Washington Post

★ ★ ★ ★ ★ (5-star rating) "Crisply written and remarkably personable. Cleverly organized so you can pluck out the minutest fact in a moment. Satisfyingly thorough."
Réalités

"The information they offer is up-to-date, crisply presented but far from exhaustive, the judgments knowledgeable but not opinionated."   *New York Times*

"The individual volumes are compact, the prose succinct, and the coverage up-to-date and knowledgeable . . . The format is portable and the index admirably detailed."
John Barkham Syndicate

". . . An abundance of excellent directions, diversions, and facts, including perspectives and getting-ready-to-go advice — succinct, detailed, and well organized in an easy-to-follow style."   *Los Angeles Times*

"They contain an amount of information that is truly staggering, besides being surprisingly current."
Detroit News

"These guides address themselves to the needs of the modern traveler demanding precise, qualitative information . . . Upbeat, slick, and well put together."
Dallas Morning News

". . . Attractive to look at, refreshingly easy to read, and generously packed with information."   *Miami Herald*

"These guides are as good as any published, and much better than most."   *Louisville* (Kentucky) *Times*

Stephen Birnbaum Travel Guides

Canada
The Caribbean, Bermuda, and the Bahamas
Disneyland
Europe
Europe for Business Travelers
Florida for Free
France
Great Britain
Hawaii
Ireland
Italy
Mexico
South America
Spain and Portugal
United States
USA for Business Travelers
Walt Disney World

CONTRIBUTING EDITORS

Tony Bartlett, Michelle Bearden, Cathy Beason, Janet Bennett, Helena Bentz, Ron Berler, Paul Bird, Tina Blackshare, Robert Bone, Al Borcover, James Bready, David Breakstone, Bob Brooke, Patricia Brooks, Anita Buck, Jeff Burger, William Burk, Marda Burton, Robert Butler, Lynn Byers, Carol Campbell, Michael Carlton, Stacey Chanin, Don Chapman, Marie Chesny, Shirley Christian, Jay Clarke, Thomas Coffey, Stephen Coleman, James Cortese, Jeanne Cowan, Karen Cure, Sally Davy, Teresa Day, Katherine Dinsdale, John Doherty, Mike Dolan, Natilee Duning, Vicky Elliott, Thomas Ellis, Luise M. Erdmann, Walter Evans, Kathryn Fanning, Brenda Fine, John Firestone, Sam Fletcher, Robin Fowler, James Frank, Janet Fullwood, Mary Ann Castranovo Fusco, Phil Gallo, Joel A. Glass, Jon Goldman, Mark Gottlieb, Paul Hagerman, Ben Harte, Susan Hawser, Willard Hazelbush, Patricia Hetrick, Rosemary Peters Hinkle, Martin Hintz, Barbara Horngren, Arline Inge, Bill Jamison, Sam Jannerone, Irene Jerison, Lou Johnson, Steve Kaplan, Laura Kelly, Michael Konon, Elliot S. Krane, Lori G. Kranz, Linda Lampman, Claudia Lewis, Pamela Marin, Antoinette Martin, Carole Martin, Timothy McEnroe, Donald McMillin, Erica Meltzer, Sandra Miller, Anne Millman, Bill Millman, Jeanne Muchnik, Laurie Nadel, Brooke Ramey Nelson, Marty Olmstead, Richard J. Pietschmann, Daniel C. Pinger, Ann Pleshette, Patricia Tunison Preston, Mike Pulfer, Grace Renshaw, Steve Roberts, Dawna Robertson, Michael Robertson, Allan Rokach, William Ryan, Marie Rychman, William Schemmel, Allan Seiden, Ellen Sherberg, Art Siemering, Douglas Smith, Ronald Smith, Victoria Sprague, Wendy Spritzer, Michael Steege, Janet Steinberg, Jean Stewart, Jack Swanson, Rick Sylvain, Karen Tenney, Warren Thompson, Charles Thurston, Diana Tittle, Robert Trumbull, Nikki Tureen, Ginny Turner, Jan Walker, Katharine Walker, Susan Walters, Hesh Weiner, Robert Wells, Loralee Wenger, Mimi Whitefield, Robert Wintner, Cathy Wood, Donald Woodward, Ann Woolman, Bill Wrenn, Sonya Zalubowski, Christine Zust

MAPS	COVER	SYMBOLS
B. Andrew Mudryk, Paul J. Pugliese	Robert Anthony	Gloria McKeown

A Stephen Birnbaum Travel Guide

Birnbaum's UNITED STATES 1990

Stephen Birnbaum
Alexandra Mayes Birnbaum
EDITORS

Lois Spritzer
EXECUTIVE EDITOR

Laura Brengelman
Managing Editor

Kristin Moehlmann
John Storch
Senior Editors

Catherine J. Langevin
Julie Quick
Associate Editor

Stephen Coleman
Assistant Editor

HOUGHTON MIFFLIN COMPANY/BOSTON 1989

For Sam and Edith Grafton, who were there at the beginning.

This book is published by special arrangement
with Eric Lasher and Maureen Lasher.

For information about permission
to reproduce selections from this
book, write to Permissions,
Houghton Mifflin Company, 2 Park Street,
Boston, Massachusetts 02108.

ISBN: 0-395-51147-X (pbk.)
ISSN: 0749-2561 (Stephen Birnbaum Travel Guides)
ISSN: 0883-2501 (United States)

Printed in the United States of America

WP 10 9 8 7 6 5 4 3 2 1

Contents

GETTING READY TO GO

All the practical travel data you need to plan your vacation down to the final detail.

When and How to Go

Preparing

On the Road

Sources and Resources

THE CITIES

Thorough, qualitative guides to each of the 44 cities most often visited by vacationers and businesspeople. Each section offers a comprehensive report of the city's most compelling attractions and amenities, designed to be used on the spot. Directions and recommendations are immediately accessible because each guide is presented in consistent form.

DIVERSIONS

A selective guide to 31 active and/or cerebral vacation themes, including the best places to pursue them. The intent is to point out where your quality of experience is likely to be highest.

For the Body

For the Mind

For the Experience

DIRECTIONS

This country's most spectacular routes and roads, most arresting natural wonders, most magnificent parks and forests, all organized into 66 specific driving tours.

East

South

Midwest

West

A Word from the Editor

The growing sophistication of travelers has made it essential that guidebooks also evolve, if only to keep pace with their readers. So we've tried to create a guide to the United States that's specifically organized, written, and edited for the knowledgeable traveler, for whom qualitative information is infinitely more desirable than mere quantities of unappraised data. We think that this guide — and the series of which it is a part — is the leader in a new generation of travel guides that are uniquely responsive to the needs and interests of today's travelers.

For years, dating back as far as Herr Baedeker, travel guides have tended to be encyclopedic, seemingly much more concerned with demonstrating expertise in geography and history than with any real analysis of the sorts of things that actually concern a typical tourist. But today, when it is hardly necessary to tell a traveler where New Orleans is or that it was an important element in the development of the United States, it is hard to justify endless pages of historic perspective. In many cases, the traveler has been to New Orleans nearly as often as the guidebook editor, so the editor must provide new perceptions and suggest new directions to make the guide genuinely valuable.

That's exactly what we've tried to do in the Birnbaum Travel Guide series. I think you'll notice a fresh tone to the text as well as an organization and focus that are distinctive and different. And even a random examination of what follows will demonstrate a substantial departure from previous guidebook orientation, for we've not only attempted to provide information of a different sort, we've also tried to present it in an environment that makes it particularly accessible.

Needless to say, it's difficult to decide what goes into a guidebook of this size — and what to omit. Early on, we realized that giving up the encyclopedic approach precluded the inclusion of every route and restaurant, and this fact helped define our overall editorial focus. Similarly, when we discussed the possibility of presenting certain information in other than strict geographic order, we found that the new format enabled us to arrange data in a way that we think best answers the questions travelers typically ask.

Large numbers of specific questions have provided the real editorial skeleton for this book. The volume of mail I regularly receive continually seems to emphasize that modern travelers want very precise information, and so we've tried to address this need and have organized the text in the most responsive way possible. If you want to know the best restaurant in Chicago or the best tennis camp for improving an erratic backhand, you will be able to extract that data easily.

Travel guides are, above all, reflections of personal taste, and putting one's name on a title page obviously puts one's preferences on the line. But I think

I ought to amplify just exactly what "personal" means. I am not at all a believer in the sort of personal guidebook that's a palpable misrepresentation on its face. It is, for example, hardly possible for any single travel writer to physically visit a thousand restaurants (and nearly that number of hotels) in any given year and provide accurate appraisals of each. And even if it were physically possible for one human being to get through such an itinerary in a single year, it would of necessity have to be done at a dead sprint, and the perceptions derived therefrom would probably be even less valid than those of any leisurely layman visiting the same establishments. It is, therefore, impossible (especially in an annually revised guidebook series such as ours) to have only one person provide all the data on the entire world.

I also happen to think that such individual orientation is of substantially less value to readers. Visiting a single hotel for one night, or eating one hasty meal in a restaurant, hardly equips anyone to provide meaningful appraisals that are of more than passing interest. No amount of doggedly alliterative or oppressively onomatopoeic text can camouflage a technique that is specious on its face. We have, therefore, chosen what I like to describe as the "thee and-me" approach to restaurant and hotel appraisal and, to a somewhat more limited degree, to the sites and sights we have included in the other sections of the text. What this really reflects is personal sampling tempered by intelligent counsel from informed local sources, for these friends-of-the-editor are almost always residents of the city and/or area about which they are consulted.

We have also tried to be sure that our contributors have had a fair access to visitors so that they may better solicit individual tourist reactions to the areas about which they contribute. It doesn't take long to discover whether a prospective contributor's tastes coincide with our own, and by the time we have assembled all the editors, researchers, writers, stringers, correspondents, and consultants that it takes to create a guide of this size, we have a fairly homogeneous group. We also find that these informed, insightful local correspondents are far more apt to hear about (or uncover) hard-to-locate gems that so often turn an ordinary visit into an exciting adventure. Furthermore, they are usually in the very best position to recognize and report on local consensus and consistency, and they represent a far better barometer of ongoing excellence than would any random encounter.

Despite this considerable number of contributors, very precise editing and tailoring keeps our text fiercely subjective. So what follows is designed to be the gospel according to Birnbaum, and it represents as much of my own tastes and instincts as humanly possible. It is probable, therefore, that if you like your steak medium rare, routinely ask to have the MSG left out of Chinese food, and can't tolerate fresh fish that is overcooked, then we're likely to have a long and meaningful relationship. Readers with dissimilar tastes may be less enraptured.

I also think I ought to point out something about the person to whom this guidebook is directed. Above all, he or she is a "visitor." That means that such elements as restaurant choices have been specifically picked to give that visitor a representative, illuminating, hopefully stimulating, and above all pleasant experience, rather than to provide an insider's guide for a constituency that already knows a city quite well. Since so many extraneous considerations can affect the reception and service accorded a regular restaurant patron, our choices can in no way be construed as a definitive guide to resident dining. We think we've got all the best in various price ranges, but they were chosen with a visitor's viewpoint in mind.

Just one example of how such choices were made is shown by the battle that waged over which French restaurant in New York City would be designated "best." Objective appraisals of the comparative cuisines of half a dozen perfectly marvelous Gallic establishments indicated that any one of them could reasonably qualify for the designation, and there was hardly a perceptible difference in the quality of the quenelles or the hauteur of the hollandaise. But there *was* a perceptible difference in how unknown diners were received and treated by the staffs of these various restaurants, and our final choice of *Lutèce* was as much due to its unusual hospitality to strangers as it was a nod to an extraordinary group of cuisineurs. We think this is especially precious information for a traveler to have at hand.

Other evidence of how we've tried to modify our text to reflect changing travel habits is most apparent in the section we call DIVERSIONS. Where once it was common for travelers to routinely take a 2-week summer vacation — one likely to be spent at some ocean or lakeside where the vacationer's most energetic activity was scratching his or her stomach — travel has changed enormously in recent years. Such is the amount of perspiration regularly engendered by today's "leisurely" vacationer that the by-product of a modern holiday is often the need to take another vacation to recover from it. So we've selected every meaningful activity we could reasonably evaluate and have organized this material in a way that is especially accessible to activists of either an athletic or cerebral bent. So whether your preference is breaking your body in a downhill hurtle over America's most difficult ski terrain or you have a particular penchant for music festivals around the countryside, we've organized lots of practical information about just that particular activity. It is no longer necessary, therefore, to wade through several hundred pages of extraneous text to find the best golf resort within a reasonable radius of where you'll be vacationing.

If there is one single thing that best characterizes the revolution and evolution of current holiday habits, it is that Americans now consider travel a right rather than a privilege. No longer is a trip to the far corners of this country — or to Europe or the Orient — necessarily a once-in-a-lifetime thing; nor is the idea of visiting exotic, faraway places in the least worrisome. Travel today translates as the enthusiastic desire to sample all of the world's opportunities, to find that elusive quality of experience that is not only enriching but comfortable. For that reason, we've tried to make what follows not only helpful and enlightening but also the sort of welcome companion of which every traveler dreams.

Finally, I should point out that every good travel guide is a living enterprise; that is, no part of this text is in any way cast in bronze. In our annual revisions, we refine, expand, and further hone all our material to better serve your travel needs. To this end, no contribution is of greater value to us than your personal reaction to what we have written, as well as information reflecting your personal experiences while trying our suggestions. We earnestly and enthusiastically solicit your comments on this book and your opinions and perceptions about places you have recently visited. In this way, we are able to provide the best sorts of information — including the actual experiences of the travel public — to make that experience more readily available to others. Please write to us at 60 E. 42nd St., New York, NY 10165.

We sincerely hope to hear from you.

STEPHEN BIRNBAUM

How to Use This Guide

A great deal of care has gone into the special organization of this guidebook, and we believe it represents a real breakthrough in the presentation of travel information. Our aim has been to create a new, more modern generation of travel books, and to make this guide the most useful and practical travel tool available today.

Our text is divided into four basic sections in order to present information on every possible aspect of an American vacation. This organization itself should alert you to the vast and varied opportunities available in this country, as well as indicate all the specific data necessary to plan a trip in the United States. You won't find much of the conventional "swaying palms and shimmering sands" text here; we've chosen instead to use the available space for more useful and practical information. Prospective American itineraries tend to speak for themselves, and with so many diverse travel opportunities, we feel our main job is to explain them and to provide the basic information — how, when, where, how much, and what's best — to let you make the most intelligent possible choices.

What follows is a brief summary of our four basic sections, and what you can expect to find in each. We believe that you will find both your travel planning and en-route enjoyment enhanced by having this book at your side.

GETTING READY TO GO

This mini-encyclopedia of practical travel facts is meant to be a sort of know-it-all companion that has all the precise information you need to understand how to go about creating a journey through America. There are entries on nearly three dozen separate topics, including how to travel, what preparations to make before you leave, how to deal with possible emergencies while away from home, what to expect in the different regions of the US, what the trip is likely to cost, and how to avoid prospective problems. The individual entries are specific, realistic, and, where appropriate, cost-oriented.

We expect that you will use this section most in planning your trip, for its ideas and suggestions are intended to facilitate this often confusing time. Entries are intentionally concise, in an effort to get to the meat of the matter with little extraneous prose. This information is augmented by extensive lists of specific sources from which to obtain even more specialized information, and some suggestions for obtaining travel information on your own.

THE CITIES

The individual reports on the 44 US cities most visited by tourists and businesspeople have been researched and written with the help of residents and professional journalists who serve as consultants on their own turf. Useful at the planning stage, THE CITIES is really designed to be used on the spot. Each report offers a short-stay guide within a consistent format: an essay, introducing the city as a contemporary place to live and visit; *At-a-Glance,* a site-by-site survey of the most important (and sometimes most eclectic) sights to see and things to do; *Sources and Resources,* a concise listing of pertinent visitor information, meant to answer a myriad of potentially pressing questions as they arise — from something simple like the address of the local tourist office to something more difficult like where to find the best nightspot, to see a show, to play tennis, or to get a taxi; and *Best in Town,* our cost-and-quality choices of the best places to eat and sleep on a variety of budgets.

DIVERSIONS

This section is designed to help travelers find the very best locations in which to satisfy their fondest vacation desires, without having to wade through endless unrelated text. This very selective guide lists the broadest possible range of vacation activities, including all the best places to pursue them.

We start with a list of possibilities that will require some perspiration — sports preferences and other rigorous pursuits — and go on to report on a number of more cerebral and spiritual vacation opportunities. In every case, our suggestion of a particular location — and often our recommendation of a specific resort — is intended to guide you to that special place where the quality of experience is likely to be highest. So whether you opt for golf or tennis, scuba or whitewater rafting, tours of spectacular resorts or epic shopping excursions, each entry is the equivalent of a comprehensive checklist of the absolute best in America.

DIRECTIONS

Here is a series of 66 American itineraries, from Maine's coastal islands to Hawaii's hidden beaches, to take you along this country's most beautiful routes and roads, most spectacular natural wonders, through our most magnificent national parks and forests. DIRECTIONS is the only section of the book organized geographically, and its itineraries cover the highlights of the entire country in short, independent segments that each describe journeys of one to three days' duration. Itineraries can be "connected" for longer trips or used individually for short, intensive explorations. Whether you are planning a major family vacation to cover thousands of miles or simply want to escape to the country, the format is adaptable to your end.

Each entry includes a guide to sightseeing highlights; a qualitative guide to accommodations and food along the road (small inns, out-of-the-way restaurants, country hotels, and off-the-main-road discoveries); and suggestions for activities.

Although each of the sections has a distinct format and a unique function, they have all been designed to be used together to provide a complete package of travel information. Sections have been carefully cross-referenced, and you will find that as you finish an entry in one section, you are directed to another section and another entry, with complementary information. To use this book to full advantage, take a few minutes to read the table of contents and random entries in each section. This will give you an idea of how it all fits together.

Pick and choose information that you need from different sections. For example, if you are interested in a camping trip of some sort — but have never been camping and don't really know where to go or how to organize yourself — you might well begin by reading the short, informative section on camping in GETTING READY TO GO. This will provide plenty of ideas on how to find a campsite, how to organize the trip, where to go for more information, what to take along. But where to go? Turn to DIVERSIONS for a listing of the best backpacking and camping sites in the country; a look through the selections will direct you to a route and a distance equal to your expertise. Perhaps you will choose a walk along the Appalachian Trail in the Great Smoky Mountains. Turn next to DIRECTIONS for suggestions on what to see along the way, including the Cumberland Gap. Once there, you might well decide to take a break to visit some of the nearby cities, Nashville or Louisville, Atlanta or even Memphis; all are fully covered in THE CITIES.

In other words, the sections of this book are building blocks designed to help you put together the best possible trip. Use them selectively as a tool, a source of ideas, a reference work for accurate facts, and a guidebook to the best buys, the most exciting sites and sights, the most pleasant accommodations and delicious food, *the best travel experiences* you can have.

GETTING READY TO GO

When and How to Go

When to Go

 The decision of exactly when to travel may be imposed upon you by the requirements of a rigid schedule; more likely, there will be some choice, and the decision will be made on the basis of precisely what you want to see and do, what activities or events you'd like to attend, and what suits your mood.

CLIMATE: Below is a general description of the climate in various American regions to help in planning. Note that all temperatures are given in the Fahrenheit scale. For a brief, city-by-city review of weather, see the *Climate* entry in each city report in THE CITIES.

New England and Upstate New York: Connecticut, Maine, Massachusetts, New Hampshire, Upstate New York, Rhode Island, Vermont – The seasons are sharply defined: cold, snowy winters with temperatures in the 20s or lower (much lower in the northern regions of Maine, Vermont, New Hampshire, and upstate New York); short, temperate springs; warm summers predominantly in the 70s and 80s, and into the 90s in the latter part of the season, often clear but sometimes humid, especially along the coasts; clear, crisp autumns with brilliant red, yellow, and orange foliage. Tourist season extends throughout the year: in winter, for skiing and winter sports; summer, for the lakes, coastal resorts, and historic areas; autumn (especially the last 2 weeks of September and first 2 weeks of October), for foliage. Least crowded is spring (except for students' spring vacation week in March). Best foliage routes: Vermont's Route 9; northwest Connecticut around Litchfield; the White Mountains and lakes of New Hampshire; the Mohawk Trail in Massachusetts.

Mid-Atlantic: Delaware, District of Columbia, Maryland, New Jersey, New York City, Pennsylvania, Virginia, West Virginia – Temperatures range from below freezing in winter to the upper 80s and into the 90s in summer, with cold, damp winters that can be brutal in windswept cities like New York. In the summer, humidity is high along the rivers, which is where many of the area's largest cities are located. Fall is pleasant, with moderate temperatures. A long, temperate, flowering spring begins as early as March, continues into June, and is the region's finest season. Tourists visit the metropolitan areas in summer, when city dwellers spend their weekends in the country, making the cities pleasantly uncrowded for visitors.

South: Alabama, Arkansas, Florida, Georgia, Kentucky, Louisiana, Mississippi, North Carolina, South Carolina, Tennessee – Anytime is a good time to visit the South, but fall and spring are the most temperate seasons. Winters range from the 40s inland to the 60s along the coast. Summer temperatures are in the 70s, 80s, and go into the 90s and are often very humid. Events in the South are usually scheduled from January to May and from mid-September to October.

Midwest: Illinois, Indiana, Michigan, Missouri, Ohio, Wisconsin – Cold winters and hot summers mark the entire region. The northern states suffer the harshest winters, with heavy snowfalls and temperatures in the 0 to 20 range. In the more southerly parts of states — the Ohio River valley section of Indiana, Illinois, Ohio, the southern tip of Illinois, and much of Missouri — winter temperatures average in the 30s. Summers across the region are hot, in the 80s and 90s, and can be oppressively humid. Even so, summer is the most popular tourist season, when the colossal state fairs get into gear and ethnic festivals are planned by towns large and small. Though the Midwest isn't as famous as New England for foliage, the leaves change just as dramatically and are at their peak in mid-October in Manistee National Forest near Cadillac, Michigan, and in Mohican State Park in Ohio.

Plains: Iowa, Kansas, Minnesota, Nebraska, North Dakota, South Dakota – The Plains states offer short, pleasant springs and autumns. In the northern areas, the summer days are warm, nights cool, and winters are often bitter cold and snowy. Farther south the winters become milder, and the risk of hot, dry, days in the 100s in July and August increases. Tourist season is generally spring through the end of summer.

Rockies: Colorado, Idaho, Montana, Utah, Wyoming – A region of great diversity, the Rocky Mountain states include mountains, deserts, and flatlands. Except in the deserts of Colorado and Utah, evenings even in summer are cool. Low humidity and dependable sunshine distinguish the entire area. November to mid-April is skiing season; sightseeing and touring begin in spring and continue until the snows announce winter. In summer, desert temperatures can reach 110 and more, and it is best to visit early in the summer season. The Rockies are most famous as a winter — skiing — destination, but a marvelous and uncrowded western vacation can be a summer tour of those famous ski resorts: *Aspen/Snowmass, Steamboat Springs,* and *Vail* in Colorado; *Big Sky,* Montana; *Jackson Hole,* Wyoming; *Park City* and *Sun Valley,* Utah.

Southwest: Arizona, New Mexico, Oklahoma, Texas – This region boasts year-round sunshine and low humidity (with some exceptions — as in Houston), as well as high temperatures. In Arizona and New Mexico, it can reach 115 in the summer, though temperatures in the northern sections are more likely to be in the 90s. The tourist season is December through April.

Far West: Alaska, California, Hawaii, Nevada, Oregon, Washington – For our purposes, the Far West is a rather artificially contrived category that comprises everything from Southern California and the Hawaiian islands to the great expanses of Alaska in the Arctic Circle. Not only is the vast range of temperature, climate, and geography within this huge area impossible to characterize neatly, but even along the Pacific coast, from California to Washington, weather and temperatures are unpredictable because of the various sea currents that affect weather conditions. In general, California north of Sacramento, Oregon, Washington, and Alaska are best seen in late spring through summer, when outdoor temperatures are warm. The winters can be quite cold and, in some coastal regions, rainy. Plan to visit Nevada, which is mostly desert, from October through April. Southern California and Hawaii are pleasant throughout the year, offering spring-like weather almost anytime.

SPORTS: In the Southeast and Southwest, from Palm Springs to South Carolina, virtually any season is a warm-weather-sports season — although snow occasionally falls even in the desert. For the rest of the country, games are played according to the weather.

Tennis and golf are under way by March in most of the country and last well into October. In the North — New England and Minnesota, for example — it is often as late as May before the mud firms, and cold sometimes stiffens knuckles as early as late September.

Since the most famous mountain climbing, hiking, and wilderness trips are in the Rockies, the Pacific Northwest, and northern New England, participants usually wait until summer, when the snow is gone, the mountain air is warmer, and less gear is required. Canoeing and rafting seasons follow much the same schedule, though whitewater rafting enthusiasts take to the rivers following the first snowmelt in April or May.

Water sports, such as boating and sailing, get under way in the Northeast in late spring and continue through early fall, with most regattas and other events scheduled from July 4 through Labor Day. On the West Coast north of San Francisco, the season lasts longer, with regattas beginning in June and continuing into September.

The New England ski season starts in earnest around Christmas (although snowfalls as early as Thanksgiving are common) and lasts through March. A good year will bring skiers out much earlier, and if the snow lasts, the slopes will be busy into April. The season in the West is usually longer, beginning pretty dependably at Thanksgiving and lasting until early or mid-April. However, skiing conditions depend on snow, and the determined skier should be prepared to plan around the weather. Newspapers and radio stations in ski areas carry detailed daily ski reports, often updated several times a day. If you are planning to go a long distance and are not certain of the conditions at your destination, call the management of the resort to get a complete report.

PARKS: Most national parks are open all year, closing only for Christmas and New Year's Day. However, many camping facilities in the parks close from October to April. For a complete list of camping facilities and their opening and closing times, contact the Superintendent of Documents, US Government Printing Office, Washington, DC 20402 (phone: 202-783-3238), requesting a copy of *National Parks: Camping Guide 1989-90* (doc. no. 024-005-01028-9, $3.50). For a list of camping directories, guides, and other useful resources, see *Camping and Hiking, Biking and RVs,* in this section. The most popular national parks, such as Grand Canyon, Zion, and Yosemite, keep some camping facilities open all year.

Parks will be most crowded in the summer. Heaviest use is in July and August. To avoid crowds, consider a spring trip, when wildflowers are in bloom; or autumn, for changing leaves and clear weather. Parks in regions with temperate winters — such as the Everglades in Florida and Big Bend in Texas — are at their best in winter.

CULTURAL EVENTS: The season for concerts, plays, art exhibitions, dance, and other cultural events across the United States is October through April. New plays open on Broadway; regional theaters bring up their lights (see *Regional Theaters,* DIVERSIONS); major orchestras perform several nights a week; and art museums hold major exhibitions, lectures, and film series (see *Great Museums,* DIVERSIONS). Schedules of events are available from the tourism and convention bureaus in most cities (addresses are given in THE CITIES).

Summer programs are less formal, often held outdoors, and usually less expensive (sometimes even free). Major cities offer full schedules of concerts and theater, as well as puppet shows and other entertainment for children. Many impromptu programs are set up in city parks. Summer events that cause national excitement include performances at the *Saratoga Performing Arts Center* in Saratoga Springs, New York, *Wolf Trap Farm Park* in Vienna, Virginia, the *Tanglewood Music Festival* in Lenox, Massachusetts, and the *Aspen Music Festival* in Aspen, Colorado. For a broader list of events, see *Music Festivals,* DIVERSIONS.

FAIRS AND CELEBRATIONS: Tobacco chewing and frog jumping contests, flower festivals, state fairs, rodeos, horse shows, Indian ceremonies, ethnic festivals, and an endless number of similar events bring people together in all parts of the country. To find out about the events along your route, write to the state tourist boards, most of which publish a calendar of events (for the addresses, see *State Tourist Offices,* in this section). *A Guide to Fairs and Festivals in the United States* by Frances Shemanski (Greenwood Press, 88 Post Road W., Box 5007, Westport, CT 06881; phone: 203-226-3571; $36.95) describes events alphabetically by state. *The Guide to Fairs, Festivals and Fun Events* by Janice and Stephen Gale (Sightseer Publications, 7400 N. Kendall Dr., Miami, FL 33156; $6.95) has a description and contact number or address for events in 18 eastern states from Maine to Florida. Though these guides are recommended, be sure to check dates and times, as they are not always current. For a selection of some of the craziest and most interesting celebrations, contests, and festivities in the US, see *Oddities and Insanities,* DIVERSIONS.

Touring by Car

 DRIVING YOUR OWN CAR: Automobile travel is the most popular mode of transportation in the US, though not necessarily the least expensive. It costs about 31¢ a mile to drive an automobile (the cost varies with the size and condition of your car, the price of gasoline, and whether you're doing city or highway driving); only about 12¢ a mile to fly by commercial airline. Driving, however, becomes more economical with more passengers and gives travelers the opportunity to explore inaccessible regions at their own pace and on their own schedule. Rather than just the means to an end, a well-planned driving route can be an important part of the adventure.

Before setting out, make certain that everything you need is in order. Read about the places you intend to visit and study relevant maps. If at all possible, discuss your intended trip with someone who has already driven the route to find out about road conditions and available services. If you can't speak to someone personally, try to read about others' experiences. The automobile clubs listed below also offer a wealth of information regarding specific driving routes.

Automobile Clubs – To protect yourself in case of on-the-road breakdowns, you should consider joining a reputable national automobile club. The largest one is the *American Automobile Association (AAA)*, with over 30 million members in chapters around the country, but numerous other clubs offer similar services. Any club should offer three basic services:

1. On-the-road insurance covering accidents, personal injury, arrest and bail bond, and lawyer's fees for defense of contested traffic cases.
2. Around-the-clock (24-hour) emergency breakdown service (including reduced rates on towing to nearest garage). For instance, *AAA* has a toll-free number for emergency road service; members are referred to the nearest service facility. Other clubs allow members to call any local mechanic and be reimbursed for the cost of towing at a later date.
3. Travel and vacation planning service, including advice and maps.

These are the basic forms of service; specific policies and programs vary widely from club to club. Before joining any one, get information and brochures from several and compare benefits and costs to find the services that best match your travel needs. Most clubs cost between $17 and $60 a year. Listed below are several of the largest US auto and travel clubs:

Allstate Motor Club: A member of the Sears family, run by Allstate Insurance. Join through any Allstate agency or contact Customer Service, PO Box 3096, Arlington Heights, IL 60006 (phone: 800-323-6282).

American Automobile Association: Affiliates throughout the US provide a wide variety of services to members, including a travel agency, trip planning, traveler's checks, and roadside assistance. Although *AAA* members receive a discount, non-members can also order from an extensive selection of highway and topographical maps available. For 24-hour emergency service throughout the US, members can call 800-336-HELP. Join through a local chapter or contact the national office, 8111 Gatehouse Rd., Falls Church, VA 22047 (phone: 703-222-6000).

Amoco Motor Club: Join at any Amoco dealer or contact the national office, PO Box 9014, Des Moines, IA 50306 (phone: 800-334-3300).

Exxon Travel Club: Provides a wide range of services including trip routing, maps and atlases, reimbursement for towing, discounts on car rentals and accommodations, and a variety of insurance packages. Ask for information from the national office, PO Box 3633, Houston, TX 77253 (phone: 713-680-5723).

Ford Auto Club: Contact the Membership Services Division, PO Box 224688, Dallas, TX 75222 (phone: 800-348-5220).

Montgomery Ward Auto Club: Open to (but not limited to) people with a Montgomery Ward charge account. Join through the credit manager at any Montgomery Ward store or contact the national office, 200 N. Martingale Rd., Schaumburg, IL 60173 (phone: 312-490-7485 in Illinois; 800-621-5151 elsewhere in the US).

Motor Club of America: National office, 484 Central Ave., Newark, NJ 07107 (phone: 201-733-1234; 800-222-6288 in New York; 800-435-7622 elsewhere in the continental US).

United States Auto Club Motoring Division: Ask for information from the national office, PO Box 660460, Dallas, TX 75266-0460 (phone: 215-541-4246 or 800-348-2761).

Oil Company Credit Cards – Most major oil companies offer credit cards that can be used to pay for gas, repairs, and most car parts at their respective service stations nationwide. A credit card will reduce the amount of cash you must carry on your trip. Applications for cards are available at service stations (*Mobil* stations have applications for *Mobil* cards only, and so on), and you will be granted a card if you can establish credit-worthiness. Issued free, they usually take about a month to process.

Charges are handled in two ways, and it is important to be aware of the system under which your card is operated. A few companies — *Amoco,* for example — allow some cardholders (depending on the kind of account) to carry charges from month to month. The cardholder pays only a minimum amount each month, and the balance is carried over. For this privilege the cardholder is charged an interest rate (usually about 1½% a month, 18% a year — this varies for different cards and from state to state) on the balance carried over. If you spent $300 on gasoline during a 2-week trip, you could spread the payment of this $300 over several months — virtually a "travel now, pay later" system — but you would end up paying more than the basic $300 when the interest charge was included.

Other companies — an example is *Gulf* — insist that the cardholder pay the full balance at the end of each billing period (usually a month) if it's under $50. On any balance over $50, if only partial payment is made, revolving credit is then extended to the unpaid balance, but interest charges will be added. There are advantages to both systems; when you consider a credit card, know which way it works and decide which is best for you.

Maps – Consult road maps. Many automobile clubs offer their members free maps and precise routings. Other travelers can get road maps free by writing to the state tourist boards (see *State Tourist Offices,* in this section). Maps are available at service stations, but due to budget cutbacks in the oil industry, most companies now charge for them. The *Rand McNally Road Atlas: US, Canada and Mexico* ($6.95) is excellent.

Preparing Your Car – Before heading off on the road, always make certain that your car is in the best possible condition. Have it inspected very carefully, paying special attention to brakes and tires, and be sure that your spare tire is in good shape. If you have room, a full-size spare is preferable to the small, solid rubber spares provided with many new cars. The days when every gas station had a mechanic on the premises have given way to self-service gas "stops" with convenience stores — so if you need a tire repaired, ask at your hotel or refer to the yellow pages to find a service station that can do it. Always carry liability insurance. Other suggestions include the following:

1. In addition to the spare tire, bring the following equipment: a flashlight with an extra set of batteries, jack, wrench, two wooden blocks; an extra set of keys (well hidden); jumper cables; gloves; a white towel (useful for signaling for help as well as for wiping the car); flares and/or reflectors; a first-aid kit; a container of water for the radiator; and a steel container of gasoline. (Plastic containers tend to break when the car is bouncing over rocky roads. This, in turn, creates the danger of fire should the gasoline ignite from a static electricity spark. Plastic containers also tend to burst at high altitudes.).

   If traveling in an isolated area, you may also want to carry a couple of extra fan belts, distributor points, a fuel pump replacement kit, condensers, and spark plugs. If you are driving at a high altitude, change cold spark plugs for hot, and advance the spark to prevent the engine from stalling. When driving a foreign car through rural areas, it is advisable to carry a basic selection of spare parts (ask your mechanic for a list of essentials), as service stations in small towns are not likely to stock them. This can prevent a wait of up to several days for parts to be sent from a foreign parts distributor in a distant metropolitan area.

2. Make the first days of your trip the shortest, and plan to drive no more than 300-400 miles per day (6-7 hours); this is a comfortable pace for most travelers. When traveling with children, plan on 200-250 miles a day (4-5 hours) at the most. Stop to rest when you are tired.

3. For current information on weather and road conditions, call the nearest *AAA*.

Breakdowns – If you break down on the road, immediate emergency procedure is to get the car off the highway, raise the hood as a signal that help is needed, and tie a white rag to the door handle or radio antenna. Don't leave the car unattended, and don't try any major repairs on the road.

Mechanics and Car Care – For any but the most simple malfunctions, you will probably need a mechanic. (Reliable mechanics are listed in THE CITIES.) An excellent series of booklets on car care, mileage, and mechanical problems and their sources is published by *Shell Oil Company* in its *Come to Shell for Answers* series, available from some *Shell* dealers or directly from the company at PO Box 2463, Houston, TX 77252 (phone: 713-241-6161). Other suggestions for breakdowns and on-the-road car care:

1. Look for mechanics with certification. The *Automotive Service Association* offers accreditation through its *National Institute for Automotive Service Excellence* (*ASE*) and has certified over 235,000 mechanics, many of whom work for local stations. Repair shops that are members of the *Automotive Service Association* abide by a code of ethics regarding fair business practices. For a list of employers of *ASE*-certified technicians, write to ASE, Local Listings, 1920 Association Dr., Reston, VA 22091, and specify the areas in which you're interested. For more information, call 817-283-6205.

2. Have some idea of what needs to be done. Oil needs to be changed approximately every 3,000 miles; a tune-up is needed every 12,000 miles (every 24,000 miles for transistorized ignition cars); spark plugs need to be changed every 25,000 miles, fan and air conditioning belts every 5,000 miles.

3. Get an estimate in writing on major repairs, and make sure there is a firm understanding that the mechanic will call if any other problems arise. The average cost for labor is between $18 and $40 per hour, with costs in some areas running as high as $70 per hour.

4. Be aware of dishonest practices. Some mechanics will cheat you. While checking oil they can "short-stick" the dipper so that the full amount of oil in your engine doesn't register; so be sure to watch while oil is being checked. When buying gas, make sure the attendant resets the pump, moving the counter back to zero. The best way to avoid being cheated is to know your car's oil and gas consumption.
5. Recognize warning signals.
   • Fluid leaks: Spread paper and look for brown or black fluid, which usually means an *oil leak;* straw-colored fluid near a wheel is likely to be *leaking brake fluid;* pink or reddish fluid means an *automatic transmission leak;* colorless or greenish fluid near the front, a *radiator or hose leak.*
   • Car has trouble starting: May be a vapor lock caused by hot weather; a cold, wet rag on the fuel line and pump may help.
   • Engine missing after quick acceleration: Could be a fleck of carbon lodged between electrodes of a spark plug. Clean plugs.
   • Rattle in rear: Loose muffler or tailpipe.
   • Rattling noise: Bent fan blade or loose pulley.
   • Loud squealing noise when wheel turns: Low power-steering fluid.
6. If your car needs to be towed, agree in advance on the price and on the station to which it will be towed. If you ask *AAA,* it will often name stations it considers reliable.

SPEED TRAPS: Watch the speedometer closely, especially in small towns. Speed traps mean expensive tickets that may also affect your insurance rates.

SAFETY BELTS: Be aware that many states now require the use of safety belts. At press time, the following states had laws requiring you to use seat belts: California, Colorado, Connecticut, Florida, Georgia, Hawaii, Idaho, Illinois, Indiana, Iowa, Kansas, Louisiana, Maryland, Michigan, Minnesota, Missouri, Montana, Nevada, New Jersey, New Mexico, New York, North Carolina, Ohio, Oklahoma, Pennsylvania, Tennessee, Texas, Utah, Virginia, Washington, and Wisconsin, as well as the District of Columbia. In some states, the law covers not just front-seat passengers but all passengers. In all 50 states and the District of Columbia, young children must either ride in a child carrier or use safety belts. Check individual state laws for details on age requirements; for example, in California, Montana, Washington, and Wisconsin, children age 4 and up must wear seat belts; in Nevada, age 5 and up. For more information on highway safety, write to the National Highway Safety Administration, Office of Public and Consumer Affairs, 400 7th St. SW, Room 3252, Washington, DC 20590.

SAVING ON GAS: Begin by planning an itinerary and making as many reservations as possible in advance so that you don't waste gas figuring out where to go or stay. Drive early in the day, when there is less traffic and heat. Then leave your car at the hotel and use local transportation within cities.

Make sure that your tires are properly inflated and your engine is tuned correctly to cut gas consumption. Avoid speeding; at 55 miles per hour (the fact that certain states are raising their speed limits to 65 notwithstanding) a car gets 25% better mileage than at 70. The number of miles per gallon is also increased by driving smoothly. Accelerate gently, anticipate stops, get into high gear quickly, and maintain a steady speed.

RENTING A CAR: No matter what the advertisements imply, renting a car is rarely as simple as signing on the dotted line and roaring off into the night. If you are renting for personal use, you must have a valid driver's license and will have to convince the renting agency that (1) you are personally credit-worthy and (2) you will bring the car back at the stated time. This will be easy if you have a major credit card; all national agencies (see below) and most local companies accept credit cards in lieu of a cash deposit, as well as for payment of your final bill. If you have a credit card but prefer to pay in cash, leave a credit card imprint as a "deposit," then pay your bill in cash when you return the car.

If you don't have a major credit card, call the renting company several days in advance, give them your name, home address, information on your business or employer; the agency then runs its own credit check. This check can be time consuming, so you should try to have it done before you leave home. In addition, you will have to leave a hefty deposit when you pick up the car — one major firm charges a minimum of $100 for a 1-day rental and, for a 1-week rental, the total week's payment plus 40%. Any unused portion of the deposit will be refunded.

Costs and Requirements – Renting is not inexpensive, but it is possible to economize by determining your own needs and then shopping around among companies until you find the best deal. As you comparison-shop, keep in mind that rates vary considerably, not only from city to city, but also from location to location within the same city. It might be less expensive to rent a car in the center of a city rather than at the airport. *Hertz* might be less expensive in Tulsa, while *Avis* is more reasonable in New York. Usually, locally based companies are less expensive than the national giants. Ask about special rates or promotional deals, such as weekend or weekly rates, bonus coupons for airline tickets, or 24-hour rates that include gas and unlimited mileage. There are two typical car rental deals:

1. Per-day charge, unlimited mileage: You pay a flat fee for each day you keep the car, but are not charged for mileage (an increasingly common alternative is to be granted only a certain number of free miles each day and then be charged on a per-mile basis over that number). If you plan to drive more than 100 miles, an unlimited mileage, flat fee is almost always the most economical arrangement.
2. Per-day, per-mile charge: You pay a flat fee for each day you keep the car (usually between $25 and $70) plus a per-mile charge of 12¢ to 40¢ or more.

Electing to pay for collision damage waiver protection will add considerably to the cost of renting a car. The renter may be responsible for up to the full value of the vehicle being rented, but you can dispense with the possible obligation to pay even this amount by buying the offered waiver at a cost of about $10 a day. If your personal auto policy covers rented vehicles, you probably won't need to pay for the waiver. That's why it's very important to check your existing coverage with your own insurance agent before making any decision about optional rental car waivers. Be aware, too, that increasing numbers of so-called premium credit cards — gold or platinum American Express cards, gold Visa or MasterCards — automatically provide collision damage waiver coverage when the cost of the car rental is paid using the appropriate credit card. Check with the credit card company for information on the amount of coverage provided; also see *Credit Cards and Traveler's Checks* in this section.

Most rental firms require clients to be at least 21 years old, but requirements vary in different locations. An 18-year-old can rent an *Avis* car in most cities, but not in Los Angeles. *Hertz*'s minimum age requirement is 25 unless the renter's employer has a contract with *Hertz* stating that drivers can be under 25. Also, *Hertz* reserves the right to charge a rate differential, and luxury models may not be available to young renters.

Major national rental companies with toll-free telephone numbers:

Alamo: 800-327-9633, nationwide
American International Rent-A-Car: 800-225-2529 in Boston, MA, and Portland, ME; 800-527-0202 elsewhere in the US
Avis: 918-664-4600 in Oklahoma; 800-331-1212 elsewhere in the US
Budget Rent-A-Car: 800-527-0700, nationwide
Dollar Rent-A-Car: 800-421-6868, nationwide
Hertz: 800-654-3131, nationwide

National Car Rental: 800-328-4567 in the continental US; 800-CAR-RENT in Alaska and Hawaii

Sears Rent-A-Car: 800-527-0770 or 800-268-8900, nationwide

Thrifty Rent-A-Car: 800-367-2277, nationwide

To economize on a car rental, consider one of the firms that rents 3- to 5-year-old cars that are well worn but mechanically sound. One such company is *Rent-a-Wreck* (phone: 800-421-7253). While these cars often rent for half of what major companies charge, they probably consume more gas than would a new, economy-size car.

Although the cost of gasoline has remained relatively stable over the past year, it's something motorists often forget to budget into their car rental expenses. On the road, remember that self-service (where you do the pumping) is usually less expensive than full service. Similarly, gas paid for in cash usually costs less than when paid for with a credit card. Also, when picking up a rental car, be sure to confirm the policy regarding the gas tank level on return. Some agencies include a charge for the initial tank of gas in the rental fee and suggest that you return the car with a close to empty tank. In other cases, if you do not return the car with a full tank, you will have to pay to refill the tank, and gasoline at the car rental company's pump is always much more expensive than gasoline from a service station.

Traveling by Plane

It *sounds* expensive to travel across the country via air, but it could be the most economical way to go if you must get to your destination quickly, and it may be preferable if you want to spend the maximum amount of time at your vacation destination. Plane travel is also less expensive per mile than travel by car (12¢ per mile to fly on a commercial airline; 31¢ to drive your own car).

If you decide to fly, you should know what kinds of flights are available; the rules and regulations pertaining to air travel; and the options for special packages offered by airlines and tour operators.

SCHEDULED FLIGHTS: A number of airlines offer regularly scheduled flights in the US. Within their ranks are all the well-known major companies and many smaller, regional lines that are not so familiar.

Tickets – When traveling on one of the many regularly scheduled flights, a full-fare ticket provides maximum travel flexibility (although at considerable expense), because tickets are sold on an open reservation system. This means that there are no advance booking requirements — a prospective passenger can buy a ticket for a flight right up to the minute of takeoff if seats are available. If your ticket is for a round trip, you can make the return reservation any time you wish, months before you leave or the day before you return. You are not required to stay at your destination for any specified amount of time. (Tickets are generally good for a year and can be renewed if not used.) You can also cancel your flight at any time without penalty. However, while it is true that this category of ticket can be purchased at the last minute, it is advisable to reserve well in advance during popular travel periods and around holiday times.

No matter what kind of ticket you buy, it is wise to reconfirm that you will be using your return reservation. Some airlines no longer require reconfirmation; others recommend that you confirm your return flight 48 or 72 hours in advance. If you do not call the airline to say you will be using the return leg of your reservation, it (or its computer) may assume you are not coming and automatically cancel your seat.

Fares – Air fares are changing so rapidly that even the experts find it difficult to keep up with them. This volatile situation is due to a number of factors, including airline deregulation, high labor costs, and vastly increased competition. Before the Airline Deregulation Act of 1978, airlines had no choice but to set their rates and routes within the guidelines of the Civil Aeronautics Board (CAB), and they could compete for passengers only by offering better service than their competitors. With the loosening of controls (and the elimination of the CAB), airlines are now engaged in a far more intense competition over prices and schedules, which has opened the door to a wide range of discount fares and promotional offers. Intensifying the competitive atmosphere has been the creation of several new carriers offering fewer frills and far lower prices. These carriers seem to appear and disappear with dismaying regularity. They have, however, served to drive down fares and make older, more entrenched carriers aware that they are in a genuine contest for travelers' dollars.

In general, the great variety of domestic air fares can be reduced to three basic categories: first class, coach (sometimes called economy or tourist class), and excursion or discount fares. A fourth category, called business class (an intermediate class between first and coach with many of the amenities of first class and more legroom than coach), has been added by many airlines in recent years.

A first class ticket is your admission to the special section of the aircraft with larger seats, more legroom, sleeperette seating on some wide-body aircraft, better food (or more elaborately served food, in any case), free drinks and headsets for movies and music channels, and, above all, personal attention. First class fares are about double those of full-fare economy, although both first class passengers and those paying economy fares are entitled to reserve seats and are sold tickets on an open reservation system. Business class is also available on a number of airlines and flights.

Coach passengers sit more snugly, as many as 10 in a single row on a wide-body jet, behind the first class section and receive standard meal service. Alcoholic drinks are not free, nor are the headsets. Like first class passengers, however, travelers paying the full coach fare are subject to none of the restrictions that are usually attached to less expensive discount fares. There are no advance booking requirements, no minimum stay requirements, and no cancellation penalties. Tickets are sold on an open reservation system: They can be bought up to the minute of takeoff if seats are available, and if the ticket is round-trip, the return reservation can be made any time you wish — months before you leave or the day before you return. Both first class and coach tickets are generally good for a year, after which they can be renewed if not used, and if you ultimately decide not to fly at all, your money will be refunded. Stopover privileges on both tickets are unlimited or extremely generous.

Excursion and other discount fares are the airlines' equivalent of a special sale and usually apply to round-trip bookings. These fares generally differ according to the season and the number of travel days permitted. They are only a bit less flexible than economy tickets and are, therefore, useful for both business travelers and tourists. Most round-trip excursion tickets include strict minimum and maximum stay requirements, and reservations can be changed only within the prescribed time limits, so don't count on extending a ticket beyond the prescribed time of return or staying less time than required. Different airlines may have different regulations concerning the number of stopovers permitted, and sometimes excursion fares are less expensive during midweek. Needless to say, these reduced-rate seats are most limited at busy times such as holidays, when full-fare coach seats sell more quickly than usual. Passengers fortunate enough to get a discount or excursion fare ticket sit with the coach passengers and for all intents and purposes are indistinguishable from them. They receive all the same basic services, even though they have paid anywhere between 30% and 55% less for the trip. Obviously, it's wise to make plans early enough to qualify for the least expensive transportation.

These discount or excursion fares may masquerade under a variety of names and they may vary from city to city (and from the East Coast to the West Coast, especially), but they inevitably have strings attached. A common requirement is that the ticket be purchased a certain number of days before departure — usually no fewer than 7 or 14 days — though it may be booked weeks or months in advance (it has to be "ticketed," or paid for, shortly after booking, however). The return reservation usually has to be made at the time of the original ticketing and cannot be changed later than a certain number of days (again, usually 7 or 14) before the return flight. If events force a passenger to change the return reservation after the date allowed, the difference between the round-trip excursion rate and the round-trip coach rate will probably have to be paid, though most airlines allow passengers to use their discounted fares by standing by for an empty seat, even if they don't otherwise have standby fares. Another common condition is the minimum and maximum stay requirement; for example, 6 to 14 days, or 1 to 6 days, but including at least a Saturday night. Last, cancellation penalties of up to 50% of the full price of the ticket are currently being assessed — check the specific penalty in effect when you purchase your discount/excursion ticket — so careful planning is imperative. At even greater risk — and bearing the lowest price of all the current discount fares — is the ticket where no change at all in departure and/or return flights is permitted, and the ticket price is totally nonrefundable. Even if none of the above conditions applies, prospective passengers can be fairly sure that the number of discount seats per flight at this lowest price is strictly limited or that the fare offering includes a set expiration date — which means it's absolutely necessary to move fast to enjoy the lowest possible prices.

There are also group inclusive tour fares available to many destinations. The requirements vary as to number of travel days, number of stopovers permitted, and number of passengers required for a group. (The last can be as few as two full fares.) The group fare always requires that a specified dollar amount of ground arrangements be purchased in advance, along with the ticket.

Most major airlines have traditionally offered their most attractive special fares to encourage travel in slow seasons and to inaugurate and publicize new routes. But in today's economic climate, increasingly the stimulus for special fares is the appearance of airlines consistently associated with bargain rates. These tend to be smaller carriers that can offer more for less because of lower overhead, uncomplicated route networks, and other limitations in their service. On these airlines, all seats on a given flight generally sell for the same price, which is somewhat below the lowest discount fare offered by the larger, more established airlines, even after they cut their fares in response. This gap, too, may disappear in the future, but it is important to note that tickets offered by the smaller airlines specializing in low-cost travel frequently are not subject to the same restrictions as the lowest-priced ticket offered by the more established carriers. They may not require advance purchase or minimum and maximum stays, may involve no cancellation penalties, may be available one way or round-trip, and may, for all intents and purposes, resemble the competition's high-priced full-fare coach. But never assume this until you know it's so.

The leading carriers now also offer a bonus system to frequent travelers. After the first 10,000 miles, for example, you might receive a first class ticket for the coach fare; after another 10,000 miles, you might receive a discount on your next ticket purchase. The value of the bonus continues to increase as you log more miles.

Given the frequency with which the air fare picture changes, it is more than possible that by the time you are ready to fly, the foregoing discussion may be somewhat out of date. That's why it is always wise to comparison-shop, and to do a good job of it, it's necessary to read the business and travel sections of your local newspaper regularly and to call the airlines that serve your destination from your most convenient gateway. The potential savings are well worth the effort.

Ask about discount or promotional fares and about any conditions that might restrict booking, payment, cancellation, and changes in plans. Check the prices from other cities. A special rate may be offered in a nearby city but not in yours, and it may be enough of a bargain to warrant your leaving from that city. If you have a flexible schedule, investigate standby fares. But remember that, depending on your departure point, they may not work out to be the rock-bottom price. Ask if there is a difference in price for midweek versus weekend travel, or if there is a further discount for traveling early in the morning or late at night. Also be sure to investigate package deals, which are offered by virtually every airline. They may include a car rental, accommodations, and/or dining or sightseeing features in addition to the basic air fare, and the combined cost of packaged elements is usually considerably less than the cost of the same elements when purchased separately.

When you're satisfied that you've found the lowest possible price for which you can conveniently qualify (you may have to call each airline more than once, since different clerks have been known to quote different prices), make your booking. Then, to protect yourself against fare increases, purchase and pay for your ticket as soon as possible after you've received a confirmed reservation. Airlines generally will honor their tickets, even if the operative price at the time of your flight is higher than the price you paid; if fares go up between the time you *reserve* a flight and the time you *pay* for it, you likely will be out of luck. Finally, with excursion or discount fares, it is important to remember that when a reservation clerk says that you must purchase a ticket by a specific date, this is an absolute deadline. Miss the deadline and the airline may automatically cancel your reservation without telling you.

If you don't have the time and patience to investigate personally all possible air departures and connections for a proposed trip, remember that a travel agent can be of inestimable help. A good agent should have all the information about which flights go where and when and which categories of tickets are available on each. Most have computerized reservation links with the major carriers so that a seat can be reserved and confirmed in minutes. An increasing number of agents also have fare-comparison computer programs, so they are often very reliable sources of detailed competitive price data. (For more information, see *How to Use a Travel Agent.*)

Reservations – When making plane reservations through a travel agent, ask the agent to give the airline your home phone number as well as a daytime business number. All too often the agent uses the agency's number as the official contact for changes in flight plans. During the winter, especially, weather conditions hundreds or even thousands of miles away can wreak havoc with flight schedules. Aircraft are constantly in use, and a plane delayed in the Orient or on the West Coast can miss its scheduled flight from the East Coast the next morning. The airlines are fairly reliable about getting this sort of information to passengers if they can reach them; diligence does little good at 6 PM if the airline has only the agency or an office number.

If you look at the back of your ticket, you'll see the need for reconfirmation of return flights stated explicitly. Some (though increasingly fewer) return reservations from international destinations are automatically canceled after a required reconfirmation period (typically 72 hours) has passed — even if you have a confirmed, fully paid ticket in hand. Reconfirmation is not required on domestic flights, but it is still a good idea, allowing you to make sure in plenty of time that the airline did not slip up in entering your original reservation, or in registering any changes you may have made since, and that it has your seat reservation request in the computer. Every travel agent or airline ticket office should give each passenger a reminder to reconfirm flights, but this seldom happens, so the responsibility rests with the traveler. Don't be lulled into a false sense of security by the "OK" on your ticket next to the number and time of the return flight. It only means that a reservation has been entered; a reconfirmation may still be necessary.

If you plan not to take a reserved flight, by all means inform the airline. Because the problem of "no-shows" is a consistently annoying one for airlines, they are allowed to overbook flights, a practice that often contributes to the threat of denied boarding for a certain number of passengers (see *Getting Bumped,* below). Let the airline know you're not coming and you'll spare everyone some confusion. Bear in mind that only certain kinds of tickets allow the luxury of last-minute changes in plans; those sold on an open reservation system (first class and full-fare coach) do, while excursion and other discount fares are often restricted in some way. Even first class and coach passengers should remember that if they do not show up for a flight that is the first of several connecting ones, the airline will cancel all of their reservations unless told not to do so.

Seating – For most types of tickets, airline seats are assigned on a first-come, first-served basis at check-in, although some airlines make it possible to reserve a seat at the time of ticket purchase. Always check in early for your flight, even with advance seat assignments.

Most airlines furnish seating charts, which make choosing a seat much easier, but in general, there are a few basics to consider. You must decide if you want a smoking or no smoking section and a window, aisle, or middle seat, or plan your seating in relation to a movie screen.

The amount of legroom you'll have (as well as chest room when the seat in front of you is in a reclining position) is determined by pitch, a measure of the front to rear spacing between seats. Since airplanes have tracks along which this spacing can be adjusted, the amount of pitch is a matter of airline policy, not the type of plane you fly. First class and business class seats have the greatest pitch, a fact that figures prominently in airline advertising. In economy class or coach, the standard pitch ranges from 33 to as little as 31 inches — downright cramped. The number of seats abreast, another factor determining comfort, depends on a combination of airline policy and airplane dimensions. First and business classes have the fewest seats per row. Economy generally has 9 seats per row on a DC-10 or an L-1011, making either one slightly more comfortable than a 747, which has 10 seats per row. However, charter flights on DC-10s and L-1011s can have 10 seats per row and be noticeably more cramped than 747 charters, on which the seating remains at 10 per row.

Airline representatives claim that most craft are more stable toward the front and midsections, while the seats farthest from the engines are quietest. Passengers who have long legs and are traveling on a wide-body aircraft might request a seat directly behind a door or emergency exit, since these seats often have greater than average pitch, or a seat in the first row of a given section, since these seats have extra legroom. It is often impossible, however, to see the movie from these seats, which are directly behind the plane's exits. Be aware that the first row of the economy section (called a "bulkhead" seat) on a conventional aircraft (not a wide-body) does not offer extra legroom, since the fixed partition will not permit passengers to slide their feet under it, and that watching a movie from this first row seat can be difficult and uncomfortable. A window seat protects you from aisle traffic and clumsy serving carts and also allows you a view, whereas an aisle seat enables you to get up and stretch your legs without disturbing your companions. Middle seats are the least desirable, and seats in the last row are the most undesirable of all, since they seldom recline fully. If you want peace and quiet, it is probably a good idea to request a seat in the first section of coach. Some airlines have designated this area as the "quiet" or "business" zone. Not all airlines have such special sections on all routes, however. If you wish to avoid children on your flight, remember that families generally do not sit in smoking areas. Once in the air, if you find that you are sitting in an especially noisy section, you are usually free to move to any empty seat — if there is one.

If you have a weight problem, you may face the prospect of a long flight with special trepidation. Center seats in the alignments of wide-body 747s, L1011s, and DC-10s are about 1½ inches wider than those on either side, so heavyweights tend to be more comfortable there.

Simply reserving an airline seat in advance, however, may actually guarantee very little. Most airlines require that passengers arrive at the departure gate at least 30 minutes (sometimes more) ahead of time to hold a seat reservation. A far better strategy is to visit an airline ticket office (or one of a select group of travel agents) to secure an actual boarding pass for your specific flight. Once this has been issued, airline computers show you as "checked in," and you effectively own the seat you have selected. This is also good insurance against getting bumped from an overbooked flight and is, therefore, an especially valuable tactic at peak travel times.

Smoking – The US government has adopted minimum standards to ensure that non-smokers will not be "unreasonably burdened" by passengers who smoke. For a wallet-size guide, which notes in detail the rights of non-smokers according to these regulations, send a stamped, self-addressed envelope to ASH (Action on Smoking and Health), Airline Card, 2013 H St. NW, Washington, DC 20006 (phone: 202-659-4310). The US Department of Transportation has determined that no smoking sections must be enlarged to accommodate all passengers who wish to sit in a no smoking section. According to a recently added proviso, however, the airline does not have to shift seating to accommodate non-smokers who arrive late for the flight or travelers flying standby. Cigar and pipe smoking are prohibited on all flights, even in the smoking sections. Some US carriers have banned smoking entirely from their flights; on all flights within the US that are scheduled to take only 2 hours or less, no smoking whatsoever is permitted.

Flying with Children – On longer flights, the bulkhead seats are usually reserved for families traveling with small children. Infants under 2 years of age travel free on most domestic flights, provided they do not occupy a seat (a second infant without a second adult would pay the fare applicable to children ages 2 through 11, generally 75% of the adult fare). Most airlines make complimentary bassinets available. Ask about obtaining one when you make your reservation, and when checking in, request a bulkhead or other seat that has enough room in front to use it. On some planes they hook into a bulkhead wall; on others they are placed on the floor in front of you. Even if you do use a bassinet, babies must be held during takeoff and landing. (For more information on flying with children, see *Hints for Traveling with Children.*)

Meals – If you have specific diet requirements (vegetarian, kosher, low calorie, low sodium, and so on), make sure to tell the airlines well before departure time. There is no extra charge for this option. It is, however, advisable to request special meals when you make your reservations — check-in time is too late. It's also wise to reconfirm that your request has made its way into the airline's computer — the time to do this is 24 hours before departure.

Getting Bumped – A special air travel problem is the possibility that an airline will accept more reservations (and sell more tickets) than there are seats on a given flight. This is entirely legal and is done to make up for "no-shows," passengers who don't show up for a flight for which they have made reservations and bought tickets. If the airline has oversold the flight and everyone does show up, there simply aren't enough seats. When this happens, the airline is subject to stringent rules designed to protect travelers.

In such cases, the airline first seeks ticketholders willing to give up their seats voluntarily in return for a negotiable sum of money or some other inducement, such as an offer of upgraded seating on the next flight or a voucher for a free trip at some other time. If there are not enough volunteers, the airline may bump passengers against their wishes. Anyone inconvenienced in this way, however, is entitled to an explanation of the criteria used to determine who does and does not get on the flight, as well as to compensation if the resulting delay exceeds certain limits. If the airline can put the bumped passengers on an alternate flight that gets them to their planned destination within 1 hour of their originally scheduled arrival time, no compensation is owed. If the delay is more than an hour — but less than 2 hours on a domestic US flight and less than 4 hours on an international flight — they must be paid denied-boarding compensation equivalent to the one-way fare to their destination (but not more than $200). If the delay is more than 2 hours beyond the original arrival time on a domestic flight or more than 4 hours on an international flight, the compensation must be doubled (but not more than $400). The airline may also offer bumped travelers a voucher for a free flight instead of the denied-boarding compensation. The passenger can choose either the money or the voucher, the dollar value of which may be no less than the monetary compensation to which the passenger would be entitled. The voucher is not a substitute for the bumped passenger's original ticket; the airline continues to honor that as well. Keep in mind that the above regulations and policies are for flights leaving the US only; they do not apply to charters or to inbound flights from abroad, even on US carriers.

To protect yourself as best you can against getting bumped, arrive at the airport early, allowing plenty of time to check in and get to the gate. If the flight is oversold, ask immediately for the written statement explaining the airline's policy on denied-boarding compensation and its boarding priorities. If the airline refuses to give you this information or if you feel it has not handled the situation properly, file a complaint with both the airline and the appropriate government agency (see *Consumer Protection*, below).

Delays and Cancellations – The above compensation rules also do not apply if the flight is canceled or delayed, or if a smaller aircraft is substituted due to mechanical problems. Each airline has its own policy for assisting passengers whose flights are delayed or canceled or who must wait for another flight because their original one was overbooked. Most airline personnel will make new travel arrangements if necessary. If the delay is longer than 4 hours, the airline may pay for a phone call or telegram, a meal, and in some cases a hotel room and transportation to it.

Deregulation of the airlines has meant that travelers must find out for themselves what they are entitled to receive. A useful booklet, *Fly Rights, A Guide to Air Travel in the US,* is available for $1 from the Superintendent of Documents, US Government Printing Office, Washington, DC 20402-9325 (phone: 202-783-3238). When ordering, specify the stock number of this publication, 050-000-00513-5, and allow 3 to 4 weeks for delivery.

■ **Caution:** If you are bumped or miss a flight, be sure to ask the airline to notify other airlines on which you have reservations or connecting flights. When your name is taken off the passenger list of your initial flight, the computer automatically cancels all of your reservations unless you take steps to preserve them.

Baggage – Though airline baggage allowances vary slightly, in general all passengers are allowed to carry on board, without charge, one piece of luggage that will fit easily under a seat of the plane or in an overhead bin and whose combined dimensions (length, width, and depth) do not exceed 45 inches. A reasonable amount of reading material, camera equipment, and a handbag are also allowed. In addition, all passengers are allowed to check two bags in the cargo hold: one usually not to exceed 62 inches when length, width, and depth are combined, the other not to exceed 55 inches in combined dimensions. No single bag may weigh more than 70 pounds. Most airlines will allow you to check the 45-inch bag in the hold if you prefer not to carry it with you, but a few require that it be stowed in the cabin under a seat. Airlines' policies regarding baggage allowances for children vary and are usually based on the percentage of full adult fare paid. Charges for additional, oversize, or overweight bags are usually made at a flat rate, the actual dollar amount varying from carrier to carrier. If you plan to travel with a bike, surfboard, scuba diving equipment, or other sports gear, be sure to check with the airline beforehand. Most have procedures for handling such baggage, but you will probably have to pay for transport regardless of how much other baggage you have checked.

To reduce the chances of your luggage going astray, remove all airline tags from previous trips, label each bag inside and out, and lock them. Double-check the tag that the airline attaches to make sure that it is correctly coded for your destination. If your bags are not in the baggage claim area after your flight or if they're damaged, report the problem to airline personnel immediately. Keep in mind that policies regarding the specific time limit in which you have to make your claim vary from carrier to carrier. Fill out a report form on your lost or damaged luggage and hold on to a copy of it and your claim check. If you must surrender the check to claim a damaged bag, get a receipt for it to prove that you did, indeed, check your baggage on the flight. If luggage is missing, be sure to give the airline your destination and/or the telephone number where you can be reached. Also take the name and number of the person in charge of recovering lost luggage. Most airlines have emergency funds for passengers stranded away from home without their luggage, but if it turns out that your bags are truly lost and not simply delayed, do not then and there sign any paper indicating you'll accept an offered settlement. Since the airline is responsible for the value of your bags within certain statutory limits ($1,250 for a lost bag on a domestic flight; $9.07 per pound on an international flight), you should take the time to assess the extent of your loss (see *Insurance* in this section). It's a good idea to keep records indicating the value of the contents of your luggage. Another idea is to take a Polaroid picture of the most valuable of your packed items just after putting them in your suitcase.

Considering the increased incidence of damage to baggage, it's now more than ever a good idea to keep the sales slips that confirm how much you paid for your bags. These are invaluable in establishing the value of damaged baggage and eliminate any arguments. A better way to protect your precious baggage from the luggage-eating conveyers is to try to carry your gear on board whenever possible.

Airline Clubs – US carriers often have clubs for travelers who pay for membership. These clubs are not solely for first class passengers. Membership (which, by law, now requires a fee) entitles travelers to use the private lounges at airports along their route, to refreshments served in these lounges, and to check-cashing privileges at most of their counters. Extras include special telephone numbers for individual reservations, embossed luggage tags, and a membership card for identification. Two airlines that offer membership in such clubs are: Pan American — the *Clipper Club,* single yearly membership $150, spouse an additional $45, 3-year and lifetime memberships also available — and TWA — the *Ambassador Club,* single yearly membership $150, spouse an additional $25, and lifetime memberships also available. However, these companies do not have club facilities in all airports. Lounge privileges are also offered to first class passengers, and other airlines also offer a variety of special club and lounge facilities in many airports.

CHARTER FLIGHTS: By booking a block of seats on a specially arranged flight, charter tour operators offer travelers air transportation, often combined with a hotel room, meals, and other arrangements, for a substantial reduction over full economy fare on scheduled flights.

Charters were once the best bargain around, but this is no longer necessarily the case. Various promotional fares on scheduled airlines are often just as low, especially on the most competitive routes, and they are usually more flexible. As a result, charter flights have been discontinued in many areas, but to some popular vacation spots, they can still be a good buy. They are especially attractive to people living in smaller cities or out-of-the-way places, because they frequently take off from nearby airports, saving travelers the inconvenience and expense of getting to a major gateway. Where demand persists, charter operators will continue to rent planes or seats from scheduled airlines (or from special charter airlines) and offer flights to the public directly through advertisements or travel agents. You buy the ticket from the operator or the agent, not from the airline owning the plane.

Charter travel once required that an individual be a member of a club or other "affinity" group whose main purpose was not travel. But since the approval of "public charters" years ago, operators have had some of the flexibility of scheduled airlines, making charters more competitive. Public charters are open to anyone, whether belonging to a group or not, and have no advance booking requirements or minimum stay requirements. One-way arrangements are permitted, though charters are almost always round-trip, and it is unlikely that you would be sold a one-way seat on a round-trip flight. Operators can offer air-only charters, selling transportation alone, or they can offer charter packages — the flight plus a combination of land arrangements such as accommodations, meals, tours, or car rental. Some things to keep in mind about the charter game are:

1. It cannot be repeated often enough that if you are forced to cancel your trip, you can lose much (and possibly all) of your money unless you have cancellation insurance, which is a *must* (see *Insurance*). Frequently, if the cancellation is well in advance (often 6 weeks or more), you may forfeit only a $25 or $50 penalty. If you cancel only 2 or 3 weeks before the flight, there may be no refund at all unless you or the operator can supply a substitute passenger.
2. Charter flights may be canceled by the operator up to 10 days before departure for any reason, usually underbooking. Your money is returned in this event, but there may be too little time for you to make new arrangements.
3. Most charters have little of the flexibility of regularly scheduled flights regarding refunds and the changing of flight dates; if you book a return flight, you must be on it or lose your money.
4. Charter operators are permitted to assess a surcharge, if fuel or other costs warrant it, of up to 10% of the air fare up to 10 days before departure.
5. Because of the economics of charter flights, your plane almost always will be full, so you will be crowded, though not necessarily uncomfortable.

Booking – If you do take a charter, read the contract's fine print carefully and pay particular attention to the following:

1. Instructions concerning the payment of the deposit and its balance and to whom the check is to be made payable. Ordinarily, checks are made out to an escrow account, which means the charter company can't spend your money until your flight has safely returned. This provides some protection for you. To ensure the safe handling of your money, make out your check to the escrow account, the number of which must appear by law on the brochure, though all too often it is on the back in fine print. Write the details of the charter, including the destination and dates, on the face of the check; on the back, print "For Deposit Only." Your travel agent may prefer that you make out your check to the agency, saying that it will then pay the tour operator the fee minus commission. It is perfectly legal to write the check as we suggest, however, and if your agent objects too vociferously (he or she should trust the tour operator to send the proper commission), consider taking your business elsewhere. If you don't make your check out to the escrow account, you lose the protection of escrow should the trip be canceled. Furthermore, recent bankruptcies in the travel industry have served to point out that even the protection of escrow may not be enough to safeguard a traveler's investment. More and more, insurance is becoming a necessity (see *Insurance*). The charter company should be bonded (usually by an insurance company), and if you want to file a claim against it, the claim should be sent to the bonding agent. The contract will set a time limit within which a claim must be filed.

2. Note specific stipulations and penalties for cancellations. Most charters allow you to cancel up to 45 days in advance, but some cancellation dates are 50 to 60 days before departure.
3. Stipulations regarding cancellation and major changes made by the charterer. Flights may not be canceled within 10 days of departure except when circumstances — such as natural disasters or political upheavals — make it physically impossible to fly. Charterers may make "major changes," however, such as in the date or place of departure or return, but you are entitled to cancel and receive a refund if you don't accept these changes. A price increase of more than 10% up to 10 days before departure is considered a major change; no price increase is allowed during the last 10 days before departure.

DISCOUNT TRAVEL SOURCES: An excellent source of information on economical travel opportunities is the *Consumer Reports Travel Letter,* published monthly by Consumers Union. It keeps abreast of the scene on a wide variety of fronts, including package tours, rental cars, insurance, and more, but it is especially helpful for its comprehensive coverage of air fares, offering guidance on all the options, from scheduled flights on major or low-fare airlines to charters and discount sources. For a year's subscription, send $37 to Consumer Reports Travel Letter, PO Box 2886, Boulder, CO 80322 (phone: 800-525-0643). Another source is *Travel Smart,* a monthly newsletter offering information on a wide variety of trips, with additional discount travel services available to subscribers. For a year's subscription, send $37 to Communications House, 40 Beechdale Rd., Dobbs Ferry, NY 10522 (phone: 914-693-8300 in New York; 800-327-3633 elsewhere).

Still another way to take advantage of bargain air fares is open to those who have a flexible schedule. A number of organizations, usually set up as last-minute travel clubs and functioning on a membership basis, routinely keep in touch with travel suppliers to help them dispose of unsold inventory at discounts of between 15% and 60%. A great deal of the inventory consists of complete tour packages and cruises, but some clubs offer air-only charter seats and, occasionally, seats on scheduled flights. Members pay an annual fee and receive the toll-free number of a telephone hot line to call for information on imminent trips. In some cases, they also receive periodic mailings with information on upcoming trips for which there is more advance notice. Despite the suggestive names of the clubs providing these services, last-minute travel does not necessarily mean that you cannot make plans until literally the last minute. Trips can be announced as little as a few days or as much as 2 months before departure, but the average is from 1 to 4 weeks' notice. It does mean that your choice at any given time is limited to what is offered and, if your heart is set on a particular destination, you might not find what you want, no matter how attractive the bargain. Among these organizations are the following:

Discount Club of America, 61-33 Woodhaven Blvd., Rego Park, NY 11374 (phone: 718-335-9612 or 800-321-9587). Annual fee: $39.

Discount Travel International, Ives Bldg., 114 Forrest Ave., Suite 205, Narberth, PA 19072 (phone: 215-668-2182 in Pennsylvania; 800-824-4000 elsewhere). Annual fee: $45 per household.

Encore Short Notice, 4501 Forbes Blvd., Lanham, MD 20706 (phone: 301-459-8020 or 800-638-0930 for customer service). Annual fee: $36 per family.

Last-Minute Travel Club, 132 Brookline Ave., Boston, MA 02215 (phone: 617-267-9800 or 800-LAST-MIN). Annual fee: $30 per person; $35 per couple or family.

Moment's Notice, 40 E. 49th St., New York, NY 10017 (phone: 212-486-0503). Annual fee: $45 per family.

On Call to Travel, 14335 SW Allen Blvd., Suite 209, Beaverton, OR 97005 (phone: 503-643-7212, members may call collect). Annual fee: $39 per family, first year; $29 yearly thereafter.

Spur-of-the-Moment Tours and Cruises, 10780 Jefferson Blvd., Culver City, CA 90230 (phone: 213-839-2418 in California; 800-343-1991 elsewhere). No fee.

Stand Buys Limited, 311 W. Superior St., Suite 414, Chicago, IL 60610 (phone: 800-331-0257 for membership information; 800-848-8402 for customer service; 800-433-9383 for reservations). Annual fee: $45 per family.

Worldwide Discount Travel Club, 1674 Meridian Ave., Miami Beach, FL 33139 (phone: 305-534-2082). Annual fee: $50 family; $40 individual.

NET FARE SOURCES: The newest notion for reducing the costs of travel services comes from travel agents who offer individual travelers "net" fares. Defined simply, a net fare is the bare minimum amount at which an airline or tour operator will carry a prospective traveler. It doesn't include the amount that would normally be paid to the travel agent as a commission. Traditionally, such commissions amount to about 10% on domestic fares and from 8% to 20% on international tickets — not counting significant additions to these commission levels that are paid retroactively when agents sell more than a specific volume of tickets or trips for a single supplier. At press time, at least one travel agency in the US was offering travelers the opportunity to purchase tickets and/or tours for a net price. Instead of making its income from individual commissions, this agency assesses a fixed fee that may or may not provide a bargain for travelers; it requires a little arithmetic to determine whether to use the services of a net travel agent or those of a conventional agent.

McTravel Travel Services (130 S. Jefferson, Chicago, IL 60606-3691; phone: 312-876-1116 in Illinois; 800-333-3335 elsewhere) is a formula fee-based agency that rebates its ordinary agency commission to the customer. For domestic flights, an agent will find the lowest retail ticket price, then rebate 8% of that price minus an $8 ticket-writing charge. The rebate percentage for international flights varies from 8% to 20%, depending on the airline, and the ticket-writing fee is $20. *McTravel* will rebate on all tickets, including max savers, super savers, and senior citizen passes. Available 7 days a week, reservations should be made far enough in advance to allow the tickets to be sent by first class mail, since extra charges accrue for special handling as well as for reservations that require any significant amount of research. It's possible to economize further by making your own airline reservation, then asking *McTravel* only to write/issue your ticket. For travelers outside the Chicago area, business may be transacted by phone, and purchases may be charged to a credit card.

One of the potential drawbacks of buying from agencies selling travel services at net fares is that your options may be limited. *McTravel* recently lost a court battle with American Airlines, which refused to do business with the discounter. A US District Court in Chicago ruled in the airline's favor, and other carriers are expected to follow suit.

BARTERED TRAVEL SOURCES: Say a company buys advertising space in a newspaper for a hotel. As payment, the hotel gives the company a number of hotel rooms in lieu of cash. This is barter, a common means of exchange among hotels, airlines, car rental companies, cruise lines, tour operators, restaurants, and other service companies. When a bartering company finds itself with excess hotel rooms (or empty airline seats or cruise ship cabin space, and so on) and offers them to the public, considerable savings can be realized.

Bartered-travel clubs can often give discounts of up to 50% to members, who pay an annual fee (approximately $50 at press time) that entitles them to select from the flights, cruises, hotels, that the company obtained by barter. Members usually present a voucher, club credit card, or scrip (a dollar-denomination voucher negotiable only for the bartered product) to the hotel, which in turn subtracts the dollar amount from the bartering company's account.

Selling bartered travel is a perfectly legitimate means of retailing. One advantage to club members is that they don't have to wait until the last minute to obtain room or flight reservations. However, hotel rooms and airline seats are usually offered to members on a space-available basis. Ticket vouchers are good only for a particular hotel and cannot be used elsewhere. The same rule applies to car rentals, cruises, package tours, and restaurants. The following clubs offer bartered travel at a discount to members.

IGT (In Good Taste) Services, 22 E. 29th St., New York, NY 10016 (phone: 212-725-9600 or 800-444-8872). Annual membership fee of $48 includes $25 credit toward future charges.

The Travel Guild, 18210 Redmond Way, Redmond, WA 98052 (phone: 206-885-1213). Annual membership fee: $48.

Travel World Leisure Club, 225 W. 34th St., Suite 2203, New York, NY 10122 (phone: 212-239-4855 or 800-444-TWLC). Annual membership fee: $50 per family.

CONSUMER PROTECTION: Consumers who feel that they have not been dealt with fairly by an airline should make their complaints known. Begin with the customer service representative at the airport where the problem occurred. If he or she cannot resolve your complaint to your satisfaction, write to the airline's consumer office. In a businesslike, typed letter, explain what reservations you held, what happened, the names of the employees who were involved, and what you expect the airline to do to remedy the situation. Send copies (never the originals) of the tickets, receipts, and other documents that support your claims. Ideally, all correspondence should be sent via certified mail, return receipt requested. This provides proof that your complaint was received.

If you still receive no satisfaction, the US Department of Transportation can help. Passengers with consumer complaints — lost baggage, compensation for getting bumped, smoking and no smoking rules, deceptive practices by an airline, charter regulations — should write to the Consumer Affairs Division, Room 10405, US Department of Transportation, 400 7th St. SW, Washington, DC 20590, or call the office at 202-366-2220. DOT personnel stress, however, that consumers should initially direct their complaints to the airline that provoked them.

To avoid more serious problems, always choose charter flights and tour packages with care. When you consider a charter, ask your travel agent who runs it and carefully check out the company. The Better Business Bureau in the company's home city can report on how many complaints, if any, have been lodged against it in the past. As emphasized above, protect yourself with trip cancellation and interruption insurance, which can help safeguard your investment in the event that you or a traveling companion is unable to make the trip and must cancel too late to receive a full refund from the company providing your travel services. (This is advisable whether you're buying a charter flight alone or a tour package for which the air fare is provided by charter or scheduled flight.) Some travel insurance policies have an additional feature, covering the possibility of default or bankruptcy on the part of the tour operator or airline, charter or scheduled.

Should this type of coverage not be available to you (state insurance regulations vary, there is a wide difference in price, and so on), your best bet is to pay for airline tickets and tour packages with a credit card. The federal Fair Credit Billing Act permits purchasers to refuse payment for credit card charges where services have not been delivered, so the onus of dealing with the receiver for a bankrupt airline falls on the credit card company. Do not rely on another airline to honor the ticket you're holding, since the days when virtually all major carriers subscribed to a default protection program that bound them to do so are long gone. Some airlines may voluntarily step forward to accommodate the stranded passengers of a fellow carrier, but this is now an entirely altruistic act.

Touring by Train

 Almost all of the regularly scheduled passenger trains in the US are run by *Amtrak,* which serves most of the country's major cities and has made dramatic improvements in equipment and service. Some specially equipped trains now have telephone service. Routes, schedules, and stations are given in the *National Timetable,* available at any *Amtrak* station or sales office. There are three timetables a year, covering the periods January to May, May to September, and September to January. Before you plan your trip, note that there is no direct transcontinental train service. All passengers must connect in Chicago or New Orleans.

Amtrak and travel agents can also provide information on tours, trains that connect with buses, and rail trips in Canada, and even help with hotel reservations and car rental details. For rail fares, seat availability, route and other information, contact *Amtrak*'s computerized reservation service by calling 800-USA-RAIL. *Amtrak's America* is a helpful planner, with information on all of *Amtrak*'s long-distance routes, pictures of sleeping accommodations, and advice on such matters as packing for your trip. Write to Amtrak's America, PO Box 7717, Itasca, IL 60143. (You can also request timetables and route guides from this address.)

ACCOMMODATIONS AND FARES: *Amtrak* fares are based on the quality of accommodation the passenger enjoys on the journey. Least expensive is the basic transportation fare. Ordinarily this will buy a coach seat for the duration of the trip, but it guarantees only that the passenger has a right to transportation. Seats are allocated on a first-come, first-served basis on unreserved coach trains, which usually only operate on short runs. In addition to the seats, long-distance, eastern-route trains offer three types of sleeping accommodations, for which the passenger pays significantly more: slumber coaches, private rooms with lounge seats that convert to beds and a toilet and washstand; roomettes, larger rooms with chairs and fold-down beds; and full-size bedrooms that can be combined into suites. On routes west of the Mississippi, the new Superliners have deluxe bedrooms with shower, washbasin, and toilet; economy, double-occupancy bedrooms; and family bedrooms, which accommodate five people. Accommodations for wheelchair-bound passengers are available on all trains, although a special service request must be made at least 12 hours before departure.

The cost of a coach seat — basic transportation fare — on a train will generally be something more than the cost of a bus ticket and something less than coach fare on a plane to the same destination — except on such competitive routes as Boston to Washington, DC, where very inexpensive flights are available. However, the plane makes the trip in a few hours; the train takes 2 days, and it is likely that anyone making the trip by train will want some kind of sleeping accommodation rather than just a coach seat. When comparing costs, however, take into account that the extra expense of accommodations on the train are offset by the comparable cost you would be paying for a hotel room. The cost of a train compared with that of a plane is very much connected to the level of comfort. From time to time, *Amtrak* also offers special promotional fares, such as a round-trip ticket for $7 more than the one-way fare.

BOOKING: Tickets may be obtained from *Amtrak* stations, travel agents, or on board an unreserved coach train (for an extra $5), and can be purchased with most major credit cards, personal check, or cash. Reservations are mandatory for all club cars, sleeping cars, slumber coaches, *Metroliner* coaches (high-speed electric trains that provide fast service between major cities in the Northeast Corridor), *Superliners,* for custom class, and on a number of other regular runs. Trains that require reservations are so marked in the *Timetable.* If you have difficulty reaching the reservation number, try early in the morning or late at night. Always allow extra time to make connections because trains are often late. If you have confirmed reservations and miss a connection because of a delayed train, *Amtrak* will provide alternate arrangements if necessary. Sleeping car attendants should be tipped at least $1 a night, assuming that you're pleased with the service.

BAGGAGE: In most stations, baggage can be checked through to destination up to 1 hour before departure (and should be claimed within 30 minutes after arrival). On long-distance runs, you will be allowed to carry on only enough baggage for essentials during the journey; you are allowed to check three pieces of luggage weighing a total of 150 pounds. Attendants on the train, or Red Caps in most stations, will give you free help with your luggage (tip about $1). *Amtrak* urges you to use only Red Caps.

TOURS: The USA Railpass is *Amtrak*'s excursion rate, but it is not available to US citizens and can only be purchased in Europe. The pass entitles the holder to unlimited coach travel on *Amtrak* trains and routes for a period of 45 days. For US citizens, *Amtrak* sometimes offers Circle Fares, unlimited mileage and stopovers for a given time at a fixed fee. At press time, *Amtrak*'s All Aboard America fare was $299. It allows the user to travel anywhere in the US with up to three stopovers and is good for 45 days. Recently, *Amtrak* has introduced a number of worthwhile tours, some connecting with boat, bus, or car packages. Brochures and details on *Amtrak* tours are available from *Amtrak* stations or from travel agents. Call 800-USA-RAIL and ask for the tour desk or write to Amtrak's America, PO Box 7717, Itasca, IL 60143.

America by Rail offers several itineraries for those who want to explore the US by train. An 11-day "Magic of the Midwest" package includes stops in Chicago, Memphis, Nashville, and St. Louis, plus a 3-day Mississippi River cruise. For information on this and other packages, write to America by Rail, 808 W. Lake Lansing Rd., East Lansing, MI 48823 (phone: 800-351-7411).

Touring by Bus

Crisscrossing America's highways to serve nearly 10,000 cities and towns, bus companies are easily the country's most comprehensive transport system. You can almost always get there by bus. *Greyhound Lines* was formed when *Greyhound* acquired the routes of *Trailways Lines*. At press time, the newly formed company had 3,904 buses and serviced 140,000 miles of routes, with depots in most cities across the country (listed in the yellow pages under "Bus"). This giant company and the many smaller independent firms make bus travel the most frequent and most economical mode of transportation in America. Buses, however, are undeniably slower than trains, planes, or private cars, and there is a tradeoff of money saved for time spent en route.

ACCOMMODATIONS AND FARES: The cost of a bus trip is about 9¢ a mile, compared to 12¢ a mile by plane and 31¢ a mile by private car. Long-distance, round-trip bus journeys were once the most economical way to go, though deregulation and competition have inched up the cost of bus travel. The competitive atmosphere affecting all modes of transportation makes it worthwhile to ask about promotional fares and to check with more than one company.

Bus passengers are allowed to stop anywhere along their route as long as their entire journey is completed before the ticket expires. Regular one-way bus tickets are good for 60 days. If you don't use the ticket within that time, it may be returned for a full refund or replaced by another ticket. Round-trip tickets are good for one year with the exception of some special fares; for instance, round-trip Supersaver tickets are good for 60 days; one way, for 30 days.

BOOKING: Reservations are not necessary on most bus routes; companies usually send as many buses as are needed to handle all passengers. Sightseeing tours and special programs (see below) require reservations and are subject to slightly different stopover rules. *Greyhound* has unlimited travel tickets that allow the ticketholder to travel anywhere in the US on company routes (and often on the routes of smaller, connecting bus lines) for specified periods of time (7, 15, and 30 days). Special prices for these unlimited travel deals represent considerable savings. *Greyhound*'s program is called Ameripass. At press time, a 7-day Ameripass fare was $189; 15-day, $249; 30-day, $349. Top savings can be enjoyed through the special promotional fares (to any place *Greyhound* travels) that require 30 days' advance purchase and a $25 penalty in case of cancellation. If you depart Monday through Thursday, the one-way fare is $59; round-trip is $118. If you leave Friday through Sunday, a one-way and a round-trip ticket cost $68 and $136 respectively. Note that holiday blackout periods exist in both cases. If you pay $75 one way, or $150 round-trip, you can leave any day of the week and there are no holiday blackout restrictions. Note that these promotional fares are offered only at certain times of the year.

SERVICES: Most buses are not equipped for food service. On long trips they make meal stops, and there is always food service of one kind or another in the terminals. It is not a bad idea to bring some food aboard. Almost all interstate, long-distance buses have air conditioning, heating, toilets, adjustable seats, and reading lamps.

FOR COMFORTABLE TRAVEL: Dress casually in loose-fitting clothes. Be sure you have a sweater or jacket (even in the summer, air conditioning can make buses quite cool). Passengers are allowed to listen to radios or cassette players, but must use earphones. Choose a seat in the front near the driver for the best view, in the middle between the front and rear wheels for the smoothest ride. Avoid the back near the toilet unless you smoke. Smoking is prohibited in a number of jurisdictions. When it is allowed, smokers are restricted to the last rows of any bus.

TOURS: *Greyhound* offers a wide variety of sightseeing tours that include overnight accommodations. For information on these programs, check with your nearest *Greyhound* office. Dozens of tour operators offer a wide variety of bus or motorcoach tours in the US. One directory is the *Travel Agent Domestic Tour Manual,* published by the *Travel Agent* magazine, which is available in some libraries. Some travel agents also have this information.

Package Tours

 If the mere thought of buying a travel package conjures up visions of a trip spent marching in lockstep with a horde of frazzled fellow travelers, remember that packages have come a long way. For one thing, not all packages are necessarily escorted tours, and the one you buy does not have to include any organized touring at all — nor will it necessarily include traveling companions. If it does, however, you'll find that people of all sorts — many just like yourself — are taking advantage of packages today because they are economical and convenient, save the purchaser an immense amount of planning time, and exist in such variety that it's virtually impossible not to find one that suits at least the majority of any traveler's preferences. Given the high cost of travel these days, packages have emerged as a good buy.

There are hundreds of package programs on the market today, offered by airlines, *Amtrak,* and the bus companies, as well as car rental companies, hotels, and travel companies. Many are built around sports such as skiing. In essence, a package is a combination of travel services that can be purchased as a single booking. It may include any or all of the following: round-trip air transportation, local transportation (and/or car rentals), accommodations, some or all meals, sightseeing, entertainment, transfers to and from the hotel at each destination, taxes, tips, escort service, and a variety of incidental features that might be offered as options at additional cost. In other words, a package can be any combination from a fully escorted tour offered at an all-inclusive price to a simple fly-drive booking allowing you to function totally on your own. Its principal advantage is that it saves money: The cost of the combined arrangements invariably is well below the cost of all the elements bought separately, and (particularly if transportation is provided by charter or discount flight) it could even be less than a round-trip economy airline ticket on a regularly scheduled flight. A package tour provides more than economy and convenience: It releases the traveler from having to make individual arrangements for each separate section of the tour.

The lower prices are possible through package travel as a result of high-volume commerce. The tour packager negotiates for services in wholesale quantities — blocks of airline seats or hotel rooms, group meals, dozens of rental cars, busloads of ground transportation, and so on — and they are made available at a lower per-person price because of the large quantities purchased for use during a given period. Most packages, however, are subject to restrictions governing the duration of the trip and require total payment by a given time before departure.

Tour programs generally can be divided into two categories — "escorted" and "independent" — depending on the arrangements offered. An escorted tour means that a guide will accompany the group from the beginning to the end of the tour. On independent tours, you generally have a choice of hotels, meal plans, and sightseeing trips in each city as well as a variety of special excursions. This plan is for people who do not want a set itinerary but who prefer confirmed reservations. Whether you choose an escorted or independent tour, always bring along full contact information for your tour operator in case problems arise, although US tour operators often have local affiliates throughout the country who are available to give additional assistance or make other arrangements on the spot.

To determine whether a package — or, more specifically, which package — fits your travel plans, start by evaluating your interests and needs, deciding how much and what you want to spend, see, and do. Gather whatever package tour information is available for your time schedule. Be sure that you take the time to read the brochure *carefully* to determine what is included. Keep in mind that travel brochures are written to entice you into signing up for a package tour. Often the language is deceptive and devious. For example, a brochure may quote the lowest prices for a package tour based on facilities that are unavailable during the off-season, undesirable at any season, or just plain nonexistent. Information such as "breakfast included" or taxes (which can add up) are important items. Note, too, that prices quoted in brochures are almost always based on double occupancy, that is, for each of two people sharing a double room. If you travel alone, the supplement for single accommodations can raise the price considerably (see *Hints for Single Travelers*).

Increasingly, in this age of rapidly rising air fares, the brochure will not include the price of the airline ticket in the price of the package, though sample applicable fares from various gateway cities will usually be listed separately as extras to be added to the price of the ground arrangements. Before doing this, get the latest fares from the airline, because the samples will invariably be out of date by the time you read them. If the brochure gives more than one category of sample fares per gateway city — such as an individual tour-basing fare, an excursion or other discount fare, or a group fare — your travel agent or airline tour desk will be able to tell you which one applies to the package you choose depending on when you travel, how far in advance you book, and other factors. (An individual tour-basing fare is a fare computed as part of a package that includes land arrangements, thereby entitling a carrier to reduce the air portion almost to the absolute minimum. Though it always represents a saving over full-fare coach or economy, lately it has not been as inexpensive as the excursion and other discount fares that are also available to individuals. The group fare is usually the least expensive fare, and it is the tour operator, not you, who makes up the group.) When the brochure does include round-trip transportation in the package price, don't forget to add the cost of round-trip transportation from your home city to the departure city to come up with the total cost of the package.

Finally, read the responsibility clause (usually in fine print at the end of the descriptive literature) to determine the precise elements for which the tour operator is — and is not — liable. Here the tour operator frequently expresses the right to change services or schedules as long as equivalent arrangements are offered. This clause also absolves the operator of responsibility for circumstances beyond human control, such as hurricanes or forest fires, or injury to you or your property. In reading, ask the following questions:

1. Does the tour include air fare or other transportation, sightseeing, meals, transfers, taxes, baggage handling, tips, or any other services? Do you want all these services?
2. If the brochure indicates that "some meals" are included, does this mean a welcoming and farewell dinner, two breakfasts, or every evening meal?
3. What classes of hotels are offered? If you will be traveling alone, what is the single supplement?
4. Does the tour itinerary or price vary according to the season?
5. Are the prices guaranteed; that is, if costs increase between the time you book and the time you depart, can surcharges unilaterally be added?
6. Do you get a full refund if you cancel? If not, be sure to obtain cancellation insurance.
7. Can the operator cancel if too few people join?

One of the consumer's biggest problems is finding enough information to judge the reliability of a tour packager, since individuals seldom have direct contact with the firm putting the package together. Usually, a retail travel agent intervenes between customer and tour operator, and much depends on his or her candor and cooperation. So ask a number of questions about the tour you are considering. For example: Has the agent ever used the package provided by this tour operator? How long has the operator been in business? Is the operator a member of the *United States Tour Operators Association* (*USTOA*)? (The *USTOA* will provide a list of its members upon request and also offers a useful brochure, *How to Select a Package Tour.* Contact the USTOA, 211 E. 51st St., Suite 12B, New York, NY 10022; phone: 212-944-5727. Also check the Better Business Bureau in your area to see if any complaints have been filed against the operator.) Which and how many companies are involved in the package? If air travel is by charter flight, is there an escrow account in which deposits will be held, and, if so, what is the name of the bank?

This last question is very important. The law requires that tour operators deposit every charter passenger's deposit and subsequent payment in a proper escrow account. Money paid into such an account cannot legally be used except to pay for the costs of a particular package or as a refund if the trip is canceled. To ensure the safe handling of your money, make your check payable to the escrow account — by law, the name of the depository bank appears in the operator-participant contract; it's usually found in that mass of minuscule type on the back of the brochure. Write the details of the charter, including the destination and dates, on the face of the check; on the back, print "For Deposit Only." Your travel agent may prefer that you make your check out to the agency, saying that it will then pay the tour operator the fee minus commission. But it is perfectly legal to write your check as we suggest, and if your agent objects too vociferously (the agent should have sufficient faith in the tour operator to trust him to send the proper commission), consider taking your business elsewhere. If you don't make your check out to the escrow account, you lose the protection of escrow should the trip be canceled or the tour operator or travel agent fail. Furthermore, recent bankruptcies in the travel industry have served to point out that even the protection of escrow may not be enough to safeguard a traveler's investment. Increasingly, insurance is becoming a necessity (see *Insurance*), and payment by credit card has become popular since it offers some additional safeguards if the tour operator defaults.

Camping and Hiking, Biking and RVs

CAMPING: Fifty-eight million Americans go camping every year, and that can mean anything from backpacking with a pup tent to living in comfort in a plush recreational vehicle. There are almost 17,000 campgrounds serving these campers, some private, many in national or state parks and forests.

Where to Camp – Campsites range from private facilities to state and national parks. For information on the national parks, send $1.25 to Consumer Information Center-J, PO Box 100, Pueblo, CO 81002, and request *National Park System Map and Guide* (doc. no. 151V). Another worthwhile booklet is *The National Parks: Camping Guide 1989-90* (doc. no. 024-005-01028-9), available for $3.50 from the Superintendent of Documents, US Government Printing Office, Washington, DC 20402. Most national parks (even the famous ones like Yosemite, Grand Canyon, and Yellowstone) have adjacent extensive national forests with the same beautiful country. A complete list of national forests appears in the free Forest Service brochure FS 13, *Field Offices of the Forest Service.* Write to US Forest Service, Publications, USDA, 12th and Independence St. SW, Room 3107, PO Box 96090, Washington, DC 20090-6090.

The National Park Service also encourages campers to use lesser-known national parks in its brochure *Lesser Known Areas of the National Park System* (doc. no. 024-005-00911-6; $1.50) from the Superintendent of Documents, US Government Printing Office, Washington, DC 20402.

Some excellent guides to both public and private campgrounds are: from Rand McNally: *Campground and Trailer Park Directory,* covering all of North America, including the US, Canada, and Mexico ($12.95); Prentice-Hall: *Allstate Motor Club: RV Park and Campground Directory* (national edition $14.95; western US $9.95; eastern US $9.95); Simon & Schuster: *Woodall's North American Campground Directory* ($12.95), *Eastern Campground Directory* ($8.95), and *Western Campground Directory* ($8.95). *Guide to the National Park Areas,* by David L. Scott and Kay W. Scott, is published in two editions, western and eastern (Globe Pequot Press, 138 W. Main St., Box Q, Chester, CT 06412; $10.95 each plus $2 postage and handling).

In addition, the *AAA* will provide its members with free camping guides that give practical hints and list campgrounds and facilities. It is now possible to reserve campsites at several national parks through Ticketron as well as through many National Park Service offices — a wise move in popular areas and during peak holiday times such as *Memorial Day, Independence Day,* and *Labor Day.*

Necessities – For outdoor camping, necessities include a tent with flyscreens (the lighter and easier to carry and assemble the better), a sleeping bag, foam pad or air mattress, waterproof ground cloth, first-aid kit (including insect repellent and sunscreen), sewing and toiletry kits, backpack stove (building fires is prohibited in many areas, especially during dry seasons), fuel (particularly where there is little wood, as in the desert), matches, nested cooking pots and utensils, canteen, jackknife, three-quarter ax (well sharpened and sheath-protected), and flashlight with an extra set of batteries.

Keep food simple. Unless backpacking deep into the wilderness, you will probably be close enough to a store to stock up on perishables; staples such as sugar, coffee, and powdered milk can be carried along. Most parks do not allow glass or tin containers. Dehydrated food has consequently become more popular, but it is also more expensive. An economical option for the more enterprising camper is to dry a variety of food at home; camping supply stores and bookstores carry cookbooks covering this simple process. Keep in mind that many national forest rangers warn about the dangers of leaving food in an area accessible to animals, repeating countless stories of scavenging bears and other wildlife invading tents and vehicles. As a basic safety precaution, it is advisable to hang foodstuffs from a tree some distance from your sleeping area.

Organized Trips – If you want to go far afield with an experienced guide and other campers, contact these organizations:

American Forestry Association, PO Box 2000, Dept. B, Washington, DC 20013-2000 (phone: 202-667-3300 or 800-368-5748)

American Wilderness Alliance, 7600 E. Arapahoe Rd., Suite 114, Englewood, CO 80112 (phone: 303-771-0380 or 800-322-WILD)

Appalachian Mountain Club, 5 Joy St., Boston, MA 02108 (phone: 617-523-0636)

Mountain Travel, 6420 Fairmont Ave., El Cerrito, CA 94530 (phone: 415-527-8100)

Nature Expeditions International, PO Box 11496, Eugene, OR 97440 (phone: 503-484-6529)

Outdoor Woman's School/Call of the Wild, 2519 Cedar St., Berkeley, CA 94708 (phone: 415-849-9292)

Sierra Club, 730 Polk St., San Francisco, CA 94109 (phone: 415-776-2211)

Yosemite Institute, PO Box 487, Yosemite, CA 95389 (phone: 209-372-4441)

HIKING: If you would rather eliminate all the gear and planning and take to the outdoors unencumbered, park the car and go for a day's hike. There are fabulous trails in the United States (some of the very best are listed in *Wilderness Trips on Foot,* DIVERSIONS). Backcountry Publications (PO Box 175, Woodstock, VT 05091) has a 15-book *Fifty Hikes* series covering New England, New York, New Jersey, Pennsylvania, and West Virginia, with maps, photos, and descriptions ($9.95 and $10.95). Globe Pequot Press (138 W. Main St., Box Q, Chester, CT 06412) also offers a series of hiking and walking guides; write for a catalogue.

To make outings safe and pleasant, find out about the trails you plan to hike and be realistic about your own physical limitations. Choose an easy route if you are out of shape. Stick to defined trails unless you are an experienced hiker or know the area well. If it is at all wild, let someone know where you are going and when you expect to be back, at least by leaving a note on your car if the hike is impromptu.

All you need to set out are a pair of sturdy shoes and socks, jeans or long pants to protect your legs, a waterproof poncho for rain showers, a canteen of water, a hat to protect you from the sun, and, if you like, a picnic lunch. It is a good idea to dress in layers so that you can add or remove clothing according to the elevation and weather. Make sure, too, to wear clothes with pockets or bring a pack to keep your hands free. Some useful and important pocket or pack stuffers include trail mix, a jackknife, first-aid kit, map, compass, and sunglasses. In areas where snakes are common, include a snake bite kit.

BIKING: In choosing bike routes, long or short, look for ways to escape the omnipresent automobile and its fumes and noise. Stick to back roads; use state highway maps which list secondary roads that the gas company maps ignore. Especially good riding is found along old canal roads, abandoned railroad right-of-ways, and hard, packed beaches. Two sources of bike routes and roads are *The Bicycle Touring Book* by Glenda and Tim Wilhelm (Rodale Press) and *American Biking Atlas & Touring Guide* by Sue Browder (Workman). Both are out of print, but check your library. For general biking information, try *The Complete Book of Bicycling* by Eugene A. Sloane (Simon & Schuster; $24.95) and *Anybody's Bike Book* by Tom Cuthbertson (Ten Speed Press; $7.95 paperback). For bicycle tours in New England and on the eastern seaboard, write for a catalogue from Backcountry Publications (PO Box 175, Woodstock, VT 05091) or from Globe Pequot Press (138 W. Main St., Box Q, Chester, CT 06412).

Road Safety – While the car may be the bane of cyclists, cyclists who do not follow the rules of the road strike terror into the hearts of drivers. Follow the same rules and regulations as automobile drivers. Stay to the right side of the road. Ride no more than two abreast — single file where traffic is heavy. Keep three bicycle lengths behind the cycle in front of you. Stay alert to sand, gravel, potholes, and wet or oily surfaces, all of which can make you lose control. Wear bright clothes and use lights or wear reflective material at dusk or at night, and, above all, always wear a helmet.

Choosing and Renting a Bike – Although many bicycling enthusiasts choose to take along their own bike, there are five basic types of bicycle available for rent — the children's fun bike, the domestic one-gear bike, the three-gear bike with caliper brakes, the touring bike with dropped handlebars and 5, 10, or even 15 gears, and the lightweight competition bike — although the 10-speed touring bike is the most common. Bike rental agencies are listed in the yellow pages of the phone directory. Bicycles must be picked up and dropped off at the same point, and the rental fee for a 10-speed generally runs between $10 and $15 a day. For these reasons, it may be a better idea to bring along your own bike.

A bicycle is the correct size if you can straddle its center bar with feet flat on the ground and still have an inch or so between your crotch and the bar. (Nowadays, because women's old-fashioned barless bikes are not as strong as men's, most women use men's bicycles.) The seat height is right if your leg is just short of completely extended when you push the pedal to the bottom of its arc. Experienced cyclists keep the tires fully inflated (pressure requirements vary widely, but are always imprinted on the side of the tire; stay within 5 pounds of the recommended pressure) and pedal at an even pace. For roadside repairs, and especially on longer rides, carry a tool kit that contains a bike wrench, screwdriver, pliers, tire repair kit, cycle oil, and work gloves. All are available in any bike shop.

To be completely comfortable, divide your weight; put about 50% on your saddle and about 25% on your arms and legs. To stop sliding in your seat and for better support, set your saddle level. A firm saddle is better than a soft springy one for a long ride. Do not use the top (usually the tenth) gear all the way; for most riding the middle gears are best. On long rides, remember that until you are very fit, short efforts with rests in between are better than one long haul.

If you are planning to travel by plane with your bicycle, be sure to check with the airline beforehand. It may require that the bike be partially dismantled and packaged and, although most carriers have procedures for handling such special baggage, you will probably have to pay for transport regardless of how much other baggage you have checked. As with other baggage, make sure that the bike is thoroughly labeled with your name, a business address and phone number, and the correct airport destination code (for further information, see *Traveling by Plane* in this section).

Tours – Cycling is a pleasant way to take in the scenery and get some exercise at the same time. In recent years, the cycling scene has considerably expanded in the US to include everything from competition rallies to long-distance guided tours. For information on variety of bicycle tours, contact one of the following:

Backroads Bicycle Touring, PO Box 1626-Q405, San Leandro, CA 94577 (phone: 415-895-1783), for Yellowstone, Glacier, Grand Canyon, and Bryce-Zion national parks, as well as California, Colorado, Alaska, Idaho, Oregon, New Mexico, Arizona, Montana, Washington, Wyoming, and Hawaii.

Country Cycling Tours, 140 W. 83rd St., New York, NY 10024 (phone: 212-874-

5151), for greater New York, Pennsylvania, Vermont, Maryland, Massachusetts, Rhode Island, Virginia, and Louisiana. One program combines bicycling with a windjammer cruise.

Vermont Bicycle Touring, Box 711, Bristol, VT 05443 (phone: 802-453-4811), for Vermont, Maine, New Hampshire, Connecticut, New York, California, and Hawaii.

Additional information on tours as well as general biking is available through biking clubs in almost every city in the country (listed in the yellow pages under "Clubs"). A national biking organization is the *League of American Wheelmen (LAW)*, which publishes a magazine for members, *Bicycle USA.* Contact LAW, Suite 209, 6707 Whitestone Rd., Baltimore, MD 21207 (phone: 301-944-3399).

RECREATIONAL VEHICLES: The term *recreational vehicles* — RVs — is applied to all manner of camping vehicles, whether towed or self-propelled. The level of comfort in an RV is limited only by the amount of money you choose to spend. They range from simple, fold-down campers providing shelter similar to a large tent to luxurious RVs, fully equipped homes on wheels, requiring electrical hookups at night to run the TV set and kitchen appliances.

RVs will appeal most to the kind of person who prefers the flexibility of accommodation — there are countless private, state, and national campgrounds throughout the country that provide RV hookups — and enjoys camping with a little extra comfort. An RV undoubtedly saves a traveler a great deal of money on accommodations and, if cooking appliances are part of the unit, on food as well. However, it is important to remember that buying or renting an RV is a major expense; also, any kind of RV increases gas consumption considerably.

Towable RVs – Tow vehicles are hitched to cars or trucks and pulled. At their simplest, they are fold-down campers, tents on wheels that unfold into sleeping spaces. Fold-down camping trailers weigh about 1,100 pounds and cost between $1,500 and $8,000, with an average price of $4,000. More elaborate are travel trailers, 10 to 30 feet long (average is about 22 feet), weighing up to 10,000 pounds and costing from $5,000 to $37,000, with an average price of $12,500. Fifth-wheel models, built to be towed by a pickup truck, range from $9,000 to $36,000, with an average price of $17,700. The park trailer, designed for seasonal or temporary living, sleeps up to 8 people and costs $14,000 to $26,000, with an average price of $16,900. The trailer should be equipped with brakes unless you expect that the combined weight of the trailer and its load will never exceed 3,000 pounds.

Motorized RVs – There are three styles of motorized vehicles:

1. The motor home is a recreational vehicle built on or as part of a motorized vehicle chassis. It usually has kitchen, dining, bathroom, and sleeping facilities, all accessible from the driver's area. Electricity, heat, air conditioning, water, and propane-gas systems are generally included. Prices for compact models average $30,000; larger, more luxurious models cost an average of $51,000.

2. Van conversions are vans manufactured by auto makers and modified for recreation by customization specialists. Among the custom features are side windows, carpeting, paneling, and sofas. These vehicles, which usually sleep 2 to 4 but have no cooking facilities, sell for an average of $20,600.

3. Also in this category are truck-campers — camping units that are loaded onto the bed of a pickup. They sleep 2 to 6, often have kitchen facilities, and range from $2,000 to $10,000. This may seem like the most economical option of the three; however, keep in mind that this cost is in addition to the initial investment in the pickup truck.

Gas Consumption – Although an RV undoubtedly saves the traveler a great deal of money on food and accommodations, the major expense is its high gas consumption.

It is most expensive to tow a large trailer camper, which decreases auto mileage by 50%. More economical, because it's smaller, is the fold-down tow camper, which will reduce normal car mileage by only about 10% to 15%. Self-propelled RVs have no better mileage records. A truck-camper gets about 20% less mileage than the same truck without a camper, and an average Class A motor home gets only 7 to 12 miles per gallon of gas. Only in a converted van will you find that your gas consumption does not change too drastically.

To reduce gas consumption, travel lightly (for every 100 pounds of weight, you use one percent more gas). Carry only the water you need on the road. Put everything inside your RV to reduce wind resistance and thereby save on gas.

Renting – RVs are a poor choice for people who do not like to drive. They are also not for people who want to leave housekeeping chores behind when they set off on vacation. They are sure to sour a person who cannot stand to do any maintenance or simple handyman chores, nor are they for people who need lots of privacy. The best way to introduce yourself to traveling by RV is to rent one. Some dealers will apply rental fees to the eventual price of purchase (check the yellow pages, then shop around for the best terms). A complimentary packet of information on how to operate, maintain, choose, and use a recreational vehicle is available from the *Recreational Vehicle Industry Association* (PO Box 2999, Reston, VA 22090).

You might also want to subscribe to *Trailer Life,* published by TL Enterprises, 29901 Agoura Rd., Agoura, CA 91301 (phone: 818-991-4980). A 1-year subscription costs $11.98; TL Enterprises also provides discounts on a variety of services for RV owners. For further information on how to operate, choose, and use a recreational vehicle, see Richard A. Wolters's *Living on Wheels* (Dutton; currently out of print; check your library).

Preparing

Calculating Costs

$ Estimating the cost of travel expenses in the US depends on the mode of transportation, what part of the country you plan to visit, how long you will stay there, and, in some cases, what time of the year you plan to travel. In addition to the basics of transportation, hotels, meals, and sightseeing, you have to take into account seasonal price changes that apply on certain air routings and at popular vacation destinations as well as inflation and corresponding price fluctuations. While the guidelines in this book will probably remain useful, costs for both facilities and services may have changed in the months since publication.

DETERMINING A BUDGET: A realistic appraisal of your travel expenses is the most crucial bit of planning before any trip. It is also, unfortunately, one for which it is most difficult to give precise practical advice. Travel styles are intensely personal, and personal taste determines cost to a great extent. Will you stay in a hotel every night and eat every meal in a restaurant, or are you planning to do some camping and picnicking, thus reducing your daily expenses? Base your calculations on your own travel style, and estimate your expenses from that. If published figures on the cost of travel were always considered gospel, many trips would not be taken. But in reality, it's possible to economize. On the other hand, don't be lulled into feeling that it isn't necessary to do some arithmetic before you go. No matter how generous your travel budget, without careful planning beforehand — and strict accounting along the way — you will spend more than you anticipated.

When calculating costs, start with the basics, the major expenses of transportation, accommodations, and food. However, don't forget such extras as local transportation, shopping, and miscellaneous items such as laundry, taxes, and tips.

The expenses for certain types of recreational activities may also figure heavily in your budgeting. Are you planning to spend time sightseeing and going to museums? Do you intend to rent a catamaran or take windsurfing lessons? Is daily tennis a part of your plan? Will your children be disappointed if they don't take a whale watching cruise? If so, charges for these attractions and recreations must be taken into account. Finally, don't forget that if haunting discos is an essential part of your vacation or you feel that one dinner show may not be enough, allow for the extra cost of nightlife.

Throughout the US, there is a great divergence in prices between metropolitan and rural areas. Any popular tourist destination is bound to be more expensive than areas off the beaten track. Sometimes venturing a bit farther afield can provide substantial economies; however, this may require more careful research and planning, as accommodations and facilities are likely to be more limited. For specific guidance on what is worth budgeting for where, see the individual city listings in THE CITIES as well as information in DIRECTIONS.

If at any point in the planning process it appears impossible to estimate expenses, consider this suggestion: The easiest way to put a ceiling on the price of some or all of the above is to buy a travel package. A totally planned and escorted one, with almost all transportation, rooms, meals, sightseeing, local travel, tips, and a dinner show or two included and prepaid, allows you to know beforehand almost exactly what the trip will cost, and the only surprise will be the one you spring on yourself by succumbing to some irresistible, expensive souvenir.

The various types of packages available are discussed under *Package Tours* in this section, but a few points bear repeating here. Not all packages are package *tours*. There are loosely organized arrangements that include nothing more than a stay at a hotel, transfers between hotel and airport, baggage handling, taxes, and tips, which leave the entire matter of how you spend your time and where you eat your meals — and with whom — up to you. Equally common are the condominium-plus-car packages, which take care of accommodations and local transportation. On such independent or hosted "tours," there may be a tour company representative available at a local office to answer questions, or a company host may be stationed at a desk in the hotel to arrange optional excursions, but you will never have to travel in a group unless you wish to. More and more, even experienced travelers are being won over to the idea of package travel, not only for the convenience and planning time saved, but above all for the money saved. Whatever elements you choose in your package, the organizer has gotten them for you wholesale, and they are prepaid, thus eliminating the dismal prospect of returning to your hotel room each night to subtract the day's disbursements from your remaining cash.

TRANSPORTATION: In earlier sections of GETTING READY TO GO, we discussed different modes of transportation and the myriad special rates available through package tours and charter flights. See each of the relevant sections for specific information. Transportation is likely to represent one of the largest items in your budget (cumulatively, only food and accommodations are likely to be higher), but the encouraging aspect of this is that you will be able to determine most of these costs before you leave. Fares — for plane, train, or bus — generally will have to be paid in advance, especially if you take advantage of charter air travel or other special deals.

Air fare is really the easiest cost to pin down precisely, though the range and variety of flights available may be confusing initially. The possibilities are outlined fully in *Traveling by Plane*. Essentially, you can choose from various types of tickets on scheduled flights, ranging in expense from first class and excursion fares to discount tickets and charters. Except for breakdown or repairs (for which you should budget something), car costs can be calculated by figuring mileage and average gas prices, based on your own experience.

FOOD: Meals are more difficult to estimate. If you stay in a condominium, you will be able to prepare some meals yourself. Depending on where you're staying, groceries can be more expensive than they are at home, but they will certainly be less expensive than eating out. Independent travelers eating all of their meals in restaurants should allow roughly $60 to $80 a day per couple for food. That includes breakfast (about $10 to $15 for two), lunch (about $15 to $20 for two), and an average dinner for two in a moderate, neither-scrimp-nor-splurge restaurant, not including alcoholic beverages or tips. You could easily add a beer and a glass of house wine to the dinner tab without wreaking havoc with these figures, but if you want the pick of the wine list or have a tendency to order lobster, expect the check, even in a moderate establishment, to run much higher. A steady diet of better restaurants will drive the average up higher still, but the figures can be revised downward, too, if you choose fruit for breakfast rather than bacon and eggs, put together your own picnic lunches for the beach, and frequently visit fast-food outlets. Our restaurant selections, chosen to give the best value for money — whether expensive or dirt cheap — are listed in the *Eating Out* section of each city chapter.

ACCOMMODATIONS: There is a wide range of choice and a substantial difference in degrees of luxury provided among the expensive, moderate, and inexpensive hotels.

Generally, all hotels of international chains in any given city are priced equally. In the larger cities (such as New York, Los Angeles, Chicago, and Miami), this ranges around $150 and up, although elsewhere deluxe hotels run from about $90 to $120 for a double. There is a big jump from these international class hotels to those in the moderate category in the same cities, and accommodations will generally be about $20 to $40 less per night. Inexpensive yet acceptable hotels in major cities charge about $50 for a double room. In small towns and rural areas these price ranges will be substantially lower. Also watch for budget motels, designed to offer basic accommodations at economy prices, where a double room may cost as little as $20 to $25 (for a list of some nationwide chains see *On the Road,* in this section). When inquiring about hotel rates, be certain to ask if they include local taxes and service charges. For specific information on accommodations throughout the US, see *Best in Town,* THE CITIES.

In addition to standard hotel accommodations, there is a wide range of camping facilities, rural inns, bed-and-breakfast establishments, and package options, including resorts catering to a variety of special interests and vacations on farms and ranches. For information on these and other adventures across the US, see DIVERSIONS.

■ **A note on our hotel/restaurant cost categories:** There are a great many moderate and inexpensive hotels and restaurants that we have not included in this book. Our *Best in Town* and *Best en Route* listings include only those places we think are best in their price range. We have rated our listings by general price categories: expensive, moderate, inexpensive. The introductory paragraph of each listing explains just what those categories mean within the context of local prices.

Planning a Trip

123 Travelers fall into two categories: those who make lists and those who do not. Some people prefer to plot the course of their trip to the finest detail, with contingency plans and alternatives at the ready. For others, the joy of a voyage is its spontaneity; exhaustive planning only lessens the thrill of anticipation and the sense of freedom.

However, for most travelers, a week-plus trip can be too expensive for an "I'll take my chances" type of vacation. Even perennial gypsies and anarchistic wanderers have to take into account the logistics of getting around, and even with minimal baggage, they need to think about packing. So at least some planning is crucial. This is not to suggest that you work out your itinerary in minute detail before you go; however, you still have to decide certain basics at the very start: where to go, what to do, and how much to spend. These decisions require a certain amount of consideration and planning. So before rigorously planning specific travel details, you might want to establish your general objectives:

1. How much time do you have for the entire trip, and how much of it do you want to spend in transit?
2. What interests and activities do you want to pursue? Do you want to visit one, a few, or several different places?
3. At what time of year do you want to go?
4. What kind of geography or climate would you like?
5. How much money can you spend for the entire vacation?
6. Do you want peace and privacy or lots of action and company?

Obviously, your answers will be determined by your personal tastes and lifestyle. These will resolve the degree of comfort you require; whether you will select a tour or opt for total independence; and how much responsibility you want to take for your own arrangements (or whether you want everything arranged for you, with the kinds of services provided in a comprehensive package trip).

There is no lack of travel information in and on the United States. You can turn to travel agents, who specialize in planning and arranging trips (see *How to Use a Travel Agent,* in this section), to travel clubs such as *AAA* and other motoring organizations that have tour centers, and to general travel sources like books, guidebooks, brochures, and maps. State tourist boards and city convention centers provide vast amounts of literature of this sort for the asking (for details on getting travel information and a bibliography of travel books and sources, see this section, *For More Information* and *State Tourist Offices;* for city convention and tourist centers, see the *Sources and Resources* section of each city report in THE CITIES).

You can now make almost all of your own travel arrangements if you have the time to follow through with hotels, airlines, tour operators, and so on. But you'll probably save considerable time and energy if you have a travel agent make the reservations and arrangements for you. The agent should also be able to advise you about alternative arrangements of which you may not be aware. Only rarely will a travel agent's services cost any money, and they may even save you some (see *How to Use a Travel Agent*). Well before departure (depending on how far in advance you make your reservations), the agent will deliver a packet that includes all your tickets and hotel confirmations and often a day-by-day outline of where you'll be when, along with a detailed list of whatever flights you're taking.

Make plans early. If you are flying and hope to take advantage of the considerable savings offered through discount fares or charter programs, you may need reservations as much as 3 months in advance. In high season, and in popular destinations, hotel and resort reservations are required months in advance. The more specific your requirements, the farther ahead you should book. (To get your first choice of accommodations inside *Walt Disney World,* for example, you might need to book as much as a year in advance if your vacation falls during one of the three or four busiest weeks of the year.) Hotels require deposits before they will guarantee reservations. Be sure you have a receipt for any deposit.

While making vacation arrangements is fun and exciting, don't forget to prepare for your absence from home. Before you leave, attend to these household matters:

1. Arrange for your mail to be forwarded, held by the post office, or picked up daily at your home. Someone should check your door occasionally to collect any unexpected deliveries. Piles of mail or packages announce to thieves that no one is home.
2. Cancel all deliveries (newspapers, milk, and so on).
3. Arrange for your lawn to be mowed and plants to be watered at regular intervals.
4. Arrange for the care of pets.
5. Etch your social security number on all appliances (television sets, radios, cameras, kitchen appliances). This considerably reduces their appeal to thieves and facilitates identification.
6. Leave a house key, your itinerary, and your automobile license number (if you are driving your own car) with a relative or friend. Notify the police, the building manager, or a neighbor that you are leaving and tell them who has the key and your itinerary.
7. Empty the refrigerator and lower the thermostat.
8. Immediately before leaving, check that all doors, windows, and garage doors are securely locked.

To discourage thieves further, it is wise to set up several variable timers around the house so that lights and even the television set go on and off several times in different rooms of the house each night.

Make a list of any valuable items you are carrying with you, including credit card numbers and the serial numbers of your traveler's checks. Put copies in your purse or pocket and leave copies at home. Put a label with your name and home address inside your luggage to provide identification in case of loss. Put your name and business address — *never your home address* — on a label on the outside of your luggage.

Review your travel documents. If you are traveling by air, check to see that your ticket has been filled in correctly. The left side of the ticket should have a list of each stop you will make (even if you are stopping only to change planes), beginning with your departure point. Be sure that the list is correct, and count the number of carbons to see that you have one for each plane you will take. If you have confirmed reservations, be sure that the column marked Status says "OK" beside each flight. Have in hand vouchers or proof of payment for any reservation for which you've paid in advance; this includes hotels, transfers to and from the airport, sightseeing tours, car rentals, and special events.

If you are traveling by car, bring your driver's license, auto registration, proof of insurance, gasoline credit cards and auto service card if you have them, maps, guidebooks, flashlight, an extra set of batteries, emergency flasher, container of water, jack and spare tire, first-aid kit, extra car keys, and sunglasses. (For more information on preparing for a journey by car, see *Touring by Car,* in this section).

If you are traveling by plane, call to reconfirm your flight 72 hours before departure, both going and returning. This will not prevent you from getting bumped in case the flight is overbooked (see *Traveling by Plane*).

Finally, you should always bear in mind that despite the most careful plans, things do not always occur on schedule. If you maintain a flexible attitude at all times, shrug cheerfully in the face of postponements and cancellations, you will enjoy yourself a lot more.

How to Use a Travel Agent

T.A. A reliable travel agent remains your best source of service and information for planning a trip, whether you have a specific itinerary and require an agent only to make reservations or need extensive help in sorting through the maze of air fares, tour offerings, hotel packages, and the score of other elements that may be involved in your trip.

You should know what you want from a travel agent so that you can evaluate what you are getting. It is perfectly reasonable to expect your travel agent to be a thoroughly knowledgeable travel specialist, with information about your destination and, even more crucial, a command of current air fares, ground arrangements, and other wrinkles in the travel scene. Most travel agents work through computer reservations systems (CRS) to assess the availability and rates of flights, hotels, and car rental firms, and can book reservations through the CRS. Despite reports of "computer bias," in which a computer may favor one airline over another, the CRS should provide agents with the entire spectrum of alternative flights to a destination and the complete range of fares in considerably less time than it takes to telephone the airlines individually — and at no extra charge to the client.

To make the most intelligent use of a travel agent's time and expertise, you should know something of the economics of the industry. As a client, you traditionally pay nothing for the agent's services; with few exceptions it's all free, from advice on package tours to hotel bookings. Any money that the travel agent makes on the time spent arranging your itinerary — booking hotels, resorts, or flights or suggesting activities — comes from commissions paid by the suppliers of these services — the airlines, hotels, and so on. These commissions generally run from 8% to 20% of the total cost of the service, although suppliers often reward agencies that sell their services in volume with an increased commission called an override.

Among the few exceptions to the general rule of free service by a travel agency are the agencies beginning to practice *net pricing*. In essence, these agencies return all of their commissions and overrides to their customers and make their income by charging a flat fee per transaction (thus adding a charge after a reduction has been made). Sometimes the rebate from the agent arrives later, in the form of a check. Net pricing, however, has become rather controversial since a major airline refused to do business with a leading proponent of net pricing and the courts supported this action (see *Net Fare Sources*).

Net fares and fees are a very recent and not very widespread practice, but even a conventional travel agent may sometimes charge you a fee for such special services as long-distance telephone or cable costs incurred in making a booking, for reserving a room in a place that does not pay a commission (such as a small, out-of-the-way hotel), or for special attention such as planning a highly personalized itinerary. A fee may also be assessed in instances of deeply discounted air fares. In most instances, however, you'll find that travel agents make their time and experience available to you at no charge, and you pay no more for an airline ticket, package tour, or other product bought from a travel agent than you would for the same product bought directly from the supplier.

The commission system implies two things about your relationship with any travel agent.

1. You will get better service if you arrive at the agent's desk with your basic itinerary already planned. Know roughly where you want to go, what you want to do, and how much you want to spend. Use the agent to make bookings (which pay commissions) and to advise you on facilities, activities, and alternatives within the limits of your itinerary. You get the best service when you are requesting commissionable items. Since there are few commissions on camping or driving-camping tours, an agent is unlikely to be very enthusiastic about helping to plan one. The more vague your plans, the less direction you can expect from most agents. If you walk into an agency and say, "I have two weeks in June; what shall I do?" you will most likely walk out with nothing more than a handful of brochures. So do a little preliminary homework.

2. Be wary. There is always the danger that an incompetent or unethical agent will send you to the place offering the best commissions rather than the best facilities for your purposes. The only way to be sure you are getting the best service is to pick a good, reliable travel agent, one who knows where to go for information if he or she is unfamiliar with an area — although most agents are familiar with destinations throughout the US.

You should choose a travel agent with the same care with which you would choose a doctor or lawyer. You will be spending a good deal of money on the basis of the agent's judgment, so you have a right to expect that judgment to be mature, informed, and interested. At the moment, unfortunately, there aren't many standards within the travel agent industry to help you gauge competence, and the quality of individual agents varies enormously. At present, only seven states have registration, licensing, or other form of travel agent–related legislation on their books. Rhode Island licenses travel agents; Florida, Hawaii, and Ohio register them; and California, Illinois, and Washington have laws governing the sale of transportation or related services. While state licensing cannot absolutely guarantee competence, it can at least ensure that an agent has met some minimum requirements.

Perhaps the best-prepared agents are those who have completed the CTC Travel Management program offered by the *Institute of Certified Travel Agents* and carry the initials CTC (Certified Travel Counselor) after their names. This indicates a relatively high level of expertise. For a free listing of CTCs in your area, send a self-addressed, stamped, #10 envelope to ICTA, 148 Linden St., Box 82-56, Wellesley, MA 02181 (phone: 617-237-0280).

An agent's membership in the *American Society of Travel Agents (ASTA)* can be a useful guideline in your selection. But keep in mind that *ASTA* is an industry organization, requiring only that its members be licensed in those states where required; be accredited to represent the suppliers whose products they sell, including airline and cruise tickets; and adhere to its Principles of Professional Conduct and Ethics code. *ASTA* does not guarantee the competence, ethics, or financial soundness of its members, but it does offer some recourse if you feel you have been dealt with unfairly. Complaints may be registered with ASTA, Consumer Affairs Dept., PO Box 23992, Washington, DC 20026-3992 (phone: 703-739-2782). But first try to resolve the complaint directly with the supplier. For a list of *ASTA* members in your area, send a self-addressed, stamped, #10 envelope to ASTA, Public Relations Dept., at the address above. There is also the *Association of Retail Travel Agents (ARTA)*, a smaller but highly respected trade organization similar to *ASTA.* Its member agencies and agents similarly agree to abide by a Code of Ethics, and complaints about a member can be made to ARTA's Grievance Committee, 25 S. Riverside Ave., Croton-on-Hudson, NY 10520 (phone: 914-271-HELP).

Agencies listed with the *National Association of Cruise Only Agencies (NACOA)* have demonstrated professionalism in the selling of cruises. For a listing of cruise-only agencies in your state (requests are limited to three states), send a self-addressed, stamped envelope to NACOA, PO Box 7209, Freeport, NY 11520. Agencies that belong to a travel consortium, such as *Associated Travel Nationwide* and *Travel Trust International,* have access to preferred rates, as do the huge networks of *American Express* and *Ask Mr. Foster* agencies.

A number of banks own travel agencies, too, that provide the same services as other accredited commercial travel bureaus. Anyone can become a client, not only the bank's customers. You can find out more about these agencies, which belong to the *Association of Bank Travel Bureaus,* by inquiring at your bank or looking in the yellow pages.

Perhaps the best way to find a travel agent is by word of mouth. If the agent (or agency) has done a good job for your friends over a period of time, it probably indicates a certain level of commitment and competence. Always ask not only for the name of the company but for the name of the specific agent with whom your friends dealt, for it is that individual who will serve you, and quality can vary widely within a single agency. There are some superb travel agents in the business, and they can greatly facilitate vacation or business arrangements.

Once you've made an initial selection, be entirely frank and candid with the agent. Budget considerations rank at the top of the candor list, and there's no sense in wasting the agent's (or your) time poring over itineraries that you know you can't afford. Similarly, if you like a fair degree of comfort, that fact should not be kept secret from your travel agent, who may assume that you wish to travel on a tight budget even when that's not the case.

Insurance

 It is unfortunate that most decisions to buy travel insurance are impulsive and usually made without any real consideration of your existing policies. Too often the result is the purchase of needlessly expensive short-term policies that duplicate existing coverage and reinforce the tendency to buy coverage on a trip-by-trip basis rather than to work out a total and continuing travel insurance package that might well be more effective and economical.

Therefore, the first person with whom you should discuss travel insurance is your own insurance broker, not a travel agent or the clerk behind the airport insurance counter. You may well discover that the insurance you already carry — homeowner's policies and/or accident, health, and life insurance — protects you adequately while you travel, and that your real needs are in the more mundane areas of excess value insurance for baggage or trip cancellation insurance.

To make insurance decisions intelligently, however, you should first understand the basic categories of travel insurance and what they are designed to cover. Then you can decide what you should have in the broader context of your personal insurance needs, and you can choose the most economical way of getting the desired protection: through riders on existing policies; with one-time short-term policies; through a special program put together for the frequent traveler; through coverage that's part of a travel club's benefits; or with a combination policy sold by insurance companies through brokers, automobile clubs, tour operators, and travel agents.

There are seven basic categories of travel insurance:

1. Baggage and personal effects insurance
2. Personal accident and sickness insurance
3. Trip cancellation and interruption insurance
4. Default and/or bankruptcy insurance
5. Flight insurance (to cover death or injury)
6. Automobile insurance (for driving your own or a rented car)
7. Combination policies

Baggage and Personal Effects Insurance – Ask your agent if baggage and personal effects are included in your current homeowner's policy or if you will need a special floater to cover you for the duration of a trip. The object is to protect your bags and their contents in case of damage or theft any time during your travels, not just while you're in flight and covered by the airline's policy. Furthermore, only limited protection is provided by the airline. Baggage liability varies from carrier to carrier, but generally speaking, for domestic air travel, luggage is insured to $1,250 — that's per passenger, not per bag. On international flights, the liability limit is $9.07 per pound of baggage (which comes to about $360 per 40-pound suitcase) and up to $400 per passenger for unchecked baggage. These limits should be specified on your airline ticket, but to be awarded even this amount, you'll have to provide an itemized list of lost property, and if you're including new and/or expensive items, be prepared for a request that you back up your claim with sales receipts or other proofs of purchase.

If you are carrying goods worth more than the maximum protection offered by the airline, you should consider excess value insurance, available from the airlines at an average, currently, of $1 per $100 worth of coverage. This insurance can be purchased at the airline counter when you check in, though you should arrive early to fill out the necessary forms and to avoid holding up other passengers checking in. Excess value insurance is also included in some of the combination travel insurance policies discussed below.

■ **A Note of Warning:** Be sure to read the fine print of any excess value insurance policy; there are often specific exclusions, such as cash, tickets, furs, gold and silver objects, art, and antiques. And remember that insurance companies ordinarily will pay only the depreciated value of the goods rather than their replacement value. The best way to protect the items in your luggage is to take photographs of your valuables, and keep a record of the serial numbers of such items as cameras, typewriters, radios, and so on. This will establish that you do, indeed, own the objects. If your luggage disappears en route or is damaged, deal with the situation immediately, at the airport or bus station. If an airline loses your luggage, you will be asked to fill out a Property Irregularity Report before you leave the airport. If your property disappears elsewhere, report it to the police at once.

Personal Accident and Sickness Insurance – This covers you in case of illness during your trip or death in an accident. Most policies insure you for hospital and doctor's expenses, lost income, and so on. In most cases it is a standard part of existing health insurance policies, though you should check with your broker to be sure that your policy will pay for any medical expenses incurred. If not, you can take out a separate vacation accident policy or an entire vacation insurance policy that includes health and life coverage.

Trip Cancellation and Interruption Insurance – Although modern public charters have eliminated many of the old advance booking requirements, most charter and package tour passengers still pay for their travel well in advance of departure. The disappointment of having to miss a vacation because of illness or any other reason pales before the awful prospect that not all (and sometimes none) of the money paid in advance might be returned. So cancellation insurance for any package tour is a must. Although cancellation penalties vary (they are listed in the fine print in every tour brochure, and before you purchase a package tour you should know exactly what they are), rarely will a passenger get more than 50% of this money back if forced to cancel within a few weeks of leaving. Therefore, if you book a package tour or charter flight, you should have trip cancellation insurance to guarantee full reimbursement or refund should you, a traveling companion, or a member of your immediate family get sick, forcing you to cancel your trip or *return home early*. The key here is not to buy just enough insurance to guarantee full reimbursement for the cost of the package or charter in case of cancellation. The proper amount of coverage should be sufficient to reimburse you for the cost of having to catch up with a tour after its departure or having to travel home at the full economy air fare if you have to forgo the return flight of your charter. There is usually quite a discrepancy between a charter air fare and the amount necessary to travel the same distance on a regularly scheduled flight at full economy fare.

Trip cancellation insurance is available from travel agents and tour operators in two forms: as part of a short-term, all-purpose travel insurance package (sold by the travel agent); or as specific cancellation insurance designed by the tour operator for a specific charter tour. Generally, tour operators' policies are less expensive, but also less inclusive. Cancellation insurance is also available directly from insurance companies or their agents as part of a short-term, all-inclusive travel insurance policy.

Before you decide which policy you want, read each one carefully. (Either can be purchased from a travel agent when you book the charter or package tour.) Be certain that the policy you select includes enough coverage to pay your fare from the farthest destination on your itinerary should you have to miss the charter flight. Also, be sure to check the fine print for stipulations concerning "family members" and "pre-existing medical conditions," as well as allowance for living expenses if you must delay your return due to bodily injury or illness.

Default and/or Bankruptcy Insurance – Although trip cancellation insurance usually protects you if you are unable to complete — or depart on — your trip, a fairly recent innovation is coverage in the event of default and/or bankruptcy on the part of the tour operator, airline, or other travel supplier. In some travel insurance packages, this contingency is included in the trip cancellation portion of the coverage; in others, it is a separate feature. Either way, it is becoming increasingly important. Whereas sophisticated travelers have long known to beware of the possibility of default or bankruptcy when buying a charter flight or tour package, in recent years more than a few respected scheduled airlines have unexpectedly revealed their shaky financial condition, sometimes leaving hordes of stranded ticketholders in their wake. Moreover, the value of escrow protection of a charter passenger's funds has lately been unreliable. While default/bankruptcy insurance will not ordinarily result in reimbursement in time to pay for new arrangements, it can ensure that you will eventually get your money back, and even independent travelers buying no more than an airplane ticket may want to consider it.

Should this type of coverage not be available to you (state insurance regulations vary, there is a wide variation in price, and so on), the best bet is to pay for airline tickets and tour packages with a credit card. The federal Fair Credit Billing Act permits purchasers to refuse payment for credit card charges where services have not been delivered, so the potential onus of dealing with a receiver for a bankrupt airline falls on the credit card company. Do not assume that another airline will automatically honor the ticket you're holding on a bankrupt airline, since the days when virtually all major carriers subscribed to a default protection program are long gone. Some airlines may voluntarily step forward to accommodate stranded passengers, but this is now an entirely altruistic act.

Flight Insurance – Airlines have carefully established limits of liability for the death or injury of passengers. For international flights, they are printed right on the ticket: a maximum of $75,000 in case of death or injury. For domestic flights, the limitation is established by state law, with a few states setting unlimited liability. But remember, these limits of liability are not the same thing as insurance policies; they merely state the *maximum* an airline will pay in the case of death or injury, and every penny of that is usually subject to a legal battle.

This may make you feel that you are not adequately protected, but before you buy last-minute flight insurance from an airport vending machine, consider the purchase in light of your total existing coverage. A careful review of your current policies may reveal that you are already amply covered for accidental death, sometimes up to three times the amount provided for by the flight insurance you're buying in the airport.

Be aware that airport insurance, the kind typically bought at a counter or from a vending machine, is among the most expensive form of life insurance coverage available, and that even within a single airport, rates for approximately the same coverage vary widely. Often the vending machines are more expensive than coverage sold over the counter, even when policies are with the same national company.

If you buy your plane ticket with an American Express, Carte Blanche, or Diners Club credit card, you are automatically issued life and accident insurance at no extra cost. American Express automatically provides $100,000 in insurance; Carte Blanche provides $150,000 and Diners Club provides $350,000. Additional coverage can be obtained at extremely reasonable prices, but a cardholder must sign up for it in advance. With American Express, $4 per ticket buys an additional $250,000 worth of flight insurance; $6.50 buys $500,000 worth; and $13 provides an added $1 million worth of coverage. Carte Blanche and Diners Club each offer an additional $250,000 worth of insurance for $4; $500,000 for $6.50. Both also provide $1,250 free insurance — over and above what the airline will pay — for checked baggage that's lost or damaged. American Express provides $500 coverage for checked baggage; $1,250 for carry-ons.

Automobile Insurance – If you have an accident in a state that has "no fault" insurance, each party's insurance company pays his or her expenses up to certain specified limits. When you rent a car, the rental company is required to provide you with collision protection. In your car rental contract, you'll see that for about $10 to $12 a day, you may buy optional collision damage waiver (CDW) protection to relieve you of all responsibility for any damage to the rental car. If you do not accept the CDW coverage, you may be liable for as much as the full retail cost of the car you're renting. Before agreeing to this coverage, however, check your own auto insurance policy. It may very well cover your entire liability exposure without any additional cost, or you automatically may be covered by the credit card company (American Express, or premium cards from Visa or MasterCard) to which you are charging your rental.

Combination Policies – Short-term insurance policies, which may include any combination or all of the types of insurance discussed above, are available through retail insurance agencies, automobile clubs, and many travel agents. These combination policies are designed to cover you for the duration of a single trip.

One such policy available to US and Canadian residents is offered by *Travel Guard International*. Endorsed by the *American Society of Travel Agents* (*ASTA*) and underwritten by the Insurance Company of North America, the comprehensive combination policy is available through authorized travel agents or by calling *Travel Guard International* directly at 800-826-1300 or 715-345-0505.

How to Pack

 No one can provide a completely foolproof list of precisely what to pack, so it's best to let common sense, space, and comfort guide you. Keep one maxim in mind: Less is more. You simply won't need as much clothing as you think, and though there is nothing more frustrating than arriving at your destination without just that item that in its absence becomes crucial, you are far more likely to need a forgotten accessory — or a needle and thread or scissors — than a particular piece of clothing.

As with almost anything relating to travel, a little planning can go a long way. There are specific things to consider before you open the first drawer or fold the first piece of underwear:

1. Where are you going (city, country, or both)?
2. How many total days will you be gone?
3. What's the average temperature likely to be during your stay?

The goal is to remain perfectly comfortable, neat, clean, and adequately fashionable wherever you go, but actually to pack as little as possible. The main obstacle to achieving this end is habit: Most of us wake each morning with an entire wardrobe hanging in our closets, and we assume that our suitcase should offer the same variety and selection. Not so; only our anxiety about being caught short makes us treat a suitcase like a mobile closet. This worry can be eliminated by learning to travel light and by following two firm packing principles:

1. Organize your travel wardrobe around a single color — blue or brown, for example — that allows you to mix and match clothes. Holding firm to one color scheme will make it easy to eliminate items of clothing that don't harmonize, and by picking clothes for their adaptability and compatibility with your basic color, you will put together the widest selection with the fewest pieces of clothing.
2. Use laundries to replenish your wardrobe. Never overpack to ensure a supply of fresh clothing — shirts, blouses, underwear — for each day of a long trip. Businesspeople routinely use hotel laundries or dry-cleaning services to wash and clean clothes. If these are too expensive, opt for local self-service laundries.

CLIMATE AND CLOTHES: Exactly what you pack on your trip will be a function of where you are going and when and the kinds of things you intend to do. As a first step, however, find out about the general weather conditions — temperature, rainfall, seasonal variations — at your destination, as a few degrees can make all the difference between being comfortably attired and very real suffering. This information is included in the individual city reports of THE CITIES; other sources of information are airlines, travel agents, state tourist offices, and local convention and visitors bureaus.

Keeping temperature and climate in mind, consider the problem of luggage. Plan on one suitcase per person (and in a pinch, remember that it's always easier to carry two small suitcases than to schlepp one roughly the size of the *QE2*). Standard 26- to 28-inch suitcases can be made to work for 1 week or 1 month, and unless you are going for no more than a weekend, never cram wardrobes for two people into one suitcase.

Throughout the United States life is quite casual, and only at the most elegant resorts will you be required to have dressy clothes. Accessorize everything beforehand so you know exactly what you will be wearing with what. If you are planning to be on the move — either in a car, bus, train, or plane — consider loose-fitting clothes that do not wrinkle. Perishable clothes — of pure cotton and linen — are hard to keep up and should be left behind. Lightweight wools, manmade fabrics such as jerseys and knits, and drip-dry fabrics travel best (although in very hot climates cotton clothing may be the most comfortable, and prints look fresher longer than solids.

Women should figure on a maximum of five daytime and three late afternoon–evening changes. Whether you are going to be gone for a week or a month, this number should be enough. Again, before packing, lay out every piece of clothing you think you might want to take. Eliminate items that don't mix, match, or interchange within your color scheme. If you can't wear it in at least two distinct incarnations, leave it at home.

Men will find that color coordination is crucial. Solid colors coordinate best, and a sport jacket that also goes with a pair of pants from a suit provides an added option. Hanging bags are best for suits and jackets, and shirts should be chosen that can be used for both daytime and evening wear. Double-duty shoes are also preferable.

Finally, prepare for changes in the weather or for atypical temperatures; for instance, if you're going on a day's outing in the mountains, where it is cooler, dress in layers so that as the weather changes you can add or remove clothes as required.

Pack clothes that have a lot of pockets for traveler's checks, documents, and tickets. If your bag gets lost or stolen, you will still have the essentials. It is a good idea to wear loose-fitting clothes that can be rinsed in Woolite or a similar cold-water detergent and hung to drip dry. And be sure to have comfortable shoes. Pack lightweight sandals for beach and evening wear. It is permissible to wear your most comfortable shoes almost everywhere.

Your carry-on luggage should contain a survival kit with the basic things you will need in case your luggage gets lost or stolen: a toothbrush, toothpaste, medication, a sweater, nightclothes, and a change of underwear. With all of your essential items at hand at all times, you will be prepared for any unexpected occurrence that separates you from your suitcase. If you have many 1- or 2-nighters, you can live out of your survival case without having to unpack completely at each hotel.

Sundries – If you are heading for a sunny climate, pack special items so you won't spend your entire vacation horizontal in a hotel room (or hospital) because of sunburn. Be sure to take a sun hat (to protect hair as well as skin), sunscreen, and tanning lotion, which is available in graduated degrees of sunblock corresponding to the level of your skin's sensitivity. (The quantity of sunscreen is indicated by number: the higher the number, the greater the protection.) A good moisturizer is necessary to help keep your skin from drying out and peeling. The best advice is to take the sun's rays in small doses — no more than 20 minutes at a stretch — increasing your time as your vacation progresses. Also, if you are heading for a vacation on skis, don't underestimate the effect of the sun's glare off snowy slopes, especially in higher altitudes — the exposed areas of your face and neck are particularly susceptible to a painful burn.

PACKING: The basic idea of packing is to get everything into the suitcase and out again with as few wrinkles as possible. Simple, casual clothes — shirts, jeans and slacks, permanent-press skirts — can be rolled into neat, tight sausages that keep other suitcase items in place and leave the clothes themselves amazingly unwrinkled. The rolled clothes can be retrieved, shaken out, and hung up at your destination. However, for items that are too bulky or too delicate for even careful rolling, a suitcase can be packed from bottom up to ensure the most protection for everything. Put heavy items on the bottom toward the hinges so that they do not wrinkle other clothes. Candidates for the bottom layer include shoes (stuff them with small items to save space), a toiletry kit, handbags (stuff them to help keep their shape), and an alarm clock. Fill out this layer with things that will not wrinkle or will not matter if they do, such as sweaters, socks, a bathing suit, gloves, and underwear.

If you get this first, heavy layer as smooth as possible with the fill-ins, you will have a shelf for the next layer, or the most easily wrinkled items, like slacks, jackets, shirts, dresses, and skirts. These should be buttoned and zipped and laid along the whole length of the suitcase with as little folding as possible. When you do need to make a fold, do it on a crease (as with pants), along a seam in the fabric, or where it will not show, such as shirttails. Alternate each piece of clothing, using one side of the suitcase, then the other, to make the layers as flat as possible. On the top layer put the things you will want at once: nightclothes, an umbrella or raincoat, and a sweater.

With men's two-suiter suitcases, follow the same procedure. Then place jackets on hangers, straighten them out, and leave them unbuttoned. If they are too wide for the suitcase, fold them lengthwise down the middle, straighten the shoulders, and fold the sleeves in along the seam.

SOME PACKING HINTS: Some travelers like to have at hand a small bag with the basics for an overnight stay, particularly if they are flying. Always keep necessary medicine, valuable jewelry, and travel or business documents in your purse, briefcase, or carry-on bag, not in the luggage you will check. Tuck a bathing suit into your handbag, too; in case of lost baggage, it's frustrating to be without one. And whether in your overnight bag or checked luggage, cosmetics and any liquids should be packed in plastic bottles or at least wrapped in plastic bags and tied.

Golf clubs and skis may be checked through as luggage (most airlines are accustomed to handling them), but tennis rackets should be carried onto the plane. Aqualung tanks, appropriately packed with padding and depressurized, and surfboards (minus the fin and also padded) may also go as baggage. Snorkeling gear should be packed in a suitcase. Some airlines require that bicycles be partially dismantled and packaged. Check with the airline before departure to see if there is a specific regulation for any special equipment or sporting gear you plan to take.

It is always a good idea to add an empty, flattened airline bag or similar piece of luggage to your suitcase; you'll find it indispensable as a beach bag. Keep in mind, too, that you're likely to do some shopping, and save room for those items.

For more information on packing clothes, send your request with a #10 stamped, self-addressed envelope to *Samsonite Travel Advisory Service* (PO Box 39609, Dept. 80, Denver, CO 80239) for its free booklet, *Getting a Handle on Luggage*.

Hints for Handicapped Travelers

From 35 to 50 million people in the US have some sort of disability, and at least half this number are physically handicapped. Like everyone else today, they — and the uncounted disabled millions around the world — are on the move. More than ever before, they are demanding facilities they can use comfortably, and they are being heard. The travel industry has dramatically improved services to the handicapped in the past few years, and though accessibility is far from universal, it is being brought up to more acceptable standards every day.

PLANNING A TRIP: Good planning is essential: Collect as much information as you can about your specific disability and about facilities for the disabled in the area you're visiting, make your travel arrangements well in advance, and specify to all services involved the exact nature of your condition or restricted mobility; your trip will be much more comfortable if you know that there are accommodations and facilities to suit your needs. The best way to find out if your intended destination can accommodate a handicapped traveler is to write or phone the local tourist association or hotel and ask specific questions. If you require a corridor of a certain width to maneuver a wheelchair or if you need handles on the bathroom walls for support, ask the hotel manager. A travel agent or the local chapter or national office of the organization that deals with your particular disability — for example, the American Foundation for the Blind or the American Heart Association — will supply the most up-to-date information on the subject. In addition, the following sources offer general information on access:

Access to the World by Louise Weiss, published by Facts on File, 460 Park Ave. S., New York, NY 10016 (phone: 212-683-2244), costs $16.95 and can be ordered by phone with a credit card. Henry Holt also now publishes Weiss's excellent book in paperback; check with your bookstore.

Access Travel: A Guide to the Accessibility of Airport Terminals, published by the Airport Operators Council International, provides information on more than 200 airports worldwide with ratings according to 70 features, including accessibility to bathrooms, corridor width, and parking spaces. For a free copy, write to the Consumer Information Center, Access America, Dept. 571T, Pueblo, CO 81009, or call 202-293-8500 and ask for Item 571T–Access Travel. To help travel agents plan trips for the handicapped, this material is reprinted with additional information on tourist boards, city information offices, and tour operators specializing in travel for the handicapped (see "Tours," below) in the North American edition of the *Official Airline Guides Travel Planner,* issued quarterly by Official Airline Guides, 2000 Clearwater Dr., Oak Brook, IL 60521 (phone: 312-574-6000).

Information Center for Individuals with Disabilities (ICID), Ft. Point Pl., 1st Fl., 27-43 Wormwood St., Boston, MA 02210 (phone: 617-727-5540/1 or 800-462-5015 in Massachusetts only; both voice and TDD — telecommunications device for the deaf). *ICID* provides information and referral services on disability-related issues and will help you research your trip. The center publishes fact sheets on vacation planning, tour operators, travel agents, and travel resources.

The Itinerary is a travel magazine for people with disabilities. Published bimonthly, it includes information on accessibility, tour listings, news of adaptive devices, travel aids, and special services as well as numerous general travel hints. A subscription is $10 a year; write to The Itinerary, PO Box 1084, Bayonne, NJ 07002-1084 (phone: 201-858-3400).

A List of Guidebooks for Handicapped Travelers is a free listing of useful publications for the disabled, compiled by the President's Committee on Employment of People with Disabilities, 1111 20th St. NW, Suite 636, Vanguard Bldg., Washington, DC 20036.

Mobility International/USA (MIUSA), the US branch of Mobility International, a nonprofit British-based organization with affiliates in some 35 countries, offers advice and assistance to disabled travelers, including information on accommodations, access guides, and study tours. Among its publications are a quarterly newsletter and a comprehensive sourcebook, *World of Options, A Guide to International Educational Exchange, Community Service, and Travel for Persons with Disabilities.* Individual membership is $20 a year; subscription to the newsletter alone is $10 annually. For more information, contact MIUSA, PO Box 3551, Eugene, OR 97403 (phone: 503-343-1284, voice and TDD — telecommunications device for the deaf).

National Rehabilitation Information Center provides general information and referral services to the disabled. For information, write or call the center, 8455 Colesville Rd., Suite 935, Silver Spring, MD 20910 (phone: 301-588-9284).

The Paralyzed Veterans of America (PVA) is a national organization that offers information and advocacy services for veterans with spinal cord injuries. *PVA* also sponsors *Access to the Skies,* a program that coordinates the efforts of the national and international air travel industry in providing airport and airplane access for the handicapped. Members also receive several helpful publications as well as regular notification of conferences on subjects of interest to the handicapped traveler. For membership information, contact PVA/ATTS Program, 801 18th St. NW, Washington, DC 20006 (phone: 202-USA-1300).

Society for the Advancement of Travel for the Handicapped (SATH), 26 Court St., Penthouse, Brooklyn, NY 11242 (phone: 718-858-5483). To keep abreast of developments in travel for the handicapped as they occur, you may want to join *SATH,* a nonprofit organization whose members include travel agents, tour operators, and other travel suppliers, as well as consumers. Membership costs $40 ($25 for students·and travelers who are 65 and older), and the fee is tax deductible. *SATH* publishes a quarterly newsletter, an excellent booklet, *Travel Tips for the Handicapped,* and provides information on travel agents and tour operators in the US and overseas who have experience (or an interest) in travel for the handicapped. *SATH* also offers a free 48-page guide, *The United States Welcomes Handicapped Visitors,* that covers transportation, accommodations, insurance, and customs regulations. Send a self-addressed, #10 envelope to *SATH* at the address above, and include $1 for postage.

The *Travel Information Service* at Moss Rehabilitation Hospital is designed to help physically handicapped people plan trips. It cannot make travel arrangements but, for a nominal fee per package, it will supply information from its files on as many as three cities, countries, or special interests. Write to the Travel Information Service, Moss Rehabilitation Hospital, 12th St. and Tabor Rd., Philadelphia, PA 19141 (phone: 215-456-9600).

TravelAbility, by Lois Reamy, is a vast database with information on locating tours for the handicapped; coping with public transport; and finding accommodations, special equipment, and travel agents. It also offers a step-by-step planning guide for the handicapped traveler. Previously published by Macmillan, *TravelAbility* is currently out of print but may be available at your library.

It should be noted that almost all of the material published with disabled travelers in mind deals with the wheelchair-bound traveler, for whom architectural barriers are a prime concern. For travelers with diabetes, a pamphlet entitled *Ticket to Safe Travel* is available for 50¢ from the New York Diabetes Association, 505 8th Ave., 21st Fl., New York, NY 10018 (phone: 212-947-9707). Another, *Travel for the Patient with Chronic Obstructive Pulmonary Disease,* is available for $2 from Dr. Harold Silver, 1601 18th St. NW, Washington, DC 20009 (phone: 202-667-0134). For blind travelers, *Seeing Eye Dogs as Air Travelers* can be obtained free from the Seeing Eye, Box 375, Washington Valley Rd., Morristown, NJ 07960 (phone: 201-539-4425).

A few more basic resource directories to look for are *Travel for the Disabled* by Helen Hecker ($9.95), and by the same author, *The Directory of Travel Agencies for the Disabled* ($12.95). *Wheelchair Vagabond* by John G. Nelson is another useful guidebook for travelers confined to a wheelchair (softcover, $9.95; hardcover, $14.95). All three are published by Twin Peaks Press, PO Box 129, Vancouver, WA 98666; to order, call 800-637-CALM. Additionally, *The Physically Disabled Traveler's Guide* by Rod W. Durgin and Norene Lindsay is helpful and informative. Available from Resource Directories, 3361 Executive Pkwy., Suite 302, Toledo, OH 43606 (phone: 419-536-5353), for $9.95, plus $2 for postage and handling.

PLANE: Advise the airline that you are handicapped when you book your flight. The Federal Aviation Authority (FAA) has ruled that US airlines must accept disabled and handicapped passengers as long as the airline has advance notice and the passenger represents no insurmountable problem in the emergency evacuation procedures. As a matter of course, American airlines were pretty good about helping handicapped passengers even before the ruling, although each airline has somewhat different procedures. Ask for specifics when you book your flight.

Disabled passengers should always make reservations well in advance and should give the airline all the relevant details of their condition at that time. Such details include information on mobility, toilet needs, special oxygen needs, and requirements for airline-supplied equipment such as a wheelchair or portable oxygen. Be sure that the person you speak to understands fully the degree of your disability: the more details provided, the more effective the help the airline can give you. On the day before the flight, call back to make sure that all arrangements have been taken care of, and on the day of the flight, arrive early so that you can board before the rest of the passengers. Carry a medical certificate with you, stating your specific disability or the need to carry a particular medicine. (Some airlines require the certificate, and you should find out the rules of the airline you'll be flying with well beforehand.)

Because most airports have jetways (corridors connecting the terminal with the door of the plane), a disabled passenger can usually be taken as far as the plane, and sometimes right onto it, in a wheelchair. If not, a narrow boarding chair may be used to take you to your seat. Your own wheelchair, which will be folded and put in the baggage compartment, should be tagged as escort luggage to ensure that it's available at planeside upon landing rather than in the baggage claim area. Travel is not quite as simple if your wheelchair is battery-operated: Unless it has non-spillable batteries, it might not be accepted on board, and you will have to check with the airline ahead of time to find out how the batteries and the chair should be packaged for the flight. Usually people in wheelchairs are asked to wait until other passengers have disembarked. If you are making a tight connection, be sure to tell the attendant.

Passengers who use oxygen may not use their personal supply in the cabin, though it may be carried on the plane as cargo when properly packed and labeled. If you will need oxygen during the flight, the airline will supply it to you (there is a charge) provided you have given advance notice — 24 hours to a few days, depending on the carrier.

Several airlines now have booklets describing procedures for accommodating the handicapped on their flights. For example, United Airlines has a list of travel tips for the handicapped; contact United Airlines, Consumer Affairs Dept., PO Box 66100, Chicago, IL 60666 (phone: 312-952-6796). Useful information on every stage of air travel, from planning to arrival, is provided in the booklet *Incapacitated Passengers Air Travel Guide*. To receive a free copy, write to Senior Manager, Passenger Services, International Air Transport Assn., 2000 Peel St., Montreal, Quebec H3A 2R4, Canada (phone: 514-844-6311). For an access guide to over 200 airports worldwide, write for *Access Travel: A Guide to the Accessibility of Airport Terminals*, published by the Airport Operators Council International (see listing above). *Air Transportation of Handicapped Persons* explains the general guidelines that govern air carrier policies. It is available free when requested in writing: Ask for Free Advisory Circular #120-32 from the Distribution Unit, US Department of Transportation, Utilization and Storage Section, M-443.2, Washington, DC 20590). For speedy service, enclose a self-addressed mailing label with your request.

The following airlines have TDD (telecommunications device for the deaf) toll-free lines for the hearing-impaired: American (phone: 800-543-1586; in Ohio, 800-582-1573); Pan American (phone: 800-722-3323); Piedmont (phone: 800-334-5874); TWA (phone: 800-421-8480; in California, 800-252-0622); and United (phone: 800-323-0170; in Illinois, 800-942-8819).

GROUND TRANSPORTATION: Perhaps the simplest solution to getting around is to travel with an able-bodied companion who can drive. If you are accustomed to driving your own hand-controlled car and want to rent one, you are in luck. Some rental companies will fit cars with hand controls. *Avis* can convert a car to hand controls with as little as 24 hours' notice, though it's a good idea to arrange for one earlier (phone: 800-331-1212). *Hertz* requires a minimum of 5 days to install the controls, and makes the additional stipulation that the car be returned to the office from which it was rented (phone: 800-654-3131). Neither company charges extra for hand controls, but both will fit them only on a full-size car, and both request that you bring your handicapped driver's permit with you. Other car rental companies provide hand-control cars at some locations; however, as there are usually only a limited number available, call well in advance.

Taking taxis or hiring a chauffeured car are other solutions to the mobility problem. Contact local transportation authorities for information on special van or bus services for disabled travelers.

TRAIN: *Amtrak* offers handicapped travelers a 25% discount on round-trip full-fare tickets. Whether you're riding a reserved or unreserved train, call in advance to make special arrangements or to reserve *Amtrak*'s special seats for disabled travelers. The newer *Amtrak* cars, such as the *Amfleet* trains and *Metroliners* (on the New York–Washington, DC, route), are boarded on the level at most stations. In other parts of the country, you will need to get *Amtrak* personnel to help with steps. Wheelchairs are available at most stations. Most of *Amtrak*'s fleet consists of new cars with special seats, properly equipped bathrooms, and special sleeping compartments for the handicapped. Older equipment, however, presents many barriers, and a traveling companion can make the trip much easier. If necessary, *Amtrak* will recommend a professional traveling companion. Seeing Eye and hearing-guide dogs may ride in the passenger cars at no extra charge, but a seat must be reserved for the dog. *Access Amtrak,* a brochure, can be requested from the Amtrak Distribution Center, PO Box 7717, Itasca, IL 60143 (phone: 800-USA-RAIL). To request a wheelchair or other assistance, call 800-USA-RAIL 24 hours before departure.

BUS: *Greyhound Lines* offers special tickets whereby the disabled passenger and a companion travel for the price of only one fare if they have the same itinerary. The disabled passenger must have a doctor's letter certifying the disability and stating that one companion is enough to help with getting on and off the bus. (If you can manage the bus steps on your own, you are not required to have a companion.) *Greyhound* will carry nonmotorized folding wheelchairs for free; call for information regarding motorized wheelchairs. A free brochure, *Helping Hand Services for the Handicapped,* is available from Greyhound Lines, Customer Relations Office, 901 Main St., Suite 2500, Dallas, TX 75202 (phone: 800-345-3109).

If you are traveling to national parks and are receiving or are eligible to receive federal benefits to the disabled, ask for the Golden Access Passport at any park that charges an entrance fee. The passport (good for life, but not available by mail) entitles you and your traveling companions to free admission and a 50% discount on such facilities as camping and boat launching.

TOURS: Programs designed for the physically impaired are run by specialists who have researched hotels, restaurants, and places of interest to be sure they present no insurmountable obstacles. The following travel agencies or tour operators specialize in making group or individual arrangements for travelers with physical or other disabilities. Because of the requirements of handicapped travel, however, the same packages may not be offered regularly.

Access: The Foundation for Accessibility by the Disabled, PO Box 356, Malverne, NY 11565 (phone: 516-887-5684). Travelers referral service that acts as an intermediary with tour operators and agents worldwide. Also provides information on accessibility at various locations.

Accessible Tours/Directions Unlimited, 720 N. Bedford Rd., Bedford Hills, NY 10507 (phone: 914-241-1700 in New York State; 800-533-5343 elsewhere). Arranges group or individual tours for disabled persons traveling in the company of able-bodied friends or family members. Accepts the unaccompanied traveler if completely self-sufficient.

Evergreen Travel Service, 19595L 44th Ave. W., Lynnwood, WA 98036-5699 (phone: 206-776-1184; 800-562-9298 in Washington State; 800-435-2288 elsewhere in the US). The oldest company in the world offering worldwide tours and cruises for the disabled (Wings on Wheels) and sight impaired/blind (White Cane Tours). Most programs are first class or deluxe and include escort by the owner or his family.

Flying Wheels Travel, 143 W. Bridge St., Box 382, Owatonna, MN 55060 (phone: 507-451-5005 or 800-533-0363). Handles both tours and individual arrangements.

The Guided Tour, 555 Ashbourne Rd., Elkins Park, PA 19117 (phone: 215-782-1370). Arranges tours for persons with developmental and learning disabilities, and sponsors separate tours for members of the same population who are also physically disabled or who simply need a slower pace.

Handi-Travel, First National Travel Corporation, 300 John St., Thorn Hill, Ontario L3T 5W4, Canada (phone: 416-731-4714). Handles tours and individual arrangements.

InterpreTours, Ask Mr. Foster, 16660 Ventura Blvd., Encino, CA 91436 (phone: 818-788-4118 for voice; 818-788-5328 for TDD — telecommunications device for the deaf). Arranges independent travel, cruises, and tours for the deaf, with an interpreter as tour guide.

Sprout, 204 W. 20th St., New York, NY 10011 (phone: 212-431-1265). Arranges travel programs for mildly and moderately disabled adults, 18 years of age and over.

Travel Horizons Unlimited, 11 E. 44th St., New York, NY 10017 (phone: 212-687-5121 in New York; 800-847-4257 elsewhere). Travel agent and registered nurse Mary Ann Hamm sets up individual trips for travelers requiring all types of kidney dialysis and handles arrangements for the dialysis.

Whole Person Tours, PO Box 1084, Bayonne, NJ 07002-1084 (phone: 201-858-3400 or 800-462-2237). Handicapped owner Bob Zywicki travels the world with his wheelchair and offers a lineup of escorted tours (many by himself) for the disabled. Also the publisher of *The Itinerary,* a bimonthly newsletter for disabled travelers (a 1-year subscription costs $10).

Hints for Single Travelers

 Just about the last trip in human history in which the participants were neatly paired was the voyage of Noah's Ark. Ever since, passenger lists and tour groups have reflected the same kind of asymmetry that occurs in real life, as countless individuals set forth to see the world unaccompanied (or unencumbered, depending on your outlook) by spouse, lover, friend, or relative.

There are some things to be said for traveling alone. There is the pleasure of privacy, though a solitary traveler must be self-reliant, independent, and responsible. Unfortunately, traveling alone can also turn the traveler into a second class citizen.

The truth is that the travel industry is not very fair to people who vacation by themselves. People traveling alone almost invariably end up paying more than individuals traveling in pairs. Most travel bargains, including package tours, hotel accommodations, resort packages, and cruises, are based on *double-occupancy* rates. This means that the per-person price is offered on the basis of two people traveling together and sharing a double room (which means they will each spend a good deal more on meals and extras). The single traveler will have to pay a surcharge, called a single supplement, for exactly the same package. In extreme cases, this can add as much as 30% to 50% to the basic per-person rate. As far as the travel industry is concerned, single travel has not yet come into its own.

There are, however, countless thousands of individuals who *do* travel alone. Inevitably, their greatest obstacle is the single supplement charge, which prevents them from cashing in on travel bargains available to anyone traveling as part of a pair. The obvious, most effective alternative is to find a traveling companion. Even special "singles' tours" that promise no supplements are based on people sharing double rooms. If you are interested in finding another traveler to help share the cost, consider contacting the travel agents listed below. Some charge fees, others are free, but the basic service offered by all is the same: to match the unattached person with a compatible travel mate. The better established among these agencies are:

Cosmos: This agency offers a guaranteed-share plan whereby singles who wish to share rooms (and avoid paying the single supplement) are matched by the tour escort with like-minded individuals of the same sex. Contact *Cosmos* at one of its three North American branches: 95-25 Queens Blvd., Rego Park, NY 11374 (phone: 800-221-0090 from the eastern US); 150 S. Los Robles Ave., Pasadena, CA 91101 (phone: 818-449-2019 or 800-556-5454); 1801 Eglinton Ave. W., Suite 104, Toronto, Ontario, Canada M6E 2H8 (phone: 416-787-1281).

Grand Circle Travel: Arranges escorted cruise/air packages for "mature" travelers, including singles. Membership, which is automatic when you book a trip through *Grand Circle,* includes a free subscription to its quarterly magazine, discount certificates on future trips, and other extras. Grand Circle Travel, 347 Congress St., Boston, MA 02210 (phone: 617-350-7500 or 800-221-2160).

Jane's International: This service puts potential traveling companions in touch with one another. No age limit, no fee. Jane's International, 2603 Bath Ave., Brooklyn, NY 11214 (phone: 718-266-2045).

Saga International Holidays: An organization for seniors over 60, including singles. Members receive the club magazine, which includes a classified section aimed at helping lone travelers find suitable traveling companions. A 3-year membership costs $5. Saga International Holidays, 120 Boylston St., Boston, MA 02116 (phone: 617-451-6808 or one of the following nationwide toll-free numbers: for reservations, 800-343-0273; for customer service, 800-441-6662; for brochure requests, 800-248-2234).

Singleworld: About two-thirds of this agency's clientele are under 35, and about half this number are women, but *Singleworld* organizes tours and cruises with departures categorized by age group. The annual membership fee is $20. Singleworld, 401 Theodore Fremd Ave., Rye, NY 10580 (phone: 914-967-3334 or 800-223-6490 in the continental US).

Travel Companion Exchange: Every 8 weeks this company publishes a directory of singles looking for traveling companions and provides members with full-page profiles of likely partners. Membership fees range from $3 to $11 per month (with a 6-month minimum enrollment), depending on the level of service required. Travel Companion Exchange, PO Box 833, Amityville, NY 11701 (phone: 516-454-0880).

Travel Mates International: Will search for and arrange shares on existing package tours for men and women of any age; will also organize group tours for its clients. Annual fee is $15. Travel Mates International, 49 W. 44th St., New York, NY 10036 (phone: 212-221-6565).

Womantours: Run by feminist Estilita Grimaldo. As its name implies, this agency puts together group and individual travel programs for women exclusively. Womantours, 5314 N. Figueroa St., Los Angeles, CA 90042 (phone: 213-255-1115).

A special book by Eleanor Adams Baxel, *A Guide for Solo Travelers Abroad* (Berkshire Traveller Press; out of print, so check your library), offers information on how to avoid paying supplementary charges, how to pick the right travel agent, how to calculate costs, and much more.

CRUISES: Certain cruise lines have a sort of standby service for singles; you pay only the usual per-person charge for a double cabin if it has not been sold to a couple. *Cunard* offers this service on the *Princess* and the *Countess* (phone: 212-661-7777 in NY; 800-221-4770 elsewhere). *Royal Cruise Line,* 1 Maritime Plaza, Suite 1400, San Francisco, CA 94111 (phone: 415-956-7200; 800-622-0538 in California), offers a guaranteed share rate for singles.

WOMEN AND STUDENTS: Two specific groups of single travelers deserve special mention: women and students. Countless women travel by themselves, and such an adventure need not be feared. You will generally find people very courteous and welcoming, but remember that crime is a national problem. Keep a careful eye on your belongings while on the beach; lock your car and hotel doors; deposit your valuables in the hotel's safe; and don't hitchhike.

One lingering inhibition many female travelers still harbor is that of eating alone in public places. The trick here is to relax and enjoy your meal and surroundings; while you may run across the occasional unenlightened waiter, solo diners are no longer an uncommon sight or scorned. *The Women's Travel Guide: 25 American Cities* by Jane Lasky and Brenda Fine (G. K. Hall; $24.95 hardcover; $12.95 paperback) is aimed at the growing number of women travelers. Another useful book, offering lively, helpful advice on female solo travel, is *The Traveling Woman,* by Dena Kaye. Though out of print, it may be found in your library.

Students traveling on a strict budget have a few accommodation options. They can stay at one of the many *YMCA* or *YWCA* residences throughout the country. But note that membership is often required if you plan to stay more than a day or two. Students and singles should also keep in mind that youth hostels exist in many cities throughout the US. They are run by the hosteling associations of some 60-plus countries that make up the *International Youth Hostel Federation* (*IYHF*); membership in one of the national groups allows access to hostels all over the world. *IYHF* hostels serve travelers of all ages under a self-help system. Visitors carry their own gear, provide their own services, and contribute to the upkeep of the hostel by performing a small domestic chore. To join the American affiliate, *American Youth Hostels* (*AYH*), write to the national office, PO Box 37613, Washington, DC 20013-7613 (phone: 202-783-6161). The cost of membership in *AYH* varies, depending on the type of membership and age category, but generally annual fees are $10 for Youth memberships (17 and under), $20 for Adult (18-54), and $10 for Senior (55 and up). A $1 mailing charge should be added to each membership fee cited above. The *AYH Handbook,* which lists hostels in the US, comes with your *AYH* card. Information on international hostels is not included with membership.

Travelers who are (or have been) students of accredited colleges and universities elsewhere might consider taking some college courses in the state they're visiting, which may qualify them for campus housing. For full details, contact the department in charge of summer semester programs at the school you'd like to attend. Typically, summer semester bulletins go out in February.

Hints for Older Travelers

 Special package deals and more free time are just two factors that have given Americans over age 65 a chance to see the world at affordable prices. Senior citizens make up an ever-growing segment of the travel population, and the trend among them is to travel more frequently and for longer periods of time. No longer limited by 3-week vacations or the business week, they can take advantage of off-season, off-peak travel, which is both less expensive and more pleasant than traveling in high season. Particularly attractive are cruises, wherein the crew takes care of all details, and special programs like *Greyhound*'s Ameripass, which offers unlimited travel for a fixed period of time (see *Touring by Bus*).

When planning a vacation, prepare your itinerary with one eye on your own physical condition and the other on a topographical map. Keep in mind variations in climate, terrain, and altitudes, which may pose some danger for anyone with heart or breathing problems.

An excellent book to read before embarking on any trip is Rosalind Massow's *Travel Easy: The Practical Guide for People Over 50,* available for $8.95 (plus $1.75 postage and handling per order, not per book) from AARP Books, c/o Scott, Foresman, 1865 Miner St., Des Plaines, IL 60016 (phone: 202-728-4313 or 800-238-2300). It discusses a host of subjects, from choosing a destination to getting set for departure, with chapters on transportation options, tours, cruises, avoiding health problems, and handling dental emergencies en route. Another book, *The International Health Guide for Senior Citizens,* covers such topics as trip preparations, food and water precautions, adjusting to weather and climate conditions, finding a doctor, motion sickness, and jet lag. The book also discusses specific health and travel problems, and includes a list of resource organizations that can provide medical assistance for travelers; it is available for $4.95 postpaid from Pilot Books, 103 Cooper St., Babylon, NY 11702 (phone: 516-422-2225). A third book on health for older travelers, Rosalind Massow's excellent *Now It's Your Turn to Travel*, has a chapter on medical problems. Previously published by Collier Books, it is out of print but available in libraries. Also, see *Medical and Legal Aid* in this section. An excellent guide for the budget-conscious older traveler is *The Discount Guide for Travelers Over 55* by Caroline and Walter Weintz (Dutton; $7.95).

Travel Tips for Senior Citizens (State Dept. publication 8970), a booklet with general advice, is available for $1 from the Superintendent of Documents, US Government Printing Office, Washington, DC 20402 (phone: 202-783-3238). The booklet *101 Tips for the Mature Traveler* is available free from Grand Circle Travel, 347 Congress St., Suite 3A, Boston, MA 02210 (phone: 617-350-7500 or 800-221-2610).

HEALTH: Be sure to take along any prescription medication you need, enough to last *without a new prescription* for the duration of your trip; pack all medications separately in a carry-on bag in case your luggage is lost or detoured, along with a note from your doctor for the benefit of airport authorities. It is also wise to bring a few common over-the-counter medications with you: aspirin and something for stomach upset may come in handy. Keep in mind that Medicare coverage operates nationwide. If you have specific medical problems, bring prescriptions and a "medical file" composed of the following:

1. A summary of your medical history, current diagnosis.
2. A list of drugs to which you are allergic.
3. Your most recent electrocardiogram if you have heart problems.
4. Your doctor's name, address, and telephone number.

■ **A word of caution:** Don't overdo it. Allow time for some relaxing each day to refresh yourself for the next scheduled sightseeing event. Traveling across time zones can be exhausting, and adjusting to major climatic changes can make you feel dizzy and drained. Plan on spending at least one full day resting before you start touring. If you're part of a group tour, be sure to check the planned itinerary thoroughly. Some package deals sound wonderful because they include all the places you've ever dreamed of visiting. In fact, they can become so hectic and tiring that you'll be reaching for a pillow instead of your camera.

DISCOUNTS AND PACKAGES: Senior citizens with identification are eligible for a huge variety of discounts in every city across the country. Although the rules change from place to place and city to city, acceptable proof of eligibility (or age) is usually a driver's license, a membership card in a recognized senior citizens' organization such as the *American Association of Retired Persons* (see below), or a Medicare card. Because senior citizen discounts are common but by no means standard, always ask about them before you pay — whether it's for a subway in Philadelphia or a campsite in Colorado. Discounts are available at hotels, for local transportation in most American cities, for concerts, movies, museums, and dozens of other activities.

The National Park Service has a free Golden Age Passport, which entitles people over 62, and those in the car with them, to free entrance to all national parks and monuments as well as to discounts on campsites (available by showing a Medicare card or driver's license as proof of age at any national park). Some states also offer free hunting and fishing licenses to retired persons.

Many hotel and motel chains, airlines, car rental companies, bus lines, and other travel suppliers offer discounts to older travelers. Some of these discounts, however, are extended only to bona fide members of certain senior citizens organizations. Because the same organizations offer package tours to both domestic and international destinations, the benefits of membership are twofold. Those who join can take advantage of discounts as individual travelers and also reap the savings that group travel affords. In addition, because the age requirements for some of these organizations are quite low (or nonexistent), the benefits can begin to accrue early. Among the organizations dedicated to helping you see the world are:

American Association of Retired Persons (*AARP*): The largest and best known of these organizations, membership is open to anyone 50 or over, whether retired or not. *AARP* offers travel programs, designed exclusively for senior citizens, that cover the globe and include a broad range of escorted tours, hosted tours, and cruises. Dues are $5 a year, or $12.50 for 3 years, and include spouse. For membership information, contact the AARP at 1909 K St. NW, Washington, DC 20049 (phone: 202-347-8800); for travel information and reservations, contact AARP Travel Service, PO Box 29233, Los Angeles, CA 90009 (phone: 213-322-7323 or 800-227-7737).

Grandtravel: This agency specializes in trips for older people and their grandchildren (aunts and uncles are welcome, too), helping to bring the generations together through travel. Ten itineraries that coincide with school vacations emphasize historic and natural sites. Transportation, accommodations, and activities are thoughtfully arranged to meet the needs of the young and the young at heart. Grandtravel, 6900 Wisconsin Ave., Suite 706, Chevy Chase, MD 20915 (phone: 301-986-0790 in Maryland; 800-247-7651 elsewhere).

Mature Outlook: This organization has replaced the *National Association of Mature People.* Through its *Travel Alert,* last-minute tours, cruises, and other vacation packages are available to members at special savings. Hotel and car rental discounts and travel accident insurance are also available. Membership is open to anyone 50 years of age or older, costs $9.95 a year, and includes its bimonthly newsletter and magazine as well as information on package tours. Mature Outlook, Customer Service Center, 60001 N. Clark St., Chicago, IL 60660 (phone: 800-336-6330).

National Council of Senior Citizens: Here, too, the emphasis is always on keeping costs low. The roster of tours offered is different each year and its travel service will also book individual tours for members. Although most members are over 50, membership is open to anyone, regardless of age, for an annual fee of $12 per person or $16 per couple. Lifetime membership costs $150. National Council of Senior Citizens, 925 15th St. NW, Washington, DC 20005 (phone: 202-347-8800).

Certain travel agencies and tour operators specialize in group travel for older travelers. For example, *Gadabout Tours,* 700 E. Tahquitz Way, Palm Springs, CA 92262 (phone: 619-325-5556; 800-521-7309 in California; 800-952-5068 elsewhere), operated by Lois Anderson, offers a variety of tours throughout the US. *Grand Circle Travel* and *Saga International Holidays* are two other such operators that cater to the over-50 market (see *Hints for Single Travelers*).

Many travel agencies, particularly the larger ones, are delighted to make presentations to help a group select destinations. A local chamber of commerce should be able to provide the names of such agencies. Once a time and place are determined, an organization member or travel agent can obtain group quotations for transportation, accommodations, meal plans, and sightseeing. Groups of 40 or more usually get the best breaks.

Another choice open to older travelers is a trip that includes an educational element. *Elderhostel,* 80 Boylston St., Suite 400, Boston, MA 02116 (phone: 617-426-7788), a nonprofit organization, offers educational programs at a huge number of schools throughout the US. Programs run for one week and usually feature three different courses of study. Accommodations are in residence halls, and meals are taken in student cafeterias. Elderhostelers must be at least 60 years old (younger if a spouse or companion qualifies), in good health, and not in need of special diets.

Hints for Traveling with Children

 What better way to be receptive to new experiences than to take along the young, wide-eyed members of your family? Their company does not have to be a burden or their presence an excessive expense. The current generation of discounts for children and family package deals can make a trip together quite reasonable.

A family trip will be an investment in your children's future, making geography and history come alive to them and leaving a sure memory that will be among the fondest you will share with them someday. Their insights will be refreshing to you; their impulses may take you to unexpected places with unexpected dividends. The experience will be invaluable to them at any age.

It is necessary to take some extra time beforehand to prepare children for travel. Here are several hints for making a trip with children easy and fun.

1. Children, like everyone else, will derive more pleasure from a trip if they know something about the places they will see. Begin their education about a month

before you leave, using maps, travel magazines, and travel books, giving them a clear idea of where you are going and how far away it is. Part of the excitement of the journey will be associating the tiny dots on the map with the very real places the children visit a few weeks later. You can show them pictures of streets and scenes in which they will stand within a month. Don't shirk history lessons, but don't burden them with dates. Make history light, anecdotal, pertinent, but most of all, fun. If you simply make materials available and keep your vacation destination and your travel plans a topic of everyday conversation, your children will absorb more than you realize.

2. Children should help plan the itinerary, and where you go and what you do should reflect some of their ideas. If they know enough about the sites they'll visit beforehand, they will have the excitement of recognition when they arrive and the illumination of seeing how something is or is not the way they expected it to be.

3. Give children specific responsibilities. The job of carrying their own flight bags and looking after their personal things, along with some other light chores, will give them a stake in the journey. Tell them how they can be helpful when you are checking in or out of hotels.

4. Give each child a travel diary or scrapbook to take along. Filling these with impressions, observations, and mementos will pass the time on trains and planes and help the children to assimilate their experiences.

PACKING: Choose your children's clothes much as you would your own. Select a basic color (perhaps different for each child) and coordinate everything with it. Plan their wardrobes with layering in mind — shirts and sweaters that can be taken off and put back on as the temperature varies. Take only drip-dry, wrinkle-resistant items that they can manage themselves and comfortable shoes — sneakers and sandals. Younger children will need more changes, but keep it to a minimum. No one likes to carry added luggage (remember that you will have to manage most of it!).

Take as many handy snacks as you can squeeze into the corners of your suitcases — things like dried fruit and nut mixes, hard candies, peanut butter, and crackers — and moist towelettes for cleaning. Don't worry if your supply of nibbles is quickly depleted. Airports and bus and train stations are well stocked with such items.

Pack a special medical kit (see *Medical Assistance*), including children's aspirin or acetaminophen, an antihistamine or decongestant, Dramamine, and diarrhea medication. Diapers are available at department stores and children's stores. A selection of baby foods is available in most supermarkets, but in the event that you may not be able to find the instant formula your child is accustomed to, bring along a supply in the 8-ounce "ready-to-feed" cans. Disposable nursers are expensive but handy. If you breast-feed your baby, there is no reason you can't continue on your trip; be sure you get enough rest and liquids.

Good toys to take for infants are the same things they like at home — well-made, bright huggables and chewables; for small children, a favorite doll or stuffed animal for comfort, spelling and counting games, and tying, braiding, and lacing activities; for older children, playing cards, travel board games with magnetic pieces, and hand-held electronic games. Softcover books and art materials (crayons, markers, paper, scissors, glue sticks, stickers) ward off boredom for children of most ages, as do radio-cassette players with headphones. Take along a variety of musical and storytelling cassettes, extra batteries, and maybe even an extra set of headphones so that two children can listen. *Advice:* Avoid toys that are noisy, breakable, or spillable, those that require a large play area, and those that have lots of little pieces that can be scattered and lost. When traveling, coordinate activities with attention spans; dole out playthings one at a time so you don't run out of diversions before you get where you're going. Children become restless during long waiting periods, and a game plus a small snack —

such as a box of raisins or crackers — will help keep them quiet. It is also a good idea to carry tissues, Band-Aids, a pocket medicine kit, and moistened washcloths.

GETTING THERE AND GETTING AROUND: Begin early to investigate all available discount and charter flights, as well as any package deals and special rates offered by the major airlines. Booking is sometimes required up to 2 months in advance. You may find that charter plans offer no reductions for children, or not enough to offset the risk of last-minute delays or other inconveniences to which charters are subject. The major scheduled airlines, however, almost invariably provide hefty discounts for children (for specific information on fares and flight accommodations for children, see *Traveling by Plane*).

PLANE: When you make your reservations, let the airlines know that you are traveling with a child. Generally, infants under 2 years of age fly free if they sit on the lap of an obliging adult. However, on longer flights, this may not be comfortable. (A second infant without a second adult would pay the fare applicable to children 2 through 11, usually 75% of the adult fare.) For children 2 to 11, prices vary for promotions when children with an adult fly free or at a deep discount (usually during January and February) or when family fares extend discounts to spouses as well.

If traveling with an infant, request a bulkhead seat, and ask for a bassinet. Request seats on the aisle if you have a toddler or if you think you will need to use the bathroom frequently. (Try to discourage children from being in the aisle when meals are served.) Carry onto the plane all you will need to care for and occupy your children during the flight — diapers, formula, "lovies," books, sweaters, and so on. (Never check as baggage any item essential to a child's well-being, such as prescription medicine.) Dress your baby simply, with a minimum of buttons and snaps, because the only place you may have to change a diaper is at your seat. The flight attendant can warm a bottle for you.

Just as you would request a vegetarian or kosher meal, you are entitled to ask for a hot dog or hamburger in lieu of the airline's regular dinner if you give at least 24 hours' notice. Some, but not all, airlines have baby food aboard. While you should bring along toys from home, you can also ask about children's diversions. Some carriers, such as United, Delta, and Pan American, have terrific free packages of games, coloring books, and puzzles.

When the plane takes off and lands, make sure your baby is nursing or has a bottle, pacifier, or thumb in its mouth. This sucking will make the child swallow and help to clear stopped ears. A piece of hard candy will do the same thing for an older child.

Avoid night flights. Since you probably won't sleep nearly as well as your kids, you risk an impossible first day at your destination, groggily taking care of your rested, energetic children. Nap time is, however, a good time to travel, especially for babies, and try to travel during off-hours, when there are apt to be extra seats. If you do have to take a long night flight, keep in mind that when you disembark, you will probably be tired and not really ready for sightseeing. The best thing to do is to head for your hotel, shower, have a snack, and take a nap. If your children are too excited to sleep, give them some toys to play with while you rest.

■ **Note:** Newborn babies, whose lungs may not be able to adjust to the altitude, should not be taken aboard an airplane. And some airlines may refuse to allow a pregnant woman in her 8th or 9th month aboard, for fear that something could go wrong with a birth during the flight. Check with the airline ahead of time and carry a letter from your doctor stating that you are fit to travel and indicating the estimated date of birth.

CAR: Traveling by car, you can be flexible — making any number of stops at souvenir shops or snake farms and meeting moods and emergencies as they arise. You can also take more with you, including items like ice chests and charcoal grills for picnics. Keep your car supplied with dried fruits, crackers, candy bars, bottled water, and facial tissue and/or toilet paper. Games and simple toys, such as magnetic checkerboards or drawing pencils and pads, can also provide a welcome diversion. Frequent stops so that children can run around make car travel much easier. Along most major highways, there are well-spaced rest areas where you can pull over and have a meal. If a break is in order between these facilities, the next best alternative is to get off at an exit and follow the signs to a nearby park or town.

TRAIN: *Amtrak* allows children under 2 (accompanied by an adult) to travel for free anytime; children 2 to 12 accompanied by an adult traveling on an excursion fare are charged half the adult fare. *Amtrak* also offers economical family plans; ask about current special packages when making reservations to determine the best deal for your family. All long-distance trains with dining car service offer children's dishes.

BUS: On *Greyhound,* children 5 through 11 are charged half price (accompanied by an adult); one child under 5 may travel free on an adult's lap. Be sure any bus on which you travel with children — even on short runs — has a bathroom.

FAMILY TRIPS: An alternative to long car trips are holidays specifically planned for families, based on some adventure or activity exciting for all. A few examples are the following:

A riverboat trip down the Mississippi on the *Delta Queen,* Delta Queen Steamboat Co., 30 Robin Street Wharf, New Orleans, LA 70130 (phone: 800-458-6789 or 800-543-1949).

A combination bus/train trip to Yosemite National Park organized by *Yosemite Gray Line,* PO Box 2188, Merced, CA 95344 (phone: 209-383-1563).

Rafting, hiking, camping with the *Sierra Club,* which runs special family outings. Write to the Sierra Club, 730 Polk St., San Francisco, CA 94109 (phone: 415-776-2211).

Wagon train trip put together by *L. D. Frome, Wagons West,* PO Box 47, Afton, WY 83110 (phone: 307-886-3872 or 800-433-1595).

These are just a few of literally hundreds of vacations available throughout the country. One book of ideas, with the names and addresses of the companies that feature such adventures, is *Adventure Travel North America* by Pat Dickerman (Holt; out of print, but check your library). Also see *Traveling with Children in the USA* by Leila Hadley (Morrow; $12.95) and *What to Do with the Kids This Year: One Hundred Family Vacation Places with Time Off for You!* by Jane Wilford and Janet Tice (Globe Pequot Press; $8.95).

Travel With Your Children publishes a newsletter, *Family Travel Times,* that focuses on the child traveler and offers helpful hints for parents. Membership is $35 a year. For a sample copy of the newsletter, send $1 to Travel With Your Children, 80 8th Ave., New York, NY 10011 (phone: 212-206-0688).

Special programs for children run the gamut from children's movies at museums and puppet shows in city parks to storytelling at a public library. Listings of these events, many of which are free, can usually be found in Friday's or Sunday's newspapers or at the city's visitors bureau or information center. Local or regional festivals, fairs, rodeos, parades, and other special events capture children's imaginations. For a list of such events, write to the tourist bureaus in the states you plan to visit. And ask about discounts; children often get discounts on everything from movies to monuments.

ACCOMMODATIONS: Often a cot will be placed in a hotel room at little or no extra charge; some places do not charge for children under a certain age. Special rates are sometimes available for families in adjoining rooms. Try to find hotels that welcome children — that don't charge for children under a certain age, for example. In many of the larger chain hotels, the staffs are more used to noisy or slightly misbehaving children. These hotels are also likely to have swimming pools or gamerooms — both popular with most young travelers. Write the hotel in advance to discuss how old your children are, how long you plan to stay, and to ask for suggestions on sleeping arrangements. Among the hotels known to welcome kids are the *Grand* hotel on Mackinac Island in Michigan (phone: 906-847-3331) and the *Hyatt Regency* at Peachtree Center in Atlanta (phone: 404-577-1234). The *Grand* (whose rates include breakfast and dinner) charges a nominal amount to cover children's meals and offers babysitting, supervision, and entertainment — including movies, golf, croquet, volleyball, tennis, and a gameroom. The *Hyatt Regency* welcomes children year-round and offers periodic specials for young families. The *Chocolate Lovers' Hyatt Fest* includes an event guaranteed to win points with the kids — fingerpainting with chocolate. Children 18 and under get a free stay when sharing a room with two adults.

Westin hotels also offer children under 18 a free stay if they share a room with their parents, and depending on the hotel, a family of five can pay the single rate for each of two adjoining rooms. Westin properties with especially good locations for children are the *Westin Crown Center* in Kansas City (phone: 816-474-4400) and Houston's *Westin Oaks* and *Westin Galleria* (phone: 713-623-4300). All three are adjacent to malls: The mall in Kansas City has an arts and crafts center and a children's theater; the Houston mall has gamerooms and ice skating.

Walt Disney World hotels do not charge for children under 18 sharing a room with their parents (maximum of five people per room). The *Polynesian Village* (phone: 407-824-2000) and *Contemporary Resort* (phone: 407-824-1000) start the kids' day with a breakfast at which various *Walt Disney World* characters table-hop, meeting the guests and signing autographs.

For another family pleaser, consider staying as a guest on a farm or dude ranch, lists of which can be obtained from state departments of agriculture (see *Vacations on Farms and Ranches*, DIVERSIONS). Write to state tourist bureaus for the names of parks with overnight accommodations and marinas where families can rent houseboats. Theme parks make good family vacations. They offer entertainment, rides, and games for the whole family and accommodate the hamburger-and-ice-cream tastes of children (see *Amusement Parks and Theme Parks*, DIVERSIONS).

Consider trading houses or apartments with people in the area where you would like to vacation. Join an organization that fosters such arrangements, such as the *Vacation Exchange Club* (12006 111th Ave., Youngtown, AZ 85363; phone: 602-972-2186). For further information on home exchanges, see *Accommodations* in this section.

Many colleges and universities open campuses to travelers during traditional academic vacations and in the summer. Some offer accommodations only (usually very cheap, in dormitory rooms); others open their recreational facilities and sports centers to visitors.

The many resort condominium apartments available for rent provide excellent accommodations for families. The apartment becomes a "home away from home," and a considerable sum can be saved by preparing meals yourself rather than taking the entire crew out to restaurants three times a day. In addition, many complexes do not charge for children under 12, and a few permit anyone under 18 to stay with their families for free. (Some condos don't allow children, so before you set your heart on a particular one, find out all the details of its rental policy.) Many of the condominium vacation packages include a rental car; these combination deals can be quite economical. If your family won't fit into the standard compact car offered, a few dollars more per day will usually buy a larger model.

■ **A final word of advice:** If you are spending your vacation traveling, rather than visiting one spot or engaging in one activity, pace the days with children in mind. Break the trip into half-day segments, with running around or "doing" time built in; keep travel time on the road to a maximum of 4 or 5 hours a day. First and foremost, don't forget that a child's attention span is far shorter than an adult's. Children don't have to see every museum or all of any museum to learn something from their trip; watching, playing with, and talking to other children can be equally enlightening experiences. Also, remember the places that children the world over love to visit: zoos, country fairs, amusement parks, beaches, and nature trails. Let your children lead the way sometimes — their perspective is different than yours, and they may lead you to things you would never have noticed on your own.

Hints for Traveling with Pets

 You may wish to bring your pet along on your vacation. There are no restrictions on traveling with your pet throughout the continental US, although it should be fully vaccinated in advance (bring written documentation from the veterinarian with you). Some restrictions do apply when traveling to Hawaii or Alaska — they vary, depending on the type of animal.

DOGS, CATS, AND BIRDS: Hawaii strictly enforces its anti-rabies laws. Therefore, all dogs and cats (except those coming from Australia, New Zealand, and Great Britain) must be quarantined for 120 days. This includes dogs and cats from the mainland, and Seeing Eye dogs are not exempt. Animals are kept at the US Department of Agriculture Animal Quarantine Station in Aiea, Hawaii, or at the Animal Quarantine Substation at the Honolulu airport. Also, you must bring a valid interstate health certificate from the pet's state of origin, signed by an accredited physician and dated no more than 10 days prior to shipping. You can obtain this form at your pet's veterinary office. According to Hawaiian Department of Agriculture authorities, you won't require any special permits to bring your dog or cat — or even a dog or cat you purchased on the Hawaiian Islands — back to the mainland.

Many birds, including cockatiels, parakeets, and canaries, can be brought into Hawaii. But to do so, you need a special entry permit and a valid Interstate Health Certificate signed by an accredited veterinarian and dated no more than 10 days prior to shipping. The latter form is available directly from your bird's veterinarian; the former, by contacting the Plant Quarantine Branch, US Dept. of Agriculture, 701 Ilalo St., Honolulu, HI 96804 (phone: 808-548-7175). Some birds, such as lories, are prohibited from entering Hawaii; call a Plant Quarantine Branch for details. If you'd like to bring a bird back to the mainland from Hawaii, check with your state's Department of Agriculture. Some states have rules against bringing in certain types of birds — usually those that may jeopardize the future of local crops.

In order to take your dog, cat, or bird into Alaska, you will need a valid Interstate Health Certificate signed by an accredited veterinarian issued no more than 10 days prior to entering Alaska. Rabies and other standard vaccination documentation is also required. Additionally, you must provide a written statement from a veterinarian certifying not only that your pet is rabies-free but also that it has never been quarantined for rabies; if it has, official permission to enter the state is required. Restrictions regarding returning with animals from Alaska vary from state to state — it is best to check with the local branch of the US Department of Agriculture.

BIRDS and OTHER ANIMALS: When traveling to and from Alaska and Hawaii, turtles and guinea pigs must be accompanied by the same papers required for importing birds (see above for details). Hamsters and gerbils, however, are prohibited, as are such harmful creatures as alligators, snapping turtles, and coyotes. Other states have restrictions regarding crossing state lines with certain protected species — one example is alligators in Florida. Before considering taking any wild animal home as a "pet," check with the local branch of the Department of Agriculture for state regulations as well as health and safety considerations. The best advice is: Don't.

For further information on interstate pet transportation, write to Dr. Schwindaman of the Import/Export Staff, USDA-APHIS-VS, Federal Bldg., 7th Fl., 6505 Belcrest Rd., Hyattsville, MD 20782, or call 301-436-6491.

BY PLANE AND CAR: Many airlines require a health certificate for your pet. United, for example, requires that Interstate Health Certificates be signed by an accredited veterinarian and dated no more than 30 days before travel. Check with your air carrier well before your departure.

It's a good idea to buy a traveling kennel if your dog is being transported by plane or car. Most airlines sell them, as do pet stores. Any animal must be boxed for the plane trip; in a car, a kennel is a good safety measure. The most important features of a kennel are size, comfort, and cleanliness. Your kennel should be large enough to permit room for your pet to walk around, turn around, and lie down; it should be constructed completely of non-chewable materials — metal or high-grade plastic. Chewable materials such as cardboard or fiberboard can be toxic. The kennel should have a sanitized pad on the bottom with a wire mesh floor that is raised at least 1 inch above the pad. The box should lock, be thoroughly ventilated, and be easy to handle and transport.

If your pet is traveling by plane, label the kennel with your name, address, destination, pet's name, and special handling instructions. Remove the animal's collar before putting it in the kennel. Dogs should not be muzzled. Put a few toys and familiar objects in the kennel to acquaint the animal with its box before the start of the trip.

Airlines will usually allow one kenneled pet to fly in the passenger compartment for a standard fee, if the kennel fits underneath the seat. This space should be reserved when you reserve your own seat. If there is no space in the passenger compartment, or the animal is too large to be brought in, it must fly as cargo, in a special area reserved for live cargo. Charges are established on the basis of the weight and size of the animal.

Don't ship your pet during very hot or very cold weather; animals are sometimes left on the runway during the loading of the hold. Afternoon and evening flights are best in hot weather. Fly in off-peak times, when the hold has less baggage and more ventilation and the personnel have more time to watch your pet. Pets should be the last cargo loaded, and the boxed pet should be given to the cargo officer, not to the person at the ticket counter, who will place the kennel on a conveyor belt. Avoid flights with stopovers and transfers lest your pet be misplaced.

When you land, retrieve your pet as soon as possible. Return it to its normal feeding schedule slowly.

If you decide to drive with an animal, be aware that animals can suffer motion sickness. You can ascertain if your pet is susceptible by taking it for short trips before you undertake the real journey. Here are a few tips to make your trip with your pet as much fun as possible:

1. Bring along a kennel or sleeping box for a dog or cat.
2. Make plenty of exercise and feeding stops. You may want to set a new record for the distance — your pet does not.
3. Take along some of your pet's toys or most adored objects.
4. Don't let your dog ride with its head out of the window. Cinders, dirt, and rocks can injure its eyes and head, and the wind can irritate its nasal and respiratory passages. Keep the windows almost closed, allowing enough ventilation for comfort.
5. If you have to leave your pet alone in the car, park in the shade and leave the windows down an inch or two for air. But don't leave the car unlocked. People all across the country like dogs, too.

But it is best to leave your pet at home. That way you won't miss the thrill of finding out how glad it is to see you when you get back.

Staying Healthy

The surest way to return home in good health is to be prepared for medical problems that might occur on vacation. Below, we've outlined everything you need to think about before you go.

Obviously, your state of health is crucial to the success of a vacation. There's nothing like an injury or illness, whether serious or relatively minor, to dampen or destroy a holiday. And health problems always seem more debilitating when you are away. However, most problems can be prevented or greatly alleviated with intelligent foresight and attention to precautionary details.

Older travelers or anyone suffering from a chronic medical condition, such as diabetes, high blood pressure, cardiopulmonary disease, asthma, or ear, eye, or sinus trouble, should consult a physician before leaving home. A checkup is advisable. A dental checkup is not a bad idea, either.

FIRST AID: Put together a compact, personal medical kit including Band-Aids, antiseptic, nose drops, insect repellent, aspirin, an extra pair of prescription glasses, sunglasses, or contact lenses (and a copy of your prescription), over-the-counter remedies for diarrhea, indigestion, and motion sickness, a thermometer, and a supply of those prescription medicines you take regularly. In a corner of your kit, keep a list of all the drugs you have brought and their purpose as well as copies of your doctor's prescriptions (or a note from your doctor). These copies could come in handy if you were ever questioned by police or airport authorities about any drugs you are carrying and if you need to refill any prescriptions in the event of loss. It is also a good idea to ask your doctor to prepare a medical identification card that includes such information as your blood type, your social security number, any allergies or chronic health problems you have, and your medical insurance number. Considering the essential contents of this kit, keep it with you, rather than in your luggage.

SUNBURN: Depending on where you're vacationing, the burning power of the sun in can be phenomenal and can quickly cause severe sunburn or sunstroke. To protect yourself, wear sunglasses, take along a broad-brimmed hat and cover-up, and use a sunscreen lotion. When choosing a sunscreen, look for one that has a PABA (para-amino-benzoic acid) base. PABA blocks out most of the harmful ultraviolet rays of the sun.

Some tips on tanning:

1. Allow only 20 minutes or so the first day; increase your exposure gradually.
2. You are most likely to get a painful burn when the sun is the strongest, between 10 AM and 2 PM.
3. When judging if you've had enough sun, remember that time in the water (in terms of exposure to ultraviolet rays) is the same as time lying on the beach.
4. A beach umbrella or other cover doesn't keep all the rays of the sun from reaching you. If you are sensitive to light, be especially careful.
5. As many ultraviolet rays reach you on cloudy days as on sunny days. Even if you don't feel hot, you are still exposed to rays.

If, despite these precautions, you find yourself with a painful sunburn, take a cooling bath, apply a first-aid spray or the liquid of an aloe plant, and stay out of the sun. If you develop a more serious burn and experience chills, fever, nausea, headaches, or dizziness, consult a doctor at once.

WATER SAFETY: The US boasts many beautiful beaches, but it's important to remember that they can also be treacherous. A few precautions are necessary. Beware of the undertow, that current of water running back down the beach after a wave has washed ashore; it can knock you off your feet and into the surf. Even more dangerous is the riptide, a strong current of water running against the tide, which can pull you out toward sea. If this happens, don't panic or try to fight the current, because it will only exhaust you; instead, ride it out while waiting for it to subside, which usually happens not too far from shore, or try swimming away parallel to the beach.

Sharks are sometimes sighted, but they usually don't come in close to shore. Should you meet up with one, just swim away as quietly and smoothly as you can, without shouting or splashing. The tentacled Portuguese man-of-war and other jellyfish drift in quiet waters for food and sting whatever they touch. If stung, do not wash the area because fresh water aggravates the stinging; instead, pour alcohol (rubbing alcohol, liquor, or perfume) over the stung area or apply meat tenderizer. Hot salt water is another effective treatment. Hawaii and other coastal regions of the US have extensive and often razor-sharp coral reefs. Treat all coral cuts with an antiseptic and then watch carefully since coral is a living organism and may cause an infection. If you step on a sea urchin, you'll find that the spines are very sharp, pierce the skin, and break off easily. Like splinters, the tips left embedded in the skin are difficult to remove, but they will dissolve in a week or two; in the meantime, rinsing with vinegar is said to dissolve them more quickly.

If complications or allergic reactions such as vomiting, breathlessness, or cramps result from any of the above circumstances, *see a doctor.*

INSECTS AND OTHER PESTS: Flies and mosquitoes can be troublesome, so as we have said, be sure to pack a repellent. If you are bitten by a snake, a poisonous centipede, or a scorpion, call a doctor immediately. Cockroaches and termites thrive in warm climates but pose no serious health threat.

FOOD AND WATER: The tap water in the US is considered among the purest to be found, so feel free to drink it; fruit, vegetables, and dairy products are likewise completely safe. However, you should avoid drinking water from streams or freshwater pools. In campgrounds, water is usually indicated as drinkable or for washing only; if you're not sure, ask.

Following all these precautions will not guarantee an illness-free trip, but should minimize the risk. As a final hedge against economic if not physical problems, make sure your health insurance will cover all eventualities while you are away. If not, there are policies designed specifically for travel. Many are worth investigating. As with all insurance, they seem like a waste of money until you need them (see *Insurance*, in this section).

HELPFUL PUBLICATIONS: Practically every phase of health care — before, during, and after a trip — is covered in *The New Traveler's Health Guide* by Drs. Patrick J. Doyle and James E. Banta. It is available for $4.95, plus $2 postage and handling, from Acropolis Books Ltd., 2400 17th St. NW, Washington, DC 20009-9964 (phone: 800-451-7771).

For more information regarding preventive health care for travelers, contact *IAMAT* (*International Association for Medical Assistance to Travelers*), 417 Center St., Lewiston, NY 14092 (phone: 716-754-4883), or write to the US Government Printing Office, Washington, DC 20402, for the US Public Health Service's booklet *Health Information for International Travel* (HEW Publication CDC-86-8280; enclose check or money order for $4.75 payable to Superintendent of Documents).

On the Road

Credit Cards and Traveler's Checks

 CREDIT CARDS: Two different kinds of credit cards are available in the United States, and travelers must decide which one best serves their interests — although they often elect to carry both types. "Convenience" or "travel and entertainment" cards — American Express, Diners Club, and Carte Blanche — are widely accepted. They cost the cardholder a basic annual membership fee ($35 to $50 is typical for these three), but put no strict limit on the amount that may be charged on the card in any month. However, the entire amount charged must be paid in full at the end of each billing period (usually a month), so the cardholder is not actually extended any long-term credit.

"Bank cards" are also rarely issued free these days (with the one exception of Sears's Discover Card), and certain services they provide (check cashing, for example) can carry an extra cost. But this category comprises real credit cards, in the sense that the cardholder has the privilege of paying a small amount (1/36 is typical) of the total outstanding balance in each billing period. For the privilege, the cardholder is charged a high annual interest rate (currently three to four times the going bank passbook savings rate) on the balance owed. Many banks now charge interest from the purchase date, not from the first billing date (as they used to do); consider this when you are calculating the actual cost of a purchase. In addition, a maximum is set on the total amount the cardholder can charge, which represents the limit of credit the card company is willing to extend. The major bank cards are Visa and MasterCard, with Discover growing rapidly.

Getting any credit card will involve a fairly extensive credit check; to pass, you will need a job (at which you have worked for at least a year), a minimum salary, and a good credit rating.

Note that some establishments you encounter in your travels may not honor any credit cards and some may not honor all cards, so there is a practical reason to carry more than one. The following is a list of credit cards that enjoy wide domestic and international acceptance:

American Express: Emergency personal check cashing at American Express or representatives' offices (up to $200 cash in local currency, plus $800 in traveler's checks); emergency personal check cashing for guests at participating hotels and, for holders of airline tickets, at participating airlines in the US (up to $250). Extended payment plan for cruises, tours, and train and airline tickets as well as other prepaid travel arrangements. $100,000 free travel accident insurance on plane, train, bus, and ship if ticket was charged to card; up to $1 million additional low-cost flight insurance available. As we went to press, American Express had just announced a 3-hour replacement of lost or stolen traveler's checks. Contact American Express Card, PO Box 39, Church St. Station, New York, NY 10008 (phone: 800-528-4800 throughout the US, except New York; 212-477-5700 in New York).

Carte Blanche: Extended payment plan for air travel (up to $2,000). $150,000 free travel accident insurance on plane, train, and ship if ticket was charged to card, plus $1,250 checked or carry-on baggage insurance and $25,000 rental car insurance. Contact Carte Blanche, PO Box 17326, Denver, CO 80217 (phone: 800-525-9135).

Diners Club: Emergency personal check cashing for guests at participating Citibank branches, and other designated banks worldwide (up to $1,000 in a 14-day period) and at participating hotels and motels (up to $250 per stay). Qualified card members are eligible for extended payment plan. $350,000 free travel accident insurance on plane, train, and ship if ticket was charged to your card, plus $1,250 checked baggage insurance and $25,000 rental car insurance. Contact Diners Club, PO Box 17326, Denver, CO 80217 (phone: 800-525-9135).

Discover Card: Created by Sears, Roebuck and Co., it provides the holder with cash advance at more than 500 locations nationwide and offers a revolving credit line for purchases at a wide range of service establishments. Other deposit, lending, and investment services are also available. For information, call 800-858-5588 (if you can't reach this number by dialing directly, dial for an operator who will be able to place the call).

MasterCard: Cash advance at participating banks worldwide and a revolving credit line for purchases at a wide range of service establishments. Interest charge on unpaid balance and other details are set by issuing bank. Check with your bank for information.

Visa: Cash advance at participating banks worldwide and a revolving credit line for purchases at a wide range of service establishments. Interest charge on unpaid balance and other details are set by issuing bank. Check with your bank for information.

TRAVELER'S CHECKS: It's wise to carry traveler's checks while on the road instead of (or in addition to) cash, since it is possible to replace or obtain a refund for them if they are stolen or lost; in the US, travelers can usually receive partial or full replacement funds the same day if they have their purchase receipt and proper identification. Issued in various denominations, traveler's checks are as good as cash in most hotels, restaurants, retail stores, and banks. More and more establishments are, however, beginning to restrict the amount of traveler's checks they will accept or cash, so it is wise to purchase at least some of your checks in small — say, $20 — denominations.

To avoid complications should you need to redeem lost checks, keep the purchase receipt and an accurate list, by serial number, of the checks that have been spent or cashed. Always keep these records separate from the checks themselves (you may want to give them to a traveling companion to hold).

Every type of traveler's check is legal tender in banks around the world, and each company guarantees full replacement if checks are lost or stolen. After that the similarity ends. Some charge a fee for purchase, others are free; you can buy traveler's checks at almost any bank, and some are available by mail. Most important, each traveler's check issuer differs slightly in its refund policy — the amount refunded immediately, the accessibility of refund locations, and the availability of a 24-hour refund service. Here is a list of the major companies issuing traveler's checks and the numbers to call in the event that loss or theft makes replacement necessary:

American Express: To report lost or stolen checks in the US, call 800-221-7282.

Bank of America: To report lost or stolen checks in the US, call 800-227-3460 or 415-624-5400, collect.

Citicorp: To report lost or stolen checks in the US, call 800-645-6556 or 813-623-1709, collect.

MasterCard: To report lost or stolen checks in the US, call 800-223-9920 or 212-974-5696, collect.

Thomas Cook MasterCard: To report lost or stolen checks in the US, call 800-223-9920 or 212-974-5696, collect.

Visa: To report lost or stolen checks in the US, call 800-227-6811 or 415-574-7111, collect.

No matter what you are using — traveler's checks, credit cards, or cash — plan ahead. Also, carry your travel funds carefully. You might consider carrying your money (cash and traveler's checks) in more than one place. Never put money in a back pocket or an open purse. Money should be kept in a buttoned front pocket, in a money purse pinned inside your shirt or blouse, or in one of the convenient money belts or leg pouches sold by many travel shops. It may be quaint and old-fashioned, but it's safe.

Accommodations

Americans who travel frequently to Europe complain that the United States has few of the centuries-old, privately owned, and personally run tradition-conscious "little hotels" that can so enhance a European visit. To a great degree, this is a fair observation, but there are fine old hotels in the US — New England inns, southwestern haciendas, frontier stagecoach rest stops (you will find our pick of them listed in *Best in Town* in THE CITIES, *Special Havens* in DIVERSIONS, and *Best en Route* in DIRECTIONS) — which have been in continuous operation for a century or more and which can match the amenities of any European hostelry. Yet, most travelers in the US will be staying at hotels and motels that are not too many years old, which are often part of national (or international) chains, and which are, to some degree, standardized in price and quality.

There is at least one benefit to this standardization: The basic level of acceptable accommodations in the US is much higher than anywhere else in the world. The tourist in America, arriving in an unfamiliar town (or driving through a new region), can assume that there will be safe, clean, comfortable accommodations nearby, in an acceptable price range.

You can choose for yourself just what price range is acceptable. Some chains — like the Hyatts and Hiltons — offer a broad range of facilities and amenities. The hotels are modern and comfortable, the service is competent, and the facilities complete; and the prices, as you would expect, are relatively high — as much as $200 or more a night for a double. Other chains may be more reasonably priced.

RESERVATIONS: It is best to make advance reservations for accommodations in any major US city, even if you are traveling during the off-season. Most cities have convention centers, and hotel space can be scarce if a large convention is being held at the same time you visit. All the hotel entries in the *Best in Town* sections of THE CITIES include phone numbers for reservations. Resorts, country inns, dude ranches, theme park hotels, and other special places should always be booked in advance, regardless of the season. Most major hotel and motel chains list their toll-free (800) reservation numbers in the white pages of the telephone directory, and any hotel within a chain can assure reservations for you at sister facilities.

OVERBOOKING: The worldwide travel boom has brought with it some abuses that are pretty much standard operating procedure in any industry facing demand that frequently outstrips supply. Anticipating a certain percentage of no-shows, hotels routinely overbook rooms. When cancellations don't occur and everybody with a reservation arrives as promised, it's not impossible to find yourself with a valid reservation for which no room exists.

There's no sure way to avoid all the pitfalls of overbooking, but you can minimize the risks. Always carry evidence of your confirmed reservation. This should be a direct communication from the hotel — to you or your travel agent — and should specify the exact dates and duration of your accommodations and the price. The weakest form of confirmation is the voucher slip a travel agent routinely issues, since it carries no official indication that the hotel itself has verified your reservation.

Even better is the increasing opportunity to *guarantee* hotel reservations by giving the hotel (or its reservation system) your credit card number and agreeing that the hotel is authorized to charge you for that room no matter what. It's still usually possible to cancel if you do so before 6 PM of the day of your reservation (sometimes 5 PM in resort areas), but when you do cancel under this arrangement, make sure you get a cancellation number to protect you from being billed erroneously.

If all these precautions fail and you are left standing at the front desk with a reservation that the hotel clerk won't honor, you have a last resort: Complain as long and as loud as necessary to get satisfaction! The person who makes the most noise usually gets the last room in the house. It might as well be you.

What if you can't get reservations in the first place? This is a problem that often confronts businesspeople who can't plan months ahead. The word from savvy travelers is that a bit of currency (perhaps attached discreetly to a business card) often increases your chances with recalcitrant desk clerks. There are less venal ways of improving your odds, however. If you are making reservations for business, ask an associate at your destination to make the reservations for you.

There is a good reason to do this above and beyond the very real point that a resident has the broadest knowledge of local hotels. Often a hotel will appear sold out on its computer when in fact a few rooms are available. The proliferation of computerized reservations has made it unwise for a hotel to indicate that it suddenly has five rooms available (from cancellations) when there might be 30 or 40 travel agents lined up in the computer waiting for them. That small a number of vacancies is much more likely to be held by the hotel for its own sale, so a local associate is an invaluable conduit to these otherwise inaccessible rooms.

BUDGET MOTELS: The budget motel is designed to offer basic accommodations (a comfortable bed, clean bathroom, central heating and air conditioning) without frills or ancillary services, bar or restaurant, or elaborate lobby. A double for a night can cost as little as $20 to $25. If you're traveling on a tight budget, watch for the following nationwide chains:

> *Budget Host Inns* (over 200 throughout the US); phone: 817-626-7064
> *Days Inn* (600 throughout the US); phone: 800-325-2525
> *Econo-Lodge* (almost 500 throughout the US); phone: 800-446-6900
> *Imperial 400* (52 throughout the US); phone: 800-368-4400
> *Motel 6* (500 throughout the US); phone: 214-386-6161
> *Red Roof Inns* (over 200 throughout the East, South, and Midwest); phone: 800-848-7878
> *Regal 8* (about 50 throughout the South, West, and Midwest); phone: 800-851-8888

At hotels and motels in all price ranges, ask about minimum rates, weekend discounts, weekly rates, commercial discounts for business travelers, special promotions, and special rates for children staying in the same room as their parents.

CONDOMINIUMS: Many travelers are opting to spend all or part of their vacation in a resort condominium. The difference between a condominium complex and an apartment hotel is not always immediately apparent (and many apartment hotels are now being converted to condominiums). In either case, the vacationer is renting not a hotel room but a studio or 1- or 2-bedroom (or larger) apartment with a full kitchen or a kitchenette and private bath(s). The apartment hotel, however, is designed entirely for transient rental, whereas the condominium complex is designed to be sold unit by unit to private owners for whom, these days, it is usually not a permanent residence but an investment and a part-time vacation home; the rest of the year it may be rented to a series of transient vacationers. Like apartment hotels, condominiums appeal to travelers because they provide the convenience and cost-saving feature of a kitchen. At their most modest, their appeal may go no farther, and in the past, travelers renting condominiums sight unseen could not always be sure they would get their money's worth. But recent trends — the development of ever more properties in prime locations and the tendency of professional management companies to take over the day-to-day operation of them — have imposed standards of quality and introduced a certain consistency in the equipment and services offered.

In appearance, topnotch resort condominium complexes vary from high-rise blocks to cottage clusters, just as resort hotels do. Some may provide all the facilities of a hotel — restaurants, lobbies, and lounges where you will bump into your fellow guests; and others may stress quiet or seclusion, with a definite lack of bustle. Some, with a view to easy maintenance, require that each unit be finished exactly like every other unit; others allow free rein to the individual owner's personal touches. (Most have at least a minimum standard of furnishings and equipment before any unit is accepted in the transient rental pool.) First class condominiums of this sort, whatever the subtle differences in atmosphere, have spacious, tastefully furnished rooms and fully equipped kitchens (all dishes, pots and pans, and tableware are supplied, and most have dishwashers). Linens are supplied, and a washer and dryer will be in your own unit or nearby. A TV set is almost always provided; air conditioning and room phones may or may not be. Most resorts have daily maid service (or can arrange it), and there is usually some arrangement for babysitting services. Tennis courts, golf courses, swimming pools, saunas, outdoor barbecue grills, and grocery and liquor stores on the premises are some of the added amenities found at many such condo complexes.

The cost of all this for one traveler alone or even one couple is not inexpensive. But for a family, two or more couples, or a group of friends, the picture is quite different. A 1-bedroom condominium rented to two people at $65 per person a night, for instance, may rent to four people at $77 a night; that is, only $6 more per additional person (and if the extra two are children under 12, they may be accommodated free at quite a few resorts). At another resort, a 2-bedroom apartment may cost $124 per night, the same for four through six people, whether children or adults. (In either case, the two extra guests sleep in the living room on a sofabed, a standard furnishing.) Weekly and monthly rates are available to reduce costs still more. As with hotels, the rates at some condominium resorts are seasonal, while at others they remain the same year-round. Above all, renting a resort condominium provides the luxury of space on a scale not normally available in a conventional hotel at any price.

There are several ways of finding a suitable condominium. They are sometimes listed along with other accommodations in each state's accommodations guide, but perhaps the best course is to consult a travel agent. Many tour wholesalers regularly include a few condominium packages among their more conventional offerings. In addition, certain companies specialize in condominium vacations. Their plans typically include a rental car and rental of the condominium, to which can be added an excursion, individual tour-basing, or group air fare (whichever is least expensive when and from where you travel), just as it could be added to any other package. If your travel agent doesn't have the brochures of these specialists, contact the companies listed below.

Condo Resorts International, PO Box 3008, Suite K8, Costa Mesa, CA 92628 (phone: 800-854-3823)

Condominiums Unlimited, PO Box 6085, Hayward, CA 94540 (phone: 800-227-1196 in the continental US except California; 415-785-5880 or 800-972-5900 in California)

Creative Leisure, 951 Transport Way, Petaluma, CA 94952 (phone: 800-4-CONDOS in the US and Canada)

While perusing the brochures, look for answers to the following questions: How do you get from the airport to the condominium? How far is the nearest beach? Is it sandy or rocky and is it safe for swimming? What size, type, and quantity of beds are provided? How far is the property from whatever else is important to you, such as a golf course or nightlife? If there is no grocery store on the premises (which may be comparatively expensive, anyway), how far is the nearest market? Are babysitters, cribs, bicycles, or anything else you may need for your children available? Is maid service provided daily? If you want air conditioning or a phone, does the apartment have them? Before deciding which resort is for you, make sure you have satisfactory answers to all these questions; ask your travel agent to find out or, if necessary, call the company involved directly.

BED-AND-BREAKFAST AND OTHER ACCOMMODATIONS: A relatively new phenomenon in the United States, bed-and-breakfast establishments provide precisely what the name implies. The bed may be in an extra room in a family home, in an apartment with a separate entrance, or in a free-standing cottage elsewhere on the host's property, and a private bath often comes with it, as does, occasionally, a kitchenette. The breakfast will probably be a version of the continental breakfast: fruit plus juice, toast or roll or homemade bread and marmalade, and coffee or tea. Or, if you're in a studio with a kitchen, you may be furnished the makings of a breakfast you'll have to prepare for yourself.

Beyond these two fundamentals, nothing else is predictable about the bed-and-breakfast route. You may have a patio, garden, pool, and barbecue pit at your door or only the bare necessities. Accommodations range from private homes and lovely mansions to small inns and guesthouses. A private bath isn't always offered, so check before you reserve. Also, there can be a fine line between "bed-and-breakfast establishment" and "boarding house," so find out as much as you can before you book to avoid disappointment. *Bed & Breakfast Reservations Services Worldwide* (the trade association), PO Box 14797, Dept. 174, Baton Rouge, LA 70898 (phone: 504-346-1928), publishes an annual brochure for $3 listing its members. The *American Bed and Breakfast Association,* 16 Village Green, Suite 203, Crofton, MD 21114 (phone: 301-261-0180), also can send you information. Or consult any of several guidebooks on the subject; see the list in *For More Information,* in this section. The *Bed and Breakfast Registry Ltd.,* PO Box 8174, St. Paul, MN 55108-0174 (phone: 612-646-4238), has nationwide listings. *Bed and Breakfast Registry* travelers can participate in the *Alamo Associate Membership Program,* which entitles them to low car rental rates, unlimited free mileage, a free upgrade coupon, and frequent flier points with United Airlines or Delta. Request plan B4-193122. Here is a list of regional groups to contact for bed and breakfast information and reservations:

Northeast

Bed & Breakfast Associates of Bay Colony, Ltd., PO Box 166, Babson Park, Boston, MA 02157 (phone: 617-449-5302)

Bed & Breakfast of New Jersey, 103 Godwin Ave., Suite 132, Midland Park, NJ 07432 (phone: 201-444-7409)

House Guests–Cape Cod and the Islands, Box 1881, Orleans, MA 02653 (phone: 508-896-7053 or 800-666-HOST)

New England Bed & Breakfast, 1045 Centre St., Newton Centre, MA 02159 (phone: 617-244-2112 or 617-498-9819)

Nutmeg Bed & Breakfast, PO Box 1117, West Hartford, CT 06107 (phone: 203-236-6698)

Pineapple Hospitality, 47 N. 2nd St., Suite 3A, New Bedford, MA 02740 (phone: 508-990-1696)

Spirit of Massachusetts Bed & Breakfast Guide, Massachusetts Office of Travel and Tourism, 100 Cambridge St., 13th Floor, Boston, MA 02202 (phone: 617-727-3201)

Mid-Atlantic

Bed & Breakfast (& Books), 35 W. 92nd St., New York, NY 10025 (phone: 212-865-8740)

The Bed and Breakfast League, Ltd./Sweet Dreams & Toast, PO Box 9490, Washington, DC 20016 (phone: 202-363-7767)

Bed & Breakfast of Philadelphia, PO Box 252, Gradyville, PA 19039 (phone: 800-733-4747)

New World Bed and Breakfast, 150 5th Ave., Suite 711, New York, NY 10011 (phone: 212-675-5600 or 800-443-3800)

The Traveller in Maryland, PO Box 2277, Annapolis, MD 21404 (phone: 301-269-6232; 301-261-2233, DC area)

Urban Ventures, PO Box 426, New York, NY 10024 (phone: 212-594-5650)

South

A & A Bed & Breakfast of Florida, PO Box 1316, Winter Park, FL 32790 (phone: 407-628-3233)

Bed & Breakfast Atlanta, 1801 Piedmont Ave. NE, Suite 208, Atlanta GA 30324 (phone: 404-875-0525)

Bed & Breakfast Birmingham, Rte. 2, Box 275, Leeds, AL 35094 (phone: 205-699-9841)

Bed & Breakfast Co., PO Box 262, South Miami, FL 33243 (phone: 305-661-3270)

Bed & Breakfast, 1360 Moss St., Box 52257, New Orleans, LA 70152-2257 (phone: 504-525-4640)

Bed & Breakfast of the Florida Keys and Florida East Coast, PO Box 1373, Marathon, FL 33050 (phone: 305-743-4118)

Bed & Breakfast Montgomery, PO Box 886, Millbrook, AL 36054 (phone: 205-285-5421)

Guest Houses, B&B Reservation Service, Box 5737, Charlottesville, VA 22905 (phone: 804-979-7264)

Historic Charleston Bed & Breakfast, 43 Legare St., Charleston, SC 29401 (phone: 803-722-6606)

Kentucky Homes Bed & Breakfast, 1431 St. James Ct., Louisville, KY 40208 (phone: 502-635-7341)

King William Bed & Breakfast Registry, 201 E. Rische, San Antonio, TX 78204 (phone: 512-227-1190)

Lincoln Ltd. Bed & Breakfast, PO Box 3479, Meridian, MS 39303 (phone: 601-482-5483)

Ohio Valley Bed & Breakfast, 6876 Taylor Mill Rd., Independence, KY 41051 (phone: 606-356-7865)

Princely Bed & Breakfast, 819 Prince St., Alexandria, VA 22314 (phone: 703-683-2159)

Southern Comfort Bed & Breakfast Reservation Service, 2856 Hundred Oaks, Baton Rouge, LA 70808 (phone: 504-346-1928; 800-375-1928 in Lousiana; 800-523-1181, dial tone, then 722, elsewhere)

The Travel Tree, PO Box 838, Williamsburg, VA 23187 (phone: 804-253-1571)

Midwest

Bed & Breakfast Chicago, PO Box 14088, Chicago, IL 60614-0088 (phone: 312-951-0085)

Bed & Breakfast in Michigan, PO Box 1731, Dearborn, MI 48121 (phone: 313-561-6041)

Buckeye Bed & Breakfast, PO Box 130, Powell, OH 43065 (phone: 614-548-4555)

West

American Family Inn/Bed & Breakfast San Francisco, PO Box 349, San Francisco, CA 94101 (phone: 415-931-3083)

Bed & Breakfast in Arizona, PO Box 8628, Scottsdale, AZ 85252 (phone: 602-995-2831)

Bed & Breakfast Innkeepers of Southern California, PO Box 15425, Los Angeles, CA 90015-0385 (phone: 714-659-3202)

Bed & Breakfast International, 1181B Solano Ave., Albany, CA 94706 (phone: 415-525-4569)

Bed & Breakfast of Southern California, 1943 Sunny Crest Dr., #304, Fullerton, CA 92635 (phone: 714-738-8361)

California Houseguests International, 18653 Ventura Blvd., #190B, Tarzana, CA 91356 (phone: 818-344-7878)

Digs West, 8191 Crowley Cir., Buena Park, CA 90621 (phone: 714-739-1669)

Eye Openers Bed & Breakfast, PO Box 694, Altadena, CA 91003 (phone: 213-684-4428 or 818-797-2055)

Mi Casa–Su Casa Bed & Breakfast, PO Box 950, Tempe, AZ 85280-0950 (phone: 602-990-0682 or 800-456-0682)

Northwest Bed & Breakfast, 610 SW Broadway, Portland, OR 97205 (phone: 503-243-7616)

Pacific Bed & Breakfast Agency, 701 NW 60th St., Seattle, WA 98107 (phone: 206-784-0539)

Travellers B&B Reservation Service, PO Box 492, Mercer Island, WA 98040 (phone: 206-232-2345)

Visitors Advisory Service, 1516 Oak St., #327, Alameda, CA 94501 (phone: 415-521-9366)

Hawaii

Bed & Breakfast Hawaii, Box 449, Kapaa, HI 96746 (phone: 808-822-7771 or 800-367-8047, ext. 339)

HOME EXCHANGES: Another accommodations option may be of special interest to families. The home exchange is an exceptionally inexpensive way to ensure comfortable, reasonable living quarters with amenities that no hotel could possibly offer, often including a car. Moreover, it allows you to live in a new community in a way that few tourists ever do: For a little while, at least, you will become something of a resident. Several companies publish directories of individuals and families willing to trade homes with others for a specific period of time. In some cases, you must be willing to list your own home in the directory; in others, you can subscribe without appearing in it. Arrangements for the actual exchange take place directly between you and the other homeowner. There is no guarantee that you will find a listing in the area in which you are interested, but each of the directories below has hundreds or even thousands of foreign and domestic properties.

International Home Exchange Service/Intervac US: Part of the Intervac network of 22 countries, which publishes three books containing 7,000 listings per year. The $35 annual subscription entitles you to the three books and the opportunity to be listed. PO Box 3975, San Francisco, CA 94119 (phone: call collect, 415-435-3497).

Vacation Exchange Club: Through its affiliates in the Directory Group Association, this organization offers some 6,000 listings, in 40 countries. For $24.70 a year, the subscriber receives two directories, one in late winter and one in the spring. For a free brochure describing the program, write to 12006 111th Ave., Youngtown, AZ 85363 (phone: 602-972-2186).

World Wide Exchange: The $45 annual membership fee includes one free listing (for house, yacht, or motorhome) and three free guides. 1344 Pacific Ave., Suite 103, Santa Cruz, CA 95060 (phone: 408-425-0531).

Dining Out

American cities have undergone something of a restaurant revolution. In the last 10 years, cities across the country — from Portland, Maine, to Portland, Oregon — have initiated renovation programs of the oldest sections of town. Often these are former port or warehouse districts, mercantile neighborhoods filled with fine 19th-century ironwork buildings that 100 years ago were in their prime and have since fallen into disrepair. Renovated, they become distinctive shopping areas, filled with fine food stores, art galleries, clothing or crafts boutiques, and . . . restaurants.

Built of simple wood and bricks to accentuate the often stunning architecture of the original buildings, these restaurants — whether in Boston or St. Louis — sometimes seem strikingly similar in look and design, but they represent a new era for the traveler. America's largest cities have always had a diverse collection of restaurants, but eating out in smaller American cities, especially in the South, Midwest, and Plains states, used to offer little variety. The new generation of restaurants is beginning to change that. Generally moderately priced and run by owner-managers who care about food, they offer an eclectic selection of menus (Oriental and traditional American, vegetarian and barbecue, haute cuisine and down home simple) with great care and real pride. We have listed our favorites in the *Eating Out* section in THE CITIES reports.

RESERVATIONS: Restaurants vary widely on reservation policies. At some, it is absolutely required (especially at more expensive and popular places in larger cities). Other equally fine restaurants refuse to take reservations at all; the patron simply waits until a table is free. If you are planning a big night out, it certainly is advisable to call the restaurant early in the day (or a few days in advance) to make a reservation or find out its policy. Every restaurant listing in *Best in Town* gives its reservation policy and a telephone number if possible.

If you plan to eat in your hotel, find out the scheduled serving times. These are usually noted in the information in your room describing the hotel's services. At some resort hotels, dining rooms may have set meal times, whereas coffee shops and room service operate more flexibly (often 24 hours a day).

Time Zones, Business Hours, Holidays

TIME ZONES: East to west, the United States is divided into four time zones: Eastern, Central, Mountain, and Pacific. Each zone is an hour apart; when it is 8 PM in New York, it is 5 PM in Los Angeles. Alaska and Hawaii are both two hours behind Los Angeles time. To discover how these zones divide the country, check the map in the front of your telephone directory. Daylight Saving

Time begins on the first Sunday in April and continues until the last Sunday in October. The only places that do not convert to Daylight Saving Time are Arizona, Hawaii, and parts of Indiana.

BUSINESS HOURS: Business hours throughout the country are fairly standard: 9 AM to 5 PM, Mondays through Fridays. While an hour lunch break is customary, employees often take it in shifts so that it rarely interrupts service, especially at banks and other public service operations. Days tend to begin earlier as you move west across the US: In Hawaii, business hours run from 7:30 or 8 AM to 5 PM.

Banks are traditionally open from 9 AM to 3 PM, weekdays, although the trend is toward longer hours. In some areas, they now open at 8 AM and stay open until 6 PM, especially at the end of the week. In addition, they may remain open one evening a week until 8 or 9 PM, and some have hours on Saturdays.

Retail stores are usually open from 9:30 or 10 AM to 5:30 or 6 PM, Mondays through Saturdays. Most large stores, particularly department stores, are open at least one night a week until 9 PM. Blue laws, which close some stores, restaurants, and bars on Sundays, are controlled by municipalities in some areas, by states elsewhere. In major cities, grocery stores, delicatessens, and supermarkets are usually open Mondays through Saturdays from 9 AM to 9 PM, and some are open on Sundays as well. In fact, 24-hour supermarkets are now operating in most regions. Drugstores are usually open from 8 AM to 9 PM, on weekdays and Saturdays. In major cities, at least one is usually open until midnight, or all night, and on Sundays; check the yellow pages.

HOLIDAYS: National holidays, when banks, post offices, libraries, most stores, and many museums are closed, include: January 1, *New Year's Day;* third Monday in January, *Martin Luther King Jr. Day;* third Monday in February, *Presidents' Day;* last Monday in May, *Memorial Day* (except in Alabama, Mississippi, and South Carolina, where it is not a legal holiday); July 4, *Independence Day;* first Monday in September, *Labor Day;* second Monday in October, *Columbus Day* (except in Alaska, Iowa, Mississippi, Nevada, North Dakota, Oregon, South Carolina, and South Dakota, where it is not a legal holiday); fourth Thursday in November, *Thanksgiving;* December 25, *Christmas.*

Mail, Telephone, and Electricity

MAIL: Most main post offices are open 24 hours a day, with at least a self-service section for weighing packages and buying stamps. In smaller cities and towns, hours are usually from 8 AM to 5 PM on weekdays and 8 AM to noon on Saturdays. Branch offices have shorter hours.

Stamps are also available at most hotel desks. There are vending machines for stamps in drugstores, transportation terminals, and other public places. Stamps cost more from these machines than they do at the post office, however.

Before you take an extended trip, fill in a change of address card (available at post offices) in order to get the post office to hold your mail or send your first class mail to your vacation address. Generally, this free service lasts for a month, longer at the discretion of the post office. You can also have your third class mail sent on, but you will have to pay for this service.

If you want to receive mail in another city but do not know your address there, have it sent to you in care of General Delivery in the city or town you will visit. This is always the main post office in any large city. Have the sender put "Hold for 30 Days" on the envelope, and make sure that a return address is on the envelope so that the post office can return it if you cannot pick it up. The post office will keep it only for 30 days. To claim this mail, go to the main post office in that city or town, ask for General Delivery, and present identification (driver's license, credit cards, birth certificate, passport). Mail must be collected in person.

If you belong to *AAA* or are an American Express customer (either a cardholder or carrier of American Express traveler's checks) you can have mail sent to their offices in cities on your route. American Express will hold mail for 30 days; letters must be marked "Client Mail Service." Any *American Express Travel Service* office can provide information on its mail service as well as a directory of American Express offices throughout the US. Letters sent to *AAA* offices should be marked "Hold for Arrival." For information regarding *AAA*'s mail service and branch locations, contact your local chapter or the national office (see *Traveling by Car,* in this section).

TELEPHONE: Public telephones are on hand just about everywhere if you are in a city or town. This includes transportation terminals, hotel lobbies, restaurants, drugstores, sidewalk booths, and along the highways. For a local call, the cost is between 10¢ and 25¢.

Long-distance rates are charged according to when the call is placed: weekday daytime; weekday evenings; and nights, weekends, and holidays. Least expensive are the calls you dial yourself from a private phone at night and on weekends and major holidays. It is always more expensive to call from a pay phone than it is to call from a private phone (you must pay for a minimum 3-minute call). If the operator assists you, calls are more expensive. This includes credit card, bill-to-a-third-number, collect, and time-and-charge calls as well as person-to-person calls, which are the most expensive. Rates are fully explained in the front of the white pages of every telephone directory.

If you are planning to be away for more than a month, you may be able to save money by asking the telephone company to temporarily suspend your home telephone service. You can also arrange to have your calls forwarded to another number.

Hotel Surcharges – When you are calling from your hotel room, inquire about any surcharges the hotel may have. These can be excessive, but can be avoided by calling collect, using a telephone credit card (free from the phone company), or calling from a public pay phone.

Emergencies – In most cities, 911 is the number to dial in an emergency. Operators at this number will get you the help you need from the police, fire department, or ambulance service. It is, however, a number that should be reserved for real emergencies only. If you are in one of the rare areas where 911 has not been adopted, dial "0" for the operator, who will connect you directly with the service you need.

ELECTRICITY: All 50 states have the same electrical current system: 110 volts, 60 cycles, alternating current (AC). Appliances running on standard current can be used throughout the US without adapters or converters.

Medical and Legal Help on the Road

MEDICAL HELP: You will discover, in the event of an emergency, that most tourist facilities — transportation companies, hotels, theme parks, and resorts — are equipped to handle the situation quickly and efficiently. All hospitals are prepared for emergency cases, and even the tiniest of US towns has a medical clinic nearby. If you are on your own, you can get emergency help by dialing 911 or "0" (for Operator). You will be put into immediate contact with the service you require.

If you have a medical condition that may require attention on your trip, have your doctor at home recommend a physician in the areas you plan to visit. If you need a doctor unexpectedly but it is not a severe emergency, you can call your own doctor for a recommendation in the area. If you are staying in a hotel or motel, ask for the house physician, who may visit you in your room or ask you to visit an office. (This service is apt to be expensive, especially if the doctor makes a "house" call to your room.) In larger cities, many hospitals have walk-in clinics designed to serve people who do not really need emergency service but who have no place to go for immediate medical attention. You can also go directly to the emergency room. A phone call to a local hospital requesting the name of a doctor will usually turn up a name; some hospitals actually have referral services for this purpose. The medical society in most towns (or counties) will refer you to a member physician in the specialty you need (listed in the telephone book under the city or county medical society; for example, Des Moines Medical Society).

Emergency assistance is also available from the various medical programs designed for travelers who have chronic ailments or whose illness requires them to return home. The *Medic Alert Foundation* sells identification emblems that specify that the wearer has a health condition that may not be readily apparent to a casual observer. A heart condition, diabetes, epilepsy, or severe allergy are the sorts of thing that these emblems were developed to communicate, conditions that can result in tragic errors if not recognized when emergency treatment is necessary and when you may be unable to speak for yourself. In addition to the identification emblems, the foundation maintains a computerized central file from which your complete medical history is available 24 hours a day by telephone (the phone number is clearly inscribed on the ID badge). The one-time membership is tax deductible and runs from $25 to $45; it is based on the type of metal from which the emblem is made, the choices ranging from stainless steel to 10K gold-filled. For information, contact the Medic Alert Foundation, Turlock, CA 95381-1009 (phone: 209-668-3333 or 800-ID-ALERT).

International SOS Assistance also offers a program to cover medical emergencies while traveling. Members are provided with telephone access — 24 hours a day, 365 days a year — to a worldwide, monitored, multilingual network of medical centers. A phone call brings assistance ranging from a telephone consultation to transportation home by ambulance or aircraft, and in some cases transportation of a family member to wherever you are hospitalized. The service can be purchased for a week ($15), a week plus additional days ($15, plus $2 for each additional day), a month ($45), or a year ($195). For information, contact International SOS Assistance, PO Box 11568, Philadelphia, PA 19116 (phone: 215-244-1500 or 800-523-8930).

Practically every phase of health care — before, during, and after a trip — is covered in *The New Traveler's Health Guide* by Drs. Patrick J. Doyle and James E. Banta. It is available for $4.95, plus $2 postage and handling, from Acropolis Books Ltd., 2400 17th St. NW, Washington, DC 20009-9964 (phone: 800-451-7771).

LEGAL AID: The best way to begin looking for legal aid in an unfamiliar area is with a call to your own lawyer. If you don't have, or cannot reach, your lawyer, most cities offer lawyer referral services (sometimes called attorney referral services) maintained by county bar associations. There are over 335 such referral services in the US, and they see that anyone in need of legal representation gets it at a reasonable fee. (They are listed in the yellow pages under "Attorney" or "Lawyer." In smaller towns, you will usually find a toll-free number that connects you to the service in the nearest larger city.) The referral service is almost always free. If your case goes to court, you are entitled to court-appointed representation if you can't get a lawyer or can't afford one.

Once you have found a lawyer, ask how many cases of this type the lawyer has worked on and the arrangements to be made regarding fee and additional costs, such as medical or ballistics experts, transcripts, or court fees. For most violations, you will receive a citation at most. There are, however, the rare occasions when travelers find themselves in jail. Since obtaining a bond can be difficult away from home, the bail bonds offered by *AAA* and other automobile clubs are extremely useful (see *Touring by Car*). If you do not have this protection, ask to see a copy of the local bail procedures, which differ from state to state. A lawyer will be able to advise you on the your alternatives in the state in which you are incarcerated.

The *SafeTravel Network* provides 24-hour emergency access to a worldwide network of physicians, lawyers, and other specialists. The service is available to purchasers of Bank America Travelers Cheques for 45 days of coverage; the cost is $8.50. For information, call 800-227-3333; or call collect, 415-624-2222. Some credit card companies offer similar services (see *Credit Cards and Traveler's Checks*).

Drinking and Drug Laws

DRINKING: In all fifty states, the legal drinking age is 21.

Laws on the availability of liquor run the gamut from Nevada's policy of "anytime, anywhere, for anyone of age" to localities where drinking is strictly prohibited. Liquor laws are set by states, counties, and municipalities and towns, making generalizations terribly difficult. Regulations on the hours that bars and restaurants can serve liquor vary, though traditionally closing time in bars is between midnight and 4 AM.

Retail store sales are also restricted to certain hours in many states. Many states require liquor stores to close on holidays and Sundays. Some alcoholic beverages, however, may be purchased on Sundays (most often in restaurants) in almost all states. The following states, however, do not allow any Sunday sales: Connecticut, Louisiana (except where prescribed by local ordinance), Mississippi (except in resort areas), and South Carolina (except in nonprofit clubs from 10 AM to 2 PM).

Some states maintain their own system of state liquor stores, which are usually the only place where you can buy hard liquor, and sometimes wine and beer as well. They include Alabama, Idaho, Iowa, Maine, Michigan, Mississippi, Montana, New Hampshire, North Carolina, Ohio, Oregon, Pennsylvania, Utah, Vermont, Virginia, Washington, West Virginia, and Wyoming.

It is possible to find dry counties or towns in all corners of the country. Usually, however, you will find a town just a few minutes away where the sale of liquor is legal.

Where the laws are tight, there are often private clubs. In states such as Kansas and Oklahoma, you can join private clubs through hotels and motels. Often you join the club with the price of your first drink. In localities that prohibit the serving of liquor but not bottle sales, restaurants or clubs often furnish glasses, ice, and mix if the patron brings a bottle. This practice is also common in states where restaurants have difficulty getting liquor licenses.

Arkansas and Michigan forbid the import of liquor. Some other states have quotas limiting imports to a quart or gallon. These are among the drinking laws least likely to be enforced. However, it is important to be aware of them, because if a state decides it is losing too much tax revenue to a neighboring state where liquor prices are lower, it will begin to crack down. It is wise, for example, not to buy a case of liquor in Missouri in front of a policeman at the last liquor store before crossing into Arkansas.

DRUGS: The best advice we can offer is: Don't carry, use, buy, or sell illegal drugs. The dangers are clear enough when indulging in your own home; if you take drugs while traveling, you may endanger not only your own life but also put others in jeopardy. And if you get caught, you may end up spending your hard-earned vacation funds on bail and attorney's fees — and end up in jail.

Under the federal drug trafficking penalties in effect at this writing, if you are charged with possession with intent to distribute, you can face 5 years to lifetime imprisonment and fines of up to $4 million *for a first offense,* depending on the substance. Don't assume that you're safe by carrying only small amounts of controlled substances for "personal use." According to a spokesman for the Drug Enforcement Administration, some states' penalties for possession of even small amounts of illegal drugs may be stiffer than the federal penalties for possession with intent to distribute. If you value your life and reputation, don't get mixed up in the illicit drug trade.

Tipping and Shopping

 TIPPING: While tipping is at the discretion of the person receiving the service, 25¢ is the rock-bottom tip for anything, and 50¢ is the current customary minimum for small services. In restaurants, tip between 10% and 20% of the bill. Waiters and captains in top restaurants expect a total of 20%; for average service in an average restaurant, 15% is reasonable. If you serve yourself, as in a cafeteria, no tip is expected. Coat checks are worth about 50¢ to $1 a coat. For carrying luggage, tip bellboys $1 per person or couple, $2 if you have a lot of luggage. The doorman who unloads your car should receive $1. For any special service you receive in a hotel, a tip is expected — again 50¢ for a small service, ranging upward to $1 or more if someone does something especially time consuming or out of the ordinary. Leave a hotel maid at least $1 a day.

Train personnel do not usually expect tips, but the exceptions are dining car waiters (who expect 15% of the bill), sleeping car attendants (who should get $2 to $5, depending on the service you require), and porters (who expect 50¢ a bag, $1 if they do something extra). Taxi drivers should get about 15% of the total fare.

SHOPPING: Regional Specialties – In New England, New York, and Pennsylvania, look for good antiques. In addition to shops on Madison Avenue in New York City or Pine Street in Philadelphia, you can find good buys in small antiques stores along country roads if you are prepared to look through the junk and have a good sense of what items are worth. Vermont cheese and maple syrup, saltwater taffy along the New Jersey shore, and shoofly pie and pretzels in the Pennsylvania Dutch country are all specialties of their respective regions.

In the South there are interesting crafts, especially in the inland mountains. West Virginia is noted for handstitched quilts and quilted clothing and toys. In Williamsburg, Virginia, reproductions of pewter, furniture, and other 18th-century items are justly famous. In Georgia, there is basketware, wood carving, handwoven wool, and ceramics. In the Blue Ridge Mountains, look for cornhusk dolls and a small wooden musical instrument called the Gee-Haw-Whimmy-Diddle. The Cherokee at Ocunaluftee Indian Village in North Carolina (see *A Short Tour of Indian America,* DIVERSIONS) sell handmade tomahawks, bows and arrows, pottery, basketwork, rugs, and feather headdresses.

In the Great Lakes region, consider homemade jams and relishes (especially in Iowa's country stores); American antiques in Illinois; hand-painted ceramics in Clay County, Indiana; wheel cheese, summer sausage, and lace in Wisconsin; and pipes, moccasins, and handwoven Indian tribal rugs in Minnesota.

In the Southwest, Mexican, Indian, and "Old West" items are especially good buys. Serapes, tree-of-life candlesticks, and wool rebozos from across the border make nice gifts. The Indian specialties are pottery, Kaibab squaw boots, Navajo rugs, and silver and turquoise jewelry, as well as drums, dolls, and headdresses. Cowboy items include hats, boots, and other ranch clothes from Arizona, New Mexico, and Texas. In the

Rockies, the same "Old West" focus prevails in many of the shops. Consider buckskin jackets or pants and tooled leather belts, boots, or hats. The region is not without its Indian specialties, but most special is Rocky Mountain jade jewelry.

The Far West, Alaska, and the northwestern states are the places to buy Eskimo crafts, which include ceremonial masks, dolls, carved whalebone sculpture, and jade items. American Indian crafts are available in Oregon and Idaho as well as in northern Nevada. Merchandise from the Orient is available in New York's and San Francisco's Chinatowns and in Hawaii.

Ask any store about mailing your purchases home; it may save on local sales taxes and will mean less to carry with you.

■ **A Special Hint:** For some particularly interesting souvenirs and gifts, look in museum shops, which often carry beautifully made reproductions from their collections — anything from prints and posters to jewelry, silver goods, and sculpture.

Factory Outlets – Outlets are huge warehouse stores where companies unload their overruns and canceled orders at dramatically reduced prices — from 20% to 75% off the retail price. They also sell irregulars (slightly flawed pieces) and seconds (more severely flawed or damaged goods). These will be appropriately marked. Some companies, like *Bass* shoes and *Dansk* housewares, have many stores, others just one or two. Factory outlets tend to be outside major urban areas, and several cities around the country have become known for having clusters of outlets nearby. The best known of these are Reading, Pennsylvania; Rochester, Minnesota; Sylvania, Ohio; Manchester, Vermont; Cohoes, New York; and Louisville, Kentucky. Two urban areas known for outlets are Orchard Street in Lower Manhattan, New York City, and Fashion Row in Miami, Florida. The New England states are famous for blankets, leather, linen, and textiles; the Carolinas for furniture, linen, textiles, and towels; and Virginia and West Virginia for glassware and pottery.

At any factory outlet, be prepared for crowds, especially on Saturdays. Bear in mind that outlets are rarely centrally located and may take some time to find. (Usually you will need a car.) Some outlets accept credit cards, but they are the ones that are likely to charge higher prices.

Two directories of factory outlets, compiled by two aptly "named" editors, A. Miser and A. Pennypincher, are *Factory Store Guide to All of New England*, listing over 350 factory outlet stores, and *Factory Store Guide to All of New York, Pennsylvania, and New Jersey*, covering over 850 factory outlets. Both are available for $6.95 from Globe Pequot Press/Affiliated Publishing, Old Chester Rd., Chester, CT 06412 (phone: 203-526-9571 or 800-243-0495). When using these guides, don't forget to call ahead; factory outlets regularly change their standard merchandise and can go out of business on short notice.

Flea Markets – A growing phenomenon, all across the country, is that of flea markets, where all kinds of goods are offered in open stands. Found in country fields or empty parking lots, stadiums or skating rinks, some are occasional events advertised locally (watch the daily or weekly paper in the area in which you are traveling); others, usually in larger cities, are run on a permanent or semi-permanent basis and advertised regularly in local papers. Among the directories of flea markets in the US are the following:

Clark's Flea Market U.S.A. covers over 3,000 flea markets, swap meets, and auctions nationwide. Published four times a year by Clark's Publications (2156 Cotton Patch La., Milton, FL 32570; phone: 904-623-0794), a single copy costs $7.50; a year's subscription, $25.

Great American Flea Market Directory lists 1,400 flea markets, swap meets, and trade shows throughout the US and includes some listings in Canada. Issued twice a year (November and June) by the Independent Dealers Association (PO Box 455, Arnold, MO 63010; phone: 314-464-2616) for $5 a copy plus $1.25 for postage and handling.

The Official Directory to U.S. Flea Markets describes in detail over 500 regularly scheduled flea markets across the country, ranging in size from under 50 to over 1,000 dealers. It also offers practical advice on how to shop at flea markets, when to haggle, and how to become a seller. Published by the House of Collectibles (a division of Random House) for $5.95, plus $1 for shipping and handling; to order call 800-638-6460.

Religion on the Road

 The surest source of information on religious services in any town is the desk clerk of the hotel or motel in which you are staying. In most cities, joint religious councils print circulars with the addresses and times of services of all the churches, synagogues, and temples in the city. These are often printed as part of general tourist guides provided by the tourist and convention center or as part of a "what's on" guide to the city. The tourist council certainly can provide the information you need on services. Many newspapers also list religious services in their area in weekend editions. Often an entire page will be devoted to church and religious news.

You may want to use your vacation to broaden your religious experience by joining an unfamiliar faith in its service. This can be a moving experience, especially if the service is held in a sanctuary that is historically significant or architecturally notable. You will almost always find yourself made welcome and comfortable.

Sources and Resources

General Notes on Sports

 From Tampa, Florida, to Green Bay, Wisconsin, you can take in major seasonal sporting events during your travels. Here is some background on teams and events. See individual city reports in THE CITIES for specific ticket information.

AUTO RACING: There are five major automobile races in the US each year:

The Indianapolis 500 takes place on *Memorial Day* weekend each year at the *Indianapolis Motor Speedway,* 4790 W. 16th St., Indianapolis, IN 46224 (phone: 317-241-2500).

The Daytona 500 is held yearly in February at the *Daytona International Speedway,* 1801 Volusia Ave., Daytona Beach, FL 32014 (phone: 904-254-6767).

The Toyota Grand Prix of Long Beach is held each April in Long Beach, California; information from 110 W. Ocean Blvd., Suite 22, Long Beach, CA 90802 (phone: 213-437-0341).

The Detroit Grand Prix is held in June (usually the third weekend). For information write to Detroit Renaissance, 100 Renaissance Center, Suite 1760, Detroit, MI 48243, or call 313-259-5400.

The Grand Prix of Miami is run in February or March on the streets of downtown Miami. For information, write to Miami Motorsports, 7254 SW 48th St., Miami, FL 33155, or call 305-662-5660.

For information on other important races: the Automobile Competition Committee for the United States, FIA, 1500 Skokie Blvd., Suite 101, Northbrook, IL 60062 (phone: 312-272-0090).

BASEBALL: Baseball is known as the national pastime, and with good reason. Its season opens in April and continues daily through the World Series in October. The professional teams are divided into two leagues, the National League and the American League. The National League (at 350 Park Ave., New York, NY 10022; phone: 212-371-7300) includes Atlanta, Chicago *Cubs,* Cincinnati, Houston, Los Angeles, Montreal, New York *Mets,* Philadelphia, Pittsburgh, St. Louis, San Diego, and San Francisco. In the American League (at 350 Park Ave., New York, NY 10022; phone: 212-371-7600) are Baltimore, Boston, California, Chicago *White Sox,* Cleveland, Detroit, Kansas City, Milwaukee, Minnesota, New York *Yankees,* Oakland, Seattle, Texas, and Toronto.

BASKETBALL: Professional basketball gets under way each year in October and keeps its fans watching the hoops through the playoffs in late May or early June. The National Basketball Association (NBA) oversees the sport and is divided into two conferences. The Eastern Conference includes Atlanta, Boston, Charlotte, Chicago, Cleveland, Detroit, Indiana, Milwaukee, New York, New Jersey, Orlando, Philadelphia, and Washington, DC. In the Western Conference are Dallas, Denver,

Golden State (Oakland), Houston, Los Angeles *Clippers* and *Lakers,* Miami, Minnesota, Phoenix, Portland, Sacramento, San Antonio, Seattle, and Utah. Information: the NBA, Olympic Tower, 645 5th Ave., New York, NY 10022 (phone: 212-826-7000).

FOOTBALL: This popular American spectator sport is under the aegis of the National Football League (NFL). The NFL season opens in September and culminates in the Super Bowl, which is held in mid-January between the top teams of the two NFL conferences. The National Conference is made up of the Atlanta, Chicago, Dallas, Detroit, Green Bay, Los Angeles *Rams,* Minnesota, New Orleans, New York *Giants,* Phoenix, Philadelphia, San Francisco, Tampa, and Washington, DC. The American Conference consists of Buffalo, Cincinnati, Cleveland, Denver, Houston, Indianapolis, Kansas City, Los Angeles *Raiders,* Miami, New England, New York *Jets,* Pittsburgh, San Diego, and Seattle. Information: the NFL, 410 Park Ave., New York, NY 10022 (phone: 212-758-1500).

College football competition also takes place throughout the country from September through December. The Rose Bowl, which is the championship game between the winner of contests among the Midwest Big Ten universities and the top team in the Pacific Conference schools, is held January 1. For tickets, which are assigned by lottery, send a postcard from September 1 through October 1 to Rose Bowl Ticket Drawing, PO Box 91386, Pasadena, CA 91109 (phone: 818-449-4100). Another famous college contest is the Yale-Harvard game, which takes place either in New Haven (odd years) or Cambridge (even years) in November. It closes the Ivy League football season. For tickets, contact the Yale Ticket Office, PO Box 402A, Yale Station, New Haven, CT 06520 (phone: 203-432-1400), or Athletic Ticket Office, Harvard Hall Basement, Harvard University, Cambridge, MA 02138 (phone: 617-495-2211).

GOLF: Professional golf tournaments are held under the aegis of the Professional Golfers' Association of America (PGA). The four biggest tournaments on its tour include the Players Championship, held in March in Ponte Vedra, Florida; the Masters Golf Tournament, held in April in Augusta, Georgia; the US Open, held in June at a different select course around the country each year; and the Professional Golfers' Association (PGA) Championship, held at a different premier layout every August. Contact the PGA of America for details, PO Box 109601, 100 Avenue of Champions, Palm Beach Gardens, FL 33410-9601 (phone: 407-626-3600).

HOCKEY: From October through May the ice is hotly contested by the National Hockey League, whose membership is composed of Boston, Buffalo, Calgary, Chicago, Detroit, Edmonton, Hartford, Los Angeles, Minnesota, Montreal, New Jersey, New York *Islanders,* New York *Rangers,* Philadelphia, Pittsburgh, Quebec, St. Louis, Toronto, Vancouver, Washington, and Winnipeg. Its best teams compete for the Stanley Cup in May. For more information, contact: NHL, 650 Fifth Ave., 33rd Floor, New York, NY 10019 (phone: 212-398-1100); or NHL, 1155 Metcalfe St., Suite 960, Montreal, Que., H3B 2W2 (phone: 514-871-9220).

HORSE RACING: Among the most prestigious national horse races are the Triple Crown races for three-year-olds. The Kentucky Derby is the first, held in early May at *Churchill Downs,* 700 Central Ave., Louisville, KY 40208 (phone: 502-636-3541). Second is the Preakness Stakes, run later in May at *Pimlico Race Course*, Baltimore, MD 21215-9945 (phone: 301-542-9400). The final leg is the Belmont Stakes, held each year in June in *Belmont Park*, Elmont, NY 11003 (phone: 718-641-4700).

TENNIS: The major event in US tennis is the US Open Tennis Championships at *Flushing Meadow Park,* held each year around Labor Day weekend. For information, write to US Open Tennis Championships, National Tennis Center, Flushing Meadow, Queens, NY 11368 (phone: 718-271-5100). Tickets go on sale in June but are very difficult to obtain.

Weights and Measures

At some time in the future, the US may convert from the familiar units of measure (feet, yards, quarts, etc.) to the far easier and more logical metric system. Some highway signs, weight scales, and grocery labels already list both measurements. Metric conversions and equivalents are listed below.

APPROXIMATE EQUIVALENTS		
Metric Unit	**Abbreviation**	**US Equivalent**
LENGTH		
millimeter	mm	.04 inch
meter	m	39.37 inches
kilometer	km	.62 mile
AREA		
square centimeter	sq cm	.155 square inch
square meter	sq m	10.7 square feet
hectare	ha	2.47 acres
square kilometer	sq km	.3861 square mile
CAPACITY		
liter	l	1.057 quarts
WEIGHT		
gram	g	.035 ounce
kilogram	kg	2.2 pounds
metric ton	MT	1.1 tons
ENERGY		
kilowatt	kw	1.34 horsepower

CONVERSION TABLES: METRIC TO US MEASUREMENTS		
Multiply	**by**	**to convert to**
LENGTH		
millimeters	.04	inches
meters	3.3	feet
meters	1.1	yards
kilometers	.6	miles
CAPACITY		
liters	2.11	pints (liquid)
liters	1.06	quarts (liquid)
liters	.26	gallons (liquid)
WEIGHT		
gram	.04	ounces (avoir)
kilograms	2.2	pounds (avoir)

US TO METRIC MEASUREMENTS		
Multiply	**by**	**to convert to**
LENGTH		
inches	2.5	millimeters
feet	.3	meters
yards	.9	meters
miles	1.6	kilometers
CAPACITY		
pints	.47	liters
quarts	.95	liters
gallons	3.8	liters
WEIGHT		
ounces	28.	grams
pounds	.45	kilograms

TEMPERATURE

$$°F = (°C \times 9/5) + 32 \qquad °C = (°F - 32) \times 5/9$$

For More Information

Every city or region has at least one local guide — rarely available outside the area — which provides information on the nearby scene that is topical, detailed, and often amusing. While you are on the road, it will be well worth your time to browse the shelves of local bookstores. Before you leave on your journey, however, you can prepare by writing to city, regional, and state tourist authorities for information (see *State Tourist Offices* in this section and *Sources and Resources* in THE CITIES); and by perusing books relevant to your special travel interests. The variety and scope of travel information in the United States today is astounding; below, a partial list of publications we have found particularly useful. Refer to individual chapters of GETTING READY TO GO for further lists of sources on specific topics.

NEWSLETTERS: A variety of newsletters provide up-to-date travel information in a simple format; most of the ones on the market today are monthly, eight-page reports that offer inside tips, detailed reports on destinations, and frank evaluations of travel bargains and opportunities in the US and abroad. Newsletters take no advertising, and can be good sources of disinterested — if subjective — judgments.

Consumer Reports Travel Letter (Subscription Dept., Box 53629, Boulder, CO 80322; phone: 303-447-9330; 12 issues per year, $37)

Entree (PO Box 5148, Santa Barbara, CA 93150; phone: 805-969-5848; 12 issues per year, $59 includes 24-hour information hotline)

First Class Confidential (Agora, 824 E. Baltimore St., Baltimore, MD 21202; phone: 301-234-0515; 12 issues per year, $75)

The Hideaway Report (Harper Assocs., PO Box 50, Sun Valley, ID 83353; phone: 208-622-3183; 12 issues per year, $85)

BOOKS: The list below comprises books we have seen and think worthwhile; it is by no means complete. Check the card catalogue of your library for other titles. Prices may have increased slightly in most recent editions.

Travel in the US

Adventure Travel North America by Pat Dickerman (Adventure Guides, 36 E. 57th St., New York, NY 10022; phone: 212-355-6334; $12 postpaid)

America by Train by Ira Fistell (Burt Franklin, PO Box 856, New York, NY 10014; phone: 212-627-0027; $10.95)

Guide to the National Wildlife Refuges by Laura and William Riley (Doubleday). Out of print; check your library.

Pictorial Travel Guide of Scenic America by E. L. Jordan (Hammond). Out of print; check your library.

Scenic Wonders of America (Random House). Out of print; check your library.

Wilderness U.S.A. (National Geographic Society, Washington, DC 20036; phone: 202-857-7000; $9.95 plus $2 postage and handling; cloth)

Facts and Information

National Parks: Index, 1987 (#024-005-01024-6; $3). Write to Superintendent of Documents, US Government Printing Office, Washington, DC 20402 (phone: 202-783-3238).

Rand McNally Road Atlas: US, Canada and Mexico (Rand McNally; $6.95)

Forests, Parks, and Camping

Allstate Motor Club: National Park Guide (Prentice-Hall; $12.95)

Allstate Motor Club: RV Park and Campground Directory (Prentice-Hall; $14.95)

Wheelers RV Resort and Campground Guide (Print Media Services, 1310 Jarvis Ave., Elk Grove, IL 60007; phone: 312-981-0100; $10.95)

Woodall's North American Campground Directory (Simon & Schuster; $12.95)

Walking and Backpacking

Backpacking in North America: The Great Outdoors by Hilary J. Bradt and George N. Bradt (Bradt Enterprises). Out of print; check your library.

Guide to Backpacking in the United States by Eric Meves (Macmillan). Out of print; check your library.

Walking: A Guide to Beautiful Walks and Trails in America by Jean Calder (Morrow). Out of print; check your library.

Bicycling

American Biking Atlas and Touring Guide by Sue Browder (Workman). Out of print; check your library.

Anybody's Bike Book by Tom Cuthbertson (Ten Speed Press; $7.95, paper)

The Bicycle Touring Book by Glenda and Tim Wilhelm (Rodale Press). Out of print; check your library.

Complete Book of Bicycling by Eugene A. Sloane (Simon & Schuster; $24.95)

Twenty Bicycle Tours in the Finger Lakes by Mark Roth and Sally Walters (Backcountry Publication; $7.95)

Twenty Bicycle Trips in and Around New York City by Dan Carlinsky and David Heim (Backcountry Publications; $7.95)

Canoeing

Back to Nature in Canoes: A Guide to American Waters by Rainer Esslen (Columbia; $6.95)

Theme Vacations

Experiencing America's Past: A Travel Guide to Museum Villages by Gerald and Patricia Gutek (John Wiley; $12.95)

Farm, Ranch, & Country Vacations by Pat Dickerman (Farm & Ranch Vacations, 36 E. 57th St., New York, NY 10022; phone: 212-355-6334; $12 postpaid)

Sobek's Adventure Vacations (Running Press; $12.95)

Food

Roadfood and Goodfood by Jane and Michael Stern (Random House; $12.95, paper)

Where to Eat in America by William Rice and Barbara Goldman (Scribner's; $12.95)

Historic Inns and Inexpensive Accommodations

Bed and Breakfast America: The Great American Guest House by John Thaxton (Burt Franklin, PO Box 856, New York, NY 10014; phone: 212-627-0027; $10.95)

The Bed & Breakfast Guide, 1989-90 Edition (National Bed & Breakfast Assn., Box 332, Norwalk, CT 06852; phone: 203-847-6196; $13.95, plus $2 postage)

Bed & Breakfast USA by Betty Rundback and Nancy Kramer (Dutton; $12.95)

The Complete Guide to Bed & Breakfast, Inns, and Guesthouses in the U.S. and Canada by Pamela Lanier (John Muir Publications, Box 613, Santa Fe, NM 87505; phone: 505-982-4078; $14.95)

Country Inns of the Middle Atlantic States by Anthony Hitchcock and Jean Lindgren (Burt Franklin, PO Box 856, New York, NY 10014; phone: 212-627-0027; $10.95)

Historic Country Inns of California by Jim Crain (Chronicle Books; phone: 415-777-7240; $8.95)

The 1989-1990 National Directory of Budget Motels (Pilot Books, 103 Cooper St., Babylon, NY 11702; phone: 516-422-2225; $4.95)

COMPUTER SERVICES: Anyone who owns a personal computer can subscribe to a database service providing everything from airline schedules and fares to restaurant listings. Three such services to try:

CompuServe (5000 Arlington Center Blvd., Columbus, OH 43200; phone 614-457-8650 or 800-848-8199)

Prodigy Services (445 Hamilton Ave., White Plains, NY 10601; phone 914-993-8000)

The Source (1616 Anderson Rd., McLean, VA 22102; phone: 703-821-8888 or 800-336-3330)

State Tourist Offices

Below is a list of state tourist offices in all the US states (city tourist and convention centers are listed in THE CITIES section of this guide). These state offices offer a wide variety of useful travel information, most of it free for the asking. For best results, request general information on state facilities (several states have "travel kits" which include lists of hotels, tourist attractions, maps, and more) as well as specific information relevant to your interests: facilities for specific sports, tours and itineraries of special interest, accommodations in specific areas. Because most of the material you receive will be outsized brochures, there is little point in sending a self-addressed, stamped envelope with your request.

Alabama: Bureau of Tourism and Travel, 532 S. Perry St., Montgomery, AL 36130 (phone: 205-261-4169; 800-392-8096 in Alabama; 800-ALABAMA elsewhere except Alaska and Hawaii)

Alaska: Division of Tourism, PO Box E, Juneau, AK 99811 (phone: 907-465-2010)

Arizona: Office of Tourism, 1100 W. Washington St., Phoenix, AZ 85007 (phone: 602-542-3618)

Arkansas: Department of Parks and Tourism, 1 Capitol Mall, Little Rock, AR 72201 (phone: 501-682-1511; 800-482-8999 in Arkansas; 800-643-8383 elsewhere)

California: Department of Commerce, Office of Tourism, 1121 L St., Suite 103, Sacramento, CA 95814 (phone: 916-322-1396)

Colorado: Tourism Board, 1625 Broadway, Suite 1700, Denver, CO 80202 (phone: 303-592-5410 or 800-433-2656)

Connecticut: Department of Economic Development, Tourism Division, 210 Washington St., Hartford, CT 06106 (phone: 203-566-3385; 800-842-7492 in Connecticut; 800-243-1685 elsewhere on the east coast, Virginia to Maine)

Delaware: Tourism Office, Delaware Development Office, PO Box 1401, Dover, DE 19903 (phone: 302-736-4271 or 800-441-8846)

District of Columbia: Washington, DC, Convention and Visitors Association, 1212 New York Ave. NW, Suite 600, Washington, DC 20005 (phone: 202-789-7000)

Florida: Visitor Inquiry, Department of Commerce, 126 Van Buren St., Tallahassee, FL 32399-2000 (phone: 904-487-1462)

Georgia: Tourist Division, Department of Industry and Trade, PO Box 1776, Atlanta, GA 30301 (phone: 404-656-3590)

Hawaii: Visitors Bureau, PO Box 8527, Honolulu, HI 96830 (phone: 808-923-1811)

Idaho: Travel Council, Hall of Mirrors, 2nd Floor, 700 W. State St., Boise, ID 83720 (phone: 208-334-2470 or 800-635-7820)

Illinois: Tourist Information Center, 310 S. Michigan Ave., Suite 108, Chicago, IL 60604 (phone: 312-793-2094 or 800-223-0121)

Indiana: Tourism Division, Department of Commerce, 1 N. Capitol, Suite 700, Indianapolis, IN 46204-2288 (phone: 317-232-8860 or 800-2-WANDER)

Iowa: Department of Economic Development, 200 E. Grand Ave., Des Moines, IA 50309 (phone: 515-281-3100 or 800-345-IOWA)

Kansas: Department of Economic Development, Kansas Tourism Division, 400 SW 8th St., 5th Fl., Topeka, KS 66603 (phone: 913-296-2009 or 800-252-6727 in Kansas)

Kentucky: Department of Travel Development, Capital Plaza Tower, 22nd Fl., Frankfort, KY 40601 (phone: 502-564-4930 or 800-225-TRIP)

Louisiana: Office of Tourism, PO Box 94291, Baton Rouge, LA 70804-9291 (phone: 504-342-8119 or 800-33-GUMBO)

Maine: Publicity Bureau, 97 Winthrop St., Hallowell, ME 04347 (phone: 207-289-2423 or 800-533-9595)

Maryland: Department of Economic and Employment Development, Office of Tourism Development, 217 E. Redwood St., 9th Fl., Baltimore, MD 21202 (phone: 301-333-6611 or 800-543-1036)

Massachusetts: Office of Travel and Tourism, 100 Cambridge St., Boston, MA 02202 (phone: 617-727-3201)

Michigan: Travel Bureau, Department of Commerce, PO Box 30226, Lansing, MI 48909 (phone: 517-373-0670 or 800-543-2937)

Minnesota: Office of Tourism, 375 Jackson St., Room 250, St. Paul, MN 55101 (phone: 612-296-5029; 800-652-9747 in Minnesota; 800-328-1461 elsewhere)

Mississippi: Department of Economic Development, Tourism Development Division, PO Box 849, Jackson, MS 39205-0849 (phone: 601-359-3414 or 800-647-2290/1)

Missouri: Division of Tourism, Truman State Office Bldg., PO Box 1055, Jefferson City, MO 65102 (phone: 314-751-4133)

Montana: Travel Promotion Division, Department of Commerce, 1424 9th Ave. Helena, MT 59620 (phone: 406-444-2654 or 800-541-1447)

Nebraska: Division of Travel and Tourism, Department of Economic Development, PO Box 94666, 301 Centennial Mall S., Lincoln, NE 68509 (phone: 402-471-3796; 800-742-7595 in Nebraska; 800-228-4307 elsewhere)

Nevada: Commission on Tourism, Capitol Complex, Carson City, NV 89710 (phone: 702-885-4322 or 800-NEVADA-8)

New Hampshire: Office of Vacation Travel, PO Box 856, Concord, NH 03301 (phone: 603-271-2343)

New Jersey: Department of Commerce and Economic Development, Division of Travel and Tourism, CN 826, Trenton, NJ 08625 (phone: 609-292-2470)

New Mexico: Economic Development and Tourism Dept., Joseph M. Montoya Bldg., 1100 St. Francis Dr., Rm. 1057, Santa Fe, NM 87503 (phone: 505-827-0291 or 800-545-2040)

New York: Division of Tourism, State Department of Economic Development, 1 Commerce Plaza, Albany, NY 12245 (phone: 518-474-4116 or 800-CALL-NYS)

North Carolina: Travel and Tourism Division, 430 N. Salisbury St., Raleigh, NC 27611 (phone: 919-733-4171 or 800-VISIT-NC)

North Dakota: Tourism Promotion Division, Liberty Memorial Bldg., Capitol Grounds, Bismarck, ND 58505 (phone: 701-224-2525; 800-472-2100 in North Dakota; 800-437-2077 elsewhere)

Ohio: Division of Travel and Tourism, PO Box 1001, Columbus, OH 43266-0101 (phone: 614-466-8844 or 800-BUCKEYE)

Oklahoma: Tourism and Recreation Department, 500 Will Rogers Building, Oklahoma City, OK 73105 (phone: 405-521-2409 or 800-652-6552)

Oregon: Tourism Division, Economic Development Dept., 595 Cottage St. NE, Salem, OR 97310 (phone: 503-378-3451; 800-543-8838 in Oregon; 800-547-7842 elsewhere)

Pennsylvania: Department of Commerce, Bureau of Travel Marketing, Forum Building, Harrisburg, PA 17120 (phone: 717-787-5453 or 800-VISIT-PA)

Rhode Island: Department of Economic Development, Tourism and Promotion Division, 7 Jackson Walkway, Providence, RI 02903 (phone: 401-277-2601; 800-556-2484 on Eastern seaboard, Maine to Virginia and northern parts of Ohio)

South Carolina: Department of Parks, Recreation and Tourism, Division of Tourism, PO Box 71, Columbia, SC 29202-0071 (phone: 803-734-0122)

South Dakota: Governor's Office of Economic Development, Department of Tourism, Capitol Lake Plaza, 711 Wells, Pierre, SD 57501 (phone: 605-773-3301 or 800-843-1930)

Tennessee: Department of Tourist Development, PO Box 23170, Nashville, TN 37202 (phone: 615-741-2158)

Texas: Travel and Information Division, Department of Highways and Public Transportation, PO Box 5064, Austin, TX 78763 (phone: 512-465-7401)

Utah: Travel Council, Council Hall, Capitol Hill, Salt Lake City, UT 84114 (phone: 801-538-1030)

Vermont: Travel Division, 134 State St., Montpelier, VT 05602 (phone: 802-828-3236)

Virginia: Division of Tourism, 202 N. 9th St., Suite 500, Richmond, VA 23219 (phone: 804-786-4484 or 800-248-4833)

Washington: Tourism Development Division, Department of Trade and Economic Development, 101 General Administration Bldg., Olympia, WA 98504 (phone: 206-586-2088 or 800-544-1800)

West Virginia: Department of Commerce, Marketing/Tourism Division, State Capitol Complex, Charleston, WV 25305 (phone: 304-348-2766 or 800-CALL-WVA)

Wisconsin: Division of Tourism, Box 7606, Madison, WI 53707 (phone: 608-266-2161; 800-ESCAPES in Illinois, Iowa, Michigan, Minnesota, and Wisconsin)

Wyoming: Travel Commission, I-25 and College Dr., Cheyenne, WY 82002 (phone: 307-777-7777 or 800-225-5996)

Camera and Equipment

 Vacations are everybody's favorite time for taking pictures. After all, most of us want to remember the places we visit — and show them off to others — through spectacular photographs. Here are a few suggestions to help you get the best results from your travel picture taking.

BEFORE THE TRIP: If you're taking your camera out after a long period in moth-balls, or have just bought a new one, check it thoroughly before you leave to prevent unexpected breakdowns and disappointing pictures.

1. Shoot at least one test roll, using the kind of film you plan to take along with you. Use all the shutter speeds and f-stops on your camera, and vary the focus to make sure everything is in order. Do this well in advance of your departure so there will be time to have film developed and to make repairs, if necessary. If you're in a rush, most large cities have custom labs that can process film in as little as an hour. Repairs, unfortunately, take longer.

2. Clean your camera thoroughly, inside and out. Dust and dirt can jam camera mechanisms, scratch film, and mar photographs. Remove surface dust from lenses and camera body with a soft camel's-hair brush. Next, use at least two layers of crumpled lens tissue and your breath to clean lenses and filters. Don't rub hard and don't use water, saliva, or compressed air on lenses or filters because they are so easily damaged. Persistent stains can be removed by using a Q-tip moistened with liquid lens cleaner. Anything that doesn't come off easily needs professional attention. Once your lenses are clean, protect them from dirt and damage with inexpensive skylight or ultraviolet filters.

3. Check the batteries for the light meter and take along extras just in case yours wear out during the trip. They can be a nuisance to find.

EQUIPMENT TO TAKE ALONG: Keep your gear light and compact. Items that are too heavy or bulky to be carried comfortably on a full-day excursion will likely stay in your hotel room.

1. Most single lens reflex (SLR) cameras come with a 50mm, or "normal," lens, a general purpose lens that frames subjects within an approximately average angle of view. This is good for street scenes taken at a distance of 25 feet or more and for full-length portraits shot at 8 to 12 feet. You can expand your photographic options with a wide-angle lens such as a 35mm, 28mm, or 24mm. These give a broader than normal angle of view and greater than normal "depth of field," that is, sharp focus from foreground to background. They are especially handy for panoramas, cityscapes, and for large buildings or statuary from which you can't step back. For extreme close-ups, a macro-lens is best, but a screw-on magnifying lens is an inexpensive alternative. Telephoto lenses, 65mm to 1000mm, are good

for shooting details from a distance (as in animal photography), but since they tend to be heavy and bulky, omit them from vacation photography equipment unless you anticipate a frequent need for them. A zoom, which is a big lens but relatively light, has a variable angle of view so it gives a range of options. Try a 35mm to 80mm; beware of inexpensive models that give poor quality photographs. Protect all lenses with skylight or ultraviolet filters, which should be removed for cleaning only. A polarizing filter helps to eliminate glare and reflection and to achieve fully saturated colors in very bright sunlight. Take along a couple of extra lens caps (they're the first things to get lost) or buy an inexpensive lens cap "leash."

2. Travel photographs work best in color. Good slide films are Kodachrome 64 and Fujichrome 50, both moderate- to slow-speed films that provide saturated colors and work well in most outdoor lighting situations. For very bright conditions, try slower film like Kodachrome 25. If the weather is cloudy, or you're indoors with only natural light, use a faster film, such as Kodachrome or Ektachrome 200 or 400. These can be "pushed" to higher speeds. There are even faster films on the market for low-light situations. The result may be pictures with whiter, colder tones and a grainier image, but high-speed films open up picture possibilities that slower films cannot.

   Films tend to render color in slightly different ways. Kodachrome brings out reds and oranges. Fujichrome is noted for its yellows, greens, and whites. Agfachrome mutes bright tones, producing fine browns, yellows, and whites. Anticipate what you are likely to see, and take along whichever types of film will enhance your results. You might test films as you test your camera (see above).

   If you prefer film that develops into prints rather than slides, try Kodacolor 100 or 400 for most lighting situations. Vericolor is a professional film that gives excellent results, especially in skin tones, but suffers shifts in color when subjected to temperature extremes; take it along for people photography if you're sure you can protect it from heat and cold. All lens and filter information applies equally to print and slide films.

   How much film should you take? If you are serious about your photography, pack one roll of film (36 exposures) for each day of your trip; leftovers can be bartered away or brought home and safely stored in your refrigerator. If you are concerned about airport security X-rays damaging your undeveloped film (X-rays do not affect processed film), store it in lead-lined bags sold in camera shops. This possibility is not as much of a threat as it used to be, however. In the US, incidents of X-ray damage to unprocessed film (exposed or unexposed) are minimal because low-dosage X-ray equipment is used virtually everywhere. As a rule of thumb, photo industry sources say that film with speeds up to ASA 400 can go through security machinery in the US five times without any noticeable effect. One type of film that should never be subjected to X-rays is the new, very high speed film with an ASA rating of 1,000. Ask to have your photo equipment inspected by hand; Federal Aviation Administration regulations in the US require that if you request a hand inspection, you get it. Finally, the walk-through metal detector devices at airports do not affect film, though the film cartridges will set them off.

3. A small battery-powered electronic flash unit, or "strobe," is handy for very dim light or at night, but only if the subject is at a distance of 15 feet or less. Flash units cannot illuminate an entire scene, and many museums do not permit flash photography, so take such a unit only if you know you will need it. If your camera does not have a hot-shoe, you will need a PC cord to synchronize the flash with your shutter. Be sure to take along extra batteries for the flash.

4. Invest in a broad camera strap if you now have a thin one. It will make carrying the camera much more comfortable.

5. A sturdy canvas or leather camera bag, preferably with padded pockets — not an airline bag — will keep equipment organized and easy to find.

6. For cleaning, bring along a camel's-hair brush that retracts into a rubber squeeze bulb. Also, take plenty of lens tissue and plastic bags to protect equipment from dust.

SOME TIPS: For better pictures, the following pointers will help.

1. *Get close.* Move in to get your subject to fill the frame.

2. *Vary your angle.* Shoot from above or below — look for unusual perspectives.

3. *Pay attention to backgrounds.* Keep it simple or blur it out.

4. *Look for details.* Not just a whole building, but a decorative element; not just an entire street scene, but a single remarkable face.

5. *Don't be lazy.* Always carry your camera gear with you, loaded and ready for those unexpected moments.

THE CITIES

ATLANTA

Until the 1960s, the world at large knew Atlanta mainly through the pages of Margaret Mitchell's *Gone With the Wind*. But then a pragmatic leadership steered it calmly through the stormy seas of social change, and an avalanche of favorable press turned the city — almost overnight — into America's urban sweetheart. Waves of ambitious entrepreneurs rushed in from across the country and around the world. Up went urban towers, ritzy hotels, glitzy restaurants, modern sports arenas, and shopping galleries where before there had been mostly red earth, pines, and kudzu.

In the early 19th century, the city was nothing but a section of frontier forest coaxed away from the Creek Indians by the state of Georgia. A proposed rail route into the area from Tennessee was determined in 1837. A surveyor for the Western & Atlantic Railroad staked the southern terminus for the new right of way near where the CNN Center, formerly the Omni International complex, now stands, calling the railroad workers' camp that grew on the site simply the Terminus.

Pretty soon they started calling it Marthasville, after the daughter of the governor who boosted the rail project. Then someone with the railroad feminized Atlantic into Atlanta and started using that name on train schedules. The city was chartered as Atlanta in 1847.

By the eve of the War Between the States, the city was a humming juggernaut whose 10,000 industrious citizens ran banks and stores and turned out munitions, railroad cars, food, and clothing for the Confederacy. Punished by devastation, Atlantans swiftly put their town back together and even invited the archfiend himself, General William Tecumseh Sherman, to witness the resurrection personally. Crusty old "War Is Hell" returned three times, was wined and dined, and was so impressed, he invested in the city's reconstruction effort.

Today's Atlanta, strung together by an overburdened network of freeways, is the financial, administrative, and distribution center and the cultural, retail, entertainment, transportation, and communications focus for a flourishing Sunbelt domain counting more than 34 million heads.

More than 30% of Georgia's manufacturing takes place in metropolitan Atlanta, and, at the latest reckoning, all but a handful of *Fortune* magazine's 500 largest corporations maintain national or regional offices and production facilities here. Attesting to the city's newest slogan, "The World's Next Great International City," about 35 nations operate consulates and trade offices.

And the city still thrives as a distribution point for travelers. After the Civil War, there was a familiar complaint about Atlanta: "Whether you're going to heaven or hell," people used to say, "you'll have to change trains in Atlanta." Today it's a change of planes, but the city's role is the same. Hartsfield International Airport, physically the world's largest jet terminal

CENTRAL
ATLANTA

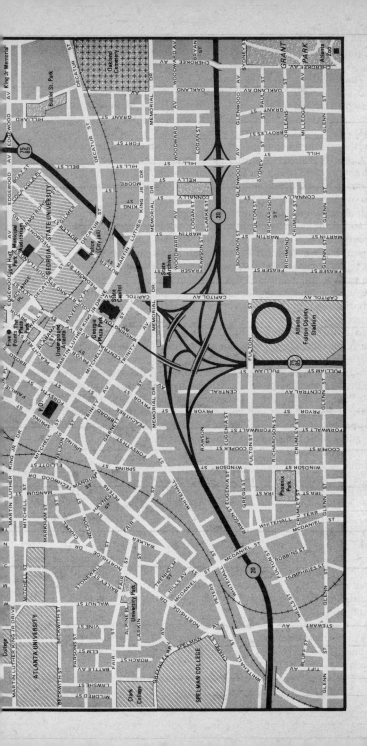

complex, annually runs neck and neck with Chicago's O'Hare in the number of passengers transported by aircraft. Every year, more than 41 million passengers — half again as many as Europe's largest airports — pass through Hartsfield's color-coded concourses to and from Nashville, Seattle, Amsterdam, Mexico City, and a thousand and one other destinations.

Thanks to a transplanted Cincinnatian named Robert Edward (Ted) Turner III, Atlanta has also made a very big name for itself in the world of communications. Launched from a bankrupt UHF station in the early 1970s, Turner's Cable News Network and superstation WTBS are now beamed across the country and to Europe and Japan as well. As a side effect, Turner's Atlanta *Braves* baseball team and Atlanta *Hawks* basketball team have fan clubs in some very unlikely out-of-state locales.

For shoppers from the far corners of Dixie, Peachtree Street is Fifth Avenue; here and in the suburban malls are found Atlanta's own retailers as well as trendy carpetbaggers from Beverly Hills, New York, and Paris. For Southerners in search of a good time, Atlanta is not known as "Hot-lanna" simply because a fellow named Sherman once burned it down.

Atlanta may be a hard-headed business giant, but it's also a town with a very large heart in which enlightened urban planning has integrated human needs and priorities into the civic structure. Clean-lined, functional skyscrapers are designed so that the inner space makes people comfortable rather than intimidated by overpowering monolithic anonymity. Sometimes, those designs even fulfill their aims. Older, inner-city neighborhoods like Midtown, Virginia/Highland, and Inman Park, once afflicted by urban blight, have been brought back to life largely by young Atlantans who thrive on urban diversity.

Culturally, the bleak days when Atlanta reigned unhappily over H. L. Mencken's "Sahara of the Bozarts" have passed into history. The *High Museum of Art,* a feast of light and contemporary angles, has been highly acclaimed by art critics. The *Atlanta Ballet* and *Atlanta Symphony* are also well esteemed, and a score of lively companies have turned the town into a major center of regional theater.

A continuous influx of newcomers from across the US, Latin America, Europe, the Orient, Asia, Africa, and Canada has radically altered the city's personality through healthy infusions of diverse lifestyles and cultures. Philosophically, Atlantans span the spectrum from button-down conservative to ultra-hip. A once-provincial town — where seldom was heard a non-Southern word — it no longer turns a surprised head at the sound of Korean or Thai or the sight of a sari on a MARTA bus or train.

Although natives have not, by a long shot, forsaken their passion for *Varsity Drive-In* chili dogs and fried peach pies or the barbecue and Brunswick stew at *Harold's,* it's far easier now to sample Oriental, Mexican, Italian, French, and even Ethiopian cuisine than it is to track down a traditional Southern table.

Atlantans can't figure for the life of them why anyone, for mere wealth and renown, would choose to live anywhere else. And in early spring, when dogwood and azalea cover the city's hillsides, residents insist that even Paris pales by comparison.

First-time visitors invariably feel at least a passing wave of disappointment.

Were they subconsciously hoping to glimpse Miss Scarlett parading down Peachtree in a flouncy frock, smuggled through the Yankee blockade by the outrageous Captain Butler? Southern belles may have gone the way of the steam locomotive, but Old Atlanta hasn't sashayed entirely out of existence. Way down in its heart it remains faithful to its Southern roots. Behind the modern skyscrapers, the nouvelle cuisine and sushi bars, expensive department stores and trendy European boutiques, there's an age-old code of soft speech and polite manners, along with a sense of fierce regional pride that can turn politics and football games into replays of the Crusades.

Atlanta is the sort of city that requires more than just one look. An oft-repeated story about *Atlanta Stadium* says a great deal about the city's character. Ivan Allen, Jr., the mayor who shepherded the stadium's construction in 1965, was fond of saying: "We built a stadium in 52 weeks on land we didn't own, with money we didn't have, for a baseball team we weren't at all certain was coming."

As it turned out, the old Milwaukee *Braves* thoughtfully migrated south the next year to become the stadium's first major league tenant. Although they have yet to fulfill their promise to win a World Series, Atlantans have never questioned their initial good judgment.

ATLANTA AT-A-GLANCE

SEEING THE CITY: The view from the 70th floor of the *Peachtree Plaza* hotel's revolving *Sun Dial* restaurant is, in a word, spectacular. When the weather is clear, your eye sweeps from the planes arriving and taking off at Hartsfield International Airport (to the south) to the Blue Ridge Mountains (in the north). The *Sun Dial* can be reached only by an 80-second ride in one of the two glass elevators that skim up and down in the glass tubes affixed to the outside of the building. You will have to order something to eat or drink to spend any time there, and it's a good idea to make a reservation first. Open daily till 1:45 AM for cocktails. Peachtree at International Blvd. (phone: 589-7505).

SPECIAL PLACES: You can walk around downtown Atlanta without much difficulty, but be warned, the streets aren't laid out in a neat, orderly grid. They roughly follow the paths of early — and now extinct — rail lines, because the early streets ran parallel to the old tracks. The result is a tangled web that often leaves visitors confused, as much by the erratic pattern as by the fact that at least half the streets seem to be named Peachtree, Circle, or Hills.

The good news is that the public transportation system — MARTA — is excellent, especially if you are downtown or near Peachtree Street. Most of MARTA's bus routes begin at rapid-rail stations in the downtown area. Call 848-4711 for information.

DOWNTOWN

Peachtree Center – Designed by celebrated local architect John Portman, Peachtree Center is the heart of modern Atlanta. The ensemble of contemporary buildings includes several office towers; the Atlanta Merchandise Mart and Apparel Mart; and the *Marriott Marquis, Hyatt Regency,* and *Westin Peachtree Plaza* hotels, all linked by aerial skyways and landscaped plazas. The 3-story Peachtree Center Gallery offers a variety of shopping, dining, and entertainment options. MARTA's Peachtree Center rapid-rail station is also part of the complex.

Woodruff Park – A few blocks south of Peachtree Center, Woodruff Park is a gift from Atlanta's best-known anonymous donor, the late Coca-Cola millionaire Robert W. Woodruff, whose considerable civic generosity has done more to change the face of the city than cosmetic surgery has done for Hollywood. (Emory University's medical school is another major beneficiary of his largesse.) At lunch, hundreds of officeworkers, street people, wandering preachers, and Hare Krishna folk swarm into the park — a gentle crowd. Grab a hot dog or plate of shrimp fried rice at *Tokyo Shapiro's*, 62 Peachtree St., across from the park, and settle down on the grass. Peachtree, Edgewood, Pryor, and Auburn Sts.

Martin Luther King Jr. Historic District – Within a 5-block National Historic District near downtown are sites associated with the life and times of the late Nobel Peace Prize winner. These include his birthplace; Ebenezer Baptist Church, where he preached with his father; his tomb, guarded by an eternal flame and inscribed with the words "Free At Last"; the Interfaith Peace Chapel; a community center; and the Center for Social Change, which displays related papers, films, and memorabilia. Auburn Ave. at Boulevard NE (phone: 524-1956).

Georgia Capitol – Completed in 1889 and crowned by a dome of North Georgia gold, the classically styled capitol contains the governor's office and museums of history, science, and agriculture. Visitors may watch democracy in action when the Georgia Assembly convenes from January through March. Guided tours on weekdays. No admission charge. Capitol Sq. (phone: 656-2844).

Federal Reserve Bank – Remember when dollar bills were silver certificates, not Federal Reserve notes? The dollar was worth a dollar in silver then. Not these days. But we're not complaining much — Federal Reserve notes seem to work just as well. To see where they're made, walk over to Marietta Street, 2 blocks east of the CNN Center, and look at the Corinthian-columned Federal Reserve Bank. Although the building is new, the Federal Reserve System's Sixth District headquarters has been here since 1914. Tours of the bank's operations and its *Money Museum* are available on Tuesdays, Wednesdays, and Thursdays, but you must call in advance to schedule a visit. No admission charge. 104 Marietta St. NW (phone: 521-8500).

Fox Theater – One of the last of the opulent 1920s "picture palaces," the beautifully restored *Fox* is a fabulous blend of Egyptian-Moorish-Byzantine-Hollywood design. A vintage movie series, with newsreels and cartoons, is a summer highlight, but the *Fox*'s calendar is mostly taken up with touring Broadway musicals and concerts of all sorts. A portion of every ticket sold goes toward ongoing restoration costs. The *Fox* seats 4,518, making it the country's second largest operating theater after *Radio City Music Hall* in New York. Tours of the hall are conducted daily except Sundays, April through October. Admission varies with the event. Peachtree St. at Ponce de Leon Ave. (phone: 881-1977).

CNN Center, Omni Coliseum, Georgia World Congress Center – Clustered at the southern edge of downtown, the three large structures are the center of the city's convention industry. At CNN Center — a modern megastructure formerly known as Omni International — visitors may tour the Cable News Network studios, watch CNN newscasts, and then enjoy a glass of ale at cheery *Reggie's British Pub*. The deluxe *Omni International* hotel at the center's southern end is connected with the Georgia World Congress Center, Atlanta's major convention complex. The adjacent *Omni Coliseum* is the scene of basketball games, rodeos, circuses, and other events (CNN, phone: 827-1500; Coliseum, phone: 681-2100; Congress, phone: 656-7600).

Carter Presidential Center – Opened in 1986, this is Atlanta's newest major attraction. The four connected circular buildings, set among 30 acres of trees, lakes, and Japanese gardens 2 miles east of downtown, contain documents, photos, and memorabilia of Jimmy Carter's White House years. Highlights include a re-creation of the Oval Office, elaborate state gifts to the Carters and other first families, and multimedia presentations on the presidency, human rights, and the environment, among other topics. A gift shop and an attractive restaurant overlook the gardens. Open daily. Admission charge. N. Highland and Cleburne Aves. (phone: 331-3942).

Underground Atlanta – The city's most eclectic shopping and amusement area — housing a total of 100 stores and an assortment of 22 bars, restaurants, and nightclubs, and 20 fast food establishments — reopened in 1989 at a cost of $142 million. After a dismal debut 20 years ago (intended as a symbol of revitalization, the original Underground became a haven for rowdy teenagers and undesirables and was closed down in 1982), the three-level (one above ground, two underground) complex, done in turn-of-the-century style, takes up 2 city blocks. We hope the new incarnation is on the right track this time. Shops are open daily from 10 AM to 9:30 PM; Sundays from noon to 5 PM. Bars and restaurants open for lunch and most remain open to the early morning hours. Martin Luther King, Jr., Dr. and Peachtree St.

ENVIRONS

The Wren's Nest – The charming name was given to this Victorian cottage by its famous owner, Joel Chandler Harris, best known as the creator of Brer Fox, Brer Rabbit, and the other immortal Southern animal characters of the Uncle Remus stories. The house has original furnishings and lots of memorabilia from the life of the Atlanta storyteller. Open daily. Admission charge. 1050 Gordon SW (phone: 753-8535).

Chattahoochee Nature Center – The center is actually a 7-acre nature preserve on the peaceful banks of the Chattahoochee River, with animal exhibits and classes for both children and adults. Open daily. Voluntary admission charge. 9135 Willeo Rd., Roswell, 20 miles north of downtown (phone: 992-2055).

Piedmont Park – Three miles north of downtown, Piedmont is a spacious green place for swimming, tennis, jogging, picnics, and observing Atlantans at leisure. The *Atlanta Arts Festival* is held here annually in early May, and the *Atlanta Symphony* presents outdoor concerts in summer. The Atlanta Botanical Garden, on 60 acres in the park, has greenhouses, a Japanese garden, rose gardens, a Fragrance Garden for the blind, and a visitors center with classes and special programs. Open daily. No admission charge. Piedmont Ave. between 10th and 14th Sts. (phone: 876-5858).

Cyclorama – The dramatic circular painting of the Civil War Battle for Atlanta (50 feet high and 400 feet in circumference) has been beautifully restored and enhanced by new sound and lighting effects. An ambitious rehabilitation program has turned the once-depressing Atlanta Zoo into a pleasant attraction. Admission charge for both the Cyclorama and the zoo. Grant Park, 800 Cherokee Ave., 3 miles from downtown (phone: 658-7625).

Fernbank Science Center – Often overlooked by non-parents, the Fernbank has the Southeast's third largest planetarium, an observatory, and a nature trail leading through 70 acres of unspoiled forest. A see-and-touch museum, an electronic microscope laboratory, a meteorological laboratory, and an experimental garden also on the premises make this a fascinating place to spend an afternoon. Open daily. Admission charge. 156 Heaton Park Dr. NE (phone: 378-4311).

High Museum of Art – In 1983, the *High Museum* moved from the Woodruff Arts Center into a spectacular new home next door. The magnificent building is an architectural masterpiece in its own right, with an exterior of dazzling white enamel tiles and a central atrium flooded with natural light. It contains collections of American, European, and African art and a fine assemblage of decorative arts. Peachtree and 16th Sts. (phone: 892-3600). The *High*'s downtown branch, in the Georgia-Pacific Center, has changing exhibitions of regional, national, and international art. Open weekdays. No admission charge. 133 Peachtree St. (phone: 577-6940).

Robert W. Woodruff Arts Center – Originally dedicated to the 122 Atlanta art patrons who died in a 1962 air crash in Paris, the center has been renamed in honor of the Coca-Cola patriarch and arts benefactor. Its art collection has moved to the *High Museum of Art* (see above), and it is now the home of the *Atlanta Symphony Orchestra*, the *Alliance Theater,* the *Atlanta Children's Theater,* and the Atlanta College of Art. It also offers traveling art exhibitions. 1280 Peachtree St. NE (phone: 892-3600).

Atlanta Historical Society – Proceed north along Peachtree Road to West Paces Ferry Road. Turn left and look for Andrews Drive, site of the society's 18-acre complex. Its showpiece is Swan House, built in 1928 and designed by well-known Atlanta architect Philip Shutze in the Anglo-Palladian style. A magnificent exercise in a popular Italian Renaissance mode, it is handsomely furnished in 18th-century antiques, many of which belonged to the former owners, prominent Atlantans Mr. and Mrs. Edward Inman. Also on the grounds is the Tullie Smith house, an authentic 1840s "plantation plain" Georgia farmhouse reconstructed on the property with all its attached buildings. Nearby is the Inmans' coach house, now a pleasant restaurant, gift shop, and art gallery. The *McElreath Memorial Hall,* which houses the society's museum and its extensive collection on Atlanta's history, most of which is available to the public, is here, too. A nature trail has been marked so that you can learn about the region's ecology. Open daily. Admission charge for Swan and Tullie Smith houses. 3101 Andrews Dr. NW (phone: 261-1837).

Six Flags Over Georgia – Just outside the Perimeter Highway (I-285), this 276-acre amusement park has over 100 rides and live shows, including the Great American Scream Machine (fastest, tallest, and longest roller coaster in the world — until 1976) and the Great Gasp parachute jump (666 feet tall), which lets you free-fall for 30 feet. During the summer, there's a free fireworks display at closing time (11 PM). Open daily, late May through Labor Day; weekends, late March through November. Admission charge. 12 miles west of Atlanta on I-20 (phone: 739-3400).

Stone Mountain Park – There's a bit of something for everybody here: a cable car ride to the top, an old steam train, hiking trails, a lake where you can ride a riverboat or canoe, an 18-hole golf course, and an antebellum plantation. And that's not all. This is Mt. Rushmore South. The Confederate heroes Jefferson Davis, Robert E. Lee, and Stonewall Jackson have been drilled into the sheer face of a giant mass of exposed granite. The enormous bas-relief was begun — but not finished — by Gutzon Borglum, who went on to carve Mt. Rushmore. Resort facilities include campgrounds, restaurants, and motels. Open daily. Admission charge. 16 miles northeast of Atlanta on Rte. 78 (phone: 498-5690).

White Water Park – A relaxing relief from Atlanta's steamy summers, this attractive, well-maintained oasis offers a variety of cooling experiences, headed by an enormous wave pool and water slides designed for the adventurous as well as the timid. A children's area has numerous activities for youngsters. There are lockers, showers, snack bars, and a picnic area. Open daily from May to September. Admission charge. At 250 N. Cobb Pkwy. (US 41), Marietta (phone: 424-9283).

Kennesaw Mountain National Battlefield Park – The mountain and 2,800-acre park were the scene of one of the most important engagements in the Battle of Atlanta campaign. Attractions include a Civil War museum and defense lines. Open daily. No admission charge. Off I-75; 25 miles from downtown, near Marietta (phone: 427-4686). Also in the vicinity is the *Big Shanty Museum* in Kennesaw. Its locomotive *General* was involved in a famous Civil War spy chase and was the subject of the Walt Disney movie *Great Locomotive Chase.* Open daily. Admission charge (phone: 427-4686).

DeKalb Farmers Market – One of this aspiring international city's most international experiences. This truly enormous indoor market is piled high with exotic fruits and other produce, seafood, sausages, cheeses, spices, breads, and scores of other delicacies from every corner of the world. Speaking a Babel of languages, patrons and clerks are themselves a mini–United Nations. Open Tuesdays through Sundays, 10 AM to 9 PM. Recorded phone messages give directions from every part of the metro area. No credit cards. 3000 E. Ponce de Leon Ave., Decatur (phone: 377-6400).

Tara – Just about everybody comes to Atlanta looking for the legendary white-columned mansion. But, alas, Tara never existed, except in Margaret Mitchell's imagination and on David O. Selznick's movie sets. *Gone With the Wind* is shown frequently at CNN Cinemas, CNN Center downtown (phone: 577-6928). Memorabilia and foreign editions of *GWTW* are on display in the Margaret Mitchell Room of the Atlanta Public Library, Peachtree and Forsyth Sts. (phone: 688-4034).

■ **EXTRA SPECIAL:** Just 35 miles northeast of Atlanta, Lanier Islands have been developed into a resort area. The 1,200 acres of hills and woods contain golf courses, tennis courts, and horseback riding and camping facilities. There are also sailboats and houseboats for rent. (Manmade Lake Lanier has 540 miles of shoreline.) Stouffer's *Pine Isle Resort* hotel is on the grounds, too. Open daily. A parking permit is $3 daily. On I-85 (Lanier Islands information, phone: 945-6701).

SOURCES AND RESOURCES

TOURIST INFORMATION: For general information, brochures, and maps, contact the Atlanta Chamber of Commerce, 235 International Blvd., Atlanta, GA 30303 (phone: 586-8400); or Atlanta Convention and Visitors Bureau, 235 Peachtree St. NE, Suite 1414 (phone: 521-6600). Exhibitions on Georgia tourism and industry are at the World Congress Center, Marietta and Magnolia Sts. NW (phone: 656-7000). A covered pedestrian bridge links the center to the *Omni International* hotel. Foreign visitors information is available from the Georgia Council for International Visitors, *Habersham* hotel, 330 Peachtree St. (phone: 577-2248).

A Marmac Guide to Atlanta (Marmac Publishers; $8.95) is the most comprehensive guide to the city, with detailed chapters on sightseeing, dining, nightlife, museums, cultural activities, shopping, and other areas of interest.

Television Stations – WAGA Channel 5–CBS; WSB Channel 2–ABC; WIIA Channel 11–NBC.

Radio Stations – AM: WGST 920 (news/talk); WEB 750 (contemporary). FM: WABK 90 (classical/news); WVEE 103.3 (urban contemporary); WCLK 91.9 (jazz).

Local Coverage – *Atlanta Constitution,* morning daily; *Atlanta Journal,* evening daily; *Atlanta* magazine, monthly.

Food – *Atlanta* magazine contains listings of most of the established restaurants and some newcomers. The Weekend section of the Saturday *Atlanta Journal-Constitution* offers complete dining, entertainment, and special events listings.

Telephone – All telephone numbers are in the 404 area code unless otherwise indicated.

Sales Tax – State and local sales tax is 5%; the hotel tax is 6%.

CLIMATE: Atlanta's temperatures vary from moderate winters to comfortable springs and falls to hot and humid summers. Winter is generally mild, but temperatures do occasionally drop to near zero, with sleet and light snow. May, September, October, and November tend to be the sunniest months. While Atlanta isn't exactly what you'd call dry, the average humidity hovers at 60%, which isn't intolerable either.

GETTING AROUND: Airport – Atlanta is served by Hartsfield International Airport, one of the world's largest and busiest. The airport's two terminals (North and South) are connected by a speedy and efficient subway system with trains that run every 2 minutes. Except during rush hours, it's about a 20-minute trip between the airport and downtown. (Changing traffic patterns make it easier to get *to* the airport in the morning and *from* the airport to downtown in late afternoon.) The flat taxi rate from the airport to downtown hotels is $13.50 for one person, $14 for two, $15 for three. *Atlanta Airport Shuttle* vans (phone: 766-5312) charge $7 one way, $12 round trip to downtown hotels, and $10 one way, $18 round trip to Emory University and Lenox Square. *Northside Airport Express* (phone: 455-1600) has bus service to several suburban terminals for $9.75 to $15 one way, $17.75 to $25 round trip. Travelers without much luggage can take MARTA (Metropolitan Atlanta Rapid Transit Authority) trains from the airport to downtown in about 12 minutes for 85¢ one way (call 848-4711 for information).

Bus – MARTA is the backbone of Atlanta's public transportation system. Bus routes interlace the city, with frequent stops at downtown locations. Exact fare required. A new rapid-rail system now runs 12 miles east-west and 12 miles north-south, connecting at the Five Points station downtown. When complete, the system will have 60 miles of tunnel and grade-level track. Each station has been designed by a different architect and decorated with murals, photos, and collages. MARTA maintains information booths at the intersection of Peachtree and West Peachtree, near the *Hyatt Regency* hotel and at Broad and Walton NE (phone: 848-4711).

Taxi – Atlanta isn't known for its efficient taxi services. Many are unclean, mechanically suspect, and often manned by drivers unfamiliar with local geography. *Yellow Cab* (phone: 522-0200) and *London Taxi* (phone: 681-2280) are among the more reliable.

Car Rental – All major national firms are represented.

LOCAL SERVICES: Business Services – *Team Concept,* 1925 Century Center NE (phone: 325-9754).
   Mechanics – *Don Davis Gulf Service,* 359 W. Ponce de Leon Ave., Decatur (phone: 378-6751); *Joe Winkler's Gulf Station,* 2794 Clairmont Rd. NE (phone: 636-2940).

MUSEUMS: The *High Museum of Art,* the *Woodruff Arts Center,* the *Hall of Fame* and *Museum of Science and Industry* in the capitol, and the *Fernbank Science Center* are described in *Special Places.* Other museums of note are:

Emory University Museum of Art and Archaeology – Greek and Roman coins, amphora, an Egyptian mummy; art ranging from the American Southwest to Southeast Asia, China, and Japan; and works by Dali, Kandinsky, and Matisse are displayed in this attractive museum. Closed Sundays and Mondays. No admission charge. Emory University, N. Decatur and Oxford Rds. (phone: 727-7522).

MAJOR COLLEGES AND UNIVERSITIES: There are nine important institutions of higher education in the metro area, each contributing to the cultural, as well as the academic, climate. They are Atlanta University, 223 Chestnut SW (phone: 522-8980); Atlanta College of Art, 1280 Peachtree NE (phone: 898-1164); Atlanta College of Business, 1280 W Peachtree NW (phone: 873-1701); Agnes Scott College, E. College Dr., Decatur (phone: 371-6285); Emory University (famous for its medical program), 1380 S. Oxford Rd. NE (phone: 727-6123); Georgia Institute of Technology, 225 North Ave. NW (phone: 894-2000); Georgia State University, University Plaza NE (phone: 651-2000); Interdenominational Theological Center, 671 Beckwith SW (phone: 527-7700); Oglethorpe University, 4484 Peachtree Rd. NE (phone: 261-1441).

SPECIAL EVENTS: The best time to visit Atlanta is during the spring *Dogwood Festival,* the second week in April, when the city explodes in color and celebration (phone: 525-6145). During the summer months, the *Atlanta Symphony Orchestra* plays outdoors in Piedmont Park on Sunday evenings.

The *Arts Festival of Atlanta* takes place in Piedmont Park in September, as does the *Atlanta Greek Festival*, a potpourri of Greek costumes, movies, gifts, art, dances, and food; Greek Orthodox Cathedral of the Annunciation, 2500 Clairmont Rd. NE (phone: 633-5870).

SPORTS AND FITNESS: A major league city, Atlanta is the home of the *Braves* and the nest of the *Falcons* and *Hawks.*

Baseball – Atlanta *Braves* play at *Atlanta–Fulton County Stadium,* 521 Capitol Ave. SW. It can be difficult to get tickets, but try calling 577-9600.

Basketball – The Atlanta *Hawks'* home games are played at the *Omni,* 100 Techwood Dr. NW (phone: 681-3605).

Bicycling – Bikes (and roller skates) may be rented at *Skate Escape,* 1086 Piedmont Ave. NE, across from Piedmont Park (phone: 892-1292).

Fishing – There's good fishing at Lake Allatoona, Lake Lanier, and Lake Jackson.

Fitness Centers – The *YMCA* (phone: 631-3666) has modern health centers throughout the metro area. *Colony Square Athletic Club* offers racquetball and aerobics classes, 1197 Peachtree at 14th St. (phone: 881-1632).

Football – The Atlanta *Falcons* (phone: 261-5400) play at the *Atlanta–Fulton County Stadium.*

Golf – The best public courses are at *Stone Mountain Park* (phone: 498-5690) and *Bobby Jones Golf Course,* 384 Woodward Way (phone: 355-1009).

Jogging – Run along Peachtree Street or Piedmont Road to Piedmont Park, about 1½ miles, and enter at 10th or 14th streets; roads in the park are closed to traffic. You can also run just past 14th Street to the Ansley Park and Sherwood Forest areas of Atlanta and along the wide residential streets. For more information, call *Atlanta Track Club* (phone: 231-9064).

Tennis – The best clay courts are at the *Bitsy Grant Tennis Center,* 2125 Northside Dr. NW (phone: 351-2774). Lanier Islands and Stone Mountain have good outdoor tennis courts, too. There are excellent public courts at the *Blackburn Tennis Center,* 3501 Ashford-Dunwoody Rd. (phone: 451-1061), and at the *DeKalb Tennis Center,* off Clairmont Rd., in suburban Decatur (phone: 325-2520).

Whitewater Rafting – Burt Reynolds (with some help from poet and novelist James Dickey) made North Georgia whitewater famous in the movie *Deliverance.* For an urban alternative, rent a raft at the Chattahoochee River Park at Hwy. 41 in NW Atlanta during the summer.

THEATER: For complete performance schedules, check the local publications listed above. Among the best-known theatrical companies are the *Alliance Theater* and *Studio Theater* at the Woodruff Arts Center, Peachtree and 15th Sts. (phone: 892-3600); *Academy Theater,* a trailblazer of new and experimental plays, 1337 Peachtree St. (phone: 892-0880); and *Theatrical Outfit,* Peachtree and 10th Sts. (phone: 872-0665). The *Center for Puppetry Arts,* 1404 Spring St. (phone: 873-3089), has performances and exhibitions.

MUSIC: The *Atlanta Symphony Orchestra* (phone: 892-3600) plays virtually year-round at the Woodruff Arts Center and gives a variety of indoor and outdoor concerts. Chamber music groups include the *Atlanta Virtuosi* (phone: 938-8611) and *Atlanta Chamber Players* (phone: 872-3360). The nationally honored *Atlanta Ballet* (phone: 873-5811) has a repertoire of classical and contemporary works. The *Ruth Mitchell Dance Company* (phone: 237-8829) performs originally choreographed ballet and jazz dancing at the *Peachtree Playhouse,* Peachtree and 13th Sts.

NIGHTCLUBS AND NIGHTLIFE: Atlanta's nightlife covers the spectrum, with most places open nightly until 3 or 4 AM. There's excellent jazz at *Walter Mitty's Jazz Café,* 816 N. Highland Ave. NE (phone: 876-7115). Blues heads the menu at *Blues Harbor,* 3179 Peachtree Rd. (phone: 261-6717). Name comedians are featured at *The Punch Line,* 280 Hildebrand Dr. (phone: 252-LAFF). *Blind Willie's,* 830 N. Highland Ave. (phone: 873-2583), highlights New Orleans blues and food; *County Cork Pub,* 52 E. Andrews Dr. (phone: 262-2227), has Irish singers. British ales, darts, and a sing-along piano draw big crowds to *Churchill Arms,* across the street from the *County Cork* (phone: 233-5633). Cabaret-style shows are presented at *Upstairs at Gene and Gabe's,* 1578 Piedmont Rd. (phone: 874-6145). The best places to meet and mingle are *Peachtree Café,* 268 E. Paces Ferry Rd. (phone: 233-4402); and *Élan,* 4505 Ashford-Dunwoody Rd. (phone: 393-1333). The most convivial old-fashioned neighborhood bars are *Manuel's Tavern,* 602 N. Highland Ave. (phone: 525-3447), and the *Stein Club,* 929 Peachtree St. (phone: 892-9466). *Reggie's British Pub* in the CNN Center, downtown (phone: 525-1437) is a jolly good spot for a glass of ale, a steak-and-kidney pie, and a rousing game of darts. The *Cotton Club,* 1021 Peachtree St., (phone: 874-2523), is a high-energy forum for the latest pop, rock, blues, and jazz.

BEST IN TOWN

CHECKING IN: Today, Atlanta visitors can pick and choose from one of the broadest assortments of hotels in the country. It's also possible to stay in a bed-and-breakfast establishment very inexpensively. These are private homes, all of which rent rooms with adjacent baths, and they're scattered throughout the city. For information and reservations: *Bed & Breakfast Atlanta,* 1801 Piedmont Ave. NE, Suite 208, Atlanta 30324 (phone: 875-0525). Expect to pay $95 and up for a double in hotels we've classified as expensive; between $50 and $75 at places in the moderate category; under $50 in inexpensive places. All telephone numbers are in the 404 area code unless otherwise indicated.

Atlanta Hilton & Towers – The 3-winged, 30-story, 1,250-room building has a group of small courtyards, each 7 stories tall. At the top are *Another World* and *Nikolai's Roof* (see *Eating Out*). The hotel provides 144 rooms for guests in wheelchairs or with other disabilities. Courtland and Harris NE (phone: 659-2000). Expensive.

Atlanta Marriott Marquis – This predictably splashy property from local architect and developer John Portman is one of the nation's largest hotels, with 1,647 rooms in a 50-story tower. It teems with restaurants, lounges, and shops, and includes spacious convention facilities. Peachtree Center (phone: 521-0000 or 800-228-9290). Expensive.

Atlanta Marriott Peachtree Corners – A new 6-story, 224-room hotel with restaurant, lobby lounge, meeting rooms, indoor heated pool, hydrotherapy pool, sauna, and health club. 141 Peachtree Pkwy. at Technology Dr., 5 minutes north of I-285 exit 23 (phone: 263-8558 or 800-228-9290).

Hyatt Regency – Each of the 1,358 rooms in the main building has an outside balcony as well as a window overlooking the inner atrium. The adjoining tower has 200 additional rooms. The 327-foot-high revolving rooftop restaurant, *Polaris,* is reached via glass elevator. 265 Peachtree NE (phone: 577-1234, 800-233-1234, or 800-228-9000). Expensive.

Omni International – Attached to the CNN Center complex, the hotel has a refined atmosphere. Many of the 471 rooms have balconies overlooking all or part of the

14-story, 5½-acre *Omni* atrium. 1 CNN Center NW (phone: 659-0000 or 800-241-5500). Expensive.

Ritz-Carlton, Atlanta – With many elegant extras, this authentic luxury hotel attracts travelers with very discerning taste. Very close to the downtown financial district and right next door to the Georgia-Pacific Center, there are 472 rooms, along with the *Dining Room* for continental dishes and the *Café* for lighter meals. 181 Peachtree St. NE (phone: 659-0400 or 800-241-3333). Expensive.

Ritz-Carlton, Buckhead – Probably Atlanta's most fashionable hotel, the plush dining rooms and lounges are *the* places to see and be seen by local and visiting celebrities. The 573 rooms and suites are handsomely appointed with numerous luxuries. In the heart of the city's most upscale shopping, dining, and nightlife neighborhood. 3434 Peachtree Rd. NW (phone: 237-2700 or 800-241-3333). Expensive.

Waverly – In the heart of a suburban shopping and office complex, this deluxe, 533-room Stouffer hotel features a health club and several good restaurants among its amenities. 100 Galleria Pkwy. NW (phone: 953-4500). Expensive.

Westin Lenox – Opened in 1988, with 375 rooms, this address is right in the heart of the city's most fashionable shopping, dining, and entertainment district. There's fine dining in the *Swan Room,* live entertainment, and a health club. 3300 Lenox Rd. (phone: 262-3344 or 800-228-3000). Expensive.

Westin Peachtree Plaza – The world's tallest hotel, this 70-story structure has a ½-acre lake in its 7-story lobby. Regrettably, its 1,100 rooms are far less spacious and barely adequate. Atop the cylindrical structure is the *Sun Dial* restaurant and lounge, our choice for the best bird's-eye view of the city and the surrounding countryside. Peachtree at International Blvd. NW (phone: 659-1400 or 800-228-3000). Expensive.

Atlanta Peachtree TraveLodge – For those looking for a smaller place, this 56-room facility might do. It's not elegant, but it is comfortable. A swimming pool, too. 1641 Peachtree St. NE (phone: 873-5731). Moderate.

Ibis – Here is a new, upbeat French-owned hotel in the downtown convention district, with 260 attractive rooms, a restaurant, bar, and small meeting facilities. 10 International Blvd. (phone: 524-5555). Moderate.

Radisson Inn Atlanta – Some 14 miles northeast of downtown, it has 2 heated swimming pools, a café and lounge, lighted tennis courts, racquetball courts, and a barber. Only one room is equipped for handicapped guests; the other 399 are standard. Pets are welcome. I-285, Chamblee-Dunwood Rd. exit (phone: 394-5000 or 800-333-3333). Moderate.

Days Inn – The Atlanta-based chain offers basic, clean accommodations at very reasonable rates. Most inns (actually motels) have a swimming pool, playground, family restaurant, color TV sets; some have kitchenettes. Ten Atlanta locations, and the high-rise downtown, a block from Peachtree Plaza (300 Spring St.; phone: 761-6500), may be the best value in the city. For information on the others, call 320-2000 or 800-325-2525. Inexpensive.

 EATING OUT: Atlanta's hundreds of restaurants, cafés, and trendy grilles and bistros specialize in everything from traditional southern home cooking to American regional dishes and an astonishing variety of international cuisines. Two people can expect to pay between $80 and $100 for dinner in restaurants in our expensive category; from $40 to $60 in the moderate range; and $20 to $30 in the inexpensive category. Prices do not include cocktails, wine, or tips. All telephone numbers are in the 404 area code unless otherwise indicated.

Bone's – The place in town for prime beef and fresh seafood in clubby, convivial surroundings. It's very popular among executives and savvy out-of-towners.

Closed for lunch on Saturdays. Reservations advised. Major credit cards. 3130 Piedmont Rd. (phone: 237-2663). Expensive.

Brass Key – One of Atlanta's most distinguished restaurants, serving very good French/continental cuisine in a setting reminiscent of Old Vienna. Closed Sundays. Reservations advised. Major credit cards. Peachtree Battle Shopping Center, 2355 Peachtree Rd. (phone: 233-3202). Expensive.

Buckhead Diner – Gleaming stainless steel, neon, and leather are the signatures of this sleek, super-chic 1990s eatery that has become a haven for the city's movers and shakers and hip out-of-towners (unlike the less glamorous, low-tab versions found in many other US cities). The menu is a trendy array of pasta, salads, seafood, and meat entrées. Valet parking. Lunch and dinner daily. No reservations. Major credit cards. 3073 Piedmont Rd. (phone: 262-3336). Expensive.

La Grotta – An elegant Northern Italian dining room. Delicious veal, pasta, and seafood dishes are matched by some of Atlanta's most professional service. Dinner only; closed Sundays and Mondays. Reservations recommended. Major credit cards. Two locations: 2637 Peachtree Rd. NE (phone: 231-1368) and 647 Atlanta St. (US 19), Roswell (phone: 998-0645). Expensive.

Hedgerose Heights Inn – Pheasant, veal, beef, seafood, and fowl are served with either a French, Swiss, or German flair, and complemented by a fine wine list and very good service. Dinner only; closed Sundays and Mondays. Reservations advised. Major credit cards. 490 E. Paces Ferry Rd. (phone: 233-7673). Expensive.

Nikolai's Roof – With decor and atmosphere suggesting Czarist opulence, the *Atlanta Hilton*'s rooftop restaurant was originally intended to heighten the establishment's prestige, not to serve as a big money-making operation — which is why it seats only 67 diners. Reservations are necessary far in advance, but if you want personal service by waiters in Cossack attire (who have memorized the evening's five-course menu), you'll find it worth the necessary advance planning. The food is French, but then the old Russian courts were also shamelessly Francophilic. Open daily, dinner only. Major credit cards. *Atlanta Hilton,* Courtland and Harris NE (phone: 659-2000). Expensive.

103 West – A creative array of richly sauced dishes and superior wines are complemented by Victorian floral prints, potted palms, and marble-topped tables. A memorable dining experience. Dinner only; closed Sundays. Reservations advised. Major credit cards. 103 West Paces Ferry Rd. (phone: 233-5993). Expensive.

Pano's & Paul's – A classy restaurant hidden in a shopping center. Continental and American cuisine is served, but the kitchen promises it will prepare anything if requested far enough in advance. Dinner only; closed Sundays. Reservations advised. Major credit cards. West Paces Shopping Center (phone: 261-3662). Expensive.

Ritz-Carlton, Buckhead – Dinner here is a carefully orchestrated affair, with menus composed by Chef Guenter Seeger. The food is creative and memorable — melon soup with lobster and mint, rack of lamb with Vidalia onions and tomato coulis, and for dessert, cherries gratinéed with cinnamon ice cream. Closed Sundays. Major credit cards. 3340 Peachtree Rd. NE (phone: 237-2700). Expensive.

Savannah Fish Company – Fish and shellfish, flown in fresh from the Gulf of Mexico, the Pacific, and the North Atlantic, are the hallmark of this cozy restaurant in the *Peachtree Plaza* hotel. Open daily. Major credit cards. Reservations for lunch only. Peachtree St. and International Blvd. (phone: 589-7456). Expensive.

Café Babalu – Atlanta's Latin community and others who enjoy Spanish food and ambience flock to this lively restaurant and tapas bar in suburban Decatur. The menu also features paella, fresh seafood entrées, and black bean and garbanzo soups. Lunch weekdays; dinner daily except Sunday. Major credit cards. Reservations necessary. 515 N. McDonough St., Decatur (phone: 371-0002). Expensive to moderate.

Morton's of Chicago – Steak and lots of it is the raison d'être of this Chicago steakhouse offshoot. The porterhouse weighs in at 24 ounces and comes with a suitably sized doggie bag. The grilled fish, veal, and lamb chops are all excellent. Closed Sundays. Reservations accepted. Major credit cards. Marquis One Tower, 245 Peachtree Center Ave. (phone: 577-4366). Expensive to moderate.

Patio – Enviably situated on the banks of the Chattahoochee River, the *Patio* marries a pretty setting of Regency antiques and white lace napery to expert French cooking. Grilled salmon with shallot brown butter sauce and triple cut lamb chops are standouts. Open daily. Reservations advised. Major credit cards. 4199 Paces Ferry Rd. NW (phone: 432-2808). Expensive to moderate.

A Taste of New Orleans – Delectable Créole and Cajun dishes done with a traditional French Quarter flair in a casually sophisticated atmosphere. Dinner only; closed Sundays. No reservations. Major credit cards. 889 W. Peachtree St. (phone: 874-5535). Expensive to moderate.

Camille's – Perpetually packed, very New Yorkish Italian café, serving big platters of pasta, seafood, veal, and chicken dishes in rich red sauces. In warm weather, take a sidewalk table and watch the crowd go by. Lunch, dinner daily. No reservations. Major credit cards. 1186 N. Highland Ave. (phone: 872-7203). Moderate.

Chef's Café – One of Atlanta's exemplary small eating places, with sensational crab cakes, homemade soups, rich pasta, unusual sandwiches, and salads. Lunch Tuesdays through Fridays; dinner Tuesdays through Sundays. Reservations necessary. Major credit cards. 2115 Piedmont Rd. (phone: 872-2284). Moderate.

Dante's Down the Hatch – A late-night niche with a faithful coterie. Jazz lovers come to hear *Paul Mitchell's Trio* and assorted combos. The fondue/wine/cheese menu is an attraction on its own, and so is owner Dante Stephenson, who's usually there to reeommend a vintage from his personally selected list. Open daily. Reservations advised. Major credit cards. 3380 Peachtree Rd. (phone: 266-1600). Moderate.

Gojinka – It's Atlanta's most authentic Japanese restaurant, claim local and visiting Asians, who rave about the sushi and sashimi. Very good tempura, sukiyaki, and yakitori, too. Diner only; closed Sundays. No reservations. Major credit cards. 5269 Buford Hwy., Pinetree Plaza Shopping Center, Doraville (phone: 458-0558). Moderate.

Indigo – Like a laid-back trip to the Caribbean, this spiffy little neighborhood café specializes in fresh seafood, conch chowder, and key lime pie. Dinner daily except Sundays. No reservations. Major credit cards. 1409 N. Highland Ave. (phone: 876-0676). Moderate.

Little Bucharest – Atlanta's expanding international horizons are reflected in this charming suburban restaurant that highlights Romanian and other central European dishes. Among the specialties are Romanian smoked sausage, duck soup, chicken paprikash, and luscious cream-filled desserts. Lunch weekdays; dinner daily except Sunday. Reservations necessary. Major credit cards. 3200 Northlake Pkwy. (phone: 934-9811). Moderate.

The Peasant Group – Some of Atlanta's favorite dining places are the locally owned *Peasant* restaurants, which feature innovative American/continental meals served in a stylish and relaxed atmosphere. The group includes: the *Pleasant Peasant,* 555 Peachtree St. (phone: 874-3223); the *Country Place,* Colony Sq., Peachtree and 14th Sts. (phone: 881-0144); *Dailey's,* 17 International Blvd., downtown (phone: 681-3303); *Winfield's,* 100 Galleria Pkwy., Smyrna (phone: 955-5300); the *Peasant Uptown,* Phipps Plaza, Peachtree and Lenox Rds. (phone: 261-6341); and the *Public House,* 605 Atlanta St., Roswell (phone: 992-4646). Open daily. No reservations. Major credit cards. Moderate.

Pentimento – A smart little café that's popular with patrons of the *High Museum* and *Woodruff Arts Center.* The menu includes imaginative soups, salads, seafood, and chicken dishes, nicely complemented by a large selection of wines by the glass. Open daily. Reservations advised. Major credit cards. In the *Woodruff Arts Center,* 1280 Peachtree St. (phone: 875-6665). Moderate.

Skeeter's Mesquite Grill – This is a Texas steakhouse, complete with country and western on the jukebox and faded denim on the patrons. Though the emphasis is on steak, the grilled Cajun redfish is pretty tasty. Open daily. No reservations. Major credit cards. 2892 N. Druid Hills Rd. (phone: 636-3817). Moderate.

Tito's – Good old Italian cooking draws crowds to this snug Virginia/Highland neighborhood eatery. Saltimbocca, veal marsala, garlicky mussels, and pasta draped with rich sauces are among the specialties. Closed Sundays. No reservations. Major credit cards. 820 N Highland Ave. NE (phone: 874-8364). Moderate.

Honto – Hong Kong–style seafood dishes lure local Asians and other fanciers of Asian cuisine for such delicacies as Dungeness crab with ginger and scallions, mussels in black bean sauce, and salt-and-pepper squid. No reservations. Major credit cards. 3295 Chamblee-Dunwoody Rd. (phone: 458-8088). Moderate to inexpensive.

Blue Nile – Atlanta's most exotic little café, it treats the adventurous to spicy meat and vegetable dishes from Ethiopia. In the heart of a lively, diverse midtown neighborhood. Open daily. Reservations accepted. Major credit cards. 810 N. Highland Ave. (phone: 872-6483). Inexpensive.

Colonnade – A cheerful local landmark that's renowned for its friendly service and delicious steaks, seafood, fried chicken, vegetables, and other American and Southern favorites. Open daily. No reservations or credit cards. 1879 Cheshire Bridge Rd. (phone: 874-5642). Inexpensive.

Harold's Barbecue – This quintessential Southern barbecue shack is a local legend for its grilled pork and beef sandwiches and hearty Brunswick stew. Closed Sundays. No reservations or credit cards. 171 McDonough Blvd. (phone: 627-9268). Inexpensive.

Huey's – An upbeat café with an outdoor terrace, featuring New Orleans gumbo, po' boys, coffee, and beignets (deep-fried New Orleans doughnuts). Popular late-night retreat. Open daily. No credit cards. 1816 Peachtree Rd. (phone: 873-2037). Inexpensive.

King & I – Spicy, exotic Thai dishes have made this friendly place a popular destination for adventurous Atlantans. Open daily. No reservations after 7 PM. Ansley Sq. at Piedmont Ave. and Monroe Dr. (phone: 892-7743). Inexpensive.

Korea House – Zesty soups, grilled meats, stews, and seafood dishes, accompanied by kimchee, that fiery Korean staple. Open daily. Reservations accepted. Major credit cards. Peachtree and 6th Sts. (phone: 876-5310). Inexpensive.

Pilgreen's – Tasty steaks, world class onion rings, great drinks, and service in a nostalgic roadhouse atmosphere have kept this a favorite with generations of Atlantans. Closed Sundays and Mondays. No reservations. Major credit cards. 1081 Lee St. (phone: 758-4669). Inexpensive.

El Toro – The zippiest enchiladas, tacos, burritos, and other Tex-Mex dishes served hereabouts. Open daily. No reservations. Major credit cards. 4300 Buford Hwy. NE (phone: 321-9502); 5288 Buford Hwy. NE (phone: 455-9677); 1775 Lawrenceville Hwy., Decatur (phone: 294-9906); and eight other locations. Inexpensive.

Touch of India – This is the place to go for the city's most expertly prepared tandoori dishes and curries. Open daily. Reservations advised. Major credit cards. 962 Peachtree St., near 10th St. (phone: 876-7777). Inexpensive.

Varsity – It's a scene right out of *American Graffiti* — a drive-in with singing car hops, an air of bedlam, and a menu of such all-American favorites as hot dogs, hamburgers, and sandwiches. Open daily. No reservations or credit cards. 61 North Ave. NW (phone: 881-1706). Inexpensive.

BALTIMORE

You might expect to find residents a shade defensive about Baltimore. Slipped quietly between the great cities of the Atlantic seaboard, like a note between the pages of a novel, the world just didn't think much about it. Commerce among Washington, Philadelphia, and New York went by on Baltimore's Beltway and Harbor Tunnel; people were so favorably impressed by the smooth efficiency of the freeway system that they used to bypass the city every time.

But Baltimore has changed its image. Over the past decade, the city has undergone a miraculous transformation. The town has suddenly sparked to life with its dazzling Inner Harbor, promenades, and marinas; a modern downtown business district; myriad new restaurants, pubs, and hotels; an expanded airport; and a new tunnel.

The striking modern buildings and plazas of Charles Center, Baltimore's heart of business, Ft. McHenry, the tiered iron stacks of the Peabody Library, the Sunpapers (among the nation's most distinguished newspapers), and the Johns Hopkins University and medical institutions give the city a contemporary cosmopolitan atmosphere as well as a link to historic tradition. Perhaps best in Baltimore is the cuisine — the riches of the bay, so to speak, in hard or soft-shell crabs, oysters (raw and stewed), clams, and shad roe — prepared in traditional Maryland style.

Baltimore's deep-water port on the Chesapeake Bay — the major Atlantic port for grain, coal, and spice — has always given residents a touch of smug satisfaction. Now its 45 miles of waterfront are further enhanced by a bright centerpiece — Harborplace. This complex is the proud achievement of a long and concerted campaign to turn the city's decaying dock and pier area into Baltimore's biggest asset. Once populated by derelict warehouses, debris, and pollution, the Inner Harbor is now the site of a pair of double-decker glass pavilions, enclosing about 140 restaurants, cafés, and specialty shops, and the spectacular National Aquarium, with its wonderful displays of marine life and even a tropical rain forest.

South of the harbor, the city's neighborhoods are being rejuvenated and restored into elegant residential areas. During the early 1970s, these blocks of row houses were the epitome of urban disaster. Through a city program, countless row houses have been sold for $1 each to anyone who will restore the home and occupy it for 18 months. This successful homesteading program now extends across the city into Fell's Point, Stirling Street, Otterbein, Patterson Park, and Ridgely's Delight.

Baltimore residents are busy these days toasting the new charms of their town and, as ever, celebrating the old. The city is proud of its architecturally impressive City Hall, completed in 1875 in French Empire style. It represents something of the city's style. For the building's centennial, Baltimore spent

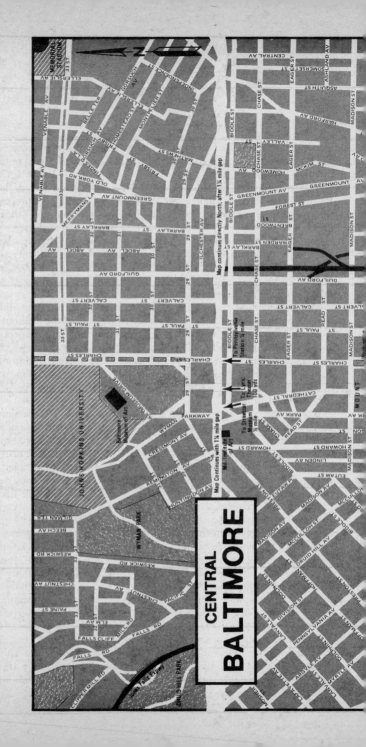

CENTRAL BALTIMORE

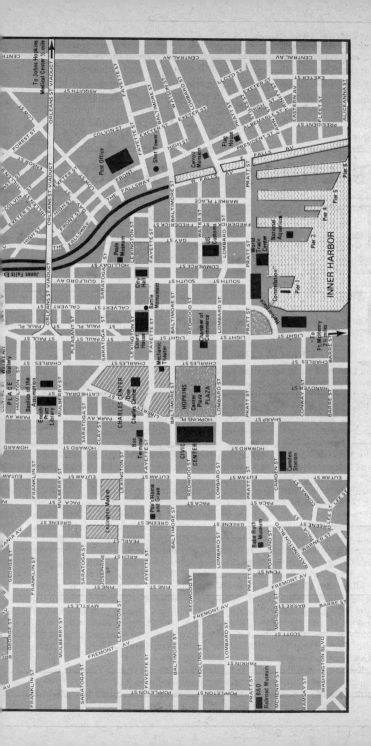

some $11 million renovating the interior while preserving the best aspects of the old decor. Outside, the only change is that the small round dome now gleams with gold leaf. Like the building itself, the city's assets can be perceived and appreciated most readily from the inside — which explains why so many people who happen upon Baltimore for one reason or another like what they find and stay. But you don't have to be a resident to like Baltimore. You simply have to visit.

BALTIMORE AT-A-GLANCE

SEEING THE CITY: Baltimore offers its finest panoramic view from the Top of the World Trade Center at the Inner Harbor, Pratt St. between South and Gay Sts. Downstream lies Fort McHenry, where the successful American repulsion of British forces in 1814 inspired Francis Scott Key to compose "The Star-Spangled Banner." To the northwest, the buildings and plazas of Charles Center stand out against the surrounding cityscape.

SPECIAL PLACES: Most of the notable sights in Baltimore are concentrated in a few nicely designed areas. Consequently, the best way to see the city is by walking. Buses and taxis, which serve the entire city, are convenient, but parking in the lots downtown isn't too difficult or expensive.

CHARLES CENTER AND DOWNTOWN

Charles Center – Built during the past two decades, Charles Center is a 33-acre plot of new office buildings, luxury apartment towers, overhead walkways, fountains, and plazas. Bounded by Lombard Street on the south, Saratoga Street on the north, Hopkins Place and Liberty Street on the west, and Charles Street on the east. (One of the city's oldest and grandest thoroughfares, Charles Street is also being revitalized, with shops and restaurants opening their doors to new business.)

Within the complex is One Charles Center, a 24-story tower of bronze-covered glass designed by Mies van der Rohe. Inside the *Morris Mechanic Theater,* such contemporary stars as Rudolph Nureyev and Lauren Bacall have performed. Charles and Baltimore Sts.

Hopkins Plaza is the scene for many events, ranging from concerts by the *Baltimore Symphony Orchestra* to performances by lesser-known jazz ensembles and chamber groups (between Hopkins Pl., Charles, Baltimore, and Lombard Sts.). Center Plaza features a 33-foot bronze sculpture in the shape of a flame, designed by Francesco Somaini and presented to the city by the Gas and Electric Company (north of Fayette St. between Liberty and Charles Sts.). Pedestrian ramps link Charles Center to the Convention Center and to the *Civic Center,* a sawtooth-roofed building that hosts circuses, ice hockey games, and rock concerts (201 W. Baltimore St.).

Edgar Allan Poe Home and Grave – Poe lived here in the 1830s; he visited Baltimore again in 1849 long enough to die and be buried. His grave is nearby, in the Westminster Presbyterian Church Cemetery at Fayette and Greene Sts. Home visiting hours are noon to 3:45 PM Wednesdays through Saturdays. Small admission charge. 203 N. Amity St. (phone: 396-7932, for information); graveyard tours are given on the 1st and 3rd Friday evenings of the month and on Saturday mornings from April through October (phone: 528-2070).

City Hall – Still in use, the domed building is a monument to mid-Victorian design and craftsmanship. 100 N. Holliday St. For tour information, call 396-1151.

Lexington Market – Since 1782 this colorful indoor marketplace has provided stalls for independent merchants, who sell a variety of goods. An addition, the Arcade, opened in October 1982, as the market celebrated its 200th anniversary. Today, 100 kiosks and shops are in operation. Lunch on Maryland seafood at its best — in the rough and at little expense — at *John W. Faidley Seafood,* one of the largest raw oyster bars in the world. The crab cakes are divine, the clam chowder superb, and the beer is cold from the tap. Market is closed Sundays. 400 W. Lexington and Eutaw Sts.

MOUNT VERNON PLACE

This 19th-century bastion of Baltimore aristocracy now houses much of the 20th century's counterculture, with an array of boutiques, plant stores, restaurants, and natural food shops. Reminders of bygone days remain in the lovely 19th-century merchant prince housefronts, the stately squares, and outstanding cultural institutions.

Walters Art Gallery – This extensive collection, owned by the Walters family (who also owned railroads) and bequeathed to the city, offers an impressive span of art from Ancient Near Eastern, Byzantine, and Classical archaeological artifacts to Medieval European illuminated manuscripts and painted panels, Italian Renaissance paintings, and 20th-century works. Closed Mondays; no admission charge on Wednesdays. Charles and Centre Sts. (phone: 547-9000).

Maryland Historical Society – Examples of 18th- and 19th-century clothing, furniture, and silver, and general exhibitions. Closed Mondays. Library rich in genealogical material. Admission charge. 201 W. Monument St. (phone: 685-3750).

Peabody Institute and Conservatory of Music – Worth a visit simply for a look at the magnificently designed library. Amid pillars and balconies, this 19th-century interior holds 300,000 volumes on tiered iron stacks that spiral upward 6 stories. Free student concerts. Mount Vernon Pl. at Monument and N. Charles Sts. (phone: 659-8164; for concert information, 659-8124).

Washington Monument – The very first Washington Monument, designed by Robert Mills and completed in 1842. Washington's statue stands atop the monument's long shaft (a 228-step climb — there's no elevator) commanding an excellent view of the city, the harbor, and Mount Vernon Place. Admission charge. Mount Vernon Pl. (phone: 396-7939).

NORTH

Baltimore Museum of Art – the home of the new *Harbor City Ballet* and noted for two especially fine collections: the Cone Collection of the French post-Impressionist period, with a wealth of Matisse's work (the Cone collection also includes much of the art collection of Gertrude Stein); and the Wurtzburger collections of primitive art and modern sculpture. Also has restored rooms from 17th- and 18th-century Maryland mansions, and a wing featuring American decorative arts and an outdoor sculpture garden. Closed Mondays. Admission charge for those 22 and over; no charge on Thursdays. Art Museum Dr. near N. Charles and 31st Sts. (phone: 396-7101).

INNER HARBOR

Harborplace – The dazzling kingpin in Baltimore's renaissance, Harborplace is carrying the heart of the city's business southward. A plethora of shops, restaurants, and market stalls — about 140 in all — fill its two glass-enclosed pavilions. On the first floor of the Light Street Pavilion is a marketplace where vendors hawk all manner of comestibles, while the upper level is chockablock with small eateries serving a diverse range of foodstuffs — everything from hot dogs to knishes. And whether you're looking for a crab mallet or a collector's comic book, chances are it's in the *Sam Smith Market,* where merchants sell a raft of unusual wares from their pushcarts and kiosks (also on the 2nd floor). The Pratt Street Pavilion has its share of restaurants, boutiques, and specialty stores. Pratt and Light Sts. (phone: 332-4191).

National Aquarium – The aquarium has an impressive series of audio-visual displays on marine life, with a total of 5,000 specimens on 7 different levels. "People movers" carry visitors between levels, which include shark and dolphin pools, puffins living in a reproduction of their natural habitat, the largest coral reef in the US, and a reconstruction of Maine's coast with a hands-on display of shellfish and other shoreline creatures. Finally, on the top floor, visitors can wander through a tropical rain forest. Open daily. Admission charge. Pier 3, Inner Harbor (phone: 576-3810).

Fort McHenry National Monument and Historic Shrine – Here in 1814, a young Maryland lawyer witnessed the successful resistance of American forces to heavy British mortar bombardment and was so inspired by the sight of the Stars and Stripes still fluttering against the morning sky that he wrote "The Star-Spangled Banner." Visitors can see the fort, the old powder magazine, the officers' quarters, the enlisted men's barracks, and then walk along Francis Scott Key's famed ramparts overlooking the harbor. Open daily. During the summer on weekend afternoons, drills and military ceremonies modeled after those of 1814 are performed by uniformed soldiers and sailors. No admission charge. South of Inner Harbor, at the end of Fort Ave. (phone: 962-4299).

US Frigate *Constellation* – The US Navy's oldest warship (1797), the *Constellation* (named by George Washington) defeated the French frigate *L'Insurgente* in America's first important victory at sea and was in service through World War II. Now the ship has daily tours. Admission charge. Pier 1, Inner Harbor (phone: 539-1797).

Maryland Science Center and Planetarium – One of 25 full-size science centers in the country, covering everything from the vastness of outer space in the planetarium to the complexity of inner space in the walk-through model of a single human cell. The newest feature here is a 400-seat IMAX (maximum image) movie theater with a 5-story screen capable of producing vivid sensations of movement so that the viewer feels part of the action. At the southwest corner of the Inner Harbor (phone: 685-2370).

The Power Plant – Once the source of power for the city's streetcars, this is Baltimore's newest family entertainment center. A Victorian fantasyland filled with special effects, the highlight is the Sensorium, a 3-D theater where visitors are bombarded with the sights, sounds, and scents of turn-of-the-century Baltimore. Also notable are the Dungeon of the Mysterious, Laboratory of Scientific Wonders, the Magic Lantern Theater, P. T. Flagg's Nightclub, and a live musical revue. Pier 4, Inner Harbor (phone: 244-7377).

■**EXTRA SPECIAL:** Just 30 miles south of Baltimore on Route 2 (Ritchie Hwy.) lies Annapolis, Maryland's capital, where the charm of the first peacetime capital of the US is still preserved. Around town are lovely 18th-century buildings, including the old State House, still in use today, the Hammond-Harwood House, a Georgian home designed by William Buckland, and the campus of St. John's College, which appears much as it did to its most famous alumnus, Francis Scott Key. Also interesting is the US Naval Academy. The remains of John Paul Jones lie in the crypt of the chapel. The full brigade of midshipmen passes in formal parade review most Wednesdays at 3:30 PM on Worden Field. In town, the harbor is flanked by boutiques and restaurants.

SOURCES AND RESOURCES

TOURIST INFORMATION: The Baltimore Office of Promotion and Tourism offers useful tourist information, such as directions, maps, and brochures and daily events listings. Suite 310, 34 Market Pl. (phone: 752-8632 or 837-4636). The new *Infotouch* travelers' directory, at computerized kiosks around the city, offers information on restaurants and hotels, plus maps and directions; a free printout is issued at the touch of a button.

Baltimore, Annapolis and Chesapeake Country Guidebook by James F. Waesche (Bodine and Associates; $4.95) is a good guide to Baltimore and the surrounding area.

Television Stations – WBAL Channel 11–CBS; WJZ Channel 13–ABC; WMAR Channel 2–NBC; WMPB Channel 67–PBS.

Radio Stations – AM: WBAL 1090 (news/talk); WFBR 130 (pop music; WWIN 1400 (urban contemporary); FM: WLIF 101.9 (easy listening/news); WJHU 88.1 (classical/jazz); WYST 92.3 (adult contemporary/light rock).

Local Coverage – The *Baltimore Sun,* published twice daily and on Sundays, lists upcoming events. The weekly *City Paper,* which is free, offers a refreshing alternative and great classifieds. *Baltimore* is a monthly magazine with features on city life, restaurant listings, and calendars of events. All are available at newsstands. *Baltimore* and *Baltimore Good Times* are comprehensive, free, tourist publications, available in hotels and from the Office of Tourism, respectively.

Telephone – All telephone numbers are in the 301 area code unless otherwise indicated.

Sales Tax – The basic Maryland sales tax is 5%.

 CLIMATE: Baltimore weather is fickle, neither the rigorous clime of the North nor the mild South. Unpredictable rain and frequent changes in wind direction make umbrellas advisable, particularly in the summer and early fall. In the summer, the weather can be hot and muggy, though the Chesapeake Bay exerts a modifying influence and brings relief with nighttime breezes. The winter is cold with moderate snowfall. Spring is windy and pleasant.

 GETTING AROUND: Airport – Baltimore/Washington, DC International Airport (or BWI) is usually a 20-minute ride from downtown Baltimore via the Baltimore-Washington Expressway; taxi fare should run about $12. Train service is available from the airport to the city's downtown station for $2.70 one way; a shuttle bus transfers passengers from the air terminal to the airport train station. Trains run twice in early morning and five times in late afternoon. *Airport Connection* (phone: 859-3000), with a desk on the airport's lower level, charges $5 for transportation to most downtown hotels.

Bus – The Mass Transit Administration covers the entire metropolitan area. Route information and maps are available at MTA's main office, 300 W. Lexington St. (phone: 539-5000; for the hearing impaired, 539-3497). The MTA Tourist Passport is a 1-day pass, good from midnight to midnight for unlimited downtown travel on buses, the subway, and trolleys. The $2.25 pass is available, along with a comprehensive map, from many downtown hotels and at the visitors center on Pier 4 in Inner Harbor.

Subway – The Metro Rail system offers limited access to much of the downtown area. Free parking and bus shuttle service is available from most stations. Trains operate from 5 AM to 10:30 PM on weekdays, from 8 AM to 10:30 PM on weekends. Fare is 90¢ plus zone fares (phone: 333-2700).

Taxi – Cabs may be hailed on the street but are usually called by phone. Major companies are *Yellow Cab* (phone: 685-1212), *Diamond* (phone: 947-3333), *Sun* (phone: 235-0300), and *BWI Airport Cab* (phone: 859-1100).

Car Rental – All the major national firms are represented. Reliable local service is provided by *Baltimore Car and Truck Rental,* 2303 N. Howard St. (phone: 467-2900).

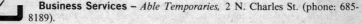 **LOCAL SERVICES: Babysitting** – *Elizabeth Cooney Personnel Agency* (phone: 323-1700).

Business Services – *Able Temporaries,* 2 N. Charles St. (phone: 685-8189).

Mechanic – *Plotkin's of Franklin Street,* 600 W. Franklin St. (phone: 728-5533).

MUSEUMS: The fine collections of the *Baltimore Museum of Art,* the *Walters Art Gallery, Maryland Historical Society,* and *Maryland Science Center* are described in *Special Places.* Some other museums of note are the following:

Baltimore Maritime Museum – The submarine USS *Torsk* and the lightship *Chesapeake* are open for tours Thursdays through Mondays in winter, daily in summer. Admission charge. Pier 4 at Pratt St. (phone: 396-5528).

B&O Railroad Museum – The most extensive collection of railroad memorabilia in the US and the second largest train exhibition in the world. It includes the nation's first passenger and freight station as well as related exhibits. Closed Mondays and Tuesdays. Admission charge. 901 W. Pratt St. (phone: 237-2387).

Babe Ruth Birthplace and Maryland Baseball Hall of Fame – Cooperstown, New York, may have the fame, but baseball buffs will find everything authentic here, from photos of the Babe to taped interviews and *Orioles* memorabilia. Open daily. Admission charge. 216 Emory St. (phone: 727-1539).

Baltimore City Life Museums – Baltimore has organized its small museums into an integrated collection, each one representing a facet of the city's culture and history. At the *Peale Museum,* 225 Holliday St., enjoy the collected works of the Peale family, early American portrait painters, and see how Baltimore grew during the 19th and 20th centuries in the exhibition "Rowhouse: A Baltimore Style of Living." Get acquainted with Baltimore's most famous literary son at the *H. L. Mencken House* on Union Square, 1524 Hollins St. Stroll through the *Carroll Mansion,* the elegant townhouse of a signer of the Declaration of Independence (800 E. Lombard St.). Dig into the city's past at the *Center of Urban Archaeology,* 802 E. Lombard St., and visit a 19th-century artisan's family through a dramatic living history presentation at the *1849 House* at 50 Albermarle St. (corner of E. Lombard). Celebrate Baltimore's renaissance at the *Courtyard Exhibition Center,* 44-48 Albemarle St. For more information, call 396-3523.

City Fire Museum – Once the oldest engine house in the nation, now filled with old equipment, artifacts, and photos of the aftermath of the Great Baltimore Fire of 1904. Open Sundays from 1 to 4 PM. 414 N. Gay St. (phone: 727-2414).

Lacrosse Hall of Fame Museum – Baltimore is the cradle of lacrosse, and displayed here are memorabilia and records of all levels. Closed on weekends. On Johns Hopkins' Homewood Campus in *Newton H. White Athletic Center* (phone: 235-6882).

Streetcar Museum – Home of the nation's first electric streetcar, this museum features a mile-and-a-quarter ride on a vintage streetcar, an exploration of the original carhouse, and exhibits of antique vehicles. Open Sundays from noon to 5 PM, and Thursdays and Saturdays in summer. 1901 Falls Rd. (phone: 547-0264).

 MAJOR COLLEGES AND UNIVERSITIES: Johns Hopkins University, at 34th and Charles Sts. (phone: 338-8000), and Johns Hopkins Hospital and Medical School, 600 N. Wolfe (phone: 955-5000), are internationally renowned. Other notable schools are the Peabody Institute and Conservatory of Music, Mount Vernon Pl. (phone: 659-8100), Morgan State University, Hillen Rd. and Cold Spring La. (phone: 444-3333), and Loyola, Charles St. and Cold Spring La. (phone: 323-1010). Goucher College is in suburban Towson on Dulaney Valley Rd. (phone: 337-6000).

 SPECIAL EVENTS: The *Maryland House and Garden Pilgrimage* lavishly demonstrates Baltimoreans' pride in their own backyards. This statewide event for garden lovers, held during the last week of April and the first week of May, is a series of self-guided tours through a group of outstanding homes and gardens. For details, contact the *Pilgrimage* offices: 1105A Providence Rd., Towson, MD 21204 (phone: 821-6933). Merriment abounds in May during the *Preakness Festival Week* of outdoor concerts, exhibitions, and performances preceding the famous horse race. Numerous ethnic fairs take place in warm weather and are held at a variety of locations (see newspapers for listings). These festivities culminate in September in the *City Fair,* with everything from Old Country food to top-name entertainers. The *Harborlights Music Festival* is held every summer, usually June through August, at Baltimore's 2,000-seat Pier 6 Pavilion. Many concerts — from symphony to pop — are given. The *Baltimore Jazz Festival,* dedicated to Eubie Blake, is held in early September. Pier 6 at Pratt St. (phone: 625-4230).

 SPORTS AND FITNESS: Baseball – The *Orioles* play their home games at *Memorial Stadium.* Tickets for good seats may be hard to get (phone: 338-1300).

Bicycling – A brochure describing several tours through the countryside is available at the Physical Fitness Commission, 201 W. Preston St. (phone: 383-4040).

Boating – Middle Branch Park is the site of the *Baltimore Rowing and Resource Center,* a unique facility that includes boat storage and a fishing pier (phone: 396-3838).

Fitness Center – The *Druid Hill YMCA* opens its pool and equipment to visitors, 1609 Druid Hill Ave. (phone: 728-1600).

Golf – Best public course is the 18-hole *Pine Ridge,* 3 miles north on Dulaney Valley Rd. (exit 27 on the Baltimore Beltway; phone: 252-1408). There are others at Forest Park, Hillside and Forest Park Aves. (phone: 448-0300), Carroll Park, Monroe and Washington Blvd.

Hockey – The *Skipjacks* (minor league) play at the *Civic Center.* 201 W. Baltimore (phone: 727-0703).

Horse Racing – The season runs from March through June, and September through mid-October. The high point is the running of the Preakness, which, along with the Kentucky Derby and the Belmont Stakes, make up the Triple Crown for 3-year-olds. At the *Pimlico Race Course,* Belvedere and Park Heights Aves. (phone: 542-9400).

Jogging – Run around the lake in Druid Hill Park. The Baltimore Office of Promotion and Tourism can provide a list of other routes.

Lacrosse – The Johns Hopkins *Blue Jays* (*Homewood Field,* Charles St. and University Pkwy.; phone: 235-6882) are among the tops in the ranks of collegiate stickmen. Seats are usually available.

Soccer – Watch the *Blast* indoors from January to April at the *Civic Center.* 201 W. Baltimore (phone: 837-0903).

Steeplechase – As for another specialty, point-to-point races (with timber barrier jumps) are run in the valleys north of the city (Western Run, Worthington, Long Green) on Saturday afternoons during April and May.

Tennis – There are many courts in the city's parks. The best are at Clifton Park, Harford Rd. and 33rd St. (phone: 396-6101 for permit).

 THEATER: For complete listings, see the publications cited above. Baltimore's theatrical offerings range from Broadway tryouts or road shows at the *Morris Mechanic Theater,* Charles Center (phone: 625-1400) to resident productions at *Center Stage,* the state theater of Maryland, 700 N. Calvert St. (phone: 332-0033), to the *Vagabond Players,* the oldest continuously operated "little theater" in the US, 806 S. Broadway (phone: 563-9135) and experimental works at the *Theatre Project,* 45 W. Preston St. (phone: 752-8558). There are also eight dinner theaters presenting Broadway shows. *Shalimar's Dinner Cabaret* features professional entertainment at Baltimore Travel Plaza (phone: 539-3091).

MUSIC: The *Baltimore Symphony Orchestra,* which is highly regarded nationally, performs at the *Joseph Meyerhoff Symphony Hall,* where the music can be appreciated in series concerts throughout the year, 1212 Cathedral St. (phone: 837-5691). The *Harbor City Ballet* performs at the *Baltimore Museum of Art* (phone: 488-4500). The *Baltimore Opera* performs in the *Lyric Opera House* (phone: 685-5086). For those more attuned to a syncopated beat, try to catch the *Left Bank Jazz Society* (call 945-2266 to learn where they're performing) or go to *Ethel's Place* (see below). Other musical programs are presented by well-known visiting artists; check the newspapers.

NIGHTCLUBS AND NIGHTLIFE: The city's hottest new nightspot, the *Fish Market,* is a converted warehouse containing five nightclubs (phone: 576-2222). *P. T. Flagg's* is in the Power Plant, the refurbished 1895 Baltimore and Electric Company building at 601 E. Pratt St., on Pier 4 (phone: 244-7377). The club features an extravaganza of lights, lasers, and popular music in an ornate interior. The entertainment varies, with dinner cabaret Wednesdays through Saturdays, including a champagne buffet. Closed Mondays; reservations. *Ethel's Place,* a contemporary jazz club founded by jazz singer Ethel Ennis, features contemporary music and jazz by local and national talents, 1225 Cathedral St. (phone: 727-7077). The city's only comedy club, the *Charm City Comedy Club,* presents stand-up comics from New York and LA, including those from top late-night TV shows, 102 Water St. (phone: 576-8558); closed Sundays, cover charge Fridays and Saturdays. The *Thirteenth Floor* in the *Belvedere* hotel has a romantic piano bar and a great view of the city, 1 E. Chase St. (phone: 547-8220). Harborplace also has a number of restaurants and pubs with live entertainment.

BEST IN TOWN

CHECKING IN: There are an increasing number of luxury hotels and several less costly ones downtown. Expect to pay $80 and up for a double; $45 to $70 in the moderate range; and $30 to $65 at those we list as inexpensive. Note that there is free parking at many of the hotel chains downtown. For bed and breakfast accommodations, contact *Amanda's Bed and Breakfast and Reservation Service,* 1428 Park Ave. (phone: 225-0001). All telephone numbers are in the 301 area code unless otherwise indicated.

Baltimore Marriott Inner Harbor – Within walking distance of Harborplace downtown, this 356-room property is ideal for business travelers and, due to its convenient location, also a good bet for tourists. It has several restaurants and lounges with entertainment. Pratt and Eutaw Sts. (phone: 962-0202 or 800-654-2000). Expensive.

Cross Keys Inn – Five miles from downtown (12 minutes via I-83, Jones Falls Expressway). A stop on the airport limousine run, the inn has a quiet atmosphere and is adjacent to the boutiques and specialty shops of Cross Keys Village Square. It has a good restaurant, coffee shop, lounge with entertainment, and a pool. 5100 Falls Rd. (phone: 532-6900). Expensive.

Hunt Valley Inn – In a suburban industrial complex where office buildings and factories are attractively landscaped and discreetly set apart from one another, this 392-room spot is the place to stay if embarking on the *Maryland House and Garden Pilgrimage* or attending the spring's timber races in hunt country. In addition to the restaurant, bar, and breakfast-luncheon parlor, recreational facilities are available — a pool, golf and tennis courts. A Marriott hotel. Shawan Rd. at I-83, in the Hunt Valley Cockeysville Business Park (phone: 785-7000). Expensive.

Hyatt Regency, Baltimore – This glossy waterfront hostelry has 500 rooms, 27,000 square feet of meeting space, and a path connecting it to Harborplace and the Baltimore Convention Center. It's also only a short walk to the National Aquarium and the Maryland Science Center. Recreational facilities include tennis courts, jogging track, and swimming pool, and there's a coffee shop (with a waterfall) for snacks, a dining room in a park-like setting, and a formal restaurant on the rooftop level. 300 Light St., Inner Harbor (phone: 528-1234 or 800-228-9000). Expensive.

Peabody Court – The same people responsible for the splendid restoration of Washington, DC's *Hay-Adams* hotel have brought similar distinctive qualities to this property in Baltimore's historic Mount Vernon Square. It has been transformed into a European-style hotel with fine service, antique decor, and a very good restaurant. Mount Vernon Pl. (phone: 727-7101 or 800-732-5301). Expensive.

Stouffer Harborplace – A contemporary high-rise, containing 622 rooms, on the Inner Harbor at Harborplace, it is convenient to the Aquarium, Science Center, and other attractions. *Windows* restaurant looks out over the harbor and features local seafood and continental dishes; 2 lounges (one with a piano bar) have live entertainment nightly. The decor is typically Stouffer's — elegant. 202 E. Pratt St. (phone: 547-1200, 800-325-5000, or 800-HOTELS-1). Expensive.

Tremont – Four blocks south of Mount Vernon Square, just off Charles Street, this hostelry caters to a clientele consisting mostly of executives looking for the privacy and amenities of an "all suites" hotel. Another attractive feature is guest privileges at the nearby *Downtown Athletic Club*. 8 E. Pleasant St. (phone: 576-1200). Expensive.

Admiral Fell Inn – A new contemporary bed and breakfast establishment with 37 rooms of various shapes and sizes carved out of 3 buildings. All rooms are named for famous city residents and feature four-poster beds. There's a small restaurant, continental breakfast, honor bar, and all-day coffee service for guests. Free van to town or summer ferry to Inner Harbor. Fell's Point, 888 S. Broadway (phone: 522-7377 or 800-292-4667). Expensive to moderate.

Belvedere – Halfway between Pennsylvania Station and the Inner Harbor, this recently renovated grand hotel has an enormous lobby with elegant fixtures, a rooftop lounge with live entertainment, beautifully appointed rooms, and 2 excellent restaurants. 1 E. Chase St. (phone: 332-1000 or 800-692-2700). Moderate.

Sheraton Johns Hopkins Inn – This is the most convenient, respectable hotel for visitors to Johns Hopkins Hospital or School of Medicine, near colorful Fell's Point. The 162-room property has a restaurant, a lounge, and a pool. 400 N. Broadway (phone: 675-6800). Moderate.

Shirley House – This 1880s hotel has been restored to its former elegance. Run as a bed and breakfast establishment, it offers guests a continental breakfast each morning and a complimentary glass of wine before bed. Spacious rooms have high ceilings, antique furnishings, and imported Victorian wallpaper. Connecting doors facilitate a variety of room arrangements. 205 Madison St. (phone: 728-6550). Moderate.

 EATING OUT: Dedicated eaters find happiness in Baltimore. From its regional specialty, seafood in the rough, to the authentic dishes of its Little Italy, there are restaurants to suit most palates and pocketbooks. Our selections range in price from $60 or more for a dinner for two in the expensive range, $35 to $50 in the moderate range, and $30 or less in the inexpensive range. Prices do not include drinks, wine, or tips. All telephone numbers are in the 301 area code unless otherwise indicated.

Conservatory at the Peabody Court – Even if the cuisine were merely mediocre, a meal here would be enjoyable simply for the lovely view overlooking Mount Vernon's cultural institutions. Fortunately, the menu is quite commendable. One specialty is Virginia squab with poached quail eggs. Closed Mondays. Reservations necessary. Major credit cards. Mount Vernon Pl. (phone: 727-7101). Expensive.

Orchid – Baltimore's first French and Oriental restaurant offers an award-winning menu of fresh meat, seafood, and crisp vegetables, in a marriage that combines the best of both worlds — creamy French sauces and fresh Oriental seasonings. Downtown near all attractions, 419 N. Charles St. (phone: 837-0080). Expensive.

Prime Rib – A hangout for figures in the city's political and entertainment worlds. Its prime ribs are great, but no more so than the crab imperial. This is a surprisingly dressy place; jackets (not ties) required. Dinner nightly. Reservations recommended. Major credit cards. 1101 N. Calvert St., in Horizon House (phone: 539-1804). Expensive to moderate.

Haussner's – Everything abounds in this German restaurant, from the fat Tyrolean dumplings to the draft Bavarian beer to the Barbizon paintings and busts of Roman emperors that cover the walls. The museum downstairs has a ball of string 300 miles long. Don't ask; we're just reporting the facts. Open Tuesdays through Saturdays for lunch and dinner. Reservations accepted for lunch only. Major credit cards. 3242 Eastern Ave. (phone: 327-8365). Moderate.

Marconi's – The interior may not be pleasing to the eye, but the artistry is on the plate. The restaurant where, in a steady stream, Baltimoreans themselves go. The specialty of this Franco-Italian restaurant is fillet of sole prepared in a variety of delicious ways. Lunch and dinner; closed Sundays and Mondays. No reservations. 106 W. Saratoga St. (phone: 727-9522). Moderate.

Olde Obrycki's Crab House – Roll back your sleeves, put on your bib, grab a mallet, and you're ready for a bout at *Obrycki's*. Here you spend all evening battling steamed crabs. There's plenty of support along the way in the warm family atmosphere. Open April through November only; closed Mondays; weekends, dinner only. Major credit cards. 1729 E. Pratt St., Fell's Point. (phone: 732-6399). Moderate.

Sabatino's – A good late-night dining spot in the heart of Baltimore's Little Italy. Veal and shrimp marsala are the specialties, appreciated by the locals, who refer to the place familiarly as *Sabby's*. Spiro T. Agnew and Marvin Mandel both ate here right after their respective court convictions. You'll doubtless do better. Open daily for lunch and dinner. Major credit cards. 901 Fawn St. Little Italy (phone: 727-9414). Moderate.

John W. Faidley Seafood – In the past hundred years, *Faidley's* has established itself as the place for oysters, crabs, and clams brought in fresh daily from the bay. The downtown lunch crowd regards a visit to *Faidley's* in Lexington Market — a vast assemblage of butchers and merchants — as the ultimate adventure. Open from 9 AM to 6 PM daily except Sundays. No credit cards. Paca at Lexington St. (phone: 727-4898). Inexpensive.

Harborplace – In addition to 33 food stalls, where visitors can find everything from Buffalo wings to chocolate-covered strawberries, the following restaurants have good food, harbor views, and moderate prices. In the Light Street Pavilion are: *The American Café,* with a light American menu and frequent live entertainment (phone: 962-8800); *City Lights,* featuring French cuisine and homemade desserts (phone: 244-8811); *Jean-Claude's Café,* also with French food (phone: 332-0950); *Phillips Harborplace,* with Chesapeake Bay seafood and a piano bar (phone: 685-6600); and *The Soup Kitchen,* with homemade soups, good salads, and desserts (phone: 539-3810). In the Pratt Street Pavilion are: *Mariner's Pier One,* with light fare, daily specials, weekend entertainment (phone: 962-5050); *Tandoor,* featuring Northern Indian cuisine cooked in tandoori ovens (phone: 547-0575); *Taverna Athena,* with authentic Greek cuisine (phone: 547-8900); *Bamboo House,* with Chinese food (phone: 625-1191); and *Gianni's,* for North Italian (phone: 837-1130).

BOSTON

No matter how you approach Boston, it's hard not to be struck by the lovely siting of this city, which juts into the island-studded harbor and graces the banks of the Charles River with its riverside parks and distinctive skyline — a poetic melding of the old and the new. Here are the narrow cobblestones where Boston's colonists walked, the Common where their cattle grazed, the churches they prayed in, and the tiny burying grounds that shelter their bones to this day. Here, too, are the bold buildings of government, the fortresses of finance, the colorful chaos of the open market, and the freewheeling spirit of the waterfront.

Anyone walking briskly could traverse this eventful terrain in an hour, but instead take the time to explore Boston at leisure, keeping an eye out for the little things — the odd quirks of architecture, the bright spots of whimsy and caprice. Spend a couple of hours in the North End, wandering along twisting streets barely wider than the ancient cowpaths they follow, or in the Back Bay, strolling down the broad avenues lined with stately townhouses, and you will see much that is lovely or curious or amusing. Look for the famous brass nameplates and gas lamps of Beacon Hill, the intricate wrought-iron balconies along Commonwealth Avenue, the market refuse set into the pavement near Haymarket, and the grasshopper atop Faneuil Hall.

This grasshopper has had one of the best views of history in the making, for Faneuil Hall was the site of many Revolutionary protest meetings. Indeed, if it has been dubbed the Cradle of Liberty, Boston itself could be considered the hotbed of dissent in which the American Revolution was spawned. It is here that the impassioned protest "Taxation without representation is tyranny" was voiced; where Sam Adams roused the citizenry and organized the Boston Tea Party; and where Paul Revere began his midnight ride when the British approached.

The 19th century saw the rise of commerce in Boston; and the flowering of arts and letters — represented by such figures as Emerson, Hawthorne, Longfellow, and Thoreau — led to its reputation as the Athens of America. The boom of population and wealth combined with the increasing noxiousness of the Back Bay caused it to be filled in to provide land for the city's expansion. Though the affluent and influential clamored to build on its wide avenues and live in its grand homes, Henry James was less impressed: "It is all very rich and prosperous and monotonous . . . but oh, so inexpressibly vacant." Today, however, that barren landscape has been transformed by a century's growth of elms, magnolias, and fruit trees, and its houses have come to represent exceptional examples of Victorian architecture in America.

After half a century of neglect and deterioration, Boston has again been experiencing a renaissance, beginning with the creation of Government Center and the restoration of the city's historic neighborhoods. With the past

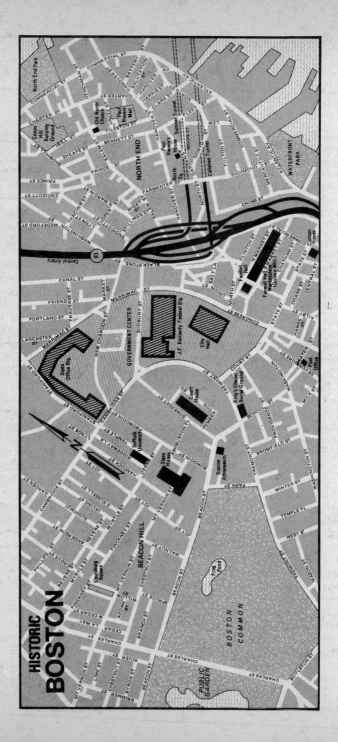

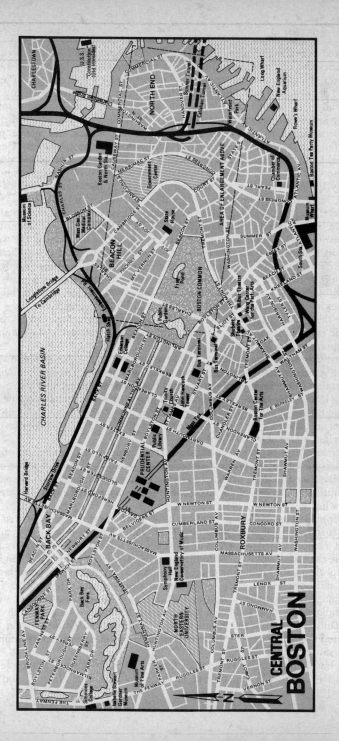

CENTRAL BOSTON

revived for posterity, city planners turned their sights to the needs —
or fancies — of a new generation of residents and visitors. During the 1970s,
Faneuil Hall Marketplace became the prototype for a new concept of urban
retail development when Benjamin Thompson and the Rouse Company successfully transformed the old, largely abandoned market buildings into a
lively and congenial gathering place that thrives in a carnival atmosphere of
jugglers, magicians, musicians, and street vendors outside, and eateries plain
and fancy, trinket shops, and unusual boutiques inside. More recently, Copley
Place, Lafayette Place, and Cambridge's Charles Square have added vitality
to the city. By now, Boston's reputation as a bastion of conservatism and
chilly Brahmins (remember "banned in Boston"?) has gone the way of history, replaced by an upbeat avant-garde image that is also reality.

Yet a civilized urbanity remains, a sense of ease combined with an abundance of opportunity. Step out of your hotel and Boston showers you with
riches. Do you like art? Boston's museums are among the finest in the world
and its galleries — both on Newbury Street and along Fort Point Channel
— are worth a day in themselves. Music? The *Boston Symphony* is only the
beginning. Baroque chamber music concerts are often sold out, jazz fans can
sit through three sizzling sets in intimate underground cafés, and the biggest
names in current folk and rock come back faithfully to sing in the clubs that
gave them their start. There are drum and bugle corps, rock groups, early
music ensembles, swing bands, and choral groups of all descriptions, not to
mention the ever-popular *Boston Pops*.

The *Opera Company of Boston* and the *Boston Ballet* are world-renowned,
and a variety of contemporary dance companies present frequent, innovative
programs. Many Broadway shows come here, and theater groups stage everything from Shakespeare to experimental plays. Beside the many commercial
movie houses showing first- and second-run films, the colleges and cultural
centers are always sponsoring film festivals where you can catch your favorite
Chaplin or Dietrich or Bogart epic.

These same colleges and cultural centers provide virtually unlimited opportunities for education and self-improvement, from the large academic communities like Harvard, MIT, and Boston University to the dozens of smaller
institutions. The list of lectures open to the public on any given day is
overwhelming.

For many people, Boston is, above all, a sports town. It's easy for *Red Sox*
fans to indulge themselves at *Fenway Park*, which has ardent admirers nationwide. *Fenway* is one of the last of the great old urban ball parks, a cozy field
where the stands are so close to the action that between pitches you can hear
the tobacco juice hitting the grass — and that's real grass, mind you. Basketball and hockey fans flock to the *Boston Garden*, just a few blocks from
Haymarket, where the *Celtics* and *Bruins* have been not infrequent world
champions. Football followers have to drive to Foxboro to watch the New
England *Patriots*, but the distance doesn't deter them. (Visitors should bear
in mind that loyalties are intense in Boston. If you must cheer for the opposi-
tion, do so softly.)

Politics often seems like another favorite sport in Boston. Mayor James
Michael Curley will live forever in the novel *The Last Hurrah*, and the

grandson of another mayor, "Honey Fitz" Fitzgerald, became the 35th president of the US, John F. Kennedy. Such names as Elliot Richardson and Henry Cabot Lodge loom large in our national consciousness, and Tip O'Neill, a North Cambridge boy, has stepped down after a lengthy tenure as Speaker of the House. But some run for more than election — Mayor Ray Flynn keeps in shape for the Boston Marathon as well.

Boston has long been known as "the home of the bean and the cod," but though scrod (as cooked cod fillets are called here) is found on many menus, it is harder and harder to find authentic baked beans. Local fishermen pride themselves in providing Boston's tables with the finest fresh fish and shellfish — especially lobster and clams. Two ethnic neighborhoods long known for their restaurants and groceries are Chinatown and the Italian North End. But today you can satisfy your desire for most any kind of cooking, be it Thai, Japanese, Portuguese, Indian, Mexican, or Greek, to name a few, and there has been an exciting proliferation of restaurants dedicated to creative nouvelle cuisine using the freshest seasonal produce. Bostonians bargain for their own at Haymarket, the traditional farmers' market adjacent to Faneuil Hall Marketplace. If you're in town on a Friday or Saturday, don't miss this chance to experience high-pitched excitement and local color.

For more peaceful and possibly healthful recreation, you are never more than a few blocks from a green oasis suitable for strolling, jogging, picnicking, or simply people watching. Thanks to the genius and foresight of Frederick Law Olmsted, Boston enjoys several miles of continuous parkland known as the Emerald Necklace. Perhaps the prettiest jewel of them all is the Public Garden, with its ever-changing displays of luxuriant blooms arranged in intricate patterns and its graceful Swan Boats cruising the quiet pond. One of the best places for jogging — and Bostonians jog everywhere! — is the path along the Embankment (also called the Esplanade) of the Charles River, which provides plenty of aquatic as well as terrestrial scenery and in summer is the site of performances in the Hatch Shell, among them the famous July Fourth extravaganza of the *Boston Pops Orchestra,* led by John (*Star Wars*) Williams.

Boston has made the journey from its staid, Puritan beginning to its vibrant, cosmopolitan present, treasuring its past but eager to experience the new.

BOSTON AT-A-GLANCE

 SEEING THE CITY: There are two unparalleled posts from which to view Boston: the John Hancock Tower's 50th-floor Observatory, and the 50th-floor Prudential Skywalk. The Hancock Tower gives you a spectacular panorama that even includes the mountains of southern New Hampshire (weather permitting), telescopes, recorded commentaries, a topographical model of Boston in 1775 (which is a must — we promise you'll be surprised), and a 7-minute film of a helicopter flight over the city. (Take the subway, the Green Line, to Copley Square.) Open daily. Admission charge. 200 Clarendon St., Copley Sq. (phone: 247-1977). Like the Hancock, the Prudential Skywalk offers an excellent 360-degree view, but the Pru also has a restaurant and bar on the 52nd floor. (Green Line, Auditorium or Prudential stop.) Skywalk and restaurant are open daily. Admission charge. Prudential Center, between Huntington Ave. and Boylston St. (phone: 236-3318).

SPECIAL PLACES: Boston is best seen on foot; the city is compact, and driving, even for residents, is hair-raising.

Freedom Trail – The city has made it both easy and fun to track down the important sites from its colonial and Revolutionary past. Just follow the red brick (or red paint) line set into the sidewalk; it takes about 2 hours to walk its length without stops or side trips. To begin, take the Green or Red Line to Park Street and go to the Visitor Information Center on the Common, which has maps available. Or you can take a double-decker bus tour (see *Getting Around*).

Boston Common – A pastoral green, this is the nation's oldest park, set up in 1634. The earliest Bostonians brought their cows and horses here to graze. Today, you'll find their descendants engaging in free-form pastimes that range from music making to baseball and skateboarding. We suggest starting your walking tour here. (It's advisable not to walk alone — and especially not at night — since the Common is often inadequately patrolled; you can park underneath the green in the Underground Parking Garage, open 24 hours daily.) For information on activities on the Common, call 800-858-0200.

State House – Facing the Beacon Street entrance to the Common, the gold-domed State House designed by Charles Bulfinch dates to 1795. The gold leaf was added in 1874. You can enter through the side door of the right wing (the main door is hardly ever used). Inside, you can pick up pamphlets in Doric Hall and visit the *Archives Museum* in the basement. It contains American historical documents, among them the original Massachusetts constitution, the oldest written constitution in the world (phone: 727-2816). There is also a library (phone: 727-2590). Closed weekends. No admission charge. Beacon St. (phone: 727-2121).

Park Street Church and Granary Burying Ground – Built in 1809, the church witnessed William Lloyd Garrison's famous antislavery address in 1829 and heard the first singing of "My country, 'tis of thee" 2 years later. Open Tuesdays through Saturdays, July and August; otherwise by appointment. 1 Park St. (phone: 523-3383). In the 1660 cemetery next door are the graves of such Revolutionary notables as John Hancock, Samuel Adams, Thomas Paine, and Paul Revere and the parents of Benjamin Franklin. Look for the grave of Mary Goose, believed to be Mother Goose. Open daily.

City Hall – The focal point of Government Center, Boston's spacious new City Hall (1968), designed by Kallmann, McKinnell, & Knowles, sits in the middle of an 8-acre plaza that is often the scene of civic celebrations and politicking. Congress St. (phone: 725-4000).

Old State House – Sitting in the middle of State Street, surrounded by modern towers of law and finance, is this 18th-century seat of government, which served both the English colony and American state of Massachusetts until Bulfinch's State House was built. Now it is a museum of Boston history. Open daily. Admission charge. 206 Washington St. (phone: 242-5655). Across the street is a National Park Service visitors center, which provides useful information about Boston and sites in outlying areas. There are free guided tours April through November. Open daily. No admission charge. 15 State St. (phone: 242-5642).

Faneuil Hall Marketplace – These three large buildings have been a market since 1826 and still house 11 of the original tenants. Redesigned and opened between 1976 and 1978, the market has become a much-copied prototype of urban renewal. Over a million people per month — natives and tourists — partake of its multiplicity of stalls, restaurants, and shops. Plan to spend time wandering around and sampling its food, drink, and chic wares. The market takes its official name from adjacent Faneuil (pronounced Fan'l) Hall, a historic meeting house. Open daily (phone: 523-2980).

Beacon Hill – Walk along Mt. Vernon Street to see the stately old townhouses that were (and are today) the pride of the first families of Boston. Look for the famous brass knockers, the charming carriage houses, and the intimate backyard gardens. A few blocks down is Louisburg Square, a rectangle of terribly proper houses facing a tiny park; this was once home to Louisa May Alcott and Jenny Lind, among others. Cobblestoned Acorn Street, parallel to Mt. Vernon and Chestnut, is the most photographed in town.

North End – Paul Revere's House and Old North Church are both snugly tucked away among the narrow red brick streets of the North End, a colorful, Italian-American community with a lively street life and some excellent little restaurants (see *Eating Out*). To experience *la dolce vita*, stop at the *Café Paradiso* (255 Hanover St.) for cannoli, cappuccino, and people watching.

Paul Revere's House – In addition to having housed the legendary Revolutionary hero, this place has the distinction of being the oldest wooden house in Boston. Before Revere lived here, one of the previous occupants was a sea captain who spent time in a Puritan pillory for "lewd and vicious behavior." Revere moved here in 1770 with his wife, mother, and five children. He had seven more children by his second wife, which is why his house was the only one on the block that didn't have to quarter British soldiers. Open daily. Admission charge. 19 North Sq. (phone: 523-2338).

Old North Church – Affectionately known as Old North, the official name of the church is Christ Church, built in 1723. On the night of April 18, 1775, sexton Robert Newman hung two lanterns outside to warn Bostonians that the British were coming by sea. His action and Paul Revere's famous ride were later immortalized by poet Henry Wadsworth Longfellow in a poem that you probably read in school. (The line you will want to remember is: "One if by land, two if by sea.") The church's original clock still ticks in the back and services are still held every Sunday. Open daily. No admission charge. 193 Salem St. (phone: 523-6676).

Waterfront – Walk along Waterfront Park, with its invigorating views of the harbor and browse in the many new shops set in the renovated wharf buildings. On Long Wharf, the pier behind the Aquarium, you'll find the Custom House, built between 1845 and 1847, the ferry (summer only) across Cape Cod Bay to Provincetown (see *Cape Cod,* DIRECTIONS), and boats for harbor cruises and fishing excursions. For information, contact *Provincetown Steamship Company* (phone: 723-7800) or *Boston Harbor Cruises,* Long Wharf (phone: 227-4320). The *Massachusetts Bay Line* leaves from Rowe's Wharf (phone: 542-8000).

New England Aquarium – One of the world's top collections of marine life, it served as the model for the National Aquarium in Baltimore. Taking center stage is the 180,000-gallon Giant Ocean Tank, the home of 1,000 aquatic specimens and a 4-story coral reef. Divers regularly feed the multitudes of turtles, fish and sharks so they don't dine on each other. Exhibits re-creating environments such as tropical marine, northern waters and tidepool surround the saltwater tank. Penguins cavort in their own habitat called the Penguin Tray, and seals and dolphins perform aboard the floating pavilion *Discovery,* next door to the main building. A variety of films are shown in the auditorium, and there's an interesting gift shop. Blue Line, Aquarium stop. Open daily. Admission charge; children under 5 free. Central Wharf, Waterfront (phone: 973-5200).

BACK BAY

Arlington is the first of an alphabetically ordered series of streets created when the Back Bay was filled in during the mid-1800s. Broad streets and avenues were laid out in an orderly fashion, and along them wealthy Bostonians built palatial homes, churches, and public institutions. This area is a joy to walk and gives a better feeling of Victorian Boston than any other part of the city.

Public Garden – A treasure among city parks and a Boston tradition since 1861, the Garden has fountains, formal gardens, and trees labeled for identification. A special treat is a ride on the Swan Boats, past the geese and ducks on the lake (open daily, mid-April through Labor Day, except on windy or rainy days; admission charge, group rates available; call 323-2700). Across Charles Street from the Common. Open daily. No admission charge.

Commonwealth Avenue – Intended to replicate the broad boulevards of 19th-century Paris, with their mansard-roofed and stately homes, Commonwealth Avenue has fulfilled its early promise. Stroll down the shady mall, with its statues of famous Bostonians. In April, the magnolias are a special treat. On the corner of Clarendon Street stands the First Baptist Church, a splendid Romanesque structure designed by H. H. Richardson and completed in 1882. Open daily. No admission charge. 110 Commonwealth Ave. (phone: 267-3148).

Newbury Street – This is where fashionable Bostonians shop. There are many art galleries and boutiques as well as a variety of restaurants and several outdoor cafés.

Copley Square – Seagoing vessels used to drop their anchors in Copley Square; now it harbors Richardson's magnificent Trinity Church. Open daily. No admission charge (phone: 536-0944). The Boston Public Library (1885) is the oldest in the country. Step inside the Copley Square entrance for a quiet moment in the lovely central courtyard. Closed Sundays (phone: 536-5400). Across Dartmouth Street from the *Copley Plaza* is Copley Place, a complex of hotels, fashionable shops (*Neiman Marcus, Tiffany,* and the like), restaurants, eight movie theaters, and an indoor waterfall (phone: 375-4400).

OTHER SPECIAL PLACES

John F. Kennedy Library – This presidential library opened in 1979. Designed by I. M. Pei, it sits on the edge of a point of land projecting into Dorchester Bay, with a magnificent view of the Boston skyline and out to sea. The museum includes a half-hour film and an exhibit of documents, photographs, and memorabilia of JFK and his administration. There's also a section on his brother Robert F. Kennedy. By car, take the Southeast Expressway south to the JFK Library/UMass exit. The route to the library is well marked. Or take the Red Line (Ashmont or Quincy train) to Columbia; a shuttle bus takes you to the library. Open daily except certain holidays. Admission charge for adults; children under 16 free (phone: 929-4567).

Museum of Fine Arts – This is one of the world's great art museums, with comprehensive exhibits from every major period and in every conceivable medium. Special shows come and go frequently, many of them mounted in the West Wing, designed by I. M. Pei. The Monets are especially dazzling. Films, classical music, lectures, and superb activities for children make this a multimedia magnet for everyone. Restaurant, snack bar, museum shop, and library. Arborway train (Green Line) Ruggles St. stop. Closed Mondays. Admission charge except Saturday mornings. 465 Huntington Ave., along the Fenway (phone: 267-9377 or 267-9300).

Isabella Stewart Gardner Museum – Mrs. Gardner, the widow of a Boston Brahmin, built this lovely Venetian palazzo, which she filled with her extraordinary collections of tapestries, stained glass, fine furniture, and paintings by masters like Rembrandt, Titian, and Corot. The courtyard is filled with blooms year-round. Free chamber music concerts are held frequently in the tapestry room, except in July and August (call ahead for the schedule). A small café serves light lunches, in the garden in summer. Arborway train (Green Line), Ruggles St. stop. Closed Mondays. Suggested donation. 280 The Fenway (phone: 734-1359).

Institute of Contemporary Art – Exciting contemporary art in several media, including frequent series of interesting films. It's set in the halls of a 19th-century police station. Green Line, Auditorium stop. Hours vary seasonally; check before you go. Admission charge. 955 Boylston (phone: 266-5151).

Museum of Science and the Charles Hayden Planetarium – A wide variety of superb exhibitions illustrate the fields of medicine, technology, and space. Many of them involve viewer participation. You can watch a model of the ocean and a simulated lunar module in action. There's a special medical wing with anatomical and medical history and nutrition displays. The centerpiece of a lovely new wing is the *Omni Theater,* where a gigantic screen nearly surrounds viewers with images and sounds from scientific or scenic films. There's also a splendid new gift shop and cafeteria. Lechmere train (Green Line), Science Park stop. Closed Mondays. Admission charge; separate admission for *Omni Theater,* advance reservations suggested. Science Park, Charles River Dam (phone: 742-6088).

Boston Tea Party Ship and Museum – Board the *Brig Beaver II,* a full-size working replica of one of the three original ships in the Boston Tea Party. If you feel like it, you can even throw a little tea into Boston Harbor. The adjacent museum houses historical documents relevant to the period, as well as films and related exhibits. Red Line, South Station stop. Open daily. Admission charge. Congress St. Bridge at Fort Point Channel (phone: 338-1773).

USS *Constitution* – View famous "Old Ironsides," the oldest commissioned ship in the US Navy and the proud winner of 40 victories at sea (phone: 242-5670). The adjacent shoreside museum displays related memorabilia and a slide show. City Square bus stop. Museum open daily. Admission charge. Boston Naval Shipyard, Charlestown (phone: 241-9078).

Bunker Hill Pavilion – Witness a vivid multimedia reenactment of the Battle of Bunker Hill on 14 screens, with 7 sound channels. Bet you thought the Americans won. Open daily, with shows every half-hour. Admission charge. Adjacent to USS *Constitution* (phone: 241-7575).

Arnold Arboretum – Contained in these 265 acres of beautifully landscaped woodland and park are over 6,000 varieties of trees and shrubs, most of them labeled by their assiduous Harvard caretakers. Green Line, Arborway stop, or Orange Line, Forest Hills stop. Open daily. No admission charge. The Arborway, Jamaica Plain (phone: 524-1717).

Frederick Law Olmsted National Historic Site – Olmsted, the premier 19th-century landscape designer best known for Central Park in New York City and Prospect Park in Brooklyn, is honored through archives that include plans, drawings, and photographs. There are tours of the house occupied by Olmsted and his two sons as well as a slide program. Olmsted also designed the nearby Brookline Reservoir and Boston's "Emerald Necklace" of green spaces, which tie the city to the suburbs. Donations are requested. 99 Warren St., Brookline (phone: 566-1689).

CAMBRIDGE

Harvard Square – Just across the Charles River from Boston, Cambridge has always had an ambience and identity all its own. Catering equally to the academic and professional communities, the Square is a lively combination of the trendy, traditional, and "upscale." It has the greatest concentration of bookstores in the country (many are open daily until late into the evening), movie options that range from vintage films like *Casablanca* to the latest from Hollywood and abroad, and the ever-present street musicians. When hunger pangs strike, everything from muffins to nouvelle cuisine awaits — with an authentic Italian ice to top it off. Red Line, Harvard Square stop.

Harvard Yard – This tree-filled enclave is the focal point of the oldest (1636) and most prestigious university in the country (the Law School is nearby, the Business School just across the river, the Medical School a bus ride away in Boston). Notice especially Massachusetts Hall (1720; Harvard's oldest building), Bulfinch's University Hall, and in the adjoining quadrangle Widener Library and Richardson's Sever Hall. Campus tours are given year-round; check at the information office in Holyoke Center (phone: 495-1573).

Arthur Sackler Museum and Fogg Museum – The *Sackler*'s 1985 postmodern building designed by James Stirling joins the *Fogg*'s neo-Georgian building to house Harvard's impressive collection of paintings, drawings, prints, sculpture, and silver, as well as changing exhibitions. Open daily; closed weekends in summer. Admission charge. 32 Quincy St. (phone: 495-5573).

Harvard Museum of Natural History – On one short block parallel to Oxford Street is this complex housing the *Natural History* (comparative zoology), *Peabody* (anthropology), *Geology,* and *Botanical* museums. The *Peabody* houses extensive anthropological and archaeological collections, with an emphasis on South American Indians. There are also exhibitions on Africa and evolution as well as a fine gift shop. Reservations must be made for either group (phone: 495-2341) or individual (phone: 495-3045) tours. Open daily. Admission charge except on Saturdays from 9 to 11 AM. 24 Oxford St. (phone: 495-1910).

Longfellow House – George Washington and his troops billeted at this Tory Row house, built in 1759, at the beginning of the Revolutionary War. Longfellow bought it when he was a professor at Harvard and lived here until his death in 1882. (His children lived in neighboring Brattle Street homes.) Now it's a National Historic Site. Open daily; summer concerts. Admission charge. 105 Brattle St. (phone: 876-4491).

Radcliffe Yard – One of the Seven Sister colleges, Radcliffe has evolved from its historical role as Harvard's Annex to its current position, with its undergraduates fully integrated into the life of the university. Radcliffe focuses on special alternative programs for women at the graduate level and those involved in career changes. Its Schlesinger Library has one of the country's top collections on the history of women in America as well as an important culinary collection. Open weekdays. No admission charge. 10 Garden St. (phone: 495-8647).

Old Burying Ground – Back on Garden Street, walk past Christ Church to the Old Burying Ground, also known as God's Acre, where the graves go back to 1635. Many Revolutionary War heroes and Harvard presidents are buried here. On the Garden Street fence, there's a mileage marker dating to 1754.

Massachusetts Institute of Technology – The foremost scientific school in the country, MIT opened its doors in Boston in 1861 and moved across the river to its Cambridge campus in 1916. In addition to its world-famous laboratories and graduate schools in engineering and science, its professional schools include the Sloan School of Management, the Center for Urban Affairs (with Harvard), and the School of Architecture. The architect I. M. Pei is an alumnus; next to his Green Building for the earth sciences is Calder's stabile *The Great Sail,* one of a superb collection of outdoor sculpture on the campus. Also worth noting are Saarinen's chapel and Kresge Auditorium, just off Mass. Ave. The *Compton Gallery* features changing technical exhibitions (77 Mass. Ave.; open weekdays; free) and the *Hayden Gallery* displays contemporary painting, photography, sculpture, and design (Memorial Dr.; closed Sundays; free). The new *Wiesner Visual Arts Center,* in the List Building, is another I. M. Pei landmark and worth a visit for its interesting interior and its often provocative changing exhibitions (20 Ames St.; open daily; no admission charge). MIT campus tours are given year-round on weekdays at 10 AM and 2 PM. Red Line, Kendall Square/MIT stop. 77 Mass. Ave. (phone: 253-4795).

Mt. Auburn Cemetery – The first garden cemetery in the United States, this rural retreat in the midst of Cambridge is bliss to the senses. Founded in 1831, Mt. Auburn's 174 beautifully landscaped acres include hills, ponds (4), trees (over 2,000), and an observation tower. Visitors are encouraged to walk or drive around, and bird watchers find it especially appealing. Among the many famous people buried here are Mary Baker Eddy, Henry Wadsworth Longfellow, Julia Ward Howe, Oliver Wendell Holmes, and Winslow Homer. An hour's stroll might be the pinnacle of a sightseeing day. Open daylight hours year-round; tower open daily only in fair weather. Stop for a map at the north entrance, 580 Mt. Auburn St. (phone: 547-7105).

■**EXTRA SPECIAL:** About 12 miles north of Boston on Route 107 is the town of Salem. The capital of the Massachusetts Bay Colony from 1626 to 1630, Salem earned a bitter name in American history as the scene of the witch trials, in which a group of women and children accused 19 villagers of witchcraft. The hysterical allegations resulted in the deaths of the accused. Several of the judges bitterly regretted their roles subsequently. Salem is also the site of Nathaniel Hawthorne's House of the Seven Gables (54 Turner St.). Hawthorne worked in the Salem Customs House and wrote his classic *The Scarlet Letter* at 14 Mall St. You can pick up a self-guiding cassette tour at the Chamber of Commerce, 32 Derby Sq. (phone: 508-744-0004). Like Boston, Salem has a history trail winding through its streets and port. The information booth provides maps and brochures. Open daily. 18 Washington Sq. (phone: 508-744-0004).

While you're in the neighborhood, be sure to stop at the *Witch Museum,* 19½ Washington Sq. N. Closed Thanksgiving, Christmas, New Year's. Admission charge (phone: 508-744-1692). The Witch House, site of some of the interrogations, radiates a claustrophobic, spooky feeling still, especially at night. (Some of the accused witches were confined here.) Open daily March to mid-December; other times by appointment. Admission charge. 9 North St. (phone: 508-744-0180). (You can get in the mood for this tour by picking up a copy of Arthur Miller's play *The Crucible.*)

For a cruise in the harbor, walk down to Salem Willows Pier; *Pier Transit Cruises* (phone: 508-744-6311). The *Peabody Museum* has fascinating scrimshaw carvings and nautical regalia from the early days of shipping and far-off ports. Closed Thanksgiving, Christmas, New Year's. Admission charge. 161 Essex St. (phone: 508-745-9500).

A few miles east of Salem, the sailboating town of Marblehead has myriad colonial houses, places to sit and look at the harbor, and lots of boats. Toward evening, you can watch fishermen unloading the day's catch.

SOURCES AND RESOURCES

TOURIST INFORMATION: For tourist information, maps, and brochures, visit one of the Visitor Information Centers — at City Hall, Boston Common, or the Hancock Tower — or call 536-4100 or 800-858-0200. The Convention and Tourist Bureau has multilingual maps and brochures and is open weekdays. PO Box 490, Prudential Plaza W., Boston, MA 02199.

A comprehensive guidebook is *In and Out of Boston (With or Without Children)* by Bernice Chesler (Globe Pequot Press; $9.95).

Television Stations – WBZ Channel 4–NBC; WCZB Channel 5–ABC; WNEV Channel 7–CBS.

Radio Stations – AM: WEEI 590 (news); WBZ 103 (pop). FM: WROR 93.5 (pop); WJIB 98 (pop).

Local Coverage – *Boston Herald,* morning daily; *Christian Science Monitor,* weekday mornings; *Boston Globe,* morning daily; *Boston Phoenix,* weekly; *Boston* magazine, monthly.

Food – *Robert Nadeau's Guide to Boston Restaurants* by Mark Zanger (World Food Press; $3.95) and *Boston* magazine's listings.

Telephone – The area code for Boston is 617 unless otherwise indicated. *Note:* Much of the North Shore and South Shore is served by the 508 area code.

Sales Tax – The sales tax is 5%, as is the hotel tax.

CLIMATE: Autumn is the best time to see Boston. Days are generally clear and brisk, with temperatures in the 50s and 60s. At night it can drop into the 40s, with chilly winds. Winter can be formidable, with icy winds, snow, and sleet. If you intend to drive, make sure your car is properly equipped. Spring is brief and cool, and temperatures are usually in the 60s. In summer, the mercury climbs into the 70s and 80s, although nights can be breezy and cooler.

GETTING AROUND: Airport – Just 3 miles from the center of the city, Logan International Airport handles both international and domestic traffic. The ride from the airport to downtown usually takes from 10 to 30 minutes, depending on traffic; taxi fare usually runs $12. *Airways Transportation Co.* (phone: 267-2981) charges $5.50 for its bus service to major hotels in downtown Boston. Buses run on the hour and half-hour from 7 AM to 11 PM (Saturdays, hourly only). The most practical means of getting to Logan from virtually anywhere in the Boston area is by the MBTA (Massachusetts Bay Transit Authority) Blue Line trains, which cost 60¢ and run every 8 minutes (every 15 minutes on weekends) from 6 AM to midnight. From the train stop at downtown's Government Center station at City Hall Plaza, travel time to the airport is about 30 minutes. A water shuttle operated by *Marina Bay Commuter* (phone: 847-1800) also connects the downtown area with Logan (except in winter, when service is suspended). Boats sail across the harbor from Rowes Wharf (400 Atlantic Ave.) to the airport every half-hour during rush periods; the trip takes about 10 minutes and costs $5.

Bus, Trolley, and Train – The Massachusetts Bay Transit Authority (MBTA) operates a network of subways (the Red, Blue, Green, and Orange lines) that are coordinated with a system of surface buses and trolleys. Exact change required. Service is fairly frequent during the day, less frequent at night, and nonexistent after about 12:30 AM. MBTA stations are marked with large, white circular signs bearing a giant T. For schedules, directions, timetables, and maps, call 722-3200. For charter tours, complete with sightseeing guides, call *Complete Transportation Services,* 661-6565.

Taxi – Boston has several taxi fleets, and you can hail them on the street, pick them up at taxi stands downtown, or call for them. *Boston Cab* (phone: 536-5010); *Independent Taxi Operators Assn.* (phone: 426-8700); *Town Taxi* (phone: 536-5000); *Checker* (phone: 536-7000); *Yellow Cab,* Cambridge (phone: 547-3000); *Ambassador/Brattle Taxi,* Cambridge (phone: 492-1100).

Car Rental – All major national firms are represented. Among the least expensive are *Budget,* 1029 Commonwealth Ave. (phone: 254-0727) or Mass. Ave., Cambridge (phone: 547-4980); and *American International,* Logan Airport (phone: 569-3550) or 200 Stuart St. (phone: 542-4196).

LOCAL SERVICES: Babysitting – *International Sitting Service,* 1354 Hancock St., Quincy (phone: 472-7789); *Child Care Resource Center,* 552 Mass. Ave., Cambridge (phone: 547-9861); *Parents in a Pinch,* 45 Bartlett Crescent, Brookline (phone: 739-5437).

Business Services – *Bette James & Associates,* 1430 Mass. Ave., Cambridge (phone: 661-2622).

Mechanic – Ray and Tom Magliozzi, at the *Good News Garage,* will repair anything for a fair price. 75 Hamilton St., Cambridge, between Central Square and MIT (phone: 354-5383).

MUSEUMS: For a description of the *Museum of Science, Fogg Museum, Museum of Fine Arts, Institute of Contemporary Art, Gardner Museum, Harvard Museum of Natural History,* and *Bunker Hill Pavilion,* see *Special Places.* Other fine museums worth visiting include the following:

Boston Center for the Arts – Multi-use arts complex in a city block of historic buldings. 539 Tremont St. (phone: 426-5000).

Carpenter Center for the Visual Arts – Le Corbusier's only building in the US. 24 Quincy St., Harvard University, Cambridge (phone: 495-3216).

Children's Museum – Museum Wharf, 300 Congress St. (phone: 426-8855).

Ralph Waldo Emerson Memorial House – 28 Cambridge Turnpike, Concord (phone: 369-2236).

Gibson House – Victorian era. 137 Beacon St. (phone: 267-6338).

Museum of Afro-American History – 149 Roxbury St., Roxbury (phone: 445-7400).

Society for the Preservation of New England Antiquities – 141 Cambridge St. (phone: 227-3956).

 MAJOR COLLEGES AND UNIVERSITIES: Boston is the country's consummate college town, with tens of thousands of students, professors, and visitors from all over the world pouring onto the campuses every academic year. There are literally dozens of educational institutions, including many of the aristocratic New England prep schools. Harvard University (see *Special Places*) is the most prestigious in the country (Harvard Sq., Cambridge, phone: 495-1000). MIT (see *Special Places*) produces scientists in all fields, many of whom continue in government research and consulting positions (77 Mass. Ave., Cambridge, phone: 253-1000). In Boston itself, Boston University emphasizes the humanities. Check the bulletin boards and college newspapers for listings of campus events; Charles River Campus (phone: 353-2000). Boston College is a sports hub in Chestnut Hill (phone: 552-8000). Other schools: Emerson College (130 Beacon St., phone: 262-2010); University of Massachusetts/Boston (Park Sq. and Columbia Point, phone: 287-1900); Brandeis University (415 South St., Waltham, phone: 647-2000); Emmanuel College (400 The Fenway, phone: 277-9540); Endicott College (376 Hale St., Beverly, phone: 927-0585); Tufts University (Medford-Somerville, phone: 628-5000); Lesley College (29 Everett St., Cambridge, phone: 868-9600); Wellesley College (Wellesley, phone: 235-0320); Suffolk University (41 Temple St., phone: 723-4700); Wheaton College (Norton, phone: 508-285-7722); Simmons College (300 The Fenway, phone: 738-2000); Wheelock College (150 The Riverway, phone: 734-5200).

 SPECIAL EVENTS: The *Chinese New Year* is celebrated in Chinatown every February. *Patriots' Day* is observed the third Monday in April, which is also when the famous *Boston Marathon* is run. The *Battle of Bunker Hill* is commemorated on June 17. *Saint's Day* celebrations occur every weekend during July and August on Hanover St. in the North End. Male and female rowers compete in the *Head of the Charles Races* the last Sunday in October. In even-numbered years, the *Harvard-Yale football game* is held in Cambridge.

SPORTS AND FITNESS: No doubt about it, Boston is one of the all-time great professional sports towns.

Baseball – The *Red Sox* play at *Fenway Park,* 24 Yawkey Way. Green Line, Kenmore stop (phone: 267-8661).

Basketball – The *Celtics* play at *Boston Garden,* 150 Causeway St. Green and Orange lines, North Station stop (phone: 523-3030; 523-6050).

Fishing – Deep-sea fishing boats leave from Long Wharf. Contact *Boston Harbor Cruises* (phone: 227-4320). You can rent boats, bait, and tackle from *Hurley's Boat*

Rental, Houghs Neck, 136 Bay View, Quincy (phone: 479-1239); and *Gamble's Landing,* 15 Bayswater Rd., Quincy (phone: 471-8060).

Fitness Center – *Fitcorp* has a track and workout equipment available, 133 Federal St. (phone: 542-1010). There's also the *Boston Health and Swim Club,* 1079 Commonwealth Ave. (phone: 254-1711).

Football – The New England *Patriots* play at *Sullivan Stadium,* Rte. 1, Foxboro (phone: 508-262-1776).

Golf – There's a city course in Hyde Park, where the Parks and Recreation Department offers golf instruction. Contact *George Wright Pro Shop,* 420 West St., Hyde Park (phone: 364-9655). You can also take lessons at the *Fresh Pond Golf Club,* 691 Huron Ave., Cambridge (phone: 354-9130).

Hockey – The *Bruins* play at *Boston Garden* (phone: 227-3200).

Jogging – Run along the banks of the Charles River on Memorial or Storrow Drive.

Racing – Thoroughbreds race at *Suffolk Downs,* Rte. C1, East Boston. Daily except Tuesdays and Thursdays (phone: 567-3900).

Sailing – You can rent boats from *Marblehead Rental Boat Co.,* 83 Front St., Marblehead (phone: 631-2259); and in Boston at the *Boston Sailing Center,* 54 Lewis Wharf (phone: 227-4198).

Skiing – There's cross-country skiing at Weston Ski Track on *Leo J. Martin Golf Course,* Park Rd., Weston (phone: 894-4903), and at Lincoln Guide Service, Lincoln (phone: 259-9204). Lessons available.

Tennis – There are courts at *Charles River Park Tennis Club,* 4 Longfellow Pl. (phone: 742-8922).

 THEATER: For information on performance schedules, check the local publications listed above.

Catch a Broadway show before it gets to Broadway. Trial runs often take place at the *Shubert Theatre,* 265 Tremont St. (phone: 426-4520); the *Colonial Theatre,* 106 Boylston St. (phone: 426-9366); the *Wilbur Theatre,* 246 Tremont St. (phone: 423-4008); and the *Wang Center for the Performing Arts,* 268 Tremont St. (phone: 800-223-0120). Or check out the *Charles Playhouse,* 74 Warrenton St. (phone: 426-6912). This is a much smaller and often livelier place, hosting consistently interesting contemporary plays. The *Lyric Stage,* 54 Charles St. (phone: 742-1790) performs new, experimental works — often satiric and political — with aplomb. The *American Repertory Theatre,* 64 Brattle St., Cambridge (phone: 547-8300), is based at Harvard's *Loeb Drama Center* and features an ever-changing bill of plays during the school year. In addition, there are dozens of smaller theater groups, including several affiliated with colleges, such as Boston University's *Huntington Theatre Company,* 264 Huntington Ave. in Back Bay (phone: 266-3913). *Boston Ballet Company* gives performances at the *Wang Center* (see above; call 542-3945 for ballet information). Tickets for theatrical and musical events can be purchased through the Out of Town Ticket Agency, in the center of Harvard Square, now on the mezzanine level of that subway station of the Red Line (phone: 492-1900); Ticketron (phone: 720-3400); Bostix, Faneuil Hall Marketplace (phone: 723-5181).

 MUSIC: Almost every evening, Bostonians can choose from among several classical and contemporary musical performances, ranging from the most delicate chamber music to the most ferocious acid rock. The *Boston Symphony Orchestra* performs at *Symphony Hall,* September through April, 301 Mass. Ave. (phone: 266-1492). (In summer, it performs at *Tanglewood Music Festival* in Lenox, Massachusetts.) Selected members of the *Boston Symphony* make up the *Boston Pops Orchestra,* which performs lighthearted orchestrations of popular music under the direction of John Williams at *Symphony Hall,* April through July (phone:

266-1492), and gives free outdoor concerts in the *Hatch Shell* on the Charles River Esplanade in June and July. The *Opera Company of Boston,* with Sarah Caldwell, finally has an elegant home at 539 Washington St. (phone: 426-2786). For jazz, try *Harpers Ferry,* 158 Brighton Ave. (phone: 254-9734), *Ryles,* Inman Sq., Cambridge (phone: 876-9330), and the *Regattabar* in the *Charles* hotel, Cambridge (phone: 864-1200), now the premier jazz club in the area. Top-name blues and pop musicians play here, too. For folk music, visit *Passim's,* 47 Palmer St., Cambridge (phone: 492-7679), or *Nightstage,* 823 Main St., Cambridge (phone: 497-8200).

 NIGHTCLUBS AND NIGHTLIFE: A sophisticated and well-heeled crowd gathers nightly in the elegant *Plaza Bar* to listen to topnotch entertainers, *Copley Plaza* hotel (phone: 267-5300), or at the *Palm Court* at *Cricket's,* 101 Faneuil Hall Marketplace (phone: 720-5570). TV celebrities, professional athletes, and those who want to meet them hang out at tiny, cozy *Daisy Buchanan's,* 240A Newbury St. at Fairfield St. (phone: 247-8516). *Narcissus* features dancing to new wave music, has a video performance center, and is available for private parties; 535 Commonwealth Ave., Kenmore Square (phone: 536-1950). Devotees of hard rock should try the *Channel Club,* 25 Necco St., right beside the Fort Point Channel of the harbor (phone: 451-1050).

BEST IN TOWN

 CHECKING IN: Boston has some fine, old, gracious hotels with the history and charm you'd expect to find in this dignified New England capital. But Boston is in the midst of a hotel building boom, and there are now many modern places offering standard contemporary accoutrements. Expect to pay $120 or more for a double room at those places noted as expensive; between $75 and $95 in the moderate category; and inexpensive, under $75. Many of these hotels offer special weekend packages for relatively low rates. Reservations are always required, so write or call well in advance. For bed and breakfast accommodations, contact *Bed & Breakfast Associates of Bay Colony,* PO Box 166, Babson Park, Boston, MA 02157 (phone: 449-5302); *Greater Boston Hospitality,* Box 1142, Brookline, MA 02146 (phone: 277-5430); *Bed and Breakfast Cambridge & Greater Boston,* Box 665, Cambridge, MA 02140 (phone: 576-1492); or write to the Massachusetts Division of Tourism (100 Cambridge St., 13th Floor, Boston, MA 02202) for its *Spirit of Massachusetts Bed & Breakfast Guide.* All telephone numbers are in the 617 area code unless otherwise indicated.

Boston Harbor – A distinctive new tower rising 15 stories above the bustle of Rowes Wharf, right on the waterfront, overlooking the harbor and the airport. There are 230 rooms, the glass-enclosed *Harborview Lounge,* and the elegant paneled *Rowes Wharf Bar and Restaurant* for refreshment, plus a spa with sauna and 60-foot pool. Business communications facilities, concierge. Water taxi zips guests to and from the airport in less than 10 minutes. 70 Rowes Wharf (phone: 439-7000). Expensive.

Bostonian – Understated and small (155 rooms), this beautifully appointed hotel is across from the shopping and entertainment activities of Faneuil Hall Marketplace and just 2 blocks from the North End and the revitalized waterfront. The *Bostonian's* glass-enclosed rooftop *Seasons* restaurant discreetly overlooks the colorful bustle below, and is one of the best in Boston. Faneuil Hall Marketplace (phone: 523-3600 or 800-343-0922). Expensive.

Charles – Between the Charles River and Harvard Square, this handsome red brick building is the centerpiece of the Charles Square complex. The 300 rooms are beautifully appointed, and those on the 10th floor have teleconferencing and telecommunications facilities as well. Relaxation can be sedentary in the pleasant *Courtyard Café* and elegant *Rarities* restaurant or more active at the lavish *Le Pli* health spa, complete with an indoor pool. The *Regattabar* features live jazz by top names nightly Tuesdays through Saturdays. Full conference facilities. 840 Memorial Dr., Cambridge (phone: 864-1200). Expensive.

Colonnade – The management at this distinguished 294-room hotel tries very hard to emulate the tradition of European luxury. There are large rooms, a (seasonal) rooftop pool, *Zachary's* restaurant, and the classy *Promenade Café*. Near the Prudential Center and Newbury Street. 120 Huntington Ave. (phone: 424-7000). Expensive.

Copley Plaza – This large (450 rooms), old hotel is on one of Boston's handsomest squares, convenient to Copley Place, Prudential Center, and Newbury Street shopping. Among its restaurants, *Copley's* offers very good food in a series of rich Victorian rooms, while the *Plaza Bar* features some of the great names in jazz. Copley Square (phone: 267-5300 or 800-225-7654). Expensive.

Omni Parker House – Right on the historic Freedom Trail, this splendid 500-room hostelry is within easy walking distance of Beacon Hill, the Common, and Faneuil Hall Marketplace. The hotel's main restaurant (there are three) is *Parker's* (where Boston cream pie and Parker House rolls were invented); the *Last Hurrah,* a jolly Victorian room in the basement, is perhaps the liveliest, with good food and a terrific swing band. Tremont and School Sts. (phone: 227-8600 or 800-THE-OMNI). Expensive.

Four Seasons – Over $80 million was spent on this 15-story luxury property across from the Public Garden. Fresh flowers fill the rich wood and marble lobby, and 19th-century artwork complements the decor. Its 288 elegant rooms and suites each have a bar and 3 phones. There are also 2 restaurants, exercise rooms, and a pool. 200 Boylston St. (phone: 338-4400 or 800-268-6282). Expensive.

Guest Quarters Suites – A distinctive property on the Charles River, it has 10 conventional guestrooms and 310 luxurious suites. Amenities include complimentary breakfast, seven meeting rooms, restaurant, pool and sauna, and garage. At the junction of two major traffic arteries, it is particularly attractive to businesspeople traveling by car. 400 Soldiers Field Rd., at the Allston exit of I-90, the Mass. Pike (phone: 783-0090). Expensive.

Hyatt Regency, Cambridge – Some 500 rooms surround an atrium with fountains, greenery, and glass-walled elevators. The revolving rooftop lounge offers a spectacular view of Boston, especially at sunset. On the Charles River, near MIT and Harvard (not easily accessible by public transportation). 575 Memorial Dr., Cambridge (phone: 492-1234, 800-233-1234, or 800-228-9000). Expensive.

Lafayette – Centrally located in Downtown Crossing and part of the Lafayette Place complex of shops, restaurants, and an outdoor skating rink, this new luxury hotel reflects Old World elegance. The 500 beautifully appointed rooms are grouped around four atriums. As befits a member of the Swissôtel group, the main dining room is the *Café Suisse;* for formal dining, the classic *Le Marquis de Lafayette* restaurant offers creative continental cuisine. Indoor pool, sun terrace, and saunas; 9 meeting rooms. 2 Ave. de Lafayette (phone: 451-2600). Expensive.

Marriott, Cambridge – The newest Marriott — the fifth in Greater Boston — is in the heart of the Kendall Square construction boom near MIT. This understated yet posh 431-room hotel features a comfortable restaurant and lounge, indoor pool, health club with saunas, complete business facilities, and concierge level. 2 Cambridge Center (phone: 494-6600 or 800-228-9290). Expensive.

Marriott, Copley Place – This 1,147-room giant is a focal point of the Copley Place development. Among its premium facilities are 3 restaurants, 3 bars, 36 meeting rooms, and the largest ballroom and most expansive exhibition area in any Boston hotel. For relaxation, there's an indoor pool, health club, and gameroom. 110 Huntington Ave. (phone: 236-5800 or 800-228-9290). Expensive.

Marriott, Long Wharf – A nautical motif envelops this red brick luxury liner on the water at the foot of State Street. Its striking 5-story atrium is a highlight and provides the focus for the *Palm Garden* restaurant. Two other restaurants, a ballroom, 5 conference rooms, an indoor-outdoor pool, and a health club offer multiple diversions. 296 State St. (phone: 227-0800 or 800-228-9290). Expensive.

Meridien – Distinctive red awnings mark this splendid 1981 renovation of the landmark Federal Reserve Bank Building in the heart of the financial district. The 1922 Renaissance revival structure was transformed with as little exterior alteration as possible; hence, there are 326 chic rooms and 22 stylish suites, in 153 styles. Surrounded by greenery in a 6-story atrium is the French bistro *Café Fleuri;* its Sunday brunch is among Boston's best. *Julien,* the elegant dining room, honors the city's first French restaurant of 1794. Its nouvelle-inspired menu is the creation of Gerard Vie, owner of *Les Trois Marches* in Versailles. Health club with indoor pool, concierge, and lobby shops. 200 Franklin St., Post Office Sq. (phone: 451-1900 or 800-223-9918). Expensive.

Ritz-Carlton – The great lady of Boston hotels, quietly elegant, impeccably correct, and conveniently across from the Public Garden, its 265 rooms a few steps from Newbury Street shops. The bar is the best place in town for a drink, and the upstairs dining room is superb. 15 Arlington St. (phone: 536-5700). Expensive.

Royal Sonesta – Tasteful renovations and sparkling additions to this flagship of the Sonesta chain have boosted its room count to 400. There are also 5 new eye-catching suites along with 3 restaurants, bars, pool, health club, the well-equipped *Royal Sonesta* Business Center, and conference rooms facing Boston across the Charles River. 5 Cambridge Pkwy. (near Kendall Sq.), Cambridge (phone: 491-3600 or 800-343-7171). Expensive.

Sheraton Boston – A huge, 1,400-room modern hotel in the Prudential Center, surrounded by fine places to shop. Its 4 restaurants, 3 cocktail lounges, and a year-round pool and health club provide plenty of diversion. Prudential Center (phone: 236-2000). Expensive.

Westin – The opulent 36-story, 804-room property is one of three hotels in burgeoning Copley Place, a $500-million development adjacent to Copley Square. The hotel also has 2 ballrooms, 3 restaurants, and a meeting capacity of 2,000. 10 Huntington Ave. (phone: 262-9600 or 800-228-3000). Expensive.

57 Park Plaza Howard Johnson's – They're pretty much the same everywhere. This one offers free parking, a year-round pool, and a location convenient to downtown. 351 rooms. 200 Stuart St. (phone: 482-1800 or 800-654-2000). Moderate.

Sheraton Commander – Here is a mellow, old 178-room hotel directly on the Cambridge Common, within easy walking distance of Harvard University and Harvard Square. 16 Garden St., Cambridge (phone: 547-4800 or 800-325-3535). Moderate.

Quality Inn, Downtown Boston – Small and centrally located, this is a newly refurbished and restored landmark in the theater district. Boasting 251 rooms and 35 suites, it also features 7 conference rooms, 2 clubs, (*Roxy's* and the *Juke Box*) and an already famous *Stage Deli* (of New York) eatery. The *Quality Inn* is the outstanding example of its national chain. 275 Tremont St. (phone: 426-1400 or 800-228-5151). Moderate.

Chandler Inn – Modest and comfortable, conveniently located between Copley and Park Squares, near Copley Place. Recently renovated, it has 56 rooms and pro-

vides a continental breakfast in its *Fritz Café,* where a light menu, cocktails, and
weekend brunch are also available. 26 Chandler St. at Berkeley St. (phone: 482-
3450). Inexpensive.

Howard Johnson's – Right on the Charles River, this modern, 205-room facility
is a few minutes' drive from both Harvard and MIT (not easily accessible by public
transportation). Sauna and paddle tennis court. 777 Memorial Dr. (phone: 492-
7777). Inexpensive.

 EATING OUT: Bostonians dine out less frequently than their New York
friends, but when they do, they have their choice of several excellent restaurants. Our selection is based on outstanding quality, reliable service, and
value. Expect to pay $85 or more for two at one of the places we've noted
as expensive; between $40 and $85, moderate; and $40 or under, inexpensive. Prices
do not include drinks, wine, or tips. All telephone numbers are in the 617 area code
unless otherwise indicated.

Le Bocage – This restaurant has some of the most consistently good French food
available in New England. Both regional and classic entrées grace the menu, which
changes to suit the season. A bright, efficient staff and a fine wine cellar add to
the pleasurable dining. Closed Sundays. Reservations advised. Major credit cards.
72 Bigelow Ave., Watertown (phone: 923-1210). Expensive.

Bay Tower Room – This restfully elegant dining room, featuring a breathtaking
view of Boston Harbor from 33 stories high, is the perfect setting for special
occasion suppers and banquets. Among the American and continental specialties,
which change seasonally, are rack of lamb, chateaubriand, and seafood-stuffed
brook trout. Piano music is featured during early evening hours, with a live combo
taking over later. Open Mondays through Saturdays, 5:30 to 10 or 11 PM; open
on Sundays for special occasions. Reservations necessary. Major credit cards. 60
State St. (phone: 723-1666). Expensive.

Jasper – Chef Jasper White has an inventive touch, manifested skillfully in his
unique treatment of such items as squab breasts and venison. He also makes his
own pasta and serves it with equal flair — try the ricotta-filled tortellini in rabbit
sauce. Closed Sundays. Reservations advised. Major credit cards. 240 Commercial
St. (phone: 523-1126). Expensive.

Panache – A sparsely decorated place enlivened by bouquets of fresh and silk
flowers, it serves some of the city's best continental cuisine. Among the most
successful dishes are grilled beef in red wine sauce, roast veal with a pesto sauce,
and chocolate mousse. Closed Sundays and Mondays. Reservations necessary.
Major credit cards. 798 Main St., Kendall Sq., Cambridge (phone: 492-9500).
Expensive.

Ritz-Carlton Dining Room – Large, lovely, serenely elegant, and one of only two
places in town where you can enjoy a view of the Public Garden while dining with
old-fashioned formality. The cuisine is continental and very good and is served by
an expert staff. Men must wear jackets and ties. Open daily. Reservations advised.
Major credit cards. 15 Arlington St. (phone: 536-5700). Expensive.

Skipjack's Seafood Emporium – With a dazzling new location in Copley Square,
the menu still features an extensive array of innovative seafood dishes (complemented by a quartet of steak and fowl entrées). Snapper Veracruz, grilled cilantro
shrimp, and blackened redfish are just three of the outstanding choices. The wine
list is extensive and carefully assembled. Special Sunday jazz brunch is a treat
(from 11 AM to 3 PM). Open daily, 11AM to 11PM. Reservations necessary. Major
credit cards. 500 Boylston St., Back Bay (phone: 536-3500); 2 Brookline Pl.,
Brookline (phone: 232-8887). Expensive.

Wild Goose Rotisserie and Grill – Guests may catch a glimpse of their goose being roasted to crisp, succulent perfection before enjoying it with game bird sausage, caramelized vinegar sauce, and braised red cabbage. Specials include whole roasted quail with chestnut stuffing and a thyme-scented duck ravioli made with fresh noodles. Open daily for lunch and dinner except Sundays, when only brunch is served. Reservations advised. Major credit cards. 300 N Market Bldg., Faneuil Hall Marketplace (phone: 227-9660). Expensive.

Another Season – An intimate spot on Beacon Hill with murals evoking turn-of-the-century Paris. The menu changes every 2 weeks and features inventive continental cuisine. Fresh seafood, a vegetarian entrée, and a marvelous array of desserts are always available. Closed Sundays; dinner only on Mondays and Saturdays. Reservations advised. Major credit cards. 97 Mt. Vernon St. (phone: 367-0880). Expensive to moderate.

Anthony's Pier 4 – This massive place right on the harbor is predictably rigged out in a nautical motif. There's a commodious waterfront deck where you can have drinks and enjoy the view while you wait for your table. Good seafood, generous servings. Open daily. No dinner reservations. Major credit cards. At 140 Northern Ave. (phone: 423-6363). Expensive to moderate.

Café Budapest – Decorated in the lavish Eastern European tradition, and renowned for fine continental and Hungarian cuisine. Avoid it on Saturday nights, when no reservations are accepted and hordes of hungry diners sometimes wait hours for tables. On weeknights this is a wonderful place to linger over superb strudel and some of the best coffee anywhere. Open daily. Reservations necessary. Major credit cards. 90 Exeter St. (phone: 266-1979). Expensive to moderate.

Davio's – The crown prince of Northern Italian cuisine in this area. Regional and continental entrees are consistently well prepared, highlighted by veal chops, homemade pasta, and upscale, luscious pizza combinations. Good wines, good service. Lovely, elegant surroundings. Open daily. Reservations necessary. Major credit cards. Two locations: 269 Newbury St. (phone: 262-4810); 202 Washington St. in Brookline Village (phone: 738-4810). Expensive to moderate.

Dover Sea Grille – An understated, relaxed, beautifully appointed seafood restaurant and lounge in Brookline, just a clamshell's throw from both Fenway Park and the medical area. Marvelous grilled entrées, especially salmon and swordfish, are specialties, as well as bountiful salads and superb desserts. "Early Catch" specials are available weeknights from 5 to 6 PM. Closed Sundays. Reservations accepted. Major credit cards. 1223 Beacon St. (phone: 566-7000). Expensive to moderate.

Hampshire House – Thoroughly evocative of 19-century Boston is this former mansion overlooking the Public Garden. The paneled, clubby café-bar has piano music nightly, moose heads on the wall, and a fire blazing in the winter. It offers a simple continental menu and a range of lighter fare. Upstairs, in the refined, eminently Victorian dining room, more elegant, traditional dishes are served. The basement houses the *Bull and Finch Pub*, a boisterous meeting, eating, and drinking place that was the inspiration for the television series "Cheers." Open daily. Reservations desirable. Major credit cards. 84 Beacon St. (phone: 227-9600). Expensive to moderate.

Harvest – A colorful dining room, lively bar, and (weather permitting) a secluded outdoor patio, all tucked into a back corner of the former Design Research complex in Harvard Square. The menu features nicely executed international dishes in the nouvelle cuisine repertoire and fine salads and desserts. Open daily. Reservations advised. Major credit cards. 44 Brattle St. (phone: 492-1115). Expensive to moderate.

Locke-Ober Café – A splendid, albeit somewhat stuffy, tradition in probably the best known of Boston's top restaurants. Though it was once an exclusive male bastion, today both sexes can eat in the handsome *Men's Grill,* with its glowing mahogany bar lined with massive silver tureens, its stained glass, snowy linens, and indefatigable gray-haired waiters. The food is identical in the less distinguished upstairs room — heavy on continental dishes and seafood. Closed Sundays. Reservations necessary. Major credit cards. 3 Winter Pl. (phone: 542-1340). Expensive to moderate.

Maison Robert – Among the finest French restaurants in the country, with food, drink, ambience, and service all worthy of top ranking. Owner-chef Lucien Robert has taught many of the French chefs in Boston and continues to prepare sauces for fish, fowl, and meat that defy imitation. Two dining areas, *Ben's Café* downstairs (on the patio in summer) and the elegant *Bonhomme Richard* upstairs, are open for lunch and dinner. Brunch only on Sundays. Reservations necessary. Major credit cards. 45 School St. in the old City Hall (phone: 227-3370). *Bonhomme Richard,* expensive; *Ben's Café,* moderate.

Chart House – This restaurant occupies the oldest building on the waterfront, and the interior is a strikingly handsome arrangement of lofty spaces, natural wood, exposed red brick, and comfortable captain's chairs. The menu lists abundant portions of steaks and seafood, with all the salad you can eat included in the reasonable prices. Open daily. No reservations, but the line moves pretty fast. Major credit cards. 60 Long Wharf (phone: 227-1576). Moderate.

Cornucopia – Off the beaten track between the Common and Lafayette Place is the historic home of the Peabody family. Here Nathaniel Hawthorne married Sophia, and Elizabeth opened the bookstore that became the meeting place for such literati as Emerson and Thoreau. Today, it has been renovated to accommodate a striking restaurant that features an eclectic blend of regional and ethnic dishes. The menu changes every two weeks. Lunch, weekdays only; dinner, Tuesdays through Saturdays. Reservations advised. Major credit cards. 15 West St. (phone: 338-4600). Moderate.

Genji – An intimate Japanese restaurant in the Back Bay that serves beautifully prepared traditional fare, including tantalizing tempura and sushi. A picturesque, private tearoom can be reserved for special occasions. The service is friendly and informative. Try the complete dinner, which is sumptuous and very reasonably priced. Open daily except Sundays for lunch and dinner. Reservations advised. Major credit cards. 327 Newbury St. (phone: 267-5656). Moderate.

Legal Sea Foods – If you don't mind waiting in line (no reservations), you'll find fresh and well-prepared seafood that we think is the best in Boston. Open daily. Major credit cards. *Park Plaza* hotel, corner of Columbus and Arlington (phone: 426-4444); in the Chestnut Hill shopping mall, 43 Boylston St. (phone: 277-7300); and 5 Cambridge Center, Kendall Sq., Cambridge (phone: 864-3400). Moderate.

Milk Street Café – Its original home sandwiched into a sparkling niche of the financial district, this bustling vegetarian and fish cafeteria presents superb breakfasts and lunches. The muffins, smoked salmon platter, flavorful soups, and generous, artful quiches are perennial pleasers. Open weekdays. No credit cards. Two locations: 50 Milk St. (phone: 542-2433); 101 Main St., Kendall Sq., Cambridge (phone: 491-8286). Moderate.

St. Botolph – Actually a restored 19th-century brick townhouse, this 2-story restaurant sports a contemporary interior with exposed brick walls and a continental menu with good, fresh seafood. Lunch served weekdays; dinner nightly; brunch on Sundays. Reservations advised. Major credit cards. 99 St. Botolph St. (phone: 266-3030). Moderate.

Durgin-Park – Famed for generous servings of traditional Yankee roast beef, prime ribs, oyster stew, Boston baked beans, and Indian pudding (among the reasons Native Americans lost this land). It's equally famous for its long, communal tables crowded with convivial diners and brusque, no-nonsense waitresses. One of Boston's best values. (Another Durgin-Park has opened up in Copley Place, but we prefer the original.) Open daily. No reservations or credit cards. 340 Faneuil Hall Marketplace (phone: 227-2038) and Copley Place (phone: 266-1964). Moderate to inexpensive.

Rebecca's – White walls, blond wood furniture, and works by local artists dominate the comfortable, modern decor. The menu, described as new American, borrows from French, Greek, Indian, and Italian cuisines. Samplings include duck in green peppercorn sauce and shrimp sautéed with feta cheese, tomatoes, and olives. Open daily. No reservations. Major credit cards. 21 Charles St. (phone: 742-9747). Moderate to inexpensive.

Rubin's Kosher Delicatessen & Restaurant – One of only two true kosher restaurants in Boston, its chopped liver, potato latkes, and lean pastrami (hot or cold) are the genuine articles. Open Sundays through Thursdays; closes Fridays at 3 PM. Major credit cards. 500 Harvard St., Brookline (phone: 731-8787). Moderate to inexpensive.

Tapas – This informal, cheerful, continental restaurant in a refurbished auto factory and showroom near Porter Square in Cambridge is the place to go when you want to eat less than a full meal or sample several offerings on the menu. *Tapas* (Spanish for "small servings") offers fine soups, salads, appetizers, entrées, and unusually imaginative desserts on a bill of fare that changes seasonally. A large, relaxed bar attracts a friendly crowd. Open daily; Sunday brunch. Reservations accepted for 5 or more. Major credit cards. 2067 Mass. Ave., Cambridge (phone: 576-2240). Moderate to inexpensive.

Ye Olde Union Oyster House – It's the real thing: Boston's oldest restaurant. Daniel Webster himself used to guzzle oysters at the wonderful mahogany oyster bar, where skilled shuckers still pry them open before your eyes. Full seafood lunches and dinners are served upstairs, amid well-worn colonial ambience. (One booth is dedicated to John F. Kennedy, once a frequent diner.) Don't miss the seafood chowder. Open daily. No reservations. Major credit cards. 41 Union St. (phone: 227-2750). Moderate to inexpensive.

Elsie's Lunch – This incomparable restaurant and sandwich shop has been serving food and drink to famished Harvard students for longer than anyone can remember. A great place to go when your feet are tired, or when you just want to fill up. Open daily. No reservations or credit cards. 71 Mt. Auburn St., Cambridge (phone: 354-8781 or 354-8362). Inexpensive.

North End Restaurants – Modestly priced Italian meals are available in dozens of little restaurants in Boston's oldest section, the North End. *Felicia's* is popular with Hub celebrities, and Felicia herself, a well-known personality, oversees the preparation of the food. Open daily. Reservations advised. Major credit cards. 145A Richmond St. (phone: 523-9885). *Lucia's* is a warm neighborhood restaurant that unfailingly provides satisfying Italian food. Open daily. Reservations advised. Major credit cards. 415 Hanover St. (phone: 523-9148). Many locals swear the town's best pizza is tossed and baked at *Circle Pizza,* 361 Hanover St. (phone: 523-8787). Others claim the *European* restaurant produces an even better pie. The *European* also has a large menu designed for the entire family. Open daily. Reservations advised. Major credit cards. 218 Hanover St. (phone: 523-5694). *Mother Anna's,* 211 Hanover St. (phone: 523-8496), and *Ida's,* 3 Mechanic St. (phone: 523-0015), are small, home-style restaurants noted for a fiercely loyal clientele and for authentic dishes cooked to order. Both are open daily, take reservations, and do not accept credit cards. All are moderate to inexpensive.

CHARLESTON, SC

Charleston residents used to joke that their city was "the best-preserved secret on the Eastern seaboard." Standing on a peninsula where the Ashley and Cooper rivers flow into the Atlantic, Charleston's harbor is guarded by Ft. Sumter, where the first shots of the Civil War were fired. (Charlestonians still refer to the War Between the States as "the Great War," and Robert E. Lee's birthday is observed as a holiday, as it is throughout much of the South.) With its architecturally gracious, historic buildings and magnificent gardens, Charleston had retained the flavor and charm of the Old South. But slow economic growth has been one of the consequences of this sleepy elegance. Charlestonians (like Bostonians or Virginians), however, tended to accept their city's lack of development as just another one of the continuing hardships of the post-Reconstruction era.

In their attempts to stimulate the local economy, city leaders tried to induce industry into the area, offering prime locations, tax incentives, and embroidered statistics about the available work force. But environmentalists opposed razing choice property for industrial parks. The conflict raged for years. The only common opinion was that tourism was not desirable. Charlestonians viewed tourists as long-necked, nosy people forever searching for bathrooms.

Then, early in 1975, Charleston was "discovered," like a rare, colorful, slightly chipped mollusk. Boosterism spread faster than the yellow fever in 1864. In the brief course of a year, "the best-preserved secret on the Eastern seaboard" metamorphosed into a national tourist attraction.

A new alliance of tourism-oriented entrepreneurs started a quarter-million-dollar promotion campaign. Abandoned warehouses near Market Street were converted into boutiques, art galleries, studios, restaurants, and expensive townhouses. Thirty restaurants opened in 1976 (only a third to a half are still prospering), and the overall success of the Market Square renovation began to stimulate similar projects in other sections of the city.

About that time, Gian Carlo Menotti, producer of the annual Festival of Two Worlds in Spoleto, Italy, wandered into Charleston. He felt that the manifestly evident pride that residents had in their past made it the perfect site for an American version of his internationally acclaimed arts festival.

From its inaugural in 1977, *Spoleto Festival USA* — with its varied offerings of opera, orchestral and chamber music, dance, and theater — has been a resounding success, drawing more visitors each year. (Regulars know it's best to secure tickets in January for the May-June performances.) Charlestonians are more than pleased at the response to *Spoleto,* because it gives visitors a chance to see that their city has a lot of substance to its style.

CHARLESTON AT-A-GLANCE

 SEEING THE CITY: Charleston is set in that sea level peninsula of southeastern South Carolina known as the Lowcountry. There are no hills from which to get a good view of the city. Nicknamed the Holy City because of its many church spires, Charleston's best view is from the ground, looking up, especially at night, when floodlights illuminate the church spires.

Guided bus or van tours are available from *Adventure Sightseeing* (phone: 762-0088), *Talk of the Towne* (phone: 577-0634), and *Gray Line Bus Tours* (phone: 722-4444). To see the city from the harbor, take a *Gray Line* water tour, departing at 2 PM daily (more often in summer) from the City Marina on Lockwood Blvd. (phone: 722-1112). It's also possible to rent a tape cassette from *Charles Towne Tours* (phone: 723-5133) for a walking or driving tour. Narrated tours in horse-drawn carriages are provided by *Charlestown Carriage Co.* (phone: 577-0042), *Palmetto Carriage Tours* (phone: 723-8145), and *Old South Carriage Co.* (phone: 723-9712) from 9 AM to dusk, with night rates as well; reservations accepted. Walking tours are conducted by *Charleston Strolls* (phone: 766-2080) and *Civil War Walking Tours* (phone: 722-7033). Take a bicycle tour with a map and a bike from the *Bicycle Shop* (phone: 722-8168).

 SPECIAL PLACES: The old city is approximately 7 square miles, and even a 5-day visit could be spent walking without covering the same street twice. An evening stroll is most popular with residents.

Ft. Sumter – A national monument, the fort where the first shots of the Civil War were fired sits on a small manmade island at the entrance to Charleston's harbor. Under federal attack from 1863 to 1865, Ft. Sumter withstood the longest siege in warfare. The Confederates gave up the fort in February 1865. To the Union, it represented secession and treachery; to the Confederates, it meant resistance and courage. The fort can be reached only by boat. *Ft. Sumter Tours* leave City Marina (17 Lockwood Blvd.) at 2:30 PM in winter, five times daily in summer. One tour leaves Patriot's Point daily at 2 PM; three times daily in summer. Admission charge (phone: 722-1691).

Charles Towne Landing – Charleston was called Charles Towne in 1670 when the first permanent English settlers arrived. Now a state park, Charles Towne Landing has a number of restored houses, a full-scale replica of a 17th-century trading vessel, open-air pavilion with underground displays of artifacts found during archaeological excavations, and an Animal Forest with indigenous animals. Plenty of picnic tables, bike trails, and tram tours, too. Open daily 9 AM to 5 PM. Admission charge. 1500 Old Towne Rd. (phone: 556-4450).

Magnolia Plantation and Gardens – World famous for its abundance of colors and scents, Magnolia Gardens' 30 acres abound with 900 different varieties of camellias, 250 varieties of azaleas, and dozens of different exquisite plants, shrubs, and flowers. Listed in the National Register of Historic Places, Magnolia Plantation has been the home of the Drayton family since the 1670s. In addition to the boat tours, a small zoo, and a ranch exhibiting a breed of miniature horse, Magnolia Gardens offers canoeing, bird watching, and bike trails through its 400-acre wildlife refuge. Open all year, from 8 AM to 5 PM, except Christmas. Admission charge. 10 miles northwest on Rte. 61 (phone: 571-1266).

Boone Hall – If you ever imagined yourself as one of those romantic characters in *Gone With the Wind,* Boone Hall is the place to live out your dream. This 738-acre estate, formerly a cotton plantation, closely resembles MGM's movie set (or is it the other way around?). Settled by Major John Boone in 1681, Boone Hall has original

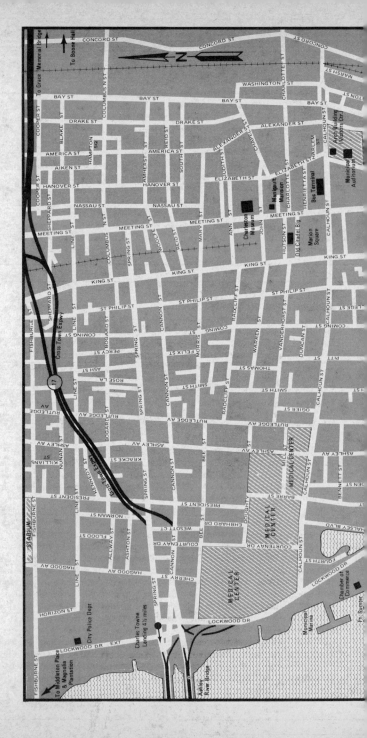

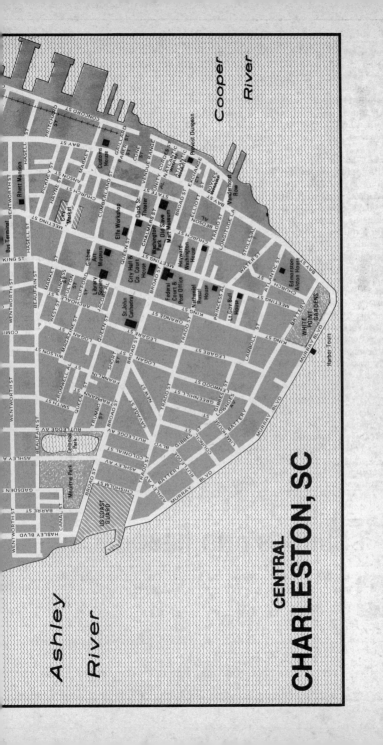

CENTRAL
CHARLESTON, SC

Ashley River

Cooper River

Bus Terminal

Rhett Mansion

Customs House

City Market

Dock St Theater

Elf's Workshop

Gibbes Art Museum

Library

Jacob Society

City Hall & Co. Court House

St. John Cathedral

Federal Court & Post Office

Old Slave Mart Museum

Hayward Washington House

Nathaniel Russel House

Lt. Gov Bull House

Edmunston Alston House

Provost Dungeon

Exchange

Vanderhorst Row

WHITE POINT GARDENS

Moultrie Park

Colonial Park

US COAST GUARD

Harbor Tours

WENTWORTH ST
HASELL ST
PRITCHARD ST
CONCORD ST
BAY ST
PINCKNEY ST
HAYNE ST
MARKET
ANSON ST
CHURCH'S ST
CUMBERLAND ST
GADSBEN ST
HASELLS ST
KING ST
MEETING ST
BEAUFAIN ST
MARKET
PRINCESS ST
WEST ST
ARCHDALE ST
FULTON ST
CLIFFORD ST
QUEEN ST
SOCIETY ST
BROAD ST
CHALMERS ST
QUEEN ST
VENDUE RANGE
STATE ST
STATE ST
UNITY AL
N. ATLANTIC
ATLANTIC
S. ATLANTIC
ELLIOTT ST
BEDONS AL
TRADD ST
WATERS ST
ATLANTIC ST
CHURCH ST
CHURCH ST
MEETING ST
LONGITUDE LA
BAY ST
STOLLS AL
ORANGE ST
LEGARE ST
TRADD ST
KING ST
PRINCESS AL
LAMBOLL ST
LEGARE ST
MAGAZINE ST
LOGAN ST
QUEEN ST
SHORT ST
BROAD ST
NEW ST
MURRAY BLVD
BATTERY
BALTERY
GREENHILL ST
LENWOOD ST
COUNCIL ST
GIBBES ST
SMITH ST
QUEEN ST
BEAUFAIN AV
RUTLEDGE AV
WILSON ST
CROMWELL AL
FRANKLIN ST
TRUMBO ST
BRAHMANN ST
SAVAGE ST
TRADD ST
GIBBES ST
LOGAN ST
ASHLEY AV
COLONIAL ST
CHISHOLM ST
BROAD ST
RUTLEDGE AV
ASHLEY AV
TRADDS AV
COUNCIL ST
LIMEHOUSE ST
MURRAY BLVD
CANAL ST
BARRE ST
WENTWORTH ST
HASLEY BLVD
RUTLEDGE AV
ASHLEY AV
COMI
KING ST
WENTWORTH ST
GABEL CARD
CONE
CORD's SP
EXCHANGE
BOYCES WHARF

slave houses intact. The ¾-mile Avenue of Oaks, planted in 1743, the famous reconstructed mansion, and the 140-acre pecan groves attract visitors from all over the world. Open daily except Thanksgiving and Christmas. Admission charge. 7 miles north on Rte. 17 (phone: 884-4371).

Drayton Hall – The only pre-Revolutionary mansion remaining on the Ashley River, this National Historic Landmark is one of the finest surviving examples of Georgian Palladian architecture. It offers a special look at colonial South Carolina and is preserved in virtually original condition. Open daily, except Thanksgiving, Christmas, and New Year's Day. Admission charge. 9 miles northwest of downtown on Hwy. 61 (phone: 766-0188).

Charleston Museum – This oldest municipal museum in the country has moved from its original facility, built in 1773, to a new complex and courtyard. It has impressive collections of arts, crafts, furniture, textiles, and implements from South Carolina's early days. Special film shows. Open daily except holidays. Admission charge. 360 Meeting St. (phone: 722-2996).

Old Exchange and Provost Dungeon – Another grim reminder of what history was really like. The Provost Dungeon dates to 1780. Here, the British imprisoned American patriots during the Revolutionary War, and exhibits show how they were treated during their detention. Attached to the Provost are excavations from the Half Moon Battery (c. 1690), the original city wall built by the British. Open daily except Sundays and major holidays. Admission charge. The 42-minute historical film *Dear Charleston* is shown several times a day and involves an additional charge. East Bay St. at Broad, under the Exchange Bldg. (phone: 792-5020).

Elfe Workshop – Thomas Elfe was an 18th-century cabinetmaker whose individual pieces now sell for as much as $80,000. Built between 1750 and 1760, the mansion has small rooms and reproduction furnishings that may make you wonder if Thomas Elfe really was one. You can ask. The guides are friendly and well informed and give five tours daily. Closed Sundays. Admission charge. 54 Queen St. (phone: 722-2130).

■**EXTRA SPECIAL:** At Middleton Place, about 15 miles north of Charleston via Rte. 61, the self-sustaining world of a Carolina Lowcountry plantation is re-created daily by people in 18th-century costume. Built in 1755, Middleton Place features the oldest landscaped gardens in the country, laid out by Henry Middleton in 1741. The 1,000-year-old Middleton Oak and the oldest camellias in the New World flourish on the lush grounds. Arthur Middleton, a signer of the Declaration of Independence, is buried here. A national historic landmark, Middleton House is the site of the *Spoleto Festival Finale* in June and *Plantation Days* (a dramatization of life on a plantation) in November. Open daily from 9 AM to 5 PM. Admission charge (phone: 556-6020).

SOURCES AND RESOURCES

 TOURIST INFORMATION: The Arch Building used to be a public house for wagon drivers entering the city, a tradition of hospitality that has carried over to the present. It now houses the Visitors Information Center (PO Box 975, Charleston, SC 29401), where you can get advice or brochures on tours, hotels, and restaurants. The staff will assist you in making reservations. Open daily. 85 Calhoun St. (phone: 722-8338). A half-hour multimedia presentation about the city, *Charleston Adventure,* is shown frequently at the Visitors Information Center. Admission charge (phone: 723-5225).

For information on events and performance schedules, call the Visitor Information

Center (phone: 722-8338) or the Charleston County Parks and Recreation Commission (phone: 762-2172).

Television Stations – WCBD Channel 2–ABC; WCIV Channel 4–NBC; WCBD Channel 2–ABC; WITV Channel 7–PBS.

Radio Stations – AM: WTMA 1250 (country); WBAL 730 (rhythm & blues). FM: WAVF 96.1 (rock 'n' roll); WXLY 102 (classic rock); WSCI 89.3 (classical/jazz).

Local Coverage – *Charleston News & Courier,* morning daily; *Evening Post,* evening daily.

Telephone – The area code for Charleston is 803.

Sales Tax – The basic sales tax in Charleston is 5%.

 CLIMATE: Charleston's average temperature is 65F. Winters are mild, summers hot. March and April are the best spring months to visit, when the city is most accessible by foot and everything green and growing is abloom. In the fall, October and November are ideal.

 GETTING AROUND: Airport – Charleston International Airport is a 20-minute drive from downtown; taxi fare should run about $15. *Low Country Limousine* provides van service from the airport to the downtown hotels for $7 (phone: 767-7117).

Bus – The South Carolina Electric and Gas Company operates the city bus system. 665 Meeting St. (phone: 722-2226). The Downtown Area Shuttle (DASH) operates on weekdays (phone: 724-7368).

Taxi – Taxis are rather inexpensive and a better bet than buses; they must be ordered by phone. Call *Yellow Cab* (phone: 577-6565) or *Eveready Cab Co.* (phone: 722-8383).

Car Rental – Major national agencies are represented at the airport.

 LOCAL SERVICES: For information about local services, call the Chamber of Commerce (phone: 577-2510).

Business Services – For any work involving office automation, call *Norell Temporary Services* (phone: 554-4933).

Mechanics – *Jennings Exxon,* 102 E. Bay St. (phone: 722-3957) or *Import American Auto Service,* 610 Hwy. 17 Bypass (phone: 884-0009).

MUSEUMS: The *Charleston Museum* is described under *Special Places.* Some other notable museums include the following:

Beth Elohim Archives Room – Artifacts relating to the oldest continuous Hebrew congregation in the US. 90 Hasell St. (phone: 723-1090).

Gibbes Art Gallery – 135 Meeting St. (phone: 722-2706).

Patriots Point Maritime Museum – On Highway 17N, just across the Cooper River, this US naval history museum features the aircraft carrier USS *Yorktown* and several other ships (phone: 884-2727).

HISTORIC HOUSES: Aiken-Rhett Mansion (1817) – 48 Elizabeth St. (phone: 723-1159).

Calhoun Mansion (1876) – 16 Meeting St. (phone: 722-8205).

Edmonston-Alston House (1828) – 21 E. Battery St. (phone: 722-7171).

Heyward-Washington House (1770) – 87 Church St. (phone: 722-0354).

Joseph Manigault House (1803) – 350 Meeting St. (phone: 722-2926).

Nathaniel Russell House (1808) – 51 Meeting St. (phone: 723-1623).

Candlelight tours of historic houses are conducted by the Preservation Society in October (phone: 722-4630). The *Historic Charleston Foundation* offers several walking tours of historic houses by day or candlelight. Admission charge. 51 Meeting St. (phone: 723-1623).

 MAJOR COLLEGES AND UNIVERSITIES: The Citadel Military College of South Carolina, founded in 1842, is one of the few state-run military schools in the country. A full-dress parade takes place Fridays at 3:45 PM. West end of Hampton Park (phone: 792-5006). The Citadel Memorial Archives has Civil War memorabilia relating to its graduates. Open daily except holidays. No admission charge (phone: 792-6846).

 SPECIAL EVENTS: *Spoleto Festival USA,* 17 days of chamber music, dance, jazz, opera and theater, begins every year in late May. For tickets, call 577-7863; for schedule information, call 722-2764. An array of local events, many free, make up *Piccolo Spoleto,* which coincides with the main festival (phone 724-7305). During the *Festival of Houses,* in March and April, more than 80 private homes and gardens are open to the public. Admission charge (phone: 722-3405).

 SPORTS AND FITNESS: Biking – Many of Charleston's parks have bike trails. Bikes may be rented from the *Bicycle Shop,* 283 Meeting St. (phone: 722-8168), or *Charleston Carriage Co.* , 96 N. Market St. (phone: 577-0042).

Fishing – The Isle of Palms fishing pier is open spring through fall; it's generally crowded, but in fact, the fishing is unexceptional. For really good surf fishing, try Capers Island and Dewees Island. Charter boats for deep-sea fishing are available through the Municipal Marina, but the best fishing is in the estuarine creeks that swim with bass, sheepshead, flounder, and trout (in fall and winter). In summer and fall the creeks are full of crabs. Crab, oyster, and creek fishing are especially good on Capers, Dewees, Bulls, Kiawah, and Seabrook Islands. There are some public oyster beds closer to Charleston. For fishing and hunting regulations, write: South Carolina Wildlife Resources Dept., PO Box 167, Columbia, SC 29202.

Fitness Centers – *Living Well Fitness Center* has exercise equipment, whirlpool bath, swimming pool, sauna, aerobic dancing, and exercise classes from 6 AM to 9 PM weekdays, shorter hours on weekends. 1650 Sam Rittenburg Blvd. (phone: 571-0130) and six other locations.

Golf – There are public courses at Patriots Point (phone: 881-0042) and Shadowmoss (phone: 556-8251). *Kiawah* and *Seabrook Islands* have fine resort golf courses, but one of the most popular golfing areas in the country, *Myrtle Beach,* is only 98 miles north of Charleston on Rte. 17. This year-round resort, though increasingly tacky, has 28 golf courses, many of them first rate. Even better is *Hilton Head Island,* with more than 20 golf courses of its own, including *Harbour Town Golf Links,* home of the annual *Heritage Golf Classic.* The resort accommodations offered on *Hilton Head* are far classier and more comfortable than those in and around *Myrtle Beach.*

Jogging – Run around Colonial Lake, on Ashley Avenue; for a nice 5-mile loop, run from Lockwood Drive to Battery, up East Bay Street, turn left onto Broad Street, right onto Meeting Street, and left onto Calhoun, which intersects with Lockwood.

Sailing – Both crewed and bareboat sailboat charters, as well as sport fishing excursions, are available through *Bohicket Yacht Charters,* 20 miles from Charleston, between Kiawah and Seabrook islands (phone: 768-1280).

Swimming – Close to the city, Sullivan's Island and the Isle of Palms have fairly nice beaches, crowded in summer. Folly Beach, at the end of Folly Road (Rte. 171), usually gets a good crowd even though it's not well kept. North of Charleston, Capers Island and Dewees Island have more secluded beaches, probably because they're only accessible by boat. Both are state wildlife refuges.

Tennis – The courts at the resorts on *Kiawah* and *Seabrook Islands* are open to the public but can be expensive, and resort guests have priority. Try *Shadowmoss Plantation Golf & Country Club*, 20 Dunvegan Dr. (phone: 556-8251), for inexpensive public courts.

 THEATER: Built in 1736, the 463-seat *Dock Street Theater* — the oldest in the country — stages frequent performances of original drama, Shakespeare, Broadway, and 18th-century classics. It's advisable to call in advance for up-to-date information and performance times. Tours of the theater are conducted sporadically during the week. Admission charge. On the corner of Church and Queen Sts. (phone: 723-5648).

 MUSIC: For *Community Concert Association, Symphony Orchestra*, and *Civic Ballet* schedules, call the Visitor Information Center (phone: 722-8338). The *Robert Ivey Ballet* presents major concerts in the spring and fall (phone: 556-1343).

 NIGHTCLUBS AND NIGHTLIFE: A great "happy hour" in town is at the *Jukebox*, 4 Vendue Range (phone: 723-3431). Charleston's newest nightspot is *Watercolors*, at the *Omni* hotel, 130 Market St. (phone: 722-4900), where an upscale, professional crowd steps out on the dance floor. Also downtown is *Ashley's*, in the new *Sheraton Charleston* hotel, 170 Lockwood Dr. (phone: 723-3000); and, for an intimate atmosphere, try the *Best Friend Bar* in the *Mills House* hotel, 115 Meeting St. (phone: 577-2400). *Myskyn's Tavern*, 5 Faber St. (phone: 577-5595), hosts jazz groups. *East Bay Trading Company* (corner of E. Bay and Queen Sts.; phone: 722-0722) is a converted warehouse filled with fun antiques and an unusual bar. Right next door at 159 E. Bay St. is *Fanigan's* (phone: 722-6916), a favorite spot for businesspeople. The best nightspot north of town is the *Windjammer*, 1008 Ocean Blvd. (phone: 886-8596), a beer-and-billiards beach bar on the Isle of Palms. Centrally located *Café 99* features an outdoor patio, raw bar, and live entertainment, 99 Market St. (phone: 577-4499).

BEST IN TOWN

 CHECKING IN: Expect to pay $80 and up for a double room in one of the places we've noted as expensive; and $50 to $75 at places listed as moderate; and under $50, inexpensive. For bed and breakfast accommodations, contact Historic Charleston Bed & Breakfast, 43 Legare St., Charleston, SC 29401 (phone: 722-6606). All telephone numbers are in the 803 area code unless otherwise indicated.

Battery Carriage House – On the Battery and facing the harbor, this elegant inn provides guests with canopied beds, a fully stocked bar in each room, and continental breakfast in bed. Free bicycles, and complimentary wine to be sipped in the wisteria-draped, walled garden. There are only 10 rooms; make reservations well in advance. Price includes breakfast, all services. 20 S. Battery (phone: 723-9881). Expensive.

Indigo Inn – In a restored tobacco warehouse, the *Indigo* is furnished with 18th-century reproductions, and 29 of its 40 rooms have 2 four-poster queen-size beds. Very service-oriented staff. Centrally located at 1 Maiden La. (phone: 577-5900). Expensive.

Lodge Alley Inn – This quiet, tasteful hostelry is in Charleston's best shopping and sightseeing area. It has 34 rooms, each with a fireplace, as well as 37 one- and two-bedroom suites and a penthouse. There's also a good French restaurant and a lounge. 195 E. Bay (phone: 722-1611). Expensive.

Mills House – A topnotch 214-room property operated by Holiday Inn, it is a Charleston classic. Its antebellum decor reflects its 19th-century history, and, fittingly, it's in the center of the historic district. Try the *Barbadoes Room* restaurant for its continental cuisine; make reservations for its famous Sunday buffet. 115 Meeting St. (phone: 577-2400 or 800-HOLIDAY). Expensive.

Omni, Charleston Place – The newest hotel in town boasts 27 retail shops and adds 443 rooms to the historic district. It also has a pool, spa, and other fitness facilities. Its *Shafetsbury* restaurant features fine continental dining, and the *Watercolors* lounge is a popular nightspot. 130 Market St. (phone: 722-4900). Expensive.

Planters Inn – In Charleston's historic district, this is the city's most elegant new inn. The building dates to the 1800s and was thoroughly renovated, under strict government rules, to maintain its original appearance. The public rooms are filled with antiques and the 43 spacious guestrooms (some with fireplaces) are furnished in period reproductions, including four-poster beds. *Eli's,* the inn's very fine restaurant, features American cuisine. 112 N. Market St. (phone: 722-2345 or 800-845-7082). Expensive.

Sword Gate Inn – In the heart of the old residential area, in a restored, antique-furnished mansion. There are only 6 small rooms, so make reservations well in advance. The young innkeepers work hard to enhance your stay. Full breakfast and use of bicycles are included in the room rate. 111 Tradd St. (phone: 723-8518). Expensive.

Two Meeting Street Inn – A real "find" in Charleston, built in 1891 and similar to a European pension. The inn has been a guest home for more than 50 years. Eight spacious rooms and a wide 2nd-floor verandah overlook White Point Gardens and the harbor. It's furnished with family antiques, silver, and Oriental rugs. 2 Meeting St. (phone: 723-7322). Expensive.

Sheraton Charleston – Near the historic district, this new *Sheraton* is set on the banks of the Ashley River, and some of its 350 rooms have balconies with river views. Its restaurant, *Albemarle's,* emphasizes seafood and beef and offers a good selection of wines. Other facilities include pool, tennis courts, and jogging track. 170 Lockwood Dr. (phone: 723-3000 or 800-325-3535). Expensive to moderate.

Best Western King Charles Inn – In the center of the historic district, this inn reflects old Charleston in the decor of its 90 rooms. There's free parking and a dining room for breakfast. 237 Meeting St. (phone: 723-7451 or 800-528-1234). Moderate.

Days Inn, Meeting St. – This 124-room hotel with a restaurant is in a very good location if seeing the city is top priority. Free parking. 155 Meeting St. (phone: 722-8411). Moderate.

Heart of Charleston – Well run and conscientiously managed, the best thing about this 100-room contemporary motel is the people who own it. Within easy walking distance of the historic, residential, and shopping districts, with a swimming pool and restaurant for breakfast and lunch. 200 Meeting St. (phone: 723-3451). Inexpensive.

 EATING OUT: Charleston used to be known as the kind of place where "you couldn't get a decent hot dog unless you knew somebody," but the times they are a-changin', and there are now more than enough interesting restaurants to whet any palate. Prices range from expensive ($40 or more for dinner for two without drinks, wine, or tips) to moderate ($25 to $35) to inexpensive (under $25). All telephone numbers are in the 803 area code unless otherwise indicated.

Cotton Exchange – Although it features a continental menu of beef, veal, and fresh seafood, most folks come here for live Maine lobster or duck, the house specialty, which the kitchen prepares in any of eight different ways. Open daily. Reservations advised. Major credit cards. 36 Market St. (phone: 577-7137). Expensive.

82 Queen – There used to be just one restaurant at this address, but its popularity prompted the management to annex the building next door. Now, in addition to the seafood specialties served in *82 Queen*'s lovely 18th-century townhouse, the *82 Queen Café and Deli* offers lighter fare such as pasta salad and sandwiches. The *Wine Bar* serves no meals but is a nice spot for a pre- or post-dinner glass of wine. Open daily. Reservations advised. Major credit cards. 82 Queen St. (phone: 723-7591). Expensive.

Robert's of Charleston – One of the city's top restaurants, the chateaubriand prix fixe dinners are served by the owner-chef Robert Dickson. No extra charge for arias he sings as he serves. Closed Sundays. Reservations required 2 weeks ahead. Major credit cards. 42 N. Market St. (phone: 577-7565). Expensive.

Wine Cellar – Each night the chef prepares a different prix fixe menu of new American cuisine, featuring 10 entrées, plus daily specials. A la carte dining is also offered. Closed Sundays. Reservations necessary. Major credit cards. 35 Prioleau St. (phone: 723-9463). Expensive.

Colony House – In the same converted warehouse as the *Wine Cellar,* this moderately priced restaurant serves the best broiled and baked seafood in town. Open daily. Reservations advised. Major credit cards. 35 Prioleau St. (phone: 723-3424). Moderate.

East Bay Trading Company – Whimsical antiques decorate this converted warehouse. The menu features beef dishes, seafood, soups, and homemade desserts (including ice cream). Closed Sundays in winter. Major credit cards. Corner of E. Bay and Queen Sts. (phone: 722-0722). Moderate.

Garibaldi's – This small Italian café serves what may be best described as Italian home cooking. Pasta dishes are offered daily, as are regular specials, including seafood. Open daily. Major credit cards. 49 S. Market St. (phone: 723-7153). Moderate.

Jilich's – In a restored warehouse, this restaurant specializes in southern regional cuisine, with emphasis on charcoal-grilled seafood. About 10 to 12 entrées are offered each evening. Closed Sundays. Reservations advised on weekends. Major credit cards. 188 E. Bay St. (phone: 577-4342). Moderate.

Marianne – The regular dinner menu is French and excellent: beef, veal, seafood, and lamb. A late supper is also available from 11 PM to 1:30 AM and features appetizers, soups, steaks, and omelettes. On Sundays, dinner is served from 5 to 11 PM. A good wine list is available. Reservations advised. Major credit cards. 235 Meeting St. (phone: 722-7196). Moderate.

Le Midi – The first thing diners see as they walk in this country-style French restaurant is the chef at work in his exhibition kitchen. All 20 to 25 entrées are served with sauces made to order; the flounder in brown butter sauce is a perennial favorite. Closed Sundays. Reservations advised for parties of 6 or more. Major credit cards. 337 King St. (phone: 577-5571). Moderate.

Poogan's Porch – Fresh seafood and low country fare in an old Charleston house, with floral wallpaper and ceiling fans. Grilled alligator is a popular appetizer. Open daily. Reservations advised. Major credit cards. 72 Queen St. (phone: 577-2337). Moderate.

Shem Creek Bar and Grill – Grilled seafood, along with chicken and prime ribs, in a casual atmosphere overlooking the creek. Open daily for lunch and dinner, with late-night offerings from 10:30 to 2 AM. Major credit cards. 508 Mill St. (phone: 884-8102). Moderate.

Joe's Seafood Emporium – Overlooking Shem Creek and specializing in charcoal-grilled, broiled, or fried seafood dishes. Chicken and prime ribs are also offered, and there's a good selection of sandwiches at lunchtime. Open daily. Major credit cards. 130 Mill St., Mt. Pleasant (phone: 884-3410). Inexpensive.

CHICAGO

Ask a resident if Chicago has a soul, and you're likely to be greeted with a laugh. The third largest city in the country (the city proper has more than 3 million people; the metropolitan area, more than 6 million), ninth largest in the world, Chicago carries a long-standing reputation as a tough meat-and-potatoes town. "Hog Butcher to the World," Carl Sandburg sang; yet it is one of the world's great cities. Despite its greatness, however, Chicago suffers from an inferiority complex, one that stems from the endless, inevitable comparisons to New York and, more recently, to Los Angeles, which has wrested away its "Second City" title.

In fact, there is a unique allure to Chicago. It has inspired a Broadway musical comedy, countless popular songs, and has been the subject of endless numbers of Hollywood films. All of which may seem especially ironic if you consider that nobody really knows whether the Indian word checagou means "great and powerful," "wild onion," or "skunk." This long-standing linguistic controversy did not, however, inhibit the composers who created that legendary tribute to "Chicago, Chicago, that toddling town."

Chicago spreads along 29 miles of carefully groomed lakeshore. Respecting Lake Michigan, the people of Chicago have been careful not to destroy the property near the water with heavy manufacturing or industry. The lake is a source of water as well as a port of entry for steamships and freighters coming from Europe via the St. Lawrence Seaway. More than 82 million tons of freight are handled by Chicago's ports every year. The city is also the world's largest railroad center. The Chicago grain market is the nation's most important, and O'Hare Airport, one of its busiest. Nuclear research and the electronics industry came of age here. In 1942, the world's first self-sustaining nuclear chain reaction was achieved at the University of Chicago. Half the radar equipment used during World War II was made here, too. Today, Chicago's Association of Commerce and Industry proudly lists an amazing assortment of "number ones" in addition to those the city is most noted for: convention business, steel production, export trade, furniture marketing, tool and die making, metal products, industrial machinery, household appliances.

People from all over the world have come here to live. In 1890, 80% of all Chicago residents were immigrants or children of immigrants. There are more Poles in Chicago than in any Polish city except Warsaw as well as sizable contingents from Germany, Italy, Sweden, and Ireland. People talk about "ethnic Chicago," which means you can find neighborhoods that will make you think you're in a foreign country. Chinatown stretches along Wentworth Avenue. Vietnamtown occupies several blocks of Argyle Street, and Koreatown fills West Lawrence Avenue. Enclaves of Ukrainians and Sicilians live in West Chicago. The Greeks can be found on South Halsted and West Lawrence; Irish and Lithuanians around Bridgeport and Marquette Park;

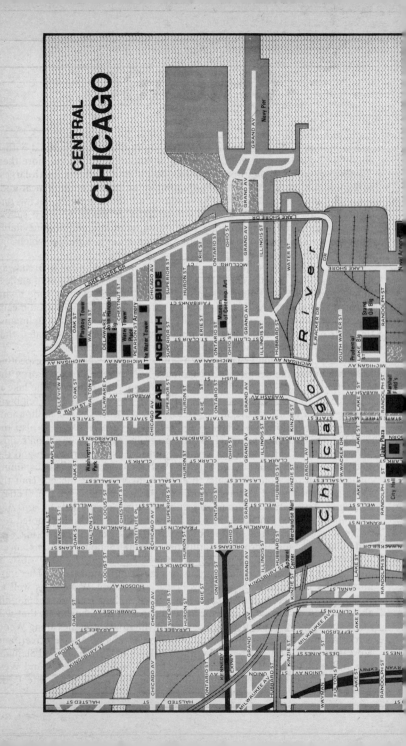

CENTRAL CHICAGO

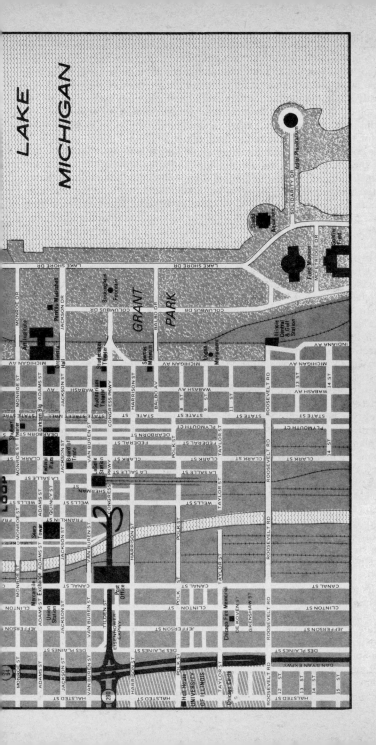

Latinos in Pilsen; Italians in an area bounded by the University of Illinois at Chicago, the Eisenhower Expressway, and the West Side Medical Center. Polonia, which looks like a set for a 1930s Polish version of *West Side Story,* is mostly along Milwaukee. Nearly every nationality has a museum, and at least some of its customs have become public domain as well. There's a splendid array of inexpensive ethnic restaurants where you can get a whole meal for the price of an appetizer in a ritzier joint.

This cosmopolitan center had unprepossessing beginnings. Marquette and Joliet, the French explorers who provided the first record of the area, knew it as the Chicago Portage, one landmark on their route to the Chicago River from the Mississippi. A trading post was established in 1679. In the 1812 Fort Dearborn Massacre, 53 people were killed by Indians. Eighteen years later, the first parcels of land were sold — $40 to $60 per 15,000-square-foot plot. The city, incorporated in 1837, began to look as if it might amount to something when the Union Pacific Railroad connected it to San Francisco in 1869; two years later, on October 8, 1871, it was in ashes. Burning at the rate of 65 acres per hour ($125,000 damage per minute) and aided by a furious southwest wind, the Great Fire melted 15,000 water service pipes, took 250 lives, left 90,000 homeless, and left 1,688 acres in rubble. The total damage was estimated at $196 million.

Like San Francisco after its earthquake, Chicago simply began to rebuild. And in the process, in the course of the following 50 years, a new urban architecture was born. Building quickly and furiously upon 4 square miles of charcoal, and abetted by simple clients whose aesthetics derived from their interests in the profits to be gained from efficient buildings rather than the glory to be garnered from neoclassical palaces, the Chicago architects *invented* the skyscraper; Frank Lloyd Wright pioneered the ground-hugging, prairie-style houses that became the prototypes for the suburban, single-family dwelling units we know today. In 1909, architect Daniel Burnham laid out a plan for the city's parks. Today, 563 of them stretch across 6,766 acres, not to mention 31 clean public beaches and 35,350 acres of trail-crossed forest preserves on the outskirts.

That the beaches are still clean and the forest acreage still pretty much unspoiled is a credit to the city planners, who have, over the years, managed to keep Chicago alive and vibrant even as other downtown areas around the country have declined. While buildings elsewhere were pulled down to make way for parking lots, Chicago got a handful of skyscrapers set on pedestrian plazas studded with magnificent pieces of sculpture by Alexander Calder, Marc Chagall, Pablo Picasso, Claes Oldenburg, Joan Miró, and others. Lively lunchtime programs keep the plazas thronged with sightseers and Loop office workers alike in the summer.

In the same vein is the renovation of the venerable Marquette Building and the completion of the federally and city funded $17-million modernization of the State Street shopping area. So if you haven't seen Chicago for a while, you're likely to be astounded. Cars have been banned; only buses are permitted on State Street — what's left of it. Sidewalks have been widened to nearly 50 feet and covered with hexagonal, battleship-gray paving blocks; open-air cafés have sprouted; and modern bus stops, subway entrances, light poles, and newsstands have been constructed of Cor-Ten steel. As part of the general face-lifting, even *Carson Pirie Scott,* the turn-of-the-century department store designed by the celebrated Louis Sullivan, has restored its interior to match the rococo splendor of its well-cared-for façade. Chicago has also been experiencing an architectural renaissance with the construction of major new office buildings, such as One Park Place, 333 Wacker Drive, One Magnificent Mile, and Helmut Jahn's State of Illinois Building.

If Chicago's modern face has improved with age, the same cannot be said of local politics. The successors to Mayor Richard J. Daley have not been able to maintain Chicago's old reputation as "the city that works," and municipal discord has become much more the order of the day. On April 4, 1989, Richard M. Daley, the first son of the late mayor, was elected to the office his father held for 21 years. Citing improvement of the troubled public school system and a war against crime as top priorities, Daley sends a message far different than any heard from his father. But although he promises "to set a positive tone" for Chicagoans, his critics doubt that he can bind a racially polarized, divided city.

Still, Chicago is quite a city, even if you consider just the ritzy Gold Coast and all those magnificent apartment buildings along the shore of Lake Michigan; the lecture programs at the University of Chicago; the program of choral works at the neo-Gothic Rockefeller Chapel; the Rush Street bars; and the Magnificent Mile — broad Michigan Avenue, lined with shops and galleries. There are the *Chicago Symphony Orchestra,* the *Lyric Opera,* and the *Art Institute,* with its world-famous collection of Impressionist and post-Impressionist paintings. There's jazz and blues till the wee hours of the morning. And if it's the kind of place that makes you want to sing — well, you won't be the first.

CHICAGO AT-A-GLANCE

SEEING THE CITY: The 110-story Sears Tower maintains a Skydeck on the 103rd floor. Open daily from 9 AM to midnight. Admission charge. Wacker and Adams Sts. (phone: 875-9696). For a view from the north, visit the John Hancock Building (fifth largest in the world), fondly nicknamed "Big John." On the 95th floor are a bar and restaurant. Open daily. Admission charge. 875 Michigan Ave. (phone: 751-3681). For a river view, *Wendella Sightseeing* takes you by boat on the Chicago River and into Lake Michigan. Daily, May through September. Admission charge. 400 N. Michigan Ave. (phone: 337-1446). For an enjoyable, informative custom tour of Chicago (individuals or groups), contact *Charlotte Kirshbaum,* 399 Fullerton, Chicago 60614 (phone: 477-6509).

SPECIAL PLACES: A sophisticated public transport system makes it easy to negotiate Chicago's streets. You can explore the Loop, the lakefront, and suburbs by El train, subway, and bus.

THE LOOP

The Loop generally refers to Chicago's business district, which is encircled by the elevated train known as the El.

ArchiCenter – The *Exhibition Gallery,* opened in 1982, has changing shows that span a wide range of architectural topics. Guided walking tours of the Loop (and other neighborhoods) daily, May through November; Tuesdays, Thursdays, and weekends the rest of the year. Chicago Highlights bus tours, Saturdays, April through November. Fees range from $5 to $17. 330 S. Dearborn, 1st floor (phone: 922-3431).

Art Institute of Chicago – Founded as an art school in 1879, the *Art Institute* houses an outstanding collection of Impressionist and post-Impressionist paintings, Japanese prints, Chinese sculpture and bronzes, and Old Masters. In the new Columbus Drive Addition, you can see the reconstructed trading room of the old Chicago Stock Exchange. In the west wall of the upper level *McKinlock Court Galleries* are Chagall's stained glass America windows. The new, $23-million Rice Building houses Edward Hopper's *Nighthawks,* Grant Wood's *American Gothic,* Vincent van Gogh's *Bedroom at Arles* and Toulouse-Lautrec's *Ballet Dancers* as well as exhibitions of European and American decorative arts and sculpture. Open daily. Admission charge except on Tuesdays. Michigan Ave. at Adams St. (phone: 443-3500 for recorded information or 443-3600).

Chicago Board of Trade – The largest grain exchange in the world. Stand in the visitors gallery and watch traders gesticulating on the floor, runners in colored jackets delivering orders, and an electronic record of all the trades displayed overhead. A new trading floor has been built to accommodate expanding markets. Open weekdays, 8 AM to 2 PM. Explanations begin at 9 AM, movies at 10, 11, 12, and 12:30. No admission charge. Jackson at La Salle St. (phone: 435-3590).

Chicago Mercantile Exchange and International Monetary Market – The show is much the same, only here you can sit down. Trading here does not stop suddenly. Each commodity has its own opening and closing time. Open weekdays, 7:30 AM to 3:15 PM. No admission charge. 30 S. Wacker Dr. (phone: 930-8249).

Marshall Field's – Chicago's most famous department store. When it was built in 1892 — before electric lighting was common — it was designed in sections, with shopping areas on balconies overlooking a skylit central courtyard. Later, the skylights were covered, one by a vivid blue and gold Louis Tiffany mosaic you can see by entering on the corner of Washington and State Sts. The *Crystal Palace,* on the 3rd floor, serves unbelievable ice cream sundaes. Frango mint ice cream (a subtle mix of coffee, chocolate, malt, and mint) is a tradition. Open Mondays through Saturdays and the first Sunday of every month. Wabash, State, Randolph, and Washington Sts. (phone: 781-1000).

NEAR SOUTH SIDE

Adler Planetarium – Exhibitions on everything from surveying and navigation instruments to modern space exploration devices, plus a real moon rock and an antique instrument collection that is one of the three best in the world — the best in the Western Hemisphere. You can see it all before or after the sky shows, which are what most people come for. There are new shows every 3 months, one for adults and one for children 5 and younger. Open daily, 9:30 AM to 4:30 PM Mondays to Thursdays, until 9 PM Fridays, and until 5 PM weekends. Free; admission charge to the sky shows. 1300 S. Lake Shore Dr. on Museum Point (phone: 322-0304).

Field Museum of Natural History – Of the endless exhibitions on anthropology, botany, zoology, and geology, one of the most famous is the pair of fighting elephants in the Main Hall. Other standouts include the hands-on Place for Wonder, where youngsters can touch a fish skeleton from the dinosaur age and try on ethnic masks;

the Plants of the World hall; with reproductions of about 500 plants from around the globe; the renovated Gem Hall; the full-scale model of a Pawnee earth lodge, where there are daily programs on Indian life; a full-size, 3-level ancient Egyptian tomb; and an exhibition, Maritime Peoples of the Northwest Coast. The Hall of Chinese Jade and the display of Japanese lacquerware are also outstanding. Open daily. Admission charge except on Thursdays. S. Lake Shore Dr. at Roosevelt Rd. (phone: 922-9410).

Shedd Aquarium – The largest aquarium in the world, this one has more than 200 fish tanks and a collection of over 7,000 specimens: sturgeon from Russia, Bahamian angelfish, Australian lungfish, and a coral reef where divers feed the fish several times a day. Open from 9 AM to 5 PM daily except Christmas and New Year's. Admission charge. Museum Point at 1200 S. Lake Shore Dr. (phone: 939-2426).

NEAR NORTH SIDE

Chicago Academy of Sciences – Particularly lively exhibitions on the natural history of the Great Lakes area, especially the reconstruction of a 300-million-year-old forest that once stood near the present site, complete with gigantic insects and carnivorous dragonflies. There are also a "walk-through" cave and canyon. Open daily. Admission charge except on Mondays. In Lincoln Park at 2001 N. Clark St. (phone: 549-0606).

Chicago Historical Society – Pioneer crafts demonstrations and a Chicago Fire slide show make this one of Chicago's most fascinating museums. New galleries focus on the city's beginnings and explore 19th-century American life through furniture and decorative objects. Open daily. Admission charge except on Mondays. Clark St. and North Ave. (phone: 642-4600).

International College of Surgeons Hall of Fame – Full of medical curiosities: old examining tables, artificial limbs, an amputation set from the Revolution, a "bone crusher" used for correcting bow legs between 1918 and 1950 (!). Finally, there's a fascinating display of prayers and oaths taken by doctors in different countries. Open from 10 AM to 4 PM Tuesdays to Saturdays, 11 AM to 5 PM Sundays; closed Mondays. No admission charge. 1524 N. Lake Shore Dr. (phone: 642-3555).

Lincoln Park Conservatory – Changing floral displays and a magnificent permanent collection that includes orchids, a 50-foot fiddle-leaf rubber tree from Africa with giant leaves, fig trees, and more ferns than you could ever imagine. Open daily. Free. In Lincoln Park, Stockton Dr. at Fullerton (phone: 294-4770).

Lincoln Park Zoo – The best thing about this zoo is that it has the largest group of great apes in captivity, now in a new Great Ape House (the rest of the zoo is undergoing extensive remodeling as well). There are, of course, the standard houses of monkey, tiger, lion, bear, and bison, plus the zoo's popular farm. Open daily from 9 AM to 5 PM. No admission charge. 2200 Cannon Dr., Lincoln Park (phone: 294-4660).

Museum of Contemporary Art – This small museum offers lively changing exhibitions, both retrospectives of contemporary artists and surveys of 20th-century art movements and avant-garde phenomena. The museum also features shows by Chicago artists, symposia, and other special events. Closed Mondays. Admission charge except on Tuesdays. 237 E. Ontario (phone: 280-2660).

Water Tower – Now a landmark, the sole survivor of the Great Fire of 1871 serves as a visitors center. Open daily except holidays. N. Michigan and Chicago Aves.

Water Tower Place – This incredible, vertical shopping mall gets busier and better every year. Asymmetrical glass-enclosed elevators shoot up through a 7-story atrium, past shops selling dresses, books, gift items plus restaurants and a movie theater. Branches of *Marshall Field, FAO Schwarz,* and *Lord & Taylor* are here, along with the lovely *Ritz-Carlton* hotel, stretching 20 stories above its 12th-floor lobby in the tower. Its skylit *Greenhouse* is great for tea or cocktails after a hard day of shopping. Michigan Ave. at Pearson St.

NORTH SIDE

Graceland Cemetery – Buried here are hotel barons, steel magnates, architects Louis Sullivan and Daniel Burnham — enshrined by tombs and miniature temples, and overlooking islands, lakes, hills, and views. A photographer killed while recording the controversial demolition of Sullivan's celebrated Chicago Stock Exchange is buried in a direct line with the grave of Sullivan himself. Guidebooks and maps may be obtained from the gatekeepers for a small fee. Closed Sundays. 4001 N. Clark St. (phone: 525-1105).

SOUTH SIDE

Museum of Science and Industry – Some 2,000 exhibits explain the principles of science in such a lively way that the museum is Chicago's number one attraction. The newest draw is the *Omnimax Theater,* which has an admission charge. Longtime favorites: Colleen Moore's fairy castle of a dollhouse with real diamond "crystal" chandeliers, the cunning Sears circus exhibit, a working coal mine, a walk-through human heart, and a captured German submarine. Open daily except Christmas, but a madhouse on weekends. No admission charge. S. Lake Shore Dr. at 57th St. (phone: 684-1414).

Pullman Community – Founded by George Pullman in 1880 as the nation's first company town, this early example of comprehensive urban planning is now a city, state, and national landmark. Walking tours conducted on the first Sunday of the month from May through October give you the story in detail; at other times you can find the Greenstone Church and other important sites on maps available at the *Florence* hotel, a Pullman-era structure that serves as a visitors center of sorts (and provides lunch on weekdays, breakfast and lunch on Saturdays, and brunch on Sundays). A number of the many privately owned row houses are open for special house tours held annually on the second weekend in October. West of the Calumet Expy. between 111th and 115th Sts. (phone: 785-8181).

WEST

Garfield Park Conservatory – Here are 4½ acres under glass. The Palm House alone is 250 feet long, 85 feet wide, and 65 feet high; it looks like the tropics. There's a fernery luxuriant with greenery, mosses, and pools of water lilies. The Cactus House has 85 genera, 400 species. At Christmas, poinsettias bloom; in February, azaleas and camellias; at Easter, lilies and bulb plants; and in November, mums. Open daily, 9 AM to 5 PM. No admission charge. 300 N. Central Park Blvd. (phone: 533-1281).

OUTSKIRTS

Brookfield Zoo – Some 200 acres divided by moats and natural-looking barriers make this one of the most modern zoos in the country. There is an indoor rain forest, special woods for wolves, a bison prairie, a replica of the Sahara, and a dolphin show. The Tropic World features South American, Asian, and African birds, primates, and other animals. Open daily. Admission charge except on Tuesdays. 1st Ave. at 31st St. in Brookfield, 15 miles west of the Loop (phone: 242-2630).

Six Flags Great America – An extravagant roller coaster and a double-tiered carousel are the highlights of this theme park featuring over 130 rides, shows, and attractions. Musical shows are performed throughout the season, and there's a special giant participatory play area for kids. It is also home to the world's largest motion picture experience. Open daily beginning the week before Memorial Day through Labor Day; weekends May through September. Admission charge. I-94 at Rte. 132 in Gurnee (phone: 249-1776 or, for recorded information, 249-2020).

Lizzadro Museum of Lapidary Art – The collection of Oriental jade carvings is one of the most extensive in the US. About 150 exhibits show off cameos, gemstones, minerals, and fossils. Closed Mondays. Admission charge except on Fridays. 220 Cottage Hill, Elmhurst (phone: 833-1616).

Oak Park – Twenty-five buildings in this suburb, most of them remarkably contemporary looking, show the development of Frank Lloyd Wright's prairie-style architecture. The architect's residence/workshop and Unity Temple are open to the public, and there are daily tours (except on holidays). Admission charge. Edgar Rice Burroughs's and Ernest Hemingway's homes are here, too, along with numerous gingerbread and turreted Queen Anne palaces. The Oak Park Tour Center, based in the Frank Lloyd Wright Home and Studio, operates most area walking tours as well as a visitors center at 158 N. Forest, where you can see photo exhibitions and take in an orientation program. At the *Wright Plus Festival,* the third Saturday in May, ten private homes are open to the public. For more information, phone the Oak Park Visitor Center (phone: 848-1500).

■ **EXTRA SPECIAL:** You don't have to go very far from downtown to reach the North Shore suburbs. Follow US 41 or I-94 north. US 41 takes you past Lake Forest, an exquisite residential area, and Lake Bluff, site of the Great Lakes Naval Station. In Waukegan, *Mathon's* seafood restaurant has been delighting crustacean addicts since before World War II; two blocks east of Sheridan Rd. near the lake on Clayton St. (closed Mondays; phone: 662-3610). Heading inland from Waukegan on Rte. 120 will take you directly to lake country, past Gages Lake and *Brae Loch Golf Course,* Grays Lake, and Round Lake where Rte. 120 becomes Rte. 134, continuing on to Long Lake, Duck Lake, and the three large lakes — Fox, Pistakee, and Grass, near the Wisconsin border. All of these lakes offer water sports, fishing, golf, and tennis. On the northern border with Wisconsin, the 4,900-acre Chain O'Lakes State Park has campsites and boat rental facilities. Pick up Wilson Rd. north at Long Lake, then take Rte. 132 past Fox Lake. This will take you to US 12, which runs to Spring Grove and the state park (phone: 587-5512).

SOURCES AND RESOURCES

TOURIST INFORMATION: The Chicago Tourism Council's Visitor Information Center, in the historic Water Tower at 806 N. Michigan Ave. and Pearson St. (phone: 280-5740), Chicago, IL 60611, distributes a downtown map that pinpoints major attractions and hotels. Chicago Visitor Eventline gives taped information on theater, sports, and special events (phone: 225-2323). Also get copies of the Chicago Transit Authority brochures: the *Chicago Street Directory,* which locates streets by their distance from State or Madison; the *CTA Route Map* of bus, subway, and El routes; and the *CTA Downtown Transit Map.* These are available at El and subway stations. For details, contact the Illinois Travel Information Center, 310 S. Michigan Ave. (phone: 793-2094).

The best guidebook is *Chicago Magazine's Guide to Chicago* (Chicago Guide; $8.95), an insider's look at the city for residents and visitors alike. For self-guided walking tours, see Ira J. Bach's architecturally oriented *Chicago on Foot* (Chicago Review; $14.95).

Television Stations – WBBM Channel 2–CBS; WMAQ Channel 5–NBC; WLS Channel 7–ABC; WTTW Channel 11–PBS.

Radio Stations – AM: WBBM 780 (news); WGN 720 (talk/sports); WLUP 1000 (rock). FM: WBBM 96.3 (talk/news); WBEZ 91.5 (news); WFMT 98.7 (classical).

Local Coverage – *Sun-Times,* morning daily; *Tribune,* morning daily; *Reader,* weekly; *Chicago* magazine, monthly.

Food – *The New Good (But Cheap) Chicago Restaurant Book* by Jill and Ron Rohde (Ohio University Press; $4.95) and *Chicago* magazine's section of restaurant reviews.

Telephone – The area code for Chicago is 312.

Sales Tax – City sales tax is 8%.

CLIMATE: They don't call it the Windy City for nothing. Fierce winter winds can knock you down, and wind-chill factors occasionally measure 47 degrees below zero! The optimal visiting season is autumn, when temperatures are in the 60s and 50s; second best is spring. Summers are muggy, but the temperatures don't usually get higher than the 80s.

GETTING AROUND: Airport – O'Hare International Airport is about 25 miles west of the Loop and, depending on traffic, a 30- to 60-minute ride by cab; the fare should run about $25. *Continental Air Transport* (phone: 454-7800) charges $10 for its bus service to the airport from 24 city locations (including all the major hotels). The trip takes almost an hour, and buses run approximately every 30 minutes. It also offers luxury 10-seat van service for the same price; reservations required. Ask your hotel concierge for Continental's return schedule. Chicago Transit Authority (phone: 836-7000; 800 972-7000) O'Hare Line trains run from several downtown and North Side spots to O'Hare's main terminal in approximately 35 minutes; the fare is $1.

Midway Airport, which handles an increasing volume of domestic traffic, is 8 miles south of the Loop. A taxi ride to Midway from the Loop will take from 10 to 20 minutes and cost about $10. The #62 Archer Express bus (heading south) can be picked up from any stop along State St. in the Loop; transfer at Cicero Ave. to any southbound bus — they stop inside the airport. This ride takes about 30 minutes and costs $1.25. *Continental Air Transport* also provides bus service to the airport from the *Palmer House, Hyatt Regency,* and *Marriott* hotels; schedules vary according to flights. The run to the airport takes about 40 minutes, and the cost is $8.

Bus, Subway, and El – Chicago Transit Authority operates bus, subway, and El services. For information, call 836-7000. There's also a do-it-yourself tour on public transport. One good round trip by public transportation starts in the Loop, goes through Lincoln Park, past the Historical Society, and into New Town on the #151 bus. When you've ridden enough, get off and catch the same bus going in the opposite direction. On Sundays and holidays, there is also a Culture Bus, which stops at the *Art Institute,* the *Field Museum,* the Shedd Aquarium, the Adler Planetarium, the *Museum of Science and Industry,* the *Oriental Institute,* and the *DuSable Museum of African-American History.* It operates every half-hour from 11 AM to 5 PM, May through September.

Taxi – Cabs can be hailed in the street or picked up from stands in front of the major hotels. You can also phone one of Chicago's taxi services: *Yellow* and *Checker Cabs* (phone: 829-4222); *Flash Cab* (phone: 561-1444); *American United* (phone: 248-7600).

Car Rental – All major national firms are represented.

LOCAL SERVICES: Babysitting – Check at your hotel for reliable services.

    Business Services – *Typing Unlimited,* 400 N. Michigan Ave. (phone: 321-0516).

    Mechanic – *Amoco* station, 665 N. Dearborn (phone: 787-8164).

MUSEUMS: Chicago is paradise if you like going to museums. Those described in *Special Places* have plenty of company, including the following:

    Balzekas Museum of Lithuanian Culture – 6500 S. Pulaski Rd. (phone: 582-6500).

Chicago Architecture Foundation, Glessner House – 1800 S. Prairie Ave. (phone: 326-1393).

DuSable Museum of African-American History – In Washington Park, at 740 E. 56th Pl. (phone: 947-0600).

Jane Addams's Hull House – A National Historic Landmark. 800 S. Halsted St. at Polk St. (phone: 413-5353).

Oriental Institute at University of Chicago – 1155 E. 58th at University (phone: 702-9521).

Polish Museum of America – 984 N. Milwaukee Ave. (phone: 384-3352).

Spertus Museum of Judaica – 618 S. Michigan Ave. (phone: 922-9012).

Ukrainian Institute of Modern Art – 2320 W. Chicago Ave. (phone: 227-5522).

Great sculpture and art can also be seen in the plazas of downtown skyscrapers. Bertoia's spellbinding *Sounding Sculpture,* at the Standard Oil Bldg., 200 E. Randolph; *Flamingo,* a stabile by Alexander Calder, at Federal Center Plaza, Adams and Dearborn; Calder's gaily colored mobile *Universe,* in the Sears Tower lobby, Wacker and Adams; sculptor Claes Oldenburg's 101-foot-high baseball bat, *Batcolumn,* at 600 W. Madison; Chagall's *Four Seasons* mosaic, at First National Plaza, Monroe and Dearborn. (If you're there at noon, you might catch a free concert.) *Chicago's Picasso* (its formal title because no one could agree on a name), a giant sculpture, is at the Richard J. Daley Plaza, on Washington and Clark near the Chagall. (There are also free concerts at the plaza every weekday, weather permitting.) Joan Miró's *Chicago* sculpture mural is across the street from Daley Plaza. Buckingham Fountain, a Chicago landmark in Grant Park at Congress Parkway, is illuminated from May to September.

 SPECIAL EVENTS: Summertime is festival time. In June, the beat of rhythm and blues fills the air at the *Chicago Blues Festival* in Grant Park. Also in June is the *Old Town Art Fair,* held in Lincoln Park. In July, sailboats race on Lake Michigan; and in August, the *Western Open Golf Tournament* is played at *Butler National Golf Club* in Oakbrook. The *Arlington Million,* the world's richest thoroughbred race, is held the last week of August at *Arlington Park.* The *Ravinia Festival,* a series of outdoor concerts by the *Chicago Symphony Orchestra* and other headliners, runs throughout the summer in Highland Park (phone: 728-4642). The first week in September heralds a *jazz festival* to the Grant Park Bandshell (free). September also brings former *Tribune* columnist Mike Royko's annual *Ribfest,* the largest spareribs cooking competition in the country. Grant Park, north of the *Field Museum of Natural History* (no admission charge).

SHOPPING: Some of Chicago's best sights are indoors, along the aisles of the city's many shops and department stores. Los Angeles boasts Rodeo Drive, and New York has Fifth Avenue. In Chicago, the chic shopping district is North Michigan Avenue, between the Chicago River and Oak Street — a stretch known as the Magnificent Mile — where you can find *Burberrys* (phone: 787-2500), *Bonwit Teller* (phone: 751-1800), *Gucci* (phone: 664-5504), *Hammacher Schlemmer* (phone: 664-9292), *Saks Fifth Avenue* (phone: 944-6500), *Lord & Taylor* (phone: 787-7400), *I. Magnin* (phone: 751-0500), *Tiffany & Company* (phone: 944-7500), *Neiman Marcus* (phone: 642-5900), *Bloomingdale's* (phone: 440-4460), and Chicago's doyenne, *Marshall Field* (phone: 781-1234). The last of these is in Water Tower Place (845 N. Michigan Ave.), a 7-story shopper's paradise that houses, among others, *Eddie Bauer* (phone: 337-4353), *FAO Schwarz* (phone: 787-8894), *Laura Ashley* (phone: 951-8004), and *Banana Republic* (phone: 642-7667).

Although much of the city's best downtown shopping is concentrated along the Magnificent Mile, the burgeoning loft area west of the Loop is increasingly being filled with eclectic shops. One of the most interesting is *City,* 361 W. Chestnut St. (phone:

664-9581), which sells avant-garde furniture. The *Mallers Building* at 67 E. Madison has 13 floors of retail and wholesale jewelers, and the *5 N. Wabash Building* has 17 floors of stores specializing in watches, necklaces, and precious stones.

MAJOR COLLEGES AND UNIVERSITIES: Although far too big to be called a college town, Chicago has many fine universities. The University of Chicago, known for its economics and social science departments, has its main entrance at 5801 S. Ellis Ave. (phone: 753-1234); University of Illinois at Chicago, 601 S. Morgan (phone: 996-3000); Illinois Institute of Technology, 3300 S. Federal (phone: 567-3000); Loyola University, 820 N. Michigan (phone: 670-3000) and 6525 Sheridan Rd. (phone: 274-3000); De Paul University, 25 E. Jackson and in Lincoln Park at 2323 N. Seminary (phone: 341-8000); Northwestern University, at Chicago Ave. and Lake Shore Dr. (phone: 908-8649) and in Evanston (phone: 491-5000); Roosevelt University, 430 S. Michigan Ave. (phone: 341-3500); Lake Forest College, Sheridan Rd., Lake Forest (phone: 234-3100).

SPORTS AND FITNESS: Plenty of major league action in town.

Baseball – The *White Sox* play at *Comiskey Park,* 35th and Shields, off the Dan Ryan Expy. (phone: 924-1000). The *Cubs* play at *Wrigley Field,* Addison and Clark (phone: 281-5050), now occasionally at night.

Basketball – The NBA *Bulls,* 1800 W. Madison (phone: 943-5800) play at *Chicago Stadium* (phone: 733-5300).

Bicycling – Chicago has a glorious bike path along the shore of Lake Michigan, running from the Loop to Evanston — about 11 miles. You can rent bikes in summer from the concession at Lincoln Park.

Fishing – After work, people flock to the rocks along the shore, casting nets for smelt. The rocks around Northwestern University at Evanston are especially popular. There's also an artificial island, attainable by footbridge, around Northwestern.

Fitness Centers – *Body Elite,* 445 W. Erie (phone: 664-5710), and *Combined Fitness Centre,* 1235 N. LaSalle (phone: 787-8400), both allow non-members for a fee.

Football – The NFL *Bears* (phone: 663-5100) play at *Soldier Field.*

Golf – Chicago has 18 public golf courses, some along the lakeshore. The most accessible municipal course is *Waveland* in Lincoln Park. The Chicago Park District offers golf instruction. For information, call 294-2274.

Hiking – Windy City Grotto, the Chicago Chapter of the National Speleological Society, organizes frequent field trips to cave country in southern Indiana and Missouri. For information, contact Windy City Speleonews, c/o Bill Mixon, 5035 N. South Drexel, Chicago 60615. Chicago Mountaineering Club organizes weekend expeditions and teaches safe climbing techniques. They meet at the *Field Museum* every second Monday. For information, write to PO Box 1025, Chicago 60690. Sierra Club, 53 W. Jackson (phone: 431-0158), also organizes outings.

Hockey – The NHL *Black Hawks* play in *Chicago Stadium* from September through April (phone: 733-5300).

Horse Racing – Horses race at four tracks in the Chicago area:

Arlington Park, Euclid Ave. and Wilke Rd., Arlington Heights (phone: 255-4300)
Hawthorne, 3501 S. Laramie, Cicero (phone: 780-3700)
Maywood Park, North and 5th Aves., Maywood (phone: 343-4800)
Sportsman's Park, 3301 S. Laramie, Cicero (phone: 242-1121)

Jogging – Run along Lake Shore Drive to Lincoln Park; there is a 5-mile track inside the park. Or simply do as many Chicagoans do and jog along the lakefront, accessible via numerous pedestrian walkways.

Polo – Summers at the *Oak Brook Polo Club,* 1000 Oak Brook Rd., Oak Brook (phone: 571-7656); during winter you can play indoors at the *Chicago Armory,* Chicago Ave. and Fairbanks.

Sailing – Lake Michigan offers superb sailing, but as experienced sailors can tell you, the lake is deceptive. Storms of up to 40 knots can blow in suddenly. Check with the Coast Guard before going out (phone: 219 949-7440). You can rent boats and take sailing lessons from *City Sailors* (phone: 975-0044). There are a few marinas between the Loop and Evanston; others, along suburban shores. Highland Park is one of the most popular city marinas.

Skiing – There are more than 50 ski clubs in the Chicago area. For information, contact the Chicago Metro Ski Council, PO Box 7926, Chicago 60680 (phone: 346-1268).

Swimming – Beaches line the shore of Lake Michigan. Those just to the north of the Loop off Lake Shore Drive are the most popular and often the most crowded. Oak Street Beach along the "Gold Coast" is the most fashionable beach. If you go farther north, you'll find fewer people. The Chicago Park District offers swimming lessons at some of the 72 city pools. The best are at Wells Park and Gill Park. For information, call 294-2333.

Tennis – The city has 706 outdoor municipal courts. The best are at Randolph and Lake Shore Drive, just east of the Loop (phone: 294-4792). For other tennis information, call 294-2314.

THEATERS: For schedules and ticket information, consult the publications noted above or visit the HOT TIX booth at State St. and Madison (phone: 977-1755), where theater tickets can be purchased at half price on the day of the performance. Many Broadway shows play Chicago before heading to the Big Apple. The main Chicago theaters are: *Shubert,* 22 W. Monroe (phone: 977-1700); *Civic,* 20 N. Wacker Dr. (phone: 346-0270); *Goodman,* 200 S. Columbus Dr. (phone: 443-3800); *Blackstone Theater,* 60 E. Balbo (phone: 977-1700); and the *Apollo Theater Center,* 2540 N. Lincoln (phone: 935-6100).

Among Chicago's thriving Off-Loop theaters are *Organic Theater,* 3319 N. Clark (phone: 327-5588); *Goodman Studio Theater,* 200 S. Columbus (phone: 443-3800); *Victory Gardens Theater,* 2257 N. Lincoln (phone: 549-5788), which is dedicated to the promotion of Chicago playwrights; *Steppenwolf Theater,* 2851 N. Halsted (phone: 472-4141); *Wisdom Bridge Theater,* 1559 W. Howard (phone: 743-6442); and *The Body Politic Theater,* 2261 N. Lincoln (phone: 871-3000).

There are several good dinner theaters as well: *Drury Lane South,* 2500 W. 95th, Evergreen Park (phone: 779-4000); *Pheasant Run Theater,* Pheasant Run Lodge, Rte. 64, St. Charles (phone: 584-1454); and the *Candlelight Playhouse,* 5620 S. Harlem Ave. in Summit, the first dinner theater in the country (phone: 496-3000).

MUSIC: Chicago isn't the musical desert that the Midwest is generally thought to be. Good music (and lots of it) can be heard all over the place. The world-renowned *Chicago Symphony Orchestra* plays at *Orchestra Hall,* 220 S. Michigan, from September through June (phone: 435-8111), and at *Ravinia Park* in Highland Park, late June through September (phone: 433-8800;). Outdoor concerts are also played in the new *Petrillo Musicshell,* behind the *Art Institute* between Jackson and Monroe on Columbus Dr. (phone: 294-2420). The *Lyric Opera of Chicago* performs at *Civic Opera House,* 20 N. Wacker (phone: 332-2244). The *Auditorium Theatre,* a landmark designed by Louis Sullivan at 70 E. Congress (phone: 922-2110), is another major hall.

NIGHTCLUBS AND NIGHTLIFE: Take in Chicago's blues, folk, and jazz scene in informal pubs, cafés, and taverns. Among them are *Park West,* 322 W. Armitage (phone: 929-5959); *B.L.U.E.S.,* 2519 N. Halsted (phone: 528-1012); *Old Town School of Folk Music,* 909 W. Armitage (phone: 525-7793);

The Vic, 3145 N. Sheffield (phone: 472-0366); and *Byfields,* in the *Omni Ambassador East* hotel, 1301 N. State Pkwy. (phone: 787-6433). *The Second City* revue ensemble performs original, improvisational, and satirical skits, 1616 N. Wells (phone: 337-3992). *Limelight* — in a former Romanesque museum nicknamed the Castle — is an outrageous New York–style dance club, 632 N. Dearborn (phone: 337-2985). *Jukebox Saturday Night,* 2251 N. Lincoln (phone: 525-5000), is the place to dance to vintage 1950s and 1960s rock 'n' roll.

BEST IN TOWN

 CHECKING IN: There are quite a number of interesting hotels in Chicago, varying in style from the intimate clubbiness of the *Tremont* and *Whitehall* to the supermodern elegance of the *Ritz-Carlton.* Unless otherwise noted, all listed here have at least one restaurant; the choice of eating places normally increases with the price of a room and the size of the hotel. Big hotels have shops, meeting places, nightly entertainment. Rates in Chicago are higher than in most other midwestern cities: Expect to pay $150 to $220 for doubles in expensive hotels; $85 to $135 in those classified as moderate; and only as low as about $40 in those listed as inexpensive. If money is no object, ask for a room with a view. "Near North Side" hotels are close to New Town, Lincoln Park, and Water Tower Place; Loop locations (about 10 minutes away by taxi) are convenient to businesses and the fine, old downtown department stores. For bed and breakfast accommodations, contact *Bed and Breakfast Chicago,* PO Box 14088, Chicago, IL 60614 (phone: 951-0085). All telephone numbers are in the 312 area code unless otherwise indicated.

Chicago Hilton and Towers – Some $180 million — the most ever spent on a hotel renovation — has transformed this 30-story landmark building into a good-looking, modern property. The former *Conrad Hilton* features 1,620 rooms, the most lavish of which is the 2-story Conrad Hilton Suite for $4,000 a night. Restored to their 1927 grandeur are the Great Hall and the Versailles-inspired Grand Ballroom. New facilities include a fitness center with an indoor running track, sundeck, exercise equipment, swimming pool, saunas, and whirlpool baths; there's also a computerized business center. Sometimes large groups of enthusiastic convention goers make it difficult to feel comfortable without a name tag. The Tower rooms are the most elegantly furnished and have the added convenience of their own registration and check-out desk (on the 24th floor), not insignificant when the hordes line up at the lobby cashier each AM. Amenities also include a 140,000-square-foot convention center, a self-parking garage, and 21 barrier-free rooms for handicapped guests. For a fee, a telephone answering machine can be hooked up to your room phone. 720 S. Michigan Ave. (phone: 922-4400). Expensive.

Drake – A 535-room institution, with a graciousness not often found in hotels these days. The *Cape Cod Room* is Chicago's finest seafood eatery (see *Eating Out*). Near North Side. N. Michigan Ave. at Lake Shore Dr. and Walton Pl. (phone: 787-2200). Expensive.

Fairmont – This opulent, sophisticated addition to the Fairmont chain opened in December 1987. Its 700 rooms and suites look out at the city skyline and Lake Michigan, and feature such luxury amenities as marble bathrooms equipped with a TV set, telephone, and lighted dressing table. The hotel's supper club, *Moulin Rouge,* features top-name entertainment. There's also a bank of meeting rooms with teleconference facilities and a spectacular penthouse boardroom with a panoramic view of the lake. 200 N. Columbus Dr. (phone: 565-8000). Expensive.

Four Seasons – Opened in March 1989, one of the city's newest luxury hotels occupies 19 floors of a stunning high-rise that also houses *Bloomingdale's.* There are 344 rooms (more than a third boast separate parlors), an opulent Presidential Suite, and 16 residential apartments in this member of what is arguably the best managed hotel group in the world. Guest facilities include 24-hour room service, two-line telephones, lighted makeup mirrors, a spa, sauna, and indoor swimming pool. This is a luxury hotel worth the adjective. 120 E. Delaware (phone: 280-8800 or 800-332-3442). Expensive.

Hyatt Regency Chicago – The 2,000 rooms in its two ultramodern towers have recently undergone a $20-million refurbishment. Conveniently located between the Loop and N. Michigan Ave. Fine dining at *Truffles.* 151 E. Wacker Dr. (phone: 565-1000, 800-233-1234, or 800-228-9000). Expensive.

Hyatt Regency O'Hare – Ideal for a comfortable overnight stop between planes. Health club. 1,100 rooms. South River Rd. exit off Kennedy Expy. (phone: 696-1234, 800-233-1234, or 800-228-9000). Expensive.

Mayfair Regent – Unlike most of the new high-rise hotels opening these days, the recently renovated *Mayfair* (formerly the *Lake Shore Drive* hotel) is small enough to offer the ultimate in comfort and style — the ratio of employees to guests is 1 to 1. Dinner here is an elegant affair: The rooftop *Ciel Bleu* offers classic French cuisine and romantic views of Lake Michigan (particularly pleasant at breakfast); the *Palm,* on the ground floor, has steaks as prime as those served by its New York counterpart. 181 E. Lake Shore Dr. (phone: 787-8500; 505-243-6466, collect, from Alaska; 800-545-4000 elsewhere in the US). Expensive.

Nikko Chicago – This elegant, new, 425-room hotel overlooking the Chicago River was built by Nikko Hotels International, Japan's largest hotel chain. Japanese touches abound — landscaped indoor gardens, native artwork, even Japanese suites with tatami sleeping rooms. A 3-floor amenity area includes a 2-story executive lounge, a business center with computer terminals, a business library, and a health club. 320 N. Dearborn St. (phone: 744-1900). Expensive.

Omni Ambassador East – Now part of the Omni Classic chain, this lovely old hotel was recently renovated but hasn't lost an ounce of charm. It also houses the famous *Pump Room* restaurant (see *Eating Out*), a Chicago institution whose entryway is lined with photos of famous guests, who always dine in booth one. Convenient location in the Gold Coast area, close to Lincoln Park, Rush Street, and the Magnificent Mile of Michigan Avenue. (Not affiliated with the *Ambassador West,* across the street.) 1301 N. State Pkwy. (phone: 787-7200). Expensive.

Palmer House – A busy, 1,800-room giant, this is another Chicago tradition. The sumptuous, recently restored *Empire Room* is a visual delight. You can also dine here at the *Palmer Steak House* and *Trader Vic's.* In the Loop on the new State Street mall. Monroe St. between State and Wabash (phone: 726-7500). Expensive.

Park Hyatt – Small, with 255 elegant rooms and suites, and as convivial as it is convenient to N. Michigan Ave. and the historic Water Tower. 800 N. Michigan Ave. (phone: 280-2222). Expensive.

Ritz-Carlton – Contemporary and chic, this beautifully appointed 430-room luxury establishment, a member of the fine Four Seasons chain, rises 20 stories above its 12th-floor lobby. In the spectacular Water Tower Place complex, it has all the accoutrements of elegance, including a fine health club and skylit indoor swimming pool. Near North Side. 160 E. Pearson (phone: 266-1000). Expensive.

Sheraton-Plaza – This 334-room gem, with 100 suites, was remodeled recently. Just off Michigan Avenue. 160 E. Huron St. (phone: 787-2900). Expensive.

Tremont – The paneled lobby, with its elaborate moldings and chandeliers, is more like a private sitting room than a public foyer. The 139 rooms offer traditional elegance. Hotel operation (as at the *Whitehall*) has suffered some from owner John Coleman's financial problems. The hotel is also the home of *Cricket's,* one of

Chicago's best restaurants (see *Eating Out*). 100 E. Chestnut (phone: 751-1900 or 800 621-8133). Expensive.

21 East Kempinski – Chicago's newest Magnificent Mile hostelry boasts an elegant 4-story atrium lobby and 247 rooms, including 6 duplex penthouse suites, overlooking the city and Lake Michigan. There is a piano bar and formal dining in *Café 21,* which serves southwestern cuisine. 24 E. Bellevue Pl. (phone: 266-2100). Expensive.

Westin Chicago – Built in 1963, this deluxe, near North Side hotel has 742 rooms and a health club with sauna and steam room. The *Chelsea* restaurant serves continental fare and the *Lion Bar* is a popular spot that's generally crowded with businesspeople. Near the *Drake* and the Hancock Center. N. Michigan Ave. at Delaware (phone: 943-7200). Expensive.

Whitehall – Small, devoted to detail, and known for its elegance and its careful, courteous service — a bit erratic of late, since its owner went into bankruptcy. Its excellent restaurant is open only to members and registered guests. 226 rooms. 105 E. Delaware Pl. (phone: 944-6300). Expensive.

Richmont – Formerly the *Eastgate,* this property was completely overhauled and reopened in 1980 as a moderately priced alternative near the Magnificent Mile. There are 193 guestrooms, a meeting room, and the *Rue St. Clair* lobby bar, which looks like a French bistro but serves American fare. 162 E. Ontario St. (phone: 787-3580 or 800 621-8055). Expensive to moderate.

Allerton – Close to museums and shopping on Michigan Avenue, 10 minutes from the Loop. The 380-room *Allerton* is an economical but quite pleasant choice — and a steal in this location. 701 N. Michigan Ave. (phone: 440-1500). Moderate.

Best Western Congress – Not as large as the nearby *Palmer House* (800 rooms), this unit of the Best Western chain has a well-deserved reputation for personal attention. It also boasts fine views of Lake Michigan and Grant Park. 520 S. Michigan Ave. (phone: 427-3800). Moderate.

Bismarck – The *Walnut Room* serves breakfast and lunch, and the *Chalet* is where guests go for dinner. There are 525 recently renovated rooms and some nice suites. 171 W. Randolph at La Salle (phone: 236-0123). Moderate.

Day's Inn Lake Shore – The best things about this 586-room property are its setting opposite the lake and Navy Pier and its relatively low rates, which are even more reasonable considering the outdoor pool. 644 N. Lake Shore Dr. (phone: 943-9200). Moderate.

Holiday Inn City Centre – Architecturally more interesting than you might expect. Swimming pools and health club, indoor tennis courts, racquetball, and free parking make this establishment's 500 rooms almost a bargain. 300 E. Ohio (phone: 787-6100). Moderate.

Holiday Inn of Elk Grove – Convenient to O'Hare. With 159 rooms and a domed indoor pool, it's an economical choice for an overnight stop. Small pets welcome. Transportation to the airport. 1000 Busse Rd. (phone: 437-6010). Moderate.

Avenue – This budget motel has only 78 rooms and few amenities, but it's close to town. 1154 S. Michigan Ave. (phone: 427-8200). Inexpensive.

Grove – An outdoor pool and low (for Chicago) prices make this 40-room motel a real find. Restaurant nearby. A half-hour drive from the Loop (longer in rush hour). 9110 Waukegan Rd., Morton Grove (phone: 966-0960). Inexpensive.

 EATING OUT: The city's restaurant business is booming, and some of the finest cooking in America can be found here. Expect to pay from $60 and up for two at those restaurants we've noted as expensive; between $40 and $60, for moderately priced meals; and under $40 at our inexpensive choices. Prices do not include drinks and wine, tips or taxes. All telephone numbers are in the 312 area code unless otherwise indicated.

Ambria – Everything about this restaurant charms, from the comfortable setting to the menu's sophisticated variations on nouvelle cuisine. Dinner might begin with a salad of sliced duck, pine nuts, and fresh pears with red currant dressing, or a tropical lobster salad. Desserts are simply remarkable. There's also a *dégustation* dinner for 4 or more with samplings of many dishes. Closed Sundays. Reservations necessary. Major credit cards. 2300 N. Lincoln Park W. (phone: 472-5959). Expensive.

Biggs – In a restored Victorian mansion. The prix fixe menu changes every day, but the selection often includes beef Wellington, duck à l'orange, roast rack of lamb persillade, fettuccine with lobster and scallops, and tenderloin tips sautéed with fresh mushrooms and served on wild rice. There's an extensive wine list. Open daily for dinner. Reservations necessary. Major credit cards. 1150 N. Dearborn (phone: 787-0900). Expensive.

Café Provençal – An intimate room on a quiet north suburban Evanston street. It offers some of the most painstakingly prepared French dishes in the area — the Wisconsin pheasant with rosemary-honey glaze and the New York foie gras with Cortlandt apples are particularly recommended. Closed Sundays. Reservations advised. Major credit cards. 1625 Hinman St., Evanston (phone: 475-2233). Expensive.

Cricket's – In the style of the *"21" Club* in New York, with red-checkered tablecloths, bare floors, low ceilings, and walls festooned with corporate memorabilia, and a menu that includes chicken hash Mornay and various daily specials. A very good choice for Sunday brunch. Reservations necessary. Major credit cards. *Tremont* hotel, 100 E. Chestnut (phone: 280-2100). Expensive.

Le Français – For years, Jean Bouchet made this one of America's finest French restaurants, but the kitchen is now in the hands of Roland and Mary Beth Liccioni. They were taking over as we went to press, and based on their work as chef and pastry chef at *Carlos'* (in nearby Highland Park) we expect the menu to turn a bit more *nouvelle.* Closed Sundays. Reservations necessary. Major credit cards. 269 S. Milwaukee, Wheeling; take Kennedy Expy. to Rte. 294 north, Willow exit (phone: 541-7470). Expensive.

Jackie's – This intimate 50-seat neighborhood restaurant offers some of the finest nouvelle cooking in the city. Consider delicate orange-honey-glazed squab served with Chinese vermicelli and napa cabbage garnished with cashews and cloud-ear mushrooms. Closed Sundays and Mondays. Reservations necessary. Major credit cards. 2478 N. Lincoln (phone: 880-0003). Expensive.

Nick's Fishmarket – The number of choices on the menu is bewildering, but the work of choosing is worth the effort. The cold appetizer assortment of shellfish is always a good bet, and try the pan-fried whole baby salmon or an abalone dish for an entrée. Closed Sundays. Reservations necessary. Major credit cards. First National Plaza, Monroe St. (phone: 621-0200). Expensive.

95th – For food with a view, this is your best bet. An American regional cuisine menu that changes seasonally. Open daily; dinner Saturdays; brunch and dinner Sundays. Reservations advised. Major credit cards. 95th floor, John Hancock Center, 172 E. Chestnut St. (phone: 787-9596). Expensive.

Palm – Owned by the same people who run the well-known New York restaurants called *Palm* and *Palm, Too,* this eatery has a similar decor of sawdust-covered floors and walls hung with drawings of famous patrons. Also like its East Coast counterpart, the kitchen here specializes in producing great steaks and lobster. Closed Sundays. Reservations necessary. Major credit cards. *Mayfair Regent* hotel, 181 E. Lake Shore (phone: 944-0135). Expensive.

Le Perroquet – Subtle, sumptuous; one of the best restaurants around. Expect a parade of delectable wonders such as *moules* or a *soufflé de crevettes Madras* as hors d'oeuvres; salmon mousseline, venison filet, or quail as entrées; pastries to follow. Closed Sundays. Reservations necessary. American Express, Diners Club, Discover, and Carte Blanche. 70 E. Walton (phone: 944-7990). Expensive.

Pump Room – A winning formula of fine cuisine, diligent service, and lovely decor have made the *Pump Room* a legend among Chicago restaurants. Continental dishes are the mainstays, but there are some nouvelle cuisine specialties; both are complemented by the restaurant's good wine list. Open daily. Reservations necessary. Major credit cards. 1301 N. State Pkwy. (phone: 266-0360). Expensive.

Spiaggia – Expertly prepared North Italian cuisine — including unique pasta dishes, veal, and a grilled fish of the day — served in a beautiful setting. Open daily except Sunday lunch. Reservations advised. Major credit cards. 980 N. Michigan (phone: 280-2750). Expensive.

Charlie Trotter's – The menu changes daily in this adventuresome, 2-room nouvelle cuisine restaurant, the civilized home of some of the city's most imaginative dishes. Appetizers range from caviar-topped sea scallops to sweetbreads with pancetta, radicchio, shredded potato, sweet peppers, and sharp cilantro butter presented in a crisp potato shell. Entrées are equally varied: tender venison, smoked quail with hazelnuts. Service is excellent; the wine list is extensive. Closed Sundays and Mondays. Reservations necessary. Major credit cards. 816 W. Armitage (phone: 248-6228). Expensive.

Printer's Row – Sophisticated American cuisine served in an elegant room. The hallmark vegetable and seafood pâtés are very good, and a roast breast of duck with corn crêpes is a standout entrée. Closed Sundays. Reservations advised. Major credit cards. 550 S. Dearborn (phone: 461-0780). Expensive to moderate.

Butcher Shop Steakhouse – A unique dining experience, where you have your steak and cook it, too. In this latest, growing trend, guests select a filet or T-bone and pop it on the grill themselves. For those who prefer full service, the kitchen will happily oblige (there's an additional $2 charge if you leave the cooking to them). Open daily. Reservations advised. 358 W. Ontario (phone: 295-4444). Moderate.

Cape Cod Room – An institution. This seafood restaurant serves reliable fresh pompano, lobster, and other fish. Open daily except Christmas. Reservations necessary. Major credit cards. *Drake* hotel, 140 E. Walton (phone: 787-2200). Moderate.

Chestnut Street Grill – The Frank Lloyd Wright and Louis Sullivan ornamentation are as distinctive as the house specialty, grilled seafood. Try the swordfish or the tuna. The desserts are sinful, especially the cappuccino-candy ice cream. Open daily. Reservations advised. Major credit cards. Mezzanine level, Water Tower Place (phone: 280-2720). Moderate.

L'Escargot – Unpretentious and pleasant, with an emphasis on provincial French cooking, including a cassoulet — white beans, sausage, pork, and goose. There's always fresh fish and homemade pastries on the menu. Open daily. Reservations advised. Major credit cards. *Allerton* hotel, 701 N. Michigan (phone: 337-1717). Moderate.

Hatsuhana – Delicious sushi and sashimi; tables as well as counter seating available. Open daily. Reservations advised. Major credit cards. 160 E. Ontario (phone: 478-2486). Moderate.

Lawry's The Prime Rib – The specialty here is prime ribs, served in three thicknesses with Yorkshire pudding and a big fresh salad with *Lawry's* special Famous French dressing and *Lawry's* seasoning salt. Open daily; weekdays for lunch. Reservations necessary. Major credit cards. 100 E. Ontario (phone: 787-5000). Moderate.

Salvatore's – Diners at this handsome Italian restaurant may sit in a garden atrium or in one of two dining rooms. The menu features 14 kinds of homemade pasta and fresh fish specials that change daily, but the kitchen is most proud of its *castelle di vitello* (roasted milk-fed veal) and *fettuccine alla Caroline* (green noodles with pine nuts, mushrooms, spinach, and cheese). Among the choices on the wine list are 114 varieties from Italy. Open daily. Reservations advised. Major credit cards. 525 W. Arlington Pl. (phone: 528-1200). Moderate.

Scoozi – A cavernous former garage that's been turned into a smashing gathering place with evocative period decor. Besides the chef's daily specials, the unusually large menu includes provincial Italian specialties such as 3-foot-long pizzas served on wooden planks (calorie counters, fear not; they do come smaller), ossobuco (braised veal shanks), and pheasant that is smoked on the premises and served with a choice of soft, baked, or sautéed polenta (the Italian version of grits). Open weekdays for lunch, daily for dinner. Reservations for lunch only. Major credit cards. 410 W. Huron (phone: 943-5900). Moderate.

Shaw's Crab House – A mammoth, immensely popular pre–World War II–style seafood house. Don't miss the stone or soft-shell crabs if they're in season. The pecan pie may be Chicago's best. Open daily. Reservations for lunch only. Major credit cards. 21 E. Hubbard (phone: 527-2722). Moderate.

La Strada – An Italian restaurant with a reputation for its tableside preparation of such specialties as veal Forestiera, rich with mushrooms and artichokes in wine sauce. Other highlights include eggplant involtini and carpaccio. Closed Sundays. Reservations advised. Major credit cards. 151 N. Michigan (phone: 565-2200). Moderate.

Szechwan House – The hot and sour soup and the crispy duck are just as appetizing as the chef's more unusual dishes, such as snails in spicy sauce and deep-fried ground shrimp wrapped in seaweed. Open daily. Reservations advised. Major credit cards. 600 N. Michigan (phone: 642-3900). Moderate to inexpensive.

Ann Sather's – The original of these two institutions may be the world's only Swedish restaurant in a former funeral home. It is on West Belmont Avenue near other Chicago institutions, such as *Wrigley Field* and the *Steppenwolf Theater*. The menu varies from time-honored Swedish dishes to hearty American fare: pork sausage patties and rich country gravy, beefsteak and eggs with cinnamon rolls. Brunch is particularly good. 929 W. Belmont Ave. (phone: 348-2378) and 5207 N. Clark St. (phone: 271-6677). Inexpensive.

Beau Thai – Lincoln Park's newest addition to the city's fine collection of Southeast Asian restaurants. Specialties include pad thai, a warm noodle dish; duck Beau Thai, cooked with cashews and vegetables; and sweet, creamy cold Thai coffee for dessert. Closed Mondays. Reservations on weekends only. Major credit cards. 2525 N. Clark (phone: 348-6938). Inexpensive.

Berghoff – Another Chicago tradition. Although the service is rushed, the meals are bountiful and the selection wide-ranging: ragout, schnitzel, steaks, and seafood. Closed Sundays. Reservations accepted for 5 or more. Major credit cards. 17 W. Adams (phone: 427-3170). Inexpensive.

Blue Mesa – Southwestern cooking is this city's latest dining craze, and Santa Fe style reigns in this comfortable room of whitewashed adobe and bleached pine. Lovers of wonderfully pulpy guacamole and steaks smothered in green chilies and onions will be quite content. Open daily. Reservations necessary for parties of 8 or more. Major credit cards. 1729 N. Halsted (phone: 944-5990). Inexpensive.

Café Ba-Ba-Reeba! – A boisterous, informal Spanish tapas restaurant/bar with an authentic feel. Dining here involves tossing back dry sherry with bites of hot and cold tapas. The tender squid, stuffed with its own ground meat and crunchy pistachios, is especially good. Open Tuesday through Saturday for lunch, daily for dinner. Reservations for lunch only. Major credit cards. 2024 N. Halsted (phone: 935-5000). Inexpensive.

Carson's – Probably the best spareribs in the city. Salads with a creamy, anchovy-flavored dressing and tangy au gratin potatoes are the other lures. Don't dress up, for bibs (supplied) are essential. Open daily. No reservations, so expect to wait. Major credit cards. 612 N. Wells St. (phone: 280-9200). Inexpensive.

Ed Debevic's – The creation of Rich Melman, king of Chicago restaurateurs — a 1950s diner that has crowds lining up outside. Burgers, chili, malts, fries, and a rollicking *American Graffiti* atmosphere. Open daily. No reservations or credit cards. 640 N. Wells (phone: 664-1707). Inexpensive.

Febo's – A real "old neighborhood" restaurant where the Northern Italian cooking tastes as if it came out of a family kitchen. Try the antipasto, followed by linguine Alfredo, cannelloni, tortellini, or chicken Alfredo in mushrooms and lemon-herb wine sauce. Closed Sundays. Reservations necessary on weekends. Major credit cards. 2501 S. Western (phone: 523-0839). Inexpensive.

Greek Islands – A simple place where you can find thoughtfully prepared dishes such as gyros, squid, lamb, and fresh broiled red snapper. The decor isn't elegant, but the food is delicious. Open daily. Reservations unnecessary. Major credit cards. 200 S. Halsted (phone: 782-9855). Inexpensive.

Hard Rock Café – Yes, Chicago has one, too. The walls of this hip hamburger emporium are covered with an assortment of rock music artifacts and declarations of world peace. Chili and grilled burgers lead the menu. Wash it all down with a fruit and honey "health shake." At the very least, a good addition to any trendy T-shirt collection. Open daily. No reservations. Major credit cards. 63 W. Ontario (phone: 943-2252). Inexpensive.

Jerome's – The room is warmly decorated and the service draws little complaint, but the food is the real attraction. In addition to a regular selection of meat, poultry, and fish, the kitchen turns out fresh bread and desserts and six to eight special dishes every day. Open daily. Reservations advised. Major credit cards. 2450 N. Clark (phone: 327-2207). Inexpensive.

CINCINNATI

Since most travelers seem to know little about Ohio's geography, it's worth stating that Cincinnati is not Cleveland. Cleveland is in the north, on Lake Erie. Cincinnati sits snugly in a basin of the north bank of the Ohio River, in the southwestern corner of the state, surrounded by tree-lined hills festooned with stately homes, on the border of Kentucky. Although resolutely businesslike and the headquarters of an unusually large number of well-known companies for a city its size (1.7 million people in the metropolitan area), Cincinnati is not as industrial as the cities of northern Ohio.

Originally called Losantiville, Cincinnati was founded in 1788 and was renamed in honor of the Society of the Cincinnati in 1790 by General Arthur St. Clair, who happened to be passing through as the new governor of the Northwest Territory. "Losantiville!" he reportedly exclaimed. "What an awful name." The rest, as they say, is history.

Like river cities everywhere, Cincinnati has a lusty past. Soldiers were dispatched to protect its earliest settlers from the Indians, but the settlers soon came to fear the soldiers more than the Indians. William Henry Harrison visited not long before he became president and pronounced it "the most debauched place I ever saw." As late as 1901, Carrie Nation arrived on a temperance crusade, but failed to smash a single saloon window. "I would have dropped from exhaustion before I had gone a block," she told curious reporters. But, in succeeding years, seemliness somehow got the upper hand and lust was banished.

Longfellow called it the "Queen City of the West," and Winston Churchill said it was "the most beautiful of America's inland cities." In 1976, the *Saturday Review* called Cincinnati "one of the five most livable cities in the United States." Why the accolades? For one thing, Cincinnati's downtown is congenially vibrant, alive during the day and night. This is partly the result of substantial, continuing investment by the business community in an effort to stave off urban decay, the common enemy of cities. Leisure-conscious Cincinnati residents enjoy music, art, good food, and sports. Many are active volunteers on civic projects. In the center of town is 20th-century Fountain Square, which surrounds the majestic 19th-century Tyler-Davidson Fountain. Modern office buildings and ground-level shops line Fountain Square on the north and east. Across the street, Fountain Square South, one of the city's most ambitious private projects, is a high-rise complex that has provided much-needed space for offices, hotels, and shops. The compact downtown area is easy to navigate. Because of its generally uncrowded streets and the 16-block-square Skywalk that connects many buildings, downtown Cincinnati can be easily explored on foot. Innumerable small restaurants, bars, and fast-food establishments exist to succor the footweary. Also within easy walking distance from downtown are *Riverfront Stadium* (home of the Cincinnati

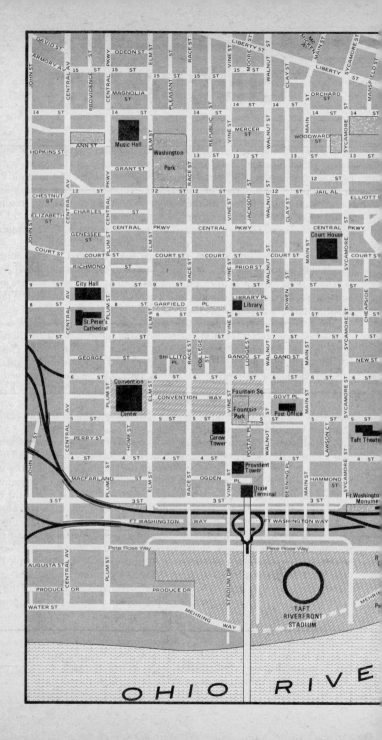

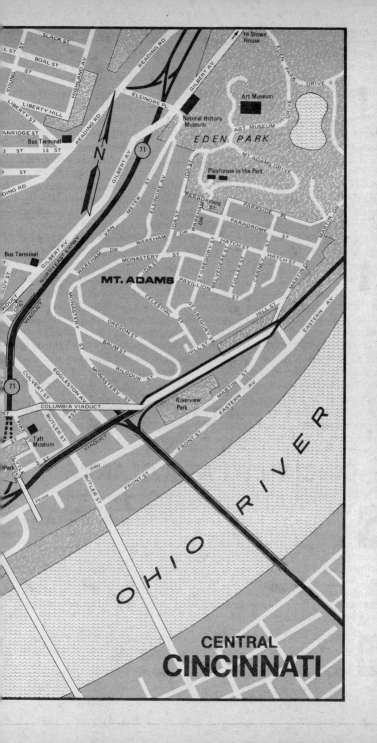

CENTRAL
CINCINNATI

Reds baseball team and the NFL *Bengals*) and *Riverfront Coliseum* (host to circuses, ice shows, rock concerts, and University of Cincinnati basketball).

Some 370,000 of the Cincinnati area's residents live in the city, many on the hillsides that ring the business district. Mt. Adams, to the northeast, and Clifton, directly north, are especially interesting. Mt. Adams is to Cincinnati what Greenwich Village and SoHo are to New York and Georgetown is to Washington: Bohemia at a price. Its slopes are covered by new and restored row houses, shops, and restaurants. Just north of Mt. Adams is Eden Park, where the *Cincinnati Art Museum, Museum of Natural History,* and *Playhouse in the Park* are found. Clifton is the site of the 36,000-student University of Cincinnati, a campus set in a residential district of baronial homes and interesting shops. Between Mt. Adams and Clifton, Mt. Auburn is undergoing extensive restoration in an effort to recapture some of the area's previous grandeur. Cincinnati residents are justifiably proud, too, of the superb *Cincinnati Symphony, Opera Company,* and *Cincinnati Ballet,* all housed in the historic *Music Hall.* The university's *College Conservatory of Music* also offers impressive musical programs.

Cincinnati people are friendly but reserved, sedately satisfied with their lives. Although there are many excellent, expensive shops in the downtown, Hyde Park, and Kenwood areas, "fashionably dressed" in Cincinnati is conservative by many other big-city standards. There are a few colloquialisms exclusive to Cincinnati. For instance, the expressions "three-way" and "four-way" do not refer to traffic signs; they refer to toppings that embellish the chili unique to the city. "Please" is used to indicate that the listener did not understand a question and would like to have it repeated or clarified. "Square" is used interchangeably with "block" when describing directions or distances, as in *"Lazarus's* is three squares north of *L. S. Ayre's."* A "pony keg" is a convenience store, mostly for the dispensing of beer for off-premises consumption. Although newcomers or visitors may say "Cincinnata," the pronunciation used by Cincinnatians is "Cincinnati."

CINCINNATI AT-A-GLANCE

SEEING THE CITY: For the best view of Cincinnati, go to the top of the Carew Tower. You may see the original seven hills on which the town is said to have been built. Admission charge. Children under 6 free. Groups of 20 or more get in for half price but must call at least 1 week in advance. 5th and Vine Sts. (phone: 381-3448).

Another popular way to see the city is by riverboat. *BB Riverboats'* vessels are available for 1- to 2-hour sightseeing, luncheon, dinner, and moonlight cruises, or daylong adventures. They are moored at the foot of Greenup St., Covington, Kentucky (just across the river from Cincinnati; phone 606-261-8500). Or try *Barleycorn's Riverboats,* Ludlow, Kentucky (phone: 606-581-0300).

SPECIAL PLACES: Pedestrians can traverse the city above the traffic via a covered Skywalk system that is totally covered. In many areas, it is enclosed and climate-controlled.

Cincinnati Art Museum – This outstanding collection of paintings, sculpture, prints, and decorative arts fills more than 118 galleries and exhibition rooms (with an exceptionally fine section on ancient Persia). Ancient musical instruments, costumes, and textiles are also on view. Closed Mondays and holidays. Admission charge except on Saturdays. Eden Park (phone: 721-5204).

Natural History Museum – The cavern and waterfall display here is the largest of its kind in the world. A wilderness trail features animals in their natural habitat. An Indian exhibition depicts early Ohio Indian life in life-size dioramas. Next door is the Planetarium. Closed Mondays. Admission charge. In 1991, the museum, along with the Cincinnati Historical Society, will move into Union Terminal, which will be renamed the *Museum Center at Union Terminal*. The current address is 1720 Gilbert Ave. (phone: 621-3889).

Harriet Beecher Stowe House – The author of *Uncle Tom's Cabin* resided here for 4 years. In addition to a collection of Stowe memorabilia, the house has a number of exhibitions on black history. Open Tuesdays through Thursdays, 10 AM to 4 PM. No admission charge. 2950 Gilbert Ave. (phone: 632-5120).

Taft Museum – William Howard Taft used this house, the home of his older half brother, for formal occasions during his presidency. Once nicknamed "the Little White House," it is now a museum of paintings, Chinese porcelain, and Duncan Phyfe furniture. Portraits and landscapes by Rembrandt, Turner, Goya, Gainsborough, and Corot line the walls. Open daily. Contributions requested. 316 Pike (phone: 241-0343).

Riverfront Stadium – Cincinnati is the self-proclaimed baseball capital of the world, and sports fans will enjoy touring the dugouts and back rooms of this 60,000-seat, artificial turf stadium. Tours by appointment during baseball season. Admission charge. 201 E. Pete Rose Way (phone: 352-6333).

Contemporary Arts Center – "What is art?" is a puzzler as old as the Cincinnati hills, and the *Contemporary Arts Center* keeps many people in this good city wondering. Not only are there constantly changing modern paintings and sculpture, the center features multimedia exhibits aimed at dazzling the mind, the eye, and the mind's eye. Closed Sundays. Admission charge except on Mondays. 115 E. 5th St. (phone: 721-0390).

Cincinnati Fire Museum – All kinds of old fire engines and paraphernalia in a 1907 firehouse listed on the National Register of Historic Places. Closed Mondays and holidays. Children under 3 free. 315 W. Court St. (phone: 621-5553).

Cincinnati Zoo – The second oldest zoo in the nation, known for its expertise in the propagation of rare and endangered species. There are more than 6,000 animals here. The most popular exhibits are the rare white Bengal tigers, the Bird of Prey Flight Cage, Outdoor Gorilla Exhibit, Children's Zoo, Insectarium, and the new Cat House. Open daily. Admission charge. 3400 Vine St. (phone: 281-4700).

College Football Hall of Fame – A new collection of memorabilia of college football greats. The emphasis is on audio-visual displays and entertainment, including films and computerized information banks. Open daily April through December, except on Thanksgiving, Christmas, and New Year's Day; open weekends off-season. Admission charge. Minutes from *Kings Island Theme Park* complex on I-71, 20 miles north of the city (phone: 398-5410).

Sharon Woods Village – Life in 19th-century Ohio, with a representative group of pre-1880 buildings in a village setting. Open Wednesdays through Sundays, May through October and during the post-Thanksgiving and pre-Christmas holidays. Admission charge. Sharon Woods, off Rte. 42 (phone: 563-9484).

Vent Haven Museum – This unique, entertaining museum across the state border in Kentucky has the largest known collection of ventriloquists' material in the world, including about 500 puppets. The owner also has an extensive collection of books in eight languages dating to the 18th century, but this private library is unfortunately not open to the public. The museum is open from May through September on weekdays, but call at least 2 weeks in advance. Maximum of 40 people per tour; no minimum. Admission charge. 33 W. Maple Ave., Fort Mitchell, KY (phone: 606 341-0461).

Krohn Conservatory – One of the largest public greenhouses in the world, it contains 1,500 labeled specimens of tropical plants and seasonal flowers. Displays change six times a year. Open daily from 10 AM to 5 PM, with extended hours during Christmas and Easter seasons. Voluntary admission charge. Eden Park (phone: 352-4086).

■**EXTRA SPECIAL:** Just 25 miles north of Cincinnati is small-town America at its best. Lebanon, Ohio — where the movie *Harper Valley PTA* was shot — is the home of the *Golden Lamb Inn,* Ohio's oldest operating inn, now also a Shaker museum and a first-rate restaurant (phone: 621-8373). While in Lebanon, visit the *Warren County Historical Society Museum* (phone: 932-1817), which also has a major Shaker collection.

Just a couple of hours south of Cincinnati lies the best horse-breeding region in the US — Kentucky bluegrass country. The drive on I-71/75 takes you through very green rolling hills and beautiful breeding farms. Stop for lunch (except Mondays) or dinner (first seating is at 6 PM) at the relaxing *Beaumont Inn,* just west of Lexington, Kentucky, in Harrodsburg. Reservations recommended. Open mid-March through mid-December (phone: 606-734-3381).

SOURCES AND RESOURCES

TOURIST INFORMATION: For maps and brochures, write or visit the Greater Cincinnati Convention and Visitors Bureau, 300 W 6th St., Cincinnati, OH 45202 (phone: 513-621-2142). It can also provide self-guided walking tour maps.

The best guide to events and places of interest is *Cincinnati* magazine, monthly, available at newsstands.

Television Stations – WCPO Channel 9–CBS; WKRC Channel 12–ABC; WLWT Channel 5–NBC; WCET Channel 48–PBS.

Radio Stations – AM: WLW 700 (sports/talk); WKRC 550 (adult contemporary/sports); WCKY 1530 (talk). FM: WRRM 98 (adult contemporary); WWEZ 92.5 (easy listening); WUBE 105 (country); WGUC 90.9 (classical).

Local Coverage – *Cincinnati Enquirer,* morning daily and Sundays; *Cincinnati Post,* afternoon daily.

Food – *Cincinnati* magazine's annual restaurant guide, available from the Chamber of Commerce, gives the best information on where to dine. The *Cincinnati Enquirer, Post,* and the city magazine feature occasional restaurant columns and guides, too.

Telephone – The area code for Cincinnati is 513.

Sales Tax – Cincinnati sales tax is 5½%.

CLIMATE: Cincinnati has four distinct seasons. Crisp winter temperatures average 31F, and summer temperatures average 75.6F. Blossomy springs and blazing falls, however, are more amenable, and a drive through the surrounding countryside in either season is a joy. Keep raingear handy in the spring and fall.

GETTING AROUND: Airport – Greater Cincinnati International Airport is about 13 miles southwest of the city in Kentucky. A trip to the airport by cab takes from 20 to 30 minutes and should cost around $20 for 1 to 5 passengers. *Jet Port Express* (phone: 606-283-3702) provides both bus and limo transportation between the airport and Cincinnati's leading hotels. Buses shuttle between the airport and downtown hotels every half hour (every hour on Saturdays) and the fare is $8 one way or $12 round trip.

Bus – Queen City Metro operates an excellent bus service. The bus stop signs carry numbers of the routes that stop there. Route maps are available from Queen City Metro, 6 E. 4th St. (phone: 621-4455).

Taxi – Call *Yellow Cab,* 1110 Kenner St. (phone: 241-2100), or go to any of the major hotels, where cabs line up.

Car Rental – Major car rental agencies are represented at the Greater Cincinnati International Airport.

Horse-drawn Carriages – Four companies operate nonmotorized transport in the Fountain Square area. Rates vary with the carriage and route. Board carriages at Fountain Square.

LOCAL SERVICES: Babysitting – *Rock-a-Bye Sitters Registry,* 432 Walnut St. (phone: 721-7440).

   Business Services – *Secretarial Office Services,* Provident Bank Bldg. (phone: 651-1161) and *Carew Tower* (phone: 381-2277).

Mechanic – *Certified Car Care,* 413 Liberty St., between Central Ave. and John St. (phone: 721-2886).

MUSEUMS: Cincinnati's major museums — *Cincinnati Art Museum, Natural History Museum, Taft Museum, Contemporary Arts Center, the Cincinnati Fire Museum,* and *Vent Haven Museum* — are described in detail under *Special Places.*

MAJOR COLLEGES AND UNIVERSITIES: The University of Cincinnati, Clifton (phone: 475-8000), has 36,000 students. Other notable schools are Xavier University, 3800 Victory Pkwy. (phone: 745-3000); the College of Mount St. Joseph, 5701 Delhi Rd. (phone: 244-4200); and the Art Academy of Cincinnati, Eden Park, (phone: 721-5205).

SPECIAL EVENTS: Ever since 1873, Cincinnati has been holding its annual *May Festival,* a series of choral and instrumental musical concerts at Music Hall, 1243 Elm (phone: 381-3300). In June, the *Ladies' PGA Championship* is held at *Kings Island* theme park, *Jack Nicklaus Sports Center,* 3565 Kings Mills Rd. (phone: 398-5200). In August, the *ATP Tournament* is held annually at the *Jack Nicklaus Sports Center.* In mid-September, Cincinnati celebrates its German heritage with an *Oktoberfest,* along the lines of the famous Munich festival, in and around Fountain Square.

SPORTS AND FITNESS: Not only is Cincinnati one of the country's most enthusiastic baseball cities, it also has an NFL team, the *Bengals. Riverfront Stadium* is easily accessible to downtown.

   Baseball – Cincinnati *Reds* (phone: 421-4510) play at *Riverfront Stadium* (phone: 421-7337).

Basketball – University of Cincinnati (phone: 556-5847); and Xavier University (745-3418).

Bicycling – There is a 6.2-mile (10-km) bike trail at *Airport Playfield,* Lunken Airport, Wilmer Ave. (phone: 321-6500). Call to see if rental bikes are available in summer months.

Fishing – There's moderately good fishing at Lake Isabella, Winton Woods (the largest of the county lakes), and in the Ohio River. Serious Cincinnati sportfishers drive 4 hours to Lake Cumberland and Kentucky Lake in southern Kentucky.

Fitness Center – The *YMCA* provides a pool, sauna, equipment, and a track, as well as an outdoor jogging map. 1105 Elm St. (phone: 241-5348).

Football – The *Bengals* play at *Riverfront Stadium* (phone: 621-3550).

Golf – For spectators and golfers, the *Jack Nicklaus Sports Center,* 3565 Kings Mills Rd. (phone: 398-5200), is among the best. Also consider the *Glenview* and *Neumann* city courses or county links in Winton Woods and Sharon Woods Parks.

Horse Racing – Enthusiasts should check out the action at *River Downs,* 6301 Kellogg Ave. (phone: 232-8000), and *Turfway Racecourse,* 7500 Turfway Rd., Florence, KY (phone: 371-0200).

Jogging – For a 6-mile jaunt, follow tree-lined Central Parkway to Ludlow Street and come back; or run back and forth across the Ohio River Suspension Bridge, designed by Brooklyn Bridge builder John A. Roebling. The Cincinnati Recreation Commission publishes a free brochure, *Healthline Fitness Course,* available at the Convention and Visitors Bureau.

Swimming – A good public pool is Sunlite Pool at Coney Island just before River Downs on Rte. 50 (phone: 232-8230). Call first to make sure it's open. There are lake beaches at nearby Hueston Woods in Butler County and Caesar's Creek in Warren County.

 THEATER: Cincinnati has two major theaters. The *Taft* features touring companies, and has a spring, fall, and winter season, 5th and Sycamore (phone: 721-0411). *Playhouse in the Park* is a professional regional theater specializing in modern American and European plays and stages several musicals during the summer. Mt. Adams Circle, Eden Park (phone: 421-3888). The University of Cincinnati produces plays during the spring, summer, and fall on its *Showboat Majestic,* moored downtown (phone: 556-4183).

 MUSIC: The internationally famous *Cincinnati Symphony Orchestra,* founded in 1895, has a September-May season at *Music Hall,* 1243 Elm (phone: 381-3300); its summer home is the *Riverbend Music Center,* 6295 Kellogg Ave. (phone: 232-5882). The *College Conservatory of Music* is one of the nation's oldest and most prominent professional music schools, on the University of Cincinnati campus, Clifton and Calhoun (phone: 556-6638). The *Cincinnati Opera,* the second oldest opera company in the US, performs at the downtown *Music Hall,* as does the *Cincinnati Ballet,* whose performance of *The Nutcracker* each December adds to Cincinnati's holiday tradition. *Music Hall,* 1243 Elm St. (phone: 621-5219).

 NIGHTCLUBS AND NIGHTLIFE: Cincinnati is pretty much a couples' town. The most popular nightspots are *Caddy's* (phone: 651-4446), *Flanagan's Landing* (phone: 421-4055), *January's* (phone: 241-7700), and *Club Paradise* (phone: 241-3088); all are on West Pete Rose Way. Just across the Ohio River, on the Kentucky riverfront, are *Barleycorn's* (phone: 606-291-8504), *Crockett's* (phone: 606-581-2800), *Newport Beach* (phone: 606-581-9000), and the *Waterfront* (phone: 606-581-1414). Cincinnati hotel bars that swing into the wee hours: *Joe's Bar* (*Terrace Hilton*), *Fifth and Vine Street Bar* (*Westin*), *Champs* (*Hyatt*), *Palm Court* (*Netherland*), *Top of the Crown* (*Clarion*), and the *Cricket* (*Cincinnatian*). There are also numerous nightspots atop Mt. Adams.

BEST IN TOWN

CHECKING IN: During the past decade, the Cincinnati hotel scene has dramatically improved, and accommodations now rival those of any comparable US city. Expect to pay between $100 and $195 for a double at any hotel listed as expensive; $70 to $100 at any in the moderate category. For bed-and-breakfast lodging, contact: *Ohio Valley Bed and Breakfast,* 6876 Taylor Mill Rd., Independence, KY 41051 (phone: 356-7865). All telephone numbers are in the 513 area code unless otherwise indicated.

Cincinnatian – This restored hundred-year-old landmark, reopened in early 1987, provides European-style elegance that has earned it a reputation as the city's premier hotel. There are 147 well-appointed rooms, some with balconies overlooking the 8-story atrium. Its *Palace* restaurant serves American regional food. One block from Fountain Square. 601 Vine St. (phone: 381-3000). Expensive.

Hyatt Regency – Opened in 1984, it has 485 rooms and 22 suites. *Champs* restaurant features seafood and steaks; *Findlay's* has more casual dining and a country breakfast on weekends.. There's also a complete health club, including a swimming pool. Valet parking. 151 W. 5th St. (phone: 579-1234). Expensive.

Omni Netherland Plaza – One of the finest hotels in the city, after a $30-million total restoration in 1983. Connected by the Skywalk to the Convention Center, with lots of meeting space of its own (capacity for 1,200). In addition to its 621 rooms, suites are available (some are lovely duplexes). Dining can be either formal at *Orchids at the Palm Court* or a bit more casual at the *Café at the Palm Court.* 24-hour room service. 35 W. 5th St. (phone: 421-9100). Expensive.

Terrace Hilton – In addition to 342 rooms and suites, this attractive hotel has several restaurants: the *Gourmet* restaurant on the top floor, the *Terrace Garden* on the 8th floor, and the very popular *Joe's Bar,* an intimate, rustic place on ground level that serves delicious deli sandwiches. 15 W. 6th St. (phone: 381-4000). Expensive.

Westin – Overlooking Fountain Square, this 17-story downtown hotel has 450 rooms and 18 suites. *Delmonico's* restaurant is one of the city's best. Fountain Sq. (phone: 621-7700). Expensive.

Clarion – Corporate executives stay at this very modern, 887-room downtown hotel with a heated outdoor swimming pool, health club, sauna, lounge, restaurant, barber, beauty shop, and valet parking. Panoramic view from the *Top of the Crown* restaurant. 141 W. 6th St. (phone: 352-2100). Moderate.

Holiday Inn, Queensgate – Longtime residents remember this *Holiday Inn* as the one across the street from the former stadium and the old railroad station. It's not in the greatest neighborhood, but if you're looking for a 246-room, functional place to rest your head, this could be it. It has a swimming pool, dining room, bar, and nightclub. 8th and Linn (phone: 241-8660). Moderate.

Kings Island Inn – A favorite of golfers, since it's near the *Jack Nicklaus course,* this Alpine chalet–style hostelry offers good accommodations in an attractive setting. In addition to its 288 rooms with queen-size beds, it has indoor and outdoor pools, playground, tennis courts, gameroom, cocktail lounge with entertainment, dining room, and bus service to Kings Island Theme Park. There's also a new conference center. 5691 Kings Island Dr., Mason (phone: 241-5800). Moderate.

Vernon Manor – A tasteful restoration of a once-faded beauty. Handsome modern decor in the bar, restaurant, and other public space; 166 elegant sleeping rooms; barbershop and flower shop. No pets. 2 miles from downtown, at 400 Oak St. (phone: 281-3300). Moderate.

EATING OUT: Cincinnati's most notable gastronomic eccentricity is its chili, which is usually served over spaghetti, to which may be added cheese ("three-way"), cheese and raw onions ("four-way"), or cheese, raw onions, and beans ("five-way"). Many of the city's finest restaurants are found in its hotels. (See *Best In Town, Checking In*). At our expensive listings, expect to pay at least $50 to $75 for two; between $25 and $50 at those places designated moderate; under $25 at places listed as inexpensive. Prices do not include drinks, wine, or tips. All telephone numbers are in the 513 area code unless otherwise indicated.

Maisonette – It may be in an unlikely spot, but it's one of the best French restaurants in the country. Its cuisine has consistently won major food awards since its opening. The service is friendly and warm. Jacket and tie required. Lunch weekdays; dinner nightly except Sundays. Reservations required. Major credit cards. 114 E. 6th St. (phone: 721-2260). Expensive.

Newport Beach – A glitzy, glass-walled barge moored across the Ohio River from downtown. The food is pricey, the view spectacular. Dinner nightly. 301 Riverboat Row (phone: 581-9000). Expensive.

Pigall's – A rival of *Maisonette*'s, it, too, has won many awards since its debut in 1956. It has its detractors, mainly regarding the service and the wine list, but remains a popular meeting place. Its formal red-gray interior with teardrop chandeliers is reflected in smoked-glass mirrors. Jacket and tie required. Closed Sundays. Reservations required. Major credit cards. 127 W. 4th St. (phone: 721-1345). Expensive.

Restaurant at the Phoenix – Opened in September 1988 in what was once an exclusive turn-of-the-century men's club. Elegant dining in the *President's Dining Room* (the former library) or the spacious, less formal *Chef's Dining Room* (adjoining the glass-walled kitchen, through which diners can watch the food being prepared). Excellent contemporary American menu. Jacket and tie required. Lunch weekdays; dinner Tuesdays through Saturdays. Major credit cards. 812 Race St. (phone: 721-2255). Expensive.

Waterfront – Afloat directly across the Ohio River from downtown Cincinnati, it offers a spectacular skyline view along with its culinary specialties — fresh grilled seafood, a seafood raw bar, a salad bar for lunch daily, and other rotisserie selections. 14 Pete Rose Pier, Covington, KY (phone: 606-581-1414). Expensive.

Forest View Gardens – Waiters and waitresses sing your favorite operatic arias and serve tasty German food in a garden setting. Its *Dining Room/Showplace* is open for dinner only, Thursday through Sunday; reservations necessary. Its *Edelweiss Bier Stube* is open for lunch on weekdays from 11 AM to 2 PM, and for light fare Thursdays through Sundays from 5 to 7 PM; reservations unnecessary. Live entertainment Thursdays through Sundays. Major credit cards. 4508 N. Bend Rd., a 20-minute drive from downtown (phone: 661-6434). Moderate.

Mike Fink – An authentic riverboat, moored on the Kentucky side of the Ohio River, it is famous for its raw bar, in addition to traditional tableside service. Open daily for lunch and dinner. At the foot of Greenup St., Covington, KY (phone: 606-261-4212). Moderate.

La Normandie Taverne and Chop House – Adjacent to the *Maisonette,* this steakhouse is renowned for its chops and fresh seafood. Casual conviviality is its hallmark. Closed Sundays. Major credit cards. 118 E. 6th St. (phone: 721-2761). Moderate.

Precinct – A good choice for an evening of dining and chatting with friends over what some say are the best steaks in town. Other selections include veal, pasta, prime ribs, and fresh seafood. The *Precinct* is also a lively nightspot, with a 2nd-floor disco and a disc jockey playing something for everyone. Open daily for dinner only. Reservations necessary. Major credit cards. 311 Delta Ave. at Columbia Pkwy., 5 minutes from downtown (phone: 321-5454). Moderate.

Izzy's – A unique Cincinnati experience for eight decades, serving world-famous corned beef, potato pancakes, homemade soups, kosher dill pickles, and sauerkraut. The original is at 819 Elm St. — serving lunch only — (phone: 721-4241), with another at 610 Main St. (phone: 241-6246), which is open until 9 PM; both are closed Sundays. Inexpensive.

Rookwood Pottery – Atop Mt. Adams, in the original kilns of the historic Rookwood Pottery building, patrons devour gigantic burgers and overindulge at the do-it-yourself ice cream sundae bar. 1077 Celestial (phone: 721-5456). Inexpensive.

CLEVELAND

If you think there are no more chapters being written in the muscle and toil history of immigrant labor in America — that the story ended several decades ago with a final wave and the third generation — there is a book you should consult with some attention. It is called Cleveland, and you may find it a good deal more compelling than you'd expect.

Cleveland is a working city, and it always has been. Laid out in 1796 with strict attention to order and propriety by the surveyors of the Connecticut Company (led by Moses Cleaveland), its tidy New England pattern of straight streets around a public square was knocked into a cocked hat with the coming of industrialization. Cleveland's location at the confluence of Lake Erie and the Cuyahoga River provided a waterway that stimulated the growth of heavy industry — shipping, steel, iron, and construction. The city sprawled. Famous fortunes got their start. John D. Rockefeller parlayed an oil business into wealth beyond imagining; shipping magnates Sam Mather and Mark Hanna began their rise; the Van Sweringen brothers created a vast railroad and construction empire. But behind all this boom, and most of the money, was the muscle power of a largely immigrant work force that earned little more for its labor than the sweat of its own brow.

The workers have stayed, and so have the industries, and it is the continuing saga of their fortune together that makes Cleveland today something of a bellwether among middle-sized industrial US cities. For one thing, heavy industry is no longer the only game in town. Cleveland is now among the top 15 US cities for major corporate headquarters. Rockefeller's Standard Oil (now BP America) has shown a continuing civic pride by spending $2 million on its headquarters complex on Public Square, part of a $1-billion building surge in Cleveland. Restoration work is booming as well. Tower City is a multimillion-dollar project that includes the Terminal Tower complex and its surrounding riverfront area. Playhouse Square, the largest restoration of its kind in the country, has revived four 1920s theaters, while the restoration of historic buildings in the Flats/Warehouse District has created lofts, shops and cafés. The Nautica riverfront development has brought life to the "left bank" of the Cuyahoga River. Today, Cleveland has a population of 600,000; Cuyahoga County, which includes the greater Cleveland area, a ring of wealthy suburbs, has 1.5 million people. Among the 59 suburbs in the county is Shaker Heights, considered one of the most affluent towns in the country. There, where the Shakers once threw off American industrial life to set up a rural commune, reside the most prosperous industrial and business leaders; it is a haven of sorts still.

But don't think Cleveland is getting effete or being abandoned by its industry. A drive along the Detroit-Superior Bridge over the Flats shouldering the twists and turns of the Cuyahoga River — the steel mills belching flames into the sky, barges plunging up and down the river — shows Cleveland's muscles still flexing.

And that might be why there's something interesting about Cleveland. It's a city of the American Dream, bothered and bewildered, but with much to admire between the fret lines. Ethnocentricity is strong. Sons and daughters of immigrants who gladly took the toughest jobs at the poorest pay own their piece of the suburbs, but the old neighborhoods live on. Little Italy is an East Side enclave; Chinatown is on the fringes of downtown; and Tremont is a mixed ethnic neighborhood where God accepts the worship of a bewildering number of denominations and faiths. When you get right down to it, there's something genuinely American about the crazy-quilt ambience of Cleveland's neighborhoods.

You can buy anything you want in Cleveland, as a matter of fact, because somewhere, someone is selling it. The city has the attributes of a major cosmopolitan center. Besides the revitalized downtown shopping district with its upscale Galleria, there's Coventry Road in Cleveland Heights, which resembles New York's Greenwich Village, and Beachwood Place, a posh shopping mall in the suburb of Beachwood. The *Cleveland Orchestra* is world-renowned, and the *Cleveland Museum of Art* has one of the richest collections in the country.

You might hear along the way that Cleveland isn't the town it used to be, and in many ways it's not. It seems to be redefining and reshaping itself. After having survived industrialization, immigration, exploitation, and every other cultural shock wave to rattle urban America, Cleveland is a city not only still on its feet, but enthusiastic. It's a city where martinis for lunch are beginning to outnumber shots-and-beers at the bar; wing tips are becoming more evident than steel-toed work boots. More people carry briefcases than lunch buckets to work.

What does it all add up to? Cleveland has diversity, history, energy, and a very friendly citizenry. It definitely deserves a close look.

CLEVELAND AT-A-GLANCE

SEEING THE CITY: Stouffer's *Top of the Town* restaurant offers a panoramic view of Cleveland, the downtown, the nearby Galleria, and Lake Erie with its recreation and shipping activity. 100 Erieview Plaza (phone: 771-1600). The Terminal Tower observation deck is open weekends from 11 AM to 3:30 PM and on holidays. Small admission charge. Public Sq. (phone: 621-7981). *Trolley Tours* (phone: 771-4484) conducts city tours daily, April to December. Reservations required.

SPECIAL PLACES: Many of Cleveland's most interesting sights are concentrated in the few areas served by public transportation. You'll want to stroll around, particularly in the University Circle area, which is the cultural heart of Cleveland, and in the lovely suburbs of Shaker Heights and Chagrin Falls.

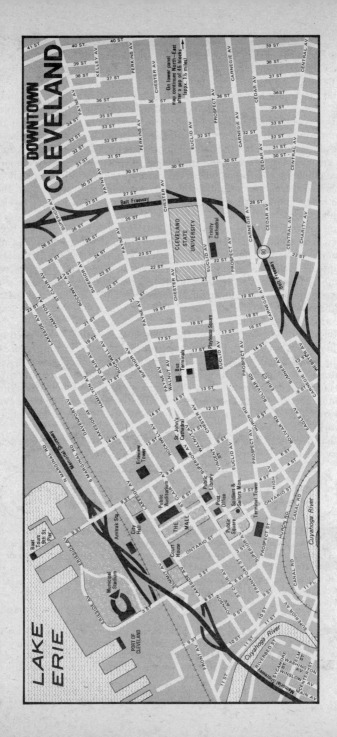

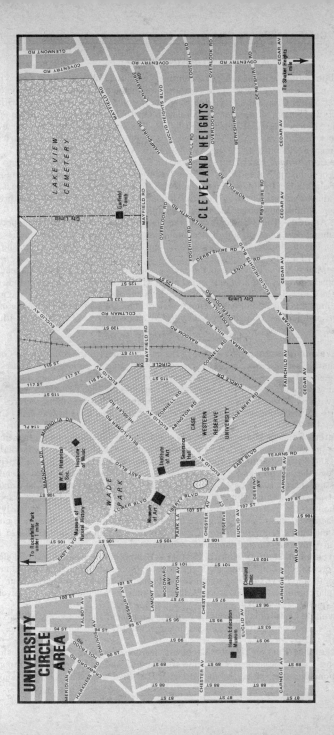

UNIVERSITY CIRCLE AREA

CLEVELAND HEIGHTS

LAKEVIEW CEMETERY

Garfield Tomb

WADE PARK

W.R. Historical Soc.
Institute of Music
Museum of Natural History
Institute of Art
Severance Hall
Museum of Art

CASE WESTERN RESERVE UNIVERSITY

Cleveland Clinic

Health Education Museum

To Rockefeller Park under 1 mile

To Shaker Heights 1 mile

DOWNTOWN

Public Square – In the heart of the business area, the Public Square is a good place to get one's bearings in Cleveland past and present. Statues pay tribute to the city's founder Moses Cleaveland, Tom Johnson, the populist reform mayor, and, with the Soldiers and Sailors Monument, to Cleveland's Civil War dead. Dominating the square are the 52-story Terminal Tower, built by the Van Sweringen brothers on the eve of the stock market crash that leveled their vast empire, and the world headquarters of BP America. Bounded by Euclid Ave., Superior Ave., and Ontario St.

The *Goodtime II* Boat Tour – The tour on the river is the best introduction to "the Flats" or industrial valley along the river basin where Rockefeller and shipping magnates Sam Mather and Mark Hanna made their fortunes. The 500-passenger boat goes down the Cuyahoga as far as the steel mills. Departures daily from May through October. Admission charge. E. 9th St. Pier (phone: 481-5001).

The Arcade – This 19th-century marketplace is a multitiered structure topped by a stunning block-long skylight of steel and glass. Bookstores, boutiques, eateries, and galleries line the arcade. At lunchtime, local musicians offer free classical, pop, and jazz concerts. 401 Euclid Ave. (phone: 621-8500).

The Mall – A spacious rectangular mall is the location of all the government and municipal buildings and a well-designed plaza with a fountain. Buildings include City Hall, the Court House, the Public Library (which has over 3 million volumes and many WPA murals), and Public Auditorium overlooking *Cleveland Stadium,* home of the *Indians* and *Browns.* Bounded by Lakeside Ave., St. Clair Ave., E. 6th and E. 4th Sts.

UNIVERSITY CIRCLE AREA

Cleveland Museum of Art – Among the best museums in the country, this Greek-style marble building contains extensive collections of many periods and cultures; it's particularly strong on the medieval period, Oriental art, and paintings of Masters including Rembrandt, Rubens, and Picasso. Overlooks the Fine Arts Gardens of Wade Park, with its seasonal flower displays. Auditorium features free films, lectures, and concerts. Closed Mondays. No admission charge. 11150 East Blvd. at University Circle (phone: 421-7340).

Western Reserve Historical Society – The largest collection of Shaker memorabilia in the world is here, including inventions such as the clothes pin, the ladderback chair, and various farming implements and furnishings. There's also an extensive genealogical collection and exhibitions on Indians and pioneers. Closed Mondays. Admission charge. 10825 East Blvd. (phone: 721-5722). Associated with the *Crawford Auto Aviation Museum,* with 200 antique autos and old airplanes. Displays trace the evolution of the automobile and describe Cleveland's prominence as an early car manufacturing center. Visitors can see how the old cars are given a new lease on life at the museum's restoration shop. Closed Mondays. Admission charge. 10825 East Blvd. at University Circle (phone: 721-5722).

Cleveland Museum of Natural History – Exhibitions of armored fish and sharks found preserved in Ohio shales, a 70-foot mounted dinosaur, skeletons of mastodon and mammoth, and Lucy, the most complete fossil evidence of early man. The museum also has a planetarium and observatory. Admission charge. Wade Oval Dr. at University Circle (phone: 231-4600).

Cleveland Children's Museum – Features permanent and temporary exhibits that explore science and nature. Admission charge. At 10730 Euclid Ave. (phone: 791-KIDS).

Rockefeller Park – This 296-acre park features the Shakespeare and Cultural Gardens, a series of gardens, landscape architecture, and sculptures representing the 20 nationalities that settled the city. Between East Blvd. and Martin Luther King Jr.

Dr. The City Greenhouse displays include a Japanese Garden, tropical plants, and a Talking Garden (with taped descriptions of plants for blind visitors.) Open daily. No admission charge. 750 E. 88th St. (phone: 664-3103).

EAST SIDE

Cleveland Health Education Museum – A first of its kind, the museum has exhibitions on the workings of the human body and health maintenance. You can see everything here from the walk-through model of a human eye to Juno, the transparent woman, and the inspiring Wonder of New Life display. Admission charge. 8911 Euclid Ave. (phone: 231-5010).

Lakeview Cemetery – The plantings here are beautiful, the view fine, and the company illustrious. Among the natives buried here are President Garfield (you can't miss the monument), Mark Hanna (the US senator), John Hay (secretary of state under McKinley), and John D. Rockefeller (father of the fortune). The Garfield Monument offers a great view of downtown. Open daily, April through November. No admission charge. 12316 Euclid Ave. (phone: 421-2665).

Coventry Road – Cleveland's answer to New York's Greenwich Village. Boutiques and shops offer unique fashions and arts. Sip unusual teas and coffees at *Arabica,* 2785 Euclid Heights Blvd., late at night, or try a sandwich and a milk shake at *Tommy's,* a local institution. 1820 Coventry Rd.

WEST SIDE

West Side Market – One of the largest Old World indoor markets in the country and a historic landmark. Fresh produce, meats, and baked goods are sold year-round on Mondays, Wednesdays, Fridays, and Saturdays. 1979 W. 25th St. at Lorain Ave. (phone: 664-3386).

NASA Lewis Research Center – The NASA complex and its visitors center offer exhibitions, lectures, and films on aeronautics, energy, space travel, and communications. There are also tours of a propulsion systems laboratory and a supersonic wind tunnel. Open daily. No admission charge. 21000 Brookpark Rd. (phone: 267-1187).

SHAKER HEIGHTS

One of the most affluent suburbs in America, Shaker Heights was developed in the early 1900s by brothers O. P. and M. J. Van Sweringen and now houses Cleveland's elite in lovely old homes on wide, winding, tree-lined streets. The area was originally Shaker Lakes, the rural commune established by the 19th-century religious sect that left American industrial life for a religious regime featuring strict celibacy. Today, all that remains of the Shakers is the *Shaker Historical Museum,* with its collection of artifacts (16740 South Park, phone: 921-1201) and the Shaker Cemetery (Lee Rd. at Chagrin Blvd.).

■**EXTRA SPECIAL:** The Pro Football Hall of Fame, in Canton, is 53 miles south of Cleveland on I-77. Inside there are all kinds of mementos of the game and its players — uniforms, helmets, team pictures, a recording of Jim Thorpe's voice, a film on football, and a research library. Open daily. Admission charge. 2121 Harrison Ave. (phone: 456-8207). On the way, you may want to stop at Hale Farm Village, where you'll find homesteads, craft shops, and a working farm typical of those of the Western Reserve between 1825 and 1850. Closed Mondays. Admission charge. 2686 Oak Hill Rd., Bath (phone: 575-9137, Cleveland; 666-3711, Akron). You can also stop in Akron, rubber manufacturing capital of the world, for a tour of the Stan Hywet Hall and Gardens. Completed in 1915 by Frank A. Seiberling, founder of the Goodyear and Seiberling Rubber companies, the building is an excellent example of Tudor revival architecture, and the 65-room house contains original antique furnishings and artworks of the 14th through 18th centuries. The 70 acres of gardens are best in spring, when thousands of tulips bloom. Closed Mondays. Admission charge for house tour. 714 N. Portage Path, Akron (phone: 836-5533).

SOURCES AND RESOURCES

TOURIST INFORMATION: The Cleveland Convention and Visitors Bureau is best for brochures, maps, and other information. 3100 Tower City Center, Cleveland, OH 44113 (phone: 621-4110; for events, 621-8860).

Television Stations – WKYC Channel 3–NBC; WEWS Channel 5–ABC; WJW Channel 8–CBS; WVIZ Channel 25–PBS.

Radio Stations – AM: WWWE 1100 (talk); WERE 1360 (talk). FM: WMMS 100.7 (album rock); WCLV 95.5 (classical).

Local Coverage – *Cleveland Plain Dealer,* morning daily; *Northern Ohio LIVE,* monthly; *Cleveland Magazine,* monthly. All are available at newsstands.

Food – Check the monthly restaurant listings in *Northern Ohio LIVE* and *Cleveland Magazine.*

Telephone – The area code for Cleveland is 216.

Sales Tax – The sales tax in Cleveland is 7%.

CLIMATE: Cleveland has cold and snowy winters that are followed by brief springs that give brief respite from damp winters and humid summers. Fall is generally the most pleasant season, with mild, sunny weather that often extends through November.

GETTING AROUND: Airport – Cleveland Hopkins International Airport is a 20- to 30-minute drive from downtown; taxi fare should run about $15. The Regional Transit Authority's Airport Rapid Transit train runs from the airport to downtown's Terminal Tower in the same amount of time but costs only $1.

Bus – Regional Transit Authority (RTA) serves both downtown and the outlying areas. Complete route and tourist information is available from the downtown office, 615 W. Superior Ave. (phone: 621-9500).

Train – RTA Rapid Transit trains serve the city's east and west sides.

Taxi – Cabs can be hailed in the street in the downtown area around Public Square or ordered on the phone. *Yellow-Zone Cab* (phone: 623-1500) and *AmeriCab* (phone: 881-1111) are the major operators.

Car Rental – Cleveland is served by the major national firms.

LOCAL SERVICES: Babysitting – *Ba-B-Sit Service Enterprises,* 592 Cahoon Rd. (phone: 871-9595).

Business Services – *Kelly Services,* 1111 Superior Ave. (phone: 771-2800).

Mechanic – *Park Auto Repair Co.,* 2163 Hamilton Ave. (phone: 241-7390).

MUSEUMS: The *Cleveland Museum of Art,* the *Western Reserve Historical Society,* the *Cleveland Museum of Natural History,* the *Cleveland Health Education Museum,* and the *Shaker Historical Museum* are all described above in *Special Places.* In the future, visitors will be able to view the memorabilia of the likes of Elvis Presley, Chuck Berry, and Buddy Holly — Cleveland has been chosen as the site of the *Rock 'n' Roll Hall of Fame,* which will be part of the Tower City Development between 2nd and 3rd Sts., downtown.

 MAJOR COLLEGES AND UNIVERSITIES: Cleveland has close to 20 colleges and universities, including Case Western Reserve University (University Circle), one of the nation's leading research institutions (phone: 368-2000); Cleveland State University (downtown) (phone: 687-2000); Baldwin-Wallace College (Berea) (phone: 826-2900); and John Carroll University (University Heights) (phone: 397-1886).

 SPECIAL EVENTS: The *May Show Exhibit* at the *Museum of Art* kicks off spring and summer events, followed by the *All Nations Festival* in June, and the *Budweiser Grand Prix, Annual Rib Burn-Off,* and *Riverfest* on the river, in July. In August, the *Feast of the Assumption* is celebrated in Little Italy. Fall festivities include the *Cleveland Air Show* and *Oktoberfest.*

 SPORTS AND FITNESS: Baseball – The American League's *Indians* play at *Cleveland Municipal Stadium* from April to September. W. 3rd St. and Erieside Ave. (phone: 861-1200).

   Basketball – The *Cavaliers* play at the *Coliseum* from mid-October to early April. I-271 and Rte. 303 (phone: 659-9100).

   Bicycling – You can rent bikes from *U-Rent-Um of America,* 188 Front St. (phone: 234-8546), or *Easy Rider Bicycle Shop,* 3974 E. 131st St. (phone: 752-1748). The Cuyahoga Falls Reservation nearby has good biking trails.

   Fitness Centers – The *13th Street Racquetball Club* has exercise equipment and a track. 1901 E. 13th St. (phone: 696-1365). *One Fitness Center,* 1375 E. 9th St., has a track, a swimming pool, and exercise equipment (phone: 781-5510).

   Football – The *Browns* play pro ball at the *Municipal Stadium* from August to January (phone: 696-3800).

   Golf – Punderson State Park has the best public 18-hole golf course, at Rtes. 44 and 87 (phone: 564-5465).

   Jogging – Run along Euclid Avenue to Public Square and on to the Flats; stop in at *Koening Sporting Goods at the Galleria* (phone: 575-9900). Run at Cleveland State University at Euclid and Prospect.

   Tennis – The best public courts are at Cain Park in Cleveland Heights, Superior Rd. at Lee Rd. (phone: 371-3000).

 THEATER: For current offerings and performance times, check the publications listed above. Cleveland has a variety of theatrical offerings, some locally produced, others traveling shows. Best bets for shows: *Hanna Theatre,* 2067 E. 14th St. (phone: 621-5000), which also features movies and other entertainment; *Cleveland Play House,* 8500 Euclid Ave. (phone: 795-7000); *Karamu House,* 2355 E. 89th St. (phone: 795-7070); *Great Lakes Theater Festival, Ohio Theatre,* 1501 Euclid Ave. (phone: 241-5490); *Eldred Theatre,* Case Western Reserve University campus (phone: 368-2858).

 MUSIC: The *Cleveland Orchestra* performs with noted soloists and guest conductors from October to mid-May in *Severance Hall,* 11001 Euclid Ave. at East Blvd. (phone: 231-1111). From June to September, it plays at *Blossom Music Center,* 1145 W. Steels Corner Rd., Cuyahoga Falls (phone: 566-9330), as do pop and rock bands. Also, the *Cleveland Ballet,* 1 Playhouse Sq. (phone: 621-2260), is a must for dance lovers.

NIGHTCLUBS AND NIGHTLIFE: Favorites are *Peabody's,* for folk or blues, 2140 S. Taylor Rd. (phone: 321-4072); *Club Isabella,* for jazz, 2025 Abington Rd. (phone: 229-1177); and *Aquillon,* a European-style disco at 1575 Merwin (phone: 781-1575).

For big-name entertainment, try the *Front Row Theatre,* 6199 Wilson Mills Rd. in Highland Heights (phone: 449-5000), or the *Play House Square Center,* 1511 Euclid Ave. (phone: 241-6000). The *Cleveland Comedy Club,* 2230 E. 4th St. (phone: 696-9266), is open Wednesdays through Saturdays.

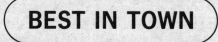

BEST IN TOWN

 CHECKING IN: Cleveland has many accommodations that are attractive, comfortable, and reasonably priced. In addition to the usual chains, there is an assortment of modern, locally owned hotels. Our selections range in price from $85 or more for a double room in the expensive category, $50 to $80 in the moderate range, and under $45 in the inexpensive list. A company called *Private Lodgings,* PO Box 18590, Cleveland, OH 44118 (phone: 321-3213), finds private residences in a variety of price ranges for those who'd rather not stay at a hotel. All telephone numbers are in the 216 area code unless otherwise indicated.

Bond Court – With a 22-story tower commanding a good view of Lake Erie, this luxury hotel is near the convention center. The attentive service includes indoor parking, coffee shop, lounge with entertainment, color TV sets, and a pleasant dining room. 526 rooms. 777 St. Clair Ave. (phone: 771-7600). Expensive.

Marriott Inn – Near the airport, Cleveland's best motor inn. Its many recreational features include an indoor pool, therapy pool, sauna, miniature golf, putting green, volleyball, badminton. Also has free airport bus, lounge with entertainment, color TV sets, coffee shop, 2 dining rooms. 400 rooms. 4277 W. 150th St. (phone: 252-5333 or 800-228-9290). Expensive.

Stouffer Tower City Plaza – Always a surprise to guests, since its look and feel are so unlike most other members of this chain. Special feature: a 10-story atrium complete with waterfall and swimming pool. There are 493 rooms and luxury suites, and 3 eating facilities; very good Sunday brunch. 24 Public Square (phone: 696-5600, 800-325-5000, or 800-HOTELS-1). Expensive.

Clinic Center – This modern 358-room high-rise is near the famous Cleveland Clinic. Features include foreign-language interpreters, color TV sets, a coffee shop, bistro, and an exquisite dining room. E. 96th St. and Carnegie Ave. (phone: 791-1900). Expensive to moderate.

Harley West – Close to the airport, this 235-room hostelry also has in- and outdoor swimming pools, sauna, basketball, and free airport limousine service. 17000 Bagley Rd., near I-71 (phone: 243-5200 or 800-321-2323). Moderate.

Holiday Inn, Lakeside City Center – A downtown high-rise overlooking Lake Erie and close to the stadium and Galleria. It has 400 rooms and features a pool, sauna, exercise room, 2 restaurants, a café and cocktail lounge, free parking, and airport shuttle. Special services for Executive Floor guests. 1111 Lakeside Ave. (phone: 241-5100 or 800-HOLIDAY). Moderate.

Alcazar – A European-style residential property nestled in the trendy Cedar Hill area, 4 miles east of downtown. The 110 rooms and 180 suites are available for overnight, weekly, and monthly stays. Features also include a full-service restaurant, heated garage, beauty salon, and laundromat. Surrey and Derbyshire Rds., Cleveland Heights (phone: 321-5400). Inexpensive.

EATING OUT: Cleveland caters to the taste of more than 100 different nationalities that have distinctive old country recipes and appetites. Restaurants reflect this background with fine ethnic cuisine and a wide range of styles: haute cuisine in shimmering elegance to solid hamburgers in a casual atmosphere. Our selections range in price from $60 or more for a dinner for two in the expensive range, $30 to $60 in the moderate, and $30 or less in the inexpensive range. Prices do not include drinks, wine, or tips. All telephone numbers are in the 216 area code unless otherwise indicated.

Giovanni's – Pasta is prepared in delectable ways; the veal and sweetbreads are equally satisfying. The decor is quite elegant, so dress accordingly. Closed Sundays. Reservations required. Major credit cards. 2550 Chagrin Blvd., Beachwood (phone: 831-8625). Expensive.

Z Contemporary Cuisine – Delectable West Coast–inspired fare, emphasizing grilled meats and fish. A house specialty is grilled chicken breast and skinny fried potatoes. Salads, pasta, and rich desserts are also worthwhile. Closed Sundays. Reservations necessary. Major credit cards. 20600 Chagrin Blvd., Shaker Heights (phone: 991-1580). Expensive.

Hyde Park Grille – The place for hearty meat eaters. Choose from tender steaks, filet mignon with king crab and béarnaise sauce, or an elegantly presented chateaubriand for two. All steaks are served with delicate deep-fried onion crisps. Dark green upholsltery and dark paneling complete the clubhouse atmosphere. Open daily. Reservations advised. Major credit cards. 1825 Coventry Rd., Cleveland Heights (phone: 321-6444). Expensive to moderate.

Lopez y Gonzalez – Hearty portions of all-time Mexican favorites — *tacos al carbón,* for example — are washed down with a glass of Mexican beer or, better still, an oversize margarita. Mesquite-smoked game hen and duck and fresh fish dishes round out the menu. Closed Sundays. Major credit cards. 2066 Lee Rd., Cleveland Heights (phone: 371-7611). Moderate.

Pearl of the Orient – Chinese cuisine carefully presented, particularly the house specialty, Peking duck; also worth noting is the hot and sour soup. Open daily. Reservations necessary. Major credit cards. 20121 Van Aken Blvd., Shaker Heights (phone: 751-8181). Moderate.

Shujiro – Japanese simplicity is the keynote here, as demonstrated by such dishes as a delicate shrimp tempura and the house specialty, scampi. Sushi is also popular. Open daily. Reservations advised. Major credit cards. 2206 Lee Rd., Cleveland Heights (phone: 321-0210). Moderate.

Café Brio – Fresh California-style food blends perfectly with an open, airy decor. Make a meal of the raw bar and appetizers or enjoy an excellent Ceasar salad, southwestern pizza, grilled chicken breast, or the house specialty, linguine with pesto and pine nuts. Nice selection of international wines. Open daily. Reservations advised. Major credit cards. 5433 Mayfield Rd., Lyndhurst (phone: 473-1670). Moderate.

That Place on Bellflower – Set in a charming century-old carriage house, this is the fleur-de-lis of Cleveland's French restaurants. Specialties are veal Oscar and fresh salmon renaissance. In the summer, dining is alfresco. Closed Sundays. Reservations advised. Major credit cards. 11401 Bellflower Rd., at University Circle (phone: 231-4469). Moderate.

Mad Greek – Moussaka, pastitsio, shish kabob, and Greek wine and liqueurs. Rustic inn atmosphere, with dining in the courtyard, weather permitting. Open daily. No reservations. Major credit cards. Cedar Rd. at Fairmont Blvd. (phone: 421-3333). Moderate to inexpensive.

Noggins – The eclectic menu includes homemade pasta and fresh seafood; good wines. Open daily. Major credit cards. 20110 Van Aken Blvd., Shaker Heights (phone: 752-9280). Moderate to inexpensive.

Balaton – The atmosphere isn't much — bright lights and paper placemats — but the Hungarian food is the real thing. Specialties include homemade soups and strudel, dumplings, and Wiener schnitzel. No alcoholic beverages. Closed Sundays and Mondays. No reservations. No credit cards. 12523 Buckeye Rd. (phone: 921-9691). Inexpensive.

Corky & Lenny's – With a name like this, it could only be a deli, and it is. Cleveland residents claim that it's the best kosher-style deli outside New York City. Has the standard deli fare and plenty of the hustle-bustle as well. No reservations. No credit cards. 13937 Cedar Rd., University Heights (phone: 321-3310). Inexpensive.

Miracles – A friendly, simple neighborhood eatery, with fast service and good food. The eclectic menu ranges from Central European kielbasa and potato pancakes to Middle Eastern fare and hearty, unusual soups. The frozen vanilla custard is a must. Closed Mondays. Reservations advised. Major credit cards. 2391 W. 11th St. (phone: 621-6419). Inexpensive.

DALLAS

Dallas is a paradox — both big city and small town. Gleaming glass monstrosities appear to rise daily in the downtown area, but Dallasites are just down-home good ol' boys at heart.

That is, if you can find a native Texan to talk to. Migration from the northern climes (with such major corporations as American Airlines relocating in the city) has doubled Dallas's population in 10 years. In less than 140 years, it has grown from a cabin on the banks of the Trinity River to a metropolitan area of almost 2 million (counting neighboring Ft. Worth and surrounding suburbs). If Texas were a nation, Dallas would be its capital. More controversial is just how Texan it is; some residents claim it is quintessential Texas — the epitome of bigness and wealth. That claim has gained the city some enmity from other parts of Texas.

A few statistics: Dallas has more Cadillacs per capita than any major city outside the Arab world. Its gross annual sales exceed $2.5 billion, and its airport is larger than the island of Manhattan. These facts point to one thing: extraordinary wealth. Where does it come from? Oil, cotton, electronics, furniture, clothing, and insurance. It is this wealth, more than any other single factor, which determines what might be called the Dallas lifestyle. Historically, money was used to entice the railroads into the city. Today, it pays for glass skyscrapers that shine golden in the setting, rush-hour sun. It also stimulates leisure businesses, like discos and restaurants. At its best, the wealth has generated a number of progressive civic programs to improve the general quality of life. At its worst, it has led to a tasteless extravagance and a preoccupation with power and influence.

But there are indications that the traditional ostentation and preoccupation with wealth may be waning. The profligacy so long associated with Dallas has been tempered by the reality of the recent decline in oil prices, the downslide in local real estate values, bank failures (more than 100 Texas banks failed in 1988), and the general softness in the cattle business. The preeminence of business in Dallas political life was given a final jolt in April 1987, when a nonbusiness candidate — and a woman, no less — beat the business council's candidate for mayor. It was the first loss of power that Dallas business leaders had suffered in years.

In 1940, an unpublished book written as part of the Texas Writers' Project (for the WPA) described the typical Dallas resident as someone who "wants the latest fashions from Fifth Avenue, Bond Street, and Rue de la Paix; the newest models in cars; and the best in functionally constructed, electrified, air conditioned homes, but prefers old-time religions with comfortable, modern trimmings and old-fashioned Jeffersonian democracy." If that picture is a touch too complacent to represent contemporary residents fairly, it nonethe-

CENTRAL
DALLAS

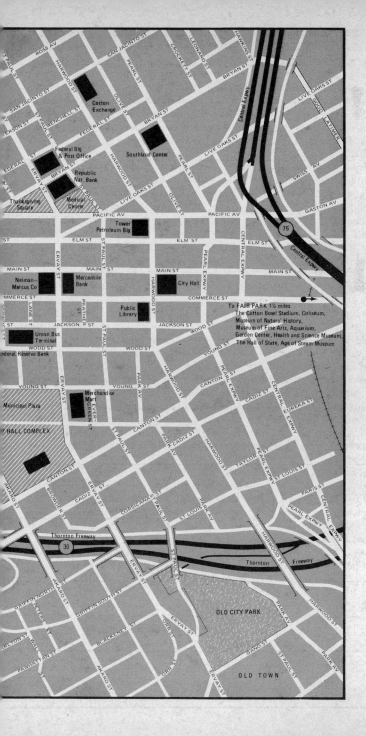

less hits close to home. Dallas residents do have a fine sense of the good life, pursue it actively — and often achieve it.

There is a dark side to the dream, and though its impact diminishes year by year, it will not disappear. To millions of people throughout the world, Dallas is the city where President John F. Kennedy was killed on a November day in 1963. Memphis and Los Angeles bear no equivalent stigma for similar tragedies — the assassinations of Martin Luther King, Jr., and Robert Kennedy. But politically conservative, laissez-faire Dallas still suffers. Until recently, the mention of Dallas in any city outside Texas brought an automatic response of "Kennedy" or "assassination."

Nowadays, the image of Dallas the city is as likely to be drawn from the "Dallas" television series. It is one that, however unflattering, Dallasites prefer, and Southfork has become at least as popular among visitors as the Texas School Book Depository, where Lee Harvey Oswald allegedly took aim.

Dallas was founded in 1841 by a Tennessee lawyer named John Neely Bryan, who built a cabin at the junction of three forks of the La Santissima Trinidad River (the Most Holy Trinity) and then set about building it into a city with circulars and much enthusiastic word-of-mouth advertising. Within 9 years, 430 people had joined him. In later years he was committed to an insane asylum — not, it should be said, for his part in the Dallas venture, though putting a city in such a flat, arid, landlocked place might have been used as evidence. But it worked. With the help of a lot of oil, cattle, manufacturing, and several fortuitous technological revolutions, Dallas has become the seventh largest city in the country.

That is not to say that all is perfect with the world beneath the Dallas sun. Unemployment is low, but those without work are just as unemployed as those in high unemployment areas. The rate of crime is high enough to worry anybody but the criminally intent, and city politics are still, for some, a gentleman's diversion. The Dallas County commissioners, by contrast, are viewed as ruffians because they comport themselves with the bellicosity and street savvy of Chicago aldermen.

Significantly, Dallas has never had the kind of racial turmoil other cities have suffered, and when the school desegregation plan was implemented here in 1976 there were few problems. But the racial tensions and separations that exist elsewhere exist here, too. They smolder and steam on street corners of this city's south side, and they are a cold undercurrent flowing beneath the manicured lawns of affluent white Dallas.

Perhaps, in all, it is not so surprising to discover that, at the heart of the bluff self-promotion that is so typically Texan and such standard Dallas-ese, there is a reflective reticence about the real nature of the city. Dallas is Texan,. no doubt (the rest of the country can see that even if Texans can't agree); it is certainly American — in the problems it shares and the successes it enjoys and the future it mulls over. But the sum of these things does not quite equal the parts of the city itself. And it is this intangible "more" that fascinates residents — and keeps them thoughtfully silent.

DALLAS AT-A-GLANCE

 SEEING THE CITY: For the best view of Dallas, go to the *Hyatt Regency Tower* with its revolving cocktail lounge, restaurant, and observation deck. Admission charge. 400 S. Houston St. (phone: 651-1234).

 SPECIAL PLACES: Although attractions in Dallas are spread out, the museums are clustered together at Fair Park. Several amusement park complexes are in Arlington, 15 miles west of Dallas.

Fair Park – For two incredibly jammed weeks in October, Fair Park is the scene of the *Texas State Fair,* with all the superlatives you would associate with such an event: biggest, best, highest, widest, etc. In 1989, the fair will be held October 6-22. For the rest of the year, Fair Park is the home of the *Cotton Bowl,* the site of the New Year's Day college football game, and Fair Park Coliseum. The Fair Park grounds and buildings were renovated for Texas's sesquicentennial celebration in 1986. Grand Ave. For information on State Fair activities, call 565-9931.

Museum of Natural History – In order to attract the Texas Centennial Exposition to Dallas in 1936, the city fathers built a group of museums at Fair Park. The *Museum of Natural History,* a neoclassic, cream limestone building, contains a variety of fauna and flora from the Southwest. There are some interesting zoology and botany exhibitions, too. Open daily. No admission charge. Ranger Circle, Fair Park (phone: 670-8457).

Dallas Museum of Art – The keystone of Dallas's new downtown Arts District houses the permanent collection of pre-Columbian art, African sculpture, and 19th-century modern and contemporary works that have been moved from the old museum at Fair Park plus some surprises. The Sculpture Garden, featuring works by Henry Moore and Ellsworth Kelly, is an urban oasis, replete with cascades and shade trees. The Reeves Collection, hung in a reconstructed Italian villa within the museum, and the Bybee Collection (furniture) are worth investigating. The Dallas skyline is an impressive backdrop to the building designed by Edward Larrabee Barnes. Closed Mondays. No admission charge, although a fee is charged for the Reeves Collection and special exhibits. 1717 N. Harwood (phone: 922-0220).

Aquarium – This one isn't the biggest or the best in the country, but it's the only one in Dallas. There are more than 300 species of native freshwater fish, cold- and tropical-water creatures — finned, scaled, and amphibious. If you like watching the fish and sea animals being fed, be sure to get here early — around 9 AM. Open daily. No admission charge. 1st St. and Martin Luther King Ave. (phone: 670-8441).

Garden Center and Science Place I and II – Next to the Aquarium, the Garden Center has delightful tropical flowers and plants with braille markers. Open daily. No admission charge (phone: 428-7476). Just down the street, Science Place features exhibitions on technology, energy, ecology, and health. A planetarium show enraptures planet watchers and stargazers. Closed Mondays. Admission charge. Fair Park (phone: 428-5555).

Midway and the Hall of State – As you walk along the Midway during the week, you will find it hard to imagine the frenetic carnival activity for which it is known. If you're here during the *State Fair* or on weekends May through September, you'll probably be swept into the frenzy, stopping only long enough to try winning a stuffed animal or doll at a shooting gallery or pitch 'n' toss. There is an assortment of spine-chilling, scream-inducing, turn-you-upside-down-and-inside-out rides for those who like thrills. There are also great food stands here — Greek, barbecue, and Mexican. At one end of the Midway, the *Hall of State* has paintings devoted to the heroes of Texas. It was built in 1936, for the Texas centennial. Open daily. No admission charge. The Midway.

Age of Steam Museum – Will bring a lump to the throat of anyone who ever loved an old train, with steam engines and other railroad nostalgia. Open Thursdays and Fridays 9 AM to 1 PM, Saturdays and Sundays 11 AM to 5 PM. Admission charge. The Midway (phone: 421-8754).

Neiman Marcus – The shrine of commercial elegance, the *Neiman Marcus* specialty store has been known to induce orgies of spending. If you have an insatiable craving for wave making machines, a computer chess game, or a biorhythm calculator, this is the place to satisfy it. These games, however, are among the more conservative items in stock. The really exotic stuff is offered in the Christmas catalogue. Three locations: Main and Ervay (downtown), NorthPark, and the Prestonwood Mall (phone: downtown, 741-6911).

Farmers' Market – This is raunchy, down-home, earthy Texas. From 6 AM, farmers drive into town in their trusty ole pickups to sell the fruit and vegetables of their labor. The market consists of a tin-roof shelter and dozens of stalls, with any number of colorful characters standing around. The vegetables are fresher and a bit cheaper than anywhere else in town. Open daily. In May, there's a flower festival, in September a fall harvest, and in November an arts and crafts fair. 1010 S. Pearl (phone: 748-2082).

Texas Stadium – *Cowboys* fans go crazy here. This open 65,100-seat stadium packs 'em in during home games. It's constructed to give you the feel of being in a theater or auditorium rather than a stadium, but critics point out that with the dome partially open, part of the field is always in shadow. Hwy. 183 at Loop 12 in Irving (phone: 438-7676).

Dallas Zoo – At one time an unkempt, run-down animal park, the Dallas Zoo has been rebuilt with newer facilities. It's now considerably more comfortable for the 1,600 mammals, reptiles, and birds that live within its 50 acres. Open daily. Admission charge. Marsalis Park, 621 E Clarendon Dr. (phone: 946-5154).

Texas School Book Depository – Known to millions of people around the world as the place where Lee Harvey Oswald hid, the Texas School Book Depository is the most-photographed site in Texas. It's now the home of the Dallas County Commissioners Court. In February 1989, the *Kennedy Museum* opened on the 6th floor. It is 9,000 square feet of exhibitions, featuring 6 films, 350 photographs, and artifacts dealing with the late president, his family, his presidency, his assassination and its investigation, and his legacy. There is an additional charge for a 35-minute audio tour. Open daily except major holidays. Admission charge. 506 Elm, at Houston (phone: 653-6659, 653-6657 for groups).

John F. Kennedy Memorial – A 30-foot monument near where Kennedy fell. It has an indoor room for meditation, with the roof open to the sky. Main and Market Sts.

Which Way to Southfork? – The question most asked by visitors is how to get to the mythical home of the Ewings. The building seen on TV's "Dallas" actually does exist. Formerly a private home, it was purchased by a real estate investor to be transformed into a hotel of sorts — you can't rent a room, but you can rent the entire house for $2,500 a night! The ranch itself is now a tourist attraction, replete with party barns and other amusements. Take Hwy. 75 north to Parker Rd. in Plano, then drive 5½ miles east to FM 2551. Open daily. Admission charge (phone: 442-6536).

ARLINGTON

Six Flags Over Texas – A theme amusement park, *Six Flags Over Texas* motifs are based on different periods in Texas history: Spanish, Mexican, French, Republic of Texas, Confederacy, and the period since the Civil War. You can get a panoramic view of the Dallas and Ft. Worth skylines from a 300-foot-high observation deck on top of an oil derrick. A narrow-gauge railway runs around the 145-acre grounds. Open weekends spring and fall, daily June through August. Admission charge. I-30 at Hwy. 360 (phone: 640-8900).

GRAND PRAIRIE

International Wildlife Park – A drive-through wildlife preserve, the only one of its kind in the Southwest. Thousands of animals roam freely around the 350-acre tract, and visitors can stop at many points along the 6 miles of safari trails. Open daily. Admission charge. I-30 and Belt Line (phone: 263-2203).

GARLAND

Wet 'n Wild – This Texas-size family recreation park attracts huge crowds on blistering summer weekends (weekdays are a bit less jammed). Waterslides, inner-tube chutes, surfing pools, and children's play areas provide heat relief for all ages. Open daily, May through August; weekends only, April and September. Admission charge. Two locations: across I-30 from *Texas Stadium* at 1800 E. Lamar Blvd. (phone: 265-3356) and 12715 LBJ Expy., near the intersection of I-635 and Northwest Hwy. (phone: 271-5637).

■**EXTRA SPECIAL:** Dallas before its skyscrapers and highways was a simpler place whose lifestyle was reflected in unique architectural styles that combined Victorian grace with the less refined influence of the prairie. One of the few places still able to convey a sense of those earlier, unhurried days is Old City Park, an oasis of greenery and history close to downtown. Restored Victorian houses, a railroad depot, pioneer log cabins, and other historically significant structures have been moved in from various locales in North Texas and are open for exploration. Closed Mondays. Admission charge. Gano and St. Paul (phone: 421-5141).

SOURCES AND RESOURCES

 TOURIST INFORMATION: For brochures, maps, and general information, contact the Dallas Convention and Visitors Bureau, 1201 Elm St., Suite 2000, Dallas, TX 75270 (phone: 214-746-6677, or the Dallas Visitor Information Center in Union Station (400 S. Houston; phone: 746-6603), a restored 1924 railroad terminal that also houses restaurants and Amtrak headquarters.

The best guides are Guide, a section in Friday's *Dallas Morning News,* and Datebook, in the *Dallas Times Herald* every Friday. Another good source of information is the *Dallas Observer* weekly tabloid.

Television Stations – KDFW Channel 4–CBS; KERA Channel 13–PBS; KXAS Channel 5–NBC; WFAA Channel 8–ABC.

Radio Stations – AM: KLIF 1190 (talk); KRLD 1080 (news). FM: WRR 101.1 (classical); KLUV 98.7 (light); KHYI 94.9 (top 40).

Local Coverage – *Dallas Times Herald,* morning and evening daily; *Dallas Morning News,* morning daily; and *D* magazine, monthly.

Food – *D* magazine's restaurant section (monthly); the Dallas restaurant guide in *Texas Monthly* magazine; and listings in Friday's newspapers.

Telephone – The area code for Dallas is 214.

Sales Tax – There is an 8% sales tax on most goods and services, including dining.

CLIMATE: Summers are blisteringly hot and humid, with temperatures over 100. Sudden thunderstorms punctuate the dry, blazing heat. From October to January, the weather is mild, although it can be in the 70s one day and in the 30s the next. From January to March, there are occasional sharp cold snaps and high winds, and between March and June you can expect rain and dust storms.

 GETTING AROUND: Airport – Dallas/Ft. Worth Airport (or D/FW), the country's largest, is approximately 20 miles from downtown Dallas. In light traffic, the drive into the city takes about a half-hour; cab fare will run about $25. The inner-city Love Field Airport serves Texas and surrounding states. Cab fare between Love Field and downtown is about $10. Companies providing transportation to area hotels include *Bluebird* (phone: 267-4101), *TBS* (phone: 361-7637), *VIP* (phone: 637-5781), *Super Shuttle* (phone: 817-329-2000), and *Limaxi* (phone: 748-6294).

Bus – Dallas Area Rapid Transit (DART) operates the bus service. For information, call 979-1111.

Taxi – There are taxi stands at most major hotels, but the best way to get one is to call *Yellow Cab* (phone: 426-6262).

Car Rental – All major national firms are represented.

 LOCAL SERVICES: Babysitting – *Babysitters of Dallas,* 5622 Dyer (phone: 692-1354).

Business Services – *Kelly Services,* Downtown, 1 Main Pl. (phone: 740-3666).

Mechanics – For American cars, *Exxon Car Care,* 5748 Live Oak (phone: 823-1351); for foreign cars, *Fischer's Foreign Car Service,* 4770 Memphis (phone: 630-2807). In emergencies, *AAA Emergency Road Service* (phone: 528-7481).

 MUSEUMS: The *Dallas Museum of Art,* the *Museum of Natural History,* the *Science Place,* and the *Age of Steam Museum,* are all discussed in detail in *Special Places.*

 MAJOR COLLEGES AND UNIVERSITIES: Southern Methodist University (SMU) has a large campus with many activities (University Park; phone: 692-2000). The University of Dallas campus is at 1845 E. Northgate in Irving (phone: 721-5000). The University of Texas has a Dallas branch at N. Floyd Rd. in Richardson (phone: 690-2111).

 SPECIAL EVENTS: The *Texas State Fair* runs for 2 weeks in October in Fair Park (October 6-22 in 1989; phone 565-9931). Other special events in 1990: the *Virginia Slims Women's Tennis Tournament* in February (phone: 352-7978); *World Championship Tennis Finals* in early April (phone: 969-5556); the *Byron Nelson Golf Classic* in early May (phone: 742-3896); and *Artfest* at Fair Park, May 26-29 (phone: 361-2011). Also in May, *St. Seraphin's Annual Festival,* featuring Ukrainian dancing and food at *European Crossroads,* 2829 Northwest Hwy. (phone: 358-5574); and the *Flower Festival* at Farmers' Market, 1010 S. Pearl (phone: 748-2082). *Dallas Summer Musicals* are held from June through August (phone: 691-7200). In September, Dallas's Greek Orthodox community sponsors a well-attended *Greek Food Festival* on the grounds of the Holy Trinity Church, 4005 Swiss Ave. (phone: 823-3509). College football teams face off annually at the *Cotton Bowl* on New Year's Day.

SPORTS AND FITNESS: Dallas has enough professional sports to satisfy just about everyone:

Baseball – The Texas *Rangers* play at *Arlington Stadium,* 1600 Copeland Rd., Arlington (phone: 273-5100).

Basketball – Dallas's NBA team, the *Mavericks,* plays at *Reunion Arena,* 777 Sports St. (phone: 658-7068).

Bicycling – Dallas has some pretty trails in the White Rock Lake–East Dallas area and at Bachman Lake, off Northwest Highway near Love Field.

Fitness Centers – The *Downtown YMCA* has an indoor and an outdoor pool, tracks, squash and racquetball courts, exercise equipment, and a sauna. 601 N. Akard at Ross, across from the *Fairmont* (phone: 954-0500).

Football – The *Cowboys* play at *Texas Stadium,* Texas 183 at Loop 12 (phone: 556-2500). The *Cotton Bowl* is held every New Year's Day at Fair Park (phone: 565-9931).

Golf – There are several municipal courses in Dallas. *Tenison Memorial* is best known as the home of Lee Trevino. 3501 Samuell (phone: 670-1402).

Jogging – For a 6-mile stint, head north on Akard, right onto Cedar Springs, then take Turtle Creek Boulevard, left onto Avondale, left onto Oak Lawn, left onto Irving, back to Turtle Creek, and retrace your steps home. Or take a bus (40 Bachman Bank or 43 Park Forest) to Bachman Lake for a 3-mile course, or to White Rock Lake (60 White Rock North on Commerce or East St.) for a 10-mile course.

Soccer – The *Sidekicks* play at *Reunion Arena,* 777 Sports St. (phone: 787-2000).

Tennis – Tennis is a year-round sport here, and it's terrifically popular. There are around 204 municipal courts. The best are at Samuell Grand at 6200 Grand Ave. (phone: 821-3811) and at Fretz Park, Hillcrest and Beltline (phone: 233-8921).

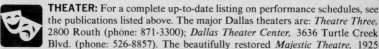 **THEATER:** For a complete up-to-date listing on performance schedules, see the publications listed above. The major Dallas theaters are: *Theatre Three,* 2800 Routh (phone: 871-3300); *Dallas Theater Center,* 3636 Turtle Creek Blvd. (phone: 526-8857). The beautifully restored *Majestic Theatre,* 1925 Elm (phone: 880-0137), stages a variety of fine arts events. Several "underground" theater companies perform in the Deep Ellum area.

 MUSIC: Dallas's new *Morton H. Meyerson Symphony Center,* designed by architect I. M. Pei, was completed in 1989 at a cost of $81.5 million. It is home to the *Dallas Symphony Orchestra,* which gives concerts in the center's 2,066-seat *Eugene McDermott Concert Hall,* 2301 Flora St. (phone: 670-3600). For information on opera, call the *Dallas Opera* (phone: 871-0090); and Rainbow-Ticketmaster (phone: 787-2000) for pop-rock concerts.

 NIGHTCLUBS AND NIGHTLIFE: Dallas crowds are so notoriously fickle that between the time of writing and the time of printing, everyone may have boogied on down the road to another hangout. Regardless of what's hot and what's not, there's never far to go. Nightlife in Dallas finds four major centers. One is Greenville Avenue, a north-south artery chockablock with restaurants and nightclubs on the east side. *Poor David's,* at 1924 Greenville (phone: 821-9891), features every style of music, from reggae to jazz; *Bowley & Wilson's,* 4714 Greenville (phone: 692-6470), features raunchy and rowdy comedy; *Max's 403 Club* in Old Town Shopping Center (phone: 361-9517), and *Studebakers* with a fifties theme at NorthPark East Shopping Center (phone: 696-2475) are three of the Greenville area's popular discos. There's also country-and-western dancing at the *Belle Starr* at Southwestern and Central (phone: 750-4787) and *Borrowed Money,* 9100 N. Central (phone: 361-9996).

A second area is the West End Historical District, a downtown district of renovated warehouses (one, Dallas Alley, contains six clubs). Here, too, is the popular *Starck Club* at 703 McKinney (phone: 720-0130). McKinney Avenue is the third major nightlife center. It runs south to downtown and features some of the best restaurants, along with private nightclubs such as *San Simeon* at 2515 McKinney (phone: 871-7373), and the tourists' favorite *Hard Rock Café* at 2601 McKinney (phone: 827-8282).

For something more avante garde, head down to the fourth area, Deep Ellum/Near Ellum, a bohemian district where many blues musicians performed in the 1930s. At *Club Dada,* 2720 Elm (phone: 744-3232), poetry, classical guitar, rockabilly, and Middle Eastern jazz can be heard. The *Video Bar,* 2610 Elm (phone: 939-9113), offers the best in music videos. *Club Clearview,* 2806 Elm (phone: 939-0006), is the place for underground music. The *Empire Club,* 2424 Swiss (phone: 828-1879), is a renovated Victorian dinner theater that is now a nouveau dance club. Down the street, near Fair Park, where some of the uprooted artists moved, are the *State Bar,* 3611 Parry (phone: 821-9246), a restaurant/gathering place for the "in" crowd; and *Bar of Soap,* 3615 Parry, is a bar/laundromat with live music (phone: 823-6617).

BEST IN TOWN

 CHECKING IN: Dallas is the third most popular convention city in the country and has a considerable number of comfortable accommodations. Some hotels cater almost exclusively to conventions, so it may be difficult to book as an individual. It will save a lot of trouble if you inquire ahead of time. For something different and a little less expensive, try *Bed & Breakfast Texas Style,* a fast-growing service that offers lodging in private homes. Contact *Ruth Wilson,* 4224 W. Redbird La., Dallas 75237 (phone: 298-5433 or 298-8586), for information. At the hotels below, expect to spend $105 and up a night for a double at those places we call expensive; between $60 and $90, moderate; $40 and under, inexpensive. All telephone numbers are in the 214 area code unless otherwise indicated.

Adolphus – An elder giant among Dallas hotels. The decor is turn-of-the-century elegant; rooms are large and individually appointed in the finest of taste. Its *French Room* (see *Eating Out*) is one of the city's classiest restaurants, and the *Palm Bar* is a favorite lunch spot. 1321 Commerce (phone: 742-8200; 800-441-0574 in Texas; 800-221-9083 elsewhere in the US). Expensive.

Crescent Court – Designed by award-winning architect Philip Johnson, this Rosewood hotel lives up to its reputation for high style and excellent service. The soaring Great Hall lobby of this impressive 190-room, 28-suite extravaganza links an 18-story office tower (with the hottest private club in town) to an elegant courtyard of ultra-chic shops and galleries whose centerpiece is a 5-story fountain. The spacious, airy rooms were designed with style as well as comfort in mind. And to ensure the enjoyment of its guests, the hotel offers a wide range of amenities and services, among them a 24-hour concierge, 24-hour room service, phones in bathrooms, babysitting service, pool, spa, a lobby lounge, the *Beau Nash* for formal dining, and the *Conservatory* for breakfast and lunch, in addition to extensive conference facilities. Free shuttle service to downtown. 400 Crescent Court (phone: 871-3200 or 800 654-6541). Expensive.

Fairmont – This Dallas favorite celebrated its 20th anniversary in 1989 by renovating throughout. Its white marble façade was replaced with Texas pink granite and there's an elegant new entrance and porte cochere. All 550 rooms have been redone, and the restaurants are as fine as ever. In the Arts District, within walking distance of the West End. 1717 N. Akard St. (phone: 720-2020 or 800-527-4727). Expensive.

Four Seasons – This 315-room property has won numberous awards for its conference facilities. Other amenities on its 400 acres include a spa and sports club, two 18-hole golf courses, 4 restaurants, tennis courts and a tennis stadium, racquetball and squash courts, a jogging track, 2 pools and 24-hour room service. There are also special golf and fitness packages. Near the airport at 4150 N. MacArthur Blvd., Irving (phone: 717-0700 or 800-332-3442). Expensive.

Grand Kempinski – In far North Dallas and an attraction in itself. Tennis courts, indoor and outdoor pools, and fine restaurants lend it a resort ambience. 15201 Dallas Pkwy. (phone: 386-6000 or 800-228-9000). Expensive.

Hyatt Regency – One of Dallas's most popular hotels, it has an eye-catching silver-burnished exterior, a soaring atrium lobby, and a rooftop restaurant with a dynamite view. 300 Reunion Blvd. (phone: 651-1234 or 800-228-9000). Expensive.

Hyatt Regency DFW – This hotel is a popular convention spot. In addition to meeting rooms, it has a swimming pool, bar, and 24-hour café. Kids under 18, accompanied by an adult, free. The Hyatt's golf and racquet sports facility, just 10 minutes away, includes 2 topnotch 18-hole golf courses, 4 outdoor lighted tennis courts, 3 indoor courts and 10 racquetball courts. Free shuttle service is provided between the hotel and its sports facilities. Dallas/Ft. Worth Airport (phone: 453-8400 or 800-228-9000). Expensive.

Loews Anatole – The red brick exterior doesn't look much like a Dallas hotel, but many residents find it a welcome change from monolithic rectangles of sparkling tinted glass. Its 2 atriums house 18 restaurants and lounges (it's *L'Entrecôte* — see *Eating Out* — is one of the best French restaurants in the city) and 13 shops, tennis and racquetball courts and *Verandah Club Spa* on grounds that cover 50 acres. 2201 Stemmons Fwy. (phone: 748-1200 or 800-223-0888). Expensive.

Mansion on Turtle Creek – Dallas's most elegant address exudes the kind of luxury and taste that make it worthy of its membership in the Leading Hotels of the World group. Custom-made furnishings, opulent bathrooms, attentive service, and the *Mansion* (see *Eating Out*), make this the best of the city's deluxe hotels. 2821 Turtle Creek Blvd. (phone: 559-2100; 800-442-3408 in Texas; 800-527-5432 in other states). Expensive.

Marriott Mandalay at Las Colinas – This 27-story enclave dedicated to luxury is in Las Colinas, a business center west of Dallas. Convenient to both the Dallas/Ft. Worth Airport and downtown, it has a fine restaurant, *Enjolie.* 221 E. Las Colinas Blvd., Irving (phone: 556-0800 or 800-228-9290). Expensive.

Plaza of the Americas – Part of the British Trusthouse Forte chain, its management was given carte blanche to hire the best help available — and that they did, from the staff at the coffee shop to the chef in the posh *Café Royal,* which features nouvelle cuisine and a well-stocked wine cellar. 650 N. Pearl Expy. at Bryan St. (phone: 979-9000 or 800-CALL-THF). Expensive.

Stouffer Dallas – Likened by some local pundits to a giant tube of lipstick, this 30-story, elliptically shaped hotel of Texas pink granite occupies an enviable site between Market Hall and the Apparel Mart. Its 542 rooms include 30 suites; there are also 2 restaurants, 24-hour room service, a rooftop health club, and heated lap pool, non-smoking rooms, morning coffee and newspaper with wake-up call. Shuttle to D/FW Airport. 2222 Stemmons (phone: 631-2222 or 800-HOTELS-1). Expensive.

Westin Galleria – This luxury hotel, with 440 balconied rooms, opens onto that large and elegant shopping mall, the Galleria, which houses some 200 stores and cinemas. Its amenities include a pool, jogging track, saunas, exercise facilities, parking garage, and 3 restaurants. Convenient to North Dallas business districts. 13340 Dallas Pkwy. (phone: 934-9494). Expensive.

Aristocrat – An old downtown establishment built by Conrad Hilton in 1925 and recently renovated, with sparkling results. Suites only, many designed for a business clientele. Reasonably priced for its location. 1933 Main St. (phone: 741-7700). Expensive to moderate.

Omni Melrose – A small, premier hotel dating from the 1920s, its 185 rooms give it the hospitable feel of a country estate. A cozy, English-style lounge and an Art Deco restaurant, the *Garden Court,* add to its appeal. 3015 Oak Lawn Ave. (phone: 521-5151; 800-635-7673 in Texas; 800-527-1488 in other states). Expensive to moderate.

Embassy Suites – Suites with kitchens are standard in this Spanish-style hotel built around a soaring atrium. Convenient to downtown and Market Center. 2730 Stemmons Fwy. (phone: 630-5332). Also at 3880 W. Northwest Hwy. at Love Field (phone: 357-4500 or 800-EMBASSY). Moderate.

La Quinta Motor Inns – If you're looking for a clean, inconspicuous place to sleep, try any of their motels. 4400 N. Central Expy. (phone: 821-4220); 8303 E R.L. Thornton Fwy. (phone: 324-3731); 10001 N. Central Expy. (phone: 361-8200); 1625 Regal Row (phone: 630-5701); 13235 Stemmons Fwy. (phone: 620-7333). Also at Dallas/Ft. Worth Airport and several other locations (phone: 800-531-5900 for all locations). Inexpensive.

EATING OUT: Restaurant dining in Dallas has become as sophisticated as that in any major American city in the last few years, with an emphasis on Southwest cuisine (which Dallas restaurants lead the way in). Expect to spend $60 or more for two in those places we've listed as expensive; between $30 and $60, moderate; under $30, inexpensive. Prices do not include wine, drinks, or tips. (Parts of Dallas are "dry," but alcoholic beverages generally are available with an inexpensive club membership.) All telephone numbers are in the 214 area code unless otherwise indicated.

Actuelle – The American-inspired menu changes seasonally in this dining oasis under a glass cupola. The atmosphere is distinctly modern and the food artistically presented. Lunch weekdays. Closed Sundays. Reservations advised. Major credit cards. 2800 Routh, in the Quadrangle (phone: 855-0440). Expensive.

Café Royal – The 4-course, *prix fixe* meal is very French and very refined. Quiet and elegant, the dining room is suited for both romance and business. Open for lunch weekdays, dinner daily. Closed Sundays. Reservations advised. Major credit cards. 650 N. Pearl, in the *Plaza of the Americas* hotel (phone: 979-9000). Expensive.

L'Entrecôte – The menu has a pronounced French accent, with entrées garnished with a garden of edible flowers. Dinner only. Closed Tuesdays. Reservations necessary. Major credit cards. 2201 Stemmons Fwy., in the *Loews Anatole* hotel (phone: 748-122). Expensive.

French Room – The most lavish dining room in the city, swathed in rich Louis XIV decor. The menu is classic French and slightly nouvelle. Closed Sundays. Reservations advised. Major credit cards. 1321 Commerce in the *Adolphus* hotel (phone: 742-8200). Expensive.

Mansion – As implied in the name, it's a handsomely refurbished private mansion. Quiet elegance, southwestern cuisine, polished service, and a VIP crowd make dining here a memorable experience. In the *Mansion on Turtle Creek* hotel. 2821 Turtle Creek (phone: 526-2121). Expensive.

Mario's – This delightful restaurant offers a mixture of Italian and French dishes. Try the scaloppine alla marsala — tender escallops of veal sautéed in butter and drenched in a rich wine and mushroom sauce. Major credit cards. 135 Turtle Creek Village (phone: 521-1135). Expensive.

Old Warsaw – One of the oldest restaurants in Dallas, it features continental cuisine with such selections as Dover sole, chateaubriand, and rack of lamb. Various pâtés are also offered. Open daily. Reservations required. Major credit cards. 2610 Maple (phone: 528-0032). Expensive.

Pyramid Room – Newly refurbished, this restaurant in the *Fairmount* hotel has expanded its predominantly French menu by adding a number of southwestern dishes. Open daily. Reservations a must. Major credit cards. 1717 N. Akard St. (phone: 720-2020). Expensive.

Riviera – The South of France is the inspiration for this superb restaurant with a distinct — but not overwhelming — continental atmosphere. Open daily. Reservations advised. Major credit cards. 7709 Inwood (phone: 351-0094). Expensive.

Routh Street Café – This wonderfully innovative restaurant uses regional produce in preparing southwestern cuisine. The 5-course, prix fixe menu changes daily. Open for dinner Tuesdays through Saturdays. Reservations advised well in advance. Major credit cards. 3005 Routh St. (phone: 871-7161). Expensive.

Café Pacific – An interesting variety of American and European dishes are served in an attractive brass and glass setting. The clam chowder and seafood sauté are especially good. One of the most extensive and reasonably priced wine lists in town. Open daily. Reservations advised. Major credit cards. 24 Highland Park Shopping Village (phone: 526-1170). Expensive to moderate.

Uncle Tai's – Some of the best Oriental food in Dallas is served at this elegant spot in the city's glitziest shopping mall. The crispy beef is a must; the two-color chicken Hunan style is extraordinary. Open daily. Reservations advised. Major credit cards. The Galleria, near Dallas Pkwy. at LBJ (phone: 934-9998). Expensive to moderate.

Baby Routh – More casual than its older sister, the *Routh Street Café*, it serves excellent southwestern fare, including catfish, a regional favorite. Open daily. Reservations advised. Major credit cards. 2708 Routh (phone: 871-2345). Moderate.

Chimney – Swiss-Austrian establishment with one of the more esoteric menus found in the Southwest. Tournedos of Montana venison is a specialty, along with Wiener schnitzel, veal Zürich, and naturschnitzel. Closed Sundays. Reservations advised. Major credit cards. 9739 N. Central Expy. at Walnut Hill, in Willow Creek Shopping Center (phone: 369-6466). Moderate.

Deep Ellum Café – Casual, comfortable atmosphere, located in a one-time hot spot for jazz — hence the name. The menu is broad, everything from Vietnamese salads to chicken with dill dumplings, to superb Southern-fried steaks. Lunch weekdays; brunch Sundays; dinner daily except Sunday. Reservations advised. Major credit cards. 2704 Elm St. (phone: 741-9012). Moderate.

Mario's Chiquita – This isn't a Tex-Mex Americanized food joint — everything here is really Mexican. The carne asada Tampico-style is a filet sliced to triple its usual length and broiled over a hickory fire, then served with green peppers, onions, and soft tacos topped with ranchero sauce. Far and away one of the finest Mexican restaurants north of the border. No reservations. Some credit cards. 4514 Travis, Suite 105 (phone: 521-0721) or 221 W. Parker Rd., Plano (phone: 423-2977). Moderate.

Newport's – In a remodeled brewery in downtown's West End, this is a wharfside seafood restaurant with pier. The brewery's old well remains open in the brick interior, with scuba divers occasionally searching for purses lost by patrons. Grilled seafood is especially good. Lunch weekdays; dinner daily. Reservations advised. Major credit cards. 703 McKinney (phone: 954-0220). Moderate.

Ranchman's Café – About an hour's drive north of Dallas is the town of Ponder (pop. 208) and one of the most splendid little hometown cafés in Texas; it's less than 40 years old. The small restaurant's old wooden screen doors open into a room with longhorns and stirrups on the wall and an authentic country-and-western jukebox. Specialties are chicken-fried steaks, T-bone steaks, French fries, and possibly the best pecan pie in the country, along with other home-baked fruit pies. Open daily. No credit cards. Bailey St. (phone: 817-479-2221). Moderate.

St. Martin's – A well-chosen, reasonably priced wine list coupled with imaginatively prepared seafood specialties make this intimate restaurant a favorite with those who like to linger over a meal. Open daily. Major credit cards. 3022 Greenville (phone: 826-0940). Moderate.

San Simeon – The kitchen here was built without a freezer! That's because only the freshest ingredients are served at this elegant eatery on the outskirts of downtown. Arched ceilings, wrought iron fixtures, and mirrored walls are the highlights of the decor. The menu changes seasonally and can include smoked tenderloin of pork and apple-bacon pancakes with maple-sage sauce, and Alaskan salmon and spinach croquettes with three-cabbage coleslaw. A neighboring bakery, *Petaluma*, prepares fresh desserts and pastries. Brunch is particularly popular and includes a banana macadamia waffle with apricot syrup and herb sausage. Dinner nightly; Sunday brunch. Reservations recommended. Major credit cards. 2515 McKinney Ave. (phone: 871-7373). Moderate.

Lombardi la Trattoria – Great food and good service have made this perhaps the most popular Italian restaurant in Dallas. The pasta and seafood dishes are stand-outs. Closed Sundays. Reservations advised. Major credit cards. 2916 N. Hall St. (phone: 528-7506). Moderate.

Trail Dust Steak House – Exactly the kind of place visitors expect in Texas. The waitresses wear cowgirl garb, a country-and-western band entertains, and the food is straight off the ranch: steaks, red beans, potatoes, and salad. Don't wear a tie; if you do, the staff will cut it off and add it to the collection on the walls. Open daily. Reservations for large parties only. Major credit cards. 10841 Composite, at the Walnut Hill exit off Stemmons Fwy. (phone: 357-3862). Moderate to inexpensive.

Dickey's Barbecue – An unpretentious decor, but superior barbecued meats. The ribs, sausages, and beef are outstanding. Closed Sundays. No reservations. Several locations: 4610 N Central (phone: 823-0240); E. 14th and Ave. M, Plano (phone: 423-9960); 7770 Forest (phone: 223-3721); and 14885 Inwood, Addison (phone: 239-8547). Inexpensive.

Dixie House – This chain of amiable eateries serves such down-home staples as chicken-fried steaks, fried chicken, pot roast, and fresh vegetable dishes including black-eyed peas, okra, and greens. Homemade bread and pastries top off the satisfying menu. Several locations: 2822 McKinney (phone: 824-0891); 3647 W. Northwest Hwy. (phone: 353-0769); 6400 Gaston Ave. (phone: 826-2412); and 14925 Midway (phone: 239-5144). Open daily. No reservations. Major credit cards. Inexpensive.

Hoffbrau – At this popular, casual steakhouse, the beef is served drenched in butter sauce and accompanied by salad, bread, and potatoes. Open daily. No reservations. Major credit cards. 3205 Knox St. (phone: 559-2680). Inexpensive.

Mia's – A casual, family-run place well-known for Tex-Mex specialties, particularly chiles rellenos. Closed Sundays. No reservations. No credit cards. 4418 Lemmon (phone: 526-1020). Inexpensive.

On the Border – Visit this place for a taste of Tex-Mex, particularly the fajitas, which are served sizzling on a hot platter and accompanied by a host of condiments. Outdoor tables placed on a good people watching corner supplement those in the spacious dining rooms inside, where a sometimes boisterous atmosphere prevails. Special Sunday brunch menu. Open daily. No reservations. Major credit cards. 3302 Knox St. (phone: 528-5900). Inexpensive.

S&D Oyster House – The restaurant's decor will remind you of almost every cozy little seafood joint you ever found along the Gulf Coast. It's almost always crowded; no reservations. Offerings include raw oysters, boiled and fried shrimp, and three kinds of broiled fresh fish. A house specialty is seafood gumbo. Only beer and wine. Major credit cards. 2701 McKinney Ave. (phone: 823-6350). Inexpensive.

Sonny Bryan's – Few would argue that *Sonny Bryan's* serves the best barbecue in Dallas, although some might take exception to the small, drab interior where school desks substitute for tables. Open daily. No reservations. No credit cards. 2202 Inwood Rd. (phone: 357-7120). Inexpensive.

DENVER

A few years back, the rage in Denver was a bumper sticker that resembled the green and white Colorado license plate and had just one word: NATIVE. But the company making them soon realized it was selling to a rather limited market and quickly rushed into production with a sequel: SEMI-NATIVE. Clearly, Denver is a city where most of the population appears to be from somewhere else. Every section of the country is well represented. There is such a balanced cross section of America that many of the major movie studios regularly hold "sneak previews" in Denver to judge how a film will be accepted around the country. The comments of first-time visitors explain why people from all over feel at home here. They usually include remarks such as "clean," "friendly," and "relaxed."

The city's population has been holding steady at about 500,000 lately, but the entire metropolitan area has grown tremendously over the years and now numbers some 1.8 million. The economy appears to be on the mend after suffering a slump in the mid-1980s, fueled primarily by the faltering oil industry; this is — or was — a big oil town.

Although the city streets have a reputation for being clean, the same cannot be said for its air. Denver's infamous "brown cloud," first reported more than 100 years ago, lingers over the city on cold winter days, sometimes obstructing the view of nearby mountains. Fortunately, though, it's more of a visual and image problem than a health one. The city has mounted an all-out attack on the brown cloud, and it's working. Although uncontrollable weather conditions are the main culprit, a combination of voluntary no-drive days, wood burning restrictions, and oxygenated gasoline have helped to clean the air and win widespread praise.

Progress is also being reported on another local issue that has national impact — a new airport to replace undersized and overused Stapleton International. Tens of millions of dollars have been spent at Stapleton in recent years to add new concourses, spiff up existing ones, and improve baggage handling facilities. While the renovations have helped somewhat, voters have approved the construction of a new facility, scheduled to open by 1995.

New visitors to Denver will be pleasantly surprised by the weather. Summer in Denver, and throughout Colorado, is spectacular. As for the rest of the time, those who think the city is covered in snow 6 months a year are in for a shock. Golf courses are open year-round. It does snow from time to time, and it can be ferocious. Even then, however, it melts fairly quickly because winter days are sunny and pleasant: temperatures in the 60s are not uncommon.

Keep in mind that most of Colorado's snow falls in the nearby mountains, not in Denver, which is out on the plains. Denver weather can be clear and spring-like, while the ski resorts, just 75 miles away, are getting a foot of fresh snow. So reports of huge snowstorms in Colorado seldom include Denver. Conversely, warm and dry weather in Denver tells nothing about ski conditions at the resorts, which can be covered in waist-deep powder. Mountains, especially the spectacular Colorado Rockies, do strange things to the weather.

Another of Denver's pleasant surprises is that shoppers can have a very good time here. The section known as Cherry Creek, east of downtown, is popular for its quaint shops and boutiques, intimate restaurants, and one of the world's truly great bookstores, *The Tattered Cover*. It also offers one of Denver's original shopping centers, which had a facelift in 1989 with the additions of such specialty stores as *Lord & Taylor, Neiman Marcus*, and *Saks Fifth Avenue*.

Downtown boasts the 16th Street Mall, anchored by historic Larimer Square and the Tabor Center. Larimer Square, a block of renovated turn-of-the-century buildings, certainly qualifies as the most charming locale in Denver. Close by is the recently completed Tabor Center, a unique 2-block-long shopping mall that brought Denver its first *Brooks Brothers* store.

From the Tabor Center, there are antique-style buses that provide free service to the Tivoli nearby. What was once a sizable brewery is now a stunning and popular shopping mall. This is one place to go with an appetite because, in addition to the great shops, the Tivoli houses some of Denver's best restaurants (see *Eating Out*).

No discussion of Denver can be complete without a look at the city's favorite excuse for mass hysteria, the Denver *Broncos* football team. Many National Football League cities claim the best fans, but Denver has the numbers to back it up. Except for the strike games in 1987 (which still drew some 40,000 each), every home game has been sold out for 20 years, in a stadium that now holds more than 70,000. About the only way to get season tickets is to have a dying fan name you in his or her will.

If you have any questions about the city's loyalty to the team, drive around the usually crowded highways during a game. It looks as if they're shooting the sequel to *The Day After*. With everyone glued to television sets, it's the perfect time to do things like the laundry. Not only can you easily find open machines at deserted laundromats, you can probably wash the clothes you're wearing with no fear of being caught.

Now, if only major league baseball would catch on and put a team here, Denver could assume its rightful place as a truly major league city.

DENVER AT-A-GLANCE

SEEING THE CITY: The best view of Denver is from the top of the capitol rotunda, where you can see the Rockies to the west, the Great Plains stretching, like an ocean, to the east, and Denver itself sprawled below. On the 13th step of the capitol is an inscription noting that you are exactly one mile above sea level. Between E. 14th and E. Colfax Aves. (phone: 866-2604).

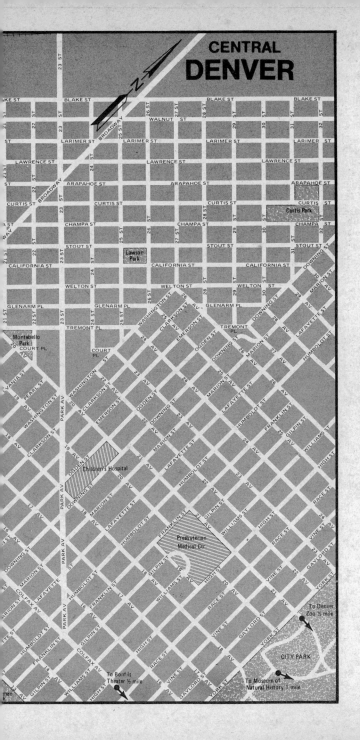

SPECIAL PLACES: It's a pleasure to walk around Denver. The downtown section has a number of Victorian mansions as well as the city's public institutions and commercial buildings.

US Mint – Appropriately enough for a city that made its fortune in gold, Denver still has more of it than anyplace else in the country (except Ft. Knox). On the outside, the Mint is a relatively unimpressive white sandstone Federal building with Doric arches over the windows. Inside, you can see money being stamped and printed and catch a glimpse of gold bullion, although the stuff on display is only a fraction of the total stored here. Most impressive is the room full of money just waiting to be counted. Open from 8:30 AM to 3 PM (9:30 AM to 3 PM on Wednesdays), closed on weekends; 20-minute tours begin on the half-hour. No admission charge. Delaware St. between Colfax and 14th (phone: 844-3582).

Denver Art Museum – That imposing, rather odd building sparkling in the sun down the street from the Mint is the *Denver Art Museum*, a supermodern structure covered with a million glittering glass tiles. Designed by Gio Ponti, its interior is just as spectacular as its exterior. Be sure to visit the American Indian collection on the 2nd floor — it has superlative costumes, basketry, rugs, and totem poles. Stop for lunch or a snack at the terrace restaurant, weather permitting. Closed Mondays. Admission $1.50 to $3; children under 6, free; Saturday mornings, no charge for Colorado residents. W. 14th Ave. and Bannock St. (phone: 575-2793).

Denver Public Library – This $3-million building houses a vast collection, including books, photographs, and historical documents related to the history of the West. The lower level, known as the basement, contains a splendid children's collection. Exhibitions on western life are on the main floor, and rare book lovers willing to hunt for the special collections will be delighted. Open daily. No admission charge. 1357 Broadway (phone: 571-2345).

Colorado State History Museum – This popular attraction features exhibitions on people who've contributed to Colorado history, period costumes from the early frontier days, and Indian relics. Many of the costumes were donated by members of old Denver families whose ancestors actually wore them. Life-size dioramas show how gold miners, pioneers, and Mesa Verde cliff dwellers used to live. Open daily. Admission $1 to $3; no charge for children under 6. 1400 Broadway (phone: 866-3682).

Capitol – The rotunda looks like the dome of the Capitol in Washington, DC, coated with $50,900 worth of Colorado gold leaf; the impressive marble staircases rate a look even if you don't want to climb to the top. There are 45-minute tours between 9:30 AM and 3:30 PM. Closed Saturdays (December through May) and all Sundays. No admission charge. Between E. 14th Ave. and Colfax, at Sherman Ave. (phone: 866-2604).

Molly Brown House – When gold miner Johnny Brown and his wife Molly moved into their Capitol Hill mansion, Denver society snubbed them as nouveau riche. But Molly earned her place in city history, and, ironically, it's her former house that is now high on the "most visited" list. She is remembered for her earthy flair and keen intelligence and for taking charge of a lifeboat when the *Titanic* sank, commanding the men to row while she held her chinchilla cape over a group of children to keep them warm — which is how she came to be known as the "unsinkable Molly Brown." Closed Mondays, September through May. Admission $1 to $3; no charge for children under 6. 1340 Pennsylvania St. (phone: 832-4092).

Financial District – Seventeenth Street is the center of Denver's financial district, and there are quite a number of tall, modern bank buildings that will give you a proper sense of the economic stability and strength that characterizes such areas. During summer lunch hours, street musicians give concerts in the plazas outside the United Bank Center and the First Interstate Bank of Denver.

Larimer Street – Walk along the new 16th Street Mall to Larimer, Denver's most interesting shopping street. You'll pass the Daniels and Fisher Tower, a 1920s land-mark said to be a copy of the campanile of Venice. It used to be the tallest building in town, but it has been overshadowed by more modern edifices. Larimer Street is lined with fascinating art galleries, curio shops, silversmiths, and cafés. Most interesting is Larimer Square, where various restaurants, crafts shops, and wine bars have been restored so that they retain the flavor of Denver's past (between 14th and 15th Sts.).

City Park – A 640-acre park with two lakes, spreading lawns, Denver's *Museum of Natural History* (known for its exhibitions of animals in natural settings) and the Denver Zoo. The museum was the first in the country to use curved backgrounds with reproductions of mountain flowers, shrubs, and smaller animals to give a feeling of the natural environment. Displays of fossils, minerals, gold coins, and birds. Open daily. Admission charge (phone: 370-6363). The museum also houses the popular Gates Planetarium (phone: 370-6351) and the *IMAX Theatre* (phone: 370-6300), its newest addition. Both closed Mondays. Admission charge. The Denver Zoo (phone: 575-2754) has designed a number of natural mountain environments for its animals. Open daily. Admission $2 to $4; children under six, free.

Highland Hills Water World – Colorado is not the place for an ocean vacation, but this is one spot where you can body-surf a mile above sea level. There are 22 exciting rides, 2 ocean-wave pools, and a special area for small children. Open daily from Memorial Day to Labor Day. Admission $10 to $12. 1850 W. 89th Ave. (phone: 427-7873).

Elitch Gardens – This is one of America's oldest amusement parks, and it has retained all of its charm over the years. The park is clean, the gardens are attractive, and the rides will have the kids asking for more. Grounds-only and all-rides admissions available. Open May through September. 4620 W. 38th Ave. (phone: 455-4771).

■**EXTRA SPECIAL:** There are so many gorgeous places to explore around Denver that it's almost unfair to single out any one in particular. Rocky Mountain National Park is, however, one of the most spectacular scenic areas of the US, and it's a perfect choice for a day trip. Within its 264,000 acres are dozens of mountains over the 12,000-foot mark, among them Bighorn Mountain and Longs Peak. The interior of the park offers the opportunity to cross the Continental Divide. You can rent horses and camping equipment in the town of Estes Park, at the northeast corner of the national park. To get there, take I-25 north for 50 miles, then Rte. 34 west. (See *Rocky Mountain National Park,* DIRECTIONS, for more information.)

SOURCES AND RESOURCES

TOURIST INFORMATION: For brochures, maps, and general information, contact the Denver Metro Convention and Visitors Bureau, 225 W. Colfax Ave., Denver, CO 80202 (phone: 892-1112). For information on skiing, contact Colorado Ski Country USA, 1560 Broadway, Suite 1440, Denver, CO 80202 (phone: 837-0793), or at its airport booth.

Denver magazine is the best guide to the Denver area; it's available at newsstands. Friday editions of the *Denver Post* and *Rocky Mountain News* have complete entertainment and activity guides.

Television Stations – KCNC Channel 4–NBC; KUSA Channel 9–ABC; KMGH Channel 7–CBS; KRMA Channel 6–PBS.

Radio Stations – AM: KOA 850 (talk/sports); KHOW 630 (music/talk); KDEN 1340 (news). FM: KVOD 99.5 (classical); KHIH 94.7 (jazz/new age); KBPI 105.9 (rock).

Local Coverage – *Denver Post* and *Rocky Mountain News,* morning dailies; *Denver* and *Colorado* magazines, monthly.

Food – *Denver* magazine has a complete listing of area restaurants.

Telephone – The area code for Denver is 303.

Sales Tax – The city sales tax is 7.1%, and the hotel tax is 11.7%.

CLIMATE: Because of the altitude, Denver is pretty dry. Even when the temperature hits the 90s in summer (it hits 100 every five years!), it's not intolerable. Nights cool to the 70s. In winter, the days are often sunny and in the 40s or 50s, but it does snow on occasion, although Denver is not usually hit by those mountain blizzards that the Weather Service reports as "sweeping the Rockies." And it only gets an average of 14 inches of precipitation a year, so visitors hardly ever need an umbrella.

GETTING AROUND: Airport – Denver's Stapleton International Airport is about a 20-minute drive from downtown; taxi fare to downtown runs $8 to $9. RTD (Regional Transportation District) buses leave for downtown Denver every half-hour from the airport terminal's east entry; fare is 75¢ during rush periods, 50¢ at other times.

Bus – RTD runs buses throughout the Denver area. For information, contact the Downtown Information Center, 626 16th St. (phone: 628-9000).

Taxi – Taxis cannot be hailed in the streets. Call *Yellow Cab* (phone: 777-7777), *Zone Cab* (phone: 861-2323), or *Metro Taxi* (phone: 333-3333). There are cab stands at the airport, bus station, Union Station, and at most major hotels.

Car Rental – All major national firms are represented.

LOCAL SERVICES: Babysitting – *Family Care,* 365 S. Newcombe (phone: 980-9090).

 Business Services – *Record Executive Services,* 11000 E. Yale Ave. (phone: 771-8686).

Mechanic – *May D & F Goodyear Auto Center,* 14th St. and Tremont Pl. (phone: 573-1502).

MUSEUMS: For a complete description of the *Denver Art Museum, Colorado State History Museum, Molly Brown House,* and *Museum of Natural History,* see *Special Places.* Other notable museums to visit:

 Buffalo Bill Museum – Interesting, especially for children. Buffalo Bill is buried on the grounds. Lookout Mountain (phone: 526-0747).

Children's Museum – 2121 Crescent Dr., I-25 at 23rd Ave. (phone: 433-7433).

Colorado Railroad Museum – 17155 W. 44th Ave. (phone: 279-4591).

MAJOR COLLEGES AND UNIVERSITIES: The University of Denver makes its home in the city proper, at S. University Blvd. and E. Evans Ave. (phone: 871-2000). The University of Colorado is 20 miles northwest of the city, on Rte. 36, in Boulder (phone: 492-0111). The US Air Force Academy's bright, clean, spacious campus is 60 miles south of Denver on I-25, near Colorado Springs (phone: 719-472-1818).

SPECIAL EVENTS: The *National Western Stock Show and Rodeo* in January lasts 2 weeks and attracts cowfolk from all over. The *Denver Art Museum*'s annual exhibition of western art runs from January through March. Easter Sunrise Service at *Red Rocks Natural Amphitheater* attracts thousands. In July and August, the University of Colorado at Boulder presents its annual *Shakespeare Festival.* And Larimer Square is the site of the *Oktoberfest* in guess what month? September!

SPORTS AND FITNESS: Baseball – The *Zephyrs* play at *Mile High Stadium,* 1700 Federal Blvd. (phone: 433-8645).

Basketball – The *Nuggets* play at *McNichols Sports Arena,* 1635 Clay St. (phone: 893-3865).

Bicycling – Bikes can be rented from *J & E Sports,* 4365 S. Santa Fe Dr. (phone: 781-4415).

Fishing – There's good fishing at Dillon Reservoir, west of Denver on I-70, and Cherry Creek Reservoir, just southeast of the city on I-225.

Fitness Centers – The *Indian Springs Resort* has relaxing, hot mineral baths, 302 Soda Creek Rd., 1 block south of Miner St., in Idaho Springs (phone: 623-2050). The *International Athletic Club* welcomes guests from several downtown hotels; it has exercise classes, tracks, racquetball and squash courts, sauna, massage; 1630 Welton (phone: 623-2100).

Football – The NFL *Broncos* (phone: 433-7466) play at *Mile High Stadium,* 1700 Federal Blvd. (phone: 433-7466).

Golf – Among the 50 golf courses in the area, the best public courses are *Kennedy,* 10500 E. Hampden Ave. (phone: 751-0311); *Park Hill,* 3500 Colorado Blvd. (phone: 333-5411); and *Wellshire,* 3333 S. Colorado Blvd. (phone: 756-6318).

Hockey – The University of Denver *Pioneers* play at the *DU Arena,* E. Jewell Ave. and S. Gaylord Way (phone: 871-2336).

Jogging – Follow the Highline Canal trail; or run in Washington Park, which is 4½ miles from downtown, or in City Park, 2 miles from downtown.

Racing – Greyhounds race at *Mile High Kennel Club* from June through August, 6200 Dahlia Rd. (phone: 288-1591). No one under 21 is admitted.

Skiing – Colorado ski country is famous all over the world. The slopes closest to the city are in *Loveland Basin,* 60 miles west on I-70; *Keystone and Arapahoe Basin, Breckenridge,* and *Copper Mountain,* all from 15 to 25 miles farther on I-70; and *Winter Park,* west on I-70, then north on Rte. 40. Former President Ford used to give news conferences on the slopes at *Vail,* a resort 100 miles west of Denver on I-70, and now has a house at Beaver Creek. Internationally acclaimed *Aspen* and *Snowmass* are about 190 miles southwest of Denver on I-70 and Hwy. 82. *Crested Butte,* 237 miles southwest, and *Steamboat Springs,* 163 miles northwest, are growing in popularity (see *Downhill Skiing,* DIVERSIONS).

Tennis – The best public courts are at *Gates Tennis Center,* 100 S. Adams St. (phone: 355-4461).

THEATER: For complete up-to-the-minute listings on theatrical and musical events, see local publications listed above. The University of Colorado at Boulder hosts a *Shakespeare Festival* every summer (see *Special Events*). The *Denver Center for the Performing Arts* presents Broadway productions as well as those of local companies, 14th and Curtis Sts. (phone: 892-0987). The *Country Dinner Playhouse,* a dinner theater, presents light offerings and musicals throughout the year, at 6875 S. Clinton in Englewood, just south of Denver (phone: 799-1410). *STAGEWEST* offers offbeat local productions in an intimate cabaret setting, with shows Wednesdays through Sundays, 1385 Curtis (phone: 623-6400).

MUSIC: Two outdoor ampitheaters feature summer rock concerts: *Red Rocks* provides a spectacular mountain setting 12 miles west of Denver off I-70 (phone: 575-2637), and *Fiddler's Green* is 12 miles south of downtown, off I-25 in the Denver Tech Center (phone: 741-5000). Most large indoor concerts are held at *McNichols Arena*, 1635 Clay St. (phone: 572-4703). The *Denver Symphony* plays from October through May at *Boettcher Hall*, 14th and Arapahoe Sts. (phone: 592-7777), with summer concerts at *Fiddler's Green*.

NIGHTCLUBS AND NIGHTLIFE: The well-dressed crowd can find jazz at the *Bay Wolf*, 231 Milwaukee (phone: 388-9221). Comedy is king at *Comedy Works*, 1226 15th St. (phone: 595-3637). Singles and rockers have an almost limitless choice all over town. Among the best are *NEO* (phone: 320-0117) in the Glendale bar district, *Panama Reds* (phone: 695-1750) and the *Wharf* (phone: 671-5111) in the eastern suburb of Aurora, and *Basin's Up* (phone: 623-2104) in Larimer Square.

BEST IN TOWN

CHECKING IN: Denver's ailing economy and plentiful hotel facilities mean great lodging values compared to those in other major US cities. Expect to pay betweeen $90 and $150 at those places we've listed as expensive; between $50 and $90 at those in the moderate category; and about $45 at places noted as inexpensive. All telephone numbers are in the 303 area code unless otherwise indicated.

Brown Palace – Built in the 1890s, it was one of the first hotels to have a multi story atrium lobby with balconies rimming it on every floor. The 231 rooms have been remodeled several times. 17th St. and Tremont Pl. (phone: 297-3111). Expensive.

Hyatt Regency Denver – In the middle of downtown, this 26-story, 540-room hotel boasts superior restaurants, a rooftop recreational complex with pool, tennis court, and jogging track, and lavish room amenities. 1750 Welton St. (phone: 295-1200). Expensive.

Loews Giorgio – The only Colorado member of the Loews chain, it boasts 200 rooms and an Italian motif. From the imported Italian marble and original artwork in the public areas to the romantic Italian atmosphere of the guestrooms, this is one of Denver's best. The library, bar, and *Tuscany* restaurant are quiet and relaxed, and all guests have free access to the nearby *Cherry Creek Sporting Club*. Close to Cherry Creek shopping area. S. Colorado Blvd. and E. Mississippi Ave. (phone: 782-9300). Expensive.

Oxford Alexis – A short stroll from the shopping attractions of the Tabor Center, Writer Square, and historic Larimer Square, the *Oxford* is a bit of history unto itself, having opened in 1891. A $12-million restoration (in 1979) turned this 82-room hotel into a Denver showplace. Restaurant, bar. 17th St. and Wazee (phone: 628-5400). Expensive.

Sheraton DTC – The Denver Tech Center's largest hotel and one of its better values, with 623 rooms, racquetball courts, a deli, and *Campari's* Italian restaurant, which is highly recommended. There is also a commercial airport shuttle. 4900 DTC Pkwy. (phone: 779-1100). Expensive.

Stouffer Concourse – The best of the bunch along "Airport Row," with 400 rooms. Its bars and restaurants offer a stylish atmosphere, though the food is not quite so good. 3801 Quebec St. (phone: 399-7500). Expensive.

Westin Tabor Center – The centerpiece of the Tabor Center, this office-hotel-retail complex is on Denver's 16th Street Mall. Its *Augusta* restaurant has been called "the best hotel restaurant in Denver;" few would dispute the fact that it is at least in the top three. There is also a pool, sauna, racquetball courts, and a fitness center. 16th and Lawrence Sts. (phone: 572-9100). Expensive.

Clarion Hotel/Denver Southeast – Across from Centennial Airport, a popular roost for executives with private planes, the *Clarion* offers beautiful southwestern decor and room appointments for a relatively low price. Amenities include use of a nearby athletic club, an outdoor pool, and helicopter shuttle to the airport. 7770 Peoria St. (phone: 790-7770). Moderate.

Comfort Inn-Downtown – Originally part of the *Brown Palace*, this 230-room structure was converted into a separate establishment for budget-conscious travelers. Complimentary breakfast and access to health club provided. 17th St. and Tremont Pl. (phone: 296-0400). Moderate.

Queen Anne Inn – Denver's best-known bed and breakfast inn is just 4 blocks from the dowtown 16th Street Mall. Proprietors Charles and Ann Hillestad restored this 1879 Victorian home into a 10-unit bed and breakfast accommodations treasure: each unit has a unique decor, private bath, and telephone. The historic surrounding neighborhood is re-emerging after years of decline. No smokers or children under 15. 2147 Tremont Pl. (phone: 296-6666). Moderate.

Marriott Courtyard – A "few frills" entry on the Denver lodging scene that's not to be overlooked. If you can forgo a bellman or room service, you can secure a Marriott-style room and access to a restaurant for a lot less money. Two-room suites are only about $20 more than a standard room. Two locations: Airport, 7415 E. 42st Ave. (phone: 333-3303); Southeast, I-25 and Arapahoe Rd.(phone: 721-0300). Moderate to inexpensive.

EATING OUT: Denver seems to be a magnet for great chefs and adventurous restaurateurs. While beef is king, there are enough places featuring nouvelle cuisine, southwestern fare, pizza, and just plain good eats to keep everyone happy. For two people, expect to pay $50 or more for dinner at restaurants listed as expensive, $30 to $45 at places in the moderate category, and $25 or less at those listed as inexpensive. Prices do not include wine, drinks, or tips. Except where noted otherwise, all restaurants are open for lunch and dinner and accept major credit cards. All telephone numbers are in the 303 area code unless otherwise indicated.

Bay Wolf – Denver's popular jazz club also boasts intimate dining. The continental fare features medallion of tenderloin, rack of lamb, grilled swordfish, and a variety of other specialties. Reservations suggested. In the heart of the Cherry Creek shopping district. 231 Milwaukee (phone: 388-9211). Moderate.

Buckhorn Exchange – Established in 1893 by a former scout for Buffalo Bill Cody, the *Buckhorn* is on the National Register of Historic Places. Festooned with scores of hunting trophies, the restaurant's game dishes — elk, buffalo, and quail, among others — continue to make history today. For those who aren't "game," more standard fare, such as generous beef cuts, are available. Don't pass up the navy bean soup or homemade apple pie with ice cream and hard cinnamon sauce. Open daily for dinner, lunch weekdays. Reservations suggested. Major credit cards. Near downtown, 1000 Osage (phone: 534-9505). Moderate.

The Fort – Near the foothills southwest of Denver, it's where locals take out-of-towners to show off Denver's pioneer spirit. Frontier recipes have been adapted to modern tastes, including elk, Buffalo Boodie Sausage, and Rocky Mountain Oysters (bull's testicles). Try a combination to get a sampling. The restaurant is a replica of Colorado's famous Bent's Fort. In warm weather, make sure you get a seat on the patio: the scenery is fantastic. Dinner nightly. Reservations necessary. Major credit cards. US 285 at Colorado Hwy. 8. (phone: 697-4771). Expensive.

Fresh Fish Company – What's in a name? Everything. The seafood here is so fresh you might think they pulled the swordfish from the Colorado River. The truth is that the fish is flown in daily from all over, so the menu items include Maine lobster, Florida stone crab claws, Canadian walleye, and Hawaiian *ahi*, among others. Everything is cooked over imported Mexican mesquite wood. Those who are health and weight conscious can choose "Healthmark" entrées, which are low in fat, cholesterol, and sodium. No Saturday lunch. Reservations accepted for 5 or more. Major credit cards. 7800 E. Hampden Ave. (phone: 740-9556). Moderate.

Beau Jo's – Ideal for a family outing, this chain of pizza places serves up the Rockies' best mountain pie. Diners choose the ingredients of their "pie," beginning with style of pie and thickness of dough, right down to variety and quantity of cheese. Pies are "weighed" and charged accordingly. Beer and wine available. Takeout available. Idaho Springs (phone: 573-6924) branch is popular as an après-ski stopover. Other locations include 2700 S. Colorado Blvd. (phone: 758-1519) and 1165 13th St., Boulder (phone: 449-3090). Inexpensive.

Bonnie Brae Tavern – In a city where most pizza seems to come from a "hut" or a "domino," this is one pizza place Denverites like to boast about. The setting is rustic and there's usually a wait for a table, but no one seems to mind. No reservations. 740 S. University Blvd. (phone: 777-2262). Inexpensive.

Le Central – Casual, affordable, and French. A real local favorite, where the menu — written on large blackboards — changes daily and the accepted dress ranges from blue jeans to suits and dresses. The service is wonderful, although some may feel rushed by the way one course quickly follows the last. Entrées include chicken, veal, filet, and lots of fish, with prices of just $6.50 to $12. Save room for dessert. Opt for the non-smoking sections and ignore the vinyl tablecloths. No credit cards. Near downtown, 112 E. 8th Ave. (phone: 863-8094). Inexpensive.

La Loma – Started in 1974 as a family enterprise, the intimate, friendly atmosphere and authentic Mexican fare still prevail. *La Loma* offers diverse Mexican selections, from enchiladas and tacos to more ambitious fare, including Mexican camarone, large Gulf shrimp sautéed in seasoned butter, and fajitas, charbroiled chicken or steak bits with grilled onions, marinated in salsa and served with corn tortillas and beans. Try the fried ice cream. Near downtown, 2527 W. 26th Ave. (phone: 433-8307). Inexpensive.

Pour La France Cafés – There are five of these comfortable, casual, bistro-like eateries in Colorado. Menus combine the best of French and American cooking and brunch is special: Grand Marnier French toast, garnished with bananas and strawberries; shrimp and crabmeat quiche; and eggs Arnold (poached eggs on a butter croissant, wtih avocado and hollandaise sauce). All the cafés have bakeries. Closed Sunday and Monday evenings. No reservations. Three locations: 730 S. University Blvd. (phone: 744-1888); 8101 E. Belleview Ave. (phone: 220-8820) and at the Pearl St. Mall in Boulder (phone: 449-3929). Inexpensive.

DETROIT

Poor mercurial Detroit. When its auto industry is percolating, there is dancing in the streets. When it isn't, the breadline forms to the right. Gluttonous prosperity or hard times — Detroit has tasted both, and usually in larger doses than other big cities — with a more diversified industrial underpinning. Cars have been Detroit's lifeblood and its curse.

The inbound drive along I-94 from Metropolitan Airport provides more than subtle shadings of the Motor City, capital of the US auto industry. Low-slung buildings of auto suppliers crowd the banks of the highway. At one bend is a giant tire the size of a ferris wheel. Farther along, the freeway skirts the leviathan Rouge manufacturing complex of Ford Motor Company, the largest industrial complex in the world, and billboards tick off auto production. More than just a digital readout, they are Detroit's electrocardiogram. But whether its vital signs are weak or strong, Detroit always manages to hang in there.

Like most of the Great Lakes country, Detroit's roots are French. When the King of France started wearing a beaver hat late in the 17th century, everyone in French society had to have one, too. This made trapping and exporting beaver fur a very lucrative venture for French trappers around Montréal and Québec. Like any successful business, the beaver trade fell prey to unscrupulous operators, and entire canoeloads of pelts were hijacked along the Great Lakes. In 1701, Antoine de la Mothe Cadillac — who was to have an automobile named after him 200 years later — arrived in Detroit to protect legitimate voyageurs and their cargoes. Cadillac picked the strait between Lake St. Clair and Lake Erie for Fort Pontchartrain d'Etroit ("on the Straits"). After the French and Indian War, the fort became British, then was taken over by the Americans in 1796, 13 years after the Revolutionary War.

If its roots are French, subsequent Detroit history — its tree and branch — is indomitably American. Detroit's destiny was charted for it at the turn of this century when Henry Ford took the horseless carriage concept and applied mass production techniques. Detroit — and the world — hasn't been the same since. A historical plaque marks the site of the little two-story plant in uptown Highland Park where Model T's first sputtered to life. Detroiters worship not only cars but the gods behind them. In the 1960s and 1970s, it was Henry Ford II; in the 1980s, Chrysler's Lee Iacocca.

Detroit's brontosaurus carmaking plants went from wheels to weapons during World War II. Tides of war workers poured into the city and population zoomed. There was plenty of everything for everybody. That was, until Detroit fell into the same lockstep of other American cities. In the quietude of the 1950s, a middle class exodus from the city began, and by the 1960s Detroit had become a case of classic American malaise: rings of wealthy suburbs around a neglected inner city — and its even more neglected resi-

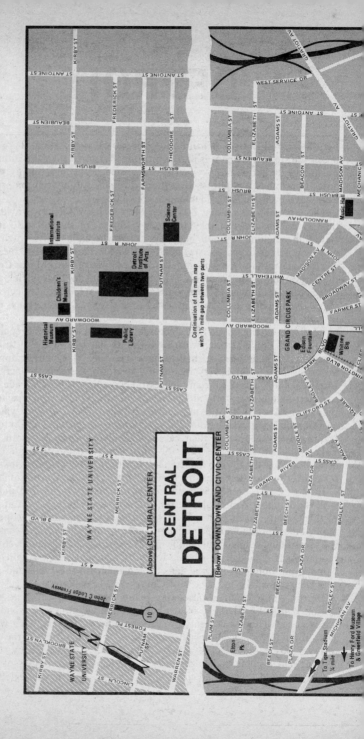

CENTRAL DETROIT

(Above) CULTURAL CENTER

(Below) DOWNTOWN AND CIVIC CENTER

Continuation of the main map
with 1½ mile gap between two parts

WAYNE STATE UNIVERSITY

International Institute

Children's Museum

Historical Museum

Public Library

Detroit Institute of Arts

Science Center

GRAND CIRCUS PARK

Edison Fountain

Whitney Blg

Music Hall

John C Lodge Freeway

To Tiger Stadium ¼ mile

To Henry Ford Museum & Greenfield Village

KIRBY ST · ST ANTOINE ST · BEAUBIEN ST · FREDERICK ST · BRUSH ST · FARNSWORTH ST · THEODORE ST · PUTNAM ST · JOHN R ST · CASS ST · 2 ST · MERRICK ST · WARREN ST · LINCOLN ST · FOREST PL · BROOKLYN ST · 3 BLVD · 4 ST

COLUMBIA ST · ELIZABETH ST · ADAMS ST · BEACON ST · MADISON AV · RANDOLPH AV · JOHN R AV · CENTRE ST · BROADWAY ST · FARMER ST · WHITEHALL ST · WOODWARD AV · PARK BLVD · CLIFFORD ST · MIDDLE ST · GRAND RIVER AV · PLAZA DR · BAGLEY ST · BEECH ST · PLUM ST · MICHIGAN AV · WEST SERVICE DR · GRATIOT AV · MECHANIC · WASHINGTON BLVD · Eaton Pk

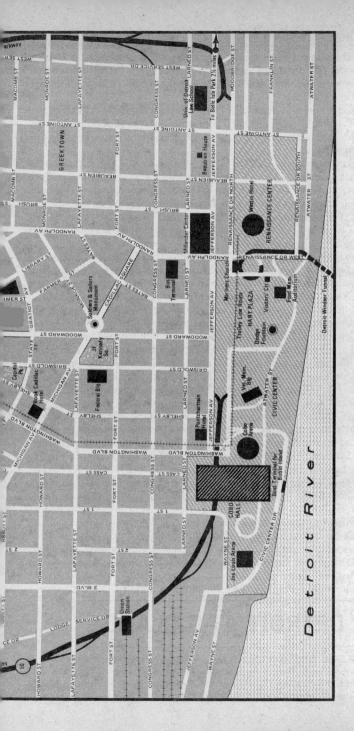

dents. Degeneration of the core city has had severe consequences for Detroit. The mass exodus spurred city planners to allocate funds for endless concrete miles of freeways to connect the suburbs around the city, leaving the downtown area to shrivel.

At last something was done, and Detroit began coming back. Downtown districts left for dead were reborn. There was a profusion of building, especially on the riverfront, along with new restaurants, and a recharged feeling among Detroiters.

Lording over modern Detroit is the Renaissance Center (known as RenCen), six circular towers of dark reflective glass surrounding an even taller tower, the 73-floor *Westin* hotel. The dramatic office-shopping-hotel complex soars regally on the lip of the Detroit River, which separates the city from Canada. Trollies bounce down Washington Boulevard to the riverfront and the doorstep of RenCen. An elevated, automated people mover threads around the central business district.

Although RenCen has had its share of troubles both financially (it defaulted on its mortgage back in 1983) and architecturally (its space age design isolates it both physically and emotionally from the surrounding downtown area), it was a necessary first step in the area's revitalization. Neighborhoods in RenCen's shadow are getting well again, and the Riverfront, a new twin-tower apartment complex, is leading a resurgence in downtown living. Across from RenCen is the $71-million Millender Center of shops, restaurants, apartments, and an *Omni International* hotel. In Bricktown and Rivertown there are new restaurants hopping inside old buildings; Greektown is a long downtown block of some of Detroit's best restaurants, as Greek as Zorba and as energized as *Walt Disney World*. At its heart is gleaming Trappers Alley: five levels of restaurants, specialty shops, and night spots.

After cars, Detroit is a sports town. Basketball fans are justifiably proud of their newly crowned NBA World Champion *Pistons* who shoot hoops at the *Palace* at nearby Auburn Hills. Baseball fans boast the *Tigers* and venerable *Tiger Stadium.* The *Joe Louis Arena,* named for one of Detroit's native sons, is the home of Detroit's pro hockey team, the *Red Wings,* and boxing. It's also on the revitalized riverfront alongside sprawling Cobo Hall, the city's cavernous convention center. There's the *Pontiac Silverdome,* with the world's largest inflated roof, for football. Detroit's Cultural Center and its Medical Center hug the city's main thoroughfare, Woodward Avenue, which separates Detroit's east and west sides.

Detroiters have a lot of good reasons to like themselves and where they live. After all, Detroit gave the world the Motown sound and the first ice cream soda, the first jazz club and "cold duck", not to mention (we will, anyway) Tom Selleck, Aretha Franklin, Lily Tomlin, and author Elmore Leonard.

DETROIT AT-A-GLANCE

SEEING THE CITY: The best view of the city is from the top of the 73-story *Westin* hotel. Part of the Renaissance Center, it is one of the city's most dramatic creations. Views are from the hotel's top three floors, called the *Summit,* with a revolving restaurant and cocktail lounge and an observation deck ($2.50 if you're not dining or a hotel guest). Ever-changing views are possible from the People Mover (phone: 962-7245); fare 50¢. There are great skyline views of Detroit from rooms in the *Hilton International Windsor* and from Dieppe Gardens, a riverside park at the foot of Ouellette Avenue, Windsor's main street.

 SPECIAL PLACES: Down on the ground, Civic Center is a good place to begin sightseeing. We've divided the city into Civic Center, Cultural Center, and other Special Places.

CIVIC CENTER

Renaissance Center – Detroit's very own Oz, this city-within-the-city dominates Detroit's skyline. Dining, entertainment, designer boutiques, and more have made RenCen tick since it opened in 1977. The fortress-like berms that surround the building add to its isolation from the rest of downtown. The huge complex is tied together by a maze of walkways, atriums, gardens — even an indoor lake. Prediction: With seven circular buildings to stroll around, first-timers will get lost. Everybody does. Group tours are available (phone: 591-3611). Jefferson Ave. between Randolph and Beaubien Sts.

Millender Center – Tethered to RenCen by an arcing skywalk over Jefferson Avenue, Millender is a smaller version of the office-shopping complex without the dizzying confusion. Both the Millender Center and the abutting *Omni* hotel boast quality shops and restaurants.

Philip A. Hart Plaza – This once ragtag area of waterfront is now an upbeat people-place designed by the international sculptor Isamu Noguchi. What it lacks in grass, this paved esplanade makes up for in action. The $30-million Dodge Fountain spouts 30 computer-controlled water displays. It's also the home of Detroit's summer riverfront festivals of food and entertainment. In winter, there's an ice skating pavilion, à la Rockefeller Center. The Detroit River is alongside, with Windsor, Ontario, on the far bank.

Detroit People Mover – An elevated, 2.9-mile cement ribbon wraps around downtown, carrying pedestrians in automated, weatherproof cars from city squares to RenCen, Cobo Hall to Greektown. Complete 13-station loop takes 14 minutes and costs 50¢.

Washington Boulevard Trolley – A charming, antique trolley car wends its way south from Grand Circus Park along Washington Boulevard and east to RenCen. (The conductor wears 1890 regalia.) The trolley runs through a new downtown section of sidewalk cafés, specialty shops, and covered parkways, past St. Aloysius Church, Cobo Hall, the Visitor Information Center, and Mariner's Church.

CULTURAL CENTER

Detroit Institute of Arts – An unusual collection of Great Masters and modern artists lines the walls, halls, and gardens here. Visitors can examine Peter Breughel's Flemish masterpiece *Wedding Dance* and Mexican artist Diego Rivera's gripping, provocative frescoes on the industrial life of Detroit. In the garden is a bust of Lincoln by Gutzon Borglum, Mt. Rushmore's sculptor. Closed Mondays. Donations accepted. 5200 Woodward Ave. (phone: 833-7900).

Detroit Public Library – This Italian Renaissance, white Vermont marble building houses books, paintings, stained glass windows, and mosaics. The *Burton Historical Museum,* an archive of material related to Detroit history, is one of the library's special collections. Closed Sundays and holidays. No admission charge. Woodward and Kirby Aves. (phone: 833-1000).

Detroit Historical Museum – The early days of Detroit are shown by models of early streets and railroads, period rooms, and exhibitions on horseless carriages and automobiles. In the basement stands a permanent display of actual storefronts from bygone eras. Closed Mondays, Tuesdays, and holidays. Donations accepted. Woodward and Kirby Aves. (phone: 833-1805).

Wayne State University – Known for its innovative architecture rather than its football. A lot of buildings have gone up since 1960, among them a new medical center attached to the Wayne State Medical School, reputed to be one of the best in the country. If you enjoy a college atmosphere, take a stroll on the campus. 650 W. Kirby (phone: 577-2424).

Detroit Science Center – The hands-on displays here allow visitors to demonstrate scientific principles for themselves. This $5-million complex also features a domed space theater. Closed Mondays. Admission charge. 5020 John R St. (phone: 577-8400).

Children's Museum – A planetarium and collections of puppets and small animals. Kids love the life-size sculpture of the horse near the entrance — it's made out of automobile bumpers. Closed Sundays. No admission charge. 67 E. Kirby Ave. (phone: 494-1210).

Museum of African American History – Black heritage explored through art and artifacts. No admission charge. 301 Douglass (phone: 833-9800).

OTHER SPECIAL PLACES

Belle Isle – This beautiful island park in the middle of the Detroit River was originally allocated for pasture by M. Cadillac himself. About 2 miles long, Belle Isle has a children's zoo; the *Dossin Great Lakes Museum,* with displays of model ships (phone: 267-6440); and an Aquarium (267-7159). It's also a good place for picnics, biking, canoeing, and jogging. South of Jefferson, across the Gen. Douglas MacArthur Bridge (recreation office, phone: 224-1100).

Boblo Boats – Every day between Memorial and Labor days, two 1,200-passenger steamers leave downtown Detroit for Boblo Island. The 26-mile boat ride takes about 1½ hours each way — the most pleasant way to see industrial Detroit and Canada. At Boblo Island, there's a large amusement park and local craftwork. At the foot of Clark Ave., 2 blocks south of I-75 (phone: 843-8800).

Cranbrook – Stroll through 49 acres of gardens surrounding an English manor. Catch a laser light show in a planetarium. Visit a nature center or browse through an art museum or science exhibition. It's all part of this internationally known center for the arts, education, science, and culture. A maple sugar festival, concerts, and other special events make Cranbrook a compelling place, worth the 25-mile drive north from Detroit. Lone Pine Rd., Bloomfield Hills (phone: 645-3000).

Star of Detroit – Restaurants/bars that are tugboats, sidewheelers, or otherwise waterbound are anchored in the Detroit River between Detroit and Windsor. The *Star* one-ups the rest by offering lunch, dinner, Sunday brunch, and cocktail cruises. Entertainment and dancing. Operates in the summer from the foot of Hart Plaza (phone: 259-9160).

Greenfield Village and Henry Ford Museum – Legend has it that when Henry Ford couldn't find a copy of McGuffey's *Reader,* he feared such examples of Americana would disappear entirely unless he founded a museum. The result is here — and as you might expect, it has hundreds of splendid, antique automobiles and thousands of 19th- and 20th-century machines. Next-door Greenfield Village is a collection of transplanted houses of historical interest. Henry Ford couldn't be stopped — he bought McGuffey's school and had it reconstructed, along with Thomas Edison's Menlo Park laboratory and the first boardinghouse to have electricity. An English shepherd's cottage and Noah Webster's house are also here. Separate admissions for Greenfield Village and *Henry Ford Museum;* combination tickets available. South of Michigan Ave. between Oakwood Blvd. and Southfield Fwy., Dearborn (phone: 271-1620).

Eastern Market – A carnival of sights, smells, and sounds, this has been a farmers' market since 1892. Saturdays are great fun, watching shoppers haggle over prices with merchants selling the freshest produce, meats, fish, poultry, and cheeses. Russell at Fisher Fwy. (phone: 833-1560).

Greektown -- A downtown enclave of restaurants serving authentic Greek fare. Quaint shops, bakeries, and Old St. Mary's Church make an interesting stroll. Trappers Alley, a 5-level mall full of restaurants, specialty shops, and *Monroe's* disco, is the new kid on the block. Monroe St. between Beaubien and St. Antoine.

Motown Museum -- To pop music fans, this brick and stucco building, called Hitsville, USA, turned out more gold than Ft. Knox. Motown memories abound in the museum including Berry Gordy Jr.'s original studio, where *The Supremes,* Stevie Wonder, *The Temptations, The Four Tops,* and others recorded. Michael Jackson, the museum's biggest benefactor, donated $125,000 to fund more displays. Open daily. Admission charge. 2648 W. Grand Blvd. (phone: 875-2264).

Plant Tours – General Motors' Lake Orion plant (phone: 377-5507) and its Buick City Assembly Center in Flint (phone: 1-236-4494) offer tours by reservation only. Tours of Windsor's Hiram Walker Canadian Club Distillery are offered twice daily, summer only (call 965-6611 for reservations).

■**EXTRA SPECIAL:** Detroit's biggest tourist attraction is just a mile away: Canada. In just a few minutes, you can enter a different country, and you don't even need a passport if you're a US citizen — just a birth certificate. Don't expect any drastic change from Detroit, however. Windsor, Ontario, just across the river, is another automobile-producing city, with Canadian GM, Chrysler, and Ford plants. If you're looking for bargains, Ontario is a great place to buy English woolens, glassware, and china. The city is literally on Detroit's doorstep, and you can get there by bus or taxi to the tunnel or by the Ambassador Bridge.

SOURCES AND RESOURCES

TOURIST INFORMATION: The Metropolitan Detroit Convention and Visitors Bureau maintains a 24-hour "What's Line" directory of events (phone: 298-6262) and distributes free brochures and maps. 2 Jefferson Ave., Detroit, MI 48226 (phone: 259-4333).

Detroit Visitor's Guide (Metropolitan Detroit Convention and Visitors Bureau; free) is the best guide to the area. Pick up a free *Detroit Monitor* or *Metro Times* for about-town happenings and attractions.

Television Stations – WJBK Channel 2–CBS; WBIV Channel 4–NBC; WXYZ Channel 7–ABC; WTVS Channel 56–PBS.

Radio Stations – AM: WJR 760 (news/talk); WWJ 950 (news); WXYT 1270 (talk). FM: WQRS 105.1 (classical); WJZZ 105.9 (jazz); WCZY 95.5 (adult contemporary).

Local Coverage – *Detroit Free Press,* morning daily; *Detroit News,* morning and afternoon daily; *Royal Oak Tribune* and *Oakland Press* (Pontiac, both afternoon). *Key* (free) and *Travel Host* magazines are available at hotels. *Detroit Monthly* is the popular city magazine.

Telephone – The area code for Detroit is 313.

Sales Tax – Detroit has a 4% sales tax; hotel tax ranges from 5% to 11%, depending on the size and location of the establishment.

CLIMATE: Seasons usually procrastinate in Detroit. You might miss spring if you blink, and summer doesn't really peak until July. Autumn can be a day. The local joke is that if you don't like the weather, stick around because it'll change again in about five minutes. Temperatures range into the 70s and

80s in summer, and a light wrap might help for cool nights. Subfreezing temperatures are often the rule in January and February, so bundle up.

GETTING AROUND: Airport – Detroit Metropolitan Wayne County Airport handles most of the city's air traffic and is about a 30-minute drive from downtown; taxi fare to downtown runs approximately $25. Commuter Transportation (phone: 941-3252) provides bus transport to the downtown area from the airport's north and south terminals for $11; for information on routes and schedules, call the Dept. of Transportation (phone: 833-7692).

Southwest Airlines (phone: 562-1221 or 800 531-5601) serves 24 cities from the regional City Airport, 7 miles from downtown. *Commuter Services* (phone: 372-0690) operates vans ($5) and limos ($17.25) between the airports and hotels. Cab fare runs $12.

Taxi – Cabs can be hailed in the street or picked up at the stands in front of hotels. Some of the cabs are licensed to cross over to Canada. If you prefer to call for a cab, we suggest *Checker* (phone: 963-7000).

Car Rental – All the major national firms are represented.

LOCAL SERVICES: Business Services – For photocopying, try *NRC,* at RenCen (phone: 259-5066); *Silver's,* 151 W. Fort (phone: 963-0000), has stationery and supplies.

    Mechanic – *Downtown Auto Service,* 1200 Cass Ave. (phone: 963-2744).

MUSEUMS: Detroit's major museums — the *Detroit Historical Museum, Institute of Arts, Children's Museum* — are described under *Special Places.*

    Four of the majestic homes created by Detroit's automotive wealth are open for public inspection in the Auto Barons Tour: Henry Ford's Fairlane mansion, Dearborn (phone: 593-5590); his son Edsel's home (where Henry II grew up), the Edsel & Eleanor Ford House, Grosse Pointe Shores (phone: 884-3400); the ornate riverfront entertainment estate of Lawrence P. Fisher, now the Bhaktivedanta Cultural Center in Detroit (phone: 331-6740); and Meadow Brook Hall in Rochester, which cost Matilda Dodge Wilson $4 million to complete in 1929 (phone: 370-3140).

MAJOR COLLEGES AND UNIVERSITIES: Wayne State University and medical complex, 650 W. Kirby Ave. (phone: 577-2424); University of Detroit, 4001 W. McNichols (phone: 927-1000); University of Michigan, 4901 Evergreen Rd., Dearborn (phone: 593-5000); Oakland University, Walton Rd., Rochester (phone: 370-2100).

SPECIAL EVENTS: The *Detroit Grand Prix* sends Indy-type cars thundering through the downtown canyons every June. The friendship between Windsor and Detroit is celebrated in the *International Freedom Festival,* a series of events during Fourth of July week, highlighted by spectacular fireworks over the river. The *Montreux Jazz Festival* has become quite an annual event the week surrounding Labor Day weekend. Concerts are held in Hart Plaza and at many other locations. Call Detroit Renaissance (phone: 259-5400) for details on the *Grand Prix, Freedom Festival,* and *Jazz Festival. Michigan's Thanksgiving Day Parade,* a Detroit tradition since 1926, still marches on every Turkey Day (phone: 923-7400).

SPORTS AND FITNESS: Detroit wouldn't be Detroit without its top major league professional teams: the *Lions,* football; *Pistons,* basketball; *Red Wings,* hockey; and *Tigers,* baseball.

    Baseball – Home base for the American League *Tigers* is *Tiger Stadium,* Michigan at Trumbull (phone: 962-4000).

Basketball – The 1989 NBA world champion *Pistons* shoot hoops at the *Palace of Auburn Hills* (phone: 377-8200).

Fishing – Fishing is pretty good in the Detroit River, especially around Belle Isle. There are hundreds of lakes in the area; we recommend Orchard Lake.

Fitness Centers – The downtown *Westin* (phone: 568-8000), *Omni* (phone: 222-7700), and *Pontchartrain* (phone: 965-0200) hotels run spas for the exercise-minded.

Football – The *Lions* (phone: 335-4151) play in the 80,000-seat, covered *Silverdome*. M-59 at Opdyke, Pontiac.

Golf – Two of the better public courses are *Rackham,* 10100 W. Ten Mile, Huntington Woods (phone: 398-8430), and *William Rogell,* 18601 Berg Rd. (phone: 935-5331).

Hockey – *Red Wings* action is on the ice at *Joe Louis Arena,* Civic Center Dr. (phone: 567-6000).

Horse Racing – Thoroughbreds race at *Ladbroke DRC* (phone: 525-7300); *Schoolcraft at Middlebelt,* Livonia (phone: 421-7170); *Hazel Park Harness Raceway,* 1650 E. Ten Mile, Hazel Park (phone: 566-1595); *Windsor Raceway,* fall and winter harness racing, Hwy. 18, Windsor, Ont. (phone: 519-961-9545).

Jogging – The ideal spot is Belle Isle Park. To get there, run 2½ miles east along Jefferson and a half mile over the arched bridge; or take the Jefferson bus, then jog around the island's perimeter. A group called "People Who Run Downtown" meets every Tuesday at a downtown saloon before or after walking or jogging a route that varies each week (phone: 961-1403).

Tennis – The City of Detroit operates several public courts. The best are at Palmer Park and Belle Isle. Call Parks and Recreation (phone: 224-1100) for schedule information.

 THEATERS: Detroit's active theatrical life provides audiences with entertaining choices. There may be a Broadway-bound hit breaking in at the *Fisher Theater* year-round. 2nd at Grand Blvd. (phone: 872-1000). The *Birmingham Theater,* 211 S. Woodward, Birmingham (phone: 644-3533), features straight drama and comedy, as does the *Meadow Brook Theatre* on the Oakland University campus. Its season runs from September to May at University Dr. east of I-75, Rochester (phone: 377-3300). Also very good are the *Hilberry Classic Theater,* 4743 Cass (phone: 577-2972), and the *Attic Theater,* 2990 W. Grand Blvd. (phone: 875-8284).

 MUSIC: Just about any kind of music thrives in Detroit — symphonic, jazz, or soul. Detroit is the birthplace of Motown, the sound epitomized by the music of Stevie Wonder, the Supremes, and the Temptations. Today rockers like Bob Seger call Detroit home. Rock and soul concerts are played at the spanking new *Palace of Auburn Hills* (also the home of the *Pistons*), 3777 Lapeer Rd. (phone: 377-8200), *Cobo Arena,* Jefferson at Washington Blvd. (phone: 567-6000), and at *Joe Louis Arena,* Civic Center Dr. (phone: 567-6000); *Pontiac Silverdome,* M-59 at Opdyke, Pontiac (phone: 857-8000); *Masonic Auditorium,* 500 Temple (phone: 832-2232); *Ford Auditorium,* Jefferson at Woodward (224-1055); *Royal Oak Music Theatre,* 318 W. 4th St. (phone: 546-7610); and the *Fox Theatre,* 2211 Woodward (phone: 567-6000). The *Detroit Symphony,* whose concert season runs from September to May, performs at *Orchestra Hall. Orchestra Hall* offers dance and classical and jazz concerts, 3711 Woodward (phone: 833-3700). *"Brunch with Bach"* is presented Sundays at the *Detroit Institute of Arts,* 5200 Woodward Ave. (phone: 833-7900). *Meadow Brook Music Festival* offers summer symphonies and pop and jazz artists, Oakland University campus (phone: 377-2010). Top-name entertainers perform at the outdoor *Pine Knob Music Theater,* Sashabaw, north of I-75, Clarkston (phone: 423-6666). The summer jazz series, *P'Jazz,* begun in 1972, is held every Friday on the terrace of the *Pontchartrain* hotel (phone: 965-0200). *Music Hall Center for the Performing Arts* (phone:

963-7680) hosts traveling dance and music concerts. The *Fisher Theater* is the home of the *Michigan Opera Theater,* 6519 2nd Ave. (phone: 874-SING).

NIGHTCLUBS AND NIGHTLIFE: *Gino's Surf Lounge* is a low-budget spot that has dancing and a floor show; 37400 E. Jefferson, Mt. Clemens (phone: 468-2611). *Midtown Café,* Birmingham (phone: 642-1133), and *Galligan's,* downtown (phone: 963-2098), are the places where singles mingle. *Baker's Uptown,* N. Saginaw at Pike, Pontiac (phone: 338-7337), has great jazz. At the *Soup Kitchen Saloon,* there's blues from Wednesdays through Sundays; 1585 Franklin (phone: 259-1374). *Windsor's Top Hat* has first-rate lounge acts; 73 University (phone: 963-3742). *Alexander's* has soothing decor and all that jazz daily except Sundays, 4265 Woodward (phone: 831-2662); *Taboo,* 1940 Woodbridge (phone: 567-6140), is Detroit's reigning New York–style disco. *Mark Ridley's Comedy Castle* presents national acts with local openers, and there's an open mike on Mondays; Woodward at Catalpa, Berkley (phone: 542-9900).

BEST IN TOWN

CHECKING IN: By expensive, we mean between $80 and $120 for a double room. Our moderate selections are in the $60 to $80 range; inexpensive lodging (less than $60) is available at various chain hotels such as *Days Inn, Budgetel, Red Roof Inn,* and *Knights Inn.* For inexpensive bed and breakfast accommodations, contact *Betsy Ross Bed & Breakfast,* 23522 Lawrence, Dearborn, MI 48128 (phone: 561-6041). All telephone numbers are in the 303 area code unless otherwise indicated.

Hyatt Regency Dearborn – Its 800 spacious, airy rooms overlook the landscaped park of the Ford World Headquarters in Dearborn. Round glass elevator pods, lit up like rockets, whisk guests to the upper floors. Nearby are Fairlane Shopping Center, Greenfield Village, *Henry Ford Museum,* and a University of Michigan campus. Michigan and Southfield Fwy., Dearborn (phone: 593-1234, 800-233-1234, or 800-228-9000). Expensive.

Omni International – Abutting the Millender Center of shops, restaurants, and apartments, this new 25-floor hostelry with 258 spacious and imaginatively appointed rooms fills Detroit's need for more downtown hotel space. There's also an exercise room and health club, meeting rooms, and restaurants. 333 E. Jefferson, at the junction of RenCen and the Detroit-Windsor Tunnel (phone: 222-7700 or 800-228-2121). Expensive.

Pontchartrain – Detroiters call it "the Pontch." Built on the site of Ft. Pontchartrain, this landmark property has emerged from a $15-million face-lift of its public areas and 420 rooms. Heavy reds, greens, and velvets have given way to soothing mauves, jades, and plums and a decidedly residential feel. And they've added a new health club. *Top of the Pontch* is a nightclub from Thursdays to Saturdays; on Sundays it's open for brunch. *Elaine's,* the fine dining room, serves continental fare; lighter meals can be taken in the *Garden Court,* with its greenhouse atmosphere. *P'jazz* concerts happen here every Friday during the summer. 2 Washington Blvd. (phone: 965-0200 or 800-537-6624). Expensive.

Ritz-Carlton Dearborn – From the outside, it looks like an imposing French château. All 11 floors, decorated in 18th- and 19th-century art and antiques, radiate unbridled warmth and elegance. Traditional decor defines the guestrooms, including those on the 2 executive floors. Fine dining is at *The Restaurant; The Grill and Bar* is a fine steaks-and-chops restaurant, with wood-burning fireplace. Full exercise room including indoor lap pool. 300 Town Center Dr., across from Ford's headquarters, Dearborn (phone: 441-2000 or 800-241-3333). Expensive.

St. Regis – Detroit's elegant, European-style hotel. Its rooms and public areas are gracefully appointed, and the French Regency exterior is done in limestone and glazed brick with wrought-iron work and bay windows. The midtown location is ideal for guests with business with the corporate giants in the New Center area, 10 minutes from downtown. 3071 W. Grand Blvd. (phone: 873-3000). Expensive.

Townsend – Here are 87 rooms (including executive and 2-room suites) in a surprisingly traditonal new building. A harpist holds court in the lobby and executive suites feature a formal dining room, living and sleeping area and 1 ½ baths. Tasteful furnishings include marble bathrooms with brass fixtures; morning delivery of newspaper; the *Rugby Grille* serves everything from beef to seafood. Use of local health club (transportation provided). 100 Townsend St., Birmingham (phone: 313-642-7900 or 800-548-4172). Expensive.

Troy Hilton – On the lip of Detroit's big north-south interstate (I-75), convenient to K-Mart headquarters, chic shopping at Somerset Mall, and the *Meadow Brook* and *Pine Knob* theaters. Guests in any of the 401 rooms also have access to an indoor/outdoor pool, sauna, and jogging track. 1455 Stephenson Hwy. (phone: 583-9000 or 800-482-3940). Expensive.

Westin Renaissance Center – This 1,400-room, 73-story round building has considerable drama in its public areas. The lobby takes up the first 8 stories, with fountains, trees, aerial walkways, specialty shops, and cocktail lounges. Three levels of bars and restaurants revolve. Unfortunately, the rooms are not nearly up to the standard of the public spaces. At the east end of Hart Plaza, on Jefferson at St. Antoine (phone: 568-8000 or 800-228-3000). Expensive.

Radisson Plaza – A 392-room hotel, with indoor pool and health club, is at the doorstep of the office towers of Southfield. Prudential Town Center, Southfield (phone: 827-4000). Expensive to moderate.

Barclay Inn – Trendy Birmingham draws its roots from this site, where John West Hunter, Birmingham's founder and first innkeeper, maintained a tavern and log cabins. The 128 rooms are divided between a 5-story tower where a Queen Anne style prevails and a motel-like building where washed pine furnishings and hunter green walls evoke a country flair. Tower hallways are a gallery of early Birmingham photos. Relax by the fireplace in the lobby with a complimentary breakfast of yogurt, fresh fruit, and scones; tea and cookies in the afternoon. At Hunter and Maple Rds., Birmingham (phone: 646-7300 or 800-521-3509). Moderate.

Berkshire – A European-style operation, with amenities such as continental breakfast and newspapers delivered to each of the 109 rooms. 26111 Telegraph at 10½ Mile Rd., Southfield (phone: 356-4333). Moderate.

Botsford Inn – The original 151-year-old stagecoach stop still serves hearty American fare in the *Coach Room.* Expansion 4 years ago increased the number of modern, spacious rooms to 75. 28000 Grand River Ave. at 8 Mile, Farmington Hills (phone: 474-4800). Moderate.

Dearborn Inn – On a 23-acre site, just a few hundred yards down the road from the historic *Henry Ford Museum* and Greenfield Village, and only a 20-minute journey from downtown Detroit, stands this Georgian-style mansion, built by Henry Ford in 1931 and later joined in 1937 by five reproductions of historic colonial homes and in 1960 by two motel-style wings. The charm and beauty of a bygone era have been re-created in the rooms and suites with early American-style furniture, hand-painted wallpaper, and old-fashioned hospitality. Guests can choose from 3 dining rooms, all of which offer tasty, albeit rather homogenous, American fare, and for those who wish to put history aside in favor of activity, there are tennis courts nestled between several of the colonial homes. Other amenities include valet, laundry, airport limousine, and babysitting service. 20301 Oakwood Blvd., Dearborn (phone: 271-2700; 800-221-7236). Moderate.

Embassy Suites – "Rooms to roam" is the concept behind this all-suite hotel group. Each of the 240 suites consists of a bedroom, parlor, and wet bar. Registered guests receive a free full breakfast cooked to order and complimentary cocktails. Indoor pool, sauna, whirlpool, and meeting rooms. Ideally situated if your business or pleasure is in the Southfield area. 27754 Franklin Rd., Southfield (phone: 350-2000 or 800-EMBASSY). Moderate.

Hilton International Windsor – Just across the Detroit River and commanding a sparkling view of Detroit's skyline from all of its 307 rooms, this new hotel features mini-bars in every room and two executive floors with concierge service. 277 Riverside Dr. W. (phone: 962-3834, 800-HILTONS, or 519-973-5555). Moderate.

Mayflower Bed & Breakfast – This cozy, family-owned inn offers full, complimentary breakfast to guests. On the town square in quaint Plymouth. 827 Ann Arbor Trail (phone: 453-1620). Moderate.

 EATING OUT: Detroit has a number of moderately priced restaurants serving everything from steaks, crêpes, and pheasant to natural foods and Coney Island hot dogs. And the nationalities represented include French, Middle Eastern, and Alsatian. Expect to pay $40 or more for two at expensive restaurants listed here; between $20 and $35, moderate; and under $20 in our inexpensive range. Prices are for two, and do not include drinks, wine, or tips. All telephone numbers are in the 313 area code unless otherwise indicated.

Les Auteurs – Cozy bistro where pictures of great chefs and autographed menus make up the wall art. A constantly changing menu features vegetable sauces and other noteworthy items such as black bean cake with smoked chicken, tomato salsa, and sour cream. Inventive toppings of rock shrimp, fresh basil, and duck confit crown thin-crusted pizza. Specials are listed on a blackboard above the open kitchen. Closed Sundays. Reservations advised. Major credit cards. 222 Sherman Dr., Washington Square Plaza, Royal Oak (phone: 544-2887). Expensive.

Golden Mushroom – The menu changes with the mood of Milos Cihelka, one of the top chefs in town. Hope you're there when he's inclined to prepare his veal Oscar, calves' liver with green peppercorns, or roast rack of lamb persillade. Mushroom specials are displayed like jewelry at your table. Closed Sundays. Reservations advised. Major credit cards. Ten Mile at Southfield (phone: 559-4230). Expensive.

Joe Muer's – Some people say this place serves the best seafood west of the Atlantic. Others say it's even better. Extravagant praise, no matter how sincere, can never substitute for firsthand experience, especially where seafood is concerned. Be prepared to wait in line, though. *Joe Muer's* doesn't take reservations. (A waiter will bring you a drink while you're standing.) Closed Sundays and holidays. No reservations. Major credit cards. 2000 Gratiot (phone: 567-1088). Expensive.

The Lark – A charming dining spot, this country inn features continental cuisine. In fair weather, a mesquite barbecue is prepared outdoors. Closed Sundays and Mondays. Reservations necessary. Major credit cards. 6430 Farmington Rd., W. Bloomfield (phone: 661-4466). Expensive.

London Chop House – No longer the top table in town, this well-known downstairs den still has its loyalists, who come for its 300-bottle wine list and changing specials (anchored, natch, by steaks and chops). Barkeeps who haven't been here more than 30 years are considered rookies. Booths by the bar are reserved for visiting celebrities. We wish they'd resolve the management battles and get back to concentrating on the food. Closed Sundays. Reservations necessary. Major credit cards. 155 W. Congress (phone: 962-0278). Expensive.

1940 Chop House – Art Deco, supper-clubbish decor, and a menu to please any beef lover. Of 20 main courses, a dozen involve red meat — certified Angus beef from Kansas, succulent and seared over leaping flames by white-clad chefs in the exhibition kitchen. Closed Sundays. Reservations advised. Major credit cards. 1940 E. Jefferson near RenCen (phone: 567-1940). Expensive.

Opus One – The latest gem in a growing necklace of downtown-area restaurants, its finely tuned menu features breast of duck, roulades of salmon, sea bass in a subtle champagne sauce, salads that are arranged, not tossed, and inventive soups led by a crayfish bisque. The decor is classical, with tapestry-covered banquettes, varying shades of white, and etched glass. Reservations advised. Major credit cards. 565 E. Larned, Bricktown (phone: 961-7766). Expensive.

Rattlesnake – Formerly called the *Rattlesnake Club* (no, that was not on the menu), this lively, contemporary room, with wide windows looking out on the Detroit River, features highly acclaimed and ever-changing appetizers and sinful desserts. Main courses tend toward dishes like pickerel with spiced crust and green papaya, and pork with leeks, apples, and cider. Save room for the caloric ball of chocolate ice cream rolled in cocoa powder. Atmosphere can best be described as "theatrical." Main dining room and grill open daily for lunch and dinner. Reservations advised. Major credit cards. 300 Stroh River Pl., foot of Joseph Campau (phone: 567-4400). Expensive.

Summit – Perched on the 72nd floor of the *Westin* and revolving to give diners a 360-degree view of Detroit, the river, and Canada. Char-grilled steaks, seafood, salads tossed right at your table, and a first-rate wine list. Open daily. Reservations advised. Major credit cards. Renaissance Center (phone: 568-8000). Expensive.

333 East – A menu that can only be described as American trendy: grilled Pacific salmon, sautéed veal, breast of duck or chicken with herb and wine sauces for dinner; sandwiches, seafood pasta, and pizza at lunch. Elegant yet unpretentious, with mirrors, American artwork, and Austrian shades to veil the glass wall overlooking Brush Street. Recommended for late dining downtown. Open daily. Major credit cards. 333 E. Jefferson at the *Omni International* hotel (phone: 222-7404). Expensive.

Van Dyke Place – Detroit's most handsome restaurant is an old house decorated with walnut woods, marble fireplaces, and silk brocade draperies. Also an attraction is the delicious French cuisine. Closed Sundays and Mondays. Reservations necessary. Major credit cards. 649 Van Dyke Pl. (phone: 821-2620). Expensive.

Whitney – De rigueur dining in Detroit in an opulent jewelbox of a midtown mansion, circa 1894. The owners insisted on American cuisine for an American house, and so the menu is replete with Michigan trout, Florida Keys shrimp, Maryland crabmeat, grilled or poached Maine lobster, California mussels, and farm-raised game. Save room for the chocolate taco: a raspberry mousse–filled walnut tuile (a super-thin cookie) topped with kiwi and grated white chocolate and napped in raspberry, lemon, and lime purée. Major credit cards. Woodward at Canfield (phone: 832-5700). Expensive.

Money Tree – The kitchen here turns out interesting soups, fresh pasta, quiche, and crêpes. There's also an impressive pastry cart and one of Detroit's liveliest after-work bars. Closed Sundays. Reservations advised. Major credit cards. 333 W. Fort (phone: 961-2445). Expensive to moderate.

Cajun Quarter – Rich seafood gumbo, shrimp Créole, blackened prime ribs, followed by sweet potato pecan pie. Sweetly Southern decor, too — pink walls, rosy table linens, and lace-paper doilies, with framed posters celebrating the food and music of New Orleans. And you only have to go as far south as Windsor, Canada (that's right, Canada is south of here), across the Detroit River. Reservations suggested. 3236 Sandwich St., Windsor, Ontario (phone: 519-258-8604). Moderate.

Charley's Crab – The seafood menu and the ragtime piano player are real crowd pleasers. Open daily. Reservations advised. Major credit cards. 5498 Crooks Rd. at I-75, Troy (phone: 879-2060). Moderate.

La Cuisine – The chef of this mite-sized French restaurant whistles up heavenly three-mustard kidneys, tasty fish soup, and more from his kitchen smack in the middle of the room. Closed Sundays and Mondays. Reservations necessary. Most major credit cards. 417 Pelissier, Windsor, Ontario (phone: 519-253-6432). Moderate.

Lelli's – Start with the best minestrone in town, served by black-tied waiters, in a romantic warren of dining rooms. Tenderloin, broiled red snapper, veal kidneys, etc., but the tour de force is solid Italian fare. The Monday lunchtime crowd is treated to a fashion show. Closed Sundays. Major credit cards. 7618 Woodward (phone: 871-1590). Moderate.

Pontchartrain Wine Cellars – Where "cold duck" was invented, with a unique French/New York style. Closed Sundays. Reservations recommended. Major credit cards. 234 W. Larned (phone: 963-1785). Moderate.

Chez Vins – Pleasing little storefront bistro in Windsor. Very French, very romantic. Take a table by the front windows or behind the blackboard menu (baked brie, snails in herb sauce, crêpes, and shrimp Créole are mainstays). Salads and crusty French bread — *bien sûr.* Numerous French wines by the glass, and courteous, pleasant service. Closed Sundays. Major credit cards. 26 Chatham St. E., Windsor, Ontario (phone: 519-252-2801). Inexpensive.

New Hellas – The hub of Detroit's 1-block Greek community is as Greek as Greek can be, with moussaka, calamari (squid), and baklava. Open daily until 3 AM. No reservations. Major credit cards. 583 Monroe (phone: 961-5544). Inexpensive.

Wong's – Windsor's most popular Oriental restaurant got that way because of good food and the caring attention of owner Raymond Wong. Heaven, for lovers of this cuisine, is the luncheon buffet. Seafood — fresh abalone, mussels, and sea snails — is showing up more and more often on the voluminous menu. Choices range from Cantonese and Hong Kong style to Szechwan. Major credit cards. 1457 University Ave. W., Windsor (phone: 961-0212 or 519-252-8814). Inexpensive.

FT. LAUDERDALE

For many Americans, the mere mention of Ft. Lauderdale immediately conjures images of the 1960 movie *Where the Boys Are* (or its 1984 successor),
which immortalized the seasonal migration of the nation's college students to
Ft. Lauderdale during spring break in search of sun and fun. The migration
has been quelled, however, by city fathers, who've discouraged that rite of
spring in order to improve Ft. Lauderdale's overall appeal to adults and to
beef up family tourism. It seems to have worked: collegians now flock to
Daytona Beach while mom, pop, and the kids populate Ft. Lauderdale's
beaches. And with good reason: Ft. Lauderdale claims to receive 3,000 hours
of sunshine a year — more than anywhere else in the continental US —
and the year-round average temperature is in the mid-70s.

In addition to its benign climate, Ft. Lauderdale's proximity to the water
has formed its character as a prime resort area. The city is virtually afloat:
It and surrounding Broward County are bordered on the east by 27 miles of
Atlantic Ocean coastline and beaches, on the west by that "river of grass,"
the Everglades. Between the two are 300 miles of navigable Intracoastal
Waterway and an intricate network of canals that have led to Ft. Lauderdale's
being dubbed the "Venice of America." Relaxed and informal, Ft. Lauderdale
is best enjoyed in shorts and sandals except at night, when things are a touch
more formal.

While other resort areas count only their visitors, the Ft. Lauderdale area
also counts boats. Nearly 30,000 are permanently registered, and 10,000 or
so more join their ranks during the winter months as the yachting crowd from
as far away as Canada cruises to the area's warm waters. (Author John D.
MacDonald's readers will recognize the Bahia Mar Yacht Basin as the place
where the laid-back sleuth Travis McGee moors his houseboat, the *Busted
Flush*.) Moreover, thousands of smaller craft — sailboats and powerboats
— knife through these waters throughout the year. Even the Christmas holiday is celebrated in special Ft. Lauderdale fashion: hundreds of elaborately
decorated and lighted boats and yachts take to the Intracoastal Waterway for
the unusual Boat Parade from Port Everglades to Pompano Beach.

The city is named after Major William Lauderdale, who arrived in 1838
to quell the Seminole Indians and build a fort on the New River in an area
of mosquito-infested, inhospitable mangrove swamps. The door for development first opened in the late 1890s, when the entrepreneur Henry Flagler
began extending his Florida East Coast Railroad south from Palm Beach. A
swamp drainage and reclamation project was undertaken in 1906, and canals
were dug to create "finger islands," thus maximizing the city's waterside real
estate. Ft. Lauderdale was incorporated in 1911 and has welcomed millions
of visitors ever since.

Today Ft. Lauderdale is the largest — and by far the best known —

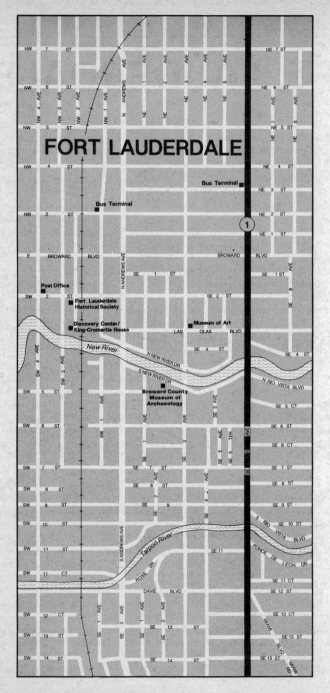

FORT LAUDERDALE

NW 7 ST
NE 7 ST

NW 6 AVE
NW 4 AVE
NW 3 AVE
NW 2 AVE
NW 1 AVE
N ANDREWS AVE
NE 1 AVE
NE 2 AVE
NE 3 AVE
NE 4 AVE
NE 5 AVE

NE 6 ST
NE 7 AVE
NE 8 AVE

NW 5 ST
NE 5 ST

NW 4 ST
NE 4 ST

NE 3 ST

Bus Terminal ■

NW 2 ST
Bus Terminal ■
NE 2 ST

① 1

NE 1 ST

E BROWARD BLVD
N ANDREWS AVE
BROWARD BLVD

SE 1 ST
SE 1 AVE
SE 8 AVE

SW 2 ST
Post Office ■

Fort Lauderdale ■
Historical Society
SE 2 ST

Discovery Center/ ■
King-Cromartie House
Museum of Art ■
LAS OLAS BLVD

SE 4 ST
SE 4 ST

SW 4 AVE
SW 3 AVE
New River
N NEW RIVER DR
S NEW RIVER DR
N RIO VISTA BLVD

SW 5 ST
Broward County
Museum of
Archaeology ■
SE 5 AVE
SE 5 CT

SW 1 AVE
SE 1 AVE
SE 3 AVE
SE 5 AVE
SE 5 TER
SE AVE

SW 6 ST
SE 6 ST
SE 6 CT

SW 7 ST
SE 7 ST
SE 7 ST

SW 8 ST
SE 6 ST
SE 2 AVE
SE 4 AVE
SE 8 ST

SW 9 ST
SE 9 ST
SE 9 ST

SW 10 ST
Tarpon River
SE 10 ST
S RIO VISTA BLVD

SW 11 ST
SE 11
PONCE DE LEON DR

SW 11 CT
ROSE DR
SE 11 CT

DAVIE BLVD
SE 12 ST

SW 12 CT
SE 1 AVE
SE 2 AVE
SE 2 AVE
SE 13
MAMI BLVD MIAMI
SE 12 CT

SW 13 ST
SE 2 AVE
SE 13 ST

SW 14 ST
SE 14 ST
SE 13 ST RD

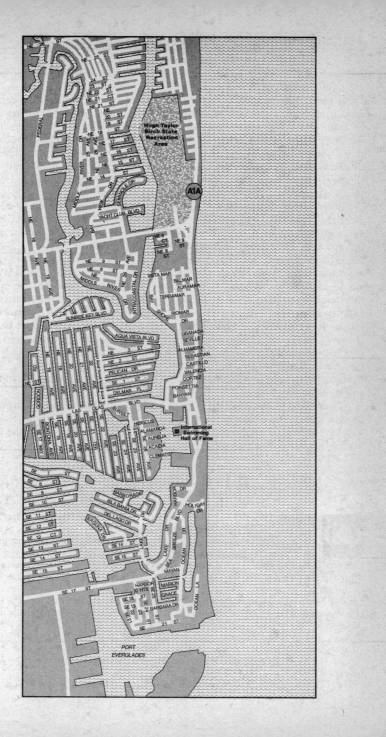

of the 28 municipalities that constitute Broward County, the second most populous of Florida's 67 counties. The permanent population of just over 1.2 million swells each season as more than 3 million tourists pour in. To these guests, Ft. Lauderdale and vicinity offer a wide choice of places to stay, from tiny motels to huge luxury hotels; more than 28,000 rooms can be found in the five major oceanfront communities. Even the most demanding diner will find satisfaction in one of the area's more than 2,500 restaurants, while its many nightclubs, discos, and theaters provide ample evening diversion. And in the sun-splashed daytime, those who tire of frolicking on the beach may work out on the approximately 50 golf courses and 550 tennis courts.

But Ft. Lauderdale is not just sunshine and surf. It's also a bustling commercial city, and its pride, Port Everglades, is one of the nation's busiest cargo and passenger ports. City fathers recently undertook a refurbishment and expansion of Ft. Lauderdale's downtown core, and a number of high-rise office buildings have sprung up, attracting new business. Furthermore, the cities that make up the greater Ft. Lauderdale area are a diverse lot: Davie, whose residents prefer jeans and cowboy boots and hats, is one of the most "western" towns this side of the Pecos; it has dozens of farms, stables, saloons, country stores, and even a weekly rodeo. In Hollywood, there's a Seminole Indian Reservation, and Hallandale is the home of the well-known *Gulfstream Race Track*. Dania, whose name reflects its early Danish settlers, is now called "the antiques center of the South," in recognition of its proliferation of antiques shops. Stretching away to the west of Ft. Lauderdale are 3,700 fertile acres of fruit and vegetable farms, adding an agricultural side to the city's personality.

As more and more people discover its enviable lifestyle, the area continues to grow and evolve. Progress has its price, however, and Ft. Lauderdale lovers will have to remain vigilant as developers draw closer and closer to the last available land — the eastern fringe of the Everglades.

AT-A-GLANCE

SEEING THE CITY: The most commanding view is from the *Pier Top Lounge* of the 17-story *Pier 66* hotel (2301 SE 17th St.). As the lounge makes one complete revolution each 66 minutes, a sweeping panorama unveils of the Atlantic Ocean and its beaches to the east, Port Everglades and Ft. Lauderdale International Airport to the south, the city's many canals, sprawling suburbs, and the Everglades to the west, and more canals and the Intracoastal Waterway to the north.

Boat Tours – Ft. Lauderdale is most easily and attractively seen by boat. The best cruises are offered by *Paddlewheel Queen,* whose owners have spent $500,000 updating this sightseeing and party boat. There are 7 sailings a day, including breakfast, lunch, cocktail, and early and late dinner cruises; 2950 NE 32nd Ave. (phone: 564-7659). Another cruise boat is the *Jungle Queen,* at Bahia Mar Yacht Basin on Rte. A1A (phone: 462-5596). To get from one point on the intracoastal to another, try *Water Taxi* (phone: 565-5507).

Tram Tours – A wonderful way to sightsee is aboard the open-air *Voyager Sightsee-*

ing Train, which winds along an 18-mile route through old and new Ft. Lauderdale, Port Everglades, "Millionaires Row," and some residential areas. 600 Seabreeze Blvd. (phone: 463-0401).

SPECIAL PLACES: The best way to get around Ft. Lauderdale is by car.

Port Everglades – Because it has the deepest water of any port between Norfolk and New Orleans, Port Everglades attracts a lot of cargo and marine outfitting business, but it's also a popular port for luxury cruise ships, especially those that sail into the Caribbean, the Gulf of Mexico, or through the Panama Canal. Its eight passenger terminals each boast a different and bold design, the result of remodeling of former warehouses and new construction. The port has two restaurants, one co-owned by Burt Reynolds, and a cocktail lounge. While there are no organized tours, visitors are free to roam at will from 8 AM to 6 PM. State Rd. 84, east of US 1 (phone: 523-3404).

Discovery Center – An integral part of downtown Ft. Lauderdale's rejuvenated historic Himmarshee Village area, featuring 22 exhibitions in three buildings. The main facility is devoted to hands-on learning of things historic, artistic, and scientific; a second building houses the new Creativity Under the Sun exhibition. Tours are offered from the Center of the King-Cromartie House, a restored turn-of-the-century residence replete with antiques and set on the New River. Closed Mondays. Admission charge. 231 SW 2nd Ave. (phone: 462-4115).

Everglades Holiday Park – Savor what the famed ecological area is all about by bird watching, taking airboat rides and special tours, or by renting boats or RVs. There's also a campground. Open daily. No admission charge. 21940 Griffin Rd. (phone: 434-8111).

Flamingo Gardens – This unique jungle environment, with a botanical garden, two museums, orange groves, peacocks, alligators, monkeys, flamingos, tram ride, and a petting zoo remains basically undisturbed by man. There is also a snack bar, a sizable souvenir shop, and a large fruit stall for purchasing and shipping citrus fruit. Open daily. Admission charge for zoo, museums, and ride; no fee to enter grounds or for parking. 3750 Flamingo Rd., Davie (phone: 473-0010).

Hugh Taylor Birch State Recreation Area – Just across the street from the beach is this lush, tropical park with 180 acres ideal for picnicking, playing ball, canoeing, hiking. Open daily. Admission charge. 3109 E. Sunrise Blvd. (phone: 564-4521).

John U. Lloyd Beach State Recreation Area – Many Ft. Lauderdale residents consider this to be *the* place for picnicking, swimming, fishing, canoeing, and other recreation. There are 244 acres of beach, dunes, mangrove swamp, and hammock (a raised area of dense tropical vegetation). Park rangers lead nature walks during winter months. Open daily. Admission charge. 6503 N. Ocean Dr., Dania (phone: 923-2833).

Ocean World – All the requisite aquatic creatures — sharks, alligators, sea lions, turtles, and dolphin — are featured here in continuous 2-hour water shows. Visitors may also watch the dolphin show off in Davy Jones' Locker, a 3-story circular tank, or the more than 40 sharks, sea turtles, and other fish in the Shark Moat. Boat tours and deep-sea fishing are also available. Open daily. Admission charge. 1701 SE 17th St. (phone: 525-6611).

Hollywood Broadwalk – A 2-mile, 24-foot-wide concrete ocean promenade bordered by a bicycle path. Bikes may be rented on the Broadwalk, and there's often music and dancing at the bandstand. Lifeguard stations manned all year from 10 AM to 4 PM.

Spyke's Grove & Tropical Gardens – Florida is famous for its citrus; here's a chance to see a working grove up close. In the winter, you can also hop aboard one of the hourly 15-minute tractor-pulled tram rides through the groves and peek at various tropical birds and animals in their natural environment. Open daily. No admission charge. 7250 Griffin Rd., Davie (phone: 583-0426).

Stranahan House – One of the area's most visited attractions is a history museum — the restored 1913 home and Indian trading post of early settler Frank Stranahan. Open Wednesdays and Fridays through Sundays. Admission charge. 1 Stranahan Pl. (Las Olas Blvd. at New River Tunnel) (phone: 524-4736).

International Swimming Hall of Fame – Many of the world's top swimming and diving competitions are held here, but its Olympic pool is open to the public when there's no meet. The adjoining museum houses unusual aquatic memorabilia from more than 100 countries. Open daily. Admission charge. 1 Hall of Fame Dr. (phone: 462-6536).

Topeekeegee Yugnee Park – With 150 acres, this is one of the area's larger parks. Visitors can enjoy all kinds of activities — swimming, boating, canoeing, picnicking, barbecuing, hiking, and biking. One of its two waterslides is said to be the fastest in Florida. Open daily. Admission charge. 3300 N. Park Rd., just off I-95, Hollywood (phone: 961-4430).

Seminole Indian Reservation – The Native Village includes a museum, gift shop, demonstrations of alligator wrestling, and snake and turtle shows. Although commercial, for-profit bingo is not legal in Florida, it is here on the reservation. The bingo hall holds up to 1,400 people and is often full; winners have pocketed as much as $110,000 in a single game. There's an admission charge for the village and another for the bingo hall (this includes four bingo cards). Both open daily; the village is at 3551 N. State Rd. 7, Hollywood (phone: 961-4519); the bingo hall is at 4150 N. State Rd. 7, Hollywood (phone: 961-3220).

■ **EXTRA SPECIAL:** To experience fully the tropical beauty and laid-back ambience that is Ft. Lauderdale, drive east on Las Olas Boulevard past its chic boutiques and palm-lined streets. Continue through the Isles of Las Olas area, which is laced with canals and filled with fancy homes nestled among royal palm trees. Proceed on past the sailboat cove, where towering masts grope for the blue sky, and cruise over the small bridge to Route A1A, along the Atlantic Ocean. Turn north and drive along A1A and, at about 4 PM, stop at one of the hotel patio bars facing the ocean for a cocktail with the "end of the day" beach people. As it nears 5 o'clock, the beach will become nearly deserted, yet the ocean is filled with the multicolored sails of boats returning to safe harbor and cruise ships steaming out to distant corners of the world. Take off your shoes, walk along the sand at the water's edge — and let the images soak in.

SOURCES AND RESOURCES

TOURIST INFORMATION: The Greater Ft. Lauderdale Convention & Visitors Bureau is now in an easily accessible streetfront space downtown, 500 E. Broward Blvd., Ft. Lauderdale, FL 33394. Stop in or phone (phone: 765-4466) for information on accommodations, activities, attractions, sports, dining, shopping, touring, and special events, as well as destination literature in French, Spanish, German, and Japanese. The Broward County Hotline (phone: 765-4468) is updated weekly and provides recorded information on dates, times, and additional sources of information about current events and visitor attractions.

Television Stations – WTVJ Channel 4–NBC; WPTV Channel 5–NBC; WCIX Channel 6–CBS; WSVN Channel 7–FOX. (*Note:* ABC/Capital Cities has no Ft. Lauderdale affiliate.)

Radio Stations – AM: WNWS 790 (news/talk); WINZ 940 (news/talk). FM:

WTMI 93.1 (classical); WZTA 94.9 (classic rock); SHE 103.5 (album rock); WJOY 107 (mellow).

Local Coverage – *Fort Lauderdale Sun-Sentinel,* morning daily, and *Fort Lauderdale News,* afternoon daily, carry the following week's events in their Showtime section on Fridays.

Telephone – The area code for Ft. Lauderdale is 305.

Sales Tax – The sales tax in Ft. Lauderdale is 6%, and there is a 3% tourist tax.

CLIMATE: With the exception of occasional days in late December through February, when it can be chilly, the area generally enjoys warm weather, with daily temperatures averaging 75F. Swimming is possible almost every day.

GETTING AROUND: Airport – Ft. Lauderdale/Hollywood International Airport is a 10- to 15-minute drive from downtown; taxi fare should run about $10. Broward County Transit's #1 bus runs between the airport (pickup at terminals: Delta Dash pull-in area and next to terminal 3, both Lower Level) and the downtown bus terminal at NW 1st St. and 1st Ave.; fare is 75¢.

Bus – Broward County Transit services most of the area. A special 7-day, unlimited-use tourist pass can be purchased for a nominal sum at most hotels. For information, call 357-8400.

Taxi – While you can hail one on the street, it's best to pick one up at one of the major hotels and restaurants, or phone for one. The major cab company is *Yellow Cab* (phone: 565-5400).

Car Rental – Ft. Lauderdale is served by all the major national firms, two of which have their corporate headquarters in the city: *Alamo,* 1401 S. Federal Hwy. (phone: 522-0000); and *General Rent A Car,* 110 SE 6th St. (phone: 463-9410). There are also several regional agencies; look in the yellow pages.

LOCAL SERVICES: Babysitting – *Baby Sitters,* 1840 Coral Ridge Dr. (phone: 564-4201).

Business Services – *First Business Services,* 1750 E. Commercial Blvd. (phone: 491-3733).

Mechanics – *Cork's,* 1041 NE 30th Court, Oakland Park (phone: 565-0630), for foreign cars; *Chuck's Oceanside Exxon,* 3001 N. Ocean Blvd. (phone: 561-3120), for American makes.

MUSEUMS: The *Stranahan House* and *Discovery Center* are described in *Special Places.* Other museums include the following:

Broward County Museum of Archaeology – 203 SW 1st Ave. (phone: 525-8778).

Ft. Lauderdale Historical Society – 219 SW 2nd Ave. (phone: 463-4431).

Museum of Art – 1 E. Las Olas Blvd. (phone: 525-5500).

MAJOR COLLEGES AND UNIVERSITIES: Broward Community College (phone: 475-6500) has three campuses: central, 3501 SW Davie Rd., Davie; north, 1000 Coconut Creek Blvd., Pompano Beach; and south, 7200 Hollywood Blvd., Hollywood.

SPECIAL EVENTS: The *Seminole Indian Tribal Fair* is normally held during the first 2 weeks in February — it is a showcase of Indian crafts, entertainment, and food. During February and March, the *Florida Derby Festival* hits town: activities include a beauty pageant, the Derby Ball and parades, culminating in the race itself, Florida's richest thoroughbred race, with a purse of

$500,000. The *Honda Golf Classic,* one of the biggest PGA tournaments, is also held in late February or early March at *Eagle Trace;* it attracts the PGA's top players. In April, seafood is king at the *Ft. Lauderdale Seafood Festival* at Bubier Park, where over 30 leading restaurants provide tastes of house specialties. Anglers get to test their skills in May during the *Pompano Beach Fishing Rodeo,* where more than $250,000 in cash is awarded for the largest catches. *Oktoberfest* falls (naturally) in October and features lots of German food, drink, and music. The *Ft. Lauderdale Boat Show,* the nation's largest in-water display of all types and sizes of watercraft, is held in November. Also in November is the *Promenade in the Park,* which showcases artwork, arts and crafts, food, and entertainment at Holiday Park. The year's activities are capped by the month long *Winterfest,* culminating in the Ft. Lauderdale and Pompano Beach boat parades, with processions of about 100 boats, festooned with colored lights and Christmas decorations, plying the Intracoastal Waterway.

 SPORTS: Baseball – Fans can watch spring training and pre-season games from the first week in March through the first week in April. The New York *Yankees* play at *Ft. Lauderdale Stadium,* 5301 NW 12th Ave. (phone: 776-1921).

Fishing – There are lots of charter boat fishing operators at Bahia Mar Yacht Basin, 801 Seabreeze Blvd., across A1A from the beach (phone: 525-7174). Landlubbers fish 24 hours a day from the 1,080-foot Pompano Beach Fishing Pier, 2 blocks north of E. Atlantic Blvd.

Fitness Centers – *Nautilus Fitness Center,* with certified instructors, offers all the standard Nautilus exercise equipment plus whirlpool bath, aerobic conditioning, and juice bar. 1624 N. Federal Hwy. (phone: 566-2222).

Golf – There are more than 50 golf courses in the area. Among those open to the public are *American Golfers Club,* 3850 N. Federal Hwy. (phone: 564-8760); *Bonaventure,* 200 Bonaventure Blvd. (phone: 389-8000); *Rolling Hills,* 3501 W. Rolling Hills Circle, Davie (phone: 475-3010); and *Jacaranda,* 9200 W. Broward Blvd., Plantation (phone: 472-5836).

Horse and Dog Racing – There's thoroughbred horse racing at *Gulfstream Park* on US 1, Hallandale (phone: 454-7000); and harness racing at *Pompano Park Harness,* 1800 SW 3rd St., Pompano Beach (phone: 972-2000). You can "go to the dogs" at *Hollywood Greyhound Track,* 831 N. Federal Hwy., Hallandale (phone: 454-9400). Phone for racing dates.

Horseback Riding – There are many stables in the area. Among the larger ones are: *Bar-B Ranch,* 4601 SW 128th Ave. (phone: 434-6175); *Briarwood Farm,* 13607 Stirling Rd. (phone: 434-6640); *Saddle Up Stables,* 5000 S. University Dr. (phone: 434-1808); all in Davie. The county also operates stables at *Tradewinds Park,* 3600 W. Sample Rd., Coconut Creek (phone: 973-3220).

Jai Alai – This Basque import is the area's most action-packed sport, with pari-mutuel betting adding spice. The season is year-round, except for 5 weeks in April and May. At *Dania Jai-Alai,* 301 E. Dania Beach Blvd., Dania (phone: 927-2841).

Nature Hikes – The Broward Parks & Recreation Dept. sponsors a different nature walk each Friday and Saturday, October through May. Call for a schedule (phone: 357-8101).

Rodeo – The "Wild West" can be found at the *Rodeo Arena* in Davie, where cowboys compete in bronco riding, calf roping, and other activities. Wednesday and Friday evenings. Admission charge. 4201 SW 65th Way (phone: 797-1166).

Skating – It seems incongruous in a tropical city, but Ft. Lauderdale residents love to ice skate. A favorite locale is *Sunrise Ice Skating Center,* 3363 Pine Island Rd. N., Sunrise (phone: 741-2366).

Swimming – The most crowded beach is along "the Strip," from Sunrise Boulevard to Bahia Mar. The Galt Ocean Mile is quieter, with an older crowd. Perhaps the quietest strand is the stretch between Galt Ocean Mile and NE 22nd St., and if you search you may find small pockets of peace in John U. Lloyd Beach State Recreation Area, 6503 N. Ocean Dr., Dania.

Tennis – A number of the major hotels have tennis courts. Otherwise, only a few are open to the public. Among them are *Crystal Lake Country Club,* 3800 Crystal Lake Dr., Pompano Beach (phone: 943-3700); and *Holiday Park Tennis Center,* 1200 Holiday Park Circle (phone: 761-5378).

 THEATER: The area's major theaters are *Parker Playhouse,* 707 NE 8th St. (phone: 764-0700), which stars name actors in Broadway productions, and *Sunrise Musical Theater,* 5555 NW 95th Ave. (phone: 741-8600), which features Broadway musicals and individual stars in concert. Theatrical and cultural events are also staged at *War Memorial Auditorium,* 800 NE 8th St. (phone: 761-5381), and *Broward Community College,* 3501 SW Davie Rd. (phone: 475-6880). For current offerings, check the newspapers.

 MUSIC: The *Philharmonic Orchestra of Flòrida* usually plays at the *War Memorial Auditorium* (phone: 561-2997), which is also the site for performances of the *Opera Guild* (phone: 728-9700) during winter months; the latter often features visiting artists from New York's *Metropolitan Opera.* The *South Florida Symphony Orchestra* stages several major productions at various sites; 1822 N. University Dr., Plantation (phone: 474-7660). Student and guest chamber, jazz, opera, and symphonic performances are staged throughout the year at *Broward Community College* (phone: 475-6500).

 NIGHTCLUBS AND NIGHTLIFE: Most hotels and larger motels offer music and/or comedy acts nightly. The *Diplomat,* 3515 S. Ocean Dr., Hollywood (phone: 457-8111), features well-known stars during the winter. Growing in popularity are comedy clubs such as *The Comic Strip,* 1432 N. Federal Hwy. (phone: 565-8887), which showcases New York and Los Angeles comics. *Musician's Exchange Café,* 729 W. Sunrise Blvd. (phone: 764-1912), is the place to go for jazz and blues. For dance music, try *Riverwatch* in the *Marriott,* 1881 SE 17th St. (phone: 463-4000); *Confetti's,* 2660 E. Commercial Blvd. (phone: 776-4080); *Mr. Laff's,* 1135 N Federal Hwy. (phone: 561-3440); and *Banana Boat,* 2650 State Rd. 84 (phone: 791-5660). There's dancing and dinner at *Stan's,* 3300 E. Commercial Blvd. (phone: 772-3777).

BEST IN TOWN

 CHECKING IN: Ft. Lauderdale's busiest period is winter, when reservations should be made as far in advance as possible. During high season a double room listed in the very expensive range could run $180 to $260 per night; a room in the expensive range will cost $140 to $180; in moderate, $95 to $145; and $80 to $115 in inexpensive. In the summer, occupancy (and room rates) drop. Note that a 3% tourist development tax and a 6% sales tax are added to all hotel bills. All telephone numbers are in the 305 area code unless otherwise indicated.

Marriott's Harbour Beach – The city's most expensive resort sits on 16 beachfront acres. Stunning public areas include 4 restaurants, 2 lounges, a pool bar, 5 tennis courts, and exercise facilities. There's also an 8,000-square-foot free-form pool with a waterfall and 50 cabanas. By contrast, the 645 rooms are disappointing, especially in view of the rates; however, suites are super. Free transport to the *Bonaventure Country Club* for golfers. Heavy meeting and convention clientele. 3030 Holiday Dr. (phone: 525-4000 or 800-228-9290). Very expensive.

Palm-Aire – It's Ft. Lauderdale's original spa — over 1,500 acres with 191 rooms, 6 tennis courts, 2 championship and one executive golf course, several racquetball courts, 3 dining rooms. Special 1-, 3-, 7-, and 14-day packages may be booked at the spa, whose programs include beauty, health, relaxation, and full spa experiences. See also *Resort Hotels,* DIVERSIONS. 2501 Palm-Aire Dr. N., Pompano Beach (phone: 972-3300; 800-336-2108). Very expensive.

Pier 66 – The 17-story octagonal tower alongside the Intracoastal Waterway was the city's first luxury high-rise hotel. A multimillion-dollar expansion and refurbishing project completed in 1988 has greatly enhanced its appeal. The 156 rooms in the tower have private balconies, and there are also 232 lanai rooms, 132 of them brand-new. Amenities include 2 tennis courts, 2 swimming pools, a 40-person Jacuzzi, a fitness center, 4 restaurants, and 3 lounges. The new conference center includes a 350-seat restaurant and an entertainment center. A fleet of 50 vessels of varying sizes is available for overnight lodging, business meetings, and sailing trips. The luxuriously furnished boats are moored at the hotel's own marina, and guests "rooming" aboard have full access to all the hotel's facilities. 2301 SE 17th St. (phone: 525-6666 or 800-327-3796). Very expensive.

Embassy Suites – The chain's largest property to date offers 363 suites at prices equivalent to a standard hotel room. Facilities include a restaurant and lounge, pool, sauna, steamroom, and Jacuzzi. Breakfast and cocktails are free. Saluted by *Consumer Reports* magazine, the accommodations also feature a wet bar with refrigerator, microwave oven, coffeemaker, and dining table; complimentary beach shuttle service, free parking, and free 24-hour airport transportation are also available. 1100 SE 17th St. Cswy. (phone: 527-2700). Expensive.

Marriott Cypress Creek – Here is a 321-room property adjacent to an 8-acre aquatic preserve in the burgeoning Cypress Creek area, north of the city. Facilities include an outdoor pool, a health club with saunas and lockers, a gift shop, and parking for 450 cars. The 16-floor structure features a restaurant, 2 lounges, a 5,082-square-foot Grand Ballroom, and 7 smaller meeting facilities. In the Cypress Park West complex (phone: 771-0440 or 800-228-9290). Expensive.

Westin Cypress Creek – This 294-room luxury property was the Westin chain's first foray into Florida. The 14-story property overlooks a 5-acre manmade lake and features a health club, large outdoor pool, and a lakeside putting green; tennis and golf are a 5-minute drive away. There are 2 restaurants — one for fine dining, a second for casual food — and a bar complex as well as an entertainment lounge. Two floors offer special concierge services. In the Radice Corporate Center (phone: 772-1331 or 800-228-3000). Expensive.

Bahia Mar Quality Royale – This nautically oriented hotel and marina, at the Bahia Mar Yacht Basin at the southern end of "the Strip," has 300 rooms, 2 restaurants, the *Schooners Lounge,* and 4 lighted tennis courts. 801 Seabreeze Blvd. (phone: 764-2233). Moderate.

Royce Resort – All of its 220 rooms have balconies that overlook either the Atlantic or the Galt Ocean Mile, and are beautifully decorated in soothing rose and mauve tones. Its *Ocean Café* offers a mostly continental menu, and the patio-bar features live music and dancing on weekends. The hotel is on the beach, has a pool, and offers sailboat rentals. 4060 Galt Ocean Dr. (phone: 565-6611). Moderate.

Sheraton Yankee Clipper – "Moored" directly on the beach, its unusual architecture makes this landmark look like a ship, and the nautical theme — which provides a warm, clubby feeling — is also carried through indoors, too. Heated swimming pools, 505 rooms, and a restaurant; 2 lounges provide entertainment. 1140 Seabreeze Blvd. (phone: 524-5551). Moderate.

Bahia Cabana – This small, unpretentious hotel, nestled next door to the Bahia Mar Yachting Center, is informal and very Floridian. There are 116 rooms and apartments with kitchenettes; 3 swimming pools; a 36-person Jacuzzi; saunas; a dining room; and an outdoor patio bar/restaurant that overlooks the marina and is a popular gathering spot for locals. 3001 Harbor Dr. (phone: 524-1555). Inexpensive.

Marina Bay – An unusual place, with all 80 rooms in 2-story houseboats on the New River, providing a tropical setting and maritime ambience. Two restaurants, one lounge with dancing, 9 tennis courts, a swimming pool, and boat slips complete the guest facilities. 2175 State Rd. 84 (phone: 791-7600). Inexpensive.

Riverside – Some 116 rooms in one of the city's oldest structures. The hotel has a sedate ambience and cozy lobby, with chandeliers, armchairs, touches of wicker, and a fireplace. There is one restaurant and an intimate restaurant/lounge decorated with etched glass as well as a swimming pool amid tropical landscaping. 620 E. Las Olas Blvd. (phone: 467-0671). Inexpensive.

EATING OUT: There are nearly 2,500 restaurants in Broward County. Many of these are well known, and most get quite crowded during the winter season, so it's always a good idea to make reservations. Casual dress is accepted in most restaurants, though a few of the more expensive ones prefer gentlemen to wear jackets. Expect to pay $60 or more for dinner for two in a restaurant listed in the expensive range; $35 to $50 in the moderate range; and $25 or less for inexpensive. Prices do not include wine, drinks, or tips. All telephone numbers are in the 305 area code unless otherwise indicated.

Café Max – This trendy, California-style eatery is credited with pioneering new American cuisine in South Florida. The casual ambience and innovative menu are complemented by an excellent wine list — emphasizing California vintages — including many available by the glass. Open daily. Reservations recommended. Major credit cards. 2601 E. Atlantic Blvd., Pompano Beach (phone: 782-0606). Expensive.

Casa Vecchia – Fine Northern Italian cuisine is served inside this lovely old house (built in the 1930s by the Ponds cold cream family), decorated with lots of plants, ceramics, and wrought iron. A courtyard adds to the charm, as does the view overlooking the Intracoastal Waterway. Open daily. Reservations recommended. Major credit cards. 209 N. Birch Rd. (phone: 463-7575). Expensive.

Down Under – The kitchen at this spot alongside the Intracoastal Waterway prepares an eclectic menu of French, American, and seafood dishes. The atmosphere and decor seem similarly haphazard — plants abound, the brick walls are lined with old posters, and the large rooms are filled with tables placed rather closely together. Open daily. Reservations recommended. Major credit cards. 3000 E. Oakland Park Blvd. (phone: 564-6984). Expensive.

La Reserve – This French/continental restaurant has a 2-tiered, beam-ceilinged, candlelit dining room with sensational picture windows overlooking the Intracoastal Waterway. Adjoining *La Reserve* is the less formal bistro, *Ginger's*. Open daily. Reservations recommended. Major credit cards. 3115 NE 32nd Ave. (phone: 563-6644). Expensive.

Christine Lee's – It's a branch of the popular Miami Beach restaurant serving Szechwan, Mandarin, and Cantonese dishes. Surprisingly, it also has some of the best American-style steaks in South Florida. Open daily. Reservations for 3 or more. Major credit cards. 6191 Rock Island Rd., Tamarac (phone: 726-0430). Moderate.

La Ferme – Marie-Paul Terrier welcomes customers with a smile and closely watches over their well-being while husband Henri tends to the kitchen, whipping up traditional and nouvelle delights. The restaurant is small and cozy, with a French Provincial decor and lace tablecloths. Closed Mondays. Major credit cards. 1601 E. Sunrise Blvd. (phone: 764-0987). Moderate.

Mai-Kai – The large, rambling main dining room has a Polynesian decor, serves exotic drinks with its Polynesian, American and Cantonese food, and features Polynesian entertainment nightly (cover charge). The grounds boast lushly landscaped tropical vegetation. Open daily. Reservations accepted. Major credit cards. 3599 N. Federal Hwy. (phone: 563-3272). Moderate.

Bobby Rubino's – The original rib joint has now expanded into a national chain, but it still serves the leanest barbecued ribs in town, usually accompanied by a delicious fried onion ring loaf. Barbecued chicken, steaks, and "combo platters" are also served. There are now five branches of this easygoing eatery; all are open daily and accept major credit cards: 4100 N. Federal Hwy. (phone: 561-5305); 1430 SE 17th St. (phone: 522-3006); 6001 Kimberly Blvd., North Lauderdale (phone: 971-4740); 3806 N. University Dr., Sunrise (phone: 748-2000); 4520 W. Hallandale Beach Blvd., Hallandale (phone: 987-5500). Moderate to inexpensive.

Manero's – This family-run restaurant is large, noisy, and crowded; the walls are adorned with autographed photos of many of the celebrities who have eaten here. Steaks and seafood are featured. Open daily. Reservations accepted. Major credit cards. 5681 W. Atlantic Blvd., Margate (phone: 971-4995). Moderate to inexpensive.

Old Florida Seafood House – It's a real find, where the seafood is consistently good and the prices reasonable. Try the raw bar — a selection of clams, oysters, shrimp, and other favorites. Open daily. No reservations. Major credit cards. 1414 NE 26th St., Wilton Manors (phone: 566-1044). Moderate to inexpensive.

Carlos & Pepe's – The clientele at this popular hangout is eager and hungry; the setting is crowded but pleasant (light woods, green plants, and tile tables); and the menu is lighthearted Mexican (tacos, tortillas, and tostadas). Open daily. Major credit cards. 1302 SE 17th St. (phone: 467-7192). Inexpensive.

Papa Leone's – Papa Leone plays the organ every night at this small (only 18 candlelit booths and tables), old-fashioned, family-run, neighborhood Italian restaurant. Open daily. American Express only. It's virtually invisible, next to *Publix,* at 2735 N. Dixie Hwy., Wilton Manors (phone: 566-1911). Inexpensive.

Two Guys – Many natives will swear that these two guys serve the best pizza in Florida; both locations are casual, with cedar paneling, hanging plants, and ceiling fans. Open daily. Major credit cards. 701 S. Federal Hwy. (phone: 462-7140); 391 N. State Rd. 7, Plantation (phone: 792-8888). Inexpensive.

FT. WORTH

First, what Ft. Worth is not: Ft. Worth is not sleek, Ft. Worth is not snooty, and Ft. Worth is not the subject of any steamy television series. Ft. Worth is not, to put it plainly, Dallas. And if ever on some feverish, less confident day long ago, its citizens wished it were, they've long since come to their senses. Ft. Worth stands far apart from its flashy big sister 30 miles to the east, and its personality could not be more distinctly its own.

On the banks of the Trinity River, 50 miles south of the Oklahoma state line and 250 miles north of the Gulf of Mexico, Ft. Worth acts as a geographic and cultural boundary between two very different parts of Texas. To the west of the city is raw and flat prairie, hardly more developed than it was a century ago, while to the east is Dallas, a flamboyant and wealthy town endowed with more pine trees and more pizzazz. A successful blend of both worlds, Ft. Worth has a natural and rugged charm. Ft. Worth writer Jerry Flemmons describes the difference between the two cities thus: "Dallas grew into a huckster city of contrived haute culture. Ft. Worth became a comfortable, ambitious town with a high society always one generation removed from flour sack underwear."

Comparisons aside, the history of Ft. Worth is an interesting one. Founded as a frontier army post in 1849 by Major Ripley Arnold to provide protection against frequent and ferocious Indian attacks, Ft. Worth was named for the Mexican War hero William Jenkins Worth. The settlers who took refuge in this stronghold considered it the very edge of civilization, since all that existed west of Ft. Worth were hundreds and hundreds of wild, dry miles of Indian territory. After the Civil War, Ft. Worth emerged as a key stop on the Chisholm Trail, a route cut through Texas and Oklahoma along which millions of longhorns were driven north to market in Kansas. Enormous stockyards were built in what is now North Ft. Worth, and entrepreneurs wasted no time in building an assortment of saloons and dance halls to accommodate the wants and needs of the weary cowhands and smooth-talking cattle barons who came to trade. These moneyed cattlemen became the first incarnation of Ft. Worth gentry; they built mansions along Pennsylvania Avenue in which entire floors were devoted to ballrooms and ladies' dressing rooms were filled with gowns bought in the East.

When the first of nine railroads came to Ft. Worth in 1876, the city acquired a new role as a meat packing and shipping center. Then in 1917 oil was discovered and Ft. Worth experienced a new boom — in population and wealth. And while cattle and oil have remained the bedrock of Ft. Worth's economy, since World War II many technological and defense industries have prospered here; three such corporate giants are the Tandy Corporation, Bell Helicopter, and General Dynamics.

Ft. Worth's broad-based economy is just one example of the city's real

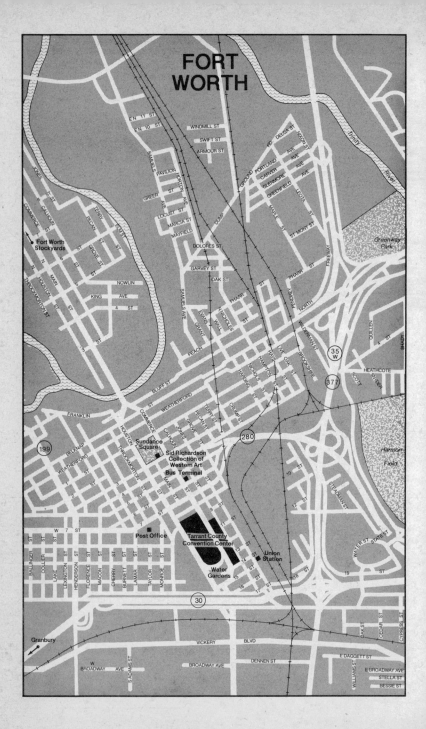

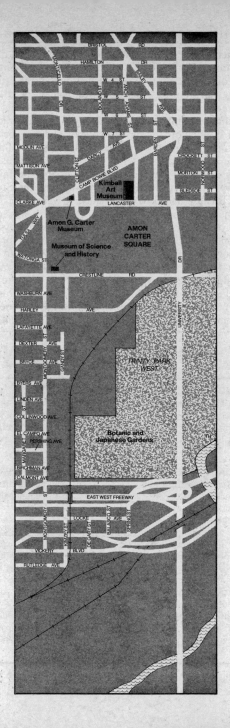

drawing card, its diversity. Another example is the several different faces of the city. Downtown Ft. Worth has the look of a city being built simultaneously in two different centuries: refurbished turn-of-the-century structures stand just a few feet from modern high-rises. And in North Ft. Worth the stockyards have been declared a National Historic District. Although the stockyard area has certainly been duded up for the tourist trade, it hasn't lost its original Old West charm, its for-real cowboy clientele, or its earthy smell and soft background music of braying livestock. Due west of downtown is Ft. Worth's artistic and cultural center, Amon G. Carter Square, a cluster of museums that's among the best west of the Mississippi. Sustained completely by family money, Ft. Worth's museums grew up with the city, supported by a citizenry not because it had to but because it wanted to.

Despite its many facets, "Cowtown" (as Ft. Worth was nicknamed) suffered for many years from a whopping identity crisis. Always overshadowed by supposedly more sophisticated Dallas, it simply settled for playing second fiddle. Then, slowly, visitors started coming to Ft. Worth to see the historic stockyards; the *Amon G. Carter* and *Kimbell Museums* began to gain acceptance and acclaim in the international art market; and the city's business leaders were acknowledged "big dogs" by anybody's standards. Suddenly, the people of Ft. Worth realized that their city's idiosyncratic mix of cattle, culture, and commerce is just what makes it a very special place.

FT. WORTH AT-A-GLANCE

 SEEING THE CITY: Panoramic views of Ft. Worth turn up serendipitously over a hill or around a corner, but the best one is from the esplanade from the east entrance of the *Amon G. Carter Museum.* Get a king-size scoop of homemade ice cream from the *Front Porch* (across Camp Bowie Blvd.), then enjoy the rolling lawn of the *Kimbell Art Museum* as well as a spectacular view of downtown.

 SPECIAL PLACES: One of the nicest things about Ft. Worth is that sightseeing is easy. All the museums are within walking distance of one another; the stockyard area is best seen on foot; and the botanical gardens and zoo are across the street from each other.

Ft. Worth Stockyards – Wear your jeans to prowl around the north side of Cowtown. If any one area best embodies the city's latest promotional slogan, "Texas the way you want it to be," the Ft. Worth Stockyards is it. After years of neglect, this isolated enclave of history is in the full throes of a renaissance, its historical integrity preserved with National Historic District status. Once the center of Ft. Worth's cattle culture, the Stockyards area developed after the Civil War as a rest stop for cowboys driving their herds north to Kansas on the Chisholm Trail. Its turn-of-the-century heyday saw millions of cattle processed through the Armour and Swift meat-packing plants. Disaster struck the Stockyards many times during the first half of this century, but the district of saloons, hotels, and western outfitters that grew up in the area thrived until the packing industry's demise. In the 1960s and early 1970s, the area deteriorated into a near-slum.

A sluggish economy saved what was left after the meat packing plants were demolished; revived interest in things Texas — and considerable financial investment —

brought the area back. Today, residents and tourists alike come to soak up the district's still authentic western flavor.

To get to the Stockyards, take Main Street north from downtown three miles to the corner of North Main and Exchange Avenue. Park your car anywhere you can; everything is within walking distance. The Stockyards area includes the newly restored *Cowtown Coliseum,* which hosts live rodeo performances on weekends; the Livestock Exchange Building, housing several fine arts galleries; and dozens of stores where you can pick up a Stetson, a pair of lizard-skin boots, or a bridle for your bronco. Any Monday or Tuesday at 9 AM you can do some shopping at a cattle auction. But most people come to the Stockyards to party: on weekend nights, the district is crowded with denim-clad folks meandering from one watering hole or country-and-western dance hall to the next. There are about two dozen nightspots from which to choose, including the century-old *White Elephant Saloon.* And if you happen to get hungry, there's no problem finding a meal — so long as you're satisfied with Tex-Mex or steaks.

Kimbell Art Museum – Architect Louis Kahn's last work opened in 1973 and is considered one of the most important and beautiful small art museums in the country. Its permanent collection dates from pre-Columbian America to the early 20th century, with an emphasis on European art. Closed Mondays. Admission charge. 3333 Camp Bowie Blvd. (phone: 332-8451).

Amon G. Carter Museum of Western Art – Best known for its paintings by Frederic Remington and Charles M. Russell, the museum also features an extensive collection of photography, sculpture, and paintings by many other 20th-century artists. Closed Mondays. No admission charge. 3501 Camp Bowie Blvd. (phone: 738-1933).

Museum of Science and History – Formerly called the *Children's Museum,* it includes the Hall of Medical Science, Man and His Possessions, and Computer Technology. Also part of the museum is the *Omni Theater,* a remarkable computerized 70mm multi-image projection and sound system — the largest of its kind in the world. Closed Mondays. No admission charge. 1501 Montgomery (phone: 732-1631).

Sundance Square – This charming square is formed by Commerce, Houston, 2nd, and 3rd streets downtown and is bordered by an interesting collection of boutiques, craft shops, restaurants, and art galleries. Main Street, which bisects the square, is notable for its red brick sidewalks, period streetlamps, and turn-of-the-century buildings. At 309 Main Street is the well-known *Sid Richardson Collection of Western Art* (phone: 332-6554), which features more than 100 paintings by the western artists Frederic Remington and Charles M. Russell. Fire Station No. 1, at 201-203 Commerce, houses a museum showcasing the city's history with the exhibition "150 Years of Ft. Worth." No admission charge..

Water Gardens – The opening scenes of the science fiction movie *Logan's Run* were shot at this water wonderland, where some 19,000 gallons of water pour over pebbled concrete sculptures every minute. Open daily. No admission charge. South of the convention center between Commerce and Houston Sts.

Log Cabin Village – Six cabins from the 1850s have been restored and furnished with period antiques. Costumed "villagers" demonstrate typical pioneer crafts — weaving, quilting, etc. Open daily. Admission charge. 2100 Log Cabin Village La. near the zoo and botanical gardens (phone: 926-5881).

Botanic and Japanese Gardens – The Botanic Gardens encompass several acres for exploring and studying hundreds of different plant species and varieties of roses. Within are the Japanese Gardens, tranquil arrangements of trees and shrubs, bridges, pools, waterfalls, and teahouses. Closed Mondays. Admission charge for Japanese Gardens only. 3220 Botanic Garden Dr., off University Dr. (phone: 870-7686).

Ft. Worth Zoological Park – Part of Forest Park, with picnic tables and a small amusement park, the Ft. Worth zoo contains America's largest herpetarium, a lovely rain forest with rare and exotic birds, and an outstanding collection of mammals.

Adjacent to the zoo is the longest miniature train ride in the country. It's a leisurely and scenic 5-mile trip covering the length of several parks. Open daily. Admission charge. 2727 Zoological Park Dr., off University Dr. (phone: 870-7050).

Thistle Hill – Built in 1903, this elegant old house is the last one remaining from the days when the rich cattle barons built their flashy mansions along Pennsylvania Avenue. Closed Saturdays. No admission charge. 1509 Pennsylvania Ave. (phone: 336-1212).

Six Flags Over Texas – About 30 minutes east of Ft. Worth, in Arlington, this famous amusement park features more than 95 rides, shows, and other attractions. Open daily June through August; weekends only in spring and fall. Admission charge. I-30 at Hwy. 360 (phone: 640-8900).

Wet 'n Wild – A great place to spend a blistering Texas day. Attractions include a body-surfing pool, waterslides, inner tube rapids, and a children's play area. Open daily, June through August; weekends only, April, May, and September. Admission charge. Across I-30 from *Arlington Stadium* at 1800 E. Lamar Blvd., Arlington (phone: 265-3013).

■ **EXTRA SPECIAL:** Ft. Worth may be typically Texan, but you really haven't seen the state until you've visited at least one of its small towns. Granbury, an easy 30 minutes southwest of Ft. Worth on Hwy. 377, has admittedly taken advantage of its charming eccentricities and attracted some tourist trade. But the appeal of the agricultural community has only been heightened. A limestone courthouse dominates a town square ringed with craft shops, ice cream parlors, and restaurants, all in 19th-century buildings. In fact, Granbury is so full of Old West buildings that it's entered in the National Register of Historic Places. The *Granbury Opera House* (on the Square on Pearl St.) features drama, comedy, and music. (Reservations are advised: PO Box 297, Granbury, TX 76048; phone: 573-9191.) Surrounding Granbury is a manmade lake of the same name with beautiful camping and picnicking facilities; the Chamber of Commerce (phone: 573-1622) may provide further information. For a country-style buffet, try the local favorite, the *Nutt House* restaurant. "Country-style buffet" means you go through a line, cafeteria style, pick yerself up some grits (pronounced *gree*-uts), red beans, and maybe some ham, and set down at a long table. The *Nutt House,* like many establishments in Granbury, is closed Mondays (121 E. Bridge St.; phone: 573-9362).

SOURCES AND RESOURCES

TOURIST INFORMATION: For brochures, maps, and general information, contact the Ft. Worth Convention and Visitors Bureau, 100 E. 15th St., Suite 400, Ft. Worth, TX 76102 (phone: 336-8791). They may also be picked up at the Visitor Information Center (phone: 682-4741), at 123 E. Exchange in the Stockyards district.

Television Stations – KDFW Channel 4–CBS; KXAS Channel 5–NBC; WFAA Channel 8–ABC; KERA Channel 13–PBS.

Radio Stations – AM: KLIF 1190 (talk/news); KFJZ 870 (jazz); KAAM 1310 (adult contemporary); KBEC 1390 (news). FM: KEGL 97.1 (top 40); KLUV 98.7 (oldies); KSCS 96.3 (country); WRR 101.1 (classical).

Local Coverage – The *Fort Worth Star-Telegram* is published mornings, evenings, and Sundays.

Food – *Texas Monthly,* the state magazine, publishes reviews of Ft. Worth's best restaurants. *D* magazine also lists Ft. Worth restaurants.

Telephone – The area code for Ft. Worth is 817.
Sales Tax – There is a 7¼% sales tax on all purchases except food.

CLIMATE: The official word is that Ft. Worth's average daily temperature during the spring is 65F; summer, 84F; fall, 66F; and winter, 47F. But don't let rumor or averages fool you: you can plan on summer scorchers and some pretty nippy winter days.

GETTING AROUND: Airport – Dallas/Ft. Worth Airport (or D/FW), the country's largest, is usually about a 40-minute drive from downtown Ft. Worth; cab fare should run about $37. Bus transportation between D/FW, the downtown hotels, and the downtown Greyhound bus terminal is provided by the city-owned T Charter Service (phone: 870-6200); fare is $6, and *Supershuttle* (phone: 329-2000); fare is $18, door-to-door, and reservations are required.

Bus – T Charter Service provides bus service throughout Ft. Worth; to check on routes and schedules, call 870-6200.

Taxi – The best way to get a cab is to phone for one. Try *Yellow Cab* (phone: 534-5555).

Car Rental – The major national agencies are represented.

Train – Amtrak serves Ft. Worth along two passenger routes, from Chicago via Houston and from St. Louis via San Antonio. 15th St. and Jones (phone: 332-2931).

Tours – For bus tours, call *Gray Line* (phone: 429-7563) or *Trailblazing Tours* (phone: 624-8687). There are also tours of the downtown area in a horse-drawn carriage, so let a Clydesdale show you the sights (phone: 870-1464).

LOCAL SERVICES: Babysitting Services – *Luv-N-Care,* 4451 Boatclub Rd. (phone: 237-5683).
   Business Services – *Kelly Services* (phone: 332-7807).
   Mechanics – American cars: *Pep Boys,* 4621 E. Lancaster (phone: 534-2227). For foreign cars: *Overseas Motors,* 2824 White Settlement Rd. (phone: 332-4181).

MUSEUMS: The *Kimbell Art Museum,* the *Amon G. Carter Museum,* and the *Museum of Science and History* are described under *Special Places.* Also of interest is the *Modern Art Museum of Fort Worth,* 1309 Montgomery (phone: 738-9215), a collection of 20th-century sculpture and paintings.

MAJOR COLLEGES AND UNIVERSITIES: Texas Christian University has especially distinguished drama and music departments and offers performances year-round in *Ed Landreth Auditorium.* 2800 S University Dr. (phone: 921-7000). Texas Wesleyan College is also in Ft. Worth, 3101 E. Rosedale (phone: 534-0251), as is the Southwestern Baptist Theological Seminary, the largest Baptist seminary in the world, 2001 W. Seminary Dr. (phone: 923-1921).

SPECIAL EVENTS: Any child who spent any time at all in the Ft. Worth Independent School District can attest that the highlight of the year comes during the 12 days in late January or early February when the *Southwestern Exposition and Livestock Show and Rodeo* comes to town. Schoolchildren have one day designated as Stock Show Day and receive free tickets, but the world's oldest indoor rodeo, midway, and stock show is fun for anyone. Contact the Southwestern Exposition, PO Box 150, Ft. Worth, TX 76101 (phone: 877-2420), for more information.

Ft. Worth's restored Main Street becomes a marketplace of food, arts and crafts, and entertainment during the *Main Street Fort Worth Arts Festival* on April 8-10. Other special events are *Mayfest,* an annual celebration with food, music, and games on the banks of the Trinity River the first weekend in May; the *Chisholm Trail Roundup,* a 3-day festival of street dances, chili cook-offs, and gunfights staged in the Stockyards area in June; the *Shakespeare in the Park* series at the *Trinity Park Playhouse* in late June, when spectators bring picnic suppers and enjoy the free performances; *Pioneer Days,* a 3-day western wingding held in September in the Stockyards; *Oktoberfest,* the first weekend in October; and the *National Cutting Horse Futurity,* held the first week in December at *Will Rogers Coliseum,* one of the premier western events in the country, with some of the highest monetary awards anywhere outside the racetrack.

 SPORTS AND FITNESS: Baseball – The Texas *Rangers* play at *Arlington Stadium,* 1700 Copeland Rd. (phone: 273-5100).
   Bicycling – The Dept. of Parks, 2222 W. Rosedale (phone: 870-6000), provides maps of scenic biking trails that circle Forest and Trinity parks.
   Fitness Centers – The coed *YMCA* downtown provides a pool, track, and all courts, 512 Lamar (phone: 332-3281). Another fitness center is *President's,* 6833 Green Oaks Rd. (phone: 738-8910).
   Golf – There are 11 country clubs and 9 municipal courses in Ft. Worth. The *Colonial National Invitation* is held at *Colonial Country Club,* 3735 Country Club Circle, in May (phone: 927-4200).
   Jogging – Maps of the jogging trails around Forest and Trinity parks are available from the Dept. of Parks, 2222 W. Rosedale (phone: 870-6000). The Trinity trail winds 8.2 miles through 3 city parks.
   Tennis – The *Mary Potishman Lard Tennis Center* near Texas Christian University offers 22 outdoor and 5 indoor courts to the public. Open daily. Admission charge. 3609 Bellaire (phone: 921-7960). The *McLeland Tennis Center* in southern Ft. Worth has 14 outdoor courts, 2 covered courts, and 1 practice court, all lighted. Open daily, 9 AM to 9 PM. The fee for 1½ hours of play outdoors is $1.50 per person before 5 PM, $2 per person after 5 PM; $12 per person on covered courts. Instruction available. 1600 W. Seminary Dr. (phone: 921-5134).

 THEATER: *Casa Mañana* ("the house of tomorrow") is probably Ft. Worth's best-known playhouse, 3101 W. Lancaster at University Dr. (phone: 332-6221). A theater-in-the-round, it mounts a variety of dramatic productions. Others include the *William E. Scott Theater,* 3505 Lancaster (phone: 738-6509); the *Circle Theater,* 227 W. Magnolia (phone: 921-3040); *Stage West,* 821 W. Vickery (phone: 332-6238); and the *Hip Pocket Theater,* which performs outdoors, 1620 Las Vegas Trail N. (phone: 927-2833). The *Caravan of Dreams Theater* stages an eclectic repertoire of drama, dance, and film at 312 Houston (phone: 877-3000).

 MUSIC: The *Fort Worth Opera,* the *Fort Worth Symphony* Orchestra, and the *Fort Worth Ballet* all give performances at the *Tarrant County Convention Center,* 1111 Houston. It's also the site of the *Van Cliburn International Piano Competition,* held every 4 years (1993 is the next competition year). For ticket information, contact Central Tickets (phone: 214-988-7250), Ticketron (phone: 640-7500), or Rainbow-Ticket Master (phone: 787-1500). Ft. Worth's Grammy-winning *Texas Boys Choir* was once called the best in the world by composer Igor Stravinsky; concerts are given in a variety of places (phone: 738-5420). The *Schola Cantorum of Texas* is a 50-member chorus that also performs in different venues (phone: 737-5788). For a very different kind of music that will appeal to the whole family, check out *Johnnie High's Country Music Revue* in *Will Rogers Auditorium,* 3001 W. Lancaster (phone: 481-4518).

NIGHTCLUBS AND NIGHTLIFE: The *White Elephant Saloon,* 106 E. Exchange (phone: 624-1887), is a popular watering hole that features barbecue, buffalo sweat margaritas, and country music; it's in the historic Stockyards area. Also worth visiting in the Stockyards is *Billy Bobs,* 2520 Rodeo Plaza (phone: 624-7117), which is open for music and dancing weekends only, and the *Longhorn Saloon,* 121 W. Exchange (phone: 624-4242). *Caravan of Dreams,* downtown at 312 Houston (phone: 877-3000), an avant-garde performing arts center, has a jazz and blues nightclub and a theater. Its *Rooftop Garden and Grotto Bar* is the city's most unusual. At *MacArthur's,* on Anderson Rd. off Camp Bowie (phone: 735-8851), the music is more eclectic; the *Hop,* 2905 W. Berry (phone: 923-7281), has a mixed bag of jazz, rock, and good food. *J & J Blues Bar,* 937 Woodward (phone: 870-2337), offers the best in regional blues, country, and jazz. *West Side Stories* offers five eclectic clubs in an entertainment complex at the former Ft. Worth Athletic Club, 3900 Hwy. 377 (phone: 560-SODA).

BEST IN TOWN

 CHECKING IN: At the hotels listed below, expect to pay $80 or more for a double room for a night in the expensive category, $45 to $80 for moderate; we found no establishments that met our standards in the inexpensive category. While Ft. Worth has no shortage of traditional hotels, another alternative, *Bed and Breakfast Texas-Style,* offers lodging and either continental or Texas-style breakfasts in private homes in the city's most desirable neighborhoods. Rates vary from budget to comfortable to deluxe, $20 to $60. Write to *Ruth Wilson,* 4224 W. Red Bird La., Dallas 75237 (phone: 214-298-5433). All telephone numbers are in the 817 area code unless otherwise indicated.

Hyatt Regency DFW – Big, convenient, and busy, this attractive property in the airport complex is a good place to stay if you're planning to divide your time between Dallas and Ft. Worth — or to visit the amusement parks between the two cities. It has 1,390 rooms, 4 restaurants, 36 holes of golf, 10 racquetball courts, 7 tennis courts, and an outdoor swimming pool. Ask about summer family rates. PO 619025, D/FW Airport (phone: 214-453-8400, 800-233-1234, or 800-228-9000). Expensive.

Stockyards – Dating to cowboy boomtown days, this historic 3-story hotel reopened in 1984 after extensive renovations. Much is made of the time Bonnie and Clyde put up here. Smack in the middle of the Stockyards district, it's a popular choice among tourists since the *White Elephant Saloon*, numerous restaurants, and other attractions are all within walking distance. Check out the saddles that serve as barstools in the *Booger Red Saloon.* 109 E. Exchange (phone: 625-6427). Expensive.

Worthington – This lovely European-style hostelry is downtown, across the street from Sundance Square. There are 508 rooms, including 70 luxury suites, 2 outdoor tennis courts, indoor pools, fully equipped athletic club, 24-hour private dining service, and a fine restaurant called *Reflections.* 200 Main St. (phone: 870-1000, 800-77205977 in Texas, 800-433-5677, in other states). Expensive.

Hyatt Regency – A renovated old Texas hotel, it has retained more of the city's original western flavor than any of the others. One block north of the convention center, 815 Main St. (phone: 870-1234, 800-233-1234, or 800-228-9000). Expensive to moderate.

Ft. Worth Hilton – It's right in the heart of downtown, near the convention center and overlooking the Water Gardens. There are 435 rooms in twin high-rise towers, an indoor pool, and the *Greenery* restaurant. 1701 Commerce St. (phone: 335-7000 or 800-HILTONS). Moderate.

Green Oaks Inn – This older hotel is a bit out of the way but conveniently across the street from an 18-hole golf course, and its 282 rooms share the grounds with 2 swimming pools, and a winding brook that falls to a fish-stocked pond. 6901 W. Freeway at State Hwy. 183 (phone: 738-7311, 800-772-2341 in Texas, 800-433-2174 elsewhere). Moderate.

 EATING OUT: In a city once called Cowtown, you'd naturally expect good beef, but natives pride themselves more on ferreting out superior Tex-Mex and chicken-fried steaks. Both are available in Ft. Worth, along with some better-than-average continental fare and a surprising assortment of ethnic eats. Expect to spend more than $50 for a meal for two in a restaurant listed as expensive; $30 to $50 for moderate; and less than $30 for inexpensive. Prices do not include drinks, wine, or tips. All telephone numbers are in the 817 area code unless otherwise indicated.

Carriage House – This longtime favorite of the Ft. Worth establishment combines a continental menu with a comfortably elegant decor. Open daily; Saturdays for dinner only, brunch only on Sundays. Reservations advised. Major credit cards. 5136 Camp Bowie (phone: 732-2873). Expensive to moderate.

Tours – This mainstay of local continental cooking has moved from a shopping center into its own building, offering atmosphere more compatible with its food and a sparkling view of downtown from its upstairs bar. Closed Sundays. Reservations advised. Major credit cards. 3500 W. 7th St. (phone: 870-1672). Expensive to moderate.

Balcony – This dressy, romantic restaurant overlooks Camp Bowie Boulevard and serves continental cuisine. Broiled lamb chops and lobster are the specialties. Closed Sundays. Reservations advised. Major credit cards. 6100 Camp Bowie (phone: 731-3719). Moderate.

Le Café Bowie – An intimate eatery, where the beef, veal, and poultry dishes are served with a crisp salad, the soup of the day, and warm, buttery bread. Open daily. Reservations advised. Major credit cards. 4930 Camp Bowie Blvd. (phone: 735-1521). Moderate.

Saint-Emilion – Creatively prepared meats, fish, and fowl are featured at this country French restaurant. Two- and four-course prix fixe meals are offered for dinner. Extensive wine selection. Closed Sundays. Reservations advised. All credit cards. 3617 W. 7th (phone: 737-2781). Moderate.

Angelo's – Hearty barbecue with the finest of trimmings is all this Ft. Worth institution offers. But what more could one ask for than an icy beer and a paper plate heaped with tangy ribs (served after 4:30 PM only) or barbecued beef plus a scoop of potato salad, coleslaw, a pickle, some onion sauce, and bread. Closed Sundays. No reservations. No credit cards. 2533 White Settlement (phone: 332-0357). Inexpensive.

Benito's – This is the best place in Ft. Worth to sample a variety of Mexican dishes. The standard Tex-Mex combos are available, but the more authentic Mexican fare — *menudo* (tripe), homemade tamales, and chiles relleños — hasn't been tamed for American tastebuds. They're delicious. Open daily. Reservations advised. Major credit cards, but no checks. 1450 W. Magnolia (phone: 332-8633). Inexpensive.

Carshon's – Split-pea soup and corned beef on rye aren't exactly the stuff of Ft. Worth's fame, but this spruced-up deli is touted statewide. Closed Mondays. No reservations. No credit cards. 3133 Cleburne Rd. (phone: 923-1907). Inexpensive.

Cattleman's Steak House – The portraits of blue-ribbon beef that grace the walls in this Stockyard stronghold are a little-needed reminder of each T-bone's heritage. Many of the cowboy customers are urban, but look carefully, since old-timers still like to splurge here. Open daily. No reservations on Saturdays. Major credit cards. 2458 N. Main (phone: 624-3945). Inexpensive.

Edelweiss – German food and an oompah band are the draws at this popular family place. The sauerbraten comes highly recommended. Closed Sundays and Mondays. No reservations. Major credit cards. 3801A Southwest Blvd. (phone: 738-5934). Inexpensive.

Hedary's – Everything is fresh and flavorful at this Lebanese restaurant, where customers may watch their dinners being prepared. Try the chicken with lemon, veal sausages, grilled lamb chops, and fresh pita bread. Closed Mondays. No reservations. All credit cards. 3308 Fairfield in Ridglea Center (phone: 731-6961). Inexpensive.

Joe T. Garcia's – This famous North Ft. Worth dive serves Tex-Mex food family-style to crowds that arrive fully expecting to line up out front for more than an hour on weekends. The wait is eased (and the food improved) by a couple of stout, delicious frozen margaritas. Open daily. Reservations advised. No credit cards. 2201 N. Commerce (phone: 626-4356). Inexpensive.

Juanita's – A tony Tex-Mex place in Sundance Square. One of the owners is June Jenkins, wife of Ft. Worth–raised author Dan Jenkins, and the place is named for his *Baja Oklahoma* heroine. Try a margarita and nachos at the bar before settling down to a Southwest meal. Dressier than most Tex-Mex eateries. Open daily. Reservations accepted. All credit cards. 115 W. 2nd (phone: 335-1777). Inexpensive.

Szechuan – If you hanker for Chinese food in Cowtown, this is the place to go — heaping portions, helpful service, and an extensive menu. The house specialties are heartily recommended. Open daily. Reservations advised. Major credit cards. 5712 Locke (phone: 738-7300). Inexpensive.

Massey's – No theory of evolution has been more often debated than how *Massey's* chicken-fried steaks came to be. To date, it's an unsurpassed delight — tender beef and a crunchy crust topped with thick and creamy gravy. Open daily. Reservations advised. Major credit cards. 1805 8th Ave. (phone: 924-8242). Inexpensive.

HARTFORD

East Coast residents used to joke that Hartford was an oasis on the highway between New York and Boston, for Hartford's unexpected beauty surprises many visitors. At first glance, the city's crystal skyscrapers, rising suddenly on the flat Connecticut River valley horizon, sparkle like Disney fantasy castles. However, the glitter is disarming. The majestic exterior of Connecticut's most dramatic cityscape masks one of the most pragmatic urban identities in the country. Hartford is the insurance capital of the United States. It is here, amid the graceful towers, that nearly every major domestic insurance company decides its policy regarding premiums and payments, decisions that, in some way or another, probably affect you. This bit of news is hardly likely to be first in your mind when you enter Hartford, however. Initial impressions are likely to be more aesthetic. But Hartford is more than just a pretty city or the state capital or a thriving business center; it is beginning to generate a lot of excitement as a place in which to enjoy oneself.

Although the Dutch visited and established a trading post in the area in the 1620s, Hartford was permanently settled by malcontents from Cambridge, Massachusetts, in 1636. For many years a lively port, here molasses, coffee, spices, and tobacco were stored in large warehouses, then shipped to other destinations on the Connecticut River. An important tobacco growing region, the Connecticut River valley was the site of the first cigar factory in the United States. Even today, the broad, green banks of the river stretch away, checkered by an intriguing patchwork of white cloth squares that shield the sensitive tobacco leaves from too much light. Hartford is still the marketing center for Connecticut Valley tobacco.

In the middle of this productive agricultural area, Hartford retains the essence of a historic New England township, a source of joy for anyone curious about American architecture during our nation's formative years. Colonial, post-Revolutionary, and 19th-century houses sit in spacious gardens. The renovated *Old State House,* where statesmen gathered to debate issues of the day as far back as 1796, is open to visitors. Mark Twain, creator of Tom Sawyer and Huck Finn, spent many years in Hartford, and his home, as well as the nearby house of *Uncle Tom's Cabin* author Harriet Beecher Stowe, are favorite stopping points along Hartford's literary trail.

And juxtaposed in the same city is a dramatic, revitalized downtown area. About 134,000 people live in Hartford, with over 800,000 in the greater Hartford area. This includes 32 New England towns within a 50-mile radius of the city center. Among them are urban centers such as East Hartford and picturebook hamlets like Avon and Old Wethersfield.

Hartford's insurance business alone employs around 50,000 people. The Connecticut state government employs even more. Bradley International Airport, between Hartford and Springfield, gives western New Englanders an alternative to the frenzy of Boston and New York airports. Visitors arriving from Canada or the Caribbean can also be spared the more chaotic environment of the larger cities.

Hartford's *Civic Center* has sparked a proliferation of new restaurants and cafés, some in creatively restored buildings. Streets that used to fold up at nightfall are now alive with bar hoppers, diners, tourists, and residents of downtown apartments. Among the new projects still sprouting like mushrooms in the district around the *Civic Center* is Goodwin Square, once the home of millionare J. P. Morgan. This historic building is being converted into a 124-suite luxury hotel connected to a high-rise offic tower. Renovation should be complete by the time this book is in your hands.

With its new image, Hartford is fast becoming a sophisticated, enthusiastic visitors' center with a magnetism all its own.

HARTFORD AT-A-GLANCE

SEEING THE CITY: The top of the Travelers' Tower offers the best view of the city, 527 feet above the madding crowd in the Travelers' Insurance Company building. There are 72 steps to climb before reaching the very top. Open weekdays from May until the last Friday in October. No admission charge, but call in advance. 700 Main St. (phone: 277-0111).

SPECIAL PLACES: Walking through Hartford can be highly enjoyable, especially since the city combines classical and contemporary architectural styles. Capitol Hill is a good place to begin.

Connecticut State Capitol – Guided tours daily, except December and January. Open weekdays, 9 AM to 3:30 PM (phone: 240-0222).

Baldwin Museum of Connecticut History – Three and a half centuries of Connecticut's heritage are packed into this museum with exhibitions tracing the growth of major manufacturers in the state. Most notable are the collection of Colt firearms and a Columbia automobile, built when Hartford's auto industry rivaled Detroit's. Closed Sundays and holidays. 231 Capitol Ave. (phone: 566-3056).

The Pavilion – This Palladian-style building at State House Square is the newest downtown landmark. Housing a warren of trendy shops and fast-food restaurants, its softly lit pink, rose, and aquamarine interior encourages strolling.

Bushnell Park – Bushnell is to Hartford what Central Park is to New York. In fact, Frederick Law Olmsted, who designed Central Park, also worked on Bushnell. The Knox Foundation, a private charitable organization, has donated an antique carousel with Wurlitzer band organ to the Bushnell Park Carousel Society, a nonprofit corporation that sells annual $10 individual and $25 family memberships to support the carousel; members can then ride free. Non-members need only spend a quarter for a ride. Private parties can have the carousel to themselves for $85 per hour. Open mid-May to August, 11 AM to 5 PM; mid-April through mid-May and September, weekends only. Closed Mondays. Bounded by Trinity, Elm, Ford, Wells, and Jewell Sts. (phone: 728-3089).

Butler-McCook Homestead – Within strolling distance of downtown's modern hotels and corporate headquarters is the oldest private home in the city, built in 1792. It has an extensive collection of 18th-century furnishings, vintage American paintings, and a fascinating collection of Japanese armor and other curios. Open Tuesdays

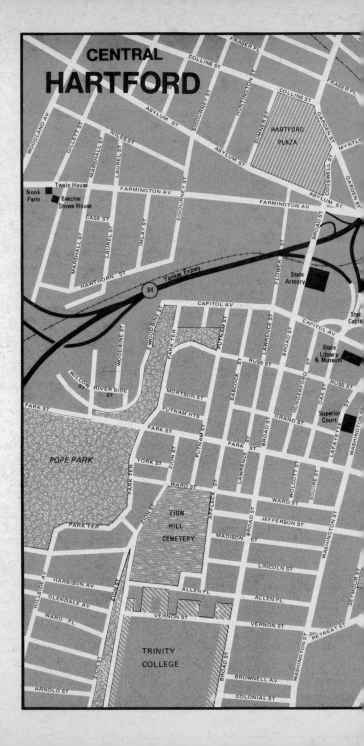

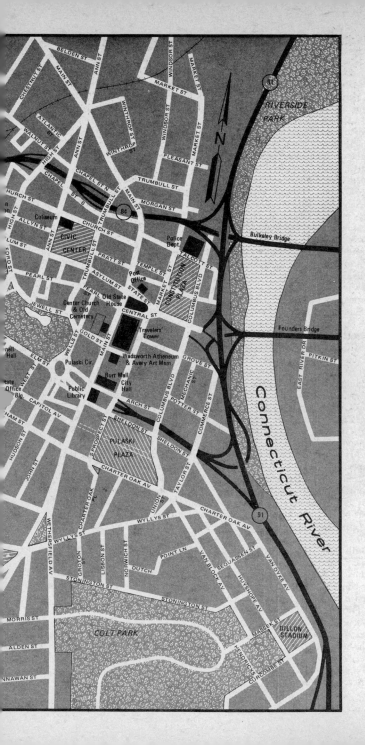

through Thursdays and Sundays, noon to 4 PM, May 15 to October 15. Special Victorian Christmas display in December. Adults, $2; children, 50¢ (phone: 522-1806).

Center Church – In 1636, the Reverend Thomas Hooker of Cambridge, Massachusetts, led a group of 100 men, women, and children and 160 head of cattle to Hartford, at the time a Dutch trading post. On the site of the *Old State House,* in 1638, he preached a revolutionary doctrine: "The foundation of authority is laid, first, in the free consent of the people." Hooker's ideas were incorporated into Connecticut's royal charter in 1662, and the minister became known as the founding father of the state. Outside the church is a cemetery, in use from 1640 to 1803. Open daily, noon to 3 PM. First Church of Christ on Main St. (phone: 249-5631).

Hartford Civic Center – This "city within a city" has about 50 shops, 13 restaurants, the 407-room *Hartford-Sheraton* hotel, plus 79,000 feet of exhibition space for the Boat Show, the Auto Show, and other large events. The Hartford *Whalers* hockey team plays in a 16,200-seat arena, which hosts other sporting events and concerts in the off-season. For concert ticket information call 727-8080; For *Whalers'* tickets call 728-3366 or 800-WHALERS.

Old State House – At one time an active meeting house for statesmen, this Federal building designed by Charles Bulfinch is now a museum. Colonial furniture and other artifacts date to 1796, when the *Old State House* was built. Now privately owned, the museum was refurbished in 1979 and a new souvenir and craft shop added. There is also information here about local attractions and special events. Open Mondays through Saturdays, 10 AM to 5 PM; Sundays, noon to 5 PM. No admission charge. Main and State Sts. (phone: 522-6766).

Wadsworth Atheneum – The oldest continually operating public art museum in the country, with eclectic collections of paintings, sculpture, ceramics, costumes, textiles, furniture, and firearms housed in five connecting buildings, the *Atheneum* features one of the largest collections of American art in the country, with more than 1,000 objects. There are important works by the Americans Church, Sargent, Whistler, and Wyeth. Also represented are such European masters as Rembrandt, Picasso, Monet, and Miró. The Lions Gallery presents special "hands-on" exhibitions accessible to the disabled. In the *MATRIX* galleries are changing shows of contemporary art. Admission charge except on Thursdays and Saturdays from 11 AM to 1 PM. 600 Main St. at Atheneum Sq. N. (phone: 247-9111).

Avery Art Memorial – Attached to the *Wadsworth Atheneum, Avery* has an important independent collection, including works by Rembrandt, Wyeth, Daumier, Picasso, Goya, Cézanne, Whistler, and Sargent. 25 Atheneum Sq. N. (phone: 278-2670).

Morgan Memorial – Also part of the *Wadsworth Atheneum,* this museum was started by J. P. Morgan, a Hartford citizen who left home to make his fortune. Fine collections of Middle Eastern and Oriental archaeological relics, Meissen china, and firearms, especially those made by Colt, a local enterprise. 590 Main St. (phone: 278-2670).

Elizabeth Park – Another of Hartford's "firsts" is this botanical wonderland, the first municipally owned rose garden in the country. More than 900 varieties and 14,000 other plants are displayed every summer, while the greenhouses stay open year-round. Open-air concerts are performed in summer. In winter, the park's pond is a popular place for ice skating. Prospect and Asylum Sts.

Nook Farm – A 19th-century writers' community, the former Nook Farm estate contains several authors' houses. Mark Twain lived in a riverboat-shaped brick, stone, and wood 3-story house with brown and orange brick patternwork. Harriet Beecher Stowe, the author of *Uncle Tom's Cabin,* lived only slightly less elaborately in a brick house next door. A 2-hour tour takes you through both houses. Closed holidays. Admission charge. Mark Twain Memorial, 351 Farmington Ave. (phone: 525-9317); Harriet Beecher Stowe House, 77 Forest St. (phone: 525-9317).

Science Museum of Connecticut – Visitors to this progressive science museum are greeted by a life-size replica of a 60-foot sperm whale. Includes an aquarium, hands-on tank, mini-zoo, and planetarium. Open Mondays through Saturdays 10 AM to 5 PM, Sundays 1 to 5 PM. 950 Trout Brook Dr., West Hartford (phone: 236-2961).

■**EXTRA SPECIAL:** For a diverting day trip that can include outdoor activities, visits to historic houses, and shopping for antiques, head west on Rte. 44. This scenic road travels over thickly forested Avon Mountain to the Farmington Valley. There, a plethora of natural attractions awaits, including canoeing, fishing, and exploring the hiking and cross-country ski trails in the Talcott Mountain State Park and Connecticut Blue Trail System. Heublein Tower, the area's key landmark, offers a panorama of five states to those who hike the 1½-mile trail starting at Rte. 185. Lining Rte. 44 are Avon, Farmington, and Simsbury, cozy New England hamlets with numerous craft boutiques and antiques shops. Farmington's *Hillstead Museum* is an imposing neo-Colonial mansion designed by architect Stanford White. The superb collection of early French Impressionists amassed by original owner Alfred Pope and the exquisite furnishings make it worth a visit (671 Farmington Ave.; phone: 677-9064). In Simsbury, dine in 19th-century elegance at the recently restored *Simsbury House,* which also has 35 rooms, each individually decorated with antique furnishings (731 Hopmeadow St.; phone: 658-7658). Farther south on Rte. 202 is Litchfield, a charming village of huge white mansions set around a classic New England village green. Just outside Litchfield, 3½ miles south on Rte. 63, is *White Flower Farm,* a perennial nursery that is a magnet for countless New England gardeners. Even for non-gardeners, it is worth a visit to see the display gardens, which peak in May and June; in July and August, a greenhouse full of magnificent English tuberous begonias share the limelight with fields of flowering shrubs and perennials. Open April through October. For more information, call 569-8789.

SOURCES AND RESOURCES

TOURIST INFORMATION: The Greater Hartford Convention and Visitors Bureau distributes brochures, maps, and general tourist information. 1 Civic Center Plaza, Hartford, CT 06103 (phone: 728-6789). It operates a visitors center at the Old State House. 800 Main at State St. (phone: 522-6766).

Television Stations – WFSB Channel 3–CBS; WVIT Channel 30–NBC; WTNH Channel 8–ABC; CPTV Channel 24–PBS.

Radio Stations – AM: WPOP 1410 (news) WTIC 1080 (news). FM: WIOF 104 (adult contemporary); WDRC 102.9 (solid gold).

Local Coverage – The *Hartford Courant* (the oldest daily newspaper in continuous circulation), morning daily; *Connecticut Magazine,* monthly; the *Hartford Advocate,* a free alternative news and entertainment publication, weekly, and *Hartford Monthly,* the city magazine, featuring events, restaurant, and entertainment listings.

Telephone – The area code for Hartford is 203.

Sales Tax – Local sales tax is 7½%.

CLIMATE: Hartford's humidity is a problem in the summer, when temperatures reach the 80s and 90s; winters are snowy, generally in the 20s and 30s; spring and fall are delightful.

GETTING AROUND: Airport – Bradley International Airport is about 12 miles from downtown Hartford. The drive usually takes 20 to 30 minutes, and taxi fare should run about $21. *Airport Taxi* (phone: 627-3210) provides hourly bus service to the downtown area from 6:35 AM to 11:20 PM (less often on weekends) for $7.25.

Bus – The state-owned Connecticut Transit Company operates the municipal bus service. 53 Vernon St. (phone: 525-9181).

Car Rental – All major national firms are represented at the airport as well as downtown. *Budget Rent-a-Car* is the least expensive local outlet. 455 Farmington Ave. near Asylum Ave. (phone: 236-2551).

Taxi – It's very difficult to get a cab in the street. Pick one up during the day in front of the *Sheraton Hartford, Parkview Hilton,* and *Summit* hotels, or call *Yellow Cab* (666-6666.)

Train – AMTRAK trains to New York and Boston pull in and out of the newly renovated Union Station Transportation Center (phone: 525-4580), which also served Greyhound Bus. Outside the station is a colorful mural by Connecticut artist Gleve Grey.

LOCAL SERVICES: Babysitting – *Care-At-Home,* 243 Farmington Ave. (phone: 728-1165)

    Business Services – *Headquarters Companies,* 1 Corporate Center (phone: 247-8300) and City Place (phone: 275-6500)

Mechanic – *Hartford Auto Repairs,* 12 S. Whitney St. (phone: 232-2236)

MUSEUMS: Museum aficionados will love the abundance of art and historical collections in Hartford. *Wadsworth Atheneum,* the *Avery Art Memorial, Morgan Memorial,* the *Science Museum of Connecticut,* and the *Old State House* are described above in *Special Places.* Another museum worthy of mention is:

Connecticut Historical Society – Open from noon to 5 PM; closed Sundays and Mondays. 1 Elizabeth St. (phone: 236-5621).

MAJOR COLLEGES AND UNIVERSITIES: Trinity College, at Summit, Vernon, and Broad Sts. (phone: 527-3151); St. Joseph College, Asylum Ave., West Hartford (phone: 232-4571); University of Hartford, 200 Bloomfield Ave., West Hartford (phone: 243-4100).

SPECIAL EVENTS: The *Festival of Lights* is held every year on Constitution Plaza the day after Thanksgiving, when thousands of tiny white lights are turned on by a child picked through a lottery. Santa Claus always makes a dramatic appearance, arriving on top of the Connecticut Bank and Trust Building in a helicopter and descending in a window-washer's gondola that looks surprisingly like a sleigh. *Wintertainment,* a 2-day festival in February, features events ranging from fireworks to snow sculpture contests and dogsled races. *A Taste of Hartford,* held at Constitution Plaza in the spring, is a giant block party with music, dancing, and booths set up by over 60 restaurants offering samples of their specialties. Hartford's *July 4th Festival* features concerts, sporting events, and fireworks displays along the Connecticut River. The *Connecticut Family Folk Festival* fills Elizabeth Park on the city's west side with the sounds of guitars, fiddles, and dulcimers during the second weekend of August.

SPORTS AND FITNESS: Fishing – For the best fishing, try Wethersfield Cove.

Fitness Center – The *YMCA* has a pool, squash and racquetball courts, and a track, 160 Jewell at Ann St. (phone: 522-4183).

Golf – There are 24 golf courses in the Hartford area. The best public course is in Goodwin Park. PGA Tour pros compete in the *Greater Hartford Open* every July at *Tournament Players Club,* Cromwell.

Hockey – The NHL *Whalers* team plays at the *Hartford Civic Center* (phone: 800-WHALERS).

Jogging – The perimeter of Bushnell Park, across from the YMCA, is ⅞ mile; other running courses include Goodwin Park, 1½ miles from downtown, with a 2-mile perimeter; and Elizabeth Park, 2 miles from downtown, with a 2½-mile perimeter.

Skiing – There's excellent cross-country skiing at the Metropolitan District Commission reservoir in West Hartford. Downhill enthusiasts like *Mt. Southington,* 20 minutes south on I-84; *Powder Ridge Ski Area,* 20 minutes south on I-91; and *Mt. Tom,* 45 minutes north on I-91.

Swimming – The Connecticut River is acceptable for boating but is not clean enough for swimming, even though it may look tempting on a hot day, Hartford residents recommend swimming at the *YWCA.* Admission charge. 135 Broad St. (phone: 525-1163). *YMCA,* 160 Jewell at Ann St. (phone: 522-4183).

Tennis – The best public courts are at Elizabeth Park, Prospect and Asylum Aves.; at the State Armory on Capitol Hill; there are indoor courts at *In-town Tennis* (phone: 246-7448).

THEATER: For complete performance schedules, check the newpapers listed above. Hartford's main theater is the *Hartford Stage Company,* 50 Church St. (phone: 527-5151); touring companies frequently bring Broadway productions to *Bushnell Memorial Hall,* 166 Capitol Ave. (phone: 246-6807).

MUSIC: Concerts, operas, symphonies, and ballets are performed at *Bushnell Memorial Hall,* 166 Capitol Ave. (phone: 246-6807); and the *Goodspeed Opera House* in East Haddam, 30 minutes south on Rte. 9 (phone: 873-8668). The *Civic Center,* 1 Civic Center Plaza (phone: 727-8080), features rock concerts.

NIGHTCLUBS AND NIGHTLIFE: Hartford's cafés are great places for listening to music. The selection varies from place to place, from night to night, so call ahead. At *Boppers,* 22 Union Pl. (phone: 549-5801), a DJ plays oldies but goodies from the back of a real 1957 convertible, parked in the center of the dance floor. *Shenanigans* restaurant, at 1 Gold St. (phone: 522-4117), has live music daily and serves dinner until midnight weekdays, until 1 AM weekends. Its bar is an authentic Art Deco diner that's been taken apart and rebuilt inside the restaurant. For disco dancing, try *Lorien,* 187 Allyn St. (phone: 525-1919), or the *Club Car,* S. Union Pl. (phone: 549-5444), which has a new upstairs dance floor and video screens, Tuesdays through Saturdays ($5 cover); there is no cover to listen to jazz in the downstairs lounge. Just across from the *Civic Center,* the *Russian Lady,* on Union Place, rocks with live music Thursdays through Saturdays for a mostly young crowd (phone: 525-3003); there is a $4 cover. *Citi Lites,* 70 Union Plaza (phone: 525-1014), is a popular yuppie hangout featuring live music and dancing to contemporary rock bands, Tuesdays through Saturdays for a small cover charge

BEST IN TOWN

 CHECKING IN: Hartford has an unexceptional collection of comfortable hotels. The *Parkview Hilton* does offer free local calls, and serves free coffee in guestrooms (some of which have waterbeds). The *Sheraton-Hartford, Summit,* and *Holiday Inn* offer in-room movies. Expect to pay $90 and up at places noted as expensive, $60 to $80 in the moderate category; we found no establishments that met our standards in the inexpensive category. For bed and breakfast accommodations, contact *Nutmeg Bed & Breakfast,* 222 Girard Ave., Hartford, CT 06105 (phone: 236-6698). All telephone numbers are in the 203 area code unless otherwise indicated.

Parkview Hilton – Overlooking Bushnell Park and the capitol, it was completely refurbished in 1981 and offers 383 rooms, and 3 restaurants. The Sunday brunch is a local favorite: for $13.95 you can stuff your face with unlimited portions of such treats as seafood newburg while enjoying that park view. Ford and Pearl Sts. (phone: 249-5611 or 800-HILTONS). Expensive.

Sheraton-Hartford – Connected to the *Civic Center,* this 407-room hotel gives the indoor sports enthusiast a wider range of facilities than any other Hartford hotel. The indoor heated pool has a lifeguard on duty. There's also a whirlpool baths, sauna, exercise room, and recreation room. The café-bar features nightly entertainment and dancing. In-room movies are also available. Cribs for infants are free. Trumbull St. at *Civic Center* (phone: 728-5151 or 800-325-3535). Expensive.

Summit – In the middle of Hartford's ultramodern, exceptionally well landscaped raised mall, Constitution Plaza, it offers 285 rooms, a café-bar, and dining room; parking in the hotel garage costs just $1 a day. 5 Constitution Plaza (phone: 278-2000). Expensive.

Holiday Inn – On the fringe of downtown, with easy access to I-84 and I-91, this high-rise property was refurbished in 1989 and now has an outdoor pool and inexpensive parking. It's a popular choice among corporate travelers. 50 Morgan St. (phone: 549-2400 or 800-HOLIDAY). Moderate.

Ramada–Capital Hill – A central hotel with basic conveniences at an attractive price, this is a good bet. Its 96 rooms have recently been refurbished and there is a restaurant and café. Parking is free. 440 Asylum St. (phone: 246-6591 or 800-2-RAMADA). Moderate.

 EATING OUT: The number and varieties of foreign cuisines available in the city are gradually increasing, but most of the best restaurants still feature traditional Hartford fare: American-Italian cooking, or the steaks-chops-seafood routine. Expect to pay between $30 and $50 at restaurants designated as expensive; between $25 and $35 at those we've listed as moderate; $25 or less at inexpensive places. Prices do not include drinks, wine, or tips. All telephone numbers are in the 203 area code unless otherwise indicated.

L'Américain – On the fringe of downtown, this eclectic restaurant inside a renovated factory is a favorite of the business community. Open daily. Reservations advised. Major credit cards. 2 Hartford Sq. (phone: 522-6500). Expensive.

Arne's – This 3-tiered restaurant on the 1st floor of the *Pavilion* is a seafood lover's delight. Newly refurbished, it's a popular lunch spot, featuring informal dining and a café-style menu. Skylights and big picture windows provide good views of downtown for diners at lower-tier tables. Closed Sundays. Reservations advised. Major credit cards. 30 State House Sq. (phone: 549-4747). Expensive.

Carbone's – Northern Italian dishes are featured at this family-owned restaurant, a Hartford fixture for more than 45 years in the city's south end, which holds a lively Italian festival in the summer. Reservations advised. Closed Sundays. 588 Frontline Ave. (phone: 249-9646). Expensive to moderate.

Max on Main – Currently the trendiest downtown dining spot, it calls itself an American bistro, perhaps because Saratoga water is served instead of Perrier. The fare is nouvelle American, featuring seafood and meat dishes made with ingredients raised locally. For lunch, try chicken pot pie, a regional specialty. Open daily. Major credit cards. 205 Main St. (phone: 522-2530). Expensive to moderate.

Peppercorns Grill – A block from the *Wadsworth Atheneum,* this eatery doesn't look like much from the outside, but it offers a unique dining experience. The eclectic menu, described as "Southwestern Italian," features pasta specialties such as spicy fettuccine and seafood dishes such as brochettes of scallops, shrimp, and calamari. Reservations advised, particularly on weekends. Major credit cards. 357 Main St. (phone: 547-1714). Expensive to moderate.

Spencer's – In the restored Linden apartment building (one of the city's most exclusive), this is actually two restaurants in one. The formal, Edwardian dining room features a continental bill of fare, while the *Tavern* serves lighter meals in a more casual atmosphere. Open daily. Reservations advised. Major credit cards. 10 Capitol Ave. (phone: 247-0400). Expensive to moderate..

Frank's – A favorite of state politicians, serving traditional Italian-American dishes. The manicotti is considered excellent and the veal superb. Especially busy before and after hockey games and *Civic Center* events, so make reservations. Specialties include fresh seafood delights, such as San Francisco cipiano. The largest wine selection in the city. Open daily except Sundays in July and August. Major credit cards. In the Cityplace Complex at 185 Asylum St., across from the *Civic Center* (phone: 527-9291). Moderate.

Hot Tomato's – This popular new downtown eatery in Union Station features Northern Italian specialties such as *giabotto* (chicken, veal, and hot sausage, with hot peppers and cheese) and shrimp piccata, made with lots of love — and garlic. The atmosphere is lively and cheeful. No reservations. Major credit cards. 309 Asylum St. (phone: 249-5100). Moderate.

Brown Thomson & Co. – In the Richardson Building complex, which also includes a shopping mall, this antiques-encrusted restaurant offers the most extensive menu in town — 125 separate items. Sandwiches, Mexican food, and delicacies such as fried ice cream are included. This is where the young people of Hartford meet these days. A comedy club operates in the back room on Friday and Saturday nights, for an $8 cover; shows are at 8:30 and 11 PM. Major credit cards. 942 Main St. (phone: 525-1600). Inexpensive.

HONOLULU

Honolulu stretches along a 20-mile strip of land between the Pacific Ocean and the 3,000-foot mountains of Oahu, the major island of the state of Hawaii. In the past 30 years the city has outgrown this narrow strip and risen up the mountains along ridges and deeply cleft valleys; it reaches into the sea with a multitude of docks and marinas that run, off and on, from Pearl Harbor to the first grand sweep of magnificent Waikiki Beach — and magnificent it is, even poised against a backdrop of high-rise hotels several blocks deep. At night the homes up in the heights glitter above the city, and beyond them — 15 minutes from downtown — are the tropical mountain rain forests, as prolific and luxuriant as ever.

Private sailors and yachtsmen know Honolulu as one of America's trimmest, cleanest port cities. To landbound Americans it is something more — the country's most foreign metropolis, an American city that stubbornly refuses to feel quite like America. Small wonder, when you consider that less than 100 years ago — until 1893, to be exact — it was the capital of a foreign country, a monarchy ruled by a queen: a Pacific Ocean island nation with its own distinct culture, arts, and world view rooted in the South Seas. In 1893, reigning Queen Liliuokalani was overthrown by Americans living in the islands, and 5 years later the islands were annexed as a US territory. They became American, but they were — are — still the islands, and that ain't canned pineapple. About 2,500 miles southwest of Los Angeles, Honolulu is about a third of the way between the continental US and Tokyo, a relationship that more than once has given rise to awe and some misgivings.

The sense of disorientation is not all one-sided. The "mainland" is what residents call the rest of the United States (and if you want to keep their respect you will never refer to it as "stateside" since Hawaii, too, is a state, and proud of it), and to many residents the other 49 states represent the strange and sometimes rather frightening culture of the *haoles*. Pronounced "*how*-lees," this old Hawaiian word for outsiders has, in the 20th century, come to mean Caucasians — a segment of the population well outnumbered by Orientals and Polynesians in Hawaii. To native Hawaiians, haoles in the past have represented Yankees who don't understand pidgin and who seem eager to bull their way into business and social success. The fact that they no longer automatically succeed in these objectives represents a change not uniformly felt, and sometimes overlooked, in the islands today.

Islanders in general, and Honolulu residents in particular, are unabashedly fond of dubbing their island home "paradise." But it is sometimes an uneasy Eden, with a history that has often been violent and tragic. Early-19th-century American missionaries experienced severe hardships here; but in the pitched battles between missionaries and western shippers and merchants for the hearts and minds of the native population, it was the Hawaiians who lost almost everything. They were converted to Christianity and lost their culture; they were taught to read, write, and count, and were decimated by foreign diseases to which they had no immunity. Only today is the long-dormant pride of culture emerging among descendants of the original Polynesian Hawaiians.

Other groups came to live in the islands, too, gradually making Honolulu a cosmopolitan city. When the economy required hard labor for the sugar plantations in the late 19th century, unskilled workers were recruited from all over, especially from Japan and China. When their contracts expired, many stayed on, marrying and spawning the lovely racial mix that characterizes contemporary Honolulu society. More than half the marriages in Hawaii today are interracial.

With the attack on Pearl Harbor — December 7, 1941 — Honolulu entered the consciousness of most mainland Americans. Martial law was declared throughout the islands, and for millions of American servicemen Hawaii became the jumping-off point for the Pacific theater. They called Oahu "the Rock," and they hated it.

They don't hate it anymore. More than 6 million visitors a year pour into the Honolulu airport and drop more than $7 billion into the Hawaiian coffers. Honolulu's green outback may be carpeted with sugar and pineapple plantations, but plantations no longer support the economy. Tourism is the vital juice of Hawaii, and much of it gets squeezed out in Honolulu. (And among the visitors are a good number of former GIs who once upon a time hated the Rock. The most popular attraction is the beautiful memorial that floats over the sunken USS *Arizona*. One million people a year visit it.)

Honolulu — the eleventh largest city in the country — is a modern metropolis struggling with modern problems. A few decades ago Waikiki was a sparsely settled peninsula along a swamp, 4 miles southeast of town. There was an unobstructed view of Diamond Head, and the tallest structure in town was the 10-story Aloha Tower, from which ship traffic in the harbor was controlled. No more, no more. Forests of high-rises dwarf the Tower and Waikiki has its share of dope dealers, pickpockets, and prostitutes. But Chinatown, while slowly being gentrified, is still in the center of town, with its noodle factories and small restaurants reminiscent of a port town 100 years ago. And within Honolulu is a taste of everything Hawaiian and a flavor of seas far beyond.

HONOLULU AT-A-GLANCE

SEEING THE CITY: For an eye-popping view of the shoreline, take the outdoor glass elevator to the top of the *Ilikai* hotel (1777 Ala Moana Blvd.; phone: 949-3811). There are equally spectacular views from the *Hanohano Room* atop the *Sheraton Waikiki* (2255 Kalakaua Ave.; phone: 922-4422) and from *Nicholas Nickolas,* atop the *Ala Moana* hotel (410 Atkinson St.; phone: 955-4811). For another good perspective, visit the 10th-floor observatory in the Aloha

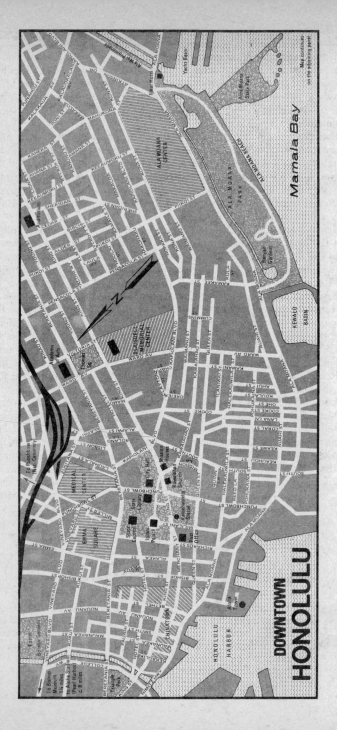

DOWNTOWN
HONOLULU

Mamala Bay

Map continues on the adjoining panel

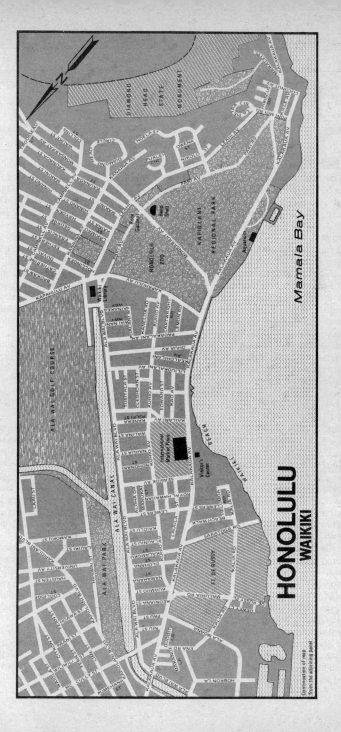

HONOLULU
WAIKIKI

Mamala Bay

Continuation of map
from the adjoining panel

Tower, with a panorama that stretches from the airport to Diamond Head; at the bottom of Fort Street Mall (phone: 537-9260). The popular Tantalus Lookout provides a sweeping perspective that takes in much of Honolulu, Waikiki, Diamond Head, and Manoa Valley, wherein lies the campus of the University of Hawaii.

 SPECIAL PLACES: Although it is now considerably overbuilt, Waikiki is nonetheless an interesting place to wander. We suggest getting to know your neighborhood first with a 3-mile walking tour.

Diamond Head – Guarding the southeasternmost boundary of Waikiki, this 760-foot volcanic crater is a world-famous landmark. You can climb around the slopes of Diamond Head along the tricky trail that begins at a gate off Makalei Place. It is also possible to drive into the crater through a tunnel to a state park inside, where there is an easy trail to the summit, which passes by World War II bunkers. Open 6 AM to 6 PM. For park information, call the State Parks Dept. at 548-7455.

Kapiolani Park – This 220-acre park, named for the wife of Kalakaua, the last king of Hawaii, has enough special places to keep you busy for more than a few hours. Just off Monsarrat Ave., the Kodak Hula Show (phone: 833-1661) is performed at 10 AM Tuesdays through Thursdays. Get there early if you want a good seat. Drift along toward the scent of the Kapiolani Rose Garden on the corner of Paki and Monsarrat. Other attractions in the park include the Waikiki Aquarium, Honolulu Zoo (recently upgraded), tennis courts, beaches, jogging trails, and the Shell, featuring entertainment under the stars. Kalakaua Ave., named after the good king, begins here. Pronounced "ka-la-*cow*-wah," it is the principal thoroughfare of Waikiki.

Waikiki Beach – Just outside the park, alongside Kalakaua Ave., begins the famous, 2½-mile-long curve of Waikiki Beach, one of the most famous beaches and surfing spots in the world. The 2- to 5-foot waves that are standard along the shoreline for much of the year are perfect for novices and amateurs. (On the few days in the summer when they reach 15 feet, Waikiki's waves should be avoided by all but experts.) Several hotels along Waikiki — for example, the *Outrigger,* 2335 Kalakaua Ave. (phone: 923-0711; ask for Beach Services) — provide instruction and surfboards.

International Marketplace – A great place to poke around outdoor stalls underneath a giant banyan tree festooned with lanterns. (A souk, Hawaiian-style, is what we call it.) You can pick up all kinds of exotic junk and treasures you just can't live without. As we went to press, plans were under way to build a large convention center on the Marketplace acreage. 2330 Kalakaua Ave.

Royal Hawaiian Shopping Center – Stretching 3 blocks along the ocean side of Kalakaua Avenue, this 3-level outdoor mall is Waikiki's largest shopping complex, with everything from Hawaiian crafts to designer clothes, plus daily performances of music and Hawaiiana as well as several restaurants serving a variety of cuisines. 2201 Kalakaua Ave. (phone: 922-0588).

Ft. DeRussy Army Museum – Weapons used by ancient Hawaiians, weapons captured from the Japanese, and weapons used by US soldiers in campaigns from the Spanish-American to the Korean War are on display here. In addition, there are uniforms worn at various times by US forces as well as those of the enemy. The most fascinating items are the Hawaiian weapons made long ago from shark's teeth and the newspaper accounts of the US involvement in World War II following the invasion of Pearl Harbor. Closed Mondays. Kalia Rd. (phone: 438-2818).

Tantalus Drive – The country road that winds its way up Mount Tantalus provides some of the most beautiful urban scenery found anywhere. The panoramas from lookouts en route through lush rain forest include Waikiki, Diamond Head, downtown Honolulu, and the distant Waianae Mountains. A state park provides one of several places to relax, picnic, or hike.

DOWNTOWN

Mission Houses Museum – This museum complex contains the earliest American buildings in Hawaii. The white frame house was shipped around Cape Horn in pieces, then reassembled in 1821 by the first missionaries. The buildings have been intelligently restored, and excellent guides are available (and give a good thumbnail sketch of basic Hawaiian history). Open daily. Admission charge. 551 S. King St. (phone: 531-0481).

Kawaiahao Church – Across from the *Mission Houses,* Kawaiahao Church is also known as the Westminster Abbey of Hawaii. It was designed by Hawaii's first minister and constructed out of 14,000 coral blocks cut from a local reef. King Lunalilo is buried in the front yard. Services are conducted in English and Hawaiian at 10:30 AM on Sundays. Open daily. No admission charge. King and Punchbowl Sts. (phone: 522-1333).

Chinatown – Chinatown is on the easternmost fringe of downtown and spills across the Nuuanu Stream into Aala Triangle Park. There are open-air meat, fish, and vegetable markets; herb shops selling age-old medications; and elderly people who still dress in traditional costume. This is also the "sin" quarter of Honolulu, where sleazy sex shows compete for customers with family-style chop suey houses. A walking tour of Chinatown with an optional lunch (a real bargain) takes place on Tuesdays at 9:30 AM, starting from the Chinese Chamber of Commerce, 42 N. King St. (phone: 533-3181).

Hawaii Maritime Museum – Pier 7 is the home of the four-masted *Falls of Clyde* and the outrigger voyaging canoe *Hokulea,* returned from its three trans-Pacific voyages along Polynesian migration routes. There are also displays related to Hawaii's maritime history, plus a library and photo archive. Pier 7, near Aloha Tower (phone: 536-6373).

Iolani Palace – With elaborate surroundings, Iolani Palace sits in state, receiving tribute from admirers. Highly revered by historians and sentimentalists alike, the palace was the royal residence of monarch and songwriter Queen Liliuokalani. In fact, she was imprisoned there following the 1893 revolution and wrote some of her famous songs, including "Aloha Oe," while in detention. Iolani was built by her brother, King David Kalakaua, between 1878 and 1882. In 1883, he placed a crown on his own head in what is now *Coronation Bandstand,* where, every Friday at noon, the *Royal Hawaiian Band* gives free, informal concerts. Palace tours are given Wednesdays through Saturdays. King and Richards Sts. (phone: 538-1471; for reservations, 523-0141).

State Capitol – Built in 1969, for $25 million, the capitol takes its inspiration from the natural history of the islands. All of its features — columns, reflecting pools, courtyard — reflect aspects of Hawaii's environment. Outside the capitol stands a beautiful bronze statue of Queen Liliuokalani and the controversial modern statue of Father Damien, the hero of the leprosy settlement at Kalaupapa on the island of Molokai. 415 S. Beretania St. (phone: 548-2211).

OTHER SPECIAL PLACES

Ala Moana Center – This is one of the world's largest shopping centers. Built in 1959, when Hawaii achieved statehood, and recently expanded and updated for the 1990s, it has more than 220 stores selling quality clothing, furniture, fabrics, and art made at home and imported from other countries. Ala Moana Blvd. across from Ala Moana Park.

Arizona Memorial – More than a million people a year come to honor the American sailors who perished on the USS *Arizona,* sunk when the Japanese bombed Pearl Harbor on December 7, 1941. Something of a surprise is the number of Japanese among the group. The only boat tour of the memorial departs from the visitors center daily except Mondays. The National Park Service operates a large museum, with exhibitions and films. The *Hilton Hawaiian Village* catamaran departs for Pearl Harbor midday from Waikiki. Most other boats leave from Kewalo Basin (hotel transfers are included) for the half-day tour that passes the memorial but does not allow for a visit.

Bishop Museum – Near the beginning of Likelike (pronounced *leekay-leekay*) Highway, in the working class neighborhood called Kalihi, this prestigious museum houses the greatest collection of Hawaiiana in the world. Founded in 1899, it is the center for most of the anthropological research done throughout Polynesia and the Pacific. In addition to excellent displays, the museum, which has been expanded recently, features daily performances of Hawaiian music and dance. Shows are also featured at the adjacent planetarium. Open daily. Admission charge. 1525 Bernice St. (phone: 848-4129).

Foster Botanic Gardens – Often overlooked by tourists, this cool, tranquil retreat in the middle of the city is a living museum of growing things. The #4 bus from Waikiki will bring you close to the garden at Nuuanu and Vineyard. Open daily. Admission charge. 180 N. Vineyard Blvd. (phone: 531-1939).

Honolulu Academy of Arts – Across Thomas Square from *Blaisdell Center,* the *Academy of Arts* has Oriental art and some European and American works. Interesting items include a Japanese ink and color handscroll dating to 1250, John Singleton Copley's *Portrait of Nathaniel Allen,* and Segna di Bonaventura's *Madonna and Child.* Lunch is served in the museum garden Tuesdays through Fridays at 11:30 AM and 1 PM. Thursday evenings dinner is served at 6:30 PM. Reservations required. Closed Mondays. No admission charge. 900 S. Beretania St. (phone: 538-3693).

National Memorial Cemetery of the Pacific – Also known as Punchbowl crater, this cemetery is the Arlington of the Pacific. In prehistoric times it was the site of human sacrifices. Now, more than 26,000 servicemen lie buried among its 112 peaceful acres overlooking downtown Honolulu. Commercial bus and van tours visit Punchbowl, but if you're on your own, you'll need a car or taxi. Take Puowaina Drive to its end.

The Contemporary Museum – Hawaii's newest museum, on the Tantalus hillside with a beautiful view of the city, features contemporary sculpture, painting, watercolor, graphics, and more, most of it in well-displayed, changing exhibitions. There's a major permanent display of the works of David Hockney. In addition, a satellite gallery is in the news building of the Honolulu Newspaper Agency on Kapiolani Blvd. Open daily from 10 AM to 4 PM except Sundays, from noon to 4 PM, and Tuesdays, when it is closed. Donations requested. 2411 Makiki Heights Dr. (phone: 526-1322).

■**EXTRA SPECIAL:** Honolulu is the great jumping-off point for island-hopping expeditions. Hawaiian Air (phone: 537-5100) flies to the islands of Kauai, Maui, Hawaii, and Molokai daily, and less frequently to Lanai; Aloha Airlines (phone: 836-1111) serves all but Lanai; Aloha Island Air (phone: 833-3219) is the largest of several commuter airlines that fly between the islands. Commuter flights link both major airports as well as more isolated communities like Hana, Maui, or Waimea on the Big Island. On some runs, commuter fares are lower than those charged for the jet service of the majors; on some they are higher. Kauai, the oldest of the islands, is known for golf at the *Princeville* and *Kauai Lagoons* resort courses, sunny Poipu Beach, and the spectacular Na Pali coast. Maui offers valleys, waterfalls, beaches, and the crater of the dormant Haleakala Volcano. The Kapalua airport makes direct flights to Lahaina, Kaanapali, Kahana, Napili, and Kapalua resorts. Hawaii is the home of Mauna Loa and Kilauea, two of the most active volcanoes in the world. On Lanai, only 17 miles long, the main draws are plenty of pineapples and two new resort hotels. The Dole Company owns most of the island, and its land is devoted to cultivating the spiny, delicious fruit. Molokai, 37 miles long, a relatively untouched ranchers' island, offers tourists the opportunity to see a rural side of Hawaii, or visit the isolated leper's settlement at Kalaupapa, now administered as a National Historic Park. There is also a resort at Kaluakoi and several small condos and hotels along the east coast for those who wish to stay awhile.

SOURCES AND RESOURCES

 TOURIST INFORMATION: For information, maps, and brochures, contact the Hawaii Visitors Bureau, 2270 Kalakaua Ave., Room 804, Honolulu, HI 96815 (phone: 923-1811).

This Week, Spotlight Hawaii, and the pocket-size *Beach Guide* series are the best of the numerous free publications aimed at visitors, and they are available in most hotel lobbies. Also see our own *Birnbaum's Hawaii 1990*.

Television Stations – KHON Channel 2–NBC; KGMB Channel 9–CBS; KITV Channel 4–ABC; KHET Channel 11–PBS.

Radio Stations – AM: KSSK 590 (oldies); KHVH 990 (news). FM: KHHH 98.5 (jazz and popular); KHPR 88.1 (classical); KQMQ 96.3 (soft rock); KMAI 93.9 (soft rock).

Local Coverage – *Honolulu Advertiser,* morning daily; *Honolulu Star-Bulletin,* evening daily; *Honolulu* magazine, monthly.

Telephone – The area code for Honolulu is 808.

Sales Tax – There is a 4% sales tax in Honolulu and a statewide 5% hotel tax.

 CLIMATE: In ancient times, the Hawaiians had no word for weather. They did, however, have words for two seasons — winter and summer. Winter, which runs from about October through April, means daytime highs reaching the mid-70s and low 80s, dropping into the low 60s at night. There can be several short rains in a day. You can count on 11 hours of daylight — short by Hawaiian standards. Summer temperatures hover around the mid- to upper 80s; rains are less frequent, and you get about 13 hours of daylight, more vacation for your money.

 GETTING AROUND: Airport – Honolulu International Airport is about a 20- to 25-minute drive from Waikiki (in moderate traffic), slightly less from the downtown area. Cab fare to Waikiki should run $12 to $14, $18 to $20, downtown. The *Gray Line* (phone: 834-1033) provides bus service from the airport to Waikiki hotels and condos for $5; buses leave from outside the baggage claim area every 20 minutes during most of the day (hourly in the morning and at night). The *Gray Line* trip to Waikiki can take anywhere from 30 minutes to 1 hour, depending on the location of your hotel. *Airport Motorcoach* (phone: 926-4747) provides limousine service for $5 between the airport and Waikiki.

Bus – TheBus, as the municipal transit line is called, is the least expensive, most convenient way to get around Honolulu. You can get a map of bus routes at your hotel, at Ala Moana Center, or from the Honolulu Dept. of Transport, Mass Transit Lines (MTL), 725 Kapiolani Blvd. (phone: 531-1611).

Taxi – Although taxis can sometimes be hailed on the street, most are on call. To be sure of getting a cab, call for one. Some reliable companies are: *SIDA* (phone: 836-0011), *Charley's* (phone: 955-2211), and *Aloha State Taxi* (phone: 847-3566).

Car Rental – There are several that provide quality service: *Tropical* (phone: 836-1041), *Budget* (phone: 922-3600), *National* (phone: 800-227-7368), *Avis* (phone: 834-5536), *Hertz* (phone: 836-2511), and *Dollar* (phone: 926-4200). Most serve 4 or 5 islands, and multi-island rates are offered. Check for special rates that are available when business is slow. Rental offices are at the airport and in Waikiki.

Helicopter Tours – *Royal Helicopters* (phone: 836-2868) and *Papillon Hawaii Pacific* (phone: 836-1566), depart from a Waikiki helipad on a series of aerial tours. *Cherry Helicoper* (phone: 833-4339) departs from the *Turtle Bay* resort on the north shore.

Trolley – The *Waikiki Trolley* provides open-air links in modified turn-of-the-century style between Waikiki (pick-ups at the *Hilton Hawaiian Village* and the Royal Hawaiian Shopping Center), and shops (Ala Moana Center, Ward Warehouse, Ward Center, Dole Cannery Square), and attractions eleswhere in Honolulu (*Honolulu Academy of Arts,* Iolani Palace, Chinatown, *Maritime Museum, Mission Houses Museum*) between 7:30 AM and 5 PM. An all-day pass costs $7 (phone: 526-0112).

 LOCAL SERVICES: Babysitting – *Wesley Ministries,* 1350 Hunakai St. (phone: 732-3273).
 Business Services – *Una May Young,* Suite 3206, Manor Wing, *Sheraton-Waikiki* hotel, 2255 Kalakaua Ave. (phone: 922-4422).
 Mechanic – *Toguchi Chevron Service Station,* 825 N. Vineyard Blvd. (phone: 845-6422).

 MUSEUMS: The *Ft. DeRussy Army Museum, Bishop Museum, Hawaii Maritime Museum, Mission Houses Museum,* and *Honolulu Academy of Arts* are described under *Special Places.* Another notable museum is the *Polynesian Cultural Center,* 1½ hours from Waikiki in Laie (phone: 923-1861). Each of the seven model villages on the 42-acre grounds represents a Pacific Island culture: Maori, Tahitian, Samoan, Fijian, Tongan, Marquesan, and Hawaiian. People live and work as they would on their native islands. Throughout the day there is Polynesian entertainment featuring the villagers. (The *This Is Polynesia* revue, evenings at 7:30, is the best of its kind in Hawaii.) Closed Sundays. Admission charge (phone: 923-1861 or 293-3333).

 MAJOR COLLEGES AND UNIVERSITIES: The University of Hawaii, in Manoa Valley (phone: 948-8855); Brigham Young University, at Laie (phone: 293-3211); Chaminade University of Honolulu (phone: 735-4711); Hawaii Pacific College, downtown (phone: 544-0239); Hawaii Loa College (phone: 235-3647).

 SPECIAL EVENTS: Special events are held year-round. Here are a few highlights:
 January: The annual *Hula Bowl* College All-Star Football Classic is played in *Aloha Stadium* and the *Chinese New Year* is celebrated in Chinatown (sometimes in February).
 February: Early in the month, the nationally televised 4-day *Hawaiian Open International Golf Tournament,* at the *Waialae Country Club* in the Kahala District (sometimes late in January).
 June: On June 11, *Kamehameha Day* honors the conqueror of the islands with a long parade and floats.
 July: In even-numbered years, the *Trans-Pacific Yacht Race* finishes off Diamond Head.
 September: The *Waikiki Rough Water Swim* is held over a 2-mile course, ending at Duke Kahanamoku Beach in front of the *Hilton Hawaiian Village* hotel. *Aloha Week* is Honolulu's biggest celebration. It features canoe races, luaus, balls, athletic events, parades and more. *Symphony* season begins.

October: The *Honolulu Orchid Society Show* is held at the *Neal S. Blaisdell Center,* with lei making and flower arranging demonstrations as well as floral displays.

December: Contestants in the *Honolulu Marathon* run from the Aloha Tower to the bandshell in Kapiolani Park. The *Triple Crown* of surfing competitions is held along Oahu's north shore. December 7 is *Pearl Harbor Day,* commemorated by a service at the *Arizona* Memorial. Early in the month, the *Pacific International Film Festival* presents a week of free movies.

 SPORTS AND FITNESS: Hawaii is one of the world's great centers for water sports. Surfing and swimming contests are held often. *Aloha Stadium* is the site of the *Hula Bowl* college football game each January; football and baseball games at other times are in Halawa Heights (phone: 488-7731). Basketball and boxing events are held at the *Neal S. Blaisdell Center,* 777 Ward Ave. (phone: 521-2911).

Bicycling – Bikes can be rented from *Aloha Funway Rentals,* 1984 Kalakaua Ave. (phone: 947-4579).

Fishing – Fishing enthusiasts from all over the world flock to Hawaiian waters. Fishing boats can be chartered from *Coreene C's Sport Fishing Charters* (phone: 536-7472), or *Island Charters* (phone: 536-1555). Most boats leave from Kewalo Basin, at the end of Ward Ave., on Ala Moana Blvd.

Fitness Centers – The *Honolulu Tennis Center* has tennis and racquetball courts, S. King St. between Isenberg and McCully (phone: 944-9696). The *YMCA* has a pool, racquetball court, sauna, exercise machines, and weights, 401 Atkinson Dr., across from Ala Moana Center (phone: 941-3344). For a treat, set up an appointment with the massage (shiatsu) specialist at the *Sheraton Moana Surfrider,* 2365 Kalakaua Ave. (phone: 922-3111).

Gliding – *Hawaii Glider Rides* has 3-seat sailplanes departing about every 20 minutes daily from 10:30 AM to 5 PM at the north shore's Dillingham Airfield (phone: 677-3404).

Golf – There are 16 public golf courses on Oahu and several more in the planning stage. These include *Ala Wai,* the closest to Waikiki (phone: 296-4653); *Pali,* in Kaneohe (phone: 261-9784); *Sheraton West Course* (phone: 695-9544) and *Makaha Valley Country Club* (phone: 695-7111), both in Makaha; and the *Turtle Bay Hilton* (phone: 293-8811), near Kahuku on the north shore.

Jogging – Run along Kalakaua Avenue to Kapiolani Park, where a group meets at the bandstand at 7:30 AM every Sunday from March through December for a short lecture and a run. The distance around the park is 1.8 miles; to tack on more mileage, continue along Kalakaua to Diamond Head Road and circle the base of Diamond Head. The road turns into Monsarrat Avenue, which leads back to Kalakaua (4½ miles altogether). Or take Diamond Head Road as far as Kahala Avenue, one of the island's most beautiful runs. Also popular, the 2-mile perimeter of Ala Moana Beach Park.

Kayaking – *Adventure Kayaking International* conducts a series of kayak tours, including 2-hour sunset and full-moon excursions, along the Diamond Head–Waikiki coast. They also offer day trips for beginners, starting at $30 a day, and 1- to 5-day overnight kayaking excursions to all five islands plus Tahiti, Fiji, Tonga, Samoa, and the Cook Islands. Prices for overnight trips start at $125 a day and include kayaks, guides, gear, and food (but not air fare to or from the final destination). Excursions arranged for groups of 4 to 12 (children welcome, too). Two locations: Nawiliwili Small Boat Harbor, Lihue, Kauai (phone: 245-9662); and 2608 Kuahine Dr., Honolulu (phone: 988-5515 or 800 634-7537).

Skin Diving – *Dan's Dive Shop,* 660 Ala Moana Blvd. (phone: 536-6181), rents diving gear, offers instructions for beginners, and has brush-up courses for those with some experience. Out near Makaha, call *Leeward Dive Center* (phone: 696-3414). On the north shore, call *Aquaventure* at the *Turtle Bay Hilton* (phone: 293-8811) for lessons, or *Surf and Sea* in Haleiwa for rentals. Snorkelers can take an inexpensive day trip to Hanauma Bay with *Ocean Snorkel Rental* (phone: 955-5680) or *Blue Water Divers* (phone: 955-1066).

Surfing – The quest for the perfect wave attracts surfers from all over the world. Most hotels along the Waikiki Beach have surfing instructors and concessions that rent surfboards, canoes, and catamarans. The most famous surfing beaches are Sunset, the Pipeline, and Waimea, on the north side of the island. Major international competitions are held here in December and January.

Swimming – With Waikiki Beach generally very crowded, an alternative is to head to nearby Ala Moana or Diamond Head beach parks, or to beaches on the other side of the island. Equally spectacular settings include Sandy Beach and Makapuu, where just about everyone body-surfs; Waimanalo and Kailua, where swimming and wind-surfing are popular; and on up the coast to Kahana and the legendary surfing beaches of the north shore. Many beaches are dangerous for swimming; stick to those with lifeguards.

Tennis – There are public courts at 40 places around Oahu. Try the ones at the *Ilikai* hotel, Ala Moana Park, *Diamond Head Tennis Center, Kapiolani Tennis Courts,* or *Honolulu Tennis Center.*

Windsurfing – *Aloha Windsurfing* (phone: 926-1185) and *Naish Hawaii* (phone: 261-6067) feature rentals and lessons in Waikiki or windward Oahu.

 THEATER: You can get tickets at the door for most plays and musicals in Honolulu. The main theaters are *Blaisdell Memorial Center Concert Hall,* Ward and King Sts. (phone: 537-6191); *Honolulu Community Theater,* Makapuu and Aloha Aves. (phone: 734-0274); and *Hawaii Performing Arts Company's Manoa Theatre* (phone: 988-6131). Also check for under-the-stars perform-ances at the *Waikiki Shell* (phone: 521-2911).

 MUSIC: The *Honolulu Symphony* plays at the *Blaisdell Center Concert Hall* (phone: 537-6191). Rock musicians appear at the *Blaisdell Center Arena* (phone: 521-2911) or sometimes at *Aloha Stadium* (phone: 487-7731) or the *Waikiki Shell* (phone: 521-2911). If the *Brothers Cazimero* are performing at the *Royal Hawaiian,* it's worth a visit.

 NIGHTCLUBS AND NIGHTLIFE: With a large tourist industry to support it and a Hawaiian musical tradition to provide the raw material, the Kala-kaua Avenue area swings from about 8 PM until 1 AM, with some clubs open until 4 AM, most nights of the week. Hawaii's most famous singer and entertainer, Don Ho, plays the *Hilton Dome,* 2005 Kalia Rd., in the *Hilton Hawaiian Village* (phone: 949-4321). The *Brothers Cazimero* frequently perform at the *Royal Hawaiian's Monarch Room* and are the most popular and enduring of Hawaii's musical entertainers. There's also a piano bar at the *Sheraton-Waikiki,* 2255 Kalakaua Ave. (phone: 922-4422), and, for jazz, try *Trapper's* at the *Hyatt Regency,* 2424 Kalakaua Ave. (phone: 922-9292). Popular discos include *Annabelle's,* atop the *Ilikai* hotel (phone: 949-3811); *Bobby McGees,* at the *Colony Surf,* 2885 Kalakaua Ave. (phone: 922-1282); *Rumours,* at the *Ala Moana Americana* (phone: 955-4811); *Pink Cadillac,* 478 Ena Rd. (phone: 942-5282); *Wave Waikiki,* 1877 Kalakaua Ave. (phone: 941-0424); *Masquerade,* 224 McCully (phone: 949-6337); *Cilly's,* 1909 Ala Wai Blvd. (phone: 942-2952); *Spats,* at the *Hyatt Regency Waikiki* (phone: 922-9292); and *Hula's,* 2103 Kuhio Ave. (phone: 923-0669), with a mixed crowd ranging from punk to gay. The *Hard Rock Café,* 1837 Kapiolani Blvd. (phone: 955-7383), attracts cognoscenti and commoners alike. At *Studebaker's,* in Restaurant Row (on the outskirts of downtown Honolulu), crowds line up to enter and enjoy music of the 50s and 60s with let-it-all-hang-out dancing by waiters and waitresses as well as patrons, 500 Ala Moana Blvd. (phone: 526-9888).

BEST IN TOWN

 CHECKING IN: Honolulu hotels vary in personality, so do a bit of careful checking before picking one. Remember, it's not just a place to sleep; it will also serve as your tropical headquarters during your visit. Expect to pay $250 or more for a double at those places we've listed as very expensive; around $160 and up at hotels classed as expensive; between $70 and $150 at those designated moderate; under $70 at hotels listed as inexpensive. For a "superior double" room in a Waikiki condominium, expect to pay around $90 to $125 a night. Unless otherwise stated, the same rate applies for one to four people, though there is often a nominal (under $10) charge for each person after the first two. For bed-and-breakfast accommodations, contact *Bed & Breakfast Hawaii,* Box 449, Kapaa, HI 96746 (phone: 822-7771), or *Bed and Breakfast Honolulu,* 3242 Kaohinani Dr., Honolulu, HI 96817 (phone: 595-6170). All telephone numbers are in the 808 area code unless otherwise indicated.

HOTELS

Halekulani – This contemporary mid-rise incorporates the old Lewers home, which served as the original hotel. Among its features are 456 rooms, a library, and an open-air, oceanfront lounge — *House Without a Key* — featuring Hawaiian music and fine views of Diamond Head and sunsets. Its restaurants, *Orchids* and *La Mer* (see *Eating Out* for both), are among Honolulu's best. The hotel, designed to reestablish Waikiki as a destination for the carriage trade, is the essence of contemporary elegance. This is a hotel for which the adjective "luxury" is no exaggeration. 2199 Kalia Rd. (phone: 923-2311; 800-367-2343). Very expensive to expensive.

Hawaii Prince – Waikiki's newest luxury hotel is the second Hawaii property for Japan's Prince hotel chain (the other is on Maui). Attention to detail, carefully prepared cuisine, and panoramic views of the neighboring Ala Wai Yacht Tower are the main justifications for top-of-the-scale rates. On the western edge of Waikiki, it is just a short walk from Ala Moana Beach and Waikiki Beach. 1697 Ala Moana Blvd. (phone: 800-321-6284). Very expensive to expensive.

Hilton Hawaiian Village – The $100 million devoted to upgrading the rooms, public areas, and the grounds of the 22-acre Hilton complex has been well spent, catapulting the decor out of the 1960s and into the present day. The result is a more open and appealing resort. With close to 2,600 rooms, it is Hawaii's largest hotel, as well as the western terminus of Waikiki Beach. Standing between the Duke Kahanamoku Lagoon and the beach, it boasts a colorful shopping center, its own post office, and a catamaran that offers both day and night cruises. The Rainbow Tower, famed for its 30-story rainbow mosaic, and the Tapa Tower, with 250 corner suites, have the best views. The Alii Tower features its own pool and full concierge services. The village has lots that visitors want from a Hawaiian vacation — pools, beaches, fine dining, luaus, and Polynesian extravaganzas featuring Don Ho — but lacks the peace and serenity of rural Oahu. 2005 Kalia Rd. (phone: 949-4321; 800-445-8667). Very expensive to expensive..

Kahala Hilton – Operated by Hilton International (which is now run by Britain's Ladbrooke group), this is one of the chain's prime showpieces. Queen Elizabeth

II spent a couple of nights here, and King Juan Carlos of Spain came for part of his honeymoon with Queen Sophia. The main structure of this lavish hostelry is 12 stories high and overlooks a glorious 800-foot stretch of beach that loses nothing by being manmade. Additional beachside bungalows and a 2-story wing watch over a large lagoon in which dolphins, turtles, and penguins cavort. Rooms in the main building have charming semicircular lanais decorated with bougainvillea. Although the room furnishings and decorations are obviously expensive, the bed headboards and the lamps never quite manage to lose the Hilton look. The lobby, however, is an absolute masterpiece — with handsome chandeliers and a stunning circular carpet — that manages to look plush and airy at the same time. Guests are greeted with chilled pineapple, and an orchid is laid on each pillow when beds are turned down in the evening. Besides ocean and pool swimming, the hotel provides kayaks and snorkeling equipment and can arrange deep-sea fishing and scuba diving. European efficiency at the executive level and island good humor at the service level are the keynotes here. They work together like a charm. 5000 Kahala Ave., Kahala (phone: 734-2211; 800-367-2525). Expensive.

Hawaiian Regent – Just across the road from the beach, the two tall towers possess little architectural distinction. The interiors, however, are a bit more appealing, with inner courtyards paved in tile and marble, and an outdoor-café atmosphere in the main lobby. The Ocean Terrace pool area is also inviting, and the rooms are large and comfortable. There are several first class restaurants in the hotel, including the prestigious *Third Floor* (see *Eating Out*), which underwent a renovation in 1988 that included the addition of a 6,000-bottle wine room. *The Library,* where there's not a book in sight, has some unusually good soft music starting at 8:30 PM. 2552 Kalakaua Ave. (phone: 922-6611; 800-367-5370). Expensive.

Sheraton Moana Surfrider – This beautifully restored Victorian hostelry has been standing at the edge of the Waikiki surf since 1901. Until its exotic neighbor, the *Royal Hawaiian,* was opened in 1927, the *Moana* was the only hotel in the area. Brass headboards, white wicker chairs, antique lamps, and Victorian armoires adorn many of the rooms. These touches, and in many cases a ceiling fan, manage to make you forget the more modern iconography of Waikiki outside. A recently completed multimillion-dollar face-lift has restored the *Moana*'s turn-of-the-century charm. When making reservations, it is wise to specify a room in the old building, if that is what you want, as the *Surfrider* wing is more contemporary in style and decor. 2365 Kalakaua Ave. (phone: 922-3111; 800-325-3535). Expensive.

Colony Surf – A true Hollywood-style condominium right on the beach, it is one of the most delightful places to stay in Honolulu. Apartments are decorated in the plush, off-white tones that many people associate with seaside living. There are no lanais, but large windows with glorious views. Kitchens are modern and fully equipped, and there is daily maid service and adequate laundry facilities. The lobby is small and elegant and chiefly famous for being the entrance to *Michel's* restaurant (see *Eating Out*). Studios with lanais and kitchenettes are available in the adjacent *Colony East* hotel, which is owned and operated by the same company at the same address. 2895 Kalakaua Ave. (phone: 923-5751; 800-252-7873). Expensive to moderate.

Diamond Head Beach – This 14-story structure on the beach was completely refurbished in 1982 to make it one of the more attractive places in terms of price and location in Honolulu. Units range from hotel rooms to 1-bedroom apartments. Rooms are smallish but comfortable, with good-size lanais. Although there is little in the way of a lobby and no shops, pool, or tour desks, these are available close by, in the *New Otani.* 2947 Kalakaua Ave. (phone: 922-1928; 800-367-6046). Expensive to moderate.

Holiday Inn Waikiki Beach – Although the rooms here provide the standard Holiday Inn level of style and comfort, this hotel boasts magnificent views of the ocean and Diamond Head. It also has a terrific site: just outside the hustle-bustle of the strip, next door to Kapiolani Park and the Honolulu Zoo, and across the street from the loveliest stretch of Waikiki Beach. Its *Captain's Table,* an easygoing eatery that looks out at the sea, is a good place to sample your first mahimahi. 2570 Kalakaua Ave. (phone: 922-2511; 800-877-8666). Expensive to moderate.

Hyatt Regency – The two octagonal towers atop the ritzy Hemmeter Center are a visual landmark among the concrete blocks along Kalakaua Avenue. The Great Hall, with its outdoor tropical garden, 3-story waterfall, and massive hanging sculpture, is a sightseeing spot in its own right. Each of its 1,234 rooms is handsomely furnished, and the art on the walls is invariably worth looking at. In the suites, which feature some exceptional antiques, there are also original oil paintings. Guests in the Regency Club, as the 39th- and 40th-floor accommodations are known, have their own private, complimentary bar, and a concierge. The pool deck is one of the most attractive in Honolulu, and the bars, cafés, and restaurants in the complex — they include *Bagwell's* restaurant, *Trapper's* (a jazz club), and *Spats* restaurant (see *Eating Out*) and disco — are among the very best in Waikiki. The service here is exemplary. At the Hemmeter Center, 2424 Kalakaua Ave. (phone: 923-1234; 800-228-9000). Expensive to moderate.

Ilikai – This 3-pronged hotel on the *ewa* (western) edge of Waikiki includes Waikiki's best tennis facilities, with 6 courts and pros available to provide instruction. The open area at the lobby level has pools, terraces, and fountains. The beach, Duke Kahanamoku Lagoon, and the yacht marina are just a stone's throw away. The 800 rooms are among the most spacious in Waikiki, and some have kitchenettes. Atop the hotel sits *Annabelle's,* a disco reached via a spectacular ride in an exterior elevator that opens up vast panoramas of the Pacific as you ascend. 1777 Ala Moana Blvd. (phone: 949-3811; 800-367-8434). Expensive to moderate.

New Otani Kaimana Beach – The location is the thing here: on the Diamond Head side of Kapiolani Park, just a few minutes away from Waikiki by foot or bus. The beach is right outside, and beautiful reefs are within easy snorkeling distance. A hotel-wide renovation and refurbishing was completed in 1988. The terrace restaurant overlooks the beach and is edged by (and named for) large hau trees. Oceanside rooms have stunning views. Families seem to like the *New Otani,* and women traveling alone have found it a friendly, hospitable, and safe haven. 2863 Kalakaua Ave. (phone: 923-1555; 800-421-8795). Expensive to moderate.

Outrigger Reef – With 800 rooms, this is one of the largest moderately priced hotels in Waikiki. All rooms and public areas have recently been upgraded, resulting in somewhat higher rates. Popular with young couples and singles traveling in pairs, it's right on the beach, with most of the rooms facing either toward Diamond Head or across Ft. DeRussy Beach Park to the ocean. Guests here seem to use their lanais more than those at any other hotel in the neighborhood; it's a friendly sight. 2169 Kalia Rd. (phone: 923-3111; 800-367-5170). Expensive to moderate.

Pacific Beach – Standing on the site of the summer home of Queen Liliuokalani, this property is famous for its 280,000-gallon indoor oceanarium, which can be viewed from the hotel's bars and restaurants. Along with the swimming pool, there are tennis courts, shuffleboards, and a Jacuzzi to ensure a feeling of well-being. A good buy. 2490 Kalakaua Ave. (phone: 922-1233; 800-367-6060). Expensive to moderate.

Royal Hawaiian – "The Pink Lady," as this flamingo-colored, 6-story landmark of Spanish-Moorish design is best known, is flanked by two other Sheraton properties that seem to stand in an adversary, rather than a neighborly, stance. And indeed, rumor has it along the beach that there are entrepreneurs who would not object to seeing the Lady deposed in favor of something more modern (and anonymous).

Never mind. While it lasts — and one hopes it will last a long time — this is one of the two grand old hotels in Waikiki (the *Moana* is the other). The pink color scheme runs, perhaps a smidgin too obviously, throughout the hotel. Most of the rooms have either a pink sofa, quilt, or drapes. Usually it works, sometimes it doesn't. In any case, once away from the bustle of the lobby, which attracts ten times more spectators than guests, this remains the most charming hotel in Waikiki. Reservations through the *Sheraton Waikiki*, 2259 Kalakaua Ave. (phone: 923-7311; 800-325-3535). Expensive to moderate.

Sheraton Waikiki – The largest hotel in Waikiki — 1,852 rooms — until it was surpassed by the *Hilton Hawaiian Village* in early 1982, the *Sheraton* still has the greatest number of units in one building of any hotel on the beach. Lanais on the Pacific side loom over the ocean as precipitously as a cliff. It's a splendid sensation if you don't suffer from vertigo, and the sunsets can be memorable. Happily, subtle tans and casually tropical styling have replaced the garish greens and floral designs that made the rooms and lobby rather hard on the eyes. The *Sheraton* has all that's expected from a big hotel: There is never a dearth of taxis, it's a pickup point for every major tour operator, TheBus stops nearby, and there is just about every kind of restaurant you could crave, except a truly first class one. 2255 Kalakaua Ave. (phone: 922-4422; 800-325-3535). Expensive to moderate.

Aston's Waikiki Gateway – Looking like an unfinished pyramid, it stands sentinel at the western end of Kalakaua Avenue, about 5 minutes' walk from the beach. Rooms, which tend to get smaller the higher up you go, have recently been renovated. Its restaurant, *Nick's Fishmarket*, is one of Honolulu's most famous. 2070 Kalakaua Ave. (phone: 955-3741; 800-367-5124). Moderate.

Ilima – Near the Ala Wai Canal, about 3 blocks from the *Royal Hawaiian Beach,* it offers the additional convenience of full kitchens in all rooms, as well as a restaurant, cocktail lounge, sauna, and pool. 445 Nohonani St. (phone: 923-1877; 800-352-6686 in California, 800-421-0767 in other states). Moderate.

Manoa Valley Inn – This may be Hawaii's most complete bed-and-breakfast facility, with 7 bedrooms in a beautifully restored turn-of-the-century Manoa Valley home, and it is highly recommended. Rates include an ample continental breakfast, afternoon pupus, and sunset cocktails. Bus connections to Ala Moana center, and from there to all other parts of Oahu, are also available. About 2 miles from Waikiki, at 2001 Vancouver Dr. (phone: 947-6019). Moderate.

Outrigger Prince Kuhio – Quietly set on Kuhio Avenue, just 1 block from the beach, it manages to feel like a small hotel despite its 620 rooms on 37 floors. There are a maximum of 18 rooms to a floor, and each room is individually decorated and furnished, with its own wet bar and marble bathroom. The lobby is a graceful and airy place where complimentary coffee is poured from a silver samovar every morning. Rooms high on the Diamond Head side have stunning views of the crater. The top 3 floors are part of the exclusive Kuhio Club. 2500 Kuhio Ave. (phone: 922-0811; 800-367-5170). Moderate.

Waikiki Beachcomber – Whether you look toward the ocean, Diamond Head, or downtown, the lanais of the *Waikiki Beachcomber* are a pleasant spot for breakfast or cocktails. For the price, its rooms are surprisingly large, with separate dressing areas and capacious closets, and their layout and color scheme give them a feeling of coolness and comfort. The lobby has facilities for booking tours, and the hotel is a short walk from the beach. 2300 Kalakaua Ave. (phone: 922-4646; 800-622-4646). Moderate.

Reef Towers – Although it is hard to believe that a street of concrete blocks can have character, the section of Lewers Street between Kalia Road and Kalakaua Avenue does — it's narrow and shaded by very tall, spindly coconut palms. One of the concrete blocks is the *Reef Towers.* Though gorgeous vistas are not a selling point here, some people find it an excellent buy. Rooms with kitchenettes are available. 227 Lewers St. (phone: 923-3111; 800-367-5170). Moderate.

Waikiki Parc – Recently opened by the same Japanese company that owns the neighboring *Halekulani,* this hotel focuses its attention on service and high-tech features like computer-coded room locks on its 298 rooms.. It's an easy walk to Waikiki Beach, a fact that isn't immediately obvious from its towering proximity to the *Halekulani* and the *Sheraton Waikiki.* 2198 Kalia Rd. (phone: 921-7272; 800-422-0450). Moderate.

Waikiki Shores Apartments – By a stroke of luck, this apartment hotel stands next to the *Ft. DeRussy Army Museum* and has an unobstructed view across the museum grounds. From each wide lanai there is a panorama of both ocean and mountains. Studios convert easily from living to sleeping accommodations, and suites have very comfortable, bright, and "homey" living rooms. Linens, cooking utensils, and dishes are provided. There are fully equipped kitchens and weekly maid service. Cost and location combine to make this one of the best buys on the beach, especially for families. 2161 Kalia Rd. (phone: 926-4733; 800-367-2353). Moderate.

Waikikian – For many returning visitors, the torches that blaze outside each night signal that they are once more entering the fabled resort area. More torches line the narrow path that passes between the Polynesian cabanas that are the hotel's salient feature. These are decorated in Hawaiian motifs, with ceiling fans, rattan carpets, exposed timber ceilings, and wooden lanais, all contributing to the South Seas atmosphere. Some units also have kitchenettes. An adjacent 6-story contemporary building offers more conventional accommodations. The beach, a romantic lagoon, and a particularly attractive palm-fringed poolside area with a popular outdoor café called the *Tahitian Lanai* complete the amenities. 1811 Ala Moana Blvd. (phone: 949-5331; 800-367-5124). Moderate.

Ala Moana – Bright, sunny rooms in lively tropical colors and just about every kind of hotel service imaginable are two of the things that help this 36-story property compensate for not being close enough to the Waikiki beaches to be in the swing. Unfortunately, the hotel's size can sometimes be a disadvantage: Although the room staff and managers seem very helpful, a somewhat impersonal feeling pervades. 410 Atkinson Dr. (phone: 955-4811; 800-367-6025). Moderate to inexpensive.

Hawaii Dynasty – Set on the extremely busy Ala Moana Boulevard, on the western perimeter of Waikiki (where the high-rises are), this property is within walking distance of the beach and the more hectic attractions of Kalakaua strip. The accommodations are large but not luxurious, and the swimming pool is one of the biggest in Waikiki. 1830 Ala Moana Blvd. (phone: 955-1111; 800-421-6662). Moderate to inexpensive.

Outrigger Edgewater – This small hostelry manages to look more like a seaside apartment house than a hotel and exudes an air of calm and quiet. For those who find the hurly-burly of large establishments either intimidating or just plain exhausting, this is the ideal spot at an ideal price. An added attraction is the *Trattoria,* a well-regarded Italian restaurant. 2168 Kalia Rd. (phone: 922-6424; 800-367-5170). Moderate to inexpensive.

Outrigger Waikiki Village – Brightly decorated with an emphasis on greens and blues, this member of the Outrigger chain is popular with young couples making a first visit to Hawaii. The poolside area is, if anything, busier than many others in the district, considering that the ocean is just 2 blocks away. Perhaps what attracts so many is its underwater viewing area. Some rooms have kitchenettes. 240 Lewers St. (phone: 923-3881; 800-367-5170). Moderate to inexpensive.

Pagoda – Some people prefer to keep away from "the strip," but still within striking distance of Waikiki's sands. This is one place to fulfill both aims. A block and a half north of the Ala Moana Center, it's quiet and pleasant with an informal staff that is surprisingly professional. On the hotel grounds is an attractive tropical garden with a pond of over 3,000 beautifully colored carp, as well as the *Pagoda* floating restaurant, which is quite popular with residents. 1525 Rycroft St. (phone: 941-6611; 800-367-6060). Moderate to inexpensive.

Pleasant Holiday Isle – Right in the heart of Waikiki and just a block from the beach, this is a compact hotel where both the decor and the service are casually cheerful. This, plus reasonable rates, more than compensates for the fact that from most of the lanais, the view is less than indelible, and the street noise is occasionally audible. 270 Lewers St. (phone: 923-0777). Moderate to inexpensive.

Quality Inn Waikiki – Just 1 block from 220-acre Kapiolani Park at the foot of Diamond Head, it has always enjoyed a good reputation for service and comfort. Some rooms in the older Diamond Head Tower and all the rooms in the newer Pali Tower have kitchenettes, although the newer accommodations tend to be larger and more subdued in decor. There are 2 swimming pools for people who find the 3-minute stroll to the beach too strenuous. 175 Paoakalani Ave. (phone: 922-3861; 800-228-5151). Moderate to inexpensive.

Royal Islander – Another stopping place where smallness is an advantage. The front desk personnel usually manage to remember guests' names. Recently renovated rooms are on the small side, though not oppressively so, and each has a lanai, refrigerator, and coffee-making facilities. Street noise may prove bothersome. The property is now managed by the Outrigger chain and is opposite the *Reef* hotel, behind which is the beach. 2164 Kalia Rd. (phone: 922-1961; 800-367-5170). Moderate to inexpensive.

Viscount Waikiki – Overlooking Ft. DeRussy and Ala Moana Boulevard, it offers complimentary indoor parking with shopping, restaurants, and the beach minutes away. 1850 Ala Moana Blvd. (phone: 955-1567; 800-255-3050). Moderate to inexpensive.

Royal Grove – This is a small apartment hotel with personality. Like the *Royal Hawaiian*, it is painted pink. There are very comfortable, cheerful studios as well as 1-bedroom units. Although the ocean, a block and a half away, is visible from some of the lanais, many people prefer to look out on the pool and tropical gardens. All rooms have air conditioning and kitchenettes. There is maid service but no room service. 151 Uluniu Ave. (phone: 923-7691). Inexpensive.

Town Inn – This 26-room downtown property offers the basics at appropriate rates of $35 a day without air conditioning, $37 with it. Weekly rates are also available. Just beyond Chinatown in a totally un-Hawaiian setting. 250 N. Beretania St. (phone: 808-536-2377). Inexpensive.

Waikiki Surf – This is one of the "finds" of Honolulu. In a semi-residential part of Waikiki, it's friendly, clean, decorated in blue and green, quiet, and delightfully inexpensive. Some rooms have kitchenettes. Perhaps best of all, the 288-room *Waikiki Surf* has two companions — the 102-room *Waikiki Surf East* (422 Royal Hawaiian Ave.) and the 110-room *Waikiki Surf West* (412 Lewers St.) — owned and run by the same very friendly people. The original *Waikiki Surf* is at 2200 Kuhio Ave. (switchboard for all three: 923-7671; 800-367-5170). Inexpensive.

CONDOMINIUMS

Aston Waikiki Beach Tower – With only four 2-bedroom apartments to a floor, this is Waikiki's most exclusive rentable condominium. The views, particularly on floors 25 to 40, are magnificent, with large lanais offering front-row seats as the sun slides into the Pacific. Another prime asset is privacy — the perfect antidote to the street energy of Waikiki. Full concierge service, with the beach just across the street. 2470 Kalakaua Ave. (phone: 926-6400; 800-922-7866). Very expensive to expensive.

Waikiki Sunset – Given the facilities, good-looking accommodations, and location just 2 blocks from the beach, this place is an authentic bargain. Besides swimming in the large pool, guests can play tennis or shuffleboard. Daily maid service. 229 Paoakalani Ave. (phone: 922-0511; 800-367-5124). Expensive to moderate.

Foster Tower – For location alone — right across Kalakaua Avenue from the beach — this is one of Waikiki's better buys. All rooms have color TV sets, and on the property are a restaurant, pool, and shops. No maid service. 2500 Kalakaua Ave. (phone: 523-7785; 800-367-7040). Moderate.

Island Colony – Another luxury high-rise looking out on the Koolau Mountains and the canal, it is decorated with bleached-wood furniture, light brown walls and textiles, and beige carpets, giving it a pleasantly restful appearance. It also has a restaurant, pool, sauna, and hydromassage facilities, as well as shuffleboard. Daily maid service. 445 Seaside Ave. (phone: 923-2345; 800-367-5124). Moderate.

Pacific Monarch – Close to the Kings Alley shopping bazaar and a few minutes from the beach, the property offers spectacular views from its upper-floor 1-bedroom and studio units and the rooftop pool area. Laundry facilities and daily maid service. 142 Uluniu Ave. (phone: 923-9805; 800-367-6046). Moderate.

Royal Kuhio – Two blocks away from the beach and the International Market Place, it has upper-floor units that offer some of the best views of Diamond Head in Waikiki. On the 7th-floor deck are barbecue facilities, a pool, and shuffleboard. Weekly maid service. 2240 Kuhio Ave. (phone: 923-1747; 800-367-5205). Moderate.

Waikiki Banyan – One of the largest condos in Waikiki, it's a short walk from the beach, zoo, and the *Ala Wai Golf Course*. The living rooms are handsomely decorated and have attractive breakfast counters that separate them from the kitchen. The building contains a sauna, a large recreation area with tennis courts and a swimming pool, laundry facilities on each floor, and daily maid service. From the top floor on the Diamond Head side, you see beyond the crater to Maunalua Bay. 201 Ohua Ave. (phone: 922-0555; 800-367-8047). Moderate.

Waikiki Lanais – With attractively furnished 1- and 2-bedroom apartments on one of Waikiki's quieter streets, this well-maintained condominium features a mix of vacation rentals and full-time residences that adds to its appeal, as does its location near the beach and the commercial heart of Waikiki. 2452 Tusitala St. (phone: 531-7595; 800-367-7042). Moderate.

EATING OUT: Strange as it seems, and disappointing though it is, there are few restaurants serving authentic Hawaiian food in Honolulu. However, there are a number of very good ethnic and continental eating places to sample. Overall, the quality of dining in the city has improved immensely in the past few years, and there's an ample selection of restaurants where visitors can enjoy a delightful meal in pleasant surroundings. Expect to pay $60 or more at those places we've described as expensive; between $25 and $55 at those places listed as moderate; under $20, inexpensive. Prices don't include drinks, wine, or tips. All telephone numbers are in the 808 area code unless otherwise indicated.

Bagwell's – Luxury is the watchword here, with sculpted and etched glass and rich pastel hues combining to create a chic tropical atmosphere made all the more appealing and private by semicircular banquettes and raised dining platforms. The service is first class and, although always conscientious and friendly, it sometimes reaches a point where it can seem choreographed. The presentation is every bit as appetizing as the food itself, which includes such distinctive entrées as double breast of roast duck in a purée of island bananas, and broiled lamb chops dressed with a sauce of red bell peppers and caramelized garlic cloves. There is also a good selection of cheeses (unusual in Honolulu) and a distinguished wine list. Jackets are not necessary, but the atmosphere is such that a gentleman may feel more comfortable wearing one. Open daily for dinner. Reservations advised. In the *Hyatt Regency* hotel, 2424 Kalakaua Ave. (phone: 922-9292). Expensive.

Bali by the Sea – Contemporary elegance, enhanced by a mix of cool whites and Mediterranean pastels, sets the scene for seaside dining. The food is excellent, with appetizers like coquille of shrimp and scallops with ginger sauce, enticing entrées such as Kaiwi Channel opakapaka with fresh basil, and a concluding irresistible dessert tray. Open daily for dinner. Reservations advised and valet parking is available. *Hilton Hawaiian Village Rainbow Tower,* 2005 Kalia Rd. (phone: 949-4321). Expensive.

Chez Michel – The same Michel who lent his name to the *Colony Surf* hotel also created this restaurant. He's retired, but the restaurant remains popular. Just outside the *Hilton Hawaiian Village* end of Waikiki in Eaton Square, it is lush with plants and boasts a rich French decor. The menu is varied, well prepared, and nicely presented. 444 Hobron La. (phone: 955-7866). Expensive.

John Dominis – One of the best restaurants in Honolulu, albeit expensive, at the end of an unpromising street of warehouses and light industries on a promontory overlooking the Kewalo Basin and the Pacific. Inside the dining room, at a central island lavishly laden with fruits of the sea, a chef shucks oysters, steams clams, and makes broth. In saltwater pools spiny lobsters and fresh local fish clamber and swim around. Mainland specialties such as Maine lobster arrive fresh, but this is also the ideal place to sample island seafood: ono (wahoo), onaga (red snapper), and opakapaka (white snapper) are all available in season. The cioppino (stew) of seafood and fresh fish cooked in tomatoes, herbs, and spices is unbeatable. Open daily for dinner. Reservations necessary. 43 Ahui St. (phone: 523-0955). Expensive.

La Mer – The distinctive menu suits one of Hawaii's most refined restaurants. Start with an appetizer of grilled filet with steamed asparagus and orange sauce, then move on to roast duck with cherries marmalade and port wine sauce. The service is excellent and the decor an appealing blend of Oriental styles. Open daily from 6 to 9:30 PM. Reservations necessary. *Halekulani,* 2199 Kalia Rd. (phone: 923-2311). Expensive.

Maile – Guests descend through a minor jungle of anthuriums, yellow heliconia, and orchids into this restaurant beneath the lobby of the *Kahala Hilton,* where kimono-clad waitresses provide expert, unobtrusive service. The award-winning menu includes roast duckling Waialae (with bananas, peaches, litchi, and oranges) and fresh island chicken (poached in white wine with tarragon). Local fish treated somewhat exotically here include mahimahi glazed with banana and served on creamed mushrooms and baked kumu with fennel and a dash of Pernod. A classical guitarist or a pianist plays during dinner. Live dance music begins at 9 PM. Open daily for dinner only. Brunch is served Sundays on the Maile Terrace. Reservations necessary. *Kahala Hilton,* 5000 Kahala (phone: 734-2211). Expensive.

Nicholas Nickolas – Find dining amid soft lights and elegant at this place atop the 40-floor *Ala Moana Americana* hotel, which affords magnificent views. The extensive menu focuses on both American and continental specialties, ranging from veal to lamb, with pasta, soups, salads, and catch-of-the-day entrées in between. Open daily from 5:30 to 11:30 PM, with live entertainment from 9:30 PM to 2:30 AM weekdays, to 3:30 AM on weekends. Reservations necessary. 410 Atkinson Dr. (phone: 955-4466). Expensive.

Nick's Fishmarket – This is one of the best fish restaurants in Honolulu. Don't let the earthy name confuse you; *Nick's* is a plush establishment with individually controlled lighting systems for those customers seated at banquettes and rather too many staffers per customer — the attention can occasionally be stifling. Live Maine lobsters are available at substantial cost, but this is also the ideal place to sample fresh island fish, such as opakapaka, mahimahi, and ulua. The combination seafood Louis salad is enormous and beautifully prepared. Open daily for dinner. Reservations necessary. In the *Waikiki Gateway* hotel, 2070 Kalakaua Ave. (phone: 955-6333). Expensive.

Third Floor – One of the top restaurants in Honolulu, it has consistently won prizes for its cooking. Guests dine in a setting of high-backed rattan chairs with red velvet cushions, strolling musicians, a carp pool, and a fountain. Among the house specialties are medallions of veal forêt noire and rack of spring lamb. For dessert there are Polynesian fruits with kirsch, followed by well-made Irish coffee. Open daily for dinner; there is a $15 minimum charge. Reservations advised. In the *Hawaiian Regent* hotel, 2552 Kalakaua Ave. (phone: 922-6611). Expensive.

Andrews – The steamed clams in herbs and spices and the veal dishes are particularly noteworthy at one of Honolulu's less touted Italian restaurants. Linens, crystal, and silver set the tone for a relaxed evening in pleasant surroundings. Open daily for lunch and dinner. Reservations advised. Ward Centre, 1200 Ala Moana Blvd. (phone: 523-8677). Expensive to moderate.

Black Orchid – Tom Selleck and the owners of *Nick's Fishmarket* have teamed up to manage this new restaurant, serving American cuisine — both indoors and alfresco. There's also a dance floor and a large, beautifully designed lounge. Open weekdays for lunch, daily for dinner. Reservations advised. Restaurant Row (phone: 521-3111). Expensive.

Bon Appetit – Perhaps Honolulu's best French restaurant, it has the look of an elegant bistro in the French provinces with its cane-back chairs and light pink linen. The menu is imaginative and includes an unusual scallop mousse, bouillabaisse, and snails in puff pastry. Closed Sundays. Reservations advised. In the Discovery Bay complex at 1778 Ala Moana Blvd. (phone: 942-3837). Expensive to moderate.

Furusato – There are two branches of this Japanese restaurant in Waikiki. Each has its own menu and ambience; both are comfortable if not elegant. The kitchens generally offer a range of steaks, seafood, and sushi. Open daily for lunch and dinner. Reservations advised. *Hyatt Regency* (phone: 922-4991) and *Foster Tower* condominium (phone: 922-5502). Expensive to moderate.

Golden Dragon – Perhaps Hawaii's most elegant Chinese restaurant, the food happily lives up to the surroundings. For example, one specialty, Imperial Beggar's chicken, is wrapped in lotus leaves with spices, then cooked for 6 hours inside a sealed clay pot to retain natural juices and flavor. Another specialty is the Peking roast duck, and be sure to leave room for pastry chef Gale O'Malley's celestial desserts. Thanks to the exquisite decorative flourishes, dining indoors is as appealing as alfresco. Reservations advised; valet parking available. *Hilton Hawaiian Village Rainbow Tower*, 2005 Kalia Rd. (phone: 949-4321). Expensive to moderate.

Hy's Steak House – Entering *Hy's* is like walking into a magnificent Victorian private library, full of velvet chairs and etched glass. But the gleaming brass broiler inside a glassed-in gazebo, where steaks and chops are prepared with loving care, demonstrates that it is something more. Although the menu indicates that chicken and seafood are available, the main attraction is steaks, which are merely superb. Open daily for dinner. Reservations advised. 2440 Kuhio Ave. (phone: 922-5555). Expensive to moderate.

Matteo's – Low lighting, pleasant decor, and high-backed banquettes all conspire to make this restaurant a place for quiet dining. The service is good, as is the food which includes such highly recommended dishes as calamari, chicken, and veal. Open daily for dinner, from 6 PM to midnight; the bar is open until 2 AM. Reservations advised. In the *Marine Surf* hotel, 364 Seaside Ave. (phone: 922-5551). Expensive to moderate.

Michel's – At most beachfront restaurants in Honolulu, the cooking takes a back seat to the view. Not here. For a start, the decor does not suggest a mere extension of sand and ocean. The dining room is elegant and subdued. Although there are occasionally deft local touches, such as prosciutto served with papaya, most of the dishes tend to be classic. Even the opakapaka is served Véronique style with a champagne sauce added. Jacket required for dinner. Reservations necessary. In the *Colony Surf* hotel, 2895 Kalakaua Ave., Diamond Head (phone: 923-6552). Expensive.

Miyako – Shabu shabu–style cooking (meat, vegetables, and seafood prepared in boiling water at the table) has the emphasis here. Seating is either in the main dining room with its rooftop, oceanside views, or in small tatami rooms where guests sit on mats on the floor. Two days' notice will procure the special Kaiseiki dinner of 7, 8, or 9 courses, all using the freshest produce, fish, and seafood available that day. Open daily for dinner. *New Otani Kaimana Beach* hotel, 2863 Kalakaua Ave. (phone: 923-1555). Expensive to moderate.

Orchids – Sliding French doors that open onto a green lawn and expansive views of Diamond Head and the sea are a perfect backdrop for crisp white linens and tables elegantly set with silver, crystal, and fresh flowers. Breakfast is a highlight, as is the Sunday brunch, though lunch and dinner are also first rate. Reservations necessary. *Halekulani* hotel, 2199 Kalia Rd. (phone: 923-2311). Expensive to moderate.

Willows – This is one of the most famous restaurants in the state, and the place to sample traditional Hawaiian dishes. The celebrated poi supper offers many of these, including poi itself, steamed laulau, sweet potato, chicken luau, and lomilomi salmon. If all this seems too exotic, the curry dishes, leavened with coconut milk, are superb. This is also the perfect place for wearing an aloha shirt or muumuu for the first time; the rural tropical atmosphere of palm trees and thatched roofs seems to call for it, and strolling musicians provide the perfect accompaniment. Open daily. Reservations necessary. 901 Hausten St. (phone: 946-4808). Expensive to moderate.

Baci – Linens, flatware, and crystal harmonize with the chic decor to provide an appropriate setting for the Italian specialties. Meals are complemented by a fairly priced selection of bottled wines. Open for lunch and dinner daily. Reservations advised for dinner and lunch groups. Ground level, Waikiki Trade Center, 2255 Kuhio Ave. (phone: 924-2533). Moderate.

Café Cambio – Contemporary northern Italian cuisine combines with southern highlights like cioppino and an antipasto misto. The owner is from Turin, which helps make *Café Cambio* the real thing. Open for lunch weekdays and dinner daily; closed Mondays. Reservations necessary for lunch only. 1680 Kapiolani Blvd., next to the *Kapiolani Theater* (phone: 942-0740). Moderate.

Café Che Pasta – Homemade pasta is only part of a menu that includes fresh grilled fish, calamari, and other nouvelle-style dishes. *Che Pasta*'s original eatery in Kaimuki established the good reputation that's maintained at this downtown branch. Open weekdays until 8 PM for lunch, snacks, and dinner. Reservations advised. 1001 Bishop St. (phone: 524-0004). Moderate.

Castagnola's – A New York–style Italian restaurant that has drawn rave reviews from the day it opened in the Manoa Marketplace. Delicate flavorings make for some good veal, pasta, and seafood dishes. Open daily except Sundays for lunch and dinner; lunch only on Mondays. 2752 Woodlawn Ave. (phone: 988-2969). Moderate.

Che Pasta – A casual café with good food. Pasta, veal, and chicken dishes are the specialties. Open weekdays for lunch and dinner, weekends for dinner only. Reservations unnecessary. 3751 Waialae Ave. (phone: 735-1777). Moderate.

Fisherman's Wharf – Tuna and charter boats tie up at the dock beside this seafront restaurant, where you'll be charmed by the nautical atmosphere. Open daily. Reservations unnecessary. 1009 Ala Moana Blvd., Kewalo Basin (phone: 538-3808). Moderate.

Il Fresco – The high tech design and tables laden with linen and crystal are consistent with the location in the chic Ward Center, an upscale shopping mall between Waikiki and downtown Honolulu. The menu is varied, with specialties ranging from blackened *ahi* (tuna) to pasta. Open daily. Major credit cards. Ward Center (enter on Auahi St.), 1200 Ala Moana Blvd. (523-5191). Moderate.

Great Wok – Cantonese-style Chinese cuisine is prepared at your table, and the menu features such delicately flavored specialties as 1000 Happiness Lobster and Blush of Empress Shrimp. Open daily from 5:30 PM. Reservations advised. Royal Hawaiian Center (phone: 922-5373). Moderate.

Hala Terrace – A *Kahala Hilton* restaurant and a lovely lunchtime spot. Sit in the shade and watch the Pacific across one of the loveliest beaches on Oahu. Meals here are on the light side, so it's worth ordering vichyssoise or a spring salad to start with. Elegant sandwiches are the main item on the menu, in addition to which there are daily specials such as Kahuku prawns, which are delicious. Open daily for breakfast, lunch, and dinner. Reservations advised. *Kahala Hilton,* 5000 Kahala Ave., Kahala (phone: 734-2211). Moderate.

Hau Tree Lanai – The food is good, but the beachfront setting, especially at breakfast or at dusk, is its own reward. 2863 Kalakaua Ave. (phone: 923-1555). Moderate.

Horatio's – The nautical decor is most appropriate in this tavern overlooking the Kewalo Boat Basin. Among the house specialties worth trying are mahimahi stuffed with shrimp and crab, and beef Wellington glazed with Madeira sauce. Freshly baked Russian rye bread accompanies each entrée. Open daily. Reservations necessary Fridays and Saturdays. Ward Warehouse, 1050 Ala Moana Blvd. (phone: 521-5002). Moderate.

Keo's Thai Cuisine – This is a fine place to sample Thai cuisine, which can be flavorful and fiery, although the kitchen will prepare milder versions of its hot specialties if requested. Mint-flavored spring rolls make a delicious appetizer, and cold sweet tea is a good accompaniment for the spicier dishes. The setting is elegant and nearly drenched in orchids; the crowd, Honolulu's cognoscenti. Reservations necessary. 441 Kapahulu Ave. (phone: 737-8240). Moderate.

Monterrey Bay Canners – The Waikiki branch of this restaurant, in the *Outrigger* hotel, offers a limited number of alfresco tables that take full advantage of the beachfront location. The best bet on the menu is one of the catch-of-the-day specials, which are reasonably priced and delicious. 2335 Kalakaua Ave. (922-5761). Moderate.

Murphy's – A pleasant eatery in the revitalized Merchant Square area and a good choice for people who are tired of exotic restaurant grub. From potato skins to salads and pasta, the menu offers many tasty specials. Live sports events are beamed in courtesy of a satellite dish. Open daily except Sundays for lunch and dinner to 9 PM. Reservations advised. 2 Merchant St. (phone: 531-0422). Moderate.

Phillip Paolo's – Set in an eclectically decorated private home, a 5-minute drive from

Waikiki, the Italian specialties by owner-chef Phillip Paolo Sarubbi earn this restaurant the high praise it receives. Daily specials complement standard features like fettuccine Vigario (pasta with mushrooms and spinach in light basil cream sauce) and shrimp parmigiana. 2312 Beretania St. (phone: 946-1163). Moderate.

Pottery Steakhouse – People actually throw and fire pottery here, and many of the eating and drinking utensils are made in the workroom-cum-boutique in the front of the restaurant. Steaks are properly aged, juicy, and flavorful. Mahimahi, cooked till it is too dry at many restaurants, is still moist when it reaches the table here. Handmade pottery is made and sold — as well as used here: If you choose the Cornish game hen, you get to keep the pot in which it was cooked. About a 10-minute drive from Waikiki. Open daily for dinner only. Reservations advised, especially on weekends. 3574 Waialae Ave. (phone: 735-5594). Moderate.

Richard's Stuffed Potato – Despite its name, this inconspicuous eatery with indoor and patio seating is most notable for the delicious meat, fish, and pasta dishes prepared by the owner-chef. Bring your own beer and wine, easily obtained at a nearby convenience store, and be prepared for a bit of a wait for dinner to reach the table. Open daily except Sundays. No reservations. 2109 Kuhio Ave. (phone: 922-0102). Moderate.

Seafood Emporium – Flavorful food makes up for the relative austerity of decor that recalls New England; clearly, the pleasure here is not in adornment but in eating. Open daily for lunch and dinner. Reservations advised for dinner. Royal Hawaiian Shopping Center, 2201 Kalakaua Ave. (phone: 922-5547). Moderate.

Sergio's – Excellent Italian and continental specialties include a full range of pasta, plus veal, chicken, and shrimp in a variety of styles. Open daily for dinner. Reservations necessary. 445 Nohonani St. (phone: 926-3388). Moderate.

Siam Inn – There has been high praise for this Thai restaurant in the heart of Waikiki, where imported spices and fresh local produce and seafood are combined to advantage. Normally fiery Thai dishes are prepared with Western tastebuds in mind. Open daily for lunch and dinner. Reservations unnecessary. 407 Seaside (phone: 926-8802). Moderate.

Spats – Dinner in a well-known disco might not sound very promising, but don't let what goes on after 9 PM deter you from coming here. The decor recalls a rather lavish speakeasy, with beveled glass, highly polished wood, and waiters in cutaways and suspenders. Try the chicken alla cacciatore or shrimp all' aglio e olio (with garlic and oil). Fettuccine Alfredo is the star attraction among the pasta. Open daily. Reservations advised for dinner. *Hyatt Regency* hotel, 2424 Kalakaua Ave. (phone: 922-9292). Moderate.

Swiss Inn – *Kahala Hilton* chef Martin Wyss has opened one of Hawaii's best restaurants in the suburban Niu Valley Shopping Center. It's well worth the 20-minute drive from Waikiki for standards like veal Florentine, trout amandine, and baked chicken. With 24 hours' notice, you can also order a meat or cheese fondue. Open evenings daily; Sundays for brunch. Reservations necessary. 5730 Kalanianaole Hwy. (377-5447). Moderate.

Sunset Grill – The style is California-casual; the food is cooked over kiawe wood to provide a distinctive flavor. Specialties include chicken, veal, lamb, and fish with rotisserie, oven, and grill preparations. Open for lunch and dinner daily, breakfast on weekends. Reservations unnecessary. Restaurant Row (phone: 521-4409). Moderate.

Trattoria – The chef doesn't overload the menu with tomato paste, and many dishes are cooked al burro — delicately, in butter — instead of doused in olive oil. The lasagna in this charmingly decorated restaurant is well worth tasting. So are *cotoletta di vitello alla parmigiana* and *pollo alla romana*. The *cannelloni milanese* is definitely a "don't miss." Open daily. Reservations necessary on weekends. *Outrigger Edgewater* hotel, 2168 Kalia Rd. (phone: 923-8415). Moderate.

Yanagi Sushi – Two Tokyo-style sushi bars serve a sushi lover's abundance of specials. The atmosphere is upbeat, the decor simple but appealing, and the sushi first-rate. Open daily. Reservations necessary. 762 Kapiolani Blvd. (phone: 537-1525). Moderate.

China House – The cavernous dining room of this Honolulu favorite is often full, usually with customers who return again and again. If shark fin or bird nest soup is your thing, you can have it here. Four varieties of the former and three of the latter are offered. The dim sum is famous throughout the island and is served daily from 11 AM to 2 PM. Open daily. Reservations advised. At the top of the ramp from Kapiolani Blvd. in the Ala Moana Center (phone: 949-6622). Moderate to inexpensive.

Compadres – Delicious Mexican food, a comfortable setting, and good prices helped make this restaurant a success at Ward Center. Mexican pizza is truly worthy of a cheese lover's praise. 2500 Kuhio Ave. (523-1307). Moderate to inexpensive.

Hard Rock Café – The Honolulu branch of this trendy international chain attracts a young crowd out to be part of "the scene." Food is good, crowds are standard day or night, and the noise level is decibels higher than that which allows comfortable conversation. But, then, that's intended to be part of the appeal. Guitars of famous rockers are part of the decor, as are other blasts of rock 'n' roll memorabilia, and patrons come as much to buy T-shirts and other signature souvenirs as to eat or drink. Valet parking. Open daily from 11:30 AM to midnight. No reservations. 1826 Kalakaua Ave. (phone: 955-7383). Moderate to inexpensive.

It's Greek To Me – The setting amid the shops of the Royal Hawaiian Center is more convenient than charming, but the food is recommended for quality, price, and the speed with which you're served. Open daily from 9 AM to 10:30 PM. Reservations necessary. On the ground floor of the Royal Hawaiian Center (phone: 922-2733). Moderate to inexpensive.

Orson's – Downstairs is a coffee shop called the *Chowder House,* which serves fresh salads as well as seafood; upstairs, a dining room decorated with beautifully stained woods offers more fine seafood. Open daily for lunch and dinner. Reservations advised. Ward Warehouse, 1050 Ala Moana Blvd. (phone: 521-5681). Upstairs moderate; downstairs inexpensive.

Pearl City Tavern – This Japanese-American restaurant is famous for its Monkey Bar, at the back of which is a long glassed-in alley where denizens of the simian world prance and preen playfully. The Japanese dishes here tend to be better than the American, and the teriyaki and tempura are especially good. The middle-aged waitresses are downright motherly. Open weekdays for lunch, daily for dinner. Reservations necessary. 905 Kamehameha Hwy., Pearl City (phone: 455-1045). Expensive to moderate.

Ryan's Parkplace – Popular for its pasta, vegetable, and fish dishes, desserts, and custom-brewed coffee. Open daily; dinner only on Sundays. Reservations advised. Ward Warehouse, 1050 Ala Moana Blvd. (phone: 523-9132). Moderate to inexpensive.

TGI Friday's – The Honolulu version of the New York original features antique furnishings, a friendly bar, and surprisingly good food at modest prices (especially for the enormous portions served, which can easily be shared). Best known for its potato skins, this eatery also serves an array of quiches, omelettes, salads, desserts, and more. It's always lively and usually noisy. Open daily. No reservations. 950 Ward Ave. (phone: 523-5841). Moderate to inexpensive.

Bavarian Beer Garden – Bratwurst, knockwurst, sauerkraut, and warm German potato salad are among the house specialties. So, too, is dancing to a 5-piece Bavarian band on the largest dance floor in Waikiki. Open nightly from 5 PM to 1 AM. Royal Hawaiian Shopping Center, 3rd floor (phone: 922-6535). Inexpensive.

Bernard's of New York – Typical New York deli offerings — from delicious cheese blintzes to matzo ball soup to lean pastrami and a weekend brunch — are the main reasons for heading this way. Near the University of Hawaii Manoa Campus, 2633 S. King St. (phone: 946-7477). Inexpensive.

Big Ed's Deli – This is the place to head if you've got a craving for New York–style pastrami or corned beef. Popular with the lunch crowd, it's much easier to go at dinnertime. Open daily from 7 AM to 10 PM. Reservations unnecessary. In Ward Center (phone: 536-4591). Inexpensive.

Bueno Nalo – The coconut wireless (as the local grapevine is called) gives this eatery high marks for its Mexican cooking — chiles relleños, chimichangas, and such. It's a casual place, where guests bring their own wine or beer and wait for tables. No reservations. Open Tuesdays through Sundays, 5 to 9 PM. 41–865 Kalanianaole Hwy., Waimanalo (259-7186). Inexpensive.

Caffè Guccini – The warm welcome at this low-key café is followed by fine pasta, rich cappuccino, and tempting desserts. Guests may bring their own wine or beer, but there's also a full bar. Open daily from 3 to 11:30 PM. Reservations unnecessary. 2139 Kuhio Ave. (phone: 922-5287). Inexpensive.

Chinese Cultural Plaza – Though not quite as successful as planned, this ethnic enclave does offer a wide range of good Oriental restaurants and cuisines — Cantonese, Hakka, Mandarin, or Mongolian barbecue — as well as shops purveying Oriental bric-a-brac that are fun to browse through. Off S. Beretania and River Sts. Inexpensive.

King Tsin – This spicy favorite serves up very tasty hot and sour soup. The crackling chicken is chopstick-lickin' good, as is the Hunan pork sautéed with broccoli. Open daily. Reservations advised. Major credit cards. 1110 McCully St. (946-3273). Inexpensive.

Wo Fat – This granddaddy of Chinese restaurants in Honolulu will soon be 100 years old. Hong Kong chicken, beef in oyster sauce, and *Wo Fat* noodles draw people here from all over the island for lunch and dinner. Open daily. Reservations advised. 115 N. Hotel St. (phone: 537-6260). Inexpensive.

HOUSTON

Houston is dazzling to the newcomer. Its downtown mushrooms unexpectedly from the flat Texas prairie in a striking display of modern architecture. The city stretches for miles in all directions, apparently without limits. Massive expressway systems, always busy, pump traffic in and out of the metropolis that's been called the "golden buckle of the Sunbelt." Although Houston is a century and a half old, its past has been all but wiped out, overrun by a sense of newness and a determination to prosper despite lagging oil prices that have sharply set back the fortunes of the oil capital of the world. It is the 20th century's incarnation of the 19th-century dream of industrial progress.

Houston is the fourth-largest city in the country (with a metropolitan population of 1.7 million) and had been one of the fastest growing. The oil boom once brought 1,500 newcomers into Houston each week, but by 1982, the sparkle was already starting to fade: That year, oilfield equipment manufacturers began their massive layoffs, and Houston's unemployment rate rose. The city began losing population at a rate of 1,100 weekly and the drain has continued, though currently at less than half that rate.

The worldwide oil glut has compounded problems, and at the moment Houston is fighting hard to emerge from an energy-based depression. Fortunately, however, in recent years several hundred companies not connected with the oil industry have relocated major operations to Houston and continue to consolidate their state and even national operations here.

These problems were added to the chaos that was one price of Houston's boom years during the 1970s. The city grew lots faster than its civic services, and every sort of urban trauma was magnified as a result. There are still no zoning laws, little evidence of city planning beyond the downtown, insufficient mass transit, congested traffic, and consequently often oppressive air pollution.

When a 19th-century traveler described Houston as a place "where one can no longer rationalize or explain what he sees," he spoke honestly not only of Houston past but of Houston present and, undeniably, of Houston future. It's the place where there are no state or city income taxes, but you still have to register cowbrands at the courthouse.

In Houston, the original bit of good luck came in the form of oil, and that was as true in the founding of the city as residents wish it would be today. In 1836, even before the first street existed, founders J. K. and A. C. Allen, brothers from New York, were advertising their new town nationwide as the state's garden spot. In reality it was humid, marshy, and mosquito-infested. People came anyway, enticed by the Allens' grandiose descriptions, cheap land, and the promises of great money-making opportunities.

Little did the newcomers realize how closely luck was following them. At

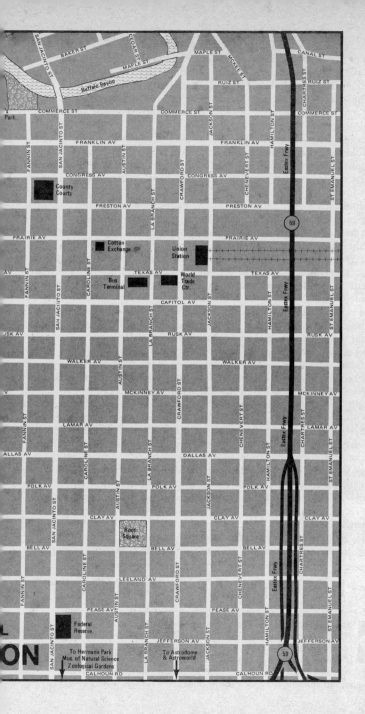

the turn of the century, oil was discovered 90 miles away, and Houston found itself in the middle of the great Texas oil boom. In 1914, civic leaders built a ship channel 32 miles inland to the city, creating a fairweather port. By the 1960s the two — oil and port — combined to make Houston one of the world's major petrochemical centers, creating the backbone of the city's economic strength.

Pure science, as well as technology, has reinforced this strength. The Lyndon B. Johnson Space Center has been the focal point of almost every manned space flight and has earned Houston the moniker "Space City." The Texas Medical Center, noted for cancer research, is one of the largest medical facilities in the country.

But Houston's growth extended to more than science and business. Similar cultural enrichment has taken place, in large part due to those who made fortunes here. Their bullish attitude has provided the city with some of the best facilities for the performing arts in the Southwest. The *Grand Opera, Houston Symphony,* and *Alley Theater,* the established resident company, are highly acclaimed nationally. The arts are thriving, patronized by a citizenry that seems to be dedicated to making its home as renowned for cultural achievement as for boldness in business.

It's been said that Houston has two seasons — eternal summer outside and winter inside, borne on gusts from ubiquitous air conditioners. The climate is hot, but being outdoors is a way of life, not a seasonal occupation. Municipal parks equipped with fine facilities for swimming, golf, tennis, and hiking are abundant. Open-air concerts, Shakespeare in the park, and sidewalk art festivals occur frequently year-round. Just 50 miles away, Galveston Bay and the Gulf of Mexico are a haven for water enthusiasts.

The city's emergence as an international business center has lent it a cosmopolitan image unique to the South. About 50 foreign consulates have offices here. In the streets, Texas drawls are still heard, but many foreign accents are also detectable. Restaurants, especially those in the Montrose district, offer exotic dishes from all over the globe.

Things are still happening at an unpredictable pace. Houston is a city once more in the process of finding itself, a feisty frontier that draws people like a magnet — where hard work is more the measure of success than family ties. Despite recent setbacks, Houstonians still think of their city as one of America's greatest, and it's hard for a newcomer not to sense this pride even after only a day here. Given the energetic human forces at work, it's hard to believe that Houston cannot weather the current slump to emerge stronger than ever.

HOUSTON AT-A-GLANCE

SEEING THE CITY: The revolving *Spindletop* cocktail lounge atop the *Hyatt Regency* hotel turns on the Houston panorama. One revolution takes in all of Space City. To the south stands downtown, to the north an industrial area and the ship channel, industrial sprawl to the east, and Houston's residential neighborhoods to the west. 1200 Louisiana (phone: 654-1234).

Stationary, but splendid for a view of the downtown skyline, is Sam Houston Park,

515 Allen Pkwy. Dominating the cityscape are the futuristic Pennzoil Towers, designed by Philip Johnson, and the city's other big oil headquarters, Shell and Tenneco.

SPECIAL PLACES: A car is a necessity for mobility in the Houston sprawl. Mass transit is unreliable and not always accessible. Several of the attractions are concentrated in a few areas, so you can park and walk, but otherwise, you'll be driving from place to place.

Museum of Natural Science – Each of the 13 halls in the largest such institution of the Southwest pertains to a different natural science including two subjects near and dear to the wallets of Houstonians — oil and space. You can learn how oil is formed, see a model of an offshore oil rig, or manipulate a working model of a fault — by turning a wheel you can create an earthquake. The space exhibit includes reproductions of the lunar Rover (the real one is still up there) and a model of the space capsule used by John Glenn. Not as endearing, but also on display, are Ecuadorian shrunken heads and a Diplodocus dinosaur skeleton. The *Museum of Medical Science* displays the human body — yours. You can listen to the rhythm of your heartbeat or test your lung capacity, or, if you're too modest to put yourself on display, skip it and visit the Burke Baker Planetarium. Open daily. Admission $2 for adults, $1 for children age 5-11. Planetarium fee $3 for adults, $1.50 for children 5-11 (50¢ for children 4 and under) includes admission to the museum. 5800 Caroline St., in Hermann Park (phone: 526-4273).

Houston Zoological Gardens – One of the best zoos around, this abounds with some rarely seen animals in unusual settings. Vampire bats, flying squirrels, and bush babies inhabit a red light district where time is reversed and you can see the bats feeding on blood at 2:30 in the afternoon. The Tropical Bird House has over 200 exotic birds in a rain forest. But our favorite is the Gorilla House, where the royal couple of the jungle swing in primordial splendor complete with waterfalls, vines, moats, and skylighting. There's also a children's zoo where kids can make contact with creatures from four regions of the world. Open daily except Mondays from 10 AM to 6 PM. Children's Discovery Zoo is open from 10 AM to 3:45 PM, Tuesdays through Saturdays and from 10 AM to 4:45 PM on Sundays. Admission charges. S. Main at Bissonnet in Hermann Park (phone: 523-5888).

Children's Museum – Don't look for antique toys here. This is a modern, hands-on experience center designed for kids 3 to 12 years old. Children use computers to assemble dinosaurs and to work math and science problems. There's even a closed-circuit TV station, complete with costumes and sets, where kids can stage their own impromptu performances. For old-fashioned fun, they can play store in a nearly real setting, draw postcards, and cut out paper dolls. The major culture display changes each year (currently featured is a Chinese village, with demonstrations by Chinese cooks, artists, and musicians). Closed 3 weeks in September for refurbishing. The rest of the year, open daily except Mondays and Fridays from 10 AM to 5 PM Tuesdays and Saturdays; 1 to 5 PM Wednesdays, Thursdays, and Sundays. Admission $2 for adults, $1 for seniors and children. 3201 Allen Pkwy. between Shepard and Waugh (phone: 522-6873).

Museum of Fine Arts – With neoclassical beginnings and finishing touches by Mies van der Rohe, this structure could house most anything — and it does, including the Ima Hogg collection of Southwestern Indian art with pottery and kachina dolls, an extensive collection of Frederic Remington's works, a pre-Columbian gallery, and a modern sculpture garden with Alexander Calder's *Crab*. Closed Mondays. Admission is $2 for adults, $1 for senior citizens and college students, free for those under 18. Thursdays are free for all. 1001 Bissonnet (phone: 526-1361).

International Strip – On the main drag of Montrose, one of the city's oldest residential neighborhoods, natives and visitors come to browse through antique shops, foreign bazaars, art galleries, boutiques, flea markets, and off-beat book shops. The art festivals held in October and April are the largest in the South. Sidewalk cafés and restaurants allow patrons to try dishes from around the world, linger in a wine tasting shop, or just hang out in a tree house bar. *A Moveable Feast* is great for health food sandwiches (3827 Dunlavy; phone: 528-3585). The Strip is also the showplace for exotic nightlife, everything from bellydancing to body painting. More sedate, but also in the neighborhood, is the Rothko Chapel, a meditation chapel with works by Russian-born painter Mark Rothko (3900 Yupon; phone: 524-9839). The Strip extends from the 100 to 1800 block of Westheimer.

River Oaks – If you're wondering where all that old oil money went, you'll find that no one's tried to hide it. Here are the palatial mansions and huge estates of Houston's super-rich, who still have it and flaunt it. River Oaks Blvd. between Westheimer and the Country Club.

Galleria Center – This stunning, glass-domed, 3-level edifice shows how the wealth is spread, Houston-style. Among the stores here are *Sakowitz* (a Houston native), *Neiman Marcus, Lord & Taylor, Tiffany's,* and *Macy's;* across the street is *Saks Fifth Avenue.* There's also a skating rink on the ground floor. Open daily. 5015 Westheimer (phone: 622-0663).

Sam Houston Park – One of the few signs that there was an old Houston, this project of the Harris County Heritage Society encompasses a restored country church, homes, and shops, depicting the lifestyle of 19th-century Houstonians. The Kellum-Noble House, the oldest brick house in Houston, contains pioneer equipment and furnishings, and the Cherry House is a Greek Revival home furnished with American Empire antiques. Tours begin at the office, 515 Allen Pkwy. Open daily. Tour charge. Allen Pkwy. and Bagby St. (phone: 655-9539).

Astrodome – Besides serving as home for the *Astros, Oilers,* and the University of Houston *Cougars,* this $36-million domed stadium, big enough to accommodate an 18-story building (standing) or 66,000 spectators, with the world's largest and most dazzling scoreboard (474 feet long and 4 stories high, complete with pyrotechnical display when the home team scores), is Texas's most popular attraction. There are guided tours at 11 AM, 1, and 3 PM, featuring a multimedia blowout on the scoreboard. Open daily. Admission charge. 4¾ miles southwest at I-610 and Kirby Dr. (phone: 799-9544).

Astroworld – Also part of Astrodomain, Houston's version of a theme park offers 70 acres of entertainment, including 11 theme amusement parks, water skiing spectaculars, and high-diving feats. The Texas Cyclone Roller Coaster induces its share of rave reviews, screams, and nausea. Open daily June through August, weekends during spring and fall. (Check locally for shortened or extended hours.) Admission charge. 9001 Kirby Dr., across from the *Astrodome* (phone: 799-1234).

San Jacinto Battleground – The 570-foot-tall San Jacinto Monument marks the spot where Sam Houston defeated Mexican General Santa Anna to win Texas's independence. The 460-acre state park also includes a *Museum of Texas History,* which traces the region's development from the Indian civilization through Texas's annexation by the US; it also houses the battleship *Texas,* veteran of both world wars. No admission charge. Farm Road 134, off Hwy. 225, 21 miles east of downtown Houston (phone: 479-2431).

Port of Houston – From an observation platform atop Wharf 9, visitors can see the turning basin area of this country's third largest port. To inspect some of the elaborate industrial-shipping developments, take an excursion along the ship channel aboard the MV *Sam Houston* (make reservations well in advance). No trips on Mondays or in September. No admission charge. Gate 8, off Clinton Dr. (phone: 225-4044).

Lyndon B. Johnson Space Center – Until you actually fly Trans-Universe to the moon, this is the closest you can get to the experience. This 1,620-acre campus-like facility was the training ground for the Gemini, Apollo, and Skylab astronauts and is the monitoring center for the NASA manned space flights. The visitors center displays craft that have flown in space, moon rocks, and a lunar module, and the Mission Control Center houses some of the most sophisticated communications computer data equipment in the world. Visitors are welcome at the Control Center and the Skylab Training Room on guided tours, available by reservation. NASA films are shown throughout the day in the auditorium. Open daily. No admission charge. 25 miles SE of downtown Houston via I-45 (phone: 483-4321).

■ **EXTRA SPECIAL:** Just 51 miles south of Houston along I-45 is Galveston Island, a leading Gulf Coast resort area. Stewart Beach is the principal public beach, and there's good swimming, surfing, sailing, water skiing, and deep-sea fishing (reservations taken at boats on Piers 18 and 19 of the Galveston Yacht Basin). Seafood restaurants, art galleries, and restored turn-of-the-century homes are in the former vacation destination of the oil magnates clustered around Strand Blvd.

SOURCES AND RESOURCES

 TOURIST INFORMATION: The Houston Convention and Visitors Council is best for brochures, maps, and general information. 3300 Main St., Houston, TX 77002 (phone: 523-5050). Many banks also provide free visitor information kits, as does the Chamber of Commerce. 1100 Milam (phone: 651-1313).

The revised edition of *Texas Monthly's Guide to Houston* by Felicia Coates and Harriet Howle (Mediatex Communications Corp.; $3.95) is a comprehensive guide. The *Intrepid Walker's Guide to Houston* by Eli Zal and Doug Milburn ($2.95) is the best guide to the network of underground tunnels connecting major downtown buildings and other off-the-beaten-track walking tours.

Television Stations – KHOU Channel 11–CBS; KTRK Channel 13–ABC; KPRC Channel 2–NBC; KUHT Channel 8–PBS.

Radio Stations – AM: KTRC 950 (news/talk); KTRH 740 (news/sports). FM: KRTS 92.1 and 104. 9 (classical); KLTR 93.7 (adult contemporary); KTSU 90.9 (jazz/urban contemporary).

Local Coverage – The *Post,* morning daily, and the *Chronicle,* evening daily, are both available at newsstands.

Food – Check Andrea Henley's *Restaurant Reference Book for Houston,* which lists almost all of the city's restaurants ($2.95), and the *Texas Monthly Guide.*

Telephone – The area code for Houston is 713.

Sales Tax – There is no city or state tax in Houston; sales tax is 8%.

 CLIMATE: In the summer, Houston is hot and humid. Winds from the Gulf of Mexico create warm summer nights, and keep the winters and the rest of the year relatively warm.

 GETTING AROUND: Airport – The city's main airports are Houston Intercontinental and William P. Hobby Airport. Those familiar with Houston traffic allow at least 45 minutes to reach either one from downtown (note that it is not unusual for rain, fog, or the nightly rush hour to double this time). *Yellow Cab* charges a flat rate of $26 for the trip between Intercontinental and downtown. Taxi fare into the city from Hobby should run about $15. *Trailways* (phone:

523-8888) operates shuttle service from Intercontinental ($7.70) and Hobby ($5) to its four downtown terminals. Buses leave every half-hour, and tickets may be purchased at stands outside each terminal.

Bus – Metropolitan Transit Authority of Harris County serves downtown and the suburbs, but the system can be confusing and unreliable. Mini-buses run in the downtown shopping area. For route information contact the main office, 401 Louisiana (phone: 635-4000).

Taxi – Cabs can be ordered on the phone, picked up in front of hotels and terminals, or, with some difficulty, hailed in the street. Major companies are *United Taxicab* (phone: 699-0000) and *Yellow Cab* (phone: 236-1111). Be warned, however, that taxi rates are rather high.

Car Rental – Because Houston is a huge, sprawling city whose backbone is its extensive freeway system, a car is the most practical mode of travel. Try to avoid being caught in Houston's rush hour, when traffic is impossibly snarled. All the major national firms serve Houston. Local service is provided by *Greater Houston Leasing,* 3231 Audley (phone: 528-0873), and *Thrifty Rent-A-Car* at Hobby Airport (phone: 947-9121) and Intercontinental Airport (phone: 449-0126).

 LOCAL SERVICES: Business Services – *Associated Executive Services,* 6250 Westpark (phone: 783-1872).

Mechanics – For American cars, *Lightsey's Auto & Diesel Repair,* 7000 Synott (phone: 498-3535); for foreign cars, *Freeman's Auto Service,* 3540 Oak Forest Dr. (phone: 681-9484).

 MUSEUMS: The *Museum of Natural Science* and the *Museum of Fine Arts* are described under *Special Places.* Other notable Houston museums worth a visit:

Bayou Bend – Early American furnishings. 1 Westcott St. (phone: 529-8773).

Contemporary Arts Museum – 5216 Montrose at Bissonnet (phone: 526-3129).

 MAJOR COLLEGES AND UNIVERSITIES: Among Houston's educational institutions are Rice University (6100 S. Main St.; phone: 527-8101), which has a good reputation for its engineering and science schools; University of Houston (4800 Calhoun Rd.; phone: 749-1011); and the Texas Medical Center (between Fannin St. and Holcombe Blvd.; phone: 797-0100).

 SPECIAL EVENTS: Check the publications noted above for exact dates. For 2 weeks in late February and early March, Houston cowboys come out in full force and descend on the *Astrodome* complex for the *Houston Livestock Show and Rodeo*. There's plenty of action — rodeo events and country and western concerts. During April and October, local and regional artists show their stuff in the *Westheimer Art Show,* an outdoor arts and crafts festival on Westheimer Rd. Most area hotels are filled for the 4-day *Offshore Technology Conference,* the world's biggest oil industry show, in late April and early May.

 SPORTS AND FITNESS: Tickets to professional games can be picked up at Ticket Connection, 2031 Southwest Fwy. (phone: 524-3687).

Ballooning – The *Rainbow's End Balloon Port* sends 'em up weekend mornings at dawn when the winds are calm. You can watch the balloonists rise to the occasion, and if they don't, join them for breakfast. 7826 Fairview (phone: 466-1927).

Baseball – The National League's *Astros* play at the *Astrodome* from April to September, I-610 and Kirby Dr. (phone: 799-9555).

Basketball – The NBA's *Rockets* play from December to April at the *Summit,* 10 Greenway Plaza (phone: 627-2115).

Bicycling – There are apparently no outlets offering bicycles for rent in the entire city of Houston. But if you find one, bring one, or borrow one, there's a good bike trail running from the Sabine Street Bridge (just east of Allen's Landing) along Buffalo Bayou to Shepherd, and back along the Memorial side of the Bayou. The City of Houston Parks and Recreation Dept. offers a list of other bike routes. 2999 S. Wayside (phone: 641-4111).

Fishing – Best for fishing is Galveston, where you can wet a line in the Gulf of Mexico off piers or from deep-sea charters that leave from Piers 18 and 19 of the Galveston Yacht Basin.

Fitness Center – The *YMCA* has a pool, indoor and outdoor tracks, exercise classes, and handball and racquetball courts, 1600 Louisiana (phone: 659-8501).

Football – The *Oilers* play at the *Astrodome* (phone: 797-1000).

Golf – Best public course for the duffer is in Hermann Park, 6201 Golf Course Dr. (phone: 529-9788). The most challenging of the municipal courts is in Brock Park, 8201 John Ralston Rd., off Old Beaumont Hwy. (phone: 458-1350).

Jogging – Most running is done along a 3-mile loop in Memorial Park, 4 miles from downtown and reached on foot from Buffalo Bayou or by taking the #16 Memorial or the #17 Tanglewood bus. Other possibilities are Hermann Park, via South Main, and the well-used trails along Ellen Parkway.

Rodeo – On Saturday nights year-round, the *Simonton Rodeo* rounds 'em up with real live rodeo followed by country-and-western dancing, on Westheimer Rd., 45 minutes west of the city (phone: 346-1534). *Gilley's Club* also has a Saturday night rodeo, followed by admission to the world's largest honky-tonk, 4500 Spencer Hwy. in Pasadena (phone: 946-9842).

Swimming – There are 42 municipal pools in Houston, open from June through Labor Day. The Hermann Park pool is convenient. 2020 Hermann Dr. (phone: 522-0403).

Tennis – The municipally run *Memorial Tennis Center* has 18 Laykold courts, showers, lockers, tennis shop, and practice court. 600 Memorial Loop Dr. (phone: 520-7056). There are free courts in most of the city parks.

 THEATER: For current offerings, check the daily and weekly publications listed above. The *Alley Theater,* Houston's established and acclaimed resident company, performs everything from classical drama to experimental plays, October to May, at 615 Texas Ave. (box office, 228-8421). During the summer, the *Miller Outdoor Theater* offers a variety of entertainments, all free, ranging from pop concerts, *Theater Under the Stars* musical extravaganzas, to a *Shakespeare Festival;* 100 Concert Dr. in Hermann Park (phone: 622-8887). Colleges and universities in the area produce plays and musicals.

 MUSIC: *Jones Hall for the Performing Arts* is the home of the nationally acclaimed *Houston Symphony Orchestra* and offers concerts and performances throughout the year by internationally renowned guest artists and companies; 615 Louisiana (phone: 237-1439). The *Houston Grand Opera* and the *Houston Ballet,* the only resident professional ballet company in the Southwest, perform at the new *Gus S. Wortham Theater Center,* 501 Texas Ave. (phone: 237-1439 for general information; 227-2787 for ballet and opera tickets), from September to March. All give free performances at the *Miller Theater* in the summer. Big rock and occasional country-and-western concerts are held at the *Summit* throughout the year; 10 Greenway Plaza (phone: 961-9003).

 NIGHTCLUBS AND NIGHTLIFE: Depending on what you want, you can unwind or recharge at one or more of Houston's nightspots. Current favorites for progressive country music, Texas-style, and local color: *San Antone Rose,* 1641 S. Voss Rd. (phone: 977-7116), or *Gilley's Club,* 4500 Spencer Hwy. in Pasadena, on Houston's southeast perimeter (phone: 941-7990); for jazz, *Rockefeller's,* 3620 Washington (phone: 861-9365); *Melody Lane Ballroom,* for ballroom dancing, 3027 Crossview (phone: 785-5301); for disco, the *Ocean Club,* 1885 St. James (phone: 963-9314), or *Studebakers,* 2630 Augusta Dr. (phone: 783-4142).

(BEST IN TOWN)

 CHECKING IN: Houston's hotel industry rode the crest of the city's boom during the 1970s, with new — and usually luxurious — hotels springing up almost daily. As a result, hotels are now the most overbuilt segment of the city's real estate industry, and it is no longer impossible to get a room during the annual Offshore Technology Conference. But even though many hotels are having problems filling their available inventory of rooms, rates are still increasing. Expect to pay $100 or more a night for a double at a hotel we list as expensive; $75 in the moderate range, and about $50 in the inexpensive category. All telephone numbers are in the 713 area code unless otherwise indicated.

La Colombe d'Or – This converted mansion, next to St. Thomas University in the heart of Houston's Montrose area, is known for its haute French restaurant. The hotel features 5 antiques-filled suites with private dining rooms and also has a penthouse for $400 a night. The walnut paneling of the bar and public areas is enhanced with original artwork. 3410 Montrose Blvd. (phone: 524-7999). Expensive.

Inn on the Park – In the new Riverway complex and part of the superb Four Seasons chain, the hotel overlooks a scenic bayou area populated by live swans and features an interesting sculpture garden. Amenities include 2 restaurants, a cabaret, health club, outdoor jogging track, 4 tennis courts, and garage. In Riverway at Post Oak La. and Woodway Dr. (phone: 871-8181). Expensive.

Lancaster – A small, elegant hostelry, set in a restored 1926 brick building with the air of a private British club. Oriental carpets and original oils fill the lobby; each of the 85 rooms and 8 suites is done up with antiques and a four-poster bed. Guests and the theater crowd (*Jones Hall for the Performing Arts* and the *Alley Theater* are across the street) enjoy the nouvelle accents on Gulf Coast seafood in the *Lancaster Grille.* Other features include a multi-lingual staff, concierge, 24-hour room service, access to health club. 701 Texas Ave. (phone: 228-9500 or 800-231-0336). Expensive.

Remington – Considered the top of the line in Houston. Built by Rosewood Hotels and now owned by Southmark Corp., it offers all the attention and amenities normally found in a top European hotel, plus 3 restaurants, a bar, lounges, a swimming pool, recreational deck, boutique, and more. 1919 Briar Oaks Dr. (phone: 840-7600). Expensive.

Westin Oaks and Westin Galleria – Smack in the middle of the luxurious Galleria Mall, the ideal spot for a shopping spree. The *Oaks* at 5011 Westheimer Rd. (phone: 623-4300 or 800-288-3000), with 400 rooms, is the older (but no less grand) facility. At the other end of the mall is the 400-room *Galleria,* 5060 W.

Alabama (phone: 960-8100), which is every bit as fine. Really big spenders can splurge on the Crown Suite at the *Oaks,* a penthouse with 2 fireplaces, 2½ baths, a banquet table for 14, and a grand piano — all for only $1,200 a night. Other features include a pool, cafés, entertainment and dancing, and access to ice skating, a running track, and indoor tennis. Pay garage. Expensive.

Allen Park Inn – Just outside the downtown area, this picturesque property is a favorite of film crews shooting in Houston. It's decorated with antiques throughout. A comfortable inn with a 24-hour restaurant and health club facilities. 2121 Allen Pkwy. (phone: 521-9321). Moderate.

Embassy Suites – All 2-room suites, with a complimentary full breakfast and 2-hour open bar daily. Free shuttle bus to downtown terminal. Health club and gameroom. 9090 Southwest Fwy. (phone: 995-0123). Moderate.

Rodeway Inn at Greenway Plaza – Another well-sited property with modest accommodations. Features include a restaurant, meeting, and banquet facilities. 3135 Southwest Fwy. (phone: 526-1071). Inexpensive.

There are several moderate to inexpensive motel chain facilities scattered about Houston, including *Ramada, Best Western, La Quinta, Days Inn, TraveLodge,* and *Texian Inn.* Features and rates are standard for what one has come to expect from such chains. The deciding factor then is location: along the Katy Freeway or Southwest Freeway if you're visiting the outlying suburbs; along Buffalo Speedway or South Main to be near the *Astrodome;* inside Loop 610 of the Southwest Freeway to shop at the Galleria; North and Eastex freeways for the Intercontinental Airport area; and Galveston Freeway for Hobby Airport and — much farther out — the Johnson Space Center.

EATING OUT: Besides offerings of fine regional foods — chili parlors and Mexican restaurants abound — Houston has a great variety of cuisines, including seafood fresh from the Gulf of Mexico, continental, Chinese, Greek, and down-home Southern meals. Expect to spend about $60 for a dinner for two at restaurants in the expensive range, $20 to $40 in the moderate range, and $20 or less in the inexpensive range. Prices do not include drinks, wine, or tips. All telephone numbers are in the 713 area code unless otherwise indicated.

Brennan's – A bit of New Orleans' Vieux Carré in Houston. Patio tables and a lovely pillared dining room are the setting for fine food. Louisiana-style and Créole specialties make this branch as pleasurable as its counterparts in New Orleans, Dallas, and Atlanta. Open daily. Reservations advised. Major credit cards. 3300 Smith (phone: 522-9711). Expensive.

Cadillac Bar – The current Houston favorite for fine Mexican cuisine. Try the *queso flameado con chorizo* (melted white cheese with sausage) with tender tortillas for starters. Ask about house specialties, which include such exotic dishes as mesquite-smoked kid. Open daily. Reservations advised. Major credit cards. 1802 Shepherd at I-10 (phone: 862-2020). Expensive.

Harry's Kenya – This lushly formal restaurant (with a safari motif) is named for the legendary African hunter Harry Selby, the model for the Peter McKenzie character in Robert Ruark's novel *Something of Value.* Its excellent continental cuisine is enlivened with dishes such as venison and wild boar. Only a few steps from downtown hotels, complimentary shuttle service takes diners to performances at *Jones Hall,* the *Alley Theater,* and the *Music Hall.* Closed Sundays. Reservations advised. Major credit cards. 1160 Smith (phone: 650-1980). Expensive.

Maxim's – Consistently fine food of the haute cuisine category, and what is probably the most extensive wine cellar in the Southwest. The decor is somewhat overwhelming, but once the meal begins, diners forget all about the pink and green overtones. The menu is weighted toward Gulf seafood, which is prepared well, but the beef is also prime. Chocolate mousse or brandy freeze for dessert are excellent. Closed Sundays. Reservations advised. Major credit cards. 3755 Richmond (phone: 877-8899). Expensive.

Ruth's Chris Steak House – A true Texas establishment, redolent with the aroma of fine beef cooking; decorated with oil company paraphernalia, and much appreciated for its prime cuts: filet, porterhouse, and strip steaks. Reservations advised. Major credit cards. 6213 Richmond (phone: 789-2333). Expensive.

Tony's – Owner Tony Vallone is on hand most of the time to oversee this stronghold of elegance in this otherwise purposely informal city. Punctilious service by waiters in black tie, understated wood-paneled decor, and fresh flowers provide the backdrop for excellent continental food. The pâtés and salads are impeccable. Of the entrées, veal piccata with truffles and mushrooms and red snapper noisette, with hazelnuts, are the best. Try the Grand Marnier soufflé for dessert, but remember to order it at the beginning of the meal. Closed Sundays. Reservations advised. Major credit cards. 1801 Post Oak Blvd.. (phone: 622-6778). Expensive.

Uncle Tai's Hunan Yuan – Uncle Tai made his name and reputation in New York City, then headed south to start his own place, and people in Houston couldn't be happier. This family-run restaurant offers impeccable service, and from the Tricolored Lobster to Uncle Tai's Texas-Hunanese-style chicken, the food is uniformly wonderful. Open daily. Reservations advised. American Express and Diners Club accepted. 1980 Post Oak Blvd. (phone: 960-8000). Expensive.

Bombay Palace – Indian cuisine is enjoying growing popularity in Houston, and this place is a great favorite. The best dishes prepared in the tandoor — the special Indian clay oven — are chicken, lamb, and prawns. Open daily. Reservations advised. Major credit cards. 3901 Westheimer (phone: 960-8472). Moderate.

La Bonne Auberge – Formerly *Foulard's,* this fine restaurant has the same chefs and the same wonderful French cuisine with added continental dishes in a romantic setting. You won't be disappointed by the five-course prix fixe dinner (for the truly hungry only). Open daily. Reservations advised. Major credit cards. 10001 Westheimer, in the Carillon West Mall (phone: 789-1661). Moderate.

Ninfa's – A local must for Mexican fare that seems to be on everyone's list, so you may have to wait in line. But it's worth it, particularly for the tacos al carbon (tortillas wrapped around barbecued pork or beef) and chilpanzingas (ham and cheese wrapped in pastry, fried, and topped with sour cream). There are seven locations now, but the downtown site is still the best. Open daily. No reservations on weekends. Major credit cards. 2704 Navigation (phone: 228-1175). Moderate.

Ouisie's Table and Traveling Brown Bag Lunch Company – Fresh, excellent ingredients coupled with an imaginative, constantly changing menu make *Ouisie's* more than a fad. The homemade soups and the chilled crisp salads, a peppery onion pâté, and the perfectly cooked fresh fish are among the best in town. Closed Sundays and Mondays. Major credit cards. 1708 Sunset (phone: 528-2264). Moderate.

Romero's – Tasty and interesting Italian and continental dishes are complemented by a good list of wines. Some favorites on the menu are veal piccata, blackened redfish, and angel-hair pasta with shrimp and crabmeat. Closed Sundays. Major credit cards. 2400 Midlane (phone: 961-1161). Moderate.

Zorba the Greek Café – Fried shrimp and seafood platters, and Greek dishes like tiropitakia (phylo filled with feta cheese), leg of lamb, and a great Greek salad. The place looks like a beer parlor, and is, but they also have retsina. No reservations. MasterCard and Visa. 202 Tuam (phone: 528-1382). Moderate.

Captain Benny's Half Shell – Boiled shrimp, freshly shucked oysters, juicy crayfish in season, and lightly fried shrimp are all dished out to the crew of regulars who jam the place. You may have to stand, but you'll find the people watching and the food worth it. Closed Sundays. No reservations. No credit cards. 7409 S. Main (phone: 795-9051). Inexpensive.

Chili's – It's easy to guess the house specialty — the real hot stuff, served steaming, spicy, and thick, concocted from a secret Texas recipe. Otherwise, the jumbo hamburgers and homemade French fries make a solid meal at an easy price. Open daily. No reservations. Major credit cards. 5930 Richmond (phone: 780-1654). Inexpensive.

James Coney Island – Here are hot dogs the way lots of folks like them to be served — with loads of chili and onions. About 15 locations around town, but the most fun spot is a 1950s-style diner with a free jukebox that plays top-40 tunes from 1959. Checks, but no credit cards. 5745 Westheimer (phone: 785-9333). Inexpensive.

Last Concert Café – This Tex-Mex restaurant is one of Houston's best-kept secrets. It's located in a rough-looking industrial section, there's no name outside, and you have to knock to get in. But once inside, you'll enjoy lots of atmosphere, delicious food, and good entertainment on the patio. Major credit cards. 1403 Nance (phone: 226-8563). Inexpensive.

Otto's – Aficionados argue over the merits of various styles of barbecue sauce. If you crave the East Texas sweet variety, ride over to *Otto's* and sample good beef, ribs, links, or ham awash in the delightful stuff. No credit cards. 5502 Memorial (phone: 864-2573). Inexpensive.

Ragin' Cajun – If you prefer the down-and-dirty spice and rice of Cajun cooking to highfalutin' Créole sauces, then this is the place to go. It's a hole in the wall, but the atmosphere is great and the gumbo and red beans with rice are delicious. No credit cards but will take checks. 4302 Richmond (phone: 623-6321). Inexpensive.

INDIANAPOLIS

Like quite a few other midwestern cities, Indianapolis is not likely to excite a visitor at first glance. There are those endless handsome neighborhoods — big trees, big yards, big houses — in an endless procession above 38th Street. Posh suburbs. Elegant shopping malls. The kind of city that might make you assume that it'd be a nice place to live — though only for a while.

But, as in other cities, first impressions are deceptive. This is partly because of the widespread lack of information about the out-of-the-ordinary places that keep the citizens happy, partly because a lot of vociferous visitors left before they got to the heart of the place under the placid surface, partly because residents took their pleasures for granted. But in the last few years, all that taking for granted has come to a halt. At just about the same time the residents of cities all over the Midwest were realizing that this part of the country was a pretty fine place to live after all, and talking up their cities, and patting themselves on the back for living there, and feeling smug, Richard Lugar took over as Indianapolis's mayor.

The city's modern revitalization began with Lugar in 1970, when he consolidated the city and county governments in an effort to ease the strain on city finances. Lugar was succeeded by William H. Hudnut III, who has since been elected to an unprecedented fourth term under a law that has come to be known as the "Hudnut Forever Law," which abolished any limits on the number of terms a mayor can serve.

Lots has happened in the last two decades: The downtown area — which had begun to decline to the extent that the movie houses had nearly all relocated to the suburbs, and the better part of the most affluent shops and shoppers had followed — began to blossom again. The old city market — vaulted in cast iron and chock-a-block with stands selling fresh produce, fish, meat, sausages, cheese, spices, coffee, and tea — was among the first of the historic local institutions to get a face-lift instead of being torn down. Then came the Convention Center and a new *Hyatt Regency* hotel, along with an arena nearby; the latter now serving as home for the Indiana *Pacers* basketball team and lots of special events such as concerts and ice shows. Monument Circle is now a clean, appealing park that's neatly surrounded by red bricks, and the new 63,000-seat *Hoosier Dome* complex welcomes sports events, conventions, and trade shows. Its facilities were the main lure to the NFL *Colts,* who left Baltimore for Indiana in one of sports' most controversial franchise transfers.

The sum of these new facilities has been to enhance Indianapolis's reputation as a major sports center. During the 1980s, the city played host to over 100 major international sports competitions. In 1987, the Pan American Games attracted more than 4,000 athletes to the city, and there were more trials for the 1988 Olympic Games held in Indianapolis than any other city in the country. Of even greater benefit to local residents and visitors, most of these world class sports facilities are open to the public when no formal competitions are scheduled.

So Indianapolis has come to be recognized as something more than the one-day-a-year town that enjoyed national recognition only on the day when the big 500-mile auto race was held. It's probably not yet accurate to put the city in the same class as Miami or New York or San Francisco, but there's little doubt that the quality of local life and the appeal it holds for visitors has grown exponentially in just about 2 decades.

INDIANAPOLIS AT-A-GLANCE

SEEING THE CITY: Indianapolis has some breathtaking vantage points. The highest point is in Crown Hill Cemetery, at the grave of author James Whitcomb Riley. (John Dillinger and Benjamin Harrison are also buried at Crown Hill, which is a National Historic Site.) 3402 Boulevard Pl. (phone: 925-8231). The Soldiers and Sailors Monument gives you the best overview of the layout of the city. Monument Circle, downtown. The view from *Teller's Cage*, the 35th-floor restaurant at the top of the Indiana National Bank Tower, is also exceptional. 1 Indiana Sq. (phone: 266-5211). Another stunning view is from the 28th floor of the City County Building Observatory on (phone: 236-4345).

SPECIAL PLACES: You'll find Indianapolis an easy place to get around. Washington Street is the north-south dividing line; Meridian Street is the east-west dividing line. Numbered streets always run east and west, and the number of the street represents the number of blocks north of Washington Street. Most of the great places are spread out north of Washington Street.

Union Station – One of the state's most popular attractions is the revitalized historic Union Station. In the mid-1980s, the once-decrepit railroad terminal was transformed into an eating-entertainment-shopping area like Faneuil Hall Marketplace in Boston and South Street Seaport in New York. Centrally located across from the Convention Center and *Hoosier Dome,* the 3-block structure opened in 1986 and features nearly 40 restaurants, 5 nightclubs, and a variety of shops. The highlight is the 276-room *Holiday Inn* — the first ever placed in an existing structure — with even a few Pullman cars available for lodging (phone: 631-2221).

Indiana State Museum – This entertaining museum relates the natural and cultural history of the state. No admission charge. 202 N. Alabama, at Ohio (phone: 232-1637).

Scottish Rite Cathedral – A vast Tudor Gothic structure with a 54-bell carillon, two organs, and an interior that looks like 3-D lace turned into wood. Free tours on weekdays only. 650 N. Meridian (phone: 635-2301).

James Whitcomb Riley Home – Indiana's underrated poet laureate lived in this comfortable house between 1892 and 1916; the whole neighborhood has been restored recently to look as it might have then. Found on a cobblestone street, the home is considered one of the finest Victorian preservations in the country. Admission charge. 528 Lockerbie (phone: 631-5885).

Benjamin Harrison Memorial Home – This 16-room Victorian-Italianate mansion, built in 1875 for the 23rd president, has been fitted out with many of the original furnishings. Admission charge. 1230 N. Delaware (phone: 631-1898).

Indianapolis Motor Speedway – Minibuses will take visitors around the 2½-mile oval on which the 500-mile race is held every year on the last Sunday in May. You can

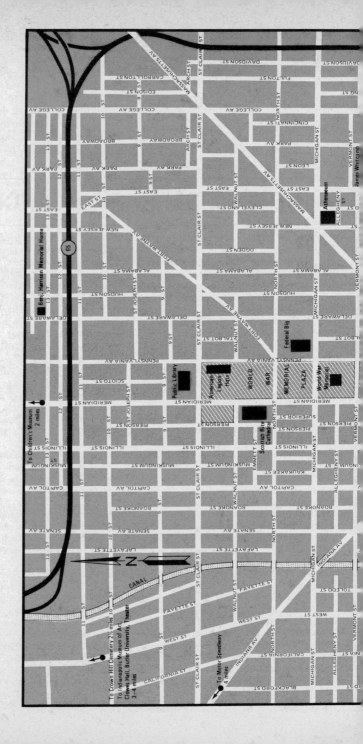

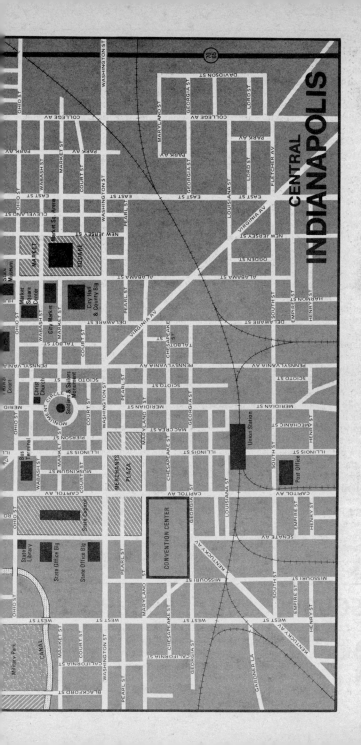

CENTRAL
INDIANAPOLIS

also visit the *IMS Museum,* where race cars from the early days are on display. Admission charge. 4790 W. 16th (phone: 241-2500).

Indianapolis Museum of Art – By any standards, a truly remarkable museum. Its Krannert Pavilion contains a wide-ranging collection of American, Oriental, primitive, and 18th- and 19th-century European art. The Clowes Pavilion, adjacent, has rooms full of medieval and Renaissance art, plus some watercolors by Turner, ranged around a skylit, plant-filled courtyard. In the gardens are modern sculptures, including Robert Indiana's *LOVE,* and a wonderful, geometrical fountain. The grounds were originally the riverview estate of the Lilly family. Their mansion now shows off a collection of English, French, and Italian 18th-century decorative art. The 154 beautifully landscaped acres also feature a greenhouse, botanical gardens, the biggest children's playhouse you've ever seen; and, as we went to press, a new wing to house the Eiteljorg Collection of African Arts was nearing completion. Admission charge for the 3rd-floor and mansion exhibitions; the pavilions are free. 1200 W. 38th St. (phone: 923-1331).

Children's Museum – This is the largest children's museum in the world. Kids and adults can ride a turn-of-the-century carousel, spelunk in a simulated limestone cave, and see a real mummy and the largest collection of toy trains on public display. Also featured are antique fire engines, a furnished Hoosier log cabin, folk art toys from around the world, a furnished Hoosier log cabin, and two major galleries full of hands-on displays exploring the natural and physical sciences. Special programs are held regularly. Here, too, expansion is under way: a $14-million Center for Exploration and a planetarium should be complete by the time you read this. Closed Mondays from Labor Day through Memorial Day. No admission charge. 3000 N. Meridian (phone: 924-5431).

Indianapolis Zoo – The $64-million, 64-acre world class Indianapolis Zoo, the nation's first major zoo in decades to be built from the ground up, opened in 1982. More than 2,000 animals are now housed in simulated natural habitats, including the world's largest totally enclosed Whale and Dolphin Pavilion. Admission: $7, adults, $4, children. 1200 W. Washington St. (phone: 630-2000).

Zionsville – A mid-19th-century restored village. The streets are now full of ritzy shops. Good for a long afternoon. 86th St. north to Zionsville Rd.

Conner Prairie Pioneer Settlement – Step back in time to 1836 and see the daily life of the era re-created. Interpreters portray villagers in this 25-building settlement: a doctor, a potter, a blacksmith, and an innkeeper talk as they perform their duties. Also on the premises is a restaurant featuring 19th-century country-style dinners. Indiana Spring (late April), an old-fashioned Fourth of July bash, and quaint Christmastime festivities. Closed Mondays. Admission charge. 13400 Allisonville Rd., about 20 miles northeast of Monument Circle via Rte. 37 and I-465 (phone: 776-6000).

Garfield Park Conservatory – More than 500 tropical plants are on display in addition to a large collection of cacti and a 15-foot waterfall. Closed Mondays. Admission charge. 2450 S. Shelby (phone: 784-3044).

Lilly Center – Through exhibitions, the research activities of the Eli Lilly Company — including genetic engineering — are highlighted. Some Lilly family memorabilia is also on display. 893 S. Delaware St. (phone: 276-3514).

SOURCES AND RESOURCES

TOURIST INFORMATION: The Indianapolis City Center, Pan American Plaza, 201 S. Capitol Ave., Indianapolis, IN 46225 (phone: 237-5200, or 800-323-INDY), and the Indiana Tourism Development Division, 1 N. Capitol, Suite 700 (phone: 232-8860 or 800-2WANDER), supply brochures and general tourist information.

Television Stations – WRTV Channel 6–ABC; WISH Channel 8–CBS; WTHR Channel 13–NBC; WFYI Channel 20–PBS.

Radio Stations – AM: WIRE 1430 (news/sports); WMLF 1310 (easy listening). FM: WIAN 90.1 (news/jazz); WENF 97 (top 40); WZPL 99.5 (album oriented).

Local Coverage – *Indianapolis Star,* morning daily and Sundays; *Indianapolis News,* afternoon daily.

Telephone – The area code for Indianapolis is 317.

Sales Tax – There is a 5% sales tax as well as a 5% hotel tax, and a 6% beverage tax in Marion Country (Indianapolis).

CLIMATE: Indianapolis has typical midwestern weather — beautiful springs, steamy summers, mild autumns, and moderately cold winters with varying amounts of snow.

GETTING AROUND: Airport – Indianapolis International Airport is a 15-minute drive from downtown; taxi fare should run about $10. *AAA Limousine Service* (phone: 247-7301) offers frequent van service from the airport to most downtown hotels for $7.25 or less, depending on the number of passengers. Metro Transit's #8 Washington St. bus provides public tranportation between the airport and downtown; for the return trip, catch the bus on Washington between Illinois and Meridian streets. The fare is $1.05; exact change is required.

You can get around by public transportation, but a car is more convenient since Indianapolis is a sprawling city.

Bus – Service has improved in recent years, and some lines operate 24 hours — but check before you go. Metro Transit (phone: 635-3344).

Taxi – Phoning *Yellow Cab* (phone: 637-5421) is the surest way to get one.

Car Rental – All the big national companies are represented here.

LOCAL SERVICES: Babysitting – Most hotels can help you arrange for sitters. Failing that, contact *Kinder Care,* with several locations in the city (phone: 844-3096, headquarters).

Business Services – *Manpower Inc. of Indianapolis,* 251 N. Delaware (phone: 635-1001).

Mechanics – *Emergency Road Service* (phone: 923-3311); *Approved Auto Repair Service* (phone: 924-5687), affiliated with AAA Motor Club, gives locations and phone numbers of reputable shops.

MUSEUMS: The *Indianapolis Museum of Art, Indiana State Museum, Children's Museum,* and the *Conner Prairie Pioneer Settlement* are described in *Special Places.*

MAJOR COLLEGES AND UNIVERSITIES: The combined campus of Indiana and Purdue universities is modern and beautifully designed; 1100-1300 W. Michigan (phone: 274-5555). The campus of Butler University is farther north, at Sunset Ave. and W. 46th St. (phone: 283-8000). The J. I. Holcomb Observatory and Planetarium sits at the campus's north end (phone: 283-9333). The private University of Indianapolis is at 1400 E. Hanna (phone: 788-3368), while Marian College is at 3200 Cold Spring Rd. (phone: 929-0123).

SPECIAL EVENTS: The *Indianapolis 500-Mile Race* — the world's biggest single-day sporting event — is held at the *Indianapolis Motor Speedway* every Memorial Day weekend; myriad activities surrounding the Indy 500 are held during May as part of the *500 Festival.* One Saturday night in June, thousands crowd Monument Circle downtown for the *Mid-Summer Fest,* a music fair. During July, *Indiana Black Expo,* the nation's largest exposition of black culture, history, and enterprise, takes place. September brings *Circlefest,* the city's largest festival of food and live entertainment. Almost as exciting are the *Indiana State Fair,* in August, and the *Indiana Avenue Outdoor Jazz Festival,* featuring jazz, blues, and an array of food vendors, both in August. Indianapolis also offers the *GTE/US Men's Hardcourt Championships* in a modern tennis stadium in August; and the *National Championship Drag Races* are held at *Raceway Park* every Labor Day weekend. *Christmas on the Circle* is a month of festivities in the heart of the city.

 SPORTS AND FITNESS: Baseball – The Indianapolis *Indians* of the AAA American Assocation have a working agreement with the Montréal *Expos.* The *Indians* play in *Bush Stadium* at 1501 W. 16th (phone: 632-5371).

Basketball – The NBA Indiana *Pacers* play in the *Market Square Arena,* 300 E. Market (phone: 639-2112).

Bicycling – *Major Taylor Celodrome* (bicycle racing track) has a smooth, 28-degree, banked track open from mid-March to early November (except when sporting events are in progress), depending on the weather. Helmet and bicycle rental available for a nominal fee. 3649 Cold Spring Rd. (phone: 926-8356).

Fishing – Panfish at Eagle Creek Reservoir, 7602 Walnut Point Rd. (phone: 293-5555). Farther out of town: Geist and Morse Reservoirs and, about 2 hours south and much larger, Monroe Reservoir, near Bloomington.

Fitness Centers – *Silhouette National Health Spa,* 6407 E. Washington (phone: 356-7223) and three other locations. The pool at the *YMCA* is also available, 860 W. 10th (phone: 634-2478).

Football – The Indianapolis *Colts* of the NFL play in the *Hoosier Dome,* 100 S. Capitol (phone: 262-3389).

Golf – There are three good public courses near Riverside Park, 3501 Cold Spring Rd., and eight others around the city. For information on all of them, call the Parks and Recreation Dept. (phone: 924-9151).

Hockey – The Indianapolis *Ice* play at the *Coliseum,* State Fairgrounds (phone: 632-5151).

Ice Skating – November to March at Ellenberger City Park, 5301 E. St. Clair (phone: 353-1600), and Perry City Park, 541 E. Stop 11 Rd. (phone: 888-0070). Also, October through March at the *Coliseum,* State Fairgrounds (phone: 927-7536), and year-round at the *Carmel Skadium,* 1040 3rd SW (phone: 844-8888). The *Indiana/World Ice Skating Academy and Research Center* is at Pan American Plaza, near Union Station. Indoor skating and skate rental are available to the public except when a competition is going on. 201 S. Capitol (phone: 237-5555).

Jogging – Take advantage of the walkways around the capitol, at Capitol and Washington Street, in the early morning and evening. Joggers also use Military and University parks and the World War Memorial area downtown. Another possibility is the campus of Indiana and Purdue universities, 1100 W. Michigan. Still other joggers use the IUPUI campus to the ½-mile River Promenade, a pedestrian walkway at White River State Park.

Swimming – The *Indiana University Natatorium* (IUPUI), one of the premier aquatic facilities in the world, has two 50-meter pools. 901 W. New York St. (phone: 274-3517).

Tennis – One of the most popular spots is at the *Indianapolis Sports Center,* 815 W. New York St. (phone: 632-3250). Most high school courts are open to the public. Municipal courts can be found throughout the city. For specific locations, call 924-9151.

THEATER: The professional *Indiana Repertory Theater* has grown by leaps and bounds in the last few years; 140 W. Washington St. (phone: 635-5252). Indianapolis also has the *Indianapolis Civic Theater,* 1200 W. 38th (phone: 923-4597), the oldest continuously active civic theater in the US. Community theater can be found at the *Christian Theological Seminary,* 1000 W. 42nd (phone: 924-1331). For dinner theater, *Beef & Boards,* 9301 N. Michigan Rd. NW (phone: 872-9664), features stars of TV, Broadway, and Hollywood. In July and August there are musicals under the stars at *Starlight Musicals,* 304 W. 49th (phone: 926-1581). The *Indiana Repertory Theatre Cabaret Club,* 140 W. Washington St. (phone: 635-5252), features an intimate nightclub setting and professional musical entertainments, Wednesdays through Saturdays.

MUSIC: The *Circle Theater* is where the *Indianapolis Symphony Orchestra* plays most of its concerts (phone: 639-4300). The *Indianapolis Opera Company* (phone: 283-3531) and the *Butler Ballet* perform primarily at *Clowes Hall* (phone: 283-9231).

NIGHTCLUBS AND NIGHTLIFE: Like every other aspect of city life, nightlife in Indianapolis has grown. For dancing: *Ike & Jonesy's,* 17 Jackson Pl. (phone: 632-4553); *Lauderdale's* is trackside at Union Station (phone: 638-8181), *Safari Bar,* with its marble dance floor, lightshow and top 40 hits, is at 5910 E. 82nd St. (phone: 842-2968). Young singles patronize *Friday's,* 3502 E. 86th (phone: 844-3355). *Crackers Comedy Club,* 8702 Keystone Crossing (phone: 846-2500), features nationally known comedians Wednesdays through Saturdays; reservations recommended. Comedy is also king (or queen) at *Indianapolis Comedy Connection,* 247 S. Meridian St., 2nd floor (phone: 631-3536), reservations required; and at the *Broad Ripple Comedy Club,* 6281 N. College (phone: 255-4211), reservations required. There are also some promising nightclubs in the rejuvenated Union Station, across from the Convention Center. Jazz can be heard at *Madame Walker Urban Life Center* on Friday nights, 617 Indiana Ave. (phone: 635-6915), and at the *City Taproom,* 28 S. Pennsylvania St. (phone: 637-1334).

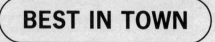

BEST IN TOWN

CHECKING IN: All the expected national chains are here — most of them immediately off I-465, which rings the city, or I-65, which run diagonally through it. Inexpensive doubles run under $45, moderately priced rooms range from $45 to $70, expensive rooms from $90 to $130, and very expensive from $130 up. Rates are usually higher during Indianapolis 500 weekend and the National Drags. Call the *Indiana Tourism Development Division* (phone: 800-2WANDER) for a list of local bed and breakfast facilities. All telephone numbers are in the 317 area code unless otherwise indicated.

Canterbury – A small, European-style luxury hostelry, two blocks from Union Station. It offers 102 rooms, skylighted penthouse suites, and a Mercedes stretch limo (once owned by Frank Sinatra) to whisk guests to the airport. Its romantic *Beaulieu* restaurant specializes in French cuisine. 123 S. Illinois St. (phone: 317-634-3000). Very expensive.

Embassy Suites Downtown – All accommodations here are fully equipped suites — 360 of them — each with bedroom, living room, and kitchenette. The hotel also has a pool, 2 hot tubs, and a sauna and steamroom. Complimentary services include full cooked-to-order American breakfast and limousine service to and from the airport. The first 3 floors of the building make up the Claypool complex of shops and restaurants. Illinois and Washington Sts. (phone: 236-1800). Expensive.

Hilton at the Circle – The glass elevator that rises and falls through the 370-room hotel allows riders to look out at Monument Circle. 34 W. Ohio (phone: 635-2000). Expensive.

Hyatt Regency Indianapolis – An imposing red brick edifice built around a 20-story central atrium lobby. With 496 rooms, 6 restaurants, lounges, and shops. 1 S. Capitol Ave., opposite the Convention Center (phone: 632-1234). Expensive.

Radisson Plaza – Within walking distance of some of the city's best shops and restaurants, it's convenient as well as comfortable. Amenities include a pool, Jacuzzi, exercise room, and men's and women's saunas. 8787 Keystone Crossing (phone: 846-2700 or 800-333-3333). Expensive.

Westin – Now the largest hotel in the state (572 rooms), it opened in 1989 across from the Indiana Convention Center. The restaurant features an open grill and buffet, and the lobby lounge has an espresso counter. The 39,000 square feet of meeting and banquet space can handle receptions for up to 1,000. 50 S. Capitol Ave. (phone: 262-8100 or 800-228-3000). Expensive.

Riverpointe – Just 2 miles from the center of downtown, this hotel features 1-, 2-, and 3-bedroom suites with fully equipped kitchens and separate living and dining areas. Complimentary coffee in the lobby. Pool and exercise facilities available. 1150 N. White River Pky., West Dr. (phone: 638-9866 or 800-445-4005). Expensive to moderate.

Holiday Inn North – Features a beautiful Holidome, a small sports complex with a pool, Jacuzzi, saunas, and other facilities for rest and relaxation. 3850 DePauw Blvd. (phone: 872-9790 or 800-HOLIDAY). Moderate.

Sheraton Meridian – In a neighborhood of older, well-maintained apartment buildings, this 294-room property is close to the *Children's Museum.* Pleasant and modern, it has an indoor-outdoor swimming pool, a sundeck, and a health club. 2820 N. Meridian (phone: 924-1241 or 800-325-3535). Moderate.

Tower Inn – Approximately 5 blocks from I-65, just north of downtown, and one of the best bargains near downtown. Spacious rooms include sofas that open into queen-size beds. Meeting rooms handle up to 75 people. 1633 N. Capitol Ave. (phone: 925-9831). Moderate.

Days Inn South – The pleasant swimming pool makes the typical low rates especially noteworthy. On US 31 south and I-465 (phone: 788-0811 or 800-325-2525). Inexpensive.

Indianapolis Motor Speedway Motel – Next to the racetrack, it has many amenities, including a golf course next to the *Speedway Museum* and an outdoor heated pool. 4400 W. 16th St. (phone: 317 241-2500). Inexpensive.

 EATING OUT: Indianapolis has always had more than its share of steak-and-baked-potato places and very few notable ethnic eateries. But this situation is changing. In addition to the variety of foods available at the places listed below, the revamped Union Station (phone: 637-1888) features over 40 eateries with every imaginable type of fare. You'll pay $40 and up for a meal for two in restaurants listed below as expensive, $25 to $30 at those marked moderate, and less than $20 at inexpensive places. Prices do not include drinks, wine, or tips. All telephone numbers are in the 317 area code unless otherwise indicated.

Chanteclair sur le Toit – Entrées and desserts are flambéed at the table while strolling violinists entertain. Veal Oscar is among the continental specialties. Open for dinner only; closed Sundays. Reservations recommended. Major credit cards. At the *Holiday Inn–Airport,* 2501 S. High School Rd. (phone: 243-1040). Expensive.

Glass Chimney – Some of the city's best continental fare appears on the carefully set tables of this consistently fine establishment in a charming old house. Open for dinner daily except Sundays. Reservations necessary. Major credit cards. 12901 N. Meridian (phone: 844-0921). Expensive.

Jonathon's – English country accents fill the four dining rooms of this tasteful place specializing in American cuisine. They also do a fine New York strip, veal Oscar, and prime ribs. Darts, backgammon, and chess are played in the Old English-style pub. Open for lunch and dinner daily; brunch served from 10:30 AM to 2 PM on Sundays. Reservations advised. Major credit cards. 96th and Keystone Ave. (phone: 844-1155). Expensive.

New Orleans House – Visit this relatively plain establishment with a very empty stomach. Unless you're ravenous, it's impossible to do justice to the extravagant all-you-can-eat seafood buffet. Allow 2½ to 3 hours to consume your fill of oysters and clams on the half shell, chowders and Créole dishes, crab legs and lobster. Open daily for dinner only. Reservations required. Major credit cards. 8845 Township Line Rd. (phone: 872-9670). Expensive.

Peter's – Dining here is more than a nutritional experience. An exclusive, small (only 52 seats) place with a constantly changing menu, it features fresh seasonal Midwest cuisine prepared with an innovative flair. Dinners include lamb, veal, Black Angus beef, game meats, and fresh fish. There's also an extensive wine list. Reservations advised. Major credit cards. 936 Virginia Ave. (phone: 637-9333). Expensive.

San Remo – The 20-minute drive from downtown is worth the effort for the Northern Italian dishes, elegant and cheery atmosphere, and excellent wine selection. Dinner is not complete without a dessert of zabaglione. In the *Holiday Inn North*, 3850 DePauw Blvd. (phone: 872-3434). Expensive.

Tower at the Heliport – One of the specialties of the house is the special dining package for couples that includes a ride in an executive helicopter before dinner. 51 S. New Jersey St. (phone: 262-3020). Expensive.

Waterson's – Entrées prepared by this kitchen vary, based on what's freshest and best at the market. Always on the menu, however, is the house's special sinful dessert, the Chocolate Concord. Closed Sundays. Reservations advised. Major credit cards. *Radisson Plaza,* 8787 Keystone Crossing (phone: 846-2700). Expensive.

Adam's Rib – Prime ribs are the specialty, but fresh fish is flown in daily, and the menu always lists one exotic viand like venison, rattlesnake, or antelope. The salad bar is one of the best in town. Open for lunch on weekdays, for dinner except Sundays. Reservations advised. Major credit cards accepted. 40 S. Main, in Zionsville (see *Special Places;* phone: 873-3301). Expensive to moderate.

Fletcher's American Grill & Café – *Fletcher's* has two dining concepts: the *Grill* specializes in food grilled over mesquite charcoal and served in an informal setting; the *Café* specializes in new American cooking, in a more formal setting. Reservations adivsed. Major credit cards. 107 S. Pennsylvania St. (phone: 632-2500). Expensive to moderate.

St. Elmo's – A local tradition since 1902 for steaks, chops, the hottest shrimp cocktails this side of Hades, and fine wines, and as wonderful as ever. Open for dinner daily except Sundays. Reservations advised. Major credit cards. 127 S. Illinois (phone: 635-0636). Expensive to moderate.

Forbidden City – The menu here is extensive; in fact, it's several pages long. Chinese, Hunan, Szechwan, and Mandarin food is prepared by a top chef and tastefully served in an elegant Oriental atmosphere. Open daily for lunch and dinner. Reservations recommended. Major credit cards. 2605 E. 65th St. at Keystone Ave. (phone: 257-7388). Moderate.

Hollyhock Hill – One of Indianapolis's several family-style restaurants. Steaks, fried chicken, and vegetables in generous portions. Open Tuesdays through Sundays for dinner, for lunch on Sundays. Reservations advised. Major credit cards. 8110 N. College Ave. (phone: 251-2294). Moderate.

Key West Shrimp House – The seafood and steaks are as good now as when the place opened 40 years ago. Closed Sundays. Reservations advised. Major credit cards. 2861 Madison Ave. (phone: 787-5353). Moderate.

Milano Inn – The best place for Italian fare. Open daily for lunch and dinner. Reservations advised. Major credit cards. 231 S. College Ave. (phone: 632-8834). Moderate.

Bar-B-Q Heaven, Inc. – Carry-out and delivery of barbecue to downtown hotels and motels from 10 PM to 4 AM daily except Sundays. Hickory-smoked ribs, rib tips, chicken, shoulder, corn beef, giant barbecue on a bun sandwiches, salads, and sweet potato pie. 2515 Martin Luther King St. (phone: 926-1667). Moderate to inexpensive.

City Taproom & Grille – From hand-cut steaks, grilled chicken, and seafood to artichokes or hearty sandwiches, the camaraderie of this downtown pub is enhanced nightly with live jazz. Reservations advised. Major credit cards. 28 S. Pennsylvania St. (phone: 637-1334). Moderate to inexpensive.

Mark Pi's China Gate – Gourmet Mandarin, Hunan, and Szechuan dishes, reasonably priced. No MSG. Reservations advised. Major credit cards. 135 S. Illinois St. (phone: 631-6757). Moderate to inexpensive.

Parthenon – Surrounded by the boutiques of Broad Ripple Village, diners feast on absolutely authentic Greek and Middle Eastern cuisine. The spanokopita, a pastry filled with spinaeh and feta cheese, is especially good. On Friday and Saturday nights, a belly dancer entertains the patrons. Open daily for lunch and dinner. Reservations advised. Major credit cards. 6319 Guilford Ave. (phone: 251-3138). Moderate to inexpensive.

Shapiro's – Indianapolis's best deli, with food served cafeteria style. Open daily for lunch and dinner. No reservations or credit cards. 808 S. Meridian (phone: 631-4041). Moderate to inexpensive.

Acapulco Joe's – Potent spices and five flavorful cheeses make this Tex-Mex restaurant's servings of enchiladas, soft tacos, burritos, enchiladas, and tostadas a cut above the rest. 365 N. Illinois St. (phone: 637-5160). Inexpensive.

MCL Cafeterias – Ten locations in the city offer homemade fried chicken, vegetables, cinnamon rolls, and pies. Open daily. No reservations. No credit cards. For general information, phone 257-5425. Inexpensive.

Paramount Music Palace – A lively family pizza place and ice cream parlor that features "the mighty Wurlitzer theater pipe organ," which plays all kinds of music. The sing-alongs and silent movies are also popular. Closed Mondays. No reservations or credit cards. I-465 at E. Washington St. (phone: 352-0144). Inexpensive.

KANSAS CITY, MO

Surrounded by rich farmlands and grazing fields, Kansas City owes a lot to its agricultural heritage, and agribusiness is the backbone of its economy. Kansas City is first in the nation as a farm distribution center and hard wheat market; second in grain elevator capacity; third as a feeder cattle market. However, don't expect to hear any of these sterling statistics from the average — and always helpful — Kansas City person-in-the-street. Residents are skittish as wild horses about anything that seems to reinforce Kansas City's ingrained "cowtown" image.

For most of its 130-year history, travelers have regarded Kansas City as a one-night stand between the Rockies and Chicago. Residents, naturally, don't see it that way. With more than a million people tucked away in the urban area of rolling woodland, limestone bluffs, and the Kansas and Missouri rivers, Kansas City is the heart of the "breadbasket of the world." It is called the City of Fountains, because of its hundreds of beautiful fountains, many of them European; some, centuries old. It is also a city of art. J. C. Nichols, developer of the Country Club Plaza and residential district, imported more than a million dollars' worth of statuary and other art in the 1920s, not for museums, but for the boulevards and parkways. In fact, Kansas City has more boulevards than Paris — 140 miles of wide, graceful, tree-lined streets and parkways.

But the resemblance to Paris does not extend to the cold, haughty condescension that Parisians show to outsiders. A visitor to Kansas City will inevitably be asked — and asked — what he or she thinks of the place. It may even get a little annoying, but Kansas City folk are self-conscious about their hick-town image and go out of their way to ask a lot of well-meaning questions to reassure you and make sure you're having a good time.

The *Nelson-Atkins Museum of Art is* one of the top museums in the United States. Classical music events, repertory drama, and a wide range of pop concerts provide enough entertainment to keep anybody busy. Kansas City's breezy, contented lifestyle has a lot to do with its increasing popularity. Dynamic, without succumbing to a frantic pace, Kansas City has been experiencing a rapid but orderly growth cycle — one, however, that has not disturbed its fluid rhythm of life. It is a center of gracious living, magnificent mansions, and old wealth.

The city has certainly come a long way from the days of Rodgers and Hammerstein's musical *Oklahoma!* In those days, according to the song, Kansas City "went and built a skyscraper seven stories high — about as high as a building ought to go." A number of private building ventures are still changing the skyline with complexes like the Crown Center, the overwhelming "city within a city," and Westport Square, which is filled with young shopkeepers and artisans who have re-created the charm of old Kansas City

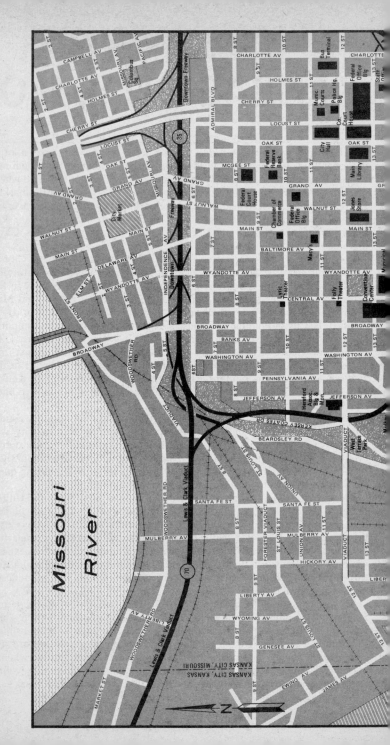

CENTRAL
KANSAS CITY, MO

by restoring the century-old buildings. The nation's first shopping center, Country Club Plaza, resembles a tile-roofed Moorish city rather than an impersonal suburban behemoth of glass and brick. But some things Rodgers and Hammerstein wrote still apply. Everything is "up to date in Kansas City," and visitors are more often than not delightfully surprised to find it beautiful as well.

KANSAS CITY AT-A-GLANCE

SEEING THE CITY: One of the best views of Kansas City is from the Observation Tower on the 30th floor of City Hall. Open weekdays. No admission charge. Oak between 12th and 13th Sts. (phone: 274-2000). Even more dramatic is the view from atop the Liberty Memorial, the great limestone column at the south edge of the downtown area, from which you'll see massive Union Station (second in size only to New York's Grand Central), the downtown skyline, and Crown Center. Closed Sundays and Mondays. Admission charge. Memorial Dr. just west of 27th and Main Sts.

SPECIAL PLACES: Kansas City's three major shopping complexes are self-contained units in which a visitor can be immersed for an entire day.

Crown Center – This $300-million development is the brainchild of the late Joyce Hall, founder of Hallmark Cards. We suggest starting out from the lobby of the super-elegant *Westin Crown Center* hotel, dominated by a tropical rain forest and waterfall that winds its way down the limestone hillside on which the hotel was built. Then move on to the shops, where more than 50 stores offer everything from fine art to frivolities. 2450 Grand (phone: 274-8444).

Westport Square – "Westward, ho!" used to echo across the field that is now Westport Square. It was here that pioneers outfitted themselves for the great journey west. Although times have changed, the tradition of seeking out supplies at Westport Square is solidly implanted in the consciousness of Kansas City residents. A lot of work has gone into restoring the old buildings, many of which date to the 1850s. Broadway at Westport Rd. (phone: 931-2855).

Country Club Plaza – A few blocks south of Westport Square, Country Club Plaza is an adult's Disneyland. More than $1 million worth of statues, fountains, and murals line the shaded walks of this spectacular Spanish- and Moorish-style residential shopping center with over 150 shops, restaurants, and nightclubs. 4629 Wornall Rd. (phone: 753-0100).

Nelson-Atkins Museum of Art – The *Nelson* is renowned for its comprehensive collection of art, from the ancient Sumerian civilization (3000 BC) to works by contemporaries. Egyptian, Greek, Roman, and medieval sculpture and a reconstructed medieval cloister make this more than just a museum of Old Masters, although there are plenty of classics on the walls — Titian, Rembrandt, El Greco, Goya, the Impressionists, Van Gogh — and contemporary Andy Warhol. It also houses a fine Oriental collection and the largest collection of works by British sculptor Henry Moore in the US. Closed Mondays, major holidays. Admission charge. 4525 Oak St. (phone: 561-4000).

Swope Park – This 1,772-acre park has two golf courses, a swimming pool, picnic areas, a zoo, and the *Starlight Theater* (phone: 333-9481), where popular musicals and concerts are performed in the summer under the stars. 5600 E. Gregory.

Kansas City Stockyards – At the nation's largest stocker and feeder market, you can see what a Kansas City steak looks like on the hoof. Depending on how you react to the cattlemen in action, you may or may not look forward to a hefty meal of the beef that helped make Kansas City famous. There are frequent cattle auctions at the stockyards. Visitors are welcome at the Sales Pavilion of the Livestock Building on Tuesdays, Wednesdays, and Thursdays. 16th and Genesee (phone: 842-6800).

Benjamin Stables on the Santa Fe Trail – This complex of barns, fields, and a blacksmith's shop re-creates an early western town. Horse-drawn carts, wagons, and carriages are visible everywhere. There are sleigh rides and hayrides, and horseback riding for those who want to ride the old Santa Fe Trail. Call one day in advance for a tour. Open 365 days a year. 6401 E. 87th at I-435 (phone: 761-5055).

Worlds of Fun – This 140-acre family theme park has more than 60 rides. The adjacent Oceans of Fun (phone: 459-9283) is a huge aquatic park that's open in the summer. Worlds of Fun is open daily from June until early September; weekends only from mid-April to late May and in September and October. Admission charge. On I-435, just north of the Missouri River, at Parvin Rd. (phone: 454-4545).

Missouri River Excursions – A relaxing way to spend a few hours. Riverboat cruises leave from Kaw Point in Kansas City, Kansas, just a few blocks west of downtown. Cruises usually operate from April through mid-December. (phone: 842-0027).

■**EXTRA SPECIAL:** Just 8 miles east of downtown Kansas City, in Independence, Missouri, is the *Harry S. Truman Library and Museum.* Remember "The buck stops here"? So should you if you're a Truman fan. Even if you're not, you might become one after a visit. Open daily except Thanksgiving and New Year's Day. Admission charge for adults; children and educational groups free. On US 24 at Delaware (phone: 833-1225). While you're there, stop for a meal at *Stephenson's Apple Farm.* Just up the road a piece from the *Truman Library and Museum* is Ft. Osage, a reconstruction of the trading post established by explorer William Clark of the famous Lewis and Clark team. Open daily during daylight hours. About 22 miles northeast of Independence on US 24, in Sibley, Missouri (phone: 249-5737).

SOURCES AND RESOURCES

TOURIST INFORMATION: The Kansas City Convention and Visitors Bureau has a 24-hour hotline (phone: 474-9600) for the latest information on city activities. It also provides brochures, maps, and a restaurant and hotel guide. City Center Square Bldg., Suite 2550, 1100 Main St., Kansas City, MO 64105 (phone: 221-5242).

Television Stations – KCTV Channel 5–CBS; KMBC Channel 9–ABC; WDAF Channel 4–NBC; KCPT Channel 19–PBS.

Radio Station – AM: KCMO 810 (news/talk).

Local Coverage – *Kansas City Times,* morning daily; *Kansas City Star,* afternoon daily.

Food – *The Kansas City Restaurant Guide,* free from the Convention and Visitors Bureau.

Telephone – The area code for Kansas City, Missouri, is 816.

Sales Tax – The sales tax in Kansas City is 6⅛%.

CLIMATE: Kansas City's midwestern climate is notorious. It's fine in the spring and fall, but the winters are rough (frequently the thermometer never rises above freezing in January), and the summers are hot and humid. Rain is particularly likely in spring.

GETTING AROUND: Airport – Kansas City International Airport is usually a 30- to 40-minute drive into the city; cab fare should run about $25 to $30. If cabs are not readily available at the airport, call the dispatcher at 471-5000. The green KCI Airport Express buses run from the airport to the major downtown and Plaza area hotels every 30 minutes, on the hour and half-hour. Tickets are $10 and can be purchased at Gate 63 in Terminal C (take the inter-airport red buses to this terminal). Return schedules vary; ask for a timetable at your hotel or call 243-5950.

Bus – The Kansas City Metro Bus covers the downtown area (phone: 221-0660).

Taxi – Call *Yellow Cab* (phone: 471-5000).

Car Rental – The best way to see Kansas City is by car. Major rental firms are represented.

Trolley – One of the best ways to see major sites is from the open-air trolleys that go from the Plaza, through Westport and Crown Center shopping centers, to downtown and back again. The trolleys (named Molly, Dolly, Polly, etc.) stop at the special trolley signs in the aforementioned shopping districts between March and December. A ride costs $2. The chatty drivers will fill you in on sights along the way. Kansas City Trolley Corp. (phone: 221-3399).

LOCAL SERVICES: Business Services – *AAA Secretarial Service*, 406 W. 34th St. (phone: 531-4615).

    Mechanic – *Glenn Freely Auto Repair*, 1922 Baltimore (phone: 421-2436).

MUSEUMS: The *Nelson-Atkins Museum of Art* and the *Harry S. Truman Library and Museum* are described in *Special Places*. Other fine Kansas City museums include the following:

    Agriculture Hall of Fame – I-70 to Bonner Springs (phone: 721-1075).

1859 Jail and Museum – 217 N. Main St., Independence (phone: 252-1892).

Kansas City Museum of History and Science – 3218 Gladstone (phone: 483-8300).

Liberty Memorial Museum – The country's only museum devoted to World War I. Memorial Dr. just west of 27th and Main Sts.; no admission charge.

Shawnee Methodist Mission and Indian Manual Labor School – Indian Mission, 53rd and Mission Rd., Fairway, Kansas (phone: 913-262-0867).

Wornall House – Civil War restoration, 61 Terrace and Wornall (phone: 444-1858).

MAJOR COLLEGES AND UNIVERSITIES: The University of Missouri–Kansas City, 51st and Rockhill Rd. (phone: 276-1000).

SPECIAL EVENTS: The *American Royal Horse and Livestock Show*, November, at *Kemper Arena*, 1700 Wyoming (phone: 421-6460). The *Renaissance Festival of Kansas City* runs for 6 weekends each fall, beginning Labor Day. The *RenFest*, a popular re-creation of 16th-century life, features musicians, courtiers, knights, actors, acrobats, craftspeople, and lots of food and drink. It takes place on 40 wooded acres at the *Agricultural Hall of Fame* in Bonner Springs, just 20 minutes west of downtown on I-70 (phone: 561-8005).

SPORTS AND FITNESS: Kansas City has professional baseball, indoor soccer, and football teams.

    Baseball – The *Royals, Harry S. Truman Sports Complex*, I-70 and Blue Ridge Cutoff (phone: 921-8000).

Basketball – The fightin' *Kangaroos* of the University of Missouri–Kansas City play home games in *Municipal Auditorium,* downtown (phone: 276-2700).

Bicycling – Bikes can be rented in summer at *Shelter House One* in Swope Park, at the main entrance, Swope Pkwy. and Meyer Blvd.

Fitness Centers – *Meadowbrook Athletic Club* offers pools, exercise equipment, aerobics classes, and a track, 5030 Main St., on the plaza (phone: 753-6767); *Town & Country Health Club,* on the 5th floor of the *Crown Center* hotel, has a pool, steam room, sauna, and coed whirlpool, 1 Pershing Rd., in Crown Center (phone: 474-4400).

Football – The NFL Kansas City *Chiefs, Harry S. Truman Sports Complex,* I-70 and Blue Ridge Cutoff (phone: 924-9400).

Golf – The best is at *River Oaks,* 140 and US 71, in Grandview (phone: 966-8111).

Horseback Riding – *Benjamin Ranch on the Old Santa Fe Trail,* 6401 E. 87th at I-435 (phone: 761-5055).

Indoor Soccer – The *Comets,* of the National Indoor Soccer League, hold forth in *Kemper Arena* from November through March (phone: 421-7770).

Jogging – Penn Valley Park, near the *Crown Center* hotel (25th to 33rd St. and Pershing Rd.); Jacob L. Loose Park inner and outer loops, 1½ blocks from the Alameda Plaza; Ward Parkway, a large, lovely boulevard (pick it up at the Alameda and run south). An excellent jogging and exercise trail is in Mill Creek Park, just east of the Plaza.

Tennis – There are more than 200 public tennis courts in the Kansas City metro area. Most are free. Swope Park has good courts at the picnic area north of the *Starlight Theater.* At 4747 Nichols Parkway, there are year-round courts.

 THEATER: For the latest information on theater and musical events, call 474-9600. The city's *Theater League* (phone: 421-7500) presents touring companies of Broadway hits in the *Midland Center for the Performing Arts,* 1228 Main, and produces its own shows in the intimate *Quality Hill Playhouse* at 10th and Central Sts. Dramatic and musical productions are also booked into the *Music Hall* in the *Municipal Auditorium,* 200 W 13th (phone: 421-8000); at the *Lyric Theater,* 10th and Central (phone: 471-7344); and the *Folly Theatre,* 12th and Central (phone: 842-5500). From July to September and January to March, the *Missouri Repertory Theatre* performs in the *Spencer Theater* on the UMKC campus (phone: 276-2704). The *Starlight Theater* in Swope Park, an under-the-stars amphitheater, features musical comedy and concerts with top-name stars from May to mid-September (phone: 333-9481). Kansas City has two dinner playhouses, *Tiffany's Attic,* 5028 Main (phone: 561-7921); and the *Waldo* (*not* Waldorf) *Astoria,* 7428 Washington (phone: 561-9876). The newest addition to the city's theater inventory is the *American Heartland Theater,* in Crown Center (phone: 842-9999). Fans of Off-Broadway shows should check out the *Unicorn Theater,* 3820 Main (phone: 531-7529). There are two fine children's theaters: *Theater for Young America,* 7204 W. 80th in suburban Overland Park (phone: 648-4600), and the *Coterie* in the Crown Center complex (phone: 474-6552).

 MUSIC: For up-to-date data on concert happenings, call 474-9600 or check the newspapers. The *Kansas City Symphony* season, from November through May, features internationally known conductors and soloists. Performances are held on Friday and Saturday nights and Sunday afternoons in the *Lyric Theater,* 11th and Central (phone: 471-7344). There are two opera seasons, in April and October at the *Lyric.* The operas are sung in English. Jazz still thrives in Kansas City; call the *Municipal Jazz Commission* hotline (phone: 931-2888) for information on jazz events. Another good source of information on current musical offerings is the *Concert Connection* (phone: 276-1171), sponsored by the UMKC Conservatory of Music. To find out who's playing at the clubs, check the arts section of the Sunday *Kansas City Star* or pick up a copy of the *Penny Pitch,* free at most record stores.

NIGHTCLUBS AND NIGHTLIFE: In the last decade, Kansas City's after-dark scene has picked up so that now it's one of the most lively in the Midwest. Because of its bistate location, liquor laws in Kansas City are a bit confusing. In Missouri, bars may remain open until 1 AM; clubs with cabaret licenses, until 3 AM. Bars are closed on Sundays, but hotels and restaurants may still serve liquor. Kansans approved a liquor-by-the-drink referendum in the fall of 1986, but counties may implement it at any time. This means that in Kansas you encounter taverns selling only 3.2 beer, restaurants with full-service bars, or private clubs requiring memberships. Singles action is liveliest at *Houlihan's Old Place,* 4743 Pennsylvania (phone: 561-3141), and at the *Longbranch Saloon,* (phone: 931-2755) in nearby Seville Square, 500 Nichols Rd. Best bet for out-of-towners is to park on the Plaza or near Westport Square and barhop. There are dozens of clubs and bars — some with live entertainment — within easy walking distance of each other. Westport Square is very casual; the Plaza is a bit more formal, and some restaurant-bars require a coat and tie. The best gay bars are on Main St. between 50th and 51st Sts.

BEST IN TOWN

CHECKING IN: Expect to pay $90 and up for a double in hotels categorized as expensive; and $70 to $80 in those places designated as moderate. All telephone numbers are in the 816 area code unless otherwise indicated.

Alameda Plaza – A sumptuous building with 392 elegantly appointed rooms in beautifully landscaped grounds on Country Club Plaza. Wornall Rd. at Ward Pkwy. (phone: 756-1500). Expensive.

Westin Crown Center – Built on a huge chunk of limestone known as Signboard Hill, because of the commercial embellishments that used to decorate it, this 730-room ultramodern hotel is part of the Crown Center complex. It integrates the limestone face of the hill into the lobby, where there is a winding stream, 5-story waterfall, and tropical rain forest. It has several restaurants, including *Trader Vic's,* and numerous shops and boutiques. 1 Pershing Rd. in Crown Center (phone: 474-4400 or 800-228-3000). Expensive.

Hyatt Regency – Kansas City's fanciest hotel is also its most notorious since the collapse, in July 1981, of two of the three skywalks that spanned its huge, glass-topped lobby. The rubble is gone, the three suspended walks have been replaced by a single elevated ramp resting solidly on pillars, and probably no other public building in America has undergone more inspections and safety tests. South of the downtown loop; McGee at Pershing Rd. (phone: 421-1234, 800-233-1234, or 800-228-9000). Expensive.

Allis Plaza – Built on what used to be known as "the strip," where jazz and bootleg gin flowed all night in the many clubs along its length, this hotel has recaptured the spirit of this bygone era in its own ambience. Part of the major face-lift of the downtown Convention Center area, it has 572 rooms and suites, the formal *Harvest* restaurant, *Lilly's Restaurant and Wine Bar,* and the *12th Street Rag* nightclub. Features include a no smoking floor, 2 outdoor tennis courts, and a health club with indoor pool, sauna, Nautilus and David equipment, and aerobics. 200 West 12th St. (phone: 421-6800). Expensive.

Marriott Plaza – The city's newest hotel has 296 rooms and is 2 blocks from the Plaza, one block from the *Nelson Gallery,* and smack-dab on the Main Street corridor. *Reunion,* a nostalgia-themed nightclub; indoor swimming; and hydro-therapy pools and a health club are among the offerings. 4445 Main (phone: 531-3000 or 800-228-9290). Moderate to expensive.

Doubletree – The once-sleepy bedroom community of Johnson County, Kansas, is now buzzing with business thanks to the industrial growth along I-435 and I-35 southwest of downtown Kansas City. The sumptuous *Doubletree* is geared to the needs of visitors with business in that part of town. 10100 College Blvd. (phone: 913-451-6100). Moderate.

Hilton Airport Plaza Inn – Ideal if you're more interested in traveling than down-town sightseeing. In addition to 360 comfortable rooms, there are 2 heated swim-ming pools — indoor and outdoor; a sauna, a whirlpool bath, a health club, putting green, and tennis courts, as well as 2 dining rooms, a coffee shop, and bar with entertainment. I-29 and NW 112th St. (phone: 891-8900 or 800-HILTONS). Moderate.

EATING OUT: Kansas City has great steaks and good French food. Its pride and joy, however, is barbecue. Visitors can select a high-priced haute cuisine restaurant or one that will provide superb food at more moderate prices — although you'll find Kansas City prices reasonable everywhere. We rec-ommend calling ahead for reservations at all the places listed below. Expect to pay $45 or more for dinner for two at those places listed as expensive; $25 to $35 at those places listed as moderate; under $20 at restaurants listed as inexpensive. Prices do not include drinks, wines, or tips. All telephone numbers are in the 816 area code unless otherwise indicated.

Alameda Rooftop – This is a great place from which to see the glittering city spread below while dining on excellent roast rack of lamb, seafood, and beef. Reservations are especially necessary if you want to sit near a window. Open daily. All credit cards. Ward and Wornall on the plaza (phone: 756-1500). Expensive.

American – Many Kansas City people say this is the best in town. Certainly, it's the fanciest. The *American* has French moderne decor and a menu featuring bluepoint oysters on the half shell, veal medallions sautéed with shrimp and artichokes, pheasant and quail, rainbow trout with pan-fried walnuts, and carpet-bagger steaks filled with oysters. Open daily. Major credit cards. In the *Crown Center* hotel, 25th and Grand (phone: 471-8050). Expensive.

Bristol Bar and Grill – One of the best seafood restaurants in the Midwest is found at the Country Club Plaza. A New York actress who eats here when she's in town says the fish is better than back home on Long Island. The decor is a pleasant blend of Victorian architecture and modern art; ask to be seated in the back room beneath the huge Tiffany leaded glass dome. The bar is a popular after-work watering hole for KC's upwardly mobile bunch. Major credit cards. 4740 Jefferson (phone: 756-0606). Expensive to moderate.

Jasper's – Not much flash, but lots of substance. In unpretentious Waldo, this may be the only eatery in town to score big on the national list of top dining spots. The cuisine is Northern Italian and extremely tasty, the decor quietly dignified, and the service impeccable. Major credit cards. 405 W. 75th St. (phone: 363-3003). Expensive.

Peppercorn Duck Club – A knockout eatery in the *Hyatt Regency.* The decor is Olde English and the food is sumptuous, especially the roast duckling. The choco-late dessert bar is appropriately sinful and the service is attentive almost to a fault — it's hard to sniffle without someone handing you a hankie. Major credit cards. McGee at Pershing Rd. (phone: 421-1234). Expensive to moderate.

Café Allegro – Kansas City's nod to affordable fine dining, the *Allegro* has a Bohemian feel and an ever-changing menu to weep over. Be on the lookout for the black and blue salmon, veal loin stuffed with wild mushrooms, baby baked halibut in phyllo, and the breast of chicken Mougin. 1815 W. 39th St. (phone: 561-3663). Moderate.

Golden Ox – In the heart of the stockyards, near *Kemper Arena,* where the wranglers who work the steer take their food breaks. Good, solid American cooking here, and arguably the best steaks in town, served with potato, garlic bread, and salad. Open daily. Call to see if reservations are necessary. All credit cards. 1600 Genesee (phone: 842-2866). Moderate.

Savoy Grill – A turn-of-the-century restaurant cherished by Kansas City residents that serves very fine seafood and steaks. The most outstanding feature of the *Savoy* is its 1903 Victorian mirrored bar and stained glass windows, giving you the feel of early Kansas City. Closed Sundays. Major credit cards. 9th and Central (phone: 842-3890). Moderate.

Stephenson's Apple Farm – Down-home cooking has made this fine restaurant's reputation. Hickory-smoked pork ribs, chicken gizzards, beef brisket, steaks, and homemade pie in a rustic American setting make this well worth a trip out to Independence, even if you have no interest in Harry S. Truman. Open daily. Major credit cards. US 40 at Lea's Summit Rd., South Independence (phone: 373-5400). Moderate.

Houlihan's Old Place – A casual dining spot serving trendy, "fun foods": blackened Cajun dishes, barbecue, teriyaki, quiches, omelettes, and croissant sandwiches. Lavishly decorated in Gay '90s style, some people say it looks like a Wild West bordello. Decide for yourself. Open till the wee hours, daily. Major credit cards. 4743 Pennsylvania, Country Club Plaza (phone: 561-3141). Moderate to inexpensive.

And finally, a note on barbecue: Kansas Citians are a peaceful lot, but you can always start a fight about who has the best ribs in town. Calvin Trillin, in his book, American Fried, claimed that *Arthur Bryant's Barbecue,* on the east side of town, was America's best restaurant. Trillin's pronouncement may have been rib-in-cheek, but there's no doubt that, given their druthers, Kansas Citians would just as soon eat barbecue as anything else. Our advice is to check the phone book, snoop around and ask locals what they prefer — and why. There's a wide choice, from *Gates & Sons* to *Richard's Famous Bar-B-Q, Heyward's Pit, Zarda's,* and a dozen more. Most are differentiated by their sauces, which range from sweet and thick to thin and peppery. There's surely a perfect one for your taste. Don't forget the dental floss.

LAS VEGAS

There may be no other place on earth so forbidding and yet so alluring as Las Vegas, that glittering oasis in the midst of mountainous Nevada desert. To some it's a 24-hour city of fantasy, to others an unending nightmare. How you feel about it may just depend on your tolerance for the phantasmagorical. But whether it's loved as a vacation paradise or damned as "Sin City," the maze of contradictions that are bred here make the place fascinating.

With the legalization of gambling in Atlantic City and the probability of legalization elsewhere, a new age is dawning. Since the 1940s, Las Vegas has reigned as the unchallenged gambling resort of the world, and it is not about to surrender its throne without a fight. A sense of competition has swept the city, and several of the older hotels have received dramatic face-lifts while the new structures that continue to spring up place special emphasis on extras and freebies. Bring along a sweater for the indoors; powerful air conditioners are at work everywhere. Dress is casual during the day; at night the showtime dress can be formal and elegant, but it's optional.

Visitors are shown one face of Las Vegas: the façade of "Entertainment Capital of the World." But this doesn't begin to describe it. The cavernous air conditioned vastness of countless Strip casinos aims at total sensory bombardment with a maelstrom of sights and sounds: the ringing bells and flashing lights of the slot machines, the rolling wheels of fortune, the dice dancing on the green tables, the smoke-filled air mixed with a heavy undercurrent of free-flowing alcohol. Throngs of people crowd the casinos at every hour of the day and night. In Las Vegas, time doesn't matter. There are no clocks in the casinos, and many places serve breakfast and dinner 24 hours a day at such bargain prices that it might make sense to eat both at one sitting. Cocktail waitresses keep the thirst quenched by bringing drinks on the house for those gambling steadily. The casinos offer these extras so that Vegas visitors can spend their time indulging in the town's one overwhelming obsession — the desire to gamble. If gratification is not found instantly, there is a choice of a few hundred other places whose neon signs blare bigger and better attractions. By the way, it is considered the height of gauche insensitivity to forget to tip a dealer working for you on your big win. Local protocol dictates that you toss a few largish chips his or her way. Never openly hand over money. This could be considered even worse than doing nothing, and the dealer will not be able to accept the gratuity.

Just venture outside on the Strip (in Las Vegas, going outside is a big step) and you will see one after another huge hotel-casino: *Caesars Palace,* the *Sahara,* the *Sands, Aladdin, Bally's.* The names promise magic, but it's mostly an optical illusion. Underneath those opulent exteriors and plush decors is a foundation of sand. Certainly, some of the biggest names in entertainment perform here and everyone flocks to see them, but the real

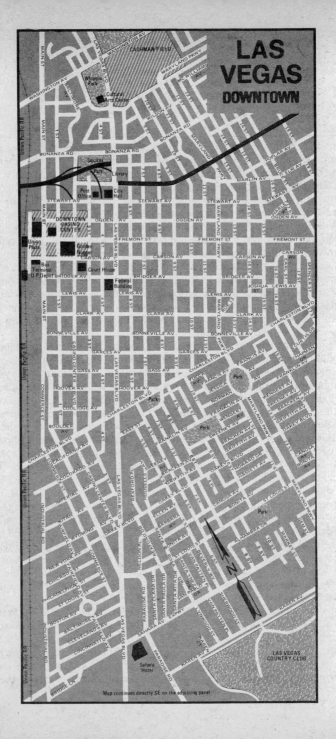

LAS VEGAS DOWNTOWN

Map continues directly SE on the adjoining panel

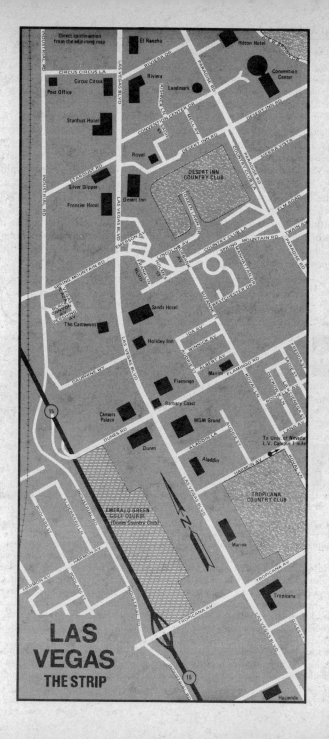

Direct continuation from the adjoining map

El Rancho

Hilton Hotel

JOE W. BROWN AV

Convention Center

CIRCUS CIRCUS LA

Circus Circus

Riviera

RIVIERA DR

PARADISE RD

Post Office

LAS VEGAS BLVD

INDUSTRIAL RD

Landmark

Stardust Hotel

KISHNER LV. CENTER DR

CONVENTION CENTER DR

DESERT INN RD

HILLWAY

Royal

Silver Slipper

STARDUST RD

Desert Inn

DESERT INN COUNTRY CLUB

SIERRA VISTA

COUNTRY CLUB LA

Frontier Hotel

LINCOLN AV

GREEN LAWN DR

ELY ROAD

INDUSTRIAL RD

EMERSON AV

FRANKLIN

HOLMES

COUNTRY CLUB LA

SPRING MOUNTAIN RD

TWAIN AV

PARADISE RD

LISBON

SPRING MOUNTAIN RD

MANHATTAN ST

SWEENEY ST

WESTCHESTER DR

BLACK CANYON

PERSHING AV

Sands Hotel

The Castaways

IDA AV

WINNICK AV

Holiday Inn

ALBERT AV

DAUPHINE WY

DUCHESS ST

KOVAL LN

LAS VEGAS BLVD

Flamingo

Maxim

FLAMINGO RD

ROCHELLE AV

DECKOW LN

PADRE ST

LINK ST

Barbary Coast

Caesars Palace

MGM Grand

AUDRIE ST

LANA AV

DUNES RD

Dunes

ALADDIN LA

To Univ. of Nevada L.V. Campus 1 mile

KOVAL LN

Aladdin

HARMON AV

ALDERMAN LN

INDUSTRIAL RD

EMERALD GREEN GOLF COURSE (Dunes Country Club)

LAS VEGAS BLVD

TROPICANA COUNTRY CLUB

PODLANG ST

HARMON AV

Marina

POOLANG ST

TROPICANA AV

HARMON AV

Tropicana

GILES ST

LAS VEGAS BLVD

LAS VEGAS

TROPICANA AV

INDUSTRIAL RD

15

Hacienda

business is gambling; anything else is done simply to draw people to the casinos. That's the real trick and that's what keeps Las Vegas going. Money is the god here, and it created poker chips in its own image. It also created some vast resort complexes — castles built on the desert that promise paradise at the next throw of the dice.

But if you do manage to break the spell of the casinos and get outside — outside the Strip and outside town — you will discover that the world outside is worth a good deal more than the few rounds of golf or tennis between poker games. Contrary to preconceived notions of the desert as a lifeless, joyless, uniformly bland stretch of rock and sand, you will value the treeless expanse for its incredible beauty — a magnificent variety of colors, and the utter freedom of its open spaces. Within miles of Las Vegas, but on the other side of the barrier of unreality, lie the dramatic red and white sandstone formations of Red Rock Recreation Area and the subtle desert colors of the Valley of Fire. These, with the nearby cool green mountains of Mt. Charleston and the manmade Lake Mead, make the desert as attractive a proposition as the Strip.

LAS VEGAS AT-A-GLANCE

SEEING THE CITY: The *Skye Room* restaurant in *Binion's Horseshoe* hotel, 100 E. Fremont St. (phone: 387-6468), offers a panoramic view of Las Vegas. As you ascend in the glass elevator, all of downtown Las Vegas glitters around you. As you reach the top, the expanse of surrounding desert appears, and your eye is drawn to the neon of the Strip, a long stream of hotels and casinos, and, to the west, the green heights of Mt. Charleston. You can also try the *Top of the Landmark,* 364 Convention Center Dr. (phone: 733-1110), for a spectacular 360-degree view.

SPECIAL PLACES: Gambling is the name of the game in Las Vegas. The cultural aspects of the city are limited, and its history has been all but obliterated by its rapid growth. But the surrounding area is rich in outdoor diversions that can fill your days with a wide variety of non-casino pleasures, leaving the nights for the air conditioned paradise of green felt, dazzling neon, and showgirl entertainment.

THE STRIP

If gambling is the game, the Strip is the place. Shining brightly in the desert sun, this 5-mile boulevard just south of town glows more intensely at night, ablaze with the glittering opulence of a seemingly never-ending stream of hotels. The sky's the limit here, and one after another of the big hotels offer it — the *Sahara, Circus Circus, Flamingo Hilton, Holiday Casino, Riviera, Sands, Caesars Palace, Tropicana,* and *Dunes.* From slot machines, poker, and blackjack to the esoteric keno and baccarat of the casinos, to the production spectaculars with a cavalcade of stars in the main showrooms, to 24-hour breakfasts or dinners, it's all here and rolling around the clock. Las Vegas Blvd., just south of the city along US 91. A few highlights are:

Caesars Palace – Las Vegas's stab at ancient Rome, *Caesars Palace* outdoes its namesake in gaming. The only other similarities are the Romanesque names of casino areas and showroom, and the fact that cocktail waitresses and keno runners dress in distinctive mini-togas. Otherwise, it's the plushest of the plush, with more red velvet carpets than the total number of Caesar's battles. Superstars perform often; be sure to make reservations. 3570 Las Vegas Blvd. (phone: 731-7110).

Circus Circus – There's gambling on the ground and gamboling up above in this tent-shaped casino where trapeze and high-wire artists, clowns, acrobats, and dancers perform to the music of a brass band. The observation gallery at circus level is lined with food and carnival stands. Children are permitted in the gallery but not on the casino floor, so bring them along and everybody can have his or her own circus. Circus open 11 AM to midnight. No admission charge. 2880 Las Vegas Blvd. (phone: 734-0410).

Wet 'n Wild – A 26-acre family-oriented water playground with a surf lagoon, water chutes, rapids, flumes, and even pearl diving. Family rates and discount tickets are available at the Strip hotels. Open daily, May through October. On the Strip between the *Sahara* and *El Rancho* hotels.

Convention Center – One of the world's major convention destinations, this is Las Vegas's center. This modern steel structure is a million-square-foot complex that can seat 7,200 in the rotunda. On Paradise Rd., next to the *Las Vegas Hilton,* off the Strip (phone: 733-2323).

DOWNTOWN

Golden Nugget Hotel and Casino – The most spectacular hotel downtown and one of the most glamorous in Las Vegas, it has undergone a $75-million expansion and renovation. Additions include the $50-million Town House Tower with just 27 duplex suites, *Elaine's* and *Stefano's* restaurants for fine dining, the 500-seat alfresco *Carson Street* restaurant, and a 500-seat theater-ballroom. The exterior of the building has been encased in Italian marble and all the old neon is but a memory. A must-see during your visit. 129 E. Fremont St. (phone: 385-7111).

THE OUTDOORS

Hoover Dam and Lake Mead – Completed in 1936, Hoover Dam is an awesome monument to man's engineering capabilities, a 726-foot-high concrete wall that tamed the mighty Colorado River and supplies electricity to Las Vegas and California. Daily tours. Modest admission charge; no admission for children under 15. Lake Mead, produced when the Colorado backed up behind the dam, is, at 115 miles long, one of the largest manmade lakes in the world. Fishing (bass, crappie, and catfish), swimming, and boating are available year-round. The visitors center for Hoover Dam (phone: 293-8367) and headquarters of Lake Mead National Recreation Area (phone: 293-4041) are 30 minutes south of the city on Boulder Hwy. (US 93).

Mt. Charleston – Just 35 minutes north of the city, Mt. Charleston dramatically exhibits the effect of increased elevation with a wide variety of trees and wildlife. Plenty of cool fresh mountain air. During the winter months, snow covers the ground and temperatures often hover below freezing at the Lee Canyon ski slopes while vacationers swim in Las Vegas hotel pools just half an hour away. Tonopah Hwy. north to Rte. 39.

Red Rock Recreation Area – A beautiful desert locale featuring red and white hues of sandstone formations, and spectacular views of steep canyons. Just a few miles farther west, the Spring Mountain State Park has Old West buildings on a ranch that has belonged to such well-known capitalists as Howard Hughes and the German Krupp family (of armament notoriety). State rangers lead tours through the old buildings. W. Charleston Blvd., 15 and 20 miles west of the city.

■**EXTRA SPECIAL:** Just 2 hours northwest of Las Vegas lies Death Valley, the hottest, driest, and lowest area in the US. It is also starkly beautiful. The high mountains surrounding the 120-mile-long valley have isolated it, and of the 600 species of plants that have been identified there, 21 grow nowhere else on earth. The variety of the colors and textures of nature in the raw is remarkable, from the jagged bluish rock salt formations of Devil's Golf Course, to the smoothly sculpted golden dunes of Mesquite Flat, to the rich reds and purples of Telescope Peak at sunrise. Scotty's Castle, an eccentric and intricate mansion built in the middle of this expanse by a Chicago millionaire, is the area's most incongruous wonder. Because of extremely high temperatures in the summer, the best time to visit the valley is from November through April. Tonopah Hwy. north (I-95) to Beatty, then take the Death Valley Junction cutoff straight into the park. (See also *Death Valley,* DIRECTIONS.)

SOURCES AND RESOURCES

 TOURIST INFORMATION: The Las Vegas Chamber of Commerce is best for brochures, maps, suggestions, and general tourist information. 2301 E. Sahara Ave., Las Vegas, NV 89104 (phone: 457-4664).

Television Stations – KLAS Channel 8–CBS; KTNV Channel 13–ABC; KVBC Channel 3–NBC; KLVX Channel 10–PBS.

Radio Stations – AM: KORK 920 (big band); KENO 1460 (oldies). FM: KOMP 92.3 (rock 'n' roll); KYRK 97.1 (top 40); KLUC 98.5 (top 40).

Local Coverage – *Review Journal,* morning and evening daily; *Las Vegas Sun,* morning daily. Several weekly entertainment guides are available at newsstands.

Telephone – The area code for Las Vegas is 702.

Sales Tax – A tax of 6% is levied on all purchases except groceries.

 CLIMATE: In the middle of the desert, Las Vegas summers are hot and dry. Winters are pleasant and mild (but cold at night), and outdoor activity takes place year-round.

GETTING AROUND: Although Las Vegas is not really a large city, the heat, dust, and wind make walking difficult. If you are going any farther than a hundred yards or so, you'll probably do better on wheels.

Airport – McCarran International Airport is a 20-minute drive and $8 cab ride from the Strip; allow 10 minutes and $5 more to reach downtown. *Whittlesea-Bell Co.* (phone: 384-6111) provides transportation to Strip hotels for $10; to downtown hotels for $16. For return service, call 2 hours before flight time. Plan to arrive at the airport at least an hour before flight time, since the distances between the main entrance and the check-in gates are great, and the newness of the facility — which has recently undergone a $300-million expansion — can cause a bit of confusion in matching passengers with their flights.

Bus – The Las Vegas Transit System covers the downtown area and the Strip. The discount commuter ticket offers a real savings if you expect to use the buses frequently. Route information is available at 1550 Industrial Rd. (phone: 384-3540). All fares are $1.

Taxi – Cabs can be hailed in the street, ordered on the phone, or picked up at taxi stands in front of hotels. Major companies are *Whittlesea Cab* (phone: 384-6111); *Yellow Cab* (phone: 873-2227); *Checker Cab* (phone: 873-2227).

Car Rental – The large national firms serve Las Vegas, though the cheapest local service is provided by *Dollar Rent-A-Car,* at McCarran Airport (phone: 739-8408);

Abbey Rent-A-Car, 3745 Las Vegas Blvd. S. (phone: 736-4988); and *Allstate,* 5175 Rent Car Rd. (phone: 736-6147).

LOCAL SERVICES: Babysitting – *Sandy's Sitter Service,* 24-hour service, 953 E. Sahara (phone: 731-2086).

Business Services – *Manpower Temporary Services,* 314 Las Vegas Blvd. N. (phone: 386-2626).

Mechanic – *Stiver's,* 2300 Western (phone: 385-2407).

Wedding Bells Are Always Ringing in Las Vegas – If you are at least 18 (16 with parental consent), and you feel a sudden urge to legally merge, it's easy to tie the knot on the spot. Just apply at the Las Vegas Marriage License Bureau; there's not even a blood test or waiting period. Pay a modest fee, say "I do," and the deed is done. They don't call this place the "Wedding Capital of the World" for nothing. Open round the clock on Fridays and Saturdays; till midnight Sundays through Thursdays. Clark County Courthouse, 3rd and Carson Sts. (phone: 455-3156; after hours, 455-4415).

MUSEUMS: Las Vegas hotels have commercial art exhibitions with works of well-known artists. *Herigstad's Gallery* has art shows as well as works for sale. Open from 10 AM to 6 PM; closed Sundays. 2290 E. Flamingo Rd. (phone: 733-7366). Also worth a visit is *Minotaur Fine Arts Ltd.* (phone: 737-1400) in the Fashion Show Mall. Open weekdays 9:30 AM to 9 PM, Saturdays 9:30 AM to 7 PM, Sundays 11 AM to 6 PM.

The University of Nevada at Las Vegas has a *Museum of Natural History* with collections of Indian artifacts and live desert reptiles. Open weekdays from 9 AM to 5 PM; closed Sundays. No admission charge. 4505 S. Maryland Pkwy. (phone: 739-3381).

The *Mineral Collection,* which is also on the campus, displays 1,000 specimens from the area and around the world. Closed weekends. No admission charge. Geoscience Hall, Room 103. (phone: 739-3262).

Other museums worth visiting are the *Las Vegas Art Museum,* 3333 W. Washington Ave. (phone: 647-4300); the *Las Vegas Museum of Natural History,* 3700 Las Vegas Blvd. S. (phone: 798-7757); the *Liberace Museum,* 1775 E. Tropicana Ave. (phone: 798-5595); and the *Lost City Museum of Archaeology,* in the Valley of Fire area 20 miles north (phone: 1-397-2193)

MAJOR COLLEGES AND UNIVERSITIES: The University of Nevada at Las Vegas is the largest school in the area, with an enrollment of 12,900; 4505 S. Maryland Pkwy. (phone: 739-3011).

SPECIAL EVENTS: The *Panasonic Invitational Golf Tournament* takes place in April. During the *Helldorado Festival,* held for 4 days in May, the city celebrates its Western heritage with rodeos, parades, beauty contests, and, for those who want some slower-paced action, a beard growing contest. The *Jaycees State Fair* takes place in August at the Convention Center and has carnival acts, magic shows, rides, livestock and craft exhibits. The *National Finals Rodeo* opens with a Cowboy Christmas Trade Show in early December at the *Tropicana* and continues at the *Thomas and Mack Center* for 10 more days.

SPORTS AND FITNESS: Las Vegas offers a wide variety of sporting events and fine facilities.

Basketball – The University of Nevada at Las Vegas has fielded one of the finest collegiate basketball teams in the nation for several years. They play from November to February in the *Thomas & Mack Center,* an 18,000-seat arena.

Tickets are usually available, but for good seats, your hotel bell captain or casino pit boss would be helpful (phone: 739-3900).

Betting – If you want to bet on almost any athletic event taking place outside of Nevada, numerous race and sports books dot the city. The facilities in *Caesars Palace,* 3570 Las Vegas Blvd. S. (phone: 731-7110), the *Stardust* hotel, 3000 Las Vegas Blvd. (phone: 732-6111), and the *Las Vegas Hilton,* 3000 Paradise Rd. (phone: 732-5111), are the most lavish on the Strip. *Union Plaza's Book* tops the downtown locales. 1 Main St. (phone: 386-2110).

Boxing – If punching is your bag, the major hotels promote many boxing matches. Major bouts between professional heavyweight contenders are held from time to time at *Caesars Palace,* the *Riviera,* the *Las Vegas Hilton,* and the *Showboat.*

Fitness Centers – The health club at *Caesars Palace* has a whirlpool bath, steam room, and exercise equipment, but no pool, 3570 Las Vegas Blvd. S., 15th floor (phone: 731-7110). The *Aristocrat Health Spa,* in the *Hilton,* has a sauna, whirlpool bath, and massage, 3000 Paradise Rd., 3rd floor on the pool deck (phone: 732-5111). A multimillion-dollar facility has been added to the *Desert Inn,* 3145 Las Vegas Blvd. (phone: 733-4571), and the *Golden Nugget* hotel sports a coed gym with sauna, whirlpool bath, and exercise equipment, 129 E. Fremont St. (phone: 385-7111).

Golf – Dozens of courses dot the desert landscape. Most of the Strip hotels have championship-quality courses, but the *Sahara Country Club,* 1911 E. Desert Inn Rd. (phone: 796-0016), and the *Desert Inn Country Club,* 3145 Las Vegas Blvd. S. (phone: 733-4444), are the best. For lower prices, try the public courses. Best bet is the *Municipal Golf Course,* which offers a reasonable challenge and good greens. Washington Ave. and Decatur Blvd. (phone: 646-3003).

Jogging – It's possible to run right along the Strip between Flamingo Road and Spring Mountain, where there are no cross streets to slow the pace (about ½ mile each way); stay on the *Caesars Palace* side. Another possibility is Squires Park, ½ mile from downtown; or drive to Sunset Park, 7 miles from downtown, or Bob Baskin Park, W. Oakey Blvd. at Rancho Dr.

Tennis – Almost all the Strip hotels have good tennis facilities open to the public. Indoor courts are available at the *Players World International,* 3890 Swenson Ave. (phone: 735-8153).

 THEATER: For current performances, check the publications listed above. Outside of the entertainment at the Strip hotels, there is not that much in the way of theater. But a few new additions and old standbys keep the curtains raised. The best bet for shows is the *Repertory Theater* at *Judy Bayley Hall,* University of Nevada at Las Vegas campus (phone: 739-3641). The Clark County Community College and other local companies are featured in *Theatre Under the Stars,* outdoors at the *Spring Mountain Ranch* in late June and early July. The creative sets make fine use of the environment, and the acting is first-rate. Tickets at the ranch, on Spring Mountain Rd., 18 miles west on Charleston Blvd. (phone: 875-4141).

 MUSIC: Symphony concerts, opera, jazz, and the *Nevada Dance Theatre* are featured throughout the year at *Artemus W. Ham Concert Hall* and the *Judy Bayley Theatre* on the UNLV campus. For tickets, call 739-3011.

 NIGHTCLUBS AND NIGHTLIFE: When it comes to nightlife, Las Vegas is king. The city never sleeps, and can keep visitors who want to keep the same hours entertained all night. The Strip hotels offer a wide variety of entertainment. There are nightly production spectaculars, with dancing girls, lavish costumes and sets, and all kinds of specialty acts. *Jubilee* at *Bally's,* 3645 Las Vegas Blvd. S. (phone: 739-4111), is most extravagant. Other notables of this genre are *Lido de Paris* at the *Stardust,* 3000 Las Vegas Blvd. S. (phone: 732-6111); *Splash* at the *Riviera,* 2901 Las Vegas Blvd. S. (phone: 734-5110); *Folies Bergère* at the *Tropicana,* 3801 Las Vegas Blvd. S. (phone: 739-2222); and *City Lites* at the *Flamingo Hilton,* 3555 Las Vegas Blvd. S. (phone: 733-3111).

In the main showrooms of all the other hotels on the Strip, a constant parade of stars perform twice nightly to audiences of 800 to 1,200 people in the *Union Plaza, Tropicana,* and *Flamingo Hilton*, either at the early show, when dinner is available, or later, when drinks are the rule. There's no cover charge, but the minimum runs about $10 to $35 per person for dinner shows and $6 to $35 for late shows. Keep a few things in mind when you are trying to get reservations to these big productions: House guests get first priority for many shows, so consider staying at the hotel which has the show you most want to see. Always call early in the morning, or better still, go in person. Most hotels do not take show reservations more than two days in advance. The reservation booths open in the morning and stay open till show time, and the earlier you get there the better. If you've been gambling a good deal, ask the pit boss for assistance, and if you haven't you might try tipping the bell captain and hoping for the best.

Often overlooked are the casino lounges, where lesser-known performers (many of whom soon become better known) perform for just the cost of your drinks.

Favorite non-hotel clubs are: *Botany's,* 1700 E. Flamingo Rd. (phone: 737-6662); *Tramps,* 4405 W. Flamingo Rd. (phone: 871-1424). Try *State Street,* 2570 State St. (phone: 733-0225); and the *Silver Dollar Saloon,* 2501 E. Charleston Blvd. (phone: 382-6921), for live country-and-western music.

Las Vegas presents the best-known burlesque/striptease artists in the world. Tops (or topless, more likely) are: the *Crazy Horse Saloon,* 4034 Paradise Rd. (phone: 732-1116); *Palomino Club,* 1848 Las Vegas Blvd. N. (phone: 642-2984); and the *Pussy Cat,* 4416 Paradise Rd. (phone: 733-8666).

BEST IN TOWN

 CHECKING IN: In Vegas, the hotel's the thing. The Strip (Las Vegas Blvd. South) is a 3-mile stream of hotel-casinos and motels, nearly matched in number — though usually not in quality — by the downtown "Glitter Gulch" area. Competition is fierce among the major hotels and keeps room costs modest and on a par with one another. Expect to pay $95 and up for a double room per night in the expensive range; $40 to $60, moderate; around $20 to $35, inexpensive. All telephone numbers are in the 702 area code unless otherwise indicated.

Bally's Grand – Rebuilt after a fire in 1980, it is now more grandiose than ever, with an overall Golden Era movie theme. There are 6 restaurants, a shopping mall, the *Ziegfeld Room* for production numbers, and the *Celebrity Room* for top-name entertainment. 3,000 rooms. 3645 Las Vegas Blvd. (phone: 739-4111). Expensive.

Caesars Palace – The current quality leader, this is the ultimate Las Vegas hotel. Even the most basic of its 1,600 rooms are ornate, while the high roller suites are especially sumptuous, with large classical statues to make you feel right at home — if you've just flown in from ancient Rome. The service is excellent, and the location — midway on the Strip — puts guests right in the middle of the action. It has big-name entertainment, cafés, bars, restaurants, pool, tennis, golf privileges, meeting rooms, shops, and free parking. Reservations are a must during the summer, especially on holiday weekends. 3570 Las Vegas Blvd. S. (phone: 731-7110). Expensive.

Golden Nugget – The most glamorous downtown hotel, it combines an overall turn-of-the-century look with a dazzling decor of marble, brass, and crystal in its casino, entertainment rooms, and restaurants. 129 E. Fremont St. (phone: 385-7111). Expensive to moderate.

Las Vegas Hilton – With 3,100 rooms, it surpasses even *Bally's* for the title of "Biggest in Vegas." The *Hilton* is a small city, with even a "children's hotel" to occupy younger guests while their parents attend to casino business. Off the Strip next to the Convention Center, it's not in the middle of the glitter, but neither is it in the center of traffic. With star entertainment, café, bars, restaurants, large recreation center with pool, tennis, health club, putting greens and golf privileges, shops, free parking. 3000 Paradise Rd. (phone: 732-5111 or 800-HILTONS). Expensive to moderate.

Aladdin – This hotel's new owners have ditched the Arabian theme and spent $30 million to give all its 1,100 rooms, 8 restaurants, and reception and public areas an elegantly modern look. The *Florentine Room* features fine dining, and *Fisherman's Port* has a Cajun/seafood menu. Other facilities include the 7,000-seat *Aladdin Theater,* the Bagdad showroom, pools, meeting rooms, shops, and tennis courts. 3667 Las Vegas Blvd. S. (phone: 736-0111). Moderate.

Sahara – First stop on the Strip, and notable for its quietly elegant decor and traditional sense of taste. This friendly sophistication characterized Las Vegas a long time ago but exists in fewer hotels each year. Here the service is personalized and excellent. Entertainment, café, bar, pools, health club, meeting rooms, shops. 1,000 rooms. 2535 Las Vegas Blvd. S. (phone: 737-2111). Moderate.

Union Plaza – A large (1,020-room) hotel, with the most complete facilities downtown, at the entranceway to the downtown "Glitter Gulch" action. Facilities include a pool, tennis courts, café, bar, restaurant, shops, meeting rooms, and casino. 1 Main St. (phone: 386-2110). Moderate.

Circus Circus – Of all the hotels on the Strip, the only one really dedicated to family entertainment (at family prices). With a full-scale circus operating complete with sideshows, there's something for everyone. Lots for the children — carousel, clown-shaped swimming pool; for the adults, cafés, bars, meeting rooms, health club, sauna. 2,500 rooms. 2880 Las Vegas Blvd. S. (phone: 734-0410). Inexpensive.

Motel 6 – Good clean accommodations at the best prices in town. The bargain is worthwhile since hotel-motel rooms get little use in Las Vegas, and most of the time you're in them, you're asleep. Also, you get a pool for your money. 758 rooms. 196 E. Tropicana (phone: 798-0728). Inexpensive.

EATING OUT: Probably the only sure bet in Vegas is the food. Between hotels, restaurants, and casinos there's plenty to eat, and the food is much better than standard hotel or nightclub fare. From the continental cuisine of the hotels' main restaurants to "all-you-can-eat" buffets, Las Vegas features quantity and quality. Though the offerings are basically American — steaks and seafood — there are a number of good ethnic restaurants. So eat up, and take advantage of the bargains in the casinos that are subsidized by gambling revenues; you're probably paying for them anyway. Our restaurant selections range in price from $55 or more for a dinner for two in the expensive range; $30 to $45 in the moderate range; and $20 or less, inexpensive. Prices do not include drinks, wine, or tips. All telephone numbers are in the 702 area code unless otherwise indicated.

André's – A French restaurant in an old home, this is a favorite of the crowd in the downtown area. Open daily. Reservations advised. Major credit cards. 401 S. 6th St. (phone: 385-5016). Expensive.

Aristocrat – A charming 80-seat restaurant featuring continental cuisine in the

Rancho Circle area. Open daily. Reservations advised. Major credit cards. 850 S. Rancho Dr. (phone: 870-1977). Expensive.

Claudine's – This posh room is a welcome relief from the gaudy atmosphere of the *Holiday Casino's Riverboat*. Specialties such as escargots bourguignonne with Pernod and hazelnut butter, and oysters Florentine precede the excellent charcoal-broiled steaks. Closed Mondays and Tuesdays. Reservations advised. Major credit cards. 3740 Las Vegas Blvd. S. (phone: 369-5000). Expensive.

Michael's – A gem of a restaurant in the Times Square section of the Strip. Among the offerings are shrimp served on frosted globes and double-dipped chocolate desserts. Outstanding service. Barbary Coast, 3595 Las Vegas Blvd. (phone: 737-7111). Expensive.

Palace Court – Considered the ultimate in dining grace in Las Vegas. Candelabra, vermeil flatware, and hand-blown crystal are the accoutrements of an unforgettable experience. Sommeliers pour wine from the hotel's distinguished wine cellar. Dinner nightly. Reservations advised. Major credit cards. 3570 Las Vegas Blvd. S. (phone: 731-7110). Expensive.

Pegasus – An elegant dining room in one of only two major hotels (the other being the *St. Tropez*) without gaming. Specialties of the house include roast duckling flambé, steak tartare, and sea bass, accompanied by attentive service and background harp music. In the *Alexis Park* hotel, 375 E. Harmon (phone: 796-3300). Expensive.

Chin's – An expanded version of the original, now nestled in the glittering Fashion Show Mall on the Strip. It serves crisp salads, *Chin's* beef, and pudding. A special elevator delivers diners from the parking garage. Fashion Show Mall (phone: 733-8899). Expensive to moderate.

Hugo's Cellar – One of two "basement" restaurants in Las Vegas, its decor creates a grotto effect and its menu is outstanding. Steaks, veal, seafood, and an imaginative salad cart are all exemplary, and there's an excellent wine list. Reservations advised. Major credit cards. In the *Four Queens* hotel, 202 E. Fremont St. (phone: 385-4011). Expensive to moderate.

Alpine Village Inn – Best are the portions of good Swiss and German food — the wurst plates of all varieties, and the huge kettles of thick, dark German chicken soup that are meant for two but could actually feed the entire Swiss Family Robinson. Restaurant also features a ratskeller with a piano player and lots of German beers. Open nightly. Reservations advised. Major credit cards. 3003 Paradise Rd. (phone: 734-6888). Moderate.

Battista's Hole in the Wall – Plentiful Italian pasta for dinner, helped along by all the wine you can drink, and an occasional Italian aria by Battista himself, to create the proper mood. Closed Sundays. Reservations advised. Major credit cards. 4041 Audrie, across from *Bally's* (phone: 732-1424). Moderate.

Bootlegger – Cozy, nestled in a quiet area about 3 miles from the Strip and specializing in Italian dishes. The sunken pit lounge area is a good place to relax after a day at the casinos. Closed Mondays. Reservations advised. Major credit cards. 5025 S. Eastern Ave. (phone: 736-4939). Moderate.

Carlos Murphy's Mexican Café – Sounds strange, but with a touch of American nostalgia and multitudes of memorabilia, this warmly decorated café offers specialties such as quiche, crêpes, and Mexican dishes. Open daily. No reservations. Major credit cards. 4770 S. Maryland Pkwy. (phone: 798-5541). Moderate.

Château Vegas – Continental cuisine in elegant surroundings, backed up by soft music and a harpist. Best bets are the Italian veal and any of the steaks. Open daily. Reservations advised. Major credit cards. 565 Desert Inn Rd. (phone: 733-8282). Moderate.

Flamingo Room – A large, attractive, Art Deco room, dominated by a savory salad bar, overlooking the hotel pool and the "Bugsy Siegel" gardens. The extensive menu features American dishes. In the *Flamingo Hilton* hotel, 3555 Las Vegas Blvd. S. (phone: 733-3311). Moderate.

Golden Steer – In a town that has to revise the phone books twice a year just to keep up with the comings and goings of things, 18 years in the same place attest to a strong tradition. The decor is luxurious western and the offerings topnotch, from the steaks (try the Diamond Lil prime ribs) to the toasted ravioli, and the extensive wine list. With a day's notice, they'll serve up a special delicacy: pheasant, goose, quail, chukar (partridge), or roast suckling pig. Open daily. Reservations advised. Major credit cards. 308 W. Sahara Ave. (phone: 384-4470). Moderate.

Limelight – A lively family-run Italian establishment, serving such specialties as chicken Florentine, veal scalloppine marsala with demi-glaze, and sea bass poached with chablis, leeks, and cream. Dinner nightly. Major credit cards. 2340 E. Tropicana (phone: 739-1410). Moderate.

Rafters – A San Francisco–style restaurant with some of the best seafood in town. Joe Thompson, a native of the Golden Gate city, has shipments flown in daily from Fisherman's Wharf. Try the splendid bouillabaisse, which comes topped with a whole soft-shell crab. Dinner nightly. Reservations advised. Major credit cards. 1350 E. Tropicana (phone: 739-9463). Moderate.

Starboard Tack – For years, a local favorite. Now a sister restaurant, the *Port Tack*, also offers romance and good food in a larger setting with an attractive sunken fireplace. Open 24 hours. Reservations advised. Major credit cards. *Starboard*, 2601 Atlantic St. (phone: 457-8794); *Port*, 3190 W. Sahara Ave. (phone: 873-3345). Moderate.

State Street – This late-night restaurant, with an atmosphere reminiscent of Chicago in the 1930s, is run by Gianni Russo, who was in the film *The Godfather*. Delicious Italian food is served until dawn. Open daily. Reservations advised. Major credit cards. 2570 State St. (phone: 733-0225). Moderate.

Viva Zapata – A cut above most Mexican places in price, but worth the difference. The atmosphere is modern and informal, decorated with baskets, fresh flowers, and posters. The food is excellent, and the flautas (tortillas stuffed with beef, vegetables, and cheese, then sautéed with avocado sauce) are really something special. Open daily. Reservations advised. Major credit cards. 3540 W. Sahara (phone: 873-7228). Moderate.

Waldemar's – In a setting reminiscent of a German grotto, chef Waldemar prepares goulash, beef shashlik, and, for dessert, wife Janina's homemade plum cake, heaped with freshly whipped cream. Open daily for lunch and dinner. Reservations advised. Major credit cards. 2202 W. Charleston (phone: 386-1995). Moderate.

El Burrito Café – This small authentic Mexican restaurant seats only 30, but the quality of the food would keep it full if it were twice as big. Offers several fine combination plates. The chicharrones, burritos stuffed with fried pork bits, are extra special. Open daily. Reservations advised. No credit cards. 1919 E. Fremont St. (phone: 387-9246). Inexpensive.

Golden Wok – This Chinese restaurant has been so successful that it now has a second location. Open daily. 4760 S. Eastern (phone: 456-1868); 504 S. Decatur (phone: 878-1596). Inexpensive.

Vineyard – On the exterior of the Boulevard, one of Las Vegas's three enclosed shopping malls, this quaint Italian eatery offers a fine antipasto salad bar and specialties such as chicken cacciatore and veal cutlet Parmigiana. Open daily.

Reservations for 6 or more. Major credit cards. 3630 S. Maryland Pkwy. (phone: 731-1606). Inexpensive.

If all-you-can-eat sounds good to you, you can spend all your time in Las Vegas doing just that. Virtually every Strip hotel and most of the downtown hotels have buffet lunches and dinners, where, for a couple of dollars, you can have as much as you can handle from an array of salads, fish, chicken, pasta, occasionally roast beef, and dessert. Best bets are the *Golden Nugget,* 129 E. Fremont St. (phone: 385-7111); *Caesars Palace*'s *Palatium,* 3570 Las Vegas Blvd. S. (phone: 731-7110); the *Riviera,* 2901 Las Vegas Blvd. S. (phone: 734-5110); the *Sahara,* 2535 Las Vegas Blvd. S. (phone: 737-2111); *Holiday Casino,* 3475 Las Vegas Blvd. S. (phone: 732-2411); *Frontier,* 3120 Las Vegas Blvd. S. (phone: 794-8200).

For something really special, try the weekend Champagne Brunch at *Caesars Palace* — a feast for the eyes as well as the tastebuds with its beautifully arranged selections of fresh pastries, fresh melons, eggs, bacon, ham, sausage, and all the champagne you can drink. 3570 Las Vegas Blvd. S. (phone: 731-7110). Inexpensive.

LOS ANGELES

Whatever you have heard — or think you know — about Los Angeles is probably wrong. Or misleading. Or hyperbole. This is a city that leads the league in misconceptions. To set the record straight on a few points:

- Despite the palm trees, Los Angeles is not tropical.

- Los Angeles is not countless suburbs in search of a city, but rather a vast metropolis encompassing the City of Los Angeles and a sprawl of municipalities and unincorporated areas.

- One cannot swim comfortably in the Pacific during the winter, when cold Alaskan currents often drop the water temperature into the 50s.

- Debilitating smog is rare, most often occurs in summer, and is usually confined to a small area.

- It is possible to visit Los Angeles happily without spending all one's time driving a car.

- The arts — music, theater, dance — can be readily enjoyed and are flourishing.

- The city has more people than swimming pools.

- Gang violence and other street crimes do occur, but Los Angeles's inner-city ills are no worse than those of other major metropolises. (If you're using this book as a guide, chances are you won't be touring the barrios anyway.)

- Sunglasses are not issued to residents at birth.

Los Angeles, like it or not, is a city of dreams, myths, and misunderstandings. It is our nation's Olympus, where certain of our gods live and cavort, and where both good and bad are inflated to larger-than-life proportions. Rarely have a city's virtues, excesses, shortcomings, and sins been exaggerated with such glee and small regard for current fact. Yes, certainly there is glitter and foolishness and often much about which to chuckle. Yes, admittedly there are the curses of occasionally snarled traffic, torrential rains, and eye-tearing smog.

But much of the rest can be sublime.

To begin with, the 8 million or so people who live in the LA metropolitan area care little about their city's skewed — and skewered — reputation. They are there, most of them, not for the glitz and the hijinks but for the quality of life.

There is no doubt that Los Angeles is one of the most beautifully situated and climate-blessed of the world's metropolises. Because of the mile-high San

Gabriel Mountains that skirt Los Angeles on the north and the Santa Monica Mountains that bisect it, it enjoys magnificent vistas and offers the unusual opportunity for secluded hillside living in the midst of a vast metropolis. Such lofty ranges also give rise to the accurate statement that this is one of the few places on the globe where it is possible in the same day both to ski and surf (though you'd better wear a wetsuit while surfing to avoid freezing).

On the other hand, many visitors are stunned to learn that Los Angeles isn't always favored with blue skies and perpetual sunshine. Late summer and early fall are usually the hottest times of year, when the dust-dry Santa Ana winds blow out of the nearby eastern desert to elevate temperatures into the 90s — and sometimes 100s — and escalate temperaments into the danger zone. This is when, wrote LA crime novelist Raymond Chandler, wives finger the sharp edges of knives and study the contour of their husbands' necks. Oddly enough, spring and early summer can bring the dullest weather of the year — chill fog and overcast skies. Winter is the rainy season and can be glorious or awful — and normally is both, in spurts — depending on the weather patterns churning out of the Pacific. Rainfalls can be quick and violent and give way to clear warm days and cool nights.

Despite these vicissitudes, it is virtually inevitable that New Year's Day will dawn bright and sunny, with temperatures in the 80s, and that the achingly beautiful panoramas seen by the tens of millions watching the Rose Bowl game on television will only reinforce the LA legend.

Los Angeles traces its origins to a dusty little settlement founded in 1781 by order of a Spanish colonial governor. The settlers gave it the monumental name of El Pueblo de Nuestra Señora la Reina de los Angeles de Porciuncula. By 1850, after California was ceded to the United States after the Mexican-American War, it had a population of a mere 1,610, and at the turn of the century it was the home of only a few more than 100,000 residents. Still largely citrus groves and bean fields, it retained much of the character of its Spanish and Mexican roots — and remained that way until the massive American migration to the West Coast began in the 1920s. California was the country's last frontier, a chance to start a new life and make one's fortune, and the city, along with the state, boomed. In the 1930s, the area attracted those rendered homeless and near hopeless by the Great Depression; in the 1940s, servicemen on their way home from World War II stopped here to put the past behind them. The 1950s and 1960s saw LA develop into a center for new industries — the technological and aerospace industries of the future.

In spite of such dynamic growth (or perhaps because of it), Los Angeles continued to derive its perceived civic persona from the sunny weather, from a beach culture that embraced only a tiny fraction of the population, and from its association with the sometimes bizarre world of the motion picture industry. The film industry had also begun to develop in the 1920s, with the arrival of the early movie moguls drawn from New York by the sun, which permitted outdoor filming year-round. Later it came to include the television and music businesses as well. LA found it difficult to be taken seriously. To much of the rest of the nation, Los Angeles was "the Coast," a place dismissed laughingly and almost by rote as provincial and self-absorbed.

Meanwhile, however, things were rapidly changing in the City of the

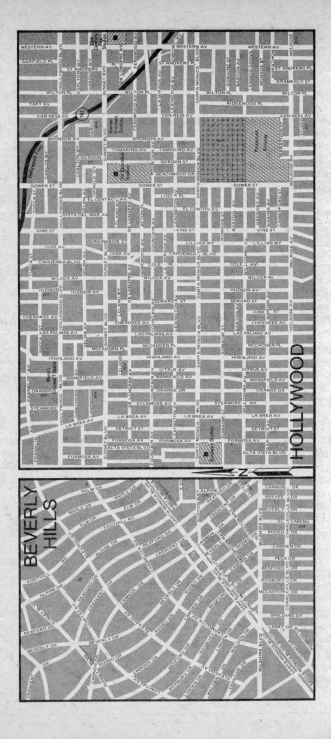

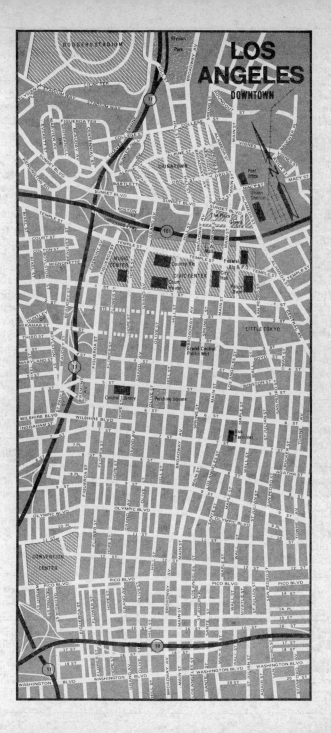

Angels. Spearheaded by local leaders frustrated by the lopsided, frivolous image of their home town, Los Angeles began an effort to shed its second class mantle. The archaic ordinance that limited downtown buildings to the height of City Hall (presumably for earthquake protection) was scrapped, and a skyline began to rise. Major league sports arrived in 1946 with the *Rams* from Cleveland, followed by professional teams in the top rank of baseball, basketball, and hockey. Finally, in 1964, the city proudly opened the ambitious, multi-theater complex called the *Music Center*.

No longer "Double Dubuque" (though to some, it's "La-La-Land," where life is a beach), LA has grown up in the last decades. It has become a sophisticated city that boasts some of the finest hotels, restaurants, shopping, nightlife, museums, and cultural events in the nation.

Over the years, Los Angeles has also become a favorite vacation destination and now welcomes more than 41 million visitors annually from all over the world. They are lured to LA, not only by its salubrious weather and the chance of glimpsing a movie or TV personality, but also by its theaters offering stage productions, symphony orchestras, opera and light opera companies, dance companies, museums, and scores of top professional and college sporting events. Specific areas of Los Angeles have become attractions in themselves: Hollywood and its *Mann's Chinese Theatre,* with cement footprints and handprints of the stars; Beverly Hills and its expensive shops and Rolls-Royce lifestyle; Westwood, with its footloose university town ambience; the casual but wealthy beach communities stretching from Malibu to the Palos Verdes Peninsula. In addition, the more traditional tourist sites and activities continue to draw many visitors to Los Angeles and its environs — Disneyland, Universal Studios, Movieland, Knott's Berry Farm, Six Flags Magic Mountain, Marineland, the *Queen Mary,* and so on.

Los Angeles still has its critics, to be sure. Its vast size (the city itself is almost half as big as the entire state of Rhode Island) may make it seem uncomfortably spread out and sometimes difficult to negotiate for those accustomed to more compact and centralized places. But most people find LA a pleasant and easy city in which to live and to visit. Beneath the official municipal veneer, away from the sunshine and removed from the artificial glitter of show biz, Los Angeles has an essentially solid and All-American soul. Add the fascination of the ethnic mix — European and African stock, plus Mexican, Chinese, Japanese, Korean, Vietnamese, and Thai — as well as its environmental meld of sea, mountain, and desert, and Los Angeles emerges from its shroud of fable to assume its logical position as one of the great cities of the world.

LOS ANGELES AT-A-GLANCE

SEEING THE CITY: There are at least three great places to go for a fantastic view of Los Angeles. The most famous is Mulholland Drive, a twisting road that winds through the Hollywood Hills. Another is the top of Mt. Olympus, in Laurel Canyon, near Sunset Boulevard. The 27-story, 454-foot City Hall Tower has a sweeping view of downtown, the mountains, and the Pacific Ocean. Open weekdays. City Hall, near south end of Los Angeles Mall (phone: 485-2891).

SPECIAL PLACES: A walk along Hollywood Boulevard from Vine Street to Highland Avenue will delight the heart of anyone who loves the era of those great movies that made Hollywood famous. However, Hollywood is no longer the physical center of film production, and its glamour is, sadly, long gone. X-rated movies now seem to outnumber the kinds of films that made the area world-renowned. Keep in mind that most residents would never contemplate walking down Hollywood Boulevard after dark. During the daytime, however, most Hollywood streets are crowded, bustling, and safe. There is a lot to enjoy here, much of it for little or no cost.

OLD HOLLYWOOD: MEMORIES AND EMPTY BUILDINGS

Mann's Chinese Theatre – Known to movie fans around the world as Grauman's Chinese Theatre, this is probably the most visited site in Hollywood. If you wander down Hollywood Boulevard toward Highland Avenue looking for the Grauman's sign, you'll never find it, though. Several years ago, Ted Mann took over the theater and added it to his movie chain. As the new proprietor, he felt within his rights to take down the sign that had made Syd Grauman famous and replace it with his own. But he caused considerable controversy. The *Chinese Theater* forecourt is world-famous for its celebrity footprints and handprints immortalized in cement. If you join the crowd of visitors outside the box office, you'll probably find imprints of your favorite star from the 1920s to the present. If you buy a ticket to get in, you'll be treated to one of the world's most impressive and elaborate movie palaces. The ornate carvings, the very high, decorative ceiling, the traditionally plush seats, the heavy curtains that whoosh closed when the film ends, and the enormous screen itself are all part of a Hollywood that no longer exists. The *Chinese Theater* is one of those movie theaters that give children some idea of what parents mean when they talk about how moviegoing has changed since their own childhoods. The less opulent *Chinese Twin* next door also shows films. 6925 Hollywood Blvd. (phone: 464-8111).

Hollywood Wax Museum – If the *Chinese Theater* makes you nostalgic for the faces belonging to the disembodied prints, stop in at the *Hollywood Wax Museum.* If you've been leery of wax museums ever since you watched Vincent Price coat his victims in wax in the famous flick *House of Wax,* we hasten to reassure you that there is no such hanky-panky going on in the back rooms here. Marilyn Monroe, Clark Gable and Jean Harlow, Paul Newman, Gary Cooper, Barbra Streisand, Raquel Welch, Sylvester Stallone as Rambo, and many more fill the star-studded display cases. There's also a horror chamber, a re-creation of *The Last Supper,* and a documentary about the history of the Academy Awards, with film clips from winners like *Gone With the Wind* and *Mary Poppins.* Open daily: weekdays to midnight, Fridays and Saturdays to 2 AM. Admission charge; no charge for children under 6. 6767 Hollywood Blvd. (phone: 462-8860).

Hollywood Studio Museum – If nostalgia is what you seek, you can also find it at the largest single historical movie artifact in existence. Called the De Mille Barn, it was designated a California Cultural Landmark in 1956 and presently houses the *Hollywood Studio Museum.* Cecil B. De Mille used this structure, a rented horse barn, as a studio when he made the first feature — *The Squawman* — ever shot in the town of Hollywood. Inside today are a replica of De Mille's office and stills from silent motion pictures. The outside of the building is interesting, too: When it was on the back lot of Paramount Studios, it often was used in Westerns and for many years was seen as the railroad station in the "Bonanza" TV series. Closed Mondays. Admission charge. 2100 N. Highland (phone: 874-2276).

Paramount Pictures – At one time, RKO studios adjoined the Paramount lot. After RKO folded in 1956, its studio became the home of television's Desilu Productions, which in turn sold its property to next-door Paramount. Close to the Bronson Avenue intersection with Melrose is the famous Paramount Gate, the highly decorative studio entrance that many people will remember from the film *Sunset Boulevard*. The Gower Street side of today's Paramount was the old front entrance to RKO. At what used to be 780 Gower Street, you will now find simply an unimpressive back door to Paramount, painted in that dull, flat beige many studios use to protect their exterior walls. The door no longer bears its old marquee with distinctive Art Deco neon letters spelling out RKO, the numbers have been torn from the front steps, and the Art Deco front doors are gone. RKO is just a memory now. Paramount extends from Melrose Ave. on the south to Gower St. on the west, Van Ness Ave. on the east, and Willoughby Ave. on the north (phone: 468-5000).

Gower Street – This was once the center for so many small film studios that it became known in the film business as Gower Gulch. It was also nicknamed Poverty Row because so many of its independent producers were perpetually strapped for production money. Poverty Row's most famous studio was Columbia Pictures, which ultimately grew healthy enough to acquire most of the smaller parcels of studio real estate in the neighborhood. Columbia's old studios still stand at Gower Street and Sunset Boulevard, although Columbia moved out several years ago. It found a new home in Burbank at the Warner Brothers Studio, which was then renamed The Burbank Studios (TBS). The two film companies operate TBS as a rental facility for film and TV production today. When Columbia vacated its Hollywood property, some of its sound stages were used for a time as indoor tennis courts. Today they have become film studios once more, available for rent to independent production companies.

Warner Brothers – During the late 1920s, when Warner's was introducing "talkies" to America, its pictures were filmed here. It was also the home of Warner's radio station at the time, KFWB. Today the old studio is the headquarters for KTLA-TV and KMPC radio. The stately southern mansion that served as Warner's administration building still stands on Sunset Boulevard. Sunset Blvd. and Van Ness Ave.

Max Factor Beauty Museum – The only museum in the world devoted to makeup is housed in the famous Max Factor Building, just off Hollywood Boulevard, where (since the 1930s) the stars came to have their faces painted, to have their hair styled, and to be fitted for wigs or toupees. The displays document the history of the company, which is synonymous with the history of makeup in film. One of the most unusual is a collection of special head blocks of famous stars, used to create wigs and toupees without the actors and actresses having to spend hours being fitted and styled. Closed Sundays. No admission charge. 1666 N. Highland Ave. (phone: 463-6668).

Hollywood Bowl Museum – Celebrating some 60 years of the bowl through pictures and artifacts, this collection includes *Beatles* memorabilia, mementos of some of the 150 world-famous conductors who have led the *Los Angeles Philharmonic Orchestra* here (especially Otto Klemperer), and the first recording equipment used on the West Coast (in 1921). Closed Sundays and Mondays. No admission charge. 2301 N. Highland Ave., on the grounds of the *Hollywood Bowl* (phone: 850-2059).

"HOLLYWOOD": ALIVE AND WELL

"Hollywood," meaning the film business, is no longer geographically in the district bearing that name. If your nostalgic walking tour of Old Hollywood has made you curious about modern production methods, we suggest a tour of one of the following Los Angeles studios:

Universal Studios – The combination movie studio tour and theme park has been attracting more than 3 million people a year. In 1915, Universal Pictures established a mammoth studio on 420 acres of what was then a chicken farm. Land in the eastern part of the San Fernando Valley was pretty cheap, and Universal's founder, Carl Laemmle, was smart enough to buy a lot of it. As a result, the modern Universal, a division of MCA, found itself with more than enough room to make movies and television shows, as well as build a theme park. The Universal Studio tours, launched in 1964, are conducted on trams, complete with guides, and take about 175 people per tour. Some of the highlights include a special stunt show, the Battle of Galactica, where you're captured by Cylons; a look at some of the 34 sound stages and other production facilities; a special-effects demonstration; a burning house; a collapsing bridge; and an earthquake simulation (called "The Big One") where the ground shakes beneath the wheels of passenger trams as riders experience shock waves in the high ranges of the Richter scale. You'll also see the house used in Alfred Hitchcock's *Psycho*, a street from *The Sting*, a flash flood, a runaway train, the parting of the Red Sea, an attack on the tour tram by the 24-foot "shark" from *Jaws*, another attack by a 30-foot-tall, computer-controlled King Kong, who tries to hurl your tram into a river, and the Doomed Glacier Expedition, where you get to plunge down an Alpine avalanche. If you're ready for all that, visit Universal Studios any day of the week. Admission charge; no charge for children under 3. Hollywood Fwy. to Lankershim exit, Universal City (phone: 818-508-9600).

Burbank Studios – To take a look at real filmmaking rather than the Universal extravaganza, try The Burbank Studios. It's now the home of Warner Brothers and Columbia Pictures, as well as many independent production companies. Nothing on the tour is staged, so visitors watch whatever is happening on that particular day. Not only do you get to see some actual shooting whenever possible, you also see a lot of behind-the-scenes action — scenery construction, sound recording, and prop departments. Since TBS tours are limited to 12 people (with children under 10 not permitted), reservations are required a week in advance. Open weekdays. Admission charge. 4000 Warner Blvd. (phone: 818-954-1744).

NBC Television Studios – Another traditional behind-the-scenes tour, NBC offers you the chance to see television studios, set construction, makeup and wardrobe departments, and to participate in some of the magic of TV in the new Sound and Special Effects Center. Tours are escorted by NBC pages, who take you, when possible, to such sets as Johnny Carson's "Tonight" show. There are 15 people on each tour, which takes about 1¼ hours. Open daily except Easter, Thanksgiving, Christmas, and New Year's Day. Admission charge. 3000 W. Alameda Ave., Burbank (phone: 818-840-3537).

Hollywood On Location – You don't have to visit the studios to see the stars. Hollywood On Location publishes a daily list of where and when current TV series, movies, and videos are filming in and near LA. On most days, shooting goes on well past midnight, and often until dawn. The TV series shoot from June through March; movies are filmed year-round. The list, which includes times and street address, is available weekdays from 9:30 AM to 4:30PM at Hollywood On Location, 8644 Wilshire Blvd., Beverly Hills (phone: 659-9165).

Beverly Hills – After a hard day on the lot, movie stars still living in Beverly Hills return to their mansions for a good night's sleep. Even during the sunshiny daylight hours, Beverly Hills is remarkably tranquil, with nary a person walking on the residential streets. Without a doubt the most affluent and elegant suburb in Southern California, Beverly Hills is a must-see. If you want to window-shop or purchase high fashion clothing, stroll along Rodeo Drive between Santa Monica and Wilshire Boulevards. If you want to make sure you don't succumb to an impulse to buy anything, go on Sunday, when many stores are closed. *Gray Line* offers van and limousine tours (phone: 481-2121). During the week, an old-fashioned trolley tours Beverly Hills (no admission charge).

DOWNTOWN LOS ANGELES

To see a Los Angeles that most people don't know about, take a walking tour downtown.

The Plaza – If you ever wondered what the place looked like before shopping centers were created, step across the Plaza and marvel. The Plaza is a wide square, the scene of monthly fiestas. The Old Plaza Church, which dates to 1822, has a curious financial history: It was partially paid for by the sale of seven barrels of brandy. The city's first firehouse is here, too. For a complete repertory of colorful local anecdotes, take a narrated walking tour of the Plaza. For information, contact El Pueblo de los Angeles State Historic Park on the Plaza, 845 N. Alameda St. (phone: 628-1274).

Olvera Street – Music from the Plaza fiesta spills into Olvera Street, a block-long pedestrian alley filled with colorful Mexican shops, restaurants, and spicy food stalls. The oldest house in Los Angeles is here — the 1818 Avila House, made of adobe. The first brick house is also here, but now it's a restaurant. There is a Visitor Center in the Sepulveda House (1887) and a free 18-minute film on the history of Los Angeles.

Los Angeles Civic Center and Mall – An unusually quiet, well-landscaped city mall, with tropical plants, gentle splashing fountains, and sculpture half hidden among the lush greenery. It's the first mall of shops and restaurants to be built on City Hall property (at Main and Los Angeles Sts.). Stop in the rotunda to see a rotating art show. Make sure you get to the top of City Hall Tower at the south end of the mall for one of the best views of the city. Mall open daily (phone: 485-2891 and 485-2121).

Third and Broadway – Several places in this area are worth noting. First is the skylit, 5-story indoor court of the Bradbury Building, now a registered historic landmark. You can ride an old hydraulic elevator to the top balcony and walk down a magnificent staircase guaranteed to evoke visions of bygone splendors. Across the corner from the Bradbury Building is the *Million Dollar Theatre* — Syd Grauman's first; it's currently a Spanish-language picture palace inside but it has a fascinating exterior. Just south of the theater is the entrance to the Grand Central Public Market, a conglomerate of stalls selling food from all over the world amid the sounds and smells of a Mexican mercado.

Little Tokyo – This is the social, economic, cultural, and religious center of the largest Japanese-American community in the US. There's a specialty shopping center here as well as many restaurants. 1st and San Pedro Sts. (phone: 620-8861).

Music Center – The best time to visit the *Music Center* is during a concert or performance, but it's worth seeing anytime. The *Ahmanson Theatre* is the base for a branch of the *Center Theatre Group* and hosts classical dramas, comedies, and international premières with big-name stars. The *Mark Taper Forum,* a small, award-winning theater, houses the branch of the *Center Theatre Group* that specializes in new works and experimental material. The glittering *Dorothy Chandler Pavilion,* a 3,200-seat auditorium, is the home of the *Los Angeles Philharmonic,* the *Joffrey Ballet,* and the *Los Angeles Master Chorale.* It's also the setting for most of the season of the new *Los Angeles Opera Company.* The orchestra season runs from October to May; musical theater is presented generally in summer, when the orchestra moves to the *Hollywood Bowl.* Take the free guided tour of the theaters. 1st and Grand Sts. (phone: 972-7483 for tour information; 972-7211 for general information).

Chinatown – Chinatown has the usual assortment of restaurants, vegetable stores, and weird little shops selling ivory chess sets and acupuncture charts. The 900 block of N. Broadway.

Museum of Contemporary Art – This is one museum in two buildings: the brand-new *MOCA* at California Plaza, designed by Arata Isozaki, a modern art exhibit in itself, and the *Temporary Contemporary,* a renovated warehouse about 10 blocks away, on Bunker Hill downtown. At both are artworks from the 1940s to the present. Also, in *MOCA*'s Ahmanson Auditorium, there is a Media and Performing Arts Program, which looks at performance — contemporary dance, theater, film, and video — as an art form. Closed Mondays. Admission charge (except Thursdays from 5 to 8 PM, when entry is free). One ticket covers admission to both buildings on the same day. *MOCA:* 250 S. Grand Ave. at California Plaza (phone: 621-2766); *Temporary Contemporary:* 152 N. Central Ave. (phone: 626-6222).

MIDTOWN

Farmers Market – "Eat your liver." No, we're not quoting your mother, we're quoting Yossarian, the hero of *Catch-22* (book by Joseph Heller, movie by Mike Nichols). Yossarian used to say "eat your liver" all the time, and at the Farmers Market you can do just that. You can also eat anything else within the realm of gastronomic imagination. You'll find over 150 stalls of American, Mexican, Italian, Chinese, and vegetarian food, and any number of exquisite bakeries and fruit and candy shops. If you don't like to eat standing up, there are tables set among the aisles of this indoor, covered market. It's a great place to be hungry. Open daily. 6333 W. 3rd St. at Fairfax (phone: 933-9211).

Hancock Park – A midtown green space, the gift of an early oil magnate. The *Los Angeles County Museum of Art* keeps building over remaining deposits where Hancock's oil pumps once bobbed. There are galleries of drawings, prints, photographs, and temporary exhibitions in the Frances and Armand Hammer Building and a dazzling, eclectic, permanent collection in the Ahmanson Building. American art is the focus of the Robert O. Anderson Building. Newest is the world's fair Oriental Pavilion for Japanese Art, which contains paintings, sculpture, and decorative arts. The *Leo S. Bing Theatre* offers special films and concerts. Closed Mondays. Admission charge. 5905 Wilshire Blvd. (phone: 857-6000). The colorful *George C. Page Museum of La Brea Discoveries* displays some of the fossilized remains of prehistoric animals trapped in the tar pits, along with movies, dioramas, and a glassed-in laboratory where paleontologists work. Closed Mondays. Admission charge. 5801 Wilshire Blvd. (phone: 936-2230). Combination *Museum of Art/Page Museum* tickets available.

FARTHER AFIELD

Griffith Park – If you thought Texas had the biggest of everything, you're mistaken. This is the largest municipal park in the country. Griffith has three golf courses, a wilderness area and bird sanctuary, tennis courts, three miniature railroads, a carousel, pony rides, and picnic areas within its 4,043 acres. Not only that — this is where you'll find the famous Los Angeles Zoo, home to 2,500 mammals, birds, and reptiles. Open daily except Christmas. Admission charge except for children under 2. 5333 Zoo Dr. (phone: 666-4650). If you like railroads, you'll love *Travel Town,* a unique outdoor museum of old railroad engines, cars, railroad equipment, and fire trucks. The Griffith Observatory, 2800 E. Observatory Rd. (phone: 664-1191), near Mt. Hollywood houses a 500-seat planetarium theater, a twin-refracting telescope, and the Hall of Science. At the new, architecturally innovative *Gene Autry Western Heritage Museum,* memorabilia, films, and visual displays trace the history of the western movement since the 1700s, prominently including the filmmakers' West. Closed Mondays. Admission charge. 4700 Zoo Dr. (phone: 667-2000). Most park facilities are open daily (phone: 665-5188).

Six Flags Magic Mountain – A 260-acre family theme park, featuring more than 100 rides, shows, and other attractions, this is the home of Bugs Bunny and his Looney Tunes friends in Bugs Bunny World. In addition to the mighty Colossus (a huge, wooden roller coaster) and the spine-tingling Revolution (a 360-degree vertical loop coaster), there's also the challenge of Roaring Rapids (a whitewater rafting experience), the Shock Wave (a stand-up looping roller coaster), the Z Force mock starship ride, and a magic show run by the wily rabbit. New is Ninja, the first overhead suspended roller coaster on the West Coast. The dolphin show and a children's village and petting zoo are also worthwhile. Open daily from Memorial Day to Labor Day, weekends the rest of the year. Admission charge except for children under 3. 25 minutes north of Hollywood on the Golden State Fwy., Magic Mountain exit in Valencia (phone: 818-367-2271 or 805-255-4100; for recorded information, 805-255-4111 or 818-367-5965).

Ports o' Call Village – Some 59 specialty shops here feature merchandise from around the world. You can relax by taking a boat or helicopter tour of Los Angeles Harbor and dining in your choice of 25 restaurants and snack shops. Open daily. Berths 76-79 at the foot of the Harbor Fwy., San Pedro (phone: 831-0287).

Redondo Beach Marina – A delightful waterfront recreation showplace, the marina offers a pier restaurant extending over the ocean, boat cruises, and sportfishing. Open daily. 181 N. Harbor Dr., Redondo Beach. Take the Harbor Fwy. to the Torrance Blvd. exit and proceed west to the ocean (phone: 374-3481).

Forest Lawn Memorial Park – A major tourist attraction, Forest Lawn is a huge cemetery calling itself a memorial park; it advertises on huge billboards overlooking the freeways. Humphrey Bogart, Walt Disney, W. C. Fields, and Clark Gable are buried here, among others. On the grounds you'll find a stained glass window depicting *The Last Supper* and the largest religious painting in the world, Jan Styka's 195-by-45-foot *The Crucifixion.* Donations appreciated. Open daily. 1712 S. Glendale Ave., Glendale (phone: 818-241-4151).

Queen Mary – Now permanently docked in Long Beach. When she was launched in 1936, a transatlantic voyage on the *Queen* was the ultimate travel experience of the time. She was "relaunched" in this picturesque harbor in 1971, after retiring from a long, exciting career on the high seas. You can tour the 81,000-ton ship stem to stern and can even spend the night — nearly 400 converted staterooms now make up the *Queen Mary* hotel. Also at the site is Howard Hughes's *Spruce Goose,* the world's largest all-wood airplane. Both open daily. Admission charge. Long Beach Fwy. to *Queen Mary* exit (phone: 435-3511).

Catalina Island – It's 2 hours by boat from San Pedro or Long Beach to Catalina Island, where you can spend the day wandering around the flower-filled hills, looking at the ocean, swimming, sightseeing, playing golf, or riding horses. There are places to stay overnight, but be sure to reserve in advance during the summer. Boats to Catalina leave daily from Catalina Landing, 320 Golden Shore Blvd., Long Beach, and from the Catalina Terminal Building, foot of Harbor Fwy., Berths 95 and 96, San Pedro. Boats are operated by *Catalina Cruises* (phone: 775-6111).

ORANGE COUNTY

Disneyland – For many people, this is the most compelling magnet in all of Southern California — and the inspired creation that forever changed the image of theme and amusement parks. If you've ever wished upon a star and longed to make your way toward the glittering spires of Fantasyland, a trip to this incredibly clean, colorful, and diversified amusement park is essential. You will undoubtedly encounter one of your favorite Disney characters promenading down Main Street, a re-creation of a typical 1890s American street. 40 minutes from downtown LA, Disneyland is open daily. Admission charge. 1313 Harbor Blvd., Anaheim (phone: 714-999-4565). Also see *Amusement Parks,* DIVERSIONS.

Movieland Wax Museum – About a 10-minute drive from Disneyland, with more than 200 movie and television stars in wax, molded into stances from their most famous roles. The original props and sets from many films are here, too. Recently opened is the Chamber of Horrors, 15 sets with wax figures re-creating the special effects that made movies such as *Psycho* and *The Exorcist* famous. Open daily. Admission charge. 7711 Beach Blvd., Buena Park (phone: 714-522-1154).

Medieval Times – Across the street from the *Movieland Wax Museum* is a castle-like structure that houses an arena and one of the area's newer attractions — an evening of 11th-century entertainment during which colorfully attired knights on horseback compete in medieval games, jousting, and sword fighting. The show comes with dinner (roast chicken flambé, spareribs, herb-basted potatoes, and various other finger foods, since people in those days didn't use forks). Open daily. Admission charge. 7662 Beach Blvd., Buena Park (phone: 714-521-4740).

Knott's Berry Farm – The theme is the Old West. An old-fashioned stagecoach and authentic steam coach will take you around the grounds, past rides called the Cork-screw, Whirlwind, Log Ride, Sky Jump, Loop Trainer, Tumbler, Slammer, and Sling-shot, as well as bumper cars. There are also a mine train, Montezooma's Revenge (a forward/backward loop roller coaster), Camp Snoopy (an entertainment area for kids), and the exciting Kingdom of the Dinosaurs. Knott's Berry Farm has top country-and-western artists performing frequently, and a great ice show at Christmastime. Open daily. Admission charge. 10 minutes from Disneyland at 8039 Beach Blvd., Buena Park (phone: 714-827-1776 or, for recorded information, 714-220-5200). Also see *Amusement Parks,* DIVERSIONS.

■**EXTRA SPECIAL:** For one of the most spectacular drives in California, follow the Pacific Coast Highway (Rte. 1) north to Santa Barbara, about 95 miles from LA. Santa Barbara is a picturesque California mission town facing the Pacific, where bright bougainvillea flowers purple and magenta against classic white adobe houses, and small clapboard buildings recall the 19th-century settlers. A "red tile" walking tour zigzags through the historic district and runs along downtown State Street — Spanish to the last tile-enclosed trash bin and mailbox. The Spanish-Moorish courthouse is worth a visit for its opulent interior and the incomparable panorama from the tower. The city center owes its harmonious Spanish look to the strict architectural guidelines for reconstruction that were imposed after the devastating earthquake of 1925. Overnighters can opt for a hacienda-style hostelry, such as the *Four Seasons Biltmore* (phone: 805-969-2261) and the *Montecito Inn* (phone: 805-969-7854); a hill resort, such as the *San Ysidro Ranch* (phone: 805-969-5046); or one of many period bed-and-breakfast establishments. The *Cold Spring Tavern,* about 10 miles northwest of Santa Barbara on Rte. 154, goes back to the old stagecoach days. Chili is popular at lunch. At dinner, the menu tends more toward chicken, steaks, and game. Open daily. 5995 Stagecoach Rd. (phone: 805-967-0066).

SOURCES AND RESOURCES

TOURIST INFORMATION: For free information, brochures, and maps, contact the Greater Los Angeles Visitors and Convention Bureau, 515 S. Figueroa St., Los Angeles, CA 90012 (phone: 624-7300). For the best (albeit most expensive) maps of the Los Angeles area as well as travel books, try *Thomas Bros. Maps & Books,* 603 W. 7th St. (phone: 627-4018).

The best individual city guides to Los Angeles are *LA/Access* by Richard Saul Wurman (Access Press; $11.95) and *Hidden LA and Southern California* by Ray Riegert (Ulysses Press Travel; $12.96).

Television Stations – KNBC Channel 4–NBC; KCBS Channel 2–CBS; KABC Channel 7–ABC; KCET Channel 28–PBS.

Radio Stations – AM: KFWB 980 (news); KABC 790 (talk); KRTH 930 (oldies). FM: KKGO 105 (jazz); KISS 102.7 (top 40); KFAC 92.3 (classical).

Local Coverage – *Los Angeles Times,* morning daily; *Los Angeles Herald-Examiner,* morning daily; *Daily News,* published in the San Fernando Valley, morning daily; *Los Angeles* magazine, monthly; *California* magazine, monthly.

Food – To keep absolutely up to date, check the restaurant listings in *Los Angeles* or *California* magazines.

Telephone – All telephone numbers are in the 213 area code unless otherwise indicated. The 818 area code covers the San Fernando Valley and the upper half of the San Gabriel Valley. The 805 area code covers the Santa Barbara area; the 714 area code, Orange County.

Sales Tax – Los Angeles has a 6½% sales tax and an 12% hotel tax.

 CLIMATE: Summers are hot and dry, with temperatures reaching the 90s during the day, but cool enough for sweaters after sundown. In winter, there are rainy days and hot days, with an average temperature of 68.

 GETTING AROUND: It's always more convenient to have a car for exploring Los Angeles; however, there are buses, taxis, and tour operators.

Airports – Los Angeles International Airport (known as LAX) is the city's major airport and handles all international and most domestic traffic. There are some services at LAX worth noting: *Skytel,* a 13-room facility that is neither a lounge nor a hotel, but a little bit of both. Each room has a bed, a private bath with amenities such as blow dryer/toiletries, color TV set, work table, and phone service. The rooms are for one person only (even Mr. and Mrs. would have to rent two) and are soundproof. They rent for $8.95 plus tax per half-hour; $16 plus tax per hour; $24 plus tax per 2 hours and up. Wake-up service is available. *Skytel* is in the Tom Bradley International Terminal, upper level (phone: 417-0200). Helpful, too, especially for business travelers, are the three business centers, in Terminals 1, 4, and 7. They have secretarial services, telexes, even conference rooms for up to 8 persons for a small charge. Also available there·are automatic teller machines. At the ABC Baggage Center, departure level of the Tom Bradley Terminal (phone: 646-7889 or 646-9143), travelers can store luggage for a day or more; price diminishes as time passes (for example, 1 bag/1 day is $8; 1 bag/7 days is about $5 per day or $36 total). They also wrap packages and ship them at their own UPS desk. For handicapped travelers, the airport provides van service with wheelchair lift for transport between terminals or to and from outlying Parking Lot C (phone: 646-6402 or 646-8021).

The drive downtown from LAX takes about an hour, depending on traffic, and taxi fare should run about $25. Although city buses do stop at the airport, a more efficient alternative is one of the private transport companies. *Supershuttle* (phone: 777-8000) offers transportation by van from LAX to the Wilshire district and downtown hotels for $11 and $10, respectively. At the airport, *Supershuttle* and several other companies can be summoned through the courtesy phones in the baggage claim area or by calling 417-8988. For the return trip, call at least 4 hours ahead for a pickup at your hotel.

Bus – For route information on scheduled city buses, call the Southern California Rapid Transit District (phone: 273-0910 in the Beverly Hills/West LA area; 626-4455 in Hollywood/central LA; and 818-781-5890 in the San Fernando Valley).

Car Rental – All major firms are represented throughout Greater Los Angeles. The least expensive is *Bob Leech Auto Rental,* with Toyota Tercels and Corollas at $15.95 a day with 100 free miles, 10¢ a mile thereafter. Sports coupes run $19.95. Free airport pickups. 4490 W. Century Blvd. (phone: 673-2727).

Taxi – Check at your hotel desk; different firms serve different areas.

Tours – *Gray Line* offers tours of downtown LA (*Music Center,* Chinatown, Little Tokyo, Olvera St., and more) and the Hollywood–Beverly Hills area, as well as Disneyland, Universal Studios, and Knott's Berry Farm. 1207 W. 3rd St. (phone: 481-2121).

 LOCAL SERVICES: Babysitting – *Babysitters Guild Agency,* PO Box 3418, South Pasadena 91030 (phone: 469-8246); *Weston's Services Agency,* 8230 Beverly Blvd., LA (phone: 274-9228); *Community Service Agency,* 18341 Sherman Way, Ste. 207, Reseda (phone: 818-345-2950).

Business Services – *HQ,* 2121 Ave. of the Stars, 6th floor, Century City (phone: 551-6660); *Century Secretarial Service,* 2040 Ave. of the Stars, Suite 400, Century City (phone: 277-3329); *Just-a-Sec,* 500 S. Sepulveda, Suite 400 (phone: 472-9521).

Mechanics – The best bet is membership in one of the major automobile clubs.

 MUSEUMS: The *Los Angeles County Museum of Art* and the *Museum of Contemporary Art* are described in *Special Places.* Other fine museums in LA are the following:

J. Paul Getty Museum – Parking reservations are mandatory (if you're driving) at this replica of a Roman villa buried at Herculaneum, now filled with antiquities and more recent art treasures. 17985 Pacific Coast Hwy., Malibu (phone: 458-2003).

Los Angeles Children's Museum – 310 N. Main St. (phone: 687-8800).

Museum of Science and Industry – 700 State Dr. (phone: 744-7400).

Natural History Museum – 900 Exposition Blvd. (phone: 744-3466).

Norton Simon Museum of Art – The rich industrialist's collection, worth $750 million. 411 W. Colorado Blvd., Pasadena (phone: 818-449-6840).

Southwest Museum – Devoted to the anthropology of the Southwest. 234 Museum Dr. (phone: 221-2163).

SHOPPING: No single street on this planet so typifies consumer excess as Rodeo Drive in Beverly Hills. Few mortals will be able to afford the prices, but window-shopping along this avenue for the affluent makes for as much fun as studying the boutiques along Paris's Rue du Faubourg-St.-Honoré, London's Bond Street, or Chicago's Michigan Avenue. In fact, many of the shop names are the same. Only a few are home-grown, such as the former *Giorgio.* This supposed model for the title store of Judith Krantz's steamy novel *Scruples* sold its name and wildly successful fragrance to Avon. Now *Fred Hayman* is the boutique. Here is a list of the top emporia along Rodeo and environs.

Abercrombie & Fitch – A trendy new version of the aristocratic old sporting goods store. 9424 Wilshire Blvd.

Alfred Dunhill of London – Tobacco and smoking accessories. 210-B N. Rodeo Dr.

Bally of Switzerland – High-style shoes for men, 340 N. Rodeo Dr.; for women, 409 N. Rodeo Dr.

Bijan – Where the rich and famous shop for men's clothing; by appointment only. 420 N. Rodeo Dr.

Carroll & Co. – Ivy league clothing for men and women. 466 N. Rodeo Dr.

Cecil Gee – British clothing for men. 346 N. Rodeo Dr.

Dyansen Galleries – Fine art. 339 N. Rodeo Dr.

Fred Hayman – Chic clothing for men and women; has a stand-up bar and complimentary drinks for shoppers in what used to be *Giorgio's.*. 273 N. Rodeo Dr.

Gucci – Italian leather goods, jewelry, clothing, accessories. 347 N. Rodeo Dr.

Hermès – Fine leather goods from France. 343 N. Rodeo Dr.

Fred Joaillier – Expensive jewelry. 401 N. Rodeo Dr.

Jurgensen's – Fine foods. 409 N. Beverly Dr.

Frances Klein – Antique jewelry. 310 N. Rodeo Dr.

I. Magnin – Branch of the well-known chain. 9634 Wilshire Blvd.

Neiman Marcus – The department store for those who have almost everything. 9700 Wilshire Blvd.

David Orgell – Crystal, china, antique and modern silver, and jewelry. 320 N. Rodeo Dr.

The Rodeo Collection – The world's poshest mall, representing *Gianni Versace,*

Sonia Rykiel, Nina Ricci, Merletto, Fogal, and *Furla,* and a good place to taste LA's most acclaimed ice cream at *Robin Rose.* 421 N. Rodeo Dr.

Scriptorium – Autograph gallery. 427 N. Canon Dr.

Sharper Image – The very latest in high tech toys. 9550 Santa Monica Blvd.

Superior Stamp & Coin – Gold coins and rare stamps. 9478 W. Olympic Blvd.

Tiffany & Co. – Fine jewelry. 9502 Wilshire Blvd.

Williams-Sonoma – Dining table and kitchen outfitters. 317 N. Beverly Dr.

For specialty shopping with more native character, browse in several burgeoning areas, such as:

Melrose Avenue – It runs an eastward gamut from upscale to funky to weird, with Gallery Row found roughly between Doheny Drive and Fairfax Avenue. *LA Impressions,* 8318 Melrose Ave., specializes in Mexican art. At *Gemini Gel,* 8365 Melrose Ave., a superb maker and exhibitor of limited edition prints, customers watch the printing through upstairs gallery windows. Antiques and gift shops, fashion boutiques, restaurants, and small theaters prosper all the way to La Brea Blvd.

Montana Avenue – This cornucopia of small shops, springing up between 7th and 17th Streets along this Santa Monica thoroughfare, has become a window-shopper's delight. Among the pricey and super-specialized boutiques, there's silk lingerie at *Lisa Norman,* 1134 Montana Ave.; bovine collectibles at *Udderly Perfect,* 740 16th St. at Montana Ave.; ditto for cat lovers at *Montana Paws,* 1025 Montana Ave.; and masks at *Thoraya,* 1205 Montana Ave. Take out superb bread and pastries at a branch of Italy's *Il Fornaio* chain or try haute Pritikin cuisine at the *Joy of Saks,* both at 1627 Montana Ave., or join celebrities sipping cappuccino at *Oggi Café,* 1518 Montana Ave.

 MAJOR COLLEGES AND UNIVERSITIES: There are three major university sity campuses spread through the LA area, in addition to dozens of colleges and junior colleges. The University of California (UCLA) is known to college football and basketball fans as the *Bruins.* UCLA's main campus is at 405 Hilgard Ave. (phone: 825-4321). The University of Southern California (USC) has the *Trojans.* USC's campus is at Exposition Blvd. and Hoover St. (phone: 743-2983). California Institute of Technology's main campus is at 1201 E. California Blvd., Pasadena (phone: 818-356-6326).

 SPECIAL EVENTS: There are more special events than we could possibly list here. For complete listings, check the local publications listed above or call the Greater Los Angeles Visitors and Convention Bureau (phone: 624-7300). Annual attractions include: *Pasadena Rose Bowl,* the traditional New Year's Day gridiron spectacle; *Los Angeles Open Golf Tournament,* Pacific Palisades, in February; *Camelia Festival,* Temple City, in February; *Los Angeles Marathon,* in March; Disneyland's *Easter Parade; UCLA Mardi Gras and Manhattan Beach Art Festival,* in May; *Westwood Arts and Crafts Show,* Westwood, in May and October; *Fourth of July* fireworks at *Anaheim Stadium* and Pasadena *Rose Bowl; All-Star Shrine Football Game,* usually held in Pasadena *Rose Bowl,* in July; *Festival of Arts and Pageant of the Masters,* Laguna Beach, in July; *SeaFest,* Long Beach, in August; *International Surf Festival,* Redondo Beach, in August; *Los Angeles County Fair,* Pomona, in September; *Hollywood Christmas Parade,* Hollywood, in November.

 SPORTS AND FITNESS: There is no question that Southern California is a paradise for sports lovers.

Baseball – The Los Angeles *Dodgers, Dodger Stadium,* 1000 Elysian Park Ave. (phone: 224-1500); California *Angels, Anaheim Stadium,* 2000 State College Blvd., Anaheim (phone: 625-1123 or 714-937-6700).

Basketball – The 1989 NBA Western Conference champion *Lakers* play at the

Great Western Forum, Manchester Blvd. and Prairie Ave., Inglewood (phone: 673-1300, 674-6000). The NBA *Clippers* play at the *Sports Arena,* 3939 S. Figueroa (phone: 748-6131).

Bicycling – Biking is great around the Westwood UCLA campus, Griffith Park, and on the bike path between the city of Torrance and the Santa Monica Pier.

Fishing – Power and sailing boats can be rented from *Rent-A-Sail,* 13560 Mindanao Way, Marina del Rey (phone: 822-1868). Fishermen catch halibut, bonito, and bass off the LA shores. Sportfishing boats leave daily from San Pedro, 22 minutes from downtown Los Angeles, site of the LA port, and from the Redondo Beach Marina in Redondo Beach.

Fitness Centers – *Nautilus and Aerobics Plus,* on the ground floor of the International Tower building, offers aerobics classes and has a Jacuzzi and sauna. 888 9th St. at Figueroa (phone: 488-0095), with branches all over the metropolitan area. Many hotels have their own health clubs (see *Checking In*).

Football – Champions of the Big 10 and Pacific 8 college conferences meet in the *Pasadena Rose Bowl* every New Year's Day. UCLA plays its home games at the *Rose Bowl,* and USC plays at the *Coliseum,* 3911 S. Figueroa (phone: 747-7111). The NFL *Rams* play at *Anaheim Stadium* (phone: 625-1123 or 714-937-6767) and the *Raiders* at the *Coliseum.*

Hockey – The *Kings* make their home at the *Great Western Forum* (phone: 673-1300, 674-6000).

Horse Racing – If you like to spend your nights at the track, make tracks for *Los Alamitos.* There's harness, quarterhorse, and some thoroughbred racing year-round. Take Fwy. 605 south to Katella Ave. exit in Orange County (phone: 431-1361 or 714-995-1234). If you prefer daytime action, try *Hollywood Park* between mid-April and late July and from early November to Christmas Eve. Near Los Angeles International Airport between Manchester and Century Blvds. (phone: 419-1500). There's also racing at *Santa Anita Park,* Huntington Dr. and Baldwin Ave., Arcadia (phone: 818-574-7223), from late December to mid-April and October through November.

Jogging – Downtown, run around Echo Park Lake (a little less than a mile); get there by going up Sunset and taking a right onto Glendale. In Griffith Park, run in the woodsy Ferndale area near the Vermont Avenue entrance; get to the park via the Golden State Freeway and watch for the sign to turn off. In Westwood, UCLA has a hilly 4-mile perimeter course and a ¼-mile track. Four blocks from Century City, Cheviot Hills Park, at 2551 Motor Ave., has a runners' course. And in Beverly Hills, jog in Roxbury Park, entrance at 471 S. Roxbury Dr. and Olympic, or along the 1½-mile stretch of Santa Monica Boulevard between Doheny and Wilshire. Jogging is also popular along the oceanside bike path between Marina del Rey and the Palos Verdes Peninsula and in Santa Monica's Palisades Park on Ocean Avenue.

Swimming and Surfing – The best beaches for swimming: El Porto Beach in Manhattan Beach, Santa Monica Beach, Will Rogers State Beach in Pasadena, and Zuma Beach, north of Malibu. For surfing, Malibu Surfrider Beach, Hermosa Beach, El Porto Beach, and Zuma Beach, are tops.

 THEATER: There is no shortage of stages in LA, despite the overshadowing presence of the film industry. The *Center Theatre Group* performs at the *Music Center*'s *Ahmanson Theatre* and *Mark Taper Forum.* For information about either, call 972-7211. Also downtown is the *Los Angeles Theatre Center,* 514 S. Spring St. (phone: 627-5599). The recently revived *State Theatre of California* is back at the *Pasadena Playhouse,* 39 S. El Molina Ave. (phone: 818-536-7529). Other Los Angeles theaters include: the *Doolittle Theatre,* 1615 N. Vine St., Hollywood (phone: 462-6666). The *Shubert Theater* is in the ABC Entertainment Center, 2020 Ave. of the Stars, Century City (for information and credit card reservations, call 800-233-3123). The *Westwood Playhouse* is near the UCLA campus at

10886 Le Conte Ave., Westwood (phone: 208-5454). The *Pantages Theatre* is at 6233 Hollywood Blvd. (phone: 642-4242). Tickets for all major events can be ordered over a telephone charge line called Teletron (410-1062) or from Ticketron outlets at most *Sears* and *Tower Records* stores; call 642-4242 for the nearest location.

MUSIC: All kinds of music can be heard in LA's concert halls and clubs. The *Los Angeles Philharmonic* plays at the *Dorothy Chandler Pavilion, Music Center* (phone: 972-7211). The *Hollywood Bowl,* 2301 N. Highland Ave., Hollywood (phone: 850-2000), is a 17,630-seat hillside amphitheater that features famous guest entertainers as well as being the summer home of the *Philharmonic.* Leading popular performers in a wide range of musical styles play year-round at the *Universal Amphitheatre,* Hollywood Fwy. at Lankershim Blvd. (phone: 818-980-9421). The *Greek Theatre,* 2700 N. Vermont Ave. (phone: 410-1062), is a 6,200-seat indoor theater with concerts by top names. The *Roxy Theatre,* 9009 Sunset Blvd. (phone: 276-2222), is also good for concerts. For country-and-western music, check out the *Palomino Club,* 6907 Lankershim Blvd., North Hollywood (phone: 818-983-1321). Rock and jazz buffs should try the *Palace,* at 1735 N. Vine, near Hollywood and Vine (phone: 462-3000), where the rock theater–dance club downstairs often has live shows as well as dancing. Upstairs, the *Palace Court* has live jazz on weekends.

NIGHTCLUBS AND NIGHTLIFE: Anything goes in LA, especially after dark. Swinging nightspots open and close quickly, since the restless search for what's "in" keeps people on the move. *Doug Weston's Troubador Club* pioneered a number of top rock music acts, at 9081 Santa Monica Blvd., West Hollywood (phone: 276-6168). Another place that seems to be able to hold its own is *Whisky A Go Go,* 8901 Sunset Blvd. (phone: 652-4202). For a quiet, more elegant late evening drink (the popular one here is champagne), try *Nippers,* 439 N. Rodeo Dr., Beverly Hills (phone: 859-8107). With Movietown's pool of talent, comedy clubs are a better bet than elsewhere. Among the options: *Improvisation,* the grandparent of them all, at 8162 Melrose Ave. (phone: 651-2583); and the *Comedy Store,* another survivor, at 8433 Sunset Blvd. (phone: 480-3232).

BEST IN TOWN

CHECKING IN: Los Angeles is the city where mere mortals stand the best chance of checking in alongside a movie star, although, obviously, it costs more for the possible privilege of rubbing shoulders with cinematic royalty. If you're looking for someplace simply to shower and sleep, you'll be happier at one of the smaller hotels or motels sprinkled throughout the area. Generally speaking, accommodations are less expensive in the San Fernando and San Gabriel valleys than in Hollywood or downtown. Expect to pay $180 and up for a double room at those places we've bracketed as very expensive; between $125 and $180 at those places listed as expensive; between $80 and $125 at moderate places; and under $80 at inexpensive places. For statewide bed-and-breakfast accommodations, contact *Eye Openers Bed & Breakfast,* PO Box 694, Altadena, CA 91001 (phone: 684-4428 or 818-797-2055), or *California Houseguests International,* 605 Lindley Ave., Suite 6, Tarzana, CA 91356 (phone: 818-344-7878). All telephone numbers are in the 213 area code unless otherwise indicated.

Bel Age – A sister property to the fine *L'Ermitage,* this hotel is also European in tone. Its 198 suites are gracefully decorated with hand-carved rosewood and pecan wood furnishings complemented by pastel color schemes. *La Brasserie* is the hotel's casual French café; *Bel Age,* its more formal dining room, serves nouvelle

Russe cuisine. Other amenities include a heated rooftop pool and limousine service to the Beverly Hills and Century City areas. 1020 N. San Vicente Blvd., West Hollywood (phone: 854-1111). Very expensive.

Bel-Air – A beautiful California ranch–style hotel, splashed with purple and magenta bougainvillea and surrounded by splendid gardens, it has been completely renovated by Rosewood Hotels, who (sadly) sold it to Japan's Sekitei Kaihatsu Company in the spring of 1989 — though Rosewood will continue to manage. It offers 52 rooms, 36 suites, and lovely public areas. Set in 11½ acres in a canyon, it's as private as you're likely to want, and you'll need a car if you plan to leave the plush premises. 701 Stone Canyon Rd., LA (phone: 472-1211). Very expensive.

Beverly Hills – The *Polo Lounge* is a famous watering spot for movie moguls and producers — a place to be seen if you're someone who people will know they've seen once they see you. The hotel is under new ownership, and renovation is freshening up the 268 rooms without destroying the old charm. Show-biz action is pretty heavy at poolside. Stargazers can watch enraptured from a cabana while eating lunch ordered from room service. 9641 Sunset Blvd., Beverly Hills (phone: 276-2251). Very expensive.

Checkers – Geared to the particular needs of the business traveler, this 190-room hotel in the center of Los Angeles's financial district has conference rooms, parlor rooms for smaller meetings, 24-hour catering service, secretarial and courier services, and interpreters. Rooms are fitted with 3 telephones with direct international dialing and call waiting capabilities. To ease the stress of the work day, the hostelry offers a rooftop spa with sauna, steamroom, and exercise equipment. And for mixing business with pleasure, Checkers' restaurant serves everything from "power" breakfasts to late-night suppers. 535 South Grand Avenue, Los Angeles (phone: 624-0000). Very expensive.

L'Ermitage – No relation to the restaurant of the same name, this hotel has a European ambience, 112 suites with kitchens, a rooftop Jacuzzi and pool, a piano lounge, and its own fine *Café Russe*, open only to guests and their guests. It is very well run and blissfully low key. Should provide better pillows, however. Parking available. 9291 Burton Way, Beverly Hills (phone: 278-3344). Very expensive.

Four Seasons – In a residential area on the Los Angeles–Beverly Hills border, just a mile from Rodeo Drive, this luxurious property offers an unusual location. But then, there is very little about this hotel that could be considered "usual." With formal gardens and lifelike J. Seward Johnson statues outside and marble floors, antiques, fresh flowers, and plants inside, it has the feel of a plush manor house, despite its being a modern 16-story high-rise. The 285 rooms are ample, luxuriously appointed, and soothingly pastel, offering such amenities as a lighted makeup mirror in each bathroom, overnight clothes pressing and shoeshines. On the 4th-floor rooftop terrace, there's a heated pool/spa area surrounded by palm trees and lounge chairs and a small exercise area nearby. Topping off the impressive list are 2 restaurants, including *Gardens,* one of the more interesting hotel restaurants. 300 S. Doheny Dr. (phone: 273-2222). Very expensive.

J. W. Marriott – On spacious grounds in Century City, this is Marriott's West Coast luxury flagship, in fashionable château style. The lobby is opulent yet somehow intimate, with art objects, plants, and two live parrots. The hotel features 375 rooms, of which more than half are suites, and indoor and outdoor pools. Room decor runs to warm beige and peach. Among the special touches in amenities: loofahs and natural sponges on tub edges. 2151 Ave. of the Stars (phone: 277-2777). Very expensive.

Loews Santa Monica – The first hotel to be built in Santa Monica in 20 years and Loews' first venture on the West Coast, this 350-room beachfront property provides 20th-century comfort in a setting reminiscent of the Victorian era, when the area flourished as a resort community. A 5-story atrium affords spectacular Pacific views; there is also an extensive fitness center, an indoor/outdoor swimming pool, and a Jacuzzi. There are 2 restaurants, the contemporary Italian *Riva,* and the more casual *Coast Café,* and a lobby bar that also serves afternoon tea. All rooms have TV sets, minibars, 2 telephone lines, hair dryers and other amenities expected of a fine hotel. 1700 Ocean Ave., Santa Monica (phone: 458-6700). Very expensive.

Regent Beverly Wilshire – Just walk out the front door into the middle of the elegant Beverly Hills shopping district. The mood of this Regent Group hotel is more businesslike and subdued, less Hollywood flash, than at the Beverly Hills. In the new tower wing, all the rooms are done in different color schemes, furniture styles, and themes. The recently reopened, newly renovated Wilshire Wing has 147 units, as well as new restaurants and bars. There are 459 rooms in all. 9500 Wilshire Blvd., Beverly Hills (phone: 275-4282 or 800-545-4000). Very expensive.

St. James Club – This lavishly restored apartment tower is an Art Deco gem that once played host to Clark Gable and Marilyn Monroe, among others. To rub shoulders with today's celebrities (Joan Collins and Quincy Jones are members) and feel like English nobility in an exclusive clubs, non-members may check into the 40 rooms and 34 suites at $8 per day above members' rates or buy a meal at the *Members' Room.* Fred Astaire in top hat and tails would have felt right at home in the stylish 1930s lobby, tapping down stairs carved out of a block of marble. 8358 Sunset Blvd. (phone: 654-710). Very expensive.

Sheraton Grande – Pampering on a *Grande* scale — with butler service, a fully stocked pantry on every floor, and other amenities beyond the call of duty. The 469 rooms are tastefully decorated, with plenty of living and work space. Conference and entertainment space is all first class and includes a ballroom, meeting rooms, teleconferencing, and, during the day, use of a 4-movie-theater complex in the building. There's a pool (but no health club), and the downtown *YMCA,* with its gym, running track, and courts, is right across the street via a pedestrian bridge. 333 S. Figueroa (phone: 617-1133). Very expensive.

Westwood Marquis – A favorite among businessfolk who appreciate quality. Originally built to house UCLA students, it has been converted to first class digs. The attractive high-rise holds 258 suites, and the bustling college town of Westwood is all around. The *Garden Terrace Room* offers a terrific brunch, and the UCLA running track is not a half-mile away. 930 Hilgard Ave., Westwood (phone: 208-8765). Very expensive.

Century Plaza and Tower – A 1,072-room property with a lot of convention business. Its new wing, the Tower, has luxurious lodgings, and the hotel has a full-service business center. There are several fine restaurants on the premises, the best being French (*La Chaumière*), and plenty of shops to browse in. In Century City, near the ABC Entertainment Center, the hotel has a complimentary town car service for trips within a 5-mile radius. 2025 Ave. of the Stars, Century City (phone: 277-2000). Very expensive (the Tower) to expensive.

Bel Air Summit – This spot underwent an extensive renovation and now has added amenities and a light, breezy atmosphere. All 162 rooms have balconies, and there are 2 swimming pools, a tennis court, cocktail lounge, and dining room. Free parking. 11461 Sunset Blvd. (phone: 476-6571). Expensive.

Beverly Hilton – Many fans say this is the best of the whole Hilton lot. It's not quite as convenient to downtown Beverly Hills as the *Wilshire,* but if you plan to spend a lot of time in the hotel you'll be happy here, since this is another one of those self-contained hotels that caters to every need. *Trader Vic's* is a consistently good restaurant, and *L'Escoffier* offers good food plus entertainment and dancing. 9876 Wilshire Blvd., Beverly Hills (phone: 274-7777). Expensive.

Biltmore – The grande dame of downtown hotels offers dramatic interiors that combine the classical architecture typical of European palaces with contemporary luxury. There are 700 well-appointed rooms, an indoor pool, and Jacuzzi. Other plusses include the fine French restaurant *Bernard's* and the *Grand Avenue* bar, with great jazz nightly. 506 S. Grand Ave. (phone: 624-1011). Expensive.

Hyatt Regency – Top-to-bottom renovation has reduced the scale of the Hyatt signature atrium and created two new restaurants. This 487-room super-modern hotel is another convention favorite. 711 S. Hope St. (phone: 683-1234). Expensive.

Los Angeles Registry – In this gray glass Art Deco tower, every room has expansive views of either the Hollywood Hills or the San Fernando Valley. The tower's top 5 floors are strictly butler-serviced suites; there are 450 rooms in all. There is also a good setup for conventions. Other features include 2 restaurants, 2 lounges, an outdoor heated pool, spa, concierge, staff, and a garage for 700 cars. 555 Universal Terrace Pkwy., Universal City (phone: 818-506-2500). Expensive.

Ma Maison Sofitel – The tail wagged the dog in the decision to build a château-style hotel as the proper setting for the reincarnation of the noted *Ma Maison* restaurant. The broad, carved staircase, warm woods, country French furniture, and gaily patterned wall and window treatments create a fittingly homey atmosphere in this 311-room property called "My House." The bistro, *La Cajole,* is an approximate re-creation of an old Parisian artists' hangout. On the Beverly Hills–Los Angeles border, the hotel offers complimentary limousine service to the airport and shopping within a 5-mile radius. 8555 Beverly Blvd. (phone: 278-5444). Expensive.

Marina Beach – Across the road from Marina del Rey, the world's largest pleasure boat harbor, this seaside resort stands a short ride (by free shuttle) from the airport. Sailing, jogging, swimming, and bicycling are among the relaxing amenities available near this cheery 300-room hotel, with 2 restaurants, a pastel color scheme, and ocean and mountain views. 4100 Admiralty Way (phone: 301-3000). Expensive.

Sheraton Plaza–La Reina – This conference center is Sheraton's largest California hotel. It features 810 rooms, comprehensive convention facilities, and *Landry's,* a fine restaurant. 6101 W. Century Blvd. (phone: 642-1111). Expensive.

Westin Bonaventure – This 1,474-room giant is a major downtown convention hotel. Its mirrored towers are an LA skyline landmark, and it is especially convenient for downtown activities. Rooms are pretty pedestrian for the high prices. 404 S. Figueroa St. (phone: 624-1000). Expensive.

Barnabey's – Possibly the best value in Southern California, with the charm of an English country inn, less than 3 miles from the airport and within walking distance of Manhattan Beach. All rooms are furnished with antiques and come with breakfast. Dine in *Barnabey's* restaurant and drink in *Rosie's Pub.* Complimentary 24-hour shuttle service to the airport, beach, and shopping. Sepulveda Blvd. at Rosecrans Ave., Manhattan Beach (phone: 545-8466). Moderate.

Century Wilshire – In Westwood, the movie theater capital of LA and home of UCLA, this 99-room hotel offers kitchen units, complimentary coffee, and continental breakfast. 10776 Wilshire (phone: 474-4506). Moderate.

Mikado Best Western – The twisting canyon roads separating Hollywood from the San Fernando Valley are among the most scenic parts of LA. The *Mikado* is set between Coldwater and Laurel canyons, where cottages and modern glass and wood homes hang dramatically from cliffs, propped up only by stilts. The 58-room *Mikado* has a pool, Jacuzzi, restaurant, and cocktail lounge. Guests receive complimentary American breakfast. Pets are welcome, too. 12600 Riverside Dr. (phone: 818-763-9141). Moderate.

New Otani – Conveniently within walking distance of the *Music Center,* the *New Otani* has 448 rooms featuring Japanese luxury and service in a lovely garden-like setting. Amenities include a shopping arcade and a Japanese health club. 120 S. Los Angeles St. (phone: 629-1200). Moderate.

Best Western Farmer's Daughter – Across the street from the Farmers Market and CBS television studios, this 66-room motel offers you the chance to be in the middle of an active part of town. There's also a heated pool, and all of the rooms have refrigerators. 115 S. Fairfax (phone: 937-3930). Inexpensive.

Figueroa – Downtown's best buy, this venerable, still gracious Spanish hotel has tile floors, patio dining, a pool, and large guestrooms. 939 S. Figueroa St. (phone: 627-8971). Inexpensive.

Safari Inn – If you're planning to visit The Burbank Studios, this will be more convenient than the Beverly Hills or downtown LA hotels. The spacious valley environment also provides more of a sense of being in the open. 105 rooms. 1911 W. Olive Ave., Burbank (phone: 818-845-8586). Inexpensive.

EATING OUT: These days, Los Angeles may be the country's most exciting restaurant town. Only the purest of purists still go completely by Escoffier's book. Through and through, ethnic places abound in all price ranges, while imaginative chefs meld superb raw materials, ethnic ingredients, and nutritional caveats into pots of culinary gold. Though popularity with the show-biz crowd is often inversely proportional to the quality of a kitchen and the maître d's treatment of non-celeb guests, good manners are creeping back. Regrettably, dining in din is still in, even when the food is exquisite, but some new restaurants have rediscovered the joy of calm. Our choices are below. Expect to pay $60 or more for two at those places we've listed as expensive; $30 to $60 at places in the moderate category; and under $30 at places in the inexpensive category. Prices do not include drinks, wine, or tips. All telephone numbers are in the 213 area code unless otherwise indicated.

Bistro Garden – The very same Beverly Hills celebrities who have parked their Rolls-Royces up the street at the *Bistro* for years are now making its sister restaurant the "in" spot. Lunch is especially chic with fare like bratwurst with hot potato salad. Closed for lunch Sundays. Reservations necessary. Major credit cards. 176 N. Canon Dr., Beverly Hills (phone: 550-3900). Expensive.

Le Chardonnay – Dark carved woods, arched mirrors, and delicate French tiles replicate a romantic Parisian bistro from the Belle Epoque. Chardonnays by the dozen star on the wine list, and the array of desserts would fill the windows of a Parisian pâtisserie. The menu is cosmopolitan, though with emphasis on the French. Closed Sundays and for lunch Saturdays. Reservations recommended. Major credit cards. 8284 Melrose Ave. (phone: 655-8880). Expensive.

Chasen's – A Beverly Hills institution for about 50 years. People come here more for echoes of old Hollywood than for the food, although specialties such as hobo steaks, chicken pot pie, and chili have become downright trendy. Dinner only; closed Mondays. Reservations advised. American Express only. 9039 Beverly Blvd. (phone: 271-2168). Expensive.

La Chaumière – Despite its location — the 5th floor of the *Century Tower* hotel in a bustling area off Santa Monica Blvd. — this dining room successfully evokes a French country manor, where diners can look out over Santa Monica Bay while enjoying such California-French inspirations as cold lobster stew with Japanese cucumbers or roast rack of Sonoma lamb with dried figs and peanut sauce. In addition to some of the best California vintages, the wine list offers fine French and German selections as well. Open nightly for dinner, weekdays only for lunch. Reservations advised. Major credit cards. 2025 Ave. of the Stars (phone: 277-2000). Expensive.

Le Dôme – One of the most interesting of LA's French restaurants. It opened as a brasserie with various grilled dishes (the thick veal chop is a wonderful introduction) but added more traditional haute cuisine in response to patron pressure. The atmosphere is chic, understated, comfortable. Closed Sundays. Reservations necessary. Major credit cards. 8720 Sunset Blvd. (phone: 659-6919). Expensive.

Dynasty Room – Continental French food is served in a restaurant that showcases original artwork and artifacts from China's T'ang Dynasty. The chicken breast with black angel hair pasta is one of several winning combinations. We also recommend veal and lamb chops and fresh swordfish. But much of the restaurant's popularity is probably owed to its "menu minceur," which offers health-conscious dinners — appetizer, main course, and dessert — that total less than 500 calories. Open daily for dinner. Reservations advised. Major credit cards. *Westwood Marquis* hotel, 930 Hilgard Ave., Westwood (phone: 208-8765). Expensive.

L'Ermitage – Successfully combining French chic with California casual, it remains a fine, classic French restaurant. Among the many excellent choices on the menu are such familiar standards as lobster consommé with oyster flan, salmon paillard, scallops and shiitake mushrooms, and, for a proper finale, poached pear, Burgundy-style, with homemade vanilla ice cream. Too special a place to waste on just an ordinary night, so celebrate something — anything — while you're here. (Maybe you could celebrate that you're willing to spend $120 for a dinner for two.) Closed Sundays. Reservations necessary. Major credit cards. 730 N. La Cienega Blvd. (phone: 652-5840). Expensive.

Ivy – A favorite venue for lunchtime power deals, it is an anomaly — an old brick farmhouse on bustling Robertson Boulevard in Beverly Hills whose rustic decor suits the eclectic American menu with a southern accent. The owner grows herbs, peppers, deep-red beefsteak tomatoes, and citrus for the kitchen. Corn chowder with fresh tarragon, warm mesquite-grilled salad with chicken or shrimp, and twice-cooked Cajun steaks — first oven-seared and then grilled — are standouts on the changing menu. Desserts are the likes of which mama could only dream of making. Open daily except Sundays for lunch and dinner. Reservations necessary. Major credit cards. 113 N. Robertson Blvd. (phone: 274-8303). Expensive.

Joss – With austere decor and waiters in high-collared white jackets, this is a high-style, high-price showcase for unfamiliar regional Chinese delicacies, such as "spicy shrimp with nuts of olive mellow and Chinese red cheese." The waiter shows off the whole perfectly crisped, golden brown Hong Kong Pin-Pei chicken before carving and preparing it in the style of Peking duck on a side table. Tangerine beef marinated in liqueur and garnished with peel is a novel taste. Open daily for dinner, daily except Saturdays for lunch. Reservations recommended. Major credit cards. 8255 Sunset Blvd. (phone: 276-1886). Expensive.

Ma Maison – The celebrated chef-owner Patrick Terrail wears a boutonnière and practically kisses ladies' hands, but the reborn *Ma Maison* retains a cozy feeling. The garden-like room is restful; service is attentive yet unobtrusive. The David Hockney covers of the menu, which changes daily, are for sale. The fare is French-Californian, expertly and lightly sauced. You would never guess that the flourless raviolis enveloped with goat cheese and herbs are made of turnips. Open daily except Sundays for lunch and dinner. Reservations advised. Major credit cards. 8555 Beverly Blvd. (phone: 278-5444). Expensive.

L'Orangerie – Under high ceilings and among the potted palms you'll find one of the city's most attractive dining rooms and some of the most exciting dishes as well. The mostly French menu offers soft scrambled eggs topped with caviar, Atlantic bass and other fish flown in from Brittany twice a week, and first class desserts like the apple tart or a puff pastry filled with raspberries and sweet cream. Open daily for dinner. Reservations necessary. Major credit cards. 903 N. La Cienega Blvd. (phone: 652-9770). Expensive.

Pacific Dining Car – Steaks — cut on the premises from aged, corn-fed beef — are the house specialty, although the menu also offers four types of fresh fish every day. The restaurant is a real dining car (plus an additional building) that's been in its downtown location since 1921. This is a good place for early dinner or late supper en route to or from a show at the *Music Center.* Open 24 hours daily. Reservations necessary. Visa and MasterCard only. 1310 W. 6th St. (phone: 483-6000). Expensive.

Le Restaurant – A quaint and unassuming decor provides the backdrop for yet another of LA's fine French establishments. All entrées, as well as appetizers, are carefully prepared. Service is just as meticulous. Closed Sundays. Reservations necessary. Major credit cards. 8475 Melrose Pl. (phone: 651-5553). Expensive.

Rex II Ristorante – In an Art Deco building in the heart of downtown and filled with Lalique, oak paneling, and brass, it duplicates the dining room of the *Rex,* an Italian passenger liner popular during the 1920s. Each evening there's a six-course special dinner or à la carte dining. On the mezzanine level there's a full bar featuring soft dance music. Open weekdays for lunch and dinner; Saturdays for dinner only. Reservations necessary. Major credit cards. 617 S. Olive (phone: 627-2300). Expensive.

St. Estephe – The Southwestern cooking fad may be fading, but the chef who raised it to artistic heights in the Southland is not. Both the food and the beauty of presentation are still worth the pricey tab and the trip to remote Manhattan Beach. Closed Sundays and for lunch Saturdays. Friday and Saturday dinner reservations advised. Major credit cards. 2640 Sepulveda Blvd., Manhattan Beach (phone: 545-1334). Expensive.

Scandia – *Scandia* is returning to its former glory after years of decline. A typical meal might begin with the Viking Platter (tiny blinis flavored with aquavit and topped with Danish caviar and sour cream), followed by virgin lobster (tiny fried Norwegian lobster tails) or tournedos Theodora (filet mignon split and garnished with goose liver). Closed Mondays. Reservations necessary. Major credit cards. 9040 Sunset Blvd., West Hollywood (phone: 278-3555). Expensive.

La Serre – The chef at this garden-like stronghold of classic French in the San Fernando Valley whips up unusual sauces, such as cream of whiskey and coffee to accompany fish, and concocts a fragrant sorbet of home-grown mint, jasmine, and roses. Lobster with different sauces is the most popular choice. Closed Sundays and for lunch Saturdays. Reservations necessary. Major credit cards. 12969 Ventura Blvd., Studio City (phone: 818-990-0500). Expensive.

Spago – Owner Wolfgang Puck describes his unusual menu as California cuisine. Although entrées include roasted baby lamb, grilled salmon and tuna, and pasta that's made daily, this restaurant is best known for its unusual and changeable pizza — with toppings like duck sausage, goat cheese, oregano, and tomato, or smoked lamb, eggplant, and roasted peppers. Baked in a wood-burning brick oven, they arrive at the table sizzling hot and crispy. Open daily. Tops among the trendy set, so it's necessary to reserve about 3 weeks ahead. Major credit cards. 1114 Horn Ave. at Sunset Blvd. (phone: 652-4025). Expensive.

La Toque – A fine French restaurant, arguably (and if there's one thing devotees of fine food and wine like to argue about, it's this) the best in the city. Small, intimate, very romantic, with a menu rewritten daily. Since only the freshest ingredients are used, the menu changes to reflect seasonal availability and quality. Usually at least four fish dishes; another four or more meat dishes, including, each autumn, game. Plus an extensive wine list — about half California labels — with some real treasures (for instance, the 1974 Diamond Creek Red Rock Terrace cabernet). Open weekdays for lunch; daily except Sundays for dinner. Only 20 tables, so reservations are advised. Major credit cards. 8171 Sunset Blvd. (phone: 656-7515). Expensive.

Valentino – Devotees generally describe the cuisine as Italian, and the homemade pasta certainly bears them out. But there's also a world of other choices on the eclectic menu — starters such as timballo (rolled baby eggplant) or crespelle (corn crêpes stuffed with seafood) and entrées like grilled fresh shrimp wrapped with swordfish and dressed with lime juice. The casually elegant spot boasts an impressive wine cellar: more than 50,000 bottles, including Italian, French, German, and California labels. Open daily except Sundays for dinner; Fridays for lunch as well. Reservations necessary. Major credit cards. 3115 Pico Blvd., Santa Monica (phone: 829-4313). Expensive.

Windsor – This award-winning restaurant is noted for its wide variety of beef dishes. Though the atmosphere is somewhat formal, it's particularly popular with the *Dodger Stadium* crowds. Closed Sundays. Reservations advised. Major credit cards. 3198 W. 7th St. (phone: 382-1261). Expensive.

Café Jacoulet – A mini-UN of influences: nouvelle French with a soupçon of Japanese in the food and in the spare, subtle decor, in a restored red brick precinct of old Pasadena. Sashimi salad is a lunch favorite, along with warm duck and chicken salads. Fish in light sauces is the specialty. Closed Mondays; no lunch Saturdays. Brunch with live jazz Sundays. Reservations recommended. Major credit cards. 91 N. Raymond Ave., Pasadena (phone: 818-796-2233). Moderate.

Le Cellier – A restaurant once notorious for overbooking, but the prices are good and the quality makes it superior to many more expensive restaurants. Daily specials, which include soup and salad, are splendid buys. Closed Mondays. Reservations advised. Major credit cards. 2628 Wilshire Blvd. (phone: 828-1585). Moderate.

Gingerman – Hollywood celebrities have really taken to Patrick O'Neal and Carroll O'Connor's local branch of New York's *Gingerman* pub. At dinner, the specialties are a good choice, and the country pâté makes a fine starter. Closed Sundays. Reservations advised for dinner; not necessary for supper. Major credit cards. 369 N. Bedford Dr., Beverly Hills (phone: 273-7585). Moderate.

Lawry's the Prime Rib – What's billed is what you get, with trimmings, at this legendary reliable — delicious prime ribs of beef with horseradish sauce, perfect Yorkshire pudding, a huge baked potato, and salad. The room is paneled but bright, the better to see the immense portions. Dinner daily. Reservations advised. Major credit cards. 55 N. Cienega Blvd., Beverly Hills (phone: 652-2827). Moderate.

Mandarin – Northern Chinese cooking in elegant surroundings instead of the usual plastic, pseudo-Oriental decor. Not on the menu, but well worth remembering as an appetizer, is the minced squab wrapped in lettuce leaves; also, be sure to try the spicy prawns. Open daily for dinner; weekdays for lunch. Reservations advised. Major credit cards. 430 N. Camden Dr., Beverly Hills (phone: 272-0267). Moderate.

Monty's – An all-around, mouth-watering favorite, *Monty's* serves great steamed clams, barbecued spareribs, the thickest, juiciest prime ribs in LA, tempting scampi, and shrimp Monty (bacon-wrapped and stuffed). The charcoal-broiled swordfish is habit-forming. Open daily. Reservations advised. Major credit cards. 1100 Glendon Ave., Westwood (phone: 208-8787), and 502 S. Fair Oaks Ave., Pasadena (phone: 818-892-7776). Moderate.

Musso & Frank Grill – It really is a grill, in Hollywood since 1919, and apparently not redecorated once (not that its regulars — film people, journalists, the moiling LA middle class — want it to change one iota). Orthodox American food and the kind of place the cachet of which is having no cachet; it's okay if you like nostalgia and rude waiters. Closed Sundays. Reservations advised. Major credit cards. 6667 Hollywood Blvd. (phone: 467-7788). Moderate.

Pane Caldo Bistrot – An unpretentious Italian ristorante with a great view of the city's famed hills. What it lacks in fancy appointments it more than makes up for with careful food preparation, generous portions, and reasonable prices. A complimentary appetizer and basket of focaccia arrive with the menu to ease the difficult task of choosing among Tuscan specialties such as warm bell pepper salad, risotto with asparagus, tagliatelle with porcini, spinach tortelloni with butter and sage, ossobuco (veal shank with vegetable sauce), and a selection of 14 individual pizza. Try the ultra-rich tiramisù or a wedge of sinfully good crème caramel for dessert. Open daily for lunch and dinner. Reservations advised. Major credit cards. 8840 Beverly Blvd. (phone: 274-0916). Moderate.

Peppone – Possibly the best Italian restaurant in LA, tucked away in a tiny West Los Angeles shopping center. Splendid pasta and veal dishes are the cornerstones of the evening. Open daily for dinner, weekdays for lunch. Reservations necessary. Major credit cards. 11628 Barrington Ct. (phone: 476-7379). Moderate.

Siamese Princess – This Oriental eatery, which predates the Thai proliferation, looks most like a second-hand antiques shop. European furniture and collectibles vie for space with Siamese gift items and photos of British, Thai, and show-biz royalty. The food, billed as "Royal Thai" and beautifully presented, ranks high above run-of-the-mill. Slivers of orange peel raise crisp rice noodles to a delicacy. Dinner daily; lunch Wednesdays through Fridays. Major credit cards. 8048 W. 3rd St. (phone: 653-2643). Moderate.

Stratton's Grill – Although it's in the heart of bustling Westwood, there is a country lodge feeling about this place, decorated as it is with lots of wood pillars and paneling and the heads of elk on the walls. Food is good, substantial grill fare with a flare. In addition to mesquite-broiled pork chops, lamb chops, and swordfish, there are lighter dishes such as sautéed shrimp in lime sauce and clams steamed in white sauce. On the lower level, diners sit in booths; upstairs, at tables overlooking the usually busy bar. Open daily for lunch and dinner. Reservations unnecessary. Major credit cards. 1037 Broxton Ave., Westwood (phone: 208-0488). Moderate.

Tamayo – Here's Old Mexican elegance in an airy, spacious hacienda, where paintings by Mexican master Rufino Tamayo are displayed and a cabrito (kid) grills to a glistening brown on the open rotisserie. The popularity of Yucatán-style sea bass, enchiladas, puntas (Monterrey-style fajitas), and mole poblano demonstrates the wisdom of using outstanding regional recipes. Dinner daily, lunch weekdays. Reservations recommended. Major credit cards. 5300 Olympic Blvd., East Los Angeles (phone: 260-4700). Moderate.

A Thousand Cranes – Besides having such a beautiful name, this Japanese restaurant is well versed in the traditional art of serving beautiful food. It has several tatami rooms and a Western dining room. Reservations advised. Major credit cards. *New Otani* hotel, 120 S. Los Angeles St. (phone: 629-1200). Moderate.

Tracton's – Eastern beef — in the form of prime ribs and various prime cuts of steak — cooked to perfection, is what draws the crowds in here. Also try the green goddess dressing on the tomato and anchovy salad. Open daily. Reservations advised. Major credit cards. 16705 Ventura Blvd., Encino (phone: 818-783-1320). Moderate.

California Pizza Kitchen – This small chain is a *Spago* disciple's pop version of pizzeria à la California. Bright, sunny interiors with yellow ceilings and flowering plants show off the big, white-tiled wood ovens, which turn out the crusts for "design" toppings from Peking-style duck to goat cheese. Chrome-accented chairs and black tables recall Milan modern, but neither pizzerias nor pizza have ever been dressed like these in their ancestral land. Pasta, salads, and desserts are also on the menu. Open mid-morning to late evening daily. Major credit cards. 207 Beverly Dr., Beverly Hills (phone: 272-7878) and other locations. Inexpensive.

Chicago Pizza Works – The pizza are deep-dish style and served with your choice of a wide range of toppings. Other offerings include lasagna, spaghetti, salads, and desserts. There are also over 100 beers from which to choose, with a brewer's dozen offered at weekly tastings. Open daily. Reservations unnecessary. Visa and Master-Card only. 11641 Pico Blvd. (phone: 477-7740). Inexpensive.

El Cholo – LA is glutted with places promising authentic south-of-the-border cooking, but this is the best, without question. Around for more than 50 years, and its burritos and combination plates are real knockouts. Open daily. There's usually a wait even with reservations; they're advised anyway. Major credit cards. 1121 S. Western Ave. (phone: 734-2773). Inexpensive.

Hamayoshi – This restaurant, one of the reasons Japanese diplomats request an appointment in Los Angeles, is a sushi bar for connoisseurs, favoring flatfish of all kinds — a list not to be equaled at almost any other sushi house. The place is small and simple, and customers sometimes have to wait outside for a spot. Open daily; no lunch on weekends. Reservations advised. Major credit cards. 3350 W. 1st St. (phone: 384-2914). Inexpensive.

Nate 'n' Al's Delicatessen – Where unrepatriated Easterners go for a hot pastrami or corned beef fix. A block or so from the *Regent Beverly Wilshire* hotel. Open daily from 7:30 AM to 8:45 PM, Saturdays to 9:30 PM. No reservations. Diners Club only. 414 N. Beverly Dr., Beverly Hills (phone: 274-0101). Inexpensive.

Original Pantry – The decor is early greasy spoon — the food, waiters, and prices ditto — yet long lines at lunch have forced expansion after 60 years. A potful of raw vegetable sticks precedes big portions of basic food. If the mood for a big American breakfast strikes at 3 AM, one might even find a parking place outside. Open nonstop. No credit cards. 877 S. Figueroa (phone: 972-9279). Inexpensive.

Panache – An elegant Belgian restaurant that pioneered saltless cooking. The chef relies on fresh herbs to season an extensive range of seafood, poultry, and meat dishes, which come with different sauces, depending on the state of the diner's diet. American Heart Association seals mark the approved items. Salt shakers, on the table for such Belgian specialties as stew with beer and trout garnished with prosciutto, cater to the uninhibited. Dinner daily, lunch weekdays. Reservations recommended. Major credit cards. 233 Wilshire Blvd., Santa Monica (phone: 451-8621). Inexpensive.

Panda Inn – Another superior small chain, with branches in upscale shopping malls and in the San Gabriel Valley. It features well-seasoned Chinese dishes with an emphasis on rather spicy Mandarin and Szechwan. The ambience is Californian rather than mom-and-pop Oriental, with white tablecloths and good light. Lunch and dinner daily. Reservations accepted. Major credit cards. 10800 W. Pico Blvd., Westside Pavilion (phone: 470-7790), and other locations. Inexpensive.

Sida – Rather difficult to find in Canoga Park, and woefully short on charm, but it makes up for it with excellent Thai food, such as noodles made on the spot to complement chicken, cold meat, and vegetable dishes. A wonderful introduction to Thai cuisine. Open daily. Reservations necessary. Major credit cards. 21109 Sherman Way, Canoga Park (phone: 818-703-9480). Inexpensive.

Twin Dragon – As inexpensive as Chinese food used to be, with a solid repertoire of topnotch northern Chinese food. A lot of families bring their children here, and it's pretty noisy. Open daily. Reservations advised. Major credit cards. 8597 W. Pico Blvd. (phone: 657-7355). Inexpensive.

And finally, for dessert, try the luscious ice cream made by *Robin Rose,* at 215 Rose Ave. in Venice and sold at the Rodeo Collection on Rodeo Dr.; in Old Pasadena at 35 S. Raymond St.; and at 333 S. Grand Ave., downtown in the Wells Fargo Center.

LOUISVILLE

Everyone knows one thing about Louisville: Once a year the town is host to that amazing horse race and attendant carousal called the Kentucky Derby. There are two seasons in Louisville: Derby Week (the first week in May) and the rest of the year. But there is a good deal to that "other" season, and Kentucky's largest city is too often dismissed as a one-horse-race town.

Louisville (pronounced *loo-ee-ville* by visitors, and *loo-a-vul* — sounding a little like *interval* — by residents) combines aspects of the big city and the small town in its character. It is a blend of urbanity and provincialism, tradition and progressivism — the product of the city's traditional role as fence-sitter between North and South.

The fence the city sits on is the Ohio River, which also serves as the boundary between Kentucky and Indiana. The city has a population of 298,000, but the metropolitan area extends into four Kentucky counties and three in southern Indiana, so Louisville is the economic, social, and cultural center of 965,000 people.

Louisville's development as an industrial town is impressive. The city was actually settled in 1778 as an informal military base; it was the point from which George Rogers Clark drove the British and the Indians from the Midwest. The appearance of steamboats on the Ohio in the early 19th century turned a lazy river town into a booming port, and today more tonnage passes through Louisville than through the Panama Canal. The city itself produces more than half the world's bourbon as well as substantial amounts of such varied products as cigarettes, chemicals, and appliances.

It's a city of "has and has not." *Actors Theatre of Louisville* has been called the "Broadway of the Midwest" by national critics. The *Louisville Orchestra* is the only city orchestra in the world with its own recording label. And don't forget the lovely parks, the good old country cookin', or the leisurely cruises up the Ohio on the steamboat *Belle of Louisville.*

What it hasn't got is a variety of places to go after — or for that matter, before — the cruise. It's hard to find a good meal after midnight. In the city named for Louis XVI of France, good French restaurants are few.

Louisville keeps trying, though. Visitors will find its will to improve itself as inspiring as they find its reverence for tradition charming. In recent years, there's been a veritable renaissance downtown. The Riverfront Plaza/Main Street area is now the home of the new *Kentucky Center for the Arts,* a natural history museum, and an array of fine shops and restaurants. And don't overlook — as if you could — the Louisville Falls Fountain, a water and light show in the middle of the Ohio River.

You get the feeling that Louisville wants to be a big city. In the southern tradition, though, it's just been taking its time.

LOUISVILLE AT-A-GLANCE

SEEING THE CITY: The *Spire* restaurant and cocktail lounge on the 19th floor of the *Hyatt Regency Louisville* revolves to show views of downtown Louisville, the Ohio River, and, when it's not too hazy, southern Indiana across the river. 320 W. Jefferson (phone: 587-3434).

SPECIAL PLACES: The best way to get around Louisville is by car. You can walk around downtown, but attractions like *Churchill Downs,* historic old homes, and the lovely surrounding countryside a few miles from the center of town require transportation.

Museum of History and Science – Space Hall, a 360-degree IMAX movie theater, the "mummy's tomb," and exhibitions on caves and the Ohio River Valley, will appeal to children as well as adults. Open daily. Admission charge. 727 W. Main St. (phone: 561-6100).

Louisville Falls Fountain – In the middle of the Ohio River, "the world's largest floating fountain" creates 375-foot-high sprays, watery fleur-de-lis (the city symbol), and other special water and light effects. Daily, April through October. Best viewing is from Riverfront Plaza/Belevedere, north of Main St., between 4th Ave. and 6th St.

Kentucky Center for the Arts – Music, dance, and theater are on the bill at the city's new performing arts center. There's also a restaurant and gift shop, and visitors are welcome. 5 Riverfront Plaza, at 6th and Main Sts. (phone: 584-7777).

Kentucky Botanical Gardens – An ever-growing collection of rare plants from around the world, plus one of the largest displays of tropical ferns in the Midwest. Closed Tuesdays and Fridays. 814½ Cherokee Rd. (phone: 452-1121).

KentuckyShow! – An entertaining multimedia presentation shown in a restored 1920s movie house that aims to convince viewers that Kentucky is a lot more than tobacco, horses, and bourbon. Closed Sundays. Admission charge. 651 4th Ave. (phone: 561-6123).

Louisville Zoological Gardens – The zoo offers a pleasant afternoon outing for the whole family, but be prepared to do some walking. Instead of cramped cages, the animals' terrain is spacious and attractive. There's also a children's zoo. Closed Mondays in winter. Admission charge. 1100 Trevilian Way (phone: 459-2184).

Louisville Galleria – The 40 stores and 10 restaurants in the city's most elegant shopping complex offer everything from high fashion to fast food. It's all under glass — 12,392 panes, to be exact. 4th Ave. between Liberty St. and Muhammad Ali Blvd. (phone: 584-7170).

Belle of Louisville – Board a 19th-century-style steamboat for a nostalgic, scenic cruise on the Ohio River. Afternoon cruises daily, Memorial Day through Labor Day (except Mondays), with Saturday evening dance cruises. Tickets available at the steamer office (4th Ave. and River Rd.) or in the boarding line at the foot of 4th Ave. (phone: 625-2355 or 582-2547).

Farmington – Built according to Thomas Jefferson's plans, the 19th-century home of Judge John Speed is an outstanding example of Federal architecture. Open daily. Admission charge. 3033 Bardstown Rd. (phone: 452-9920).

Old Louisville – The homes in Old Louisville (2nd to 6th Streets and Ormsby to Eastern Parkway) are fine examples of 19th-century Victorian architecture. You can visit the Information Center year-round for a free walking tour. 1340 S. 4th St. in Central Park (phone: 635-5244).

Locust Grove – Another fascination for architecture fans, this Georgian plantation

CENTRAL LOUISVILLE

was the last home of George Rogers Clark. Open daily. Admission charge. 561 Blankenbaker La. (phone: 897-9845).

Churchill Downs – By far Louisville's most popular attraction, the Kentucky Derby draws over 100,000 people to *Churchill Downs* on the first Saturday in May. The twin-spired track is packed with fans sipping mint juleps, shedding a few tears at the sound of "My Old Kentucky Home," and if they're lucky, catching a glimpse of some of the world's most expensive horseflesh. If you can stand the unabashed sentimentality, the crowds, and the expense (accommodations are sold at a substantial premium on Derby weekend), the Derby is worth the trip — at least once. Reserved seats for the race are hard to come by (they're held by box owners), but all you need to join the general admission party in the infield is $20 — and a lot of nerve. For information, write to Churchill Downs, Derby Ticket Office, 700 Central Ave., Louisville, KY 40208 (phone: 636-3541).

The spring meet begins in May; closing dates vary. The fall meet varies from year to year. At other times the grounds are open. At the *Kentucky Derby Museum,* you can view racing memorabilia, watch a 360-degree panorama on the race, and through "hands-on" exhibits test your Derby trivia skills and explore the mysteries of pari-mutuel betting. Daily except Derby Day. Admission charge. 700 Central Ave. (phone: 637-1111).

■**EXTRA SPECIAL:** Kentucky history comes to life in Bardstown, about 40 miles south of Louisville. At My Old Kentucky Home State Park, visitors can tour the Federal mansion that inspired Stephen Foster to write what is now the state song. Open daily except Mondays in January and February; admission charge (phone: 348-3502). An outdoor drama, *The Stephen Foster Story,* is presented from June through September in the park. The *Oscar Getz Museum of Whiskey* chronicles the history of one of Kentucky's most famous products. Open daily, except Mondays in winter (phone: 348-2999). You can see how whiskey is made today at Maker's Mark Distillery, weekdays (phone: 865-2881). Traditional Kentucky food can be found at the *Old Talbott Tavern,* whose previous patrons include Abraham Lincoln and Andrew Jackson (phone: 348-3494). Take I-65 south out of Louisville, exiting to Rte. 245. En route to Bardstown, you'll encounter Clermont, where you can view a complete collection of Jim Beam decanters at the *American Outpost Museum,* open daily year-round (phone: 543-9877).

SOURCES AND RESOURCES

TOURIST INFORMATION: The Jefferson County Convention and Visitors Bureau, 400 S. 1st St., Louisville, KY 40402 provides lists of current events, maps, and other tourist information. Ask for the excellent Louisville Information Kit, Founder's Square at 5th St. and Muhammad Ali Blvd. (phone: 582-3732).

Television Stations – WHAS Channel 11–CBS; WAVE Channel 3–NBC; WLKY Channel 32–ABC; WKET Channel 68–PBS.

Radio Stations – AM: WHAS 840 (talk/sports/news); WAVG 970 (oldies/news/sports). FM: WLRS 107.3 (rock); WUOL 90.5 (classical); WFPL 89.3 (jazz/information).

Local Coverage – *Louisville Courier-Journal,* morning daily; *Scene* magazine on Saturdays with highlights of the coming week's events; *Louisville* magazine, a monthly that includes a calendar of events. All are available at newsstands.

Telephone – The area code for Louisville is 502.

Sales Tax – A state tax of 5% is added to all purchases except groceries.

CLIMATE: The general tendency is toward mild winters, brief but exquisite springs and falls, and overbearingly humid, long, and polluted summers. But save the bets for the thoroughbreds; snow in April or a 40F day in December isn't too long a shot.

 GETTING AROUND: Airport – Louisville's Standiford Field airport, 5 miles south of downtown, handles only domestic flights. Depending on the traffic, the drive to the airport can take anywhere from 10 to 30 minutes and taxi fare will run about $10. The airport limousine service costs $4.50 and makes stops at a few downtown hotels, but most hotels in town offer courtesy vans to pick up registered guests. The city's TARC buses stop near the airport's main entrance and travel downtown for 35¢ or 60¢, depending on the time of day; for the return trip, buses can be picked up along the southbound side of 1st Street. For airport information, call 367-4636.

Bus – TARC bus system serves the downtown area adequately during the day but is limited in the suburbs and after dark downtown. Route information is available at the Transit Authority Office, 1000 W. Broadway (phone: 585-1234).

Taxi – Cabs must be ordered by phone and are often slow to respond. The major company is *Yellow Cab* (phone: 636-5511).

Car Rental – Most national firms have offices at the airport, and *Hertz* has an office downtown in the *Hyatt Regency* hotel, 320 W. Jefferson (phone: 589-0951).

 LOCAL SERVICES: Babysitting – *We Sit Better of Louisville*, Starks Bldg., 455 4th Ave. (phone: 583-9618).

   Business Services – *Private Secretary*, Starks Bldg., 455 4th Ave. (phone: 581-1444).

Mechanics – *Lee's Gulf Service*, 301 E. Breckinridge (phone: 583-6912); *Smith Imported Car Service*, 1250 E. Broadway (phone: 583-4724).

 MUSEUMS: Museums not mentioned in *Special Places* include the following:

   Kentucky Railway Museum – Open May through October. La Grange Rd. and Dorsey La. (phone: 245-6035).

Rauch Planetarium – On the U. of L. campus, behind the museum (phone: 588-6664).

J. B. Speed Art Museum – 2035 S. 3rd St., next to the U. of L. (phone: 636-2893).

Zachary Taylor National Cemetery – 4701 Brownsboro Rd. (phone: 893-3852).

 MAJOR COLLEGES AND UNIVERSITIES: The University of Louisville, a four-year state school, is the area's oldest educational institution (between Eastern Pkwy. and Floyd St. south of 3rd St.; phone: 588-5555).

 SPECIAL EVENTS: The week preceding the race, the *Kentucky Derby Festival* unwinds with a parade, music, hot-air balloons, and a race between the *Belle of Louisville* and *Delta Queen* steamboats. Many events are free; write to 137 W. Muhammad Ali Blvd., Louisville 40202 (phone: 584-6383). The *Kentucky State Fair* is held in mid-August at the *Kentucky Fair & Exposition Center* (phone: 366-9592).

 SPORTS AND FITNESS: Baseball – The Louisville *Redbirds*, members of the American Association, play at the *Kentucky Fair and Exposition Center*. Off I-264 (phone: 367-9121).

   Bicycling – Rent from *Highland Cycle*, 1737 Bardstown Rd. (phone: 458-7832). Cherokee Park has good bike trails in hilly terrain.

College Sports – The University of Louisville's basketball and football teams play at the *Kentucky Fair and Exhibition Center,* off Watterson Expy. (I-264) (phone: 588-5151).

Fitness Centers – The *Louisville Athletic Club* has a lot to offer: a rooftop pool, exercise classes, steam room, sauna, whirlpool bath, and racquetball and squash courts; towels are provided, and there's a lounge and restaurant as well; 5th and Muhammad Ali, at the red awning (phone: 583-3871; call ahead). The *YMCA* has a pool, gym, racquetball court, and indoor track, 2nd and Chestnut (phone: 587-6700).

Golf – There are two good 18-hole courses: *Iroquois Park* (Newcut Rd. and Southern Pkwy.; phone: 363-9520) and *Seneca Park* (Taylorsville Rd. and Cannons La.; phone: 458-9298).

Horse Racing – In addition to racing at *Churchill Downs* (May through July, November), the *Louisville Downs* has trotting races January through April and July through October. 4520 Poplar Level Rd. (phone: 964-6415).

Jogging – For a 3-mile run, start at the *Hyatt Regency Louisville* on 4th Ave. Run north to Main St., turn right onto Main St., turn left at 2nd St., and head across Clark Memorial Bridge; then retrace your tracks.

Tennis – The *Louisville Tennis Center* has the best outdoor courts in the area. Open during spring and summer, Trevilian Way, across from the Louisville zoo (phone: 452-6411). Indoor courts are available right across the river at the *Louisville Indoor Racquet Club,* 8609 Westport Rd. (phone: 426-2454).

THEATER: For current offerings, check the papers noted above. The *Actors Theatre of Louisville* (ACT), one of the nation's prominent theater companies and the birthplace of the Pulitzer Prize–winning *Crimes of the Heart,* performs traditional productions and avant-garde plays from September through May, 316-320 W. Main St. (phone: 584-1205). Touring repertory groups, including Broadway road shows, play at the *Kentucky Center for the Arts,* 5 Riverfront Plaza (phone: 584-7777).

MUSIC: The *Louisville Orchestra,* the *Kentucky Opera Association,* and the *Louisville Ballet Company* perform at the *Kentucky Center for the Arts,* 5 Riverfront Plaza (phone: 584-7777).

NIGHTCLUBS AND NIGHTLIFE: Current favorites include the *Phoenix Hill Tavern,* which features popular music and a large rooftop beer garden, 644 Baxter Ave. (phone: 589-4630); *Butchertown Pub* for a variety of "hot" bands, plus a lively, friendly atmosphere, 1335 Story Ave. (phone: 583-2242); *Rascals* for meeting, mingling, and dancing, 1930 Bishop La. (phone: 452-1031)

BEST IN TOWN

CHECKING IN: Louisville's broad selection of accommodations ranges from standard large hotels to a resort-style motel with a lake and wave-making swimming pool. The more expensive hotels cost $100 to $150 per night for a double room, though they may have some less expensive accommodations in the moderate category ($65 to $85). Inexpensive hotels are in the $40 to $65 range. For bed-and-breakfast accommodations, contact *Kentucky Homes Bed & Breakfast,* 1431 St. James Ct., Louisville, KY 40208 (phone: 635-7341). All telephone numbers are in the 502 area code unless otherwise indicated.

Brown – Built in the 1920s, this architectural landmark has found new life as a Hilton. From the marble-floored lobby and archway-filled mezzanine to the wood interior of the *English Grille,* it's a real piece of Louisville history. Two restaurants (try a Hot Brown turkey sandwich, invented at the hotel), cocktail lounge. 4th and Broadway (phone: 583-1234). Expensive.

Hyatt Regency Louisville – One of the city's best stopping places, it features an 18-story atrium, spacious rooms, and several restaurants, including *Stetson's* and the revolving *Spire.* It also has a pool, Jacuzzi, and tennis courts. 320 W. Jefferson (phone: 587-3434). Expensive.

Seelbach – The charm of a bygone era is combined with modern amenities here. A showplace in the early 1900s, the hotel has undergone extensive renovation aimed at re-creating its turn-of-the-century appearance. There are 324 rooms in all, a restaurant, 3 bars, a Georgian-style ballroom, 24-hour room service, and valet parking. Adjoining the Galleria shopping complex. 500 4th Ave. (phone: 585-3200). Expensive.

Executive Inn – English manor decor sets the tone for this comfortably appointed motel adjacent to both the airport and the *Kentucky Fair and Exposition Center.* Amenities include a health club, barber/beauty shops, and fine food prepared by an award-winning chef. Watterson Expy. at fairgrounds (phone: 367-6161). Moderate.

Galt House – Though the decor is imitation extravagant — felt wallpaper, red plush carpets, and new "antiques" — the hotel is next to Riverfront Plaza, has a fine view of the Ohio, and is convenient for downtown shopping. Facilities include 2 cocktail lounges, an outdoor swimming pool, and 3 restaurants, one with a revolving section (the view is better than the food). 140 N. 4th St. (phone: 589-5200). Moderate.

Louisville In-Towne – Good value, with all the standard features: pool, color TV sets, restaurant, and cocktail lounge. 100 E. Jefferson St. (phone: 582-2481). Inexpensive.

Sheraton Lakeview – This resort-style hotel features some unusual extras: a "Wave-Tek" ocean, which is really a huge swimming pool with mechanically created waves; a real 11-acre lake with boating and fishing; 10 lakefront villas; and a floating bridal suite on the lake. It also has health club access, babysitting service, and a restaurant and cocktail lounge. 2 miles north of downtown off I-65 at 505 Marriott Dr., Clarksville, Indiana (phone: 812-283-4411). Inexpensive.

 EATING OUT: Our restaurant selections range in price from $60 to $90 for dinner for two in the expensive range, $35 to $60 in the moderate range, and $35 and below in the inexpensive range. Prices do not include drinks, wine, or tips. All telephone numbers are in the 502 area code unless otherwise indicated.

Casa Grisanti – Louisville's best restaurant offers carefully prepared Italian cuisine (try especially the veal), a good wine list, and attentive service. Closed Sundays. Reservations advised. Major credit cards. 1000 E. Liberty St. (phone: 584-4377). Expensive.

Oak Room – Antique furnishings combine with a continental menu and formal service to make dining here an elegant affair. Try the medallions of venison with quail or grilled swordfish. Open daily, including a sumptuous Sunday brunch. Reservations a must. Major credit cards. *Seelbach* hotel, 500 S. 4th Ave. (phone: 585-3200). Expensive.

610 Magnolia – Beautiful table settings, discreet service, and a chef who sometimes wanders through the dining room in shorts — that's the combination of elegance and eccentricity that typifies this deliciously daring eatery, tucked away on an Old

Louisville side street. The menu changes weekly according to the chef's whims, ranging from such items as crayfish salad with saffron sauce to tenderloin with Cognac. Desserts are a must — try the three-chocolate pecan marjolaine. Open Fridays and Saturdays only. Closed January and February. Reservations advised. No credit cards. 610 W. Magnolia Ave. (phone: 636-0783). Expensive.

Kienle's – The food is wonderful — and heavy. Wiener schnitzel, sauerbraten, and the homemade mushroom and cauliflower soups are highlights. Beer only. Closed Sundays and Mondays. No jeans or children under 12. Reservations advised. No credit cards. Shelbyville Rd. Plaza (phone: 897-3920). Moderate.

Bristol – An informal bar and grill in the heart of downtown. Continental entrées include trout meunière and tenderloin seasoned in beer, as well as lighter fare. Open daily. No reservations. Major credit cards. *Kentucky Center for the Arts* (phone: 583-3342). Moderate to inexpensive.

Hasenour's – Steaks are the specialty, but the seafood and daily specials are also reliable in this popular neighborhood restaurant. There's a wide variety in both food and price, and the drinks are among the most masterfully mixed in town. Open daily. Major credit cards. 1028 Barret Ave. (phone: 451-5210). Moderate to inexpensive.

Old Stone Inn – Take a half-hour's ride in the country to this 18th-century landmark, which serves good, old-fashioned southern food like fried chicken, country ham, and fresh vegetables. Closed Mondays and Tuesdays and December through March. No liquor. Reservations advised. Major credit cards. Take I-64 East to US 60N in Simpsonville (phone: 722-8882). Moderate to inexpensive.

Train Station – Built in 1901, this station in suburban Anchorage once served passengers heading to Louisville and nearby communities. Today, people come to enjoy the pleasant atmosphere, well-prepared food, and topnotch wine list. The menu ranges from traditional burgers and steaks to veal and chicken dishes with imaginative sauces. Closed Tuesdays. Reservations advised. Major credit cards. 1500 Evergreen Rd. (phone: 245-7121). Moderate to inexpensive.

MEMPHIS

A modern southern city in the southwestern corner of Tennessee, Memphis is much more economically and psychologically in tune with the Mississippi and Arkansas cotton-and-soybean belt than with Tennessee mountain country. During the early 1970s, the press gave the city a bum rap by calling it "a backwater river town." Residents took offense at what seemed to them a willful misrepresentation of a quite genuine Memphis trait — that slow, unflustered approach to life entirely fitting in a town with the southern credentials Memphis carries. But there was an element of truth in the snipe which residents recognized and set out to correct.

Everyone has heard the cliché that New York City is a great place to visit but you wouldn't want to live there. For a good while, Memphis — named in 1819 for the Egyptian city of Memphis — was known as just the reverse: a great place to live, but you wouldn't necessarily want to visit. Today, Memphis is a good place to live and is fast becoming a good place to visit, too. It has become one of the nation's top distribution centers and been labeled a "boom town" by economic authorities.

The 850,000 people in the Memphis area do live at a somewhat slower pace than people in other parts of the country. Sitting high on the bluffs overlooking the Mississippi at the mouth of the Wolf River, the 19th-century city was one of the busiest ports in the United States and the site of the largest slave market in the central South. Memphis lost its city charter for a year in 1878 when the yellow fever epidemic forced more than half its population to move to St. Louis (the half that could afford to move), but it survived as a shipping center. Today, more than one-third of the US cotton crop is still marketed through Memphis.

Memphis is basically a conservative town, both in politics and economics. One theory for this, advanced by residents, is that because the wealth in Memphis was accumulated over the decades through cotton, and because the process of accumulation was so slow, the community leaders are reluctant to spend. Memphis is not like Houston, with its fast-flowing oil money, or Atlanta, which leaped ahead of all southern cities to become a tourist haven, in Memphis terms, almost overnight.

Memphis is a beautiful city with thousands of trees, magnificently landscaped lawns, and spacious parks, sitting atop the Mississippi bluff and surrounded by scores of fishing lakes. Outdoor activities (hunting, fishing, golf, water skiing, speedboat racing, auto racing, tennis, etc.) abound.

A few uniquely American phenomena are headquartered in Memphis. Elvis Presley, the late King of Rock 'n' Roll, lived in and is buried on the grounds of Graceland, his Memphis mansion. It draws more visitors to the city than any other single attraction. And Holiday Inns and Federal Express were born and are based in Memphis, organizations built on a bedrock of

shrewd business judgment and old-fashioned southern faith. Not an unusual combination in this very southern city.

MEMPHIS AT-A-GLANCE

SEEING THE CITY: The best way to see Memphis is by drifting along the legendary Mississippi. Captain Jake Meanley's *Memphis Queen* paddleboat takes you along the river. The cruise takes about an hour and a half. It leaves daily from March through December, from Memphis Downtown Harbor, Monroe Ave. and Riverside Dr. (phone: 527-5694).

SPECIAL PLACES: A natural place to start a tour of Memphis is by the riverbanks. From there, you can wander through downtown, wending your way out to the suburbs.

Mud Island – Legend has it that Mud Island, measuring 1 by 5 miles, was formed by mud deposits clinging to a gunboat sunk during the Civil War. Residents are sure it was a Union gunboat, because, they say, Confederate gunboats were unsinkable. Mud Island is the site of a $63-million tribute to the history and heritage of the Mississippi, with exhibits on its legends, music, and people; a 5,000-seat outdoor amphitheater; a 5-block scale model of the river; and restaurants, shops, a river museum, marina, and picnic area. Enter on Front St. between Poplar and Adams (phone: 576-6595); Mud Island is accessible by monorail.

Beale Street – Renovated buildings along this historic street, which saw the birth of the blues in the early 1900s, contain specialty shops, restaurants, bars, and offices. At the corner of Beale and 3rd is W. C. Handy Park, and at Beale and Main, Elvis Presley Plaza; both feature statues honoring these two international artists from Memphis. At 329 Beale is the *Old Daisy Theater,* where the Center for Southern Folklore, which serves as the interpretive center for the new Beale Street, presents the show *If Beale Street Could Talk* each Friday at 2 PM or by appointment. Admission charge (phone: 726-4205).

Victorian Village – Homes and churches in this downtown area date to the 1830s and feature a variety of architectural styles, among them late Victorian, neoclassic, Greek Revival, French, and Italianate. The Fontaine House and the Mallory-Neely House are open to the public daily. 100 to 700 block of Adams St.

Overton Square – A 15-minute drive from downtown, the square has restaurants and bistros, jazz trios and rhythm and blues bands, specialty shops, an art gallery, and a professional theater. Madison at Cooper.

Libertyland – At the Fairgrounds, a mile from the square on East Parkway, this theme park reflects nostalgia and patriotism (its roller coaster is aptly named the Revolution). Open weekends beginning in the spring, daily from mid-June through August. Admission charge; children under 3 free. Fairgrounds (phone: 274-1776).

Memphis Pink Palace Museum and Planetarium – The museum is built of pink Georgia marble, and features exhibitions on the natural and cultural history of the mid-South. Closed Mondays. Admission charge. 3050 Central Ave. (phone: 454-5600).

Chucalissa Indian Village – A reconstructed village where Choctaw Indians live and work. Grass huts and a ceremonial house and museum are on the site, and Indian tools, weapons, and pottery are displayed. Closed Mondays. Admission charge. 6 miles south of downtown, adjoining Fuller State Park on Indian Village Dr. (phone: 785-3160).

Memphis Zoo and Aquarium – The complete range of lions, tigers, monkeys, and birds can be found in this well-designed city zoo. An aquarium adjoins the animal sections. Closed Thanksgiving, Christmas Eve, Christmas, and icy days. Admission charge except Mondays from 3 to 4:30 PM in winter and 3:30 to 5 PM in summer. Overton Park, off Poplar Ave. (phone: 726-4775, recording; for further information, 726-4787).

Graceland – Elvis Presley's home is the most popular site in Memphis. The white-columned southern mansion is now open to the public, and Elvis fans can also stroll through the 14-acre estate, well shaded by oak trees, and pay respects at the grave of Elvis, his mother, father, and grandmother. Don't forget to look closely at the Musical Gate at the foot of the winding circular driveway. It has a caricature of Elvis with guitar and a bevy of musical notes in ornamental iron. Elvis's plane, the *Lisa Marie,* is also on display. Closed Tuesdays, November through February; and Thanksgiving, Christmas, and New Year's Day. Admission charge; make tour reservations in advance. 3764 Elvis Presley Blvd. in Whitehaven, South Memphis (phone: 332-3322 in Tennessee; 800-238-2010 elsewhere).

Sun Recording Studio – Elvis, Johnny Cash, Jerry Lee Lewis, Carl Perkins, and other recording artists cut their first records here. Restored and operated by Graceland Division of Elvis Presley Enterprises. Tours daily from 10 AM to 6 PM. Admission charge. 706 Union (phone: 332-3322).

■**EXTRA SPECIAL:** About 2½ hours away by car, Shiloh National Military Park lets visitors follow the sequence of the famous Civil War Battle of Shiloh, in 1862. Points of interest are clearly marked, and visitors can walk or drive along a 10-mile route. Pre-Columbian Indian mounds are also visible along the way. A 25-minute movie about the battle is shown in the visitors center. Closed Christmas Day. Off US 64 in Shiloh (phone: 1-689-5275).

SOURCES AND RESOURCES

TOURIST INFORMATION: The Memphis Visitor Information Center, 207 Beale St., Memphis, TN 38108 (phone: 526-4880), the Memphis Convention and Visitors Bureau, 50 N. Front St., Morgan Keegan Tower, Memphis, TN 38103 (phone: 576-8181), and the Memphis Area Chamber of Commerce, 203 Beale St. (phone: 526-4880), are all good places for general information.

Key magazine and the *Convention and Visitors Guide* are the best sources for Memphis activities.

Television Stations – WREG Channel 3–CBS; WMC Channel 5–NBC; WHBQ Channel 13–ABC; WKNO Channel 10–PBS.

Radio Stations – AM: WHBQ 56 (news/talk); WBIA 1070 (rhythm & blues); WMPS 1380 (news/talk/sports). FM: WKNO 91 (classical/news); WEZI 94 (easy listening); WEGK 103 (rock).

Local Coverage – *Memphis Commercial Appeal,* morning daily; *Memphis* magazine, monthly.

Telephone – The area code for Memphis is 901.

Sales Tax – There is a city and state sales tax of 7¾%.

CLIMATE: Memphis humidity is formidable. Even though temperatures seldom drop below the 30s in winter, it's wet. The worst month is February, when it occasionally snows. July and August get dripping hot as the temperature climbs into the 90s and 100s; dress coolly.

GETTING AROUND: Airport – Memphis International Airport is usually about a 30-minute drive from downtown and midtown; taxi fare should run about $14. The *Airport Limousine Service* (phone: 346-1300) meets incoming flights and takes passengers to the city for $6. When returning to the airport, call in advance for a pickup. Although public bus #20 stops at the terminal building, a transfer to bus #13 is required to get downtown. The fare is 95¢.

Bus – Memphis buses generally run between 5 AM and 8 PM during the week, with limited service on the weekend. Information, routes, from Memphis Area Transit Authority, 1370 Levee Rd. (phone: 274-6282).

Taxi – There are taxi stands near the bus station and at the airport. It's best to call *Yellow Cab* (phone: 526-2121).

Car Rental – The major national firms have agencies in Memphis. A reliable local firm is *Thrifty Rent-A-Car,* 2230 E. Brooks (phone: 345-0170).

LOCAL SERVICES: Babysitting – *Crosstown Christian Daycare and Elementary School* provides 24-hour, 7-day service for children 15 months and older. 1258 Harbert (phone: 725-4666).

   Business Services – *Business Services Network,* 5100 Poplar (phone: 763-2974).

Mechanic – *Lamb's Auto Service,* 3343 Millbranch (phone: 345-5875); *A. S. Martin & Sons,* 411 Monroe (phone: 527-8606).

MUSEUMS: The *Memphis Pink Palace Museum* is famous for natural history exhibitions (see *Special Places*). Other museums are the *Memphis Brooks Museum of Art* (American and European art), Overton Park (phone: 722-3500); and *Dixon Gallery and Gardens* (French and American Impressionist art) 4339 Park Ave. (phone: 761-5250). Both are closed Mondays.

MAJOR COLLEGES AND UNIVERSITIES: Memphis State University (phone: 454-2040); Rhodes College (phone: 274-1800); University of Tennessee, Memphis (phone: 528-5500).

SPECIAL EVENTS: The *Volvo Tennis Championships* are held in February. The *Memphis in May International Festival* stretches from late April into early June. Highlights of the festival are the *International Children's Festival, International Cooking Contest* (barbecue), *Beale Street Musical Festival* and a *Sunset Symphony* on the banks of the Mississippi. *Great River Carnival* (formerly the *Cotton Carnival*) in early June, has parades, a midway, music and a riverside pageant. In September one of the ten largest fairs in the country, the *Mid-South Fair,* takes place. In December is college football's *Liberty Bowl.*

SPORTS AND FITNESS: Baseball – The Memphis *Chicks* (short for Chickasaw Indians, who once lived in the area) play at *Tim McCarver Stadium,* renamed for the Memphis-born former catcher for the Philadelphia *Phillies.* The *Chicks* are a Southern League farm club for the Kansas City *Royals.* Tim McCarver Stadium, Fairgrounds (phone: 272-1687).

Fishing – There are fish in the lakes, mostly bass, bream, crappies, and catfish. Sardis Lake is a good bet; Meeman-Shelby Forest, a 14,000-acre park with two large lakes.

Fitness Center – The *Peabody Athletic Club,* in the *Peabody* hotel, offers aerobics classes and a sauna, 149 Union (phone: 529-4161).

Golf – The $300,000 *PGA–Federal Express St. Jude Classic* is played in late July or early August at the *Colonial Country Club,* a private course 10 miles east on I-40. The best public golf course is *Galloway,* 3815 Walnut Grove Rd. (phone: 685-7805).

Jogging – Run in Audubon Park on Park Avenue, and Overton Park on Poplar Avenue.

Soccer – The Memphis *Storm* play November through March at *Mid-South Coliseum* (phone: 767-4000).

Swimming – Some of the lakes are polluted. The nearest good swimming pool is *Maywood,* just across the state line in Olive Branch, Mississippi. Admission charge. 422 S. Maywood Dr. (phone: 601-895-2777).

Tennis – The best year-round public courts are at *Audubon Tennis Center,* 4145 Southern (phone: 685-7907), and *John Rodgers Tennis Complex,* Midtown (phone: 523-0094).

 THEATER: *Playhouse on the Square,* 51 S. Cooper (phone: 726-4656); *Theater Memphis,* 630 Perkins Ext. (phone: 682-8323); *Orpheum Theater,* 89 Beale St. (phone: 525-3000); *Circuit Playhouse,* 1705 Poplar Ave. (phone: 726-5521).

 MUSIC: Big-name country and rock concerts are played at *Mid-South Coliseum,* Fairgrounds (phone: 274-7400), and *Dixon-Meyers Hall* at the *Cook Convention Center,* 255 N. Main (phone: 523-7645). Headliners appear at the *Mud Island Amphitheater* from May through September (take the monorail on Front St. between Poplar and Adams; phone: 576-6595) and at the *Orpheum Theater,* 89 Beale St. (phone: 525-3000), year-round.

 NIGHTCLUBS AND NIGHTLIFE: Memphis blues originated on Beale Street, with W. C. Handy, and is performed nightly at *Rum Boogie,* 182 Beale (phone: 528-0150). There's fifties and sixties music at *Proud Mary's,* 326 Beale (phone: 525-8979). Other popular downtown nightspots include *Alfred's,* 197 Beale (phone: 525-3711), and the *Anchor Bar* at *Captain Bilbo's* (phone: 526-1966), both in the Beale Street Landing shopping and restaurant complex at the corner of Beale and Wagner. In midtown, the Overton Square area at Madison and Cooper, try the *Public Eye* (phone: 726-4040) or the *Bombay Bicycle Club* (phone: 726-6055). Best bets elsewhere are *Etcetera*, 4730 Poplar Ave. (phone: 761-2880); *Silky Sullivan's,* 2080 Madison (phone: 725-0650); and *Bad Bob's Vapors* (country and rock), 1743 Brooks Rd. E. (phone: 345-1761).

BEST IN TOWN

 CHECKING IN: Restoration of the 400-room *Peabody* is finished, and the construction of a new *Holiday Inn Crowne Plaza* convention center has also been completed. There's an abundance of *Holiday Inns* (six, to be exact) — hardly surprising since the chain makes its headquarters in Memphis. Other chains, such as *Ramada, TraveLodge, Hilton,* and *Sheraton,* are also represented. Expect to pay between $60 and $100 for a double at the hotels mentioned here. All telephone numbers are in the 901 area code unless otherwise indicated.

Peabody – In 1935, Mississippi author David Cohn wrote that "the Delta begins in the lobby of the *Peabody* and ends on Catfish Row in Vicksburg." Built in 1925, the 13-story, 400-room hotel reopened in 1981 after a $20-million renovation. A focal point of the elegant Renaissance lobby is a travertine marble fountain to which the *Peabody* ducks — trained mallards — march and swim each day. Sixteen square marble columns support a mezzanine balcony; the ceiling is graced by ornate woodwork and stained glass skylights. *Chez Philippe* is the hotel's fancy restaurant; *Dux,* its theme restaurant (see *Eating Out*). (Incidentally, neither restaurant serves duck.) For music and dancing, there's the *Skyway,* a rooftop nightclub. The *Plantation Roof* affords splendid views of the river and city. The hotel's lower level has a pool, snack bar, health club, beauty shop, barber shop, and shoeshine parlor. 149 Union Ave. (phone: 529-4000). Expensive to moderate.

Holiday Inn Crowne Plaza – Part of the new executive-oriented group of Holiday Inn hotels, focusing on the affluent business traveler, this hotel, adjacent to the Memphis Convention Center, offers 415 rooms, pool, health club, and sauna. *Chervil's* is the ambitious restaurant, and there's a coffee shop and 24-hour room service. 250 N. Main (phone: 527-7300). Moderate.

Hyatt Regency – This circular, 27-story, all-glass structure is known affectionately as "the glass silo." The 400-room hotel, on the eastern outskirts of town, has a swimming pool, café, and bar with nightly entertainment and dancing, free parking, free cots, and cribs. Pets welcome. Children under 18 free. 939 Ridge Lake Blvd. (phone: 761-1234). Moderate.

EATING OUT: The city's natives are sometimes quick to say "There ain't no good eatin' places in Memphis," but this is a bum rap. While it's true there are hundreds of fast-food franchise outlets in every section of the city, a visitor still can dine well, feast on some of the best barbecue anywhere, or enjoy home-cooked meals. Our restaurant selections range in price from $38 for two in the expensive range; around $20 for two, moderate; under $20, inexpensive. Prices do not include drinks, wine, or tips. All telephone numbers are in the 901 area code unless otherwise indicated.

Dux – A delightful place in the *Peabody* hotel, serving American and continental cuisine. 149 Union Ave. (phone: 529-4199). Expensive.

Folk's Folly – This is a steakhouse supreme, serving the largest bits of beef in Memphis. Vegetables are prepared Cajun-style. Try the sautéed mushrooms or fried dill pickles. Humphrey Folk, a John Wayne type, owns the restaurant. According to local legend, he opened it to help his girlfriend, who always wanted to run a restaurant. Open daily. Reservations advised. Major credit cards. 551 S. Mendenhall (phone: 762-8200). Expensive.

Justine's – Often acclaimed as one of the nation's notable restaurants, and deservedly so. The French cooking here is first rate. Baking is done on the premises. A rather formal ambience prevails in this antebellum mansion, however. Jacket and tie are required. So are reservations. Closed Sundays. Major credit cards. 919 Coward Pl. (phone: 527-3815). Expensive.

Captain Bilbo's – Have a drink at the bar and listen to nightly entertainment while viewing beautiful sunsets on the Mississippi River. And don't be surprised if an Illinois Central Gulf Railroad train rumbles past — the railroad track is only 22 feet from the restaurant's windows. Next, enjoy the excellent salad bar, seafood gumbo, steaks, and fish. Open daily. Reservations accepted for groups of 12 or more. Major credit cards. 263 Wagner (phone: 526-1966). Moderate.

Grisanti's – This Northern Italian restaurant features spicy food and a chance to swap insults with owner Big John Grisanti, a legend on the city's nightlife circuit. The cannelloni, manicotti, and veal are highly recommended. The blind can order from a braille menu. Closed Sundays. Reservations accepted for 10 or more. Major credit cards. 1489 Airways Blvd. (phone: 458-2648). Moderate.

Pete and Sam's – Pound for pound, the best all-around restaurant in town; serves dynamite Italian-American food. Order anything, the steaks are as good as the pizza. There are two locations, but try the original on Park Avenue. Open daily. Reservations are a good idea. Major credit cards. 3886 Park (phone: 458-0694). Inexpensive.

Rendezvous – In a basement in a back alley, this classic little place is chock full of Memphis memorabilia. It's as much a museum as a restaurant, and it serves the best barbecue ribs, beef, and pork in town. Closed Sundays, Mondays, and holidays. No reservations. Major credit cards. General Washburn Alley, off S. 2nd and behind the Ramada Inn (phone: 523-2746).Inexpensive.

Memphis is a major league barbecue town, so everyone has his or her own favorite barbecue spot. One is *Gridley's* at 4101 Summer and three other locations about town (phone: 452-4057). Another is *John Wills Bar-Be-Q Pit,* 2450 Central (phone: 274-8000). There's also *Smokey Ridge Barbecue,* near the airport at 3333 Winchester Rd. (phone: 795-7534); and *Willingham's World Champion Bar-B-Que,* 2707 Perkins Rd. (phone: 362-7427). If you don't mind driving 40 miles for maybe the best barbecue of them all (and under $5), try *Bozo's* at Mason, out Summer Ave. and Hwy. 70.

MIAMI-MIAMI BEACH

Difficult as it is to find adults actually born in Miami, practically all residents regard themselves — somehow — as natives. The year-round population of Miami is 1.8 million. This figure swells immensely during the winter months, when millions of "snowbirds" arrive. ("Snowbird" is a tricky term as used in Miami; it refers primarily to tourists escaping the northeastern freeze, but could just as easily describe South Americans in town for a midsummer shopping spree.) Sprawling across 2,054 square miles of land (the metropolitan area also encompasses 354 square miles of water), Miami is a huge and cosmopolitan metropolis; yet it has managed to maintain a provincial quality in spite of commercialized efforts to identify it as a tropical New York City.

This is in part due to the way in which the metropolitan area is organized. Greater Miami (actually metropolitan Dade County) comprises 28 municipalities and a scattering of totally unincorporated areas. This breeds something of a small-town attitude in residents who have a chauvinistic interest in their own enclaves. They identify with the whole city — it is, after all, all Miami — but they live where they live.

In even larger part, it is due to a deeply rooted tradition of hospitality and neighborliness that can only be described as somehow "Southern" — even while admitting that a large number of those residents who display it most openly are either recent arrivals or part-time snowbirds.

From an early small settlement consisting primarily of Indians, Miami only began to grow after one Julia Tuttle tickled the fancy of a railroad tycoon with some orange blossoms. According to the story told here, Tuttle was an early settler who was eager to see Miami become part of a railroad hookup with the rest of the state. She petitioned railroad magnate Henry Flagler to extend his Florida East Coast Railroad from Palm Beach to Miami. He seemed in no great hurry to do so until the Big Freeze of 1894 devastated most of Florida's fruit and vegetable crops. Most, but not all. When he received a box of frost-free orange blossoms from Tuttle, he suddenly got her point. Soon enough Miami had rail access to the rest of the world.

It wasn't long until the rest of the world was glad of access. Attracted by year-round warmth and sunshine, thousands of new residents began pouring into the area, only one step behind hundreds of shrewd and even occasionally honest entrepreneurs. Miami and Miami Beach became glittering wintertime destinations, and later began drawing vacationers in summer as well. While Miami Beach still remains tourist-oriented, Miami has developed into a flourishing international business hub. They are together an attractive combination that lures a wide variety of visitors.

Jolted a few years ago into the realization that their fun and sun city had begun to lose its good reputation, the local government began implementing a series of major programs dedicated to restoration and redevelopment. Renewing the beaches, sprucing up oceanfront hotels, cleaning up the Miami River, expanding the park system, dressing up the historic hotel district, and enforcing strict environmental laws to protect the delicate marine ecology reflected a determination to keep the good life good.

That Miami still has the image of offering the good life is attested to by the waves of new residents who settle in one or another of Miami's municipalities each year (a fact that sits uneasily with long-time residents, torn as they are between the need for steady economic growth and the desire to maintain a familiar quality of life). Today, most of these new residents are Spanish-speaking, many from the steady flow of refugees from Cuba, others fleeing violence in Central America, while still others are affluent Venezuelans and Colombians who occupy their homes only part of the year. This has turned metropolitan Miami into a city where you can buy anything from fried bananas to Chilean wine, and where Spanish is the first language of more than 50% of the year-round inhabitants. However, there is also an only slightly smaller tide of new resident and regular visitors from the Caribbean, Britain, and Europe, bringing Miami such things as Jamaican-Chinese restaurants, Haitian grocery stores, and elegant French cuisine.

Coral Gables is Miami's prestigious planned community, conceived and built by entrepreneur George Merrick. Elegant gates to the city are still standing in various spots around the Gables, relics of Merrick's grand scheme to build "a place where castles in Spain are made real." Strict building codes prevail, and woe to the newcomer who tries to put a flat roof on his home. In a county where almost all the streets are laid out in a simple north-south-east-west numbered grid, Coral Gables sticks to its Spanish and Italian street names and layout. Just 10 minutes from the airport, it has also become the favored locale for multinational corporations doing business in Latin America.

South Miami, adjacent to the Gables, is reminiscent of an Anywhere, USA, crossroads town. Farther south, in an unincorporated part of Dade County called Kendall, lie expensive estates with pools and tennis courts where not so long ago there were only extensive mango and avocado groves.

Closer to downtown Miami is the area known as Coconut Grove, a base for wealthy year-round and winter residents and not so wealthy colonies of artists and writers. Here, crafts shops stand next to expensive boutiques, health food stores sit alongside posh restaurants, and old Florida houses of coral rock nestle close to modern high-rises. Luxurious yachts and sailboats lie in Biscayne Bay, and the Grove's younger generation lies all over Peacock Park. Little Havana is part of the center city, but is really a small world unto itself, with its Latin culture intact. Increasingly, it dominates Miami's political and commercial life.

Also in a class by themselves are the communities of Miami Beach and Key Biscayne. Besides its glittering hotel row, the Beach (and the small manmade islands between it and the mainland) houses some of the most luxurious waterfront homes in Greater Miami. The South Beach section has undergone a tremendous renaissance, with rehabilitation of many classic Art Deco apart-

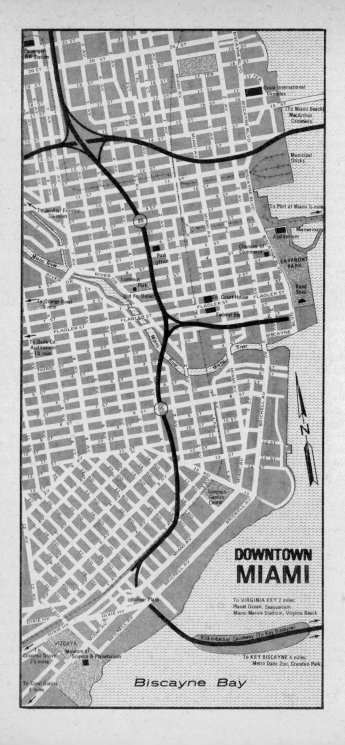

DOWNTOWN
MIAMI

To VIRGINIA KEY 2 miles:
Planet Ocean, Seaquarium,
Miami Marine Stadium, Virginia Beach

To KEY BISCAYNE 4 miles:
Metro Dade Zoo, Crandon Park

Biscayne Bay

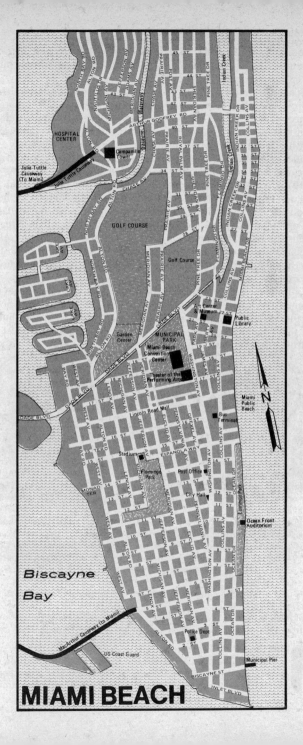

MIAMI BEACH

ment buildings and hotels, as well as construction of new high-rise condominiums. Key Biscayne has rows of luxury high-rises, simple bungalows, and excellent beaches.

With a mean annual temperature of 75F, 60,000 plus registered boats, miles of improved beaches, 57 marinas, 11,829 acres of parks, 354 square miles of protected waters, and 3,200 more of sheltered waters, Miami's vital statistics support its reputation as a sunny, water-oriented resort. Yet in recent years, the city has become a major urban area, with an economic diversity associated with cities of comparable size. To a large extent, this is a result of the Latin American–Caribbean connection. Population has grown by 40% since the early 1970s, and employment has doubled in local business and industry. Indeed, the export trade is expected soon to overtake tourism as the number one industry. Traditional tourist migration from the Northeast has slowed; a good part of it is stopped midstate by the growing attractions of the Tampa–Walt Disney World–Orlando–Daytona axis. Reports of Miami's drug- and race-related flare-ups have made headlines across the country (most recently during the week before the 1989 Super Bowl) and have doubtless discouraged some potential visitors.

Still, this area was once a small village stuck on the side of a swamp, and it became America's single greatest tourist magnet. It's probably not true, as an old Florida legend claims, that a race of giants once lived here, but it surely is true that Miami today possesses a gigantic will that wants most to grow. It's hard to believe it will not have its way.

MIAMI–MIAMI BEACH AT-A-GLANCE

 SEEING THE CITY: The *Rusty Pelican* (3201 Rickenbacker Cswy.) looks across Biscayne Bay at the spectacular Miami skyline; the *Roof Garden* restaurant atop the *Doral-on-the-Ocean* (4833 Collins Ave.) offers vistas of the bay and the Atlantic; the *700 Club* atop the *David William* hotel (700 Biltmore Way) in Coral Gables offers a panorama of the area; and the rooftop *Club Casablanca* at the *Coconut Grove* hotel (2649 S. Bayshore Dr.) commands a fine vista of Biscayne Bay.

Miami is largely a waterfront city, and one of the best ways to get to know it is by boat. Besides the *Island Queen,* which leaves from Miamarina (see *Special Places,* below), *Nikko's Gold Coast* cruises set sail out of Haulover Marina, 10800 Collins Ave. (phone: 945-5461), and the *Spirit* — with lunch, dinner, and "moonlight party" cruises at 2:30, 7, and 10:30 PM respectively — departs from the *Fontainebleau Hilton,* 4441 Collins Ave. (phone: 1-458-4999).

A bus tour of Miami highlights is given by *American Sightseeing Tours,* 4300 NW 14th St. (phone: 871-4992).

For a different view of the city, you can take *Miami Helicopter*'s flight over Miami Beach from Opalocka Airport. Open year-round (phone: 685-8223).

 SPECIAL PLACES: The best way to see Greater Miami is by car.

Port of Miami – Every week thousands of people depart on Caribbean cruises from here, making Miami the world's largest cruise port. Cruises aren't free, but watching the tourist-laden ocean liners turn around in the narrow channel that leads to the open sea is. Open daily. Ships leave Fridays, Saturdays, Sundays, and Mondays from 4 to 7 PM.

Bass Museum – Its Art Deco motif complements the outstanding collection of Renaissance, baroque, and rococo works. Admission charge except for children under 16. 2121 Park Ave., Miami Beach (phone: 673-7533).

Bill Boggs Cape Florida State Park – A 406-acre spread of bike paths, woodlands, picnic areas, and a mile-long beach. The 45-foot lighthouse here is South Florida's oldest landmark. Admission charge. 1200 Crandon Blvd. (phone: 361-5811).

Miamarina – Sightseeing and charter boats berth in this downtown marina. You can board the *Island Queen* for a 2-hour circle cruise of Biscayne Bay, viewing waterfront estates and residential islands daily (phone: 379-5119). Admission charge. 400 SE 2nd Ave.

Bayside Marketplace – Opened in 1987 on 20 acres of Biscayne Bay shoreline, this $93-million complex includes 165 shops, restaurants, entertainment areas, and a life-size reproduction of the HMS *Bounty*, built for the 1960 film *Mutiny on the Bounty*. Open daily. Admission charge to the *Bounty*. Entrance at NE 4th St. and Biscayne Blvd. (phone: 577-3344).

Little Havana, Calle Ocho (8th Street) – The real Latin Flame, however, burns in this community, founded by Cubans who left after Castro's takeover. Shops feature handmade jewelry, dolls, and works of art. Fruit stands, bakeries, restaurants, and coffee stalls offer authentic Latin food. Try *Málaga* or *Versailles* for lunch or dinner — roast pork with rice and black bean sauce, then flan (a custard covered with caramel syrup) for dessert (740 SW 8th St.; phone: 858-4224), followed by a cup of espresso at a sidewalk stall. You can watch cigars being hand-rolled by Cuban experts in exile at *Padron Cigars* (1566 W. Flagler St.; phone: 643-2117).

Metro-Dade Cultural Center – This huge $25-million downtown complex, designed by Philip Johnson, houses the *Center for the Fine Arts* (phone: 375-1700; admission charge), which features traveling exhibitions, the *Historical Museum of South Florida* (phone: 375-1492; admission charge), with exhibitions on Spanish exploration, Indian civilization, and maritime history, and the Miami-Dade Public Library (phone: 375-BOOK). The cultural center is at 101 W. Flagler St.

Metrozoo – Here, in Miami's cageless zoo, Bengal tigers lounge before a replica of a Cambodian temple; and the mountains, streams, and bridges inside the new free-flight aviary evoke the natural habitat of the Asian birds inside. The air conditioned monorail whisks through the aviary. There is a special combined fare with Metrorail on weekends. Open daily. Admission charge. 12400 SW 152nd St. (phone: 251-0401).

Planet Ocean – The International Oceanographic Foundation maintains this multimillion-dollar permanent exhibition that tells the story of the world's oceans in films and exhibitions (including a real submarine and a real iceberg). Open daily. Admission charge. 3979 Rickenbacker Causeway, Virginia Key (phone: 361-9455 or 361-5786).

Miami Seaquarium – Once you've learned all about the oceans, you can see who lives there at South Florida's largest tropical marine aquarium. Among the 10,000 creatures swimming around the tidepools, jungle islands, and tanks under a geodesic dome are killer whales, sharks, sea lions, and performing seals and dolphins. The real stars, though, are Flipper, of TV fame, and Lolita, a killer whale. Open daily. Admission charge. On Rickenbacker Causeway across from Planet Ocean (phone: 361-5705).

Miami Marine Stadium – This 6,500-seat roofed grandstand on Biscayne Bay hosts Miami's big shows as well as powerboat races, water shows, outdoor concerts, and fireworks displays. Check newspapers. 3601 Rickenbacker Cswy. (phone: 361-6732).

Miccosukee Indian Village – Just 25 miles west of Miami, descendants of Florida's original settlers are maintaining the lifestyle of their forebears. Among the attractions are alligator wrestling, crafts demonstrations, and airboat rides. US 41 (phone: 223-8388).

Vizcaya Museum and Gardens – A palatial estate, where International Harvester magnate James Deering reaped his personal harvest. The 70-room Venetian palazzo, with 35 rooms open to the public, is furnished with European antiques, precious china, and artworks from the 15th to the 19th century and is surrounded by 10 acres of formal gardens. Closed Christmas Day. Admission charge. 3251 S. Miami Ave., just off US 1 (phone: 579-2708; 579-4626).

Museum of Science and Space Transit Planetarium – Exhibitions on a coral reef and the Everglades are enlightening, and there's a participatory science arcade. The planetarium has several shows daily, and if you are really inspired you can search for the stars yourself with the Southern Cross Observatory telescope atop the building in the evenings. Open daily. Admission charge. 3280 S. Miami Ave. (phone: 854-4242).

Fairchild Tropical Gardens – Founded by a tax attorney with a touch of the poet in him, this might just be one of the most lyrical tax shelters imaginable — 83 acres of paradise with tropical and subtropical plants and trees, lakes, and a rare plant house with an extensive collection of unusual tropical flora. Tram rides are available through the grounds complete with intelligent commentary. Closed Christmas Day. Admission charge. 10901 Old Cutler Rd. (phone: 667-1651).

Parrot Jungle – More of the tropics, but this time, screaming, colorful, and talented. Not only do these parrots, macaws, and cockatoos fly, but they also ride bicycles, roller skate, and solve math problems. If you don't believe it, just wait till you see the flamingos on parade — all amid a jungle of huge cypress and live oaks. Open daily. Admission charge. 2 miles south off US 1 at 11000 SW 57th Ave. (Red Rd.) and Killian Dr. (phone: 666-7834).

Monkey Jungle – The monkeys wander, run free, go swimming, and swing from trees while visitors watch from inside a wire cage. Naturally, some chimp stars perform, and there are also orangutans, gibbons, and an Amazonian rain forest with South American monkeys in natural habitats. Open daily. Admission charge. 14805 SW 216th St. (phone: 235-1611).

Orchid Jungle – Jungle trails wind through this huge orchid display, more species and colors than you thought existed. Open daily. Admission charge. South of Miami off US 1 in Homestead, 26715 SW 157th Ave. (phone: 247-4824).

Mary A. Heinlein Fruit and Spice Park – Some 20 tropical acres feature over 500 species of fruit, nut, and spice trees and plants. Guided tours by Parks Dept. naturalists include samplings of seasonal fruits. Tours are conducted Saturday and Sunday afternoons for a nominal charge. Open daily. 35 miles southwest of Miami, at 24801 SW 187th Ave., Homestead (phone: 247-5727).

Miami Beach – At one time, this 8-mile-long island east of the mainland was renowned for its glittering seaside resorts, but over the years its image has been tarnished by crime and racial unrest. Recent efforts at renewal and redevelopment have improved the situation, bringing tourists back to the flashy *Fontainebleau Hilton* and the other big hotels that line Collins Avenue, the main drag. A $64-million beach renourishment program created a 300-foot strand extending from Government Cut to Haulover Inlet, and a beach boardwalk runs 1.8 miles from 21st to 46th St. One Miami Beach attraction (besides the sun, sand, and star-studded nightlife) is the Miami Beach Garden and Conservatory, with a beautiful display of Florida's native flora, 2000 Convention Center Dr. The southern end of the island, between 5th St. and 20th, known locally as "South Beach" or SoBe, has been designated a National Historic District because of its many Art Deco buildings.

■ **EXTRA SPECIAL:** For a refreshing change, drive south along US 27 through miles of Miami's little-known farmland. Stock up on fresh fruits and vegetables at numerous stands or go right out into the U-Pic fields and choose your own. Forty miles south of Miami (turnoff on US 1) is Everglades National Park, a unique and extremely diverse subtropical wilderness with some of the best naturalist-oriented activities anywhere in the world. This 1½-million-acre preserve features alligators, raccoons, manatees, mangroves, and thousands of rare birds, all in their natural habitats. For complete details see DIRECTIONS. Farther south along US 1 stretch the Florida Keys, a chain of islands connected by an Overseas Highway. Here is everything from the only living coral reef in the continental United States (which you can see in all its glory only by skin diving, snorkeling, or in a glass-bottom boat) at John Pennekamp State Park (the only underwater park in the country) in Key Largo to great fishing possibilities and better food: conch chowder, and Key lime pie. For complete details see DIRECTIONS.

SOURCES AND RESOURCES

TOURIST INFORMATION: The Greater Miami Convention and Visitors Bureau at 701 Brickell Ave., Suite 2700, Miami, FL 33131 (phone: 539-3000), is best for brochures, maps, and general tourist information. For information on fairs, art shows, and events in the area's parks, call the Parks and Recreation Department's information line (phone: 579-2568).

Television Stations – WCIX Channel 6–CBS; WPLG Channel 10–BAC; WTVJ Channel 4–NBC; WPBT Channel 2–PBS.

Radio Stations – AM: WIOD 610 (news); WNWS 94 (news/talk); WINZ 1060 (talk). FM: WTMI 93.1 (classical); WMXJ 102.7 (oldies); WAVE 95.7 (jazz); WJQY 107.5 (easy listening).

Local Coverage – *Miami Herald,* morning daily, publishes the Weekend section on Fridays with a schedule of upcoming events; *South Florida* magazine, monthly; *New Times,* an alternative weekly, includes "The Wave," a listing of weekly happenings.

Telephone – The area code for Miami is 305.

Sales Tax – There is a 5% statewide sales tax and a 5% hotel tax.

CLIMATE: Miami is warm all year, with average daily temperatures of 81F in summer and 69F in winter, and lots of sunshine. Temperatures can also get cool indoors, where air conditioning prevails.

GETTING AROUND: Airport – Miami International Airport is usually a 15-minute drive from downtown and about a half-hour from Miami Beach, longer during rush periods (8:30-9:30 AM and 4:30-6PM). Taxi fares average $12 to downtown, $16 to mid–Miami Beach. *Red Top* (phone: 526-5764) has van service every 20 to 30 minutes from the airport to hotels in downtown Miami for $6.75, to those in Miami Beach for $8. Call *Red Top* 24 hours in advance when returning to the airport; pickups are made 2 hours before flight time.

Metrorail – Metrorail, an elevated rail system, went into operation in 1984 from the Dadeland shopping mall in the Kendall area to downtown Miami, beyond to the Civic Center and Hialeah; fare, $1. The Metromover rail system is a 1.9-mile downtown loop that began service in 1986; fare, 25¢. For information, call 638-6700.

Bus – Metrobus serves downtown Miami, Collins Avenue on Miami Beach, Coral Gables, and Coconut Grove fairly well, but service to other areas tends to be slow and complicated. For information on routes, schedules, and fares, call 638-6700.

Taxi – You can sometimes hail a cab in the street, but it's better to order one on the phone or pick one up in front of any of the big hotels. Major cab companies are *Yellow Cab* (phone: 444-4444), *Super Yellow Cab* (phone: 888-7777), *Metro Taxi* (phone: 888-8888), and *Central Cab* (phone: 532-5555).

Car Rental – Miami is served by the large national firms; rates here are among the least expensive in the country.

LOCAL SERVICES: Business Services – *Stephan Secretarial Services,* 3132 Ponce de León Blvd., Coral Gables (phone: 446-9500).

Mechanics – *Martino,* for foreign and American cars, 7145 SW 8th St. (phone: 261-6071); *Lejeune-Trail Exxon,* for American makes, 801 SW 42nd Ave. (phone: 446-2942).

MUSEUMS: *Vizcaya Museum and Gardens,* the *Museum of Science and Space Transit Planetarium,* the *Bass Museum of Art,* and the museums in the Metro-Dade Cultural Center are described in some detail in *Special Places.* Other museums to see:

Cuban Museum of Arts and Culture – The cultural heritage of Miami's Cuban community. 1300 SW 12th Ave. (phone: 858-8006).

Lowe Art Museum – 1301 Stanford Dr., on the University of Miami campus in Coral Gables (phone: 284-3535).

MAJOR COLLEGES AND UNIVERSITIES: The University of Miami in Coral Gables (1200 San Amaro Dr.; phone: 284-2211) has an enrollment of 17,000. Florida International University is a 4-year college with two separate campuses (SW 8th St. and 107th Ave., NE 151st St. and Biscayne Blvd.; phone: 554-2363). Miami Dade Community College, with three campuses, is the largest junior college in the country (11380 NW 27th Ave., 11011 SW 104th St., and 300 NE 2nd Ave.; phone: 347-3135).

SPECIAL EVENTS: Miami is the site of the annual *Orange Bowl Parade,* nationally televised from Biscayne Blvd. each New Year's Eve as a prelude to the *Orange Bowl* football classic played on New Year's night. Two of the country's largest boat shows are held here each year, the *Dinner Key Boat Show* in Coconut Grove, in October, and the *International Boat Show* at the Miami Beach Convention Center in February. Miami Beach hosts the *Art Deco Weekend* every January on Ocean Avenue in the historic Art Deco district on South Beach, the *Festival of the Arts* each February, and the *Coconut Grove Art Festival* in the same month draws many away from the beach to stroll the shady lanes of this artists' haven. February also hosts the *Miami Film Festival,* a week of premières of national and international films with visiting directors, producers, and stars. Also in late February or early March, the *Miami Grand Prix* attracts top racing drivers to the downtown "track" on Biscayne Blvd. between Flagler and NE 8th Sts. (phone: 662-5660). In March, in Little Havana, natives and visitors alike head for Calle Ocho (8th St.) for *Carnaval Miami,* a 9-day festival featuring the largest conga line in the world. In April, the *Greater Miami Billfish Tournament* attracts more than 500 anglers vying for South Florida's richest fishing purse. In November, the *Miami Book Fair International* welcomes authors, publishers, booksellers, and street vendors to one of the world's largest week-long celebrations of the printed word.

SPORTS AND FITNESS: Baseball – Fans can watch preseason games of the Baltimore *Orioles,* whose spring training camp is in Miami; they often play the New York *Yankees,* who train in nearby Ft. Lauderdale (phone: 635-5395). The University of Miami *Hurricanes* play at *Mark Light Stadium* on campus at 1 Hurricane Dr., corner of Ponce de León and San Amaro (phone: 284-2655).

Basketball – The *Heat,* Miami's NBA entry, burns up the court at the *Miami Arena,* 721 NW 1st Ave. (phone: 530-4400, 577-HEAT).

Bicycling – Rent from *Dade Cycle Shop,* 3216 Grand Ave. in Coconut Grove (phone: 443-6075). There are more than 100 miles of bicycle paths in the Miami area, including tree-shaded lanes through Coconut Grove and Coral Gables. A self-guided bicycle tour of Key Biscayne originates in Crandon Park. Dade County Parks & Recreation Dept. has information (phone: 579-2676).

Boating – Greater Miami is laced with navigable canals and has many private and public marinas with all kinds of boats for rent. Sailboats are available from *Dinner Key Marina,* Pan American Dr., Coconut Grove. Windsurfer and Hobie Cat rentals, some with free instruction, are available from *Easy Sailing* shops on Key Biscayne (phone: 361-2021). Charter boats for sport fishing are available at *Crandon Park Marina* (phone: 361-1281), *Miami Beach Marina* (phone: 673-6000), and *Miami Marina* downtown (phone: 374-6260).

Fishing – Surf and offshore saltwater fishing is available year-round. The boardwalks on the Rickenbacker and MacArthur causeways and the Haulover Beach Fishing Pier (10800 Collins Ave., Miami Beach; admission charge) are popular fishing spots. There's also plenty of freshwater action in canals and backwaters, including the Everglades and Florida Bay. Charter boats offer a half day and full day of deep-sea fish, snapper, grouper, yellowtail, pompano, and mackerel trips from *Crandon Park Marina* (phone: 361-1281) and *Haulover Marina,* 10800 Collins Ave. (phone: 947-3525).

Fitness Centers – Staying in shape is no problem in Dade County. Try the *YMCA* at the downtown World Trade Center (phone: 577-3091); it allows free visits for out-of-town guests. *Bodyworks* in South Miami (phone: 665-5468), and *Body and Soul* in Coral Gables (phone: 443-8688) are also good places.

Football – The NFL *Dolphins* and Dolphin-mania infect the entire city during the football season, so for good seats call the new *Joe Robbie Stadium* in North Dade in advance (phone: 620-2578). The University of Miami *Hurricanes* play at the *Orange Bowl;* for tickets, contact the University of Miami ticket office, 1 Hurricane Dr., Coral Gables (phone: 284-2655), or go to the Orange Bowl.

Golf – More than 35 golf courses are open to the public. Some of the best are *Kendale Lakes,* 6401 Kendale Lakes Dr. (phone: 382-3930); *Biltmore,* 1210 Anastasia Ave., Coral Gables (phone: 442-6485); *Miami Springs,* 650 Curtiss Pkwy., Miami Springs (phone: 888-2377); *Bayshore,* 2301 Alton Rd., Miami Beach (phone: 532-3350); *Palmetto,* 9300 SW 152nd St., Miami (phone: 238-2922); and *Key Biscayne,* 6700 Crandon Blvd., Key Biscayne (phone: 361-9129).

Horse and Dog Racing – Betting is big in Miami. *Hialeah Race Track,* 2200 E. 4th Ave., Hialeah (phone: 887-4347), is worth a visit just to see the beautiful grounds and clubhouse and the famous flock of pink flamingos (they're in the opening of TV's "Miami Vice"). There is also thoroughbred horse racing at *Gulfstream Park,* 901 S. Federal Hwy., Hallandale (phone: 944-1242), and at *Calder,* 21001 NW 27th Ave. (phone: 625-1311). Greyhound racing is held at *Flagler,* 401 NW 38th Ct. (phone: 649-3000), and at *Biscayne,* 320 NW 115th St. (phone: 754-3484). Check the racing dates before heading to the track.

Jai Alai – From December through April there's jai alai (a Basque game resembling a combination of lacrosse, handball, and tennis) and betting action nightly at the *Miami Jai-Alai Fronton,* the country's largest. You can pick up tickets at the gate or reserve them in advance, 3500 NW 37th Ave. (phone: 633-6400).

Jogging – Run along South Bayshore Drive to David Kennedy Park, at 22nd Avenue, and jog the Vita Path; or jog in Bayfront Park, at Biscayne and NE 4th St. On Miami Beach, run on a wooden boardwalk that extends along the ocean from 21st to 51st St., or run toward the parscours on the southern tip of South Beach.

Nature Walks – There are nature walks at Fairchild Tropical Gardens and the Fruit and Spice Park, but the Parks & Recreation Dept. offers frequent guided tours through natural hammocks, tree forests, bird rookeries, and even through water (a marine walk and nature lesson and dousing are at Bear Cut, Key Biscayne). For information contact the Parks Dept. office (phone: 662-4124).

Skating – Hard-hit snowbirds can head north to Broward County for year-round ice skating at *Sunrise Ice Skating Center,* 3363 Pine Island Rd. (phone: 741-2366).

Swimming – With an average daily temperature of 75F, and miles of ocean beach on the Atlantic, Miami Beach and Key Biscayne offer some great places for swimming, all water sports, and another prime activity, sun worshiping. Some of the best beaches include the following:

> *Bill Baggs Cape Florida State Park.* This long beach with sand dunes, picnic areas, fishing, boat basin, restored old lighthouse, and museum is a favorite of residents. At Cape Florida, the far south end of Key Biscayne.
>
> *Crandon Park Beach,* a 2-mile stretch lined with shade trees, picnic tables, barbecue pits, ample parking. Drive to the far end for private cabanas rented by the day or week. Rickenbacker Causeway to Key Biscayne.
>
> *Haulover Beach* is a long stretch of beautiful beach, good for surfing and popular with families. Marina, sightseeing boats, charter fishing fleets, restaurants, and fishing pier. A1A north of Bal Harbour.
>
> *Miami Beach.* Several long stretches of public beach at various places, including South Beach for surfers (5th St. and Collins Ave.), Lummus Park with lots of shaded beaches (South Beach on Ocean Ave.), and North Shore Beach with landscaped dunes and oceanfront walkway (71st St. and Collins Ave.). There are also small public beaches at the ends of streets in the midst of Hotel Row.

Tennis – Many hotels have courts for the use of their guests, and there are also public facilities throughout the county. Some of the best are the *Abel Holtz Tennis Stadium* in Flamingo Park in Miami Beach with hard and clay courts, 1200 12th St. (phone: 673-7761); *Biltmore,* 1150 Anastasia, Coral Gables (phone: 442-6565); *Tamiami,* 10901 Coral Way, (phone: 223-7076); *North Shore Center,* 350 73rd St., Miami Beach (phone: 993-2022); and *Tropical Park,* 7900 SW 40th St., Miami (phone: 223-8710).

 THEATER: For current offerings, check the publications listed above. The *Coconut Grove Playhouse,* 3500 Main Hwy. (phone: 442-4000) imports New York stars for its classic season from October to May. The *Jackie Gleason Theater of the Performing Arts* offers touring plays and musicals, including some pre- and post-Broadway shows, 1700 Washington Ave. (phone: 673-8300). The *Gusman Cultural Center,* 174 E. Flagler St. (phone: 374-2444), and the *Dade County Auditorium,* 2901 W. Flagler St. (phone: 545-3395), book theatrical and cultural events year-round. The *Miami City Ballet,* 905 Lincoln Rd., Miami Beach (phone: 532-7713), headed by Edward Villella, is considered one of the country's best young companies and performs a full season beginning each fall.

 MUSIC: Visiting orchestras and artists perform in Miami at the *Gusman Cultural Center,* 174 E. Flagler St. (phone: 374-2444), and at *Dade County Auditorium,* 2901 W. Flagler St. (phone: 545-3395), or in Miami Beach at the *Theater of the Performing Arts,* 1700 Washington Ave. (phone: 673-8300). The *Greater Miami Opera Association,* 1200 Coral Way (phone: 854-7890), stages a full complement of major productions in the winter season, as does the *New World Symphony,* 101 E. Flagler St. (phone: 371-3005).

 NIGHTCLUBS AND NIGHTLIFE: Miami's nightlife runs the gamut. For a Vegas-style "flesh and feathers" revue, head for the *Sheraton Bal Harbour,* 9701 Collins Ave., Miami Beach (phone: 865-7511), or to *Les Violins,* for a flashy show with a Cuban twist, 1751 Biscayne Blvd. (phone: 371-8668).

For live blues and a bit of history, stop in at *Tobacco Road,* 626 S. Miami Ave. (phone: 374-1198), Miami's oldest bar. If jazz is your bag, try *Greenstreets,* 2051 LeJeune Rd., Coral Gables (phone: 445-2131). For tunes from the 1950s and '60s, two spots in Coconut Grove are popular: *Biscayne Baby,* 3336 Virginia St. (phone: 445-3751), and *Village Inn,* 3131 Commodore Plaza, (phone: 445-8721). The south end of Miami Beach is the latest "in" spot for nightlife. Head to *Woody's* (owned by Rolling Stones guitarist Ron Woods) for rock 'n' roll, 455 Ocean Dr. (phone: 534-1744), *Club Nu* for chic crowds and dance music, 245 22nd St. (phone: 672-0068), and *Paris Modern,* 550 Washington Ave. (phone: 538-8801).

BEST IN TOWN

CHECKING IN: Winter is the busy season, and reservations should be made well in advance. In winter, a double room in the very expensive range will run $195 and up per night; $145 and up in expensive; $120 and up in moderate; and about $70 in inexpensive. In summer, most hotels cut their rates, so shop around. For information about bed-and-breakfast accommodations, contact: *Bed & Breakfast Co.,* PO Box 262, South Miami, FL 33243 (phone: 661-3270). All telephone numbers are in the 305 area code unless otherwise indicated.

Alexander – An elegant, yet surprisingly homey, place metamorphosed from former luxury apartments. A chandeliered portico, a grand lobby with a curving stairway and antiques from the Cornelius Vanderbilt mansion in New York, and 211 spacious, antiques-filled suites are all impressive, as is *Dominique's* French restaurant (see *Eating Out*), with a main dining room overlooking the ocean. Roasted rack of lamb and exotic appetizers such as rattlesnake salad, alligator tails, and buffalo sausage are specialties. A $15-million expansion in 1987 added a second restaurant and a ballroom. The grounds include an acre of tropical gardens, 2 lagoon swimming pools — 1 with its own waterfall — and 4 soothing whirlpool baths; a private marina and golf and tennis facilities are nearby. 5225 Collins Ave., Miami Beach (phone: 865-6500 or 800 327-6121). Very expensive.

Fisher Island – Just off the southern tip of Miami Beach, this exclusive 216-acre island was once the private playground of William Vanderbilt. Recently turned into a private club and elite resort refuge, *Fisher Island* has extravagantly furnished resort apartments, villas, and a couple of historic cottages available for transient rental — though the cost is significant. It's worth it to many for the island's unique serenity and distance from "the outside world." Facilities include superb tennis courts (including a couple of grass ones), a marina, 2 restaurants, and several shops. Accessible only by private ferry (phone: 535-6020 or 800-624-3251). Very expensive.

Grand Bay – Run by the Aga Khan's CIGA chain and done in high style, the 181-room hotel overlooks Biscayne Bay and is near the equally tony Mayfair Mall. It houses the fashionable *Régine's* nightclub, 3 restaurants and lounges, and a pool. 2669 S. Bayshore Dr., Coconut Grove (phone: 858-9600). Very expensive.

Mayfair House – This all-suite hotel, part of the Mayfair Mall complex in the heart of Coconut Grove, has 181 suites, each with a terrace, Jacuzzi, and small dining area where a complimentary continental breakfast (with lots of tropical fruit) is served each morning. There is one restaurant, the private *Ensign Bitter's Dining Club* (for hotel guests only), and a rooftop pool with bar. 3000 Florida Ave. (phone: 441-0000 or 800-433-4555). Very expensive.

Sonesta Beach – On the beach at Key Biscayne, this top class resort's facilities include a tennis club with 10 Laykold courts (3 lighted) and instruction by two pros, an Olympic-size swimming pool, and a fitness center. In addition to the 300 rooms, there are also 4 restaurants and villas with from 2 to 5 bedrooms. 350 Ocean Dr. (phone: 361-2021). Very expensive.

Biltmore – A majestic landmark, dating to 1926 and topped by a replica of the Giralda Bell Tower of Seville, it reopened a few years ago after a multimillion-dollar restoration and modernization. There are 286 rooms and suites; 2 restaurants; a lounge; the exclusive and private *Biltmore Club;* a spa; swimming pool with whirlpool bath; 10 lighted tennis courts; and the 18-hole *Biltmore Golf Course.* 1200 Anastasia Ave., Coral Gables (phone: 445-1926). Expensive.

Biscayne Bay Marriott – On the marina, it offers 605 coral or mint-green rooms in the original building, a majority with bay views, and 150 rooms in the Venetia building, an extension added in 1987. The brass and marble lobby is comfortably welcoming, and the 2 restaurants serve fresh seafood, as does the hotel's oyster bar. A 3rd-floor skybridge connects the *Marriott* to the *Venetia* and to the *Omni International* shopping and hotel complex. 1633 N. Bayshore Dr. (phone: 374-3900 or 800-228-9290). Expensive.

Doral Ocean Beach Resort – Recently, $70 million have been spent on the *Doral,* its sister, the *Doral Country Club,* and the new *Doral Saturnia International Spa Resort* next to the country club. The effort shows. On the 18th floor of this 420-room high-rise is the *Doral Roof Garden* restaurant (worth the trip for the baby coho and chocolate linguini alone). Other highlights include a presidential suite, exclusive shops, Olympic-size pool, numerous water sports, tennis courts, an 80-foot executive yacht available for meetings, and the only FAA-licensed helipad on Miami Beach. There is shuttle service to the country club (built around 5 championship 18-hole golf courses) and the spa. Relaxed elegance and friendly staff. 4833 Collins Ave., Miami Beach (phone: 532-3600). Expensive.

Fontainebleau Hilton – The famous Miami Beach landmark, on 18 acres of beachfront real estate, is far more glitzy than glittering. The hotel's lagoon-like pool has a grotto bar inside a cave, and there are 12 restaurants and lounges as well as a kosher kitchen. The award-winning *Dining Galleries* restaurant is especially popular for Sunday brunch. Fully equipped spa; 1,206 rooms; 7 tennis courts. 4441 Collins Ave., Miami Beach (phone: 538-2000 or 800-HILTONS). Expensive.

Place St. Michel – This charming, European-style small inn in the heart of Coral Gables is cozy and elegant. On the premises is *Stuart's,* a jazz bar, an excellent restaurant, and a charcuterie, and a snack bar that is popular with the local lunch crowd. 162 Alcazar Ave., Coral Gables (phone: 444-1666). Moderate.

Hyatt Regency – Here is a 615-room riverside hostelry that's part of Miami's convention and conference complex in the heart of downtown. The top 2 floors feature Hyatt's Regency Club service, with complimentary continental breakfast, private lounge, and other extras. Two restaurants, one of which features a continental menu. 400 SE 2nd Ave. (phone: 358-1234, 800-233-1234, or 800-228-9000). Moderate.

Inter-Continental Miami – Formerly the *Pavillon,* this city-center hotel is built in the grand old hotel tradition. The 646 rooms have marble baths and Oriental furniture along with other luxurious appointments. Facilities include 4 restaurants, a lounge, a swimming pool, tennis and racquetball courts, a jogging trail, and a 200-seat auditorium. 100 Chopin Plaza (phone: 577-1000, 800-332-4246, or 800-327-0200). Moderate.

Omni International – This 10½-acre downtown complex includes 165 shops, 10 movie theaters, 21 restaurants, an amusement area, a sundeck, and rooftop pool. The *Omni* has 535 rooms and suites. 1601 Biscayne Blvd. (phone: 374-0000 or 800-THE-OMNI). Moderate.

Sofitel – A member of the French hotel chain, it is a relative newcomer to the States, and this sleek example is strictly international business in flavor. It offers 285 rooms, 2 French restaurants, a French bakery, lobby bar, health club, pool, Jacuzzi, and boating on a 100-acre freshwater lake. 5800 Blue Lagoon Dr., Miami (phone: 264-4888). Moderate.

Cavalier – The atmosphere and decor of this 44-room beachfront hotel are more camp than luxury. In the heart of the Art Deco district, it's a favorite with the fashion crowd, who flock to the ocean for photo shoots. Request one of the 4 rooms with ocean views and don't count on valets, porters, or room service. 1320 Ocean Dr., Miami Beach (phone: 531-6424). Inexpensive.

EATING OUT: Much of Miami socializing centers around restaurant dining, so beware the long lines during the winter season (December through April), when snowbirds swell the ranks of regulars. Residents always make reservations. Expect to pay $70 or more for a dinner for two in the very expensive range; $50 to $60 in the expensive; $35 to $50 in the moderate; and $25 or less in the inexpensive range. Prices do not include drinks, wine, or tips. Many establishments in the expensive category require that men wear jackets; it's wise to call ahead to inquire. All telephone numbers are in the 305 area code unless otherwise indicated.

Café Chauveron – Transplanted from New York City to Bay Harbor without the slightest disturbance of its famous soufflés, it's a French restaurant in the grand manner. Everything is beautifully prepared, from *coquille de fruits de mer au champagne* to soufflé Grand Marnier. Docking space if you arrive by boat. Open daily but closed from June through early October. Reservations necessary. Major credit cards. 9561 E. Bay Harbor Dr., Bay Harbor Island, Miami Beach (phone: 866-8779). Very expensive.

Dominique's – It's known for its outré dishes, such as rattlesnake and alligator, but regulars prefer the always excellent rack of lamb or filet of beef or veal, done in a classic French manner. For dessert, try the pistachio soufflé, named for a famous patron, Don Johnson. Open daily. Reservations necessary weekends and advised weekdays. Major credit cards. In the *Alexander* hotel, 5225 Collins Ave., Miami Beach (phone: 861-5252). Very expensive.

Pavillon Grill – For diners seeking creative cookery, here is American cuisine with a decidedly nouvelle bent: Everglade frogs' legs cakes with chilled vermouth mayonnaise, marinated and mesquite-grilled lamb chops, lobster and chicken fanned over black beans and sweet red pepper sauce. The setting is stylishly formal, so men will need jacket and tie. Dinner only; closed Sundays. Reservations advised. Major credit cards. In the *Inter-Continental* hotel, 100 Chopin Plaza (phone: 577-1000). Very expensive.

Forge – Prime ribs and Java steaks are the specialties on the otherwise continental menu here, with an extensive wine list. This gaudily decorated restaurant is filled with Tiffany lamps, carved ceilings, and chandeliers. There's also a lounge with entertainment. Open daily. Reservations necessary. Major credit cards. 432 Arthur Godfrey Rd., Miami Beach (phone: 538-8533). Expensive.

Gatti – In Miami Beach since 1924, this family-owned restaurant remains in its original stucco house. The Northern Italian cuisine is excellent. Jackets required. Closed Mondays and May through October. Reservations advised. Major credit cards. 1427 West Ave., Miami Beach (phone: 673-1717). Expensive.

Grand Café – This place oozes good taste, from the European elegance of the dining room and attentive service to the beautifully presented dishes, such as rack of lamb, she-crab soup, and black linguine (made with squid ink). Jacket required. Reservations a must for dinner, suggested for breakfast and lunch. Open daily. Major credit cards. In the *Grand Bay* hotel, 2669 S. Bayshore Dr., Coconut Grove (phone: 858-9600). Expensive.

Reflections on the Bay – The waterfront setting is spectacular, the glass and beam structure stunning, and the food carefully prepared and artistically presented. The menu changes frequently, but always features fresh ingredients and an intriguing tropical/Caribbean flair. Try the smoked mallard duck with fruit and summer greens; peppered prawns with callaloo greens and plantains; or spicy crabcakes with lobster sauce and okra. Open daily. Reservations advised. Major credit cards. Bayside Market Pl., 401 Biscayne Blvd., Miami (phone: 371-6433). Expensive.

Vinton's – Spread across the ground floor of the old *La Palma* hotel, an elegant choice, with foot pillows and fresh flowers for the ladies and sorbet served midway through dinner to refresh the palate. Superb duck with raspberry sauce, salmon in sorrel sauce, and lots of fresh seafood. Some dishes flambéed tableside. Closed Sundays. Reservations advised. Major credit cards. 116 Alhambra Circle, Coral Gables (phone: 445-2511). Expensive.

English Pub – The *Pub,* dismantled in England and shipped here, is dark, atmospheric, and . . . pubbish. Prime ribs are the specialty. Open daily. Reservations advised. Major credit cards. 320 Crandon Blvd., Key Biscayne (phone: 361-5481). Expensive to moderate.

Café Tanino – What with white lights twinkling overhead, mirrors, fresh flowers, and peach and white napery, *Café Tanino* is as festive as the Venice carnival prints on the walls. The cuisine is pan-Italian, with dishes from Sicily and Naples as well as the north. Open daily. Reservations accepted. Major credit cards. 2312 Ponce de León Blvd., Coral Gables (phone: 446-1666). Moderate.

Casa Juancho – Country hams hang over the bar and troubadours stroll and serenade at this lively Spanish restaurant. The parrillada en mariscos (shrimp, scallops, squid, and lobster cooked on the big open grill) is a house specialty, as are the tapas (small appetizers), served straight from the bar. Open daily. Reservations not accepted after 7:30 PM on weekends. Major credit cards. 2436 SW 8th St. (phone: 642-2452). Moderate.

Charade – Continental food in a charming Coral Gables landmark. Portions are large, and an oversize salad is included in the price of an entrée. Major credit cards. 2900 Ponce de León Blvd., Coral Gables (phone: 448-6077). Moderate.

Christy's – *Christy's* feels like a private club, with its leather armchairs, brass sconces, and dark wood — and for the pinstripe-suit types who entertain here, it practically is. The aged Iowa steaks and Caesar salad are tops; lobster, veal, duck, and chicken are also first rate. Open daily. Reservations necessary. Major credit cards. 3101 Ponce de León Blvd., Coral Gables (phone: 446-1400). Moderate.

Joe's Stone Crab – By now, this famous old (since 1913) South Beach restaurant is a Miami tradition, big, crowded, noisy, and friendly (get there by 6:30 or you'll have to wait). The stone crabs are brought in by Joe's own fishing fleet. People come here for serious eating, ordering tons of the coleslaw, hash brown potatoes, and Key lime pie that can keep dedicated diners waiting in line for up to two hours. Open daily; closed from mid-May to mid-October. No reservations. Major credit cards. 227 Biscayne St., Miami Beach (phone: 673-0365). Moderate.

Le Manoir – Very good traditional French food at reasonable prices in a former bakery. Big hit is the Friday night bouillabaisse. Closed Sundays. Reservations necessary. Major credit cards. 2534 Ponce de León Blvd., Coral Gables (phone: 442-1990). Moderate.

Monty Trainer's – A casual atmosphere pervades this bayside eatery in Coconut Grove. Guests can arrive either by car or boat (100 dock spaces are available for diners), then enjoy a meal on a palm-fringed terrace or indoors. Its pricier twin, *Monty's Stone Crab* at Mayfair in the Grove, serves those delectable crustaceans year-round (they're brought in from Virginia off-season), as well as a wide array of fresh seafood. Open daily. Reservations advised. Major credit cards. *Monty*

Trainer's, 2560 S. Bayshore Dr. (phone: 858-1431). *Monty's Stone Crab,* 3390 Mary St. (phone: 448-9919). Both moderate.

Raimondo's – In a plain brick building in Coral Gables, *Raimondo's* doesn't offer much atmosphere, but the food is as good as ever. Daily specials are posted, but spaghetti carbonara and red snapper meunière are also excellent. Open daily. Reservations advised. Major credit cards. 4612 S. LeJeune Rd. (phone: 666-9919). Moderate.

The Strand – This Miami Beach hot spot caters to an artsy, chic clientele, and suffers from uneven service, but is still recommended for the opportunity to glimpse Miami's see-and-be-seen crowd. Try the fried goat cheese with marinara sauce, Caesar salad, and the (incredibly wonderful) meatloaf. Reservations advised. Major credit cards. 671 Washington Ave., Miami Beach (phone: 532-2340). Moderate.

Big Fish – A funky, friendly converted gas station on the working Miami River is now a popular lunchtime eatery. The appeal is casual dining, a panoramic view of downtown, and fresh seafood on a menu chalked on a blackboard. Try the grouper sandwich on pita, with collard greens and black-eyed peas as accompaniments. No credit cards or reservations. 55 SW Miami Ave. Rd., Miami (phone: 372-3725). Inexpensive.

Blackie's Café – The food here is hickory-grilled — steaks, ribs, chicken, duck, lobster, stone crabs, and so on. Everything comes with homemade bread, salad, and potato, and all the grilling is done over the barbecue pit. The restaurant's new home has lots of waterside dining. Open daily. Very casual, with a mostly post-beach crowd. Major credit cards. 5005 Collins Ave., Miami Beach (phone: 866-7818). Inexpensive.

Centro Vasco – Next to jai alai, this is Miami's favorite Basque import. Specializes in filet madrilene de Centro Vasco, seafood paella, and arroz con mariscos. A great sangria is made right at your table. Open daily. Reservations advised. Major credit cards. 2235 SW 8th St. (phone: 643-9606). Inexpensive.

Málaga – This traditional Cuban restaurant in Little Havana is a good place to get acquainted with the cuisine. Best are standards like fried whole snapper, spiced pork, or arroz con pollo. Flamenco shows downstairs start at 9:30 PM every night but Tuesday. Open daily. Major credit cards. 740 SW 8th St. (phone: 858-4224). Inexpensive.

Marshall Major's – Some people call Miami the Bronx with palm trees. Whether or not that's true, *Major's* ranks with New York delis — pastrami, corned beef, home-style flanken, boiled chicken and vegetables, all served in huge portions. There's an Early Bird Special for dinner. Open daily. No reservations. Major credit cards. 6901 SW 57th Ave. (phone: 665-3661). Inexpensive.

Versailles – Authentic Cuban food and a lively ambience characterize this Little Havana landmark. A favorite of Latins and knowledgeable gringos. Wonderful Cuban sandwiches, black beans, and rice. Open daily till the wee hours. No reservations. Major credit cards. 3555 SW 8th St. (phone: 445-7614). Inexpensive.

Wolfie's – A Miami Beach institution that might be described as a deli, whose eclectic, 500-item menu carries everything from knishes to chicken parmigiana. Open daily. No reservations or credit cards. 2038 Collins Ave. (phone: 538-6626). Inexpensive.

Woody's Famous Steak Sandwich – Many residents swear by this little eatery. It's strictly no-nonsense — just thinly sliced steaks and grilled onion, peppers, and mushrooms, topped with melted cheese, on a toasted roll. Closed Sundays. No credit cards. 13105 Biscayne Blvd., North Miami (phone: 891-1451). Inexpensive.

MILWAUKEE

Milwaukee is the kind of place that grows on you gradually, like contentment with a cold glass of beer. And beer is the word you immediately associate with Milwaukee. Only in 1889 was brewing the city's principal industry, but Milwaukee residents loyally claim they consume more beer than anyone else in America. Two of the nation's six largest breweries are making beer in the city that grew up around a French-Canadian trading post.

The city's role as a lake port was primarily responsible for its early growth. Here, Lake Michigan receives the waters of the Milwaukee, Menominee, and Kinnickinnic rivers. With so much water around, it's easy to see why Milwaukee used to be a swamp. But the resourceful pioneers who arrived in 1833 discovered plenty of gravel left by a departing glacier ten thousand years earlier. They were fast with a shovel, and before long, New Englanders were parceling off Milwaukee real estate and selling it to each other.

The sailing ships brought loads of immigrants in the 19th century — first the Irish, fleeing the potato famine; then the Germans, including those who left home after the abortive revolutions of 1848; and in years following a variety of ethnic groups, among them the Poles, now Milwaukee's second largest ethnic group. (The Poles gave the city kielbasa sausage, a dietary staple on the South Side.)

During the latter half of the 19th century, Milwaukee called itself the German Athens. As late as the 1880s, two out of every three Milwaukee residents who bought a daily paper chose to read the news in the language of Goethe. The city's Germanic era ended in a flurry of divided loyalties and ill will during World War I. The Deutscher Club changed its name to the Wisconsin Club, sauerkraut became liberty cabbage, and the Germania Building was called the Brumder Building until recently, when it took back its original name.

Although Milwaukee's European heritage has been considerably diluted over the years, stubborn local conviction insists that food ought to be piled high on the plate, that no one ought to thirst for long, and that a householder who doesn't keep his lawn cut is a menace to civilization. With a downtown district that seems too small for a metropolitan population of 1.4 million and an Old World respect for homey virtues and tidy streets, Milwaukee impresses a lot of people as an overgrown small town. Where else but in Milwaukee would everyone quit work for a sausage break, as employees of Usinger's wiener works do each morning, to sample the product? Where but at *County Stadium* would a bratwurst be nearly as popular with hungry fans as a hot dog? A bratwurst on a poppy seed roll in one hand, a beer in the other, and the home team hitting homers — now that's Milwaukee living!

But there is lots more to the place than sauerbraten and suds. Milwaukee's lakefront has been compared to the Bay of Naples — not, it must be admitted, by the Neopolitans, but by the people who live here. Much of the shore belongs to the local taxpayers, including those who fish there for everything from smelt to coho salmon. (Milwaukee residents claim that no one lives more than half an hour from where the fish are biting.) When the weather is warm, the beaches within 5 minutes of downtown are crowded, even though Lake Michigan is generally too chilly for leisurely swimming. (Even in July and August sweaters are not uncommon).

Everyone celebrates the annual opening of Wisconsin's deer season, with thousands of hunters scurrying toward the woods and North Country taverns. Milwaukee County is proud of its park system, its zoo, its golf courses, and horticultural exhibits in glass domes that rise south of the Menominee Valley. The *Milwaukee Symphony* plays at the *Performing Arts Center,* and there are first-rate repertory and ballet companies. A downtown natural history museum and an art museum on the lakefront augment the city's cultural life. Urban problems are less severe in Milwaukee than in other cities of comparable size. The odds are pretty good you won't get mugged walking downtown after dark, and any political scandals you hear about are likely to be mild in comparison to those of other major cities. Milwaukee works hard to uphold its tradition of honest politicans and upright public servants.

Still, as nearly anyone you ask will admit, the city is no San Francisco, New Orleans, or New York. And ever since the early days, when a certain rival lakeport pulled ahead in the competition to attract settlers, it's been clear it's no Chicago. But the people who live in the community that made beer famous take comfort in that.

MILWAUKEE AT-A-GLANCE

SEEING THE CITY: The 41-story First Wisconsin Center, Milwaukee's second tallest building, anchors the eastern end of Wisconsin Avenue at Lake Michigan. Arrange a free visit to the top-floor observatory deck by calling 765-5733. 777 E. Wisconsin Ave.

SPECIAL PLACES: Milwaukee River divides the downtown area into east and west segments of unequal size (walking east you soon run into the beautiful Lake Michigan shoreline).

DOWNTOWN WEST

Wisconsin Avenue West – Walking west from the bridge along Wisconsin Avenue, Milwaukee's principal shopping street, you pass *Marshall Field's* (formerly *Gimbel's*), on the same site that John Plankinton, a pioneer butcher, started his career with one cow and boundless ambition. He became a millionaire, and gave a start to packing tycoons Philip Armour and Patrick Cudahy. The blocks between *Marshall Field's* and the *Boston Store* have been converted into the Grand Avenue shopping mall.

Joan of Arc Chapel – On the campus of Marquette University. This is the medieval chapel where Joan of Arc prayed before being put to torch — not here in Milwaukee, but in the French village of Chasse, from whence the chapel was transported stone by stone. One of those stones reputedly was kissed by Joan before she went to her death,

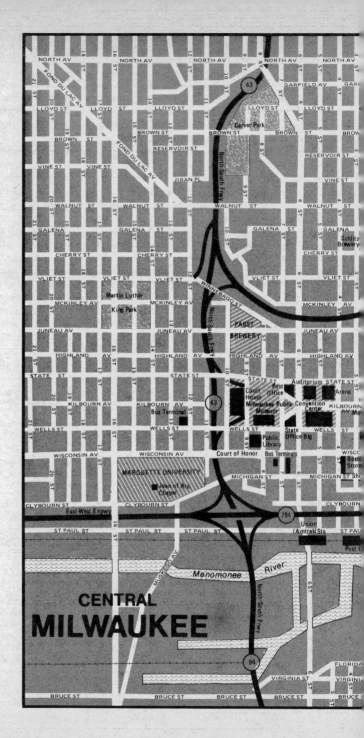

CENTRAL MILWAUKEE

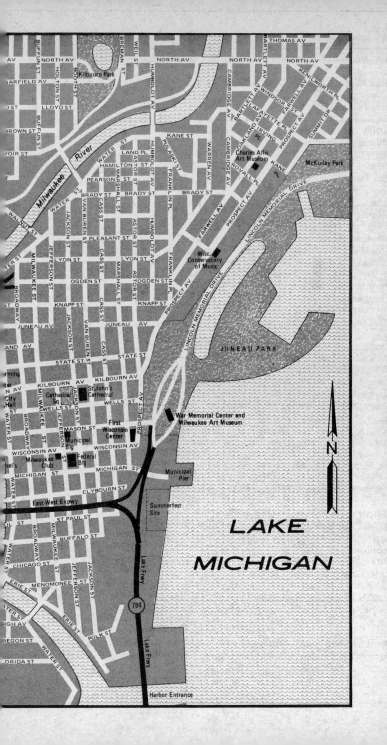

and is said to be discernibly colder than the others. Open daily. No admission charge. 601 N. 14th St. (phone: 224-7700).

Alex Mitchell Home – Now quarters of the Wisconsin (formerly Deutscher) Club, this was originally the house of General Billy Mitchell's grandparents. A Scot, Alex Mitchell arrived in Milwaukee with a carpetbag full of money and established the first bank. Banks were illegal at the time, but that didn't stop him. He called it an insurance company. Later he became a railroad president. 900 W. Wisconsin Ave.

Milwaukee Public Museum – Has the fourth largest collection of natural history displays in the country, plus a "Streets of Old Milwaukee" section, showing the city in the 19th century. The museum has some excellent dioramas: Northwest Coast, Great Plains, East Africa. Discreetly hidden away in an upstairs bedroom is the sink that once belonged to Kitty Williams, a famous Milwaukee madam. Open daily except major holidays. Admission charge. 800 W. Wells St. (phone: 278-2700).

Milwaukee County Historical Museum – Built in a bank once run by beer barons, it is near the MECCA Complex, whose amenities include a sports arena and facilities for conventions and meetings. The *Bradley Center,* just to the north, opened just in time for the 1988-89 pro basketball season. The museum has an archive and numerous exhibitions on the city's history, several of which are especially entertaining for children. Open daily. No admission charge. 910 N. 3rd St. (phone: 273-8288).

Père Marquette Park – Between the museum and the river, this park is named after the explorer-priest who stopped briefly in Milwaukee during a canoe trip through the Great Lakes area. Local legend insists that he landed here, although the site was then part of an extensive tamarack swamp along the Milwaukee River.

DOWNTOWN EAST

Wisconsin Avenue East – Wisconsin Avenue, east of the river, is a shopper's haven, with numerous fine stores. Shops on several nearby cross streets have been lovingly restored to their 19th-century origins. Across from the *Pfister* hotel is the Milwaukee Club, whose members are the city's ruling elite.

Milwaukee War Memorial, Milwaukee Art Museum – On the lakefront, where Lincoln Memorial Drive crosses Wisconsin Avenue, the original building was designed by Eero Saarinen. The *Art Museum* has recently doubled its size; its permanent collection includes Old Masters, contemporary art, and primitive painting and sculpture. It also runs the *Villa Terrace Decorative Arts Museum* at 2220 N. Terrace Ave. Outside, Lake Michigan provides a powerful backdrop for sculpture. The museum is closed Mondays. Admission charge. 750 N. Lincoln Memorial Dr. (phone: 271-9508).

Cathedral Square – Between Jackson and Jefferson Streets, this square dates to Wisconsin's territorial days. Except for the tower, St. John's Cathedral was nearly destroyed by fire in 1935. On the west side of the square, *Skylight Theater* offers musical plays and vest pocket operas. If you feel like a snack, turn left on Jefferson to #761, where *George Watts & Son*'s interesting silver shop has a restaurant tucked away on the 2nd floor.

City Hall – Milwaukee's best-known landmark, this building with the tall tower (393 feet) was designed in 1895 so that taxpayers could drive their buggies up in the rain to pay real estate taxes without getting wet. In the tower above the arched entry, Old Sol, a 20-ton bell, gathers dust. In 1922, citizens complained about the noise of Old Sol tolling, and city fathers ordered it stilled. N. Water St. at Wells St.

OTHER SPECIAL PLACES

Annunciation Greek Orthodox Church – The last major building designed by Wisconsin-born architect Frank Lloyd Wright. You can tour the saucer-shaped structure daily except Sundays. Admission charge. 9400 W. Congress St. (phone: 461-9400).

Whitnall Park – One of the larger municipal parks in the country, Whitnall includes the 689-acre Boerner Botanical Gardens, with sunken gardens, nature trails, and exhibitions. Open daily. No admission charge (phone: 425-1130). Also on the park grounds is the Todd Wehr Nature Center, a wildlife preserve for hikers and strollers. Open daily; closed Sundays in winter. No admission charge (phone: 425-8550).

Milwaukee County Zoo – Among the most famous zoos in the country, this one allows the animals to roam free in natural habitats. Kids adore the miniature railroad and children's zoo. Open daily. Admission charge. 10001 W. Blue Mound Rd. (phone: 771-5500).

Schlitz Audubon Center – The 180 acres of undisturbed grazing area once provided pasture to brewery horses weary from pulling beer wagons. It's a good place to wander and wonder at days gone by. A 60-foot wooden tower built on a 100-foot bluff offers a bird's-eye view of the city and countryside. Be warned — there is no elevator. Closed Mondays. Admission charge; free to members of Audubon Center. 1111 E. Brown Deer Rd. (phone: 352-2880).

Harbor Cruises – *Iroquois Boat Line* offers 2-hour trips along the Milwaukee River. Daily from Memorial Day through Labor Day. Admission charge. Clybourn St. Bridge dock (phone: 354-5050). From early June to mid-October, dinner cruises of the harbor are offered daily aboard the *Star of Milwaukee,* departing from the municipal pier at the east end of E. Michigan St. (phone: 273-7827). The *Emerald Isle* also offers cruises of the harbor and the Milwaukee shoreline (phone: 786-6886).

■ **EXTRA SPECIAL:** For an interesting day trip, take I-94 west 78 miles to Madison, the state capital and home of the University of Wisconsin's 1,000-acre, Big Ten campus. Drop in at the information center at Memorial Union on Park and Langdon Streets to pick up a map and find out what's happening on campus. There's more than enough to keep you busy, with an art center, geology museum, planetarium, observatory, and arboretum to see. The four lakes in Madison — Mendota, Monona, Waubesa, Wingra, and nearby Kegonsa — are great for fishing and swimming. If you continue driving west (toward the Iowa border), you'll find yourself in Wisconsin cheese country.

SOURCES AND RESOURCES

TOURIST INFORMATION: For information, maps, and brochures, contact the Visitor Information Centers at 828 N. Broadway and 161 W. Wisconsin (phone: 273-3950, 276-6080). Also, the Greater Milwaukee Convention and Visitors Bureau, 756 N. Milwaukee St., Milwaukee, WI 53202 (phone: 273-3950). The public service bureau in the lobby of the Journal Building, 4th and State, is also helpful.

Television Stations – WIFN Channel 12–ABC; WITI Channel 6–CBS; WTMJ Channel 4–NBC; WMVS Channel 10–PBS.

Radio Stations – AM: NAUK 1510 (country); WBKU 1470 (adult contemporary); WTMJ 620 (talk). FM: WUWM 89.8 (jazz/news); WKLH 96.5 (classic rock); WKTI 94.5 (top 40).

Local Coverage – *Milwaukee Sentinel,* morning daily; *Milwaukee Journal,* afternoon daily; *Shepherd Express* and *Milwaukee Weekly,* weeklies; *Milwaukee* magazine, monthly.

Telephone – The area code for Milwaukee is 414.

Sales Tax – Sales tax is 5% statewide.

CLIMATE: Summer and fall are generally pleasant, but expect sudden change when the wind shifts to the east. In winter, be prepared for bitter winds. The sub-zero cold is formidable.

GETTING AROUND: Airport – General Mitchell International Airport handles the city's domestic and international air traffic and is a 15-minute drive from downtown; taxi fare should run about $12. An economical share-a-ride program is available to those heading to the same destination; make arrangements through the Ground Transportation Coordinator, directly outside the baggage claim area. Milwaukee County Transit buses also provide service downtown for $1 (exact change required). *Airport Limousine* (phone: 282-8200) leaves every half-hour for downtown hotels ($4.70) as well as hotels in the western and northern metro areas ($9.50).

Bus – During the summer, a shuttle bus runs from the lakefront to the courthouse, mostly along Wisconsin Avenue. For information on bus schedules, contact Milwaukee County Transit System, 4212 W. Highland Blvd. (phone: 344-6711).

Taxi – There are taxi stands at most major hotels, but we recommend calling *City Veterans Taxi* (phone: 933-2266) or *Yellow Cab* (phone: 271-1800).

Car Rental – Most major car rental firms are represented. For a reliable local agency, contact *Selig Chevrolet,* 10200 W. Arthur Ave., West Allis (phone: 327-2300), or *Econo-Lease,* 3504 W. Wisconsin Ave. (phone: 933-1040).

LOCAL SERVICES: Babysitting – *Sara Care Services,* 9730 W. Bluemound Rd., (phone: 774-7272).

Business Services – *National Business Offices,* 1033 N. Mayfair Rd. (phone: 259-9110), also at 2040 W. Wisconsin Ave. (phone: 933-0636); *National Bookkeeping Service,* 759 N. Milwaukee St. (phone: 276-6655).

Mechanics – *Midtowne Mobil Servicenter,* 714 N. 27th St. (phone: 344-9229); *Bodden's Service,* 136 N. Water St. (phone: 272-3777); for foreign cars, *Tosa Imports,* 6102 W. North Ave. (phone: 771-2340).

MUSEUMS: The *Milwaukee Public Museum, Milwaukee County Historical Society Museum,* and *Milwaukee War Memorial and Art Center* are described in *Special Places. Discovery World,* a museum of science, economics, and technology where visitors can manipulate exhibits, is open weekends in the main library building, 818 W. Wisconsin Ave. (phone: 765-9966). Milwaukee has other museums a-plenty, among them:

Charles Allis Art Museum – 1630 E. Royall Pl. (phone: 278-8295).

Captain Frederick Pabst Mansion – 2000 W. Wisconsin Ave. (phone: 931-0808).

Brooks Stevens Auto Museum – 10325 N. Port Washington Rd. (phone: 241-4185).

MAJOR COLLEGES AND UNIVERSITIES: Marquette University (13,000 students), 11th and 18th Sts. on Wisconsin Ave. (phone: 224-7700); University of Wisconsin–Milwaukee (27,000 students), Kenwood Blvd. and Downer Ave. (phone: 963-1122).

SPECIAL EVENTS: At the end of January is *Icebreaker,* Milwaukee's annual winter festival. *Summerfest* is held every June and July on the lakefront. Amusement park rides, rock and jazz concerts are part of the celebrations. It is followed by a series of ethnic festivals featuring appropriate food and entertainment at the *Henry W. Maier Lakefront Festival Park* grounds. *Lakefront*

Festival of the Arts is held outdoors near the *Milwaukee Art Center* in the middle of June with music, food, arts and crafts exhibits. The *Great Circus Parade,* revived in 1985, is now an annual July event. The *Wisconsin State Fair* takes place for 2 weeks in mid-August on the fairgrounds adjoining I-94, west of downtown. The weekend before Thanksgiving, *Holiday Folk Fair* features ethnic food, music and entertainment. MECCA complex, Kilbourn Ave.

 SPORTS AND FITNESS: Baseball – The *Brewers* play at *County Stadium,* 201 S. 46th St. (phone: 933-9000).

Basketball – The Milwaukee *Bucks* and Marquette *Warriors* play at the new *Bradley Center,* 4th and State (phone: 227-0400).

Bicycling – Bikes can be rented from *East Side Cycle and Hobby Shop,* 2031 N. Farwell Ave. (phone: 276-9848); *Wilson Park Schwinn Cyclery,* 2033 W. Howard Ave. (phone: 281-4720).

Fishing – Salmon and trout as big as 30 pounds are caught in Lake Michigan, from shore and breakwater. You can use launching ramps at McKinley Marina and near South Shore Yacht Club for $3 to $5. Half-day boat charters cost about $160 for a party of six, including bait and tackle, and are offered by numerous firms (see the yellow pages under Fishing Parties — Charter).

Fitness Center – The *YMCA* has a pool, track, sauna, weights, and massage, 9250 N. Green Bay Rd. (phone: 354-9622).

Football – Green Bay *Packers* play their games at *County Stadium,* 201 S. 46th St. (phone: 342-2717).

Golf – The best public golf course is at Mee-Kwon Park, 6333 W. Bonniwell Rd., Mequon (phone: 242-1310).

Hockey – The Milwaukee *Admirals* play at the *Bradley Center* (phone: 227-0700).

Ice Skating – In winter, many parks open rinks. For year-round ice skating (indoors), try *Wilson Park Center,* 4001 S. 20th St. (phone: 281-4610) and *Eble Ice Arena,* 19700 W. Blue Mound Rd. (phone: 784-2900).

Jogging – Run in Lake Front Park, near War Memorial Center, on the beach, sidewalk, or oval track.

Nature Walks – The Schlitz Audubon Center, at 1111 E. Brown Deer Rd., has plenty of nature walks, highlighted by an amazing variety of birds.

Polo – Sundays in summer Milwaukee's polo teams compete at *Uihlein Field,* Good Hope Rd. and N. 70th St. (no phone).

Skiing – Currie, Dretzka, and Whitnall parks have ski tows, and mostly beginners' trails. Cross-country skiers may use all county parks. The Whitnall Park trails are particularly good.

Swimming – Seven public beaches along the lakefront have lifeguards and dressing facilities. The water is usually chilly, even in August. For information on the 17 public pools, call 278-4343.

Tennis – Try *North Shore Racquet Club,* 5750 N. Glen Park Rd. (phone: 351-2900), or *Le Club,* 2001 W. Good Hope Rd. (phone: 352-4900). In warm weather, numerous county parks have courts available for nominal fee.

 THEATERS: For complete listings on theatrical and musical events, see local publications listed above. *Milwaukee Repertory Theater* (phone: 224-9490), in a former power station on E. Wells St., just east of the Milwaukee River, is linked to the *Wyndham Milwaukee Center,* which includes a new hotel, office tower, and shops. The *Pabst Theater,* at 144 E. Wells St. (phone: 278-3663), which stages a variety of shows, is also connected to the center as part of what is called the Theater District. Across E. Kilbourn Ave. is the *Performing Arts Center,* home of *First Stage Milwaukee,* a children's theater. *Riverside Theater,* 116 W. Wisconsin Ave.

(phone: 271-2000), features stage shows by top performers. Other theaters include: *Skylight Theater,* 813 N. Jefferson St. (phone: 271-8815); *Theatre X,* 820 E. Knapp St., for experimental drama (phone: 278-0555).

MUSIC: *Milwaukee Symphony, Pennsylvania and Milwaukee Ballet,* and *Florentine Opera Company* perform at the *Performing Arts Center,* 929 N. Water St. (phone: *273-7121). "Music Under the Stars"* concerts are held in Washington and Humboldt parks on Friday and Saturday nights in July and August.

NIGHTCLUBS AND NIGHTLIFE: For jazz, visit *John Hawk's Pub,* Broadway and Michigan (phone: 272-3199). *Park Avenue,* 500 N. Water St. (phone: 765-0891), is a a lively disco for the under-30 crowd; *Rumors,* in the *Marriott* at 375 S. Moorland Rd. in Brookfield (phone: 786-1100), has dancing to top 40 hits and caters to well-dressed young professionals; *La Playa,* atop the *Pfister* hotel (phone: 272-5444), has touch dancing to a 10-piece combo plus a spectacular view. For dinner with piano music, try *Chip & Py's,* 815 S. 5th (phone: 645-3435).

BEST IN TOWN

CHECKING IN: Milwaukee's hotels range from the traditional, older *Pfister* and the modern *Hyatt Regency* to the functional *Grand* hotel, formerly the *Red Carpet Inn* near the airport. Expect to pay between $80 and $105 for a double at those places designated expensive; between $55 and $75 in the moderate category; about $45 or $50 at inexpensive places. Several offer weekend bargain rates. All telephone numbers are in the 414 area code unless otherwise indicated.

Hyatt Regency – This new $28-million, 18-story hotel was the first large hotel to be built in Milwaukee in many years and has helped to end a chronic shortage of rooms for conventions. And, by no coincidence, it is next to the downtown convention center. Topping the 485-room structure, with its atrium lobby, is the *Polaris,* a revolving restaurant. 4th and Kilbourn (phone: 276-1234, 800-233-1234, or 800-228-9000). Expensive.

Pfister – Catering to visiting and local elite since the 1890s. For a while, it looked as if the 330-room establishment was sliding gently downhill, but the present owners have brought it back to the level that enchanted Enrico Caruso and several presidents. The bronze lions in the lobby are named Dick and Harry, by the way, and the best views of the lake are from rooms 8, 9, 10, or high up in the new tower in the romantic lounge, *La Playa.* 424 E. Wisconsin Ave. (phone: 273-8222). Expensive.

Wyndham – In the heart of downtown, this is the latest accommodations entry on the local scene. Opened in July 1988, the facility is connected to the Theater District complex and is across the street from City Hall and the *Performing Arts Center.* The 10-story high-rise has 221 rooms, the *Kilbourn Café* for steaks and fowl, plus 2 nice bars. Rides in horse-drawn carriage are another feature. 139 E. Kilbourn Ave. (phone: 276-8686). Expensive.

Marc Plaza – The largest hotel in Milwaukee since 1927, its 540 rooms have gone through extensive renovation during their long career. Updated facilities include a heated indoor swimming pool and sauna. 509 W. Wisconsin Ave. (phone: 271-7250). Expensive to moderate.

Hilton Inn – Overlooking the Milwaukee River, this 164-room hostelry includes such amenities as king-size beds and an indoor pool. The adjoining *Anchorage* restaurant is noted for its seafood. On the Milwaukee River, near the Hampton Ave. exit of I-43 (phone: 962-6040 or 800-HILTONS). Moderate.

Marriott Inn – Stands out among the many motels on the outskirts of town. It has 254 rooms (one especially equipped for paraplegics), an indoor heated pool, and a popular disco, *Rumors.* 375 S. Moorland Rd., Brookfield (phone: 786-1100 or 800-228-9290). Moderate.

Grand Hotel – Near the airport, next to a convention hall, this property has 400 rooms, 2 heated swimming pools, and handball, tennis, and racquetball courts. If you're intrigued by Milwaukee's favorite sport, you'll be delighted to find out it's close to a bowling alley. 4747 S. Howell Ave. (phone: 481-8000). Moderate to inexpensive.

EATING OUT: Visiting Milwaukee without sampling the Wiener schnitzel would be like going to New Orleans's French Quarter and living on Big Macs. It was once said that visitors could get any kind of food in Milwaukee as long as it was German, but these days it's easy to feast at Polish, Chinese, Italian, Greek, Japanese, Serbian, and American restaurants as well. Expect to pay between $40 and $60 for two at those places listed as expensive; between $30 and $40 in the moderate category; under $20 in the inexpensive bracket. Prices don't include drinks, wine, or tips. All telephone numbers are in the 414 area code unless otherwise indicated.

English Room – Fairly exotic for Milwaukee, this is the place if you suddenly develop an overwhelming craving for crêpes flambées or pheasant with truffles. Flaming dishes are prepared at your table with appropriate theatrical flourish. Open daily. Reservations necessary on weekends. Major credit cards. In the *Pfister* hotel, 424 E. Wisconsin Ave. (phone: 273-8222). Expensive.

John Ernst – Even older and still a favorite of members of the brewing aristocracy, serving since 1878. Decorated with steins, German clocks, and posters. You can get steaks, but to do as the local populace does, it's better to order "sauerbraten mit dumplings, ja?" Closed Mondays. Reservations advised on weekends. 600 E. Ogden Ave. (phone: 273-5918). Expensive.

Karl Ratzsch's – Ranked as one of Milwaukee's top dining spots for many years, specializing in Teutonic cuisine since the days when the city called itself the German Athens. Open daily. Reservations advised on weekends. Major credit cards. 320 E. Mason St. (phone: 276-2720). Expensive.

La Rôtisserie and Polaris – These two restaurants are in the *Hyatt Regency* hotel. The former overlooks the 18-story lobby/atrium and specializes in duck roasted on a spit. The latter, revolving slowly atop the *Hyatt*'s roof, offers a more limited menu but a better view. Open daily. Reservations advised. Major credit cards. 4th and Kilbourn (phone: 276-1234). Expensive.

Beer Baron's – In the elegant former headquarters of the brewery once run by Valentin Blatz, this popular downtown eatery suits diners in the mood for anything from a fancy meal to a sandwich or an elaborate salad. An adjoining saloon matches the high standards of the pioneer brewers. In July and August, lunch is served on the sidewalk café. Reservations advised. Major credit cards. 1120 N. Broadway (phone: 272-5200). Expensive to moderate.

Mader's – Another family-run place going back to shortly after the century's turn, decorated in Bavarian style. For years, the late Gus Mader offered a reward to anyone who could finish his 3½-pound pork shank. The prize? Another 3½-pound pork shank, to be eaten in the same sitting. Open daily. Reservations advised on weekends. Major credit cards. 1037 N. 3rd St. (phone: 271-3377). Expensive to moderate.

Old Town – At this Serbian restaurant you can dine to the tune of tinkling tamburitzas. Fine, you say, but what is Serbian food? Well you might ask. We did, and were delighted to find it means sizzling lamb dishes cooked somewhat spicier than similar Greek and Turkish dishes. Closed Mondays. Reservations advised on weekends. Major credit cards. 522 W. Lincoln Ave. (phone: 672-0206). Moderate.

Toy's Chinatown – The family that owns this elaborate downtown Chinese restaurant has been serving Milwaukee residents for three generations, so when you eat here, you're not just getting egg rolls, you're getting tradition. Unless you order hundred-year-old duck eggs, you can be sure of fresh Cantonese dishes, like sweet and sour shrimp, spareribs, and chow mein. Open daily. Reservations advised on weekends. Major credit cards. 830 N. 3rd St. (phone: 271-5166). Moderate.

Bavarian Inn – This inn sits in a park owned by Germanic clubs, but its dining room is open to the public daily except Mondays. The food is good, the atmosphere informal, and Sunday buffet is one of the best bargains in town. You can help yourself to as much as you like. Be sure to bring a big appetite to do it justice. Closed Mondays. Reservations advised on weekends. Major credit cards. Take the Silver Spring exit from I-43 north, turn south on N. Port Washington Rd., then west on Lexington to 700 W. Lexington Ave. (phone: 964-0300). Inexpensive.

Jake's Delicatessen – If corned beef on rye appeals to you more than goose à la Tivoli or souvlaki, head for *Jake's*. All kinds of people eat here, from local millionaires to penniless kreplach lovers. You can sit at a booth, at a counter, or take your pastrami sandwich with you in a paper bag. Try the specials — they're giant knockwurst-like sausages. Open daily. Reservations advised. No credit cards. 1634 W. North Ave. (phone: 562-1272). Inexpensive.

■**THE BEERS THAT MADE MILWAUKEE FAMOUS:** If you're wondering where the smell of malt is coming from, follow your nose to one of the big breweries, where you'll be escorted through the facilities and given samples of the frothy wares (unless you're a child, in which case you only get to look): *Miller,* 3939 W. Highland Blvd. (phone: 931-2153), *Pabst,* 915 Juneau Ave. (phone: 223-3709), and a smaller one, *Sprecher's,* 730 W. Oregon St. (phone: 272-BEER). All welcome visitors except on holidays, when everyone stays home testing the product.

MINNEAPOLIS-
ST. PAUL

Describing the Twin Cities is like describing your children: They can be very different and yet you love them for their unique qualities. Vibrant and culturally eclectic, Minneapolis and St. Paul complement one another, each lending something extra to the other's character.

The Twin Cities share the Mississippi River, a common history, and great pride in the Minnesota *Twins,* who did much to unify the spirit of the two cities by defying the odds and winning the World Series in 1987. Still, there are Minneapolitans who speak of St. Paul as a foreign country, and St. Paulites who shy away from the "big city" of Minneapolis.

Minneapolis has been the larger of the two cities for almost a century, but St. Paul, the state's capital and the older of the two, has been playing "catch-up" in recent years and adopting some of the sophistication of its younger sister. Little by little, the differences between the cities have diminished.

In the past decade, St. Paul has enjoyed an enthusiastic revival. A large-scale redevelopment brought $903 million in new buildings to the downtown area. Town Square Park is a 4-level, glass-enclosed park filled with streams, waterfalls, and trees. The World Trade Center, completed in 1987, brought additional vigor to the downtown revival. The 40-story building is the tallest in the city and the hub of international business in the region. Fine shops and enticing eateries are just a skywalk away from 100 retail stores, professional services, entertainment centers, and government offices. Grand Avenue and the Ramsey Hill redevelopment combine 2 miles of epicurean delights and innovative shops with restorations of Victorian architecture in F. Scott Fitzgerald's old stomping ground.

The flamboyant twin, Minneapolis, has embarked on a renewal program. Nicollet Mall, the heart of downtown shopping and business, is having its face lifted. Some old eyesores have disappeared, while historic architectural gems are being preserved and put to new uses. The former Munsingwear plant now houses the upper Midwest's largest design center and is listed in the National Register of Historic Places. The riverfront area has new vitality since the resuscitation of the warehouse district, with its attractive shopping, living, and dining areas. The city retains its natural beauty through an outstanding park system while at the same time creating residential neighborhoods of distinct character and ethnic variety.

Both cities now benefit from a broad economic base. Major employers are in high-technology electronics and communications fields. Fortune 500 companies include Minnesota Mining, Honeywell, General Mills, Control

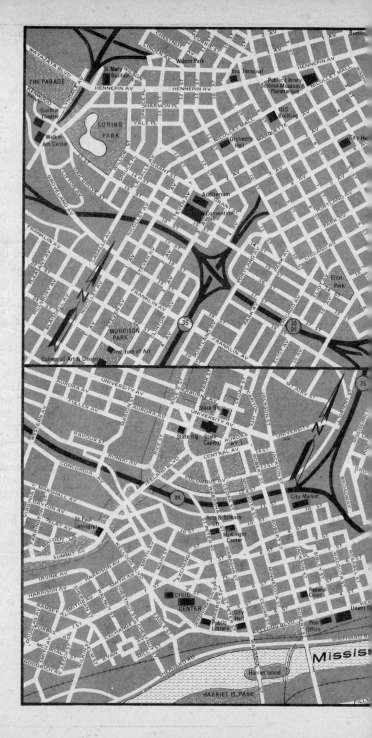

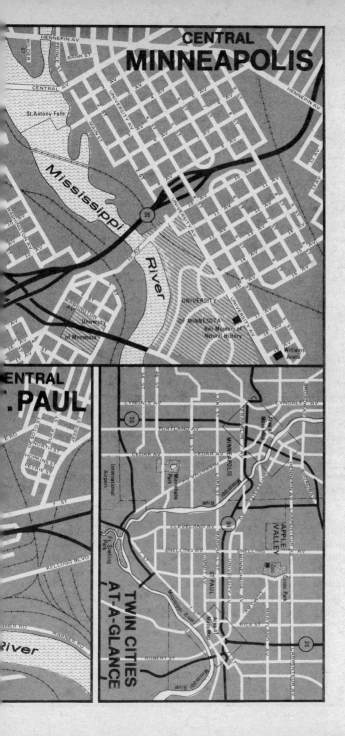

Data, Pillsbury, Land O' Lakes, International Miltifoods, and Bemis. There has also been a steady increase in moviemaking in recent years, making the Twin Cities now the fourth largest film production center nationally. They are seventh in the fields of advertising and public relations. St. Paul has attracted more of the steel and chemical plants over the years, while Minneapolis has cleaner industries like electronics. With some 139 municipalities in the seven-county area and dozens of neighborhoods in each municipality, the Twin Cities have opted for a joint approach in solving mutual urban problems.

At the junction of the Mississippi and Minnesota rivers, the Twin Cities region was discovered by French explorers in the late 17th century but remained relatively undeveloped until the 1850s, when the Indian territory west of the Mississippi was opened for settlement. Situated at the first navigable point on the Mississippi, Minneapolis and St. Paul became major shipping points for timber, flour, furs, and other natural resources.

Although St. Paul initially led in population, Minneapolis surpassed its twin around 1880 and has been Minnesota's largest city ever since. With a population of 2.2 million, the Twin Cities metro area is the third fastest growing urban region in the United States — and the fifteenth largest. South of Franklin Street, St. Paul and Minneapolis are divided by the Mississippi, but Twin Cities residents don't perceive the river as the boundary. The University of Minnesota campus spans both sides of the river but retains a Minneapolis address.

Some 936 lakes and 513 parks contribute to Minneapolis–St. Paul's unusual pastoral beauty. The cities also rank high in health care and in the arts. Part of the charm of the metro area can be directly attributed to an almost religious sense of tithing on the part of the more responsible corporations and their principals. Business leaders undoubtedly realize that the relative isolation of the Twin Cities (at least 400 miles from another major city) requires a full measure of cultural and sports activities to attract talented employes.

The world-famous *Guthrie Theater* makes its home here, as does the *Minnesota Orchestra* — a full-time symphony. The only full-time chamber orchestra in the United States, the *St. Paul Chamber Orchestra*, performs to packed houses. The *Minneapolis Institute of Arts*, the *Walker Art Center*, the *Ordway Music Theater*, two science centers, the *Minnesota Opera*, and the many historical collections and art galleries are responsible for the Twin Cities' reputation as a cultural center. In St. Paul, Noah Adams hosts National Public Radio's "Good Evening," featuring songs, stories, guests, and humor, originating from the *World Theater*, the city's oldest surviving theater, restored in 1986.

Minneapolis–St. Paul residents don't even mind the severe winter weather. They enjoy it with a vigor by snowmobiling, ice fishing, and skiing. Twin Citians like where they live no matter what the season.

MINNEAPOLIS–ST. PAUL AT-A-GLANCE

SEEING THE CITY: Although the IDS and Multi-Foods buildings are taller, the best view of the area is from the observation deck of the 32-story Foshay Tower (9th St. at 2nd Ave) in Minneapolis; closed in winter. St. Paul is built on seven hills, like Rome. Cherokee Park, overlooking the Mississippi River, affords a spectacular panorama of both cities. Another good view is that from Pennsylvania Avenue Hill.

SPECIAL PLACES: The most extraordinary feature of downtown Minneapolis and St. Paul is their interior skyways, an interconnected belt of pedestrian malls and escalators lacing in and out of shops, banks, and restaurants at the 2nd-story level. When it's below zero, you may still walk around comfortably without a coat. At street level, courtyards, gardens, fountains, and sculpture form attractive plazas. In Minneapolis, travelers may check in at one of two hotels connected to the skyway, the *Radisson Plaza* and the *Marriott City Center.* St. Paul's skyway connects to the *Holiday Inn, Radisson St. Paul,* and St. Paul hotels (see *Checking In*).

MINNEAPOLIS

Minneapolis Institute of Arts – Architecturally classical, the museum houses Old Masters, Chinese and Egyptian art, Revere silver, and historical exhibitions. In addition, its Society for Fine Arts presents classical films, recitals, and lectures. A model for other arts institutions around the country, the institute is also the home of the Minneapolis College of Art and Design and the *Children's Theater Company.* Open daily. Admission charge. 2400 3rd Ave. S. (phone: 870-3131).

Guthrie Theater – Internationally acclaimed for its superb productions, the *Guthrie* features a resident professional repertory company that presents ensemble productions of classical and modern drama. The contemporary theater building can seat more than 1,400 people in a 200-degree arc around an open stage. After a nationwide search for a hospitable metropolitan environment in which to locate a repertory theater, Sir Tyrone Guthrie selected Minneapolis. His choice has been borne out by the enthusiastic, loving support of audiences and patrons. The theatrical season generally runs from May to February; 1990 is the theater's 25th anniversary. Concerts are given throughout the year. 725 Vineland Pl. (phone: 377-2224 or 347-1100).

Walker Art Center – Named after T. B. Walker, a local patron of the arts, the center, in the *Guthrie* building, complements the classical *Institute of Arts* by focusing on post-Impressionist and contemporary art. The *Walker* also features alternating exhibitions, innovative film programs, and concerts. The restaurant is open from 11:30 AM to 3 PM. Closed Mondays. Admission charge. 725 Vineland Pl. (phone: 375-7636 or the box office, 375-7622).

Minnehaha Park – In his poem "Hiawatha," Longfellow immortalized the "laughing waters" of Minnehaha Falls along the Mississippi. In addition to the splendor of the Falls, you can picnic near a statue of Minnehaha herself and brave Hiawatha. No admission charge. Minnehaha Pkwy. and Hiawatha Ave. S.

Minneapolis Grain Exchange – An ornate hall the size of a large school gym, the exchange is a loud, hectic place where futures and samples of actual grains are bought and sold. You can take a guided tour through the world's largest grain exchange, but you must make reservations in advance. Visitors balcony open daily. Tours given on weekdays. 400 4th St. S. (phone: 338-6212).

Orchestra Hall – Music has had an appreciative audience in the Twin Cities since the turn of the century. The hall houses the *Minnesota Orchestra* (formerly the *Minneapolis Symphony*), which played its first concert in 1903 and has been playing classical and symphonic pop music to responsive audiences ever since. Though spartan in appearance, the new *Orchestra Hall* is renowned for its superior acoustics. 1111 Nicollet Ave. (phone: 371-5656).

Minnesota Zoo – Set in the rolling hills of Apple Valley, this 500-acre, state-funded zoological park provides a natural environment for Siberian tigers, musk oxen, moose, and other northern animals. There are many aquatic species in the Aquarium, and a 5-story indoor tropical environment houses jungle fauna and flora. In winter, cross-country skiers can enjoy 10 km of groomed trails that meander past musk oxen, caribou, and other Minnesota wildlife. Zoo lovers will find this one among the nation's best. Open daily. Admission charge. 12101 Johnny Cake Ridge Rd., Apple Valley, 25 minutes south of the city on Hwy. 35 (phone: 431-9200).

ST. PAUL

Como Park – St. Paul has a multitude of parks. The largest is St. Paul's Como Park, which dates to Victoria's reign. A 70-acre lake, a small zoo, a golf course, and children's rides contribute to its popularity. In addition, there are special floral gardens, a year-round conservatory, and a lakeside pavilion where summer concerts are held. Open daily. No admission charge. University Ave. between Park and Cedar Sts. (phone: 488-7291 or 292-7400).

State Capitol – St. Paul is Minnesota's political center, and its capitol is one of the most important buildings in the state. Set on a hill, its giant dome — a replica of one designed by Michelangelo in Rome — is one of the state's outstanding landmarks. More than 25 varieties of marble, limestone, sandstone, and granite were used to construct the building. Free guided tours given daily. The Minnesota Historical Society building is on the edge of the capitol grounds. Founded in 1849, ten years before Minnesota became a state, the society houses records of pioneer days. Open daily. No admission charge. University Ave. between Wabasha and Cedar Sts. (phone: 297-3521).

Governor's Residence – This English Tudor residence, built in 1910-11, is on the National Register of Historic Sites. Donated to the state by the daughters of lumberman Horace Irvine, it is open for tours the third Thursday of each month, from 10 AM to 2 PM. Reservations required. No admission charge. 1006 Summit Ave. (phone: 224-9735).

St. Paul's Cathedral – The center of the Roman Catholic archdiocese, this cathedral is a replica of St. Peter's in Rome. Architecturally notable for its 175-foot-high dome and a central rose window, it has a special Shrine of the Nations, where visitors can meditate and pray. Open daily. No admission charge. 239 Selby Ave. (phone: 228-1766).

Science Museum of Minnesota – This $3.5-million complex combines a 635-seat theater for the performing arts, a 300-seat auditorium, an art gallery, a rooftop lounge, and the pièce de résistance, the science museum. Featuring natural history, environmental, and geological exhibitions and films, the science center is immensely popular with residents. Open daily during the summer; closed Mondays in winter. No admission charge. 30 E. 10th St. (phone: 221-9488).

William L. McKnight Science Center – The Science Center — named after the founding father of the 3M Company — is among the most advanced science centers in the US. Part of the *Science Museum of Minnesota,* the high point of this new science complex is its "omnitheatre" — a floor-to-ceiling hemispheric screen surrounding the audience and tilted at 30 degrees so that viewers will see the screen in front of them rather than above, as in conventional planetariums. Closed Mondays. Admission charge. 505 Wabasha (phone: 221-9400).

Ft. Snelling State Park – The oldest landmark in the Twin Cities, one of the first military posts west of the Mississippi. Not very far west, however: Ft. Snelling sits high on a bluff overlooking the junction of the Mississippi and Minnesota rivers. You can see what life was like here during the 1820s. People in costume demonstrate early crafts, and parade in military formation. Fife and drum bands perform in summer. The history center is open weekdays year-round. Ft. Snelling is open daily, May through October. Free admission to the history center and museum; admission charge for the fort. Hwy. 5 and 55, 6 miles southwest of the city (phone: 726-9430 or 726-1171).

■**EXTRA SPECIAL:** The St. Croix Valley, 25 miles northeast of Minneapolis–St. Paul, offers several stops for a day's outing. Stillwater, birthplace of Minnesota, is within easy striking distance of the *Afton Alps, Welch Village,* and *Wild Mountain* for skiers. In Stillwater, visit the Grand Garage and Gallery on Main Street, with its shops and galleries. It has restaurants, but a better eating stop is *Brine's Meat Market and Lunchroom,* which has the *Employees Lunchroom* upstairs, open to anybody employed anywhere, with great bratwurst, pastrami, and chili. On the Wisconsin side of the tour is Somerset, which has one of the greatest summer activities in the entire world: tubing down the Apple River. You get carted upriver about 4 miles, plunked into an inner tube, and sent drifting back to Somerset. The river flows quickly at the outset, but widens and slows down, and the ride into town is tranquil.

SOURCES AND RESOURCES

TOURIST INFORMATION: The Greater Minneapolis Chamber of Commerce and the Minneapolis Convention and Visitors Association are at 1219 Marquette, Minneapolis, MN 55403 (phone: 348-4330). The St. Paul Chamber of Commerce and Convention Bureau are at 445 Minnesota St., St. Paul, MN 55101 (phone: 223-5000 and 297-6985, respectively).

Minnesota Explorer, a 24-page guide to events throughout the state published three times a year, is free from the Minnesota Office of Tourism, 250 Farm Credit Bldg. at 5th and Robert, St. Paul 55101 (phone: 296-5029 or 800-328-1461).

Television Stations – KSPT Channel 5–ABC; WCCO Channel 4–CBS; KARE Channel 11–NBC; KTCA Channel 2–PBS.

Radio Stations – AM: WCCO 830 (talk/news); KSPT 1450 (talk/easy listening). FM: KTCZ 97.1 (jazz); KS95 95 (top 40).

Local Coverage – The *Star-Tribune,* daily; *St. Paul Pioneer Press/Dispatch,* daily. The *Reader* and *City Pages* (both distributed free in the Mall and downtown hotels) list activities in the Twin Cities. *Mpls.–St. Paul* and *Twin Cities* magazines, available monthly at newsstands, give full details on what's what.

Food – The *Twin Cities Directory,* published monthly, is distributed free throughout the metro area, especially at hotels. It contains reviews of restaurants and a listing of the month's events. The *Official Visitors Guide* (free from the Convention and Visitors Bureau) lists eateries, casual to elegant.

Telephone – The area code for Minneapolis–St. Paul is 612.

Sales Tax – The sales tax in Minneapolis is 6½%; in St. Paul, 4%.

CLIMATE: In winter, be prepared for the worst. The average temperature is 19F, but it can drop to 35F below zero, and snow has been known to fall as early as October. Summer temperatures are generally in the 70s and 80s.

 GETTING AROUND: Airport – Minneapolis–St. Paul International Airport is a 20- to 30-minute drive from the downtown area of either Twin City; cab fare should run about $15-$20. *Airport and Airline Taxi-Cab Corp.* (phone: 721-6566) provides metered cab transportation from the airport to Minneapolis hotels; *A-Plus Cab* (phone: 228-9460) handles St. Paul hotel transfers for $10. Metropolitan Transit Commission buses 7C and 7D run between the airport and downtown Minneapolis, stopping along Washington Avenue every 40 minutes; to get to the airport from downtown St. Paul, take bus 9B on 6th St. and transfer to the 7C or 7D at Ft. Snelling. The fare is 75¢. Limousines leave both the airport and downtown hotels in both cities about every 15 minutes. One-way fare: $5.50 (St. Paul) and $6.50 (Minneapolis); round-trip fare is $9.50 in both cities. Two good companies are *St. Paul Airport Limousine* (phone: 726-5479) and *Minneapolis Airport Limousine* (phone: 726-6400).

Bus – Minneapolis–St. Paul bus systems are a model of efficiency. They run from 6 to 1 AM. Express buses make the trip between Minneapolis and St. Paul in 20 minutes. Passengers' queries are handled by an extensive switchboard. Metropolitan Transit Commission, 560 6th Ave. N., Minneapolis (phone: 827-7733). Fares are 75¢ off peak, 90¢ peak..

Taxi – As in many other cities, taxis are impossible to get when you really need them and plentiful when you don't. Most are radio-dispatched. There are some taxi stands. The largest cab company is *Yellow Cab*, 2812 University Ave. SE (phone: 331-8294); in St. Paul (where it's known as *Town Taxi*), 167 Grand Ave. (phone: 222-4433).

Car Rental – All major firms are represented. A good local agency is *Dollar Rent-A-Car,* at the airport (phone: 726-9494).

 LOCAL SERVICES: Babysitting – The *YWCA* cares for children from 3 months to 5 years old; make reservations 24 hours in advance. Minimum sitting assignment is 4 hours. 1130 Nicollet Ave. (phone: 332-0501). There's also *New Horizon Child Care,* 1385 Conway St., St. Paul (phone: 778-9441); *Ramsey County Day Care Referral* (phone: 298-4260); and *Jack and Jill Sitting Service,* 1651 4th St., at White Bear Lake (phone: 429-2963).

Business Services – *A-1 Secretarial Services,* Pioneer Bldg., Suite 219, St. Paul (phone: 228-1907); *Executive Business Services* (word processing and copying), 1111 3rd Ave. S., Minneapolis (phone: 332-5903).

Mechanics – *Fisher Tire and Auto* provides excellent 24-hour road service at extremely reasonable prices. 1022 Hennepin Ave. (phone: 338-6953). *DJ's Towing,* 842 University Ave., St. Paul (phone: 291-2637), provides complete auto repair and 24-hour towing at competitive prices.

MUSEUMS: The pride of Minneapolis–St. Paul is the Twin Cities' cultural wealth, and a visit to the many fine museums is well worth it. The *Minneapolis Institute of Arts,* the *Walker Art Center,* the *Science Museum of Minnesota,* and the *McKnight Science Center* are described in *Special Places.* Some others to see:

American Swedish Institute – 2600 Park Ave., Mpls. (phone: 871-4907).

Bell Museum of Natural History – 10 Church St. SE, Mpls. (phone: 624-1852).

James J. Hill House – 240 Summit Ave., St. Paul (phone: 297-2555).

Landmark Center – 75 W. 5th St., St. Paul (phone: 292-3272).
Minneapolis Planetarium – 300 Nicollet Mall, Mpls. (phone: 372-6644).
Minnesota Museum of Art – 305 St. Peter, St. Paul, with additional galleries in the Landmark Center, 75 W. 4th St., St. Paul (phone: 292-4355).
Ramsey House – 265 S. Exchange St., St. Paul (phone: 296-0100).
Schubert Club Keyboard Instrument Museum – Landmark Center, 75 W. 5th St., St. Paul (phone: 292-3267).

 MAJOR COLLEGES AND UNIVERSITIES: About 55,000 students attend the University of Minnesota, one of the Big Ten universities; the campus sprawls across the east and west banks of the Mississippi. Escorted tours are available. University Ave. SE (phone: 624-6868).

 SPECIAL EVENTS: The *Aquatennial Festival* in late July features sailboat races, a torchlight parade, and "Queen of the Lakes" beauty contest. *Minnesota State Fair,* 11 days, ending Labor Day at Como and Snelling Aves., St. Paul. *St. Paul Winter Carnival,* late January or early February, is a citywide celebration.

 SPORTS AND FITNESS: Professional Sports – The new 60,000-seat *Hubert H. Humphrey Stadium* (500 11th Ave. S.) houses major league baseball, basketball, and football teams. For information on games call: *Twins* (baseball; phone: 375-1116), *Timberwolves* (basketball; phone: 337-3865), *Vikings* (football; phone: 333-8828). The *Metropolitan Sports Center,* 7901 Cedar Ave. S., is the home of the *North Stars*; (hockey; phone: 989-5151).
Biking – There are bike trails around Lake Harriet, Lake Calhoun, and Lake of the Isles in Minneapolis; Lakes Como and Phalen in St. Paul. Bicycles may be rented from the *Bike Shop,* 215 Oak St. SE, Minneapolis (phone: 331-3442), and at Lake Como, St. Paul (phone: 735-1333).
Fishing – Twelve fishing lakes are in the Twin Cities metro area; the best is Lake Minnetonka, which has 177 miles of shoreline. 15 miles west on Hwy. 12. Within the city limits, Lake Calhoun has a fishing dock.
Fitness Centers – The *Medalist Sports Clubs,* Como and Snelling Aves., St. Paul (phone: 646-1165), and *Northwest Racquet, Swim and Health Clubs* (phone: 546-5474), have exercise equipment, sauna, whirlpool bath, and running tracks.
Golf – There are 18 courses in Minneapolis–St. Paul. Best is *Meadowbrook Golf Course,* 201 Meadowbrook Rd. at Goodrich Ave., Mpls. (phone: 929-2077).
Horse Racing – *Canterbury Downs,* 25 miles west of downtown Minneapolis, has thoroughbred and harness racing from mid-April through November (phone: 445-RACE).
Ice Skating – The cities clear, test, and maintain outdoor rinks on many of the lakes. Indoor ice arenas offer some free time for public skating. Consult the telephone directory for locations and numbers.
Jogging – Run to Loring Park via Marquette Avenue and West Grant Street (about 1½ miles) and then around the park (.8 mile). A more ambitious run leads to Lake of the Isles, 2½ miles from downtown, and from there to several other lakes: Cedar Lake to the west or Lakes Calhoun and Harriet to the south; the perimeter of each lake is about 3 miles. Another route is along the Mississippi on East or West River Road, by the University of Minnesota. In St. Paul, joggers take to the trails around Lake Como and Lake Phalen. The most popular and beautiful spot for runners in St. Paul is Summit Avenue.
Skiing – Best are *Afton Alps Ski Area, Inver Hills,* and *Buck Hill.*

Swimming – There are public swimming beaches at 23 lakes in and around the Twin Cities area. Open June to August.

Tennis – There are many lighted, outdoor courts as well as indoor courts (ranging from $6.50 to $9 per hour) available throughout the cities.

THEATER: In addition to the *Guthrie,* Minneapolis–St. Paul has more than a dozen theaters. The universities and colleges also produce plays and musicals. Best bets: *Guthrie* (phone: 377-2224) and *Children's Theater Company* (phone: 874-0400).

MUSIC: For a complete schedule of musical happenings, check the newspapers, especially *St. Paul Pioneer Press/Dispatch* ETC on Thursdays; *Star-Tribune* Variety Weekend on Fridays. The copper-capped, glass-walled *Ordway Music Theater,* 345 Washington St. (phone: 224-4222), presents performances by the *St. Paul Chamber Orchestra,* the *Minnesota Opera,* the *Schubert Club,* and the *Minnesota Orchestra.* There are outdoor summer concerts at Lake Harriet in Minneapolis and at Lake Como in St. Paul.

NIGHTCLUBS AND NIGHTLIFE: *Gallivan's Downtown* in St. Paul, 354 Wabasha (phone: 227-6688), features professional entertainment. *The Manor,* 2550 W. 7th St. (phone: 690-1771), provides ballroom dancing Wednesdays through Saturdays. *Cleo's,* at IDS Center, Mpls., (phone: 349-6250) offers a panoramic 50th-floor view, a happy-hour buffet. The *Normandy Inn Piano Bar,* 405 S. 8th St., Mpls. (phone: 370-1400), is a French-style pub with live entertainment on weekdays. The *Continental Room* at *McGuire's Inn* of Arden Hills, 1201 W. County Rd. E., St. Paul (phone: 636-4123), also presents well-known entertainers. Bob Dylan began his singing career in the West Bank area near the University of Minnesota, where there are a number of small clubs and cafés.

Rupert's, 5410 Wayzata Blvd., Mpls. (phone: 544-5035), boasts a 10-piece band cranking out jazz, swing, and pop tunes Tuesdays through Saturdays, plus top Minnesota acts on Wednesdays. Singles flock to *McCormick's Saloon and Deli* in the *Radisson University,* 615 Washington Ave. (phone: 379-8888). The former Greyhound Bus Depot in Minneapolis is now *First Avenue & 7th Street Entry,* 29 W. 27th St. a nightclub featured in local rock star Prince's film *Purple Rain* (phone: 332-1775). *The Fine Line Music Café,* 318 1st Ave. N., Minneapolis (phone: 338-8100), presents some of the best local talent to a "hip" audience. *St. Paul's Hearthrob Café and Nightclub* (phone: 224-2783), 30 E. 8th St., draws a young, energetic crowd who dance to loud recorded music.

BEST IN TOWN

CHECKING IN: There are a number of places near the Minneapolis–St. Paul International Airport, in the suburb of Bloomington, as well as some new and newly renovated hotels downtown. Expect to pay $90 or more for a double room in one of the hotels we've listed as expensive; $70 to $90 in the moderate range; and around $50 in inexpensive places. *Days Inns, Best Western,* and *Quality Inns* are a few chains providing inexpensive lodging. All telephone numbers are in the 612 area code unless otherwise indicated.

Hyatt Regency – In Nicollet Mall, just a short hop from the airport. There are 540 tasteful rooms and suites, and a Regency Club floor for extra-special service. *The*

Terrace is the hotel's more casual eating spot; the *Willows* restaurant has fancier, continental fare; the *Willows Lounge* features entertainment every night but Sunday. 1300 Nicollet Mall (phone: 370-1234, 800-233-1234, or 800-228-9000), Mpls. Expensive.

Luxeford Suites Minneapolis – An all-suite hotel at the edge of downtown, with a European feel. Each room has a wet bar, refrigerator, and microwave, and a fresh glass of orange juice is served in the room each morning along with a copy of *USA Today*. A complimentary continental breakfast is laid out on the English sideboard of the club room, just off the lobby. 1101 La Salle Ave., Mpls. (phone: 332-6800). Expensive.

Marriott City Center – This new 32-floor glass tower (which is linked to the city's enclosed skyway system) is as modern and up-to-date as the many services it offers guests. It's particularly suited for those in town on business, since one whole floor is like a small convention center, with rooms appropriate for both small and large functions. The hotel also has 2 notable restaurants: *Gustino's* for Northern Italian cuisine and the *Fifth Season* for American dishes from all around the country. 30 S. 7th St., Mpls. (phone: 349-4000 or 800-228-9290). Expensive.

Sofitel – The first North American link in the French hotel chain offers a concierge, the latest issues of Parisian magazines, and authentic croissants for breakfast. Many of the 287 deluxe rooms have bidets. Continental elegance includes an indoor heated pool, sauna, babysitting service, bars, and piano bar. Children under 12 admitted free, but for the rest of us it's pricey. I-494 and Hwy. 100, Bloomington (phone: 835-1900). Expensive.

St. Paul – A beautifully restored Victorian hotel that's shining again after a $20 million face-lift. Crystal chandeliers sparkle in the lobby and elegant Biedermeier-style furniture decorates the guestrooms, some of which have lovely views over Rice Park. The hotel also has a notable and pricey restaurant, *L'Etoile*. The St. Paul is connected by a skyway to department stores, banks, boutiques, and travel agencies, and is across Rice Park from the *Ordway Theater*. 350 Market St., St. Paul (phone: 292-9292). Expensive.

Vista Marquette – Connected to the interior skyway in the IDS center and offering gracious, spacious accommodations in the middle of downtown. Presidents Ford and Carter have stayed here. Bar and restaurant, heated parking; 281 rooms. 710 Marquette Ave., Mpls. (phone: 332-2351; 800-328-4782). Expensive.

Radissons – The *Radisson South* is the tallest and largest hotel in Bloomington, with 578 rooms, an indoor heated pool, sauna, restaurants, bar, dancing, entertainment, shopping mall, and free parking. 7800 Normandale Blvd. (phone: 835-7800). *Radisson St. Paul* has 485 rooms (2 for the disabled), a revolving rooftop restaurant, a café, lobby bar/lounge, indoor heated pool and garden court, entertainment, dancing, barber and beauty shops, sundeck, in-room movies. 11 E. Kellogg Blvd. (phone: 292-1900). The *Radisson Plaza* has 357 rooms, including 18 for disabled guests, restaurants, a lounge, and access to Plaza VII exercise equipment, sauna, and whirlpool bath. 35 S. 7th St., Mpls. (phone: 339-4900). Two other Radisson properties are the *Radisson Minnetonka,* 12201 Ridgedale Dr., Minnetonka, with 222 rooms (phone: 593-0000), and *Radisson University,* 615 Washington Ave. SE, Mpls., with 308 rooms (phone: 379-8888). All are expensive to moderate.

Normandy Inn – In the heart of downtown Minneapolis, this cozy hostelry offers 228 cozy rooms. It occupies a full block and has a pool, conference and banquet rooms, whirlpool bath, sauna, and adequate parking. Two dining rooms; one serves full dinners, the other light lunches. 405 S. 8th St., Mpls. (phone: 370-1400). Inexpensive.

EATING OUT: Almost any kind of food can be found in the Twin Cities area, from high-priced, exquisitely prepared continental cuisine to Japanese food or kosher delicatessen. In fact, Minneapolis–St. Paul is considered a great eating-out town. Prices range from $50 or more for a dinner for two in the expensive range, $30 to $50 in the moderate, and $25 or less, inexpensive. Prices do not include drinks, wine, or tips. All telephone numbers are in the 612 area code unless otherwise indicated.

Blue Horse – Winner of innumerable awards over the years, this gracious, intimate restaurant is consistently cited as one of the Twin Cities' finest. The chef devotes full, loving attention to every dish. The pasta is specially prepared and comes highly recommended. The wine list is extensive. Closed Sundays. Reservations necessary. Major credit cards. 1355 University Ave., St. Paul (phone: 645-8101). Expensive.

510 – An evening couldn't be better spent partaking of the eight-course tasting menu at this elegant restaurant next door to the *Guthrie Theater.* The preparation is French, and the results are largely terrific, whether it's veal chops with wild mushrooms, pork tenderloin with fig coulis, smoked goose, or one of the praiseworthy dessert soufflés. Closed Sundays. Reservations a must. Major credit cards. 510 Groveland Ave., Mpls. (phone: 874-6440). Expensive.

Forepaughs – The charm and elegance of the Victorian age is preserved in this restaurant, where French cuisine is served in a gracious 19th-century former home. Free parking and shuttle service to the *Ordway Theater* provided. Open daily. Reservations advised. 276 Exchange St., St. Paul (phone: 224-5606). Expensive.

Lowell Inn – The closest thing to a New England inn that you'll find in the Midwest. The menu includes beef fondue, and gigantic drinks are another special feature. The emphasis here is on elegant surroundings and gracious service rather than great food. Open daily. Reservations necessary. Major credit cards. 102 N. 2nd St., Stillwater (a northeast suburb of St Paul; phone: 439-1100). Expensive.

Murray's – Well known for its hickory-smoked shrimp appetizers, award-winning silver butterknife steaks, and homemade rolls and dressing. The decor is in the 1940s tradition, and there is music later in the evening. Open from 4 PM on Sundays. Reservations advised. Major credit cards. 26 S. 6th St., Mpls. (phone: 339-0909). Expensive.

New French Café – A white brick storefront provides a simple setting for some fine French cooking. The menu changes seasonally (look for duck and pheasant in winter, wild mushrooms in spring) but always includes fresh fish, gorgeous desserts, and the café's own bread, for which it's justly famous. Open daily for breakfast, lunch, dinner, and late supper. Reservations advised. Major credit cards. 128 N. 4th St., Mpls. (phone: 338-3790). Expensive.

Orion Room – High atop the IDS Center, 50 stories up, the view from three seating levels is magnificent. Specialties, including rack of lamb, chateaubriand, wild rice soup, and Dover sole, and impressive tableside presentation enhance the spectacular setting. Open daily. Reservations advised. Major credit cards. IDS Center, 80 S. 8th St., Mpls. (phone: 349-6250). Expensive.

Black Forest Inn – Near the *Institute of Arts,* the inn serves bratwurst and sauerkraut dinners, Wiener schnitzel, and other honest, substantial German fare. The restaurant evolved from a tavern that used to serve only beer. It still offers German beers, and you can enjoy drinking in the outdoor beer garden. Open daily. Reservations advised. Major credit cards. 1 E. 26th St., Mpls. (phone: 872-0812). Moderate.

Figlio – The cooking is Italian via California — pizza and pasta topped with unusual combinations, as well as fresh fish and meats from the wood-fired oven and grill in the open kitchen. It's a high-energy restaurant and one of the hottest spots in the Twin Cities. Open daily. Reservations. Major credit cards. 3001 Hennepin Ave. S., Mpls. (phone: 822-1688). Moderate.

Fuji Ya – If you're in the mood to sample the gentle, tranquil mood and food of Japan, then this is the place. Reiko Weston, who came to the Twin Cities as a war bride, charmed discriminating diners first with conventional Japanese fare, then with showbizzy teppan yaki cuisine, and most recently with a sushi bar. The view of Lock #1 on the Mississippi complements the settling effects of the food and service. Closed Sundays. Reservations advised. Major credit cards. 420 1st St., Mpls. (phone: 339-2226). Moderate.

Lexington – This landmark restaurant has attracted politicians and business leaders for half a century. The decor leans toward formal, the cooking traditional, with short ribs of beef, lamb shanks, prime ribs, lobster newburg. Closed Sundays. Reservations advised. No credit cards. 1096 Grand Ave., St. Paul (phone: 222-5878). Moderate.

Pronto – In addition to Northern Italian cuisine of a very high standard, this smart-looking restaurant offers floor-to-ceiling views of the city greensward from both of its dining rooms. Go for the classics — *carpaccio, paglia e fieno, saltimbocca alla romana, zuppa inglese.* Sunday's brunch buffet is a hit, and deservedly so. Open daily. Reservations advised. Major credit cards. *Hyatt Regency,* 1300 Nicollet Mall, Mpls. (phone: 333-4414). Moderate.

Café Brenda – Some call this sunny downtown spot a health food restaurant, but the fare is so tasty and sophisticated you forget it's also good for you. Try the Wisconsin rainbow trout, warming winter casseroles, and meal-size salads. Closed Sundays. Reservations advised. Visa and MasterCard. 300 1st Ave. N., Mpls. (phone: 342-9230). Inexpensive.

Chi Chi's – No matter where one springs up, you're certain to find them lining up to partake of the Mexican cuisine done with American know-how. *Chi Chi's* popularity is due in no small part to the pleasant atmosphere (rotating fans, sprawling plants, and stucco walls), hefty margaritas and the chain's knack for using the freshest ingredients available. Specialties include chimichangas and Mexican fried ice cream. Expect a wait because the portions are large and reasonably priced. Open for lunch and dinner. Reservations advised. Major credit cards. Five locations: 7717 Nicollet Ave., Richfield (phone: 866-3433); 389 N. Hamline, St. Paul (phone: 644-1122); 40 S. 7th St. (phone: 339-0766); 15550 Wayzata Blvd., Minnetonka (phone: 473-0770); and 7355 Regent Ave. N., Mpls. (phone: 561-0550). Inexpensive.

Ciatti's – There's a good selection of Italian dishes, including a variety of pasta served with different sauces, and a menu listing over 30 entrées; some non-Italian dishes are also available. Desserts, like the amaretto torte, are delicious. Open daily. Reservations advised. Major credit cards. 1346 La Salle Ave. S., Mpls. (phone: 339-7747), and 850 Grand Ave., St. Paul (phone: 292-9942). Inexpensive.

Leeann Chin's – This cavernous space used to be the Union Depot. Now lofty columns, smoked mirrors, and a rosy beige decor provide a warm backdrop for stunning Oriental vases, jade, ivory carvings, and whimsical modern Chinese paintings. A buffet with everything from fun kin soup and cream cheese wontons to lemon chicken and almond cookie ice cream is served for both lunch and dinner. Open daily. Reservations advised. Major credit cards. Union Depot Pl. at 4th and Sibley, St. Paul (phone: 224-8814); 900 2nd Ave., Mpls. (closed Sundays; phone: 338-3488). Inexpensive.

St. Anthony Main – An entire development of eating establishments and specialty shops on rustic Main Street, on the Mississippi. *Anthony's Wharf:* East Coast cuisine comes to Minneapolis, offering fresh lobster, fresh scallops, rainbow trout, and swordfish. Reservations accepted. Major credit cards. 201 SE Main St., Mpls. (phone: 378-7058). Moderate. For dessert, stop by *Häagen-Dazs* for all-natural, out-of-this-world ice cream.

What's the best place for barbecue? That question has always been followed by lively debate in Minneapolis. Current favorites include *Market BBQ* (1414 Nicollet Ave. S., Mpls., phone: 872-1111) preferred by longtime residents for ribs cooked to dry, smoky perfection over a wood fire. And then there's *Rudolph's Bar-B-Que* (1933 Lyndale Ave. S., phone: 871-8969; 815 E. Hennepin Ave., phone: 623-3671; or 366 Jackson in St. Paul, phone: 222-2226), which took top honors in the National Rib Cook-Off in 1985 for its sloppy, piquant-sauced ribs served up with a great side of coleslaw.

NASHVILLE

Hundreds of thousands of hero-worshiping country music fans from around the country come to Nashville every year, by the busload, for the afternoon or the weekend, to take a tour of the homes of the stars and cruise past the houses where Minnie Pearl, Barbara Mandrell, and dozens of others live. Afterward, when the final "ooh" is "aahed," they take in a performance of the Opry.

The "Grand Ole Opry," a 2½-hour country music extravaganza that takes the title as the longest-running radio program in the US, is justifiably Nashville's biggest drawing card. Something that inspires so many people can't be all bad, and even if you hate country music, you can't fail to be amused by the spectacle. Onstage in the very fancy *Grand Ole Opry House* — which in 1974 replaced the original downtown auditorium (not air conditioned) where the show was recorded for more than 30 years — there are guitarists in glittery, rhinestoned polyester suits; busty female vocalists with curly manes and slinky dresses (or little-girl outfits that seem strangely incongruous with the bodies underneath), or cloggers who stomp up a storm in a blizzard of ruffly white petticoats. Every time a new performer comes onstage, the fans whistle, clap, jump up and down in their seats, then scramble up the aisles to be the first to get an autograph or snap a picture. Sometimes so many flashbulbs pop off at once that it seems as if a giant strobe is flickering over the audience. Onstage, friends and families of the performers look on from church pews moved from the old *Ryman Auditorium,* where the Opry spent the better part of 30 years, or mill around in the wings, never bothering to make themselves inconspicuous. It's hard to tell the hangers-on from the stars, who, meanwhile, are twanging away onstage or signing autographs backstage, in the manner of true professionals.

Which they all are. If you've seen Robert Altman's film *Nashville,* you've got a pretty fair idea that this city is far from being the simple hillbilly heaven portrayed in the songs that pour out of the one-square-mile area of South Nashville known as Music Row. The country music business, which is concentrated here, is a multimillion-dollar industry, getting bigger all the time. There are scores of large recording studios, a number of major music publishers, more than a hundred talent agencies, and countless record pressing plants, marketing firms, and production houses. The *Opry House* is the largest broadcast studio in the world. TV shows by the score are taped in Nashville. The odds are even that when you come for a visit you can sit in on a taping, and when you do, you'll find out why audiences you hear at the beginning of some live TV shows are clapping so madly: Studio people close to the stage urge them on like cheerleaders.

But for all that, Nashville is also a southern city, with all the traditions of gentility that characterize the breed, and you don't have to stay here for

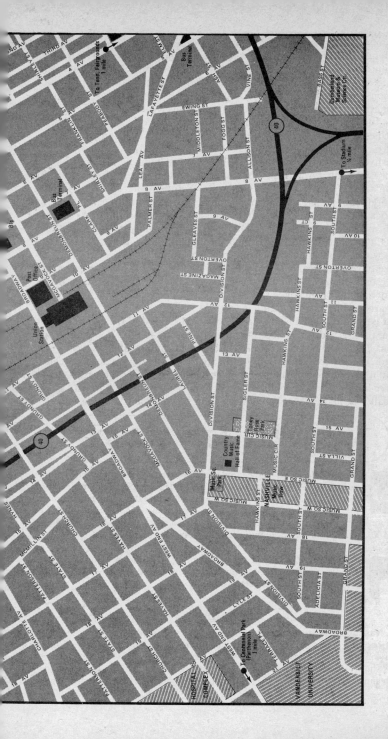

very long before you understand whence came the nickname "the Athens of the South." The town that annually goes berserk for the *Country Music Fan Fair* is also home to many colleges and universities, countless plantation mansions, and the world's only full-scale replica of the Greek Parthenon. There are symphony orchestra concerts and lovely old suburban neighborhoods that by no stretch of the imagination could you call nouveau riche. The Cheekwood Botanical Gardens boasts one of the finest growths of boxwood in the country.

Nashville is also the base of a number of other industries. There's Nissan Motor Company's American truck assembly plant, which produces all the Nissan trucks sold in the US; GM's new Saturn plant; and the Hospital Corporation of America, the world's largest for-profit health care company. American Airlines also has made Nashville a southeastern hub. As a result of this expanded commercial activity, the city has grown rapidly. That also means it's wise to avoid its freeways during rush hour; the traffic jams are made worse by seemingly unending roadwork.

Like other American cities of half a million, Nashville has its slums. And its eyesores: highways lined with what seems like an endless procession of fast-food joints, chain coffee shops with plastic signs, streams of neon lights, and garishly illuminated used car lots.

But beyond that, and beyond the occasional silliness of the country music mania, there is something about the place that can't fail to catch your imagination. There's unabashed, unpretentious good humor almost everywhere you go. There are dozens of nifty little Southern-cooking restaurants (called "meat 'n' threes" because their entrées generally consist of meat with a choice of three home-cooked vegetables) and hole-in-the-wall nightclubs with stages so small that fiddlers can barely keep from bowing the banjo players.

NASHVILLE AT-A-GLANCE

SEEING THE CITY: The *Polaris Room* atop the *Hyatt Regency* hotel downtown (7th and Union), makes a complete rotation each half hour, providing an excellent view of the city. The view is well worth the cost of lunch, dinner, or a drink. Visitors can also get a good lay of the land by picking up a free brochure at the Nashville Area Chamber of Commerce, 161 4th Ave. N. (phone: 259-3900), which outlines a walking tour of the downtown area.

SPECIAL PLACES: Most of the outstanding attractions are clustered within a couple of miles of the downtown area, and ranged along the southern and eastern outskirts of the metropolitan area.

DOWNTOWN

Ft. Nashborough – A partial reconstruction of the pioneer fort where Nashville began back in 1779, when a small band of settlers under the leadership of James Robertson arrived on the west bank of the Cumberland River. In five cabins, costumed guides show how the settlers chopped wood, tended gardens, carded and spun wool, made candles and lye soap, cooked meals (in pots hanging from iron hooks in immense stone fireplaces), and entertained themselves with singing. Closed Sundays and Mondays. Admission charge. 170 1st Ave. N (phone: 255-8192).

Ryman Auditorium – Home of the "Grand Ole Opry" between 1943 and 1974. Climb up onto its creaky wood stage and see mementos of the stars of days gone by. The *Ryman,* Mecca to country music lovers, was built in 1891 by a riverboat captain, Tom Ryman, who had found religion and wanted to help others do the same. Open daily. Admission charge. 116 Opry Pl. (phone: 254-1445).

Tennessee State Capitol – Designed by architect William Strickland, who was entombed in the building after he died, at his request. Completed in 1859. Guided tours available. Open daily. No admission charge. 505 Deaderick (phone: 741-3211).

MUSIC ROW

Country Music Hall of Fame and Museum – Memorabilia of country music stars — Elvis Presley's solid gold Cadillac, comedienne Minnie Pearl's straw hat complete with dangling price tag, Chet Atkins's first guitar, rare film footage of Patsy Cline and earlier country singers. A new exhibition celebrates 60 years of the "Grand Ole Opry." Open daily. Admission charge. Music Row at 4 Music Sq. E. (phone: 256-1639).

Studio B – Elvis Presley, Chet Atkins, Charley Pride, Eddy Arnold, and a score of other greats recorded for RCA at this famous studio in the 1950s and 1960s. Guides will tell you its history, talk about the Nashville recording industry, and let you act as a recording engineer at a "mix-down" session, in which the 16 tracks recorded by the artists are put onto 2 tracks before delivery to the record presser. Admission charge to Studio B is included in the *Hall of Fame* entry fee. Open daily. 17th Ave. at Roy Acuff St. (phone: 242-9414).

Riverfront Park – Recently renovated by the Metro Parks Department, this park on the Cumberland is a little heavy on the concrete, but Metro hires local bands to play on Saturday nights during the summer, and sheltered tables make for nice noon picnicking on cooler days (phone: 259-6399 for entertainment information).

EAST

Grand Ole Opry – This long country-music-star-studded spectacular is well worth the planning it takes to get tickets. More than a third of the 60-odd acts under contract to the Opry will perform on a given night, and you're bound to like some if not all of them. There are shows Fridays at 7:30 PM and Saturdays at 6:30 and 9:30 PM, matinees Tuesdays, Thursdays, Saturdays, and Sundays, and a second Friday show during the peak months, when Opryland USA is open. Reserved-seat tickets sell out months in advance for summer shows. General admission tickets go on sale Tuesdays at 9 AM the week of the show, at the Opryland box office only. The nearer to summer, the earlier you must arrive to get a ticket. Information Center, 2802 Opryland Dr. (phone: 889-3060).

Opryland USA – Music from Broadway and the hit parade and just about any other kind of melody that has ever been called music, including foot-tapping bluegrass, carry out the American-music-is-great motif at this new-style family theme park. In addition to the shows, Opryland features a number of adventure and amusement rides. The *General Jackson* — a re-creation of an old showboat — carries passengers from Opryland to downtown Nashville and back. Open daily in summer, and weekends in spring and fall. Admission charge. Information Center, 2802 Opryland Dr. (phone: 889-6611 or 889-6700).

Hermitage – Once the home of President Andrew Jackson, the old plantation home is now a museum devoted to the Jackson family. Tulip Grove, a Greek revival house completed in 1836, is also on the grounds. Open daily; last tour at 4:30 PM, without fail. Admission charge. About a 30-minute drive from downtown in Hermitage (phone: 889-2941).

SOUTH

Belle Meade Mansion – Inside the century-old rock walls that edge the 24-acre estate, Belle Meade is just a shadow of its former self, but even its shadow is impressive: immense pillars and ornate plaster cornices outside and, inside, Adamesque moldings and a splendid double parlor. Open daily. Admission charge. Harding Rd. at Leake Ave., US 70S (phone: 356-0501).

Parthenon – A full-scale replica of the ancient Greek building; the building material is not marble but a steel-reinforced conglomerate. Its four bronze doors are the largest in the world. Recently remodeled, the interior features an impressive replica of the statue of Athena that graced the original Parthenon. Displays include reproductions of the Elgin marbles, plus pre-Columbian art and various changing exhibitions. Closed Mondays. Admission charge. In Centennial Park at 25th Ave. N. and West End Ave. (phone: 259-6358).

Travellers' Rest – The remarkably finely detailed home of John Overton, one of Nashville's first settlers, restored, expanded, and filled with furniture, letters, and memorabilia that tell the story of Tennessee's settlement and civilization. Open daily. Admission charge. 636 Farrell Pkwy. 6 miles south of downtown via Franklin Rd., which is US 31 (phone: 832-2962).

Tennessee Botanical Gardens and Cheekwood Fine Arts Center – *Cheekwood,* a Georgian mansion built in the 1930s, is now a museum with art shows and traveling exhibitions. You may be more impressed, though, by the elegant Palladian window, or the chandelier (once the property of a countess), or the swooping spiral staircase (which used to be a fixture of Queen Charlotte's palace at Kew in England). Outdoors: formal gardens, a wisteria arbor, wildflower gardens, a Japanese sand garden, greenhouses, horticultural exhibits, and an outstanding boxwood garden. Closed Mondays except in December. Admission charge. Forrest Park Dr., 7 miles west of town via West End Ave., then Belle Meade Blvd. (phone: 352-5310).

■**EXTRA SPECIAL:** You'll see the announcements for tours of the homes of the stars on big billboards on the way into town, and even if you ordinarily hate group excursions, you may like these. While you're getting a glimpse into what makes Nashville tick, you can also enjoy some delightful southern-accented speech and the colorful language that seems to be the mark of Nashville citizenry. Each of the following offers several all-day, half-day, or evening tours: *Country Western/ Gray Line,* 501 Broadway and 2614 Music Valley Dr. (phone: 244-7330, 883-5555, or 800-251-1864); *Grand Ole Opry Tours,* 2808 Opryland Dr. (phone: 889-9490); *Nashville Tours,* 2626 Music Valley Dr. (phone: 889-4646); and *Stardust Tours,* 1504 Demonbreun St. (phone: 244-2335).

SOURCES AND RESOURCES

TOURIST INFORMATION: For brochures, maps, general tourist information, and all kinds of other help, your best bet is to write the Nashville Area Chamber of Commerce, 161 4th Ave. N., Nashville, TN 37219; to phone 259-3900; or to stop by the Tourist Information Center at exit 85 on I-65N, just east of downtown.

The *Nashville Visitor's Guide,* on sale at most newsstands, is as comprehensive a city guide as you'll see anywhere.

Television Stations – WSMV Channel 4–NBC; WTVF Channel 5–CBS; WKRN Channel 2–ABC; WDCN Channel 8–PBS.

Radio Stations – AM: WLAC 1510 (news/talk); WSIX 980 (country). FM: WWKX 104 (contemporary hits); WPLN 90 (classical/jazz).

Local Coverage – *The Tennessean,* morning daily; the *Nashville Banner,* afternoon daily. The former publishes a complete events listing on Fridays and Sundays; the latter on Thursdays. *Nashville* magazine publishes a monthly events calendar. All are available at newsstands.

Food – Check the *Nashville City Guide* or the *Nashville Visitor's Guide* for complete restaurant listings.

Area Code – The area code for Nashville is 615.

Sales Tax – The sales tax for most goods is 7¾%; the hotel tax is 11¾%.

 CLIMATE: Nashville's temperatures hover around the 80s and 90s in summer, dropping into the 40s and 30s (occasionally into the 20s or lower) between November and February. It gets humid in the summer, and you can expect thunderstorms from March through late summer. Expect rain in the spring and in October and November.

 GETTING AROUND: Airport – The Nashville Metropolitan Airport is a 15- to 20-minute drive from downtown (30 minutes or more during rush hours), and cab fare will run $10 to $15. Many hotels provide free transportation from the airport; check with your hotel when making reservations.

Bus – You need a car to manage conveniently. However, buses are available (route information, phone: 242-4433).

Taxi – Nashville's principal cab companies are *Yellow* (phone: 256-0101) and *Checker* (phone: 254-5031).

Car Rental – Major national car rental agencies can be found in Nashville. Four have rental offices at the Metro Airport; two more (*Thrifty* and *American International*) offer airport pickup.

 LOCAL SERVICES: Babysitters – If you think you might need one, ask your hotel or motel to make the arrangements when you book your room.

Business Services – *Executive Park Office Services* (typing services), 4741 Trousdale Dr. (phone: 331-2300); *Diamond Personnel,* 1 Maryland Farms (phone: 377-3344).

Mechanics – People come from all the way across town to have their domestic cars fixed at *Garrett Amoco Service,* 2600 Lebanon Rd., Donelson, near Opryland (phone: 883-1386); for foreign cars, try *Stubblefield Brothers,* 317 6th Ave. S. (phone: 255-5453). Also good are *Robinson's Chevron,* 2801 McGavock Pike, at exit 96 of I-65, about 5 miles north of downtown (phone: 883-2261), and *J&L Auto Service* (American cars only) at the Texaco at 2508 Nolensville Rd. (phone: 331-4249).

 MUSEUMS: In addition to those described above in *Special Places,* the following are worth investigating:

Cumberland Museum and Science Center – Closed Mondays. Admission charge except Tuesdays. 800 Ridley Ave. (phone: 259-6099).

Tennessee State Museum – In the *Tennessee Performing Arts Center* (phone: 741-2692), with a branch devoted to military history in the War Memorial Bldg. Frequent exhibitions of local arts and crafts. No admission charge. 7th and Union Sts. (phone: 360-0197).

Van Vechten Gallery – Houses the Stieglitz Collection, over 100 works of 20th-century art donated to Fisk University by artist Georgia O'Keeffe after the death of her husband, photographer Alfred Stieglitz. Closed Mondays. Admission charge. Fisk University campus, 17th Ave. N. (phone: 329-8543).

MAJOR COLLEGES AND UNIVERSITIES: Of the dozen-plus colleges and universities in Nashville, Vanderbilt, West End at 21st Ave. (phone: 322-7311), is perhaps the most famous, as its nickname, "the Harvard of the South," would suggest. The city is also the home of Fisk University, 17th Ave. N. (phone: 329-8500), one of the US's most noted predominantly black colleges.

SPECIAL EVENTS: The *Opryland Gospel Jubilee* brings gospel bands, choruses, and lots of extra music to the theme park every year over Memorial Day weekend (see *Special Places*). Also in May is the *Tennessee Crafts Fair,* one of the largest shows in the South. For information, write PO Box 150704, Nashville, TN 37215 (phone: 383-2502). The second Saturday of May is the *Iroquois Steeplechase,* the daylong series of eight races that's the oldest amateur steeplechase meet in the US; Old Hickory Blvd. in Percy Warner Park, 11 miles south of Nashville. For information: PO Box 22711, Nashville 37202 (or call 373-2130, beginning in February). The *International Country Music Fan Fair,* usually scheduled for the first week of June, brings thousands for 5 days of spectacular shows, autograph sessions, concerts and a Grand Masters Fiddling Contest. For more information, write to Fan Fair, 2804 Opryland Dr., Nashville 37214 (phone: 889-7503). In late September or October, there's the *National Quartet Convention,* 5 days of top-name gospel singing at the Nashville Municipal Auditorium. For information: National Quartet Convention, Dept. N, 54 Music Sq. W., Nashville 37203 (phone: 320-7000). In late summer or early fall, Charlie Daniels holds his annual *Volunteer Jam,* with surprise guest artists (past performers include Billy Joel, Willie Nelson, and Crystal Gayle) at *Starwood Amphitheater.* For tickets and schedule, call the amphitheater (phone: 793-5800).

SPORTS AND FITNESS: Baseball – The Nashville *Sounds,* a AAA farm team for the Cincinnati *Reds,* play in *Greer Stadium* on Chestnut, between 4th and 8th Aves. S. (phone: 242-4371).

Fishing and Boating – Two manmade lakes — Old Hickory (phone: 822-4846) and Percy Priest (phone: 889-1975) — are a 20-minute drive from downtown, and several others are within an hour or so. Black bass, rock bass, striped bass, walleye, sauger, northern pike, crappie, bluegill, and sunfish are the standard catch. Call the Resource Management office at each lake for boat and equipment rental details. The Tennessee Wildlife Resources Agency, PO Box 40747, Ellington Agricultural Center, Nashville 37204 (phone: 781-6500), can provide details about other lakes in the area.

Fitness Centers – For members (including those from other cities) and guests of local members, the *YMCA* offers an indoor and a roof track, racquetball, exercise equipment, and a sauna, 1000 Church (phone: 254-0631).

Golf – There are ten public courses in Nashville. Best 18- or 27-holers are at *Harpeth Hills,* Old Hickory Blvd., off Rte. 431 S. (phone: 373-8202); *McCabe Park,* 46th Ave. N. at Murphy Rd. (phone: 269-6951); *Nashville Golf and Athletic Club,* Moore's Lane in Franklin (phone: 794-6646); *Shelby Park Golf Course,* 20th Ave. and Fatherland St. (phone: 259-6455); and *Two Rivers Course,* Two Rivers Pkwy. near Opryland (phone: 889-9748).

Jogging – Follow Church Street (which turns into Elliston Place) to Centennial Park, about 1½ miles from downtown and near Vanderbilt University; or drive or take the West End Belle Meade bus (from 6th and Church, or Deaderick at 4th or 6th) to Percy Warner Park. Jogging in either area after dark is not recommended.

Stock Car Racing – Local racing on a ⅝-mile track at the *Tennessee State Fairgrounds* every Saturday night from April through mid-October, Wedgewood Ave. between 4th and 8th Aves. S. (phone: 726-1818).

Swimming – *Wave Country,* on Two Rivers Pkwy., near Opryland, is the Southeast's largest surf-producing swimming pool. Open May through September. Admission charge (phone: 885-1052).

Tennis – The major public facility is in *Centennial Park,* West End and 25th Aves. N., where 13 courts are open from March through October. Admission charge. For more information, call 259-6399. Indoor tennis at *Nashboro Village Racquet Club,* 2250 Murfreesboro Rd. (phone: 361-3242). It also has outdoor clay courts, open during the summer months.

THEATER: For touring Broadway shows and regional companies: the *Tennessee Performing Arts Center,* 505 Deaderick St. (phone: 741-2787). Lively children's theater and classics for adults: the *Nashville Academy Theatre* (the city's resident professional company), 724 2nd Ave. S. (phone: 254-9103). The *Tennessee Repertory Theatre* performs four plays yearly in the *Polk Theater* of the *Tennessee Performing Arts Center* (see above). Two small companies that perform recent works are *Actors Playhouse,* 2318 West End (phone: 327-0049), with performances from September through May; and *The Circle Players* (phone: 383-7469), who present several plays each year, either at the *Johnson Theatre* of the *Tennessee Performing Arts Center* or at the *Alternate Circle Theater,* 1703 Church St. For dinner theater, try *Chaffin's Barn Dinner Theater,* 8204 Hwy. 100 (phone: 646-9977).

MUSIC: The *Nashville Symphony Orchestra* holds concerts from September through May in the *Tennessee Performing Arts Center.* The symphony box office is at 208 23rd Ave. N. (phone: 329-3033). On Friday and Sunday nights during June, July, and August, there are musical programs at *Centennial Park.* For information, call the Parks and Recreation Dept.'s activities number (phone: 259-6399). Chamber music is offered at *Cheekwood* on weekends, at *Fisk,* and at *Blair School of Music* on the Vanderbilt campus. Often it's free.

TV SHOW TAPINGS: The Nashville Network (TNN), a cable TV network originating in Opryland, tapes a number of programs before live audiences. For information about how to attend a TNN taping, contact the Nashville Network, Information Services, 2806 Opryland Dr., Nashville, TN 37214 (phone: 883-7000). The nationally syndicated "Hee Haw" variety hour is also taped at TNN's studios during June and October. Inquire by calling Opryland Customer Service (phone: 889-6700).

NIGHTCLUBS AND NIGHTLIFE: For music, this is a hard town to beat. Even motels can sometimes turn up good entertainers. Check newspapers and the *Nashville Visitor's Guide* for a thorough rundown of places to hear country music.

For the best in a concentrated area, however, visit Printer's Alley downtown, where, along with some striptease joints and seedy-looking bars, there are standouts like the *Captain's Table,* a silver-and-white-linen-tablecloth sort of place (phone: 256-3353), and *Boots Randolph's,* which features Boots (when he's in town), comedy acts, and a house band (phone: 256-5500). For bluegrass, try the *Bluegrass Inn,* at the rear of 1914 Broadway at the edge of the Vanderbilt campus (phone: 329-1112), or the *Station Inn,* 402 12th Ave. S. (phone: 255-3307). Hear local talent play jazz, rock, country, and folk music at the *Bluebird Café,* 4104 Hillsboro Rd. (phone: 383-1461), which frequently hosts Writers Nights to give local songwriters a chance to try out their compositions; *Bogey's,* 5133 Harding Rd., in the Belle Meade Galleria (phone: 352-2447); the *Bullpen Lounge* at the *Stock Yard* restaurant, 901 2nd Ave. N. (phone: 255-6464); the *Cannery,* 811 Palmer Pl. (phone: 726-1374); and *Exit/In,* Elliston Pl. (phone: 321-4400). The city's most active singles bar is the *Heartthrob Café* at Fountain Square (phone:

259-3502), with good music and a big dance floor. Most major hotels have entertainment in their lounges; the *Opryland* hotel has three lounges that offer good live country music. The *General Jackson* showboat at Opryland offers dinner and an excellent musical show as well as entertainment in the lounge before dinner (phone: 889-6611 for reservations). *Zanies Comedy Showplace,* 2025 8th Ave. (phone: 269-0221), features stand-up comedians nightly.

BEST IN TOWN

CHECKING IN: There are dozens of new motels in Nashville — some parts of large chains, some parts of small chains, and a few independents. Prices generally range from $80 and up per night for a double room in an expensive hotel; $45 to $75 for accommodations in hostelries we've classified as moderate; and as low as $30 in an inexpensive place. All numbers are in the 615 area code unless otherwise indicated.

Hermitage – Built in 1910, this showpiece structure of Beaux Arts classic design is now a luxury hotel featuring 112 suites — with 3 phones and 2 color TV sets in each. It also has an oak-paneled bar and a fine dining room. 231 6th Ave. N., downtown (phone: 244-3121 or 800-342-1908). Expensive.

Hyatt Regency – Like so many members of this chain, this 476-room hotel has glass elevators to whisk guests up through a vast skylit lobby. Also notable here are *Speaker's,* for casual dining, and the *Polaris Room,* which rotates each half-hour, providing a stunning view of the city. 623 Union St., downtown (phone: 259-1234, 800-233-1234, or 800-228-9000). Expensive.

Opryland – Here are 1,891 rooms and 120 suites quite near the *Opry* and Opryland (but 20 minutes from downtown). Good entertainment at its *Stagedoor, Saloon, Cascade,* and *Staircase* lounges. The *Old Hickory Room* is one of the city's better (and more expensive) restaurants. The hotel also has a beautiful indoor park with suspended walkways. 2800 Opryland Dr. (phone: 889-1000). Expensive.

Stouffer's Nashville – A downtown high-rise with 673 rooms, next to the Convention Center. There is casual dining at the *Commerce Street Bar and Grill,* and the *Bridge Deli* features sandwiches. Also near mall shopping. 611 Commerce St. (phone: 255-8400 or 800-468-3571). Expensive.

Hermitage Landing Beach Cabins – On Percy Priest Lake, with lake activities — fishing, boating, swimming — at your doorstep. 20 units with kitchenettes (5 have fireplaces). Rte. 2 on Bell Rd. (phone: 889-7050). Moderate.

Holiday Inn Vanderbilt – A standard 300-room chain high-rise, close to Vanderbilt University and a horde of good restaurants, across the road from the Parthenon and Centennial Park and near some good nightspots. 2613 West End Ave. (phone: 327-4707). Moderate.

Knights Inn South – This no-frills motel has 115 rooms; some units have kitchenettes. I-24 at Harding Pl. (phone: 834-0570). Inexpensive.

EATING OUT: Nashville is, as they say, a good eating town, with lots of small, unpretentious restaurants where you'll find fried chicken and shrimp, steaks, home-style vegetables, and the like. An inexpensive meal for two will cost $20 or less, a moderate one about $20 to $30, and an expensive one anywhere from $30 up. Prices do not include drinks, wine, or tips. All numbers are in the 615 area code unless otherwise indicated.

Arthur's – Seven-course continental dining and plush decor characterize this chic eating place. The menu changes daily. Open daily. Reservations recommended.

Major credit cards. The Mall at Green Hills, off Abbott-Martin Rd. (phone: 383-8841). Expensive.

Julian's – Sophisticated French cuisine with seasonal specials along with the regular menu. The restaurant is in an old house, complete with white columns and plants. Dinner only. Diners can order à la carte or enjoy the prix fixe dinner. Closed Sundays. Reservations recommended. Major credit cards. 2412 West End Ave. (phone: 327-2412). Expensive.

Mario's – Owner Mario Ferrari serves Northern Italian specialties, pasta, seasonal specials, interesting appetizers, and a variety of Italian veal dishes. Dinner only. Closed Sundays. Reservations recommended. Major credit cards. 2005 Broadway (phone: 327-3232). Expensive.

Ciraco's – Pasta, pizza, and a variety of veal dishes are available in either the intimate back room, with formal, white-tablecloth decor (where dishes and prices tend to be fancier), or the front section, on plastic red-and-white-checked tablecloths. Reservations recommended for back room. Open daily. 212 21st Ave. S. (phone: 329-0036). Expensive to moderate.

Chinatown – An escape from the red plastic tablecloths found at almost every other Chinese restaurant in Nashville, it's a good spot for quiet conversation and tasty Hunan, Szechwan, and Mandarin food. Open daily. Major credit cards. 3813 Hillsboro Rd. (phone: 269-3275). Moderate.

Faison's – Daily specials include fresh fish, pasta dishes, and soups, as well as a selection of specialty sandwiches. Yuppies pack in to soak up the pleasant atmosphere and well-executed entrées. 2000 Belcourt Ave. (phone: 298-2112). Moderate.

Garcia's of Scottsdale – Good Mexican food and margaritas, in an accessible location at the Harding Road exit off I-65. Expect a wait on weekends unless you go early. 4285 Disco Dr. (phone: 331-9040). Moderate.

12th and Porter – Daily specials of fresh fish, either grilled or served in a sauce over fettuccine or rice. The eclectic menu also includes special pizza, calzone, plus beef and chicken dishes with interesting sauces. Casual, bohemian atmosphere. Closed Sundays. 114 12th Ave. N. (phone: 254-7236). Moderate.

Cakewalk – A small, pleasant café serving excellent lunches and dinners — fish and shrimp dishes, salads, quiche, good burgers, and an attractive weekend brunch menu. 3001 West End Ave. (phone: 320-7778). Moderate to inexpensive.

Miss Daisy's – For refined Southern entrées and desserts. Open daily for lunch; dinner Tuesdays through Saturdays. 4029 Hillsboro Rd. (phone: 269-5354). Moderate to inexpensive.

Cooker – This chain offers some of the best Southern cooking in town — nothing fancy, but plenty of big salads and stick-to-your-ribs main courses in a pleasant atmosphere. Open daily for lunch and dinner. Major credit cards. 2609 West End Ave. (phone: 327-2925); 4770 Lebanon Rd., Hermitage (phone: 883-9700); 1195 Murfreesboro Rd. (phone: 361-4747). Inexpensive.

Elliston Place Soda Shop – Good lunches and dinners served by waitresses who look as if they're about to tell you to eat all your vegetables. The tile and chrome decor is beautifully intact from the 1940s. Closed Sundays. Reservations not necessary. No credit cards. 211 Elliston Pl. (phone: 327-1090). Inexpensive.

Fuddrucker's – Good fast food in a busy setting that appeals to singles. Do-it-yourself burgers, hot dogs, wurst, and salads. 2020 West End Ave. (phone: 329-1331). Inexpensive.

Gaslight Beef Room – At Opryland USA, this steaks and baked potato place is convenient if you're going to the *Opry*. Best are the homemade rolls. Open any time Opryland is open (see *Special Places*). Reservations not necessary. Major credit cards. 2802 Opryland Dr. (phone: 889-6611). Inexpensive.

Loveless Motel – Fried chicken, homemade biscuits, and peach and blackberry preserves, plus country ham (salty, the way it's supposed to be) with gravy. Breakfast anytime; reservations recommended. Closed Mondays. No credit cards. Rte. 5, Hwy. 100 (phone: 646-9700). Inexpensive.

Swett's Dinette – Excellent Southern cooking, including home-cooked pork chops, barbecue, meatloaf, and vegetables, ranging from traditional Southern green beans to stewed apples. 28th and Clifton (phone: 320-9210). Inexpensive.

NEW HAVEN

To most visitors, New Haven is Yale, and Yale is New Haven. Certainly, the university dominates the city center, with 200 buildings spreading across much of New Haven's downtown section. And as the city's largest single employer, Yale could qualify as New Haven's major industry, if the production of literate graduates can be properly called an industry.

But there was a New Haven long before there was a Yale. The city was established in 1638; Yale moved to New Haven from Old Saybrook, Connecticut, in 1716 and wasn't even called Yale until 2 years later. And the city has always had the kind of diverse population that Yale discovered as a goal to work toward in the late 1960s.

An early trading center with a good harbor on Long Island Sound, New Haven established its true character in the 19th century, when the construction of the New Haven Railroad and the arrival of Irish, Italian, Polish, and Eastern European Jewish immigrants provided all the ingredients for heavy industry (the first repeating rifle was a New Haven product, which, like a number of young, ambitious Yale students, helped settle the frontier).

Today New Haven is a city of strong contrasts. There is the "Hill Section," a miserable slum of ugly old wooden buildings, once occupied by Irish railroad workers; but there is also Hillhouse Avenue, described by Dickens as the loveliest street in America. The avenue is flanked by beautiful Victorian mansions of red brick, set back from the street by spacious landscaped gardens. One of the homes, the Aaron Skinner house, is an outstanding example of Greek Revival architecture.

Many of New Haven's neighborhoods have retained their particular ethnic characteristics, although the city has undergone a population loss in recent decades, down about 25,000 from a high of 163,000 in the late 1930s. Neat wooden houses line the streets of Fair Haven, where many Irish live, and the Wooster Square area, with its large Italian population. Lace-curtain Irish and aristocratic Yankees live in the exclusive homes in Westville and on Wooster Square itself. The efforts of city officials were the principal factor in keeping these neighborhoods intact and desirable during the 1950s and 60s, when New Haven was confronted with deterioration and the threat of wholesale suburban exodus. New Haven was not allowed to degenerate into a massive slum surrounding an Ivy League enclave.

New and modern buildings standing side by side with the genteel 19th-century homes create a sharp contrast of architectural styles. But the presence of Yale creates an even more distinct mixture of cultures. The university and city have coexisted for two and a half centuries, sometimes on good terms, sometimes not. Town and gown relations are improving, mostly due to the efforts of A. Bartlett Giamatti, Yale's president from 1978 to 1986, who originally went to Yale on a scholarship.

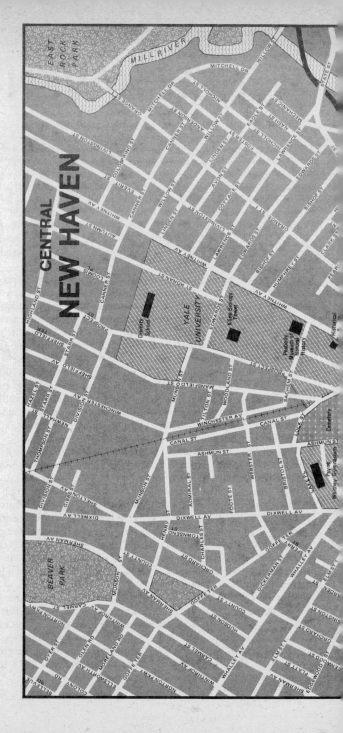

Yale gives the town a number of its valuable libraries and galleries — the *Peabody Museum of Natural History,* the *Yale Collection of Musical Instruments,* the *University Art Gallery,* and the *Center for British Art.* The town, in turn, supplies the university with workers and complements its collections with three beautiful churches on the Green, the New Haven Historical Society, and a score of good restaurants. Like an old married couple that has suffered bitter disappointments in the past and still harbors ancient grievances, the bond between town and university is hardly perfect; but if this particular marriage wasn't made in heaven, it was most certainly contracted on the New Haven Green, around which town and gown are intertwined, presumably forever. Despite what others may think, both "Yalies" and "townies" know that New Haven wouldn't be New Haven without Yale and Yale really wouldn't be Yale outside New Haven.

NEW HAVEN AT-A-GLANCE

SEEING THE CITY: Once used by the Quinnipiac Indians for smoke signals, the 359-foot summit of New Haven's eastern cliff in East Rock Park still commands a panoramic view of the area — the city centered around the Green, the Yale campus, the harbor, and, on a clear day, 18 miles down Long Island Sound to Bridgeport.

SPECIAL PLACES: New Haven, the first architecturally planned city in the US, was designed for walking. Laid out in nine squares, New Haven is centered around The Green, still its main square. Almost everything of interest is nearby, in a 30-block area whose cultural and historic scope transcends its geographic limits.

The Green – The 16-acre square of grass, trees, and shrubbery in the city center remains today the focal point of New Haven activity as it was for early-17th-century settlers. Originally all public buildings were on the Green, as well as cows and pigs to keep the grass down. All the animals are now gone. The only buildings left are three churches, two of Georgian and Federal style and one Episcopal church of Gothic Revival, all built between 1812 and 1815.

New Haven Colony Historical Society and Museum – A large model offers a look at New Haven of 1640, and other collections span the city's historical development over the past three centuries. Closed Mondays. No admission charge. 114 Whitney Ave. (phone: 562-4183).

Yale Campus and Facilities – Named for East India trader and donor Elihu Yale, the university, founded in 1701, is one of the most distinguished educational institutions in the world. The campus is lovely with its ivy-covered Gothic buildings, charming green courtyards, and examples of contemporary architecture. The best way to see the campus is to take a free university tour led by student guides well versed in college lore and anecdotes. The tour begins at the Old Campus with its Gothic and Romanesque structures, including the oldest of the ivy-covered buildings, Connecticut Hall, and proceeds to Memorial Quadrangle, Harkness Tower, Mory's, and the newer Yale structures such as the Ezra Stiles and Morse colleges and the Beinecke Rare Book Library. Tours are given at 10:30 AM and 2 PM weekdays and at 1:30 PM on weekends throughout the year, starting at the University Information Office, Phelps Archway, 344 College St. (phone: 432-2300).

Peabody Museum of Natural History – Exhibits on evolutionary history: a huge skeleton of a brontosaurus, the Pulitzer Prize–winning *Age of Reptiles* mural by Rudolph Zallinger, the Hall of Mammals. Open daily. Admission charge; no charge on Tuesdays. 170 Whitney Ave. (phone: 432-5050).

University Art Gallery – This fine collection includes John Trumbull's original paintings of the American Revolution and samples of ancient Greek and Roman art and architecture. Closed Mondays. No admission charge. 1111 Chapel St. (phone: 432-0600).

Yale Center for British Art and British Studies – Designed by Louis I. Kahn, it features works of Hogarth, Constable, Turner, Stubbs, and Blake. The paintings are hung in bright, open galleries that create the atmosphere of an English country house and provide optimal viewing. There are more British works here than anywhere outside Great Britain. Closed Mondays. No admission charge. 1080 Chapel St. (phone: 432-2800).

Shubert Performing Arts Center – This historic theater, once the preeminent staging ground for Broadway plays and musicals, has been restored to its original 1914 elegance, thus spurring a performing arts and retail renaissance in the College and Chapel streets area. Productions include both national touring groups and local performers. 247 College St. (phone: 624-1825).

Palace Performing Arts Center – Directly across College St. from the *Shubert Center,* this concert hall complements New Haven's performing arts scene with an impressive musical performance schedule including everything from rock 'n' roll to classical. Children's shows are also regularly scheduled. 246 College St. (box office phone: 624-8497).

■**EXTRA SPECIAL:** Some 60 miles east of New Haven on I-95 is the town of Mystic, where the fastest clipper ships and the first ironclad vessels were built in the 19th century. The town has been restored as a 19th-century seaport. You can stroll along the waterfront of the Mystic River or down the cobblestone streets lined with reproductions of quaint seaport homes. The *Mystic Seaport Museum* has an outstanding collection featuring the *Charles W. Morgan,* a large wooden whaling ship in service for more than 80 years, and the *Joseph Conrad,* one of the last square-riggers ever built. For more information, see DIRECTIONS.

SOURCES AND RESOURCES

TOURIST INFORMATION: The New Haven Convention and Visitors Bureau is best for maps, brochures, and general information; downtown at 900 Chapel St., New Haven, CT 06510 (phone: 787-8367). You can also visit the Long Wharf Information Office at Exit 47 of I-95 (phone: 787-8318) from mid-April through mid-October. Yale has its own information center at Phelps Archway, 344 College St. (phone: 432-2300), which offers hour-long architectural and historical walking tours of the campus weekdays at 10:30 AM and 2 PM, weekends at 1:30AM (free).

Enjoying New Haven, A Guide to the Area by Jane Byers and Ruth McClure ('Round-the-Town Publications; $4.95) is a good guide to the city.

Television Stations – WVIT Channel 30–NBC; WFSB Channel 3–CBS; WTNH Channel 8–ABC; WEDH Channel 65–PBS.

Radio Stations – AM: WAVZ 1300 (oldies); WNHC 1340 (urban contemporary). FM: WKCI 101 (rock).

Local Coverage – The *New Haven Register,* mornings and Sundays; the Friday *Register* lists the coming week's attractions. Available at newsstands.

Food – *Best Restaurants in Southern New England* by Patricia Brooks (101 Productions; $4.95) has many New Haven listings.

Telephone – The area code for New Haven is 203.

Sales Tax – Connecticut has a 7.5% sales tax on most consumer goods and a meals tax of 10%.

CLIMATE: Umbrellas are an important item in New Haven. On Long Island Sound, the city gets a lot of rain. The sea breeze, which gives some pleasant relief during the humid summers, the spring, and the fall, becomes raw during the cold and snowy winters.

GETTING AROUND: Airport – Tweed–New Haven Airport is a 15-minute drive from downtown, and taxi fare will run about $12. The Connecticut Transit bus that heads this way is not recommended for those with luggage, since it stops 2 blocks away. Tweed–New Haven handles only domestic flights. Those with international connections can get to JFK and La Guardia in New York City and Newark International in northern New Jersey by contacting *Connecticut Limousine* (phone: 878-2222); the ride to any of the three from its terminal on Brewery St. at Long Wharf (behind the New Haven post office) will take approximately 2 hours and cost from $24 to $27.

Bus – Connecticut Transit serves the downtown area and the suburbs. Route information and guides are available at 470 James St. (phone: 624-0151).

Taxi – Cabs can be ordered on the phone. The largest company is *Metro Cab* (phone: 777-7777).

Car Rental – New Haven has offices of all the national firms.

LOCAL SERVICES: Business Services – *Audubon Copy Shoppe,* 48 Whitney Ave. (phone: 865-3115).

Mechanic – *Libby's Sales and Service,* 60 Printer's La. (phone: 772-1112).

SPECIAL EVENTS: The *New Haven Jazz Festival,* a series of concerts featuring well-known artists, runs from early July through mid-August. The *20-kilometer Road Race* takes place annually on Labor Day, and the *New Haven Bed Race* is held in early September. The weekend before Thanksgiving of odd-numbered years, the *Yale-Harvard football game* takes place, with all the fanfare of a traditional rivalry, at the *Yale Bowl.*

MUSEUMS: With Yale's fine collections and New Haven's *Historical Society,* the city touches all cultural bases. Two special collections reach interests further afield:

Beinecke Rare Book and Manuscript Library – 121 Wall St. Closed Sundays (phone: 432-2977).

Yale Collection of Musical Instruments – Open Tuesdays through Thursdays, 1 to 4 PM, and Sundays, 2 to 4 PM.; closed in August. 15 Hillhouse Ave. (phone: 432-0822).

MAJOR COLLEGES AND UNIVERSITIES: Yale University (see *Special Places*). Other educational institutions in the area are the University of New Haven, 300 Orange Ave. in West Haven (phone: 932-7000), and Southern Connecticut State College, 501 Crescent St. (phone: 397-4000).

SPORTS AND FITNESS: Fitness Center – The *Downtown Racquet Club* has racquetball, squash, and basketball courts, sauna, and Nautilus equipment, 230 George St. (phone: 787-6501).

Football – Yale has teams in all major sports, but the most followed are the *Bulldogs,* who play football at the *Yale Bowl.* Rte. 34, between Derby Ave. and Chapel St. Call the Athletic Association for tickets (phone: 432-1400).

Hockey – The New Haven *Nighthawks* of the American Hockey League play from October to April at the *New Haven Coliseum,* 275 S. Orange St. (phone: 787-0101).

Horse Racing – Although there is no racetrack nearby, OTB has taken on a new meaning here with an $8 million racing theater, complete with a 24-by-32-foot screen and 40 betting windows. The "grandstand" seats 1,800. Open six afternoons (not Tuesdays) and six evenings (not Sundays) a week, it's called *Teletrack* (phone: 789-1943) in the Long Wharf area.

Jogging – Run along Whalley Avenue, which is hilly, to Edgewood Park, about 2 miles north; Amity Road provides a more rural setting; Fountain Street and Litchfield Road are other options. Every Monday at 6:15 PM a Fun Run leaves from Running Start, 93 Whitney Ave. and Trumbull St. (phone: 865-6244).

Skiing – Best facilities nearby are at *Powder Ridge* in Middlefield, 21 miles on I-91 (exit 16) to E. Main St. in Meriden; from there follow the signs to Powder Ridge.

Tennis – There are many good outdoor courts for the public in the city. Municipal courts at Bowen Field (Munson St. between Crescent St. and Sherman Ave.) and at Wilbur Cross High School (Orange St. and Mitchell Dr.) are free, while the *College Wood Courts* (Orange and Cold Spring Sts.) charge a small fee. Yalies get preference at university courts, but the public is welcome. Derby and Central Aves.

THEATER: For up-to-date offerings and performance times, check the publications listed above. New Haven is the home of a well-known professional repertory company, the *Long Wharf Theatre Company,* with productions of classics, musicals, contemporary works, and experimental theater, in a former warehouse in the meat and produce terminal. Closed in the summer. 222 Sargent Dr. (phone: 787-4282; see *Regional American Theater,* DIVERSIONS). *Yale Repertory Theatre,* 1120 Chapel St. (phone: 432-1234), also has experimental theater and classic plays. Under the direction of Lloyd Richards, its productions have received great acclaim in recent years, and many have moved to Broadway. The *Shubert Theater,* 247 College St. (phone: 562-5666), serves Broadway touring companies, and the *Palace Theater,* 264 College St. (phone: 624-8497), features everything from jazz shows to wrestling.

MUSIC: The *New Haven Symphony Orchestra* gives concerts from October through April at *Woolsey Hall* on the Yale campus (For ticket information call 776-1444). For information about the *Yale Chorus,* student groups, and visiting artists, call university information at 432-2300. Opera buffs should check out the *Shubert,* 247 College St. (phone: 562-5666), which features opera when a Broadway touring company is not in residence.

NIGHTCLUBS AND NIGHTLIFE: Nightspots come and go in New Haven. For the yuppie crowd, *Bopper's of New Haven,* at 239 Crown St. (phone: 562-1957), offers a lively disc jockey, oldies from the 1950s and '60s, and good dance music. Adding a touch of class to New Haven's nightlife is the *Palms,* the renovated ballroom of the old *Taft* hotel, at 265 College St. (phone: 776-3316). *Toad's Place,* 300 York St. (phone: 777-7431), features national and local rock acts; disco dancing Wednesdays, Fridays, and Saturdays. *Partners,* mostly for gays, is at 365 Crown St. (phone: 624-5510), and *The Pub,* also gay, is at 168 York St. (789-8612).

BEST IN TOWN

CHECKING IN: Everything is easy to find in New Haven, but visitors will certainly be frustrated in their search for a grand old traditional hotel — it's simply not there. What does exist is as easy to find in New Haven as anywhere else — branches of the familiar chains, which offer moderately priced accommodations ($80 to $90 per night for a double room). There are also expensive and inexpensive rooms downtown (ranging from a high of $150 a night to a low of $40 to $50 per night). For bed-and-breakfast accommodations, contact *Bed & Breakfast Ltd.*, PO Box 216, New Haven, CT 06513 (phone: 469-3260). All telephone numbers are in the 203 area code unless otherwise indicated.

Inn at Chapel West – A welcome relief to travelers tired of the same old hotel chains. It offers 10 tastefully decorated rooms in a newly refurbished house in the heart of the downtown renovation. Rates include continental breakfast. 1201 Chapel St. (phone: 777-1201). Expensive.

Colony Inn – The old *Midtown Motor Lodge,* completely refurbished and as close to Yale as you can get without being enrolled. 1157 Chapel St. (phone: 776-1234). Moderate.

Holiday Inn – Also downtown, with a pool and a restaurant. 30 Whalley Ave. (phone: 777-6221). Moderate.

Park Plaza – Downtown, with a rooftop restaurant that features a view of New Haven at night, plus music and dancing. 155 Temple St. (phone: 772-1700). Moderate.

Duncan – A small, old hotel near Yale (so near, in fact, that students sometimes live here). But there are rooms available for visitors, travelers, and the student-at-heart. 1151 Chapel St. (phone: 787-1273). Inexpensive.

EATING OUT: For folks who consider eating far more important than sleeping, New Haven is the place for you. What the city lacks in fancy overnight accommodations, it makes up for in an abundance and variety of restaurants. A 2-minute walk through the center of town will turn up several worthwhile eateries tucked away in basements and other unlikely corners. Because there are many potential diners in the city, restaurants are highly competitive, and prices are generally reasonable. Most of the restaurants are in the moderate ($20 to $30 for a dinner for two) to inexpensive range ($15 and under) though there are a few that are more expensive ($40 and up). Prices do not include tax, drinks, or tip. All telephone numbers are in the 203 area code unless otherwise indicated.

Delmonaco's – The decor is strictly Valentino — Valentino posters on the wall and sometimes an old Valentino silent film to dine by. And the food is southern Italian. Inspired by the atmosphere, the chef has created two dishes designed to raise passions in the blood: fresh fish on linguine topped with a whole lobster, and a variety of meats mixed with peppers and onions, cooked in a secret sauce. Both terrific, both called the Chef's Specials. Closed Tuesdays. Reservations advised. Major credit cards. 232 Wooster St. (phone: 865-1109). Expensive.

Leon's – This family-run restaurant is rich in Italian food. The specialty is chicken Eduardo, prepared in a light butter and garlic sauce, but mussel and clam dishes are also good. Closed Mondays. Reservations for large parties in private rooms only. Major credit cards. 321 Washington Ave. (phone: 777-LEON). Expensive.

Robert Henry's – Centrally located near Yale University in the beautifully restored Sherman Building, *Robert Henry's* brings more than a simple touch of class to downtown New Haven dining. Award-winning French chefs prepare a sophisticated menu combining the finest French culinary technique with only the freshest native ingredients. The menu changes frequently to keep pace with the chefs' creativity and the seasonal availability of fish, game, native vegetables, and herbs. All desserts are homemade, including the sorbets, ice creams, and chocolates. Elegant decor features original turn-of-the-century woodwork, marble, and hand-painted windows. No lunch on weekends. Reservations advised. Major credit cards. 1032 Chapel St. (phone: 789-1010). Expensive.

Azteca's – A welcome addition to yet another reawakening New Haven neighborhood (the Upper State Street District), *Azteca's* offers the finest Mexican cuisine in the area: tacos, enchiladas, chimichangas, and salads served in a cheerful, southwestern ambience. Closed Sundays. Reservations advised. MasterCard and Visa. 14 Mechanic St. (phone: 624-2454). Moderate.

Bruxelles – Next door to the *Shubert* and *Palace* theaters, this lively bar and brasserie matches the upbeat mood of this rejuvenated New Haven quarter. Contemporary cuisine from roast duck to fancy pizza. Open daily. Reservations for 8 or more. Major credit cards. 220 College St. (phone: 777-7752). Moderate.

Elm City Diner – An atypical Art Deco diner, favored by theatergoers for its late night menu. Nouvelle cuisine. Piano bar Friday and Saturday nights. Open daily. No reservations. Major credit cards. 1226 Chapel St. (phone: 776-5050). Moderate.

Hatsune – This Japanese restaurant, recently moved to much larger quarters, offers a wide variety of Japanese dishes, including sushi and sashimi. Closed Mondays. Major credit cards. 993 State St. (phone: 776-3216). Moderate.

Hunan Wok – New Haven's best Chinese restaurant, serving Hunan, Szechwan, and Mandarin cuisine in a warm and friendly atmosphere. Open daily. Take-out service. Major credit cards. 142 York St. (phone: 776-9475). Moderate.

Miya – A fine Japanese restaurant with the best sushi in town, as well as fresh fish specials, tempura, and teriyaki. Two tatami rooms are available for 6 or more by reservation. Open daily except Mondays; lunch Wednesdays through Fridays. Major credit cards. 1217 Chapel St. (phone: 777-9760). Moderate.

Old Heidelberg – One of the city's basement restaurants, this one has a real Yale flavor, complete with students, beers, steaks, and pictures of generations of varsity heroes lining the walls. Open daily. Reservations advised. Major credit cards. 1151 Chapel St. (phone: 777-3639). Moderate.

Scoozi – New Haven's hottest new Italian restaurant, offering generous portions of pasta and a fine wine selection in a bright, contemporary atmosphere. Two flights below street level, next door to the *Yale Repertory Theatre*. Open daily. No reservations. Major credit cards. 1104 Chapel St. (phone: 776-8268). Moderate.

Claire's Corner Copia – Even after expanding and redecorating, *Claire's* is still packed at mealtimes, with good reason. Here you'll find the best homemade food away from home. Soups are nothing short of wonderful, as are the breads and cakes (the carrot cake is widely acknowledged to be the finest in the city). Open daily. No reservations or credit cards. 1000 Chapel St. (phone: 562-3888). Inexpensive.

Gentree's – A favorite with both students and townies, it offers a sumptuous California salad bar at lunchtime, all-you-can-eat barbecued ribs and chicken Monday nights, and great potato curls anytime. Open daily. Reservations unnecessary. Major credit cards. 194 York St. (phone: 562-3800). Inexpensive.

Louis' Lunch – This tiny place, which looks like an English pub, claims to be the birthplace of the hamburger. Whether this is true or not, the burgers are great

— big, juicy, and charcoal grilled. And don't ask for ketchup — they don't have it and to ask is considered an affront to the quality of the product. Open weekdays till 4:30 PM. No reservations. No credit cards. 263 Crown St. (phone: 562-5507). Inexpensive.

Pepe's – Pepe claims to have invented the pizza. You might not believe him, but you'll have to agree that in an area where pizza making is fine art, *Pepe's* takes the pie. Closed Tuesdays. No reservations. No credit cards. 157 Wooster St. (phone: 865-5762). Inexpensive.

Picnic on the Green – Part of the redesigned Chapel Square Mall with over a dozen eateries. Seating is along a window wall overlooking the New Haven Green. Open daily. Chapel Square Mall mezzanine. 900 Chapel St. Inexpensive.

NEW ORLEANS

Jazz musicians call it the Big Easy, and if anyone can transmit a feeling for New Orleans, they can. Some can't even read music — but they can improvise; and in New Orleans, that's what it's all about.

The past has been a double-edged sword for New Orleans. Not even its port on the Mississippi — second in trade only to New York City harbor — has shaken it out of a certain Old South torpor. The city (with a metropolitan population of about 1,190,000) lacks manufacturing and heavy industry, and throughout its long history as a center of trade and source of great wealth for some, it has maintained a European, 18th-century air. For the rich, it has ever been a sophisticated, cultured haven; for the poor — many of whom are black — it has offered little hope of betterment over the years. The poverty just seems to roll along like the river; and little has appeared to change it. But at the same time, this torpor has managed to protect the city's charms, where in a different place they might have fallen long ago before the trumpet of civic progress.

Initially, New Orleans was something of a hot property, traded back and forth between governments. The French were first attracted in the early 1700s by the area's deep, swift harbor; named for the regent of France, Philippe, Duc d'Orléans, it served as the capital of the French territories in America from 1723 to 1763, when a Bourbon family pact transferred it to Spanish rule, until it was ceded back to France in 1800. Two important things developed from all this swapping and ceding: the Créole culture, unique to the New World and descended from French and Spanish parents; and one of the greatest bargains of the century. Napoleon sold New Orleans and the entire Louisiana Purchase to the United States for $15 million in 1803, doubling the size of the country's territory. In 1815, to protect this wily investment, General Andrew Jackson and his Kentucky militiamen teamed with anyone and everyone — including the pirate Jean Lafitte, the Choctaw Indians, numerous Créoles, and some black slaves — to defeat the British in the Battle of New Orleans. The War of 1812, unfortunately, had ended, some time earlier, somewhat dampening the victors' spirits. (News of the peace had not yet reached the combatants.) Jackson secured the Mississippi River for America, and New Orleans began to grow as a major port for the cotton, sugarcane, and indigo crops grown on surrounding plantations and as a kind of Old World cosmopolitan center in the midst of the deep South. The terrain is basically flat plains of the river delta — the Mississippi flows to the south, and the sea-sized Lake Pontchartrain borders the city on the north.

Today, the Vieux Carré, or French Quarter, the main area of interest in New Orleans, reflects and preserves the New Orleans style. Protected by a powerful Vieux Carré Commission, which regulates construction and modification of the area, the architecture is a blend of French and Spanish

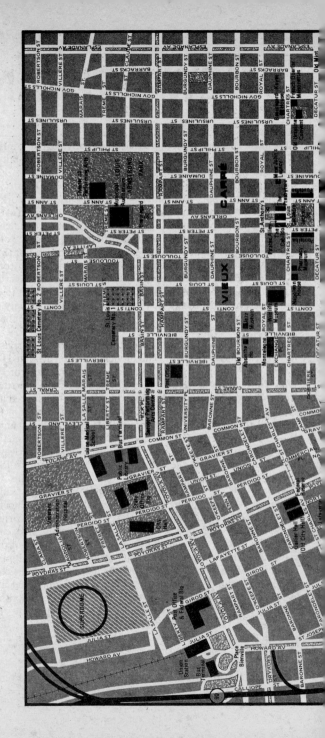

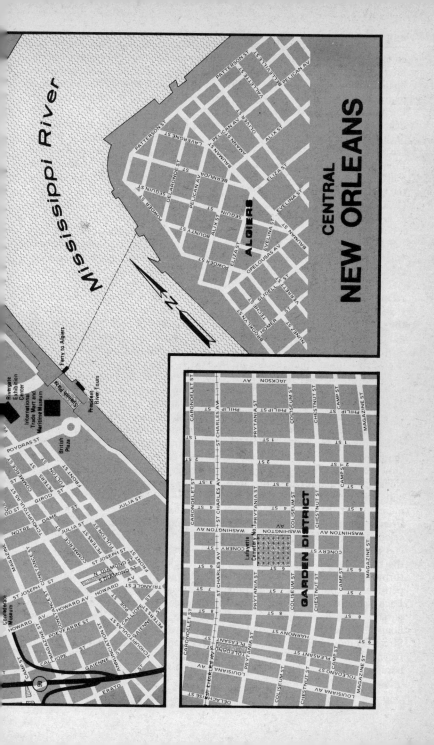

CENTRAL
NEW ORLEANS

Mississippi River

ALGIERS

PATTERSON ST
VALLETTE ST
BELLEVILLE ST
PELICAN AV
PATTERSON ST
LAVERGNE ST
OLIVIER ST
ALIX ST
PELICAN AV
BAUMAN ST
MANN ST
DELARONDE ST
BERMUDA ST
PELICAN ST
SEGUIN ST
SEGUIN ST
BOUNTY ST
ALIX ST
POWDER ST
ELIZA ST
EVELINA ST
BAUMAN ST
OPELOUSAS AV
EVELINA ST
ELIZA ST
EVELINA ST
VERRET ST
HOMER ST
SLIDELL ST
TEICHE ST
NUNEZ ST
BROOKLYN AV

Ferry to Algiers.

Spanish Plaza

President River Tours

British Plaza

Rivergate Exhibition Center
International Trade Mart and Maritime Museum

Confederate Museum

POYDRAS ST
NOTRE DAME
MAGAZINE ST
CONSTANCE ST
TCHOUPITOULAS ST
CONSTANCE ST
COMMERCE ST
FULTON ST
FRONT ST
PETERS ST
GIROD ST
JULIA ST
JULIA ST
ST JOSEPH ST
ST JOSEPH ST
DIAMOND ST
DIAMOND ST
TRIANGLE N
JULIA ST
HOWARD
HOWARD AV
HOWARD AV
POEYFARRE ST
CALLIOPE ST
CALLIOPE ST
MAGAZINE ST
CONSTANCE ST
TCHOUPITOULAS ST
ANNUNCIATION ST
PETERS ST
GAIENNE ST
GAIENNE ST
CALLIOPE
ERATO
CAMP ST
9B

GARDEN DISTRICT

Lafayette Cemetery No. 1

CARONDELET ST
ST CHARLES AV
PHILIP ST
PRYTANIA ST
COLISEUM ST
CHESTNUT ST
PHILIP ST
CAMP ST
MAGAZINE ST
JACKSON AV
1 ST
2 ST
3 ST
4 ST
WASHINGTON AV
CONERY ST
6 ST
7 ST
8 ST
HARMONY ST
TOLEDANO ST
PLEASANT ST
LOUISIANA AV
DELACHAISE ST
LOUISIANA AV
CHESTNUT ST
COLISEUM ST
PRYTANIA ST
CONERY ST
WASHINGTON AV
CARONDELET ST
ST CHARLES AV
CORONDELET ST
MAGAZINE ST
CAMP ST
CHESTNUT ST
COLISEUM ST
PRYTANIA ST

colonial (and their hybrid, Créole) standing side by side. Fine examples of the mixture of cultures and styles are the Cabildo, once the headquarters of Spanish colonial rule, and the Presbytère. (The Cabildo's top floor was gutted by fire in 1988 and, as we went to press, was still closed for reconstruction). Each of the impressive structures features wide Spanish arches and a French mansard roof. Flanking the European-style Jackson Square are the imposing St. Louis Cathedral and the Pontalba apartments, which have a French arcade and beautiful cast ironwork on the balconies, seen throughout the French Quarter. And there is a lot more; the renovated French Market, with a history dating back 200 years, still has a colorful atmosphere and some of the best café au lait on either side of the Atlantic. The way to see the French Quarter is also old-fashioned — riding in a mule-drawn carriage, a streetcar, or just strolling down the cobblestone streets. It's the kind of place where you relax and take it easy — the charms surround you.

In New Orleans, though, you don't just see and feel the city, you must taste what it has to offer — Créole food, a highly developed regional style blending classical French cuisine with Spanish and American Southern, enhanced by spices and seasonings from American Indian, African, and West Indian recipes. The results are so good that they say down in New Orleans when a Créole goes to heaven, the first thing he asks Saint Peter is where he can find the jambalaya (a fragrant stew of shrimp, oysters, tomatoes, and rice) or filé gumbo (a spicy soup of shrimp, crabmeat, okra, oyster, herbs, and rice). Seafood is a Créole staple, as are fresh vegetables and veal, and the city is rich in fine restaurants that serve it up in style.

And then there is the *Carnival Season* — an extravagant blowout that begins shortly after Christmas and builds up steam till *Mardi Gras* (Fat Tuesday), preceding Ash Wednesday. The tradition of *Mardi Gras* in New Orleans was begun over 100 years ago by a social club, the Mystick Krewe of Comus. Other private clubs picked up the idea, and thus began a series of elaborate balls and parades whose tradition continues today. The balls are still the principal event of New Orleans society. A well-known businessman is crowned King; the Queen is a debutante from a prominent family. But all the world loves a parade, and the *Mardi Gras* has gone public (though private balls still are held). In addition to the traditional parades with elaborate floats, marching jazz bands, doubloons and trinkets tossed to the crowds, the entire French Quarter, St. Charles Avenue, and Canal Street are jammed. And celebrate they do in all manner of the word. Also parading on *Mardi Gras* is a black krewe, led by King Zulu, who shares some of the spotlight with the Big Shot of Africa. Zulu meanders throughout downtown New Orleans throwing painted coconuts, doubloons, and beads. The annual costume competition for transvestites colorfully jams already jammed Bourbon Street. Each year, two parades of magnificently decorated trucks follow the Rex parade, with the occupants throwing trinkets just like the maskers on the floats. Costumed marching clubs dance and weave their way toward Canal Street behind small Dixieland jazz bands before Rex takes to the streets. In recent years, new krewes parade in the suburbs on *Mardi Gras* after the Rex parade.

Mardi Gras is both the best and the worst of times to visit New Orleans. The revelry and spectacle reach great heights, but so, too, do the hotel prices and the frenetic pace. There are other festivals which offer New Orleans in a different mood, without the crowds of *Mardi Gras* (see *Special Events*). Don't expect to witness a substantially different mood if you visit in January 1990, however. New Orleans will play host to Super Bowl XXIV.

The *Jazz and Heritage Festival* is a special event, but there's no dearth of music anytime. The place that started off such great jazzmen as Louis Armstrong, Buddy Bolden, Joe "King" Oliver, Kid Ory, and Jelly Roll Morton still swings. The Old Mint, which has been renovated, is the permanent home for excellent exhibitions on how it all began with a merging of Afro-American and European rhythms. At *Preservation Hall,* Dixieland jazz is played every night; and in countless honky-tonks on Bourbon Street the beat goes on. New Orleans still has brass band funerals where a marching band accompanies the procession from the church to the cemetery, playing solemn marches and hymns. As soon as the services are over, the rhythm picks up and the theme changes to something like "I'll Be Glad When You're Dead You Rascal You." The mourners begin prancing and cavorting behind the band, picking up others who join in the "Second Line" though they probably don't even know who died. But it doesn't really matter because when you leave the Big Easy, New Orleans folk act like you're on your way to the Bigger Easy, and send you off easily. Regardless of where you go afterward though, while you're there, it's hard not to join in. And why not? As they say in New Orleans, if you ain't gonna shake it, what did you bring it for?

NEW ORLEANS AT-A-GLANCE

SEEING THE CITY: The revolving bar in the *Top of the Mart* restaurant, on the 33rd floor of the World Trade Center of New Orleans, offers the best view of the city, the Mississippi River as it cuts the crescent shape of New Orleans, and the barges, ocean liners, and ferries as they move up and down the river. 2 Canal St. at the river (phone: 522-9795).

River Tours – On the free ferry you can ride back and forth to Algiers. The *Bayou Jean Lafitte* motor vessel gives a tour from the Toulouse Street Wharf (behind Jax Brewery) through the bayou country to Bayou Barataria, home of the famous pirate. The paddlewheel steamboat *Natchez* has daily runs from the Toulouse Street Wharf up and down the river. A small paddlewheeler, the *Cotton Blossom,* makes three runs daily from the Canal St. docks to Audubon Zoo. Admission charge for all three (phone: 586-8777). The motorized, 3-decker *Cajun Queen* and the sternwheeler *Créole Queen* offer both daytime and dinner cruises, which depart from behind Riverwalk (phone: 524-0814). The *Voyageur,* a sightseeing boat, cruises from the foot of Canal Street into bayou country, with a stop at Chalmette Battlefield (phone: 523-5555).

SPECIAL PLACES: Nestled between the Mississippi River and Lake Pontchartrain, New Orleans's natural crescent shape can be confusing. North, south, east, and west mean very little here; New Orleans residents keep life simple and use "lakeside" or "riverside" as directions.

VIEUX CARRÉ

Jackson Square – This stately square was once the town square of the French colonial settlement, and the scene of most of New Orleans's history, from hangings to the transfer ceremony of the Louisiana Purchase. Rebuilt in the 1850s with the equestrian statue of Andrew Jackson, the hero of the Battle of New Orleans, the square is a pleasant place to sit and watch New Orleans go by, against a setting of charming brick façades of the surrounding buildings. Heads no longer roll here, but an occasional open-air jazz concert does, and the only hangings are on the iron fence bounding the area, where local artists display their work, and some draw portraits. Traffic has been removed from the area, leaving a pedestrian mall. 700 Chartres St. bordered by Chartres, St. Ann, St. Peter, and Decatur Sts.

St. Louis Cathedral – Built in 1794, this beautiful Spanish building features towers, painted ceilings, an altar imported from Belgium, and markers for those buried in the sanctuary in French, Spanish, Latin, and English. Tours given daily except Sunday. Donations requested. 700 Chartres St., across from Jackson Square (phone: 525-9585).

Presbytère – Used as a courthouse during the Spanish colonial period, it is also part of the *Louisiana State Museum* and features mostly touring exhibitions. Closed Mondays and Tuesdays. Admission charge. Corner of Chartres and St. Ann Sts. (phone: 568-6968).

Pontalba Apartments – Built in the 1850s, this row of townhouses features distinctive cast ironwork on the balconies and a French-style arcade. Rich in New Orleans history, the apartments and shops have seen the comings and goings of the French aristocracy, Jenny Lind, Sherwood Anderson, and William Faulkner. Today, ice cream parlors and small shops line the ground floors, and some very fortunate New Orleans residents live above. Jackson Square at St. Ann and St. Peter Sts.

Moon Walk – Named for former mayor Moon Landrieu, the title's a bit misleading. But this promenade alongside the Mississippi River shows "Ol' Man River" at its best as it winds its way along the crescent shape of the city (the only resemblance Moon Walk has with the moon). The Mississippi is deep and swift at New Orleans and the port, which can accommodate oceangoing vessels, is second in tonnage only to New York. Across the levee from Decatur St. at Jackson Square.

French Market – A farmers' market for 2 centuries, the French Market still has a colorful atmosphere with stands under large old arches offering everything in the way of fresh vegetables and fruits (try the Louisiana oranges, sugarcane, and the sweet midget bananas), meats, and fish including live crab, turtle, shrimp, catfish, and trout. The covered section has cafés, candy shops, and gift shops. *Café du Monde* is a New Orleans institution featuring marvelous café au lait (half coffee and chicory, half hot milk) and beignets (square French donuts). The café never closes, and the market is open daily. Extending down Decatur St. from St. Ann to Esplanade.

Beauregard-Keyes House – Although George Washington never slept here, almost everyone else lived in this Federal house, including the novelist Frances Parkinson Keyes, chess player Paul Morphy, and Confederate General P.G.T. Beauregard; quite a few of another sort died here in a Mafia battle in 1909. The house has period furniture, a collection of dolls, and Keyes memorabilia. Closed Sundays. Admission charge. 1113 Chartres St. (phone: 523-7257).

Royal Street – There really was a streetcar named *Desire,* and in the 19th century it used to run along Royal Street. Though the streetcar is gone, desire for the old days remains and some of it can be fulfilled by a stroll down this street, famous for its antiques shops and highly distinctive architecture.

Historic New Orleans Collection – Scholarly archives, a preserved French Quarter residence, gift shop, and historic exhibitions. Closed Sundays and Mondays. 533 Royal St. (phone: 523-4662).

Old Mint – Opened in 1982 and part of the *Louisiana State Museum,* the Mint contains a *Mardi Gras* exhibition, a jazz exhibit, and archives. Jazz lovers will find souvenirs of the patron saints of jazz — Louis Armstrong's first horn, Bix Beiderbecke's cuff links, and instruments played by members of the *Original Dixieland Jazz Band.* Fine displays trace the development of jazz from its Afro-American rhythms and the European brass band tradition to current progressive strains. Open Wednesdays through Sundays. Admission charge. 400 Esplanade Ave. (phone: 568-6968).

Preservation Hall – What's recorded in the jazz collection at the Mint still happens every night at *Preservation Hall;* featured is traditional New Orleans Dixieland played by a different band from a group of six. No booze is allowed, sparse surroundings, but the real jazz thing. Open nightly. Admission charge. 726 St. Peter St. (phone: 523-8939).

Bourbon Street – Though the street was named for the French royal family, it actually has a lot more in common with the drink, which, along with anything else potable, can be found here in abundance (and New Orleans establishments have added many drinks to the bartender's list, including the absinthe frappe and the Hurricane). Round-the-clock honky-tonks offer live jazz, which gets wild in the wee hours, and live booze, which gets wicked the morning after. A hot strip since the postwar years, Bourbon Street also has lots of strip joints and peep shows, where, even if you stay outside, you'll get more of an eyeful than a peep as the hawkers swing the doors open to lure customers. Among the hottest spots is *Lafitte's Blacksmith Shop,* 941 Bourbon St., where pirate Jean Lafitte is purported to have had a blacksmith shop, now a bar where the forge is still flaming; others are the *Old Absinthe House,* 240 Bourbon St., a barroom since 1826, for rhythm and blues, and *Lulu White's Mahogany Hall,* for Dixieland jazz. 309 Bourbon St.

St. Louis Cemetery Number One – The Last stop in the Vieux Carré, this old New Orleans cemetery with its tombs designed by earlier architects is literally a diminutive necropolis. The marshy ground dictated aboveground burial, and the monuments are interesting for their structure, inscriptions, and number of remains inside (to solve overcrowding, tombs are opened, and the remaining bones are moved deeper into the vault to accommodate new arrivals). If you're interested, the caretaker will give you a tour. Among the prominent buried here are Etienne de Boré, the first mayor of New Orleans; Paul Morphy, the chess player; and Marie Laveau, a 19th-century voodoo queen. Open daily. No admission, but small charge for tours. (It's best not to wander around alone.) 400 Basin St.

DOWNTOWN AND THE GARDEN DISTRICT

Canal Street – Where the French Quarter ends, the business district begins, and the transition is sharp, from narrow cobblestone streets to a wide, main boulevard. The World Trade Center of New Orleans, a glass skyscraper, is the center for companies dealing in foreign trade.

Garden District – Above Canal Street and the business district is the lovely Garden District, once the center of 19th-century American aristocracy, still preserving its old style. The houses, mainly Victorian and Greek Revival in design, are set back from the street with wide, shady gardens of oak, magnolia, camellia, and palm trees. The district is a great place to stroll anytime (or take the St. Charles Ave. streetcar).

CITY PARK AND LAKE PONTCHARTRAIN

New Orleans Museum of Art – This attractive Greek Revival building has fine permanent collections including the Samuel H. Kress Collection (Italian renaissance and baroque masterpieces), 19th-century French salon paintings, works by Degas, pre-Columbian art, African art, Spanish colonial paintings, and a splendid collection of Fabergé. Closed Mondays. Admission charge. In City Park (phone: 488-2631).

Lake Pontchartrain – New Orleans's other body of water, this large saltwater lake has fishing from the sea wall as well as on the lake. Best is the drive over the Lake Pontchartrain Causeway, the longest overwater highway bridge in the world — 24 miles across open water, and for 8 miles in the center, you are completely out of sight of land; there's only Lake Pontchartrain as far as the eye can see. I-10 leads to the Causeway. Toll.

■**EXTRA SPECIAL:** Somewhere out there in Louisiana country was once the heart of the Old South, and it still beats faintly along the banks of the Mississippi. A little over 100 years ago sugarcane was king in Louisiana, and large plantations established commercial empires, as well as an entire social system, around it. A few of these plantations have been restored and are open to visitors who want to see what that period was like, at least for the people on top. And the life that the southern gentry created for themselves really is something to see. The most interesting plantations are within an hour's drive of New Orleans. Houmas House (72 miles west on River Rd.), which was used for the filming of *Hush, Hush, Sweet Charlotte,* looks just like a plantation should — a big, white mansion with stately columns and lovely grounds with huge, old oak trees and formal gardens. There is an excellent tour through the house, which has a circular staircase, rare antiques, a widow's walk for river gazing, and outside, garçonnières, little windmill-shaped structures where young men were sent to live independently when they came of age. San Francisco (42 miles west along River Rd.) is an attractive structure — Flamboyant Steamboat Gothic with lots of Victorian trim, elaborate ceiling paintings, and, over the front door, a mirror that reflects the Mississippi River. Other impressive plantations are *Oak Valley* (phone: 523-4351), 60 miles west on River Rd., whose magnificent miles of ancient oak trees predate the splendid brick edifice, and *Madewood* (phone: 524-1988), 2 miles from Napoleonville, where Spanish moss hovers over an old graveyard and beautifully restored manor house and outbuildings. Both plantations welcome overnight guests.

SOURCES AND RESOURCES

TOURIST INFORMATION: The New Orleans Tourist Information Center, in the French Quarter, provides a wealth of information on the city's attractions, including maps, brochures, and personal help. 529 St. Ann St., New Orleans, LA 70116. (phone: 566-5031).

New Orleans by Carolyn Kolb (Doubleday; $3.95) is the most comprehensive guide to New Orleans and the surrounding area. Another good source is *The Pelican Guide to New Orleans* by Tommy Griffin (Pelican; $2.95).

Television Stations – WDSU Channel 6–NBC; WVUE Channel 8–ABC; WWL Channel 4–CBS; WYES Channel 12–PBS.

Radio Stations – AM: WWL 87 (talk/news); WNOE 1060 (country); WSMB 1450 (talk). FM: WEZB 97.1 (contemporary); WLTS 106 (light rock); WRNO 99.5 (rock).

Local Coverage – The *New Orleans Times-Picayune,* daily.

Food – Check the *New Orleans Eat Book* by Tom Fitzmorris (New Orleans Big Band and Pacific Co., $6.95).

Telephone – The area code for New Orleans is 504.

Sales Tax – Citywide sales tax is 9%.

CLIMATE: New Orleans weather is subtropical with high humidity, temperatures, and substantial rainfall. Moderated by the Gulf of Mexico winds, summer temperatures hover around 90F, while winter temperatures rarely drop to freezing. Summers can get unbearably sticky.

 GETTING AROUND: Airport – New Orleans International Airport is a 45-minute drive from the downtown area, and taxi fare is set at $18. The *Louisiana Transit Co.* (phone: 737-9611) runs an Airport-Downtown Express bus on a 10- to 25-minute schedule from downtown at the corner of Elks Pl. and Tulane Ave.; fare, $1.10. *Airport-Rhodes Transportation* (phone: 469-4555) also provides service from the airport to downtown hotels for $7.

Bus – New Orleans Regional Transit Authority provides efficient bus and streetcar service throughout the city. The St. Charles Ave. streetcar offers a scenic ride through the Garden District (board at Canal and Baronne Sts.). A new streetcar line that runs along the riverfront and through the Central Business District and the French Quarter, from Julia St. to Esplanade, also makes a good sightseeing excursion. Complete information is available at the Regional Transit Authority office, 101 Dauphine (phone: 569-2600), or by calling RideLine at 569-2700.

Taxi – Cabs can be ordered on the phone, hailed in the streets, or picked up at stands in front of hotels, restaurants, and transportation terminals. Major cab companies are *Yellow-Checker Cab* (phone: 525-3311) and *United Cab* (phone: 522-9771).

Car Rental – All of the major national car rental companies have offices in New Orleans.

 LOCAL SERVICES: Business Services – *Dictation Incorporated,* open 24 hours daily, 500 Valence St. (phone: 895-8637).
Mechanic – *Doody and Hank's Service,* 719 O'Keefe (phone: 522-5391).

 MUSEUMS: The *New Orleans Museum of Art,* the *Old Mint,* the *Louisiana State Museum,* and the *Historic New Orleans Collection* are described above in *Special Places.* Other notable New Orleans museums are:
Confederate Museum – 929 Camp St. (phone: 523-4522).
Pharmacy Museum – 514 Chartres St. (phone: 524-9077).

 MAJOR COLLEGES AND UNIVERSITIES: Tulane University, 6400 St. Charles Ave. (phone: 865-5000), is New Orleans's most prominent educational institution, known primarily for its medical and law schools. Loyola University, 6300 St. Charles Ave. (phone: 865-2011), with an enrollment of over 10,000 students, is also in the city. The University of New Orleans, the Lakefront (phone: 286-6000), is the area's largest school.

 SPECIAL EVENTS: When it comes to special events, none tops New Orleans's *Mardi Gras,* an extravagant succession of parades, carnivals, and balls that begin January 6 and continue through Ash Wednesday. (For a fuller description, see the New Orleans essay).

As if *Mardi Gras* merriment were not enough, the old river city begins to celebrate again soon after Ash Wednesday. Irish-Americans and Italian-Americans take to the streets on *St. Patrick's Day* and *St. Joseph's Day,* March 17 and 19, respectively. The *Tennessee Williams/New Orleans Literary Festival* takes place in mid-March. The new, family-oriented *French Quarter Festival,* during the second weekend of April, is quickly gaining in popularity. It is a weekend of food, parades, and free musical entertainment in the Vieux Carré.

Since 1969, New Orleans has been driving home the point that there just ain't no better place for jazz than the *New Orleans Jazz and Heritage Festival,* held for 2 weeks each April and May. The top names in jazz perform at a number of places throughout the city, while all kinds of bands — ragtime, traditional New Orleans Dixieland, Cajun — and folk and blues musicians entertain at the Fair Grounds on weekends. All come together as jazz stars join in late-night jam sessions in the French Quarter. More than just music for the soul, the *Heritage* includes something for the stomach and plenty of it. All kinds of Créole and Cajun food, the New Orleans specialties, are available on the Fair Grounds.

The *New Orleans Food Festival, Bastille Day,* and *La Fête* (phone: 525-4143), all held every July, celebrate the city's heritage with musical, sports, cultural, and culinary events.

 SHOPPING: New Orleans offers an abundance of shopping opportunities. Local specialties in the French Quarter include gorgeous papier-mâché and porcelain masks from *Mardi Gras,* superb jazz posters and records, harlequin dolls, antiques (especially jewelry), and used books (try the *Librairie* or *Old Books* on Royal St.). While the Vieux Carré is something of a tourist trap, the quality of the shops jammed into its streets and the friendliness of their proprietors make it a magnet for shoppers seeking the unusual. For both shopping and dining, the Jax Brewery Complex, next to Jackson Square and the river, is a popular option. Outside the Quarter, there are art galleries and antiques shops on Magazine St. in the Garden District and boutiques in Canal Place and the Riverwalk, both at the foot of Canal Street by the river. Large department stores are also on Canal Street and in several malls. The latest is the New Orleans Centre, with branches of *Macy's* and *Lord & Taylor,* plus three levels of the finest shops and eateries in the Central Business District.

 SPORTS AND FITNESS: The biggest thing in New Orleans sports is the *Superdome,* the world's largest domed stadium. There are daily 45-minute tours of the 27-story arena (capacity: 76,000). It hosts the New Year's Day *Sugar Bowl* football classic (phone: 587-3810) and in 1990 will host *Super Bowl XXIV*.

Bicycling – Both City Park and Audubon Park are good for riding.

Fishing – On Lake Pontchartrain, and within easy distance of the Gulf of Mexico, New Orleans is a fishing paradise (for fishermen, not fish). The best spot is Empire, 52 miles south on Rte. 23 where you can rent boats or take a charter to go after king mackerel, white trout, and red snapper, at *Battistella's Marina* (phone: 657-9811). You can fish in Lake Pontchartrain for bass, speckled trout, and red fish off the seawall along Lake Shore Drive or rent a boat from *Ed Lombard's* bait center at Chef Menteur.

Fitness Center – In the *Hilton,* the *Rivercenter Tennis Club* has a sauna, whirlpool bath, outdoor track, aerobic classes, and tennis and racquetball courts, 2 Poydras St., at the river (phone: 587-7242).

Football – The NFL's *Saints* play at the *Superdome* from August to December. Tickets are available at the box office, 1500 Poydras St. at La Salle St. (phone: 522-2600). The Tulane University *Green Wave* team plays at the *Superdome* from late September through November (phone: 861-9283).

Golf – Golf is popular year-round, and the best courses for the public are the four 18-hole courses at City Park, Esplanade Ave. southwest of the French Quarter (phone: 483-9397), and the course at Audubon Park, 473 Walnut (phone: 861-9511).

Horse Racing – There are two seasons for racing and pari-mutuel betting: winter season at *Fair Grounds Race Track,* 1751 Gentilly Blvd. (phone: 944-5515) from Thanksgiving Day to mid-April; summer season at *Jefferson Downs,* Kenner La. (phone: 466-8521) from mid-April to early November.

Jogging – Audubon Park, 3 miles from downtown, has a popular 3-mile course; run or take the streetcar on St. Charles Avenue to get there.

Swimming – You can swim during the summer at the Olympic-size pool in Audubon Park, St. Charles Ave. (phone: 587-1920).

Tennis – City Park has 45 good public courts of various composition, open year-round; there's a small fee (phone: 483-9383).

THEATER: For up-to-date offerings and performance times, check the *New Orleans Times-Picayune.* New Orleans has several theaters that offer performances, some locally produced, others traveling shows. Colleges and universities in the area also produce plays and musicals. Best bets for shows: *Theatre of the Performing Arts,* 801 N. Rampart St. (phone: 522-0592); *Saenger Performing Arts Center,* 143 N. Rampart St. (phone: 888-8181); *Le Petit Théâtre du Vieux Carré* (the oldest continuously operating community theater in the nation), 616 St. Peter St. (phone: 522-9958).

MUSIC: Classical concerts and opera are heard at *Theatre of the Performing Arts,* 801 N. Rampart St. (phone: 522-0592); *New Orleans Opera Guild* has 8 productions from September to May (phone: 529-2278); the *New Orleans Philharmonic Symphony* performs from September to May at the *Orpheum Theater,* 129 University Pl. (phone: 525-0500). Jazz is the big story in New Orleans music, and when it comes to jazz, it's time for:

NIGHTCLUBS AND NIGHTLIFE: New Orleans is a night town, and the jazz gets better and the drinks stronger (at least it seems that way) as the night wears on. At any one time there is an astonishing array of jazz being played in the city: top names and talented local musicians playing traditional New Orleans jazz, progressive, blues, rock, or folk music.

Current favorites are: *Pete Fountain's Night Club,* in the *Hilton* on Poydras St. (phone: 523-4374), featuring the renowned jazz clarinetist; *Tipitina's,* 501 Napoleon (phone: 895-8477), for blues, Cajun, rock, and rhythm and blues; *Snug Harbor,* 626 Frenchmen (phone: 949-0696), for local favorites; *Storyville Jazz Hall,* 1104 Decatur (phone: 525-8199), for a great variety of artists; *Lulu White's Mahogany Hall,* 309 Bourbon St. (phone: 525-5595), for Dixieland music by the Dukes of Dixieland; and the *Maple Leaf Bar,* 8316 Oak St. (phone: 866-9359), for ragtime, rhythm and blues, and Cajun dancing on Thursday nights. *Preservation Hall* is the place for pure jazz (no drinks) by traditional New Orleans bands, 726 St. Peter St. (phone: 523-8939). Favorite bars: *Napoleon House,* 500 Chartres St. (phone: 524-9752); *Lafitte's Blacksmith Shop,* 941 Bourbon St. (phone: 523-0066); *Old Absinthe Bar,* 400 Bourbon St. (phone: 525-8108); *Pat O'Brien's* (home of the Hurricane), 718 St. Peter St. (phone: 525-4823); *Harry's Place,* corner Dumaine and Chartres (phone: 524-7052), *Bombay Club,* 1019 Dumaine St. (phone: 586-0972); and *Fritzel's,* a place frequented by Europeans at 733 Bourbon St. (phone: 561-0432).

BEST IN TOWN

CHECKING IN: Hotels in New Orleans are usually more than just places to stay after spending a day (and half the night) seeing the city. Many of the hotels reflect the influence of French, Spanish, and/or Louisiana colonial architecture and often a full measure of charm. The service in these hotels is generally excellent. No matter where you stay or what you pay, make reservations well in advance, particularly during *Mardi Gras* season, from Christmas to Ash

Wednesday (this includes Sugar Bowl Week, which precedes the football classic on New Year's Day). Slightly higher rates prevail during these periods. In general, however, the spate of hotel building that coincided with New Orleans's ill-fated World's Fair of 1984 has tended to keep the hotel business very competitive and rather reasonable — especially on weekends. Expect to pay $100 to $160 a night for a double room (and way up — particularly for suites) in the expensive range, $75 to $95 in the moderate scale, and $45 to $70 in the inexpensive category. Many of the more expensive hotels have excellent weekend promotional packages. All telephone numbers are in the 504 area code unless otherwise indicated.

Fairmont – They say New Orleanians wept when its predecessor, the *Roosevelt,* was sold to the Fairmont interests. But they weep no more. The *Fairmont*'s owners have successfully wedded the charms of San Francisco and New Orleans and produced an efficient, 750-room enterprise. At the fine *Sazerac* restaurant, topers can sample the Sazerac cocktail or the famed Ramos gin fizz. The *Blue Room* has dinner dancing and top acts. *Bailey's* is a 24-hour restaurant-bar. Facilities also include a heated pool and 2 tennis courts. University Pl. (phone: 529-7111 or 800-527-4727). Expensive.

Inter-Continental New Orleans – An imposing presence in the business district, with 497 comfortable rooms, New Orleans musicians entertaining in the public rooms, and the *Veranda* restaurant. 444 St. Charles Ave. (phone: 525-5566, 800-332-4246, or 800-327-0200). Expensive.

Maison de Ville – This fine small hotel in the French Quarter is actually a variety of accommodations: the main house, with wonderfully restored former slave quarters; and, most notable, the *Audubon Cottages* (named for the naturalist, who lived and painted here a century ago), each of which has a patio with access to a small swimming pool. It is in these cottages that the best of French Quarter ambience is felt. The hotel's new restaurant, the *Bistro,* guided by an award-winning chef, has been acclaimed by both food critics and patrons. 727 Toulouse St. (phone: 561-5858 or 800-634-1600). Expensive.

Méridien – Here is a 497-room hotel on Canal Street in the shopping district, directly on the *Mardi Gras* parade routes. The French atmosphere is thick, especially in the casual *La Gauloise* restaurant as well as in the more elegant and expensive *Henri* restaurant. Health club, pool. 614 Canal St. (phone: 525-6500). Expensive.

New Orleans Hilton – A downtown 1,602-room resort by the river, with a fine view and the International Rivercenter, an entertainment development that includes a cruise ship terminal, a tennis club, and a luxury shopping mall. Also has a pool, health club, sauna, and garage. Special features are *Le Café Bromeliad*'s Sunday champagne brunch; *The Rainforest* nightclub; *Pete Fountain's* nightclub, featuring the famous jazz clarinetist; *Winston's,* offering continental dining; and *Kabby's Seafood* restaurant, with a Sunday seafood brunch and Dixieland jazz. 2 Poydras St. at the Mississippi River (phone: 561-0500 or 800-HILTONS). Expensive.

Omni Royal Orleans – On the site of the famous St. Louis Hotel, amid the hustle and bustle of the Vieux Carré. The lobby is luxurious Italian marble, most of the 350 rooms are elegantly furnished, and there is conscientious service. Features the *Esplanade Lounge,* popular with the late-night crowd, *Café Royale, Touche-Bar,* a 3-level nightspot, the fine *Rib Room* for dining, a rooftop pool, a fitness center, shops, garage. 621 St. Louis St. (phone: 529-5333 or 800-THE-OMNI). Expensive.

Pontchartrain – With 100 tastefully decorated rooms, each done individually, and suites with many French provincial antique furnishings, this hotel is a favorite of celebrities and traveling dignitaries. Its service is truly worth the name. It has an excellent restaurant, the *Caribbean Room* (see *Eating Out*), serving Créole specialties and a bar with a jazz pianist nightly. 2031 St. Charles Ave. (phone: 524-0581). Expensive.

Soniat House – This remarkable pair of townhouses has been beautifully restored, and everything possible has been done to reinforce the feeling that guests are living in the New Orleans of 150 years ago. Rooms are filled with antique furniture, often including canopied beds and Victorian loveseats. 1133 Chartres St. (phone: 522-0570 or 800-544-8808). Expensive.

Westin Canal Place – There are remarkable panoramic city views from the 11th-floor lobby of this hotel atop Canal Place — the shopping mall — with 438 top-quality rooms and suites of varying sizes and views. 100 Rue Iberville (phone: 566-7006 or 800-228-3000). Expensive.

Windsor Court – A luxuriously British-style hotel with 58 deluxe rooms and 266 suites. Its afternoon tea is so popular that a reservation may be necessary. Every room, public and private, is richly decorated and comfortable. Its *Grill Room* is one of the highest-rated restaurants in New Orleans. 300 Gravier St. (phone: 523-6000). Expensive.

Cornstalk – This old Victorian home is surrounded by a New Orleans landmark — a wrought-iron fence showing ripe ears of corn shucked on their stalks, ready for harvest, and pumpkin vines. The interior is something of a landmark, too — a grand entrance hall and lobby with antique mirrors and crystal chandeliers. The 14 rooms feature four-poster beds, and you can take continental breakfast there, in the front gallery, or on the patio. 915 Royal St. (phone: 523-1515). Expensive to moderate.

LaMothe House – Surrounded by moss-draped oaks on the Boulevard Esplanade at the edge of the French Quarter, this 150-year-old double townhouse exudes Old World charm with elaborate late Victorian furnishings and ambience. Careful attention to detail is a hallmark here. The 11 rooms and 9 suites are furnished with period antiques. 621 Esplanade Ave. (phone: 947-1161 or 800-367-5858). Expensive to moderate.

Monteleone – At the gateway of the Vieux Carré, this old 600-room hotel maintains a friendly atmosphere while offering the amenities of a larger operation. Features rooftop pool and bar, revolving lounge, formal dining at *Le Chasseur,* a coffee shop, *Le Café,* an oyster bar, and a garage. 214 Royal St. (phone: 523-3341). Expensive to moderate.

Ste. Helene – A carefully preserved historic building, this guest house has a courtyard pool and 3 floors with 16 rooms, 7 with balconies overlooking the pool or busy Chartres Street. Conveniently located 2 blocks from Jackson Square and the popular *Napoleon House* bar/restaurant, it features reproductions of 19th-century antiques; each room has a full bath, color TV set, central air conditioning, and telephone. 508 Chartres St. (phone: 522-5014). Expensive to moderate.

Place d'Armes – Right off Jackson Square, this tastefully decorated hostelry has a lovely courtyard with a pool, fountains, magnolia and banana trees, and outdoor tables. There are 74 rooms and 8 antiques-furnished suites in eight 18th-century renovated buildings. Rooms have color TV sets, and many have ceiling fans and balconies. 625 St. Ann St. (phone: 524-4531; 800-535-7791). Moderate.

Le Richelieu – A gem nestled at the end of the French Quarter, it offers 71 rooms and 17 suites, all pleasantly furnished. Refrigerators are found in 56 of the rooms, and most have brass ceiling fans. The lush, tropical patio with pool and *Terrace Café and Lounge* is a popular gathering spot for locals. 1234 Chartres St. (phone: 529-2492; 800-535-9653). Moderate.

Columns – An unusual hotel in the Garden District, perfect for travelers who care less about creature comforts (not every room boasts a private bath) and more about immersing themselves in the ambience of early New Orleans. A recent refurbishment has modernized rooms. If the bar looks familiar, you know it from films like *Pretty Baby* and *Tightrope.* The St. Charles Ave. streetcar runs by the front door. 3811 St. Charles Ave. (phone: 899-9308). Moderate to inexpensive.

French Quarter Maisonnettes – A converted Vieux Carré mansion with a carriage-way drive of flagstones and a spacious patio, the inn is a quaint and friendly place to stay. Each of the 7 rooms is luxuriously private, some right on the patio. The owner presents each guest with a printed, personal folder listing places to go and offering advice and suggestions for activities. 1130 Chartres St. (phone: 524-9918). Inexpensive.

Quality Inn Midtown – Convenient and modestly priced, with an award-winning restaurant featuring Maine lobster, boiled Créole beef brisket, and shrimp cocktail. Pool, café, bar, meeting rooms. 102 rooms. 3900 Tulane Ave. (phone: 486-5541). Inexpensive.

EATING OUT: The city abounds with restaurants. Most are good. Many are excellent. And all reflect the distinctive cuisine of New Orleans, Créole cooking — shaped through the years by the cultures of France, Spain, America, the West Indies, South America, African blacks, and the American Indian. Seafood is king in Créole recipes, and the nearby waters are a rich kingdom, providing crab, shrimp, red snapper, flounder, Gulf pompano, and trout. Vegetables in season, fowl, veal, and fresh herbs and seasonings are culinary staples that fill out the court and have made this strongly regional style a royal art. There are many fine expensive and moderately priced restaurants. Inexpensive restaurants and even department stores serve up New Orleans specialties, gumbo, po' boy sandwiches, and red beans and rice on Mondays, a New Orleans tradition. Our selections range in price from expensive at $65 or more for a dinner for two, $35 to $45 in the moderate range, and $20 or less in the inexpensive range. Prices do not include drinks, wine, or tips. All telephone numbers are in the 504 area code unless otherwise indicated.

Antoine's – Established in 1840, and one of the oldest restaurants in the country, it still offers a grand gastronomic experience, although some say the service is slipping. The waiters know the daily fare well and it pays to listen to their suggestions. Specialties include tournedos with Créole red wine sauce, *pompano en papillote,* oysters Rockefeller, *filet de boeuf Robespierre,* soufflé potatoes, and baked Alaska. Though the decor is somewhat sparse — white tiled floors and mirrored walls — *Antoine's* has a great wine cellar and picturesque private dining rooms. Closed Sundays. Reservations advised. Major credit cards. 713 St. Louis St. (phone: 581-4422). Expensive.

Bistro at Maison de Ville – Tiny and wonderfully intimate, it's a favorite of locals. Chef Susan Spicer (we don't know if that's her real name) is a devotée of Provençal cuisine: wild game dishes, such as grilled breast of duck, panéed rabbit, sautéed sweetbreads, and venison. Lunch daily except Sundays; dinner nightly. Reservations necessary. Major credit cards. 733 Toulouse St. (phone: 528-9206). Expensive.

Caribbean Room – The *Pontchartrain* hotel's exceptional dining room serves French and Créole cuisine. The menu is imaginative, and specialties are beautifully presented — trout Véronique (poached and topped with green grapes and hollandaise sauce), crabmeat Biarritz (lump crabmeat with whipped cream dressing and topped with caviar), and, if you can go the distance, Mile-High Ice Cream Pie for dessert. An elegant brunch is served Sunday mornings. Open weekdays for lunch; daily for dinner. Reservations and jackets required. Major credit cards. 2031 St. Charles Ave. (phone: 524-0581). Expensive.

Christian's – A quaint place known for its French and Créole menu. The redfish au poivre vert (a broiled filet served with green peppercorn cream sauce) is highly recommended. Closed Sundays. Reservations necessary. Major credit cards. 3835 Iberville (phone: 482-4924). Expensive.

Eiffel Tower – When folks talk about the Eiffel Tower, don't assume they mean the one in Paris: when the French landmark's 2nd-floor restaurant was removed for structural reasons in 1981, it was transported to New Orleans and painstakingly reconstructed. It is not only an excellent dining place but a stunning sightseeing attraction. Don't miss the oysters Rockefeller soufflé and fresh hearts of palm salad. Delicious desserts are served until the wee hours. On Friday evenings, 1940s music is played for a 9-12 dinner dance with no cover charge. Lunch weekdays; dinner nightly. Reservations advised. Major credit cards. 2040 St. Charles Ave. (phone: 524-2555). Expensive.

K-Paul's Louisiana Kitchen – Though out of favor with many local diners and food critics, who label it "overrated and overpriced," grouse about the lines at the door, community seating, and unpredictable hours, no New Orleans restaurant listing is complete without mention of this Paul Prudhomme eatery. In spite of the aforementioned caveats, it is still worth a visit. Lunch and dinner weekdays. No reservations. American Express only. 415 Chartres St. (phone: 942-7500). Expensive.

Le Ruth's – Owner and chef Warren Le Ruth spent his career in New Orleans preparing French and Créole food, and his children now serve consistently fine dishes — oysters and artichoke soup, soft-shell crab with lump crabmeat and meunière sauce, veal Marie with crabmeat, frogs' legs meunière, homemade desserts, mandarin ice, or the exquisite almond torte. The restaurant also bakes its own bread. Closed Sundays and Mondays. Reservations necessary. Major credit cards. 636 Franklin St. in Gretna, 4½ miles across the Mississippi River Bridge from Canal St. (phone: 362-4914). Expensive.

Alex Patout's – One of the state's most respected and innovative chefs has opened a popular new French Quarter restaurant, especially good for lunch. Impeccably prepared "haute Cajun" dishes, such as duck smothered with oyster dressing, sweet potatoes with pecans, tasso pasta with shrimp, and superb gumbos. Lunch weekdays; dinner nightly. Reservations advised. Major credit cards. 221 Royal St. (phone: 525-7788). Moderate.

Arnaud's – This once-noble Vieux Carré restaurant, founded in 1918 by Count Arnaud Cazenave, has rejoined the ranks of New Orleans's best. Its traditional menu has been shortened and strengthened: Many dishes were eliminated; some that originated here and became famous were retained; a few were added. You can't miss with shrimp Arnaud (a spicy remoulade), trout meunière, and caramel custard. The dining areas also have been refurbished, but not at the sacrifice of the old France–old New Orleans decor — crystal chandeliers and flickering gas lanterns. Open daily. Reservations advised. Major credit cards. 813 Bienville St. (phone: 523-5433). Moderate.

Brennan's – Although the food is as good as ever, it's become so popular that the atmosphere is very hectic and the service declining. However, the saying goes that you haven't really had a full day in New Orleans unless you've started it with breakfast at *Brennan's* — poached eggs with hollandaise and marchand de vin sauce, creamed spinach, or New Orleans style with crabmeat, turtle soup, and maybe bananas Foster (bananas with ice cream and liqueur) for a flaming dessert, and certainly café Brulot (coffee with Curaçao and orange rind). Open daily. Reservations necessary. Major credit cards. 417 Royal St. (phone: 525-9711). Moderate.

Commander's Palace – This longtime favorite in an old mansion in the Garden District has been operated for the past several years by a branch of the *Brennan's* restaurant family. The unusual "jazz brunch" offered on Saturdays and Sundays features traditional and exotic poached egg dishes accompanied by New Orleans jazz. Dinner specialties include trout pecan, crabmeat imperial, turtle soup, lemon crêpes, and filet mignon. Open daily. Reservations advised. Major credit cards. 1403 Washington Ave. (phone: 899-8221). Moderate.

Feelings – A fetching local favorite renowned for its duck, fresh seafood specials, and peanut butter pie. Seafood-baked eggplant is always popular, along with a delicious appetizer of shrimp and crawfish etouffée. Piano music enhances Friday and Saturday nights and Sunday brunch. Lunch weekdays; dinner nightly. Reservations advised. Major credit cards. 2600 Chartres St. (phone: 945-2222). Moderate.

Galatoire's – No matter who you are or who you think you are, you stand in line on the sidewalk like everyone else when the house is full. But both the wait and the possible humiliation (depending on who you think you are) are worth it. This favorite of New Orleans residents has great French and Créole dishes, a distinctive atmosphere with ceiling fans and mirrored walls, and knowledgeable waiters. Specialties include trout Marguery with shrimp, shrimp remoulade, oysters en brochette, eggs Sardou (artichokes and spinach over poached eggs), and crêpes maison filled with currant jelly. Open for lunch and dinner; closed Mondays. No reservations or credit cards. 209 Bourbon St. (phone: 525-2021). Moderate.

Masson's Restaurant Français – An elegant French restaurant near the lakefront that has a strong local following. Chef-owner Ernest Masson visits France frequently to bring back recipes for the latest in haute cuisine. He tries them out for a while and if they are *assez haute,* he adds them to the offerings on the already fine menu — oysters LaFourche, veal Vivian, and marinated rack of lamb. Closed Mondays. Reservations advised. Major credit cards. 7200 Pontchartrain Blvd. (phone: 283-2525). Moderate.

Torey's – Owned by the Le Ruth family, (see *Le Ruth's,* above), it is in the heart of the French Quarter and run by the younger generation with the same exacting — and delicious — standards established in their original restaurant. Dinner only; closed Sundays and Mondays. 430 Dauphine (phone: 561-8133). Moderate.

Upperline – Off the beaten path, but always filled with diners who come here for the charcoal-grilled fish and the "Taste of New Orleans Créole Dinner," an entrée consisting of small portions of 3 different New Orleans specialties: blackened fish, chicken etouffée, and barbecued shrimp. Dinner nightly. Reservations necessary. Major credit cards. 1413 Upperline (phone: 891-9822). Moderate.

Versailles – This relative newcomer to the New Orleans scene improves each year. Its menu is a good mix of French, German, and Créole. One fine appetizer is the Versailles escargots en croute, classic snails bourguignonne served in a hollowed-out bun made of New Orleans French bread. Main course specialties include duck à la Flamande, rack of lamb persillade, veal financière with sweetbreads, bouillabaisse Marseillaise, and veal farci with crabmeat. On the ground floor of the Carol Apartments at the edge of the Garden District. Closed Sundays. Reservations advised. Major credit cards. 2100 St. Charles Ave. (phone: 524-2535). Moderate.

Alonso's – This typical New Orleans neighborhood restaurant and bar specializes in seafood. The main attraction is the very large, very good, and very inexpensive seafood platter. It contains the traditional hot seafood, plus a few seasonal items like crayfish or soft-shell crab, and some boiled shrimp or crab tossed in for good measure. Don't expect your party to be served together — you get it while it's hot. Extremely crowded on Friday nights. Closed Sundays. No reservations. No credit cards. 587 Central Ave. (about 6 miles from Canal St.) (phone: 733-2796). Inexpensive.

Central Grocery Company – Its grocery store has been here since 1906 and still stocks flour, beans, and other staples in barrels to sell by the pound. More popular, however, are the great take-out Italian sandwiches, cheeses, and salads. Open daily. No credit cards. 923 Decatur (phone: 523-1620). Inexpensive.

D. H. Holmes – You can get a good and filling lunch or snack at this department store for just a few dollars. The daily specials are usually good, and the turtle and vegetable soups are great. Closed Sundays. No reservations. Major credit cards. 819 Canal St. (phone: 561-6321). Inexpensive.

Mandina's – Of the vast number of places that offer po' boy sandwiches, this small family-style restaurant does it best with Italian sausage and roast beef. The large servings of meatballs and spaghetti, gumbo, and jambalaya will not take too big a bite out of your pocket. Open daily. No reservations. No credit cards. 3800 Canal St. (phone: 482-9179). Inexpensive.

Ye Olde College Inn – In the university section, daily dinner plates, shrimp remoulade, red beans and rice, oyster loaf, French-fried onion rings, and a good bar. The Créole vegetables, especially the eggplant and stewed okra, are at the top of their class. Open daily. No reservations. Major credit cards. 3016 S. Carrollton Ave. (phone: 866-3683). Inexpensive.

Gumbo Shops – Gumbo, a culinary essential of Louisiana life, is a thick, spicy soup based on either seafood or chicken, and no two cooks make it exactly alike. According to locals, the best seafood gumbo is served at the *Gumbo Shop,* 630 St. Peter St. (phone: 525-1486), and at *Ralph and Kacoo's,* 519 Toulouse St. (phone: 522-5226). The best places to sample chicken gumbo are *Mr. B's,* 201 Royal St. (phone: 523-2078), and *Bozo's,* 3117 21st St., Metairie (phone: 831-8666). Inexpensive.

NEW YORK CITY

Any visitor's first impression of this enormously diverse city can easily be distorted by the specific neighborhood in which he or she happens to land. An uninitiated tourist in the Tottenville section of Staten Island would likely surprise neighbors back home with descriptions of rolling farmland, rural ambience, and settings seemingly more appropriate to Iowa than to this country's most cosmopolitan center. That same stranger standing in parts of the South Bronx would horrify friends with tales of a "war zone" reminiscent of Dresden after the bombings. And seeing the corner of 59th Street and 5th Avenue for the first time, our fledgling traveler couldn't help but be impressed with the incredible elegance of surroundings whose gaudy opulence has few equals in the world. The question, then, is which is the real New York?

The answer is that New York is all these things. In a way, visitors have their choice of the New York City they wish to visit, and it's a simple matter to be insulated from most potential unpleasantness. A tourist's terrain in New York is traditionally limited to Manhattan and, indeed, generally bordered by the Hudson and East rivers and 34th and 96th Streets. Within this relatively narrow geographic area stand New York's most famous hotels, its elegant restaurants, and its most celebrated theaters, cinemas, museums, and fine shops.

It is, therefore, sometimes difficult for a visitor to reconcile the entertaining New York of his or her own experience with the troubled and troublesome New York described in the newspapers. It is hard to understand matters of want and welfare while window-shopping in the chic, dramatic boutiques of Madison Avenue or craning one's neck up the canyons of Park Avenue. But the tourist's New York and the most crowded residential areas of the city seldom intersect and unless the tourist specifically sets out to see the city's other faces, the only aspect of New York's malaise likely to intrude will be the growing number of homeless people and panhandlers — they are found literally all over the city.

New York offers an array of distractions unequaled anywhere on earth. Nowhere are there more museums of such a consistently high quality. Nowhere are there restaurants of such striking ethnic diversity. Nowhere is there more varied shopping for more esoteric paraphernalia, and nowhere in the world does the pace of city life and the activities of the populace more dramatically accent a city's vitality and appeal.

Just as Americans hardly ever refer to themselves simply as Americans — they are southerners, Texans, Californians, and the like — New York's nearly 8 million residents are similarly chauvinistic about the specific enclaves of their city. Though in theory New York is composed of five boroughs — Manhattan, Queens, Brooklyn, the Bronx, and Richmond (Staten Island) — everyone understands that Manhattan is "The City."

So a visitor to New York should not feel at all self-conscious about his or her insular orientation, since some residents of Flushing (in Queens) talk of going to the city with the same undertone of long-distance travel adventure as residents of Kansas City. Brooklynites have been known to avoid crossing the East River for years at a time, and many think of themselves as living in some relatively rural hamlet quite separate and entirely distinct from the evils of the Big Town. And there are truck farmers on Staten Island who haven't ventured into Manhattan in a generation. Yet all are lifetime New Yorkers, and all are filled with especially fierce pride in the area of the city in which they live.

Indeed, New York is truly the capital of this country in almost every way, and the presence of the United Nations complex in the middle of Manhattan makes it possible to describe the city as the capital of the world as well. It is likely that more French people can be found in Paris, more Japanese in Tokyo, and more Africans in Dakar, but it is unlikely that any other city in the world boasts so large a population of all these cosmopolitan cultures, races, and ethnic entities as New York. And one has only to pick any of a broad range of midtown restaurants to experience dining elbow-to-elbow with the very same figures who, just hours before, were deciding everything from the future of world commerce to the maintenance of world peace.

New York is also the communications capital of the planet. From the Avenue of the Americas come most of the decisions that determine television viewing — not only in this country, but around the world — and while the majority of TV production facilities are firmly based in California, the decisions about what will be produced (and seen) are usually made in executive offices in Manhattan. New York has the same dominance in radio broadcasting and magazine publishing, and though the city is now down to only four citywide daily newspapers, one of them — *The New York Times* — is considered a standard-bearer of contemporary journalism. Books, records, and even motion pictures all depend on decisions originating in New York for everything from creativity to advertising and financing, and they reflect what has often been described as the bias of the eastern establishment. The capital of that establishment is clearly New York.

There is, in addition, widespread perception that for any creative artist to succeed, she or he must gain recognition in New York. In the theater, every actor, writer, director, designer, singer, dancer, musician, and composer feels the magnetic pull of Broadway. Painters, sculptors, writers of every description, cartoonists, jingle rhymers, artists, and charlatans all focus their creative and financial yearnings on New York. Whether one wants to make it on the stage, on the screen, on the airwaves, in bookstores, or on billboards, the path to success must eventually traverse New York.

Just as hard to characterize as the geography of this city is the attempt to stereotype a typical New Yorker. The city is notable, first of all, for its immense ethnic diversity, and there are large segments of the city where the English language is hardly ever heard. From the obvious examples of Spanish Harlem, Chinatown, and Little Italy to the less apparent Slavic and Hasidic enclaves, centuries-old tradition is maintained through rigid authoritarianism and purposeful segregation. Though New York's ethnic ghettos are initially

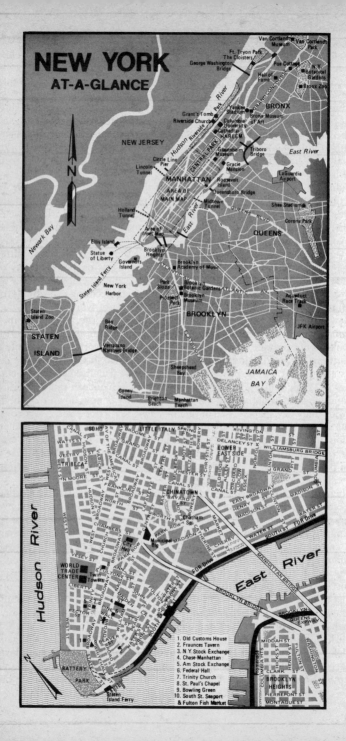

CENTRAL MANHATTAN

Metropolitan Museum of Art

Hayden Planetarium

Museum of Natural History

N.Y. Historical Society

UPPER WEST SIDE

CENTRAL PARK

Whitney Museum

Frick Collection

UPPER EAST SIDE

Juilliard Bldg.

Avery Fisher Hall

Lincoln Center

Metropolitan Opera

N.Y. State Theater

Aerial Tramway to Roosevelt Isl.

Bloomingdale's

QUEENSBORO BRIDGE

N.Y. Coliseum

Columbus Circle

CENTRAL PARK SOUTH

Plaza Hotel

Grand Army Plaza

GM Bldg.

Bergdorf-Goodman's

Tiffany's

Carnegie Hall

Museum of Modern Art

ROCKEFELLER

St. Patrick's

Radio City

Saks Fifth Av

Waldorf-Astoria Hotel

McGraw-Hill Bldg.

CENTER

UNITED NATIONS

THEATER

MIDTOWN

DISTRICT

AV OF THE AMERICAS

Pan Am Bldg.

Ford Foundation

Bryant Park

N.Y. Public Library

Grand Central Station

Chrysler Bldg.

Tudor City

Port Auth. Bus Terminal

Lord & Taylor

MURRAY HILL

GARMENT DISTRICT

Macy's

Morgan Library

B. Altman's

Madison Sq. Garden

Gimbels

Penn Station

Empire State Bldg.

N.Y.U. Medical Center

Kips Bay Plaza

Gen. Post Office

Bellevue Hospital

Madison Sq

East River

FDR Drive

Gen. Theological Seminary

CHELSEA

Gramercy Park

Union Sq

New School

Salmagundi Club

Jefferson Market Library

St. Mark's Church

GREENWICH VILLAGE

Cooper Union

EAST VILLAGE

Tompkins Square Park

Washington Square

University

Cherry

HOUSTON

invisible and completely unofficial, they are often most stringently maintained by their residents.

Other New Yorkers use these districts to their own benefit and regularly visit ethnic neighborhoods to attend "foreign" festivals during the year. The *Chinese New Year* is nowhere more intensely celebrated than on Mott Street, and one would be hard pressed to develop a more authentic case of Italian indigestion than can be suffered during the *San Gennaro Festival* on Mulberry Street each fall. New Yorkers, whose culinary horizons probably reach farther afield than those of any other civic population on earth, regularly feast on such exotica as Greek specialties wrapped in grape leaves, Lebanese shish kebabs, Slavic pirozhkies, spicy Latin dishes, and German wursts. A visitor who does not sample as many ethnic cuisines as possible is indeed wasting a special opportunity.

New York's cultural and gastronomic leadership is only slightly less important to the nation and the world than its financial ascendancy. Just walking through the Wall Street area provides a dramatic impact and reaffirms that the city has a firm hold on world commerce. Visitors' galleries at the New York Stock Exchange and some of the commodity exchanges provide a unique opportunity to watch capitalism in action in its wild state, and nowhere is the sense of the enormity of American industry and the scope of commercial trading more keenly felt.

Trading has a long history in New York City, for it was here that the original $24 worth of trinkets and baubles bought the island of Manhattan from the Indians who may (or may not) have been its owners. Depending on one's point of view, the Indians were either boldly deceived on the price or they made one of the best real estate deals in the city's history.

That original island of Manhattan, a near wilderness traversed by several streams and rivers, bears little resemblance to the island as it presently exists. Various landfill and reclamation projects have enlarged it over the years, and just a brief glance today at the Battery Park area (at Manhattan's southernmost tip) indicates that expanding the island's real estate is still very much an active enterprise.

Through the years, New York has resisted identification with any exclusive European heritage, and its current cast betrays very little of the passage from Dutch hands to English and the subsequent domination of first one group of immigrants and then another. In this sense, it is a singularly liberated city, feeling little allegiance to any one ancestor or antecedent. From this polyglot past springs the New York feeling that it is really a nation unto itself.

In all the world, New York has no equal. Its ability to prosper in spite of its monumental problems testifies to its strength and resilience more dramatically than can any analytic essay. That its residents choose to continue to live amid its many municipal shortcomings highlights the fact that its excitement and challenges far outweigh its imperfections, and the inclination of tourists from all over the world to visit its buildings and byways continues to make it the single most popular city for tourists. This ongoing appeal amply justifies New York's avowed preeminence and ensures its continued attraction as the greatest magnet in America. It is, above all, a city that revels in its ability to

tantalize the curious and strongly attract the interest of those who live elsewhere.

NEW YORK AT-A-GLANCE

SEEING THE CITY: New York is, to put it simply, the most complex city
in the world. People who have lived here all their lives don't even know all
of it — its size and diversity challenge even the most ambitious. The best bet
for the visitor who wants to feel the magic of New York and to understand
how the city is laid out is to take it all in from one of several vantage points.

Brooklyn Promenade – Standing on this walkway at dusk, with the lights of
Manhattan shimmering across the East River, you'll get an idea of the magnitude and
beauty of the city. In lower Manhattan the towers of the World Trade Center rise before
you, and the Brooklyn Bridge spans the river to your right. Farther north stand the
Empire State Building and the UN Secretariat Building, landmarks of midtown. The
easiest way to get here is via the IRT 7th Avenue subway line, Clark St. stop.

World Trade Center – The elevator to the observation deck of Two World Trade
Center whisks you more than a quarter of a mile above the street. There is an enclosed
deck on the 107th floor and a promenade on the roof above the 110th floor. Manhattan
spreads out to the north, Brooklyn is to the east, to the west is New Jersey, and to the
south lies New York Harbor, leading to the Atlantic Ocean. Open daily from 9:30 AM
to 9:30 PM. During winter months, the deck may be closed; check beforehand. Tickets
are sold on the mezzanine level of Tower Two. Liberty and West Sts. (phone: 466-7397).

Empire State Building – Although many tourists prefer the newer and higher
World Trade Center observation deck, the old queen of New York attracts more than
2 million people a year — the Art Deco design is more romantic than anything in the
World Trade Center (even if Deborah Kerr never kept her appointment with Cary
Grant here in *An Affair to Remember*). You can feel the breeze from the 86th floor or
ascend to the glass-enclosed 102nd floor. Don't be surprised if in the evening the top
of the building is bathed in colored lights — it's the city's way to commemorate
holidays and special occasions. Open daily from 9:30 AM to midnight (the last elevator
is at 11:25 PM). Admission charge. 34th St. and 5th Ave. (phone: 736-3100).

Views from Above and Below – Some of the most dramatic views of New York
are visible when entering the city by car. The three western access routes have special
features: the Holland Tunnel access road from the New Jersey Turnpike, leading into
lower Manhattan, offers a panorama of the southern tip of the island; the Lincoln
Tunnel access road offers a view of Manhattan's West Side; and the George Washington
Bridge, linking New Jersey and the Upper West Side, has spectacular views of the
Hudson, the city's long shore along the river, and the New Jersey Palisades, as well
as being a work of art itself, best seen from a distance, from the river, or while driving
north on the West Side Highway.

Tours – Many of the tour companies in the city will help you get your bearings before
setting out on your own. *Gray Line,* 900 8th Ave., between 53rd and 54th Sts. (phone:
397-2600), provides good bus tours. *Circle Line Sightseeing Yachts* offers an interesting
3-hour guided boat trip around Manhattan from early March until mid-November.
Boats leave from Pier 83 at the foot of W. 42nd St. and the Hudson River (phone:
563-3200). Most spectacular is *Island Helicopter*'s ride around Manhattan. Though the
price is considerable ($30-$139 for flights ranging from 5 to 40 minutes), you won't
forget this trip soon. At E. 34th St. and the East River (phone: 718-895-1626). Also
try *Manhattan Helicopter Tours* (phone: 247-8687) and *Adventures on a Shoestring*
(phone: 265-2663).

Seeing New York on foot is probably the best way to get acquainted with this complex city. A number of excellent walking tours are available, led by guides who are knowledgeable about everything from architecture and ethnic neighborhoods to literary history, the jazz circuit, movie locations, and noshing spots. Try the *New-York Historical Society* (phone: 873-3400), the *Municipal Art Society* (phone: 935-3960), the *Museum of the City of New York* (phone: 534-1672), the *92nd Street YMHA* (phone: 996-1105), *New York Walk-About* (phone: 914-834-5388), and the *New School for Social Research* (phone: 741-5600).

 SPECIAL PLACES: Manhattan is a 12½-mile-long island stretching 2½ miles at its widest point. Avenues run north and south, streets run east and west. Fifth Avenue is the dividing line between addresses designated east and those designated west. For example, 20 E. 57th Street is in the first block of 57th east of 5th Avenue; 20 W. 57th Street is in the first block west of 5th Avenue. New York grew from south to north, street by street and neighborhood by neighborhood. The oldest parts of the city are around the docks in lower Manhattan and in the financial district.

The best way to discover the city and enjoy its incredible variety and ethnic diversity is by direct contact — walking through the neighborhoods. You will want to take taxis or public transport between areas — distances can be great — but have no hesitation about walking once you've arrived. The much-touted reputation of New Yorkers for aloofness and unfriendliness simply isn't true. Just watch what happens when you ask directions on a bus or subway (except during rush hours, when things are, admittedly, a bit primitive). We suggest a copy of *Flashmaps! Instant Guide to New York* (Flashmaps; $4.95), which has the most accessible and best-organized series of maps of New York neighborhoods we've seen.

LOWER MANHATTAN

Statue of Liberty – Given by France as a symbol of friendship with the United States, this great lady has been guarding the entrance of New York Harbor since its dedication in 1886. To celebrate its centennial in 1986, "Liberty Enlightening the World" was given a major face-lift, and a new museum was added to its base. New lighting makes the statue even more dazzling than ever after dark. The *Circle Line* (phone: 269-5755) runs from Battery Park to Liberty Island; there is no admission charge to the statue or to the *American Museum of Immigration* (phone: 422-2150) at the base, though there is a fee for the boat trip. You can see the statue from a distance and the southern tip of the city by riding the *Staten Island Ferry,* still one of the world's great transportation bargains at 25¢. The Ferry Terminal is next to Battery Park (the South Ferry stop on the IRT 7th Ave. line).

Ellis Island – Visible from the Statue of Liberty or Battery Park, Ellis Island served as a processing center for immigrants from 1892 to 1954. More than 17 million people passed through this island on their way to a new life in the land of opportunity. These aging shells of buildings were the sites of joy and heartbreak; many immigrant families were separated here when some members were refused entry to the US because of bad health or lack of money. A boat leaves from Battery Park (April through September). Ellis Island, now run by the National Park Service (phone: 732-1286), has been closed for renovation since 1984. The Great Hall — the centerpiece of the immigration process — is expected to open as part of a restored complex sometime in 1990.

Governors Island – Groups can visit this island in New York Harbor from April through November. Now a Coast Guard base, the island's two pre-1800 structures are the Governor's House and Ft. Jay. Soviet leader Mikhail Gorbachev visited here in late 1988. Free tours for groups of 15 to 30 (no individual tours) can be arranged by writing to the Special Services Division, Building 110, Governors Island, NY 10004 (phone: 668-7255).

Battery Park – Twenty-one acres of green, overlooking New York Harbor, this is the spot for picnics on hot summer days. There's a statue of Giovanni da Verrazano, who piloted the *Dauphine,* the ship that reached Manhattan in 1524 (Verrazano was later killed by cannibals in the Caribbean). There's also a monument to World War II dead. Castle Clinton, built as a fort in 1812, has functioned as an opera house, an immigrant landing depot, and an aquarium at various times. Its latest incarnation is as a ticketing center for the Statue of Liberty ferry. Bordered by State St., Battery Pl., and the river (phone: 344-7220).

Battery Park to Wall Street – This area is a lovely place to wander on weekends, when the empty streets emphasize the incongruity of the Chase Manhattan building and the World Trade Center surrounded by the 17th- and 18th-century buildings on Pearl Street, Bowling Green, and Hanover Square. Two buildings of particular note are the India House on the south side of Hanover Square (1837) and the old US Custom House (the new Custom House is in the World Trade Center), which was built in 1907 in neoclassic style. Another turn-of-the-century building at 56 Beaver St. until recently housed *Delmonico's* restaurant, the meeting place of lower Manhattan's elite.

Fraunces Tavern Museum – This building, the site of Washington's farewell to his officers in 1783, contains memorabilia of the American Revolution (including Washington's hat). The *Fraunces Tavern* restaurant occupies the ground floor. Most of the buildings and streets are designated as a historic area. Open weekdays from 10 AM to 4 PM and, from October to May, noon to 5 PM Sundays. No admission charge from 10 AM to noon on weekdays. At the corner of Pearl and Broad Sts. (phone: 425-1778).

New York Stock Exchange – A tree stands in front of the stock exchange to commemorate the tree under which the first transaction took place in 1792. Today, more than 1,600 corporations are listed on the big board. You can observe the action from a glass-enclosed gallery reached via the visitors' entrance at 20 Broad St. Open weekdays from 9:20 AM to 3 PM. No admission charge (phone: 656-5167). Cameras are prohibited. The American Stock Exchange (86 Trinity Pl.) no longer has a visitors gallery. If you want to see real emotion, head for the Coffee, Sugar, and Cocoa Exchange, 4 World Trade Center (phone: 938-2800), which makes the Stock Exchange seem like a London tea party. Open weekdays from 9 AM to 3 PM. No admission charge.

Federal Hall – This National Historic Site served as the British headquarters during the Revolution and was later the seat of American government. George Washington was sworn in as president here in 1789. Open weekdays from 9 AM to 4:30 PM. No admission charge. At the corner of Wall and Broad Sts. (phone: 264-8711).

Trinity Church and Museum – The church faces Wall Street, which is appropriate, because it has been a wealthy parish since it was first granted a charter by William III in 1697. One of the citizens who aided in building the church was Captain Kidd, the notorious pirate who was hanged in London in 1701. The present building was completed in 1846, but the graveyard beside the church is even older. William Bradford, Jr., Robert Fulton, and Alexander Hamilton are buried here. For years, the Trinity Church steeple was the highest point on the New York skyline. During the summer, the church sponsors lunch-hour entertainment, called the *Noonday Café,* for downtown workers in the south courtyard. Classical concerts are held year-round on Tuesdays at 12:45 PM in the church, and on Mondays and Thursdays at 12:10 PM in St. Paul's Chapel. At Broadway and Wall Sts. (phone: 602-0800).

St. Paul's Chapel – The oldest church building in Manhattan, this fine example of Colonial architecture was erected in 1766 on what was then a field outside the city. George Washington worshiped here. On the corner of Broadway and Fulton St. (phone: 602-0874).

Battery Park City – A $4-billion complex including apartments, tree-lined streets, public parks and squares, and a sumptuous centerpiece, the World Financial Center (not related to the neighboring World Trade Center). It's also home of the *Winter*

Garden (not to be confused with the Midtown theater of the same name), where a variety of free concerts are held and artworks displayed. A true city within a city, this landfill development in the Hudson River is logically designed and decidedly not ostentatious. There are a wealth of other diversions: among them, a spa, a 1950s rock 'n' roll club, and numerous shops. The views from Battery Park City are spectacular, and the *Winter Garden* is a must. Browsing is free. The *Winter Garden* is open from 7 AM to 1 AM (phone: 416-5300). For general Battery Park City information, call 945-2600.

World Trade Center – A world in itself. At 1,350 feet each, its two towers are not the tallest buildings in the world (the CN Tower in Toronto is, at 1,821 feet), but close to it. In order to build the center, 1.2 million yards of earth and rock were excavated (they're now in the Hudson River). The concourse has shops and some excellent restaurants (see *Best in Town*), including the *Big Kitchen,* the *Market Dining Room,* and the 107th-floor *Windows on the World.* Not all World Trade Center businesses involve trade, but the Custom House is here, as are the Commodity Exchange and the Cotton and Mercantile Exchanges. Open daily. No admission charge. Bounded by West, Church, Liberty, and Vesey Sts. (phone: 466-4170).

City Hall – This is the third City Hall of New York; it was built in 1803 and contains the office of the mayor and the City Council chamber. The original construction cost half a million dollars, and in 1956 the restoration cost some $2 million (times change). The building was a site of great importance to New York's and America's history: Lafayette visited in 1824; Lincoln's body lay in state in 1865; and, in the 1860s, City Hall and Tammany Hall (Park Row and Frankfort St.) were controlled by Boss Tweed, the powerful corrupt politician who dominated New York politics until the 1870s.

Other city government buildings nearby include the Municipal Building on the northeast corner of City Hall Park, the United States Court House, across from Foley Square, the New York County Courthouse next door, the Federal Office Building on the other side of Lafayette St., and the Hall of Records. City Hall Park has a statue of Nathan Hale, the patriot of the Revolution, who was executed here in 1776. Today, protestors of every persuasion gather in the park to "fight City Hall." Open weekdays from 10 AM to 3 PM. No admission charge. In a triangular park between Park Row, Broadway, and Chambers St.

South Street Seaport and the Fulton Fish Market – In July 1983, stage one of the South Street Seaport renovation was completed, enlivening the area with new shops and restaurants and additional space for the *South Street Seaport Maritime Museum.* The Museum Block is an entire row of rejuvenated buildings (some dating to the 1700s) with room for exhibitions, shops, and offices. The Schermerhorn Row of renovated 19th-century warehouses is also alive with retail outlets and the South Street Seaport Museum Visitors Center. All of these changes have not substantially altered the area's famous old *Fulton Fish Market,* where, from about 2 to 8 AM, trucks still deliver fresh fish to the wholesale outdoor market. But the old market is now joined by another building called the Fulton Market, with restaurants, cafés, and food stalls. Among the many eateries are two of New York's oldest seafood restaurants, *Sweets* (2 Fulton at South St.; phone: 344-9189 or 825-9665; closed weekends), and *Sloppy Louie's* (92 South St.; phone: 509-9694). For years, these veterans of the *Fulton Fish Market* served the freshest seafood at rock-bottom prices in simple quarters. When the seaport was renovated, the restaurants moved into more sanitized surroundings, with proper dining rooms and higher prices — and, unfortunately, lost their boisterous atmosphere and earthy appeal. At least the portions remain hearty and the fish is as fresh as ever. Also of interest are the historic boats docked at Piers 15 and 16, where summertime pop and jazz concerts are staged. The new 3-story Pier 17 Pavilion adds even more shops and restaurants to the riverside complex. Fulton St. between South and Water Sts.

Brooklyn Bridge – You can stroll from Manhattan to Brooklyn by crossing the

Brooklyn Bridge on a pedestrian walk. You'll get a good view of the city, and a close look at this engineering feat. The 6,775-foot bridge, which spans the fast river at a height of 133 feet and is considered by many to be one of the most beautiful bridges in the world, was completed in 1883 and cost $25 million. Many workers were seriously injured during its construction, and a number of people have since committed suicide by jumping from it. Always open. Free (unless someone succeeds in selling you title to the bridge). Take the IRT Lexington Ave. line to Worth St.–Brooklyn Bridge station.

Chinatown – The best way to get the feel of New York's Chinese neighborhood is to hit the streets, especially Mott, Bayard, and Pell. More than 100,000 people live in this small area of crowded, narrow streets, and the Chinese population spills into neighboring Little Italy. Although the Chinese community here is not as large as the one in San Francisco, it is authentic. You'll know when you reach Chinatown by the pagoda-shaped telephone booths and stores that sell shark fins, duck eggs, fried fungi, and squid. Herbs are lined up next to aspirin in the pharmacies. This is where Chinese shop, and uptowners and out-of-towners follow their lead. Don't miss the good, inexpensive restaurants, the tea parlors, or the bakeries. Try the dim sum at lunchtime (steamed or fried dumplings filled with seafood, pork, or beef). Favorite spots among New Yorkers are *Peking Duck House* (22 Mott St.) and *Sun Hop Kee* (13 Mott St.). Sundays are a good time to visit the area, but if you can, come during the Chinese New Year (held on the first full moon after January 21). The celebration is wild and woolly, with fireworks, dancing dragons, and throngs of people. While you'll get the best sense of Chinatown from the streets, if you want historical perspective, stop by the *Chinese Museum,* which houses exhibitions from the first dynasty to the present. Open daily from 10 AM to 1 AM. Admission charge. 8 Mott St. (phone: 964-1542).

Little Italy – Italian music from tenement windows, old men playing *bocce,* old women dressed in black checking the vegetables in the markets, store windows with religious articles, pasta factories, and the ubiquitous odor of Italian cooking fill this neighborhood, which has the reputation of being one of the safest areas in the city. Mulberry Street is the center of Little Italy, but the area stretches for blocks around and blends into parts of SoHo and Greenwich Village. Even Bleecker Street, toward 7th Avenue, has a decidedly Italian flavor, with bakeries selling cannoli and cappuccino sandwiched between Middle Eastern restaurants and stores selling Chinese window shades. Little Italy is thronged during the festivals of *San Gennaro* and *St. Anthony.* In late September, *San Gennaro* covers Mulberry Street from Spring to Park. *St. Anthony* fills Sullivan Street, from Houston to Spring, in mid-June. The festivals attract people from in and out of the city with game booths, rides, and most of all, enough food and drink (both Italian and "foreign") for several armies. Bordered by Canal and Houston Sts. and the Bowery and Ave. of the Americas.

Bowery – There is nothing romantic about New York's Skid Row. On this strip are people who are decidedly down on their luck — both old and young. If you drive west on Houston Street, you'll get a look at some of the inhabitants — they'll wipe your windshields whether you like it or not and expect some change for their trouble. Recently, however, the Bowery has had some new settlers; a few theaters and music places have moved in. The area also has some good places to shop; specialties include lamps and restaurant supplies. The stores have relocated here because of the proximity to one of the most interesting shopping markets in the world: the Lower East Side. Between 4th St. and Chatham Sq.

Lower East Side – This area is probably the largest melting pot in the city. Its Sunday market is an experience that shouldn't be missed. Eastern European Jews, many of whom are Hasidim (an ultra-religious sect, recognizable by the men's ear-locks, called *peyes,* and their fur hats and long black coats), sell their wares for rock-bottom prices; you'll have to bargain if you want the best prices, and these merchants are formidable opponents. The area is also houses Hispanics, Blacks, and various other minority groups; you will hear Yiddish, Spanish, and even some Yiddish-accented Spanish.

The Lower East Side was where the Eastern European Jews, fleeing czarist persecution and deadly pogroms, first settled during their massive migration from 1880 to 1918. Many of the streets, including Rivington, Hester, Essex, and Grand, still look as they did then. To really get a taste of the area, try the food at the *Grand Dairy* restaurant (341 Grand St.; phone: 673-1904), knishes at *Yonah Schimmel's* (137 E. Houston St.; phone: 477-2858), hot dogs at *Katz's* delicatessen (205 E. Houston St.; phone: 254-2246), or the Romanian "broilings" at *Sammy's* (157 Chrystie St.; phone: 475-9131 or 673-5526).

SoHo – The name stands for "South of Houston Street" (pronounced *how*-stun). SoHo leads a double life. On weekends, uptown New Yorkers and out-of-towners fill the streets to explore its trendy stores, restaurants, and art galleries. During the week, SoHo is a very livable combination of 19th-century cast-iron buildings, spillovers from Little Italy, off-off-Broadway theater groups, and practicing artists. At night, the streets are empty and you can see into the residential lofts of the old buildings; some are simple, open spaces, others are jungles of plants and Corinthian columns. *Fanelli's*, on the corner of Mercer and Prince Streets, is one of the oldest bars around and a hangout for residents. Many artists are now moving to TriBeCa, which is south and west of SoHo and has better loft pickings. SoHo is between Canal and Houston Sts., Broadway and Hudson St.

TriBeCa – Long neglected, TriBeCa (the name stands for "triangle below Canal Street") is riddled with abandoned warehouses, cast-iron hulls, and lonely cobblestone streets, but is enjoying a flashy comeback. The current artist residents have spawned a plethora of trendy art galleries on White and Franklin Streets and lower Hudson Street. There are also many discount clothing stores, nightclubs, restaurants, and theaters. Historical oddities worth visiting include the *Bond* hotel, at 125 Chambers St., reputedly Manhattan's oldest hotel; Stanford White's "Clocktower" building, at 346 Broadway; the Art Deco Western Union Building; and the *Market Diner,* at West and Laight streets. TriBeCa extends from Canal Street to Chambers Street and from Broadway to the East River.

East Village – Famous during the 1960s as the center of the New York counterculture, this section has become gentrified, with a growing number of art galleries, restaurants, and night spots competing for space with poor artists and various ethnic groups (the largest of which is Ukrainian, but there are also Armenians, Czechs, Germans, Russians, Poles, Jews, Blacks, and Hispanics, many of whom live in low-income housing projects). St. Mark's Place, between 2nd and 3rd Avenues, was once the city's psychedelic capital. It is still a lively block, clogged with inexpensive restaurants and shops featuring styles from hippie to punk, and generally hops at all hours of the day and night. Two streets south is what could be considered India Row: numerous Indian restaurants line East 6th Street between 1st and 2nd avenues. Astor Place, on the border of the East and West villages, is the site of *Cooper Union* (good for free concerts and lectures) and the *Public Theater,* 425 Lafayette St. (phone: 598-7150), Joe Papp's creation, where you'll find some of the best serious drama (both contemporary and classical) and experimental theater as well as progressive jazz. You can have a drink at *McSorley's Old Ale House,* 15 E. 7th St. (phone: 473-9148), a fixture in the East Village for years. A few blocks north is the spiritual home of the village, St. Mark's-in-the-Bouwerie, on the corner of 2nd Ave. and 10th St. The church still sponsors community activities, especially poetry readings by some of the best poets in New York. The East Village has housed many writers, from James Fenimore Cooper (6 St. Mark's Pl.) to W. H. Auden (77 St. Mark's Pl.) to LeRoi Jones — now Imamu Baraka (27 Cooper Sq.). Bounded by Lafayette St. and the East River, Houston and 14th Sts. (Some parts of the East Village, especially east of Avenue A, remain seedy; don't wander here after dark unless you know where you're going.)

GREENWICH VILLAGE

You can and definitely should stroll around the West Village (as residents know it) at night. The area is filled with surprises. You've probably heard of Bleecker Street, the slightly tawdry gathering place of tourists and the high school crowd from the suburbs, or of Washington Square Park, with its musicians, mimes, and street people. But you might not have pictured Grove Court, the lovely and secluded row of 19th-century houses near the corner of Grove and Bedford Streets (where O. Henry lived), or the Morton Street pier on the Hudson River, from which you can see the Statue of Liberty on a clear day. But the Village is more than this. It is a neighborhood of activists, struggling to maintain control of their beloved community. There are meatpacking factories from the 1920s, old speakeasies turned into restaurants, a miniature Times Square on West 8th Street, and immaculate (and expensive) brownstones on quiet, tree-lined streets. Get a map (you'll need it — there's nowhere else in Manhattan where West 4th Street could bisect West 12th) and wander. Or you can ask directions — villagers love to help and it's a nice way to meet them. You can eat, go to the theater, sip cappuccino in an outdoor café, hear great jazz, and find your own special places. Bounded by 5th Ave. on the east, the Hudson River on the west, Houston St. on the south, and W. 14th St. on the north.

Washington Square – A gathering place for students from New York University, frisbee aficionados, volleyball players, modern bohemians, and people who like to watch them all. The Arch is New York's answer to the Arc de Triomphe. Buildings surrounding the square include the New York University library, administration buildings, and law school. The north side of Washington Square has some lovely homes, including #7, where Edith Wharton lived. Bounded by extensions of W. 4th St., MacDougal St., Waverly Pl., and University Pl.

Bleecker Street – Strolling down Bleecker Street from La Guardia Place to 8th Avenue you'll pass outdoor cafés, head shops, falafel parlors, jazz clubs including the *Village Gate* (Bleecker and Thompson Sts.), Italian specialty stores, and myriad restaurants. You should also wander down some of the side streets, like Thompson, MacDougal (Bob Dylan's old stomping ground), and Sullivan. Have a cappuccino at *Caffè Dante* (79 MacDougal), then pay homage to Eugene O'Neill at the *Provincetown Playhouse,* 133 MacDougal. Beyond 7th Avenue, the side streets become more residential; try Charles Street, West 10th Street, and Bank Street for examples of how the upper middle class lives in the Village. You'll also pass Christopher Street, the center of gay life in Manhattan (although the toughest part of it comes alive on West Street, by the West Side Highway, on weekend nights).

Fifth Avenue – Where the wealthy Villagers live. The Salmagundi Club, built in 1853 at 47 5th Avenue (near 12th Street), is the last of the imposing private mansions that once lined the avenue. On the streets between 5th and the Avenue of the Americas (which the natives call 6th Avenue) you can see expensive brownstones. The New School for Social Research, 66 W. 12th St., has courses on everything from fixing a leak to ethnomusicology. From Washington Sq. north to 14th St.

Avenue of the Americas – New Yorkers know it as 6th Avenue. One of the most unusual buildings in the village is the Jefferson Market Library, on 6th Avenue and 10th Street, with a small garden alongside. Built in 1878 in Italian Gothic style, it served as a courthouse for many years. Across the street is *Balducci's,* 424 6th Ave. (phone: 673-2600), an Italian market with an incredible selection of exotic foods, plus meats, seafood, poultry, cheeses, breads, pastries, fresh fruit, and vegetables. *Famous Ray's of Greenwich Village,* 465 6th Ave. at W. 11th St. (phone: 243-2253) — the place on the corner with the long lines — is considered the source of some of the best pizza in the city. (Note that many pizza places in the city have "Ray's" in their names, but this is the one that gets the raves.)

Farther west (between 6th Ave. and Hudson St. and W. Houston and Christopher

Sts.) is a series of small winding streets with some especially interesting places to visit. At 75½ Bedford Street is the house in which Edna St. Vincent Millay and John Barrymore once lived (not at the same time) — it's only 9 feet wide. *Chumley's,* 86 Bedford St. (phone: 675-4449), used to be a speakeasy during Prohibition and still has no sign on the door — but it does have good food and poetry readings inside. Commerce Street is a small side street lined with lovely old buildings, including the *Cherry Lane Theater,* one of the city's oldest. Morton Street, one block south, is often mistaken for Hester Street, because it was the site of the filming of *Hester Street,* a 1975 film about the Lower East Side Jewish immigrants. (Hester Street begins in Little Italy.) Another block south is Leroy Street with St. Luke's Place, a row of 19th-century houses. No. 6 Leroy was built in 1880 and was the home of Mayor Jimmy Walker. If you walk to the end of the block and north on Hudson, you'll come to the *White Horse Tavern,* 567 Hudson St. (phone: 243-9260), Dylan Thomas's hangout on his trips to New York City. Go in and have a drink.

14TH STREET TO 34TH STREET

Union Square – For many years, this was a place to avoid — particularly at night, when it was populated by drug pushers and other undesirables. Now it has been given a major face-lift, and its open-air produce market on Wednesdays, Fridays, and Saturdays harks back to the halcyon days of the 19th century when the square was the core of upper-crust Manhattan life. A number of cafés, discos, antiques and old bookstores, and theaters fill the side streets; stop in at the *Metropolis Café* (31 Union Sq. W.) or the *Union Square Café* (21 E. 16th St.).

Gramercy Park – A few blocks north of Greenwich Village, Gramercy Park is one of the few places where visitors can get a feel for what Manhattan used to be like. The park itself is open only to residents (they have their own keys), but on a sunny day you can see nannies with their privileged young charges sitting on the benches in the shadows of the 19th-century mansions that surround the park. Stop in for a beer at the cozy, historic *Pete's Tavern,* 129 E. 18th St. (phone: 473-7676). Teddy Roosevelt's birthplace, at 28 E. 20th St. on Gramercy Park (phone: 260-1616), is a museum, open from 9 AM to 5 PM Wednesdays to Sundays. Other well-known native sons and daughters include Herman Melville, Stephen Crane, Edith Wharton, and O. Henry. A few blocks north of Gramercy Park on Lexington Avenue are dozens of little East Indian shops selling splendid assortments of spices, saris, cotton blouses, jewelry, and food. E. 21st St. and Lexington Ave.

Chelsea – An eclectic residential neighborhood in the West 20s, between 7th and 10th Aves., where you can find elegant brownstones next door to run-down, 4-story, walk-up tenements. The *Chelsea* hotel, W. 23rd St. between 7th and 8th Aves., has earned an important place in literary history. Thomas Wolfe, Brendan Behan, Dylan Thomas, and Arthur Miller slept and wrote in its rooms. Andy Warhol made a 4-hour movie about its raunchier inhabitants. For a sojourn into tranquillity, step into the inner courtyard of General Theological Seminary, a gift to the city in 1817 by Clement C. Moore, author of *A Visit from Saint Nicholas.* Open daily (except when special use is being made of it), noon to 3 PM weekdays, 11 AM to 3 PM Saturdays, and 2 to 3 PM Sundays. No admission charge. 175 9th Ave. (phone: 243-5150).

MIDTOWN (34TH STREET TO 59TH STREET)

West 34th Street – A major shopping street, this is the home of the traditional mercantile giant, *Macy's,* as well as *B. Altman's* (technically on East 34th Street) and scores of boutiques selling blue jeans, blouses, underwear, shoes, records, and electronic gear. The main shopping district runs along 34th Street from 8th Avenue east to Madison Avenue, with a number of smaller, shops lining the street as far east as 3rd Avenue. The hub of 34th Street is Herald Square, where Broadway intersects the Avenue of the Americas (6th Avenue).

Madison Square Garden, Felt Forum, and Penn Station – A huge coliseum-arena, office building, and transportation complex. The *Garden*'s 9,500 seats are usually fully packed when the New York *Knicks* (NBA basketball) and the New York *Rangers* (NHL hockey) play home games, when the *Ringling Brothers and Barnum & Bailey Circus* comes to town, or whenever there is a major exhibition, concert, or convention. The *Felt Forum,* a 5,000-seat subsidiary hall that's part of the *Garden* complex, is the site of boxing matches, concerts, and smaller exhibitions. Penn Station is Amtrak's major New York terminal (for Amtrak information, phone: 736-4545). No guided tours. 1 Pennsylvania Plaza, W. 33rd St. between 7th and 8th Aves. (phone: 564-4400 or 563-8300 for Garden and Forum information).

Garment District – The center of the clothing and fashion industries. On any weekday during office hours, racks of the latest apparel are pushed through the terrifically hectic streets. Along 7th and 8th Aves. from 30th to 39th Sts.

Empire State Building – The first skyscraper in New York to be attacked by King Kong. The 102-story Art Deco edifice was erected in 1931 and became the symbol of the city for decades. There is an open-air observation deck on the 86th floor to which millions of tourists have been whisked over the years to gaze in awe at the surrounding New York skyline and another glass-enclosed viewing area on the 102nd floor. Open daily, 9:30 AM to midnight. Admission charge. W. 34th St. and 5th Ave. (phone: 736-3100).

Jacob K. Javits Convention Center – Much delayed and over budget, this glass and steel monolith designed by I. M. Pei, covering 22 acres along the Hudson River, hosts the bigger synods and conventions that outgrew the soon to be demolished New York Coliseum. The complex runs for 5 blocks between 11th and 12th avenues and encompasses 1.8 million square feet of space, making it one of the world's largest buildings. It has more than 900,000 square feet of indoor exhibition space, another 50,000 square feet outside, and a 15-story atrium. The kitchens produce banquet meals for up to 10,000, while the cafeteria serves 1,500 people an hour. State-of-the-art meeting facilities include a sophisticated audio-visual system and soundproofing throughout its 131 separate meetings rooms, with simultaneous interpretation in up to 8 languages. There's also a VIP lounge, a press room, a video information center, and a cocktail lounge. The only thing missing is a garage. 655 W. 34th St. (phone: 216-2000).

Times Square – Every New Year's Eve, Times Square is where thousands of New Yorkers and visitors welcome in the New Year. Although the height of mad celebration reaches its pinnacle at that time, Times Square is always crowded. The quality of the crowds, however, leaves much to be desired. In spite of its reputation as one of the major crossroads of the world, Times Square is mainly the hangout of drug pushers, pimps, hookers, junkies, religious fanatics, and assorted street peddlers attempting to fence stolen goods. It is also the center of the city's tackiest sex industry. To the naked eye, it is nearly wall-to-wall porn shops and hard-core movies. Proposals for rehabilitation have been almost as numerous as the prostitutes on parade. A sign of a possibly brighter future comes in the form of the new 50-story *Marriott Marquis* convention hotel (see *Checking In*) built — over protests from the theater community — on the site of the *Helen Hayes* and *Morosco* theaters, at W. 44th St., where Broadway crosses 7th Ave.

Broadway and the Theater District – Just north of Times Square, you'll find the colorful marquees and billboards for which New York is famous. The lights are still pretty dazzling, twinkling on and off in a glittering electric collage. On most nights, the side streets are jammed with people from 7:30 to 11 PM. The legitimate theaters are mostly clustered between W. 42nd and W. 50th Sts. to the east and west of Broadway. Sixty- to 90-minute backstage tours, conducted by directors, actors, and other theater pros, can be reserved by calling *Backstage on Broadway* (phone: 575-8065).

New York Public Library – A couple of blocks east of Times Square, this dignified old building is a good place to sit and catch your breath. Sit on the front steps, between the famous lion statues. As we went to press, Bryant Park, behind the library, was closed for renovation. Inside the library is New York's largest reference collection of books, periodicals, and exhibits of graphic art, as well as a gift store; there are also various exhibitions and public programs. Tours are given daily except Sundays at 11 AM and 2 PM. Closed Sundays. No admission charge. E. 42nd St. and 5th Ave. (phone: 930-0501).

Grand Central Station – This magnificent Beaux Arts relic is worth seeing. It has just been cleaned and spruced up, and even if you don't have time for the free 1-hour tour Wednesdays at 12:30 PM (phone: 935-3960), at least check out the zodiac dotting the immense vaulted ceiling. Main entrance on 42nd St. between Madison and Lexington Aves.

Chrysler Building – The princess of the skyline. Its distinctive, graceful spire, decorated with stainless steel, now sparkles with more than its usual brilliance since the installation of hand-blown fluorescent lights around its peak. Although it has long ceded the title of tallest on the skyline, this twinkling, Art Deco building of the 1930s remains, to many New Yorkers, the most beautiful of all. There are no tours or observatories, but a visit to the small lobby, with its exquisite inlaid elevator doors, is worth a trip. 405 Lexington Ave. at 42nd St.

Ford Foundation Building – If you happen to be wandering through New York at sunrise and climb the stairs between 1st and 2nd Avenues on 42nd Street, you'll see the bronzed windows of the Ford Foundation building catch the first rays of the sun, reflecting copper-colored light into the sky. At other times, the building is just as dramatic. Built around a central courtyard containing tropical trees and plants, it is the only place in Manhattan where you can feel as if you're in a jungle. It's one of the great New York experiences — especially on snowy afternoons. Open weekdays. No admission charge. 320 E. 43rd St. (phone: 573-5000).

Tudor City – A nearly forgotten pocket of the city, this 1920s neo-Tudor apartment complex is one of its most romantic parts. An esplanade overlooks the East River and the United Nations. The home of many diplomats and UN employees, Tudor City serves as an international campus. (According to local legend, Tudor City used to be where executives and industrialists housed their mistresses in the 1930s and 1940s.) The long, curved staircase leading to the sidewalk opposite the United Nations is known as the Isaiah Steps because of the biblical quote carved into the wall. Between E. 41st and E. 43rd Sts. at Tudor City Place (near 1st Ave.).

United Nations – Although the UN is open all year, the best time to visit is between September and December, when the General Assembly is in session. Delegates from nearly 160 nations gather to discuss the world's problems, and there are a limited number of free tickets available to the public. The delegates' dining room is also open to the public for lunch weekdays throughout the year. Overlooking the East River, it offers a lovely international menu and the chance to overhear intriguing conversations. Reservations are essential; pick up a pass in the lobby. There are guided tours of the UN. Open daily. Admission charge for tour. 1 Dag Hammerskjold Plaza, E. 45th St. and 1st Ave. (phone: 963-4440).

Rockefeller Center – A group of skyscrapers originally built in the 1930s, Rockefeller Center is best known for the giant Christmas tree in December, for its ice skating rink, and for *Radio City Music Hall,* a theatrical landmark and home of the *Rockettes* (phone: 757-3100). There are tours of the center and the observation tower as well as tours of NBC television studios ($6) from 30 Rockefeller Plaza (the RCA Building) daily except Sundays. 5th Ave. between 48th and 51st Sts. (phone: 664-4000 or 246-4600).

St. Patrick's Cathedral – A refuge from the crowds of 5th Avenue, it's the most famous church in the city. Dedicated to Ireland's patron saint, it stands in Gothic splendor across the street from Rockefeller Center in the shadow of the skyscrapers.

Resplendent with gargoyles on the outside, stained glass windows and magnificent appointments on the inside, St. Patrick's is a good place for rest, contemplation, and prayer. Catholic services are held daily. 5th Ave. between E. 50th and E. 51st Sts. (phone: 753-2261).

Sixth Avenue – Officially known as Avenue of the Americas, but no true New Yorker calls it that. Sixth Avenue between 42nd and 57th Streets is particularly breathtaking at dusk, when the giant glass and steel buildings light up.

Museum of Modern Art – A must. The masterpieces of modern art hanging on the walls include Wyeth's *Christina's World*, Monet's *Water Lilies,* and Van Gogh's *Starry Night.* A renovation project completed in 1984 gave *MOMA* twice as much gallery space and expanded study and library facilities. The most dramatic alteration is a 4-story glass Garden Hall overlooking the sculpture garden. The museum's permanent collection is now installed in chronological order, and, by following a suggested route, visitors can see the history of modern painting and sculpture unfold. Closed Wednesdays except to members. Admission charge; on Tuesday evenings, admission is on a pay-as-you-wish basis. 11 W. 53rd St. (phone: 708-9480).

Fifth Avenue – Although the street runs from Washington Square straight up to Spanish Harlem, when New Yorkers refer to 5th Avenue they usually mean the stretch of the world's most sophisticated shops between Rockefeller Center at 49th Street and the *Plaza* hotel at the southeastern corner of Central Park at Central Park South (59th St.). *Saks, Gucci, Tiffany, Cartier, Bergdorf Goodman,* and, for children, *FAO Schwarz* make walking along the street an incredible test in temptation. Stop in at *Steuben Glass* on the corner of 56th Street and marvel at its permanent collection of sculpted glass depicting mythological and contemporary themes. Fifth Avenue is the dividing line between east and west in New York street addresses. It is the only New York avenue that runs perfectly straight along a north-south axis.

Grand Army Plaza – This baroque square, with its central fountain just across the street from the southeast corner of Central Park, faces the regal *Plaza* hotel, the General Motors Building, and the hansom cabstand where horse-drawn carriages (some guided by drivers in top hats and tails) wait to carry clients through Central Park. If you have a lover, be sure to arrange to meet here at least once. Be sure, too, to take at least one ride through the park in a hansom cab, preferably at dusk or very, very late. Central Park South and 5th Ave.

Central Park – More than 50 blocks long but only 3 blocks wide, this beloved stretch of greenery designed by Frederick Law Olmsted and Calvert Vaux in the 1860s is now a National Historic Landmark. New Yorkers use it for everything — jogging, biking, walking, ice skating (at renovated Wollman Rink), riding in horse-drawn hansom cabs, listening to concerts and opera, watching Shakespearean plays, demonstrating, flying kites, boating, gazing at art, and playing all kinds of ball games. You should, however, avoid the park at night. The long-neglected Central Park Zoo, between E. 61st and E. 65th Sts. on 5th Ave., was taken over by the New York Zoological Society (phone: 367-1010), which also runs the Bronx Zoo, and major changes were made in the habitats for this mid-Manhattan menagerie. It finally reopened in 1988 to rave reviews (admission charge). Central Park is bounded by Central Park South (W. 59th St.) on the south, W. 110th St. on the north, 5th Ave. on the east, and Central Park West on the west. Urban rangers offer free walking tours of the park (phone: 860-1353), and there are even guides who describe which items growing in the park are edible. For information on park events, call 360-1333.

UPPER EAST SIDE

Metropolitan Museum of Art – Perhaps the finest museum this side of the Louvre; more than 2 million people visit every year. You could easily spend days walking through the impressive sections displaying the costumes, ceramics, metalwork, armor, mummies, paintings, drawings, sculpture, photographs, and mosaics of dozens of different periods and countries. The special exhibitions are really special. There is a good cafeteria and two gift shops. Films and lectures are presented throughout the year, and a distinguished concert series (phone: 570-3949) is held from September through May. Closed Mondays. Suggested admission: $5. 5th Ave. at 82nd St. (phone: 535-7710 or 879-5500).

Solomon R. Guggenheim Museum – Designed in 1959 by Frank Lloyd Wright, this white circular building has spiraling ramps along its inner walls so you can travel through the collections by following the curves of the building. While it is given over primarily to exhibitions of contemporary art, some patrons feel that its architecture is more impressive than the collection it houses. Closed Mondays. Admission charge except Tuesday evenings. 1071 5th Ave., between E. 88th and E. 89th Sts. (phone: 360-3500).

Yorkville and Gracie Mansion – An interesting ethnic neighborhood of mostly German and Eastern European families. There are plenty of restaurants, beer halls, and delicatessens selling Wiener schnitzel, sauerbraten, wurst, and kielbasa. Gracie Mansion, dating to 1799, is the official residence of the mayor of New York and sits in a garden that is part of Carl Schurz Park alongside the East River. The park is popular with joggers and dog-walkers and is most attractive at dawn, when the eastern sky comes to life. Yorkville stretches from E. 80th to E. 89th Sts. between Lexington and York Aves. Gracie Mansion and Carl Schurz Park are at E. 88th St. and East End Ave. The mansion can be visited by appointment only, from April to October (phone: 570-4751).

Roosevelt Island – A self-contained housing development in the middle of the East River. Roosevelt Island, accessible from Manhattan by tramway or bus from Queens, offers a unique view of midtown Manhattan. A loop bus encircles the island, which has restricted automobile traffic. Visitors can also stroll the attractive main street from end to end, stopping at shops and eateries along the way. A landscaped riverside promenade has benches for relaxing while enjoying the view. The aerial tramway leaves each side every 15 minutes daily except during rush hours, when it leaves every 7½ minutes. The tram costs $1 (subway tokens are also accepted). Manhattan terminal at E. 60th St. and 2nd Ave. (phone: 753-6626).

UPPER WEST SIDE

Columbus Circle and New York Coliseum – The southwestern corner of Central Park is dominated by a statue of Christopher Columbus and a traffic circle. On the western side of the circle stands the New York Coliseum, once the site of major events such as the annual auto, boat, and antiques shows.

Lincoln Center – If you have ever seen Mel Brooks's film *The Producers,* you have probably retained an image of the glowing lights of a fountain shooting into the air with an exuberance to match the enthusiasm of actors Zero Mostel and Gene Wilder. That's the Lincoln Center fountain, and it's just as magnificent in real life. The pulsing water and light are dramatically framed by the *Metropolitan Opera House,* a contemporary hall with giant murals by Marc Chagall. The performing arts complex also contains *Avery Fisher Hall* (home of the *New York Philharmonic*), the *New York State Theater* (home of the *New York City Ballet*), the *Vivian Beaumont Theater,* the *Mitzi E. Newhouse Theater,* the Juilliard Building, and the Library and *Museum of the Performing Arts* (see *Theater* and *Music* sections, below). Guided tours through the major buildings are conducted daily and last about an hour. Admission charge for tour. 140 W. 65th St. and Broadway, in the Lincoln Center Concourse (Lincoln Center: phone: 877-1800; Metropolitan Opera House: phone: 582-3512).

American Museum of Natural History – Though it could use a face-lift, the museum is a cornucopia of curiosities. The anthropological and natural history exhibitions in the form of life-size dioramas showing people and animals in realistic settings have made this one of the most famous museums in the world. The dinosaurs on the 4th floor are the stars of the show. New is the Hall of South American Peoples, with more than 2,300 objects produced by aboriginal cultures of South America over a period of 12,000 years. Exhibitions include polychrome pottery, intricate gold and silver ornaments, and spectacular, brilliantly colored textiles. The museum has a cafeteria, a restaurant, and three gift shops. Free guided tours leave from the main floor information desk. Open daily except Thanksgiving and Christmas. Donations accepted; no admission Fridays and Saturdays after 5 PM. Central Park West and W. 79th St. (phone: 769-5100 for recording or 769-5000).

Hayden Planetarium – An amazing collection of astronomical displays on meteorites, comets, space vehicles, and other galactic phenomena. The sky show, in which constellations are projected onto an observatory ceiling, is one of the great New York sights. Subjects include lunar expeditions, the formation of the solar system, and UFOs. Open daily. Admission charge. W. 81st St. between Central Park West and Columbus Ave. (phone: 769-5920).

Cathedral of St. John the Divine – The largest Gothic cathedral in the world, with a seating capacity of 10,000. It is irreverently nicknamed St. John the Unfinished, for a chronic shortage of funds has allowed only two-thirds of the impressive church to be completed since work began in 1892. Stonemasons, who most recently put down their trowels in the late 30s, picked them up again in 1979, with plans to finish the interior of the Crossing and the two towers' spires by the year 2000. There is a stunning collection of Renaissance and Byzantine art inside, and an exquisite time to see it all is on Christmas Eve at midnight mass. Guided tours of the cathedral and the stoneyard are conducted daily. The well-stocked gift shop rivals many for its variety of souvenir and gift items. Open daily. No admission charge. Amsterdam Ave. and W. 112th St. (phone: 316-7540).

Columbia University – The Big Apple's contribution to the Ivy League. Although more than 27,000 students attend classes here, the campus is spacious enough to dispel any sense of crowding. Around the campus are a number of interesting bookstores, restaurants, and bars. The *West End Café*, 2911 Broadway and W. 113th St. (phone: 666-8750), is a long-standing student favorite, and it was from here that Jack Kerouac went forth to lead the Beat Generation of the 1950s. On weekdays at 3 PM, from September through May (except during finals), free guided tours of the campus leave from 201 Dodge Hall. Open daily. No admission charge. Broadway and W. 116th St. (phone: 854-2845).

Riverside Church – Perched on a cliff overlooking the Hudson River, Riverside is an interdominational Christian church with a functioning carillon tower and an amazing statue of the Angel Gabriel blowing the trumpet. The white building next to the church is known as "the God Box" because many religious organizations (among them, the National Council of Churches and the Interfaith Council on Corporate Responsibility) are based here. The carillon tower is open daily; free guided tours of the church Sundays at 12:30 PM. W. 120th St. between Riverside Dr. and Claremont Ave. (phone: 222-5900).

Grant's Tomb – Who is buried in Grant's tomb? Suffice it to say, You-Know-Who and his wife, Mrs. You-Know-Who, are entombed here in a gray building topped with a rotunda and set in Riverside Park. A word about the park: Don't wander in after dark. Grant's tomb is officially known as General Grant National Memorial. Closed Mondays and Tuesdays. No admission charge. Riverside Dr. and W. 122nd St. (phone: 666-1640).

Cloisters and Ft. Tryon Park – Without a doubt one of the most unusual museums in the country, if not the world. The *Cloisters,* a branch of the *Metropolitan Museum,* consists of sections of cloisters that originally belonged to monasteries in southern

France. It houses an inspiring collection of medieval art from different parts of Europe, of which the Unicorn Tapestries are the most famous. Recorded medieval music echoes through the stone corridors and courtyards daily; medieval and Renaissance concerts are held on selected Sundays throughout the year. As part of its 50th anniversary celebration in 1988, the Cloisters Treasury on the ground floor was expanded. Set in Ft. Tryon Park along the Hudson River, the *Cloisters* offers a splendid view of the New Jersey Palisades, the George Washington Bridge, and the Hudson River. Closed Mondays. Suggested admission: $5. Closest intersection is Washington Ave. and W. 193rd St. (phone: 923-3700).

Harlem – Some visitors to New York — black or white — are uncomfortable at the thought of entering Harlem, and, like any unfamiliar place, it can be intimidating. But there is much to see there, and a visit has the undeniable effect of shattering the monolithic association with threat and violence that attends most people's image of the community. Starting in earnest at 110th Street and stretching to about 160th Street, it is a community filled with neighborhoods of families as concerned about community problems as families in other neighborhoods throughout the city.

The nicest part of Harlem is the landmark block called "Strivers Row" — 138th Street between 7th and 8th Avenues — a string of turn-of-the-century brownstones designed by Stanford White. Quite a lot of Harlem, however, is undergoing a revival. *Mart 125* (phone: 870-4100) is a new shopping center offering handicrafts from developing countries, and the annual *Harlem on the Hudson Festival*, held on Harlem's 10-block waterfront, specializes in Black, Latin, and Caribbean arts and entertainment. In August there is *Harlem Week*, 20 days of music, food, and cultural happenings, and in the fall, the *Harlem Jazz Festival*. As we went to press, the new *Harlem Symphony Orchestra* was seeking incorporation. The famous *Apollo Theater* has been made over, condos are going up, and a multi-screen cinema has opened. The area's ambitious projects also include a *National Cultural Arts Center*, a marina, a hotel, and several new restaurants.

In the words of a New York police officer: "The best way to see Harlem is by driving or in a cab. Take a bus rather than a subway if you are using public transportation." Among the reliable tour operators are *Harlem Spirituals* (phone: 302-2594), *Harlem Tours* (phone: 410-0080), *Harlem Your Way* (phone: 690-1687 or 866-6997), and *Harlem Renaissance Tours* (phone: 722-9534). Worthwhile sights include the Morris-Jumel Mansion, once Washington's headquarters (W. 160th St. at Edgecombe Ave.; phone: 923-8008); the Schomburg Center for Research in Black Culture (515 Lenox Ave. at W. 135th St.; phone: 862-4000); the *Studio Museum* (144 W. 125th St.); and the *Black Fashion Museum*, the country's only museum devoted to Black contributions to fashion (155-57 W. 126th St.; phone: 666-1320). For more information on Harlem, contact the Uptown Chamber of Commerce (phone: 427-7200) or the Convention and Visitors Bureau (phone: 662-6500).

BROOKLYN

Mention Brooklyn to most Manhattanites and you'll probably hear "Oh, I never go to Brooklyn" or some smart-aleck remark. People who do not know the borough think purely in terms of the book *A Tree Grows in Brooklyn* or 1930s gangster movies in which Brooklyn-born thugs make snide remarks out of the sides of their mouths while chewing on cigars. Actually, Brooklyn has a lot of trees (more than Manhattan) and some charming neighborhoods that are more European than American in character. Not only is it greener, it is also considerably more peaceful than Manhattan, even though it has more than 4 million people and bills itself as "the Fourth Largest City in America."

Brooklyn Heights – The most picturesque streets of classic brownstones and gardens can be found in this historic district. Not only does the Promenade facing the skyline offer the traditional picture-postcard view of Manhattan, but the area behind it retains an aura of dignity that characterized a more gracious past. Montague Street, a narrow thoroughfare lined with restaurants and shops selling ice cream, candles, old prints, flowers, and clothing, runs from the East River to the Civic Center, a complex of federal, state, and municipal government buildings. To get to Brooklyn Heights from Manhattan, take the IRT 7th Avenue line to Clark Street; or, better yet, walk across the Brooklyn Bridge and bear right. The district extends from the Brooklyn Bridge to Atlantic Avenue and from Court Street to the Promenade. For information on events in the Heights, contact the Brooklyn Heights Association, 55 Pierrepont St. (phone: 718-858-9193).

Atlantic Avenue – Lebanese, Yemeni, Syrian, and Palestinian shops, bakeries, and restaurants line the street, where purveyors of tahini, Syrian bread, baklava, halvah, assorted delicious foodstuffs, Arabic records, and books are also to be found. There is even an office of the Palestinian Red Crescent, an official branch of the International Red Cross that has been helping victims of the wars in Lebanon. Occasionally, women in veils make their way to and from the shops, some incongruously carrying transistor radios. The most active street scene takes place between the waterfront and Court Street along Atlantic Ave.

Park Slope – An up-and-coming restoration district, the Slope resembles London's borough of Chelsea, with many beautiful, shady trees and gardens. It feels more like a town than part of the city, especially at night, when the only sounds are the birds and the wind rushing through the trees. A large part of Park Slope has been designated a historic district, and there are some truly impressive townhouses here. Grand Army Plaza, a colossal arch commemorating those who died in the Civil War, stands at the end of the Slope that extends along the western edge of Prospect Park. Seventh Avenue, 2 blocks from the park, is an intriguing shopping street where you can get old furniture, stained glass, ceramics, houseware, flowers, health food, vegetables, and toys. Saturday afternoons get pretty lively. To get to Park Slope from Manhattan, take the IRT 7th Avenue line to Grand Army Plaza or the IND D train to the 7th Avenue exit.

Prospect Park and the Brooklyn Botanic Gardens – Prospect Park, an Olmsted and Vaux creation, has more than 500 acres of gracefully landscaped greenery with fields, fountains, lakes, a concert bandshell, an ice skating rink in winter, a bridal path, and a zoo. The Botanic Gardens, 1000 Washington Ave. (phone: 718-622-4433), contain serene rose gardens and hothouses with orchids and other tropical plants, as well as an impressive bonsai collection, cherry trees, a Zen meditation garden, and hundreds of flowers and shrubs. Closed Mondays. No admission charge. From Manhattan, take the IRT 7th Avenue line to Eastern Parkway or take the IND D or Q train to Prospect Park.

Brooklyn Museum – In addition to its outstanding permanent anthropological collections on American Indians of both the northern and southern hemispheres, this museum hosts terrific traveling exhibitions. In the permanent collection are fine exhibits of Oriental arts, American painting and decorative arts, and European painting. The roster of artists whose work is permanently displayed includes Van Gogh, Rodin, Toulouse-Lautrec, Gauguin, Monet, and Chagall. It is also noted for its Egyptian and primitive art collections. Closed Tuesdays. Suggested donation: $3. From Manhattan, take the IRT 7th Avenue line to Eastern Parkway. 200 Eastern Pkwy. and Washington Ave. (phone: 718-638-5000).

Bay Ridge – Although Brooklynites have been fond of this Scandinavian waterfront community for years, it took the film *Saturday Night Fever* to bring it to national attention. Bay Ridge is dominated by the world's longest suspension bridge, the Verrazano-Narrows Bridge, which connects Brooklyn with Staten Island. (Some people say this bridge goes from nowhere to nowhere else, but they fail to appreciate its finer aesthetics.) Although chances are you won't see John Travolta tripping down 4th

Avenue, you will see a lot of people who look like the character he played in the film, and you'll also get to see the bridge rising over the tops of houses, shops, restaurants, and discos. A bike path runs along the edge of the Narrows from Owls Head Pier, the pier of the now-defunct Brooklyn–Staten Island ferry, all the way to the Verrazano-Narrows Bridge. The pier has recently been renovated and is a great place for fishing, watching the ships come in, and looking at a wide-angle view of lower Manhattan. To get to Bay Ridge from Manhattan, take the BMT RR train to 95th St.

Coney Island – If you've seen the classic film *The Beast from 20,000 Fathoms,* you no doubt remember the climactic final scene in which the beast is shot down from the top of a roller coaster called the Cyclone. As the monster falls, he destroys half of Coney Island. But fear not, gentle reader, Hollywood's illusion is a far cry from reality — although some disenchanted residents wish it were a lot closer to the truth. Now a long strip of garish amusement park rides, penny arcades, hot dog stands, and low-income housing complexes, Coney Island is jam-packed in summer, eerily deserted in winter. Weekends in the summer are the worst time to visit. Weekday evenings are considerably less frenetic. You can ride the Cyclone, one of the most terrifying roller coasters on the East Coast, and the Wonder Wheel, a giant Ferris wheel alongside the ocean, but the parachute jump, which is Coney Island's landmark and can be seen for miles, is no longer operational. Astroland Park: phone: 718-372-0275 or 718-265-2100. There are honky-tonk bars along the boardwalk, where country-and-western singers compete with the sound of the sea. If you get a sudden craving for Italian food, head for *Gargiulo's,* 2911 W. 15th St. (phone: 718-266-0906) for some good Neapolitan dishes. The ultimate offbeat New York treat is to have hot dogs at *Nathan's* at 2 in the morning. The area's newest ethnic flavor is provided by Russian immigrants. Surf and Stillwell Aves. Take IND F, D, or B trains to Coney Island from Manhattan. For further information, contact the Chamber of Commerce (phone: 718-266-1234).

Sheepshead Bay – More like a New England fishing village than part of New York, fishermen sell their catch on the dock in the early afternoon. Charter boats that take people out for the day leave very early in the morning. For the best view of the scene, cross the wooden footbridge at Ocean Avenue and walk along the mile-long esplanade. A few blocks south of the bay is Manhattan Beach, one of the smaller city beaches. Brighton Beach, a few blocks to the east, joins Manhattan Beach with Coney Island. To get to Sheepshead Bay from Manhattan, take the IND D train to Sheepshead Bay.

THE BRONX

If you intend to visit the Bronx, don't ask for directions from someone from Brooklyn. Because of local prejudice, residents of these boroughs often look down on each other. With almost 2 million inhabitants, the Bronx is smaller than Brooklyn; it's the only borough in the City of New York that is on the mainland. Although all the points of interest listed here are safe for visitors, some sections of the Bronx are the most dangerous parts of New York City. The South Bronx has been nicknamed Ft. Apache by the police, and one officer advises staying clear of any place south of Fordham Road.

Bronx Zoo – One of the most famous zoos in the world, it has 250 acres that house more than 3,000 animals. Elephants, tigers, chimps, seals, rhinos, hippos, birds, and buffalos are the favorites. To get there from Manhattan, take the IRT 7th Ave. #2 Express to Pelham Pkwy.; walk west to the Bronxdale entrance (for other routes, call the zoo). Open daily from 10 AM to 4:30 PM. Admission charge Fridays through Mondays; other days, donation suggested; parking, $4. At Fordham Rd. and Bronx River Pkwy. (phone: 367-1010).

New York Botanical Gardens – Adjoining the zoo to the north, the 250-acre gardens are set in an unspoiled natural forest. The site comprises the only surviving remnants of the original woodland that covered the city. The Enid A. Haupt Conservatory (closed Mondays) with its 11 pavilions — each with a totally different environment

— is a special treat. Other highlights include a rose garden, azalea glen, daffodil hill, conservatory, botanical museum, and restaurant. Well worth the trip, especially in the spring. From Manhattan take the IND D train to Bedford Park Station and walk 8 blocks east. Open daily 8 AM to 7 PM. Admission charge for the Conservatory except Saturdays before noon; parking, $4. Southern Blvd. and 200th St. (phone: 220-8700).

Bronx Museum of the Arts – This museum moved into its new permanent home in 1983. Its changing exhibitions have two themes: contemporary art and the artistic expression of the many ethnic groups who live in the borough. Classical music concerts, film programs, poetry readings, and dance performances are held throughout the year. From Manhattan, take the IRT 4 to 161st St. or the IND D to 167th St. Closed Fridays. Suggested donation: $1.50. 1040 Grand Concourse at 165th St. (phone: 681-6000).

Edgar Allan Poe Cottage – A tiny cottage, adequately cramped to inspire claustrophobia in anyone larger than a raven, sits incongruously in the middle of the Grand Concourse. Poe lived here during his last years; the cottage contains his personal belongings. Closed Mondays and Tuesdays. Admission charge. E. Kingsbridge Rd. at Grand Concourse (phone: 881-8900).

Wave Hill – A country mansion where Mark Twain, Teddy Roosevelt, and Arturo Toscanini once lived. It features a Gothic Armor Hall and beautiful gardens. Open daily. No admission charge weekdays. In the elegant, residential Riverdale section of the Bronx, 675 W. 252nd St. (phone: 549-2055).

Yankee Stadium – A landmark, the home of the Bronx Bombers. Here, in this renovated 55,000-seat stadium, Babe Ruth, Lou Gehrig, Joe DiMaggio, and dozens of other baseball stars batted. Take the IND D train from Manhattan to 161st St. Open during baseball season. 161st and River Aves. (phone: 293-6000).

Hall of Fame of Great Americans – Bronze-cast busts of great American presidents, poets, and people noted for achievement in the sciences, arts, and humanities. About 100 busts stand on podiums set atop columns. The Hall is outdoors on the Bronx Community College campus; from Manhattan take the IND D train to 183rd St. or the IRT 4 train to Burnside Ave. Closed in winter, open daily the rest of the year. No admission charge. W. 181st St. and University Ave. (phone: 220-6003 or 220-6920).

QUEENS

Manhattanites used to think of Queens as outer suburbia — until Manhattan's skyrocketing rents prompted many middle class folks to take a second look. Actually, Queens is less than 5 minutes away from Manhattan by subway and has a population of nearly 2 million. It boasts major sports facilities, 196 miles of waterfront, numerous parks, cultural centers, universities, and even a growing motion picture industry. Queens is also one of the most ethnically diverse areas in the nation, though nationalities tend to congregate in specific pockets. Greeks have settled in Astoria; Hispanics in Corona and Jackson Heights; Asians in Flushing. The largest Hindu temple in North America is found on Bowne Street in Flushing, and Flushing's Chinatown now rivals Manhattan's. These neighborhoods offer a fascinating assortment of restaurants, groceries, and bakeries — Filipino, Italian, Peruvian, Ecuadorian, Colombian, Argentinian, Greek, German — and also sponsor a number of festivals featuring their own foods, crafts, music, and dancing. For information on these activities, call Queens Borough Hall (phone: 718-520-3220).

Queens's architectural ambience can change literally from block to block — from pretty Kew Gardens to opulent Jamaica Estates and Bayside Hills, and from the quiet row houses of Flushing to the Victorian houses in Richmond Hill, Old Woodhaven, and College Point. The earliest settlement in Queens dates to 1642. It was named for Queen Catherine of Braganza and was formally incorporated in 1898. Historical sites abound, including the Friends Meeting House in Flushing. Built in 1694, it is the oldest house of worship in the US.

Sports buffs flock to Queens to see the *Mets* at *Shea Stadium,* the horse races at *Aqueduct* and *Belmont,* and the *US Open Tennis Championships* at the *USTA National Tennis Center* at the World's Fair site in Flushing Meadow Park. There are also abundant facilities for golf, tennis, swimming, ice skating, horseback riding, boating, hiking, and bird watching. Lovers of the great outdoors enjoy the borough's wetlands and woodlands, including the 2-mile Pitobik Trail, Turtle Pond, and Alley Pond Creek (phone: 718-229-4000); Forest Park (phone: 718-520-5905/6/7); Jamaica Bay Wildlife Refuge (phone: 718-474-0613); and the Queens Botanical Gardens, in Flushing (phone: 718-886-3800).

Bowne House – This "shrine to religious freedom," dating from 1661, was the home of John Bowne, a Quaker credited with winning freedom to worship in the Dutch West Indian colony from Governor Peter Stuyvesant. The house is now a museum, featuring 17th- and 18th-century furnishings, pewter, and paintings. Open 2:30 to 4:30 PM, Tuesdays, Saturdays, and Sundays. Admission charge. 37-01 Bowne St., Flushing (phone: 718-359-0528).

Kingsland House – The sole survivor of what was once the prevalent architectural style in Queens, this Dutch Colonial/English house dating to 1774 contains antique china and assorted memorabilia. Open 2:30 to 4:30 PM Tuesdays, Saturdays, and Sundays. Donations encouraged. 143-35 37th Ave., Flushing (phone: 718-939-0647).

King Mansion – Built in 1730 for Rufus King, one of the signers of the Constitution, it is a fine example of Georgian-Federal architecture. Open 1 to 4 PM, Thursdays only. Admission fee. Jamaica Ave. at 153rd St., Jamaica (phone: 718-523-1653).

Astoria Motion Picture & Television Foundation – Built on the site of the Famous Players–Lasky Studios, where the Marx Brothers films (among others) were produced, the Foundation offers filmmaking classes, lectures, and film series. An excellent permanent exhibit, "Making Movies in New York: 1896-1982," includes costumes, posters, props, old cameras, and other displays. By appointment only. 34-31 35th St., Astoria (phone: 718-784-4520).

American Museum of the Moving Image (AMMI) – A new, $15-million, multi-level museum at the site of Astoria Studios (now Kaufman Astoria Studios), which launched such stars as Clara Bow, Douglas Fairbanks, and Gary Cooper and produced the first "talkies." Visitors can tour a full-scale movie set, learn to mix sound for movies and television, and view displays of some 60,000 artifacts — costumes, scenery, posters, toys, scripts, props, fan magazines. The museum/studio will also screen major films, videos, and TV programs in two theaters on the first floor. For additional information, contact AMMI (phone: 718-784-4520).

Flushing Meadows–Corona Park – The site of the 1939 and 1964 World's Fairs and the original headquarters of the UN, the park is now a center for sports, cultural, and outdoor activities. The *Queens Museum* has a variety of changing exhibitions as well as a permanent collection that includes a 15,000-square-foot scale model of New York City. Open from 10 AM to 5 PM Tuesdays through Fridays, noon to 5:30 PM weekends. Admission charge (phone: 718-592-2405). The park's New York Hall of Science opened in 1987; its permanent exhibitions include laser displays and cow's-eye dissections. Open from 10 AM to 5 PM Wednesdays through Sundays. Donations encouraged (phone: 718-699-0005). The *Queens Theater-in-the-Park,* near *Shea Stadium,* presents musicals, plays, concerts, and dance ensembles (phone: 718-592-5700). There is also a Children's Zoo, open daily from 9:30 AM to 4:30 PM. No admission charge (phone: 718-699-4275).

STATEN ISLAND

Much closer to New Jersey than New York, Staten Island is the Big Apple's most remote borough and, with about 375,000 people, its least populous. Since the Verrazano-Narrows Bridge opened in 1964, Staten Island has been filling up with suburban housing developments and shopping centers. However, a few farms remain in southern

Staten Island. To find them, take the bus marked Richmond Ave. at the ferry terminal. Getting around Staten Island by public transportation takes a long time. Driving is recommended if at all possible.

Staten Island Zoo – Considerably smaller than the Bronx Zoo, this zoo is near a lake in Barret Park. Its specialty is reptiles, and snakes of all descriptions. Open daily 10 AM to 4:45 PM. Admission charge: donation suggested. 614 Broadway and Clove Rd. (phone: 718-442-3101).

Jacques Marchais Center for Tibetan Art – One of the esoteric treasures of the city, this is also one of the best-kept secrets in the metropolitan area. A reconstructed Tibetan prayer hall with adjoining library and gardens with Oriental sculpture, the center sits on a hill overlooking a pastoral, un–New York setting of trees. *The Tibetan Book of the Dead,* other occult tomes, prayer wheels, statuary, and weavings are on display. Open only Fridays through Sundays in April, October, and November; extended hours May through September. Admission charge. 338 Lighthouse Ave. (phone: 718-987-3478).

Conference House – This manor house was built in 1670 and hosted such Revolutionary War notables as Benjamin Franklin. Crafts demonstrations are usually offered on the first Sunday of each month; call ahead. Open from 1 to 4 PM Wednesdays to Sundays. Admission charge. 7455 Hylan Blvd. (phone: 718-984-2086).

Richmondtown Restoration – A 96-acre park, with exhibits and crafts demonstrations harking back to the early Dutch settlers. Open from 10 AM to 5 PM weekdays, 1 to 5 PM weekends and holidays. Admission charge. 441 Clarke Ave. (phone: 718-351-1617).

SOURCES AND RESOURCES

TOURIST INFORMATION: The New York Convention and Visitors Bureau, 2 Columbus Circle, New York, NY 10019 (phone: 397-8222), is an excellent source for tourist information and assistance. Its office carries hotel and restaurant information, subway and bus maps, descriptive brochures, and current listings of the city's entertainment and activities, and it is staffed by multilingual aides. The New York Chamber of Commerce and Industry can mail informative brochures and pamphlets to people planning to move to the New York area. Some of the details may be out of date, but the literature can be helpful. Contact the Chamber at 200 Madison Ave., New York, NY 10016 (phone: 561-2020). For further information, contact the New York State Department of Economic Development, Division of Tourism, 1515 Broadway, 51st Floor, New York, NY 10036 (phone: 827-6250).

Visitors who require assistance in an emergency — anything from a lost wallet to a lost child — should stop at the Traveler's Aid Services office at 158-160 W. 42nd St. (phone: 944-0013); open weekdays 9 AM to 6 PM (Wednesdays to 1 PM), weekends 9:30 AM to 3 PM. There is also a branch at the International Arrivals Building at Kennedy Airport (phone: 718-656-4870); open weekdays 10 AM to 8 PM, weekends 1 to 8 PM.

Numerous excellent guides to the city's architecture and history are available at most good-size bookstores.

Television Stations – Channel 2–WCBS; Channel 4–WNBC; Channel 5–WNYW; Channel 7–WABC; Channel 13–WNET.

Radio Stations – AM: WOR 710 (news/talk); WCBS 880 (news/talk); WFAN 660 (sports/talk); WQXR 1560 (classical music). FM: WNYC 93.9 (classical); WQXR 96.3 (classical); WBGO 88 (jazz); WNEW 102.7 (rock); WBLS 107.5 (urban contemporary).

Local Coverage – *The New York Times,* the *Daily News,* and *New York Newsday* are all morning dailies. The *New York Post* comes out twice daily, and the *Village Voice* weekly. Other publications include the weekly *New Yorker* and *New York* magazines.

Telephone – The area code for Manhattan and the Bronx is 212; the area code for Brooklyn, Queens, and Staten Island is 718.

Food – *Restaurants of New York,* by Seymour Britchky ($10.95); *Zagat New York City Restaurant Survey* ($8.95); and Mimi Sheraton's *Favorite New York Restaurants* (Simon & Schuster; $9.95).

Sales Tax – New York City's sales tax is 8¼%; hotel tax is 13¼%.

CLIMATE: The best times to visit New York are in the spring — April to mid-May — and in the fall — mid-September through October — when temperatures are comfortable, in the high 60s to low 70s. Winter and summer are extreme, averaging in the 80s and up in July and August, in the 30s or below during the months of hard winter. However, the weather should not determine your visit, since most of what makes New York great takes place indoors, and air conditioning and central heating are standard. New Yorkers dress informally for many events; anything in good taste goes. Remember, there is no rainy season as such — it can happen any day of the year. Be prepared. And during the warm months, a sweater or a wrap is usually welcome after an hour or so of sitting in an air conditioned place. Wintertime can be quite cold; boots, hats, gloves, and a heavy coat are necessities.

GETTING AROUND: Airports – New York City is served by three major airports: John F. Kennedy International (JFK) and La Guardia (for domestic flights) — both in the borough of Queens — and Newark International, across the Hudson in New Jersey. It takes 50 to 60 minutes to reach JFK from midtown Manhattan by cab and costs about $30. La Guardia from midtown is a 30- to 45-minute ride, with a fare of around $20. Newark International from midtown is the meter amount (usually about $40), plus $10 and tolls; one fare covers up to four or five passengers and their luggage (except trunks, which are 50¢ extra).

Quick and relatively inexpensive transportation is available via several bus lines. *Carey Transportation* (phone: 800-AIR-RIDE or 800-247-7433) provides service from 125 Park Ave. between 41st and 42nd Sts., the Air Trans Center at the Port Authority Bus Terminal, and the *Hilton, Sheraton City Squire*, and *Marriott Marquis* hotels to JFK and La Guardia airports. Buses leave every 20 or 30 minutes. One-way fare to JFK is $8, $6 for La Guardia; Carey also runs a shuttle between these two airports ($7). *New Jersey Transit* handles service to Newark International out of the Port Authority Bus Terminal (phone: 564-8484), on 8th Ave. between 40th and 42nd Sts. Purchase tickets ($5) at the Air Trans Center desk on the ground floor of the terminal's North Wing. Buses depart every 15 to 30 minutes and the trip takes about a half hour. *Olympia Trails* (phone: 964-6233 in New York, 201-374-6660 in New Jersey) provides coach service every 20 minutes on weekdays from Newark International's North, A, B, and C terminals to the World Trade Center and Grand Central Terminal, and hourly from La Guardia and Kennedy to the World Trade Center only; the fare is $5. *Newark International Airport–New York City Mini Bus Service* (phone: 201-961-2535) is yet another alternative. It takes passengers from Newark to midtown Manhattan hotels for $12.

New York Helicopter (phone: 800-645-3494) offers daily flights from midtown's 34th St. Heliport to JFK in 10 minutes. One-way fare is $58 plus tax.

Pan Am's *Water Shuttle* (phone: 800-54-FERRY) sails hourly from Pier 11 at South and Wall Sts. to La Guardia's Marine Air Terminal; the fare is $20.

If luggage is light, travelers headed for JFK from Manhattan or Brooklyn can take the JFK Express, a combination bus and subway airport connection. The service operates every 20 minutes and is $6.50. For a subway map and more information see *Subways,* below.

The fare on New York City buses and subways (and the Roosevelt Island tramway) is $1, no matter how far you travel. Tokens are required on the subway.

Bus – New York City buses run frequently. There are more than 220 routes and over 3,800 buses in operation. Although slower than subways, buses bring you closer to your destination, stopping about every two blocks. The main routes in Manhattan are north-south on the avenues, and east-west (crosstown) on the streets, as well as some crisscross and circular routes. Check both the sign on the front of the bus and the one at the bus stop to make sure the bus you want stops where you are waiting. Be sure to have exact change for the basic fare (subway tokens are preferred), and ask for a transfer, should you need one, when you board the bus. *Bus drivers do not make change nor do they accept bills, but they do accept tokens.* Transfers should be obtained from the bus driver at the time of paying your fare; they are free. Most bus routes operate 24 hours a day, 7 days a week, but a few do not run late at night or on Sundays. For information on buses to points outside Manhattan from the Port Authority Bus Terminal, call 564-8484. Free bus maps are available at Grand Central and Penn Stations or by sending a stamped, self-addressed #10 envelope to the New York Transit Authority, Room 875, 370 Jay St., Brooklyn, NY 11201, Attn.: Maps. For information, call 718-330-1234.

Subways – No doubt about it, the New York subway system is confusing and became more so with the December 1988 opening of the Archer Avenue Extension, a long-delayed improvement project. Designed to reach inaccessible parts of Queens, the extension affected service in the other boroughs as well, and as we went to press, the changes — some extensive — were not reflected on the maps posted in subway stations. But this is no reason to avoid the subway. Its convenience and speed can't be duplicated by any other form of transportation, and the intelligence of its overall design is awesome. Pick up a free subway map at any token booth or at the Convention and Visitors Bureau.

Basically, there are three different subway lines, with express and local routes serving all city boroughs except for Staten Island (reached via the Staten Island Ferry). The most extensive line is the IRT, which originates in Brooklyn and traverses Manhattan en route to the Bronx. The IRT has two main divisions: the 7th Avenue line, which serves the West Side of Manhattan, and the Lexington Avenue line, which covers the East Side. You can go from east to west (crosstown) on the shuttle (SS) or IRT 7 train between Grand Central Station and Times Square. The IND serves Brooklyn, Queens, Manhattan, and the Bronx. The BMT serves Brooklyn, Queens, and Manhattan. The subway is the most heavily used means of city transportation (almost 4 million people ride it daily on 230 miles of track) and is mobbed during rush hours, weekdays from 7:30 to 9 AM and from 4:30 to 7 PM. Buy tokens at booths in the subway stations and insert them in turnstiles to enter the subway. Buy a 10-pack of tokens to save time. The subway system operates 24 hours a day. At night, the lights outside many stations indicate accessibility: A red light means the station is closed; a yellow light indicates that a token is required for entry (no clerk on duty at the token booth); and a green light means both the station and token booth are fully open. For further information, call the NY Transit Authority (phone: 718-330-1234).

Taxi – The handiest and most expensive way to get around the city is by cab. Cabs can be hailed almost anywhere and are required to pick you up and deliver you to your specified destination. Cabs can be identified by their yellow color and are available if their roof light is on. Cabbies expect a 20% tip. There is a 50¢ surcharge on some cab fares between 8 PM and 6 AM.

Car Rental – New York is served by all the major car rental companies as well as a host of small local firms.

LOCAL SERVICES: Babysitting – Ask at the hotel desk for recommended babysitting services.

Business Services – *A Steno Service* (phone: 682-4990) and *Ann H. Tanners Co.* (phone: 687-2870) for secretarial services; *QED Transcription Service* (phone: 563-0740) or *Wordflow* (phone: 725-5111), for taping and immediate transcription of meetings and seminars.

Limousine Service – *London Town Cars* (phone: 988-9700 or 800-221-4009).

SPECIAL EVENTS: January–February, *Chinese New Year Celebration and Dragon Parade,* Chinatown; March 17, *St. Patrick's Day Parade,* 5th Ave.; Easter Sunday, *Easter Parade,* 5th Ave.; May, *Ninth Avenue International Festival;* May, *Washington Square Outdoor Art Show,* Greenwich Village; first Sunday in June, *Puerto Rican Day Parade,* 5th Ave.; June, *JVC Jazz Festival,* throughout city; July-August, free *Shakespeare Festival, Delacorte Theater,* Central Park; free performances, *NY Philharmonic, Metropolitan Opera,* all boroughs; August, Harlem Week; late August–September, *US Open Tennis Championships, USTA National Tennis Center,* Queens; September, *African-American Day Parade;* September, the 10-day *Festival of San Gennaro,* patron saint of the Neapolitans, Mulberry St., Little Italy; September–October, *New York Film Festival,* Lincoln Center; October, *Columbus Day Parade,* 5th Ave.; October 31, *Halloween Parade,* Greenwich Village; October or November, *NYC Marathon;* November, *Veterans Day Parade; Macy's Thanksgiving Day Parade,* Broadway, Herald Square; December, *Christmas Tree Lighting,* Rockefeller Plaza; November–January, the *Great Christmas Show,* Radio City Music Hall.

For borough-by-borough information on parades, festivals, exhibits, and free events, call 360-1333 (Manhattan); 718-783-4469 (Brooklyn); 590-3500 (Bronx); 718-447-4485 (Staten Island); and 718-291-1100 (Queens).

MUSEUMS: The city boasts more than 100 museums. The *Guggenheim, Museum of Modern Art, Metropolitan Museum, Hayden Planetarium, American Museum of Natural History, Cloisters, Brooklyn Museum, Jacques Marchais Center for Tibetan Art,* and *Fraunces Tavern Museum* are described in *Special Places.* Other notable New York museums include the following:

American Craft Museum – 40 W. 53rd St. (phone: 956-6047).

Asia Society – 725 Park Ave. (phone: 288-6400).

Center for African Art – 52–54 E. 68th St. (phone: 861-1200).

Cooper-Hewitt Museum – A branch of the Smithsonian Institution, featuring textiles and material arts. 2 E. 91st St. (phone: 860-6868).

Forbes Galleries – World's largest collection of Fabergé Imperial Easter eggs, plus toy boats and soldiers. 62 5th Ave. at 12th St. (phone: 620-2389).

Frick Collection – The Pittsburgh industrialist Henry Clay Frick's collection of paintings, sculpture, porcelains, furniture, and antiques. 1 E. 70th St. at 5th Ave. (phone: 288-0700).

Guinness World of Records – In the Empire State Bldg., 350 5th Ave. (phone: 947-2335).

International Center of Photography – 1130 5th Ave. at E. 94th St. (phone: 860-1777) and 77 W. 45th St. (phone: 869-2155).

Intrepid Sea–Air Space Museum – World War II aircraft carrier has exhibits on the Navy, pioneers of aviation, and technology. Permanently moored at Pier 86 on the Hudson River, W. 46th St. at 12th Ave. (phone: 245-0072).

Jewish Museum – 1109 5th Ave. at E. 92 St. (phone: 860-1888).

Museo del Barrio – Hispanic art. 1230 5th Ave. at E. 104th St. (phone: 831-7272).

Lower East Side Tenement Museum – 97 Orchard St. (phone: 431-0233).

Museum of American Folk Art – 49 W. 53rd St. (phone: 581-2475).

Museum of the American Indian – 3753 Broadway at W. 155th St. (phone: 283-2420).

Museum of Broadcasting – 1 E. 53rd St. (phone: 752-7684).

Museum of the City of New York – 5th Ave. at E. 103rd St. (phone: 534-1672).

Museum of Holography – 11 Mercer St. (phone: 925-0526).

New York Historical Society – 170 Central Park West at W. 77th St. (phone: 873-3400).

Pierpont Morgan Library – Old Masters drawings, early printed books, and music manuscripts, plus a public research library. 29 E. 36th St. at Madison Ave. (phone: 685-0008).

Studio Museum in Harlem – Exhibitions of works by Black artists; workshops by artists in residence. 144 W. 125th St. (phone: 864-4500).

Whitney Museum of American Art – 945 Madison Ave. at E. 75th St. (phone: 570-3676); new branches in the Philip Morris Bldg., 120 Park Ave. at E. 42nd St. (phone: 878-2550); and at Equitable Center, 787 7th Ave. at W. 51st St. (phone: 554-1113).

SHOPPING: This city is like no other for acquiring material possessions. It is the commercial center and the fashion capital of the country, and styles that originate here set the trends for fashionable folk from Portland, Maine, to Portland, Oregon. The scope of merchandise available approaches the infinite, and there's a price range for every budget.

Bloomingdale's, A World unto Itself – Considered by many to be the ultimate in Upper East Side chic; it's lost some of its cachet, though many still flock here. Whether you want satin running shorts or a sequined evening gown, you'll find it here. Saturdays on the main floor is something of a social event, particularly for suburban teenagers. E. 59th St. between Lexington and 3rd Aves. (phone: 355-5900 or 705-2073).

Bookstores – The publishing capital of the world, New York is a bibliophile's delight. Leaders among its outlets include *Barnes and Noble,* 105 5th Ave. at 18th St. (phone: 807-0099), 600 5th Ave. at 48th St. (phone: 765-0590), and several other locations, which carries a wide selection at bargain prices. *B. Dalton,* 666 5th Ave. at W. 52nd St. (phone: 247-1740), and at two other Manhattan locations (open daily); and *Doubleday,* 673 5th Ave. at E. 53rd St. (phone: 223-6550) and 724 5th Ave. at 56th St. (phone: 397-0550), all carry a broad variety of new titles and trade books. The *Strand,* 828 Broadway at E. 12th St. (phone: 473-1452), has a huge collection of old and used books and even some rare manuscripts. For an unusual selection of out-of-print books in an out-of-the-way location, visit *Isaac Mendoza Book Co.,* 15 Ann St. (phone: 227-8777). *Rizzoli,* 31 W. 57th St. (phone: 759-2424) and 454A W. Broadway (phone: 674-1616), is best known for its collection of art, music, and photography books. *Gotham Book Mart,* 41 W. 47th St. (phone: 719-4448), specializes in contemporary literature and poetry, and sells books on theater and film. *Kitchen Arts & Letters,* 1435 Lexington Ave. at E. 93rd St. (phone: 876-5550), is a bookstore and gallery exclusively devoted to food and wine. *Forbidden Planet,* 821 Broadway at E. 12th St. (phone: 473-1576), with a branch at 227 E. 59th St. (phone: 751-4386), has the wackiest bunch of comics, science fiction, masks, and monsters you're liable to find this side of Mars. *New York Astrology Center,* 63 W. 38th St., 5th Floor (phone: 719-2919), claims to have the country's largest selection of books on astrology. The *Complete Traveller Bookstore,* 22 W. 52nd St. (phone: 685-9007); *Traveller's Bookstore,* 75 Rockefeller Plaza at W. 52nd St. (phone: 664-0995); and *Banana Republic,* 2376 Broadway at W. 87th St. (phone: 874-3500), all have enviable troves of travel literature. Architecture buffs should head to *Perimeter,* 146 Sullivan St. (phone: 529-2275). And bookish-minded toddlers will be delighted by *Eeyore's Books for Children,* 25 E. 83rd St. (phone: 988-3404) and 2212 Broadway at W. 79th St. (phone: 362-0634).

Boutiques and Specialty Shops – Fifth Avenue in the East Fifties and Madison Avenue in the East Sixties and Seventies are lined with boutiques that carry haute couture at hauts prix, but looking is free. The names are an encyclopedia of style: *Versace, Kenzo, Sonia Rykiel, Daniel Hechter, Emanuel Ungaro, Saint Laurent, Armani, Valentino, Gucci, Ralph Lauren, Tahari, Jaeger, Chanel,* and the like. Other interesting, superb merchandise can be found in shops such as *Alcott & Andrews,* 335 Madison Ave. at E. 44th St. (phone: 818-0606) and 1301 6th Ave at W. 52nd St. (phone: 315-2796), for fine, color-coordinated classics and business attire for women. Also on the cutting edge of fashion are the styles at *Charivari Workshop,* 441 Columbus Ave. at W. 81st St. (phone: 496-8700), and at five other locations around town. For casual Italian sweaters in the latest styles, visit one of the city's many *Benetton* stores (there are a few on Fifth Avenue in the forties). For the finest in raincoats, there's *Burberrys,* 9 E. 57th St. (phone: 371-5010); and *Aquascutum of London,* 680 Fifth Ave. at E. 54th St. (phone: 975-0250). *Ashanti,* 872 Lexington Ave. at E. 65th St. (phone: 535-0740), specializes in stylish clothes for larger women. *Polo/Ralph Lauren,* 867 Madison Ave. at 72nd St. (phone: 606-2100), in the Rhinelander Mansion (1884), is a showcase for the designer's men's, women's, and boys' collections.

Indoor urban malls are a new phenomenon in New York City; they arrived in 1984 with the glitzy Trump Tower, 725 5th Ave. between 56th and 57th Sts. The tenants in the tower's 6-story marble and mirrored atrium are among the world's most opulent (and most expensive) vendors: *Harry Winston's Petit Salon, Asprey's, Boehm Porcelain, Buccellati* (silversmiths), *Charles Jourdan* (men's and women's shoes), *Martha* and *Lina Lee* (both for women's fashions), *Loewe* (leather goods), *Pineider* (stationery and fine writing implements), and *Norman Crider Antiques.*

Herald Center, opened in 1985, spans the block between W. 33rd and 34th Sts. on 7th Ave.; about 70 retail and restaurant outlets are in operation. The directory is less exclusive than Trump Tower's, but many prestigious names are in residence, such as *Ann Taylor, Alfred Dunhill,* and *Charles Jourdan.*

In lower Manhattan, Pier 17 at the *South Street Seaport* is another shopper's paradise.

Department Stores – *Macy's,* Broadway at 34th St. (phone: 695-4400), is the quintessential New York department store. You can buy what you need and choose from a large assortment of high-quality, stylish goods, but most people come here for the total experience of shopping — browsing, watching, and buying. *Macy's* basement emporium, the *Cellar,* is designed as a street lined with shops that carry everything from fruits and vegetables to housewares, and restaurants, including the *Cellar Grill,* which serves a variety of pizza, pasta, and grilled meats. *B. Altman,* at 5th Ave. and 34th St. (phone: 679-7800), has a good selection of women's and men's clothing and housewares. *Lord & Taylor,* 5th Ave. and 39th St. (phone: 391-3344), has stylish, rather conservative clothing and a bright, airy atmosphere that makes browsing enjoyable. *Saks Fifth Avenue,* 5th Ave. and 49th St. (phone: 753-4000), is where you can be sure to get whatever is chic this season. *Bonwit Teller,* 4 E. 57th St. (phone: 593-3333), seems to be a cross between *Lord & Taylor* and *Saks. Bergdorf Goodman,* 5th Ave. and 58th St. (phone: 753-7300), is the epitome of elegant shopping. In some haute couture salons, you sit in a parlor overlooking Central Park while salespeople bring merchandise for you to examine, then escort you to the fitting room. *Henri Bendel,* 10 W. 57th St. (phone: 247-1100), carries an impressive selection of trendy clothes, accessories, and miscellany. The new *Barney's for Women,* 7th Ave. at W. 17th St. (phone: 929-9000), is a major fashion player. *Abraham and Straus,* 420 Fulton St. in downtown Brooklyn (phone: 718-875-7200), carries a complete stock of moderately priced goods.

Jewelry and Gems – Diamonds are a girl's best friend, they say, and so as not to limit ourselves, we'll include emeralds, rubies, sapphires, gold, silver, and other precious metals. And so as not to discriminate, we'll include men, too. Without a doubt, the most famous of all luxury emporiums is *Tiffany & Co.*, 727 5th Ave. at 57th St. (phone: 755-8000). If you must have something from *Tiffany's* but can't afford a necklace or ring, you can purchase a novelty like a silver bookmark or toothpaste roller. Across the street, *Harry Winston,* 718 5th Ave. at 56th St. (phone: 245-2000), has display cases, but most of the jewels are kept in an inner sanctum. After conferring with .a salesperson, the items you wish to see are brought for your inspection. *Cartier,* 653 5th Ave. at 52nd St. (phone: 753-0111) and in Trump Tower (phone: 308-0840), is renowned for highly polished silver and some of the world's finest jewelry and accessories. *Fortunoff,* 681 5th Ave. at 59th (phone: 758-6660), has a variety of fine gems, sterling, gold, and porcelain in a wide range of prices. For bold Brazilian jewelry, stop in at *H. Stern Jewellers,* 645 5th Ave. at 51st St. (phone: 688-0300) and also at several hotels. *Fred Leighton,* 773 Madison (phone: 288-1872), is known for its antique, deco designs. For splendid glass sculpture, bowls, trays, and goblets, go to *Steuben Glass,* 715 5th Ave. at 56th St. (phone: 752-1441).Known for quality and quantity in pearls is *Mikimoto,* 608 5th Ave. at 49th St. (phone: 586-7153). Other noted jewelers are *David Webb,* 7 E. 57th St. (phone: 421-3030); *Van Cleef & Arpels,* 744 5th Ave. at 57th St. (phone: 644-9500) and also in *Bergdorf Goodman;* the new *Black, Starr & Frost,* in the *Plaza* hotel (phone: 838-0720); and for watches, *Tourneau Corner,* 500 Madison Ave. at E. 52nd St. (phone: 758-3265) and also in *Bonwit Teller.*

If your budget is limited, do your gem shopping along 47th Street between 5th and 6th Avenues. That's the heart of New York's wholesale jewelry district, and the best place to find sparkling stuff at mortal prices. And if you're planning to get married (or even reaffirm your vows), *Bill Schifrin* (Booth 86 at the National Jewelers Exchange, 4 W. 47th St. (phone: 944-1713) is a good place to stop; it has the largest collection of wedding rings in the world.

Kitchen Equipment – The Bowery is New York's kitchenware and lamp district, where large wholesale houses such as the *Federal Restaurant Supply Co.,* 202 Bowery St. (phone: 226-0441), offer some commercial products at very reasonable prices. The *Bridge Co.*, 214 E. 52nd St. at 3rd Ave. (phone: 688-4220), has four floors of kitchenware. You can find every possible domestic and imported item here, from cherry pitters to egg slicers. Selecting a single pot or pan could occupy several hours or a full day, given the number and variety on display.

Knickknacks – *Jenny B. Goode,* 1194 Lexington Ave. at E. 81st St. (phone: 794-2492) and 11 E. 10th St. (phone: 505-7666), sells amusing nostalgia and contemporary adaptations (soft-sculpture, mugs with gorgeous gam handles, watches disguised as giant Oreo cookies) that are a serendipitous delight. *Mythology,* 370 Columbus Ave. at W. 77th St. (phone: 874-0774), has a wonderful selection of antique toys, modern robots, rubber stamps with hundreds of designs, unusual jewelry, and plastic food that looks good enough to eat. *Belle Epoch,* 211 E. 60th St. at 3rd Ave. (phone: 319-7870), has very interesting tabletop antiques as well as a lovely collection of antique jewelry.

Round the world in a unique way with a trip to the *United Nations Gift Shop,* UN Bldg., 1st Ave. at E. 46th St. (phone: 754-7700), featuring handicrafts, ethnic clothing, native jewelry, indigenous toys — lots of beautiful things from many UN member states. Also visit *Liberty of London*'s new shop, featuring the popular textiles and notions of one of Britain's leading stores; it's at 108 W. 39th St. (phone: 391-2150), not far from *Lord & Taylor.* It also has an uptown location: 229 E. 60th (phone: 888-1057).

Luggage and Leather Goods – You'll have no trouble finding a wide selection of high- and low-priced luggage and leather goods in New York. *Hermès,* 11 E. 57th St. (phone: 751-3181), is known the world over for spectacular silk scarves and ties, saddles and other fine leather goods in a variety of exotic skins, all at heart-stopping prices. *Louis Vuitton,* 51 E. 57th St. (phone: 371-6111), has a large selection of leather goods (made in France) sporting the famous "LV" logo. However, if you prefer interlocking "G"s, visit *Gucci,* 685 and 689 Fifth Ave. at 54th St. (phone: 826-2600). For elegant, high-quality merchandise that's only slightly less pricey, try *Crouch & Fitzgerald,* 400 Madison Ave. at E. 48th St. (phone: 755-5888); *Mark Cross,* 645 5th Ave. at 51st St. (phone: 421-3000); or *T. Anthony,* 480 Park Ave. at E. 58th St. (phone: 750-9797). Along less expensive lines, you will run into several reasonable leather goods and luggage stores during your strolls around the East and West Sides and the Lower East Side.

Men's Clothes – Manhattan has fashions to fit every man's taste, from the ultra-expensive chic at *Bijan* (by appointment only), 699 5th Ave. between 54th and 55th Sts. (phone: 758-7500); to *Billy Martin's Western Wear,* 812 Madison Ave. at E. 68th St. (phone: 861-3100); to the discounted conservative styles at *Mernsmart,* 1 Vesey St., 75 Church St. (phone: 227-5471) and 2 W. 46th St. (phone: 840-3310). *Brooks Brothers,* 346 Madison Ave. at E. 44th St. (phone: 682-8800) and 1 Liberty Plaza downtown (phone: 267-2400); *J. Press,* 16 E. 44th St. (phone: 687-7642); and *F. R. Tripler,* 366 Madison Ave. at E. 46th St. (phone: 922-1090), all offer expensive, high-quality conservative business suits and other classic menswear. *Burton's Natural Cloth,* 14 E. 41st St. (phone: 685-3760); and *St. Laurie,* 897 Broadway at E. 20th St. (phone: 473-0100), carry similar merchandise with slightly lower price tags. *Paul Stuart,* Madison Ave. at E. 45th St. (phone: 682-0320), offers an expensive but less strictly traditional collection of top-quality clothing, while *Barney's,* 106 7th Ave. at W. 17th St. (phone: 929-9000), has an eclectic array of goods that ranges from Hickey Freeman and Bill Blass to the top European designers. For Italian alta moda in SoHo, try *Di Mitri,* 110 Greene St. (phone: 431-1090).

Poster and Print Shops – *The Old Print Shop,* 150 Lexington Ave. at E. 29th St. (phone: 683-3950), has a huge collection of early American prints, watercolors, and paintings ranging in price from $10 to $20,000. For contemporary theater posters and some collector's items, try the *Triton Gallery,* 323 W. 45th St., between 8th and 9th Aves. (phone: 765-2472). Rare movie posters are available at *Poster America,* 138 W. 18th St. (phone: 206-0499), and *Jerry Ohlinger's,* 242 W. 14th St. (phone: 989-0869).

Records and Tapes – There are a number of places where you can get good prices. *Sam Goody's,* at 51 W. 51st St. (phone: 246-8730) and 666 3rd Ave. at E. 43rd St. (phone: 986-8480), stocks new labels, classical, jazz, and foreign music as well as audio equipment. Two chain stores, *King Karol* and *Disc-o-mat,* carry a lot of labels at prices lower than standard retail stores. *Disc-o-mat*'s main store is at 716 Lexington Ave. at E. 58th St. (phone: 759-3777). *King Karol*'s main store is at 1521 3rd Ave. at 85th St. (phone: 988-9557). *Tower Records,* at 692 Broadway and E. 4th St. (phone: 505-1500), is the world's largest record store and is open until midnight every day of the year; there's also a branch uptown at 1965 Broadway and 66th St. (phone: 799-2500). *J&R Music World* at 33 Park Row (phone: 349-0062) has the best selection of new and hard-to-find jazz records at good prices. *House of Oldies* at 35 Carmine St. (phone: 243-0500) specializes in discs from the past. *Gryphon Record Shop,* 251 W. 72nd St., #2F, between Broadway and West End Ave. (phone: 874-1588), has 60,000 out-of-print records. *Colony Records,* at Broadway and 49th St. (phone: 265-2050), has a limited but diverse selection of music, most notably Broadway cast albums.

Sheets and Pillowcases – For good buys on top-brand and designer sheets and pillowcases, New York is definitely the place. At *Ezra Cohen,* 307 Grand (phone: 925-7800); *H & G Cohen Bedding Co.,* 306 Grand St. (phone: 226-0818); and *J. Shachter,* 115 Allen St. (phone: 533-1150), you can find all the major brands at a 25% to 30% discount. *J. Shachter* also specializes in making comforters from any fabric you wish. (All are closed Saturdays and open Sundays, typical of the stores on the Lower East Side).

Shoes – All of the expensive, top shoe designers are represented: *Ferragamo,* 730 5th Ave. at 57th St. (phone: 246-6211), for men, and 717 5th Ave. at 56th St. (phone: 759-3822), for women; *Bally of Switzerland,* 711 5th Ave. between 55th and 56th Sts.

(phone: 751-9082) and at three other Manhattan locations for men, and 689 Madison Ave. at E. 62nd St. (phone: 751-2163), for women; *Bruno Magli,* 681 5th Ave. (phone: 355-3280), for men only; *Charles Jourdan,* 725 5th Ave. in Trump Tower (phone: 644-3830) and 769 Madison Ave. at E. 66th St. (phone: 628-0133); *Carrano,* 677 5th Ave. (phone: 752-6111) and 750 Madison Ave. at E. 65th St. (phone: 570-9020); and *Maud Frizon,* 49 E. 57th St. (phone: 980-1460). For well-made men's boots and shoes, stock up at *McCreedy & Schreiber,* 37 W. 46th St. between 5th and 6th Aves. (phone: 719-1552) or 213 E. 59th St. between 2nd and 3rd Aves. (phone: 759-9241). *Shoetown,* 291 7th Ave. at W. 26th St. (phone: 675-3100), has a wide selection of women's designer shoes at discount prices.

Special Shopping Districts – The ultimate shopping experience is on the Lower East Side of Manhattan, if you're up to it. Along Orchard Street, Delancey Street, and all the side streets, you'll find incredible bargains in all manner of clothing, housewares, foam padding; but finding them is only half the battle. Then you have to fight for them, and the haggling begins. The merchant says something along the lines of, "I couldn't give you this for a penny less than $12," to which you respond that it's not worth more than 50¢, and usually you come to terms, apparently unsatisfactory to both of you. A lot of the selling is done in a mixture of Yiddish, English, Russian, and Spanish — particularly the counting — and if you know any or all four, you'll do better than wholesale. See *Special Places* for more on the Lower East Side.

Sporting Goods – The most elegant sporting goods store is *Abercrombie & Fitch* at South Street Seaport (phone: 809-9000) and at Trump Tower (phone: 832-1001). *Herman's,* New York's best-known sporting goods chain, has everything, but *Paragon* says it has more. At either one, you can find just about every piece of sporting gear and wear under the sun. *Herman's* stores are at 110 Nassau (phone: 233-0733), 135 W. 42nd St. (phone: 730-7400), 39 W. 34th St. (phone: 279-8900), and 845 3rd Ave. at E. 53rd St. (phone: 688-4603). *Paragon* is at 867 Broadway at E. 18th St. (phone: 255-8036). Serious joggers should stop in at the *Super Runners Shop* in Herald Center, at 7th Ave. between 33rd and 34th Sts. (phone: 564-9190) and three other locations. *Gerry Cosby's,* 3 Penn Plaza (phone: 563-6464), outfits professional teams and offers top-of-the-line sporting goods and souvenirs. *Orvis,* at 355 Madison Ave. (phone: 697-3133), has fishing and hunting gear.

Thrift Shops – Most thrift shops carry a variety of merchandise, from men's and women's clothing to household items and appliances to furniture. The best area for thrifting in New York is the upper East Eighties along 1st, 2nd, and 3rd Aves. Unfortunately, many of the secondhand clothes stores in New York carry the price tags of fine antiques stores. Some interesting places to try are *Stuyvesant Square Thrift Shop,* 1704 2nd Ave. at E. 96th St. (phone: 831-1830); *Irvington House Thrift Shop,* 1534 2nd Ave. at E. 80th St. (phone: 879-4555); *Thrift Shop East,* 336 E. 86th St. between 1st and 2nd Aves. (phone: 772-6868); and *Spence-Chapin Thrift Shop,* 1424 3rd Ave. at E. 80th St. (phone: 737-8448).

Toys – Once immersed in the enchanting world of children's toys at *FAO Schwarz,* GM Bldg., 5th Ave. at 58th St. (phone: 644-9400), adults have as difficult a time as children leaving empty-handed. It has every kind of toy — from precious antiques and mechanical spaceships to simple construction sets and building blocks. The prices are very high. *The Enchanted Forest,* 85 Mercer (phone: 925-2677), and *Toy Park,* 112 E. 86th St. (phone: 427-6611), also have fine merchandise.

Trendy Gear – There are several large outlets in New York for the stylish military attire that has put practical army surplus clothes and gear on the fashion pages. The best stores for work shirts, pea jackets, navy pants, jeans, combat boots, and other surplus attire, which have the unique combination of being both "in" and inexpensive, are *I. Buss,* 738 Broadway (phone: 529-4655); *Parachute,* 121 Wooster St. (phone: 925-8630); *Unique Clothing Warehouse,* 718 Broadway between Waverly and

Washington Sts. (phone: 674-1767), and *Hudson's,* 97 3rd Ave. at E. 12th St. (phone: 473-7320).

Uniquely New York – Probably nowhere else on earth could you find everything from earplugs to fine silver under one roof. *Hammacher Schlemmer,* 147 E. 57th St. between 3rd and Lexington Aves. (phone: 421-9000), has it all. And what it doesn't have, whether it's a chotchka or a real white elephant, it'll try to order.

47th St. Photo, 67 W. 47th St. (phone: 398-1410), is a bare-bones bargain center for cameras, computers, and other electronic gear with excellent discounts and a huge selection (some 5,000 items in stock). The tiny 2nd-floor headquarters, as well as its branches at 115 W. 45th St. and 116 Nassau St., tend to be chaotic with customers; know what you want before you go, because salespeople will not spend time helping you decide. Closed Friday afternoons and Saturdays; open Sundays.

 MAJOR COLLEGES AND UNIVERSITIES: New York City has a variety of leading institutions of higher education, some offering a broad-based liberal arts curriculum, others concentrating in areas of specialization, and all of them enriching New York as a center of culture and learning. Among them are: Barnard College, Broadway at W. 117th St. (phone: 280-5262); Brooklyn College, Bedford Ave. and Ave. H (phone: 718-780-5485); the City College of City University, Convent Ave. at W. 138th St. (phone: 690-6741); Columbia University, Broadway and W. 116th St. (phone: 280-1754); Cooper Union, 3rd Ave. and 7th St. (phone: 254-6300); Fashion Institute of Technology, 227 W. 27th St. between 7th and 8th Aves. (phone: 760-7700); Fordham University, Columbus Ave. at W. 60th St. (phone: 841-5100) and E. Fordham Rd. at 3rd Ave., Bronx (phone: 579-2000); Hunter College, 695 Park Ave. (phone: 772-4000); Jewish Theological Seminary of America, Broadway at W. 122nd St. (phone: 678-8000); Juilliard School of Music, Lincoln Center Plaza (phone: 799-5000); Mannes College of Music, 105 W. 85th St. (phone: 580-0210); Marymount Manhattan College, 221 E. 71st St. (phone: 517-0555); New School for Social Research, 66 W. 12th St. (phone: 741-5600); New York Institute of Technology, 1855 Broadway at 61st St. (phone: 399-8300); New York University, Washington Sq. (phone: 598-1212); Pace University, 1 Pace Plaza (phone: 488-1200); Parsons School of Design, 5th Ave. at 12th St. (phone: 741-8900); Pratt Institute, 200 Willoughby Ave., Brooklyn (phone: 718-636-3600); Queens College, 65-30 Kissena Blvd., Flushing, Queens (phone: 718-520-7000); Union Theological Seminary, 3041 Broadway at Reinhold Niebuhr Pl. (W. 120th St.; 662-7100); University of St. John's, in Jamaica, Queens (phone: 718-990-6750); and Yeshiva University, 500 W. 185th St. at Amsterdam Ave. (phone: 960-5400).

 SPORTS AND FITNESS: New York is a sports-minded city, offering a great variety of spectator and participatory activities. It is the home of the *Yankees* and *Mets, Jets* and *Giants* (though the latter two now play in New Jersey), *Rangers* and racetracks, and countless tennis players, swimmers, bikers, runners, joggers, and walkers, to name but a few.

Baseball – The season, April through early October, features the *Mets* (National League) at *Shea Stadium,* Flushing, Queens (phone: 718-507-8499), and the *Yankees* (American League) at *Yankee Stadium,* Bronx (phone: 293-6000). Tickets are usually available at the many Ticketron outlets throughout the city (central ticket information, phone: 977-9020).

Basketball – The area features the *Knicks,* playing at *Madison Square Garden* (phone: 563-8300), and the *Nets,* whose home is the *Brendan Byrne Arena* at the Meadowlands Sports Complex in East Rutherford, New Jersey, during the regular season from late October to early April (phone: 201-935-8500, for ticket and schedule information).

Bicycling – There are over 50 miles of bike paths in the city, with Central Park in

Manhattan and Prospect Park in Brooklyn the two most popular areas. Most roadways within the parks are closed to traffic from May through October, except in rush hour on weekdays. They are closed on weekends year-round. Bikes can be rented in the parks or on nearby side streets.

Billiards and Bowling – Extremely popular with many New Yorkers. Pool halls and bowling alleys are plentiful throughout the city. Consult the yellow pages for the nearest location.

Boxing – Major bouts are still fought at *Madison Square Garden* (phone: 563-8300), and the *Daily News* continues to sponsor the Golden Gloves competition every winter.

Fitness Centers – *Polygym* is a personal training center open around the clock at 428 E. 75th St. (phone: 628-6969). On the West Side, the *Hudson Health Club,* in the *Henry Hudson* hotel, has a pool, track, steam room, gym, and yoga and other classes; 353 W. 57th St. near 9th Ave. (phone: 586-8630). Also consult the phone book for the various Y's around the city.

Football – During the September–December season, the *Jets* and the *Giants* play at *Giants Stadium* at the Meadowlands Sports Complex in East Rutherford, New Jersey (about 6 miles from midtown). Tickets to any of the NFL games are hard to get due to the great number of season subscribers. For *Giants* ticket information, call 201 935-8500; for *Jets* tickets, call 421-6600. Columbia University leads (in a manner of speaking) the collegiate football scene, with its games played at *Baker Field* (phone: 280-2541, ext. 2546).

Golf – For up-to-date information on current golf tournaments, call the Metropolitan Golf Assn. (phone: 914 698-0390). The Dept. of Parks public information office (phone: 360-8141) can provide a complete list of public courses and how to get on them.

Handball – Try Central Park's courts, north of the 97th St. transverse.

Hockey – Tickets are expensive and scarce during the early October to early April season, featuring the *Islanders,* at the *Nassau Coliseum* (phone: 516-794-9300), and the *Rangers, Madison Square Garden* (phone: 563-8300).

Horseback Riding – Horses can be rented and boarded at the *Claremont Riding Academy,* 175 W. 89th St. at Amsterdam Ave. (phone: 724-5100). There are almost 50 miles of bridal paths in the city, most in Central Park.

Horse Racing – Harness racing is at *Yonkers Raceway,* in lower Westchester County, nightly except Sundays (phone: 562-9500), and at *Roosevelt Raceway* in Westbury, Long Island (phone: 516-222-2000). The *Meadowlands,* East Rutherford, New Jersey (phone: 201-935-8500), has both harness and flat racing nightly, except Sundays. Thoroughbreds also run during the day at *Aqueduct Race Track* in Queens (phone: 718-641-4700), or *Belmont Park Race Track* in Elmont, Long Island (phone: 718-641-4700). *Aqueduct* and *Belmont* are closed Tuesdays. Each track has a separate season; they are never open at the same time.

Jogging – Undoubtedly the most popular sport in New York, with enthusiastic runners in all the city parks; paths at Riverside Park, near W. 97th St., around the Central Park Reservoir, 85th St., and the promenade along the East River, between E. 84th and 90th Sts. Either the New York Road Runners Club (phone: 860-4455) or Convention and Visitors Bureau (phone: 397-8222) can supply information on routes.

Ice Skating – From October to April, you can show off your figure eights at the famous *Rockefeller Center* rink (phone: 757-5730); from November through April at the recently reopened *Wollman Rink* in Central Park (phone: 517-4800); and from early November through February at *Lasker Rink,* Central Park (phone: 397-3142). The small rink in front of the Rivergate Apartments, 401 E. 34th St. at 1st Ave. (phone: 689-0035), is open from November through March. For indoor skating year-round, try *Skyrink,* 450 W. 33rd St. (phone: 695-6555). For information about skating conditions, call 397-3098 or 517-4800.

Roller Skating – Central Park on summer weekends is one huge skating rink, with rentals available from *Peck & Goodie* on 8th Ave. between 54th and 55th Sts. (phone: 246-6123).

Swimming – Several dozen indoor and outdoor pools are operated by the Parks Dept. Indoor pools are open most of the year, except Sundays and holidays, and usually until 10 PM weekdays. Call the Parks Dept. public information office (phone: 360-8141) for particulars. Check the yellow pages for pools at the YMCA and YMHA.

Ocean swimming is a subway or bus ride away. Jones Beach State Park, Wantagh, Long Island, 30 miles outside the city, is the most popular. It is a beautifully maintained, enormous stretch of sandy beach, and includes surf bathing, swimming and wading pools, lockers, fishing, outdoor skating rinks, paddleball, swimming instruction, restaurants, and day- and nighttime entertainment. Beaches maintained by the city are Orchard Beach in the Bronx; Coney Island Beach and Manhattan Beach, Brooklyn; and Riis Park and Rockaway Beaches in Queens.

Tennis – Courts maintained by the Parks Dept. require a season permit. One of the larger privately owned clubs that will rent by the hour is the *Midtown Tennis Club*, 341 8th Ave. at W. 27th St. (phone: 989-8572). Check the yellow pages for other locations.

 THEATER: There are devoted New York theatergoers who wouldn't dream of stepping inside a Broadway theater. They prefer instead the city's prolific off-Broadway and off-off-Broadway circuit, productions less high-powered but no less professional than the splashiest shows on Broadway. On the other hand, there are theater mavens who've never seen a performance more than three blocks from Times Square and who can remember every detail of the opening night of *A Chorus Line.* If their reminiscences don't have you running to the nearest box office for front-row seats to the season's biggest hit, you are made of stone.

Broadway signifies an area — New York's premier theater district, the blocks between Broadway and 9th Avenue running north of Times Square from 42nd Street — and a kind of production — the "big show" that strives to be the smash hit of the season and run forever. The glitter of the area has turned a bit tacky since the halcyon days of the Great White Way, but a renovation of the area is in the planning stage and may eventually turn things around. In any case, the productions remain as stellar (and pricey) as ever.

Off-Broadway and off-off-Broadway signify types of theater (playhouses producing shows that qualify as off-Broadway are strewn from the Lower Village to the Upper West Side) that have developed in response to the phenomenon of Broadway. Off-Broadway productions are often smaller in scale, with newer, lesser-known talent, and are likely to feature revivals of classics or more daring works than those on Broadway. Off-off-Broadway is more experimental still, featuring truly avant-garde productions with performances in coffee houses, lofts, or any appropriate makeshift arena. Off-Broadway often approaches the price of a Broadway ticket, though the price of a seat for an off-off-Broadway production is usually much less.

You should take advantage of all three during a visit. The excitement of a Broadway show is incomparable, but the thrill of finding a tiny theater in SoHo or the West Village in which you are almost nose to nose with the actors is undeniable. Planning your theater schedule is as easy as consulting any of the daily papers (they all list theaters and current offerings daily, with comprehensive listings on Fridays or Saturdays) or looking in the "Goings On About Town" column in *The New Yorker* or "Cue" Theater Guide in *New York* magazine, which lists current theater fare under headings of "Broadway," "Off-Broadway," and "Off-Off-Broadway."

Broadway tickets can be quite expensive (they average $15 to $50, depending on where you sit and when you go), but that needn't be a deterrent to seeing as many shows as you can. The *TKTS* stands, 47th St. at Broadway in Times Square and 2 World

Trade Center in lower Manhattan (phone: 354-5800), sell tickets at half price, plus a service charge of a dollar or two, for a wide range of Broadway and off-Broadway productions; tickets are sold on the day of performance after 3 PM for evening shows, after noon for matinees. You must line up for the tickets — there are no reservations — and payment must be made in cash or traveler's checks.

Theater Companies – *Circle Rep,* 99 7th Ave. South (phone: 924-7100); *Jean Cocteau Repertoire,* 330 Bowery (phone: 677-0060); the *Joyce,* 175 8th Ave. (phone: 242-0800); *La Mama ETC,* 74A E. 4th St. (phone: 475-7710); *Manhattan Theatre Club,* at *City Center,* 131 W. 55th St. (phone: 645-5590); *National Black Theatre,* 2033 5th Ave., 2nd Floor (phone: 427-5615); *The Public,* 425 Lafayette St. (phone: 598-7150); *Repertorio Español,* 138 E. 27th St. (phone: 889-2850); *Ridiculous Theatrical Company,* 1 Sheridan Sq. (phone: 691-2271); and *Roundabout,* 100 E. 17th St. (phone: 420-1360 or 420-1883). All can provide a schedule of offerings and performance dates. Alternatively, call the Theatre Development Fund's hot line (phone: 587-1111; out of state, 800 782-4369 or 800 STAGE-NY) or *New York* magazine's hot line, weekdays from 10:30 AM to 4:30 PM (phone: 880-0755).

 MUSIC: New York is a world center for performing artists. It presents the best of classical and nonclassical traditions from all over the world, in a variety of halls and auditoriums, filled with appreciative, knowledgeable audiences.

Lincoln Center for the Performing Arts, completed in 1969, represents the city's devotion to concerts, opera, and ballet, and is on Broadway and 65th St. (general information, phone: 877-2011). It consists of: *Avery Fisher Hall,* home of the *NY Philharmonic* (phone: 874-2424); *NY State Theater,* featuring the *NY City Ballet* and *NY City Opera* (phone: 870-5570); *Metropolitan Opera House,* for the opera and the *American Ballet Theatre* (phone: 362-6000); *Damrosch Bandshell,* an open-air theater used for free concerts; the *Juilliard School* for musicians, actors, and dancers (phone: 799-5000); and *Alice Tully Hall,* home of the *Chamber Music Society* (phone: 362-1911). In addition, all the auditoriums in *Lincoln Center* present other musical events and recitals. While in the area, visit the *NY Public Library at Lincoln Center,* a unique library and museum of the performing arts (phone: 870-1630). Guided tours of *Lincoln Center* are available daily (phone: 877-1800, ext. 512).

Other major halls are *Carnegie Hall,* recently renovated, at 57th St. and 7th Ave. (phone: 247-7800); *City Center,* 131 W. 55th St. (phone: 246-8989); *Grace Rainey Rogers Auditorium,* 5th Ave. and 82nd St. (phone: 570-3949), in the *Metropolitan Museum; Kaufmann Auditorium,* at the 92nd St. Y, 92nd St. and Lexington Ave. (phone: 427-4410); *Symphony Space,* 2537 Broadway at 95th St. (phone: 864-5400); and *Brooklyn Academy of Music,* 30 Lafayette Ave. (phone: 718-636-4100). Also check music and dance listings in the newspapers *New York* and *The New Yorker* magazines. The *TKTS* booth in Times Square, which sells discount theater tickets, now has a counterpart on West 42nd Street for those interested in buying half-price tickets to music and dance events on the day of the performance. The booth, open daily from noon to 7 PM, is on the 42nd Street side of Bryant Park, behind the NY Public Library, just east of 5th Ave. (phone: 382-2323).

Many pop, rock, rhythm and blues, and country artists perform at *Madison Square Garden,* 7th Ave., at 33rd St. (phone: 563-8300).

NIGHTCLUBS AND NIGHTLIFE: The scope of nightlife in New York is as vast as the scope of daily life. Cultural trends strongly affect the kinds of clubs that are "in" at any given time and their popularity has a tendency to peak, then plunge rather quickly. Old jazz and neighborhood clubs, on the other hand, remain intact, catering to a regular local clientele. They offer various kinds of entertainment, and many stay open until the wee hours of the morning serving drinks and food. It is a good idea to call all the clubs in advance to find out when they are open and what shows or acts they are offering; or consult the "Cue" listings in *New York* magazine. Many of the city's nightclubs with live entertainment and/or dancing have cover charges of about $15 and up; most accept major credit cards.

The current focus of the trendy crowd is on clubs that offer rock and contemporary or new wave music with some disco mixed in as well. In addition to their lavish stereo systems, many of these clubs also feature videos, live bands, a few bars, and lots of room for dancing. Most popular are: the *Ritz,* 54th St. between 8th Ave. and Broadway (phone: 541-8900); *Heartbreak,* 179 Varick St. (phone: 691-2388); the *Cat Club,* 76 E. 13th St. (phone: 505-0090); *Limelight,* 47 W. 20th St. and around the corner at 660 6th Ave. (phone: 807-7850); and dance palace extraordinaire, the *Palladium,* 126 E. 14th St. (phone: 473-7171).

Possibly the swankest place in town is *Nell's,* 246 W. 14th St. between 7th and 8th aves. (phone: 675-1567). This Victorian-style nightclub has been immortalized by *People* magazine. *Warning:* It's very difficult to get in. Other trendy spots at press time include the *Tunnel,* 220 12th Ave. at W. 27th St. (phone: 244-6444), very big and very funky; *Octagon,* new, huge, and high tech, 555 W. 43rd St. at 11th Ave. (phone: 947-0400); *1018,* at the corner of 10th Ave. and W. 18th St. (phone: 645-5156); the *Saint,* 105 2nd Ave. at E. 8th St. (phone: 477-0959); *Shout,* 124 W. 43rd St. (phone: 869-2088); and *Stringfellow's,* 35 E. 21st St. (phone: 254-2444), a new Art Deco disco, imported from London. For everything from swing to disco, try the *Red Parrot,* 617 W. 57th St. at 11th Ave. (phone: 247-1530), with its own 20-piece orchestra.

Among the nightclubs with food and drink that feature live music — including rock, soul, rhythm and blues, reggae, jazz, and top 40 music — are *Sweetwaters,* 170 Amsterdam Ave. at W. 68th St. (phone: 873-4100); *El Morocco,* a legend at 307 E. 54th St. (phone: 750-1500); and *Mikell's,* 760 Columbus Ave. at W. 97th St. (phone: 864-8832). You can dine and dance to country music and bluegrass at *O'Lunney's Steak House,* 915 2nd Ave. at E. 48th St. (phone: 751-5470). The *Bitter End,* 149 Bleecker St. (phone: 673-7030); *Club Oasis,* 40 E. 58th St. (phone: 688-3365); and the *Bottom Line,* 15 W. 4th St. (phone: 228-7880), often offer traditional blues and jazz. Country music notables entertain, and are entertained, at the *Lone Star Café Roadhouse,* 240 W. 52nd St. (phone: 245-2950), when they come to New York. The *Eagle Tavern,* 355 W. 14th St. between 8th and 9th Aves. (phone: 924-0275), is good for country, bluegrass, and Irish music.

Even though discos are no longer the city's hottest spots, there are still a fair number of chic places where the beat goes on, such as *Regine's,* 502 Park Ave. at E. 59th St. (phone: 826-0990). The famous Brooklyn hangout where the movie *Saturday Night Fever* was filmed, *2001 Odyssey,* 802 64th St. (phone: 718-238-8213), still draws a crowd. For dancing to a Latin beat, try the *Sounds of Brazil* (*S.O.B.*) supper club, 204 Varick St. (phone: 243-4940). If you prefer disco on wheels, check out *Empire Roller Disco,* 200 Empire Blvd., Brooklyn (phone: 718-462-1570). As for good, clean traditional ballroom fun with American and Latin live dance music, the famous *Roseland Dance City,* 239 W. 52nd St. (phone: 247-0200), definitely deserves a whirl — it holds up to 4,000 dancers.

For a low-key, elegant evening of dancing to live music, a good show and dinner, try *Jimmy Weston's,* 131 E. 54th St. (phone: 838-8384); or *Freddy's Supper Club,* 308 E. 49th St. (phone: 888-1633). *Au Bar,* a supper club with all the lofty but cozy accoutrements of London's Belgravia, opened in 1988 to great critical acclaim; it's at 41 E. 58th St. (phone: 308-9455). The *Rainbow Room,* 30 Rockefeller Plaza (phone: 757-9090), reopened in late 1987 after a $20-million renovation that restored the splendor of its 1930s heyday. It has good cheek-to-cheek dance music and dazzling views of the city from the 65th floor of the RCA Building. The adjacent *Rainbow Promenade* is a café for midnight snacks.

Among the small, intimate supper clubs with good food, a nice, informal atmosphere, and low-key, quality entertainment, we recommend the *Café Carlyle,* in the *Carlyle* hotel, 35 E. 76th St. at Madison Ave. (phone: 744-1600), and the *Ballroom,* 253 W. 28th St. (phone: 244-3005). Lively, casual "showcase" clubs, where singers, comedians, and performers of all kinds test their new material on reliably loud but not always appreciative audiences, include *Caroline's,* 332 8th Ave. at W. 26th St. (phone: 924-3499) and 89 South St., Pier 17 (phone: 233-4900); the *Improvisation* (the *Original*), 358 W. 44th St. (phone: 765-8268); and *Catch a Rising Star,* 1487 1st Ave. (phone: 794-1906). The *Magic Towne House,* 1026 3rd Ave. (phone: 752-1165), is a unique weekend spot offering skilled magic acts by appointment only.

The largest concentration of singles bars in New York can be found on 1st and 2nd (some on 3rd) Avenues, between 61st and 80th Streets. If you walk along either one of these you will probably find a likely looking place. Be sure to check out *Adam's Apple,* 1117 1st Ave., between 61st and 62nd Streets (phone: 371-8650); and *B. Smiths,* where the crowd is more interesting than the food, 771 8th Ave. at 47th St. (phone: 247-2222). If you like sitting around a piano, listening to, requesting, and even singing your favorite tunes, the *Village Green,* 531 Hudson St. (phone: 255-1650); *Knickerbocker Saloon,* 33 University Pl. (phone: 228-8490); and *Oliver's* restaurant, 141 E. 57th St. (phone: 753-9180), can fill the bill as well as satisfy your appetite.

The *Village Vanguard,* 178 7th Ave. S. (phone: 255-4037); the *Village Gate,* Bleecker and Thompson Sts. (phone: 475-5120); *Sweet Basil,* 88 7th Ave. S. (phone: 242-1785); and the *Blue Note,* 131 W. 3rd St. (phone: 475-8592), feature top jazz artists. Some of the more casual, neighborhood-type jazz clubs with reasonable prices and a relaxed atmosphere are *Arthur's Tavern,* 57 Grove St. (phone: 675-6879); the *Angry Squire,* 216 7th Ave. at W. 22nd St. (phone: 242-9066); *Bradley's,* 70 University Pl. (phone: 228-6440); the *West End Jazz Room,* 2911 Broadway at W. 114th St. (phone: 666-9160). For nostalgia and more traditional jazz sounds, try *Fat Tuesday's,* 190 3rd Ave. (phone: 533-7902), or *Michael's Pub,* 211 E. 55th St., where Woody Allen still plays his clarinet on Monday nights; reservations necessary (phone: 758-2272).

Cabarets and floor shows have been making something of a comeback. *Café Versailles,* 151 E. 50th St. (phone: 753-3884), is the place for gorgeous showgirls and flashy production numbers, while popular comedy revues are featured at *Palsson's,* 158 W. 72nd St. (phone: 595-7400). *Chippendales,* 1110 1st Ave. at E. 61st St. (phone: 935-6060), offers all-male strip shows "for women only" Wednesday through Saturday nights.

Gay bars are scattered throughout New York, but the Upper West Side in the seventies and Christopher Street in the West Village distinguish themselves as gay areas. Christopher Street, especially, is noted for its cruising bars.

BEST IN TOWN

CHECKING IN: New York City is still one of the hardest places in the world to find an empty hotel room between Sunday and Thursday nights, even though a rash of new properties have opened. However, don't expect this increased supply to offset inflation's upward push on room rates in the foreseeable future. Do expect to pay $200 or more — often lots more — for a very expensive room for two in Manhattan; $150 to $200 for an expensive one; $100 to $150 for a moderately priced room; and $100 or less for an inexpensive one. These prices include no meals. Note: Many of these hotels offer special weekend packages for relatively low rates. The packages include a variety of amenities — from just a room to a room plus breakfast/dinner, champagne, theater tickets, and parking. Reservations are always necessary, so write or call for information well in advance.

An alternative to taking a standard hotel room is a new Bed & Breakfast plan run by *Urban Ventures*. Accommodations are in private homes, include a continental breakfast, and cost from $34 to $75 per night. For a brochure, contact *Urban Ventures*, PO Box 426, New York, NY 10024 (phone: 594-5650). Other organizations providing similar services are the *B&B Group* (*New Yorkers at Home*), 301 E. 60th St., New York, NY 10022 (phone: 838-7015); *At Home in New York*, PO Box 407, New York, NY 10185 (phone: 956-3125 or 265-8539); the *Bed and Breakfast Network of New York*, 134 W. 32nd St., Suite 602, New York, NY 10001 (phone: 645-8134); and *Bed and Breakfast* (*and Books*), 35 W. 92nd St., New York, NY 10025 (phone: 865-8740).

Another option: YMCAs throughout the city are about $45 a night. Most are coed. All telephone numbers are in the 212 area code unless otherwise indicated.

Carlyle – The leader among luxurious uptown hotels, where the Kennedy family traditionally stays. Noted for its quiet and serenity, with prices to match the high level of service. Predominantly a residential hotel. 35 E. 76th St. (phone: 744-1600). Very expensive.

Doral Tuscany – In the middle of attractive Murray Hill, it is a name not often known outside the city's immediate environs. Guests who know it well treasure the service and atmosphere (there are 125 rooms). 120 E. 39th St. (phone: 686-1600 or 800-847-4078). Very expensive.

Drake Swissôtel – A Swiss-owned property that is both smart and conservative. In addition to 640 beautifully appointed rooms and 49 suites, it boasts a topnotch French restaurant, the *Lafayette*, supervised by chef Louis Outhier of Cannes' famed *L'Oasis*, which has earned a three-star rating from Michelin for 17 consecutive years. Swiss chocolates on your pillow each night; lavish lobby and champagne/wine bar. 440 Park Ave. at E. 56th St. (phone: 421-0900 or 800-DRAKE-NY). Very expensive.

Grand Hyatt – A tourist's idea of how a New York City hotel should look, the old *Commodore* has been reincarnated with sleek modern lines, mirrored exterior glass, and shiny chrome. The centerpiece of the multilevel lobby is the tiered, marble fountain crowned by a 77-foot bronze sculpture. On the lobby's upper level is the *Sungarden*, a glass-enclosed bar and cocktail lounge that overhangs the hotel's entrance and the busy 42nd Street traffic. The 1,400 smallish rooms are dressed in rich, earthy tones that are brightened daily with fresh flowers. 109 E. 42nd St. at Park Ave. (phone: 883-1234, 800-233-1234, or 800-228-9000). Very expensive.

Helmsley Palace – The midtown property combines the landmark Henry Villard houses with a 51-story high-rise and has beautifully restored, elegant public rooms decorated in marble, crystal, and gold as well as modern guestrooms. Guests must use the 50th Street side entrance for checking in, but thereafter can enter through the wrought-iron gates on Madison Avenue. 455 Madison Ave. at E. 50th St. (phone: 888-7000 or 800-221-4982). Very expensive.

Howard – One of New York's newer hotels, it has 107 rooms, furnished with a distinctly British accent in oak and marble. Health club on the premises. 127 E. 55th St. (phone: 826-1100 or 800-221-1074). Very expensive.

Inter-Continental – The latest addition to the former *Barclay* hotel is the sleek, oak-paneled *Barclay* restaurant. Facilities include a health club. A large (686 rooms), distinguished property on a quiet East Side street. 111 E. 48th St. (phone: 755-5900, 800-332-4246, or 800-327-0200). Very expensive.

Lowell – Little expense has been spared in turning this once undistinguished property into an authentic gem, an Art Deco delight — with mostly 1- and 2-bedroom suites. The smallish rooms are perfect for a modestly proportioned king, and each suite has a working fireplace (a log costs $3.50). The overall feeling is one of being a guest in a very well-bred New York townhouse — on what could very well be the most stylish block in Manhattan. 28 E. 63rd St. (phone: 838-1400). Very expensive.

Peninsula – Formerly *Maxim's de Paris,* this 250-room hotel features oversize marble bathtubs, a health club with jogging track, and a swank French restaurant and bistro. 700 5th Ave. at W. 55th St. (phone: 247-2200). Very expensive.

Mayfair Regent – For those who stay at the *Gritti* in Venice and the *Hôtel du Cap* in the south of France. There are just 80 rooms and 120 suites, plus the nonpareil *Le Cirque* restaurant. Uncompromising elegance and superb service. 610 Park Ave. at E. 65th St. (phone: 288-0800 or 800-223-0542 in New York State; 800-545-4000 in other states). Very expensive.

Morgans – The ultimate contemporary hotel, without so much as a sign out front. Stereo cassette players and component TV sets with stereo sound are standard amenities in every room (VCRs and movies are also available), bathrooms are pure high tech, and artwork is by avant-garde photographer Robert Maplethorpe. The only traditional touch here is the *Brooks Brothers*–style linens. All things considered, it's not surprising that the hotel's 154 rooms are usually occupied by a trendy, young, international clientele. 237 Madison Ave. at E. 37th St. (phone: 686-0300 or 800-334-3408). Very expensive.

New York Marriott Marquis – A predictably pedestrian convention hotel designed by John C. Portman, this 50-story, 1,876-room addition to Times Square tries to make up for a lack of distinction in room design with a 37-floor open atrium that is long on glitz, short on class. *The View,* a 3-tier rotating rooftop restaurant, overlooks the city, and the 8th-floor revolving lounge overlooks Broadway. 1535 Broadway (phone: 398-1900 or 800-228-9290). Very expensive.

Omni Berkshire Place – Built in 1926, the old *Berkshire* hotel has been resuscitated by the Omni chain with dash and considerable understated flair. Most impressive is the Atrium Lobby, a mirrored lounge accented with soft shades, creating a quite comfortable and intimate atmosphere. Gaining momentum on the culinary scene is the pretty *Rendez-vous* restaurant serving both classic French and nouvelle cuisine. 21 E. 52nd St. (phone: 753-5800 or 800-THE-OMNI). Very expensive.

Parker Meridien – Billing itself as New York's "first French hotel," this establishment provides guests with the elegance of a European hostelry. There are 600 luxurious rooms, plus apartments, bars, and *Le Restaurant Maurice,* serving superb nouvelle cuisine. The sports-minded will enjoy *Club Raquette* for racquetball, handball, and squash; the rooftop running track that encircles the enclosed pool, where the views of Central Park are lovely; and the health club. 118 W. 57th St. (phone: 245-5000 or 800-543-3000). Very expensive.

Pierre – The most luxurious stopping place in midtown, with the most august clientele. The elegance is low key but consistent, and the rooms with a park view command the highest of already heady prices. Operated by the superb Four Seasons group, on one of the most attractive corners of the city, it is the place to stay. 5th Ave. at E. 61st St. (phone: 838-8000 or 800-268-6282). Very expensive.

Plaza – The hotel was recently sold to Donald Trump, and he and Mrs. T. have ambitious plans, including reopening the famed *Persian Room.* This is the only New York City hotel designated as a historic landmark and the first hotel NYC visitors think of when they imagine a luxurious urban hostelry. Erratic, but mostly elegant. 5th Ave. at W. 59th St. (phone: 759-3000). Very expensive.

Plaza Athénée – Small and sumptuous, this is the US edition of the celebrated *Plaza Athénée* in Paris. The Trusthouse Forte management strives to look as unlike a hotel as possible and prides itself on personal attention to its guests. There are 160 rooms and 34 suites, all furnished with French antiques. 37 E. 64th St. (phone: 734-9100 or 800-225-5843). Very expensive.

Regency – Where the movers and shakers of America now stay when they're in New York. More business is probably conducted in the dining room here at breakfast than in all of the rest of the country during a normal business day. Its modern architecture does not detract at all from its appeal, and a recent basement-to-roof restoration and refurbishing has only added to its luster. Facilities include a health club. 540 Park Ave. at E. 61st St. (phone: 759-4100 or 800-223-0607). Very expensive.

Ritz-Carlton – Brought to you by the same people (lately in bankruptcy) responsible for the *Tremont* and *Whitehall* hotels in Chicago and the *Ritz-Carlton* in Washington, DC. The luxury touches here (in the shell of the old *Navarro*) are chintz and Chippendale in the rooms, Courvoisier and chocolates on the nightstand at bedtime, leather banquettes and firelight in the *Jockey Club* restaurant, and a park view for guests in front rooms. 112 Central Park South (phone: 757-1900 or 800-223-7990). Very expensive.

Royalton – The management of super-chic *Morgans* set out to impress New York once again, this time with a 205-room property a major boost to the ongoing rejuvenation of its Times Square locale. The block-long lobby, with areas specifically designed for reading, conversation, billiards, and board games, is a popular gathering spot (and the men's room has to be seen to be believed). Many of the rooms come with a wood-burning fireplace, sleeping loft, and living area, which includes a VCR, color TV set, and stereo cassette deck. All baths have a phone, and many sport a 5-foot round tub. Guests can opt for either casual or more formal dining or just for pre-theater cocktails in the bar. 44 W. 44th St. (phone: 869-4400). Very expensive.

Stanhope – Recently bought by the Japanese Tovishima group, this posh, upper Fifth Avenue hotel with 118 rooms, most of them 1- or 2-bedroom suites and all affording views of Central Park or Manhattan's spectacular skyline. Guests meet and relax in the hotel's opulent public rooms and enjoy a wide range of dining options, including an outdoor café in summer and afternoon tea in the sitting room. Special services can be arranged through the concierge. Complimentary limousine to midtown weekday mornings and evening transportation to *Lincoln Center, Carnegie Hall,* and the theater district. 995 Fifth Ave. (phone: 288-5800 or 800-828-1123). Very expensive.

United Nations Plaza – In addition to its beautifully integrated modern design, from the sleek, green-tinted glass exterior through the dark green marble reception area to the top 10 floors, it also offers rooms with magnificent city views. Managed by Hyatt International, it has both a truly international staff and exceptional facilities — including a tennis court, heated pool, and exercise room — to pamper all guests. E. 44th St. at 1st Ave. (phone: 355-3400 or 800-228-9000). Very expensive.

Vista International New York – The first hotel to be built in Manhattan's Wall Street vicinity in over 100 years, it sits between the World Trade Center towers facing New York Harbor. A full range of special services is available for business travelers in reliable Hilton Hotels style. Other highlights include the indoor *Executive Fitness Center,* with first-rate sports equipment; the *Greenhouse* and *American Harvest* restaurants, offering very good American regional specialties; and the *Tall Ships Bar,* a popular after-work meeting place. 3 World Trade Center (phone: 938-9100 or 800-HILTONS). Very expensive.

Westbury – The tapestries at the entrance are Belgian; the soft pink carpeting in the marble lobby, Irish — as befits this tranquil, European-style hotel with its large international clientele (part of the Trusthouse Forte group). Completely refurbished and redecorated over the past few years, the *Westbury* has retained its crystal chandeliers in the lobby and its brass doorknobs engraved with the hotel's address. Its *Polo* restaurant serves nouvelle cuisine. 15 E. 69th St. at Madison Ave. (phone: 535-2000 or 800-223-5672). Very expensive.

Essex House – Since Nikko Hotels of Japan took over in mid-1985, this 40-story landmark overlooking Central Park has undergone a multimillion-dollar enhancement program and a distinct transformation in style. 160 Central Park South (phone: 247-0300 or 800-NIKKO-US). Very expensive to expensive.

The Mark – Recently reopened and refurbished, the former *Madison Avenue* hotel is noted for understated elegance. Its 100 rooms and 85 suites all feature a separate glass shower stall, tub, and vanity, cable TV sets, two-line phones, pantry with refrigerator, sink, and stove, heated towel bars and heating lamps in bathrooms, overstuffed chairs, credenzas, and sofas, all in neoclassical Italian motif. Suites are large and offer a bidet, library, vanity, wet bar, large terrace, and separate living, dining, and bedroom areas. Also here are the 3-tiered *Lobby Lounge,* which serves afternoon tea as well as meals, the classic *Sant Ambroeus* restaurant, serving pasta, pastries, and gelati, the *Café Grill,* and sophisticated boutiques. Quiet elegance throughout. Madison Ave. at E. 77th St. (phone: 744-4300 or 800-THE-MARK). Very expensive to expensive.

New York Helmsley – A shining glass skyscraper on 42nd Street, this executive-oriented facility has special services available for the business traveler — with secretaries, telex, photocopying, and meeting rooms among them. For dining, there's *Mindy's,* a continental restaurant, and for drinks and piano music try *Harry's New York Bar.* 212 E. 42nd St. (phone: 490-8900 or 800-221-4982). Very expensive to expensive.

New York Hilton & Towers – An enormous modern structure near Rockefeller Center. One of New York's largest hotels, it's a bit antiseptic in ambience, but about as efficiently run as any hotel with more than 2,000 rooms can be. A favorite meeting and convention site. Pets allowed. 1335 Ave. of the Americas between W. 53rd and 54th Sts. (phone: 586-7000 or 800-HILTONS). Very expensive to expensive.

Sherry-Netherland – It's a little less renowned than the *Plaza* and the *Pierre* (its immediate neighbors), but hardly less elegant. The location is superb, and this is a luxurious stopping place truly worthy of the description. 5th Ave. and E. 59th St. (phone: 355-2800 or 800-223-0522). Very expensive to expensive.

Waldorf-Astoria and Waldorf Towers – A legend on Park Avenue, divided between the basic hotel and the more opulent (and more expensive) Towers. The degree of comfort delivered here is consistent with the hotel's reputation; it is also a popular convention property. *Peacock Alley* is a lively cocktail rendezvous, and the clock in the middle of the lobby may be New York's favorite meeting place. 301 Park Ave. at E. 50th St. (phone: 355-3000 or 800-HILTONS). Very expensive to expensive.

Beekman Tower – A small, pleasantly old-fashioned all-suite hotel (convenient to the United Nations) with a cocktail lounge, the *Top of the Tower,* boasting splendid skyline views. 1st Ave. and E. 49th St. (phone: 355-7300 or 800-ME-SUITE). Expensive.

Golden Tulip Barbizon – Not to be confused with the *Barbizon Plaza,* this East Side establishment was recently bought by Steve Rubell, owner of *Morgans* and the *Royalton.* It was formerly a residential hotel for women only, but a thorough refurbishing has turned it into one of New York's newer tourist hotels, with 368 rooms and a café. 140 E. 63rd St. (phone: 838-5700 or 800-223-1020). Expensive.

Halloran House – Since 1924, *Halloran House* has kept one foot in the past and one in the future. Gothic, Byzantine, and Italian architechture complement 1990s sophistication. There are 652 rooms and 14 suites, many with a view of Manhattan and the East River, AM/FM radios, color TV sets, room safes, extra phones in the bathrooms, and 3 no smoking floors. Dining options are *Norman's* restaurant, open for breakfast, lunch and dinner; *Green Thumb Café;* and *Biff's Place* nightclub — a softly lighted hideaway featuring luncheon buffet, as well as dancing and live entertainment. The hotel has just completed the first phase of a $20-million renovation that resulted in the reopening of the 6 meeting and conference rooms. Special packages. (phone: 755-4000 or 800-223-0939, 800-854-3355 in Canada). Expensive.

Sheraton Centre – This 50-story modern monolith, once the *Americana,* has been taken over by the Sheraton chain. It's always busy; the rooms are quite comfortable and it's only a short walk to the theater. The top 5 floors, called the Sheraton Towers, are for more exclusive "business class" clients. 7th Ave. at W. 52nd St. (phone: 581-1000 or 800-325-3535). Expensive.

Loews Summit – A large, commodious hotel, well located for businesspeople and conventioneers with midtown East Side interests, the *Summit* offers a full range of meeting and banquet facilities accommodating groups of 20 to 300 people, plus a health club. Its restaurant, *Maude's,* features an excellent luncheon buffet — a good value. E. 51st St. at Lexington Ave. (phone: 752-7000 or 800-522-5455 in New York; 800-223-0888 in other states). Expensive to moderate.

New York Penta – Having undergone a $35-million renovation and under the direction of a dynamic new management team, the hotel in the heart of Manhattan offers elegance and comfort. Executive meeting facilities make it a first class business hotel. 401 7th Ave. at W. 33rd St. (phone: 736-5000 or 800-223-8585). Expensive to moderate.

Roosevelt – The hotel has recently changed ownership and undergone redecoration and restoration. The accommodations are clean and comfortable and its *Crawdaddy* restaurant has one of the area's most popular after-work bars. A good value (and location) for business travelers. Madison Ave. at E. 45th St. (phone: 661-9600 or 800-442-8420 in New York State; 800-223-1870 in other states). Expensive to moderate.

Algonquin – Long a favorite among literary types, the hotel's reputation is most closely connected to the days of the "round table" in one of its fine restaurants. The personal attention accorded by the management is visible everywhere, and, if anything, the hotel has improved with age. It was recently acquired by a Japanese investment firm. 59 W. 44th St. between 5th and 6th Aves. (phone: 840-6800 or 800-548-0345). Moderate.

Mayflower – A favorite with ballet and concert buffs as well as celebrities from the arts world. Guests enjoy a relaxed atmosphere and large, comfortable rooms with pantries that once served the permanent residents. This hotel deserves to be better known. Quite close to *Lincoln Center.* 15 Central Park West, between W. 61st and 62nd Sts. (phone: 265-0060 or 800-223-4164). Moderate.

Milford Plaza Best Western – Out-of-towners usually come to Manhattan for Broadway's bright nightlife, and the *Milford* is smack in the center of New York's theater district. All kinds of money-saving tour packages are available, and while rooms are small, they're not a bad value for the money. *Mama Leone's* restaurant has just been added to the hotel inventory. The neighborhood, however, is the pits! 270 W. 45th St. at 8th Ave. (phone: 869-3600 or 800-221-2690). Moderate.

Salisbury – Owned by the Calvary Baptist Church, this hotel has a small, welcoming lobby and newly painted, nicely sized pastel rooms (all with refrigerators and pantries, but no stoves). It's a favorite with buyers and musicians, who like the hotel's location near 5th Avenue and *Carnegie Hall.* 123 W. 57th St. (phone: 246-1300 or 800-223-0680). Moderate.

Wyndham – Though admittedly overshadowed by better-known neighbors like the *Pierre, Plaza,* and *Sherry-Netherland,* this extremely convenient hotel has been fondly described as a posh country inn; a fine, small London hotel; and a private club. It's a particular favorite among actors. It takes a certain self-sufficiency to enjoy the *Wyndham*'s special appeal; there's no room service, the hotel restaurant is closed on weekends, and the front door is locked at night. 45 W. 58th St. between 5th Ave. and Ave. of the Americas (phone: 753-3500). Moderate.

Empire – Across the street from *Lincoln Center,* accommodations here are suffi-ciently comfortable and clean, and the food service is pretty good. 44 W. 63rd St. (phone: 265-7400 or 800-545-7400). Moderate to inexpensive.

Chelsea – A New York architectural and historic landmark where Dylan Thomas, Arthur Miller, Lenny Bruce, Diego Rivera, Martha Graham, and others have made their New York home. The atmosphere in this 19th-century structure is distinctly unmodern, unhomogenized, and unsterilized. There is a large permanent occupancy, with about 35 rooms available for transients. Rooms vary in structure, price, and facilities — some have a kitchen, a fireplace, and a bathroom, and others have none of the above. For the adventurous only; make reservations well in advance. 222 W. 23rd St. (phone: 243-3700). Inexpensive.

Gorham – The variety of room-and-bed combinations possible, together with the fact that all units contain a kitchenette, dining table, and color TV set, make the *Gorham* a great boon to families traveling with children. 136 W. 55th off Ave. of the Americas (phone: 245-1800). Inexpensive.

Olcott – By no means plush, but certainly comfortable and adequate, this is a typical New York residential hotel that offers some transient accommodations. Spacious facilities and a homey atmosphere are its advantages. Most rooms are suites, with a living room, bedroom, kitchen, and bathroom. All rooms have air conditioning. Reservations should be made several weeks in advance. 27 W. 72nd St., only one block from Central Park (phone: 877-4200). Inexpensive.

Shoreham – On a fashionable block off Fifth Avenue, this small hotel has 75 good-size rooms that are pleasantly decorated and have modern bathrooms and cable TV. Although the hotel has no dining room, each guestroom has an electric coffeemaker and small refrigerator. 33 W. 55th St. (phone: 247-6700). Inexpensive.

Wales – This comfortable, reasonably priced hotel is in a very appealing neighbor-hood, close to Central Park and the *Metropolitan* and *Guggenheim* art museums. It offers more than 50 individually decorated rooms and suites, some with kitchen-ette, four-poster bed, or tile fireplace, all with cable TV. 1295 Madison Ave. at E. 92nd St. (phone: 876-6000). Inexpensive.

EATING OUT: New York City is, plain and simply, the culinary capital of the world. It is possible that there are more good French restaurants in Paris or more fine Chinese eating places in Taiwan, but no city in the world can offer the gastronomic diversity that is available in New York. If there is one compelling reason to come to New York, it is to indulge exotic appetites that cannot be satisfied elsewhere, and it is not unusual for dedicated eaters to make several pilgrimages to New York each year simply to satisfy their sophisticated pal-ates.

Regrettably, New York's tastiest cuisine does not come cheap, though there are places to dine around the city where you need not pay in 30-, 60-, and 90-day notes. But as in most places, you get what you pay for, and you should expect to pay $100 or more for two in the restaurants that we've noted as expensive. Moderate restaurants will run between $70 and $100 per couple, and in inexpensive establishments, expect to spend from $30 to $70 for a meal for two. These price ranges do not include drinks, wine, or tips. Unless otherwise noted, reservations are necessary. All telephone num-bers are in the 212 area code unless otherwise indicated.

Aquavit – In the old Rockefeller townhouse, Manhattan's newest Scandinavian restaurant is a current favorite with local foodies. It's actually two restaurants: a formal dining room set around an atrium and waterfall, with a prix fixe dinner; and a more casual room upstairs featuring simpler cooking. There are many varieties of salmon and game, such as arctic venison (reindeer) and snow grouse. Try the smorgasbord, caviar bank, and "aquavit chiller," consisting of 8 flavored vodkas. Open weekdays for lunch and dinner; Saturdays for dinner only; closed Sundays. Major credit cards. 13 W. 54th St. (phone: 307-7311). Expensive.

Aurora – A very posh, very stylish place designed by Milton Glaser in Art Deco style, with a lighting scheme that changes with the hour. The American-cum-French cuisine, supervised by the legendary Joe Baum, revolves around grilled meats and fish. You've never sat more comfortably in an elite eatery. Closed Sundays. Major credit cards. 60 E. 49th St. (phone: 692-9292). Expensive.

Le Bernardin – Gerard and Maguy de la Coze have moved their headquarters from Paris to the sparkling new Equitable Life Building, where they occupy subtly elegant premises. The menu is fiercely seafood-oriented, and no one prepares the products of the world's oceans more imaginatively or deliciously. Since the doors opened here in 1986, such unusual specialties as tuna tartare and sea urchin soup have become staples of the NYC restaurant scene, and it's worth a visit just to see what new wonders are swimming out of the kitchen. Lunch and dinner daily (prix fixe menu); closed Sundays. Reservations necessary, 3 weeks in advance. Major credit cards. 155 W. 51st St. (phone: 489-1515). Expensive.

Café Luxembourg – The interior here runs to Art Deco, bright lights, and noise, with everyone appearing to be looking around for someone famous. Not far from *Lincoln Center,* it is especially welcome to concertgoers. The cuisine is nouvelle, though the specials tend to be uneven. For the best look at the chic crowd, come late (between 11 PM and 3 AM). There's also a Sunday brunch featuring *boudin blanc,* a white pork sausage. Open daily. Major credit cards. 200 W. 70th St. (phone: 873-7411). Expensive.

Il Cantinori – A welcome addition to New York's stable of Northern Italian restaurants that's on one of the city's loveliest blocks. A beamed ceiling, terra cotta floor, and chairs of wood and straw create the charming ambience inside. Begin with *risotto nero* (a rice delicacy in squid ink) or *ravioli alla fiorentina* (dumplings of spinach and ricotta cheese) before an entrée of excellent fish or game. For dessert, try the restaurant's version of the popular Italian confection *tirami sù,* espresso-soaked ladyfingers and sweet mascarpone cheese. Open daily. American Express and Diners Club only. 32 E. 10th St. (phone: 673-6044). Expensive.

La Caravelle – A traditional bastion of classic French cuisine with all of the attendant hauteur, this is often the choice of New York's smartest set. Menus are unalteringly interesting, and the kitchen is not merely competent but innovative. The pre-theater menu is a bargain. Closed Sundays. Major credit cards. 33 W. 55th St. (phone: 586-4252). Expensive.

Chanterelle – Its dingy SoHo corner has been abandoned but not its commitment to seriously elegant dining. The prix fixe menu leans toward nouvelle dishes. Begin with seafood sausage, then choose from such entrées as salmon en papillote, rack of lamb, duck in sherry vinegar, or sautéed soft-shell crabs, all accompanied by crisp stir-fried squash mixed with zucchini blossoms and other vegetables. A cheese board is offered, and dessert might be chocolate pavé, a dense, rich, mousse-like cake. Closed Sundays and Mondays. Make reservations about 2 months in advance. Major credit cards. 2 Harrison St., corner of Hudson (phone: 966-6960). Expensive.

Christ Cella's – A creditable eatery that specializes in sirloin steaks and seafood. The decor is unimpressive, the service is indifferently efficient, and it's a favorite of advertising and publishing types. Not quite up to its old standards, but still worth a visit. Closed Sundays. Major credit cards. 160 E. 46th St. (phone: 697-2479). Expensive.

Le Cirque – The tables are too close together, the noise level can be deafening, and reservations are as hard to come by as an invitation to Buckingham Palace. Still, the remarkable French food that comes out of the kitchen is enough to make legions of dedicated diners put up with the less than perfect atmosphere. Everything on the menu is special and prepared perfectly. Remember, however, that the main reason for dining here is to taste the sublime crème brûlée for dessert. Nowhere in the world is it prepared better. Closed Sundays. American Express and Diners Club only. 58 E. 65th St. (phone: 794-9292). Expensive.

Coach House – Not as highly regarded as it once was, but still generally considered one of New York's best "American" restaurants. The black bean soup is a tradition here, as are the rack of lamb and the superb chocolate cake. Another attraction is its Greenwich Village location, across from some interesting Federal row houses. Closed Mondays. Major credit cards. 110 Waverly Pl. (phone: 777-0303). Expensive.

Four Seasons – The *Pool Room* is perhaps the most beautiful dining room in the city, with a proprietorship that is not only creative but extremely able. This is arguably the best restaurant in the US, not just because of its accomplishments, but because of its innovation and boldness. Although the menu is interesting from top to bottom, desserts deserve special mention, and there's one called Chocolate Velvet that is simply ecstasy. Special "spa cuisine" provides careful calorie and sodium monitoring for the health-conscious. The *Grill Room* is currently the luncheon favorite of New York's power elite, and is a good choice for dinner as well. Prices are stunningly high. Closed Sundays. Major credit cards. 99 E. 52nd St. (phone: 754-9494). Expensive.

Gloucester House – The most expensive seafood center in the city. Fresh biscuits are a particular delight and help soften the blow of some frankly staggering prices. A fine place to dine, but a real budget-bender. Closed Sundays. Major credit cards. 37 E. 50th St. (phone: 755-7394). Expensive.

La Grenouille – Soft green walls and glorious floral arrangements provide a romantic setting in which to sample such house masterpieces as *les grenouilles provençales* (frogs' legs); thin, sautéed calves' liver Bercy; and roast duck (prix fixe). Be prepared, however, for a very haughty, condescending attitude if you're not known to the staff. Closed Sundays and Mondays. American Express and Visa only. 3 E. 52nd St. (phone: 752-1495). Expensive.

Lutèce – New York's (and perhaps this country's) finest classic French restaurant, with service and atmosphere to match the extraordinary cuisine. Of all the premier restaurants in New York, this is the one most hospitable to strangers willing to pay the high price for deluxe French food. If you have the option, dine in the comfortable upstairs room, though the garden room downstairs is a treat in New York City. André Soltner runs this bastion of gastronomic delight with a firm hand, though it's been a bit erratic of late. Best be prepared for a check that will total well into three figures. To sample the combination of classic dishes, innovative nouvelle creations, and Alsatian specialties, order the *menu de dégustation,* a tasting of six or seven courses. Make reservations a month in advance. Closed Sundays. All major credit cards. 249 E. 50th St. (phone: 752-2225). Expensive.

Manhattan Ocean Club – Both the lower-level and upstairs dining rooms of this fine seafood house near *Carnegie Hall* are reminiscent of a museum, with white walls, Grecian columns, and Picasso plates and prints displayed behind glass. The real attraction is the fresh, delicious fish and shellfish — the Hawaiian wahoo and melt-in-your-mouth kumomoto oysters are particularly good. The new *pâtissier* is winning awards with such sumptuous treats as calvados ice cream on apple tarts. Open daily. Major credit cards. 57 W. 58th St. (phone: 371-7777). Expensive.

Il Nido – A superb menu of northern Italian specialties and the highest standards of service are the hallmarks of Adi Giovannetti's attractive, if somewhat cramped, East Side establishment. *Crostini di polenta* with a sauce of mushroom and chicken liver is the perfect starter, to be followed by *fritto misto* (mixed fried fish), *crostacei marinara* (shellfish in marinara sauce), or any of a host of other house specialties. Closed Sundays. Major credit cards. 251 E. 53rd St. (phone: 753-8450). Expensive.

Oyster Bar – This is the place for oysters: On any given day, there will be 10 varieties from which to choose. There's also Maine lobster, North Atlantic salmon, Dover sole, mako shark steaks, pompano, pink snapper, swordfish, Florida stone crabs, and Mediterranean seafood. The huge volume assures fresh product. Open weekdays. Major credit cards. Grand Central Terminal (phone: 490-6650). Expensive.

Palio – An elegant entry into New York's abundant inventory of fine Italian eateries. The street-level bar is surrounded by a mural of the exciting medieval horse race that gives the restaurant its name, and the upstairs dining room is spacious and elegant. Perfect for pre- or after-theater dinners. Open nightly except Sundays for dinner; only weekdays for lunch. Major credit cards. 151 W. 51st St. (phone: 245-4850). Expensive.

Quilted Giraffe – Among the prime temptations at this highly regarded restaurant are entrées such as grilled Norwegian salmon and moist, crisp-skinned confit of duck with garlic potatoes. An alternative to the prix fixe dinner is a tasting menu offering five small courses. Similarly, the Grand Dessert provides a sampling of such pleasures as a hazelnut waffle with vanilla ice cream and maple sauce. The two intimate dining rooms have only 17 tables; for weekends, be sure to reserve about a month in advance. Open Mondays through Saturdays for dinner, Tuesdays through Fridays for lunch. American Express only. 550 Madison Ave. (phone: 593-1221). Expensive.

River Café – Set on a barge on the Brooklyn shore of the East River, with spectacular views of the lower Manhattan skyline. One of the top American restaurants, with an especially good weekend brunch menu featuring lobster baked in horseradish oil with oyster risotto, poached eggs on smoked salmon waffles, and duck confit with roasted garlic and white beans. Open daily. Reservations necessary 2 weeks ahead. Major credit cards. 1 Water St. (phone: 718-522-5200). Expensive.

Riveranda/Empress of New York – The food may not be the best in town, but the experience of dining on the city's only restaurant-yacht is worth the tab. It's delightful to have dinner and dance while cruising the Hudson River and New York Harbor past the glittering Manhattan skyline. There are luncheon and Sunday brunch cruises as well. Advance reservations and tickets necessary. Open daily in summer. Major credit cards. Sailings from Pier 62 on the Hudson River at W. 23rd St. (phone: 929-7090). Expensive.

Russian Tea Room – With enough blinis to float diners down the Volga, this festive restaurant is an almost obligatory stop for any visitor who plans to attend a concert at adjacent *Carnegie Hall.* Try the borscht or chicken Kiev, abide by the waiter's suggestions, or let your Slavic instincts have free rein. Open daily. Major credit cards. 150 W. 57th St. (phone: 265-0947). Expensive.

Spark's – Nothing (except the food) is admirable: the entry to the dining room is the most cramped and uncomfortable in town, the decor is early bordello, and the service is oppressive at best. Still, the steaks are superb, the wine list is genuinely extraordinary, and it's a chance to experience at first hand the level of abuse that is an integral part of New York City life. Closed Sundays. Major credit cards. 210 E. 46th St. (phone: 687-4855). Expensive.

Tavern-on-the-Green – The food is less famous than the decor and location at one of New York's most beautiful dining establishments. In winter, the snow-covered trees trimmed with tiny white lights outside the *Crystal Room* make a dazzling display. Best of all at Christmastime, but only slightly less spectacular in summer. Open daily. Major credit cards. Central Park West and 67th St. (phone: 873-3200). Expensive.

"21" Club – The legendary atmosphere and unquestionable cachet are what lure most visitors, but when the original owners sold out, there was a discernible decline in camaraderie. A refurbishing spruced up the place, and the menu was overhauled — to the dismay of most former patrons. Happily, more than a touch of the old ambience (and favorite foods) has returned recently. Ties are always required, and if you're not a regular or a celebrity, sometimes the welcome isn't very warm. The upstairs dining room is more elegant and quiet, but those who wish to see and be seen usually adorn the section on the left as you enter the downstairs bar. Closed Sundays. Major credit cards. 21 W. 52nd St. (phone: 582-7200). Expensive.

Windows on the World – Somewhat overpriced (though interesting) menu that is extremely ambitious, but the food is less alluring than the best view of the city. Try to sit along the north wall, where you'll have all of glittering Manhattan spread out at your feet. If you don't care to spend the price of dinner, stop for a drink in the bar and enjoy the superb hors d'oeuvres. There's also a reasonably priced all-day Sunday buffet. The *Cellar in the Sky* room here serves an interesting prix fixe menu with a wide choice of wines — but no view. Open daily; for weekends, reservations a month in advance are advised. Major credit cards. 1 World Trade Center (phone: 938-1111). Expensive.

Café des Artistes – One of New York's most romantic restaurants, in a West Side apartment house. Appetizers and main dishes (French country style) are all first rate, but the real lures are the desserts. Save room, for they've an unusual special offering that includes a sample of every dessert on the menu. For those with a sweet tooth, it's like visiting paradise. The most beautiful weekend brunch in town (reservations necessary). Open daily. Major credit cards. 1 W. 67th St. between Columbus Ave. and Central Park West (phone: 877-3500). Expensive to moderate.

Kitcho – Soups are notably delicate, and teriyaki grills of meat or fish are perfectly seasoned at this authentic Japanese restaurant. Try such delicacies as *kushi-katsu* — crisp, deep-fried chunks of pork — or *to-banyaki* — marinated and grilled meat or fish with broiled vegetables. With all the grilling going on, *Kitcho* needs better ventilation. Closed Saturdays. American Express and Diners Club only. 22 W. 46th St. (phone: 575-8880). Expensive to moderate.

Palm – The best sirloin steaks in New York in an atmosphere so unattractive that it's the restaurant's prime appeal. Sawdust covers the floor, tables and chairs are refugees from a thrift shop, but the steaks are just great. The largest (and most expensive) lobsters in New York are served here. *Palm Too,* across the street, is a branch serving identical food that takes care of the overflow. Closed Sundays. Major credit cards. 837 2nd Ave. (phone: 687-2953). Expensive to moderate.

Parioli Romanissimo – Ensconced in an attractive East Side townhouse and frequented by the "beautiful people," the tables at this classy spot are among the most difficult to book in the city. Those who succeed dine on pricey but delicious Italian specialties. Opt for a meaty main course like veal chop giardiniera and then splurge on the chocolate torte for dessert. Service is notoriously chilly, and even when reservations are in hand, expect a wait. Closed Sundays and Mondays. American Express, Diners Club, and Carte Blanche only. 24 E. 81st St. (phone: 288-2391). Expensive to moderate.

Parker Lighthouse – In addition to a spectacular waterfront view just across the Brooklyn Bridge and sophisticated decor, there's an interesting selection of Cajun and seafood dishes. Open daily. Major credit cards. 1 Main St. at Fulton Landing, Brooklyn (phone: 718-237-1555). Expensive to moderate.

Peter Luger – The best porterhouse (T-bone) steaks in the country, lurking in the shadows under the Brooklyn side of the Williamsburgh Bridge. The neighborhood is hardly fashionable, but the food is first class. No menu, but try the thick-sliced onions and tomatoes under the special barbecue sauce, and be sure to taste the best home fried potatoes the city has to offer. Open daily. No credit cards. 178 Broadway, Brooklyn (phone: 718-387-7400). Expensive to moderate.

Water Club – The decor at this restaurant/barge in the East River is naturally nautical, but with restraint, since the view is decorative enough: river traffic and the twinkling lights of the Manhattan and Queens skylines. The menu, too, is nautical, with similar restraint. Appetizers range from oysters and smoked salmon to Beluga caviar, entrées from Maryland crab cakes to Dover sole (with a delicately flavored beurre blanc) and lobster — but diners can also order pâté plus filet mignon or the lovely roast duck with chestnuts and poached pear. Open daily; Sunday brunch. Major credit cards. It's tricky to get there, so take a cab. East River at 30th St., on the northbound service road of the FDR Drive (phone: 683-3333). Expensive to moderate.

America – The menu is as big (and varied) as its namesake — a staggering 175-plus dishes, representing every corner of the country and the ethnic groups that inhabit it — including dishes like the American-as-apple-pie Blue Plate Special and a peanut butter and jelly sandwich. The food ranges from good to fair, and the service is best described as leisurely. With its high, exposed ceiling and mural-covered walls, America looks like a warehouse-cum-loft, with an elevated bar that, despite its football field dimensions, is jammed most nights. Open daily. Major credit cards. 9-13 E. 18th St. (phone: 505-2110). Moderate.

American Festival Café – In Rockefeller Center and cheery and very American. Reasonably priced and varied menu, including prime ribs, steaks, salad, roast chicken, and warm and cold seafood. Noted for its desserts, including Mississippi Mud pie, New York cheesecake, and key lime pie. Open daily. Major credit cards. 20 W. 50th St. (phone: 246-6699). Moderate.

Pierre au Tunnel – Onion soup, mussels, frogs' legs, and minute steaks typify the French provincial dishes featured by this theater district bistro since 1950. Try the *noisette de veau* or *tripes à la mode de Caen.* Closed Sundays. American Express, Visa, and MasterCard only. 250 W. 47th St. (phone: 582-2166). Moderate.

Azzurro – A tiny, modern storefront on the Upper East Side demonstrates the unexpected delicacy of Sicilian cooking. Grilled fish, fine pasta specials, and delectable vino santo. The waiters are all cousins; Mama is in the kitchen. Open daily. American Express and Diners Club only. 1625 Second Ave. (phone: 517-7068). Moderate.

Ballroom – When it opened a few years ago, this very pretty bistro in the Garment District introduced a new twist to Manhattan dining — the tapas bar. A changing, varied menu of *tapas* (Spanish for "appetizer") is spread along a lengthy bar, and patrons either nibble their way through dinner at the bar or head for the dining room, where waiters circulate with trays of tapas. There's also a very tempting menu of main courses, a reasonable and tasty buffet lunch, and a dessert table that's as much a feast for the eyes as the tastebuds. Cabaret-type entertainment is another reason to go. Closed Sundays and Mondays. Major credit cards. 253 W. 28th St. (phone: 244-3005). Moderate.

Black Sheep – Utterly charming French country inn atmosphere with regional cuisine. Owner Michael Safdiah, who studied under French master chefs, is especially proud of the duckling braised over an open fire with Armagnac, prunes, and apricots; the loin rack of lamb, Tuscan-style; and subtly flavored seafood specials. Vegetarian dishes are imaginative and tasty (try the artichokes with potatoes). A traditional Provençal aioli sauce (mayonnaise made with garlic, olive oil, and anchovies) served with crudités welcomes all diners. Extensive wine list. Open daily. Major credit cards. 342 W. 11th St. (phone: 242-1010). Moderate.

Café Un Deux Trois – In this lively theater district bistro, patrons draw on the paper tablecloths with crayons while waiting to sample carefully prepared daily specialties that include fresh sea trout, steaks with pommes frites, and couscous with chicken, lamb, and chickpeas. Theatergoers should plan to dine early to be sure to make curtain time. Open daily from noon to midnight (to 11 PM Sundays). Reservations necessary for 5 or more. Major credit cards. 123 W. 44th St. (phone: 354-4148). Moderate.

Café 43 – A welcome addition to the theater district, this French brasserie-style restaurant offers an array of interesting dishes, beautifully presented — chicken with pine nuts, duck confit, swordfish in tarragon sauce — and a wide selection of good wines by the glass. There's a prix fixe menu for those who are particularly budget conscious. Closed Sundays. Major credit cards. 147 W. 43rd St. (phone: 869-4200). Moderate.

Carolina – Southern and southwestern dishes grilled over hickory and mesquite are specialties. Although the red pepper shrimp can be disappointingly mild, the crab cakes are light and succulent, the corn bread flavorful, and the slaw creamy and delicious. The green chile soufflé is a tasty starter and the chocolate mud pie and tangy lime pie tempting finales. Note that the rear "garden room" can be noisy and traffic through the front room disconcerting; ask for a table to the right of the entrance. Open daily. Major credit cards. 355 W. 46th St. near 9th Ave. (phone: 245-0058). Moderate.

Cockeyed Clams – The best seafood-per-dollar value in New York. Tables are close and the dining room can get quite noisy, but you won't find a better lobster or piece of snapper in the city for these prices. Open daily. American Express only. 1678 3rd Ave at 94th St. (phone: 831-4121). Moderate.

Gage & Tollner – Holding forth at this stand since 1889, it's worth a visit, if only to watch the gaslight glowing in the evening. Specialties include lobster newburg and crabmeat Virginia. Among the specialties are 15 separate styles of potatoes. Open daily. Major credit cards. 374 Fulton St., Brooklyn (phone: 718-875-5181). Moderate.

Grotta Azzurra – Neapolitan specialties are served in a basement in the heart of Little Italy. Lobster fra diavolo exacts a high price, but it's worth the tariff. The garlic bread is like no other in this world, and it guarantees that you won't be bothered by vampires for years. Closed Mondays. No reservations. No credit cards. 387 Broome St. (phone: 925-8775). Moderate.

Hatsuhana – A Japanese restaurant that's still winning kudos from some of New York's toughest restaurant critics. The sushi, sashimi, and tempura are about the tastiest in town. Closed Sundays. Reservations necessary for dinner only. Major credit cards. 14 E. 48th St. (phone: 355-3345). Moderate.

Jean Lafitte – As accurate an evocation of a cozy Parisian neighborhood bistro as exists in New York. For French folk feeling homesick, this will cure their blues. Excellent tripe, and the best place to sample an authentic choucroute (on specials only) or steak au poivre. Superb soups, which change daily, are a special treat during a cold New York winter. Open nightly for dinner; lunch on weekdays only. Major credit cards. 68 W. 58th St. (phone: 751-2323). Moderate.

Odéon – Opened in 1980 in a gray cast-iron building, this refurbished cafeteria is in the midst of TriBeCa. Look for entrées such as squab with shiitake mushrooms and wild rice, and roast loin of lamb with white peppercorns. A dessert worth trying is crêpes with praline butter and apricot liqueur. Open daily; Sunday brunch. Major credit cards. 145 W. Broadway (phone: 233-0507). Moderate.

Periyali – In this cool Aegean oasis, patrons enjoy traditional Greek fare prepared with an exceptionally light touch. Specialties include lima bean salad with *skordalia*, a tangy potato-based purée; baked sea bass with garlic, tomato, and white wine; and moussaka with grilled zucchini. For dessert, don't miss the luscious custard-filled *galaktoboreko*. Open weekdays for lunch and daily except Sundays for dinner. Major credit cards. 35 W. 20th St. (phone: 463-7890). Moderate.

Provence – The perfect restaurant for its neighborhood. The spices and tomato-based sauces of southeastern France are nowhere better prepared, and the chicken with garlic gives a whole new meaning to the serving of fowl. A huge vat of aging brandy adorns the bar and provides a perfect digestif at the conclusion of a meal. Closed Mondays. American Express only. 38 MacDougal St. (phone: 475-7500). Moderate.

Quatorze – On the periphery of Greenwich Village, this is an attractive, convivial bistro. Diners may eat either at the marble-topped bar or in the pale yellow dining room with oak floor, white linen-draped tables, and a wall of red velvet banquettes. Try the chicory and bacon salad drenched in a hot vinaigrette dressing, then the grilled salmon in choron sauce or the grilled chicken. Choose the crispy, warm apple tart for dessert. The short wine list includes some interesting, reasonably priced offerings. Open daily. American Express only. 240 W. 14th St. (phone: 206-7006). Moderate.

Raga – A carved wooden gateway, tall carved columns, heavy silk fabrics, and antique musical instruments mounted on the walls provide the opulent setting for one of New York's finest Indian restaurants. Lobster Malabar, gosht vindaloo, and meat, poultry, and seafood specialties broiled in the stone tandoor are particularly good here. Most evenings musicians play the sitar, tabla, and flute for an unobtrusive background. Open daily. Major credit cards. 57 W. 48th St. (phone: 757-3450). Moderate.

Sabor – A tiny, unprepossessing eatery in the heart of Greenwich Village that serves up simple, Cuban-based cuisine, such as white bean soup, red snapper in green sauce, baked chicken scented with cumin, and shrimp in lime sauce. The baked coconut dessert, with cinnamon, sherry, and a dollop of whipped cream, is a must. Open daily. Major credit cards. 20 Cornelia St. (phone: 243-9579). Moderate.

Sammy's Roumanian Steak House – The last survivor of a long, Lower East Side tradition of ethnic meat restaurants. Traditional Eastern European favorites are featured, as is old country music of a sort you're not likely to hear in any other establishment. The makings for egg creams are set right on the table — an experience you don't usually find this side of Anatefka. Open daily. American Express and Diners Club only. 157 Chrystie St. (phone: 475-9131). Moderate.

Santa Fe – Less trendy than many of the new Mexican eateries that have sprung up around the city; there are no hanging plants, no neon signs, no ear-splitting conversational roar. Instead, crisp linens and salmon-colored walls hung with Mexican weavings provide a serene setting for nicely tart margaritas and well-prepared southwestern dishes. Just a few blocks from *Lincoln Center*. Open daily. Major credit cards. 72 W. 69th St. (phone: 724-0822). Moderate.

Shun Lee Palace – Chef T. T. Wang is one of New York City's most talented Chinese cooks, and his menu here includes some exciting Oriental temptations. If you can somehow round up a group of 10 to dine together, you might be interested in ordering Wang's special Chinese feast. Open daily. American Express and Diners Club only. 155 E. 55th St. (phone: 371-8844). Moderate.

Shun Lee West – Same as above, this time very near *Lincoln Center*. Actually, this recently refurbished dining room is the better of the two *Shun Lee* emporiums run by Michael Wong, and its prices are about 20% lower. Open daily. Major credit cards. 43 W. 65th St. (phone: 595-8895). Moderate.

Village Green – This 19th-century row house was recently renovated, but the new owners have kept the 2-story dining room elegant yet cozy: linen-draped tables shining with crystal and silver, and a fire snapping away in the hearth. The menu is continental, the food always well prepared, and the service friendly. Closed Sundays and Mondays. Major credit cards. 531 Hudson St. (phone: 255-1650). Moderate.

Carnegie Delicatessen – The quintessential New York deli. The sandwiches are enormous, far too big to put in a normal human mouth. Corned beef and pastrami are king; waiters provide entertaining banter (to help pass the time). Communal tables; no atmosphere save the frantic 7th Avenue scene. Open daily. No reservations. No credit cards. 854 7th Ave. (phone: 757-2245). Moderate to inexpensive.

Harvey's Chelsea Restaurant – Etched-glass windows, polished brass rails, and baroque wood paneling make this turn-of-the-century bar a delightful oasis in an otherwise dreary neighborhood. The best choice on the menu is the tasty fish and chips, accompanied by a frosty draft. Open daily. American Express only. 108 W. 18th St. (phone: 243-5644). Moderate to inexpensive.

Málaga – Delicious, reasonably priced Spanish specialties such as paella, shrimp in garlic sauce, and fish in salsa verde make this a neighborhood favorite. Try to sit in the front room, because the tin ceiling in the back room reverberates with noise when it's crowded. Open daily. Major credit cards. 406 E. 73rd St. (phone: 737-7659 or 650-0605). Moderate to inexpensive.

One Fifth Avenue – A popular, casual place whose weekend brunch (with piano player) comes highly recommended. Sirloin and lamb chops are good bets for lunch and dinner. Open daily. Major credit cards. 1 5th Ave. (phone: 260-3434). Moderate to inexpensive.

Il Bocconcino – The celebrity photographs in the window date back to *la dolce vita* days, when Gilberto was a *papparazzo* in Rome. Now he and co-owner Giorgio run this modest but congenial Greenwich Village spot, with lace curtains, white tablecloths, and some murals of Italianate architecture to remind them of home. Sample the bruschetta (Roman garlic bread), then follow with pasta, chicken, veal, seafood, or a meal of Gilberto's pizza. Sidewalk tables in summer. Open daily. Major credit cards. 168 Sullivan St. (phone: 982-0329). Inexpensive.

Green Tree – For a taste of the old country, head to this family-run Upper West Side establishment. Hungarian waiters load down your table with specialties of their homeland — chicken or cold cherry soup, stuffed cabbage, and Hungarian goulash. For dessert try the palacsintas, crêpes filled with cheese or apricot jam. Open daily. No credit cards. 1034 Amsterdam Ave. at W. 111th St. (phone: 864-9106). Inexpensive.

Hard Rock Café – More a monument to rock 'n' roll than a restaurant, this funky spot — akin to the original in London — sports all manner of memorabilia: the guitars of Eric Clapton, Pete Townsend, and Bo Diddley, gold records of the Rolling Stones, and Prince's purple coat. Check out the 45-foot guitar-shaped bar and the 1959 Cadillac Biarritz jutting out from the 2nd floor. The menu is your basic hamburgers and shakes; the music can be very loud. Popular with the younger set, the café draws between 1,500 and 2,400 patrons a day. Open daily. Major credit cards. 221 W. 57th St. (phone: 489-6565). Inexpensive.

Hunan House – Among Chinatown's best, this pleasant restaurant specializes in the subtly spiced food of the province of Hunan. Start off with fried dumplings or hot and sour soup, then have Hunan lamb, prepared with scallions; Changsha beef, done in a hot sauce with broccoli; or Confucius prawns with cashews. Open daily. No reservations. American Express and Diners Club only. 45 Mott St. (phone: 962-0010). Inexpensive.

Manhattan Brewing Company – A newly renovated 3-level restaurant-cum-shopping complex features authentic barbecued, smoked, and grilled dishes — served at the *Tap Room* and the *Ocean Grill* — as well as a raw bar, liquor bar and brewed-on-the-premises beers. Open daily. MasterCard, Visa, and American Express. 40-42 Thompson St. (phone: 219-9250). Inexpensive.

Pamir – A small, family-run restaurant specializing in Afghan (much like Indian) cooking. The delicately seasoned lamb dishes are very good. Closed Mondays. MasterCard and Visa only. 1437 2nd Ave. (phone: 734-3791). Inexpensive.

Tennessee Mountain – Some of the meatiest baby back ribs in town come from this casual SoHo outpost. The gentle tomato-based sauce is also used to flavor the barbecued chicken, and don't miss the fried onion rings. Seafood is also served. Open daily; weekend brunch. Major credit cards. 143 Spring St. (phone: 431-3993). Inexpensive.

Sunday brunch is a cherished tradition among New Yorkers (who usually take along a copy of the Sunday *New York Times*). Some popular brunch spots are *Sarabeth's Kitchen,* 423 Amsterdam Ave. (phone: 496-6280) and 1295 Madison Ave. (phone: 410-7335); *Provence,* 38 MacDougal St. (phone: 475-7500); *Man Ray Bistro,* 169 8th Ave. (phone: 627-4220); *Odéon,* 145 W. Broadway (phone: 233-0507); *Cadillac Bar,* 15 W. 21st St. (phone: 645-7220); *Brasserie,* 100 E. 53rd St. (phone: 751-4840); and *Florent,* 69 Gansevoort St. (phone: 989-5779). Most of these cost under $20 per person. Hotel dining rooms with copious, and more costly, brunch buffets are the *Café Pierre* at the *Pierre; Ambassador Grill* at *UN Plaza; Peacock Alley* at the *Waldorf-Astoria;* and the *Palm Court* at the *Plaza.*

 TAKING TEA: New Yorkers have become quite fond of the British tradition of afternoon tea, and a number of the city's poshest hotels have jumped on the bandwagon: the *Mayfair Regent, Lowell, Pierre, Helmsley Palace, Regency,* and *Stanhope* all offer superlative service to shoppers and browsers, with a variety of teas, scones, sandwiches, and condiments. Taking tea is a great way to experience the elegant ambience of these hotels without having to stay the night. Prices are mostly under $20; À la carte service is also available at some hotels.

OKLAHOMA CITY

On April 22, 1889, the United States opened the theretofore protected federal lands of central Oklahoma to settlement by white men. Between dawn and dusk more than 10,000 people poured across these unrelieved prairie midlands staking claims and laying out homesteads as if pursued by the Furies. By nightfall a city of flickering campfires and roughly marked claims outlined the farthest extents of the city born so abruptly, and in such a fever, on the open prairie.

If it was a moment of dreams fulfilled for the settlers, it was the bitter end of a promise to the Indians who had been "given" Oklahoma years before. The area had become American in 1803 as part of that most fabulous of real estate deals, the Louisiana Purchase. Almost immediately, it was declared Indian Territory, and what remained of Native American tribes throughout the US, from the forests of New England to the bayous of the South, were arbitrarily and compulsorily moved there (see *A Short Tour of Indian America*, DIVERSIONS). The land was owned and administered by the federal government, but dedicated to use for, and by, the Indians. This commitment lasted about 60 years. By the end of the Civil War, the area was halved, the western half becoming Oklahoma Territory, the eastern half remaining Indian Territory. From then until 1907, when both territories became the State of Oklahoma, the Indians lost land as the open and to-be-settled areas were extended.

But for the settlers, the area that was to be Oklahoma City represented one precious commodity — space, inexpensive land on which to establish homes. Just how ambitious they were, and how many of them there were, is still evident: In terms of area, Oklahoma City is one of the largest American cities, with 621 square miles within its municipal borders. And more than ambitious, it was lucky: Beneath the surface of jealously guarded homesteads percolated a sea of oil, and Oklahoma became the city with oil derricks downtown (even in front of the capitol). Oil meant money, and with the money came a level of sophistication that a prairie town scarcely could have expected otherwise. In the last couple of years, the bounty of black gold has been less apparent as the worldwide oil glut cut revenues and severely increased unemployment. As a result, Oklahomans avidly seek other sources of income as they wait for the energy industry to stabilize and oil prices to rise.

Today Oklahoma City has a population of close to 1 million people. Oil is still a mainstay — a rather shaky one of late — of the economy, but the giant Oklahoma City Air Materiel Area (Tinker Air Force Base) employs more than 35,000 civilians and 4,800 military personnel. The FAA Aeronautical Center, including the Civil Aeromedical Institute, is at the city's bustling Will Rogers World Airport. More than 2 million passengers fly to and from Oklahoma City annually. The city is also a major distribution center for

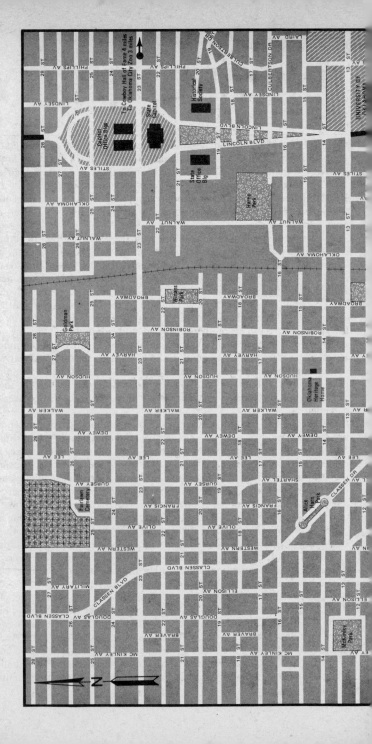

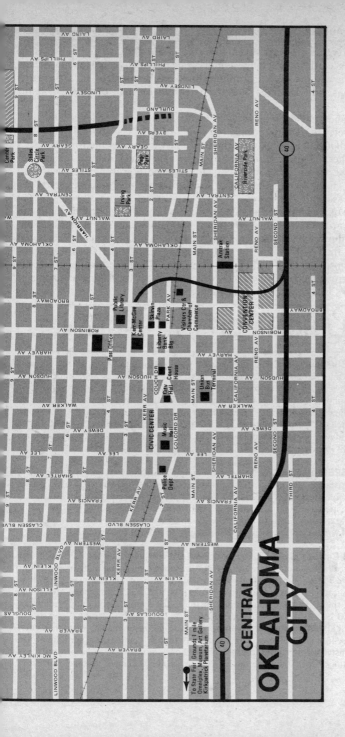

CENTRAL OKLAHOMA CITY

wheat and cotton grown in surrounding areas. The OKC feeder market is the third largest cattle market in the country. The University of Oklahoma School of Medicine with its affiliate hospitals, Research Building, Medical Research Foundations, and Veterans Hospital is considered one of the best in the nation.

Sports and religion play a big part in the lives of residents. OKC (as residents refer to it) is practically the center of what is commonly known as the Bible Belt. More than 45 denominations are represented in the city's 500 churches, from Zen Buddhist to Baptist (lots more Baptists than Buddhists). The fervor of spirit is not all religious, however. Every autumn, "Big Red" fever sweeps the city as the University of Oklahoma starts the football season.

Because of its wide-open spaces, Oklahoma City is mainly residential, with plenty of yard to mow between homes. Local real estate is a relative bargain, especially during the current economic malaise. A house and land that would cost more than $200,000 in the eastern or far western parts of the country currently costs less than half that amount here. What's more, the residential area is surrounded by lovely lakes, which are great for fishing and some of the nation's best sailing (even ice sailing).

OKLAHOMA CITY AT-A-GLANCE

SEEING THE CITY: The *Eagles Nest* restaurant, on top of the 20-story United Founders Life Tower, offers a view of the city as well as fine seafood specialties. 5900 Mosteller Dr. (phone: 840-5655). *Carriages for Hire* (phone: 235-1303) offers daily tours through downtown by horse-drawn carriage; tours also run Friday and Saturday nights, 6PM until midnight. *Territorial Tours Limited,* by Carol Jordan, 1636 SW 79th. Terrace, Oklahoma City, OK 73159, offers individual and group tours across the state. Most popular tours are through metro area, Guthrie and Norman. Call 681-6432.

SPECIAL PLACES: Most of the major attractions are not within walking distance. The city's Masstrans system provides bus service to all points of interest. For bus information, call 235-RIDE. You can also rent a car; most national car rental agencies are represented.

Arts Annex – Ongoing exhibitions, classes, and 1-day workshops (in art, dance, and professional writing). Open daily. 3000 Pershing Blvd. State Fairgrounds (phone: 948-6400).

National Cowboy Hall of Fame and Western Heritage Center – Hi-ho, Silver! Cowboys, real and fictional, line the halls of this outstanding museum. In addition to the extensive collection of Western art and sculpture, there are dioramas, relief maps showing migration paths, and a model Western village. Also represented are famous cowboys of the silver screen and heroes of the rodeo circuit. Open daily. Admission charge. 1700 NE 63rd St. (phone: 478-2250).

Kirkpatrick Center Museum Complex – A single price enables visitors to enjoy all the museums and galleries comprising this unique complex. In addition to the attractions listed below, the *Kirkpatrick Center* houses numerous exhibitions and historical collections. Open daily. Admission charge. 2100 NE 52nd St. (phone: 427-5461).

Air Space Museum – Over 500 exhibits, including reproductions of the Wright Brothers' airplane and the space shuttle, tell the exciting story of aviation in Oklahoma and across the nation (phone: 424-1443).

Center of the American Indian – Donated to showcase Native American culture, the museum's permanent collection includes paintings, artifacts, crafts, and jewelry (phone: 427-5228).

International Photography Hall of Fame – Experience the world through the eyes of world-famous master photographers; of special note is the breathtaking photo-mural of the Grand Canyon (phone: 424-4055).

Omniplex Science Museum – One of the largest science and technology museums in the Southwest; hands-on participation is encouraged to make science fun for all ages (phone: 424-5545).

Kirkpatrick Planetarium – The most exciting way yet to discover the universe. Take a backyard look at the night skies on a voyage to the planets, stars, and galaxies (phone: 424-5545).

Enterprise Square, USA – A unique learning center that uses contemporary educational techniques, entertainment, and audience participation to communicate the fundamentals of the US economic system. Admission charge. 2501 E. Memorial Rd. (phone: 425-5030).

Oklahoma City Zoo – Captivity seems to agree with the more than 2,000 animals, birds, and reptiles here, perhaps because they're left to wander freely in natural settings. The zoo's newest attraction, Aquaticus, features live dolphin shows and marine life exhibits. A safari train transports visitors over 500 acres of exhibits. Open daily except Christmas and New Year's Day. Admission charge. Martin Luther King Blvd. and NE 50th St. (phone: 424-3344).

State Capitol – This is one of the few capitols in the nation that does not have a dome. It's also the only one with active oil wells on the grounds. The capitol complex consists of several buildings. Most interesting is the main building, of granite and limestone, with pillars and a wide staircase in front. A cowboy statue greets visitors entering the lobby, and murals of Oklahoma history hang in the halls. Open daily. Lincoln Blvd., between 22nd and 23rd Sts. (phone: 521-2011).

State Museum of Oklahoma – A fascinating collection of Indian artifacts chronicling Indian history from diggings that go back to AD 400 and to the days of Custer and Buffalo Bill. The library has one of the most complete archives of historical documents on American Indians in the US. Open daily. No admission charge. On the capitol grounds, in the Oklahoma Historical Society, 2100 N. Lincoln Blvd. (phone: 521-2491).

Frontier City Theme Park – Visitors enjoy thrilling rides and view exciting live and animated shows at this "western-style" theme park. Open daily, May through September. Admission charge. Rte. 35N and 122nd St. (phone: 478-2412).

White Water – At this amusement park, visitors can body-surf in the Wave Pool, take a slow ride over the rapids in an inner tube, or slide down the Bermuda Triangle (the tallest water slide in the world). Open May through September. Admission charge. 3908 W. Reno (phone: 943-9687).

Metro Concourse – Beneath downtown Oklahoma City is an extensive network of tunnels and skywalks connecting dozens of unique restaurants and retail shops to hotels, office buildings, and the Myriad Convention Center. Stretching over 1½ miles, it is one of the most comprehensive enclosed pedestrian systems in the country. Open daily. No admission charge.

■**EXTRA SPECIAL:** Myriad Gardens, one of Oklahoma City's unique attractions, is in the heart of downtown. Originally patterned after Tivoli Gardens in Copenhagen, this attractive park features spectacular landscaped hills, gardens, and water-falls, enhanced by the Crystal Bridge — a huge glass and steel structure conceived as a greenhouse, containing exotic plants from all over the world. Live entertainment featured regularly on the *Water Stage* (phone: 232-9903). Open daily. No admission charge Saturday mornings from 10 AM to noon. Other times: $1 adults; 50¢ children 6-12 and senior citizens.

SOURCES AND RESOURCES

TOURIST INFORMATION: Oklahoma City Convention and Tourism Bureau has brochures and maps; 4 Santa Fe Plaza, Oklahoma City, OK 73102 (phone: 278-8912).

Television Stations – KOCO Channel 5–ABC; KTVY Channel 4–NBC; KWTV Channel 9–CBS; OETA Channel 13–PBS.

Radio Stations – AM: KTOK 1000 (news/talk); KOMA 1520 (easy listening); WKY 930 (country). FM: KJYL 103 (top 40); KKNG 92.5 (news/talk); KMGL 104 (classical).

Local Coverage – *Daily Oklahoman,* morning daily; *Journal Record,* daily for business and law news.

Food – *Downtowner* magazine, weekly.

Telephone – The area code for Oklahoma City is 405.

Sales Tax – Local sales tax is 5¼%.

CLIMATE: The weather is very changeable. Changeable means that in winter it can be 12F in the morning and 45F or 50F in the afternoon. In the summer it sometimes gets up to 100F or higher, but the wind and low humidity keep it from being totally unbearable. The winds sometimes gust to 35 to 40 miles an hour.

GETTING AROUND: Airport – Will Rogers World Airport is a 15-minute drive from the downtown area; taxi fare should cost about $13. *Airport Express* (phone: 681-3311) provides transportation from the airport to downtown for $6 per person, plus $3 for each additional passenger.

Bus – Masstrans operates frequent buses; 300 E. California (phone: 235-RIDE).

Taxi – There are taxi stands in front of the big hotels and at major intersections. For dependable service, call *Yellow Cab* (phone: 232-6161) or *Safeway Cab* (phone: 235-1431).

Car Rental – Every major national firm is represented.

LOCAL SERVICES: Business Services – *Kelly Services,* 6303 N. Portland, Suite 105 (phone: 946-4309).

Mechanic – *Ray's Tire and Auto Service,* 5201 N. Pennsylvania (phone: 842-1427).

MUSEUMS: In addition to the variety of museums described in *Special Places,* other Oklahoma City museums include the following:

1899er Harn Museum and Gardens – 312 NE 18th St. (phone: 235-4058).

45th Infantry Division Museum – 2145 NE 36th St. (phone: 424-5313).

Governor's Mansion – 820 NE 23rd St. (phone: 521-2342).

Museum of the Unassigned Lands – 4300 N. Sewell (phone: 521-1889).

National Softball Hall of Fame – 2801 NE 50th St. (phone: 424-5266).
Oklahoma Art Center – 3113 Pershing Blvd., State Fair Park (phone: 946-4477).
Oklahoma Firefighters Museum – 2716 NE 50th St. (phone: 424-3440).
Oklahoma Heritage Center – 201 NW 14th St. (phone: 235-4458).
Oklahoma Museum of Art – 7316 Nichols Rd. (phone: 840-2759).
Oklahoma Museum of Natural History – 1335 Asp Ave., Norman (phone: 325-4711).
Overholser Mansion – 405 NW 15th St. (phone: 528-8485).

MAJOR COLLEGES AND UNIVERSITIES: Central State University (Edmond; phone: 341-2980): University of Oklahoma (Norman; phone: 325-0311); Oklahoma State University (Stillwater; phone: 744-5000); Oklahoma City University (2501 NW Blackwelder; phone: 521-5000); Bethany Nazarene College (6729 NW 39th Expy.; phone: 789-6400).

SPECIAL EVENTS: *Wintertales,* storytelling festival, January; *Festival of the Arts,* April; *Paseo Festival,* arts festival, Memorial Day weekend; *Red Earth,* Native American celebration, June; *Aerospace America,* air show, June; *Indian Hills Pow Wow,* August; *Festifall,* arts festival, September; *Oklahoma State Fair,* September; *World Championship Morgan Horse Show,* October; *World Championship Quarterhorse Show, World Championship Appaloosa Horse Show,* November; *American Bicycle Association "Grand National,"* December; *All-College Basketball Tournament,* December.

SPORTS AND FITNESS: Baseball – The *'89ers* play at *All Sports Stadium,* Fairgrounds Park, 10th and May (phone: 946-8989).
  Fishing – Anglers will find excellent fishing at any of the beautiful lakes in the Oklahoma City area: Lake Hefner (Hefner Rd. & N. Portland), Lake Overholser (NW 36th & County Line Rd.), Lake Stanley Draper (I-240 & Douglas Blvd.), and Lake Thunderbird (Hwy. 9, east of Norman).
  Fitness Center – The *YMCA* has a pool, track, weights, and squash, handball, and racquetball courts, 125 NW 5th St. (phone: 232-6101).
  Football – College games are held at *Owen Stadium,* at the University of Oklahoma in Norman (phone: 325-0311), and *Lewis Field* at Oklahoma State University, Stillwater (phone: 744-5746).
  Golf – The best city course is at Lincoln Park, Eastern Ave. and NE 50th St.
  Horse Racing – *Remington Park,* the state's first major pari-mutuel racetrack, is an $81-million facility featuring 153 days of thoroughbred, quarterhorse, and mixed-breed racing. For information and schedules, call 424-1000.
  Jogging – It's possible to run to Memorial Park, at NW 32nd and Classen; in the park is a posted map showing 2- to 8-mile routes. Run around Lake Hefner, in Stars and Stripes Park, off Hefner Road, or the less traveled Lake Overholser, west of downtown and reachable only by car; or take the #11 or #12 bus to Westwood and run around Woodson Park (1½ miles).
  Sailing – There's good sailing (and ice sailing) on Lake Hefner, Lake Overholser, Lake Stanley Draper, and Lake Thunderbird.
  Tennis – Good public courts are at Memorial Park, 32nd and Classen, and Will Rogers Park, 36th and Portland.

THEATER: The *Lyric Theater* hosts a professional summer stock company that performs musicals from June through August, NW 25th and Blackwelder (phone: 528-3636). The *Jewel Box Theatre,* 3700 N. Walker (phone: 521-1786); and *Carpenter Square Theater,* 840 Robert S. Kerr (phone: 232-6500), present innovative, contemporary productions year-round.

MUSIC: The *Oklahoma City Philharmonic Orchestra* plays at the Civic Center Music Hall, 201 Channing Sq. (phone: 232-7575). *Oklahoma City University music school* frequently sends opera singers to the Metropolitan Opera in New York City. Check out its performance schedules by calling 521-5000.

NIGHTCLUBS AND NIGHTLIFE: *Fritzi's* has top-of-the-chart entertainers, 3034 N. Portland (phone: 949-1880); and *Jokers, The Comedy Club,* 2925 W. Britton Rd., features nationally acclaimed comedians (phone: 752-5270).

BEST IN TOWN

CHECKING IN: Over 75 hotels and motels in Oklahoma City offer travelers a wide range of accommodations and prices. Expect to pay $70 and up for a double room at hotels listed as expensive and about $50 in the moderate category. A number of inexpensive hotels may be found in the $30 range. All telephone numbers are in the 405 area code unless otherwise indicated.

Embassy Suites – A modern hotel offering 236 1- and 2-bedroom suites opening onto balconies overlooking a central atrium. Dining room, spa, whirlpool bath, concierge, free airport transportation. Meridian and SW 18th (phone: 682-6000 or 800-EMBASSY). Expensive.

Waterford – Features include 196 rooms and suites that are graciously appointed with lovely cherry wood armoires and other traditional pieces. The *Waterford* restaurant offers formal continental dining; the *Veranda Room* serves lighter fare. For relaxation, guests enjoy a well-equipped health spa, including Nautilus, sauna, whirlpool bath, outdoor pool, tennis courts, jogging track, and squash courts. Free airport transportation. 63rd at Pennsylvania (phone: 848-4782). Expensive.

Marriott Oklahoma City – The city's newest hotel offers modern decor along with the late-night hot spot, *Russell's*. Free airport transportation, spa, whirlpool bath, concierge. 3233 NW Expy. (phone: 842-6633 or 800-228-9290). Expensive to moderate.

Sheraton Century Center – In the heart of downtown, this modern building has 400 rooms, renovated in elegant decorator colors. Outdoor pool, disco, and restaurants. 1 N. Broadway (phone: 235-2780 or 800-325-3535). Expensive to moderate.

Skirvin Plaza – An Oklahoma City historic landmark, this beautiful hotel has maintained its elegance and grace through the years. In the heart of downtown, near the *Civic Center Music Hall* and theaters. Free airport transportation, concierge. 1 Park Ave. (phone: 232-4411). Expensive to moderate.

Fifth Season Inn – One of the city's newest hotels, it is centrally located and offers beautifully decorated rooms opening onto a central atrium. Along with a full complimentary breakfast and cocktails, special services include a Jacuzzi, hot tub, sauna, and free transportation to the airport or *Remington Park* racetrack. 63rd St. at Broadway Extension (phone: 843-5558). Moderate.

Hilton Inn West – With 4 clubs under its roof, it has become a popular gathering place for visitors as well as locals. In addition to 508 guestrooms, there are 4 pools (1 indoor), tennis, volleyball, and paddle tennis courts, exercise room, and sauna. 401 S. Meridian (phone: 947-7681 or 800-HILTONS). Moderate.

Saddleback Inn – In the heart of the I-40 and Meridian area, adjacent to many of the finest restaurants and city nightlife spots, it features a restaurant, lounge, outdoor pool, and spa. Free airport transportation. 4300 SW 3rd (phone: 947-7000). Moderate.

EATING OUT: Oklahoma City is known for its steaks. Restaurants are spread out across the city, rather than concentrated into one area. Expect to pay $40 at an expensive restaurant; between $15 and $20 at those we've classed as moderate; under $15 at the inexpensive one. Prices are for a meal for two, without drinks, wine, or tip. Liquor by the drink is available in Oklahoma County. All telephone numbers are in the 405 area code unless otherwise indicated.

Eagle's Nest – In addition to an elegant atmosphere and a magnificent view of the city, menu features include steaks, lobster, and veal. Open daily. Major credit cards. 5900 Mosteller Dr., United Founders Tower (phone: 840-5655). Expensive.

Haunted House – Dine in a relaxed atmosphere in a lovely old country inn serving steaks and seafood. Closed Sundays. Major credit cards. Reservations necessary. 1 mile east of the Cowboy Hall of Fame, just off I-44 (phone: 478-1417). Expensive to moderate.

Hungry Peddler – Noted for its outstanding prime ribs and seafood specialties, it offers a deluxe salad bar and family atmosphere. No reservations. Open daily. Major credit cards. 4500 W. Reno (phone: 947-0779). Expensive to moderate.

Alberta's Tea Room – A restaurant with a quiet atmosphere and fine food and service. *Alberta's* menu is the culmination of years of creative cooking, with homemade rolls, steaks, fresh shrimp in a luscious rémoulade sauce, and other specialties. Open for lunch only; closed Sundays. Reservations necessary for parties of five or more. Major credit cards. French Market Mall at 63rd and N. May (phone: 842-3458). Moderate.

Applewoods – Moderately priced, excellent food in an elegant setting. All you can eat of the best apple fritters and dinner rolls found anywhere. Open daily. Major credit cards. 4301 SW 3rd (phone: 947-8484). Moderate.

Bayou – Popular for specialties such as fresh seafood, jambalaya, and shrimp Créole. Live entertainment evenings. Closed Sundays and Mondays. Major credit cards. 2301 S. Meridian (phone: 682-8200). Moderate.

Harrigans – The tastiest, widest variety of food in Oklahoma City: prime ribs, steaks, chicken, quiche, hamburgers, potato casserole, salads, homemade desserts, all served in attractive, brass-appointed dining rooms. Drinks served in club area. Open daily. Three locations: 2125 N. Memorial (phone: 751-7322), 6420 NW Expy. (phone: 728-1329), and 2203 SW 74th (phone: 686-1012). Moderate.

Magnolia Café – Authentic Cajun-Créole cooking, direct from Acadia, Louisiana. Live Dixieland band Friday and Saturday evenings. Fun atmosphere. Open daily. 6714 N. Western (phone: 848-1026). Moderate.

Molly Murphy's House of Fine Repute – Waiters and waitresses here are actually performers who dress up like comic and storybook characters. The menu features steaks and chicken, and the Bacchus feast, a platter of steak, chicken, vegetables, and fruit. Open daily. No reservations. Major credit cards. 1100 S. Meridian (phone: 942-8588). Moderate.

Santa Fe Crossing – A good choice for lovers of Mexican food, it also has a charming Southwestern desert decor. Open daily. Reservations unnecessary. MasterCard and Visa only. 36 W. Memorial Pkwy. (phone: 755-9030). Moderate.

Sullivan's – This is the place for straightforward American food — prime ribs, choice steaks, and seafood — prepared to perfection. Private dining rooms available. Reservations advised. Major credit cards. Corner of Reno and Meridian (phone: 943-5740). Moderate.

Texanna Reds – Sizzling mesquite-broiled fajitas and other Mexican specialties. Adult gameroom upstairs. Open daily. Major credit cards. 4600 W. Reno (phone: 947-8665). Moderate.

Sleepy Hollow – The next best thing to eating a home-cooked meal. All meals are served family style. Entrées include chicken, steaks, shrimp, ribs, and catfish. Open daily. Major credit cards. 1101 NE 50th (phone: 424-1614). Moderate to inexpensive.

Johnnie's Charcoal Broiler – Absolutely the best charcoal-broiled burgers in the region and excellent steaks served in a casual, family atmosphere. Open daily. 2652 W. Britton Rd. (phone: 751-2565) and 421 SW 74th (phone: 634-4681). Inexpensive.

Oklahoma County Line – Barbecue is king here, a hearty variety stirred up from beef ribs, brisket, and smoked sausages. Prime ribs, pork loin, and duck and chicken are also well prepared. There's even homemade ice cream for dessert. 1226 NE 63rd St. (phone: 478-4955). Inexpensive.

La Roca – Besides the attractive, casual atmosphere, devotees (as well as newcomers) also enjoy some of the best Mexican food outside of Mexico. Closed Sundays. Major credit cards. 412 S. Walker (phone: 235-0703). Inexpensive.

OMAHA

Whenever a stand-up comic wants to take a shot at a cowtown, he invariably aims at Omaha. Omaha has a lot of cows, and cows are a sure laugh. The blizzards and thundershowers are funny, too, but they obscure the target. What the comic fails to mention is that the Wizard of Oz also came from Omaha (as he admits when he's been debunked), and though it's no Emerald City, it has considerable appeal.

Nebraska's largest city (metropolitan population of 377,000) strikes a nice compromise between the friendly ways of a small town and the cultural sophistication of a far larger city. Omaha is the industrial center of the Great Plains and maintains one of America's largest shopping centers, but also has relatively clean air, a low crime rate, and free-flowing traffic. A good art museum, an ambitious opera, a symphony, and a zoo, provide evidence that Omaha is no longer just an overgrown cowtown, though the cows continue to be pretty important citizens.

Omaha is on the west bank of the Missouri River, and, with its suburbs, spreads out across 89 square miles of rolling midwestern terrain. The river, which runs 2,723 miles from southwest Montana to join the Mississippi north of St. Louis, has played an important role in the city's historic and economic development. Founded in 1854 by a ferryman from Council Bluffs, the raw young river town bristled with gunfighters and gamblers. In 1868, saloon keepers outnumbered teachers, and undertakers outnumbered clergymen. But its location on the river and the naming of the city by President Lincoln as the eastern terminus of the transcontinental railroad in 1862, assured Omaha's future prosperity. During the following decades, the prairie gave way to stockyards, plants, and warehouses. Today barges transport grain, farm products, and machinery on the Missouri, and the transcontinental railway lines converge in the home of Union Pacific. Omaha is a major center of grain and livestock markets, meat packing, insurance, and is the headquarters of the Air Force's Strategic Air Command.

Despite its advantageous position, Omaha's collective ego is sensitive about being so far removed from America's cultural capitals. But this situation, too, has its assets. Residents are proud that many silly notions ballyhooed elsewhere never really catch on in Omaha. And some of them never even arrive. Swinging nightspots are not that common, but the sunsets are beautiful. The Gerald Ford Birthsite is now a pleasant park. And there are many places to rustle up an Omaha steak, which is a carnivore's justly celebrated slab of pleasure.

Though the downtown area has been in a slow state of decline for twenty years, and many of the businesses have moved out to West Omaha, which sprawls with shopping centers, fast-food chains, and apartment complexes, a relatively recent "Return to the River" movement has generated renewed

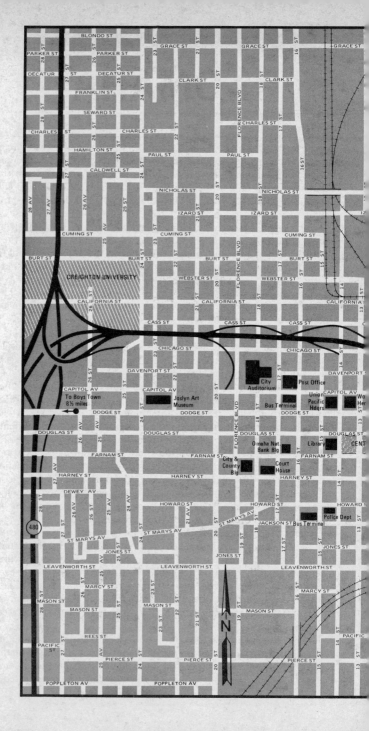

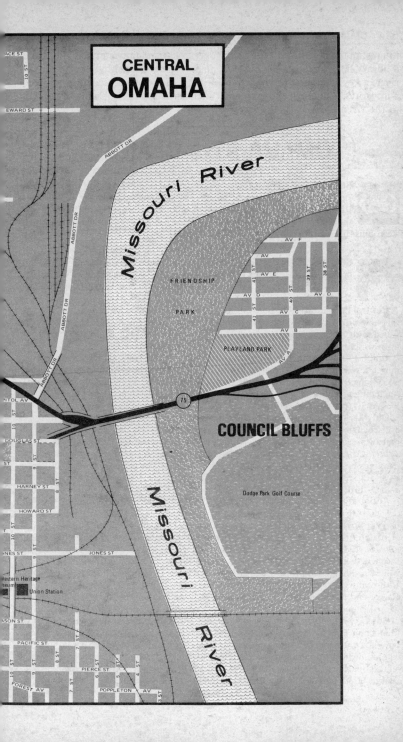

CENTRAL
OMAHA

Missouri River

FRIENDSHIP

PARK

PLAYLAND PARK

75

COUNCIL BLUFFS

Dodge Park Golf Course

Missouri River

Missouri River

ACE ST

10 ST

EWARD ST

ABBOTT DR

ABBOTT DR

ABBOTT DR

ABBOTT DR

PITOL AV

ST

10 ST

DOUGLAS ST

ST

9 ST

HARNEY ST

8 ST

HOWARD ST

10 ST

9 ST

JNES ST

JONES ST

western Heritage
seum

Union Station

ASON ST

PACIFIC ST

10

9 ST

8 ST

7 ST

PIERCE ST

6 ST

5 ST

4 ST

FOREST AV

POPPLETON AV

3 ST

AV F

AV

AV E

41 ST

39 ST

38 ST

AV D

40 ST

AV D

41 ST

AV C

AV B

AV A

interest in the downtown area. New government and university buildings and a library have already been built. In place of deteriorated buildings near the river, a key section of the new Central Park Mall has been completed, lined with stores, fountains, and even an artificial stream that will someday stretch to the river.

OMAHA AT-A-GLANCE

SEEING THE CITY: *Maxine's,* a restaurant and lounge atop the *Red Lion Inn,* offers the best view of Omaha — the metropolitan area, the Missouri River, and farther east to the small industrial town of Council Bluffs and the bluffs themselves, which are windblown deposits of soil that have formed steep hills, unusual for midwestern terrain.

SPECIAL PLACES: Omaha is spread out. You can walk around downtown or take the bus, but it's best to have a car to visit the places of interest on the outskirts of town, and in West Omaha, which is the thriving business center.

Central Park Mall – Reclaimed from a decayed commercial and warehouse district, this new urban park will stretch a mile east to the Missouri River when completed. Lined with an artificial stream, pond, and waterfall, the Mall is already the site of festivals and free concerts in nice weather. 14th and Douglas Sts.

Union Pacific Historical Museum – In Union Pacific National Headquarters, the museum recalls this line's colorful history as a transcontinental trailblazer, displaying everything from artifacts from the driving of the Golden Spike to Lincoln memorabilia (including a replica of his funeral car). Closed Sundays. No admission charge. 1415 Dodge St. (phone: 271-3530).

Old Market – Once Omaha's wholesale produce center, the market is now an ever-changing collection of small shops, restaurants, pubs, art and craft galleries, pinball arcades, and plant stores. Among the most interesting of the galleries is the *Artists' Cooperative,* which features contemporary and abstract prints, sculpture, and paintings by 30 of the area's best artists. The *Spaghetti Works* serves lunch and dinner — all the spaghetti and as much of the works (bread, salad, sauces) as you can eat for a song. 11th and Howard Sts.

Antiquarium – Near but not part of the Old Market, the *Antiquarium* has the real old stuff, from rare 19th-century manuscripts to over a half-million used books at bargain prices. Closed Sundays. 1215 Harney St. (phone: 341-8077).

Joslyn Art Museum – This monolithic chunk of pink marble holds one of the finest midwestern and western collections around, as well as exhibitions of international art through the ages. It features the Maximilian-Bodmer Collection of paintings, done while on the Belgian prince's Upper Missouri River Expedition of 1833-34. Also has 19th-century western landscapes of Albert Bierstadt, paintings by Remington, Russell, Catlin, and the Stewart-Miller Collection, focusing on the Great Plains of the 1830s. Closed Mondays. Admission charge. 2200 Dodge St. (phone: 342-3300).

Boys Town – An internationally famous institution for homeless boys, it was founded in 1917 by Father Flanagan in the belief that there is no such thing as a bad boy, given a good Christian upbringing and education. Self-conducted tours of the campus, which has 65 buildings including grade and high schools, a trade school, gyms, a fine philatelic and numismatic center, and 350 good boys. Open daily. No admission charge. 138th and W. Dodge Rd. (phone: 498-1140).

■**EXTRA SPECIAL:** Fifty miles southwest of Omaha along I-80 is Lincoln, the state's capital and second largest city. The *University of Nebraska State Museum* (14th and U Sts., in Morrill Hall) has excellent displays of the geology and animal life of the Great Plains from prehistoric to modern times, as well as the world's largest mammoth. The 400-foot capitol is an impressive sight, visible for miles around, and features a glazed dome with the Indian Thunderbird design, topped by a 32-foot statue of *The Sower.*

SOURCES AND RESOURCES

TOURIST INFORMATION: The Omaha Convention and Visitors Bureau, 1819 Farnam, suite 1200, Omaha, NE 68183 (phone: 444-4660) publishes brochures and maps of attractions that are available in all the hotels. For timely information on scheduled cultural events, call the bureau's Events Hotline (phone: 444-6800).

Television Stations – KETV Channel 7–ABC; KMTV Channel 3–CBS; WOWT Channel 6–NBC; NETV Channel 12–PBS.

Radio Stations – AM: KFAB 1110 (adult contemporary); KOIL 1290 (oldies); KKAR 1180 (news/talk). FM: KGOR 99.9 (1960s and '70s music); KEFM 96.1 (adult contemporary); KQKQ 98.5 (contemporary hits); KUNO 90.7 (classical/jazz/new age).

Local Coverage – *Omaha World-Herald,* morning and evening daily, publishes a Sunday *Entertainment* magazine, which lists the coming week's events.

Food – Weekend editions of the *Omaha World-Herald* are the best bet for current information.

Telephone – The area code for Omaha is 402.

Sales Tax – The sales tax in Omaha is 5.5%; across the river in Council Bluffs, shoppers pay a 4% tax.

CLIMATE: Seasons are distinct and there is daily variety, perhaps a bit too much for some when the mercury drops to 15F below or rises to 105F above. Omaha is mostly sunny, with evening showers and thunderstorms occurring frequently between April and September.

GETTING AROUND: Airport – Omaha's Eppley Airfield is a 10-minute drive from downtown; cab fare should run about $6. Most hotels offer free airport shuttle transportation for guests.

Bus – Metropolitan Area Transit provides efficient service for the city and Council Bluffs. For route information contact Metro Area Transit, 2615 Cuming St. (phone: 341-0800).

Taxi – Cabs can be picked up at taxi stands in front of major hotels or at the airport, or can be ordered on the phone. Major companies are *Happy Cab* (phone: 339-0110 or 331-8294); *Checker Cab* (phone: 342-8000); *Safeway Cab* (phone: 342-7474); and *Yellow Cab* (phone: 341-9000).

Car Rental – Omaha has offices of the major national firms and inexpensive service is provided by *Thrifty,* 2323 Abbott Dr. (phone: 345-1040).

LOCAL SERVICES: Business Services – *Professional Typing Services,* 900 S. 74th Plaza (phone: 397-0309).

Mechanic – *Anderson's Amoco Service,* 3423 S. 72nd St., (phone: 391-8611).

MUSEUMS: In addition to the *Joslyn Art Museum* and the *Union Pacific Historical Museum* (see *Special Places*), you ought to visit:

Omaha History Museum – Closed Mondays. 801 S. 10th St. (phone: 444-5071).

Strategic Aerospace Museum – Open daily. 12 miles south on US 75 (phone: 292-2001).

MAJOR COLLEGES AND UNIVERSITIES: The University of Nebraska at Omaha at 60th and Dodge Sts. (phone: 554-2800), with an enrollment of 15,000, and the Medical Center, 42nd St. and Dewey Ave. (phone: 559-4000) are both part of the University of Nebraska system. Creighton University (enrollment 5,000) is a private institution founded in 1878 by the Creightons, early settlers of the territory, 2500 California St. (phone: 280-2700).

SPECIAL EVENTS: The *Ak-Sar-Ben World's Championship Rodeo* in late September features bull riding, calf roping, wild broncos, livestock collections, and country-and-western entertainers.

SPORTS AND FITNESS: Baseball – The American Association's Omaha *Royals* play their home games at *Rosenblatt Stadium* from May to September; 13th St. and Murphy Ave. (phone: 734-2550). In June, the stadium is the site of the *NCAA Baseball World Series;* tickets available at *City Auditorium,* 1804 Capitol Ave. (phone: 444-4750).

Dog Racing – The enclosed grandstand at *Bluffs Run* offers pari-mutuel bettors all-season comfort. Races daily except Thursdays from early January through mid-December. Take the S. 24th St. exit in Council Bluffs off I-80 (phone: 712 323-2500).

Fitness Centers – The *YMCA* provides a pool, track, and racquetball courts, 20th St. and Howard (phone: 341-1600).

Golf – There are two excellent public golf courses: *Benson* at 5333 N. 72nd St. (phone: 444-4626) and *Applewood* at 6111 S. 99th St. (phone: 444-4656).

Horse Racing – For racing and pari-mutuel betting, *Ak-Sar-Ben* is ranked among the country's finest tracks. The season is from May through August, 63rd and Center Sts. (phone: 554-8800).

Jogging – Run in Memorial Park; on the University of Nebraska at Omaha or Creighton University campuses; or in the Dundee area, off Dodge, especially along Underwood Street, which is lined with lovely, old homes.

Tennis – Dewey Park has fine outdoor public tennis courts, at 500 Turner Blvd. (phone: 444-4980), and Hanscom Park offers indoor public courts, 3200 Creighton Blvd. (phone: 444-5584 or 444-5585).

THEATER: For current offerings, check the publications listed above. The *Omaha Community Playhouse,* where Henry Fonda got his start, puts on a large variety of productions year-round, using amateur performers and a professional staff, 6915 Cass St. (phone: 553-0800). The *Firehouse Dinner Theater,* 514 S. 11th St. (phone: 346-8833), has professional local and outside actors who perform in comedies and dramas throughout the year.

MUSIC: The *Omaha Symphony* performs with featured guest artists from September to May, and *Opera/Omaha* presents three operas from November to April, both at the *Orpheum Theater,* a restored vaudeville palace at 409 S. 16th St. The *City Auditorium* has entertainment all year. Tickets for all *Orpheum* and *Auditorium* events are available at the Auditorium Box Office, 1804 Capitol Ave. (phone: 444-4750), or at *Younkers Stores* ticket centers.

NIGHTCLUBS AND NIGHTLIFE: The *Howard Street Tavern* is a two-fisted bar with the best in blues, jazz, rock, and bluegrass music, at 11th and Howard Sts. (phone: 341-0433). Other hot spots are *Arthur's Le Grille,* 8025 W. Dodge Rd. (phone: 393-6369); *Chicago,* 3529 Farnam St. (phone: 346-7300), for chatting up; and *Club 89,* 89th and H Sts. (phone: 339-8989), for cabaret.

BEST IN TOWN

 CHECKING IN: Several of the national chains have good representatives in Omaha. Our selections range in price from around $85 and up for a double room per night in the expensive category, $50 and up in the moderate range, and $45 and under, inexpensive. All telephone numbers are in the 402 area code unless otherwise indicated.

Embassy Suites – A Spanish-style building with a gleaming tiled fountain courtyard and an indoor garden. The 188 suites have kitchens, living rooms, hide-a-bed couches, complimentary full breakfasts. Facilities also include wet bars, a heated indoor pool, whirlpool baths, and a sauna. Free airport service. 7270 Cedar St., 1½ miles north of I-80, exit 72nd St. (phone: 397-5141 or 800-EMBASSY). Expensive.

Omaha Marriott – Within walking distance of the city's largest shopping center, the Westroads, it offers 303 rooms. 10220 Regency Circle, just southeast of the I-680 Dodge St. exit (phone: 399-9000 or 800-228-9290). Expensive.

Red Lion Inn – Its location across the street from *City Auditorium* makes it Omaha's busiest convention hotel, with 456 rooms. The revolving bar of the rooftop restaurant, *Maxine's,* offers a panoramic view of the city. Free parking in adjacent garage. 1616 Dodge St. (phone: 346-7600). Expensive.

Dillon Inn – Offers upscale accommodations, but dispenses with a pool and other extras. Complimentary continental breakfast plus a 24-hour restaurant next door. Westroads Mall is directly across the street. 9720 W. Dodge Rd., just northeast of I-680 Dodge St. exit (phone: 391-5300 or 800-253-7503). Moderate.

Holiday Inn – Nebraska's largest hostelry (phone: 504 rooms) features 2 restaurants, 2 lounges with live entertainment, "Holidome" (enclosed swimming pool), putting green, electronic games, shuffleboard, and bar. 3321 S. 72nd St., just north of I-80, exit 72nd St. (phone: 393-3950). Moderate.

New Tower – Centrally located, this 340-room hotel has good standard accommodations with modern furnishings and design. Features a domed indoor pool, saunas, whirlpool baths, and a cocktail lounge. 7764 Dodge St. (phone: 393-5500). Inexpensive.

Rodeway Inn – In one of the city's busiest hotel areas, this chain's brand of basic motel hospitality includes color TV sets, complimentary continental breakfast, and a *Perkins' Cake and Steak* restaurant next door. 7101 Grover, just north of I-80, 72nd St. exit (phone: 391-5757). Inexpensive.

 EATING OUT: There really are a lot of cows out here, and when visitors eat out they quickly learn why. Omaha restaurant offerings run the gamut from prime ribs to hamburgers. Steaks are big here, and folks are proud of the local product — the beef is terrific. This is not fertile ground for vegetarians. Besides steakhouses, there are several ethnic eateries, plus a handful of continental restaurants. Our selections range in price from $50 up for a dinner for two in the expensive range, $30 to $45 in the moderate, and $25 and under in the inexpensive range. Prices do not include drinks, wine, or tips. All telephone numbers are in the 402 area code unless otherwise indiated.

Blue Fox – The continental menu with a sprightly Greek accent is the creation of owner/chef George Kokkalas. Everything — from appetizers to desserts — is made from scratch, and the fish and other seafoods are flown in fresh. The veal dishes and rack of lamb are very good. Closed Sundays. Reservations advised. 11911 Pierce Court; just off 119th and Pacific Sts. in the Boardwalk Shopping Center (phone: 330-3700). Expensive.

French Café – Of Omaha's restaurants that specialize solely in French food, this one adds a bit of glamour and buzzes with excited conversation. Specialties include onion soup, veal, rack of lamb, a daily fresh fish dish, rich desserts, and an extensive wine list, all served in an elegant, comfortable atmosphere. It's decorated with antiques, brassworks, and fresh flowers. Open daily. Reservations advised. Major credit cards. 1017 Howard St. (phone: 341-3547). Expensive.

Indian Oven – Tandoori cooking, done over an open fire in a clay oven, makes this Old Market–area restaurant the city's most exotic. Carefully spiced Indian dishes, only some of which are "hot," range from rogan josh, a traditional North Indian lamb curry, to several chicken entrées and an even longer list of vegetarian dishes. Closed Mondays. Reservations advised. Major credit cards. 1010 S. Howard St. (phone: 342-4856). Expensive to moderate.

Salvatore's – The menu offers a wide range of Italian dishes as well as other fine continental food. There's a good wine list, and the owner sometimes sings operatic arias. Closed Sundays. Reservations advised. Major credit cards. 4688 Leavenworth St. (phone: 553-1976). Expensive to moderate.

Firmature's Sidewalk Café – At this green oasis within the city's most elegant shopping center, the all-encompassing menu ranges from lighter fare — omelettes, crêpes, and such — to steaks and seafood. Specialty of the house is Omaha's most coveted prime ribs. The New Orleans Brunch served on Sundays is worth missing a sermon for. Open daily. Reservations advised. Major credit cards. 153 Regency Fashion Court (phone: 397-9600). Moderate.

Gallagher's – The long menu runs the gamut from light to hearty fare — burgers to quiche. Opulent decor is set off by a stained glass skylight. Open daily. Reservations advised. Major credit cards. 10730 Pacific St. (phone: 393-1421). Moderate.

Imperial Palace – An artfully decorated alternative to the usual Chinese storefront eating place, it has gained a reputation as Omaha's best Oriental restaurant. The menu embraces several of the cuisines of Northern China and the sinus-clearing specialties of Szechwan. Open daily. Reservations accepted. Major credit cards. 11200 Davenport St. (phone: 330-3888). Moderate to inexpensive..

Mister C's – Although the decor here might be a little tacky — twinkling lights reminiscent of Italian street carnivals, an iridescent mural of Venice on one wall, a backlighted diorama of a Sicilian village on another — the food is quite good. Specialties are Omaha steaks and Italian pasta; homemade soup appears on every table nightly except Saturdays, and strolling musicians play requests nightly. It may well be the busiest steakhouse in Omaha, and despite its formidable capacity, there's often a wait to get in. Mister C himself greets one and all. Open daily. Reservations advised. American Express and Diners Club only. 5319 N. 30th St. (phone: 451-1998). Moderate to inexpensive.

Neon Goose – This glitzy café/bar covers an entire block facing the city's old Union Station, just a short walk south of the Old Market area. Its menu runs from burgers to fresh seafood and it is known for a very good Sunday brunch. Closed Mondays. No reservations. Major credit cards. 1012 S. 10th St. (phone: 341-2063). Moderate to inexpensive.

Bohemian Café – Besides an impressive collection of Jim Beam bottles, which speaks for itself, the café features a full line of Eastern European specialties, like boiled beef in dill gravy, sweet and sour cabbage, roast duck, liver-dumpling soup, and kraut. Open daily. Reservations advised. Major credit cards. 1406 S. 13th St. (phone: 342-9838). Inexpensive.

Michaels' II – When mamacitas do the cooking, they do it right. Consistently excellent Mexican food — spiced to sting, but not to start a fire — served in an unpretentious bar atmosphere. Open daily. No reservations. No credit cards. 1919 Missouri Ave. (phone: 733-9666). Inexpensive.

To corral a prime Omaha steak, try either of Omaha's classic steakhouses, *Johnny's* or *Ross'.* In both places all is the way it should be, big and heavy, from the cowtown decor, where huge tables and chairs leave plenty of room to rassle with the beef to that pure slab of well-marbled pleasure itself, which can weigh in at as much as 20 ounces (not including the potato, spaghetti, bread, and salads that normally come along with the main ingredient). *Johnny's* (4702 S. 27th St.; phone: 731-4774). *Ross'* (909 S. 72nd St.; phone: 393-2030). Both closed Sundays. Both take reservations and credit cards. Expensive to moderate.

ORLANDO

Orlando was just another good-size American city until 1971, when Walt Disney's dream park opened nearby. The number of hotel and motel rooms shot from 6,300 to more than 50,000 during the next few years, and it now ranks second only to New York in total number of hotel rooms. The $300-million Orlando International Airport, whose glass, concrete, and steel structure is considered the state of the art in airport design, was constructed within a decade to handle the dramatically increased traffic, and it soon became the fastest-growing airport in the US.

In short, Orlando had come a long way since it started out as a campground for soldiers fighting the bloody Seminole Indian War in the early 19th century, and it was formally established in 1857. But despite several growth spurts — in 1880, when a railroad line was run from the city of Sanford; in the 1920s, just before the Great Depression; in 1956, with the opening of an important defense plant; and in 1961, when President Kennedy declared that the US would place a man on the moon within the next 10 years and thereby launched the space industry in Central Florida — Orlando drifted into and through the 20th century on the commerce of oranges and cows. And since the area was always more or less farmland, much of Orlando today is short on antique charm and long on look-alike apartment developments, fast-food restaurants, used car lots, and other none-too-lovely marks of the modern age.

What many people don't realize until they spend a little more time here is that the city has its beauty spots as well. Though parts of its downtown may seem sad and decaying, other sections have recently been renovated and spruced up. The city also boasts the ambitious *Harley* hotel and the lively Church Street Station entertainment complex, which attracts residents from the little towns around Orlando for a night out. The entire area is neat and clean as a pin, and as Church Street Station caught on, a number of other buildings in the neighborhood were turned into atmospheric restaurants and clubs.

Then there's Winter Park, one of Orlando's small towns-cum-suburb. There are lovely neighborhoods where the lawns are broad and velvety and dotted with palms or huge old live oaks thickly veiled with Spanish moss. Many of the houses are sprawling and of gleaming white stucco, with roofs of red-orange ceramic tile in the Spanish style. The shops and restaurants in the small "downtown" commercial center rival those anywhere in the country. In fact, many of the older shops have given way to nationwide chains such as *The Gap* and *Victoria's Secret*.

Moreover, Orlando is something of an outdoors paradise. The more than 2,000 spring-fed lakes in the area take care of the water sport scene, and the 85 publicly owned and operated parks and recreation facilities offer golf, tennis, jogging, and lots more. Residents (as well as visitors) take advantage of the abundant recreational facilities at Walt Disney World, about 20 miles southwest of downtown, especially after-dark entertainment and the three championship golf courses.

ORLANDO AT-A-GLANCE

 SEEING THE CITY: For most visitors, the Orlando area's premiere panorama is the one from *Top of the World* in Walt Disney World's *Contemporary Resort.* Whether you see it at sunset, when rosy light gilds the spires of Cinderella Castle, or at night, when tiny white lights glitter along the rooflines, it's absolutely stunning.

 SPECIAL PLACES: Walt Disney World alone requires a minimum of 3 to 4 days — and even twice that time would not do total justice to all its shows, sporting facilities, restaurants, and other attractions. When the rest of Orlando is also considered, it's easy to see how time can really fly during a visit.

ORLANDO AND ENVIRONS

Florida Cypress Gardens – It's said that you'd have to visit 70 countries at different times of the year to see all the plants that can be viewed in a single day at this 223-acre attraction developed back in the mid-1930s. The famous water ski shows, in which athletes ski barefoot and backward, are also well worthwhile. There is also an Animal Forest, with displays of various species of exotic animals. *Kodak's* revolving Island in the Sky offers spectacular views from 150 feet up, and Cypress Junction, an elaborate model railroad exhibit, is well worth a look. Open daily. Admission charge. Rte. 540, Winter Haven (phone: 813-324-2111).

Gatorland Zoo – In a couple of hours here you see thousands of alligators. Open daily. Admission charge. 14501 S. Orange Blossom Trail near Kissimmee (phone: 855-5496).

Sea World – The world's largest marine park ranks among Orlando's must-sees thanks to the high quality of the animal displays. Don't miss the *Legend of Shamu* show, a living documentary exploring the complex personality of killer whales; the Shark Encounter exhibit, which includes a film showing an incredible shark-feeding frenzy sequence and a glass tunnel that lets you walk "through" a huge pool full of sharks; and the new Penguin Encounter, where more than 200 feisty penguins waddle, hop, leap, and dive to the delight of onlookers. Open daily. Admission charge. 7007 Sea World Dr., Orlando (phone: 351-0021).

Wet 'n Wild – Among connoisseurs of water slides, this aquatic play park full of water-based thrill rides gets top marks. Bring a bathing suit, and prepare for long lines on summer afternoons. Varying hours, depending on the season. Admission charge. 6200 International Dr., Orlando (phone: 351-3200).

Boardwalk and Baseball – Orlando's family entertainment park is on the site formerly occupied by Circus World. Features include exhibits on loan from the *Baseball Hall of Fame* in Cooperstown, New York, 30 thrill rides, a midway, several restaurants and shops, and a mile-long boardwalk. Live entertainment and an IMAX film are featured daily. There are also six major league baseball fields and a 6,500-seat stadium. The Kansas City *Royals* hold spring training here. Admission charge. I-4 and US Hwy. 27, 28 miles southwest of Orlando (phone: 800-826-1939 or 800-367-2249 in Florida).

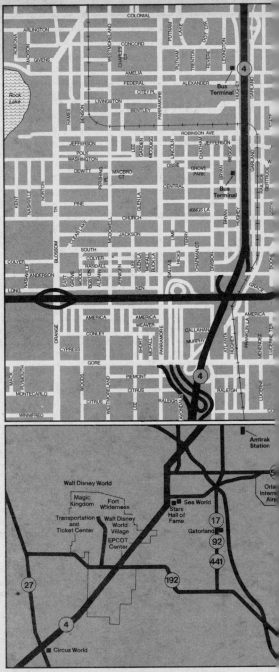

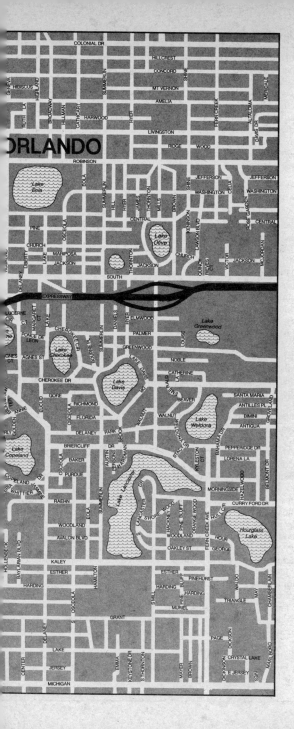

Universal Studios Florida – Moviemaking comes to central Florida. Along with Disney–MGM Studios Theme Park, this attraction, scheduled to open in mid-1990, lets visitors immerse themselves in the world of movie and television production. A sister attraction to the Hollywood institution, the Orlando studios also allow guests to witness a wide range of trade secrets while participating in scriptwriting, set design, casting, costuming, makeup, sound effects, editing, and special effects. The 444-acre property also offers a tour that re-creates scenes from some of Universal's most memorable films. An earthquake simulation, measuring 8.3 on the Richter scale, that recently debuted in Hollywood is being built here as well. Several restaurants, shops, and a branch of the *Hard Rock Café* are also planned. Admission charge. 1000 Universal Studios Plaza (phone: 363-8000).

WALT DISNEY WORLD

The fact that Walt Disney World attracts over 26 million visitors annually says just about everything that anyone needs to know about the basic appeal of Walt Disney's greatest dream-come-true. Less obvious is the sheer size of the place. For instance, the Magic Kingdom, the well-known rides and attractions area with the Cinderella Castle and other landmarks of American pop culture, occupies just 98 of the 27,400 acres of WDW's property. EPCOT Center, which opened in the fall of 1982 to great fanfare, is more than twice as large — and that still leaves 27,000 acres for the villas and hotels, shopping, a nonpareil swimming hole, a state-of-the-art water park, a nighttime entertainment complex, a working movie and TV production studio and theme park, three golf courses, tennis courts, several lakes, and a huge nature preserve. The main telephone number at WDW is 824-4321.

Magic Kingdom – The glittering Cinderella Castle, the magical heart of the Magic Kingdom, sets the mood for this marvel of a park full of nooks and crannies, lush landscaping, restaurants, shops, shows, and "adventures" — boat rides, roller coasters, and other amusements that transcend themselves because they're incorporated into elaborate sets full of artificial plants, robotic people, and sound effects.

Top attractions include Pirates of the Caribbean and Jungle Cruise in the park's Adventureland section; the implacably cute Country Bear Vacation Hoedown and Big Thunder Mountain Railroad in Frontierland; the beautiful Haunted Mansion in Liberty Square; the wild Space Mountain in-the-dark coaster in Tomorrowland; a special celebration with Mickey Mouse at Mickey's Birthdayland; Fantasyland's It's A Small World, with mechanical dolls and folk costumes; and the Hall of Presidents in Liberty Square, where a Disney-manufactured Abraham Lincoln stands up and talks as though he were Abe in the flesh.

During summer evenings and school holiday periods, be sure to see the Main Street Electrical Parade. The floats, made of metal frameworks studded with a million twinkling lights, are stupendous; the music, very tuneful. The fireworks presented shortly after the end of the first of the two runnings of this parade are equally impressive.

EPCOT Center – Something like a world's fair, but executed with the considerable technical skills, creativity, and financial resources of the Disney organization, EPCOT Center has two "entertainment worlds": Future World and World Showcase. Future World examines often controversial concepts such as energy and agriculture, while World Showcase brings nations of the world to life with the same extraordinary devotion to detail that makes the Magic Kingdom so enchanting. Appropriate entertainment, ethnic food, and lively shops stocked with wares made in the featured nations round things out.

At EPCOT Center, as in the Magic Kingdom, there are a few attractions that visitors simply must not miss. In Future World, these include the entire Living Seas pavilion, the ride inside the round ball known as Spaceship Earth, the Listen to the Land boat ride in The Land pavilion, the Journey into Imagination ride, the 3-D movie *Captain EO* (starring Michael Jackson), the new ride through the human body in the Wonders of Life pavilion, and the electronic funhouse known as the Image Works (all in the Journey into Imagination pavilion); and the shows in the World of Motion, Horizons, and Energy pavilions. In World Showcase, make a point to see the movies in the Canada, China, and France pavilions, which take the travelogue to new heights, and the technologically diverting show at the American Adventure.

Disney–MGM Studios Theme Park – The newest major Disney attraction opened to rave reviews in May 1989. For the first time in history, a fully functioning television and motion picture production facility now offers guests the opportunity to spend a day at the movies — on both sides of the camera. The studios have several components. There's a backlot and soundstage tour like no other, where soundproof catwalks allow visitors to watch a movie being filmed. Hollywood Boulevard, with its shops, restaurants, and Art Deco architecture, is reminiscent of old Hollywood. A ride-through attraction allows guests to see some famous film scenes: Gene Kelly in *Singin' in the Rain,* Julie Andrews and Dick Van Dyke in *Mary Poppins,* and Sigourney Weaver in *Aliens* come to life as Audio-Animatronic actors set in remarkably realistic movie set re-creations. A stunt theater, several restaurants, a sound effects studio, and an animation building round out the offerings. Star Tours, the much-acclaimed thrill attraction at California's Disneyland, is slated to open in 1990.

Disney Village Marketplace – The shops here stock everything from baby bonnets to silk dresses, from thousand-dollar bottles of wine and toy soldiers to stuffed animals — and then some. You can sit on a bench and watch the boats on the lagoon — or rent one yourself on the spot. Best of all, for R&R, there's the wonderful *Baton Rouge Lounge,* aboard the gleaming white riverboat known as *Empress Lilly,* and *Cap'n Jack's,* across the lagoon, where you can get huge, tart, unique-to-WDW strawberry margaritas.

Typhoon Lagoon – The ultimate water-fun park. Set on a 50-acre site, it boasts the world's largest manmade watershed mountain, plus pools for snorkeling, surfing, swimming, and sliding.

Pleasure Island – Adjacent to the Disney Village Marketplace, this complex features movies, nightclubs, restaurants, a roller-skating rink, and shops that stay open well past midnight to fill the local void of late-night entertainment.

River Country – It's next to impossible to go through childhood without developing a few fantasies about the perfect swimming hole. River Country is just such an animal, and it's full of curvy water chutes where even blasé grownups can't help but grin, even roar, with delight.

Discovery Island – Crisscrossed by footpaths, this tranquil 11½-acre landfall in Bay Lake is the home of dozens of birds — some in cages or huge aviaries, others running free; their chirps, tweets, crows, and caws nearly drown out the sounds of the little motorboats zipping across surrounding Bay Lake.

Hoop-Dee-Doo-Revue – Perhaps the most memorable of all WDW's lively live entertainment is this dinner show, wherein a round of singing, dancing, and wisecracking keeps audiences whooping it up until their sides are as sore from laughing as their stomachs are full of country-style vittles. Reservations are required well in advance (phone: 934-7639).

Behind the Scenes – There isn't a Magic Kingdom visitor around who wouldn't like to see Disney character costumes being made or talk to a Disney artist in person. The Wonders of Walt Disney World program makes precisely this kind of experience available to youngsters, and Disney Learning Adventures does the same for adults. For information, call 828-2405.

SOURCES AND RESOURCES

TOURIST INFORMATION: For details, contact the Greater Orlando Visitor Information Center, 8445 International Dr., Suite 152, Orlando, FL 32819 (phone: 363-5871); Orlando Convention and Visitors Bureau, 7208 Sand Lake Rd., Suite 300, Orlando, FL 32819 (phone: 363-5800); and Walt Disney World Co., Box 10,000, Lake Buena Vista, FL 32830 (phone: 824-4321).

Television Stations – ABC Channel 9–WFTV; CBS Channel 6–WCPX; NBC Channel 2–WESH; PBS Channel 24–WMFE.

Radio Stations – AM: WWNZ 740 (news/talk); WDBO 580 (news/talk/easy listening). FM: WSTF 101 (top 40); WBJW 105.1 (top 40); WDIZ 100.3 (rock).

Local Coverage – There are what's-doing sections in Friday's *Orlando Sentinel,* a daily, and in *Orlando* magazine. We immodestly believe that the best guide to the area is our own volume, *Steve Birnbaum Brings You the Best of Walt Disney World* (Houghton Mifflin; $9.95).

Telephone – The area code for Orlando is 407.

Sales Tax – The sales tax is 8%, as is the hotel tax.

CLIMATE: Spring and fall enjoy temperatures averaging in the mid-70s. From November through March, warmer clothing is a must for evening. Summer can be hot and humid. Always pack something for unseasonably warm or cool weather.

GETTING AROUND: Airport – Orlando International Airport is 12 to 15 miles from the city's downtown area and 28 miles from the gates of Walt Disney World. Cab fare from the airport to Orlando averages around $12, $30 to WDW. *Airport Limousine* (phone: 423-5566) provides transportation from the airport to the major downtown hotels for $10 and to WDW for $12. Reserve a seat upon landing at the airport; a van should depart about 20 minutes later. City buses run hourly between the airport and Orlando's downtown terminal at Pine and Central; the fare is 75¢. Call 841-8240 for more information.

Bus – *Gray Line* (phone: 422-0744) and *Rabbit* (phone: 291-2424) are among the operators providing transportation from hotels all over the city to the major attractions. Hotel desks can provide details.

Taxi – Several firms provide service, among them *City Cab* (phone: 422-4561), *Yellow Cab* (phone: 699-9999), and *Ace Taxi* (phone: 859-7514).

Car Rental – Most major car rental firms are represented. Orlando has one of the largest number of fleet vehicles of any US city, and the rates (most with unlimited mileage) are relatively modest.

LOCAL SERVICES: Babysitting – Both *Polynesian Village Resort* and *Contemporary Resort* have child care facilities. *Kindercare,* the children's center at WDW, is suitable for youngsters age 2 through 12 (phone: 827-KIDS). The *Hilton at Walt Disney World Village* offers a "Youth Hotel" where children age 3 through 12 can be accommodated.

Business Services – *Blumberg Communications,* 7101 Presidents Dr., Orlando (phone: 857-4747).

Mechanics – *College Park Auto Service,* 2610 Edgewater Dr., Orlando (phone: 425-7372); *Car Care Center,* Floridian Way, Walt Disney World (phone: 824-4813).

MUSEUMS: Orlando has a handful of noteworthy small institutions:
Charles Hosmer Morse Museum of American Art – Noted for its collection of Tiffany stained glass. 133 E. Welbourne Ave. in Winter Park (phone: 644-3686).

Orlando Museum of Art – Permanent displays of paintings and sculpture and frequent special exhibits. 2416 N. Mills Ave. (phone: 896-4231).

Orlando Science Center – Houses the John Young Planetarium. 810 E. Rollins St. (phone: 896-7151).

MAJOR COLLEGES AND UNIVERSITIES: University of Central Florida, Alafaya Trail (phone: 275-2000); Rollins College, Winter Park (phone: 646-2000).

SPECIAL EVENTS: The *Scottish Highland Games* in January draw huge crowds for Highland dancing and bagpipe competitions. The *Winter Park Sidewalk Art Festival,* the third weekend of March, is one of the Southeast's most prestigious such events. The *Florida State Air Fair,* held in nearby Kissimmee in October, has performances by the US Navy's Blue Angels, the Army's Golden Knights, or the Air Force's Thunder Birds. At Walt Disney World, beautiful decorations are put up at Christmastime, and there are parties and extra-large fireworks displays on New Year's Eve. The Fourth of July also occasions additional pyrotechnics.

SPORTS AND FITNESS: Baseball – The Minnesota *Twins* hold their spring training at Orlando's *Tinker Field* in late February and early March. The Orlando *Twins,* a farm team, play here in summer (phone: 849-6346). The Houston *Astros* prepare for the season at *Osceola Stadium* in Kissimmee (phone: 933-5500). The Kansas City *Royals* hold their spring training at *Boardwalk and Baseball,* 28 miles southwest of Orlando (phone: 648-5151).

Basketball – Orlando has been awarded one of the new franchises by the NBA, and its entry, the *Orlando Magic,* began play during the 1989-90 season.

Fishing – Bass anglers flock to Florida's third largest lake, Tohopekaliga. To find out about nearby fishing camps, contact the Kissimmee–St. Cloud Convention and Visitors Bureau (phone: 847-5000).

Fitness Centers – The *YMCA,* 433 N. Mills Ave., Orlando (phone: 896-6901), has an indoor pool, weight room, gymnasium with Nautilus equipment, outdoor track, and racquetball facilities. In addition, many hotels have health clubs for guests.

Football – The University of Central Florida *Knights* (phone: 849-2105) play at *Orlando Stadium* in the fall.

Golf – Walt Disney World has three public courses: *Magnolia* and *Palm* at the *Disney Inn* and *Lake Buena Vista Golf Course* (phone: 824-2270).

Jogging – Around Lake Eola in downtown Orlando, and on a trail at Ft. Wilderness and on the roads of WDW.

Swimming – Wet 'n Wild and WDW's River Country and Typhoon Lagoon (see *Special Places*) are good bets for a dip, and most hotels have pools. Within the boundaries of WDW, there are especially good-size pools at *Contemporary Resort* (phone: 824-1000), *Royal Plaza* (phone: 828-2828), and *Buena Vista Palace* (phone: 827-2727).

Tennis – It's possible to play on the many lighted Walt Disney World courts (where court reservations, lessons, rental rackets, and even a partner-finding service are available; phone: 824-3578). Or you can play for a small fee on Orlando parks courts (phone: 849-2161). The *Grosvenor* resort, *Royal Plaza, Buena Vista Palace, Hilton at Walt Disney World Village, Holiday Inn Main Gate-East, Hyatt Orlando, Ramada Resort,*

Sheraton-Lakeside Inn, Grand Cypress Hyatt Regency, Marriott's Orlando World Center, Court of Flags, Orlando Vacation Resort, Orlando Marriott, Stouffer Orlando resort, and *Sheraton World* are among the hotel establishments with courts for guests.

THEATERS: *Mark Two* features a buffet meal followed by a Broadway-style musical with a professional cast, 3376 Edgewater Dr. (phone: 422-3191). At *King Henry's Feast,* a five-course repast is served in true Elizabethan style (no forks), while some of the Bard's characters perform, 8984 International Dr. (phone: 351-5151). The *Civic Center of Central Florida* features musicals, dramas, and mysteries, 1001 E. Princeton St. (phone: 896-7365).

MUSIC: Programs of dance, music, and theater are often presented at the *Mayor Bob Carr Performing Arts Centre,* 401 W. Livingston St. (phone: 843-8111).

NIGHTCLUBS AND NIGHTLIFE: Once a pair of decaying hotels in a depressed section of none-too-lively downtown Orlando, the Church Street Station complex of bars and restaurants is now a very big deal, and nobody grumbles too much — on the way home — about the cover/entrance charge. The area has proven so popular that an upscale shopping mall and a new hotel are slated to open here in the not-too-distant future. There's Dixieland to keep things lively at vast, wood-floored *Rosie O'Grady's Good Time Emporium,* bluegrass at the brick-floored, plant-and-wicker-decked *Apple Annie's Courtyard,* disco in *Phineas Phogg's Balloon Works,* ballroom dancing at *Orchard Garden,* traditional American and continental food at *Lili Marlene's,* oysters and other seafood at *Crackers,* and barbecue and all the fixings at the *Cheyenne Saloon & Opera House.* Be aware that the charge for many specialty drinks includes the price of the glass (you turn it in at the gift shop for a refund). Children are welcome. 129 W. Church St. (phone: 422-2434).

In Winter Park, there's *Cheek to Cheek,* in the *Villa Nova* restaurant, 839 N. Orlando Ave. (phone: 644-2060), a good place for dancing to top 40 music. *Park Avenue,* 4315 N. Orange Blossom Trail (phone: 295-3750), has a huge dance floor and great sound system.

And WDW itself has a variety of nightspots, from the elegant, intimate *Empress Lilly Lounge* and the comfortable *Village Lounge,* which attracts top jazz entertainers, to the mad, merry *Baton Rouge Lounge,* which features Disney's own more than competent musician-comedians. At Pleasure Island, try *The Comedy Warehouse,* the *Neon Armadillo,* and the *Mannequin Dance Theater.*

BEST IN TOWN

CHECKING IN: Most Orlando-area accommodations are clustered along International Drive and nearby Sand Lake Road at the Orlando city limits, 10 to 15 minutes' drive from WDW; along US 192, which runs east and west and intersects I-4 near WDW (actually in Kissimmee, and closer to WDW); and inside WDW itself. Expect to pay $125 to $210 for a double at those places designated as expensive; $80 to $120 for those identified as moderate; and $50 to $75 at inexpensive spots — occasionally less during quiet periods in winter. All telephone numbers are in the 407 area code unless otherwise indicated.

***Walt Disney World–owned Properties* –** For both facilities and convenience, the hotels and villas owned by the Disney organization can't be beat, and the addition of the moderately priced *Caribbean Beach Resort* means that even budget-conscious travelers can enjoy staying right on the Walt Disney World property. The *Contemporary Resort,* a bustling high-rise with a pair of 3-story wings, has magical views, a lake's-edge location, 2 terrific swimming pools, and one of the biggest gamerooms anywhere. The *Polynesian Village*, on lushly landscaped grounds in several buildings by a lake, is only slightly more tranquil. Both are right on the monorail line — and exceptionally convenient to both the Magic Kingdom and EPCOT Center. The *Grand Floridian Beach Resort* is between the *Polynesian Village* and the Magic Kingdom and is also on the main monorail route. Its Victorian style is reminiscent of old Florida and is the first authentic luxury (and expensive) hotel at WDW. The understated *Disney Inn* is nearby, not on the monorail, but has a pleasantly relaxed atmosphere. The *Caribbean Beach Resort,* near EPCOT Center and the new Disney–MGM Studios Theme Park, is composed of 5 brightly colored villages surrounding a 42-acre lake.

Not far from the *Caribbean Beach Resort,* two new Disney-owned hotels are slated to open during 1990. The 634-room *Disney Yacht Club* and the 580-room *Disney Beach Club* have a New England theme and were designed by noted architect Robert A. M. Stern. The *Yacht Club* opens during the spring and the *Beach Club* will follow late summer. Close to the array of shops at the Disney Village Marketplace are the *Walt Disney World Resort Villas,* where 1-, 2-, and 3-bedroom villas overlook a lake and a golf course. All of them are especially good values for families. The octagonal treehouse-type villas — built on top of a central "pole," surrounded by pines and peacocks, and equipped with kitchens — are utterly delightful. Also lovely are the luxurious trailers at *Fort Wilderness Campground,* which come complete with bathrooms, color TV sets, and fully equipped kitchens.

The Southeast's largest hotel and convention complex is now on Disney property as well. The *Swan* resort, which opened late in 1989, has 760 rooms, and the *Dolphin,* slated to open during the summer of 1990, will have 1,510 rooms. The hotels wil share spacious convention facilities measuring some 200,000 square feet.

All properties, except the *Caribbean Beach Resort,* which is inexpensive to moderate, are expensive. For details, phone WDW Central Reservations (934-7639).

Walt Disney World Hotel Plaza – The seven hotels here, within walking distance of the Disney Village Marketplace, are nearly as convenient as the WDW-owned properties, and a couple of them are a bit less pricey. Also, small discounts on WDW admission tickets are available to guests at plaza hotel properties. Our favorites in the complex are the *Buena Vista Palace,* which boasts 870 handsomely decorated rooms embellished with Mickey Mouse telephones and old-fashioned ceiling fans (as well as air conditioning), plus outstanding sporting facilities (phone: 827-2727 or 800-327-2990); the 814-room *Hilton at Walt Disney World* has a Youth Hotel that recommends it to guests with children (phone: 827-4000); also attractive is the *Royal Plaza* hotel, a 17-story high-rise with a pair of 2-story wings, plus tennis courts and a good swimming pool (phone: 828-2828 or 800-327-2990). The *Howard Johnson Resort,* another high-rise with a 6-story annex, is also handsome (phone: 828-8888 or 800-654-2000). The newest hotel here is the *Pickett Suite,* where all 229 suites feature a bedroom, living room, wet bar, refrigerator, built-in hair dryer, and 2 TV sets. There's also a pool, tennis courts, and a gameroom (phone: 934-1000 or 800-742-5388). Note that reservations for all of these properties can be made through WDW Central Reservations (phone: 934-7639). All are expensive.

Hyatt Regency Grand Cypress – This glittering, $110-million, 750-room luxury hotel, with a 170-foot atrium lobby modeled after the *Hyatt Regency Maui* in

Hawaii, is the star of an 800-acre complex that has more facilities than most visitors can ever use, including one of the largest free-form swimming pools anywhere. The golf course, restricted to guest use, is a Jack Nicklaus gem. Some 48 luxury villas surround the course's fairways. 1 Grand Cypress Blvd., Lake Buena Vista (phone: 800-228-9000; 239-4700 for the villas). Expensive.

Marriott's Orlando World Center – Here is a 1,503-room, 27-story resort hotel that commands nearly 200 beautifully landscaped acres, just minutes away from Walt Disney World's EPCOT Center. Features include a 6-story lobby atrium, 4 swimming pools, 12 lighted tennis courts, an 18-hole Joe Lee golf course, a fully equipped health spa, a gameroom, 10 restaurants and lounges, and lots of specialty shops. World Center Dr., Orlando (phone: 239-4200 or 800-228-92920). Expensive.

Stouffer Orlando – This $86-million, 782-room property rises 10 stories above an enormous atrium complete with free-flying birds and exotic fish. A fitness center, 6 tennis courts, pool, 4 restaurants, and convention facilities round out the offerings. 6677 Sea Harbor Dr. (phone: 351-5555, 800-325-5000, or 800-HOTELS). Expensive to moderate.

Orlando Marriott – Arranged in 2-story stucco villas scattered around landscaped grounds, the 1,076 smart rooms here are popular with business travelers but ideal for any visitor in search of serenity. 8001 International Dr. (phone: 351-2420, or 800-228-9290). Moderate.

Park Plaza – Orlando's answer to New England's country inns has plenty of charm, even if the rooms don't always measure up to the palm-and-antique-decked lobby. 307 Park Ave. S., Winter Park (phone: 647-1072). Moderate.

Days Inn–Lake Buena Vista – An especially good value very close to the Disney Village Marketplace. There are 203 rooms, a pool, restaurant, and gameroom. 12799 Apopka-Vineland Rd., Lake Buena Vista (phone: 239-4441 or 800-325-2525). Inexpensive.

 EATING OUT: The last decade's growth has attracted chefs from all over the world, so first class dining experiences are easy to find. Expect to pay between $50 and $80 for two at those places listed as expensive; between $40 and $50 in the moderate category; and under $40 in the inexpensive bracket — excluding drinks, wine, and tips. All telephone numbers are in the 407 area code unless otherwise indicated.

Chefs de France – Three of France's finest chefs — Paul Bocuse, Roger Vergé, and Gaston LeNôtre — firmly based the menu here on nouvelle cuisine, with very good results. Gleaming napery, sparkling brass, etched glass, and all manner of turn-of-the-century touches make the decor as appealing as the food. There's also a separate menu "for the little gourmet" (for kids under 12) at reduced prices. A first-rate bistro thrives upstairs. Open daily. Reservations necessary (they are available to Walt Disney World hotel guests by telephone — check with the hotel desk clerks; otherwise reservations are available only in person at EPCOT Center). Major credit cards. World Showcase, EPCOT Center, Walt Disney World. Expensive.

Le Cordon Bleu – The unpretentious decor here gives no hint of the quality of the artichoke bottoms filled with crabmeat and glazed with Mornay sauce, snails in garlic butter, rack of lamb, and other specialties at this favorite eating spot. Closed Sundays. Reservations necessary on weekends. Major credit cards. 537 W. Fairbanks, Winter Park (phone: 647-7575). Expensive.

Empress Room – Elegant (but cordial) service and Louis XV surroundings, replete with crystal and gold leaf, make this WDW room in the *Empress Lilly* riverboat a favorite among Orlando residents out for a big celebration. Jackets required for men. Open daily. Reservations necessary well in advance. Major credit cards. Disney Village Marketplace, Walt Disney World (phone: 828-3900). Expensive.

Maison & Jardin – An elegant spot with high ceilings, widely spaced tables, and vast windows that take in the surrounding formal gardens, this restaurant that local wags have nicknamed "Mason Jar" serves ambitious fish, meat, and fowl preparations. Major credit cards. 430 S. Wymore Rd., Altamonte Springs (phone: 862-4410). Expensive.

Park Plaza Gardens – Garden-like awnings, skylights, and greenery make a lovely backdrop for tasty meals. Open daily. Reservations accepted for dinner only. Major credit cards. 319 Park Ave. S., Winter Park (phone: 645-2475). Expensive.

Victoria & Albert's – In Walt Disney World's *Grand Floridian Beach Resort,* this small dining room seats only 53, and elegant touches include Royal Doulton china, Sambonet silver, and Schott-Zweisel crystal. The menu varies nightly. One oddity of note: Every host or hostess is named Victoria or Albert (we have no idea why). Major credit cards. *Grand Floridian Beach Resort,* Walt Disney World (phone: 824-2391). Expensive.

Chatham's Fifth Avenue – Two talented young chefs (who happen to be brothers) have opened this small, 35-seat restaurant in Windermere. The menu changes daily, and specials created in the open kitchen include roast duck with fresh raspberries; red snapper in pecan butter; and delectable five-onion soup. The chefs' mother serves as hostess, and their grandmother does all the baking (try her lemon cake). Closed Sundays. Reservations a must. No credit cards — and no smoking. 503 Main St., Windermere (phone: 876-6131). Expensive to moderate.

La Cantina – Orlando residents line up for as much as an hour for the huge steaks and Italian specialties here. Closed Sundays and Mondays. Major credit cards. 4721 E. Colonial Dr., Orlando (phone: 894-4491). Moderate.

Ming Garden – Sophisticated Mandarin, Szechwan, Hunan, and Cantonese dishes with an emphasis on Florida seafood. Decorated in shades of plum, with elaborate plum blossom chandeliers, the dining room is filled with greenery. Reservations advised. Major credit cards. 6432 International Dr., Orlando (phone: 352-8044). Moderate.

East India Ice Cream Company – Imaginative breakfasts, big sandwiches at lunch and dinner, unusual flavors of ice cream made on the premises, and an antique-like, brick-floored setting are the drawing cards. Open daily. No reservations or credit cards. 327 Park Ave. S., Winter Park (phone: 628-2305). Inexpensive.

Walt Disney World Restaurants – Most first-time visitors are surprised to discover just how far the WDW food offerings surpass the well-trod hamburgers-and-hot-dogs path — and then dive right into steak and kidney pie, fettuccine all' Alfredo, amaretto-flavored soufflés, or any number of other exotic foodstuffs served at EPCOT Center's World Showcase eateries. Another pleasure is that even cafeterias and fast-food stops have a bit of atmosphere that makes them just a little special. Where you eat at WDW will be determined by where you are at mealtimes. Below are a few of the more noteworthy spots.

In the Magic Kingdom, *Crystal Palace,* an old-fashioned glass-and-plant-filled cafeteria on Main Street, is very pretty. *Town Square Café* nearby serves delicious Monte Cristo sandwiches. *King Stefan's Banquet Hall* in Cinderella Castle has service by waitresses (but you must reserve in person, first thing in the morning).

EPCOT Center offers even greater variety. In Future World, try The Farmers Market in The Land, where each of a half-dozen stands serves soups or salads, barbecue, cheese items, baked potatoes, and other savory specialties. Upstairs, at *The Land Grille Room,* are unusual American foods and scrumptious cheese bread. At the Living Seas Pavilion, try the fresh seafood at *Coral Reef* restaurant, complete with a panoramic view of a living underwater coral reef. *Stargate* serves unique breakfast pizza. In World Showcase, don't miss Canada's low-ceilinged, stone-walled *Le Cellier,* a cafeteria that offers a tasty Canadian pork and potato pie called tourtière; Italy's *Alfredo's,* for tasty Italian food; Germany's *Biergarten,* for its hearty food and oom-pah entertainment; Mexico's *San Angel Inn,* which takes Mexican food far beyond tacos; and China's *Nine Dragons,* where meals are prepared in a variety of provincial Chinese cooking styles. Dinner reservations, a must at many restaurants, must be made in person in Earth Station. (Walt Disney World hotel guests can make reservations by telephone; check with the hotel desk clerks.) Otherwise, arrive at the front gate a half-hour before the published park opening, decide where to eat, and send the speediest member of your group to book your table when the park opens. (Be aware that by an hour later most restaurants are usually booked for prime dinner hours.) Lunch reservations can be made at the restaurant in person on the day of the seating or at Earth Station. Booking procedures sometimes change, so confirm the preceding information on arrival at WDW (phone: 824-4321).

At the *Contemporary Resort,* consider the viewful *Top of the World* for its bountiful breakfast and Sunday brunch buffets. The superb banana-stuffed French toast served in *Polynesian Village's Tangaroa Terrace* is worth a detour. At *Disney Inn's Garden Gallery,* there's delicious French-fried ice cream at lunch and dinner. At the *Grand Floridian,* the octagonal *Narcoosee's* offers seafood and steaks in a delightful setting.

At the Disney Village Marketplace, the comfortable, unassuming *Village* restaurant has fine lake views. Aboard the *Empress Lilly* riverboat, there's the charming *Fisherman's Deck,* with a picture-window view of a churning paddlewheel. At *Pleasure Island,* there's the *Fireworks Factory, Spinners,* and a variety of stands at *Merriweather's Food Fare.*

Travelers with children should make note of the special breakfasts with Disney characters in attendance (phone: 824-4321; 934-7639 for reservations). Moderate.

PHILADELPHIA

An American visiting Philadelphia for the first time is bound to leave with a new appreciation of what the United States stood for when it was founded. It's not merely a question of the neatly preserved pockets of historic buildings. It has to do with the Philadelphians themselves. They have a way of talking about "our history" that naturally seems to include a visitor, even if your first reaction is to think "Our history? I don't live here." A few hours spent walking through streets that look like illustrations in history books you read as a child will bring home the notion that this is, truly, the America you learned about in school.

But it's not a textbook experience. The tradition in which the city was born, the inextricable marriage of politics and conscience, is everywhere evident. Even on bitterly cold days, you are likely to see human rights vigils at Independence Mall, across the street from the buildings in which the Bill of Rights and the Constitution were drafted, and where the Declaration of Independence was signed. Residents don't pass even small demonstrations without at least slowing down to read the signs; and a protest too small to warrant media attention in New York is often reported in detail here. A longtime resident, who opposed the Vietnam War, says he often comes to gaze at the Tomb of the Unknown Revolutionary Soldier in Washington Square. "I just come to read the inscription ('Freedom is a light for which many men have died in darkness'). I ask myself what I would have done then. Of course, I can't say. But I do know that those people acted on their conscience. They had to fight. They weren't heroes so much as real people making ethical decisions. Like we did during the Vietnam War."

When William Penn founded Philadelphia in 1682, on a flat, fertile site between the Delaware and Schuylkill rivers, he advertised his colony as a place of religious freedom, christening it "The City of Brotherly Love." Thousands of persecuted Europeans left their homes and came to this New World city to create lives for themselves that would enable them to live in accord with their beliefs. By 1750, Philadelphia was the leading city in the colonies. In 1752, the Liberty Bell emerged from a foundry in England. It had been designed to mark the 50th anniversary of William Penn's Charter of Privileges. A precursor of later documents, such as the Universal Declaration of Human Rights, the Charter declared, "Proclaim liberty throughout all the land, unto all the inhabitants thereof." When the colonies broke away from Great Britain in 1776, the Bell cracked upon being put to use. (It was recast by a Philadelphia foundry.) From 1790 to 1800, the first Congress of the United States met in Congress Hall. Philadelphia only relinquished its role as the nation's capital when the District of Columbia became the permanent headquarters of the federal government.

The city now has a population of 1.6 million (4.7 million in the metropoli-

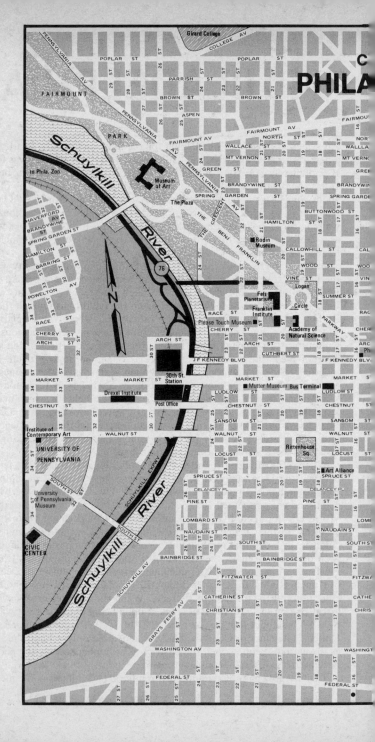

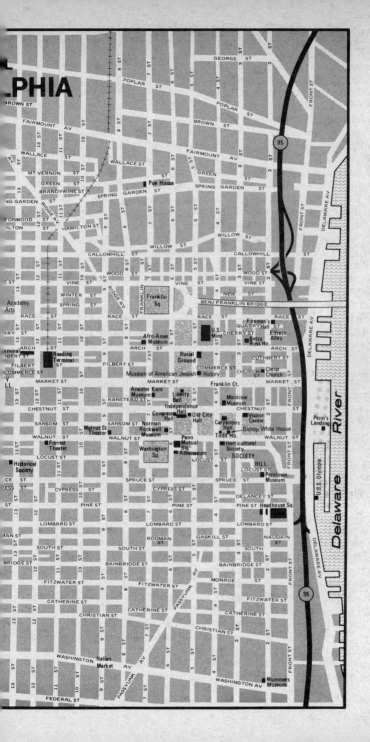

tan area). To this day it follows Penn's original plans, laid out around four spacious parks (one in each quadrant of the city). Today's Philadelphians still live in the city's 18th-century townhouses, trimmed with cream-colored wooden shutters, and they pray in the same churches as did George Washington, Benjamin Franklin, and John Adams. You begin to discover Philadelphia as you walk along the narrow red brick, dovetail-patterned sidewalks that lead through narrow alleys to reveal hidden gardens and courtyards. These parts of the city look remarkably like the 18th-century sections of London.

But Philadelphia is not without modern charm. Between 1986 and 1988, the city undertook an ambitious $14-million project to restore its famed, centuries-old Market Street, which had declined gradually over recent decades. Essentially, Market Street's east end, running from historic Independence Mall at 5th Street to City Hall at Broad Street, was transformed from a seedy, crumbling section into what has been called the "Champs-Elysées de Philly." A maze of overhead traffic lights and pedestrian islands were removed while sidewalks were widened, repaved in brick and concrete, and lined with stately trees to enhance the historic atmosphere. Clusters of junk shops and decaying buildings were razed to make way for attractive office and retail buildings, while larger, historic buildings were saved by businesses that moved in to give them new life.

One such complex of buildings that survived — due to many hard-fought battles by history-conscious local groups — had been owned and operated since the mid-1800s by the once-prosperous *Lit Brothers* department store. A complete restoration, including replacement of no less than 1,000 windows, led to a grand reopening celebration in 1987. Now known as Mellon Independence Center, the complex, on Market Street between 7th and 8th, houses a combination of shops, restaurants, and offices, and is one example of the city's effort to breathe life back into its cherished historical buildings. As one local columnist noted, although "it is not an architectural masterpiece, it is a crucial piece of the fabric and history of the city that has now been reclaimed."

Another historic building that survived the decline is *Wanamaker's,* one of the city's oldest and most prominent department stores. A delightful place for shopping and browsing, it boasts the city's most famous meeting place — the bronze bald eagle statue on the main floor of the building's 7-story atrium. During the holiday season, people congregate around the eagle to gaze at a brilliant show of lights and listen to the resounding strains of the grand court organ, allegedly the largest functioning organ in the world. The best places from which to enjoy the Christmas shows are from either the main floor or the 2nd-floor balcony, where you can behold the architectural splendor of the six layers of white balconies trimmed in gold.

Almost directly behind *Wanamaker's* is the city's most famous landmark, William Penn's statue on City Hall. The city's founder crowns a dome that, in turn, caps what can only be described as an architectural extravaganza of portholes, turrets, wedding cake statuettes, Ionic, Doric, and Corinthian columns and pillars. Until 1984, Billy Penn's statue (as residents call it) was, by law, the tallest fixture on the skyline. After a lengthy debate, the rule declaring that nothing in the city exceed the 548-foot height of the statue was overturned, and a contractor was allowed to erect two taller buildings. However, the 26-ton, 37-foot-high bronze Billy Penn should be able to hold his own after undergoing a revolutionary process to remove nearly 100 years of grime and restore his original patina. Soon the historic City Hall below will shed several years of scaffolding to reveal its $18.5-million restoration.

Philadelphia mixes the historic with the modern in sometimes amusing ways. Thus, diagonally behind Penn's left shoulder stands a giant clothespin — yes, a sculpted clothespin — which dominates the plaza in front of the Atlantic Richfield building. The old-fashioned wooden clip clothespin towers several stories above street level, in funny juxtaposition to the solid, ornate City Hall.

In recent years, the city has also attempted to revitalize once crumbling areas and thereby entice people to return from the suburbs. The Society Hill riverfront restoration project is a case in point. Named for the Free Society of Traders, an early British company, Society Hill had deteriorated over the years. But with ingenuity, determination, and creative use of space, it was transformed into what has since been called "the textbook example of how to improve urban environment in America." Concern for keeping the city livable has resulted in rezoning some of the downtown streets into traffic-free pedestrian malls. Now you can browse along Chestnut Street, Philadelphia's popular shopping street, without breathing exhaust fumes or dodging in and out of traffic to cross to the other side. You can also wander along the Delaware River, taking in the sights and sounds of the riverfront shops on Front Street, and the ships berthed in the docks. And, if you're feeling extravagant or just want to delight your shopping eye, be sure to visit the Bourse. Standing not 500 feet from the Liberty Bell, this restored, turn-of-the-century building offers elegant shops and restaurants.

Philadelphia's sense of humor cuts loose every New Year's Day, when the *Mummers Parade* struts down Broad Street, playing tunes like "Oh, Dem Golden Slippers." A tradition since 1901, it is Philadelphia's Mardi Gras, incorporating the ebullient New Year's customs of several ethnic communities. Mummers' suits (don't call them costumes) are extraordinary fantasies of brightly colored silk, sequins, gold braid, feathers, pointed hats, and veils. Prizes are awarded for the best, some of which are on display at the *Mummers Museum,* where you can also listen to recordings of parade music. How do you get to be a Mummer? According to a former resident, you have to be invited to participate by one of the Mummers Clubs — usually a storefront social club in the ethnic neighborhoods of South Philly (where the *Rocky* movie series has been filmed). Because of the competitiveness among rival clubs and neighborhoods, coming from West Philly makes you ineligible. Once you're in the club, you can spend the rest of the year practicing an instrument like the ukulele or banjo, learning the songs and steps to the Mummers Strut. Mothers in the neighborhood often spend the year designing and sewing the suits, although there are some commercial establishments like *Pierre's* on Walnut Street that supply outfits.

Every July, Philadelphia celebrates the signing of the Declaration of Independence. The bicentennial celebrations of 1976 focused national attention on the place where it all began. But when the firecrackers stopped and the

200-year anniversary became just another page in the calendar, the bicentennial displays were not torn down; they were, instead, integrated into the network of historic sites that people come from all over the world to see. The same sort of thinking prevailed during the 1987 celebration of the 200th anniversary of the US Constitution.

Philadelphia residents used to joke that the next-door state of New Jersey had been created only so that Philly residents would have somewhere to go on the weekend. But nowadays people joke, "I went to Philadelphia on Sunday — and it wasn't closed."

PHILADELPHIA AT-A-GLANCE

 SEEING THE CITY: You don't have to run up the steps of the *Philadelphia Museum of Art* the way Sylvester Stallone did in *Rocky*. You can walk up to get the same far-reaching view of the skyline. Inside is an impressive collection of paintings, drawings, sculpture, and graphic art from all periods and countries. Closed Mondays and holidays. Admission charge (for the museum, not the view). 26th and Parkway (phone: 763-8100).

A different, but equally appealing, view of Philadelphia is afforded from the observation deck of City Hall Tower. The vistas from this vantage point encompass the city, its surrounding rivers, and the New Jersey shoreline. Open weekdays. Tours at 12:30 PM or by appointment. No admission charge. At Broad and Market Sts. (phone: 567-4476).

You can also see Old Philadelphia by horse-drawn carriage. Tours depart from the carriage stand on Chestnut between 5th and 6th streets daily, weather permitting. After 6 PM, carriages depart from Head House Square on 2nd Ave., between Pine and South Sts. Charge for carriage tours (phone: 922-6840).

 SPECIAL PLACES: Philadelphia's tight city blocks and narrow streets make it great for walking, not driving. Streets, laid out in checkerboard fashion, are easy to understand, but they are always choked with traffic. It's best to park your car at your hotel. Philadelphia's main places of interest are clustered in Independence Hall National Historical Park and around Fairmount Park in West Philadelphia.

INDEPENDENCE HALL HISTORICAL AREA

Visitor Center – This is a good place to launch a tour of the historical area and pick up maps and brochures. There's also a half-hour film that provides helpful historical background. Open daily. No admission charge. 3rd and Chestnut Sts. (phone: 597-8974).

Independence National Historical Park – "The most historic square mile in America." This is what everyone comes to see. Within the park, you'll find the major Colonial and Revolutionary era buildings, which we've listed separately below. Open daily. No admission charge. The general park area runs from 3rd to 7th St. between Chestnut and Walnut Sts. (phone: 627-1776 for a 24-hour recording).

Independence Hall – When you think of Philadelphia, this is probably the first image that comes to mind. The solid tower, massive clock, and graceful spire are unmistakable. Early colonists called it the State House. Here, the Declaration of Independence was signed and, 11 years later, the Constitution was written. Open daily, with guided tours, beginning in the East Wing. No admission charge. 5th and Chestnut Sts. (phone: 597-8974).

Congress Hall – The first US Congress met here, between 1790 and 1800. George Washington delivered his final congressional address in these halls; here, too, the Bill of Rights was adopted. In 1800, the seat of federal government moved to the District of Columbia. Open daily. No admission charge. 6th and Chestnut Sts. (phone: 597-8974).

Old City Hall – The first US Supreme Court issued judgments from the bench inside this building. The court moved to new headquarters in Washington, DC, in 1800.

Independence Mall – Across the street from the Halls, this leafy stretch of grass, fountains, and tree-lined walks contains the glass pavilion housing the Liberty Bell. It was moved from Independence Hall so more people could see it and touch it. Open daily. No admission charge. Market and 5th Sts. (phone: 597-8974).

Carpenters' Hall – So named because it housed the Carpenters' Company Guild during the colonial era (before unions). The oldest building organization in the US still owns the hall, and early carpentry tools are on display. In 1774, the First Continental Congress met here. Closed Mondays; also closed Tuesdays in January and February. No admission charge. 320 Chestnut (phone: 925-0167).

Army-Navy and Marine Corps Memorial Museums – In Pemberton House and New Hall, respectively, the exhibitions and collections focus on Revolutionary War history in these military branches from 1775 to 1805. The buildings are on Carpenters' Court (leading back to Carpenters' Hall). Open daily. No admission charge. Chestnut, between 3rd and 4th Sts. (phone: 597-8974).

Second Bank of the United States – One of the earliest buildings designed by noted architect William Strickland, this early-19th-century building is an outstanding example of Greek Revival architecture. It houses "The Portraits of the Capitol City," which highlights people who were important in government, industry, the arts, and religion during the late 1700s. Open daily. No admission charge. Chestnut, between 4th and 5th Sts. (phone: 597-8974).

Todd House – Before she became Dolley Madison — wife of fourth president James, famed as First Lady and society hostess — she was Dolley Payne Todd, whose husband, the young Quaker lawyer John Todd, died in the yellow fever epidemic of 1793. Their home, built in 1775, is typical of middle class residences of the period. Free guided tours, by reservation only, must be arranged in person at the Visitor Center on the day of the tour (see above). Open daily. 4th and Walnut Sts. (phone: 597-8974).

Bishop White House – While the Todd House reflects a middle class lifestyle, this home typifies the affluence of people such as Bishop William White, a politically active Episcopalian minister (from the 1770s to the 1790s) who served as rector of both Christ Church and St. Peter's. Open daily. No admission charge. 3rd and Walnut Sts. Must be combined with a tour of the Todd House. Sign up at the Visitor Center (phone: 597-8974).

Christ Church – Benjamin Franklin sat in pew 70. George Washington prayed here, too. The original church was built in 1695; this, a larger one, was erected in 1745 and is still in use. Open daily. Donation suggested. 2nd St. above Market St. (phone: 922-1695).

Christ Church Burial Ground – Throw a penny on the grave of Benjamin and his wife, Deborah Franklin — it's a Philadelphia custom. Tours by appointment (phone: 922-1695). Open daily, mid-spring through summer. 5th and Arch Sts. (phone: 922-1695).

Betsy Ross House – Where, tradition says, George Washington directed Elizabeth Ross, an upholsterer's widow, in the stitching of the first American flag. According to the Philadelphia Historical Commission, however, Betsy Ross never lived here and had nothing to do with the first US flag. Make up your own mind, after you've seen this tiny cottage filled with household items and memorabilia allegedly pertinent to that famous seamstress. Open daily. No admission charge. 239 Arch (phone: 627-5343).

Elfreth's Alley – The oldest continuously occupied residential street in America, dating to 1690. Only 1 block long, 6 feet wide, it is lined with 200-year-old houses. Usually the first weekend in June, Elfreth's Alley holds its annual pageant with house tours and craft shows. Closed in January. North of Arch St., running between Front and 2nd sts. For more information, call the museum house (phone: 574-0560).

Headhouse Square – Only survivor of the many middle-of-the-street markets that once flourished in the city. Built in 1775, it is surrounded by good restaurants and revitalized shops. In summer, it hosts crafts demonstrations and concerts. 2nd and Pine.

Mummer's Museum – The city's pop history is lovingly preserved in this memorial in South Philadelphia, in the heart of where Mummery began. The outside is tile as dazzling as a Mummer's suit. Inside are memorabilia, history, sound recordings. Closed Mondays. Admission charge. 2nd St. at Washington Ave. (336-3050).

Franklin Court – Benjamin Franklin came to Philadelphia in 1723. In his later years Franklin resided in a brick house on this site. He died here in 1790. Although the house itself is no longer standing (it was demolished in 1812), three of the surrounding houses designed by Franklin are here, along with an 18th-century garden with a mulberry tree (planted by the National Park Service in 1976 because Franklin had one), a print shop, and a post office. An underground museum has Franklin stoves and a phone where you can "dial-an-opinion" from Benjamin Franklin. Open daily. No admission charge. Running from Chestnut to Market between 3rd and 4th Sts. (phone: 597-8974).

USS *Olympia* – The oldest steel-hulled American warship afloat, the *Olympia* was Commodore George Dewey's flagship at Manila Bay in the Spanish-American War. Open daily. Admission charge. Penn's Landing, near Delaware Ave. and Spruce St. (phone: 922-1898).

Penn's Landing Trolley – After leaving the USS *Olympia,* buy a ticket for a 20-minute ride on a restored trolley that served the Delaware Valley between 1904 and 1958. The conductor provides commentary as passengers tour the neighborhoods of Queen Village, Society Hill, and the Olde City, and ride along the Delaware River, where many tall ships are berthed. Fare charge. Tickets valid for the entire day. Weekends and holidays from April through December. Also check on extended summer schedule. Board at Delaware Ave. at Dock or Spruce St. (phone: 627-0807).

Boathouse Row – A collection of Victorian boathouses used by collegiate and club oarsmen. The hub of many national competitions. East River Dr., running along the east bank of the Schuylkill River, north of the *Museum of Art.* If you're driving just west of the museum on the Schuylkill Expressway (Route 76) after dark, don't miss the view across the river of the historic boathouses outlined in white lights.

WEST PHILADELPHIA

Fairmount Park – Approximately 8,000 acres of meadows, gardens, creeks, trails, and 100 miles of bridle paths for joggers, bicyclists, softball players, fishermen, and picnickers. For a small price, pick up a detailed park map at Memorial Hall, 42nd and Parkside. Then be sure to take in the Japanese House and Garden (where tea is served in season), Glendinning Rock Garden, and, if children are along, Smith Memorial Playground. The *Fairmount Park Trolley Bus* (phone: 879-4044, for information), a replica of a Victorian conveyance, is a pleasant way of getting around the park and also seeing some of Philadelphia. It starts out at the Visitors Center, 16th and John F. Kennedy Blvd. On Mondays and Tuesdays (daily December through March) there is a 2½-hour narrated tour of the Society Hill section of the city, Center City, and parts of the park, stopping at one of the seven restored historic mansions: Cedar Grove, Sweetbriar, Lemon Hill, Mount Pleasant, Strawberry, Woodford, and Laurel Hill. Wednesdays through Sundays, April through early December, the bus makes 90-minute rounds of the park with on-off privileges at all of the mansions. Don't miss the Christmas tour the first weekend in December, which takes in the mansions and

Horticultural Society, decorated in colonial holiday styles. (Mansions closed Mondays and Tuesdays. Admission charge. For guided tours, call 787-5449.) Park open daily. No admission charge. The park begins at the *Philadelphia Museum of Art* and extends northwest on both sides of the Wissahickon Creek and Schuylkill River.

Philadelphia Zoo – Established in 1874, this is the nation's oldest zoo and is considered one of the best run. More than 1,600 animals, reptiles, and birds make their home within its 42 acres. There are several natural habitat displays, a children's zoo, and a safari monorail aerial tram. Don't miss the tree house, where children can interact with nature. Open daily, except holidays. Admission charge except on Mondays from November through February. 34th St. and Girard Ave. (phone: 387-6400).

Philadelphia Museum of Art – Outstanding collections of all periods and schools, housed in a sweeping Greco-Roman building. Closed Mondays, Tuesdays, and holidays. Admission charge except on Sundays until 1 PM. 26th and Parkway (phone: 763-8100).

Franklin Institute Science Museum – Ben Franklin would have traded his kite for one day in this remarkable science museum, with Fels Planetarium and four huge floors jammed with exhibitions on anatomy, aviation, and space exploration. Open daily except holidays. Admission charge. 20th St. and Parkway (phone: 448-1200; planetarium (closed Mondays), 448-1292).

Rodin Museum – Sculpture, sketches, and drawings make up the largest collection of Auguste Rodin's work outside France. An afternoon can easily be spent wandering through the halls and gardens. Foreign language tours are available by appointment. Closed Mondays, Tuesdays, and holidays. No admission charge; donations accepted. 22nd and Parkway (phone: 763-8100).

OTHER SPECIAL PLACES

City Hall – The most distinctive landmark in Philadelphia. Critics have called it "an architectural nightmare." Others praise its elaborate decor: sculpture, marble pillars, alabaster chandeliers, ceilings with gold leaf, carved mahogany, and walnut paneling. The Tower, at William Penn's feet, looks out to the Delaware and Schuylkill rivers. The business district fans out from City Hall. Guided tours of the tower and offices are offered weekdays. No admission charge. Broad and Market Sts. (phone: 686-2250).

Rittenhouse Square – Named after David and Benjamin Rittenhouse, who designed the first astronomical instruments in the US toward the end of the 18th century. Today, Rittenhouse Square is one of the loveliest, most elegant residential areas of the city. Handsome brownstones and high-rise apartment houses surround a green park, where people from all over town congregate. Art shows, flower shows, and concerts take place here in spring and summer. 18th and Walnut Sts..

US Mint – Watch coins being minted. This facility can produce 10,000 coins per minute. At each marked observation post, a pushbutton activates a taped commentary on the different stages of the minting process. Historic coins are exhibited in the Relic Room, and a special counter sells proof sets and medals. Accessible to people in wheelchairs. Closed Sundays, October through April, and on Saturdays, January through March, and national holidays; coinage machines not in operation on Saturdays. No admission charge. 5th and Arch Sts. (phone: 597-7350).

Edgar Allan Poe House – The poet composed his epic to the raven, and his chilling story *The Murders in the Rue Morgue* in these quarters. He lived here for 3 years, with his mother-in-law and young bride. A must for Poe addicts. Closed only on major holidays. No admission charge. 532 N. 7th (phone: 597-8780).

Pennsylvania Horticultural Society – The formal gardens of the 18th century are re-created here, with flowers, shrubs, and pruned trees typical of the era. This is the oldest horticultural association in the US, with a library devoted to botanical subjects. Open weekdays. No admission charge. 325 Walnut (phone: 625-8250).

Reading Terminal Market – Shoppers of all persuasions come to foray for fresh ground horseradish, study French brie, and snack at oyster bars. Check out the homemade soups and hot-from-the-oven shoofly pie. Ice cream at *Bassett's* is a must. Closed Sundays. 12th and Arch Sts. (phone: 922-2317).

Italian Market – Also known as Rocky's market. This is part of Sylvester Stallone's famous jogging trail, in South Philly. 9th St. and Washington Ave.

■**EXTRA SPECIAL:** Even if you've never played the song "Washington at Valley Forge" on a kazoo, you've undoubtedly heard of the place. General George Washington and 11,000 Revolutionary troops retreated to Valley Forge during the winter of 1777-78. The site of their camp and training grounds is now a state park. The visitors center has a film and museum (open daily), and the park itself has a number of interesting historical buildings and brigade huts. There is also a 10-mile, self-guided auto tour; information is available at the visitors' center. Closed Christmas. No admission charge. Take the Schuylkill Expressway (Rte. 76) to the Valley Forge exit (about 20 miles). Take Route 363 north to the park (phone: 783-7700).

SOURCES AND RESOURCES

TOURIST INFORMATION: Right in the heart of the city, only steps from City Hall, is the Philadelphia Visitors Center, with maps, brochures, and other information. Ask specifically for a vacation kit containing the "Official Visitor's Guide" of restaurants, hotels, tours, maps, etc., a seasonal "Calendar of Events," and other helpful information. 16th St. at John F. Kennedy Blvd. (phone: 636-1666) or write: 1515 Market St., Philadelphia, PA 19102. For a recording on what to see and where to go, call the Philly Fun Phone (phone: 568-7255; 24 hours). For discount tickets to theater, music, and other cultural events, call the Cultural Connection Information Hotline (phone: 564-4444).

Disabled people can obtain information by calling the Mayor's Office for the Handicapped (phone: 686-2798); ask for the guide *Access to Philadelphia*. Foreign visitors can stop in at the Council for International Visitors (with 24-hour emergency language translation), Civic Center Blvd. at 34th St. (phone: 879-5248).

Television Stations – WPVI Channel 6–ABC; WCAU Channel 10–CBS; KYW Channel 3–NBC; WHYY Channel 12–PBS.

Radio Stations – AM: KYW 1060 (news); WCAU 1210 (news/talk); WFIL 560 (oldies). FM: WHYY 90.0 (news/talk/public affairs); WEAZ 101.1 (easy listening); WXPN 88.9 (folk, classical, news).

Local Coverage – The *Inquirer,* morning daily; the *Daily News,* afternoon daily; *Philadelphia* magazine, monthly.

Food – *Philadelphia* magazine's restaurant listings or the "Official Visitor's Guide."

Telephone – The area code for Philadelphia is 215.

Sales Tax – There is a 6% sales tax on most purchases, excluding many items of clothing.

CLIMATE: Winter temperatures in Philadelphia generally hover in the 20s and 30s. Spring and autumn are the best times to visit — temperatures then are usually in the 50s to 70s. Summer tends to be hot and sticky, with temperatures in the 80s and 90s.

GETTING AROUND: Airport – Philadelphia International Airport is a 30-minute drive to Center City (up to an hour during rush periods); taxi fare should run about $18. The SEPTA (Southeastern Pennsylvania Transportation Authority) Airport Express train (phone: 574-7800) makes the 20-minute trip to the city's main terminal, 30th St. Station, for $4. Trains stop at most of the airport terminals every half hour.

Bus, Rail, and Subway – SEPTA (Southeastern Pennsylvania Transportation Authority) will take you everywhere, by bus, trolley, train, or subway. A good SEPTA map showing routes for all public transportation is available at newsstands (call 574-7800 for information). The #76 bus runs daily except Sundays and takes you up and down the city's main shopping thoroughfare on Chestnut Street between 18th and 6th Sts.; 60¢.

Taxi – Costly, but for short hops to transport three or four people, it's worth it. Hail them in the street or do as Philadelphians do and pick them up in front of the 30th Street train station, the Greyhound bus terminal, or the nearest hotel, which is where most of them wait for customers. Call *Yellow Cab* (phone: 922-8200), *Quaker City Cab* (phone: 728-8000), or *United Cab Association* (phone: 625-2881).

Car Rental – Philadelphia is served by all the national firms. *Thrifty Car Rental* is particularly worth noting: its inexpensive fleet ranges from mini-vans to executive no-smoking cars (phone: 365-3900 or 800-367-2277).

 LOCAL SERVICES: Business Services – *CPS Services,* 1700 Walnut St., Suite 809 (phone: 985-9535).
    Mechanic – *Center City Service* (24-hour garage), 427 N. Broad (phone: 922-7021).

MUSEUMS: The *Philadelphia Museum of Art, Rodin Museum,* and the *Franklin Institute Science Museum,* described in *Special Places,* are only a few of Philadelphia's museums. Some of the other notable museums include the following:

Academy of Natural Sciences – Particularly known for its dinosaur exhibits. 19th St. and the Parkway (phone: 299-1000).

Afro-American Historical and Cultural Museum – Closed Sundays. 7th and Arch St. (phone: 574-0380).

Athenaeum – Library and historic documents; architectural history and decorative arts of the 19th century. 219 S. 6th St., Society Hill (phone: 925-2688).

Attwater Kent Museum – Local history. 15 S. 7th St. (phone: 922-3031).

Barnes Foundation – French Impressionist art (Fridays through Sundays only; reservations helpful). 300 N. Latch's La., Merion Station (phone: 667-0290).

Civic Center – Variety of exhibitions and events. 34th and Civic Center Blvd. (phone: 823-7400).

Fireman's Hall Museum – 2nd and Quarry Sts. (phone: 923-1438).

Historical Society of Pennsylvania – 1300 Locust St.(phone: 732-6200).

Institute of Contemporary Art – U. of Pennsylvania, Meyerson Hall, 34th and Walnut Sts. (phone: 898-7108).

Library Company of Pennsylvania – Rare books. 1314 Locust St.(phone: 546-2465).

Museum of American Jewish History – 55 N. 5th St. (phone: 923-3811).

Mutter Museum – Medical history. 19 S. 22nd St. (phone: 563-3737).

Pennsylvania Academy of Fine Arts – The oldest art school and museum in the country. Broad and Cherry Sts. (phone: 972-7600).

Perelman Antique Toy Museum – 270 S. 2nd St. (phone: 922-1070).

Philadelphia Maritime Museum – 321 Chestnut St. (phone: 925-5439).

Please Touch Museum – Terrific hands-on exhibitions for children 7 years and under. 210 N. 21st St. (963-0667).

Port of History Museum – Walnut St. and Delaware Ave. (phone: 925-3804).

Print Club – Prints and photography. 1614 Latimer St., between Locust and Spruce Sts. (phone: 735-6090).

Norman Rockwell Museum – Complete collection of *Saturday Evening Post* covers. In Curtis Center at 6th and Walnut Sts. (phone: 922-4345).

Rosenbach Museum and Library – Former private house containing porcelains, antiques, graphic art, and rare books. 2010 Delancey Pl., between Spruce and Pine Sts.(phone: 732-1600).

University of Pennsylvania Museum – Anthropology and archaeology exhibitions. 33rd and Spruce Sts.(phone: 898-4000).

Wagner Free Institute of Science – A Victorian building housing natural history exhibitions. 17th St. and Montgomery Ave. (phone: 763-6529).

MAJOR COLLEGES AND UNIVERSITIES: Philadelphia's colleges and universities are among the best in the country. Foremost is the University of Pennsylvania, founded by Benjamin Franklin in 1740. 34th and Walnut Sts. (phone: 898-5000). Others include: Temple University, Broad St. and Montgomery Ave. (phone: 787-7000); Drexel University, 32nd and Chestnut Sts.(phone: 895-2000); La Salle College, 20th and Olney (phone: 951-1000); St. Joseph's College, 5600 City Line Ave. (phone: 879-7300); Haverford College, Haverford (phone: 896-1000); Swarthmore College, Swarthmore (phone: 328-8000); Bryn Mawr College, Bryn Mawr (phone: 526-5000); Villanova University, Villanova (phone: 645-4500).

SPECIAL EVENTS: The *Mummers Parade,* a Philadelphia tradition on January 1, is 8 hours of string bands strutting up Broad Street in elaborate costumes. Spring comes to the city during the second week in March when the *Philadelphia Flower and Garden Show* is held at the Civic Center, 34th and Civic Center Blvd. Come fall, *Super Sunday,* usually the second Sunday in October, is a day of free culture at institutions along the Benjamin Franklin Parkway, with folk dancing, flea markets, music, food, and mobs of people. The *Philadelphia Craft Show,* held the first or second weekend in November at the 103rd Engineers Armory at Drexel University, is a jury show that displays and sells a wide variety of crafts by artisans from around the state.

SPORTS AND FITNESS: Whether you like to watch or do it yourself, there's enough sports activity to satisfy even the fanatics.

Baseball – From April to September, the *Phillies* chase the pennant at *Veterans Stadium,* Broad St. and Pattison Ave. (phone: 463-1000).

Basketball – Pro basketball's *76ers* pack them in at the *Spectrum,* Broad St. and Pattison Ave., from October to April (phone: 339-7676).

Bicycling – Rent year-round from the *Fairmount Bicycle Rental* (closed Sundays) behind the *Art Museum,* Boathouse Row and E. River Dr. (phone: 978-8545). Some 10.6 miles of Fairmount Park are devoted to bike paths.

Boating – Within the city you can rent rowboats and canoes for the Schuylkill River at the *East Park Canoe House* on E. River Dr. (phone: 225-3560).

Fitness Centers – Your hotel facilities are your best bet.

Football – The NFL *Eagles* play at *Veterans Stadium,* Broad St. and Pattison Ave. (phone: 463-5500)

Golf – Try to get invited to a private country club. If you can't, your next best bet is to try the public city course at Cobbs Creek, 7800 Lansdowne Ave. (phone: 877-8707).

Hockey – Hardest to get are tickets to the *Flyers,* who play at the *Spectrum* from October to May. Best bet is to try a center city ticket agency (or call 755-9700).

Horse Racing – *Philadelphia Park* has thoroughbred racing at Street and Richlieu Rds. (phone: 632-5770).

Jogging – In Fairmont Park, run along the banks of the Schuylkill River; enter the park at Eakins Oval.

Skiing – Everybody goes to the Pocono Mountains, 2 hours away in northeastern Pennsylvania. Best bets: *Camelback Mountain,* Tannersville (phone: 717-629-1661), *Big Boulder,* Lake Harmony (phone: 717-722-0101), and *Jack Frost,* Whitehaven (phone: 717-443-8425).

Tennis – The nation's number one indoor event, the *US Pro Indoor,* is held annually at the *Spectrum* in late January. The city owns more than 200 all-weather courts and Fairmount Park also has that many. Call the City Recreation Dept. at 686-3600, or the Fairmount Park Commission at 686-0052.

THEATER: Broadway- and off-Broadway-bound shows, or post-Broadway reruns, are all performed at two major houses and a dozen other theaters. *Forrest Theater* at 1114 Walnut St. (phone: 923-1515) has year-round offerings, as does the *Walnut Street Theater,* 9th and Walnut Sts. (phone: 574-3550). The *Wilma Theater,* 2030 Sansom St. (phone: 963-0345), offers a series of plays, as does the *Society Hill Playhouse* at 507 S. 8th St. (phone: 923-0210). The *Annenberg Center* at 3680 Walnut St. (phone: 898-6791) has three theaters that present a wide variety of plays and musicals and house the *Philadelphia Drama Guild,* the *Annenberg Subscription Series,* and the *Philadelphia Festival Theater for New Plays.*

MUSIC: The *Philadelphia Orchestra,* under conductor Riccardo Muti, performs at the *Academy of Music,* a classic 1847 building at Broad and Locust Sts. (phone: 893-1930). In summer, they play at the *Mann Music Center,* Fairmount Park (phone: 567-0707), where rock concerts are also held. In summer, call 878-7707 for rock and pop concert tickets. Free tickets to orchestra concerts are available at the Visitors Center (16th and John F. Kennedy Blvd.) on the day of a performance. The *Opera Company of Philadelphia,* the *Pennsylvania and Milwaukee Ballet,* and the *Soloists Chamber Orchestra of Philadelphia* also perform at the *Academy of Music* at various times throughout the year.

NIGHTCLUBS AND NIGHTLIFE: Philadelphians prefer cabarets to Las Vegas–type shows. Best bets: *Café Borgia,* 406 S. 2nd St. (phone: 574-0414), a café with Left Bank ambience and sophisticated jazz; *Chestnut Cabaret,* 3801 Chestnut St.(phone: 382-1201), ranging from rock 'n' roll to rhythm and blues; and *Middle East,* 126 Chestnut St. (phone: 922-1003), with belly dancers. Comics perform upstairs from Middle East at *Comedy Works* (phone: 922-5997), at *The Comedy Factory Outlet,* 31 Bank St. (phone: 386-6911), and at *Going Bananas,* 2nd St. between South and Bainbridge (phone: 925-3470). *Palumbo's,* 824 Catherine St. (phone: 627-7272), has long been a staple of family entertainment.

■ **TAKE SOME PHILADELPHIA HOME WITH YOU:** "Tastykakes" are what exiled Philadelphia residents dream about. The little packages of cakes and pies are available at most grocery stores. But the biggest food thrill is Bassett's ice cream, available all around the city.

BEST IN TOWN

 CHECKING IN: Hotels range from durable, famous places to sleek, new spots with loud, lively lobbies. But there are very few really good inexpensive hotels. Expect to pay $100 to $150 or more for a double in any of those places we've listed as very expensive; between $75 and $100, expensive; between $50 and $75, moderate. Most hotels offer weekend packages at significantly reduced rates. For bed and breakfast accommodations, contact *Bed and Breakfast Connections,* PO Box 21, Devon, PA 19333 (phone: 687-3565), or *Bed & Breakfast of Philadelphia,* PO Box 630, Chester Springs, PA 19425 (phone: 827-9650). All telephone numbers are in the 215 area code unless otherwise indicated.

Barclay – A quiet, stylish stalwart, only steps from Rittenhouse Square and the Walnut Street shops. Its French restaurant is a favorite with the monied Main Line crowd. Though the 240 rooms are not regal, they are comfortable and tastefully furnished. Good to request a renovated room when making your reservation. Conference facilities for up to 300. Guests also have use of the adjacent *Rittenhouse Fitness Center.* 237 S. 18th St. (phone: 545-0300). Very expensive.

Four Seasons – The height of local elegance, with 371 authentically luxurious rooms. Features include such touches as a mini-bar and a hair dryer in each room, twice-daily maid service, terrycloth robes, and a complimentary shoeshine, as well as 3 restaurants: the most gracious *Fountain,* very highly praised for its menu, which changes frequently and emphasizes local favorites; the *Swan Café* for all-day cuisine, and a courtyard café open during the summer. Other amenities include meeting rooms, 24-hour valet and room service, concierge, and a health spa with pool, exercise room, sauna, and whirlpool bath. Typical first-rate *Four Seasons* service. One Logan Sq. (phone: 963-1500 or 800-332-3442). Very expensive.

Hershey Philadelphia – A first class 450-room contemporary hotel in the center of the city, it features extensive meeting facilities, a restaurant, 3 cocktail lounges, nightly entertainment, and valet and room service. The athletically inclined can use the indoor pool, jogging track, racquetball courts, exercise room, and gameroom or relax in the suntanning salon, sauna, and whirlpool baths. Broad and Locust Sts. (phone: 893-1600). Very expensive.

Holiday Inn, Midtown – Small, scrupulously maintained 161-room motor inn with a good location and an outdoor pool. Near theaters, and just a stroll away from all the best shops. Free indoor parking, with valet. Restaurant and bar. 1305 Walnut (phone: 735-9300 or 800-HOLIDAYS). Very expensive.

Hotel Atop the Bellevue – One of the nation's grandest hotels when it opened in the 1890s, it fell on hard times in the 1970s. However, after extensive renovations, this landmark reopened in 1989 in an 11-story retail/office complex. The 121 rooms and 51 spacious suites, decorated in turn-of-the-century style, offer many modern amenities: bathroom TV sets and hairdryers; an entertainment center with VCR, stereo, and mini-bar; and 3 phones with two lines each, and a computer hookup. Fine dining is available in the *Founders* and *Ethel Barrymore* rooms. The *Library* lounge and rooftop sundeck are perfect for lazing. 1415 Chancellor Court (phone: 893-1776). Very expensive.

Latham – The $1-million refurbishment completed in 1988 included redecorating the 139 rooms with bright floral bedspreads, marble-topped bureaus and nightstands, graceful French writing desks and equipping them with hair dryers, makeup mirrors, and remote-control cable TV sets. Chocolates on the pillow at night are one of the ways the hotel pampers its guests. A favorite of businesspeople who seek a central location and good service. There are 2 phones in each room, with call waiting and computer hookups, and a complimentary *Wall Street Journal* is delivered to rooms every business day. Guests may use the health club a block away. The hotel restaurant, *Bogart's* (see *Eating Out*), and the *Crickett Lounge* are places to see and be seen. Concierge, valet, and room service. 17th and Walnut (phone: 563-7474). Very expensive.

Palace – Another relative newcomer to the city's hotel scene, this 280-suite British-owned property is furnished in 18th-century English reproduction pieces and carved French-style beds. Features include meeting facilities, restaurant and lounge, valet and room service, outdoor pool, and reciprocal arrangements through concierge with city health clubs. 18th and Parkway (phone: 963-2222 or 800-223-5672). Very expensive.

Rittenhouse – Appointed in classic European style, it has 88 rooms, 11 suites, and 9 condominiums for business travelers. Amenities include spacious marble bathrooms with tub and stall showers, phones with 2 lines and a computer hookup, VCR, and twice-daily maid service. A restaurant and café, both 2-story, overlook famous Rittenhouse Square. There are also 2 lounges, a health spa with sundeck, indoor pool, sauna, workout equipment, and an aerobics room. 210 W. Rittenhouse Sq. (phone: 546-9000 or 800-474-1700). Very expensive.

Sheraton Inn, Society Hall – In the historic district, within walking distance of Penn's Landing and Independence Mall. Its brick and wood decor lend colonial overtones to its rooms and lobby, where balconies overlook a verdant atrium. Restaurant and nightclub, indoor pool, and health club. 365 rooms with computerized snack bars (you select your items from a machine and they are billed to your room). One Dock St., near Walnut (phone: 238-6000 or 800-325-3535). Very expensive.

Wyndham Franklin Plaza – This large, lavish hostelry is one of the city's best and only 4 blocks from City Hall, a few steps from the parkway. Facilities include 720 modern rooms and 38 suites, racquetball courts, a fully equipped health club with indoor pool, underground parking, meeting rooms, 3 restaurants, a lounge, valet and room service, and concierge. 17th and Vine Sts. (phone: 448-2000). Very expensive.

Adams Mark – This 515-room property was completely refurbished in 1983 to no great effect. The decor, featuring furnishings from around the world, remains ordinary and dull. Facilities include 2 restaurants, 3 lounges, nightly entertainment, meeting rooms, indoor and outdoor pools, sauna, whirlpool bath, racquetball courts and exercise rooms, room service, and free parking. City Line Ave. and Monument Rd. (phone: 581-5000). Very expensive to expensive.

Guest Quarters, Philadelphia Airport – One mile from the main terminal and 15 minutes from the city center, it offers 250 suites, each with living room, bedroom, and bath; also an exercise room and indoor swimming pool, whirlpool bath, and sauna; an 8-story atrium that includes the *Atrium Café and Lounge;* meeting and banquet facilities for up to 250 people; courtesy airport transportation and free hotel parking. 1 Gateway Center (phone: 365-6600 or 800-424-2900). Very expensive to expensive.

Penn Tower – Slightly away from the mainstream with its Civic Center location, but close enough to most sites to remain convenient. It has 227 rooms, a restaurant, cocktail lounge, meeting rooms, and executive amenities. Guests have use of athletic facilities at the University of Pennsylvania. Civic Center Blvd. at 34th St. (phone: 387-8333). Very expensive to expensive.

Holiday Inn, Center City – Good location, near the Penn Center complex, within walking distance of major museums, a mile from Independence Mall. It offers 443 recently renovated rooms, a restaurant, lounge, lobby bar, meeting facilities, and an outdoor pool. 18th and Market (phone: 561-7500 or 800-HOLIDAY). Expensive.

Holiday Inn–City Line – A total of 350 rooms, plus an indoor/outdoor pool, exercise room, restaurant, lounge, discount limousine service to and from the airport, and free parking. It's also convenient to City Line shops and restaurants. City Line and Presidential Blvd. (phone: 477-0200 or 800-HOLIDAY). Expensive.

Howard Johnson's – Near Valley Forge, with 168 rooms (some designated no smoking), cable TV, and an outdoor pool; convenient to area restaurants. Rte. 202, N. and S. Gulph Rd., King of Prussia (phone: 265-4500 or 800-654-2000). Expensive.

Sheraton Inn, University City – Convenient to the University of Pennsylvania campus, with 377 rooms; an outdoor pool; a restaurant called *Smart Alex,* whose disc jockeys provide evening entertainment; and the *36th Street Deli,* which serves breakfast and lunch. 36th and Chestnut Sts. (phone: 387-8000). Expensive.

George Washington – We're certain George Washington would have preferred staying at this motor lodge during his cold Valley Forge encampment. Its facilities include 330 rooms, cocktail lounge, and indoor/outdoor pool. Restaurant next door. Rte. 202 and Warner Rd., King of Prussia (phone: 265-6100). Moderate.

Quality Inn, Center City – With 279 rooms in the heart of the museum district and within walking distance of most major city attractions, the style is casual comfort. Amenities include a restaurant, lounge, outdoor pool, and free parking. 22nd and Parkway (phone: 568-8300 or 800-228-5151). Moderate.

 EATING OUT: The city boasts quite a few outstanding restaurants. In fact, Philadelphia has been enjoying a restaurant renaissance in recent years, with both spacious and intimate places opening their doors, many offering very fine dining experiences. Expect to pay $75 or more for two in those places we've listed as very expensive; $50 to $70 in the expensive category; $20 to $40, moderate; under $20, inexpensive. Prices do not include drinks, wine, or tips. All telephone numbers are in the 215 area code unless otherwise indicated.

Le Bec Fin – Usually the best in town and, at its best, one of the finest restaurants in the country. Imaginative French food by Georges Perrier, the proprietor and master chef from Lyon. Constantly changing menu, but always a selection of lavish desserts. Closed Sundays. Make weekend reservations well in advance as the restaurant seats only 60. Lunch served weekdays. Prix fixe dinner, around $80 per person; lunch around $24 per person. Major credit cards. 1523 Walnut (phone: 567-1000). Very expensive.

DiLullo Centro – Opened in 1985 in a renovated theater, this large establishment has world class atmosphere and small restaurant quality. Opulence is everywhere, from a bronze food-presentation table and glass elevator to Impressionist murals. The menu features a wide variety of homemade pasta as well as veal and seafood dishes and fresh pastries. Closed Sundays. Reservations advised. Major credit cards. 1407 Locust St. (phone: 546-2000). Very expensive.

Bogart's – Like the movie set of *Casablanca,* with wooden ceiling fans and tinkling piano. You won't find Bogie belting one down at the bar, but you will find continental dishes, some with fruit-flavored sauces that exhibit the chef's southern touch, and a well-dressed crowd. Open daily. Reservations advised. Major credit cards. *Latham* hotel, 17th and Walnut (phone: 563-9444). Expensive to moderate.

Bookbinder's Seafood House – The better (and less expensive) of the two restaurants bearing this famous name. Happy, bustling, serving the same well-prepared, simple food, fresh from the ocean. Open daily. Reservations advised. Major credit cards. 215 S. 15th (phone: 545-1137). Expensive to moderate.

Dickens Inn, Philadelphia – In the historic Harper House, whose architecture bespeaks the Federal period; the imported authentic period pieces from England create an English inn right out of Charles Dickens's day. In fact, Dickens's great-grandson Cedric Charles Dickens has given his stamp of approval on numerous visits. Begin an enjoyable evening by sipping a yard of ale and nibbling shepherd's pie in the inn's tavern. Then move on to the restaurant proper to choose from a menu that features traditional English cuisine, including the famous roast beef and Yorkshire pudding or a leg of lamb. Delicious desserts come from a bakery on the premises. Lunch and dinner daily. Reservations advised. Major credit cards. 2nd between Pine and Lombard Sts. (phone: 928-9307). Expensive to moderate.

Downey's – A local favorite where diners come to relax and party, this Irish eatery in the heart of Society Hill is noted for both its corned beef dinners and liquored cakes. The continental menu includes a variety of steak dishes, and an oyster bar features seafood and soups. The wood and brass decor is complemented with Irish artifacts, including a mahogany bar brought over from a bank in Cork. Entertainment ranges from a strolling string ensemble (weekend brunches) to a Dixieland band (Sunday evenings). Open daily. Reservations advised. Major credit cards. Front and South Sts. (phone: 629-0525). Expensive to moderate.

Garden – A continental menu with a French influence, along with fresh seafood and game in season, all served in a stylish old townhouse. Patrons can dine outdoors in the courtyard when the weather's good, or station themselves at the cozy Oyster Bar in the front room. Closed Sundays. Reservations advised. Major credit cards. 1617 Spruce St.(phone: 546-4455). Expensive to moderate.

Old Original Bookbinder's – Philadelphia's best known restaurant, with mahogany and gleaming leather. Many love it, many hate it. The seafood is as much of a legend as many of the celebrities who dine here. Open daily. Reservations advised. Major credit cards. 125 Walnut St. (phone: 925-7027). Expensive to moderate.

Top of Center Square – Expansive windows in each of the four dining rooms on the 41st floor of the First Pennsylvania Bank building provide a panorama of the city. Request the east dining room to see the beautifully lighted City Hall and Billy Penn statue towering above. There is a varied and delicious menu of meats and seafoods. Open daily. Reservations advised. Major credit cards. 1500 Market St. (phone: 563-9494). Expensive to moderate.

Fishmarket – Always crowded at lunch, so get there early. The featured seafood entrées vary according to the day's catch, but the high quality of preparation never wavers. The shrimp, tomato, and cheese pie is fabulous, as is the yellowtail snapper and bouillabaisse. Open daily. Reservations advised. Major credit cards. 124 S. 18th St. (phone: 567-3559). Moderate.

Head House Inn – Complete a tour of historic Philadelphia with a meal at this quaint corner inn. The atmosphere is colonial, but the menu is strictly contemporary, with a good selection of pasta, steaks, veal, and seafood. Lighter fare includes French onion soup, quiches, and salads. Open daily except Tuesdays. Reservations advised. Major credit cards. 2nd & Pine Sts. (phone: 925-6718). Moderate.

Apropos – A place for those seeking an upbeat bistro atmosphere with sophisticated ambience; but be warned — it can get noisy here. The menu ranges from mesquite-grilled chicken, fish, and meat entrées to lighter fare, such as salads, pasta, and sandwiches. All breads and desserts are freshly baked. Dining is available in the large, open dining room or the glass-enclosed street café. Open daily. Reservations advised. Major credit cards. 211 S. Broad St. (phone: 546-4424). Moderate to inexpensive.

Imperial Inn – One of the best-known Chinese restaurants in Chinatown. Its menu features Szechwan, Mandarin, and Cantonese dishes. Lunches are more casual;

lights are dimmed and linen tablecloths are added at dinner. Cocktails are served here, and parking is available at nearby 11th and Race Sts. Open daily; no lunch on Saturdays. Reservations advised. Major credit cards. 146 N. 10th St. (phone: 627-5588). Moderate to inexpensive.

Marabella's – A contemporary Italian restaurant featuring mesquite-grilled seafood, great pizza, and Italian delicacies including handmade pasta. Try the tortellini with goat cheese, sun-dried tomatoes, and olives; or a huge salad entrée of grilled chicken cutlet on a bed of radicchio, endive, and Bibb lettuce. Follow up (if you still can) with the chocolate and raspberry torte. Reservations for lunch only. Major credit cards. 1420 Locust St. in Academy House (phone: 545-1845). Moderate to inexpensive.

Famous Delicatessen – Famous among Philadelphia residents, and for its celebrity customers, to which the picture-lined walls will attest. Monstrous hot pastrami, roast beef, and corned beef sandwiches. No-frill eating; the food comes on paper plates. Open Mondays through Saturdays until 6 PM; Sundays until 4 PM. No reservations. No credit cards. 700 S. 4th St. (phone: 627-9128). Inexpensive.

Melrose Diner – With its 50-year history, fanatically devoted staff, and round-the-clock crowds, this is as much a Philly institution as the scrapple it serves. Food preparation is fastidious, right down to the refiltered water and the coffee specially brewed in a custom-made urn. Waitresses wearing coffee-cup-shaped pins with clock faces (the diner's logo; a tiny knife and fork form the hands) serve up scrapple and eggs, cutlets, burgers, creamed chipped beef on toast, and other no-frills fare. The homemade desserts are popular takeout items. Open 24 hours. No reservations. No credit cards. In South Philly at Broad St. and Snyder Ave. (phone: 467-6644). Inexpensive.

Pete's Pizza – Convenient to the *Franklin Institute, Please Touch,* and other museums, the menu here includes Philadelphia hoagies, grinders, and burgers in addition to pizza. It also claims to have the city's best stromboli. Open daily from 6 AM until 1 AM. 116 N. 21st St. (phone: 567-4116). Inexpensive.

USA Café at The Commissary – Specializing in "the cuisine of the American Southwest with some Louisiana overtones," the café has a look as modern as its menu: streamlined tubes of orange neon run along the deep blue ceiling. The food is tasty and imaginatively prepared, from the batter-fried peppers stuffed with crabmeat and Monterey Jack cheese to the barbecued ribs. *The Commissary,* downstairs, is a handsome cafeteria with a simpler menu — mostly salads, omelettes, and pasta. *Café:* weekday lunch only; reservations advised; moderate to inexpensive. *Commissary:* with adjoining piano bar open daily; inexpensive. Both accept major credit cards. 1710 Sansom St. (phone: 569-2240).

H. A. Winston & Co. – Dozens of burger permutations in an atmosphere that's warm, cozy, and comfortable. Open daily. Reservations unnecessary. Major credit cards. 1500 Locust St. (phone: 546-7232). Inexpensive.

PHOENIX

Phoenix: the Los Angeles of the future? If it sounds unthinkable, consider these facts: In 1960, the Phoenix metropolitan area had a population of 439,000; now its citizenry numbers about 1.9 million. It's among the fastest growing metropolises in the US. Its major industries are electronics and aerospace, both businesses coming of age with the next millennium — not just future-oriented, but damn near futuristic. People are flocking to the Southwest, and in many cases landing in Phoenix and its environs. If residents view this turn of events with some satisfaction, they are not oblivious to the dangers ahead. Most people come here for two things — the 8 months of nearly perfect weather and the environment. Phoenix is craggy mountains against cerulean skies, and palm trees lining wide, clean streets. By day, the sun fairly sparkles; as evening nears, the sunset paints splashes of deep purple and blazing orange across the horizon. This, residents say, is what heaven is all about. But nothing threatens the environment like numbers, and the numbers of Phoenicians keep growing. It's apparent that a substantial segment of the populace is nonetheless willing to sacrifice a pristine environment in the interest of economic growth. On the worst days you can see smog during the morning rush hour. But just as you're ready to chuck it all, the winds sweep the air clean again, and Phoenix rises like the mythical bird of its namesake, from the ashes. The shiny coppers, cool turquoises, silver sages, and verdant greens return, and are visible for miles.

The scenery is frankly spectacular. The city takes a back seat to the awesome beauty of the Valley of the Sun (as the area around Phoenix is called). From the top of nearby South Mountain one sees the Valley stretch away in all directions, with the checkerboard of Phoenix's main avenues crisscrossing far into the northern horizon. East and west, suburbs extend for 50 miles (Glendale, Avondale, Sun City, and Youngtown to the west; Scottsdale, Tempe, and Mesa eastward toward the fabled Superstition Mountains). In the northeast, there's no mistaking the Valley's most distinctive landmark, Camelback Mountain. If you were to draw an imaginary line down its rugged, red haunches, you'd have the boundary between Phoenix and Scottsdale, the city's fashionable, artistic suburb.

As the eye follows the palisades of the Superstitions along the eastern horizon, it picks out the far mountain chain which cradles the crashing Salt River, lifeblood of the city and the Valley. The Salt has been irrigating the Valley for more than 1,000 years, and some of its canals follow water paths created by ancient Hohokam Indians.

What ancient history Phoenix has is associated with its first residents, the Indians. The city itself is little more than 100 years old, and Arizona has only been a state since 1912. But it cherishes its Indian past. Ringed by reserva-

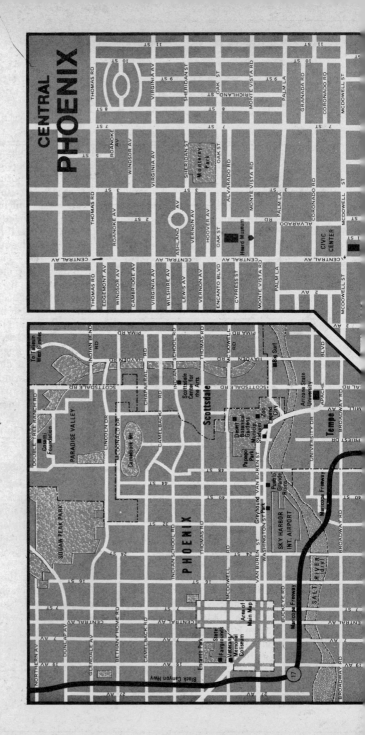

CENTRAL PHOENIX

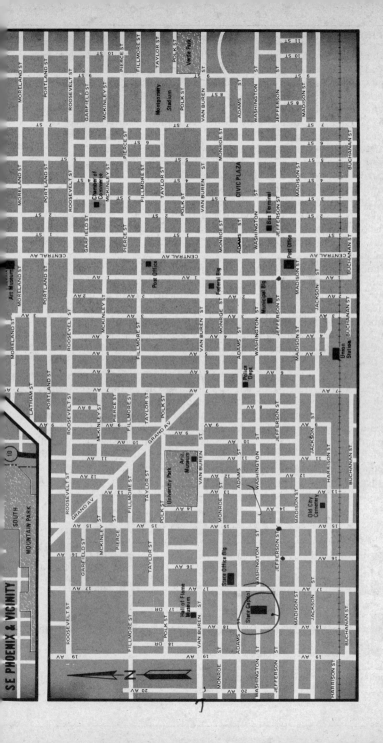

tions, the Valley has a number of museums devoted to indigenous cultures, as well as art galleries featuring the work of local Indian artists.

If you think the desert is all sand dunes, you'll be delightfully surprised by the abundance of plant life. There are at least a dozen species of cactus, one of which, the saguaro, with its thick, tall torso and upraised arms, is the state symbol. You'll also be surprised by residents' attitude toward distance. They consider it nothing to drive 200 miles for a picnic or a swim. (By the way, you'll need a car to get around here. Everything is spread out.)

Everything is also dependent on the weather, generally fantastic in winter and incredibly hot in summer. In winter, the Valley bustles with thousands of "snowbirds" escaping the northern and eastern cold. Except for the occasional cold snap or cloudburst, it's possible to play tennis and golf all winter. But make no mistake. It gets cold after dark. Sometimes, the temperature drops below freezing. Even during the daytime, coats or sweaters are often necessary. Oddly enough, though, Phoenix gets most of its rain in the summer — what little there is.

By June, Phoenix metamorphoses into an oven. The snowbirds forsake the mountain-rimmed bowl to return to their spring gardening, and residents scurry from air conditioned house to air conditioned car to air conditioned office. Daytime temperatures climb over the century mark most days through September. On a really cool night the mercury might plunge to 70F! On weekends, Phoenix becomes a ghost town as people flee to the cooler mountain forests. You'll understand why Arizona is one of the few states in the nation that doesn't have daylight saving time. Arizonans can't wait for the sun to go down.

The heat also generates some tall local legends. One of the hottest-selling items in souvenir shops is an ordinary-looking twig called a "lizard stick." An accompanying tag informs the buyer that this stick is used by Arizona lizards during the summer. The crafty critters, it alleges, carry the stick in their mouths as they run from burrow to burrow. When their feet get too hot, they jam the stick into the sand, and climb it to give their feet a rest. It won't be taken amiss if you raise a skeptical eyebrow at these gadgets. They sell a lot of them here, but save your wonder for the fabulous Phoenix desert.

PHOENIX AT-A-GLANCE

SEEING THE CITY: As you look out on Phoenix from South Mountain ponder on the words of an Indian prayer to Corn Mother and Sun Father: "Oh, it is good, you provide. It is the ability to think. It is the wisdom that comes. It is the understanding."

SPECIAL PLACES: Street numbers start at zero in the center of downtown. Central Avenue, the business and financial district, runs north and south, bisecting the city into east and west. Numbered avenues lie to the west of Central, numbered streets to the east.

State Capitol – The building will give an idea of what granite from the Salt River Mountains looks like when put to constructive use. It has now has been restored to its original appearance in 1912, at the time of statehood. The murals inside depict Arizona's discovery and exploration in the 16th century and life in the region through the 1930s. Closed weekends and holidays. No admission charge. W. Washington and 17th Ave. (phone: 542-4675).

Heard Museum of Anthropology and Primitive Arts – A fascinating anthropological collection of artifacts from ancient Indian civilizations in Arizona. The kachina doll collection, donated by Senator Barry Goldwater, is consistently interesting for neophytes as well as experts. Changing exhibitions feature contemporary American Indian sculpture, paintings, and drawings. Gift shop carries fine Indian jewelry, crafts, and artwork. Open daily except holidays. Admission charge. 22 E. Monte Vista (phone: 252-8840 or, for recorded information, 252-8848).

Phoenix Art Museum – Specializes in contemporary art from the Southwest; other collections lean toward North American art in general (including Mexican), with a small exhibition of Renaissance, 17th-, and 18th-century material. Closed Mondays and major holidays. Admission charge except Wednesdays. 1625 N. Central (phone: 257-1222).

Pueblo Grande Museum and Indian Ruins – *Pueblo Grande* is on the site of a former Hohokam Indian settlement. By climbing to the top of a mound marked into seven stations, you can see the ruins which are believed to have been occupied from 200 BC to AD 1400, when the Hohokam vanished without a trace. Phoenix municipal archaeologists are continuing their excavations. Open daily except holidays. Admission charge. 4619 E. Washington (phone: 275-3452).

Desert Botanical Gardens – Half of all the varieties of cactus in the world are planted on the grounds, and self-guiding tours and booklets help identify the prickly flora. Open daily. Admission charge. Papago Park (phone: 941-1217).

Phoenix Zoo – When you're done walking around the Botanical Gardens, take a leisurely drive through desert rock formations to the Phoenix Zoo, which covers more than 125 acres in another section of Papago Park. (You can stop to picnic in the park.) Two of the most popular attractions are the oryx herd and Hazel, the gorilla. There are more than 1,200 animals altogether. Open daily. Admission charge. 5810 E. Van Buren (phone: 273-7771).

Scottsdale – This re-created western community with hitching posts is a haven for artists and art lovers. Scottsdale's Fifth Avenue is lined with galleries (see *Museums and Galleries*) featuring Indian art, handicrafts, and jewelry. Every Thursday evening from 7 to 9, October through May, the community sponsors an "art walk" through town. In Scottsdale, taking a walk is an aesthetic adventure. Take McDowell Rd. east to Scottsdale Rd. north.

Cosanti Foundation – The architect Paolo Soleri maintains a workshop here, with a model of Arcosanti, his megalopolis of the future. His sculpture and windbells are on display, too. Open daily except major holidays; call for tour information. Donation. 6433 E. Doubletree Rd., Scottsdale (phone: 948-6145).

Taliesin West – The future owes much of its shape to the innovative imagination and technical expertise of the master architect Frank Lloyd Wright. His former office and school, Taliesin West (pronounced tal-ly-*ess*-en), offers the chance to see what goes into planning and designing those marvelous, ultramodern structures. Closed on rainy days and holidays; limited, varying hours from June to mid-October. Admission charge. Scottsdale Rd. north, to Shea Blvd. east, to 108th St. north, to Taliesin West in Scottsdale (phone: 860-8810).

Borgata – Not the place for bargain-priced jeans or a pound of sugar, it's one of the most opulent retail operations this side of Beverly Hills — and one of the most unusual anywhere. The Borgata houses about 50 boutiques and restaurants in a setting redolent of an old Italian village. It's well worth a visit, even if you can only afford to cast amazed glances at the price tags. Open daily. 6166 N. Scottsdale Rd., Scottsdale.

Heritage Square – This Victorian complex in the heart of downtown is a refreshing change in this relatively young city. Spend an afternoon in the museums, shops, restaurants, and open-air lathe house. Rosson House (1894) is particularly notable. Open Wednesdays through Sundays. Admission charge. 127 N. 6th St. (phone: 262-5071).

Rawhide's 1880s Western Town – Mosey on over to the valley's most authentic Wild West town, complete with gunfights, gold panning, a museum, a specialty zoo, steakhouse and saloon, and sunset cookouts. With the McDowell Mountains as a backdrop, it's a glimpse into how the West really was. Open daily. Admission charge. 23023 N. Scottsdale Rd. (phone: 563-5111).

Dolly's **Steamboat on Canyon Lake** – A unique way to tour the desert. Board this nostalgic replica of a historic steamboat to cruise Canyon Lake, in the breathtaking Superstition Wilderness. Guides give an informal history and geography lesson along the way. Cruises depart at noon and 2 PM daily, with sunset charter rides available. Call for summer hours. Admission charge. 5106 E. Emilita, Mesa (phone: 827-9144).

■**EXTRA SPECIAL:** For a picturesque day trip through open desert, take the Black Canyon Highway north, to Cordes Junction, then travel west through the old territorial capital of Prescott to Sedona, famous for its dramatic red cliffs. At Sedona, take a breathtaking drive up Oak Creek Canyon to Flagstaff, or complete the circle by driving back to Verde Valley, returning via the Black Canyon Highway. Be sure to stop in Jerome, the ghost town too ornery to die. A community of artists now lives in the old wooden buildings that cling precariously to the steep mountainside of this former copper mining town. Jerome has great curio and antiques shops specializing in mining paraphernalia and one of the best restaurants in Arizona, the *House of Joy.* The food is continental, the prices are reasonable, and it's open only on weekends (so reservations are a must; phone: 634-5339).

SOURCES AND RESOURCES

TOURIST INFORMATION: For maps, brochures, and information, contact Phoenix and Valley of the Sun Convention and Visitors Bureau, 505 N. 2nd St., Phoenix, AZ 85004 (phone: 254-6500), or Arizona Office of Tourism, 1100 W. Washington Ave., Phoenix, AZ 85003 (phone: 542-3618).

The best guide is *Phoenix Metro* magazine's *City Guide* (Phoenix Publishing; $3.95).

Television Stations – KTVK Channel 3–ABC; KTSP Channel 10–CBS; KTAR Channel 12–NBC; KAET Channel 8–PBS.

Radio Stations – AM: KFYI 910 (news/talk); KLFF 1360 (big band); KAMJ 1230 (contemporary). FM: KMEŎ 96.9 (easy listening); KOY 95.5 (adult contemporary); KSLX 100.7 (nostalgia).

Local Coverage – *Arizona Republic,* morning daily; *Phoenix Gazette,* evening daily except Sundays; *Scottsdale Progress,* afternoon daily; *New Times, Business Journal,* and *Arizona Business Gazette,* all weekly; *Phoenix Metro* magazine, *Arizona Trend, Phoenix Home & Garden,* all monthly.

Food – *100 Best Restaurants in Arizona,* by John and Joan Bogert (ADM; $3.95).

Telephone – The area code for Phoenix is 602.

Sales Tax – In Phoenix, the sales tax is 6.7%.

CLIMATE: Try not to visit in summer, when it's more than 100F. Fall, winter, and spring are dry, warm, and sunny. Temperatures range from daytime highs of between 60F and 80F to nighttime lows of about 35F to 50F.

GETTING AROUND: Getting around Phoenix is next to impossible without a car.

Airport – Sky Harbor International Airport is just a 10-minute drive from downtown, and, depending on the cab company, taxi fare will run from $7 to $14. (Fares have been deregulated and now vary widely, so be sure to agree on a price before getting into a cab.) *Supershuttle* (phone: 244-9000) offers transportation from the airport to downtown for $5 and to most other Valley locations for $16 maximum. For rides to the airport, call 24 hours in advance. *Phoenix Transit* (phone: 257-8426) buses stop at terminals 2 and 3 at Sky Harbor every half hour. One goes downtown and one to the east valley. Fare is 75¢ and transfers are free.

Bus – There are buses, but service is sketchy, with interminable waiting periods, erratic schedules, very limited nighttime service, and no buses at all on Sundays. However, you can call Phoenix Transit System (phone: 257-8426) for schedule information. *Greyhound* runs buses to Tempe and Mesa (phone: 248-4040).

Taxi – Call *Yellow Cab* (phone: 252-5071) or *Triple A* (phone: 437-4000)..

Car Rental – All major national firms are represented. *Rent A Wreck* (phone: 252-4897) is among the least expensive.

LOCAL SERVICES: Babysitting – *Ace Babysitting Service,* 3737 E. Turney Ave. (phone: 956-2848).

Business Services – *Alison's Secretarial Service,* 3270 E. Camelback Rd. (phone: 955-3542).

Mechanic – *Western States Tire Co.,* 201 W. Van Buren (phone: 254-4131).

MUSEUMS: The *Heard Museum, Phoenix Art Museum,* and *Pueblo Grande Museum* are described in *Special Places.* Other museums worth a visit:

Arizona Mineral Museum – 1826 W. McDowell (phone: 255-3791).

Hall of Flame Museum – No kidding. A collection of firefighting paraphernalia from 1725. 6101 E. Van Buren (phone: 275-3473).

ART GALLERIES: Although Phoenix does have some interesting art galleries, most of the finest are in Scottsdale, within walking distance of one another. They exhibit a rich and vast array of art forms — paintings, sculpture, graphics — and many are devoted to American Indian art and contemporary western art. Some of the best are:

Artistic Gallery – Artists include the nationally acclaimed R. C. Gorman. 7077 E. Main St., Scottsdale (phone: 945-6766).

Suzanne Brown Gallery – Contemporary western art, from abstract to representational. 7156 E. Main St., Scottsdale (phone: 945-8475).

Marilyn Butler Fine Art – Fritz Scholder is among the gallery's artists. 4160 N. Craftsman Court, Scottsdale (phone: 994-9550).

Hand and the Spirit – Tapestries, ceramics, jewelry, and other American crafts. 4222 N. Marshall Way, Scottsdale (phone: 946-4529).

Elaine Horwitch Galleries – Contemporary sculpture and paintings by a wide variety of artists. 4211 N. Marshall Way, Scottsdale (phone: 945-0791).

Gallery McGoffin – The country's only batik gallery. 902 W. Roosevelt, Phoenix (phone: 255-0785).

Lovena Ohl Gallery – Indian arts and crafts, from primitive to contemporary. 4251 N. Marshall Way, Scottsdale (phone: 945-8212).

MAJOR COLLEGES AND UNIVERSITIES: The largest and most active campus is Arizona State University, Apache Blvd., Tempe (phone: 965-9011). Phoenix College, 1202 W. Thomas Rd. (phone: 285-7418), and American Graduate School of International Management, 59th Ave. and Greenway Rd., Glendale (phone: 978-7011), sponsor concerts and activities, too.

SPECIAL EVENTS: The *Phoenix Open Golf Tournament* takes place in January (phone: 263-0757 for information); other golf tournaments are played throughout the year. In February, the million-dollar Arabians prance into town for a spectacular equestrian event of pageantry at the *Arabian Horse Show and Sale* (phone: 264-5691). In March, the *Veterans Memorial Coliseum,* 1826 W. McDowell, is the site of the *Phoenix Jaycees Rodeo of Rodeos* (phone: 264-4808). In May, one of the city's most vibrant celebrations is the *Cinco de May,* an annual holiday celebrating the Mexican victory over French troops in 1862. In October, the *Arizona State Fair* fills up the State Fairgrounds (phone: 252-6711) and the *Cowboy Artists of America* bring their works to town for this nationally recognized sale and exhibition at the *Phoenix Art Museum* (phone: 257-1880). November finds hundreds of colorful balloons dotting the turquoise skies in the annual *Thunderbird Balloon Race* at the American Graduate School of International Management in Glendale (phone: 978-7208). Watch for the month-long schedule of activities that begin in December for the *Sunkist Fiesta Bowl,* capped by a New Year's weekend that brings a parade, a national high school band pageant, and two of the country's top collegiate football teams together for a bowl title.

 SPORTS AND FITNESS: The year-round sun makes Phoenix ideal for watching or participating in outdoor athletics.

Basketball – NBA Phoenix *Suns* play at *Veterans Memorial Coliseum,* 1826 W. McDowell (phone: 258-6711). The Arizona State University *Sun Devils* play at the *University Athletic Center* on the campus in Tempe (phone: 965-2381).

Bicycling – Rent bikes from *Airplane and Bicycle Works,* 4400 N. Scottsdale Rd., Scottsdale (phone: 949-1978).

Dog Racing – *Greyhound Park,* 40th and E. Washington Sts. (phone: 273-7181).

Fishing – Trout, bass, and crappie can be caught at Apache Lake and Salt River.

Football – The NFL Phoenix (formerly St. Louis) *Cardinals* and the Arizona State *Sun Devils* play at *Sun Devil Stadium.* Call the ticket office for seat availability (phone: 965-2381).

Golf – There are about 90 courses in Phoenix. The best public course is Encanto Municipal (phone: 253-3963).

Horseback Riding – Hourly rentals at *Ponderosa Stable,* 10215 S. Central (phone: 268-1261), and *South Mountain Stable,* 10005 S. Central (phone: 276-8131). *All Western Stables,* 10220 S. Central (phone: 276-5862), also rents horses by the hour.

Horse Racing – *Turf Paradise* (from October to May), 19th Ave. and Bell Rd. (phone: 942-1101).

Inland Surfing – If you've always wanted to surf but can't quite brave the force of the ocean, *Big Surf* (phone: 947-2478) at 1500 N. Hayden Rd. in Tempe is a good place to break in. There are artificial beaches and waves, and you can rent the entire facility for parties. Closed Mondays except holiday weekends and October through March; open weekends only in September. Admission charge.

Jogging – An enclosed haven for fast walkers on scorchingly hot days is the air conditioned Paradise Valley Mall (Mondays through Saturdays 6 to 10 AM, Sundays 8:30 AM to noon) before it is officially open to shoppers; in northeast Phoenix at the intersection of Tatum and Cactus (phone: 996-8840). Under the sun run along the banks of the Arizona Canal (pick it up beside the *Biltmore* hotel) or the Grand Canal, reachable by jogging about a mile north along Central Avenue; Encanto Park, about three-quarters of a mile from downtown, also attracts runners.

Swimming – The Salt River is good for swimming, too. There are 23 municipal pools in Phoenix. Every large park has one. Try the pool at Coronado Park, N. 12th St. and Coronado Rd.

Tennis – *Phoenix Tennis Center* has 22 lighted courts for night games, 6330 N. 21st Ave. (phone: 249-3712). In all, there are more than 1,000 courts in the Phoenix area.

Tubing – Arizona's most popular summer sport. On any given weekend, as many as 20,000 residents strap beer-filled ice chests and their bottoms to old inner tubes and float down 5 or 10 miles of free-flowing Salt River, below Saguaro Lake, just north of Mesa. The trip is free and you can buy tubes — the bigger the better — at gas stations and stands along the route. This utterly relaxing pastime is called "tubing down the Salt." For tube rental and shuttle service, contact *Salt River Recreation,* Mesa (phone: 984-3305).

THEATER: There's quite a lot of drama in Phoenix and Scottsdale. A lot of plays take place on campuses, and world-renowned performers like the late Sir Michael Redgrave have come to play Shakespeare. Check the local publications listed above for schedules. The major theaters include: *Phoenix Little Theater,* 25 E. Coronado Rd. (phone: 254-2151); *Gammage Auditorium,* a Frank Lloyd Wright building on the campus of Arizona State University in Tempe (phone: 965-3434); and *Scottsdale Center for the Arts,* Civic Center Plaza, Scottsdale (phone: 994-2787).

MUSIC: The *Phoenix Symphony* (phone: 264-4754) and *Arizona Opera Company* (phone: 254-1664) play at *Symphony Hall,* 225 E. Adams; the *Scottsdale Symphony* and *Arizona Ballet Theater* perform at *Scottsdale Center for the Arts,* 7383 Scottsdale Mall (phone: 994-2787). Traveling dance troupes play *Gammage Auditorium* and *Scottsdale Center for the Arts.* Nationally known rock performers and classical musicians appear at *Gammage Auditorium.* Rock groups also give concerts at *Veterans Memorial Coliseum,* 1826 W. McDowell (phone: 258-6711). Good music is also found on college and university campuses (see *Major Colleges and Universities*).

NIGHTCLUBS AND NIGHTLIFE: One of the most popular nightspots in Phoenix is *Oscar Taylor* at Biltmore Fashion Sq. (phone: 956-5705), which offers a great happy hour and a decor that's reminiscent of Chicago during Prohibition. Another good meeting place is *Timothy's,* 6335 N. 16th St. (phone: 277-7634), where jazz artists appear nightly. If you crave a little Mexican food with your nightclubbing, don your dancing shoes and head to *Acapulco Bay Beach Club,* 3837 E. Thomas (phone: 273-6077). And for margaritas and music that will knock your socks off, try *Depot Cantina,* 300 S. Ash, Tempe (phone: 966-6677).

BEST IN TOWN

CHECKING IN: If you're going to Phoenix on business, you'll probably want to stay downtown. If it's a vacation, you can't beat the resorts, which offer full recreational activities and valley tours. Meals are usually included in the room rate at a resort, but be sure to check first. Expect to pay between $120 and $280 for a double room at an expensive resort; between $75 and $100 at an expensive hotel; $25 to $75 in moderate; and around $25 at an inexpensive listing. For bed and breakfast accommodations, contact *Bed & Breakfast in Arizona,* PO Box 8628, Scottsdale, AZ 85252 (phone: 995-2831), or *Mi Casa, Su Casa,* PO Box 950, Tempe, AZ 85280 (phone: 990-0682). All telephone numbers are in the 602 area code unless otherwise indicated.

Arizona Biltmore – The first, and still among the best in the valley, this 502-room resort is first class in every way. Golf and tennis facilities are outstanding, and so are the pools. Individual guests may be put off by the hordes of convention and meeting goers, who always seem to dominate the premises. The dining rooms serve fine continental food. 24th St. and Missouri (phone: 955-6600). Expensive.

Boulders – Opened in 1985 by the Rockresort group (but no longer managed by them), this is a "rock resort" in another sense, too: It's set on 1,300 acres of desert foothills at the base of a towering pile of boulders. The 120 adobe-colored casitas blend beautifully with the surroundings, and each contains a room with a wet bar and working fireplace. There are also tennis courts, golf courses, and horseback riding. Carefree, about 30 miles north of Phoenix (phone: 488-9009). Expensive.

Camelback Inn – This is among the largest resorts in the state — 423 rooms, mostly in 2-story cottages. It's set among the beautiful Camelback Mountain foothills and has swimming pools, golf, and tennis facilities. The cowboy cookouts are great fun. 5402 E. Lincoln Dr., Scottsdale (phone: 948-1700). Expensive.

Camelview – The desert landscaping here provides a placid retreat from the hustle-bustle of nearby downtown Scottsdale. There are 200 rooms, including suites and casitas, plus a pool, 8 lighted tennis courts, an exercise parcourse, and numerous other amenities. The main restaurant, *Café on the Lakes,* serves steaks and sea-food. 7601 E. Indian Bend Rd., Scottsdale (phone: 991-2400 or 800-228-9822). Expensive.

Doubletree Inn – A nice hotel that's convenient to *Scottsdale Center for the Arts,* the Scottsdale Mall, and the town's numerous boutiques. An added bonus is the *Rotisserie Bar & Grill,* which features southwestern cuisine and a stylish piano bar that's open late every night but Sunday. 7353 E. Indian School Rd., Scottsdale (phone: 994-9203). Expensive.

Embassy Suites – Run by a hotel chain whose goal is to provide guests with a homey atmosphere, and since 95% of the guests return, it appears that the management is successful. Accommodations are in 2-room suites with kitchens; breakfasts and late afternoon cocktails are free; and tipping is not permitted. 5001 N. Scottsdale Rd., Scottsdale; 1515 N. 44th St., 2333 E. Thomas Rd., 2630 E. Camelback Rd., and 3210 NW Grand Ave., Phoenix; 4400 S. Rural Rd., Tempe (phone: 800-362-2779). Expensive.

Hermosa Inn – Long one of the valley's most exclusive guest ranches and tennis resorts, it advertises that it is "not just a resort, it's an attitude." That sounds like hype until you check in and find rooms with gas-fired fireplaces, wet bars, Jacuzzis, and a staff that gives VIP treatment to every guest. The setting seems far removed from the rat race, but civilization is only minutes away — if you want it. 5532 N. Palo Cristi Rd., Paradise Valley (phone: 955-8614). Expensive.

Hyatt Regency – Play tennis after dark, swim, or relax those aching muscles in the whirlpool bath. This elegant, 711-room newcomer has a fine restaurant and an overpriced coffee shop. 122 N. 2nd St. (phone: 257-1110 or 800-228-9000). Expensive.

Hyatt Regency Scottsdale – Built on the Gainey Ranch development, this new, $75-million, 497-room luxury resort offers all the basic recreational facilities (swimming pool with swim-up bar, 8 tennis courts, 27 holes of championship golf, health club, and Jacuzzi) as well as a few extras (lawn tennis and croquet). After all that exercise, guests can sate their hunger and quench their thirst at the 2 restaurants, entertainment lounge, or lobby bar. 7500 E. Doubletree Ranch, Scottsdale (phone: 800-228-9000). Expensive.

Marriott's Mountain Shadows – With a 1,500-seat grand ballroom and 10 meeting rooms, it's no wonder this place is popular with convention groups and business travelers. And after all those meetings, guests can relax by taking advantage of the 3 pools, 2 Jacuzzis, 8 tennis courts, and three 18-hole golf courses. There are 2 informal restaurants, *Cactus Flower Café* and *Shells Oyster Seafood Bar.* 5641 E. Lincoln Dr., Scottsdale (phone: 800-228-9290). Expensive.

Phoenician Golf and Tennis Resort – This brand-new $300-million property at the base of legendary Camelback Mountain has 605 rooms, individual casitas, several restaurants, an 18-hole championship golf course and clubhouse, tennis, and health spa. 6000 E. Camelback Rd., Scottsdale (phone: 941-8200). Expensive.

Phoenix Crescent – A 344-room hotel that caters to the business traveler. Features include a pool, tennis courts, health club, and restaurant, as well as a location that is convenient to the rapidly expanding North Phoenix commercial center. 2620 W. Dunlap Ave. (phone: 943-8200). Expensive.

Pointe at Squaw Peak – Lovely southwestern decor characterizes this mountainside resort, which manages to remain almost fully booked even during the summer. *Pointe of View* (see *Eating Out*), which features Northern Italian cuisine, is one of several good restaurants here. 7677 N. 16th St. (phone: 997-6000 or 800-528-0428). Expensive.

Pointe at Tapatio Cliffs – Patterned after the successful *Pointe at Squaw Peak,* this mountainside resort has attractive Spanish-southwestern architecture and luxurious amenities. The dazzling *Etienne's Different Pointe of View* restaurant is a high-tech mountaintop facility that serves fine French cuisine. 11111 N. 7th St. (phone: 997-6000 or 800-528-0428). Expensive.

Registry Resort – A good choice for those who want to go first class, this busy place borders several golf courses and has 3 pools, a complete fitness center, and nightly entertainment. Its *La Champagne* (see *Eating Out*) restaurant is considered one of the valley's best, and Sunday brunch in the *Phoenician Room* combines live music with a remarkable array of food. 7171 N. Scottsdale Rd., Scottsdale (phone: 991-3800). Expensive.

Scottsdale Princess – Built on 450 acres of desert, this resort provides the best of the Southwest, with 363 rooms and 37 suites in its main building, plus 125 casitas. There's a full range of sports facilities, including two championship 18-hole golf courses (they play the Phoenix Open on the TPC Stadium course), 10 tennis courts (6 lighted), 3 heated pools, and a health club/spa with racquetball and squash courts, as well as restaurants, lounges, bars, and shops. 7575 E. Princess Dr., Scottsdale (phone: 585-4848 or 800-223-1818). Expensive.

Sheraton Phoenix – A Phoenix fixture, previously known as the *Adams* hotel. The 534 large rooms all have magnificent views and there's an old-time feeling at the quaint bar, with swimming pool, good coffee shop, and a good dining room. 111 N. Central (phone: 257-1525, or 325-3535). Expensive.

Stouffer-Cottonwoods – It's easy to relax at this resort while admiring Camelback Mountain in the distance, sniffing the piñon-perfumed air, and basking in the bright Arizona sun. The 170 fresh and comfortable rooms have a southwestern decor. A jitney connects the hotel with nearby shopping, and there's a pool, putting greens, and jogging trails. Golf and horseback riding are nearby. 6160 N. Scottsdale Rd., Scottsdale (phone: 991-1414, 800-325-5000, or 800-HOTELS-1). Expensive.

SunBurst – A Santa Fe decor enhances the refurbished *SunBurst,* which has as much to offer outdoors as in. Amenities include a free-form pool, a spa, a lively lounge, and a restaurant (the *Desert Rose*) with very good American and continental cuisine. 4925 N. Scottsdale Rd., Scottsdale (phone: 945-7666). Expensive.

Westcourt – Ultramodern, boasting more original artworks in its 284 luxury rooms and suites than many galleries. In the city next to the gargantuan Metrocenter — packed with shops and restaurants — it also has a dining room called *Trumps.* 10220 N. Metro Pkwy. E. (phone: 997-5900). Expensive.

Wyndham Paradise Valley – This 20-acre, $40-million facility offers 380 rooms, including 27 suites, as well as 2 pools, a health club and spa, 2 racquetball courts, 6 tennis courts, and 2 restaurants, one of which features very creative American nouvelle cuisine. 5401 N. Scottsdale Rd., Scottsdale (phone: 947-5400). Expensive.

Holiday Inn – A modern 292-room hotel near the financial district has 2 swimming pools, whirlpool bath, and a good restaurant. Pets are welcome. 3600 N. 2nd Ave. (phone: 248-0222 or 800-465-4329). Moderate.

Fiesta Inn – This venerable favorite is a true Southwest delight, with Mexican tiles and room-size fireplaces. Complimentary airport transportation, health club, and jogging trails are included. 2100 S. Prest Dr., Tempe (phone: 967-1441). Moderate.

Lexington – This is a good place for an extended visit. All 139 suites come with kitchens, continental breakfast, and hospitality hour. Discounts for long stays/relocation. 1660 W. Elliot Rd. (phone: 345-8585 or 800-53-SUITE). Moderate.

Travel Inn 9 – Smaller and quieter than the others, this 68-unit motel (with pool) is also kinder to your budget. 201 N. 7th Ave. (phone: 254-6521). Inexpensive.

EATING OUT: Best bets in Phoenix are Mexican restaurants and steakhouses. Expect to pay $60 or more for a meal for two at an expensive restaurant; between $35 and $50 at a moderate restaurant; under $25 at a selection noted as inexpensive. Prices do not include drinks, wine, or tips. All telephone numbers are in the 602 area code unless otherwise indicated.

Avanti – This place has a 6-page menu of Northern Italian and continental dishes. Open daily except Christmas. Reservations advised. Major credit cards. Two locations: 3102 N Scottsdale Rd., Scottsdale (phone: 949-8333); 2728 E. Thomas Rd., Phoenix (phone: 956-0900). Expensive.

La Champagne – Part of the prestigious *Registry Resort,* this ambitious restaurant offers American nouvelle and French cuisine, black tie service, an extensive wine list, and piano music. Closed Sundays and Mondays. Reservations advised. Major credit cards. 7171 N. Scottsdale Rd., Scottsdale (phone: 991-3800). Expensive.

Golden Eagle – Although this restaurant is expensive, the view over the valley and the quick and attentive service make you feel it's worth it. The continental menu features some southwestern specialties. Closed Sundays, Christmas, and New Year's. Reservations advised. Major credit cards. 201 N. Central, atop the Valley Bank Center, Phoenix (phone: 257-7700). Expensive.

La Hacienda – This authentic Mexican mansion at the *Scottsdale Princess* features Mexican specialties as well as a roast of the day, which may be juicy lamb or crackling crisp suckling pig. The bar and lounge serve Mexican hors d'oeuvres and Spanish tapas during cocktail hours to the strains of live mariachi music. Open daily for lunch and dinner in season. Reservations advised. Major credit cards. 7575 E. Princess Dr., Scottsdale (phone: 585-4848). Expensive.

Pointe of View – As its name implies, this restaurant affords an impressive panorama of the valley. Charcoal-broiled steaks and pasta are house specialties. Open daily. Reservations advised. Major credit cards. 7677 N. 16th St., Phoenix (phone: 997-5859). Expensive.

Mancuso's – The decor at the Scottsdale location will transport you to an Italian Renaissance castle, and the continental cuisine merits applause, as do the service and the prices of entrées, which include soup, salad, and more. Closed major holidays. Reservations recommended. Major credit cards. 6166 N. Scottsdale Rd., Scottsdale (phone: 948-9988); 4949 E. Lincoln Dr., Paradise Valley (phone: 840-8670). Expensive.

Palm Court – Tuxedoed waiters prepare much of the food at your table at this dining room in the Scottsdale Conference Resort. While gazing out on Camelback Mountain and Lake McCormick, you can select from the brief but tempting à la carte continental menu. Recommended are the Bibb lettuce salad, the lobster bisque, and the rack of lamb. Sunday brunch here is considered among the valley's finest. Open daily. Reservations advised. Major credit cards. 7700 E. McCormick Pkwy., Scottsdale (phone: 991-3400). Expensive.

Le Relais – Surrounded by a $3-million collection of artwork, all catalogued and up for sale, diners savor French specialties, such as veal with forest mushrooms and fresh fish flown in from France, from a menu that changes nightly. Closed Sundays and all of late July and August. Reservations advised. Major credit cards. 8711 E. Pinnacle Peak Rd., Scottsdale (phone: 998-0921). Expensive.

Ruth's Chris Steak House – There's no cowboy atmosphere at all, but *Ruth's Chris* does serve the best steaks in the state, in a sleek, contemporary dining room. Prices are high, but portions are gigantic. Closed Christmas. Reservations advised. Major credit cards. 2201 E. Camelback Rd., Phoenix (phone: 957-9600). Expensive.

Tomaso's – The latest effort of a successful valley restaurateur, this eatery and its siblings are known for their Northern Italian cuisine. Closed Thanksgiving and Christmas. Reservations advised. Major credit cards. 610 E. Bell Rd., Phoenix (phone: 866-1906); 3225 E. Camelback Rd., Phoenix (phone: 956-0836); and 1954 S. Dobson Rd., Mesa (phone: 897-0140). Expensive.

Voltaire – The most popular entrée is sand dab — a white fish from the sole family that the chef blankets with egg batter and sautés with lemon butter — but the rack of lamb, medallions of veal, and boned breast of duck are just as gratifying. Closed Sundays, Mondays, and June through September. Reservations advised. Major credit cards. 8340 E. McDonald, Scottsdale (phone: 948-1005). Expensive.

Rick's Café Americana – The kitchen at this loving re-creation of the nightclub in *Casablanca* turns out dependable, diverse continental fare. A pianist plays and takes requests in the lounge. Closed on Christmas. Reservations advised. Major credit cards. 8320 N. Hayden, Scottsdale (phone: 991-2233). Expensive to moderate.

Alexilion – Understated and elegant, *Alexilion* is where Phoenix's elite meet. To find out why, sample the international cuisine, that embraces everything from sand dabs provençale to *bah mie goreng* (an Indonesian blending of chicken, pork, and shrimp). Closed Thanksgiving, Christmas, and New Year's Day. Reservations advised. Major credit cards. 4017 E. Indian School Rd., Phoenix (phone: 957-6957). Moderate.

El Chorro Lodge – Old Arizona charm at its best. By night, cozy up to the fireplace for a romantic interlude; by day, bask in the sun on the patio overlooking the majestic Camelback Mountain. No matter what time of day, don't miss the basket of hot sticky buns. Open daily, but closed during the summer. 5550 E. Lincoln, Scottsdale (phone: 948-5170). Moderate.

Don & Charlie's – If your appetite is bigger than your budget, try this restaurant. The menu's American dishes may seem standard, but just wait till they arrive at your table. Steaks are huge and perfectly cooked, and the meaty pork ribs are good, too. Closed on Thanksgiving. Reservations advised. Major credit cards. 7501 E. Camelback Rd., Scottsdale (phone: 990-0900). Moderate.

Famous Pacific Fish Co. – Good service and bargain prices are simply extras. This place is really special for its combination of Mexican mesquite charcoal broiling and fresh seafood. The nautical ambience is delightful, too. Don't miss the New England clam chowder, which may not be the "world's finest" (as the menu claims) but certainly comes close. Closed on major holidays. Lunch reservations only. Major credit cards. 4321 N. Scottsdale Rd., Scottsdale (phone: 941-0602). Moderate.

Lunt Avenue Marble Club – If the name isn't enough to draw you in, it has great deep-dish pizza, too, and one of the best sandwich selections in the state. Closed on Thanksgiving and Christmas. Reservations advised. Major credit cards. Three locations: 2770 W. Peoria (phone: 863-9791); 2 E. Camelback Rd. (phone: 265-8997), Phoenix; 1371 N. Alma School Rd., Chandler (phone: 899-6735). Moderate.

Monti's La Casa Vieja – A valley landmark. Serves some of the best steaks anywhere. It's always crowded, but the service is good. Side dishes are plentiful. Open daily. Reservations for lunch only. Major credit cards. 3 W. First, Tempe (phone: 967-7594). Moderate.

The Moroccan – It doesn't look like much from the outside, but inside, diners are transported to another place and time. The exotic menu features meat pastries topped with sugar and cinnamon, marinated vegetables, and an array of spicy lamb dishes. Entrées come with five courses and are eaten with the hands. For an added treat, there's Moroccan music and hip-rolling belly dancers. 4228 N. Scottsdale, Scottsdale (phone: 947-9590). Moderate.

Pinnacle Peak Patio – No trip to Arizona would be complete without a visit to a real, by-God western cowboy steakhouse. This one's the oldest and most famous, with 2-pound Porterhouses broiled over mesquite coals and served with sourdough bread and pinto beans. Don't wear a tie! Closed Thanksgiving, Christmas Eve, and Christmas. Reservations for large groups only. Major credit cards. 10426 E. Jomax Rd., Scottsdale (phone: 967-8082). Moderate.

Piñon Grill – Who said hotel restaurants had to be boring or uncreative? If you hunger for authentic southwestern fare, head to the *Piñon Grill* at the *Inn at McCormick Ranch*. The lakeside setting and the copper and cactus decor only enhances the cuisine of the topnotch and daring kitchen. 7401 N. Scottsdale Rd., Scottsdale (phone: 948-5050). Moderate.

T-Bone – A real out-of-the-way find that's never crowded. It has basically the same menu as *Pinnacle Peak*, with a fantastic night view of the valley. Food is brought by entertaining, gun-totin' waitresses, and you can help yourself to a filling salad. Closed on Thanksgiving, Christmas, and the first 2 weeks in July. Reservations unnecessary. Major credit cards. End of 19th Ave. south of Dobbins, Phoenix (phone: 276-0945). Moderate.

What's Your Beef – A valley favorite, serving beef and fresh fish; the super salad bar with fruits, vegetables, and breads is a big favorite. An adjoining bar offers entertainment nightly with no cover charge. 8111 E. McDowell, Scottsdale (phone: 998-1987). Moderate.

RoxSand – One of the most talked-about restaurants to open in the valley in years, this stylishly decorated dining spot features "intercontinental" dishes that vary widely in price, complexity, and origin. There are enticing entrées from Italy, Korea, Mongolia, Morocco, Sweden, and Russia, but nothing beats the desserts. Closed on major holidays. Reservations accepted. Major credit cards. 2594 E. Camelback Rd., Scottsdale (phone: 381-0444). Moderate to inexpensive.

Aunt Chilada's – Authentic Mexican cuisine is the specialty here. Try the Whole Aunt Chilada: chimichangas, bean burritos, tamales, guacamole, sour cream, and homemade flour tortillas served with fideo (Mexican pasta) instead of rice. Don't worry; it serves two. Open daily except Thanksgiving. Reservations advised. Major credit cards. 7330 N. Dreamy Draw Dr., Phoenix (phone: 944-1286); 2021 W. Baseline Rd., Tempe (phone: 438-0092). Inexpensive.

Herman's – So you're miles from home and feel the need for a sports fix coming on. Don't despair — just head to *Herman's,* a neighborhood bar and grill that combines good food with more television sets than an appliance store. The comfortable atmosphere and diverse menu score high with all fans. 3223 S. Mill, Tempe (phone: 967-0568). Inexpensive.

Los Olivos – A family operation for more than 3 decades, this is the valley's oldest Mexican restaurant. A thoroughly modern decor belies its age, but the food explains its longevity. Try such house specialties as sour cream enchiladas and carne asada, then walk off the meal by strolling over to the adjacent *Scottsdale Center for the Arts*. Closed major holidays. Reservations accepted. Major credit cards. 7328 E. 2nd St., Scottsdale (phone: 946-2256). Inexpensive.

Original Hamburger Works – If all you want is a good burger, wander over to the vicinity of Phoenix College and partake of giant hamburgers with all the fixin's. The decor is rustic 1880s, with advertising posters from the turn of the century on the walls. Open daily except Thanksgiving and Christmas. No reservations. No credit cards. 2801 N. 15th Ave., Phoenix (phone: 263-8693). Inexpensive.

Pink Pepper – A few years ago, the valley had only one Thai restaurant; now there are about two dozen. The ultramodern *Pink Pepper* is the prettiest of the lot, and since it uses moderation when sprinkling on the spices, it's a good place for the uninitiated to try this often hot-as-fire cuisine. The soups with lemon grass and coconut milk are tops, as are the meat dishes with Phonaeng curry. Open daily. Reservations advised. Major credit cards. 2003 N. Scottsdale Rd., Scottsdale (phone: 945-9300). Two other locations: 4967 W. Bell, Phoenix (phone: 843-0070); 1941 W. Guadalupe, Mesa (phone: 839-9009). Inexpensive.

PITTSBURGH

Like the mythical phoenix, Pittsburgh has risen from its ashes — almost literally. For more than a hundred years, it was one of the most important industrial cities in the world, producing one-fifth of all the steel made in the United States. But with prosperity came pollution and the image of a one-industry town; it had become something of an urban slag heap dubbed Steel Capital, USA.

Then, having lost ground to fierce competition from abroad, the domestic steel industry declined, forcing Pittsburghers to adapt. Over the past three decades civic leaders and residents have made a concerted effort to clean up the air, put some green underfoot, and promote the city as a vital and vibrant place to live. To some degree, they have succeeded. Once-smoggy skies are now clear, revealing stunning skylines, healthy rivers, and more trees per capita than any other city in the US.

Pittsburgh is also an important city commercially. It has the third largest number of Fortune 500 companies' headquarters in the country, with 16 of them maintaining offices in the downtown area, known as the Golden Triangle. The top 6 bring in more than $1 billion in annual revenue. In recent years, nearly 200 additional foreign and domestic companies have settled here, making Pittsburgh an international center in the fields of chemical, plastic, nuclear, and general scientific research.

A metropolis of 1.5 million people, the city is spread out around the confluence of the Allegheny and Monongahela rivers. The Point, where the rivers join to form the Ohio River, has been strategically important as far back as the years before the French and Indian War. This confluence was a point of contention and, later, the site of vicious conflict between France and Great Britain, at that time colonial rivals. It was not far from the Point, in 1754, that the young George Washington, then an ardent British officer, ordered an attack on a French encampment, thereby inadvertently triggering the Pennsylvania phase of the French and Indian War. In 1758, British troops managed to secure control of the river forks, which enabled them to ensure their domination of North America. They built the formidable Ft. Pitt at the Point, naming the battlement in honor of England's prime minister, William Pitt.

Even as Ft. Pitt's military importance declined, Pittsburgh developed as a commercial town and river port. As the center for transporting westward-bound pioneers and supplies, the "Key to the West" did a thriving business, selling flatboats loaded with glass, home furnishings, hardware, dry goods, and farm products. In 1760, the largest coal seam ever struck in the United States was discovered on Mt. Washington. With this coal and the iron ore that was shipped from nearby, Ft. Pitt became industrial as well as commercial.

Iron foundries multiplied, and during the Civil War Pittsburgh was the "arsenal of the North." It was also a magnet for magnates. The roster of tycoons who made their fortunes in Pittsburgh includes Thomas Mellon, Andrew Carnegie, and Henry Clay Frick.

As the industries flourished, the immigrants flocked to this burgeoning center of employment. Besides future tycoons like Frick and Carnegie, stonemasons and other Old World artisans also came, craftsmen who created much of the ornate stone and metal work found in Pittsburgh's older buildings and bridges. And there are many bridges in Pittsburgh — 1,700 at last count.

The cleaner current environment heightens the enjoyment of Pittsburgh's cultural activities, many of which are the legacy of the giants of industry. Thomas Mellon and Andrew Carnegie endowed several art institutions; Henry Clay Frick gave the city a museum, and the Henry Heinz family of the famous "57 varieties" contributed a performing arts center. The wealth also helped underwrite education, recreation, and health care. Today Pittsburgh has 28 colleges, 4 universities, 170 research and development facilities, an internationally acclaimed symphony, and more golf courses per capita than any other city in the country. For a city its size, Pittsburgh is an amazingly friendly place. It is not uncommon for strangers to wish each other a good day on their way to work or for visitors asking directions to be personally escorted to their destination — or given an ad lib tour. Pittsburghers are very proud of their city, a pride that is well justified.

PITTSBURGH AT-A-GLANCE

SEEING THE CITY: Go to the top of Mt. Washington via the Duquesne or Monongahela inclines for a sweeping 17-mile view of the confluence of the Allegheny, Monongahela, and Ohio rivers. Duquesne (75¢ each way) is at W. Carson St. (phone: 381-1665); Monongahela (60¢ each way), in operation since 1870, is at E. Carson St., behind the Freight House Shops of Station Square (phone: 237-1000). Exact change (75¢) is required. Pittsburgh's original blast furnace can be seen on the south side of the Monongahela River, between the two inclines.

For a more down-to-earth view, take one of several different cruises on the Gateway Clipper fleet, from the dock at Station Square. The captain aboard the 2-hour sightseeing cruise ($6 for adults, $4 for children), will highlight points of interest along all three rivers. The *Goodship Lollipop* has clowns to keep children occupied while parents enjoy the sights on its 1-hour cruise (adults $4; children $3). Reservations are required for the dinner cruise ($17 to $20 per person), which leaves the dock daily at 7 PM. Specialty cruises include a tour of the river lock system and an excursion to *Waterford Race Track*, Wheeling, West Virginia. Some cruises are seasonal; call 355-7980 for information.

SPECIAL PLACES: There are three main sections of the city in which you'll find most of Pittsburgh's places of interest. The Golden Triangle encompasses the downtown area; North Side, old homes, the restored "Mexican War Streets," and parks; Oakland, museums and cultural institutions.

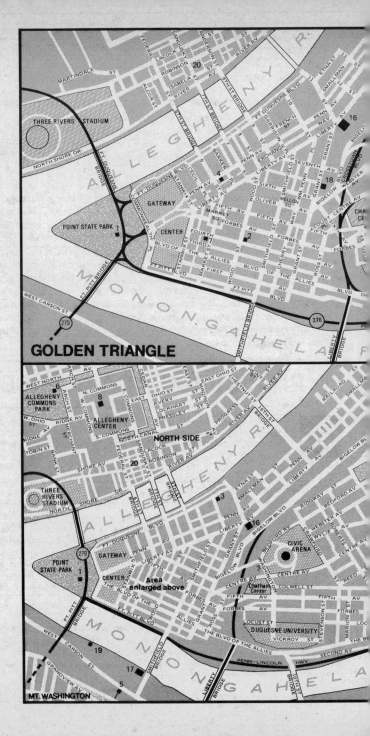

GOLDEN TRIANGLE

THREE RIVERS STADIUM

NORTH SHORE DR

POINT STATE PARK

GATEWAY CENTER

WEST CARSON ST

279

376

A L L E G H E N Y R.

M O N O N G A H E L A R.

MARTINDALE

FEDERAL ST
LACOCK ST
ROBINSON ST
ISABELA ST
RIVER

ANDERSON ST
SANDUSKY ST
9TH ST BRIDGE
7TH ST BRIDGE
6TH ST BRIDGE

RIVER AV

ALCOR ST

FT. DUQUESNE BRIDGE

FT. DUQUESNE BLVD
CECIL

PENN AV
STANWIX ST

COMMONWEALTH

BLVD OF
THE ALLIES
FT. PITT BLVD
FT PITT BRIDGE

MARKET ST

SMITHFIELD BRIDGE

20

FT DUQUESNE BLVD
GARRISON
FRENCH ST
EXCHANGE
PENN AV
LIBERTY AV

BARKER

6TH ST
WOOD ST
LIBERTY AV

SIXTH AV
FIFTH AV
MARKET SQ
FORBES
FOURTH
THIRD
FIRST

SMITHFIELD ST
WM. PENN
SEVENTH AV
OLIVER
MELLON SQ
FIFTH AV
CHERRY WAY
GRANT ST

ETNA ST
SMALLMAN
PENN WAY
LIBERTY

BIGELO

16

18

COURT CENTRE AV
FIFTH
FORBES

ROSS AV

CHA
CE

FT PITT
BLVD

4

1

2

7

NORTH SIDE

WEST NORTH AV
ARCH AV

ALLEGHENY COMMONS PARK

ALLEGHENY CENTER

N. COMMONS
W. COMMONS
E. COMMONS
S. COMMONS
RIDGE AV
MERCHANT
W. OHIO ST
RIDGE
TOBIN ST
BANK ST
SHORE AV

THREE RIVERS STADIUM

NORTH SHORE DR

POINT STATE PARK

GATEWAY CENTER

EAST ST
CEDAR
OHIO ST
EAST OHIO ST
CHESTNUT ST
RIVER AV
16TH ST

AVERY
LOCKHART
PRESSLEY ST
NORTH CANAL
LACOCK
ROBINSON
RIVER AV

EAST
E. RANDOLPH ST
FEDERAL ST

8

20

279

FT. DUQUESNE BLVD
PENN

LIBERTY AV
FIFTH AV

STANWIX ST

Area enlarged above

THE BLVD OF THE
FORBES
FT. PITT BLVD
ALLIES

WEST CARSON ST

GRANDVIEW AV

MT. WASHINGTON

SMITHFIELD BRIDGE

FT. DUQUESNE BRIDGE

SIXTH ST BRIDGE

ETNA ST
SMALLMAN
LIBERTY
PENN AV

RIVER AV
PROGRESS

16TH ST

RAILROAD
SMALL

RIDGWAY ST
BEDFORD AV
WEBSTER AV
WYLIE AV
BIGELOW BL

1

3

16

BIGELOW BLVD

GRANT BLVD

BIGELOW BLVD
CENTRE AV
WASHINGTON

BEDFORD AV

CIVIC ARENA

ROBERTS
CENTRE AV
REED

CRAWFORD

SMITHFIELD ST

CENTRE AV
COLWELL ST

FIFTH AV
FORBES

Chatham Center

LOCUST ST
VICKROY ST

DUQUESNE UNIVERSITY

FIFTH AV
FORBES

STEVENSON ST
MARION ST

LOC
THE B

19

17

5

WEST CARSON ST

PENN LINCOLN HWY
SECOND AV

M O N O N G A H E L A R.

LIBERTY BRIDGE

CENTRAL
PITTSBURGH

LANDMARKS

1. Fort Pitt Museum
2. Bank Center
3. David L. Lawrence Convention Center
4. Heinz Hall
5. Monongahela Incline
6. West Park Conservatory—Aviary
7. PPG Place
8. Buhl Planetarium
9. Cathedral of Learning
10. Carnegie Museum and Library
11. Mellon Institute
12. Phipps Conservatory
13. Historical Society of Western Pennsylvania
14. Frick Fine Arts Building
15. Pittsburgh Playhouse Theater Center
16. Penn. Central Station
17. Pittsburgh & Lake Erie Station
18. U.S. Steel Building
19. First Blast Furnace
20. "Mexican War" District

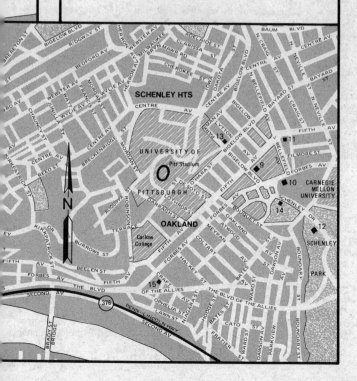

GOLDEN TRIANGLE

Though most of the major attractions are within walking distance, use the subway for quick crosstown transportation.

Point State Park – At the tip of the Golden Triangle, it covers 36 acres of broad walks and spacious gardens on the banks of the river junction, Point State Park contains Ft. Pitt Blockhouse, a 1764 fortification, and *Ft. Pitt Museum,* with exhibitions on the French and Indian War and early Pennsylvania history. The park is free and open daily (phone: 281-9284); the museum is open Wednesdays through Sundays. Admission charge.

Bank Center – Once a financial hub, these four turn-of-the-century buildings are now an indoor bazaar. Under a stained glass skylight and amid marble columns and gleaming brass are shops, cinemas, and restaurants. After browsing in the boutiques, have espresso, antipasto, or quiche in the atrium's café as you watch the parade pass by. 307 4th Ave.

PPG Place – The "crown jewel" in Pittsburgh's skyline is a plaza surrounded by six modern Gothic buildings, all with a mirrored glass façade, designed by Philip Johnson and John Burgee. On the ground floor of PPG 1 is the Wintergarden, open to the public for civic functions. An array of international food establishments and retail boutiques runs throughout buildings 2 through 6. Summer concerts are given in the plaza. Off Stanwix St.

One Oxford Centre – This office tower at Grant Street and 4th Avenue has three lower floors dedicated to designer shops including *Charles Jourdan, Gucci,* and *Bill Blass.* Elegant restaurants, some featuring live jazz, are there when you've had your fill of shopping.

Civic Arena – Recognizable by its stainless steel roof — the largest retractable dome in the world — this is the home of the Pittsburgh *Penguins* hockey team and the Pittsburgh *Spirit* soccer team. The circus, dog show, and top-name concerts are also held here. Bordered by Washington and Crawford Sts., Bedford and Centre Aves.

David L. Lawrence Convention Center – The city's newest exposition hall (opened in 1980), it has 131,000 square feet of space and hosts the home show and the *Pittsburgh Folk Festival* every May. Call 565-6000 for a schedule of upcoming events. Penn Ave.

Liberty Center – Pittsburgh's newest retail and office complex, adjoined to the convention center by a bridge, features four floors of retail shops, two international restaurants, a luxury hotel, a fitness center, and 20,000 square feet of garden space.

Heinz Hall – A very classy movie theater in 1926, *Heinz Hall* is now an acoustically balanced, stately auditorium, home of the *Pittsburgh Symphony, Pittsburgh Opera,* and *Civic Light Opera,* and host to performing arts troupes. Worth a look for its ornate decorations. Guided tours by appointment. Admission charge. 600 Penn Ave. (phone: 392-4800 for tour; 281-5000 for tickets).

Station Square – Beautifully restored Pittsburgh and Lake Erie Railroad complex includes an outdoor museum with antique rail cars and Bessemer converter, an elegant restaurant and saloon in the old station, and a complete shopping mall in the adjacent freight house. The *Gateway Clipper* dock is also here.

NORTH SIDE

To get to the North Side from the Golden Triangle, cross the 6th Street Bridge, then proceed north to the Allegheny Center Mall. Crosstown buses leave from *Horne's,* at Penn Ave. and Stanwix St.

Allegheny Observatory – With a 30-inch-diameter refractory lens — a very powerful telescope — this observatory is acclaimed as one of the world's best. Amateur astronomers can scan the heavens or partake in the illustrated lectures. Open Wednesday, Thursday, and Friday evenings by appointment, April through October. No admission charge. Riverview Park off Perrysville Ave. (phone: 321-2400).

Pittsburgh Aviary/Conservatory – Close to 260 species of birds chatter away in walk-through and enclosed exhibitions. A good place to escape from 20th-century urban America with the advantage that you can slip back into it once you've recharged your battery. Open daily. Admission charge. Ridge Ave. and Arch St., Allegheny Commons (phone: 323-7235).

Children's Museum – Tots and preteens can play with video equipment, operate puppets they know from television, and participate in a kid clinic where they are the doctor to an injured dummy. Admission charge. Open daily. Seasonal hours. Call 322-5058 for recording of hours and special events. Old Post Office Bldg., Allegheny Square.

Buhl Science Center – One of the first and best sky shows in the country. Entertaining exhibitions on astronomy and other branches of science allow you to pedal a bicycle to generate electricity, push a button to activate the rotation of planets in our solar system, and monitor voice patterns on an oscilloscope. A weird-looking Zeiss projector is used for "Sky Dramas" in the *Theater of the Stars*. Open daily. Admission charge. Allegheny Square (phone: 321-4302).

OAKLAND

Cathedral of Learning – Part of the University of Pittsburgh, this imposing 42-story Gothic tower is the only skyscraper of classrooms in the country. A special attraction is the 19 Nationality Rooms on the first floor, devoted to each of the city's major ethnic groups. Open daily. No admission charge. Bigelow Blvd. and 5th Ave. (phone: 624-6000).

The Carnegie – Cultural complex comprising the main branch of the Carnegie Libraries, a music hall, a museum of art with a magnificent collection of French Impressionist works, and the *Carnegie Museum of Natural History*, featuring 10,000 objects on display from all fields of natural history and anthropology. Closed Sunday mornings and Mondays. Donation. 4400 Forbes Ave. (phone: 622-3172).

Phipps Conservatory – Rare tropical and domestic fragrant blossoms flourish in the greenhouses and gardens of this 2½-acre publicly owned conservatory. Annual flower shows are in spring, fall and during Christmas. The 13 greenhouses are only a fraction of the greenery of surrounding Schenley Park, which covers 422 acres. Schenley has a lake, tennis courts, baseball fields, a golf course, an ice skating rink, picnic areas, and nature trails. Conservatory (admission charge) and park open daily. Schenley Park (phone: 255-2375).

Historical Society of Western Pennsylvania – Curious bottles of antique glass, hand-carved furniture, and other memorabilia line the halls, walls, and shelves. You can peruse old documents on Pennsylvania history in the library. Closed Sundays and Mondays. No admission charge. 4338 Bigelow Blvd. (phone: 681-5533).

Pittsburgh Zoo – Not only does this zoo have more than 2,000 animals spread over 75 acres but there's an indoor Aquazoo as well, with tanks full of domestic trout and pike, and esoteric species like penguins and piranhas. Nocturnal animals are on display in the Twilight Zoo (a children's zoo that operates from May to October). Open daily. Admission charge. Highland Park (phone: 441-6262).

Frick Art Museum – A magnificent Renaissance mansion houses Great Masters from the Renaissance through the 18th century. Marie Antoinette's furniture is on display in an ornate living room. The eclectic collection comprises Russian silver, Flemish tapestries, and Chinese porcelains. Closed Mondays and Tuesdays. No admission charge. 7227 Reynolds St. and S. Homewood Ave., Point Breeze (phone: 371-7766).

■**EXTRA SPECIAL:** For a change of scene, try the Laurel Highlands, just an hour's drive from the city. Take Rte. 22/30 east from downtown via Penn Lincoln Parkway to Ligonier, where you'll find the *Compass Inn,* an old coaching inn used by travelers in the 18th century. Lively tours are given Sundays from noon to 4:30 PM from the end of May to the end of October, with special candlelight tours in November and December; admission charge. Also nearby is Ft. Ligonier, a restored fort from the French and Indian War. Open daily from 9 AM to 5 PM from April 15 to November 15; admission charge (phone: 412 238-9701). The *Mountain Playhouse,* one of the oldest summer theaters in the country, is a half-mile north of Jennerstown on Rte. 985 off Rte. 30. Hungry theatergoers can dine next door at the excellent *Green Gables* restaurant. For reservations and information, call 814-629-9201.

SOURCES AND RESOURCES

TOURIST INFORMATION: For information on places of interest and events contact the Visitor Information Center in Gateway Center, the Golden Triangle. The VIC is run by the Greater Pittsburgh Convention and Visitors Bureau, 4 Gateway Center, Pittsburgh, PA 15222 (phone: 281-7711), which offers a variety of city guides. For recorded information on daily events, call 800-255-0855 in Pennsylvania; 800-821-1888 elsewhere.

Television Stations – WPXI Channel 11–NBC; KDKA Channel 2–CBS; WTAE Channel 4–ABC; WQED Channel 13–PBS.

Radio Stations – AM: KDKA 1020 (contemporary/oldies); WTAE 1250 (contemporary/oldies); WKQV 1410 (news/talk). FM: WBZZ 94.6 (top 40); WYDD 104.7 (top 40/jazz weekends); WDUQ 90.5 (classical).

Local Coverage – *Post-Gazette,* morning daily; *Press,* evening daily; *Business Times-Journal,* weekly.

Food – See the restaurant sections of *Pittsburgh* magazine.

Telephone – The area code for Pittsburgh is 412.

Sales Tax – There is a 6% sales tax on everything except clothing.

CLIMATE: Pittsburgh has a moderate climate with frequent precipitation year-round. Summer temperatures climb into the 80s; winters drop into the 20s. About 200 days of the year are cloudy, and winters are snowy.

GETTING AROUND: Airport – Greater Pittsburgh International Airport is a 40-minute ride from downtown; taxi fare should cost about $25. *Airport Transportation Co.* (phone: 471-2250) provides bus service every 20 or 30 minutes from the airport to the *Westin William Penn, Pittsburgh Hilton & Towers,* and *Vista International* hotels for $8.

Bus – Port Authority Transit provides efficient bus service (phone: 231-5707, for information).

LRT Subway – New PAT underground service has expanded to South Hills; it operates from downtown to South Hills, through Station Square, across the Monongahela River, from 5 AM (6:30 AM on Sundays), to 1 AM daily. Ultramodern trains run frequently during the day and every 15 to 30 minutes at night. They are free in the downtown Golden Triangle until 7 PM; all other route fares range from $1 to $1.25.

Taxis – *People's Cab* (phone: 681-3131; for 24-hour service, 441-5334) or *Yellow Cab of Pittsburgh* (phone: 665-8123).

Car Rental – All major national firms are represented.
Van Service – *Peoples Cab* (phone: 441-5334).

LOCAL SERVICES: Babysitting – All hotels have babysitting services.
There are no independent child care services, however.
    Business Services – *Allegheny Personnel Services,* Arrott Bldg. (phone:
391-2044).
Mechanic – *Drugmand's Texaco,* 304 Virginia Ave. (phone: 431-1130).

MUSEUMS: The *Ft. Pitt Museum, Children's Museum, Buhl Science Center,*
the *Carnegie, Historical Society of Western Pennsylvania,* and *Frick Art
Museum* are described in *Special Places.* Other museums worth noting:
    Art Institute of Pittsburgh – 536 Penn Ave. (phone: 263-6600).
Old Economy Museum and Village – 14th and Church Sts., Ambridge (phone:
266-4500). See DIVERSIONS.
Pittsburgh Center for the Arts – 5th and Shady Aves. (phone: 361-0873).

MAJOR COLLEGES AND UNIVERSITIES: University of Pittsburgh,
Forbes Ave., Oakland (phone: 624-4141); Chatham College, 5th Ave. and
Woodland Rd. (phone: 365-1100); Duquesne University, Blvd. of the Allies
(phone: 434-6000); Carnegie-Mellon University, Schenley Park (phone: 578-
2000).

SPECIAL EVENTS: The *Three Rivers Arts Festival,* displaying the work of
over 600 artists, spans 17 days in June. Performing arts and a film festival
are a small part of the Carniegie-sponsored festivities. The *Pittsburgh Folk
Festival,* an ethnic fair and entertainment spectacular, takes place the weekend before Memorial Day weekend at the David L. Lawrence Convention Center. The
Shadyside Art Festival takes place in Shadyside in early August. The festive *Three
Rivers Regatta,* the first weekend in August, features the Grand Prix of Formula I boat
racing, *Steamboat Races for the Mayors Cup,* the race of the River Belles, and the
not-to-be-missed "Anything That Floats" race. A hot-air balloon race, live music, and
aerobatic and water ski shows enliven the event. Schenley Park becomes a racetrack
of yesteryear during the *Pittsburgh Vintage Grand Prix* the third weekend in August.
And from the end of May through mid-August, the *Three Rivers Shakespeare Festival*
stages three productions at the Stephen Foster Memorial. Point State Park is the site
of celebrations over July 4th and Labor Day weekends.

SPORTS AND FITNESS: Baseball – The *Pirates* play at *Three Rivers
Stadium,* Stadium Circle, North Side (phone: 323-5000).
    Bicycling – There are no bike rental shops in town, but the county parks
(like North and South parks) have rental facilities.
Canoeing, Kayaking – You can canoe and kayak through exciting whitewater
rapids in the Laurel Highlands. *Canoe, Kayak and Sailing Craft* offers lessons and
guided tours, 712 Rebecca Ave., Wilkinsburg (phone: 371-4802).
Fishing – The City Parks and Recreation Dept. runs a group fishing program at
Panther Hollow in summer. You can rent rods and reels (phone: 255-2355).
Fitness Center – The *YMCA* has a pool, racquetball courts, track, and exercise
classes, 304 Wood St. (phone: 227-3800).
Football – The *Steelers'* home grid is at *Three Rivers Stadium* (phone: 323-1200).
Golf – Three golf courses within the city limits offer good facilities. *Schenley Park
Golf Course,* in Oakland, has 18 holes (phone: 682-9848), as does *North Park Golf
Course,* off Rte. 19 (phone: 935-1967). The 27-hole *South Park Golf Course* is off Rte.
88 (phone: 835-3545).

Hiking – There are quite a few hiking programs. For information on Parks Dept. nature tours and programs for the handicapped, contact Schenley Nature Center, Schenley Park (phone: 681-2272). For information on hiking, backpacking, canoeing, and camping in the area, contact the Sierra Club (phone: 561-0203).

Hockey – The *Penguins* play at *Civic Arena,* Washington Pl., Center and Bedford Ave. (phone: 642-1800).

Horse Racing – Fans have a choice of the *Meadows,* Washington, Pennsylvania (phone: 563-1224), or *Waterford Park,* Chester, West Virginia (phone: 304-387-2400).

Horseback Riding – Hit the trail in South Park. You can rent a horse or sign on for a hayride at *Valleybrook Stables* (phone: 835-9687). If you bring your own horse, you can board it at *Morning Star Stables* (phone: 655-9793).

Ice Skating – Gliding's good from October to March at an outdoor rink in Schenley Park (phone: 521-8579) or indoors year-round at *Mt. Lebanon Ice Rink* (phone: 561-3040).

Jogging – Point State Park, where the Allegheny and Monongahela meet; Schenley Park; and North Park (get there by car).

Scuba Diving – In Pittsburgh? Check it out. *Sub-Aquatics* gives a 36-hour course in essentials with tips on local lakes and water-filled quarries, 1593 Banksville Rd. (phone: 531-5577).

Soccer – The Pittsburgh *Spirit* Soccer Club also plays at the *Civic Arena* (phone: 642-1800).

Swimming – There are swimming pools throughout the city. Ream Playground has a good one, Merrimac and Virginia (phone: 431-9285).

Tennis – The best municipal courts are at Mellon Park. There are excellent suburban courts at North and South parks.

THEATER: Pittsburgh's theatrical scene is pretty lively, especially in summer when *Park Players* and *Pittsburgh Puppet Theater* take to the parks. For information, call 255-2354. The *Pittsburgh Public Theater,* 1 Allegheny Sq. (phone: 321-9800), and *Heinz Hall,* 600 Penn Ave. (phone: 392-4800), are the city's most prestigious theaters. *Pittsburgh Playhouse Theater Company* produces plays for both children and adults, 222 Craft Ave. (phone: 621-4445). The *Benedum Center for the Performing Arts,* 207 7th St., presents Broadway shows, drama, rock concerts, and films in its restored auditorium (phone: 456-2600). *Syria Mosque,* 4423 Bigelow Blvd., features popular artists and stage productions in an ornate theater (phone: 621-3333). The *Pittsburgh Ballet Theatre,* 2900 Liberty Ave., features classical and modern ballets (phone: 281-0360).

Carnegie-Mellon Theater Co. performs at *Kresge Theater,* Carnegie-Mellon University, Schenley Park (phone: 578-2407). *Chatham College Theater* presents modern classics (phone: 365-1100). There are dinner theaters at *Apple Hill Playhouse, Lamplighter Restaurant,* Delmont (phone: 468-4545), and *Little Lake Dinner Theater,* Rte. 19S, Donaldson's Crossroads (phone: 745-6300, 745-9883).

MUSIC: The world-famous *Pittsburgh Symphony Orchestra* performs from September through May at *Heinz Hall,* 600 Penn Ave. (phone: 392-4800). In summer, the air fills with music. The *American Wind Symphony* performs at Point State Park (phone: 681-8866). Jazz can be heard at the *Aviary,* string ensembles at the *Conservatory,* and folk music on *Flagstaff Hill.* The Parks Dept. coordinates schedules (phone: 255-2390). For jazz events, dial MUS-LINE.

NIGHTCLUBS AND NIGHTLIFE: *Chauncy's at Station Square* was voted the best dining and dancing spot in the city by *Pittsburgh* magazine. It's very dressy, and the crowd, food, and entertainment are tops. The DJ plays classics from the 1950s and '60s nightly (phone: 232-0601). *Mirage* is a

European-style nightspot with 4 different environments, 7 cocktail bars, and dancing in the marble rotunda with its grand staircase. It features the newest top 40 music by a DJ, with the hottest videos on 10 screens and monitors. Open Fridays and Saturdays only (phone: 281-0349).

BEST IN TOWN

CHECKING IN: With the city's second renaissance has come an influx of much-needed hotel space, mostly in the nearby suburbs of Greentree, Coraopolis, and Monroeville. All hotels listed below are downtown and are in the expensive category; this means expect to pay $80 or more for a double. We could find no hotels that met our standards in less expensive categories. All telephone numbers are in the 412 area code unless otherwise indicated.

Bigelow – Downtown's only all-suite apartment hotel, it has 200 studios and 1-, 2-, and 3-bedroom units. The quiet *Ruddy Duck* restaurant serves complimentary breakfast on weekdays. Fitness center next door. Steel Plaza (phone: 281-5800). Expensive.

Hyatt Pittsburgh – Conveniently near the *Civic Arena* and Exhibit Hall, the 400 rooms here have all been redecorated. The improvement is very apparent, and the top two Regency floors offer excellent accommodations. *Hugo's Rotisserie* serves a moderately priced lunch and buffet dinner, with roast duckling the specialty of the house. You can get an inexpensive meal at *QQ's Café*. Both open daily. Chatham Center (phone: 471-1234, 800-233-1234, or 800-228-9000). Expensive.

Pittsburgh Greentree Marriott – Facilities that liven up this 500-room hostelry include a swimming pool, a putting green, a whirlpool bath, sauna, and exercise room. Guests can enjoy entertainment or disco nightly in the *Trolley Bar* or dinner at *Ashley's*. 101 Marriott Dr., Crafton (phone: 922-8400 or 800-228-9290). Expensive.

Pittsburgh Hilton & Towers – Standing at the edge of Point State Park, overlooking the Monongahela and Allegheny rivers, it has undergone a dramatic renovation. The lobby has been redesigned and computerized, and parlor suites with wet bars have been added. Some of the 700 rooms, all totally refurbished, overlook the park. Gateway Center (phone: 391-4600 or 800-HILTONS). Expensive.

Sheraton Inn, Station Square – A 300-room riverside hotel with cocktail lounges and 2 restaurants: *River's Edge,* with a good seafood buffet on Fridays; and *Mr. C's,* which serves a sumptuous Sunday brunch. Near Station Square's shops and restaurants. Smithfield and Carson Sts. (phone: 261-2000 or 800-325-3535). Expensive.

Vista International – Pittsburgh's newest and most comfortable hotel has a contemporary design, with a 4-story atrium lobby, 616 rooms, and a fitness center. Guests can dine informally at the *Orchard Café* or more sumptuously at the *American Harvest* restaurant. At Liberty Center on Grant St. (phone: 281-3700 or 800-367-8478). Expensive.

Westin William Penn – A $30-million renovation by Westin management has reinstated this property's status. Because the building was declared a National Historic Landmark, the exterior remains unchanged; the most striking alterations are found in the 595 enlarged and modernized rooms. There are 2 restaurants — one a coffee shop serving food all day, one for dinner only. Mellon Sq. (phone: 281-7100 or 800-228-3000). Expensive.

EATING OUT: The city offers a wide choice of restaurants, with a variety of ethnic eateries all over town. These are, for the most part, highly rated, for they offer a quality of food and diversity of dishes far greater than those found at anonymous "continental" restaurants. Many places are more dressy in the evening. Expect to pay $65 or more for two at a restaurant we've noted as expensive; between $35 and $50, moderate; under $25 at a place listed as inexpensive. Prices don't include drinks, wine, or tips. All telephone numbers are in the 412 area code unless otherwise indicated.

Christopher's – An unusual restaurant with a fantastic view. Ride the exterior glass elevator up to dine luxuriously on steak Diane, chateaubriand, seafood, and specialties cooked tableside. Very dressy, with live entertainment on Friday and Saturday evenings. Closed Sundays. Reservations necessary. 1411 Grandview Ave., Mt. Washington (phone: 381-4500). Expensive.

Hyeholde – Just a few minutes from the Pittsburgh airport is a medieval castle, or at least what looks like one, with wooden beams, slate floors, European tapestries, and spacious grounds. The dinner menu changes daily but usually consists of classic dishes — filet mignon, trout, breast of fowl — prepared with the freshest ingredients. Bread and desserts are homemade, and don't pass up the Hyeholde trifle. The wine list is the most extensive in the area. Closed Sundays. Reservations advised. Major credit cards. 190 Hyeholde Dr., Coraopolis (phone: 264-3116). Expensive.

Louis Tambellini's – The outstanding selection here includes lemon sole, lobster tail, scallops, shrimp, oysters, crabmeat, and frogs' legs. The spinach salad is crunchy, and the homemade gnocchi irresistible. Closed Sundays. No reservations or credit cards. 860 Saw Mill Run Blvd. (phone: 481-1118). Expensive.

Top of the Triangle – Atop the 64-story, triangular US Steel Building, this restaurant provides diners with a gorgeous 3-mile panoramic view. The oak walls add a certain warmth that modern decor often lacks. There's nightly entertainment in the glass-enclosed cocktail lounge. *Stouffer's* provides the food. Open daily. Reservations advised. Major credit cards. 600 Grant St. (phone: 471-4100). Expensive.

Arthur's – This small restaurant in the city's oldest office building provides an attractive early American decor with four working fireplaces. The menu includes continental and American dishes; the smoked meats and fish are excellent (all smoking is done on the premises). Some specialties are onion soup with a German beer base, and veal stuffed with smoked scallops and mozzarella cheese, served with spinach noodles in a marsala wine and mushroom sauce. Closed Sundays. Reservations advised. Major credit cards. 209 4th Ave. (phone: 566-1735). Expensive to moderate.

Common Plea – One of the best downtown restaurants, popular with city officials and lawyers and known for its house appetizers. The atmosphere is relaxed; the array of fresh seafood, splendid. Lunch weekdays; dinner daily. Reservations advised for lunch. Major credit cards. 308 Ross St. (phone: 281-5140). Expensive to moderate.

Grand Concourse – This elegant remake of the old Pittsburgh and Lake Erie Railroad Terminal is the best thing to happen to Pittsburgh's restaurant scene in years. Beautiful wood, stained glass, and gleaming brass surround diners who devour excellent seafood — oysters, shrimp, clams, crab — and especially a tangy seafood chowder that is served in a pewter tureen. Lunch and dinner daily. Reservations for dinner only. Major credit cards. 1 Station Sq. (phone: 261-1717). Expensive to moderate.

Le Mont – A classic, contemporary eatery with French and Italian specialties and a spectacular view of the Golden Triangle. House specialties include prime ribs and veal. Dinner only; jackets required. Closed Sundays. Reservations advised.

Major credit cards. 1114 Grandview Ave., Mt. Washington (phone: 431-3100). Expensive to moderate.

Le Pommier – Everything is made on site at this elegant (yet homey) restaurant in the heavily Slavic South Side — from starter stocks and sourdough country bread to ice cream and bountiful apple desserts (*le pommier* means "apple tree"). Proprieters Jim (he's a doctor) and Christine Dauber (she's chief cook, he handles everything else) serve a cross between classic French fare and nouvelle cuisine: chicken breast stuffed with chèvre is a favorite as is the chocolate cake filled with Grand Marnier–laced chocolate mousse. There's also an exceptional wine list. Closed Sundays. Reservations necessary. Major credit cards. 2104 E. Carson St. (phone: 431-1901). Expensive to moderate.

Landmark Tavern (1902) – Return to the early part of the century in Pittsburgh's best period tavern, in the heart of Market Square. Sample the oyster bar (the city's first), calimari, prime ribs, veal dishes, imported beer, and distinctive wines. Lunch and dinner daily. Casual; reservations recommended for dinner. Major credit cards. 24 Market Sq., next to PPG Place (phone: 471-1902). Moderate.

Shadyside Balcony – A charming restaurant in Shadyside's shopping quarter serving soups, fresh fish, vegetarian dishes, and imaginative sandwiches with a homey touch. Live jazz entertainment. Closed Sundays. Reservations advised. Major credit cards. 5520 Walnut St. (phone: 687-0110). Moderate.

Tequila Junction – A short walk from the city, across the Smithfield Street Bridge, will take you to the Freight House Shops at Station Square, where you can lunch or dine south of the border. In a romantic brick and adobe inn, sip a strawberry margarita followed by one of the many tasty Mexican entrées, such as crabmeat enchilada or chili Colorado. Open daily. No reservations. Major credit cards. Freight House Shops, Station Square (phone: 261-3265). Moderate.

PORTLAND, OR

The most important thing to bear in mind while visiting Portland is that it's very likely that you will be made to feel welcome. Under no circumstances, however, should you let on that you'd actually like to live here. You will want to live here, if you've got any sense, even after just one visit; but better to lie about it. Portland residents are that sensitive.

They're not unfriendly, mind you. It's simply that the city is beautiful — always ranking high on metropolitan "quality of life" surveys — and with an enlightened government and determined citizenry, it's getting better all the time. Even the 1980 eruptions of Mt. St. Helens haven't left any scars. Quite the contrary — the Mt. St. Helens National Volcanic Monument has become a topnotch tourist draw.

Portland stretches along the Willamette River (one of the few rivers in the country that flows north) just below the point where it joins the Columbia. The confluence provides Portland with a deep, freshwater port that serves oceangoing vessels, and because the city straddles the Willamette, ships dock beneath downtown bridges. By river some 110 miles from the ocean, Portland is a seaport. Around the whole metropolitan area, like the brackets of parentheses, are the Northwest's two most imposing mountain ranges — the Cascades in the east, the Coast Range to the west.

The city is divided neatly into its east and west sides by the Willamette; each side has its own atmosphere (east side, homey; west side, posh. The elegant, downtown shopping district is very west side). The two segments of the city are connected by 11 bridges. The whole city is then divided into five large sections: North, Northeast, Northwest, Southeast, Southwest. Sounds confusing, but it actually makes finding places very easy with a local map, since every address includes an area designation (SW, NE, N., and so on).

For the most part, the city is flat, hugging its major waterways, lakes and ponds, with hundreds of parks spread across its metropolitan area. Now and then, a group of forested hills raises an imperious eyebrow — some residential, others intentionally undeveloped. In the east, the city holds up three fingers of small, residential mountains, as if pointing to the great mountains to the east, and 11,235-foot Mt. Hood in the Cascades, an hour away.

Greater Portland stretches from the foothills of Mt. Hood to the western plains of the Coast Range; more than 1 million people live in this four-county area.

The city was incorporated in 1845 by New England settlers — it's named for Portland, Maine. When the great crash of 1893 closed banks across the country, one pioneer Portland merchant, Aaron Meier, took his bags of gold to banker Henry Corbett. The next morning, as the rest of the nation's banks failed, Corbett stood tall and firm in the middle of his bank's lobby — properly attired in frock coat and top hat — with Meier's gold piled conspicuously around him. There was no closure in Portland that day.

When Scottish shipper Donald Macleay bequeathed 107 acres to the city at the turn of the century, it was with the stipulation that no wheeled vehicle ever be allowed to enter the premises. The city agreed, and has even expanded Macleay's trust. Today, Macleay Park stands in the middle of the city, untouched by exhaust fumes or bicycle tread, part of nearly 5,000 acres of dense forest — a green velvet buffer for hikers, bird watchers, and nature lovers.

Macleay anticipated the attitude of modern Portlanders with admirable skill. In recent years, the city has torn up some 24 blocks right out of the heart of the west side business district to build a brick-covered, tree-lined pedestrian mall, spotted with fountains and sculpture. Along the Willamette River, which creates the city's natural seaport, the old factories have been razed, and greenways are spreading out with smug brilliance. By order of the people, the Willamette River has been cleaned up, and riverboating, salmon fishing and water skiing are now commonplace.

Along with the rest of the state, Portland has banned the use of fluorocarbons in aerosol sprays, abolished the sale of beer and soda in non-returnable cans and bottles, and requires the use of automobile seat belts by all. Portland is a potent force in civic activism, and in this environment-conscious city, it's considered almost unpatriotic not to recycle everything — from newspapers to plastic cups.

After taking a long look at the first 40-story building to go up in its business area, Portland moved swiftly to assure that no other such building would be built higher. It has thus saved its panorama of mountains and wooded hillsides for succeeding generations.

The City of Roses, Portland has also been a thorn in the side of some industry. All new buildings must pass inspection as early as the initial planning stages, and the powerful Historical Landmarks Commission works constantly to protect Portland's historic buildings. On its list of protected properties are several iron-fronted buildings, plus one sycamore and one elm tree, each planted by founding parents and each continually bursting the seams of downtown sidewalks.

PORTLAND AT-A-GLANCE

SEEING THE CITY: Portland offers several exceptional vantage points from which to see the city, the valley in which it lies, and the mountains beyond. Pittock Acres Park, the grounds of the former Pittock Mansion (see below), sits 1,000 feet above the city. At your feet are the port, business section, the Willamette River, and the southeast residential areas. In the distance are the Cascade Mountains — Mt. Hood in Oregon, Mt. Rainier, Mt. Adams, and Mt. St. Helens in Washington. 3229 NW Pittock Dr. And Washington Park; the best view is from the International Rose Test Gardens, looking east toward mountains in the background. 400 SW Kingston.

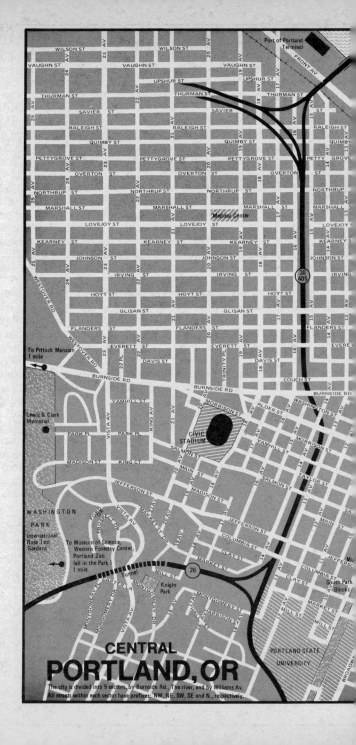

CENTRAL
PORTLAND, OR

The city is divided into 5 sectors, by Burnside Rd., The river, and by Williams Av.
All streets within each sector have prefixes: NW, NE, SW, SE and N., respectively.

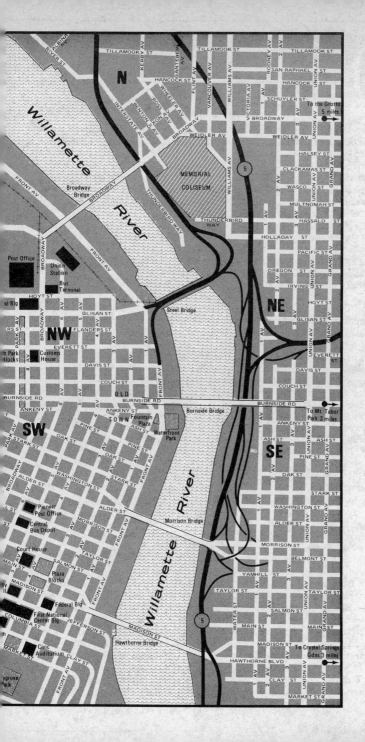

SPECIAL PLACES: Portland was made for walking. Her founders frequently built homes in the west hills and walked to work along the waterfront. Especially on the west side, major points of interest are within walking distance of one another.

WEST SIDE

Portland Center for the Performing Arts – The brightest dazzler on the city's roster of flourishing arts institutions is the 2,776-seat *Arlene Schnitzer Concert Hall* in the former Paramount. The ornate detail of the 1928 vaudeville–movie palace has been lovingly refurbished. Home of the *Oregon Symphony Orchestra,* the hall also holds pop, country, and jazz concerts; shows films, and hosts conventions. Next door are two plush smaller theaters, which opened in the fall of 1987. The *Oregon Shakespearean Festival* performs here, as do other local theater and dance groups. SW Broadway at Main (phone: 248-4335, for tours; 248-4496, for tickets).

Oregon Historical Society – Exhibitions on Oregon history, before and after the arrival of the white man. Also a fine series of dioramas on Indian life, plus a research library with open stacks for browsing; pioneer craft demonstrations for children. Changing exhibitions vary from the Magna Carta to country quilts. Closed Sundays. No admission charge. 1230 SW Park (phone: 222-1741).

Ira Keller Fountain (and Civic Auditorium) – A series of pools and waterfalls a block wide, facing the *Civic Auditorium.* In hot weather, people splash around in its tons of swirling water. Designed by Lawrence Halprin, it is called *Ira's Fountain.* SW 3rd Ave at Clay. Though several blocks removed from its three sisters, *Civic Auditorium* is considered the fourth theater of the *Portland Center for the Performing Arts* (phone: 248-4496 for tickets).

Pioneer Courthouse – The first federal building in the Pacific Northwest, completed in 1875 and now restored to its original Victorian splendor. The interior includes a working post office, an elegant Victorian courtroom (where the US Court of Appeals meets), and adjoining rooms for the judges. The courtroom can be seen by asking the security guard to unlock the door. Enter at 555 SW Yamhill (no phone). Across the street is Pioneer Courthouse Square, an open city block that has become the hub of downtown. This is a place for music, flowers, food, and fanfare.

Portlandia – The cookie-tin Portland Building (designed by the postmodern architect Michael Graves) is now crowned in glory. Over the main portico kneels a copper lady of heroic proportions. The new symbol of the city, the sculpture is by Raymond Kaskey. 1120 SW 5th Ave.

Old Town – When the Pioneer Courthouse was brand new, some folks thought it much too far from the downtown business section — a whole six blocks. Now "downtown" is called Old Town, a restored shopping and browsing area filled with craft, art, and antique shops. The area runs from 1st to 5th Avenues, on both sides of Burnside. Artists from all over the state sell their work at the Sunday and Saturday markets, under Burnside Bridge, from 10 AM to 5 PM, Saturdays; 11 AM to 4:30 PM Sundays; March, through the weekend before Christmas.

Worth noting on Ankeny, south of Burnside: *Dan and Louis Oyster Bar* (see *Eating Out*), and *Le Panier,* on SW 2nd, whose Parisian chefs serve fresh French bread and croissants every day. North of Burnside, Couch Street, and beyond are numerous specialty shops. Best buys are Indian artifacts, toys, spinning and weaving supplies, original jewelry.

Washington Park – One of the city's oldest parks, it has 145 acres, all part of the 40-mile park system that thrives within the city limits. There are six points of special interest on the grounds: the Rose Test Gardens, the Japanese Garden, the *Oregon Museum of Science and Industry,* the World Forestry Center, the Vietnam War Memorial, and Tera One, a totally solar home, as well as some magnificent views of the city and countryside. Plan to spend some extended periods of time here, but note: The only food is the hot dogs and hamburgers at the zoo, so think about taking along a picnic lunch (*Elephant's Delicatessen* will prepare one for you; 13 NW 23rd Pl., phone: 224-3955).

The Rose Test Gardens offer hundreds of varieties of roses, all generously identified. June through September is the best time to see them. In summer, a zoo train runs from the Gardens to the zoo (admission charge), which (among other displays) has a children's petting zoo. At the Penguinarium you can see Humboldt penguins at close range. Open daily.

The zoo is part of a complex that includes the *Oregon Museum of Science and Industry* (*OMSI*), the Planetarium, and World Forestry Center. *OMSI,* closed only on Christmas, offers the world's largest kaleidoscope, an outer space demonstration area, hands-on computers, and various traveling exhibitions. Admission charge. World Forestry Center has displays, exhibitions on Oregon's largest industry. Admission charge. The entire complex is on SW Canyon (phone: 228-OMSI; zoo, 226-1561; Forestry Center, 228-1367).

Pittock Mansion – The imposing French Renaissance home built by Henry Pittock, a poor boy who made good as publisher of *The Oregonian* at the turn of the century. The grounds are open daily and are free; the house is open every afternoon from 1 to 5 PM, for a fee. The *Gate Lodge* serves lunch and tea on weekdays. 3229 NW Pittock Dr. (mansion, phone: 248-4469; lodge, 221-1730).

Tryon Creek State Park – The state's first metropolitan park, 2 miles south of central Portland, with 600 acres of wilderness for biking, hiking, and naturalists (horses are welcome, but there are none for rent). Adjoining Lake Oswego, at 11321 SW Terwilliger Blvd. (phone: 653-3166).

Powell's Books – Owner Mike Powell says visitors have been known to stop here before they go to their hotel! Among the reasons: more than a million new and used books, espresso, pastries, and readings by local authors at the *Anne Hughes Coffee Shop,* part of the store. One of the largest bookstores in the country, (it's a block long), *Powell's* has thoughtfully produced maps so that book lovers can find their way through the funky, cavernous store. Open 9 AM to 11 PM, Mondays through Saturdays; 9 AM to 9 PM on Sundays. 1005 W. Burnside St. (phone: 228-4651).

Weather Machine – Check out the forecast every day at noon, when this whimsical mechanical sculpture predicts the weather for the following 24 hours with a trumpet fanfare and a spray of water. Up pops one of three metal sculptures: a gold leaf sun for fair skies; a blue heron for clouds and drizzle; a fire-breathing copper dragon for stormy weather. A series of lights indicates the temperature and air quality. Pioneer Courthouse Square.

EAST SIDE

The Grotto – An outdoor chapel, built in a grotto with a 10-story cliff, monastery, and gardens at the top. The 64 acres of grounds are open for contemplation, quiet walks, solitude. Sunday mass is celebrated in the chapel at 10 AM. 8840 NE Skidmore (phone: 254-7371).

Crystal Springs Gardens – More than 2,000 rhododendron plants, maintained by the Portland chapter of the American Rhododendron Society. No Portlander would miss the gardens during April and May, when first the azaleas, then the rhododendrons, reach their peak. Adjacent is the campus of Reed College. SE 28th Ave. near SE Woodstock.

Mt. Tabor Park – Believed to be the only extinct volcano within a US city's limits. Some of the best views of the city. Between Yamhill and Division, east of SE 60th Ave.

■**EXTRA SPECIAL:** Sauvie Island, the largest island in the Columbia River, is just north of Portland on US 30. Devoted primarily to farmland, the island is ideal for biking, hiking, picnicking, fishing, or just lolling about for a day. Here, the Oregon

Historical Society maintains the Bybee-Howell House, a restored pre–Civil War farmhouse, open to the public from June to Labor Day (free; donations appreciated). The last Saturday of September is the "Wintering-In" picnic and celebration at the house, when farmers sell harvest goods.

The Columbia River Highway runs east and west of Portland. Drive east for a view of the Columbia River Gorge, with its 2,000-foot cliff and 11 waterfalls.

SOURCES AND RESOURCES

 TOURIST INFORMATION: The Visitors Information Center at the Convention and Visitors Association is best for brochures, maps, general tourist information and personal help; if you arrive after hours, outdoor map dispensers and kiosks can provide a basic orientation. 26 SW Salmon (phone: 222-2223).

The Oregon Welcome Center offers travel information at 12345 N. Union Ave. (phone: 285-1631).

The Portland Guidebook by Linda Lampman and Julie Sterling (The Writing Works; $5.95) is the most comprehensive guide to Portland and its environs.

Television Stations – KATU Channel 2–ABC; KOIN Channel 6–CBS; KGW Channel 8–NBC; KOAP Channel 10–PBS.

Radio Stations – AM: KGW 620 (adult contemporary); KUPL 1330 (country); KXL 750 (news/talk). FM: KMJK 106.7 (classic rock); KINK 101.9 (adult contemporary); KGON 92.3 (rock).

Local Coverage – *Oregonian,* morning and afternoon daily; *Willamette Week* offers a liberally opinionated study of the city.

Food – Check *The Portland Guidebook* and the weekly newspaper restaurant reviews.

Telephone – The area code for Portland is 503.

Sales Tax – At this writing, there is no sales tax in Oregon. But buyer beware — a sales tax measure is on the ballot in almost every election.

 CLIMATE: The good news: It doesn't get too cold in Portland (snow is pretty rare); it doesn't get too hot here, either (summer temperatures above 90F only last 2 or 3 days). However, it certainly does rain. The months from October through May are the worst. June, July, August, and September are fairly clear, and the average temperature is in the 70s. That's the time when tourists visit the Portland area, so book ahead.

 GETTING AROUND: Airport – Portland International Airport is a 20- to 30-minute drive from downtown, and cab fare should run $18 to $22. The *Raz Tranz Portland Airporter* bus (phone: 246-4676) provides transportation to downtown's major hotels for $5; $1 for children 6-12, children under 6, free. The trip takes about 45 minutes, 60 minutes during rush hour. Buses depart from in front of the airport every 20 minutes from 5:30 AM to midnight, every 30 minutes on weekends and holidays. Tri-Met city bus #12 also stops in front of the airport and connects to buses going downtown; the fare is 85¢ to $1.35.

Bus – Portland's Tri-Met system covers three counties; exact-change-only fare is zoned except within the 340-block downtown shopping area (including Old Town, major shopping malls, Art Institute and Historical Society, riverfront) which is free and called Fareless Square. Complete route and tourist information (and map of Fareless

Square) is available from the downtown Customer Assistance Office, 1 Pioneer Courthouse Square (enter under the waterfall).

Light Rail – The bus system is complemented by MAX, the light rail network of streetcars serving downtown and the eastern suburbs. Schedules are available at light rail stops along the streets as well as at the Pioneer Courthouse Square transit office.

Taxi – Cabs must be called by phone or picked up at taxi stations in front of the major hotels. They cannot be hailed in the street. Most hotels have direct phone connections to the two largest companies, *Broadway Cab* (phone: 227-1234); *Radio Cab* (phone: 227-1212).

Car Rental – National and local firms are represented in abundance. Everything from rental Lincolns to *Rent A Wreck;* check the yellow pages. *General Rent A Car,* 7101 NE 82nd (phone: 257-3451), has one of the lowest weekly rates.

LOCAL SERVICES: Babysitting – *Wee-Ba-Bee Attendants* (phone: 661-5966); *Rent-a-Mom of Oregon* (phone: 222-5779).

    Business Services – *Business Service Bureau,* 1208 SW 13th Ave. (phone: 228-4107); *Business Communication Center,* 200 SW Market (phone: 226-1007).

Mechanics – *Tune Up Specialties,* 8060 NE Glisan (phone: 252-8096), ask for Tony; *Alliance Goodyear,* 333 SW 10th Ave. (phone: 227-2443).

MUSEUMS: The *Oregon Historical Society* and the *Pittock Mansion* are both noted in *Special Places.* Other interesting museums include the following:

    American Advertising Museum – The nation's best collection of persuasive media, from sandwich boards to videos. Through the evolution of advertising much of our country's history and progress is revealed. Closed Mondays and Tuesdays. Admission charge. NW 2nd Ave. at Couch (phone: 226-0000).

Oregon Art Institute – With an outstanding permanent collection of Northwest Indian art, the museum also features a representative group of Oregon's prolific contemporary artists and a wide variety of traveling shows. Also part of the *Institute* is an outdoor Sculpture Mall, the Pacific Northwest College of Art, and the Northwest Film and Video Center. Closed Mondays. Admission charge. SW Park and Madison (phone: 226-2811).

Portland Carousel Museum – With more working carousels than any other US city, Portland also claims one of the only carousel museums. Inside, examine the intricately carved and painted horses; outside, ride the carousel away into magical nostalgic wonderlands. Open daily from 11 AM to 5 PM. Admission charge. NE Holladay St. between 7th and 9th Aves. (phone: 235-2252).

Portland Children's Museum – The place to be on a rainy day. Kids amuse themselves for hours with dozens of hands-on displays, exploring a cave and a tunnel, and more. Closed Mondays. Admission charge. 3037 SW 2nd Ave. (phone: 248-4587).

MAJOR COLLEGES AND UNIVERSITIES: The jewel in Portland's academic crown is Reed College, 3203 SE Woodstock Blvd. (phone: 771-1112), a private, liberal arts college of the highest caliber. Other institutions of learning are the University of Portland, 5000 N. Willamette Blvd. (phone: 283-7911); Lewis and Clark College, 0615 SW Palatine Hill Rd. (phone: 244-6161); and Portland State University, 724 SW Harrison (phone: 229-3000).

PARKS AND GARDENS: Even the freeways into Portland are divided by banks of wild roses and iris; the city is surrounded by green mountains and garlanded with 7,608 acres of parkland. Washington Park, Pittock Acres Park, Mt. Tabor Park, Crystal Springs Gardens, and Tryon Creek State Park are all described in Special Places. Other notable Portland parks are:

Council Crest Park – above Portland Heights, SW Fairmount Blvd.
Hoyt Arboretum – 400 SW Fairview Blvd.
Rocky Butte – I-84 east to NE 102nd.
Westmoreland Park – SE 22nd Ave. at Bybee.

SPECIAL EVENTS: The *Portland Rose Festival,* featuring everything from beauty queens to bicycle races, runs during the first half of June. *Wintering-In Celebration,* on Sauvie Island, is a harvest festival on the last Saturday of September. The *Mt. Hood Festival of Jazz* brings the best jazz musicians to town every August.

SPORTS AND FITNESS: Baseball – The Portland *Beavers,* the top farm team for the Minnesota *Twins,* play at *Portland Civic Stadium,* April to September. Tickets are sold at the stadium, 1844 SW Morrison (phone: 248-4345 or 2-BEAVER).

Basketball – The *Trail Blazers* play their home games at *Memorial Coliseum* from October through April; tickets at the Coliseum, 1401 N. Wheeler (phone: 239-4422).

Bicycling – Rent from *Tailwind Outfitters,* Canyon Rd. at 117th (phone: 641-2580). Numerous city and country rides are described in *The Portland Guidebook.*

Fishing – For chinook salmon, try the lower Willamette or Willamette Slough from March through early May. Steelhead are found in the Clackamas River, and its tributary, Eagle Creek, from December through February. But best of all (for fly fishermen) are the Washougal and Wind rivers in southwest Washington state, where you can do battle with the warrior steelhead.

Fitness Centers – The *YMCA* has branches at 6036 SE Foster Rd. (phone: 294-3311), 1630 NE 38th St. (phone: 294-3377), and 2831 SW Barbur Blvd. (phone: 294-3366).

Golf – The metropolitan area has 20 public courses. The best is *Forest Hills Country Club,* 20 minutes from downtown in Cornelius (a plus: it has showers; phone: 357-3347).

Horse and Dog Racing – For racing and pari-mutuel betting, *Portland Meadows Horse Race Track,* 1001 N. Schmeer Rd. (phone: 285-9144), with a season from October to April; and *Multnomah Kennel Club Dog Race Track,* 220 3rd Ave., Fairview (12 miles from city) (phone: 667-7700), from May to September.

Jogging – Run up Broadway or 5th Ave. to Duniway Park, then follow the bike path along Terwilliger Blvd.; this route can range from 5 to 30 miles, as time or stamina permits. Upcoming running events are listed with the Oregon Road Runners Information Hotline (phone: 223-7867).

Skiing – The closest is *Mt. Hood Meadows;* better is *Mt. Bachelor,* 180 miles from Portland at Bend.

Tennis – The Park Bureau runs 7 indoor and dozens of outdoor courts. The indoor courts may be reserved by calling 233-5959 or 248-4200. Otherwise, first come, first served. The major tennis center is in Buckman Park, *Portland Tennis Center,* 324 NE 12th Ave.

THEATER: For up-to-date offerings and performance times, check the publications listed above. Portland has 15 theaters that offer performances, some locally produced, others traveling shows. Colleges and universities in the area also produce plays and musicals. Best bets for shows: *Portland Civic Auditorium* (phone: 248-4496), *Portland Civic Theatre* (phone: 226-3048), *New Rose Theater* (phone: 222-2487), *Storefront Actors' Theatre* (phone: 224-4001), and *Portland Repertory* (phone: 224-4491).

MUSIC: Concerts and opera are held by *Oregon Symphony Orchestra* (phone: 228-1353); *Portland Opera Association* (phone: 241-1401); summer concerts in Washington Park between mid-July and mid-August, and free concerts at *Waterfront Park* from late August to mid-September (phone: 796-5100).

NIGHTCLUBS AND NIGHTLIFE: Portland has become a genuinely great jazz town. Homegrown groups like the Tom Grant Band and the Mel Brown Quintet are gaining national attention. Current favorite clubs: *Brasserie Montmartre,* 626 SW Park (phone: 224-5552), where the jazz is mellow weeknights and heats up on weekends; *Café Vivo,* 555 SW Oak St. (phone: 228-8486), where Tom Grant can be found at the keyboard most weekends; *Remo's,* 1425 NW Glisan (phone: 221-1150), an old firehouse now converted to a sophisticated supper club. Pop music, Dixieland, folk, and rock are also offered at Portland's many pubs, taverns, and nightclubs. Try *Starry Night,* 8 NW 6th Ave. (phone: 227-0071), for danceable new wave; *Key Largo,* 31 NW 1st Ave. (phone: 223-9919), for blues and rock; *Shanghai Lounge,* 0309 SW Montgomery (phone: 220-1865), for rock music and for meeting everyone in town. The place to wear saddle shoes and string ties for rock 'n' roll of the 1950s and '60s is *Bebop USA,* 11753 SW Beaverton-Hillsdale Hwy. (phone: 644-4433). The *Goose Hollow Inn,* 1927 SW Jefferson (phone: 228-7010), is a singularly Oregonian pub whose owner, the mayor of Portland, frequently can be seen in the crowd of plaid shirts and raincoats.

BREW PUBS: Portland, with its many micro-breweries, boasts the most breweries of any US city. The largest is *Blitz Weinhard Brewing Co.*, 1133 W. Burnside. Nearby are *Columbia River Brewery,* 1313 NW Marshall St., *Widmer Brewing Co.*, 1405 NW Lovejoy St.; and the *Portland Brewing Co.*, 1331 NW Flanders St. In downtown Portland, there's the *B. Moloch/Heathman Bakery and Pub,* 901 SW Salmon, and farther out of town are the *Hillsdale Brewery and Public House,* 1505 SW Sunset Blvd., and *Fulton Pub and Brewery* at 0618 SW Nebraska St.

■ **TAKE SOME PORTLAND HOME WITH YOU:** Fresh chinook and silver salmon are two of Portland's best known exports, and airlines are accustomed to seeing passengers board an outbound flight with a cold fin under one arm. *Troy's Seafood Market,* 816 NE Grand (phone: 231-1477), will supply fresh salmon and crab, specially packed to travel.

BEST IN TOWN

CHECKING IN: The choice of Portland hotels has become more interesting of late. With the addition of the *Heathman* and the *Riverplace Alexis,* it is now possible to slumber in splendor as well as in the comfort and convenience always offered by the city's better hotels. Expect to pay $100 or more for a double room in one of the hotels we've categorized as expensive; $60 to $100 in the moderate range; and under $60 in the inexpensive category. For bed and breakfast accommodations, contact: *Northwest Bed & Breakfast,* 610 SW Broadway, Suite 609, Portland, OR 97205 (phone: 243-7616). All telephone numbers are in the 503 area code unless otherwise indicated.

Riverplace Alexis – The city's newest inn is one of its smallest: only 74 rooms and suites clustered on the waterfront. (Ten condos are available for rent in the complex next door.) In the morning, guests awaken to views of the marina and to continental breakfast. Marble, brass, fresh flowers, and classic furnishings produce an easy elegance. Six suites have wood-burning fireplaces and wet bars. Concierge, 24-hour room service, access to adjacent health club. The *Esplanade* restaurant prepares Northwest regional cuisine. 1510 SW Harbor Way (phone: 228-3233). Expensive.

Heathman – Adjoining the *Performing Arts Center* are 152 of the most luxurious rooms and suites in town. After a 2-year restoration and renovation, done by the same designer as San Francisco's *Stanford Court,* the *Heathman* has emerged as an authentic first class property. Amenities include complimentary video movie library for room use, concierge, valet parking, and access to a nearby health club. Its main restaurant is noted for its selections of fresh Pacific Northwest seafood and game. SW Broadway at Salmon (phone: 241-4100 or 800-551-0011). Expensive.

Portland Marriott – More than a million dollars' worth of millwork went into this Northwest incarnation. It has 504 rooms, a concierge level, 2 restaurants (one with a view of the Willamette River), banquet facilities, indoor pool, whirlpool bath, sauna, and exercise rooms. 1401 SW Front Ave. (phone: 226-7600 or 800-228-9290). Expensive.

Westin Benson – Built in 1913 by wealthy logger Simon Benson to be Portland's premier hotel. Although the lobby maintains a feeling of Old World luxury, the 321 rooms and suites don't really offer the kind of traditional atmosphere you might expect. Now managed by Westin Hotels and Resorts, it is comfortable and convenient, with a quite good *London Grill* restaurant (open daily) and a respectable *Trader Vic's* as well (closed Sundays). Concierge; access to health club; 24-hour room service. Valet parking. 309 SW Broadway (phone: 228-9611 or 800-228-3000). Expensive.

Portland Hilton – Sitting snugly between the major streets of the downtown shopping district, the 455-room *Hilton* sports a skylit atrium lobby and a health club. *Alexander's* restaurant on the top floor offers good food with a glittery view. Amenities include room service, seasonal pool, and banquet facilities. 921 SW 6th (phone: 226-1611 or 800-HILTONS). Moderate.

Red Lion Motor Inns – This giant complex on the Columbia River, just between Portland and Vancouver (Washington), is 10 minutes from the airport and comprises 3 inns: the *Red Lion Columbia River, Red Lion Jantzen Beach,* and *Red Lion Inn at the Quay* (on the Washington side) — with a total of 830 rooms. Fine restaurants, free parking, live entertainment, a large convention center, 2 grand ballrooms, and room service. Pool, tennis, and mini-golf at *Red Lion Jantzen Beach. Red Lion Columbia River,* 1401 N. Hayden Island Dr. (phone: 283-2111); *Red Lion Jantzen Beach,* 909 N. Hayden Island Dr. (phone: 503-283-4466); *Red Lion Inn at the Quay,* 100 Columbia St., Vancouver, WA 98660 (phone: 206-694-8341). Moderate.

Mallory – A step down from the Jacuzzi tubs and poolside cabanas, but a comfortable, quiet 144-room hotel that offers a good room and adequate restaurant facilities at a reasonable price. Just across the street from the *Civic Theater.* Free parking. 729 SW 15th Ave. (phone: 223-6311). Inexpensive.

 EATING OUT: Portland shines pretty brightly as an eating place. The impact of a certain style of restaurant — small, personal, with creative cuisine and inviting decor — has had dramatic effects on local eating habits. Residents are out of their own kitchens and around town as never before. Many new restaurants are specializing in Pacific Northwest cuisine, which puts to delicious use the abundant local seafood, farm fresh vegetables, and regional wines. Our restaurant selections range in price from $50 or more for a dinner for two in the expensive range, $20 to $40 in the moderate, and $20 or less in the inexpensive range. Prices do not include drinks, wine or tips. All telephone numbers are in the 503 area code unless otherwise indicated.

Atwater's – Occupying the entire 30th floor of the US Bancorp Tower, one of the main lures is the only 360-degree view over all downtown. The restaurant does justice to the striking panorama, with a Northwest menu that relies on only the freshest local products. The menu undergoes revision seasonally. Dinner daily, plus brunch on Sunday. Reservations advised. Major credit cards. 111 SW 5th Ave. (phone: 220-3600). Expensive.

Alexis – This is the place to be on Greek Independence Day (March 25), when Portlanders of all ethnic backgrounds join in the festivities. But a convivial atmosphere prevails every day at this casual, family-owned Greek eatery. A selection of the delectable appetizers, from grape leaves to spicy chunks of octopus, accompanied by a basket brimming with homemade bread can be a meal in itself. Dinner daily, lunch weekdays. Reservations accepted. Major credit cards. 215 W. Burnside St. (phone: 224-8577). Moderate.

Café des Amis – The name of this restaurant is reflected in its lace curtains and candlelight setting and in the delightfully personable waiters. The menu is slightly French, more Pacific Northwest. Stuffed quail, poussin, fettuccine with mussels, salmon, and halibut are all done in a distinct style. Dinner only. Closed Sundays. Reservations advised. Major credit cards. 1987 NW Kearny (phone: 295-6487). Moderate.

Cajun Café and Bistro – The current chef has introduced the best of Southwest cooking to the menu. Take your taste buds on a journey of serveral thousand miles at one sitting, sampling blackened seafood from the Pacific Northwest and, as a chaser,a bowl of "Terminator green chili stew." Dinner daily, lunch weekdays. Reservations advised. Major credit cards. 2074 NW Lovejoy St. (phone: 227-0227). Moderate.

Chen's Dynasty – For Chinese specialties like stir-fried pork with pickled mustard greens and peanuts or cracked crab with Hunan black beans, this is the place. The menu of Chinese delights seems endless. Open daily. Reservations advised. Major credit cards. 622 Washington (phone: 248-9491). Moderate.

Harborside – The eclectic, 100-item menu ranges from Cajun pizza to peanut butter truffle cake, with a stop at fresh salmon along the way. The proprietors miraculously manage very high quality throughout. Tables on three tiers give all diners a view of the waterfront. Open daily. Reservations advised. Major credit cards. 0309 (really) SW Montgomery (phone: 220-1865). Moderate.

Jake's Famous Crawfish – Serving crawfish and other seagoing delectables since 1892, *Jake's* has occupied its current premises since 1908. Worth a visit for both quality food and interesting surroundings. Open daily. Reservations advised. Major credit cards. 401 SW 12th St. (phone: 226-1419). Moderate.

Plainfield's Mayur – East Indian dishes prepared in full dramatic view at the tandoor, a deep clay oven with a 1,000° fire at the bottom. Tandoori chicken, lamb, breads, and other Indian specialties are served in pleasant surroundings of soft blue and white, complemented by chandeliers and mahogany chairs. Dinner daily except Sundays. Reservations advised. Major credit cards. 852 SW 21st Ave. (phone: 223-2995). Moderate.

Rheinlander – A good spot to feed the kids on grand portions of good German food. Not the place to go for an intimate rendezvous, since it's filled with families who enjoy being serenaded by a strolling accordian player. Open daily. Reservations advised. Major credit cards. 5035 NE Sandy Blvd. (phone: 288-5503). Moderate.

Ringside – Portland's premier steakhouse has been serving the finest cuts of beef since 1944. The loyal patronage knows the longtime waiters by name, and vice versa. Though mostly known for steaks and prime ribs, some cognoscenti wouldn't dream of going anywhere else for fried chicken or hamburgers. The crisp onion rings are legendary. Dinner daily; lunch weekdays. Reservations advised. Major credit cards. 2165 W. Burnside St. (phone: 223-1513). Moderate.

Thirty-One Northwest – The second level of an urban shopping center is the unlikely location of this enclave of dusty rose elegance, where the salmon melts in your mouth and the vegetables are never overdone. This is the best of all possible escapes from the hubbub below. Closed Sundays. Reservations advised. Major credit cards. 31 NW 23rd Pl. (phone: 223-0106). Moderate.

Carnival – Decorate your own hamburger and sample creamy milkshakes in an enticing variety of flavors. Indoor booths in a circus tent atmosphere or picnic tables in the back garden are all family-pleasers. Closed Sundays. No credit cards. 2805 SW Sam Jackson Park Rd. (phone: 227-4244). Inexpensive.

Casa-U-Betcha – Standard Mexican fare, well prepared, with a number of delicous house specialties and a low-cost children's plate. Dinner daily; lunch weekdays. Major credit cards. 612 NW 21st Ave. (phone: 222-4833). Inexpensive.

Dan and Louis Oyster Bar – A Portland institution. Clams, crab, oysters — quickly, simply, and deliciously prepared. Opened in the days when restaurants didn't worry about decor, and it's still the same today (which means it has a distinct, turn-of-the-century style). Open daily. Reservations for 5 or more. Major credit cards. 208 SW Ankeny (phone: 227-5906). Inexpensive.

Delphina's – Choose anything from pizza to tender milk-fed veal in this cozy Northwest neighborhood restaurant. The bread and pasta are Delphina's own, and justly famous throughout the city. Open daily. Reservations advised. Major credit cards. 2112 NW Kearney (phone: 221-1195). Inexpensive.

Organ Grinder – Not so much a restaurant as a performance at which you can buy pizza and beer. The place has at least seven pipe organs connected to one keyboard, at which pop tunes are played to accompany silent films. Open daily. No reservations. Some credit cards. 5015 SE 82nd Ave. (phone: 771-1178). Inexpensive.

Original Pancake House – No kin to the national chain of nearly the same name. From lingonberry to German pancakes, these are Portland's best, and well loved in the city. Closed Mondays and Tuesdays. No reservations. No credit cards. SW Barbur Blvd at 24th (phone: 246-9007). Inexpensive.

Papa Haydn – Select dessert first, then order a light meal that won't spoil it. There's almost always a crowd gathered around the pastry case, where delights ranging from "autumn meringue" to *boccone dolce* are on display. Dinners feature light, continental cuisine, with an emphasis on seafood and chicken. Lunch and dinner Tuesdays through Saturdays; Sunday brunch. No reservations. Major credit cards. 5829 SE Milwaukee Ave. (phone: 232-9440) and 801 NW 23rd Ave. (phone: 228-7317). Inexpensive.

Rose's Delicatessen – Delicate blintzes, delicious cakes, gigantic sandwiches. The food isn't kosher, but the atmosphere — and the quality of the sandwiches — is vintage New York City. Open daily. Make reservations or expect a wait during prime meal times. Major credit cards. 315 NW 23rd Ave. (phone: 227-5181). Inexpensive.

ST. LOUIS

Long known as a great city in which to raise a family, the Gateway to the West is finally growing up and expanding in new directions. As the economic landscape flourishes and the cultural and social communities expand, St. Louis is rapidly becoming a thriving metropolis and now offers more than baseball and a scenic view of the Arch to both visitors and residents.

Founded as a fur trading post by Pierre Laclede in 1764, St. Louis has become the fourteenth largest metropolitan area in the US. It's also the country's second largest inland port, the third largest mail center, and the sixth busiest air center. Ten of the Fortune 500 companies have their headquarters here, and a total of 357 maintain offices here. Recently the city school system, where the country's first kindergarten was established, celebrated its 150th anniversary.

This city, which in the 1940s was said to be "First in shoes, first in booze, and last in the American League" (referring to the hapless, now defunct St. Louis *Browns*), is moving back into the limelight. St. Louis is home of major league teams: the baseball *Cardinals* and hockey *Blues.* The Bowling Hall of Fame, next to *Busch Stadium,* stands as a testimonial to yet another sport. Residents hail the achievements of its performing artists as well as its athletes. The *St. Louis Symphony,* the nation's second oldest symphony orchestra, was recently acclaimed as number 2 in the nation by *Time* magazine. The *Fabulous Fox,* a movie palace resuscitated in all its glitzy greatness, has led to big-name entertainment and the best of Broadway touring companies coming to St. Louis's own Grand Boulevard.

The city's cultural and entertainment rejuvenation has been spurred by an infusion of capital into the real estate market, especially downtown, where the entire skyline has changed significantly. Due to a strict city ordinance, no building near the famous Arch is allowed to tower above the gleaming steel structure's 630 feet, but the new, 42-story Metropolitan Square building stands 618 feet and is among the city's first real skyscrapers. (Actually, the Wainwright Building, designed by Louis Sullivan, was known as the first skyscraper in the nation and was renovated by the State of Missouri as a state office building several years ago.)

A spirit of revitalization captured the city early in the 1980s. Neighborhoods such as DeBaliviere Place, Soulard, Lafayette Square, Shaw Park, Compton Heights, Washington Heights, and Benton Park have been given a face-lift and renovated by urban pioneers who turned their new blood and ideas to these old, abandoned areas. Today they have become national landmarks and offer an architectural history lesson of the Midwest. Walking tours and home tours are offered regularly by the Landmarks Association.

At the centerpiece of St. Louis's rebirth is newly revived Union Station, an enormous train depot that served passengers from 1894 until the late 1970s.

ST. LOUIS
WEST END

PAGE BLVD
PAGE BLVD
PAGE BLVD
COOK A
MAPLE AV
MAPLE AV
BAVARD AV
WALTON AV
NEWBERRY TER
FINNEY AV
FINNEY A
CABANNE
GATES AV
LEWIS PL
MARCUS AV
FAIRFAX AV
FAIRFAX AV
GATES AV
MC MILLAN AV
WEST BELLE PL
CLARENDON AV
AUBERT AV
ENRIGHT AV
ENRIGHT AV
ENRIGHT AV
ENRIGHT AV
KINGSHIGHWAY BLVD
EUCLID AV
WALTON AV
TAYLOR AV
NEWSTEAD AV
PENDELTON AV
WHITTIER ST
ENRIGHT AV
ENRIGHT AV
DELMAR BLVD
DELMAR BLVD
ENRIGHT AV
LAKE AV
DELMAR BLVD
WASHINGTON BLVD
DELMAR BLVD
To Powell Hall
100 yds
ENRIGHT AV
DELMAR BLVD
WASHINGTON BLVD
OLIVE ST
OLIVE ST
WASHINGTON BLVD
WESTMINSTER PL
WESTMINSTER TER
WALTON AV
MC PHERSON AV
MC PHERSON
WESTMINSTER PL
LENNOX PL
MC PHERSON AV
PRIVATE STREETS DISTRICT
MARYLAND
PLAZA
PERSHING AV
MARYLAND AV
WHITTIER ST
PORTLAND PL
LAKE PL
KINGSHIGHWAY BLVD
MARYLAND AV
MARYLAND AV
WESTMORELAND PL
EUCLID AV
LINDELL BLVD
LINDELL BLVD
LINDELL BLVD
BOYLE AV
LINDELL BLVD
PINE BLVD
St. Louis
Cathedral
PINE BLVD
PINE BLVD
TAYLOR AV
NEWSTEAD AV
LACLEDE AV
LACLEDE AV
LACLEDE AV
PARK AV
PARK AV
PARK AV
EUCLID AV
DUNCAN AV
DUNCAN AV
AUDUBON AV
BOYCE AV
FOREST PARK
CLAYTON
TAYLOR AV
NEWSTEAD AV
BOYLE AV
KINGSHIGHWAY BLVD
EUCLID AV
PAPIN ST
To Municipal Opera House
Jefferson Memorial
St Louis Zoo
Art Museum
All in the Park within 1 mile
Planetarium
CHOUTEAU AV
CHOUTEAU AV
40
GIBSON AV
ARCO AV
ARCO
MANCHESTER A
Daniel Boone Expwy
OAKLAND AV
OAKLAND AV
WICUITA AV
MANCHESTER AV
TOWER GROVE AV
BOYLE AV
VANDEVENT
OAKLAND AV
MC KLIND AV
BERTHOLD AV
EAST RD
SWAN AV
NORFOLK AV
NEWSTEAD AV
Checkerdome
WEST PARK AV
WEST PARK AV
MANCHESTER AV
KINGSHIGHWAY BLVD
TAYLOR AV
VANDEVENT AV
MC CREER AV
MANCHESTER AV
MC KLIND AV
MC CREE AV
TOWER GROVE AV
44
DE TONTY ST
SUBLETTE AV
LILLY AV
NORTHRUP AV
BOARD AV
SHAW AV
SHAW AV
SHAW AV
PIERCE
JANUARY AV
PATTISON AV
SHAW AV
MAURY
ALFRED AV
MANCHESTER AV
SHAW AV
EDWARDS
SCOPER AV
HEREFORD ST
Missouri
Botanical Gdns
MC KLIND AV
LILLY AV
DOGGETT AV
WILSON AV
VANDEVENT AV
WILSON AV
THE HILL
WILSON AV
BISCHOFF
SHENANDOAH AV
Chimatron

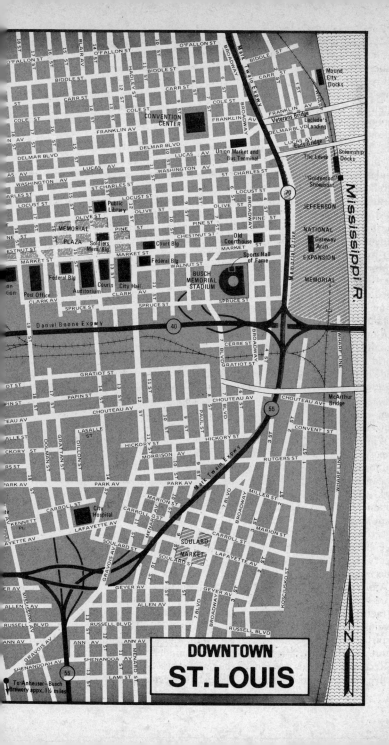

DOWNTOWN
ST. LOUIS

The largest and busiest train station in the world during World War II, Union Station was designated as a National Historic Landmark in 1976 and restored and renovated in grand style by the Rouse Company — developers of Baltimore's Harborplace and Boston's Faneuil Hall. It is now a shopping/restaurant/entertainment/hotel complex with its own lake as an added attraction; the main lobby and lounge of the *Omni* hotel occupies the original station's Grand Hall.

St. Louis grew up along the river, and the mighty Mississippi has left its indelible mark on the city's music — jazz, gospel, and bluegrass are part of regularly held festivals. Another reminder of the city's river heritage is the warehouse district, where once goods were shipped en route to the rugged West. Restored right down to its original cobblestone streets, Laclede's Landing draws office traffic during the day, restaurant and bar patrons at night. The development is particularly appealing to conventioneers and college students. An unusual public plaza with fountains, trees, and old-fashioned cast-iron lampposts lends distinction to this area.

More sophisticated palates travel to St. Louis's Central West End, very near Forest Park, for a little more diversity and, frankly, better food. Dedicated diners also know that a good meal may be found in the city's various ethnic neighborhoods, prime steakhouses downtown, and many new French restaurants scattered throughout the metropolitan area.

Along with good food, St. Louisans like good beer. They know that only a tourist orders anything that isn't an Anheuser-Busch product. The world's biggest brewery calls St. Louis home and the city takes as much pride in its beer heritage as in its architecture and sports teams. Not surprisingly, the brewery (which offers free tours) owns both the baseball team and the stadium. Grant's Farm, August Busch's home, is also a tourist attraction, complete with buffaloes and, at the end of the ride, what else — pretzels and beer.

While St. Louis looks to its future, there remain the living monuments to its past. The 1904 World's Fair gave birth to the ice cream cone and hot dog and inspired a great Judy Garland flick, but, more important to St. Louisans, the fair brought to prominence Forest Park, one of the nation's largest urban parks, and the St. Louis Zoo. On the south side of town, the Missouri Botanical (Shaw's) Garden literally grew out of British immigrant Henry Shaw's generosity and dedication to beauty. In addition to being a botanical research center, it is also the home of the Climatron (a geodesic-domed greenhouse), a peaceful Japanese garden, rose gardens, the Desert House, Henry Shaw's townhouse, his herb garden, and the scented garden — especially popular with the visually handicapped.

Along the river, where St. Louis began, sits the stately Old Cathedral. Built in 1834 on the site of the first log cabin chapel west of the Mississippi, it attracts members of all faiths. Its museum contains an 800-year-old Spanish crucifix and the original church bell from 1770. The immense and awe-inspiring building stands next to the Arch, a gleaming symbol of St. Louis's future, and near the Mississippi itself, a reminder of the strength of its past.

Recently, St. Louis was ranked the seventh best city in the country in which to live, and Partners for Livable Places has selected the city as one of the 26 most livable in America. At one time its citizenry would have been skeptical of the rating. Today they have faith in their city and its future.

ST. LOUIS AT-A-GLANCE

 SEEING THE CITY: A tour of St. Louis must begin along the Mississippi River, where the city began, and the riverfront offers an irresistible focal point: the Gateway Arch, soaring 630 feet above the levee. From its top, you can see most of St. Louis and miles of countryside beyond, on both sides of the river. Ride to the top of the Arch in one of two capsule trams, train-like vehicles running on special tracks to the 70-foot observation room, which affords a truly spectacular 30-mile view. While waiting for the tram, visit the *Museum of Westward Expansion* (11 N. 4th St.; phone: 425-4465), see a film on the construction of the Arch in the *Tucker Theater,* or browse in the *Museum Shop,* on the plaza beneath the Arch. Admission to the museum is free with a $1 park pass, good for 7 days. Built in 1966 by architect Eero Saarinen, the Arch is so delicately engineered that its last segment — that bit of the arch that's farthest off the ground and connects the two columns — had to wait to be installed until the weather was perfect, so that the steel would neither contract nor expand a fraction until it was in place.

 SPECIAL PLACES: Though it's most convenient to get around St. Louis by car, most areas lend themselves to a walking tour. You can park along the waterfront, for example, and explore on foot the levee, Laclede's Landing, and downtown. For the less energetic, *Tram Tour* (516 Cerre St.; phone: 241-1400) offers a 2-hour narrated tram tour of the downtown area, which runs about every 30 minutes in summer; once in the morning and once in the afternoon in winter.

RIVERFRONT AND DOWNTOWN

The Levee – Moored on the river side of the cobblestone levee are St. Louis's most famous riverboats: the *Goldenrod Showboat,* for dinner and old-fashioned "meller-dramers," and the *Huck Finn* and *Tom Sawyer,* for day and night trips up and down the Mississippi. You'll also find the New Orleans–based *Delta Queen* (phone: 800-543-1949) and the *Robert E. Lee* (phone: 241-1282), luxurious sternwheelers from the golden era of steamboats, as well as the only floating *McDonald's* and the *President,* the world's largest excursion boat (phone: 342-7200 or 621-4040).

On the city side of the levee is Jefferson Expansion Memorial Parkway, with the Arch at its center, and in one corner, the Old Cathedral, which is, naturally, the oldest cathedral west (just west) of the Mississippi, 2nd and Walnut Sts. (phone: 231-3250). It started as a log cabin in 1764 when the city was founded and took its present form in 1834.

Laclede's Landing – In the 50 years after the Civil War, St. Louis became rich as well as famous, and the entire downtown section boomed and bloomed. What's left of the bloom is Laclede's Landing, a 10-block area just north of the levee on the far side of massive Eads Bridge with some fine examples of cast-iron-fronted buildings (Raeder Place, formerly the *Old Missouri* hotel at 806 N. 1st, is best of all). It's now the home of a new generation of restaurants and galleries, and one of the few areas in the city where liquor can be served until 3 AM. Some suggestions while wandering the area are *Kennedy's 2nd Street Company,* 612 N. 2nd St. (phone: 421-3655), for a lunch of chili, burgers, and sandwiches, and a great place to hear local bands; *Mississippi Night,* 914 N. 1st St. (phone: 421-3853), which features local as well as national bands (the

Ramones and the *Psychedelic Furs* have played here); *The Old Spaghetti Factory,* 727 N. 1st St. (phone: 621-0276), for inexpensive Italian dishes and an old European decor; or, for a good catfish dinner or oyster appetizer, *2nd Street Diner and Fish Market,* 721 N. 2nd St. (phone: 436-2222). For food as well as entertainment, try *Hannegan's Restaurant and Pub,* 719 N. 2nd St. (phone: 241-8877), or *Bogart's on the Landing,* 809 N. 2nd St. (phone: 241-9380).

Old Courthouse – At one time a site of slave auctions, this courthouse was just 2 years old in 1847 when an American slave named Dred Scott tested the legality of slavery by suing his owner. The case was heard here; when he lost, the course of slavery was set. Inside are displays of Old St. Louis and courtrooms where great lawyers such as Thomas Hart Benton tried their cases. Most interesting today is the building's cast-iron dome, completed in 1859, and the mural that adorns its interior. Open daily. No admission charge. 4th St. at Market (phone: 425-4465).

National Bowling Hall of Fame and Museum – A haven for bowling aficionados, it traces the history and development of bowling from 5200 BC to the present. Headquarters of the American Bowling Congress and the Women's International Bowling Congress. Old-time bowling alley, videodisc program, wide-screen theater, and restaurant. Admission charge. 8th and Walnut, across from *Busch Stadium* (phone: 231-6340).

Eugene Field House – Primarily an antique toy collection, with some artifacts of the famous St. Louis author Eugene Field, who wrote *Little Boy Blue.* At Christmastime, the house prepares a complete Victorian Christmas display. Closed Mondays. Admission charge. 634 S. Broadway (phone: 421-4689).

Campbell House Museum – A stately mid-Victorian townhouse containing original furnishings. 1508 Locust (phone: 421-0325).

Mercantile Money Museum – Here is everything you've ever wanted to know about money, including counterfeiting. A talking mannequin introduces you to the witticisms of Benjamin Franklin. No admission charge. Mercantile Tower, 7th and Washington Sts. (phone: 425-2050).

St. Louis Centre – One of the country's largest urban shopping complexes, a 4-level glass-enclosed mall consisting of 150 shops and 20 restaurants that connects two of the city's largest department stores, *Dillard's* and *Famous-Barr.* Between 6th St., 7th St., Washington Blvd., and Olive Blvd.

Union Station – Eleven acres of history successfully masquerading as a shopping center. Originally built in the glory days of railroads, and once the busiest train station in the country, it has been restored at a cost of $135 million. Carefully preserved, it now features myriad exclusive shops and deluxe restaurants, a free theater, a luxury hotel, and authentic peeks into its rich past. Also two hot nightspots: *Menage: A Dance Café,* in Union Station at the corner of 20th Street (phone: 241-4770), features moderate lunch and dinner along with nightly disco dancing; *Whitey Herzog's Restaurant and Powerhouse Nightclub,* just south of the train shed (phone: 421-2770), features lunch, dinner, and dancing. Conference areas are available during the day. A 10-screen movie theater operates at the far south end of Union Station. Old and new St. Louis meet here. 18th and Market Sts.

Union Market – Once the largest public market in the city, this landmark currently features an international food court with produce, grocery items, a deli, and take-out shops. 6th and Convention Plaza Dr., adjacent to St. Louis Centre.

Dental Health Theatre – The props are 3-feet-high fiberglass teeth and a carpeted pink tongue, the characters are marionettes, and the show's all about teeth and dental health. This unique theater is a good place to take the kids. Open weekdays from 9 AM to 4 PM; call ahead for show times. No admission charge. 727 N. 1st St., Suite 103, on Laclede Landing (phone: 241-7391).

SOUTH ST. LOUIS

South St. Louis is primarily German, Italian, and Eastern European. The most determinedly ethnic neighborhood in the area is the Hill (between South Kingshighway and Shaw). From its *bocce* courts and front yard shrines to its green, white, and red hydrants, the Hill is 20 blocks of solid Italian consciousness — great for walking and snacking. Two suggestions: *John Volpi & Co.*, 5256 Daggett (phone: 772-8550), closed Mondays, for salami, prosciutto, and Italian sausage; *Amighetti Bakery,* 5141 Wilson (phone: 776-2855), closed Sundays and Mondays, for fresh bread and carry-out "po' boys." This area is particularly noted for its fine Italian restaurants.

Anheuser-Busch Brewery – The makers of Michelob and Budweiser offer free 1-hour tours of the brewery and grounds, featuring, naturally, a healthy sampling of the King of Beers. Best on the tour: the stables, a registered landmark building, where the mighty Clydesdale horses reside when they're not on parade. Closed weekends and holidays. No admission charge. 610 Pestalozzi St. (phone: 577-2626).

Missouri Botanical Garden (Shaw's Garden) – After Henry Shaw got very rich with a hardware store in downtown St. Louis, he decided to repay the city by opening his Southside garden estate to the public. Since 1860 its reputation and its collection have grown apace. Highlights of the 79-acre park: the Climatron, a geodesic-domed tropical greenhouse; Seiwa-En, a beautiful Japanese garden; and the Scented Garden, a special collection of scented plants for the blind that may be touched and handled, with descriptions and explanations in braille. Henry Shaw's home is open for tours. Other features include the *Boehm Porcelain Gallery,* a gift shop, and the *Garden View* restaurant. Open daily. Admission charge. 2101 Tower Grove (phone: 577-5100).

Soulard Market – Soulard is the name of both the market and the neighborhood which surrounds it. Since 1847, when the ground was given to the city to be used as a public farmers' market, Soulard Market has been open for business — busiest on Saturday mornings, when everything from live rabbits to homemade apple butter is for sale to city slickers. The outside stalls around the main building open whenever fresh goods — meat or poultry, vegetables, fruit, farmers' canned goods or home specialties — come into the city. Closed Sundays and Mondays; most active Fridays and Saturdays. 7th St. and Lafayette (phone: 622-4180).

CENTRAL WEST END

Named for its location near famous Forest Park at the western edge of the city limits, Central West End is St. Louis's most sophisticated and elegant section — a warren of small shops, pleasant restaurants, and ornate mansions in the fashionable "places" (private boulevards maintained by the residents; grandest of the grand are Portland and Westmoreland places). All is grist for the walkers' mill, even the private "places," so spend some time just exploring.

Maryland Plaza – A stroller's delight, between Kingshighway and Euclid Avenue, just around the corner from the *Chase* hotel (see *Best in Town*). With the best people watching in town, this area is a magnet for politicians, media types, and other glitzy characters. A potpourri of shops and restaurants makes for good food and great buys, too. Visit 26 Maryland Plaza, an arcade of boutiques featuring everything from seashells and antique clothing to herbs. For a bite to eat, if you have money enough left over, try *Duff's,* 392 N. Euclid (phone: 361-0522), for a lunch of sandwiches and imported beer, or the *Forest Park Deli,* 4910 W. Pine at Euclid (phone: 367-1634), a 24-hour, full-service eatery with good coffee. Sample *Dressel's,* 392 N. Euclid (phone: 361-1060), for hearty Welsh pub fare (and the city's best selection of beer and ale). The *Central West End* also sports several establishments that can satisfy more hearty appetites: *Balaban's,* 405 N. Euclid (phone: 381-8085), for a dinner of seafood, French cuisine, or their unusual dinner crêpes; *Culpeppers,* 300 N. Euclid (phone: 361-2828), a trendy bar-café whose spicy chicken wings, club sandwiches, and soups are well-known; *Flamingo Café,* 313 N. Euclid (phone: 361-7811), an attractive Pasta House outlet decorated in an Art Deco motif; and the *Magic Wok,* 1 Maryland Plaza (phone: 367-2626), a Hunan restaurant with the best Chinese food in town. If you're at the *Chase* hotel and elegant dining is what you want, you need go no farther; its *Tenderloin Room,* 212 N. Kingshighway (phone: 361-2500), is the place for prime ribs, chops, and seafood in a Victorian setting. For monthly shows of photography and contemporary art, stop by the *Greenberg Gallery of Contemporary Art,* 44 Maryland Plaza (phone: 361-7600); *Vaughn Cultural Center,* 1408 N. Kingshighway (phone: 361-0111); and the *Center of Contemporary Arts,* 524 Trinity Ave. (phone: 725-6555).

St. Louis Cathedral – It is not just the size of the cathedral — immense — that is awesome; it is the mosaics that adorn almost the whole interior space — beautiful, ethereal, light bearing; millions of pieces of stone and glass in thousands of shades depicting saints, apostles, and religious scenes. Considered one of the finest examples of mosaicwork in this hemisphere, and not to be missed. Tours conducted on Sundays (except Easter) at 1 PM. Lindell at Newstead (phone: 533-2824).

Fabulous Fox Theater – This recently restored 1929 movie palace now has all the gilt and glitz of its yesteryears. At night the house lights come on, and the *Fox* presents some of the biggest entertainment names in the country — Las Vegas–style shows and pop concerts at midwestern prices. Tours of the theater are given Wednesdays, Thursdays, and Saturdays at 10:30 AM for $2. 527 N. Grand Blvd. (phone: 534-1678, for entertainment information).

University City Area – On Delmar Avenue, in the University City loop area (where the streetcars turn around), just west of the Central West End, there's a "strip" of happenings: resale shops, modern boutiques, art galleries, and bookstores. *Blueberry Hill,* a bar/restaurant where Chuck Berry, Elvis Presley, and Bo Diddly are held in esteem, serves Rock 'n' Roll beer, a local brew (6504 Delmar; phone: 727-0880). The *Tivoli Theatre,* 6350 Delmar (phone: 725-0220), features a repertory of foreign, classical, and modern films, as does the *High Pointe Cinema,* nearby, at 1001 McCausland (phone: 781-0800).

■**EXTRA SPECIAL:** An hour south from St. Louis just off Rte. 55 is Ste. Genevieve, one of the oldest permanent settlements west of the Mississippi (established in 1735) and a town that has maintained its bounty of old homes with admirable care. A number of the oldest homes are open daily, as is an excellent old inn, *St. Gemme Beauvais,* 78 N. Main St. (phone: 883-5744). It's a beautifully furnished, 8-room village inn with the best food in town. And not to be missed, if you are in the area during the second weekend of August: *Ste. Genevieve's Jour de Fête,* when all the old homes are open for a festive 2 days.

For the young, or just the young at heart, take a day trip to Six Flags Over Mid-America, a 200-acre theme park with Looney Tunes Town (where you can shake hands with Bugs Bunny), the shooting rapids of Thunder River, the Screamin' Eagle, and all sorts of unique shows and shops. Open daily, late May through late August, it's about a 20-minute drive from downtown, at I-44 and Allenton Rd. in Eureka (phone: 938-4800 or 938-5300). Or visit the locale of Huck Finn and Tom Sawyer — Hannibal, Missouri (phone: 221-0114). Described as the "World's Most Famous Small Town," it was the home of Samuel Clemens, better known as Mark Twain. Another unusual attraction is Silver Dollar City. Tucked away in the heart of 2,000 acres overlooking Table Rock Lake, it is a unique community of good-time shows, old-time crafts, fun-time rides, and plenty of farm-fresh food in a variety of good restaurants.

Other nearby attractions: Meramec Caverns, one of the largest cave formations in the world and once a hideout of Jesse James. Camping and canoeing on the Meramec River are available April through October. The caverns themselves are open from March through December. Take I-44 west to the Stanton exit (phone: 468-3166). *Cahokia Mounds State Historic Site and Museum* displays artifacts dating from AD 700 to 1450, when Indians inhabited the area, and conducts tours, craft classes, and a variety of seasonal events. Open daily from 9 AM to 5 PM. Donations accepted. 7850 Collinsville Rd., Collinsville, IL (phone: 618-346-5160)

SOURCES AND RESOURCES

 TOURIST INFORMATION: The Convention and Visitors Commission (10 S. Broadway, Suite 300, St. Louis, MO 63102; phone: 421-1023 or 800-247-9791), publishes a free guide that lists special events (festivals, street fairs, house tours); it also has maps and other tourist information. A free Travel Plan Kit featuring a group tour manual, a 35-page visitor's guide, and a calendar of events is available. The St. Louis Visitors Center, at 445 N. Memorial Dr. (phone: 241-1764), also has brochures, baseball schedules, and other information of interest.

The St. Louis Annual Guide (*St. Louis* magazine; $3.50) is comprehensive. The *St. Louis Symphony Society* arranges special group (20 or more) tours of any part of the city, with proceeds going to the society's treasury; 712 N. Grand Blvd. (phone: 533-2500). The *American Institute of Architects* has architectural maps of the city, pinpointing interesting buildings (phone: 621-3484). The *Landmarks Association* has information on neighborhoods and restoration projects (phone: 421-6474).

Television Stations – KTVI Channel 2–ABC; KMOV Channel 4–CBS; KSDK Channel 5–NBC; KECT Channel 9–PBS.

Radio Stations – AM: KMOX 1120 (talk/sports); KGLD 1380 (oldies); KUFA 55 (classic country); KOOL 590 (1950s music). FM: KSD 93.7 (classic rock); KEZK 102.5 (adult contemporary).

Local Coverage – *St. Louis Post-Dispatch,* daily (Thursday's edition carries a calendar of coming events); the *St. Louis American,* published each Thursday, the city's most informative black community newspaper; *St. Louis* magazine, monthly. The *St. Louis Business Journal* is a weekly update on the business scene, and the weekly *Riverfront Times* focuses on city happenings.

Telephone – The area code for St. Louis is 314.

Sales Tax – There is a 6.1% sales tax on general merchandise. In addition, restaurants charge a 1.5% tax, and hotels charge a 3.75% tourism tax.

 CLIMATE: St. Louis weather is unpredictable, with temperatures ranging from −10F to +103F. From mid-June through September, the heat and humidity are high, particularly in August. Dress coolly, but be aware that most places are air conditioned. Autumn is crisp, cool, and beautiful. Suits and sweaters or light wraps are necessary. Winters are very cold, with snow and ice. Spring is wonderful, but be prepared for occasional rain and very strong winds from April to June.

GETTING AROUND: Airport – Lambert–St. Louis International Airport is usually a 30-minute drive from downtown (up to an hour during rush periods), and cab fares should run $18. The airport limo service to downtown costs $5.90 and leaves the airport every 15 minutes. The city's Natural Bridge Airport bus leaves for downtown from the air terminal's main entrance every 45 minutes to an hour and costs 85¢.

Bus – The Bi-State bus system serves most of the metropolitan area. Route information, maps, 707 N. 1st St. (phone: 231-2345). Fare 85¢; 15¢ for transfers.

Taxi – Cabs can be picked up at the major department stores and hotels, hailed in the streets, or ordered by phone. Major companies are *Laclede Cab* (phone: 652-3456); *Yellow Cabs* (phone: 361-2345); *County Cab* (phone: 991-5300); *Allen Cab* (phone: 531-4545).

Car Rental – St. Louis is served by all the major national companies; several have booths at the airport as well as around the city. A reliable local service is *Enterprise Leasing,* with nine locations around the city (phone: 231-4440).

LOCAL SERVICES: Babysitting – A number of agencies are listed in the yellow pages, but most will be more expensive than the nonprofessional organization that provides conscientious babysitters. *Missouri Baptist Hospital* (phone: 569-5193) supplies nursing students with good references and their own transportation; tightly run, relatively strict, and careful.

Business Services – *Bradley Business Service,* 34 N. Brentwood (phone: 721-3842).

Mechanics – *Domian Standard Service,* 814 S. Lindbergh (phone: 993-4025), has 24-hour road service and can work on most foreign cars as well as all American automobiles. Closest to the downtown area are *Stringer's Amoco Station,* 7th and Russell (phone: 776-0092), with 24-hour service, and *Overturf's,* 902 S. Broadway (phone: 436-2540).

MUSEUMS: The story of the movement west is told in murals, graphic displays, and film sequences at the *Museum of Westward Expansion* under the Arch (see *Special Places*). Other museums of interest in St. Louis:

Dog Museum – Moved from New York City in 1987, the museum rotates selections from its permanent art collections. On hand are items depicting the dog throughout history. Open Mondays through Saturdays from 9 AM to 5 PM, Sundays from 1 to 4 PM. Admission charge. 1721 S. Mason Rd., in Queeny Park in West County (phone: 821-DOGS).

The Magic House – Dares children to have a good time and learn something, too. Closed Mondays. Admission charge. 516 Kirkwood (phone: 822-8900).

McDonnell Douglas Prologue Room – At the world headquarters of the aerospace giant, the room displays some of McDonnell Douglas's achievements, including the first Gemini and Mercury space capsules ever built. Open daily (except Sundays) from 9 AM to 4 PM, June through August. No admission charge. McDonnell Blvd. and Airport Rd. (on the northeast side of the airport (phone: 232-5421).

Missouri Historical Society and History Museum – It's easy to get lost amid the colorful displays describing the history of St. Louis, the State of Missouri, and the American West. Of particular interest are the exhibits depicting 100 years of St. Louis advertising and of the 1904 World's Fair; Charles Lindbergh memorabilia; and the extensive collections of firearms and period costumes. Open Tuesdays through Sundays from 9:30 AM to 4:45 PM. Guided tours offered on weekdays; make an appointment. No admission charge. Forest Park, Lindell Blvd., and De Baliviere (phone: 361-1424).

National Museum of Transport – The many vehicles on which Americans have relied, from horse-drawn buggies to Bobby Darin's dream car, are on display. The museum's train collection is heralded as one of the greatest collections of locomotives in the nation. Open daily (except holidays) from 9 AM to 5 PM. Admission charge. 3015 Barrett Station Rd., in West County (phone: 965-7998).

St. Louis Art Museum – Forest Park (phone: 721-0067). Closed Mondays.

St. Louis Science Center (McDonnell Planetarium) – The McDonnell Planetarium and the *Museum of Science and Natural History* are both part of one entertainment and educational complex. The Planetarium now features a Star Theater, hands-on science and natural history exhibitions, and a Discovery Room. Open daily. Exhibitions are free; admission charge for Star Theater. 5100 Clayton Ave., Forest Park (phone: 289-4400).

St. Louis Wax Museum – Over 130 lifelike wax figures, including those of movie stars, presidents, sports celebrities, religious leaders, and public figures. Open daily (call for hours). Admission charge. 2nd and Morgan Sts. (phone: 241-1155).

MAJOR COLLEGES AND UNIVERSITIES: There are five major universities in the St. Louis area: St. Louis University, founded by the Jesuits in 1818 and the oldest college in the US west of the Mississippi, Grand at Lindell (phone: 658-2222); Washington University, founded by an ancestor of T. S. Eliot, too shy to name the school for himself (at the western end of Forest Park on a beautiful campus; phone: 889-5000); the University of Missouri, St. Louis, 8001 Natural Bridge Rd. (phone: 553-0111); Webster University, 470 E. Lockwood in the quaint hamlet of Webster Groves (phone: 968-6900); and Southern Illinois University–Edwardsville, in Edwardsville, Illinois, about 30 minutes east of downtown St. Louis (in St. Louis, phone 621-5168).

PARKS AND GARDENS: Forest Park is America's third largest city park (Central Park and the Portland, Oregon, park system are larger) and it offers far too much to see in even a long day. Highlights are the zoo, whose exhibits — "Big Cat Country," the famous Monkey House, the walk-through Bird Cage — can be visited on foot or by zoo train. The newest addition is a grand Jungle of the Apes House. The Children's Zoo charges a modest admission price, and you must buy a ticket for the train; all else free (phone: 781-0900). The *Art Museum,* on Art Hill (closed Mondays), maintains a wide-ranging collection and hosts traveling exhibitions (phone: 721-0067). Laumeier International Sculpture Park, 12580 Rott Rd. (phone: 821-1209), features huge outdoor sculptures in a woodsy setting. St. Louis RV Park, 900 N. Jefferson (phone: 241-3330), is an urban park for recreational vehicles. Pool. Closed December through February. For information on the Missouri Botanical Garden, see *Special Places.*

SPECIAL EVENTS: The *International Festival* (phone: 997-1445) is held at Steinberg Rink in Forest Park during the 3-day Memorial Day weekend. Authentic music, dance, food, and crafts of 35 nationalities are featured. The *Huck Finn* and the *Tom Sawyer* riverboats are the contestants in the *Memorial Day Riverboat Race.* On the *Goldenrod Showboat,* St. Louis ragtimers host the *National Ragtime and Jazz Festival* (phone: 621-3311) in June. The *Japanese Festival* (phone: 577-5100) at Missouri Botanical Gardens is an annual summer celebration of Japanese culture through music, dance, food, and crafts. The *Veiled Prophet Fair* (phone: 367-FAIR) on the Arch grounds is a 4-day entertainment extravaganza, featuring a parade of 20 or more lavishly outfitted floats, fireworks, marathons, music, and air and water events, that takes place during the July 4 holiday. German food and culture are celebrated during the *Strassenfest,* a weekend celebration usually held the end of July in the area bordered by 11th, 13th, Pine, and Clark Sts. The *Great Forest Park Balloon Race* (phone: 726-6896), an annual St. Louis tradition since 1904, begins in Forest Park and ends wherever the wind carries. Contact the Visitors Bureau (phone: 421-1023) for exact dates.

SPORTS AND FITNESS: St. Louisans love their professional teams, and sports events are well attended.

   Baseball – *Busch Memorial Stadium* (Broadway at Walnut St., downtown) is the home of the National League *Cardinals* (phone: 421-3060).

Tickets are available at the stadium and from *Famous-Barr* and *Dillard* department stores.

Bicycling – The largest biking event in St. Louis is the Moonlight Ramble, a 17-mile bike ride that starts at 2 AM on the last Sunday of every August and lasts until dawn. American Youth Hostel will have information (phone: 421-2044).

Fitness Center – The *YMCA* has a pool, racquetball courts, track, and exercise equipment, 1528 Locust St. (phone: 436-4100).

Golf – Forest Park has two public courses, 9 and 18 holes respectively. The 18-hole course has a reputation for being tough, but greens and tees are not in the best condition, though work is being done to improve the grounds. The only other public golf course is in Ruth Park, 8211 Groby Rd., in St. Louis County. Modest fees (phone: 727-1800).

Hockey – The *Blues* play NHL hockey at the *Arena,* 5700 Oakland (phone: 644-0900).

Horse Racing – Thoroughbred racing at *Cahokia Downs,* Rte. 460, about 20 minutes from St. Louis; harness racing at *Fairmount Park,* Rte. 40 East, Collinsville, Illinois (phone: 436-1517).

Jogging – Start at Wharf Street below the Gateway Arch and run the 2-mile stretch along the river; jog the 6-mile perimeter of Forest Park; or follow Wydown Road by the Washington University campus for about a 2-mile residential run.

Tennis – Best for the visitor are the courts at *Dwight F. Davis Tennis Center* in Forest Park, open during daylight hours; permits for daily play obtained at the center (phone: 367-0220).

 THEATER: For up-to-date offerings and performance times, check the publications listed above. For dinner and a show, especially if you are with children, visit the *Goldenrod Showboat,* protoype for Edna Ferber's *Showboat,* where nightly melodramas demand boos and hisses for the villain. Moored at the levee (information, phone: 621-3311). Other choices are the fine *Repertory Theatre of St. Louis,* 136 Edgar Rd. (phone: 968-4925); the *Fabulous Fox,* 527 N. Grand Blvd. (phone: 534-1111), winter home of traveling Broadway shows and name entertainers; and the *Westport Playhouse,* 600 West Port Plaza (phone: 878-2424), one of St. Louis's newest and most attractive theaters, for productions ranging from plays to well-known entertainers. The *Municipal Opera House* in Forest Park offers its summer stock program of musicals. About 1,400 seats every performance are free; line up outside the Muny about 6:30 PM (phone: 361-1900). *St. Louis Black Repertory's 23rd Street Theatre,* 2240 St. Louis Ave. (phone: 231-3706), is entering its 13th season.

 MUSIC: Concerts and opera from the *St. Louis Symphony* at *Powell Hall* (information, phone: 533-2500); *Opera Theater of St. Louis, Loretto-Hilton Theater* (phone: 961-0171); and *Sheldon Memorial,* 3648 Washington (phone: 533-9900).

 NIGHTCLUBS AND NIGHTLIFE: There's been a recent shot in the arm of St. Louis's nightclub scene. After dark from Laclede's Landing to the suburbs, night crawlers can enjoy live jazz at *Gene Lynn's,* 9th and Washington (phone: 241-3833), and *Standing Room Only,* 75 Maryland Plaza (phone: 361-3733). In Union Station, there's disco dancing at *Menage,* at the corner of 20th St. (phone: 241-4770), and *Whitey Herzog's,* just south of the train shed (phone: 421-2770). Elsewhere, try *Mike Talanya's Jukebox Diner and Party Club,* 2410 Schuetz in West County (phone: 993-5449); 64 West, 5130 Oakland, south of Forest Park (phone: 535-6464), where the yuppies hang out; and *Tavern on the Plaza,* 14 Maryland Plaza (phone: 361-8505). *Mississippi Nights,* 914 N. 1st St. (phone: 421-3853), the only "nightclub" on Laclede's Landing, features a large dance floor and music from local as well as nationally known concert bands. For stimulating conversation and popular happy hours, there's *Café Balaban,* 405 N. Euclid in the Central West End (phone: 361-8085), where St. Louis's old money rubs elbows (literally) with the nouveau riche; and *Cardwell's,* 8100 Maryland, in the suburb of Clayton (phone: 726-5055), a mixture of business and cocktail chatter. Local and nationally known comedians appear at the *Funny Bone Comedy Club,* 940 W. Port Plaza (phone: 469-6692).

(BEST IN TOWN)

 CHECKING IN: Whether you want to be within walking distance of the levee, smack-dab downtown, on either end of Forest Park, or conveniently near Lambert Field Airport, high quality hotels are available. Prices range from $80 and up for a double in our expensive category, $55 to $75 in the moderate range, and $50 and under for an inexpensive hotel. These prices do not include the 3.75% tourism tax tacked on to the 6.1% St. Louis sales tax or the $2 fee on all hotel rooms. All telephone numbers are in the 314 area code unless otherwise indicated.

Adam's Mark – In the shadow of the Gateway Arch, with 17th-century Flemish tapestry, French crystal chandeliers, Russian lithographs, and an Italian marble lobby, *Adam's Mark* reflects the grand tradition of Europe's finest hotels. One of the city's best. 4th and Chestnut (phone: 241-7400). Expensive.

Airport Marriott – At Lambert Field Airport, half an hour from downtown, this 433-room spot features extensive recreational facilities — 2 pools, tennis courts, putting greens, sauna and exercise rooms — and is good both for business people on short visits and families on the road who'd like to stretch after a day of travel. Free parking. I-70 at the airport (phone: 423-9700). Expensive.

Majestic – This distinctively European hotel sets the standard for fine service and the most luxurious accommodations in downtown St. Louis. Each of the 91 guestrooms or mini-suites is unique in design and appointments. Full-service concierge. Pampering from check-in to check-out includes evening turn-down service. *M & B's Bar and Grille* features fine, unhurried dining. 1019 Pine St. (phone: 436-2355). Expensive.

Marriott Pavilion – In the midst of rebuilt downtown St. Louis. The "Pavilion" of its title is the Spanish Pavilion, jewel of the 1964 New York World's Fair, dismantled and moved to St. Louis by Mayor Alfonso Cervantes amid great controversy. It now makes up the 2-story lobby of the 671-room *Marriott,* where it is a great success. The hotel offers a coffee shop, 2 restaurants, a bar, a pool, a sauna, and free parking. 1 Broadway (phone: 421-1776). Expensive.

Omni International – More than just a hotel, it's an event — part of the complex that includes the beautifully restored Union Station, originally built in 1894. Of its 546 rooms, 68 are in Head House, which was actually part of the station, and the remainder under the original roof of the train shed. All have phones and TV sets in the bathrooms. There are 2 restaurants, the elegant *American Rotisserie* and the less formal *Café Potpourri,* and the *Grand Hall* bar. Surrounded by more than 11 climate-controlled acres of fine shops and marketplaces, it is truly an experience. 1820 Market St. (phone: 241-6664). Expensive.

Sheraton St. Louis – On the banks of the Mississippi, the hotel has many rooms with river views. All of them have color TV sets, telephones, and other standard amenities. There are also bars, a dining room and a café, and a swimming pool. 910 N. 7th St. (phone: 231-5100). Expensive.

Stouffer Concourse – Striking contemporary design, dramatic grand entrance with landscaped terraces, 393 well-appointed rooms, spa, fitness center, indoor and outdoor pool, superb restaurants, lounges, and exclusive club floors. 9801 Natural Bridge Rd. (phone: 429-1100). Expensive.

Chase – The grand old hotel of St. Louis, where limousines routinely line the entrance drive and celebrities are regular guests. Made an official landmark in 1977, the *Chase* is beautiful to behold. It isn't an intimate little hotel, with 821 rooms carved from an original 1,192, but it does have all the amenities one would expect of a grand hotel. Barber shop, 3 restaurants, 4 bars, shops, garage for guests next door. 212 N. Kingshighway (phone: 361-2500 or 800-325-8989). Moderate.

Cheshire Inn and Lodge – Aspires to an image of an English country inn, 1 block west of Forest Park. Close neighbors are no longer surprised by the English double-decker bus that fetches hotel guests from the airport; the theme is embellished with reproductions of English antiques in its 110 rooms. Beds set very high off the floor. Pool, good restaurant, free parking. Clayton Rd. at Skinker (phone: 647-7300). Moderate.

Clarion – For comfort as well as convenience, this impressive 855-room riverfront establishment is the place. In addition to luxury suites with Jacuzzi, features include indoor and outdoor pools, health club, gameroom, 24-hour coffee shop, delicatessen, 2 bars, and the revolving *Top of the Riverfront* restaurant, which treats diners to a 360-degree panorama of the city. 200 S. 4th St. (phone: 241-9500). Moderate.

Clayton Inn – This modern 220-room hotel in one of St. Louis's wealthy suburbs provides good service, spacious rooms decorated in contemporary style, and fine facilities. There are 2 restaurants, including the *Top of the Sevens* (closed Sundays), with a panoramic view of the city, a piano bar, health club with indoor and outdoor pools, sauna, exercise room, and whirlpool bath. 7750 Carondelet Ave. (phone: 726-5400). Moderate.

Forest Park – An older hotel undergoing successful renovation, just two blocks from the *Chase* in the Central West End. Half the hotel is given over to permanent residents, leaving about 100 rooms available for visitors. Hotel has a dining room, coffee shop, barber and beauty shops, cleaner's, outdoor pool, and free parking. 4910 W. Pine Blvd. (phone: 361-3500). Inexpensive.

 EATING OUT: Considering St. Louis's large Italian community, it is hardly surprising that the city's premier restaurant serves Italian haute cuisine or that its name is *Tony's.* What is more surprising is the host of good restaurants that complement it and the wide variety of cuisines and reasonable prices charged. Our choices below are grouped into broad price categories — expensive, about $60 for a meal for two; moderate, $30 to $40; inexpensive, $15 to $25 — and are guaranteed to get you into the most interesting corners of the city for lunch or dinner. Prices do not include drinks, wine, tips, or the 1.5% restaurant tax added to the 6.1% St. Louis sales tax. All telephone numbers are in the 314 area code unless otherwise indicated.

Al's – Just north of Laclede's Landing, an unlikely but successful combination of riverboat decor and Italian (and American) dishes. Arguably, it has the best steaks in town as well as a very respectable rack of lamb and an excellent shrimp de jonghe. Dinner only; closed Sundays. No reservations on Saturdays. Major credit cards. 1st St. at Biddle (phone: 421-6399). Expensive.

Anthony's – Without knowing, you might be justified in assuming that Anthony's owner was trying to steal Vince Bommarito's thunder; you might even suspect bad blood between the two. Blood there is, but not bad, one hopes; Anthony's is owned and run by Tony Bommarito, Vince's brother and partner in that original spaghetti-house-that-became-king. It's dedicated to light, French cuisine, fresh sea-food (a rarity in St. Louis), and service that matches brother Vince's place. Open for lunch weekdays as well as dinner daily except Sundays. Most major credit cards. 10 S. Broadway (phone: 231-2434). Expensive.

Richard Perry – This restaurant serves as the dining room of the quaint *Majestic* hotel in the heart of downtown and has the air of an English club. The menu features nouvelle, California modern, and regional cuisines prepared by chef Richard Perry. Sunday brunch offerings are among the finest in the Midwest. Open daily. Major credit cards. In the *Majestic* hotel, 1019 Pine St. (phone: 771-4100). Expensive.

Tony's – According to the *Wall Street Journal,* owner Vince Bommarito is the Vince Lombardi of the restaurant world — a stickler for detail and a perfectionist. What began as a spaghetti house has grown into a first-rate eatery, with waiters who study food and drink the way medical students cram for finals. Winner of the "Pasta Restaurant of the Year" award from the National Pasta Association, *Tony's* takes no reservations, and the wait on Saturday night can last more than 3 hours. Dinner only; closed Sundays and Mondays. Major credit cards. 862 N. Broadway (phone: 231-7007). Expensive.

Cardwell's – Seasonal dishes served in an atmosphere of relaxed elegance. Grilled meats cooked over pecan wood, mouth-watering pasta. Sunday brunch. Daily happy hour with complimentary hors d'oeuvres. Valet parking. 8100 Maryland, in the suburb of Clayton (phone: 726-5055). Moderate.

Cunetto's House of Pasta – On The Hill, where everything Italian prospers, and where the heart and soul of good food is pasta, hot, fresh, in a variety of styles, augmented by veal, steaks, and Italian specialties. Weekdays, lunch and dinner; Saturdays, dinner only. No reservations (long waits at dinnertime). Major credit cards. 5453 Magnolia (phone: 781-1135). Moderate.

House of Jamaica – Jerked beef, pork, chicken, goat, and fish are done up in tasty fashion and served with Red Stripe beer (the Jamaican brew). The decor is very native, as is the service — slow. Open daily except Sundays for lunch and dinner. Major credit cards. 6235 Delmar, in University City (phone: 725-4308). Moderate.

Lettuce Leaf – A former business school professor decided to put his marketing theories into practice and opened up a few restaurants that serve tasty salads, sandwiches, and soups, and a very good cheesecake. Open daily. Major credit cards. Three locations: 7823 Forsyth (phone: 727-5439); 107 N. 6th (phone: 241-7773); and 600 W. Port Plaza (phone: 576-7677). Moderate.

Miss Hulling's Cafeteria – A St. Louis tradition, serving healthful foods. The menu features 26 different salads. All breads and desserts are baked on the premises. Open daily except Sundays from 6 AM to 8:15 PM. Major credit cards. 11th and Locust Sts. (phone: 436-0840). Moderate.

La Patisserie – The quiche and house coffee cake are the most sought-after treats at this European café. Weekends there may be a wait, but it's worth it. Open daily for breakfast and lunch only. Major credit cards. 6269 Delmar (phone: 725-4902). Moderate.

Riddles Penultimate Café – American modern cuisine with a dash of Cajun makes this a favorite among the business set and college students. The wine bar ranks high. Try the daily "chalkboard specials." Open for lunch weekdays, dinner daily; closed Mondays." Reservations advised on weekends. Major credit cards. 6307 Delmar, in University City (phone: 725-6985). Moderate.

Edibles – Not much to look at, but the food more than makes up for appearances. A cafeteria by day and café by night. Try the beef bourguignonne or a spinach pita, and don't miss the chocolate cheesecake for dessert. Closed Sundays. No credit cards. 7816 Forsyth (phone: 721-0822). Inexpensive.

Original Restaurant – Popular soul food kitchen just a few blocks northeast of Union Station. Good eating. Open daily for breakfast, lunch, and dinner. 2217 Olive (phone: 421-7048). Inexpensive.

Salad Bowl Cafeteria – Home cooking, cafeteria-style, with a focus on the family. Open daily except Saturdays from 11 AM to 7:30 PM. 3949 Lindell Blvd. (phone: 535-4274). Inexpensive.

SALT LAKE CITY

Salt Lake City was born when two great natural forces, history and geology, came together in an accident of fate. To its current residents, it was a fortuitous cosmic collision. This kind of epic overview has a particular appeal to the residents of this gleaming oasis in the desert, since Salt Lake City is the headquarters of the Church of Jesus Christ of Latter-Day Saints. Known to most of us as Mormons, disciples of this church believe in divine revelation. And they believe God guided them here. Although the church tries to keep a low profile, evidence of its past work is everywhere, and visitors are immediately aware of the influence of its teachings. All the streets, for example, run at right angles to each other, and are numbered in a grid scale from the center point of Temple Square. This is the plan ordered by Mormon leader Brigham Young in 1847, when he followed the plans envisioned by Mormon prophet Joseph Smith years before.

It was Brigham Young who led persecuted and desperately weary Mormons across 1,000 miles of wind-swept prairie and mountains in search of a refuge where no one would bother them. When they arrived, Salt Lake City was a place no one else would covet. The transformation of barren desert into a habitable urban environment was the Mormons' major task, and their history is the legacy of the city.

Geology played its part by placing the Wasatch Mountains to the west of the Great Salt Lake basin. Rising abruptly from the Great Salt Lake Desert, their peaks snatch eastward-bound clouds and wring water from them. This makes the mountains good for skiing, but creates problems for the valley-bound city. The mean precipitation for Salt Lake City itself is 16 inches a year, while the mountains annually reap about 450 inches of precipitation in the form of snow. Even so, Utah is the second driest state in the nation. (First is next-door Nevada.) But the scarcity of water has stimulated irrigation engineers to come up with a number of ingenious, creative solutions. Now there are dams in the mountains to trap the winter snowfall so that upon melting it can be delivered to the farmers in the valleys, who desperately need water to harvest their crops.

Although the lack of water is a problem, scarcity of population is not. In fact, it's quite an advantage, infinitely preferable to the overcrowding which is characteristic of most cities. The heart of the Intermountain area, Salt Lake City absorbs a sizable number of Utah's 1,650,000 residents. The largest city in the state, the city proper houses 167,000 people. More than 700,000 live in the larger Wasatch Front metropolitan district, sandwiched between the mountains to the east, the Great Salt Lake, and its desert to the west.

For a city of its size and relative isolation, the cultural scene is surprisingly

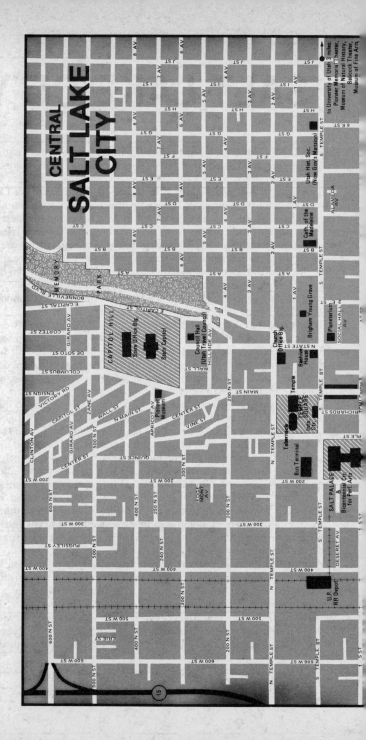

CENTRAL
SALT LAKE CITY

to University of Utah 3 miles:
Pioneer Memorial Theater,
Museum of Natural History,
Babcock Theater,
Museum of Fine Arts

Utah Hist. Soc.
(New Gov't Mansion)

Cath. of the Madeleine

Brigham Young Grave

Planetarium

SOCIAL HALL AV

Church Office Bldg.

Beehive House

Temple

TEMPLE SQUARE

SALT PALACE &
Bicentennial Cnt.
for Perf. Arts

Tabernacle

Bus Terminal

Council Hall
(Utah Travel Council)

State Office Bldg.

State Capitol

CAPITOL HILL

MEMORY PARK

BONNEVILLE BLVD

Pioneer Museum

U.P.
RR Depot

DESERET AV

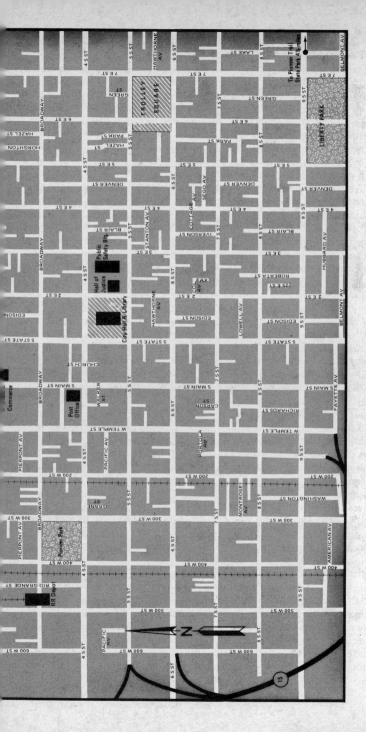

active. The *Utah Symphony,* an important North American orchestra, tours Europe regularly. *Ballet West* is one of the outstanding ballet groups in the country, and the illustrious *Mormon Tabernacle Choir* is so well known it needs no description. Several modern dance companies, the *Utah Opera Company,* and half a dozen theater groups perform throughout the year. The new Salt Lake County arts complex has three special buildings designed for concerts, ballet, and art exhibitions. Monday, a slow night in most cities, is a lively time in Salt Lake City, thanks to the Mormon Church. Mormon families are asked to set aside Monday as Family Home Evening, which makes it a good night for family movies and visits to local ice cream parlors. (Mormons have large families, so the emphasis on family togetherness is good for business.)

Brigham Young designed the city so its wide streets and tree-lined boulevards would be its most prominent features. His architectural foresight has stood the test of time, although the home of the Mormon pilgrims, like most other places, has yielded to the tyranny of progress. Ten years of intense building programs have changed the face of Salt Lake City. Main Street was torn up and completely redesigned, with sparkling fountains, patterned sidewalks, hundreds of new trees, and flower planters. Other streets have received the same treatment, and run-down areas have given way to new buildings like the *Salt Palace* arena, convention center, and ZCMI and Crossroads malls, enclosed downtown shopping centers. Some delightful, old Victorian mansions remain; portions of others have found a new home at Trolley Square, a shopping center patterned after San Francisco's Ghirardelli Square. The ten beautifully landscaped acres of Temple Square surrounding the Salt Lake Temple and Tabernacle still attract more than 4 million visitors a year, making it Utah's most popular tourist site.

Although 60% of Salt Lake City residents are Mormons, other ethnic communities exert strong cultural influences. The Guadalupe Center provides a base for the Mexican-Americans' civic activities. The Japanese community's *Obon Festival* and the annual *Greek Festival* contribute that eclectic, cosmopolitan flair generally associated with much larger cities. Even in other neighborhoods, many Salt Lake City residents are multilingual. Independent, pragmatic, and idealistic, Salt Lake City people prefer to do things themselves rather than ask for help. However, when other people need help, they will go out of their way. On a larger scale, their civic sense and altruism are almost legendary. When neighboring Idaho's Teton Dam burst in 1976, thousands of people from Salt Lake City turned out in force to clean up the muck.

An attractive, well-organized city of good-natured people should be enticing enough for just these qualities alone, without the added incentive of the Great Salt Lake, without which, obviously, nothing would be the same. Swimming in its briny, warm water is as much a part of the Salt Lake City experience as immersing oneself in its streets and buildings. Salt Lake City is unquestionably a splendid collaboration of nature, civilization, and people who refuse to accept the notion that kindness and what we commonly refer to as progress are mutually exclusive concepts.

SALT LAKE CITY AT-A-GLANCE

SEEING THE CITY: From the top of Capitol Hill, you can look out over the whole city. For a less panoramic view, try the horse-drawn carriages through downtown Salt Lake City. The fare is $20 for 2 to 4 passengers for half an hour, $25 for 5 or 6 passengers. Reservations cost an additional $5. Pick up the carriages on the south side of Temple Square at 6 PM. Contact *Carriage Horse Livery, Ltd.* (phone: 521-3331).

SPECIAL PLACES: Salt Lake City's grid pattern is simplicity itself. Everything radiates from Temple Square. For example: 18 blocks south is 18th South, 5 blocks west is 5th West. Most of the city's attractions are within walking distance, except for the lake and the university.

CENTRAL CITY

Temple Square – The logical place to start a tour of the city, as it's the heart of the worldwide Mormon Church. Enclosed within a 15-foot wall, the 10 acres of Temple Square's grounds draw about 4 million visitors a year. Within the grounds are the Salt Lake Temple, a granite structure that took 40 years to build; the dome-shaped, acoustically perfect Tabernacle, home of the *Mormon Tabernacle Choir;* and an information center, where you can join any one of many free, daily guided tours. The great Tabernacle organ conducts public recitals every day at noon. *Tabernacle Choir* rehearsals are open to the public on Thursday evenings. Organ recitals and choir rehearsals are free (phone: 240-2534).

Church Office Building – Across the street at Temple Square East is Utah's tallest structure, the Church Office Building, housing the general offices of the Church of Jesus Christ of Latter-Day Saints. Its Family History Library is used by thousands of people daily. It houses the world's largest genealogical collection of family histories, parish registers, biographies, and so on; chances are you or your ancestors are listed. Members of the staff will be happy to help you find out. Temple Square (phone: 240-2331).

Beehive House – Built by Brigham Young as his official residence in 1854, *Beehive House* is now a museum run by the Church. It was the first governor's mansion and is open Mondays through Saturdays from 9:30 AM to 4:30 PM (except Thanksgiving, Christmas, and New Year's Day); Sundays from 10 AM to 1 PM. The patriarch himself is buried half a block northeast in a quiet park. No admission charge. 67 E. South Temple and State Sts. (phone: 240-2671).

Capitol Hill – Capitol Hill contains the capitol, *Pioneer Museum,* and Council Hall, all within easy reach. The granite and marble capitol is a splendid piece of Corinthian architecture, and it houses many exhibitions of Utah products and art. Council Hall, across the street to the south, was moved to the hill stone by stone and now houses the Utah Travel Council, where you can pick up brochures and maps (see *Sources and Resources;* phone: 538-1030). Daughters of the *Utah Pioneers Museum,* west of the capitol, has one of the most complete collections of pioneer relics in the West. Open Mondays through Saturdays from 9 AM to 5 PM, Sundays in June, July, and August from 1 to 5 PM; closed on major holidays. Donations accepted. 300 N. Main St. (phone: 538-1050).

Salt Palace and Salt Lake County Center for the Performing Arts – Almost anything goes on at the 28,000-seat *Salt Palace* — conventions, sports events, rock concerts (100 S. West Temple; phone: 363-7681 or 534-6370). The *Salt Lake County*

Arts Center and a concert hall are on the same grounds. The *Capitol Theater,* a restored vaudeville playhouse, is nearby at 50 W. 200th South (phone: 363-7681).

ZCMI Center and Crossroads Plaza – Returning to tree-lined Main Street, you'll find two of the largest downtown covered shopping malls in the West. The ZCMI Center, on the east side of the street (15 S. Main St.), has over 60 stores inside, some of which serve old-fashioned refreshments like phosphates and iron port (made of a shot of every soda flavor). Across the street to the west is the new Crossroads Plaza, with 70 stores and numerous theaters and fast-food eateries. 18 S. Main St.

MID-CITY

South Temple – Start at the Cathedral of the Madeleine, a Roman Gothic church completed in 1909, which has a beautiful series of German stained glass windows (331 E. South Temple). Farther along the street are dozens of exquisite old mansions built by mining magnates at the turn of the century. One of them, the marble, stone, and wood Governor's Mansion, has been restored and is at 603 E. South Temple.

Trolley Square – This interesting square has won national acclaim as a restoration project. Ingeniously rebuilt in abandoned trolley barns, this collection of shops, theaters, restaurants, and boutiques attracts a fascinating stream of people. Wandering artists and troubadors entertain in the turn-of-the-century entries and courtyards. Open daily. 5th South and 7th East Sts. (phone: 521-9877).

Liberty Park – Three blocks south on 7th East is 80-acre Liberty Park, with bowers, picnic areas, tennis and horseshoe courts, a swimming pool, a playground, the Tracy Aviary home for birds, an amusement park, and a boating center. 1302 South and 900 East Sts. (phone: 972-6714).

EMIGRATION CANYON

Pioneer Trail State Park – "This is the place," Brigham Young said when he and his entourage caught their first glimpse of the Valley of the Great Salt Lake. And this is where you'll now find the new Pioneer Trail State Park, with 12 renovated buildings from pioneer times, including the Brigham Young Farm Home and the Social Hall. This is also the site of This Is The Place Monument and visitors center, with audio-visual exhibits showing the Mormon trek from Illinois to Utah. Tours of the buildings are available. The park is open daily except on Martin Luther King Day, Presidents' Day, Thanksgiving, Christmas, and New Year's Day. Guided tours through homes from Memorial Day weekend through Labor Day weekend only. Hours vary; call in advance (phone: 533-5881). Emigration Canyon, 2601 Sunnyside Ave.

GREAT SALT LAKE

Great Salt Lake – The most important natural feature of the region, the 73-mile long lake is marshy, salty, sticky, and warm. As you approach it, it may look like nothing more than marshes and weird salt flats. Runoff causing the lake waters to rise and the beaches to flood was a major problem until 1987, when the State of Utah began pumping lake water out to the desert. New beaches have been constructed and the boat harbor at Saltair Beach State Park (at the southern end of the lake) was saved, so there is some water access and minimal facilities. The rising waters have diluted the salt concentration, so while floating is still a unique experience, it's not the fantasy it once was. The water tastes awful and stings terribly if it gets in your eyes, so don't splash. We warn you, too, that the brine flies are sometimes ferocious. 17 miles west on US 40, I-80.

■ **EXTRA SPECIAL:** The 848,000-acre Wasatch National Forest is one of the busiest forests in the country. In the High Uintas Primitive Area, it is full of mountain lakes, rugged spruce, dramatic canyons, and mountain peaks as high as 13,400 feet.

The Utah State Fish and Game Dept. operates a winter elk feeding ground at Hardware Ranch in Logan (phone: 533-9333). There are camping and picnic grounds at Little Cottonwood and Big Cottonwood canyons, only picnicking in Mill Creek. Call the Salt Lake Ranger Station for information (phone: 524-5042). Those closest to the city are the most crowded. Hunting conditions are excellent here. Deer, elk, and moose can be hunted in the fall. A variety of trout swim the streams. Call the Utah Division of Wildlife Resources: 533-9333 for general information; 530-1295 for recorded fishing information; 530-1297 for recorded hunting information. In winter, skiers flock to *Alta,* 25 miles southeast of the city on Rte. 210; *Brighton,* 27 miles southeast on Rte. 152; and *Snowbird,* in Gad Valley, 2 miles from *Alta* (see *Sports*). To get to the eastern section of Wasatch, take US 40, and Rtes. 152, 210; to reach the northern part, follow US 89 and 91. For further information, contact the Supervisor's Office, Wasatch-Cache National Forests, 125 S. State St., Salt Lake City 84138 (phone: 524-5030 for campground information; 364-1581 for avalanche information).

SOURCES AND RESOURCES

TOURIST INFORMATION: For brochures and maps, write, call, or visit the Salt Lake City Convention and Visitors Bureau, 180 S. West Temple, Salt Lake City, UT 84161 (phone: 521-2822). For additional information on Salt Lake City and the State of Utah, contact the Utah Travel Council, Council Hall, Capitol Hill, Salt Lake City, UT 84114 (phone: 538-1030). Information centers are also at Salt Lake City International Airport and Great Salt Lake State Park. For information on winter skiing and summer recreation, call 521-8102.

The best guide to Salt Lake City is the *Salt Lake Visitor's Guide,* a free brochure available from the convention and visitors bureau.

Television Stations – KSL Channel 5–CBS; KTVX Channel 4–ABC; KUTV Channel 2–NBC; KBYU Channel 11–PBS.

Radio Stations – AM: KALL 910 (adult contemporary); KSUN 1490 (news/talk); KSOP 1370 (country). FM: KLVV 99.5 (adult contemporary); KCPX 98.7 (top 40); KISN 97.1 (adult contemporary); KSOP 104.3 (country).

Local Coverage – *Salt Lake Tribune,* morning daily; *Deseret News,* evening daily; *Utah Holiday,* monthly magazine.

Food – The *Deseret News* carries restaurant reviews and listings each Friday evening.

Telephone – The area code for Salt Lake City is 801.

Sales Tax – The sales tax is 6.25%; hotel room tax is 3%.

CLIMATE: Wintertime is for skiing. Spring is beautiful but fickle, with apricot blossoms sometimes covered in snow. Summer is hot and dry, with temperatures climbing into the 90s. Fall is gorgeous, especially in the nearby canyons.

GETTING AROUND: Airport – Salt Lake City International Airport is a 15- to 20-minute ride from downtown; taxi fare should run $9 to $11. Utah Transit Authority buses run hourly from the airport terminals into the city center for 50¢.. Special Downtowner buses run from the airport to downtown hotels on a regular basis.

Bus – For information on bus schedules in and around Salt Lake, call Utah Transit Authority (phone: 287-4636).

Taxi – The best way to get a cab is to call *Yellow Cab* (phone: 521-2100).

Car Rental – All major firms are represented; an inexpensive local alternative is *Holiday/Payless Rent-a-Car,* 1974 W. North Temple (phone: 596-2596).

Trolley – An old-fashioned trolley circles the downtown area and major hotels, with pickup points at Trolley Square and Temple Square. Fare is 50¢. Contact the Utah Transit Authority (phone: 287-4636).

 LOCAL SERVICES: Business Services – *Aztec Typing Service,* 211 E. 3rd South (phone: 364-6806).

Mechanic – *Andy Stevens Automotive,* 458 Montague Ave. (phone: 328-9222).

 MUSEUMS: *Beehive House* is described under *Special Places. Hansen Planetarium* features exhibitions on astronomy and natural science (phone: 538-2098). On the University of Utah campus are the *Utah Museum of Natural History* (phone: 581-6927) and the *Utah Museum of Fine Arts* (phone: 581-7332). Other notable museums are the *Salt Lake Arts Center,* 20 S. West Temple (phone: 328-4201), and the new *Museum of Church History and Art,* 45 N. West Temple (phone: 240-3310).

 MAJOR COLLEGES AND UNIVERSITIES: The University of Utah campus has several theaters, a special events center, and two museums (see *Museums,* above). The university enrolls 25,000 students. Between 14th East and 20th East, 1st South and 5th South (phone: 581-7200).

 SPECIAL EVENTS: On July 24, Salt Lake City celebrates *Pioneer Day,* marking the arrival of the Mormon pioneers. In April and October, thousands of Mormons from all over the world converge on Temple Square for the conferences of the LDS Church. In July, the *Japanese Obon Festival* is held at the Buddhist Temple, 211 W. 1st South. In September, the *Greek Festival* takes place at the Hellenic Memorial Building. For information on other special events, call 521-2822.

 SPORTS AND FITNESS: Baseball – The minor league Salt Lake *Trappers* play from mid-June to Labor Day at *Derks Field,* 65 W. 1300 South (phone: 484-9900).

Basketball – The NBA Utah *Jazz* play in the *Salt Palace* (phone: 363-7681).

Fishing, Hunting, Camping, Backpacking, River Running – At Wasatch National Forest (phone: 524-5030), you can fish, hunt, camp, and backpack (see *Extra Special*). For hunting and fishing regulations, contact the Utah Division of Wildlife Resources, 1596 W. North Temple (phone: 533-9333). For information on backpacking, river running, and primitive wilderness areas in general, call the Bureau of Land Management Office of Public Affairs, 136 E. South Temple (phone: 524-5330).

Fitness Centers – The *Deseret Gym* has a pool, sauna, steam room, track, and basketball, racquetball, and squash courts, 161 N. Main (phone: 359-3911). *Sports Mall Metro* (phone: 328-3116) features a track, sauna, exercise equipment and classes, and squash, racquetball, and handball courts in Crossroads Plaza, near the *Marriott.*

Golf – There are 8 public courses in the Salt Lake valley. The best is *Mountain Dell* (phone: 582-3812), in Parley's Canyon.

Hockey – The Salt Lake *Golden Eagles* play at the *Salt Palace* (phone: 363-7681).

Ice Skating and Sleigh Riding – *Bountiful Recreation Center,* 150 W. 6th North, Bountiful (phone: 298-6120) for ice skating year-round, or *Triad Center* outdoor ice rink, 50 S. 300 West, November through March (phone: 575-5423). *Sugarhouse Park,* 21 S. 16th East, for sleigh riding.

Jogging – Run in Memory Grove Park, half a mile from downtown, or in Liberty Park (1-mile perimeter), about 2 miles from downtown.

Skiing – Utah claims to have the "Greatest Snow on Earth." And certainly, downhill and cross-country skiers from all over the world enthusiastically attest to its excellence. The season runs from mid-November to May or June. For a recorded ski report, call 521-8102. The major ski resorts within half an hour's drive of Salt Lake City are the following.

Alta – The granddaddy of them all, in Little Cottonwood Canyon, has the best and most consistent snow conditions. 25 miles southeast of city on Rte. 210 (phone: 742-3333).

Brighton – At the top of Big Cottonwood Canyon. The average annual snowfall here is 430 inches. 27 miles southeast on Rte. 152 (phone: 943-8309).

Deer Valley – Utah's newest and most stylish ski resort, where the number of skiers is limited, making for short lift lines. Reservations advised. 2 miles south of *Park City* (phone: 649-1000; 649-2000 for ski conditions).

Park City – The US Ski Team's National Training Center, with the longest night-skiing run in the nation. 20 miles east on I-80, up Parley's Canyon (phone: 649-8111).

Snowbird – Also in Little Cottonwood Canyon, *Snowbird* is a jet set resort, with a spectacular tram lift to Hidden Peaks at 11,000 feet. The lift runs in summer, too. Gad Valley, 2 miles from *Alta* (phone: 521-6040).

Swimming – Beaches are open at the Great Salt Lake. Take I-80 west of town. For freshwater swimming try the Raging Waters, a huge aquatic park at 1200 W. 1700 South (phone: 973-9900).

Tennis – There are 17 parks in the city with tennis courts. The most popular are the 16 courts (14 lighted) at Liberty Park. Lessons are available spring and summer only (phone: 538-2165). The University of Utah has quite a few outdoor public courts.

THEATER: The *Pioneer Memorial Theater* on the University of Utah campus is an important regional theater featuring Equity actors in leading roles. The *Babcock Theater,* in the same building, stages more intimate productions (phone: 581-6961 for both). Downtown, the *Salt Lake Acting Company* produces lively drama at 168 W. 500 North (phone: 363-0525). *Theater 138* and *Walk Ons* share a building at 3350 S. Highland Dr. (phone: 484-9801), where they put on newer productions. Check local listings for other groups.

MUSIC: Salt Lake City has many concerts and dance events. For information, call 533-8477. The *Mormon Tabernacle Choir* rehearsals are open to the public on Thursday evenings. No admission charge. Temple Square. The *Utah Symphony Orchestra, Ballet West, Ririe-Woodbury Dance Company,* and *Repertory Dance Theater* perform at *Symphony Hall* and the *Capitol Theater.* Big-name rock and country artists perform at the *Salt Palace,* 100 S. West Temple (phone: 363-7681).

NIGHTCLUBS AND NIGHTLIFE: *Room at the Top* in the *Salt Lake Hilton,* 150 W. 5th South, has a piano bar and fine food (phone: 532-3344). The *Zephyr,* 301 S. West Temple (phone: 355-9913), features live jazz and blues. More comfortable but less trendy is Salt Lake City's oldest private club, *D. B. Cooper's,* 19 E. 200 South (phone: 532-2948). Utah liquor laws require that tourists buy a 2-week membership ($5) for clubs, which entitles you to bring four friends.

BEST IN TOWN

 CHECKING IN: Since more than 10 million people a year visit Utah, it's logical to expect a decent selection of hotels in Salt Lake City. You won't be disappointed. Tourism is Utah's largest single industry, and accommodations are plentiful and varied. Expect to pay between $60 and $110 for a double room in those places we've listed as expensive; between $45 and $60 for those we've designated as moderate; and between $35 and $45 in inexpensive places. All telephone numbers are in the 801 area code unless otherwise indicated.

Salt Lake Hilton – Exuding an aura of contemporary sophistication, this 351-room property has suites with sunken baths; there is an outdoor swimming pool, therapy pool, sauna, 2 dining rooms, and 2 clubs. A package store on the premises sells liquor. Pets are welcome. 150 W. 5th South (phone: 532-3344 or 800-HILTONS). Expensive.

Salt Lake Marriott – The 515-room hotel has 2 restaurants, a lounge, an indoor pool, saunas, a liquor store, and direct access to the Crossroads Mall. Guests have privileges at an adjoining health spa for racquetball, squash, and tennis. The 16-story structure is opposite the *Salt Palace* on the corner of West Temple and 1st South (phone: 531-0800 or 800-228-9290). Expensive.

Little America – On the city's main thoroughfare, within walking distance of the downtown shopping area and convention center, this 850-room hotel has year-round swimming in an indoor-outdoor pool, plus another outdoor pool, wading pool, saunas, and weight-lifting room. Children under 12 free. Free bus service to the airport. 500 S. Main St. (phone: 363-6781). Expensive to moderate.

Carlton – A small (56 rooms), older hotel in the downtown area. Recently remodeled, it offers a refrigerator and recliner in each room, plus sauna, Jacuzzi, and small exercise room. 140 E. South Temple (phone: 355-3418). Moderate.

Peery – The oldest hotel in the city, completely renovated in 1985, it is small (just 77 rooms) but elegant, with the charm of the early 1900s. Amenities include an outstanding café, complimentary continental breakfast, newspaper, shoeshine, and social hour from 5 to 7 PM Mondays through Thursdays. Two restaurants; free airport transportation. 110 W. 3rd South (phone: 521-4300). Moderate.

Tri Arc – A 13-story high-rise built in an unusual arc to give every one of the 380 rooms a view of the valley. The panoramic view from the top is spectacular. Amenities include satellite TV, an outdoor pool, and a heliport. The *13th Floor Supper Club* and the *Golden Spike* restaurants are popular with residents (open daily). Children under 14 free. 161 W. 6th South (phone: 521-7373). Moderate.

Comfort Inn–Salt Lake Airport/International Center – Conveniently located just 7 miles from downtown and 2½ miles from the airport, it has 160 rooms (some of which are do not allow smoking) and 4 executive suites. Other features: remote-control color TV sets, a heated pool (open in season), a spa (open year-round), a restaurant serving 3 meals daily, and complimentary coffee and tea. 200 N. Admiral Byrd Rd. (phone: 537-7444 or 800-228-5151). Inexpensive.

Temple Square – Another centrally located hotel, this is the city's best modest hostelry. Remodeled in 1989, it offers free parking and has a coffee shop on the premises. The keynote here is function rather than fancy. Across the street from Temple Square at 75 W. South Temple (phone: 355-2961). Inexpensive.

TraveLodge Salt Palace – Within walking distance of downtown, it features 130 rooms, a restaurant, an outdoor pool open year-round, a sauna, a whirlpool bath, and complimentary shuttle to the airport. Kids under 12 free. 215 W. North Temple (phone: 532-1000 or 800-255-3050). Inexpensive.

EATING OUT: Salt Lake Valley restaurants offer a number of different cuisines, from continental to seafood, steaks, and chops. Expect to pay between $40 and $50 for two at those places we've listed as expensive; between $20 and $30 at those places designated moderate; under $20, inexpensive. Prices do not include drinks, wine, or tips. All telephone numbers are in the 801 area code unless otherwise indicated. Special note: The larger restaurants have liquor licenses; otherwise diners have to bring their own from the nearest state liquor store (closed on Sundays). You can expect a small setup fee at many restaurants.

La Caille at Quail Run – One of Utah's finest restaurants, in a château (styled as an 18th-century French maison) a few miles from the city, serves food commensurate with its well-appointed surroundings. The dining room, overlooking the formal gardens of the estate, features French cuisine and a popular Sunday brunch. Open daily for dinner, Sundays for brunch. Reservations necessary. Major credit cards. 9565 Wasatch Blvd. (phone: 942-1751). Expensive.

La Fleur de Lys – A downtown dining spot featuring traditional French cuisine in an elegant, unhurried atmosphere. Open from 5:30 to 10 PM; closed Sundays. Reservations advised. Major credit cards. 165 S. West Temple St., in Arrow Press Square (phone: 359-5753). Expensive.

Bird's Café – Pleasant dining amid San Francisco–style grill decor. They handle the basics — fresh fish, pasta, beef, and lamb — with deft and tempting touches. Open for lunch and dinner daily; brunch only on Sundays. Evening reservations advised. Major credit cards. 1355 E. 21st South (phone: 466-1051). Moderate.

Market Street Grill – A popular gathering spot, especially at lunchtime, it's in a handsomely renovated old building. The menu features fresh seafood (flown in daily) as well as steaks, prime ribs, and lamb. There's also an oyster bar. Open daily. Reservations advised for breakfast and lunch in the grill. Major credit cards. 60 Post Office Pl. (phone: 322-4668; oyster bar, 531-6044). Moderate.

Lamb's – In business since the early 1900s, this old-fashioned downtown restaurant has become an institution. This is where the city's power brokers power lunch. A surprisingly extensive menu, good seafood. Open daily except Sundays from 7 AM to 9 PM. Reservations accepted. Major credit cards. 169 S. Main St. (phone: 364-7166). Moderate to inexpensive.

Café Pierpont – A south-of-the-border restaurant that caters to families, near downtown in a renovated old school. Try the fajitas or the huge mesquite-broiled T-bone. Open for lunch weekdays, for dinner Saturdays and Sundays. Major credit cards. 122 W. Pierpont (phone: 364-1222). Inexpensive.

Marianne's Delicatessen – For fans of German specialties, from homemade sausages to scrumptious desserts. Besides brimming delicacies to go, there are hot specials and a long list of sandwiches. Be prepared for a bit of a wait if you arrive between noon and 1 PM. Open Tuesdays through Saturdays for lunch from 11 AM to 3 PM; deli open 9 AM to 6 PM. 149 W. 2nd South (phone: 364-0513). Inexpensive.

Old Spaghetti Factory – One of the more popular inexpensive eating places in town, it has lots of friendly ambience. You may find yourself dining on an old brass bed or in a trolley car, with turn-of-the-century furnishings and memorabilia around. Spaghetti comes in all styles, but try the clam sauce. Open daily. No reservations. 189 Trolley Square (phone: 521-0424). Inexpensive.

Windows on the Square – In *Weinstock's* department store, this eatery offers basic American food, good family atmosphere, and an unbeatable view of Temple Square (ask for a window seat). Open 11 AM every day; closing times vary with store hours. In the Crossroads Mall (phone: 524-2677). Inexpensive.

SAN ANTONIO

Fed up with politics after failing to win reelection to Congress in 1835, Davy Crockett told his Tennessee constituents, "You kin all go to hell, I'm a-goin' to Texas." And so he did. He ended up in San Antonio just in time to join the Texians at the Alamo in their struggle to gain independence from Mexico. (The citizens became "Texans" after severing their ties with Mexico.) He fought alongside Colonels William Travis and James Bowie, who showed Crockett the original bowie knife and said, "You might tickle a fellow's ribs a long time with this instrument before you'd make him laugh." And certainly Santa Anna and his 5,000 soldiers did not go away laughing when the 187 Texas heroes withstood their might, and greatly weakened their ranks, before finally succumbing to the greater force. Though all the fighters for Texas went down in the battle, Crockett (among the last surviving) made his final stand with a lunge at the Mexican general and was promptly dispatched by the swords of the Mexican soldiers.

Today the Alamo still stands, at the center of a cosmopolitan area that blends the old Texas, with its classic Spanish influence, and the largely Texan-Mexican (Tex-Mex) style of today. Alongside numerous well-preserved reminders of days gone by, the missions and lovely adobe buildings, stand modern steel skyscrapers. Established in 1718 by Spanish missionaries who came to convert the Indians, San Antonio drew thousands of pioneers from around the world. Many ethnic groups remain today, but the largest is the Mexican Americans, who make up over half of the city's population of just over 1 million. The city is largely bilingual, but beyond this mix of cultures is a great disparity in economics; San Antonio is a city of poverty and wealth, with pockets of posh suburbs sharing the same pair of pants with pockets of poverty. Here, where the great post–Civil War cattle boom originated, rich Texas ranchers and bankers live in fabulous homes, which are as far as you can get from the public housing units occupied by the poor. But in recent years, the Mexican-Americans have gained political power. Two congressmen and over half of San Antonio's state legislative delegation and City Council are of Mexican descent.

Military tradition runs deep in the city's blood. Teddy Roosevelt recruited his famous Rough Riders in the bar of the *Hotel Menger*. Several aviation "firsts" were established at Ft. Sam Houston in 1910 by Lt. Benjamin D. Foulois when he reported, "My first takeoff, my first solo, my first landing, and my first crash on the same day." San Antonio's current military record is somewhat more stable if less flamboyant. Five military installations with more than 60,000 active duty personnel and civilian employees make the federal government the city's major employer. More than 70,000 enlisted men and women a year undergo basic training at Lackland Training Center, the cradle of the Air Force.

Since 1968, San Antonio has been an authentic tourist magnet. That was the year of HemisFair, a World's Fair celebrating San Antonio's 200th birthday, which left the city with a valuable convention center, the *Lila M. Cockrell Theater for the Performing Arts,* and the Institute of Texan Cultures. Even more important, the year long celebration focused attention on the city's forgotten architectural treasures. La Villita, San Antonio's oldest residential neighborhood, was restored with lovely adobe buildings housing authentic Mexican artisan shops. Homes in the King William District, where the German community lived in grandeur in the 19th century, were restored and feature German stonemasonry as well as almost every notable style of American architecture of the past century. And to walk on the Paseo del Río, the river walk that traces the horseshoe course of the San Antonio River in town, is to step into a people-scale tropical paradise of banana palms and bougainvillea only steps away from apartments, shops, cafés, and San Antonio's business center.

SAN ANTONIO AT-A-GLANCE

SEEING THE CITY: The Tower of the Americas, San Antonio's most visible landmark, at 622 feet, offers the best vantage point from which to view the city and the surrounding countryside. From the observation deck you see flatland stretching to the south and gently rolling hills to the northwest, leading to the Texas Hill Country. Directly below are the buildings of HemisFair Plaza, the site of the 1968 World's Fair, and a tributary of the San Antonio River that cuts a horseshoe path through town and branches into HemisFair Plaza and Rivercenter Mall.

SPECIAL PLACES: The heart of San Antonio is great for walking, with the lovely Paseo del Río (River Walk) tracing the course of the river, and short distances between many of the attractions. Visitors can also take a slow-paced, horse-drawn carriage tour of downtown and the King William District. Carriages are available daily, from 10 AM to about 10 PM, and leave from the Alamo. Other sights, including the missions along Mission Trail and the zoo, are best reached by car or bus.

CENTRAL CITY

The Alamo – Where Davy Crockett, Col. James Bowie, Col. Travis, and the 184 other Texas heroes fought against Mexican dictator Santa Anna and his force of 5,000 in Texas's 1836 struggle for independence. Established in 1718 by Spanish priests as Mission San Antonio de Valero, the original mission has been restored and the site turned into a block-square state park that includes a museum with displays on the Alamo and Texas history, with an excellent weapon collection of Mexican folk art featuring derringers, swords, and an original bowie knife. Open daily. No admission charge. Alamo Plaza (phone: 222-1693). After visiting the Alamo, it's easy stroll along the Paseo del Río, which now reaches the west side of S. Alamo St., directly across from the park; the steps from street level are bounded by a series of waterfalls that lead to the *Hyatt* hotel.

La Villita – This little Spanish town in the center of the city looks very much as it did 250 years ago, when it was San Antonio's first residential area. Girded by a stone

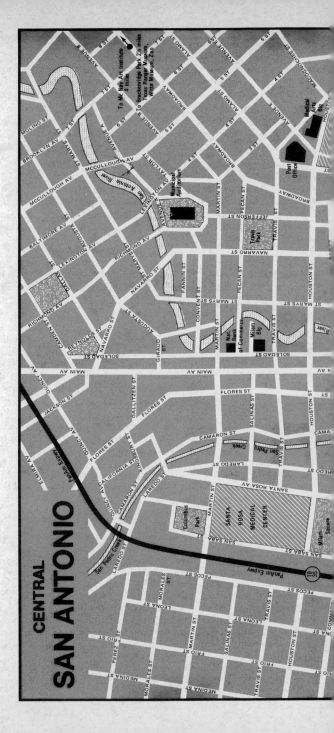

CENTRAL
SAN ANTONIO

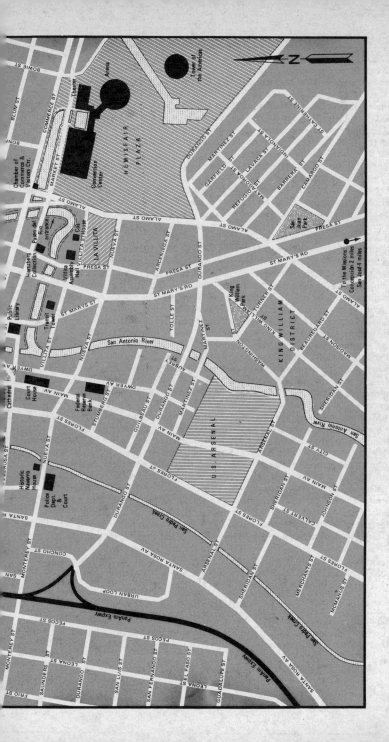

wall and surrounded by banana palms and bougainvillea, the stone patios and adobe dwellings have been authentically restored and now house artisans' shops where many of the old crafts — glass blowing, weaving, dollmaking, and pottery — are still practiced. Among the buildings are the restored Cos House (1835), where General Cos, commander of the Mexican forces, surrendered to the Texians; and the *Old San Antonio Museum,* featuring displays on Texas history and pleasant outdoor cafés. Open daily. No admission charge. One square city block bounded by the river on the north, Nueva St. on the south, S. Alamo St. on the east, and Villita St. on the west. Main office, 416 Villita St. (phone: 299-8610).

Paseo del Río – A branch of the San Antonio River winds like a horseshoe through the central business district. Stone stairways lead down to the River Walk which, only 20 feet below street level, is as far from the world of the business district as you can get. Tall trees, tropical foliage, and banana palms line the walks dotted with curio and craft shops, night spots and cafés, and an increasing number of fashionable apartments. You can experience the river on a barge and dine by candlelight aboard some. Make arrangements through the barge office, 430 E. Commerce St. (phone: 222-1701).

HemisFair Plaza – A legacy of the 1968 World's Fair, HemisFair Plaza features the Tower of the Americas with its panoramic view of Texas countryside, a convention center, the *Lila M. Cockrell Theater for the Performing Arts,* shops, and several modern buildings that have exhibitions. The Institute of Texan Cultures examines the influence of 26 different ethnic groups — including the Mexicans, Germans, Poles, Hungarians, and Irish — who developed the state. There are films, slide shows, and exhibitions of artifacts including Mexican stone cooking equipment and examples of the dress of each of the groups. Closed Mondays. No admission charge (phone: 226-7651).

San Antonio Museum of Art – Rapidly gaining recognition as one of the Southwest's best museums, *SAMA* occupies the buildings that once housed the Lone Star Brewing Company. Its most recent permanent display is Con Cariño (with affection), a Mexican folk art collection. Nelson A. Rockefeller's extensive private collection comprises the bulk of Con Cariño, reported to be the largest such collection in the US. Open daily. 200 W. Jones Ave. (phone: 226-5544).

El Mercado – Though the original marketplace has been renovated, it is still lined with Spanish buildings and retains its old market flavor, with Mexican merchants who do their best to lure you into shops offering handcrafted objects like baskets, piñatas, pottery, silver jewelry. Open daily. 515 W. Commerce St. (phone: 299-8600).

Spanish Governor's Palace – The only Spanish colonial mansion remaining in Texas. Built in 1749 for the Spanish governors when Texas was a province of Spain, the palace has 3-foot-thick walls, a keystone above the door bearing the Hapsburg coat of arms, original Spanish furnishings, and a floor of native flagstone. Open daily. Admission charge. 105 Military Plaza (phone: 224-0601).

Hertzberg Circus Collection – If you're a circus fanatic, you'll go ring crazy here with displays of artifacts tracing the development of the circus from its English origins to P. T. Barnum and the American three-ring extravaganza. Particularly strong in miniatures featuring the original carriage of Tom Thumb and an entire circus in one room. Open daily; closed Sundays November to April. No admission charge. 210 W. Market St. in Library Annex (phone: 299-7810).

SOUTH SIDE

Missions – The Alamo was the first of five missions established under Spanish rule. All except the Alamo are still active parish churches and are located along the well-marked Mission Trail, starting at the southern tip of the city. The most notable to see are the following:

Mission Concepción – The oldest unrestored church in the country is remarkably well preserved, with original frescoes made by the padres and Indians from a mixture of vegetable and mineral dyes. Open daily. 807 Mission Rd. (phone: 229-5732).

Mission San José – Called the Queen of the Missions, it's the finest and largest example of early mission life. The original parish church, built of limestone and tufa, features Rosa's Window, an impressive stone carving, and is surrounded by a 6-acre compound including a restored mill, Indian quarters, and granary. Open daily. 6539 San José Dr., 6 miles south on US 281 (phone: 229-4770).

Buckhorn Hall of Horns – Once an old shoot-'em-up saloon, this hall was transported lock, stock, and barrel by the Lone Star Brewing Company to tamer grounds. The collection is as wild as ever — some of the fastest guns in the West, and hunting trophies of everything imaginable from horns and antlers of elk, buffalo, and antelope to whole polar and grizzly bears. Open daily. Admission charge. 600 Lone Star Blvd. on the company's grounds (phone: 226-8303).

NORTH SIDE

Brackenridge Park – This 343-acre park includes the Southwest's largest zoo. Rock cliffs provide a backdrop for fine displays of animals in their natural settings. Over 3,500 specimens of 800 species are represented and best are the Monkey Island, an outdoor hippo pool, open bear pits, and a children's zoo nursery. Open daily. Admission charge. 3903 N. St. Mary's (phone: 734-7183).

San Antonio Botanical Gardens – A living museum of diverse plant life, ranging from desert to tropical, is presented in lovely formal gardens on this 33-acre site near downtown. The gardens' centerpiece is the Lucile Halsell Conservatory, a 90,000-square-foot belowground central courtyard surrounded by a complex of greenhouses. Open daily except Mondays from 9 AM to 6 PM; conservatory to 5 PM. Admission charge. 555 Funston (phone: 821-5115).

McNay Art Institute – Small but fine collections include works by Picasso and Chagall among displays of international scope and exhibitions of regional artists. Open daily. No admission charge. 6000 N. New Braunfels (phone: 824-5368).

WEST SIDE

Sea World of Texas – The world's largest marine entertainment showplace, on 250 acres of rolling hills 20 miles west of San Antonio. It features spectacular performances of killer whales, sea lions, and dolphins; professional water skiing and speed boat shows; concerts; and other events. Open Wednesdays through Sundays in winter, daily the rest of the year. 10500 Sea World Dr., reached by city bus service (phone: 225-4903).

■**EXTRA SPECIAL:** The *Grey Moss Inn,* in Grey Forest, a wildlife sanctuary only a few minutes from downtown, offers outdoor dining on a shaded patio where you can have charcoal-broiled steaks, seafood, or chicken prepared on an open grill. You may see a white-tailed deer grazing nearby as you dine. Indoor dining centers around a fireplace (see *Eating Out*). Open daily for dinner only. Reservations advised. Major credit cards. Scenic Loop Rd., 12 miles from the Bandera Rd. Loop 410 Interchange (phone: 695-8301).

SOURCES AND RESOURCES

TOURIST INFORMATION: General tourist information, brochures, maps, and events calendars are available at the San Antonio Convention and Visitors Bureau, 121 Alamo Plaza, San Antonio, TX 78205 (phone: 299-8123; or write: PO Box 2277, San Antonio, TX 78298). More convenient is the San Antonio Visitor Information Center, directly across from the Alamo, at 317 Alamo Plaza, San Antonio, TX 78205 (phone: 299-8155). The *San Antonio Convention & Visitor's Guide* (free) is a good area guide.

Television Stations – KEWS Channel 5–CBS; KMOL Channel 4–NBC; KSAT Channel 12–ABC; KLRN Channel 9–PBS.

Radio Stations – AM: WOAI 1200 (news/talk); KTSA 550 (pop music); KKYX 68 (country). FM: KTFM 102.7 (top 40); KMMX 106 (soft rock); KITY 92.9 (top 40); Y100 100.3 (country).

Local Coverage – The *San Antonio Express-News,* morning and afternoon daily and the *San Antonio Light,* morning and afternoon daily. Both papers are available at newsstands. Paseo del Río Association's *Showboat* lists upcoming events and is available at the convention and visitor's bureau and in hotel lobbies.

Telephone – The area code for San Antonio is 512.

Sales Tax – The basic sales tax is 7.5%; hotel room tax is 13%.

 CLIMATE: Known as the place where "sunshine spends the winter," San Antonio winters are, naturally, sunny and mild with temperatures averaging above 50F. If you like hot weather, summers are blistering and humid, with temperatures over 90F and lots of sunshine except for an occasional tropical storm from the Gulf of Mexico.

 GETTING AROUND: Airport – San Antonio International Airport is about a 15-minute drive from downtown; a taxi ride will run about $12. Buses also run between the airport and downtown during certain hours in the morning and afternoon for 75¢; call VIA Metropolitan Transit (phone: 227-2020) for schedules. Limousine service is provided by most major hotels.

Bus – San Antonio Metropolitan Transit System serves all sections of the city. The basic fare is 40¢; second-zone (outside I-410) is an additional 10¢; and express buses are 75¢. Complete route and tourist information is available from the Transit Office, 800 W. Myrtle St. (phone: 227-2020).

Streetcar – Attractive reproductions of antique trolleys (on rubber wheels) follow five distinct tourist and traffic loops to and through major points of interest around the city. The fare is 10¢. Free maps are available from any visitor center.

Taxi – Cabs may be ordered by phone or picked up at taxi stations in front of major hotels. Some will answer a hail in the street, most will not. Two of the largest companies are *Checker* (phone: 222-2151) and *Yellow* (phone: 226-4242).

Car Rental – All national firms are represented, but one of the best for the budget-minded is *Budget Rent-A-Car,* at San Antonio International Airport, 9245 John Saunders (phone: 828-5693).

 LOCAL SERVICES: Babysitting – *Northside Sitters Club,* 2500 Jackson Keller (phone: 341-9313).

Business Services – *Manpower,* Interfirst Plaza Bldg., 300 Convent (phone: 224-9251).

Mechanic – *Faulk's Exxon Car Care Center,* 802 San Pedro Ave. (phone: 224-9531).

MUSEUMS: The *Alamo Museum,* the *Hertzberg Collection,* the *McNay Institute,* the *Buckhorn Hall of Horns,* and the *Institute of Texan Cultures* are described in *Special Places.* Other interesting museums to visit:

San Antonio Museum of Art – Open daily. 200 W. Jones Ave. (phone: 226-5544).

Texas Ranger Museum – Closed Mondays, Tuesdays. 3805 Broadway (phone: 822-9011).

Witte Memorial Museum – Open daily. 3801 Broadway (phone: 226-5544).

ART GALLERIES: Artists and craftsmen from all over the world are finding that San Antonio is an accommodating place to live and work. The art colony is growing rapidly, and galleries are numerous. Try the *Raul Gutierrez Gallery of Fine Arts* for Western oils, acrylics, and bronzes (8940 Wurzbach; phone: 696-5356), and *La Villita*, where well-known Southwest craftsmen ply skills ranging from glass blowing to weaving (420 Paseo de la Villita; phone: 299-8610). At the *Southwest Craft Center* (300 Augusta; phone: 224-1848), you can also watch art objects being created.

MAJOR COLLEGES AND UNIVERSITIES: With ten colleges and universities, San Antonio has a large student population. The major educational institutions are the University of Texas at San Antonio, Loop 1604, 17 miles north of downtown (phone: 691-4011); St. Mary's University, 1 Camino Santa Maria (phone: 436-3011); Trinity University, 715 Stadium Dr. (phone: 736-7011); the University of Texas Health Science Center, 7703 Floyd Curl (phone: 567-7000); Incarnate Word College, 4301 Broadway (phone: 828-1261); and Our Lady of the Lake University, 411 SW 24th (phone: 434-6711).

SPECIAL EVENTS: A city of fiestas, the most elaborate blowout is the 10-day *Fiesta San Antonio* in mid-April, celebrating Sam Houston's victory over Santa Anna with parades, the *Battle of the Flowers,* the *Fiesta Flambeau* in the streets, and the *Fiesta River Parade* with lighted floats on the river, a king and queen, and lots of food and drink for the subjects. The *Starving Artists Show* in early April has works of art by hungry local artists for nothing much more than $20; everyone is trying to make ends meet so they can eat at the fiesta. San Antonio celebrates the Mexican defeat of the French in the Battle of Puebla in true Mexican form during the *Cinco de Mayo* festival, at Market Square during the first weekend in May.

SPORTS AND FITNESS: Baseball – The San Antonio *Dodgers* minor league team plays at *V. J. Keefe Field,* St. Mary's University (phone: 434-9311).

Basketball – The NBA *Spurs* play at the *Convention Center Arena* from October through March; tickets at the Arena in HemisFair Plaza (phone: 224-9578).

Fitness Center – The *YMCA* has a pool, track, weights, and handball and racquetball courts. 903 N. St. Mary's and Lexington (phone: 227-5221).

Golf – There are 17 courses in the city in constant use all year round. Best for visitors is *Olmos Basin Municipal Course,* 7022 McCullough (phone: 826-4041).

Jogging – Run along the River Walk early or late in the day; up Broadway to Brackenridge Park; or follow the Mission Trail, along Mission Road (the marathon route), to the missions.

Swimming – There are 17 municipal pools open May through Labor Day (phone: 299-3000). Best is Alamo Heights Pool, 229 Greeley St. For serious lap swimmers, two 50-meter pools are open year-round: Northside Aquatics Center, 7001 Culebra (phone: 681-4026); and Blossom Athletic Center, 12002 Jones-Maltsberger (phone: 494-3775).

Tennis – *McFarlin Tennis Center* is a municipal facility. Courts are $2 per person per hour before 5 PM, $3 afterward. Reservations advised. 1503 San Pedro Ave. (phone: 732-1223).

THEATER: More than a dozen theaters offer a continuing and varied fare of traveling and locally produced shows, the most impressive of which is the *Majestic Theater,* 214 E. Houston St. (phone: 226-2626). This incredibly ornate structure has been restored to its 1920s grandeur and now hosts everything from traveling national theater companies to rock concerts. The area's colleges and universities also produce plays. For shows: *San Antonio Little Theater,* off the 1500 block of San Pedro (phone: 733-7258); *Harlequin Dinner Theater,* Ft. Sam Houston (phone: 221-5953); *Melodrama Playhouse,* 300 HemisFair Plaza (phone: 271-0300); *Alamo Community Theater,* 339 W. Josephine (phone: 734-4646); and *Arneson River Theater* on Villita St. and the river (phone: 299-8610), where the stage and terraced hillside of the audience are separated by the river, and an occasional passing barge upstages the actors.

 MUSIC: The *San Antonio Symphony* performs with guest stars from September through May. Offices at 109 Lexington Ave. (phone: 225-6161).

 NIGHTCLUBS AND NIGHTLIFE: Pop music, jazz, Dixieland, folk, rock, and country-western are all offered at San Antonio's many pubs, taverns, and nightclubs. For a little country, try the *Farmer's Daughter,* 542 North W. W. White Rd. (phone: 333-7391). For jazz, try *Jim Cullum's Landing,* 522 River Walk (phone: 223-7266). You may want to try the nostalgia of *Larry Herman's Roaring 20's,* 13445 Blanco Rd. (phone: 492-1353).

BEST IN TOWN

 CHECKING IN: You can find all of the things you're probably looking for in San Antonio's hotels, like comfortable and convenient accommodations. Expect to pay $95 or more for a double room for a night in the expensive category and $60 to $85 in the moderate range. All telephone numbers are in the 512 area code unless otherwise indicated.

Hilton Palacio del Río – Right on the riverside, at the liveliest corner of Paseo del Río, the *Hilton* makes the best use of its prime location. The *El Comedor Dining Room* serves alfresco on the River Walk, half of the 484 rooms in this attractive Spanish-style building have river views, and there is an elevator stop that lets you off at river's edge. Also features a rooftop pool, free coffee in rooms, meeting rooms, shops, and *Durty Nellie's* pub, where you can let loose with an Irish lullaby. 200 S. Alamo St. (phone: 222-1400). Expensive.

Hyatt Regency, San Antonio – Most of the 633 rooms in this 16-story hotel built around an atrium have views of the San Antonio River and Old San Antonio. For dining and drinking, there's *La Puerta on the River Walk,* and *Caps* and the multilevel *River Terrace Lounge* in the atrium. Pool. 123 Losoya (phone: 222-1234). Expensive.

La Mansion del Río – This hotel combines a Spanish-style building with a restored 1852 building that was originally part of St. Mary's University. Nicely designed, with 335 rooms overlooking either the river or an inner courtyard and a pool. Features the *Capistrano Room* and *Las Canarias* restaurants and the *El Colegio* bar. 112 College St. (phone: 225-2581). Expensive.

Plaza – A spacious garden hotel on nearly 5 acres, accented by tropical gardens, tall native Texas trees, and sparkling fountains. Its 252 rooms have balconies overlooking La Villita Historic District. The *Anaqua* restaurant has a distinctive international menu. Incorporated into the complex are 3 restored 19th-century bungalows, which are a functional part of the hotel's entertainment facilities. Pool, exercise rooms, sauna, and tennis courts. 555 S. Alamo (phone: 229-1000). Expensive.

Wyndham – This 328-room property, with an exterior of polished pink granite, opened in 1985. With its 20,000 square feet of meeting space, the hotel is a boon to business travelers, though anyone can appreciate its 2 large swimming pools, exercise room and sauna, and attractive 2-story lobby with brass sculptures and a marble bar. 9803 Colonnade (phone: 691-8888). Expensive.

Crockett – Behind the Alamo since 1909, it recently emerged from a $15-million renovation as one of the nicest of San Antonio's "old" hotels. Some of the 200 rooms are small, but all are beautifully decorated. The most impressive accommodations are the luxurious 7th-floor suites overlooking the Alamo grounds. *Lela B's* restaurant serves meat salads (turkey, duck, steak) and the like at lunch, weekdays, and continental fare for dinner, daily. 320 Bonham (phone: 225-6500). Expensive to moderate.

Inter-Continental, San Antonio – Richness envelops guests who enter the lobby, a by-product of the Empire chandeliers, Oriental rugs, marble and hand-painted Mexican tiles, and a rosewood and gold-leaf grand piano. This is the old, landmark *St. Anthony,* handsomely restored. The *Jefferson Manor* restaurant (one of the city's best) serves traditional American specialties in the setting of a Monticello estate; the hotel also has another restaurant, several bars, a rooftop garden, 24-hour room service, and a pool. 300 E. Travis St. (phone: 227-4392). Expensive to moderate.

San Antonio Marriott Rivercenter – Directly across the street from the convention center and nestled in a bend of the San Antonio River, it is one of the city's newest and largest hotels. Most striking is its 7-story atrium with an indoor-outdoor heated swimming pool. *Gambits* on the River Walk, a 2-story nightclub, opens up onto the river; the *Cabrillo* features live entertainment; and the *Cactus Flower Café* has riverside dining on its patio. 711 E. River Walk (phone: 224-4555). Expensive to moderate.

La Quinta – Two blocks from the river, this 2-story Spanish building offers comfortable, convenient accommodations at good prices. Pool, TV sets, café. 130 rooms. 1001 E. Commerce St. (phone: 222-9181). Also La Quinta Airport, 333 NE Loop 410 (phone: 828-0781). Both moderate.

Radisson Gunter – Opened in 1909, this hotel was twice declared a Texas landmark. A turn-of-the-century atmosphere still pervades the lobby, with its crystal chandeliers, marble floor, and dark mahogany paneling. More modern are the 326 high-ceilinged rooms with tile baths. International and Texas specialties are served in the *Café Suisse* restaurant; *Pâtisserie Suisse* is a European-style bakery; and there's dancing at *Padre Muldoon's,* a Victorian saloon. 205 E. Houston St. (phone: 227-3241). Moderate.

El Tropicano – Six blocks from the heart of downtown, at the north end of the River Walk, and thus a good place from which to tour the river on foot or by water taxi. 110 Lexington Ave. (phone: 223-9461). Moderate.

EATING OUT: Some 26 ethnic groups pioneered Texas, and its current large military population has brought back a taste for exotic dishes from remote areas of the globe, resulting in a wide variety of restaurants. However, most folks would agree that San Antonio's best restaurants are Mexican. Non-Texans (outlanders, as they're called down here) are generally surprised (happily) by the prices. Our selections range in price from $50 or more for dinner for two in the expensive range, $25 to $40 in the moderate range, and under $20 inexpensive. Prices do not include drinks, wine, or tips. All telephone numbers are in the 512 area code unless otherwise indicated.

Arthur's – Expert service amid stylish surroundings, with a menu of seafood, meat, and poultry dishes. Shipments of white asparagus from France, fish from Boston, and strawberries from Peru arrive daily, adding further gustatory interest. The *Cabaret Bar* is a good spot for jazz. Open daily for dinner only. Reservations advised. Major credit cards. 4001 Broadway on the Boardwalk (phone: 826-3200). Expensive.

Fig Tree – Long, leisurely dinners with excellent service are the rule at this 19th-century adobe house. In the rare event that you have to wait for a table, have a drink on the balcony overlooking the San Antonio River. Specialties are seafood and beef. La Villita section, a few blocks from the Alamo site. Open daily for dinner only. Reservations advised. Major credit cards. 515 Paseo de la Villita (phone: 224-1976). Expensive.

La Louisiane – When it opened in 1935, this fine French and Créole restaurant offered full dinners for 75¢ to $1.25. Imminent failure was forecast by residents, who said it was too expensive for San Antonio. Today, a couple can go all out with an elegant $65 to $75 production that includes pompano en papillote (poached with oyster and shrimp in white wine sauce), frogs' legs sauté meunière, and three vintage wines; or some excellent dishes on a less grand scale. *La Louisiane* has won many national awards for its food and service. Closed Sundays and Mondays. Reservations advised. Major credit cards. 2632 Broadway (phone: 225-7984). Expensive.

PJ's – A table at this sophisticated hangout is the best seat in town for watching the River Walk scene. The cuisine is French nouvelle and excellent, with an emphasis on fresh fish and lightly sauced meats. The service, by tuxedoed waiters, wins constant praise. *PJ's* can be reached by river taxi from the Casa Río boat dock. Closed Sundays. Reservations advised. Major credit cards. 1 River Walk Pl., at St. Mary's (phone: 225-8400). Expensive.

Grey Moss Inn – To get to this historic inn in Texas hill country, you have to drive through some of the loveliest scenery around (see *Extra Special*). Mesquite-grilled steaks are the specialty. Open daily for dinner only. Reservations — and directions — essential. Major credit cards. On Scenic Loop Rd., about 15 miles northwest of town (phone: 695-8301). Expensive to moderate.

Café du Vin – As its name implies, wine is the star here. It covers one entire wall of this bright and pleasant café, and since it's sold at retail with only a 20% corkage fee, diners can afford to indulge more than a little. There's wine by the glass, too. The food is American nouvelle, with dishes like blackened shrimp, veal tortellini, and bacon, lobster, and tomato sandwiches. Open daily. Reservations advised. Major credit cards. Castle Oaks Village, 8055 West Ave. (phone: 349-4672). Moderate.

Cappy's – This is the kind of place where folks head after work on Fridays to let down their hair. It's comfy and familiar, with exposed brick walls and lots of natural wood, and choices include everything from light salads and burgers to more elaborate fish and meat entrées. Open daily. Major credit cards. 5011 Broadway, Alamo Heights (phone: 828-9669), and 123 Northwest Loop 410 (phone: 366-1700). Moderate.

Crumpets – Soothing is the word for the atmosphere here: It's the classical music, quietly elegant room, and superlative desserts turned out by the restaurant's pastry shop next door. Try the buttercream cake or fresh fruit tart. Preceding dessert is some very good light continental fare. Open daily. Major credit cards. 5800 Broadway, Alamo Heights (phone: 821-5454). Moderate.

L'Etoile – This lively bistro turns out the kind of solid cooking that has given French food a good name — salmon in pastry shell, pâté, beef Wellington, and bouillabaisse. Inside, it's all light wood and soft colors under a skylit cathedral ceiling. There's also dining outdoors. Open daily. Reservations advised for dinner. Major credit cards. 6106 Broadway, Alamo Heights (phone: 826-4551). Moderate.

Mama's – Good food in a family atmosphere with everything from burgers to steaks. Specialty of the house is chicken-fried mushrooms. A volleyball court and basketball hoop are set up in the fenced backyard so kids can work off their energies while Mom and Pop have a leisurely after-dinner drink. Open daily till the wee hours. Major credit cards. 9907 San Pedro (phone: 349-2314). Moderate.

El Bosque – Excellent Mexican food in a country setting 15 minutes from downtown. Try the menu's Extra Special No. 1, which includes the works: enchiladas, refried beans, Spanish rice, tamales, tortillas, chiles con queso, guacamole salad. The chiles rellenos are a house specialty. Cocktails and Mexican beer. Open daily. Major credit cards. 12656 West Ave. (phone: 494-2577). Inexpensive.

Cadillac Bar – An import from Nuevo Laredo, featuring dishes most often found in Mexican border towns. Beware of the salsa sitting innocently on the table; it has vaporized more than one palate. Ramos gin fizzes are the drink of choice; fish dishes are the best menu items. Strolling mariachis add to the atmosphere of this very friendly, informal eatery. Lunch and dinner daily except Sundays. Major credit cards. 212 S. Flores (phone: 223-5533). Inexpensive.

Church's Fried Chicken – Fast food with a hot twist — chicken and jalapeños. Both spicy and cheap. The headquarters of the national chain, San Antonio has more than 30 *Church's* so you can't miss them. Open daily. Inexpensive.

Earl Abel's – After feeding hungry families for almost half a century, Earl has gotten pretty good at it. The place is a godsend for those who have been watching the ravenous animals at the nearby zoo. Offers big servings of standard American fare — freshwater catfish, a chicken liver dinner, a full line of hamburgers, big T-bones, and terrific homemade pecan pie. No reservations. Major credit cards. 4200 Broadway (phone: 822-3358). Inexpensive.

La Fogata – Authentic recipes and foods from Mexico. Cooking is exclusively by charcoal, and though the menu sounds exotic, the prices are down to earth. (No liquor is served.) Open daily. No reservations. Major credit cards. 2427 Vance Jackson (phone: 340-1337). Inexpensive.

Mario's – A popular West Side eatery often described as a piece of Mexico that mistakenly strayed across the border. It's a 24-hour operation where patrons warm up on a breakfast of chilaquiles (scrambled eggs with tortilla strips) and tackle grilled sweetbreads and a dessert of capirotada (bread pudding) for lunch. Mariachis keep the place lively. Two blocks from El Mercado. A second *Mario's,* at 4429 Walzem Rd. (phone: 599-2920), is open from 11 AM to 10 PM. Visa and Master-Card accepted. 325 S. Pecos (phone: 223-9602). Inexpensive.

Mi Tierra Café and Bakery – When you tire of souvenir hunting at El Mercado, head for the heart of the market square for the real thing — great Mexican food at low prices. The cheese enchiladas are terrific, and the cabrito (kid) is good here too. Open 24 hours a day. No reservations. Major credit cards. 218 Produce Row (phone: 225-1262). Inexpensive.

El Mirador – Citizens say the best (and most authentic) Mexican food in the city is served here. It's a special favorite at lunchtime on Saturdays, when the entire citizenry seems to visit. Caldo Xochitl (a chicken-cum-vegetable soup) is a special treat. Breakfast 6:30 to 10:45 AM. Closes at 4 PM on weekdays and 3 PM Saturdays. No credit cards. 722 S. St. Mary's (phone: 225-9444). Inexpensive.

Schilo's Delicatessen – This downtown favorite has been around since the 1920s, and it's still where the locals go for stick-to-your-ribs German fare. Open daily except Sundays from 10 AM to 7 PM. No reservations. Major credit cards. 424 E. Commerce (phone: 223-6692). Inexpensive.

SAN DIEGO

Sunlit against a sapphire sea, clean and glowing with self-satisfaction, San Diego is archetypal Southern California. Residents call it paradise. (Really.)

Strangers in paradise are usually flabbergasted by the terrific climate. This is one place that really lives up to its outrageously positive reputation. Residents in this land of eternal spring (70F is the average annual temperature) tend to gripe when even the merest wisp of cumulus mars the clear blue heaven. Never mind that days without sunshine are few and far between; nothing short of perfect weather will do. You can get spoiled living in Eden.

A lot of people do. More than 1 million live in the city, while the San Diego metro area has 2.3 million people. Technicolor visions of splendid afternoons spent lounging on the beach attract newcomers by the thousands. The city is among the country's fastest growing. Detractors used to gripe that San Diego was nothing but resorts and conservative suburbs, its downtown lifeless except when the Navy came in. No more. With a vibrant, revitalized central core and public transportation on wheels, tracks, and water, San Diego is becoming the ideal city. Green and open between the sea and the mountains, it contains all the makings of urban good life within easy reach: sophisticated comforts, history, lively arts — even the airport is close to downtown. No wonder 32 million people visit San Diego every year.

Tourism is the city's third largest industry. The US government is number two. In fact, 24% of the San Diego labor force works for Uncle Sam. The San Diego navy complex includes the largest naval air station on the West Coast. First is the aerospace equipment and missile industry. About 1,000 firms manufacture aviation equipment. (The military-industrial complex thrives in Southern California as much as anything else.) San Diego's present size is a direct consequence of the incredible mobilization during World War II. After the Japanese attack on Pearl Harbor, the US moved its Pacific naval headquarters from Honolulu to San Diego. Here were manufactured thousands of B-24 Liberators, which, in turn, pounded thousands of tons of high explosives into the very heart of occupied Europe. Millions of people passed through town during the war years, and many returned to settle when there was peace. This influx swelled the city to the bursting point, necessitating a series of building projects. Then, as America entered the space age, thousands more engineers, rocket specialists, and physicists poured into the area. San Diego gave birth to the Atlas missile, one of the earliest of the sophisticated rockets used to launch man into space.

And originally, it is the place where California began. In 1542, Juan Rodriguez Cabrillo, the Portuguese explorer sailing under a Spanish flag, pulled into the natural shelter formed by San Diego Bay. Cabrillo was later to become known as the "Columbus of California." The first settlement came more than two centuries later, however, when explorer Gaspar de Portolá and a group of Spanish settlers planted San Diego's first European roots. The oldest city in California includes on its list of original settlers the legendary Franciscan, Fray Junipero Serra, founder of the 21-mission trail known as El Camino Real. The first of Fray Serra's missions, San Diego de Alcala, forms the southern end of the chain that lines the coast as far as Sonoma, north of San Francisco. (One wonders what the gentle, pacifist disciple of St. Francis would think of the missiles that are manufactured here now.) Spaced about a day's journey apart, each mission housed about 1,000 Indian converts to Catholicism. The Indians worked as farmers and craftspeople. Food, clothing, and medical care were dispensed by the priests, who also taught the Indians how to irrigate the fields. The missions were established in the 18th century with the aim of proselytization, but military priorities were also in mind. As the Russians pushed into Alaska, the Spanish government looked toward its string of religious settlements and outposts as strategic bulwarks in the event of an invasion. To the north of San Diego de Alcala, San Luis Rey de Francisco and San Juan Capistrano stood between California's southernmost city and Los Angeles.

In 1810, Mexicans gained control of San Diego after a successful revolution in the northern Mexican town of Querétaro, led by a revolutionary priest named Hidalgo. The United States seized the land from Mexico in 1846 during its expansionist "manifest destiny" period. Under American rule, San Diego grew slowly, taking a back seat to the mercantile centers of Los Angeles, San Francisco, and Sacramento, the state capital, located on major railroad lines and at the juncture of two of the state's major rivers. San Diego remained an insular village until the center of population moved from "Old Town" to the "New Town" (designed by sugar heir John Spreckels) at the turn of the century. Modern San Diego follows Spreckels's plan, but it has expanded more than 20 miles to the north, south, and east. San Diego County contains mountains with enough snow for winter skiing and fertile agricultural land. In fact, agriculture is San Diego's fourth largest industry. The area is the world's largest producer of avocados. The majority of the more than 500 million avocados grown in California last year came from San Diego. Many eventually found their way into guacamole consumed by visitors and residents. Guacamole, a Mexican hors d'oeuvre, is a culinary influence that is just one of the many Mexicanisms permeating the San Diego atmosphere. San Diego's Mexican-Spanish heritage is also reflected in its large Mexican-American population and in its modern architecture as well as in its remarkable old buildings. The Mexican border is only 17 miles to the south, and because of it, San Diego retains a unique character: a blend of American hospitality, traditional border-town sensuality, and the best climate this side of paradise.

SAN DIEGO
DOWNTOWN

N

PARK BLVD

PARK BLVD

SAN DIEGO ZOO

Balboa

Park

Balboa

Cabrillo Bridge

El Prado

Plaza Panama

All in this section of Balboa Park
Timken Art Gallery
Fine Arts Gallery
Shakespearean Theater
Museum of Man
Aerospace Museum
R.H.Fleet Space Theater
Museum of Natural History

Balboa
Stadium

6 AV

5 AV

QUINCE ST

OLIVE ST

PALM ST

NUTMEG ST

MAPLE ST

4 AV

LAUREL ST

KALMIA ST

3 AV

JUNIPER ST

IVY ST

FRONT ST

HAWTHORNE ST

GRAPE ST

FIR ST

ELM ST

DATE ST

BEECH ST

ASH ST

CEDAR ST

8 AV

7 AV

6 AV

5 AV

4 AV

3 AV

2 AV

1 AV

FRONT S

ALBATROSS ST

BRANT ST

CURLEWS ST

RAYNARD WY

FALCON ST

GOLDFINCH
ST

HAWK ST

IBIS ST

SPRUCE ST

REDWOOD ST

PALM ST

NUTMEG ST

DOVE
ST

EAGLE ST

ARROYO ST

RAYNARD WY

MAPLE ST

KALMIA ST

ALBATROSS ST

JUNIPER ST

IVY ST

US
Customs

STATE ST

COLUMBIA ST

INDIA ST

KETTNER BLVD

FRONT ST

UNION ST

CALIFORNIA ST

PACIFIC HWY

INDIA ST

CEDAR ST

BEECH ST

ASH ST

STA

FRONT S

HARBOR DR

County
Bldg

OLD TOWN
SAN DIEGO

SAN DIEGO RIVER

TAYLOR ST

TAYLOR ST

HOTEL CIRCLE N.

HOTEL CIRCLE S.

VALLE VISTA

ST JAMES ST

LINDEN
PL

ALMEDA DR

LINWOOD
ST

Juniper Serra
Museum

PRESIDIO PARK

PRESIDIO DR

JACKSON ST

MASON ST

WALLACE ST

HARNEY ST

TWIGG ST

CONGRESS ST

SAN DIEGO AVE

Casa De
Estudillo

Old Town
Plaza

Historic
District

To El Campo

Santo 200 Yds.

Heritage
Park

Mormon
Memorial

JUAN ST

SUNSET RD

HARBOR DR

WITHERBY ST

ARISTA ST

ARISTA DR

AMPUDIA ST

CONDE ST

MORELAND
ST

JEFFERSON ST

CALHOUN ST

MOORE ST

SAN DIEGO AVE

WASHINGTON ST

INGLE
SIDE
ST

CALHOUN ST

ROSECRANS ST

GAINES ST

BANDINI ST

INGLESIDE

PINE ST

STEWART ST

PRINCE

RISS ST

LOMA ST

CORTEZ PL

ALCOTT ST

TRIAS ST

TITUS
ST

TOYNE ST

CORONADO DR

VALENTINO

STOCKTON
ST

ST JAMES ST

5

8

SAN DIEGO
AT-A-GLANCE

University of California

Scripps Institute
of Oceanography
Sea Caves

Bear Rock
Country Prose St. Park

SAN DIEGO AT-A-GLANCE

 SEEING THE CITY: The Cabrillo National Monument, where Juan Rodriguez Cabrillo first saw the West Coast in 1542, still offers the most spectacular view of San Diego. It's the most visited national monument in the US — more popular than the Statue of Liberty. Museum and Visitor Center open daily. No admission charge. Catalina Blvd. on the tip of Point Loma (phone: 557-5450).

 SPECIAL PLACES: San Diego stretches from the fashionable northern suburb of Del Mar to the Mexican border: all in all, a span of more than 30 miles along the Pacific Coast. It's advisable to concentrate your sightseeing efforts in one particular area at a time. There's no way you can see everything in just a day. Each of the Big Four (Balboa Park, Old Town, San Diego Zoo, and Sea World of California) are all-day propositions.

SAN DIEGO

Shelter Island – A manmade resort island in the middle of San Diego Bay lined with boatyards, marinas, and picturesque, neo-Polynesian restaurants. Between July and November, marlin sportfishers haul their giant catches into port here to be weighed and photographed. Stop off at Marlin Club Landing, 2445 Shelter Island Drive. If the sight of these monsters makes you yearn for the tug of a giant fish on the line, sign on for a marlin expedition at any of the sportfishing marinas two blocks away on Fenelon Street. You can also fish for albacore and yellowtail. To get to Shelter Island, follow Rosecrans Street until you see signs pointing to Shelter Island.

Harbor Island – This is a super-deluxe, $50-million resort island. Actually, it started as a landfill project in 1961 when the US Navy offered surplus harbor muck to the Port of San Diego. The navy was deepening a channel through the Bay. Port officials took them up on their offer and used the 3½ million tons of waste to create Harbor Island. You'd never know, to look at the place. Humble beginnings have yielded fancy beachside promenades, traffic-free malls, restaurants, and hotels. Take Rosecrans to Harbor Drive, then follow signs to Harbor Island.

Mission Bay Park – A 4,600-acre waterfront recreation area. Here you'll find manmade tropical islands, channels, and specific areas where you can water-ski, swim, and sail. There are golf courses, hotels, and restaurants here, too. The 2-mile stretch of Mission Beach, along the western edge of the park, is one of San Diego's oldest beach communities. The Visitor Information Center is open daily. Take Rte. 5 to Mission Bay Drive exit. The Information Center is right off the exit ramp (phone: 276-8200).

Sea World of California – This 135-acre oceanarium is the highlight of the Mission Bay recreation complex. Performing dolphins and Shamu, the 3-ton killer whale, entertain regularly. The shows include performing seals and otters, and a water-light extravaganza. Penguin Encounter is a glassed-in bit of Antarctica, where penguins from Emperors to fledglings flourish at zero degrees. Backstage you can feed the dolphins and meet the walruses. Yes, there are sharks, too. Open daily. Admission charge. Mission Bay Park (phone: 226-3901).

Old Town San Diego State Historic Park – The site of California's first permanent Spanish settlement, preserved by the State Department of Parks and Recreation. Tours, daily at 2 PM, leave Town Plaza and include the Seeley Stables, with exhibits on Californian and Western history and children's displays; the Stuart House, an early adobe structure where volunteers demonstrate candlemaking, spinning and weaving, and cook corn tortillas on adobe bricks; the Machado-Silvas House, another adobe structure; the Casa de Estudillo (see below); and an early dentist's office. Living history programs take place on the fourth Saturday of each month. The Bazaar del Mondo, an area of shops and restaurants, is also in the park proper, plus an old-fashioned general store, tobacconist, and confectionery. As we went to press, the first California Courthouse was being restored and an archaeology museum was under construction. For further information, contact the visitor information center (phone: 237-6770) or the State Parks district office (phone: 237-6766). Some of the park's other highlights:

Old Town Plaza – The best way to see Old San Diego is by walking through it. Old Town Plaza (also known as Washington Square) used to be the scene of violent cockfights and bullfights. Duelists chose this as their site for shooting it out. No admission charge. San Diego Ave., Mason, Calhoun, and Wallace Sts. in Old Town San Diego State Historic Park, the site of California's first permanent Spanish settlement. For general park information, call 237-6770.

Casa de Estudillo – A former *commandante* of San Diego, José Maria Estudillo, lived here while the city was under Mexican control. It was also the site of Helen Hunt Jackson's book *Ramona,* which describes how the Indians were mistreated. It was built in 1829. Open daily. Admission charge. San Diego Ave. and Mason St. (no phone).

San Diego Union Newspaper Museum – Still going strong, the *San Diego Union* started out in this small 1850s building. In fact, the newspaper is responsible for restoring it and for setting up the editorial offices and printing press. Copies of the first *Union* ever printed are still on sale for 25¢. Closed Mondays. No admission charge. 2626 San Diego Ave. (phone: 297-2119).

Old California Museum – Right in back of the *Newspaper Museum,* here's a good place to get an idea of what Old Town looked like a hundred years ago. A diorama is on display. Across the alley, there are the Seeley Stables, barns, and a fine collection of horse-drawn wagons and carriages. There's also a slide show of San Diego history. Open daily. Admission charge. 2626 San Diego Ave. (phone: 297-2119).

Whaley House – The first brick house in San Diego, built by New Yorker Thomas Whaley. The house is supposed to be haunted by a man who was hung on the grounds in 1852. Haunted or not, the house was the scene of many lively high society parties in its day. Ornate 19th-century furnishings still fill the halls. Closed Mondays and Tuesdays. Admission charge. 2482 San Diego Ave., in Old Town (phone: 298-2482).

El Campo Santo – At the southern end of San Diego Avenue is a cemetery containing the graves of many pioneers, soldiers, and bandits. One of the latter, Antonio Garra, was actually executed next to his grave. Unfortunately, many of the headstones are missing, but there's enough history here to make a visit compelling. San Diego Ave. and Noell St., in Old Town (no phone).

Mormon Battalion Memorial Visitors Center – This military museum marks the longest infantry march in US history: 1846 to 1847, when 500 Mormons left their home in Illinois and trekked more than 2,000 miles to San Diego. Only 350 made it. It also has a number of exhibitions of the Church of Jesus Christ of Latter-Day Saints and historical displays. Open daily. No admission charge. In Heritage Park at 2510 Juan St. (phone: 298-3317).

Heritage Park – A pocket of preserved Victoriana. The County Parks and Recreation Dept. has its offices in the Sherman-Gilbert House. There are several other mansions to explore. Open daily. No admission charge. Heritage Park Row, in Old Town (phone: 565-3600).

Junipero Serra Museum – Named after Fray Junipero Serra, this lovely mansion contains documents, books, and artifacts on the history of the region during its Spanish colonial, Mexican, and early US periods. The tower gallery is especially fascinating.

The museum is on the site of the original European settlement. Open daily. No admission charge. Presidio Park, in Old Town (phone: 297-3258).

Horton Plaza – The first major project in San Diego's downtown redevelopment program, this multilevel shopping plaza comprises major department stores, movie theaters, restaurants, entertainments, and 150 specialty shops. The legendary *U. S. Grant* hotel is across the street on Broadway. Stretching from Broadway to G St. between 1st and 4th Aves.

Balboa Park – A definite must — the cultural heart of the city. Within its 1,200 acres of lawns, groves, lakes, and paths are a complex of fine museums, set in an area of the park known as the Prado, a Shakespearean theater, and the world-famous San Diego Zoo (each listed below). Open daily. No admission charge. Park Blvd. (phone: 239-0512).

San Diego Zoo – Incomparable. One of the finest zoos in the world. For more than 60 years, San Diego has been home to more than 4,000 animals. The zoo covers more than 125 acres, with animals ranging from Australian koalas to the only New Zealand kiwis in captivity in the country to Indonesian Komodo dragons. Very few of the animals are caged in. The Skyfari Aerial Tramway gives you a great bird's-eye view of everything. Guided bus tours leave frequently from the gate. Open daily. Admission charge. Balboa Park (phone: 234-3153 or 231-1515).

Timken Art Gallery – Controversial when it was built in 1965 because some people felt it clashed with the prevalent Spanish adobe architecture, the modern *Timken* houses French, Spanish, Flemish, Russian, and Italian Renaissance art. You'll find Rembrandt, Bruegel the Elder, and Cézanne on the walls. Open daily. No admission charge. 1500 El Prado, Balboa Park (phone: 239-5548).

San Diego Museum of Art – Donated by the Appleton Bridges family in 1926, the original section of the gallery was built to resemble the university at Salamanca, Spain. Two newer wings have since been added. Diego Rivera, Rubens, Rembrandt, and Dali are represented. Closed Mondays. Admission charge. Plaza de Panama, Balboa Park (phone: 232-7931).

San Diego Museum of Man – Concerning itself primarily with anthropology and archaeology, this museum bears the distinction of being the only remaining permanent structure from San Diego's 1915 Exposition. Its Spanish colonial tower is remarkable in itself. Exhibitions focus on the Southwest Indians. Open daily. Admission charge except Wednesdays. El Prado, Balboa Park (phone: 239-2001).

Aerospace Historical Center – Containing the *San Diego Aerospace Museum* and the International Aerospace Hall of Fame, it has a notable collection of antique planes and gliders. Open daily. Admission charge. Ford Bldg., Balboa Park (phone: 234-8291).

Reuben H. Fleet Space Theater – The first of its kind. Simulated space travel is the attraction here. Images projected on the 360-degree screen give you the impression you're moving in zero-gravity conditions. The Science Center also has exhibitions on astronomy and technology, and a free demonstration of lasers. Open daily. Admission charge. Off Park Blvd., Balboa Park (phone: 238-1223).

Natural History Museum – More than a century old, this museum has a collection of birds that nest in the San Diego area, and sharks, whales, and fish who make their home in the surrounding seas. A Sefton seismograph measures tremors and earth movement. Open daily. Admission charge. Across from the *Fleet Space Theater,* Balboa Park (phone: 232-3821).

Seaport Village – The city's new waterfront complex of restaurants and specialty shops built around three main plazas edging San Diego Bay is designed to look much like a New England fishing village. A main attraction is the wonderfully restored Flying Horses Carousel, with its hand-carved wooden animals, originally constructed around 1900 for the amusement park at Coney Island, New York. It's nice to stroll through the village in the evening and have dinner in one of the restaurants here. *Papagayo's* (phone: 232-7581) has very good Mexican seafood dishes and reasonable prices. Seaport Village, 849 Harbor Dr. at Pacific Hwy. (phone: 235-4014).

Embarcadero – Another interesting place to walk. From the pier you can see the activities on North Island Naval Air Station across the bay and watch the hundreds of sailboats cruising. Navy ships are open to visitors on weekends, off the Broadway Pier.

Maritime Museum – The oldest square-rigged merchantman afloat, the 125-plus-year-old *Star of India,* is berthed here, along with the turn-of-the-century ferryboat *Berkeley* and steam yacht *Medea.* Open daily. Admission charge. Broadway Pier at Harbor Dr. (phone: 234-9153).

LA JOLLA

Tidepools – La Jolla, an uncommercial beach 12½ miles north of San Diego, offers opportunities to observe marine life in a natural setting. Visit the tidepools just beyond Alligator Head at La Jolla Cove at low tide to see a veritable profusion of hermit crabs, anemones, and starfish clambering over one another. Make sure you wear tennis shoes — the jagged rocks can cut your feet. From San Diego, take Rte. 5 to Ardath Rd. exit. Follow Ardath west until it becomes Torrey Pines Rd. Take Torrey Pines west, turn right on Prospect and follow it to Coast Boulevard. Follow signs to La Jolla Cove.

Whale Point – If you visit La Jolla during December, January, or February, visit Whale Point. Every year the giant whales migrate south along this route. Since they've been doing this for the past 8 million years or so, we have no reason to believe they'll stop before you read this chapter. To get to Whale Point, follow the shore south from Alligator Head. Opposite the only large building on the beach, there's a small cove known as Seal Rock. From Seal Rock, you'll be able to see another cove, marked by a lifeguard stand and a wall. That's Whale Point.

La Jolla Museum of Contemporary Art – Dramatically situated near the beach, between Seal Rock and Whale Point, the gardens and building are well worth a look. You'll find paintings and sculpture from all over the world. A good place to contemplate art and nature. Closed Mondays. Admission charge. Prospect and Silverado (phone: 454-0267).

Sea Caves – A natural formation of seven caves hollowed out by the waves. You reach them by walking along the cliffs facing the ocean. Take Coast Boulevard to the tunnel leading to Coast Walk.

Scripps Institute of Oceanography – One of the most highly esteemed marine study institutes in the world. You can stroll through the grounds, or relax on the Scripps beach. You can't walk on the pier, but the *Scripps Aquarium Museum* is open to the public. You can watch the fish being fed at 1:30 PM Wednesdays and Sundays. Open daily. No admission charge. 8602 La Jolla Shores Dr. (phone: 534-6933).

Torrey Pines State Reserve – In order to avoid crowding, admission is limited. Get there early. The strange-looking bent pine trees, which are the outstanding feature, date to the period when Southern California was a vast pine forest. On the northern side of the park, Los Penasquitos Lagoon offers a spectacular vantage point for watching blue herons and rare egrets. Mule deer come to the southern part of the lagoon to feed. Open daily. Admission charge. Torrey Pines Rd. (phone: 755-2063).

■**EXTRA SPECIAL:** No tour of San Diego would be complete without a visit to Mexico. The bustling border city of Tijuana is just 17 miles south of downtown. Many visitors and residents drive there, park their cars on the US side of the border, and walk into Tijuana. (The Tijuana taxis are infamous for overcharging. If you refuse to pay, you can end up in jail.) San Diego's new trolley system is a good alternative to driving. The trip to Tijuana takes about 40 minutes and costs $1.50 each way. It's possible to hop on the trolley at various points along the route, but the trip originates at the Amtrak Terminal, C St. and Kettner Blvd., and terminates at San Ysidro (200 feet from the border). Trolleys leave the main stations (in either direction) every 15 minutes from 5 to 1 AM daily; tickets are purchased at vending machines at all pickup points. Tijuana has many crafts shops selling finely wrought ironwork, pottery, and jewelry. Prices are a fraction of what the same items cost in the US. You can bring back $400 worth of goods duty-free, once every 30 days. Goods must be declared at retail value at the checkpoint for reentering the US, but certain items — such as Mexican national treasures — are prohibited. Upon reentering, you may be asked for proof of citizenship (it often depends on how Latino and/or nervous you look), but it's wise to carry some sort of identification. Also, if you're driving into Mexico, it's wise to purchase insurance at one of the many insurance offices near the border. It will prevent you from unpleasant detention should you happen to have an accident. Conventional US auto insurance is not valid in Mexico. The Tijuana Cultural Center has an *Omnimax Space Theater*, a museum, a performing arts center, shopping, and a restaurant (Paseo de los Heroes; phone: 706-684-1111 or 706-684-1132). Tijuana also offers year-round thoroughbred racing, dog racing, jai alai, and bullfighting.

A short drive down a scenic toll road from Tijuana is Ensenada, a resort and fishing village. From Ensenada, the road stretches south to the most famous Mexican Pacific coast resort cities or to Baja California. No visas or tourist cards are needed for US citizens in the border areas. You do need a tourist card to travel south of Ensenada.

SOURCES AND RESOURCES

 TOURIST INFORMATION: The San Diego Convention and Visitors Bureau, 1200 3rd Ave., Suite 824, San Diego, CA 92101 (phone: 232-3101), distributes brochures and maps. The main International Visitor Information Center is at Horton Plaza downtown, at 1st Ave. and F St. (11 Horton Plaza, San Diego, CA 92101; phone: 236-1212). Another information center is on E. Mission Dr., off Rte. 5 (phone: 276-8200). For maps and brochures on walking tours of the historic district, stop at the State Park Visitor Center at Old Town Plaza (phone: 237-6770).

Barry Berndes' *The San Diegan* (San Diego Guide; $1.95) is the most complete guide to the area; write to *The San Diegan,* PO Box 99127, San Diego 92109, or call 275-2213.

Television Stations – KGTV Channel 10–ABC; KFMB Channel 8–CBS; KNSD Channel 39–NBC; KPBS Channel 15–PBS.

Radio Stations – AM: KFMB 760 (adult contemporary); KSDO 1130 (news/talk/sports); KSON 1240 (country). FM: KFSD 94.1 (classical); KCBQ 105.3 (rock); KIFM 98.1 (jazz).

Local Coverage – *Evening Tribune,* evening daily; *Union,* morning daily; *Del Mar News-Press,* weekly; *San Diego Magazine,* monthly.

Food – Barry Berndes' The *San Diegan*; *Epicurean Rendezvous,* Maya Madden, Editor (AM/PM Publishing; $6.50).

Telephone – The area code for San Diego is 619.

Sales Tax – The sales tax is 7%. The tax on hotel rooms is 7%.

CLIMATE: Rainstorms are few and far between, and almost invariably occur in December, January, and February. During these months, the temperature might drop down into the high 40s at night, so bring a sweater. Daytimes are generally in the 60s. The rest of the year, you can expect bright days and coo enings with daytime highs in the 70s, lows at night in the 50s. Bathing suits are de rigueur all year round.

GETTING AROUND: Airport – San Diego International Airport is within sight of downtown. The cost of a cab ride between the airport and downtown varies but should run $6 or $7, $11 or $12 to Mission Valley. San Diego Transit (phone: 233-3004) bus #2 leaves from the airport every 20 minutes and runs along Broadway, downtown; fare, $1. *KO-AM Transportation* (phone: 233-0470) and *Rainbow Ride Shuttle Service* (phone: 695-3830) also operate airport transfer service by mini-van.

Bus – The San Diego Transit System operates frequent buses connecting downtown with the suburbs (phone: 233-3004).

Taxi – You can get a cab by calling *Yellow Cab* (phone: 234-6161); *Radio Cab* (phone: 232-6566); *Checker Cab* (phone: 234-4477); *Co-Op Cab* (phone: 280-9381).

Car Rental – The best way to see everything at your convenience is by car. Most major national car rental firms are represented at the airport. For lower rates, try *Ladki International* (phone: 233-9333 or 800-367-9796).

Trolley/Ferry – The San Diego Trolley originates at the Amtrak Terminal, C St. and Kettner Blvd. It runs between the terminal and Tijuana, with pickup stops downtown, while the bayside line serves the convention center and coastal hotels and attractions. Tickets, available from machines at all stops, cost 50¢ to $1.50, depending on distance (phone: 231-8541). The trackless *Molly Trolley Express,* with siblings Polly, Dolly, and Ollie, makes frequent loops with stops at major hotels and attrractions for $5 for an all-day pass. There is a ferry, which costs $1.50, between the Broadway Pier in San Diego and the Old Ferry Landing on Coronado, whence the *Coronado Trolley* makes the rounds of the island's major hotels (phone: 437-1861).

Water Taxi – Water taxis serve Coronado, the convention center, bayside hotels, shopping destinations, and attractions (phone: 437-1861). The fare is $5 to $8, depending on distance, with tokens available at hotels.

LOCAL SERVICES: Babysitters – *Baby Sitter Service,* 4138 30th St. (phone: 281-7755); *Reliable Babysitter Agency,* 3368 2nd Ave., Suite B (phone: 296-0856).

Business Services – *Economic Development Corp. of San Diego,* 701 B St. (phone: 234-8484).

Mechanics – *Dean's Tenth Avenue Garage,* 843 10th Ave. (phone: 232-1428); *Jimmy on the Spot Mobile Service* — he comes to you (phone: 560-1140).

MUSEUMS: Balboa Park contains most of the city museums: the *Timken* and *Fine Arts Galleries, Museum of Man, Aerospace Museum, Reuben H. Fleet Space Center,* and *Museum of Natural History.* The *Maritime Museum, Serra Museum, San Diego Union Newspaper Museum, Heritage Park,* historic *Old Town* houses, and *La Jolla Museum of Contemporary Art* are given fuller descriptions in *Special Places. Palomar Observatory*'s giant telescope was, for many years, the most powerful in the world. It's still in use. Photographs of the cosmos are on display. Open daily. County Rd. S6, east of Escondido (phone: 742-3476).

MAJOR COLLEGES AND UNIVERSITIES: Scripps Institute of Oceanography (see *Special Places*) is only a part of the University of California at San Diego. The rest of the campus is at University City, La Jolla (phone: 452-2230). Other colleges and universities include the following: US International University, Pomerado Rd. (phone: 271-4300); San Diego State University, Alvarado Freeway (phone: 265-5200); University of San Diego, Alcala Park (phone: 260-4600).

SPECIAL EVENTS: San Diego is a summer festival almost all y

January: Mission Bay Marathon, from Quivira Basin loop in Mission Bay (phone: 437-4667); *MONY Tournament of Champions* (PGA golf tournament), *La Costa Country Club,* Costa del Mar Rd., Carlsbad (phone: 438-9111).

February: Shearson Lehman Bros. or *Andy Williams Open,* at *Torrey Pines Golf Course,* La Jolla (phone: 281-4653); wildflowers bloom in the desert at Borrego State Park, February through April (phone: 767-5311).

March: St. Patrick's Day Parade (phone: 299-7812).

April: San Diego Crew Classic, West Mission Bay (phone: 488-1039).

May: Fiesta de la Primavera, celebrating San Diego's historical past, in Old Town State Park (phone: 237-6770); *Cinco de Mayo Festival* (phone: 296-3161 or 299-6055).

June: Del Mar County Fair, Del Mar Fairgrounds (phone: 259-1355 or 755-1161); *Annual Camp Pendleton Rodeo,* Camp Pendleton, Area 16 (phone: 725-4905).

July: Festival of the Bells, celebrating the founding of California's first mission, Mission San Diego de Alcala, 101818 San Diego Mission Rd. (phone: 281-8449); *Mission San Luis Rey Fiesta,* at Mission San Luis Rey (phone: 757-3651); *Sand Castle Days* at Imperial Beach Pier (phone: 429-4757); *World Championship Over-the-Line Tournament,* a beach softball game at Mission Bay (phone: 294-8484).

August: Annual celebration of America's *Finest City Week* (phone: 234-0331); *N.A.S. Miramar Air Show* at the naval air station (phone: 537-4082).

September: Cabrillo Festival commemorating the discovery of the West Coast (phone: 557-5450); *Fiddle and Banjo Contests,* Frank Lane Memorial Park in Julian (phone: 765-1857).

October: Oktoberfest, La Mesa Blvd. (phone: 465-7700); *San Diego Zoo Founder's Day,* free admission, first Monday in October (phone: 231-1515).

November: Mother Goose Parade, El Cajón (phone: 444-8712).

December: Mission Bay Christmas Boat Parade of Lights, from Quivira Basin to Sea World of California (phone: 488-0501); *San Diego Harbor Parade of Lights* (phone: 222-0301); *Las Posadas,* Mexican Christmas ceremony, Mission San Luis Rey (phone: 757-3250); Old Town's *Las Posadas* (phone: 297-1183); *Christmas on the Prado,* Balboa Park (phone: 291-4903).

SPORTS AND FITNESS: There's just about everything for everybody.

Baseball – The National League *Padres* (phone: 283-4494) play at *Jack Murphy Stadium,* 9449 Friars Rd. (phone: 281-1330).

Bicycling – *Hamel's Action Sports Center,* 704 Ventura Pl., Mission Beach (phone: 488-5050); *California Bicycle,* 633 Pearl St., La Jolla (phone: 454-0316); *Wheels 'n Things,* 2910 Navajo Rd., El Cajon (phone: 465-3976).

Fishing – The longest fishing pier on the West Coast is at Point Loma. There are also piers at Mission Bay, San Diego Harbor, and Shelter Island. You don't need a license, and there is no fee for pier fishing. For deep-sea fishing, however, you do need a permit. Write to the California Dept. of Fish and Game Resources Bldg., 1350 Front St., Room 2041, San Diego, CA 92101 (phone: 237-7311). Marlin, yellowtail, and sailfish run in the spring. *Bass Guides of San Diego,* 777 Broadway, El Cajón (phone: 588-5488), guides fishermen on San Diego's lakes.

Fitness Centers – *San Diego Sports Medicine Center* offers aerobics classes and workout equipment, 6699 Alvarado Rd. (phone: 287-4446); the *YMCA* has a pool and weight room, 5505 Friars Rd. (phone: 298-3576).

Flying – You can rent a Cessna or take flying lessons at *Gibbs Flying Service,* Montgomery Field (phone: 277-0310).

Football – The NFL *Chargers* (phone: 280-2111) and San Diego State *Aztecs* (phone: 283-7378) play home games at the *Jack Murphy Stadium.*

Golf – For tournaments, see *Special Events,* above. *Torrey Pines* municipal golf course alongside the ocean is the site of the annual Shearson Lehman Bros. or Andy Williams Open (phone: 453-3530). It's also the most famous of the more than 60 public courses in San Diego County. *Mission Bay Golf Course* is lit up for night games, Mission Bay Park (phone: 273-1221).

Ice Skating – The *House of Ice,* 11001 Black Mountain Rd. off Mira Mesa Blvd. W. (phone: 265-5163), has day and night skating.

Jai Alai – Jai alai is played at *Fronton Palacio,* Tijuana, Fridays through Wednesdays (phone: 011-52-668-51612).

Jogging – Run along Laurel Street to Balboa Park, where there are six different courses, ranging from less than ½ mile to 9 miles. It's possible to jog along Harbor Drive in the direction of the airport, but avoid rush hours because of the fumes. Mileage (8 miles' worth) is marked around Mission Bay. In La Jolla, run along the shore and boardwalk or the La Jolla cove.

Racing – Thoroughbreds race at *Del Mar Race Track,* July to September, I-5 to Fairgrounds exit (phone: 259-1355; or contact Del Mar Thoroughbred Club, 755-1141). There's also racing at *Caliente Race Track,* Tijuana (phone: 011-52-668-62001; see *Extra Special*).

Sailing and Boating – The *City Recreation Dept.* rents motorboats and rowboats for use on lakes (phone: 236-5740). They also give sailing courses (phone: 488-1004). *Seaforth Boat Rentals* has sailboats, rowboats, and power boats as well as boats rigged for water skiing; they also rent fishing gear and windsurfing equipment. 1641 Quivira Rd., Mission Bay (phone: 223-1681). You can rent sailboats and take sailing lessons at *Harbor Island Sailboats,* 2040 Harbor Island Dr., Harbor Island (phone: 291-9568) and *Vacation Village Boat Rentals,* 1404 W. Vacation Rd. (phone: 274-4630).

Skiing – The Torrey Pines Ski Club organizes trips to nearby mountains; write to PO Box 82087, San Diego, CA 92138.

Surfing and Scuba Diving – La Jolla Cove is the most popular scuba diving spot because the water is particularly clear. Boomer Beach, so named because of the rumbling sound of surf crashing to shore, is the body-surfers' first choice. Surfboarders ride the waves at La Jolla Shores.

Swimming – There are 70 miles of public beaches, not to mention Mission Bay Park's manmade lagoons. La Jolla and Torrey Pines State Park beaches are especially beautiful (see Special Places). There are ten municipal swimming pools: Kearney Mesa, Kearns Memorial Park, Vista Terrace, Swanson, King, Colina del Sol, Mission Beach Plunge, Memorial, Clairemont, and Allied Gardens. For information call the Aquatics Department of the City Recreation Office (phone: 270-3932).

Tennis – For special tennis tournaments, see *Special Events,* above. Public courts are at La Jolla Recreation Center, 615 Prospect St. (phone: 454-2071); Morley Field, 2221 Morley Field Dr., Balboa Park (phone: 295-9278); Standley Park, 3585 Governor Dr. (phone: 452-LOVE); and Robb Field, 2525 Bacon St. (phone: 224-7581).

Whale Watching – Watch the migrating sea mammals from Cabrillo National Monument, Whale Point in La Jolla, or take a whale watching excursion from *H & M Landing,* 2803 Emerson St. (phone: 222-1144), or *Fisherman's Landing,* 2838 Garrison St. (phone: 222-0391), December, January, and February.

 THEATER: The *Old Globe Theatre* stages Shakespearean festivals every summer. The Elizabethan theater reproduction housing the festival was destroyed in 1978 by arson but has been rebuilt with public donations (phone: 239-2255). The rest of the year, the company performs modern musicals and dramas at the next-door *Cassius Carter Center Stage,* in Balboa Park (phone: 239-2255). *San Diego Repertory Theatre* performs in the new *Lyceum Theater* (two stages) in Horton Plaza (phone: 235-8025). *Gaslamp Quarter Theatre Company*

offers eight plays per season at the *Gaslamp Quarter Theatre,* 547 4th St., and *Hahn Cosmopolitan Theatre,* 444 4th Ave. (phone: 234-9538 and 232-9608). The *La Jolla Playhouse,* at the Mandeville Center of the University of California–San Diego campus, presents a variety of plays from May through November (phone: 534-6760).

 MUSIC: The *San Diego Convention and Performing Arts Center* consists of three separate theaters. *San Diego Symphony Hall (Fox Theatre)* is the new home of the *San Diego Symphony* (phone: 699-4200). The *San Diego Opera Company* performs at the *Civic Theatre* (phone: 232-7636). *Golden Hall* and the *San Diego Stadium* are the stages for big-name rock artists. *Plaza Hall* hosts trade expos and exhibitions like the annual antiques show. All at 202 C St. (phone: 236-6510). The *California Ballet* performs the *Nutcracker Suite* at Christmas, other classics the rest of the year, 8276 Ronson Rd. (phone: 560-5676). The *Ballet Society of San Diego* performs classics, too, at its home, 337 W. Washington St. (phone: 299-9001). *San Diego Youth Symphony* also performs at *Civic Theatre* (phone: 233-3232). Free organ concerts are played every Sunday afternoon at the *Spreckels Organ Pavilion,* Balboa Park. For jazz, visit the *Catamaran,* 3999 Mission Blvd., Mission Beach (phone: 488-1081).

 NIGHTCLUBS AND NIGHTLIFE: The *Halcyon* is a very popular disco in town at 4258 W. Point Loma Blvd., Ocean Beach (phone: 225-9559), as is *Confetti,* 5373 Mission Center Rd. (phone: 291-8635). *Bali Hai* has a Hawaiian nightclub act, 2230 Shelter Island Dr. (phone: 222-1181). *Bacchanal* has live music nightly throughout the week during the summer and also offers a panoramic view from a circular dining room, 8022 Clairemont Mesa Blvd. (phone: 560-8022). *Old Del Mar Café,* 273 Via de la Valle, Del Mar (phone: 755-6614), is a popular venue for live jazz, country, and rock, as is the *Old Pacific Beach Café,* 4287 Mission Blvd., Pacific Beach (phone: 755-6614). *Croce's* restaurant, 802 Fifth Ave., features live jazz nightly, as does the *Palace Bar* at the *Horton Grand* hotel.

■ **WHEN THE SWALLOWS COME BACK:** Yes, the swallows come back to Capistrano. Every year, though not necessarily on March 19. Stop in at the Mission of San Juan Capistrano in March for a serenade. It's open daily and fascinating. No admission charge. Follow Rte. 5 north for 47 miles to the Capistrano exit (phone: 493-4700).

(BEST IN TOWN)

 CHECKING IN: San Diego is growing, and so are the number of fine hotels and resorts, with outdoor athletic facilities and super views. Expect to pay $120 and up for a standard double at those places noted as expensive; between $80 to $120, moderate; and under $80 at places listed as inexpensive. For accommodations at bed-and-breakfast establishments, contact *Bed & Breakfast Directory for San Diego,* PO Box 3292, San Diego, CA 92112 (phone: 297-3130). All telephone numbers are in the 619 area code unless otherwise indicated.

Del Coronado – One of the world's most picturesque hotels. When it opened in 1888, it was the largest wooden building in the country and the first hotel in the world to have electrical lighting and elevators. Thomas Edison himself supervised the electrical installation. Today, this turreted, rambling, 339-room resort is such a landmark that the management offers tours on Saturday afternoons. Rooms in the historic building are regrettably less impressive than the exterior architecture, and there is a modern annex that's downright pedestrian. Then there are those early morning flights buzzing out of the naval air station . . . The nearby *Chart House* restaurant is very good. There are 2 health clubs, 2 pools, tennis courts. On the Coronado Peninsula, 1500 Orange Ave. (phone: 435-6611). Expensive.

Humphrey's Half Moon Inn – On Shelter Island, overlooking the bay and the marina with all its sleek and shining boats, this inn has 137 luxury rooms and a pool, and is within walking distance of boatyards and sportfishing operations. Also known for its jazz. 2303 Shelter Island Dr. (phone: 224-3411; 800-532-3737 in California; 800-854-2900 elsewhere). Expensive.

Marriott – Two elliptical towers rise 25 floors above San Diego Bay and the hotel's own 19-acre marina. Inside are 681 rooms and suites, a shopping arcade, and half a dozen restaurants and bars. Also on the premises are 4 lighted tennis courts and a large outdoor pool. 333 W. Harbor Dr. (phone: 234-1500 or 800-228-9290). Expensive.

Le Meridien San Diego at Coronado – The French put up this fresh, airy, *très gai* luxury resort in a South Seas island setting, with tropical plantings, lagoons, and exotic birds on the Coronado Peninsula. The rooms are bright, the atmosphere relaxing. An on-site spa soothes the strains of a full range of resort activities, and a spa menu is always available. Food at both the elegant *Marius* and the casual brasserie, *L'Escale,* is exquisite (see *Eating Out* for both). Cars can be rented at the hotel, and the *Coronado Trolley* and water taxi both pick up passengers here. 2000 2nd St., Coronado (phone: 435-3000 or 800-453-4300). Expensive.

Omni San Diego – Right inside the whimsical, postmodern Horton Plaza shopping center, this hotel has managed to fit in an outdoor swimming pool and 2 tennis courts, plus a health club. The interior is done in softened tones of Santa Fe adobe, and the menu at the *Festival* restaurant is also southwestern. With theaters and shopping right outside the door, the *Omni* is in the thick of the action, and the bustle, too. 910 Broadway Circle (phone: 939-2200 or 800-THE-OMMI). Expensive.

Sheraton Grand on Harbor Island – This 500-room resort and convention hotel has tennis courts, saunas, a swimming pool, and complete convention facilities. Harbor Island has more of the same. 1380 Harbor Island Dr. (phone: 291-2900 or 800-325-3535). Expensive.

U. S. Grant – Restored to its 1910 ambience, the grand property is a registered National Historic Place. The downstairs could be a museum. The lobby, with pillars and a green and white marble floor, is awesome, and public rooms glitter with gold leaf and chandeliers. The 283 rooms are discreetly luxurious and equipped with modern amenities, but vestiges of the past remain, such as windows that open. A health club is another concession to today. Light lunch and tea is served in the *Grant Grill Lounge,* and breakfast, lunch, and dinner at the excellent *Grant Grill.* The central location can't be beat in the redeveloping downtown. Complimentary van transportation to and from the airport. 326 Broadway (phone: 232-3121 or 800-221-3802). Expensive.

Westgate – A modern, deluxe, 225-room property considered among the finest in the US. Its downtown location makes it convenient as well. Consistent with the $1 million worth of antiques decorating the premises, the hotel also offers superb service. The *Fontainebleau Room* is one of the best restaurants in town (see *Eating Out*). 1055 2nd Ave. (phone: 238-1818 or 800-522-1564). Expensive.

Hacienda Old Town – Here is an all-suite hostelry with microwave ovens, refrigerators, and coffeemakers; outdoor barbecue grills are available for guests' use. A swimming pool and fitness center are on the premises, as are 2 restaurants. Guests can also sign for their meals at the neighboring *Brigantine*. 4041 Harney St. (phone: 298-4707 or 800-888-1991). Moderate.

Horton Grand – Ironically, an old bordello rebuilt in rampant Victorian style is considered the city's most romantic hostelry. Joined by a sunny atrium is the hotel's second half, once a saddlery. The concierge dresses like a madam in a Western. Guilded mirrors swing open to reveal TV sets, and toilets flush with a chain from an overhead wood tank. Amenities are modern, the service cheerfully solicitous. At the *Ida Bailey* (the original madam's name), the Viennese chef cooks up wild boar and alligator Créole as well as less exotic fare. Jazz nightly. 311 Island Ave. (phone: 544-1886). Moderate.

Horton Park Plaza – Another downtown National Historic Landmark, it's a tastefully converted former office building with a beautiful 2-level restaurant of the same name. All units are suites with cable TV. There's an exercise room and a Jacuzzi. 901 5th St. (phone: 232-9500 or 800-443-8012). Moderate.

Somerset – Sunny apartments with kitchens, close to Balboa Park and the lively restaurant row on 5th Ave. Pool, Jacuzzi, complimentary continental breakfast, and cable TV are among the amenities. 606 Washington St. (phone: 692-5200; 800-356-1787 in California; 800-962-9665 elsewhere). Moderate.

Clarion – Also convenient to Balboa Park, this renovated hotel looks like a sun-filled Mediterranean Tara. Several rooms and suites have libraries, and 2 suites come with white tile wood-burning fireplaces, incongruous but cozy. The pool is Olympic-size, and there is a spa and a restaurant, the *Red Fox*. Complimentary continental breakfast, parking, and shuttle to the airport and rail terminal. 2223 El Cajón Blvd. (phone: 296-2101; 800-423-1935 in California; 800-843-9988 elsewhere). Inexpensive.

Torrey Pines Inn – A spectacular location overlooking the Pacific and right next door to the famous *Torrey Pines Golf Course*. Surfers and hang gliders are visible from the hotel, and La Jolla's beaches are just out the door. Swimming pool and lounge with entertainment on the premises. 67 rooms. 11480 Torrey Pines Rd., La Jolla (phone: 453-4420; 800-448-8355 in California; 800-44U-TELL elsewhere). Inexpensive.

Town and Country – One of the best in Mission Valley. Its 1,000 rooms make this the largest hotel in the city. A popular convention hotel; facilities include pools, saunas, barber shop, beauty parlor, and 24-hour coffee shop. 500 Hotel Circle (phone: 291-7131; 800-542-6082 in California; 800-260-8USA elsewhere). Inexpensive.

EATING OUT: San Diego has a wide range of restaurants, the most prevalent menu items being Mexican and seafood. Two local chains are excellent — *Anthony's Fish Grottos* and *Chart House*. Expect to pay $55 or more at those places listed as expensive; $30 to $55, moderate; under $30, inexpensive. Prices are for a meal for two, not counting drinks, wine, or tips. All telephone numbers are in the 619 area code unless otherwise indicated.

Anthony's Star of the Sea Room – One of the best on the West Coast. Overlooking San Diego Harbor, *Anthony's* serves fresh-from-the-ocean abalone, and other fish and shellfish. The clams Genovese is often ordered as an entrée. Open daily except major holidays. Reservations necessary a day or two in advance. Major credit cards. 1360 Harbor Dr. at foot of Ash St. (phone: 232-7408). Expensive.

Avanti – A showcase for Northern Italian specialties in an Art Deco setting. The menu features superb pasta, including fettuccine in a salmon sauce and tortellini with walnuts and cream; also sophisticated veal dishes, including marsala and piccata. Open daily. Major credit cards. 875 Prospect St., La Jolla (phone: 454-4288). Expensive.

Fontainebleau Dining Room – Waiters wearing white gloves quietly serve superlative continental dishes such as veal with bay shrimp. The dessert cart is fabulous.

One of San Diego's very best. Open daily. Reservations necessary. Major credit cards. *Westgate* hotel, 1055 2nd Ave. (phone: 238-1818). Expensive.

George's at the Cove – This pleasant restaurant with big windows overlooking the La Jolla coast features French preparation of American food with international seasonings. Examples: prawns with tapenade, tuna with wasabi. Open daily for lunch and dinner; Sunday brunch. Major credit cards. 1250 Prospect St., La Jolla (phone: 454-4244). Expensive.

Grant Grill – A classic grill, specializing in fish, steaks, and roasts grilled on a spit in the kitchen. The dining room retains its original men's club atmosphere. Open daily, Sunday brunch. Major credit cards. *U. S. Grant* hotel, 326 Broadway (phone: 239-6806). Expensive.

Lubach's – In the face of stiff new competition, this old favorite shows its staying power. Shrimp brochette and calf's sweetbreads financière highlight a menu that includes some fabulous beef and duck dishes. Closed Sundays and holidays. Reservations advised. Major credit cards. 2101 N. Harbor Dr. (phone: 232-5129). Expensive.

Marius and L'Escale – The roots of the cuisine are in Provence, home of the consulting chef, applied here with a light hand and a touch of whimsy by a resident chef barely old enough to order a drink legally in the dining room. Spa menu dishes are lean and spare but neither look nor taste it. Pastries are as ethereal as fairy dust. Open daily. Major credit cards. *Meridien* hotel, 2000 2nd St., Coronado (phone: 435-3000). Expensive.

Prince of Wales – Named after the *Del Coronado*'s illustrious visitor, this restaurant is designed like an English club room. We suggest the crown roast rack of lamb — it's appropriately regal. Open daily. Reservations necessary. Major credit cards. *Del Coronado* hotel, 1500 Orange Ave. (phone: 435-6611). Expensive.

Sheppard's – Another hotel restaurant with an excellent reputation. The chef was trained in France and around San Francisco, and his cooking shows these twin influences. The wine list may also be the best in town. Dinner nightly except Sundays and Mondays. Major credit cards. *Sheraton Grand* hotel, 1380 Harbor Island Dr. (phone: 291-2900). Expensive.

Top o' the Cove – Looking out onto La Jolla Cove, a favorite of show biz types from LA, and consistently voted the most romantic restaurant in the area. It features squab, venison, and fresh pasta dishes. Open daily. Reservations necessary. Major credit cards. 1216 Prospect St., La Jolla (phone: 454-7779). Expensive.

Butcher Shop – If, after the theater or other late activity, you crave a good steak, this is the place. Meals are served until 1 AM. Closed Sundays. Reservations advised. Major credit cards. 5255 Kearny Villa Rd. (phone: 565-2272). Moderate.

Café Pacifica – A seafood place that has pulled ahead in popularity. The fish is fresh; the seasoning cosmopolitan in the modern manner. An alternative to Mexican in Old Town. Dinner nightly, lunch weekdays. Major credit cards. 2414 San Diego Ave. (phone: 291-6666). Moderate.

China Camp – Not the usual Chinese menu, specialties include "gold miner's chicken" and "beggar's hen," based on the recipes of the Chinese immigrants who came to California in 1849 to pan for gold. Dinner nightly, lunch weekdays. Reservations advised. Major credit cards. Pacific Hwy. at Hawthorne (phone: 232-1367). Moderate.

Nino's – Unpretentious surroundings and superior food. The deep-fried zucchini and eggplant are served as an appetizer with every meal. Follow that with spaghetti in butter and garlic and veal fiorentina and you've got a meal to remember. Closed Mondays and Tuesdays. Reservations advised. Major credit cards. 4501 Mission Bay Dr. (phone: 274-3141). Moderate.

Pacifica Grill – A more casual downtown sibling of the *Café Pacifica* overlooks the ground level of a warehouse fetchingly converted into a mini-mall next to the Amtrak terminal. The restaurant features familiar dishes concocted on the principle that anything goes as long as it's southwestern. The wild mushroom fajitas with fresh herbs and Maui onion work beautifully, and the sourdough bread and coffee are exceptional. Dinner nightly, lunch weekdays. Major credit cards. 1202 Kettner Blvd. (phone: 696-9226). Moderate.

Croce's and Croce's Top Hat – The two form a unit as a memorial to a jazz player who was a great cook. Both are casual and simple and serve good food until midnight. Breakfast, lunch, and dinner at *Croce's;* weekend brunches and lighter fare at the *Top Hat.* Jazz performances nightly at the *Jazz Bar.* Major credit cards. Two blocks from Horton Plaza in the Gaslamp district. Corner of 5th Ave. and F St. (phone: 233-4355). Moderate to inexpensive.

Alfonso's of La Jolla – The Mexican dishes here are probably the most popular in town. Try carne asado Alfonso or one of the burrito or taco combination plates. Ask for Alfonso's Secret — it changes every day, and it's not on the menu. Open daily for lunch and dinner. Reservations advised. Major credit cards. 1251 Prospect St., La Jolla (phone: 454-2232). Inexpensive.

Calliope's – A Greek café and take-out place, where both the aromas and the prices are pleasing. Marinated fish, fowl, and meats are roasted or skewered for the grill, there are phyllo specialties and classic Greek appetizers and salads. Open daily, brunch on Sunday. Major credit cards. 3958 Fifth Ave. (phone: 291-5588). Inexpensive.

Chez Beat and Ralph – The Swiss-owned, cozy, arty neighborhood restaurant has a devoted following. The food is continental except on occasional Swiss nights, when fondue is the prima donna and yodelers the chorus. The desserts are irresistible anytime. Lunch weekdays, dinner daily, breakfast Sundays; closed Mondays. Visa and MasterCard only. 762 Garnet Ave. (phone: 463-2600). Inexpensive.

Corvette Diner – A fire engine red classic Corvette holds the place of honor in this noisy, jumping '50s bar and grill. It features excellent hamburgers with a variety of trimmings, mid-American nostalgic fare, and pure corn entertainment. Open from 11 AM to 11 PM weekdays, to midnight weekdends. $10 minimum on Visa and MasterCard. 3946 5th Ave. (phone:452-1076; or 542-1001 for recording). Inexpensive.

Old Town Mexican Café y Cantina – The Mexican favorite of most eaters in Old Town. Carnitas are the specialty. There is patio dining, and the bar stays open to 2 AM. Dinner nightly, lunch daily except Sundays, brunch Sundays. Major credit cards. 2489 San Diego Ave. (phone: 297-4330). Inexpensive.

Point Loma Seafoods – Hickory-smoked foods attract diners and gulls. Especially popular for take-out lunch. You pick up your meals, sit where you are, and throw what is left over to the birds. Lunch and dinner daily. No credit cards. Inexpensive.

SAN FRANCISCO

"San Franciscans are the luckiest people on earth; they not only get a vacation with pay, they have San Francisco to come home to." A Chamber of Commerce press release? No, just the sentiments of one of the lucky ones, *San Francisco Chronicle* columnist Herb Caen, who, like most of its residents, is in love with this city. It is a characteristic of genuine San Franciscans, whether native or transplanted, that they simply can't hear enough praise of the place. And such is the nature of San Francisco that they are very rarely disappointed. A visitor commented on her last day in the city, "I feel sorry for children born here. How sad to grow up and find out the whole world isn't like this." And even Billy Graham has stated publicly that "the Bay Area is so beautiful I hesitate to preach about heaven while I'm here."

Any place that can give pause to Billy Graham must be a remarkably well-endowed piece of geography. And so San Francisco is. The city occupies a hilly peninsula of 47 square miles, shaped something like a slightly crooked thumb pointing northward. On its western border is the Pacific Ocean; to the east is huge, beautiful San Francisco Bay. The waters of the Bay join the Pacific through the narrow northern strait that Golden Gate Bridge spans so spectacularly. When the Bay fills with fog, as it often does, the bridge becomes a single strand of lights riding over clouds. By choosing an inland suburb or an area on the coast, residents can have either the Sun Belt warmth of California's eternal spring or the sharper, foggier weather bred along the shoreline.

Either way, the city's climate is universally desirable for walking, if you can handle the incredibly steep hills. Hidden lanes, small houses circled by picket fences and surrounded by large commercial buildings, stately Victorian façades, stunning murals and other public art, and historical plaques reward even a casual stroll. Grant Avenue provides a tour of Chinatown; Columbus, a glimpse of Italian North Beach and the birthplace of the Beat Generation; and Post Street, a taste of San Francisco's fashionable shops and art galleries.

More demanding is a climb up the city's hills. To live "uphill" in any part of town is more prestigious than downhill, and to live on a famous hill tops all. Nob Hill, original home of the railroad nabobs and now site of several of the city's luxury hotels, is a most elegant address, and Russian Hill has renowned views of the city and the Bay. Along Telegraph Hill's eastern side, Filbert and Greenwich Streets create a series of steps that become wooden sidewalks fronting New England–style cottages, surrounded by gardens and filled with an impressive quiet.

For a city so generously festooned with views, vistas, and vantage points, San Francisco was a long time being discovered. Explorers seeking a northern strait and new lands, among them Sir Francis Drake and Juan Ro-

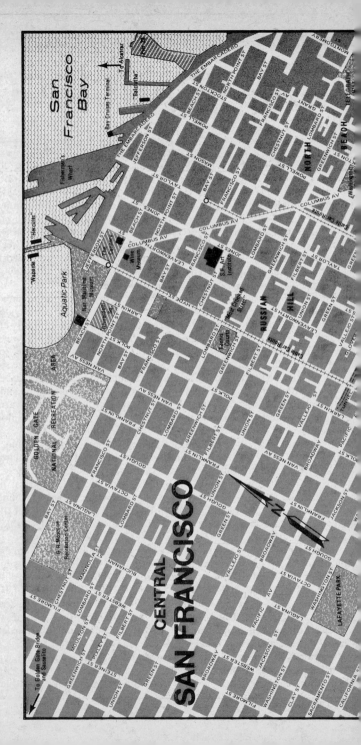

dríguez Cabrillo, sailed up and down the California coast without spying the great, but hidden, inner bay. In 1769, a Spanish land expedition led by Gaspar de Portolá blundered onto San Francisco Bay on a trek north from Mexico. Their goal had been Monterey, and their excitement at discovering one of the world's finest natural harbors was exceeded only by their confusion. The discovery, once made, did not go unexplored. In 1775, another Spaniard, Juan Manuel de Ayala, sailed through the rugged portals that had hidden the bay for so long, and for the first time the full potential of the inlet was realized.

Soon after, the area was fully incorporated into Spain's American empire when Father Junipero Serra built Mission Dolores. San Francisco was an early center for the Pacific fur trade, and the 19th century brought New England whalers, Russian trappers, and, when gold was discovered at Sutter's Mill in 1849, nearly everyone else and his brother. By 1850, the population of San Francisco had grown from 900 to 56,000 — prompting Will Rogers to observe a century later that it was "the city that never was a town." (The population is 750,000 today.) Ten years after the gold strike, silver was found in the Comstock Lode, and San Francisco was caught in a second wave of prosperity that carried it to the end of the century. While Levi Strauss made a minor fortune providing Nevada miners with blue jeans, Leland Stanford, Charles Crocker, Collis P. Huntington, and Mark Hopkins financed the transcontinental railroad.

In many ways, this uncompromising history influences the city's character today. The Gold Rush brought adventurers from around the world; they were violent, hard men, but they lived together with a certain graceless tolerance. The railroad brought Chinese into the city, and later came Japanese. Russians, Greeks, Mexicans, Filipinos, Scandinavians — all settled in larger and smaller communities around the city over the years. The result is an admirable harmony, and a kind of hodgepodge culture both pleasing and natural: In what other city is the longtime chef of the town's best pizza parlor Chinese? The basis for this culture is respect and tolerance among individual citizens. The city gives birth to new lifestyles, in part, because the civic body politic doesn't get choleric over diversity. It is a natural center of gay life, for example, and gays have been incorporated into the city's mainstream.

What is life like here? Consider this anecdote: In this city of hills, full buses occasionally have trouble negotiating the steepest inclines. A bus driver with a full load may be forced to stop before beginning ascent, to ask a few passengers to get off. Remarkably enough, some always do. This is an absolutely true story, but it is also a parable of sorts, a conundrum to contemplate when standing on Golden Gate Promenade. From there you will see the fine spires of the bridge, with the gold dome of the *Palace of Fine Arts* shining below, and in the distance, framing the picture, the blue Pacific. If that's not a sight worth getting off the bus for, you're just not resident material.

SAN FRANCISCO AT-A-GLANCE

SEEING THE CITY: Coit Tower, on the summit of Telegraph Hill, offers a spectacular panorama of San Francisco and the surrounding area: to the north are the waterfront and San Francisco Bay, the Golden Gate Bridge, Alcatraz Island, and on the far shore, Sausalito; downtown San Francisco lies to the south; to the east are Berkeley and the East Bay hills; and Nob Hill and Russian Hill rise to the west. The tower itself, a 210-foot cylindrical column built in 1934 under the Work Projects Administration, is a striking landmark against the city's skyline. Open daily. Small admission charge. Follow Telegraph Hill Blvd. to the top from Lombard and Kearny Sts. Twin Peaks is another excellent vantage point from which to view the city. Follow Twin Peaks Blvd. to the top. Several cocktail lounges offer fine views, too; the highest, at 779 feet, is the *Carnelian Room,* the restaurant and bar atop the Bank of America building, open nightly for dinner and on Sundays for brunch, 555 California St. (phone: 433-7500).

SPECIAL PLACES: San Francisco is a compact city and easy to get around. Most of the attractions are concentrated within a few areas, and the mild weather year-round makes walking pleasant, but you can sightsee by almost anything that rides, flies, or floats, from cable cars and their motorized facsimiles to buses, bicycles, carriages, boats, helicopters (in the wine country), to a beautifully preserved DC-3. Send $1 to the San Francisco Convention and Visitors Center, PO Box 6977, San Francisco, CA 94101, for the indispensable *San Francisco Book,* which lists many tour operators and videocassettes. The *Rides Guide–Auto Tape Tours,* 484 Lake Ave., Oakland (phone: 653-2553), has audiocassettes for do-it-yourself touring between Big Sur and the Napa and Sonoma valleys. *San Francisco Discovery Walks* offers visitors a close look at the city's fine architecture, gardens, views, and Victorian interiors. Contact Fred Baumeister, 1200 Taylor St., #32 (phone: 673-2894). For unusual field trips and informative insider's tours, call *Near Escapes* (phone: 921-1392).

DOWNTOWN

Civic Center – This 7-square-block area encompasses several attractive buildings and a nicely designed fountain and plaza. Among the buildings are City Hall, a notable example of Renaissance grandeur with a 300-foot-high dome; the *War Memorial Opera House,* site of the signing of the UN Charter in 1945 and current home of the *San Francisco Opera* and *Ballet;* the *Civic Auditorium,* scene of cultural and political events since 1915; and the *Louise M. Davies Symphony Hall.* The War Memorial Veterans Building houses the *San Francisco Museum of Modern Art.* Its fine permanent collections include works by Matisse, Klee, Calder, and Pollock, while changing exhibitions include works by internationally known modern and contemporary artists. Closed Mondays. Admission charge except Tuesdays from 10 AM to 5 PM; reduced on Thursday nights. McAllister St. and Van Ness Ave. (phone: 863-8800). Bounded by Van Ness Ave. and Hyde, McAllister, and Grove Sts., the Civic Center is also a good place to start the 49-Mile Drive, a well-marked trail that takes in many of the city's highlights. Just follow the blue, white, and orange seagull signs.

Union Square – Right in the shopping area, Union Square offers respite from the crowds of people in its throngs of pigeons. You can feed the pigeons, relax on the benches, and watch the fashion shows, concerts, and flower displays that are held here in good weather. The elegant *St. Francis* hotel is on the west side of the square, while the surrounding area contains sidewalk flower stands and the city's finest shops. Among the most interesting of these is *Gump's,* which has a beautiful collection of jade pieces among its many rare imports (250 Post St.; phone: 982-1616). Bordered by Geary, Post, Powell and Stockton Sts.

Bank of California Museum – The bank maintains a *Museum of Money of the American West,* a collection of Gold Rush artifacts, silver ingots, and privately minted gold coins. Open weekdays during banking hours. No admission charge. 400 California St. (phone: 765-0400).

Wells Fargo History Museum – The history room features more of Old California, with photographs and relics from Gold Rush days, and the Wells Fargo Overland Stage, the wagon that brought pioneers west, as well as coins, placer, and hard rock gold from mother lode mines. Open weekdays from 9 AM to 5 PM. Free. 420 Montgomery St. (phone: 396-2619).

Embarcadero Center – This 8½-acre area, housing shopping malls and offices, between the financial district and the waterfront features several notable sculptures, including the Vaillancourt Fountain (100 abstractly arranged concrete boxes with water pouring out of the ends) and a 60-foot sculpture by Louise Nevelson. At noon, street merchants set up stalls and you can pick up a variety of handcrafted goods — leather items, jewelry, macramé, paintings, and sculptures. At the foot of Market St.

Chinatown – The largest Chinese community outside of the Orient, Chinatown is an intriguing 24-block enclave of pagoda-roofed buildings, excellent restaurants, fine import shops featuring ivory carvings and jade jewelry from the Orient, temples, and museums. Grant Avenue is the main thoroughfare — enter through an archway crowned with a dragon (Grant at Bush St.). Best to go on foot or take the California Street cable car, because the area is too congested for easy parking. The Old St. Mary's Church, built in 1854 of granite from China, is the city's oldest cathedral. It survived the earthquake, perhaps because of its warning on the façade above the clock dial: "Son Observe the Time and Fly from Evil" (Grant Ave. and California St.). More words of wisdom, as well as regional artifacts, including tiny slippers used for the bound feet of Oriental ladies, pipes from Old Chinatown opium dens, and photographs of some famed telephone operators who memorized the names and numbers of 2,400 Chinatown residents in the old days, can be found at the *Chinese Historical Society of America Museum.* Open Tuesdays through Saturdays, 1 to 5 PM. No admission charge. 17 Adler Pl. off Columbus Ave. (phone: 391-1188). For information on walking tours of Chinatown, contact the Chinese Cultural Center, 750 Kearny St. (phone: 986-1822), Tuesdays through Saturdays.

You haven't really experienced Chinatown fully until you've had dim sum, a brunch or luncheon feast of a variety of delicate morsels — chopped mushrooms in half-moons of rice dough, deep-fried sweet potato, meat dumplings; try either *Yank Sing,* 427 Battery St. (phone: 362-1640), or the *Hong Kong Tea House,* 835 Pacific Ave. (phone: 391-6365). Bordered by Kearny, Mason, Bush Sts. and Broadway.

North Beach – There is no longer a beach here, but this traditional neighborhood remains colorful and diverse — mostly Italians, Basques, and Chinese. The area's great for strolling and eating — there are bakeries and bread shops selling cannolis, rum babas, marzipan, and panettone (a round, sweet bread filled with raisins and candied fruit). There are numerous restaurants and cafés where you can have dinner, espresso, or cappuccino. For lunch or dinner, the *Washington Square Bar and Grill,* 1707 Powell St. (phone: 982-8123), has great pasta, fresh fish, and veal as well as a popular bar. Or if you want to make it yourself, you can pick up art imports and majolica espresso pots at *Biordi's,* 412 Columbus Ave. (phone: 392-8096). At night, the district around Broadway offers everything from rock music and jazz to Italian opera on the jukebox at *Tosca Café,* 242 Columbus (phone: 391-1244), to excellent shows by female impersonators at the legendary *Finocchio's,* 506 Broadway (phone: 982-9388). Day or night, *Enrico's Sidewalk Restaurant,* 504 Broadway (phone: 392-6220), is perfect for sipping, snacking, and people watching. One of the best times of year to visit North Beach is in early June, during the street bazaar, when local artists display their wares along Upper Grant Avenue. Other times, numerous galleries and studios exhibit crafts, paintings, jewelry, and unusual clothing. Washington Square is a nice place to sit in the sun or have lunch with the paisanos under the statue of not the square's namesake but Benjamin Franklin (Columbus and Union Sts.). Extends north and northwest from Chinatown to San Francisco Bay.

Japan Center – This attractive modern complex is the focal point in culture and trade of San Francisco's substantial Japanese community. The 5-acre area contains the *Kabuki Theater,* teahouses, restaurants, sushi and tempura bars, art galleries, shops selling everything from pearls to stereo equipment, a school where you can learn Japanese dollmaking and flower arranging, and the Japanese consulate. The elegantly landscaped Peace Plaza with its 5-tiered Peace Pagoda in the center of a reflecting pool is the scene of the April *Cherry Blossom Festival* and traditional Japanese celebrations, like the Mochi-Pounding Ceremony (in which much preparation and even more pounding result in delicious rice cakes). Speaking of pounding, the recently renovated *Kabuki Hot Springs and Japanese Spa* offers shiatsu massage, traditional Japanese baths, whirlpool baths, saunas, steambaths, and other services; the works will make you feel good as a newly made rice cake (1750 Geary Blvd.; phone: 922-6000). Bounded by Laguna, Fillmore, Geary, and Post Sts.

FISHERMAN'S WHARF AND VICINITY

Fisherman's Wharf – This rambling waterfront section is at once the center of the commercial fishing industry and California's major tourist attraction, second only to Disneyland. On the wharf at Jefferson Street you walk through an open-air fish market where you can partake in an old San Francisco tradition. Buy a loaf of freshly baked sourdough bread at *Boudin's Bread Company* and create the ultimate urban picnic by adding Dungeness crab purchased at one of the numerous sidewalk stalls. The fishing boats return in the afternoon and hoist their crates of fish to the pier at the foot of Jones and Leavenworth Sts. If you're up late (about 3 AM), there are few sights at that hour more impressive than the San Francisco fleet leaving the harbor for a day's catch. The wharf restaurants are often crowded and expensive, and you would do better to have a seafood dinner elsewhere (see *Eating Out*). But the wharf vicinity does have many sidewalk stalls selling handcrafted items, and interesting sights have sprung up around this fishing base. Among things to see:

Pier 39 – Reconstructed with wood salvaged from other (demolished) piers, Pier 39 is a popular entertainment complex on the northern waterfront. A pleasant hour or two can be spent ambling through the plethora of shops — crafts, bakery, import, clothing, specialty, toy, jewelry, camera, fine food, crystal and silver, and many others. Meanwhile, mimes, jugglers, and other street performers provide continuous entertainment. For lunch or dinner, there's an international roster of cuisines from which to choose — Mexican, Italian, Japanese, Chinese, Swiss, French, Polynesian; grab a bite at one of the numerous, stand-up, take-out fresh seafood booths; or simply indulge your sweet tooth at *Swensen's,* a member of the famous ice cream chain. Children can run off excess energy at the Pier's playground and park or take a ride on the double-decker Venetian carousel at the end of the pier; weekend sailors and fishermen can charter boats at the marina. Pier 39, on the Embarcadero, just east of Fisherman's Wharf. (Parking garage across the way on Beach St.)

San Francisco Maritime National Historic Park – A huge, ship shape building at the foot of Polk St., the park's *Museum Exhibits Building* is a treasure trove of photographs tracing shipping development from Gold Rush days to the present: with figureheads, massive anchors, shipwreck relics, and beautiful model ships. Open Wednesdays through Fridays. No admission charge. Aquatic Park (phone: 556-6435 or 556-9870). Berthed off Hyde Street Pier nearby, three old ships welcome the public. The *Balclutha* was a British cargo ship that had rounded Cape Horn 17 times carrying rice and wine to San Francisco, worked as an Alaskan salmon trader, and even did a stint in Hollywood as a rather oversized prop in sea films. The *Eureka* used to shuttle across the bay, carrying passengers and cars in the early decades of the century. The antique automobiles displayed on the car deck are sure to delight car buffs. Aboard the schooner CS *Thayer*, "sailors" demonstrate raising sails and tying knots against the background of sea chanteys. Open daily. Admission charge. Hyde St. Pier (phone: 556-6435).

Pier 45/USS *Pampanito* – A project of the National Maritime Museum Association. Historical photographs of this World War II submarine, including its role in the sinking of two Japanese ships with 2,000 British and Australian POWs aboard and the rescue of 73 survivors 2 days later, are on display on the pier. On board, a narrated tape guides visitors through the operations and life of a submersible, where every inch of space had to be put to life-and-death use. Open daily. Pier 45 (phone: 929-0202).

Bay Cruises – The *Blue and Gold Fleet* (Pier 39; phone: 781-7877) and the *Red and White Fleet* (Pier 43½, near Fisherman's Wharf, and Pier 41 (phone: 546-2896 or 800-445-8880), cruise year-round past Alcatraz Island and the Golden Gate Bridge and then to the shoreline of Marin County, rimming the bay. Departures every day, all day, year-round. Admission charge. For evening vistas of the Bay Area from the water, *Hornblower Yachts* offers luxury dining cruises (phone: 434-0300).

Alcatraz Island – This famed escape-proof federal penitentiary stands out grimly in the bay, 1½ miles from Fisherman's Wharf. Such notorious criminals as Al Capone, "Machine Gun" Kelly, and Doc Barker never returned from their stays here. The prison was closed in 1963 because of exorbitant operating costs and has been open to the public since 1973. The National Park Service runs tours of the prison block, where you see the "dark holes" in which rebellious prisoners were confined in solitude, and the tiny steel-barred cells. Two-hour tours depart daily on a first-come, first-served basis; tickets may be purchased in advance through Ticketron. Departs from Pier 41 (phone: 546-2896 or 800-445-8880).

Ghirardelli Square – Originally a chocolate factory and a woolen mill, which turned out uniforms for the Union Army during the Civil War, these stately red brick buildings now house import shops where you can find anything from Persian rugs to Chinese kites, outdoor cafés, art galleries, and fine restaurants. The *Mandarin* serves excellent Chinese food; *Maxwell's of San Francisco* (phone: 673-8812) has a flashy setting and a stunning bay view; but perhaps sweetest of all is the *Ghirardelli Chocolate Manufactory* (phone: 771-4903), where you can watch chocolate being made and then eat the spoils afterward, and, if you're truly inspired, the Golden Gate banana split, which tops all — three scoops of ice cream, three flavors of syrup, and a banana bridge rising above mountains of whipped cream. Open daily. Bounded by Beach, Larkin, North Point, and Polk Sts.

The Cannery – Similar to Ghirardelli Square, canned fruits and vegetables were the products here. Today this 3-level arcade features chic boutiques and restaurants and an olive tree–shaded central courtyard where street musicians and mimes strut their stuff. Open daily. Bounded by Beach, Leavenworth, and Jefferson Sts.

Lombard Street – Often referred to as the most twisting urban street in the world, Lombard St. has eight switchbacks in a single block. Drive down slowly or, better yet, stroll, taking time to appreciate the lovely residential façades, colorful flowers, and lush plantings. Between Hyde and Leavenworth Sts.

GOLDEN GATE — THE PROMENADE AND THE PARK

Golden Gate Promenade – This 3½-mile shoreline trail is among the most spectacular walks (or jogging paths) in America. You meander from Aquatic Park past lush green trees, eroding rocky points, a classy yacht harbor in front of the St. Francis Yacht Club, a grassy park beside an old cobbled sea wall, all the while approaching that ultimate of spans, the Golden Gate Bridge. Near the seawall, the incoming tide fills the pipes of the Wave Organ, creating music by the sea. A number of interesting museums line the way. *Ft. Point,* completed in 1861 as the West Coast's only Civil War outpost, is now a National Historic Site. No admission charge (under the bridge, phone: 556-1693). The *Presidio Army Museum,* established in 1776 as a Spanish garrison, has artifacts illustrating its whole history. Closed Mondays. No admission charge. Lincoln and Funston Ave. (phone: 561-4115). Most unusual is the *Palace of Fine Arts,* a grand Beaux Arts building constructed for the Panama-Pacific Exhibition of 1915. It houses the Exploratorium, a collection of 400 displays on science, technology, and the reaches and limits of human perception. Closed Mondays and Tuesdays. Admission charge for adults. 3601 Lyon St. (phone: 563-7337).

Golden Gate Bridge – The loftiest and one of the longest single-span suspension bridges ever constructed, the bright-orange Golden Gate marked its 50th anniversary in 1987 with a huge civic celebration that culminated in the permanent lighting of its towers. To enjoy a stunning view, follow the handicapped-accessible walk up to the toll plaza level, where you'll also find new gardens landscaped with native flowering plants. From here you have several options: You can catch a bus back downtown; turn around, and walk back with the view of the city skyline accompanying you all the way; or follow in the footsteps of great coast trekkers across the Golden Gate Bridge and beyond — north along trails on the ridges and shoreline for 60 miles to Tomales Point. You can walk across the bridge (or under it); if you are driving, take the very first exit north of the bridge, park, and enjoy the terrific view of San Francisco.

California Palace of the Legion of Honor – A memorial for America's World War I dead, modeled after its namesake in Paris, this beautiful classic Greek building houses a fine collection of European art from medieval to Impressionist, represented by Monet, Manet, and Degas and Rodin sculptures. Closed Mondays and Tuesdays. Admission charge includes entry to the *de Young Museum* (see below). Lincoln Park (phone: 750-3600).

Golden Gate Park – Developed from 1,000 acres of rolling sand dunes, Golden Gate Park has all the amenities of a large recreation area. There are bike paths, hiking and equestrian trails, three lakes (where you can sail model boats, or rent real ones, or practice casting), sports fields, and a 25-acre meadow. The park also features a Rose Garden, a lovely Rhododendron Dell, the Strybing Arboretum — over 70 acres rich with 5,000 species of plants and trees from all over the world — and the Conservatory of Flowers, a greenhouse with lush tropical growth. (Arboretum and Conservatory open daily. Free. Along South Drive and Conservatory Drive respectively.) The *Japanese Tea Garden* is a masterpiece of Oriental landscaping with a half-moon wishing-well bridge, a bronze Buddha, a temple, a teahouse serving jasmine and green tea, and, in the spring, magnificent blooms of cherry blossoms. Open daily. Admission charge. (Off South Drive just west of the *de Young Museum.*) No such lyrical setting could be complete without music, and the Music Concourse offers this with free open-air *Municipal Band* concerts on Sunday afternoons when weather is good (between the *de Young Museum* and the *California Academy of Sciences*). The park also has three fine museums:

M. H. de Young Memorial Museum – One of the West Coast's major art museums, it houses paintings, sculpture, and decorative arts from more than 300 cultures and an outstanding collection of American art. Closed Mondays and Tuesdays. Admission charge (phone: 750-3600).

Asian Art Museum of San Francisco – The bulk of this 6-century array of jades, bronzes, ceramics, paintings, woodwork, and art from India, Korea, and Southeast Asia was donated by Avery Brundage. Closed Mondays and Tuesdays. Admission charge (phone: 668-8922).

California Academy of Sciences – The state's oldest scientific institution offers a wide variety of exhibitions ranging from the Steinhart Aquarium, with dolphins, piranhas, talking fish, penguins, and 14,000 other species, to the farthest reaches of space in the Morrison Planetarium's changing shows. Open daily. Admission charge. On the Music Concourse (phone: 221-5100).

Cable Car Museum – This lovely brick building is the powerhouse for the current system and the storehouse for cable car history. The first cable car, invented in 1873 by Andrew Hallidie, and exact scale models of cars servicing all the various lines are on display here at their middle stop. Open daily. Free. Washington and Mason Sts., near Chinatown (phone: 474-1887).

San Francisco Zoo – The addition of Koala Crossing and an ultramodern Primate Discovery Center make a visit here more worthwhile than ever. More than 1,000 birds and animals can be viewed on foot or from aboard the motorized tour train. Adjacent to the main zoo is the Children's Zoo, a 7-acre nursery where children can stroke barnyard animals or watch baby lions being bottle fed (phone: 661-7777). The spectacular primate center has dozens of exotic and/or endangered species as well as a sophisticated discovery center full of hands-on experiments and informative, fun-to-do computer/slide programs. Open daily. Admission charge. Sloat Blvd. and 45th Ave. (phone: 661-4844).

■**EXTRA SPECIAL:** Within an hour's drive of San Francisco (north along US 101, Rte. 37, then Rte. 21) begins the number one wine-producing region in the US, the gently rolling Sonoma County and, beyond, the Napa Valley. The most interesting wineries for tours and tastings are Beringer (St. Helena), where you tour cellars dug into a hillside and then attend a tasting at Gothic Rhine House; the Christian Brothers (Mont LaSalle); and the Sterling Vineyards (south of Calistoga), with its striking Aegean-style architecture. The mild weather encourages not only grape production but also outdoor activity. Pick up some bread and cheese along Highway 29 en route to Bothe–Napa Valley State Park. Its 1,000 acres of broad-leaved trees, pines, and redwoods are lovely for picnicking, biking, and swimming in summer. In Yountville, you can shop on three levels at Vintage 1879, a bevy of specialty stores housed in a renovated brick warehouse, or take a hot-air balloon ride (contact *Adventures Aloft,* phone: 707-255-8688). Calistoga, to the north, is a health spa with its own "Old Faithful" geyser, a 60-foot shower of steam erupting about every 40 minutes. If time permits, try one of Napa Valley's charming bed-and-breakfast establishments, such as *La Residence* in Napa, 4066 St. Helena Hwy. N., Napa, CA 94558 (phone: 707-253-0337), or lovely resorts. *Meadowood,* 900 Meadowood La., St. Helena, CA 94574 (phone: 707-963-3646), and *Auberge du Soleil,* 180 Rutherford Hill Rd., Rutherford, CA 94573 (phone: 707-963-1211), both have renowned restaurants.

South of San Francisco and about 1½ hours away (via US 101, then Rte. 156, then Rte. 1; or via the slow, scenic coastal Rte. 1 all the way) lies the Monterey Peninsula, an area rich in history and natural beauty. The town of Monterey was the military capital of California under three flags, and many of its adobe buildings survive in the State History Park. In Cannery Row, where gift shops and restaurants have taken over defunct sardine canneries, the Monterey Bay Aquarium is a spectacular re-creation of the region's marine life. The peninsula's pines and broad white beaches, bright with flowering succulents, are breathtaking. Famous for golf on Pebble Beach, the area attracts nature lovers who come to see monarch butterflies wintering in Pacific Grove, sea otters, seals, and the wild shorelands of Point Lobos State Preserve, south of Carmel. In this inexplicably faux-Bavarian resort town is a blessedly Mediterranean retreat with gorgeous gardens, the *La Playa* hotel, El Camino Real at 8th, Carmel-by-the-Sea, CA 93921 (phone: 408-624-6476 or 800-582-8900), the place to stay.

SOURCES AND RESOURCES

TOURIST INFORMATION: The San Francisco Convention and Visitors Bureau, at 1390 Market St. (PO Box 6977, San Francisco, CA 94101), is best for brochures, maps, general tourist information, and personal help. If you write ahead, it will send you a valuable package of information, including a 3-month calendar of events. Call 391-2000 anytime for the lowdown on what's going on in town. Its downtown Visitor Information Center on the lower level of Halladie Plaza (just downstairs from the cable car turnaround) provides multilingual service. 900 Market St. at Powell St. (phone: 974-6900).

San Francisco at Your Feet by Margot Patterson Doss (Grove Press; $7.95) is a good walking guide.

Television Station – KGO Channel 7–ABC; KCBS Channel 5–CBC; KRON Channel 4–NBC; KQED Channel 9–PBS.

Radio Station – AM: KGO 810 (news/talk); KCBS 740 (news/talk); KFRC 610 (oldies). FM: KQED 88.5 (classical); KXXX 99.7 (top 40); KJAZ 92.7 (jazz).

Local Coverage – *San Francisco Chronicle,* morning daily; *San Francisco Examiner,* evening daily. Sundays, the two publish a joint edition, including a comprehensive entertainment section, the Datebook.

Food – Check *Restaurants of San Francisco* by Patricia Untermann and Stan Sesser (Chronicle Books; $7.95).

Telephone – The area code for San Francisco is 415.

Sales Tax – The basic sales tax is 6.5%, and the hotel tax is 11%.

CLIMATE: Daytime temperatures average 60F to 65F in summer and 45F to 57F in winter, so residents vary their spring-like wardrobes of knits and lightweight woolens only slightly from season to season. In summer, morning and evening fogs make parts of the day very cool, so a jacket or sweater is essential. Traditional summery cottons are still useful outside the city, however, because while it is 65F in San Francisco, it can be in the 80s in the suburbs. In winter, a topcoat — preferably a lined raincoat (downpours are common between November and March) — should be adequate.

GETTING AROUND: Airports – San Francisco International Airport is about 16 miles south of the city, a 30-minute drive when it's not rush hour. Taxi fare from downtown to the airport should run about $25. A number of shuttle operators provide transportation to and from the airport for about $7 each way. Pick one up at the airport and reserve your return trip 6 hours ahead. SFO Airporter buses run every 20 minutes between the airport and downtown for $4 one way, $7 round trip. SAMTRANS buses (phone: 761-7000) serve both the peninsula and downtown San Francisco (the Transbay Terminal at Mission and 1st Sts.). Buses depart from the airport every half-hour during the day, hourly at night; the fare is $1.25. For more information on the airport's facilities, consult one of its teleguide terminals.

Oakland International Airport is a 30-minute drive from San Francisco's financial district during non-commuter hours; cab fare should run about $30. Bus transportation into downtown San Francisco is provided by AC Transit (phone: 839-2882) for $1.50. Rail service is available via the BART system (phone: 464-6000 or 788-2278); take a shuttle bus to the *Oakland Coliseum Arena* ($1), and then pick up BART to Montgomery St. in downtown San Francisco ($1.90). For airport information, call 444-4444.

Bus – Efficient and inexpensive buses serve the entire metropolitan area. Bus maps appear at the front of the yellow pages in the telephone book. For detailed route information contact MUNI (Municipal Transit) of San Francisco, 949 Presidio Ave. (673-MUNI).

Streetcar – Five lines of the MUNI Metro streetcar system run under Market Street, one level above BART, and branch off toward various parts of the city. For route information, call 673-MUNI.

Cable Car – The best way to travel up and over the hills of the city is aboard these famous trademarks; they are pulled along at 9½ miles an hour. There are three lines, and the most scenic is the Hyde Park line, which you can pick up at the turntable at Powell and Market Sts. It will take you over both Nob and Russian Hills to gaslit Victorian Square. For route information call 673-MUNI.

BART – If you really want to move, this ultramodern, high-speed rapid transit rail network will whisk you from San Francisco to Oakland, Richmond, Concord, Daly City, and Fremont at up to 80 miles an hour. The system is easy to use, with large maps and boards in each station clarifying routes and fares. For information, contact Bay Area Rapid Transit, 800 Madison St., Oakland (phone: 788-2278).

Taxi – Cabs can be hailed in the street or called on the phone. Major cab companies are *Yellow Cab* (phone: 626-2345); *Veterans Cab* (phone: 552-1300); *Luxor Cab* (phone: 282-4141).

Car Rental – There are a few things to remember if you plan to drive in San Francisco: Cable cars and pedestrians always have the right-of-way; curb your wheels when parking on a hill to prevent runaway cars. The national firms all serve San Francisco. Least expensive is *Bob Leech Autorental*, with Toyota Tercels and Corollas at $15.95 a day with 100 free miles, 10¢ for each mile thereafter. Sports coupes run $19.95. Five minutes from the airport at 435 S. Airport Blvd., South San Francisco (phone: 583-3844).

LOCAL SERVICES: Babysitting – *Bay Area Baby Sitters Agency,* 758 San Diego Ave., Daly City (phone: 991-7474).

Business Services – *Red Carpet Services,* 821 Market St. (phone: 495-1910).

Mechanics – *California Garage,* for American cars, 1776 Green St. between Gough and Octavia Sts. (phone: 474-0279). *Foreign Car Repair,* for imports, 6027 Geary between 24th and 25th Sts. (phone: 752-8305).

MUSEUMS: The city's major museums are all described in *Special Places.* Others worth a visit:

Archives for the Performing Arts – Weekdays (appointments preferred). War Memorial Opera House, near Fulton and Franklin Sts. (phone: 431-0717).

California Historical Society – 2090 Jackson St. (phone: 567-1848).

Mexican Museum – Wednesday through Sunday afternoons. Ft. Mason Bldg. D, Laguna St. and Marina Blvd. (phone: 441-0404).

Museo Italo-Americano – Wednesday through Sunday afternoons. Ft. Mason Bldg. C (phone: 673-2200).

SHOPPING: Shopping the neighborhoods as well as downtown is easy in a compact city. For Japanese wares one can go to Japantown; for Chinese, Chinatown. With Ghirardelli Square, the Cannery, and Pier 39, San Francisco revived the age-old combination of marketplace and fun fair. When serious buying is the object — and money is not — the place to be is Union Square and the streets that frame it. In the square stand department stores: *Macy's, Saks Fifth Avenue, I. Magnin,* and *Neiman Marcus.* Specialty shops include firms from Britain, France, Italy, Denmark, and Switzerland, and native competitors. Not to be confused with Union Square is a stretch of Union Street on the old dairyland, Cow Hollow, and another on Fillmore Street. On Victorian Union Street, exotic and unusual gift shops predominate, while Fillmore's specialty is fashion, both new and vintage. Here's a window-shopper's sampler. For more bargains in high fashion, explore the factory outlets south of Market Street, which open to the public on weekends.

Alfred Dunhill of London – Classic men's wear from a once-and-present tobacconist. 290 Post St. (phone: 781-3368).

Bally of Switzerland – Europe's most popular high-quality shoe chain. 238 Stockton St. (phone: 398-7463).

The Collector – Private label and other designer fashions for women. 537 Sutter St. (phone: 981-8570).

Coup de Chapeau – An anachronistic custom milliner. 1906 Fillmore (phone: 931-7793).

L'Essentiel de Provence – A wide selection of herbs, fragrances, and potpourris from France. 1728 Union St. (phone: 928-4483).

Eileen Geary – A local designer's retail shop. 90 Grant St. (phone: 982-7737).

Gump's – Found here are art, jewelry, crystal, china, sculpture, furniture, stationery and food. *Gump's* also hosts an annual thematic "event," with proceeds going to benefit cultural and social organizations. Close to Chinatown. 250 Post St. (phone: 982-1616).

Hermès – The familiar signature on high-priced silk scarves belongs to this Frenchman, who began as a harnessmaker and branched out to leather and other accessories. 1 Union Square (phone: 391-7200).

Jessica McClintock – Beaded, lacy original fashions. 353 Sutter St. (phone: 397-0987).

Laura Ashley – The nostalgic Victorian recently relocated. 253 Post St. (phone: 788-0190) and 1827 Union St. (phone: 920-7200).

Louis Vuitton – Accessories with the familiar royalist-French logos. 317 Sutter St. (phone: 391-6200).

N. Peal Cashmere – A branch of a shop in London's Burlington Arcade. It stocks the finest sweaters, and shares the premises with Swaine Adeney, which sells men's clothing. 434 Post St. (phone: 421-2713).

Next to New Shop – The name says it all. 2226 Fillmore (phone: 567-1627).

Oggatte – A large selection of Florentine papers and other gift items. 1846 Union St. (phone: 346-0631).

Paris 1925 – For old watches and Art Deco jewelry. 1954 Union St. (phone: 567-1925).

Paul Bogner – European sportswear. 400 Sutter St. (phone: 434-3888).

Repeat Performance – Almost-new clothing. 2223 Fillmore (phone: 563-3123).

Seconds-to-Go – Another good, used-clothing store. 2252 Fillmore (phone: 563-7806).

Smile – A gallery with "tongue in chic:" art and crafts with a sense of humor. 750 Union St. (phone: 799-1901).

A. Sulka & Co. – Famous for ties, it also sells men's shirts, slacks, and robes. 188 Post St. (phone: 362-3450).

The Way We Wore – Vintage clothing. 2238 Fillmore (phone: 346-1386).

Victoria's Secret – For romantic, frilly underclothes. 395 Sutter (phone: 397-0521) and 2245 Union St. (phone: 921-5444).

Wilkes-Bashford – High-priced men's clothing; sip Perrier while making selections. 375 Sutter St. (phone: 986-4380).

Williams-Sonoma – San Francisco is the home of this expensive kitchenware chain. 576 Sutter St. (phone: 982-0295).

Zoe – Far-out, expensive clothes. 2400 Fillmore (phone: 929-0441).

 MAJOR COLLEGES AND UNIVERSITIES: Two of the country's most prestigious universities are near San Francisco: University of California at Berkeley, Sproul Hall, Berkeley (phone: 642-6000), and Stanford University in Palo Alto (phone: 723-2300). San Francisco State University, 1600 Holloway Ave. (phone: 338-1111), and the University of San Francisco, Golden Gate Ave. and Parker Ave. (phone: 666-6886), are in the city.

 SPECIAL EVENTS: The *Chinese New Year,* a week-long celebration in January or February (depending on the fullness of the moon) begins with numerous private observances — settling of debts and honoring of ancestors — and then Chinatown goes public with festivals that draw thousands to the streets for the colorful Dragon Parade, featuring a block-long dragon, Miss Chinatown USA pageant, marching bands, and elaborate fireworks. To buy reserved bleacher seats, contact the Chinese Chamber of Commerce, 730 Sacramento St. (phone: 982-3000).

The *Cherry Blossom Festival,* held on 2 weekends in April at Japan Center (Post and Buchanan Sts.; phone: 922-6776), features traditional tea ceremonies, flower arranging and dollmaking demonstrations, bonsai displays, and performances by folk dancers from Japan. The crosstown parade highlights the events with over 50 Japanese performing groups and intricate floats of shrines and temples.

Fleet Week celebrates the birthday of the US Navy with a parade of ships under the Golden Gate Bridge and several days of open house on the vessels, plus aerial events, fireworks, and boat rides.

The *Grand National Livestock Exposition, Horse Show, and Rodeo,* held in late October and early November at the Cow Palace (6 miles south of the city on Rte. 101), is one of the biggest events in the country, with all manner of rodeo events, equestrian competitions, and the best livestock in the West.

 SPORTS AND FITNESS: The Bay Area has everything in professional sports.

 Baseball – The San Francisco *Giants* play from April to October in *Candlestick Park* (phone: 467-8000). Gilman Ave., on the southern edge of the city on Rte. 101. The Oakland *A's* play at the *Oakland Coliseum Stadium* (phone: 638-0500).

Basketball – The NBA's *Golden State Warriors* play from October to March at the *Oakland Coliseum Arena* (phone: 638-6000).

Bicycling – Rent from any of the three *Avenue Cyclery* locations (phone: 387-3155): 756 Stanyan St., 1269 9th Ave., or 1865 Haight St. All are near Golden Gate Park, which has good bike trails.

Fishing – Fine salmon fishing in the sea beyond the bay. Season is mid-February to mid-October. Charter boats leave daily early in the morning and return in the afternoon. For information contact *Captain Ron's Pacific Charters,* 300 Jefferson St. at Fisherman's Wharf (phone: 771-2800). You can also cast off San Francisco's municipal pier at Aquatic Park, anytime. No license required.

Fitness Centers – *Fitness Break,* 30 Hotaling Pl. near Washington and Montgomery Sts. (phone: 788-1681), has weekday aerobic workouts, mornings, noons, and evenings; showers and lockers available. The *YMCA,* 166 Embarcadero (phone: 392-2191), has a pool, sauna, and weight room, along with racquetball and handball courts. The *YWCA,* 620 Sutter (phone: 775-6500), has a pool as well as a hotel.

Football – The San Francisco *49ers* play at *Candlestick Park* from August to December (phone: 468-2249).

Golf – There are fine courses at Golden Gate Park (phone: 751-8987), Lincoln Park (phone: 221-9911), and Harding Park (phone: 664-4690).

Horseback Riding – Rent from *Golden Gate Stables,* Kennedy Dr. at 36th Ave. (phone: 668-7360). Seven miles of equestrian trails wind through the park.

Jogging – Run along the Embarcadero to the Marina Green; jog back and forth across the Golden Gate Bridge (1½ miles each way) and enjoy the fore and aft views as well as the one directly below. Take the #5 bus, which stops on Market, out to Golden Gate Park, where there are numerous dirt and concrete trails, not to mention plenty of other joggers. (It's not recommended to run alone in the park).

Racing – For horse racing, *Bay Meadows* is the place, in San Mateo (phone: 574-7223). Seasons are: quarter horse racing — third week of February through the third week of April; thoroughbred racing — first week of September through the first week of February. In the East Bay, *Golden Gate Fields* features thoroughbred racing from early February through late June (phone: 526-3020).

Skating – Roller skating is very popular in San Francisco, especially in Golden Gate Park on Sundays, when traffic is detoured off the park's main roads. You can rent skates from *Magic Skates* (phone: 668-1117), 3038 Fulton St. at 6th Ave., right across from the Park.

Swimming – Though much of San Francisco's waters are too rough and cold for swimming, Phelan Beach is good when the weather permits and the current is safe, at Sea Cliff Ave. and El Camino Del Mar.

Tennis – Good public tennis courts are in Golden Gate Park on John F. Kennedy Dr. (phone: 566-4800).

Yacht Racing – The Yacht Racing Association holds several races each year in San Francisco Bay. Good observation points are the Marina and the Vista Point area on the north side of the Golden Gate Bridge (for information, call 771-9500).

 THEATER: The *American Conservatory Theater* is an excellent resident repertory company and performs classical productions and modern plays from October to June at the *Geary Theater,* 415 Geary St. (phone: 673-6440). The *Curran Theater* is best for musicals and often stages traveling Broadway productions, 445 Geary St. (phone: 776-5080). The *Orpheum Theater,* 1192 Market St. (phone: 474-3800), and the *Golden Gate Theater,* Golden Gate and Taylor Sts. (phone: 474-3800), also feature Broadway shows. *Club Fugazi,* an old North Beach landmark, has camp productions in a nightclub setting, 678 Green St. (phone: 421-4222).

 MUSIC: The *San Francisco Opera Company,* featuring celebrated guest artists, performs at the *War Memorial Opera House* (Civic Center) from September to early December. Since tickets are difficult to get, it's best to write in advance: War Memorial Opera House, Box Office, San Francisco 94102 (phone: 864-3300). The *San Francisco Ballet,* the country's oldest company and among the finest, moves into the *Opera House* with its *Nutcracker* production in December, followed by a repertory season from January through May (phone: 621-3838). The *San Francisco Symphony* season runs from September through May at *Davies Symphony Hall* in the Civic Center (phone: 431-5400), but the orchestra can be heard at other times, too, such as during its *June Beethoven Festival* or its July *Pops Concerts* in the *Civic Auditorium*. The *Midsummer Music Festival* is a series of free Sunday ballet, symphony, opera, jazz, and ethnic programs from mid-June to mid-August at *Stern Grove,* 19th Ave. and Sloat Blvd.

Tickets for most music, dance, and theater events can be obtained through BASS ticket centers (phone: 762-2277) and Teletron (phone: 329-SHOW). In addition, half-price tickets to many events can be bought (cash or traveler's checks only) on the day of performance at the STBS booth on the Stockton Street side of Union Square, Tuesdays through Saturdays from noon to 7:30 or 8 PM (phone: 433-STBS for recorded information).

NIGHTCLUBS AND NIGHTLIFE: San Francisco is alive at night and can keep you going whether you're inclined toward jazz or high camp. Much of the nightlife glitters around North Beach, but there's also plenty of activity all around the city. Current favorites: the *Venetian Room* in the *Fairmont* hotel (phone: 772-5163) for big-name entertainment; *Great American Music Hall,* 859 O'Farrell (phone: 885-0750), for major jazz and folk artists; *Milestones,* 376 Fifth St. (phone: 777-9997), for jazz; *Finocchio's,* 506 Broadway (phone: 982-9388), for female impersonators. For comedy: *Cobb's Comedy Club,* 2801 Leavenworth St., in the Cannery (phone: 928-4320); *Club Fugazi,* with the hilarious "Beach Blanket Babylon," the longest-running show in local history, which may just never close, 678 Green St. (phone: 421-4222); *Lipps Bar and Grill,* so called since "Phil" at the sign's beginning burned out, 201 9th St. (phone: 552-3466); and *Punch Line,* 444 Battery St. (phone: 397-7573). For cabaret, try the *Plush Room,* 940 Sutter St. (phone: 885-6800). For a view of San Francisco at night try: *Top of the Mark,* 1 Nob Hill in the *Mark Hopkins* hotel (phone: 392-3434); *Oz,* a nightclub atop the *St. Francis* hotel (phone: 397-7000); or *Starlite Roof,* in the *Sir Francis Drake* hotel (phone: 392-7755). The district south of Market — known as SoMa — is the trendiest for dancing. Hottest are: *Club DV8,* 55 Natoma St. (phone: 777-2217); *DNA Lounge,* 375 11th St. (phone: 626-1409); and *Slim's,* 333 11th St. (phone: 621-3330).

BEST IN TOWN

CHECKING IN: President Taft called San Francisco the town that knows how, and though he probably wasn't talking about hotels, his statement nonetheless applies. A pleasant embarrassment of riches confronts visitors, from luxurious mammoths to ritzy mid-size establishments to dozens of intimate "boutique" hotels, which mimic European small hotels of character. Expect to pay from $140 and up for a standard double room in the expensive bracket; $80 to $140, moderate; and under $80, inexpensive. For bed-and-breakfast lodgings, contact *American Family Inn/Bed & Breakfast San Francisco,* PO Box 349, San Francisco, CA 94101-0349 (phone: 931-3083), or *Bed & Breakfast International–San Francisco,* 1181-B Solano Ave., Albany, CA 94706 (phone: 525-4569). All telephone numbers are in the 415 area code unless otherwise indicated.

Campton Place – A small hotel in the European tradition, it opened in 1983 half a block north of Union Square. Its sumptuously decorated (if smallish) 125 rooms and suites offer armoires, writing desks, remote-control cable TV, a telephone in the marble and brass bath, and even padded coat hangers. There's a roof garden for sunning and small receptions, and two conference rooms. On the lobby level, wonderfully innovative and impeccably prepared American cuisine is served at breakfast, lunch, and dinner in the *Campton Place* restaurant (see *Eating Out*); cocktails and coffee are available in the adjacent bar. Other amenities include concierge, telex, cable, and valet services. 340 Stockton St. (phone: 781-5555 or 800-235-4300). Expensive.

Donatello – One block west of Union Square, this elegant hotel offers 140 spacious rooms (including 9 suites), a serene atmosphere, and special touches such as live plants, terrycloth robes, complimentary local telephone calls, parking facilities, conference rooms, and a concierge. On the mezzanine level is a restaurant — also called *Donatello* — highly regarded for its Northern Italian cuisine. 501 Post St. (phone: 441-7100 or 800-792-9837). Expensive.

Fairmont – Just on the other side of the cable car tracks, but on Nob Hill neither side is the wrong one. Adjoining the distinctive old-fashioned main building is a modern tower topped by the *Fairmont Crown,* which serves lunch, dinner, and Sunday brunch. The façade is best known for its appearance on TV's "Hotel" series. Among the other features are the *Squire Room* for outstanding continental cuisine, the *Tonga Room* for Polynesian fare and dancing, *Mason's* restaurant, the ornate *Venetian Room* (closed Mondays) for supper and top-name entertainment, the *New Orleans Room* for nightly jazz, the *Bella Voce* coffee shop, and the *Sweet Corner* for ice cream. 700 rooms and suites. California and Mason Sts. (phone: 772-5000). Expensive.

Four Seasons Clift – A multimillion-dollar renovation has polished this traditional favorite to near perfection. An air of subdued elegance prevails, from the lobby sitting areas, reminiscent of an Edwardian salon, to the traditionally furnished guestrooms. No hotel in San Francisco provides friendlier service. The *Redwood Room* bar and lounge is a 1933 Art Deco original, paneled in redwood burl and set off with smart chandeliers, wall sconces, and Gustav Klimt prints. Its restaurant, the *French Room,* serves French cuisine in an innovative California translation, plus a menu of low-calorie, low-cholesterol, low-sodium alternatives, and it has an award-winning list of predominantly California wines. Many of the 332 rooms are unusually spacious, with color TV sets, extension phones in baths; gift shop, garage. Geary and Taylor Sts. (phone: 775-4700). Expensive.

Grand Hyatt San Francisco – With a grander name, after a top-to-bottom renovation, the hotel is well spruced up. The view from the lavish suites on the 34th floor is simply breathtaking. *One-Up* is a top-floor restaurant and cocktail lounge; *Nappers Too,* off the plaza deck, is popular for weekday lunches; and the *Plaza* restaurant on the mezzanine is the place for Sunday brunch. 700 rooms. 345 Stockton St. (phone: 398-1234 or 800-228-9000). Expensive.

Huntington – A red-carpeted lobby, crystal chandelier, white woodwork, windows that open in guestrooms and baths give an elegant yet homey air to this former apartment building. A chauffeured Rolls-Royce Silver Shadow provides complimentary transportation within downtown. One of the best values on Nob Hill, with an atmosphere of understated elegance. The 151 rooms are each distinctively decorated and comfortable, and many have good views. The *Big Four* restaurant (the name refers to the four Gold Rush millionaires) looks like a turn-of-the-century men's club and serves fish, chops, and steaks, plus a fillet of buffalo. *L'Etoile* is a fine French restaurant (closed Sundays). 1075 California St. (phone: 474-5400). Expensive.

Hyatt Regency – Inside this futuristically designed structure is an 18-story atrium lobby with all the activity of a three-ring circus, plus glass elevators that whisk you to the top, where a revolving bar looks out on San Francisco. The 803 rooms are attractive and modern, and the *Hyatt* offers all the amenities: convention facilities, shops, color TV sets, and, for a small extra fee, in-room movies. The lobby is particularly lively, with Dixieland jazz concerts on weekend afternoons, big-band dancing on Friday evenings, and the *Regency Strings* nightly. 45 Embarcadero Center (phone: 788-1234 or 800-228-9000). Expensive.

Mandarin Oriental – This luxurious hostelry occupies the top 11 floors of the 48-story California Center, in the heart of the financial district, affording each of the 160 rooms unobstructed views of the city and portions of the bay. Decorated in soothing beige and white, the rooms are graced with Oriental-motif art, fresh flowers, and marble bathrooms, each of which comes complete with robe, slippers, digital scale, and hair dryer. The larger Mandarin rooms include screened sitting areas and floor-to-ceiling windows. The marble-walled lobby, the reception area, and the Business Center, along with the outstanding restaurant, *Silks,* are all on the ground level. 222 Sansome St. (phone: 885-0999 or 800-792-9837). Expensive.

Mark Hopkins – In the heights of extravagance at Number 1 Nob Hill, with some of the original gables and turrets of railroad magnate Mark Hopkins's 19th-century mansion and a guest list that has included everyone from Haile Selassie to Frank Sinatra. The 400 suites and rooms feature either classical or contemporary decor, commodious baths and closets, possibly a grand piano (the Presidential Suite has one). The tower rooms have especially fine views, but the glass-walled *Top of the Mark* lounge is best for a 360-degree panorama of the city. The *Nob Hill* restaurant serves noteworthy French cuisine, with outstanding lamb and duck dishes. Open daily. 1 Nob Hill (phone: 392-3434). Expensive.

Meridien – The epitome of commercial luxury, with a distinctly French atmosphere, this 36-floor, 700-room hotel is in the spruced-up South of Market area, just a block from the Moscone Convention Center. It features a fine restaurant, *Pierre,* which serves contemporary California-French cuisine in an elegant lobby-level setting. There is also a hotel brasserie, *Café Justin,* open from 6:45 AM to 11 PM. 50 3rd St. (phone: 974-6400 or 800-543-4300). Expensive.

Nikko – San Francisco's close ties with the Pacific Rim are nowhere more evident than in this new hotel midway between Union Square and the theater district. The 525 rooms in this 25-story building include 2 traditional Japanese suites and 3 Nikko floors, with private lounges offering continental breakfast, an honor bar, and express check-out service. This is the only downtown hotel with a heated, glass-enclosed swimming pool, part of the extensive health club that includes a workout room, Jacuzzi, sauna, and massage rooms. Foreign visitors or Americans doing business abroad may take advantage of the language skills of the multilingual staff. 222 Mason St. (phone: 394-1111 or 800-NIKKO-US). Expensive.

Portman–San Francisco – Glittering with rosy marble, brass, chrome, and garlands of lights, this 300-room hotel combines an American look with Asian-style service. Three valets per floor are prepared to unpack, bring tea on arrival, offer bath soaps, press clothes, polish shoes, draw baths, and prop broom bristles against room doors (a toppled bristle signals that the guests may be out and their rooms should be tidied up). Computers with software and exercise machines are available for room use upon request. The *Portman Grill* achieves the high standard set by several new hotel restaurants in the city. Four Rolls-Royces to shuttle guests, free within downtown, at a charge to and from the airport. 500 Post St. (phone: 771-8600 or 800-533-6465). Expensive.

Sherman House – This ornate, white 19th-century mansion, overlooking San Francisco Bay from Pacific Heights, has been transformed into one of the city's most luxurious small inns. Gaudy Victorian antiques, marble wood-burning fireplaces, four-poster beds swathed in tapestries, deep window seats, wet bars, wall safes, TV sets and cassette systems, whirlpool baths, and down comforters are standard amenities in most of the 15 rooms and suites. One even has a large deck with a

300-degree bay view, and one of the three carriage house rooms has its own gazebo. Dining rooms, open to guests and their guests, look out on the bay and a formal garden designed by Thomas Church. 2160 Green St. (phone: 563-3600). Expensive.

Spreckels Mansion – Actually two adjoining 19th-century houses, offering 10 distinctive guestrooms furnished with French and English antiques, oversize brass beds, and eye-lingering views through leaded-glass windows. Fantasize about the days when Jack London frequented the place as you savor a sumptuous breakfast in bed or the late-afternoon wine hour. On a hill overlooking Buena Vista Park, at 737 Buena Vista (phone: 861-3008). Expensive.

Stanford Court – Recently acquired by the Stouffer hotel chain, it is built on the site of 19th-century Governor Leland Stanford's mansion. Designed in the tradition of Nob Hill elegance and with a touch of original flair, the drive-in courtyard is covered by a Tiffany-esque glass dome; the 402 rooms and suites have rattan furniture, canopied beds, etchings of old San Francisco, and private baths complete with miniature TV sets and heated towel racks. The restaurant, *Fournou's Oven,* specializes in contemporary American cuisine, with meats roasted over an oakwood fire, while the more casual *Café Potpourri* offers breakfast and lunch. The well-stocked wine cellar features private wine bins where patrons store their personal favorites. Coffee and tea are served in the lobby bar. 905 California St. (phone: 989-3500 or 800-227-4736). Expensive.

Westin St. Francis – A San Francisco landmark. Since 1904 this grand old hotel has entertained royalty, presidents, and international celebrities with its Old World charm. As a 75th birthday present, the *St. Francis* underwent a massive renovation and added the 32-story Tower, which keeps to the hotel's theme of red velvet, glimmering crystal, and polished rosewood. At the top of the Tower are *Victor's* restaurant, featuring nouvelle cuisine, and the chic *Oz* disco; both have lovely panoramic views of the city. The older sections of the hotel house the restaurants, cocktail lounges, and convention facilities. Union Square (phone: 397-7000 or 800-228-3000). Expensive.

White Swan Inn – This conversion of an old hotel into a 27-room "boutique" English inn is a success. The personal welcome, lounge, and library with fireplaces, card rooms, and garden are so very British, it's hard to believe the hostelry is American-owned. Rooms are spacious and bright, amenities luxurious. Complimentary breakfast and afternoon tea, which also includes wine, sherry, and hors d'oeuvres. 845 Bush St. (phone: 775-1755). Expensive.

Inn at Union Square – Four floors of tranquillity in the middle of downtown San Francisco, this stylish hotel has 30 rooms graced with Georgian antiques and brass fixtures, warm printed fabrics and pastel colors, down pillows and thick bathrobes. The penthouse suite has a sauna, whirlpool bath, and fireplace. Each day of one's stay here is punctuated with breakfast (in bed, if you wish), tea and cucumber sandwiches, and wine and hors d'oeuvres. 440 Post St. (phone: 397-3510 or 800-2-THE-INN). Expensive to moderate.

Mansion – This Queen Anne–style historical landmark will provide a stay unlike any other, with larger-than-life murals of local personages on some walls, a pervasive pig motif (ask for the story behind this one) on others (not in the 16 bedrooms, fortunately), a nightly musical hour or magic show that features Claudia the Ghost on piano, and a huge dining room dwarfed by a backlit stained glass window. Beyond (or despite) this, the food and service are excellent. 2220 Sacramento St. (phone: 929-9444 or 800-424-9444). Expensive to moderate.

Union Street Inn – This Edwardian inn in a chic neighborhood has 5 distinctly different guestrooms — all feature either a brass or a canopied bed and two have a private bath — plus a separate, quite lovely, and potentially very romantic carriage house. On pretty days, breakfast can be taken in the pleasant back garden. 2229 Union St. (phone: 346-0424). Expensive to moderate.

Andrews – A recently renovated Victorian building that retained some original brass fixtures and beveled glass windows, as well as a sense of old-fashioned hospitality, in its 48 rooms. Continental breakfast included. The *Post Street Bar and Café* off the lobby serves California favorites at lunch and dinner. 624 Post St. (phone: 563-6877 or 800-622-8557). Moderate.

Bedford – Another transformation: plain on the outside, cheerful with garden colors inside. Close to Union Square, with original late 1920s bath tiles and fixtures. Amenities include a video library, valet parking, pre-dinner wine, and weekday morning limousine service to the financial district. The *4-Star Café* serves breakfast and dinner. 761 Post St. (phone: 673-6040 or 800-227-5642). Moderate.

Canterbury/Whitehall Inn – Plenty of charm and greenery, including a florist's shop. In the lobby there is a grandfather clock, a terrarium, 2 aquariums, and lots of human life as well — most on its way to or from *Lehr's Greenhouse,* a tropical garden restaurant with emphasis on seafood, steaks and pasta; the shrimp Créole is excellent and Sunday brunch is very popular. 250 rooms. 750 Sutter St. (phone: 474-6464; 800-652-1614 in California, 800-227-4788 elsewhere). Moderate.

Diva – Italianate meets high tech in 7 floors of stunning guestrooms, all furnished with chrome, glass, and bright lacquered furniture and fixtures. The bare floor in the lobby feels cold, and the ultramodern rooms look like a decorator's dream of a with-it office. The Italian theme softens with traditional down comforters and pillows, snacks and cold drinks in the mini-fridge, and complimentary continental breakfast that includes Italian coffee. New *Crocodile* restaurant. Perhaps best of all is the location: right near the theaters and just a couple of blocks from Union Square. 440 Geary St. (phone: 885-0200 or 800-553-1900). Moderate.

Galleria Park – An affordable European-style hotel in the heart of the shopping and financial district is just what the city needed. For starters, there's a 3rd-floor park, a jogging track, an Art Nouveau lobby, and an 8-story atrium. Other features, like concierge, bar, morning coffee, wine on Fridays (TGIF), milk and cookies, Wednesday movies and 2 restaurants (*Bentley's* for fresh seafood and *Chambord Brasserie*), make this hotel quite impressive for the price. 177 rooms (with refrigerators) and 20 suites. The rooms on the lower floors may induce claustrophobia. 191 Sutter St. (phone: 781-3060 or 800-792-9639). Moderate.

Handlery Union Square – A family-run establishment, recently renovated and now merged with the *Stewart*. It offers 378 rooms, a tour desk, multilingual staff, a whole floor for non-smokers, heated outdoor pool, sauna, restaurant, and ample parking. 351 Geary St. (phone: 781-7800). Moderate.

Inn at the Opera – This inn is so close to the cultural pulse of the city that several of its 48 rooms and suites overlook the rehearsal studios of the *San Francisco Ballet*. All feature small refrigerators, microwave ovens, large baths, armoires and other antique furnishings, and unusual architectural details that distinguish each room. On the ground floor, *Act IV* resembles an English hunt club and serves breakfast and dinner until 10 PM, then post-theater lighter fare until after midnight. 333 Fulton St. (phone: 863-8400 or 800-325-2708). Moderate.

Kensington Park – This 1924 building, which housed the Elks Club, is now an elegant hotel with a liveried host; a marble lobby with a high, painted ceiling; and spacious rooms furnished with mahogany Queen Anne reproductions. Complimentary coffee and croissants are served buffet style on each floor in the morning; afternoon tea and sherry in the lobby. 450 Post St., a block from Union Square (phone: 788-6400 or 800-553-1900). Moderate.

Majestic – Convenient to midtown, this 5-story Edwardian mansion has been lavishly restored, with spacious rooms and suites upstairs and an elegant lobby lounge sharing the ground floor with the *Café Majestic* and its cozy adjacent bar. The sunlit restaurant won instant acclaim with its innovative California-French cuisine at lunch, dinner, and Sunday brunch. 1500 Sutter St. (phone: 441-1100 or 800-252-1155). Expensive to moderate.

Miyako – The renovated *Miyako* in Japantown is the place for a plunge into the Orient — and a Japanese bath — especially during the *Cherry Blossom Festival.* The decor is Japanese, and both Japanese and Western suites with saunas are available, as is cable TV and a restaurant. 1625 Post St. (phone: 922-3200 or 800-228-3000). Moderate.

New Richelieu – In downtown San Francisco, where old hotels never die, this one has been lovingly restored to the just-post-earthquake style of its birth. The lobby is rich with cardinal-red plush carpets, white settees, mirrors, dark woods, inverted dome chandeliers, and Tiffany-style stained glass. Period clothes are on display, as is the house cat, on its favorite settee. A rumpus room has a bar and a pool table. A small exercise gym is on the premises. The hotel offers complimentary breakfast and afternoon tea, though there's no restaurant. Complimentary chauffeured limousine, manager's hospitality hours. 1050 Van Ness (phone: 673-4711 or 800-227-3608). Moderate.

Orchard – Another restored property near Union Square, built in 1907 and now sporting a Mediterranean look with class. Italian custom-made rosewood furniture with a silky finish stars in attractive rooms overlooking a garden. Breakfast isn't free, but the *Sutter Orchard* restaurant serves a delicious and reasonably priced one, with unusually good coffee. 562 Sutter St. (phone: 433-4434 or 800-433-4343). Moderate.

Petite Auberge – Near Union Square but closer to the heart of France, this less pricey Gallic sister of the *White Swan,* complete with an antique carousel horse in the foyer, manages to be both rustic and elegant. A sweeping staircase (and a small elevator for the less athletic) leads to 26 rooms on 5 floors, furnished with French country antiques. Full concierge service is provided. Reserve a month or more in advance. 863 Bush St. (phone: 928-6000). Moderate.

Regis – Across the street from two theaters and very close to others, it celebrates life upon the wicked stage in its Thespian decor and memorabilia and by keeping late hours at *Regina's,* an outstanding Créole restaurant. Furnishings are French and English antiques, and, as in other "boutique" hotels, amenities are deluxe but prices aren't. 490 Geary St. (phone: 928-7900 or 800-345-4443). Moderate.

Villa Florence – Out front there is the hustle, bustle, and cable car clanging of Powell Street, and indoors the aroma of garlic and the pleasant noises from the trendy, first-rate restaurant, *Kuleto's.* This hostelry exudes overdone Italian atmosphere, with a trompe l'oeil mural that doesn't quite deceive the eye and Renaissance marble commingled with Art Nouveau. This ambience extends upstairs, to the 177 vividly decorated rooms. 225 Powell St. (phone: 397-7700 or 800-243-8700). Moderate.

Washington Square Inn – Within walking distance of Ghirardelli Square and Chinatown. Only 15 rooms, each individually decorated, in a turn-of-the-century house in the North Beach area. Three rooms overlook Washington Square Park and are more expensive. 1660 Stockton St. (phone: 981-4220). Moderate.

Victorian Inn on the Park – Known as the *Clunie House,* it was built in 1897 in honor of Queen Victoria's Diamond Jubilee and now has guests reserving 2 or 3 weeks in advance for one of its 12 bedrooms. Inlaid oak floors, mahogany woodwork, charming period pieces, a handsome oak-paneled dining room (which serves an excellent continental breakfast), and a lavish parlor are only some of the drawing cards of this registered historic landmark. Across from Golden Gate Park, at 301 Lyon St. (phone: 931-1830). Moderate to inexpensive.

Beresford – For British charm at a reasonable price. Old-fashioned service, a writing parlor off the Victorian lobby, flower boxes in the street windows, and pleasant rooms. Even the lamppost in front has a white and blue Wedgwood-esque frieze. The *White Horse* tavern uses fresh vegetables from the hotel's garden and fish caught by its own boat. 112 rooms. 635 Sutter St. (phone: 673-9900 or 800-533-6533). Inexpensive.

Lombard – Built in 1925, this 99-room hotel has recently undergone an extensive face-lift that, ironically, evokes the past — in this case, the elegant turn-of-the-century hotels in London. The main public room has a fireplace, piano, and marble floors, and hand-etched glass doors open into the high-ceilinged lobby. Complimentary limousine service, a redwood sun deck, and a restaurant, the *Gray Derby,* are among the amenities. 1015 Geary St. (phone: 673-5232; 800-327-3608 in California; 800-227-3608 elsewhere). Moderate to inexpensive.

Pensione International – This refurbished 46-room stopping place boasts an incredible location for the price (as little as $25 for a double with shared bath, $40 with private bath), plus color TV sets and complimentary continental breakfast. About halfway between Union Square and Japantown, it is within easy walking distance from the theater district. 875 Post St. (phone: 775-3344). Inexpensive.

 EATING OUT: San Francisco has almost 4,300 eating places, serving a wide variety of food, from haute cuisine to ethnic fare, and taking fine advantage of the wonderful seafood and fresh produce so readily available from the ocean and the surrounding countryside. Along with the longtime favorites like *Ernie's* and *Jack's,* San Franciscans welcome trendy new restaurants that show up on the horizon at an astonishing rate. One notable trend is toward first-rate food in hotel restaurants, starting with *Campton Place* and extending to much newer establishments like *Silk's* at the *Mandarin Oriental* hotel and the *Portman Grill.* At the other end of the spectrum are the neighborhood places that specialize in Chinese, Japanese, Vietnamese, Thai, or Mexican food at very affordable prices. Our restaurant selections range in price from $60 or more for a dinner for two in the expensive range; $30 to $60, moderate; $30 or less, inexpensive. Prices do not include drinks, wine, or tips. All telephone numbers are in the 415 area code unless otherwise indicated.

Blue Fox – The setting may be downtown San Francisco, but the mood is definitely Northern Italian. Piemontese-born restaurateur John Fassio has brought the foods of his region to these shores in grand style, making such delicacies as *risotto* with quail, venison with white truffles, and pumpkin *gnocchi* with sage butter feel very much at home on the West Coast. Open for dinner only, Monday through Saturday. Reservations advised. Major credit cards. 659 Merchant St. (phone: 981-1177). Expensive.

Campton Place – In the *Campton Place* hotel, but a legitimate magnet for diners in its own right. A relatively small room, decorated in soft shades of rose and gray, with a menu that is an outstanding example of American dishes done to perfection — without excessive fuss or fanfare. Breakfast, lunch, and dinner are served daily, and each is marvelous. Reservations at least a week in advance are necessary. Major credit cards. 340 Stockton St. (phone: 781-5555). Expensive.

Chez Panisse – Alice Waters gained national prominence when she began using the best, freshest local ingredients in classic French recipes in this 2-story, brown shingle house in the heart of Berkeley. Since only one meal is served in the downstairs dining room each evening, it's a good idea to call ahead to find out what it includes: perhaps spring lamb, grilled salmon, ravioli stuffed with potatoes, or something even more innovative. Upstairs, the more casual and less expensive *Chez Panisse Café* specializes in pizza, calzone, and imaginative salads and soups. Closed Sundays and Mondays. Reservations advised. Major credit cards. 1517 Shattuck Ave., Berkeley (phone: 548-5525). Expensive.

Donatello – Among the first of the new crop of local restaurants to dispel the myth that fine dining and downtown hotels are mutually exclusive, this one serves what is arguably the best Italian food in town. Here you'll find two dining rooms, the *Marble Room,* with its arched mirrors and needlepoint murals, and the *Fortuny Room,* named after its apricot-colored silk wall coverings. A prix fixe dinner ($65) includes appetizer, entrée, and dessert, accompanied by wines from a cellar of some 250 selections. But the regular menu — which features such specialties as wild mushrooms, a very tender veal, a bounty of exquisite pasta, and a sinful supply of desserts — is usually irresistible. Open daily for lunch and dinner. Reservations necessary, as far ahead as possible. Major credit cards. 501 Post St. (phone: 441-7182). Expensive.

Ernie's – Perhaps the best known name on the local scene. Dining here is a leisurely affair, so you have plenty of time to enjoy the atmosphere — Victorian yet tasteful. Traditional French dishes share the menu with nouvelle cuisine. Open daily. Reservations necessary. Major credit cards. 847 Montgomery St. (phone: 397-5969). Expensive.

Fleur de Lys – Behind its heavy, ornate doors, the place blossoms with floral draperies. This is a bastion of French cuisine — with California insistence that natural flavors come through. Among the highest prices in town, but habitués say it's worth it. Dinner daily except Sundays. Major credit cards. 777 Sutter St. (phone: 673-7779). Expensive.

Fog City Diner – A sleek chrome and neon restaurant with a creative approach toward food called American dim sum — an array of American-style (from Cajun to Tex-Mex) appetizers meant to be passed around the table — that include deep-fried catfish fingers and Buffalo chicken wings. Entrées for diners who prefer a plate to themselves range from spicy chicken adobo to homemade sausage with polenta. Like any self-respecting establishment that calls itself a diner, *Fog City* has milk shakes, hamburgers, and similar fare, but even these are done differently. Open daily for lunch and dinner. Major credit cards. 1300 Battery St. (phone: 982-2000). Moderate.

Masa's – Although Masa Kobayshi died in 1985, his namesake restaurant, now headed by his protégé Julian Serreno, still ranks as one of the city's finest. Masa was a master of perfect presentation, extravagant sauces, and creative combinations, and Serreno carries on that tradition. Dinner only, Tuesdays through Saturdays, 6 to 9 PM. Reservations necessary; call 3 weeks ahead. Visa and MasterCard only. 648 Bush St. (phone: 989-7154). Expensive.

Stars – The stars have to do with the founding chef, Jeremiah Tower, a culinary luminary, as well as the patrons, all of whom are visible and audible in this large, glamorous restaurant. Stars is broken into various levels for dining, drinking, and sampling seafood at the oyster bar. The changing menu might list an appetizer of marinated salmon or warm duck salad, Tower's stock-in-trade main course of grilled tuna served with baby vegetables, or hearty meat dishes. The wine list numbers in the hundreds, including California wines from $15 and imports up to $900. It's slightly noisy, exciting, open late, and within walking distance of the *Opera House* and *Symphony Hall.* Open daily. Reservations necessary. Major credit cards. 150 Redwood Alley, between Polk St. and Van Ness Ave. (phone: 861-7827). Expensive.

Buca Giovanni – Very Italian in decor and menu, this brick cellar is reminiscent of a Northern Italian trattoria, as is the food. A longtime favorite with locals, strong on veal, pasta, and Italian wild mushrooms. Closed Sundays. Reservations advised. Major credit cards. 800 Greenwich St. (phone: 776-7766). Moderate.

Caffè Sport – Another nostalgic bit of Italy, with three sittings per evening for dinners served family style and the kind of food you find in Italy. Closed Sundays and Mondays. Reservations accepted. No credit cards. 974 Green St. (phone: 981-1251). Moderate.

California Culinary Academy – Primarily involved in teaching classic French cuisine to prospective chefs, the public is invited to sample the students' creations. Sumptuous four-course dinners are served Mondays, Tuesdays, and Wednesdays. We gluttons prefer the Thursday and Friday night buffets — especially the table laden with more than 40 desserts. Open weekdays for lunch and dinner. Reservations necessary, about a month ahead, if possible. Major credit cards. 625 Polk St. near Turk (phone: 771-3500). Moderate.

Celadon – This Chinese restaurant is an elegant eating place where the napkins and carpet are celadon green, the chairs are graceful and highly polished, and Oriental decor shows a light touch. The food is Cantonese, which the Chinese consider their haute cuisine. A set multiple-course meal, such as the "Scholar's Dinner," is an excellent introduction to the chef's versatility. Open daily. Major credit cards. 881 Clay St. (phone: 982-1168). Moderate.

Le Central – For a variation on the continental theme, a brasserie-style restaurant with bright lights, brick walls hung with French art and the menu written on mirrors and blackboards. Food is in the best brasserie fashion: cassoulet (navy beans simmered with sausages, duck, pork, and lamb), choucroute Alsacienne (sauerkraut cooked in wine with bacon, pork, and sausage), and saucisson chaud (thinly sliced sausage with hot potato salad). Closed Sundays. Reservations advised for lunch and dinner. Major credit cards. 453 Bush St. (phone: 391-2233). Moderate.

China Moon – In a cleverly disguised coffee shop setting, the owner/chef has succeeded in presenting her singular brand of Chinese food. In what other "Chinese" restaurant would you expect to find such appetizers as chile-spiked spring rolls, spicy lamb, fresh water chestnuts, and Peking antipasto plates side by side with a California wine list and Western-style desserts? Dim sum, the traditionally Chinese lunch of 20 or so choices, takes a detour here by offering such unusual fare as glazed pecans, carmelized tofu, and marinated chicken nuggets. No smoking permitted. Closed Sundays. Reservations advised. Visa and MasterCard only. 639 Post St. (phone: 775-4789). Moderate.

Elite Café – Informal and very busy, it bills itself as a seafood place and has an oyster bar to prove it. But the tone is Créole, and many other Southern specialties figure on the menu. Dinner nightly and Sunday brunch. Major credit cards. 2049 Fillmore (phone: 346-8668). Moderate.

Empress of China – The Szechwan, Hunan, and Cantonese dishes served here are tasty (Peking duck is the house specialty), and the rooftop garden adds spectacular views to the dining experience. Open daily. Reservations advised. Major credit cards. 838 Grant Ave. (phone: 434-1345). Moderate.

Garibaldi Café – An intimate double dining room tastefully decorated in high-tech neon and an equally tasteful, clever kitchen make this restaurant a standout. Specialties such as roast pork loin stuffed with apricots and veal-stuffed tortellini in a creamy Champagne pesto change daily, but they're always excellent. Open for lunch weekdays; for dinner Tuesdays through Saturdays. Reservations advised. Visa and MasterCard only. 17th and Wisconsin Sts. (phone: 552-3325). Moderate to inexpensive.

Hayes Street Grill – In a city famous for its seafood, this is one of the best seafood restaurants it has to offer. Everything is fresh, nothing is overcooked, and there is always a long list of daily specials. Along with great sourdough bread and an unusually good crème brûlée for dessert, it is a quintessential San Francisco dining experience. Open for lunch and dinner weekdays; dinner only on Saturdays. Reserve at least a week ahead. Visa and MasterCard only. 324 Hayes St. (phone: 863-5545). Expensive.

Tung Fong – This tiny teahouse in Chinatown serves remarkable dim sum, and weekend brunch is a wonderful experience. Carts come laden with Cantonese delicacies, such as a paper-wrapped chicken with barbecue sauce, dumplings with black-mushroom centers, and succulent spareribs. Both the pickled mustard greens and the hot black bean sauce are available by the bottle. Open daily except Wednesdays. No credit cards. 808 Pacific Ave. (phone: 362-7115). Moderate.

Jack's – A landmark for nearly as long as San Francisco has been on the map. Because of its location in the financial district, many visitors don't know about it and its excellent American and French food. All the grilled entrées are recommended, but the banana fritters with brandy sauce are unbeatable. The decor is unpretentious, as are the prices (particularly the dinner special), and the service is good. Open daily. Reservations necessary. American Express only. 615 Sacramento St. (phone: 421-7355). Moderate.

Janot's – A stone's throw from formidable culinary competition, this French-Californian eatery manages top quality at medium prices. The atmosphere is nostalgic-modern, with the bricks, brass, and banquettes of yesterday in an up-to-date combination. The menu features such standards as steaks and calf's liver, imaginative French dishes, and scrumptious hot and cold salads. Lunch and dinner daily except Sundays. Major credit cards. 44 Compton Pl. (phone: 392-5373). Moderate.

Jil's – This Jil is not Jack's friend misspelled but the acronym of the initials of three young transplanted Dutch people who own it. The "I" of the trio, Ilona, cheerfully presides over the dining room, bright with primary colors and splashes of modern art. The eclectic food, with borrowings from Indonesia, Europe and California, is zippy and fresh. Dinner daily; lunch Mondays through Saturdays. Jazz on Sundays. Major credit cards. 242 O'Farrell St. (phone: 983-9353). Moderate.

Lanzone and Son – Beloved local restaurateur Modesto Lanzone renamed this eating place to acknowledge his son's increased participation in the business. The spectacular bay view is surpassed only by the food, particularly the pasta. (The menu is much the same as that at *Modesto Lanzone,* near the Civic Center, where, instead of a view, diners are treated to a stunning selection of sculpture.) Among the most intriguing pasta dishes is pansotti, a concoction of delicate ravioli stuffed with spinach and ricotta and served with a creamy hazelnut sauce. Closed for Saturday and Sunday lunch. Reservations advised. Major credit cards. 601 Van Ness Ave. (phone: 928-0400). Moderate.

MacArthur Park – Fresh seafood, barbecued steaks and spareribs, and a good California wine list. One of the better breakfasts in town. Open daily. Reservations advised. Major credit cards. 607 Front St. (phone: 398-5700). Moderate.

Mandarin – A Chinese palace with thick beamed ceilings, a delicate cherrywood lotus blossom carving, Mandarin antiques and embroideries — and excellent Chinese food which you watch being barbecued in the Mongolian fire pit. To be set up in style, call owner and hostess Madame Cecilia Chiang a day in advance and order the Mandarin duck (a whole duck prepared with scallions and plum sauce), beggar's chicken, sharkfin soup, or anything she may recommend. Open daily. Reservations advised. Major credit cards. 900 North Point, in Ghirardelli Square (phone: 673-8812). Moderate.

Maye's Original Oyster House – The other traditional seafood favorite in San Francisco. After 100 years, owned by the same family using the same secret recipes for broiled calamari, baked creamed crabmeat, and poached salmon in egg sauce. The decor's also original, though there's not much to it (large leather booths). Open daily. Reservations advised. Major credit cards. 1233 Polk St. (phone: 474-7674). Moderate.

Rings – A straightforward café of the kind locals try to keep to themselves. House standards include dishes such as chicken breast marinated in orange juice and achiote; the ever-changing list of specials might have corn, pepper, and goat cheese frittata or grilled king salmon with honey-pepper glaze. Open for lunch weekdays; for dinner Tuesdays through Saturdays. Reservations for 5 or more. Visa and MasterCard only. 1131 Folsom St. (phone: 621-2111). Moderate.

Tadich's Grill – San Francisco's oldest restaurant (since 1849), and still going strong with what clientele maintain is the freshest seafood in town. Best bets: baked avocado with shrimp diablo, rex sole, salmon, sea bass. Don't pass up the home-made cheesecake for dessert. Closed Saturdays, Sundays, and major holidays. No reservations. No credit cards. 240 California St. (phone: 391-2373). Moderate.

Le Trou – An intimate, storefront restaurant serving exquisitely prepared food in classic country French style, this is the kind of place San Franciscans dream of discovering. Chef Robert Reynolds explores the cooking of various regions for his prix fixe dinners and, since there are no choices, it is a good idea to call ahead to see what is being offered on a given evening. For example, you might be presented with an appetizer of duck liver on a mound of sweet red cabbage and currants, an entrée of tender rolled veal breast with an eggplant-and-red-pepper timbale, and a dessert of homemade raspberry cake with espresso — all accompanied by a 1984 Bordeaux. Closed Sundays and Mondays. Reservations advised. No credit cards. 1007 Guerrero St. (phone: 550-8169). Moderate.

Yoshida-Ya – This stunning Japanese restaurant is known for its excellent yakitori — a selection of meats, fish, and vegetables, all marinated, skewered, and grilled over charcoal. Upstairs and weekends are less crowded. Open daily. Reservations advised. Major credit cards. 2909 Webster at Union (phone: 346-3431). Moderate.

Balboa Café – A glass-enclosed San Francisco tradition, very popular, very crowded, and very noisy. It serves timeless American fare, including first class burgers, until 11 PM. Open daily. Major credit cards. 3199 Fillmore St. (phone: 921-3944). Inexpensive.

Buena Vista – This saloon has built its reputation on Irish coffee — which some say is the best in the world — and an extensive imported beer selection. The diverse clientele comes to drink, be merry, and then eat. Food, although a secondary consideration, is very good here and ranges from steaks and veal to hot dogs and enchiladas; breakfasts are a treat and are served all day. Community tables are half the fun. Overlooks the bay, with views of Alcatraz and Marin County. Open daily. No reservations. No credit cards. 2765 Hyde St. (phone: 474-5044). Inexpensive.

Caffè Trieste – A relaxed and homey place, immortalized in *The Golden Gate,* a novel by Vikram Seth in sonnet form, that is a popular early morning hangout. Customers start the day with strong Italian coffee and fresh sticky pastries. Around noon, the clientele comes to eat simple meals — quiche, sandwiches — or simply linger over cappuccino. Impromptu operatic arias are sung by the Giotto family on Saturday afternoons, and fresh coffee beans are sold at the next-door annex. Open daily. No reservations. No credit cards. 601 Vallejo (phone: 392-6739). Inexpensive.

David's – Cheese blintzes with sour cream and jam, stuffed cabbage, gefilte fish with challah, chicken liver with schmaltz, or hot pastrami on Siberian soldiers' bread. And if you really can't get enough, you can move in — adjoining the restaurant is *David's* hotel, where guests receive a 10% discount on all meals. Open late daily. No reservations. Major credit cards. 474 Geary St. (phone: 771-1600). Inexpensive.

Far East Café – Don't let the neon-lit exterior fool you — inside there are ornate Chinese lanterns and private, curtained booths. The extensive Cantonese menu features all the old classics and, if you call in advance, an excellent family banquet. Open daily. Reservations advised. Major credit cards. 631 Grant Ave. (phone: 982-3245). Inexpensive. .

Isobune – At this sushi and sashimi restaurant there's counter service only —

but what counter service! Japanese-style wooden boats glide by bearing all sorts of Japanese wonders, and customers take what they want. Each dish contains two or three pieces of sushi and costs from $1 to $2. The tab is figured by counting plates. Count on a worthwhile wait. Open daily. No reservations. Visa and Master-Card. 1737 Post St. (phone: 563-1030). Inexpensive.

Khan Toke Thai House – The most ornate and, many think, the best, Thai eatery in town. It goes to show that the best needn't be the dearest. Waitresses wear the national costume, and Thai dancers perform on Sundays. Open daily. Major credit cards. 5937 Geary (phone: 668-6654). Inexpensive.

Magic Pan – For late supper or brunch, featuring hearty soups, avocado or melon salad, and crêpes filled with ratatouille, creamed chicken, beef bourguignonne. Best of all is the Southern praline crêpe, with vanilla ice cream, spiced whipped cream, toasted pecans, and hot praline sauce. There's also a spacious bar up front. Open daily. Reservations advised. Major credit cards. 341 Sutter St. (phone: 788-7397). Inexpensive.

Pier 23 – With all the charm of an authentic waterfront dive but with food that makes up for the absence of fancy surroundings. A perfect lunch stop for weary Fisherman's Wharf sightseers. The menu generally features a few fresh seafood specials, such as crab salad with lemon basil dressing, as well as regular items like Mexican-style quesadillas stuffed with cheese and walnuts. Open daily for lunch and Sunday brunch only. On the Embarcadero (phone: 362-5125). Inexpensive.

La Rondalla – Christmas decorations are left in place all year at this usually festive corner "Mexicatessen." A mariachi band makes Saturday nights particularly lively. Beyond all the tinsel is good, hearty food, and specials like the beef dishes and chiles rellêños are deserving of the name. Open daily; on Sundays, brunch only. Reservations only for 10 or more. No credit cards. 901 Valencia St. (phone: 647-7474). Inexpensive.

San Francisco Bar-B-Q – The aroma of Thai spices wafts over Potrero Hill when the cooks fire up the grill to barbecue spareribs, chicken, duck noodles, salmon, trout, lamb, or even oysters. The meats can be ordered à la carte or as part of a dinner that includes sticky rice and grated carrot salad, with sourdough bread. A bowl of noodles comes cooked in sesame and soy, with crisp grilled pieces of duck. Just about everything on the menu can be ordered to go. Closed Sundays for lunch and all day Monday. No credit cards. 1328 18th St. (phone: 431-8956). Inexpensive.

SANTA FE

The Pueblo Indians had a village on the site of Santa Fe several centuries before Europeans settled in the New World. According to legend, they called the town "the dancing ground of the sun," an apt description of a splendid setting. The city sprawls across a 7,000-foot-high plateau in the middle of the vast sagebrush-swept southwestern desert. To the east rise the massive, forested peaks of the Sangre de Cristo mountains, and to the west, those of the Jemez Mountains. The sky is a shimmering turquoise blue and the air, clear and dry. Sunlight, which is dazzling in intensity, dominates the perspective, casting ever-shifting patterns of light and shadow across the monumental landscape.

The ancestors of the Pueblo, the Anasazi people, settled in this area thousands of years ago. Anthropologists are uncertain of their origins, but the Pueblo believe they came from an underworld beneath the earth's surface. This place was dark, ugly, and damp, and they struggled to get out. After many vicissitudes, they finally emerged through the earth's navel onto the land and into the light. The point of emergence is represented by a small opening, or sipapu, constructed in the sacred underground ceremonial chambers called kivas, which are still found in pueblos today.

The Spanish established modern Santa Fe a decade before the Pilgrims landed at Plymouth Rock. In contrast to the English settlers, who came to America to escape poverty and religious persecution at home, the Spanish came to the New World to reshape it in the image of the Old. Their interests were, quite simply, God, gold, and glory; however, their settlement here was a serious miscalculation. La Villa Real de la Santa Fe de San Francisco, the Royal City of the Holy Faith of St. Francis, yielded little gold or glory, and the Pueblo took to the Spanish ways of worshiping God in only limited and frustrating ways. When Spanish demands and oppression became too great, the Indians rose up in the Pueblo Revolt of 1680, when they burned most of Santa Fe and drove the Spanish away. They did not return until 12 years later, and even then the Reconquest, led by Don Diego de Vargas, was bloody and many Indians were killed. Although the Palace of the Governors was intact and the walls of the San Miguel Mission were standing, everything else had been razed. The Spanish colonists had to rebuild Santa Fe totally, using construction concepts borrowed from the Pueblo. Many of these early-18th-century structures have survived to the present.

The frontier period of Santa Fe life, which began in 1821, with the opening of the Santa Fe Trail, had less influence on the city than the Spanish, but looms large in America's mythology of the West. At its peak of activity, trade on the Santa Fe Trail employed 10,000 men a year and grossed millions of dollars. When American traders reached Santa Fe at the end of the 70-day journey from Missouri, they poured into the gambling halls that lined the plaza to drink, play monte, and dance fandangos with lavender-scented señoritas in black veils. The trail made Santa Fe a natural target for the US Army in its march westward to fulfill the country's Manifest Destiny. In 1846 General S. W. Kearny seized the city from Mexico, and 2 years later the Treaty of Guadalupe Hidalgo was signed, giving the territory of New Mexico to the US. Santa Fe at first resisted then gradually adapted to the change.

Shortly thereafter, a new breed of settler began to arrive from the East. Anthropologists came here to continue the work of Adolph Bandelier, a Swiss scholar of international reputation who lived in Santa Fe in the 1880s. Bandelier's studies of the Pueblo stimulated considerable interest in North American prehistory. By the first decade of the 20th century, the anthropologists had established Santa Fe as a research center for Indian culture and had initiated a successful campaign to preserve the city's historic adobe architecture as well.

They were energetically assisted in their preservation efforts by the painters and writers who settled in the area beginning around 1910. These artists, attracted by the serenity and primitive charm of New Mexico and by the quality of its light, were the single most important outside influence on the city in this century. Through them, Santa Fe became nationally known as an art colony, where young artists were developing new techniques as well as working in traditional styles. The Museum of Fine Arts was founded with the philosophy that any local artist might exhibit his work there.

The leading figures of the first decade were Robert Henri and John Sloan, both of whom continued to live mainly in New York, though Sloan maintained a summer home in Santa Fe for more than 30 years. In the 1920s, Mabel Dodge Luhan moved her radical salon from New York City to Taos, bringing such visitors as the English novelist D. H. Lawrence and the early American modern painters Max Weber, John Marin, Georgia O'Keeffe, Marsden Hartley, and Andrew Dasburg. Two of Luhan's guests, O'Keeffe and Dasburg, stayed in the area and became legendary presences. Georgia O'Keeffe, who lived in Abiquiu, was known for her elemental New Mexico landscape paintings. Andrew Dasburg, who settled in Taos, once compared the pureness of the light to that in the Garden of Eden. Seldom given to understatement, D. H. Lawrence wrote that "the moment I saw the brilliant, proud morning shine high up over the deserts of Santa Fe, something stood still in my soul and . . . the old world gave way to a new." And Marsden Hartley claimed the area was the only place in America where true color exists. For these artists, and for anyone who cares to linger, Santa Fe remains, as the original settlers knew it, "the dancing ground of the sun."

SANTA FE AT-A-GLANCE

SEEING THE CITY: Visitors with lots of time and stamina should hike the trail up Tesuque Peak (12,040 feet) from the Aspen Vista Picnic Area. The trailhead is on the paved road to the Santa Fe Ski Area, a drive that also provides fine views for those who prefer to stay in the car.

SPECIAL PLACES: The downtown area of Santa Fe is very compact and can easily be explored on foot. A car would be helpful for visiting the museums on Camino Lejo or for taking day trips to Taos, Acoma, and other nearby places of interest.

The Plaza – The plaza has been the center of Santa Fe life for almost four centuries, ever since the day in 1610 when mounted Spanish soldiers in medieval armor first used it as a parade ground. Throughout the centuries the plaza has been the scene of the most important public events in the city: markets, fiestas, proclamations, parades, and even, at one time, bullfights. An obelisk now marks the center of the lovely, tree-shaded square. Along the footpaths emanating from the obelisk are benches where weary shoppers rest, sightseers fiddle with their cameras, and office workers enjoy picnic lunches. The Palace of the Governors dominates the north side of the square; the three other sides are lined with shops, restaurants, and galleries.

Palace of the Governors – Built by Spanish settlers in 1609-10, eleven years before the Pilgrims landed at Plymouth Rock, this is the oldest continuously used government building in the country, serving as the seat of government for four "nations": Spain, Mexico, the Confederacy, and the US. Originally, all of the palace was made of mud except for the roof beams, or vigas. The walls, then as now, were adobe. The dirt floor was mixed wih animal blood to pack it down and produce a sheen. Following the Pueblo Revolt of 1680, the Indians enlarged the structure and used it as a large pueblo. It was again occupied and further enlarged by the Spanish following the Reconquest in 1694. The palace became a museum in 1909, housing historical exhibitions for the *Museum of New Mexico.* This makes it a natural starting point for a tour of the city. Closed Mondays during January and February. On the Plaza (phone: 827-6483).

Museum of Fine Arts – Next door, moving west from the palace, this museum houses a collection of more than 8,000 works of art. Over 20 exhibitions a year feature 20th-century art and photography, prints, and sculpture with a strong emphasis on the Southwest. Completed in 1917, some 300 years after the palace, the building is an outstanding example of Pueblo Revival architecture. It became a model for the architectural style that still dominates Santa Fe, combining traditional adobe design and materials with modern comfort and efficiency. Closed Mondays during January and February. On the Plaza, W. Palace Ave. (phone: 827-4455).

Museum of International Folk Art – Housing the world's largest collection of folk art from around the globe, the museum was founded in 1953 by Florence Dibell Bartlett, who believed craft to be a bond among the peoples of the world. The collection includes traditional costumes and textiles, masks, folk toys, items of everyday use, and Hispanic folk art from the Spanish colonial period. The famed Girard Foundation Collection, with selections from more than 100 countries, is on permanent exhibit. Closed Mondays in January and February. Camino Lejo (phone: 827-8350).

Museum of Indian Arts and Culture – Opened in 1987, it serves as the exhibition facility for the adjacent 61-year-old Laboratory of Anthropology. The laboratory's collection includes more than 50,000 pieces of prehistoric and historic basketry, pottery, textiles, jewelry, clothing, and other items crafted by the native peoples of the Southwest. Artifacts from this collection are shown in rotating exhibitions. With the inclusion of Southwest Indians on the staff and in the museum's many public programs, visitors see traditional art forms being carried forward in vibrant and innovative ways. Closed Mondays in January and February. Camino Lejo (phone: 827-8941).

Sena Plaza – East of the palace is this charming, tree-shaded and flower-brightened courtyard surrounded by the four wings of the 19th-century Sena hacienda. The 33-room adobe structure is now divided into shops and offices. E. Palace Ave.

St. Francis Cathedral – Directly across Palace Avenue, this structure built between 1869 and 1886 is the legacy of the French bishop Jean Baptiste Lamy, the most influential person in local history and the subject of Willa Cather's *Death Comes for the Archbishop.* The Romanesque style of the building is, like many of Lamy's ideas, imported and a little out of place. Its most interesting feature is the adobe chapel that existed here before the cathedral, most of which was incorporated into the larger structure built of local quarry stone. In continuous use since 1718, the chapel is dedicated to La Conquistadora (Our Lady of the Conquest), protector of the early Spanish settlers. The carved wooden statue of Conquistadora, said to be the oldest madonna in North America, was brought here from Mexico by the Spanish in 1625. Cathedral Pl.

Barrio de Analco – The Santa Fe River is as slow, irregular, and inexpedient as the town it crosses, yet because it was the main source of water in the early days, almost all the homes were built along it. Noting how the town followed the path of the river, one 19th-century visitor described Santa Fe as "three streets wide and a mile long." Many of the old homes on the narrow streets in the Barrio de Analco (as the quarter on the other side of the river was called) have been preserved, particularly on East De Vargas. Although these homes are still private residences, visitors can stroll by for a look.

"Oldest House" – The foundations of this structure are thought to have been laid by the Pueblo Indians in the 13th century, although the tree rings in the ceiling beams only date to about 1750. However accurate the claim to be the "oldest house in the US," the western portion of this structure is in fact a good example of primitive adobe construction. Most early Santa Fe residents had similar dwellings, with low log ceilings, dirt floors, thick mud walls, and a corner fireplace for heating and cooking. 215 E. De Vargas.

Chapel of San Miguel – This chapel is as old as the Palace of the Governors. Originally built in 1610-12, it was practically razed by the Pueblo Indians in the 1680 Revolt. When the Spanish rebuilt it in 1710, they covered over what remained of the earlier walls, placed the windows up high, and added adobe battlements to the roof. The most prominent feature of the interior is a fine old reredo, or colonial Spanish altar screen, made in 1798. Most of the paintings on the altar screen were done in Mexico in the 18th century. Old Santa Fe Trail and De Vargas St.

State Capitol – A bit south of San Miguel's Chapel is this unusual structure, which residents call the "Round House." It is intended by architects to evoke a Pueblo kiva (the ceremonial chamber in which religious rites are performed). Old Santa Fe Trail.

Canyon Road – One of the most romantic and picturesque streets in the US, it's also the oldest still in use; it was well established as a Pueblo trail long before the Spanish arrived. By the 18th century, residents were building adobe homes and cultivating farms along Canyon Road, which follows the river east from downtown. Sections of some of the current buildings date from that period, and the style of the street's architecture was established in a way that has not changed substantially since. In the early 20th century, Canyon Road became the center of the Santa Fe art colony. Though few artists can afford to live here today, the street is still zoned for "residential arts and crafts," limiting its use to galleries, studios, restaurants, and homes. It's an ideal place to see both the residential character of the old city and the latest work of Santa Fe artists.

Cristo Rey Church – Built in 1940, this church was designed by architect John Gaw Meem in classical Spanish mission style. Nearly 200,000 adobe bricks were used in its construction, all made from soil on the site — the traditional practice. One of the largest adobe structures in existence, it was scaled to house the most famous piece of Spanish colonial art in New Mexico, an ornately carved stone reredo, commissioned in 1760. Upper Canyon Rd.

■**EXTRA SPECIAL:** Santa Fe is the best place in New Mexico (and perhaps in the entire Southwest) to shop for Indian art: jewelry, pottery, weavings, paintings, kachina dolls, beadwork, and baskets. As you travel, even a cursory browse will quickly reveal that Indian art can be very expensive: Pueblo pottery may cost several hundred dollars, while Navajo rugs can run into the thousands. We recommend that you begin by visiting the area's museums — the *Indian Pueblo Cultural Center* in Albuquerque as well as the *Wheelwright Museum of the American Indian* and the *Museum of Indian Arts and Cultures* in Santa Fe. They all display the very distinctive work produced by the various tribes and you'll soon learn to recognize the traditional patterns and techniques each one employed. You'll also become familiar with the names of certain families or individuals who have become well known for a particular style. The museum shops at the *Indian Pueblo Cultural Center,* the *Palace of the Governors,* and the *Wheelwright Museum* all carry fine Indian art as well as numerous books on the subject. They are also usually attended by salespeople who are willing to part with a few pointers about how to tell the real from the fake (some cheaper, imitation crafts are imported from Taiwan), what's special about the pieces they carry, and how to care for what you buy. In addition to the museum shops, there are a number of stores and galleries along the plaza and elsewhere in the city that sell Indian art. Among those to look for are: *Wind River Trading Co.* (112 E. Palace; 113 E. San Francisco), *Cristof's* (106 W. San Francisco), *Dewey Galleries, Ltd.* (74 E. San Francisco), *Morning Star Gallery* (513 Canyon Rd.), *Mudd-Carr Gallery* (229 Otero), *Packard's Indian Trading Co.* (61 Old Santa Fe Trail), and *Santa Fe East* (200 Old Santa Fe Trail). It's possible to buy directly from the Indians under the portico of the Palace of the Governors or by visiting the several pueblos in the area — Jemez, Zia, Santa Clara, San Ildefonso, Acoma, Zuni, Taos — to buy pottery and jewelry directly from the Indians. Two final bits of advice: Buy what you like when you see it; each piece is handmade and unique, and if you hesitate, you will not find it elsewhere. Also, bring lots of cash if you shop in the pueblos, because Indians selling from their living rooms won't be equipped to take credit cards.

SOURCES AND RESOURCES

TOURIST INFORMATION: For a free copy of the Santa Fe Convention and Visitors Bureau's *Visitors Guide,* call 800-528-5369, or pick one up at the Sweeney Center, 109 W. Marcy St., Santa Fe, NM 87504. A better but more expensive alternative is the newsstand at *La Fonda* hotel (100 E. San Francisco), just off the plaza, which carries all available guides and major works of fiction and nonfiction about the area. For a lively literary introduction to the city and vicinity, pick up Willa Cather's *Death Comes for the Archbishop* and John Nichols's *The Milagro Beanfield War*, a film version of which is also available on videocassette.

Television Stations – KOB Channel 4–NBC; KGGM Channel 13–CBS; KOAT Channel 7–ABC; KNME Channel 5–PBS.

Radio Stations – AM: KREO 920 (oldies); KFMG 1080 (rock); KRZY 1450 (country); KZSS 610 (rock). FM: KHFM 96.3 (classical); KLSK 104 (jazz); KFMG 108 (rock); KISS 97 (rock).

Local Coverage – The *New Mexican* is published daily; look at Friday's Pasatiempo section for information on events of the coming week. Do not, however, rely on the paper for restaurant recommendations.

Telephone – The area code for Santa Fe is 505.

Sales Tax – Local sales tax is 5.625%.

CLIMATE: Santa Fe's climate is shaped by both the Rocky Mountains and the southwestern desert. The sun is usually shining, the air is very dry, and the sky is very clear and turquoise blue. During the day, the air temperature always feels warm, even when there's snow on the ground, although as soon as the sun sets the air cools quickly. The average daily temperature in the summer is about 80F and about 40F in the winter.

 GETTING AROUND: Santa Fe Municipal Airport is serviced by Mesa Airlines (phone: 800-MESA-AIR), which flies from Albuerque to Santa Fe. Visitors usually fly into Albuquerque International Airport, about 65 miles south, and then either rent a car or rely on the bus service provided by a firm called *Shuttlejack* (phone: 243-3244, 982-4311 from Santa Fe). Departures are from the east end of the airport approximately every 2 hours; the trip costs $15 and takes about 80 minutes.

There is limited public transportation in Santa Fe, and although the downtown area is small enough to see enjoyably by foot, a car is needed to visit the farther-flung points of interest.

Car Rental – All the major car rental agencies are represented at Albuquerque airport. Cars may be rented in Santa Fe after arrival, but the rental offices are scattered and rather inaccessible. *Avis* has an office at *Garrett's Desert Inn,* 311 Santa Fe Trail (phone: 800-331-1212 or 982-4361), and *Hertz* at the *Hilton Inn,* 100 Sandoval (phone: 800-654-3131 or 982-1844).

Taxi – There is no central taxi stand, but you can call *Capital City Cab Co.* , 825 Early Rd. (phone: 988-1211).

 MUSEUMS: The *Palace of the Governors* and *Museum of Fine Arts* are described in *Special Places.* Also of interest are the following, all of which are on Camino Lejo, just off the Old Santa Fe Trail:

Museum of Indian Arts and Culture – An extensive collection of southwestern Indian art dating back many centuries (phone: 827-7355).

Wheelwright Museum of the American Indian – Indian arts and artifacts (phone: 982-4636). *Note:* The *Case Trading Post* downstairs sells high-quality and award-winning Indian pottery, jewelry, and weavings. (See also *Indian America,* DIVERSIONS.)

 MAJOR COLLEGES AND UNIVERSITIES: College of Santa Fe, St. Michael's Dr. (phone: 473-6011); St. John's College, Camino de Cruz Blanca (phone: 982-3691).

 SPECIAL EVENTS: Summer is the performing arts season, with cultural events staged by the *Santa Fe Opera* and the *Santa Fe Chamber Music Festival* nightly in July and August. The annual *Indian Market* is held the third week in August in the plaza; at this very popular juried event, Indians from the surrounding pueblos sell a wide variety of crafts — jewelry, pottery, sand paintings, weavings, kachina dolls, and so on. The *Fiesta de Santa Fe,* celebrated the weekend after Labor Day, originated in 1712. It opens with the ritual burning of a 40-foot marionette, called Zozobra, representing Old Man Gloom. After 2 days of parades, dancing, eating, and partying, the fiesta ends with mass at St. Francis Cathedral. The eight northern pueblos near Santa Fe have very different but equally interesting fiestas and other celebrations; the Santa Fe Convention and Visitors Bureau (phone: 984-6760) usually has information about the ones visitors are allowed to attend.

 SPORTS AND FITNESS: Camping and Hiking – For maps and advice about the Santa Fe area, write to the US Forest Service, PO Box 1689, Santa Fe, NM 87504, or call 988-6940. For information about the Bandelier National Monument, write to the Superintendent, Bandelier National Monument, Los Alamos, NM 87544 (phone: 672-3861). Also refer to the book *Day Hikes in the Santa Fe Area,* published by the local chapter of the Sierra Club.

Fitness Centers – *Santa Fe Spa,* 786 N. St. Francis Dr. (phone: 984-8727); *Carl Miller's Conditioning Center,* 560 Montezuma (phone: 982-6760).

Golf – The *Santa Fe Country Club,* at Airport Rd., (phone: 471-0601), is popular.

Horse Racing – The season at the *Downs,* just south of the city on I-25, extends from late May to Labor Day, with races on Wednesdays and weekends (phone: 471-3311).

Jogging – The most pleasant run is along the Santa Fe River, on Palace Avenue or Canyon Road. A more strenuous route is up Bishop's Lodge Road, into the Tesuque valley.

Skiing – Northern New Mexico usually has good powder from mid-December until early March and sunny spring skiing for several weeks after that. The *Santa Fe Ski Area* is close, moderate in size and challenge, and relatively uncrowded (phone: 983-5758, or 982-4429). Advanced skiers often prefer the long, steep runs at the *Taos Ski Valley,* 1½ hours away (phone: 776-2291).

Tennis – There are 32 courts in nine locations around town (phone: 984-6860, for information). Non-guests are sometimes allowed to use (for a fee) the courts at the *Bishop's Lodge* and *Rancho Encantado* resorts.

 MUSIC: The *Orchestra of Santa Fe* performs at the *Lensic Theatre* downtown (phone: 988-4640) from October to May; in February the orchestra performs a Bach or Mozart Festival, alternating composers every year. A newer orchestra, the *Santa Fe Symphony* (phone: 983-3530), performs a similar season. In July and August the *Santa Fe Chamber Music Festival,* widely recognized for its posters reproducing the work of Georgia O'Keeffe, takes place at the *St. Francis Auditorium* in the *Museum of Fine Arts on* W. Palace Ave. The 8-week festival begins in early July and features eminent artists from around the world (phone: 983-2075). The internationally acclaimed *Santa Fe Opera* offers lavish, adventuresome performances in a dramatic outdoor theater from early July to late August (phone: 982-3851). Lectures and backstage tours are available by appointment. The theater is on Hwy. 84/285, about 8 miles north of town.

 NIGHTCLUBS AND NIGHTLIFE: Santa Fe is not known for its throbbing nightlife; the summertime arts festivals can be exciting, but for the most part, it's a pretty quiet town. There are, however, some diversions. Maria Benitez, one of the world's great flamenco artists, dances most summer nights at the *Sheraton de Santa Fe* (phone: 982-5591). Live music (usually rock) and dancing can be found at *Club West,* 213 W. Alameda (phone: 982-0099). If you're not up for dancing, consider soaking at *Ten Thousand Waves,* a Japanese bathhouse in the mountains with communal and private hot tubs, Ski Basin Rd. (phone: 982-9304).

BEST IN TOWN

 CHECKING IN: Santa Fe sees a tremendous influx of visitors every summer, so it's best to book well in advance. Expect to pay up to $200 a day in the hotels listed in the expensive category, $60 to $100 in moderate, and under $50 in inexpensive. In the winter, rates are usually 10% to 25% lower. All telephone numbers are in the 505 area code unless otherwise indicated.

Bishop's Lodge – Originally the retirement home of Bishop Lamy in the late 19th century, this comfortable hotel has its own stables and breakfast horseback rides, tennis courts, pool, and sauna, trap and skeet shooting range, and an all-day program for children. The tariff in the summer includes two meals a day, with ample buffets of American and continental food and a steak fry on Friday nights. Open April to November. Bishop's Lodge Rd. (phone: 983-6377). Expensive.

Eldorado – Santa Fe's newest hotel, opened in 1986, is the most luxurious choice in the downtown area. A member of the Clarion chain, it also has the best facilities in town for business and large group functions. 309 W. San Francisco (phone: 988-4455).

La Fonda – A Santa Fe landmark just off the plaza, it's less notable for service than for a striking appearance and historic character: Though the present hotel was built in 1920, an inn called *La Fonda* has existed on this site since the opening of the Santa Fe Trail, almost 200 years ago. The recently refurbished rooms have Spanish Colonial accents. 100 E. San Francisco St. (phone: 505 982-5511). Expensive.

Inn at Loretto – The exterior of this modern hotel near the plaza is distinctively Spanish pueblo in style, although the rooms are quite standard, with no surprises. It's named for the historic spot it occupies, that of the old Loretto Academy, established in the 1850s by Bishop Lamy and the Sisters of Loretto. 211 Old Santa Fe Trail (phone: 988-5531). Expensive.

Rancho Encantado – The "Enchanted Ranch" is a gracious small resort in the Tesuque hills. Within the original adobe buildings are Santa Fe–style rooms, the most attractive in the area, with fireplaces, vigas, Indian rugs, and hand-painted tiles. Recently built condominiums can also be rented: 1 or 2 bedrooms, with living and dining rooms as well as a kitchen. The ranch offers facilities for a range of outdoor activities, such as horseback riding, tennis, archery, and swimming. Rte. 22 in Tesuque, 8 miles north of Santa Fe (phone: 982-3537). Expensive.

La Posada – A few blocks from the plaza, this southwestern inn is spread out over 6 landscaped acres. The center of the complex is the Staab House, a Victorian home dating from 1882 that's been tastefully converted into a good restaurant and a popular lounge. Rates depend on the size and charm of the room, some of which are fairly conventional and some romantically southwestern, with adobe fireplaces, vigas, and Indian rugs. 330 E. Palace (phone: 983-6351). Expensive to moderate.

Grant Corner Inn – One of several small bed-and-breakfast inns recently opened in old homes in the downtown area. This one may be the nicest, with 9 comfortable rooms and a terrific breakfast. 122 Grant Ave. (phone: 983-6678). Moderate.

Preston House – Another good bed-and-breakfast option downtown. Two of the 5 rooms have fireplaces. 106 Faithway (phone: 982-3465). Moderate.

St. Francis – Built in the 1920s and restored to its original style, this small downtown hotel features 81 rooms decorated in period furnishings and fixtures, the whole reflecting a simple, romantic elegance. 210 Don Gaspar (phone: 983-5700). Moderate.

El Rey Inn – The best bargain in town for Santa Fe charm; if downtown (instead of on motel row), prices would at least double. Many of the individually decorated rooms have adobe fireplaces, vigas, and tile murals; some are solar heated and overlook a garden. 1862 Cerrillos (phone: 982-1931). Moderate to inexpensive.

 EATING OUT: Expect to pay $40 or more for a meal for two (without drinks, wine, or tip) in a restaurant listed below as expensive; between $20 and $40 at moderate; and around $15 in inexpensive. All telephone numbers are in the 505 area code unless otherwise indicated.

Compound – Santa Fe's best known restaurant may no longer be depended upon to deliver consistently excellent meals on every occasion, but the (continental) food served usually is very good and there's a fine wine list. In a converted 19th-century hacienda, the eatery also provides a delightful dining environment. Coat and tie required for men. Closed Sundays, Mondays and January and February. Reservations necessary. American Express. 653 Canyon Rd. (phone: 982-4353). Expensive.

Periscope – Although lunch is available Tuesdays through Saturdays, dinner is only served here on Saturday nights, and these seven-course extravaganzas — featuring dishes from around the world — are always carefully prepared and usually delicious. The set lunches are a bargain. Reservations necessary. Visa and MasterCard only. 221 Shelby (phone: 988-2355). Dinner expensive; lunch moderate.

Coyote Café – Chef/owner Mark Miller, who established a national reputation in the San Francisco Bay area, opened this fashionable restaurant in 1987. The southwestern nouvelle cuisine uses regional ingredients in imaginative ways. Closed weekends for lunch. Reservations advised. Visa and MasterCard only. 132 W. Water (phone: 983-1615). Expensive to moderate.

Pink Adobe – One of the city's best restaurants for many years, "the Pink" (as it's known) features an unusual menu that includes steaks, Créole dishes, and New Mexican specialties. Try the steak Dunnigan, with green chile, or the chicken enchiladas with green chile and sour cream. Reservations necessary. Major credit cards. 406 Old Santa Fe Trail (phone: 983-7712). Expensive to moderate.

Santacafé – Locally popular for its casual elegance and fine food, it offers a sophisticated menu that changes daily and ranges around the globe. Closed weekends for lunch. Reservations advised. Visa and MasterCard only. 231 Washington (phone: 984-1788). Expensive to moderate.

Shohko Café – One of several Japanese restaurants that have become very popular in Santa Fe, it offers what must be the only green chile tempura in the world. The rest of the menu includes more traditional dishes — sukiyaki, teriyaki, and so on — and there's a large, crowded sushi bar. Closed Sundays and for lunch on weekends. Reservations advised for dinner. Visa and American Express only. 321 Johnson St. (phone: 983-7288). Expensive to moderate.

La Tertulia – The classiest of the city's restaurants serving New Mexican cuisine, housed in a converted convent. The native dishes tend to be mild but tasty, and the homemade sangria is excellent. Closed Mondays. Reservations necessary. Major credit cards. 416 Agua Fria, near Guadalupe (phone: 988-2769). Expensive to moderate.

Las Brazas – Topnotch Mexican fare, including superb relleños, served in several dining areas, including a patio. The decor is very Santa Fe — high beamed ceilings, stucco walls, carved chairs, marble-topped tables, and numerous artifacts. Open daily except major holidays. MasterCard and Visa only. About 11 miles north of town, on Rte. 11/Hwy. 285 (phone: 455-2111). Moderate.

Rancho de Chimayo – Generally agreed to be the best New Mexican–style restaurant anywhere, it's in an old adobe hacienda about 25 miles north of Santa Fe. The drive, the setting, and the food are all delightful. Those who especially like hot dishes should try carne adovada, pork cooked in red chile. The flan (custard with caramel syrup) may be the area's best. Closed Mondays in winter and January. Major credit cards. Reservations necessary. Rte. 4 in Chimayo (phone: 351-4444 or 984-2100 from Santa Fe). Moderate to inexpensive.

Josie's Casa de Comida – A rare example of a dying breed — the small, plain, downtown luncheon café. The chiles relleños, enchiladas, and other regional dishes are terrific, and the more standard American lunches are pretty good, too. *Josie's* is so popular that people will line up and wait patiently on the street for a table. Lunch only. Closed weekends. 225 E. Marcy St. (phone: 983-5311). Inexpensive.

Shed – It's the most popular place in town for lunch. There is usually a line after 11:30 AM, but the wait is pleasant in the front courtyard, originally the central patio of a large hacienda. The red chile served on blue corn enchiladas, tacos, and burritos is unmatched, the posole and beans very good, and the desserts fine.

Lunch only. Closed Sundays. No reservations or credit cards. 113½ Palace Ave. (phone: 982-9030). Inexpensive.

Tecolote Café – Despite the inauspicious location, it serves the best breakfast in town, complete with a basket of homemade biscuits and blueberry muffins. The Santa Fe omelette — filled with green chile and cheese — will get anyone moving. Breakfast, lunch and dinner. Closed Mondays. No reservations. Visa and Master-Card only. 1203 Cerrillos Rd. (phone: 988-1362). Inexpensive.

Tomasita's – At this local favorite, the selection of dishes is limited but the flavors authentic, the portions large, and the service friendly. Unless you arrive early, the wait for a table can easily be as long as your dinner. Closed Sundays. No reservations. Visa and MasterCard only. 500 Guadalupe (phone: 983-5721). Inexpensive.

SAVANNAH

New England's first families trace their bloodlines to the manifest of the *Mayflower*. Georgians trace theirs to the good ship *Ann*, which sailed up the Savannah River on February 12, 1733, with a cargo of 114 English men and women, good and true. They were Bowlings, Cannons, Hodges, Milledges, Parkers, Warrens, and Youngs: basket makers, peruke makers, cider traders, carpenters, tailors, shopkeepers, servants, a surgeon, a gardener, a silk weaver. A few First Georgians had been rescued from English jails, where they had been languishing for failure to pay their bills.

Ashore on Yamacraw Bluff, expedition leader General James Edward Oglethorpe laid out his plans for the seat of His Majesty's Crown Colony of Georgia. Under Oglethorpe's plan, Savannah unfolded on an orderly grid of 24 squares, which provided mustering points for troops when danger threatened and gossiping nooks when times were peaceful.

During the halcyon days before the Civil War (known as the War Between the States in the South), when the cotton bound for the mills of Worcester and Liverpool flowed through Savannah's busy harbor, wealthy brokers and merchants turned the squares into flowering public gardens and erected around them splendid mansions of English Regency, Georgian, and Neo-Gothic styles. Today, the squares are green oases that distinguish Savannah from other American cities.

History, benign neglect, and a late-blooming restoration movement conspired to save the city for future generations to enjoy. Near the close of the war, with General William Tecumseh Sherman's Union army at the gates, city fathers marched out and surrendered. Instead of being put to flames à la Atlanta, Savannah was presented, intact, as a Christmas gift to President Lincoln. But what Sherman didn't destroy, "progress" nearly did.

By the mid-1950s, the city's precious architectural heritage was in grave danger of extinction. When the century-old City Market was bulldozed for an unsightly parking garage, and the owner of a mortuary eyed the *Isaiah Davenport House* — an especially fine early-19th-century Georgian townhouse — for a parking lot, outraged Savannahians united and formed the Historic Savannah Foundation. Over the past 30 years, the foundation has spearheaded restoration of close to 2,000 endangered structures in the 2.2-square-mile National Historic District, which is the largest in the nation.

The mortuary is closed now, and the *Davenport House* has become a museum. The parking garage that replaced the Old City Market has itself been replaced by a new City Market. Opened in late 1986, the reborn market has transformed four woebegone downtown blocks into a colorful commercial center and visitor attraction, with interesting shops, fresh produce and seafood, a flea market, craftspeople and artists, restaurants, entertainment, and vendors hawking their wares. Outside the handsome stucco and brick buildings, trees, landscaping, awnings, and kiosks extend the festive atmosphere. Visitors reach the area in horse-drawn carriages.

The City Market is the newest and most exciting example of a compatible partnership between history and sensitive progress. A few years ago, blocks of brick warehouses along the Savannah River, which had held cotton for shipment, were transformed into pubs, seafood restaurants, art galleries, shops, and nautical museums. The lively enterprises are flanked by a brick esplanade called Riverfront Plaza, with benches that invite passersby to sit a spell and watch the mighty cargo ships glide up and down the river.

Some of the city's most gracious old mansions have been resurrected in the form of inns and guesthouses, the most elaborate of which are rich in antiques and art, four-poster beds, wood-burning fireplaces, and modern accouterments such as saunas and hot tubs. Tours of private homes are given in spring and at Christmas, and at historic houses throughout the year. These include the *Isaiah Davenport House;* the *Owens-Thomas House,* with a balcony from which the Marquis de Lafayette addressed the populace in 1825; the Green-Meldrim House, where General Sherman quartered during the Union occupation; and the Juliette Gordon Low House, birthplace of the woman who founded the Girl Scouts.

The town's Visitors Bureau is based in the restored 18th-century Central of Georgia Railroad Depot. The Great Savannah Exposition, a dazzling multimedia presentation of the city's history, takes place in the train sheds behind the center.

Savannah loves nothing better than a rousing party. On March 17, heartfelt Irish tears and laughter flower into kelly green exuberance. Whether it's really the second largest St. Patrick's Day celebration in all North America may be a matter of debate, but there's no arguing with the enthusiasm of 250,000 revelers (about the size of the city's year-round population), who down green grits with green beer and cavort, green from head to toe, through the old streets and squares.

In summer, residents and visitors alike take to the beaches. The Atlantic sands of Tybee Island are only a half-hour's drive from downtown. Georgia's "Golden Isles," the resort havens of St. Simons Island, Sea Island, and Jekyll Island, are 80 miles down the coast. The shopping, dining, tennis, golf, and posh villas of South Carolina's Hilton Head Island are only 35 miles away from Savannah.

For its rich heritage and its architectural and natural beauty, Savannah is an opportunity not to be missed — a truly special corner of America.

SAVANNAH AT-A-GLANCE

SEEING THE CITY: Driving into Savannah across Talmadge Bridge offers a fine introductory view of the city. For a bird's-eye view of the Savannah River's busy cargo traffic, have lunch, dinner, or drinks at *Windows* restaurant in the *Hyatt Regency* hotel, 2 W. Bay St. (phone: 238-1234).

For a pleasant introduction to Savannah, take a cruise on one of the *Cap'n Sam Cruise Line* sightseeing boats. Cap'n Sam runs regular daily tours of the harbor (a

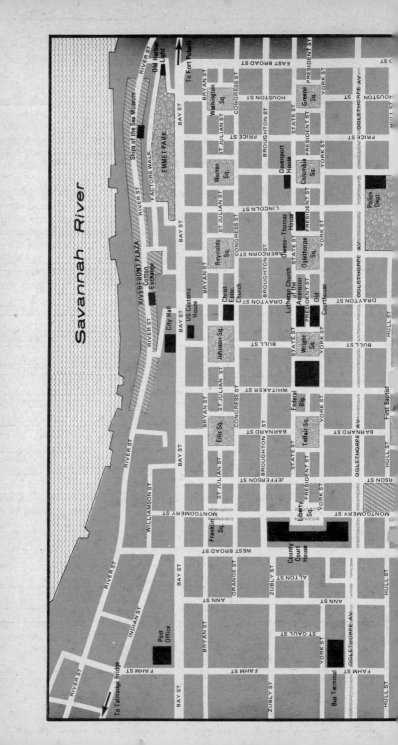

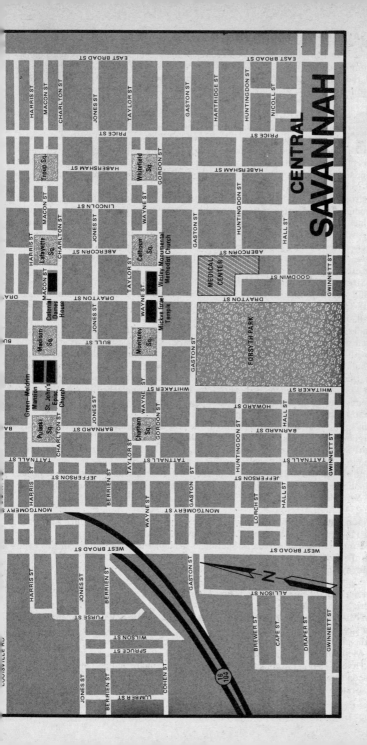

CENTRAL
SAVANNAH

20-mile, 2-hour trip); twilight cocktail cruises in the evenings; and on summer nights, special dinner/dance cruises. The boats — *Harbor Queen I, Waving Girl, Harbor Queen II,* and the *Cap'n Sam* — depart from the foot of Bull Street behind city hall. Call 234-7248 for the cruise schedule and reservations.

SPECIAL PLACES: Historic Savannah is appealingly negotiable on foot. We recommend at least four walking tours; and count on a minimum of 2 days to see everything. To see it from an insider's perspective, call *Square Roots* (phone: 232-6866), a dynamic little tour company that offers escorted walking tours of gardens, hidden shops, and private homes, spiced with amusing anecdotes and scandals of the past and present. For walking on your own, here are the city's most favored routes.

Riverfront Plaza – A logical place to start, Riverfront Plaza leads eastward along the Savannah River shoreline. Bordering the thriving seaport's 40-foot-deep channel, the 9-block, brick plaza is alive with commercial establishments in the 19th-century buildings which were formerly cotton warehouses. Waterfront browsers may be treated to a rock concert or a chamber music recital by an ensemble from the *Savannah Symphony.* A Riverfront Plaza day tour will undoubtedly whet the appetite for an evening excursion.

Bull Street – If you spend a morning at the Plaza, the afternoon can be spent walking down Bull Street, from City Hall to Forsyth Park, 12 blocks south. Savannah's principal north-south street, Bull contains the city's five most beautiful squares. The 6-story City Hall, on River and Bay Streets, stands alongside two brass cannons captured from Cornwallis at Yorktown. The cannons were presented to the Chatham Artillery, a Savannah military unit, by George Washington, in 1791. East of City Hall, Factors Walk, with its iron bridges and narrow street, runs along the city side of the former cotton buildings. After passing City Hall, you will come to the US Customs House, built in 1852 on the same site where Georgia's founder, James Edward Oglethorpe, lived in 1733. It's also where evangelist John Wesley first preached in America. The five squares, not to be missed, are listed below:

Johnson Square – Here, two fountains flow and decks of azaleas are in dazzling flower in spring. Christ Episcopal Church, the first church established in the Colony of Georgia (1773), stands here, too. The present building dates to 1838.

Wright Square – The exquisite Ascension window of the Lutheran Church of the Ascension (1878) is internationally known as a work of art.

Chippewa Square – Here you'll find the First Baptist Church, the oldest of its denomination in Georgia; the Barrow Mansion, which now houses an insurance firm; and the *Savannah Theater,* one of the oldest theaters in continuous use in the country (phone: 233-7764).

Madison Square – The carillons and stained glass windows of St. John's Episcopal Church (1840) are well known to church lovers. Here, too, is the former Green-Meldrim mansion, which served as Sherman's headquarters after Savannah was captured in the Civil War.

Monterey Square – Temple Mickve Israel, consecrated in 1878 for Georgia's oldest Jewish congregation (1773), contains a Torah scroll more than 800 years old. The Gordon and Taylor Street houses facing Monterey Square are outstanding examples of historic preservations.

From Abercorn to St. Julian Street – Starting at Calhoun Square, at Abercorn and Gordon streets, walk north toward *Massie School* (1885), a Greek Revival structure that is the public school system's education museum. Alongside stands Wesley Monumental Methodist Church. Four blocks north, at Lafayette Square, is the Colonial Dames House (1849). Two blocks east, beside Troup Square and on parallel Charlton and Macon Streets, are Savannah's two best examples of slum conversion properties, now first-rate townhouses. A block and a half north of Troup Square, Colonial Park

Cemetery contains the graves of Georgia colonists, with priceless tombstone inscriptions. From the cemetery, it's a 2-block walk up Abercorn Street to the *Owens-Thomas House* (1816) at the corner of State Street, hailed as "America's finest example of English Regency architecture." Now a museum, the house was visited in 1825 by Revolutionary hero Marquis de Lafayette. One block east, facing Columbia Square, *Davenport House,* now a museum, is the first architecturally important structure to have been reclaimed by the Historic Savannah Foundation. From here, it's a 3-block walk north to St. Julian Street, which splits three squares: Reynolds Square at Abercorn Street, Warren Square at Habersham Street, and Washington Square at Houston Street. This section has one of Savannah's largest clusters of restored 18th- and 19th-century homes. Facing Reynolds Square is the *Pink House* (c. 1790), now a restaurant.

Ft. Pulaski – A national monument named for the Revolutionary hero killed in the 1779 Battle of Savannah. Built between 1829 and 1847, the fort was captured by Union forces in 1862. Open daily. No admission charge. US 80 near Savannah Beach (phone: 786-5787).

■**EXTRA SPECIAL:** The Great Savannah Exposition, a new multimillion-dollar attraction in the former train yards behind the Savannah Visitors Center, is a pleasant way to absorb a little history. Two theaters feature films, animated historical characters, and sound-and-light effects; Exposition Hall contains a 19th-century steam locomotive, a replica of the cotton gin (invented in Savannah), and many other interesting artifacts. Open daily. Admission charge (phone: 238-1779).

Hilton Head Island, a luxury resort area in South Carolina about 40 miles northeast of Savannah, has 16 golf courses, pretty beaches, deep-sea fishing, tennis courts, a private airstrip, and plenty of nightlife. Hilton Head has become overcrowded, and reservations are advised if you plan to stay overnight. *Sea Pines Plantation,* a resort community of private villas and a 204-room, oceanfront inn, has beaches, 3 championship golf courses (including famed Harbour Town), tennis courts, bicycle paths with rental facilities, swimming pools, marinas, and a 625-acre forest preserve. For information, contact Sea Pines Plantation, Hilton Head Island, SC 29928 (phone: 800-845-6131 or 803-785-3333). Reservations islandwide may be made through the Hilton Head Reservation Service (phone: 800-845-7019). For information on Hilton Head activities, call the Chamber of Commerce (phone: 803-785-3673).

About 80 miles down the Atlantic coast from Savannah lie Georgia's "Golden Isles" — Sea Island, Jekyll Island, and St. Simons Island. Reached by causeway from Brunswick, Georgia, each has its own personality, and together they lay out an enormous spread of golf, tennis, beaches, lodgings, and dining. St. Simons offers the widest range of accommodations, shopping, and dining. Neighboring Little St. Simons is a privately owned, mostly primeval sanctuary, with a comfortably rustic lodge, dense forests, and 6 miles of unspoiled beaches and dunes (phone: 638-7472). Sea Island is the site of the fine *Cloister* hotel, with world class golf, elegant dining, and comfortable accommodations (phone: 638-3611). Jekyll Island's newest star is the *Jekyll Club* hotel, a gorgeously restored Victorian clubhouse, operated as a Radisson resort, where the elite once lodged (phone: 635-2600).

SOURCES AND RESOURCES

TOURIST INFORMATION: Your first stop should be the Savannah Visitors Center, 301 W. Broad St. (phone: 944-0456). Housed in the railway station, which dates to the 1860s, the center has maps, information, tours, and a free slide show and is also the starting point for city tours. Before leaving home, write to the Savannah Convention and Visitors Bureau, 222 W. Oglethorpe Ave., Savannah, GA 31499 (phone: 944-0456).

Sojourn in Savannah by Betty Rauers and Franklin Traub (Historic Savannah Foundation; $3) offers detailed information on places of interest around town.

Television Stations – WJCL Channel 22–ABC; WSAV Channel 3–NBC; WTOL Channel 11–CBS; WVAN Channel 9–PBS.

Radio Stations – AM: WSOK 1230 (gospel/R&B); WSGA 1400 (nostalgia); WBMQ 630 (oldies/talk); WCHY 1290 (country); FM: WSVH 91 (classical and jazz); WAEZ 97.3 (adult contemporary); WCHY 94.1 (country).

Local Coverage – *Savannah Morning News* and *Savannah Evening Press,* dailies.

Telephone – The area code for Savannah is 912.

Sales Tax – State and local sales tax is 5%. There is an additional hotel and motel tax of 5%.

 CLIMATE: Warm and sunny is the forecast for Savannah most of the year, with temperatures mostly in the 70s. From December through March, you can expect the mercury to drop into the 50s and 40s, and in the height of summer, to climb to the high 80s or low 90s. You can also be pretty sure of afternoon thunderstorms between June and September. Apart from the rains, however, the humidity is hardly ever greater than 60%.

 GETTING AROUND: Airport – Savannah International Airport is about 8 miles from the downtown area; taxi fare between the airport and downtown hotels is a flat rate of $15 for one passenger, $3 for each additional passenger. For $8 per person, *Coastal Express* (phone: 964-0332) takes passengers to downtown hotels. Two other companies provide service to Hilton Head Island, an hour's drive away, for $16: *Low Country Adventures* (phone: 803-681-8212) and *Regal Limousine* (phone: 803-785-5466).

Bus – Savannah Transit Authority operates the municipal bus system, 900 E. Gwinnett St. (phone: 233-5767).

Taxi – Cabs can be hailed in the streets, downtown. There are taxi stands at the main hotels, but you may prefer to call *Adam Cab* (phone: 927-7466).

Car Rental – *Avis* and *Hertz* have offices in town. *Thrifty Rent-a-Car* is a reliable local service (phone: 964-2341).

 LOCAL SERVICES: Babysitting – *Angels and Imps,* 614 Jackson Blvd. (phone: 355-1068).

   Business Services – *Norrell Services,* 7203 Hodgson Dr. (phone: 354-0044).

Mechanic – *Jackson Brothers Car Care Center,* 1141 W. Gwinnett St. (phone: 236-0631).

 MUSEUMS: Savannah is a treasury of historic and cultural elegance. On your way through the streets of the historic district, the *Telfair Academy of Arts and Sciences* on Barnard St. (phone: 232-1177) recommends itself as one of Savannah's outstanding museums. Other notable museums to visit:

Juliette Gordon Low Girl Scout National Center – 142 Bull St. (phone: 233-4501).

Savannah Science Museum – 4405 Paulsen (phone: 355-6705).

Ships of the Sea Maritime Museum – 503 E. River St. (phone: 232-1511).

Tybee Island Museum and Lighthouse – Tybee Island (phone: 786-5801).

MAJOR COLLEGES AND UNIVERSITIES: Armstrong State College, 11935 Abercorn St. Extension (phone: 927-5211); Savannah State College, Thunderbolt (phone: 356-2186). Both are four-year colleges within the Georgia state university system.

SPECIAL EVENTS: *Georgia Day,* February 12, commemorates the founding of the colony, and festivities last for a week. *St. Patrick's Day* (March 17) features the biggest street parade south of New York and traditionally kicks off Savannah's high spring season. Against a Technicolor background of millions of flowering azaleas, dogwood, and forsythia, the annual *Christ Episcopal Church Tour of Homes,* the end of March and early April, draws awestruck visitors into more than three dozen private mansions and gardens and to candlelight suppers at historic places around the city. *Night in Savannah,* the third weekend in April, is a 3-night festival of Dixieland and jazz and a culinary extravaganza prepared by the city's numerous ethnic communities. Christmas is a special season, when homes, churches, and public buildings are dressed in colonial finery. Music, parades, and festivities punctuate the month of December, and the city ushers in the New Year with typical exuberance.

SPORTS AND FITNESS: Savannah is at the head of one of the country's most popular vacationing areas. Names like Hilton Head, Sea Island, St. Simons, and Jekyll Island are all familiar to lovers of the outdoor life, and all are less than a day's drive from Savannah.

Bicycling – Cycling through the historic district can be an unforgettable experience. The *De Soto Hilton* hotel rents bikes.

Fitness Center – An outdoor pool, weight machines, indoor track, and tennis courts at the *YMCA* at 6400 Habersham (phone: 354-6223).

Golf – The *Sheraton Savannah Resort* course, one of the best known in the South, is also open to the public on Wilmington Island (phone: 897-1612). The best municipal course is at *Bacon Park,* Skidaway Rd. and Shorty Cooper Dr. (phone: 354-2625). (Shorty Cooper was one of the original golf caddies at Bacon Park.)

Jogging – Run around the perimeter of Forsyth Park, 1 mile, or along the waterfront in the early morning or evening when it isn't heavily trafficked; Lake Mayer, reachable by car, has an asphalt track. A jogging map is available at the *De Soto Hilton.*

Swimming and Fishing – Tybee Island (formerly Savannah Beach), nostalgically remembered as one end of a rollicking railroad that connected the mainland to the beach, has been a favorite haunt for many years. Here, you can indulge your penchants for swimming, fishing, surfing, crabbing, boating, picnicking, or beachcombing among the dunes. It's 18 miles from downtown Savannah.

Tennis – Best public tennis courts are at Bacon Park, Lake Mayer, Forsyth Park, and Daffin Park.

THEATER: For complete performance schedules, check the publications listed above. *Savannah Civic Center* is the largest auditorium in the city, Orleans Sq. (phone: 234-6666). *Little Theater,* Chippewa Sq. downtown (phone: 233-7764), is another place for good drama. It occupies the historic *Savannah Theater,* the oldest theater in continuous use in the US.

MUSIC: The *Savannah Civic Center* is the home of the *Savannah Symphony Orchestra,* and offers the best concerts, ballets, touring Broadway productions, and dance theater performances, in Orleans Sq. (phone: 234-6666).

NIGHTCLUBS AND NIGHTLIFE: Riverfront Plaza is alive with discos and clubs. Three of the most popular are *Emma's* (phone: 232-1223), *Kevin Barry's Irish Pub* (phone: 233-9626), and *Corky's* (phone: 234-0113).

BEST IN TOWN

CHECKING IN: Savannah has over 3,600 rooms for guests, most of them scattered among the motels within and around the fringe of the city. The city also has four hotels that offer a special elegance. Expect to pay between $80 and $100 or more for a double at those places we've listed as expensive; between $60 and $80 in the moderate range; under $50 for an inexpensive hostelry. For reservations at many of Savannah's historic inns, phone these central numbers: *Savannah Historic Inns and Guest Houses* (phone: 800-262-4667) and *R.S.V.P. Savannah* (phone: 232-7787). All telephone numbers are in the 912 area code unless otherwise indicated.

Comer House – A grand Victorian mansion on one of the city's most picturesque squares, it offers guests the seclusion of 2 garden suites with kitchenettes and tours of the mansion's beautifully furnished main rooms. 2 E. Taylor St. (phone: 234-2923). Expensive.

DeSoto Hilton – In the heart of the historic district, this 264-room property blends modern pleasures with Savannah's Old World charms and retains much of the decor that made its predecessor the queen of the gaslight era's carriage trade. Amenities include the *Pavilion Room* for fine dining, the *Red Lion* lounge, and recreation facilities. Liberty and Bull Sts. (phone: 912 232-9000). Expensive.

Eliza Thompson House – This quaint 3-story 1847 townhouse in the Historic District has been restored and converted to an inn. Some of the 25 rooms are filled with antiques as well as with Savannah history books. Others also have fireplaces, kitchenettes, or private entrances. Complimentary sherry makes things even cozier. 7 W. Jones St. (phone: 236-3620). Expensive.

Gastonian Inn – One of the city's newest and loveliest inns, it offers 13 rooms, rich in antiques and historic Savannah decor, in a pair of mid-19th-century townhouses. Many rooms have whirlpool baths. Tariffs include full southern breakfast, afternoon tea, and late-night cordials. 220 E. Gaston St. (phone: 232-2869). Expensive.

Hyatt Regency Savannah – This 350-room hotel rises above the Riverfront Plaza, giving guests a view of the oceangoing ships cruising in and out of the harbor. *Windows* restaurant, overlooking the river, has quickly become a favorite dining spot, along with the more casual *MD's Lounge* and *Patrick's Porch.* Guests can arrange tours and other activities at the concierge's desk in the lobby. Indoor parking. 2 W. Bay St. (phone: 238-1234 or 800-233-1234). Expensive.

Magnolia Place Inn – Facing Forsyth Park, the 13-room inn is in the heart of Old Savannah and has antique furnishings along with Jacuzzis, limousine service, and videodisc players. 503 Whitaker St. (phone: 236-7674). Expensive.

Mulberry – Lavishly refurbished in 1988, with 101 rooms and 28 suites, it is the classiest and most service-oriented of Savannah's historic inns. Facilities include 24-hour valet service, an excellent restaurant, a clubby bar, and a chintz-filled living room for afternoon tea. Rooms are furnished with bottles of Perrier, terrycloth robes, deluxe toiletries, and down pillows. The Executive Conference Center has computers, fax machines, and other commercial conveniences. 601 E. Bay St. (phone: 238-1200). Expensive.

Planters Inn – Built in 1920, this 7-story hotel has recently journeyed back in time to become a 19th-century-style inn, with antiques, Georgian furnishings, and all the modern comforts. The penthouse rooms even have working fireplaces. 29 Abercorn St. (phone: 232-5678). Expensive.

Sheraton Savannah – Ten miles from Savannah on the Wilmington River, this was one of the Roaring Twenties' great resort hotels, and succeeding owners have kept it in first class condition. Its 210 deluxe rooms are distributed among the 8-story hotel, a number of small cottages, and some villas. It has a restaurant, nightly dancing, swimming pool, sauna, tennis, fishing, and boating. Its pride is its 18-hole golf course, one of the South's finest. A modified American plan is available. Wilmington Island Rd. (phone: 897-1612 or 800-325-3535). Expensive.

Best Western/Savannah Riverfront – This 142-room motel overlooks River Street. Its *Bottle Works* restaurant is open for all meals. Pool and bar. 412 W. Bay St. (phone: 233-1011). Moderate.

Courtyard by Marriott – Attractive, contemporary guestrooms and a good restaurant and bar make this an excellent suburban choice. 6703 Abercorn St. (phone: 354-7878 or 800-228-9290). Moderate.

Downtown Ramada Inn – Built of Savannah gray bricks salvaged from older buildings and ornamented with wrought iron balconies, the 204-room, 6-story hotel harmonizes with the architecture of the surrounding historic landmark district. It has a swimming pool, and its *Regency Restaurant and Tavern* is a local favorite. Next to the Savannah Civic Center. 201 W. Oglethorpe (phone: 233-3531 or 800-2-RAMADA). Moderate.

Bed-and-Breakfast Inn – A restored 1853 townhouse that offers historic inn charm at moderate prices. 117 W. Gordon St. (phone: 238-0518). Moderate to inexpensive.

Days Inn Savannah – Across the street from Riverfront Plaza, it's a good choice for families since there's a swimming pool, gameroom, and a 24-hour restaurant where kids under 12 eat for free. 253 attractive rooms. 201 W. Bay St. (phone: 236-4440 or 800-325-2525). Moderate to inexpensive.

Quality Inn/Heart of Savannah – Its romantic name and size (53 rooms) create a certain intimacy, in contrast to larger hotels. The two great things about it, though, are the free continental breakfast and the price, about $40 for two. 300 W. Bay St. (phone: 236-6321 or 800-228-5151). Inexpensive.

EATING OUT: Savannah's restaurants range from elegant to home style. Chefs at fine restaurants do wondrous things with fresh shrimp, oysters, flounder, and blue crabs. Two people can eat very well for about $50 or less. Anything between $25 and $35 is moderate; under $20, inexpensive. Prices do not include drinks, wine, or tips. All telephone numbers are in the 912 area code unless otherwise indicated.

Pirates' House – In Savannah's oldest standing building, this made literary history in Robert Louis Stevenson's *Treasure Island.* In any of its 23 dining rooms, a meal is an authentic experience. Choices include oysters Savannah, several flaming dishes, local seafood, steaks, red rice, and exotic desserts. Open daily. Reservations advised. Major credit cards. 20 E. Broad St. (phone: 233-5757). Expensive.

River's End Seafood – Lovely, upscale dining room on the Thunderbolt yacht harbor specializes in fresh local seafood, live Maine lobster, steaks, and prime ribs. Closed Sundays. Reservations advised. Major credit cards. 3122 River Dr., Thunderbolt (phone: 354-2973). Expensive.

Windows – This exquisite restaurant in the *Hyatt Regency Savannah* overlooks the Savannah River. Diners can watch merchant ships come and go while choosing from a continental menu featuring seafood, duck, and stir-fried Oriental dishes.

Open daily; brunch only on Sundays; no lunch on Saturdays. Reservations advised. Major credit cards. 2 W. Bay St. (phone: 238-1234). Expensive.

Elizabeth on Thirty-Seventh – In a lovely old Savannah mansion, the dining room has been widely acclaimed. Freshly prepared seasonal foods are offered along with sumptuous desserts. Closed Sundays and Mondays. Reservations advised. Some credit cards. 105 E. 37th at Drayton (phone: 236-5547). Expensive to moderate.

La Toque – This popular dining spot features continental cuisine and fresh local seafood. All entrées are cooked to order, and there's a good wine list. A specialty food shop, *Swiss Affair Ltd.*, is also on the premises and serves light dinners (omelettes, soups, and salads). Closed Sundays. Reservations advised. Major credit cards. 420 E. Broughton St. (phone: 238-0138). Expensive to moderate.

Chart House – Loads of nautical paraphernalia, first-rate seafood and steaks, a cozy bar, and balconies overlooking the Savannah River and Riverfront Plaza make this one of the most popular dining spots in town. Open daily. Reservations. Major credit cards. 202 W. Bay St. (phone: 234-6686). Moderate.

Garibaldi's – An 1870s firehouse has been cunningly refashioned into a comfortable Italian café serving first rate pasta, veal, seafood, grilled duck, lamb, and lobster. Dining is enhanced by the decor: marbletop tables, lace curtains, mirrors and antiques. Dinner daily. Reservations advised. Major credit cards. 315 W. Congress St. (phone: 232-7118). Moderate.

Johnny Harris – Specialties here are steaks, prime ribs, barbecue, and chicken. They do their own baking on the premises. In its third generation of continuous ownership, this is where the nationally marketed Johnny Harris Barbecue Sauce originated. Jacket and tie are required on Friday and Saturday nights, but surprisingly, reservations are not necessary. Closed Sundays. Major credit cards. 1651 E. Victory Dr. (phone: 354-7810). Moderate.

Pavilion – Another well-known Savannah restaurant, featuring traditional "Old South" recipes from land and sea, with a great buffet. Open daily. Reservations advised. Major credit cards. *De Soto Hilton* hotel, Bull and Liberty Sts. (phone: 232-0171). Moderate.

Sebastian's – In a restored old tavern, this cozy dining room offers creative Low Country, American, and European cuisine. Reservations advised. Major credit cards. Closed Sundays. 321 Jefferson St., downtown (phone: 234-3211). Moderate.

Bodi's Café and Bakery – A cheery little suburban bake shop and café is a nice drop-in spot for lunch, continental breakfast, fresh croissants, breads, desserts, and wines. Open early morning to late night daily except Sundays. No reservations. Major credit cards. 7135 Hodgson Memorial Dr. (phone: 354-3733). Inexpensive.

Crystal Beer Parlor – For the last half-century this place has been famous for its sandwiches, burgers, and casual, friendly atmosphere. Closed Sundays. Major credit cards. 301 W. Jones St. (phone: 232-1153). Inexpensive.

Love's Seafood – On the Ogeechee River, south of the city, this simple seafood place has for many years been known for its shrimp, oysters, crabs, and channel catfish. Open for lunch and dinner daily except Mondays. No reservations. Major credit cards. US 17S (phone: 925-2232). Inexpensive.

Palmers Seafood House – On Wilmington Island, just 15 minutes from downtown; many residents and visitors consider this the best place in the area for fresh seafood. The atmosphere is casual, and no reservations are taken. Open daily. Major credit cards. 80 Wilmington Island Rd. (phone: 897-2611). Inexpensive.

Wall's BarBQ – Housed in a shack in an unpaved alley, this old Savannah favorite still dishes out the best deviled crab cakes in town. These piquantly seasoned patties cost $2 each and are available only on Fridays and Saturdays from noon to 6:30 PM. Take them out for gobbling elsewhere, since the shack's interior leans toward the gloomy. Between Houston and Price Sts. (phone: 232-9754). Inexpensive.

Mrs. Wilkes' Boarding House – This is one of Savannah's culinary landmarks. Mrs. Wilkes advertises by word of mouth, and while some people are critical, they admit that it is only because when they want home cooking they eat at home. When you walk into *Mrs. Wilkes'*, you'll find set out on dining room tables food enough to stagger Sherman's army: grits, biscuits, sausage, and eggs for breakfast, or fried chicken, swordfish steaks, potatoes, rice, peas, cornbread, and other down-home treats for lunch. To serve yourself, just spread your arm in that proverbial boarding-house reach. Open weekdays for breakfast and lunch. No reservations or credit cards. In the basement of 107 W. Jones St. (phone: 232-5997). Inexpensive by any standards — about $5 for all you can eat.

SEATTLE

Visitors often feel they have "discovered" Seattle: Because the Emerald City is less well known than many of its West Coast counterparts, travelers are surprised and delighted to find a booming city with a striking skyline, a surfeit of green spaces, lovely residential neighborhoods, lots of cultural events, and a host of outdoor and adventure activities, all very accessible. The nearby mountains offer skiing, and Puget Sound provides sailing and salmon fishing.

Seattle occupies a rich corner of the western frontier, six hills tucked away by imposing mountain ranges to the east and west. The Olympic Mountains lie on the western horizon line, and the Cascades, with their jagged cliffs crowned by the snow-capped summit of 14,410-foot Mt. Rainier, on the eastern. Immediately to the west is Elliott Bay off Puget Sound, which leads outward to the vast expanse of the Pacific, and on the east is a 24-mile length of fresh water, Lake Washington.

The earliest inhabitants of the region were the Northwest Indians, who were generally more content to trade than to make war with neighbors. Their territory was covered with thick forests, the waters of Puget Sound and Lake Washington filled with fish, and they lived in harmony with their surroundings. They had fish and clams for the taking, a moderate climate year-round, and plenty of cedar for the construction of their superb, long canoes.

The European settlers who came in the 1850s couldn't leave well enough alone. They harvested the readily available timber and sent it south to San Francisco. Then they leveled a couple of the more prominent hills to make north-south travel easier. One of those hills, now a concrete canyon in Seattle's downtown, was the lumberjacks' principal source of timber. When teams of oxen skidded the new-cut logs down the street to the sawmill, a new American expression was born — Skid Road (now Row). On either side of the Road, you can now hear the strains of rock and jazz from nightclubs where once only the music of box-house bands played. Lumbering is still one of Washington Sstate's major industries, but the oxen are gone.

Seattle seems to owe its rise to having been in the right place at the right time. There was nothing inevitable about its growth. Olympia, to the south, was an established town when Seattle was little more than a collection of rude huts; Port Townsend was better situated on the Sound; and Tacoma, though it didn't develop as early, was named as the terminus of the Northern Pacific Railroad. Seattle had a fine deep water harbor on the Sound, but so did several other 19th-century Washington towns. But in 1897 a "ton of gold" was brought back from Alaska aboard a ship that docked at a Seattle pier, and the town was, well . . . golden. Gold fever spread, and the city naturally became a boom town because of its easy access to riches — a protected inland passage to Alaska. Vice flourished in this raw frontier town, if you consider brothels a way of flourishing. The confluence of Seattle lumberjacks and miners on their way to find their fortune in gold in the Klondike brought about a demand for prostitution, which was best satisfied in all the West along Seattle's Skid Road.

After the Gold Rush days, Seattle seemed almost ashamed of itself for its extravagances. It was quick to embrace Prohibition in 1916, three years before the rest of the nation capitulated. It was a conservative town, and after World War II it became a one-industry town, depending far too heavily on airplane production.

Things began to change in 1962, when a group of businessmen put together an audacious undertaking, a World's Fair in Seattle. The Alaska-Yukon Pacific Exposition in 1909 had created quite a stir, but this was something else. Even the backers were dubious of its success. But the venture turned out profitably and left the city with a different attitude toward itself — a feeling that the city could be first class in more ways than it thought possible.

The World's Fair gave the city a real boost culturally, too, leaving it with the valuable legacy of the Seattle Center, a complex that includes an opera house, playhouse, the *Bagley Wright Theater, Arena Coliseum,* the *Pacific Science Center* with its wide-ranging exhibitions, and the futuristically designed Space Needle. The *Seattle Repertory Theater* is a strong professional group; the *Seattle Symphony* under the direction of Gerard Schwarz is of world class; and the *Seattle Opera*.

In sports, too, Seattle hit the big league. The basketball *SuperSonics* play their games at the *Coliseum,* the football *Seahawks* and baseball *Mariners* play at the *Kingdome,* which sits on land reclaimed from Elliott Bay.

With all of its progress toward the future, Seattle still is concerned with its heritage and has maintained the "old town" alongside the new. Pioneer Square, where the city was founded in 1852, has been renovated and designated a historic preservation area. The old brick buildings surrounding the square are protected from the ruthless movements of progress and the bulldozer. Beyond the stately façades lie galleries, boutiques, and restaurants.

The inner city is unusually healthy; the plane manufacturing industry is booming, and people are moving back into the city to enjoy a new sense of belonging. Off in the distance, the snow-capped peaks of the Cascades and Olympic Mountains and the expansive stretch of Puget Sound and Lake Washington create a magnificent backdrop. But it is the scene of current Seattle — the dynamic activity of a rising city — that is attracting residents.

SEATTLE AT-A-GLANCE

SEEING THE CITY: The best view of Seattle and the magnificent Washington landscape is from the top of the Space Needle (phone: 443-2111). The observation deck and revolving restaurant offer 360-degree views of the city, Puget Sound, Lake Washington, and beyond to the snow-covered peaks of the Cascade and Olympic Mountains. Admission charge unless dining. Seattle Center.

SPECIAL PLACES: Don't be confused by the geographical designations in street addresses, like north or south. The directions that follow avenue names and precede street names (5th Ave. N. or N. 5th St.) give location in relation to downtown (where only street names and numbers are used).

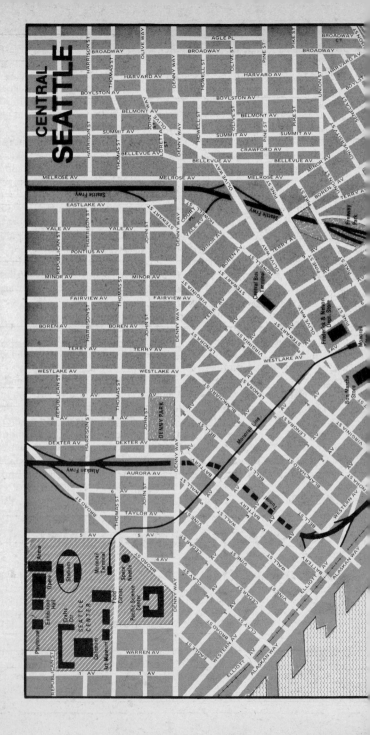

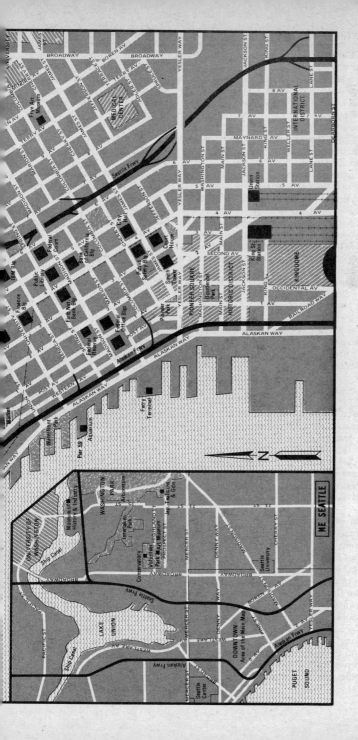

Seattle Center – The legacy of the 1962 World's Fair, this 74-acre area contains some of the city's finest facilities. Dominating the 50 buildings and the grassy plazas is the Space Needle, a futuristic steel structure that spires 605 feet upward from its tripod base. Among the other highlights are the Food Circus (Center House, 305 Harrison St.) where you can sample inexpensive international delicacies, two playhouses, the *Opera House* and *Arena* (adjoining buildings on Mercer St.), and Fun Forest Amusement Park (370 Thomas St.) for a variety of entertainment. Information for Seattle Center theater tickets and activities at booth in Center House Bldg., 5th Ave. N. between Denny Way and Mercer St. (phone: 684-7200). There are two notable museums in the Center:

Pacific Science Center – Designed by Minoru Yamasaki, the center features astro-space displays, with a large fiberglass moon and a full-scale model of a lunar module, an operating oceanographic model of Puget Sound that simulates waves, a laserium that uses laser beams to form images, a reconstruction of a Northwest Indian longhouse, and a popular science playground with hands-on exhibitions for children. Open daily. Admission charge. 200 2nd Ave. N. (phone: 443-2001).

Seattle Art Museum Pavilion – Changing exhibitions of photography and regional and contemporary artists, including Harry Callahan and Andy Warhol. Closed Mondays. Admission charge. 2nd Ave. N. and Thomas St. (phone: 625-8901).

Seattle Aquarium – Next to the public fishing pier at Waterfront Park, the aquarium offers a close view of what's swimming in Puget Sound. In the domed viewing room — actually a 400,000-gallon tank — you are surrounded by octopus, starfish, dogfish sharks, rock cod, red snapper, scallops, shrimps, anemones, and sea pens. There are also tropical fish, a touch-me exhibition, and a wonderfully captivating family of sea otters. Open daily. Admission charge. Pier 59 (phone: 625-4357). All along the waterfront, there are seafood bars where you can pick up a good lunch.

Puget Sound Ferry Ride – If looking out at the Sound and up at its marine life isn't enough, you can have the full Sound experience by taking the 45-minute ride to Winslow or to Bremerton or as far as Victoria, British Columbia. Ferry Terminal (phone: 464-6400).

Pike Place Market – Founded in 1907, this public market is now a historic site full of lively vendors and a colorful array of produce, flowers, and fresh fish. There are also musicians, craftspeople, and specialty restaurants. Closed Sundays except in summer. 1st Ave. between Pike St. and Virginia St.

Seattle Art Museum – The exceptional Oriental collection of Richard E. Fuller features beautiful Chinese jade and bronzes, delicately crafted pottery and snuff bottles, and Indian stone sculptures. Also changing displays of modern and Northwest Indian art. Closed Mondays. Admission charge except Thursdays. Volunteer Park (phone: 625-8900).

Museum of History and Industry – Extensive collection of Pacific Northwest artifacts traces the history of Seattle's first 100 years. A mural depicts the fire that leveled the city in 1889, and the displays include almost everything that came afterward — mementos of the Gold Rush, old fire fighting equipment, a maritime display, and a Boeing exhibit that follows its development over the past 60 years. Open daily. Admission charge except Tuesdays. 2700 24th Ave. E. (phone: 324-1125).

Westlake Center – This $110-million retail and office project now forms the heart of downtown Seattle. The airy 4-level glass and steel retail pavilion features upscale specialty shops, pushcarts, and the Pacific Picnic food court, offering ethnic dishes. It is flanked by a 25-story office tower and Westlake Park, with its granite plaza designed in contrasting colors to resemble a woven Indian basket. The center, open daily, is connected to the city's main department stores and is served by a monorail terminal. Pine St., between 4th and 5th Aves.

Pioneer Square – The site where the city was founded in 1852 has become a historic preservation area and remains in all its Victorian grandeur today. The classic brick buildings house some of the city's best boutiques, galleries, and restaurants (for seafood at a moderate price, try lunch at *La Galleria;* see *Best in Town,* below). When fire ravaged the district in 1889, the city rebuilt atop the rubble, leaving an underground town 10 feet below. *Bill Speidel's Underground Tours* guide visitors through the subterranean 5-block area, which has some storefronts, interiors, and old waterlines intact. Tours daily. Admission charge. Reservations advised (610 1st Ave.; phone: 682-4646). For gold rush nostalgia, visit the Klondike Gold Rush National Historic Park (117 S. Main; phone: 442-7220), which traces the history of Klondike gold fever with murals, exhibitions, movies, and a slide show.

International District – Often called the Gateway to the Orient, Seattle has a large Chinese and Japanese community concentrated in this interesting old section of the city. There is a Buddhist temple, many craft shops, and Asian restaurants. Shop at *Uwajimaya* (6th Ave. S. and S. King; phone: 624-6248), the West Coast's largest Asian retail store, for gifts and specialty food items. The *Wing Luke Memorial Museum* features a permanent exhibition tracing the immigration of the Chinese to the Northwest from the 1860s on, a folk arts gallery, and a fine arts gallery. Closed Mondays. Admission charge. 407 7th Ave. S. (phone: 623-5124).

University of Washington Arboretum – Some 200 lakeside acres contain over 5,000 species of plant life from all over the world. Features one of the largest Japanese tea gardens outside Japan. Open all year. Admission charge for Japanese Garden. Lake Washington Blvd. between E. Madison and Montlake (phone: 543-8800).

■**EXTRA SPECIAL:** Just an hour and a half south of Seattle is the spectacular Mt. Rainier National Park, with its 14,410-foot summit of the Cascade range. There are over 300 miles of trails, ranging from the super-rough, 90-mile Wonderland trail, which circles the peak, to short nature walks for mere earthlings. On the way home, stop at the *Wild Berry* restaurant in Ashford (phone: 569-2628) for a colossal club sandwich made with three slices of homemade whole wheat or rye bread and a jar of delicious mountain blackberry jam. Also on Route 161 is the Northwest Trek Wildlife Park (phone: 847-1903), where moose, elk, buffalo, mountain goat, and caribou roam free. The zoo belongs to the animals; visitors tour from a tram and are not allowed off.

SOURCES AND RESOURCES

TOURIST INFORMATION: The Seattle/King County Convention and Visitors Bureau offers daily events schedules, maps, and information. 666 Stewart St. (phone: 447-4240).

    The Seattle Guidebook by Archie Satterfield, available at the Elliott Bay Book Co. (phone: 624-6600) for $9.95, is a good guide to Seattle and the surrounding area.

Television Stations – KING Channel 5–NBC; KIRO Channel 7–CBS; KOMO Channel 4–ABC; KCTS Channel 9–PBS.

Radio Stations – AM: KING 1090 (news/talk); KLSY 1540 (soft rock); KIXI 880 (1940s, '50s, and '60s). FM: KING 98.1 (classical); KLSY 92.5 (soft rock); KMGI 107.7 (adult contemporary).

Local Coverage – *Seattle Post-Intelligencer,* morning daily, publishes What's Happening on Fridays with coming week's events; *Seattle Times,* afternoon daily, publishes Tempo magazine on Fridays. Both are available at newsstands. *Seattle Visitors Guide* is available at hotels and some restaurants.

Food – *Seattle's Best Places* by David Brewster (Weekly Press; $14.95).
Telephone – The area code for Seattle is 206.
Sales Tax – Local sales tax is 8.1%, except on groceries.

 CLIMATE: Seattle's proximity to Puget Sound keeps the climate mild and moderately moist. Winters are relatively warm, with temperatures averaging around 40F; it seldom snows. The wet season is from October to April, so carry an umbrella. Seattle is best in summer and early fall, when city and countryside are most accessible.

 GETTING AROUND: Airport – Seattle-Tacoma International Airport (known as Sea-Tac) is about a 25-minute drive from downtown; taxi fare from the center of the city will run about $18 to $20. *Gray Line Airport Express* (phone: 626-6088) offers service every half hour and costs $5. Stops are made at the *Stouffer Madison, Holiday Inn Crowne Plaza, Four Season Olympic, Westin, Sheraton,* and *Warwick* hotels. *Shuttle Express* (phone: 286-4800) offers service to your home from the airport for $9 and from downtown locations to the airport. Metro buses #174 and #194 leave for Sea-Tac from 9th Ave. and Stewart St. via 2nd Ave.; fare, 85¢ ($1 during rush hours).

Bus – Metropolitan Transit provides extensive service in the metropolitan area with an added attraction: Metro's Free Ride Service in the downtown-waterfront area. Route information is available at its office, 821 2nd Ave. (phone: 447-4800).

Monorail – The quickest and most exciting way to get from downtown to Seattle Center is via the World's Fair monorail. Leaves every 15 minutes from Westlake Center.

Taxi – Cabs can be hailed in the street or ordered on the phone. Major companies are *Farwest* (phone: 292-0569) and *Yellow Cab* (phone: 622-6500).

Car Rental – Seattle is served by the major national firms.

 LOCAL SERVICES: Business Services – *Secretarial Assistants,* Columbia Center (phone: 682-6072).
    Mechanic – *Salmon Service Center,* 25th and 65th NE (phone: 523-9400).

 MUSEUMS: Exhibitions on the history, art, industry, and even marine life of the Pacific Northwest and the world are well represented in Seattle's cultural institutions. The *Seattle Art Museum,* the *Pacific Science Center,* and the *Museum of History and Industry* are described under *Special Places.* Other interesting museums are the following:

Bellevue Art Museum – American and regional art. Bellevue Sq. (phone: 454-3322).

Frye Art Museum – Contemporary regional works. Terry Ave. and Cherry St. (phone: 622-9250).

Museum of Flight – This aviation museum features a soaring glassed-in gallery with more than 20 full-size planes suspended from the ceiling, including a DC-3 and the first supersonic jet. Admission charge. 9404 E. Marginal Way S., near Sea-Tac Airport (phone: 764-5720).

MAJOR COLLEGES AND UNIVERSITIES: The University of Washington, founded in 1861, is the area's oldest and largest educational institution, at 17th Ave. NE and NE 45th St. (phone: 543-9198). Also in the city are Seattle University, 12th Ave. and E. Columbia St. (phone: 296-6000), and Seattle Pacific University, 3rd Ave. W. and W. Nickerson St. (phone: 281-2000).

SPECIAL EVENTS: The *Seattle Seafair* is a citywide celebration in late July and early August featuring everything from a hydroplane race, a torchlight parade, a beauty contest, and a marathon to a special appearance by the Pacific Fleet. Check the papers for exact dates.

SPORTS AND FITNESS: Seattle is in the big leagues, with three professional teams. The best bet is to order tickets by phone and later pick them up at the team's ticket office.

Baseball – The *Mariners'* season runs from April through September at the *Kingdome* (phone: 628-3555).

Basketball – The NBA *SuperSonics* play from October through April at the *Seattle Center Coliseum* (ticket office, at the west entrance, phone: 281-5800).

Bicycling – Rent from *Gregg's Green Lake Cycle,* 7007 Woodlawn Ave. NE (phone: 523-1822). Green Lake Park and Burke-Gilman Trail are good areas for biking.

Fishing – You can wet a line from the public pier of Waterfront Park or go after the big salmon by renting a boat or taking a charter into the deep sea from Pier 54 (Ivar's Pier) on the Seattle waterfront (phone: 783-8873).

Fitness Centers – The *Clark Hatch Fitness Center* (phone: 728-1500) has a pool, Jacuzzi, sauna, steamroom, exercise equipment, and weights; athletic clothing is provided; 2001 6th Ave., across from the *Westin* hotel; The *YMCA* has a pool, weight room, and track, 909 4th Ave. and Madison (phone: 382-5000). The private *Seattle Club* (2020 Western Ave.; phone: 443-1111) is open to guests of several downtown hotels. Among the many facilities are racquetball courts, track, pool, Nautilus, massage, tanning, exercise classes, and a restaurant.

Football – The NFL *Seahawks* play from August through December at the *Kingdome,* 201 S. King St. (phone: 827-9777).

Golf – The city has three good 18-hole municipal courses: *Jackson Park,* 1000 NE 135th St. (phone: 363-4747); *Jefferson Park,* 4101 Beacon Ave. S. (phone: 762-4513); *West Seattle Municipal Course,* 4470 35th Ave. SW (phone: 935-5187).

Horse Racing – *Longacres Racetrack* is 11 miles southeast via I-5 and I-405 in Renton (phone: 226-3131). The season is from early April through mid-October.

Jogging – Run the 3-mile course at Myrtle Edwards Park on the waterfront, at Alaska Way between W. Bay and W. Thomas. Or follow many Seattle residents and run around Green Lake (2.8 miles); to get there, take the #6 or #16 northbound bus from 3rd and Pine.

Skiing – Close by is *Alpental* on the Snoqualmie Pass via I-90 (phone: 434-6112). Also popular is *Crystal Mountain*, 120 miles away near Mt. Rainier (phone: 663-2265).

Tennis – City parks have outdoor courts.

THEATER: For current offerings check the publications listed above. The *Seattle Repertory Theater* performs classical and modern productions from October through May at the *Bagley Wright Theater* at the Seattle Center, 155 Mercer St. (phone: 443-2222). *Intiman Theatre Co.* performs at the *Seattle Center Playhouse,* 155 Mercer St. (phone: 624-4541). *A Contemporary Theater* plays at 100 W. Roy (phone: 285-5110). The *5th Avenue Theater,* 1308 5th Ave. (phone: 625-1900), features pop concerts and touring Broadway plays; and the restored *Paramount Theater,* 907 Pine St. (phone: 682-1414), brings in top concert artists. The *Empty Space Theatre,* 95 S. Jackson (phone: 587-3737), showcases new plays. The *Bathhouse Theatre,* 7312 W. Green Lake Dr. N. (phone: 524-9108), stages experimental productions, the *New City Theatre,* 1634 11th Ave. (phone: 323-6800), features works by up and coming playwrights, and the *Group Theatre,* 3940 Brooklyn Ave. NE (phone: 543-4327), focuses on ethnic plays.

MUSIC: The *Seattle Symphony* and the *Seattle Opera Association* perform at the *Opera House* from September through April. The Opera's *Wagner Ring Festival* is in August. The ticket offices for both are in Center House, Seattle Center (For Symphony phone: 443-4747; Opera 443-4711).

 NIGHTCLUBS AND NIGHTLIFE: Some of the area's hottest nightspots are *Dimitrou's Jazz Alley,* 6th and Lenora (phone: 441-9729), for jazz; and *Swannie's,* 222 S. Main St. (phone: 622-9353), for headline comedy acts. Another popular spot is *Celebrity's Bar and Grill,* 315 2nd Ave. S. (phone: 467-1111).

BEST IN TOWN

 CHECKING IN: Seattle has an abundance and wide variety of accommodations. Those we rate as expensive begin at $100 for a double room; moderate, from $60. We could find no hotels that met our standards in the inexpensive category. For information about bed and breakfast accommodations, contact: *Pacific Bed & Breakfast Agency,* 701 NW 60th St., Seattle, WA 98107 (phone: 784-0539). All telephone numbers are in the 206 area code unless otherwise indicated.

Alexis – For the sophisticated traveler who needs to be pampered, this 51-room hotel is the place. The management claims service to be its top priority and it shows, from the optional butler who will do your unpacking to the free shoeshines. 1st and Madison (phone: 624-4844). Expensive.

Four Seasons Olympic – A splendid restoration of a historic city landmark, it blends the old and new seamlessly. Highlights include the guestrooms, decorated in Henredon furnishings; the *Solarium,* a sparkling new health spa; and the *Georgian* restaurant, a favorite for special occasions. Many of the city's most popular attractions are within walking distance. 411 University (phone: 621-1700 or 800-332-3442). Expensive.

Seattle Sheraton – With one of the region's most extensive permanent collections of contemporary Northwestern art, valued at more than $1 million, this is the place for those who enjoy culture along with their comfort. Many of the more than 2,000 original works, including a fantastic glass collection, are displayed in the lobby and other public spaces. Many of the 880 rooms offer great views. The hotel has a pool room on the 35th floor (the Cirrus level); 3 restaurants, *Banners, Fullers Gallery Seafood Bar* (see *Eating Out*), and *Gooey's Lounge;* shops; airport bus; and valet parking. 6th and Pike (phone: 621-9000 or 800-325-3535). Expensive.

Sorrento – This small first class hotel, with just 76 rooms, offers many extras: terrycloth bathrobes, plants and potpourri in every room, a hot water bottle in your bed in winter, and complimentary limousine service into downtown. Dine at the highly acclaimed *Hunt Club* or enjoy English tea in the afternoon. Terry Ave. and Madison St. (phone: 622-6400). Expensive.

Westin Seattle – Two imposing 40- and 47-story towers in the heart of the shopping district that are difficult to overlook. The 875 rooms offer spectacular views of Puget Sound, Mt. Rainier, and the Cascade and Olympic Mountains. Restaurants include a *Trader Vic's,* the *Market Café,* and the *Palm Court.* Shops, airport bus. 5th Ave. at Westlake (phone: 728-1000 or 800-228-3000). Expensive.

Inn at the Market – Accommodations in French country style above the Pike Place Market. Most of the 65 rooms feature a view of Elliott Bay. Guests enjoy complimentary coffee, limousine service around downtown, and *Campagne* restaurant for French country cuisine. Coffee shop; athletic facilities nearby. 86 Pine St. (phone: 443-3600). Expensive to moderate.

Mayflower Park – In the downtown shopping district, adjacent to Westlake Center, providing recently refurnished and renovated accommodations in a convenient setting. Children under 17 stay free with their parents. Inexpensive parking, a coffee shop, and a cocktail lounge, *Oliver's.* 4th Ave. and Olive Way (phone: 623-8700). Moderate.

Pacific Plaza – An older hotel, smartly updated to appeal to businesspeople and others who want to be in the center of downtown at a reasonable price. It features 168 quiet rooms and complimentary continental breakfast. 400 Spring St. (phone: 623-3900). Moderate.

EATING OUT: Seattle's food industry did not really get moving until the 1962 World's Fair. Being in the international spotlight spawned a wide variety of ethnic restaurants and boosted the quality of existing establishments. Our selections run from $60 and up for a dinner for two in the expensive range to $40 to $55 in the moderate and $35 or less in the inexpensive category. Prices do not include drinks, wine, or tips. All telephone numbers are in the 206 area code unless otherwise indicated.

Canlis' – Features excellent dishes, including several cuts of charcoal-broiled steaks, poached fresh salmon in hollandaise sauce, pan-fried Quilcene oysters from nearby Quilcene Bay, and a sweeping view of Lake Union. Closed Sundays. Reservations advised. Major credit cards. 2576 Aurora Ave. N. (phone: 283-3313). Expensive.

Daniel's Broiler – A small, intimate, and usually crowded restaurant on the shores of Lake Washington, *Daniel's* has a pretty view and some of the finest stir-fried vegetables and prawns you'll find in the Northwest. Steaks are also favorites. Open daily for dinner only. Reservations advised. Major credit cards. 200 Lake Washington Blvd. (phone: 329-4191). Expensive.

Fullers – In the *Seattle Sheraton,* this is one of Seattle's best, if not the best restaurant in the city. Elegant peach- and buff-colored recessed booths showcase original artwork by Northwest artists. Villeroy & Boch china, crystal, silver-plated tableware, and hand-blown glass vases with fresh flowers are the prelude to splendid cuisine. The menu celebrates the special wealth of Northwest foods with selections such as grilled salmon with truffles, baby leeks and herb port cream, or seared tuna with macadamia nuts and pineapple tamarind jalapeño butter. The wine list showcases the best the state has to offer, which is quite a lot. Closed Sundays. Reservations advised. Major credit cards. 6th and Pike (phone: 621-9000 or 800-325-3535). Expensive.

Baffert's – Actually, three places in one: a New York–type bar where young Seattleites gather; the *Garden Court* for casual dining; and the *Club Room,* with a more intimate and formal atmosphere. The menu features creative Northwest cuisine, and the wine list is extensive. Open daily. Reservations advised. Major credit cards. 314 Broadway E. (phone: 323-1990). Expensive to moderate.

La Galleria – The decor of this Pioneer Square restaurant will make you feel as if you were dining on a street in Italy. Fresh seafood, pasta, and veal specialties are served in the indoor garden; and set aside some time for wine tasting in the underground wine cellar. Closed Sundays. Reservations suggested. Major credit cards. 83 King St. (phone: 467-1660). Expensive to moderate.

Ray's Boathouse – On the waterfront at Shilshole Bay, a great place to have a leisurely dinner while watching the sun go down behind the Olympic Mountains. Seafood offerings are fine and varied. Open daily. Reservations advised. Major credit cards. 6049 Seaview Ave. NW (phone: 789-3770); also *Ray's Downtown,* 950 2nd Ave. (phone: 623-7999). Expensive to moderate.

Jake O'Shaughnessey's – A taste of the old Seattle, with booze bottles lining the mirrored bar walls, the decor of the turn-of-the-century saloon, and six beef and seafood entrées. Specialties are fresh salmon roasted over alder wood, saloon beef, roasted for 8 hours in a cast of pure grain roasting salt, and Puget Sound sea stew with ten Sound ingredients. Open daily. Reservations suggested. Major credit cards. 100 Mercer St. in Hansen Baking Co. (phone: 285-1897). Moderate.

Metropolitan Grill – Aged beef, served a variety of ways, is the chef's specialty, as is the ever-popular salmon. Special *Seahawks* brunch during football season. Open daily. Reservations advised. Major credit cards. 820 2nd Ave. (phone: 624-3287). Moderate.

Mikado – From its sushi bar, with delectable raw fish, through a dinner menu featuring shioyaki seafood, the *Mikado* is an experience. Tatami rooms, where you feel a part of the Japanese culture, are available for 6 or more. Dinner only; closed Sundays. Major credit cards. 514 S. Jackson St. (phone: 622-5206). Moderate.

Settebello – Northern Italian cuisine is featured here, with daily pasta, veal, and seafood specialties. Red floor tiles brighten the room, and, though not noisy, the restaurant has an appealing liveliness. Closed Sundays. Reservations advised. Major credit cards. 1525 E. Olive Way (phone: 323-7772). Moderate.

Bahn Thai – Near the Seattle Center, featuring art and artifacts from Thailand, plus mouth-watering Thai specialties such as Pahd Thai (noodles with peanut sauce). Service is gracious and attentive. Reservations advised. Major credit cards. 409 Roy St. (phone: 283-0444). Inexpensive.

Ivar's Indian Salmon House – With lovely views of Lake Union, this is a favorite restaurant with out-of-towners. Designed to look like an Indian longhouse, it features heavy timbers, canoes hanging overhead, and totem poles inside. The menu includes alder-smoked salmon and black cod, prepared in Northwest Indian style, as well as mouth-watering prime ribs. Open daily. Reservations advised. 401 NE Northlake Way (phone: 632-0767). Inexpensive.

Trattoria Mitchelli's – The *"Tratt"* is great for an omelette and morning cappuccino, lunch, dinner, or late-night dining. Whether you choose a stool at the counter or a seat in the dining room, you'll enjoy the rich colors and warm ambience of a European café. The menu includes a tasty antipasto, Caesar salad, a range of pasta dishes, and a variety of rich desserts; specials are listed on chalkboards. Open daily except Mondays until 4 AM. No reservations on Friday and Saturday nights, Gallery Walk night (the first Thursday of each month, when galleries stay open late and people walk through the area), or during *Seahawks* games. Major credit cards. 84 Yesler Way (phone: 623-3883). Inexpensive.

WASHINGTON, DC

In the 1950s, during one of the thaws in the Cold War, President Eisenhower was showing the visiting Nikita Khrushchev around Washington. Every time Eisenhower pointed out a government building, the Soviet leader would claim that the Russians had one bigger and better that had taken only half as long to build. Eisenhower, so the story goes, got pretty weary of this civic one-upsmanship, and when they passed the Washington Monument he said nothing, forcing Khrushchev to ask what the structure was. Eisenhower replied, "It's news to me. It wasn't here yesterday."

Well, the story may be somewhat apocryphal, but it does indicate something important about Washington: It is a city filled with imperial architecture — grand, expansive, deliberate — of a kind that simply doesn't happen overnight or by chance. And yet it is a city that did, indeed, happen almost by chance; a city that until World War II seemed to resist almost in its bones being what it has become today: the international showplace of the United States.

A walk along the Mall will remove any doubts you have about the quality of Washington's cityscape. The Mall is the grand promenade of the capital, connecting the Capitol to the Lincoln Memorial by 2 miles of open green and reflecting pools, lined by the excellent *Smithsonian* museums. Gleaming marble and massive, columned buildings on and surrounding this expanse signify that this is the seat of the sovereign power of the United States of America. These structures, familiar to everyone from picture postcards, take on real dimensions and fulfill the promise of grandeur (particularly at night, when they are bathed in floodlights). But this city of wide tree-lined avenues offers enough open space for varied architectural styles to appear highly consistent. Newer government buildings of modern design and neat rows of townhouses fit in with Federal and Greek Revival structures. And Washington will retain its impressive mien. A city ordinance limits the height of buildings to 13 stories, so the Capitol remains the city's tallest building. Though others approach it, none surpasses the splendor of this domed edifice.

The fact that Washington is so impressive is especially remarkable if you consider its stormy birth at the turn of the 18th century. Its future then couldn't have looked more bleak. Were it not for a band of disgruntled Continental soldiers who marched into Philadelphia on June 20, 1783, to demand back pay, Congress might well have remained in that most civilized of American cities, and Washington would probably still be a marshy swamp.

For the next 7 years, Congress wrangled over the location of the new federal city. In 1790, as a result of a compromise between the North and the South, a site on the Potomac shore was selected, far enough inland to protect against surprise attack, yet accessible to ocean vessels and at the head of a tidewater. Maryland agreed to give 69.25 square miles of land and Virginia

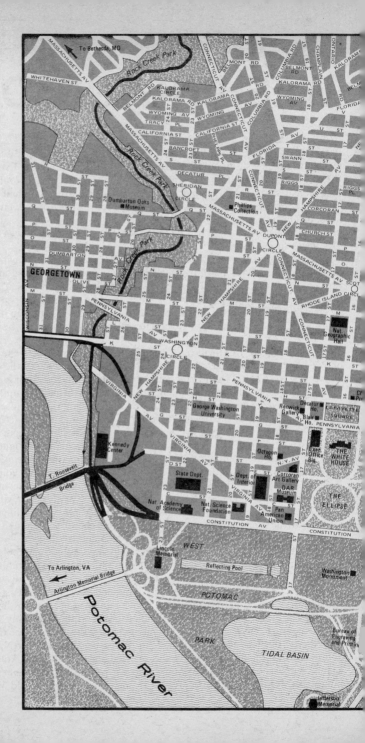

CENTRAL
WASHINGTON D.C.

30.75 square miles to form the square to be known as the District of Columbia. The city was named for George Washington, who as first president was authorized to oversee its development.

Washington appointed Major Pierre L'Enfant, a French engineer, to lay out the city. L'Enfant arrived on the scene in 1791 and on viewing Jenkins's Hill, the present Capitol Hill, he pronounced it "a pedestal waiting for a monument." He also set about designing avenues 160 feet wide which were to radiate out from circles crowned with sculpture. The city's two focal points were to be the Capitol and the president's house, with Pennsylvania Avenue the principal ceremonial street between.

L'Enfant soon became involved in a controversy over the sale of lots which were to have raised money to finance construction of government buildings, and was fired before the year was out. He spent the rest of his life in relative obscurity, living off the charity of friends. George Washington died in 1799 before the development of the federal city was assured. But President Adams's resolve was firm and Congress was pried from its comfortable surroundings in Philadelphia to the howling wilderness of Washington in November of 1800. Abigail Adams was none too happy with the choice, and wrote to her sister from the new White House: "Not one room or chamber of the whole is finished. . . . We have not the least fence, yard or other convenience without, and the great unfinished audience room I make a drying room of, to hang the clothes in." Abigail was displeased by the White House, and nobody was pleased with the city. The streets were unpaved and mud-rutted, the sewers, nonexistent, and the swampy surroundings infested with mosquitoes (better to stay in the drying room).

During the War of 1812 the city underwent a devastating setback when British troops marched in and succeeded in burning the White House and gutting the Capitol. A torrential thunderstorm saved the city from total destruction, but much was burned beyond repair.

Ironically, for the showplace of democracy, just about the most constructive period of the capital's history took place 50 years later, when Alexander "Boss" Shepherd, Governor of the District of Columbia, decided to make Washington worthy of being the capital city in fact as well as in name. Between 1871 and 1874 he succeeded in having the streets paved, gas, sewer mains, and street lights installed, and parks laid out. He thought big, lived high, and used cronyism as his modus operandi. The results were spectacular, as was the debt — $20 million — which left the city bankrupt. The "Boss" was fired; he fled to Mexico, but returned later to a hero's welcome.

Events did not turn out so badly after all for Pierre L'Enfant — or at least for his plans (he, unfortunately, died a pauper in 1825). In 1901 the McMillian Commission was instituted to resurrect L'Enfant's original plans and treat the capital as a work of civic art. Railroad tracks were removed from the Mall, plans were made for the construction of the Lincoln Memorial and Arlington Bridge, and 640 acres of swampland were converted into Potomac parklands. The remains of Pierre L'Enfant were transferred to a grave in Arlington National Cemetery overlooking the city that still bears the stamp of his magnificent design.

First-time visitors to Washington may well wonder if there's a life in

Washington beyond the monuments, buildings, fountains, and statues. Behind the handsome façades lie many Washingtons, but it would take the combined skills of a historian, political analyst, city planner, expert on international, race, and social relations, and a master satirist to explain each one. The writer Ben Bagdikian observes: "In many respects, Washington, DC, is a perfectly normal American city. Its rivers are polluted. The air is periodically toxic from exhaust fumes. It has traffic jams, PTA meetings, and other common hazards of urban life. . . . Beyond its official buildings the natives rise each morning, crowd into buses and car pools, go to work, return at night, to the naked eye no different from the inhabitants of Oklahoma City or Pawtucket, Rhode Island."

All true, but Washington has something no other city has — the federal government. The District is something of a one-industry town, but the industry is government, and that makes all the difference. Nearly half of the 640,000 people living in Washington and its immediate surroundings work for some branch of government (the population of the entire metropolitan area is close to 3.5 million). As civil servants, they earn relatively high incomes, a factor that provides a solid economic base for the city. Contrary to popular opinion, the population is relatively stable. Even during a change of administration, only about 3,000 officeholders are unseated. In addition to the permanent government employees, diplomats from more than 150 countries serve in Washington — considered to be the world's top post. The embassies lend a cultural sophistication to the capital and further diversify the population.

In response to these influences, Washington has developed as a major cosmopolitan center. Restaurants offer nearly as wide a representation of nationalities as do the embassies, and in some cases, even wider — you can eat in a Cuban restaurant, but try to find the Cuban embassy (if you do, it's news to us; it wasn't there yesterday). In the *Smithsonian Institution*'s museums you can see anything and everything, from the US's only Leonardo da Vinci painting to something even da Vinci, in his wildest dreams, never imagined: the film *To Fly* (at the *National Air and Space Museum*), projected on a huge screen with dazzling camerawork that scans the countryside and the globe from dizzying heights, as if the viewer were in the cockpit of a plane or a spacecraft. (Perhaps this *was* da Vinci's wildest dream.) The cultural picture has never been brighter (remember that it used to be an "event" to have a visiting ballet troupe squeeze onto the stage of a downtown movie theater or a post-Broadway road show visit Washington's only theater, the *National*). But today the *Kennedy Center* draws star artists and provides a home for music, theater, and dance companies. And what better proof of being an established cultural center than having branches of *Bloomingdale's, I. Magnin's,* and *Neiman Marcus*?

Still, there are some long shadows across the Washington horizon. The city has a sufficiently high crime rate to have caused it to be dubbed "Murder City," though the business and tourist areas, as well as most of the western end of the city, are relatively safe. The District's resident population, which is largely black, suffers from a distressingly high rate of unemployment, particularly among unskilled workers and teenagers, and the drug problem is epidemic. The combination of distrust in local elected officials and high crime figures precipitated a "white flight" to the suburbs, but recently there is some evidence of families returning to the city to renovate homes in once-seedy neighborhoods that are becoming more stable, integrated communities. Many of the city's worst slums, particularly in the southwest section, have been torn down and replaced by apartment houses, theaters, restaurants, townhouses, and a redeveloped waterfront area.

The forecast remains murky. With home rule a reality (since 1973), Washington abandoned its status as "the last colony." Though residents now vote for president, a mayor, a city council, and a non-voting representative to Congress, civic corruption has meaningfully impeded reform and renewal. Still, the city a visitor sees has never been more vital and vibrant.

And so it goes with Pierre L'Enfant's city. It is the Washington he envisioned that you see today. Every visitor to the Capitol should stand on its west terrace and appreciate one of the finest cityscapes in the world. And as you gaze, you might contemplate the words of Henry Adams. Over a century ago, he wrote, "One of these days this will be a very great city if nothing happens to it." Something has, but nevertheless it is.

WASHINGTON AT-A-GLANCE

 SEEING THE CITY: The 555-foot Washington Monument commands a panorama of the capital in all its glory. To the north stands the White House, below stretches the green Mall, with the Lincoln Memorial in the west and the Capitol perfectly aligned with it to the east. Beyond to the south and west flows the Potomac River, and across the river lies Virginia.

 SPECIAL PLACES: In Washington, all roads lead to the Capitol. The building marks the center of the District. North/south streets are numbered in relation to it, east/west streets are lettered, and the four quadrants into which Washington is divided (NW, NE, SW, SE designated after addresses) meet here.

An easy way to get around the principal sightseeing area is by *Tourmobile.* These 88-passenger shuttle trams allow you to buy your ticket (good for all day) as you board, get on or off at any of the 18 stops, listen to highlights of the sights along the way, and set your own pace. Tourmobiles pass each stop every 30 minutes. For complete information contact the office at 1000 Ohio Dr. SW (phone: 554-7950).

Old Town Trolley Tours offers 3-hour group charter tours or individual tours of the District (phone: 554-5100). *Gray Line* offers narrated bus tours of the District and outlying areas (phone: 386-8300). Museum tours as well as special group tours emphasizing historic Washington are run by *National Fine Arts Associates,* 4801 Massachusetts Ave. NW (phone: 966-3800). The *Spirit of Washington* runs sightseeing boats from March to December on the Potomac and from March to mid-October to Mount Vernon. 6th and Water Sts. SW (phone: 554-8000 or 554-1542). *Washington à la Carte,* 1706 Surrey La. NW (phone: 337-7300), offers tailor-made tours for any size group.

CAPITOL HILL AREA

The Capitol – The Senate and House of Representatives are housed in the Capitol, which is visible from almost every part of the city. When the French architect L'Enfant first began to plan the city, he noted that Jenkins's Hill (now called Capitol Hill) was "a pedestal waiting for a monument." And though Washington laid the cornerstone in 1793, the pedestal had to wait through some 150 years of additions, remodelings, and fire (it was burned by the British in 1814) to get the monument we know today. The 258-foot cast-iron dome, topped by Thomas Crawford's statue of Freedom, was erected during the Civil War; beneath it, the massive Rotunda is a veritable art gallery of American history featuring Constantino Brumidi's fresco, *The Apotheosis of Washington* in the eye of the dome, John Trumbull's Revolutionary War paintings on the walls, and statues of Washington, Lincoln, Jefferson, and others. The rest of the building also contains many artworks, and though you are free to wander about, the 40-minute guided tours that leave from the Rotunda every quarter hour are excellent and provide access to the visitors galleries of Congress (congressional sessions start at noon). Open daily from 9 AM to 4:30 PM (last tour at 3:45). Between the first week of May and Labor Day, the Rotunda is open until 8 PM. Free. You can also ride the monorail subway that joins the House and Senate wings with the congressional office buildings and try the famous bean soup in the Senate Dining Room. 1st St. between Constitution and Independence Aves. (phone: 224-3121). Metro: Capitol South.

Supreme Court Building – This neoclassical white marble structure, surrounded by Corinthian columns and with the inscription on its pediment "Equal Justice Under Law," was designed by Cass Gilbert and completed in 1935. Until then, however, the highest judicial body in the nation and one of three equal branches of government met in makeshift quarters in the basement of the Capitol. Now the Court receives equal treatment under the law and meets in an impressive courtroom flanked by Ionic columns when it is in session intermittently from October through June. Sessions are open to the public on a first-come, first-served basis. Open weekdays; courtroom presentations are on the half-hour from 9:30 AM to 3:30 PM except when court is in session. No admission charge. 1st St. between Maryland Ave. and E. Capitol St. NE (phone: 479-3211). Metro: Capitol South.

Library of Congress – These magnificent Italian Renaissance buildings house the world's largest and richest library. Originally designed as a research aid to Congress, the Library serves the public as well with 80 million items in 470 languages, including manuscripts, maps, photographs, motion pictures, and music. The exhibition hall displays include Jefferson's first draft of the Declaration of Independence and Lincoln's first two drafts of the Gettysburg Address. Among the Library's other holdings are one of three extant copies of the Gutenberg Bible, Pierre L'Enfant's original design for Washington, and the oldest known existing film — the 3-second *Sneeze* by Thomas Edison. The *Coolidge Auditorium* has regular concerts and literary events. For program and ticket information, call 707-5502. Forty-five-minute guided tours are offered on weekdays 10 AM to 3 PM. Open weekdays from 8:30 AM to 9:30 PM, Saturdays from 8:30 AM to 5 PM, Sundays from 1 to 5 PM. No admission charge. 1st St. between E. Capitol and Independence Sts. SE (phone: 707-5000). Metro: Capitol South.

Folger Shakespeare Library – The nine bas-reliefs on the façade depict scenes from Shakespeare's plays, and inside you can find out anything you want to know about Shakespeare and the English Renaissance. The world's finest collection of rare books, manuscripts, and research materials relating to the foremost English-language playwright is here. The library, an oak-paneled, barrel-vaulted Elizabethan palace, also has a model of the *Globe Theater* and a full-scale replica of an Elizabethan theater complete with a trap door (called the "heavens" and used for special effects). Visitors can see how productions were mounted in Shakespeare's day and how they are done today. Poetry, concerts, and plays by Renaissance and modern authors are presented here. The bookstore features the fine Folger series on the Elizabethan period as well as editions of Shakespeare's plays. Open 10 AM to 4 PM (tours 11 AM to 1 PM) daily except Sundays. No admission charge (phone: 544-4600). For information on attending a play, see "Theater," *Sources and Resources*. 201 E. Capitol St. SE (phone: 546-4000).

Botanic Gardens – If you feel as if you are overdosing on history, the Botanic Gardens provides a pleasant antidote with its azaleas, orchids, and tropical plants, and we're not even going to tell you how big they are or where they're from. Open daily, 9 AM to 5 PM; until 9 PM from June through August. No admission charge. 1st St. and Maryland Ave. SW, at the foot of Capitol Hill (phone: 225-8333). Metro: Federal Center SW.

THE WHITE HOUSE AREA

White House – Probably the most historic house in America because George Washington never slept here, though every president since has. It has been the official residence of the head of state since 1800. Designed originally by James Hoban, the White House still looks like an Irish country mansion from the outside; inside there are elegant parlors decorated with portraits of the presidents and first ladies, antique furnishings of many periods, and many innovations added by various presidents, like the revolving tray in the Green Room — an invention of Thomas Jefferson's that revolved between pantry and dining room, allowing him to serve such novelties as macaroni and ice cream and waffles without fear of eavesdropping servants. The five state rooms on the first floor are open to the public, and though you won't actually see the business of government going on, you'll be very close to it.

Visitors line up at the East Gate on E. Executive Ave. Open Tuesdays through Saturdays from 10 AM to noon. (Tickets, required during summer months, are available from the kiosk on the Ellipse.) Congressional tours of seven rooms, instead of the usual five, are available by writing to your congressman in advance. Be sure to specify alternate dates. Tuesdays through Saturdays from 8 to 10 AM. No admission charge. 1600 Pennsylvania Ave. NW (phone: 456-7041). Metro: McPherson Square.

Lafayette Square – If you do not enter the White House, you can get a fine view of it from this square, which was originally proposed by city planner L'Enfant as the mansion's front yard. Statues commemorate Andrew Jackson and the foreign heroes of the American Revolution — Lafayette, de Rochambeau, von Steuben, and Kosciusko. Flanking the square are two early-19th-century buildings designed by Benjamin Latrobe, Washington's first public architect. St. John's Church, constructed along classically simple lines, is better known as the Church of Presidents because every president since Madison has attended services here. Open daily. No admission charge. 16th and H Sts. NW (phone: 347-8766). The Decatur House, built for Commodore Stephen Decatur and occupied after his death by a succession of diplomats, is a Federal townhouse featuring handsome woodwork, a spiral staircase, and furniture of the 1820s. Open Tuesdays through Fridays, 10 AM to 2 PM; weekends, noon to 4 PM. Admission charge. 748 Jackson Pl. NW (phone: 842-0920). Near the southwest corner of the square at 1651-1653 Pennsylvania Ave. NW is Blair House, the president's official guesthouse since 1942 (not open to the public).

Ellipse – This grassy 36-acre expanse is the location of the zero milestone from which all distances in Washington are measured, the site of everything from demonstrations and ball games to the national Christmas tree. 1600 Constitution Ave. NW.

Corcoran Gallery of Art – If you think you've seen the Athenaeum portraits of George Washington before, you're probably not experiencing déjà vu. Check your wallet and with luck you'll see several more reproductions and maybe a few of Jackson, too. This outstanding collection of American art contains some less familiar works as well, including a beardless portrait of Lincoln (a $5 bill won't help you here). The *Corcoran* also offers the opulent Grand Salon from the *Hôtel d'Orsay* in Paris, built by Boucher d'Orsay during the reign of Louis XVI and moved and reconstructed here in its entirety. Open 10 AM to 4:30 PM, Tuesdays through Sundays; until 9 PM on Thursdays. No admission charge. 17th St. and New York Ave. NW (phone: 638-3211). Metro: Farragut N. or W.

Renwick Gallery – The nation's first art museum, this beautiful French Second Empire building was designed by Smithsonian "Castle" architect James Renwick in 1859 to house W. W. Corcoran's art collection. Now run by the *Smithsonian Institution,* it is worth a visit for its changing exhibitions of contemporary American crafts and design. The gallery's other noteworthy sights are the entrance foyer, with its impressive staircase, and the 1870 Grand Salon, with overstuffed Louis XV sofas and potted palms. Open daily, 10 PM to 5:30 PM. No admission charge. Pennsylvania Ave. at 17th St. NW (phone: 357-2531). Metro: Farragut N or W.

Daughters of the American Revolution Museum – Though any member of the DAR must prove that she is descended from those who served the cause of American independence with "unfailing loyalty," the museum is open to everyone regardless of the color of his or her blood. Exhibitions feature 33 period rooms, including the parlor of a 19th-century Mississippi River steamboat. There's also an extensive genealogical library. Open weekdays from 8:30 AM to 4 PM, Sundays from 1 to 5 PM (closed Saturdays). No admission charge. 1776 D St. NW (phone: 628-1776). Metro: Farragut W.

Octagon House – This stately red brick townhouse is a notable example of Federal architecture. The house in which President James and Dolley Madison lived for 6 months after the British burned down the White House in 1814 is maintained as a museum to give a picture of the high style of the early 19th century and features American antique furnishings from the Federal period. Open Tuesdays through Fridays from 10 AM to 4 PM, weekends noon to 4 PM. Donations suggested. 1799 New York Ave. NW (phone: 638-3105). Metro: Farragut W.

Organization of American States – In the Pan American Union Building. Its architects, Paul Cret and Albert Kelsey, have blended the styles of North and South America in this building of imposing formality and inviting elegance. Open 9 AM to 5 PM weekdays. The *Museum of Modern Latin American Art* is just behind the Aztec Garden. Open daily except Sundays from 10 AM to 5 PM. No admission charge. 17th St. and Constitution Ave. NW (phone: 458-6016).

THE MALL

This 2-mile stretch of green from the Lincoln Memorial to the Capitol forms something of the grand avenue envisioned by Pierre L'Enfant in his original plans for the city.

Lincoln Memorial – From the outside, this columned white marble building looks like a Greek temple; inside the spacious chamber with its colossal seated statue of Lincoln, sculpted by Daniel French, it is as inspiring. Carved on the walls are the words of the Gettysburg Address and Lincoln's Second Inaugural Address. National Park Service guides present brief talks at regular intervals. Open 24 hours a day. Memorial Circle between Constitution and Independence Aves. (phone: 426-6841).

Washington Monument – Dominating the Mall is the 555-foot marble and granite obelisk designed by Robert Mills (completed in 1884) to commemorate George Washington. The top (reached by elevator) commands an excellent panoramic view of the city. You can ride down or descend the 897 steps, where you see many stones donated by such groups as the "Citizens of the US residing in Foo Chow Foo, China." Open daily, 8 AM to midnight, from the first Sunday in April through Labor Day; 9 AM to 5 PM the rest of the year. No admission charge. 15th St. between Independence and Constitution Aves. (phone: 426-6839). Metro: Smithsonian.

Vietnam Veterans Memorial – Maya Ying Lin, a Yale architecture student, designed this simple but immensely moving memorial to the American soldiers who died or are missing as a result of the Vietnam War. The two arms of the long, V-shaped polished black granite walls point toward the Washington Monument and the Lincoln Memorial. On the 492-foot-tall wall are inscribed the names of the men and women who were killed in the war or are still missing. A sculpture by Frederick Hart, depicting three soldiers, stands a short distance from the memorial. Constitution Ave. NW and Henry Bacon Dr. (phone: 634-1568).

US Navy Memorial Plaza – The new plaza, dedicated in October 1987, has a statue of a lone US sailor overlooking the US portion of a granite world map. The visitors center, scheduled to open this year, will include a gift shop, IMAX theater, and museum. Military bands perform during spring and summer evenings; pick up a brochure at any hotel or call for schedule. Pennsylvania Ave. between 7th and 9th Sts. NW (phone: 524-0830).

Bureau of Engraving and Printing – If you're interested in money and how it is really made, the 25-minute self-guided tour that follows the entire process of paper currency production will prove enlightening if not enriching. Everything of a financial character from the one-cent postage stamp to the $500-million Treasury Note is designed, engraved, and printed here. Though it costs only a penny to produce a single note, there are no free samples. Open weekdays, 9 AM to 2 PM. No admission charge. 14th and C Sts. SW (phone: 447-9709). Metro: Smithsonian.

National Archives – The repository for all major American records. The 76 Corinthian columns supporting this handsome building designed by John Russell Pope are nothing compared to the contents. Inside, in special helium-filled glass and bronze cases, reside the very pillars of our democracy — the Declaration of Independence, the Constitution, and the Bill of Rights. Open daily, 10 AM to 5:30 PM; extended hours April through Labor Day decided annually. No admission charge. Constitution Ave. between 7th and 9th Sts. NW (phone: 523-3000). Metro: Archives.

Jefferson Memorial – Dominating the south bank of the Tidal Basin, this domed temple-like structure (also designed by John Russell Pope) is a tribute to our third president and the drafter of the Declaration of Independence. The bronze statue of Jefferson was executed by Rudulph Evans and inscribed on the walls are quotations from Jefferson's writings. This is the place to be for the most dramatic view of the cherry blossoms in early April. Open daily. No admission charge. South Basin Dr. SW (phone: 426-6822). Metro: L'Enfant Plaza.

J. Edgar Hoover Building – If you want to find out a little more about an organization that already knows everything about you, take a tour of the FBI. In addition to a film on some past investigative activities, you'll get to see the laboratory and a firearms demonstration. Open weekdays, 8:45 AM to 4:15 PM. This popular tour takes 45 minutes. Line up early. No admission charge. Pennsylvania Ave. between 9th and 10th Sts. NW (phone: 324-3447). Metro: MetroCenter or Gallery Place.

National Gallery of Art – One of the larger jewels in Washington's rich cultural crown, this gift to the nation by Andrew Mellon, financier and former Secretary of the Treasury, houses one of the world's finest collections of Western art from the 13th century to the present. Among the masterpieces in this huge and opulent white marble gallery are a grand survey of Italian painting including da Vinci's *Ginevra de' Benci,* Fra Filippo Lippi's *The Adoration of the Magi,* Raphael's *Saint George and the Dragon,* works of French Impressionists, a self-portrait by Rembrandt, Renoir's *Girl With a Watering Can,* Picasso's *The Lovers,* and an extensive American collection. The 7-story East Building, designed by I. M. Pei, is something of an architectural masterpiece itself. An intriguing structure of interlocking triangular forms, it houses the Center for Advanced Study in the Visual Arts as well as exhibition halls. Several visits are necessary to see the whole gallery; there are also tours, films, lectures, and weekly concerts. Open Mondays through Saturdays from 10 AM to 5 PM, Sundays from noon to 9 PM. No admission charge. Between 3rd and 7th Sts. and Constitution Ave. NW (phone: 737-4215 weekdays; 842-6188 weekends). Metro: Judiciary Square Federal Center or Archives.

Smithsonian Institution – Before James Smithson died in 1829 he willed his entire fortune of half a million dollars "to found in Washington, an establishment for the increase and diffusion of knowledge among men." The wealthy English scientist had never even been to America and probably had no idea how much knowledge would be increased and diffused here in his name. Today the *Smithsonian* administers numerous museums, galleries, and research organizations; has an operating budget of over $90 million, a staff of over 4,000, and 75 million items in its total collection. The *Smithsonian*'s newest contribution, a $73-million 3-floor complex, just south of the Castle on Independence Ave. SW, is a bit controversial because it is underground. Opened in autumn 1987, it houses two museums — the *Arthur M. Sackler Gallery,* featuring Asian art (including bronzes, jades, paintings, lacquerware, and sculpture), and the *National Museum of African Art* (see below), which was moved from its former Capitol Hill location. The 3rd floor houses the International Center for exhibitions, and atop it all is the Enid A. Haupt Garden, a $3-million Victorian delight built around a 100-year-old linden tree. Entry to the museums is through kiosks in the garden. The Romanesque red sandstone building known as the Castle is the best place to get visitor information on any of the *Institution*'s activities. All buildings are open daily, 10 AM to 5:30 PM. Extended summer hours. No admission charge. 1000 Jefferson Dr. SW (phone: 357-1300, for information on all 14 Smithsonian museums).

Among the Smithsonian Museums on the Mall are the following:

National Museum of African Art – The most extensive collection of African art in this country, and the only one dedicated exclusively to the arts of sub-Saharan Africa. Exhibitions include figures, masks, and sculptures in ivory, wood, bronze, and clay from 20 African nations; also color panels and audiovisual presentations on the people and environment of Africa. One gallery has an intriguing display concerning the influence of Africa's cultural heritage on modern European and American art. Delightful gift shop. Open all day weekdays and weekend afternoons. No admission charge. New location in the Quadrangle on the Mall, next to the *Sackler Gallery of Art* (phone: 357-4600).

National Museum of Natural History – Only 1% of the museum's collection is on display but, with a total of some 60 million specimens, there's still plenty to see. Features eyefuls of the biggest and the best of most everything from the largest elephant on record — 12 tons from the African bush — to the precious Hope Diamond, at a hefty 44.5 karats, the largest blue diamond known (its only flaw is that it has brought tragedy to all its possessors). The Hall of Dinosaurs has mammoth skeletons. And there's even Martha, who died in the Cincinnati Zoo in 1914 and is now stuffed, the last of the extinct passenger pigeons. Open daily. No admission charge. Constitution Ave. at 10th St. NW. Metro: Smithsonian or Federal Triangle.

National Museum of American History – Everything that has to do with American ingenuity in craftsmanship, design, and industry can be found here along with some things that bear only the most tenuous link. (That's where the real fun begins.) Hall after hall features such items as Eli Whitney's cotton gin, a gargantuan pendulum which was used by French physicist Jean Foucault to demonstrate the rotation of the earth, and a full gallery of First Lady mannequins dressed in Inaugural Ball gowns. Open daily. No admission charge. Constitution Ave. at 14th St. NW. Metro: Smithsonian or Federal Triangle.

National Air and Space Museum – The largest of the Smithsonian's museums, with displays of aircraft in its vast, lofty interior. Exhibitions include the Wright Brothers' plane, Charles Lindbergh's *Spirit of St. Louis,* the Apollo 11 command module, and a walk-through model of a Skylab orbital station. The films *To Fly, The Dream Is Alive, Living Player,* and *Flyers,* shown on a huge screen, are as spectacular as they are dizzying. Planetarium shows are presented in the Albert Einstein Spacearium. Open daily. No admission charge. Independence Ave. between 4th and 7th Sts. SW. Metro: L'Enfant Plaza.

Hirshhorn Museum and Sculpture Garden – Smaller but also superb is this collection donated in 1974 by a Latvian immigrant and self-made millionaire. The *Hirshhorn,* designed by Gordon Bunshaft, is worth a visit not only for its fine collection but also for the building itself, a circular concrete structure with an open core in which a bronze fountain shoots water 82 feet into the air. Displays include 19th- and 20th-century European and American works, and an attractive sculpture garden that features Rodin's *The Burghers of Calais* and Picasso's *Baby Carriage.* Open daily. No admission charge. Independence Ave. at 8th St. SW. Metro: L'Enfant Plaza.

Freer Gallery of Art – This prime collection of Far and Near Eastern art was amassed by the Detroit industrialist Charles L. Freer. Includes Chinese bronze, jade, and porcelain pieces, Greek biblical manuscripts, Japanese ceramics, and Egyptian glassworks. Freer also gathered over 1,000 works of James Whistler. The Peacock Room, Whistler's only known attempt at interior decorating, should not be missed. Open daily. No admission charge. 12th St. and Jefferson Dr. SW. Metro: Smithsonian.

Arts and Industries Building – Just east of the Castle, this is the second oldest Smithsonian building on the Mall. The Centennial Exhibition, displayed in Philadelphia in 1876, has been re-created with marvelous displays of fashions, furnishings, and machinery. Open daily. No admission charge. Jefferson Dr. and Independence Ave. at 9th St. SW. Metro: Smithsonian.

DOWNTOWN

National Portrait Gallery and National Museum of American Art – Inside the *National Portrait Gallery,* an excellent example of Greek Revival architecture, many Americans who have gone down in the history of this country have gone up on the walls (in portrait form, that is). Among those hanging are all the American presidents, Pocahontas, Horace Greeley, and Harriet Beecher Stowe. The *National Museum of American Art* features American painting, sculpture, and graphic arts, including Catlin's paintings of the Indians and a choice group of works of the American Impressionists. Both museums (also administered by the *Smithsonian*) are open daily. No admission charge. 8th St. at F and G Sts. Metro: Gallery Place.

Ford's Theatre – The site of Lincoln's assassination in 1865 by John Wilkes Booth is a national monument, and in the 1960s it was restored and decorated as it appeared on the fatal night of April 14, 1865. In the basement is a museum of Lincoln memorabilia, including displays showing his life as a lawyer, statesman, husband and father, and president, and the clothes he was wearing when he was shot, the derringer used by Booth to shoot him, and the assassin's personal diary. Theater performances are held throughout the year. For theater tickets, call 347-4833. Open daily, 9 AM to 5 PM. Admission $1; no admission charge for those under 12, over 62, or handicapped. 517 10th St. NW (phone: 426-6924). Metro: Metro Center, 11th St. exit.

Peterson House – Directly across the street from the theater and museum is the house in which Lincoln died the morning after the shooting. The small, sparsely furnished house appears much the way it did in 1865. Open daily from 9 AM to 5 PM. No admission charge. 516 10th St. NW (phone: 426-6830).

GEORGETOWN

There's not much tobacco left in this area, once the Union's major tobacco port. It's particularly nice in the spring when it's pleasant to walk along the Chesapeake and Ohio Canal. The whole area's great for strolling. Besides the Canal (between Jefferson and 31st Sts.) the streets off Wisconsin Avenue house the city's social and political elite in beautiful restored townhouses with prim gardens and lovely magnolia trees. The main drags are Wisconsin Avenue and M Street, with boutiques and restaurants. Most of the action, including the city's hottest nightlife, takes place here. In the area at the top of the hill (along R St. east of Wisconsin Ave.), large 18th-century country estates survive and mingle with smaller row houses. The Dumbarton Oaks Garden has beautiful formal gardens, and in the *Dumbarton Oaks Museum* is a fine collection of early Christian and Byzantine art. The entrance to the museum is at 1703 32nd St. NW; the entrance to the gardens is at 31st and R Sts. NW. The museum is open Tuesday through Sunday afternoons; no admission charge. The gardens are open daily from 2 to 5 PM; admission charge from April to October (phone: 338-8278).

■**EXTRA SPECIAL:** Just 16 miles south of Washington on George Washington Memorial Parkway is Mount Vernon, George Washington's estate from 1754 to 1799 and his final resting place. This lovely 18th-century plantation is interesting because it shows a less familiar aspect of the military-political man — George Washington as the rich southern planter. The mansion, overlooking the Potomac, and the outbuildings that housed the shops that made Mount Vernon a self-sufficient economic unit have been authentically restored and refurnished. Some 500 of the original 8,000 acres remain; all are well maintained, and the parterre gardens and formal lawns provide a magnificent setting. There's also a museum with Washington memorabilia; the tomb of George and Martha lies at the foot of the hill. In the spring or the summer, start out early to avoid big crowds. Bicycle paths lead from the DC side of Memorial Bridge to Mount Vernon — a lovely ride along with Potomac. Open daily, 9 AM to 5 PM, March through October; to 4 PM the rest of the year. Admission charge (phone: 703-780-2000).

Also beautifully landscaped and overlooking the Potomac, but with many more tombs and monuments is Arlington National Cemetery, a solemn reminder of this country's turbulent history. Here lie the bodies of many who served in the military forces, among them Admiral Richard Byrd, General George C. Marshall, Robert F. Kennedy, Justice Oliver Wendell Holmes, and John F. Kennedy, whose grave is marked by the Eternal Flame. The Tomb of the Unknown Soldier, a 50-ton block of white marble, commemorates the dead of World Wars I and II and the Korean and the Vietnam wars and is always guarded by a solitary soldier. Changing of the guard takes place every hour on the hour (every half-hour during summer months). The grounds of the cemetery were once the land of Robert E. Lee's plantation but were confiscated by the Union after Lee joined the Confederacy. Lee's home, Arlington House, has been restored and is open for public inspection. Cars are not allowed in the cemetery, but you can park at the visitor center and go on foot or pay and ride the *Tourmobile.* The house is open daily, 9:30 AM to 4:30 PM from October to March, to 6 PM the rest of the year (phone: 703-557-0613). The cemetery is open daily from 8 AM to 5 PM; April to September to 7 PM (phone: 703-697-4967). Directly west of Memorial Bridge in Arlington, Virginia.

SOURCES AND RESOURCES

TOURIST INFORMATION: The Washington Convention and Visitors Assn., 1212 New York Ave. NW, Washington, DC 20005, coordinates all Washington tourism information and runs the Visitor Center at 1455 Pennsylvania Ave. NW (phone: 789-7000). The center (open daily except Sundays, 9 AM to 5 PM) provides free maps and information on where to stay, eat, and shop. Volunteers from the Travelers Aid Society (phone: 347-0101) and International Visitors Information Service (phone: 783-6540) are on hand to assist foreign visitors. The Visitors Association also has toll-free numbers for individual travelers (phone: 800-422-8644) and for meeting planners (phone: 800-635-MEET).

Television Stations – WJLA Channel 7–ABC; WUSA Channel 9–CBS; WRC Channel 4–NBC; WETA Channel 26–PBS.

Radio Stations – AM: WNTR 1050 (news/talk); WTOP 1500 (news); WFUD 930 (adult contemporary). FM: WPFW 89.3 (jazz); WKYS 93.9 (urban contemporary); WGAY 99.5 (easy listening).

Local Coverage – The *Washington Post,* morning daily; The *Washington Times,* morning daily; *City Paper,* a free weekly; and *Washingtonian* magazine, monthly.

Food – *The Shoestring Gourmet* by Erik Kanin, Nancy Turner, and Andrea Lubershane (Andrik Associates; $5.95) describes where two can dine for $20 or less.

Telephone – The area code for the District is 202; for Maryland, 301; and for Virginia, 703.

Sales Tax – The sales tax is 6%; hotel rooms carry an 8% tax.

 CLIMATE: Washington has four distinct seasons. Summers are Amazonian, falls New Englandish and lovely, winters cold with some snow and lots of slush (wear boots or suffer), and spring — when the cherry blossoms bloom and all is sublime.

 GETTING AROUND: Airports – Washington is served by three major airports. National is the city's primary facility, and the 20-minute drive to downtown by taxi will cost about $8 one way. The *Washington Flyer* (phone: 685-1400) provides limo service every half-hour from National to most downtown and Capitol Hill hotels for $7. The Metro's Blue and Yellow Lines connect downtown with the airport; Metro Center, at 11th and G Sts. NW, is the system's main terminal (phone: 637-7000).

Dulles International Airport is about 25 miles west of the city, in Virginia. The ride from downtown DC to Dulles usually takes about an hour, and cab fare should run about $35. The *Washington Flyer* (phone: 685-1400) leaves Dulles about every half-hour from the *Mayflower,* the *Capitol Hilton,* and the *Washington Hilton* hotels; fare $12 one way, $20 round-trip.

Baltimore/Washington International Airport (BWI) also serves the DC area and is a 45-minute trip from downtown by car. Cab fare from BWI to DC should run about $40. The *Washington Flyer* (phone: 685-1400) airport limo runs between BWI and the *Capitol Hilton* hotel for $22. BWI Airport Transportation (phone: 441-2345) also offers bus service from DC to BWI for $12.

Amtrak – More than 50 Amtrak trains daily pull into historic Union Station on Capitol Hill, including the Metroliner, linking the capital to New York and other northeast-corridor cities. For reservations and information, call 800-872-7245.

Bus – The Metro Bus system serves the entire District and the surrounding area. Transfers within the District are free and the rates increase when you go into Maryland and Virginia. For complete route information call the Metropolitan Area Transit Authority office (phone: 637-7000).

Subway – The fastest way to get around Washington is by Metrorail, the subway system. The lines that are in operation provide a quick and quiet ride. New lines to the suburbs and other areas of the city open as they are completed, and buses deposit or pick up passengers at these stations. Metro hours are 6 AM to midnight, weekdays; 8 AM to midnight, Saturdays; and 10 AM to midnight, Sundays. For complete route and travel information and a map of the system, contact the Washington Metropolitan Area Transit Authority office, 600 5th St. NW (phone: 637-7000).

Taxi – Cabs in the District charge by zone. Sharing cabs is common, but ask the driver whether there is a route conflict if you join another passenger. Cabs may be hailed in the street, picked up outside stations and hotels, or ordered on the phone. By law, basic rates must be posted in all taxis. Major cab companies are *Yellow* (phone: 544-1212) and *Diamond* (phone: 387-6200).

Car Rental – All the national firms serve Washington.

Tourmobile – This shuttle bus operates in the downtown sightseeing area between the Lincoln Memorial and Capitol area (the Mall). Tickets can be purchased from the driver or from a booth near the tour sites. Passengers get on and off as often as they wish. The *Tourmobile* also goes to Arlington Cemetery.

LOCAL SERVICES: Babysitting – *Child Care Agency,* 733 15th St. NW (phone: 783-8573).

　　Business Services – *WSS Secretarial Service,* 2020 K St. NW (phone: 457-1848).

Mechanic – *Call Carl* (24-hour service), 1112 Half St. SW (phone: 479-7200).

MUSEUMS: When it comes to museums, Washington is one of the nation's major showplaces, with the *Smithsonian Institution*'s outstanding museums leading the way. Described in some detail in *Special Places* are the *National Gallery of Art,* the *Smithsonian* (including the new Quadrangle containing the *Arthur M. Sackler Gallery* and the *National Museum of African Art*), *Hirshhorn Museum, Freer Gallery of Art, National Air and Space Museum, Arts and Industries Building, National Museum of Natural History, National Museum of American History, National Portrait Gallery, National Museum of American Art,* the *Renwick Gallery,* and the *Corcoran Gallery.* Other notable museums include the following:

Columbia Historical Society – A museum devoted to Washington, DC, history, housed in the spectacular Victorian mansion of brewer Christian Heurich. Library open to the public Wednesdays, Fridays, and Saturdays from 10 AM to 4 PM; tours Wednesdays through Saturdays from noon to 4 PM. 1307 New Hampshire Ave. NW (phone: 785-2068).

Hillwood – Russian icons, portraits, and Fabergé creations are housed in the elegant former home of Marjorie Merriweather Post. Tours by appointment only; call well in advance for reservations. 4155 Linnean Ave. NW (phone: 686-5807).

National Building Museum – A new museum in the old but wonderful Pension Building. 4th St. and Judiciary Sq. NW (phone: 272-2448).

National Geographic Society Explorers Hall – 17th and M Sts. NW (phone: 857-7588 for recorded information; 857-7000 for general information).

National Museum of Women in the Arts – Opened in April 1987, this museum in a former Masonic temple has a permanent collection of 500 pieces of pictorial, sculpted, and ceramic art spanning 400 years. New York Ave. and 13th St. NW (phone: 783-5000).

Phillips Collection – 19th- and 20th-century art. 1600 21st St. NW (phone: 387-0961).

Textile Museum – A diverse collection of fabrics from around the world, in a large former mansion. Open Tuesdays through Saturdays from 10 AM to 5 PM and Sundays from 1 to 5 PM. 2320 S St. NW (phone: 667-0441).

Washington Doll's House and Toy Museum – 5236 44th St. NW (phone: 244-0024).

Woodrow Wilson House – A memorial to our 28th president and his wife. 2340 S St. NW (phone: 673-4034).

SHOPPING: Washington has spruced up its shopping districts, inspired by a $100-million campaign to renovate the nation's main street, the stretch of Pennsylvania Avenue from the White House to the Capitol. The effort spilled over to nearby downtown, where a convention center was built in

1982, department stores were rebuilt and renovated, a new mall installed, the *Willard* hotel refurbished, and shops added. Always a bit pokey about moving into the 20th century, the city now sprouts pockets of well-known fashionable shops in its business and midtown area to complement other long-established shopping draws, such as trendy Georgetown, the bohemian Dupont Circle, and the Watergate complex (across from the *Kennedy Center for the Performing Arts*). For unique gifts, the city's myriad museums are the best bet. Most museums, shrines, and churches have their own shops, some offering reproductions of treasures at very affordable prices. Here's a sampling of what's available, by area:

Downtown – The "F Street Corridor," a few blocks east of Pennsylvania Avenue, features Washington's traditional department stores (*Hecht Co., Woodward & Lothrop,* and the more upscale *Garfinckel's*) as well as the new glitzy shops at the National Press Building (at 13th and F Sts.). The collection of more than 80 specialty shops and restaurants on 3 glassed-in levels includes *Thornton's* British chocolate store and the *Sharper Image,* with expensive gadgets. Nearby, the *Willard* hotel (at Pennsylvania Ave. and 14th St.) houses designer boutiques. Along Pennsylvania itself, at 11th St. NW, the Old Post Office Pavilion is a festive marketplace of 50 shops and restaurants in the city's oldest Federal building. The renovated multistory complex provides daily entertainment free.

K Street/Business District – A few blocks to the northwest of downtown, the business district has blossomed with malls and shops. International Square (1850 K St. NW), set in a 12-story atrium with a cascading fountain, is filled with restaurants, fast-food eateries, and 30 retail shops. Just a few blocks away (at Connecticut Ave. and L St. NW), atop the Farragut North metro station, is the Connecticut Connection, a 3-story shopping and dining emporium. At the intersection of Connecticut Avenue and K Street north is an array of famous-name stores, ranging from Washington's own *Raleigh's* department store to *Burberrys Ltd.*

Georgetown – The latest addition to the boutiques and shops that line the historic area is Georgetown Park Mall (at Wisconsin Ave. and M St.). The red brick building resembles the other Victorian structures but was built only a few years ago. Among its 85 shops are *Abercrombie & Fitch, Liberty Silk,* and *FAO Schwarz* toy store. The eclectic collection of shops along Georgetown's streets includes *Hats in the Belfry* (1237 Wisconsin Ave. NW), the Irish shop *Threepenny Bit* (3122 M St. NW), and *Orpheus Records* (3249 M St. NW; phone: 337-7970), which specializes in obscure recordings. A few blocks north on Wisconsin Avenue are four intriguing shops: The *Phoenix* (Mexican jewelry, crafts, and clothing; 1514 Wisconsin), *Santa Fe Style* (crafts and art from the American Southwest; 1525 Wisconsin), *Little Caledonia* (unusual furnishings, fabrics, and stationery; 1419 Wisconsin), and *Appalachian Spring* (handmade crafts, quilts, and jewelry from all over the US; 1415 Wisconsin).

Dupont Circle – In the northern part of downtown, where Connecticut Avenue intersects Massachusetts Avenue, lies Dupont Circle. Browsers will discover art galleries, book shops, and boutiques, along with chic cafés and restaurants. *Kramerbooks & Afterwords* (1517 Connecticut Ave. NW) is known as a singles hangout, since the bookstore encourages its patrons to linger at the café in back.

Museums – The *Smithsonian* museums are a good place to start looking for one-of-a-kind gifts, though nearly every monument, shrine, and church in Washington offers such a shop. The shop at the *Museum of Natural History* (at 14th St. and Constitution Ave. NW), has everything from a reproduction of the Hope Diamond to First Lady dolls. The Arts and Industries Building (Jefferson Dr. and Independence Ave. at 9th St. NW) stocks items shown in the *Smithsonian* mail-order gift catalogue. Other finds and their respective museums include: NASA flight jackets, US rocket model kits, and astronaut freeze-dried dinners (*Air and Space*); contemporary jewelry (Hirshhorn); and busts of past presidents (*National Portrait Gallery*). *Dumbarton Oaks'* (R and 23rd St.

NW) private collection of Byzantine and pre-Columbian jewelry is reproduced for sale. The National Cathedral (Massachusetts and Wisconsin NW), has an extensive gift shop, and the National Geographic Society (17th and M Sts. NW) offers some of the best bargains around in atlases and maps.

 MAJOR COLLEGES AND UNIVERSITIES: Washington has several universities of high national standing — George Washington University, 19th to 24th Sts. NW, F St. to Pennsylvania Ave. (phone: 994-1000); American University, Massachusetts and Nebraska Aves. NW (phone: 885-1000); Georgetown University, 37th and O Sts. NW (phone: 625-0100); Howard University, 2000 6th St. NW (phone: 636-6100); and Gallaudet University (for the deaf), 7th St. and Florida Ave. NE (phone: 651-5000).

 SPECIAL EVENTS: Any town that inaugurates a new president every 4 years is in good standing when it comes to special events. The president takes the oath of office every 4th year on January 20. Usually the swearing-in is followed by a parade down Pennsylvania Ave.

In between inaugurations there's plenty to keep the District going for four more years. The publications above list exact dates. When you start noticing white single blossoms and a flood of pink double blossoms, it's *Cherry Blossom* time in Washington. In early April, a big festival celebrates the coming of the blossoms and the spring with concerts, parades, balls, and the lighting of the Japanese Lantern at the Tidal Basin.

Around the same time (give or take a few blossoms), is the *Easter Monday Egg Rolling,* when scads of children descend on the White House lawn; adults are admitted only if accompanied by a child.

House, garden, and embassy tours are given in April and May, allowing entrance to some of Washington's most elegant interiors. For information on the tours, see the Weekend section in Friday's *Washington Post.*

During the summer, the *American Folklife Festival* sponsored by the *Smithsonian Institution* sets up its tents on the Mall near the reflecting pool, and groups from all regions of the country do their stuff with jug bands, blues, Indian dance and handicraft demonstrations.

The city is especially festive at Christmas. Special music programs are presented at the *Kennedy Center* and at many other spots around town.

 SPORTS AND FITNESS: Basketball – The NBA's *Bullets* hold court from October to April at the *Capital Centre,* Capital Beltway and Central Ave. in Landover, Md. (phone: 301-350-3400). Tickets are available at Ticketron outlets.

Bicycling – Rent from *Thompson Boat Center,* Rock Creek Pky. and Virginia Ave. NW (phone: 333-4861). The towpath of the Chesapeake and Ohio Canal, starting at the barge landing in Georgetown, is a good place to ride.

Fitness Center – *Office Health Center* has separate exercise classes and whirlpool baths for men and women; its assistants all have master's degrees in health education or related fields; 1990 M St. and 20th, off Connecticut (phone: 872-0222).

Football – The NFL's *Redskins* play at *Robert F. Kennedy Stadium* from September to December. Tickets during the season are hard to come by and there is usually a waiting list for season tickets, but if you're in town during late July or August for pre-season games, chances are much better. Try the Ticketron outlet, 51 N St. NE (phone: 659-2601), or the stadium box office, E. Capitol and 22nd Sts. SE (phone: 546-2222).

Golf – The best public golf course is the *East Potomac–Hains Point Course.* In East Potomac Park off Ohio Dr. (phone: 863-9007).

Hockey – The *Capitals,* Washington's pro hockey team, play at *Capital Centre* from October to April. Tickets are available at Ticketron outlets or by calling 301-350-3400.

Jogging – Join plenty of others in making a round trip from the Lincoln Memorial to the Capitol (4 miles); also run in Rock Creek Park and in Georgetown, along the C & O Canal.

Skating – From November to April you can skate on the rink on the mall between 7th and 9th Sts. NW (phone: 371-5343).

Swimming – Year-round facilities are available at the *East Capitol Natatorium,* 635 North Carolina Ave. SE (phone: 724-4495).

Tennis – Washington has some fine public courts; the best bets are the District tennis facilities at 16th and Kennedy Sts. NW (phone: 722-5949).

THEATER: The opening of the *Kennedy Center* in 1971 gave the District a real cultural boost; it's off Virginia Ave. NW (phone: 254-3600). The center's *Eisenhower Theater* offers musical and dramatic productions, including Broadway previews and road shows (phone: 254-3670). The *Terrace Theater,* on the top floor, offers many different productions — modern dance, ballet, dramas, poetry recitals, and so on (phone: 254-9895). The *National Theater* presents major productions throughout the year, 1321 Pennsylvania Ave. NW (phone: 628-6161). The *Arena Stage* and the *Kreeger Theater* host classical and original plays year-round, 6th St. and Maine Ave. SW (phone: 488-3300), and the *Ford's Theatre* offers American productions at 511 10th St. NW (phone: 347-4833). The *Folger Theatre Group* offers innovative interpretations of Shakespeare's plays as well as more contemporary works at the Folger Library's classical theater, 201 E. Capitol St. SE (phone: 544-7077). Washington also has what one theater critic calls the "Off-off Kennedy Center movement" — a network of small avant-garde houses on or near the stretch of 14th Street NW above Thomas Circle: *Studio Theater* (1333 P St. NW; phone: 332-3300); *Woolly Mammoth Theater Company* (phone: 393-3939) and *Horizons Theater* (phone: 342-5503), which have separate stages at the same address (1401 Church St. NW); and *Source Theater* (1835 14th St. NW; phone: 462-1073). During the summer the *Olney Theater,* about a half-hour drive from the District, offers summer stock and well-known casts (Rte. 108, Olney, Md.; phone: 301-924-3400) and the *Wolf Trap Farm Park for the Performing Arts* presents musicals, ballet, pop concerts, and symphonic music in a lovely outdoor setting (Rte. 7 near Vienna, Virginia, accessible via Dulles Airport toll road Rte. 267 and by subway to West Falls Church; phone: 703-255-1860). In winter, the *Barns at Wolftrap,* a 350-seat theater, holds performances indoors (phone: 938-2404). Unsold theater and concert tickets are available on the day of the performance at half price from the TICKETplace stand in F Street Plaza, 12th and F Sts. NW (phone: 842-5387).

MUSIC: The *National Symphony Orchestra,* conducted by Mstislav Rostropovich, performs at the *Kennedy Center Concert Hall* from September through June (phone: 254-3776). The *Opera Society of Washington* (phone: 857-0900) presents four operas a year at the *Kennedy Center Opera House.* The *Juilliard String Quartet* and other notable ensembles perform chamber music concerts on Stradivarius instruments at the *Library of Congress Auditorium,* 1st St. between E. Capitol St. and Independence Ave. SE, Thursday and Friday evenings in the spring and fall (for tickets, call 707-5502). During the summer there's music under the stars at *Wolf Trap Farm Park* (phone: 703-255-1860) and free concerts by the service bands on the plaza at the West Front of the Capitol or in front of the Jefferson Memorial. Consult newspapers for where and when. *Army and Navy Band* concerts are presented at different locations in the winter. For information on *Army Band* concerts call 696-3399; for *Navy Band* concerts, 433-2394.

NIGHTCLUBS AND NIGHTLIFE: For some, Washington is an early-to-bed town, but there's plenty of pub crawling, jazz, bluegrass, soul, rock, and folk music going on after dark. You just have to know where to look for it, and best bets are Georgetown, lower Connecticut Ave., and the Capitol Hill areas. Current favorites: *F. Scott's,* one of the classiest bars in town, 1232 36th St. NW (phone: 342-0009, evenings); *Blues Alley,* for mainstream jazz and Dixieland, 1073 Wisconsin Ave. NW (phone: 337-4141); *Jenkins Hill,* for the District's longest bar, where everyone from public servants to students slake their thirst, 223 Pennsylvania Ave. SE (phone: 544-6600); the *Dubliner Restaurant and Pub,* with old Irish and Celtic tunes and jigs, 520 N. Capitol St. NW (phone: 737-3773); and *Cities,* a watering hole-cum-restaurant-cum-nightclub in what once was a 3-story auto dealership, 2424 18th St. NW (phone: 328-7194), at the heart of Washington's newest nightlife scene — Adams Morgan, a funky melange of bars, dance clubs, ethnic restaurants, and shops radiating from the intersection of Columbia Road and 18th Streets NW. In recent years Adams Morgan has come to rival Georgetown as "the" place to see and be seen after dark in the capital.

BEST IN TOWN

CHECKING IN: Hotel building is currently going on at a dizzying pace, relieving the midweek room shortages that have prevailed for years. Still, accommodations at the best stopping places can dwindle fast, so reservations should be made in advance. Visitors in town for only a few days should stay downtown to make the best use of their limited time; weekends offer the best package deals. Inexpensive taxis, the Metro system, and buses facilitate getting around without a car, which is difficult and expensive to park. However, if you have a car, major motel chains have facilities at all principal entry points to the district — Silver Spring and Bethesda in Maryland, Arlington, Rosslyn, and Alexandria in Virginia. Expect to pay $125 and up (sometimes way up) for a double room in the expensive range, $75 to $100 in the moderate range, and $40 to $70 in the inexpensive category. For information about bed and breakfast accommodations, contact: *The Bed and Breakfast League,* 3639 Van Ness St. NW, Washington, DC 20008 (phone: 363-7767), or *Sweet Dreams & Toast,* PO Box 4835-0035, Washington, DC 20008. Washington, DC, Accommodations provides assistance with hotel reservations according to the vistor's needs. This free service is available by calling 800-554-2220. All telephone numbers are in the 202 area code unless otherwise indicated.

Canterbury – Near the downtown business district and not far from the White House, this small hotel has 99 suites with a stocked bar in each. Amenities include a complimentary continental breakfast, underground parking, nightly turndown service with a Godiva chocolate placed on your pillow, and *Chaucer's* restaurant. Lower weekend package rates are available. 1733 N St. NW (phone: 393-3000). Expensive.

Four Seasons – On the edge of Georgetown, this hotel looks a lot like a penitentiary from the outside, but the interior is bright and beautiful, and the appeal of its rooms has got visitors returning whenever possible. The *Aux Beaux Champs* restaurant also deserves high praise. A traditional concierge offers many personal services including mail delivery. 2800 Pennsylvania Ave. NW (phone: 342-0444). Expensive.

Georgetown Inn – In the middle of one of Washington's most historic areas, this handsome brick building is unusually classy for a motor inn. All 95 rooms are well appointed with large beds and bathroom phones. Free parking. 1310 Wisconsin Ave. NW (phone: 333-8900). Expensive.

Grand – A distinctive copper dome wedged between walls of brick and granite marks this West End hostelry (formerly the *Regent*). In architecture and ambience, it is reminiscent of a small European hotel: a white marble staircase cascades through the lobby, the inner courtyard is meticulously landscaped, and all 262 rooms feature Italian marble baths, 3 phones, remote-control TV sets, and working fireplaces in some suites. The elegant *Mayfair* serves *cuisine courante,* a step beyond nouvelle, with a menu that changes daily; the *Promenade Lounge* features lunch, brunch, and high tea in a more informal atmosphere. Besides a multilingual concierge and currency conversion service, there is 24-hour room service, valet and dry cleaning, valet parking, and Godiva chocolates accompanying the nightly turndown service. 2350 M St. NW (phone: 429-0100 or 800-848-0016). Expensive.

Hay-Adams – An incomparable location just off Lafayette Square, within a silver dollar's throw of the White House. This 143-room hotel retains its Old World dignity and maintains the standards of the neighborhood with antique furnishings, a paneled lobby, a fine dining room, cocktail lounge, and good service. The entire hotel was renovated in 1984. 16th and H Sts. NW (phone: 638-6600). Expensive.

JW Marriott – A significant step above other members of this chain. Connected to a mall complex of 160 stores and the *National Theater,* it has 744 rooms, a pool, and a health spa. The Marquis floors (14 and 15) are especially nice. 1331 Pennsylvania Ave. NW (phone: 393-2000). Expensive.

Loews L'Enfant Plaza – This imposing, modernistic structure is one of Washington's best hotels, occupying the top floors of an office complex. A huge fountain cascades on the plaza; below there is a large shopping mall with chic boutiques and a Metro station, and on the 12th story there's an outdoor swimming pool. The service is high quality, the location conveniently near the Mall, and there are 372 rooms, 2 restaurants, and a cocktail lounge. 480 L'Enfant Plaza SW (phone: 484-1000). Expensive.

Madison – With 374 luxurious rooms, excellent service by a well-trained staff, amid gracious Federal decor; extras including interpreters, refrigerators, saunas, and bathroom phones. The *Montpelier Room* is quite a good restaurant. Open for buffet on weekdays and Sunday brunch. There are also 2 more informal restaurants and a cocktail lounge. 15th and M Sts. NW (phone: 862-1600). Expensive.

Mayflower – Four blocks from the White House, this 724-room hotel, which hosted Calvin Coolidge's inaugural ball, has undergone a very satisfying face-lift. The lobby and public areas are light, airy, and filled with flowers. Two excellent new restaurants: the elegant *Nicholas* specializes in nouvelle cuisine with a wide variety of seafood, and the less formal *Café Promenade* has a buffet lunch and scrumptious desserts. The cocktail lounge also serves a light lunch. 1127 Connecticut Ave. NW (phone: 347-3000). Expensive.

Ritz Carlton – Restored to an elegance beyond even its original standard. This is as close to an evocation of a classic European hotel as exists in Washington. Facilities include the *Jockey Club* restaurant, the *Fairfax Bar,* as well as a ballroom and 7 meeting rooms. A new addition brings the room total to 230. 2100 Massachusetts Ave. NW (phone: 293-2100 or 800-241-3333). Expensive.

Sheraton Carlton – Host to many presidents and dignitaries. Truman used to hold his affairs of state here while the White House was being redone, and Jimmy Carter announced his intention to run here. The hotel's Italian Renaissance lobby is elegant, the 235 rooms comfortable, the Sunday brunch terrific, and the bar good enough to win approval from Jimmy Breslin. There are 2 excellent dining rooms and a cocktail lounge. 923 16th St. NW (phone: 638-2626). Expensive.

Vista International – François Mitterrand and Elizabeth Taylor are among those who have stayed at this 413-room hotel, only six blocks from the White House. Its six 1-bedroom suites, designed by Givenchy, sport full-length mirrors and bathrooms in opalescent tile (cost: $425 a night). Favorite recipes of past presidents are on the menu at the *American Harvest* restaurant; cardiovascular fitness gear is available at the health club. 1400 M St. (phone: 429-1700). Expensive.

Washington Court – A 268-room luxury hostelry with a 4-story atrium; moderately priced restaurant, the *Café;* picturesque views; complimentary limousine service; and other amenities, such as TV sets and phones in both bedroom and bath, and exercise equipment delivered to rooms on request. Two blocks from the Capitol, 525 New Jersey Ave. (phone: 628-2100). Expensive.

Watergate – Though this modern hotel-apartment-office complex doesn't look too historic, appearances can be deceiving (as can small pieces of tape). With 238 large contemporarily furnished rooms, indoor swimming pool and health club, the excellent *Watergate* restaurant (open daily), cocktail lounge, Les Champs shopping mall with even more dining possibilities, and a location adjacent to the *Kennedy Center.* 2650 Virginia Ave. NW (phone: 965-2300). Expensive.

Westin – This new member of the Westin chain is as elegant inside as it is outside. In addition to its lovely interior garden and 416 luxuriously appointed rooms — they even have bathroom speakers for the cable TV and 3 phones — there is a fine restaurant, the *Colonnade,* for formal dining, a more casual brasserie, and a lobby lounge in a glass loggia just off the garden. As if all this were not enough, there is a professionally staffed fitness center, complete with pool, Jacuzzi, sauna, squash courts, aerobics room, weights, and state-of-the-art exercise equipment, plus a beauty salon and juice bar. 24th and M Sts. NW (phone: 429-2400 or 800-228-3000). Expensive.

Willard Inter-Continental – Nine president-elects stayed at this Beaux Arts landmark while awaiting completion of the White House, and Charles Dickens and Julia Ward Howe were regulars. But the "crown jewel" of Pennsylvania Avenue fell into disrepair (and was almost razed during the late 1960s). New manager Inter-Continental recently completed a thorough $70-million renovation and modernization of all public spaces and 394 rooms, restoring it to its turn-of-the-century grandeur. Amenities include a mini-bar, direct-dial telephone, and hair dryer in all rooms. The hotel dining room is one of DC's most elegant eateries. Corner Pennsylvania Ave. and 14th St. NW (phone: 628-9100). Expensive.

Wyndham-Bristol – It's all suites — 240 of them. There's also a the *Bristol Grill* restaurant, as well as the *Metro Café* for snacks and sandwiches. Cordials and chocolates that appear in the suites at night are among the hotel's appealing touches. It's also one of the rare hotels with a female concierge, Dixie Eng. 2430 Pennsylvania Ave. NW (phone: 955-6400). Expensive.

Georgetown Dutch Inn – Near the C&O Canal and within a block of the best restaurants and shopping that Georgetown has to offer, this small inn has 47 housekeeping units. 1075 Thomas Jefferson St. NW (phone: 337-0900). Moderate.

Tabard Inn – On a charming semi-residential street near the heart of the business district. Guests enjoy an ambience rare in an American city; there is a library and small dining room on the first floor. The rooms are furnished with antiques and some of them share baths. 1739 N St. NW (phone: 785-1277). Moderate.

Washington – One of the city's older hotels, recently refurbished and offering an incomparable view from its rooftop restaurant. Between April and early November, the hotel's rooftop verandah offers the best view in town over which to sip drinks. Always comfortable, but great during an inaugural parade. The 370 rooms feature TV sets and bathroom phones; nearby downtown shopping. 15th St. and Pennsylvania Ave. NW (phone: 638-5900). Moderate.

Kalorama Guest House – Bed and breakfast (and complimentary afternoon sherry) in 6 comfortable turn-of-the-century row houses decked out with antique furnishings. Four units in Kalorama, 1854 Mintwood Place NW (phone: 667-6369), and two units at Woodley Park near the National Zoo, 2700 Cathedral Ave. NW (phone: 328-0860). Moderate to inexpensive.

Windsor Inn – Small, unpretentious hostelry in the up and coming Adams Morgan district. Attracts relocating embassy employees as well as government workers preferring a modest, homey atmosphere. All 40 rooms have color TV sets and air conditioning; the staff is personable and attentive. Continental breakfast comes with a newspaper; and for a European touch, there is afternoon sherry. 1842 16th St. NW (phone: 667-0300 or 800-423-9111). Moderate to inexpensive.

Allen Lee – At this hotel in the heart of the George Washington University campus near the downtown area, some of the rooms don't have private baths, but it's a popular spot with young people. 2224 F St. NW (phone: 331-1224). Inexpensive.

Harrington – A 310-room, older hotel in the center of Washington's commercial area, it has seen better days but provides clean accommodations and is within walking distance of the Mall. Popular with high school students and family groups, who are drawn because the *Kitcheteria* makes feeding the troops easy and inexpensive. 11th and E Sts. NW (phone: 628-8140). Inexpensive.

Rock Creek – This small, 54-room hotel is a well-kept secret. Not too far from downtown, adjacent to Rock Creek Park, it offers quiet lodging with few amenities. 1925 Belmont Rd. NW (phone: 462-6007). Inexpensive.

Savoy Suites – This pleasant hotel between Georgetown and the Washington Cathedral has 150 rooms, 120 of them efficiencies. 2505 Wisconsin Ave. NW (phone: 337-9700). Inexpensive.

Windsor Park – A modest 43-room property within walking distance of the subway and near the French Embassy. Convenient and basic. 2116 Kalorama Rd., NW (phone: 483-7700). Inexpensive.

 EATING OUT: Considering the international aspects of Washington — 2,000 diplomats and a large number of residents who have lived abroad and brought back a taste for foreign cuisines — it's not too surprising that the District can provide an international gastronomic tour de force. What is surprising is that this wasn't the case until just a few years ago. The greatest local meals even two decades ago were served in private homes or in embassies (Jefferson was known to treat his guests to such delicacies as ice cream and imported French wines). The change began when the Kennedys brought a French chef to the White House, and this awakened a broad interest in food and spawned a restaurant boom that hasn't stopped yet. Though it's always helpful to have an ermine-lined wallet or, better yet, a generous expense account, those who have only the yen for good food needn't go hungry. Our restaurant selections range in price from $100 or more for a dinner for two in the very expensive restaurants to between $75 and $90 in expensive places, $40 to $60 in the moderate ones, and $35 and under in the inexpensive bracket. Prices do not include drinks, wine, or tips. Reservations are a must at the top-flight restaurants. All telephone numbers are in the 202 area code unless otherwise indicated.

Aux Beaux Champs – This handsome dining room in the *Four Seasons* hotel is distinguished by a highly creative menu that changes daily, stylish service, and a very cosmopolitan clientele. Open daily. Reservations advised. Major credit cards. 2800 Pennsylvania Ave. NW (phone: 342-0810). Very expensive.

Jean-Louis – Named for its chef, this is a small (only 14 tables) and elegant restaurant with gracious service and fine nouvelle cuisine. Fixed price dinners. Closed Sundays. Reservations necessary. Major credit cards. In the *Watergate* hotel, 2650 Virginia Ave. NW (phone: 298-4488). Very expensive.

Le Lion d'Or – Reputed to have the finest French food in town, although some say that the service isn't up to par. Don't leave without tasting one of the spectacular desserts. Open Saturdays for dinner only; closed Sundays. Reservations necessary. Major credit cards. 1150 Connecticut Ave. NW (phone: 296-7972). Very expensive.

Le Pavillon – Though this restaurant may have the highest prices in town, French chef Yannick Cam offers nouvelle cuisine to those who know and appreciate the best. Closed Sundays. Reservations necessary. Major credit cards. 1050 Connecticut Ave. NW (phone: 833-3846). Very expensive.

Cantina d'Italia – Still the longest running hit among Italian restaurants (Northern Italian cuisine), the changing menu offers new culinary delights but retains the old showstoppers like *fettuccine con salsa di noci* (homemade noodles with puréed walnuts, pine nuts, ricotta cheese, and parmesan). The only drawback is the small and somewhat confining basement location. Closed weekends. Reservations necessary. Major credit cards. 1214A 18th St. NW (phone: 659-1830). Expensive.

Dominique's – This restaurant has elegant French food, a lively and friendly atmosphere, and, if you insist, such exotic items as wild boar, rattlesnake, and buffalo. For a great bargain, try the pre- and post-theater prix fixe menu. Closed Sundays. Reservations necessary. Major credit cards. 1900 Pennsylvania Ave. NW (phone: 452-1126). Expensive.

Jockey Club – Originally (but no longer) operated under the direction of the management of New York's *"21" Club*, this *Ritz Carlton* restaurant is a favorite meeting and eating spot for local movers and shakers. The decor looks more like *"21"* than the original. Open daily. Reservations necessary. Major credit cards. 2100 Massachusetts Ave. NW (phone: 659-8000). Expensive.

Maison Blanche – The "in" spot for the Reagan White House, where Washington's famous and powerful met amid an elegant Parisian dining room decor. Classical French dishes are served, but there are touches of nouvelle cuisine as well. An extensive list of lunch and dinner specials is offered daily. Closed Sundays. Reservations necessary. Major credit cards. 1725 F St. NW (phone: 842-0070). Expensive.

Morton's of Chicago – This is one of the best places in Washington to get steaks with all the trimmings. Dinner only; closed Sundays. Reservations advised. Major credit cards. 3251 Prospect St. NW (phone: 342-6258). Expensive.

Adams Room – There's not a better place to start the day than this beautiful room with views of the White House and Lafayette Square. Breakfast choices range from French pastries and fresh berries to pecan waffles or corned beef and eggs. Open daily for breakfast and lunch. Reservations required. Major credit cards. *Hay-Adams* hotel, 16th and H Sts. NW (phone: 638-6600). Moderate.

American Café – A DC institution, this café is popular for informal but imaginatively prepared meals of grilled fish, sandwiches, salads, and soups. There are also some luscious desserts and homemade breads. Open daily. Major credit cards. Three of the establishment's eight locations: 1211 Wisconsin Ave. NW, Georgetown (phone: 944-9464); on Capitol Hill at 227 Massachusetts Ave. NE (phone: 547-8500); and National Pl., 1331 Pennsylvania Ave. NW (phone: 626-0770). Moderate.

Broker – A bit off the beaten track in southeast Washington, this stunning restaurant deserves a visit for its unusual and beautifully prepared Swiss dishes. Sunday brunch is a specialty. Open daily. Reservations advised. Major credit cards. 713 8th St. SE (phone: 546-8300). Moderate.

Clyde's – A lively place frequented by Georgetown students and trendy types. *Clyde's* serves omelettes, pasta, and steaks but is known mostly for its terrific bacon cheeseburgers and its weekend brunch. There's also Guinness stout on tap that's served at just the right temperature. Open daily. Reservations advised, although none are taken for weekend brunch. Major credit cards. 3236 M St. NW (phone: 333-0294). Moderate.

La Colline – Charming and moderately priced, this restaurant serves adventurous French food and daily specials as well as wonderful desserts. Open daily. Reservations advised. Major credit cards. 400 N Capitol St. (phone: 737-0400). Moderate.

Dar es Salam – An intimate jewel in Georgetown that serves Moroccan food in an authentic Arabic setting, featuring a fine traditional *couscous*. Moderate; reservations advised. Downstairs, the *Scheherazade* nightclub offers live music and the best belly dancing in town. Major credit cards. 3056 M St. NW (phone: 342-1925). Moderate.

Le Gaulois – Though small and sometimes overcrowded, it has a topnotch French menu including a full page of daily specials. Closed Sundays. Reservations advised. Major credit cards. 2133 Pennsylvania Ave. NW (phone: 466-3232). Moderate.

Germaine's – A varied Oriental menu — including Japanese, Korean, Vietnamese, and Indonesian foods. Specialties are lemon chicken and squirrel fish. Open daily. Reservations advised. Major credit cards. 2400 Wisconsin Ave. NW (phone: 965-1185). Moderate.

Gusti's – A downtown standby with consistently good service and traditional Italian specialties. Open daily. Reservations unnecessary. Major credit cards. 19th and M Sts. NW (phone: 331-9444). Moderate.

Harvey's – A fixture in Washington since 1858, it's reputation for fine seafood is well deserved. Try the crab imperial, lobster and shrimp Norfolk, or the shad roe in season. Closed Sundays in July and August. Reservations advised. Major credit cards. 1001 18th St. NW (phone: 833-1858). Moderate.

Lafitte – Classic French and authentic Créole specialties are served in an atmosphere reminiscent of 18th-century New Orleans. The chocolate raspberry torte is a must. Brunch only on Sundays. Reservations advised. Major credit cards. 1310 New Hampshire Ave. NW (phone: 466-7978). Moderate.

Marrakesh – A few minutes from Capitol Hill in a cumin-colored cube of a building, this spacious Near Eastern restaurant has excellent traditional food accompanied by belly dancing. Reservations advised. No credit cards. 617 New York Ave. NW (phone: 393-9393). Moderate.

Old Ebbitt Grill – An old-timer in a new and elegant Victorian setting. Tasty appetizers lead off a menu ranging from hamburgers to filet mignon. Try the hot fudge sundae for dessert. Open daily. Reservations advised. Major credit cards. 675 15th St. NW (phone: 347-4800). Moderate.

Old Europe – Features the best German wine list in the District with some French and American labels; standard German dishes as well. Open daily. Reservations advised. Major credit cards. 2434 Wisconsin Ave. NW (phone: 333-7600). Moderate.

Suzanne's – Owner and chef Suzanne calls this tiny bistro occupying the second floor of a turn-of-the-century townhouse a "casual, friendly joint." There's nothing casual about the food, though, which is American contemporary (chicken salad with poblano chilies and salsa or stuffed veal en papillote) are excellent. Don't miss the desserts. Closed Sundays. Visa and MasterCard only. 1735 Connecticut Ave. NW (phone: 483-4633). Moderate.

Tabard Inn – The nouvelle-influenced menu at this charmingly quirky inn is strong on fresh seafood such as grilled tuna and swordfish. Sunday brunch is a popular affair and a good excuse to try the terrific Bloody Marys. Open daily. Reservations advised. Visa and MasterCard only. 1739 N St. NW (phone: 785-1277). Moderate.

Au Pied de Cochon – An informal place for a good meal at a decent price 24 hours a day. If *pieds de cochon* (pigs' feet) aren't your style, try asparagus vinaigrette, coq au vin, and other bistro specialties. No reservations. Major credit cards. 1335 Wisconsin Ave. NW (phone: 333-5440). Moderate to inexpensive.

Astor – Consistently good Greek food at consistently rock-bottom prices. Known more for its food (try the *poililia* hors d'oeuvre platter, *moussaka, pastitsio,* or *styfado* — beef stew) than its atmosphere, the restaurant provides belly dancers upstairs amid electric blue vinyl and marbled Formica. An inexpensive wine list has Greek and Mediterranean offerings. Open daily. Reservations advised. Major credit cards. 1813 M St. NW (phone: 331-7994). Inexpensive.

City Café – A warm, upbeat new spot not far from Washington Circle in the West End with a blend of light and nouvelle dining. Individual pizza topped with sun-dried tomato, onion, and goat cheese, or chicken, tomato, and mozzarella are especially gratifying. Interesting soups, stir-fried scallops with vegetables, and hearty hamburgers are other worthy offerings. Open daily. Reservations advised. No credit cards. 2213 M St. NW (phone: 797-4860). Inexpensive.

Enriqueta's – The Mexican fare at this compact Georgetown favorite is always first-rate. Try the *pollo en salsa poblana* or chiles rellenos. Open daily. Reservations for large groups only. Major credit cards. 2811 M St. NW (phone: 338-7772). Inexpensive.

House of Hunan – Relatively new in town, this restaurant already ranks among the finest in the city. Unusual appetizers include shrimp balls and vegetable curls, and special main dishes are crisp whole fish Hunan style, and honeyed ham. Open daily. Reservations necessary for dinner. Major credit cards. 1900 K St. NW (phone: 293-9111). Inexpensive.

Iron Gate Inn – A former stable now dedicated to Middle Eastern food: shish kebab, couscous, and stuffed grape leaves. Speaking of which, there's a charming little grape arbor over the outdoor dining area where you can be served in warm weather. Open daily. Reservations advised. Major credit cards. 1734 N St. NW (phone: 737-1370). Inexpensive.

Roma – Solid Italian family-style place, best in warm weather when the large outdoor garden is open and musicians and singers add to the relaxed ambience. All the old favorites are there from pasta to pizza. Open daily. Reservations advised. Major credit cards. 3419 Connecticut Ave. NW (phone: 363-6611). Inexpensive.

Scholl's Colonial Cafeteria – A 62-year-old Washington institution, serving generous portions of fresh, well-cooked food at more than reasonable prices. Tour groups welcome. Open daily except Sundays for breakfast, lunch, and dinner. No credit cards. 1990 K St. NW (phone: 296-3065). Inexpensive.

Vietnam Georgetown – Small and intimate, this simple restaurant serves the best Vietnamese food in town. Specialties include deep-fried crispy rolls, shrimp with sugarcane, and beef in grape leaves. Open daily. No credit cards. 2934 M St. NW (phone: 337-4536). Inexpensive.

For the sweet of tooth, Washington has a home-grown ice cream empire founded by renegade attorney Bob Weiss. *Bob's Famous Ice Cream* has stores on Capitol Hill (236 Massachusetts Ave. NE; phone: 546-3860), near the Cleveland Park Metro station (3510 Connecticut Ave. NW; phone: 244-4465), and in Bethesda (4706 Bethesda Ave.; phone: 301-986-5911). Bob's ice cream also is sold just above Georgetown at *The Ice Cream Shop* (2416 Wisconsin Ave. NW; phone: 965-4499).

DIVERSIONS

For the Body

Downhill Skiing

 You don't have to be particularly athletically inclined to ski or even particularly rich. People all over the US have taken to the hills, with some 1,200 ski areas around the country to practice their art. For no other reason than the sheer number of runs, knowing where to go can be a problem.

If you're going for only a day or a weekend, the primary consideration will be to find a nearby resort that meets your budget and doesn't have long lift lines. For a list of those near you, write to the state travel directors or see magazines like *Ski* and *Skiing; Ski*'s monthly "Where to Ski in Your Region" is full of information on lift rates, kids' programs, tips on avoiding lift lines, and more. If you have a week to spend, the problem of choosing an area becomes more difficult. California, Colorado, Idaho, Montana, New Hampshire, New Mexico, Utah, Vermont, and Wyoming all have resorts with terrain that is diverse enough and nightlife, restaurants, and other amenities that are abundant enough to prove alluring. The *White Book of Ski Areas, U.S. & Canada* (Inter-Ski Services, PO Box 3635, Georgetown Station, Washington, DC 20007; phone: 202-342-0886) lists all the ski areas in the US and Canada, with detailed information. It's revised annually and can be found in ski shops and bookstores ($13.95) or obtained by mail from the publisher ($16).

The first decision involves choosing the particular part of the country where you most want to ski — East, Midwest, Rockies, or the Far West. California and the Pacific Northwest get the most snow, with hundreds of inches' accumulation every winter, but because of the high moisture content of the clouds that bring it from the sea, it is often heavy and slushy. The East often endures long lift lines, and the relatively low altitudes at which most skiing there (and in the Midwest) is done, combined with weather patterns, result in a lot of between-snowfall freezing and thawing that often make for icy trails.

For the kind of powder snow that makes for the best skiing, there's no place like the Rockies. That these mountains are the only great land barrier for storms moving inland from the West Coast means that they get huge quantities of snow, and the area's basic overall dryness makes the moisture content low, so that the snow is light and skis skim across it with almost no resistance. Because the water density per cubic centimeter is high (particularly in Utah), the snow has enough body to support a skier through deep powder. The northern Rockies get more snow than the southern Rockies, but snow in the south is drier.

Mountains are smallest in the Midwest, where vertical drops (the perpendicular height from the highest lift-served point to the base of the ski area) may amount to only a few hundred feet, but midwestern resorts are just the place if you are learning. Also good for newer skiers — especially southeastern residents with limited time to spare — are the somewhat greater vertical drops (up to 1,600 feet) of the resorts scattered from West Virginia all the way down to Alabama.

The mountains are highest in the West; the vertical drops are steeper and the runs somewhat longer. In the West, too, you will find wide-open bowls. Though their slopes are steep at the top, most intermediates can get down them in good shape by taking long traverses. In the East, trails have been cut narrow to keep snow from blowing off and to provide shelter from the wind. As a result, skiing that is already difficult because of the snow conditions can be even more demanding because the skier must always ski the fall line. Not all the fall lines are horrendously steep, of course, but going straight down takes fortitude even on a gentle slope.

Eastern mountains range in size between the hills of the Midwest and the Western giants. As a rule, if you're just learning to ski, you won't need access to difficult terrain that only a big mountain can provide; what matters will be whether the beginners' area has terrain varied enough to keep you interested. You don't want to spend a week on the slope with a view of the world's biggest parking lot.

Where you go will also depend on what sort of lodging you like: not all resorts have condominiums or housekeeping units. Not all have inexpensive ski dorms or, for that matter, those friendly, rustic old inns where everybody eats in the lodge every night. Most resort towns have modern motels and ski lodges with private baths, saunas, swimming pools, and the like. In New England, in addition, you'll find old country inns — long on charm but not much for plumbing and not always as convenient as some people like.

Some resorts are better for families. Most families are made up of skiers of varying abilities, and if all the hard runs are in one place, and all the easy runs are a 5-minute drive away, families are going to have a hard time getting together for lunch or at the end of the day, even if there's some sort of shuttle bus. If you're taking your family, pick a resort that has a centralized lift layout on one mountain. (Check the trail map in the area's brochures.) Check, too, to see whether nurseries and children's ski schools in which you want to park your kids for the afternoon require that you pick them up for lunch; some resorts provide all-day supervision, and some don't.

The resorts listed below include a few of the major destinations in the country. At all of them, you'll find an abundance of lifts, with rates from $10 to $35 a day (considerably less when you purchase a full week's pass), lodging places in all price ranges, a variety of packages, and seasons that run generally from mid-November into April. Note that most resorts are extremely crowded at Christmastime, over the Washington's Birthday holiday, and during the Easter holidays. Always reserve well in advance.

EAST

SUGARLOAF USA, Carrabassett Valley, Maine: With a 2,637-foot vertical drop, plus 70 trails and slopes and above-timberline skiing in the spring, this is the third biggest ski mountain in the East. There are 400 acres of skiable terrain, almost evenly divided among novice, intermediate, and expert trails. Recent additions include two high-capacity quad chair lifts, increased snowmaking coverage, and a new Half Pipe for snowboarding. More emphasis has also been placed on recreational racing. In addition, a major expansion of the base lodge has been completed; guests will now find convention facilities, a new nightclub for teens, and better storage areas. Best skiing is in February, March, and April. There's a definite Down East feel to the place, and you can stay right on the mountain in condos or comfortable lodges. Information: Sugarloaf USA, Carrabassett Valley, ME 04947 (phone: 207-237-2000; 800-THE-LOAF from eastern US; or 800-THE-AREA for the Sugarloaf Chamber of Commerce reservation service).

MT. WASHINGTON VALLEY, North Conway and Jackson, New Hampshire: With four ski mountains (and interchangeable lift tickets), better than half a dozen ski villages (including Jackson, which one ski writer called the most beautiful in all New

England), a bounty of country inns, one of the region's best XC trail networks, and striking scenery at the base of the Northeast's tallest mountain, this is quite a ski area. Black Mountain, with a 1,200-foot vertical, offers easy, family-type skiing. At Attitash, the narrow, looping trails draw a fashion-oriented family crowd, and limited lift-ticket sales keep down the weekend crowds. Mt. Cranmore, friendly, easy, and wide open, is great for intermediates; its oddball Skimobile is one of the oldest lifts in New England. Wildcat has narrow, hair-raising trails (built to keep Mt. Washington's winds from denuding the slopes) and a 2,100-foot vertical. All have snowmaking; and since the area is not well known outside Boston, it's not as crowded as some others, and many good packages are available. Information: Mt. Washington Valley Chamber of Commerce, PO Box 385, North Conway, NH 03860 (phone: 603-356-3171).

WATERVILLE VALLEY, Waterville Valley, New Hampshire: Known for its snow-making and its carefully groomed slopes, this resort also boasts varied terrain on a maximum 2,020-foot vertical; a self-contained "village" full of spiffy condos; daytime shuttle bus service; reciprocal lift privileges with eight other New Hampshire ski areas midweek; and a friendly ski week program for adults as well as children. And the village is growing. A 5-building retail and commercial center, with 37 shops and 7 restaurants, plus offices and housing units for employees, is now complete. The resort also has added the High Country Express — New Hampshire's only detachable quad lift — which carries 3,000 skiers an hour over a distance of 7,000 feet. Other additions include the *Golden Eagle Lodge,* a 139-room hotel designed to resemble New Hampshire's grand old resort hotels, and a children's ski center, which offers various programs for young-sters age 3 and up. In the indoor sports center are racquet sports and a health spa; outdoor activities are also available. Information: Waterville Valley Ski Areas, Waterville Valley, NH 03215 (phone: 603-236-4144 for snow information; 800-552-4767 from New Hampshire; 800-468-2553 from the rest of the East; 603-236-8371 elsewhere for reservations).

BOLTON VALLEY, Bolton Valley, Vermont: One of the most accessible resorts in Vermont, this self-contained haven (a real family pleaser) is in the center of the state, about 20 miles east of Burlington, Vermont's largest city; it is the closest ski resort to Burlington International Airport. There are two interconnected mountains here: Ricker, with slopes down to the main village, and Timberline Peak. Five lifts, including one quadruple chair, serve 40 trails on a vertical rise of 1,600 feet. The village includes a cross-country touring center. Bolton Valley's biggest claim to fame, however, is its children's facilities: It recently expanded the size of its nursery (for children from 3 months to 5 years) and added an activity room for children from age 5 to 12. There is also an area specially landscaped to help young beginners adopt correct skiing positions naturally. Information: Bolton Valley, Bolton Valley, VT 05477 (phone: 802-434-2131; 800-451-3220 in the Northeast).

KILLINGTON, Killington, Vermont: The home of the longest ski lift in North America and the longest trail in the US, this trail-veined basin offers a huge variety of terrain. There are long wide runs, steep and narrow ones (107 trails in all), six intercon-nected peaks, six base lodge facilities, one of the best novice slopes in the East, and Vermont's longest vertical drop (3,175 feet).The Bear Mountain area, where the US Alpine Ski Team trained for the 1980 Olympics, offers New England's steepest skiing terrain. Killington also has fantastic snow conditions (which mean skiing from Novem-ber to June), and the standout snowmaking operation, now the world's most extensive, has been expanded every year so that 62% of the skiable terrain is now covered, 40 miles in all. Killington also has some of the East's best learn-to-ski weeks, a children's center, and good packages. *The Inn of the Six Mountains* (phone: 802-422-4302; 800-228-4676) is the newest addition to the lodging in the Killington area. It has 103 rooms and a dining room lighted solely by candles. Shuttle bus service to the slopes is available. Information: Killington Ski and Summer Resort, Killington, VT 05751 (phone: 802-422-3333; 802-773-1500 for general information; 802-773-1330 for lodging and reservations).

MAGIC MOUNTAIN, near Londonderry, Vermont: The miniature Switzerland that Hans Thorner established as a ski resort in 1960 never grew as quickly as nearby Stratton and Bromley. But it is a friendly place and notably smooth-running. The lower half of the mountain is for novices or intermediates; the top will challenge the very best skiers, particularly now that there are two mountains connected over the top and the two steepest glades in the East are here; and there's snowmaking from top to bottom on both the east and west sides, with coverage of 100% of the terrain. Five hostelries are available, each with its own personality and all within walking distance of the slopes; also available for rental are 17 condos, most of them with three or four bedrooms. Information: Magic Mountain, RFD #1, Box 32, Londonderry, VT 05148 (phone: 802-824-5566; for snow information, 800-222-7545).

BROMLEY, Manchester Center, Vermont: Bromley, one of Vermont's original ski mountains and the only major ski area in the East with a southern exposure, is a traditional favorite among skiers, offering a casual, comfortable atmosphere and a wide variety of skiing terrain. It has a 1,344-foot vertical drop; 35 wide, well-groomed trails for all skill levels; snowmaking that covers more than 84% of the terrain; one of the best ski schools in the East, and slopeside accommodations. The 9 lifts and all trails are laid out to maintain a central base area — a convenient focal point, especially for families. State-accredited nursery facilities are at the base. Information: Bromley Mountain, PO Box 1130, Manchester Center, VT 05255 (phone: 802-824-5522).

STOWE, Stowe, Vermont: When one journalist poked fun at *Stowe's* lift lines and its variable snow conditions, letters of indignation poured in. *Stowe* is close to an airport and interstate highways and is served by Amtrak. This is the East's premier ski resort, and its regulars don't take that position lightly. Nowadays, they have even more to puff up about. A massive snowmaking installation covering 60% of the resort's terrain and a new detachable quad chair lift (reducing base-to-summit ride time from 13 to 6½ minutes) have resolved situations that most skiers were willing to tolerate only because the skiing on the 2,350-foot vertical was so good. Meanwhile, a well-coordinated children's ski school–day care setup has added terrific appeal for young families; the famous tough runs share the limelight with the 70% of the slopes and trails rated for novices and intermediates; cross-country skiing is also available. The restaurants, night-life, and accommodations are as varied and lively as ever. Information: Stowe Area Assn., PO Box 1320A, Stowe, VT 05672 (phone: 802-253-7321; outside Vermont, reservations, 800-24-STOWE); Stowe Ski Resort, Stowe, VT 05672 (phone: 802-253-7311, or 800-253-4SKI).

STRATTON, Stratton, Vermont: With its 2,003-foot vertical drop, Stratton's mountain, in the Green Mountains of southern Vermont, is the tallest in the region. It is a smooth classic cone divided into two separate areas, each with steep sections that are wide, interestingly contoured, and unfailingly well groomed. Its improved snowmaking system, 90 trails, and 11 lifts offer something for skiers at every level. There are four lodges within walking distance of the base and a number of condominiums at the area. It also offers a special carousel that tows beginners around in circles until they get the feel of their skis, and, in the glittering Sports Center, indoor tennis, racquetball, swimming, and Nautilus equipment. The new *Stratton Mountain Village,* a $75-million expansion, features a hotel, luxury villas and townhouses, conference facilities, covered parking, 30 shops along a pedestrian path, several restaurants, a bank, and a movie theater. Spa enthusiasts should check out the *Liftline Lodge*'s ski and spa program. Also new is Starship XII, a futuristic gondola designed in France. The first of its kind in the US, it has 64 snug units, each of which can hold 12 passengers, that zip from base to summit in 7½ minutes, transporting 2,400 passengers per hour — sightseers as well as skiers. Information: Stratton Corporation, Stratton Mountain, VT 05155 (phone: 802-297-2200).

SUGARBUSH SKI RESORT, Warren, Vermont: One resort with two lift-laced mountains, separated by 2 miles of road, it offers some of the best expert terrain in the East. It also boasts some of the nicest scenery, as many intermediate runs and trails are clustered amid some of New England's most photographic inns. The only problem here is in getting used to the nomenclature. Thanks to a host of successive owners — as well as further expansions — in recent years, longtime fans may do a few double-takes getting used to the new names. The original 4,000-foot-high mountain, previously known as Sugarbush, is now called South Basin. And its sister mountain is no longer Glen Ellen but Mt. Ellen. What hasn't changed is the diversity: Along with 71 trails and a 2,600-foot vertical, there is a giant sports center with indoor tennis courts and a swimming pool. Nearby *Schaffer Farm* provides winter riding. New to the resort are snowboarding lessons and rentals. Accommodations in the valley — guesthouses and inns, condominiums, motels, hotels, the slopeside, 3,000-bed *Sugarbush Village* (phone: 802-583-3000 or 800-451-4326), and the posh *Sugarbush Inn* (phone: 802-583-2301) — overlap; each resort has a housing office that can place you. Be sure to check out the après-ski merriment at the *Sugarbush Inn,* or try *Phoenix* or *Chez Henri* for lunch. Information: Sugarbush Ski Resort, Box 350, Warren, VT 05674-9993 (phone: 802-583-2381; reservations, 800-53-SUGAR, or 802-583-3333).

MT. SNOW, near West Dover, Vermont: Mt. Snow is a big, 3,600-foot mountain with 1,700 vertical feet of skiing. A network of 77 trails is spread over four separate, but interconnected, mountain areas. There are 15 lifts, including a high-speed quad chair. Snowmaking covers 80% of all skiable terrain, ensuring reliable skiing from early November through early May. Especially popular are Mt. Snow's theme weeks, including a guaranteed "learn to ski the summit" program. The area includes a ski school, day care, nursery, and ski rentals. Cross-country skiing, snowmobiling, and sleigh rides are nearby. Dozens of restaurants and nightspots provide plenty of après-ski entertainment. Mt. Snow's location in southern Vermont makes it the closest major ski resort to eastern metropolitan centers. Information: Mt. Snow Resort, Mt. Snow, VT 05356 (phone: 802-464-3333; lodging, 802-464-8501; ski report, 802-464-2151).

WEST

SKI LAKE TAHOE, near Lake Tahoe, California: Within an hour's drive of incredibly deep-blue Lake Tahoe are 16 ski resorts, together offering the greatest concentration of skiing available in America. The five largest are *Heavenly, Northstar-at-Tahoe, Alpine Meadows, Squaw Valley USA* (for more about which, see below), and *Kirkwood.* Alone, each of the five resorts offers magnificent, varied terrain; the combination is simply mind-boggling. *Heavenly* (phone: 800-2-HEAVEN), straddling the California-Nevada state line, is America's largest ski resort, covering 20 square miles. The intermediates' haven is on the Nevada side, the beginner/intermediate terrain mainly in California, with plenty of expert terrain on each. This is also the resort closest to major-league gambling and low-cost, high-quality lodging in South Lake Tahoe. *Alpine Meadows* (phone: 800-TAHOE-4U) offers over 2,000 skiable acres, with a smooth lift layout, a respectable 1,800-foot vertical, 125 acres covered by snowmaking machines, and the longest ski season at Tahoe — through Memorial Day. The upper mountain is full of steep bowls and narrow chutes, but there's usually enough space for traversing; the lower slopes are wide, gentle, beautifully groomed. *Kirkwood* (phone: 209-258-7000), with a 2,000-foot vertical, has become one of Tahoe's fastest-growing destination ski resorts by recently doubling its lodgings. It also has a Nordic operation with 45 miles of groomed track. Olympic and Sentinel bowls and the snow-filled saddles of the ridges have established Kirkwood's reputation as a place for experts and intermediates. *Northstar* (phone: 800-533-6787), with a 2,200-foot vertical, is a self-contained resort community with ski-in/ski-out condominiums, excellent beginner and intermediate terrain, and a full-service cross-country and Telemark center. Information: Ski Lake Tahoe, PO Box BN, Incline Village, NV 89450 (phone: 702-831-3993).

MAMMOTH/JUNE SKI RESORT, Mammoth Lakes, California: Mammoth it is. This 11,053-foot blown-out volcano is skiable from late October until early July; the bottom sections are excellent for beginners. Elsewhere, there are rugged runs designed to chill experts on 3,100 feet of vertical served by 30 lifts. Facilities include 3 day lodges, 4 ski shops, 2 rental shops, a ski school, and a race department as well as 2 restaurants and cafeterias and on-hill snack bars. The complex also has 3 indoor spas, day care facilities, a free shuttle around the mountain, and 400 lodging rooms. The town of Mammoth, at the base, has 34 miles of cross-country ski trails, horse-drawn sleighs, hot-air balloon rides, snowmobiles, dogsledding, and ice skating, in addition to shopping, dining, and lodging. The Mammoth Lakes Resort Assn. (phone: 619-934-2712) will put together vacation packages tailored to individual needs. Information: Mammoth/June Ski Resort, PO Box 24, Mammoth Lakes, CA 93546 (phone: 619-934-2571).

SQUAW VALLEY USA, Olympic Valley, California: Experts, intermediates, and novices enjoy 8,300 acres of wide-open bowl skiing, with 27 lifts, including a 150-passenger aerial cable car and a 6-passenger gondola. The 1960 Winter Olympics site and its bustling Olympic Village are still lively — and lots of fun. The "No waiting in line or your money back" policy guarantees skiers their money back if the average lift-line wait is over 10 minutes. Recently completed is the Opera House, a complex at the base of the mountain housing a 250-seat movie theater, a general store, conference rooms, a Nordic center, and a French restaurant, *Chez Fritsch.* The Papoose Area for youngsters has been expanded and now includes the Ten Little Indians Snow School (ages 3 to 5), which also looks after nonskiers (6 months to 3 years). The resort has also widened from top to bottom its popular Mountain Run, a beginner-intermediate slope, to eliminate late afternoon congestion. Information: Squaw Valley, PO Box 2007, Olympic Valley, CA 95730 (phone: 916-583-6985; 800-545-4350; 24-hour snow phone 916-583-6955).

ASPEN, Aspen, Colorado: The biggest action town in ski-dom, an old mining center, and the granddaddy of American ski resorts, Aspen has a little something for everyone. Aspen Mountain, with its 3,267-foot vertical, is known for its powder, its steep runs, and celebrated toughies like Silver Queen. Aspen Highlands, with its 3,800-foot vertical, has runs of up to 3½ miles. Its terrain is well balanced, with half intermediate and the other half divided equally between beginner and expert. Buttermilk Mountain, with its 2,030-foot vertical, is a beginners' and intermediates' paradise, not only for the quality of the snow, but also for the width and gentleness of its trails. And there's nightlife and good eating in a quantity and variety that you'll find at few other ski resorts in the world, as well as excellent family packages. Information: Aspen Mountain and Buttermilk Mountain, PO Box 1248, Aspen, CO 81612 (phone: 303-925-1220); Aspen Highlands, PO Box T, Aspen, CO 81612 (phone: 303-925-5300; reservations 800-525-8955).

BRECKENRIDGE, Breckenridge, Colorado: Some 85 miles (90 minutes) west of Denver and associated with Copper Mountain and Keystone through a "Ski the Summit" (Summit County) lift ticket exchange program, Breckenridge, one of Colorado's first great skiing finds, does a brisk business among skiing families — and everybody else lucky enough to have discovered it. There are three mountains (with a fourth being planned), three base areas, a 2,613-foot vertical rise, 1,519 skiable acres comprising over 60 miles of trails (which even on the busiest days can seem empty), 430 acres of snowmaking, and a Nordic center. Snowmobiling, ice skating, dogsledding, and other winter activities are nearby. Besides all of this, Breckenridge resort has the distinction of being part of a town that is nearly 130 years old, with its own history, character, and appearance. The town boasts 350 historic Victorian structures as well as many newer homes designed to harmonize with their older neighbors — perfect for a walking tour to loosen up sore muscles. There is a variety of available lodgings, including 3 bed-and-breakfast establishments, and an active nightlife. In town, free public transportation is plentiful, but a car is better for real mobility. Information: Breckenridge Ski Area, PO Box 1058, 1599 Summit County Rd., #3, Breckenridge, CO 80424 (phone: 303-453-2368).

COPPER MOUNTAIN RESORT, Copper Mountain, Colorado: About 75 miles west of Denver, the mountain soars above a compact condominium village, including the only cold-weather *Club Med* in North America. Three base lift areas, within walking distance of accommodations, lead, respectively, to beginner, intermediate, and advanced terrain. The vertical is 2,760 feet; and there is a high-speed quad chair lift. The addition of the 20-acre Liberty Trail brings the total to 76 trails and 1,180 acres. Copper Mountain offers a $3-million racquet and athletic club and extensive cross-country activities and is in the midst of a $40-million expansion. Together with *Breckenridge* and *Keystone,* this resort is part of the "Ski the Summit" (Summit County) exchange program. Information: Copper Mountain Resort, PO Box 3001, Copper Mountain, CO 80443 (phone: 303-968-2882; 800-I-LUV-FUN outside Colorado).

KEYSTONE and ARAPAHOE BASIN, Keystone, Colorado: Only 68 miles from Denver, *Keystone* offers four unique skiing experiences: *Keystone Mountain, North Peak, Arapahoe Basin,* and *Keystone Night Ski.* Even the easy slopes, like the 3-mile "Schoolmarm," are interesting, and the difficult slopes, while hard, are not impossible. The snowmaking system, which can cover 100% of Keystone Mountain and 50% of North Peak, is the Rockies' most extensive. Top-to-bottom night skiing is available on 40% of the mountain, reached via gondola. *Arapahoe Basin,* the longtime favorite of Denver day-trippers that is now owned by Keystone, is the highest lift-served area in North America. It has added late (into June) skiing to Summit County's offerings. Its vertical is 1,640 feet; *Keystone*'s is 2,340. *Keystone*'s third, newest mountain, *North Peak,* with 200 acres of advanced intermediate and expert terrain, brings the resort's skiable acreage to 1,050. *Keystone* and *North Peak* can be reached by six-passenger gondola, another part of *Keystone*'s expansion program. All three areas participate in the "Ski the Summit" lift exchange program with *Copper Mountain* and *Breckenridge.* Shuttle buses are available, but a car is helpful. The Olympic medal–winning Mahre twins, Phil and Steve, run the training center here. The 5-day programs are held for recreational racers or for skiers who just want to improve their skills. Information: Keystone Resort Reservations, PO Box 38, Keystone, CO 80435 phone: 800-222-0188).

CRESTED BUTTE MOUNTAIN, Mt. Crested Butte, Colorado: Lots of skiing, no crowds, and friendly people are the reasons this has become one of the most popular of Colorado's mid-size resorts. Mt. Crested Butte offers 11 lifts and 51 trails, while the surrounding mountains offer a vast system of ski touring trails. The Old West town of Crested Butte is a National Historic District with beautiful Victorian buildings. Lodging choices include condominiums and the luxurious, 262-room *Grande Butte* hotel, just 20 yards from the base lifts. American, United, Continental, and Delta airlines serve the county airport in Gunnison, 30 miles away. Information: Crested Butte Mountain Resort, Box A, Mt. Crested Butte, CO 81225 (phone: 303-349-2333; 800-525-4220 for reservations).

SNOWMASS RESORT, Snowmass Village, Colorado: Snowmass is the ideal ski resort for an intimate getaway or a family vacation. It has one of North America's largest mountains, offering immense diversity for every level of skier. Plus, 95% of the accommodations are located slopeside. Improvements include a third high-speed SuperChair on the Big Burn; kids' half-price lift tickets; a children's nursery–ski school program called the Big Burn Bears; toll-free reservation numbers and a computerized reservation system connecting all of Snowmass's properties; and direct nonstop flights to Aspen/Snowmass from Chicago, Dallas, Los Angeles, Long Beach, and San Francisco. In addition to Snowmass, three other ski mountains — *Aspen, Aspen Highlands,* and *Buttermilk* — are within a 12-mile radius and they're all linked by an interchangeable multi-day lift ticket as well as free shuttle bus service. Everything is easy at Snowmass, with slopeside lodging, a pedestrian mall, a complete self-contained community and free village shuttle service. Snowmass's 20-plus restaurants offer a variety of food, and shopping options include furriers, boutiques, jewelry stores, children's shops, and T-shirt outlets. Recent additions include a transit plaza, an 8,000-square-foot day care center for children from 18 months to 3½ years, and 30 shops and restaurants. A full health spa has also been added to *Silvertree* hotel. Other activities range from sleigh-ride barbecues, dogsled rides, cross-country skiing, and snowmobiling to hot-air ballooning. All of these special features make this charming village community a perfect ski destination. Information: Snowmass Resort Assn., Box 5566, Snowmass Village, CO 81615 (phone: 303-923-2000).

STEAMBOAT, Steamboat Springs, Colorado: This relaxed family area is on the outskirts of an archetypal Old West town named for its whistling hot springs. The runs (100 of them) are roomy and varied; there are trails, bowls, and powder fields for skiers of all skills; good children's programs; and a 3,600-foot vertical. An 8-passenger, high-speed gondola shoots skiers up to Thunderhead Terminal (where there is also a restaurant and barbecue sun deck) in just 9 minutes. Steamboat's celebrated, ultra-light "champagne powder" is best experienced in January and February; March and April are good for sunny, warm spring skiing. Information: Steamboat, PO Box 774408, Steamboat Springs, CO 80477 (phone: 303-879-0740; 800-332-3204 in Colorado).

TELLURIDE, Telluride, Colorado: This former mining town, a National Historic District, is more than 100 years old. Both Butch Cassidy and Sundance launched their bank-robbing careers at the Bank of Telluride. One of Colorado's fastest growing resorts, Telluride offers not only great skiing but a beautiful natural setting and accommodations in lovely Victorian-style buildings. Since 1985, it has almost doubled in size both in its accommodations and ski facilities. About 80% of the lodgings are within walking distance of either of the resort's two base facilities. And there are plans to build more. As for the skiing, there are 756 acres of skiable terrain divided among 45 trails: 26% expert, 50% intermediate, and 24% beginner. There is a new 2½-mile beginners' run, the Galloping Goose, and a new 9-mile Nordic ski track; snowboarding is also available. The vertical is 3,155 feet. Information: The Telluride Ski Resort, 562 Mountain Village Blvd., PO Box 307, Telluride, CO 81435 (phone: 303-728-3856 or 800-525-3455).

VAIL, Vail, Colorado: One of the most magnificent ski complexes in the US, this pioneer of modern American skiing takes up 10 square miles of a mountain up and down a 3,200-foot vertical. There's so much skiing that even experts can spend a week at Vail and continue to find new challenges. The resort's already vast slopes recently doubled in size when it opened China Bowl, a mouth-watering expanse on the back side of the main skiing area. The area actually includes four bowls — China, Tea Cup, Siberia, and Mongolia — making Vail the largest single mountain resort in North America. Also new is the Orient Express ski lift, a high-speed quad that takes skiers out of China Bowl. A new poma lift at the eastern end of the mountain takes skiers off to Mongolia; the Born Free Express helps eliminate congestion in the primarily intermediate Lionshead area. Facilities are also being expanded at Beaver Creek, Vail's sister resort, about 7 miles down the valley. Trails with western and mining town themes take kids on skis through tepees, mines, and mogul gardens. The newest Vail experience is an overnight at the isolated *Trapper's Cabin* in Beaver Creek. Guests can either ski to the rustic log cabin or be chauffeured by Snowcat. Lodging in the area ranges from small, simple inns and lodges to full-service hotels within skiing distance of the lift bases. With Cadillac limousines and complimentary champagne at the end of the day, Beaver Creek is becoming the most elegant mountain resort in the nation. There's also ice skating, sleigh rides, cross-country skiing, snowmobiling, and more. Information: Vail Resort Assn., 241 E. Meadow Dr., Vail, CO 81658 (phone: 303-476-1000; 800-525-3875 outside Colorado); or Avon/Beaver Creek Resort Assn., PO Box 912, Avon, CO 81620 (phone: 800-525-2257).

SUN VALLEY, Sun Valley, Idaho: The ne plus ultra of destination ski resorts, this grande dame offers something for everyone on its 3,400 vertical feet — steilhangs for the brave and ballroom slopes for the tyro. Baldy, famous for steep-bowl skiing, now boasts an equal variety of intermediate terrain, more like that of Dollar (Sun Valley's other mountain — accessible by shuttle bus). The news here is that Sun Valley is modernizing to enable hard-core skiers to get to the top quicker and easier. A new, high-speed quad has replaced two slower lifts and now ferries skiers to the top of Baldy, dropping them near the *Lookout* restaurant. And the Christmas quad has replaced two side-by-side lifts that ferried skiers from the *Roundhouse* restaurant. Lodging is in Sun Valley proper, both at the base of Dollar, where there's a self-contained village full of shops and restaurants, and at Baldy's base, in the old mining town of Ketchum. Information: Sun Valley, Sun Valley, ID 83353-0010 (phone: 208-622-4111; 800-635-8261; 800-635-4150 for snow reports).

BIG MOUNTAIN, Whitefish, Montana: It's often been said that the farther you have to go to get to a resort, the friendlier it's bound to be. And though remarkably *accessible* thanks to decent transportation, the Big Mountain is a good example. Singles can have a great time because of the coziness of the lodges (within walking distance of lifts) and a schedule of parties, and families enjoy it because of the centralized, manageable layout of its 50 miles of runs. Because the mountain is in the northern Rockies, it gets enough snow so that you can ski from Thanksgiving until mid-April. *Whitefish,* 28 miles from the west entrance to Glacier National Park, is an old logging town turned resort; après-ski can be lively. Information: The Big Mountain, Box 1400, Whitefish, MT 59937 (phone: 406-862-3511).

TAOS SKI VALLEY, Taos, New Mexico: Featherlight powder, brilliant sunshine, notably absent lift lines, and some startlingly steep expert runs are what have made Taos famous. Another welcome feature is that beginner, intermediate, and expert slopes are all accessible from the top of each lift. The vertical drop is 2,613 feet, base elevation is 9,207 feet, and the 71 runs encompass powder glades, bowls, chutes, and well-manicured expanses. Snowmaking covers 80% of the beginner and intermediate terrain. Après-ski centers on several cozy American-plan lodges at the mountain's base. The ski school was ranked the best in the country in 1988 by a panel of ski industry experts. Information: Taos Ski Valley, Taos Ski Valley, NM 87525 (phone: 505-776-2291; 800-992-SNOW for reservations; 505-776-2916 for snow reports).

ALTA, Alta, Utah: Two things are generally known about this rustic resort hidden away in Little Cottonwood Canyon since 1938, not far from Snowbird and Salt Lake City. First, this is the mother nest for powder skiers (snowfall averages 500 inches yearly); second, the famous Alf's High Rustler run, a ¾-mile chute with a 40-degree slope, no trees, and challenging terrain, is possibly the most sought-after trail in the West. However, not all the runs on these 1,750 skiable acres are steep, and the novice and intermediate bowls offer wonderful views of jagged peaks and forests. The base is 8,500 feet and the top is over 11,000. Alta is also one of the cozier of American ski resorts, since all après-ski life revolves around the several lodges at base. Lift rates are among the lowest you'll find at any major ski resort. Information: Alta Ski Area, 3332 E. Little Cottonwood Rd., Alta, UT 84092 (phone: 801-742-3333; 801-942-0404 for lodging information; 801-572-3939 for current snow conditions).

DEER VALLEY, Park City, Utah: This highly unusual ski resort believes that skiers care as much about the flakiness of their croissants as they do about the grooming quality and steepness of their slopes; it's like a superb big resort at which a major ski mountain is just one of the amenities. Accordingly, the base lodge and the midmountain lodge are tastefully done up with pine, cedar, fir, and real antiques; the restrooms are fitted out with pink Carrara marble and brass fixtures. Accommodations are in the luxurious fieldstone and stucco *Stein Eriksen Lodge* and in superb condos with hillside views, big Jacuzzis, sun porches, and the like. As for the skiing, it's ideal — thanks to an annual 300 inches of the type of powdery snow only Utah can deliver, trails that unfold like a good novel, and a limited lift ticket sales policy that keeps lift lines down to 5 minutes. The vertical here is 2,200 feet. Add the great cuisine (the preparation and serving of which require the effort of a third of all Deer Valley employees), and you've got a ski vacation option like no other in the US. Information: Deer Valley Resort, Box 1525, Park City, UT 84060 (phone: 801-649-1000; 800-424-3337).

PARK CITY, Park City, Utah: With its many varied trails, night skiing, and snowmaking, Park City has always been terrific for skiers of all levels, with some of the steep snowfields a particular challenge to experts. It's the US Ski Team's National Training Center and has the longest night skiing run in the country. On the eastern slopes of the Wasatch Mountains, it is Utah's largest ski area, with some 2,200 acres of skiable terrain. The maximum vertical is now 3,100 feet. The town is an erstwhile mining settlement full of shops, health food emporiums, saloons, fancy steak joints — and lots of atmosphere to spare. Information: Park City Ski Area, PO Box 39, Park City, UT 84060 (phone: 801-649-8111; lodging reservations, 800-222-PARK; 801-649-9571 for snow conditions).

SNOWBIRD, Snowbird, Utah: Like Alta, well known for powder skiing. Where Alta is old-fashioned and home-grown, Snowbird, just a mile to the west, is high tech and elegant; the fact that it's a multimillion-dollar project shows in the slick condominium lodges of unadorned concrete and in the aura of luxury that surrounds the whole scene. As for the 1,900 acres of skiing, there are superb runs for experts on Snowbird's 3,100 vertical feet, and a respectable quota of runs for novices and intermediates as well. Among the resort's special ski programs are the Mountain Experience (5 hours of steep going off-trail for experts), free guided skiing tours, and helicopter skiing in the backcountry with the *Wasatch Powderbird Guides.* There's also a full-service health and beauty spa. Information: Snowbird Ski and Summer Resort, Snowbird, UT 84092 (phone: 800-453-3000 for reservations; 801-532-1700 from Salt Lake City; 800-882-4766 for groups and conferences; 801-742-2222 for information; 801-521-6040 from Salt Lake City).

SUNDANCE, Sundance, Utah: Owned and operated by actor Robert Redford, it is meant to appeal to folks with a special interest in the environment. There are few crowds at this 2,150 vertical: When the 450-car parking lot is full, the lift ticket office closes. Overnight guests stay in nearby cottages or private homes tucked in the trees alongside the slopes. Accommodations include single bedrooms, studio apartments, and *Sundance Mountain Inns,* which hold up to 12 people. In keeping with Mr. Redford's goals, films are presented regularly at the Sundance Screening Room. The area also serves as the home for the Sundance Institute, a center for promising artists, and for the Institute for Resources Management, an organization dedicated to preserving America's natural resources. Information: Sundance, RR #3, Box A-1, Sundance, UT 84604 (phone: 800-225-4107).

JACKSON HOLE, Teton Village, Wyoming: That the resort has America's greatest vertical drop (4,139 feet) and its longest runs does not explain why it also ranks among the country's least crowded. That is because the first lifts here went up on redoubtable Rendezvous Mountain, and its first reputation was as not only the steepest, but also the toughest. Energetic development of the 2,200 vertical feet of Après Vous, the resort's other, far more forgiving giant, is only beginning to dispel the scare stories. High time: half of Jackson Hole's skiable acreage is rated for experts, its nonexpert terrain is bigger than the entirety of 90% of other US ski resorts. That, plus a compact lift-base arrangement of resorts (so that cars are optional) makes Jackson Hole a good vacation bet for any skier. Information: Jackson Hole Central Reservations, PO Box 510, Teton Village, WY 83025 (phone: 307-733-4005 or 800-443-6931).

Cross-Country Skiing

 You can go striding and gliding across almost anywhere when there's even a little snow on the ground. Or you can spend an afternoon tooling down a frozen river or canal, around the edge of a cemetery, or through a city park. You can cross-country in most forests, national and state parks, and even in wildlife management areas. All you need is a pair of cross-country skis. As long as there is enough snow to cover the grass, the pavement, or the underbrush, those long, skinny skis will glide right along.

The special cross-country skiing centers springing up around the country not only offer lessons and cross-country ski rentals but also suggest marked trails that are tracked by machines to make the going easier and distribute trail maps. In very wild areas, some will also provide guides.

EAST

ACADIA NATIONAL PARK, Bar Harbor, Maine: The 50 miles of carriage roads on Mt. Desert Island, which are not plowed in winter, take you up and down the rugged mountains of the interior and along the coast, and when conditions are right, this is a winter wonderland par excellence. The total trail mileage is 85. However, because the ocean moderates the temperatures, you can't count on snow; call before traveling. Information: Acadia National Park, Box 177, Bar Harbor, ME 04609 (phone: 207-288-3338).

SUGARLOAF AREA, Kingfield, Maine: Two miles from Sugarloaf USA, Maine's largest downhill skiing area, the Carrabassett Valley Touring Center has some 52 miles of trails along old logging roads, through forests, down an old narrow-gauge railroad track, to a pond surrounded by hills and mountains, and around some condominiums at Sugarloaf. Lodgings are in cabins, condominiums, and motels nearby. Information: Carrabassett Valley Touring Center, Carrabassett Valley, ME 04947 (phone: 207-237-2205).

BERKSHIRES, around Lenox, Massachusetts: There are miles and miles of trails through the forests here, some in state parks, some at resorts, and some maintained by special touring centers. Country inns are like hotels with personality or else intimate resorts or house parties at somebody's exceptionally wonderful country home. You'll find a number of major touring centers with ski rental shops and special activities — some of them adjoining state forest lands that also have trails. For general information on the area, contact Berkshire Visitors Bureau, Berkshire Common, Plaza Level, Pittsfield, MA 01201 (phone: 800-237-5747, Northeast except Massachusetts; 413-443-9186, Massachusetts and rest of US.).

MT. WASHINGTON VALLEY, around North Conway, New Hampshire: Inns, a couple of ski centers, *Appalachian Mountain Club* (*AMC*), and the *Jackson Ski Touring Foundation* maintain over 150 miles of trails at the base of some of the highest peaks in the East. *The Jackson Ski Touring Center* has more than 90 miles of trails within the city limits, plus 24 miles maintained at the *Intervale Nordic Center* and additional trails at the *Whittaker Woods*. Most of the trails are groomed, which means that the snow has been compacted to form a uniform surface for skiing, and some are "groomed and tracked," meaning that a set of machine-molded depressions has been added to the snow surface. In addition, there are 40 miles of ungroomed trails. A large information booth in town tells ski tourers the current condition of virtually every trail mile, including descriptions of the easiest, more difficult, and most difficult terrain. Some curl through the valley, weaving between country inns and art galleries, shops, and quaint restaurants; some plunge into the forests. The most distinctive lodging is at the AMC's *Pinkham Notch Camp,* off by itself at the northern end of the valley, beloved of rugged outdoor types (although with thick wool blankets and freshly ironed sheets on the narrow bunk beds and shiny tile in the bathroom down the hall, it's not all that spartan). The AMC also maintains two backcountry huts (supply your own food and sleeping bag); reservations are required. Information: Appalachian Mountain Club, PO Box 298, Gorham, NH 03581 (phone: 603-466-2727); Mt. Washington Valley Chamber of Commerce, PO Box 385, North Conway, NH 03860 (phone: 603-356-3171).

ADIRONDACKS, around Lake Placid, New York: This 6-million-acre region offers some of the most varied touring in the eastern US; the area around the site of the 1980 Olympics at Lake Placid is one of its centers. The *Bark Eater* — a small country inn (Alstead Mill Rd., Keene, NY 12942; phone: 518-576-2221) — offers skiing on its own 9-mile trail system, rentals, and personalized lessons; guided wilderness ski tours, via a nearby trail, connect with the newly developed Adirondack Ski Touring Council's trail system. Rustic mountain lodge offering backcountry ski packages, workshops, seminars, lodge-to-lodge tours, rentals, and instruction (PO Box 867, Lake Placid, NY 12946; phone: 518-523-3441). Both systems connect with the 33 miles of set track at the Mt. Van Hoevenberg Cross-Country Center, where each trail has been very carefully designed to help skiers of varying ability levels perfect their skills. Various sections of the Northville–Lake Placid Trail, a famous wilderness hiking trail through the valleys between the two towns, are also suitable for cross-country skiing. For a free booklet describing them as well as others in the Adirondacks, write the New York Dept. of Environmental Conservation, 50 Wolf Rd., Albany, NY 12233-4255 (phone: 518-457-7433). Also contact the Lake Placid Chamber of Commerce, Olympic Arena, Lake Placid, NY 12946 (phone: 518-523-2445), or Olympic Regional Development Authority, Lake Placid, NY 12946 (phone: 518-523-1655).

NORTHEAST KINGDOM, Vermont: A still quiet, unspoiled section of the Green Mountain State, it is one of the US's up-and-coming ski touring areas. You can ski-tour through woods and fields, on old logging roads or unplowed secondary roads, or along hiking trails or hunting trails — as well as on a number of trails that are prepared and maintained as part of the ski touring at *Burke Mountain Recreation,* a downhill ski resort with a 35-mile cross-country trail network (PO Box 247, East Burke, VT 05832; phone: 802-626-3305). The *Inn on the Common,* a fancy, antiquey establishment on the green in one of those picture-postcard towns presided over by a white-steepled clapboard church (Craftsbury Common, VT 05827; phone: 802-586-9619), uses the extensive facilities — including over 30 miles of trails — at the 2½-mile-distant *Craftsbury Ski Center* (phone: 802-586-7767) as well as the network of 50 miles of groomed and tracked and 45 miles of worked wilderness trails that encompass the entire town.

STOWE, Vermont: The more-Austrian-than-in-Austria chalet that was always such an attraction of the *Trapp Family Lodge* (owned by the *Sound of Music* Trapp family) burned in 1980. But the Trapps never took setbacks lying down, and the cross-country ski center reopened within a week of the fire — much to the satisfaction of Stowe XC-ers: The center is the oldest in the US and one of the finest (Stowe 05672; phone: 802-253-8511, or 800-826-7000). Linking up with its 37 miles of especially well-groomed trails are the paths at prim and proper *Edson Hill Manor* (Stowe 05672; phone: 802-253-7371); those at the *Mt. Mansfield Touring Center* at the base of the alpine facilities; and 20 miles of trails at *Topnotch-at-Stowe,* a very fancy, well-done contemporary resort (Stowe 05672; phone: 802-253-8585 or 800-451-8686). Various other trails connect the Stowe network to the *Smugglers' Notch* ski area. Information: Stowe Area Assn., PO Box 1320A, Stowe, VT 05672 (phone: 802-253-7321; 800-24-STOWE for reservations).

INN-TO-INN XC, Vermont: Through the woods, fields, and high country, a car shuttle takes care of your luggage. *Country Inns Along the Trail* offers guided and self-guided trip packages that include accommodations, meals, car shuttles, and directions. *Vermont Voyageur Expeditions* offers guided tours. Individualized trips for those who wish to bicycle from inn to inn are available for a $40 trip fee. Both guided and self-guided hiking trips from inn to inn are also available. Information: Country Inns Along the Trail, c/o Churchill House Inn, RD 3, Box BTG, Brandon, VT 05733 (phone: 802-247-3300); Vermont Voyageur Expeditions, Montgomery Center, VT 05471 (phone: 802-326-4789).

MIDWEST

SUPERIOR NATIONAL FOREST, north of Duluth, Minnesota: Some of Minnesota's most concentrated touring opportunities are on the eastern edge of this vast forestland on the Canadian border. There are hundreds of miles of groomed and ungroomed trails in the forest, most of them maintained by ski clubs or the rustic lodges and inns of the region. Many are connected; the "Ski Thru" program lets you travel from inn to inn while the owners take care of your luggage. For a list of lodges and details, contact Minnesota Office of Tourism, Northeastern Region, 320 W. 2nd St., Room 707, Box 204, Duluth, MN 55805 (phone: 218-723-4692 or 800-62-NORTH outside Minnesota).

CHEQUAMEGON NATIONAL FOREST, Park Falls, Wisconsin: This north-central Wisconsin woodland has about 64 miles of mapped and marked loop trails, ranging in length from about 1 mile to about 10, designed primarily for cross-country skiers. But it's also possible to set out along hundreds of miles of unplowed roads or along the 60-mile section of the North Country National Scenic Trail that runs through the forest. This is a straight-line affair, but you can camp en route at Adirondack-style shelters; the scenery certainly warrants the efforts. Information: Chequamegon National Forest, 1170 S. 4th Ave., Park Falls, WI 54552 (phone: 715-762-2461).

WEST

LASSEN VOLCANIC NATIONAL PARK, Mineral, California: There are about 30 miles of trail marked for cross-country skiing around the park. It's also possible to ski on just about any of the 150 miles of hiking trails (with topography map and compass or guide) or to glide along the park roads (which aren't plowed or groomed). These features, along with a comfortable warming hut, make this an especially great place for a cross-country ski vacation. Cross-country rentals available at the Lassen Park Ski area. Open Fridays through Sundays including holidays; Wednesdays and Thursdays by reservation (phone: 916-595-3376; snow conditions, 916-595-4464). The trip through the deep pine woods to the Bumpass Hell thermal area — where mud pots and hot springs roar, bubble, and throw great clouds of warm steam into the cold air — is especially memorable. It's important to check with the park rangers upon entering. Information: Lassen Volcanic National Park Headquarters, PO Box 100, Mineral, CA 96063 (phone: 916-595-4444 or 916-595-3302).

SEQUOIA AND KINGS CANYON NATIONAL PARKS, near Visalia, California: *Sequoia Ski Touring*'s extensive trail network takes you through groves of the magnificent giant sequoia trees, across white-carpeted meadows, and to overlooks that give you wonderful vistas of the Sierra high country. Day long guided tours are available out of two centers. Information: Sequoia Ski Touring, Sequoia & Kings Canyon Guest Services, Sequoia National Park, CA 93262 (phone: 209-565-3435).

YOSEMITE NATIONAL PARK, Yosemite, California: The sequoias drown in the snow, the waterfalls freeze into fantastic sculptures, and everything sparkles. *Yosemite Mountaineering School* (phone: 209-372-1244; October to May) takes groups on easy overnight trips through just such wonderlands. Special clinics teach you touring, winter camping, touring survival, cross-country racing techniques, ice climbing — and how to handle that cross-country anathema, a real downhill run. The first weekend in March, the whole place is overrun for 2 days of anyone-can-do-it "citizens' races" and the Nordic Holiday Race. For lodgings, it is possible to book anything from the primitive cabins at *Curry Village* to the posh, high-ceilinged *Ahwahnee*. Information: Reservations Office, 5410 E. Home Ave., Fresno, CA 93727 (phone: 209-252-4848).

STEAMBOAT SPRINGS, Colorado: Some of the best tours in the state can be found around the *Scandinavian Lodge,* one of the country's first to emphasize cross-country skiing, and the *Steamboat Ski Touring Center;* Sven Wiik, the former US Olympic Nordic Team coach who set up both of them, knew what he was doing when he planned them. Especially on Rabbit Ears Pass, you've got the advantages of being up at 10,000 feet — the great views and November-to-May powder — and none of the steep pitches or, for that matter, avalanche danger. The lodge — where you'll eat Scandinavian favorites and après-ski in big public rooms decorated with the weavings and the pottery of Mrs. Sven Wiik — manages to stay low-key despite the fact that there's a downhill resort practically within schussing distance. Information: Scandinavian Lodge, PO Box 774484, Steamboat Springs, CO 80477 (phone: 303-879-0517; 800-233-8102, except Colorado and Hawaii).

VAIL, Colorado: The *Vail Cross Country Center,* directed by Jean Naumann, has been the focus of ski touring in the area; it now shares the spotlight with its companion resort 10 miles west, *Beaver Creek Cross Country Center;* both have complete ski schools. At Vail, there are easy marked and packed trails on the gentle terrain of a golf course east of town. Guides are available to take beginners through the aspen forests in the valley not far away, and to lead better skiers into the steep country up the valley to the high country of the White River National Forest for half- and full-day tours. At *Beaver Creek,* there's an 18-mile double machine set track with a skating lane at McCoy Park and a complete instruction and touring program. Rental equipment available at both locations. Information: Vail/Beaver Creek Cross Country Ski Centers, 458B Vail Valley Dr., PO Box 7, Vail, CO 81658 (phone: 303-476-5601, ext. 4380, or 303-949-5750, ext. 4312), and the Vail Resort Assn., 241 E. Meadow Dr., Vail, CO 81658 (phone: 303-476-5677, or 800-525-3875).

SUN VALLEY, Idaho: This is one place you don't have to climb to get to the high country: Helicopters take you up to the Douglas fir–covered mountains for trips to Boulder Basin or Corral Creek, or you can go on your own to the Pioneer Cabin near Hyndman Peak, where you can picnic in the sun. In addition there are some hundred miles of marked trails that you can do on your own or with guides. At *Elkhorn Resort,* with up to 150 annual inches of snow on 750 acres of trails, daily skiing in Sun Valley is an adventure for every level of skier. *Elkhorn* has its own cross-country ski tracks, providing skiing for the novice and the expert. Information: Nordic Ski Touring Center, Box 272, Sun Valley, ID 83353 (phone: 208-622-4111); Elkhorn Resort, PO Box 6009, Sun Valley, ID 83354 (phone: 208-622-4511 or 800-635-8261).

GRAND TETON NATIONAL PARK, near Jackson, Wyoming: There are miles and miles of touring in this park — along roads as well as on countless trails around and in the Jackson Hole Valley, with splendid views of the jagged-tooth mountains; up gentle hills and across frozen flatlands. More experienced skiers may register at park headquarters for trips into the canyons, up the steeper slopes, and through high-country tundra. *Flagg Ranch Village,* at the south entrance of nearby Yellowstone National Park, is open for lodging, meals, and cross-country skiing from December 15 to March 15. The Jackson Hole valley contains a handful of special cross-country ski areas, with lodges, restaurants, rentals, tours, and instruction. You can also find helicopter skiing through *High Mountains Helicopter Skiing* (PO Box 2217, Jackson, WY 83001; phone: 307-733-3274). Teton Pines and Spring Creek Ranch have good beginner terrain. Especially nifty and away-from-it-all is the *Togwotee Mountain Lodge,* on a pass about 45 miles from Jackson in the middle of some of the snowiest forests and meadows anywhere (PO Box 91, Moran, WY 83013; phone: 307-543-2847). With 25 miles of groomed, marked, and set track at its full-service cross-country ski area, Togwotee is now the largest cross-country ski area in Wyoming. The average yearly snowfall is 500-600 inches, and there is unlimited backcountry and telemark skiing in the surrounding Bridger-Teton National Forest (PO Box 1888, Jackson, WY 83001; phone: 307-733-2752) and the neighboring Teton Wilderness Area. Or you can stay in a sleek condominium in *Teton Village* at the base of Jackson Hole Ski Resort, 12 miles from town, which also has a cross-country touring center (Box 290, Teton Village, WY 83025; phone: 307-733-2292). And these organizations are only some of the options. Information: Jackson Hole Chamber of Commerce, PO Box E, Jackson, WY 83001 (phone: 307-733-3316); Grand Teton National Park, PO Drawer 170, Moose, WY 83012 (phone: 307-733-2880).

YELLOWSTONE NATIONAL PARK, Yellowstone, Wyoming: There's an otherworldly look to the place in winter — partly because of the clouds of steam rising from the flats almost everywhere, partly because of the overwhelming emptiness of it all: Geysers roar, fumaroles rumble, and blue pools mild as morning glories explode into showers of scalding water, without a soul to witness the spectacle. There are bison, Canada geese, and elk in such profusion that you stop noticing them after a while. You can make cross-country tours out of the *Old Faithful Snow Lodge* or *Mammoth Hot Springs* hotel in the northern section of the park. Rental snowmobiles are available to get you to more distant trailheads. Information: TW Recreational Services, Yellowstone National Park, WY 82190-0165 (phone: 307-344-7311).

The Best Tennis Vacations

Got some vacation time coming and want to work on your game? You can visit a camp or clinic, or just hole up at a resort with good tennis facilities and play away.

The 5-to-8-hour-a-day programs known as camps are particularly intensive. Usually held at colleges, private schools, or camps that cater to children in other seasons, they don't offer much in the way of accommodations, but there's always plenty of tennis. Cost for room, board, and instruction is about $90 per day. Clinics, usually held at hotels or resorts, are special weekend or week-long programs with instruction provided by the establishment's own pros or by visiting experts. Clinics may cost $30 to $100 per day more than camps.

But in either case you're guaranteed a certain number of hours of court time every day. At the beginning of the program you're graded, grouped with others of similar ability, and then worked — hard — by instructors who drive you like boot camp drill sergeants. Usually you tackle one stroke at a time. First there will be a demonstration, then simple hitting drills, then more complicated hitting drills in which the stroke is made part of a more complex sequence of moves. You'll end each day with varying degrees of sunburn, blisters, and sore muscles. (One New York jogger arrived at his camp feeling smug and fit; he ended his first day so bushed he could hardly focus on his *Times.*) How successful the course is will depend on where you start. Intermediates who want to add some muscle and bite to their game probably will. But beginners won't leave ready to challenge Ivan Lendl.

Resorts are probably the most relaxing places to spend a tennis vacation. Sign up for a couple of lessons, play tennis when you want, and use the resort's saunas, whirlpool baths, swimming pools, golf courses, and activity programs the rest of the time. In other than clinic situations it's often true that larger resorts catering to groups attract so many beginners that advanced players may be bored; that older, more established resorts attract more advanced players and may not be much fun for beginners; and that a high courts-to-rooms ratio and the presence of a tennis host who arranges games usually means that the tennis program is well enough organized that you won't spend all your time waiting around for a court.

Find out where the resort you're considering fits into this scheme. Also look into the court situation. How many are there, and what kind? How many are lighted? (In some areas, it's just too hot to play during the day.) Can you reserve courts? How far in advance? Can you do it on the phone or must you present yourself in person? Is there any limit to how long you can play? And if you're not taking your own partner, is it easy to scare up a game?

For a complete and up-to-date list of clinics and camps, check the annual January issue of *Tennis* ($1.75 from *Tennis* magazine, 5520 Park Ave., PO Box 395, Trumbull, CT 06611; phone: 203-373-7000). For tennis resorts, see *Tennis*'s annual November listing of the US's 50 greatest or its annual February treatment of places to play.

Described below are some good bets for a first-rate tennis vacation.

TENNIS CLINICS

These organizations sponsor clinics and camps at a number of resorts, schools, and college campuses. Each outfit has its own teaching style and methods.

RAMEY TENNIS SCHOOLS: Based in Owensboro, Kentucky, this organization puts on spring and summer clinics for youth and adults in stroke development and, for better players, tournament camps and competitive play and drill programs at the college campus in Valparaiso, Indiana, as well as at Springfield, Ohio, and at the corporate headquarters in Owensboro. Adult weekend programs and ladies-only programs are held at an indoor club, with deluxe hotel housing, in Owensboro. There are junior "tournament camps" at Valparaiso and Owensboro. One of the unique features of the program at the headquarters is that campers are housed in cottages on a 100-acre working farm and have home-cooked, farm-fresh food. The cottages are used off-season for bed-and-breakfast guests. Computer stroke charting and videotape analyses are other special features. Information: Ramey Tennis Schools, 5931 Ky. 56, Owensboro, KY 42301 (phone: 502-771-5590 or 502-771-4723).

VAN DER MEER TENNIS CENTER: Billie Jean King's onetime coach Dennis Van der Meer, one of the most knowledgeable and influential of the nation's teaching pros, personally supervises programs for players at all skill levels at his Hilton Head Island, South Carolina, headquarters. Programs are also conducted at Sweet Briar, Virginia; Gray Rocks Inn, Canada; Lake Ozark, Missouri; and in California as well as Europe and Asia. Information: Van Der Meer Tennis Center, PO Box 5902, Hilton Head Island, SC 29938 (phone: 803-785-9602 in South Carolina; 800-845-6138 elsewhere).

ALL AMERICAN SPORTS: Adult programs emphasizing strategy and stroke development, and featuring intensive drill sessions and liberal use of video replay equipment and ball machines, are offered at resorts in Scottsdale, Arizona; Boulder, Colorado; Amelia Island, Orlando, and Naples, Florida; Kona, Hawaii; Hancock, Massachusetts; Windham, New York; Stowe, Vermont; plus one in Loreto, Mexico, and three in the Caribbean. Participants may opt for anywhere from 2 to 4 hours of court work per day. On the other hand, at the camp in Amherst, Massachusetts, the tennis program is very intensive, with five hours of instruction daily. Information: All American Sports, 116 Radio Circle, Mt. Kisco, NY 10549 (phone: 914-666-0096 in New York; 800-223-2442 elsewhere).

JOHN GARDINER'S: The celebrated ranches in Scottsdale, Arizona, and Carmel Valley, California, have spawned a new tennis clinic at Teton Pines Resort, Jackson, Wyoming, and a junior summer camp in Sun Valley, Idaho. The method has you hitting lots of balls under the supervision of well-trained and well-disciplined instructors who hammer the basics into you as you hammer balls. Information: John Gardiner's Tennis, 5700 E. McDonald Dr., Scottsdale, AZ 85253-5268 (phone: 602-948-2100).

TENNIS RESORTS

EAST

MT. WASHINGTON, Bretton Woods, New Hampshire: This classic grand resort, housed in an turn-of-the-century, white Edwardian structure, gives you spectacular views into the Presidential Range of the White Mountains. Private and group lessons (some using video) are available, and facilities include 12 clay courts; court reservations are possible. Information: Mt. Washington Hotel, Bretton Woods, NH 03575 (phone: 603-278-1000).

WATERVILLE VALLEY, Waterville Valley, New Hampshire: Condominiums and country inns, snuggled in the White Mountain National Forest, popular with families. Facilities: clinics and private instruction; 18 clay courts and 2 indoor courts; court reservations possible. Also pools, horseback riding, golf, a summer music festival, a health/fitness spa, a new 5-building retail and commercial center, with 37 shops and 7 restaurants. Information: Waterville Valley Resort, Waterville Valley, NH 03215 (phone: 603-236-8371).

CONCORD, Kiamesha Lake, New York: With 1,200 rooms scattered through several high-rise hotel structures on 4,000 acres in the Catskills, this place is like a city — but you can play all winter long. Facilities: 40 Latexite courts, 16 of them indoor and open 24 hours a day; ball machines and other teaching aids; courts available by reservation only; private and group lessons. Information: The Concord, Kiamesha Lake, NY 12751 (phone: 914-794-4000, ext. 1655; 800-431-3850).

TOPNOTCH-AT-STOWE, Stowe, Vermont: An elegant, modern resort. Facilities: All-American Sports clinics; 4 courts indoors, and 10 out; reservations possible. Information: Topnotch-At-Stowe, PO Box 1260, Stowe, VT 05672 (phone: 802-253-8585 or 800-451-8686).

STRATTON, Stratton Mountain, Vermont: Tennis is booming at Stratton Mountain Resort, with 19 courts available: 2 Plexi-Cushion indoors and 17 outdoors (9 Har-Tru, 2 red clay, and 6 Deco-Turf II). The *Stratton Mountain Inn* itself is a modern, renovated 125-room ski and summer resort. Featuring the Stratton Teaching Method, the tennis school offers instruction for all ability levels. Available in 2-day weekend and 5-day midweek programs from May through mid-September, this school matches students of similar skills and concentrates on stroke instruction through videotaping and drills. The Stratton tennis package includes use of the Stratton Sports Center, court privileges, and complimentary lunch. The sports center is the site of the Volvo International Tennis Tournament. Information: Stratton Mountain Resort, Stratton Mountain, VT 05155 (phone: 802-297-2200).

SUGARBUSH INN, Warren, Vermont: A gracious yet casual country inn in the heart of the Green Mountains. The food is wonderful, and facilities include 11 courts (5 clay, 6 Har-Tru); video replay and ball machines; and private instruction and clinics. Reservations possible. Information: Sugarbush Inn, Warren, VT 05674 (phone: 802-583-2301; 800-451-4320 for reservations).

GREENBRIER, White Sulphur Springs, West Virginia: One of the few turn-of-the-century resorts that hasn't lost even a little of its class. Facilities: 20 courts — 15 Har-Tru outdoors, 5 air conditioned Dynaturf courts indoors; private lessons and clinics. See also *Resort Hotels.* Information: Greenbrier, White Sulphur Springs, WV 24986 (phone: 304-536-1110; 800-624-6070).

SOUTH

AMELIA ISLAND PLANTATION, Amelia Island, Florida: This 1,250-acre development offers terrific beaches, wonderful subtropical forest scenery, plenty of peace and quiet, and facilities outstanding enough to have put the place on *Tennis* magazine's list of America's top 50 tennis resorts. You'll find 25 clay composition courts (3 lighted), 2 Deco-Turf hard courts, 4 Omni courts, video replay and ball machines, clinics by All American Sports, and private and group lessons. Court reservations are available. See also *Golf* and *Beaches.* Information: Amelia Island Plantation, Hwy. A1A, Amelia Island, FL 32034 (phone: 904-261-6161 or 800-874-6878).

GRENELEFE, Grenelefe, Florida: A four-star, four-diamond, 1,000-acre resort development in the pines and citrus country a half-hour southwest of Walt Disney World. The tennis facilities and services include 21 courts (9 Har-Tru, 5 Laykold, 11 lighted); videotape and ball machines; and clinics and private lessons. In addition, it offers a range of activities guaranteed to divert even a tennis fanatic: three 18-hole golf courses; five swimming pools; 6,400-acre Lake Marion, with its full-service marina; saunas and Jacuzzis; bike rentals and jogging trails. Information: Grenelefe Resort and Conference Center, 3200 State Rd. 546, Grenelefe, FL 33844-9732 (phone: 800-237-9549; 800-282-7875 in Florida).

SHERATON ROYAL BISCAYNE BEACH, Key Biscayne, Florida: The courts at this tropical island resort, off the Miami shore, draw locals as well as vacationers; you can almost always find a tennis partner. Facilities: 10 Laykold courts (4 lighted); video replay and ball machines; court reservations necessary; private and group lessons. Information: Sheraton Royal Biscayne, 555 Ocean Dr., Key Biscayne, FL 33149 (phone: 305-361-5775 or 800-325-3535).

DORAL, Miami, Florida: A veritable city of a resort, this ultra-posh establishment on a 2,400-acre estate offers just about any diversion (including five 18-hole championship golf courses and one 9-hole course) that you could ask for, except a beach of its own. But there's one just 15 minutes away at its sister property, the *Doral Ocean Beach Resort,* not to mention a swimming pool, fishable lakes, 3 restaurants, and a cocktail lounge with dancing. Tennis facilities: 15 well-kept clay and hard-surface courts; backboard and ball machines; court reservations available; tennis hostess; private and group lessons. Arthur Ashe is director of tennis. See also *Golf.* Information: The Doral Resort & Country Club, 4400 N.W. 87th Ave., Miami, FL 33178 (phone: 305-592-2000 in Florida; 800-327-6334 elsewhere).

INNISBROOK, Tarpon Springs, Florida: Near the famous sponge market, a thousand acres of pine woods, citrus groves, moss-hung cypress trees, lots of golf, and 1,000 condo suites make this quite a big place — but it's well managed and friendly all the same. Facilities: 18 courts — 11 Har-Tru, 7 Laykold — 7 lighted; video replay and ball machines; backboards; court reservations possible; clinics, and private and group lessons. Home of Terry Addisen's *Australian Tennis Institute.* Information: Innisbrook, PO Drawer 1088, Tarpon Springs, FL 34688-1088 (phone: 813-942-2000; 800-456-2000).

HILTON HEAD, South Carolina: Along with its stunning white beaches, quietly elegant villas, homes, and marinas, and subtropical forests, this island also has lots of tennis. You'll find most of it at two resorts: the *Palmetto Dunes* and the *Sea Pines Vacation Resorts. Palmetto Dunes* has 25 courts, 19 of them clay and 6 of them lighted, and offers *Rod Laver Tennis* clinics in addition to private and group instruction; the emphasis is on the Australian method, which brought up so many great players of Laver's generation. At *Sea Pines* — the largest tennis-oriented resort in the world — there are 43 courts (most Har-Tru) clustered primarily in three locations, each a short distance from the beach; shopping; restaurants; and swimming pools. Private lessons are available if you don't want to join one of the resort's own impressive roster of tennis clinics, which include a "Tiny Tots" program for children aged four to seven (life-size cartoon characters are incorporated into the drills), and clinics that focus on singles and doubles strategy, the contact point, preparation, and the like. There are full-time tennis hostesses at both resorts and almost daily round-robin tourneys for players of all ages and skill levels. The difference is mainly a matter of style and layout: *Sea Pines* is big, spread out enough that you need at least a bike to get around, whereas at the smaller *Palmetto Dunes* (with also a *Hyatt Regency* and the *Mariner's Inn*), nearly everything is within walking distance. Information: Palmetto Dunes, PO Box 5606, Hilton Head Island, SC 29938 (phone: 803-785-7300 or 803-785-1161 in South Carolina; 800-845-6130 elsewhere); and the Rod Laver Tennis Center, PO Box 4798, Hilton Head Island, SC 29938 (phone: 803-785-1152 in South Carolina; 800-845-6130 elsewhere); or Sea Pines Vacation Resorts, PO Box 7000, Hilton Head Island, SC 29938 (phone: 803-785-3333 in South Carolina; 800-845-6131 elsewhere).

WORLD OF TENNIS AT LAKEWAY, Austin, Texas: Townhouses cluster around the groups of courts in the Texas hill country. Facilities include 26 Laykold courts — 12 lighted, 2 indoors; reservations necessary. Private lessons and clinics as well as health club facilities are available. Information: World of Tennis at Lakeway, One World of Tennis Sq., Austin, TX 78738 (phone: 512-261-6000 or 800-LAKEWAY).

JOHN NEWCOMBE'S TENNIS RANCH, New Braunfels, Texas: Quiet and unpretentious — but the video replays are in color. At John Newcombe's home base, where he appears five or six times yearly, you lodge in comfortable condos or motel rooms. Facilities: 24 Laykold courts — 8 lighted and 4 covered; video replay; practice alleys; many clinics. Information: John Newcombe's Tennis Ranch, PO Box 469, New Braunfels, TX 78130 (phone: 512-625-9105; 800-292-7080 in Texas; 800-262-NEWK elsewhere).

MIDWEST

FRENCH LICK SPRINGS, French Lick, Indiana: This venerable resort in the hills of the southern part of the state, once *the* spot to sip mineral waters and take a cure and the first place in America where a chef served tomato juice, is now doing a booming business in conventions, golf — and tennis. Facilities include 18 courts — 8 indoor, 10 outdoors, all lighted — ball machines, and video aids. Court reservations possible; some limits may apply. Private and group lessons. Information: French Lick Springs, French Lick, IN 47432 (phone: 812-935-9381).

BOYNE MOUNTAIN LODGE, Boyne Falls, Michigan: A complex of villas, chalets, and lodges in the northern Michigan hills that caters to skiers in winter and to golfers and tennis players in summer. Tennis at *Boyne Mountain* and *Boyne Highlands* is now under the direction of Peter Burwash International. The tennis program was originally designed by the Laver organization, and *Tennis Digest* magazine rated it among the top 50 private tennis facilities in the country. Tennis weeks and weekends are scheduled May through September. Facilities: 12 Laykold courts; ball machines; reservations possible; clinics and private lessons. Information: Boyne Mountain Lodge, Boyne Falls, MI 49713 (phone: 616-549-2441).

WEST

ARIZONA BILTMORE, Phoenix, Arizona: This ultra-posh, large-scale, superstar resort is well known for the fact that the gold leaf dining room ceiling, the glass mural in the lobby, and the texture of the walls in the lobby were all inspired by or based on the designs of Frank Lloyd Wright; the tile-bottomed Olympic-sized swimming pool compares favorably to the no-holds-barred paradise at San Simeon. Facilities include 17 Plexipave courts (15 lighted); plus video replay and ball machines; reservations possible; private lessons and clinics. Information: Arizona Biltmore, PO Box 2290, Phoenix, AZ 85002 (phone: 602-955-6600; 800-528-3696 outside Arizona).

JOHN GARDINER'S, Scottsdale, Arizona: Some people call this Papa Bear of the tennis world the most complete and professional training establishment in the world — and there's good reason for that. Facilities and services include 22 Plexipave outdoor courts and 2 Omni courts; video replay and ball machines (plus other instructional aids); tennis clinics; private lessons; complimentary court time for guests. You can lodge in small casitas or in three- or four-bedroom casas, some with their own pool and court; the court at the Casa Rosewall is on the roof. Champagne on the house when it rains. Information: John Gardiner's Tennis Ranch, 5700 E. McDonald Dr., Scottsdale, AZ 85253-5268 (phone: 602-948-2100; 800-245-2051 for reservations).

LA COSTA, Carlsbad, California: This super-spa, a favorite among stars of all stripes, has equally well developed tennis facilities: 23 hard-surface courts (17 grass, 4 clay, 5 lighted); ball machines; reservations recommended; private lessons by members of a pro staff headed by Pancho Segura. Information: La Costa, Costa Del Mar Rd., Carlsbad, CA 92009 (phone: 619-438-9111 or 800-854-5000).

JOHN GARDINER'S, Carmel Valley, California: Luxurious. The first *Gardiner* ranch is still the ultimate tennis resort; and Gardiner himself is on hand with his team of top instructors to take care of the 28 guests who can be accommodated at any given time in the week-long clinic programs (offered April through November). There are 14 Plexipave courts and computerized ball machines. Information: John Gardiner's Tennis Ranch, PO Box 228, Carmel Valley, CA 93924 (phone: 408-659-2207).

VIC BRADEN TENNIS COLLEGE, Coto de Caza, California: The licensed psychologist and tennis ace whom no less than Jack Kramer called the greatest tennis teacher in the world holds forth here, delivering pre-drill lectures that some stand-up comics would envy. ("Get to know your navel." "Air your armpits.") The facilities are equally impressive: 16 concrete courts — all lighted; ball machines; specially designed hitting lanes; a tall teaching tower and video screening rooms; and a huge array of newfangled teaching devices. Classroom lectures are also part of the program. Information: Vic Braden Tennis College, 1 Coto de Caza Dr., Coto de Caza, CA 92679 (phone: 714-581-2990; 800-CALL-VIC in California; 800-42-COURT elsewhere).

SUN VALLEY, Idaho: Guests at the *Sun Valley Inn,* the *Sun Valley Lodge,* and condominiums in Sun Valley and in *Elkhorn* (the smaller resort community a mile away) have access to more than 50 Laykold courts. *Elkhorn* offers year-round tennis to guests, with clinics and lessons conducted by a staff of professional instructors. Reservations are available, as are videotaping and closed-circuit TV facilities. Information: Elkhorn Resort at Sun Valley, PO Box 6009, Sun Valley, ID 83350 (phone: 208-622-4511 or 800-635-9356), and Sun Valley Co., Sun Valley Rd., Sun Valley, ID 83353 (phone: 208-622-4111; 800-632-4104 in Idaho; 800-635-8261 elsewhere).

Golf: The Greening of America

 Golf can be a most frustrating sport for travelers in America, especially those who've spent any appreciable time in front of a television set watching the pros cavort in all their glory on some of the world's finest courses. Not only are the courses attractive to the point of distraction, but seeing them so temptingly displayed only heightens their allure.

One would think that the willingness to travel to each course's locale would permit a golfer to satisfy his or her fondest longings. Not so. The fact is that only about half a dozen of the golf courses listed by *Golf Digest* magazine among the country's top 50 are open for public play on any regular basis, and tourists don't do that much better with the rest.

Nonetheless, there are still a host of top courses that are open to traveling players.

What follows is a list of a few of those that are truly worth traveling a significant distance to experience.

EAST

TACONIC, Williamstown, Massachusetts: One of the least-known championship courses in the US, in the northwest corner of Massachusetts. Though it is the home of the Williams College golf team and the preferred turf of an active membership, it is open to transient players on weekdays (except from noon to 1:30) and on weekend and holiday afternoons after 1 PM. Especially on a fall afternoon, with the leaves just turning on the trees covering the beautiful Berkshire hills, this landscape is right out of America's past, although the very real teeth of this course are apparent in any season. Information: Taconic Golf Club, PO Box 183, Meacham St., Williamstown, MA 01267 (phone: 413-458-3997).

CONCORD, Kiamesha Lake, New York: One of the very best courses in the country is part of the three-course *Concord* resort hotel complex on Kiamesha Lake in the Catskill Mountains. It is a track well worth its nickname, "the Monster." It is nearly unconscionably long and almost intolerably difficult, and that's probably why great numbers of masochistic golfers from New York City and points north trudge up to its first tee every weekend. These crowds usually include a number of Japanese players (the most avid, most polite, and sometimes, it seems, most painstakingly slow golfers in the world), so you should plan your own assault for a weekday. Information: The Concord, Kiamesha Lake, NY 12751 (phone: 914-794-4000; 800-431-3850).

HERSHEY, Hershey, Pennsylvania: It's difficult to take seriously a course so close to Cocoa and East Chocolate Avenues, but that doesn't change the fact that the two courses at the *Hershey Country Club* are among the best in the Northeast. The West course is especially challenging. Chocolate freaks may find the scent in the air a bit distracting, but no one can quarrel with the quality of the golfing challenge. Information: Hershey Country Club, 1100 E. Derry Rd., Hershey, PA 17033 (phone: 717-533-2360).

HOMESTEAD, Hot Springs, Virginia: Three superior courses are the focus of attention at this magnificently kept dowager of a hotel, and the fact that the redoubtable Sam Snead makes his home nearby gives you an idea of just how good they are. The *Cascades* course, a couple of miles from the *Homestead*'s front door, is the best of the trio of tracks; it hosted the 1988 USGA National Amateur tournament. The newer *Lower Cascades* course is longer. The *Homestead Golf Course*, built in 1892 and but a nine-iron from the front door of the *Homestead*, is Virginia's oldest course and one of America's oldest as well. Information: The Homestead, Hot Springs, VA 24445 (phone: 703-839-5500).

GREENBRIER, White Sulphur Springs, West Virginia: Anyone who regularly attends any sort of meeting or seminar will inevitably trip over the immense, elegant *Greenbrier;* but golfers tend to look forward to these conferences with particular relish. The resort's trio of golf courses provide a more than adequate variety of play. A special attention-getter is the lavish buffet lunch served every day in season in the clubhouse — oh, those peach halves with the freshly whipped cream! See also *Resort Hotels.* Information: The Greenbrier, White Sulphur Springs, WV 24986 (phone: 304-536-1110; 800-624-6070).

SOUTH

AMELIA ISLAND PLANTATION, Amelia Island, Florida: Golf is just one of the many activities to be pursued here, and it is quite a challenge. The courses are a definite contrast in styles. The original 27-hole layout, designed by Pete Dye in 1972, is composed of three nines, none of which stretches much more than 3,000 yards from the regular men's tees. But golfers must contend with overhanging trees, narrow fairways, and small greens perched along salt marsh or tucked behind sand dunes. At Amelia's second layout, the *Long Point Club,* golfers will find as much water as terra firma. Still, the George Fazio design is one of the best anywhere, and was recently rated so by *Golf Digest.* See also *Beaches* and *Tennis.* Information: Amelia Island Plantation, Highway A1A, Amelia Island, FL 32034 (phone: 904-261-6161 or 800-874-6878).

WALT DISNEY WORLD, Lake Buena Vista, Florida: Veteran golfers seldom consider this resort complex for their vacations, but this ambitious attempt to be all things to all people has three courses right on the resort complex grounds. The 7,190-yard *Magnolia* was named for the 1,000 magnolia trees scattered around its lakes and elevated tees; the 6,967-yard *Palm* is rated among the nation's most challenging golf tests. There's also the 6,706-yard *Lake Buena Vista* club course. The trio hosts the Walt Disney World/Oldsmobile Golf Classic, a $600,000 PGA event, each October. Added attractions include the Golf Studio instructional program and the courses' relative removal from the frenzy of the park proper: it's not unusual for the adults in a Walt Disney World vacation group to hide out on one of the courses while their youngsters try to bring the Magic Kingdom to its knees. Having succeeded, the kids may then try their luck with the 6-hole *Wee Links,* designed to introduce the junior set to the game. Information: Walt Disney World Central Reservations, PO Box 10100, Lake Buena Vista, FL 32830-0100 (phone: 407-824-8000).

DORAL, Miami, Florida: At the moment, this 650-room resort stands like the grand dame of the Miami–Miami Beach tourist axis. But the *Doral's* superb golf facilities (five championship 18-hole layouts, plus an executive course) thus far remain unassailed, and the fabled *Blue Monster* is still the most formidable challenge in the state. It is the site of the annual $1-million Doral-Ryder Open, and the *Gold Course* offers little diminution in challenge. Touring pro: Peter Jacobsen. Information: The Doral Resort & Country Club, 4400 NW 87th Ave., Miami, FL 33178 (phone: 305-592-2000 in Florida; 800-327-6334 elsewhere).

GRAND CYPRESS, Orlando, Florida: Completed in 1984, this Jack Nicklaus course at the *Grand Cypress* resort somehow transcends its relatively flat terrain by creating dunelike rough on which high grass grows; the sense of playing in a Scottish environment is inescapable. Perhaps the most notable design element of the landscape is the number of two-tiered fairways. These unusual hazards make position play all important and add a new dimension to a round here. Double greens are another unusual aspect. The *New Course* adds 18 holes to the original 27. It's a pity that access to the course is currently restricted to hotel guests only. Information: Grand Cypress Golf Club, 1 N. Jacaranda, Orlando, FL 32819 (phone: 407-239-4700).

SAWGRASS OCEANSIDE, Ponte Vedra Beach, Florida: For 5 years this was the site of the Tournament Players Championship, and anyone who watched Jack Nicklaus pump a couple of drives into the drink during the 1979 installment knows that this is one of the premier places to play. In 1987, the *Oceanside* course hosted the Mazda Senior TPC. When the wind blows here, the task can be all but impossible. You also have the opportunity to make the experience as difficult as you choose, for two of the three 9s (the *East* and *West* courses, which made up the original 18 here) have four sets of tees from which one can play. It's one of the South's toughest golf tests. Membership is required for use of the *Sawgrass* facilities, although it is possible to obtain limited temporary access by staying at the *Marriott at Sawgrass* hotel. Information: Marriott at Sawgrass, Ponte Vedra Beach, FL 32082 (phone: 800-872-7248 or 904-285-7777).

TOURNAMENT PLAYERS CLUB, Ponte Vedra Beach, Florida: This may well be Pete Dye's consummate masterpiece. The 17th hole became a classic in 1982 after the first professional tournament here, and it remains one of the most famous holes in golf. It won't treat you any more kindly, so bring enough golf balls when you attempt to conquer the sculptured fairways and unkindly undulating greens. It's not likely that you'll score very well, but it's a comfort to know the pros do only a little better. The Valley Course, also designed by Pete Dye, with Jerry Pate as PGA Tour Player Consultant, opened in October 1987. The Senior Tournament Players Championship was held on this challenging layout in both 1988 and 1989. A private club owned and operated by the PGA Tour and hosting two major PGA tour events, The Players Championship and the Senior Players Championship, this establishment allows resort guests and visiting golfers to play the courses through reasonably priced associate memberships and guest fees. It is also possible to gain access by staying at the *Marriott at Sawgrass* hotel. Information: Tournament Players Club at Sawgrass, 110 TPC Blvd., Ponte Vedra Beach, FL 32082 (phone: 904-285-3301).

SEA ISLAND, St. Simons Island, Georgia: This is only the most important part of the 10,000-acre resort complex known as the *Cloister*. The 36 holes of golf (divided into four distinct nines) all have ocean views, and the landscape is dominated by magnolias and pampas grass. The *Seaside* nine is probably the most challenging of the available four, which may be played in any order or combination. The neighboring *St. Simons Island Club*, which has its own 18-hole course and a low country–style clubhouse, is also a part of the *Cloister* complex. Information: The Cloister, Sea Island, GA 31561 (phone: 912-638-3611).

PINEHURST, Pinehurst, North Carolina: There is no golf community in the US more devoted to the game than *Pinehurst*. Non-golfers often can't grasp what all the hushed reverence is about, but believers happily play two rounds a day on the seven courses here, visit the PGA Golf Hall of Fame in between rounds, and attend golf clinics at the *Pinehurst* hotel after dinner. Donald Ross's *Pinehurst #2*, named among the top ten courses of the world by leading golf publications, is the class of the circuits here; George and Tom Fazio built a tough but scenic #6. A #7 course, designed by Rees Jones, opened in 1986. Instruction is also available. See also *Resort Hotels*. Information: Pinehurst Hotel and Country Club, PO Box 4000, Pinehurst, NC 28374 (phone: 800-672-4644 in North Carolina, 800-334-9560 elsewhere).

HARBOUR TOWN, Hilton Head Island, South Carolina: Golfers have long known what the general public is just discovering: This island, the second largest (after New York's Long Island) among the East Coast's barrier chain, holds some of the country's best resort terrain. Golfers have their choice of two dozen courses; but the magnet is usually the *Harbour Town Golf Links*, part of the marvelous *Sea Pines Resorts* development (see *Beaches; Tennis*) and the site of the annual PGA MCI Heritage Classic. With a whopping course rating of 74 — one of the highest in the country — its difficulty needs no elaboration. Only the laid-back environment provides some small salve to soaring scores. Designed by Pete Dye with Jack Nicklaus consulting; Dye is our personal choice for the game's most creative craftsman, and his talent and handiwork are nowhere better displayed. Information: Harbour Town Golf Links, Sea Pines Plantation, Hilton Head Island, SC 29928 (phone: 800-671-2446 in South Carolina; 800-845-6131 elsewhere).

WILD DUNES, Isle of Palms, South Carolina: Although this is a very nice, very pretty, 1,600-acre golf and beach resort, its golf course is, as its name implies, wild. Off the fairways, the course has a deliberately scruffy, unkempt look, as if it had been out very late the night before. And it is full of topographical surprises. No two holes are quite the same. There's one (#14) that is built around an ancient oak, thought to be the fateful tree in Edgar Allan Poe's short story "The Gold Bug," and a pair of finishing holes that play nip and tuck with the Atlantic. Accommodations are equally diverse; guests can choose from private villas and cottages with porch views of fairways, marshes, lagoons, tennis courts, marina, or the ocean. Information: Wild Dunes, Box 388, Isle of Palms, SC 29451 (phone: 800-845-8880).

WEST

THE BOULDERS, Carefree, Arizona: Of the three 9-hole courses at this former Rockresort, which opened in 1985, the *Boulders'* nine is the most scenic and challenging. The green of #1 is set in an amphitheater of boulders, while the tee at #2 is at the very foot of a sheer, high, boulder-strewn hill. Each hole of the *Saguaro* nine offers four sets of tees, and the combination of the *Saguaro and Boulders* nines provides the opportunity to play a course of 6,851 yards from the professional tees — though only the longest-hitting, lowest-handicap players should attempt this feat. The *Lake* nine has had a substantial face-lift, making it consistent with the dramatic desert look that makes the other two courses so fascinating. See also *Resort Hotels.* Information: The Boulders, PO Box 2090, Carefree, AZ 85377 (phone: 602-488-9009).

THE WIGWAM, Litchfield Park, Arizona: In a state that is rapidly becoming one of the golfing centers of the nation, none is better than the *Gold Course,* one of a trio of courses at this Phoenix-area resort, operated by the Suncor Development Company. See also *Resort Hotels.* Information: The Wigwam, PO Box 278, Litchfield Park, AZ 85340 (phone: 602-935-3811).

SCOTTSDALE PRINCESS, Scottsdale, Arizona: A lovely setting for the *Stadium Course* of the Tournament Players Club of Scottsdale, adjacent to the impressive *Desert Course.* Both were designed by the team of Weiskopf, Morrish, and Twitty and are operated to the high standards of the PGA Tour. The 7,038-year, par 71 PGA-TPC *Stadium* is the site of the annual Phoenix Open PGA Tour event. The *Desert Course* is a challenging 6,589-yard, par 71. There is also a full-service pro shop. See also *Resort Hotels.* Information: Scottsdale Princess, 7575 E. Princess Dr., Scottsdale, AZ 85255 (phone: 602-585-4848; 800-255-0080).

LOEW'S VENTANA CANYON, Tucson, Arizona: Designed by Tom Fazio to blend easily with the natural surroundings, the course here is both a work of art and a stiff challenge. Golfers will find greens tucked against whaleback rocks as well as high grounds that provide 100-mile views south into Mexico. The front nine leads a player through the beautiful Esperero Canyon; down the #1 handicap, par 5, 552-yard 7th hole; to the challenging 9th hole, with its sweeping "hidden" green. The *pièce de résistance,* however, is the 18th, likely to become the signature hole of the resort. The approach shot on this par 5 must carry a gulley and land softly on a green with water guarding the right side. Behind it, a waterfall gently gushes. See also *Resort Hotels.* Information: Loew's Ventana Canyon Resort, 7000 Resort Dr., Tucson, AZ 85715 (phone: 602-299-2020 or 800-234-5117).

LA COSTA, Carlsbad, California: At this famous Southern California hotel and health spa, Dick Wilson and Joe Lee created courses that bedevil even the pros, so you'll probably welcome the opportunity to repair to the steamroom after your first foray. There are a total of 36 holes now. Information: La Costa, Costa Del Mar Rd., Carlsbad, CA 92009 (phone: 619-438-9111 or 800-854-5000).

TORREY PINES, La Jolla, California: San Diego is the golfing capital of Southern California, with nearly six dozen public courses to satisfy its golf-crazed citizenry. The best of these is the course at *Torrey Pines* (where the San Diego Open tournament is held every year), and both the *North and South* courses are worth attention. Information: Torrey Pines Inn, 11480 N. Torrey Pines Rd., La Jolla, CA 92037 (phone: 619-453-4420 for lodging and golf packages; call the starters, 619-453-0380, for golf course information).

PEBBLE BEACH GOLF LINKS, Pebble Beach, California: If there is a leading contender for the title of Most Photographed Golf Course, it has to be the ocean-hugging *Pebble Beach Golf Links* on the windswept Monterey Peninsula. This is one of the rare instances where a truly first class US tournament track is actually accessible to the public, and it's an opportunity not to be missed. Information: Pebble Beach Golf Links, Seventeen Mile Dr., Pebble Beach, CA 93953 (phone: 408-624-3811).

SPYGLASS HILL, Pebble Beach, California: Just 2 miles from *Pebble Beach Golf Links* and considered so difficult that even the touring pros complain about it. But tromping through the local plants is a botanical education in itself. Information: Spyglass Hill, Pebble Beach, CA 93953 (phone: 408-624-3811).

KEYSTONE, Keystone, Colorado: At first glance, *Keystone Ranch* looks like something out of a John Wayne movie — and it is. The first class golf course, opened in 1980, is laid out on a 9,300-foot plateau framed by snow-capped peaks; several holes run around old ranch buildings, while some are tree-lined like those at Hilton Head; water hazards resemble those at Pebble Beach, and the overall design bears a similarity to Pine Valley's. The *Keystone Resort* has fine condominium and hotel facilities. Perhaps the greatest attraction of all is the thin air; you'll find your shots going considerably farther than at sea level. Information: Keystone Resort, Box 38, Keystone, CO 80435 (phone: 800-222-0188).

MAUNA KEA BEACH RESORT, Kamuela, Big Island of Hawaii, Hawaii: Part of the premier resort of the same name is built on lava flows that have somehow solidified to give the course a linksland character. This is a warm, arid corner of these islands, and much care (and water) is needed to keep the terrain green and true. The spectacular volcanic peak that gives the resort its name is the backdrop for nearly every shot, and the *Mauna Kea* fairways are among the most scenic in the world. See also *Resort Hotels.* Information: Mauna Kea Beach Resort, PO Box 218, Hwy. 90, Kamuela, HI 96743 (phone: 808-882-7222; 800-228-3000).

MAUNA LANI BAY, Kohala Coast, Big Island of Hawaii, Hawaii: Built atop jagged black lava flows, using thousands of tons of imported topsoil, this is considered one of the most beautiful courses in the islands. Oceanfront hole #6 has perhaps the most dramatic setting, including a 199-yard clifftop carry over a small bay. Beauty aside, the course provides a true test of golfing skill. Hazards range from the conventional complement of sand traps to huge lava boulders that evoke images of Japanese gardens. Information: Mauna Lani Bay Hotel, PO Box 4959, Kohala Coast, HI 96743 (phone: 808-885-6655; 800-367-2323 for golf/hotel packages).

PRINCEVILLE, Hanalei, Kauai, Hawaii: The garden spot of the Garden Island, with three spectacular nines (Ocean, Woods, and Lake) in the same terrain you saw in the film *South Pacific.* The adjacent *Prince* course, an 18-holer planned by Robert Trent Jones, Jr., brings the total number of holes to 45, making *Princeville* one of Hawaii's biggest golf resorts. The weather can be uneven here — the lush forests are the by-product of plentiful rainfall — but the quality of the courses merits the risk. Information: Princeville at Hanalei, PO Box 3040, Princeville, HI 96722 (phone: 808-826-3040 or 800-367-7090).

GOLF CLINICS

Regular practice under the supervision of a pro on your own home course can't be beat for reducing your handicap. But there's no substitute for an occasional look at your weaknesses from a new point of view. That's the purpose of the golf clinics that have sprouted up all over the country.

GOLF DIGEST INSTRUCTION SCHOOLS, headquartered in Trumbull, Connecticut: The "Harvard" of golf schools holds its courses — taught by some of the best teaching pros in the business — at resorts all over the country, year-round. Information: Golf Digest Instruction Schools, 5520 Park Ave., Box 395, Trumbull, CT 06611-0395 (phone: 203-373-7130 or 800-243-6121).

WALT DISNEY WORLD GOLF STUDIO, Lake Buena Vista, Florida: Directed by WDW golf professional Eric Fredericksen, this program aims to help golfers develop their own styles by building on current skills. Videotapes help you chart improvement, and the instructor's audiotape of his pointers, which participants can take home, can add punch to subsequent practice. Unlike many other programs, WDW Golf Studio's last only 2 hours; Additional sessions magnify improvement. Information: Walt Disney World Golf Studio, Palm Magnolia Dr., Lake Buena Vista, FL 32819-1000 (phone: 407-824-2250).

GOLF SCHOOL AT MT. SNOW, Mt. Snow, Vermont: Started in 1978, the Golf School has become the most popular golfing program in the country. Keys to the school's big success are small teaching groups with a maximum of four students, and an accelerated teaching method that incorporates the use of videotape, special practice areas, and a building-block approach. The school offers 2-day weekend programs and 5-day midweek sessions that include lodging, meals, and 5 hours of daily instruction. Offered at *Plantation Resort* in Crystal River, Florida, during the winter months. Information: Golf School at Mt. Snow, Mt. Snow, VT 05356 (phone: 800-451-4211).

STRATTON GOLF SCHOOL, Stratton Mountain, Vermont: This school is one of the oldest in New England. A unique 22-acre training site, designed by noted golf course architect Geoffrey Cornish, allows students to simulate all golf shots. Director Keith Lyford and his staff focus on the basics — grip, stance, alignment, and swing — during 2- and 5-day sessions from mid-May to September. Lodging packages available. Information: Stratton Golf School, Stratton Mountain, VT 05155 (phone: 802-297-2200).

Sailing America's Coastal Waters

WINDJAMMER CRUISES

 There's no better way to get a feeling for the great age of sailing than on one of the big windjammers that were built during the first quarter of this century, mostly for oystering, fishing, or cargo and later converted to handle passengers. You spend your days swimming off the side or dozing in the sun, and you eat big meals, family style, that may include muffins and pastries cooked on old-fashioned wood stoves. You cruise at least a few hours every day, sometimes all day, then stop for a while — to go sightseeing, have a cookout, or to take hot showers at a marina. When you fall asleep at night, it's to the creaking of the ship's oak beams.

Otherwise, what a specific cruise is like depends a lot on the boat. On smaller vessels, the atmosphere is bound to be chummy (or confining, depending on your psyche) and somewhat more informal; each passenger has more say about where you go, what you do, and when you do it.

When considering the different windjammers, a selection of which follows, look into their size, ports of call, price (usually from $375 to $535 for a week aboard, including meals), means of power, and the policy on children (there may be minimum ages of, say, 14 or 16). Also investigate the plumbing facilities: many boats simply supply wash water on deck, while others have washbasins or showers right in their cabins.

ADVENTURE **AND** ***ROSEWAY,*** **Camden, Maine:** The largest windjammers that sail off the US coast. Built during the Roaring 20s, the 120-foot *Adventure* was a Gloucester fishing vessel; the 112-foot *Roseway* was built as a yacht and was used for many years as a pilot boat in Boston Harbor. Today, both cruise the Maine coast and carry 37 passengers each (no children under 16). Hot and cold showers on all cruises. In addition, there are folk music, photography, and watercolor painting "theme" sailings. Information: Yankee Schooner Cruises, PO Box 696, Camden, ME 04843 (phone: 207-236-4449; 800-255-4449 except in Maine).

MARY DAY, Camden, Maine: This 90-foot schooner accommodates 28 in single, double, and triple cabins on weekly cruises among Maine's coastal islands. Noted for her sailing ability and speed, *Mary Day* has no engine. A small powerboat provides access to shore and power in calm weather. Each cabin has fresh water; there is a shower on deck. Specialty cruises, like photography and natural history, are scheduled each season. Four non-smoking cruises are scheduled each season. Information: Coastal Cruises, PO Box 798, Camden, ME 04843 (phone: 207-236-2750).

PAULINE, Camden, Maine: The former queen of the Sardine Carrier fleet now carries passengers on weekly cruises along the Maine coast, from Campobello to Portland. Designed to island hop rather than to rely on sails alone, the 83-foot *Pauline* will take 12 passengers cruising in relaxed luxury, reminiscent of the golden age of yachting. Information: Capts. Ken and Ellen Barnes, 70 Elm St., Camden, ME 04843 (phone: 207-236-3520 or 800-999-7325).

STEPHEN TABER, Camden, Maine: This family-operated, two-masted, 68-foot gaff schooner, built in 1871, is the oldest continuously active US merchant vessel. It used to carry bricks and cord wood, but it has been cruising Maine's Penobscot Bay region with up to 22 passengers since 1946 (no children under 14). Running water in cabins. Listed in the National Register of Historic Places. Information: Schooner *Stephen Taber,* 70 Elm St., Camden, ME 04843 (phone: 207-236-3520).

AMERICAN EAGLE, Rockland, Maine: A former fishing vessel launched in 1930, this two-masted, 92-foot schooner has had a 2-year restoration and now takes 28 guests (no small children) on 3- and 6-day trips along the coast of Maine from May to October. Its captain is the former operator of the *Lewis R. French* (see below). Cabins have reading lights and sinks; there is a shower on board. Both the food and the speed of the craft are proudly featured. Information: Capt. John Foss, PO Box 482, Rockland, ME 04841 (phone: 207-594-8007 or 207-594-7617).

HARVEY GAMAGE, Rockland, Maine: Launched in 1973 and supplied with running water, this 95-foot schooner is one of the most technologically advanced of all the windjammers. The two showers aboard are cold, but only a few windjammers have any at all. The ship is also unusual in welcoming children of any age among its 30 passengers. Special rates for senior citizens available. Cruises take in the New England coast in summer, the Virgin Islands during the winter. Sailing instruction is provided. The *Rachael & Ebenezer,* Dirigo Cruises' other vessel, also sails lower New England in the summer, but in wintertime it's based in the Florida Keys. Information: Dirigo Cruises, 39 Waterside La., Clinton, CT 06413 (phone: 203-669-7068).

ISAAC H. EVANS, Rockland, Maine: Built in 1886, this 64½-foot, two-masted schooner spent most of its life oystering and freighting in Delaware Bay. Now completely rebuilt, it has fresh running water in the cabins, a potbellied stove for heat in the public room back aft, one hot- and cold-water shower, and a small push boat for going ashore (or getting to safe harbor) if there's no wind: The ship itself has no engine. Up to 22 passengers at a time (minimum age 16). Information: Capt. Edward Glaser, PO Box 482, Rockland, ME 04841 (phone: 207-594-8007).

LEWIS R. FRENCH, Rockland, Maine: This two-masted, 64-foot schooner, built in 1871 as a cargo vessel, is the oldest schooner still sailing in this country. It has been completely rebuilt so that it is essentially a new ship on an old design. The small cabins have reading lights and running water; up to 22 guests can be accommodated. Also on board is one hot shower — "to ensure lasting friendships," as the ship's brochure puts it. Information: Capt. Dan Pease, PO Box 482, Rockland, ME 04841 (phone: 207-594-8007).

***SHENANDOAH,* Vineyard Haven, Massachusetts:** An engineless square topsail schooner, launched in 1964, it is the only square-rigger in the US windjammer fleet. At 108 feet at the rail, it carries up to 29 passengers at a time in cabins for one to four. It puts in at ports throughout southern New England, between Nantucket on the east and Mystic on the west. Everybody has a washbasin; hot water comes from the galley. No children under 10. Information: Coastwise Packet Co., Box 429, Vineyard Haven, MA 02568 (phone: 617-693-1699).

***BILL OF RIGHTS,* Newport, Rhode Island:** One of the newest of America's wind-jammers, this 125-foot replica of a topsail schooner that ran contraband during the Civil War carries 32 passengers in 16 staterooms, equipped with running water. It puts in at southern New England harbors like Mystic, Nantucket, and Block Island. It also runs sail training weeks in the summer. Information: Schooner *Bill of Rights,* PO Box 477, Newport, RI 02840 (phone: 401-849-4980).

SAILING SCHOOLS

ANNAPOLIS SAILING SCHOOL, Annapolis, Maryland: Based in Annapolis, America's first and largest sailing school has branches in all parts of the country and on St. Croix in the US Virgin Islands. The basic 2-day beginners' course includes 4 hours in the classroom and 8 hours on the water; the 3- and 5-day beginners' courses give you extra time to practice your skills. Several other programs are available, including many advanced courses (handling auxiliary cruising boats, coastal navigation and piloting, racing, and preparation for bareboat chartering), but are not offered at all of the school's locations. Fees range from about $185 for the 2-day beginners' course to $375 for the 5-day course; on week-long cruises, students pay $820 to $1,450 per boat, depending on its size. Information: Annapolis Sailing School, PO Box 3334, Annapolis, MD 21403 (phone: 301-267-7205 in Maryland; 800-638-9192 elsewhere).

OFFSHORE SAILING SCHOOL, Ft. Myers, Florida: Founded by former Olympian and 12-meter sailor Steve Colgate, this school has five locations offering 3-day and/or week-long Learn to Sail courses ($395 to $650) for beginners, with classroom and on-water sailing instruction. The courses cover all the basics, including navigation and some spinnaker work on 27-foot extra-stable Olympic class Solings. Advanced courses ($415 to $1,195) are offered on the same schedule and include Advanced Sailing, Bareboat Preparation, Introductory Racing and Advanced Racing, Live Aboard Cruising for Bareboat Certification, and Racing and Intensive Racing for beginning and advanced racers. Locations include Captiva Island, Florida; Cape Cod, Massachusetts; Tortola, the British Virgin Islands; and South Street Seaport, New York. Information: Offshore Sailing School, 16731-110 McGregor Blvd., Ft. Myers, FL 33908 (phone: 800-221-4326; 813-454-1700).

GREAT SAILING AND CRUISING

Some parts of the US coastline are so sail-happy that you'd think everybody there owns a boat; if you don't, you can usually charter. Expect to be asked about your sailing experience; most are handled by brokers for private owners. Your experience will determine which boat you get; which you want will depend on how long you plan to cruise, since boats under 26 feet can be a little too cozy for a week on the water.

MARINA DEL REY, California: Ever since this marina, the largest manmade recreational-boat harbor in the world, was built in the 1960s, pleasure boaters have been passing through in droves; there are 6,400 slips and plenty of rentals and sailing schools. Transient boat rentals are available for overnight or up to 1 week. Information: Dept. of Beaches and Harbors, 13837 Fiji Way, Marina del Rey, CA 90292 (phone: 213-305-9545).

NEWPORT BEACH, California: Local celebs and some 10,000 others keep boats in this big, beautiful, busy Southern California harbor, the largest pleasure-boat harbor in the world. There are dozens of marinas; for a list, contact the Newport Harbor Area Chamber of Commerce, 1470 Jamboree Rd., Newport Beach, CA 92660 (phone: 714-644-8211).

SACRAMENTO–SAN JOAQUIN RIVER DELTA, surrounding Stockton, California: Better than 1,000 miles of sloughs, cuts, canals and other streams tunnel through the tules (the tall rushes that give this flatland its distinctive appearance), and for some local folk, weekend cruising is a way of life. Three great rivers help form the delta labyrinth — the Mokelumne, San Joaquin, and Sacramento. The delta's banks are sprinkled with over 100 handy marinas, restaurants, and river rat hangouts where you can stop to wet your whistle, take on fuel or water, buy supplies, or merely mingle with the locals. Most rentals are houseboats, which just about anyone can handle. Information: Stockton–San Joaquin Convention and Visitors Bureau, 46 W. Fremont St., Stockton, CA 95202 (phone: 209-943-1987; 800-888-8016).

SAUSALITO, California: The yachting center for San Francisco Bay, with space for over 2,000 boats in its marinas. For information on yacht rentals and brokers, contact the Redwood Empire Assn., One Market Plaza, Spear Street Tower, Suite 1001, San Francisco, CA 94105 (phone: 415-543-8334).

LONG ISLAND SOUND, Connecticut and New York: Between the notched shoreline of Connecticut and the rocks and sand edge of Long Island, there are literally hundreds of square miles of protected cruising water. The Sunday *New York Times* classified section always contains an extensive listing of boats available for charter. For crewed yachts, contact Sparkman & Stephens, 79 Madison Ave., New York, NY 10016 (phone: 212-689-9292).

MAINE COAST: Straight and bold in the southwest, deeply notched near Boothbay Harbor and scattered all over with islands like Matinicus (ultra-wild) and Monhegan (crisscrossed with walking paths that take you to bluffs and boulders where you can sun yourself) — the Maine coast offers enough variety to make it among the country's best spots for cruising — provided, that is, you can handle the frequent fogs, the tides, the rocky shores, and the scarcity of marinas. Information: Cape Dory Charters, c/o Robinhood Marine Center, Robinhood, ME 04530 (phone: 207-371-2525); and Seal Cove Boatyard, PO Box 99, Harborside, ME 04642 (phone: 207-326-4422); Sparkman & Stephens, 79 Madison Ave., New York, NY 10016 (phone: 212-689-9292), for crewed yachts.

CHESAPEAKE BAY, Maryland and Virginia: The sine qua non of cruising in America, 185-mile-long Chesapeake Bay, America's largest estuary, is broken by river mouths, little coves, and harbors where you can tie up and go ashore for a walk through 300-year-old towns; and scattered with quaint islands like Smith and Tangier, where the people started losing their Elizabethan accents in the 1960s. The cruising season, which begins in April, continues well beyond October, when the Annapolis In-the-Water Boat Show, the largest in the world, is held. For information and charters (bareboats from 27 to 40 feet): Hartge Chesapeake Charters, Church Lane, Galesville, MD 20765 (phone: 301-867-7240).

America's Most Surprising Ocean Beaches

Along America's thousands of miles of lake and ocean shores, you'll find beaches for everyone. Most of the East Coast between the brief busy coast of New Hampshire and Miami Beach is beach-edged; a dotted line of slim barrier beaches, which protect the mainland from the brunt of the ocean's force, extends from Long Island to Florida. There, and along the Gulf Coast of Florida, Texas, and Mississippi (which has bluer, warmer waters, more gently sloping bottoms, and less surf than East Coast shores), beach grass backs the sand; behind that, further inland, grow scrubby trees and, in the South, tropical vegetation. Often, incredible as it may seem, the deep roots of these fragile plants are all that keep the islands from washing away in storms (as, indeed, they sometimes do anyway).

Beaches up and down the Pacific Coast are, as a rule, better for beachwalking and fishing than for swimming because of riptides and heavy undertow. However, there are exceptions. Water at beaches below Santa Barbara is generally warm enough for dips. Above Santa Barbara it's for the hardy only because of the proximity of the Alaska Current. Around Carmel, the shore is scalloped with coves; north of Fort Ross, it's gravelly and driftwood collecting is terrific. Still farther up the coast, the beaches are edged by forests. The coastlines of Oregon and southern Washington make up one solid strip of beach cut by occasional headlands; but the best concentrations are between Pacific City and Florence, Oregon. Storm watching in winter is popular there, as is beachwalking afterward to pick up the leavings — driftwood, most commonly, but occasionally brightly colored Japanese fishing floats as well. As for Hawaii, it has some of the best beaches of all; the one on Waikiki is only the most famous.

In addition to the beaches described below, which are some of the country's best, there are still others described elsewhere in this book. Consider, for instance, Acadia National Park, in Maine; Assateague Island, Maryland; Cape Cod, Massachusetts; the New Jersey coast, including Victorian Cape May; the Outer Banks of North Carolina; Padre Island, off the Texas Gulf Coast; Carmel, California; and the entire western edge of Oregon.

EAST

OGUNQUIT, Ogunquit, Maine: This little harbor town is also the site of a 3-mile stretch of beach that is one of the best in New England — partly for its length, partly for the gentleness of the drop-off. The Atlantic is "refreshing," as you must expect in Maine. Information: Chamber of Commerce, Box 2289, Ogunquit, ME 03907 (phone: 207-646-2939).

OLD ORCHARD, Old Orchard Beach, Maine: A 7-mile strand, 700 feet wide — it is the state's longest; the low surf makes it one of the safest on the Atlantic for swimming. Motels, cottages, condos, and amusements abound. Information: Chamber of Commerce, Box 600, Old Orchard Beach, ME 04064 (phone: 207-934-2091).

CRANE BEACH, Ipswich, Massachusetts: This historic town, with several hundred colonial homes, also boasts a wonderful 7-mile-long sweep of dune-backed sand. There's not much surf, so swimming is possible. Information: Ipswich Chamber of Commerce, 46 Newmarch St., Ipswich, MA 01938 (phone: 508-356-3231).

FIRE ISLAND, New York: Walk-on ferries from Patchogue, Sayville, and Bay Shore, Long Island (May through October only), take passengers by the thousands to this slip of land, where there are communities for families and gay and heterosexual singles, and the 19,000-acre Fire Island National Seashore, where you can camp (by reservation), swim, hike, take a guided nature walk, surf cast, or just sit in the sun. Also accessible — at each end — by car. Information: Fire Island National Seashore, 120 Laurel St., Patchogue, NY 11772 (phone: 516-289-4810).

HAMPTON BAYS, Long Island, New York: The affordable Hampton, this hamlet offers superb beaches, boating, and ocean and bay fishing, plus restaurants, discos, markets, bookstores, specialty food shops, and parties that keep the area swinging until the wee hours. Rooms are difficult to come by on short notice. However, after Labor Day, the beaches are still inviting. Information: Chamber of Commerce, PO Box 64, Hampton Bays, NY 11946 (phone: 516-728-2211).

WATCH HILL BEACH, Watch Hill, Rhode Island: A fine surf beach open to the public in a town so exclusive that little else is. Presiding over the entrance to the beach is the century-old Flying Horse Carousel, one of the oldest in the nation, in use since 1879. More beaches can be found nearby at Misquamicut and Weekapaug, with its picturesque rocky overlooks. Rentals and information: Chamber of Commerce, 55 Beach St., Merchant's Square, Westerly, RI 02891 (phone: 401-596-7761).

SOUTH

GULF STATE PARK, Gulf Shores, Alabama: These 2½ miles of sugary sand, lapped by the aquamarine Gulf, make up only one short section of the 32-mile stretch between Alabama and Mobile Points — but it's the best section for vacations because of the quality of the facilities (which include cabins, campsites, an 18-hole golf course, and a saltwater fishing pier) at the modern, 144-room, well-run *Gulf State Park Resort.* Information: Gulf State Park Resort, Box 437, Gulf Shores, AL 36542 (phone: 205-968-7531), Gulf State Park information: HC 79, Box 9, Gulf Shores, Al 36542 (phone: 205-968-7544, 800-544-4853, or 800-ALA-PARK.).

FERNANDINA BEACH, Amelia Island, Florida: Along the eastern coast of Amelia Island, this lovely 13-mile beach boasts one of the finest beach resorts in existence, the *Amelia Island Plantation,* nestled among groves of live oak and surrounded by salt marshes and dunes on the south end of the island (phone: 904-261-6161 or 800-874-6878). The plantation offers 25 tennis courts, 27- and 18-hole golf courses, 14 swimming pools, a health spa, bike trails, charter fishing, horseback riding on the beach, a youth program, restaurants, and comfortable condominiums. On the north end of the island is Fort Clinch State Park, offering beachside camping, and the Municipal Fishing Pier that juts 1,500 feet into the ocean. Also along the coast are bed-and-breakfast establishments and the *Summer Beach Resort and Country Club* (phone: 800-322-7448). The nearby historic town of Fernandina is worth a visit. Information: Amelia Island–Fernandina Beach Chamber of Commerce, 102 Centre Street, P.O. Box 472, Fernandina Beach, FL 32034 (phone: 904-261-3248).

NORTHWEST COAST, Florida: This may be the whitest sand you'll ever see; it's white like snow, white like sugar. West of Panama City, in the panhandle, US 98 runs next to these beaches (but low dunes protect sunbathers from the sound of the traffic). One US government–owned 6-mile stretch, between greater Ft. Walton Beach (pop. 68,000) and Destin (pop. 8,000), is completely undeveloped; there's no parking lot — you just stop your car anyplace along the road. Between Destin and Panama City, there are all kinds of handsome new hotels, motels, and condos, many available for rent in summer. Some of the towns east of Panama City are just being discovered as the great tourist destinations they are. St. George Island, near Apalachicola, has 20 miles of beaches, a state park, and a couple of hundred beach houses on stilts, some of which are available for rent through *Alice D. Collins Realty* (Box 16, St. George Island, Eastpoint, FL 32328; phone: 904-670-2758) and *Suncoast Realty* (Box 2, St. George Island, Eastpoint, FL 32328; phone: 904-670-2247). Surf fish in the gulf or pick up oysters along the bay: The loudest noise you'll hear on a busy summer's day is the occasional banging of a screen door. Not far away, the T. H. Stone State Memorial-St. Joseph Peninsula State Park has another 20 miles of pure white sand, nice campsites in a grove of trees, and facilities for biking, boating, clamming, and fishing. As for temperatures, late March and early April begin the warm-weather season, and especially around Ft. Walton Beach, the crowds, such as they are, stay until Labor Day. But even on July 4 you can get off to yourself on the empty strands. September and October are the best months for deep-sea fishing, and November through March is known as snowbird season, when northerners come to worship the sun and swim in waters that rarely get below 58F. Information: Destin Chamber of Commerce, PO Box 8, Destin, FL 32541 (phone: 904-837-6241), and Greater Ft. Walton Beach Chamber of Commerce, PO Drawer 640, Ft. Walton Beach, FL 32549 (phone: 904-244-8191).

SANIBEL-CAPTIVA ISLANDS, Florida: The 20-mile stretch of white sand on this two-island chain off the coast of Ft. Myers offers some of the finest, perhaps even the finest, seashell collecting in the US, especially after storms with heavy northwest winds, usually following a cold snap, between January and March. Some good areas to search are around the lighthouse at the eastern tip of Sanibel; Bowman's Beach at the island's western end; the southerly tip of Captiva; and the northerly tip of Captiva. The water averages about 72F in winter, 80F in summer. Temperatures range between 65F and 86F in April, between 61F and 77F in November. Motels on the island are hidden away in groves of trees, so the atmosphere is low-key, even during the busy Christmas and spring school holidays. Always reserve in advance, however. Information: Chamber of Commerce, PO Box 166, Sanibel, FL 33957 (phone: 813-472-1080).

CUMBERLAND ISLAND NATIONAL SEASHORE, Cumberland Island, Georgia: The interior of this 16-mile-long, 3-mile-wide barrier island, the most southerly of Georgia's Sea Islands, is covered with marshes alive with fiddler crabs, oysters, long-legged wading birds like ibis and wood stork, and with groves of weirdly contorted live oak, magnolia, holly, and pine. The 18 miles of beaches that rim these wildlands are golden and (since the ferry that serves the island from St. Marys, Georgia, makes the 45-minute trip on a fairly limited basis) fairly empty as well. All you've got to do is walk a little farther from the ferry dock than anybody else and you'll be alone. Or, plan well in advance to reserve one of the handful of campsites on the island or a room at *Greyfield,* a small inn (phone: 904-261-6408; see *America's Special Havens*). Camping and boat reservations are accepted by phone only. Information: Cumberland Island National Seashore, PO Box 806, St. Marys, GA 31558 (phone: 912-882-4335).

GULF ISLANDS NATIONAL SEASHORE, near Ocean Springs, Mississippi: In this 70,800-acre portion of the Mississippi and Florida preserve there are some 52 miles of sugary sand beaches, all of them on barrier islands off the Mississippi coast — Horn, Petit Bois, and East and West Ship islands — and the Florida Coast — Santa Rosa Island and Perdido Key. The first two Mississippi islands, once national wildlife refuges because of the richness of the wildlife inhabiting the brackish and freshwater ponds and marshes and now classified as Wilderness Areas, are accessible only by private or chartered boat, as is the east section of Ship Island (split in two by Hurricane Camille in 1969); you can camp in your boat or on the shore. Island camping is very popular, especially during fall and spring. (Charter boats are available through concessions in Biloxi and Gulfport.) Ship Island is accessible by private craft or, from April through September, by a twice-daily ferry from Gulfport or Biloxi; each boat accommodates 250. That may sound like a lot of people, but once on the island the crowds scatter to the right and left of the boardwalk that leads to the Gulf Coast beach, and you can end up practically alone. Regularly scheduled tours are given during the summer months. The Florida islands are accessible by car and offer campgrounds, historic fortifications, and visitors centers. For those who prefer more company, the mainland in Ocean Springs, Mississippi, has a 51-site campground with water and electrical hookups, a boat ramp, visitor center, picnic areas, and recreational equipment. Take plenty of sunscreen, a lightweight long-sleeve shirt, and trousers: You'll need the protection since there's scarcely a bit of shade on the islands. Information: Gulf Islands National Seashore, 3500 Park Rd.; Ocean Springs, MS 39564 (phone: 601-875-9057).

HILTON HEAD ISLAND, South Carolina: The 12 miles of sugar sand beach here are clean, gently sloping, and almost completely free of crushing waves. They're also wide — 600 feet at low tide — and hard-packed. You can bicycle along them as well as, bird watch, beachcomb (best after fall and winter storms), jog, and swim (April into October). When the weather is too cold for splashing in the surf, you can always take a dip in one of the pools at the several resort developments that make this island famous; among them are *Sea Pines Vacation Resorts* (woodsy, spread out; phone: 803-785-3333 in South Carolina; 800-845-6131 elsewhere), and *Palmetto Dunes* (everything in walking distance; phone: 803-785-1161 in South Carolina; 800-845-6130 elsewhere). Some of the best golf and tennis facilities in the country are also on the island, along with sailing schools and fishing schools, bike paths, stables, shops, restaurants, and much more. Information: Chamber of Commerce, Box 5647, Hilton Head Island, SC 29938 (phone: 803-785-3673).

KIAWAH ISLAND, South Carolina: This barrier island is located southwest of historic Charleston. Nestled behind natural sand dunes bordering 10 miles of wide, sandy beach, you can stroll or bike on hard ocean beach (among the best spots on the East Coast for shelling) and pick up elegant disks and stiff pen shells, lettered olives, whelks, and such. Or play tennis (28 courts) or golf (three 18-hole courses); bike along the 12 miles of paths; or swim in the ocean or any of three large resort pools. From May through August, loggerhead turtles lay their eggs on the beach in the dark of the night. The climate is subtropical and balmy, with average highs in the 80s in August and September and in the 60s in February and March. Lodgings are available in the posh *Kiawah Island Inn* and in villas; restaurants and shops are nearby. Information: Kiawah Island Co., PO Box 294-1201, Charleston, SC 29412-0910 (phone: 800-6-KIAWAH).

GRAND STRAND, Myrtle Beach, South Carolina: Stretching for 60 miles from the North Carolina border to Georgetown, South Carolina, this strand of white beaches is one of the most popular seaside resorts on the Atlantic coast. Accommodations range from modest motels to plush oceanfront villas and condominiums, and dozens of hotels and motels crowd the boardwalk — making the atmosphere mostly tacky and touristy. The recreational possibilities are broad, what with 59 18-hole golf courses in the area, 150 tennis courts, 10 fishing piers, 1,100 restaurants, 2,000 retail shopping outlets, and all sorts of amusements and attractions. If that doesn't appeal, the Grand Strand also has 9 campgrounds and 2 state parks, with more than 7,000 sites. The Strand's peak activity period is in summer, but a mild year-round climate makes it pleasant in fall and early spring as well. Information: Chamber of Commerce, PO Box 2115, Myrtle Beach, SC 29578 (phone: 803-626-7444; 800-356-3016.

WEST

HUNTINGTON BEACH, California: "The Surfing Capital of the USA," with its 1,800-foot-long pier (built in 1902 as the Pacific's answer to Atlantic City), is one of the top spots on the coast to watch surfers catching some of the Pacific's best waves, sometimes right under the barnacle-spiked pilings; a good surfer can stay on top for the distance of two city blocks. Information: Greater Los Angeles Visitors and Convention Bureau, 515 S. Figueroa St., Los Angeles, CA 90012 (phone: 213-624-7300).

PISMO BEACH, California: The giant Pismo clams, once found in such numbers that farmers plowed them up for hog and cattle feed, are now scarce on this wide, 21-mile-long strand. But you can swim (best from August through November) and go surfing, fishing, shelling, or just drive down the beach. ATCs (all-terrain cycles) can be rented nearby, and there are dozens of special events. Motels are mainly at the north end of the strand, atop rocky cliffs; some have their own narrow beaches, accessible by twisty wooden staircases. Information: Pismo Beach Chamber of Commerce, 581 Dolliver St., Pismo Beach, CA 93449 (phone: 805-773-4382; 800-443-7778 in California).

POINT REYES NATIONAL SEASHORE, Point Reyes, California: A 40-minute drive north of San Francisco, the westernmost point of this triangle of land holds the US Weather Bureau's record for the foggiest, windiest station between Mexico and Canada. So, even though people swim at 4-mile Drake's Beach and at 3-mile Limantour, Point Reyes is not where you come for fun in the sun (or swimming, either; there are no lifeguards). Rather, you come for the solitude and great walks — especially along Pacific-pounded Point Reyes and McClure's beaches. People stop for picnics on the former, the more sheltered of the pair, then move on; McClure's is nearly deserted most of the time because of its more difficult access (a steep, though navigable, trail). Inland, where weather is less changeable, 140 miles of hiking trails show off wildflowers, marshes, and wildlife. Also visit the self-guided Earthquake Trail, Bear Valley Visitor Center, Kule Loklo (Miwok Indian Exhibition), the Morgan horse ranch, and the historic Point Reyes Lighthouse, a good spot for whale watching. Motels are in Inverness. Information: Point Reyes National Seashore, Point Reyes Station, CA 94956 (phone: 415-663-1092).

KAANAPALI, Maui, Hawaii: The longest of all Hawaii's great beaches, this one takes in about 3 miles of golden sand near Lahaina, the old whaling port; flat water makes it good for swimming. Edging the beach: an area full of hotels and golf courses on land owned by the Amfac Corporation, whose careful master plan has kept the architecture handsome and harmonious. Information: Maui Visitors Bureau, 38 Dairy Rd., Kahului, Maui, HI 96732 (phone: 808-871-8691).

Scuba: The Wild Blue Under

 Just about anyone can use a snorkel, mask, and flippers (invented, incidentally, by Benjamin Franklin) wherever the water is clear enough — in Hawaii, along the coast of Block Island, Rhode Island, or at Florida's John Pennekamp Reef State Park (see DIRECTIONS).

Scuba diving is something else. Handling everyday procedures and emergencies with equal aplomb takes training and practice. And so, to buy scuba gear, refill tanks, and rent equipment at any dive shop, you have to be able to show proof of having passed special certification courses that require one or two nights a week for four to six weeks, partly in a swimming pool and partly in open water. For details, contact the certifying organizations: the *National Assn. of Underwater Instructors* (*NAUI*), 4650 Arrow Hwy., Suite F1, Montclair, CA 91763-1150 (phone: 714-621-5801); *PADI International,* 1243 E. Warner Ave., PO Box 25011, Santa Ana, CA 92799 (phone: 714-540-7234); or your YMCA.

Longtime divers should note the recent publication of a series of wreck charts that pinpoint the locations of explorable shipwrecks in the Atlantic, the Gulf of Mexico, and the Pacific between San Diego and Vancouver. Just $15 each, the charts are accompanied by booklets that explain why the ship sank and when. Information: Wreck Charts, 11 Creek Bend Dr., Fairport, NY 14450 (phone: 716-377-1061).

SHORT COURSES

You can get your certification (or C card) on your vacation if you work at it every day. Several establishments in Hawaii offer short courses, with a good deal of work in the clear warm waters around the coral reefs. They include the *Sea Sage Diving Center,* 4-1378 Kuhio Hwy., Kapaa, Kauai, HI 96746 (phone: 808-822-3841); and *Gold Coast Divers,* 755719 Alii Rd., Room 119, Kailua-Kona, HI 96740 (phone: 808-329-1328; 800-367-8047, ext 458).

SOME GREAT DIVING SPOTS

Check local diving shops for up-to-the-minute particulars.

LA JOLLA COVE, La Jolla, California: Starting in this 50-yard-deep, 100-yard-wide notch in the Southern California coastline, the San Diego–La Jolla Underwater Park takes in about 7 miles of underwater scenery up the coast as far as Torrey Pines; within that area there's a look-but-don't-touch area where you can see vast quantities of kelp, abalone, and lobster. One of the best sites is at the edge of a 20-mile-long submarine canyon that borders the underwater park; the drop-off is 11,000 feet. Information: Parks and Recreation Dept., Coastal Division (phone: 619-236-6652), and, for details about La Jolla hostelries, the San Diego Convention and Visitors Bureau, 1200 3rd Ave., Suite 824, San Diego, CA 92101 (phone: 619-236-1212).

JULIA PFEIFFER BURNS STATE PARK, Big Sur, California: Some 42 miles south of Monterey, where the mountains shoulder down to the sea, divers in wet suits watch sea lions, some 50 varieties of fish, and occasional whales coming by to scrape barnacles from their backs on rocky chimneys in the sea floor. All this and kelp beds, too. Partington Cove, where the diving takes place, is extremely rugged, so only experienced divers should venture in. *Nepenthe,* a redwood pavilion designed by a Frank Lloyd Wright disciple on a cliff 800 feet above the sea, is the place to eat and see what's going on in the area (phone: 408-667-2345). Information: Pfeiffer Big Sur State Park, Big Sur, CA 93920 (phone: 408-667-2315).

HAWAII'S KONA COAST, Big Island of Hawaii, Hawaii: On the leeward side of Hawaii Island there's good diving in the Pine Trees area (lava-tube caves big enough to drive a Volkswagen through, plus lionfish, lobsters, and a spectacular canyon) and the Red Hills area (good caves, including one in which you'll almost always see a shark, shrimp, and banded coral). Everywhere there are arches, coral, clear warm water, and fish. This island is good for diving because it's new in geologic terms and there's not a lot of sand to cover up food for the fish. *Gold Coast Divers* sponsors several night dives, plus a unique manta ray dive that gives participants the opportunity to ride these big graceful creatures. Information: Gold Coast Divers, King Kamehameha Hotel, Suite P-1, 75-5660 Palani Rd., Kailua-Kona, HI 96740 (phone: 808-329-1328).

TRIPS

The establishments that sponsor scuba courses for beginners usually also run extensive dive trip schedules to sites accessible only by boat, for experienced divers; for lists of these operators in the area you want to visit, write the national scuba-instruction certification organizations, PADI and NAUI (above), or the YMCA. The following outfits also sponsor trips.

CALIFORNIA: *The Diving Locker,* 1120 Grand Ave., San Diego, CA 92109 (phone: 619-272-1120), sponsors dive trips to San Clemente Island and Coronado Island as well as offering scuba classes, rentals, and local beach dives.

FLORIDA: Diving trips to the Keys are sponsored by the *Reef Shop Dive Center,* 84771 Overseas Hwy., Islamorada, FL 33036 (phone: 305-664-4385); *The Diving Site,* 12399 Overseas Hwy., Marathon, FL 33050 (phone: 305-289-1021); *Hall's Diving Center,* 1994 Overseas Hwy., Marathon, FL 33050 (phone: 305-743-5929 or 800-331-HALL); and *Key West Pro Dive Shop,* 1605 N. Roosevelt Blvd., Key West, FL 33040 (phone: 305-296-3823 or 800-426-0707), specializing in personel scuba instruction, daily wreck and night dives. In the Palm Beach area, contact *Norine Rouse Scuba Club* of the Palm Beaches, 4708 N. Dixie Hwy., West Palm Beach, FL 33407 (phone: 305-844-2466), for trips to colorful reefs and to sunken ships full of porkfish, grunts, coneys, and other exotic fish. Around Ft. Lauderdale beach, where there are 50 differ- ent coral reefs and wrecks, contact *Pro Dive Charters,* Bahia Mar Yachting Center, 801 Seabreeze Blvd., Ft. Lauderdale, FL 33316 (phone: 305-761-3413).

TEXAS: Along the coast of Padre Island not far from Corpus Christi, you can dive off oil platforms or three sunken Liberty ships; the water is warm and very clear. Information from *Padre Island Dive Shop,* 6920 S. Padre Island Dr., Corpus Christi, TX 78412-6901 (phone: 512-993-6000).

Touring America's Waterways

 In the days before cities were strung together by highways, people traveled from one settlement to another along rivers and chains of lakes. Quite a few have been dammed up, polluted, or defaced by highways and factories. But there are still enough open and visible water courses to suit the needs of most recreationists, and you don't have to be an expert paddler to enjoy them. Some are easy enough for beginning canoeists in open-deck canoes. Others — whitewater torrents as wild now as they were 200 years ago — are serviced by experienced boatmen who will take you down in big rubber rafts.

FLATWATER CANOEING

The following waterways offer extensive opportunities for paddling trips easy enough for almost anyone — though you should check on conditions before you put in, since recent rainfalls or strong winds can turn normally navigable lakes and streams into trouble spots. Canoes are usually available at about $8 to $30 a day, with packages and reductions available for multi-day tours. Liveries are usually your best source of information about campsites en route. Most provide shuttle services from point of entry to final landing.

EAST

ALLAGASH, Maine: As much a region as a 92-mile-long river and chain of lakes, the Allagash sweeps and swirls through one of the mightiest woodlands in the East as it heads north from Telos Lake near Baxter State Park to its confluence with the St. John River along the Canadian border. Countless other lakes and streams, in equally wild country, are accessible by portages, so you can canoe and fish to your heart's content. May and June are high-water months; fall foliage, which flames bright in late September and early October, changes the scene once again. Information: Maine Bureau of Parks and Recreation, Dept. of Conservation, Station 22, Augusta, ME 04333 (phone: 207-289-3821).

ADIRONDACK CANOE ROUTES, New York: You feel like a 19th-century woodsman as you paddle through this hundred-mile-long chain of river-and-portage-connected lakes in New York's North Country. The waters are on the cold side, but still lovely for swimming and fishing. You can camp in a three-sided log lean-to on the shore of one of the lakes or on the islands in the middle. The terrain along the route is mountainous, rocky, forested, and, except for the shelters, virtually undeveloped. Information: New York State Dept. of Environmental Conservation, 50 Wolf Rd., Albany, NY 12233-4255 (phone: 518-457-7433).

DELAWARE RIVER, Pennsylvania, New York, New Jersey: From the foothills of the Catskill Mountains in southern New York State to the Delaware Water Gap on the border of Pennsylvania and New Jersey, the Delaware ripples through some 120 miles of dense woodlands — the sort you wouldn't expect to find so close to the East's big cities. Liveries include *Bob & Rick Lander's Delaware River Canoe and Raft Trips* (RD 2, Box 376, Narrowsburg, NY 12764; phone: 914-252-3925); *Jerry's Three River Canoe Rentals and Campgrounds* (PO Box 7, Rte. 97, Pond Eddy, NY 12770; phone: 914-557-6078); *Kittatinny Canoes* (Silver Lake Rd., Dingmans Ferry, PA 18328; phone: 717-828-2338 or 717-828-2700).

SHENANDOAH RIVER, Virginia: Snaking between the Massanutten Mountains and the Blue Ridge on this majestic stream, you will almost always have a panorama of forested hills in view — though occasionally the banks are given over to farmlands or summer homes. This goes on for nearly 100 miles, but the most popular trip is the 45-mile stretch between Luray and Front Royal, which can be paddled in a long weekend. The foliage peaks in mid-October, while the fish are most active in early June. Tube rentals are offered from June through September. Information: Shenandoah River Outfitters (Rte. 3, Luray, VA 22835; phone: 703-743-4159).

SOUTH

BUFFALO NATIONAL RIVER, Arkansas: This 148-mile-long stream in northern Arkansas is speckled by gravel bars and edged by forests and cliffs full of waterfalls, caves, and fern falls. The seasons — from the pink and white springs to the lush summers and through the stunning orange and red autumns — make each trip down the Buffalo a delight. Current is no problem; long pools alternate with rapids and riffles. Camping is permitted on the gravel bars and at most river accesses; hiking is available in wilderness areas and on developed day-use trails. Information: Buffalo National River, PO Box 1173, Harrison, AR 72602-1173 (phone: 501-741-5443).

WHITE RIVER, Arkansas: With its ghostlike morning fogs, cave-pocked shoreline bluffs, mountains, wildlife, and good trout fishing, this 100-mile stream provides a beautiful trip. Information: Batesville Area Chamber of Commerce, 409 Vine St., Batesville, AR 72501 (phone: 501-793-2378).

EVERGLADES NATIONAL PARK, Florida: In still water, the paddling is more strenuous, but the scenery — mangroves, big buttonwood trees, bays, and tunnels — is worth the effort. There are several short trails and one 100-miler that will keep you paddling for days. Winter months are best; there are fewer bugs, you see more birds, and the weather is more invigorating. You need a back-country use permit for overnight stays. Information: Everglades National Park, PO Box 279, Homestead, FL 33030 (phone: 305-247-6211).

OKEFENOKEE NATIONAL WILDLIFE REFUGE, Georgia: Leachings of decaying vegetation stain these still south Georgian waters black as a moonless night; and, smooth as glass, they reflect every twig of the moss-veiled cypress forests through which many of the canoe trails will take you. (Others cut through "prairies" — water-rooted versions of those in Kansas.) A limited-permit system ensures that when you canoe through the swamp, you'll have a campsite all to yourself each night of your trip. Information: US Fish and Wildlife Service, Rte. 2, Box 338, Folkston, GA 31537 (phone: 912-496-3331).

BLACK CREEK, Mississippi: Canoeing this stream through forests of cypress, pines, and oaks, you can simply float along on the gentle current; at night, you can camp on snow-white sandbars. The longest trip is about 40 miles, about 3 days, starting at Big Creek. About 75% of the trip runs through the National Forest. Information: De Soto National Forest, Black Creek Ranger District, PO Box 248, Wiggins, MS 39577 (phone: 601-928-4422).

MIDWEST

BLUE RIVER, Indiana: From Fredericksburg to this southern Indiana stream's confluence with the Ohio, there are 58-plus miles of clear deep green water edged by forests of redbud, oak, maple. Good rock bass fishing, especially in early summer. Information: Old Mill Canoe Rental, PO Box 60, Fredericksburg, IN 47120 (phone: 812-472-3140).

AU SABLE RIVER, Michigan: Along the 240 canoeable miles of this twisting mid-western waterway you'll find quiet wooded shores, some in the Huron National Forest, and plenty of good fishing. Information: Oscoda–Au Sable Chamber of Commerce, 100 W. Michigan Ave., Oscoda, MI 48750 (phone: 517-739-7322; 800-235-4625 in Michigan).

BOUNDARY WATERS CANOE AREA WILDERNESS, Minnesota: Wild and vast, this system of streams, narrows, and island-dotted lakes created by glaciers eons ago offers — with surrounding Superior National Forest (of which it is a part), nearby Voyageurs National Park, and Ontario's Quetico Provincial Park — some of the most extensive canoeing on the continent. Guides, liveries, and complete outfitting services are widely available in Grand Marais, Ely, and Crane Lake, Minnesota. Information: Superior National Forest, PO Box 338, Duluth, MN 55801 (phone: 218-720-5324).

OZARK NATIONAL SCENIC RIVERWAYS, Missouri: The Current River and its tributary the Jacks Fork together offer some 140 miles of woods, caves, springs, sinkholes, and pleasant, easy-to-negotiate pools and riffles. Information: Ozark National Scenic Riverways, PO Box 490, Van Buren, MO 63965 (phone: 314-323-4236).

WEST

RUSSIAN RIVER, California: Fast enough to be fun, but not too fast, the 60 miles of this California stream from the Lake Mendocino Dam to the Pacific are safe almost year-round and understandably popular. The waters — deep pools, small riffles, and moderate rapids — swirl you between steep forested banks, past shores full of vineyards, orchards, and stands of redwood that hide summer cottages, to open spaces where you can smell the salt air. And it's all just an hour north of San Francisco. Rentals and information: Burke's Russian River Canoe Rentals, PO Box 602, Forestville, CA 95436 (phone: 707-887-1222).

MISSOURI RIVER, Montana: Central Montana's wonderfully stark sagebrush-and-sandstone-cliff wilderness encompasses the 149-mile length of this National Wild and Scenic River. It's a great place for sun, and it's also among the best in the West (where most other streams are wildwater torrents) for easy canoeing on free-flowing water. May, June, and September are best for wildlife watching; the cottonwoods turn to gold in late September and October. Information: Missouri River Outfitters, PO Box 1212, Ft. Benton, MT 59442 (phone: 406-622-3295).

WHITEWATER RAFTING

When you're knifing through the 20-foot-high waves of a river racing downstream at the rate of 50,000 or 60,000 cubic feet per second, and your clothes are drenched with the spray, and you can hardly hear the screams of your fellows for the noise of the river (something like the roar of a dozen freight trains), and when the same scenario repeats itself day after day — even the wildest roller coaster seems tame.

But even when the same river is flowing at its normal 5,000 cubic feet per second, and even in the East, where the torrential stretches of wilderness rivers are so short that whitewater trips usually last only a day, it's not hard to understand why river-running can get into your blood. Few other means of wilderness travel put you so close to the forces of nature. And if you're not the rugged, hardy type, another way to get deep into the wilderness without some kind of noisy motor simply doesn't exist. Many of the following have been designated National Wild and Scenic Rivers, which means that their route passes through true wilderness and also that it is advisable to apply for a permit (or sign up with an outfitter) well in advance — at many, early in the preceding winter — as access is strictly limited, ensuring that the word "crowd" will never pass anyone's lips. Most of the country's mightiest rivers are accessible on trips run by commercial operators — both small outfits who take their craft down one or two streams in a given region and larger organizations that have developed programs nationwide. Among the latter are the *Sierra Club,* 730 Polk St., San Francisco, CA

94109 (phone: 415-776-2211); the *American River Touring Assn.,* Star Rte. 73, Groveland, CA 95321 (phone: 800-323-ARTA); and *OARS,* PO Box 67, Angels Camp, CA 95222 (phone: 209-736-4677), which specializes in Grand Canyon trips. *Adventure Bound,* 2392 H Rd., Grand Junction, CO 81505 (phone: 303-241-5633), runs 1- to 5-day trips on the Green, Colorado, Gunnison, and Yampa rivers in Colorado and Utah.

Depending on where you go and when and who takes you, you may wield a paddle (with the guide in the rear shouting out instructions) or you may go along as just a passenger. In the very wildest waters, you'll probably go in big catamaran rafts. On other trips down other rivers, the outfitter will pack along inflatable canoes or kayaks, and you can get out and do some paddling on your own, even closer to the water level, when you tire of watching the cliffs, rocky banks, and forests go by — that is, if you're not worn out from the swimming, picnicking, hiking, fishing, and other diversions that the outfitters normally program into excursions. Between the river, the sourdough pancake breakfasts, the steaks and spuds dinners, the companionable evenings around the campfires, and the lullaby the river sings to you through the quiet canyon nights — a trip down a great waterway is one of those memorable vacation adventures that brings out the poet in you.

COLORADO RIVER (GRAND CANYON SECTION), Arizona: The most challenging of all river trips, and one of the most popular, is also, some people will tell you, one of the great moments of human experience. You shoot some 100 rapids — Badger Creek, Soap Creek, 25 Mile, House Rock, Unkar, Nevills, Crystal, Lava, Sockdolager, Grapevine, and dozens of others — as you run the 277 miles between the put-in area at Lee's Ferry and the headwaters of Lake Mead. The soaring sculptured walls and the glowing colors of their rock layers are as grand when seen from below as they are when you stand on the Canyon rim. And though the flow is controlled by the Glen Canyon Dam upstream, the river itself changes all the time. Summers are busy and hot; in spring you'll find comfortable temperatures in the 70s and 80s, blooming desert plants, and smaller crowds. For a complete list of outfitters (who go downstream in everything from dories to motor-powered rafts), write the River Subdistrict, Grand Canyon National Park, PO Box 129, Grand Canyon, AZ 86023 (phone: 602-638-7843).

MAIN SALMON, Idaho: A good trip for beginning your river-running career, Lewis and Clark's "River of No Return" offers enough deep-rolling rapids to keep you interested, but not so many that you'll spend your river hours in terror. On the 100-mile stretch between Corn Creek and Spring Bar, not far from Riggins — the stretch most commonly floated by commercial outfitters — there are warm springs and quiet pools where you can get out and splash, sandy beaches, spectacular canyons, bighorn sheep and other wildlife, and, on the north-facing slopes, stands of Douglas fir. In one 10-mile stretch, the banks rise so steeply from the water's edge that there's not even a trail along the shore. Runs during high water in May or June are wildest; the following months through Labor Day are quieter on the water. Actually, the river is floatable for 237 miles between North Fork and the confluence of the Salmon and the Snake. Private parties require permits to float the Wild section, from Corn Creek to Long Tom Bar, but only from June 20 to September 7. For a list of outfitters, including some who will take you the whole route, write the Idaho Outfitters and Guides Assn., PO Box 95, Boise, ID 83701 (phone: 208-342-1438), or the Salmon National Forest, Box 780, North Fork, ID 83466 (phone: 208-865-2383).

MIDDLE FORK OF THE SALMON, Idaho: This 105-mile stretch, floated by numerous private individuals and 29 outfitters, is a wild and scenic river that flows between Boundary Creek and the Main Salmon. It takes you through the Frank Church River of No Return Wilderness, over 80 or more wild rapids, and into the second deepest gorge on the continent (Hell's Canyon on the Snake is the deepest). During rest stops and overnights, you can explore creeks, waterfalls, side canyons, petroglyphs, historic sites, and hot springs. Information: Middle Fork Ranger District, Challis National Forest, PO Box 750, Challis, ID 83226 (phone: 208-879-5204); and the American River Touring Assn., Star Rte. 73, Groveland, CA 95321 (phone: 800-323-ARTA).

SELWAY RIVER, Idaho: From Paradise Guard Station at the mouth of White Cap Creek to Selway Falls, this river drops an average of 28 feet per mile. Too rocky for floating most of the time, it is among the most challenging whitewater courses in the country during peak spring runoff in the last week in May and the first two in June (applications for permits to float from May 15 to July 31 should be submitted between December 1 and January 31 to the West Fork Ranger Station, for a random drawing.) You wouldn't want to pit yourself against the Selway on a first river trip, but it's a good bet for veterans. There are also four commercial river guides catering to the inexperienced. The river's course takes you through the 1,337,681-acre Selway-Bitterroot Wilderness, among the country's largest, most of which is passable only on foot or by boat. Information: Bitterroot National Forest, West Fork Ranger Station, Darby, MT 59829 (phone: 406-821-3269); and the Nezperce National Forest, Moose Creek Ranger Station, PO Box 464, Grangeville, ID 83530 (phone: 208-983-2712).

ROGUE RIVER, Oregon: A National Wild and Scenic River, the 33 miles between Grave Creek and Watson Creek, about 25 miles from the Pacific, offer Class III rapids, high canyons, rock gorges, wildlife, good fishing (for steelhead, chinook, and silver salmon), and historic sites — Zane Grey had a cabin at Winkle Bar. There's whitewater on rapids like Mule Creek Canyon and Blossom Bar, but since there are long stretches of smooth water between them, commercial trips on the Rogue are good for families. Most operators run between Grave Creek and Foster Bar. Information: River Permits/ Information, 14335 Galice Rd., Merlin, OR 97532 (phone: 503-479-3735).

YOUGHIOGHENY RIVER, Pennsylvania: The trip down the 7½-mile wild section of this famous eastern whitewater stream lasts only a little over half a day, but you get quite a run for your money. The scenery is beautiful: laurel and rhododendron in the spring, wraithlike mists and lush forests in summer, and bright leaves in autumn. Information: Ohiopyle State Park, PO Box 105, Ohiopyle, PA 15470-0105 (phone: 412-329-8591).

CHATTOOGA, South Carolina: This National Wild and Scenic River, considered to be among the most beautiful in the world, can be rafted from March through October. After seeing *Deliverance,* which was filmed here, a lot of people who didn't know any better tackled the whitewater in metal canoes, and the canoes usually ended up on the river's bottom, torn to pieces or wrapped around rocks. In other words, this is no trip for beginners. But in a raft, and with a guide, almost anyone can shoot the rapids. *Wildwater* (PO Box 100, Long Creek, SC 29658; phone: 803-647-9587) has guided over 200,000 people on the Chattooga since 1971 and will show you how to run them — great for helping you understand swift water. There are stretches suitable for beginners through advanced in these 47 miles (spanning two national forests). Overnight trips are available. Other outfitters include *Nantahala Outdoor Center* (*NOC*), US 19 West, Box 41, Bryson City, NC 28713 (phone: 704-488-6900), which offers whitewater rafting trips on four more rivers in the Southeast, including the Ocoee River, one of the most recently popular recreational rivers in the US; and *Southeastern Expeditions,* 1955 Cliff Valley Way, Northeast Suite 220, Atlanta, GA 30329 (phone: 404-329-0433). Canoe and kayak trips are available from all three outfitters; day outings are offered for groups of 12 or more.

RIO GRANDE, Texas: A stretch of the Rio Grande within Big Bend National Park takes you through some of the most isolated country in America. You won't find much whitewater, but the floating is spectacular. Most trips run through either Santa Elena Canyon, Boquillas Canyon, or Mariscal Canyon. Santa Elena is deepest, and, because of Rockslide Rapids, wildest; Mariscal, most remote; Boquillas, 16 miles from end to end, the longest and great for sunsets. Raft trips of at least 30 miles include non-canyon stretches. Go in April to see a spectacular wildflower display, in May to see the bird migrations, or in October, which is the residents' favorite time because of the great weather and the ordinarily reliable water flows. One portion of the river, now designated the Rio Grande Wild and Scenic River, offers an 84-mile raft trip through the extremely remote "Lower Canyons." Information: Big Bend National Park, TX 79834 (phone: 915-477-2251).

COLORADO RIVER (CATARACT CANYON SECTION), Utah: In all of the immense Colorado River system, this stretch of water in Canyonlands National Park offers some of the most technically demanding whitewater and some of the most exciting rafting in the country — even if you don't go in the spring, when the flow is many times normal. Cataract Canyon lies just downstream of the Green's confluence with the Colorado; trips through the canyon begin either on the Green or the Colorado, and continue downstream to Lake Powell. Permits required — for the Cataract Canyon section only — for private parties. Information: Canyonlands National Park, 125 W. 2nd South, Moab, UT 84532-2995 (phone: 801-259-7164).

GREEN RIVER (GRAY AND DESOLATION CANYONS), Utah: Were you to put in on the Green below Flaming Gorge and float all the way to Lake Powell, several hundred miles later, you wouldn't find more interesting river country than this stretch between Sand Wash (about 42 miles southwest of Myton) and Green River City (some 96 miles later). Gray Canyon generally has the biggest rapids, but there are some in Desolation that, in the words of one river rat, will "eat you up if you don't know what you're doing." The scale of the canyon landscape is impressive. At Rock Creek, about halfway through the trip, it is as deep as the Grand Canyon. Views from the boat take in stands of Douglas fir, cottonwood groves, and petroglyphs from the Fremont culture of 1,200 years ago. Floating season is May through late September; spring is wildest, July and August hottest. Information and permits: Bureau of Land Management, PO Drawer AB, Price, UT 84501 (phone: 801-637-4584).

WHITEWATER STREAMS, West Virginia: The Mountain State's geographical position and topography conspire to dump abundant rain and snow on the Allegheny Highlands, a region of misty mountains, ridges, and deep gorges cut by eons of runoff. Major streams born here include the Cheat, Tygart, Greenbrier, Elk, Gauley, Meadow, and the three sisters of the Monongahela National Forest — the Cherry, Williams, and Cranberry rivers. All feature whitewater stretches suitable for various skill levels. In the south, New River and its rowdy tributary, the Bluestone, drain a huge, sparsely populated, and ruggedly beautiful watershed. In eastern West Virginia, the Potomac and its tributaries, the South Branch and the Cacapon, and the gentle Shenendoah combine whitewater and stunning landscapes rich in American history. Professional outfitters run trips on many of these streams in spring, summer, and fall, and also teach paddling and kayak skills to individuals. Information: Travel West Virginia, State Capitol Complex, Bldg. 6, Room 564, Charleston, WV 25305 (phone: 800-CALL-WVA).

Goin' Fishing: The Best Spots in America

 America's number one participation sport has hooked 25% of the US population, so it's no wonder that huge amounts of money, not to mention bureaucratic time and effort, go into massive stocking programs. Just where you'll find all these fish at any given time can vary from year to year, depending on water conditions, weather, chemicals, and season.

A long familiarity with the habits of fish in a single lake is almost a guarantee of hefty stringers, but, as the professional bass fishermen who fish many different lakes can tell you, it's enough to have reliable knowledge of the species' habits, and of the water temperatures, bottom conformations, shoreline, and so on, of the area you're fishing — information that is easily obtained from local fish and game authorities and from area marinas and bait and tackle shops.

EAST

Ocean fishing is big in all the coastal states — mainly for bluefish and stripers that migrate up and down the coast as they seek out congenial water temperatures. Inland, fishermen work the lakes and stalk the wily trout in streams and rivers.

MOOSEHEAD LAKE, Greenville, Maine: A sportfishing resort for over a century, the largest body of water in Maine provides landlocked salmon and brook and lake trout; deep waters (246 feet) and good oxygenation make the fishing good throughout the season — despite some fishing pressure from a variety of fishing camps around the shores. The steamer *Katahdin* cruises the lake daily in season. Call the *Moosehead Marine Museum* for reservations (phone: 207-695-2716). Area information: Moosehead Lake Region Chamber of Commerce, Box 581, Greenville, ME 04441 (phone: 207-695-2702).

OCEAN CITY, Maryland: The white marlin capital of the world sends fishermen out to the Baltimore and Washington Canyons, about 65 miles offshore, for dolphin, bonita, tuna, wahoo, shark, porgy, bluefish, seabass, and blue marlin. Surf casting and jetty fishing can also yield good results. Information: Chamber of Commerce, Rte. 1, PO Box 310A, Ocean City, MD 21842 (phone: 301-289-8559).

LAKE WINNIPESAUKEE, near Laconia, New Hampshire: The largest body of water in New Hampshire (70 square miles) offers some of the best stringers of lake trout and landlocked salmon in New England. Some 240 miles of shoreline on the mainland, and still more on 278 scattered islands, provide good habitat for bass and pickerel. Salmon are most active in April, May, and June (at the surface); later you've got to fish deeper. Lake trout are liveliest in April and May. There's ice fishing from ice-in through March for lake trout, but not salmon and other species. Information: Lakes Region Assn., PO Box 300, Wolfeboro, NH 03894 (phone: 603-569-1117), and the New Hampshire Fish and Game Dept., 2 Hazen Dr., Concord, NH 03301 (phone: 603-271-3211).

BATTENKILL RIVER, near Manchester, Vermont: This famous Vermont fishing stream, a forest-edged, sun-dappled angler's idyll, is heavily fished, but its long, slow, waist-deep pools give the brookies and browns who inhabit it "a two-day look at every visitor" (according to one veteran), and since the fish are not hatchery-bred, they don't regard man as a friend. The upshot is that the average fisherman doesn't get much: The stream is what you'd call a challenge. A nationally known tackle company based nearby can answer your questions about when and where. Information: Orvis, 10 River Rd., Manchester, VT 05254 (phone: 802-362-3900).

NEW RIVER, near Hinton, West Virginia: This fascinating fishing stream produces good creels of trophy white bass, hybrid striped bass, smallmouth bass, muskellunge, walleye, rock bass, and channel catfish. Best spots are downstream of the Bluestone Dam and at the New/Gauley confluence. Information: Dept. of Natural Resources/Wildlife, 1800 Washington St., East Charleston, WV 25305 (phone: 304-348-2771).

SOUTH

The southern fisherman heads for the Gulf or the Atlantic, where offshore oil rigs and artificial reefs draw huge populations of big fish, or for the huge Arkansas, Kentucky, and Tennessee impoundments, which are managed with fishing in mind. Crappie and largemouth bass are usually available, but depending on the area, you'll also get smallmouth, trout, stripers. Try western North Carolina and northern Georgia for trout.

LAKE EUFAULA, near Eufaula, Alabama: One of the finest largemouth fisheries in the country, not just for the quantity of fish available for the taking but also for their size. This impoundment of the Chattahoochee River along the Georgia-Alabama line is the site of many annual tournaments. Spring and fall are best. Information: Chamber of Commerce, PO Box 697, Eufaula, AL 36027 (phone: 205-687-6664).

WHITE RIVER, Lakeview, Arkansas: Local fishermen call this wilderness Ozarks stream the trout capital of the world; the lake water released below the Bull Shoals Dam is ideal for trout propagation, and record catches of rainbows and browns are not uncommon. For a list of outfitters, request the *Ozark Mountain Region Guide* from the Arkansas Dept. of Parks and Tourism, 1 Capitol Mall, Little Rock, AR 72201 (phone: 501-682-7777; 800-482-8999 in Arkansas; 800-643-8383 elsewhere).

BOCA GRANDE PASS, Boca Grande, Florida: One of the world's most famous fishing grounds, for the silvery legions of fighting tarpon that invade the Gulf every summer, will give you the liveliest action in June; the season extends from March through October. Information: Charlotte County Chamber of Commerce, 2702 Tamiami Trail, Port Charlotte, FL 33952 (phone: 813-627-2222).

DESTIN, Florida: Residents call Destin "the world's luckiest fishing village," and with more than 100 party boats and charters (the state's largest fishing fleet) charging into the Gulf every day, they just may be right. The quarry: pompano, grouper, king mackerel, sailfish, blue marlin. The *Destin Seafood Festival* takes place the first week of October; the *Deep Sea Fishing Rodeo,* October 1-31. Information: Chamber of Commerce, PO Box 8, Destin, FL 32541 (phone: 904-837-6241).

BILLFISH ALLEY (DE SOTO CANYON), south of Ft. Walton Beach, Florida: Paralleling the coast for a hundred miles, this offshore depression offers an abundance of white and blue marlin, sailfish, tuna, dolphin, wahoo, and swordfish. (Best fishing is May through October.) Information: Chamber of Commerce, PO Drawer 640, Ft. Walton Beach, FL 32549 (phone: 904-244-8191); Panama City Beach Resort Council, PO Box 9473, Panama City Beach, FL 32407 (phone: 904-234-6575).

THE KEYS, Florida: Islamorada, Marathon, and Key West are the three main centers in the area for bonefish, permit, and tarpon; Islamorada's sportfishing fleet is one of the US's largest. And that doesn't include the deep-sea fishing — for marlin, sailfish, grouper, and the other big ones. Information: Chamber of Commerce, 3330 Overseas Hwy., Marathon, FL 33050 (phone: 305-743-5417); Greater Key West Chamber of Commerce, 402 Wall St., Key West, FL 33040 (phone: 305-294-2587); Chamber of Commerce, PO Box 915, Islamorada, FL 33036 (phone: 305-664-4503).

ALLIGATOR ALLEY, between Naples and Ft. Lauderdale, Florida: Along the canal that parallels Rte. 84, bass and bluegills feed and reproduce in nearly ideal conditions (it's said that more tolls have been paid by fisherman than by cross-state drivers). Fishing is best at low water. Information: Naples Area Chamber of Commerce, US 41, Naples, FL 33940 (phone: 813-262-6141).

TEN THOUSAND ISLANDS, near Naples, Florida: This trackless mangrove wilderness of creeks, oyster-bottomed coves, and rivers, stretching 60-odd miles along the Gulf Coast, is one of the best US spots for snook, a battling tropical fish found only in southern Florida; May through July is the season. Information: Naples Area Chamber of Commerce, 1700 N. Tamiami Tr., Naples, FL 33940 (phone: 813-262-6141).

LAKE OKEECHOBEE, Okeechobee, Florida: Some of the world's finest black crappie fishing can be found at this inland sea, the second largest body of fresh water entirely within the US; you can also take bluegill and bass, plus catfish that sometimes take two hands to display. The season runs from November to April. Information:

Okeechobee County Chamber of Commerce, 55 S. Parrott Ave., Okeechobee, FL 34972 (phone: 813-763-6464).

LAKE JACKSON, near Tallahassee, Florida: There is an interesting reason for the legendary catches of big largemouth bass at this angling hot spot. Every 25 years or so, three or four sinkholes, part of an underground river system, open up and drain the lake, thereby exposing the bottom to sunlight, rejuvenating plants, and thus improving the habitat for fish — so that they grow bigger. Information: Office of Informational Services, 620 S. Meridian St., Tallahassee, FL 32399-1600 (phone: 904-488-4676).

LAKE BARKLEY and KENTUCKY LAKE, near Cadiz, Kentucky: The 220,000 acres of water (with 3,500 miles of shoreline) shared by these two impoundments offer some of the state's most consistently fine bass fishing — with an abundance of largemouth, smallmouth, and spotted bass (the last two are especially plentiful in Kentucky Lake). The area has also been called the "crappie capital of the world." March through November is the season. Information: Land Between the Lakes, TVA, Golden Pond, KY 42231 (phone: 502-924-5602).

GRAND ISLE, Louisiana: Internationally known for its deep-sea fishing, especially around offshore oil rigs. The surf fishing — for trout, flounder, sheephead, tarpon, reds, and mackerel — is also great. Information: Nez Coupe Souvenir & Tackle Shop, PO Box 171, Grand Isle, LA 70358 (phone: 504-787-3352).

CURRITUCK SOUND, Knotts Island, North Carolina: This huge shallow expanse of water between Kitty Hawk and the Virginia line offers some of the best freshwater fishing in the country — largemouth plus rock bass, speckled trout, and white perch. The sound's size and its hundreds of islands make a guide essential. Good catches are the rule April through November, especially during southerly winds. There is a bass tournament in mid-October. Information: Elizabeth City Area Chamber of Commerce, PO Box 426, Elizabeth City, NC 27907-426 (phone: 919-335-4365).

OUTER BANKS, North Carolina: The proximity of the Gulf Stream to this slender finger of sand has brought good fishing close to shore. There are blue and white marlin, flounder, weakfish, bonito, tuna, dolphin, barracuda, wahoo, sailfish, Spanish and king mackerel, and bluefish aplenty. Best fishing is from April through November. Information: Outer Banks Chamber of Commerce, PO Box 1757, Kill Devil Hills, NC 27948 (phone: 919-441-8144).

LAKES MARION and MOULTRIE, near Santee, South Carolina: This 171,000-acre impoundment of the Santee and Cooper rivers, the first in the country with a landlocked striped bass program, offers some of the best fishing for these fighters, and has produced world-record channel catfish and warmouth as well as black crappie, and bowfin. Crappie and largemouth are especially plentiful. Information: Santee-Cooper Country, Drawer 40, Santee, SC 29142 (phone: 803-854-2131).

MIDWEST

Michigan, Minnesota, and Wisconsin together boast nearly 5 million fishing license holders, so it's not surprising that the angling is lively. The best fishing is for trout on Michigan's Au Sable, Manistee, Pine, Rifle, and upper Muskegon rivers; for steelhead in April; and for smallmouth bass in lakes in the northwest part of the lower peninsula.

In Minnesota, on the other hand, walleye is the fish — but you can also get smallmouth on the waters along the Canadian border; pike in the north, muskie in the Boy River chain, the Mantrap chain, and Big Lake and Leech Lake; and kamloops and native steelhead in the streams that empty into Lake Superior.

Missouri's fishing is mainly in the big southwestern reservoirs, but there's also float fishing for bass and panfish on the Jack's Fork, the Meramec, the Eleven Point, Niangua, James, Big Piney, and Current rivers. Ohio's western basin produces some of the US's best walleye fishing in spring and summer — off reefs, island shorelines, and submerged shoals.

Wisconsin produces salmon beginning in August around Kenosha, Milwaukee, and Racine. Fishermen troll for lake trout in summer and go for cohos and brown trout between Bayfield and Washburn. There are smallmouth in all the northern lakes, especially on the Door County peninsula in July and August.

LAKE MILLE LACS, near Brainerd, Minnesota: The fact that between opening day and late July the harvest of walleyes allegedly ran to 2½ tons of fish a day (or about 400,000 over the whole period one year) gives you an idea of the scope of the fishing here. Information: Chamber of Commerce, 6th and Washington, Brainerd, MN 56401 (phone: 218-829-2838; 800-432-3775 in Minnesota).

WEST

Salmon fishing in Alaska is the standard by which all other salmon fishing is matched; you can get kings in May and June and silver salmon in autumn. But California is the bigger fishing state, with over 2 million holders of fishing licenses and 500 charter boats leaving from ports up and down the coast — for salmon in the north, and for yellowtail, albacore, and bonito in the south.

Trout reigns as king in Colorado. Ditto for Idaho, the Black Hills of South Dakota, western Montana, and the mountain lakes of California and Washington. Idaho's Snake, Clearwater, and Salmon Rivers are visited every year by huge quantities of steelhead and chinook in October, November, March, and April.

Hawaiian catches hold more than half of the International Game Fish Association records for blue marlin — but there's also adventure to be had in going for bonefish (not in the flats as in Florida but in deep water) and surf casting.

In Oregon and Washington, charters go for salmon and tuna from June through September. Chinook and silver run in summer and early fall, and steelhead in winter.

Meanwhile, there are walleye in Missouri River impoundments in South Dakota, and in North Dakota, smallmouths around islands and flooded butte tops of the various impoundments. In Utah, 200-mile-long Lake Powell has crappie, striped bass, and walleye; bass are active March through May and late September and early November.

SACRAMENTO RIVER, Redding, California: Especially downstream from Redding to Hamilton City (August through December), this river offers excellent fine king salmon fishing. Hefty 25- to 30-pounders are common, and 40-pounders are occasionally pulled out. The Balls Ferry area south of Redding and the mouths of the American and Feather rivers are also good, as is the steelhead fishing in the Klamath River and Trinity, to name just a few: This is outdoor country par excellence. Information: Chamber of Commerce, PO Box 850, Red Bluff, CA 96080 (phone: 916-527-6220), and the Shasta-Cascade Wonderland Assn., 1250 Parkview Ave., Redding, CA 96001 (phone: 916-243-2643).

KONA COAST, Big Island of Hawaii, Hawaii: All but one of those record fish caught in Hawaii were pulled in off the Kona coast. Charters are plentiful around the port of Kailua. Information: Hawaii Visitors Bureau, 75-5719 W. Alii Dr., Kailua-Kona, HI 96740 (phone: 808-329-7787).

COLUMBIA RIVER, below the Bonneville Dam, Oregon: May and June shad runs are so huge that nearly everyone catches one of these strong-running, high-leaping fish; stringers of 25 (the limit) are not uncommon. Walleye fishing is a recent major attraction as are salmon and steelhead. There is wheelchair access at Cascade Locks, above the Dam. Information: Chamber of Commerce, Port Marina Park, Hood River, OR 97031 (phone: 503-386-2000); Columbia River Wholesale, 455 Wanapa, Cascade Locks, OR 97014 (phone: 503-374-8214); or Smith's War Surplus, 1737 Cascade St., Hood River, OR 97031 (phone: 503-386-3040).

PORT ARANSAS, Texas: Some 70 charter boats operate out of this small town on

Mustang Island, one of a handful of long, skinny islands that skim Texas's Gulf Coast. Sportsmen come by the dozen to cruise out to sea in search of finned fighters like tarpon, sailfish, tuna, marlin, and the like. But you don't have to be a diehard fisherman to have a great time here. Party boats accommodating anywhere from 18 to 100 passengers sail out to the snapper banks, about 1½ hours offshore, allowing anglers to haul in fish by the basketful. The so-called electric reels provided on the boats going out after snapper may take away some of the sport — just press a button and the reel whirls into action, bringing in a hooked fish in a trice. If you don't want to have to give away all your catch, be sure to stay in a motel with housekeeping facilities. Information: Chamber of Commerce, Box 356, Port Aransas, TX 78373 (phone: 512-749-5919; 800-242-3084 in Texas; 800-221-9198 elsewhere).

ILWACO, Washington: Each summer, a fleet of charter boats goes out into the Pacific for kings and silvers at the Salmon Capital of the World; several thousand salmon are caught offshore every year. Some fishermen, in fact, complain that they get their limit almost as soon as they leave shore, and don't know what to do with the rest of the day. The area is also famous for its razor clam digging. Information: South Pacific County Visitors & Convention Bureau, PO Box 562, Long Beach, WA 98631 (phone: 206-642-2400).

FIREHOLE RIVER, Yellowstone National Park, Wyoming: With headwaters near Old Faithful, this river is small by Western standards; the rainbows and browns that inhabit it are most commonly just 10 to 16 inches long; and the fish big enough to keep (those over 16 inches) are hard to catch, even in late May and June and again from late August until season's close in late October, when the mayfly and caddis fly hatches bring the trout into action. But the Firehole is one of the nation's great "total experience" rivers: Rarely will you fish here without seeing wildlife, and the scenery — forests, mountains, and clouds of steam rising from the great meadows that flank the stream — is superb. Information: Bud Lilly's Trout Shop, 39 Madison Ave., Box 698, West Yellowstone, MT 59758 (phone: 406-646-7801).

FISHING SCHOOLS

In the last few years, a number of fishing pros and tackle manufacturers have taken it upon themselves to teach the bumbling angler the fine art of filling up a stringer — so even if you didn't grow up in a fishing family, you can quickly begin acquiring the skills necessary to keep you hauling them in with the best. Some provide instruction in fly-fishing and concentrate on trout; others teach you bait- and spin-casting techniques.

FENWICK FLY FISHING SCHOOLS, based in Westminster, California: The company that took the lead in mass-producing first-rate fly rods some 20 years ago now turns out topnotch fishermen at the 2- to 5-day courses it offers all over the US and Mexico. The emphasis differs with the school locale; you can learn fly-fishing, bass and muskie tactics, steelhead techniques, and more. Information: Paul Brown, Fenwick/Woodstream Co., 14799 Chestnut St., Westminster, CA 92683 (phone: 714-897-1066).

BUD LILLY'S FLY-FISHING SCHOOL, West Yellowstone, Montana: Complete 2- and 3-day programs are offered. More informal programs are run daily in this scenic area; special courses are offered for women. Information: Bud Lilly's Trout Shop, 39 Madison Ave., Box 698, West Yellowstone, MT 59758 (phone: 406-646-7801).

JOAN AND LEE WULFF FISHING SCHOOLS, Lew Beach, New York: Two of the nation's most famous fishermen share their expertise with anglers of all skill levels at their school in the Catskills, just 120 miles from New York City. The Beaverkill is one of several productive waters where you can practice. Weekend courses (which include fly casting instruction) are offered in trout fishing and Atlantic salmon fishing, or you may take a course devoted entirely to just fly casting. Late April through June. Information: Joan and Lee Wulff Fishing School, Main St., Lew Beach, NY 12753 (phone: 914-439-4060).

ORVIS FLY-FISHING SCHOOL, Manchester, Vermont: This manufacturer of fine fishing gear, in business since 1856, has taught the intricacies of the sport to such luminaries as the late Supreme Court justice Potter Stewart, and in the opinion of some who know the field, its program — which includes practice in the company's stocked ponds, dry runs on the famous .Battenkill (see above), and classroom sessions — is one of the best of its kind. Students stay at the colonial *Equinox Inn.* In fall, Orvis sponsors a shooting school. Information: Orvis, 10 River Rd., Manchester, VT 05254 (phone: 802-362-3900).

Mountain Climbing and Mountains

Like all great sports, mountaineering allows the participant to choose the severity of the test — to match skills to challenge. Climbs can range from simple but rugged hikes requiring some technical work (that is, the use of chocks, nuts, ropes, ice axes, and crampons to get over vertical rock faces and icy surfaces) to high-altitude expeditions lasting weeks and requiring specialized skills, great reserves of strength and endurance, and sophisticated equipment. But one rule applies to all climbing: You are only as safe as your judgment and training are good. And it is always exhilarating.

Climbing is not a forbidding sport for a beginner, but the only way to start is with training. Best is a beginner's 1-day course; in the West, with either the *Exum Mountain Guides* in Grand Teton National Park, Box 56, Moose, WY 83012 (phone: 307-733-2297, seasonal), or at the *Yosemite Mountaineering School* in Yosemite National Park, Yosemite, CA 95389 (phone: 209-372-1335, June to mid-September; 209-372-1244, rest of the year). In the East there's a school sponsored by *Eastern Mountain Sports,* Main St., PO Box 514, North Conway, NH 03860 (phone: 603-356-5433). A 1-day course will give a not too strenuous introduction to belaying, anchoring, rappelling, and moderate-angle climbing; and even with these modest skills you will be able to take rocks which in your pre-course life you'd have judged unclimbable.

Better than a 1-day course (which is really more orientation and encouragement than adequate training for more rigorous climbs) is a week or multi-week course, which provides an active, exciting vacation. The one you pick will depend on where you want to be and what you want to learn — rock work, snow and ice techniques, or expedition planning. Some courses concentrate on one subject; others combine the three.

CLIMBING SCHOOLS

PALISADE SCHOOL OF MOUNTAINEERING, Bishop, California: Week-long courses and guided climbs are offered during summer, operating out of a base camp in the Palisades, a 10-mile-long crest of jagged peaks and glaciers. You can learn ice and snow climbing, rock climbing, and expedition planning. Also offered are expeditions to the Mexican volcanoes, the Ecuadorian Andes, and the Japan Alps. Information: Palisade School of Mountaineering, PO Box 694, Bishop, CA 93514 (phone: 619-873-5037).

COLORADO MOUNTAIN SCHOOL, Estes Park, Colorado: Basic to advanced ice, snow, and rock climbing courses and climbs in Rocky Mountains National Park, lasting from 1 to 7 days, are offered year-round by this establishment, as well as several expeditions. Information: Colorado Mountain School, PO Box 2062, Estes Park, CO 80517 (phone: 303-586-5758).

NANTAHALA OUTDOOR CENTER, Bryson City, North Carolina: This wilderness adventures center, the largest whitewater canoe and kayak instruction facility in the US, also offers a program of weekend and 5-day rock climbing clinics for beginners and intermediates, as well as regional bicycle tours, mountain-bike rentals, and hikes in the area around the Great Smokies. Information: Nantahala Outdoor Center, US 19W, Box 41, Bryson City, NC 28713 (phone: 704-488-2175).

RAINIER MOUNTAINEERING, Tacoma, Washington: Seminars in snow and ice climbing and guided summit climbs of Mt. Rainier are offered at this northwestern institution. Information: Rainier Mountaineering, 201 St. Helens St., Tacoma, WA 98402 (phone: 206-627-6242).

AMERICA'S MOUNTAINS FOR THE CLIMBING

LONGS PEAK, near Estes Park, Colorado: One way to reach this 14,255-foot summit in Rocky Mountain National Park involves a long, challenging trek from the Longs Peak Ranger Station through aspen stands and conifer forests, tundra, alpine meadows, and boulder fields through the Keyhole (about 8 miles). The north face route is less crowded, but climbing skills are required. Information: Backcountry Office, Rocky Mountain National Park, Estes Park, CO 80517-8397 (phone: 303-586-4459).

MT. KATAHDIN, near Millinocket, Maine: The 5,267-foot peak in Baxter State Park, the northern terminus of the Appalachian Trail, rises sharply as you get close to the 4,000-foot timberline. Most routes don't require ropes, and the climb takes a day — but slopes full of loose rock can make the going tough. Information: Baxter State Park, 64 Balsam Dr., Millinocket, ME 04462 (phone: 207-723-5140).

MT. WASHINGTON, near North Conway, New Hampshire: The view from the 6,288-foot summit — the "second greatest show on Earth," according to no less than P. T. Barnum — attracts hikers by the thousands. The trails up are steep, but not that steep. The danger, instead, lies in the weather, reputedly the worst in the world. It is treacherous, and ferocious snowstorms do blow up on a regular basis with practically no warning — even in summer. Information: Appalachian Mountain Club, PO Box 298, Gorham, NH 03581 (phone: 603-466-2725).

MT. MARCY, near Lake Placid, New York: This 5,344-foot Adirondack peak can be reached in a day over a variety of routes — most of them steep trails that make many climbers wish they were in better shape. The forests at the bottom — full of ferns and trees whose foliage seems almost electric green — may remind you of the Pacific Northwest rain forests. Information: New York State Dept. of Environmental Conservation, License Sales/Information Office, 50 Wolf Rd., Albany, NY 12233-0001 (phone: 518-457-3521).

MT. HOOD, near Government Camp, Oregon: The 11,235-foot summit of this inactive volcano has been conquered by many, but this climb takes technical know-how and preparation; it is the inexperienced, poorly equipped climber who is most apt to be injured (and well over a hundred people have lost their lives on the mountain). Most people follow the southside route, which departs from the *Wy'East Day Lodge,* where you can register and get current conditions at a 24-hour climbing station. Then you're off for the beautiful trip — beginning at midnight, past scenic glaciers and fumaroles. The best climbing is from May to mid-July. Information: Mt. Hood National Forest, 2955 N.W. Division St., Gresham, OR 97030 (phone: 503-666-0700).

MT. RAINIER, near Ashford, Washington: Visible on a clear day for over 100 miles in all directions, this 14,410-foot mountain, the fifth highest in the lower 48 states, is lush with wildflowers and giant forests below the 6,800-foot timberline, heavily glaciated above it. The 2-day trip to the top, which takes you over glaciers and crumbling lava, is long, strenuous, demanding, and not without hazards — but anyone in good condition can do it with a guide and the proper equipment. Information: Mt. Rainier National Park, Tahoma Woods, Star Route, Ashford, WA 98304 (phone: 206-569-2211).

GRAND TETON, near Jackson, Wyoming: Looking at it from below, you'd never think that relatively inexperienced climbers could safely scale the awe-inspiring 13,770-foot summit. However, the granite rock (solid enough that you can trust it) offers plenty of handholds and footholds — everything you need to climb a mountain, one step at a time, with some training, the proper equipment, and a guide (which more experienced climbers will be able to do without). *Exum Mountain Guides,* which operates the School of American Mountaineering (Box 56, Moose, WY 83012; phone: 307-733-2297 from June to mid-September) and *Jackson Hole Mountain Guides* (PO Box 5477, Jackson, WY 83001; phone: 307-733-4979), will take you on the 2-day climb to the top after you've spent 2 days in the climbing school. Information: Grand Teton National Park, PO Drawer 170, Moose, WY 83012 (phone: 307-733-2880).

Wilderness Trips on Foot

 Building your backpacking skills to the point that you can go deep into a trackless wilderness for a few weeks and come out none the worse for wear takes some time. But it's not impossible. Day hikes, for example, are a good introduction. All the national parks and forests, state parks and forests, and various other public lands have trails of various lengths that are perfect for simple walks. You'll be breaking in your boots so that over extended treks blisters will be less likely to develop, and you'll be building up your stamina.

From there, short trips close to home are your best bet. Or you can sign up for one of the various outdoor programs that school tenderfeet in wilderness and hiking skills. Guided trips build confidence and provide companionship. A few areas of the US have the counterparts of the hikers' huts scattered all over the Alps; you don't have to carry a tent or even food.

Then there are thousands of square miles of hikable terrain all over the country, with easy trails for novices, more rugged ones (steeper, less well maintained) for better hikers, and huge wildernesses where you can hike cross-country with just a topographic map and compass.

OUTDOOR TRAINING SCHOOLS

Some adults are lucky enough to have learned how to handle themselves in the wilderness when they were young — in the company of backpacking-loving relatives. Others must acquire camping skills on their own, and learn about everything from tree identification to backcountry first aid from books. For the very timid, however, there's no better introduction to woodcraft than one of the handful of outdoor training schools offered by a number of organizations around the country. The *National Outdoor Leadership School (NOLS)* and *Outward Bound,* listed below, are among the most important. You can find out about others in magazines like *Backpacker* (1515 Broadway, 11th Fl., New York, NY 10036; phone: 212-719-6000) and *Outside* (1165 N. Clark, Chicago, IL 60610; phone: 312-951-0990), where most advertise their services.

NATIONAL AUDUBON SOCIETY ECOLOGY CAMPS, based in Greenwich, Connecticut: These June, July, and August programs held in Connecticut, Maine, and

Wyoming focus on area ecosystems; you lodge in cabins and bungalows in each area and do your learning on field trips. Great for both adults and children. Information: National Audubon Society, 613 Riversville Road, Greenwich, CT 06831 (phone: 203-869-2017).

OUTWARD BOUND USA, based in Greenwich, Connecticut: With schools in Maine, Colorado, Minnesota, North Carolina, and Oregon; at each, the aim is to help you move beyond your self-imposed limits as well as to provide an enjoyable wilderness experience. Information: Outward Bound, 384 Field Point Rd., Greenwich, CT 06830 (phone: 203-661-0797 or 800-243-8520).

BOULDER OUTDOOR SURVIVAL SCHOOL, Provo, Utah: The mountains, deserts, and canyonlands of Utah are the setting for this small but venerable institution's 12-, 15-, and 26-day programs. You learn primitive fire building techniques, trap-and-snare construction, plant identification, primitive direction finding, shelter construction, and more. But increased self-confidence and personal awareness, and enhanced interpersonal relationships, are equally important benefits. *BOSS* also offers special courses and workshops on other similar subjects. Information: BOSS Booking Offices, PO Box 905, Rexburg, ID 83440 (phone: 208-356-7446).

AMERICAN HIKING SOCIETY, based in Washington, DC: This nonprofit hikers' association sponsors 2-week trail maintenance and construction trips from January until the end of September. Information: American Hiking Society, 1015 31st St. NW, Washington, DC 20007 (phone: 703-385-3252).

NATIONAL WILDLIFE FEDERATION CONSERVATION SUMMITS: Week-long programs with self-designed schedules in Colorado, Maine, and Washington, held in July and August, focus on natural history and outdoor recreation; the programs and activities are wonderful for families. Information: National Wildlife Federation, Conservation Summits Department, 1400 16th St. NW, Washington, DC 20036-2266 (phone: 703-790-4363).

NATIONAL OUTDOOR LEADERSHIP SCHOOL (NOLS), based in Lander, Wyoming: This organization, originally established to school wilderness-trip leaders in certain outdoor skills, offers courses in backpacking, minimum-impact camping, cross-country skiing, sea kayaking, and climbing, in Alaska, Washington, and Wyoming, as well as Mexico and Africa, all year. Information: NOLS, PO Box AA, Lander, WY 82520 (phone: 307-332-6973).

EASY LONG TRIPS

On these trips, you don't have to pack anything more than the clothes you'll need for the time you're away from home. Hikers' huts and inns provide your shelter.

YOSEMITE NATIONAL PARK, Yosemite, California: The High Sierra camps in this park are among the few places of their type in the US, where you can stay in the mountains overnight without having to camp out. The five tent-dormitory groups are roughly 9 miles apart. Hot showers, linen, blankets, soap, towels, and breakfast and dinner are provided for about $60 per person per night. Reservations (available in writing beginning December 1 and usually gone within 2 weeks) are required. Information: Yosemite Park & Curry Co., High Sierra Desk, 5410 E. Home Ave., Fresno, CA 93727 (phone: 209-454-2002).

GLACIER NATIONAL PARK, West Glacier, Montana: You can't exactly backpack from Sperry to Granite Park — the two rugged stone chalets in this park — but you can do overnight backpacks first to one and then to the other, returning to your car between times. Only the restrooms, in separate buildings, and the kitchens at both chalets have been modernized, so they're much as they were when built around World War I. Both are lit after dark by candlelight, both are in the National Register of

Historic Landmarks, and both are open only in July and August; rates are around $50 a night including three meals. Reserve well in advance. Information: Belton Chalets, PO Box 188, West Glacier, MT 59936 (phone: 406-888-5511 from April to mid-September).

WHITE MOUNTAINS NATIONAL FOREST, around North Conway, New Hampshire: In the heart of the Presidential range, a system of hikers' huts maintained by the Appalachian Mountain Club gives you almost unlimited hiking variety — both above and below tree line. No two are quite alike: Lakes of the Clouds, situated at the edge of two icy blue lakes above tree line, seems relatively new; the Madison Hut, just above tree line, is built of stone and seems almost ancient. Blankets (but not linen), dinners, and breakfasts are provided for the nightly charge, about $34 a person. Reservations are essential. Information: AMC, Pinkham Notch Camp, PO Box 298, Gorham, NH 03581 (phone: 603-466-2727).

INN-TO-INN HIKING, around Vermont: A group of country inns along an 80-mile section of Vermont's Long Trail have teamed up to offer special trips during which you sleep in big brass beds under antique quilts, soak off your sore muscles in claw-footed bathtubs, and bring your gear and car to the selected finish each morning, where it will await your later arrival as the innkeeper drives you back to the day's starting point. Information: Country Inns Along the Trail, c/o Churchill House Inn, RD 3, Box BTG, Brandon, VT 05733 (phone: 802-247-3300).

GUIDED HIKES

Not all organizations that sponsor trips for groups furnish the gear you'll need; some provide everything, while some will set you up with everything but a sleeping bag. Make sure to confirm this in advance, and find out whether the rates — usually from about $35 to $100 per day — include food, sleeping gear, lodging the night before the trip begins (if necessary), guides, equipment, and the like. For extensive lists of organizations offering group backpacking trips and hiking trips with pack stock carrying your gear, read *Outside* magazine, or consult Pat Dickerman's *Adventure Travel North America,* $14 postpaid from Adventure Guides, 36 E 57th St., New York, NY 10022 (phone: 212-355-6334 to order by credit card). Dickerman has also begun an advisory service that can book spaces on a variety of adventure outings, such as horseback trips, cattle drives, and river runs.

CAMP DENALI WILDERNESS LODGE AND NORTH FACE LODGE, Denali National Park, Alaska: Spectacular vacations in view of 20,320-foot Mt. McKinley in North America's highest national park, home of moose, caribou, grizzly bears, wolves, and white mountain sheep. Enjoy bird watching and wildflowers in early June; fall color and migrating sandhill cranes in late August and early September. Naturalist-guided hiking, canoeing, gold-panning, rafting, fishing and flightseeing, natural history evening programs, photography workshops also scheduled. *Wilderness Lodge* offers individual cabins and a central shower facility for stays of 3 to 5 nights or longer. *North Face Lodge,* in the heart of the park, with a spectacular view of the Alaska Range and Mt. McKinley, offers 1- and 2-night stays. Fees at both lodges include accommodations, transportation, meals, and access to all the activities and equipment. Information: Summer: Camp Denali, PO Box 67, Denali National Park, AK 99755 (phone: 907-683-2290); Winter: Camp Denali, Box 216, Cornish, NH 03746 (phone: 603-675-2248).

KENAI GUIDE SERVICE, Kasilof, Alaska: Offering 1- to 3-day "Touch of the Wilderness" hiking and light backpacking trips into the Kenai Mountains — walk on a glacier, see hordes of spawning red salmon, observe Dall sheep and mountain goats. Information: Kenai Guide Service, PO Box 40, Kasilof, AK 99610 (phone: 907-262-5496).

SIERRA CLUB, based in San Francisco, California: The conservation organization offers a variety of trips. Information: Sierra Club, Outing Dept., 730 Polk St., San Francisco, CA 94109 (phone: 415-776-2211).

UNIVERSITY OF THE WILDERNESS, based in Evergreen, Colorado: Its 5- to 10-day trips take you through the mountains, deserts, and river canyons of the southern and western US; workshops and classes on the Snowy Range Campus near Laramie, Wyoming, cover wilderness photography, art, music, Rocky Mountain flowers, wildlife, and related environmental subjects. Information: University of the Wilderness, PO Box 1687, Evergreen, CO 80439 (phone: 303-674-9724).

WILDERNESS SOUTHEAST, Savannah, Georgia: This active organization offers adventures for inquisitive minds via naturalist-led hiking, flatwater canoeing, sailing, and snorkeling programs in southeastern woodlands, islands, coral reefs, and swamps. Designed for all ages, year-round, and lasting 3 to 7 days. Information: Wilderness Southeast, 711 Sandtown Rd., Dept. BTG, Savannah, GA 31410 (phone: 912-897-5108).

APPALACHIAN MOUNTAIN CLUB, Gorham, New Hampshire: This group's guided overnight hikes give you insight into the White Mountains' natural and social history. Information: AMC, Pinkham Notch Camp, PO Box 298, Gorham, NH 03581 (phone: 603-466-2727).

AMERICAN FORESTRY ASSOCIATION, based in Washington, DC: Backpacking, canoeing, and rafting trips of 5 to 10 days in the wilds of both the East and West. Information: AFA Trail Riders, 1516 P St. NW, Washington, DC 20005 (phone: 202-667-3300).

BEST BACKPACKING SPOTS

There's good backpacking all over the country — even in the Midwest, where most of the forests have given way to farms and pastures. Best hiking and backpacking, however, lie in one of 11 general regions — Alaska, the Northwest Coast ranges, the Cascade range (slightly inland in Washington, Oregon, and northern California), the Columbia Plateau (just slightly inland from the Cascades), the Rockies (swooping through Idaho, western Montana, most of Wyoming and Colorado, and northern New Mexico), the Great Desert (covering most of Nevada), the Sierra (in California), the Colorado Plateau (northern Arizona, northwestern New Mexico, the southern two-thirds of Utah), the Ozarks of northern Arkansas and southern Missouri, the Appalachians (extending from northern Maine through Tennessee and Virginia), and the north woods of northern Michigan and Wisconsin and Minnesota. Each area has its particular characteristics.

Alaska's mountains, valleys, forests, and oceans are all wilderness; the climate is wet and temperate in the southern part of the state, drier and much colder (with winters that fall to 50F below) north of the Alaskan range, and drier and colder yet north of the Brooks range, where large trees simply do not exist and the vegetation has to hug the ground to survive the winds. Trails and cross-country travel are both possible, but mosquitoes, bad in June, sometimes make the wilds unpleasant.

The Northwest Coast ranges, with peaks less than 8,000 feet, are primarily distinguished by their weather — wet, with about 200 inches of rain each year — and the resultant lush growth of cedars, firs, hemlocks, spruces, redwoods, ferns, mosses, shrubs. Summer is the driest season; trail use is usually moderate. The Cascade range, paralleling the Northwest Coast range, has peaks up to 10,000 feet, somewhat lighter precipitation, dense forests except in areas covered by relatively recent lava flows, good trails — and all-around fine wilderness. The Sierra, made famous by John Muir, are known for their good hiking — and with reason. Not only are there awesome glaciated granite peaks (which are characteristic), but the climate is somewhat drier than along the coast, with low-altitude forests of ponderosa, yellow, and lodgepole pine, and white and red fir giving way to alpine lakes and lichen-covered granite boulders as you follow uphill trails (which are plentiful); in addition, mosquitoes and other pests are usually absent. It's not hard to understand why the area is heavily trafficked.

The Columbia Plateau, on the other hand, gets relatively little use. Home of some of the largest populations of cougar in the country, of eagles, hawks, salmon, and sturgeon (and relatively insect-free because of the overall aridity), it has areas of recent volcanic activity, like moonscapes; ponderosa pineland; alpine terrain; and canyons like the celebrated Hell's Canyon and Snake River Canyon. A good many people float the streams, but scarcely anyone ventures uphill. The Great Desert area, cut by mountain ranges of sculptured rock, is the wildest and least used. People think of it as hot and boring. Actually, it boasts a wide variety of terrain: handsome stands of the weird Joshua tree (in the Mojave Desert), the cactus of the Sonora Desert (archetypal desert), and sagebrush and cottonwood country in its Great Basin section. There aren't many designated backpacking trails, but if you've got the experience to go cross-country, this is a place to do it.

The Colorado Plateau is characterized by its weirdly shaped buttes, canyons, mesas, and a range of environments from desert to alpine. It's hikable so long as you're prepared.

The Rockies, on the other hand, require less experience. More than 40 monuments, forests, and parks make this Valhalla for foot travelers; there are snow-capped peaks, fields of wildflowers, alpine lakes, icy streams, slopes full of conifers and deciduous trees. With the Sierra, this is the US's prime backpacking territory.

The Ozarks offer some backpacking through dense forests in low mountains and shallow valleys, scattered with caves and underground rivers; this is especially good if you want to travel cross-country, though long trails have recently become more abundant. The north woods, on the other hand, are full of trails. Flat and rolling countryside makes the going fairly easy as well, and huge numbers of lakes offer fine campsites.

In the East, the Appalachians make for the best backpacking. The peaks are lower and more rounded than those in the West, but many of the grades are just as steep as those in the rest of the country. The Appalachian Trail runs the length of the chain for 2,100 miles from Maine to Georgia; the oldest long-distance trail in the US, the Long Trail, runs for 265 miles along the spine of the Green Mountains in Vermont. For details about these long trails, contact the *Appalachian Trail Conference,* PO Box 807, Harpers Ferry, WV 25425-0807 (phone: 304-535-6331), or the *Green Mountain Club,* PO Box 889, Montpelier, VT 05602 (phone: 802-223-3463).

In addition to these long trails, there is yet a third — the recently designated North Country National Scenic Trail, the country's longest, which runs for 3,246 miles from Crown Point, New York, across seven northern states to the Lewis and Clark National Historic Trail at Lake Sakakawea in North Dakota. Information: North Country Trail Assn., PO Box 311, White Cloud, MI 49349 (phone: 402-221-3371).

TONTO NATIONAL FOREST, Phoenix, Arizona: This is the largest national forest in the state, with more than 2.8 million acres, an 800-mile trail system, and eight wilderness areas that go from an elevation of 1,500 feet to nearly 8,000 feet. You'll find desert, grassland, piñon, a maze of box canyons, arid mountains covered with chaparral, as well as some ponderosa pine and mixed conifer at the higher elevations. Experience in desert travel and sufficient reserved water are important. Trail conditions vary from excellent to very poor. Several *Recreation Opportunity Guides and Maps* are available, which give detailed information on the specific area and its trails. Information: Tonto National Forest, PO Box 5348, Phoenix, AZ 85010 (phone: 602-225-5200).

OUACHITA NATIONAL FOREST, Hot Springs, Arkansas: Some of America's best hiking is to be found along the ridge-climbing, scenic, 186-mile-long Ouachita National

Recreation Trail and its 40-odd miles of spurs. Information: Ouachita National Forest, PO Box 1270, Hot Springs, AR 71902 (phone: 501-321-5202).

OZARK NATIONAL FOREST, Russellville, Arkansas: The Ozark Highlands Trail stretches for 130 miles across the forest, which is most beautiful in spring, when dogwoods and redbuds bloom by the thousands, and during fall foliage season. Information: Ozark National Forest, PO Box 1008, Russellville, AR 72801 (phone: 501-968-2354).

KLAMATH NATIONAL FOREST, Yreka, California: Above the California-Oregon border, this region has vast forests largely unused, because the many other national forests one must pass through on the way tend to absorb the majority of visitors. Here are outstanding backpacking possibilities (as well as river activities) in a state that is full of them, because of the size (almost 1.7 million acres) and the fine forests of pine, cedar, Douglas fir, and hemlock that cover mountains ranging up to 8,000 feet. You can hike 1,100 miles of trails, most just moderately steep, and cross-country in the roadless areas of five established Wilderness Areas (covering 500,000 acres): Salmon-Trinity Alps, Russian, Siskiyou, Red Buttes, and the Marble Mountain. The wildlife population includes elk, pronghorn antelope, black bear, couger, and wild horses, and in the spring and fall, you'll see a spectacular wildfowl show, as birds from Canada and Alaska, moving along the Pacific flyway, converge on the eastern part of the forest. The Pacific Crest Trail also runs through the Klamath. Information: Klamath National Forest, 1312 Fairlane Rd., Yreka, CA 96097 (phone: 916-842-6131).

NEZPERCE NATIONAL FOREST, Grangeville, Idaho: An incredible trail system — over 2,300 miles — makes this 2.2-million-acre forest one of the best for backpacking in the Rockies. An elevation range from 1,000 feet to 10,000 feet makes for plenty of variety — deep river canyons, rolling prairies, and rugged mountain peaks. Three Wilderness Areas (covering almost 1 million acres) and four Wild and Scenic Rivers fall within park boundaries. Information: Nezperce National Forest, Rte. 2, Box 475, Grangeville, ID 83530 (phone: 208-983-1950).

SUPERIOR NATIONAL FOREST, Duluth, Minnesota: One of the finest forest areas in the country, these 3 million acres take in a million acres of wilderness scattered with lichen-covered granite outcrops and lakes — about two thousand of them, with rocky shorelines, islands, and occasional sand beaches. And there are over 250 miles of maintained hiking trails varying in length and difficulty. The fishing — for walleye, northern pike, trout, and bass — is superb; some people come for that alone. Information: Superior National Forest, PO Box 338, Duluth, MN 55801 (phone: 218-720-5324).

TOIYABE NATIONAL FOREST, Sparks, Nevada: The largest national forest in the lower 48 states, the Toiyabe is scattered across central, southern, and western Nevada, and the eastern slopes of the Sierra Nevada in eastern California. The Toiyabe has high sierra environments with alpine lakes, icy streams, spectacular granite formations, and coniferous forests; and desert-like country with cactus, creosote bush, yucca, and juniper and piñon stands. Hundreds of miles of trails poke into every corner of its 3.4 million acres; those in California's Hoover Wilderness near Yosemite and Mt. Charleston in the Las Vegas district are heavily used, while trails in the newly established Carson-Iceberg and Mokelumne wildernesses and the high desert ranges of central Nevada are quiet. Temperatures are not as forbidding as you might expect, although snow may occur any month of the year. For a few brief weeks, generally in October, you can gather the tasty piñon pine nuts, long an important food staple for the native Americans of Nevada and California, and a great delicacy nowadays. Information: Toiyabe National Forest, 1200 Franklin Way, Sparks, NV 89431 (phone: 702-331-6444).

WILLAMETTE NATIONAL FOREST, Eugene, Oregon: You can do outstanding backpacking on good trails through over 1,675,000 acres, 379,000 of which have been designated as wilderness: the Diamond Peak Wilderness, a cluster of volcanic peaks covered with fir, hemlock, pine, and meadows, scattered with lakes; the Bull of the Woods Wilderness, a terrain of rocky ridgetops and forested dells; the Mt. Jefferson Wilderness, which surrounds an extinct, glacier-covered volcano; the Three Sisters Wilderness, whose extensive trails take you through vast forests, sub-alpine terrain, meadows, and expanses of basalt and obsidian left from recent volcanic activity; the Mt. Washington Wilderness, much of which is lava flow; and more. Information: Willamette National Forest, PO Box 10607, Eugene, OR 97440 (phone: 503-687-6521).

SISKIYOU NATIONAL FOREST, Grants Pass, Oregon: The low mountains in the southwestern corner of the state are covered by wonderful flowering bushes — wild lilac, azaleas, and rhododendrons among them — and crossed by fine fishing streams, including the celebrated Rogue. You can hike along the Rogue River Trail, a part of the 36,038-acre Wild Rogue Wilderness, through the rugged Coast Range; along the Boundary Trail through Craggie Scenic Area; to Hanging Rock on the Panther Ridge Trail; or through the rugged Kalmiopsis Wilderness, 179,650 acres of rocky hills and low canyons where you'll see interesting hardwoods and shrubs, some quite rare. Hornets, yellow jackets, poison oak, and rattlesnakes are common but not usually a problem if you take some care. Superb fishing in the Rogue River during fall's massive salmon and steelhead migration. Siskiyou is also the gateway to Oregon Caves National Monument. Information on specific trails may be obtained from the supervisor's office in Grants Pass (phone: 503-479-5301) or the following Ranger Districts: Chetco (phone: 503-469-2196); Galice (phone: 503-476-3830); Gold Beach (phone: 503-247-6651); Illinois Valley (phone: 503-592-2166). Information: Siskiyou National Forest, PO Box 440, Grants Pass, OR 97526 (phone: 503-479-5301).

ASHLEY NATIONAL FOREST, Vernal, Utah: The 460,000-acre High Uintas Wilderness — a wonderful expanse of lakes, forests, meadows, and rocky mountains, which the Ashley National Forest shares with the Wasatch National Forest — is what most people come to hike from July through September, but similar environments can be found throughout the more than 1.3 million acres of this national forest, particularly on the east, which is far less crowded. Lakes, streams full of trout, and many exposed geologic formations are also here. Information: Ashley National Forest, Ashton Energy Center, 1680 W. Hwy. 40, Suite 1150, Vernal, UT 84078 (phone: 801-789-1181).

For the Mind

Regional American Theaters

 A note in the program tells you to keep the aisles free of obstructions, and when the lights go down and the actors come whooping down the aisles around you, you know why.

Regional theater isn't always so exuberant, but it's not provincial either. The old situation, in which all you had in the hinterlands was dinner theater and summer stock of varying quality, no longer exists. Regional theater — theater outside New York City — has entered its prime, and some of the most exciting and innovative productions, the kinds that "lower the drawbridge between actor and audience," in the words of one critic, go onto stages all over the country. Regional theaters provide actors with a year-round opportunity to get back to the basics, and give talented local authors and first-timers a chance to get their works produced. Meanwhile, whether the play ends up on Broadway or never gets more than a reading, audiences get some lively dramatic experiences.

EAST

GOODSPEED OPERA HOUSE, East Haddam, Connecticut: Works of Cole Porter, George Gershwin, and Rodgers and Hart are among the classics regularly played here, as American musicals comprise this theater's repertoire. The *Goodspeed* puts on three shows during its season, April through December. Information: Goodspeed Opera House, Rte. 82, East Haddam, CT 06423 (phone: 203-873-8668).

HARTFORD STAGE COMPANY, Hartford, Connecticut: This innovative organization presents an assortment of six plays during its season (October through June) in productions that are noteworthy for their style, verve, and aesthetic vision; the focus is on presenting new works and rediscovering — and reinterpreting — the classics. Information: Hartford Stage Co., 50 Church St., Hartford, CT 06103 (phone: 203-527-5151).

LONG WHARF THEATRE, New Haven, Connecticut: This prestigious regional theater welds fine ensemble performances by some of America's best actors to what the artistic directors like to call "plays of character," which are produced in two intimate theaters. Numerous *Long Wharf* productions go on to New York stages. Among past hits: *The Gin Game, Sizwe Banzi Is Dead, The Shadow Box,* and *Joe Egg.* Information: Long Wharf Theatre, 222 Sargent Dr., New Haven, CT 06511 (phone: 203-787-4282).

TRINITY REPERTORY COMPANY, Providence, Rhode Island: Eleven major productions of modern, classic, and original dramas are staged annually in two theaters. *Trinity Rep* makes headlines for itself as much for its characteristic vigorous ensemble style as for the plays themselves. The theater won a Tony Award as the nation's best repertory company in 1981 and, in 1984, the first Ensemble Grant from the National Endowment for the Arts. Since it began in 1964, the two aims of the company have been to provide permanent employment for its resident artists and to involve the audience as participants in the theater experience. Information: Trinity Repertory

Company, 201 Washington St., Providence, RI 02903 (phone: 401-521-1100; box office, 401-351-4242).

ARENA STAGE, Washington, DC: One of the oldest and most consistently admired American theater companies and the first outside New York to receive a Tony for theatrical excellence, *Arena Stage,* founded in 1950, is noted for developing American drama and for introducing foreign (particularly Eastern European) plays to the US. The theater's three stages seat 827, 514, and 180; the last is used for small musical revues and experimental works. Robert Prosky and James Earl Jones have performed here; past productions include *After the Fall* by Arthur Miller, *Happy End* by Bertholt Brecht and Kurt Weill; *Women and Water* by John Guare, *A Lesson from Aloes* by Athol Fugard, *Tomfoolery* by Tom Lehrer, George Bernard Shaw's *Major Barbara,* and *On the Razzle* by Tom Stoppard. Reservations necessary. Information: Arena Stage, 6th St. and Maine Ave. SW, Washington, DC 20024 (phone: 202-554-9066; box office, 202-488-3300; TDD number for deaf patrons, 202-484-0247).

SOUTH

ACTORS THEATRE OF LOUISVILLE, Louisville, Kentucky: In recent years, the two stages here have become bright spots on the American theater scene. The annual *Humana Festival of New American Plays,* initiated in 1977, has gained international critical attention and has sent graduates on to successful runs on both coasts: *Agnes of God, Crimes of the Heart, Extremities,* and *Getting Out* all premiered here. The four dozen or so productions each season, both classics and innovative new works, are presented in a main auditorium and a smaller upstairs theater — both in a grand old columned building that has been designated a National Historic Landmark. Information: Actors Theatre of Louisville, 316-320 W. Main St., Louisville, KY 40202 (phone: 502-584-1265; box office, 502-584-1205).

DALLAS THEATER CENTER, Dallas, Texas: Conventional dramas and plays by contemporary authors, many of them premières, alternate between the *Kalita Humphreys Theater* and the *Arts District Theater,* the latter a flexible, open performance space. Preston Jones's *A Texas Trilogy* got its start here. Besides the six works presented each season on both stages, an additional two plays, considered by the Center to be somewhat more controversial or just plain "different" (*Cloud 9* among them), are staged at a downstairs studio theater. Information: Dallas Theater Center, 3636 Turtle Creek Blvd., Dallas, TX 75219 (phone: 214-526-8210; box office, 214-526-8857).

ALLEY THEATRE, Houston, Texas: Classical drama, notable contemporary revivals, and new works chosen for ideas and language (usually 12 each season) are presented on both a large thrust-stage theater and a smaller arena theater. Both are in a stunning concrete and glass structure downtown. The *Alley* is one of the country's oldest resident professional theaters. Information: Alley Theatre, 615 Texas Ave., Houston, TX 77002 (phone: 713-228-9341; box office, 713-228-8421).

MIDWEST

GOODMAN THEATRE, Chicago, Illinois: The second oldest regional theater in the country, the *Goodman* mounts frequent productions of works by living writers, brings classics up to date in eye-opening ways, and stages that colorful favorite, *A Christmas Carol,* at the end of the year. There are two theaters: the *Studio,* which seats 135, and the *Mainstage,* which seats 683. Information: Goodman Theatre, 200 S. Columbus Dr., Chicago, IL 60603 (phone: box office, 312-443-3800).

ORGANIC THEATER, Chicago, Illinois: Dedicated to producing world première theater. From its science fiction trilogy *Warp!* to the pirate epic *Bloody Bess,* award-winning *Adventures of Huckleberry Finn,* baseball comedy *Bleacher Bums,* long-running *E/R Emergency Room,* and surreal comedy *Rubber City,* the *Organic* has explored the full range of theatrical expression. David Mamet's *Sexual Perversity in*

Chicago started out here, too. Information: Organic Theater, 3319 N. Clark St., Chicago, IL 60657 (phone: 312-327-5588).

GUTHRIE THEATER, Minneapolis, Minnesota: With 1,441 seats, the *Guthrie* is the largest of the country's regional theaters. It also has the longest season, and its house, which shares a handsome contemporary building with the *Walker Art Center,* is one of the most unusually designed, with a unique thrust stage that gives audiences access to three sides of the production; no member is more than about 50 feet from the actors. Classical drama, European revivals, and American plays are presented Tuesdays through Sundays. Hume Cronyn, Jessica Tandy, Frank Langella, and Michael Moriarty are among scores of actors who got their start, or polished their skills, on the *Guthrie* stage. Information: Guthrie Theater, 725 Vineland Pl., Minneapolis, MN 55403 (phone: 612-377-2224).

CINCINNATI PLAYHOUSE IN THE PARK, Cincinnati, Ohio: World premières of plays by new American playwrights, classics, rarely presented works, musicals, and comedies are the staples in the two theaters of this much-praised regional professional company. Information: Cincinnati Playhouse in the Park, PO Box 6537, Cincinnati, OH 45206 (phone: 513-421-5440; box office, 513-421-3888 and, in Ohio only, 800-582-3208).

MILWAUKEE REPERTORY THEATER, Milwaukee, Wisconsin: This institution, active since 1954, presents classics and exciting contemporary plays, often with a regional emphasis. The *MRT* presents six mainstage productions in its 720-seat theater during its September/October, May/June seasons. The beloved *A Christmas Carol* is presented at the *Pabst Theater* in December. Performances are also held at the 216-seat *Stiemke Theater* and the 100-seat *Stackner Cabaret.* The *MRT* plays to nearly 200,000 people annually and its shows have toured internationally. Information: Milwaukee Repertory Theater, 100 E. Wells St., Theater Complex, Milwaukee, WI 53202 (phone: 414-224-9490).

WEST

MARK TAPER FORUM, Los Angeles, California: One of the nation's most respected resident theaters, the *Mark Taper Forum* production of *Children of a Lesser God* won Tony awards for best play, best actor, and best actress in 1979 and for overall theatrical excellence in 1977, the same year Michael Cristofer's *Shadow Box,* which was produced here, won a Pulitzer. On the main stage, you'll see many premières and an occasional revival; the subject matter tends toward the timely, the currently problematical. Also under the *Taper* wing are the *Improvisational Theatre Project,* the intimate *Taper, Too* house, and the Sunday-afternoon *Literary Cabaret.* Information: Mark Taper Forum, 135 N. Grand Ave., Los Angeles, CA 90012 (phone: 213-972-7211).

AMERICAN CONSERVATORY THEATRE (A.C.T.), San Francisco, California: A bit of Shakespeare, some Chekhov, some Shaw, works by Lanford Wilson, Sam Shepard, and Terence Rattigan, and world premières by a slew of others have played to capacity audiences at this San Francisco theater, which started out in Pittsburgh and moved to the coast in the mid-sixties. A second performing space showcases works in progress. There are also signed performances for the hearing impaired, handicapped accessibility, and the annual year-end production of *A Christmas Carol,* now a Bay Area tradition. Information: A.C.T., 450 Geary St., San Francisco, CA 94102 (phone: 415-673-6440).

SEATTLE REPERTORY THEATRE, Seattle, Washington: Modern and contemporary comedies and dramas, both classics and premières, are performed at the 860-seat *Bagley Wright Theatre* at Seattle Center and in the *PONCHO Forum,* an intimate studio theater seating 170, where fully produced, often controversial plays are presented. Information: Seattle Repertory Theatre, Seattle Center, 155 Mercer St., Seattle, WA 98109 (phone: 206-443-2210; box office, 206-443-2222).

Outdoor Dramas

Paul Green, who in his long career as a dramatist wrote some of the best of these native American epic plays, called this dramatic form "a people's theater," and anticipated the day when it would ripen into something like the outdoor drama of the Greeks. Whether or not we ever see that day, 1¾ million travelers make an annual pilgrimage to woodland amphitheaters across the country to watch these spectacles of war and peace, statesmen and villains, heroes and plain folk, prejudice, feuds, murder, night riders, love and suffering — the very stuff of American history acted out a lot larger than most of it was lived.

Outdoor drama is not a subtle art form, since it employs many pageant elements. These summer epics have two compelling virtues that would win audiences in any case: They are natively American, based on legends, stories, tall tales, and real history told in the very places where the legends occurred, the history was lived; and they are exciting — colorful, enthusiastically acted, compulsively produced with horses charging, guns and cannon exploding, flames leaping, and extravagant costuming and good music. And they are also generally inexpensive; reserved seats (which you should consider) usually cost less than $10 a head; unreserved even less. For a complete list of American outdoor dramas (there are more than 60), send a self-addressed and stamped envelope to the Institute of Outdoor Drama, LB 3240 Graham Memorial, University of North Carolina, Chapel Hill, NC 27599-3240 (phone: 919-962-1328).

EAST

TRAIL OF THE LONESOME PINE, Big Stone Gap, Virginia: The love story of a mountain girl and a mining engineer from the East, set in the days when coal and iron discoveries were changing the lives of the mountain people. It's a true story, presented not far from where the couple wooed, in this part of the state so deeply affected by mining. Mid-June through August. Information: June Tolliver Playhouse, PO Box 1976, Big Stone Gap, VA 24219 (phone: 703-523-1235).

HATFIELDS AND McCOYS and HONEY IN THE ROCK, Beckley, West Virginia: The saga of the most famous feuding families in America (complete with a runaway daughter, a stillborn baby, killings, bounties, and betrayal) alternates in repertory with the story of the formation of West Virginia during the Civil War. Indians coined the phrase "honey in the rock" to refer to natural gas which escaped from cracks in rocks and which they worshiped (as you'll see in a scene in which gas jets under the stage are ignited). Late June through early September. Information: PO Box 1205, Beckley, WV 25802 (phone: 304-253-8313; 800-642-2766 in West Virginia in summer).

SOUTH

GREAT PASSION PLAY, Eureka Springs, Arkansas: The quaint hillside town where Carry Nation made her last temperance speech also puts on a pageant about Christ's last days, complete with camels, horses, sheep, donkeys, doves, and a cast of over 200. Last Friday of April through last Saturday of October. Information: The Great Passion Play, Box 471, Eureka Springs, AR 72632 (phone: 501-253-9200).

ARKANSAW TRAVELLER FOLK AND DINNER THEATRE, Hardy, Arkansas: This evening of Ozark food, good country music, and comedy based on the 1840 legend of the Arkansaw Traveller is in its 20th successful year. (When visiting a fellow mountain man, the Traveller asks about a leaky roof; the man explains that when it's raining he can't fix it, and when it's not, he doesn't need to.) Late May through early September. Information: Arkansaw Traveller, PO Box 536, Hardy, AR 72542 (phone: 501-856-2256).

CROSS AND SWORD, St. Augustine, Florida: Paul Green's production of Pedro Menéndez de Avilés's founding of St. Augustine, the oldest permanent settlement in the US, was first seen in 1965, the year the city celebrated its 400th birthday; it now plays from mid-June through mid-August. Information: Cross and Sword, PO Box 1965, St. Augustine, FL 32085 (phone: 904-471-1965).

STEPHEN FOSTER STORY, Bardstown, Kentucky: A musical about how the composer wooed and won his Jeanie with the light brown hair (whose real name, it turns out, was Jane). Mid-June to Labor Day. Information: Stephen Foster Story, PO Box 546, Bardstown, KY 40004 (phone: 502-348-5971).

LEGEND OF DANIEL BOONE, Harrodsburg, Kentucky: This popular drama focuses on the history of the great pioneer, at the *James Harrod Amphitheatre* in Old Fort Harrod State Park — a 28-acre preserve set up to honor the first permanent white settlement in Kentucky. (*Lincoln,* the amphitheater's other outdoor drama, focuses, naturally, on the history of the great president.) Mid-June through late August. The *Trustees' Office,* the Shaker restaurant and inn at nearby Shaker Village of Pleasant Hill (phone: 606-734-5411; see *America's Special Havens*), and the lovely *Beaumont Inn,* with overnight accommodations and a restaurant serving traditional Kentucky fare (Harrodsburg, KY 40330, phone: 606-734-3381), are area musts. Information: Legend of Daniel Boone, PO Box 365, Harrodsburg, KY 40330 (phone: 606-734-3346).

HORN IN THE WEST, Boone, North Carolina: This story of how the earliest American pioneers rebelled against the royal governor and went west was written by Kermit Hunter, a celebrated creator of outdoor dramas. Late June through mid-August. Information: Horn in the West, PO Box 295, Boone, NC 28607 (phone: 704-264-2120).

UNTO THESE HILLS, Cherokee, North Carolina: Kermit Hunter also wrote this piece about the Cherokee Indians from 1540 until 1838, when they were herded westward over the Trail of Tears; it's presented mid-June through late August at the *Mountainside Amphitheater,* on the edge of the Oconaluftee Indian Village, a replica of a Cherokee settlement of 200 years ago (see *A Short Tour of Indian America*). Information: Unto These Hills, PO Box 398, Cherokee, NC 28719 (phone: 704-497-2111).

THE LOST COLONY, Manteo, North Carolina: A fixture of the summer season on the Outer Banks since 1937, America's first outdoor historical drama tells the story of the birth of Virginia Dare and of the mysterious disappearance of Sir Walter Raleigh's first English colony in 1587, with music, Indian dances, fireworks, and grand court scenes. Mid-June through late August. Information: The Lost Colony, PO Drawer 40, Manteo, NC 27954 (phone: 919-473-2127 or 919-473-3414).

TEXAS, Canyon, Texas: The struggle between farmers and cattlemen in the not-always-so-gay 1880s is presented by a cast of 80, with new sound-and-light effects, at Palo Duro State Park, near Amarillo, from mid-June through late August in a 1,000-foot-deep, 100-mile-long canyon so impressive that in many ways it turns out to be the star of the show. Information: Texas, PO Box 268, Canyon, TX 79015-9989 (phone: 806-655-2181).

THE LONE STAR, Galveston, Texas: The story of the Texas fight for independence features a cast of over 80 (including six horses), cannon and gunfire, and a couple of really spectacular battle scenes. The hero of the production is Sam Houston, general of the Texas army that defeated Mexican general Santa Anna and his forces; Alamo heroes Davy Crockett and Jim Bowie are also on hand. The drama plays in repertory with a Broadway musical (which is changed from time to time) from June through August. Information: The Amphitheatre, PO Box 5253, Galveston, TX 77554 (phone: 409-737-1744).

MIDWEST

SHEPHERD OF THE HILLS, Branson, Missouri: Harold Bell Wright's novel of this name is reenacted on the farm where the 1902 Ozarks' drought it depicts actually took place. Branson is near 43,100-acre Table Rock Lake and Silver Dollar City, an amusement park where crafts is the theme. The drama is staged from late April through October. Information: Shepherd of the Hills Homestead and Outdoor Theater, HCR 2, Box 770, Branson, MO 65616 (phone: 417-334-4191).

TECUMSEH!, Chillicothe, Ohio: The Shawnee war leader's struggle with William Henry Harrison over the Northwest Territory involves a cast and crew of 80, a dozen horses, and thirteen stages, in performance mid-June through the beginning of September. Information: Tecumseh!, PO Box 73, Chillicothe, OH 45601 (phone: 614-775-0700).

TRUMPET IN THE LAND, New Philadelphia, Ohio: Outdoor drama spectacular with missionaries, Indians, soldiers, and the Revolutionary War on America's first frontier, complete with horses, a massacre, dances, and music. It's presented from mid-June through August about a mile from Schoenbrunn Village, a restoration of the settlement where many of the events took place. Information: Trumpet in the Land, PO Box 450, New Philadelphia, OH 44663 (phone: 216-364-5111).

BLACK HILLS PASSION PLAY, Spearfish, South Dakota: Under the direction of Josef Meier, an ensemble of some 200 players present the last seven days in the life of Christ, from June through August in Spearfish and mid-February through mid-April in Lake Wales, Florida. Information: PO Box 489, Spearfish, SD 57783 (phone: 605-642-2646), or PO Box 71, Lake Wales, FL 33859-0071 (phone: 813-676-1495).

WEST

RAMONA OUTDOOR PLAY, Hemet, California: This love story is set among the rolling hills in the colorful Hemet–San Jacinto Valley and uses an entire mountainside as a setting. Some consider the beauty of this dramatization of Helen Hunt Jackson's novel to be unparalleled. Since 1923, tourists from all over the world have found it a fascinating journey into the California of yesteryear. Six performances are presented in late April and early May. Tickets go on sale in January. Information: Ramona Pageant Assn., PO Box 755, Hemet, CA 92343 (phone: 714-658-3111 after January 1).

TRAIL OF TEARS CHEROKEE HERITAGE CENTER, Tahlequah, Oklahoma: The story of the Cherokees from the end of the tragic march over the Trail of Tears until the beginning of this century. The story is presented at the *Tsa-La-Gi Amphitheatre,* where, among other attractions, you can tour a re-creation of an early 17th-century Cherokee village, where Cherokee in costume work at crafting baskets, weapons, pottery, and tools. Mid-June through late August. The *Cherokee National Museum* uses state-of-the-art technology to present the Cherokee story from man's arrival in North America to the present day; it is open year-round. You can stay nearby at the pleasant *Tsa-La-Gi Lodge* (phone: 918-456-0511). Information: Trail of Tears, PO Box 515, Tahlequah, OK 74465 (phone: 918-456-6007).

Music Festivals:
Summers of Sound

 All over the country, throughout the summer, musicians get together to regale audiences with the glorious sounds of music — not just symphonies, string trios, chorales and cantatas, but also breakdowns, rags, gospel choruses, and a lot of country fiddling and picking. They're playing in mansions and amphitheaters, rustic gardens and antique opera halls, huge band shells, and even the California vineyards. Some festivals are 1-day happenings. Some mean round-the-clock music for a weekend or more.

State tourist organizations can tell you about the ones in the area you want to visit. Or, for a list of bluegrass events, you can contact *Bluegrass Unlimited* magazine for its annual festival edition ($1.95; PO Box 111, Broad Run, VA 22014; phone: 703-349-8181).

Expect to pay from about $5 to $50 for tickets, depending upon where, what, when, and whom. Should you order in advance? By all means, most especially if the object of your trip is to hear a specific performance. Usually, you will be able to get seats at the last minute (and at the big festivals you can always sit on the lawn), but advance planning will ensure your sitting where you want. Remember, too, that tickets for seats under a sheltering roof eliminate the chance that rain will wash out your enjoyment.

EAST

TANGLEWOOD, Lenox, Massachusetts: The *Boston Symphony Orchestra*, Seiji Ozawa, director, summers at this old, 210-acre Massachusetts mountain estate in the heart of the Berkshires. The orchestra performs for 10 weeks, Thursdays through Sundays, mostly during July and August, in an enormous covered amphitheater surrounded by lawns. Chamber music concerts take place most Thursday nights and selected other weeknights. There's a bounty of great country inns in the area. Information: Boston Symphony Orchestra, Symphony Hall, 301 Massachusetts Ave., Boston, MA 02115 (phone: 617-266-1492).

CHAUTAUQUA INSTITUTION, Chautauqua, New York: Founded in 1874 as a training camp for Sunday school teachers, this lakeside community of quaint Victorian guesthouses and hotels is a learning festival where music keeps company with operas, symphony concerts, popular entertainment, plays, lectures, and courses in the fine and performing arts, psychology, politics, philosophy, crafts, and just about any other subject you can name. Late June to late August. Information: Chautauqua Institution, Colonnade Bldg., Chautauqua, NY 14722 (phone: 716-357-6200).

LAKE GEORGE OPERA FESTIVAL, Glens Falls, New York: Favorite operas and American premières are sung in English by internationally recognized performers in fully staged productions with a professional orchestra during July and August in this most delightful of American vacation areas; Sunday evenings, there are Opera-on-the-Lake cruises. Information: Lake George Opera Festival, PO Box 425, Glens Falls, NY 12801 (phone: 518-793-6641).

HUNTER MOUNTAIN FESTIVALS, Hunter, New York: Hunter Mountain is big on ethnic festivals, offering a roundup from July to early September of Italian, German, Polish, American Indian, and Celtic music celebrations, as well as polka, golden oldies, and two country festivals (with artists on past rosters including Willie Nelson, Waylon Jennings, Emmy Lou Harris, Tammy Wynette, and the *Legends of Bluegrass*), for a total of nine separate festivals at this upstate New York ski mountain. Information: Exposition Planners Ltd., Bridge St., Hunter, NY 12442 (phone: 518-263-3800).

CARAMOOR FESTIVAL, Katonah, New York: On weekends from late June through late August, chamber and orchestral concerts are presented on an Italian Renaissance–style estate an hour's drive from Manhattan — the large works in an outdoor theater surrounded by 15th-century Venetian columns, the chamber concerts in a Spanish-style courtyard. Information: Caramoor, PO Box R, Katonah, NY 10536 (phone: 914-232-5035).

JVC JAZZ FESTIVAL, New York, New York: America's first and oldest jazz festival, born in 1953 as the Newport Jazz Festival and held in New York City since 1972, is now under the sponsorship of this large electronics company. It offers mostly big-name performers, with a few up-and-comers along the way, for 10 days in June at various spots in the city, including a boat cruise. Information: JVC Jazz Festival, PO Box 1169, Ansonia Station, New York, NY 10023 (phone: 212-787-2020).

SARATOGA PERFORMING ARTS CENTER, Saratoga Springs, New York: The watering hole of the horsey set, this genteel old town is also the home of the giant amphitheater where the *New York City Ballet* performs in July and the *Philadelphia Orchestra* in August. Popular special events, including the *Newport Jazz Festival–Saratoga,* are presented from June through September. And throughout the summer programs of theater and dance are presented in SPAC's *Little Theatre.* Information: SPAC Box Office, Saratoga Springs, NY 12866-0826 (phone: 518-587-3330). The *Gideon Putnam* hotel, on the grounds of the Saratoga Spa State Park (where you can still take the waters orally or in a variety of mineral baths), is posh and comfortable in that particular way that spells affluence (phone: 518-584-3000).

NEWPORT MUSIC FESTIVAL, Newport, Rhode Island: Three times daily, for 2 weeks every July, first-rate international artists perform classical music in the gilt and marble ballrooms of Newport's glorious mansions. Newport is one of the most prestigious musical festivals in the country. For lodgings, see *America's Special Havens.* Information: Newport Music Festival, PO Box 3300, Newport, RI 02840 (phone: 401-846-1133).

MARLBORO MUSIC SCHOOL AND FESTIVAL, Marlboro, Vermont: Fine musicians playing earnestly together under the direction of Rudolf Serkin make such music every weekend from mid-July through mid-August that most tickets sell out within a couple of weeks of an early April mailing. You may latch onto one of the hundred available for seating under a canopy outdoors by presenting yourself at the box office about an hour before curtain time (8:30 PM on Saturday, 2:30 PM on Sunday). To get on the mailing list, write to the Marlboro Music School and Festival, 135 S. 18th St., Philadelphia, PA 19103 (phone: 215-569-4690), before mid-June and after mid-August, or at Marlboro, VT 05344 (phone: 802-254-8163), in the summer. *The Inn at Sawmill Farm,* PO Box 367, West Dover, VT 05356 (phone: 802-464-8131), about 20 miles from Marlboro, offers especially pleasant lodgings (see *America's Special Havens*).

OLD FIDDLERS' CONVENTION, Galax, Virginia: One of the largest and best-known festivals devoted to traditional music, this institution of half a century's duration is held annually during the second full weekend in August. Information: Old Fiddlers' Convention, Oscar Hall, 328A Kenbrook Dr., Galax, VA 24333 (phone: 703-236-6355).

HAMPTON JAZZ FESTIVAL, Hampton, Virginia: The *Hampton Coliseum,* where this event is held, sells out well in advance for performances by top names in soul and jazz, annually the last weekend in June; generally Friday through Sunday. Information: Hampton Jazz Festival, PO Box 7309, Hampton, VA 23666-0309 (phone: 804-838-4203).

FILENE CENTER AT WOLF TRAP FARM PARK, Vienna, Virginia: At this national park for the performing arts, you'll get a cross section of what's going on in the American and international music scene: Big-name performers in the world of classical and popular music, ballet, opera, and modern dance may fill up the lawns and the big open-air pavilion, while next the air reverberates with the music of folk singers or bluegrass musicians like Bill Monroe or Doc Watson, or even tap-dance groups or country-and-western performers like Tammy Wynette — all of whom have been on stage in the last few years. Early June into September. Information: Wolf Trap Foundation, 1624 Trap Rd., Vienna, VA 22180 (phone: 703-255-1916).

NATIONAL FOLK FESTIVAL, based in Washington, DC (changing locations): An annual event since 1934, this noncommercial, free festival is the oldest multicultural folk festival in the US. Crafts demonstrations and storytelling are part of the goings-on, and a few other traditional arts are represented as well; but the real emphasis is on the music — bluegrass, blues, gospel and ballad singing, old-time fiddling, Tex-Mex, ethnic, and country music — and the nation's best performers in each genre appear. Joint sponsors are the National Council for the Traditional Arts and the National Park Service; the site changes yearly, as does the date — anytime between late July through late September. Information: NCTA, 806 15th St. NW, Suite 400, Washington, DC 20005 (phone: 202-639-8370).

SOUTH

MOUNTAIN DANCE AND FOLK FESTIVAL, Asheville, North Carolina: Square dancers and cloggers keep time to the music of mountain pickers, fiddlers, ballad singers, dulcimer players every August for this event, the oldest of its type in the country — it's been going strong since 1927. Information: Chamber of Commerce, PO Box 1010, Asheville, NC 28802 (phone: 704-258-3916 or 800-548-1300 in North Carolina; 800-257-1300 from other eastern states).

SPOLETO FESTIVAL USA, Charleston, South Carolina: Gian Carlo Menotti's important Italian arts festival made its stateside debut in 1977, and has been going strong ever since, every year for 17 days beginning in late May. Performances of all types of dance, theater, jazz, opera, and symphonic, choral, and chamber music endow this event with extraordinary breadth. Information: Spoleto Festival USA, PO Box 157, Charleston, SC 29402 (phone: 803-722-2764).

MIDWEST

RAVINIA FESTIVAL, Highland Park, Illinois: The *Chicago Symphony Orchestra* holds forth in the open-air pavilion of a 36-acre woodland park beginning in late June, and stands as the star attraction of this international festival of all the arts. Visiting orchestras, recitals and chamber music programs, ballet and dance, a jazz and popular music series, and a New Perspectives series are also a part of a long and varied summer season that lasts into September. Information: Ravinia Festival, 1575 Oakland Ave., Highland Park, IL 60035 (phone: 312-RAVINIA).

BEANBLOSSOM BLUEGRASS MUSIC FESTIVAL, Beanblossom, Indiana: This blink-and-you-miss-it settlement in the hilly southern part of the state really hops in June, when bluegrass music star and festival organizer Bill Monroe brings his musicians to town for a big bluegrass marathon. Of the thousands who come to watch the scheduled concerts in the wooded amphitheater, many set up tents and park their campers in a nearby field, and the air rings with the fiddling and picking of their jam sessions into the wee hours. Information: Monroe Festivals, 3819 Dickerson Rd., Nashville, TN 37207 (phone: 615-868-3333).

CINCINNATI MAY FESTIVAL, Cincinnati, Ohio: A 200-voice chorus and opera superstars perform cantatas and other major choral works annually during the last 2 weekends in May in the oldest continuing choral festival in the Western Hemisphere. Information: Cincinnati Music Festival Assn., Music Hall, 1241 Elm St., Cincinnati, OH 45210 (phone: 513-621-1919 or 513-566-8184).

BLOSSOM MUSIC CENTER, Cuyahoga Falls, Ohio: When the *Cleveland Orchestra* isn't playing at this woods-rimmed, cedar-shingled shell halfway between Akron and Cleveland, you'll find pop concerts — everything from the *Beach Boys* and Barry Manilow to jazz and ballet. All in all, some 80 musical events are held every year from mid-May through mid-September. Full banquet facilities are available. Information: Blossom Music Center, 1145 W. Steels Corners Rd., Cuyahoga Falls, OH 44223 (phone: 216-920-8040 or 216-231-7300).

WEST

CARMEL BACH FESTIVAL, Carmel, California: Works by Bach and others are performed in recitals (sometimes two a day), daily evening concerts, and matinees at the halls and churches — such as the Sunset Cultural Center and the Carmel Mission

Basilica — of this lovely, sophisticated village on the northern California coast for 3 weeks from mid-July to early August every year. Information: Carmel Bach Festival, PO Box 575, Carmel, CA 93921 (phone: 408-624-1521). Information about the many interesting hotels and restaurants in the area is available from the Carmel Business Assn., PO Box 4444, Carmel-by-the-Sea, CA 93921 (phone: 408-624-2522).

MONTEREY JAZZ FESTIVAL, Monterey, California: The sellout concerts that make up this event held annually the third weekend in September, the oldest continuously presented jazz festival in the nation, feature some of the biggest names in the business. Season tickets ($79) sell out by May 31; ground admission available through the festival weekend. Information: Monterey Jazz Festival, PO Box JAZZ, Monterey, CA 93942 (phone: 408-373-3366).

ASPEN MUSIC FESTIVAL, Aspen, Colorado: Constant musical activity of one sort or another — jazz, choral, orchestral, and operatic pieces, chamber works, and about anything else you can name — makes this festival, which is held annually from late June through late August, one of the nation's liveliest, and the town of Aspen an important cultural center. Sometimes the performers are name soloists on the order of Pinchas Zukerman and Arleen Augér; sometimes you'll be hearing gifted students from the Aspen Music School, whose sessions run concurrently. No matter. The repertoire of baroque through contemporary works is always interesting, and the performances are thoughtful and well executed. There's plenty of backpacking, hiking, swimming, fishing, horseback riding, and other outdoor activity going on during the off-hours. Information: Aspen Music Festival, PO Box AA, Aspen, CO 81612 (phone: 303-925-3254).

CENTRAL CITY OPERA, Central City, Colorado: American talent shows its stuff in imaginative productions sung in English in a tiny, acoustically perfect 19th-century opera house during July and August. Some of America's finest operatic singers perform here. Information: Central City Opera, 621 17th St., Suite 1601, Denver, CO 80293 (phone: 303-292-6500).

NATIONAL OLD-TIME FIDDLERS' CONTEST, Weiser, Idaho: Parades, barbecue dinners — and near-nonstop fiddling at daytime and nighttime competitions, and jam sessions in between — keep this town of 4,000 hopping every year the third full week in June. Weiser is the self-styled "fiddling capital of America" and the home of the Fiddlers' Hall of Fame, and the contest attracts some 300-plus contestants age 3 to 92 and nearly 5,000 spectators from all over the US and Canada. Information: Chamber of Commerce, 8 E. Idaho St., Weiser, ID 83672 (phone: 208-549-0450).

SANTA FE OPERA, Santa Fe, New Mexico: Familiar and unfamiliar works, plus American and world premières and an abundance of unusual compositions, alternate in repertory at this open-air theater during July and August. Tickets in advance are strongly recommended: Santa Fe is staging some of the nation's best opera. Information: Santa Fe Opera, PO Box 2408, Santa Fe, NM 87504-2408 (phone: 505-982-3851; box office, 505-982-3855).

PETER BRITT FESTIVALS, Jacksonville, Oregon: In the spectacular outdoor *Britt Music Pavilion,* the northwest's oldest music festival, founded to honor pioneer vintner, horticulturist, and daguerrotypist Peter Britt, now offers five festivals every summer; classical, bluegrass, jazz, dance, and musical theater. Reserve your seats and a picnic table. Arrange lodgings well in advance because of the concurrent *Oregon Shakespearean Festival,* some 15 miles away in Ashland. Information: Peter Britt Festivals, PO Box 1124, Medford, OR 97501 (phone: 503-779-0847; 800-88-BRITT in western states).

GRAND TETON MUSIC FESTIVAL, Teton Village, Wyoming: From mid-July until late August, for 7 weeks, you'll find great music in these oft-climbed mountains — small ensembles during the week, a full symphony orchestra on Saturdays; sometimes the artist or composer talks about the pieces beforehand. *Festival Hall* is known for its fine acoustics. Information: Grand Teton Music Festival, PO Box 310, Teton Village, WY 83025 (phone: 307-733-3050).

Restored Towns and Reconstructed Villages

 Williamsburg, Virginia, is only the most famous of America's restored towns: All over the country historical villages have been reconstructed — some simply repaired and restored, others pieced together from brand-new buildings or from original structures collected from numerous sites — to graphically re-create the day-by-day life of earlier periods in American history. At the best of these, curators hire craftspeople to demonstrate everyday tasks of the era, and provide lectures, walking tours, and special events. In general, the larger the restoration, the wider the variety of special activities.

And though not all museum villages are as authentic as Williamsburg, where the quest for historical accuracy extends to making male craftspeople's shoes from the same kind of leather that would have been used in the 18th century, curators at most museum villages take considerable pains to make sure that at least the most obvious things are correct. There's no better place to enjoy yourself learning history.

EAST

MYSTIC SEAPORT, Mystic, Connecticut: Gulls wheel and cry overhead while you're walking around the 17 acres of this re-created New England sea village, where, along with blacksmithing, woodcarving, fireplace cooking, and weaving, there's a ship's chandlery, sail loft, ship model shop, printers' shop, general store, tavern, and more. You may see shipwrights at work on 19th-century ships and boats, and the restored *Charles W. Morgan,* America's last surviving wooden whaleship and a National Historic Landmark, towers proudly over it all. And there's more at this outdoor maritime museum: more ships; the US's largest collection of small boats; exhibits of scrimshaw, marine art, and figureheads; steamboat cruises; children's games; a planetarium; demonstrations of sail-setting and furling and other marine skills; special events all year; and, at Christmas, a lively program of lantern-light tours and other period merriment. Information: Mystic Seaport, PO Box 6000, Mystic, CT 06355-0990 (phone: 203-572-0711). (See also *Mystic Seaport,* DIRECTIONS.)

PLIMOTH PLANTATION, Plymouth, Massachusetts: This reconstruction of the Pilgrims' village now includes a dozen-plus houses, a fort, and farm buildings where men and women in period dress portray residents of the early colony in speech, manner, and attitude, while pursuing the daily routine of the 17th-century farming community. The Pilgrims, it turns out, did not wear somber clothes, but instead, like other working folk of the time, wore colorful garments often decorated with lace and stitchery. In the Wampanoag Summer Campsite, museum staff recount the history and traditions of the native people who befriended them. Closed from December through March. Three miles north of the plantation, on Water St., is Plymouth Rock, and at State Pier is an exact replica of the *Mayflower.* Its sails are made of flax and sewn by hand, its beams pegged together with "tree nails" made from 120-year-old cider vats. Information: Plimoth Plantation, PO Box 1620, Plymouth, MA 02360 (phone: 508-746-1622). As for actual colonial landmarks, nearby Duxbury and Kingston have street upon street of old homes. In Plymouth itself, visit the houses of the Pilgrims, their burial sites, a gristmill, and the town's two wineries (one of which, aptly enough, produces only cranberry wine). Thanksgiving is a particularly good time to go; there's a public feast at the town's Memorial Hall, and a reenactment of the Pilgrims' Progress to church. Information: Plymouth Area Chamber of Commerce, 91 Samoset St., Plymouth, MA 02360 (phone: 508-746-3377).

OLD STURBRIDGE VILLAGE, Sturbridge, Massachusetts: Things are so authentic at this re-created village that sheep help to trim the grass on the village green, and the general store is stocked with just those items an early-19th-century shopper would have expected. Hardworking ladies cook up savory goodies on open hearths, using 19th-century "receipts," and blacksmiths, broom-makers, coopers, printers, shoemakers, and other artisans go about their work the traditional way. The purpose is to show rural America turning into industrial America, and so in addition to the farm and the gristmill, there are exhibits like the water-powered wool carding mill and the 1830s sawmill. Sturbridge is one of the most respected establishments of its type, the largest living history center in the Northeast, and even without its huge assortment of period theatricals, speech makings, church services, and other special events, you could go back many times and never see it all. At Thanksgiving, *Ballard Tavern* puts on a traditional feast. Reservations are necessary. Information: Old Sturbridge Village, Sturbridge, MA 01566-0200 (phone: 617-347-3362). At the *Publick House,* a quaint inn outside the restoration area, Christmas brings a wonderful Edwardian Yule feast-cum-pageant complete with scarlet-coated beefeaters and a boar's head (phone: 617-347-3313; see *America's Special Havens*).

STRAWBERY BANKE MUSEUM, Portsmouth, New Hampshire: Beginning in the 1600s, this neighborhood flourished for some 200 years, only to sink into what seemed a lasting decline in the mid-1800s. But a 10-acre area was rescued from demolition in the 1950s and has since been largely restored. Of the 35 historic houses, 5 are furnished in different period styles, 6 contain museum exhibits, 5 house crafts workshops, and the remainder are in various stages of completion. Two major restorations opened in summer 1987. In all, there are 85 exhibition rooms in 11 different buildings as well as several period gardens. Information: Strawbery Banke Museum, PO Box 300, Portsmouth, NH 03801 (phone: 603-433-1100).

FARMERS' MUSEUM AND VILLAGE CROSSROADS, Cooperstown, New York: The message here is how, in the 75 years between the end of the Revolution and the beginning of the Civil War, the plain people of America built a nation where only forests had stood. The museum's Main Barn has displays on farm technology, village life, domestic economy, 19th-century trades, and amusements. Craftspeople work at broom-making, cabinetmaking, spinning, and weaving nearby. Outside, there's a dirt-laned village where you'll see more of the same in period buildings while sheep wander around on the green; in summer the green is the site of stilt-walking and 19th-century games. There is also open-hearth cooking at the farmhouse, herbal cure preparation in the druggist's shop, and home-roasted coffee in the tavern. Special programs include a *Harvest Festival* in the fall; 19th-century–style Fourth of July celebration; seminars dealing with American culture during a week in July; and, scattered throughout the year, craft workshops for the interested amateur as well as the professional. Lodgings in the area include the fine Georgian-style *Otesaga* (phone: 607-547-9931; see *Resort Hotels*). Information: The Farmers' Museum, PO Box 800, Cooperstown, NY 13326 (phone: 607-547-2533).

GENESEE COUNTRY MUSEUM, Mumford, New York: Some 55 19th-century American buildings gathered from upstate New York and restored on this rolling 125-acre site reflect American life in the early 1800s. New additions include an elegant Italianate home, its 2-story carriage house, and handsome sunken formal gardens, a gunsmith shop, and a 2-story Shaker building. You'll also see a pottery, bandstand, farm, parsonage, pioneer settlement, a variety of homes, an inn, a Methodist church, a score of working crafts shops, and offices, all peopled by costumed "villagers." The unusual Gallery of Sporting Art explores man and his animals. Next to the museum complex is the new Nature Center, 200 acres of trails exposing visitors to the flora and fauna of the region. Open from mid-May through the third week of October, with special events most weekends. Information: Genesee Country Museum, Flint Hill Rd., Mumford, NY 14511 (phone: 716-538-6822).

HOPEWELL FURNACE NATIONAL HISTORIC SITE, near Elverson, Pennsylvania: This settlement, dating to 1770, is the most far-ranging restoration of the kind of iron producing center that flourished in this corner of southeastern Pennsylvania in the 18th and 19th centuries. The ironmaster's home, charcoal house, waterwheel, blast machinery, casting house, cold-blast furnace, tenant houses, and barns are all open year-round. Blacksmithing, metal casting, carpentry, and other skills and crafts of the early 19th century are demonstrated from late June through Labor Day. Information: Hopewell Furnace, RD 1, PO Box 345, Elverson, PA 19520 (phone: 215-582-8773).

SHELBURNE MUSEUM, Shelburne, Vermont: In these collections of Americana housed in 37 historic buildings moved to the 45-acre site from all over New England, you'll see hundreds of carousel figures, cigar store Indians, cradles, dolls, dresses, horse-drawn vehicles, quilts, rugs, ship figureheads and shop figures, tin bathtubs, tools for farming and woodworking, and toys. The collection of decoys is the largest in the US. The massive steamship *Ticonderoga,* now landlocked, presides over it all. To see it all, go between mid-May and mid-October; only a few buildings are open in winter — and only on Sundays. The best lodgings are at the classy *Basin Harbor Club,* on Lake Champlain, open from mid-June through mid-October (phone: 802-475-2311; see *Resort Hotels*); eat at the handsome, antiques-filled *Dog Tavern* — and don't miss those great sticky buns (phone: 802-388-7651). Information: Shelburne Museum, Shelburne, VT 05482 (phone: 802-985-3344).

JAMESTOWN, Jamestown, Virginia: Foundations, property ditches, a church tower dating to 1639, and a few streets in the Jamestown National Historical Site are all that remain of the city that served as Virginia's capital and cultural center for 92 years; the liveliest area is the Glasshouse, reconstructed and fitted out so that craftsmen can make glass as they did here three centuries ago. The museum contains one of the largest collections of 17th-century artifacts in the country, part of which is on display at the visitors center. Three- and 5-mile drives provide access to the marshes and pine forests of Jamestown Island. Nearby, at the 25-acre Jamestown Festival Park, are a reconstructed fort; a 17th-century Indian village; exhibitions and demonstrations of skills as performed in the 17th century (agriculture, Indian technology, seamanship, carpentry); full-scale replicas of the three famous ships that, though hardly bigger than yachts, transported 104 men and boys to Virginia in 1607. There is also an indoor museum, expanded and renovated in 1989, which features an orientation film and exhibitions that tell the story of Jamestown's beginnings in the Old World, the Powhatan Indian culture encountered by the colonists, and the first 100 years of the colony. Information: Jamestown Settlement, PO Drawer JF, Williamsburg, VA 23187 (phone: 804-229-1607); Colonial National Historical Park, PO Box 210, Yorktown, VA 23690 (phone: 804-229-1733). (See also *Tidewater Virginia,* DIRECTIONS.)

COLONIAL WILLIAMSBURG, Williamsburg, Virginia: All the superlatives apply to this restoration of Virginia's 18th-century cultural, social, and legislative center — not just for the sheer size of the collection (150,000 items, 173 acres, 88 colonial and early-19th-century buildings, several hundred reconstructions, and 2 formal museums), but also for the variety of crafts demonstrated (36 in all), the historical authenticity, and the craftworkers' knowledge. Summer days, spring and autumn weekends, and Christmas are the busiest times here, which may mean standing in line to get into the taverns. Information: Williamsburg Area Tourism & Conference Bureau, PO Box GB, 901 Richmond Road, Williamsburg, VA 23187 (phone: 804-253-0192). (See also *Tidewater Virginia,* DIRECTIONS.)

YORKTOWN, Yorktown, Virginia: The final conflict of the War of Independence was fought here during the spring of 1781, when the British general Lord Cornwallis led his army into Virginia in the hope of conquering the southern colonies. Opposing him was the smaller American force led by General Lafayette. After several skirmishes, Cornwallis received orders to fortify Yorktown as a base for contact with the British fleet. Meanwhile, General George Washington decided that a combined land and naval battle in Virginia was now possible. On September 5, the French fleet intercepted the British outside the Virginia capes and forced it to retire: Washington and Rochambeau arrived later in the month and laid siege to the town. The Celebration of Victory, held here every October, commemorates this historic event. Like neighboring Williamsburg and Jamestown, Yorktown proper offers a number of sites that portray the Revolutionary War period and the climactic siege; they are open year-round, with extended hours in summer. Information: Colonial National Historic Park, PO Box 210, Yorktown, VA 23690 (phone: 804-898-3400).

SOUTH

HISTORIC ST. AUGUSTINE, St. Augustine, Florida: The Spanish settled in St. Augustine in 1565, making this the US's oldest permanent settlement. The plain stucco houses of the restored section line a narrow street across from the Castillo de San Marcos (the fort that protected the town) and fill a couple of side streets as well. At work in some buildings are a candlemaker, carpenter, Spanish cigarmaker with lightning-fast hands, and a weaver who crafts marvels out of the loveliest of wools. The settlement's story is told at the Visitor Information Center — a good place to begin any visit — and at the outdoor drama *Cross and Sword,* performed during summer months (see *Outdoor Dramas*). Special events include an annual Blessing of the Fleet on Palm Sunday weekend and, on Easter Sunday, a Parada de los Caballos y Coches, a parade of horse-drawn carriages. Other events include a *Days in Spain Festival* in August, a maritime festival the first weekend in October, and reenactments of various historic events year-round. Information: St. Augustine and St. Johns County Chamber of Commerce, PO Drawer O, St. Augustine, FL 32085 (phone: 904-829-5681).

WESTVILLE 1850, Lumpkin, Georgia: Life in the South wasn't all barbecues and 17-inch waistlines. Some people lived in modest homes, gathered eggs in the baskets they crafted, made pottery jugs and bowls, repaired buggies, dried fruits, stored vegetables, made syrup from sugarcane, and ginned cotton and baled it — all things you'll see demonstrated at this nifty re-created village. Extra craftsmen are on hand for the *Fair of 1850,* the first week in November, and there are Maypole dances on May Day, a barbecue on July 4, and Christmas activities every Saturday in December. Information: Westville 1850, PO Box 1850, Lumpkin, GA 31815 (phone: 912-838-6310).

MIDWEST

LINCOLN'S NEW SALEM STATE HISTORIC SITE, Petersburg, Illinois: Edgar Lee Masters's home town of Petersburg, the setting for his *Spoon River Anthology,* is a mere 2 miles from the town where Abraham Lincoln tended store, worked as a postmaster, studied law, learned surveying, and, in 1837, got himself elected to the legislature. A variety of buildings have been reconstructed next to the Onstott Cooper Shop (an original structure that has been restored) on a site presented to the state by William Randolph Hearst. There are craft workers on hand during the summer and for special events throughout the year. Information: Lincoln's New Salem State Historic Site, RR 1, Box 244A, Petersburg, IL 62675 (phone: 217-632-7953).

HENRY FORD MUSEUM & GREENFIELD VILLAGE, Dearborn, Michigan: The *Henry Ford Museum*'s phenomenal collection of American decorative arts, tools, household furnishings and appliances (whole collections of washing machines, vacuum cleaners, and sewing machines, for instance), and implements of agriculture, communications, lighting, power, and, especially, transportation cover 12 acres — but that's only what you'll see in the museum. Set in Greenfield Village, on an adjacent 240 acres, are, for starters, a courthouse where Abe Lincoln practiced law as a circuit rider; Edison's Menlo Park, New Jersey, laboratory; homes or birthplaces of the Wright brothers, Luther Burbank, Noah Webster, Harvey Firestone, Henry Ford, and William Holmes McGuffey (of McGuffey's *Reader*); and nearly 80 other structures that tell the story of American life from the colonial period to the turn of the century. Many were moved from their original sites. The emphasis is on the changes that occurred in America with the new processes and inventions of the Industrial Revolution. Depending on the season, you can ride in a horse-drawn carriage or sleigh, an antique car, a steam train, a steam-powered paddlewheel boat — or even take a spin on a 1913 carousel. Best lodgings in the area are at the Georgian-style *Dearborn Inn* (phone: 313-271-2700; see *America's Special Havens*). Information: Henry Ford Museum and Greenfield Village, PO Box 1970, Dearborn, MI 48121 (phone: 313-271-1620).

LUMBERTOWN USA, Brainerd, Minnesota: The town that calls itself Paul Bunyan's home is also the site of a re-created 1870 logging center with bunkhouse, mess hall, saloon, and nearly 30 other buildings. Closed mid-September through late May. Information: Chamber of Commerce, Brainerd, MN 56401 (phone: 218-829-2838).

STUHR MUSEUM OF THE PRAIRIE PIONEER, Grand Island, Nebraska: The cottage in which native son Henry Fonda was born is on display here along with some 60 other structures — and an operating steam train — that give a vivid impression of what life was like for the ordinary pioneers here on the south-central Nebraska prairie. The village is open May through September; you can visit two museums also on the property year-round. Nearby are Harold Warp's Pioneer Village and the 1864 Fort Kearny State Historical Park, once an important stop on the Oregon Trail. Information: Stuhr Museum, 3133 W. Hwy. 34, Grand Island, NE 68801 (phone: 308-381-5316).

HAROLD WARP'S PIONEER VILLAGE, Minden, Nebraska: This antiques collection installed in a group of 26 buildings compactly arranged on a 20-acre site shows you "man's progress since 1830." That means, in part, that you'll see not one old kitchen setup but several (from 1830, 1860, 1890, 1910, 1930, 1950, and 1980) as well as living rooms and bedrooms — 22 rooms in all. Stoves, refrigerators, 300 autos and trucks, farm machinery, farm tractors, bikes, boats, planes, fire engines, streetcars, steam engines, locomotives, and many other familiar objects get the same thorough treatment; there are 50,000 historic items at this 36-year-old institution. Information: Harold Warp Pioneer Village Foundation, PO Box 68, Minden, NE 68959 (phone: 308-832-1181; 800-445-4447 outside Nebraska).

WEST

BODIE STATE HISTORIC PARK, near Bridgeport, California: Within 20 years of the discovery of gold in 1859, Bodie was, in the words of its pastor Reverend F. M. Warrington, "a sea of sin lashed by the tempests of passion." It had 30 mines, breweries, 65 saloons, ale stoops, pothouses, restaurants, gin mills, and opium dens; and, on Maiden Lane and Virgin Alley, plenty of ladies — Eleanor Dumont (alias Madame Mustache), Nellie Monroe, French Joe, and Rosa May. Five percent of the original structures have withstood the years of fire and heavy snowstorms since the town's heyday; the 170 buildings that have survived are maintained by the California State Park system in a state of "arrested decay" — that is, minor repairs are made and walls are shored up, but no attempt is made to make Bodie look any different than it did when it was at last abandoned. Peering through windows as you take the mapped-out walking tour, you'll spot old-fashioned condiments and canned goods on a general store shelf; caskets inside the morgue; a pipe organ in the Methodist church. It can all be enormously eerie. Open all year. Information: Bodie State Historic Park, PO Box 515, Bridgeport, CA 93517 (phone: 619-647-6445).

COLUMBIA STATE HISTORIC PARK, Columbia, California: The "gem of the southern mines" never quite died out like Bodie but only decayed, so restoration was relatively simple. Walking tours mapped out by the state take you past all the important structures. After your tour, pan for gold in Matelot Gulch, ride a stagecoach, or sip sarsaparilla. Plenty of camping and hiking is available in the surrounding Stanislaus National Forest, and there are lively special events during Easter, the first weekend in May, the July Fourth weekend, and the first 2 weekends of December. Open year-round. Best lodgings are at the restored 1851 *Gunn House,* in Sonora (phone: 209-532-3421); the restored 1857 *Fallon* hotel, in the park (phone: 209-532-1470); and at its associate, the very Victorian *City* hotel (phone: 209-532-1479; see *America's Special Havens*). Information: Columbia State Historic Park, PO Box 151, Columbia, CA 95310 (phone: 209-532-4301); Tuolumne County Visitors Bureau, Box 4020, Sonora, CA 95370 (phone: 209-984-4636); Tuolumne County Chamber of Commerce, PO Box 277, Sonora, CA 95370 (phone: 209-532-4212); Stanislaus National Forest, 19777 Greenley Rd., Sonora, CA 95370 (phone: 209-532-3671).

POLYNESIAN CULTURAL CENTER, Laie, Oahu, Hawaii: Studying at the Mormon-operated Brigham Young University Hawaii Campus, students from all over the South Pacific put themselves through school by working at this 42-acre reconstruction of traditional villages of Fiji, Hawaii, New Zealand's Maori culture, Samoa, Tahiti, the Marquesas, and Tonga. The crafts, singing, dancing, and food preparation are all things the students have grown up with, so it couldn't be more authentic. Some 100 young Islanders make up the cast of *This Is Polynesia,* a special evening performance. Information: Polynesian Cultural Center, 55-370 Kamehameha Hwy., Laie, HI 96762 (phone: 808-293-3333 or 800 367-7060).

Utopias and Religious Settlements

Ever since the Pilgrims fled England for the New World, Americans have been leaving settled areas for wildernesses where they could set up their own civilizations, far from corrupting influences. Sometimes the new settlements survived. For instance, the Amana Colonies in Iowa — founded over a century ago — still thrive, even though the communal ownership of property was dissolved in the 1930s. In parts of Ohio, Pennsylvania, and Maryland, the Amish still live by the old ways, though buggies are not quite so common as they once were.

A good many others were not so successful. All through American history, religious settlements and attempted Utopias have come and gone like Christmas shoppers through a revolving door. Often, however, the communities that they built have withstood the ravages of time, and the last few years have seen a number of these settlements restored as museum villages. Some are open year-round, some only in summer; it's wise to call before you go. Admission fees are low — $10 or usually less for passes that will allow you to tour all the buildings, or 50¢ to $1 or so for each restored structure. Some are free.

BISHOP HILL, near Galesburg, Illinois: The first major Swedish settlement in the US, this community near the Mississippi River was not a big success. Erik Jansson, the dissident Swede who came here in 1846 and persuaded some 1,200 of his fellows to follow him, was assassinated in 1850 — and it was all downhill after that. In 1861, communal ownership of property was dissolved. Dissidents among the dissidents withdrew. Mismanagement of remaining property ensued. The community went into debt and Bishop Hill crumbled. However, a good many of the descendants of the original settlers stayed on, so the buildings did not all decay. By the 1960s, when people got interested in the colony, 13 of the 16 original structures were still standing, among them the *Colony* hotel, the blacksmith shop, the Steeple Building (topped by a one-handed clock), and the Colony Church, which could seat 1,000 worshipers. Early every Christmas morning, a traditional Julotta service is held by candlelight in the church sanctuary. The nearest motels are in Galesburg, where you can visit Carl Sandburg's birthplace, see the granite boulder under which his ashes were placed, and, on the campus of Knox College, tour the site of the Lincoln-Douglas debates. Information: Bishop Hill State Historic Site, Box D, Bishop Hill, IL 61419 (phone: 309-927-3345).

NAUVOO, Nauvoo, Illinois: Chicago was little more than a one-horse town when the followers of Mormon leader Joseph Smith arrived here and started building simple frame houses with wood from Wisconsin forests and brick they were soon manufacturing themselves. By 1846, the town was 20,000 strong, full of gardens, and topped by an immense white marble temple. Schisms developed, partly because of disagreements within the Mormon band itself over the polygamy issue. Joseph Smith ended up shot by a mob at the jail in Carthage, and Brigham Young, another Mormon, led the group westward — just as in the famous old grade B movie on the subject. Over the years, while Salt Lake City was abuilding, the houses in Nauvoo were falling down, one by one. But the neat grid of streets is still as clear as ever, and scattered here and there are enough restored and reconstructed buildings to provide a pretty good idea of how it all was. Most are open for free tours and manned by Mormon missionaries, who, it seems, are attempting conversion just by presenting facts (almost always interesting). Jonathan Browning, maker of the famous rifles, was a Mormon, as you'll learn; you'll tour his studio and home and see an interesting device he worked out that would churn butter and rock a baby in a cradle at the same time. The Mormons were replaced in Nauvoo by a group of French Utopian thinkers called Icarians. They did not flourish, and most left in about 10 years. Following them came a very traditional group of Germans, who found that the land would grow grapes and built 35 wine cellars, which in 1937 were discovered to be perfect for ripening blue cheese. These businesses flourish in Nauvoo today, and when you eat at the *Nauvoo* hotel, you can sample them both in one of its seven dining rooms. The hotel also has comfortable rooms with private bath (open mid-March through November; phone: 217-453-2211). A good time to visit, if you can plan for lodgings well in advance, is the weekend before Labor Day, when the annual *Grape Festival* takes place. Among the parades for grownups and kids and other small-town doings, there's a ceremony called the Wedding of the Wine and Cheese; also *City of Joseph,* a free outdoor musical, is presented the second week in August on a hillside overlooking the Mississippi. Information: Nauvoo Chamber of Commerce, PO Box 341, Nauvoo, IL 62354 (phone: 217-453-6648).

NEW HARMONY, Indiana: This quiet little town in southwestern Indiana near the confluence of the Wabash and Ohio rivers has been the home of two Utopian settlements. The first was led by Harmonist George Rapp, who, with his 700-plus followers, turned the forests and swamplands they found here in 1814 into 30,000 acres of farms, factories, and homes in a bare ten years. The later venture was led by Robert Owen, a Scottish intellectual who drew distinguished scholars, writers, and educators to New Harmony, established free kindergartens, education for women, a library, and many other firsts. That settlement declined, but many sturdy Harmonist buildings survived and are open year-round. Particularly fascinating are the Workingmen's Institute, founded in 1838 as a trade school and now filled up with Indian artifacts, lacy antique underwear, a stuffed eight-legged calf, and the oddest lot of other knickknacks you'll see in a long time; and the re-created Labyrinth, a maze made out of hedges that you can actually try to walk through. The original, built by George Rapp's Harmonists, was supposed to represent the choices taken during a lifetime. A variety of special programs take place in the striking Atheneum, designed by architect Richard Meier and opened to the public in 1979. The carefully designed *New Harmony Inn,* modern but Shaker-simple, a real symphony of polished woods, itself is worth the trip (phone: 812-682-4491; see *America's Special Havens*), and there's good food at the *Red Geranium* (phone: 812-682-4431) and the *Bayou Grill* (phone: 812-682-4431). Information: Historic New Harmony, New Harmony, IN 47631 (phone: 812-682-4474 or 812-682-4488).

AMANA COLONIES, Iowa: The Community of True Inspiration, a Lutheran splinter group, founded this group of seven villages — now a National Historic Landmark — in 1855 as a communal society in which everybody shared all goods, all gains, and even ate together. Reorganized some three quarters of a century later in 1932, the Amana Colonies today have a good deal more community feeling than you find in other parts of the US. The story of life in the good old days is told at the *Barn Museum* in South Amana (a scale-model village), and at the *Museum of Amana History* in Amana (exhibitions of potting, ice-cutting, bookbinding, woodworking, wine making, soap making, along with an Amana doctor's washhouse and woodshed, and a schoolhouse). Amana, West Amana, South Amana, Middle, High, and Homestead all have interesting little shops where you can buy local produce — fruit wines, woolens, furniture, baked goods, sausages, and other foods and crafts. And several have atmospheric restaurants that are great for German-American food served family style; *Bill Zuber's Restaurant* is one (phone: 319-622-3911). Information: Amana Colonies Travel Council, Box 303, Amana, IA 52203 (phone: 319-622-3828).

SHAKER VILLAGE OF PLEASANT HILL, near Harrodsburg, Kentucky: The third largest of 19 Shaker communities stretching from Maine to Kentucky, Pleasant Hill flourished in the early 19th century. Members of this celibate, communal society were devoted to a life of simplicity and purity. The Shaker conviction that religion should not be separated from the secular concerns of human life meant that much effort and ingenuity were expended on the tiniest details of life; every physical object was considered a prayer, and engineered for perfection. The tools and furniture that resulted fetch high prices at auctions today; they're bound to make an impression on you when you see them in this restoration's 30 original buildings. There are many crafts demonstrations and special events, including paddlewheel riverboat rides on the Kentucky River. Dining, crafts, conference facilities and 72 overnight guest rooms are available in the original buildings. Information: Shaker Village of Pleasant Hill, 3500 Lexington Rd., Harrodsburg, KY 40330 (phone: 606-734-5411).

HANCOCK SHAKER VILLAGE, near Pittsfield, Massachusetts: The best place in the East to see Shaker architecture. The standout is the 3-story Round Stone Barn, designed for efficiency but beautiful enough to bring Le Corbusier and other great architects to mind. In all, 20 buildings on the property are filled with Shaker furniture, artifacts, and "spirit drawings." The four-story Brick Dwelling House held a hundred men and women; and there's a laundry and machine shop, wash house, and icehouse. Once a year, for a week in August, the museum stages Worlds' People's Dinners, which are open to the public (by reservation only), along with cooking and craft demonstrations daily, the end-of-July *Kitchen Festival*, and other special events. Country inns are plentiful nearby. Open Memorial Day weekend through October. Information: Hancock Shaker Village, PO Box 898, Pittsfield, MA 01202 (phone: 413-443-0188).

SHAKER VILLAGE, Canterbury, New Hampshire: One of two remaining active Shaker communities. The 22 white frame structures that stand here now were once the home of 300 Shakers. Meeting House Lane is lined with enormous sugar maples planted for the orphans for whom they cared. Tours of the village lead through the Ministry, Sisters' Shop, Laundry, Schoolhouse, and Meetinghouse (with separate entrances for men and women). Friday evenings offer candelight dinners and tours. Authentic Shaker food is served at the *Creamery* restaurant. Information: Shaker Village, Canterbury, NH 03224 (phone: 603-783-9511).

OLD SALEM, Winston-Salem, North Carolina: Founded in 1766 by a group of

Moravians from Pennsylvania, Salem's church directed not just spiritual life but also secular doings — and business prospered. At the restoration, there are demonstrations of domestic skills practiced in early Salem, decorative arts and household items, plus craft shops and the immense Single Brothers House, where 14-year-old boys came to live while they learned a craft. Special events are planned throughout the year. Information: Director of Information, Old Salem, Inc., Drawer F, Winston-Salem, NC 27108 (phone: 919-721-7300).

SCHOENBRUNN VILLAGE STATE MEMORIAL, near New Philadelphia, Ohio: Concerned about spreading the Gospel to the Indians, the Moravian church sent missionaries into the wilderness, and this was the first of six separate settlements that were established in this area. David Zeisberger and his force of Christian Indians, converts, and missionaries cleared the wilderness and within a couple of years had put up some 60 log structures. But by that time, England and the colonies were at war, and Schoenbrunn was caught between the firing lines. The missionaries and their congregations departed, leaving the settlement to crumble. What you see now — a church, school, and a baker's dozen other structures — is a re-created area built by the Ohio Historical Society since the 1920s. On occasional special weekends, craftspeople are on hand to demonstrate spinning, candle-dipping, or tending the gardens, planted with red and calico corn, sweet corn, herbs, turnips, and pumpkins. *Trumpet in the Land,* an outdoor drama presented mid-June through August in an amphitheater nearby, tells the story (see *Outdoor Dramas*). Information: Schoenbrunn Village State Memorial, PO Box 129, New Philadelphia, OH 44663 (phone: 216-339-3636).

ZOAR STATE MEMORIAL, Zoar, Ohio: Another group of German Separatists who, like George Rapp, refusing to accept the Lutheran doctrine, found themselves alternately ignored and persecuted until it seemed easier to leave the Old World than to stay; and on Rapp's example, they crossed the ocean and bought a tract of land on the Tuscarawas River. The system of communal ownership under which the community eventually flourished in Zoar was not inspired by the Bible so much as by necessity imposed during the very lean times of the settlement's first years. When you visit today, you see it as it was during the lifetime of leader Joseph Baumeler: the red brick houses with their tile roofs and bright trim are spic and span; the bakery, tin shop, and garden house look for all the world as if they were still open for business; and the fantastic community garden, geometric in design, which is still so neat you'd say it had been laid out by some Prussian drill sergeant. A good time to see it all is during the *Zoar Harvest Festival,* held annually on the first weekend in August, when there are antiques, craft, and music shows. Zoar State Memorial is closed from November through March. There are small shops and several bed-and-breakfast establishments in private historic houses open all year. The nearby *Atwood* resort hotel on Atwood Lake Park is modern, comfortable, beautifully situated, and quite reasonable (phone: 216-735-2211 or 800-362-6406). Information: Zoar State Memorial, PO Box 404, Zoar, OH 44697 (phone: 216-874-3211 or 216-874-3011).

OLD ECONOMY VILLAGE, Ambridge, Pennsylvania: When Father George Rapp left New Harmony, Indiana, in 1824, he came here — and proceeded to create something even grander than the settlement he had left. There was, first of all, his own Great House, which was as imposing as the domicile of the society's leader should be. Then there was the Feast Hall, a single room that could seat 500 diners. Both structures, plus the wine cellar, shoe shop, cabinetmakers' shop, store, community kitchen, and two dwellings, have been restored and are open to the public. Why did this enormously successful settlement finally die out? The policy of celibacy eventually rang the death knell, and the society was dissolved in 1905. Information: Old Economy Village, 14th and Church Sts., Ambridge, PA 15003 (phone: 412-266-4500).

EPHRATA CLOISTER, Ephrata, Pennsylvania: This religious experiment in the heart of Pennsylvania Dutch country, begun in 1732 by a German Seventh-Day Baptist named Conrad Beissel, lasted until 1813 — despite celibacy and despite the rigorous lifestyle demanded of its practitioners: They slept on beds which were more like narrow benches, laid their heads on wooden pillows, walked down straight and narrow hallways and through doorways so low they had to stoop. There may have been plenty of symbolism behind all of it — and that, among other things, is what you learn about when you tour the handsome buildings. You'll also learn why singing was permitted, and, at the *Vorspiel* historical pageant, presented in summer, you'll hear some of the original music of Ephrata. Information: Ephrata Cloister, 632 W. Main St., Ephrata, PA 17522 (phone: 717-733-6600).

Great Museums

 Some of the best museums in the world can be found in the US — not just art museums, but natural history museums and science museums where the visitor is invited to touch, climb, experiment, try out, push buttons, and learn. Most have fascinating shops where you can buy reproductions of objects in the collections — postcards, statuary, textiles, jewelry, knickknacks.

For a complete listing of both major and minor museums of the urban areas you plan to visit, see the individual reports in THE CITIES. Herein, a distillation of the best: art museums, museums of science and industry, natural history museums — the country's very best.

Those listed here are worth some time — a half day is usually adequate — and return visits. They're popular, especially on weekends. To get the most from your time, try to visit midweek. Most have special exhibits for the holidays, changing exhibitions that supplement the permanent collections, and a schedule of concerts, lectures, and short courses that are well worth investigating, even on a short visit. Hours usually vary with the season. Most are closed one day a week; many are closed New Year's, Thanksgiving, and Christmas days, and some on other holidays. Admission prices are low; in Washington, DC, many of the museums are free; in New York City, there's often a "pay what you wish, but you must pay something" donation "requested."

EAST

BALTIMORE MUSEUM OF ART, Baltimore, Maryland: Strong on 20th-century art, thanks to the Cone Collection — paintings, prints, and sculptures of Matisse, Picasso, and other French post-Impressionists donated by the two wealthy Cone sisters — the museum also has period rooms that highlight the architectural and artistic development of Maryland, through furniture and decorative art objects, from the 1700s; the Wurtzburger collection of African, Native American, pre-Columbian, and Oceanic art; a vast print collection; fine 19th- and 20th-century American paintings and sculpture; art from the Gertrude Stein collection (also donated by the Cones); a spectacular outdoor sculpture garden; a stunning wing with galleries for changing exhibitions and a café overlooking the garden; and the Jacobs wing of Old Master paintings. Information: Baltimore Museum of Art, Art Museum Dr. (N. Charles and 31st Sts.), Baltimore, MD 21218 (phone: 301-396-7101).

MUSEUM OF FINE ARTS, Boston, Massachusetts: This great, vast old museum in the heart of Boston, not far from *Fenway Park,* sits beside a lovely 12-acre park near the bank of the Charles River; on sunny days, you can spot artists with sketch pads in hand on the green. Inside, you'll find an extensive permanent collection of Impressionists (including the most Monets outside Paris), works by American portrait and landscape painters, and American decorative arts (Duncan Phyfe chairs, Paul Revere silver, and other classic early American items). The collection of Egyptian architectural casts and artifacts is the largest outside Cairo; the Asiatic collection is the earth's largest under one roof. I. M. Pei designed the museum's west wing. Information: Museum of Fine Arts, 465 Huntington Ave., Boston, MA 02115 (phone: 617-267-9300 or, for recorded information, 617-267-9377).

ISABELLA STEWART GARDNER MUSEUM, Boston, Massachusetts: One of the world's magnificent private galleries. The collections are housed in a 15th-century-style Italianate mansion built between 1899 and 1903, with capitals, columns, fireplaces, fountains, staircases, and other architectural elements imported from Europe by the museum's founder, Mrs. Jack Gardner, a not-so-proper Bostonian who drank beer as well as tea and further disgraced herself in the eyes of Boston society by being born in New York City. Mrs. Jack — as she was called — lived on the top floor of her 4-story mansion during her lifetime, maintaining the rest of the house as a museum, which by the terms of her will is open to the public with the proviso that the arrangement of paintings, furniture, and other objects remain as it was during her lifetime. As a result, objects that seem to have as much sentimental as aesthetic value are exhibited next to Rembrandts, Titian's *Rape of Europa,* and other pieces collected with the advice of Bernard Berenson, the art scholar who coined the term "squillionaire." (The museum *Guide* is a good thing to have.) The sounds of the lovely fountain in the marble and plaster courtyard in the center of the palace, and the smell of the flowers growing around it, are almost always with you as you inspect the results of Mrs. Gardner's acquisitiveness — Tintorettos, Manets, Botticellis, Whistlers, one Corot, and one of the 36 surviving works of Vermeer. When your feet are tired, you can take lunch or tea at a café on the premises. Information: Isabella Stewart Gardner Museum, 280 The Fenway, Boston, MA 02115 (phone: 617-734-1359).

AMERICAN MUSEUM–HAYDEN PLANETARIUM, New York, New York: Adjoining the *Natural History Museum* (below), the Hayden has two floors of astronomical exhibitions and lively sky shows on astronomy and space science in the domed theater. Information: American Museum–Hayden Planetarium, Central Park West at 81st St., New York, NY 10024 (phone: 212-769-5920).

AMERICAN MUSEUM OF NATURAL HISTORY, New York, New York: In the 40 halls and galleries of this behemoth, you'll find rooms and rooms of dinosaur bones; one of the largest collections of minerals and gems in the world (including the 563-carat Star of India sapphire); fabulous life-size dioramas of animals and vegetation; a fine exhibition about reptiles from the prehistoric days to the present, and much more. Especially interesting is the Margaret Mead Hall of Pacific Peoples, which preserves aspects of these peoples' traditional cultures. Spring 1988 saw the opening of the Hall of the South American Peoples, a new permanent exhibition that covers the major regions and cultures of the continent. The hall is divided into two main sections. In the first section, Andean archaeology chronicles the history of the continent through the material remains of the people. The second section depicts Amazonian ethnology and is divided into subsections dealing with the topics of ceremonies, warfare, and technology. Don't miss the great whale — a 94-foot replica of a blue whale hanging from the ceiling of the Hall of Ocean Life. The largest meteorite ever retrieved from the earth's surface is displayed in the Arthur Ross Hall of Meteorites. And recently the museum installed a stupendous screen for showing nature films; 4 stories high and 66 feet wide, it surrounds you with images. Information: American Museum of Natural History, Central Park West at 79th St., New York, NY 10024 (phone: 212-769-5000 or, for recorded information, 212-769-5100).

FRICK COLLECTION, New York, New York: Henry Clay Frick, a coke and steel magnate who died in 1919, commissioned the architect Thomas Hastings to design a house that could function equally well, later on, as a museum, and so it's not surprising that the surroundings, sumptuous with their elegant furnishings and thick carpets, are so perfectly suited to the elegant collection of sculpture, fine furniture, porcelains, enamels, and paintings — among them Renoir's *Mother and Children,* Fragonard's *The Progress of Love,* Rembrandt's *Self-Portrait* and *Polish Rider,* Giovanni Bellini's *St. Francis in the Desert,* three canvases by Vermeer, Holbein's portraits of Sir Thomas More and Thomas Cromwell, and works by Gainsborough, Goya, Lawrence, Reynolds, Turner, and nearly everyone else (or so it sometimes seems) who ever inspired an art lover to rapture. All in all, the *Frick* is relaxing, hospitable, and among the most accessible museums anywhere. Information: Frick Collection, 1 E. 70th St., New York, NY 10021 (212-288-0700).

METROPOLITAN MUSEUM OF ART, New York, New York: The most extensive art collection in the US. There are works of great masters from the Middle Ages to the present day, an amazing collection of European Impressionist paintings, a vast assemblage of Greek and Roman sculpture, the most comprehensive collection of Islamic art anywhere, Oriental art, prints and photographs, musical instruments, decorative arts from all ages, and special exhibitions of stunning quality. The Lila Acheson Wallace Gallery has an extensive Egyptian collection; the Sackler Wing contains the Temple of Dendur. The American Wing comprises three centuries of American period rooms, paintings, sculpture, and decorative arts. The Michael C. Rockefeller Wing has works from Africa, the Pacific Islands, and pre-Columbian America. The Lila Acheson Wallace Wing has 22 galleries and a roof garden devoted to 20th-century works. Asian art galleries include a Buddhist shrine and a Chinese Garden court. A variety of tape-recorded audio tours that hit the high spots of the collections will help you handle the mind-boggling presentation. At Christmas, a tree is hung with 18th-century Neapolitan ornaments — each one a sculpture in its own right. Items relating to many of the ongoing and permanent exhibitions are sold in the museum's shops. Closed Mondays. Information: Metropolitan Museum of Art, 5th Ave. at 82nd St., New York, NY 10028 (phone: 212-535-7710 or 212-879-5500).

MUSEUM OF MODERN ART, New York, New York: The museum that is possibly the most complete museum of modern art in the world is more beautiful than ever since the completion of a major renovation in mid-1984. The permanent collections — concerned with 20th-century art — include works of abstractionists, Expressionists, conceptualists, film makers (there are daily film programs), industrial designers, photographers, and others. It is not a showplace of works of the very avant-garde; but then neither will you encounter Botticellis or Titians. Information: Museum of Modern Art, 11 W. 53rd St., New York NY 10019-5486 (phone: 212-708-9480).

SOLOMON R. GUGGENHEIM MUSEUM, New York, New York: The first visual encounter you'll have when you come to this museum will be with the Frank Lloyd Wright structure that houses the collection. Perfectly round, with a domed roof, the building is constructed so that the exhibits are ranged along the walls of a quarter-mile-long ramp that spirals upward for seven floors. Standing at the bottom, looking toward the skylight at the top, you can't help but wonder if Wright had read William Butler Yeats's "Turning and turning in the widening gyre . . ." It's also hard to understand the criticism that greeted the new building in October 1959; it was dubbed "a marshmallow" and even "a clothes washer." More charitable commentators said only that the building overpowered the art on display. Whether you agree will depend on how you feel about Wright vis-à-vis Kandinsky (one of the largest assemblages of his work in the world is here), Chagall, Delaunay, Picasso, and other Impressionist, modern, contemporary, and avant-garde artists represented in the permanent collections and in the ever-changing exhibitions that make the Guggenheim so lively. Information: The Guggenheim, 1071 5th Ave. (at 89th St.), New York, NY 10128 (phone: 212-360-3500).

WHITNEY MUSEUM OF AMERICAN ART, New York, New York: Devoted to American art, primarily that of the 20th century, with emphasis on the work of living artists, the *Whitney* presents about 15 exhibitions annually. The permanent collection includes works by Calder, de Kooning, Hopper, Johns, O'Keeffe, Nevelson, Prendergast, Segal, Sheeler, and Warhol. There are three museum branches in Manhattan and one in Stamford, Connecticut. Information: Whitney Museum of American Art, Madison Ave. at 75th St., New York, NY 10021 (phone: 212-570-3676).

FRANKLIN INSTITUTE, Philadelphia, Pennsylvania: This huge, vital, hands-on science museum has all kinds of new exhibits on subjects from aviation and astronomy to mechanics, light, math, patterns, and electricity. Watch light bend as it passes through concave and convex mirrors, walk through a 15,000-times-life-size heart, board a T-33 Jet Trainer, and take a ride on Philadelphia's beloved 350-ton Baldwin locomotive. Daily demonstrations show how lightning works and what energy is all about. Planetarium shows discuss black holes, satellite technology, and the constellations. And there's much, much more. Information: Franklin Institute, 20th St. and the Parkway, Philadelphia, PA 19103 (phone: 215-448-1200).

PHILADELPHIA MUSEUM OF ART, Philadelphia, Pennsylvania: In an imposing edifice of Minnesota dolomite, which Lord Dunsany called the most beautiful building in America, are Van Gogh's *Sunflowers,* Cézanne's *Bathers,* Marcel Duchamp's *Nude Descending a Staircase,* Picasso's *Three Musicians,* and the famous statue of Diana that topped New York City's first *Madison Square Garden.* Along with the excellent Impressionist collection, there's a Japanese Tea House, designed to convey the atmosphere as well as the art of Japan, a Chinese scholar's study, a large collection of arms and armor, and distinguished collections of china, porcelain, glass, jade, graphics, sculpture, and decorative arts. Free on Sundays before 1 PM. Information: Philadelphia Museum of Art, 26th St. and the Parkway, Philadelphia, PA 19130 (phone: 215-763-8100).

CORCORAN GALLERY OF ART, Washington, DC: In its gracious, skylit halls full of American art — among the finest collections of 18th- and 19th-century American art anywhere, in fact — are prestigious assortments of works by Sargent, Bierstadt, and Copley. You'll also find European paintings, however (some by Corot, some by the animal sculptor Antoine Barye, as well as Renaissance drawings), and a variety of changing exhibitions of contemporary art and photography. One block beyond the White House. Information: Corcoran Gallery of Art, 17th St. and New York Ave. NW, Washington, DC 20006 (phone: 202-638-3211).

HIRSHHORN MUSEUM AND SCULPTURE GARDEN, Washington, DC: One of the newer museums under the *Smithsonian's* wing and the most modern of the city's museums of modern art. The *Hirshhorn* houses the ever-astonishing collections amassed by Joseph H. Hirshhorn (1899–1981), who grew up in such poverty that he never even owned a toy. He spent much of the fortune he made in stocks and uranium buying art (the way some people buy clothes). The painting collection, much expanded and refined since the original Hirshhorn gift, focuses on American art and includes works by Estes, Golub, Gorky, Henri, Hopper, de Kooning, Noland, and Stella; European masters such as Bacon, Balthus, Kiefer, and Magritte are also represented. The extraordinary vitality of the sculpture collection reflects the greatness of Calder, Degas, Matisse, Moore, Rodin, Serra, and David Smith — many of whose works are displayed in the Hirshhorn sculpture garden — and the innovations of more recent sculptors. For this variety alone the *Hirshhorn* would be fascinating; the building itself — circular and fortress-like — is intriguing as well. Information: Hirshhorn Museum, Independence Ave. at 8th St., Washington, DC 20560 (phone: 202-357-2700).

NATIONAL GALLERY OF ART, Washington, DC: In a John Russell Pope building whose 500,000 square feet make it one of the world's largest marble structures, this museum, built to introduce Americans to the cream of European art, is what one local critic called "the sort of place paintings would aspire to if masterpieces went to heaven." Columns of Tuscan marble, floors of green marble from Vermont and gray marble from Tennessee, and walls of Indiana limestone and Italian travertine produce an effect that is unadulteratedly sumptuous, especially since a recent renovation; the museum's contents are, if possible, even more awe-inspiring. Leonardo da Vinci's *Ginevra de Benci*

(America's only Leonardo), Jan Vermeer's *Woman Holding a Balance,* a Rembrandt *Self-Portrait,* Jean-Honoré Fragonard's *A Young Girl Reading,* Auguste Renoir's *A Girl with a Watering Can,* and Claude Monet's *Rouen Cathedral, West Façade* are among literally thousands of breathtaking canvases and sculptures — gifts of hundreds of donors — housed in the original building and the striking East Building, designed as a grouping of interlocking triangles by I. M. Pei & Partners. It can all be a bit bewildering, so, as an introduction, you might want to join one of the regular tours; rent a tape tour; or pick up the excellent *Brief Guide.* A monthly calendar of events includes free films, lectures, and concerts. Information: National Gallery of Art, 4th St. and Constitution Ave. NW, Washington, DC 20565 (phone: 202-737-4215).

SMITHSONIAN INSTITUTION, Washington, DC: Completed in 1855, the red Gothic castle on the Mall now functions mainly as office space for the staff that oversees the *Smithsonian's* scattered museums and galleries — nine on the Mall, five (including the National Zoo) in other parts of DC, one in New York City, and a half-dozen scientific research facilities around the country. The total collection contains over 100 million items and gains almost a million more every year; only an infinitesimal percentage is displayed at any given time, so there's always something new to see. The museums of *American History, Natural History,* and *Air & Space* are among the most popular in Washington. Information: Smithsonian Visitor Information, 1000 Jefferson Dr. SW, Washington, DC 20560 (phone: 202-357-1300).

MIDWEST

ART INSTITUTE OF CHICAGO, Chicago, Illinois: El Greco's *Assumption of the Virgin,* Seurat's *Sunday Afternoon on the Island of le Grand Jatte,* and Grant Wood's *American Gothic* are among the works in the *Art Institute's* outstanding collections, which also include excellent Impressionist and post-Impressionist works, Japanese prints, Chinese sculpture and bronzes, European and American prints and drawings, and more. The American Galleries are wonderfully conceived to show off the development of US culture; the Chagall stained glass windows and the Trading Room, from the old Chicago Stock Exchange Building, are not to be missed. The renovated photography department is one of the most sophisticated facilities of its kind in the world. The new, $23-million Rice Building houses Edward Hopper's *Nighthawks,* Vincent van Gogh's *Bedroom at Arles,* and Toulouse-Lautrec's *Ballet Dancers* as well as exhibitions of European and American decorative arts and sculpture. Information: Art Institute of Chicago, Michigan Ave. at Adams, Chicago, IL 60603 (phone: 312-443-3600).

FIELD MUSEUM OF NATURAL HISTORY, Chicago, Illinois: Outstanding collections of more than 16 million artifacts and specimens. Through ongoing fieldwork and basic research, the museum has become not just a treasure house of specimens drawn from all corners of the globe, but also a dynamic, scholarly community resource that appeals to people with a sense of curiosity about the world in which they live. Over 9 acres of exhibitions on anthropology, botany, zoology, and geology, plus special displays, music, dance, theater performances, and "time travel" back to the age of the great dinosaurs. Information: Field Museum, Roosevelt Rd. at Lake Shore Dr., Chicago, IL 60605-2496 (phone: 312-922-9410).

MUSEUM OF SCIENCE AND INDUSTRY, Chicago, Illinois: Chicago's most popular attraction has computers to question, buttons to push, rides to ride, and so on, as part of some 2,000 exhibitions in 75 major halls examining the principles of science and technology (as well as other subjects). High points: Colleen Moore's fairy castle of a doll house; the computerized nutrition exhibit Food for Life; and the Sears circus exhibit, full of dioramas of circus scenes, piped-in circus music, and a dynamic short film (the kind you want to sit through twice in a row). The working coal mine, the walk-through human heart, and the German U-505 submarine are every bit as much fun as they always have been. And there are new exhibits on chemistry, physics, geology, the post office, anesthesiology, the life sciences, newspapers, and Nobel Prize winners, not to mention a Business Hall of Fame and the exciting and long-awaited offering from IBM on computers. The new Henry Crown Space Center features the *Omnimax Theater* and other space exhibitions. Free general admission and parking. Information: Museum of Science and Industry, 57th St. and Lake Shore Dr., Chicago, IL 60637 (phone: 312-684-1414).

MINNEAPOLIS INSTITUTE OF ARTS, Minneapolis, Minnesota: The exterior of this highly esteemed institution is architecturally classic, and it houses an equally classic variety of Old Masters and other paintings, sculpture, decorative arts, photographs, and Asian, African, Oceanic, ancient, Oriental, and American objects. In addition, the museum presents films, concerts, and lectures. Information: Minneapolis Institute of Arts, 2400 3rd Ave. S., Minneapolis, MN 55404 (phone: 612-870-3131).

WALKER ART CENTER, Minneapolis, Minnesota: Offering a vivid overview of major 20th-century art, this art center housed in a striking contemporary building complements the *Institute*'s classic collections; originates many touring exhibitions; and conducts a lively program of music, dance, film, theater, and educational activities. Information: Walker Art Center, 725 Vineland Pl., Minneapolis, MN 55403 (phone: 612-375-7636 or the box office, 612-375-7622).

DETROIT INSTITUTE OF ARTS, Detroit, Michigan: One of this country's most comprehensive collections fills the 101 galleries of the *DIA,* which is the fifth largest fine arts museum in the country. Italian art is only one of the areas in which the museum has large holdings; French painting and decorative arts and the Dutch and Flemish painters are also well represented. Diego Rivera's spectacular *Detroit Industry* frescoes cover the walls of a central court. Egyptian mummies and suits of medieval armor are on display, as well as a large collection of pre-Columbian, African, Native American, Asian, American, and 20th-century art. A photography gallery opened not long ago, and Tony Smith's contemporary *Gracehoper* straddles the lawn. On Sundays, there is Brunch with Bach, and there are frequent special exhibitions, lectures, films, music and theater performances. Information: Detroit Institute of Arts, 5200 Woodward Ave., Detroit, MI 48202 (phone: 313-833-7900).

CLEVELAND MUSEUM OF ART, Cleveland, Ohio: A major American museum and one of the few of its kind that is still free to the public, this private institution boasts an enviable collection that encompasses all periods and cultures. Under the long directorship of the renowned Oriental art scholar Sherman E. Lee, who retired in 1983, galleries were organized chronologically, with the decorative arts pieces displayed alongside paintings and sculpture of the same period and place. A new wing, organized on the same basis, presents important collections of 19th- and 20th-century European and American art. The constantly growing collection currently numbers over 48,000 objects; the arts of the Near and Far East, India, the pre-Columbian Americas, Europe, America, Africa, and ancient Egypt, Greece, and Rome are represented. The Oriental collection is one of the finest in the Western world, and the museum has particularly fine medieval, European painting, and decorative arts collections; of late, the museum has been developing its collection of contemporary art and photography. Throughout the year there are frequent concerts and films, with gallery talks every afternoon except Mondays. The original 1916 building overlooks a garden and lagoon; a 1970 wing, designed by Marcel Breuer, houses special exhibition galleries, the musical arts department, and the education department (one of the largest professionally staffed education departments in the country); a smaller 1984 addition contains an art research library, open to the public on Wednesdays. A number of Cleveland's other cultural institutions face the museum across a grassy oval. Closed Mondays. Information: Cleveland Museum of Art, 11150 East Blvd. at University Circle, Cleveland, OH 44106 (phone: 216-421-7340).

MILWAUKEE PUBLIC MUSEUM, Milwaukee, Wisconsin: The basic theme here is how man and other living creatures adapt to the environment, but there are a lot of variations, and exhibits relate not only to Indians, history, geology, and world cultures of the distant past, but also to aspects of American society. This sprawling institution really shines, however, when it comes to the making of dioramas. At a Northwest Coast Indian exhibition, for instance, smells and sounds come at you from all sides. In the Great Plains area, a rattlesnake rattles a warning, and when the buffalo charge, you can hear the thundering of their hooves on the earth — getting louder and louder. The geese honk overhead in a wildlife exhibit. In the Metasequoia Swamp, flashes of lightning illuminate hulking dinosaurs, and a loon calls out plaintively. At a portrayal of an East African bamboo forest, you hear the sounds of an elephant come crashing through the trees. Particularly interesting is the Streets of Old Milwaukee section, where the 19th-century city has been re-created, right down to flickering gaslights, telephone poles wrapped with wire to keep horses from chewing them, and a kite tangled up in the treetops. The same ingenuity is at work in the European village of shops and homes, which portrays 33 cultures of the Old World, and at the stunning exhibit that documents the history, anatomy, and behavior of the planet Earth (and stars two life-size dinosaurs). The Wizard Wing Discovery Center offers a hands-on way to learn about water, collecting, pioneering skills, and a variety of natural history and cultural subjects. The new Biology Hall exhibition is a life-size replica of a Costa Rican rain forest — with a real waterfall and abundant plant life viewable from two perspectives. Information: Milwaukee Public Museum, 800 W. Wells St., Milwaukee, WI 53233 (phone: 414-278-2700).

WEST

LOS ANGELES COUNTY MUSEUM OF ART, Los Angeles, California: With five buildings surrounding a spacious central court, this is one of the top museums in the country and the largest in the West. The permanent collection features paintings, sculpture, graphic arts, photography, costumes, textiles, and decorative arts from a wide range of cultures and periods from prehistoric times to the present. The museum's holdings include American and European painting, sculpture, and decorative arts, 20th-century arts, pre-Columbian Mexican art, selections from Dr. Armand Hammer's European master paintings collection, a unique assemblage of glass from Roman times to the 19th century, the renowned Gilbert collection of mosaics and monumental silver, and Indian and Islamic art. Major traveling loan exhibitions are also presented, along with lectures, films, concerts, and other educational events in the 600-seat theater. The recently opened Pavilion for Japanese Art houses the internationally renowned Shin'en-kan collection of Japanese paintings and a collection of Japanese ceramics, sculpture, lacquerware, screens, scrolls, and prints. Information: Los Angeles County Museum of Art, 5905 Wilshire Blvd., Los Angeles, CA 90036 (phone: 213-857-6000).

ASIAN ART MUSEUM OF SAN FRANCISCO, San Francisco, California: The Avery Brundage Collection — one of the world's finest of Oriental art — includes some 10,000 sculptures, paintings, bronzes, jades, ceramics, architectural elements, and decorative objects from China, Japan, Korea, India, Southeast Asia, Nepal, Tibet, and Iran. There are also special temporary exhibitions and free teaching tours. The museum shares an entrance with the *de Young* (below), but the two are distinct institutions. Information: Asian Art Museum of San Francisco, Golden Gate Park, San Francisco, CA 94118 (phone: 415-668-8922).

CALIFORNIA PALACE OF THE LEGION OF HONOR, San Francisco, California: The collections housed in this graceful building in the French neoclassical style (based on the Legion of Honor in Paris) are predominantly French, but you'll also find the largest graphics collection in the western US. The large collection of Rodin sculptures is outstanding. With the *M. H. de Young* (below), it is part of the *Fine Arts Museums of San Francisco*. Information: Lincoln Park, San Francisco, CA 94121 (phone: 415-750-3600 or 415-750-3659).

M. H. DE YOUNG MEMORIAL MUSEUM, San Francisco, California: One of the western US's largest art museums, its collections include paintings, sculpture, and decorative arts from ancient Egypt through the 20th century. There are galleries devoted to American painting and decorative arts; to the traditional arts of Africa, Oceania, and the Americas; and to period rooms from Europe and America. Fra Angelico, Rembrandt, Rubens, Titian, El Greco, Goya, Hals, Van Dyck, Gainsborough, and Reynolds are represented. There is also a café with garden dining. Information: M. H. de Young Memorial Museum, Golden Gate Park, San Francisco, CA 94118 (phone: 415-750-3600).

DENVER ART MUSEUM, Denver, Colorado: Besides having an excellent collection that takes in the period from AD 1100 to the present, the *Denver Art Museum* has top collections of pre-Columbian art and artifacts, native American art, Oriental art, and textiles, plus holdings in American, European, and contemporary art. The 7-story, $6.5-million structure, which looks something like a medieval castle with its slit-like windows, was designed around the exhibitions; some display halls completely re-create another time and place. Information: Denver Art Museum, 100 W. 14th Ave. Pkwy., Denver, CO 80204 (phone: 303-575-2793).

AMON G. CARTER MUSEUM OF WESTERN ART, Ft. Worth, Texas: This museum started out in 1961 chronicling America's westward expansion, with a huge collection of paintings and sculpture by Frederic Remington and Charles Russell. But gradually the museum has adopted American art from 1800 to 1950 as its theme, and, in addition to western pieces, you'll also see 19th-century landscapes and genre paintings by such artists as Winslow Homer, Albert Bierstadt, Mary Cassatt, and Thomas Moran, as well as 20th-century works by Georgia O'Keeffe and Stuart Davis. A selection of the 250,000-item American photography collection is also always on view. A theater provides a home for films, lectures, and symposia. Information: Amon G. Carter Museum of Western Art, 3501 Camp Bowie Blvd., Ft. Worth, TX 76107 (phone: 817-738-1933).

KIMBELL ART MUSEUM, Ft. Worth, Texas: This result of a bequest by Kay Kimbell contains an incredible array of works by Caravaggio, Mantegna, Cézanne, Duccio, El Greco, Holbein, Picasso, Poussin, Rembrandt, Velázquez, Watteau, and others, not to mention Egyptian, Greek, pre-Columbian, African, and Asian art. Special loan exhibitions and other public programs are regularly scheduled. Information: Kimbell Art Museum, 3333 Camp Bowie Blvd., Ft. Worth, TX 76107 (phone: 817-332-8451).

MODERN ART MUSEUM OF FORT WORTH, Ft. Worth, Texas: A collection of 20th-century paintings, drawings, sculpture, and prints, among whose highlights are major works by Picasso, Louis, Warhol, Rothko, Stella, de Kooning, Rauschenberg, Motherwell, Pollock, and other modern masters. It is also within a block of the *Amon Carter* and *Kimbell* museums. Information: Modern Art Museum of Fort Worth, 1309 Montgomery St., PO Box 907006, Ft. Worth, TX 76107 (phone: 817-738-9215).

Space Centers: The Future Now

 The Saturn V Rocket on display at the Alabama Space and Rocket Center — one of three such space centers in the US — is longer than a football field and as wide as a two-lane highway; the sheer size of it is adequate testimony to the scope of the space program. There are plenty of reasons to visit. At each center you will be given facts and figures that may give you pause the next time you start to agree with someone who calls the space exploration program a waste of money. You'll be offered the opportunity to take over the controls of a rocket, and in a dozen other ways retrace the small steps that were such giant leaps for mankind. Outside there are "rocket parks" — greenswards where mammoth spacecraft grow like so many monster asparagus stalks.

SPACE AND ROCKET CENTER, Huntsville, Alabama: The feature attractions at *Earth's Largest Space Museum* tell you what's happening on the space scene — and look into the future as well. The current emphasis is on the Space Shuttle and the Space Station, scheduled for orbit in 1993. Visitors can walk through NASA's full-scale mock-up of the Space Shuttle orbiter: the 122-foot Pathfinder used for clearance and engineering tests at the nearby Marshall Space Flight Center, where NASA develops rockets for the space program. Visitors to the *Spacedome Theater* feel as if they are riding with shuttle astronauts during presentations of the Omnimax film *The Dream Is Alive.* The thunderous roar at launch from a 48-speaker sound system and inspiring views back at Earth on the planetarium-type ceiling provide a unique experience. Because the Saturn V rocket that launched Neil Armstrong to the Moon was made in Huntsville, Apollo spacecraft, space suits, and astronaut training gear are popular museum displays. The original moon rocket — which has been designated a National Historic Landmark — dominates the 20-acre park of NASA rockets and army missiles. Bus tours that depart from the museum enter the Space Station development center and various astronaut training facilities. From February to Labor Day, the center holds the US Space Camp for young people 10-19 years old, with weekly astronaut training activities and simulated Space Shuttle missions; activities can be viewed in the new Space Camp Training Center. Information: Space and Rocket Center, 1 Tranquility Base, Huntsville, AL 35807 (phone: 205-837-3400 or 800-633-7280).

SPACEPORT USA, Kennedy Space Center, Florida: The Kennedy Space Center is on Merritt Island and is the home of all Space Shuttle launchings; Cape Canaveral, across the Banana River, is the site for launchings of Department of Defense flights and NASA unmanned launchings. This 220-square-mile spaceport is a hotbed of space-related activity — everything from data-gathering and tracking to fuel storage and manned-flight launches. The best way to see it is on the 2-hour bus tour, which takes in the launching site of the Space Shuttle, Mission Control, and more. Spaceport USA, where you meet the tours, itself offers abundant attractions, including a lunar roving vehicle, a replica of an Apollo Lunar Module, and a baker's dozen theaters, minitheaters, and tape programs that tell you about flights past and future. Its newest attraction is the *IMAX Theater,* where viewers can watch a Space Shuttle launch on a screen 5 stories high and 70 feet wide; six-track stereo delivers the audio sensation of actual takeoff. If you opt for a tour around Christmas or in summer, be sure to arrive as close as possible to the center's 9 AM opening to avoid lines.

Afterward, you can swim off unspoiled beaches along the 25-mile Canaveral National Seashore, go deep-sea fishing, and, at the Merritt Island National Wildlife Refuge, see alligators, panthers, and some 200 species of birds. Cocoa Beach, where most motels are just a shell's throw from the Atlantic, is the place to lodge. Information: Spaceport USA, Visitor Center, PW Recreational Services, Kennedy Space Center, FL 32899 (phone: 402-452-2121).

LYNDON B. JOHNSON SPACE CENTER, Houston, Texas: An important research and development center for the US's Space Shuttle flight program. You can learn about the subject at the visitors center, where you see moon rocks, space suits, rocket engines, and spacecraft from the Mercury, Gemini, Apollo, Skylab, and Apollo-Soyuz test missions, and other impedimenta of the space age. NASA films played all day long show you what each mission was like. Self-guided walking tours of the JSC take you to the Mission Simulation and Training Facility (Building 5), where astronauts practiced their complex Skylab tasks, as well as Building 9A (devoted to Space Shuttle training) and Building 31A (where lunar samples are studied). Briefings at Mission Control are also available daily on a first-come, first-served basis. Reservations recommended. Go first to the Visitors Center in Building 2. Information: NASA Johnson Space Center, AP4/Public Services Branch, Houston, TX 77058 (phone: 713-483-4321).

TO SEE A LIFT-OFF

"It's like being inside a flame — no heat, but your entire body shakes, your bones and organs shake, the earth shakes." That is one writer's description of watching a launch: They're definitely worth seeing. A good place to watch a shuttle launch is on the beach in Cocoa Beach, between Cape Canaveral and Patrick Air Force Base. (For launch information, call 800-432-2153 in Florida; 407-452-1212 in other states.) It is hard to plan a vacation around a launching, because variable weather conditions make a strict schedule impossible. There is a special viewing area, 3 miles from the launching pads, for which you can make reservations through the Kennedy Space Center.

Factory Tours: Watching the Work

 Every year, literally hundreds of companies welcome thousands of visitors to their plants. Newspapers show off their printing presses, breweries their mash tubs, distilleries their warehouses and their quality-control systems, soft-drink companies their bottling plants, wineries their vineyards and aging rooms. Each region has a specialty. There are maple sugar houses and marble quarries in Vermont, tobacco warehouses and cigarette factories in Kentucky and North Carolina, glass factories in West Virginia, petrochemical works in Louisiana, oil fields and coal mines in Wyoming, lumber mills and wood products plants in the Pacific Northwest. Most big companies have plants in several parts of the country. If you're interested in seeing how a specific product is made, write the corporate headquarters and ask about tours.

Below, you'll find a very brief sampler of some industrial tours available to the general public. There are hundreds more, however. To find out about them, contact the state tourist offices and chambers of commerce in the areas you plan to visit. More than 2,500 factory and business tours are listed and described in the *Tours and Visits Directory,* a reference book published in 1981 by the Gale Research Company, available in many libraries (but double-check before visiting, as it hasn't been updated since then).

And always phone ahead. Companies may need to line up someone to take you around, and that takes time. Even when the operation does have a regularly scheduled tour program, you've got to be sure that it will not be temporarily closed down because of vacations or model changeovers. If you have children, you need to make sure they are old enough to go on the tour. (There's usually an age limit of anywhere from 7 to 16.) This may seem like a lot of trouble, but the excitement of the factories — the speed of the machines, the clanks and the screeches, the roars and the buzzes — will make all the planning worthwhile.

EAST

SCOTT PAPER COMPANY, Skowhegan, Maine: This mill takes tree-length logs, cuts them up into sections, chops them into chips, conveys them to a digester, treats them with chemicals, cooks them, bleaches them, and then bales up the soft, whitish fibers that result — wood pulp. The resemblance of the stuff to cotton is just one of the more interesting parts of the process, the first step in the manufacture of paper. Tours run in June and July. Information: Bill Pasha, Scott Paper, Skowhegan, ME 04976 (phone: 207-453-9301).

HARRISON OYSTER COMPANY, Tilghman Island, Maryland: In the heart of the fishing country of Maryland's Eastern Shore, watch oystermen unloading their briny catch and view an assembly line of oyster shuckers — as nimble-fingered a group as you can imagine. Though the tour lasts only half an hour, the process is fascinating and offers a pleasant diversion during a journey through one of the East's quaintest corners. Afterward, sample some of the local specialty in the adjacent restaurant, *Harrison's Chesapeake House.* Mid-September to mid-March, mornings only; restaurant open mid-March to end of December. Information: Harrison Oyster Co., PO Drawer J, Tilghman Island, MD 21671 (phone: 301-886-2530).

ANHEUSER-BUSCH, Merrimack, New Hampshire: One of the Anheuser-Busch breweries where the tour is guided (rather than self-guided), this brewery is also notable for being the East Coast home of the famous Clydesdales. Information: Anheuser-Busch, PO Box 610, Merrimack, NH 03054-0610 (phone: 603-889-6631).

CORNING GLASS CENTER, Corning, New York: Journey through time on a thread of glass at the most fascinating center of its kind. Uncover the ancient treasures of a 3,500-year-old craft at the *Corning Museum of Glass.* Probe a future life through fiber optics in the Hall of Science and Industry. Witness the crystal wonders of today's glassblowing art in the Steuben Glass Factory. See a glass exhibition that changes each year in the museum, and take in Broadway theater, Western art, antiques shops, and historical sights in turn-of-the-century Corning. Information: Corning Glass Center, Corning, NY 14831 (phone: 607-974-8271).

EASTMAN KODAK, Rochester, New York: With 300 buildings and grounds that are 1 mile across and 7 miles long, this town-size plant, which houses the company's largest manufacturing operation, would probably take weeks to tour in its entirety, so the audio-visual presentation that begins a visit here and summarizes the whole operation makes a lot of sense; the bus tour that follows provides a visit to the disc film manufacturing complex. There are also tours to the Kodak Apparatus Division plant, which manufactures cameras, projectors, and copier duplicators. No children under 5 permitted. Tours are conducted from May through September. Information: Eastman Kodak Co., Kodak Park Division, Visitor Services, 200 Ridge Rd. W., Rochester, NY 14652 (phone: 716-722-2465).

JULIUS STURGIS PRETZEL COMPANY, Lititz, Pennsylvania: At America's first pretzel bakery, built in 1784, visitors are given the history of the pretzel, along with a piece of dough, which they're taught to twist into a pretzel. In the half-hour tour that follows, a machine does more or less the same thing with lumps of dough (for hard pretzels only; soft ones are still made by hand), which, newly shaped, are baked for 7 minutes, then packaged. Visitors have first crack at buying the results. Closed Sundays and major holidays. Information: Julius Sturgis Pretzel Co., 219 E. Main St., Lititz, PA 17543 (phone: 717-626-4354).

FAIRDALE FARMS, Bennington, Vermont: This is really two tours in one. First, there's plenty of pigs, goats, ducks, and chickens; then there's the processing plant, where, through windows, visitors watch cooled and pasteurized milk being bottled in gallons and half-gallons. Self-guided tours run from May through September. Information: Fairdale Farms, PO Box 9, Bennington, VT 05201 (phone: 802-442-6391).

BEN & JERRY'S ICE CREAM, Waterbury, Vermont: The ice cream factory is set in a rolling pasture in the heart of the Green Mountains. Air conditioned guided tours include a multimedia slide show about how Ben and Jerry began making ice cream; then a visit to the production room to see every stage of the manufacturing process and sample the delicious results. Afterward, visitors may stop in at the gift shop and ice cream parlor, featuring all of Ben & Jerry's flavors as well as crafts items. Visitors are also welcome to picnic on the grounds. The half-hour tours run daily, except Sundays, year-round. Expect long lines in summer. Information: Ben & Jerry's Ice Cream, Rte. 100, PO Box 240, Waterbury, VT 05676 (phone: 802-244-5641).

BUREAU OF ENGRAVING AND PRINTING, Washington, DC: At the world's largest securities manufacturing establishment, you can watch the making of currency on 25-minute self-guided tours. Information: Bureau of Engraving and Printing, Washington, DC 20228 (phone: 202-447-9709).

SOUTH

VILLAZON AND COMPANY, Tampa, Florida: Cigars, machine-made, from leaf to banding. Mornings are most active, and production peaks during September, October, and November. Closed mid-December to mid-January, during other holidays, and the first 2 weeks in July. Information: Villazon and Co., 3104 N. Armenia, Tampa, FL 33607-1480 (phone: 813-879-2291).

McILHENNY COMPANY, near New Iberia, Louisiana: An aged mash made of fermented red peppers is mixed with 100-grain vinegar in barrels, then put through three progressively finer strainers to make Tabasco brand pepper sauce, and, finally, bottled, labeled, and packed into cartons. All in the middle of Avery Island, surrounded by the mysterious Bayou Petit Anse. Information: McIlhenny Co., Avery Island, LA 70513 (phone: 318-365-8173).

FIELDCREST CANNON, Cannon Village, Kannapolis, North Carolina: Free guided tours of the textile manufacturing process are available on a limited basis. The tours are conducted by a skilled guide and are offered weekday mornings, plant schedule permitting. Always call in advance. Children under 12 are not admitted. Information: Cannon Village Visitor Center, 200 West Ave., Kannapolis, NC 28081 (phone: 704-938-3200).

MIDWEST

CATERPILLAR TRACTOR COMPANY, Peoria, Illinois: When the immense yellow tractors roar off the assembly line like so many mechanized elephants, everything shakes, even the concrete floor. By appointment only; closed weekends, holidays, and 2 weeks of July. Information: Tour Coordinator, Caterpillar, 100 NE Adams St., Peoria, IL 61629 (phone: 309-675-4578).

KARE, Minneapolis, Minnesota: The TV studios and newsroom — especially the weather department — are this tour's most popular attractions, which also includes control booths, master control, and the art department. Tours run from 9 AM to 1 PM, which avoids the most hectic part of the day but still provides a real sense of how a television station operates. No children under 10. Closed weekends. Information: KARE, 8811 Olson Memorial Hwy., Minneapolis, MN 55427 (phone: 612-546-1111, ext. 366).

HALLMARK VISITORS CENTER, Kansas City, Missouri: Although you don't go through the actual production area, you can watch employees at work: engravers creating metal dies, pressmen running greeting cards through a press that applies shiny foil, and so on. Particularly enticing is a bow making machine that visitors can activate. The visitors center features exhibitions of the company's products, including greeting cards from the Depression and World War II. Closed Sundays and some holidays. Admission is free. Information: Hallmark Cards, PO Box 419580, Kansas City, MO 64141-6580 (phone: 816-274-5672).

HOMESTAKE MINE, Lead, South Dakota: Here, you can see the aboveground operations of the oldest underground gold mine in the Western Hemisphere. No tours on Saturdays, Sundays, holidays, and from October through April. Information: Lead Civic Assn., Lead, SD 57754-0894 (phone: 605-584-3110).

KOHLER, Kohler, Wisconsin: Ball clay is piped through miles of tubing into plaster molds of toilets, sinks, and drinking fountains. After two days of drying, this "green-ware" is smoothed by hand, then sprayed with colored glazes. Thus are born the beautiful Kohler bath and kitchen fixtures on exhibit at the Kohler Design Center, a multilevel showcase of the company's past, present, and future. What comes as a particular surprise to the 12,000 to 15,000 who visit annually is how much the plant resembles the studio of a ceramic artist and how much of the work is still done by hand — the punching of the holes for the fittings, the smoothing of the edges, and even some of the glazing. The town of Kohler — a planned community, one of the first in America, with strict guidelines about green space, parks, and construction — is interesting in itself. Reservations required; children under 14 not admitted. No plant tours in late July and early August. Information: Kohler Design Center, 101 Upper Rd., Kohler, WI 53044 (phone: 414-457-3699).

WEST

HERSHEY CHOCOLATE COMPANY, Oakdale, California: This isn't the main Hershey factory, which is in Hershey, Pennsylvania, but since the main plant stopped giving public tours in 1973, this is the one to visit to see the sweet, rich stuff being mixed, molded, and packaged. Cravings can be satisfied at the store on the premises, where Hershey products are sold. Closed weekends and holidays. Information: Hershey Chocolate Co., 1400 S. Yosemite Ave., Oakdale, CA 95361 (phone: 209-847-0381).

US MINT, Denver, Colorado: Guided tours are held on weekdays (closed holidays and weekends). Visitors may view various operations of coin production, plus displays and exhibitions that include six gold bars. Tours are free. Information: US Mint, 320 W. Colfax Ave., Denver, CO 80204-2693 (phone: 303-844-3582).

PENDLETON WOOLEN MILLS, Pendleton, Oregon: Visitors to this plant watch wool production from fleece to fabric and are impressed with the huge kettles and percolators, each one holding some 500 pounds in which the stock is dyed; the special cylinders that comb the wool and turn it into yarn; and the subsequent winding of that same yarn onto bobbins or cones. The strands are then fed into sophisticated looms that transform it into the colorful plaid fabrics seen in the factory salesroom. Information: Pendleton Woolen Mills, 1307 SE Court Pl., Pendleton, OR 97801 (phone: 503-276-6911).

AUSTIN BAKING COMPANY, Austin, Texas: Thousands of loaves of bread and rolls are turned out each day, and visitors can view their creation, from the mixing of dough to baking and packaging. Tours run Wednesdays and Fridays from October to May. Information: Austin Baking Co., 5800 Airport Blvd., Austin, TX 78752 (phone: 512 453-6606).

BOEING COMPANY (747/767 PLANT), Everett, Washington: By virtue of being big enough to hold 50 planes in various stages of completion, the final assembly building that plant visitors tour is the largest building in the world by volume — 62 acres under one roof! Children under 12 not admitted. Closed weekends. Information: The Boeing Co., PO Box 3707 (OE-44), Seattle, WA 98124-2207 (phone: 206-342-4801).

For the Experience

National Parks: A Checklist

 Set aside by Congress for their exceptional array of one-of-a-kind scenic, geological, and historic features, the national parks are the Metropolitan Museums of America's natural history. You won't find all of the country's most marvelous natural features in the system — but almost.

Nevertheless, park boundaries are drawn arbitrarily, and usually take in only the areas where the marvels are found in greatest concentration. National forests, national wildlife refuges, state parks, and other government-protected preserves often surround the parks or take in similar countryside — and they're far less crowded.

Here is a list of the parks and adjacent recreation areas and attractions. Unless otherwise indicated, all of them offer camping and ranger programs; permits are usually required for overnight hiking trips into the backcountry.

Almost all parks will be crowded during a mid-July to mid-August summer "rush hour," and it may be necessary to reserve your campsite in advance. But you will also find naturalist programs scheduled with a frequency that you wouldn't encounter at other times of year — say, in other summer months, or during spring, fall, and winter. Then, on the other hand, you may have the country's most marvelous natural features almost all to yourself.

For folders on the individual areas, you can write the superintendents of the parks you're interested in, or address your query for information about more than one park to the National Park Service, Public Inquiries Office, PO Box 37127, Washington, DC 20013-7127 (phone: 202-343-4747). The Superintendent of Documents, US Government Printing Office, Washington, DC 20402, sells a good booklet on camping in the national park system as well as an interesting publication describing the dozens of less-used parks and a comprehensive listing of parks. Michael Frome's excellent *National Park Guide* (Rand McNally; $11.95) describes all 48 national parks plus the more than 300 National Park Service areas.

EAST

ACADIA NATIONAL PARK, Bar Harbor, Maine: With its towering shoreline cliffs, rocky coves, trail-crossed inland forests, and mountains, this 35,065-acre national park, the only one in New England, offers some of the most spectacular scenery in a beautiful state. Ocean Drive, the sea-hugging section of the 27-mile-long Park Loop Road, takes you to Thunder Hole, where waves crash on the shore with impressive fury when the surf is strong; to tidepools full of brightly colored marine life; to Otter Point, where the lobster boats and pleasure craft dot the horizon; to brief but golden Sand Beach; and to Cadillac Mountain, whose summit is the highest on the US's eastern seaboard. Somes Sound, the East Coast's only fjord, is also in the park. Acadia National Park, Box 177, Bar Harbor, ME 04609 (phone: 207-288-3338). See also *Acadia National Park*, DIRECTIONS.

SHENANDOAH NATIONAL PARK, Front Royal, Virginia: Crisscrossed by some 500 miles of trails — 94 of them along the Appalachian Trail — Shenandoah National

Park's 195,450 acres are about as close to paradise as a hiker can get. The 105-mile-long Skyline Drive, which crosses and recrosses the top of the ridge along which the park sprawls, makes the place wonderful for Sunday drivers as well — particularly in May, when the pink azalea is in bloom; in June, when the mountain laurel is blossoming; and from mid- to late October during the fall color display. You can go riding, cycling, or fishing, or join the rangers for nature walks and campfire talks — and even today, when you look up into the night sky, you won't have any trouble figuring out why the Indians named the area "Daughter of the Stars." The ridge drive continues for nearly 500 miles more as the Blue Ridge Parkway. You can follow it or find other diversions closer at hand in the George Washington National Forest, which flanks the park. Information: Shenandoah National Park, Rte. 4, Box 348, Luray, VA 22835 (phone: 703-999-2266 for recorded information on weather, campground, lodge, and activities, or 703-999-2229 for further details). See also *Shenandoah National Park,* DIRECTIONS.

SOUTH

HOT SPRINGS NATIONAL PARK, Hot Springs, Arkansas: Five thousand acres in the Ouachita Mountains, 47 mineral hot springs, and a spa at Bath House Row (where baths go for about $8 each) make this one of the nation's most unusual national parks. Nearby: DeGray and Ouachita lakes, immense impoundments where you can swim, fish, go boating; and the Ouachita National Forest, great for backpacking and hiking. From mid- to late May, the magnolias bloom; mid-October brings the equally spectacular fall foliage show. Information: Hot Springs National Park, PO Box 1860, Hot Springs, AR 71902 (phone: 501-624-3383). See also *Hot Springs National Park,* DIRECTIONS.

EVERGLADES NATIONAL PARK, Homestead, Florida: The park's 1.4 million acres of mangrove swamps and watery plains provide a wonderful feeding ground for waterbirds, ducks, and all manner of tropical bird life: egrets, brown pelicans, yellow-crowned and black-crowned night herons, roseate spoonbills, great white herons, wood ibis, bald eagles. Go in summer to see giant loggerhead turtles laying their eggs on the beaches at Cape Sable (it may be difficult to find them but not impossible), or in winter and early spring for the best bird watching. Nearby is the Audubon Society's 6,000-acre Corkscrew Swamp Sanctuary, home of the largest remaining stand of virgin bald cypress in the US. Information: Everglades National Park, PO Box 279, Homestead, FL 33030 (phone: 305-247-6211). See also *Everglades National Park,* DIRECTIONS.

MAMMOTH CAVE NATIONAL PARK, Mammoth Cave, Kentucky: The 52,000-plus acres of woodlands take in what used to be known as "the greatest cave that ever was." That was back in the days ladies had to don bloomers to visit, but a trip along segments of the cave's 300-plus miles of mapped corridors will convince you that it isn't far from true, even today. Information: Mammoth Cave National Park, Mammoth Cave, KY 42259 (phone: 502-758-2328). See also *Mammoth Cave National Park,* DIRECTIONS.

GREAT SMOKY MOUNTAINS NATIONAL PARK, near Gatlinburg, Tennessee: The committee who picked the area for a park site called it "exceptional, for the height of the mountains, depths of the valleys, ruggedness of the area, and unexampled variety of trees, shrubs, and plants." That this statement remains true is particularly amazing when you consider that the park lies within a day's drive of almost all the major cities in the East and the Midwest; the Smokies get the heaviest use of any national park in the system. Yet, with about 520,000 acres (half in Tennessee, half in North Carolina), 800 miles of hiking trails, and scenic parkways which never seem to end, you can usually get off by yourself, even in summer, the busiest season. Spring, fall, and winter are also lovely — spring for the wildflowers (late April) and rhododendrons and azaleas (June and early July); fall for the crisp air and flaming colors; winter for the solitude. Information: Great Smoky Mountains National Park, Rte. 2, Gatlinburg, TN 37738 (phone: 615-436-1200). See also *Great Smoky Mountains National Park,* DIRECTIONS.

BIG BEND NATIONAL PARK, on the Mexican border near Terlingua, Texas:
The park's canyons were formed as the Rio Grande wore away at the hardened sediments of an inland sea that covered the area millions of years ago. From the desert floor to the rocky, pine- and juniper-covered Chisos Mountains — which change colors as the sun moves through the sky — one finds coyotes, ringtails, mule deer and white-tail deer, lizards, snakes, and some 400 species of birds; because of the wide range in elevation, from about 1,800 feet at river level to 7,835 feet atop Mt. Emery, habitats and wildlife are exceptionally diverse. Hiking trails, primitive roads, and commercial rafting trips provide access. Information: Big Bend National Park, Big Bend, TX 79834 (phone: 915-477-2251). See also *Big Bend National Park,* DIRECTIONS.

GUADALUPE MOUNTAINS NATIONAL PARK, near Salt Flat, Texas: Just south of the New Mexico line, this 76,293-acre 1972 addition to the national park system preserves a spectacular exposure of what some geologists consider the world's most significant and extensive fossil reef, a reminder that many years ago the entire area was covered by a sea. Guadalupe Peak, Texas's highest (8,749 feet, accessible by trail), is here, as are the whitish, thousand-foot cliffs known as El Capitan; the rugged country-side takes in desert vegetation and high-country forest of ponderosa pine, southwestern white pine, and Douglas fir. The last week in October and the first 2 weeks in November, when the canyon maples, oaks, and walnuts take on their autumn colorations, are particularly beautiful. Information: Guadalupe Mountains National Park, HC60 Box 400, Salt Flat, TX 79847-9400 (phone: 915-828-3251).

MIDWEST

ISLE ROYALE NATIONAL PARK, near Houghton, Michigan, in Lake Superior:
With some 166 miles of trails, this 539,280-acre park on the largest island in Lake Superior is one of the best places for hiking in the US — and certainly in the Midwest. You can also go boating, or fish in inland streams, bays, and in Lake Superior for trout, northern pike, or perch. Information: Isle Royale National Park, 87 N. Ripley St., Houghton, MI 49931 (phone: 906-482-0984). See also *Isle Royale National Park,* DIRECTIONS.

VOYAGEURS NATIONAL PARK, International Falls, Minnesota: While it is possible to drive to the edge of this 218,000-acre park, access to most of the forests, bogs, and lakes (4 big ones and 30 smaller ones) is almost entirely by houseboat, runabout, cruiser, and canoe. More than 125 primitive, boat-in campsites await the today's explorer, as do two wilderness trails that offer access to inland lakes. The Kebetogama Peninsula is a large, roadless wilderness that is home to timber wolves, moose, bear, and numerous other animals. Powerboating, canoeing, camping, along with fishing and, in winter, cross-country skiing, snowmobiling, and ice fishing, are the park's main activities. A complete program of naturalist-guided activities is available during the summer months. Pleasant resorts and outfitters who rent anything from boats to camping gear are abundant on the park's perimeter. Information: Voyageurs National Park, PO Box 50, International Falls, MN 56649 (phone: 218-283-9821). See also *Voyageurs National Park,* DIRECTIONS.

WEST

DENALI NATIONAL PARK AND PRESERVE, Denali Park, Alaska: North America's tallest mountain, 20,320-foot Mt. McKinley, towers over the spectacular Alaska Range, which dominates the scenery in this 9,375-square-mile subarctic wilderness — but if you come specifically to see Denali, "the high one," you may be disappointed: the mountain is cloud-covered for more than half of every summer season. However, the park, set aside in 1917 for wildlife protection, does offer an excellent opportunity to hike in both tundra and taiga and to look for grizzly, moose, caribou, Dall sheep, and wolf, as well as many other species of mammals, birds, and flora. The landscape will quite simply take your breath away. Information: Denali National Park and Preserve, Box 9, Denali National Park, AK 99755 (phone: 907-683-2294). See also *Denali National Park,* DIRECTIONS.

GLACIER BAY NATIONAL PARK, Gustavus, Alaska: The 5,000 square miles here encompass rugged mountains; glaciers flowing and calving into a deep, fjord-like bay; and a variety of landscapes ranging from terrain just recovering from glacial retreat to lush, temperate rain forest. Brown and black bears, whales, and seals, as well as eagles and another 200 species of birds, may be observed here. The park is accessible only by airplane or boat. Information: Superintendent, Glacier Bay National Park, Gustavus, AK 99826 (phone: 907-697-2230).

GRAND CANYON NATIONAL PARK, Grand Canyon, Arizona: "The world's most wonderful spectacle," according to naturalist John Burroughs. True or not, no other natural formation in the US comes close to equaling the canyon's size, color, or geological significance. The Grand Canyon, carved bit by bit over millennia by the force of the Colorado River, is 277 miles long, as wide as 18 miles across, and more than a mile deep. Layer upon layer of fossilized rock, limestone, and sandstone date to Precambrian times and tell an incredible story of how this land was formed. Information: Grand Canyon National Park, PO Box 129, Grand Canyon, AZ 86023 (phone: 602-638-7888). See also *Grand Canyon National Park,* DIRECTIONS.

PETRIFIED FOREST NATIONAL PARK, near Holbrook, Arizona: Part of the Painted Desert — a vast area of bright-colored sandstone, shale, and clay formations — 93,533-acre Petrified Forest National Park is made up of numerous areas where the fallen trees of 225-million-year-old forests have gradually filled with minerals stained brilliant red, purple, and blue by traces of iron, carbon, and manganese and have fossilized. The logs of jasper, agate, and other quartzes that resulted — some 100 feet long — lie helter-skelter on the ground. The 50,000 park acres designated as wilderness make for great hiking and primitive backpack camping; best seasons are late spring and early fall, when desert wildflowers are in bloom and temperatures are moderate. Information: Petrified Forest National Park Headquarters, AZ 86028 (phone: 602-524-6228). See also *Petrified Forest National Park,* DIRECTIONS.

LASSEN VOLCANIC NATIONAL PARK, near Mineral, California: This park has mud pots, fumaroles, hot springs, and such, just like Yellowstone; but Lassen is far less crowded. The park's center, 10,457-foot Lassen Peak, is one of the most recently active volcanoes in the lower 48 states. Information: Lassen Volcanic National Park, PO Box 100, Mineral, CA 96063-0100 (phone: 916-595-4444). See also *Lassen Volcanic National Park,* DIRECTIONS.

REDWOOD NATIONAL PARK, near Crescent City, California: Northern California's 106,000-acre park, 1 to 7 miles wide, stretches for 50 Pacific-pounded miles adjoining a section of Six Rivers National Forest and takes in sand and pebble beaches, creeks, cliffs, and huge stands of virgin redwoods, including the earth's tallest tree, measured in 1963 at 367.8 feet. In 1980, UNESCO added the park to its prestigious World Heritage List of places worthy of preservation for the good of mankind. Most of the other mature redwoods reach 200 feet. Information: Redwood National Park, 1111 Second St., Crescent City, CA 95531 (phone: 707-464-6101). See also *Redwood National Park,* DIRECTIONS.

SEQUOIA AND KINGS CANYON NATIONAL PARKS, near Three Rivers, California: The two parks, administered as one, take in a 65-mile-long, 1,300-square-mile expanse of rugged canyons, peaks, and gorges that include Mt. Whitney and part of the high sierra. The parks also preserve groves of giant sequoia, which, with the coastal redwoods, are among the last surviving members of a large group which was widespread eons ago. Information: Sequoia and Kings Canyon National Parks, Three Rivers, CA 93271 (phone: general information, 209-565-3456; round-the-clock, 209-565-3341). See also *Sequoia and Kings Canyon National Parks,* DIRECTIONS.

YOSEMITE NATIONAL PARK, Yosemite, California: A 1,189-square-mile parkland, with groves of sequoias, mountain meadows, alpine vegetation, immense waterfalls (at their most thunderous in May and June), and huge monoliths. One of them, El Capitan, is among the world's largest masses of visible granite. You can take naturalist trips led by rangers or mule and horseback trips operated by the park's concessioner; go to mountain climbing school (see *Climbing Schools, Mountain Climbing and Mountains*); or take a summer photography workshop at the *Ansel Adams Gallery.* Ranger-led backpack trips are limited and are offered through the Yosemite Association. Information: Yosemite National Park, PO Box 577, Yosemite, CA 95389 (phone: 209-372-0264/5). See also *Yosemite National Park,* DIRECTIONS.

MESA VERDE NATIONAL PARK, near Durango and Cortez, Colorado: Fourteen hundred years ago, Indians came to this land; built and lived in homes on the mesa tops and in elaborate dwellings set into the cliffsides of the area canyons; and then, possibly having overused their environment, they abandoned the area. Anthropologists and archaeologists believe that they probably moved south into northern New Mexico and Arizona, where they are represented now by various groups of Pueblo Indians. Current visitors can explore some of the most dramatic of the cliff dwellings, including Long House and Step House on Wetherill Mesa; the 200-room Cliff Palace, the largest cliff dwelling in North America; Spruce Tree House, amazingly well preserved; and Balcony House. Whether you tour these on your own or in the company of a ranger will depend on which site you visit and when you travel. But either way, even history haters can't fail to get hooked on matters archaeological. Other area attractions: The old Durango and Silverton narrow-gauge railroad, which runs from Durango, through deep forested canyons, to the quaint old mining town of Silverton (call 303-247-2733 for train information); the San Juan National Forest, great for hiking and fishing; and a variety of other national monuments: the Aztec Ruins, Chaco Canyon, and other nearby towers, pueblos, and cliff dwellings scattered around the Four Corners area; Navajo, near Kayenta and Tuba City, Arizona; and Canyon de Chelly, near Chinle, Arizona, in the Navajo reservation. Lodgings are available in Cortez at *Fair View Lodge,* modern, beautifully situated, and aptly named (phone: 303-529-4543), which also offers 3-hour tours. In Durango, you'll find the famous 100-year-old *Strater* hotel, lavishly furnished with authenic Victorian antiques, yet with all modern conveniences (phone: 303-247-4431), along with some 50 other hostelries. For park information, contact the superintendent in Mesa Verde National Park, CO 81330 (phone: 303-529-4461); for details about the surrounding area, write the Cortez Chamber of Commerce, Box 968, Cortez, CO 81321 (phone: 303-565-3414).

ROCKY MOUNTAIN NATIONAL PARK, Estes Park, Colorado: The 265,193 acres — 414 square miles — of high peaks and luxuriant forests that were set aside as a park in 1915 are today virtually unspoiled and make excellent hiking. Some visitors like to make the trek to the top of 14,255-foot Longs Peak, one of the park's 113 named peaks over 10,000 feet; others like to stroll to lovely Emerald Lake, its shores framed by towering peaks. Information: Estes Park Area Chamber of Commerce, PO Box 3050, Estes Park, CO 80517 (phone: 303-586-4431 or 800-443-7837), and Superintendent, Rocky Mountain National Park, Estes Park, CO 80517 (phone: 303-586-2371). See also *Rocky Mountain National Park,* DIRECTIONS.

HALEAKALA NATIONAL PARK, on the island of Maui, Hawaii: The spectacular drive to the summit, over the highest paved road in the mid-Pacific, and the stunning emptiness of the 19-square-mile crater of this now-dormant volcano are only two of the highlights of a visit to this 28,665-acre preserve. The highway clings precariously to the mountainside and offers views of mists, cloud banks, pastureland, ocean. The vast, silent area — ribboned with hiking trails where you can stay overnight in primitive cabins or at campgrounds — is dotted by cinder cones, lava flows, and spatter vents. In the Kipahulu District of the park, on the Pacific, you can splash in waterfall pools that tumble into each other on the way to the sea. Local outfitters guide bicycle riders down the mountain on the 38 miles of paved highway. Horseback rides into the crater are also available. Information: Haleakala National Park, PO Box 369, Makawao, Maui, HI 96768 (phone: 808-572-9306; for recorded weather information, 808-572-7749; for recorded cabin and hiking information, 808-572-9177). See also *Haleakala National Park,* DIRECTIONS.

HAWAII VOLCANOES NATIONAL PARK, near Hilo, Hawaii: Rising to 4,400 feet, Kilauea has been dubbed "the drive-in volcano" because of its rare accessibility. It's just one of two that are still active in this 229,177-acre park; and between it and 13,677-foot Mauna Loa, something is usually acting up. You may see Kilauea letting out fountains of lava (once, a spurt sprayed 1,900 feet into the air). You may see rivers of lava. You may feel Mauna Loa's tremors. You will doubtless see steam; along Steaming Bluff it will swirl around you like a fog. And at the Hawaiian Volcano Observatory's *Jaggar Museum,* you can watch seismographs at work. The modern *Volcano House* is a good place to lodge; it's not fancy — but not every hotel can boast a dining room with a view of a steaming crater (phone: 808-967-7321). On the opposite side of the island, on the Kona Coast, is Puuhonua-o-Honaunau National Historic Park, at Honaunau, the reconstruction of an ancient Hawaiian temple. Information: Hawaii Volcanoes National Park, PO Box 52, Hawaii National Park, HI 96718 (phone: 808-967-7311).

GLACIER NATIONAL PARK, West Glacier, Montana: Properly called Waterton-Glacier International Peace Park, because it adjoins Canada's Waterton National Park, this Montana area's million-plus acres — a phenomenal 1,600 square miles — take in precipitous peaks, knife-edged ridges, 50 glaciers, and approximately 700 miles of hiking trails. Grizzlies live here, along with bighorn sheep, mountain goats, mule and whitetail deer, and many species of birds. Fifty-mile-long Going-to-the-Sun Road provides magnificent vistas. There are marvelous places to stay in the park as well: *Sperry* and *Granite Park Chalets,* built around World War I and hardly modernized since, are accessible only by hiking trail — but if you can get there, you can see what it feels like to live in a stone chalet without electricity. Far fancier are the bigger establishments — *Lake McDonald Lodge* and *Many Glacier* hotel inside the park, and *Glacier Park Lodge,* just outside — which are like sets for a Nelson Eddy musical. Nearby: a chair lift ride at Big Mountain, near Whitefish; Flathead Lake, south of Kalispell, the largest natural freshwater lake west of the Mississippi; Flathead National Forest; and Bigfork, a tiny artsy town. Good lodgings are available at Big Mountain and at the *Flathead Lake Lodge* (phone: 406-837-4391; open May through September), a dude ranch on the lakeshore a mile south of Bigfork. Time your visit for early summer and you'll catch the resort full of rodeo cowboys, who come to improve their skills at a special rodeo school. Information: Glacier National Park, West Glacier, MT 59936 (phone: 406-888-5441; for recorded information on weather, road conditions, camping, and park activities, 406-888-5551). See also *Glacier National Park,* DIRECTIONS.

CARLSBAD CAVERNS NATIONAL PARK, near Carlsbad, New Mexico: Lying underneath the rugged foothills of the Guadalupe Mountains, Carlsbad Cavern is only the best known of the dozens of caves in this 46,753-acre national park; the cave is as noteworthy for its immensity as for its variety of formations. From May through September, you can watch hundreds of thousands of bats leaving their underground lairs each evening. In another part of the park, lantern tours through an undeveloped cave are available. Information: Carlsbad Caverns National Park, 3225 National Parks Hwy., Carlsbad, NM 88220 (phone: 505-785-2232). See also Carlsbad Caverns National Park, DIRECTIONS.

THEODORE ROOSEVELT NATIONAL PARK, Medora, North Dakota: Some 70,634 acres of the badlands that so enchanted the future president when he first came to the area as a big game hunter in 1883 are preserved in this park, and when you visit, you'll easily comprehend the attraction that led Roosevelt to purchase two ranches in the area: The buttes and canyons, carved by wind and water into fantastic shapes, make the scenery extraordinarily beautiful, and the countryside is full of buffalo, prairie dogs, eagles, and more. Information: Superintendent, Theodore Roosevelt National Park, Medora, ND 58645 (phone: 701-623-4466).

CRATER LAKE NATIONAL PARK, near Crater Lake, Oregon: Formed by the collapse of a volcano some 6,800 years ago, 21-square-mile, 1,932-foot-deep Crater Lake is the deepest in the United States (and second deepest, next to Canada's Great Slave Lake, in the Western Hemisphere), and boasts some of the most brilliantly blue waters anywhere. Bordering the park are the Umpqua, Winema, and Rogue River National Forests; the *Oregon Shakespearean Festival* in Ashland; quaint Jacksonville, home of *Peter Britt Festivals* (see *Music Festivals*); and the whitewater raft trips down the Rogue. Information: Crater Lake National Park, PO Box 7, Crater Lake, OR 97604-0007 (phone: 503-594-2211). See also *Crater Lake National Park,* DIRECTIONS.

WIND CAVE NATIONAL PARK, near Hot Springs, South Dakota: Set in the Black Hills, this 28,260-acre park is home to bison, prairie dogs, pronghorn antelope, and an unusual cave full of exotic crystal formations — frostwork crystals made of calcite, aragonite, and boxwork, a honeycomb affair made of crystalline fins. You can see these on traditional walks through the cave, on special candlelight tours through unelectrified sections, and on spelunking tours where you do your locomoting on all fours. Neighbors include Mt. Rushmore National Memorial (where the faces of Washington, Teddy Roosevelt, Lincoln, and Jefferson are carved in granite cliffs), aptly named Jewel Cave National Monument, Custer State Park, home of one of the world's largest herds of bison, and Black Hills National Forest. You shouldn't miss the *State Game Lodge* in Custer State Park, where Coolidge and Eisenhower once summered and where you can now eat buffalo steaks and South Dakota pheasant (phone: 605-255-4541). According to one commercial buffalo rancher, buffalo tastes like beef wished it did — flavorful, but tender as a filet mignon. Information: Wind Cave National Park, Hot Springs, SD 57747 (phone: 605-745-4600); Black Hills National Forest, RR 2, Box 200, Custer, SD 57730 (phone: 605-673-2251); Custer State Park, HCR 83, Box 70, Custer, SD 57730 (phone: 605-255-4515); Custer State Game Lodge, HCR 83, Box 74, Custer, SD 57730 (phone: 605-255-4541).

BADLANDS NATIONAL PARK, Interior, South Dakota: Erosion has left the landscape of this 244,000-acre park sculpted into canyons and cliffs, spires and gullies, all banded with the bright colors of the many layers of mudstone and sandstone deposited here over millennia. On the Fossil Exhibit Trail you can see embedded in rock what remains of fleet-footed rhinos and other mammals that prowled the area from 37 million to 23 million years ago. Also preserved in the park is the mixed-grass prairie and its inhabitants — bison, pronghorn and bighorn sheep, and lots of deer. Information: Superintendent, Badlands National Park, PO Box 6, Interior, SD 57750 (phone: 605-433-5361).

ARCHES NATIONAL PARK, near Moab, Utah: Through some of the numerous arches already discovered in Arches National Park's 73,379 acres, you can see the park's vast expanse of canyons and, off in the distance, the snow-capped peaks of the LaSal Mountains. Trim, tapered Delicate Arch, the park's most celebrated landmark, is higher than most houses. Landscape Arch is among the world's longest known natural stone arches. Though only a few miles east of Canyonlands, the formations here have their own distinct character, and a visit to both will teach you a lot about how the earth came to be what it is. Information: Arches National Park, PO Box 907, Moab, UT 84532-2995 (phone: 801-259-8161), and the Grand County Travel Council, PO Box 550, Moab, UT 84532-0550 (phone: 801-259-8825; 800-635-MOAB in Utah).

BRYCE CANYON NATIONAL PARK, Bryce Canyon, Utah: The Paiute Indians called the stunning giant rock formations along the edge of the Paunsaugunt Plateau here "red rocks standing like men in a bowl-shaped canyon." But when you drive along the 18-mile-long parkway, especially while on the plateau's edge, you may think the results of 60 million years of silt and clay deposits and water action resemble castles and cathedrals, Hindu temples and skyscrapers, chessmen and such. The colors — pink, orange, and scarlet, sometimes striped with lavender and blue, or cream, white, and yellow — are even more vivid at sunset. Information: Bryce Canyon National Park, Bryce Canyon, UT 84717 (phone: 801-834-5322). See also *Bryce Canyon National Park,* DIRECTIONS.

CANYONLANDS NATIONAL PARK, near Moab, Utah: The Green and Colorado rivers, which meet in this area, have carved deep and winding gorges in the reddish-orange sandstone. The buttes, cliffs, mesas, spires, columns, and pillars — like mad Ludwig's castles in Bavaria — are truly fantastic. The still relatively untrammeled 337,570 acres, full of juniper and piñon, can be seen on jeep tours out of Moab, on float trips down the Green and Colorado rivers (see *Touring America's Waterways*), as well as on foot or horseback and by car from a number of overlooks. Nearby, you'll find Arches National Park; the cool woodlands of Manti-LaSal National Forest; the fine recreational waters of Glen Canyon National Recreation Area and Lake Powell; Natural Bridges National Monument; and Hovenweep National Monument, a chain of prehistoric Indian dwellings. Lodgings are available in Moab and Monticello. Information: Canyonlands National Park, 125 W. 2nd South, Moab, UT 84532-2995 (phone: 801-259-7164), and Grand County Travel Council, PO Box 550, Moab, UT 84532-0550 (phone: 801-259-8825; in Utah 800-635-MOAB).

CAPITOL REEF NATIONAL PARK, near Torrey, Utah: Once home of a few hardy settlers and occasionally visited by explorers, outlaws, and prospectors, this isolated area's beauty has only recently been discovered by the rest of America. The uplift known as the Waterpocket Fold, with layer upon layer of exposed rock formations, makes the area a geologist's paradise. The Fruita historic district, around the visitors center and campground, marks a pioneer Mormon settlement and forms a green oasis in the midst of the desert where visitors may pick cherries, apricots, peaches, and other fruit in season. Visitors can also enjoy a variety of desert flora and fauna, marvel at the rock art of the prehistoric Fremont Indian culture, and view the sheer-walled sandstone cliffs, canyons, and monoliths whose rich, rainbow hues seem almost luminous in the late-afternoon sun. You can see it all from your car or on foot, along short hiking trails or by carefully planned backpacking trips. Information: Capitol Reef National Park, Torrey, UT 84775 (phone: 801-425-3791).

ZION NATIONAL PARK, near Springdale, Utah: It was the Mormons, settling here in the 19th century, who called the central feature of this 229-square-mile park Zion, or "heavenly city of God," and who gave many of its features their unusual names — Kolob Canyons and Mt. Moroni. Backcountry trails can be rugged but full of marvels, like Kolob Arch, which claims to be the world's largest natural span at 310 feet, or "Hanging Gardens" — rock walls draped, in season (late April through September), with columbine, monkey flower, maiden-hair ferns, and scarlet lobelia — which you see along the Gateway to the Narrows Trail. Park roads provide terrific views of the canyon walls, colored crimson, purple, pink, orange, and yellow. Horseback trips are also available. Within a 125-mile radius, you can also visit the North Rim of the Grand Canyon; Bryce Canyon National Park; Cedar Breaks National Monument; the Dixie National Forest; and the *Utah Shakespearean Festival,* one of America's nationally known Shakespeare festivals, on the campus of Southern Utah State College at Cedar City. July, August, and September reservations recommended (phone: 801-586-7880). Information: Zion National Park, Springdale, UT 84767 (phone: 801-772-3256). See also *Zion National Park,* DIRECTIONS.

MT. RAINIER NATIONAL PARK, Longmire, Washington: The dormant ice-clad volcano that is the raison d'être of this park is only its most striking feature. The

235,404 acres also have cathedral-like forests of Douglas fir and Pacific silver fir, western red cedar, and western hemlock. The park is a wonderland of glaciers and boasts the lower 48's most extensive single-peak glacier system as well as its longest glacier (Carbon) and its largest (Emmons). Nearby are the Mt. Baker–Snoqualmie National Forest, the Gifford Pinchot National Forest, and the Crystal Mountain Resort, a ski and summer resort development that does a brisk business even when the weather is warm. There are hotels in the park; motels, inns, and lodges are along the access routes 7, 706, 410, and 12. Information: Mt. Rainier National Park, Tahoma Woods Star Route, Ashford, WA 98304 (phone: 206-569-2211). See also *Mt. Rainier National Park,* DIRECTIONS.

NORTH CASCADES NATIONAL PARK, near Sedro Woolley, Washington: Ice falls and waterfalls, hanging valleys and ice caps, and some 300 glaciers, plus canyons, granite peaks, and mountain lakes and streams make this a rugged 789 square miles. It's not for that reason only, however, that you'll find some of the most extensive opportunities for outdoor recreation in the area. In addition to the park, there's the 184-square-mile Ross Lake National Recreation Area (which lies between the park's north and south units); the 97-square-mile Lake Chelan National Recreation Area (adjoining the south unit on its southern border); and surrounding the four units, the Mt. Baker–Snoqualmie, Wenatchee, and Okanogan national forests. You'll find especially interesting rooms at the rustic *North Cascades Lodge* (phone: 509-682-4711) in Stehekin, at the north end of Lake Chelan and accessible only by boat or float plane from the town of Chelan. Lodgings can also be found at *Diablo Lake* resort (Everett operator, area code 206; ask for Newhalem 5578) and *Ross Lake* resort (Everett operator, area code 206; ask for 397-7735); *Ross Lake* is not accessible by car. Information: North Cascades National Park, 2105 Hwy. 20, Sedro Woolley, WA 98284 (phone: 206-856-5700).

OLYMPIC NATIONAL PARK, near Port Angeles, Washington: These 1,441 square miles lay claim to some of the wettest weather in America; 60 living glaciers; alpine meadows; deep lush valleys; exquisitely green rain forests full of fungi, lichens, and some 70 species of moss, draped over branches and growing on tree trunks. There are stands of Sitka spruce and Douglas fir, sometimes 300 feet tall and 1,000 years old. Huge Roosevelt elk, the largest remaining herd in the country, inhabit the park. Seals, sea lions, and whales can be seen along the beaches in the Pacific Coast section. Nearby are the Olympic Highway, which circles the peninsula; Olympic National Forest; and the San Juan Islands, a still fairly unspoiled resort area in Puget Sound, accessible by ferry from Anacortes, Washington, and Sidney, British Columbia. Information: Olympic National Park, 600 E. Park Ave., Port Angeles, WA 98362 (phone: 206-452-4501). See also *Olympic National Park,* DIRECTIONS.

GRAND TETON NATIONAL PARK, Moose, Wyoming, and environs: This 40-mile-long string of snow-capped and glaciated mountains dominates the skyline as do few other mountains in the nation. The 13,770-foot Grand Teton simply towers over Jackson Hole, the valley to the east of the Teton Range. Surrounding are Teton and Targhee National Forests, both heavily forested and trail-crossed. Thankfully, the park suffered little damage during the forest fires in the fall of 1988. Information: Grand Teton National Park, PO Drawer 170, Moose, WY 83012 (phone: 307-733-2880). See also *Grand Teton National Park,* DIRECTIONS.

YELLOWSTONE NATIONAL PARK, in the northwest corner of Wyoming: Old Faithful is the most famous thermal feature in this park full of thermal features. There are countless geyser basins, mud pots, bubbling springs, hot pools that are blue, red, orange, and yellow, depending on the temperature of the water and the plants (algae) that can survive there. What many people don't know is that Yellowstone also boasts beautiful mountains, numerous waterfalls, abundant wildlife, and rich forests that make for some of the US's finest backpacking. Yellowstone has a reputation for being crowded — and it is, during July and August at its major points of interest. Go into the backcountry, however, and you can have trails almost to yourself, but you must see the park ranger first for current trail conditions and a backcountry camping permit. Though forest fires in 1988 devastated about a fifth of the park's total acreage, Old Faithful and the other natural attractions of the park were not affected, nor were the park buildings and roads, which remain open. Information: National Park Service, PO Box 168, Yellowstone National Park, WY 82190 (phone: 307-344-7381). See also *Yellowstone National Park,* DIRECTIONS.

Amusement Parks and Theme Parks

 Seventy or eighty years ago, the American Sunday changed forever. Until then, America's amusement parks were run as sedate adjuncts to picnic groves, usually owned by the companies that ran trolleys and interurban train lines. At some unrecorded moment, a trolley line executive realized that people loved the rides a lot more than the picnics, and before long picnicking as a Sunday afternoon pastime went the way of oil lamps. Huge entertainment complexes sprang up beside piers and boardwalks across the country. Roller coasters didn't go very fast (one attendant was chided for eating his lunch on board), but they stirred the masses. "It was something dreadful," scrawled a shaken Agatha Wales on the back of a postcard after her ride on the Venice, California, roller coaster. "I was never so frightened in my life. And if the Dear Lord will forgive me this time, I will never ride it again." Most folks were simply thrilled.

Today, more time, money, and talent is going into the business than ever before — and the results are spectacular. Not only are the parks clean, green, and flowering, but you can take in zippy, chills-down-the-spine shows and even top-name entertainers after you've whirled over some of the scariest roller coaster tracks in history.

Admission fees — usually around $15, with reductions for children — generally buy all the rides and shows you want, though occasionally you'll have to pay extra to play skill games.

EAST

SIX FLAGS GREAT ADVENTURE, Jackson, New Jersey: Located between New York City and Philadelphia, this 1,700-acre facility includes a 350-acre drive-thru safari, with 1,500 free-roaming animals representing 50 species. Here, guests can drive their own vehicles through at their leisure or take an air conditioned bus ride for a nominal charge. The park contains 30 amusement rides, a special children's area called Looney Tunes Land, three live water shows, and six other live shows for your enjoyment. For those who like to get wet, there are four water rides, including Splashwater Falls. The Great American Scream Machine is one of the tallest, fastest roller coasters in the world. Information: Six Flags Great Adventure, PO Box 120, Jackson, NJ 08527 (phone: 201-928-3500).

HERSHEYPARK, Hershey, Pennsylvania: A Hershey Bar and a Reese's Cup are two of the friendly chocolate-flavored characters seen strolling the grounds of the 87-acre theme park. In Chocolate Town, U.S.A., it has eight distinct theme areas. Be sure to visit the general store in the Old West theme area Pioneer Frontier or Mimi the Mermaid in Kaptain Kid's Kove. Pennsylvania's German and English heritage is woven through an artfully reconstructed Tudor castle and food shops offering local specialties like Belgian waffles and funnel cakes; there are also personable craftspeople on hand — candlemakers, blacksmiths, and leathercrafters. The fast, old wooden roller coaster, known as the Comet, is among the best in the US; the SooperdooperLooper

— a thrill ride that shoots passengers around steeply banked turns and upside down through one enormous 360-degree vertical loop — was the first of its kind on the East Coast. The Canyon River Rapids ride gives the exhilarating feeling of whitewater rafting, and there are over three dozen other rides. Also included in the basic admission charge is a trip through ZooAmerica, an 11-acre, high-quality zoo that showcases the plants and animals of five different North American environments; its prairie dogs, pumas, bison, timber wolves, and other mammals look as exotic to most visitors as the African creatures displayed at other parks. Information: Hersheypark, 100 W. Hersheypark Dr., Hershey, PA 17033 (phone: 717-534-3900). See also *Pennsylvania Dutch Country,* DIRECTIONS.

KINGS DOMINION, Richmond, Virginia: Fun for the entire family with 42 rides, 11 live shows, and an exciting lineup of top-name concert performers every season. Scooby Doo, Yogi Bear, and other Hanna-Barbera characters roam among the visitors. Kings Dominion's four roller coasters include the Rebel Yell, one of the first double-track racing coasters in the country; the Shockwave, the East Coast's only stand-up roller coaster; the Grizzly, a giant wooden coaster rated as one of the country's top 10; and the Scooby Doo, specially designed for children. There are five water attractions to splash through, including White Water Canyon, Diamond Falls, and the all new Racing Rivers (but leave your bathing suit at home). Information: Kings Dominion, Rte. 1, Box 166, Doswell, VA 23047 (phone: 804-876-5000).

THE OLD COUNTRY, Williamsburg, Virginia: Run by the people who operate Busch Gardens, the Dark Continent, in Tampa, this is one of the most beautiful US parks. The site — 360 acres of ravine-cut woodlands — is one large reason. Not much of it has been manicured or tamed, and the rides (Rhine cruises, steam engine train trips, a log flume, and the like) have been chosen and installed to make the most of the scenery. The Loch Ness Monster — an absolutely terrifying double-looped, upside-down roller coaster that drops riders 114 feet in 5 seconds — is one of the best rides in the country, and the Big Bad Wolf roller coaster travels seemingly out of control before plunging 80 feet to a splashing finish. The food stands out, too; you'll find not only hamburgers, but also European specialties — sausages, cheeses, pasta, tortes. And, as befits a park with a 17th-century European theme, there are musical revues, oompah bands, strolling entertainers, concerts by top performers, import shops, and a giant Festhaus — a party hall like those in Munich, except that this one is twice the size of a football field. Visiting the Old Country makes a fine complement to sightseeing around Colonial Williamsburg. (See *Tidewater Virginia,* DIRECTIONS.) Information: The Old Country, PO Box FC, Williamsburg, VA 23187 (phone: 804-253-3350).

SOUTH

BUSCH GARDENS, THE DARK CONTINENT, Tampa, Florida: Africa, the Dark Continent, is the theme of this 300-acre family entertainment center, where even the names of the seven distinctly different amusement areas evoke the exotic — Nairobi, Marrakech, the Congo, and so forth. A pair of rare white Bengal tigers (2 out of less than 100 existing in zoos worldwide) are among the more than 3,000 animals here, many of whom roam freely among the park's plains and waterways. Bird gardens, bazaars, belly dancers, Broadway-style musical revues, an animal nursery, and snake charmers are among the dazzling attractions. And of course there are rides, including the Phoenix, a looping boat swing, and the Python and Scorpion roller coasters. Information: Busch Gardens, 3000 Busch Blvd., Tampa, FL 33612 (phone: 813-971-8282).

WALT DISNEY WORLD, Lake Buena Vista, Florida: Phenomenally successful after more than a decade and a half, this 43-square-mile resort complex holds even more promise today with the continuing introduction of new attractions and facilities. EPCOT Center, the "thinking man's theme park" that's more than twice the size of the Magic Kingdom — WDW's Disneyland-like rides and attractions area — examines technology and global cultures in a number of pavilions that feature some of Disney's most advanced special effects to date. The newest of these, the $100-million "Wonders of Life" pavilion in Future World, opens in late 1989. Yet the 45 attractions of the Magic Kingdom, presided over by that fairy tale castle, and River Country, the ultimate in old-fashioned swimming holes, look as terrific as ever. Now there's also the new MGM–Disney Studio Theme Park to see and enjoy, plus the three golf courses, the tennis courts, the one-of-a-kind campground, the dinner shows, the shopping village, and the several spiffy resorts. The *Grand Floridian* and *Caribbean Beach* resort opened in 1988, *Swan* and *Dolphin* hotels in 1989, and then there are *Typhoon Lagoon* and *Pleasure Island,* also new in 1989. Walt Disney World Information Center is now open on I-75 in Ocala, Florida. Information: Walt Disney World, PO Box 10,000, Lake Buena Vista, FL 32830 (phone: 407-824-4321; for reservations, 407-824-8000). See also *Orlando,* THE CITIES.

SIX FLAGS OVER GEORGIA, Atlanta, Georgia: Loosely based on the six governments whose flags have flown over Georgia, Six Flags climbs a forested hillside on the western edge of the city. There are graded paths for strolling, benches for sitting and inhaling the sweet southern air, and plenty of soda and hot dogs. The roller coaster, the Great American Scream Machine, ripples around a reflecting lake that makes it seem even higher than it really is. In addition to that, there's a triple-loop coaster, a whitewater raft trip, and 39-odd other rides, plus Looney Tunes characters, live shows, and magicians. By the way, the six flags belong to Britain, France, Spain, the US, the Confederacy, and, naturally, the state of Georgia. Information: Six Flags Over Georgia, PO Box 43187, Atlanta, GA 30378 (phone: 404-739-3400).

CAROWINDS, Charlotte, North Carolina: Nine theme areas, with a good assortment of rides and shows and five coasters, including one that turns riders upside down four times, and a wild whitewater rapids ride. There's also Smurf Island and Hanna-Barbera Land for children. Information: Carowinds, PO Box 410289, Charlotte, NC 28241 (phone: 704-588-2600).

OPRYLAND USA, Nashville, Tennessee: The 120-acre wooded site on the banks of the Cumberland River on the edge of this southern city was pretty to begin with, and the architects made the most of the landscape by leaving all but a handful of the original trees while adding dozens of their own, and thousands of flowers. The park is a treat to behold. But Opryland really shines when it comes to music — not just country and bluegrass, as you might expect, but also rock 'n' roll, gospel, Broadway show tunes, and more; up to a dozen stage shows each year, with over 400 performers. There are thrill rides, too: a twisting corkscrew roller coaster; the wild Grizzly River Rampage (a/k/a G-R-R), a huge and satisfyingly long whitewater rafting adventure; a bobsled adventure; and more. Every Memorial Day weekend, the big *Opryland Gospel Jubilee* brings some of the country's top-name gospel groups to the park; throughout the year, television specials are taped in the park (and tickets are free to park guests), and top country stars perform from spring to autumn. The park is part of Opryland USA, a complex that includes the *Grand Ole Opry* and the *General Jackson* showboat, an entertainment palace that cruises the Cumberland River. Information: Opryland Customer Service, 2802 Opryland Dr., Nashville, TN 37214 (phone: 615-889-6700 or 615-889-6611).

ASTROWORLD, Houston, Texas: Another member of the Six Flags organization, this park is big, clean, as glossy as the Space City itself, and full of rides and attractions (over 100 of them) for the entire family, including a replica of the famous Coney Island Cyclone — one of the most exciting roller coasters ever built — a stomach-churning shuttle loop coaster, a wild river-rapids ride, and a 15-acre water recreation park, WaterWorld, as well as the *Southern Star Amphitheatre,* a 9-acre concert facility. Information: AstroWorld, 9001 Kirby Dr., Houston, TX 77054 (phone: 713-799-1234).

SIX FLAGS OVER TEXAS, Arlington, Texas: Developed around the theme of the six governments that have, over the years, called Texas their colony (Mexico, Spain, France, the Republic of Texas, the Confederacy, the US), Six Flags Over Texas, halfway between Dallas and Fort Worth, was the first of the successful theme parks. When it was founded in 1961, it would have been called "Texas Under Six Flags" but for the protest of a Texas director that "Texas ain't never been under nuthin'." Summers are hot — but nearly everything that can be air conditioned is. The assortment of rides and good clean fun entertainment is similar to that at its sister park in Atlanta. Information: Six Flags Over Texas, PO Box 191, Arlington, TX 76010 (phone: 817-640-8900).

MIDWEST

SIX FLAGS GREAT AMERICA, Gurnee, Illinois: This addition to the ever-growing Six Flags chain has added some rides and attractions — in 1988, Shock Wave, the tallest and fastest steel roller coaster in the world, looping upside down seven times; in 1987, Power Dive, a looping starship thrill ride, and expansion of Bugs Bunny Land; in 1986, Splash Water Falls, a giant water ride. However, the Americana theme remains unchanged in its five areas, including Orleans Place, Yukon Territory, and so on. There's also a Farmers' Market (where you can buy Mexican and Italian specialities, Belgian waffles, deli sandwiches, made-from-scratch French fries, and more); street entertainment providing a variety of sights and sounds; a reproduction of an antique 100-foot-high double-decker carousel; and the *Pictorium,* a movie theater where the image projected measures 70 by 96 feet; plus a variety of Broadway-style original show productions. Other highlights include an exciting whitewater raft ride and one of the world's largest double-racing wooden roller coasters. Information: Six Flags Great America, PO Box 1776, Gurnee, IL 60031 (phone: 312-249-1776; for recorded information, 312-249-2020).

SIX FLAGS OVER MID-AMERICA, Eureka, Missouri: Like the other parks in the chain, this one near St. Louis will show you a something-for-everyone good time. The 200-acre park also features Thunder River, a whitewater raft ride; Colossus: the Giant Wheel; and the Screamin' Eagle roller coaster — no longer the highest and fastest of them all, but still plenty exciting. Information: Six Flags Over Mid-America, PO Box 60, Eureka, MO 63025 (phone: 314-938-5300 or 314-938-4800).

CEDAR POINT, Sandusky, Ohio: While many other old-fashioned amusement parks went into decline around 1960, this fixture of the Great Lakes summer scene was just getting renovated, with the finest of results. There's a midway that really looks like one instead of some make-believe European country and a host of nifty one-of-a-kind rides: Gemini (a traditional racing wooden coaster whose 125-foot-high first hill drops 118 feet at a 55-degree angle); one of the tallest Ferris wheels in the world (with views out over Lake Erie, which laps at the boundaries of the park); an IMAX movie theater with a 67-by-88-foot screen that makes you feel you're part of the action; four theaters of live shows; five carousels; an enormous arcade; and a marine-life complex where you can watch performing dolphins and sea lions. Cedar Point has 54 rides, the newest being Iron Dragon, a suspended roller coaster in which guests wind through trees and loop over a lagoon. With this addition, Cedar Point now has more roller coasters (7) than any other US park. Especially enjoyable for the family is Soak City, a $3-million, 5-acre water complex featuring 10 body, raft, inner tube, and speed slides. Located directly on the beach, this complex requires separate admission and includes changing rooms, showers, and more. Admission to Cedar Point is required. Soak City will operate on the same schedule as the rest of park. Stay at the big, rambling *Hotel Breakers,* built in 1905 and fitted out with Tiffany windows and chandeliers. Knute Rockne, who perfected the forward pass on the Cedar Point beach, married an employee of the hotel. Information: Cedar Point, CN 5006, Sandusky, OH 44871 (phone: 419-626-0830).

KINGS ISLAND, near Cincinnati, Ohio: A family entertainment center with more than 100 rides and attractions, Kings Island features the world's longest, wooden roller coaster, the Beast; a stand-up coaster, the incredible King Cobra; and Vortex, a new steel coaster that turns riders upside down six times. On the 1,600-acre grounds, there are also two golf courses, a tennis stadium, the College Football Hall of Fame, a 288-room resort hotel, and a campground. Information: Kings Island, Kings Island, OH 45034 (phone: 513-241-5600).

WEST

DISNEYLAND, Anaheim, California: The original dream of Walt Disney's is as fantastic as you've probably heard, as magical as Tinker Bell's fairy dust, and perfect to the last detail. Thrill rides aren't the big deal. Instead, there are "adventures" — you get bombarded by cannonballs fired by Pirates of the Caribbean, visit a haunted mansion, explore the frontier, or fly through outer space. The special effects are truly astounding. During the summer evening Main Street Electrical Parade, floats and creatures are outlined in thousands of tiny white lights — supercalifragilisticexpialidocious — and the fireworks are stupendous. Ditto for the renovated Fantasyland, whose old-fashioned kiddie attractions have been treated to some $55 million of Disney's most magical special effects. Speaking of special effects, George Lucas designed a few for one of the park's newest attractions, Star Tours, a flight simulator in which riders experience a *Star Wars*-type journey to the moon of Endor, home of the Ewoks. And then there is the brand-new Splash Mountain, the ultimate flume ride. For a list of nearby lodgings, an area map, and other vacation aids, write to the Anaheim Area Visitor and Convention Bureau, PO Box 4270, Anaheim, CA 92803 (phone: 714-999-8999). For Disneyland information: Guest Relations Office, 1313 Harbor Blvd., Anaheim, CA 92803 (phone: 714-999-4565).

GREAT AMERICA, Santa Clara, California: This 100-acre park — the largest family entertainment center in northern California — continues to offer a crowd-pleasing combination of live stage shows, games, shops, and thrill rides. Rip Roaring Rapids — a thundering new whitewater raft ride — is a popular representative of the latter. Among the other attractions are a wooden roller coaster called the Grizzly, a double-decker carousel, a dolphin and sea lion exhibition, and an IMAX film projected onto a screen that's 7 stories high and 96 feet wide. Hanna-Barbera characters and Smurfs entertain the tots. Information: Great America, PO Box 1776, Santa Clara, CA 95052 (phone: 408-988-1800).

KNOTT'S BERRY FARM, Buena Park, California: Just down the road from Disneyland, this park started out as, yes, a berry farm, then grew like Topsy when Mrs. Walter Knott began serving chicken dinners and Mr. Walter Knott took to concocting entertainments to amuse people who queued up for Mrs. Knott's chicken. It isn't another Disneyland. Nor is it an Opryland. Old things — antiques — are scattered throughout two of the four sections (a Mexican Village, a Roaring '20s area, a Ghost Town, and Camp Snoopy, a children's park), so here and there you'll spot an old wagon wheel, some airplane parts, narrow-gauge locomotives, or an antique carousel. In addition to the rides (about 30 in all, including some real white-knucklers), you can watch cancan dancers, marionettes, a summer ice show, and delightful aquatic attractions in the new Pacific Pavilion, as well as play games in the largest arcade west of the Mississippi. And there's plenty of good eating right on the grounds: Sicilian pizza, extra-juicy hot dogs, barbecued ribs, among other things — if you don't want Mrs. Knott's fried chicken, that is. Information: Anaheim Area Visitor and Convention Bureau (address above) for area information; Knott's Berry Farm, 8039 Beach Blvd., Buena Park, CA 90620-5002 (phone: 714-220-5200).

SIX FLAGS MAGIC MOUNTAIN, Valencia, California: The third in a trio of Southern California diversions, Magic Mountain is the place to go to get spun around, shaken like a rag doll, and flipped head over heels on a multitude of coasters, water rides, and spinning wheel rides. The park is green and clean as a whistle. And one area, Spillikin Handcrafter's Junction, is almost funky: You can watch craftsmen turning pots, blowing glass, working with leather and wood — and then buy the products. And since the Six Flags organization took over, the place has really blossomed, with a dolphin and dive show, Animal Antics show, fireworks, the Animal Farm and Petting Zoo, Bugs Bunny World for children, and music and dance revues, so that the offerings are more balanced than ever before; you can have a good time even if you don't go on the rides. Looney Tunes cartoon characters are the new park mascots. Lodging information: Greater Los Angeles Visitors and Convention Bureau, 515 S. Figueroa St., Los Angeles, CA 90071 (phone: 213-624-7300). Park information: Six Flags Magic Mountain, PO Box 5500, Valencia, CA 91355 (phone: 818-367-2271 or 805-255-4100; for recorded information, 805-255-4111 or 818-367-5965).

UNIVERSAL STUDIOS, Universal City, California: Only during a trip to Universal Studios can one encounter a 30-foot, 6.5-ton King Kong, beam up to the starship *Enterprise*, experience 15 minutes in the life of a "Miami Vice" cop, and get caught in an earthquake measuring 8.3 on the Richter scale. Universal Studios has been offering tours since 1964, but this is a far cry from the original tour — which consisted of a makeup demonstration, a look at Edith Head–designed costumes, threats of a push-button monster, and performances by two Western stuntmen. Today's visitor journeys via tram through the 420 studio acres and are intercepted by alien creatures who wage a laser battle before their eyes; the bridge they cross collapses; and the "Red Sea" parts before them. They also visit the sets of such movies as *All Quiet on the Western Front, Jaws,* and *The Sting;* view a multi-media special-effects show; and walk amid the larger-than-life props used in *The Incredible Shrinking Woman.* The Studios is in the midst of a $150-million expansion project that will include *E.T.: The Extra Terrestrial* and *Back to the Future* exhibits by the time it is complete in 1991. Information: Universal Studios, 100 Universal City Plaza, Universal City, CA 91608 (phone: 818-508-9600).

America's Best Resort Hotels

American resorts are playgrounds for adults — full of golf courses, tennis courts, horseback riding trails and horse stables, bike paths, hiking paths, swimming pools, lake beaches, and other facilities too costly for the average homeowner's backyard.

Any decent resort should offer these kinds of activities. The list below is a selection of American resorts that give just a bit more — more activities, better service, greater style — or simply have just a bit more panache than their competitors. For any resort you will pay more than for a hotel or motel. At our choices, prices are likely to be even higher. But remember: Rates are usually reduced — sometimes cut in half — during off-season (the timing of which will vary depending upon where the resort is, and when it experiences its heaviest crowds). When you are budgeting, be sure to ask whether greens fees, tennis court fees, and the costs of other activities are included in the price of your room. If not, they can add as much as $25 or $30 a day or more to your budget. Also ask whether any meals are included.

EAST

BALSAMS, Dixville Notch, New Hampshire: This fairy tale castle — immense and white, with red tile roofs — sits at the base of 800-foot cliffs alongside a manmade lake, surrounded by 15,000 acres of the forests and stony peaks of northernmost New

Hampshire. The 6,842-yard Donald Ross 18-hole golf course, built against the side of a mountain and full of sloping fairways, is a challenge; even the 9-hole executive course, a mere 2,020 yards long, will require every club in your bag. There's also tennis, swimming, hiking, trout fishing, and, in winter, downhill and cross-country skiing. Information: The Balsams, Dixville Notch, NH 03576 (phone: 603-255-3400 or 800-255-0800 in New Hampshire; 800-255-0600 elsewhere).

SPALDING INN & CLUB, Whitefield, New Hampshire: This snug resort in the White Mountains shares the feeling of gracious but unpretentious elegance that's encountered at few other hotels in the country. The maintenance is superb, from the lawns and gardens and white-trimmed clubhouse and cottages to the 4 clay tennis courts, the 9 holes of par 3 golf, and the heated swimming pool. Piano bar nightly except Sundays and Mondays. But the *Spalding Inn & Club* is perhaps best known for its lawn bowling green, and several national and international tournaments have been held here. The public rooms capture the charm of country living. The resort runs on the full American plan, and the food is good and interesting enough to quell any desire you may have to eat around. Information: Spalding Inn & Club, Whitefield, NH 03598 (phone: 603-837-2572).

OTESAGA, Cooperstown, New York: The building's fine turn-of-the-century Georgian exterior, with large columns and a stately colonnaded lobby, is a good deal more formal than the resort itself, which is mannerly but not straight-laced. You can swim in Lake Otsego, at the foot of the resort's lawns, or go sailing, fishing, golfing, or tennis playing. There's a wonderful noontime buffet, a heated pool, nightly dancing. Cooperstown, of course, is a village of museums: the *Farmers' Museum,* the *Baseball Hall of Fame,* the *Fenimore House.* Information: The Otesaga, Box 311, Cooperstown, NY 13326 (phone: 607-547-9931).

GROSSINGER'S, Grossinger, New York: This giant Catskill resort has undergone substantial renovation and expansion under new ownership. Included are new guest buildings, with 236 rooms and luxury suites, plus 272 completely renovated rooms, dining rooms, kitchens, a 40,000-square-foot convention center, and a new 3-story main building whose lobby showcases a 6,400-square-foot atrium. Among the recreational facilities: a 50-meter outdoor pool and a 20,000-square-foot ice skating rink (both Olympic size); a 25-meter indoor pool, health clubs, indoor and outdoor tennis courts, 27 holes of championship golf, a 30-acre private lake, a ski center (downhill and cross-country), and tobogganing and snowmobiling trails. Information: Grossinger's Resort Hotel and Spa, Grossinger, NY 12734 (phone: 914-292-5000 or 800-874-7480 in New York State; 800-431-6300 elsewhere).

BASIN HARBOR CLUB, Vergennes, Vermont: In its tenth decade of summer resort operation and in the fourth generation of the Beach Family proprietorship, the *Basin Harbor Club* sits right on the banks of Lake Champlain some 20 miles from the *Shelburne Museum* in Shelburne. It's clearly an operation designed for a well-heeled clientele but appears far more informal than most, more like an assemblage of summer homes at an exclusive lake resort. Which makes sense, since lodging is in 77 cottages (some beautifully appointed, some as modest as most people's lake resort places) and a modestly sized lodge. You'll find a 3,200-foot grass airstrip, tennis courts, swimming pool, boats for rent, and a children's program. The *Basin Harbor Maritime Museum,* while sharing the resort's name, is actually a separate entity. The museum features a broad spectrum of educational happenings, including weekly lectures, and a full-scale replica of an 18th-century bateau, the workhorse of the French and Indian Wars and the American War of Independence. The golf course was treated to a massive, 5-year reconstruction program, and the rocks along the shore of Lake Champlain are great for sunning. On July 4, the resort celebrates with a buffet breakfast, brass band performances, and a big fireworks display. Open from May to mid-October. Information: Basin Harbor Club, Vergennes, VT 05491 (phone: 802-475-2311).

WOODSTOCK INN, Woodstock, Vermont: The town, a picture-postcard affair whose village green is rimmed by colonial homes and presided over by church steeples boasting four Paul Revere bells, deserved an inn like this; but when the old *Woodstock Inn* burned, nobody really expected a new hostelry quite so fine as this Rockresort. You can swim, play tennis on any of 10 courts (2 indoors), play racquetball or squash in the new sports center, golf on a superb Robert Trent Jones course, bike — or, nearby, shop for antiques, go horseback riding, or hike in the forests. In winter, there is downhill skiing at Suicide Six, cross-country on any number of trails, sleigh rides, and more. There are special holiday celebrations for Thanksgiving, Christmas, and Washington's Birthday. Information: Woodstock Inn & Resort, 14 The Green, Woodstock, VT 05091 (phone: 802-457-1100).

HOMESTEAD, Hot Springs, Virginia: One of the very finest American resorts, this complex of impressive red brick buildings has immense colonnaded salons where piano music accompanies afternoon tea every day and health clubs where you can soak in mineral baths or take saunas or get massaged within an inch of your life. You can go swimming, play tennis, or golf on any of three wooded courses, go riding through the 15,000 acres of Alleghany Mountain forests that belong to the resort, or pass an evening dining and dancing in dressed-up style. This is a big hotel (600 rooms), but it's so well ordered that you can hardly tell when the house is full. Information: The Homestead, Hot Springs, VA 24445 (phone: 703-839-5500).

TIDES INN, Irvington, Virginia: A gracious establishment founded in 1947 on a peninsula on the western shore of Chesapeake Bay about an hour's drive from Williamsburg or Richmond, this 112-room resort follows the best tradition of family-owned resorts, with fine service and elegant facilities — yachting, all-weather and fast-dry tennis courts, a swimming pool overlooking the Rappahannock River, a putting green, a 9-hole par 3 golf course, Sir Guy Campbell's 6,500-yard 18-hole course, George Cobb's 7,000-yard championship 18, and dining salons where the cutlery is real silver. The feeling at the *Tides Lodge,* across the inlet, is rustic-modern, casual — completely different. Information: Tides Inn, Irvington, VA 22480 (phone: 804-438-5000 or 800-TIDES-INN).

GREENBRIER, White Sulphur Springs, West Virginia: Staying here will take you back to the Ginger Rogers–Fred Astaire era: You can't help but feel like dressing for dinner and going dancing in the *Old White Club* afterward — despite the fact that it's also difficult not to wear yourself out on the riding trails, hiking paths, tennis courts, and three golf courses that fill up the hotel's 6,500 acres. Everything about this place is elegant, from the endless string of parlors ornamented with Chinese vases and priceless screens, centuries-old oil paintings, real English antique furniture and such, to the long menu full of every conceivable fish, fowl, meat, salad, appetizer, dessert, to the accommodations in comfortable bedrooms and "cottages," a short walk away from the hotel, like Fifth Avenue apartments. A new spa, built in 1988, features mineral baths, steamrooms, sauna, therapeutic showers, and massage. Information: The Greenbrier, White Sulphur Springs, WV 24986 (phone: 304-536-1110 or 800-624-6070).

SOUTH

MARRIOTT'S GRAND, Point Clear, Alabama: A rambling structure of weathered cypress occupies a corner of a 600-acre expanse of live oaks and spreading pines that grow right down to the soft white sand that edges Mobile Bay. The extensive facilities include 36 holes of golf, card rooms, a swimming beach and a freshwater pool, sailboats for sailing, courts for tennis, bikes for cycling, greens for lawn bowls, and a big air conditioned yacht for Gulf of Mexico fishing trips. But the atmosphere is low-key and nobody feels obliged to scurry around to take advantage of it all. Information: Grand Hotel, Hwy. 98, Point Clear, AL 36534 (phone: 205-928-9201).

BOCA BEACH CLUB, at Boca Raton Hotel & Club, Boca Raton, Florida: You know you're entering a special place from the moment you arrive: Cozy armchairs and a goblet of champagne or a flagon of fresh orange juice are offered even before you check in; and registration is accomplished at lovely antique desks attended by a smiling, attentive staff. The rooms are large and tastefully furnished, and the club's site on a spit of land between the Intracoastal Waterway and the Atlantic guarantees a watery vista no matter where your room is. The best rooms in the house, however, are those on the ground floor: they offer lanais for lounging and direct access to the beach on the Atlantic side. There are also two large pools, and guests have access to the numerous tennis courts, the golf course, and the considerable other amenities of the sprawling 1,000-room resort complex of which it represents just one section. Information: Boca Raton Hotel and Club, 501 E. Camino Real, Boca Raton, FL 33432-6127 (phone: 305-395-3000 or 800-327-0101).

RITZ-CARLTON, Naples, Florida: The brainchild of circus fame's John Ringling, this hotel was planned in the late 1920s but never materialized because of the onset of the Great Depression. More than 50 years later, Ringling's vision became a reality. Set on 19 acres of oceanfront property, this Mediterranean-style, 14-story hotel occupies 500,000 square feet, with 463 rooms and 32 suites. The huge lobby harks back to the Old World: It is furnished with English Georgian and French Regency pieces, Italian marble floors, and paintings by European artists, representing the best of the hotel's $2.5-million art collection. All guests have a gulf view, and those with Club rooms, on the 12th and 14th floors, may enjoy concierge services and such amenities as afternoon tea and after-dinner aperitifs. There are three dining rooms — offering a range from pheasant and venison in one to Texas chili and sundaes in another — plus a health club and spa, tennis courts, and a heated swimming pool. Golfers can play on the nearby *Pelican's Nest* and *Bonita Bay* courses. Information: Ritz-Carlton, 280 Vanderbilt Beach Rd., Naples, FL 33963 (phone: 813-598-3300 or 800-241-3333).

DORAL COUNTRY CLUB, Miami, Florida: It is well-nigh impossible to accurately pick the centerpiece here: the world class golf (5 championship courses), 15 tennis courts, an equestrian center, virtually unlimited access (and free transportation) to its sister property, the *Doral–Miami Beach,* or the *Doral Saturnia International Spa Resort.* Taking into account the availability of facilities at all the Dorals, virtually no physical or spiritual need is left unattended. Information: Doral Country Club, 4400 N.W. 87th Ave., Miami, FL 33178 (phone: 305-592-2000 in Florida; 800-327-6334 elsewhere).

BREAKERS, Palm Beach, Florida: The heirs of Florida pioneer developer and Standard Oil co-founder Henry Flagler built this great palace by the sea, the third on the property, in 1925-26 to be the best resort in the world. Crystal chandeliers, hand-painted frescoes, vaulted ceilings, and polished marble floors combine with 15th-century Flemish tapestries and Italian Renaissance–influenced architecture to create an atmosphere worthy of the hotel's listing on the National Register of Historic Places. Also on the 140-acre property are an 18-hole golf course, 14 tennis courts, 2 croquet lawns, an Olympic-size swimming pool, a fitness center, and a private beach. Another 18-hole golf course and 5 other tennis courts are available for guests at *Breakers West,* 10 miles west of the resort. Supervised youth programs are available during the summer and holiday seasons. Information: The Breakers, 1 S. County Rd., Palm Beach, FL 33480 (phone: 305-655-6611; 800-833-3141).

PALM-AIRE, Pompano Beach, Florida: This low-slung white stucco hotel and spa, whose sweeping lawns are brightened by an explosion of begonias, impatiens, and orange trees loaded with ripe fruit, has been around since 1971 — and attracting spa lovers ever since. Just 15 minutes from the beach, it offers a complete range of spa facilities, from the Olympic-size pool and Nautilus equipment to the steamrooms, saunas, whirlpools, Swiss showers, and racquetball courts. Massages, salt-glow treatments, loofah scrubs, exercise classes, stress management seminars, and other special programs keep guests busy between rounds on the 5 golf courses and 37 tennis courts. Information: Palm-Aire Hotel & Spa, 2501 Palm-Aire Dr. N., Pompano Beach, FL 33069 (phone: 305-972-3300; 800-327-4960 outside Florida).

DON CESAR REGISTRY RESORT, St. Petersburg Beach, Florida: Away from the noise and traffic downtown, this pink, Moorish-style establishment, built in 1928 and listed in the National Register of Historic Places, is unsurpassed for luxury in the area. Guests' rooms are plush, and the public rooms are done in period French style. Activities include swimming in the heated pool (right on the Gulf of Mexico), health club treatments and workouts, scuba, golf, jet skiing, sailing, tennis, fishing, dinner cruises, and children's programs. Information: Don Cesar Registry Resort, 3400 Gulf Blvd., St. Petersburg Beach, FL 33706 (phone: 813-360-1881).

KING AND PRINCE, St. Simons Island, Georgia: The centerpiece of this unpretentious 1930s Spanish-style palacio-by-the-sea is the splendid dining room, a former ballroom hung with a quartet of vast brass chandeliers and lined on both sides with arched windows that look out over the surf-pounded Atlantic (illuminated after dark). The resort has beautiful oceanfront rooms with lazy ceiling fans, suites with sunken living rooms and entrances directly on the beach, contemporary villas, and lounges with period furniture and panoramic ocean views. It's all very quietly elegant, but not so stuffy that you feel embarrassed to walk barefoot outside. Activities: golf, tennis, swimming (indoors and out), riding, biking, surf fishing. Information: King and Prince Hotel, PO Box 798, St. Simons Island, GA 31522 (phone: 912-638-3631).

CLOISTER, Sea Island, Georgia: This famous old Georgia shore resort — one of the East Coast's most noteworthy — is the kind of almost clubby place to which young people who came here originally on vacation with their parents return on their honeymoon, then come back time and time again, bringing their own youngsters; where, even when guests don't know each other at the start, conversations come easily, simply because everyone shares (if nothing else) a dedication to the resort's old-fashioned good manners. That means dressy evenings of dinner and dancing, and afternoons on the tennis courts or the links (absolutely superb; see *Golf*), or riding, shooting, fishing, boating, cycling, or swimming (either at the beach or in two lovely pools). The facilities are first class all the way, the grounds are immaculately kept, and the 260-plus rooms all look so fresh that even regulars marvel. Extensive renovations have further refreshed the public rooms and guestrooms, sports facilities, and gardens. Information: The Cloister, Sea Island, GA 31561 (phone: 912-638-3611; 800-SEA-ISLAND).

PINEHURST, Pinehurst, North Carolina: Founded by a Yankee soda fountain manufacturer named James Tufts, *Pinehurst* quickly became known as a golf center. But it offers a lot more than golf (for more about which, see *Golf*): the 13,000 acres of grounds, laid out by the firm of Frederick Law Olmsted (who gave New York its Central Park), for instance. The tennis. The gun club, which is the site of more than a dozen trap and skeet tournaments annually. And the sailing on 200-acre Lake Pinehurst; the hayrides, carriage tours, and trail rides; the jogging trails; the rental bicycles; and croquet and lawn bowling. It all adds up to one of the most invigorating — as well as one of the friendliest — grand resorts around. Accommodations are in a gracious hotel furnished with antiques and in more than 125 well-appointed condominiums. Information: Pinehurst Hotel and Country Club, PO Box 4000, Pinehurst, NC 28374 (phone: 800-672-4644 in North Carolina, 800-334-9560 elsewhere).

MIDWEST

GRAND HOTEL, Mackinac Island, Michigan: The fact that there are no cars on this island gives it a turn-of-the-century feel seldom found elsewhere in the US today.

A rambling white structure with 286 rooms, set on 500 acres of lawns, gardens, and trees adjoining a 2,000-acre state park and overlooking the Straits of Mackinac, the recently renovated *Grand* is old-fashioned from the pillared verandah (so long you could barely recognize a friend standing at the opposite end) to the horse-drawn surreys that meet guests at the ferry, the afternoon teas, the ornate staircase, and the 19th-century furnishings. By some accounts, this is the world's largest summer resort. There's a big heated pool, whirlpool, and sauna; cycling, horseback riding, golf (on a completely rebuilt course), and tennis are major activities. Closed from November to mid-May. Information: Grand Hotel, Mackinac Island, MI 49757 (phone: 906-847-3331).

WEST

THE BOULDERS, Carefree, Arizona: Opened in 1985 by Rockresorts, it is set on 1,300 acres of desert foothills, at the base of towering piles of immense rocks that gave *The Boulders* its name. The resort's 120 adobe-colored casitas blend remarkably well with the surrounding stones, and while the landscape has been tamed slightly to allow for construction, the proliferation of desert vegetation has actually been enhanced. Walking from any guestroom to the nearby lodge for a meal is to stroll through an entire spectrum of cactus varieties, to say nothing of sage and desert honeysuckle. The interior landscape is equally impressive: Each casita contains a room with a wet bar and a large oval tub; easy chairs with ottomans face a mesquite-log-burning fireplace in the conversation area. For recreation, there are 6 tennis courts, 3 first class 9-hole golf courses, exercise facilities, and access to horseback riding on desert trails. Information: The Boulders, PO Box 2090, Carefree, AZ 85377 (phone: 602-488-9009).

WIGWAM, Litchfield Park, Arizona: One of the top resorts in the country, founded around World War I as an R&R spot for Goodyear Tire and Rubber Company executives, now directed by Sun Cor Development Company, this establishment offers 228 rooms in one- and two-story adobe casitas surrounded by palm- and eucalyptus-shaded gardens. Golf is the main activity because of the two excellent Robert Trent Jones courses — the 7,220-yard *Gold Course,* cleverly filled with sand traps, and the much easier 6,107-yard *Blue Course,* par 70, which offers well-bunkered fairways and many water holes. A third course designed by Robert Lawrence plays 6,861 yards (par 72). There are also 8 tennis courts (6 lighted), plus ball machines, practice alleys, and a good program of clinics and private instruction. Other activities: horseback riding, steak broils, shuffleboard, lawn sports, swimming, and full health club facilities. Closed from June to mid-September. Information: The Wigwam, PO Box 278, Litchfield Park, AZ 85340 (phone: 602-935-3811).

ARIZONA BILTMORE, Phoenix, Arizona: Frank Lloyd Wright's ideas were part of the inspiration for this grand duchess of desert resorts, designed by his admirer Albert Chase McArthur. The place sports some very Gatsbyesque features, including the gold leaf ceiling in the dining room and the glass mural in the lobby. The kitchen is good enough to bring diners from all over the valley, and there is an endless assortment of facilities — 17 tennis courts (15 lighted), two 18-hole golf courses, 3 swimming pools (one lined with Catalina tile, comparable to the one at William Randolph Hearst's San Simeon). Information: Arizona Biltmore, PO Box 2290, Phoenix, AZ 85002 (phone: 602-955-6600; for reservations, 800-528-3696 outside Arizona).

MARRIOTT'S CAMELBACK INN, Scottsdale, Arizona: This resort at the foot of Mummy Mountain, facing its namesake across the valley, was built in 1935 of adobe mud dug up for the foundation; and in recent years, the total number of rooms on the 120 acres has expanded to about 420. To accommodate all the guests there are 2 swimming pools, 10 tennis courts, 2 of the fancier of the area's 18-holers, as well as a staff big enough to make room service and overall maintenance head and shoulders above that of most far smaller establishments. You can also go biking, hiking, riding on an Indian reservation a few miles away; play Ping-Pong, billiards, shuffleboard — or get massaged by the whirlpools. Information: Marriott's Camelback Inn, 5402 E. Lincoln, Scottsdale, AZ 85253 (phone: 602-948-1700).

SCOTTSDALE PRINCESS, Scottsdale, Arizona: This $90-million property, which opened in December 1987, has quickly gained recognition as one of the premier resort destinations in the Southwest. Service is always attentive, yet not overbearing, and the facilities are diverse and pleasing. Activities include two 18-hole golf courses, world class tennis courts, 3 heated pools, a health club, spa, and numerous restaurants. Guests choose from among casitas, suites, and rooms; all room have been designed around the subtle and earthy accents of the Southwest and feature separate living and working areas, terraces, wet bars, refrigerators, telephones with call waiting, and large bathrooms; casitas offer wood-burning fireplaces. Adjacent is Horseworld, Scottsdale's 400-acre horse park. See also *Golf.* Information: Scottsdale Princess, 7575 E. Princess Dr., Scottsdale, AZ 85255 (phone: 602-585-4848; 800-255-0080).

LOEW'S VENTANA CANYON RESORT, Tucson, Arizona: Guests approach the resort via a winding road dotted with towering saguaro cacti (Tucson's trademark) amid chirping birds — over 132 species inhabit the site. With vertically textured masonry, emulating the ribbing of the saguaro, the expansive 93-acre resort subtly emerges from the foothills of the Santa Catalina Mountains. At the entrance, there's a 2-level lake formed by an 80-foot waterfall that rushes down from the Catalinas. Nearby sits a 300-year-old saguaro cactus that the resort's planners were able to preserve by shifting the hotel from its original site. Everything blends with the desert theme — from the host of outdoor activities to the earthy tones used in the rooms. There are miles of nature trails for hiking, and biking to secluded picnic areas. There are also 2 outdoor swimming pools with adjacent hot tubs; a 27-hole golf course; 10 lighted tennis courts; a croquet court; and a health spa with exercise rooms, saunas, and weight training equipment. Each guestroom and suite has a mini-bar, a stocked refrigerator, a giant bathtub, 2 TV sets, 2 phones, and a terrace with a spectacular view. See also *Golf.* Loew's Ventana Canyon Resort, 7000 Resort Dr., Tucson, AZ 85715 (phone: 602-299-2020 or 800-234-5117).

RITZ-CARLTON, Laguna Niguel, California: A haven for Southern California's jet setters and celebrities, this Mediterranean-style villa-hotel property sprawls on a bluff overlooking the Pacific. As would be expected of hotels of the esteemed Ritz-Carlton company, the rooms (393 of them) are furnished elegantly, the restaurants — the formal *Dining Room,* the clubby *Grill & Bar,* and the natural food *Café* — serve only the finest fare, and the service can't be beat. Recreational facilities include tennis courts, a health club, a pool, and an uncrowded, white sand beach; golf is available at the nearby *Monarch Links.* Information: Ritz-Carlton, 33533 Shoreline Dr., Laguna Niguel, CA 92677 (phone: 714-240-2000).

SONOMA MISSION INN, Sonoma, California: A 1980 renovation of this 97-room wine country landmark, in operation since 1927, included the addition of a world class spa. Another multimillion-dollar refurbishment and expansion in 1986 added 70 rooms, many with fireplaces and balconies, all in the mission style of the original building. The result is one of the most appealing resorts on the West Coast. The guests' quarters are inviting and contemporary, the service friendly, and the ambience casual yet distinctly luxurious. The coed spa blends fitness, beauty, and nutrition programs with relaxation, elegance, and informality. Its cuisine is almost as famous as the celebrities the resort attracts: Kurt Russell and Goldie Hawn, Tuesday Weld, Tom Selleck, Gregory Hines, Burt Bachrach, and Tom Cruise among them. Member of Preferred Hotels Worldwide; Mobil 4-Star award. Information: Sonoma Mission Inn & Spa, PO Box 1447, Sonoma, CA 95476 (phone: 707-938-9000).

THE LODGE AT PEBBLE BEACH, Pebble Beach, California: The California coast — "The finest meeting place of land and water in existence," according to one admirer

— deserves no less than this magnificent hotel. The interior is only a part of the charm. The *Pebble Beach Golf Links,* a leading contender for the title of "most photographed golf course," and the Robert Trent Jones, Sr. *Spyglass Hill* golf course are among the most famous in existence, for good reason; they're also among the few tournament class courses open to the public. And there are still other courses in Pebble Beach. If you don't like golf, you can go shopping in the Lodge arcade and in nearby Carmel; sightseeing along the celebrated Seventeen Mile Drive, with magnificent views of the rocky shore; horseback riding through the private 5,328-acre Del Monte Forest; swimming; or play tennis at the nearby *Beach and Tennis Club.* Information: The Lodge at Pebble Beach, Seventeen Mile Dr., Pebble Beach, CA 93953 (phone: 408-624-3811).

FOUR SEASONS BILTMORE AT SANTA BARBARA, Santa Barbara, California: Any of the hotel's 21 Montecito acres not taken up with the Spanish mission-style buildings that house the guestrooms are filled with gardens of eucalyptus, junipers, monkey trees, and oaks. The rooms are luxurious — with oversize beds, good mattresses, oversize showerheads, and thick bath towels. About one-quarter of the rooms have fireplaces. In the *Coral Casino Cabana Club,* there's an Olympic-size swimming pool across from the hotel, plus an additional one on the property, 3 lighted tennis courts, and a ¼-mile-long beach. In the area, there's golf, fishing, and horseback riding. Summer, when daytime temperatures in the eighties are moderated by a constant ocean breeze, is the prime season. Information: Four Seasons Biltmore, 1260 Channel Dr., Santa Barbara, CA 93108 (phone: 805-969-2261).

THE BROADMOOR, Colorado Springs, Colorado: When this magnificent hostelry was built by mining magnate Spencer Penrose and Charles Tutt in 1918, it was with the idea that this would be one of the world's most fashionable hotels, that it would be "permanent and perfect." It is. One of the interesting things about the *Broadmoor* is that in late winter and early spring you can sometimes enjoy winter and summer sports in the same day — skiing in the morning, for instance, golf or tennis in the afternoon. As for the venerable main building itself, it's everything you'd expect of a structure put up with the assistance of hundreds of European craftsmen: Not only are there art objects from around the world in all the public rooms, but incredible ornamentation embellishes walls, ceilings, and floors alike. Information: The Broadmoor, 1 Lake Ave., Colorado Springs, CO 80906 (phone: 303-634-7711).

MAUNA KEA, Kamuela, Big Island of Hawaii, Hawaii: Some say this is the most fantastic work yet of Laurance Rockefeller, the major domo of the Rockresorts group that originally developed this property, along with a handful of other luxury resort hotels. Now managed by Westin Hotels, the *Mauna Kea* seems to have grown up out of the landscape; it's an asset to the surroundings rather than an eyesore. There are many diversions: a tough Robert Trent Jones, Sr. golf course with stupendous Pacific views from every green, 13 tennis courts, a splendid white sand beach, a swimming pool, a 58-foot catamaran, riding, snorkeling, scuba diving, and windsurfing. Hunting expeditions can be arranged, as can helicopter sightseeing trips. Throughout the hotel there are over 1,600 artifacts from Asia and the Pacific cared for by art conservators from the staff of the *Bishop Museum.* Information: Mauna Kea Beach Resort, PO Box 218, Hwy. 90, Kamuela, HI 96743 (phone: 808-882-7222).

MAUNA LANI BAY, Kohala Coast, Big Island of Hawaii, Hawaii: Even before its opening in 1983, it was widely predicted that this 351-room arrow-shaped hotel, built on 3,200 acres atop a prehistoric lava flow where the early Hawaiians settled around AD 750, would be Hawaii's most luxurious. And as it has turned out, that is not far from true. Guests are greeted with fresh orange juice and leis. The lobby resembles a rain forest, complete with palm trees, waterfalls, and saltwater lagoons adorned with colorful fish. The guestrooms, done in ivory and burgundy, are no less striking. The same goes for the 4 restaurants, including the elegant *Third Floor* and *Bay Terrace.* Some 27 acres of the property have been preserved as a historic park and can be explored on a number of walking trails. Fifteen acres of ancient spring-fed fishponds (which once provided fish for the *alii* — Hawaiian royalty) offer wonderful picnic grounds, a private swimming hole, and more quiet walking paths. Those of more sociable bent may opt for swimming at the pool or beach, outrigger canoe rides, helicopter tours, tennis at the *Tennis Garden,* lawn tennis at the *Racquet Club,* or golf on 18 holes whose green fairways snake through black lava broken by coastal inlets; though the course is not quite as fierce as it may first appear, the occasional cavorting of migrating whales not half a mile from the sixth tee can be distracting. An interesting children's program, Camp Mauna Lani, is run at various times each year. Information: Mauna Lani Bay Hotel, Box 4959, Kohala Coast, HI 96743 (phone: 808-885-6622 or 800-367-2323 outside Hawaii).

HALEKULANI, Honolulu, Oahu, Hawaii: Many generations of Waikiki visitors who have noted the truth in this venerable hostelry's name, which means "house befitting heaven," should be more than pleased with the recent $125 million renovation and expansion that have transformed a rather intimate 190-room establishment into a modern, but still remarkably personable, 456-room resort. The new design incorporates the restored two-story main building of the original hotel into a complex of multilevel structures surrounding tranquil courtyards and gardens. The *House Without a Key* restaurant, immortalized in one of Earl Derr Biggers's Charlie Chan novels, has been rebuilt on the same spot, and the old bungalow rooms have been replaced by large, luxurious, expansively balconied rooms, most facing the Pacific. All 3 restaurants overlook the ocean and Diamond Head, and the famous century-old kiawe tree continues to preside. The striking tiled orchid design accenting the large oceanside pool has come to be a symbol for the hotel itself. Information: The Halekulani, 2199 Kalia Rd., Honolulu, HI 96815 (phone: 808-923-2311; 800-367-2343 outside Hawaii).

HANA-MAUI, Hana, Maui: On the eastern coast of East Maui in the isolated ranching village of Hana, a settlement with a worldwide reputation for peace, quiet, and the simple spirit of old-time Hawaii, the *Hana-Maui* embraces this ideal and elaborates on it with a definitively understated interpretation of luxury. The hotel has just undergone a massive and expensive upgrading and face-lift under the aegis of its new owners, Rosewood hotels, the same group that has turned the *Remington* (Houston), the *Mansion at Turtle Creek* (Dallas), and the *Bel-Air* (Beverly Hills), among others, into the leading bastions of transient luxury in this country. This level of luxury does not come inexpensively, though tariffs include breakfast, lunch, and dinner, since there really is only one other place to eat in Hana. Public areas are handsome, and the lawns are rife with the sort of vegetative prodigality for which Hana is famous. The *Hana-Maui* is the place for horse lovers; it has its own stables and offers an assortment of breakfast rides, cookout rides, sunrise rides, and moonlight rides, as well as English and Western riding lessons. A heated outdoor pool is on the grounds and there are private facilities at Hamoa Beach, 3 miles away and the prettiest beach in the district — albeit with seasonally rough surf. The rebuilt 1929 Packard that takes guests there is another *Hana-Maui* touch, as is the umbrella — a tip of the hat to Hana's showery weather. This is not the place for folks who crave action and excitement; it is Eden for the self-sufficient who truly wish to get away from it all. Information: Hotel Hana-Maui, PO Box 8, Hana, HI 96713 (phone: 808-248-8211 or 800-321-HANA).

KAPALUA BAY RESORT, Kapalua, Maui, Hawaii: With its fringe of pineapple fields bordered by neat rows of Cook pines, its view of Molokai (looming like a mirage on the horizon), and the landscapes distinguished by banyan trees and delicate yellow oleanders, this northwestern Maui resort hotel is the centerpiece of 750 acres as magnificent as any in Hawaii. And from the latticework of white pillars and bougainvillea-decked crosspieces out front to the grand, open-air, multilevel lobby full of hanging plants, it is as quietly luxurious as the landscape is beautiful. In addition to an array of water sports, there are 10 tennis courts, a pair of 18-hole golf courses that rank among the most distractingly scenic in existence, and a beach right on the doorstep. (The name means "arms embracing the sea.") Exercise classes, wine tastings, garden tours, afternoon tea, and inviting food and settings for lunch or dinner round things out. Information: Kapalua Bay Hotel, 1 Bay Dr., Kapalua, Maui, HI 96761 (phone: 808-669-5656; 800-367-8000 outside Hawaii).

Inn Sites: America's Special Havens

 When standardization finally overtook the hotel industry, at least one great anxiety — where to stay — was removed from travel. Travelers could be assured of finding acceptable accommodations in even the most remote corner of the country. But a new worry arose: What happened to those special places, the inns and hostelries with special charm, with atmosphere, with a personal spirit and style and history all their own?

They still exist. The trend toward cookie-cutter construction simply increased the number of hotel and motel rooms; it didn't destroy those unique lodgings that still grace this country from Maine to Oregon. They tend to become the "finds" of lucky patrons who would publish their credit card numbers before they would broadcast the name and location of their favorite hideaway.

But being made of sterner stuff, we offer a listing of our favorite places all across this country. Some are traditional New England inns, perfect for a ski weekend or a trip through the woods when the foliage is at its most brilliant; some are luxurious hideaways; some are rugged western lodges where the horses are spirited and the campfire stories tall.

EAST

GRISWOLD INN, Essex, Connecticut: For true devotees of traditional New England fare, there is no better place to find it. Built in 1776, the "Gris" is a favorite port of call for Connecticut River sailors, who may tie up just a few steps from the front door. Landlubbers arriving by car are just as welcome, and all are quickly infused with the inn's friendly spirit. There's much to catch the eye — an outstanding collection of historic lithographs, steamboat relics, historic firearms, many ships' name plaques, and a fine group of marine oils by Antonio Jacobsen. The beds, mostly brass, are in rooms that long ago developed port or starboard lists. Guests enjoy unpretentious but outstanding New England fare, with an emphasis on beef and fresh seafood delivered daily. At the inn's famous Hunt Breakfast on Sunday, children 6 years and under are served free. No less than Lucius Beebe acclaimed the *Tap Room* as "the most handsome barroom in America," and the description is not far from wrong. But it has a rival for the title in the adjacent *Covered Bridge Room,* which is hung from floor to ceiling with the prints and the paintings in the inn's standout collection. Nightly entertainment ranges from sea chanteys to Dixieland, and throughout December "A 1776 Country Inn Christmas" gives guests a taste of that era, with a special game menu, magicians and madrigal singers, and the staff outfitted in colonial costumes. Information: Griswold Inn, Essex, CT 06426 (phone: 203-767-1812). William G. Winterer, innkeeper. 18 rooms; 5 suites.

COPPER BEECH INN, Ivoryton, Connecticut: The decor of this elegant, charming, and immaculate inn in a turn-of-the-century Victorian home run by Eldon and Sally Senner looks more like your rich old aunt's country estate than a commercial enterprise. There are 4 airy rooms in the main house, and the bathrooms have huge, old-fashioned, claw-footed bathtubs; an additional 9 rooms are in a restored carriage house on the property, each with its own Jacuzzi, bathtub, TV set, and French doors leading out onto decks. A gallery displays fine antique Oriental porcelain, the old greenhouse has been converted into a lounge, and the three dining rooms are full of fresh flowers, crystal, gleaming silver, and the incredible smells of baby pheasant, beef Wellington, pâté, lobster bisque, bouillabaisse, and other delights that have put the inn on Connecticut's culinary map. Breakfasts are light, which is just as well because dinner is so good (no dinner served Mondays). Information: Copper Beech Inn, Main St., Ivoryton, CT 06442 (phone: 203-767-0330).

CURTIS HOUSE, Woodbury, Connecticut: The inn, reputedly Connecticut's oldest, is in a town with more than 30 antiques shops, 20 on Main Street alone. Original beams and fireplaces set the atmosphere in the spacious dining rooms. The bedrooms have colonial furniture, a number of them with pretty canopied beds. Specialties on the regional American menu include roast duck, sweetbreads, and roast leg of lamb. Beef and seafood are also featured. Information: Curtis House, Woodbury, CT 06798 (phone: 203-263-2101). Chester C. Hardisty, innkeeper. 18 rooms.

BLUE HILL INN, Blue Hill, Maine: In operation on Blue Hill Bay since 1840, this inn celebrates its 150th anniversary in 1990. According to the innkeepers, it is "the only inn in Maine which has never been operated as anything but an inn." Wingback armchairs, fireplaces, traditional wallpapers, period furnishings, comforters, and private baths make the bedrooms as cozy as they can be. But the real attraction here is the Maine coastline, best seen on foot, but accessible by bicycle, moped, or car. The sea reaches into the meadowland all along this crabbed and twisting shoreline, so you keep seeing bits of the Atlantic wherever you go. Craft shops in Blue Hill carry famous Rowantrees and Rackliff pottery as well as the works of local weavers, painters, and metalsmiths. Chamber music is performed several times a week in the summer by the students of Kneisel School of Music. The inn serves country-style breakfasts every morning, after which you are free to explore the coast or visit beautiful Deer Isle and Mt. Desert Island not far away. The inn's first-rate 6-course dinners are rich in chowders and fresh seafood; you'll also dine well on veal marsala, rack of lamb, beef filet, Cornish hens, and homemade breads and desserts. Information: Blue Hill Inn, Blue Hill, ME 04614 (phone: 207-374-2844). Mary and Don Hartley, innkeepers. 10 rooms.

THISTLE INN, Boothbay Harbor, Maine: It's not the rooms (which are plain and old-fashioned) that make up this inn's attraction, so much as the warm and friendly atmosphere. In the tavern, a hangout for natives as well as a drawing card for weekenders, an upturned dory supports the bar and a piano player seldom has trouble getting together a chorus. The drinks are so hearty that most people are surprised by their size. In the restaurant, specialties include extra thick lamb chops, Down East steaks, prime ribs, and broiled seafood. Information: Thistle Inn, Boothbay Harbor, ME 04538 (phone: 207-633-3541). Jim and Mary MacCormac, innkeepers. 8 rooms.

CENTER LOVELL INN, Center Lovell, Maine: This house was over 160 years old when William Bil, a graduate student in sociology and children's literature in New Haven, came up and decided to turn the place into the kind of friendly bed-and-breakfast establishment he had encountered in England. But Bil's family is Italian, and so what he ended up with turned out to be, in his words, "a typical New England home — except Italian," a place of "bed-and-breakfast friendliness with Italian food." The food, all of it cooked as his grandmothers would have done it, is a point of pride with Bil. He drives all the way to New York just to get the right cheeses and the right salami for his antipasto platters. Other specialties include Nicolo Firenze, a boneless half of chicken with an unusual stuffing, and gamberi al forno roma, baked shrimp stuffed with crab. Three or four times a year — for New Year's Eve, Memorial Day, July 4, and one evening during the week of the big, locally famous *Fryeburg Fair* every autumn — Bil lays out a seven-course banquet. Even if your timing is off for this feasting, however, there's plenty to keep you busy when you visit: hiking and antiquing in summer; craft-shopping at the *Fryeburg Fair* and leaf-peeping in the fall; and, in winter, alpine and cross-country skiing on an extensive network of old logging roads that begins right at the back door. (One Boston writer called the trails here New England's best.) Information: Center Lovell Inn, Rte. 5, #20, Center Lovell, ME 04016 (phone: 207-925-1575). William and Susan Bil, innkeepers. 11 rooms.

GREENVILLE INN, Greenville, Maine: Built by a wealthy lumber baron in 1895, this rambling Victorian mansion sits on a hill overlooking Moosehead Lake, the Squaw Mountains, and the town of Greenville. Both inside and out, the focal point is a large leaded and stained glass window that depicts a spruce tree. The rooms are furnished with intricately carved cherry mahogany and oak woodwork and fireplace mantels, gaslight fixtures, and embossed wallcoverings. Many of the elegantly appointed guestrooms have queen- or king-size beds; some have original baths with deep ceramic tubs and pull-chain toilets; one has a unique needle-spray marble shower. The breakfast and dinner menu changes daily. Dinner may include fresh Maine seafood, veal, lamb, duck, and choice steaks. Summer activities include hiking, fishing, whitewater rafting, and canoeing; visitors can also ride the steamship *Katahdin* on the lake or a chair lift up Squaw Mountain. In winter, there's alpine skiing, cross-country skiing, and snowmobiling. Autumn offers spectacular fall foliage viewing. Information: Greenville Inn, Box 1194, Greenville, ME 04441 (phone: 207-695-2206). Elfie, Michael, and Susie Schnetzer, innkeepers. 9 rooms.

ISLAND INN, Monhegan Island, Maine: The century-old frame structure sitting on a picturesque bluff overlooking the tiny harbor between Monhegan and its satellite island of Manana is open summers only. Ferry service from June through September is provided by the *Balmy Days,* from Boothbay Harbor (phone: 207-633-2284). The inn, operated by a Monhegan native and his wife, has a large, bright dining room where boiled lobster is the specialty, and fresh, simply prepared fish — striped bass, haddock, bluefish — fills the menu. An all-you-can-eat buffet on Sunday nights draws scores of Monhegan visitors who have spent the day exploring the awesome, 150-foot cliffs that face the pounding surf to the east. Although the inn has its own generator, most of the island goes without electricity. The yellow gleam of the kerosene lamps through the windows of the surrounding wood-shingled houses makes a pretty sight as you walk along the village's single dirt road. More than 600 varieties of flowering plants — including the trailing yew, unique to the island — and up to 200 species of birds may be seen along the many woodland trails. Information: The Island Inn, Monhegan Island, ME 04852 (phone: 207-596-0371). Bob and Mary Burton, innkeepers. 45 rooms.

ROBERT MORRIS INN, Oxford, Maryland: The most famous Robert Morris, Jr., used his wide connections to raise money for the American Revolution, and when other backers failed to appear, he did not hesitate to pay the troops out of his own pocket. Alas, what the war couldn't do bad speculations accomplished a few years later, when he went bankrupt from a series of frontier land deals. His father's home, carefully preserved over the years, today is Tidewater Maryland's finest inn. Many of the rooms are decorated in vintage Americana, and you may climb into a high four-poster with the aid of a small stepladder. The slate on the tavern floor was quarried in Vermont, and public rooms and guestrooms alike are decorated with a combination of country and antique furnishings. Best known to sailors, who tie up at the inn's anchorage on the Tred Avon River; to fishermen, who use the inn as a headquarters for excursions up and down the Chesapeake Bay shore; and to local gourmands, who swear its restaurant does the best things possible to bay crabs and the local oysters, the inn is a must for anyone touring the area. Information: Robert Morris Inn, PO Box 70, Oxford, MD 21654 (phone: 301-226-5111). Jay Gibson, innkeeper. Ken and Wendy Gibson, owners. 33 rooms — some no smoking. Caters to couples; no children under 10.

WHEATLEIGH, Lenox, Massachusetts: This 33-room Italianate palazzo was built in 1893 by an American railroad man and banker, and ranks as the most elegant inn in all New England — if not in North America. Surrounded by formal gardens and lawns, the structure is all blond bricks and terra cotta and limestone detailing. There are loggias and arcades, stained glass windows, a magnificent swooping staircase, lovely fireplaces, and, everywhere, ornately carved ceilings, moldings, mantelpieces, and walls. Travelers with a weakness for such things have reason to rejoice at the inn's restaurant, with cuisine appropriate to the setting. The four front bedrooms upstairs are extra special and commensurately costly. Information: Wheatleigh, PO Box 824, Lenox, MA 01240 (phone: 413-637-0610). Susan and Linfield Simon, innkeepers. 17 rooms.

JARED COFFIN HOUSE, Nantucket, Massachusetts: The gas lamps ornamenting the façade of this inn have been converted to electricity, but they still cast a flattering glow on the 1845 brickwork — and give you an inkling of the marvels you will find inside: high ceilings; wonderfully ornate moldings; elegant chests and desks in Chippendale, Sheraton, and American Federal style; many canopied beds, several draped with crewel-embroidered fabric; Oriental rugs; scrumptious seafood; and, most important of all, the extraordinary warmth and friendliness evinced by every staff member from the chambermaid to the desk clerk to the waitresses and the innkeepers themselves. Spring, summer, and fall are busy; winter — except during the year-end holidays, when the innkeeper stages a special celebration — is delightfully peaceful. This is the island's best-known and most popular inn, and you'll need reservations well in advance. But the planning always pays off when you return from a day of soaring along some cliff's-edge road on your bike, or tennis, golf, or soaking up the sun at the beach. Information: Jared Coffin House, 29 Broad St., Nantucket, MA 02554 (phone: 508-228-2405). Philip Whitney Read, innkeeper. 60 rooms in 6 buildings.

HANCOCK INN, Hancock, Massachusetts: Now that the old wooden structure of this hostelry is like new again, owner-manager Chester Gorski, who once spent a good deal of his time toiling over burst pipes and ancient wiring and other maladies of a long-neglected building, has turned his full attention to culinary matters, earning quite a reputation for himself in the process. Dinner offerings are elaborate and tasty. There's billi-bi (a cream of mussel soup) and medallions of fresh veal and jumbo shrimp in Dijon mustard sauce, duckling braised in port wine with grapes, and fresh lemon sole wrapped around a bay scallop and served in a shallot and muscadet wine sauce. Ellen Gorski has a way with salads, and the white wine vinaigrette in which she tosses some unusual mixtures of vegetables (perhaps watercress and endive with a bit of romaine and shredded raw beets) is a standout; her cheesecake, whipped-cream-filled chocolate mousse torte, and frozen white chocolate mousse rank among guests' favorites. Exactly what you'll find on the menu depends on the season and the availability of ingredients — but it will always be continental and so good that you'll pity the poor soul who comes here on a diet. The guestrooms are modest but comfortable. Information: Hancock Inn, Rte. 43, Hancock, MA 01237 (phone: 413-738-5873). Chester and Ellen Gorski, innkeepers. 7 rooms.

OLD FARM INN, Rockport, Massachusetts: When Antone Balzarini, a recent emigrant from northern Italy, rented the property that now surrounds this neat inn, he must have known about its long history and its several owners — the initials of one of them, one James Norwood, are chiseled on an old granite gate post together with a date, 1799. But he could not have foreseen its future as one of the most prosperous and popular establishments in a village where the visitors are more often discerning than not. He himself purchased the farm down the road, but one of the dozen children he raised later came back to the property, which by then was known as the Babson Farm, and began restoring the farmhouse, filling it with antiques and converting the erstwhile barn into guest accommodations. The rooms are cozy, the atmosphere very peaceful and private, and the proprietors as helpful as could be, providing guests with sightseeing pointers and dining suggestions. Information: Old Farm Inn, 291 Granite

St., Rte. 127, Rockport, MA 01966 (phone: 508-546-3237). The Balzarini family, innkeepers. 7 rooms.

RED LION INN, Stockbridge, Massachusetts: This fine old rambling four-story clapboard structure occupies a prominent place on Main Street, which looks just as if Norman Rockwell ought to have painted it. He did. His home was just across the road, and the country's largest and finest collection of his paintings can be seen just a block away, in the *Norman Rockwell Museum.* Still, there's more to Stockbridge than Rockwelliana — the *Berkshire Theater Festival,* Lenox's *Tanglewood Music Center,* and the *Jacob's Pillow Dance Festival* at Lee, among other things — and the inn hums throughout the hot-weather months with overnight guests, diners, and a good many other folk who have simply stopped in to ogle the high-ceilinged Victorian parlors and their gleaming silver and mahogany embellishments; or to sit on the long front porch, where two rows of rocking chairs bob back and forth from early morning until well after dusk. The inn is well worth seeing, even if you can't get a bed for the night (call well in advance for reservations). Certainly, the inn's restaurants — the flower-laden courtyard; the cozy *Widow Bingham's Tavern,* with its candles and checkered tablecloths; and the main dining room, full of sparkling silver and white napery — are among the most charming spots for meals in an area that is full of appealing eateries. Hearty homemade soups begin many dinners here; they conclude with one of New England's spiciest Indian puddings. Information: Red Lion Inn, Stockbridge, MA 01262 (phone: 413-298-5545). Betsy Holtzinger, innkeeper. 103 rooms.

COLONEL EBENEZER CRAFTS INN, Sturbridge, Massachusetts: In the 18th century, the finest homes were always built on the highest points of land — which gave their owners not only a commanding view of their property and herds but also the distinction of being set somewhat apart from their contemporaries. The circa 1786 farmhouse that the owners of the *Publick House* (see below) transformed into an inn a few years ago was one of those distinguished buildings. Its new role in life has not diminished its preeminence in the community, however, since this structure on the summit of Fiske Hill makes as lovely an inn as it was a farmhouse. Antiques and fine reproductions, afternoon tea or sherry in the library or the sunroom, fruit and cookies in the evening, and continental breakfasts in the morning — by the pool in warm weather — make this an exceptionally pleasant place. The inn's namesake — a strong man who studied theology at Yale, established the *Publick House* as a tavern in 1770 and equipped and drilled a cavalry company during the Revolution — later founded the town of Craftsbury, Vermont. Information: Colonel Ebenezer Crafts Inn, c/o Publick House, PO Box 187, Sturbridge, MA 01566 (phone: 508-347-3313). Patricia and Henri Bibeau, innkeepers. 8 rooms.

PUBLICK HOUSE, Sturbridge, Massachusetts: This is not one of those cozy country inns where it's you and the innkeeper against the rest of the world. Instead, this hostelry — which opened as one of our not-quite-yet-a-nation's finest restaurants in 1771 — is most popular for its food; and the hungry pour by the bus- and carload through its doors, then chow down on fresh fish and lobster pie and wonderful sticky buns. Some have had the foresight to reserve in advance, and, when they're sated on the innkeeper's savory offerings, they can simply waddle up the creaky, crooked stairs to one of the cozy rooms — or step outside to the *Country Motor Lodge* in back and collapse in one of the Colonial-style rooms. Recently purchased and totally renovated by the *Publick House,* the 100-room *Lodge* also sports an outdoor pool, tennis court, and jogging course, so visitors can work off at least some of the calories they've consumed. Some time ago the *Publick House* innkeeper initiated a splendid pageant-cum-feast, a revival of the Yuletide celebration known in merrie Olde England, with a Boar's Head Feast, a Yule Log Procession, and the telling of moving tales of the season; held thrice daily on the two Saturdays and Sundays preceding Christmas, it now sells out well in advance. A newer event, Yankee Winter Weekends, keeps the inn filled from January through March. You're welcomed with syllabub (chablis with cream) and Joe Froggers (giant ginger cookies), then fed goodies nearly around the clock: breakfasts of fried mush and deep-dish apple pie and hickory-smoked bacon; snacks of curried meatballs, aged cheddar, roasted chestnuts, codfish cakes and chowder and hot buttered rum; and dinners of roasted venison and other exotic concoctions. Then, as in summer (when a flock of sheep keep the grass short on the meadow behind the inn), you can visit Old Sturbridge Village, a reconstruction of a New England village that might have existed at about the time of the Industrial Revolution (see *Restored Towns and Reconstructed Villages*). Information: Publick House, PO Box 187, Sturbridge, MA 01566 (phone: 508-347-3313). Buddy Adler, innkeeper. 17 rooms; Country Motor Lodge, Publick House, PO Box 187, Sturbridge, MA 01566 (phone: 508-347-9555). Carol Young, manager. 100 rooms.

LONGFELLOW'S WAYSIDE INN, Sudbury, Massachusetts: Originally known as the *Red Horse Tavern*, the inn changed its name in 1863, the better to bask in the fame Longfellow created for it when he wrote *Tales of a Wayside Inn*, a series of poems whose most celebrated section begins, "Listen, my children, and you shall hear . . ." The building in which Longfellow set his work, which had been purchased by Henry Ford in the 1920s, was partially destroyed by fire, after some two and a half centuries of existence, in the mid-50s; but with Ford Foundation help it was soon restored. The former plans were somewhat modified: Many of the original guestrooms were turned into museum-like room settings showing how the inn probably looked in the early 18th century, and eight new rooms were added and fitted out with fine bathrooms and reproduction furnishings in early American color schemes. The surrounding 106 acres insulate you from the highway hubbub, and, because the inn's principal trade is in meals, when the diners are gone you it's as though you're on your own private estate. Meals consist of sturdy New England fare, including tasty breads, cakes, and pies out of the inn's own ovens, made from flour ground by the mill on the premises. Also on the grounds is the schoolhouse that inspired "Mary Had a Little Lamb" and a classic New England chapel complete with white clapboards and soaring steeple, where countless New England sweethearts have tied the knot. Information: Wayside Inn, Sudbury, MA 01776 (phone: 508-443-8846). Francis J. Koppeis, innkeeper. 10 rooms.

FITZWILLIAM INN, Fitzwilliam, New Hampshire: The "Rules of the House" provide an accurate insight into what you're likely to find: "This is a New England country inn, in the heart of a New England country village, and we have some customs that may seem strange to you. Please try to understand our ways and abide by our requests." If you find this off-putting, you'll be encouraged by rule number one: "We have no room keys to give you — everyone trusts everyone else in the country. However, we do lock the outside doors early. If you're going to be out, please pick up a house key at the desk. The innkeeper is shy about answering the door in his PJs." Modern intrusions are unwelcome in this wooden hostelry dating from 1796. The innkeeper has been quoted as saying that when a prospective guest asks if the rooms have television sets, they're referred to "the nice motel just down the road." Information: Fitzwilliam Inn, Fitzwilliam, NH 03447 (phone: 603-585-9000). John and Barbara Wallace, innkeepers. 25 rooms.

LOVETT'S INN, Franconia, New Hampshire: Built in 1784, this is an early example of a Cape Cod cottage with a central chimney. For many years, it served as the main building of a working farm that supplied dairy products, vegetables, and eggs to resorts in the area. Listed in the National Register of Historic Places, it features 7 rooms (3 with private baths), a living room with a fireplace, 2 dining rooms, and a glassed-in sunporch. In addition, there are 16 modern cottages and a carriage house on the grounds. Cross-country skiing is nearby, as are a number of walking and hiking trails, tennis courts, lakes for fishing, and factory outlets. Information: Lovett's Inn, Profile Rd., Franconia, NH 03580 (phone: 603-823-7761). Lan Findlay, general manager. 30 rooms.

JOHN HANCOCK INN, Hancock, New Hampshire: John Hancock never slept here or even stopped for a short mug of ale while inspecting the nearby landholdings left to him by a rich uncle. But the inn does boast that its 1789 opening makes it New Hampshire's oldest inn operating in the same building. In the Monadnock region, the "Currier and Ives corner of the Granite State," in one of those quintessentially New England towns with a white-steepled church, a bandstand on the green, and a half dozen bright clapboard houses stuck away in a fuzz of leaves, the inn is full of small neat rooms with twin canopy beds or white ruffled curtains and tiny-print wallpapers. But number 16 happens to be more beautiful than nearly any other room in any other inn in the region. The murals that are its most striking feature, creations of an itinerant artist named Rufus Porter, depict the scenes of the area in heavenly blues and greens. The furniture is mahogany, the bedspread and curtains are white; but the work is so lively that you get an odd, you-are-there feeling. The only other remnant of Porter's work is found inside the closet of one of the rooms down the hall. The restaurant's offerings include roast duckling, seafood casserole, and prime ribs — served daily, not just once or twice a week as in many similar small restaurants. The bar, with buggy seats for benches and giant bellows for tables, is exceptionally homey. Information: John Hancock Inn, Main St., Hancock, NH 03449 (phone: 603-525-3318). Glynn and Pat Wells, innkeepers. 10 rooms.

LYME INN, Lyme, New Hampshire: Lyme is as delightful a New England village as you'd ever want to find, with its big green common, its fine clapboard church, its well-stocked country store — not to mention its handsome inn, a favorite lodging place for parents of students at nearby Dartmouth College and a tourist attraction in its own right. All the rooms are furnished with antiques. The structure itself, put up in 1809, is full of walls that slant, hallways that narrow then inexplicably widen, and stairways that twist and climb every which way, apparently without rhyme or reason. A fascinating collection of framed samplers, hanging on the walls of the dining rooms, is worth close scrutiny, not only for the workmanship but perhaps for the messages as well, from "God Bless Our Home" to more religious aphorisms. Information: Lyme Inn, Lyme, NH 03768 (phone: 603-795-2222). Fred and Judy Siemons, innkeepers. 14 rooms.

NEW LONDON INN, New London, New Hampshire: You may travel through New England for the length of a normal lifetime and assume you've seen most of what is good and fair when, suddenly, you discover a delight like New London. Here is a perfection of New England college towns, not so much restored, one senses, as preserved. And in the middle of all this beauty, across from the town green, sits this 3-story clapboard inn furnished with antiques. Built in 1792, it has 30 rooms, all with private baths. There are wide porches, complete with rocking chairs, and fireplaces in the living rooms and dining room to ward off the New England chill. The dining room is beautifully decorated, and the food, considered the best in the area by many, is extraordinary. Each meal is prepared to order using fresh, seasonal ingredients. All of the breads and desserts are made at the inn. The homemade egg bread is used for the French toast, which is one of the breakfast selections included in your room rate. There's plenty to keep you busy: golf, tennis, hiking, water sports on three lakes, downhill and cross-country skiing. Information: New London Inn, PO Box 8, New London, NH 03257 (phone: 603-526-2791). Maureen and John Follansbee, innkeepers.

MAINSTAY INN, Cape May, New Jersey: Cape May, one of our nation's oldest seaside resorts, is a treasure of Victorian architecture, and the *Mainstay Inn* — just a few blocks from the Atlantic — is one of its gems. From the inn's buff-colored picket fence to the green wicker chairs that sit on its verandah, to the 12-foot mirror in the entrance hall, this late-19th-century former gambling house has been lovingly restored and exquisitely furnished in pure Victorian style by a dedicated young couple. Information: The Mainstay Inn, 635 Columbia Ave., Cape May, NJ 08204 (phone: 609-884-8690). Tom and Sue Carroll, innkeepers. 11 rooms.

VIRGINIA, Cape May, New Jersey: Those searching for accommodations just a notch above the typical local Victorian bed and breakfast will delight in this 24-room hostelry in a newly restored, elegant, 110-year-old landmark building. Quiet, elegant, and staffed by young and talented people, it's close to the beach, boardwalk, and shopping, and its *Ebbitt* dining room is a must, even for non-guests. Lunch and dinner menus are extensive and the dishes do the place proud, but it's the breakfasts — freshly baked muffins, frittatas, apple cinnamon pancakes and down-home porridge — that had us coming back for more. Information: Virginia Hotel, 25 Jackson St., Cape May, NJ 08204 (phone: 609-884-5700).

INN AT SHAKER MILL, Canaan, New York: When Ingram Paperny uncovered this abandoned early-19th-century mill, it had neither bedrooms nor public rooms and was sorely in need of a carpenter. But the structure, set beside a hillside waterfall, so tempted its discoverer that he set up his own wood shop and began its careful conversion to inn. The simple but comfortable rooms reflect the heritage of austerity left by the Shakers who lived in the area, including Old Chatham, New York, where there's now an extraordinary museum collection on display, and just across the state line in Hancock, Massachusetts, home of the popular Shaker Village. The inn's setting in the foothills of the Berkshires is one of great beauty, and so it attracts an interesting crowd, everyone from magazine editors to mycologists. Information: The Inn at Shaker Mill, Canaan, NY 12019 (phone: 518-794-9345). Ingram Paperny, innkeeper. 20 rooms.

1770 HOUSE, East Hampton, Long Island, New York: Like so many other American inns, the *1770 House* has had several lives (in this case, first as a home, later as a store, then as a boarding house, and finally as the dining hall of a boys' school), and over the years hardly anybody bothered to give it the care it required. And so, when Sid and Miriam Perle bought the place, the building was a wreck. Thanks to their efforts, however, the structure has never looked better. The exterior, clapboards painted white with coal-black shutters at the windows, makes the inn a creditable addition to a venerable neighborhood. Inside, the old and the new work together to delightful effect. (Especially striking: the large colonial fireplace in the *Keeping Room* giftshop, the Perles' wonderful clock collection, and the stained glass that is used as a decorative accent throughout the inn.) The *1770 House* is open year-round but serves meals only on weekends in winter. Information: The 1770 House, 143 Main St., East Hampton, NY 11937 (phone: 516-324-1770). Sidney and Miriam Perle, innkeepers. 7 rooms.

GURNEY'S INN, Montauk, Long Island, New York: If you define an inn as a colonial hostelry on an elm-shaded New England street, this may not be the place for you: You won't find the antique lamp or the ancient patchwork quilt, the spinning wheel or the stenciled wall. You lodge in cottages with fireplaces or in comfortably decorated rooms with ocean-view balconies or terraces, set among trees and country gardens; dress up for dinner and dance to live music in the lounge after you've supped; or just hole up in your room, enjoy the sunset, and gaze at the mighty ocean or take in a television show when you've had your fill of the spa facilities (excellent enough to attract the likes of Cheryl Tiegs). But *Gurney's Inn* is a personable place, and when you go out on the beach, one of those endless, surf-pounded Atlantic strands, you put civilization thousands of miles behind you. The shore is delightful for jogging or sunbathing in summer, and even better for walks in the fall — if you don't mind the whip of the wind, the tingle of the cold, and spray in the face as the price of a beach to call your own. Information: Gurney's Inn Resort & Spa, PO Box UUU, Montauk, NY 11954 (phone: 516-668-2345). Nick and Joyce Monte, innkeepers. 109 rooms.

TARA, Clark, Pennsylvania: Two Pennsylvanians brought the Old South up north in 1986, when they opened *Tara*, a Greek Revival mansion like the one in the movie. Jim and Donna Winner took their inspiration from *Gone With the Wind* when they restored the place: They named the guestrooms after Rhett, Scarlett, and other characters and hung murals depicting scenes from the movie in the dining room. The hospitality is pure Southern, too. Information: Tara, Box 475, 3665 Valley View Rd., Clark, PA 16113 (phone: 412-962-3535). Jim and Donna Winner, innkeepers. 13 rooms.

1740 HOUSE, Lumberville, Pennsylvania: Built around an early-18th-century stable by two other refugees from urban America, the *1740 House* is one of the best inns in Bucks County, which is full of inns — not so much because it's particularly quaint (because it isn't: the rooms are air conditioned, the floors are carpeted wall to wall, the baths are tiled, and the furnishings are fine period reproductions). Rather, the *1740 House* prospers year after year because it is one of those unfailingly well-managed places where everything works, and because it is in the kind of countryside where everyone dreams, at least once, of making a second home: a woodsy region that shelters antique houses, run through by a mighty river and a placid canal where you can canoe or ice skate; where the towns have grown just enough so that there are interesting shops, movie theaters or playhouses, and restaurants and snack bars where you're as apt to find quiche on the menu as hamburger. In Bucks County, as at the *1740 House,* you can have your comforts and get away from it all, too. Hearty breakfasts (served in a sunny room overlooking the canal) and dinners are available at the inn; you'll have to go elsewhere for lunches, and BYOB. Information: 1740 House, River Rd., Lumberville, PA 18933 (phone: 215-297-5661). 24 rooms.

CLIFF PARK INN, Milford, Pennsylvania: This early-19th-century farmhouse-turned-inn, a venerable mountain resort hotel set not far from a 900-foot cliff that towers over the Delaware River, has been run since 1900 by five generations of the same family — so if you come here expecting someplace homey, you won't be disappointed. The beds in one room are covered with lace spreads. And there are cushy sofas in the parlors and antiques and polished floors throughout. But *Cliff Park* also has something of the elegance of a country club, in part because, ever since the golf course was added in 1913, back when the sport was just catching hold in America, golf has been one of the guests' favorite pastimes. Most rooms are upstairs in the main building; three cottages are also available nearby. Open April through November. Information: Cliff Park Inn, RD 2, Box 8562, Milford, PA 18337 (phone: 717-296-6491). Harry Buchanan, innkeeper. 20 rooms.

1661 INN, Block Island, Rhode Island: The uniqueness of this pretty, simple structure, perched above the village that clusters about the harbor, comes mostly from the beauty of its site on a meadow rising 12 miles off Point Judith, an hour's ferry ride away. But the atmosphere — informal enough that before-dinner wine-and-nibbles hours seem to make perfect sense — figures strongly as well; the special house drinks — the Monhegan Moro, a wild combination of sweet and dry vermouth, and the Island of the Little Gods Mind Boggler, white wine with cranberry juice — are something else again. An abundant breakfast buffet offers eggs, ham, bacon, corned beef hash, home-grown potatoes, fresh fish, muffins and breads, and fruit. Lunches and dinners are served at the owners' other property, the mansard-roofed, Victorian *Manisses* hotel, inside the Garden Terrace room or on the breezy deck outside. That sister establishment now boasts 17 rooms, all with private bath and 4 with Jacuzzis. Block Island is one of the best places in the East for biking; there's also good snorkeling, picnicking, salt- and freshwater fishing, bird watching, and beachcombing — below the steep Monhegan cliffs for shells, driftwood, and other flotsam. Information: The 1661 Inn and Hotel Manisses, PO Box 1, Block Island, RI 02807 (phone: 401-466-2421). Joan and Justin Abrams, innkeepers. 25 rooms.

INN AT CASTLE HILL, Newport, Rhode Island: This 3-story Victorian mansion, built on a 32-acre water's-edge site in 1874 by the son of the Swiss-American naturalist Louis Agassiz, is one of those mansions that Newporters call, inexplicably, "cottages." However, though it's a plain sort of place by the standards of William Wetmore's Stanford White–designed Château-sur-Mer and Cornelius Vanderbilt's Richard Morris Hunt–designed the Breakers, you may have a tough time stretching your imagination to call it a cottage. In the first place, it's huge; and in the second place, it's more elegant than most Fifth Avenue apartments. The chestnut paneling gleams. Tiffany lamps shed their soft glow on fantastically carved Victorian furniture, much of it original to the house. Oriental rugs protect the polished floors. In the dining room, you'll sit on velvet-covered chairs, drink coffee poured from silver urns, and eat with silver cutlery. Innkeeper Paul McEnroe is a thoroughgoing professional and a gracious human being, and knows how to make every guest feel at home; the wonderful "New Year's" dinner dance (the first Saturday of December) sells out well in advance as a result. The menu offers a Neptune's bounty of clams, lobsters and other seafood, as well as veal, beef, and lamb prepared with a continental flair. Rooms are in the main house and in a newer area out back; for charm, the former are best. Continental breakfast served to guests only. The kitchen reopens the weekend before Easter for guests and general public. Information: Inn at Castle Hill, Ocean Dr., Newport, RI 02840 (phone: 401-849-3800). Paul McEnroe, innkeeper. 16 rooms.

OLD TAVERN, Grafton, Vermont: Restored, along with some 25 other Grafton buildings, by the Windham Foundation, as a part of one of the country's most extensive restoration projects, the *Old Tavern* is one of America's most beautiful inns. (Its guest list of historic figures is more than impressive: Ralph Waldo Emerson, Rudyard Kipling, and Henry David Thoreau are only a few of the entries.) Everything shines: the wooden floorboards throughout the main building and the annex across the street, the furniture, the tops of the tables in the dining room, the silver tableware, the glasses, and the china. All of the sleeping rooms are furnished with the loveliest sorts of antiques — lace tester beds, wing chairs covered with chintz, Chippendale highboys, and such. When you consider all that, and the delightful setting in picture-postcard Grafton, you may call the *Old Tavern* one of your favorite inns even though it's more elegant than cozy; so many people love the place so well, in fact, that you'll be hard put to get a room at the last minute. It's important to reserve well in advance and to ask the desk clerk carefully about the rooms: No two are alike, and some are more wonderful than others. The surrounding area is gorgeous, too: In Grafton alone there's the general store, the cheese company, and 2 lovely covered bridges. Information: The Old Tavern, Grafton, VT 05146 (phone: 802-843-2231). Richard Ernst, innkeeper. 42 rooms and 6 guesthouses.

GOVERNOR'S INN, Ludlow, Vermont: Built in 1890 by Vermont governor William Wallace Stickney, the inn retains the intimate feeling of a comfortable and elegant country house. Its 8 delightful guest chambers (6 with private baths) are furnished in the manner of the Victorian period with heirloom antiques, Oriental rugs, brass beds, and highly polished oak. House guests and the public enjoy elegant six-course dinners glowing with candlelight, and full English breakfast. Meals are prepared from fresh and preferably indigenous ingredients such as native pumpkin, blueberries, New England seafood, and cranberries. The preparation is inventive, and the dinner is served with panache. The award-winning kitchen also prepares wonderful picnic hampers (the outfitted basket is then yours to keep) on just a few hours' notice. All of this, coupled with friendly and accommodating innkeepers, make a stay at the *Governor's Inn* a personal experience akin to what guests of the governor may have experienced. Information: The Governor's Inn, 86 Main St., Ludlow VT 05149 (phone: 802-228-8830). Charlie and Deedy Marble, innkeepers.

NORWICH INN, Norwich, Vermont: Just across the Connecticut River from Dartmouth College, the *Norwich Inn* has been in operation since 1797, and the people of the town take a proprietary interest in the establishment. When you visit the handsome Terrace Dining Room, glassed-in porch, carpeted and filled with plants so that it seems almost like a greenhouse, you can order roast duckling, fresh salmon, or rack of lamb. And you can order from one of the most extensive wine lists in the area — fine Champagne, first-growth French wines, and reasonably priced bottles both imported and domestic, some of which you usually can't get anymore. Norwich, one of those immaculately kept towns whose clapboard and brick homes and tall trees define most people's idea of how a New England town should look, is as charming as ever; and *Dan & Whitt,* a big old general store where you can buy hardware and grain for yourself and your animals, rifles and flannel and soaps and just about anything else you can name, is still doing its booming business. In summer, you can go hiking and biking, and in winter you'll want to go for a ski. Rooms, all with private bath, are both in the inn and in a motel unit directly behind it. Information: Norwich Inn, PO Box 708, Norwich, VT 05055 (phone: 802-649-1143). Bob and Tammy Savidge, innkeepers. 27 rooms.

KEDRON VALLEY INN, South Woodstock, Vermont: In operation since the early 1800s, this pleasant, relaxing inn — under the proprietorship of Max and Merrily Comins since the end of 1985 — has been updated to the point where, among other things, all rooms now have private baths and the new chef, a Paris-trained professional, prepares local products in "nouvelle Vermont" style. Horseback riders are still able to ride the 250 miles of trails at the nearby stables — operated by the inn's former owners — which continue to make Kedron Valley one of their favorites. But even if you don't ride, there is much to do. In summer you can sit out by the spring-fed pond before taking a dip or hike on numerous trails; and golf, indoor and outdoor tennis, aerobics, a swimming pool, and other athletic facilities are just up the road. In winter, miles of cross-country trails are maintained in the area, and downhill skiing is available in almost every direction. Afterward, the innkeepers suggest you "settle back in your rocker, pull the antique quilt a little closer, and put your feet up by the potbelly stove in your room." Or you can take a horse-drawn sleigh ride through the countryside. Information: Kedron Valley Inn, Rte. 106, South Woodstock, VT 05071 (phone: 802-457-1473). Max and Merrily Comins, innkeepers. 28 rooms: 6 with fireplaces, 7 with wood-burning stoves.

HARTNESS HOUSE, Springfield, Vermont: A cockamamie jumble of dormers, arched windows, fieldstones, bay windows, and other fancies of the typical Victorian architect, this mansion was originally the home of an inventor and "machine tool genius" who at one time held the post of Governor of Vermont, one James Hartness. Some of the rooms, including a wonderfully handsome turret room, are in this house; other more modern quarters can be found in an addition in the back. The inn also has 3 stately dining rooms and the attractive *Crown Point Pub.* Outside, under a spreading maple, there's a swimming pool, with a lighted clay tennis court nearby and, just beyond, a weird object that looks like a tank turret tipped partly over — *Hartness's* telescope, a nightly attraction. The area around Springfield, along the Black River, was for many years a center for the manufacture of precision machine tools, and Springfield came to be known as "the cradle of invention." The *American Precision Museum,* in nearby Windsor, is well worth visiting to learn the story. Also in the area is the St. Gaudens National Historic Site, across the river in Cornish, New Hampshire. Information: Hartness House, 30 Orchard St., Springfield, VT 05156 (phone: 802-885-2115). Bob Staudter, innkeeper. 46 rooms.

INN AT WEATHERSFIELD, Weathersfield, Vermont: Mary Louise Thorburn spent years entertaining a house full of people (and loving it), and after the nest emptied out, running an inn seemed the natural thing to do. She and her husband, Ron, looked all over for the perfect place, and in 1978 they came to Weathersfield, a perfect gem of a New England town, some 19 miles from Woodstock. They saw this inn with its six white pillars and wavy-paned glass; fell in love with the design, the layout, and the setting on 12 acres of lawns and trees back from the road; bought the place practically on the spot; and in 1980 opened for business as one of those very special places where visitors feel like welcome guests in someone's home. And what a home: The floors are wide-planked throughout, the rooms are all furnished in antiques — some with four-posters, one with a magnificent old bedstead canopied with a single piece of hand-crocheted lace. Half the guest rooms have working fireplaces. There are enough antique quilts in the house to dazzle a museum textiles curator, and the bedsheets are flowered, ruffled, or edged with lace. (Atop every mattress, Mrs. Thorburn has laid an electric pad: just the thing to warm your toes on a cold Vermont night after the fire on your hearth has died down.) Afternoons are given over to bountiful English teas, served in sterling and accompanied by salmon mousse on bread rounds, fresh vegetables with a dip, and some wonderful sweet treat — perhaps an English trifle or a tipsy pudding. This is such a friendly occasion that guests who have met here often join up later for sightseeing, dinner company, and other activities. Breakfasts — sausage or ham and Grand Marnier–and–orange–water French toast, well-sauced fines herbes omelettes, eggs Benedict, Scotch eggs, or shredded cheddar cheese eggs — are so generous that you may be able to make tea do for lunch, especially if you know you have one of the Thorburns' delightful dinners, confected of imaginative appetizers, soups, entrées, and desserts, to look forward to. Carriage and sleigh rides are available with Dick, the inn's amiable horse. Recent additions include a fitness and recreation center with sauna and a playing field for badminton, volleyball, and croquet. Information: Inn at Weathersfield, PO Box 165, Weathersfield, VT 05151 (phone: 802-263-9217). Mary Louise and Ron Thorburn, innkeepers. 14 rooms.

INN AT SAWMILL FARM, West Dover, Vermont: Abandoned barns, uniquely adaptable because of their huge open spaces, seem to make a special sort of inn — or so you would conclude upon seeing this fine establishment, the creation of Rodney Williams, an architect, and Ione, his wife, a professional decorator. The spaces are good, to begin with: the living room is high-ceilinged, just big enough for two sitting areas, but not so big that you can't sit and see the fire burning in the huge hearth; the dining rooms are small enough that you can almost feel you're at someone's very elegant dinner party; and there are all manner of comfortable nooks and crannies where you can go to read a book or just lie down and snooze. Ione has furnished the whole place with bright fabrics, and, because the Williamses' daughter is married to a Fieldcrest executive, everything from the towels and the sheets to the blanket covers, the carpets, and the bedspreads is color-coordinated. Meanwhile, the Williamses' son Brill has become quite a chef, and the ingredients he uses are always just a little fresher and a little more perfect than the garden variety. The food reflects that fact. And there is an equally impressive wine cellar — 18,000 bottles. The *Marlboro Music Festival* is nearby, and keeps the inn full in summer; and in fall, the flaming foliage draws crowds. In winter, people come to ski on Mt. Snow, just down the road, or to cross-country over the river and through the woods. There are also 2 trout ponds open to guests as well as tennis and 2 nearby public golf courses. So, no matter when you want to visit, reserve well in advance. Information: Inn at Sawmill Farm, PO Box 367, West Dover, VT 05356 (phone: 802-464-8131). Rodney, Ione, and Brill Williams, innkeepers. 22 rooms, 10 with fireplaces.

RED FOX TAVERN, Middleburg, Virginia: Washington surveyed the land; and Civil War rebels used the building, constructed in 1728, as headquarters. (The bar is made from the table used by Jeb Stuart's surgeon.) Later, because Middleburg lies in the heart of the Virginia hunt country, the inn prospered as a social center for the horsey set. But then for some reason it went into a decline and might well have gone the way of countless other old American buildings had it not been for the energetic ministrations of a local lady who wanted to do some good for the community and have a little fun at the same time. And so it was that the *Red Fox Tavern* was filled up with Williamsburg wallpapers and with antique furniture and paintings which, like so many of the people who come here once again for their hunt breakfasts, speak of horses as if there were no other subject in the world. In the dining room (pegged floors; stone wall; fireplaces; Windsor chairs), the innkeeper serves classic southern breakfasts and wonderful lunches and dinners that mix local specialties like crab cakes and peanut soup with steaks, chops, and continental offerings such as veal with mushrooms and cream. Music and lighter fare are available in *Mosby's Tavern,* out back. There's plenty to watch — if not the National Beagle Trials, then plenty of races and shows. Information: Red Fox Tavern, Washington and Madison Sts., PO Box 385, Middleburg, VA 22117 (phone: 703-687-6301 or 800-223-1728). Turner Reuter, Jr., innkeeper. 26 rooms.

COUNTRY INN, Berkeley Springs, West Virginia: The six imposing white pillars on the front of this building suggest formality. But don't be deceived: this country inn is about as friendly as an inn can be and is a great place to stay when you come into the area — to visit 5,000-acre Cacapon State Park (where there's hiking, riding, cross-country skiing, swimming, golfing on the Robert Trent Jones course, and tennis); to tour (an hour away) Harpers Ferry National Historical Park, where John Brown staged his notorious raid, or Charlestown, with its Shenendoah Downs; or simply to take the waters in Berkeley Springs. The inn also has its own spa, featuring whirlpool mineral baths, massages, and facials. Moreover, the eating at the inn could hardly be better, and the art gallery and lobby display works from rural scenes painted by local artists to the Old Masters. The inn's adjoining Colonial-style 3-story property called *Country Inn West* offers an additional 36 rooms. Information: The Country Inn, 207 S. Washington St., Berkeley Springs, WV 25411 (phone: 304-258-2210). Jack and Adele Barker, innkeepers. 72 rooms.

GENERAL LEWIS INN, Lewisburg, West Virginia: What started out as a private home on a hilltop back in 1834 and grew over the years into a magnificent mansion, with columns in the front and a sweep of beautiful lawns all about, has been a classic inn in a lovely, old-fashioned town since 1929 — much to the delight of traveling Americans enamored of antiques-furnished rooms and hearty country meals. Information: General Lewis Inn, 301 E. Washington St., Lewisburg, WV 24901 (phone: 304-645-2600). Rodney Fisher, innkeeper. 26 rooms.

SOUTH

ROD AND GUN CLUB, Everglades City, Florida: Times have changed since the 1920s, when industrialist Barron Collier converted an 1883 gulfside house, popular with hunters and fishermen for years, into a private club, and made it a hideaway for very important persons (including a scattering of US presidents). So the club is now open to the public. But much of the flavor of the early days remains, and there are mounted sport fish and hunting specimens on the walls; the emphasis here is still on the water and its creatures. A marina serves private boats. Charters and guides are available, as are skiffs and canoes for some fine fishing — for grouper, tarpon, or the battling snook; the chef will prepare your catch for a small fee. The inn is a mile from the entrance to Everglades National Park, and in February the place hops with a special seafood festival. There's a pool (screened because of the mosquitoes), and tennis courts are nearby. Information: Rod and Gun Club, Drawer 190, Everglades City, FL 33929 (phone: 813-695-2101). Martin Bowen, innkeeper. 18 rooms in separate cottages.

CHALET SUZANNE, Lake Wales, Florida: The style of many places can be suggested in a word or phrase — Victorian, early American, motel modern. *Chalet Suzanne* is what you'd call eclectic. Left to her own devices in the depths of the Depression, with two children to care for, a tiny young widow named Bertha Hinshaw decided to start serving meals to the public. Talent and energy made this central Florida endeavor a huge success over the years, and by the time Bertha Hinshaw died not long ago, in her 90s, the inn had its own orange groves, a private airstrip, one of the finest and most original kitchens in the state, and a reputation for being one of the oddest-looking inns this side of paradise, for the *Chalet Suzanne,* as the establishment came to be called, after Mrs. Hinshaw's daughter, eventually came to reflect her passion for collecting anything and everything, but particularly tiles, and her penchant for putting together elements of architectural styles from all around the globe, everything from turrets to bare-wood decks. What could have been garish is here simply exquisite. Information: Chalet Suzanne, PO Drawer AC, Lake Wales, FL 33859-9003 (phone: 813-676-6011). Carl and Vita Hinshaw, innkeepers. 30 rooms.

GREYFIELD INN, Cumberland Island, Georgia: A one-of-a-kind inn on a one-of-a-kind island in the Atlantic, just northeast of the Georgia-Florida state line, this establishment was built by the Thomas Carnegies around the turn of the century for their daughter and her husband, and, substantially unaltered, was opened as an inn several years ago by a Carnegie granddaughter, Mrs. Lucy Ferguson. If something this far off the beaten track, accessible only by boat or chartered plane, appeals to you, then you may not mind that there are no tennis courts or swimming pool, and that the only recreation on the island, really, is reading, conversation, shelling, walking, and looking for birds, armadillos, and alligators. And when you've had enough of that, you can just sit around in the house and savor the lifestyle of one sort of turn-of-the-century rich. Information: Greyfield Inn, PO Drawer B, Fernandina Beach, FL 32034 (phone: 904-261-6408). Ferguson family, innkeepers. 9 rooms.

INN AT PLEASANT HILL, Harrodsburg, Kentucky: The Shakers — an ascetic, communal sect that originated in England in the mid-18th century — are usually associated with upstate New York and Massachusetts, where more than 200 years ago Mother Ann Lee established the country's first major Shaker settlements. However, the Shakers went west in the 19th century and eventually settled in Kentucky — at Auburn and near Harrodsburg at Pleasant Hill (see Utopias). As part of the nationwide revival of interest in the Shakers, particularly in their architecture and design, 28 of the 30 surviving buildings at Pleasant Hill have been restored, and 14 of them are fitted out with guestrooms and appropriate reproductions of Shaker furniture — chairs and trundle beds, sconces, mirrors, and, everywhere, pegs to hang things up as the Shakers did. The nonprofit organization that administers Pleasant Hill has provided every room with its own tiled bath, air conditioning, and a television set; but otherwise the feeling is one of authenticity. A dining room in the Trustees' House offers big Kentucky-style breakfasts with grits, eggs, sausage, biscuits, and the rest; lunches and dinners are also belt-looseners. Information: Inn at Pleasant Hill, 3500 Lexington Rd., Harrodsburg, KY 40330 (phone: 606-734-5411). Ann Voris, innkeeper. 72 rooms.

COLUMNS HOTEL, New Orleans, Louisiana: The unusual hotel where director Louis Malle filmed Brooke Shields's notorious film *Pretty Baby* has become no less than one of the city's most evocative stopping places thanks to a recent renovation. In the Garden District, with the St. Charles streetcar passing its front door, it started out as a wealthy tobacco merchant's home, became a boardinghouse in 1914, and was transformed into a hotel in the 1940s. Now it has a kind of luscious decadent splendor, from its Victorian lounge and ballroom-restaurant to its grand, free-standing stairwell and its abundant touches of Honduras mahogany. Information: The Columns Hotel, 3811 St. Charles Ave., New Orleans, LA 70115 (phone: 504-899-9308). Clare and Jack Creppel, innkeepers. 16 rooms.

LaMOTHE HOUSE, New Orleans, Louisiana: Built in the early 1800s by a successful planter named Jean LaMothe, this exquisite early New Orleans town house is a delightful place to call home while visiting this exciting city. From the stately foyer to the lushly planted courtyard and throughout the elegantly antiques-furnished establishment, you can't help but find yourself transported to the city's earlier, gentler days. But you won't find the discomforts: all of the rooms are air conditioned, and each has a private bath, a color TV set, and a phone. Continental breakfast, the only meal served, is always an event: everyone sits at a long banquet table and lingers over chicory coffee drawn from a Sheffield urn at least two centuries old. At night you'll find a chocolate on your pillow — and your bed turned down. New owners have refurbished the house to make a good thing even better, with American Victorian antiques and color schemes. The inn is just a few blocks from the heart of the French Quarter and its jazz, good food, and intriguing shops. Information: LaMothe House, 621 Esplanade Ave., New Orleans, LA 70116 (phone: 504-947-1161 or 800-367-5858). Ralph and Freida Lupin, innkeepers. 20 rooms.

MAISON DE VILLE, New Orleans, Louisiana: This gem of a hotel in the heart of the French Quarter offers a choice of accommodations: In the maison — where Tennessee Williams did his final draft of *Streetcar* — there are magnificent antiques-furnished rooms with balconies and street or courtyard views; out back, there are the remodeled circa 1742 slave quarters. And then, a stroll away on Dauphine Street, are the delightful *Audubon Cottages,* where John James Audubon lived and worked in 1821. Built in the Créole brick and post style (something like the old European half-timbered buildings), they have perhaps the most elegant rooms of all, with luxuriously furnished bedrooms, kitchens with stocked refrigerators, and private gardens. The entire *Maison de Ville* complex stands out, however, for the service: Tables in restaurants and space on sightseeing tours are booked by an omniscient concierge; shoes left outside your door are shined; a classic French breakfast is served on a silver tray, along with copies of *USA Today* and the *Wall Street Journal* and a rose. And when you return after a night on the town, you find a piece of chocolate on your pillow. In October 1986, an intimate, 40-seat, Parisian-style bistro was added where chef Susan Spicer prepares Provençale and Mediterranean cuisine. Information: Maison de Ville, 727 Toulouse St., New Orleans, LA 70130 (phone: 504-561-5858 or 800-634-1600). Lloyd Francis, general manager. 14 rooms, 2 suites, 7 cottages.

SONIAT HOUSE, New Orleans, Louisiana: Installed in a pair of remarkable townhouses built around 1830 and recently restored to the tune of nearly a million dollars, *Soniat House* blends the American and the Créole to the credit of both. While the bathrooms are marbled, modern, and equipped with telephones, the lofty-ceilinged bedrooms are filled with English and French antiques, including canopied or French empire beds and antique Oriental rugs; many have their own balcony or terrace, and five have Jacuzzis. The 3-story spiral staircase, the rocking chair–equipped balcony that spans the façade, the lush garden courtyard, and the location near the French Market are bonuses, as is the breakfast of biscuits with homemade strawberry preserves, fresh orange juice, and rich Créole coffee. Information: Soniat House, 1133 Chartres St., New Orleans, LA 70116 (phone: 504-522-0570 or 800-544-8808). Rodney Smith, innkeeper. 25 rooms.

HOUND EARS LODGE AND CLUB, Blowing Rock, North Carolina: Skiing down south? Yep, up here in the Blue Ridge Mountains. It can be pretty good, too, both here at the lodge and nearby. Open all year, this friendly resort has a fine 18-hole golf course as well as swimming, tennis, and other outdoor activities — for children as well as adults. The lodge operates on the modified American plan, and meals are served to overnight guests only. Information: Hound Ears Lodge and Club, PO Box 188, Blowing Rock, NC 28605 (phone: 704-963-4321). David Blust, manager. 27 rooms.

NU-WRAY INN, Burnsville, North Carolina: If you like to get high on mountains and you're east of the Rockies, this is the place. Nearby are the Pisgah National Forest, one of the wildest woodlands in the East (don't miss Linville Gorge), and Mt. Mitchell, at 6,684 feet, the highest east of the Mississippi. The inn, at about half that altitude, will keep your feelings on the up side with its good food, featuring fried chicken and country ham, served family style, and friendly atmosphere — despite the fact that you're awakened every morning without fail at 8:00 by the ringing of a bell and summoned to a country breakfast a half hour later by that same bell. The meal is worth it. The call to dinner (reservations suggested) is less jarring; a Reginaphone, an old-fashioned music box that is just one of the many Wray family antiques scattered around the inn, is your summons. Open from May through November. Information: Nu-Wray Inn, PO Box 156, Burnsville, NC 28714 (phone: 704-682-2329). Betty Souders, innkeeper. 32 rooms.

MARSHALL HOUSE, Marshall, North Carolina: Built in 1903 as a private residence for James H. White, a prominent community leader, the house retains the serenity of a bygone era. It is filled with Scotch-Irish remnants, including furniture, quilts, and musical instruments. Nearby sights include other historical homes, the Cherokee Indian Reservation, and Great Smoky Mountains National Park. Information: Marshall House, 5 Hill St., PO Box 865, Marshall, NC 28753 (phone: 704-649-9205). Susan Beshiri, innkeeper. 9 rooms.

SNOWBIRD MOUNTAIN LODGE, Robbinsville, North Carolina: As the name implies, this is a place for the birds — and those who love to watch them. From the inn's 3,000-foot setting bordering the Nantahala National Forest, the views above and below are breathtaking. Birders and hikers have their choice of trails, from the gentle to the rugged. The forest covers 450,000 acres, including a 50,000-acre Cherokee reservation with a restored village and many exhibits and demonstrations for visitors. Moreover, there are some spectacular driving tours in the area, most notably to 30-mile-distant Fontana Dam and its 30-mile-long lake. The inn serves all meals but has no bar. Information: Snowbird Mountain Lodge, Joyce Kilmer Forest Rd., Robbinsville, NC 28771 (phone: 704-479-3433). Bob and Connie Rhudy, innkeepers. 22 rooms.

RHETT HOUSE INN, Beaufort, South Carolina: The former home, not of Rhett Butler, but of Thomas Rhett and his wife, Caroline Barnwell, is warm and gracious, with fresh flowers in the rooms, homespun quilts on the beds, and the smells of baking bread and fresh coffee in the morning. Historic Beaufort and its recently restored waterfront are nearby, with tennis, golf, and swimming. The inn is also convenient for day trips to Charleston, Hilton Head, and Savannah. Information: Rhett House Inn, 1009 Craven St., Beaufort, SC 29902 (phone: 803-524-9030). Marianne and Steve Harrison, innkeepers. 8 rooms, 3 with fireplaces.

SWORD GATE INN, Charleston, South Carolina: Charleston is known for its glorious old homes, and the carefully restored *Sword Gate Inn,* in an 18th-century mansion in the heart of the city's historic section, is ideal for getting you into the spirit of the city. The furnishings were selected with sensitivity and great care for detail, and everything, from the complimentary fruit bowls to the freshly cut flowers, is directed toward your comfort and delight. A full Southern breakfast — delicious and informal — and evening wine and cheese are included in the tariff. Bicycles are available, and tours of the city are arranged upon request. Information: Sword Gate Inn, 111 Tradd St., Charleston, SC 29401 (phone: 803-723-8518). Walter E. Barton, innkeeper. 6 rooms, 3 with working fireplaces.

EXCELSIOR HOUSE, Jefferson, Texas: In the 19th century, this community 170 miles east of Dallas on the Louisiana border was a booming cotton-shipping center. But then the world, in the person of the railroads, passed it by. Business suffered, "progress" ceased, and Jefferson came into the 1950s virtually unscarred by the wrecker's ball. The brick and timber, grillework-embellished *Excelsior House,* a New Orleans–style construction that was one of the town's most prominent buildings, was bought in 1961 by the Jesse Allen Wise Garden Club, and its members set about sanding and painting, polishing and papering, to return the hotel to the grandeur it knew back in the days when it was welcoming the wealthy and the famous (even a few presidents). The rooms are now furnished with warm walnut, mahogany, and maple dressers and sleigh beds, canopy beds, and Jenny Lind–style spool beds. In the public rooms, there are Oriental rugs underfoot and chandeliers of crystal and porcelain overhead. Some of the ceilings are pressed tin, some are plaster. The windows are draped in the Victorian style. Breakfast, for which you convene on the sun porch, is the only meal served — but what a meal it is: ham and eggs, grits, and heaps of the fluffy, bite-size Orange Blossom muffins for which the hotel is famous. Also memorable are a visit to Jay Gould's luxurious private railway car, which was restored by the garden club after it was found rotting away in a field, and a leisurely tour of the town's several other historical sights. Information: Excelsior House, 211 W. Austin St., Jefferson, TX 75657 (phone: 214-665-2513). Mary Brantley, manager. 14 rooms.

MIDWEST

ABE MARTIN LODGE, Nashville, Indiana: Like many other Indiana state park lodging places, the rustic stone and log *Abe Martin Lodge* at Brown County State Park is not long on antiques-filled sleeping accommodations and fancy cuisine. Guest quarters both in the lodge and in the surrounding cabins tend toward the plain but comfortable, and food toward the homestyle; fried chicken and biscuits are the order of almost every day. But few far more sumptuously furnished hostelries can boast such a setting — in the midst of 15,000 acres of wooded hills (a landscape that gives the lie to stories about Indiana being pancake-flat); the scenery is gorgeous during the pink and white springs, when the dogwoods and redbuds deluge the hills with a rosy blizzard, and in the blazing autumns, when the hardwoods turn scarlet, yellow, and all the colors in between. The scene brings the Great Smokies to mind, if on a smaller scale. Nearby Nashville, a small town gone touristy with galleries and antiques shops, is quaint and distinctively Hoosier. Information: Abe Martin Lodge, PO Box 25, Nashville, IN 47448 (phone: 812-988-4418).

NEW HARMONY INN, New Harmony, Indiana: Associated with a restoration of two 19th-century communes that flourished here (see *Utopias)*, the *New Harmony Inn* may be the most beautiful new hostelry in America. The lines are spare and clean, like those of a Shaker building, and the variety of woods used as furniture, floors, stairways and moldings provides a visual treat, especially in combination with natural colors and subtle, serene shades of blue and green. Amenities include a unique glass-roofed swimming pool, tennis courts, a health spa, sauna, and whirlpool bath. The *Bayou Grill* offers excellent meals, including breakfast. You can also get a terrific lunch or dinner at the *Red Geranium,* a couple of minutes' walk away. Information: New Harmony Inn, PO Box 581, New Harmony, IN 47631 (phone: 812-682-4491). Patti Hoskins, sales representative. 90 rooms.

NATIONAL HOUSE INN, Marshall, Michigan: The one-man preservation drive launched by a former Marshall mayor, one Harold Brooks, over a half century ago is finally bearing fruit, and hundreds of people are now actively involved in breathing new life into the town's beauty spots. Brooks bought several choice homes — the finest examples of 19th-century architecture in the area — and held them until he found buyers willing to restore and preserve the structures in their original style. Later, thanks to an enlightened zoning code and community cooperation, more and more homes were saved, so that by now 12 of them are in the National Register and 35 more are listed by the state as historic landmarks; all are examples of fine Victorian workmanship. The *National House* (1835) is the oldest operating inn in Michigan. It started as a hotel, served as a stop on the Underground Railroad (with abandoned tunnels and a hidden cellar room to show for it), went through several transformations — once into a windmill factory and another time into an apartment house — and has in recent years been restored in the Victorian style of its distinguished neighbors. From the doorknobs to the bed linens, everything has been done with a reverence for the original. The highlight of the year is the town's annual Historic Home Tour, the first weekend after Labor Day, when thousands come here to inspect the restored houses. Information: National House Inn, 102 S. Parkview, Marshall, MI 49068 (phone: 616-781-7374). Barbara Bradley, innkeeper. 16 rooms.

LOWELL INN, Stillwater, Minnesota: Built more than half a century ago, this gracious, Colonial-style inn, with its 13 columns and high portico, has been run by the Palmer family since 1930 with a greater-than-usual degree of sensitivity to the proper care and feeding of guests. The bedrooms have been recently redone (but no TV sets were added to disturb the peace), and each of the 3 popular dining rooms has a different motif: The Garden Room, stone-floored, with wrought-iron tables and chairs, has a pretty trout pool from which you can pick your supper; the George Washington Room, full of bright napery and gleaming silver, reflects the colonial period; and the Matterhorn Room, whose specialty is fondue, is full of Swiss woodcarvings that seldom fail to evoke *oohs* and *ahs* from about everyone who sees them. Lowell, which is just about 18 miles from St. Paul, is chockablock with antiques shops, and after the bustle of the Twin Cities it seems about the most heavenly place on earth. Information: Lowell Inn,

102 N. 2nd St., Stillwater, MN 55082 (phone: 612-439-1100). Arthur and Maureen Palmer, innkeepers. 21 rooms.

ST. GEMME BEAUVAIS, Ste. Genevieve, Missouri: A number of the late-18th- and early-19th-century buildings in this surprise of a town, whose founding in 1732 makes it Missouri's first permanent settlement, have been restored — among them the Amoureaux House, which dates to 1770; the 1790 *Green Tree Tavern,* the town's first inn; and *St. Gemme Beauvais,* its only operating inn. As befits the town's French heritage, the hostelry's breakfasts and lunches (the only meals served) feature continental concoctions like quiche, crêpes, and omelettes; in keeping with the age of the structure, the parlors and guest accommodations are almost entirely done up in Victorian antiques — immense carved bedsteads that make you feel small no matter how much you ate for lunch, ornately framed mirrors, dressing tables with marble tops, a handsome old dining table and chairs. Lace curtains, flowered wallpapers, and draperies in the Victorian manner complete the effect, which is every bit as charming as the town itself. No wonder the citizens of St. Louis, less than two hours away, are so fond of the place. And for those who don't mind making the short walk to the inn for meals, a 5-room annex in an 1850 house provides equally luscious accommodations. Open all year. Information: St. Gemme Beauvais, 78 N. Main, PO Box 231, Ste. Genevieve, MO 63670 (phone: 314-883-5744). Paul Swenseon and Marsia Wilson, innkeepers. 8 rooms, with a 5-room annex.

BUXTON INN, Granville, Ohio: Granville — in the middle of the state, near Denison University, the *Heisey Glass Museum,* and the *Indian Mound Museum* — is anybody's idea of how a Middle American town should look: spotlessly clean, with tree-lined streets, graceful buildings, inviting homes, and pleasant shops. It's a perfect setting for the growing *Buxton Inn* (not to be confused with its larger neighbor, the *Granville Inn*). The rooms have been furnished with a keen eye for the right antiques; several of the chandeliers are especially worth noting. And so, too, is the food. There's a fireplace in the front dining room, which has low ceilings to enhance its cozy atmosphere. Breakfast, lunch, and dinner are served daily in its atmospheric dining rooms, among them a new greenhouse room, and include French-American specialties like seafood coquille cardinale, Louisiana chicken (rolled in seasoned flour, sautéed, and served with a cream sauce, toasted almonds, and artichoke hearts), tournedos chasseur, and chocolate mousse cake. Also don't miss the bean soup. Information: Buxton Inn, 313 E. Broadway, Granville, OH 43023 (phone: 614-587-0001). Orville and Audrey Orr, innkeepers. 4 rooms, with an 11-room annex.

GOLDEN LAMB INN, Lebanon, Ohio: Midway between Cincinnati and Dayton in a town of 10,000, Ohio's oldest inn has, since its founding in 1803, provided lodging to ten presidents, DeWitt Clinton, Henry Clay, Mark Twain, and a very cross Charles Dickens (who visited when the *Golden Lamb* was a temperance hotel and complained that he couldn't get a drink). It is smack in the middle of town on a beautiful, wide, tree-lined street that also offers a number of antiques shops and antique stores. The *Golden Lamb*'s antiques-furnished rooms, some fitted out with four-posters, are among the most pleasant in the area, and the inn makes a fine base for a couple of days' canoeing or fishing on the Little Miami River or visiting the nearby museums. The food at the inn is good, and overnight guests get preferred seating. Try some of the Shaker items on the menu. Information: Golden Lamb Inn, 27 S. Broadway, Lebanon, OH 45036 (phone: 513-932-5065). Jackson B. Reynolds, innkeeper. 18 rooms.

WHITE GULL INN, Fish Creek, Wisconsin: Fish Creek is just what it sounds like: Door County's gift to those who just want a small, far-out-of-the-way place near water where things are fairly quiet and the eating's good, something like Montauk or Cape Cod. As for the food, you can't beat the Fish Boil dinner, the best of the day's catch from Lake Michigan, with boiled potatoes, a tasty coleslaw, and homemade cherry pie. Wash it down with a beer and amble down to the harbor and then back to bed for a good night's sleep to prepare for another day of the same. All of the rooms are stuffed with antiques; 5 have fireplaces, as do all 4 cottages; and the dining room has a brick floor, open beams, and wood ceiling. The atmosphere is country warm. Information: White Gull Inn, PO Box 159, Fish Creek, WI 54212 (phone: 414-868-3517). Andrew and Jan Coulson, innkeepers. 14 rooms and 4 cottages with fireplaces.

WEST

ARIZONA INN, Tucson, Arizona: When Isabella Greenway (a bridesmaid of Eleanor Roosevelt and the state's only woman congressional delegate) opened this as an inn in 1930, it was primarily a desert oasis for the mighty, the mighty rich, and the well-heeled well-knowns — Rockefellers, Windsors, movie stars, and such. But the inn, no longer off in the desert by itself and no longer beyond the reach of lesser souls, has found itself surrounded by Tucson. No matter, it goes its own luxurious way in the manner and spirit in which it was conceived. The gardens will astonish you first: flourishing amid the arid desert environment are 14 acres of lawns and flowers scattered with bushes and trees and crisscrossed by lovely footpaths; to take care of them, the inn employs more gardeners than some inns welcome as guests. Inside, the color scheme is a Mexican-American symphony of corals, beiges, grays, and reds that harmonize with the desert surroundings. A full-time decorator keeps things looking their best. A vivid blue heated pool is shaded on one side (to the delight of those for whom the glaring sun can be too much). You can play tennis (and the courts are floodlit) or, not far away, go riding or enjoy a round of golf. A good portion of the staff has worked here for a couple of decades or more, reflected in their unfailingly professional service. The continental menu attracts diners from all over the state. Information: Arizona Inn, 2200 E. Elm St., Tucson, AZ 85719 (phone: 602-325-1541; 800-421-1093). Robert Minerich, innkeeper. 85 rooms, 8 suites.

TANQUE VERDE RANCH, Tucson, Arizona: When is a dude ranch a country inn? When the dude ranch is, like this one 12 miles outside Tucson on the edge of the 1.4-million-acre Coronado National Forest and the lovely 63,000-acre Saguaro National Monument, the last word in luxury and personable charm. No run-of-the-mill dude ranch, the *Tanque Verde,* part of which used to be a stagecoach stop, has 5 tennis courts, indoor and outdoor swimming pools and a therapy pool, saunas, exercise rooms, and other luxuries. Most rooms have fireplaces and patios, and all have phones (but no TV sets). Antiques are scattered throughout the inn. Some 200 species of birds, from the bridled titmouse to the bald eagle, have been identified in the area, and the inn is so popular with bird watchers that bird banding is a regular activity. Riding, however, is still the big deal, and you can do it to your heart's content (or your bottom's protest) on your choice of some 100 horses, on supervised trail rides that take place several times daily. And when all is said and done, there's the *Dog House* bar, a bunkhouse converted to a bottle club. Information: Tanque Verde Ranch, Rte. 8, PO Box 66, Tucson, AZ 85748 (phone: 602-296-6275). Bob Cote, innkeeper. 47 rooms, 13 suites.

VENTANA INN, Big Sur, California: Boasting a setting as stupendous as any in the country — an expanse of staggeringly beautiful meadows in the rugged Santa Lucia Mountains that drop precipitously down to the rocky shoreline of the California coast 150 miles south of San Francisco — the *Ventana Inn* is quintessentially California modern. That means pale natural cedar, plenty of wicker, patchwork quilts, Franklin stoves and window seats, patios and private balconies, cathedral ceilings with giant beams, swimming pools long enough for healthful laps, Japanese hot baths, a sauna, and complimentary wine and cheese in the lobby each afternoon. Sybarites can take the pleasure even further — by choosing one of the rooms with a hot tub or indulging in a massage or facial. Hiking in the woods is literally right outside the door; the beach, but a short walk away. Breakfast, included in the room rate, is served on a tray in your room or buffet-style in the lobby in front of the fireplace — fresh juice and fruits, homemade breads and pastries, honey, coffee, and both herbal and caffeinated tea. But perhaps best of all are the sweeping vistas that take in all that splendid natural scenery. The silence — broken only, in the breakfast rooms, by classical music and the ticking of the clock and, in the guest quarters, by the rush of the wind through the redwoods — is not bad, either. Information: Ventana Inn, Hwy. 1, Big Sur, CA 93920 (phone: 408-667-2331). Robert Bussinger, innkeeper. 59 rooms.

MOUNT VIEW, Calistoga, California: Built in 1918 and enlarged in 1938, this 2-story beige stucco wine country establishment is a showplace of the Art Deco style. A cozy lobby warmed by a large fireplace is decked out with overstuffed sofas, chrome-trimmed chairs, and exotic floral arrangements. *Fender's,* the black and silver Art Deco cocktail lounge, plays music of the '20s and '30s nightly from 11:30 PM to 1:30 AM. The dining room, where wine country cuisine is the star at breakfast, lunch, and dinner, features plum-colored walls hung with framed advertisements of the 30s. Also featured is an extensive wine list named one of the top 100 in the nation by the *Wine Spectator* magazine. Accommodations include rooms decorated in the Art Deco style and suites richly appointed with period antiques. Especially noteworthy is the Carole Lombard Suite, with a fan-shaped headboard of clear and smoked mirrors. On Sundays, there's a wonderful brunch and afternoon Dixieland jazz. Don't forget to visit the mudbaths for which the town is famous. Information: Mount View Hotel, 1457 Lincoln Ave., Calistoga, CA 94515 (phone: 707-942-6877). Scott Ullrich, general manager. 34 rooms and suites.

VAGABOND'S HOUSE, Carmel-by-the-Sea, California: It's one thing to restore a neglected but fundamentally magnificent old building. It's a trick of quite another sort to take a group of efficiency units from the early 1940s and transform them into a charming inn worthy of unique natural surroundings. But that's what the innkeepers have done here on the loveliest part of the northern California coast. Antiques collected over the years crowd the inn's rooms. The ticking of old clocks is one of their character-istic sounds, along with the chattering of the squirrels who inhabit a wonderful main garden patio centered on an immense old live oak, dotted with rhododendron and camellia bushes, and hung here and there with baskets of ferns, begonias, and fuchsias. Most rooms face that patio, and each has a character all its own, depending on the particular mix of maple and wicker, bentwood and books, brass and quilts; most of the rooms have a fireplace. The combination of such details makes the inn one of the loveliest places to stay when you come to this area to see the much-photographed Point Lobos and the redwoods at Big Sur and to browse through the Carmel shops. The inn serves only continental breakfast. Nearby, under the same management, the newly renovated *San Antonio House Inn* offers private 2- and 3-room suites with antiques and original art, a patio or garden, refrigerator, fireplaces, and fresh flowers. Information: Vagabond's House Inn, 4th and Dolores Sts., PO Box 2747, Carmel-by-the-Sea, CA 93921 (phone: 408-624-7738 or 408-624-4334). Honey Jones, manager. 11 rooms.

CITY HOTEL, Columbia, California: Thanks to a State Parks Department historic preservation project, this once fabulously prosperous Gold Rush town three hours from San Francisco is a living museum of the area's mid-19th-century boom days, and from spring through fall the town is jammed with sightseers. A highlight of nearly everyone's visit is a stop at this 2-story brick hotel, restored in the 70s to the tune of over $500,000. The gold diggers of those long-gone days liked their comforts every bit as much as the tourists do, and when they struck it rich, they would usually go all out to treat themselves. And so a hotel in a town like this was apt to be just as grand as you find the *City,* the passion for the good life reflected in the furnishings — tufted settees, marble-topped washstands and bureaus, Victorian bedsteads in burled wood or brass, Oriental rugs, a rosewood piano, brass hat racks and chandeliers gleaming at every turn. What you don't expect is a wine list as excellent and extensive as the one you find in the gorgeously furnished restaurant, or a kitchen that is not only so competent but so talented; some people come to Columbia just for the food. Information: City Hotel, PO Box 1870, Main St., Columbia, CA 95310 (phone: 209-532-1479). Tom Bender, innkeeper. 10 rooms.

ST. ORRES, Gualala, California: The shoddiness of most contemporary building notwithstanding, a renaissance of interest in fine workmanship has quietly been taking place in America. As just one example, consider this inn on the northern California coast, a Russian palace of a structure built of redwood and salvaged materials around a tumbledown old guest house by a couple of carpenters-with-a-dream, and then named for the family that homesteaded the land. The interior is an exercise in woodworking virtuosity. Redwood paneling on the bedroom walls is meticulously tongue-in-grooved and laid in intriguing patterns that are as distinguished as those of an ancient fresco, or, for that matter, the ones you find in the velvet quilts that were hand-stitched by a talented local craftswoman for the beds. And the dining room — a 3-story space walled partially in redwood-framed stained glass and topped by another copper onion dome — may be more arresting than any other restaurant in the country. In such a setting, you expect original meals, and you get them — wonderful variations on continental classics for which some people drive all the way from San Francisco; a concoction known as chocolate decadence may make a chocoholic of you even if you don't have a sweet tooth. There is even a spa next to the creekside cottages. The totality is so marvelous that the peaceful setting among the beaches, coves, and redwoods is just icing on the cake. Information: St. Orres, PO Box 523, Gualala, CA 95445 (phone: 707-884-3303). Eric Black, Ted Black, Rosemary Campiformio, innkeepers. 8 rooms, 9 cottages.

TIMBER COVE INN, Jenner, California: Set on a rocky sea-view promontory 90 miles north of San Francisco, this establishment has a lobby with a full-length window at one end, a massive "walk-in" fireplace at the other, and a beamed, 40-foot ceiling overhead. Most of the rooms have hot tubs, fireplaces, and ocean views. Throughout, natural woods, walls of stone or redwood barn siding, and exposed beams lend a rustic feel. There's a meditation pool, redwood groves, and a fern-fluffed canyon right on the grounds, and 26 acres of oceanside hiking trails. The whole place is utterly quiet and peaceful, in perfect harmony with the spectacular surroundings. Information: Timber Cove Inn, 21780 North Coast Hwy., Jenner, CA 95450 (phone: 707-847-3231; the inn itself is 14 miles north of Jenner). Richard Hojohn, innkeeper. 49 rooms.

HERITAGE HOUSE, Little River, California: Because so many early California settlers were homesick when they first arrived here from New England, they built their houses in styles that would remind them of the East Coast, and left this part of the West liberally sprinkled with New Hampshire cottages and Down East farmhouses like the one at the core of the main building of this inn on California's northern coast (which, incidentally, Baby Face Nelson once used as a hideout). But even though the original structure has been added to many times over the four decades since the present innkeeper came here in 1949, most of the rooms are not in the farmhouse but in small, medium, large, and extra-large guest cottages surrounding it. Each set of quarters is different. Some of the old ones, originally sited elsewhere in the coast region, were knocked down, transported to Little River, reassembled with varying degrees of fidelity to the original, and then luxuriously furnished; others were built from salvaged lumber. All the rooms have private baths; many have fireplaces or pot bellied stoves; and — most important of all — most have views of the ocean, which is what you come here for in the first place. As for the kitchen, it eschews the continental in favor of the best of American cuisine — everything from the tiny pancakes to the cream soups and meat and fish entrées. Information: Heritage House, 5200 N. Highway 1, Little River, CA 95456 (phone: 707-937-5885). Gay Dennen, innkeeper. 69 rooms.

UNION HOTEL, Los Alamos, California: This old hotel, originally built in 1880 and rebuilt after a fire in 1915, had gone through more than 25 owners and nearly as many incarnations — as pool hall, dance hall, rooming house, and candidate for the wrecker's ball — when, in 1972, a meat wholesaler from not-far-distant Los Angeles, casting about for a new career, discovered the place and decided that running an inn was just what he had always wanted to do. He hired a carpenter and bought a couple of old barns, a trio of old sheds, and a garage to use as lumber to re-create the façade of the first *Union Hotel* as portrayed in an old print. And then he went out antiques hunting. When he came home from his travels, he had enough furniture and knickknacks to give the empty building the cluttered look that a structure of its vintage deserved. Look around you, and marvel: Here are century-old gaslights from Mississippi and chairs hand-carved in Alabama, a mantelpiece from a Pasadena mansion and a vintage Singer sewing machine; there you see the chandeliers that once graced the home of Lee J. Cobb, a lamp used in the filming of *Gone With the Wind,* a grandfather clock, a 150-year-old bar made of African mahogany and an ivory-inlaid Brunswick pool table. Scattered around the guestrooms are a mahogany armoire that conceals a Murphy bed, a brass and iron bedstead inset with cloisonné work, and countless antique four-posters, quilts, and crocheted bedspreads. After all this Victorian clutter, the spacious dining room (where unpretentious home cooking is the order of the day) and the rough-paneled Western bar (which you enter through swinging doors that once admitted customers to a southern bordello) are a welcome change. The inn and restaurant are open only Friday through Sunday nights (year-round). Kids are charged for their food according to how much they weigh on a big butcher scale. A hundred feet west of the hotel is a 3-story Victorian house (1864) that is now open after extensive restoration work. Information: Union Hotel, 362 Bell St., PO Box 616, Los Alamos, CA 93440 (phone: 805-928-3838 or 805-344-2744). Richard Langdon, proprietor. 16 rooms.

BEL-AIR, Los Angeles, California: In the fashionable Bel-Air district of Los Angeles, this was a favorite hideaway of Gary Cooper, Howard Hughes, Grace Kelly, Sophia Loren, Marilyn Monroe, Gregory Peck, and other celebs since it opened in the '20s. The hotel's 88 rooms (36 of which are suites) are in 1- and 2-story mission-style buildings and bungalows scattered amid 11.5 acres exquisitely landscaped with rose gardens, lovely lawns, paths of poppies and palms, and streams that run into a lake where the lovely Bel-Air swans live. Executive chef George Morrone caters to the sophisticated tastes of patrons with "back to basics" cuisine: Meats are lightly marinated rather than doused in rich sauces, and herbs are grown on the premises. Information: Hotel Bel-Air, 701 Stone Canyon Rd., Los Angeles, CA 90077 (213-472-1211). Paul Zuest, managing director. 88 rooms.

MacCALLUM HOUSE, Mendocino, California: East is East and West is West and they meet here, three hours north of San Francisco. Mendocino, Nantucket West to many, is another example of how the early California settlers brought New England to the coast. The *MacCallum House* happens to be one of the prettier expressions of the Easterners' homesickness. Built in 1882 by lumber magnate William H. Kelley as a wedding present for his daughter Daisy and her husband, Alexander MacCallum, this 3-story Victorian mansion, trimmed with jigsaw-cut woodwork and fronted by a wonderful expanse of windows, was bought by two San Franciscans in 1974, about 20 years after Daisy's death. With the house, they purchased almost all of the furnishings, and so, when you visit, you can browse through Daisy's library (which includes some handsome leatherbound books, some volumes in French and German, some books on travel and religion, and a good many romantic novels) and admire the Tiffany lamps, Persian carpets, and carved footstools that belonged to the MacCallums themselves until not long ago. Some of the guestrooms are in the main building, but the old carriage house, the barn, and the greenhouse have also been rebuilt, and most guests are accommodated there. The elegant continental dinners devised by Tim Cannon have become a tradition. A short walk from town are the headlands at Russian Gulch State Park that can be described by only one word — spectacular. Information: The MacCallum House, PO Box 206, Mendocino, CA 95460 (phone: 707-937-0289). Melanie and Joe Reding, innkeepers. 20 rooms.

LÉGER, Mokelumne Hill, California: Built in 1851, restored and refurbished in 1960 and again in 1984, the pleasant Victorian interior of this former beer hall and its 2-story verandah (pillars below and railing above) seem to re-create, for a moment, the Gold Rush days of the mid-19th century, and sometimes you can almost imagine how it was in Mok' Hill that famous weekend of legend when no less than 17 hangings took place in one night. The rooms are old-fashioned, with flowered wallpaper, high Victorian beds, and plenty of rocking chairs. The surrounding Mother Lode Country is less gussied up than some other sections of California's former mining regions, and it's a welcome change. But if you don't want to go out exploring, you can just laze around the swimming pool out back among the orange trees and enjoy the fine food served in the dining room daily. There's also golf, tennis, and 2 parks nearby. Information: Hotel Léger, PO Box 50, Mokelumne Hill, CA 95245 (phone: 209-286-1401). Ron and Joyce Miller, innkeepers. 13 rooms.

SAN YSIDRO RANCH, Montecito, California: Originally owned by the Franciscan Missions, this 540-acre resort near Santa Barbara, which opened in 1893, enjoyed a long season as the choice vacation spot of the rich and the famous: Laurence Olivier and Vivien Leigh were married here; John F. Kennedy honeymooned with Jackie here; John Galsworthy, Aldous Huxley, Sinclair Lewis, Winston Churchill, Somerset Maugham, Bing Crosby, Jack Benny, and many others stayed here; and Ronald Colman owned the place from the mid-30s until his death in 1958. But in the '60s, the legend began to fade, and the inn started to fall apart and was well down the road to total ruin when Jim Lavenson, former president of New York's great *Plaza* hotel, put up the money to clean up, fix up, and paint up. And so, when you visit today, the 3 tennis courts, stables, restaurant, and swimming pool are all as spiffy as they were when Galsworthy revised his *Forsyte Saga* there (if not more so: 9 of the guest cottages have their own Jacuzzis). You can hole up in front of your fireplace, order room service, and never see the day, or mix with fellow guests in the bar and dining room. The kitchen, whose specialties include a smattering of both the French and the American, is good enough that among those who drop in to say "Hi!" to the chef is none other than Julia Child. Special meals grace the tables on holidays. The ranch is one of only 6 American inns listed in the prestigious Relais et Châteaux guide. Information: San Ysidro Ranch, 900 San Ysidro La., Montecito, CA 93108 (phone: 805-969-5046). Bob Harman and Claude Rouas, innkeepers. 43 cottages.

INN AT RANCHO SANTA FE, Rancho Santa Fe, California: It was one of those classic corporate bloopers: The Atchison, Topeka and Santa Fe Railroad bought up some 10,000 acres of cheap land to plant 3 million eucalyptus trees to provide — company officials hoped — an endless supply of railroad ties. Nobody had bothered to think, however, that the wood of eucalyptus trees is soft and splits easily — and though the trees took off, there wasn't a tie to be had in the bunch. The railroad then went into the citrus business, and later started up a residential development, one of the first planned communities in the country. The inn was first built to house prospective purchasers and it just kept on growing until it became what you find here today — a sedate and very restful complex of unpretentious cottages nestled on 20 acres of luxuriant grounds surrounding the original building. There are 3 tennis courts, a heated swimming pool, an English croquet court, and, nearby, 2 championship golf courses and Del Mar beach (7 miles away). The inn will pack you a box lunch. There's a wonderful library and a high-ceilinged living room, both with fireplaces, as well as very fine dining rooms — and all just 27 miles from San Diego. Information: The Inn at Rancho Santa Fe, PO Box 869, Rancho Santa Fe, CA 92067 (phone: 619-756-1131; 800-654-2928 in California). Daniel L. Royce, innkeeper. 75 rooms.

WINE COUNTRY INN, St. Helena, California: Here in Napa Valley, some 70 miles from San Francisco, is a rarity: a brand-new, built-from-scratch, old-fashioned country inn. Ned and Marge Smith spent years dreaming, talking, sketching, and planning inns; they traveled to classic inn country, lived there as guests, and picked the brains of innkeepers. And when they were ready a few years ago, they built their own, a marriage of the old and new made in inn heaven. Each room is different; most have fireplaces and all have character. Thanks to the careful attention to detail, it all works as it should. There's also a pool and Jacuzzi. Breakfast is the only meal, and it's served in a large, attractive common room. There are many fine restaurants in the area, and the menus for most of them are available for your perusal. Information: Wine Country Inn, 1152 Lodi La., St. Helena, CA 94574 (phone: 707-963-7077). Jim Smith, innkeeper. 25 rooms.

MANSION, San Francisco, California: Unlike many other cities of its size, San Francisco is blessed with an inn — and a highly unusual one it is. The *Mansion,* created by a former adman, boasts 19 rooms with private bath — some almost *House & Garden* charming. There's the lovely John Muir Room, for instance, and the elegant Empress Josephine Room, with its Louis XIV canopy bed and matching mirrored armoire, private sundeck, and bar; Barbra Streisand and Robin Williams have been among its guests. Some rooms have a marble fireplace, some a private terrace, some a slanted, garret-like ceiling. All are named for some historic personage (a mural on the wall depicts his or her life) and all have speakers so you can tune into classical music. Downstairs, there's more of the same elegance — crystal chandeliers, original art, and beautiful paneling, for starters. Victorian memorabilia — beaded bags, lace shawls, antique clothing — is all around. Among the most interesting features, however, are the ghostly spirits whose presence was certified by the same demonologists that exorcised the celebrated house in Amityville, New York. Room rates include fresh flowers in the room, complimentary wine upon arrival, full breakfast, coffee and tea nightly, and Mansion Magic Concerts. Other features include an attractive music parlor, game room and library, billiard room, and an elegant restaurant, open only to hotel guests and friends, where chef David Coyle, who served the Duke and Duchess of Bedford in Woburn Abbey castle for more than a decade, turns out ambitious entrées like prime New York steaks accompanied by wine, mushroom, and truffle sauce; fettuccine tossed with shrimp and a basil, garlic, and Romano cheese sauce; boneless trout stuffed with smoked roe and doused with a Chablis sauce; and venison and juniper berry pâté marinated in port and fines herbes. In a toney residential neighborhood, the *Mansion* is San Francisco's only designated Landmark Hotel. Information: Mansion Hotel, 2220 Sacramento St., San Francisco, CA 94115 (phone: 415-929-9444 or 800-424-9444). Denise Mitidieri, manager. 19 rooms.

SONOMA, Sonoma, California: This old wood and adobe structure, which started out in the 1870s as a dry goods store and meeting hall, was carefully restored in 1976 by the present owners and now has a delightful Gay Nineties ambience. All of the rooms are furnished in turn-of-the-century European and American antiques; Room 3 is named after the Mexican General Vallejo (who founded the town) and furnished with his own exquisitely carved rosewood bedroom suite, which is currently on loan from the Sonoma League for Historic Preservation. In the morning, when you go downstairs for continental breakfast in the inn's charming lobby, the management will help you plan a good tour of the surrounding wine country and nearby points of interest like the Jack London State Historic Park at Glen Ellen, where you can see the ruins of London's own Wolf House as well as the home of his widow, filled with London memorabilia. They can also help you arrange horseback or hot-air balloon rides, picnics, and massages in your room. Information: Sonoma Hotel, 110 W. Spain St., Sonoma, CA 95476 (phone: 707-996-2996). Dorene and John Musilli, innkeepers. 17 rooms.

SUTTER CREEK INN, Sutter Creek, California: One of the oldest country inns in the West, this green-shuttered bit of New England in California was built in 1859 by a wealthy merchant for his eastern bride. It came into the possession of Jane Way, a somewhat psychic palm reader, graphologist, and former housewife, in 1966, and she turned it into an inn. She installed canopy beds, queen-size beds, and beds that swing, ever so gently, by chains from the ceiling. (If you can't get used to the motion, you can stabilize your bed.) Some of the bathtubs were sunk into the floors. Fireplaces and Franklin stoves were installed. Outbuildings were converted to guestrooms, with hidden patios and gardens scattered about. Chintz by the yard was swathed around squashy sofas, draped over beds, and hung at the windows. There are plenty of antiques, but they're the kinds that look as if they don't mind being used. The place feels comfortable, reflecting (with a greater degree of fidelity than is usual) the personality of the innkeeper herself. Jane doesn't serve lunch or dinner — she leaves that to other innkeepers in the area — but instead she offers her guests the chance to congregate first thing in the morning over a big eggs and sausage breakfast in the brick-walled kitchen, a room as warm as the flash of the copper utensils hung from beams and walls alike. When the conversation lags, Jane may add brandy to your coffee (if you haven't already done so) or swirl it with a cinnamon stick, just because it's more festive that way. Or she might be persuaded to tell you how she came to terms with the ghost she encountered when she first arrived at the inn, or about her father, who is known locally for having brought France's Colombard grape to California. Or, because she is well versed in local history, she might tell you the sad tale of John Sutter, who had built up one of the state's biggest ranches when a carpenter working in the area discovered gold in one of his streams in 1848 and set off a gold rush that had prospectors killing his cattle, destroying his land, and ruining his hopes for a comfortable old age. Only the memory remains: *Sutter Creek* today is beautifully kept, an antiquer's delight. Information: Sutter Creek Inn, 75 Main St., Box 385, Sutter Creek, CA 95685 (phone: 209-267-5606). Jane Way, innkeeper. 19 rooms.

AHWAHNEE, Yosemite National Park, California: Built in 1927 in a deep, wide valley guarded by granite mountains, ostensibly to accommodate the growing number of visitors arriving in the park by automobile, this marvelous establishment is rustic but luxurious, with slate floors, beamed ceilings, a cavernous lobby, and immense windows in even the smallest sitting rooms to give you views into the park. The *Ahwahnee* is the kind of place where dressing for dinner is the order of the day. Yet the old stone structure manages at the same time to so harmonize with the surroundings that even Frank Lloyd Wright admired it. Meals in the vast and imposing dining room, especially notable for its towering picture windows and heavily beamed ceiling, are highlighted by salmon (sometimes broiled, sometimes poached in white wine) and prime ribs. Like the park, the hotel is open all year. But you'd be hard-pressed to say which season is best for a visit. In summer, there's hiking all through the Sierra, and you can sign up for rock climbing schools or special programs dealing with high-altitude ecology. In winter, the favored pastimes include downhill and cross-country skiing, snowshoeing to some of the frozen waterfalls, or races and winter games sponsored by the park concessionaire. At Christmastime, usually the high point of the *Ahwahnee*'s season, the hotel hosts the annual Bracebridge Dinner, wherein a section from Washington Irving's *Sketch Book* is reenacted in song and drama: The good Squire Bracebridge, an English country gentleman who is seated at the head of the dining room on a table set up on a dais, entertains his guests (you, a few hundred others, and assorted satin-, velvet-, and fur-clad actors and singers) over a fabulous six-course dinner that includes a flaming plum pudding and a peacock pie. The pageantry is gorgeous, so the limited number of tickets are hard to come by. Currently, they're sold by lottery during the January preceding each dinner, but the procedure changes occasionally, so write in advance for particulars. Information: Yosemite Reservations, 5410 E. Home Ave., Fresno, CA 93727 (phone: 209-252-4848). 121 rooms.

BURGUNDY HOUSE, Yountville, California: The rolling hills, bucolic landscapes, and usually sunny skies of California's three great wine producing areas — the Mendocino, Napa, and Sonoma valleys — seem a world apart from usually congested, often foggy or rainy San Francisco, even though they're just an hour or so north. And so, when you come to the Napa Valley town of Yountville, which recently celebrated its sesquicentennial, you have scenery, delightful weather, and the *Burgundy House* besides. This luxurious inn — installed in a circa 1870 former antiques shop, brandy distillery, and speakeasy with 2-foot-thick fieldstone walls — has been decorated in an eclectic style with all manner of antique pieces, many of them French. All the rooms have private baths. Many guests gather in a big common room in the late afternoons or evenings and for breakfast — this is the kind of place where strangers become fast friends. Information: Burgundy House, 6711 Washington St., Yountville, CA 94599 (phone: 707-944-0889). Dieter and Ruth Black, innkeepers. 5 rooms.

MAGNOLIA, Yountville, California: Built in 1873 and probably used as a bordello and a rumrunners' headquarters at various times during its checkered past, this small, stylish, stone-walled wine country establishment is fitted out with marble-topped tables, brass or walnut beds covered with crocheted lace bedspreads, and other French antiques; about a third of the rooms have fireplaces, and all have private baths. The breakfasts of French toast (with a special port wine syrup) or various egg dishes are excellent. The Jacuzzi and large swimming pool complete the experience. Select a bottle from the extensive wine cellar (20,000 bottles, including over 300 California selections). Information: Magnolia Hotel, 6529 Yount St., PO Drawer M, Yountville, CA 94599-1913 (phone: 707-944-2056). Bruce and Bonnie Locken, innkeepers. 12 rooms.

LODGE AT CORDILLERA, Edwards, Colorado: This European-inspired, auberge-style resort in the Colorado Rockies tries hard to harmonize with its surroundings. Designed by Belgian architect Leon Lambotte, the resort/residential community contains buildings of native stone, stucco, and forged iron. The 28 rooms in the lodge are of handcrafted post and beam design, with hardwood floors, marble fireplaces, and spectacular views of the New York Range. Another Belgian, executive chef Jacques Deluc, formerly of the Michelin two-star *Barbizon* outside Brussels, brings his expertise to the lodge's *Picasso* restaurant, whose menu features wild game, seafood, and local produce; there's a spa menu as well. Recreational facilities include a spa and a health club, 15 miles of cross-country ski trails, and trout fishing on a private 3-mile stretch of Eagle River, while downhill skiing at Vail and Beaver Creek is only 10 minutes away. Information: Lodge at Cordillera, PO Box 988, Edwards, CO 81632 (phone: 303-926-2200 in Colorado; 800-548-2721 elsewhere). 28 rooms.

RANCHO ENCANTADO, Tesuque, New Mexico: Surrounded on three sides by the Tesuque Indian Reservation and on the fourth by the Santa Fe National Forest, this topnotch Old Southwest resort hotel came into being in the 1930s as a very ordinary sort of desert lodge. But in the late '60s Betty Egan, a Cleveland widow with four children, came here to start life over again. She took the place in hand and turned it into the exciting complex it is today, a luxurious Western guest ranch — more than a hotel, more than an inn; the sort of establishment where you expect to find cowbells and dried peppers and Indian weavings hanging here and there, the occasional rawhide chair, and lots of red tile. The guestrooms, all furnished with antiques and southwestern Indian art and artifacts, all have their own patios; most have fireplaces. The tri-level dining room, walled in white adobe, looks out across the desert, some 170 acres of which make up the *Rancho Encantado* spread. For fun, you can swim in a heated outdoor pool, play tennis, go riding (on horses you hire by the hour), or join in many other indoor or outdoor activities. Food is Mexican, American, and continental. (Be sure to try the sour cream chicken enchiladas and the carne asada, steaks marinated with chili strips.) There are big feasts for Thanksgiving and Christmas. European Plan (no meals) only. Information: Rancho Encantado, Rte. 4, Box 57C, Santa Fe, NM 87501 (phone: 505-982-3537). Betty Egan, innkeeper. 22 rooms, 36 vacation condominiums.

SALISHAN LODGE, Gleneden Beach, Oregon: A dedicated environmentalist who was also a thoroughgoing sybarite couldn't find a better spot for a vacation than this unusual modern resort on the Oregon coast about 90 miles west of Portland. Here, everything harmonizes with the spectacular landscape of lagoons, woods, beach, and ocean. Every bedroom, lounge, and dining room is further testimony to the good taste of the resort's designers and the architectural integrity of the complex. The creation of Oregon manufacturer John D. Gray, *Salishan* stands as one proof that good design and reverence for the environment can also be good business. Rooms — all with fireplaces, big bathrooms, and oversize windows that frame forest or bay and ocean views — are in 15 villas that are connected by bridges and covered walkways. The dining room is also exceptionally handsome, and the kitchen is noted for its way with seafood, particularly salmon, which comes barbecued, baked in puff pastry, and fixed just about any other way you can imagine. The wine list is so extensive that it has an index; it enumerates everything from an unpretentious Beaujolais to a Lafite-Rothschild that costs more than a whole weekend's stay at some very nice places. The wine cellar stocks some 20,000 bottles and is available for tours, tastings, and even catered dinner parties. The resort even has its own art gallery and publishes a botanical guide to the flora on the grounds and in the area. And every guest is assigned his own parking space (a feature much appreciated by the Cadillac-Mercedes-BMW crowd that gravitates here). To round things out, there is an indoor swimming pool, therapy pool, and a variety of health club facilities (exercise rooms, saunas, and such); tennis courts, both indoors and outdoors; and golf. Bird and whale watching, deep-sea fishing, collecting driftwood, and studying the trees and the wildflowers on the nature trails can keep you plenty busy, however. Information: Salishan Lodge, PO Box 118, Gleneden Beach, OR 97388 (phone: 503-764-2371 or 800-452-2300). Hank Hickox, innkeeper. 201 rooms, 3 suites.

TIMBERLINE LODGE, Timberline, Oregon: Those who lived through the Great Depression remember that the WPA (Works Progress Administration) was the whipping boy of everyone who condemned the New Deal as a waste, and that the men who worked for the organization were widely considered no better than a bunch of lazy bums. *Timberline Lodge,* built by the WPA with youths from the CCC (Civilian Conservation Corps) more than halfway up snow-capped, 11,246-foot Mt. Hood, puts the lie to that notion. Hundreds of Oregonians — trained to chisel stones, blacksmith, carve, and carpenter by locals and by craftsmen imported from Europe — created a structure that is truly monumental, from its 400-ton chimney (a hundred feet high) and its 750-pound bronze and brass weather vane, to the cathedral of a lobby, the massive staircases, and the giant doorway. Even the details are dazzling: the chairs made of hardwood, wrought iron, and rawhide; the newel posts carved with animals and birds from sawed-off telephone poles; stained glass murals portraying local scenes and creatures; hand-wrought chandeliers and lamps; rugs hooked from the blankets and uniforms used by the workers; and on and on. The ensemble is a structure in harmony with the mountain it calls home, a work of unusual architectural design and impressive craftsmanship — and a monument to American determination. When you visit, you'll lodge in rooms filled up with sturdy blond furniture, handwoven rugs, and appliquéd spreads and curtains. Every room has a private bath and a good view (either of valley or peak). There's a heated pool and a sauna; you can ski in both summer and winter, and when the weather permits, you can hike or climb as well. At Christmastime, Richard Kohnstamm, who has been here since the 1950s, celebrates the season with such verve that even stay-at-homes don't miss the hearth fires back home. Information: Timberline Ski Area, Timberline Lodge, OR 97028 (phone: 503-272-3311). Richard Kohnstamm, area operator. 59 rooms.

CAPTAIN WHIDBEY INN, Coupeville, Washington: The chief claim to fame of the peaceful, wooded island 50 miles north of Seattle where venerable Coupeville is located is this resort built in 1907, high above the sea, of the reddish logs of the locally plentiful madrona tree. A fixture of the Pacific Northwest vacation scene almost since the beginning, it is popular, however, not so much because of any superabundance of activities (it's as quiet as the island itself) but because it is a personality kid, a one-of-a-kind through and through. Dominating the lobby is a huge stone fireplace surrounded by easy chairs. The shelves of the library are jammed with books. The window-walled dining room, where you can order from a wine list as distinguished as any in the area and a menu that features all kinds of fish and crustaceans fresh from the cold local waters, gives you views of Penn Cove and, beyond it to the northeast, the snowy summit of Mt. Baker. And the ceiling of the bar, a favorite watering hole in this part of the world, is hung with hundreds of empty bottles whose labels bear inscriptions testifying to the good times had during the consumption of their contents. Rooms in the main building, all of them furnished simply but with some antiques and all with down comforters, are like miniature log cabins; they share the baths down the hall. For privacy and space, you want the equally charming rooms facing the lagoon. Short summer sails with the captain are a special treat. Information: Captain Whidbey Inn, 2072 W. Capt. Whidbey Inn Rd., Coupeville, WA 98239 (phone: 206-678-4097). Capt. John Colby Stone, innkeeper. 33 rooms.

JAMES HOUSE, Port Townsend, Washington: Dreaming of a future as the West's greatest port, this community boomed as rich men working on getting richer poured into town. Of the great houses they built along the city's streets to show off their substance, Francis Wilcox James's was the most impressive. Built in 1889 at a cost of around $10,000 — at a time when $2,000 or $3,000 would pay for more than adequate living quarters, and $4,000 was all that was required to construct something really splendid — this porticoed, dormered, many-chimneyed, peak-roofed, shingle Queen Anne mansion fell on hard times in the years after the railroads passed Port Townsend by, and left the early dreams unrealizable. The ceilings were lowered, the large rooms were partitioned into cubicles. Then, in the 1960s, Bill and Frances Eaton saw the house, loved it, bought it, and over the course of a decade restored it. From the banisters and the parquet floors to the carved settees and the high-standing bedsteads, the *James House* gleams. Information: James House, 1238 Washington St., Port Townsend, WA 98368 (phone: 206-385-1238). Lowell and Barbara Bogart, innkeepers. 12 rooms.

BED-AND-BREAKFAST ESTABLISHMENTS

The day that stateside travelers had to really hunt for the inexpensive pleasures of Europe's bed-and-breakfast establishments is fast becoming a memory as the bed-and-breakfast movement continues to boom. One bed-and-breakfast reservation service has placed more than 10,000 guests in private homes in the last 5 years, and it is only one of more than 150 organizations in 1,000 American cities. In 1983, the yellow pages of the telephone book began including a heading for bed-and-breakfast reservations services.

The *American Bed and Breakfast Assn.* (PO Box 23294, Washington, DC 20026) can send you more information if you include a large, self-addressed, stamped envelope. Or you can consult any of several guidebooks on the subject: the association's *A Treasury of Bed & Breakfast* ($14.95; $17.95 postpaid first class) includes over 3,000 homes in the US and Canada, lists of reservation services, and a chapter on starting your own establishment. *Bed & Breakfast USA,* updated annually, by Betty Rundback and Nancy Kramer (Dutton; $10.95) includes some 1,000 listings; *Bed & Breakfast North America,* 4th ed. (Betsy Ross Publications, 3057 Betsy Ross Dr., Bloomfield Hills, MI 48013; $12.95; $14.95 postpaid), describes 600 small inns in the US, Canada, and Mexico, and lists reservations services; *The Bed & Breakfast Guide* (National Bed & Breakfast Assn. PO Box 332, Norwalk, CT 06852; $11.95; $13.95 postpaid) lists 1,130 bed and breakfasts in the US, Canada, Bermuda, Puerto Rico, and the US Virgin Islands, and 80 bed and breakfast reservations services; and *Bed & Breakfast America: The Great American Guest House Book* by John Thaxton (Burt Franklin, 235 E. 44th St., New York, NY 10017; $8.95) lists 350 homes and inns in 38 states, recommended through the author's personal experience.

A number of organizations can help you reserve accommodations around the country. The best to try include the following.

> *Bed & Breakfast Company — Tropical Florida,* PO Box 262, South Miami, FL 33243 (phone: 305-661-3270): Bed-and-breakfast lodgings in Florida; send a self-addressed, stamped envelope for free brochure describing the reservations service.
>
> *Bed & Breakfast International — San Francisco,* 151 Ardmore, Kensington, CA 94707 (phone: 415-525-4569): Bed-and-breakfast housing in San Francisco and the Greater Bay Area, wine country, Monterey, Los Angeles, San Diego, and other areas of travel interest in California; selected host homes in Hawaii, Las Vegas, Seattle, and New York City.
>
> *The Bed & Breakfast League/Sweet Dreams and Toast,* PO Box 9490, Washington, DC 20016 (phone: 202-363-7767): Bed-and-breakfast lodgings in Washington, DC, and its suburbs.
>
> *Northwest Bed & Breakfast,* West Coast Reservations Service, 610 SW Broadway, Suite 609, Portland, OR 97205 (phone: 503-243-7616): A call or letter will connect you with 400 delightful bed-and-breakfast homes in California, Oregon, Washington, Hawaii, and British Columbia. Descriptive directory. Help in planning itineraries — coast, mountains, farms, ranches, desert, cities. Also unique accommodations in Great Britain and France. For free information, send a self-addressed, stamped envelope.

Visitable Vineyards

Whether you're in search of the perfect cabernet or the perfect vacation, you'll find it in American wine country. Ten years ago, you might have flown to Europe. Today US wines are grabbing gold medals in blind tastings against the finest French Bordeaux, Burgundies, and many others, and winery touring is the newest American sport.

America's wine capital is the dynamic Napa–Sonoma area in northern California, with more than 150 wineries open to the public within an hour and half's drive from San Francisco. In the Pacific Northwest, particularly Washington, you can taste fine wines in spectacular surroundings. New York State has several beautiful wine routes, some right near New York City.

Outside the "big three" grape-growing states, wineries drop off sharply in number and scale, but there are still plenty to see in your travels around the US. The rolling hills of Virginia's Albermarle wine country, where Jefferson planted European vines at Monticello, are within easy driving distance of Washington, DC. In Pennsylvania, you can taste and tour near the place where Washington crossed the Delaware. The Texas hill country now invites visitors to taste both premium reds and whites. There's a flourishing wine route on the shores of Lake Erie. In more than 25 states, you can watch vintners make wines from the acclaimed European varietals and the sturdier French-American hybrids, as well as from the traditional native American grapes and local fruits and berries.

What makes wine touring the ideal travel diversion is the vine's own finicky nature.

Grapes thrive in protected valleys and on gentle hillsides that are warmed by long hours of sunshine and cooled by the mists from rivers, lakes, and coastlines — dream settings for day-trippers and vacationers as well as serious oenophiles.

Furthermore, wine makers — from the giant conglomerate to the lone vintner in a four-car garage — are anxious to showcase their products. At small wineries, you'll probably be taken through by the owner, who'll taste with you and share production secrets down to the last barrel stave. These visits require planning, since appointments usually must be made in advance. For more casual visits, try larger wineries with tasting rooms open to drop-ins (a souvenir-shop atmosphere often comes with the territory here). They're apt to be better organized for touring the vineyards, the crushing pads, and the fermentation rooms, with their giant steel tanks, endless rows of aging barrels, and clattering bottling lines.

Tastings of the company's current wines are usually complimentary (like the tour), though a few big houses, particularly the California champagne makers, have started to charge. Some wineries pour grape juice for children and for whoever is driving. Start with the whites and work up through the full-bodied reds and sweet dessert wines. Don't hesitate to spit (as professional tasters do) or to empty unconsumed wine from your glass into the crocks set along the tasting bar.

Bus trips are sometimes offered out of larger cities, but generally you'll need a car for wine touring. Bring low-heeled, rubber-soled shoes for climbing up observation ramps and stepping over hoses on wet floors. Bring a sweater, too, for chilly, damp aging cellars. Since many wineries are open only from around 10 AM to 4 PM and there may be a wait for tours, don't plan more than four winery stops a day.

CALIFORNIA

You'll find pockets of scenic wine country from Mendocino County, well to the north of San Francisco, all the way down to the Mexican border, with some good visiting in the Monterey–Carmel areas, around Santa Barbara, and inland in the Temecula Valley between Los Angeles and San Diego. But mecca is superchic Napa Valley and country-gentleman Sonoma County, both an hour north of San Francisco. These premium grape-growing areas, home to megabuck international wine companies and millionaire "farmers," serve up a trendy vacation lifestyle with calculated rusticity. Napa Valley's *Oakville Grocery Company,* in an old gas station, sells picnic pâtés and cheeses worthy of *Fauchon* in Paris. At a bakery on the sleepy little Healdsburg town square in Sonoma County, the croissants are turned out by the former pastry chef of Berkeley's famed *Chez Panisse* restaurant.

NAPA VALLEY

Some 30 miles long and 6 miles across at its widest point, cozy Napa Valley, with microclimates and soil variations at every turn, is the promised land for cabernet sauvignon, Pinot noir, chardonnay, sauvignon blanc, Johannisberg Riesling, and many more of the world's finest grape varieties. It's also a playground for winery touring, ballooning, cycling, hiking, picnicking, boutiquing, fine dining, and discovering charming inns. Its main road, Highway 29, runs the length of the valley, chockablock with vineyards and wineries, and winds through the gussied-up country towns of Napa, Yountville, St. Helena, and Calistoga, which soon become as familiar as your own home town.

Napa is California's biggest tourist attraction after Disneyland. Time your visit for spring if you want to avoid the July-through-September vacation crowds and the October weekend stampedes. With autumn's arrival, the tempo quickens, the grapes hang heavy, and the trucks line up to dump their gleaming harvest onto the crushing pads. If you come in summer, you'll face bumper-to-bumper traffic, crowds jostling for places at the tasting bar, and no room at the inns, unless you do San Francisco on the weekend and Napa midweek.

Here's a sample of the range of experiences you'll find in Napa's wineries.

DOMAINE CHANDON: Seeming to grow out of the earth, this low-slung symphony of stone arches looks out across the valley of vines to the golden, oak-studded hills on the other side. Tours of this glamorous arm of the French firm of Moët et Chandon begin in an underground wine museum and proceed through a high-production sparkling-wine making operation. You'll see the unusual sight of high fermentation tanks lying on their sides, and inspect the latest automatic riddling machines (for periodic turning of the bottles). There's no tasting with this tour, but you can buy a glass of bubbly (try the réserve) in a sunny sit-down café. Domaine Chandon also has an internationally known restaurant for lunch or dinner, which requires reservations well in advance. Information: Domaine Chandon, California Dr., PO Box 2470, Yountville, CA 94599 (phone: 707-944-2280).

CHARLES KRUG WINERY: Founded in 1861, this is the Napa Valley's oldest winery. Original stone buildings shaded by ancient oaks stand next to giant modern additions equipped with the latest technology. The lively, informative tour is like a walk through wine making history. Free tasting includes older vintage cabernets. Information: Charles Krug Winery, 2800 St. Helena Hwy., PO Box 191, St. Helena, CA 94574 (phone: 707-963-5057).

PRAGER WINERY & PORT WORKS: In a frame house behind the main highway, a dedicated wine maker is championing a port revival. His modest output is available on the premises — in bottles personally autographed in gold ink. He bottles his wines outside the front door, and his tasting room is the kitchen behind a minuscule barrel room. Call first, or you may have to get him out of his vegetable garden. Information: Prager Winery & Port Works, 1281 Lewelling La., St. Helena, CA 94574 (phone: 707-963-3720).

GRGICH HILLS CELLAR: Connoisseurs come to this attractive hacienda for its whites, particularly the handsome chardonnays. The tasting room welcomes drop-ins, but tours with the wine makers are by appointment. Information: Grgich Hills Cellar, 1829 St. Helena Hwy. PO Box 450, Rutherford, CA 94573 (phone: 707-963-2784).

HANNS KORNELL CHAMPAGNE CELLARS: Here you see traditional champagne making, the way three generations of Kornells produced Sekt in the Rhine Valley. In the long, dim cellars, Kornell's bottles are turned by hand in the age-old manner. Tour guides are particularly spirited and helpful, and the silver-haired gentleman chiming in at the complimentary tasting might be Kornell himself. Information: Hans Kornell Champagne Cellars, 1091 Larkmead La., Calistoga, CA 94515 (PO Box 249, St. Helena, CA 94574) (phone: 707-963-1237).

STERLING VINEYARDS: When locals grumble about the Disneyfication of Napa, they point to the wildly popular white ski gondolas that lift visitors from the parking lot to the white building of this imposing winery, which was modeled after a hilltop monastery in Greece. Once aloft, you get breathtaking views down-valley and a well-organized self-guided tour (follow the signs) along ramps overlooking the works. There's a sit-down tasting of cabernets, chardonnays, Pinot noirs, and merlots in a luxurious tower room. A $5 gondola fee includes tasting. Information: Sterling Vineyards, 1111 Dunaweal La., PO Box 365, Calistoga, CA 94515 (phone: 707-942-5151).

CLOS PEGASE: Napa's current eyebrow raiser is the stolid ocher-and-rust-colored many-columned complex designed by the postmodern architect Michael Graves — it's been called a cross between a nuclear reactor and a Greek temple. The winery tour, not surprisingly, devotes as much attention to architectural detail as to the process of making the well-received chardonnay and fumé blanc. Information: Clos Pagase, 1060 Dunaweal La., PO Box 305, Calistoga, CA 94515 (phone: 707-942-4981).

CHÂTEAU MONTELENA: You have to ask the way to this century-old stone palace shrouded by woods at the north end of the valley. After a tour and tasting, visitors can purchase a bottle of its famous chardonnay and picnic among the black swans on the island in the château's pond. Picnic and tour reservations are required, but the tasting room is always open. Information: Château Montelena, 1429 Cubbs La., PO Box 738, Calistoga, CA 94515 (phone: 707-942-5105).

CLOS DU VAL WINE COMPANY: This unpretentious modern French château faces Napa's Silverado Trail, the road that runs along the quieter, eastern edge of the valley, where pasturelands recall a time when Napa was dairy country. In the vineyards that lead up from the road, a rose bush has been planted (a French custom) at the end of each row of vines. Tours are informal, and you can taste a range of European varietals as well as zinfandel, a California mainstay. Information: Clos du Val Wine Company, 5330 Silverado Trail, PO Box 4350, Napa, CA 94558 (phone: 707-252-6711).

ROBERT MONDAVI WINERY: The best guided tour in the valley is at this white, V-shaped, mission-styled winery surrounded by flower gardens. There's a dramatic view of the vineyards, framed by an entrance archway, where a statue of St. Francis stands guard. Tours paced with the precision of a TV game show give comprehensive walk-throughs from vineyard to bottling line and end with a tasting that's a learning experience. In summer, be there before noon to ensure your tour ticket. Information: Robert Mondavi Winery, 7801 St. Helena Hwy., PO Box 106, Oakville, CA 94562 (phone: 707-963-9611).

VICHON WINERY: Plan to be at this hillside boutique winery around lunchtime. The shady picnic tables at the edge of their best cabernet vineyard afford a sensational view of the valley. Tours are small and personal, and tasting will include their proprietary chevrignon, a blend of semillon and sauvignon blanc. Information: Vichon Winery, 1595 Oakville Grade, PO Box 363, Oakville, CA 94562 (phone: 707-944-2811).

BERINGER VINEYARDS: It's hard to miss this turreted Rhineland mansion from the road. Stop at its lavish, paneled tasting rooms and take the fascinating tour of hand-dug caves still showing the pickax marks left by Chinese laborers in the 1800s. Beringer doesn't make its wines right here, but there's a lot to see. Information: Beringer Vineyards, 2000 Main St., PO Box 111, St. Helena, CA 94574 (phone: 707-963-7115).

BRIEFLY NOTED

CHRISTIAN BROTHERS GREYSTONE CELLARS: The largest stone building in California is now a gigantic aging cellar and a wine museum — no wine is made here. There's a highly informative lecture tour, including a lesson in tasting. You'll also see the famous Brother Timothy corkscrew collection. Information: Christian Brothers Greystone Cellars, 2555 N. Main St., PO Box 552, St. Helena, CA 94574 (phone: 707-967-3112).

FREEMARK ABBEY WINERY: After the tour here, sip cabernet in a spacious Oriental-carpeted tasting room, complete with fireplace and a concert grand. Information: Freemark Abbey Winery, 3022 St. Helena Hwy. N., PO Box 410, St. Helena, CA 95474 (phone: 707-963-9694).

FLORA SPRINGS WINE COMPANY: A real family business, with a child's swing outside the door and owners who'll show you how they saved and updated an ancient winery. Bring barbecue fixings and use the grill in their hilltop picnic patio. By appointment only. Information: Flora Springs Wine Co., 1978 W. Zinfandel La., St. Helena, CA 95474 (phone: 707-963-5711).

SPRING MOUNTAIN: For cabernets and chardonnays made on the hillside estate pictured in TV's "Falcon Crest." No charge for the winery tour or tasting, but a fee is charged for the optional walk around the famous house. Information: Spring Mountain, 2805 Spring Mountain Rd., St. Helena, CA 95474 (phone: 707-963-5233).

SONOMA COUNTY

Just over the mountains, less than a half hour from the Napa Valley, a whole new wine country offers rural calm, uncrowded roads, plentiful accommodations, and a chance to soak up California history. The Sonoma town square, for instance, was the site of the Bear Flag uprising that declared California's independence from Mexico. Sonoma County's closely linked wine valleys — Alexander, Dry Creek, Sonoma, and Russian River — still have room for pear and apple orchards, truck farms, and chicken ranches among the vineyards. There's even an organized "farm route" that leads to farmstands, llama- and pony-petting corrals, and cheese and jam making enterprises that offer a good break between wineries — ideal if you're touring with children.

SEBASTIANI VINEYARDS: There's constant hubbub in the tasting room–gift shop of this winery, which has operated in the town of Sonoma since 1900. The giant Sebastiani company offers more than a dozen bottles for tasting at several busy serving bars. Tours of the vineyards and winery are well guided and include a look at a fascinating collection of hand-carved casks. Information: Sebastiani Vineyards, 389 4th St. E., PO Box AA, Sonoma, CA 95476 (phone: 707-938-5532).

BUENA VISTA WINERY: A short drive into the hills from Sonoma takes you to the place where the scoundrel adventurer Agoston Haraszthy planted the first European wine grapes in California in the 1860s. The romantic ivy-covered stone buildings are a wine museum; the fine Buena Vista wines tasted here are made at another location. There's picnicking under giant eucalyptus trees along the stream out front. Information: Buena Vista Winery, 1800 Old Winery Rd., PO Box 1842, Sonoma, CA 95476 (phone: 707-938-1266).

GLEN ELLEN WINERY AND VINEYARDS: Down the hill from historic Jack London State Park near the tiny crossroads town of Glen Ellen, a cluster of modest white frame buildings snuggles in a hollow that looks up at a patchwork quilt of terraced vineyards. Instead of taking a formal tour, you browse among the grapes, tanks, and barrels yourself and ask your questions in the tasting room. A towering grove of redwoods shading the picnic grounds are reminders that you're at the edge of California's redwood country. Information: Glen Ellen Winery and Vineyards, 1883 London Ranch Rd., Glen Ellen, CA 95422 (phone: 707-996-1066).

IRON HORSE VINEYARDS: Call ahead to enjoy the understated elegance of this privately owned estate winery on its own hilltop, reached by a rutted narrow road. Surrounded by vine-covered hills that shut out the world, you'll stroll the winery, a glass of fumé blanc in hand, as a wine maker shows you around. You'll be given more tastes of cabernet, chardonnay, and sparkling wine in a barrel-aging room; there's no souvenir shop–tasting room here. Information: Iron Horse Vineyards, 9786 Ross Station Rd., Sebastopol, CA 95472 (phone: 707-887-1507).

LAMBERT BRIDGE: A road with lazy oxbow curves winds through a sea of vines to a redwood country lodge, where visitors step into a cavernous paneled room lit by two rows of chandeliers hanging from its cathedral ceiling. Fit for a prince's audience chamber, it's actually the room where the barrels are stacked for aging. The wine maker will pour his cabernet, merlot, and chardonnay at a table by the big stone fireplace. Only recently opened to the public, this one is worth making an appointment. Information: Lambert Bridge, 4085 W. Dry Creek Rd., Healdsburg, CA 95448 (phone: 707-433-5855).

HOP KILN WINERY: This moldering stone building out in the country provides a look back to the days before the wine boom, when Sonoma's vineyards were hop fields for a thriving beer industry. The building's three square towers are actually chimneys for the old hop-drying furnaces that stand alongside the wine making tanks and barrels. Try the zinfandel. Information: Hop Kiln Winery, 6050 Westside Rd., Healdsburg, CA 95448 (phone: 707-433-6491).

KORBEL CHAMPAGNE CELLARS: The biggest champagne maker in the US conducts one of the most thorough guided tours, ending with a generous free tasting at a block-long bar made from old barrels. Korbel, founded in 1882 near the Russian River, has its original buildings in place and an antique rose garden to visit. Information: Korbel Champagne Cellars, 13250 River Rd., Guerneville, CA 95446 (phone: 707-887-2294).

FERRARI-CARANO VINEYARDS: This showplace is new on the Sonoma scene. The Italianate winery is surrounded by vineyards and 5 acres of manicured lawns bordered by Old World rock and flower gardens. Stop by for tastings, which include a popular chardonnay. Tours of the shiny facilities can be arranged by appointment. Information: Ferrari-Carano Vineyards, 8761 Dry Creek Rd., PO Box 1549, Healdsburg, CA 95448 (phone: 707-433-6700).

VIANSA WINERY: This luxurious Tuscan hillside villa is scheduled to open early in 1990. Tours will include a wine making video and tastings of the winery's main products, cabernet sauvignon, chardonnay, and sauvignon blanc wines. Picnic grounds look down on the valley. The owners are members of the pioneer Sebastiani wine making family. Information: Viansa Winery, 461 7th St. W., Suite 5, PO Box 1849, Sonoma, CA 95476 (phone: 707-996-4448).

BRIEFLY NOTED

CHÂTEAU SOUVERAIN: The most impressive winery building dominates a Dry Creek Valley hillside and offers tours and tastings plus dining-with-a-view, at moderate prices, for lunch and dinner. Information: Château Souverain, 400 Souverain Rd., PO Box 528, Geyserville, CA 95441 (phone: 707-433-8281).

GLORIA FERRER CHAMPAGNE CAVES: This offshoot of Spain's Freixenet winery offers an informative tour through its lavish Catalonian-contemporary complex, with panoramic views of Sonoma County from the wine-bar terrace. There's a charge for tasting. Gloria Ferrer Champagne Caves, 2355 Hwy. 121, PO Box 1427, Sonoma, CA 95476 (phone: 707-996-7256).

PIPER SONOMA CELLARS: Visitors enjoy a lively tour showing the latest champagne making equipment in this California branch of France's Piper-Heidsieck. Piper Sonoma Cellars, 11447 Old Redwood Hwy., Healdsburg, CA 95448 (PO Box 650, Windsor, CA 95492; phone: 707-433-8843).

CHÂTEAU ST. JEAN: Take a self-guided tour through a fanciful winery building set well back in the vineyards. Taste its premium whites in a charming villa across a flower-filled courtyard. Information: Château St. Jean, 8555 Sonoma Hwy., PO Box 293, Kenwood, CA 95452 (phone: 707-833-4134).

For a California winery guide send $1.50 to the Wine Institute, 165 Post St., San Francisco, CA 94108 (phone: 415-986-0878).

NEW YORK STATE

You get your choice of ambience here. Take a rural vacation in the mountainous Finger Lakes region of central New York, between Rochester and Syracuse. Take a day trip from Manhattan to the quiet Hudson Valley. Combine a visit to the state's newest wineries on eastern Long Island with a weekend at a stylish Hamptons beach town.

In the Finger Lakes area, there are 40 wineries, most of them small, within minutes of each other along uncrowded roads that rim the hills around a group of glacier-cut lakes. Terraced vineyards, fields of wheat and corn, and grazing cattle flourish within sight of their sparkling waters. This is camping, boating, biking, and antiques-auction country. The farmer/wine maker takes time to direct you to your next stop as you leave his place. Most of the wineries are clustered around the biggest lakes — Cayuga,

Seneca, and Keuka — within easy reach of historic small towns, charming old inns, and bed-and-breakfast establishments. New York's prodigious wine output depended on native American labrusca grapes until the mid-1970s, when new small farm wineries found success with European varieties and hardy French-American hybrids. So you'll see a range of wines, mostly whites, from humble to haute.

In the Hudson Valley, grape farmers on both sides of the river produce premium wines with European varietals and such French-American hybrids as seyval blanc and baco noir. Long Island's vineyards, planted in what used to be potato fields, all specialize in the big-name European varieties.

FINGER LAKES

TAYLOR/GREAT WESTERN/GOLD SEAL WINERY: Not a little old wine maker but a snappy guide in a golf shirt leads your group, starting from one of the biggest visitor centers in the country. You're really seeing three venerable Lake Keuka wineries that now operate as one. On foot and by bus, you go through a mix of state-of-the-art facilities and original 19th-century buildings. Your tour of the still- and sparkling-wine making processes ends in an old champagne vault, where they'll pour fine dry champagne and five other wines, followed by sherry. You can watch a viticulture film in a theater that was once a 35,000-gallon sherry barrel. Information: Taylor/Great Western/Gold Seal Winery, County Rte. 88, Hammondsport, NY 14840 (phone: 607-569-2111).

WAGNER VINEYARDS: Estate-bottled whites, notably Johannisberg Riesling and chardonnay, draw oenophiles here, but the octagonal red pine building looking over the vineyards to Seneca Lake below is an attraction in itself. There is a good guided tour and a leisurely tasting of European varietals and native wines. Picnic or enjoy a meal in a pretty tent café. Information: Wagner Vineyards, Rte. 414, Lodi, NY 14860 (phone: 607-582-6450).

GLENORA: There's a gorgeous view of Seneca Lake. No tour, only a film, but you look into the working winery and taste the firm's fine chardonnay, Johannisberg Riesling, and seyval blanc. Information: Glenora, 5435 Rte. 14, Dundee, NY 14837 (phone: 607-243-5511).

BRIEFLY NOTED

BULLY HILL VINEYARDS: A lively winery/restaurant complex with an interesting wine museum. Information: Bully Hill Vineyards, RD 2, Hammondsport, NY 14840 (phone: 607-868-3210).

BARRINGTON CHAMPAGNE COMPANY: The sparkling wines here are made by the *méthode champenoise,* which the owner explains step by step during the tour and tasting. The wine cellar is in the historic *Red Brick Inn* in Dundee. Tour and tasting are by appoinment. Information: Barrington Champagne Co., 2081 Rte. 230, Dundee, NY 14837 (phone: 607-243-8844).

SONNENBERG GARDENS: Visitors can sample wines made by three different New York wineries — Canandaigua, Widmer, and Manischewitz — and tour late Victorian showpiece gardens all in one stop. The actual wineries are elsewhere. Tasting room and gardens (and picnic area) are open from Mother's Day through mid-October. Information: Sonnenberg Gardens, 151 Charlotte St., PO Box 663, Canandaigua, NY 14424 (phone: 716-394-4922; tasting room, 716-394-7680).

HUDSON VALLEY

Wine country begins an hour from Manhattan and meanders upstate on both sides of the river, with charming farm wineries and colonial towns for stops along the way.

BENMARL VINEYARDS: The jewel of the Hudson River is this pioneer farm winery high on the east bank. You need an appointment, but you'll be rewarded by a chat with artist and wine maker Mark Miller, the man who started the premium-wine renaissance in the Hudson Valley. Tours through Miller's rustic chalet-style buildings include a look at his 3,800-bottle collection of fine old European wines and examples of his own sculpture and painting. The tour costs $5. There's no charge for tasting his premium estate-bottled red and his red table wines or enjoying a view clear to the foothills of the Berkshires. Lovely picnic groves and a small café. Information: Benmarl Vineyards, Highland Ave., Marlboro, NY 12542 (phone: 914-236-4265).

BRIEFLY NOTED

BROTHERHOOD WINERY: Its unrivaled 150 years of continuous operation make a tour of this landmark fieldstone winery and its underground storage caves a must, especially if you're visiting nearby West Point. During Prohibition, Brotherhood made sacramental wines but produces varietals these days. Information: Brotherhood Winery, 35 North St., Washingtonville, NY 10992 (phone: 914-496-3661).

CASCADE MOUNTAIN VINEYARDS: A tiny winery among the vines at the end of a lane has intimate tours and tastings — and funky names like Pardonnay-Moi for its wines. Local cheeses, sausages, and game are served at its café. Information: Cascade Mountain Vineyards, Flint Hill Rd., Amenia, NY 12501 (phone: 914-373-9021).

LONG ISLAND

LA RÊVE: The most spectacular of Long Island's dozen wineries, this new beauty is housed in a 17,000-foot cooper-roofed building patterned after a Normandy château. The tasting rooms and terrace overlook the vineyards. Tours are free; there's a charge for tastings. Information: La Rêve, PO Box 962, 162 Montauk Hwy., Water Mill, NY 11976 (phone: 516-726-7555).

For a New York winery guide, contact the New York Wine and Grape Foundation, 350 Elm St., Penn Yan, NY 14527 (phone: 325-536-7442).

PACIFIC NORTHWEST

WASHINGTON

No matter where you happen to be in Washington, you're always no farther than an hour's drive from a winery. You're most likely, however, to do your touring around Seattle, a major wine center despite the fact that wine grapes don't do well in its cool, damp climate. Washington's well-known white wines and newly acclaimed reds come from vines grown in the sunny farmlands on the eastern side of the snow-crowned Cascade Mountains. Grapes are crushed right in the fields, and their juice is trucked over the hills to Seattle wineries. For country winery visiting, tour the Yakima Valley, three hours from the city. About a dozen wineries are open to visitors along Highway 82, running down the center of the valley.

CHÂTEAU STE. MICHELLE: Seattle's major winery welcomes visitors to a graceful, French-style château surrounded by 87 acres of manicured grounds. The vineyards here are for experimental purposes and decoration — visitors throw grapes to the ducks in the ponds. There is an expert tour of the white wine process (the reds are made in eastern Washington) and a tasting from among a dozen red and white varietals, including the popular chardonnay and Johannisberg Riesling. Lush picnic areas. Information: Château Ste. Michelle, 14111 NE 145th St., Woodinville, WA 98072 (phone: 206-488-1133). In eastern Washington, tour Ste. Michelle's older, rustic winery at Grandview (205 W. 5th St., Grandview, WA 90930; phone: 509-882-3928) and its huge, new, state-of-the-art Columbia Crest plant in an elegant château at River Ridge (Rte. 221, Paterson, WA 99345; phone: 509-875-2061). Ste. Michelle's three wineries make more than half of all Washington State wine.

COLUMBIA WINERY: The blue Victorian gingerbread building across the road from Château Ste. Michelle is a touch of luxury for this respected winery, which was formerly in a warehouse. (Columbia took over the building from Haviland in 1988.) The winery offers tours and tastings of varietals, including merlot, chardonnay, and semillon. Information: Columbia Winery, 14030 NE 145th St., PO Box 1248, Woodinville, WA 98072 (phone: 206-488-2776).

SNOQUALMIE: A short excursion from Seattle into the wooded western foothills of the Cascades (no grapes grow here either) takes you past spectacular waterfalls to this modern chalet winery with an eagle's eye view of the Snoqualmie River Valley. You'll see the latest wine making equipment at work and sample their unique, dry, Alsatian-style gewürztraminer by a comfy fire. Information: Snoqualmie, 1000 Winery Rd., Snoqualmie, WA 98065 (phone: 206-888-4000).

For a Washington winery guide, mail a self-addressed, stamped (45¢ postage) envelope to the Washington Wine Institute, 1932 1st Ave., Room 510, Seattle, WA 98105 (phone: 206-441-1892).

OREGON

The hard-to-please Pinot noir grape is the new pride of Oregon, having found ideal growing conditions in vineyards next to the familiar hazelnut groves, berry patches, and orchards. In fact, wine is being made all up and down the state. From Portland it's a short drive to the lush Willamette Valley to taste Pinot, chardonnay, and Riesling in small, friendly wineries.

KNUDSON ERATH: Even at Oregon's biggest winery, you need an appointment for a guided tour. Or simply drop by to sample the prizewinning Pinot and traditional whites, and admire the vine-covered hillsides from the tasting room patio. Information: Knudson Erath, 17000 NE Knudsen La., Dundee, OR 97115 (phone: 503-538-3318).

SOKOL BLOSSER: A noted architect designed this concrete winery built into the hillside. There's a generous tasting, a picnic pavilion, and a sweeping view of the Willamette Valley. Taste anytime, but make an appointment if you want a tour. Information: Sokol Blosser, 5000 NE Sokol Blosser La., PO Box 399, Dundee, OR 97115 (phone: 503-864-2282).

For an Oregon winery guide, contact the Oregon Winegrowers Association, 1359 W. 5th St., Eugene, OR 97402 (phone: 503-343-4078).

HILLCREST VINEYARD: Richard Sommer,the father of Oregon's modern winegrowing industry, is famous for his gewürztztraminer and Johannisberg Riesling. Tastings of these and other varietals are held in his modern-rustic winery in the rolling hills of the Umpqua River valley in Southern Oregon. Visitors can take the guided tour or look down on the winery operation from the deck. Lovely picnic area. Information, Hillcrest Vineyard, 240 Vineyard La., Roseberg, OR 97470 (phone: 503-673-3709).

AROUND THE COUNTRY

The welcome mat is out at wineries in half the states in the US. Check with state and local tourism organizations for winery guides. Some places close in winter, many receive on weekends only, and some require appointments. Phone ahead.

TEXAS

Fine red and white varietal wines are making news in the hill country near Austin and San Antonio and on the high plains around Lubbock in West Texas. Names to note: *Oberhellman Vineyards,* HC 61, Box 22, Fredericksburg, TX 78624 (phone: 512-685-3297); *Fall Creek Vineyards,* 1111 Guadalupe St., Austin, TX 78701 (phone: 512-476-

4477); *Slaughter Leftwich,* at 4300 Eck La. in Lake Travis (Box 22F, Austin, TX 78734; phone: 512-266-3331); *Llano Estacado Winery,* Box 3487, Lubbock, TX 79452 (phone: 806-745-2258).

OHIO

Fairs and festivals are a traditional part of wine touring in country that has produced native American grapes for generations. To tour the string of new wineries specializing in European varietals, drive along Lake Erie between Sandusky and Conneaut. Picturesque pre-Prohibition wineries can be found in the "wine islands" (Bass Islands) on Lake Erie, reachable by ferry from Port Clinton. Names to note: in the Lake Erie area, *Chalet Debonné Vineyards,* 7743 Doty Rd., Madison, OH 44057 (phone: 216-466-3485); in the wine islands, *Lonz,* Middle Bass Island, OH 43446 (phone: 419-285-5411) and *Heineman,* PO Box 300, Put-in-Bay, OH 43456 (phone: 419-285-2811); in the Cincinnati area, *Meier's Wine Cellar,* 6955 Plainfield Heights, Silverton, OH 45236 (phone: 513-891-2900).

VIRGINIA

From Washington, DC, it's less than a 2-hour drive to the gentle Albemarle wine country near Charlottesville, where small country vintners produce fine varietals, including some of the East Coast's better cabernets and merlots. At least 30 wineries from the Alleghenies to the eastern shore welcome visitors. Names to note: *Oakencroft Vineyards and Winery,* 2 Boar's Head La., Charlottesville, VA 22901 (phone: 804-296-4188); *Montdomaine Cellars,* Rte. 6, Box 188A, Charlottesville, VA 22901 (phone: 804-971-8947); *Meredyth Vineyards,* PO Box 347, Rte. 628, Middleburgh, VA 22117 (phone 703-687-6277).

PENNSYLVANIA

The bucolic southeast corner of the state is the home of beautiful old wineries making native American wines and newcomer European varietals. Names to note: in New Hope, *Bucks County Vineyards,* RD 3, Box 167, New Hope, PA 18938 (phone: 215-794-7449); in the Brandywine River valley, *Chaddsford Winery,* Rte. 1, Box 229, Chaddsford, PA 19317 (phone: 215-388-6221); in Amish Country, *Mount Hope Winery,* Rte. 72 in Manheim (PO Box 685, Cornwall, PA 17016; phone: 717-665-7021).

Vacations on Farms and Ranches

 In the country, city people rediscover the sound of songbirds and the smell of grass. Suburbanites get the chance to poke around an area where the nearest neighbors live miles away. Parents can say to their children, "No, milk does not start out in cartons" — and then prove it. Youngsters can see people who live differently, think differently, and have different values. But even if there were no lessons to be learned, a stay at a farm or ranch would be a decidedly pleasant way to pass a couple of weeks, so it's no wonder that all over the country there are hundreds of farms and ranches welcoming guests.

No two are quite alike. On the one hand, there are the guest farms and dude ranches with tennis courts, fancy swimming pools, square dances, hayrides, jam-packed recreation programs, and the like; guests are the main business. On the other hand, there are family farms and working ranches where raising animals or crops is the central activity, and the owners take guests only to bring in extra money.

In the sampling below, inexpensive means you'll pay about $135 to $250 per person per week, moderate about $250 to $400, and expensive about $400 and up. However, sometimes the rates include unlimited use of facilities and all the riding you want — and sometimes one or more of the activities cost extra. Most places include three meals a day in their rates. Be sure to find out exactly what's included when you price the ranches.

For a comprehensive description of farms and ranches of all kinds, plus addresses, phone numbers, rates, size, activities, and previous guests' comments, see Pat Dickerman's *Farm, Ranch & Country Vacations* ($13 postpaid from Farm & Ranch Vacations, 36 E. 57th St., New York, NY 10022; phone: 212-355-6334); for western ranches, Dickerman can also dispense advice and make reservations. Herewith, a short list of some of the most typical.

FAMILY FARMS

RODGERS DAIRY FARM, West Glover, Vermont: About 35 miles from the Canadian border in Vermont's unspoiled Northeast Kingdom, three generations of the Rodgers family run a 350-acre dairy farm on the same property which their Scottish ancestors settled in the early 1800s — and provide lodgings to city folk in a century-old, 17-room, white clapboard farmhouse surrounded by maple-shaded lawns ringed with an old-fashioned split-rail fence. Daytimes, you can watch the cows being milked by machine and learn to ride the pony and to reach under the clucking hens to gather eggs — scary but fun. You can make friends with the dogs and the kittens, pull weeds in the gardens, and gather vegetables which will appear on the big dinner table within the hour. If it's haying time you can help pick up bales of hay, stack them on the haywagons, and unload them in the barn. Or, if you want, you can drive a few miles to Shadow Lake for a swim, or to Barton, 12 miles away, to see what it's like to be in a town with 1,051 inhabitants (many more than in the villages of Glover and West Glover, pop. 650, combined), take in an auction or two, or just sit in lawn chairs under the maple trees. Information: James and Nancy Rodgers, Rodgers Dairy Farm, RFD 3, Box 57, West Glover, VT 05875 (phone: 802-525-6677). Moderate.

WILSON'S PINTO BEAN FARM, Yellow Jacket, Colorado: Everything at this southwestern Colorado establishment is comfortable and homey — but don't expect luxury: The trailer guests occupy is not a late model, and the three guest rooms in the farmhouse are not large. Yet to visit Esther, Art, and the Wilson children (in their teens and twenties) is to experience real, honest-to-goodness farm life — 1,100 acres of pinto beans, wheat, and alfalfa; an assortment of farm animals; and a shed with the huge modern farm machinery used for planting and harvesting crops. The Wilsons grow much of their own food, and Esther's home-churned butter, home-baked bread, kosher dills, sweet pickle chips, apricot jam, and chokecherry jelly turn up on the big family table like clockwork, along with apple, cherry, and plum pies. Biking and horseshoe pitching are favorite activities, as is hiking to Canyon Pasture, where you can see the remains of a settlement, now overgrown with sagebrush, that once housed more people than similar, better-preserved structures at nearby Mesa Verde National Park (see *National Parks,* DIRECTIONS). Also nearby in the red earth country of the Four Corners region are the Hovenweep and Canyon de Chelly National Monument. Open March through November. Information: Arthur and Esther Wilson, PO Box 252, Yellow Jacket, CO 81335 (phone: 303-562-4476). Inexpensive.

DUDE RANCHES

RANCHO DE LOS CABALLEROS, Wickenburg, Arizona: Visitors can take their pick of 74 horses to lead and speed along the sandy desert trails of Wickenburg. A country club atmosphere pervades "Los Cab," with its 7,000-yard golf course, 4 tennis courts, and a swimming pool. Accommodations in 74 3- and 4-unit casitas. Information: Rancho de los Caballeros, Box 1148, Wickenburg, AZ 85358 (phone: 602-684-5484). Expensive.

WHITE STALLION, Tucson, Arizona: Yot get the feeling of wide-open spaces on this 3,000-acre spread northwest of Tucson, at the foot of the rugged Tucson Mountains, within a 100,000-acre game preserve. The *White Stallion* is the only guest ranch in the area that can also claim a longhorn cattle operation — but riding is the point here — owners Allen and Cynthia True raise quarter horses, and once a week the cowboys stage a rodeo in the ranch arena. Wranglers will take you into the saguaro-dotted desert around the ranch house up to four times a day. And when you are not on horseback, the time is filled with hayrides, barbecues and cookouts, shuffleboard, and hikes. Or you can stake out a spot at poolside or in the cozy library, or visit the hot tub therapy room, or have a round of golf nearby, or a game of tennis on the ranch's Laykold courts. There's even a petting zoo. Everyone is on a first-name basis; the place is friendly and very informal, despite the size (about 45 guests). Open October through the first Sunday in May. Information: Allen and Cynthia True, White Stallion Ranch, 9251 W. Twin Peaks Rd., Tucson, AZ 85743 (phone: 602-297-0252). Expensive.

WICKENBURG INN, Wickenburg, Arizona: Under new management, this 15-year-old operation has expanded its riding program under wrangler Susan O'Day Brown and now has 80 horses, including 10 gaited horses. Other facilities include 11 all-weather tennis courts, an observatory, and 2 nearby golf courses. Nature hikes and arts and crafts make this a great place for kids. Six lodge rooms and 41 whitewashed casitas, with fireplaces and kitchenettes. Information: Wickenburg Inn, Box P, Wickenburg, AZ 85358 (phone: 602-684-7811). Expensive.

SAN YSIDRO RANCH, Montecito, California – Aptly called the ranch of the stars — Steve Martin, Bruce Springstein, and Barbra Streisand have been guests — it has undergone a remodeling and added a restaurant, *Stonehouse*, under the direction of French chef Marc Ehrler. Trails afford spectacular views of the the Pacific and the Santa Ynez Mountains. There are only 8 horses — many guests bring their own. The 43 cottages feature fireplaces, deckside Jacuzzis, and the occupant's name carved in a wooden sign by the door. Information: San Ysidro, 900 San Ysidro La., Montecito, CA 93108 (phone: 805-969-5046). Expensive.

C LAZY U, Granby, Colorado: This establishment, at about 8,200 feet just west of the Continental Divide, is the real thing: a working ranch as well as the western version of a country inn, with warm hospitality and all the amenities. The emphasis is on horseback riding, and guests are given their own personal mounts to ride during their stay. But other horsing around also figures: ranch riding competitions and rodeos, to be specific. The *C Lazy U* is also a guest ranch, though, and so you'll find a heated pool, a whirlpool bath and sauna, tennis and racquetball courts, a skeet-shooting range, Ping-Pong tables, and miles of trails for hiking (and cross-country skiing in winter). And if that won't keep you busy, you can always go fishing — or just take a drive through the mountains. The large lodge, which faces a lake where you can ice skate in winter, is surrounded by guest cottages. All the rooms are cozy and comfortable; the food is solid and plentiful; and evenings are convivial. Information: C Lazy U Ranch, PO Box 378, Granby, CO 80446 (phone: 303-887-3344). Expensive.

COLORADO TRAILS, Durango, Colorado: See the Old West, hear its tales, and get the flavor of cowboy life — and at the same time lodge in a tidy little cabin with your own bath, carpeting, and electric heat, at this 525-acre mountain ranch just outside Durango, in the southwestern corner of Colorado. With up to 75 other vacationers, you can take riding lessons (the horse operation is one of the best of its kind); go on trail rides and hayrides and overnight trips; swim in a heated pool; lounge in the whirlpool bath; play tennis; fish for trout; shoot arrows, shotguns, and rifles; water-ski on 10-mile-distant Vallecito Lake; or square dance. The staff puts on chuck wagon dinners, variety and music shows, and powwows around the campfire. But there's never any pressure to do anything, and though sing-alongs may at first seem corny, somehow everyone ends up enjoying them. Counselors take groups of kids off for riding and other activities each day; the arrangement seems to give each generation just the right amount of time together and apart. Open June to early September; plan to reserve several months in advance. Information: Ginny and Dick Elder, Colorado Trails Ranch, PO Box 848E, Durango, CO 81302 (phone: 303-247-5055, or 800-323-3823). Expensive.

HOME RANCH, Clark, Colorado: The only ranch among the 12 Relais et Châteaux properties in the US, it offers 6 rooms in the main lodge, 7 spruce-log cabins, and 40 horses for trail and pack riding. Other activities include hiking, fly fishing, and swimming. The new chef hails from the *Elk Canyon Ranch* in Montana; his hearty fare is served family style. Cabin rooms are furnished with antiques, Indian rugs, and down comforters. Information: Home Ranch, Box 822, Clark, CO 80428 (phone: 303-879-1780). Expensive.

LONE MOUNTAIN RANCH, Big Sky, Montana: A 100-horse guest ranch in summer, a cross-country ski resort in winter, it encompasses 4,000 acres in the Spanish Peaks Wilderness Area. Trail rides, limited to seven riders, vary in difficulty and often lead up into remote wilderness settings for campfire lunches beside a lake. On site are 20 cabins with fireplaces, electric heat, private baths, and queen-size beds, plus a 12-person hot tub and a saloon. On any given night, dinner might feature barbecued steaks with a flambéed dessert. Restless dudes have several options: group excursions to Yellowstone, trout fishing runs on the Gallatin River, float trips on the Madison and Yellowstone rivers, and tours of the *Museum of the Rockies* in Bozeman. Information: Lone Mountain, Box 69, Big Sky, MT 58716 (phone: 406-995-4644). Expensive.

PARADISE GUEST RANCH, Buffalo, Wyoming: Nestled in a valley at the edge of the Big Horn National Forest, the aptly named *Paradise* offers "accessible seclusion." Guests here are matched with a horse suitable to their riding ability for the duration of their stay. Scheduled rides — with wranglers — range from 1-hour, half-, and full-day outings to 3- or 4-day pack trips. There is a dining room with a lively atmosphere which serves ample portions of stick-to-your-ribs home-style cooking, a saloon with live entertainment, and a spacious meeting room. Cozy 1-, 2-, and 3-bedroom log cabins are complete with outdoor deck, fireplace, dining area, and a small kitchen area. Activities include hiking, fishing, swimming in a heated pool, spa, chuckwagon cookouts, talent shows, history and nature talks, square dances, and special programs for children, including a campout in the hills ("parents' night off"). Minimum stay is 1 week; ask about special rates for children. Information: Jim and Leah Anderson, PO Box 790, Buffalo, WY 82834 (phone: 307-684-7876). Expensive.

WORKING RANCHES

VISTA VERDE, Clark, Colorado: Owned by a couple of displaced New Yorkers, this 600-acre working ranch provides "dudes" with such creature comforts as a Jacuzzi and mints on the pillows. There's riding daily, yet with pleasant interruptions: Colorado River rafting, ballooning from nearby Steamboat Springs, and hiking. Dinners are cooked by Jacques Wilson, a creative Jamaican who works in Palm Springs during the winter. Eight roomy log cabins, with daily maid service. Information: Vista Verde, Box 465, Steamboat Springs, CO 80477 (phone: 303-879-3858). Expensive.

G BAR M, Clyde Park, Montana: One of the few remaining cattle ranches in the West to cleave to the old lifestyle and welcome vacationers, this establishment in the Bridger Mountain foothills just east of Bozeman has 3,300 acres mainly given over to cattle, plus four rooms in the ranch house and two outlying log cabins fitted out for visitors. Riding, of course, is the main feature; you'll go out to check fence and water holes, help doctor calves that got too curious about porcupines, carry salt to the cattle on summer range in the high country, and so on; and George Leffingwell, the owner, puts even the most inexperienced rider at ease. Because part of the ranch is a private game sanctuary, you'll often see mule deer, golden eagles, and coyotes, along with moose, elk, and bear on occasion. You can also go fishing or hiking, hunt fossils, and photograph wildflowers. Once every week there's an all-day ride and on Saturday nights there's music and a steak fry. Otherwise, you won't find much of an activities program — and most people like it that way: "It's like coming home after being away for a long time," one visitor explains. Everyone — ranch family, vacationers, and ranch hands — has meals (including breakfasts of sourdough pancakes and chokecherry syrup) together, and in the course of mealtime talk, you'll learn about the area's history and ecology, the economics of operating a cattle ranch, and the independent spirit of the Western rancher. Open from mid-May to mid-September. Information: the Leffingwells, the G Bar M Ranch, PO Box AE, Clyde Park, MT 59018 (phone: 406-686-4687). Moderate.

HALTER, Big Sandy, Montana: In the center of the Missouri River Wilderness Waterway, 80 miles east of Great Falls, Montana, the Halter family raises cattle, horses, hay, and barley on 3,000 acres of meadows and rugged breaks along the White Cliffs of the Missouri River, described in Lewis and Clark's journal. Gay Halter Pearson and her husband, Ron, will show you how to ride, or take you on overnight trail rides or trips in inner tubes down the Judith River. Gay's father, Jerry Halter, who is active in efforts to make the area a wild river waterway, can regale you with tales of the homesteads, forts, and Indian ruins in the area, some of which you'll see when (ranch work permitting) he takes you on float trips down the Missouri. All the guests — usually one family at a time, never more than two — seem to fit easily into the Halters' life, and they're exceptional people. Open from April into November. Information: Gay Halter Pearson, Box 408, Big Sandy, MT 59520 (phone: 406-378-2549). Moderate.

DEER FORKS, Douglas, Wyoming: It takes about an hour to drive through the rangelands of eastern Wyoming from the town of Douglas to the 5,900-acre spread where the Middleton family grazes cows, grows hay, and welcomes guests. The two rustic housekeeping cabins with private baths and fully equipped kitchens where guests stay are quite comfortable. You can eat in these guesthouses or, if you prefer, share some meals with Ben and Pauli Middleton and their two children; the fare usually includes beef from the family's cattle, vegetables from their garden, and homemade breads and pies. Besides the milk cows, there are plenty of animals here to delight children — lambs, cats, even a cowdog (an Australian shepherd with an instinctive ability to herd cattle). If you can ride, you may be rounding up cows from the far corners of this mountainous ranch, and if you can't, you'll soon learn how. Hiking, arrowhead-hunting, and trout fishing will also keep you busy. Also, depending on the season, you may find yourself stacking bales of hay, separating steers from heifers, or helping the vet do pregnancy tests. One day you may drive in to see the rodeo, or state fair, or a cattle auction; another, you may join the Middletons and their friends and relatives for a branding. Open year-round. Information: Ben and Pauli Middleton, Deer Forks Ranch, Rte. 6, 1200 Poison Lake Rd., Douglas, WY 82633 (phone: 307-358-2033). Moderate to inexpensive.

A Short Tour of Indian America

When people discuss early American history, their starting point is usually the 17th or 18th century, and the founding of Jamestown, the colonial settlements, or George Washington and the heroics of the American Revolution. But long before any of this took place, long before the white man ever arrived, the real history of this country was the story of the American Indian. During the period of the last glaciation, some 25,000 to 50,000 years ago, the area that is now the Bering Strait was a broad plain about 1,000 miles wide. Nomadic peoples wandered across this land bridge from Siberia into what is now Alaska. Before them stretched a vast uninhabited land, as diverse as it was silent, from the frozen ice caps of the north to the primordial swamp of the southeastern tropics. These people roamed freely over the land and truly discovered what we have come to call North America. They lived in direct and respectful relationship to the soil. In the far North, they became ice hunters. In the rich forests of the North, hunting bands tracked the caribou, deer, beaver, and small fur-bearing animals. In the eastern woodlands and warm southeastern region, agriculture reached a high stage of development and was the center of ceremonial life. The Great Plains was inhabited by both farmers and hunters, people who would become great warriors after the introduction of the horse in 1750. Along the Pacific coast settled tribes who were primarily fishermen. The culture of native North America reached its most sophisticated point among the Pueblo, who lived in communal villages in the Southwest and developed a hardy strain of maize capable of surviving in this arid region.

All of these people came to be known as Indians, for no better reason than that Christopher Columbus, landing one day in Santo Domingo, thought he was in the Indies, off the coast of Asia. As the Indians settled in different parts of North America, they adopted diverse lifestyles; but they remained fundamentally similar in many ways. They were a most remarkably resourceful people. Isolated from the rest of the world, they not only survived on their own, but they created rich cultures around the mysteries and miracles of nature. In addition to the wide variety of maize grown by different tribes, Indians developed pumpkins, beans, squash, tobacco, potatoes, sweet potatoes, chocolate, tomatoes, vanilla, and peanuts — all native and unique to this continent. The different tribes spoke their own languages, and though these may have derived from several parent tongues, at one time at least 200 mutually unintelligible languages were spoken by the American people. In these languages, the Indians told stories of the wonders of creation. The Navajo mythology involves a series of ascents through different worlds inhabited by spirits and beings of both good and evil. The story of emergence from the Black World that was "darker than the darkness of all the moonless nights of many winters" is as beautiful and rich as the story of Adam and Eve. Other tribes created their own legends, songs, dances, and ceremonies. Some lived in fear of nature, others praised its benevolence, but all reacted to it directly, channeling tremendous amounts of physical and emotional energy into their rituals. In New Mexico the Indians painted a series of murals with iron oxide to glorify nature. Elsewhere in the Southwest, they built subterranean chambers of worship, called kivas. In the Southeast, immense ceremonial mounds of earth were filled with sculpture, and many stand today, still protecting the secrets of the rituals for which they were created.

The European explorers who came to the Americas in the 16th, 17th, and 18th centuries came for conquest, and with their arrival, the story of the American Indian takes a tragic turn; it becomes, to a great extent, a tale of exploitation. In 1492, Columbus sailed to the New World and encountered the Indians; he remarked on the "artless and generous quality" they had "to such a degree as no one would believe but he who had seen it." In return for their good will, Columbus sent 600 Indians back to Spain to work as slaves. During the following centuries the Spanish, British, and, in their turn, Americans waged nearly constant war against the Indians. There was outright massacre, exemplified by the 1890 incident at Wounded Knee, when 300 unarmed Sioux men, women, and children, gathered to celebrate a Ghost Dance (itself a frenetic ritual which Indians believed would save them from decimation by the white invaders), were surrounded and gunned down by the Seventh Cavalry of the US Army. Less horrific, but just as pernicious, was systematic subjugation by the US government.

In 1835, the Five Civilized Tribes of the East (Cherokee, Seminole, Creek, Choctaw, and Chickasaw) were forcibly relocated to Indian Territory in Oklahoma, only to have most of the land taken away from them by the government for white homesteading after the Civil War. From 1887 to 1934 the General Allotment Act divided communal Indian lands, and reduced the total number of Indian-owned acres in America from 138,000,000 to 48,000,000. Even in pathetic reservation enclaves, civil rights were denied the Indians. (Not until 1968, with the Civil Rights Act, were the provisions of the Bill of Rights extended to reservation Indians.)

Though many tribes have become extinct, the American Indian still survives (with a population of 830,000), a testament to human dignity and endurance. Except in the Southwest, the Indian tribes no longer occupy their original lands, and their members are beset with problems — discrimination, as well as extremely high unemployment and high alcoholism and suicide rates. But the story of the real discoverers of America is not finished. In recent years, many young Native Americans have become radicalized by the plight of their people: In 1969 Indians occupied Alcatraz Island; in 1972 many marched on Washington, presenting the federal government with a list of demands (called the Trail of Broken Treaties paper); and in 1973, Indians occupied the Pine Ridge Reservation on the site of the Wounded Knee Massacre, bringing broad international recognition to their plight.

But improvement in Indian affairs demands more than recognition; the gap is one of understanding that can only be bridged by direct contact. In recent years, this has become possible with the growth of tourism in Indian communities. Even some militant members of Indian society believe that this is a positive trend, one which will allow their tribes to practice their own unique lifestyles while sustaining themselves economically. And so, from the commercialized Seminole reservations in Florida to the settlements in the Southwest, where tribes still inhabit the lands of their ancestors — some of the most beautiful country in America — you can glimpse the complex dances and ceremonies and examine the magnificent handcrafted baskets, jewelry, patchwork, and painting of these ancient civilizations. The cultures that you'll encounter in this Indian America — though at the root of our nation's heritage — are as foreign as those of remotest Egypt and the Orient.

When you enter Indian America, it is best to meet the people on their own terms. Do not take photographs of ceremonies, rituals, or individuals without express permission. Similarly, do not use recording devices, sketch pads, and notebooks. It is advisable to behave as unobtrusively as possible, refraining from applause, loud talking, or even questions about the significance of rituals. In some cases, explanations may be offered. Otherwise it is best to watch what is going on around you and do research before or afterward. Keeping these few things in mind, you will undoubtedly find an adventure in Indian America truly rewarding.

Described below are several highlights of Indian America — reservations and other Indian lands, ceremonies, beautiful natural settings, and excellent museums.

For information about arts and crafts businesses owned and operated by Native Americans, get a copy of the free *Source Directory* published by the Indian Arts & Crafts Board (US Dept. of the Interior, Room 4004, Washington, DC 20240; phone: 202-343-2773).

And for an overview of American Indian heritage, consult the following:

> *Indians of North America,* by Harold E. Driver (University of Chicago Press; $16.95, paperback), a reconstruction of the native American culture with an emphasis on the 20th century and the post-60s era.
>
> *I Have Spoken: American History Through the Voice of the Indians,* edited by Virginia L. Armstrong (Athens, Ohio: Ohio University/Swallow Press; $7.95, paperback).

EAST

MICCOSUKEE TRIBAL ENTERPRISE, near Miami, Florida: Some 550 members of the Miccosukee tribe (which was not officially recognized until 1962) live on this reservation on the northern border of the Everglades National Park. A museum has exhibits tracing the history of the tribe, which shares a language and hunting and fishing techniques with the Seminole, who also live in Florida, and craftspeople are on hand to demonstrate doll making, wood carving, and basketweaving; daily alligator-wrestling shows are presented as well. The lifestyle on the reservation is still fairly traditional. In the school system, English takes second place to Mikasuki, the tribal language. Many Miccosukee live in chickees, which are palmetto thatched-roof dwellings, and some work as artists, making baskets, cypress wood carvings, and clothing of patchwork cloth (available at the Cultural Center). A quarter-mile east of the museum is the Miccosukee restaurant, which serves traditional Indian fare — frybread, pumpkin bread, and catfish — as well as hot dogs, burgers, and such. One of the best times to visit is at the end of December during the annual *Indian Arts Festival,* when musicians and artists and craftsmen from many tribes around the world converge on the reservation to play everything from traditional music to Indian rock. On US 41, 26 miles west of Miami. Information: PO Box 440021, Miami, FL 33144 (phone: 305-223-8380 or 305-223-8388); Florida Dept. of Commerce, Div. of Tourism, 107 W. Gaines St., Tallahassee, FL 32399-2000 (phone: 904-487-1462).

CHEROKEE, North Carolina: Adjacent to the Great Smoky Mountains National Park, this beautiful area is the country where the Cherokee lived before they were forcibly relocated to Oklahoma in 1838 along a route now called the Trail of Tears. But some Cherokee remained, hiding in the mountains, and others returned later. Today, this is the center of the Cherokee people, and many work here in the tribal government, in factories that produce moccasins and quilts, and in tourist businesses. One of the best times to visit is in the fall during the *Fall Festival,* when Cherokee from all over return home and participate in traditional dances, games, and arts and crafts demonstrations. The event customarily begins the Tuesday of the first full week in October. For exact dates, check with the Cherokee Visitor Center, PO Box 465, Cherokee, NC 28719 (phone: 704-497-9195; 800-438-1601 in the eastern US; 800-222-6157 in NC). Of interest at Cherokee are the following.

Oconaluftee Indian Village – This replica of a Cherokee village depicts the life of the 18th century, with guided tours. Included are a seven-sided council house, ceremonial chambers, and lectures at various sites where members of the tribe, dressed in authentic costumes, demonstrate crafts, cooking, and weapon making. Open mid-May through October. Off Rte. 441 on Drama Rd. For a little more history come to life, see the drama *Unto These Hills,* which recounts the story of the Cherokee people in an amphitheater during the summer (see *Outdoor Dramas*). Mountainside Theater on Drama Rd. Information: Oconaluftee Indian Village, Cherokee, NC 28719 (phone: 704-497-2315 or 704-497-2111).

Museum of the Cherokee Indian – Owned by the Eastern Band of Cherokee Indians, this museum has multimedia theaters and innovative exhibitions, including a new hands-on exhibit for small children, that focus on the history of the tribe with examples of clothing and implements used for farming, hunting, and fishing. Open daily year-round. Admission charge. On Drama Rd. Information: Museum of the Cherokee Indian, PO Box 770A, Cherokee, NC 28719 (phone: 704-497-3481).

Qualla Arts and Crafts Mutual – Best of the area's many craft shops, this is the official cooperative marketing center of the Cherokee. The work is authentic, and many items here are rarely available elsewhere, such as white oak, river cane, and honeysuckle vine baskets, animal sculptures made of buckeye, walnut, and wild cherry, pottery, and beadwork. Write or call for their $2 color catalogue. Rte. 441 near the museum. Information: Qualla Arts and Crafts Mutual, PO Box 277, Cherokee, NC 28719 (phone: 704-497-3103).

WEST

Some 17 million acres in northeastern Arizona and neighboring New Mexico and Utah form the Navajo nation, the largest Indian reservation in America. The Navajo are the most populous of the Indian tribes, with over 200,000 members, many of whom live in traditional dwellings called hogans, octagonal houses built of logs, cemented with clay, and covered with earth. The Navajo were primarily a pastoral rather than agricultural people, but they did pick up farming, weaving, and sand painting from the Pueblo.

WINDOW ROCK, Arizona: The town is the seat of Navajo tribal government and is a good place to begin a trip into Navajoland. You can view displays about the tribe's history and culture at the *Tribal Museum;* learn a bit about how the Navajo see their environment and live in harmony with it at the Navajo Zoological Park; shop for crafts at the *Navajo Arts and Crafts Enterprise;* and take any number of excursions into the surrounding countryside. The Navajoland Tourism Office within the Navajo Division of Resources can suggest destinations and give you dates for various events and activities. Among the biggest festivities are the *Navajo Nation Fair,* staged in Window Rock the first Wednesday through Sunday after Labor Day, and the Fourth of July celebration and PRCA rodeo, held annually during the July Fourth weekend from Thursday through Sunday. The *Navajo Nation Inn's* restaurant offers southwestern dishes like Navajo tacos and frybread (phone: 602-871-4108). Information: Navajoland Tourism Office, PO Box 308, DOR Bldg., Window Rock, AZ 86515 (phone: 602-871-4941, ext. 1436/7).

MONUMENT VALLEY NAVAJO TRIBAL PARK, Arizona and Utah: The valley is a classic western scenic wonder with high mesas, sculptured buttes, natural bridges, earth arches, chiseled canyons and gorges, huge sandstone monoliths, and has been used in filming innumerable Westerns, including a few early John Wayne films. A 17-mile road (a 1½- to 2-hour drive) winds its way through the valley and can be negotiated by most cars, except during the winter, when four-wheel-drive vehicles are advisable. Visitors should not photograph the Navajo or their possessions without permission. Camping is available at the park headquarters, where there is also a Navajo arts and crafts shop. 25 miles north of Kayenta off Rte. 163. Information: Box 93, Monument Valley Tribal Park, UT 84536 (phone: 801-727-3287).

NAVAJO NATIONAL MONUMENT, Tonalea, Arizona: The largest and most intricate of Arizona's cliff dwellings are preserved in this rugged country. There are two areas, each of which contains a remarkable 13th-century pueblo ruin. Betatakin Area is the site of the monument headquarters, and the visitor center offers exhibitions on the Anasazi culture, a slide show and film, a Navajo arts and crafts shop, and a campground. Betatakin is the more accessible of the areas, and the ruin across the canyon may be viewed from a half-mile-long foot trail or visited on a 3-mile (round-trip), 4-hour guided hike (daily in summer; no tours in winter). The other area, Keet Seel, may be reached on horseback (reserve in advance at headquarters) or by a strenuous 8-mile hike, also in summer only. Call first for tour information and winter weather conditions. 28 miles west of Kayenta off Rte. 160. Information: Navajo National Monument, HC-71, PO Box 3, Tonalea, AZ 86044-9704 (phone: 602-672-2366).

HUBBELL TRADING POST NATIONAL HISTORIC SITE, Ganado, Arizona: Dating to the 1870s, this is the oldest continuously active trading post on the Navajo reservation. The post and Hubbell home depict the life of an unusual trader and his family, and have displays on the history of the area, and beautiful Navajo sand paintings, handwoven rugs, silver work, and other jewelry. The National Park Service runs guided tours of the site, and there are usually Navajo weaving and silversmithing demonstrations at the Visitor Center. 1 mile west of Ganado on Rte. 264. Information: Hubbell Trading Post National Historic Site, PO Box 150, Ganado, AZ 86505 (phone: 602-755-3475).

FIRST, SECOND, AND THIRD MESA, Arizona: The Hopi are exceptional jewelry makers and farmers and live in a close communal relationship in apartment villages on three isolated ridges of land high above the northeastern Arizona desert. The best place to stay is on the Second Mesa, at the *Hopi Cultural Center,* which has a motel, museum, and restaurant where traditional Hopi foods such as hominy stew, frybread, and *piki* are served along with hamburgers and such. At the *Hopi Arts and Crafts Guild,* you can purchase the finest of Hopi crafts — silver jewelry, pottery, kachina dolls, and baskets. The studio of Charles Loloma, the most prominent contemporary Indian jeweler, and Old Oraibi, the oldest continuously occupied village in the US, are on the Third Mesa. A variety of ceremonies are open to visitors, but the exact dates are usually not announced till very close to the event, so check at the cultural center. Motel reservations should be made at least 3 weeks in advance. Rte. 264 at Piñon Rd., 4 miles northwest of Rte. 87. Information: Hopi Cultural Center, PO Box 67, Second Mesa, AZ 86043 (phone: 602-734-2401).

Nowhere in the United States do you get a better sense of the Indian past than among the Pueblo, the desert peoples of New Mexico. The aridity of the climate has left many ancient ruins intact, and the tribes live among them on the land of their ancestors in pueblos, communal villages of adobe or sandstone dwellings that blend unobtrusively into their surroundings. The pueblos described below are within driving distance of Santa Fe or Albuquerque.

ACOMA, New Mexico: Perhaps the most spectacular of the pueblos, this village sits on a 367-foot-high mesa, commanding a panoramic view of the New Mexico plain. The pueblo has been inhabited for some 1,000 years, and though many of the families have homes in nearby farming villages, Acoma is open to visitors year-round except during religious ceremonies. Among the buildings are the mission of San Esteban, established in 1629 and constructed of adobe walls 10 to 14 feet thick; a subterranean ceremonial chamber known as a kiva on the main plaza (off-limits to visitors); and several small craft shops where delicate Acoma pottery with geometric and bird pattern motifs can be purchased for prices lower than at trading posts elsewhere. Tribal members lead tours daily. Small admission charge and photographic fee. On I-40, Exit 102, 60 miles west of Albuquerque. Information: PO Box 309, Pueblo of Acoma, NM 87034 (phone: 505-252-1139).

TAOS, New Mexico: Sitting at the base of the Sangre de Cristo range, which culminates in New Mexico's highest point, the Taos pueblo is a stronghold of tribal tradition. The people are devout in their religious observances, and subsist as farmers. Near the multistoried adobe dwelling, craftsmen display moccasins and drums as well as mica clay pottery. The *San Geronimo Fiesta* in late September is open to the public and features extraordinary dancing, a greased-pole climbing contest, and other festivities. The town of Taos, 2½ miles south, is primarily an artists' colony, and the work of residents and of other artists is displayed at some 55 galleries all over town. Area information: Taos County Chamber of Commerce, Drawer I, Taos, NM 87571 (phone: 505-758-3873 or 800-732-8267).

Once dominant on the northern plains, the Sioux — nomadic buffalo hunters who lived in conical tents of animal hide called tipis — were the prototype for the American Indian image. Today, the buffalo no longer roam, and the tribe is beset with economic problems, but the Sioux still maintain their dignity. The area is not highly developed commercially, but if you do visit, the rewards will be great.

OGLALA SIOUX TRIBE, PINE RIDGE RESERVATION, South Dakota: This 2.3-million acre reservation — the site of the 1890 Wounded Knee massacre in which some 300 unarmed Sioux were slaughtered (a tragedy later commemorated by a simple gravesite) — is now the home of nearly 19,000 Lakota. You can visit the Red Cloud Indian School, 4 miles north of Pine Ridge, where there are exhibits on the Lakota culture and displays of fine Lakota art: beadwork, quillwork (an intricate type of weaving employing porcupine quills), and magnificent paintings on buffalo hide that display a visionary quality; despite the fact that life in the past (not to mention the present) was beset by tragedy, they depict a happy life that might again be. The Tribal Office can provide information about powwows to which the public is welcome, among which is the *Oglala Nation Fair.* Held the last week of July, it is a celebration of both honor and achievement that involves much traditional drumming, elaborate dancing, and a parade. There are also other powwows and rodeos throughout the summer. The reservation is 120 miles south of Rapid City on Rte. 18. Information: Oglala Sioux Tribe, PO Box H, Pine Ridge, SD 57770 (phone: 605-867-5821).

MUSEUMS

HEARD MUSEUM OF ANTHROPOLOGY AND PRIMITIVE ARTS, Phoenix, Arizona: One of the world's best, this museum founded in the late 1920s focuses on the native cultures of the Southwest. The museum's award-winning exhibit "Native Peoples of the Southwest" serves as its centerpiece and is the largest exhibit of its kind in North America. Tracing the history of the region from 15,000 BC to the present, its many displays include everything from prehistoric pottery vessels to contemporary Navajo textiles. A special gallery features most of the museum's collection of Hopi kachina dolls — perhaps its best-known collection — many of which were donated by Barry Goldwater. These painted and feathered dolls, according to Hopi lore, are handed to children by the kachina spirits, who represent ancestors and things of nature. The museum also has exhibitions of jewelry, baskets, textiles, ceramics, and artifacts of the area's ancient inhabitants. Of a pair of additional galleries devoted to changing shows, one focuses on contemporary Native American fine art — the museum is one of the leading institutions of its kind concerned with the work of today's artists and craftsmen — while the other compares this native culture to others around the world. Information: Heard Museum, 22 E. Monte Vista Rd., Phoenix, AZ 85004 (phone: 602-252-8840 or, for recorded information, 602-252-8848).

WHEELWRIGHT MUSEUM OF THE AMERICAN INDIAN, Santa Fe, New Mexico: Changing exhibits focus on the history, culture, and art of Native Americans. The museum is modeled after a traditional Navajo residence, the eight-sided hogan. At the heart of the permanent collection are the stunning Klah and Manuelito sand painting tapestries. Downstairs is the museum's gift shop, a re-created 19th-century trading post where Indian arts and crafts of exceptional quality are for sale. Information: Wheelwright Museum, 704 Camino Lejo, PO Box 5153, Santa Fe, NM 87502 (phone: 505-982-4636).

MUSEUM OF THE AMERICAN INDIAN, New York, New York: One of the world's largest anthropological museums, this institution houses an immense, uniquely representative collection of the artifacts of the aboriginal peoples of North, Central, and South America; it ranks among the world's biggest such collections and represents everything from precious ornaments to commonplace tools, from paleo-Indian projectile points to abstract paintings by contemporary Indian artists, covering the hemisphere from Atlantic to Pacific, from the Arctic to the Antarctic. More than 10,000 artifacts are on display in the public galleries. Temporary exhibits and special programs are scheduled throughout the year. In the gift shop, you can buy original Indian hand-crafted objects as well as books on native American culture. The museum will be taken over by the *Smithsonian Institution* in 1991. Information: Museum of the American Indian, Broadway at 155th St., New York, NY 10032 (phone: 212-283-2420).

SIOUX INDIAN MUSEUM, Rapid City, South Dakota: This fine facility, operated by the Indian Arts and Crafts Board of the Department of the Interior, transmits a feeling for the Sioux past with its collection of 19th-century Sioux artifacts — clothing, games, moccasins, pipe bags, and baby carriers. Another gallery broadens the scope with changing exhibitions, usually shows of contemporary artists from many different tribes. Information: Sioux Indian Museum, PO Box 1504, 515 West Blvd. between Main and St. Joseph Sts., Rapid City, SD 57709 (phone: 605-348-0557).

Dam Nation

 The politics of water and the ecology of America's "big dams" are just beginning to be understood, but the bane of environmentalists can, for all that, make quite a pleasant vacation experience. First of all, dams are clean-lined and beautiful to look at; they're impressively huge. All the bigger ones — including those listed here — offer tours of the powerhouses of pumping stations, or at least have visitors centers with exhibits that explain what the dams do. Often, you can also watch boats being locked through navigation systems or see fish fighting their way up fish ladders to their upstream spawning grounds. And when you've seen the dam, you can enjoy yourself on the huge reservoirs they impound.

GLEN CANYON, near Page, Arizona: Five million cubic yards of concrete, 1,560 feet across, rise 710 feet above the bedrock across the Colorado River between sheer walls of red Navajo sandstone. Behind: Lake Powell, 186 miles long and with more than 1,900 miles of shoreline. You can fish for crappie or striped and largemouth bass; the largest stripers are nearing 40 pounds. Around the lake is the 1¼-million-acre Glen Canyon National Recreation Area. Information: Glen Canyon National Recreation Area, PO Box 1507, Page, AZ 86040 (phone: 602-645-2471).

OROVILLE, Oroville, California: Rising 770 feet above Oroville's business district, this is the highest dam in the US. Lake Oroville, with 162 miles of shoreline, backs up behind the dam and provides good camping, boating, and fishing — for king salmon, rainbow and brown trout, largemouth and smallmouth bass, crappie, bluegill, and catfish. There's a visitors center with an observation tower at 90 Kelly Ridge Rd. Information: Lake Oroville State Recreation Area, 400 Glen Dr., Oroville, CA 95965 (phone: 916-538-2200).

KENTUCKY, near Gilbertsville, Kentucky: The 206-foot height and 8,422-foot length make this structure across the Tennessee River the largest in the TVA system; together with the Barkley Dam on the Cumberland River nearby, it impounds some 220,000 acres of water with 3,400 miles of forested, cove-notched shoreline. Both Kentucky Lake and Lake Barkley are great for crappie and bass fishing as well as catfish, sauger, and bluegill; and a multitude of activities are available at Kenlake, Kentucky Dam Village, and Lake Barkley State Resort Parks, and at the TVA's own 170,000-acre Land Between the Lakes, all on the shores of the two impoundments. Information: Kentucky Dept. of Travel Development, Capitol Plaza Tower, Frankfort, KY 40601 (phone: 502-564-4930 or 800-225-TRIP).

FORT PECK, near Glasgow, Montana: The largest earth-fill dam in the US, the second largest in the world, this $75 million, 21,026-foot-long structure rises 250½ feet above the Missouri River. Fort Peck Lake, with 1,520 miles of shoreline, is the world's fourth largest reservoir. And the Glasgow mayor said it could be built for $1 million!

Information: Chamber of Commerce, 110 5th St. S., Box 832, Glasgow, MT 59230 (phone: 406-228-2222).

HOOVER, Boulder City, Nevada: This 726-foot-high structure, the Western Hemisphere's highest concrete dam, was selected by the American Society of Civil Engineers as one of the country's Seven Modern Wonders of Civil Engineering — and when you take the 528-foot, 52-story elevator ride to the power plant, you'll probably agree. Some 115 miles long, with 822 miles of shoreline when full, Lake Mead (behind the dam) is by volume one of the world's largest manmade reservoirs. Information: Lake Mead National Recreation Area, 601 Nevada Hwy., Boulder City, NV 89005-2426 (phone: 702-293-4041).

JOHN DAY, near Biggs, Oregon: For this $487 million project, the US Army Corps of Engineers rerouted highways and moved a pair of towns and parts of two others (Boardman, Roosevelt, Arlington, and Umatilla, respectively). The most impressive part of a visit is a viewing window in the fish ladder by which adult salmon and steelhead make their way upstream to spawn. But all kind of superlatives apply. Lake Umatilla stretches for about 75 miles behind the dam. Information: The Dalles–John Day Project, Resources Section, PO Box 564, The Dalles, OR 97058 (phone: 503-296-1181).

FLAMING GORGE, near Vernal, Utah: In the Green River's Red Canyon, this $80-million, 502-foot-high dam impounds a 91-mile-long (42,020-acre) reservoir in the Flaming Gorge National Recreation Area — 185,645 acres of bright red and orange rock canyons, rust-colored chimneys and spires, and pine-clad mountains. The recreation area offers 3 marinas, 9 boat ramps, river floating, fishing, numerous campgrounds, etc. Information: Flaming Gorge Ranger District, Ashley National Forest, PO Box 157, Dutch John, UT 84023 (phone: 801-885-3315).

GRAND COULEE, Coulee Dam, Washington: One of the world's largest concrete dams, this one completed in 1942 is higher than a 46-story building and nearly a mile long, used up 11,975,521 cubic yards of concrete, and has a spillway twice as high as Niagara Falls. Yet it's dwarfed by the immense granite cliffs on either side. The spillway is floodlit on summer nights. Recreational opportunities are available in the 100,059-acre Coulee Dam National Recreation Area. Information: Visitors Center, Coulee Dam National Recreation Area, PO Box 620, Grand Coulee, WA 99133 (phone: 509-633-1360).

Historic Canals

 When Charles Dickens traveled through Ohio in the 1840s, he did it on a canal boat — and returned to scribble the tale of the cramped quarters and the odoriferous companionship of the mules brought aboard between stints of pulling.

But until the advent of the railroads, the canals that linked inland cities to lakes and rivers from Maine to Chicago provided the fastest transportation. Then canal boomtowns died out, and many canals (like much of the original Erie Canal, which linked Lake Erie and the Atlantic Ocean) were filled in and paved over or left to crumble.

Still, canals have not been forgotten. Cruising on these wave-free waterways is relaxing, and several short trips are available for only a few dollars a person. Also, *Midlakes Navigation Co.*, PO Box 61, Skaneateles, NY 13152 (phone: 315-685-5722), has 2- and 3-day cruises on the canals of New York State — Champlain, Erie, Oswego, and Seneca-Cayuga. And *American-Canadian Line,* Box 368, Warren, RI 02885 (phone: 401-247-0955; 800-556-7450), runs 12-day trips between Warren, Rhode Island, and Montreal, Quebec, via the Erie and Oswego canals, the Saquenay River, and the St. Lawrence Seaway. The *American Canal Society,* 809 Rathton Rd., York, PA 17403 (phone: 717-843-4035), keeps its members posted on what they can see where with a newsletter (annual membership, $12). Here are a few canal sites you can visit:

EAST

C&D CANAL MUSEUM, Chesapeake City, Maryland: An old stone pumphouse on the Chesapeake and Delaware Canal has working models of a lock, a brief slide show that relates the story of the still-busy 150-year-old canal for which it is named, and a wooden waterwheel, a mechanical marvel fitted out with buckets that transferred water from Back Creek into the canal at the rate of 1.2 million gallons an hour. Information: US Army Corps of Engineers, Chesapeake City Project Office, Chesapeake City, MD 21915 (phone: 301-885-5622).

OLD ERIE CANAL STATE PARK, DeWitt to Rome, New York: Some 35 miles of the celebrated Erie Canal are maintained by the state for recreational use, and in summer you can go hiking and biking, and in winter, snowmobiling. Picnic areas and connecting paths to nearby recreation areas are strategically placed. Information: Central Region–New York State Office of Parks Recreation and Historic Preservation, Rte. 173, Jamesville, NY 13078 (phone: 315-492-1756).

CANAL TOWN MUSEUM, Canastota, New York: This newly expanded museum, in a yellow clapboard building directly across the street from the canal, is filled with artifacts related to canal days, models of canal boats, and displays on Canastota history. Information: Canal Town Museum, PO Box 51, 122 Canal St., Canastota, NY 13032 (phone: 315-697-3451).

ERIE CANAL VILLAGE, Rome, New York: A re-created 1840s canal village, featuring period buildings such as the *New York State Museum of Cheese, Bennett's Tavern,* and the *Harden Carriage Museum,* with over 25 carriages on view. Visitors may also enjoy a horse-drawn packetboat ride down a restored section of the Old Erie Canal or a steam engine train ride on the Fort Bull Railroad. Open mid-May through September. Information: Erie Canal Village, 5789 New London Rd., Rome, NY 13440 (phone: 315-336-6000, ext. 250, or 315-337-3999).

ERIE CANAL MUSEUM, Syracuse, New York: Changing exhibitions of life on the canals are set up in the last surviving building where canal boats were weighed to determine the tolls they'd pay. A full-size canal boat has been reconstructed, participational exhibitions organized, and a weighmaster's office re-created. The archival materials are extensive. Open Tuesdays through Sundays, 10 AM to 5 PM. Group tours available by appointment. Research library open to the public by appointment. Information: Erie Canal Museum, 318 Erie Blvd. E., Syracuse, NY 13202 (phone: 315-471-0593).

ALLEGHENY PORTAGE RAILROAD NATIONAL HISTORIC SITE, Cresson, Pennsylvania: The eastern and western divisions of the state-run Pennsylvania Canal were linked by this railroad. Visitors see some of the stone railroad ties, a quarry where they were made, one of the engine house foundations, a stone bridge, and a full-scale model of a locomotive; demonstrations of stonecutting are presented in summer. A slide program at the visitors center set up in the old *Lemon House Tavern* tells the story. Information: Allegheny Portage Railroad National Historic Site, PO Box 247, Cresson, PA 16630 (phone: 814-886-8176).

CHESAPEAKE AND OHIO CANAL NATIONAL HISTORICAL PARK, Washington, DC, to Cumberland, Maryland: A 1924 flood put an end to the uneven career of this 184-mile-long waterway between Georgetown and Cumberland, Maryland. The woodsy towpath is ideal for hiking and biking; the sections of the canal that aren't dry (22 miles above Georgetown) are great for canoeing. Exhibitions in the visitors center at Great Falls, Maryland, in an old hotel, tell the story. Visitor centers are also in Hancock and Cumberland. Information: C&O Canal National Historical Park, PO Box

4, Sharpsburg, MD 21782 (phone: 301-739-4200; 202-443-0024 in the Washington area).

MIDWEST

ILLINOIS AND MICHIGAN CANAL HEADQUARTERS BUILDING, Lockport, Illinois: What some people call the best-preserved canal town in America has a number of old canal locks (as well as a modern one), a fine 19th-century block of storefronts, some stone sidewalks — and the only canal museum in the US that illustrates the construction, operation, and demise of a single waterway. The Pioneer Settlement, the *Illinois State Museum,* Lockport Gallery, Department of Conservation facilities, and a recreation trail are additional offerings to visitors. Exhibitions relating to the history of the settlement and the lifestyle of the area's pioneers round out the extensive display. Information: Will County Historical Society, 803 S. State St., Lockport, IL 60441 (phone: 815-838-5080).

CANAL FULTON, Canal Fulton, Ohio: A full-size replica of the mule-drawn canal barges that once plied the Ohio-Erie Canal rides you up and down that same waterway today. A small museum adjoins the boat dock. Information: Canal Fulton Heritage Society, PO Box 854, Canal Fulton, OH 44614 (phone: 216-854-3808).

ROSCOE VILLAGE, Coshocton, Ohio: This once-busy 1800s community on the Ohio–Erie Canal is a fine place to get an idea of what rough-and-ready canal life was like. The restored village is open year-round and offers unique shops, old-time crafts, exhibit buildings, fine dining, and a new 51-room country inn. Visit a blacksmith shop, general store, restored period home, and an old-fashioned ice-cream parlor. You can also ride a horse-drawn trolley or canal-boat replica. Many lively special events all year. Festive, quaint Roscoe Village welcomes travelers with 19th-century American hospitality. Information: Roscoe Village, 381 Hill St., Coshocton, OH 43812 (phone: 614-622-9310).

America's Military Academies

From the establishment of West Point in 1802 to the opening of the Air Force Academy in April 1954, the academies have always provided a variety of spectacles from pomp-and-circumstance full-dress parades to museums of military equipment, cannon, and guns. The grounds are manicured, delightful for walking; the settings usually breathtaking. Be sure to time your visit to catch a parade; and ask about athletic events and guided tours which are often available.

US AIR FORCE ACADEMY, Colorado Springs, Colorado: After you've seen the visitors center and its displays about cadet life, a self-guided tour (which takes about 2 hours) of the 18,000-acre grounds will include the Academy's chapel — a "chapel of the future" when it was built in 1963 in the shape of a 17-spired tetrahedron pyramid 150 feet high, with separate chapels inside for various faiths. Every weekday at noon, weather permitting (except during summer vacations and some other breaks), the cadets — in uniform — assemble, then march in formation to the dining hall to the accompaniment of martial music. A real goose-bump raiser. You can lodge in Colorado Springs — the state's second biggest city — at any number of motels or hotels; most prestigious is the *Broadmoor,* a very posh, very old, and very famous resort (phone: 303-634-7711; see *Resort Hotels*). Information: HQ USAFA/PAV, US Air Force Academy, Colorado Springs, CO 80840-5151 (phone: 303-472-2555).

US COAST GUARD ACADEMY, New London, Connecticut: Your visit to this pretty campus begins at the modern visitors center, where you can browse through exhibits and watch a multimedia show depicting cadet life, then pick up a map for a self-guided tour that takes in the chapel; the academy's museum, notable for its intriguing collection of vessel models; and when it's in port, the sailing bark *Eagle*, now used for cadet training cruises. Once weekly in spring and fall, usually on Friday afternoons, cadets parade in review. An added attraction of this nautically minded corner of Connecticut is the interesting selection of inns, the best of which includes the venerable *Griswold Inn*, a bustling place on Main Street in Essex that has been putting up travelers for centuries (phone: 203-767-1812), and the *Copper Beech*, in Ivoryton, the former home of a Connecticut ivory trader, full of high-ceilinged, four-poster sleeping chambers (phone: 203-767-0330). See *America's Special Havens*. For academy information, contact the US Coast Guard Academy, Public Affairs Office, New London, CT 06320 (phone: 203-444-8270).

US NAVAL ACADEMY, Annapolis, Maryland: On certain Wednesday afternoons during fall and spring, and during commissioning week, the 4,500 spit-and-polished midshipmen have a 3:45 PM dress parade on Worden Field. During the academic year when the temperature is above 55F, the Brigade of Midshipmen assembles in Tecumseh Court for reports, a drum and bugle performance, and a march to lunch. There's more to see: the crypt of John Paul Jones, somewhat like Napoleon's in Paris; the chapel, really a large cathedral, complete with stained glass windows; trophies in the fieldhouse (and an explanation of how the goat came to be the navy's mascot); a museum full of naval history exhibits. Pamphlets outlining a self-guided walking tour are available, as are guided tours. Information: US Naval Academy, Annapolis, MD 21402 (phone: 301-263-6933).

US MERCHANT MARINE ACADEMY, Kings Point, New York: On Long Island's picturesque North Shore, and overlooking Connecticut, Long Island Sound, and New York City and its bridges, this academy occupies what used to be the Chrysler estate (as well as parts of others on Long Island's Gold Coast). At the Main Gate, you can get maps and information about what to see — displays about the history of the Merchant Marine and their ships at the *American Merchant Marine Museum*, and regimental reviews, held on some Saturdays in fall and spring at 10 AM. Information: US Merchant Marine Academy, Steamboat Rd., Kings Point, NY 11024-1699 (phone: 516-773-5000).

US MILITARY ACADEMY, West Point, New York: Founded on March 16, 1802, with an initial enrollment of ten, this academy is probably the most famous and most visited of the service schools, and for good reason. It fairly oozes military tradition. The campus is beautiful, as manicured as any parkland, full of Gothic buildings, and magnificent views like the one from Trophy Point, above the Hudson River. ("The fairest of the fair and lovely Highlands of the North River, shut in by deep green heights and ruined forts, and looking down upon the distant town of Newburgh," according to Charles Dickens, who visited in 1842.) The Cadet Chapel, a lofty granite Gothic structure overlooking the cadet parade field, houses the largest church pipe organ in the country. The museum — filled with military artifacts from the Stone Age to the present — is the largest military museum in the world. At Trophy Point, you can see a few links of the heavy iron chains the American revolutionaries stretched across the river to block British ships during that war. Cadet parades are held during spring and fall; for times and dates, call ahead. The *Thayer* hotel is on the grounds (phone: 914-446-4731). Country inns come and go in the area. Among the nicest are the *Bird and Bottle Inn* in Garrison (phone: 914-424-3000) and the *Beekman Arms* in Rhinebeck (phone: 914-876-7077). You can eat or lodge in any of these. Also interesting, for food: the Culinary Institute of America's *Escoffier Room* and *American Bounty* restaurants, in Hyde Park, where top chefs of the future are in rigorous training (phone: 914-471-6608; closed July). Information: Visitors Information Center, US Military Academy, West Point, NY 10996 (phone: 914-938-2638).

Great Horse Races

 Ever since President Washington closed Congress on October 24, 1780, so that he and the senators could attend the races at this country's first racetrack, Baltimore's *Pimlico*, Americans have been competing against each other on horseback.

Every breed has its set of competitive events. Standardbreds, bred to trot (with diagonal legs moving in synchronization) or, more commonly, to pace (with lateral legs moving together), pull sulkies around dirt ovals. Thoroughbreds ridden by tiny jockeys in brightly colored silks charge down flat tracks or leap their way over steeplechase courses. Quarter horses run for million-dollar purses, while Western horses work out at rodeos.

ALL ABOUT HORSES

KENTUCKY HORSE PARK, Lexington, Kentucky: World-renowned Kentucky Horse Park is the only one of its kind in the world and possibly the best place in the country to get a feeling for American horse life. This $35-million facility, which opened in September 1978 on 1,032 acres in the heart of the Kentucky bluegrass country, represents not just the thoroughbreds born and bred in the area but also Morgans, Arabians, Appaloosas, and just about any other breed you can name. With a stirring 25-minute film on the history of man and horse, and a 40,000-square-foot museum full of dioramas, computers, and various displays about horses the size of dogs, horses and Roman chariots, horses in the Wild West, and more. A motorized tram ride gives you an overview and takes you through the back paddock areas. On the Walking Farm Tour, you can see a farrier, a harnessmaker, a carriage works, and over 25 breeds of horses, and learn about their day-to-day care. The tour also features two live shows daily: the *Hall of Champions Show* with such champion thoroughbreds as John Henry (the winningest thoroughbred ever), Forego, Rossi Gold, A Letter to Harry, and Standardbred Rambling Willie (the horse that God loved, with combined winnings of over $11 million); and the ever-popular and most colorful *Parade of Breeds Show*. You can ride horses and ponies, cruise the grounds in horse-drawn omnibuses, watch appropriately costumed drivers hitch up landaus — and take in dozens of special events: polo games, steeplechase meetings, dressage exhibitions, horse pulling contests, quarter horse sprints, cross-country races.

Five newly constructed polo fields — and a commitment by the US Polo Association to move their offices to the new National Horse Center — are turning the Horse Park into a polo center. A new covered arena that seats 5,600 people will offer competition in any weather. Also available are 265 sites for camping, tennis courts, recreation areas, a fine lively activities program, and a good-size swimming pool. Information: Kentucky Horse Park, 4089 Iron Works Pike, Lexington, KY 40511 (phone: 606-233-4303).

GREAT RACES

Of the hundreds of races that give horse racing the largest paid attendance of any US sport, these are among the biggest.

BLUE GRASS STAKES, Lexington, Kentucky: With a $200,000-added purse, this is the biggest event of the 16-day spring meeting at *Keeneland Race Course* — famous, rustic, and very beautiful at this time of year with the dogwoods and flowering crabs in full bloom. Because the race is run nine days before the Kentucky Derby, over a course just an eighth of a mile shorter than the Derby's mile and a quarter, it is a steppingstone to the Triple Crown. The $200,000-added Spinster, for fillies and mares three years old and up, highlights a 16-day October season and determines, at least in part, which horse will be named champion in her respective division. Four times a year there are thoroughbred sales — yearlings in July and September, breeding stock in November, all ages in January. The highest price ever paid for a horse at public auction — $13.1 million — was paid here at Keeneland in 1985 for a colt by Nijinsky II. Tickets and information: Keeneland Assn., PO Box 1690, Lexington, KY 40592-1690 (phone: 606-254-3412).

KENTUCKY FUTURITY, Lexington, Kentucky: The *Red Mile,* named for the color of the clay on the track, has two seasons every year — the first from late April through June at night, the second from mid-September through early October. The first 2 weeks of the season are night races; the rest, afternoons. The Kentucky Futurity — a mile-long, $200,000 race for 3-year-old trotters, the third leg of the Triple Crown for trotters — comes at the end of September or early October. The fact that the fillies and colts who enter have raced against each other for months by the time they get here makes for exciting races. The *Red Mile* is known as the fastest standardbred track in the world. Right in the middle of the October meeting is the Tattersalls Sale (the equivalent of Keeneland's big yearling sale). On Show Day, the Sunday halfway through the October meeting, all the horse farms in the area hold open houses, complete with burgoo (a kind of oatmeal gruel) and music — and anyone can come. Information: The Red Mile, PO Box 420, Lexington, KY 40585 (phone: 606-255-0752; 800-354-9092).

KENTUCKY DERBY, Louisville, Kentucky: Always the highlight of the spring meet, always on the first Saturday in May, this race, modeled after England's Epsom Derby, was established in 1875 and has been run over the same course ever since (though the original mile-and-a-half distance was trimmed to 1¼ miles in 1896). It's a big deal for the horse owners because of the big purse (some $700,000); for the horses because of the competition and the distance (which is considerable for a 3-year-old so early in the season); and for all of Louisville, for which this is a social as well as a sporting event. Reserved seat tickets are sold on an invitational basis — which means that tickets rarely change hands from year to year. However, general admission tickets are sold on the day of the race. Information: Churchill Downs, 700 Central Ave., Louisville, KY 40208 (phone: 502-636-3541).

PREAKNESS, Baltimore, Maryland: The middle jewel of the Triple Crown is raced the third Saturday in May for more than $500,000 on the 1³⁄₁₆-mile dirt track at the *Pimlico Race Course.* The Preakness, one of the oldest races in America, started in 1873 and attracts the best 3-year-old thoroughbreds from all over the country — not to mention crowds of more than 80,000. The regular racing season at *Pimlico* runs from March through June, and September through mid-October on both the flat track and the ⅞-mile turf course. Information: Maryland Jockey Club, Pimlico Race Course, Baltimore, MD 21215-9945 (phone: 301-542-9400).

HAMBLETONIAN, East Rutherford, New Jersey: Named for the greatest sire of them all (every trotter and pacer is said to be related to this famous horse), this jewel in the Triple Crown for trotters was moved to the *Meadowlands* in 1981 from its home of 25 years at the Illinois Du Quoin State Fair. Held on a Saturday in August, it is one of the most prestigious races of them all, with a purse of $1 million. Information: The Meadowlands Racetrack, East Rutherford, NJ 07073-0700 (phone: 201-935-8500).

WOODROW WILSON PACE, East Rutherford, New Jersey: The richest event in harness racing, this contest for 2-year-old pacers — a midsummer annual at the *Meadowlands* — carries a purse of approximately $2 million. Information: The Meadowlands Racetrack, East Rutherford, NJ 07073 (phone: 201-935-8500).

ALL-AMERICAN FUTURITY, Ruidoso Downs, New Mexico: The richest race of its kind since the dawn of civilization, with a $2.5 million gross purse ($1 million of which goes to the winner), is not a race of thoroughbreds but of quarter horses — originally bred primarily for ranch work with powerful hind quarters that make them superb sprinters, and now infused with thoroughbred blood. Between 10,000 and 15,000 people make their way every summer to southern New Mexico to watch over 300 horses go through eliminations that leave the 10 fastest to compete on a quarter-mile dash down a straight track. Held on Labor Day. In 1986, a 7-furlong thoroughbred course was completed next to the quarter horse straightaway. Information: Ruidoso Downs Race Track, Box 449, Ruidoso Downs, NM 88346 (phone: 505-378-4431).

BELMONT STAKES, Elmont, New York: The third and final leg of the races for the Triple Crown by the best of the country's 3-year-old thoroughbreds. Called "The Test of the Champion," it is held every year in the first half of June and is the longest (1½ miles) of the Triple Crown events. Secretariat holds the record at 2:24. The regular racing season at *Belmont Park,* where the race is held, is mid-May through July, and late August to mid-October. No races on Tuesdays. Information: New York Racing Assn., PO Box 90, Jamaica, NY 11417 (phone: 718-641-4700).

TRAVERS, Saratoga Springs, New York: The nation's oldest active stakes race for 3-year-olds — a 1¼-mile run for thoroughbred colts — is held at the oldest active racetrack in the country, the *Saratoga Race Course,* where they've been racing almost every year since 1864. Many US tracks have been designed after *Saratoga.* The Travers, known as "the Midsummer Derby," usually draws the top 3-year-olds from the Triple Crown series. The season runs for four weeks in August, and there are stakes races of one sort or another almost every day, with big races on Saturdays: the Alabama, for 3-year-old fillies; the Whitney, for 3-year-olds and up; and the Hopeful, a race for 2-year-olds whose winner, historically, has often gone on to compete successfully in the Triple Crown races the following year. No races on Tuesdays. Information: New York Racing Assn., PO Box 90, Jamaica, NY 11417 (phone: 718-641-4700).

INTERNATIONAL TROT, Westbury, New York: In Europe, trotting trainers are more concerned with gait and style, and a European trotting race is a pretty race. You can see the difference between European trotters and American at the $250,000 International Trot, the world championship of trotting, held at *Roosevelt Raceway* every July or August during the summer meet (other meets are held late February through April and mid-October to early December). Information: Roosevelt Raceway, PO Box 778, Westbury, NY 11590-0978 (phone: 516-222-2000).

MESSENGER STAKES, Westbury, New York: The second most important race of the *Roosevelt Raceway* year, this one held at the end of October or beginning of November is the third leg of the Triple Crown for 3-year-old pacers and helps decide who gets divisional honors and who gets named the horse of the year. The purse is $275,000. Information: Roosevelt Raceway, PO Box 778, Westbury, NY 11590-0978 (phone: 516-222-2000).

CANE PACE, Yonkers, New York: This $500,000 race, usually held in midsummer, with the Little Brown Jug (Delaware County Fair, Delaware, Ohio) and the Messenger Stakes (see above), make up the Triple Crown of pacing; the race is similar to the Messenger in many ways, right down to the half-mile track (somewhat slower, because of the turns required, than the mile-long track at the *Meadowlands,* in East Rutherford, New Jersey). As for all other staked races, competitors have been entered (and payments made to keep their entrance status current) almost from birth. Information: Yonkers Raceway, Central Ave., Yonkers, NY 10704 (phone: 914-968-4200).

YONKERS TROT, Yonkers, New York: Worth an estimated $350,000, this is one of the three glamour events of trotting (with the Kentucky Futurity and the Hambletonian described above) held in summer at the end of the "Yonkers Trot Week" festival. Information: Yonkers Raceway, Central Ave., Yonkers, NY 10704 (phone: 914-968-4200).

MARION du PONT SCOTT COLONIAL CUP INTERNATIONAL STEEPLE-CHASE, Camden, South Carolina: The $60,000 cup makes this late fall event, first held in 1970, one of the very biggest in steeplechase racing. With the American Grand National at Charlottesville, Virginia, and the Temple Gwathmey at *Belmont Park,* New York, it is one of the jewels of the Triple Crown of steeplechasing. But unlike its fellows, the Colonial Cup is an international race, and participants come from around the world. The horses compete over special "Colonial Cup fences" made of fresh pine brush — 17 obstacles in all. The Carolina Cup, held in the spring, is older and draws bigger crowds (though the purse is not so large). Information: Colonial Cup, PO Box 280, Camden, SC 29020 (phone: 803-432-6513).

RODEOS

Beyond the fact that the rodeo cowboy's skills are rooted in the life of the Wild West, the rodeo system today has very little to do with that romantic era. In the first place, there's big money involved — hundreds of thousands of dollars in prizes for all the different events. Then, too, the cowboys are more like Olympic athletes: They train hard and work hard to get where they are. All rodeos sanctioned by the Professional Rodeo Cowboys' Association (PRCA) — the larger of the two cowboy "leagues" — include bareback, saddle bronc, and bull riding; calf roping and team roping; and steer wrestling. Often there's also barrel racing (for women), sanctioned by the Girls' Rodeo Association; plus chuck wagon races and the like. All of these rodeos — the US's biggest and most important — are associated with livestock shows or big state or county fairs.

NATIONAL WESTERN STOCK SHOW AND RODEO, Denver, Colorado: At this venerable annual event, the largest indoor rodeo in the country, some 1,000 entrants vie for over $300,000 in prize money every January. But as the biggest of the US's livestock exhibitions, it also has plenty of exhibits that tell you everything you never knew about livestock matters from saddles to beef production. All over the place there are kids grooming animals in preparation for judging, and onlookers numbering in the thousands. Livestock sales for cattle and horses total about $10 million each year. Information: National Western Stock Show and Rodeo, 1325 E. 46th Ave., Denver, CO 80216 (phone: 303-297-1166).

NATIONAL FINALS RODEO, Las Vegas, Nevada: At the end of the year, the top fifteen money-winners in seven events who have competed in the more than 640 Professional Rodeo Cowboy Association–sanctioned rodeos qualify for the National Finals — and from there they all compete for the championships in the various divisions. At stake are over $2 million in prizes and the NFR and world titles, and the competition is fierce. The 10 performances are held beginning the first Friday in December; most tickets sell out well in advance. Information: Las Vegas Events, 2030 E. Flamingo Ave., Suite 200, Las Vegas, NV 89119 (phone: 702-731-2115).

SOUTHWESTERN EXPOSITION AND LIVESTOCK SHOW AND RODEO, Ft. Worth, Texas: The world's oldest indoor rodeo, begun in 1896 and held in the heart of cowboy country. It consists of 28 performances over a period of 17 days in late January through early February every year, and pays over $450,000. Information: Southwestern Exposition, PO Box 150, Ft. Worth, TX 76101 (phone: 817-877-2420).

HOUSTON LIVESTOCK SHOW AND RODEO, Houston, Texas: This event, which runs for 2 weeks beginning in late February, features a Texas-size rodeo, complete with musical concert, held in the *Astrodome;* and the world's largest livestock show, which fills up the *Astrohall* and *Astroarena* with horses, sheep, chickens, pigs, and cattle, for display and for sale at auction. In 1983, five chickens went for $61,000, and in 1984, the grand champion steer for $150,000. Tickets and information: Houston Livestock Show, PO Box 20070, Houston, TX 77225 (phone: 713-791-9000).

CHEYENNE FRONTIER DAYS RODEO, Cheyenne, Wyoming: The biggest US rodeo and the "Daddy of 'em all" is a long-standing tradition in Wyoming. In addition to the usual competitive events, there are night shows (generally featuring country and western performers like Willie Nelson, the *Oak Ridge Boys,* or the *Judds*), chuck-wagon races; and parades, Indian dancers, and various exhibitions and entertainments at the associated 10-day celebration. Last full week in July. Information: Frontier Days, PO Box 2666, Cheyenne, WY 82003 (phone: 307-778-7200).

FOR MORE INFORMATION

There are complicated systems for the way the thoroughbreds and standardbreds race; an understanding will help you enjoy the races more and make wiser bets. The *Thoroughbred Racing Associations,* 3000 Marcus Ave., Suite 2W4, Lake Success, NY 11042 (phone: 516-328-2660), publish lists of major races. The *US Trotting Assn.*, 750 Michigan Ave., Columbus, OH 43215 (phone: 614-224-2291), publishes a history of the sport and free booklets that tell you how to pick a winner, purchase a horse, or pursue a career in racing. Steeplechasing information: *National Steeplechase and Hunt Assn.*, PO Box 308, Elmont, NY 11003 (phone: 516-437-6666). Rodeo information: *PRCA (Professional Rodeo Cowboys Assn.*), 101 Pro Rodeo Dr., Colorado Springs, CO 80919 (phone: 303-593-8840); this association is the sanctioning body of more than 600 professional rodeos annually.

Oddities and Insanities

 America is full of offbeat attractions — museums given over to one subject (cartoons, buttons, soup tureens), whole festivals entirely devoted to matters that you'd consider entirely inconsequential, big blowouts or festivals that completely take over a town, and "world's best," "world's only," "world's first," etc. Around every corner there's something unexpected. Here are some of particular note.

EAST

BARNUM FESTIVAL, Bridgeport, Connecticut: A ten-day flurry each June/July of contests, concerts, fireworks, circus parades, clowns, an antique auto show, and an air show in the great showman's hometown. Information: Barnum Festival, 1070 Main St., Bridgeport, CT 06604 (phone: 203-367-8495).

NEWSPAPER HOUSE, Rockport, Massachusetts: A cabin made entirely of pasted, folded, and pressed newspapers — with furniture made of rolled newspapers — is at 52 Pigeon Hill St., in this shop-crammed resort town north of Boston. Information: Chamber of Commerce, Rockport, MA 01966 (phone: 508-546-6575).

LAKE CHARGOGGAGOGGMANCHAUGGAGOGGCHAUBUNAGUNGAMAUGG, Webster, Massachusetts: The name, in the language of the Nipmuc Indians, means "fishing place at the boundaries; neutral meeting grounds" but is more commonly translated as "I fish on my side, you fish on your side, and no one fishes in the middle." Local fishermen call it Lake Webster. Largemouth and smallmouth bass, pickerel, and rainbow and brown trout enjoy an almost ideal environment. Sailing and water skiing are also big draws. Information: Webster-Dudley-Oxford Chamber of Commerce, Box 100, Webster, MA 01570 (phone: 508-943-0558).

LUCY THE MARGATE ELEPHANT, Margate, New Jersey: Constructed in 1881 by James V. Lafferty to help attract real estate buyers, this 38-foot-long, 65-foot-tall building in the shape of an elephant is now a National Historic Landmark. She stands on a beach south of Atlantic City and is open for tours after being restored by the Save Lucy Committee. There's a small museum inside and you can climb the spiral stairways to the howdah, an observation platform on her back, to view the ocean and surrounding areas. Open daily from June 15 through Labor Day; weekends only, spring and fall. Information: Save Lucy Committee, PO Box 3000, Margate, NJ 08402 (phone: 609-822-6519).

NATIONAL POLKA FESTIVAL, Hunter, New York: Top bands, a band competition, a dance floor that holds 1,000 in the largest tent in the US, ethnic foods, and daily dance contests. August. Information: National Polka Festival, Bridge Street, PO Box 297, Hunter, NY 12442 (phone: 518-263-3800).

MUSEUM OF CARTOON ART, Rye Brook, New York: Exhibitions of historical and contemporary cartoons, with examples of over a thousand different cartoonists — not to mention cartoon animations on film and video. The collection, the largest of its kind in the world, is housed in Ward's Castle, the first house in the world to be constructed entirely of reinforced concrete. It's a good idea to call for directions. Open Tuesdays through Fridays from 10 AM to 4 PM, Sundays from 1 to 5 PM. Information: Museum of Cartoon Art, Comly Ave., Rye Brook, NY 10573 (phone: 914-939-0234).

WORLD CHAMPIONSHIP SNOW SHOVEL RIDING CONTEST, Ambridge, Pennsylvania: You sit on shovels or spades, then slide down a 153-foot snow-covered slope; the idea is to get down before your opponents — still sitting on the shovel. In the Modified division, mock exhaust pipes, runners, and copper coatings are just a few of the alterations that have been permitted within the rules. Held every January, usually the Saturday of Super Bowl weekend, depending on snow conditions. Information: Beaver County Tourist Promotion Agency, 14th & Church Sts., Ambridge, PA 15003 (phone: 412 — 66-2226).

BEAN SOUP FESTIVAL, McClure, Pennsylvania: Thousands of gallons of bean soup are stirred up in 35-gallon iron kettles to accompany 25 roast hogs and the usual small-town festival doings every year in September. It's a great feast. Information: Bean Soup Festival, Box 8, McClure, PA 17841 (phone: 717-658-8425).

UNITED CHURCH OF CHRIST GAME SUPPER, Bradford, Vermont: A church supper where the goodies on the table are beaver, boar, bear, coon, pheasant, rabbit, buffalo, venison, moufflon ram, and whatever else is available that year; the sittings sell out within days of tickets going on sale. November. Information: United Church of Christ, Box 182, Bradford, VT 05033 (phone: 802-222-4418 or 802-222-4670).

CONVENTION OF THE AMERICAN SOCIETY OF DOWSERS, Danville, Vermont: A gathering of novice and experienced dowsers with reports, workshops, meetings, and speakers. One 4-day weekend in September preceded by a 2-day dowsing school. Information: American Society of Dowsers, Danville, VT 05828-0024 (phone: 802-684-3417).

WORLD'S FAIR, Tunbridge, Vermont: A country fair with pony and horse pulling contests, oxen judging, contra dancing, and antiques displays (among other things) — it gets pretty lively on Saturday night! Mid-September. Information: Vermont Dept. of Agriculture, 116 State St., Montpelier, VT 05602 (phone: 802-828-2418).

FEAST OF THE RAMSON, Richwood, West Virginia: The publisher of this town's newspaper once threatened to put the juice of the ramp — a wild onion-like vegetable peculiar to the shady coves of Appalachia — in the printing ink, and the townspeople panicked. Once you've eaten ramps, the smell hangs around you for days, but the annual feast devoted to the green is much loved nonetheless. There is also a mountain-related arts and crafts display and traditional musical entertainment. April. Information: Chamber of Commerce, 50 Oakford Ave., Richwood, WV 26261 (phone: 304-846-6790).

SOUTH

NATIONAL PEANUT FESTIVAL, Dothan, Alabama: Peanut recipe contests, parades, arts and crafts shows, soapbox derbies, and calf and greased-pig scrambles are the staples at this 2-week small-town bash grown to state fair size. And the nuts themselves are for sale everywhere. Mid-October. Information: National Peanut Festival Assn., 1691 Ross Clark Circle SE, Dothan, AL 36301 (phone: 205-793-4323).

WORLD'S CHAMPIONSHIP DUCK-CALLING CONTEST, Stuttgart, Arkansas: The competition for the title of Queen Mallard is followed by various duck-calling competitions, some for kids, some for women, some for men in hale, mating, feed, and comeback calls. All of this is the kick off for a week-long festival and carnival. Annually, starting the weekend of Thanksgiving. Information: Chamber of Commerce, PO Box 932, Stuttgart, AR 72160 (phone: 501-673-1602).

NATIONAL WILD TURKEY CALLING CONTEST AND TURKEY TROT FESTIVAL, Yellville, Arkansas: Miss Turkey Trot presides over this big (and cacophonous) October contest, further enlivened by dancing, a parade, live entertainment, and lots more. Information: Yellville Chamber of Commerce, PO Box 369, Yellville, AR 72687 (phone: 501-449-4676).

WORLD CHAMPIONSHIP SWAMP BUGGY RACES, Naples, Florida: With their high wheels, these homemade conveyances that can get through mud and water under nearly any conditions are a way of life in this part of the country; a flooded 125-acre park located on County Road 951 provides the racecourse twice a year, usually the last Sundays in October and February. Information: Swamp Buggy, PO Box 3105, Naples, FL 33939 (phone: 813-774-2701).

WORLD'S CHICKEN PLUCKIN' CHAMPIONSHIP, Spring Hill, Florida: Teams compete at this small community northwest of Tampa to establish new world records (to be listed in *Guinness*) the first Saturday in November. Also part of the goings-on is a Miss Drumstick Contest, in which competitors' torsos are enveloped in flour sacks; and there's plenty of music, singing, dancing, and food. Information: Spring Hill VFW–Post 10209, 15166 Spring Hill Dr., Spring Hill, FL 33573 (phone: 904-796-0398).

MULE DAY, Calvary, Georgia: Mule-judging contests here have spectators casting their ballots for the ugliest, most stubborn, and prettiest mules — but only after a big and very lively mule parade has gotten everyone in the mood. And tobacco-spitting contests, cakewalks, sugarcane grinding, greased-pig-chasing competitions, and plenty of live country entertainment round out the program. Held the first Saturday in November. Information: Chamber of Commerce, PO Box 387, Cairo, GA 31728 (phone: 912-377-MULE).

GREAT EASTER EGG HUNT, Stone Mountain Park, Georgia: One of the world's largest Easter egg hunts, with 62,000 brightly colored hard-boiled eggs hidden in a meadow. The park where it is held, on the outskirts of Atlanta, also has two Easter sunrise services, one at the mountain's base, the other at its peak. Information: Stone Mountain Park, PO Box 778, Stone Mountain, GA 30086 (phone: 404-498-5600).

INTERNATIONAL BANANA FESTIVAL, Fulton, Kentucky: The twin cities of Fulton, Kentucky, and South Fulton, Tennessee, celebrate the area's role as "Banana Crossroads of the United States" and "Banana Capital of the World" with banana-eating contests, a banana bake-off, and a 2-ton banana pudding that serves 20,000 — half to a third of the people who put in an appearance in these communities about 50 miles from Paducah and 127 miles from Memphis. And it's free — and so are the bananas handed out to all comers. There's also a 3-day arts and crafts show. September. Information: International Banana Festival, PO Box 428, Fulton, KY 42041-0428 (phone: 502-472-2975).

CRAWFISH FESTIVAL, Breaux Bridge, Louisiana: Every year a major event is involved in serving up these little crustaceans in all imaginable forms. The first full weekend of May. Information: Breaux Bridge Crawfish Festival Assn., PO Box 25, 101 Berard St., Breaux Bridge, LA 70517 (phone: 318-332-6655).

LOUISIANA FUR AND WILDLIFE FESTIVAL, Cameron, Louisiana: Trapshooting, retriever dog trials, duck- and goose-calling and oyster-shucking contests, nutria- and muskrat-skinning contests, and more. Second weekend in January. Information: Secretary, Louisiana Fur and Wildlife Festival, PO Box 366, Cameron, LA 70631 (phone: 318-775-5718).

NATIONAL HOLLERIN' CONTEST, Spivey's Corner, North Carolina: Left over from the days before telephones, when each man had his own holler. In 1976, a three-legged dog barked along with the hollerers. Third Saturday in June. Information: Ermon Godwin, PO Box 332, Dunn, NC 28334 (phone: 919-892-4133).

EASTER EGG FIGHTS, Sugar Hill, North Carolina: Descendants of this Piedmont town's early German settlers, following a 160-year-old custom, test the durability of their hard-boiled brightly colored eggs by banging the small ends together. The contestant who ends up with the least damage wins. Early on Easter Sunday. Area information: Chamber of Commerce, PO Box 305, Cherryville, NC 28021 (phone: 704-435-3451).

CHITLIN' STRUT, Salley, South Carolina: The chitlin' capital of the world serves up over 10 tons of these boiled, deep-fried hog intestines every year on the Saturday after Thanksgiving. There's also a carnival, hog calling contest, and lots of other activities. Information: E. W. Clamp, PO Box 482, Salley, SC 29137 (phone: 803-258-3331).

WORLD'S BIGGEST FISH FRY, Paris, Tennessee: Some four tons of catfish hauled out of the Tennessee River are cooked up at this big affair to serve with an equally staggering quantity of coleslaw, hush puppies, and baked beans. Late April. Information: Chamber of Commerce, Box 8, Paris, TN 38242 (phone: 901-642-3431).

ZILKER PARK KITE FESTIVAL, Austin, Texas: The oldest of America's dozen or so celebrations of this favorite childhood toy is held annually in mid-March; some 10,000 spectators usually show up to watch the 200 fliers send up craft as small as a square on a Rubik's cube and as large as a master bedroom. Information: Parks and Recreation Dept., 1500 W. Riverside Dr., Austin, TX 78704 (phone: 512-477-PARD).

EASTER FIRES PAGEANT, Fredericksburg, Texas: Costumed Easter bunnies, fireworks, and bonfires in a pageant which got its start back in the days when parents told their youngsters that what were actually the bonfires of watchful Indians were the cookfires of Easter bunnies boiling eggs. Easter Eve. Information: Chamber of Commerce, PO Box 506, Fredericksburg, TX 78624 (phone: 512-997-6523).

WURSTFEST, New Braunfels, Texas: Crowds of over 140,000 come around to gobble mettwurst, blutwurst, bratwurst, leberwurst, wurstkabobs, pork hocks, sauerkraut, dumplings and all the rest at a 10-day extravaganza that nods to the heritage of the people who settled here. Late October through November. Information: Wurstfest Assn., PO Box 310-309, New Braunfels, TX 78131-0309 (phone: 512-625-9167).

EASTERN SHORE SEAFOOD FESTIVAL, Chincoteague, Virginia: The 3,000 or so tickets to this big affair sell out nearly a year in advance, and you'll see why: The savory Chincoteague oysters are served here by the ton, along with clams (steamed, raw, in fritters), and plenty of coleslaw, French-fried sweet potatoes, hush puppies, and other goodies. Early May. Information: Eastern Shore Chamber of Commerce, 1 Court House Ave., PO Box 147, Accomac, VA 23301 (phone: 804-787-2460).

MIDWEST

NATIONAL HOBO CONVENTION, Britt, Iowa: Thousands of vacationers come to see the hobos converge on this little town every year in August — and have been doing so since 1900. A king and queen are selected, and 500 gallons of Mulligan stew are dished out for free. Information: Chamber of Commerce, PO Box 63, Britt, IA 50423 (phone: 515-843-3867).

INTERNATIONAL PANCAKE DAY, Liberal, Kansas: The main event is a foot race in which married women in housedresses, aprons, and headscarves run a 415-yard S-shaped course through town while flipping flapjacks in skillets — a strange activity that got its start some 500 years ago in England. Shrove Tuesday. Information: International Pancake Day, PO Box 665, Liberal, KS 67901 (phone: 316-624-1106).

WORLD'S LONGEST BREAKFAST TABLE, Battle Creek, Michigan: Where else but in the Breakfast Capital of the World would you find four blocks of end-to-end picnic tables laden with products of the Big Three (Kellogg's, General Foods, and Ralston-Purina)? And it's all free. June. Information: Greater Battle Creek/Calhoun County Visitor and Convention Bureau, 172 W. Van Buren St., Battle Creek, MI 49017 (phone: 616-962-2240).

MAGIC GET-TOGETHER, Colon, Michigan: After the great illusionist Harry Blackstone moved here in the '20s, the town became a magicians' colony of sorts; Abbott's Magic Company puts on this extravaganza of "illusions," as magic tricks are known in the business. August. Information: Abbott's Magic, 1204 St. Joseph's St., Colon, MI 49040 (phone: 616-432-3235).

NATIONAL CHERRY FESTIVAL, Traverse City, Michigan: One of America's greatest summertime civic celebrations. Seven days of events and activities including three parades, sporting events, childrens' events, band competitions, and free entertainment daily. July. Information: National Cherry Festival, PO Box 141, Traverse City, MI 49685 (phone: 616-947-4230).

NATIONAL FENCE PAINTING CONTEST, Hannibal, Missouri: Kids dressed up like Tom Sawyer compete as part of the Tom Sawyer Days, held every year the first week in July. Supremacy among fence-painters is determined by the judges' opinion of the authenticity of a contestant's costume — and the speed and thoroughness with which he or she applies the whitewash. There's also frog jumping, a Tomboy Sawyer contest, Tom Sawyer and Becky Thatcher contest, Main Street raft race, the Clemens Arts and Crafts Show, an over-30 fence-painting contest, fiddlers' contest, parade, fireworks show, eats, drinks, concerts, and other entertainment each night. Information: National Fence Painting Chairman, c/o Hannibal Jaycees, PO Box 484, Hannibal, MO 63401.

PUMPKIN SHOW, Circleville, Ohio: Crowds up to half a million come for what Ohioans call "the greatest free show on Earth" — and down piles of pumpkin ice cream, pumpkin pie, pumpkin fudge, pumpkin candy, pumpkin milk shakes, pumpkin cookies, and even pumpkin burgers. October. Information: Chamber of Commerce, 135 W. Main St., PO Box 462, Circleville, OH 43113 (phone: 614-474-4923).

BUZZARD DAY, Hinckley, Ohio: Buzzard Town USA got its name because of a flock of 75 or so of the big birds that spend most of the warmer months here. March 15, the approximate date of their return from their wintering grounds, is Buzzard Day, celebrated the first following Sunday. There are bazaars where you can buy chocolate buzzards, buzzard cookies, T-shirts, and bumper stickers, and a big pancake breakfast. Information: Chamber of Commerce, Box 354, Hinckley, OH 44233 (phone: 216-278-2554).

INTERNATIONAL CHICKEN FLYING MEET, Rio Grande, Ohio: An organized version of what farm boys have been doing from haylofts, trees, cliffs, and other high places for years, at the Bob Evans Farm. Third Saturday in May. Information: ICFM Secretary, 3776 S. High St., Columbus, OH 43207 (phone: 614-491-2225).

LUMBERJACK WORLD CHAMPIONSHIPS, Hayward, Wisconsin: Events in sawing (single-man bucking, two-man bucking, power sawing), log rolling, speed climbing, ax throwing, canoe jousting, lumberjack relays, and chopping contests at a museum village, Historyland, that traces the history of the area. July. Information: Historyland,

PO Box 726, Hayward, WI 54843 (phone: 715-634-8662; 800-826-3474 outside Wisconsin).

WEST

FUR RENDEZVOUS, Anchorage, Alaska: This action-packed festival features the World Championship Sled Dog Race, an Eskimo blanket-toss exhibition, fur auction, fur style show, and over 130 other events, including an outhouse ski race, Grand Prix car racing, a cross-country snowmobile race, carnival rides, the Miners and Trappers Ball, and "Monte Carlo Night" (with blackjack, Yukon poker, and roulette). One of the nation's ten largest festivals. Ten days in February. Information: Fur Rendezvous, 327 Eagle, Anchorage, AK 99510 (phone: 907-277-8615).

CALAVERAS COUNTY FAIR & JUMPING FROG JUBILEE, Angels Camp, California: This county fair features the International Frog Jump Finals, which climax a season of frog-jumping events across the country. The 2,800 contestants jump bullfrogs in an attempt to beat Rosie the Ribiter's 1986 21-foot-5¾-inch record. Frogs are available for rent. Third full weekend in May. Information: Frogtown, PO Box 96, Angels Camp, CA 95222 (phone: 209-736-2561).

MULE DAYS, Bishop, California: The Mule Capital of the World puts on the world's largest nonmotorized parade, with hundreds of mule teams, riding teams, pack strings, and comedy entries (in which mules carry outhouses or beds). Some 600 mules compete in more than 94 events, including packing contests, steer roping, jumping, driving, chariot races, and western races. Other events during the weekend include western dances, barbecues, pancake breakfast, mule sale, and an arts and crafts show. Memorial Day weekend. Information: Chamber of Commerce, 690 N. Main St., Bishop, CA 93514 (phone: 619-873-8405).

NATIONAL DATE FESTIVAL, Indio, California: A ten-day county fair with unusual entertainment: races of camels and ostrich (who behave so unpredictably that everybody else is upstaged), not to mention the Arabian Nights/Queen Scheherazade pageant and street parade — and lavish displays of dates. February. Information: National Date Festival, PO Drawer NNNN, Indio, CA 92202 (phone: 619-342-8247).

INTERNATIONAL SURF FESTIVAL, Manhattan Beach, California: Also at Hermosa, Torrance, and Redondo beaches, this event has no board-surfing competitions, but does have many other events — such as paddleboard races, a pier-to-pier swim, a sand-castle making contest, and a body-surfing contest. Late July or August. Information: Chamber of Commerce, 425 15th St., Manhattan Beach, PO Box 3007, CA 90266 (phone: 213-545-5313).

NATIONAL BASQUE FESTIVAL, Elko, Nevada: The population of this little town skyrockets as merrymakers from all over come to chorus the Basque national anthem, watch Basque games and contests (walking weight carries, tugs of war, handball, woodchopping and sheep hooking contests, and 250-pound granite-ball lifts), and enjoy Basque meals and dancing and singing. It all culminates on Sunday afternoon with the Basque "Irrintzi" (war cry) contest. Weekend of July 4. Information: Chamber of Commerce, 1601 Idaho St., PO Box 470, Elko, NV 89801 (phone: 702-738-7135).

WORLD CHAMPIONSHIP COW CHIP THROWING CONTEST, Beaver, Oklahoma: About 225 miles northwest of Oklahoma City on Highway 3, pasture-discus fans from around the world compete in this highly specialized athletic event, also known as the Organic Olympics. There's a special division for men and women champions and a very special division for politicians. Also on the schedule: country music fest, parade, carnival, dances, a Wild West shootout, and antique coin, gun, and hobby shows. Late spring. Information: Chamber of Commerce, PO Box 878, Beaver, OK 73932 (phone: 405-625-4726).

WORLD POSTHOLE DIGGING CHAMPIONSHIP, Boise City, Oklahoma: Men, women, and children compete. The event is part of the annual Santa Fe Trail Daze festival the first weekend in June. Information: Chamber of Commerce, PO Box 1027, Boise City, OK 73933 (phone: 405-544-3344).

INTERNATIONAL BRICK AND ROLLING PIN THROWING CONTEST, Stroud, Oklahoma: Hurlers from this small town compete against teams from Stroud, England, Stroud, Canada, and Stroud, Australia, for the best throws with bricks (for men) and rolling pins (for women). July. Information: Chamber of Commerce, PO Box 633, Stroud, OK 74079 (phone: 918-968-3321).

NATIONAL ROOSTER CROWING CONTEST, Rogue River, Oregon: Roosters from across the nation attempt to best the 1979 record set by White Lightning — 112 crows in 30 minutes. Additional events of the day are a mini-marathon run, a parade, and an exhibit of old cars and vans. Last Saturday in June. Information: Chamber of Commerce, PO Box 457, Rogue River, OR 97537 (phone: 503-582-0242).

LEBANON STRAWBERRY FESTIVAL, Lebanon, Oregon: Bigger than the National Strawberry Festival (Manistee, Michigan, in early July), this festival stars the World's Largest Strawberry Shortcake (a 5,700-pounder that is 36 feet long, 10 feet wide, 5 feet high and served with 25 cases of whipped cream and 3,000 pounds of strawberries, and feeds 15,000 people, free). Other events: carnival, parades, exhibits, 1-mile fitness walk. Early June. Information: Chamber of Commerce, 1040 Park St., Lebanon, OR 97355 (phone: 503-258-7164).

WORLD'S CHAMPIONSHIP SNOWSHOE SOFTBALL TOURNAMENT, Winthrop, Washington: Teams from all over the Pacific Northwest battle it out on snowshoes one day every February in this tiny, old-fashioned western town. Besides the softball, there's a sled-bed race, jousting, and a relay tourney — all on snowshoes. Information: Three Finger Jocks, PO Box 425, Winthrop, WA 98862 (phone: 509-996-2411).

DIRECTIONS

East

Mystic Seaport, Connecticut, to Providence, Rhode Island

Mystic Seaport, a restored whaling village and nautical museum, is off I-95 in Mystic, Connecticut, about 150 miles northeast of New York City. A driving tour will take you through several grimy, industrial New England towns, but you can escape the interstate at exit 71, South Lyme. Bear left at the end of the ramp, then left again at the junction of Rte. 156, going toward East Lyme (the sign is very confusing). This is a charming back road that winds through forgotten little towns of country stores, antiques shops, and boatyards fronting Long Island Sound.

NIANTIC, Connecticut: A village of New England Gothic frame homes. Cross a drawbridge flanked by marinas and restaurants. As you reach the opposite side of the bridge, you'll pass the entrance to the Millstone Nuclear Power Plant. At the Millstone Energy Center, families can play energy computer games and enjoy hands-on exhibitions and live marine aquaria; 278 Main St., Niantic (phone: 203-444-4234). One wooded interlude beyond, you'll find yourself in a long strip of curio shops, gas stations, and shopping centers. For deep-sea fishing and whale watching expeditions, contact *Captain John's Sport Fishing Center,* 15 First St., Waterford (phone: 203-443-7259). This is antiques country, too, and there are innumerable places to stop and browse. In the distance, that inviting cluster of soft spruce hills punctuated by a church spire is New London.

NEW LONDON, Connecticut: An 18th- and 19th-century whaling port, now home of the US Coast Guard Academy, so there are lot of military jeeps and rugged seamen. In all, New London has a rather faded air, similar to some of the waterfront industrial districts in London, England, for which the town was named. Follow the signs to the business district and park on Bank Street near the Fishers Point Ferry Landing, with its polished wood waiting room. In winter, a fierce, wet wind blows in from Long Island Sound, but in warmer months the cool breeze is ideal. You can stroll along the Captain's Walk, a cobblestone promenade offering a view of the water. Some of the main sites in New London are the *Lyman Allyn Museum,* a hodgepodge collection of Egyptian, Greek, Roman, medieval, Renaissance, and antique furniture (625 Williams St.; phone: 203-443-2545); the Monte Cristo Cottage, boyhood home of playwright Eugene O'Neill (325 Pequot Ave.; phone: 203-443-0051); Ocean Beach Park, with beach, mile-long boardwalk, rides, and pool, open late May through Labor Day (south of New London, off I-95; phone: 203-447-3031); the US Coast Guard Academy, where the three-masted *Eagle* is in port at various times during the year (Exit 83 off I-95; phone: 203-444-8270); Ye Olde Towne Mill, in use since 1650, with a museum room containing the grindstones and the gears operated by the waterwheel (Mill and State Pier Rd.; phone: 203-444-2206).

MYSTIC, Connecticut: Take I-95 12 miles north to Exit 90. Leaving the interstate, you'll pass the Mystic Marine Life Aquarium, with sea lions, seals, and more than 6,000 species of marine life (phone: 203-536-3323). About ½ mile south of I-95 on Rte. 27 is *Mystic Seaport Museum* (phone: 203-572-0711). Even in the winter the parking lot is crowded, but then it is possible to wander through the seaport without encountering hordes of people. In summer, the place is jammed. It takes at least three hours to see everything, including the town of Mystic, which consists of neat rows of sparkling white buildings along the banks of the Mystic River, which feeds into Long Island Sound. In the seaport itself are four major historic ships, a working shipyard, a re-created 19th-century community area with craftspeople, and a formal exhibition area. Board the 1882 training ship *Joseph Conrad;* the fishing schooner *L. A. Dunton;* and the fully restored 1841 whaling ship *Charles W. Morgan.* In summer, there are daily demonstrations of sail setting and furling, chantey singing, and other maritime skills, along with horse and carriage rides. One large display is an assortment of giant ships' figureheads. Exhibitions of scrimshaw (engraved whale's teeth) depicting old clipper and whaling ships bear testimony to years of patient craftsmanship. Also open to visitors are the chandlery, the ropemaking factory, rigging and sailmaking lofts, and model ships. The planetarium has daily shows. Be sure to stop at the Mystic Scale Model, to see the town as it was in the 19th century. Stepping outside again, you'll realize how much love and care has gone into preserving the peaceful beauty and dignity of the village. Festivals and parades are held year-round, and from May through October the 1908 steamboat *Sabino* provides half-hour cruises daily.

WESTERLY, Rhode Island: About 12 miles east of Mystic on Rte.1, this town of dignified, white Colonial mansions stretches to the coast of Block Island Sound. Westerly includes Watch Hill, an exclusive residential community, and Misquamicut State Beach. Florence Nightingale's cap is on display at Westerly Hospital, Wells St. (phone: 401-596-6000). Be careful driving around town. Westerly has only five principal streets, but you can easily get lost and end up back in Pawcatuck, Connecticut. Keep bearing right around the circle to avoid this.

PROVIDENCE, Rhode Island: The capital of Rhode Island, about 50 miles from Westerly on I-95 or Rte. 1, another delightfully empty road that hugs the coast, is a city with a low skyline. Take the Broadway exit off I-95 and bear right. Drive straight along that street and then bear left until you get to Kennedy Plaza and the US Courthouse on Exchange St., a building with several interesting classical sculptures depicting Justice. Circle the plaza, take a left on Dorrance, and when you pass the Westminster Mall, a pedestrian shopping plaza, turn left on Weybosset St. to the Crawford St. Bridge. Bear right at the intersection; at the end of the bridge, turn left and left again on S. Main St. to Waterman St. Head up the hill, past the Rhode Island School of Design's *Museum of Art* (224 Benefit St.; phone: 401-331-3511). This area, known as College Hill, includes Brown University, whose main gates are on Prospect St. (phone: 401-863-1000), and the Rhode Island School of Design, known as RISD, at 2 College St. (phone: 401-331-3511). Both campuses have concerts, films, plays, lectures, and cultural exhibitions throughout the year. Brown plays in the varsity Ivy League. Interspersed with the college buildings are a number of historical houses. These splendid Colonial estates, columned mansions, and gardens are like entering another world. Some of the houses are open daily. By the way, George Washington really did sleep in the Stephen Hopkins House (10 Hopkins St. at Benefit St.; phone: 401-885-4222 or 401-831-7440). The easiest way to return to I-95 is by following Thayer St. to I-195, which feeds into I-95. I-95 will take you back to New York or on to Boston, about 45 miles northeast.

BEST EN ROUTE

Larchwood Inn, Wakefield, Rhode Island – Built in 1831, this country inn is known for its delicious, fresh seafood, elegant yet comfortable furnishings, and cozy atmosphere. Close to swimming, boating, fishing, and surfing as well as bicycling and cross-country ski routes. 521 Main St., Wakefield, RI 02879 (phone: 401-783-5454).

Omni Biltmore, Providence, Rhode Island – A renovated, lovely old hotel. Its restaurant, *Stanford's*, features an open kitchen and open grill that produce New England seafood specialties, plus steaks, pasta, salads, and a variety of desserts. Kennedy Plaza, Providence (phone: 401-421-0700; 800-THE-OMNI).

Captain Daniel Packer Inn, Mystic, Connecticut – After wandering around the seaport, a seafood meal is a must. This restored inn, dating from 1754, has fresh fare daily, including scrod and scallops, and lobster on weekends. There's New England clam chowder, and the house specialty is shrimp Dijon. 32 Water St., Mystic (phone: 203-536-3555).

The Maine Coast and Acadia National Park, Maine

To drive along Maine's coastline is to spend some honest time with nature. Not the kind of ski lodge nature that seems to be little more than an entertainment, letting you come and go as you will and ending conveniently at the doors of a warm lodge. Nature in Maine comes mostly on its own terms, and those are terms of force — the fundamental power of the open Atlantic, the obdurate resistance of the rocky coastline against which it washes.

What makes this an honest trip, if you are observant, is a single revelation: that the forces at work here are totally oblivious to human beings. Watch eddies of the sea suck and slap against some stark slab of stone, perhaps at Acadia National Park, where the process is particularly well defined; the edge of the continent is being constantly, imperceptibly worn away, altered, but it is not an action within the scope of our time scale. It is not something that happens for any motive. It is natural force; it is nature. We don't even have language to describe such a process and its relation to us. Words like indifferent or oblivious imply knowledge, intention, will. They don't begin to represent the implacable force of water and stone, its inhuman beauty. Only by seeing it does this become comprehensible.

Perhaps the best road in the country to see this sea and stone contest — east of the California/Oregon coastal road — is Maine's Rte. 1. It stretches from Kittery to the Canadian border, but the most interesting section for a short 2- or 3-day drive is from Portland to Acadia National Park.

This route allows you to stop along the way at any number of villages and towns of unique Maine flavor. All along this craggy coast, America's history is evident. Not so much the history of great battles or the sites of events that altered destiny, but in a sense of one's own past. We are all, in some part, Yankees. There's more than a little twinge of recognition while viewing something studied but never before seen, like the widow's walks on the roofs of so many of the houses. It's this kind of familiar history that nudges your consciousness all along this coastal route.

Anyone in search of a few days' respite from the current century will hardly be disappointed by the state of Maine.

PORTLAND: A good place to begin your drive along the coast. It's a city, like countless others, with the requisite number of hotels and places to eat. The true flavor of Maine, however, lies beyond the city limits. Head out on I-95 due north, which in Maine is known as "Down East."

BATH: Now — and always — a shipbuilding center. The *Maine Marine Museum* (263 Washington St.) features several exhibition areas, including a historic shipyard and an apprentice shop where small craft are being built. You can also explore the antique fishing boat *Sherman Zwicker* during the summer.

WISCASSET: An ideal place to sample life as it was during the late 1800s. Many of the homes of that era are still occupied today. Originally built by wealthy merchants and shippers, they are lovingly maintained by their present owners. The Nickels-Sortwell House (Main and Federal Sts.), one of several homes open to the public, offers a good example of 19th-century Federal elegance — at least as it existed in Maine.

BOOTHBAY HARBOR: This town has been discovered by tourists, but that should not detract from its interest as a place to visit. It is, rather, a tribute to the Yankee ingenuity that early recognized the salability of picture-postcard scenes, incomparable lobster suppers, and singular charm. Enjoy the appealing (albeit commercial) displays that have been concocted for your amusement, among them the Railway Village (just north of town) with its narrow-gauge train that carries passengers. There's also the public aquarium (no charge) at McKown Point. And be sure to eat your fill of the local delicacy — lobster. You'll find it served in a variety of styles, delicious and relatively inexpensive.

While there are several fine places to stay right in Boothbay Harbor, there's something quite special just across the bay on Monhegan Island, the *Island Inn.* It's family-owned and over a century old, and there's a sort of time-stood-still feeling about the entire island. Most of the island has no electricity; peace and seclusion are the main elements of island entertainment, and you can explore in solitude, discovering the wildflowers and birds on your own. It's only a short ferry ride from the mainland to this gentler time.

ROCKLAND: This modern port city is the world's largest lobster distribution point and the takeoff place for the ferry to two very special Maine islands — North Haven and Vinalhaven. North Haven has a number of summer estates. Vinalhaven is a fishing village of about 1,200 Down East residents. There are no tennis courts, swimming pools, or movies; but there are church suppers (with baked beans, brown bread, and homemade pies), walks along the often foggy shores, and the constant coming and going of fishermen. Both islands are accessible via the *Maine State Ferry Service* from Rockland (phone: 207-596-2202). North Haven now has the *Pulpit Harbor Inn* (phone: 207-867-2219); Vinalhaven has the *Libby House Bed and Breakfast* (phone: 207-863-4696) and *Tidewater Motel* (phone: 207-863-4618); local families also take in travelers.

CAMDEN: Stop here between Rockland and Mt. Desert Island (described below) simply because it is such a beautiful harbor town. Surrounded by high hills (there is good skiing here in the winter, and winter sports at Camden Snow Bowl) and a number of beautiful old homes, it is a town for walking around in, for a long lunch, or for shopping — especially if you are shopping for one of Maine's 3,344 islands. The town is something of a center for real estate agents dealing in islands, and the place to start is with the ads in *Down East* magazine, published in neighboring Rockport and available throughout the state.

MT. DESERT ISLAND: An exceptional place, one of the most wildly beautiful spots in the country, with 35,000 acres devoted to spectacular Acadia National Park; the peak for which it was named (by the French explorer Champlain in 1605) is Mt. Cadillac, the highest spot on the Atlantic coast (which, at 1,530 feet, is hardly gargantuan, but offers a marvelous view of Frenchman's Bay from its height); its major town, Bar Harbor, has been synonymous with wealth and society since the 1920s.

In its heyday — from the 1890s through the 1940s — Bar Harbor was simply too posh for the likes of most folks; the old wealth, certainly, is still on the island (as you will see when you peek at the mammoth estates in the hills as you drive the park's loop road). But today Bar Harbor is far too open, too raucous, too egalitarian to appeal to its original crowd. It opens and closes with the summer season, and for people on the way to the splendors of Acadia, it offers trendy shops (wander along Main Street and note especially the *Rock Shop*), many hotels, and a host of good seafood restaurants.

But the real attraction of Mt. Desert is Acadia. It is the only national park that was purchased with private funds, an effort organized by Dr. Charles W. Eliot of Harvard and George Bucknam Dorr when lumber interests threatened the island. The nation accepted the gift in 1916. Parts of the park are off the island, on Isle au Haut and Schoodic Point on the mainland, but the main attractions are accessible from the 27-mile Park Loop Road.

Start a tour at the visitors center (at the entrance near Bar Harbor), with exhibitions on the ecology and history of the island. You can also pick up information on camping and sports (golf, cycling, horseback riding, hiking, swimming, and an array of winter activities) and maps of the driving routes as well as the hundreds of trails that score the island's "mountains." The Ocean Drive loop culminates in the crown of Mt. Cadillac; along the way there are ample opportunities to stop for a descent straight to rocky shore, where sea and stone meet.

Special treats, available at the harbors of the island's towns (Bar Harbor, Northeast Harbor, Bass Harbor), are sea cruises of nearby islands directed by naturalists. You search for eagle's nests or signs of porpoises and seals, go whale watching, learn about the lobster trade, or make forays to historical museums on out islands. Get information at the visitors center or from the companies that offer the cruises, on the harbors mentioned above. Acadia is New England's only national park and it is a major treasury of authentic wilderness. Information: Superintendent, Acadia National Park, Box 177, Bar Harbor, ME 04609 (phone: 207-288-3338).

BEST EN ROUTE

There is a delicate art to planning a trip to New England, and Maine is no exception. Summer and winter are high seasons; book well in advance. The three weeks from late September to mid-October are leaf-peeping season, a magic time to be here but crowded, especially in the delightful New England inns — themselves incentive enough for a trip. An optimal time to visit is after the leaves turn and before winter, when life has returned to non-tourist normal, and with luck the weather is fine. But that is just the period (mid-October to mid-November) when the Maine inns begin closing for the season, and you must plan in advance to get the ones you want. (An incentive: Rates during this period can be cut in half.)

Homewood Inn, Yarmouth – Beyond Portland on beautiful, foggy Casco Bay, this traditional inn has a hearty country breakfast, a popular Wednesday night clambake, tennis, pool, boating, and gameroom. Closed from mid-October to early June. Drinkwater Point, PO Box 196, Yarmouth, ME 04096 (phone: 207-846-3351).

Island Inn, Monhegan Island – This frame structure on a bluff over the tiny harbor is open summers only. Fresh fish — striped bass, haddock, bluefish — are regulars on the menu; the cooking is not fancy, but the service is cheerful and quick. An all-you-can-eat buffet on Sunday nights brings in hikers. Open June through September. See also *America's Special Havens*, DIVERSIONS. Monhegan Island, ME 04852 (phone: 207-596-0371).

Whitehall Inn, Camden – A classic Maine house, wrapped around by a deep, cool porch decorated with lots of potted plants. It was here that Edna St. Vincent

Millay (a resident of the town from the time she was 18) gave the first public recitation of *Renascence*. Open May through October. 52 High St., PO Box 558, Camden, ME 04843 (phone: 207-236-3391).

Asticou Inn, Northeast Harbor, Mt. Desert Island – An elegant but comfortable resort that maintains its style in simple ways. It encourages repeat visits and likes to get to know its visitors. Open from mid-June to mid-September. In the very backyard of Acadia National Park. Asticou Way, Northeast Harbor, Mt. Desert Island, ME 04662 (phone: 207-276-3344).

Maryland's Eastern Shore

On the eastern coast of Maryland, set between the Chesapeake Bay and the Atlantic Ocean, is the peninsula called the Eastern Shore, one of the most charming and unspoiled historic sections of the country. Dating from pre-Revolutionary times, the Eastern Shore has retained the simple elegance that characterized the region when Lord Baltimore and his followers established their settlements. Although part of the eastern seaboard, the environment is surprisingly remote from urban and suburban 20th-century America.

The Eastern Shore is more than just a few scattered plantations separated by open green. It retains a neat harmony of spreading rivers and streams, large and small farms, fine homes, with grounds that stretch to the water's edge. Mention the bay in this part of the country and you'll find it means only one thing: the Chesapeake, 200 miles long, from 4 to 30 miles wide, fed by 150 rivers, and containing more than 7,000 miles of tidewater shoreline. Here, you can taste some of the best oysters, crabs, and clams in the country, within sight of fishermen on the bay to remind you of the region's most important occupation. Take US 40 or I-95 northeast from Baltimore about 35 miles, then head 5 miles south on Rte. 213 to Chesapeake City.

CHESAPEAKE CITY: The Maryland port of the Chesapeake and Delaware Canal. Built in 1829 for $2 million, the canal shortens the water route between Baltimore and Philadelphia by more than 275 miles and has been a constant source of jobs for people in the surrounding community. The canal was purchased by the US government in 1919 and lowered to sea level in 1927 for $10 million. Since then, it has served as an important commercial line in the inland waterway connecting Maine to Florida and has been used for leisure vessels as well. One of the world's largest waterwheels can be found in the stone pumphouse, along with a scale model of the original canal, on the government property. The wheel was used to control water levels until the early 1900s. Information: Old Lock Pump House (phone: 301-885-5621).

EARLEVILLE: About 5 miles west of Rte. 213 overlooking the Sassafras River is Mount Harmon Plantation, an 18th-century tobacco plantation with a brick mansion, formal boxwood and wisteria gardens, and a tobacco house. The restored 1730 manor house is furnished with American and English antiques. The 386-acre property is almost entirely surrounded by water and recalls life and work during the 17th and 18th centuries on Maryland's Eastern Shore. More than 200 acres continue to be farmed, although tobacco no longer is raised. Owned by the Natural Lands Trust, Mount Harmon is open to the public from April through October. Information: Mount Harmon Plantation, PO Box 65, Earleville, MD 21929 (phone: 301-275-2721).

CHESTERTOWN: About 22 miles south of Warwick on Rte. 213, this tranquil, pretty, pre-Revolutionary town facing the Chester River contains several historic 2-story brick houses. Across town, away from the river, Washington College spreads over 20 acres. Founded in 1780 by the Reverend William Smith, this small liberal arts college, named after George Washington (who served on the Board of Visitors and Governors), now has an enrollment of about 800 students (Washington Ave.). Pre-Revolutionary buildings include: the Wickes House (100 E. High St.), Palmer House (532 W. High St.), Geddes-Piper House (Church Alley), and Widehall and the Customs House (both at High and Water Sts.). On the third Saturday in September, there's a candlelight walking tour that takes you past the wide, sweeping lawns of the town's homes into the public and Colonial homes decorated with ornate, carved mantelpieces and unusual Americana. For information, call Mrs. Robert Bryan at 301-778-1141. For general information on historic homes and tours, contact the Chestertown Town Hall (phone: 301-778-0500) or the Kent County Chamber of Commerce (phone: 301-778-0416).

WYE MILLS: About 25 miles south of Chestertown on Rte. 662 (via Rte. 213), this tiny colonial town grew up around an early-18th-century gristmill that has now been restored and is operated by college students. The Wye Church, built in 1721, is also in use. Nearby stands the Wye Oak, the official state tree. It has provided shade for 450 years and is one of the tallest white oaks in the country.

EASTON: About 12 miles south of Wye Mills on US 50 is the self-proclaimed "Colonial Capital of the Eastern Shore." Easton is often swamped with envious Northerners, some of whom become so enchanted that they return to purchase old estates upon retirement. Easton has some fine local antiques, artwork, and artifacts. During the second week in November, the town celebrates the *Waterfowl Festival,* which attracts wildfowl artists and carvers from all over the East Coast. Historic attractions in town include the Third Haven Meeting House, built in 1682, and the *Talbot County Historical Society and Museum.* Information: Easton Chamber of Commerce (phone: 301-822-4606).

OXFORD: Take Rte. 333 southwest from Easton until you reach the end of land. Here, you can ride on the oldest "free running" ferry in the nation. The Oxford-Bellevue ferry shuttles across the Tred Avon River, offering a fine view of the enclosed port and this small boating community.

ST. MICHAELS: When you leave the ferry, take Rte. 329 to Rte. 33 northwest about 8 miles. St. Michaels has an authentic 19th-century lighthouse at the *Chesapeake Bay Maritime Museum,* which contains maritime exhibitions, a boatbuilding workshop, and Chesapeake Bay sailing craft. Narrated cruises of the Miles River can be taken from the museum aboard the *Patriot.* Information: Chesapeake Bay Maritime Museum (phone: 301-745-2916).

TILGHMAN ISLAND: Continue southwest on Rte. 33 to its southern tip. Tilghman Island is the home port for a portion of the Chesapeake Bay skipjack fleet, the last commercial sailing fleet in North America. The island is a haven for fishermen, and fishing boats and a skipjack are available for charter.

BLACKWATER NATIONAL WILDLIFE REFUGE: Returning to Easton, pick up Rte. 50 south through Cambridge to Rte. 16, and past Church Creek to Rte. 335, about 20 miles. Blackwater is a winter refuge for Canada and snow geese, ducks, and birds of prey. There are driving tours, walking tours, and a visitors information center. For information, call the refuge at 301-228-2677.

CRISFIELD: About 55 miles south of Cambridge, this is where you can catch boats to two excellent retreats, Smith and Tangier islands. Several boats take passengers, mail, and freight to the islands, where colonies of Chesapeake Bay watermen live and work. Both islands are flat, sandy, and surrounded by marshland. Smith Island, Maryland, a miniature version of the mainland, has tiny frame houses with small gardens, wharves, crab shanties,and very little commercialism. There's no town hall here because there's no local government. Nearly everything is part of the United Methodist Church. Tangier Island, Virginia, is more developed, with a new anchorage for visiting sailors, a high school, and a local government headed by a mayor. For more information, contact the Somerset County Tourism Commission (phone: 301-651-2968).

BEST EN ROUTE

Tidewater Inn, Easton – Almost a legend, certainly a landmark. Activities in town center around this 120-room Colonial inn, especially during *Waterfowl Festival.* The restaurant is famous for fish and other local produce. Dover and Harrison Sts., Easton, MD 21601 (phone: 301-822-1300).

Robert Morris Inn, Oxford – In the former home of a financier, the inn is next to the Tred Avon River ferry. Close to tennis, golf, sailing, swimming, and bicycling. Dining room open to the public (see also *America's Special Havens*, DIVERSIONS). Oxford, MD 21654 (phone: 301-226-5111).

Chesapeake House, Tangier Island – Another secluded guest house close to nautical activities. Tangier Island is in Virginia waters. Tangier Island, VA 23440 (phone: 804-891-2331).

The Berkshires, Massachusetts

Up and down the East Coast, the Berkshires are famous for art and music in the summer, foliage in the fall, and downhill and cross-country skiing in the winter. Nobody seems to be quite sure how it all began — whether vacationers began going to the Berkshires because of the excellence of the music and art or whether artists and musicians began going because that's where the summer people went — or whether it's simply that everybody loves a vacation in the Berkshire Mountains.

More correctly referred to as the Berkshire Hills (although you'll swear they look just like mountains), Berkshire County fills the western quarter of the state, stretching from Connecticut to Vermont along the 50-mile border Massachusetts shares with New York. However, the Berkshires begin in earnest west of I-91, from Great Barrington in the south to the Mohawk Trail and Vermont in the north. Running straight through this area is Rte. 7, connecting the major towns (major in influence, not in size; only Pittsfield is a city of any size): Great Barrington, Stockbridge, Lenox, Pittsfield, Williamstown, and, slightly to the east, North Adams. Rte. 7 is a good road on which to start a trip, but remember the special advantage of Berkshire geography: The outside boundaries of the Berkshires form an almost perfect square, which in turn makes an almost perfect driving route. Follow the square and you can take in all the significant cultural, educational, and historical activities that give the Berkshires its special cachet.

Summer is, of course, prime time for artistic offerings. From the world-famous *Tanglewood* concerts and the *Jacob's Pillow* dance performances to the less well known theatrical offerings and the galleries presenting works of art and crafts, the Berkshire area is synonymous with both excellence and innovation in the arts.

A formidable rival to summer is the fall season, when the Berkshire Hills explode into color. The season starts in late September, but finding foliage at its colorful peak is about as chancy as finding perfect snow on a ski trip: You never know if nature will cooperate. Still, there are some general rules about when foliage will peak in a particular area. In late August, the harbingers stand out as solitary spots of gold or scarlet against the green hillsides. By mid-September, swamp maples are ablaze at the higher elevations and the northern part of the region. Most of the area, however, doesn't peak until October.

Snow always changes the face and appeal of a northern area, and the Berkshires are no exception. Mt. Greylock, the state's highest peak, provides a glorious setting for cross-country skiing and snowmobiling.

During the summer months there's so much going on that even old-timers have to consult the newspaper to plan their cultural days. You'll find an exhaustive list of events in local papers, divided into areas, each providing a complete rundown on what's happening in any location. For lodging referrals or information on the whole area, any season, write to the Berkshire Visitors Bureau, PO Box PR, Berkshire Common, Pittsfield, MA 01201 (phone: 413-443-9186 or 800-BERKSHR). Request the Berkshire's summer and winter guides and the *Circle Tours* booklet, which describes nine trips through the area. Information on the Mohawk Trail area: Mohawk Trail Assn., PO Box J, Charlemont, MA 01339 (phone: 413-664-6256).

STOCKBRIDGE: This beautiful town is the archetypal Berkshire village, in part because of the many famous paintings by its late resident Norman Rockwell. Its buildings and its people have graced the covers of the *Saturday Evening Post* dozens of times. You can see the originals of many famous covers at the *Norman Rockwell Museum* (Main and Elm Sts.; phone: 413-298-3822), a lovingly preserved collection of Rockwell work. Just down the street is the marvelous *Red Lion Inn,* justly one of New England's most famous hostelries. The *Berkshire Theatre Festival* (Main St.; phone: 413-298-5536), the oldest summer theater in the country, takes place in a landmark building designed by Stanford White.

Two interesting stops are Chesterwood, the home of sculptor Daniel Chester French, and the *Mission House.* Chesterwood (2 miles northwest of town off Rte. 183, Glendale; 413-298-3579) is maintained by the National Trust for Historic Preservation. You can visit the home, its gallery, and the gardens. *Mission House* (in town, Main and Sergeant Sts.; phone: 413-298-3239) was built in 1739 by the Reverend John Sergeant, who preached to the Berkshire Indians. (Relations were warm between the Indians and white settlers. Today, about a mile out of town, stands a marker reading: "The Ancient Burial Place of the Stockbridge Indians, Friends of Our Fathers.") Today the house is a museum of early Colonial life.

BECKET: Here is the home of *Jacob's Pillow,* the oldest dance festival in America. For 9 weeks in summer, it draws dance groups from all over the world; its own resident company performs as well. PO Box 287, Lee, MA 01238 (phone: 413-243-0745), for schedule and reservations.

LENOX: Generally acknowledged as the star town of the Berkshires, Lenox is the summer home of the *Boston Symphony Orchestra.* Every summer, the *Tanglewood* concerts draw crowds of thousands each weekend. And there's more than one way to take your music at Tanglewood: at the *Koussevitsky Music Shed* you can join the throngs picnicking, dreaming, and enjoying the symphony concerts; the *Chamber Music Hall* offers more intimate programs to smaller audiences. All these — and more

— take place on the 210-acre estate of Tanglewood, near where Nathaniel Hawthorne lived and wrote. You can tour the manicured grounds and the Hemlock Gardens as well. For Tanglewood's schedule: Symphony Hall, 301 Massachusetts Ave., Boston, MA 02115 (phone: 617-266-1492). The Mount, once the home of novelist Edith Wharton, is open to the public from June through October. It is also the summer home of *Shakespeare & Company,* which produces classical Shakespearean plays outdoors in July and August (south junction of Rte. 7 and 7A; phone: 413-637-1899).

Nearby is the Pleasant Valley Wildlife Sanctuary (472 W. Mountain Rd.; phone: 413-637-0320), maintained by the Massachusetts Audubon Society. Guided trails show you much of western Massachusetts nature and a beaver colony as well. There are small jewel-like lakes at almost every turn in this part of the Berkshires. One of the nicest is Stockbridge Bowl (south off Rte. 183).

PITTSFIELD: Its main summer event is the *South Mountain Concerts,* which feature opera, chamber music, and young people's concerts (call 413-442-2106 for schedules and information). Hancock Shaker Village, 5 miles west of town, is an original Shaker community built around 1790. Open from Memorial Day through Halloween, it has a restored round barn, homes and buildings, and many exhibitions and demonstrations of Shaker life. The *Berkshire Museum* (39 South St.) has an impressive collection of Old Masters, early American works, and some very modern works as well as natural history displays. If you loved *Moby Dick,* you'll want to visit Arrowhead (780 Holmes Rd.), Herman Melville's home from 1850 to 1863. The Berkshire Historical Society maintains this home, open from Memorial Day through Halloween, with its Melville memorabilia, furniture, and period costumes.

WILLIAMSTOWN: The home of Williams College also offers the *Williamstown Theater Festival* (Main St.) and the *Clark Art Institute* (South St.), a jewel box of a museum with outstanding examples of French Impressionists, old silver, porcelains, and sculpture.

It is at Williamstown that you turn the "corner" of the Berkshire route and join the Mohawk Trail toward North Adams and Greenfield. Before reaching North Adams, to the south nature provides some spectacular attractions with the proximity of Mt. Greylock and its lookout tower; the Natural Bridge formation (scientists estimate that it's been around for about 55 million years!); and the Savoy Mountain State Forest and Mohawk Trail intersection, with a host of camping, picnicking, swimming, hunting, and fishing.

NORTH ADAMS: The *Fall Foliage Festival* is held here in the last weeks of September to celebrate the coming of color with a no-holds-barred Oktoberfest blowout. It's a perfect time to visit. Contact the Northern Berkshire Chamber of Commerce, 69 Main St., North Adams (phone: 413-663-3735).

BEST EN ROUTE

Below are our choices from a wide variety of eating and lodging places. The Berkshires have some of the best inns in the country — truly an embarrassment of riches (see *America's Special Havens,* DIVERSIONS). We suggest you also examine a couple of the inn books listed in *For More Information,* GETTING READY TO GO.

Wheatleigh, Lenox – An elegant Italianate palazzo, surrounded by formal gardens and lawns, with a restaurant that serves an equally elegant cuisine. Of the 17 rooms, we recommend the 4 in front. See also *America's Special Havens,* DIVERSIONS. PO Box 824, Lenox, MA 01240 (phone: 413-637-0610).

Red Lion Inn, Stockbridge – The atmosphere here is homey, friendly, and full of small-town charm. The inn dates from 1773; some rooms have original antiques. Rates are higher during summer weekends; in winter, fewer rooms are open. The restaurant serves all meals and is noted for good, dependable, Yankee cuisine. See also *America's Special Havens,* DIVERSIONS. Main St., Stockbridge, MA 01262 (phone: 413-298-5545).

Williamsville Inn, West Stockbridge – Dating from 1797, this former farmhouse is the center of a 10-acre property that includes a pool, tennis court, pond for fishing, and skiing and antiquing nearby. The 15 rooms (only 13 in winter) include 2 with fireplaces. The inn is particularly known for its fine continental cuisine. Children over 10 welcome. Rte. 41, West Stockbridge, MA 01266 (phone: 413-274-6580).

Best Western Springs Motor Inn, New Ashford – Your hosts, the Grossos, have been feeding visitors for almost 60 years in informal, hearty style. Rte. 7, New Ashford, MA 01237 (phone: 413-458-5945).

Le Jardin, Williamstown – Country inn combines gracious surroundings with fine French cuisine. Closed in November. 777 Cold Spring Rd., Williamstown, MA 01267 (phone: 413-458-8032).

Cape Cod, Martha's Vineyard, and Nantucket, Massachusetts

When you look imaginatively at a map of Massachusetts, Cape Cod takes on the shape of a squat foot — wrapped in an elfin slipper that rises and curls at the toes — taking a step into the Atlantic. The cape is 70 miles long, from Buzzards Bay, where it leaves the mainland of southeastern Massachusetts, to the tip of its toe at Provincetown. It juts at least 30 miles into the Atlantic, far enough to be washed by the warmer waters of the Gulf Stream; consequently, the cape has cooler summers and milder winters than the mainland.

Below it, accessible by ferry and plane, are the two famous islands of Martha's Vineyard and Nantucket, where the homes and villages of America's 19th-century seafaring community are still intact and inhabited.

What is special about the cape and the islands has everything to do with the sea. It is the sea that provides the sailing, swimming, and beaches so attractive in summer. (Cape Cod has 300 miles of coastline — all clean and beautiful; the northern and eastern beaches are colder than those on the south side, which are warmed by the Gulf Stream and are about 10F milder.) It is the sea that is responsible for the cape's history. The Pilgrims landed at Provincetown about a month before they reached the mainland at Plymouth, and its beautiful, perfectly preserved 19th-century homes and villages are products of the area's successful ventures into worldwide shipping 150 years ago. (There was a time when Nantucket captains were as likely to meet one another in the Banda Islands as on the streets they shared at home.) And it is the sea — and the sand it torments — that makes Cape Cod one of the most interesting ecological studies a layman is likely to stumble across.

That's the good news. The bad news is, of course, that nasty commercialism has corrupted much of this tranquillity — filling up the open spaces with fast-food chains, assaulting the eyes and ears of the beholder with a concrete barrage. But only in some places! Two specific areas of the cape are protected by law from 20th-century excesses: the Cape Cod National Seashore, with its 40-mile stretch of untamed shoreline; and old Rte. 6A (or old Kings Highway

Historic District) along the north coast of the cape. Here you'll be able to discover villages with their heritage intact. Village elders must give their okay for so much as a shingle to be changed. Consequently, very few changes take place.

For a look at what might have happened without these protective laws, take a drive along Rte. 28 (along the south shore), which is up to its neon in the 20th century. Nothing has escaped modernization here. Rte. 28 is lined on both sides with drive-ins, stores, and restaurants with names like *Leaning Tower of Pizza.*

And so the formula for sightseeing on Cape Cod can be shaped according to your preference: If you're looking for up-to-the-minute action, follow Rte. 28; if you seek peace and a sense of history, take Rte. 6A; and if you're in a rush to get to Provincetown, take Rte. 6, which bisects the cape.

In order to see both Cape Cod and the neighboring islands, it makes sense to sweep the northern shore up to Provincetown (Rte. 6A), and return via the outer shore along the southern coast as far as Hyannis (Rte. 28). Here, pick up the ferry for the two offshore islands and later return to the cape at Woods Hole in Falmouth.

One further caveat: Everybody loves Cape Cod. In peak season, the whole area fairly groans under the weight of all its adoring visitors (Provincetown leaps from a population of 5,000 to 55,000 in summer). If you can time your trip for either spring or late fall, you'll be able to see much more nature. And you'll be able to find some local folks with time to sit and chat. However, if you want crowds, excitement, and big names, July and August are your time.

SANDWICH: The first town along Rte. 6A, it is rewardingly historic. The *Sandwich Glass Museum* (Rte. 130) has remarkable examples of the town's famous glass. The First Church of Christ (1848) features a spire that was copied from a design by England's Christopher Wren. Everything American from antique cars to a Civil War gristmill can be seen at the Heritage Plantation (Rte. 6A, Grove and Pine Sts.). And children will be delighted with the *Yesteryears Doll Museum* (River and Main Sts.).

YARMOUTH PORT: Here are three restored original houses: Captain Bangs Hallet House (18th century) on Strawberry La.; Colonel John Thatcher House (1680) on Rte. 6A; and Winslow Crocker House (1780), also on 6A.

"THE DENNISES": Four towns — Port, South, East, and West Dennis — together offer a combination of old and new: historical houses to tour, and, June through Labor Day, current theater offerings at the *Cape Playhouse* (Rte. 6A; phone: 508-385-3911 for schedule and reservations). The *Dennis Pines Golf Course,* in East Dennis, has an 18-hole course (phone: 508-385-8347).

BREWSTER: This town offers two interesting museums: *Drummer Boy* (2 miles west), a 35-acre site with Revolutionary scenes; and the *Cape Cod Museum of Natural History* (Main St.) with live animals and marine exhibitions. Sealand of Cape Cod (3 miles on 6A in West Brewster) has marineland shows and a penguin rookery.

EASTHAM: The gateway town to the Cape Cod National Seashore. The old Eastham Windmill still works. In addition, the Historical Society maintains several restored homes for touring. It is just off Rte. 6 in an 1869 schoolhouse, with exhibits.

CAPE COD NATIONAL SEASHORE: Cape Cod is a peninsula without bedrock — it is all sand. Before white men came here in any numbers, the cape had stands of hardwood and topsoil, which protected the Atlantic shoreline from the sea's fury. When the hardwood went, the sea and the wind played havoc with the sand —

shores around Truro and Wellfleet were eaten away, and the same sand was deposited along the moors surrounding Provincetown. The Cape Cod National Seashore came into being in 1961 after years of appalling disregard almost put an end to this 27,000-acre chunk of the cape. It now runs 40 miles from Chatham to Provincetown and includes six towns, much private property, and four public areas. No camping is allowed except in privately owned campgrounds. There are four picnic areas. From June through the fall, the National Park Service conducts guided tours and evening lectures. There are many self-guided trails. For more information: Superintendent, Cape Cod National Seashore, South Wellfleet, MA 02663 (phone: 508-349-3785); Province Land visitors center at Race Point Rd., Provincetown (phone: 508-487-1256); Salt Pond visitors center on Rte. 6, Eastham (phone: 508-255-3421).

WELLFLEET: Numerous beaches for swimming and a wealth of inland freshwater ponds dot the area. Fishing and sailing are also well provided for here — the town marina can accommodate 150 boats. Wellfleet Bay Wildlife Sanctuary runs a summer day camp for kids with the emphasis on natural history appreciation. The Massachusetts Audubon Society sponsors the sanctuary and maintains its many self-guided nature trails.

PROVINCETOWN: The town most familiar to first-timers on the cape, it attracts artists and celebrities and is exceedingly liberal and easy going — in rather startling contrast to the town's early history as the first landing site of the Pilgrims.

In 1899 Charles Hawthorne established the Cape Cod School of Art in Provincetown, and its reputation as an art center was established. Several leading artists summer here (including Robert Motherwell), and the town's long Commercial Street has at least a dozen good galleries side by side with museums (*Provincetown Museum* adjoins the Pilgrim Monument overlooking the town, the *Heritage Museum,* and the town's oldest house, at 27 Commercial St.). The *Provincetown Playhouse on the Wharf* gained national recognition for its excellence and innovation in theater. Unfortunately, a tragic fire in 1976 destroyed the theater as well as the *Eugene O'Neill Theater Museum.*

To return via the south shore (Rte. 6 to Orleans, then Rte. 28) you must backtrack for a period of time. An interesting stop, which you passed on your way to Provincetown, is Truro.

TRURO: A real change from Provincetown's hustle and commotion. Sparsely settled, Truro is known for the excellence of its fishing and swimming and for the Highland Light (also known as the Cape Cod Light), which dates to 1795 and can be seen 20 miles out to sea. Less well known is the fact that a large part of Truro's summer population comprises New York City and Boston psychiatrists.

CHATHAM: The three sights to see here are the Chatham Light, the fish pier, and the *Railroad Museum.*

HYANNIS: Now synonymous with the Kennedy family, but long before the clan and its compound, Hyannis drew its share of visitors because of its marvelous swimming beaches. There's an annual *Antiques Fair* in July (National Guard Armory) and musical theater-in-the-round is held in the *Melody Tent* (W. Main St.; phone: 508-775-9100 for schedule and prices). Hyannis is also a terminus for the ferry services to the islands. There are day trips for sightseeing as well as auto ferry service. You must reserve well in advance for space on the ferries by calling the *Steamship Authority* (phone: 508-771-4000). *Hy-Line* (phone: 508-775-7185) also serves the islands, and the *Island Queen* leaves from Falmouth (phone: 508-548-4800) but goes only to Martha's Vineyard.

NANTUCKET: It is not by chance that both Captain Ahab and First Mate Starbuck of the ill-fated *Pequod* were Nantucket men. Nothing could have seemed more likely to Melville's readers, and besides, one Captain George Pollard of Nantucket did lose a ship to an enraged sperm whale. Nantucket was once the whaling capital of the world, and you know it the instant the ferry gets within sight of Nantucket town. Main Street is lined with elegant 19th-century homes (many open for viewing); the *Whaling Museum* offers a whaling boat among other exhibits.

Some 30 miles south of Cape Cod, the island is only 49 square miles and can boast 50 miles of sand-dune-protected beaches. The Gulf Stream hovers offshore, warming the waters to an amazing 70F or more much of the summer. There are eight beaches, most with lifeguards, bathhouses, and food facilities. Sailing enthusiasts can rent all sizes of boats. Bicycle lanes coexist peacefully with roads for cars.

MARTHA'S VINEYARD: If you've ever heard that New Englanders are feisty and independent, consider some former goings-on on Martha's Vineyard. In 1977, the state legislature decided to take away the island's individual representation, incorporating it into a single district with Cape Cod. Natives of the island didn't take too kindly to this, and they formed a group to push for secession. They received offers from other US states for annexation — including Hawaii. A compromise was finally worked out so you won't have to say you've been to Martha's Vineyard, Hawaii!

Five miles by sea from Cape Cod, a sprawling 10 miles wide and 20 miles long, this island requires you to have some wheels to see it all. You can rent cars, bikes, or mopeds. Shuttle buses scurry between the main resort towns, and taxis and tour buses are available.

The main towns are Vineyard Haven, shopping center for the island; Gay Head, famous for its multicolored clay cliffs looming above the ocean; Oak Bluffs; Menemsha; and Edgartown.

Edgartown is the oldest settlement on the island, a fact well documented by the *Dukes Historical Society Museum* (School and Cooke Sts.). Built in 1765, it has some marvelous examples of Colonial architecture, a Jacobean fireplace, and seven open fireplaces. You return to the mainland via the ferry (remember to reserve!), this time arriving at Woods Hole on Cape Cod.

MASHPEE: Route 28A leads northward and back to mainland Massachusetts. But before leaving Cape Cod, detour inland to Mashpee, which is in the heart of the cape and in the heart of cranberry country. Descendants of the Mashpee Indians still gather cranberries from the many bogs. There's also the *Wampanoag Indian Museum* (Rte. 130), with a diorama and exhibitions of Indian lore; the Old Indian Meeting House (1648); and the Mashpee burial grounds (Rte. 28, south of town).

BEST EN ROUTE

Old Yarmouth Inn, Yarmouth Port – The oldest place (1696) on the cape, you won't find the inn advertised anywhere. It doesn't need to — its delighted clientele does it for them. It's good for rooms and meals — 5 rooms, including 2 suites, each with private bath. Open year-round. Old King's Highway, Yarmouth Port, MA 02675 (phone: 508-362-3191).

Jared Coffin House, Nantucket Island – Numerous celebrities have stayed here since 1845, when it was built. Now historically restored, the 28-room hotel (with three annexes adding another 30 rooms) offers old-time elegance to its guests — a formal dining room complete with piano during evening meals. Twin- and king-size beds are canopy-covered. See also *America's Special Havens,* DIVERSIONS. 29 Broad St., Nantucket, MA 02554 (phone: 508-228-2405).

White Mountains, New Hampshire

There's a pleasant, comfortable feeling about the White Mountains, similar to the pleasing quality of a George Gershwin tune. As you drive along roads that wind through deep, tree-lined gorges and sparkling clear mountain brooks, breathing the clean, fresh smell of pine everywhere, you get an inescapable sense that "all's right with the world."

Smack in the center of the state, some 140 miles north of Boston on I-93 (the only interstate through the area), the White Mountains offer New Hampshire countryside at its best. Our route starts at Plymouth and wanders through some of the best sightseeing and skiing land in the state.

PLYMOUTH: As you approach the White Mountains, 3,600 square miles of one of the oldest mountain ranges in the Appalachian chain, you can take a brief detour onto Rte. 25 at Plymouth, about 60 miles north of Manchester, for a quick look at the Polar Caves. As the name implies, these caves are reminders of the great glaciers that passed this way around 50,000 years ago, then retreated to the north. The Hanging Boulder, an 80-ton rock that seems to hang in midair, has been suspended that way for countless thousands of years; it isn't likely to fall on your head.

WHITE MOUNTAIN NATIONAL FOREST: As you return the 5 miles to I-93, you'll pass the southern boundary of the national forest. There are 20 campgrounds in the forest; *Pinkham Notch* is the headquarters of the Appalachian Mountain Club Huts System (for information and reservations, call 603-466-2727). If you're here in the fall, you'll be overwhelmed by the foliage, reds and oranges fanning out in all directions like spectacular flames, and you might wonder why they're called the White Mountains. In summer, the subtle green leaves of the white birch ripple with those of the sugar maple, giving the mountains an unforgettable depth and richness. Since the White Mountains are older than the Rockies, geological forces have had more time to smooth them into rounded formations. Information: White Mountain National Forest, PO Box 638, Laconia, NH 03247 (phone: 603-524-6450).

THE FLUME: The Flume is a narrow natural gorge flanked on both sides by 70-to-90-foot granite walls and set in the fir, spruce, and birch forest of Franconia Notch State Park. Intertwined along the cliffs are an intricate set of catwalks that allow you to get several unusual perspectives of the Flume Brook and its waterfall. There's also a major new visitors center here.

THE OLD MAN OF THE MOUNTAINS: As you leave the Flume, driving slowly, take in the view of Mt. Liberty. Just 3 miles north you'll see the Old Man of the Mountains, a magnificent, craggy, Lincolnesque profile carved naturally into the side of a mountain. New Hampshire's most famous landmark, it is often used as a symbol of the state. Skiers are no doubt more familiar with this part of the world as the site of the Cannon Mountain Aerial Tramway.

FRANCONIA NOTCH: Known as "the Switzerland of America," Franconia Notch is between the Kinsman and Franconia mountain ranges and is traversed by I-93. The Old Man of the Mountains is on the west side of the notch. The southern flank of the Franconia Range stretches across the horizon, sedate as those grand men of history for whom the Presidential Range is named. Mt. Lincoln and Mt. Lafayette are the closest to Franconia, but as you proceed northeast on Rte. 3, you'll pass Mt. Cleveland, then the approach to Mt. Washington, the tallest peak. Jefferson, Adams, and Madison stand to the north; Monroe, Franklin, Eisenhower, Clinton, Jackson, and Webster to the south.

MT. WASHINGTON: Ascending this mountain is an adventure whether you climb, take the cog railway or chauffeured van, or drive yourself. Many of these dramatic, rugged paths lead to the rocky summit at 6,288 feet. That might not sound high to you, and certainly it's not by Rocky Mountain standards, but Mt. Washington is the tallest peak in the Northeast. Unless you're an experienced climber, we recommend going up in a vehicle. Mt. Washington is known for its foul weather. There's the chance of snow no matter when you go. Even if you're there in mid-August, when the neighboring valleys are in the humid 80s, you'll need a heavy sweater before you get to the top of

Mt. Washington. If you're climbing, be sure to check weather conditions before setting out. The mountain has taken many lives over the years; there can be some very slippery, dangerous spots along the way. If you are driving, make sure to stop frequently while descending to let your brakes cool off. The road is so steep that it is possible to burn the lining from brake drums before reaching the bottom. If you don't want to risk it, take the Cog Railway. Working since 1869, it's a safe way to reach the stark, windswept mountain peak.

CRAWFORD NOTCH: Crawford Notch State Park has camping, fishing, hiking, and picnicking facilities (in Bartlett on Rte. 302; phone: 603-374-2272). Traveling southeast on Rte. 302, you'll pass Attitash Ski Area and Alpine Slide (a 4,000-foot-long ride down a mountain).

NORTH CONWAY: About 20 miles south of Crawford Notch you can ride up a mountain on a skimobile at the Mt. Cranmore Ski Area (phone: 603-356-5543). There's also a restored Victorian railway in town.

KANCAMAGUS HIGHWAY: North Conway and Conway have grown into resort towns of shopping centers and motels. If it seems overdeveloped for your taste, head west on Rte. 112, known as the Kancamagus Highway. This is one of the most glorious drives anywhere in the US, going into the deep recess between the mountains to take you closer to what you've already seen from a distance, returning you to I-93 about 35 miles later.

BEST EN ROUTE

Dana Place Inn, Jackson – A 27-room hotel with an indoor pool, river swimming, tennis courts, fishing; close to a golf course and cross-country and downhill skiing. Pinkham Notch Rd., Jackson, NH 03846 (phone: 603-383-6822).

Lovett's Inn by Lafayette Brook, Franconia – Guest house and cabins, some with fireplaces in the living rooms; a swimming pool, pond, and cross-country skiing. Close to golf, tennis, and fishing. Personal service and excellent cooking. 30 rooms. See also *America's Special Havens*. Profile Rd., Franconia, NH 03580 (phone: 603-823-7761 or 800-356-3802).

The Jersey Shore: Atlantic City to Cape May, New Jersey

There are good beaches all along the 127-mile intercoastal waterway of New Jersey's Atlantic Ocean shoreline, but the most famous section is the 50-mile stretch of wide, beautiful seashore and gentle surf that begins just south of Atlantic City and ends at Cape May Point. It has some of the best beaches on the eastern seaboard and an unusual geographic conformation that makes for fabulous fishing: The oceanfront land is actually a series of narrow islands that run parallel to the mainland, with a tidal bay in between. Fishermen can choose deep-sea fishing or the calmer waters of the protected bays.

This section of the Jersey shore was *the* place to summer in the late 1800s for anyone who was anyone. This popularity — exemplified most by Atlantic City, made famous by the Depression-era game of Monopoly — ultimately led to overexposure and a recession; since World War II, as successive waves of "beautiful people" flocked first to Florida and then to European and

Caribbean beaches rather than prosaic New Jersey, the major resorts suffered severe setbacks.

In desperate attempts to lure tourists back, many of these towns began casting about for other means of excitement — amusement parks, convention facilities, special activities. This is good news and bad news for the visitor today. Good news because it makes the shore — with its quiet surf and wide beaches — a great place to take small children; bad news because amid the hurly-burly you might just overlook the very best aspect of some shore towns — the lovely Victorian and Edwardian houses hidden in the streets behind the gaudy boardwalks.

These islands and mainland communities form what is called the Jersey Cape. The islands themselves, popular with many French Canadians, are connected by Ocean Drive — actually a series of bridges designed as a scenic, efficient beltway for traffic up and down the cape. The towns along Ocean Drive stir the memory of anyone raised on the East Coast — Atlantic City, Ventnor City, Margate City, Strathmore, Sea Island City, Avalon, Stone Harbor, Wildwood, Cape May. A stop at any one of them will prove entertaining, but the high points are certainly Atlantic City, America's newest gambling center; Wildwood; and beautiful Victorian Cape May. Information: Atlantic City Convention and Visitors Bureau, 2314 Pacific Ave., Atlantic City, NJ 08401 (phone: 609-348-7100); Wildwood Dept. of Tourism, PO Box 609, Wildwood, NJ 08260 (phone: 609-522-1407); Cape May County Public Affairs, PO Box 365, Cape May Courthouse, NJ 08210 (phone: 609-886-0901). Or call the New Jersey Division of Travel and Tourism's 24-hour information number: 800-JERSEY-7 or 800-537-7397.

ATLANTIC CITY: On November 2, 1976, New Jersey legalized casino gambling, and Atlantic City slammed into high gear to become Las Vegas's East Coast competition. So far, the project has received mixed reviews. While the casinos are generating high revenues and are successfully competing with their Vegas counterparts, benefits to the community such as a bolstering of the local economy and a face-lift for areas outside the Boardwalk (where the new building is concentrated) are slow in materializing. Nonetheless, Atlantic City is the only spot in the eastern two-thirds of the country in which Americans can legally gamble in a casino, and it attracts everyone from the tuxedoed high roller on down to the riffraff. The first casino to open was the lavish *Resorts International* at North Carolina and Boardwalk, followed in 1979 by the *Caesar's Boardwalk Regency* at Arkansas and Boardwalk and *Bally's Park Palace Hotel and Casino.* There are now 12 in all, with several more under way. The city's latest non-casino attraction is *Ocean One,* a sparkling new shopping complex built to resemble an ocean liner with open decks and a nautical motif, which juts out over the water on one of the Boardwalk's former piers. Of course, you can also enjoy the rest of the Boardwalk (all 6 miles of it) — its piers, teeming with amusement centers; the Miss America pageant; and of course the saltwater taffy.

WILDWOOD: This town strikes something of a balance between the quieter pleasures of a visit to Cape May and the ritz, swank, and swizzle of Atlantic City. Wildwood has a fine, wide beach, an appropriately lively boardwalk with six amusement piers, and a reputation for good evening entertainment, offered by a varied array of nightclubs with comedians and singers, jazz bands and Dixieland groups.

CAPE MAY: The clocks here all stopped somewhere toward the end of the 19th century — and that suits the townsfolk just fine. That particular time warp has proved to be a gold mine for tourism. The determined and dogged theme of this town is Victoriana. There are so many original and preserved Victorian frame buildings still in mint condition that Cape May has been declared a national landmark. Attempts at modernization are squashed as quickly as possible.

Indeed, authenticity is lovingly protected in this town. Its 600 Victorian buildings stand busily side by side, each resplendent in its gingerbread excess, scalloped widow's walks traced along scalloped rooftops, columned verandahs with latticework trims; even the gardens seem just right for a nosegay framed with a lace doily.

Visitors can enjoy this old-fashioned community in a number of ways. There's a 1¼-hour historic walking tour 4 days a week that leaves from the information booth at Washington and Ocean Streets. A horse-drawn tourist trolley covers a similar route. There's a delightful Victorian pedestrian mall and even a Victorian bandstand where weekly concerts are presented, a free offering by the community. At Convention Hall, visitors are treated to entertainment ranging from free ballroom dancing, teen discos, and concerts to antiques shows, cartoon shows, and so on. Consult the calendar of events posted at the information office just outside the hall on Beach Drive at the boardwalk.

But for pure self-indulgence and excess you just can't beat the experience of living in one of these authentic Victorian mansions during your stay. A Victorian guest house might well feature afternoon tea served on the verandah, an antique four-poster bed in your room, or a tour of the house.

Probably the most famous of these guest houses is the *Mainstay Inn,* known locally as the Victorian Mansion. Authenticity is fiercely maintained by the present owners, a young couple who delight in sharing their wealth of Victoriana with interested visitors. This house was built in 1872 as an Italian villa and has gone through some fascinating changes. Your room might be one of the "front rooms," which means you'll luxuriate in 12-foot ceilings and a splendid view. Or you might choose one in the "new wing," which was built in 1896 to accommodate the six housemaids.

At the very tip of the cape is the Cape May Point State Park. Although no swimming is allowed here due to the insidious currents, called "Cape May rips," visitors love to search the beach for "diamonds" — bits of wave-polished quartz that shine brilliantly in the sand. There's also a nearby bird sanctuary and lighthouse.

Also at the tip of the cape is the Cape May–Lewes, Delaware ferry. Passengers may embark here for the 70-mile ride to Delaware. Make reservations by writing to PO Box 827, North Cape May, NJ 08204 (phone: 609-886-2710 or 609-886-2718).

BEST EN ROUTE

Mainstay Inn, Cape May – Built in 1872, with original furnishings, a grand dining room, and verandah. A few blocks from the ocean. Rates include a continental breakfast on the porch (in summer) and afternoon tea at 4:30 PM. Open weekends November and December, then closed through March. See also *America's Special Havens,* DIVERSIONS. 635 Columbia Ave., Cape May, NJ 08204 (phone: 609-884-8690).

Seventh Sister Guest House, Cape May – A 6-room inn built in the late 1800s. Most rooms have an ocean view, and the house has a comfortable porch facing the sea. Baths are shared. 10 Jackson St., Cape May, NJ 08204 (phone: 609-884-2280).

Windward House, Cape May – A shingle cottage in the heart of the historic district with 8 rooms, all with private baths. 24 Jackson St., Cape May, NJ 08204 (phone: 609-884-3368).

Hotel-Casinos, Atlantic City – *Resorts International,* N. Carolina at Boardwalk (phone: 609-344-6000 or 800-GET-RICH, from most East Coast states); *Atlantis,*

Florida Ave. and Boardwalk (phone: 800-257-8672); *Caesar's Atlantic City,* Arkansas Ave. at Pacific (phone: 800-257-8555); *Bally's Park Place,* Park Pl. at Boardwalk (phone: 800-225-5977); *Bally's Grand,* Boston and Pacific Aves. on the Boardwalk (phone: 800-257-8677); *Harrah's Marina,* 1725 Brigantine Blvd. (phone: 800-242-7724); *Sands,* S. Indiana Ave. between Pacific Ave. and Boardwalk (phone: 800-257-8580); *Del Webb's Claridge Hotel Casino and Hotel,* Indiana and Boardwalk (phone: 800-582-7676 in New Jersey; 800-257-8585 elsewhere); *Showboat,* Delaware and Boardwalk (phone: 800-621-0200); *Trump,* Mississippi Ave. and Boardwalk (phone: 800-441-0909); *Trump Castle,* Huron Ave. and Brigantine Blvd. (phone: 800-441-5551); *Tropworld,* Brighton Ave. and Boardwalk (phone: 800-257-6227 or 800-THE-TROP).

Adirondack Park and Mountains, New York

For some people the ideal vacation is a complete return to nature. They seek out rugged wilderness locations and gently ease their "civilized" bodies into the comforting natural rhythms. The Adirondack Park offers almost unlimited challenges and opportunities for this sort of communion with the elements. Of the 6 million acres in this area, nearly half are protected by law from the "modern improvements" of man. There are mountains; more lakes than you can count, several of them very famous (Saranac Lake, Lake George, Lake Champlain, Lake Placid); many campsites tucked away in the miles of forests; and the old Indian Canoe Route.

The Adirondack Park and Mountains encompass just under 9,000 square miles, just about filling the entire northeastern section of New York State, from Lake Champlain and the Vermont border to as far south as Glens Falls. The area is popular year-round; in winter for skiing and other snow sports (Lake Placid was the site of the 1932 and the 1980 Winter Olympics); in summer for its lakes, forests, and fishing; in autumn for the spectacular foliage of its wooded mountains. It's an especially attractive vacation area because among the lakes and mountains of the interlaced villages are towns of reasonable size, which can be visited — or avoided — as you choose.

The deliberate underdevelopment of the Adirondack Park is the very foundation of its charm and appeal. Roads are few, however, and they don't always lend themselves to a straight route, especially if you really want to get a sense of the scope of the area. But with some backtracking and patience you can circle the entire parkland in a few days, allowing plenty of flexibility for stopping, looking, enjoying, and relaxing.

The Adirondack Mountains are about 4 hours from New York City. Our route starts at Lake George and makes a counterclockwise loop through the area; along the way you will have ample opportunity for exploring on your own. Information: Division of Tourism, Dept. of Economic Development, 1 Commerce Plaza, Albany, NY 12245 (phone: 518-474-4116 or 800-CALL-NYS) in all 48 contiguous states); or New York State Office of Parks Recreation, Historic Preservation, Empire State Plaza, Albany, NY 12238 (phone:

518-474-0456); for camping information: call the Summer Recreation Office (phone: 518-457-2500) or write for brochures to the New York State Dept. of Environmental Conservation, 50 Wolf Rd., Albany, NY 12233.

LAKE GEORGE VILLAGE: The most populous (30,000 accommodations for tourists) and most commercial town in the area. The lake itself is a 32-mile jewel set comfortably at the base of some very impressive mountains. There are dozens of state-owned islands in the lake. Lake George Village is an active, exciting place, with some of the drawbacks of a tourist center. The natural pleasures of swimming, boating, and fishing have almost been superseded by more profitable ventures like the Great Escape (5 miles south on Rte. 9), a theme park with six fairy tale areas.

The entire Adirondack area is a mine of early American history, especially from the French and Indian War period. Lake George is no exception. Ft. William Henry (Canada St.) is a reconstructed 200-year-old fort, with interesting displays. You will be shown a 45-minute edited version of *The Last of the Mohicans* as part of the tour. An impressive number of war relics are on display.

Explore the scenic beauty of Lake George on one of the many cruise vessels that offer daily sightseeing cruises as well as dinner, jazz, and moonlight cruises. An eagle's-eye view of the area is yours for the driving. Take Rte. 9 a half mile south to Prospect Mountain State Parkway. At the end of the 5-mile climb is a spectacular view of the southern Adirondack Mountains and upper Hudson Valley.

BLUE MOUNTAIN LAKE: Take Rte. 28 west from Lake George. In addition to the glorious scenery you'll also find the *Adirondack Lake Center for the Arts* (in the village), with an art gallery, concerts, films, and exhibitions. The *Adirondack Museum* (1 mile north on Rte. 30) has 20 buildings of treasures (mostly on the history of the area). Nearby Blue Mountain has nature trails and some overlooks at its peak.

Rte. 30 north will take you past Long Lake. Tupper Lake lies just north. The chief attraction is Big Tupper Mountain with its excellent skiing facilities, including a chair lift (which operates in summer for sightseeing), T-bar, beginners' lift, and various snack bars. There is golfing, boating, swimming, and camping all around the lake.

SARANAC LAKE: World famous as a health resort, Saranac's spas have been visited by a host of celebrities (including Robert Louis Stevenson, whose cottage is open to the public) and a lot more just plain folks. This area, too, is a winter and summer sports resort. There are boat races, art exhibitions, and concerts. The Dickert Memorial Wildlife Collection (in the Saranac Lake Free Library, 100 Main St.) has some marvelous mounted specimens of local wildlife. In winter, Mt. Pisgah Ski Center — at the end of the village — has a ski lift.

LAKE PLACID: This largest town in the Adirondacks is synonymous with the 1932 and 1980 Winter Olympics, and the sports facilities are superior here. At the *Olympic Arena and Convention Hall* (Main St.) there are winter and summer skating as well as ice shows, concerts, and other performances. On the famous Mt. Van Hoevenberg Bobsled Run (7 miles southeast on Rte. 73) you can skim down in an Olympic-type bobsled. During the winter there are afternoon races (December to March). It's also a good cross-country ski area.

Lake Placid Center for Music, Drama, and Art (Saranac Ave. at Fawn Ridge) offers concerts, performances by the repertory company, and art exhibitions (phone: 518-523-2512 for specific information).

John Brown's Farm Historical Site (John Brown Rd. off Rte. 73) gives you a glimpse into the famous abolitionist's life — his furnishings, his home, and his gravesite.

Lake Placid, too, has a variety of lake cruises. Trips leave from Holiday Harbor (north on Rte. 86 to Mirror Lake Drive). General tourist information is available from the Lake Placid Chamber of Commerce, Olympic Arena, Lake Placid, NY 12946 (phone: 800-342-9561 in New York State; phone: 800-833-2521 elsewhere).

AUSABLE CHASM: A scenic wonder on Rte. 9 north not to be missed. There are any number of ways to view this incredible gorge, which slashes from 100 to 200 feet deep along its route. Footbridges cross its 20-to-50-foot width. You can take a self-guided walking tour and see the quaintly named rock formations: "pulpit rock," "elephant's head," "cathedral rock." From May through September, you can also take a guided boat ride down a natural flume through the rapids. (Just to settle any arguments, it's pronounced Oh-*say*-bl.)

FT. TICONDEROGA: This fort played a strategic part in our nation's history. Originally built in 1755 by the French, it changed hands in its active life about a dozen times, was burned, and almost destroyed. Now restored according to the original French plans, it houses a museum with many original weapons, uniforms, and other war trappings. Live fife-and-drum performances and cannon firings add realistic touches.

Although there is much to do in Adirondack towns, there is much more to do in the Adirondack countryside, and chances are you're here to camp, fish, swim, and hike. Below are a list of some of the campgrounds in the area with telephone numbers for more information and reservations. For complete information: Division of Tourism, Dept. of Economic Development, 1 Commerce Plaza, Albany, NY 12245 (phone: 518-474-4116 or 800-CALL-NYS) in all contiguous states.

Lewey Lake at Indian Lake (206 sites). Climb Snowy and Blue Ridge mountains, fish, swim, canoe, hike (phone: 518-648-5266).

Moffit Beach at Lake Pleasant (258 sites). Camp on Sacandaga Lake. Swim, fish, hike, canoe (phone: 518-548-7102).

Luzerne at Fourth Lake (165 sites). Swim and hike (phone: 518-696-2031).

The Glen Island Group at Bolton Landing (212 sites). Register at Glen, boat to any of 55 islands. Sites all have fireplace, tent platform, semiprivate dock. Four different boat launching sites. Swim, hike, fish, canoe (phone: 518-644-9696).

Rogers Rock at Hague (301 sites). Hiking up the 1,000-foot Rogers Rock. View over Lake George. Swim, fish, hike, canoe (phone: 518-585-6746 or 518-585-9728).

Putnam Pond, 6 miles from Ticonderoga (56 sites). Miles of trails branch out from here to forest ponds and lakes (phone: 518-585-7280).

Cranberry Lake at Cranberry Lake (173 sites). Over 50 miles of wilderness trails, some with rustic lean-tos. 20 miles of Oswegatchie Inlet for boaters. Swim, fish, hike, canoe (phone: 315-848-2315).

Ausable Point at Peru (121 sites). Remote area, near rapids. Swim, fish, canoe (phone: 518 561-7080).

BEST EN ROUTE

The Lodge, Lake Clear – German food in rustic and woodsy surroundings. The lodge itself is pure old-Adirondack, with mounted moose heads hung on the walls. The menu is fixed and served family style — and everyone gets to know everyone else over a hearty meal. Reservations are a must for dinner and for the few available rooms. The Lodge on Lake Clear, Lake Clear, NY 12945 (phone: 518-891-1489).

Hotel Saranac, Saranac – Owned and operated by Paul Smith College, it's a learning laboratory for students of hotel administration, with 92 rooms, dining room, lounge, bakery, and gift shop. If you have a complaint, an army of folks will hear you out. 101 Main St., Saranac Lake, NY 12983 (phone: 518-891-2200).

Hudson River Valley, New York

Rip Van Winkle slept here. So did George Washington. And you can, too, in any number of charming inns and hotels as you explore the magnificent Hudson River and the valley that surrounds it. There is so much scenic beauty, so many historical reference points, and so many downright fascinating bits of folklore that you will find yourself totally caught up in the charm and mystery of this area.

Our route follows the east bank of the Hudson from New York City to Rip Van Winkle Bridge, about 20 miles south of Albany. This is the entry point to the Catskill Mountain area to the west and the Adirondacks to the north. At the bridge, our itinerary crosses from the east to the west bank, and returns toward New York City. For a comprehensive, mile-by-mile guide to this route, see *The Hudson River Tourway* by Gilbert Tauber (it's out of print; try your public library).

This is a compelling route for the sheer beauty of the Hudson, if for no other reason. In its 315-mile course from the Adirondacks to the sea, the Hudson changes style from a shimmering, 3-mile-wide expanse (called Tappan Zee by the early Dutch; *zee* is Dutch for "sea") to a sinuous serpent squeezed by the towering Palisades downriver nearer New York City. To see the river reflect the setting sun is one of the enchantments of New York life.

Throughout local history men have compared the Hudson to Germany's Rhine. And men of great wealth, seeking to exploit the similarities, built palatial estates along its banks. Lacking any definable style, these pseudo-villas and châteaux have been lumped together into the tongue-in-cheek category of Hudson Valley Gothic. Many of these mansions are open to the public and are well worth a look.

British and American forces fought for this area inch by inch during the Revolutionary War. The Hudson was the key to holding the great northern territories beyond, and the towns up and down the valley held in turn patriots and king's men.

Finally, less tangible but very real is the air of folklore and mystery — the delicious shiver of the supernatural — that cloaks the high mountains and heavily forested valleys. There's the goblin who sits atop Dunderberg whose churlish moods control the winds whipping up the river below. And, of course, there's the Headless Horseman; this is his turf.

TARRYTOWN: Just 25 miles north of New York City is Washington Irving's "Sleepy Hollow" country. Sunnyside, Irving's home for 24 years, is open year-round. You can see his books, manuscripts, household furnishings, and some statues of his characters (W. Sunnyside La., off Broadway/US 9). Nearby is one of those incredible Hudson Gothic mansions, Lyndhurst (635 S. Broadway), built in 1838 by Alexander Jackson Davis and the home of railroad tycoon Jay Gould from 1880 to 1893. The 67-acre estate, now run by the National Trust for Historic Preservation, offers stunning interiors and vistas as well as outdoor concerts and festivals in the warm months. Closed Mondays (phone: 914-631-0046).

GARRISON: A mansion here must not be missed. Boscobel, on Rte. 9D, built by S. M. Dyckman for his wife in 1806, remains a glorious villa housing a collection of rare and beautiful antiques. The grounds are manicured in English formal style, and the view of the Hudson is spectacular. The Manitoga Nature Center, the former estate of Russell Wright, features 200 acres of forests and trails overlooking the Hudson (on Rte. 9D; phone: 914-424-3812).

POUGHKEEPSIE: Two families have immortalized their names as well as their town: the Vassars, for their prestigious college, and the brothers Smith, for their cough drops. Be sure to visit the Glebe House (635 Main St.), built in about 1767 as a rectory for the Episcopal church, and the Clinton House (549 Main St. at White St.), home of the governor during the brief period in 1777 when Poughkeepsie was the state capital. There are also some beautiful old houses in town.

HYDE PARK: This town is familiar to most Americans as the home of Franklin Delano Roosevelt. He spent most of his life here and, with his wife, Eleanor, is buried in the rose gardens on the Roosevelt estate. Visitors may browse through FDR's books, collections, and other personal treasures in the estate's museum and library. The admission price here also entitles you to visit the Vanderbilt Mansion down the road. Designed by Stanford White and built in 1895, this Gothic home is a study in lavish excess. New for visitors is the Eleanor Roosevelt retreat and homestead, Val-kill, just a short shuttle bus ride from the FDR home and library.

RHINEBECK: For a bit of history-come-alive, don't miss the Old Rhinebeck Aerodrome (off Rte. 9 on Stone Church Rd.). In addition to a spiffy collection of World War I aircraft still in working order, there's a Waldo Pepper–type simulated dogfight overhead staged Sunday afternoons, May through September, and Saturday afternoons as well from early July to the end of the season. It's very real. And what with the aviators in goggles and flowing white scarves, you'll find yourself searching the cast for a glimpse of Robert Redford — or at least the Red Baron. Rhinebeck is a lovely 300-year-old town with, reportedly, the oldest inn in the country, the *Beekman Arms*. The Rhinebeck Chamber of Commerce has free maps for self-guided walking and driving tours, available May through October at the visitor booth between 17 and 19 Mill St.

KINDERHOOK: This is the birthplace and burial site of Martin Van Buren, eighth president of the US. Just east of Kinderhook (Rte. 66) is the Old Chatham Shaker Village, a restoration of the 18th-century community. Visitors can go into the homes and see the marvelously simple items created by these people. There are also an herb garden, bookstore, and gift shop. From this point either continue north into the Adirondacks or cross the river (via the Rip Van Winkle Bridge, 20 miles back, near Hudson) and return south along the west bank of the Hudson.

CATSKILL: The gateway to the famous mountain resort area is also the site of Mr. Van Winkle's famous nap. The Catskill Game Farm (12 miles west, off Rte. 32) delights kids with its touch-and-feed areas for tame deer and other animals (open from mid-April to late October). Catskill State Park is a forest preserve that contains six campgrounds, hundreds of miles of marked nature trails, a ski run with chair lift, and all the glories of nature. Hunter Mountain is a popular ski area here and well known for its summertime international festivals.

WOODSTOCK: Now associated with the flower children of the '60s, the town was established in 1895 by a wealthy Englishman as a colony for intellectuals and artists. The Art Students League of New York set up a summer program here a few years later. Still healthy and active today, Woodstock continues to be synonymous with the arts. Each summer cultural events are presented to the public: Woodstock Artists Association Gallery (28 Tinker St. at Village Green; phone: 914-679-2940) features traveling shows by local and nationally known artists.

KINGSTON: One of New York's oldest towns (settled in 1652), it has survived every curve ball thrown by history — and there have been a number. First a Dutch trading post, then an English colony, and finally American (the state constitution was signed here in 1777), the city suffered attacks by various parties at every juncture — Indians, Dutch, British, Americans. A century ago its major industry was cement; that played out, but today it still prospers with a diverse economy, including a large IBM complex. This town has more than 15 original early American homes in the old stockade area (the stockade was built in 1658) that can be toured. Some of the houses on the self-guided tour made up a segment of the Underground Railroad for escaped slaves headed for Canada. Afterward, you can peek into the *New York State Senate House and Museum* (269 Fair St.).

NEW PALTZ: Six restored homes and a church from the original settlement, founded by French Huguenots in 1678, are open to the public from the end of May through October. Closed Mondays and Tuesdays. An equal attraction is the marvelous *Mohonk Mountain House,* a splendid resort nearby.

NEWBURGH: For more than a year (between April 1782 and August 1783), George Washington and the Continental Army made their headquarters here, and it was from here that the successful conclusion of the war was announced. The headquarters are a fascinating place to visit — the Jonathan Hasbrouck House (Liberty St.), where Washington stayed, and the New Windsor Cantonment (Temple Hill Rd., off Rte. 32), a reconstruction of the army's winter camp. Ironically, it's not open in the winter, only from late April through October.

MOUNTAINVILLE: Not far away is the *Storm King Mountain Art Center* on Old Pleasant Hill Rd., a cut-stone French château housing some important pieces of sculpture, including some by David Smith, and 200 acres outdoors. The view is quite Alpine in feeling: The river narrows between towering mountains, and one is impressed with the distant vistas.

For a change in perspective, visit the Brotherhood Winery (35 North St. in Washingtonville, off Rte. 94). Established by monks many years ago, it remains America's oldest functioning winery. Tour the caverns where the aging casks lie in state, learn a bit about wine making, and then sample some of the products (phone: 914-496-3661 for hours).

WEST POINT: The US Military Academy, founded in 1802, was the training ground for some of our nation's top military leaders. There are some places you'll want to see, spots remembered from all those movies: the chapel with its stained glass windows, the kissing rock, and Trophy Point, with its crow's-eye view of the Hudson.

BEST EN ROUTE

Beekman Arms, Rhinebeck – This just might be the oldest continuously operating inn in the US. It is built over an original stone tavern (c. 1700); the main portion of the existing hotel was built in 1766. During the Revolution it was known as *Bogardus Tavern* to its regulars — among them Washington and Lafayette. Accommodations today include the original building, plus an American Gothic guesthouse, a renovated carriage house, and two wings of new courtyard rooms. Rhinebeck, NY 12572 (phone: 914-876-7077).

Bear Mountain Inn, Bear Mountain – Renovated a few years back at a cost of millions, this charming old inn was built to resemble a Swiss chalet. Besides the main inn, accommodations are available in the *Overlook Lodge* and in four large lakeside cabins. Open all year. Bear Mountain Inn and Conference Center, Bear Mountain, NY 10911 (phone: 914-786-2731).

Inn at the Falls, Poughkeepsie – Opened in 1985, this multimillion-dollar development combines the amenities of a luxury resort with the ambience of a bed-and-breakfast inn. Fourteen of the 36 rooms are suites, with designs ranging from

English manor home to American country, Oriental, or contemporary themes. Many rooms have four-poster, wrought-iron, or canopy beds, brass headboards, armoires, and rolltop desks. Breakfast is delivered to the rooms each morning, with silver, china, and linen service. 50 Red Oaks Mill Rd., Poughkeepsie, NY 12603 (phone: 914-462-5770).

Mohonk Mountain House, New Paltz – Open year-round, this world-famous resort offers a wide variety of sports, a relaxing, rustic atmosphere in the 1869 Victorian mansion, and overwhelming panoramic scenery. Room rates include all meals; the dining room is open to the public as well. Miles of nature trails lead guests on self-guided tours. Cross-country skiing and horseback riding are two favorite sports. New Paltz, NY 12561 (phone: 914-255-1000; 212-233-2244 in New York City).

La Crémaillère, Banksville – Though situated in a small town in New York State, this inn captures the essence of French country ambience. The rustic walls are hung with original oils depicting various French provinces, open fireplaces warm body and soul, lovely china pieces decorate the small wood bar. The food, ranging from Dover sole to seasonal game, is outstanding, worthy of the multi-star ratings the restaurant has received. Closed Mondays and the month of February. Call for directions and reservations. Banksville, NY (phone: 914-234-9647).

Culinary Institute of America, Hyde Park – Combining the best of creative cooking with a new experience in dining out, the institute offers a 2-year cooking course to serious chefs. The final phase includes cooking for the public in one of 4 dining rooms on the premises: the *Escoffier* restaurant, formal and extremely professional in its approach to haute cuisine; the *American Bounty,* for a selection of American regional fare; the *St. Andrews Café,* for spa cuisine (low-calorie, nutritionally balanced); and the *Caterina de Medici,* for Northern Italian food. Lunches and dinners are served Tuesdays through Saturdays at the *Escoffier* and *American Bounty;* weekdays at *St. Andrews* and the *Caterina de Medici.* (Dinners, it should be noted, are meticulous 3-hour affairs; reservations, a must, should be made well in advance.) Rte. 9, Hyde Park, NY 12538 (phone: 914-471-6608).

Niagara Falls and Buffalo, New York

If you're searching for an unspoiled vacation paradise far from crowds and confusion, Niagara Falls is definitely not your destination. It is, in fact, a major tourist attraction, second only to New York City in the entire eastern US. Big and bawdy, Niagara Falls generally makes things seem larger than life — its commercialism is tackier and somehow more annoying than in other areas, its industrial pollution more offensive. Despite all these excesses, Niagara Falls manages, quite literally, to rise above it all.

It is ironic that the single most devastating threat to the future of the falls comes not from the abuses of man but rather from a weakness in nature. The shale and limestone foundations of the riverbed are slowly being washed away by the sheer force of the water plunging over the falls. As this erosion continues, the falls will be forced backward until they flatten out altogether and become little more than a series of rapids in the river.

But there's still time to pack the car and leave a note for the newspaper boy to say you're leaving. (Scientists estimate that all this will take another few tens of thousands of years.) So visit the falls. And while you marvel at their massive beauty, you might even have a kind thought or two for the commercial-minded folks whose various enterprises make it so ridiculously easy for you to see the attractions.

You can also shuttle over the several bridges across the Niagara River and see the whole thing from the Canadian vantage points.

Once you've had enough of the wonders of nature and crave some intellectual stimulation, you can drive to nearby Buffalo, an upstate cultural oasis complete with major art galleries, museums, and a symphony orchestra — not to mention three professional sports teams.

NIAGARA FALLS: The falls are formed as the waters of Lake Erie race downhill to join Lake Ontario, becoming en route the Niagara River. The river gathers strength and power in the narrows, then plunges almost 200 feet to form the world-famous falls. A small island in the river splits this whitewater juggernaut at the point of its mighty dive, dividing it into two falls instead of one: the American Falls — 184 feet high and 1,076 feet wide; and the Horseshoe (Canadian) Falls — 176 feet high and 2,200 feet wide. There is a minor falls, much smaller, called Bridal Veil.

The indomitable little island responsible for this twofold masterpiece is Goat Island, named for its former residents. Its 70 acres are prime viewing locations, making it a popular attraction. In addition to scenic walks almost at the brink of the falls, the island features a heliport for sightseeing choppers and an elevator that takes visitors to the falls' base. From here the fearless may don the heavy-weather gear provided by the tour leader and walk along the path just behind the incredible wall of water — as drenching as it is deafening.

If you can dream up an offbeat angle from which you'd like to view the falls, chances are someone has already thought of it and has turned it into a prosperous business. An aerial view? The selection includes: Spanish Aerocars, cable cars that cross over the whirlpool and rapids; helicopter rides; or any of several observation towers. The two best viewing towers are on the Canadian side, on a 250-foot escarpment across from the falls. They are the 524-foot Skylon Tower (viewing height about 770 feet above the falls) and the 416-foot Panasonic Tower (viewing height about 665 feet).

At ground level there are any number of ways to view. The View-mobile offers miniature trams that run a 30-minute course between Prospect Point and Goat Island, allowing passengers to get on and off at any of several stops along the route. Of the various boat trips, the *Maid of the Mist* is the most famous. (Actually, there are four sightseeing boats named *Maid of the Mist,* so you won't have too long to wait.)

And don't forget night viewing. The Horseshoe Falls is lighted by four billion candlepower in rainbow colors every night. The energy for this Technicolor extravaganza is provided by the falls itself.

Several bridges span the river, and crossovers are made as hassle-free as both countries' Customs can manage. The Canadian side offers a wide range of falls-oriented attractions in addition to the towers already mentioned. But the American side has plenty of things to see. The Niagara Power Project (4 miles north of town, Rte. 104) uses displays and demonstrations to help the layperson understand how all this raw natural power is harnessed and put to work for us. Another learning experience is at the *Schoellkopf Geological Museum* (Niagara Reservation State Park; phone: 716-278-1780), where audiovisual presentations illustrate the various rock formations in the area, specifically how they affect the future of the falls. The museum also has a lovely rock garden and a nature trail.

At the Niagara Reservation State Park, where the falls are located, an interpretive center that opened in 1987 highlights the region's history, natural history, and geology, and shows some of the amazing stunts that have taken place in the vicinity of the falls.

Many festivals and special events are scheduled during the peak summer months. At the huge *Artpark* (7 miles north of town; Robert Moses Parkway at Lewiston) there are 200 acres where dance performances, concerts, and other artistic presentations are held (phone: 716-745-3377 for schedules; in summer, phone: 716-754-9001).

Those interested in Native American heritage should visit the *Native American Center for the Living Arts,* known as "The Turtle" because of its shape. It has cultural displays, art attractions, museum collections, and theatrical performances prepared or created by Native Americans (phone: 716-284-2427). Information: Niagara Falls Convention and Visitors Bureau, 345 3rd St., Suite 101, Niagara Falls, NY 14303 (phone: 716-278-8112 for recorded information, or 716-278-8010).

If you have time, stop by the *Rainbow Centre,* 301 Rainbow Blvd., one of the region's newest attractions. It's a one-stop fashion, dining, and entertainment experience, just a block from the American Falls, while the Wintergarden is a majestic, glass-enclosed tropical park with ponds, waterfalls, and 7,000 trees, connected to the Niagara Falls Convention Center and open year-round (phone: 716-278-8010). In winter, there is now the *Festival of Lights,* an annual celebration that includes thousands of lights and animated displays.

A 15-minute drive from the falls is Old Ft. Niagara, which was built by the French in 1725 and changed hands several times between the Americans and the British. It's the most colorful and best preserved of all the historic Great Lakes forts (phone: 716-745-7611).

BUFFALO: The second largest city in New York (pop. 358,000) has all the cultural, industrial, and other urban trappings you would expect in a large city. What's surprising is the breadth of its fine arts centers and its physical beauty. Virtually surrounded by parks, Buffalo is most proud of Delaware Park, designed by the famed landscape architect Frederick Law Olmsted (best known for New York City's Central Park). Delaware boasts not only spectacular grounds and landscaping but also a golf course, a zoo (with some buffalo, of course), and two museums: the *Albright-Knox Art Gallery* (1285 Elmwood Ave.), with an impressive collection of contemporary American and European works as well as 18th-century English and 19th-century French and American artists; and the *Buffalo and Erie County Historical Society* (25 Nottingham Court at Elmwood Ave.), which plunges you into the rich history of the area.

The Buffalo and Erie County Botanical Gardens (in South Park) has undergone major renovations to return the buildings and grounds to their original 1898 appearance. The park, the last to be designed by Olmsted, contains 12 greenhouses with tropical and exotic trees, plants, and flowers and a 30-foot waterfall. Spring and fall flower shows and a Christmas show are held here. No admission charge (phone: 716-828-1040).

There's boating and fishing on nearby waters, including Lake Erie, and skiing within an hour of the city. Buffalo also has three professional sports teams: the *Bills* (football), who play in *Rich Stadium* (Abbott Rd. and US 20); the *Bisons* (baseball; an AAA league) and the *Sabres* (hockey), who play in *Memorial Auditorium* (Main and S. Park Sts.).

Famous in its own right, the *Buffalo Philharmonic Orchestra,* conducted by Semyon Bychkov, is based in the *Kleinhans Music Hall,* known for its superior acoustics (370 Pennsylvania Ave., Buffalo, NY 14201; phone: 716-886-0067 for schedules and tickets).

The Allentown section of Buffalo is one of the largest historic preservation sites in the country, with 40 blocks of antiques and arts and crafts shops, boutiques, galleries, restaurants, Victorian homes, and do-it-yourself walking tours. The annual *Allentown Art Festival,* in June, attracts thousands. Information: Allentown Assn. (phone: 716-881-1024).

BEST EN ROUTE

Best Western Red Jacket Inn, Niagara Falls, NY – Some rooms have private patios overlooking the Niagara River (which at this point is actually an island strait). A pool and weekend entertainment. 7001 Buffalo Ave., Niagara Falls, NY 14304 (phone: 716-283-7612).

Ameri-Cana, Niagara Falls, Ontario, Canada – About 4 miles outside the hustle and bustle of downtown, amid spacious grounds with a play area, this motor inn has rooms, Jacuzzi suites, and several efficiencies. Pool, spa, tennis, basketball, volleyball, and billiards. It makes a great base for families. 8444 Lundy's La., Niagara Falls, Ont. L2H 1H4 (phone: 416-356-8444).

Old Red Mill, Clarence, NY – Some 11 miles northeast of Buffalo, this restaurant has several interesting dining areas: a lovely old house with fireplaces and a few converted railroad cars. Mailing address: 8326 Main St., Williamsville, NY 14221 (phone: 716-633-7878).

Old Orchard Inn, East Aurora, NY – Converted into a fine restaurant, this old home serves family style in a warm, rural atmosphere. 2095 Blakely Rd., East Aurora, NY 14052 (phone: 716-652-4664).

Pennsylvania Dutch Country, Pennsylvania

The Pennsylvania Dutch aren't Dutch at all. They came here in the 18th century from Germany seeking the freedom to worship as they wished, and in William Penn's country they found it. They also found natives who couldn't pronounce the word Deutsch ("German" in German) — so Dutch it has been ever since. The center of this large area — which encompasses the counties of Lancaster, York, Dauphin, Lebanon, Berks, and Lehigh — is Lancaster, the middling-size city in southern Pennsylvania almost halfway between Philadelphia and Harrisburg.

The freedom these devout people sought was the right to observe and practice Jesus's teachings as they interpreted them — their interpretation being highly literal. With typical brevity, they summed up their beliefs: "God said it/ Jesus did it/ I believe it/ And that settles it!"

In reality, what we mean by "Pennsylvania Dutch" actually incorporates three bodies of faith: the Amish, most rigid in their interpretation of the Bible, shunning all things modern and living physically austere lives based on the style of their forefathers; the Mennonites, more accepting of the outside world but still what is called in the area "plain"; and the Moravians, also called the "fancy Dutch," mainly German Lutherans and Reformed Church members whose farms are set apart by the "hex signs" that adorn their barns.

Some Amish will not speak to strangers; their homes may not be toured; they may not be photographed. Despite their refusal to use any modern technology (they travel by horse and buggy), they are superior farmers. Each

year droves of tourists sample their distinctive and now famous foods —
shoofly pie, scrapple, and chicken-corn soup.

Luckily, all is not buttoned up in Pennsylvania Dutch country. There are
many Mennonites whose source of income is the tourist trade, and it is
possible to rent rooms in a Mennonite farmhouse rather than stay in a hotel.
You can hire a Mennonite guide for a personal tour of the countryside,
thereby gaining an edge on commercial tour groups. These unusual and
interesting additions to your visit can be arranged at the Mennonite Information Center (2209 Millstream Rd., Lancaster, PA 17602; phone: 717-299-
0954). Because the area is so large, — to get a true feeling for the plain and fancy
peoples you should have a plan — an organized idea of what you want to see,
buy, or eat. Information: Pennsylvania Dutch Visitors Bureau, 501 Greenfield
Rd., Lancaster, PA 17601 (phone: 717-299-8901).

LANCASTER: The largest concentration of authentic Pennsylvania Dutch sights are
clustered here and just outside town along Rtes. 30 and 340. Farmers markets are one
of the biggest draws — with good reason. Here the prize of the crops are offered for
sale — along with flowers, plants, homemade baked goods, canned relishes, and old-
country-style sausage and bologna. There are six such markets, but the most popular
is the Central Market (Penn Sq.), open from 6 AM to 4:30 PM on Tuesdays and Fridays.
Also worth visiting is the Green Dragon Market and Auction in Ephrata, with outdoor
merchants, antiques dealers, flea markets, and indoor merchants; Fridays only, in
summer.

For a better understanding of Amish life, you can visit several simulated Amish
communities. The Amish Homestead (1½ miles east on Rte. 462) shows the farming
techniques practiced by the first Amish settlers and has a tour of an 18th-century house;
the Amish Farm and House (3 miles east on Rte. 30) offers a tour and a lecture, "The
Plain People"; and the Amish Village (7 miles east, just off Rte. 30 on Rte. 896 south)
has a tour through a farmhouse, blacksmith shop, one-room school, and smokehouse.
There are several ways to get an overall view of Lancaster. Many commercial sightseeing tours offer planned itineraries. Or you can take a self-guiding auto tape tour. The
tape and player can be rented for about $9 from many commercial establishments. (Ask
at the Information Center for one nearby.)

BIRD-IN-HAND: Here you can learn about the traditional folk-art hex signs. At the
Hex Barn (off Rte. 340) you can watch them being made and then buy some of the
finished products. At the Folk Craft Center (west on Rte. 340, north on Mt. Sidney
Rd.) there's a charming display of antique toys, dower chests, and other folk furnishings. And on many roads in this area, you'll cross ancient covered bridges, many in
their original state. Outside Bird-in-Hand is the excellent *Plain 'n' Fancy Farm* restaurant (on Rte. 340) with a representative menu of Pennsylvania Dutch favorites. Almost
anywhere you stop to eat in Pennsylvania Dutch country is an experience in overabun-
dance as well as plain good cooking, in a culture that traditionally equates well stuffed
with good health. Be prepared to be as dazzled by the sheer size of the spread as by
the flavor of the food.

HERSHEY: Milton Hershey was a Mennonite whose lifestyle appears to have been
pretty worldly — and if not his lifestyle, at least his sweet tooth, which has also affected
just about every American since the Hershey Chocolate Factory was built in 1903. The
townsfolk and descendants of Milton Hershey don't appear to be overly modest either.
Much of this town bears his name, from the Hershey Gardens to Hersheypark (a theme
park with rides and amusements), to *Hershey Stadium* (sporting events), to just about
everything else. One thing you'll want to see is the tour of Chocolate World, where

you'll watch a simulated step-by-step version of how chocolate is made, from cacao bean to Hershey Kiss.

KUTZTOWN: Famous for its *Pennsylvania Dutch Folk Festival*, held every year in early July, the town welcomes the serious shoppers who throng here to buy the many handicrafts, sample the culture and food, and enjoy historic exhibitions of the plain and the fancy Dutch. Be sure to visit the Crystal Cave, a natural phenomenon discovered in 1871 and now improved with indirect lighting and safe walkways. You'll see crystal formations, natural bridges, and caverns.

While the annual events and farmers markets are warm-weather major attractions, remember that the crowds they draw create a distraction and a disadvantage. So you might want to time your visit during the off-season (spring, fall, or winter), when the tourist traffic is lighter and you stand a better chance of fading into the background and gaining truer insights.

Regardless of season, your stay will be much more enjoyable if you do your homework in advance. Brochures and detailed maps are easily obtained from the tourist bureaus, and they are absolutely essential. There are at least 220 noteworthy sights to see and visit in Lancaster County alone.

BEST EN ROUTE

Visiting a Mennonite Farm – If you wish to do this, you must call or write ahead to the Mennonite Information Center or the Pennsylvania Visitors Bureau (address above). They will send you an up-to-date listing of the participating farms. Some serve breakfast; others do not. A double room (no private bath) costs about $20 and up. The Mennonites are afraid of publicity and are fearful to say in print that they will serve meals because of the avalanche of tourists in the area. Individual tourists are often lucky enough to form personal relationships with their Mennonite hosts. Information: Mennonite Information Center, 2209 Millstream Rd., Lancaster, PA 17602 (phone: 717-299-0954).

Sheraton Lancaster Golf Resort and Conference Center, Lancaster – A large resort for a total family vacation. Guests choose from a barrage of activities — sports, amusements, even cabaret shows — something for everyone. 2300 Lincoln Hwy. E., Lancaster, PA 17602 (phone: 717-299-5500).

General Sutter Inn, Lititz – The inn has been around since 1764 and the 12 rooms (all with private baths) are comfortable, clean, and unfancy; the food is marvelous. 14 E. Main St., Lititz, PA 17543 (phone: 717-626-2115).

Groff's Farm, Mt. Joy – In a 1750s home, the food is all made from the freshest ingredients. The wine is made here and housed in the cellar. There are two seatings: 5 and 7:30 PM Tuesdays and Fridays, 5 and 8 PM Saturdays. Copies of one of Betty Groff's cookbooks are for sale. Reservations are a must. 650 Pinkerton Rd., Mt. Joy, PA 17552 (phone: 717-653-2048).

Newport and Block Island, Rhode Island

Newport, America's first resort town, is so crammed with history that you can take a leisurely stroll past a row of 19th-century millionaires' mansions, stop by a tavern that has been in business since 1673, and visit the Old Colony House, where George Washington conferred with French strategists during the Revolutionary War. Like old sedimentary rock, the town is composed of different time layers. There is Colonial Newport — a refuge from religious intolerance; 18th-century Newport — a bustling and prosperous seaport; and late-19th-century Newport — the summer playground of the super-rich. And thanks to the work of the Preservation Society of Newport County and the Newport Restoration Foundation, they all coexist in 20th-century Newport, an architectural museum of glittering mansions, impressive 17th- and 18th-century homes, and some of the oldest houses of worship in America. Add a pleasant shoreline and snug harbor in Narragansett Bay and you have a place where history and recreation are in fine balance.

Founded in 1639 by victims of the Massachusetts elders' religious intolerance, Newport attracted settlers of all religious convictions, including Quakers and Jews. In the 17th and 18th centuries, the town prospered as a seaport and merchants built fine homes with the profits they made from transporting rum to the West Indies and slaves from Africa. It was during this period, in the 1720s, that wealthy planters and merchants from the Carolinas and West Indies began to spend their summers here, making Newport America's first resort. The British occupation during the Revolution put an end to Newport's first golden age; the second did not begin until after the Civil War, when people like the Astors, the Belmonts, and the Vanderbilts began to build their summer "cottages" — modeled after the grand palaces and châteaux of Europe.

A center for yachting and all kinds of sea sports, Newport is on the tip of the large island for which the state is named, in Rhode Island Sound. It has several excellent beaches, but even better ones are on Block Island, about 12 miles south of the mainland and accessible by ferry from Newport (as are Providence, New London, Connecticut, and Montauk Point, New York). Newport and Block Island are a morning's drive from Boston or New York.

NEWPORT: To get oriented at once, stop at the Chamber of Commerce (44 Valley Rd.) for a free visitors guide, maps, and information on current happenings. There are frequent musical programs, especially in summer. Newport's bookstores carry many guidebooks to the town; an excellent one is *Newport: A Tour Guide* by Anne Randall, which offers well-planned walking routes. Newport is so compact that you can walk or bicycle just about everywhere, but if you like your sightseeing sitting down, *Viking Tours* (phone: 401-847-6921) offers a 2-hour city bus tour and a 1-hour harbor/bay boat ride as well as walking tours.

If you have come to Newport, you have come at least in part to see its mansions. The Preservation Society of Newport (118 Mill St.) offers a very good tour of some of Newport's most stunning "summer cottages." Hunter House (54 Washington St.), built in 1748, is the only Colonial mansion on the tour. This stately home once served as the headquarters of the commander of French forces in the American Revolution. The Breakers (Ochre Point Ave.), a 70-room mansion overlooking the Atlantic, is the most splendid of Newport's great houses. Built in 1895 for Cornelius Vanderbilt, the building resembles a northern Italian Renaissance palace. In the course of a stroll down Bellevue Avenue, you will pass the finest examples of Newport's "cottages" from the Gilded Age. The Elms, built in 1901 for a Philadelphia coal magnate, was modeled after the Château d'Asnières near Paris. After touring the house, which is completely furnished with museum pieces, you can walk around the grounds and see the formal French gardens and collection of rare trees and shrubs from all over the world. Marble of all kinds and colors was used to build Marble House, completed in 1892 for William K.

Vanderbilt. This palatial home contains all of its original furnishings. Château-sur-Mer, built in 1852, is one of the finest examples of ornate Victorian architecture in America. Rosecliff, where scenes from Paramount's *Great Gatsby* were filmed, was designed by Stanford White after the Grand Trianon at Versailles and built in 1902. Also on Bellevue Avenue are the *International Tennis Hall of Fame and Tennis Museum,* an 1881 casino where the first tennis matches were played, and Belcourt Castle, with the largest stained glass collection in the world.

Another way to see Newport's mansions is to take the Cliff Walk, a 3-mile trail between the mansions and the sea.

Away from mansion row, you step back in time to the Federal and Colonial eras. At the Old Colony House (Washington Sq.), Washington conferred with Rochambeau. The Wanton-Lyman-Hazard House (17 Broadway), built in 1675, is the oldest residence in Newport. The Newport Historical Society (82 Touro St.) houses a fine collection of old Newport silver, porcelain, furniture, toys, and dolls as well as a marine museum. Nearby is the Touro Synagogue (85 Touro St.), considered an architectural gem as well as a symbol of religious liberty. Built in 1763, the synagogue is the oldest in the US (closed Saturdays and religious holidays).

At the corner of Church and Spring streets, Trinity Church, built in 1726, is the most perfectly preserved Colonial wooden structure in the country. The church, modeled after the London churches of Christopher Wren, contains many artifacts of early American life. A few blocks away is the Redwood Library, built in 1748 and a National Historic Site. Legend has it that the Old Stone Mill next to the library was built by Norsemen, but excavation dates this building to about 1673.

At the Samuel Whitehorne House (416 Thames St.), you can see some of the exquisitely crafted furniture, silver, and pewter that once graced the homes of wealthy Newport merchants.

If you crave a few of Newport's treasures for yourself, you can shop for fine reproductions of Colonial furniture, silver, and brassware at the *Brick Market* (Thames St.). Antiques shops line Franklin and Spring streets, and the boutiques on cobblestoned Bowen's Wharf at the waterfront (off Thames St.) carry everything from sweaters to scrimshaw. (Be sure to try some of the seafood restaurants, too.)

BLOCK ISLAND: An antidote to too much shopping and sightseeing, this pear-shaped bit of rolling meadowland is 12 miles at sea in Block Island Sound and just an hour's ferry ride from Newport. There are a few historical things to see on Block Island: Settler's Rock, where the first settlers landed in 1661; the Palatine Graves, where an ill-fated ship met a watery grave (commemorated in a poem by Whittier); the Block Island Historical Society, with exhibitions on the island's history. (The island has a bad reputation with sailors. The site of over 200 shipwrecks, it was for a good part of the 18th century a haven for pirates, smugglers, and sea thieves.) But mostly this is a place to loll on the beach, take long walks by the sea, or do some serious fishing. The waters off Block Island support tuna, bluefish, cod, and flounder, and there are over 300 inland ponds. Block Island is an excellent vantage point for bird watching: It is filled in fall and spring with migrations of birds on the Atlantic flyway. At the southeastern end of the island, Mohegan Bluffs, 200 feet above sea level, offer long ocean vistas. You can leave your car on the mainland and rent a bike to get around; the whole island covers only 11 square miles. It has a fine harbor, and sailors up and down the coast put up here for biking around the beaches for a day, picnicking, and shopping.

BEST EN ROUTE

Inn at Castle Hill, Newport – Formerly the home of Alexander Agassiz, the son of the famous 19th-century naturalist. Rooms have excellent views of Narragansett Bay. The inn itself has been declared a historical monument. The restaurant here is quite good; there's a varied menu, but the specialty is, of course, seafood. See also *America's Special Havens,* DIVERSIONS. Ocean Dr., Newport, RI 02840 (phone: 401-849-3800).

The 1661 Inn and Hotel Manisses, Block Island – A Block Island tradition, the inn serves only breakfast, though the owners have restored their *Manisses* restaurant to its 1870s appearance and serve breakfast, lunch, and dinner here from April through October. The inn is open from Memorial Day through Columbus Day. See also *America's Special Havens,* DIVERSIONS. PO Box I, Block Island, RI 02807 (phone: 401-466-2421).

Vermont: A Short Tour

"Winter or summer," one Vermonter says, "being here is the name of the game." It's true. You can't go wrong in Vermont, no matter when you go. From the beautiful southern villages that inspired Norman Rockwell to the elaborate ski resorts flanking the Green Mountains, it's all stunning. There are several routes to the Green Mountain State. From Boston, take I-93 to I-89 directly to Burlington, Vermont's largest city, on Lake Champlain. With Burlington as your base, you can explore the northern part of the state, wander along the Canadian border, then journey through the southern section on your way back to Boston.

BURLINGTON: This town dates back to the Revolution, and Revolutionary War hero Ethan Allen is buried here in Greenmount Cemetery. Burlington's location on Lake Champlain makes it a major navigational center for ship traffic between the US and Canada. It was the site of a major naval battle during the War of 1812. From Battery Park, you can get a marvelous view of the tranquil lake and spruce-lined shores. It's hard to believe that any place this peaceful could have been a battlefield. Lake Champlain and Vermont's inland lakes provide a variety of catch, plentiful and safe for consumption. Ferries cross Lake Champlain every hour from the end of May through mid-October to reach Port Kent, New York. The crossing takes 2 hours round-trip (contact *Lake Champlain Transportation Co.*, King St. Dock; phone: 802-864-9804). There is a swimming area at North Beach. In town, the University of Vermont (phone: 802 656-3480), Trinity College (phone: 802-658-0337), and St. Michael's College (phone: 802-655-2000) offer films, concerts, plays, and sports activities throughout the academic year.

SOUTH HERO: Just north of Burlington on one of Lake Champlain's islands. *Allenholm Farms* sell fresh apple cider and hot apple and pumpkin pies in late September–early October, when Vermont's foliage is at its height. The apples come from the Allenholm orchards. Pick up some milk at a country store and feast while gazing at the lake. To get to South Hero, take Rte. 7 to Rte. 2 northeast. You'll pass through Sand Bar Wildlife Area and State Park, another good spot for picnicking.

STOWE: If you ski, you've undoubtedly heard of Stowe. Even if you don't, it's worth a trip. Take Rte. 7 north to Rte. 104A east. (When you pass Cambridge, keep your eye out for a genuine Vermont covered bridge. No longer in use, it's now standing off to the side of the highway.) Head south on Rte. 108 at Cambridge Junction–Jeffersonville, the prettiest part of the state, according to many residents. A few miles south of the turnoff, you'll pass through Smugglers Notch, an important hideout for contraband goods passing between the US and Canada during the War of 1812. The rugged, hairpin road through the notch is impassable during winter, but you can cross-country ski (a detour to Stowe when Smugglers Notch is closed would be I-89 east to Rte. 100). There are downhill ski areas at Smugglers Notch, Mt. Mansfield — the tallest peak in the state — and nearby Bolton Valley. Mt. Mansfield explodes into view as you round a hill. When the sun is shining behind its snow-covered peak in winter, the mountain is, in the words of one resident, "most amazing." (High praise from a Vermonter.) Marking the end of the Green Mountains, Mt. Mansfield's 4,393 feet are laced with trails and caves. In August, you can pick blueberries as you hike. Stowe, one of the most famous ski areas in New England, is just down the road on Rte. 108.

HUNTINGTON GORGE: From Stowe, continue south to Rte. 89 west, toward Burlington, taking the Richmond exit. Follow Rte. 2 toward Jonesville, take a right on the steel bridge crossing the Winooski River (Winooski is an Indian word for "onion"), and follow the road to Huntington Gorge, a secluded picnic and swimming spot. Here, the Huntington River narrows to a waterfall. But be careful — there are no lifeguards.

JAY PEAK: Alternately, from Stowe, you can head north on Rte. 100 all the way to Canada. Just before you reach the border, take the turnoff for Rte. 101 north to the Jay Peak ski area. To return to Burlington, head west on Rte. 105 to St. Albans, formerly an important railroad stop along the route to Canada. Here you can pick up I-89 south to Burlington.

SHELBURNE: Just south of Burlington, this is the home of the *Shelburne Museum,* with restored Americana from the 1880s (phone: 802-985-3344). You can see what an old Vermont village used to look like. There are farm buildings, a grocery store, a pharmacy, feed shops, a dentist's office, and even the steamboat *Ticonderoga,* which used to ply its way across Lake Champlain. If you're fortunate enough to be here at sunset, go to Shelburne Point, the tip of a little finger of land pointing northwest on the shores of Lake Champlain. The sunsets are no less than magnificent from this vantage point, and there's a beach and a restaurant at the marina.

LINCOLN GAP: Wandering south along Rte. 7, through Vergennes, you'll encounter a number of good restaurants and inns. South of Vergennes, you can detour east on Rte. 17, through Bristol, to Lincoln Gap, a winding passageway.

MIDDLEBURY: On the western boundary of the Green Mountain National Forest, here is the site of Middlebury College and the Bread Loaf Writers' School, where Robert Frost taught. There's a Robert Frost Mountain, a Robert Frost Wayside Recreation Area, and Middlebury College Snow Bowl, a family ski area popular with residents but not yet familiar to out-of-staters. There's a good climbing trail at neighboring Ripton. Continue southeast on Rte. 125, which runs into Rte. 100 south, to get to the Killington and Pico Peak ski areas.

PLYMOUTH: The birthplace of President Calvin Coolidge, his former home is now a museum. His son, John Coolidge (now 84 years old), runs *Plymouth Cheese,* a small factory where everything is made by hand. Coolidge and his team of hardy Vermonters keep the place open even when the world is covered with snow. The cheddar is delicious. (Speaking of Vermont specialties, in late winter, take a special trip to St. Johnsbury, home of the *Maple Grove Maple Museum and Factory,* the world's largest maple candy factory. For Vermonters, maple sugaring time is a celebration of spring. To get to St. Johnsbury, take Rte. 2 east from Burlington.)

ROUTE 100A: This scenic road takes you past Calvin Coolidge State Forest. At Ludlow, the Okemo Mountain ski area has good conditions. From Ludlow, take Rte. 100 south to its end at South Londonderry, site of Ball Mountain Dam Recreation Area, and pick up Rte. 30 southeast to Brattleboro.

You've probably noticed by now that Vermont has no billboards on its highways and very few bottles littering the roadsides. Vermonters are very proud of their state and have passed a number of strict conservation laws designed to protect the countryside from abuse. Visitors are welcome, but must share this respect for the land.

BRATTLEBORO and STRATTON: In the winter, Stratton is a very popular ski resort and Brattleboro the biggest town near another major ski area, Mt. Snow. If you're visiting during the fall, there's Stratton's *Annual Art Festival* and also, of course, spectacular foliage displays; pack a picnic lunch and set off through the trees. For information on scenic autumn foliage tours, skiing, and more: Vermont Travel Division, 134 State St., Montpelier, VT 05602 (phone: 802-828-3236).

BEST EN ROUTE

Cortina Inn, Killington – This 98-room resort is best known for its intensive tennis school held on 8 clay and Plexipave courts, but there are also hunting, fishing, golf, horseback riding, and skiing nearby. Owners Bob and Breda Harnish have also opened a health club on the premises, with an indoor pool, sauna, whirlpool bath, and weight training. Rte. 4, Killington, VT 05751 (phone: 802-773-3331).

North Hero House, Champlain Islands – A 23-room inn with tennis and water sports facilities, with an ideal lakefront location. Bicycles provided. Open June through mid-October. Champlain Islands, North Hero, VT 05474 (phone: 802-372-8237).

Middlebury Inn, Middlebury – Close to the college and the *Shelburne Museum,* this 75-room inn is near golf, tennis, bicycling, skiing, and swimming. The dining room is open to the public. Court Sq., Rte. 7, Middlebury, VT 05753 (phone: 802-388-4961).

Waybury Inn, East Middlebury – Built in 1810 as a stagecoach stop, it has 15 rooms. This is a popular spot for hearty meals, even if you don't plan to spend the night. Rte. 125, East Middlebury, VT 05740 (phone: 802-388-4015).

Okemo Inn, Ludlow – Built in 1810, this has a homey feel, with a grand New England fireplace and 12 rooms, 10 with private bath; dining room, outdoor pool, golf and ski packages. Rte. 103, RFD 1, Box 133, Ludlow, VT 05149 (phone: 802-228-8834).

The Creamery, Danville – It's a good choice for well-prepared steaks and fresh fish and seafood as well as homemade breads and pies (the maple cream in particular has received raves). Closed Mondays during winter. Hill St., Danville (phone: 802-684-3616).

Shenandoah National Park, Virginia

For 80 miles along the spine of the Blue Ridge Mountains in northwestern Virginia, overlooking the beautiful valley of the Shenandoah River, lies Shenandoah National Park. More than 95% of the park's 190,000 acres are wooded — stands of deciduous hardwood (oak, hickory, maple) that explode into color during the first short, cold days of autumn. Through the park runs the 105-mile Skyline Drive as well as a 95-mile section of the Appalachian Trail, the entire length of which winds from Maine to Georgia.

Bounded by the Blue Ridge Mountains on the east and the Alleghenies to the west, the Shenandoah Valley is the heart of the mighty Appalachian Mountain chain, an area loved and revered by Indians and white men for centuries (Shenandoah is Indian for "daughter of the stars"). George Washington surveyed land here and was so awed by its special splendor that he became a large landowner. Eventually he required all of his tenants to plant at least four acres of apple trees — a legacy Americans can still enjoy while gazing from the park's overlooks and trails to the glorious apple orchards that blanket the valleys below. The park was established in 1935 to make inviolate a goodly portion of the Shenandoah area. It extends from the town of Front Royal in the north to just east of Waynesboro in the south, and is only a couple of hours' drive from the Washington, DC, area. Waynesboro is connected by I-64 to Richmond and the "historic triangle" towns of Williamsburg-Yorktown-Jamestown. For shorter trips, visitors can also use the park entrance at Thornton Gap on US-211. Park headquarters are on US 211, 4 miles west of Thornton.

FRONT ROYAL: Take in some of the attractions at the northern edge of the park before entering. The Blue Ridge Mountains here form the most southeasterly wave of the Appalachians, formed of lava a billion years old. The area has nature walks, picnic facilities, and crafts shops. *Warren Rifles Confederate Museum* (95 Chester St., Front Royal) has many relics of the Civil War, including furniture, rare photographs, weapons, and other typical war memorabilia.

If you're visiting in the fall, plan to attend the annual *Festival of Leaves* held in Front Royal the second or third weekend in October (when the foliage is usually at its peak). The festival, one of the largest in all Virginia, offers a wide variety of attractions, including craftsmen and an art show with over 50 artists exhibiting. Information: Chamber of Commerce, PO Box 568, Front Royal, VA 22630 (phone: 703-635-3185).

And if you find yourself seduced by the beauty of the Shenandoah River and want to get to know it better before entering the park, a short drive north into West Virginia's eastern panhandle will bring you to Harpers Ferry, where you can join a Shenandoah River whitewater rapids expedition. Each trip takes about 5 hours, including a Southern hospitality–style picnic, and is organized by *Blue Ridge Outfitters* in Harpers Ferry (phone: 304-725-3444) or *Front Royal Canoe Co.* (phone: 703-635-5440) between April and November. (See also *Harpers Ferry and Monongahela National Forest* in this section.)

SHENANDOAH NATIONAL PARK: Every autumn the park produces just about the most spectacular show of fall foliage to appear anywhere in the country. The Skyline Drive charges straight along the crest of the Blue Ridge for the entire length of the park, surrounded by successive waves of Appalachian hills — the Blue Ridge nearest, Alleghenies to the west — rising and falling into the distance. It is an unparalleled leaf-peeping experience, but keep in mind that this is a period of heavy tourism for the park. Park vistas are as beautiful in the spring and summer as they are in autumn. Flowers and blossoming trees carpet the valleys in infinite varieties of color and depth. If you want to see the foliage, by all means brave the park in October; however, it's best to make your trip on the less populous weekdays.

The park has two visitors centers: Dickey Ridge, just within the northern entrance at Front Royal, and Byrd Visitor Center at Big Meadows, where rangers have deliberately checked the growth of the forest to allow a huge, green meadow to flourish in the sunshine. There, myriad varieties of park plants — orchids, violets, wildflowers — grow in profusion. A visit to the park should include a stop at one of the centers — preferably first — to pick up literature and check out daily activities. Rangers lead nature walks through different parts of the park, advise on trails, and provide information on camping. Shenandoah has two lodges, four campgrounds, one primitive group camping area, and a policy allowing backcountry camping. However, campers must have permits, available at entrance stations, visitor stations, or park headquarters.

There are two distinct ways of seeing the park. Skyline Drive has numerous stops and overlooks, many with short trails leading from them, which allow visitors to drive the park's length, stopping where they wish. Certainly you can enjoy the many beautiful vistas along the route doing this, and with some luck even see some of the park's wildlife — deer or perhaps a bear. However, the only way to get more than a passing acquaintanceship with Shenandoah is simply to plunge into it, and with more than 500 miles of hiking trails and paths — some quite arduous, others little more than strolls — as well as the Appalachian Trail, Shenandoah is a park made for hiking.

Available at the visitors centers is a free newspaper called Shenandoah Overlook, with daily activities and a list of services and facilities and points of interest. The trail up Hawksbill Mountain is rigorous (from 1.1 to 3 miles, round trip) but very rewarding: Along its route — if you go by way of the Appalachian Trail — are numerous stopping points that offer spectacular views of the valley.

A walk around Stony Man Mountain reveals something about the underpinnings of the entire mountain chain in this area. Formed of ancient lava galvanized by eons of slow heat, along Stony Man (and elsewhere in the park) high cliffs of lava break into great columns of stone, called columnar jointings, which developed as the lava that made them cooled and separated. Here and wherever stone is exposed, you will see strange, circular bubbles of color in the rock. These were caused by gas that percolated through the lava as it cooled, nearly a billion years ago.

Though 95% forest, the park has very little virgin woodland left. When it was established in 1935 and the last of the residents were moved nearby, almost nothing was left of the original Blue Ridge forests; generations of farmers had practiced the time-honored method of quick-burning to clear forests and prepare fields for planting. Today's woodlands represent a masterwork of reforestation. A real tragedy was the loss of the area's native chestnut trees. Once the most common tree in the mountains, they were certainly the most useful. Their wood was excellent for furniture, their bark provided tannic acid required for tanning, and their nuts were a cash crop. But 70 or 80 years ago a fungus deadly to the trees entered the US from the Far East and devastated the native forests. Today scientists are trying to develop resistant breeds, but nothing has appeared to replace the thousands of acres of chestnuts.

At Limberlost, in Whiteoak Canyon, you can see some of the very few virgin trees left in the park. There is a stand of original hemlock trees and some 350-to-400-year-old white oaks. Information: Superintendent, Shenandoah National Park, Rte. 4, Box 348, Luray, VA 22835 (phone: 703-999-2266 for taped information on weather, campground, lodge, and activities, or 703-999-2229 for further details).

BEST EN ROUTE

Shenandoah has four major campgrounds for the general public, one youth campground, and seven picnic areas. It also has a unique backcountry "camp where you like" system, but, as noted above, all backcountry campers must have permits; they specify how many people are allowed in the party and how long they will be out. The park also has two excellent lodges, *Skyland* and *Big Meadows*. For reservations at either, write to ARA Virginia Sky-Line Co., PO Box 727, Luray, VA 22835 (phone: 703-743-5108). *Skyland* is a Shenandoah tradition, begun in 1894 by George Pollock. It has 158 rooms, a full dining room, a stable, and craft shops. *Big Meadows* offers the same features, with only 104 rooms. Lodging is available from March through December, with reservations required about 2 months in advance for any time except foliage season (then 8 months, minimum). South of *Big Meadows, Lewis Mountain* offers 7 furnished cottages with bath, heat, electric lights, linens, and a connecting cooking-eating area outside. Open mid-May through October. Address and phone same as lodges, or call 703-999-2255.

For accommodations outside the park, contact any of the following: Front Royal Chamber of Commerce (phone: 703-635-3185); Page County Chamber of Commerce (phone: 703-743-3915); Waynesboro/East Augusta Chamber of Commerce (phone: 703-949-8203); Shenandoah Valley Travel Assn. (phone: 703-740-3132); or Shenandoah Bed and Breakfast Reservations (phone: 703-459-8241). The state of Virginia also has excellent tourist information. Write Virginia Division of Tourism, 101 N. 9th St., Richmond, VA 23219, specifying the area you wish to visit.

Tidewater Virginia

One of the richest historical areas in the country is Virginia's coast — traditionally called Tidewater Virginia — on the Chesapeake Bay. Here, almost within call of one another, are Williamsburg, Jamestown, and Yorktown; the beautiful 18th-century plantation homes along the James, York, Rappahannock, and Potomac rivers; and to the west and north, Richmond and Fredericksburg, with a wealth of surrounding Civil War sites. There is hardly a period of early American history, from initial exploration to the War Between the States, not represented by some vital detail here.

Begin a tour of Tidewater Virginia at the beginning. The "historic triangle" between the James and the York rivers is the most highly concentrated area of historical sites in the whole country. The three points of the triangle are: Jamestown, where America began; Williamsburg, where patriots plotted the future of the nation-to-be; and Yorktown, where the Revolutionary War ended and the nation was born. And all three are conveniently linked by the Colonial Parkway.

JAMESTOWN: Williamsburg became the seat of the royal government in 1699. Before that, Jamestown had been the center of the royal colony and the site of the first successful English settlement in America. John Smith and his group of 103 settlers arrived in Jamestown in May 1607. Today it is an island; at the time, it was connected to the mainland by a narrow isthmus that the James River eventually ate away. The first years of the colony were extremely hard, with little help from the London Company, which sponsored the journey; and, in general, fate dealt the town a rather hard hand. By 1699, when the government was moved, it had been burnt down once, set afire another time, and finally abandoned.

Today the area is part of the Colonial National Historical Park. For the most part, one sees diggings indicating where buildings were and how extensive the settlement was. The one remaining building of the period is the church tower of 1639, around which the church has been reconstructed. Also reconstructed on its original site is the Glasshouse, fitted out as it was originally, with craftspeople blowing glass. But history comes most vividly alive at Jamestown Festival Park, in the harbor of the James River (not part of Jamestown itself). Here are full-scale replicas of the three tiny ships on which the first settlers made their journey: the *Susan Constant,* the *Godspeed,* and the *Discovery.* You can actually board one of them and see the cramped quarters that housed those courageous men. There is also a re-creation of James Fort, which you can tour, as well as several special exhibition houses. For more information, see *Restored Towns and Reconstructed Villages,* DIVERSIONS.

WILLIAMSBURG: The first restoration of a historical area ever undertaken in the US, it is still the best. Work was begun in 1926; no detail was too insignificant, no project too large, in this staggering task. Visitors to Williamsburg can actually experience life as it was lived in Colonial days. Craftsmen ply their trades exactly as they did then, sheep graze on the green, a horse-drawn cart takes you down Duke of Gloucester Street, with its array of taverns and shops all busy at their 18th-century businesses. Take a stroll over to Market Square and watch the militia train and drill. A good introduction to Colonial Williamsburg can be found at the visitors center (Colonial Pkwy. and Rte. 132 Y). Of the 400 buildings that have been restored there are some you won't want to miss: the Governor's "Palace," as it was called by the disgruntled colonists whose taxes paid the bills for this luxurious mansion; the College of William and Mary, built in 1693 and the second oldest college in America; and two jovial and famous meeting places, Raleigh and Wetherburn's taverns.

Make reservations well in advance, for Williamsburg is a very popular destination for families. There are a great many motels and hotels near town. In the town itself is the *Williamsburg Inn* (Frances St.), a joy to see or visit for its painstaking authenticity. (See *Restored Towns and Reconstructed Villages*, DIVERSIONS, for more information about Williamsburg.)

YORKTOWN: The third city of colonial significance, Yorktown was an important tobacco shipping port until the Revolutionary War began. In the autumn of 1781, British Commander Cornwallis got boxed in here by a combination of the French fleet along the coast and French and American ground troops, led by George Washington. On October 9 a siege began, and 10 days later Cornwallis surrendered. The Revolutionary War was over. Unlike Jamestown, however, Yorktown is a functioning city today, surrounded by the Yorktown Battlefield. The Yorktown Victory Center (on Rte. 238) has information and brochures as well as Revolutionary War exhibitions and a display of archaeological material raised from one of Cornwallis's ships that sank in the York River during the war. After a visit here, you can walk through the battlefield, which is carefully designed to explain the battle and its significance. Of special interest is the Moore House (on Rte. 238), where the capitulation papers were drawn up (they were signed in the adjacent trenches), and the *Swan Tavern* (Main St. and Ballard), a reconstruction of an early-18th-century tavern, now a shop. Before leaving the area, consider a visit to *Busch Gardens, The Old Country*, a theme park outside Williamsburg (5 miles on Rte. 60); see Amusement Parks, DIVERSIONS.

TIDEWATER PLANTATIONS: Along any and all of the rivers, inlets, bays, and peninsulas of Tidewater Virginia and the Chesapeake Bay you will find lovely Georgian homes, fully restored and inhabited, which date from the tobacco trade days of the mid-1800s. However, from Williamsburg west along the north shore of the James River are a number of the most famous plantation homes in America. Most are open to visitors, and even if one house is closed on the particular day you visit, the grounds are always open. About 8 miles outside Williamsburg is Carter's Grove, built in the 1750s and restored as part of the Colonial Williamsburg project. Across the river from Jamestown is Smith's Fort Plantation, built almost 100 years earlier, on land given by the Indian Chief Powhatan to his daughter Pocahontas and her groom John Rolfe. Nearby is Bacon's Castle, which claims the oldest documented garden in America. Just east of Smith's Fort lies Chippokes Plantation State Park, a plantation dating to 1619. Along the James River north shore route are Sherwood Forest, the home of President John Tyler; Westover, the home of William Byrd II, built in the 1730s as the focal point of his 179,000-acre fiefdom; Evelynton, home of the man who fired the first shot of the Civil War; Berkeley, the birthplace of President William Henry Harrison; and Shirley, the seat of the immensely powerful Carter family.

PORT OF HAMPTON ROADS: This port incorporates three cities — Newport News, Portsmouth, and Norfolk — and is a center for shipping and shipbuilding. It is also the entry point to Virginia's beaches, either around Cape Henry to Virginia Beach or through the Chesapeake Bay Bridge-Tunnel to the peninsula of Virginia that hangs below Maryland.

From Yorktown, Rte. 17 and I-64 lead into the center of these seafaring towns. A fitting stop is the *Mariner's Museum* (Clyde Morris Blvd., Newport News). It offers a wealth of ships' fittings, models, cannon, maps, and instruments. In Newport News you can take a the harbor cruise (from the Boat Harbor at the end of Jefferson St.) which takes you around Hampton Roads and historic Ft. Monroe, in the very waters where the *Monitor* met the *Merrimac*.

BEST EN ROUTE

Williamsburg Inn, Williamsburg – Genteel luxury in a perfectly restored and maintained 18th-century atmosphere. In the center of Williamsburg, the inn offers history outside the front door and a golf course outside the back. Reservations Office, Colonial Williamsburg Foundation, PO Box C, Williamsburg, VA 23187 (phone: 804-229-1000; 800-HISTORY for reservations).

Tides Lodge, Irvington – Primarily a golf establishment that offers numerous outdoor activities (yachting, tennis, canoeing, jogging, swimming, biking, fishing) for the family. The elegant *Tides Inn* is nearby. See also *Resort Hotels,* DIVERSIONS. Irvington, VA 22480 (phone: 804-438-6000).

Harpers Ferry and Monongahela National Forest, West Virginia

West Virginia really is the stuff that country music is made of — country roads, rocky cliffs, Blue Ridge Mountains, almost heaven. But it's much more than mountaintops and John Denver lyrics. The small towns built into these old hills are strongholds of America's history. This is where John Brown's ill-fated raid on Harpers Ferry took place, where one of the bloodiest and most crucial battles of the Civil War was fought, and where hundreds of mule-drawn barges navigated the Chesapeake and Ohio Canal, carrying coal to fuel the young nation. The towns are within a few hours' drive of each other through beautiful backcountry, including the Monongahela National Forest, a thickly wooded area with both tranquillity and wild and woolly whitewater canoeing.

HARPERS FERRY, West Virginia: Though this lovely hillside town overlooking the confluence of the Potomac and Shenandoah rivers appears tranquil today, it was the site of John Brown's raid on the federal arsenal in 1859 as part of his plan to arm a slave rebellion and to establish a free state in the Blue Ridge Mountains. The abolitionist force succeeded in capturing the arsenal, but it was surrounded by the local militia, and Brown was captured by Colonel Robert E. Lee and hung for treason and murder a month and a half later. A ½-mile walking tour through the Harpers Ferry National Historical Park (Shenandoah St.) links several restored homes, a gunmaking museum, the engine house where Brown was caught, a blacksmith shop, confectionery, tavern, and Jefferson Rock, which commands a fine view of the area's rivers and hills.

SHARPSBURG, Maryland: The headquarters of the Chesapeake and Ohio Canal National Historical Park (the park itself is 10 miles south of US 70 along Rte. 65). This 185-mile canal was begun in 1828 to link Washington, DC, and Pittsburgh. It never reached its final destination; construction was halted at Cumberland, Maryland, in 1850 because the railroad had become a more efficient means of transportation. The canal is still among the longest and best preserved canals built during the early 1800s.

It was used until 1924 to carry coal, crops, and lumber from the West Virginia mountains to Georgetown. At its peak, some 500 mule-drawn barges navigated the waterway and were raised and lowered through its 75 locks. Many of the locks and aqueducts have been restored, and interesting old buildings line the banks of the canal, now run by the National Park Service. Trails and campsites along the entire length of the canal are available for hikers and bicyclists.

The Antietam National Battlefield and Cemetery Site lies 1 mile north of Sharpsburg on Rte. 65. Here the Union forces stopped the first Confederate invasion of the North in one of the bloodiest battles of the war. Iron tablets and battlefield maps describe the events. The visitors center houses a museum; musket and cannon demonstrations, historical talks, and bicycle tours are scheduled throughout the year.

CHARLES TOWN, West Virginia: Charles Washington, brother of George, founded and designed this town in 1786. Of interest here are numerous historic homes as well as the Jefferson County Courthouse (N. George and E. Washington Sts.), the site of the 1859 trial of John Brown and his gallows (S. Samuel and Hunter Sts.). The *Jefferson County Museum* (N. Samuel and E. Washington Sts.) has everything of John Brown's that's not a-moldering in the grave. Just outside town is Harewood, an estate built by another Washington brother, Samuel, and the site of the wedding of James and Dolley Madison. Nearby are Claymount Court (Summit Point Rd.), built by George's grandnephew, Bushrod; and Happy Retreat (Blakely Pl.), an earlier home of Charles.

BERKELEY SPRINGS, West Virginia: For many years, this resort city was called Bath, after the English spa. George Washington noted the mineral springs while surveying the region for Lord Fairfax, who donated the springs to Virginia in 1756; they have been public property ever since. Not one to mingle with the commoners, Fairfax bathed in a private hollow that's known as the Fairfax Bathtub. Today, however, the hoi polloi bathe right at the center of town in the Berkeley Springs Park, a state-run facility with health baths, warm springs, a swimming pool, and even a Roman bathhouse.

Cacapon Park, 10 miles south of town (off Rte. 522), is a 6,155-acre park at the base of Cacapon Mountain with excellent facilities for golf, tennis, horseback riding, fishing, swimming, and boating.

LOST RIVER STATE PARK, near Moorefield, West Virginia: These parklands were once a vacation spot of the Lee family of Virginia and now have facilities for swimming, tennis, picnicking, and riding. One of the original cabins has been restored and turned into a museum. Nearby stands unusual Ice Mountain (it has ice at its base even on the hottest summer days). The mountain is honeycombed with cold underground passages that keep the ice frozen.

MONONGAHELA NATIONAL FOREST, West Virginia: The forest covers over 850,000 acres in the heart of the Alleghenies, stretching southwest from the Maryland border for 100 miles through the West Virginia backcountry, a region of rounded mountains and twisting valleys. Much of the Monongahela is a "reconstructed" forest. In the early part of this century, large forest fires and indiscriminate logging practices stripped it of its huge stands of timber. The regeneration and planting program began in 1920 and the region is blanketed once again with deep forests inhabited by whitetail deer, black bear, wild turkey, and many other wildlife species.

A popular route through Monongahela starts at Petersburg, at the northeast corner of the forest, and heads southwest via Rte. 28 to Bartow. The road runs along the north fork of the Potomac. Seneca Rocks, towering 1,000 feet above the river, is a major landmark (there's also a visitors center here). Mountain climbers from all over come here to claw their way up the rugged face of this immense rock cliff. Nearby is Spruce Knob, at 4,862 feet the highest peak in West Virginia. (West Virginia's average altitude is the highest of any state east of the Mississippi.) This area of the forest is being managed as a national recreation area. The 100,000 acres have facilities for hiking and camping. Starting at the Seneca Rocks, there's whitewater canoeing for 15 miles along the headwaters of the Potomac (best undertaken in the spring).

Near Greenbank is the National Radio Astronomy Observatory, a huge radio telescope with which astronomers are recharting the heavens. Tours of the complex are given during the summer and a film explains the work done at the observatory. The facility is open daily from mid-June through Labor Day; weekends only from Memorial Day to mid-June and in September and October.

At Cass (just south of Greenbank, off Rte. 7) is the depot of a state-owned railroad with a steam locomotive that runs through the rugged mountains along an old logging track up to the summit of Bald Knob, the second highest mountain in the state. The trip to the top of the mountain takes 4½ hours.

In the southwestern portion of the forest, west of Mill Point and north of Rte. 39, lies Cranberry Glades, a large outdoor botanical laboratory centered around a big cranberry bog. The area is particularly beautiful during the fall but worth a visit at any time. Nearby, the Cranberry Mountain visitors center has instructive displays.

The Monongahela National Forest now has 26 campgrounds. There are about 700 miles of streams with excellent trout and bass fishing. In season, there is hunting for bear, deer, grouse, cottontail rabbit, snowshoe hare, squirrel, and wild turkey. There are also about 600 miles of hiking trails and four wilderness areas totaling approximately 78,000 acres. Information: Monongahela National Forest Headquarters, USDA Bldg., 200 Sycamore St., PO Box 1548, Elkins, WV 26241 (phone: 304-636-1800).

BEST EN ROUTE

Greenbrier, White Sulphur Springs – Just south of Monongahela, this magnificent resort has been favored by celebrities ranging from Robert E. Lee to the Duke of Windsor and 20 American presidents since the springs were first used in 1778. Originally a mineral spa, the *Greenbrier* has been a resort for more than 200 years and is famous for having as many employees as guests — a standard few modern resorts can match. There are 600 rooms, three 18-hole golf courses, one of which was redesigned by Jack Nicklaus, 20 tennis courts, 2 Olympic-size pools, miles of riding trails, skeet and trap shooting, an art colony, theaters, nightclubs, restaurants, and a spa. There's also a notable diagnostic clinic on the premises. After roughing it in the Monongahela National Forest, nothing could be better than being pampered here for a day or two. See also *Resort Hotels,* DIVERSIONS. Station A, White Sulphur Springs, WV 24986, just west of town on Rte. 60 (phone: 304-536-1110; 800-624-6070).

Cacapon Lodge, near Berkeley Springs – This state-run facility in the park provides good standard accommodations and easy access to all the park activities. 49 rooms, plus 11 shared baths in the "old inn," dining room, 18-hole golf course, tennis, 6-acre lake, paddleboats, fishing. Deluxe cabins available year-round; the inn closes from the last week of October through April. Berkeley Springs, WV 25411 (phone: 304-258-1022).

Watoga State Park, south of Marlinton – Another state facility that offers 88 campsites, cabins, restaurant, swimming pool, picnicking, fishing, and hiking. Information and reservations: 304-799-4087.

South

Hot Springs National Park, Arkansas

If you've only thought of Hot Springs, Arkansas, as a place to bring your aching joints when they seem to creak, you're in for a huge surprise. Hot Springs is the hottest tourist attraction in Arkansas. And it's only 50 miles from Little Rock, the state capital.

A city of some 35,000, Hot Springs is the center of Hot Springs National Park. This, in itself, is unusual, since most national parks are miles from large, populated centers. The place has certainly come a long way from the day in 1541 when the explorer Hernando de Soto christened it "the valley of vapors." At that time, it was a secluded section of Indian territory, and it was supposedly the Indians themselves who led De Soto and his exhausted team to the bubbling pools of water, where they were rejuvenated after a bath. The legendary curative properties of these 47 thermal springs became known all the world over. In 1832, 4 square miles of Hot Springs were declared a federal reservation. In 1921 they became a national park, which now covers almost 5,000 acres.

The fabled Bathhouse Row has been offering regimens of baths and massages long enough to be listed on the National Register of Historic Places. There are six bathhouses, one of them on Bathhouse Row (the others are in nearby hotels). Before you step into the mineral baths, it's recommended (not required) that you be examined by a physician. You do need a referral from a licensed physician for physiotherapy sessions at any of the hydrotherapy facilities. The springs themselves are on the western slope of Hot Springs Mountain. A reservoir collects the 800,000 gallons flowing through 45 of the thermal springs daily and channels them to the bathhouses. (You can see two of the bubbling springs behind the Maurice Bathhouse on Central Avenue; another flows down the hillside above Arlington Lawn at the north end of Bathhouse Row. The rest are not visible to the public.)

You might be surprised at the blue-green algae floating on the surface of the springs, since algae traditionally make their home in colder waters. The springs puzzle geologists, too, but for other reasons. They theorize that rain seeps through an aquifer and then rises along layers of rock to bubble out through a fault at the base of Hot Springs Mountain. But how is it heated? Perhaps by molten rock deep inside the earth or by radioactive minerals. It could be the result of inner seismic friction or unexplained chemical reactions.

The spa is merely one aspect of this vacation area. From February to April, thoroughbred horses race at *Oaklawn Park,* a handsome track. The season reaches its climax during the week-long *Racing Festival of the South* in the third week of April. It culminates in the running of the Arkansas Derby on the final day. The races kick off a lively, diversified summer and fall season. In June, Hot Springs is the scene of the *Arkansas Fun Festival;* in July, the Miss Arkansas Pageant; in October, the *Arkansas Oktoberfest;* in November, the *Healthfest/Spa 10K Run.* Special performances of an outdoor drama are staged at the 1,600-seat *Mid-America* amphitheater.

Other places of interest include Arkansas Alligator Farm (847 Whittington Ave.); IQ Zoo (600 Central); Wildwood 1884 (Victorian Mansion, 808 Park Ave.); *Josephine Tussaud Wax Museum* (250 Central Ave.); the Magic Springs Family Fun Park (Rte. 70 east); Educated Animals (380 Whittington Ave.); the Fine Arts Center (815 Whittington Ave.); and the *Mid-America Museum.*

For a touch of tranquillity, follow Rte. 270 west to the gently rolling Ouachita Mountains, one of the oldest mountain ranges on the continent. Here, you'll find three manmade lakes on the Ouachita River: Lakes Ouachita, Hamilton, and the smallest, Catherine. These lakes are the pride of Hot Springs, each offering fishing, swimming, water skiing, sailing, and scuba diving. You can camp at Lake Catherine, 12 miles west of Malvern. There are also campsites along the southern shores of Lake Ouachita and an unbeatable 18 miles of hiking trails through the forests. You can join guided nature walks during the summer. Lake Ouachita offers a unique camping opportunity. If you rent a Camp-a-Float motorized barge, you can take your car or camper onto the water and travel around the 48,000-acre lake without having to land.

For complete information on accommodations and facilities, call the Hot Springs Visitor Information Center (phone: 800-543-BATH). For a free travel kit, write to the Hot Springs Convention and Visitors Bureau, PO Box 1500, Hot Springs National Park, Hot Springs, AR 71902, or contact the Arkansas Dept. of Parks and Tourism, 1 Capitol Mall, Little Rock, AR 72201 (phone: 501-371-1511 or 501-371-7777; 800-482-8999 in Arkansas; 800-643-8383 elsewhere). Since it attracts people from all over the world, Hot Springs isn't one of those national parks where you can look forward to hot dogs on stale rolls and rubbery hamburgers. There's an abundance of restaurants: American, German, Italian, Czechoslovakian, French, Mexican, and kosher. Information: Superintendent, Hot Springs National Park, PO Box 1860, Hot Springs, AR 71902 (phone: 501-624-3383).

BEST EN ROUTE

Arlington Hotel, Hot Springs – In the middle of the city, with its own hot mineral water bathhouse, the hotel has 2 swimming pools, 3 restaurants, and over 450 rooms. Central and Fountain Sts., Hot Springs, AR 71901 (phone: 501-623-7771; 800-643-1502 outside Arkansas).

The Ozarks, Arkansas

They call it "the Natural State" — down home, pickin' and strummin', come-as-you-are Arkansas. It's an unpretentious part of the world, when you get right down to it. The home of the Ozarks is one of the great capitals of American folk myth and heritage. This is the land of country roads leading through gentle, blue-green mountains, twisting along the edges of gorges that catapult into white, frothy rivers. If you can imagine a banjo or fiddle in the background, you've got the whole picture. To get to the Ozarks from Little Rock, the capital, take I-30 and Rte. 67 north about 110 miles.

NEWPORT-JACKSONPORT: On the banks of the White River, famous for its fine trout. You can stop at Jacksonport State Park, just north of Newport, to picnic. If you have enough confidence in your casting ability, you can fish in the river for your meal. Jacksonport was once a rough-and-ready frontier river town, and its old courthouse is now a museum. The *Mary Woods II,* a White River paddlewheel steamboat, is also on display. According to local history, Jacksonport citizens liked the river city so much, they refused to let the railroad come in; so the station was built 3 miles south, in Newport. As a result, Jacksonport declined.

BATESVILLE: Follow the river northwest along Rte. 14, about 35 miles up the road, and you'll be able to step back into the 19th century, since this town is very much as it was during the days when the paddlewheelers steamed into dock, full of passengers and cargo. For two weeks during the summer, Arkansas College holds Folklore Workshops in conjunction with the *Ozark Folk Center,* 40 miles away in Mountain View.

MOUNTAIN VIEW: The home of the *Ozark Folk Center,* this is a good place for first-timers to get acquainted with the crafts, customs, and music of the Ozarks. Since it opened in 1973, the center has been a country music and folk history lover's dream. In addition to mountain craft displays and workshops, the 80-acre center is alive with music. If you're visiting in April, you'll probably be swept up in a crowd of about 100,000 people, all flocking to town for the *Arkansas Folk Festival,* 2 weekends of jug band, fiddle, Jew's harp, mountain dulcimer, and banjo strummin' sessions. If you don't like crowds but hanker after that foot-stompin' music, stop by between late spring and October. The *Ozark Folk Center's* 1,043-seat auditorium has concerts almost every night. There are also free concerts at the county courthouse every Saturday night, and, in October, a two-week *Family Harvest Festival* at the center. Traditional pottery, quilting, shucking, spinning and weaving — you can see it all at the folk center. And you can take some home — from the center's shop. For information call the Ozark Folk Center, 501-269-3851.

BLANCHARD SPRINGS CAVERN: Blanchard is in the Sylamore District of the Ozark National Forest, about 15 miles north of Mountain View on Rte. 14. Considered one of the most spectacular underground natural environments in the country, it has only been open to the public since 1973. You can walk along Dripstone Trail, an intricate labyrinth that crisscrosses the palatial subterranean caverns and takes you past stalactites. More difficult is the Discovery Trail, with a Christmas-tree-shaped stalagmite, a frozen waterfall, and a cavern called the Ghost Room (open all year long). There are nature trails and camping areas here, too. Be sure to make reservations (phone: 501-757-2213) at least 3 days in advance during the summer months, even if you only want to tour. Closed Mondays and Tuesdays, November through March.

MOUNTAIN HOME: Some fabulous river and lake country lies just to the north of Blanchard Springs. If you stay on Rte. 5, you'll pass the junction of the rushing waters of the White and Buffalo rivers. About 50 miles north of Mountain View is Mountain Home, sitting between Norfork Lake and Bull Shoals, two of the Ozarks' most famous lakes. Both are great for canoeing, swimming, and water skiing. Bass, bream, crappie, catfish, stripers, and rainbow trout swim around in the clear water just waiting to be caught, and there are Ozark guides who'll take you to where the fish are biting. You can even join a night fishing expedition on a pontoon boat. On the shores of Bull Shoals Lake, Bull Shoals State Park has campsites and a dock (on Rte. 178). Near Buffalo Point National Recreation Area, on the shores of the Buffalo River, you can rent a canoe for an unforgettable trip along one of America's wild rivers. The 132-mile Buffalo River flows through spectacular blue mountains, and there are no artificial dams to obstruct the water's flow. The National Park Service maintains cabins at Buffalo Point and campsites along the riverbanks.

HARRISON: "The hub of the Ozarks," Li'l Abner country. Here you'll find Dogpatch, USA, a theme park filled with cartoonist Al Capp's notable characters (on Rte. 65).

EUREKA SPRINGS: This delightful Victorian town is just east of 28,000-acre Beaver Lake. A fashionable health spa in the 1880s, Eureka Springs has 63 natural springs within the city limits, more than Hot Springs, the state's most popular thermal spa resort. The kids will love the shuttle bus, designed to look like a trolley car. During the summer, there's an occasional concert with different types of music at the Basin Spring Park bandshell. From late April through October, the *Great Passion Play* is performed near the 7-story-tall Christ of the Ozarks statue in a 4,200-seat amphitheater (daily except Mondays and Thursdays). Information: Eureka Springs Chamber of Commerce, PO Box 551, Eureka Springs, AR 72632 (phone: 501-253-8737).

BEAVER LAKE: Rte. 62 loops around the north shore of Beaver Lake. Here you can visit Pea Ridge National Battlefield Park, site of a decisive 1862 Civil War battle, after which Missouri stuck firmly to the Union.

OZARK–ST. FRANCIS NATIONAL FOREST: On your way back to Little Rock, take Rte. 62 south to Fayetteville, home of the University of Arkansas's main campus (phone: 501-575-2000). Then follow Rte. 71 south, past Devil's Den and Lake Fort Smith state parks, to I-40 east. (There's a Travel Information Center to the west of the intersection of Rte. 71 and I-40.) On your way back to Little Rock, stop at Clarksville, gateway to the 1.1-million-acre Ozark–St. Francis National Forest. You can get off the interstate and wander north along Rte. 21 through dense, uninhabited forest. As you breathe in the scent of pine, you might find yourself humming to the tune of some banjo song you heard a few nights earlier. This is the time to enjoy the cool, rushing sounds of the forest. Information: the Forest Supervisor, Ozark–St. Francis National Forest, PO Box 1008, Russellville, AR 72801 (phone: 501-968-2354).

BEST EN ROUTE

Ozark Folk Center Lodge, Mountain View – A 60-room lodge in woodsy surroundings right next to the folk center. A good place to choose if you want a rustic environment and a chance to be where it's all happening. PO Box 500, Mountain View, AR 72560 (phone: 501-269-3871).

Scottish Inn – Near all the major attractions in Mountain View, the *Scottish Inn* features 56 ground-floor units, each with air conditioning, color TV set, and AM/FM radio. Rooms are available with 1, 2, or 3 double beds (some waterbeds). Ample free parking, restaurants (full menu and fast food) within walking distance, and playground for the kids are also among the attractions. Open year-round. Junction Hwys. 5-9-14 and 66, Mountain View, AR 72560 (phone: 501-269-3287 or 800-251-1962).

Everglades National Park, Florida

In most of America's national parks you have little more to do than arrive and open your eyes to be impressed. The Everglades is far more demanding. Here you must know something about ecology, and something about what you're looking at, to appreciate the full splendor of this magnificent swamp wilderness.

The Everglades is America's only subtropical wetlands. Fed by the waters of southern Florida's huge Lake Okeechobee, the entire southern tip of the state was once more or less like the Everglades today — a huge tract of mangrove swamps, seas of saw grass, hammocks of hardwood trees, and millions of birds, fish, snakes and alligators, and insects (especially mosquitoes). As southern Florida developed, the slow-draining waters of Okeechobee were channeled for irrigation and swamps drained. Bit by bit, southern Florida dried out.

In 1947, alarmed by the destruction of these unique wetlands, the federal government set aside 1,398,939 acres 30 miles southwest of Miami as Everglades National Park. Despite various (and continuing) threats, the park remains today: the third largest of America's national parks, 2,188 square miles of the world's most delicate ecological system, stretching to Florida's southern and western Gulf coasts.

You must understand the delicacy of the Everglades to enjoy its understated pleasures. It is actually a freshwater river (its Indian name is Pa-Hay-Okee, "River of Grass") 100 miles long, 50 miles wide, and just inches deep. This strange stream travels along an incline of only 3 inches a mile, moving so slowly that a single drop of water takes years to reach the Gulf from Lake Okeechobee. This slow river provides nourishment for a vast and complex system of life and is a perfect laboratory in which to see the interdependence and sensitivity of an ecosystem. Where the earth rises so much as three inches, the plant life in the Everglades changes from saw grass to hardwood forest. Where ripples appear in a pond, a small fish is eating mosquito larvae; a large fish, a bream perhaps, will dine on the larvae-eater; bass hunt the bream; gar will feed on the bass; and the gar is menu fodder for the alligator who originally made (or deepened) this pond with his tail in the winter.

About 200 miles north of the Tropic of Cancer, the Everglades is the meeting point of subtropical and temperate life forms. In this it is unique in the US: Here you see mangrove, West Indian mahogany, and the poisonous manchineel tree, and in a nearby hammock rising from the saw grass, pine and hardwood trees. Alligators and whitetail deer share the same stomping ground.

The entrance to the Everglades is on Rte. 9336 about 12 miles southwest of Homestead. Rte. 9336 ends at the park entrance; from here follow the main park road for a 38-mile journey through the park to Flamingo, on Florida Bay. There are several ways to see the 'glades: by car, you can drive to various stops along the road; on foot, where trails follow into the heart of things (with or without ranger guides); by small outboard or canoe, following the water routes. In any case, the first stop is the visitors center at the park entrance, where you can see exhibitions on park wildlife and ecology and pick up information on guided tours, "swamp tromps" (more about these later), and park activities and rules.

If you are driving, the next stop is Royal Palm Station (about 2 miles beyond the center), where you can follow boardwalks over the saw grass and watch for animal life. (That saw grass has mean, serrated edges on three sides. It chews clothes or flesh with equal ease, so be careful.)

Beyond Royal Palm the road runs through pine forests to Long Pine Key, a good picnicking spot. Note the pines. They manage to survive only because they are sturdily fire resistant. You may see a number of them with fire-blackened trunks. In both summer and winter fires sweep through parts of the 'glades. Many trees are killed, but pines burn only on the outside; their corky bark protects them. In summer, the saltwort marshes that flank many of the forests dry out and are torched by summer lightning, but since it is the rainy season, when water levels are high, these fires do little damage. It is the fires during the winter dry season — usually caused by man — that do the most harm.

Pa-Hay-Okee is the next stop on the car route. From here you have access to a high platform and boardwalks that overlook Shark River Basin, where alligators and fowl gather. The alligators form an important link in the chain of life in the Everglades. During the dry season — autumn through spring — they settle into sloughs and dig deep holes with their tails. In late winter, as the marshes dry out, fish get caught in these " 'gator-holes," which become teeming pools of fish life. This is crucial for the wading birds, which nest near these ample sources of food and are assured a food supply.

Seven miles beyond Pa-Hay-Okee is Mahogany Hammock, the largest stand of mahoganies in the US. Boardwalks allow you to wander into it. A bit farther is Paurotis Pond, where you encounter the first mangrove trees. Here salt and fresh water begin to mix, and the mangrove is the only tree that thrives in salt water. It is a great colonizer and lives in a constant drama of creation and destruction all along the Gulf shore. It settles into the swampy salt water of the coast, and as it drops seeds and throws out breathing roots it captures material and actually begins "building" earth bulwarks against the sea. As seagulls and other sea birds collect around it, dropping guano, this earth becomes rich and fertile. Then hurricanes sweep the coast, and everything is ripped out of the swampy ground and thrown inland.

The main park road ends at Flamingo, where you'll find a hotel, camp-grounds, and boats for hire (including houseboats) for excursions into portions of the 'glades only accessible by waterway.

Serious visitors should plan to spend most of their time out of their cars, on marked foot trails or on a "swamp tromp" into the very heart of the marshes. (There is also a tram ride available at Shark Valley off Rte. 41, which skims the northern border of the park.) For the less hardy, foot trails are a comfortable way to have an intimate experience of the 'glades.

Gumbo Limbo Trail begins at Royal Palm and explores the interior of Paradise Key, where exotic air plants and hardwood trees grow; also at

Royal Palm, Anhinga Trail is a likely route to spot a number of alligators and a variety of birds from an elevated walkway. You might just be lucky enough to spot some of the delicate Virginia whitetail deer along the Pineland Trail (beginning about 2 miles from Long Pine Key area). These little deer are the prey of the Florida panther, which, sadly, lives in dwindling numbers here in the Everglades. At the Pa-Hay-Okee Overlook you'll get a perspective of the expanse of saw grass that makes up the Shark River basin.

For the more intrepid who would like to meet nature's challenge, from December through March there are the frequent "slough slogs" or "swamp tromps" — walking expeditions led by park naturalists which get you into things. Quite literally. You'll need old clothes and shoes that you don't mind getting muddy and wet. And be sure to have plenty of mosquito repellent handy. There are several possible destinations: out to a 'gator hole, a tree island, or a major mangrove stand. Ask for schedules at the visitors center.

The Wilderness Waterway is just about the most challenging test the Everglades can cook up for the outdoors person. It is a 99-mile water trail that corkscrews through the Ten Thousand Islands area. Although the water lanes are well marked, there is sufficient room for error that travelers are asked to take all precautions when undertaking this journey. By powerboat it is quite possible to complete the course in about 6 hours. However, any serious nature observer will opt for the canoe and the serenity it offers en route. There are minimally outfitted campsites, each wryly nicknamed, along the water lanes: "Hell's Bay" ("hell to get into and hell to get out of"); "Onion Key," the bare-bones remains of a 1920s land developer's dream; and a crude pit outhouse and fireplace campsite known as "the Coming Miami of the Gulf." The waterways begin at Everglades City and extend to Flamingo.

The somewhat less athletic and daring boater might prefer to take a guided boat cruise. One such cruise departs every evening from Flamingo to tour Florida Bay; this is a good opportunity to view Florida's blazing sunsets and watch the indigenous birds returning to roost for the evening. There are also daily cruises from Everglades City to explore Upper Chokoloskee Bay.

The not-so-visible members of the Everglades family run the gamut from the lowly and much-hated mosquito all the way to the signature 'gator, who is most often spotted when his eyes break water while the rest of him hides beneath the surface. Fish are tropical and abundant, each with a role in the food cycle that maintains the Everglades. Schools of dolphin can usually be spotted from the coastal shorelines. Recreational fishing is permitted, but all plants and animals are protected by law from any molestation or harm by man. Information: Superintendent, Everglades National Park, PO Box 279, Homestead, FL 33030 (phone: 305-247-6211).

BEST EN ROUTE

Fontainebleau Hilton – Still the glittering standard by which most Miami Beach hotels are measured. Some say the hotel's lagoon-like pool is the best swimming hole in South Florida. 1,250 rooms. 4441 Collins Ave., Miami Beach, FL 33140 (phone: 305-538-2000 or 800-445-8667).

Holiday Inn – Across from the University of Miami, this motel is a good choice for visitors to the southwest area. The rooms are comfortable and there's a popular restaurant. 1350 S. Dixie Hwy., Miami, FL 33146 (phone: 305-667-5611).

Omni International – This 553-room hotel is in a large shopping mall, where there is a carousel popular with the kids. 16th St. and Biscayne Blvd., Miami, FL 33132 (phone: 305-374-0000 or 800-THE-OMNI).

Florida Keys and John Pennekamp Coral Reef State Park, Florida

Curving 150 miles out into the Gulf of Mexico from the southern tip of mainland Florida, the Florida Keys dot the waters like an ellipsis following a phrase. And in many ways this archipelago is an afterthought to that great landmass above, centered around Miami, with its glittering nightlife and crowded swimming beaches. The 45 islands that make up the Keys are generally tucked soundly away by 11 at night, have very few swimming beaches despite the availability of water (the shallow waters coupled with fierce coral discourage swimming), and few glamorous resorts. The local hotel with five stories — a midget by Miami standards — is a skyscraper hereabouts.

What the Keys do have, however, are some of the finest seascapes around — the blue waters of the Atlantic to the east and south and the green seas of the Gulf of Mexico on the northern side. As you drive along the Overseas Highway (US 1), a toll-free highway that spans the islands with 43 bridges (some only 100 feet long, one stretching as far as 7 miles), you'll be surrounded on all sides by sea and sky. Even on the Keys themselves, many of which are only a few hundred yards wide, you can see through the mangroves, Caribbean pine, and silver palmetto to the sea, which is the overwhelming presence here. And though you can't see it from the car, below the surface the view is even more dramatic. The Keys are surrounded by an offshore coral reef, a section of which can be seen close up at the John Pennekamp Coral Reef State Park in Key Largo. It is a slightly hallucinogenic underwater scene as bright blue and green tropical fish move in and out of the sculptured reefs of white, pink, and orange coral.

The story of the Overseas Highway is interesting. In the late 1880s, Henry Flagler, an associate of John D. Rockefeller, aimed to establish a "land" route to Cuba by extending the Florida East Coast Railroad line to Key West. From there he planned a ferry shuttle for the final 90 miles to Havana. He invested some $20 million in the construction of tracks, but the 1929 crash destroyed his project. Six years later, the Labor Day Hurricane of 1935 wiped out most of what remained of the tracks. At that point, the government stepped in and began building the Overseas Highway along the same route. In 1982, 37 bridges were replaced with wider, heavier spans, including the well-known Seven-Mile Bridge at Marathon.

Of the 45 keys linked by the highway, several are major islands with accommodations, restaurants, shops, and their own unique characteristics. Much of this local flavor has to do with the natives of the area. They're

Floridians, but they call themselves Conchs. Descended from the London Cockneys who settled in the Bahamas, the Conchs also incorporate Cuban, Yankee sailor, and Virginia merchant blood. Conchs have always been people of the sea — fishermen, boatsmen, underwater salvagers. (They could hardly be otherwise, living as they do, surrounded by water.) And when you are in their territory, you can easily share their pleasures. Fishing is king in these parts, with over 300 varieties of fish in the surrounding waters. Besides the challenges to anglers, the availability of fresh fish has stimulated Key chefs to dream up such creations as Conch chowder and, in their land-bound flights of fancy, Key lime pie — which must be yellow, not green, to be genuine.

JOHN PENNEKAMP CORAL REEF STATE PARK and KEY LARGO NATIONAL MARINE SANCTUARY, Key Largo: Key Largo is the first of the keys and the longest, but what is most interesting here is under water. Running parallel to the Key for 21 miles is the country's only underwater state park and the sole living coral reef in the continental US. The park is a snorkeler's and scuba diver's heaven, encompassing 170 square miles of the Atlantic Ocean, hundreds of species of tropical fish, and 40 different varieties of coral. Laws forbid taking anything from the water so that the area will be preserved for others to see.

To get an overview of the reef and surrounding sea, take the *Discovery* tour boat and look through the eye-level windows lining the hull. Though somewhat commercial, it provides valuable information on the ecological balance of the reef and journeys several miles out onto the high seas to the reef's most spectacular section, where you'll see beautifully colored coral formations and other marine life, including barracuda, giant sea turtles, and sharks, from a dry vantage point. But as the water gets bluer and bluer, the ride gets rougher and rougher, so take the anti-seasickness tablets they offer at the beginning of the trip.

You can also venture into the water under better circumstances for scuba diving tours of the reef. Gear can be rented at one of Key Largo's many dive shops or at park headquarters.

Closer to shore, water trails for canoeing in the mangrove swamp offer alternatives for those who want to stay above water. And for those who want to go in, the swimming beach has a roped-off area that is good for a dip or some casual skin diving.

There are 47 campsites, all with tables, charcoal grills, electrical hookups, and water. Reservations for the sites should be made up to 60 days in advance — the park is a very popular destination. Stop by the Visitors Center. Reservations and information: John Pennekamp State Park, PO Box 487, Key Largo, FL 33037 (phone: 305-451-1202).

ISLAMORADA, Upper Matecumbe Key: A sportfishing center in an area that's famous for fishing, the many coral reefs in the surrounding shallow waters attract scuba and skin divers as well. The Underwater Coral Gardens, two colorful coral deposits and the wreck of a Spanish galleon, offer underwater exploration and photography and can be reached by charter boat.

LONG KEY: Stop here for some underwater hunting (in season) of crawfish — lobster-like crustaceans without the pincers. There are dive shops all along the route, indicated by the red-and-white-striped divers' flags, which arrange private or group snorkeling expeditions to nearby reefs where you stalk (swim after) your prey. Long Key Park (phone: 305-664-4815).

MARATHON: This large key, midway down the archipelago, has been developed as a tourist center and has an airport and an 18-hole golf course. Nevertheless, Marathon retains much of the original character of a fishing town. There are over 80 species in the Gulf and ocean waters which can be taken with rod and reel or nets from charter boats or the key's bridges. For information on the many fishing contests held throughout the year, write to the Chamber of Commerce, 3330 Overseas Hwy., Marathon, FL 33050 (phone: 305-743-5417). The competition is tough and the fish smart. *Hall's Diving Center* (1994 Overseas Hwy.; phone: 305-743-5929) is a good place to rent gear.

BIG PINE KEY: The largest of the Lower Keys contains 7,700 acres thick with silver palmetto, Caribbean pine, and cacti. Tiny key deer were thought to be extinct until they reappeared here, and it is possible to spot rare white heron. The Bahia Honda State Recreational Area (5 miles east on US 1) has camping, boating, picnicking, and coral-free swimming.

KEY WEST: The southernmost community in the US and the point closest to Cuba (a 90-mile swim), this famous key combines Southern, Bahamian, Cuban, and Yankee influences in a unique culture that can be seen in its architecture, tasted in its cuisine, and felt in its relaxed, individualistic atmosphere. Traditionally, fishermen, artists, and writers are drawn to this tranquil slip of sand and sea. Ernest Hemingway, among its early devotees, lived here during his most productive period, when he wrote *To Have and Have Not, For Whom the Bell Tolls, Green Hills of Africa,* and one of his greatest short stories, "The Snows of Kilimanjaro." His Spanish Colonial–style house of native stone, surrounded by a lush garden of plantings from the Caribbean, is now a museum with many original furnishings and Hemingway memorabilia (907 Whitehead St.). Among others who have been attracted to Key West are Harry Truman (who established a "Little White House" here), John James Audubon, Tennessee Williams, John Dos Passos, and Robert Frost.

To get your bearings, take the Conch Tour Train, a 90-minute narrated tram ride that covers 14 miles, passing all the highlights of town. The train leaves several times a day from one of two depots: Duval and Front Streets and Old Mallory Square. Since Key West is best for strolling, afterward you can visit the places that sounded most interesting or walk to the galleries, craft, and shell shops. *Antonia's,* 615 Duval (phone: 305-294-6565), is a good place to eat.

The *Lighthouse Museum* (Truman Ave. and Whitehead St.) has many military displays, including a Japanese submarine captured at Pearl Harbor. The Audubon House (205 Whitehead St.), where the artist worked on paintings of Florida Keys wildlife in 1831 and 1832, has a complete set of *Birds of America* engravings.

Fishing dominates sports here as elsewhere in the Keys. In addition to fishing, there is a collection of local marine life at the Municipal Aquarium (Whitehead St. on Mallory Sq.). For scuba diving around the coral reefs, the *Key West Pro Dive Shop* sponsors trips and rents gear (1605 N. Roosevelt Blvd., PO Box 580, Key West, FL 33040, phone: 305-296-3823). Information: Key West Chamber of Commerce, 402 Wall St., Key West, FL 33040 (phone: 305-294-2587). Area information: Florida Keys Visitors Bureau, PO Box 1147-PR, Key West, FL 33041 (phone: 800-FLA-KEYS).

BEST EN ROUTE

Hawk's Cay Resort – This 178-room hotel has 4 dining rooms, a cocktail lounge, tennis courts, marina, and freshwater pools. Marker 61, Marathon, FL 33050 (phone: 800-432-2242 in Florida; 800-327-7775 elsewhere).

Pier House, Key West – In the heart of the restored Old Town Key West area, this 120-room hotel has 3 dining areas and a pool. 1 Duval St., Key West, FL 33040 (phone: 305-294-9541; 800-432-3414 in Florida; 800-327-8340 elsewhere).

Eden House, Key West – An old guesthouse, built back in the early 1920s, now stands as the best of traditional designs, and the price is right. 1015 Fleming St., Key West, FL 33040 (phone: 305-296-6868).

Okefenokee Swamp, Georgia

If you've ever hummed "Way Down Upon the Suwannee River," you already have a connection to the Okefenokee Swamp. In fact, you're even ahead of Stephen Foster, who'd never seen the Suwannee River when he wrote the song. He originally called it "Way Down Upon the Pedee River," but luckily for Okefenokee lovers, he switched names, thereby immortalizing a curious wandering waterway that begins in this southeast Georgia marshland and flows 230 miles through northeast Florida into the Gulf of Mexico. If you've ever hummed "Way Down Upon St. Marys River," you are already no doubt familiar with the aquatic interrelationships within the 660 square miles of the Okefenokee Swamp. St. Marys is the other Okefenokee river.

The powerful, mysterious marshland of watery caverns lined with elegant, luxurious cypress trees dripping with moss is known as the "land of the trembling earth," a name bestowed upon it by its early inhabitants, the Indians. Many thousands of years earlier, the swamp had been a vast expanse of salt water. Trail Ridge, now Okefenokee's eastern border, was then an ocean reef. But shifting land formations locked the water in, and it became a breeding ground for swamp vegetation. The first white settlers arrived in 1853 and made their living by farming, fishing, hunting 'gators, and picking wild herbs to sell. The swampers led a fairly rugged life, plying their boats up and down the Suwannee in search of cooters, the giant turtles they sold in local markets. Youngsters earned pocket money by catching snakes for people to keep as pets and crayfish for fishermen's bait. The worn, wooden porches of swamp dwellers' cabins were very often covered with the drying leaves of a plant called deer's tongue, used as a medicine and to flavor pipe tobacco.

There are several ways to get to the Okefenokee Swamp from Savannah, Georgia. If you take I-95 south along the coast, you'll find any number of interesting places to stop. At Brunswick, 60 miles south of Savannah, pick up Rte. 84 east for about 50 miles, to Okefenokee Swamp Park, the northern entrance to the Okefenokee National Wildlife Refuge.

SAPELO ISLAND: About 50 miles south of Savannah is the Sapelo Island National Estuarine Sanctuary — the island's official name. The number of visitors allowed here is restricted because it has been set aside by the Georgia Department of Natural Resources to study and protect the salt marshes — and their marine life — surrounding the island. This island is so unspoiled that ecologists use it as a base for measuring the pollution levels of other areas. Along with lots of deer and wild turkey and the University of Georgia Marine Institute laboratories, the lovely South End mansion is here. Originally built as a plantation house in the 1800s and once owned by the tobacco tycoon R. J. Reynolds, South End is sometimes used by former President Carter and his family for vacations. Tours of the island are given Fridays only from June through Labor Day; Wednesdays and Saturdays the rest of the year (reservations required; phone the Darien Chamber of Commerce, phone: 912-437-6684); you get to the island by ferry from Darien (it's a 30-minute boat ride).

MARSHES OF GLYNN: About 30 miles farther south, the Marshes of Glynn stretch west from the highway. Georgia-born poet Sidney Lanier composed an epic poem to the marsh in 1878; "The Marshes of Glynn" is not exactly something you would hum at a bus stop, but "Glooms of the live oaks, beautiful-braided and woven/With intricate shades of the vines that myriad-cloven/Clamber the forks of the multi-form boughs" gives you a pretty good idea of life in the sea-marsh.

SEA ISLANDS: Barely 10 miles farther south, these legendary islands hug the Georgia coast. Fabled for their exquisite resorts and superior outdoor sports facilities, St. Simons, Jekyll, and Sea islands have a unique charm. Jekyll, the most southerly island, was a private club for millionaires until 1946, when it became a state park, with 9 miles of beach, a wildlife refuge, and restored millionaire's cottages.

OKEFENOKEE NATIONAL WILDLIFE REFUGE: Follow I-95 south from St. Simons about 30 miles to the Okefenokee turnoff (Rte. 40), then go approximately 22 miles west to Folkston. Follow Rte. 121/23 south for 8 miles to the Suwannee Canal Recreation Area. Here, at the eastern entrance to the National Wildlife Refuge, you can take guided boat trips or rent a boat yourself. There are also hiking trails, a visitors center, and a wildlife observation drive. Interpreters out at the Chesser Island Homestead will explain how families settled the area and describe what life was like in the swamp. In 1937, the government declared Okefenokee a National Wildlife Refuge. Since then, rare species of woodpecker, reptiles, amphibians, and wading birds nest here, protected by law. Mud turtle, snapping turtle, and Florida cooter swim among the water lilies, along with an inordinate variety of frogs, toads, and snakes. Although some, like the king and black racer snake, are not dangerous, others, such as the diamondback rattler and cottonmouth, are venomous and can be hazardous. If you're taking a guided excursion in a flat-bottomed boat, the swamp guide will explain how to watch out for these and other reptiles. Most snakes are scared of people and won't go out of their way to attack. Within the boundaries of the refuge is Stephen C. Foster State Park, which offers camping, picnicking, fishing, and boat tours and rentals. Outside the northeastern refuge boundary is Laura Walker State Park, near Waycross, Georgia, which also offers recreational facilities as well as swimming. Okefenokee Swamp Park, in Waycross, offers tours by small boat. Information: Okefenokee National Wildlife Refuge, Rte. 2, Box 338, Folkston, GA 31537 (phone: 912-496-3331).

BEST EN ROUTE

The King and Prince Beach Hotel, St. Simons Island – A 96-room resort inn alongside the sea with a good beach, swimming pool, tennis courts, and bike rental. Close to golf, horseback riding, fishing, sailing, and skeet shooting. Dining room open to visitors. See also *Resort Hotels,* DIVERSIONS. PO Box 798, St. Simons Island, GA 31522 (phone: 912-638-3631).

Jekyll Inn, Jekyll Island – As you'd expect from a former millionaires' paradise, Jekyll Island resorts are still deluxe. This beachfront resort complex has a restaurant, lounge, and many other facilities. There are also 9 tennis courts and 63 holes of championship golf on the island. 975 N. Beachview Dr., Jekyll Island, GA 31520 (phone: 912-635-2531).

Mammoth Cave National Park, Kentucky

An ancient Chinese sage, believing that it is better to be soft and yielding than hard and inflexible, was fond of pointing out that stone, the most rigid of substances, always gives way to water. If Lao-tzu were around today, he would find the perfect example of his teachings in Mammoth Cave, a huge system of underground chambers and passageways in central Kentucky that has been hollowed out of stone entirely by the seepage of rainwater and the flowing and dissolving action of underground streams.

Mammoth Cave National Park is off I-65, about 100 miles from Louisville and the same distance from Nashville. The entrance to the main cave is about 9 miles west of Cave City, Kentucky. The longest known cave in the world, Mammoth contains chambers that are two thirds the length of a football field. Its tallest dome is 192 feet high; its deepest pit is 106 feet deep. Although the entire cave complex lies beneath an area only 10 miles in diameter, its known passageways and chambers wind and twist through five separate levels for more than 300 miles.

If its size alone isn't enough to impress you, consider the cave's fantastic formations: Disney-like shapes in stone that twist and turn, ripple and flow, in infinite variation. Most of these natural sculptures, like strange yet familiar objects in a dream, remind you of a hundred different things at once, but some — usually the larger ones — so strongly suggest particular objects that they have been named: King Solomon's Temple, the Pillars of Hercules, Frozen Niagara, the Giant's Coffin, the Bridal Altar (which has actually been used for weddings). Adding to the dreamlike effect, clusters of gypsum crystals, like rare flowers, hug many of the cave's walls, turning them into exotic hanging gardens.

National Park Service rangers conduct daily tours (except on Christmas Day) of the most interesting parts of the cave. (No solo exploring is allowed.) And if you weary of the park's subterranean wonders, aboveground are 52,000 acres of beautiful Kentucky woodlands to roam.

The origins of Mammoth Cave go back more than 280 million years to a time when a shallow sea covered this part of the country. The sea left layers of mud, shells, and sand that hardened into limestone and sandstone. After the sea drained away, rainwater, containing small amounts of carbonic acid, seeped into fissures in the limestone layers, dissolving some of the stone as it percolated down. Over time, the cracks widened and a system of underground streams developed which hollowed out the cave. As the streams cut deeper and deeper into their beds, they continuously lowered the floor of the cave, allowing more and more of the upper regions to dry.

Water not only carved out this mammoth house of stone, it furnished and decorated it as well. As it seeped through the limestone in the dry parts of the cave, it evaporated, leaving a mineral deposit called travertine (also known as cave onyx). Water dripping from the ceiling of the cave over centuries formed chemical icicles of travertine, or stalactites. Water flowing over rock formed waterfalls of travertine, or flowstone. In a similar way, water shaped the cave's pillars, temples, and altars. Even as you marvel at these formations and gasp at the vastness of this underground palace, water, seeping through the limestone and flowing in underground streams, continues the process begun eons ago.

Human beings knew about Mammoth Cave more than 3,000 years ago. The remains of a mummified man who was apparently killed by a falling boulder while he was chipping minerals from the cave walls indicate that the woodland Indians used to mine gypsum here.

Kentucky pioneers discovered the cave in 1798; since then it has had a varied history. During the War of 1812, saltpeter, an ingredient in gunpowder, was extracted from dirt found on the floor of Mammoth Cave. As one of the principal sources of saltpeter in the entire country, the cave played an important role in winning the war.

In the 1840s, when the cave was privately owned, a doctor attempted to cure tubercular patients by having them live in the constant temperature (54F) and humidity (87%) of the cave for several weeks. A few patients died and the rest emerged sicker than before.

Throughout the 19th century, the curious came from far and near to see the cave's wonders by the flickering light of whale-oil lamps. Occasionally, the famous were drawn as well. Edwin Booth, the celebrated Shakespearean actor, recited Hamlet's soliloquy in a chamber of the cave now called Booth's Amphitheater.

There are five main entrances to the cave: the natural or Historic Entrance and four manmade entrances known as Frozen Niagara, Carmichael, Violet City, and New Entrance. You can purchase tickets for a variety of different tours at the visitors center near the Historic Entrance or at Ticketron outlets throughout the US.

There are six main tours to choose from — one to suit just about every age and level of endurance. (All tours require sturdy shoes and a warm sweater.) The easiest trip is the Presidential (¼ mile, 1¼ hours), which takes you to a variety of formations, the largest of which is Frozen Niagara. On the Historic Trip (2 miles, 2 hours) you will see the Rotunda Room, where mineral-laden dirt was processed into saltpeter during the War of 1812, and Mammoth Dome, the highest dome in the cave.

To see some of the most beautiful gypsum formations in the cave, take the Half-Day Trip (4 miles, 4½ hours), on which you will stop for lunch in the Snowball Room, 267 feet underground. It ends at Frozen Niagara.

The Frozen Niagara Tour (¾ mile, 2 hours), a more strenuous version of the Presidential Tour, is also worth taking. Descend 280 stairs, past impressive pits and domes, to Grand Central Station, and from there to the stalactites and stalagmites of the dripstone formation area. Not for those with claustrophobia or acrophobia.

You will see the cave in an entirely different light when you take the Lantern Trip (3 miles, 3 hours). While electricity makes it easy to see everything, only lantern light creates the proper shadowy atmosphere for cave viewing.

The Echo River tour (3 miles, 3 hours) includes a boat ride on the river but is somewhat strenuous, since it also means enduring steep hills and deep sand.

Persons in wheelchairs need not miss out on Mammoth Cave. A special tour (½ mile, 1½ hours) is available for the disabled.

When you finally emerge from your tour, blinking in the sunlight and dazzled by all the wonders underground, you can restore your senses with a short (1 mile) walk on the Cave Island Nature Trail, which begins and ends near the Historic Entrance. Giant sycamores and beech trees line this trail, which leads to the bottomlands of the Green River. There, underground streams emerge from the caverns belowground. Several other trails wind through the woods on this side of the park.

The least developed and, in many ways, the most beautiful part of the park is its north side. Here, you can walk along the stream beds past waterfalls and natural bridges or meander along the steep bluffs that afford lovely views of the Kentucky hills. To get to this little-known side of the park, take the free car ferry run by paddlewheel and guided by cables across the Green River.

If you have just returned from a cave and have had enough hiking for the day, you can board the *Miss Green River* for a leisurely cruise. The twilight cruise is the best for seeing wildlife: As you sit in comfort, you glide past beaver, turtles, deer, and snakes on the riverbank. Not as exciting as the *African Queen* maybe, but a very pleasant way to pass an hour. You can buy tickets for the cruise at the visitors center.

If your fishing gear is just languishing in the trunk of the car, put it to good use in the Green River or in the scenic Nolin River, which runs along the park's western boundary. Fishing permits are not required in the park.

Before you head north to Louisville for the Kentucky Derby (held on the first Saturday of May at *Churchill Downs*), northeast to the beautiful Blue-grass Country around Lexington, or west to the lake country that borders Tennessee, don't forget to stop at the craft shop at Mammoth Cave National Park. Here you can buy woven items, pottery, metal crafts, baskets, brooms, wood carvings, and dulcimers handmade in the Kentucky hills. Information: Superintendent, Mammoth Cave National Park, Mammoth Cave, KY 42259 (phone: 502-758-2328).

BEST EN ROUTE

There are numerous hotels and motels in the area, at Cave City and Bowling Green. Farther afield in central Kentucky, in the general direction of Louisville and Lexington, are a couple of inns of interest that could be comfortably incorporated into a Mammoth Cave visit.

Doe Run Inn, Brandenburg – Close to the Indiana-Kentucky border near the Ohio River, 40 miles southwest of Louisville, the inn incorporates the remains of an early Kentucky mill, and it is simple, unadorned, and comfortable. One reason for visiting is to eat — chicken, ham, biscuits — traditional Kentucky fare done with great attention. Hwy. 448, Brandenburg, KY 40108 (phone: 502-422-2982).

Boone Tavern Hotel, Berea – Run by Berea College and staffed by students; 59 rooms, 2 dining rooms (one for private parties), and access to the college's pool, tennis and racquetball courts, and running track. About 40 miles south of Lexington. Main St., Berea, KY 40403 (phone: 606-986-9358).

Bayou Country, Louisiana

Technically, a bayou is a bit of waterway that has wandered away from — or been left by — a main river. A huge, slow river will create bayous as it flows across any flat plain, cutting new waterways as rising sediment changes its course, then abandoning them when it changes direction yet again.

That's the dictionary definition of a bayou, but it doesn't begin to describe the bayou country of southern Louisiana, where the Mississippi River flows so slowly, and over such a wide and meandering course, that it has bred bayous like bastard children, a whole world of them, filled with swampgrass patrolled by alligators and cypress forests festooned with Spanish moss. Bayou country — called Acadiana — starts west of New Orleans and covers 22 parishes (counties) from Avoyelles Parish down to the Gulf Coast.

Bayou is actually the French mispronunciation of the Choctaw word bayuk, meaning creek or stream. The Choctaw Indians were the first inhabitants of this region. In the mid-1700s they were joined by the Acadians, French inhabitants of Nova Scotia whom the British exiled from Canada. (You may remember Evangeline, Longfellow's tragic poem about their trek.) These Acadians — "Cajuns," as they came to be known down here — adapted to the temperate climate, settled in, and gradually turned the bayou country into a French-American enclave unlike anything in the world.

The marriage of bayou and French was felicitous; today the culture remains, though not untouched, still unique. Whimsical Cajun French crops up everywhere: horse races at Evangeline Downs begin with the cry *"Ils sont partis"* instead of "They're off." The unofficial motto of this part of the country is *Laissez les bons temps rouler,* which, if not authentic French, nonetheless translates into an accurate summary of Cajun attitudes — "Let the good times roll."

On a map, Acadiana is in south-central Louisiana, west of Baton Rouge. Its eight parishes include a few largish cities, some spectacular gardens, some local oddities like salt islands that you're not likely to see anywhere else, and a lot of history kept alive by the Cajuns.

Due to its sprawling size, Acadiana does not lend itself to an organized driving route. Part of the charm of a visit here is in meandering like the bayous themselves, traveling wherever highways lead you. A detailed map of Acadiana is absolutely essential, as some of the roads here will not even show up on large state maps. Request a driving map from the Lafayette Convention and Visitors Commission, PO Box 52066, Lafayette, LA 70505 (phone: 318-232-3737).

There are dozens of little towns, each with its own festival or its special claim to fame. Remember that you are in the South, where the pace is much less hectic than in other regions of the US. The people are very outgoing — friendlier and more willing to sit for a spell and chat. Add to this Southern hospitality and French charm — and you have the basic ingredients for a memorable vacation. Allow enough time to let yourself get into the slow swing. Certainly try some of the regional cuisine, like crawfish. Join in the local festivals. In short . . . *Laissez les bons temps rouler!*

ATCHAFALAYA BASIN: Running down the eastern third of Acadiana, the Basin is a good place to begin getting familiar with the country — and incredible country it is. The Basin is a swamp of 1,300 square miles, stretching from near Lafayette south to the Gulf. Three times larger than Okefenokee Swamp in Georgia, it receives little notice outside the state because it is totally undeveloped for tourists, with one exception. For an adventure through Atchafalaya Basin, you can board the boat tour that leaves from McGee's Landing near the town of Henderson (take exit 115 off Rte. I-10).

LAFAYETTE: At the intersection of US 167 and I-10, this is the undisputed center of Acadiana. A city with a population of some 90,000, it boasts the usual variety of municipal auditoriums, centers, and museums. But these are not the things that have drawn you to bayou country. There are special Cajun places and events here you'll not want to miss. The Acadian Village (1½ miles off Hwy. 167, north on Ridge Rd.) is a bayou town that has been relocated and restored to reflect life in the 19th century. Visitors can walk through town, stopping at the general store, several open houses, the trading post, and a blacksmith shop. The heart of the village is the Chapel of New Hope; the chapel remains a symbolic heart today because this village exists not only as a historic restoration but also as a fund-raising center for the Alleman Center for Louisiana's handicapped citizens.

Lafayette holds its own *Mardi Gras* celebration, the second largest such celebration in the US. The week or so of parades, live music, and general reveling culminates in the *Annual Southwest Louisiana Mardi Gras Association Pageant and Ball;* tickets are available from the Chamber of Commerce, 318-233-2705.

In March and April, Lafayette holds the *Azalea Trail* festivities, when antebellum homes throughout the area open to the public and millions of azaleas grown in the area burst into bloom; it is the perfect time to visit the town. And the annual *Festivals Acadiens,* held the third weekend of September, features Cajun music, bayou food, native crafts, and other regional curiosities.

BREAUX BRIDGE: Here the annual *Crawfish Festival* is held the first weekend of May. This "crawfish capital of the world," 9 miles northeast of Lafayette (Rte. 94 and I-10), is actually a picturesque Acadian town on the banks of the Bayou Teche. Up to 50,000 hungry visitors come to enjoy this delicacy that restaurants serve in dozens of different ways, all Cajun and all delicious.

ST. MARTINVILLE: This is the area where a great many Acadians first settled, and the town is filled with references to that epic story and Longfellow's poem. (If you read the poem before you visit, it will heighten your appreciation of the town.) In town you can visit Evangeline's grave. The city has a life-size bronze statue of Evangeline, a gift from actress Dolores del Rio after filming the movie here. The town courthouse has a small, intriguing display of early French aristocratic coats of arms, but even more interesting is the *Acadian Museum,* on the 157 acres of the Longfellow-Evangeline Commemorative Area just outside town, with live demonstrations of early crafts.

NEW IBERIA: At the junction of Hwys. 90 and 14 is the center of the sugarcane industry as well as the home of the romantic Bayou Teche. Here, too, is Shadows-on-the-Teche, a stately old mansion very much like those always associated with the Old South. It's vintage 1830 and is now one of 12 properties owned and maintained by the National Trust for Historic Preservation.

Just outside town are two of those geographical oddities mentioned earlier — islands formed by salt domes that pushed up from the sea-level marshlands millions of years ago. These dome-islands are, as you might imagine, rich in salt. In fact it is mined right there. (Salt from here served the entire Confederate army for the duration of the war.) But there is also an astonishing amount of other natural resources, including oil reserves, and some of America's most fertile earth.

AVERY ISLAND: Though small, it is packed with things to see and marvel over. Jungle Gardens and Bird Sanctuary were both developed by the late Edward Avery McIlhenny. The Gardens are a 200-acre landscaped paradise, featuring exotic growing things from all over the world. The Bird Sanctuary is famous for its huge rookery for egrets. Enormous flocks of herons and egrets and other birds protected here can be seen in warm months. Ducks and other migrating fowl can be seen in winter. Here on Avery Island grow all those tiny but fiery little peppers that go into the supersecret recipe for Tabasco sauce. You can tour the Tabasco plant if you like, but they guard their secret formula jealously.

A final note about Avery Island: It is one of the primary US producers of fur bearing nutria. Nutria, lest you ask, are fur bearing mammals also known as coypus, originally from South America. A number of years ago a hurricane allowed some domestic nutria to escape from their cages. They discovered that the bayou agreed with them and proceeded to overpopulate. They are caught today for their fur.

BEST EN ROUTE

Lafayette is basically an ordinary city when it comes to lodgings; an exception is the *Acadiana* (see below). Many hotels and motels are comfortable, reasonable, and handy but offer little more than convenience. Outside the city, you can stay in an old plantation house, which will provide a more interesting atmosphere.

Mintmere Plantation House, New Iberia – Built in 1857 and restored in 1976, the rooms in this lovely home are decorated with antiques and look out over Bayou Teche. 1400 E. Main, New Iberia, LA 70560 (phone: 318-364-6210).

Acadiana, Lafayette – A modern 6-story, 300-room hotel with a restaurant and 2 lounges, an outdoor swimming pool, and other amenities, including hot tubs. 1801 W. Pinhook Rd., Lafayette, LA 70505 (phone: 318-233-8120).

Hilton and Towers, Lafayette – Here is a property with 328 rooms, including Jacuzzi suites, a restaurant, lounge, and outdoor pool. 1521 W Pinhook Rd., Lafayette, LA 70508 (phone: 318-235-6111).

Asphodel, near Jackson – A plantation village in the heart of plantation country, close to bayou country. Asphodel is the plantation, open for tours only; the village has smaller buildings: an inn/restaurant, antique train depot used for meetings and parties (reservations necessary), gift shop, and breakfast room. The cuisine is interesting, mixing Créole cooking with the best of others. Rooms come with "Southern breakfast" (grits, eggs, bacon, and much more). 18 rooms. Asphodel Plantation, Rte. 2, Box 89, Jackson, LA 70748 (phone: 504-654-6868).

Natchez Trace Parkway, Natchez, Mississippi, to Nashville, Tennessee

For several hundred years before white men settled in the Mississippi and Ohio valleys, the Natchez, Choctaw, and Chickasaw Indians used one major trail to pass north and south. Worn down to a permanent roadbed, the trail — or Trace — wandered for 500 miles from the lower Mississippi River into what was to become central Tennessee. When Kentucky and Tennessee filled up with hunters and trappers, then settlers, the Trace entered the history of commerce. "Kaintuck" boatmen floated their goods downriver on flatboats carried by the Mississippi's currents, but they were obliged to return home on foot (sometimes on horseback). Between the late 1700s and about 1820, the Natchez Trace was a constant thoroughfare. The coming of steamboats changed the history of the Trace. By 1819 there were 20 steam-driven ships plying the Mississippi, eliminating the need for overland portage.

Parts of the Natchez Trace still exist, and today the entire route is commemorated by the Natchez Trace Parkway, a modern highway being built under the auspices of the National Park Service and still under construction, that will run from Natchez, Mississippi, northward through a slip of Alabama, to just outside Nashville, Tennessee. The parkway does not replace the

Trace, but it does follow the original route as closely as possible, and there are numerous spots along the way where travelers can park and actually walk on the Trace. The parkway's longest continuous section stretches from Jackson, Mississippi, to Shady Grove, Tennessee, 303 miles of quiet two-lane highway with numerous points of interest — Indian mounds, sites of Civil War battles, areas of natural interest, and above all, portions of the Trace that cross the parkway's route — marked by signs. You can follow the Natchez Trace Parkway from Nashville south to Natchez (realizing that the entire route is not yet completed) or from Natchez to Nashville. We start our itinerary, as did the boatmen who used the Trace, at Natchez, traveling north to Tennessee. Information: Superintendent, Natchez Trace Parkway, RR 1, NT 143, Tupelo, MS 38801 (phone: 601-842-1572).

NATCHEZ: Before beginning the journey north, spend some time in Natchez itself. When the boatmen ended their downriver journeys here in the first decades of the 19th century, they found a city on its way to getting rich, obsessed with elegance and style, supported by the profitable cotton trade. The rivermen saw little of this elegance or opulence, however. With their wages stuffed in their pockets, they spent most of their time in Natchez-Under-the-Hill, everything a shantytown river city should be. Gamblers, prostitutes, killers, adventurers, and traders gathered there to pursue their respective businesses.

There is little of Natchez-Under-the-Hill today, but there is a great deal to see and do in Natchez itself. It is known as the city "where the Old South still lives," and in town are two antebellum homes of note: Stanton Hall (401 High St.) and Rosalie (100 Orleans St.). Rosalie is the earlier of the two, built about 1820. There are a number of antebellum homes in the area open to the public; a list is available from the Pilgrimage Headquarters (PO Box 347). There's an annual Christmas Pilgrimage for a week in December and for a month every spring — early March to April (and/or 2 weeks in early October) — when the Pilgrimage and Natchez garden clubs sponsor a daily tour that includes some 30 of the finest antebellum homes in the country. Everything possible is done to create the aura of the Old South: ladies in hoop skirts greet visitors in their spacious parlors, formal gardens are pruned, preened, and open to the public, and the evenings are given over to an annual Confederate Pageant.

Within city limits is the Grand Village of the Natchez Indians (US 61, on Jefferson Davis Blvd.), a National Historic Landmark that has yielded archaeological proof that Natchez is the site of the Natchez Indians' largest village (the "Grand Village"). The Natchez culture peaked in the mid-1500s and came to a disastrous end in 1730, when the French wiped out most of the tribe.

NATCHEZ TRACE PARKWAY: When completed, the parkway will run the full 450 miles between Natchez and Nashville, crossing and recrossing the Trace many times in its course. Today, a total of 406 miles are open from near Natchez to Tennessee Hwy. 50. However, roads leading to these sections are clearly marked, so it is possible to leave from either terminus and follow the route of the Trace.

The parkway is completely free of commercialism. There are no hotels or restaurants along the road. Park rangers patrol the road to provide visitor assistance. There are picnicking facilities at frequent scenic spots and campsites at three campgrounds. Campsites can't be reserved, and there is a 15-day limit on camping. The parkway headquarters is 4 miles north of Tupelo. There you can get maps and information and see a film on the Trace and its history.

Today the significance of the Natchez Trace is the history that is buried on or near it. The parkway offers a way of following the Trace while having the most significant aspects of it pointed out as you go. Indian mounds, remains of inns or "stands," as they were called, and talks presented by rangers give a sense of what the Trace was like when it was a footpath that cut through steaming swamps and flatlands, plagued by insects, disease, roving bands of cutthroats (the boatmen who used the Trace were returning home from profitable trading ventures on the Mississippi; as they walked along the dark lane of the Trace, sometimes through sections up to 15 feet below ground level, they would be set upon by thieves), and unfriendly Indians.

Just 12 miles outside Natchez on the parkway is Emerald Mound, one of the largest Indian ceremonial mounds ever found in the US. Built sometime in the 300 years before 1600, Emerald Mound covers nearly 8 acres and is representative of the Mississippi Indians who predated the Natchez and Choctaw, who still lived in the area when white explorers discovered it. Just 12 miles north of Emerald Mound is Mount Locust, restored to its original 1810 appearance, when it served as both a home and an inn along the Old Trace.

Outside Tupelo is Chickasaw Village, the site of a fortified Chickasaw camp. Much of the country around the Trace saw action during the Civil War, and numerous markers note points of historical interest. Though it is off the parkway, anyone interested in the war will certainly want to visit the Tupelo National Battlefield, where some 10,000 Confederate horsemen met 14,000 Union troops. The cavalry engaged the Union forces three times on July 14, 1864, and was defeated each time at a ghastly price in men and horses. Finally the Union troops retreated north, after buying enough time for General Sherman to move his force by rail to begin the attack on Atlanta.

A segment of the parkway 109 miles beyond Tupelo has one special feature, a short section of the actual Trace that can be driven, called the Old Trace Loop Drive. About 2½ miles of the Trace have been paved (though very narrow) and turned into a one-way loop drive for automobiles, featuring several scenic overlooks. Trailers are not recommended to try the loop.

BEST EN ROUTE

The Burn, Natchez – Antebellum elegance; 6 rooms for guests. 712 N. Union St., Natchez, MS 39120 (phone: 601-442-1344).

Texada, Natchez – Pronounced "te-hada." This fully restored 1792 mansion, part of the yearly Pilgrimage Tour, offers accommodations for overnight guests. Rooms are in the main house, and one has twin sleigh beds. There is also a 3-bedroom guest cottage. 222 S. Wall St., Natchez, MS 39120 (phone: 601-445-4283).

Carriage House Restaurant, Natchez – In the courtyard of Stanton Hall, the restoration project of the Pilgrimage Garden Club. The menu emphasizes old-fashioned Southern cooking, and it's excellent. 401 High St., Natchez, MS 39120 (phone: 601-445-5151).

Cock of the Walk, Natchez-Under-the-Hill – The atmosphere comes from the flatboat days, when boatmen fought one another to earn the right to wear the red feather, signifying they were "cock of the walk." The tavern features red-shirted waiters who serve the Mississippi specialty of catfish — blackened, almondine, or broiled — and fried chicken, shrimp, and oysters. Natchez-Under-the-Hill, Natchez, MS 39120 (phone: 601-446-8920).

Outer Banks and Cape Hatteras National Seashore, North Carolina

The elements reign supreme on the Outer Banks, a 175-mile ribbon of sandy islands — linked by ferries and bridges — running faintly parallel to the North Carolina coast. The ocean and the wind lash at the shoreline, changing its shape, washing away and replacing sand. Storm waves falling across the sand at a particularly narrow point can make two islands where once there was one, and there are spots where only a few hundred feet separate a crashing Atlantic from the calm Pamlico Sound. The visitor will gaze in awe at what the ocean and the wind can do, because a trip to these islands (north to south: Bodie, Pea/Hatteras, Ocracoke, and Cape Lookout) is a trip not of doing but of simply being there and witnessing the ever-writing hand of nature.

Except for one stretch of superhighway — the "motel row" from Kitty Hawk to Nags Head, an area tolerated for the tourists it brings — the Outer Banks are America's seaside wilderness, where man has been defeated by nature and has admitted it. And a good thing, too. With almost all the motels in one area, the rest of the land is under the auspices of the National Park Service and is protected from development (except for some small villages on the islands).

Ghosts haunt the Outer Banks. More than 500 ships sank within just a few miles of its shores, earning it the title "Graveyard of the Atlantic." It began with Sir Richard Grenville's *Tiger* in 1585 and continues today; its most recent victim was the *Lois Joyce* in January 1982. Most famous was the Federal gunboat *Monitor;* it survived a match with the Confederacy's *Merrimac* in March of 1862, but on December 31 of that same year it went under in a Hatteras storm.

The irregular coastline and manic weather made these shores the perfect lair for pirates. In the early 1700s, Edward Teach (Blackbeard) and his band holed up in Ocracoke. It was here, in 1718, that Blackbeard was killed.

This section of ocean offers excellent sport, with scores of fish to be pulled in by surf casters: drum, bluefish, trout, and mackerel.

There's no telling what nature will do next: Birds stop here by the thousands on their way north and south in warm and cold seasons, making the Outer Banks one of the country's prime bird watching spots. The trees that held the sands in place centuries ago are gone, having been felled for New England shipbuilding by the fishermen who lived here. Today, several picturesque fishing villages remain, accented by wildflowers — thousands of them — whipping in the breezes.

Three approaches link the banks with the mainland: from the north, use the bridge at Point Harbor near the end of Rte. 158; and from the west, the extension of Rte. 64, running across Roanoke Island and through Manteo before coming out near Nags Head. From the south, a toll ferry connects Cedar Island and Swan Quarter to Ocracoke Village. Free ferry service runs from Ocracoke Island to the village of Hatteras. For more information and to make reservations on the ferry from Swanquarter call 919-926-1111; from Ocracoke, call 919-928-3841 or from Cedar Island, call 919-225-3551; reservations are accepted by phone or in person within 30 days prior to the crossing. For details on free ferry service from Hatteras, call 919-986-2353.

KITTY HAWK: A visit can start from either end of the Outer Banks islands, but we'll begin in the north, at Kitty Hawk, because there isn't a schoolchild alive who doesn't associate this little town with Wilbur and Orville Wright and that day in 1903 when a new era began. Commemorating the two bicycle makers from Dayton is a majestic monument, the Wright Brothers National Memorial, on the Rte. 158 bypass in the town of Kill Devil Hills. The memorial has a visitors center (open year-round, except Christmas; entry fee, $1 per person or $3 per car) that displays full-scale reproductions of the 1902 glider and the 1903 "flying machine"; nearby are the reconstructed hangar and living quarters.

The drive south through Nags Head is disappointing; simply ignore the motels that line the road and contemplate the scenery to come. Nags Head is the last town before the Cape Hatteras National Seashore officially begins, and the beach just south of town boasts spectacular sand dunes.

CAPE HATTERAS NATIONAL SEASHORE: The Bodie Island Lighthouse Visitor Center, near the southern end of Bodie Island (signs point the way), is open Memorial Day through Labor Day. Nearby is a nature trail with an observation platform for viewing the bird life. As we went to press, the center was closed temporarily for renovation.

Before continuing south, cross the bridge to Manteo on Roanoke Island. Just north of town is the Ft. Raleigh National Historic Site, commemorating the English colonies settled in 1585 and 1587 by Walter Raleigh and found empty and mysteriously abandoned in 1590. Historians are still puzzled by the disappearance of the colony and the single word croatoan, found carved on a palisade post. Today, visitors can tour a reconstruction of the earthwork fort and a nature trail by Roanoke Sound. The site is open daily (except Christmas). Next to the site is the Elizabethan Gardens, a memorial to the colonists, featuring an herb garden, flower gardens, and sculpted lawns. A nightly presentation (in summer, except Sundays) of the historical drama *The Lost Colony* takes place at the *Waterside Amphitheater* at Ft. Raleigh. (See *Outdoor Dramas,* DIVERSIONS.) The gardens are closed from mid-December to early January.

Pea Island is the next bit of land south of Bodie, home of the Pea Island National Wildlife Refuge, 5,880 acres maintained by the US Fish and Wildlife Service. All year long this is one of the East Coast's most populated avian roosting places, but it's especially exciting in late fall, winter, and early spring when birds head south or north. Expect to see great snow geese, gadwalls, Canada geese, loons, grebes, herons, brant, whistling swans, and countless other species of aquatic and migratory birds.

The drive south on Rte. 12 on Hatteras Island deserves unhurried attention because each spot is worth a stop. Markings along the road indicate places for swimming, fishing, viewing hulls of wrecked vessels, and spying on wildlife. At the "elbow" of the island is the village of Buxton, and just south is the Cape Hatteras Lighthouse, America's tallest at 208 feet. It is now closed for safety reasons. If you spend enough time watching the waves and the shifting sands, you'll feel that you're watching the shape of the island change, sand washing away and returning in different configurations. Nearby is the Hatteras Island visitors center, with programs and displays on the island's centuries of maritime activity and industry (open daily except Christmas).

The town of Hatteras, south of Buxton on Rte. 12, is known only as a place to stop for a bite to eat or a quick look around. Stop and talk to some natives and listen for their cockney-like accent. The story goes that Hatteras Village was settled by the survivors of a ship that left Devon, England, and capsized off the coast. To this day, villagers have a "Devon" twang to their speech. A more prosaic explanation made by some is that the sheer isolation of the colonial settlers from Virginia cemented their Elizabethan accents.

The final island in the Cape Hatteras national seashore chain is Ocracoke, physically the most beautiful. The only town is Ocracoke Village, at the island's southern tip, where ferries from Cedar Island and Swanquarter dock and pick up passengers for the return trip. Stop in the visitors center there (Memorial Day to Labor Day) to pick up brochures on the island's many walks and sights. You should also be sure to visit Cape Lookout National Seashore, the next set of islands to the south. Ferries leave from Harker's Island (passengers only) and the towns of Davis and Atlantic (passengers and four-wheel-drive vehicles) for Cape Lookout. There are no roads on this newly cited national monument to nature, but you can walk around and see unfettered vegetation and the remains of abandoned fishing villages. Of all the areas in the Outer Banks, this is one of the most fascinating and well saved for last. There is little to do, but so very much to see and experience. Information: Cape Lookout National Seashore, PO Box 690, Beaufort, NC 28516.

For more information on campgrounds and anything else in the Outer Banks: Superintendent, Cape Hatteras National Seashore, Rte. 1, Box 675, Manteo, NC 27954 (phone: 919-473-2111). National Park rangers are more than willing to help with all your questions by mail, on the phone, or in person. They'll even teach the novice how to surf cast (in summer only); just bring your own bait. For lodging information outside the park: Dare County Tourist Bureau, PO Box 399, Manteo, NC 27954 (phone: 919-473-2138).

BEST EN ROUTE

Make reservations to stay in either Kill Devil Hills or Nags Head at the northern end of the island chain outside the seashore park; there is a wide choice of motels and restaurants. (Most establishments close from mid-October to early April; be sure to call or write for exact dates.)

Chart House, Kill Devil Hills – With comfortable accommodations and a selection of recreational activities — private beach, pool, golf, picnic facilities. Also on Rte. 158 at milepost 7.5. PO Box 432, Kill Devil Hills, NC 27948 (phone: 919-441-7418).

Quality Inn Sea Ranch, Kill Devil Hills – Amenities include an indoor-outdoor pool, indoor tennis, golf privileges, and a nightclub with entertainment. It is north of town, on Rte. 158 at milepost 7, PO Box 325, Kill Devil Hills, NC 27948 (phone: 919-441-7126).

Blue Heron, Nags Head – This hostelry has its own beach and bargain rates, very near the *Sea Oatel* (see below) on Rte. 158. RR 1, PO Box 741, Nags Head, NC 27959 (phone: 919-441-7447).

Quality Inn Sea Oatel, Nags Head – Also on its own beach, with many of the rooms overlooking the sea, on Rte. 158 at milepost 16.5. PO Box 489, Nags Head, NC 27959 (phone: 919-441-7191).

Hatteras Island Resort, Rodanthe – On the north end of Hatteras Island on Rte. 12. It offers 32 rooms, cottages with 2-, 3-, and 4-bedroom apartments, pool, playground, fishing pier, restaurant, and lounge. Write to the motel at PO Box 8, Rodanthe, NC 27968 (phone: 919-987-2345).

Island Inn, Ocracoke – A surprise in the town of Ocracoke on Ocracoke Island, with very comfortable rooms overlooking the harbor and, best of all, perhaps the best food in the area. PO Box 9, Ocracoke, NC 27960 (phone: 919-928-4351).

While in the area be sure to try *Port O' Call* restaurant, an especially good seafood place with daily specials. On Rte. 158 at milepost 9 (phone: 919-441-7484).

There is a choice of clean and well-managed campsites on the Outer Banks: Oregon Inlet (on Bodie Island), Cape Point (Buxton, on Hatteras Island), in Ocracoke, in Salvo (south of Rodanthe), and in Frisco (northeast of Hatteras). The first three are open in late spring, summer, and early fall; the other two, summers only. Information from the Cape Hatteras National Seashore (address above). There are also many private camping facilities available on Hatteras Island.

Great Smoky Mountains National Park, Tennessee and North Carolina

When most people consider US national parks, their thoughts turn to nature's spectacles — shooting geysers, roaring rivers carving out vast canyons, forests turned to stone. The most popular of the national parks has no such superstars but still attracts more than 9 million visitors annually with its almost perfect serenity. Spread across the southwestern corner of North Carolina and the southeastern tip of Tennessee, the Great Smoky Mountains National Park offers 800 square miles of quiet beauty — virgin forest blanketing a third of the land; 16 rounded ancient mountains reaching 6,000 feet or higher; drives with inspiring views; more than 800 miles of marked trails for hiking and horseback riding; over 600 miles of streams for fishing; lush and varied vegetation; and a romantic, bluish mist from which the Great Smokies derive their name. They are the oldest mountains in America and among the oldest on earth, formed during the Appalachian Revolution, a period that began about 230 million years ago and which lasted many millions of years. The Great Smokies rose as the earth's crust gradually buckled and thrust upward. Whipped, worn, and shaped by eons of storms, winds, and rains, the Smokies survived the weather's onslaught, and today their altitude is better than 5,000 feet for 36 miles along the main crest. Clingmans Dome, the highest peak, arches 6,643 feet upward, and, like its neighbors, almost always wears a veil of blue "smoke." Therein lies one of the Smokies' mysteries. What the Indians once called "smoke" we now know is a mist formed by a mixture of water vapor and oils secreted by plants.

The Smokies support an incredible variety of plants. Nurtured by an average of more than 60 inches of rain a year, more than 130 species of trees flourish in the park. Some trees here were seedlings when the Europeans came to America, including giants with trunks measuring 25 feet in circumference. Hemlocks, pines, oaks, yellow poplars, mountain laurel, and rhododendrons can be seen as you drive along US 441, which becomes Newfound Gap Road as it bisects the park. As you drive or climb upward, you encounter diverse flora — southern, New England, and Canadian plant life all on one mountain. The Smokies contain nearly all the forest types one would encounter traveling the length of the Appalachian Trail from Georgia to Maine.

Mt. Le Conte (6,593 feet) is one of the Smokies to explore thoroughly. You can enjoy the view from a distance, but a mountain is more than a big thing to be seen from a car window. To fully appreciate its beauty, ascend Mt. Le Conte by foot or on horseback. There is no road. At its base, southern plants (like dogwood) abound. Higher up, New England sugar maples and yellow birches appear. And thriving near the top are spruce and fir trees, native to southern Canada. During the Ice Age, the glacier advance stopped north of the Smokies. As a result, northern plants migrated south in order to survive and mingled with local species.

On the way up Mt. Le Conte, you can follow the Alum Cave Trail or choose less traveled "quiet walkways." The park has three visitors centers, at Sugarlands, Cades Cove, and Oconaluftee, where helpful staff offer maps and brochures on available trails. A wide variety of interpretive programs are led by a ranger May through October.

If you follow Alum Cave Trail, on crossing Alum Cave Creek you confront another of the park's mysteries: the laurel hells. Laurel and rhododendron tangle together so inextricably as to be almost impenetrable. No one knows why no trees grow on this ground. But getting out of a hell can be tricky off the paths.

Did someone say bears? Yes, there are many black bears in the Smokies. The black bear is the smallest species of bear in North America, weighing 200 to 300 pounds. However, chances are you won't come across any bears, since they tend to shy away from humans, and hikers on trails rarely encounter them. Occasionally, backcountry bears will raid hikers' packs and food supplies, so when camping at night, hang your packs on tree limbs over ten feet high and four feet between the tree trunks. Bolder bears will sometimes beg for food from tourists. Avoid feeding or approaching them. Bears that rely on handouts forget how to forage for food when the tourist season ends. Certainly do not imitate the man who tried to push a bear into his car so that he could take the bear's picture next to his wife. As gentle as bears may seem, they can suddenly turn mean. But you are more likely to see other wildlife, such as the 200 bird species that frequent the park, or white-tailed deer, commonly seen at Cades Cove at dawn and dusk.

Back on the main track, the Alum Cave Trail leads not to Alum Cave (there is none) but to a bluff with a good view. Legend has it that Confederate soldiers came up here to mine alum for gunpowder. What is here is an overhang of black slate 150 feet high and about 300 feet long. On the summit there is a glorious view and a resting spot — *Le Conte Lodge* — well worth the trek up.

Clingmans Dome, the highest peak in the Smokies, is another worthwhile climb. The winding road up leads to a parking lot. From there a paved half-mile trail leads to the summit, continues spiraling up the ramp of an observation tower, and ends in a serene and beautiful view from the Smokies' highest point. The smooth asphalt trail provides access to the view for those in wheelchairs, but park officials advise that the path and ramp to the tower are steep.

Cades Cove, a green Tennessee valley in the park's western reaches, is another tranquil spot. A one-way road circles past cabins, barns, and a gristmill from the days of the pioneers. Many of the 19th-century pioneers who settled this area now rest in the Cades Cove church graveyard (as well as in numerous other graveyards in the area).

Gregory Bald is a good example of the kind of wide, green, open meadowland typical of the Smokies' mountaintops and something of a mystery. There is no obvious reason for the grassy balds, and none of the traditional explanations put forward by park naturalists — wind, fire, or prolonged dry spells killing tree life, making way for meadows — is entirely satisfactory.

Gregory Bald and Clingmans Dome are among the park sites on the famous Appalachian Trail. Stretching from Maine to Georgia, the Appalachian Trail zigzags for 70 miles along the park's crest. Altogether, there are about 900 miles of trails in the Great Smoky Mountains National Park, and many of them can be hiked easily in a day or less. Horseback riding is permitted on about half of them.

For motorists, there are 215 miles of roads in the park, 140 miles paved and 75 miles of graded gravel. The main one, Newfound Gap Road, affords splendid views of the mountains as it winds across the park between Gatlinburg, Tennessee, and Cherokee, North Carolina.

Gatlinburg, the northern entrance to the park, sees a large share of the park's visitors. This town of 3,600 permanent residents can handle more than 30,000 visitors per night in accommodations ranging from family-operated cabins and cottages to 400-room convention hotels. The city, stretching for a mile along a creek, is wall-to-wall hotels and tourist shops.

Both Gatlinburg and Cherokee, capital of the Cherokee Indian Reservation on the park's south side, have been heavily exploited for tourism, offering everything from hot tubs to haunted houses and skyview chair lifts. The latest attraction is Dollywood, in Pigeon Forge, Tennessee, just outside Gatlinburg. Named after singer and native Tennessean Dolly Parton, the theme park, which charges up to $17 admission, includes a living museum that depicts her "rags to riches" story, along with country music entertainment, crafts, and rides. Dollywood, 700 Dollywood La., Pigeon Forge, TN 37863-4101 (phone: 615-428-9401).

The Cherokee Indian Reservation has more than 70 campgrounds and motels. It features the Oconaluftee Indian Village, a replica of an 18th-century Cherokee village, and the Qualla Arts and Crafts Mutual, which has high-quality crafts. (For more information, see *A Short Tour of Indian America*, DIVERSIONS.) The North Carolina side of the park itself has a number of attractions, including the Cataloochee historic district and part of the north shore of Fontana Lake. A quieter alternative to the hubbub of the other tourist centers is Townsend, Tennessee, west of Gatlinburg on Rte. 321 S.

The Great Smoky Mountains National Park is open year-round, as are its visitors centers, except Cades Cove, which is open only from mid-April through October. The blue mist is thickest in the heat of summer, but the mountains are smoky and majestic in any season. Even on the busiest summer day you can find peace and seclusion, especially if you take the park's quiet walkways, self-guiding nature trails, and backcountry trails. Peak visiting months are July through October. The park provides short radio messages with information on 1610 on the AM radio dial. Information: Superintendent, Great Smoky Mountains National Park, Rte. 2, Gatlinburg, TN 37738 (phone: 615-436-1200).

BEST EN ROUTE

Visitors have several lodging options inside the park. Of the nine developed campgrounds, reservations are recommended in summer at those at Cades Cove, Elkmont, and Smokemont, which are open year-round. Reservations can be made at any Ticketron outlet or by writing Ticketron, Dept. R, 401 Hackensack Ave., Hackensack, NJ

07601. Permits are required for all overnight use of the backcountry, and can be reserved up to 30 days in advance by contacting Great Smoky Mountains National Park, Gatlinburg, TN 37738 (phone: 615-436-5615). The park has nearly 90 primitive backcountry campsites, most of which are simply clearings with water; there are also 17 shelters (with chain link fencing fortified against bears) along the Appalachian Trail and other trails. Listed below are other lodgings inside the park.

Le Conte Lodge, Great Smoky Mountains National Park – A secluded retreat atop Mt. Le Conte, accessible only by foot. The lodge is on park grounds but privately run, and it can accommodate up to 50 people with plenty of fresh mountain air and hearty mountain fare. Open from late March to late-November; reservations essential. PO Box 350, Gatlinburg, TN 37738 (phone: 615-436-4473).

Wonderland Hotel, Great Smoky Mountains National Park – Old-fashioned atmosphere with good service and food in a quiet setting. Similar to *Le Conte,* but this hotel at Elkland can be reached by car. Open mid-May to October 31. Rte. 2, Gatlinburg, TN 37738 (phone: 615-436-5490).

For accommodations outside the park, visitors to Tennessee can contact the chambers of commerce at Gatlinburg, TN 37738; Sevierville, TN 37864; Townsend, TN 37882; or the privately run Smoky Mountains Accommodations, which books reservations at 40 properties (Rte. 4, Box 538, Gatlinburg, TN 37738; phone: 800-231-2230). For North Carolina accommodations, try the chambers of commerce at Cherokee, NC 28719, or Bryson City, NC 28713; and on the Cherokee Reservation, Cherokee Tribal Travel and Promotion, PO Box 465-18, Cherokee, NC 28719 (phone: 800-438-1601).

Big Bend National Park, Texas

If the call of the wild has got your number, strike out for Big Bend National Park. It's as remote as you can get in the Southwest without actually setting foot into one of the more obscure sections of northern Mexico. About 240,000 visitors come to Big Bend National Park every year — not a huge crowd as parks go, but still more than the intrepid handfuls who braved it in 1944, when this area came under federal jurisdiction. But the national park is only part of a mammoth, exquisite stretch of land, known as the last surviving huge wilderness of Texas. It's still as raw here today as it was when the frontiersmen and women arrived to conquer the Wild West.

Big Bend is literally just that — a big bend in the Rio Grande in southern Texas. If you look at the map, you can see that it's set in that little pocket of Texas that sags slightly to the left of the main body of the state. Although it's not as far south or as far west as you can go by any means, it hugs an interesting corner of the state. It's also nowhere near anyplace you're likely to call civilized. The closest town is Marathon, Texas, about 41 miles north. And the only thing really noteworthy about Marathon is that you have to go through it to get to Big Bend. If you're coming from Dallas/ Ft. Worth, 545 miles northeast, take I-20 to Rte. 18 south at Monahans. Rte. 18 runs into Rte. 385 south at Ft. Stockton, which takes you through Marathon, all the way to Persimmon Gap Ranger Station. Continue on to the administration building and visitors center at Panther Junction in Big Bend National Park.

Because it's so out of the way, lots of people don't get out here. Not that the folks and wildlife in Big Bend really mind — they adore having these isolated, 740,118 acres of canyons and desert all to themselves. You might not understand why anyone would want to live here at all if you go down to the park's lower elevations in summer, when the scorching heat makes it almost too hot to breathe. Dust fills the air, whirling in conical clouds with only an occasional thunderstorm to break the dry agony. Legends about the intolerable July temperatures include the one about a Big Bend coyote chasing a Big Bend jackrabbit. Even though both are swift animals, the story goes, it was so hot, "they was both walkin'." But since the park's altitude ranges from 1,750 to 7,835 feet, there are places to cool off.

If you visit in the spring, there's a good likelihood you'll experience a jubilant awe in the presence of rocky cliffs overflowing with white and crimson blossoms. Although the scenery is a knockout, we can't promise you a sunny garden; Big Bend is notoriously unpredictable when it comes to climate. In February, it can hit the 90s on a Monday and snow 3 inches or more later in the week. And very often, the temperature climbs 40F during the day, only to drop faster than a stone falls off a cliff after dark.

Millions of years ago the entire area was covered with water. Layers and layers of sand filtered down to the bottom, forming sedimentary rock — in some places, more than 1,000 feet thick. When the ocean dried, the Rio Grande poked its wet nose into the neighborhood and began winding its way through the rocky plains, wearing a groove in the earth along its path. This same process of water eroding rock was a part of the making of the Grand Canyon.

Any trip to Big Bend should begin at the visitors center at Panther Junction. From there, continue along the road to Chisos Basin, where you can rent horses and guides for 3-hour or all-day expeditions. You can also camp here, at the Chisos Basin campground. (Since the Chisos Basin is more than 5,000 feet high, be sure to bring a sleeping bag even in the summer.) You can see spectacular sunsets from here, as the sky cascades into a medley of pink, orange, and purple. Because the desert atmosphere is especially clear, the shimmering changes of color are intense and powerfully moving. Whitetail deer occasionally wander past; skunk and javelina also make this their home. You can hear the coyote wail as it gets dark, an eerie, echoing prelude to a harmonious serenade of night birds. Lizards come out in the morning, which is really the best time for human exploration, too. The park takes in an entire mountain range — the Chisos Mountains. The shallow Rio Grande cuts its way through the gorges of Boquillas Canyon and the 1,400-foot-high Santa Elena Canyon. It's a great place to land catfish.

You don't have to rough it to see these canyons, although many people prefer the greater intimacy of traveling on foot. A good driving road leads to Santa Elena and Boquillas canyons. In fact, you can drive for 187 miles through Big Bend. If you want to hike, the rangers will tell you about the trails. There's one to Lost Mine Ridge that takes about 3 hours, round-trip, and another good one to the South Rim. Inquire at Panther Junction visitors center. Information: Superintendent, Big Bend National Park, Big Bend, TX 79834 (phone: 915-477-2251).

BEST EN ROUTE

Chisos Mountains Lodge, Big Bend National Park – A small lodge with motel-type units, restaurant, and a supply store, dramatically situated within the park at 5,400 feet. Reservations necessary year-round. Big Bend National Park, TX 79834 (phone: 915-477-2291).

Indian Lodge – This rustic inn in nearby Davis Mountain State Park has 39 air conditioned rooms, pool, restaurant, parking. State-run; access to all park facilities. PO Box 786, Ft. Davis, TX 79734 (phone: 915-426-3254).

Padre Island National Seashore, Texas

Like the coasts of New Jersey and the Carolinas, Texas's Gulf of Mexico shoreline is blessed with a series of long, lean islands that lie just offshore and follow the great arc of the Gulf Coast with almost perfect fidelity. The last and longest of these islands is Padre Island, 115 miles of sand and grass that stretch along the south Texas coast, roughly from Corpus Christi to Port Isabel, where Mexico and Texas meet like two lips puckering to kiss the Gulf.

Padre Island is really two islands separated by a tiny channel of sea: South Padre Island, the southernmost 35 miles of the island; and North Padre Island, covering 80 miles, 65 miles of which is designated as the Padre Island National Seashore. The national seashore is a stretch of sand, grass, dunes, and sea where you stand a good chance of witnessing nothing but the work of nature — waves beating against the shore, acres of grasslands, and, if you're lucky, not another human being, just the thousands of birds and shore animals that live here or visit during migrations.

Development is contained in settlements predominantly confined to the northern and southern extremities of Padre Island, where you will find the motels, hotels, restaurants, resort communities, condominiums, and highways that have made the south Texas coast famous. As if it weren't enough to have these civilizations coexisting, Padre Island is an anomaly because the two ways of life get on together very well.

The "port" cities — Port Aransas in the north and Port Isabel in the south — are the main points of development as well as being two of the three gateways to Padre; the third gateway is park road 22, which runs east out of Corpus Christi. If you've come to visit the seashore, you'll almost have to stay in or near one of the port cities; that's not so bad. If you've come to visit the cities and enjoy their very relaxed, sun-filled, pleasure-dome existence, that's not so bad, either, so long as you make some time to visit what nature has wrought.

PORT ARANSAS: Actually on Mustang Island, an "adopted" part of the Padres. The University of Texas Marine Science Institute is here, a reminder of the area's primary — if not only — industry, the sea. Charter trawlers crowd the town's small harbor, waiting to plow the bountiful Gulf waters in search of tarpon, sailfish, snapper, tuna, and countless other breeds of fighters. A hefty catch is almost guaranteed every time you set out with rod and reel. (Many of the deep-sea party boats are equipped with motorized reels: Get a nibble, flick the switch, and land your catch. If, like many people, you feel this method eliminates the sport in fishing, be sure to check out the equipment when you rent.) In July, the town is filled with anglers in for the Deep-Sea Roundup, a contest to see who can land the biggest and who can land the most. Other attractions center on the 18 miles of sparkling white beach, focal point for surfers, surf casters, swimmers, and surfside drives.

There is direct access to the national seashore from Port Aransas, but before going over, visit the Aransas National Wildlife Refuge on the mainland. To get there take Rte. 35 through Aransas Pass and go just beyond the tiny hamlet of Lamar. The 54,000 acres of the Aransas National Wildlife Refuge have been set aside for the nearly extinct whooping crane, visible in the colder months, when the cranes come down from Canada. (The refuge is open daily; admission is $2 per vehicle.) There is an observation tower and an information station as well as trails for spying on the natives by foot or car. An alternative to a park visit is a cruise up Aransas Bay past the water side of the refuge for less obstructed views of the cranes. Cruises leave from Rockport and must be arranged at its harbor.

PADRE ISLAND NATIONAL SEASHORE: Return to Port Aransas and take Rte. 53 south, the single highway that links Mustang Island with North Padre. After making the crossing, one of the first sights is Malaquite Beach, with a visitors center that's open year-round and an excellent campground for trailers and the hearty few who tent on the beach. (Up and down Padre the beaches are open for overnight guests, but camping is not allowed in the dunes or grasslands. For more information, contact the Superintendent, address below.)

There are no towns or any other signs of man's existence in the national seashore park. Once upon a time, the grasslands that cover the inland portions of the island — from the beaches of Laguna Madre in the west to the beaches of the Gulf of Mexico in the east — were grazing land for cattle. Padre Nicholas Balli, the Spanish monk after whom the island chain is named, started raising livestock here in 1800, but the cattle, cowboys, and monks are gone, and the grasses are returning to the sandy soil.

Other men have been here in the last 500 years, mostly Spaniards in the 16th, 17th, and 18th centuries, chasing or being chased by Indians. And the shallow waters of the Gulf side took their toll of vessels, including many a royal treasure ship. It's acknowledged by the residents and seashore personnel that millions of dollars in silver and gold are probably buried in the Padre sand or lost just off the coast. For this reason, the seashore is off limits to metal detectors and today's treasure hunters. The natural splendor will not be violated by fortune seekers.

To travel around the greater part of the national seashore other than on foot assumes that you own or have rented a four-wheel-drive vehicle. But note that driving on the dunes and in the grasslands is prohibited.

However you go, watch for the diverse and utterly fascinating collection of animal life. On the ground, the island is crawling with creatures like coyote, ground squirrels, gophers, and kangaroo rats. At least 12 different types of snakes are known to reside in the tall grasses, including two species of rattlers. Watch out for these unfriendly fellows. (Campgrounds and other areas designated for two-legged guests can be assumed safe from potentially dangerous visitors.) In the air and alighting everywhere are hundreds of birds of different species: herons, willets, black skimmers, marsh hawks, pelicans, avocets, horned owls, peregrine falcons, and swarms of sanderlings. They come from Mexico and Central America in the spring or pass through on their way south in fall and early winter. Year-round, Padre is an avian amusement park.

Of course, wherever you go, there is fishing. The beaches of Padre are regarded as among America's best for variety and sheer volume. Standing on the beach throwing your tackle to the surf, you may be the only person visible for miles. There may not be another soul to hear your victory shout after a half-hour fight with a shark — a fairly common catch in this part of the Gulf.

Near Malaquite Beach is the Grasslands Trail, a well-marked trek through the tall grasses (visitors are forbidden to walk on the dunes). The walk offers a look at many types of the island's native growth, including sea oats, railroad vines, croton, wild indigo, and a last vestige of Virginia live oak. The walk is also impressive for its museum-like representation of how dunes are formed. You may think that the dunes — in every stage of formation from small sand drifts to hills — have been prepared as some kind of exhibit. But no, these are real drifts, in the normal and natural process of being shaped by wind, weather, and sand shifts. For Grasslands Trail information, call 512-949-8068. As we went to press, the opening of a new visitors center at Malaquite was imminent. General information: Superintendent, Padre Island National Seashore, 9405 S. Padre Island Dr., Corpus Christi, TX 78418 (phone: 512-937-2621).

SOUTH PADRE ISLAND: Because no road runs the full length of either North or South Padre, you'll have to get back on mainland roads to reach South Padre. The southern tip of the island is being carefully developed as a vacation paradise, so hotels and motels and miles of sporting pleasures line the white-yellow beach and turquoise water. The causeway through Port Isabel comes out near Isla Blanca Park. There you'll find a bathhouse and cabanas, plus overnight accommodations for sleeping under the stars. There are also food concessions, water skiing facilities, a trailer park, and a children's recreation area.

PORT ISABEL: Just across the Laguna Madre and connected to South Padre by the Queen Isabella Causeway is Port Isabel, a growing but still peaceful resort town — one of the South's first vacation centers, the favorite of Texas society dating to the mid-1800s. Port Isabel is primarily a fishing town, with the world's largest shrimping fleet tying up here and a little farther into the bay at the port of Brownsville, and the harbor is home port for many deep-sea charter fishing boats.

Just west of town on Rte. 100 is the smallest state park in this state famous for big things, the Port Isabel Lighthouse Historic Site. The lighthouse dates to the 1850s, when gold rush fever made Port Isabel a popular stop for folks on the way west. The lighthouse also overlooks the site of Ft. Polk, a Mexican War camp and depot that was commanded by General Zachary Taylor. The last land battle of the Civil War was also fought in the neighborhood, at Palmito Hill. The lighthouse is open daily, 9 AM to 5 PM, with an admission charge.

If you're in Port Isabel, take a quick drive across the Mexican border to Matamoros, a town featuring markets for jewelry, leather, and clothing as well as some authentic Spanish restaurants and nightclubs. They accept American currency, and only proof of citizenship is necessary to cross the border.

At the end of any visit through the untamed, natural, sandy expanses of North Padre Island, you'll find South Padre, and especially Port Isabel, quiet, relaxed enclaves perfect for enjoying a warm sun, sparkling water, and deluxe accommodations. For more information on accommodations and activities on South Padre: The South Padre Island Visitors and Convention Bureau, PO Box 3500, South Padre Island, TX 78597 (phone: 512-761-6433).

BEST EN ROUTE

The Beachhead, Port Aransas – Just a boardwalk away from the beach. One- and 2-bedroom apartments available with kitchens; parking, a coin laundry, and a heated pool. Balcony views look over the Gulf. PO Box 1577, Port Aransas, TX 78373 (phone: 512-749-6261).

Executive Keys, Port Aransas – On the Gulf, with balcony views from some rooms. Recreation facilities include lawn games, golf privileges, volleyball. All of the 2- and 3-bedroom suites have dishwashers in the kitchens and similar amenities. PO Box 1087, Port Aransas, TX 78373 (phone: 512-749-6272).

Island Retreat, Port Aransas – A fisherman's delight, offering fish cleaning and freezing facilities for guests. Most apartments have balconies on the Gulf and convenience appliances. Also has 2 pools, access to the ocean, and a raft of recreational activities. PO Box 637, Port Aransas, TX 78373 (phone: 512-749-6222).

Bahia Mar, South Padre Island – The *Hilton*'s (below) competition, with 2 pools and saunas, tennis courts, and a putting green. Choice of accommodations from rooms to apartments and townhouses. PO Box 2280, South Padre Island, TX 78597 (phone: 512-761-1343).

South Padre Hilton Resort Hotel, South Padre Island – The cream of South Padre Island's hotel-apartment offerings, with a large condominium tower, a private beach, a restaurant, a lounge with live music, an Olympic-size pool, and tennis. PO Box 2081, South Padre Island, TX 78597 (phone: 512-761-6511 or 800-292-7704).

Most people on the island cook for themselves, and there is a shortage of good restaurants besides the cafés and roadhouses that line the highways. For first class meals, locals and long time summer residents drive into Corpus Christi or Brownsville. When on South Padre Island, you might try the Jetties (Rte. 100; phone: 512-761-6461) for a wide choice in seafood; its known especially for fresh jumbo Gulf shrimp.

For more information, contact these local service organizations: Corpus Christi Area Convention and Tourist Bureau, PO Box 2664, Corpus Christi, TX 78403; Cameron County Park Board, PO Box 666, Port Isabel, TX 78578.

Midwest

The Lincoln Heritage Trail, Illinois, Indiana, and Kentucky

The Lincoln Heritage Trail blazes 2,200 miles along the folkloric roads of Illinois, Indiana, and Kentucky, Abraham Lincoln's home states. Here, his voice still echoes around every bend: eloquently in government chambers, softly in great Victorian mansions, and jokingly in the backwood cabins of his close friends. Along the trail, memories of Mr. Lincoln are vividly recollected through reenactments of scenes from America's past and reconstructions of stately buildings, quaint homesteads, and entire 19th-century towns. The route that follows is a living history book, tracing Lincoln's footsteps through frontier America.

SPRINGFIELD, Illinois: Here you will see and hear more about Abraham Lincoln than anywhere else in the US. Start with Lincoln's own residence (the only house he ever owned) on 8th and Jackson Sts. One of a row of handsome period homes, it has been repainted in its original colors of Quaker brown and apple green and furnished with some Lincoln family possessions. Informative tour guides minutely detail Lincoln's home life. Open daily.

The Old State Capitol on Public Square, where Lincoln gave his famous "House Divided" speech, has been completely rebuilt, and the stunning second-floor legislative chamber looks as if a session had just adjourned. The Illinois State Historical Library is on the bottom floor. Closed Sundays.

A 117-foot granite obelisk marks the Lincoln Tomb site in Oak Ridge Cemetery. The tomb's rotunda contains a single statue of Lincoln and a few bronze plaques, creating a solemn and dignified tribute; at the rear of the memorial, a monument to Lincoln is enclosed in a semicircular chamber, flanked by flags and remnants of the longest funeral procession in history. On the opposite wall are the crypts of Mary Todd Lincoln and three of the couple's four sons.

A few miles from Springfield I-55, in the city of Lincoln, are the *Lincoln College Museum,* which houses an impressive array of memorabilia, and the historic Postville Courthouse, where the walls are covered with maps outlining the route Lincoln traveled as a lawyer of the 8th Judicial Circuit and documents about the court system in his day.

NEW SALEM, Illinois: The next site on the trail is the village of New Salem, reconstructed to look exactly as it did when Lincoln lived here in the 19th century. You'll see mammoth oxen pulling covered wagons along dirt roads lined with tiny log cabins, and a visit to the cabins finds women in period costumes kneading dough, cooking over flaming hearths, and spinning wool. During the summer months, beginning at sunset, you can watch an outdoor drama held nightly, except Mondays: *Your*

Obedient Servant, A. Lincoln. (If it rains, performances are held at the Senior Citizens Center at Petersburg, a 5-minute drive away.)

VINCENNES, Indiana: The trail through Lincoln country cuts into Indiana at the border town of Vincennes, the original capital. Called "the Birthplace of the West," it's a tribute to early American growth. Visit the George Rogers Clark Memorial and Visitors Center, an awesome structure that contains several massive murals by Ezra Winter. Headsets, distributed at the entrance, explain each mural and its relevance to the American past.

The Log Cabin visitors center provides tickets for the Trailblazer tour on a trolley-like bus that winds its way through the Mile of History in the old state capital.

HISTORIC NEW HARMONY, Indiana: Take a break from Lincoln and visit New Harmony, another landmark in American history. Originally a tract of wilderness on the banks of the Wabash, the village grew from settlements of religious and utopian communal sects. First came the Rappites (or Harmonists), led by Father George Rapp, who preached that the second coming of Christ would occur in their lifetime. Later came the Owenites, a group of experimenting intellectuals looking to improve the quality of life. Today it's a showplace for cultural triumphs both past and present. A number of famous architects and artists have put their mark on its contemporary buildings and sculpture, including Richard Meier and Philip Johnson.

The placid walkways of New Harmony are lined with restored, sparsely furnished houses and Harmonist dormitories. Ticket books purchased at the visitors center provide access to many buildings, including the Atheneum, an architectural award winner. The Roofless Church and the *Opera House* are open to the public (no admission charge). Be sure to wander through the labyrinth — a reconstruction of the sect's maze symbolizing the twisting road of life to perfect harmony. Also see *Utopias,* DIVERSIONS.

LINCOLN CITY, Indiana: Now pick up the Heritage Trail in Lincoln City (on Rte. 162, off US 231) at the Lincoln State Park and the Lincoln Boyhood National Memorial. The memorial features a museum, a working pioneer farm on the site of the farm Lincoln's father owned from 1816 to 1830, and the burial place of his mother. The state park has many recreational facilities, and both areas have self-guided history-nature trails. Entrance fee for the state park. *Young Abe Lincoln* comes home to Indiana each summer in an outdoor drama about his boyhood years, presented at the 1,500-seat *Lincoln State Park Amphitheater* in Spencer County. The grounds are open daily except Christmas and New Year's.

JEFFERSONVILLE, Indiana: Shortly before reaching Jeffersonville you can take a side trip to Wyandotte Cave in Harrison Crawford Wyandotte Woods and Cave, on Rte. 62 in Leavenworth. It is one of the largest cave complexes in North America. Then, off I-65, is the town of Jeffersonville. Perched on the banks of the Ohio River, the *Howard Steamboat Museum* (in James Howard's former home) displays intricately carved models of his 19th-century masterpieces. Outside the window, the *Belle of Louisville* steamboat still chuffs by. Also visit the Culbertson Mansion, an opulent example of post–Civil War architecture on New Albany's Mansion Row. Hillerich and Bradsby Slugger Park is the home of the world-famous Louisville Slugger bats; visitors can see a display of historic World Series bats and memorabilia and take a guided tour of the factory.

Cross the Ohio River into Louisville. For a complete report on the city and its attractions, see *Louisville,* THE CITIES.

HODGENVILLE, Kentucky: Abe Lincoln's life in Kentucky began in a tiny cabin nestled among the bluish-green, "Knob" hills of north-central Kentucky. Take I-65 to Hwy. 61 and the Abraham Lincoln Birthplace and National Historic Site in Hodgenville. A section of this national park is actually Sinking Springs Farm, where Lincoln was born in 1809. An elaborate memorial building has been erected around the original family cabin. A faulty land deed uprooted the family when Lincoln was only two and provoked their move to Knob Creek, where the family lived for 7 years. The primitive Lincoln log cabin stands reconstructed among the lushest of bluegrass hills.

BARDSTOWN, Kentucky: Continue northeast on Hwy. 31E for a pleasant stop at Bardstown, where you'll find the Federal Hill estate better known as "My Old Kentucky Home." Tour the grand estate and its mansion, where Stephen Foster supposedly wrote the famous song. Have lunch in Bardstown under the cozy brick arches of *La Taberna* restaurant, at 5th St. and Xavier Dr.

LEXINGTON, Kentucky: Next, it's northeast to Lexington via US 150 and US 68, the scenic palisades road. In Lexington, off Rte. 68 (which becomes Broadway) on West Main Street, is Mary Todd Lincoln's childhood home. This grand house personifies her life in the aristocracy and contradicts Lincoln's background completely: Meticulously crafted antiques and exquisitely detailed carpets crown the polished wooden floors. 578 W Main St. Open from April to mid-December; closed Sundays and Mondays. Admission charge.

HARRODSBURG, Kentucky: South of Lexington on US 68 is Old Fort Harrod State Park, a reproduction fort that was the first permanent pioneer settlement west of the Alleghenies, circa 1774. The cabin where Abraham Lincoln's parents were married is on the grounds. The historical dramas *Lincoln* and *The Legend of Daniel Boone* are presented in the summer in the amphitheater (see *Outdoor Dramas,* DIVERSIONS). Open year-round.

BEST EN ROUTE

New Harmony Inn, New Harmony, Indiana – This inn's 90 rooms all have simple wood furnishings and some have working fireplaces, kitchenettes, and small balconies. The atmosphere reflects the quiet, easy pace of the community, and the *Red Geranium* restaurant next door offers fine dining. PO Box 581, New Harmony, IN 47631 (phone: 812-682-4491). Also see *America's Special Havens,* DIVERSIONS.

Huber Orchard and Winery – In the rolling hills and valleys along the Ohio River, it features 18 award-winning wines. Tours, sampling, wine making, and cheese making. Open year-round. RR 1, Box 88, Borden, IN 47106 (phone: 812-923-WINE).

Joe Huber Family Restaurant – A country feast in the spacious restaurant on the Huber family's 360-acre farm includes country ham, fried chicken and biscuits, and homegrown fruits and vegetables. RR 1, Box 648, Borden, IN 47106 (phone: 812-923-5255).

Old Talbott Tavern, Bardstown, Kentucky – Operated continuously since 1779, the tavern serves lunch and dinner. 107 W. Stephen Foster Ave., Bardstown, KY 40004 (phone: 502-348-3494).

Beaumont Inn Dining Room, Harrodsburg, Kentucky – A lovely old inn offering country-style full-course meals. 638 Beaumont Dr., Harrodsburg, KY 40330 (phone: 606-734-3381).

Isle Royale National Park, Michigan

Imagine yourself on a remote island where there are no cars, no roads, and where the only sound you are likely to hear at night is the call of a loon, the cry of a wolf, or the wind in the trees. If the thought appeals, your destination should be Isle Royale, largest of the 200 islands and islets that make up Isle Royale National Park in Lake Superior. Isle Royale — the dominant island for which the park was named — lies parallel to the northwest shore of Lake Superior, like a long candle flame pointing north, 45 miles long and between 5 and 9 miles wide. Open in summer only, this isolated bit of wilderness in Lake Superior has changed little since French trappers took possession of it and named it in honor of Louis XIV.

Though closer to the Minnesota-Canada border, the park officially is part of Michigan. You can reach Isle Royale from both the Michigan and the Minnesota shores of Lake Superior. Access from Michigan is through the town of Houghton, by seaplane or ferry. (It is about a 6-hour ferry ride to Isle Royale; a splendid grace period in which to leave civilization behind and contemplate the real isolation of the island.) The route to Houghton from St. Ignace (the town at the northern end of the Mackinac Straits Bridge, which links Michigan's Upper and Lower peninsulas) takes you through the land of Hiawatha, the Ojibwa Indian immortalized in Longfellow's poem.

The shorter route to Isle Royale is from Minnesota. The ferry leaves Grand Portage, just below the Canadian border, 150 miles north of Duluth. The Duluth–Grand Portage section of US 61 offers one of the most scenic shore drives in the US. And in Grand Portage you can visit the national monument that marks the site of the "great depot" of early fur trading days.

Another ferry runs from Copper Harbor, about 50 miles north of Houghton; the trip takes about 4[12] hours. All ferries accommodate passengers only; cars and other wheeled vehicles are not allowed on the island. There are ample parking facilities. For information on ferry schedules and reservations, write the superintendent of the park.

Hundreds of millions of years ago, lava flows formed the earliest rock of Isle Royale. During the glacial period, a layer of ice a mile high covered the island, but when the ice melted and the resulting lake receded a bit, Isle Royale emerged — "an island of rock rising abruptly from the lowest depths of the lake in irregular hills to a height varying from 100 to 450 feet above the level of the lake," as Michigan's first state geologist put it in 1841. A thin layer of soil, in some places no more than a few inches deep, covers the rock like icing on a cake, but it is enough for spruce, balsam, pine, aspen, and birch to thrive.

As you make your way across the water to Isle Royale, leaving the mainland shore farther and farther behind, you will begin to get a sense of the isolation that has deeply affected the island's ecology. Only birds and animals that have been able to fly, swim, or drift across from the mainland are found on Isle Royale. Moose suddenly appeared for the first time on the island around 1912 and, without a predator, multiplied so fast that the plant browse became scarce on the island and overpopulation threatened to reduce the herds. A fire in 1936 stimulated the growth of new browse and, in the winter of 1948-49, wolves crossed the ice from Canada, restoring the ecological balance.

On Isle Royale, 166 miles of hiking trails, springy with moss and spruce needles, take the place of roads. The trails lead to lookout points with sweeping views, sheltered inlets along the pebbled shore, abandoned copper mines now buried deep in blueberry thickets, and silent inland lakes (over 20 of them), where at sunrise or sunset you are likely to glimpse a moose. More than 30 campgrounds are scattered across the island.

Hiking offers an opportunity to observe some of the island's abundant wildlife, which includes beaver, muskrat, mink, weasel, squirrels, the snowshoe hare, and red fox as well as moose. There are also wolves, but they are extremely shy of human beings. Herring gulls and warblers are plentiful, but you will also see pileated woodpeckers, osprey, and loons among the 200 species of birds on the island. There are hundreds of common wildflowers as well as such rarities as yellow lady's slipper, bog kalmia, swamp candle loosestrife, and some 30 different species of orchids.

Such unspoiled wilderness has its price. You won't, for example, find flush toilets at the campgrounds. Non-campers can stay in the comparative luxury of the *Rock Harbor Lodge* (see *Best en Route*), but in general, if you turn pale at the thought of roughing it, Isle Royale is probably not for you.

One of the best ways to explore the island's interior is to walk its length. To do this, take the Greenstone Ridge Trail, which connects *Rock Harbor Lodge* at the eastern end of the island with Washington Harbor at the western end, 40 miles away. This hike will take you several days. A much shorter but very rewarding walk is the trail to Mt. Franklin, where you can continue on to Ojibway Lookout, offering a fine view of the Canadian mainland from the tower. If you take the trail that leads to Monument Rock, a 70-foot-high natural tower that has been sculpted by waves and ice, you can continue past the rock to Lookout Louise, which offers the best views in the entire park.

A fine trail leads to the old Rock Harbor Lighthouse, built in 1855 to guide the boats sent by mining companies to take out the island's copper. The lighthouse guards what one member of the team on the US Linear Survey of 1847 called "the most beautiful harbor in Lake Superior." This same gentleman reported seeing mirages of islands and mountains off Isle Royale's coast.

On the west end of the island, a trail leads from Washington Creek to an abandoned copper prospecting site. A boat makes a full circuit around the island several times each week. (For information, write to Grand Portage–Isle Royale Transportation Line, 1332 London Rd., Duluth, MN 55805; phone: 218-728-1237.) There are shorter excursions to nearby islands, as well as boat rentals and a marina for small private craft at Rock Harbor. If you want to canoe, bring your own or rent one at Rock Harbor or Windigo. The park's canoeing brochure indicates the best routes.

Anglers will find pike, walleye, perch, and even some whitefish in the island's inland lakes, brook trout in its streams, and lake trout in Lake Superior. You don't need a license for the inland waters of the park, only for Lake Superior. If you plan to camp overnight, you must obtain a permit from the headquarters in Rock Harbor.

To learn more about the flora and fauna you have seen during the day, you can attend one of the evening programs that are given at Windigo, *Rock Harbor Lodge,* and Daisy Farm Campground. Information: Superintendent, Isle Royale National Park, 87 N. Ripley St., Houghton, MI 49931 (phone: 906-482-0984).

BEST EN ROUTE

Rock Harbor Lodge, Isle Royale – At the eastern end of the island, this offers 20 housekeeping lodges, 60 rooms, a dining room and snack bar. You can buy camping supplies and food here as well. Reservations between mid-June and Labor Day: National Park Concessions, PO Box 405, Houghton, MI 49931 (phone: 906-337-4993); the rest of the year: National Park Concessions, Mammoth Cave, KY 42259 (phone: 502-773-2191).

Isle Royale Campsites – There are 36 campgrounds along the shores and inland lakes. Some offer screened shelters and minimal facilities. There are usually enough shelters for all, but it's best to bring your own tent just in case. A park ranger or camping brochure will tell you how long you will be able to stay at each site.

St. Croix River, Minnesota and Wisconsin

Many people say the territory around the St. Croix River is haunted. They say that spirits of the Indians who lived here for many generations are still a strong presence in the birch and pine forests lining the riverbanks. There are even some who say the Indians' shadowy birchbark canoes still make their way through the tributaries and creeks feeding into the St. Croix, and that you can hear the rustle of paddles breaking water if you listen in the silence.

More prosaic travelers, less inclined to give credence to tales of ghostly wanderers, are nonetheless enchanted by the magic of the St. Croix — a 164-mile stretch of water separating Minnesota and Wisconsin that was one of the first to be granted federal protection under the Wild and Scenic River Act of 1968. It's surprising to find such a relatively unspoiled section of country close to a big city, but you don't have to travel very far from the cosmopolitan Twin Cities, Minneapolis–St. Paul, to get to the lower St. Croix. It's just 25 miles northeast of St. Paul on Rte. 36.

Although the lower St. Croix valley is dotted with attractive villages, the untamed upper St. Croix hasn't changed much from Indian times. In fact, the Ojibwa (or Chippewa), descendants of the Algonquin, still harvest wild rice from the fertile crannies hidden among the small inlets lacing the surrounding marshes. But the placid waters bear a history of conflict.

The Dakota Indians lived here first, treasuring the river for its fish, the land for its wild rice, and the forest for its many kinds of game. (Otter, beaver, raccoon, fox, and deer still make their home in these woods.) After more than 350 years of wars, the Dakota were driven out by the Ojibwa, who had moved in from the East after unsuccessfully trying to defend their land from Iroquois attack. While the Ojibwa and Dakota battled, the French explorers and traders arrived, calling the Dakota a derogatory Ojibwa name, Sioux. After the Ojibwa victory, the Sioux fled south and west, eventually to be vanquished by the whites.

The French used the St. Croix as a fur connection, establishing many trading posts along its banks and developing the waterway into a flourishing commercial route. Beaver pelts were sold and shipped to Canada, and from there to Europe, where they found their way to the haberdashers of the fashionable. The intense struggle to control this resource-rich territory was not confined to the Indians and the French. The British were avid for supremacy, too, and in 1763, when the French and Indian wars were finally over, the Union Jack flew from the masts and flagpoles along the St. Croix. The Hudson Bay Company and other trading enterprises of the period conducted a brisk business until the War of 1812, when the US imposed a ban on foreign trading activity in the area. Then the loggers arrived. Thousands of men felled hundreds of thousands, perhaps even millions, of trees, mostly white pine, and the river was used to float logs. Innumerable lumberjacks perished while dynamiting logjams that clogged the river's flow. The lumbering era is a strong part of the historic legacy of the valley, and St. Croix residents still compete in logrolling contests. The logging came to an end when there were no longer enough trees for the industry to operate profitably. Since then, the region has been marked for conservation, and many people are working through a number of organizations to prevent further exploitation and destruction of the forest.

STILLWATER: The birthplace of Minnesota is a riverfront town 25 miles from St. Paul. Stillwater's the kind of place where they consider you a newcomer unless at least one generation of your family is in the cemetery. But don't let that throw you — it's a great place to visit, full of charming old buildings, fine antiques shops, emporiums, and cafés. If you'd like to charter an old twinstack steamwheel boat, go to the Stillwater Levee in Lowell Park, where you can rent the 200-passenger *Andiamo Showboat* or the 60-passenger yacht *Andiamo Too.* If you're visiting in May, be sure to take in the Rivertown Arts Festival, at which artists from all across the US display their works; it's held for 2 days in Lowell Park on the banks of the St. Croix. For information on logrolling contests, fireworks, and the pageantry of Stillwater's annual Lumberjack Days (July), contact Stillwater Area Chamber of Commerce, 423 S. Main, Stillwater, MN 55082 (phone: 612-439-7700). For sightseeing tours of the upper and lower St. Croix, call *Valley Tours* (phone: 612-439-6110).

MARINE–ON–ST. CROIX: At one time a dynamic lumberjack town, Marine–on–St. Croix has lost much of that rip-roaring, freewheeling atmosphere that characterized its formative years during the tree-tumbling era, but you can muse about what the old days must have been like in William O'Brien State Park overlooking the river.

TAYLORS FALLS and ST. CROIX FALLS: Canoe enthusiasts will probably head straight for these two towns sitting across the river from each other about 28 miles north of Stillwater. This is the dividing line between the upper and lower St. Croix. Here, the picturesque, tranquil southern stretch becomes rugged whitewater. (Actually, it's the other way around, since the St. Croix flows from north to south, but as you're most probably driving from the south, it will seem as if the peaceful part of the river ends and the wild section begins.) The land is relatively unsettled from this point north, which makes it ideal for back-to-the-woods people. The dramatic disparity between upper and lower St. Croix has its roots in the glacial and postglacial era, which formed two great lakes out of melting ice about 10,000 years ago. The water melting from glacial Lake Grantsburg, which covered much of Minnesota, flowed south, forming the St. Croix. When the entire mass of ice covering the hemisphere began to recede, glacial Lake Duluth, the predecessor of Lake Superior, was unable to drain east because of a huge section of ice that refused to melt. The excess water began cutting its way through sand, gravel, and boulders of what is now the St. Croix Valley, in the process forming the great gorge known as the Dalles. The path of the new glacial river also bored giant kettle holes, which are responsible for the tricky currents that challenge today's canoeists. (For a list of outfitters and other information, contact State of Wisconsin Dept. of Development, Madison, WI 53707; phone: 608-266-2161; 800-ESCAPES in the Midwest.) If you are unwilling to tackle the frothy, churning waters of the northern St. Croix in a canoe, you might consider a paddlewheel excursion on the St. Croix Dalles as a safer alternative. These excursions take you past geological formations in the river while guides explain what each is and how it was formed. *Taylors Falls Scenic Boat Tours* (PO Box 225, Taylors Falls, MN 55084; phone: 612-465-6315 or 612-291-7980) runs these trips daily from May through October on the *Taylors Falls Queen* (a genuine old paddlewheeler) and the 250-passenger *Taylors Falls Princess* (also authentic). For information about a houseboat vacation on the St. Croix, write to Great River Harbor, 1009 E. Main, Box 106. Wabasha, MN 55981 (phone: 612-565-3376). For information about canoe routes on the St. Croix River and throughout Minnesota, contact the Minnesota Office of Tourism, 375 Jackson St., 250 Skyway Level, St. Paul, MN 55101 (phone: 800-652-9747 in Minnesota; 800-328-1461 elsewhere). If you enjoy looking at the great outdoors but don't care to spend the night, you can head back to Minneapolis–St. Paul on Rte. 8 west to I-35 south.

BEST EN ROUTE

Lowell Inn, Stillwater – More than 50 years old, this country inn built in red brick Colonial style is known as the Mount Vernon of the West. It has a dining room and is run by the 11 members of the Palmer family. 102 N. 2nd St., Stillwater, MN 55082 (phone: 612-439-1100).

Voyageurs National Park and Boundary Waters Canoe Area, Minnesota

Centuries before there were roads in North America, the Indians in their birchbark canoes traveled a network of lakes, streams, and connecting portage trails that stretched from the Rocky Mountains to the St. Lawrence River. In the heyday of the great fur trade, French-Canadian voyageurs plied this natural highway, paddling and portaging huge quantities of furs east to Montréal and great numbers of soldiers, explorers, and missionaries west to the frontier. The last of the voyageurs disappeared in the 1830s, but in Voyageurs National Park and the Boundary Waters Canoe Area in northern Minnesota, you can still get a taste of what it was like on the old voyageur highway in the days when the splash of a paddle was the only manmade sound on these waters and the wilderness stretched as far as the eye could see.

Voyageurs National Park and the Boundary Waters Canoe Area are part of the oldest landmass in the world. Glaciers shaped this land, scooping out its lake basins, scoring its surface with an intricate maze of waterways, polishing its ancient boulders smooth. Except for an occasional sandy beach or rocky cliff, a canopy of trees — spruce, pine, fir, balsam, aspen, and birch — covers the land to the water's edge.

Voyageurs National Park, one of the country's newest national parks (it was established in 1975), extends almost 50 miles along Minnesota's northeast border. Numerous streams and 30 lakes — ranging in size from Rainy Lake, 35 miles long, to Quarterline Lake, about 350 yards across — make up a third of the park's 218,000 acres. At the heart of the park lies the wild and scenic 75,000-acre Kabetogama Peninsula. You can hike, fish, and of course boat here, and stay in accommodations that range from tentsites accessible only by water to fine lakeside resorts. As in the days of the voyageurs, wild rice grows in the shallow waters of the park, and deer, moose, wolves, beaver, and bear inhabit its deep woods. No fees are charged for using the park and no permits are required. Motorboats are the park's most popular means of transportation; there are no restrictions on their use.

Just east of Voyageurs National Park lies the vast Boundary Waters Canoe Area (BWCA), one million acres of Minnesota's Superior National Forest, most of which have been reserved exclusively for the use of canoeists. The BWCA stretches nearly 100 miles along the border between Minnesota and Ontario's million-acre Quetico Provincial Park, another protected canoeing area. With its myriad lakes interconnected by innumerable streams and portage trails and its access to Quetico's waters, the BWCA offers the canoeist an almost infinite number of route possibilities. Motorboats and cars are allowed only in certain parts of this canoeist's paradise, and even the air space is restricted. Travel permits are required.

VOYAGEURS NATIONAL PARK: Access to the park's perimeter is from Crane Lake, Ash River, and Kabetogama Lake resort areas east of Rte. 53 and from International Falls, Minnesota, via Rte. 11 east. To enter the park, a boat or floatplane is needed. They can be hired at the many resorts surrounding the park. In the winter, ice roads, snowmobiles, and skis provide access. Voyageurs is unique to the national park system in that it provides an opportunity for visitors to motorboat and camp at one of the more than 125 primitive campsites scattered on islands and bays throughout the park.

At the east end of Rainy Lake, the well-preserved *Kettle Falls Hotel* (see *Best en Route*), built in 1913, recalls the days when only trappers, traders, fishermen, and lumberjacks passed through these parts. Because of a quirk in the boundary line here, you can stand at Kettle Falls on the Minnesota side and look south to Canada.

Canoeing is possible in the park as long as you pay attention to the weather. Fast-rising storms can generate dangerous waves on the larger lakes. Experienced canoeists use islands for shelter from the winds and avoid crossing the biggest open stretches of water. You can obtain maps and the services of a guide at local resorts, canoes and supplies from outfitters at a number of places.

Another major Voyageurs recreation is fishing. The waters of Lakes Rainy, Namakan, Sand Point, and Kabetogama are known for their walleye, northern pike, and smallmouth bass. In the smaller lakes and streams are lake trout, and Shoepack Lake on Kabetogama Peninsula has the famed muskellunge.

Park visitors may stay at one of the 60 resorts or 2 state campgrounds just outside the park. You'll also be able to arrange for anything from water skiing to backcountry fishing via floatplane.

For information on naturalist-guided activities, camping, and recreational facilities in and adjacent to the park: Superintendent, Voyageurs National Park, PO Box 50, International Falls, MN 56649 (phone: 218-283-9821).

BOUNDARY WATERS CANOE AREA: The main gateway to BWCA is through Ely, Minnesota (other routes are through Grand Marais or, by canoe, through the Voyageurs lake system). If you go by paddle and portage, it is possible to follow the Canada-US border all the way from Rainy Lake at the western end of Voyageurs to the eastern end of BWCA and beyond to Grand Portage, on the shores of Lake Superior.

This 275-mile route retraces the final leg of the 2,000-mile journey made annually by the northwestern voyageurs, who transported furs from the northwest trading posts in the Rockies to the central depot of the fur trade in Grand Portage. Here, the Montrealers, who had paddled across the Great Lakes to meet them, collected the furs to take east. The voyageurs used to paddle 18 hours a day, but assuming you will be traveling at a more leisurely pace, this trip should take about 3 weeks.

Within the BWCA, any number of routes are possible, from a day-long excursion to a summer-long voyage. Information is available from Boundary Waters Canoe Area, Forest Service, US Dept. of Agriculture, PO Box 338, Duluth, MN 55801. Maps of all major canoeing trails in Minnesota and Quetico Provincial Park in Ontario are sold at *W. A. Fisher Co.*, 123-125 Chestnut St., or PO Box 1107, Virginia, MN 55792 (phone: 218-741-9544).

Reservations for entry permits into the BWCA are recommended. These permits are available from district rangers, some canoe outfitters, and resorts anywhere in the Superior National Forest.

Like Voyageurs National Park, the BWCA doesn't offer many whitewater thrills. (Where there are rapids, they are generally too rough to navigate and you have to take a portage trail around them.) What it does offer, however, is the chance to canoe in solitude. If you choose one of the less traveled routes that require longer portages, you may be lucky enough to have almost the whole route to yourself.

The time of year can also make a difference: Peak months at BWCA are July and August, but the prime season for canoeing runs from May through September. Unfortunately, May and June are also the prime months for mosquitoes and black flies.

Canoe outfitters in Ely and Grand Marais can supply you with everything you might need for your trip, including guides, food, and the canoe itself.

After your canoeing adventure, you can rest your newly developed paddling muscles by taking a scenic drive on Honeymoon Trail or the Gunflint or Sawbill trails in the magnificent Superior National Forest. Wherever you travel in this huge wilderness preserve, you won't be far from one of its 2,000 lakes.

Not far from the eastern edge of the Boundary Waters Canoe Area in the Superior National Forest is Grand Portage and the Grand Portage National Monument, which marks the site of the central trading depot of the voyageurs. From Grand Portage, in the summer, you can take a ferry to Michigan's remote Isle Royale National Park, an island wilderness in Lake Superior. Information: Boundary Waters Canoe Area, Forest Supervisor, PO Box 338, Duluth, MN 55801 (phone: 218-720-5324).

BEST EN ROUTE

The Voyageurs National Park area abounds with fishing camps, lodges, and resorts. The Park Service will provide lists of them. Voyageurs' facilities are by no means complete; expansion continues, with many resorts and hotels still under construction or in the planning stages.

Kettle Falls Hotel, Rainy Lake – Long a favorite of fishermen, it's accessible only by boat and plane, on the east end of the 40-mile lake that stretches along the US-Canada border. Open from mid-May to October. Kettle Falls Hotel, PO Box 1272, International Falls, MN 56649 (phone: 218-374-3511).

West

Denali National Park and Preserve, Alaska

With the passage of the Alaska Lands Bill on December 2, 1980, the park's name was changed from Mt. McKinley National Park to Denali National Park and Preserve. Denali, an Athabasca Indian word meaning "the High One," refers, of course, to the commanding peak, Mt. McKinley.

Mt. McKinley is our giant. Nothing in our part of the world is higher, and at more than 20,000 feet, Mt. McKinley approaches — admittedly just barely — Himalayan altitudes. (The Greater Himalayas tower above it at 25,000 to 29,000 feet[Mt. Everest]; but McKinley competes handily with the Lesser Himalayas, whose peaks rise 7,000 to 15,000 feet above the Vale of Kashmir.) Just a couple of hundred miles from the Arctic Circle, Mt. McKinley is the heart and soul of surrounding Denali National Park and Preserve, about 6 million acres of the austere, wild tundra country that is one of the greatest natural wonders in the US.

McKinley is actually two peaks, its double summits separated by 2 miles of glacial ridge. It is an imposing sight: North Peak rises 19,470 feet, South Peak, 20,320. No matter how many pictures you see, how many articles you have read, nothing quite prepares you for it: the startled recognition, an audible gasp or sigh, unrestrained exclamations of wonder. Be forewarned, however, that Mt. McKinley makes its own weather and can be cloud-hidden as much as 75% of the summer.

Climbers have been on the South Peak since the early 1900s when "sourdoughs," gold prospectors with some free time, decided to get to the top to see what the country looked like from up there. In a show of bicentennial enthusiasm, nearly 80 climbers made it to the summit of South Peak in July 1976. The fatality rate for McKinley climbers is low, but the last 7,000 feet are covered by sheer ice and snow, which make for very difficult climbing. In 1988, there were 559 successful ascents (and 357 unsuccessful ones). Parties interested in scaling McKinley or Mt. Foraker must register with the National Park Service first. Because of the difficulty of the slope, only experienced, healthy climbers with tested skill and proper equipment should consider the challenge.

Mt. McKinley is just one of the attractions of this huge, isolated tundra world — a world, alas, few get the opportunity to visit. The park is designed to protect its year-round, native inhabitants, but no longer is man an afterthought — the park attracts 600,000 visitors a year. There is one navigable road through the park; most of it is closed to private traffic, and the rest is restricted except for park shuttle buses. The park is open year-round, but its access road is closed from October until late May due to snow. Spring arrives late, not until June or early July, when the wildflowers, nesting birds, and mosquitoes come out in full force. An added treat, as if calculated to give extra pleasure to the 3 or 4 months allowed to visitors, is that sunlight lasts 18 to 20 hours each day in the warm season; consequently, many activities are scheduled for 6 AM to take advantage of the early morning light, when the mountain shimmers cold-blue and ice-white, before clouds can obscure its uppermost heights.

The park was set aside in 1917 for the protection of wildlife: caribou, grizzly bear, surefooted Dall sheep, wolf, and a huge variety of smaller, furred, warm-blooded beasts. One of the surprises of the park is its array of flora, including a variety of miniature trees — 1-foot willows, knee-high birch — which have adapted to the incredible cold of winter and limited water by developing root systems reaching yards into the earth, where the temperature may be 50F warmer than on the surface. They literally grow down instead of up. Mosses and lichen grow like tufts of beard on the tundra's rough face, providing vital food supplies to caribou and other non-hibernating winter creatures. Visitors habitually learn to identify hundreds of plant species by their shapes and color when sighted across a broad meadow or hanging from a sheer canyon wall.

Denali National Park and Preserve is not a place to visit casually. The only road into the interior begins in the town of Denali Park, 123 miles south of Fairbanks, 240 miles north of Anchorage. For years after the park was established in 1917 it remained without direct road access to these main cities; a railroad and private aircraft linked it to the outside world (and still do, along with commercial air service from the two towns). Today, Rte. 3 passes the entrance to the park on its run from Anchorage to Fairbanks. The road into the park is almost 90 miles long, running due west past many scenic canyons, passes, and riverbanks. Only the first 15 miles are paved. The first sight of Mt. McKinley occurs a few miles in, but it isn't until mile 60, at Highway Pass, that you can get a full view of its magnificent peaks. To help protect wildlife, private vehicles are not allowed on the park road after Savage River Bridge, at mile 14.5 (except for visitors with confirmed reservations for more distant campsites).

Campsites are spread intermittently along the road, and a shuttle bus stops at them as well as at the many trails and sights. The bus is also something of a mobile social center, a place for picking up the latest on wildlife sightings. The shuttle bus runs from Riley Creek Information Center to Wonder Lake (at the northern edge of the park), making stops along the way wherever passengers request. Shuttle service runs regularly from 6 AM to 7 PM (check for exact times at the Information Center). There is also a bus stop near the railroad depot.

The Eielson visitors center sits just off the park road some 65 miles in from the entrance. At an elevation of 3,730 feet, it offers good views of the mountain's twin peaks and the awesome spectacle of the Muldrow Glacier, stretching from McKinley to within a mile of the park road. Exhibitions at the center explain glacial geology and describe past mountain-climbing expeditions. Make a point of stopping at the center, especially if you plan to hike or stay overnight. Information on weather conditions, animal activity, and other potentially lifesaving data are available from the rangers stationed there.

Along the park road you're sure to pass a number of places worthy of a stop. The Teklanika River is a classic example of the glacial rivers that flow on their curled courses north from the Alaska Range. Dall sheep, those surefooted mountain climbers, can be spotted as mere dots on the sides of Igloo Canyon. Grizzly bear activity centers around Sable Pass. (No matter where you spot grizzlies and other animals throughout the park, don't frighten them or attempt to pet or feed them. They only look friendly.) Wildflowers spreading across the vast fields of Stony Hill Overlook are a summer contribution to the scene. And at Wonder Lake, the last stop on the park road at the northern end of the park, magnificent reflections of the mountains are cast on the mirrorlike surface.

Hikers and backpackers should obtain a backcountry-use permit before setting out on their treks. Fishing licenses are not required, but a limit is imposed. A state license is now required for access to the preserve and park areas. (Fishing in the park is far from Alaska's best due to silty lakebeds and streams and shallow ponds.) Tours can be arranged at the Denali National Park hotel for a full day's excursion into the park. For information on all aspects of park life and visiting, write: Superintendent, Denali National Park and Preserve, Box 9, Denali National Park, AK 99755 (phone: 907-683-2294).

BEST EN ROUTE

Denali National Park Hotel and McKinley Chalets, Denali National Park – Filling meals are offered day and night — especially appealing to the early riser who wants to make that 6 AM appointment with nature. A combined 369 rooms, 219 of them in the newer *McKinley Chalets.* Information: ARA Outdoor World, 825 W. 8th Ave., Suite 240, Anchorage, AK 99501 (phone: 907-276-7234).

In Denali National Park and Preserve – A choice of several campgrounds along the park road offers the best opportunity to see, and feel, tundra life. The camps are Sanctuary River, Teklanika, Igloo Creek, Wonder Lake, Savage, and Riley Creek. Motorists can drive to Savage and Riley Creek without road permits, but other sites are on the controlled-access portion of the road. Bring warm clothing, a waterproof shelter, mosquito netting and/or repellent, camp stoves (no wood is available in the park). Information: Superintendent, Denali National Park and Preserve, Denali National Park, AK 99755 (phone: 907-683-2294).

Camp Denali – This wilderness vacation lodge in the heart of the park, with a commanding view of Mt. McKinley, features 3-, 4-, 5-, and 7-night stays, log cabins, and communal dining. The emphasis is on natural history and guided hiking. In summer, write Camp Denali, PO Box 67, Denali National Park, AK 99755 (phone: 907-683-2290). In winter, Box 216, Cornish, NH 03746 (phone: 603-675-2248).

North Face Lodge – For those who like things a little less rustic, the park offers modern lodging with a country-inn flavor for 2- and 3-night stays. There's also a commanding view of you-know-what. In summer, write North Face Lodge, PO Box 67, Denali National Park, AK 99755 (phone: 907-683-2290). In winter, Box 216, Cornish, NH 03746 (phone: 603-675-2248).

Tongass National Forest, Alaska

John Muir, the Scottish naturalist who wrote eloquently about Yosemite and this country's western wilderness, was rendered almost speechless by the beauty of the southeastern panhandle of Alaska. "Never before this had I been embosomed in scenery so hopelessly beyond description," he said in Travels in Alaska. His words capture the nature of this area, much of which is still preserved as a wilderness in Tongass National Forest. The Tongass is the largest of the national forests, encompassing 16.9 million acres, reaching nearly the entire length of the rugged 500-mile coastline of southern Alaska from north of Juneau to south of Ketchikan, east from the outermost islands of the Alexander Archipelago to the border of British Columbia in the west. The panhandle is also bordered by two parallel mountain ranges. To the west, the peaks of the submerged Fairweather Range form the islands of the archipelago; to the east looms the Coast Range, with many peaks between 5,000 and 10,000 feet and numerous glaciers. In between is enough land to leave even the most blasé visitor breathless: America's only remaining frontier — more than 11,000 evergreen-covered islands, fjords whose flanks rise precipitously from the water's edge, huge walls of moving ice, glaciers carving and molding the coastline, and lush, moss-blanketed rain forests rising toward the Coast Range.

The Inside Passage runs the entire length of the Tongass. This waterway, which once provided gold seekers with access to the Klondike, is well protected from the bitter northwesterly winds by the outlying islands, and it's a pleasant passage by ferry along the foot of the Coast Range. Fjords and rivers flow into the passage, and the surrounding lowlands are blanketed by thick stands of hemlock, cedar, and spruce. In the summer, wildflowers abound: Fireweed, shooting stars, iris, and anemone color the marshes and meadows of the Tongass.

This region does not conform to stereotyped notions of Arctic harshness. If you expect huskies pulling sleds and boundless snow, the weather will disappoint you. Sitka, a city with a climate typical of the region, has an average temperature of 56F in August and 32F in January. This moderation is caused by the Japanese Current, which brings warm temperatures and plenty of rain. Sitka collects an average of 97 inches of rain annually, with June the driest month and October the wettest. During the summer it gets dark around midnight, so there is plenty of light for exploration of the Tongass.

The Tongass is a "working forest" managed for a variety of uses, such as providing timber and minerals for domestic and international markets, food and shelter for wildlife and fish, and a variety of recreational opportunities and facilities for the enjoyment of thousands each year.

The national forest is a rich wildlife area. Brown and black bear, trumpeter swans, deer, wolf, moose, and mountain goats roam many of the islands and coastal regions. The bald eagle, a bird that is close to extinction in the lower 48 states, thrives in Alaska and can be readily seen. Fishing is outstanding, with salmon up to 50 pounds not uncommon. In addition, many varieties of trout inhabit the freshwater lakes and streams of the Tongass.

Even bigger and better than a 50-pound salmon is another natural phenomenon of the Tongass — the glacier. Alaska possesses the largest expanse of glacial ice in the world outside Greenland and Antarctica. The panhandle's active glacier system offers a view of a broad succession of glacial stages. The glaciers that carved, shaped, and plowed much of this region are of fairly recent origin. Geologists estimate that about a million years ago, during the Pleistocene period, the sea level was hundreds of feet lower than it is today; glaciers moved from the heights of the Coast Range toward the sea, gouging the deep fjords and river valleys visible in the Tongass today.

Glaciers originate in snowfields in the higher regions of mountains. The only prerequisite for glacier formation is a snow cover that deepens over the years as more snow accumulates than melts. As successive layers build up, the accumulated weight exerts increased pressure on the underlying layers. When pressure is sufficient, snow crystallizes into ice. Movement of the glacier begins when the weight of the accumulation exceeds the strength of the ice. The immense pressure exerted by the sheer mass of the ice makes the ice "flow," something like cold molasses; glacial ice is not brittle.

The glaciers that exist in Alaska today are reminders of a "Little Ice Age," which began around 2,500 years ago and lasted until about 200 years ago. Due to a warming trend in the climate during the latter half of the 19th and first half of the 20th century, many Alaskan glaciers are receding. There is some evidence that this warming trend is slowing, and some glaciers, such as the Taku Glacier near Juneau, are advancing. The cool climate and ample snow in the mountains every year allow the glaciers to form. The ice in most Southeast Alaska glaciers is only a couple of hundred years old — the time it takes for the snow to change to ice and flow to the front of the glaciers.

The only glacier in southeast Alaska accessible by highway, Mendenhall Glacier, is reached by Rte. 7 and Mendenhall Loop Rd., just 13 miles from downtown Juneau. Mendenhall is over 12 miles long and 1½ miles wide at its face. The National Forest Service has a visitors center (open daily) at the glacier and also maintains trails alongside so that you can view the river of ice from excellent vantage points. If you're lucky, you'll see an example of calving: when a large slab of cobalt blue ice plummets from the glacier's face into Mendenhall Lake.

The retreat of Mendenhall Glacier has left rocky deposits (glacial moraines) in its wake, illustrating how virgin forest grows on seemingly barren soil. Only lichens and moss can survive in the most recently exposed regions. However, in the areas exposed during earlier years, small willows take hold and are followed by spruce and hemlock that mature into a forest. When the glacier moves inexorably forward during the next ice age, the forest will be swept aside.

The few major cities in the panhandle serve as excellent departure points for fishing, camping, and hiking forays into the Tongass, and also provide comfortable modern accommodations. Inaccessible by highway, the cities are reached by air, cruise ship, or the Alaska Marine Highway System, a state-run ferry service linking Seattle, Washington, and Prince Rupert, British Columbia, with the panhandle. Information: Division of Marine Transportation, PO Box R, Juneau, AK 99811 (phone: 907-465-3941).

Southernmost Ketchikan is renowned for its salmon fishing, and the many sportfishing lodges in the area offer anglers a chance to go after king salmon. The *Tongass Historical Society Museum* (629 Dock St.) has a collection of Indian artifacts and items used by southeastern Alaska pioneers. Petersburg and Wrangell are the next stops on the Marine Highway. The *Clausen Memorial Museum* (2nd and Fram Sts.) in Petersburg has a good collection of historical fishing gear. The Bear Tribal House (on Chief Shakes Island) of the Tlingit Indians has a fine totem pole collection.

To the northwest lies Sitka, which was known as the Paris of the Pacific during the 19th century, when it was the major trading outpost of the Russian Empire. St. Michael's Russian Orthodox Cathedral (Lincoln St.) is one of the best surviving examples of Russian peasant cathedral architecture in the free world and contains ecclesiastical art and gifts from the czar. The Sitka National Historical Park and the Russian Bishop's House, managed by the National Park Service, interpret this Russian America period and the interaction between the Russians and the Tlingit natives of Sitka. The *Sheldon Jackson Museum* (on the Jackson College campus) has an outstanding collection of Aleut, Eskimo, and Indian artifacts. In mid to late June, the city hosts the All-Alaska Logging Championships.

Juneau, the state capital, at the northern end of the Inside Passage, has the widest range of accommodations. A walking tour links 15 points of historic interest. The *Alaska State Museum* (in the Subport area) has extensive collections of pioneer memorabilia from the Russian American period and Gold Rush era as well as Aleut, Eskimo, and Indian crafts and artifacts. Bus tours of the Mendenhall Glacier region are available from the city.

Only a boat or short plane ride away from these cities lies the wilderness of the Tongass. The Forest Service maintains campgrounds in the areas and close to cities. In addition, about 150 cabins in the outlying areas, on the seacoast, or near rivers or lakes offer excellent opportunities to get back to nature. They have no bedding, plumbing, or electricity, but most of the lakeside cabins include a skiff. Cabins, which must be reserved in advance, cost $15 per night per party. When you go this way, you see the Tongass for what it is — a spectacular and productive rain forest. For further information and reservations write to the US Forest Service Information Center, 101 Egan Dr., Juneau, AK 99811 (phone: 907-586-8751). It has exhibits, displays, and audiovisual programs on the resources and management of the Tongass National Forest; open daily in summer. For further information on the cities and the rest of the panhandle: Alaska Division of Tourism, PO Box E, Juneau, AK 99811 (phone: 907-465-2010).

BEST EN ROUTE

The Landing, Ketchikan – Some 46 rooms with restaurant and lounge, directly across from the airport and ferry terminal. 3434 Tongass Ave., Ketchikan, AK 99901 (phone: 907-225-5166).

Westmark Shee Atika Lodge, Sitka – On the waterfront, the facilities here include a restaurant and marina. 330 Seward St., Sitka, AK 99835 (phone: 907-747-6241 or 800-544-0970).

Baranof, Juneau – In the center of the city, this 199-room hotel has a restaurant, a coffee shop, and piano music. 127 N. Franklin St., Juneau, AK 99801 (phone: 907-586-2660).

Westmark Juneau, Juneau – This 106-room hotel has a restaurant, and lounge. 51 W. Egan Dr., Juneau, AK 99801 (phone: 907-586-6900).

Grand Canyon National Park, Arizona

On first looking at the Grand Canyon, even the firmest atheist may feel intimations of some higher power. An awesome force created this vast expanse of beautiful sculptures of the earth. Level upon level of rock of intricate and seemingly infinite formations rises out of this huge chasm in the earth and seems to be patterns of some master design. As your eye traces the layers and reaches the far rim of the canyon, your gaze keeps rising as if expecting to see a sign, perhaps the artist's signature emblazoned across the sky. And you may find confirmation of your beliefs. On the other hand, you may, at this point, begin searching for some scientific explanation. Whether the force was natural or supernatural, the instrument of the sculpting is right in front of you, at the bottom of the canyon. You've only to look at the Colorado River.

You may have overlooked the river, because the Colorado follows a winding course through the canyon and is not even visible at certain points along the rim, and where it is, it appears to be a narrow gentle stream. Looks have never been more deceiving. At the floor of the canyon, you see this gentle stream for what it really is — the wide and mighty Colorado. And only then do you begin to understand the tremendous force that has cut an awesome course through vast stretches of rock and time. The canyon is 277 miles long, from less than 1 mile to 18 miles wide, and more than a mile deep. While the area around it has been "under construction" for 2 billion years, the canyon itself is a relative newcomer, geologically speaking. The Colorado River began eroding layers of sediment about 10 to 20 million years ago, and its present course is no more than 6 million years old.

The story told by the multiple layers of the Grand Canyon is extraordinary. Initially, the area surrounding the canyon (long before it existed) was flat. Over millions of years heat and pressure buckled the land into mountains, which were then flattened over more millions of years by erosion. Mountains formed again, eroded, and were covered by shallow seas. All of this is recorded in the canyon, a great book written by the hands of time and force. The rock layers exposed to view are like steps in a staircase of natural history. At the bottom of the gorge is the first step, the Vishnu Group, the hard shiny black rocks of the Precambrian age, which are among the oldest exposed rocks on earth. As we move up the staircase, the changes in hue, texture, and fossil remains between layers are truly incredible; there is the Redwall limestone, a 500-foot-thick deposit of gray-blue limestone stained by higher layers, outstanding because of its sheer cliffs and traces of fossils from a warm, shallow sea; above that is the Coconino sandstone, the solid remains of sand dunes in which fossilized footprints indicate lizard life. And at the top is the pale gray Kaibab limestone (at 250 million years, the toddler of the Grand Canyon family), a rich exhibition case for fossils from the shallow sea that once covered the area — sponges, sharks' teeth, corals, and bivalves.

Though geologists could spend lifetimes exploring the area, the canyon has attractions beyond. Hikers, bikers, river adventurers, naturalists, and just plain tourists have equal claim on the wonder. Between the South Rim and North Rim (about 9 miles as the crow flies, almost 23 miles by the rugged Kaibab hiking trail, and more than 200 miles by automobile) there is a vast expanse with something to see at every point, from the magnificent views to four distinct climatic zones to many species of plants and animals.

The South Rim is the more heavily visited of the two and the best place for an introduction to the Grand Canyon. Crowded in the summer but open year-round, it has extensive facilities for visitors amid a lovely background of juniper and piñon forest and open fields of Arizona blue lupine, yellow wild buckwheat, and purple asters. The South Rim visitors center, *Yavapai Museum,* and *Tusayan Ruin and Museum* offer orientation exhibits on the geological history of the area and the peoples who lived in the canyon. At the center you can pick up information on all the daily and weekly activities, from nature hikes along the rim led by rangers to more strenuous excursions into the canyon. South Rim drives cover 35 miles and have excellent overlooks. The 8-mile West Rim drive is closed to automobile traffic from Memorial Day Weekend through mid-September but has a free shuttle bus service linking key points. Ranger-naturalists rove between Hopi Point, Maricopa Point, and Trailview for interpretive talks on the geology, botany, animal life, and peoples of the Grand Canyon. The West Rim drive provides the best overview of the canyon, and the frequent buses that run from early morning till evening allow visitors to enjoy the sights at their own pace. Scenic airplane and helicopter flights are available year-round.

Trails for hiking down into the canyon start at the South Rim and, if you know your limits, can provide more intimate acquaintance with the wonders therein. The Bright Angel Trail, with rest stations at 1½ and 3 miles, and the steep South Kaibab Trail, a 6.4-mile hike with no water facilities, are best for hiking. You can take supervised nature walks or do it on your own, but remember that the canyon gets hotter as you descend and is hottest at midday. Take your hike in the early morning or late afternoon, be sure to have plenty of water and food and a hat for protection from the sun, and don't forget that going down is the easy part. Leave twice as much time for hiking back up. Note that hiking to the Colorado River and back in one day is not recommended.

One of the most interesting and certainly less strenuous ways to see the canyon is by muleback. There are 1-day rides and overnight trips into the inner gorge; riders stay overnight at the small guest ranch alongside Bright Angel Creek, where comfortable cabins can soothe even the most saddle-sore.

There are a wide range of lodgings at the South Rim from the private concessions in the park — the rustic *Bright Angel Lodge,* the modern *Yavapai* and *Thunderbird* lodges — to several park-run or privately operated campgrounds. Since the canyon is such a popular attraction, reservations should be made well in advance, particularly in the summer (phone: 602-638-2401).

Less accessible from major highways and cities, the North Rim is also less crowded and offers different views of the canyon from a magnificent setting. Tall blue-green firs, scarlet gilias, and roaming deer can be seen on the North Rim, which is closed in the winter because of heavy snows (open from mid-May to mid-October). The 26-mile Cape Royal Drive has magnificent overlooks including Point Imperial, which at 8,801 feet is the highest point on the canyon rim and features spectacular views of the subtle hues of the Painted Desert, Marble Canyon, and the Colorado River. The North Rim has some organized activities (trail walks, talks, evening programs led by rangers, muleback trips) but is more a place for solitary communion with nature. The most outstanding vista is Toroweap Point, which, far off the beaten track (reached only by 60 miles of dirt road), offers an amazing view, 3,000 feet down a sheer vertical wall to the snake-shaped Colorado.

The *Grand Canyon Lodge* provides modest accommodations on the North Rim. A campground near the inn allows stays of up to 1 week.

Of all the ways to see the canyon, none is more exciting than rafting the roaring Colorado. Various commercial enterprises offer trips on several types of boats powered by outboard motors. On these, you get to see the canyon from the bottom up — cat's claw, yucca, blackbrush, the pink Grand Canyon rattlesnake — and above rise the sheer cliffs of rock almost older than time itself. Shooting along the rapids, you get a sense of the power that has revealed it all. Information: Superintendent, Grand Canyon National Park, PO Box 129, Grand Canyon, AZ 86023 (phone: 602-638-7888).

BEST EN ROUTE

There are a variety of accommodations in the Grand Canyon National Park. The National Park Service runs several campgrounds on a first-come, first-served basis. However, Mather Campground on the South Rim can be reserved through Ticketron from Memorial Day to Labor Day weekends. For overnight hikes you need a permit and should make reservations by contacting the Backcountry Office at the address given above. Several concessions operate motels and hotels in the park. Rooms should be reserved 3 to 4 months in advance by contacting Grand Canyon National Park Lodges at South Rim, Grand Canyon, AZ 86023 (phone: 602-638-2401).

   El Tovar – This hotel is the oldest and most luxurious of the Grand Canyon accommodations. Some suites have balconies overlooking the canyon, and there is a good dining room serving prime ribs and filet mignon. South Rim (phone: 602-638-2401).

Petrified Forest National Park, Arizona

In one of those great moments of film history, Humphrey Bogart, playing a desperate criminal in *The Petrified Forest,* allows his sensitive side to rule and frees his captive, Bette Davis, at the ultimate cost of his own life. But in this case it was more than the woman that compelled him. Certainly the desert landscape of the Petrified Forest, at once desolate and inhospitable, yet strangely beautiful in its harshness, can turn a person's head and heart. And such a change in conscience is not a special effect of the movie but part of the real life here as well. The Painted Desert Visitors Center has a display of apologetic letters, in some cases long confessionals written as many as 20 years later, from visitors who have broken the park rules and taken samples of petrified wood, only to find that the wood weighs more heavily on their minds than on their bookshelves. The Petrified Forest has a powerful impact on the minds and imaginations of those who see it.

You have simply to go there to feel its power; you will undoubtedly be surprised by what you find. The 147-square-mile Petrified Forest is nothing like a forest at all but rather a semi-arid desert and shortgrass prairie region in northeastern Arizona. Few living trees stand, and the dominant forms of vegetation are saltbush and sedges growing sparsely around mesas and buttes that bake in the unrelenting sun. But there are trees, or at least the remains of trees, and thousands of them, lying supine and glowing in the desert landscape. In fact, the park contains the richest collection of petrified wood in the world, ranging from huge prone logs to small brilliantly colored chips — burning oranges, deep reds, rusts, and yellows mixed with the dark shades of black, blue, and purple and lighter shades of white, gray, and tan. The only color you won't see much of is green, for forest has turned to stone. And the colors of the logs are part of the landscape as well. The northern portion of the park contains a portion of the Painted Desert, which really is just that, except that the colors are natural in this series of plateaus, buttes, and low mesas, remarkable for the bright reds, oranges, and browns in layers of sandstones, shales, and clays. The area is something of an outdoor gallery; the Painted Desert might more aptly be called the sculpted desert, for it exhibits nature's work in various media as the hues and forms change from minute to minute with the intensity of sun and the formidable shadows of late afternoon or early morning.

In the dawn of its history, the Petrified Forest was actually a coastal plain of marshes and swamps. About 225 million years ago, what is now a high desert plateau was a low-lying swamp basin with dense beds of ferns, mosses, and trees growing in marshlands and along streams. Groves of conifers flourished on hills and ridges above this basin. Over long periods of time, natural forces felled the trees, and flooding streams transported them to the floor of the floodplain, where they were gradually buried under thousands of feet of mud, sand, and silica-rich volcanic ash. Water carrying the silica and other minerals seeped through the sediment and filled in each wood cell, retaining the details of the wooden mold. The silica left glass-like deposits of white, gray, and tan, while traces of iron in the water colored the logs yellow, orange, red, and rust, and manganese created the blacks, blues, and purples. During a period of mountain building activity 70 million years ago, an upheaval lifted the layer high above sea level, and gradual erosion left the rainbow logs exposed. Geologists believe that more logs are buried below the surface to a depth of 300 feet. Since 1981, fossils of at least 25 animals that lived in the area have been discovered, as well as petroglyphs that acted as solar calendars. In 1985, one of the oldest dinosaur skeletons in the world was excavated from the Painted Desert.

Though more logs will be exposed in the continuing evolutionary process, what is on the surface is truly remarkable and can be seen in half a day. The park's major features, five separate forests with concentrations of chips and huge chunks of onyx, agate, and jasper, are linked by a 28-mile road. The two visitors centers, open year-round except Christmas and New Year's Day, are good places to stop first to see specimens of polished petrified wood, displays explaining the petrification process, and of course the letters from petty and grand petrified-wood thieves whose consciences got the better of them. Giant Logs, behind the Rainbow Forest Museum, is a magnificent highlight for its beautiful colors and the evidence of the petrification process; many trunks exceed 100 feet in length, and brilliant chips of onyx, agate, carnelian, and jasper tint the desert sand. At Long Logs, logs are piled on top of one another, and a partially restored Indian pueblo built of petrified wood chunks overlooks the area. One of the park's most unusual sights is Agate Bridge, a huge single log with over 100 feet exposed and both ends encased in sandstone. A parking lookout on a ridgetop above Jasper Forest provides a view of masses of logs strewn on the valley floor. Be sure to stop at Blue Mesa, where a 1-mile loop of paved trail leads along a blue-gray ridge carved by the wind into intricate sculptures. Newspaper Rock is a mammoth chunk of sandstone with intriguing uninterpreted picture writings of prehistoric Indians. The rock is permanently closed due to rock slides, although an overlook with coin-operated telescopes allows visitors to inspect the rock art. Exploration of the vast unmarked surroundings should be arranged with park rangers; without natural water sources or trails, the Petrified Forest is not for casual hiking. Modern explorers should carry hats to shade themselves from the sun and plenty of drinking water. Backpack camping is allowed with a permit from one of the visitors centers.

The Painted Desert is at the northern end of the park. After stopping at the visitors center to see displays showing how traces of iron have stained the layers of clay and sandstone many shades from bright red to pale blue, take a drive to one of the several overlooks and see it for yourself. The colors seem ever-changing and appear most vivid in early morning or late afternoon, or after rain, a most uncommon event.

There are no lodging facilities inside the park and camping is not permitted. Removing petrified wood from the park is also strictly forbidden. However, if you want a sample of petrified wood, you can purchase one taken from private lands outside the park at the Painted Desert Oasis and Rainbow Forest Curio near the park entrances. But leave the park intact as federal law, nature's law, and, as many have found, the law of the conscience dictate. The beauty of the Petrified Forest is there for all to behold. You really can't take it with you — except in your mind's eye. Information: Petrified Forest National Park Headquarters, AZ 86028 (phone: 602-524-6228).

BEST EN ROUTE

The park has no overnight facilities (backpack camping only), but there are about half a dozen motels in Holbrook, 25 miles to the west, and one in Chambers, 21 miles east.

Best Western Arizonian Inn, Holbrook – It offers 70 rooms, a pool, a casual restaurant. Reservations recommended April through October. 2508 E. Navajo Blvd., Holbrook, AZ 86025 (phone: 602-524-2611 or 800-528-1234).

Comfort Inn, Holbrook – Opened in December 1986, it has 61 rooms with queen-size beds, a pool, and complimentary coffee, tea, or cocoa in the lobby. Reservations advised. 2602 E. Navajo Blvd., Holbrook, AZ 86025 (phone: 602-524-6131 or 800-228-5150).

Best Western Chieftain, Chambers – Near the Navajo Reservation, this 52-room hotel has a pool, a service station, and a restaurant serving Spanish, American, and Indian food such as Navajo tacos — frybread sandwiches with beans and other vegetables. Reservations advised in summer. PO Box 697, Chambers, AZ 86502, on I-40 (phone: 602-688-2754).

Big Sur and the Monterey Peninsula, California

Big Sur is a 50-mile stretch of Pacific coast south of the Monterey Peninsula and Carmel-by-the-Sea; its name is a corruption of a Spanish phrase meaning "big south." California Rte. 1 hugs the rugged coastline from Monterey, through Big Sur, to Morro Bay, 125 miles south. Convict chain gangs spent almost two decades carving the twisting highway out of solid cliffs, a highway that is unquestionably the most dramatic on the entire Pacific Coast.

The Monterey Peninsula and Carmel lie 125 miles south of San Francisco, 350 miles north of Los Angeles. Carmel is 4 miles south of the town of Monterey.

MONTEREY: California's first capital has more than 40 buildings built before 1850. The Old Custom House is the oldest government building in California, dating to 1827. It has historic material on display (Custom House Sq.). The Monterey Presidio, now a Defense Department language training center, dates to 1770, when it was built by Franciscan Father Junipero Serra, founder of California's Mission Trail (Pacific St.). California's first constitution was drafted in Colton Hall in 1849; the building dates to 1848 (Pacific St. and Colton Hall Park). Enamored with what he sensed as "the haunting presence of the ocean," Robert Louis Stevenson in 1879 lived and worked at the *French Hotel,* now called the Robert Louis Stevenson House (530 Houston St.). Cannery Row, the site of John Steinbeck's famous novel, has long since given way to chic shops and elegant eateries. The Monterey Bay Aquarium (886 Cannery Row) has 100 major exhibitions and galleries, including a 3-story kelp forest, and three feeding shows daily.

SEVENTEEN-MILE DRIVE: Despite its name it's only 12 miles long, but it takes you from the beaches and cypress trees of Pacific Grove to Carmel. Stop off at Seal Rock, Cypress Point, *Pebble Beach Golf Links* (site of the ATT–Pebble Beach National Pro-Am, and Pebble Beach, enclave of the super-rich).

CARMEL-BY-THE-SEA: In this picturesque seaside artists' colony, about 25% of the permanent population are working artists. Carmel's quaint, untouched quality is attributable to some of the most stringent zoning laws in the country, passed in 1929. Since then, neon signs, traffic signals, and dozens of other garish accouterments have been prohibited. Carmel's narrow streets are lined with intriguing boutiques, shops, art galleries, and some excellent restaurants. The Carmel Mission, the most perfectly restored of all the California missions, was founded in 1770 by Father Junipero Serra, who loved it so much, he arranged to be buried here. In 1960, Pope John raised the mission to the status of a minor basilica, the second religious landmark so designated in the American West (Lasuen Dr. and Rio Rd.). South of Carmel, Point Lobos Recreation Area, a 1,255-acre park, has some of the most beautiful scenery along the California coast. Be sure to visit China Cove, Bird Island, and the wonderful stands of cypress. Colonies of seals and sea lions live on the rocks. Though there are no wolves in the area, the Spanish called it lobos (meaning "wolf") because the seals' barking reminded them of the sound of wolves. The park has a visitors center and hiking trails (4 miles south of Carmel on Rte. 1). The *Bach Music Festival* takes place every July. For information on events in Carmel-by-the-Sea, contact the Carmel Business Assn., Carmel, CA 93921 (phone: 408-624-2522).

CARMEL VALLEY: Follow the Carmel Valley Road east into the land of strawberry fields, orchards, grazing pasture, and artichoke farms. Because of its sunny, warm climate, the valley is an ideal choice for vacationers. You can play golf, ride horses, swim, play tennis, hunt wild boar and deer in season, or fish for trout in the Carmel River. Carmel Valley Begonia Gardens are ablaze with the colors of 15,000 flowers. The Korean Buddhist Temple is a good place to experience a contemplative foreign religion (Robinson Canyon Rd.). Most hostelries in the Carmel Valley are resorts. For information on accommodations and events, contact the Carmel Valley Chamber of Commerce, PO Box 288, Carmel Valley, CA 93924 (phone: 408-659-4000).

THIRTY-MILE DRIVE: The 30 miles between the Monterey-Carmel area and Big Sur are some of the most dramatic in the country. It takes about an hour to drive along the coast-hugging, twisting road where the Santa Lucia Mountains encounter the sea. Bixby Creek Bridge, just south of Carmel, is a 260-foot-high observation point where you can park, watch the ocean pound the beach, and gaze hypnotically at the Point Sur Lighthouse, which flashes every 15 seconds.

BIG SUR: This most famous piece of shoreline on the continent is so familiar to TV and movie audiences, it's almost unnecessary to talk about it. The rolling grassy hills of Big Sur end abruptly at cliffs towering high above the sea. There are many places to stop and watch sea otters, seals, and sea lions near the shore. You might even see whales spouting farther out to sea. Below the cliffs, waves crash over the boulders. You won't need to be told which spots on the road are especially scenic; when you round a hairpin curve and find yourself grabbing for your camera, you'll know you've found one.

In the town of Big Sur, you can stroll along the beach, have a picnic overlooking the water, browse in the art galleries, or visit the redwood trees, inland. Be sure to stop at *Nepenthe,* a restaurant on an 800-foot cliff that was built by a student of Frank Lloyd Wright. It has evolved over the years into Big Sur's main hangout and social center (phone: 408-667-2345). Pfeiffer–Big Sur State Park, a deep forest of redwood and other trees, provides a change of scenery from the bare, grassy hills of Big Sur. It has horseback riding, hiking trails, fishing spots, picnic areas, campgrounds, food service, and a lodge. At Jade Cove, you can hunt for jade at low tide. For information, contact Big Sur Information Center, Big Sur, CA 93920 (phone: 408-667-2100).

SAN SIMEON: About 40 miles south of Big Sur, William Randolph Hearst's fabled castle, San Simeon, contains sections of castles from other parts of the world which the newspaper tycoon shipped to his Pacific estate. Amazingly reconstructed, the majestic rooms, halls, courtyards, and swimming pools are no less than stunningly elegant.

Tours will take you through this regal $50-million treasure house, now a state historical monument of 123 acres overlooking the ocean. Tickets may be purchased in advance through Mistix reservation service, by mail or phone: PO Box 85705, San Diego, CA 92138-5705 (phone: 800-444-PARK in California; 619-452-1950 elsewhere).

MORRO BAY: Named for the massive volcanic spire jutting out almost 600 feet above the sea. Morro Bay State Park, a 1,483-acre tract with horseback riding, hiking trails, picnic areas, and campsites, also has a natural history museum on local marine biology and ecology.

BEST EN ROUTE

Ventana Inn, Big Sur – Dramatic, contemporary elegance with exposed beams, high ceilings, balconies, patios, and windows looking over the mountains and ocean. All 59 rooms have patchwork quilts or duvets and hand-painted headboards; some have hot tubs. Restaurant, 2 breakfast rooms, 2 pools, sauna, Jacuzzi, and hiking trails. See also *America's Special Havens*, DIVERSIONS. Hwy. 1, Big Sur, CA 93920 (phone: 408-667-2331).

Pine Inn, Carmel – This Victorian establishment has stained glass, electrified gas lamps, marble-topped tables, wooden chests, and brass beds. A penthouse area has 6 rooms, 1 with a fireplace. Each of the 49 bedrooms is furnished differently. PO Box 250, Carmel, CA 93921 (phone: 408-624-3851).

Sea View Inn, Carmel – Although the sea view is partially blocked by tall pines, this inn built around 1906 has retained much of its original atmosphere — if not its original $3 rate. There are 8 bedrooms, 6 with private bath; several have window seats and rocking chairs. A delicious breakfast is included. PO Box 4138, Carmel, CA 93921 (phone: 408-624-8778).

Death Valley National Monument, California

One of the largest of our national monuments, Death Valley National Monument covers 3,000 square miles, 550 of which are below sea level. It is 140 miles west of Las Vegas via Rtes. 95 and 373, 300 miles northeast of Los Angeles via I-14 to Rte. 395 to 190 or I-15 and Rte. 127, on the California side of the California-Nevada border, in the Mojave Desert. Originally, the 140-mile valley was called Tomesha ("ground afire") by the Indians, but was given its present name by a party of prospectors who got lost in the valley during the Gold Rush.

To the 49ers and the early settlers, Death Valley was a deadly obstacle to be overcome in order to reach the riches of California. Modern travelers find it an exciting, dramatic place that can be explored in relative safety. Death Valley can be a special side trip on journeys from southern California to Las Vegas, Yosemite, or Sequoia–Kings Canyon national parks.

Death Valley is part of a region of extremes. At 282 feet below sea level, it is the lowest point in the entire Western Hemisphere. Only 70 air miles away stands the highest point in the continental US — Mt. Whitney, 14,494 feet above sea level. Death Valley is also one of the hottest places on earth, with temperatures recorded as high as 134F in the shade (the all-time world record is 136F, recorded in Libya, in 1922). Summertime is a good time to stay away unless you are well prepared.

Each of the canyons and mountains surrounding Death Valley seems to have its own special colors. Golden Canyon has bright golds and rich purples; Mustard Canyon is various shades of ocher. The Black Mountains have reds, greens, and tans. One particularly interesting canyon is Mosaic Canyon, whose gray rock surfaces are embedded with colorful pebbles that have been worn down by erosion, making the canyon look as if someone decorated it with brilliant mosaics.

If a scientist were to tell you he or she was going to Death Valley to study fish, you might raise an eyebrow. However, several species of fish in the streams of Death Valley do not exist anywhere else in the world. There are, in fact, more than 40 species of life indigenous only to Death Valley. Despite its great heat and minuscule rainfall (less than 2 inches a year), Death Valley has springs and several streams that flow all year. There's even a small swamp. During migration periods, Death Valley is visited by such unlikely guests as Canadian and snow geese, herons, and ducks.

In addition to its valid claims on things that are the highest, the lowest, the oldest, and the biggest, Death Valley might also be the richest. There are many legends about the fabulous lost mines of Death Valley. They may or may not be true, but at one time it certainly had some of the nation's most lucrative mines. There were boom towns with colorful names like Bullfrog and Skidoo, towns that died when the mines played out, although today you'll pass what remains of these once-vibrant mining centers en route to monument headquarters, north of Furnace Creek. At the Furnace Creek visitors center, you can pick up brochures and maps explaining how to take self-guiding auto tours. There are also slide shows, nature exhibitions, and other activities run by the rangers.

Death Valley is actually the floor of what was once a large inland lake fed by runoff from glacial retreats in the Sierra Nevada range. With the disappearance of the glaciers, the supply of new water couldn't keep up with the evaporation rate of 150 inches per year. Little in the way of rain makes it past the formidable barrier of the Sierra. The Devil's Golf Course is the name for a bed of salt pinnacles, some of which are as high as four feet and still growing.

If there's one mineral that Death Valley is famous for, it's borax. The borax mines were established in the 1880s, when roads in Death Valley were built for the legendary 20-mule team wagons that hauled the borax out of the valley. Three of the modern roads in Death Valley follow the route of the old mule teams. At the Harmony Borax Works, 1½ miles north of the visitors center, are the remains of one of the first processing plants.

One of the most famous landmarks in Death Valley is Scotty's Castle. Walter Scott (or "Death Valley Scotty," as he was known) had once been a performer in Buffalo Bill's Wild West Show. He built an elaborate, lavishly furnished castle in Grapevine Canyon at the north end of Death Valley, claiming he had paid for it with gold from a secret mine. The castle, standing like a mirage on the edge of the desert, has been famous ever since it was built. The romantic tale of a secret gold mine is, unfortunately, false. The castle was actually built by Albert M. Johnson, a wealthy Chicago businessman who came to Death Valley and quickly became friends with the flamboyant ex-cowboy.

Other well-known Death Valley landmarks are Zabriskie Point, Titus Canyon, Telescope Peak — 11,049 feet high — and, directly below it, Badwater, the lowest point in the valley. Nine campgrounds are scattered throughout the valley, among them: Furnace Creek, Mahogany Flat, Mesquite Spring, Sunset Campground, and Texas Springs. Reservations are not accepted, but there's almost always plenty of room for everyone. The tourist season runs from mid-fall to mid-spring, and the weather is pleasant during the winter. If you're planning to do any hiking, keep in mind at all times that Death Valley got its name for a reason. You should always carry plenty of extra water.

Death Valley's stark visual appeal evokes a strong emotional response. While other western national parks and monuments allow visitors to view the beauty of the West, Death Valley invites you to experience something of the spirit of the Old West — the determination, drive, and sense of hope that made this part of America what it is today. The original pioneers knew that they faced the very real possibility of death as they started out across this valley. Most of them made it and went on to new lives in California; one lies buried beneath its sands. You can't visit Death Valley without instinctively finding yourself thinking about these settlers. It's a monument to the American spirit and to the spirit of the pioneers who traveled the American West. Information: Superintendent, Death Valley National Monument, Death Valley, CA 92328 (phone: 619-786-2331).

Within a few hours' drive of Death Valley are a number of ski resorts, among them: June Mountain, Mammoth Mountain, and Wolverton. Just 120 miles from Death Valley lies the southernmost glacier field in the Northern Hemisphere, near the town of Big Pine on Rtes. 190 and 395.

BEST EN ROUTE

Reservations at both the inn and the ranch listed below can be made through Furnace Creek Inn, PO Box 1, Death Valley, CA 92328.

Furnace Creek Inn and Ranch, Death Valley – This luxurious, 69-room inn has a swimming pool, tennis, lounge with entertainment, and palm-lined gardens; open from mid-October to early May. The 230-room ranch, open year-round, has 3 restaurants, a pool, golf, and tennis; 30 cabin units. About a quarter-mile south of the visitors center on Rte. 190 (phone: 619-786-2345).

Furnace Creek Ranch, Death Valley – More casual accommodations in cottages and motel units, with a swimming pool, golf, tennis, horseback riding, restaurant, cocktail lounge, and service station. Adjacent to trailer park and landing strip for light planes. Open all year. Next to the visitors center on Rte. 190 (phone: 619-786-2345).

Lake Tahoe, California

Lake Tahoe is so much more than a lake resort that its name is almost misleading. It is equally famous for its incomparable outdoor sports facilities, especially skiing, and for sophisticated gambling casinos offering the best nationally known entertainers. The largest alpine lake in North America,

Tahoe is 22 miles long, 12 miles wide, and has 72 miles of shoreline. At an altitude of 6,229 feet, it is 1,664 feet deep and contains enough water to cover the entire state of California to a depth of more than one foot. Despite its size and the heavily populated sections of its shoreline, the water is pure enough to drink. In fact, it could supply every person in the US with 5 gallons of water every day for 5 years.

Lake Tahoe is nestled at the notch in the California-Nevada state line where California's eastern boundary starts to slant southeast. Actually, two-thirds of the lake belongs to California, one-third to Nevada. South Lake Tahoe is 198 miles from San Francisco, on I-80 to Sacramento, then Rte. 50. At South Lake Tahoe you have a choice: Rte. 50 to Rte. 28, north, along the undeveloped eastern shore in Nevada, or Rte. 89, which runs into Rte. 28, around the northern edge of the lake in California.

There are two theories about Lake Tahoe's origins. One argues that the lake was a huge crater gouged out of the crown of the Sierra Nevada range during the Ice Age. Another puts the lake's beginnings at 3 million years ago, when volcanic lava hardened, trapping the Tahoe waters in a deep, geological cup. Modern Tahoe offers something for nearly everyone. Luxury-seekers will find ultramodern hotels and casinos at both ends of the lake. Sports enthusiasts will find skiing, boating, swimming, fishing, hiking, golf, and tennis in abundance. Campers seeking solitude and untrammeled nature have access to any of the three national forests around the lake — Tahoe, 696,000 acres to the north of the lake; Toiyabe, 3.1 million acres on the eastern edge in Nevada; and Eldorado, 886,000 acres to the southwest.

Starting at the US Forest Service visitors center (open from Memorial Day to June 28, weekends 10 AM to 6 PM; from June 28 to Labor Day, 8 AM to 6 PM daily; 916 541-0209), at the southern tip of the lake on Rte. 89, 1 mile north of Camp Richardson, you can trace the shoreline by car north and west through California or through Nevada. The corkscrew road winding through the ponderosa pine and spruce along the western edge of the lake is considerably more rugged than the strip facing the eastern shoreline. California offers much better sightseeing, since Rte. 89's intricate twists and turns reveal dramatic, panoramic views. You'll have to take it easy — the road is peppered with 10 mph zones, and, on a weekend, it's clogged with people. And take it very slow if the weather is foggy, rainy, or snowy — Rte. 89 can be treacherous.

EMERALD BAY: You might well experience déjà vu — the feeling you've been here before. This is one of the most photographed sites in the state. Eagle Falls, a canyon above the bay, has crystal-clear pools for swimming. Cruises of Emerald Bay are available aboard the *Tahoe Queen,* a glass-bottom paddlewheeler (phone: 916-541-3364) and MS *Dixie* (see *Zephyr Cove,* below).

DESOLATION VALLEY WILDERNESS: In startling contrast to Emerald Bay's fairyland splendor, these 41,000 forbidding acres of lake-dotted granite form a barren landscape laced with dozens of hiking trails. Experienced hikers have been known to gripe that the trails are as mannerly as a city park's.

TAHOE CITY: This is ski country. You can pick up interchangeable lift tickets for slopes at *Northstar, Alpine Meadows, Heavenly Valley, Squaw Valley,* and *Diamond Peak at Ski Incline, Homewood,* and *Mt. Rose.* For information, call Ski Tahoe North (phone: 800-TAHOE-4-U). Tahoe North Visitors and Convention Bureau is at 850 N.

Lake Blvd., PO Box 5578, Tahoe City, CA 95730 (phone: 800-822-5959 in California; 800-824-6348 elsewhere).

SQUAW VALLEY: Five miles north of Tahoe City, the site of the 1960 Olympics, Squaw Valley is one of the most famous ski areas in the world, with 27 chair-lifts, cable cars, and complete accoutrements. The aerial tram operates during the ski season and for two months in the summer (phone: 916-583-6985).

INCLINE VILLAGE: At the northern end of the lake, this town is in Nevada. Lakeshore Boulevard is lined with expensive houses, showy hotels, casinos, and other attractions that make this "the Entertainment Capital of Lake Tahoe." Robert Trent Jones designed the two championship 18-hole golf courses, notorious for their water hazards. *Golf Incline,* as it's called (phone: 702-832-1141), becomes *Ski Incline* from December through April (phone: 702-832-1177).

PONDEROSA RANCH: This ranch is probably as familiar to you now as your own living room, and you can catch a glimpse of the set of the TV series "Bonanza" from the Incline golf courses. More than 350,000 people visit every year. A haywagon ride leaves the Ponderosa Stables at 8 AM; breakfast is served (phone: 702-831-0691).

MT. ROSE: Detour north on Rte. 27 for a bird's-eye perspective of the lake and environs. In winter, Mt. Rose has 2 ski slopes; in summer, there are 24 campsites in the Mt. Rose Campground (phone: 702-882-2766).

TOIYABE NATIONAL FOREST: Slightly to the east of the shoreline, the forest is known for its challenging hiking trails — so "uncontrolled" that inexperienced hikers are cautioned to stay away. Reservations must be made in advance for 5 of the campsites, 18 are on a first-come, first-served basis. For information, contact Toiyabe National Forest, 1200 Franklin Way, Sparks, NV 89431 (phone: 702-331-6444).

CAVE ROCK: Once used as a natural barrier against enemy attack by the Paiute Indians, today the cave is a tunnel for cars, with a lookout point.

ZEPHYR COVE: Cruise to Emerald Bay on the MS *Dixie,* a triple-deck ship offering dinner, cocktail, and sunset cruises as well as daylight passenger excursions. The ship can be hired for special charter cruises off-season, October through April. During the spring and summer, reserve well in advance (phone: 702-588-3508).

STATELINE: This is gambling country, what Tahoe is most famous for. Take your pick — you'll find slot machines, craps and keno tables, roulette wheels, and giant names in nightclub entertainment all over town. *Harrah's, High Sierra, Harvey's,* and *Caesar's Tahoe* are the most famous casinos. *Bill's,* next to *Harrah's,* has a smaller casino and gives discount coupons to guests at other hotels. *South Tahoe Nugget* also distributes coupons. It's about ¾ mile east of *Bill's* on Rte. 50. For information and reservations, contact the Lake Tahoe Visitors Authority, PO Box 16299, South Lake Tahoe, CA 95706 (phone: 916-544-5050).

BEST EN ROUTE

River Ranch Lodge, Tahoe City, California – A 22-room inn with a cocktail lounge and restaurant. PO Box 197, Tahoe City, CA 95730 (phone: 916-583-4264).

Coeur du Lac Condominiums, Incline Village, Nevada – For information on rentals, write PO Box 7107, Incline Village, NV 89450 (phone: 800-468-2463, ext. BRAT).

Hyatt Lake Tahoe, Incline Village, Nevada – Big casino and nightclub activity, plus water sports, tennis, and golf nearby. 460 rooms. PO Box 3239, Incline Village, NV 89450 (phone: 702-831-1111).

Caesar's Tahoe Resort, Stateline, Nevada – This resort has 450 rooms, a Chinese and a continental restaurant, a showroom, cabaret, and complete gambling facilities. PO Box 5800, Stateline, NV 89449 (phone: 702-588-3515 in Nevada; 800-648-3353 elsewhere).

Del Webb's High Sierra, Stateline, Nevada – A casino with 1,200 slot machines, superstar nightclub, lounge, luxury facilities (540 rooms), and here, too, nonstop action. *Stetson's* serves filet mignon béarnaise and flambéed desserts. PO Box C, Stateline, NV 89449 (phone: 800-648-3322 from Arizona, California, Idaho, Oregon, and Utah; 800-648-3395 elsewhere).

Harrah's, Stateline, Nevada – The world-famous 546-room super-resort has a 150-yard-long casino, famous entertainers, 4 lounges, and a full range of activities 24 hours a day. The *Summit* restaurant has lake views and serves continental specialties like pheasant with choucroute and champagne sauce. PO Box 8, Stateline, NV 89449 (phone: 800-648-3773).

Harvey's, Stateline, Nevada – More than 1,600 slot machines, all gambling facilities, and several restaurants. *Top of the Wheel* serves Polynesian and American specialties. The *Sage Room* serves steaks and seafood, and the *El Dorado Room* serves a buffet. There's also the *Seafood Grotto* and *El Vaquero* Mexican restaurant. Over 700 rooms. PO Box 128, Stateline, NV 89449 (phone: 800-648-3361; 702-558-2411 in Nevada, Hawaii, and Alaska).

Christiana Inn, South Lake Tahoe, California – If you're looking for quieter accommodations close to the scene, try this small (2 rooms, 4 suites), European-style chalet a mere 100 yards from the ski lifts at Heavenly Valley. The dining room offers an extensive continental menu and wine list. PO Box 18298, S. Lake Tahoe, CA 95706 (phone: 916-544-7337). In Heavenly Valley, try the *Top of the Tram* restaurant (steaks, chicken, trout entrées). The price of Sunday brunch includes the tram. Keller Rd. (phone: 916-544-6263).

Palm Springs and Joshua Tree National Monument, California

Palm Springs is in the Coachella Valley, 100 miles southeast of Los Angeles. It was at one time an important stop on the stagecoach route from Prescott, Arizona, to Los Angeles. Today, the drive from LA to Palm Springs takes about two hours on I-10, which in LA is the San Bernardino Freeway.

The sun shines an average of 350 days a year in Palm Springs and the air is pure. The average daytime temperature is 88F; nighttime average, a comfortable 55F. Since the humidity is always low, you can enjoy the heat without suffering from that muggy, clammy feeling that can accompany high humidity.

Palm Springs was discovered hundreds of years ago by the Agua Caliente Indians. Agua Caliente means "hot water" in Spanish, and it was, in fact, the discovery of hot springs in the earth which led to the area's development into a spa and, later, a resort, for the Indians considered the springs to have miraculous healing powers. They were opened to the public around the turn of the century, and, whether or not they healed anyone, they have provided a miracle for the Agua Caliente tribe, the largest single landowner in Palm Springs. The 180 members of this tiny tribe own over 10 square miles of tremendously valuable land within the city limits.

Today, people are more attracted to Palm Springs' warm, dry climate, its desert scenery, and superb resort facilities than to the springs themselves. For the rich, Palm Springs offers all the luxurious goods and services money can buy. For anyone, rich or poor, it offers what money cannot buy — a sparkling environment and delightful climate. Although Palm Springs has over 200 hotels and welcomes about 2 million visitors annually, it is still a very small town, with a permanent population of approximately 38,000. It probably has the world's highest number of swimming pools per capita — over 7,500, one for every five people. Not everyone in Palm Springs is rich, although sometimes it seems that way. In winter, the wealthy, the famous, and the powerful come to play, and prices for everything soar as high as Mt. San Jacinto, the peak overlooking the city. During the summer, temperatures rise and prices drop.

No matter when you come, you'll find active nightclubs, hundreds of fascinating (and expensive) boutiques, and sports activities that range from horseback riding through the nearby canyons to balloon trips through the desert. Known as "the Golf Capital of the World," Palm Springs has over 70 golf courses and is the site of more than 12 major golf tournaments each year, including the Bob Hope Chrysler Classic and the Nabisco–Dinah Shore Invitational. There are about 400 tennis courts and an increasing number of important annual tennis championships. The round of constant events and festivals includes rodeos, horse shows, the Desert Circus, art festivals, major league exhibition baseball games, charity balls, and designer fashion shows. Check out the elegant specialty shops on Palm Canyon Drive, the main thoroughfare.

The main places of interest include the *Palm Springs Desert Museum,* a lavish cultural center with an excellent art museum, a history museum with unusual Indian artifacts, and outstanding facilities for the performing arts (101 Museum Dr.). The Living Desert has plants in natural settings with landscaped paths; Moorten Botanical Gardens offers more than 2,000 kinds of desert plants from all over the world (1701 S. Palm Canyon Dr.). San Jacinto Wilderness State Park, atop the 10,780-foot mountain, has more than 50 miles of hiking trails, picnic areas, and six campgrounds. Its 13,000 acres can be reached only by an aerial tram ride. Part of the larger San Bernardino National Forest, the park is the site of numerous activities — some serious and some purely fanciful — throughout the year. Information: Greater Palm Springs Convention and Visitors Bureau, 255 N. El Cielo Rd., Suite 315, Palm Springs, CA 92262 (phone: 619-327-8411).

THE INDIAN CANYONS: Filled with plants, bubbling hot springs, magnificent waterfalls, ancient Indian cliff dwellings, and pictographs on the walls, the canyons may remind you of Shangri-la — they were used as the location of the original movie version of *Lost Horizon,* James Hilton's novel about the fabled hidden paradise. The canyons, part of the Agua Caliente Indian Reservation, are closed to visitors during the summer.

INDIO: "The Date Capital of the World" (the kind that grow on trees), Indio is also the site of the *National Date Festival* in February. Decor is neo–Arabian Nights, with camel and ostrich races. A movie called *The Sex Life of a Date* plays at Shield's Date Gardens.

JOSHUA TREE NATIONAL MONUMENT: Created in 1936 over howls of protest from mining companies that wanted to exploit the region, the monument is a haven for the strange Joshua tree and other desert wildlife and plants. The Joshua tree was given its name by early pioneers who felt that it resembled the prophet Joshua raising his arms in supplication to God or perhaps pointing the way for them to go.

Start your tour at the Twentynine Palms Oasis, site of the monument's headquarters, visitors center, and museum. A hike along the short nature trail will acquaint you with the plants and animals that live here. The park spreads over 870 square miles south of the oasis, with good major roads. Split Rock, one of the monument's best-known landmarks, is a giant split boulder more than three stories high with a natural cave underneath.

Ten miles south of Pinto Wye, Cholla Cactus Gardens and nature trail cover several acres. The gardens are filled with a species of cactus known as jumping cholla, so called because it seems to jump out at you to give you a painful sting. (It's probably a good place to skip if you have young children with you.) Wonderland of the Rocks in Hidden Valley is the most popular site on monument grounds. Thousands of years of desert winds have carved the rocks into bizarre shapes resembling sailing ships, monsters, cabbages, kings, and assorted other oddities. The best examples of Joshua trees stand at Keys View, which offers impressive views of the San Bernardino Mountains, San Jacinto, and the distant waters of the Salton Sea. Information: Superintendent, Joshua Tree National Monument, 74485 National Monument Dr., Twentynine Palms, CA 92277 (phone: 619-367-7511).

BEST EN ROUTE

Gene Autry, Palm Springs – Here are 186 rooms and 12 cottages, plus 3 heated pools, tennis, restaurant, and a nightclub with entertainment. Open year-round. 4200 E. Palm Canyon, Palm Springs, CA 92264 (phone: 619-328-1171).

Palm Springs Marquis – Features here include 264 deluxe rooms and villas, pools, tennis, dining, entertainment, and free airport shuttle service. 150 South Indian Ave., Palm Springs, CA 92262 (phone: 619-322-2121).

Palm Springs Plaza Resort and Racquet Club – This luxury resort, with its award-winning restaurants, includes 256 spacious rooms, 6 lighted tennis courts, a pool, and spa. 400 E. Tahquitz Way, Palm Springs, CA 92262 (phone: 619-320-6868).

La Siesta Villas Condominium Resort, Palm Springs – Eighteen rooms in self-contained villas, all with fireplaces and kitchen units, plus condominiums. Heated pool. No children under 18. 247 W. Stevens Rd., Palm Springs, CA 92262 (phone: 619-325-2269).

Wyndham Palm Springs Hotel – This new 410-room luxury hotel has the largest swimming pool of any Palm Springs hotel, a fully equipped health club, 2 Jacuzzis, 2 restaurants, and live entertainment in its nightclub. Open year-round. 888 E. Tahquitz, Palm Springs, CA 92262 (phone: 619-322-6000).

Redwood National Park and Lassen Volcanic National Park, California

Millions of years ago, redwoods grew throughout vast areas of North America. Now they're found only in a narrow band of land along the coast of northern California and southern Oregon, and they rarely grow more than 50 miles inland since the conifer needs the coastal fog's moisture, which it absorbs through its needles.

REDWOOD NATIONAL PARK: Established in 1968, Redwood National Park consists of several fragments of land in California near the Oregon border. About a quarter of the park's 106,000 acres is divided into three state parks — Jedediah Smith State Park, 9 miles northeast of Crescent City (where Redwood National Park maintains its headquarters and visitors center); Del Norte Coast Redwoods State Park, 7 miles southwest of Crescent City; and Prairie Creek Redwoods State Park, near the southern boundary of Redwood National Park at Orick. When the national park was created, the existing parklands were augmented with other redwood groves purchased from lumber companies and private owners. It now has about 40 miles of rugged shoreline with spectacular bluffs. Altogether, Redwood National Park is roughly 50 miles long but only 7 miles wide at its widest point. If you're coming from San Francisco (326 miles to the south), you'll enter the park at Orick.

Just north of Orick is the site where the park was dedicated. Nearby stands Lady Bird Johnson Grove, a group of immense trees named in honor of the former First Lady. Along Redwood Creek are the tallest trees on earth. A redwood grove gives the feeling of a cathedral. The huge trees grow close together, shutting out the sunlight from above. The branchless trunks soar 80 to 100 feet straight up before the bows spread out to form the roof of the grove. Few smaller trees can grow in their shadow. Although redwoods are related to the giant sequoias of the High Sierra, it's quite simple to distinguish the two — the tall, slender trunk and dark brown bark of a redwood differs from the sequoia's bright reddish brown and comparatively massive trunk. The scientific name for the coast redwood is Sequoia sempervirens.

For over a century commercial logging has been active in this region, and since it began, more than 85% of the original redwood forest has been cut down. In 1978, vast new tracts of land were acquired by the park, almost doubling its size. Unfortunately, however, all but a few thousand acres had already been cut over by the lumber companies. A National Park Service study done in the 1960s estimates that virtually all of the original forest outside the parks will be gone by the 1990s. Presently, there are over 250,000 acres of redwood parks in the state.

Nature designed the redwood for durability. It can grow either from seeds or sprout from the roots and stumps of old trees. Its bark is often more than a foot thick, and there are natural chemicals in the fiber of the tree that make it incredibly resistant to decay, disease, and fire. The durable, everlasting quality of the redwood is the main reason for the demise of the original groves; it is superb for items like picnic benches and the siding of houses, and it has incredible insulation properties.

The Tall Tree is the tallest known tree on earth — 367.8 feet high and 44 feet in circumference. To the north of Redwood Creek, Prairie Creek State Park gets as much rain as an Amazon rain forest (about 100 inches a year, most of which falls in winter). The park is filled with redwood, big-leaf maple, Douglas fir, and luxuriant foliage and flowers. Fern Canyon's 50-foot-high walls are swathed with moss and lichen, and 40 miles of trails stretch through the area's 12,000-acre forest. In the broad meadows of the state park, a herd of about 200 Roosevelt elk roams free. Gold Bluffs, at the western edge of Prairie Creek State Park, faces the sea. Rugged promontories jut into the Pacific and huge waves break over the jagged rocks. There are more than 100 campsites at Gold Bluffs and Prairie Creek. South of Eureka, there are 33 miles of majestic redwood groves on the Avenue of the Giants in Humboldt Redwoods State Park.

Del Norte Coast Redwoods State Park, 7 miles southwest of Crescent City, is unusual because its virgin redwood forest extends right to the steep bluffs overlooking the rocky shore. The best views are from the coast-winding Damnation Trail. In late spring, this section is ablaze with azaleas. There are campgrounds at Mill Creek. The northernmost section of the national park, Jedediah Smith Redwoods State Park, stands at the northeastern edge of the coastal redwood belt. It contains redwoods as well as inland species like Jeffrey pine. The largest trees are in the Frank Stout Memorial Grove, where the star attraction is the 340-foot Stout Tree. There are campsites and good swimming at a sandy beach along the Smith River (9 miles northeast of Crescent City). Information: Redwood National Park, 1111 2nd St., Crescent City, CA 95531 (phone: 707-464-6101).

LASSEN VOLCANIC NATIONAL PARK: Lassen is about 160 miles southeast of Redwood National Park. Lassen Peak last erupted from 1914 to 1921, making it one of the most recently active volcanoes in the continental US. After centuries of peace, Lassen's 20th-century eruptions lasted for 7 years, highlighted by a massive explosion in May 1915 that mowed down all life on the northeast side of the mountain for several miles. Volcanic dust fell as far away as Nevada. In 1916, the volcano and the surrounding area were set aside as a national park. (You could say it opened with a bang.) The smallest of the national parks in California, 106,000-acre Lassen is a tiny Yellowstone, with bubbling mud pots, boiling hot springs, and hissing steam vents known as fumaroles. Like Yellowstone, most of Lassen's major sites are easily accessible by car. The park headquarters are in Mineral, on Rte. 36, 9 miles from the entrance, where you can stop for information. Or you can take Rte. 44 east from Redding about 40 miles to the visitor information enter at Manzanita Lake. The 30-mile Lassen Park Road winds through the western section of the park, which contains the major attractions, including 10,457-foot Lassen Peak. More than 150 miles of hiking trails lead to thermal areas and lakes. Lassen Peak Trail will take you on a 2½-mile climb to the summit of Lassen Peak; a shorter, easier trail leads to Bumpass Hell, a section of hot springs, mud pots, and fumaroles in the southwestern corner of the park. (Bumpass is named for an early guide who plunged a leg into a steaming mud pot.) Nearby is the Sulphur Works, accessible by car. In winter you can downhill ski in the southwestern corner of the park or cross-country ski anywhere in the park.

Summit Lake, in the park's center, is the embarkation point for backpacking trips to the eastern areas. Cinder Cone, in the northeast corner, was set aside as a national monument several years before Lassen became a park. The stark, black cylindrical cone is surrounded by colorful formations of volcanic ash called the Painted Dunes. To the east of Cinder Cone lie the aptly named Fantastic Lava Beds, a mass of black volcanic stone deposited when Cinder Cone erupted in 1851. If you are intimidated by the thought of visiting volcanoes, keep in mind that Cinder Cone is considered dormant. That doesn't mean, however, that new eruptions are impossible. Information: Superintendent, Lassen Volcanic National Park, PO Box 100, Mineral, CA 96063-0100 (phone: 916-595-4444).

BEST EN ROUTE

The Benbow Inn, Garberville – Built in the 1920s to resemble an English Tudor mansion, the inn has dark wood paneling, a stone fireplace, and a shaded terrace. Facilities include a 9-hole golf course, hiking trails, fishing, hunting, swimming, canoeing. Closed January through mid-April. 445 Lake Benbow Dr., Garberville, CA 95440 (phone: 707-923-2124).

Mineral Lodge, Mineral – Set in a valley with a mountain view, the lodge consists of several buildings, a swimming pool, restaurant, tennis, and gift shop. PO Box 160, Mineral, CA 96063 (phone: 916-595-4422).

Sequoia and Kings Canyon National Parks, California

Sequoia and Kings Canyon national parks are the backpackers' highway into the majestic Sierra Nevada of Southern California. By car you can see a bit — the giant sequoias, for which Sequoia is named, the forests that surround them, the lower elevation sights. But only two major roads enter the 1,300 square miles of the parks: One is frequently closed during the winter by mammoth snowfalls; the other meanders into and out of the western corner of Sequoia so quickly that one feels it is intimidated by the mountains to the east. What you don't see by car is almost everything but the trees: the largest mountain peaks, especially Mt. Whitney, tallest peak in the continental US (at 14,495 feet), the animals, the streams, and the thousands of miles of backcountry, mountain trails for hiking, camping, horse and mule packing, fishing. These are the High Sierra experience.

Geographically and administratively, Sequoia and Kings Canyon are one park, covering about 860,000 acres. But the two boast radically different physical features. Sequoia, the southwestern corner of which is accessible by car, is the site of the world-renowned giant sequoia trees, the largest living things known on earth (and not to be confused with coastal redwoods — Sequoia sempervirens — which are taller than Sequoiadendron but not nearly so broad). Forests of the giant sequoia used to cover the hemisphere; now they are found only on the western faces of the Sierra Nevada, at middle elevations (still thousands of feet above sea level, however). East of the stands of sequoia, the park begins to rise with the Sierra Nevada, culminating at the park's eastern edge in Mt. Whitney, Mt. Muir (14,045 feet), and Mt. Langley (14,042 feet). Then, as quickly as they sprouted, the great peaks fall away to lower elevations, and outside the parks the country breaks into deep, long valleys.

Kings Canyon stretches north of Sequoia, sharing with it one entire border. Made a national park in 1940 (50 years after Sequoia), Kings Canyon has the same wild, rugged mountain beauty of eastern Sequoia, with the additional attraction of sheer canyon ledges for which it gained fame. Mountains of 13,000 feet are not at all uncommon in the eastern region of Kings Canyon, and running through them, from the northern reaches of Kings Canyon to Mt. Whitney in Sequoia, is the John Muir Trail, the 220-mile walking path that threads through the most spectacular, isolated, and peaceful vistas of both parks. Immediately to the east and north of the parks is the John Muir Wilderness Area, with Inyo National Forest just beyond.

There is no more fitting tribute to the naturalist than these trails and protected areas. It seems that most of America's beautiful parks and natural wonderlands have at some time in their histories required the guardianship of a farseeing and usually heroic protector; for many that person was John Muir. Sequoia and the High Sierra are perhaps his most remarkable testaments. Muir fought the government and the lumber companies to protect the sanctity of these natural treasures in the late 1880s, long before most people recognized their beauty and spiritual importance. In 1890, thanks to Muir's devotion, Sequoia National Park was officially created, the country's second such refuge. (Yellowstone Park had been established 18 years earlier. Yosemite Park followed Sequoia by a mere 5 days.)

Automobiles are given limited access in Sequoia and Kings Canyon; there is, however, a beautiful drive along the 46 miles of Generals Highway, which begins at the park entrance, 7 miles north of Three Rivers, winds through the mighty stands of sequoia in the park's southwestern corner, and ends at Grant Grove in Kings Canyon. (Sometimes the Generals Highway is closed in winter due to snow — as much as 3 to 4 feet per snowfall in some places; call 209-565-3351 for recorded park weather and road conditions.)

If you start the driving tour at the western corner of Sequoia, you will drive past some of the most magnificent examples of sequoia in the world — several of the mightiest named for American generals. Based on its total volume, the General Sherman Tree is known as the largest living thing on this planet. It rises 274.9 feet on a 102.6-foot circumference, and it is the subject of thousands of photographs; not one expresses the sheer awe you'll feel standing next to its thick, reddish-brown trunk, wondering if it ever stops. Estimates of the age of General Sherman put it somewhere between 2,200 and 2,500 years. Estimates of the tree's weight place it at 2,000 tons, with enough wood to build 40 five-room houses. It is as high as the Capitol in Washington and no less a national treasure. The General Sherman Tree is part of Giant Forest, of special interest because it offers a view of sequoia in every stage of development, from sapling (they grow from seeds about the size of a pinhead) to high in the sky.

As you drive the full length of the Generals Highway you will pass several other magnificent trees, especially in Grant Grove (actually part of Kings Canyon), where the road joins Rte. 180 and turns north on the way to the heart of Kings Canyon. There stands the General Grant Tree, a full 7 feet shorter than Sherman, but 5 feet larger in circumference, and considered by many to be the more awe-inspiring spectacle. The Robert E. Lee Tree is nearby, and a short drive (about 5 miles) from the grove is Big Stump Basin, where you can see what remains of these colossi after loggers get to them, as they did in the late 19th century despite Muir's efforts. Another well-known tree in the range is Hart Tree, standing in the Redwood Mountain Grove, west of Generals Highway in Kings Canyon National Park.

Halfway along Generals Highway you will come to Lodgepole visitors center, with displays on the trees and other aspects of park life. By all means plan to stop for a while. The visitors center (there is also one in Grant Grove and a visitor contact station at Cedar Grove in Kings Canyon) has information on a huge array of available activities and is a starting point for guided hiking tours. There is no question that the best way to see the parks is with backpack, tent, and time to hike around. Ranger-guided trips to the mountains and through the sequoia forests give a feeling for the land that is impossible to have from the road, even with frequent stops.

Making plans and seeing exhibitions is not the only incentive for stopping at Lodgepole visitors center. Rising some 6,725 feet above sea level (4,000 feet above the Kaweah River), Moro Rock offers a magnificent view of the parks and all their treasures. The eastward view is most impressive, looking toward the spiny backbone of the Sierra. A short walk from the rock is Crescent Meadow and Tharp's Log, the log cabin headquarters of the 19th-century explorer Hale Tharp. A stroll out to Beetle Rock is best saved for late afternoon and the experience of a sunset closing out the day over the park. And the strong-winded should hike down to Crystal Cave, a marble cavern highlighted by guided tours.

For an exciting overnight trip, join a tour to Bearpaw Meadow. The walk on the High Sierra Trail is 11 miles of scenery that rivals the best of the Muir

Trail. Make reservations with the park concession for facilities there. If you are roughing it, you must get a backcountry permit from the visitors center. Past Bearpaw, the High Sierra Trail continues eastward until it meets the Muir Trail at Wallace Creek. From there, you can make side trips to Mt. Whitney, Big Arroyo, or Kern Canyon. Be sure to tell park personnel where you plan to be and when you plan to return.

The center of activity in Kings Canyon is Cedar Grove, reached by Rte. 180. This area has four campgrounds with 351 sites, and the ranger station at Cedar Grove has the most current information on hikes. From Cedar Grove, hikes can go in almost any direction on miles of trails. The least explored areas are to the north, into the heart of Kings Canyon Park. You will find lakes of all sizes and mountain after mountain. It must be done on foot or horse or muleback. There is little stopping you from tackling the miles of trails and countless opportunities for individual exploration. After all, that's why John Muir fought for it. Information: Superintendent, Sequoia and Kings Canyon National Parks, Three Rivers, CA 93271 (phone: general information, 209-565-3456; round-the-clock, 209-565-3341).

BEST EN ROUTE

Although nothing in the Sequoia and Kings Canyon area really earns a place in *Best en Route,* there are ample alternatives for accommodations — in nearby hotels and motels, in park lodges, and in campsites throughout the national parks and forests.

There are more than a dozen in the two parks. The Lodgepole Campground is run on a reservation-only basis and they can be made through Ticketron outlets during the summer. Otherwise it's first-come, first-served. Guest Services, Sequoia National Park, CA 93262 (phone: 209-565-3456), has information about the park's four lodges: *Giant Forest Lodge* in Sequoia Park, *Cedar Grove* and *Grant Grove* lodges in Kings Canyon, and *Stoney Creek Lodge* between Sequoia Park and Kings Canyon.

In the parks, a number of stores and supply stations can help outfit you for a hike or overnight. They are near the campsites and also sell the fishing licenses that are required if you plan to tackle the lakes and streams for the many varieties of native catch, especially the magnificent golden trout. Mules, burros, and horses can be rented at Giant Forest, Cedar Grove, and Mineral King for day or overnight pack trips throughout the parks.

Other campsites are available in the Sequoia National Forest, on Hume Lake (where boating, swimming, fishing, and other accommodations are the featured attractions), in Inyo National Forest, and at Stony Creek Campground (on Generals Hwy., south of Grant Grove in Kings Canyon).

Hotel and motel accommodations outside the park are limited to four nearby towns: Three Rivers, just south of Sequoia; Visalia to the west; and Porterville and Fresno.

Yosemite National Park, California

A good many of California's finest physical resources are the product of the Sierra Nevada, the mountain range that runs for 500 miles parallel to the Nevada border. The gem in this mountainous necklace is Yosemite National Park, 1,190 square miles of mountains, valleys, granite spires and monoliths, waterfalls and forests, in central-eastern California.

Yosemite was established as a national park in 1890, but its natural history spans millions of years, starting during an ancient age when a shallow arm of the Pacific covered a section of western Nevada, the Sierra Nevada, and the great Central Valley of California. The sea dried up and subsequent volcanic activity caused molten rock to infiltrate the underlying sedimentary layers. In time, these layers were eroded and the igneous rock, granite, was exposed. Later upheavals of the earth tilted these layers to the west, creating the steep eastern flank and long western slope of the mountains we know today. As a consequence of the angle of the mountains, the flow of streams became more rapid, cutting deep V-shaped valleys into the granite. Then, during Ice Ages 2 or 3 million years ago, glaciers gouged the valley into a U-shaped trough with a round bottom and sheer sides. Finally, the melting glaciers formed a lake whose bed is the present valley floor.

Today the valley is Yosemite's main attraction, though by no means all the park has to offer. Carpeted with meadows and forests and watered by the Merced River, the valley is 7 miles long and up to 1 mile wide. Its walls rise 2,000 to 4,000 feet from the valley floor, featuring some of the geological wonders of the world. First and foremost is El Capitan, at 7,569 feet the largest known single block of granite in the world, a sheer outcropping that does not have a single fracture on its entire perpendicular wall, a challenge to even veteran rock climbers. Towering above the lower end of the valley, directly across from El Capitan, are the 6,114-foot Cathedral Spires. On the north side of the valley stand the Three Brothers, a trio of leaning peaks piled on top of one another to a height of 7,779 feet. Beyond, the upper valley broadens with a semicircle of granite domes — Sentinel, Basket, North Dome, and the massive Half Dome. These huge granite deposits were formed by glaciation and exfoliation; in the latter process, the surface layers of rock released from subterranean pressures peel, chip, and crumble into rounded contours on their way toward ultimate dissolution. Though this shaping force is completely imperceptible, the valley's magnificent waterfalls demonstrate the process of gradual dissolution still at work. The most spectacular of the valley's falls is Yosemite, noted for its height; the Upper Fall plunges 1,430 feet over the north wall (a height equal to nine Niagara Falls), and the Lower Fall immediately below is a drop of more than 300 feet. Combined with the cascades in between, the fall's double leap measures 2,425 feet, making Yosemite the highest waterfall on this continent. With the valley's other waterfalls — Ribbon, the misty Bridalveil, Nevada, Vernal, and Illilouette — Yosemite offers one of the most amazing water spectacles anywhere.

Yosemite Village, the center of activities in the park, with campgrounds, lodging, shops, and restaurants, is a good place to begin a visit. The Yosemite Valley visitors center, open year-round, offers exhibits on the geological development of the area and information on the wide range of activities — ranger-guided walks, lectures, and demonstrations (the Yosemite *Guide* provides a schedule of the week's activities). After a stop at the visitors center and a tour of the valley via tram has oriented you, over 800 miles of trails outside the valley can be covered by horse, mule, or foot.

No matter how you see them, there are several highlights of the park that you should not miss. Glacier Point offers a sweeping 180F panorama of the

High Sierra. Half Dome rises in front of you, Nevada and Vernal Falls are prominent, and in the background are the snowy peaks of Yosemite's backcountry. The road to Glacier Point (closed in winter) winds through red fir and pine forest and meadow. You can hike to the valley floor along one of several trails. Four-Mile Trail (really 4.6 miles) zigzags down steeply, while Pohono Trail skirts the south rim and descends to the valley floor near Bridalveil Fall, a total of 13 miles.

Tuolumne Meadows is a major trailhead to the high country and, at 8,600 feet, the largest subalpine meadow complex in the High Sierra. Though it is closed in the winter, during the summer the park operates a campground here and a full-scale naturalist program exploring high-altitude ecological systems.

The Mariposa Grove is the largest of the park's three groves of mammoth sequoia. Over 200 of the beautiful old trees here measure more than 10 feet in diameter. Among them is the tunnel tree (now supine), which was so large that people used to drive through the hollow area at the base. The Grizzly Giant is not hollow; but if it were, a Mack truck carrying the tunnel tree could drive straight through it.

In addition to its scenic attractions, Yosemite offers a wide variety of summer and winter recreational activities. The miles of trails offer hiking for everyone from tenderfoot to trailblazer. Wilderness permits are required for overnight backcountry travel and are issued at the ranger station on a first come, first served basis or by mail reservation February through May. Tuolumne Meadows stables at *Camp Curry* and *Wawona* rent horses and mules and offer a variety of guided trips from 1-day excursions to 6-day saddle trips through the High Sierra. If you're afraid of mules and horses, bike rentals at *Yosemite Lodge* and *Camp Curry* provide wheels. For those who like to live dangerously, the vertical granite walls of the valley beckon with some of the finest climbing areas in the world. Actually, the Yosemite Mountaineering School (phone: 209-372-1244) gives lessons on scaling a sheer cliff.

In wintertime, Yosemite becomes a snow-covered paradise, with Badger Pass for downhill skiing, over 90 miles of trails for cross-country skiing, an outdoor ice-skating rink at *Camp Curry,* and magnificent mountainous vistas. Call 209-372-4605 for recorded road and weather conditions.

At every time of year Yosemite has something to offer, and while you are there, you imagine how those cliffs would appear during another — perhaps covered with snow — or how the falls thunder as the snow melts. But no matter what you imagine about Yosemite, a visit will more than fulfill its promise. Information: Superintendent, PO Box 577, Yosemite National Park, CA 95389 (phone: 209-372-0264/5).

BEST EN ROUTE

The National Park Service runs 16 developed campgrounds in the park. Group campsites must be reserved in advance. Individual campsites are assigned on a first-come, first-served basis, except between April and mid-November, when the Yosemite Valley campgrounds are on a campsite reservation system. Reservations can be made through your local Ticketron office.

Ahwahnee – This classy structure of stone and native timber dates from 1927. It has a good dining room, bar, entertainment, and lots of well-designed public areas.

See also *America's Special Havens*, DIVERSIONS. Yosemite Valley (phone: 209-252-4848).

Yosemite Lodge – A combination of cabins and modern hotel rooms built around a central area with 2 restaurants, a cafeteria, swimming pool, bike rental, shops, and, in the summer, an ice cream cone stand. Yosemite Valley (phone: 209-252-4848).

Camp Curry – Rustic tents, cabins, and hotel rooms have access to a cafeteria, public lounge, fast-food service, pool, and bike rental facility. The Mountaineering School has its headquarters here, and in the winter, there's an ice skating rink. Yosemite Valley (phone: 209-252-4848).

Wawona – A century-old Victorian structure 27 miles south of Yosemite Valley on Rte. 41. Roughly half of its 77 rooms have private baths and all are furnished with antiques. The dining room serves all meals; 9-hole golf course; tennis; swimming pool. Open April through Thanksgiving (phone: 209-252-4848).

Rocky Mountain National Park, Colorado

The North American Rocky Mountains stretch from northern New Mexico and southern Colorado to the Columbia Range and the Rocky Mountain Trench in Canada, 300 miles north of the US-Canada border. And this massive range is part of an even larger series of mountains, the North American Cordillera, which includes the Brooks Range in Alaska and Mexico's Sierra Madre, the mountains that follow Mexico's eastern and western coasts.

In the US, the highest peaks in the Rockies are those of the Front range, so named because it is the first range of the chain to rise from the Great Plains in north-central Colorado. Some 414 square miles of the Front range have been set aside as the Rocky Mountain National Park, and within its 265,193 acres are 113 named peaks over 10,000 feet, 76 above 12,000 feet, innumerable mountain valleys (averaging 8,000 feet above sea level), and Longs Peak at 14,255 feet. It is a spectacular area of glacial moraines (great piles of rocks where the advance of glaciers finally stopped), mountain lakes, alpine valleys, and tundras. The area has five small glaciers and myriad hiking and horse trails, peaks, canyons, and roads.

The Colorado Rockies began formation around 70 million years ago; they rose and were worn down by wind and water erosion over the next 30 million years. A 15-million-year period of volcanic activity and faulting threw them up once again. The mountains that appeared were at the mercy of wind and water for eons, but its present form was stamped on the chain during the past 2 million years, when the first of four glacial periods began. Portions of mountains were leveled by the incredible force of the glaciers; chasms appeared as mountain walls were cut through; cirques dug where the glaciers' heads buttressed against unyielding mountain faces. Many of the beautiful mountain lakes that dot the park today are the remnants of deep gouges dug by the inexorable force of glaciers grinding against bedrock.

The first human beings in the area were probably Indian tribes who traveled in nomadic bands more than 11 thousand years ago. In recent centuries the land was controlled by the Ute and the Arapahoe. Arrowheads, pottery, tools, and hand hammers are just some of the Indian artifacts that have been found in the park region. Some trails still in use today bear the marks of the earlier Indians who crossed this mountainous terrain.

However, the Louisiana Purchase brought ownership of this land to the US government in 1803. The first American pioneers, Colonel Stephen Long (1820), William Ashley (1825), and John C. Frémont (1843), paved the way for other adventurers. The mountains became the goal of many Easterners seeking gold in the late 1850s and early 1860s. In 1859, Joel Estes saw the Front Range and within a year had settled his family there, in Estes Park, the area now named for him (just 3 miles from the main entrance to the park). Estes loved the beauty and abundance of the area, but several years after he arrived, he became weary of the isolation and moved farther west. Within a year he was back again, unable to live without the rugged spectacle of the mountains surrounding him. He was not alone in his appreciation. An Irish earl built a huge estate in the Front Range and publicized the beauty of the area. In 1915, the region became a national park, thanks largely to the hard work and constant writing of Enos Mills, a great naturalist and author. He believed that this wonderful wilderness should be maintained, as a park, in order to preserve the clean air and lofty peaks. He once wrote: "He who feels the spell of the wild, the rhythmic melody of falling water, the echoes among the crags, the bird songs, the wind in the pines . . . is in tune with the universe."

Rocky Mountain National Park is open all year, though many facilities — and roads — within the park close during the snows, between October and May. The park is approached through the beautiful valley, Estes Park. In the town of Estes Park you can take an aerial tramway to the top of Prospect Mountain (8,900 feet) for your first, overwhelming view of the Rockies to the west. From the town, there are two possible entrances — through the Fall River entrance directly onto the Trail Ridge Road, the main driving route through the park, or through the more southerly entrance at Beaver Meadows. If it is your first visit, by all means take the slightly more roundabout route through the Beaver Meadows entrance, where you will be able to stop at the visitors center for orientation. Rangers will provide maps of the entire park. There are more than 355 miles of trails in the park, designed for amateurs as well as experienced hikers. There is a ½-mile trail at Bear Lake (at the end of the short drive south from Beaver Meadows) that circles the lake. If you are a serious hiker you may want to try the 16-mile (round-trip) route to and from the top of Longs Peak, the highest in the range. Though long, it is by no means an impossible feat; about 200 hikers a day reach the pinnacle during the summer. The view from the top is unsurpassed. Rangers at the Beaver Meadows visitors center headquarters have information on hikes, camping and campgrounds, activities, and facilities in the park.

There are two roads across the park: Trail Ridge Road, which starts at the Fall River entrance and meanders west and then south to Grand Lake (the park's western entrance point); and the shorter Fall River Road, an offshoot of the Trail Ridge that runs slightly north of the longer road. Fall River is a narrow, one-way dirt road with a 15 mph speed limit that is strictly enforced, but it offers marvelous opportunities for photographs, both of the peaks in the park, and of park wildlife. The entire park is a wildlife refuge, natural habitat of elk, deer, black bear, coyote, and the increasingly scarce mountain lion and bobcat. You may see bighorn sheep — called Rocky Mountain sheep — which are the park's emblem, and if you do any hiking, especially in spring (which comes late here), you will see the alpine wildflowers that flourish in the meadows above and below treeline. Summer is brief in the mountains — a few weeks in late July and August — and the winters are long and harsh, and above treeline flora is that of the tundra — lichen, tiny flowers, scrub trees with deep roots that can survive the freezing winters, deep snows, and rocky, barren terrain above 11,000 feet.

Trail Ridge Road, the park's main road, offers an exquisite view of Longs Peak and leads you by the Mummy Range, where you rise above the treeline and lose sight of the stands of spruce, pine, and fir. At Fall River Pass, where the road turns gradually southward, you can stop at the Alpine visitors center, where exhibitions explain the alpine tundra through which you are driving. The *Trail Ridge Store* has a snack bar for light meals. If you follow Trail Ridge Road to its end at Grand Lake you will cross the Continental Divide at Milner Pass (10,760 feet). The Divide is the weaving line that defines a basic North American watershed: all precipitation falling to the west of this ridge eventually winds up in the Pacific; to the east, it ends up in the Atlantic or the Gulf of Mexico. Farther north the Divide often appears as no more than a gentle rise in the road, but at Milner Pass, where the north fork of the Colorado River begins, you get a real sense of its significance. From here, Trail Ridge Road follows the Colorado to the western entrance and egress point of the park at Grand Lake and Lake Granby, which border the park on its southwest edge. Grand Lake has a good boat harbor. Information: Superintendent, Rocky Mountain National Park, Estes Park, CO 80517 (phone: 303-586-2371); Estes Park Area Chamber of Commerce, PO Box 3050, Estes Park, CO 80517 (phone: 800-443-7837); or Grand Lake Chamber of Commerce, Grand Lake, CO 80447 (phone: 303-627-3402).

BEST EN ROUTE

Hobby Horse Motor Lodge, Estes Park – Adjacent to a stable and golf course, with riding trails in the surrounding area. It has its own trout pool for children as well as a heated swimming pool. PO Box 40, 800 Big Thompson, Estes Park, CO 80517 (phone: 303-586-3336).

McGregor Mountain Lodge, Estes Park – At the entrance of Rocky Mountain National Park, overlooking Fall River Canyon. There are 1- and 2-room accommodations, chalet, and outdoor hot tub. 2815 Fall River Rd. MR, Estes Park, CO 80517 (phone: 303-586-3457).

Machin's Cottages in the Pines, Rocky Mountain National Park – Comfortable, well-appointed cottages that accommodate groups of up to 10 people. Cottages have completely equipped kitchens, fireplaces, and cozy living rooms. PO Box 2687, 2450 Eagle Cliff Rd., Estes Park, CO 80517 (phone: 303-586-4276).

Hawaiian Islands: A Survey

Over 5 million visitors a year are drawn to the "Aloha State" by its sunny, tropical weather and spectacular beauty. Yet many of these people never venture beyond the traditional tourist centers of Honolulu, Waikiki, Lahaina on Maui, or the Kona Coast of the Big Island. None of the major Hawaiian Islands are untouched by tourism, but several less developed sections of them genuinely reflect the original Polynesian and plantation cultures that are unique to the islands. This doesn't mean developed areas should be avoided. There is a definite allure and excitement in Honolulu and Waikiki that grab you the minute you step off the plane. Both Maui's beautiful western coast and the Kohala "Sun" Coast on the Big Island boast some of the finest resort hotels in the world, with unmatched facilities and activities. Visitors should simply keep in mind that there is another, purer Hawaii, far closer than the historic islands, just beyond the resorts. By careful planning, you can have both, and that makes Hawaii one of the most exciting vacation spots in the United States.

The state of Hawaii has a population of more than 1 million. It consists of 132 islands, some no more than bare rocks hardly above waterline, that stretch across 1,600 miles of the north Pacific Ocean from Hawaii Island in the southeast to Kure and the Midway Islands in the northwest. The largest islands are clustered together in the southeastern end of the chain, about 2,500 miles southwest of Los Angeles, and these make up what most of us think of as Hawaii: Hawaii, Kahoolawe, Maui, Lanai, Molokai, Oahu, Kauai, and Niihau.

Of the eight major islands, only six (listed below) are open to tourism. Kahoolawe, a 45-square-mile dot in the ocean between Hawaii and Maui, has been a US Navy bombing range since World War II and is uninhabited. Niihau, off Kauai's western coast, is privately owned (73 square miles) and devoted to a colony of pure Hawaiians living as did their ancestors. No tourists or journalists are allowed to visit without explicit permission from the owners.

HAWAII: Called the Big Island, with nearly twice as much land area as the rest of the chain combined (just over 4,000 square miles) and a population of 110,000. The island has two active volcanoes, Kilauea and Mauna Loa.

MAUI: A fascinating combination of sophisticated resorts (along the western coast) and rural, mountainous inlands. The 729-square-mile island is dominated by Haleakala, a 10,023-foot dormant volcano surrounded by a large national park.

LANAI: The smallest island open to tourists (140 square miles) and in the early stages of developing tourist facilities. Much of the land is devoted to growing pineapples.

MOLOKAI: Most famous for the leper colony on the isolated peninsula of Makanalua. This early colony was taken over in 1873 by Father Damien, a Belgian priest, who strove to make it a home for the people who were persecuted elsewhere. Molokai also has some of the most spectacular sea cliffs in the islands. Today it is very much the plantation island that it was in the late 1800s, although several organizations have built luxurious resorts along one coast.

OAHU: The capital island, with Honolulu and Waikiki Beach and an infinite variety of activities, sights, and nightlife. The 608-square-mile island supports four-fifths of the population of the entire state (see *Honolulu,* THE CITIES):

KAUAI: A splendid combination of plantation Hawaii and resorts, restaurants, and activities. The 533-square-mile island has some of the most beautiful country in the world, including the spectacular mountain coast of Na Pali, which is inaccessible by car. Kauai is experiencing the fastest tourist growth of all the islands.

Hawaii, Hawaii

Slightly smaller than Connecticut, Hawaii is the largest island in the Hawaiian chain — hence its nickname, the Big Island. It is also the youngest, making it a living text of how, and of what, the entire chain was formed. It is the island of active volcanoes, where periodic eruptions of Kilauea and Mauna Loa (the two living volcanoes that form Hawaii Volcanoes National Park) pour tons of lava across the countryside and into the sea. The forces at work on this island have wrought a variety of landscape that typifies the natural processes gradually shaping and reshaping the entire chain. But here, because the island is large enough to feel like a small subcontinent, you can travel from the rich earth of the sugarcane fields (and on the famous southwestern Kona Coast, America's only coffee fields) to the strange, sparse, moonlike rockbeds of lava in the park and along the verdant eastern coast. Green tropical jungle and gray, twisted rock — those are the muscle and bone that form the face of the Big Island.

Kilauea has been erupting with some measure of frequency in recent years, and Mauna Loa last erupted in 1985. Eruptions are always anticipated by the scientists living in the park, who constantly monitor the moods of the volcanoes. Hundreds of people — sightseers, photographers, journalists, and the idly curious — fly over to the island to try to catch a glimpse of eruptions when they occur. Since January 1983, a rift zone of Kilauea has erupted on and off, creating a cone called Pu'uu O'o that is now higher than Diamond Head. It is in an area of the national park inaccessible by road. In late 1986, lava reached the coast, destroying 28 homes and creating 20 additional acres for the island when it flowed into the sea. Thousands of cubic yards of lava continue to flow into the sea daily, running downhill through channels beneath the solidified crust and emerging at a temperature of about 2,000 F.

The attractions of the Big Island are manifold. It has glittering resort areas on the western side — the Kona and Kohala coasts — which offer accommodations and activities of every sort; it has many, many small communities that are untouched by commercialism and represent agricultural Hawaii as well as any in the islands; and it has the volcano areas, with a lava-torn landscape that is unique in all the world. With an airport at Hilo on the northeastern coast, and one north of Kona (Keahole Airport) on the western coast, either place can be the Hawaiian entrance or exit point for travelers.

Allow at least 4 days to see the Big Island. There are really three major areas to explore: Hilo and the northern Hamakua Coast; the Kona Coast, famous for game fishing; and Volcanoes National Park. The route described below starts at Hilo and circles counterclockwise past the Hamakua area, to the Kona Coast, and ends at the park.

HILO: The seat of Hawaii County and the fourth largest city in the state, Hilo offers an opportunity to see Hawaii's thriving orchid industry nose-to-blossom. Some nurseries are designed to give the impression of being ornate formal gardens; a few are open to the public. These include Nani Mau Gardens, 421 Makalika St.; Hilo Tropical Gardens, 1477 Kalanianaole Ave.; and Orchids of Hawaii, 2801 Kilauea Ave.

The *Lyman Mission House and Museum* (276 Haili St.), built in 1839 as the home of an early missionary, has exhibits on the ethnic makeup of the islands, as well as artifacts of early Hawaiian culture. Nearby is a very genuine, and very large, artifact: the Naha Stone, which adorns the front yard of the Hilo Library (300 Waianuenue Ave.). The stone weighs more than 2 tons. According to an ancient legend, the man who could lift the stone would become king of all the islands. The man who did so was King Kamehameha I — known to history as Kamehameha the Great because he did indeed conquer all the islands (more with the help of cannon than brute strength). Be sure to tour Banyan Drive, named for its numerous banyan trees, which were planted by celebrities visiting the island. Two of Banyan's parks worth visiting are Liliuokalani Gardens (adjacent to *Uncle Billy's Hilo Bay* hotel), a 30-acre park filled with ornamental stone structures that were gifts from Japan; and the Bicentennial Park, dedicated in 1976 to mark America's 200th birthday. At the end of Banyan Drive is the Suisan Fish Market, where fishermen auction their morning catch weekdays at 7:30 AM. Beyond the market on Pauahi Street, the Wailoa Cultural and Visitor Information Center offers free art exhibitions. While in the neighborhood, stroll down Keawe Street, where you'll find a number of pleasant shops and restaurants.

HAMAKUA COAST: North along Rte. 19 the views are staggering. Atop high pali (cliffs), the road looks over the windward coast and the not-very-peaceful Pacific Ocean. This road was constructed to accommodate nature, not man, and you will soon develop a rhythm in your driving as you curve, plunge, curve, and climb around waterfalls and valleys. All along the route you will see state Hawaiian Warrior signs that indicate scenic overviews. Don't fail to stop. When Hawaiians think a view is good enough to warrant special note, mainlanders had better take them at their word. Off the highway at the small village of Honomu is Akaka State Park, with two of the most beautiful waterfalls on the island. The highest is Akaka Falls itself — a 442-foot ribbon of water that plunges daintily down a jungle cliff; the other is Kahuna Falls, which drops 400 feet. Nearby are jungle walks among lush, if eerie, plants. Laupahoehoe Point — a small "leaf of lava" that pushes into the brutal, angry Pacific — is an excellent spot for picnicking. The point is marked by a Warrior sign, and you must drive from the road down a small, winding road to the point itself. There the picnic area is bathed in a fine sea spray, and you can watch the sometimes terrifying fury of the sea smashing against the rocks. In 1946, a school with 20 children and 3 teachers inside was lost to the sea when a giant tidal wave washed over the point. A monument commemorates the spot.

The end point of the northward Rte. 19 road is Waipio Valley, where Rte. 19 joins Rte. 25, the only navigable point through the Kohala Mountains. The largest valley on the Big Island, Waipio was once the home of the kings of old Hawaii — Kamehameha, Liloa, and Umi. Here there is a lookout tower with fine views of the northeastern end of the island, and drivers with four-wheel vehicles who offer tours through the rough roads of the valley.

PUUKOHOLA HEIAU NATIONAL HISTORIC SITE: Where Rte. 19 crosses the base of the Kohala Mountains and turns south to follow Hawaii's eastern coast stands this historic site, an ancient temple (approximately 15th century) and altar that young King Kamehameha I rebuilt in 1791 and dedicated to a god of war. Behind this act of piety was cold and cunning ambition. He invited his chief island rival to the dedication cermony and there killed him. With that act Kamehameha initiated his drive to conquer not just the island of Hawaii but all the major islands in the chain. Just down the road from the heiau lies perhaps the most elegant strand of beachfront resorts in Hawaii — the Kohala Coast's *Westin Mauna Kea, Mauna Lani,* and the *Hyatt Regency.* Beyond these is Puako, a small village with some of the best examples of Hawaiian petroglyphs. At Puako, Rte. 19 becomes the Queen Kaahumanu Highway, cutting across a lava desert and skirting a number of beautiful, and as yet relatively undeveloped, beaches.

KAILUA-KONA: The major town on the Kona Coast and the starting point of a series of resorts that stretches to Keauhou. Most of the town's contemporary attractions — hotels, shops, restaurants, and bars — are on Alii Drive. There, also, is Hulihee Palace, a summer resort built in 1837 for the Hawaiian royal family that today houses a museum of furnishings and memorabilia of the period. Directly across the street is the Mokuaikaua Church, the first Christian church in the Hawaiian Islands, built in 1836. Worth visiting on the grounds of the *King Kamehameha* hotel near Kailua Pier is the restored Kamakahonu compound — headquarters of King Kamehameha the Great, who died here in 1819 — now a national monument. Also part of the compound is Ahu'ena Heiau, a former temple that was the seat of Hawaiian government during the final 7 years of Kamehameha's reign. Kailua-Kona is a major center for deep-sea fishing along the Kona Coast (one of the best big-game fishing grounds in the world), and there are numerous charter operations, most of them based at Honokohau Harbor between the town and Keahole Airport.

KEALAKEKUA BAY: Take the Kuakini Highway (Rte. 11) south from Kona through the coffee producing uplands to Kealakekua, famed as the site where British Captain James Cook was killed in 1779. Cook was the first Western explorer to discover the Hawaiian Islands (which he called the Sandwich Islands) when he sailed into Kauai's Waimea Bay in 1778 in search of fresh water. He was greeted joyfully by the Hawaiians, who regarded him as something of a god and who recognized his courage and mastery of the sea. Cook's expedition stayed for only a few weeks, but returned in January 1779 to Kealakekua Bay on the Big Island. Here too he was accorded great respect. On February 4, 1779, Cook and his crew set sail but ran into a storm that damaged one ship and forced them to go back. This lapse in godliness, as well as the new demands for food and supplies, strained relations between the islanders and Cook, and eventually a battle erupted, ending with Cook's death. It has become legend that the islanders dismembered and ate Cook, but this is not true. They gave him a hero's burial, which involved dismemberment and special burial in the earth. The spot where Cook fell is marked by a monument, and today the bay is a marine preserve noted for its excellent snorkeling.

CITY OF REFUGE NATIONAL HISTORICAL PARK: From Highway 11, follow Rte. 160 east to Pu'uhonua O Honaunau — the City of Refuge. This ancient and sacred area was once a sanctuary for Hawaiian criminals. Fugitives had to swim the perilous Honaunau Bay to reach the City of Refuge. Once there, they were entitled to pardons from the resident priest and could then return home, free from stigma and the threat of death. Today visitors can explore this bit of antiquity, watch craftsmen carve canoes with the same tools and methods used by early Hawaiians, and marvel at the perfect remains of parts of the 6-foot-thick walls built of lava rock and locked in place without mortar, and at the royal palace grounds, heiaus, dwellings, and formidable tikis, handcrafted copies of the 16th-century originals. Brochures are available at the visitors center.

HAWAII VOLCANOES NATIONAL PARK: Back on Highway 11, head south to the island's volcano area. When the Big Island's Kilauea, 4,400 feet and 11 miles in circumference, actually erupts, people flock from around the world to watch. The eruption series that started in 1983, however, is in areas inaccessible by road. Mauna Loa, 13,677 feet, is also in the park, which is dedicated to collecting and disseminating information on volcanic phenomena. The visitors center (about 2 miles inside the park's boundaries) has volumes of material on the effects of these two volcanoes as well as information on park activities — camping and hiking within Kilauea's crater, ranger-led hikes, special events. The park service has a new $3.5-million observatory, with working seismological equipment in the adjacent building (now the *Thomas A. Jagger Museum*). At *Volcano House* (the park's inn and restaurant, just across from the visitors center) you can spend the night on the edge of Kilauea crater and have a box lunch packed for a day's hike the next morning. Information: Superintendent, Hawaii Volcanoes National Park, PO Box 52, Hawaii National Park, HI 96718 (phone: 808-967-7311).

KALAPANA: Most visitors return to Hilo via the 30-mile route on Highway 11, but others may prefer a 90-mile circular route that follows the coast. Chain of Craters Road connects to Highway 130, leading from Volcanoes National Park to Kalapana — and perhaps the most intriguing beach in all Hawaii. Its rare black sands resulted from molten lava meeting the cold Pacific. Highway 130 will take you past macadamia orchards to the town of Kea'au, or take Highway 137 to Mackenzie State Park. Turn on Highway 132 to visit Pohoiki and its new Geothermal Visitors Center. Down the road lies Lava Tree State Park and then Pahoa, with its anthurium farms and papaya orchards.

BEST EN ROUTE

Hyatt Regency Waikoloa, Kohala – Probably the most lavish property in all Hawaii, this new self-contained resort spreads along 62 acres on the sunny Kohala Coast. It features 1,244 rooms, 7 restaurants, 12 lounges, 4 swimming pools, 3 championship golf courses, tennis courts, horseback riding facilities, a spa, shops, and more. 1 Waikoloa Beach Dr., Kohala Coast, HI 96743 (phone: 808-665-1234 or 800-228-9000).

Westin Mauna Kea, Kohala – This is as close to paradise as most of us will ever get. A valuable art collection is displayed throughout the main rooms and halls for all to touch and appreciate; gardens delight the eye at every turn. It has 3 fine dining rooms, very handsomely decorated guestrooms, and a Robert Trent Jones, Sr. golf course with a world-famous water hole over the crashing Pacific. Tennis, beach, horseback riding, and pool. See also *Resort Hotels,* DIVERSIONS. PO Box 218, Kohala Coast, Hawaii, HI 96743 (phone: 808-882-7222 or 800-228-3000).

Kona Village Resort, Kona Coast – Some 100 bungalows dot the 65-acre expanse of this village, each designed and decorated in the style of one of the islands of the South Pacific. Facilities include tennis courts, water sports, sailing. The daily rate includes breakfast, lunch, and dinner. PO Box 1299, Kaupulehu-Kona, Hawaii, HI 96745 (phone: 808-325-5555 or 800-367-5290).

Volcano House, Hawaii Volcanoes National Park – This is the first place to fill up when scientists at the observatory predict a major eruption. The gracious, comfortable inn and restaurant requires reservations — even during periods of quiet. Surely it must be one of the few hotels in Hawaii that routinely lights a cozy fire in the evenings. Hawaii Volcanoes National Park, HI 96718 (phone: 808-967-7321).

Kauai, Hawaii

Kauai is a spectacular island by any standards: oldest in the archipelago — first formed, and, therefore, first to cool — most lush, verdant, and rich with soil, a land where anything will grow. Papaya, mango, coconut, hundreds of varieties of exotic plants and orchids, bougainvillea and cactus, litchi, banana trees, mimosa — an endless list. And every growing edible — as well as almost every other species — was brought by someone: the first Hawaiians, the missionaries, Western explorers, the Japanese, mainland visitors. Without human help, the islands get only one new species of plant every 10,000 years.

On the windward side, everything is green. The razor-sharp pinnacles of the volcanic fissures along Na Pali coast, the spectacular rock chasms that spill down the windward side of the island into dense jungle valleys, pouring forth myriad waterfalls, are covered with a light down of lichen. And that which is not green is red — the ferrous red of iron-permeated soil, further evidence (if any were needed) of the now utterly extinct volcanoes that heaved this island thousands of feet from the sea bed.

Even the misconceptions that visitors carry to the island are dominated by geography. Kauai is known as one of the wettest spots on earth. But, in fact, it rains only 60 to 80 inches a year on the northern — wetter and windward — side of the island; only 15 to 20 inches a year leeward. Way up on Mt. Waialeale (Why-ali-ali), it rains some 500 inches a year, and thus the source of Kauai's reputation for less than favorable weather. But Waialeale is in the middle of the island, 5,000 feet up, and it actually acts as a rain barrier for the southern half of Kauai. Windward it is wet, especially in winter, but spring and summer bring good vacation weather to the entire island.

LIHUE: By necessity most vacationers begin their visit to Kauai here, the island's commercial center and the site of its main airport (a 20-minute flight from Oahu). Whether coming for a week (advised) or a day (popular but a pity), Lihue is the point of arrival and offers the first glimpse of the marriage of sugarcane and tourism that characterizes Kauai right now. Best about Lihue is its location on Kauai's eastern coast, midway on the road that circles the island (Kauai is a slightly dented and bashed circle, 32 miles across; the road would make a complete circle around the island except for the interruption of the impassable Na Pali Cliffs).

The newest attraction in Lihue is Kilohana, a legendary plantation estate and former home of Gaylord Wilcox. Built in the 1930s, this must-see grand estate features horse-drawn carriage rides throughout its lush gardens, working farm, and old plantation camp; shops selling products of the islands; and two restaurants (open daily). Also worth seeing in Lihue is the *Kauai Museum,* with exhibits of Kauai's flora and fauna, island history, and missionary memorabilia. Just north of town is Wailua State Park and the Fern Grotto, a large, secluded cave with lush tropical foliage. Guided boat tours are available to this enchanting spot, a popular site for weddings.

Once beyond Lihue, you plunge almost instantly into old Hawaii. The towns and villages still live in the grip of the two monoliths of island life, the missionary church and the plantation. Little towns like Hanapepe (which means "working babies"), the sugar village of Kaumakani, and Makaweli are part of a genuine frontier plantation culture. Along this south and west side of Kauai, more people speak Hawaiian than in any other district in the state. Hanapepe's main street was used for the TV miniseries "The Thornbirds." Hawaiian Salt Pans and Salt Pond Park lie near the west end of town. Nearing the east side of Waimea, you'll also come upon the remains of the Russian Fort, built in 1817 by a German physician who dreamed of taking over the island for the Russians. Waimea, the site where Captain James Cook discovered the Sandwich Islands, has a statue of Cook and numerous buildings listed in the National Register of Historic Places.

Highway 550 leads through Waimea Canyon (the Grand Canyon of the Pacific), a "must see," and eventually ends at Kokee State Park — quite literally perched over a 1,000-foot drop into the westernmost valley of Na Pali. That is the final destination of the drive south (perhaps a whole 19 miles from Lihue), but along the way there is much to see.

POIPU BEACH: Its waters (like those along most of the island's beaches) are shallow a long way out and subject to fits of rock along the sea floor where sand ought to be, but it's still a lovely beach for swimming and sunning. (All island beaches, even those of the posh resorts, are public, open, and free.) Poipu Beach has two of the best posh resorts on the island, the *Stouffer Waiohai* and *Kiahuna.* The road to Poipu travels through a tunnel of trees, taking you back 150 years to Old Koloa Town, Hawaii's first sugar plantation town, now authentically restored and featuring modern shops, restaurants, and services. Nearby, at Koloa Baseball Field, a Sunshine Market (Mondays only, from noon to 3 PM) gives visitors the opportunity to meet local farmers and purchase vegetables and fruits seldom seen on the mainland.

SPOUTING HORN: An outjutting of volcanic rock, so eaten by the sea that when a strong roller comes in, the sea water spurts through a hole 10 to 15 feet into the air; a sad sigh whispers through this natural pneumatic tube with each spout. It provides a good illustration of the power the sugarcane companies have traditionally held on Kauai. Years ago, the spout shot as high as 80 feet into the air, high enough that salt spray was flung across the cane fields — perhaps 200 yards away — killing patches of cane. The plantation managers dynamited the horn, widening the hole so that the spout stayed within a reasonable height. Now the horn is protected by the state.

WAIMEA CANYON: Nowhere on the island are you so close to the staggering power of the earth itself as when peering into the depths of this 3,600-foot canyon, 10 miles long. The original Hawaiians believed this was the work of Pele, goddess of fire. It hardly makes more sense to try to imagine the force necessary to have left these huge wedges of mountain hanging just so; to have honed these cliffs to such sharp precision; to have etched such regular and undeviating patterns across miles and miles of rock. When a helicopter swings across the canyon, hanging 1,000 feet or so above the Waimea River at the bottom of the ravine and whizzing along the length of the valley, you can suffer vertigo just watching.

KOKEE STATE PARK: The 4,345-acre park has a lovely, tiny museum, a large picnic area, a restaurant (hamburgers and other sandwiches), and a dozen comfortable cabins for about $25 a day (make reservations at least 3 months in advance, *Kokee Lodge,* PO Box 819, Waimea, Kauai, HI 96796; phone: 808-335-6061). It's a good place to stop after Waimea Canyon and before going the few miles more to the road's end at Na Pali Lookout. It is also the starting point of miles of nature walks and hiking trails that will be irresistible to botanists and backpackers.

NA PALI COAST: The highlight of any trip to Kauai. Here the windward side of the island breaks into a series of splendid, jagged, jungle valleys thousands of feet deep, like patterns cut into fine crystal. They stretch from the mountains to the sea and are accessible only by foot (and some not even by foot), air, or sea. Numerous legends and superstitions surround Na Pali. It was here that an entire tribe of Hawaiians disap-

peared forever several centuries ago. And here that the legendary Menehune —
a race of dwarfs credited with building much of the stonework on the island —
are said to have hidden when they mysteriously disappeared. Some islanders believe
they still live in Na Pali. (Lest you don't quite believe in the existence of the Menehune,
Captain James Cook, who landed here in 1778, mentions in his report to the British
Admiralty seeing a group of very light-skinned, diminutive women.) Late last century,
a leper named Koolau fought off the entire state militia by guerrilla warfare waged from
the jungles of Na Pali. He refused to go to the leper colony on Molokai and took his
family into the depths of the jungle, where presumably they lived and died.

From the lookout 4,000 feet above the ocean, is a magnificent view down Kalalau
Valley to the water. There are some hiking trails into Na Pali from the eastern side of
the island, but most frequent access is from the other side, where Kauai's main, circular
road ends at Hanalei and Haena. From there you can hike to beaches 2, 6, or 10 miles
along the coast, following wave upon wave of valley. Or take the easy way out and hire
a helicopter from Lihue or Princeville (companies charge about $95 and up for an
hour's ride) to spin you through the valleys.

HANALEI: *South Pacific* was filmed here, and a marvelous old plantation town it is.
The town has a thrown-together, informal museum, the *Hanalei,* but of more interest
is Waioli Mission House, built in 1846 and filled with period furnishings. It's a piece
of genuine New England Hawaii. There's also good scuba and snorkeling in the area.

From Hanalei, a weaving, mountainous road takes travelers along spectacular sea-
cliffs. At Lumahai Beach, you can park and walk down a steep path to the beach, rated
as one of the top 10 in the world by the TV show "Lifestyles of the Rich and Famous."
Farther on, the road ends at Haena State Park, a nice swimming beach when there is
no surf.

BEST EN ROUTE

Stouffer Waiohai, Poipu Beach – This super-deluxe resort is sleek and handsome
and thoroughly devoted to pampering its guests. Bedrooms are spacious, done in
fresh, cool colors and outfitted with well-stocked wet bars and luxurious dressing
rooms. An early morning dip in one of its 3 swimming pools or a stroll along its
lovely curve of sandy beach should be followed by breakfast on your lanai overlooking the sea; ask for the house specialty — macadamia nut muffins. PO Box
174, Koloa, HI 96756 (phone: 808-742-9511 or 800-468-3571).

Sheraton Mirage Princeville, Hanalei Bay – Overlooking the bay — perhaps the
most spectacular view in Hawaii — this truly grand hotel is sheer elegance, with
both plantation grandeur and colonial charm. It has 300 luxurious rooms and
suites; 3 fine restaurants; a pool and secluded beach; golf, tennis, and horseback
riding. Hanalei Bay (phone: 808-826-9644 or 800-334-8484).

Coco Palms Resort, Wailua – Set in a 45-acre coconut grove, this 390-room hotel
with an emphasis on Hawaiiana is very much a tradition. It has a torch lighting
ceremony, thatched cottages, lagoons, museum, chapel (for weddings), petting
zoo, and 10 tennis courts. PO Box 631, Lihue, Kauai, HI 96766 (phone: 808-822-
4921 or 800-542-2626).

Westin Kauai, Kalapaki Beach – This redo and expansion of the former *Kauai
Surf* is like Disneyland both inside and out. Guests are transported by horse-
drawn carriages along a scenic 10-mile path through 800 acres of lush gardens
and by canolas (outrigger canoe–gondola hybrids) and mahogany launches
through the lagoons, whose small islands hold kangaroos, wallabies, and monkeys. Also featured: Hawaii's largest swimming pool, with a central island; 5
Jacuzzis; 8 tennis courts; two 18-hole golf courses designed by Jack Nicklaus; a
health spa; a private beach; 17 restaurants/lounges; over 90 shops and boutiques;

and over $2.5 million in art. Kalapaki Beach, Lihue, Kauai, HI 96766 (phone: 808-526-4111 or 800-228-3000).

Maui, Hawaii

The second largest island in the Hawaiian chain has a very strange shape, an even more interesting history, and topography that accounts for some of the most beautiful country in the islands. Given only a day or two, you will undoubtedly end up on the beaches of West Maui, where beautiful hotels and condominiums stretch from Kaanapali to Kapalua, or on the resort strip farther south, from Kihei to Wailea. You could do worse. But with just a couple more days, and a car to help negotiate the long — for the islands — distances between stops, you can add to that the lush valleys around Wailuku and Kahului and the heights of Haleakala National Park. The result would be almost a small survey of Hawaii's geologic and cultural history — a dormant volcano; verdant, fertile valleys devoted to cane and pineapples; and a west coast village that was a standard stop on the whaling route more than 150 years ago, when missionaries and New England whalers literally fought for the hearts and minds of the Hawaiian people.

Maui has three distinct geographic areas. Picture the island in the form of a steer's head facing east. West Maui, with the gold coast strip of hotels and beach, and the well-preserved whaling town of Lahaina form the ear of this steer. Inland, West Maui is mountainous, wild, and, in part at least, unexplored. Where the ear joins the head, at Wailuku and Kahului, the mountains break and there is much flat and fertile farmland. To the east the island rises steadily along the slopes of dormant Mt. Haleakala, its summit 10,023 feet above the sea. At the snout of the hypothetical steer is the village of Hana.

Most tourists begin their visit to Maui at Kahului airport (a 20-minute jet flight from Oahu) and from there head west for Lahaina and the resorts beyond, south for Kihei and Wailea, or east on Rte. 37 to Haleakala.

LAHAINA: The capital of the Hawaiian islands from 1795 until 1843, when King Kamehameha III moved the court to Honolulu. Of far greater impact on the town and its people were the whaling ships, which made Lahaina a regular stop from the early 1800s until petroleum replaced whale oil as a source of light at the end of the century. For the 80 or 90 years of the whaling period, life was constant turmoil. Missionaries saved souls and sailors seduced and drank, and in general the Hawaiians were harassed and harangued on all sides. A great deal of the original whaling town still exists, in part due to the hard work of Lahaina's contemporary citizens, who have spent a good part of recent years in restoration work. An interesting place to visit is *Baldwin House Museum,* the home of the medical missionary Dr. Dwight Baldwin in the mid-19th century. In the vicinity is a huge, spreading banyan tree (in the town square near Front St.). It was planted in 1873 to commemorate 50 years of missionary work on the island, and it stands still strong and hale today. Across the street from the tree is the town's most famous manmade landmark, the *Pioneer Inn,* an old rake of a hotel that opened at the turn of the century; in the harbor in front is the *Carthaginian II,* a ship of recent vintage true-rigged like a brig of the whaling era. Visit anytime during the winter months, when the annual migration of humpback whales is under way, and enjoy a wide choice of whale watching cruises. The whales breed in Hawaiian waters in the winter (in summer they live much farther north, in Arctic seas), and standing on the dock you can see them cavorting between Maui and Lanai from December through April.

The town's newest attraction is the Lahaina Cannery, built on the site of an old pineapple cannery and featuring shops and restaurants with a cannery theme. Here also is the Lahaina, Kaanapali & Pacific Railroad ("the sugarcane train"), Hawaii's only passenger train service; vintage steam engines run along 6 miles of track stretching between Lahaina and Kaanapali Beach Resort.

KAANAPALI TO NAPILI: This 4-mile stretch of beach has been called "a sort of rarefied Waikiki." Even "rarefied" does it a disservice. If the beach is not quite so spectacular as Waikiki, the resorts that line it have been far more sensitively and sensibly developed than those that pile up like a freeway crash along Honolulu's pride. The beach is neatly divided by a huge outcropping of black volcanic rock, called Black Rock in English and Kekaa in Hawaiian. At the base of this beauty is the *Sheraton Maui.* Six other hotels and an equal number of condominium complexes make up the *Kaanapali Beach Resort,* which also includes the famous *Royal Kaanapali Golf Courses* (two of eight 18-hole courses on the island) and *Whalers Village.* The full impact of the whaling industry on Maui is described in detail in a museum at the shopping center, where there are whale exhibits, including a huge skeleton at the Whalers Village entrance.

KAPALUA: Beyond Kaanapali, the coast of West Maui is almost one uninterrupted stretch of holiday condominiums to the northwest tip of the island. Two particularly beautiful beaches can be found here, the beach at Napili Bay and Kapalua Bay, perhaps the most perfect crescent beach on the island. Kapalua Bay is surrounded by the exquisite scenery of another of Maui's planned resort developments, Kapalua, set on panoramic acreage formerly used to grow pineapples. *Kapalua Bay Hotel,* condominium communities, 2 Arnold Palmer golf courses, 10 tennis courts, and a small shopping center are the central features of the resort.

WAILUKU: Another early Maui city that has survived — and thrived — in the 20th century. On Maui's northern coast, close to Kahului and its airport, Wailuku has its own remnants of early Hawaii. A staunch emblem of Maui's missionary past is Kaahumanu Church (Rte. 30), the first version of which was built in 1832 (the present structure dates to 1876). It is a simple building that reflects much of the spirit and the form of early church work here and throughout the islands. Wailuku is also a good place to make forays to Iao Valley, in the mountains of inland West Maui. Along the way on Rte. 32 is the *Maui Historical Society Museum,* with exhibitions on all aspects of Maui history. It is a good place to stop before continuing to the road's end a few miles farther west, at Iao Valley's Kepaniwai Park, which pays tribute to Maui's ethnic groups. The park also contains the dramatic Iao Needle — a lava pinnacle rising 2,250 feet from the valley floor. Pegged as "the Yosemite of the Pacific" by Mark Twain, the park is also the approximate point where King Kamehameha the Great (grandfather of the King Kamehameha who moved the royal court from Maui to Oahu) finally trapped his Mauian enemies in the basin of Iao Valley and decimated them, assuring the loyalty of all the major islands in the chain. This happened in the 1790s, and the carnage was so great that the stream that runs through the valley was named Wailuku, "Bloody River."

Another attraction near Wailuku is Maui Tropical Plantation, 60 acres of Hawaiian agriculture including bananas, mangoes, papayas, ginger, pineapples, sugar, avocados, and macadamia nuts. The visitors center features a Hawaiian marketplace as well as a restaurant, nursery, and display pavilion.

KIHEI, WAILEA, AND MAKENA: The southwestern coast of Maui is on the dry leeward side of Haleakala. Six miles of the coast are known as Kihei — and better known as "sunny" Kihei because of the sparse average annual rainfall. Kihei is almost one long strip of golden beach from beginning to end, and not too many years ago the land fronting the beach — the same land that is now chockablock with low- and high-rise condominiums — was virtually virgin territory. So while Kihei has its beach to recommend it, it is often pointed to as a worst-case example of unchecked development, while the planned resort of *Wailea,* just south, is considered a model of the way to go. Wailea, too, has glorious beaches, but they are backed by resort property irrigated to the ultimate in verdure, and the two 18-hole golf courses, a 14-court tennis center (with 3 grass courts), shopping center, three condominium villages, and two first class hotels complement rather than violate the landscape. South of Wailea, *Makena Resort* has an 18-hole golf course and the luxury 300-room *Maui Prince*.

HALEAKALA NATIONAL PARK: "The House of the Sun" — Mt. Haleakala — dominates the entire eastern half of Maui. The approaches from the west are a peaceful contrast to the tourist frenzy of the coastal resort areas. Here is countryside virtually untouched by commercialism, a series of pastoral scenes that could represent almost any mountainous region in the world. Because of the mountain, Maui enjoys a unique climate system, hot on the coasts, fertile and moist on the flat plains between West Maui and the mountain, and progressively cooler weather as the altitudes increase. Some 10,000 feet high, Haleakala is the largest dormant volcano in the world. Its crater is an immense 19-square-mile hole 3,000 feet deep, honeycombed with trails and devoted to a national park. On the way to the park's entrance you will pass (on Rte. 377) the Kula Botanical Gardens, where experts will explain how Maui's unique climate is used to grow simple garden vegetables (the best in the islands) beside exotic tropical orchids. Also in the area is Tedeschi Vineyard, on the 18,000-acre Ul'upalakua Ranch, which dates to the 1850s. A tasting room (open daily) is in the ranch's 19th-century jailhouse.

Park headquarters, at about 7,000 feet, is a necessary stop for information on campgrounds, the mountain, and activities like horseback riding, hiking, and renting simple cabins in the crater maintained by the National Park Service. Cabin rental can be reserved only through a lottery. Three months before your visit, send your name and address with your date preference to Haleakala National Park, PO Box 369, Makawao, HI 96768; you will be notified if you are selected. Camping is strictly controlled; it is restricted to three 12-person cabins and two campgrounds, with a 3-day maximum stay. Early morning and late afternoon are the best times for visiting the crater, since there's less chance of cloudiness. No matter how warm it may be at the base of Haleakala, you will need some light wrap at the summit, and heavier clothing if you go at sunrise (a popular excursion).

The view from the top is spectacular. From there you see West Maui, and the neighboring islands of Hawaii, Lanai, Molokai, and Oahu. It was from the summit of Haleakala that Maui the god lassoed the sun to force him to make his daily trip across the sky more slowly. And dawn atop the mountain is one of the finest experiences a traveler can behold.

The park extends to Maui's eastern coast in a single 8-mile strip. The area encompasses a stretch of ecologically delicate jungle, where the rangers are struggling to maintain an environment that protects and encourages the tropical growths. The area also includes the Seven Sacred Pools, a series of pools and streams that spill into one another like a pyramid of champagne glasses filled to overflowing. This eastern area of the park, which encompasses the Kipahulu Valley, can be reached by circling East Maui on the Hana Highway, a scenic route that is in itself one of the island's sightseeing attractions. The road is rough, winding, and very narrow — with an estimated 617 curves and 56 bridges — which is why the 52-mile drive takes about 3 to 4 hours and why it's difficult to stop to enjoy the views. But there are three lookout points along the way before it ends in Hana, a tiny village populated mainly by part-Hawaiians who work on the Hana Ranch and by out-of-town celebrities seeking seclusion. Beyond

Hana, another 10 miles of rutted road leads to the park again, to where the lowest of the Seven Pools spills into the sea. Information: Superintendent, Haleakala National Park, PO Box 369, Makawao, Maui, HI 96768 (phone: 808-572-9306; for recorded weather information, 808-572-7749; for recorded cabin and hiking information, 808-572-9177).

BEST EN ROUTE

Stouffer Wailea Beach Resort, Wailea Beach – This beachfront resort features 350 rooms, 2 championship 18-hole golf courses, 14 tennis courts (3 grass), and a 15-acre tropical garden with waterfalls, ponds, and streams surrounding a swimming pool and 4 whirlpool baths. There are also 3 restaurants and 2 lounges. 3500 Wailea Alanui Dr., Wailea, HI 96753 (phone: 808-879-4900 or 800-992-4532).

Hyatt Regency Maui, Kaanapali – Not just a hotel but a sightseeing attraction. Besides the 815 elegant rooms in three 7- to 9-story towers, the hotel's 20 landscaped acres contain tropical gardens, waterfalls, and Maui's largest swimming pool, fed by a 130-foot water slide. The hotel also boasts $2 million worth of Asian and Pacific art and a staff ornithologist to care for the many exotic birds on the property. 200 Nohea Kai Dr., Lahaina, HI 06761 (phone: 808-661-1234 or 800-228-9000).

Hana-Maui, Hana – This intimate hotel spreads across 50 acres on the island's far east coast; the only distractions from the perfectly blue Pacific are tennis courts, riding stables, and a pool. It recently completed a remodeling and expansion project; all 82 rooms have been renovated. Rates include all meals and activities. PO Box 8, Hana, HI 96713 (phone: 808-248-8211 or 800-321-HANA).

Kapalua Bay Resort, Kapalua – Beautifully situated on a privately owned 23,000-acre pineapple plantation on the northwest coast of Maui, the resort offers 327 hotel and villa units, two 18-hole Arnold Palmer championship golf courses, 10 tennis courts, pools, secluded beaches, water sports, 5 distinctive restaurants, and posh boutiques. One Bay Dr., Kapalua, HI 96761 (phone: 808-669-5656 or 800-367-8000).

Molokai, Hawaii

There is a distinct hierarchy of development among the Hawaiian islands, and once you understand the forces at work it is a pretty accurate measure of the state of the local agricultural economy. Most of the major islands — Maui, Hawaii, Kauai, Molokai — have been dependent on agriculture at one time or another during this century. And time and again that industry has failed, forcing the islands, one after another, to develop adequate tourist facilities to replace the lost farming income. It has happened most recently on Kauai, which for years had a thriving sugarcane industry, with plantations of thousands and thousands of acres. In the last decade, however, the island has repeatedly lost business to the Far East, where cane is produced at perhaps one-tenth the cost (primarily because of low labor costs). And so Kauai began developing tourist facilities — very cautiously and with great consideration — to replace the vacuum left by sugarcane.

All this is happening right now on Molokai. Throughout the 19th-century

Molokai was known as "the Forgotten Island." Then, early in the 20th century, pineapples were introduced and the island began a gradual renaissance; Dole and Del Monte bought large chunks of the island, and people returned to Molokai for pineapple jobs. But as in the case of sugarcane on Kauai, impossibly cheap labor in the Far East has meant that island pineapples are simply too expensive, and Dole and Del Monte ceased operations in 1975 and 1983, respectively.

Right now Molokai has only one full-fledged resort, the *Kaluakoi,* though the *Molokai* hotel, with a Polynesian flavor and convenient location in Kaunakakai, is a classy alternative. More are on the drawing boards, but for the time being the island seems almost in a state of suspension, awaiting the future. The sense of quiet and solitude that has always characterized it has never been more marked than it is right now. In some places — the closed Dole Pineapple plantation town — there is an eerie sense of history just passed, of an era having closed so recently that it still vibrates in the air; yet elsewhere on the island this solitude is splendid and serene — for example, along the jagged, wild, inaccessible cliffs east of Makanalua Peninsula, or at the many coves and beaches that swimmers have entirely to themselves for hours on end. It is certainly an island that can be visited on a day trip from Oahu; the visitor flies either to Molokai Airport (well outside the town of Kaunakakai) to see the whole island or to Kalaupapa to visit the historical site and colony on the Makanalua Peninsula. But Molokai has wild roads and beautiful vistas as yet unmapped on any standard tourist itinerary, and a 2- or 3-day visit will offer a feeling of Hawaii not available on any of the more developed islands.

KAUNAKAKAI: Eight miles east of Hoolehua Airport, through which most tourists enter Molokai, is the island's main town of Kaunakakai. It may surprise you. With its main street and the wooden façade of its stores, it looks remarkably like a western frontier town. There is a distinct "cowboy" atmosphere about it typical of many towns throughout the islands. In the case of Kaunakakai, this atmosphere is more a reflection of the general character of Molokai towns than its proximity to the island's huge Puu O Huko Ranch. With a population of less than 1,000, the town has few tourist facilities, but much about it speaks of the island's recent history. You will note, for example, the fine, long wharf — extending a half mile into the sea — which is almost empty today. It was built to accommodate the huge barges on which pineapples were shipped for processing. Today little work is done on it.

PAPOHAKU BEACH: This is the west coast site of Kaluakoi resort, with nearly 600 hotel rooms and condominium units in 7 properties. The coast tends to be rocky, with occasional underwater coral reefs that can be an unpleasant surprise for swimmers. The beach is better for sunning than swimming. Adjacent to Kaluakoi is the 2,000-acre Molokai Ranch, where some 500 animals roam for viewing. On the way to Papohaku, along Rte. 46, you will pass the former Dole plantation town of Maunaloa, where artists and craftspeople have settled. It is well worth a look as a living museum of contemporary company towns in Hawaii.

PALAAU STATE PARK: Along Molokai's northern coast, the park overlooks Makanalua Peninsula and the Kalaupapa settlement. The peninsula is 2,000 feet below the park, at the base of a series of jagged, wild cliffs that become inaccessible farther along the eastern coastline. The present view is not the original overlook. This can be found at the beginning of the Jack London Trail (also in the park), the tortuous switchback trail, navigable by foot or mule only, that leads from the overlook to the peninsula below, a trip of several hours.

HALAWA VALLEY: Filling Molokai's northeastern end. The valley is accessible only by Rte. 45, which begins in Kaunakakai and follows the island's coast east and north. At least a half-day's excursion from the airport, it offers a real sense of Molokai today — and the best views of the magnificent cliffs at road's end. (The road, by the way, becomes increasingly narrower as it heads north, twisting and turning along the mountains that rise like a ship's prow along the island's northern coast.) Immediately outside Kaunakakai on Rte. 45 are a number of ancient fish ponds. Dating as far back as the 15th century, they were built as fattening-up farms for the fish trapped inside, assuring the availability of a fresh fish meal whenever the royal whim desired one. All the major islands have ruins of these royal fish ponds, but the ones on Molokai are in the best state of preservation and are therefore worth a stop.

At the end of Rte. 45 is deserted Halawa Valley. Once a thriving community valley patchworked with taro farms, in 1946 the warnings of the giant tidal wave (tsunami) forced an evacuation from the valley. No one returned. The valley remains a tranquil, very tropical place popular with hikers and nature lovers. It's 4½ miles long, and a 2-hour hike that isn't too difficult leads to Moaula and Hipuapua Falls, which cascade 250 feet down into the head of the valley. The freshwater pool at Moaula Falls is cool but safe for swimming.

KALAUPAPA: In 1866 the entire Makanalua Peninsula was declared a leper colony by royal decree, and sufferers throughout the islands were forced to come here. Kalaupapa's isolation acted as a perfect buffer, protecting the healthy islanders from the disease they feared and shunned. The suffering inflicted on victims of the disease was intense: No provisions were made for food, shelter, clothing, or the basic necessities of life. Lepers were peremptorily dumped on the island and left to die (often with whichever family members consented to care for them in exile). In 1873 a Belgian priest, Father Damien Joseph de Veuster, chose to join the lepers, and for the next 16 years he labored to provide shelter and food for them and to build a living community where only disease and despair had ruled human relations. In 1889 he died of leprosy, but he left behind a real community. Today the peninsula is under the auspices of the Hawaii State Department of Health, and about 100 persons live here. It is their peninsula, but visitors are welcome (children under 16 are not allowed). Hansen's disease is completely under control today thanks to various sulfa drugs, and adults are completely safe. Several organizations offer tours of the peninsula, which can be approached by air, sea, or foot (a very tough hike) or mule from the overlook at Palaau State Park. One company, *Molokai Mule Rides,* offers a tour that makes its way down the 1,600-foot cliffs via a 3-mile cliff trail to Kalaupapa; PO Box 200, Kalaupapa, Molokai, HI 96757 (phone: 808-567-6088).

BEST EN ROUTE

Kaluakoi Hotel and Golf Club, Kepuhi Beach – This exclusive Polynesian-style resort is beautifully set along secluded white sand beaches. Its 288 rooms are spread over 32 buildings, with tennis courts, an 18-hole golf course, a pool, shops, and excellent dining in 2 restaurants. PO Box 1977, Maunaloa, Molokai, HI 96770 (phone: 808-523-0411 or 800-367-6046).

Molokai, Kaunakakai – In a palm grove about 2 miles from town, this resort is conveniently located in the center of the island. Rooms are distributed among buildings throughout the grounds. PO Box 546, Kaunakakai, Molokai, HI 96748 (phone: 808-553-5347 or 800-922-7866).

Oahu, Hawaii

Oahu, home of four-fifths of Hawaii's population, is quite appropriately nick-named "the Gathering Place." Since Kamehameha III moved the royal court to Honolulu from Maui in 1843, Oahu has been the social, political, and industrial center of the entire archipelago. Since World War II it has also been the center of tourism, and several Oahu sites and cities have become synony-mous with Hawaii itself: Honolulu, Diamond Head, Waikiki, and Pearl Har-bor. (For a detailed report on these sites, see *Honolulu,* THE CITIES.) Just as you must get off Oahu to the Neighbor Islands to see all of Hawaii, you must get out of Honolulu to see all of Oahu. On the other hand, simply because of Honolulu, Oahu offers an immense variety of activities.

WAIKIKI BEACH: Not unlike Miami Beach, Waikiki is a miracle of shoulder-to-shoulder tall hotels with the expected complement of souvenir shops, restaurants, discos, bars, and other tourist attractions. The beach itself is the most extravagant stretch of sand in all the islands. It was the exclusive spot of the ancient *alii* (royalty), who came here to sun and surf. The beach today remains as physically beautiful as any you will see in the world — when you can see it, that is. It is usually well hidden beneath a layer of supine bodies. Even sunrise joggers must jockey for a bare stretch of sand. Waikiki is not a deserted island paradise. There are some splendid hotels and restau-rants along this strip. There are also honky-tonk traps and tacky stores.

From Honolulu and Waikiki the route we describe below roughly follows the south-ern, eastern, and northern coasts of the island in a large 110-mile loop. The first part of this loop, Rte. 72, covers the entire eastern tip of Oahu, from Diamond Head to Kailua. Ask at your hotel or at the desk of any car rental agency for a booklet of Oahu itineraries called the *Drive Guide.* It contains helpful maps and interesting descriptions of the routes.

OAHU'S SOUTHERN TIP: The road really starts at Diamond Head, the spectacular volcanic crater that has become the symbol of Hawaii. The volcano that formed this perfect crater has been extinct for at least 150,000 years, and early Hawaiians, for whom it was just as much a landmark as it is for Hawaiians today, thought it resembled nothing so much as a fish head. There are a number of relatively tough hiking paths in the crater that can be entered from a road between Monsarrat and 18th Avenues, off Diamond Head Road.

Rte. 72 passes through two affluent neighborhoods beyond Diamond Head, the Kahala district and Hawaii Kai, a development begun by Henry Kaiser, the man who during World War II turned the making of Liberty ships into a 5-week project. Hanauma Bay Beach Park is where the Elvis Presley film *Blue Hawaii* was filmed. It has one of the most beautiful underwater parks in the country and is an excellent place for snorkeling or scuba diving because the waters are so perfectly clear. Nearby is Halona Blow Hole, a submerged lava tube that turns sea water into a saltwater geyser as waves roll in.

Here, too, is Sea Life Park (808-259-7933), with a number of standard aquatic displays (dolphins, seals, whales) as well as a fascinating see-through tank filled with coral and various forms of sea life that would normally live in a coral reef. At feeding times you can watch scuba divers plunge into the water to lead a happy parade of turtles, multicolored fish, manta rays, eels, and small and larger sharks happily intent on the food being distributed. For confirmed landlubbers it is a fascinating performance. The easternmost point on the island is Makapuu Point, marked by a lighthouse. This is the point at which the trade winds divide, some continuing north, some south, across the island. At Kailua, to the north, it is possible to cut inland and return to Honolulu through the Koolau Mountains via the Pali Highway (Rte. 61). En route are the Nuuanu Pali Tunnels and the scenic masterpiece, Pali Lookout. This is where Kamehameha I drove the defenders of Oahu over the steep cliffs to their deaths. Today the view from these heights is as grand as it is fear-inspiring. The Pali Highway is mountainous, leading through lush tropical rain forests, numerous curves, and arriving abruptly in the teeming urban Honolulu.

EASTERN OAHU: The coastal loop continues beyond Kailua as Rte. 83, the Kamehameha Highway. This road takes you along the eastern and northern coasts of the island. Each of the islands has at least one — and usually several — mountains or ridges that form some familiar shape. On Maui there is the John F. Kennedy profile in Iao Valley; on Kauai, Queen Victoria's profile. All the islands are of volcanic origin, and in the fury of an eruption lava turns, twists, and tears into a fantastic variety of shapes. Oahu's major profile is the Crouching Lion, visible from Rte. 83. Like all of these figures, the resemblance is not exact and depends as much on the viewer's perspective and good will as on the actual shape of the formation. But what is interesting is that myths always collect around these profiles. A bit beyond the Crouching Lion is the lovely Sacred Falls, an 87-foot waterfall that plunges into a pool. You are welcome to swim in the pool and cavort in the falling water, but it is a hard mile's hike beyond the parking spot, and you should be prepared for about an hour's tramp.

The culmination of the drive along the eastern shore is the Polynesian Cultural Center in Laie (phone: 808-293-3333; in Waikiki, 808-923-1861). Though it is a commercial enterprise, the center has excellent reconstructions of villages of all the major cultures of the Pacific — Marquesas, Samoan, Tongan, Hawaiian, Tahitian, Fijian, Maori — with cultural performances and arts and crafts demonstrations in each village. There are lunchtime and evening Polynesian shows. A mixture of museum and Disneyland, the center is informative and a great deal of fun as well.

NORTHERN OAHU: Where Rte. 83 rounds the top of the island and turns southwest, it runs smack dab into a spot that is guaranteed to raise goose pimples on any surfer's surface — Sunset Beach, home of the Big Waves, including the notorious Banzai Pipeline. Here, every winter, international competitions are held. More cerebral, but thrilling in its own right, is nearby COMSAT — earth station for international commercial satellite communications. Ahead on the north shore is Waimea Falls Park (phone: 808-638-8511), another natural wonder gone professional. The famous and incredibly beautiful waterfall is now made easy to see on a round-trip tram ride. The 1,800-acre park features archaeological sites with 3,500 varieties of plants, including 100 endangered species.

From here the highway turns south and heads toward Honolulu. About 11 miles west of Waikiki is Pearl Harbor. The Arizona Memorial Visitor Center (open daily) shows a film about the December 7, 1941, attack. A shuttle boat then takes visitors to the memorial that stands above the sunken battleship *Arizona*.

BEST EN ROUTE

Halekulani, Honolulu – When it comes to service and class, this luxury hotel sets the standard. Gracing Waikiki Beach, it offers 412 posh rooms and 44 suites; an orchid-tiled pool; elegant shops; 3 fine restaurants (one with award-winning French cuisine); lounges; a grand ballroom; and concierge staff. 2199 Kalia Rd., Honolulu, HI 96815 (phone: 808-923-2311 or 800-367-2343).

Kahala Hilton, Honolulu – This deluxe hotel has a magnificent setting on a tropical lagoon inhabited by dolphins and turtles. Many of the 370 rooms have separate dressing rooms and lanais overlooking the lagoon, mountains, or beach. All have large baths and are decorated with interesting handmade wall hangings. The *Maile* restaurant is one of the best in the Honolulu area. 5000 Kahala Ave., Honolulu, Oahu, HI 96816 (phone: 808-734-2211 or 800-367-2525).

Royal Hawaiian, Honolulu – Fondly known as "the Pink Palace" or "Pink Lady," this 555-room hotel was the place to stay in the 1930s, when luxury liners steamed into Honolulu with elegant passengers who stayed for months. The pink stucco Mediterranean-style building retains its glittering chandeliers and long corridors, although it has changed hands since then and is now managed by Sheraton. Avoid the new tower; it's the gracious, older rooms that really give this place its charm. 2259 Kalakaua Ave., Honolulu, HI 96815 (phone: 808-923-7311 or 800-334-8484).

Craters of the Moon National Monument, Idaho

Everyone wants to know what the moon really looks like. For centuries we lived with intense speculation, some of it informed by science, much indebted to imagination. Since 1969 we have lived with reality: those incredible pictures of a flat, gray, pockmarked surface scarred by all the flying debris of space for eons, flanked by strange, craggy rocks rising from Swiss cheese holes in the ground; and in front, standing with a flag unfurled in a vacuum, the astronaut, looking as awkward and out of place as a snowman learning to walk. These pictures have become part of our consciousness, our definition of what space travel is about. And while all the rigmarole of space is familiar — the lift-off, the orbit, the lunar module — the moon remains a mystery. What did the first astronauts feel? What would it be like to visit the moon?

It's not impossible. And no farther away than Idaho. When scientists wanted to familiarize prospective astronauts with the lunar surface, they brought them to Craters of the Moon National Monument, on the Snake River Plain. The next best thing to actually being there, Craters of the Moon will give you an understanding of that extraterrestrial splendor we spend billions of dollars trying to reach.

It's not unfamiliar territory to many people, especially skiers. Some 70 miles to the west is Idaho's Sun Valley, one of the state's finest skiing centers. Coming south from Sun Valley, or north from I-84, you must drive at least a section of Rtes. 93 and 75 before getting to the turnoff for Craters of the Moon. Along the road are two diversions worth considering.

SHOSHONE INDIAN ICE CAVES: Idaho has a number of caves — some discovered, some not — related to its volcanic origins. The Shoshone Indian Caves are a constantly cool (about 32F) series of caves (or one long cavern really) that simply won't change temperature no matter how hot it is outside. There are tours every half hour between May and October. (Be sure to bring a sweater.) On the grounds are an Indian museum and the statue of Chief Washakie of the Shoshone tribe. Admission charge. About 43 miles south of Sun Valley, 15 miles north of Shoshone on Rte. 75.

SHOSHONE FALLS: Although quite a detour — 30 miles south of the town of Shoshone — the falls are well worth the drive. Larger than Niagara, these waterfalls drop 212 dramatic, turbulent feet into the Snake River. (Evel Knievel fans will remember Snake River because of his world-famous, daredevil jump across Snake River Canyon, which is farther along the meandering Snake.) Like all parts of the Snake, the drama of the falls is affected by the flow of water, which is, in its turn, affected by rainfall and, more important, the amount of irrigation along its course through Idaho. During the heat of the summer irrigation is at its height, the falls are at their nadir.

CRATERS OF THE MOON NATIONAL MONUMENT: Craters of the Moon is 60 miles northeast of Shoshone, along Rte. 93. You'll know you're in the right part of the country a few miles before you reach Carey, Idaho, when you pass a series of lava beds. If you miss them, don't worry; there'll be plenty more coming up.

Craters of the Moon is a land of lava on lava — stark, black, and cinder-blown. Its visual impact is stunning: miles of black lava rising and falling over the otherwise broad, flat valley, with abrupt, jagged peaks and huge cinder and lava cones — one 800 feet high — dotting the landscape. The entire area was the product of a series of volcanic explosions that over eons added successive layers of lava to rock and lava already laid down. So startling is the effect of seeing the monument that its equally startling geologic history takes some time to appreciate.

The monument sits atop a 60-mile fissure in the earth known as the Great Rift. In eight great epochs of upheaval, the Great Rift exploded in waves upon waves of white-hot magma — spewing molten rock at 2,000F out of the fissure itself — throwing tons of debris and rock into the air to form the volcanic cones that appear across the area. The cones belong to one of the earlier series of eruptions; lava flows within the monument date anywhere from 2,000 to nearly 15,000 years ago.

The human history of the monument is nowhere near as intriguing as its natural history. Indians certainly knew — and passed through — the area. You will see trail markers and cairns piled in various spots; they are Indian artifacts, though we do not know exactly how they were used. But it does not seem to have been an important part of the world for them. The area was discovered by white men in 1833 and proclaimed a national monument in 1924.

The place to start any tour is at the visitors center, where there are displays on the area's amazing formations and natural history which describe the process in detail. From there, a 7-mile loop drive will take you past most of the monument's best-known landmarks. Don't miss the Indian Tunnel, an 830-foot lava tube used as a cave by the Indians on treks through the lava fields, and Devils Orchard, one of the younger lava formations. Be sure to take along water, even when you are driving. In summer, the sun bakes the lava, burns the foot, and parches the throat. (In winter, the entire area is covered in deep snow and turns into marvelous cross-country ski terrain.)

For the more adventurous, numerous trails and walks let you explore the monument on foot and bring you face to face with the lava. There is much to recommend this approach. Since much of the monument can't be reached by car, it is the only way to really see the vast area of lava fields that are virtually unexplored. And by venturing into the (relative) unknown on foot, you will discover the monument's great secret: Far from being a sterile, hostile, bleak landscape, it is alive with plants, birds, and animals. Hundreds of species of flora have adapted to the area; there are mountain bluebirds, nighthawks, and sparrows galore; and in the backcountry you will see mule deer, hear coyote, and, if you're very lucky, spot a distant bobcat. Permits are required for overnight travel into wilderness areas. Information: Superintendent, Craters of the Moon National Monument, PO Box 29, Arco, ID 83213 (phone: 208-527-3257).

BEST EN ROUTE

You will certainly have no trouble finding hotels and motels within striking distance of Craters of the Moon. However, most recommendable are several lodges in the Sun Valley/Ketchum area.

Heidelberg Inn – More in the Alps tradition of Idaho resorts, the *Heidelberg* is a kind of Austrian Alps motel, pleasanter to visit than to try to describe. Some of its 30 rooms have fireplaces and kitchenettes. PO Box 304, 1908 Warm Springs Rd., Sun Valley, ID 83353 (phone: 208-726-5361).

Sun Valley Lodge and Inn – The lodge and inn are separate physical entities, but part of the *Sun Valley Resort*. The lodge is a classic, rustic redwood ski lodge (of recent vintage) with 141 rooms, some with fireplaces. The inn is more family-oriented, with 115 rooms in a rambling, neo-Tyrolean building. Some shops and restaurants are in a mall separating the two buildings. Sun Valley Rd., Sun Valley, ID 83353 (phone: 208-622-4111; 800-632-4104 in Idaho, 800-635-8261 elsewhere).

Tamarack Lodge – A very comfortable resort lodge with 28 rooms, including suites with fireplaces and balcony rooms with mountain views, indoor heated pool (the only one in the area), Jacuzzi, and saunas. Corner of Sun Valley Rd. and Walnut Ave., PO Box 2000, Sun Valley, ID 83353 (phone: 208-726-3344).

Flint Hills, Kansas

The Flint Hills run from the Kansas-Oklahoma border into the northern third of the Sunflower state. The north-south axis of the hills lies about 45 miles east of Wichita, or about a quarter of the distance between the Missouri state line in the east and the Colorado foothills of the Rockies that form Kansas's western edge.

So named because of the chunks of flint in the soil, the Flint Hills are among the last surviving plains of prairie grassland. Although at one time the plains formed a belt that ran from Chicago to the edge of the Rockies and from Canada to Texas, now scarcely 1% of the original 400,000 square miles of tallgrass remain. Most of the land has been razed to provide homes on the range or has been reduced to stubble by machines and grazing herds.

Once the plains were subject to long droughts and brush fires — the stereotypical picture of this area of Kansas. But modern technology has changed that image of the plains, with the planting of fire lines, the building of large reservoirs, and the construction of superhighways. Also, the Flint Hills are probably not as dry and devoid of plant life as you might have thought. Trees line the area's streams, which in turn nourish wild plums; wildflowers seem to thrive on the streams' grassy slopes with blooms for every warm season; Fremont's clematis, towering sunflower, evening primrose, larkspur, cornflower, indigo, and clover mingle on the hillsides.

For the most part, this section of Kansas looks much as it did when pioneers passed through on their way west, and settlers stayed to farm the rich soil in other parts of the state. The farms are vastly larger now, the fields tended by giant clanking machines, but the prairie that served as a home for herds of buffalo and pronghorn antelope is still prime grazing territory. The area is also known for its sprawling cattle ranches and rich oil deposits.

Cattle fed on the grasses of Kansas grow exceptionally large and healthy, although it was not until the turn of the century that agricultural scientists understood why. Under the prairie lies limestone chock full of protein and minerals. The prairie roots, going down into the earth as deep as six yards, tap this remnant of an ancient seabed and bring its nourishment to the stems and leaves, making extraordinarily rich fodder. Cowboys still ride the hills on horseback and in four-wheel drives, searching for the stragglers of their grazing herds. You can join these lone sailors in a sea of golden grass by driving through Flint Hills. If you have a jeep, you can get away from the paved highways that cross the plains here, but even if you stick to the civilized paths, you cannot help being transported, for a moment, to the simpler life of the past.

The route we suggest will lead you through Flint Hills en route from Kansas City to Oklahoma City.

TOPEKA: The state capital since 1861, Topeka was the site of bitter conflict between abolitionists and proslavery factions during the Civil War. After years of being known as Bleeding Kansas, the state joined the Union. Sites in town include the State House, housing artwork depicting pioneer and Civil War years (Capitol Square; phone: 913-296-3966). The zoo has exhibitions that include a tropical rain forest and a new gorilla encounter (Gage Park; phone: 913-272-5821). Nearby, the Reinisch Memorial Rose and Rock Gardens provide an oasis of fragrant tranquillity in spring, summer, and autumn (Gage Park). The Kansas State Historical Society has a new multimillion-dollar museum complex with displays on the state's history (take the Wanamaker North exit off I-70, west of Topeka).

EMPORIA, FLINT HILLS: Take I-35 about 50 miles southwest from Topeka. This is the heart of the Flint Hills region and its major cattle market. Tens of thousands of cattle are sent to the slaughterhouse from this town every year. Emporia was the home of William Allen White, publisher of the *Emporia Gazette* and one of America's most respected editors. His bust stands in Peter Pan Park. For information on activities, call the Emporia Convention & Visitors Bureau (phone: 316-342-1600). Emporia State University presents concerts, plays, and films throughout the year (1200 Commercial). The Way College emphasizes biblical studies (1300 W. 12th). Lyons County Lake and Park, a 528-acre recreation area, has swimming, boat launching, fishing, and camping. Campsites do not have hookups (11 miles north of town on Rte. 170). For information, call the State Forestry, Fish and Game Commission office in Emporia, 316-342-0658.

FLINT HILLS NATIONAL WILDLIFE REFUGE: About 5,000 acres form this refuge, primarily devoted to waterfowl. In winter, as many as 20 bald eagles nest on the grounds, as well as many other species. Among them: snow geese, blue geese, greater and lesser Canadian geese, mallard ducks, great horned and snowy owls. Whitetail deer, coyote, red fox, and rabbit live here too. The best time to visit is fall, either before or after the hunting season, when the refuge is closed to human visitors. Open the rest of the year. No admission charge. From Emporia, take Rte. 99 south about 3 miles. After you cross the river bridge, you'll see an unnumbered county road running east to Hartford. Follow it for about 20 miles to the refuge (phone: 316-392-5553).

FALL RIVER AND TORONTO DAM AND LAKE STATE PARKS: Known as the twin reservoirs of the "Kansas Ozarks," the combined recreation area consists of 2,000 acres, with 40 miles of shoreline. Fishing, boating, swimming, hiking, and camping are available. The parks are 55 miles south of Emporia on Rte. 99, then east for 20 miles on Rte. 96 (phone: 316-658-4445).

WICHITA: Kansas's largest city and leading manufacturing center, Wichita is the headquarters of four aircraft companies. Places of interest include the *Wichita Art Museum,* containing American and European canvases and sculpture (619 Stackman Dr., Sim Park); *Wichita Art Association,* containing two modern galleries and a children's theater (9112 E. Central); *Sedgwick County Historical Museum,* containing displays on home life in the 1800s (204 S. Main); Wichita State University, with Frank Lloyd Wright buildings and a contemporary art museum (N. Hillside and 17th Sts.). Kids will enjoy the *Old Cow Town Museum,* a restored frontier village with Wyatt Earp's jail. Open daily (1871 Sim Park Dr.).

Glacier National Park, Montana

Montana's Glacier National Park is measured in millions: 1 million acres carved by the movement of massive glaciers millions of years ago, visited by about 2 million people every year. These 1,600 square miles shared by the US and Canada are known as Waterton/Glacier International Peace Park or simply Glacier, although the giant ice sheets to which the park owes its name and its geography have long since disappeared. There are still some 50 small glaciers throughout the park — snow masses deep enough to compact the lower levels into ice and heavy enough to creep downhill. The largest of these, Grinnell, covers 300 acres and contains ice 400 feet thick. In the summer, streams of water from Grinnell and the other glaciers cascade down the mountainside, gathering volume as they merge and tumble into the deep cold lakes. This spectacular descent and many other features of this alpine wilderness in the northwest region of Montana (just west of St. Mary) merit at least a 1-week visit.

Glacier's six large lakes (all at least 5 miles long) stretch from the park's edges into its interior; it has some 200 smaller lakes and glacial ponds, 1,000 waterfalls, over 50 streams, and 700 miles of trails and paths for hiking and horseback riding as well. The Blackfeet Indians considered the area sacred because of its awesome beauty.

The park is open all year long, although most roads are closed in winter due to heavy snow. Late fall brings visitors who come to observe the migrating bald eagles and other wildlife; winter brings cross-country skiers and snowshoers. Others come merely to enjoy a snowball fight in summer, fish in a mountain stream, or watch a mountain goat appear to defy gravity in search of vegetation along a mountain slope.

Enter the park from West Glacier, along US 2 or from St. Mary on the park's east end along US 89. Within park boundaries, you will be urged to follow regulations, not only because of the geography of the park, which can be treacherous, but to protect its rich and abundant animal life. The 57 species of animals include the mountain goat, deer, moose, elk, beaver, muskrat, mink, bighorn sheep, coyote, wolf, and grizzly bear. Glacier is one of the few US parks that is home to grizzlies. Hikers are encouraged to make noises along the trail, indicating their presence in order to avoid surprising and frightening the bears.

In addition to the variety of animal life, there are at least 200 types of birds, from hawks and eagles that swoop overhead to grouse and dippers that inhabit the woods and streams. As in any wildlife preserve, these creatures are not easy to spot, and it is likely that you will leave having seen only an occasional mountain goat or sleepy marmot.

The best way to see the park is on foot, on short walks from the visitors centers at Logan Pass, St. Mary, or Apgar, or on longer treks, some of which are guided. In some areas you can rent horses for horseback journeys through the park. But if you have a few days to spare, the best assurance of getting a taste of the park's resources is to hike and camp in any of the 15 roadside campgrounds. What you discover on your own can be augmented by participating in one of the daily walks or campfire programs conducted by rangers at the visitors centers or campgrounds. They will point out the myriad plants and explain how the knife-edged ridges and glacial peaks were formed eons ago, an invaluable part of your visit.

If you cannot manage more than a drive through Glacier, you will still have the experience of one of the best routes in America. The park's Going-to-the-Sun Road, starting in St. Mary on Rte. 89, is an unforgettable 50 miles of twisting, cliff-hanging mountain roadway linking the east and west sides of the park. (Vehicles over 30 feet long or over 8 feet wide are banned from the road during July and August, and even a slight snow necessitates strict regulations.)

Along the way, you skirt the edge of St. Mary Lake, with its backdrop of snow-capped peaks and Douglas firs, reaching the first of 17 parking turnouts about 5 miles beyond the lake. Here you can see Triple Divide Peak, where — as the name implies — mountain waters divide and enter three larger water systems: the Arctic via Hudson Bay, the Gulf of Mexico via the Mississippi system, and the Pacific Ocean via the Columbia River.

After many other magnificent vistas and views of the park's towering peaks (including 10,080-foot Mt. Jackson), you reach the highlight of the drive, the crossing of the Continental Divide at Logan Pass. From this 6,680-foot elevation there's a 100-mile view of the countryside — a spectacular panorama that justifies Glacier's reputation as the Alps of America.

At the visitors center here, you can get directions to Hidden Lake overlook. The 1½-mile hike, part boardwalk and part trail, offers a fine view of the calm, deep blue lake 800 feet below — a perfect finale to a lovely walk.

Your drive on the Going-to-the-Sun Road eventually leads into McDonald Valley. For more hiking, head over to Avalanche Campground and pick up an easy 2-mile trail that leads to Avalanche Basin. Technically called a "glacial cirque," this is a natural amphitheater with 2,000-foot walls and six waterfalls — a spectacular sight that gives you a sense of the park's interior without making a longer trek.

The park's largest lake, McDonald is a center of activity. You can swim, take a boat tour from the dock at *Lake McDonald Lodge,* or hike to Sperry Glacier, where *Sperry Chalets* offer overnight stays complete with prepared meals and box lunches. Reservations are required. The chalets are also a good spot from which to plan a fishing expedition (fishing permit not required).

There is also fishing at Two Medicine Lake in Two Medicine Valley, southeast of Lake McDonald. Rainbow, brook trout, and the occasional mackinaw are caught. Two Medicine Lake is a good place for camping, hiking, and boating as well.

For horseback riding, you should stay in Many Glacier Valley long enough to join one of the popular all-day trips through wildflower-filled alpine meadows to Cracker or Poia lakes. Horseback riding is also available at *Lake McDonald Lodge* and in the Apgar area.

There are many other sights in the park — Red Eagle Lake, with some spectacular falls and an impressive gorge; Flattop Mountain, near Lewis Range, where the juxtaposition of forest and meadow makes it a favorite for hiking; and Grinnell Lake, where a trail leads to the largest glacier in the park.

If you have driven through the park and would like even more wildlife adventure and/or isolation in the mountain pines, take Chief Mountain International Highway (Rte. 17) to Waterton Lakes National Park in Canada. An extension of Glacier, it offers more of the same, with fewer crowds. Information: Superintendent, Glacier National Park, West Glacier, MT 59936 (phone: 406-888-5441; for recorded information on weather, road conditions, camping, and park activities, 406-888-5551).

BEST EN ROUTE

If you prefer sheets and blankets to the stars above, there are several good hotels, motels, and lodges at the park. If you wish to stay at one of the chalets at Sperry or Granite Park, write to Belton Chalets, PO Box 188, West Glacier, MT 59936 (phone: 406-888-5511 April through Labor Day); otherwise information on accommodations at 7 different properties and around the park is available through Glacier Park, Inc., headquartered during the season in the *Glacier Park Lodge*, at the southeast corner of the park on Rte. 49, East Glacier, MT 59434 (phone: 406-226-5551), from October through May at Greyhound Tower, Reservations Dept., Station 5510, Phoenix, AZ 85077 (phone: 602-248-6000).

Lake McDonald Lodge – Built in 1913 in a setting of giant cedars, it has a cozy atmosphere with Old West flair, a lobby with a giant fireplace, 101 rooms, and a lakeside locale. A good choice for fishing, boating, or riding. Make early reservations. Open from early June to early September. 10.6 miles northeast of West Glacier on Going-to-the-Sun Rd. (phone: 406-226-5551).

Glacier Park Lodge – Over 50 years old and built of cedar and Douglas fir timbers, it offers a pool, playground, 155 rooms, and a steakhouse. Open from early June to early September. Just outside the southeast corner of the park on Rte. 49 (phone: 406-226-5551).

Carlsbad Caverns National Park, New Mexico

If you're driving across the eastern part of New Mexico and those vast horizontal stretches of land are beginning to appear endless rather than beautiful, there's something nearby that can satisfy the direction of your fancy — Bat Flight at Carlsbad Caverns. Here, every night at sunset from May through September, 5,000 bats per minute spiral out of the open-mouthed darkness of the cave, as many as 500,000 to 1 million in one viewing. For an hour or more, the bats, on their way out to feed for the night, create a blackening vortex against the sky which widens into a gray streak as they set off into the stillness of nightfall.

Carlsbad Caverns National Park is in New Mexico's southeastern corner, just 15 miles from the Texas state line to the south and 27 miles from Carlsbad, New Mexico, to the northeast. As you approach Carlsbad Caverns, you begin to sense something unique about the place; the monotony of the terrain is broken by the rise of the foothills of the Guadalupe Mountains. But it is underground in this hilly, desert region that everything spectacular is happening. Below the surrounding terrain (the national park encompasses 73 square miles) are many caves, with the main cavern one of the largest known underground cavities in the world. In the late 1800s, New Mexico residents noticed the nightly bat flights from a nearby cave and named it Bat Cave. But they left the bats and the cave alone until 1901, when the deposits of bat guano near the cave's entrance attracted commercial interest. A mining operation was set up and, from then to 1923, 200 million pounds of guano were extracted from the cave for fertilizer. During that time, James Larkin White, a cowboy and guano miner, explored the inside of the cave and discovered its marvelous limestone formations. Inside the cave lie acres of caverns and formations. Even now, some areas in the surrounding network have still not been completely explored. But the main cavern, with its stalagmite and stalactite formations of magnificent design and infinite variety — some joining and creating monumental pillars, others densely clustered in fragile and delicate patterns — is a testament to nature's artistry.

The beginnings of this subterranean gallery go back more than 200 million years when a vast inland sea covered the entire area. At the edge of this sea, limestone-secreting organisms and mineral precipitates built the massive Capitan Reef. In the course of millennia, the sea dried up and the reef was buried under several thousand feet of sediment. Then, approximately 20 million years ago, cracks appeared in the rock. Rainwater, made slightly acidic from carbon dioxide in the air and soil, seeped into the cracks and worked its way down to the water table. The acid eroded the rock and created the caverns. Mountain building activity raised the caverns above the water table, and the erosion was accelerated as massive blocks of porous rock, no longer supported by water, collapsed, increasing the size of chambers. The seepage of surface rain and melted snow from above continued, carrying dissolved limestone to the walls of the cavern, where it was deposited. Drop by drop, eon by eon, the water deposited more limestone, creating many formations — stalactites that hang like icicles from the ceiling and stalagmites that reach up from the ground. Where the two have fused stand massive pillars.

To get a good feeling for nature's work at Carlsbad Caverns, you will need about half a day. (The park is open all year except on Christmas Day.) After stopping at the visitors center to consult displays on the history of the cavern, follow a short trail to the entrance of the cavern, where a self-guided tour begins (visitors are given portable radio receivers). Remember to wear a sweater — the cave stays a pleasantly cool 56F year-round. The natural entrance to the cave is imposing — an arch 90 feet wide and 40 feet high. The walk goes a total of 3 miles, beginning with a relatively steep descent down switchback trails to a depth of 829 feet. As you progress, the main points of interest are described on your radio receiver, but look all about and take your time to appreciate the immensity and beauty of what lies around you. You walk along the main corridor through a succession of amazing chambers — the circular King's Palace, with its ornate limestone decorations and curtains of glittering cave onyx, the Queen's Chamber, noted for its delicate "elephant ear" formations, and the Papoose Room, a low-ceilinged chamber with numerous stalactites. Larger than both the King's and Queen's chambers is the Big Room, which fulfills its title with a 255-foot ceiling in an area the size of 14 football fields. The room's magnificent and huge totem poles, pillars, and domes are most striking.

If you are pressed for time or cannot make the descent by foot, there is an elevator and a shorter tour of 1¼ miles, of the Big Room.

Incongruous as it may seem after walking through the cavern's natural chambers, there is a lunchroom at the bottom where you can have a meal. Except for the lunchroom and the elevator that brings you to the surface after you complete the tour, little has been done to alter the natural state of the caverns. The lighting is well hidden in underground cables and brings out the subtle hues in the limestone formations.

Lantern-lit tours are also available at New Cave — the ultimate in underground adventure — 25 miles from the visitors center and 36 miles from the city of Carlsbad. The trip also involves a trek up a steep ½-mile trail. The tour through the cave lasts from 1½ to 2 hours. You discover the spectacular formations only with the help of the lights you are carrying. Tours are given daily during the summer and weekends the rest of the year. Reservations are required (phone: 505-785-2232). You needn't be an experienced spelunker, but you should wear sturdy walking shoes.

At the visitors center, you can stroll along a self-guided nature trail or, in the summer, take the daily guided tour and view the arid desert vegetation and large variety of cacti, and with luck some of the area's wildlife — mule deer and lizards. Walnut Canyon Desert Drive, a one-way gravel road of 9.5 miles, begins a half mile from the visitors center and travels along the top of a ridge to the edge of Rattlesnake Canyon and back down through upper Walnut Canyon to the main entrance road. For the more adventurous, there is backcountry camping with plenty of contact with the wilderness — the trails are poorly defined, and the desert, rugged and dry.

Neither trailblazer nor tenderfoot should miss the bat flight any evening from May through September (the bats migrate to Mexico in winter). Everyone sits in the amphitheater at the cave's mouth, waiting for the bats to come whirling out; a park ranger explains the flight but is usually upstaged in midsentence when thousands of bats pour out of the cave into the darkening horizon. Information: Superintendent, Carlsbad Caverns National Park, 3225 National Park Hwy., Carlsbad, NM 88220 (phone: 505-785-2232).

BEST EN ROUTE

Although you can get a permit at the visitors center for rugged backcountry camping, there are no developed overnight facilities in the park. The town of Carlsbad, 27 miles northeast of the park along US 62, offers a wide range of motels, hotels, and camping facilities. Whites City, a privately owned town 7 miles northeast of the visitors center, has a motel and a few shops as well.

Best Western Cavern Inn, White's City – This motel has 131 rooms, a restaurant, 2 pools with spas, and accepts pets. PO Box 128, White's City, NM 88268 (phone: 505-785-2291, 800-THE-CAVE in New Mexico, 800-CAVERNS elsewhere).

Best Western Motel Stevens, Carlsbad – There is a pool, an attractive restaurant, dancing and entertainment; 181 rooms. PO Box 580, 1829 S. Canal St., Carlsbad, NM 88220 (phone: 505-887-2851).

Motel 6, Carlsbad – In addition to 80 rooms, amenities here include a pool, color TV sets, and low rates. Kids under 18 free in room with parents. 3824 National Parks Hwy., Carlsbad, NM 88220 (phone: 505-885-0011).

Rodeway Inn, Carlsbad – This 107-room motel has a café, color TV sets, a heated indoor pool, whirlpool bath, sauna, exercise room, playground, dancing, and entertainment on Saturday nights. PO Box 640, 3804 National Parks Hwy., Carlsbad, NM 88220 (phone: 505-887-5535 or 800-228-2000).

Crater Lake National Park, Oregon

The Klamath Indians have their own explanation for the creation of this spectacular, brilliant blue, deep lake in the Cascade Mountains of southern Oregon. Llao, the god of the underworld who lived here, and Skell, the god who dwelt on Mt. Shasta, had a battle over an Indian maiden. Skell won and collapsed Llao's mountain. It was later filled with water to prevent Llao from escaping, thus creating the caldera that now is the focal point for more than 500,000 visitors each year.

Geologists offer an equally splendid version of the story. At least a half-million years ago, in the age of the Cascade Mountains — which include Rainier, Shasta, and Adams — Mt. Mazama began to build. Over the next 500,000 years a series of eruptions, interrupted by dormant periods, built Mt. Mazama to an estimated 12,000 feet. The eruptions came from a chamber of magma (hot molten rock) several miles beneath the mountain. A massive eruption of Mt. Mazama about 6,800 years ago virtually emptied the magma chamber and weakened the structure of the volcanic cone. The cone collapsed into the chamber, forming a caldera about 6 miles wide and nearly 4,000 feet deep. Continuing lesser eruptions within the caldera created smaller cones and helped seal off the basin with lava flows. Rain and snow began filling the basin and eventually formed a lake. Although the lake's surface temperature gets as warm as 60F to 67F in summer, its depths remain very cold; and although the water is relatively pure, rangers advise visitors not to drink it.

Whichever version makes a believer of you, Crater Lake is a sight not to be missed. Oregon's only national park (established in 1902 after long years of lobbying), it is famous for animal and plant life, miles of hiking trails, a scenic road running 33 miles around the rim of the crater, and the lake, 1,932 feet deep, the deepest in the US. The park's vistas are unparalleled both for their natural beauty and for the many natural viewing places created as if expressedly for the visitors who flock here.

Although far from southern Oregon's few big cities (Medford is about 80 miles south, Roseburg a bit farther west), Crater Lake's Rim Road is as ideal a method for viewing this wonder as any man could have devised. Almost 100 miles of trails, many starting from the Rim Road, snake through the park, up adjacent mountains for panoramic views of the lake or down to the lake's shores. There you can find boat trips around the lake and to its two islands, Phantom Ship and Wizard.

Until 1853, Crater Lake was unknown to white men. Then a gold prospector, John Wesley Hillman, stumbled upon it while searching with a party of gold diggers for the famous Lost Cabin Mine. It was called Deep Blue Lake by the few who knew of it, and the discovery wasn't made public for 31 years. Official expeditions were made during that time, and in 1886 a government geologist sounded its depths at 1,996 feet, a respectable finding for the limited equipment of the day.

The man most crucial to the lake's fate first saw it in 1885. William Gladstone Steel was a Kansan transplanted to the great new West. Once he laid eyes on this spectacle, he committed his life to its preservation. He personally led a crusade to save it from homesteaders, lumber interests, and prospectors. Teddy Roosevelt, perhaps the greatest conservationist to inhabit the White House, made Crater Lake a national park on May 22, 1902. In 1913, Steel was rewarded for his long crusade with an appointment as the park's second superintendent.

Crater Lake National Park is a 286-square-mile tract surrounded on almost every side by national forests. There are three entrances. From the south (driving north from Klamath Falls, on Rte. 97), take Rte. 62 to the southern entrance and soon enter the Rim Road. From the north, you enter from Rte. 138, passing through the park's Pumice Desert before reaching the Rim Road.

Begin at the visitors centers at Rim Village (open late May to late September) and Munson Valley (open all year), and the nearby Sinnott Memorial, an excellent orientation point. Talks on the origin of the lake are given at Rim Village daily, and exhibitions are open. Cross-country skiing is popular here during winter months; ask at the visitors center. During winter months, only the park's south and west entrances are open.

There are two reasons to go to Crater Lake: one is to take a boat tour on it (no private craft allowed), and the other is to get above it, to look down on it, as did the men — Indian and white — who discovered it. Two walking tours worth investigating start at the visitors center. A 1½-mile trail runs to the top of Garfield Peak, 1,900 feet above the lake's surface. The other trail is Discovery Point Trail, taking the modern explorer to the spot where John Hillman first laid eyes on this unexpected vision.

Fishing is allowed without a license; the lake has trout and a species of small Kokanee salmon. Nightly campfire programs are held at Mazama Campground and the Rim Center at Rim Village.

From the visitors center you enter the Rim Road — you'll have to struggle to keep your eyes on the road and off the scenery. Fortunately, nature anticipated your needs, and numerous natural stopping places mark the circular route. There are also many trails and tracks that lead from stopping places up nearby summits (for even larger views).

The first stop on the mountain is called the Watchman, with a ⅘-mile trail to its summit, overlooking the lake from 1,800 feet. Farther along, on the northeast side, you'll run across Cleetwood Trail and its 1-mile path down to the lake's shores. It is a steep path down, steeper coming back up, and don't take more than you can comfortably carry. But do go down, for at the end of the trail the boat trips on Crater Lake begin, 2-hour circles around the lake and to the islands. Boat trips have rangers on board explaining what you pass and what to look for. Inquire at the visitors centers before heading down Cleetwood Trail as to times and availability of boat trips.

Other stops along the route include the 2½-mile trail up Mt. Scott, the highest point in the park. A little farther on is the turnoff for the drive to the top of Cloudcap, 1,600 feet above the lake. All these paths and roads give different perspectives on the vastness of the lake below, views of the Cascade Range to the north, and the full scope of Oregon scenery all around.

The major drawback to Crater is winter, for when it comes, the park closes almost totally. There are 50-foot accumulations of snow by the time winter has had its say, and the north entrance is closed almost the entire season. Though park accommodations close, a choice of ski facilities is open inside the park. The Rim Road opens sometime in June — when the snow is cleared. Certain roads and trails may be closed during peak season due to conservation considerations.

A last note: Although you'll undoubtedly have the experience of sneaking up on "tame" wild animals like deer, squirrels, chipmunks, marmots, and foxes, don't feed or try to pet them. For more information on facilities, park accommodations, travel suggestions: Superintendent, Crater Lake National Park, Crater Lake, OR 97604 (phone: 503-594-2211).

BEST EN ROUTE

Crater Lake Lodge, Rim Village – Just what you'd expect of a well-managed, comfortable, but rustic national park lodge. There are 62 rooms and a number of cabins available, plus a store in Rim Village. There is nightly entertainment — campfire programs — and easy access to information on ranger tours, boat rides, lectures, and other park activities. Open from June 10 to mid-September. Reservations necessary. Crater Lake Lodge, PO Box 128, Crater Lake, OR 97604 (phone: 503-594-2511).

Also in Crater Lake National Park – Two campgrounds within the park offer a variety of camping facilities: Mazama, in the south-central area, and the primitive Lost Creek. All are run on a first-come, first-served basis. Information: Superintendent, Crater Lake National Park, Crater Lake, OR 97604 (phone: 503-594-2211).

Diamond Lake Resort, Diamond Lake, Oregon – Just 7 miles north of the park's northern entrance, this lodge has 92 rooms, on the lakefront. Diamond Lake, OR 97731 (phone: 503-793-3333).

The Oregon Coast

One of the most awesome drives in the country is along Oregon's northwest Pacific Coast, from Astoria at the mouth of the Columbia River all the way to the California border at Pelican Beach. Here you can see how land has been — and is still being — sculpted by the enormous, slow force of the sea. Very little of the land along the coast is privately owned, so you can stop at hundreds of points along the road that are part of state and federal forests. Most of the coast is lined with steep cliffs; 20 million years ago, when the coastline was formed, the land was level with the Pacific. The route can be driven north to south or south to north; we start at the northernmost point, Astoria, and work south. To get from Portland to Astoria take Rte. 30, a 75-mile drive. The coast road is Rte. 101. Information: Department of Tourism (phone: 503-378-3451).

ASTORIA: At the mouth of the Columbia River, known for its salmon, Astoria is both a river fishing and a commercial deep-sea fishing center. On the waterfront, the *Colombia River Maritime Museum* has ship models, artifacts, and — moored outside — a restored lightship. From the top of the Astoria Column on Coxcomb Hill, you can see the harbor, ocean, and, inland, the wooded mountains. Astoria Column is a monument to the area's history. Four miles south on Rte. 101, Ft. Clatsop National Memorial replicates the fort where Lewis and Clark spent the winter of 1805-6. Just west is the major charter fishing port of Warrenton. Ten miles south of Ft. Clatsop, the small town of Gearheart has an excellent 18-hole golf course.

SEASIDE: Two miles south of Gearheart, this is one of Oregon's busiest shore resorts. A sea wall along the coast forms a 2-mile boardwalk above the beach. Tillamook Head, 5 miles from Seaside on an old logging road that juts west to the ocean, stands more than 1,200 feet above sea level and provides a sweeping view of the northern territories and the offshore Tillamook Lighthouse. South of Seaside, Rte. 101 turns east along the Necanicum River, through green lowlands where commercial farms grow lettuce and peas. At Cannon Beach Junction, a road lined with towering hemlocks leads to Cannon Beach, a community becoming known for its music, art, and theater programs.

ARCH CAPE: Arch Cape is carved into a bluff at Neah-kah-nie Mountain. Barely 5 miles down the road, Manzanita is both a beach and mountain resort, tucked in a cove protected by rugged headlands to the north. From here the road cuts inland with Nehalem Bay, crosses the Nehalem River, and passes through Wheeler. Seven miles south, Rockaway has broad beaches, the arched Twin Rocks, an offshore formation, and attractive resort facilities.

TILLAMOOK BAY: The bay's main town is Tillamook, a center of Oregon's inland dairy region. The Tillamook Cheese Factory here has a viewing area and interpretive exhibits. Cape Meares, just west of town, offers a broad view of the ocean from a 700-foot-high overlook. Cape Meares is the first stop on the Three Capes Scenic Drive, which also leads to Cape Lookout and Cape Kiwanda, near Pacific City.

NESKOWIN: About 30 miles south, the beaches attract beachcombers who hunt for Japanese floats, colored glass balls used as net supports by Oriental fishermen. The floats cross the Pacific on the Japan Current. Cascade Head, southwest of Neskowin, stands 1,400 feet high and juts out to sea.

DEVIL'S LAKE: Some 14 miles south of Neskowin, the lake offers good fishing and claims to be the source of the shortest river in the world, "D" River, which flows only 400 yards from Devil's Lake to the Pacific. Just west, Lincoln City has one of the largest concentrations of resort facilities on the coast.

DEPOE BAY: Go south for 15 miles. Before reaching Depoe Bay, just south of Boiler Bay State Park, huge (up to an acre) heaps of shells mark the remains of Indian feasts. The town's harbor is nearly always filled with trawlers, and charter boat fishing is available, as are sightseeing and whale watching cruises. Offshore, water spouts from an aperture in the rocks known as Spouting Horn. Look for the geyser of spray shooting skyward from the ocean. The Depoe Bay Aquarium has displays of local marine life (Rte. 101 in the middle of town). About 4 miles south, Cape Foulweather viewpoint overlooks an impressive stretch of ocean, and just south, Devil's Punch Bowl State Park looks out to Otter Rock, a seabird rookery that was once the home of thousands of sea otters. At the base of a sandstone bluff, waves rush through two openings and boil up inside the rocky caldron, receding in a wash of foam. This is the Devil's Punch Bowl. For information on Depoe Bay parks, contact Oregon State Parks, 525 Trade St. SE, Salem, OR 97310 (phone: 800-452-5687). About 10 miles south of the Devil's Punch Bowl, Newport spreads across a steep, ridged peninsula between the ocean and Yaquina Bay. The resultant sheltered harbor offers year-round surfing, scuba diving, fishing, clamming, and crabbing. In Newport, be sure to sample the delicious Dungeness crab and Yaquina Bay oyster. Across the bay, the Mark O. Hatfield Marine Science Center has a variety of exhibitions and is popular with kids for its "handling pools."

FLORENCE: Here, the coastline alters in character. The steep, craggy headlands give way to a 50-mile stretch of sand dunes extending to the Coos Bay area. Behind the low foredunes along the shore stretches a chain of freshwater lakes. Beyond the lakes are huge dunes, some reaching as high as 250 feet and extending as far as 3 miles inland. Half-buried pine and spruce mark the dunes' eastward march. Jessie M. Honeyman State Park contains Cleawox Lake, locked in by the dunes, and a dense, evergreen forest laced with trails. Honeyman is at the northern boundary of Oregon Dunes National Recreation Area, part of Siuslaw National Forest. You can take a dune buggy ride or hike over the dunes, but be careful: It's easy to get lost. Winds can whip up and become blinding in a short time, covering your footprints. Dune hiking is also more taxing than hiking on hard-packed ground. Trail access and views of some of the highest dunes are available from the Dunes Overlook, between Florence and Reedsport. Eight miles north of Florence are the Sea Lion Caves, where a modern elevator takes visitors down to one of the world's largest sea caves. Sea lions can be seen inside primarily during the fall and winter; they live outside on the rocks in front during spring and summer.

REEDSPORT/WINCHESTER BAY: Reedsport is the headquarters for the Oregon Dunes National Recreation Area. Nearby, Winchester Bay has one of the Oregon coast's largest sport fishing fleets.

COOS BAY: South of the dunes area, mile-long McCullough Bridge crosses Coos Bay, site of the lumber town of North Bend. The Coos Bay region is the West's main lumber port. Shore Acres, Sunset Bay, and Cape Arago state parks, west of Coos Bay, overlook protected coves and Simpson's Reef offshore. Shore Acres has large formal gardens on view at a former estate. From the headland, sea otters and sea lions can be seen playing on offshore reefs.

BANDON: Some 17 miles south of Coos Bay, this diversified town features a restored Old Town, a cheese factory, and a spectacular beach. Summer sternwheeler riders are offered up the Coquille River. A few miles south, a petting zoo/walk-through safari is at the West Coast Game Park (phone: 503-347-3106).

CAPE BLANCO: Forty miles south of Coos Bay, a road leads to Cape Blanco, the most westerly point in Oregon. The flat, grassy cape juts 2 miles into the Pacific, overlooking Blanco and Orford reefs to the south. The Cape Blanco Lighthouse on the headland was built in the 1870s. Port Oxford, 6 miles south of the Cape Blanco turnoff, is a small harbor town protected by a cape to the north called the Heads. Many trails lead through underbrush to secluded beaches and tidal pools. Humbug Mountain, 6 miles farther south, rises 1,750 feet; Humbug Mountain State Park (part of Siskiyou National Forest) has fishing, swimming, and camping facilities.

GOLD BEACH: At the mouth of the Rogue River (which can be toured by jet boat), 22 miles south of Humbug Mountain, is Gold Beach. During the 1850s a good deal of gold was dredged from the Rogue, but in 1861 floods swept the deposits into the ocean. (Small amounts of gold can still be found along the beaches.) The stretch of coastline from here to the California line is probably the most rugged in Oregon. Innumerable coves and tidal pools remain, virtually untouched. Cape Sebastian, 7 miles south of Gold Beach and 35 miles from the California border, is a 700-foot promontory reaching out to the sea, with many trails branching inland from the coast. Harris State Park, 6 miles from California, has miles of beach and a view of offshore bird rookeries. For more information on the Oregon Coast, contact the Oregon Coast Assn., PO Box 670, Oregon Coast, OR 97365.

BEST EN ROUTE

Crest Motel, Astoria – Panoramic hilltop view overlooking the Columbia River, with mountains on the far shore; 36 rooms, including 2 large suites, in 3 buildings on 2½ acres of woods and lawns, with whirlpool bath, in-room coffee, and continental breakfast. 5366 Lief Ericson Dr., Astoria, OR 97103 (phone: 503-325-3141).

Salishan Lodge, Gleneden Beach – A spectacular first class resort designed to harmonize with the surrounding woods, lagoons, beach, and ocean. The 201 rooms and 3 suites are in 15 villas; resort facilities include almost the entire list of possibilities. See also *America's Special Havens,* DIVERSIONS. PO Box 118, Gleneden Beach, OR 97388 (phone: 503-764-2371 or 800-452-2300).

Tu Tu Tun Lodge, Gold Beach – On the banks of the Rogue River, all 18 rooms overlook the water. A jet boat stops to pick up passengers at the lodge dock daily. Dining room, swimming pool, fishing, wild river jet boat trips, 4-hole pitch-and-putt course, and hiking trips. 96550 N. Bank Rogue, Gold Beach, OR 97444 (phone: 503-247-6664).

Jacksonville Inn, Jacksonville – Some 100 miles inland from Gold Beach, in the heart of what was once gold rush country. Built in 1863, the inn has been through several incarnations — a bank, hardware store, professional offices, and a repair shop. Each of the 8 bedrooms is lovingly furnished with antiques. The dining room, open for lunch and dinner, serves substantial meals of steaks, seafood, and continental dishes; wine and gift shop. An interesting 19th-century town, Jacksonville has a number of frontier-era buildings to explore. PO Box 359, 175 E. California St., Jacksonville, OR 97530 (phone: 503-899-1900).

Badlands National Park, South Dakota

About 80 miles east of Rapid City, South Dakota, several miles south of I-90, Badlands National Park covers more than 380 square miles, haunting southwestern South Dakota with a presence of irregular, awesome hills carved in colors brilliant enough to make even Dorothy's magical rainbow seem commonplace. It was raised in status from a national monument to a national park in 1978.

The Indians called this region Maco Sica, or "land bad," probably because of its barren terrain and weird shapes. Later, the French-Canadian explorers and trappers who passed through labeled the barren buttes les mauvaises terres — badlands. General Alfred Sully took one look at the place and called it "a part of hell with the fires burned out."

The journey starts in Rapid City.

RAPID CITY: Settled in the late 1870s after gold was discovered in the Black Hills, Rapid City now has a population of over 50,000 and spreads across a section of Black

Hills plateau. Main sites in town include the South Dakota School of Mines and Technology, with displays of fossils and geological artifacts, including specimens of local minerals (St. Joseph St.); Dahl Fine Arts Center, with giant murals showing scenes of US history and assorted Americana (713 7th St.); Marine Life, with aquariums and dolphin and seal shows (2 miles south on Rte. 16); Bear Country USA, home of roaming buffalo, wolves, deer, mountain lion, antelope, and various smaller furry native creatures (8 miles south on Rte. 16). At Black Hills Reptile Gardens you can see rattlesnakes being milked, alligators being wrestled, and snakes from all over the world (6 miles south on Rte. 16). Chapel in the Hills is a replica of an 800-year-old Norwegian church set among rolling hills in a tranquil valley (Chapel Rd.). The *Horseless Carriage Museum* offers old-fashioned cars, clothes, musical instruments, machinery, and other nostalgia; 10 miles south on Rte. 16. And then there's Mount Rushmore (25 miles south on Rte. 16). Before heading for the national park, look at the surrounding countryside from Skyline Drive, a scenic route in the southwest part of town. Information: Rapid City Chamber of Commerce, PO Box 747, Rapid City, SD 57709 (phone: 605-343-1744; from Memorial Day to Labor Day, 605-348-2850, Visitor Information Center).

Next, pick up I-90 southeast to the park. You can enter 8 miles south of Wall, which is 55 miles from Rapid City.

BADLANDS NATIONAL PARK: Until about 65 million years ago, this area was submerged under a shallow sea. Silt and clay accumulated on the sea bottom; and as time passed, these sediments hardened into the rock known as the Pierre Shale. Eventually, the same forces that pushed up the Black Hills also lifted the seabed. By the time of the Oligocene Epoch (37 to 23 million years ago), the area had been transformed into a floodplain and resembled the Gulf Coast of today. Animals roamed the flood plain in great numbers. Many of the animals later suffered extinction, but some, such as the tiny three-toed horse, evolved into species we see today. Frequent flooding buried mammal bones with mud, permitting them to fossilize. Millions of years rolled by and the climate became cooler and drier. Finally, in the last few thousand years, a semiarid climate punctuated by downpours set off erosion. Now the land is a sweeping garden of nature's sculpture, with fantastic buttes rising above zigzag gullies. Colored layers representing ancient soils are vivid reminders of the long-lost Golden Age of Mammals, and each scouring rain uncovers fossil skulls, their empty sockets explored by sunlight after millennia of darkness.

No matter how desolate the landscape appears, there is plenty of wildlife. Occasionally, you can spot a juniper or red cedar among the stark surroundings. Likewise, yucca and rabbit brush thrive on the recently fallen slopes and valleys which hold greater moisture. Most animals in the area seek refuge in those moist prairies on the park's circumference, but in the badlands you can see buffalo, along with herds of deer and antelope. The jackrabbit, cottontail, and chipmunk attempt to avoid their predatory neighbor, the coyote. Occasionally, the golden eagle, cliff swallow, rock wren, and snowy owl make appearances.

In the late 1800s, the badlands were overrun with geologists seeking fossils. In an attempt to preserve the area, Congress passed legislation authorizing Badlands National Monument in 1929. In 1939, a presidential proclamation set aside 150,000 acres to be administered by the National Park Service. An additional 94,000 acres were added in 1968. (Collecting fossils is not permitted.)

Though there are entrances at both sides of the Badlands National Park (26 miles apart), the entrance at the northeast corner, just south of Cactus Flat, takes you to headquarters and the visitors center, which is farther down the road on the left, near Cedar Pass. Inside are displays and a recorded slide program. In the summer, nature hikes are conducted and evening programs take place in the amphitheater.

You can drive for 22 miles along a paved road lined with parking areas and lookouts with markers describing geological and botanical phenomena. There are six main hiking trails in addition to the ¾-mile Door Trail and the shorter Cliff Shell nature trail. Both take you into the middle of the multicolored plateaus and soft clay surroundings so you can see them at close range. If you are a photographer, be sure to set out in the early morning or late afternoon, when the low light intensifies the hues of the jagged hills. There are campsites at Sage Creek and Cedar Pass.

If you enter at Cedar Pass, you can drive through the park and exit at the western Pinnacles entrance, picking up I-90 at Wall for the return trip to Rapid City. Or you can stop in Kadoka, about 25 miles east of Cedar Pass. Information: Superintendent, Badlands National Park, PO Box 6, Interior, SD 57750 (phone: 605-433-5361).

KADOKA: Only 815 people live in this town, but if you're interested in looking at some of the biggest petrified logs in the neighborhood as well as fluorescent minerals, Badlands agates, prehistoric remains of mammals such as saber-tooth tigers, and fossilized fish from the period when South Dakota was partially underwater, stop in at Badlands Petrified Gardens, off Exit 152 of I-90 (phone: 605-837-2448).

BEST EN ROUTE

Cedar Pass Lodge, Badlands National Park – In the heart of the rugged badlands, not far from the park's visitors center. Accommodations consist of 24 cabins and a main building with a restaurant and a gift shop. Hwy. 240 off I-90. PO Box 5, Interior, SD 57750 (phone: 605-433-5460).

Black Hills, South Dakota

The fabled Black Hills cover about 6,075 square miles of southwestern South Dakota along the Wyoming border. Famous for mineral deposits and pure grazing land, the Black Hills are actually green: a blend of oak, elm, ash, pine, and aspen. They are, in reality, a far cry from the ominous-sounding name bestowed upon the hills by the Indians.

According to folklore, Paul Bunyan and his blue ox, Babe, created the Black Hills. Hungry, the huge Babe swallowed a stove in the hope of finding nourishment. Unfortunately, his stomach couldn't adapt to this hefty substance and he died. Unable to find a suitable burial ground, Paul Bunyan poured soil over his faithful companion. With time, the rain carved brooks and streams into the mound and brisk winds and birds brought seeds to the undeveloped hills. Thus the Black Hills. To tour the Black Hills from Rapid City, take Rte. 16 southwest for 13 miles to Rockerville.

ROCKERVILLE: This veritable ghost town was in its glory during the late 1870s, when $1 million worth of gold was mined out of the surrounding hills, but its supply of the valuable mineral ran dry as suddenly as it was found. By 1882, most residents moved farther west, leaving empty saloons and cabins to the animals that roamed the hills. But nowadays the town comes alive in summer, when tourists come to see the old-time saloon, general store, and soda parlor.

KEYSTONE: One of the first pioneer towns in the area, it is the official address of Mt. Rushmore, 3 miles from the center of town (see *Mt. Rushmore,* in this section). You can see it from the Rushmore Aerial Tramway, ½ mile south of Keystone, on Rte. 16A. Also on Rte. 16A, you can mine for gold ore and keep anything you find at Big Thunder Gold Mine.

HILL CITY: About 10 miles west of Keystone on Rte. 16 is Hill City, where an 1880s steam train takes you through the Black Hills, past the settings used in the TV series "Gunsmoke." You can go by train and connecting car to Keystone and back. To make reservations, write 1880s Train, PO Box 1880, Hill City, SD 57445 (phone: 605-574-2222). About 5 miles south stands 7,242-foot Harney Peak, the highest point in South Dakota. Two of the most popular trailheads are located at Willow Creek Horse Camp on the north of the wilderness and Sylvan Lake on the south. From these trailheads, you can hike to the summit. Harney Peak provides an elegant view of "the Needles," a section of granite pinnacles.

CUSTER: About 25 miles southwest of Keystone on Rte. 16 west and Rte. 385 south and nestled along French Creek, Custer is one of the oldest towns in the Black Hills. Though quartz, mica, beryl, and gypsum are mined in the immediate area, it was gold that brought the town its prosperity. In fact, the first gold strike in the state occurred in 1874 in Custer State Park (5 miles east on Rte. 16A, 7 miles north on Rte. 89), where you can swim, fish, and hike. Within the park's 72,000 acres roams one of the largest publicly owned buffalo herds in the world. The park has four state lodges that offer accommodations and meals and 11 campgrounds (also run by the state), four lakes, mountain streams, and many outdoor recreational facilities. Daily interpretive programs are held from Memorial Day through Labor Day. Entrance fee charged from May through September; open year-round. Information: Custer State Park, HCR 83, Box 70, Custer, SD 57730 (phone: 605-255-4515).

JEWEL CAVE NATIONAL MONUMENT: About 14 miles west of Custer on Rte. 16. Myriad crystal formations create beautiful images and designs. Walking tours and more rigorous spelunking tours are conducted during the summer, but you should be in good physical condition before considering one. The visitors center and exhibition room provide background on local geology (about 14 miles west of Custer on Rte. 16). The last weekend in July, the *Gold Discovery Days Pageant* at Custer attempts to re-create the time of the great gold discovery of 1874. Celebrations include a carnival, a rodeo, and a reenactment of Gold Rush events.

WIND CAVE NATIONAL PARK: Designated a national park by President Theodore Roosevelt in 1903, the cave got its name from the strong wind currents that blow through its entrance. The winds are believed to be caused by external atmospheric pressures. Most of the 28,260-acre park is aboveground and consists of woodlands and open prairies. Elk, bison, and prairie dogs wander freely among the wildflowers and trees, making this area a favorite of photographers. It's about 15 miles south of Custer on Rte. 385. Information: Wind Cave National Park, Hot Springs, SD 57747 (phone: 605-745-4600).

BLACK HILLS NATIONAL FOREST: The forest covers more than a million acres of dense stands of pines and open meadows seemingly wedged into the crevices of the rugged, jagged hills. Established in 1897, Black Hills National Forest is home to elk, deer, antelope, and mountain goats. Camping, hiking, fishing, and picnicking facilities are available. A visitors center at Pactola Lake is open from Memorial Day to Labor Day. Information: Forest Supervisor, Black Hills National Forest, RR2, Box 200, Custer, SD 57730 (phone: 605-673-2251).

LEAD: Unlike neighboring towns, Lead (pronounced "leed") never ran dry of gold. The largest working gold mine in the Western Hemisphere, Homestake Mine, in operation since 1877, offers tours from May through October (on Rte. 14A and Rte. 85). In winter, Lead is an active ski resort as people challenge the slopes of Terry Peak, at 7,076 feet the highest ski mountain east of the Rockies. The chair lift to the summit gives you an unparalleled view of Montana, North Dakota, Nebraska, and Wyoming (1½ miles southwest on Rte. 14A).

DEADWOOD: Less than 5 miles east of Lead on Rte. 85, Deadwood is primarily a tourist town. Once, however, it was the "get rich quick" spot after Custer ran dry. Wild

Bill Hickok, Calamity Jane, and Preacher Smith roamed the streets and caroused at the very well attended saloons. It was here that Wild Bill Hickok lost not only a game of poker but his life. He and other Wild West characters are buried at Mt. Moriah Cemetery. Every summer, the trial of Wild Bill's killer is reenacted at the Old Town Hall (Lee St.) in a play called *The Trial of Jack McCall.* The first weekend of August, Deadwood holds a rodeo and a parade on Main St. to celebrate the "Days of '76." For information call the Chamber of Commerce (phone: 605-578-1876).

BEST EN ROUTE

State Game Lodge, Custer State Park – Here are motel units and cabins, stocked fishing streams, and fine horseback riding trails. Restaurant and cocktail lounge. Pets are welcome. State Game Lodge, Custer State Park, Custer, SD 57730 (phone: 605-255-4541).

Sylvan Lake Resort, Custer State Park – Near Sylvan Lake, a popular resort area, this hotel offers fishing and riding. You can stay in cabins or in a standard hotel room in the lodge. A restaurant is on the premises. The lodge is open year-round; cabins are open from May to October. For reservations, write to Sylvan Lake Resort, PO Box 695, Piedmont Rte., Piedmont, SD 57769 (phone: 605-574-2561).

Rushmore View Motor Lodge, Keystone – Provides a terrific view of Mt. Rushmore without crowds and traffic. Open May until October. PO Box 197, Keystone, SD 57751 (phone: 605-666-4466).

Mt. Rushmore National Memorial, South Dakota

Southwest of Keystone, off Rte. 16A, Mt. Rushmore National Memorial rests in the eastern portion of South Dakota's Black Hills, surrounded by trees and streams. The portraits of Presidents Washington, Jefferson, Lincoln, and Theodore Roosevelt, which are carved into the granite cliffs, rise above all else in the area. Mt. Rushmore, fittingly known as "the Shrine of Democracy," has become a symbol of America.

Looking at the site from nearby Harney Peak, a 7,242-foot mountain, Mt. Rushmore's designer, Gutzon Borglum, spotted the rectangular block that was later to serve as the base for his presidential masterpiece and became excited with the possibility. "There's the place to carve a great national memorial," Borglum exclaimed. "American history shall march along the skyline."

Upon closer inspection, Borglum found Mt. Rushmore was, indeed, ideal for his intended project. Despite a few minor flaws, the surface was relatively smooth, rising 5,659 feet above sea level. The rock face that rested on the southeast corner of the slab was 1,000 feet long and 400 feet wide and provided maximum daylight and optimal illumination.

Curiously enough, Mt. Rushmore got its name by accident. In fact, there is no connection between the name and the shrine to the four presidents. In the late 19th century, the Black Hills became a haven for gold seekers. Inevitable land disputes followed. One miner, involved in a interminable conflict, hired the services of an eastern lawyer, Rushmore, to settle his claim.

One day, riding past the rocky plateau with his client, the lawyer asked about its name. Kidding, the miner said it was Mt. Rushmore. And 45 years later, in 1930, Mt. Rushmore became the official name.

But the idea to construct a shrine was not as easily accepted. In 1923, Doane Robinson, South Dakota state historian and poet, proposed building a monument dedicated to famous western heroes such as Lewis and Clark, Kit Carson, and the famous Sioux Indian Red Cloud. But the citizens were reticent to support the idea, failing to grasp the potential significance of such a romantic memorial. Refusing to give up, Robinson finally managed to win the support of two influential and wealthy South Dakotans, Representative William Williamson and Senator Peter Norbeck. Both agreed that the giant sculpture would bring fame and fortune to the quiet midwestern state, known primarily for its mineral-rich Black Hills and never-ending prairies. Robinson and his colleagues found the needed support, and in 1924 Gutzōn Borglum was called to survey the terrain and discuss the project. Foreseeing the possibilities and intrigued by the challenge, Borglum left Confederate Memorial, which he was carving at Stone Mountain outside Atlanta, Georgia, and headed for the Black Hills.

It was Borglum's idea to create a national memorial that would embrace the merits and symbolize the ideals of our most celebrated presidents. But many people were critical. Wanting no manmade sculpture to destroy the beauty of the rich Black Hills, they made fund-raising difficult. Traveling extensively, Borglum finally found enough money to begin his greatest work. Aware that people might only react to its size, he declared, "I did not and don't intend that this shall be just a damn big thing, a three-day tourist wonder."

On August 10, 1927, President Calvin Coolidge rode a horse 3 miles from nearby Keystone to dedicate the beginning of Mt. Rushmore's construction. Sporadic funding and inclement weather forced the project to take 14 years, the actual construction requiring 6½ years. Borglum, with the help of his son, Lincoln, supervised throughout, overseeing an average crew of 30, some of whom came from the Stone Mountain sculpture in Georgia. Between 1927 and 1941, when the project was completed, nearly $1 million was spent, all but $153,992 from the federal government. Borglum died in March 1941, just before Mt. Rushmore's completion. Nevertheless, his lifelong dream became reality only a few months later, under his son's supervision. Since that time, no addition or refinement has been made, despite numerous proposals.

When looking at Mt. Rushmore, you can see the painstaking detail that Borglum inscribed into the tough granite surface; George Washington's jacket collar and Teddy Roosevelt's spectacles are two examples. The faces weren't sculpted by traditional methods. More than 450,000 tons of rock were removed; the outer surface was removed with dynamite. Drillers, lowered in "swing seats" from above, blasted away stone to rough out the faces. The remaining rock was chipped away by hand and smoothed by a technique called "bumping," using an air hammer.

However, even with all the fine detail, it is still the dimensions of the monument that create its impressive aura. The faces measure 60 feet from top of head to chin; the mouths stretch more than 18 feet across, and the average nose is 20 feet long. The finished project is a perfect example of that love of size that swept 20th-century America. Mt. Rushmore ranks as one of the largest sculptures in the world, comparable to the ancient Egyptian pyramids and sphinxes.

The symbolism in this "Shrine of Democracy" is as grand and potent as its physical dimensions. Addressing congressional peers in 1928, William Williamson stressed the symbolic, allegorical significance of the memorial. "Washington symbolizes the founding of our country and the stability of our institutions," he said. "Jefferson, our idealism, expansion, and love of liberty; Lincoln, our altruism and sense of inseparable unity. Roosevelt typifies the soul of America — its restless energy, rugged morality, and progressive spirit."

The memorial's visitors center is open daily, from 8 AM to 5 PM. In summer it remains open till 10 PM. No camping or picnicking permitted. Information: PO Box 268, Mt. Rushmore National Memorial, SD 57751 (phone: 605-574-2523).

BEST EN ROUTE

Palmer Gulch Lodge, Hill City – Down-home ranch accommodations with horseback riding, fishing, hiking, and swimming. Cabins can accommodate between 3 and 8 guests. PO Box 295, Hill City, SD 57745 (phone: 605-574-2525).

Powder House Lodge, Keystone – Only 4 miles from Mt. Rushmore, in a mountain setting, these accommodations consist of cabins and motel units. Restaurant specializes in roast beef. Open May through September. Box 74, Keystone, SD 57751 (phone: 605-666-4646).

Great Salt Lake, Utah

There's a stretch out west, familiar to anyone who has crossed the country on I-80 — that ultimate American superhighway — where all life seems to stop. On both sides of the shimmering blacktop spread vast reaches of sand, blinding white in the unrelenting sun. The air is hot, dry, and stagnant, and the monotonous flatness inspires mirages. But sometimes the harsher a place seems, the more interesting it turns out to be, and this is the case with the Great Salt Lake Desert region in Utah.

As you continue driving you will encounter what looks like a gray-blue inland sea that is either the Great Salt Lake or the largest mirage you're ever likely to see. If you're still on I-80, west of Salt Lake City, the lake is no illusion. And as you get closer, you will find that it is no anomaly in relation to the surrounding landscape but only to our general concept of lakes and seas. This 30-by-80-mile body of water does not teem with life as one would expect. It is North America's dead sea by virtue of its high salt concentration — as much as 22% in the lake's northern reaches (almost seven times saltier than sea water). The only life that the lake supports is some primitive algae, bacteria, a kind of brine shrimp (¼ inch long and feathery, a semitransparent crustacean used for tropical fish food), and swarms of stingless brine flies that blacken the shores from June to September. Naturally, the water is unfit for drinking, hardly ideal for swimming, and not exactly a fisherman's dream. But it does offer 4.8 billion tons of salt, deposits of magnesium, lithium, gypsum, potash, boron, sulfur, and chloride compounds that have lured chemical firms to this liquid mine; and for everyone else, some of the most fantasy-fulfilling floating, wading, and bobbing imaginable.

With a little knowledge of natural history, everything begins to fall into place. The arid and desolate area that surrounds the lake appears as inhospitable as it does because it was once covered by the lake's salty waters. Today's Great Salt Lake is merely a drop in the bucket compared to this earlier sea. Only 23,000 years ago, freshwater Lake Bonneville (formed from the melting snows of successive Ice Ages) stretched from Salt Lake City west into Nevada, north into Idaho, and south into Cedar City, Utah, covering an area comparable to Lake Michigan. The lake reached depths exceeding 1,000 feet and encompassed 20,000 square miles. (The terraced striations marking its former shorelines are still visible today on the flanks of the Wasatch Mountains of the Rockies.) When the last of the glaciers waned and the ice retreated northward, weather in this region became hotter and drier. Lake Bonneville shrank below the level of its outlet, Red Rock Pass in southeast Idaho, and its feeder streams continued to bring in minerals that could not escape. Though some water flowed in, the amount was not sufficient to offset evaporation, and the lake grew saltier and saltier. Today, the remnant of this once vast inland sea is so salty that no swimmer can sink in it. The Southern Pacific's rail causeway, built in 1903, divides the lake into two sections of differing salinities. To the south of the dike-supported track, the lake appears bluer because the freshwater inflow dilutes the salinity; the north side approaches saturation. But either side of the tracks provides ample testing grounds for experiments in human buoyancy.

In 1983, highwater covered all the "beaches" and flooded the permanent facilities of Great Salt Lake State Park Saltair Beach, at the southern end of the lake (16 miles west of Salt Lake City on I-80). Restoration took place between 1986 and 1987, and both the marina and beaches reopened in 1987. The boat harbor has been saved, and there is some water access and minimal facilities. (For a full report on the city, see *Salt Lake City*, THE CITIES.) In the summer the water will be quite warm, around 80 F. Once you are in chest- or neck-deep water you can experiment as you wish (floating is still pretty easy). But there are positions you shouldn't try — any that involve putting your face in or under the water. You won't sink, but that burning sensation in your eyes and nasal and oral passages will make you wish you never set eyes on the Great Salt Lake. The park is open year-round (but keep your suit on; Utah law does not look kindly on nudity). There is a boat ramp and small sailboat rentals. Motorboats are not used because the high salt concentration will corrode the motor and metal. Those with boats can get information from the rangers on how to reach some of the lake's islands.

Antelope Island, the other point for public access, is closed now due to highway flooding. When open, the island is a good jumping-off point for boat trips because it provides access to several other lake islands — Egg and Fremont, where you can see birds and other animals including horses and sheep that are brought here for summer grazing. Gunnison Island in the northwest quadrant of the lake can only be reached via boat and is a nesting site for the great white pelican. Amid these scrubby bushes and rock heaps, you can spot this magnificent bird as well as terns and gulls.

Though you'd hardly suspect it as you lie in the warm waters of the Great Salt Lake or watch the seagulls soar, there are a dozen well-developed ski resorts within an hour's drive in the Wasatch Mountain Range east of Salt Lake City. The base elevation is 8,000 feet and the season stretches from November to May, so when it gets too cold to float (although folks of polar bear habits do immerse themselves year-round), there are plenty of places to ski in what Utahns claim is the greatest snow on earth. There's a good cover of snow, and unlike on the lake, on the slopes the law of gravity prevails — if you fall, you're down. For more information on the Great Salt Lake: Superintendent, Saltair Beach State Park, GSL, PO Box 323, Magna, UT 84044 (phone: 801-533-4081).

BEST EN ROUTE

For information on camping in the Salt Lake area, contact Utah State Parks and Recreation, 1636 W. North Temple, Salt Lake City, UT 84116 (phone: 801-538-7220; State Park Reservations, 800-328-2267). A wide range of accommodations is available in Salt Lake City.

Salt Lake Hilton, Salt Lake City – This hotel exudes an aura of contemporary sophistication. Suites have sunken baths; there is an outdoor swimming pool, therapy pool, sauna, and 3 dining rooms. 150 W. 500 South, Salt Lake City, UT 84101 (phone: 801-532-3344 or 800-421-7602).

Zion and Bryce Canyon National Parks, Utah

According to official Utah sources, one seventh of all the national parks in the US lie within a 200-mile circle in southern Utah. Two of the most spectacular, Zion and Bryce Canyon, are only 90 miles apart. From Salt Lake City, I-15 south proceeds 320 miles to Zion National Park. From there, Rte. 17 and Rte. 9 east to US 89 north and Rte. 12 takes you to Bryce Canyon National Park. Another route is from Las Vegas, only 160 miles south of Zion National Park, by way of I-15 and Rte. 9.

ZION NATIONAL PARK: A series of dramatic gorges and canyons, Zion is geologically part of the area that includes the Grand Canyon, 125 miles to the south, and Bryce Canyon, 89 miles northeast. From the air, the three canyons look like a series of steps, with Grand Canyon the first, Zion in the middle, and Bryce Canyon, the top. The middle sibling of this vast natural canyon-scape is younger than the Grand Canyon and older than Bryce. It dates to the Mesozoic era, a period familiar to us as the time when dinosaurs stalked the earth. (It is possible to see dinosaur footprints in the rocks at Zion if you ask at a visitors center.) At first a sea, then a desert, Zion's layered buttes and canyons are actually the scars of incredibly harsh climatic changes. These shifts created psychedelic purple, lilac, yellow, and pink rock walls and gorges that shimmer in the clear light. When you see it, you'll know why they call this "the land of rainbow canyons." Geologists believe Zion Canyon was formed by the Virgin River, which carved a gorge out of deep layers of sediment left from the shallow seas that covered the area. We're not sure whether the river was named after explorer Thomas Virgin or the Virgin Mary. There seems to be a running debate among historians, just as there is among geologists. The 229 square miles of Zion National Park (established in 1919) were named by a 19th-century Mormon, Isaac Behunin. To the Mormons, Zion means "heavenly resting place."

Zion is most impressive for the intense and rugged beauty of its canyons, some of which are impassable even today just as they were when explorers began visiting the area last century, and for the splendid incandescence of the color of its rock formations. There is a breathtaking drive on the Zion–Mt. Carmel Highway, which runs along the east section of the park, connecting with canyon drive, zigzagging up Pine Creek Canyon and through the 5,607-foot-long tunnel. This road connecting I-15 and US 89 is all the more remarkable when you consider that it was completed in 1930, the year Zion and Bryce canyons were first photographed from the air. Before setting out on this road, be sure to read the tunnel information.

Any visit should begin at the Zion Canyon visitors center near the southern entrance, where there's a museum of geological exhibitions and an information desk. From the lobby, you'll have an excellent view of multicolored Zion Canyon. Another visitors center is to the north, at the Kolob Canyons exit off I-15. Overnight hikes on any of the 65 miles of trails require permits, which you can pick up at the visitors centers before setting out. And be sure to check weather conditions — the trails around the canyon rim are sometimes closed due to snow. From the Zion Lodge, you can also embark on horseback trips on Sandbench Trail. For a combined driving-hiking expedition, drive to the Temple of Sinawava, 8 miles from the south entrance of the park. Inside the amphitheater-shaped temple are the two giant pillars for which the temple got its name: the Altar and the Pulpit. Once you reach the temple, the road stops, so you'll have to get out and walk. From here, it's a mile to the beginning of the Narrows, where the Virgin River, sometimes no more than 20 feet wide, races through the giant walls of rock where columbine and shooting star flowers grow in spring. You can join a guided nature hike during the summer or camp along the ash-, cottonwood-, and moonflower-lined banks of the river in the two designated areas. It's 2½ strenuous miles to Angels Landing at the top of the canyon, but the view is worth it. There is a 2-day backpacking trip along the 12-mile West Rim Trail. The southwestern section of Zion National Park is desert. Coalpits Wash is the home of lizards, cacti, and a small waterfall. Information: Superintendent, Zion National Park, Springdale, UT 84767 (phone: 801-772-3256).

KANAB: Southeast of Zion, this town of about 13 motels and a handful of restaurants has the distinction of being 20 miles east of a set of coral pink sand dunes used as a location for many a Hollywood movie.

BRYCE CANYON NATIONAL PARK: The Paiute Indians may have called the stone formations at Bryce Canyon "red rocks standing like men in a bowl-shaped canyon" and thought the twisted shapes had been cast into stone by a vengeful god. Technically, Bryce's canyons are not canyons at all but breaks in the earth, tremendous pink and white limestone amphitheaters as deep as 1,000 feet. Standing at the eastern edge of the Paunsaugunt Plateau (Paunsaugunt means "home of the beaver"), Bryce Canyon National Park is laced by a network of tributaries (usually dry) of the Paria River. You can get a great view of the splintered rock plateau stretching to the north from the 9,105-foot-high Rainbow Point. (We recommend taking it easy at Bryce Canyon. The 8,000- to 9,000-foot altitude will tire you quickly.)

As at Zion, the best place to start your explorations of Bryce Canyon's 35,835 acres is the visitors center. Here you'll find geological, natural history, and archaeological exhibits. Guided naturalist activities are offered during summer; horseback rides are available spring, summer, and fall. In summer, there is also a van tour, which leaves from *Bryce Canyon Lodge*. There are 20 miles of driving roads along the rim of the canyon and 61 miles of hiking trails for exploring either the top or the bottom of the canyon. The most popular hiking trail is the Navajo Loop Trail, a 1- to 2-hour excursion that takes you more than 500 feet into the canyon, past Thor's Hammer and other rock formations. The trail intersects with the Peekaboo Loop Trail (a 3½-mile loop) and Queen's Garden Trail. Although the Paunsaugunt Plateau was given its name because of a preponderance of beaver, they are not in the park. You should, however, be able to spot skunks, deer, marmots, chipmunks, and squirrels without too much difficulty. Hawks, swallows, and ravens are among the more prevalent winged creatures that can be seen above Bryce Canyon. This is also one of the best places in the country for photography. Light sparkles here, illuminating the canyons so that they seem to glow from an inner fire. Dawn and dusk are the best times to take pictures. Winter activities include cross-country skiing, snowshoeing (some snowshoes are loaned at the visitors center), and winter camping. Part of one campground is open all winter. Each of the park's two campgrounds has a 14-day restriction. Information: Superintendent, Bryce Canyon National Park, Bryce Canyon, UT 84717 (phone: 801-834-5322).

BEST EN ROUTE

Zion Lodge, Zion National Park – A group of cabins and motel units with a total of 120 rooms. There are horseback riding facilities and a snack bar–restaurant. Managed by TW Recreational Services, PO Box 400, Cedar City, UT 84720 (phone: 801-586-7686).

Bryce Canyon Lodge, Bryce Canyon National Park – A collection of cabins and motel units with a total of 110 rooms, some with ornamental fireplaces. Managed by TW Recreational Services, PO Box 400, Cedar City, UT 84720 (phone: 801-586-7686).

Bryce Canyon Pines Motel and Restaurant, Bryce Canyon – About 8 miles from the park. Facilities include a restaurant and coffee shop, heated swimming pool, and horseback riding. Some of the 50 rooms have fireplaces. Bryce Canyon Pines, Star Route 1, Panguitch, UT 84759 (phone: 801-834-5336).

Mt. Rainier National Park, Washington

Swathed in glaciers, Mt. Rainier reaches 14,410 splendid, icy feet into the sky. A formidable, awesome presence, it is the tallest peak in Washington state (fifth tallest in the lower 48), 60 miles southeast of Seattle. Exploring Mt. Rainier's perilous slopes might not be your idea of a holiday — not everyone likes to hang upside down from a precipice, fastened to firmament by the mere grace of rope and pick — but regardless, your first encounter with Mt. Rainier is sure to be unforgettable.

Even those who are not enamored of mountains, insisting that "when you've seen one, you've seen 'em all," almost invariably return from a visit to Mt. Rainier converted. A solitary giant laced with frosty crevasses, this mountain dominates the surrounding area. In fact, the 235,404 acres of Mt.

Rainier National Park seem to have been selected specifically to provide natural settings of pine, wildflowers, and lakes against which the craggy Rainier can be seen to best advantage.

A curious combination of glacial and volcanic activity, Mt. Rainier is the product of relatively recent geological phenomena. One would be hard put to establish its precise age, since the mountain itself is the product of those momentous eruptions occurring within the last million years, which are also responsible for Mt. Baker, near the Canadian border, Lassen Peak in northern California, and the other peaks in the Cascade Range, to which Rainier belongs.

Climbers approaching Columbia Crest, Mt. Rainier's summit, have reported tiny geysers of steam spurting through the ice, a sign of volcanic activity below. The steam has carved intricate mazes in the mountain's ice, forming a labyrinthine network of ice tunnels and caves. In 1870, the first team to reach the summit of Mt. Rainier spent the night safely nestled in one of these burrows. Without these natural caves and tunnels to provide shelter, they probably would have died from exposure. Mt. Rainier's glacial system, the most extensive "single peak" network in the country (apart from Alaska), consists of 26 named glaciers and about 50 smaller, unnamed ones. Their age is estimated to be a mere 10,000 years, a legacy of the last, massive Ice Age Retreat. Carbon Glacier is Mt. Rainier's longest — 6 miles; Emmons Glacier, almost 4½ miles long by 1 mile wide, the largest. If you're curious about geological activity, this is the best place for observing icy and subterranean thermal forces in action. The Nisqually Glacier may move between 50 feet and 400 feet a year.

Declared a national park in 1899, Mt. Rainier is surrounded by national forests. Snoqualmie National Forest forms the eastern, northern, and western boundaries. Gifford Pinchot National Forest is to the south.

To get to Mt. Rainier National Park from Seattle, take I-5 south about 13 miles to exit 42B, then follow Rte. 161 south and pick up Rte. 7 to Rte. 706, which will take you directly to Mt. Rainier. This approach is open year-round.

MT. BAKER–SNOQUALMIE NATIONAL FOREST: This forest stretches 160 miles from the Canadian border to White Pass. Spruce and fir trees cover the 1.7 million acres that include Mt. Baker, a 10,778-foot dormant volcano, 390 glaciers, and 1,200 miles of trails, including sections of the Pacific Crest Trail. There are ski centers at Snoqualmie Pass, White Pass, Stevens Pass, Mt. Baker, and Mt. Pilchuck. Campsites open in summer. On Rte. 410, just north of Mt. Rainier National Park. Forest headquarters at 1022 1st Ave., Seattle, WA 98104 (phone: 206-442-0170; Ranger Station, 206-856-5700).

CRYSTAL MOUNTAIN: A year-round resort with excellent ski facilities in winter. A year-round chair lift offers a breathtaking view, sweeping from Mt. Rainier to Mt. Hood in Oregon. The Washington Cascade Crest Trail leads to nearby mountains. Snoqualmie National Forest on Rte. 410 (phone: 206-663-2265).

MT. ST. HELENS: In August 1982, President Ronald Reagan signed a bill naming Mt. St. Helens a National Volcanic Monument and designating 110,000 acres of its surrounding area for recreation and research. Part of Gifford Pinchot National Forest, Mt. St. Helens had been dormant since 1842 until it stirred to life in March 1980. A series of earthquakes and minor eruptions culminated in a massive explosion that blasted over 1,300 feet off the top of the 9,677-foot mountain in May 1980. The story of the eruptions is presented at the Mt. St. Helens Visitors Center on Highway 504, just east of Castle Rock (Exit 49 on Interstate 5). Also in Gifford Pinchot is Mt. Adams, a 12,326-foot monster with glaciers, forests, and lava flows, the Pacific Northwest's second largest peak. At its base, the Pacific Crest Trail leads from the western side of the mountain through Goat Rocks Wilderness. There are several campgrounds in different parts of the forest; open most of the year but closed to vehicles. Gifford Pinchot borders Mt. Rainier National Park to the south. For the visitors center, call 206-274-6644; for recorded information about roads and weather conditions (24 hours), call 206-274-6644; for climbing information, 206-247-5800).

MT. RAINIER NATIONAL PARK: Enter the park via Mather Memorial Parkway, a 50-mile paved road that takes you to the White River entrance where the road forks. You can continue south, to Stevens Canyon and the Ohanapecosh visitors center and campground, or west, to the Sunrise visitors center and White River Campground, about a mile from the road. Stevens Canyon Road, a section of the 117-mile network of paved roads, takes you along the southern boundary, past the Tatoosh Range and 5,955-foot Eagle Peak. The road passes Paradise, Longmire, and the Nisqually entrance and ranger station, in the southwest corner of the park. The visitors center distributes free information on hiking and climbing. Be sure to pick up the booklet entitled *Fragile, Handle with Care* before setting out. Guides conduct interpretive walks from Paradise in summer. In winter, Paradise is headquarters for snowshoe walks and cross-country skiing. At Paradise, Longmire, or Sunrise visitors centers, you can pick up the Wonderland Hiking Trail, a 90-mile route that circles the base of Mt. Rainier. Wonderland takes you past Box Canyon, waterfalls, fields with wildflowers in season, Golden Lakes, Carbon River, Carbon Glacier, and the Mowich Glaciers. Campsites are spaced about 12 miles apart along the trail. Northern Loop Trail extends 17½ miles from Wonderland Trail through backcountry meadows to Chenuis Mountain, at an elevation of 6,400 feet. Pick up a permit at a visitors center if you intend to camp overnight only during the summer.

The 1963 US Mt. Everest Expedition trained on Mt. Rainier, but you don't have to be preparing to tackle the world's largest mountain to get to Rainier's peak. You can take a 1- or a 5-day course in mountain climbing techniques at the national park's *Paradise Guide House,* Rainier Mountaineering (201 St. Helens, Tacoma, WA 98402; phone: 206-627-6242). All climbers must register at one of the visitors centers before setting out, and there are restrictions on the number of people allowed in each party. Park officials have also set requirements for health, equipment, and leadership qualifications. All guided climbs are monitored. Even in good weather, sudden storms can envelop the mountain in gales of Himalayan ferocity, and, on quiet days, the glacial movements sometimes form new crevasses. At any moment, sudden rockfalls can tear out hunks of trail. The best time to climb is mid-July, after the summer storms have passed but before the constant summer heat wears down the ice, causing unstable mountain conditions. Generally, the climb takes two days, with an overnight stop at Camp Muir, a shelter at 10,000 feet. You can rent or buy climbing gear at *Paradise Guide House.* Information: Superintendent, Mt. Rainier National Park, Ashford, WA 98304 (phone: 206-569-2211).

BEST EN ROUTE

Crystal Mountain, Crystal Mountain – A self-contained alpine village with Silver Skis Chalet and Crystal Chalets condominiums, with heated pool, night skiing, and grocery stores. *Crystal House, Crystal Inn,* and *Alpine Inn,* the three hotels on the premises, have 120 rooms. 100 condo units available all year. Off Rte. 410. Crystal Mountain, WA 98022 (phone: 206-663-2265).

Mt. Rainier National Park, Washington – Near Paradise, elevation 5,400 feet, *Paradise Inn* has a lodge-type lobby with two open fireplaces, cocktail lounge, snack bar. Dining room. 128 rooms. Open from early June to early October. Near Longmire visitors center, elevation 2,700 feet, *National Park Inn* offers meal service and a gas station. Open daily year-round. 16 rooms. For reservations, write Manager, Paradise Inn or National Park Inn, Mt. Rainier Guest Services, PO Box 108, Ashford, WA 98304 (phone: 206-569-2275).

Olympic National Park, Washington

The heart of the Olympic peninsula in western Washington State, Olympic National Park covers 1,441 square miles of diverse terrain. On the western edge of the peninsula lies a 57-mile stretch of wild Pacific beachfront. Hundreds of offshore islands nestle among the inlets and coves that shelter many communities of seals and other marine and amphibious creatures. Inland, numerous small lakes dot the landscape, filling glacial pits that scarred the earth when giant masses of ice withdrew to the north at the end of the Ice Age about 10,000 years ago. The lakes are part of a thriving water system, and the western slope of the Olympic peninsula is the wettest spot in the continental US, with an average annual precipitation of 133+ inches. It is cloudy more than 220 days each year and wet 160 days. Temperatures are in the 70s in summer, in the 30s in winter. Here, too, are jungle-like, complex, and primeval rain forests, and not far from them glacier-capped mountains tower into the sky. The biggest is Mt. Olympus, a 7,965-foot peak in the center of the park. All told, about 60 glaciers cover some 25 square miles of mountainous terrain, in frosty juxtaposition to the lush vegetation nearby.

Discovered in 1592 by the Spanish explorer Juan de Fuca, for whom the strait connecting the Pacific with Puget Sound was later named, the Olympic Peninsula was the home of the Coast Salish Indians, an artistic civilization with an intense economic and spiritual kinship to the sea. A stream of trappers and traders found their way to the peninsula in the early 1800s, and they brought with them germs to which the Indians were not immune. A series of appalling epidemics and conflicts with the white settlers wiped out many of the original inhabitants. Today, the descendants of the Salish survivors live on reservations. The Quillayute and Hoh Indian reservations are adjacent to Olympic National Park's coastal area. The Ozette and Makah Indian reservations are in the northwestern corner of the peninsula; the Skokomish and Nisqually Indian reservations, in the southeast. Olympic National Park itself was established in 1938, and the coastal area came under federal protection in 1953, with additional coastal land added in 1976.

Some 75 miles west of Seattle, Olympic National Park is accessible from Rte. 101, which loops around the peninsula. From Seattle, you can take a Washington State Ferry across Puget Sound to the Kitsap Peninsula, then take the Hood Canal floating bridge. Or take I-5 south from Seattle to

Olympia and pick up Rte. 101 north. This road loops around the eastern, northern, and western coasts of the peninsula. You have to pick up Rte. 12 at Aberdeen to complete the circular route to Olympia, a distance of 50 miles.

The major entrance to Olympic National Park is Port Angeles, site of the largest of three visitors centers (*Pioneer Memorial Museum*) with exhibitions on local fauna and flora. Heart o' the Hills Road, an 18-mile paved road that ascends to an elevation of nearly a mile, begins here. Halfway up, at Lookout Point, you can see across the Strait of Juan de Fuca to British Columbia and to Mt. Baker when visibility is good. Perched at the top of the road, *Hurricane Ridge Lodge* (not always accessible during the winter) is a good place to catch your breath and pick up more information. If you plan to explore the wilderness or camp, you must get a permit, available at ranger stations and visitors centers. You can embark on Big Meadow Nature Trail on foot, or you can continue by car along an unpaved mountain road to Obstruction Point, at 6,450 feet. Unless it's shrouded in fog, Mt. Olympus should be staring you smack in the face. A number of hiking trails begin at Obstruction Point. One leads to Deer Park Campground. You can't reserve space at any of the campsites, so it's advisable to carry rain gear if you plan to sleep outdoors. The maximum stay permitted at any site is 14 days.

Lake Crescent is about 20 miles west of Port Angeles on Rte. 101, still in mountain country. West of the lake, you can pick up the road to *Sol Duc Hot Springs Resort,* Soleduck Campground, and the Seven Lakes Basin.

Named after the mythological home of the Greek gods and covered by six glaciers, some as thick as 900 feet, 7,965-foot Mt. Olympus gets about 200 inches of snow and rain a year.

On the western edge of the park stands the Hoh rain forest; the visitors center can give you information on the numerous species of shrubs, fungi, mosses, and trees. This is the home of the giant Sitka spruce, which often grows as high as 300 feet. Roosevelt elk, deer, bear, raccoon, and dozens of different species of birds live in this area.

One of the park's finest attributes is its Pacific Coast area, 57 miles of rugged beachfront studded with giant rocks and the home of seagulls, eagles, seals, and sea lions. Campsites are open year-round. Fishing boats can be chartered at La Push. Unlike the Makah Indians (below), the Quinault Indians at the reservation 5 miles to the south do not welcome tourists. Information: Superintendent, Olympic National Park, 600 E. Park Ave., Port Angeles, WA 98362 (phone: 206-452-4501).

MAKAH INDIAN RESERVATION: About 68 miles west of Lake Crescent, pick up a small road running north from Sappho, bearing left onto Rte. 112 northwest to Clallam Bay. Continue to the northwesternmost tip of the peninsula at Neah Bay, a fishing village where the Makah Indians operate several charter fishing companies, motels, and crafts shops. There's a museum at Neah Bay containing the archaeological material excavated by teams from Washington State University. And there are campsites at Makah Bay, 1 mile south. For information contact the travel secretary at the Makah Tribal Office, PO Box 115, Neah Bay, WA 98357 (phone: 206-645-2201).

OLYMPIC NATIONAL FOREST: The forest forms the eastern, northern, and southern borders of the national park with 651,000 acres of rain forest vegetation. Campsites in the Quinault Lake and Hood Canal area are open in summer. For information, contact Olympic National Forest Headquarters, 801 Capital Way, Olympia, WA 98507 (phone: 206-753-9534).

BEST EN ROUTE

Kalaloch Lodge – On Rte. 101 on the ocean beach, 36 miles south of Forks. Lodge rooms, motel, cabins, dining room, coffee shop, cocktail lounge, store, and service station. Open year-round. For information or reservations: Kalaloch Lodge, HC 80, Box 1100, Forks, WA 98331 (phone: 206-962-2271).

Lake Crescent Lodge – About 21 miles west of Port Angeles on Rte. 101. Lodge and motel rooms, cottages, dining room, and cocktail lounge. Open from May through October. For information or reservations: Lake Crescent Lodge, HC 62, Box 11, Port Angeles, WA 98362 (phone: 206-928-3211).

Log Cabin Resort – Some 17 miles west of Port Angeles on the northeast end of Lake Crescent, 3 miles off Rte. 101. Motel units, cabins, restaurant, cocktail lounge, groceries, RV park, camping spaces, boat rentals, boat launch, fishing tackle, and laundromat. Open from April to October. Information or reservations: Log Cabin Resort, 6540 E. Beach Rd., Port Angeles, WA 98362 (phone: 206-928-3245).

Sol Duc Hot Springs – In the Soleduck Valley, 40 miles west of Port Angeles. Motel units with kitchenettes, swimming pool, hot mineral pools and baths, dining room, grocery store, fishing tackle, camping supplies, curios and gifts. Open from mid-May to the beginning of October. Contact: Sol Duc Resort, PO Box 2169, Port Angeles, WA 98362 (phone: 206-327-3583).

There are 18 campgrounds in the park, with sites available on a first-come, first-served basis.

Devils Tower National Monument, Wyoming

In the film *Close Encounters of the Third Kind,* François Truffaut holds up a picture of Devils Tower, asking, "Have you ever seen anything like this?" "Sure," says Richard Dreyfuss. "I've got one just like it in my living room."

If you've seen the movie, you undoubtedly know that Devils Tower is the site selected for encounters of the third kind (physical contact) with beings from another planet. And you're also aware that one aspect of the initial contact is the implantation of a psychic image of Devils Tower in the minds of American men and women, who then become obsessed with visions of the tower, which they are driven to reproduce by sketching, painting, or even sculpting a giant replica.

Whether or not you've seen the film, your first encounter with Devils Tower National Monument will most probably be overwhelming. A gargantuan landmark rising suddenly in the middle of a vast Wyoming plain, Devils Tower is the only outstanding physical feature in the northeastern sector of the state. On a clear day you can see it from as far as 100 miles away.

Devils Tower is close to the western edge of the Black Hills National Forest in Wyoming. If you're coming from Rapid City or the Black Hills, take I-90 or Rte. 34 west (Rte. 34 becomes Rte. 24 when you cross the Wyoming state line). It's about 100 miles. You can also get there on Rte. 14. Devils Tower National Monument covers 1,346 acres of land between the towns of Sundance and Hulett.

Pioneers traversing the Great Plains by horse and wagon used it as a guidepost, as had the first white explorers and, before them, the Indians. Some of those Indians called it Mateo Tepee, meaning Grizzly Bear Lodge. The army misinterpreted Mateo Tepee to mean Bad God's Tower, and it was by this name the first US Geological Survey party became acquainted with it in 1875, later changing its name to Devils Tower. According to one legend, the Bad God (Satan) beats on the top of the tower as on a drum to frighten the land during thunderstorms. Kiowa Indians, however, mythologically ascribe the tower's origin to an incident in which several bears tried to attack seven young Indian maidens. The Great Spirit saved them by lifting the rock on which they were standing to a great height — thus, the tower. In this version, those deep, vertical ridges on the sides of the tower were formed by the bears' frustrated scratching in an attempt to reach their prey. When the animals died from exhaustion, the Great Spirit lifted the little girls to the sky and transformed them into the constellation Pleiades. We don't know if President Theodore Roosevelt was aware of these myths, but in 1906 he decided Devils Tower was important enough to become the country's first national monument.

Since then, it has intrigued visitors from all over the world. Geologists have come to its base at the foot of the Belle Fourche River, fascinated by the layers of sedimentary rock and vegetation. According to scientific estimates, the tower dates back about 50 million years, the product of a geological process involving molten rock bubbling up from the center of the earth and cooling. The fluted, strangely symmetrical sides of the monolith also provide a visible lesson in how plants are formed. Although the formidable, barren-looking tower hardly seems hospitable to botanical life, the rock attracts lichens that slowly erode the solid mineral surface into tiny fragments. As dust blows in from the prairie, little pockets of soil nestle in the cracks, attracting moss and liverwort. As the soil deepens, grass and wildflowers grow. Sagebrush and other shrubs cluster closer to the base while, lining the very bottom, aspen and pine trees take root. About a half mile from the base, a prairie dog community burrows intricate underground mazes. (Because they are on the grounds of a national monument, the colony at Devils Tower is one of the few protected communities of prairie dogs in the US.)

If you want to climb to the top of the tower, make sure you register at the visitors center or administrative building. Scaling the sides has become a lot more feasible since 1893, when William Rogers reached the summit. Instead of climbing, he actually wedged a wooden ladder device between the vertical ridges of the rock. In 1937, the first team of three climbers reached the top by traditional methods. If you're contemplating the climb, remember there are now more than 120 ways to reach the 1½-acre top of the giant, tree-stump-shaped tower. And when you get there, you'll probably encounter falcons' and hawks' nests. If you're not up for an assault on the tower itself, you can wander along the Tower Trail and watch the prairie dogs burrow.

You'll also catch glimpses of rabbit, chipmunk, and, if you're lucky, whitetail and mule deer. (Deer come out to feed at sunset.) There are interpretive exhibitions at the base of the nature trail. The visitors center has a color brochure with a map you can follow as you hike.

Although inclement weather tends to keep people away in winter, Devils Tower National Monument is open year-round. Because of its isolated location, you'll find yourself alone with the four staff members if you head out there between October and March. There are cross-country ski trails lacing the grounds and plenty of room to stretch, but the 51 campsites might well be closed due to snow since the rangers don't maintain the road in rough weather. Summer activities include campfire programs.

Whether you come to climb, to explore the geology and nature, or to photograph the mysterious, dramatic rock, you'll be fascinated by Devils Tower's mystique, as have thousands of others. And who knows? After seeing the real thing, you might decide that you, too, want one in your living room. Information: Superintendent, Devils Tower National Monument, Devils Tower, WY 82714 (phone: 307-467-5370), or the Wyoming Travel Commission, I-25 at Etchepare Circle, Cheyenne, WY 82002 (phone: 307-777-7777 or 800-225-5996).

BEST EN ROUTE

Dampier's Hunting Valley, Four Corners – About 45 miles southeast of Devils Tower, with ranch house, trailer hookup, and cabins. Near hiking, rodeos, and trout fishing. Accommodations for 50 guests. James and Marilyn Dampier, General Delivery, Four Corners, WY 82715 (phone: 307-746-4797).

Grand Teton National Park and Jackson Hole, Wyoming

Grand Teton National Park is just south of Yellowstone National Park in northwestern Wyoming, near the Idaho border. The park encompasses over 310,000 acres, which include the most spectacular part of the Teton Range, the "youngest" stretch of peaks in the Rockies — less than 10 million years old.

Early French-Canadian fur trappers gave the Tetons their name, French slang for "big breasts." Perhaps their naming represented wishful thinking, for there is nothing smooth, soft, or voluptuous about the jagged, irregular spires of the Teton Range. The name is doubly ironic since there are three mountains named Teton: Grand, Middle, and South Teton. According to legend, John Colter explored the Jackson Hole–Yellowstone region during the winter of 1807–8. He brought back fantastic tales of boiling springs, powerful geysers, and sulfurous fumes spouting from the earth. People back East didn't believe him and nicknamed the place "Colter's Hell." If Yellowstone is Colter's Hell, then by rights the Tetons, with their tranquil, majestic beauty, should be called Colter's Heaven. Although there are higher mountains in North America, the Tetons have a special visual impact because their sheer mass rises abruptly without foothills from the peaceful flat valley of Jackson Hole, Wyoming.

Jackson Hole ("hole" is an old fur trappers' term for an enclosed mountain valley) is about 50 miles long and 6 to 12 miles wide, with highways leading to different parts of the valley. The town of Jackson is south of Grand Teton National Park. Coming from Yellowstone National Park, take the Rockefeller Parkway, which runs beside the Snake River from Yellowstone. Most of the valley is accessible by automobile year-round.

About 1,200 acres of national parkland burned during the forest fires of 1988; Yellowstone suffered more extensive damage.

GRAND TETON NATIONAL PARK: As you head for park headquarters at Moose visitors center, be sure to stop at the spectacular Signal Mountain overlook. (The Moose and Colter Bay visitors centers and Jenny Lake Ranger Station distribute information on hiking, fishing, camping, and the history of the Tetons.) There are more than 200 miles of hiking trails in the park. One 3-hour excursion includes a boat ride across Jenny Lake and a moderate hike of 2 miles round-trip to Hidden Falls and Inspiration Point. The boat leaves the East Shore Dock at Jenny Lake about every half hour from 8 AM to 6 PM. More difficult is the Teton Crest Trail, which climbs to an elevation of 2 miles above sea level. Another strenuous hike, along the Indian Paintbrush Trail, is known for its resplendent wildflowers and wonderful views of the lakes and mountains. Both Teton Crest and Indian Paintbrush trails are suitable for people in reasonably good physical condition. (Be warned, however, that the park rangers' idea of "reasonably good physical condition" might well be considerably more rigorous than your own.) You can rent canoes and boats on Jackson and Jenny lakes or launch your own (you must buy a permit, available at the Moose and Colter Bay visitors centers). There are scheduled boat rides on Jackson Lake, the biggest lake in the valley. Guided rubber raft trips down the Snake River leave from *Jackson Lake Lodge* as well as other valley locations. There are over a dozen routes to the summit of Grand Teton Mountain, 13,770 feet high. Some are relatively easy technical climbs, but one is considered to be among the most difficult in the nation. *Exum Mountain Guides* of Jenny Lake offers a 2-day mountain climbing course, with guides to take you up many peaks in the summer (Box 56, Moose, WY 83012; phone: 307-733-2297). *Jackson Hole Mountain Guides* at Teton Village also provides climbing courses and guides (Box 5477, Jackson, WY 83001; phone: 307-733-4979). You can rent horses at Colter Bay, Jenny Lake, or *Jackson Lake Lodge.* There are six campgrounds, and permits are required for backcountry camping. Information: Superintendent, Grand Teton National Park, PO Drawer 170, Moose, WY 83012 (phone: 307-733-2880).

BRIDGER-TETON NATIONAL FOREST: Adjoins the national park to the east, and extends north to flank Yellowstone National Park. Bridger-Teton takes in more than 3.4 million acres of forest, river, mountain, and wilderness. Trout fishing in streams and mountain lakes, hunting, skiing, rafting, 2,856 miles of hiking trails, and the Teton and Bridger wildernesses are the major attractions. There are 42 campgrounds, with a total of 595 sites, and an aerial tramway that rises to 10,450 feet — great for sightseeing in summer, skiing in winter. Information: Forest Supervisor, Bridger-Teton National Forest, FS Building, PO Box 1888, Jackson, WY 83001 (phone: 307-733-2752).

TARGHEE NATIONAL FOREST: Often called the back door to Grand Teton and Yellowstone national parks because it borders them, Targhee covers 1,854,240 acres, most of it in southeast Idaho. Fishing, rafting, swimming, horseback riding, backpacking, and camping (at 28 campgrounds) are the activities in summer. The Jedediah Smith and Winegar Hole wilderness areas (on the west side and in southeast corner of the park, respectively) allow hiking, skiing, fishing, and no-trace camping. In winter, there's snowmobiling on 750 miles of groomed trails and cross-country as well as downhill skiing at Grand Targhee Winter Sports Area in Alta, Wyoming. Information on Targhee: Forest Supervisor, Targhee National Forest, PO Box 208, St. Anthony, ID 83445 (phone: 208-624-3151).

JACKSON HOLE: With the biggest vertical drop and the longest runs anywhere in the US, two world-famous ski resorts attract people to the Jackson Hole area: *Teton Village,* on Rendezvous Mountain overlooking Jackson Hole, and *Grand Targhee,* on the west side of the range, both of which are in the national forest. *Teton Village,* 12 miles west of Jackson, has more extensive beginning and intermediate slopes than those found at 90% of the major ski resorts in the country as well as some of the toughest slopes around. It's an excellent place for a family whose members ski at different levels. *Grand Targhee* is an hour's drive from Jackson over Teton Pass, on Rtes. 22 and 33, but it offers excellent skiing from the very early fall to very late spring. Jackson Hole has more than just impressive ski facilities, excellent food, and après-ski entertainment. In fact, its most important feature is something other ski areas often lack — snow. One year, the US Forest Service had already recorded 161 inches of new snow by the opening day of the ski season — more than most ski resorts get in an entire year. In summer, more than a million people come to Jackson Hole for quiet, leisurely Snake River floating excursions or more exciting whitewater trips. There are more than a dozen float trip operators in the area. Three of the best are *Barker-Ewing* (Box 100, Moose, WY 83012; phone: 307-733-1800); *Triangle X* — also a first-rate working dude ranch (Box 120T, Moose, WY 83012; phone: 307-733-5500); and *Jack Dennis Float Trips* — especially for fishing trips (PO Box 286, Jackson, WY 83001; phone: 307-733-3270). The Jackson Hole area has the best fishing in the Rockies; local cutthroat trout are legendary. Information: Jackson Hole Area Chamber of Commerce, Jackson, WY 83001 (phone: 307-733-3316).

BEST EN ROUTE

Jackson Lake Lodge, Grand Teton National Park – Boating and fishing expeditions, swimming, horseback riding, and restaurant. 385 rooms. Grand Teton Lodge Co., PO Box 240, Moran, WY 83013 (phone: 307-543-2855).

Jenny Lake Lodge, Grand Teton National Park – Log cabins in a rustic setting. Boating and fishing expeditions, hiking trips, horseback riding, and restaurant. 30 rooms. Grand Teton Lodge Co., PO Box 240, Moran, WY 83013 (phone: 307-733-4647).

Colter Bay Cabins, Grand Teton National Park – Log cabins with full water sports and horseback riding; restaurant. 209 rooms. Grand Teton Lodge Co., PO Box 240, Moran, WY 83013 (phone: 307-543-2855).

Alpenhof, Teton Village – Chalet-style mountain lodge with pool, sauna, close to skiing. Fireplaces in lounge, good American and continental restaurant. 40 rooms. PO Box 288, Teton Village, WY 83025 (phone: 307-733-3242). Jackson Hole Reservations (phone: 307-733-4005) represents all accommodations in Teton Village, including the *Alpenhof.*

Hitching Post Lodge, Jackson – Specializes in cookouts and chuck wagon breakfasts. Heated pool. 17 rooms. Open from May through September. PO Box 521, Jackson, WY 83001 (phone: 307-733-2606).

Yellowstone National Park
Wyoming

Nowhere on earth is the raw power of nature more apparent than at Yellowstone National Park. We learn as schoolchildren that the face of the earth is constantly changing — mountain ranges are formed and then eroded; lakes are born and then slowly degenerate into swamps; Ice Ages come and go, forever changing the contour of the land. But all these things take thousands, even millions of years, and the inner forces that shape the earth we live on are rarely perceptible to us.

At Yellowstone, however, the awesome grandeur of the earth's primal forces can be seen, felt, smelled, and heard. The ground rumbles as a geyser shoots thousands of gallons of scalding water into the air, steam hisses and roars from crevasses in the earth, hellish sulfurous odors fill the air, mud flats boil and bubble. Yellowstone combines the grandeur of creation with the mightiness of destruction.

Yellowstone was the first national park to be established anywhere in the world (1872). It is the largest national park in the contiguous states, covering 3,472 square miles — larger than Rhode Island and Delaware combined. Although most of the park lies in northwestern Wyoming, it also stretches into Montana and Idaho. There are entrances at Gardiner, Montana (north), West Yellowstone, Montana (west), Jackson, Wyoming/Grand Teton National Park (south), Cody, Wyoming (east), and Cooke City, Montana (northeast). The entrance at Gardiner is open all year. The other entrances are closed to cars from early November through April. The John D. Rockefeller Memorial Parkway leads from Grand Teton National Park to the south entrance of Yellowstone. Delta and Northwest airlines serve nearby cities, and bus transportation to the park is seasonally available from these airports. All entrances except the north and the northeast are open in winter to snowmobiles and heated snow coaches and are also accessible on foot — skis or snowshoes. Yellowstone's winter season runs from mid-December through mid-March.

In 1988, forest fires in Yellowstone destroyed about 440,000 acres — 20% of the park's total of 2,219,766 acres — though the park's facilities, as well as its most famous features — wildlife, geysers, hot springs, and magnificent scenery — are still in place, and all the park roads and facilities remain open. With the fertilizing effects of the ashes, however, the grasses and wildflowers in the park are expected to be more productive than ever in future summers.

The superstar of Yellowstone is Old Faithful. The geyser has been erupting on an average of once every 70 minutes ever since it was discovered over 100 years ago. The average period between eruptions is deceptive; the period between performances has varied from a record low of 30 minutes to a record high of 2 hours. Though not the largest geyser in Yellowstone, Old Faithful is among the most dependable, shooting thousands of gallons of steaming water from 106 to 184 feet into the air for periods of 2 to 5 minutes.

More than 200 active geysers in the park make Yellowstone the greatest geyser region in the world. (Only three other areas in the world have concentrations of geysers — Iceland, New Zealand, and Siberia.) Yellowstone also has an estimated 10,000 hot springs, mud pots, and fumaroles (natural vents in the earth that shoot out superheated steam). The heat source for this thermal activity is thought to lie as close as 2 to 3 miles below the surface of the earth where a chamber of magma (molten rock) heats the overlying layers of stone. A geyser occurs where groundwater seeps into underground crevasses in the red-hot rocks. The water is superheated to over twice its boiling point. At first, the pressure of the thousands of gallons of overlying water prevents the superheated liquid from turning to steam. Finally the pressure becomes so great that some of the water is pushed out through the cone of the geyser. As the pressure drops, the superheated water instantly distills into steam and blasts out of the geyser's cone.

Geyser basins cover less than 2% of Yellowstone. Even without the geysers, Yellowstone would still be an important national park. The Grand Canyon of the Yellowstone, with a waterfall twice as high as Niagara and canyon walls splashed with multicolored rock, deserves that status by itself. There's also a unique petrified forest, with trees that remained upright just as they were when they were covered with volcanic dust and turned to stone millions of years ago. Yellowstone Lake is the largest mountain lake above 7,000 feet in North America and one of the highest lakes of its size in the world; only Lake Titicaca in Peru has a higher elevation.

Many of Yellowstone's major attractions are accessible by car. The famous Grand Loop is a 142-mile-long road that traces a circular route around the park. Counting the trip into and out of the park, your visit to Yellowstone will be about 200 miles long. You should plan on a minimum of 2 or 3 days to see the major attractions.

The park's headquarters and museum and the Mammoth Hot Springs Terraces are near the Gardiner entrance. At the springs you will see bizarre-looking terraced pools formed on the side of Terrace Mountain by mineral-rich water from the hot springs. Some of the terraces are growing at the rate of a foot a year as the hot springs dissolve the subterranean limestone beds under the mountain and redeposit the minerals on the surface. Terrace Mountain is quite literally turning itself inside out. Over the course of a few years, you could watch a mountain growing before your eyes.

The Norris Geyser Basin is 21 miles south of Mammoth Hot Springs. A museum has exhibitions and guided walks through the main basin. There's also a 2-mile trail through the lower basin.

The west entrance (via Rtes. 20 and 191) joins the Grand Loop at Madison Junction. Heading south, the Grand Loop goes along the banks of the Firehole River, a stream that's fed by dozens of hot springs in its bed.

Old Faithful is just 16 miles south of Madison Junction, where there is a museum with fine exhibits. There's also a visitors center at Old Faithful. The surrounding geyser basins — Upper, Midway, and Lower — have some of the best geysers, hot springs, and mud pots in the park.

The south entrance road joins the Grand Loop 17 miles east of Old Faithful. The road hugs the shore of Yellowstone Lake all the way up to its northern end. Yellowstone Lake has great fishing for cutthroat trout (although there are strict catch limitations). Boats and tackle are available at Bridge Bay Marina on the northwest shore.

North of Fishing Bridge, the Grand Loop leads to the 24-mile-long Grand Canyon of the Yellowstone. The river has carved a twisting canyon 800 to 1,200 feet deep. The dominant color of the stone face of the canyon walls is, of course, yellow, but the canyon is also tinted with colors ranging from pale saffron to bright orange.

The Upper Falls of the Yellowstone mark the beginning of the canyon. The water moves with such force that it appears to arch through the air rather than fall. Farther along is the magnificent Lower Falls, which are twice as high as Niagara. The Upper Falls are easy to see; the best view of the Lower Falls is from a trail leading to them. Inspiration Point, which juts far out into the canyon, offers incredible views of the river raging below.

At Tower Junction, the northeast entrance road joins the Grand Loop. Nearby, the spectacular Tower Falls drop 132 feet.

Several hotels/motels are readily accessible from park roads (see *Best en Route*) and some of the major campgrounds are at Bridge Bay, Grant Village, Lewis Lake, Madison Junction, Canyon, and Tower Fall. Keep in mind, however, that Yellowstone is packed to the treetops with tourists in the summer, especially in July and August. If you would like to visit at that time, make reservations well in advance of your trip. Reservations for lodging must be made through TW Recreational Services (see below). Campgrounds are run on a first-come, first-served basis.

One message that is constantly repeated is a warning that it is illegal and dangerous to feed the animals, especially the bears. Bears can turn from seemingly tame creatures to the unpredictable wild animals they are in a split second. Buffalo, too, are swifter and more dangerous than they appear and should not be approached.

Yellowstone presents the park service with a dilemma. It is one of the most popular national parks, and millions of people visit each year, causing traffic jams and leaving behind tons of litter. Some visitors want the park service to expand the facilities, while others would prefer a moratorium on further development, fearing that some of the unique character of Yellowstone would be destroyed. The last major expansion program took place from 1955 to 1965. In 1959, Yellowstone was shaken by a series of huge earthquakes that knocked down half a mountain — almost as if the earth were reasserting its sovereignty over the area and cautioning those who wanted to exploit and commercialize this region that they should regard Yellowstone with awe and teat it with proper respect.

For more information on facilities in Yellowstone contact: National Park Service, PO Box 168, Yellowstone National Park, WY 82190, 5 miles south of the north entrance at Mammoth Hot Springs (phone: 307-344-7381).

BEST EN ROUTE

TW Recreational Services, Inc., is a concessionaire that offers lodging in nine properties, meals, and tours around the park. For further information, contact TW Recreational Services, Yellowstone Division, Yellowstone National Park, WY 82190 (phone: 307-344-7311).

Old Faithful Snow Lodge – For accommodations during the winter season (mid-December to mid-March) as well as the summer. Dining room, lounge, gift shop, and 65 cabins and rooms. Loop Rd. next to Old Faithful.

Lake Yellowstone Hotel and Cabins – Built in 1891 and remodeled several times, this matriarch has lakeview dining, a lobby bar, gift shop, and easy access to boating and fishing. There are 194 renovated rooms with bath and queen-size beds; 102 cabins. Open only in summer. 2 miles south of Fishing Bridge Jct.

Canyon Village – Centrally located, ½ mile from the Grand Canyon of the Yellowstone River. 588 cabins, open in the summer. Loop Rd. at Canyon Jct.

Mammoth Hot Springs Hotel and Cabins – With 94 rooms and 126 cabins (some with view of the springs), 2 restaurants, fireside lounge, gift shop, and activities desk. Open in summer and winter. 5 miles south of the north entrance on Loop Rd.

Grant Village – The area's newest accommodations, built in 1984. Three condo-style buildings have 299 rooms with private baths, including 12 rooms equipped for the handicapped. Separate dining room and lakeview steakhouse. Open only in summer. 18 miles from Old Faithful on Loop Rd.

INDEX

Index

GET YOUR TRAVEL ADVICE AND GO!

Stephen Birnbaum brings you the very best travel advice in the world in his series of travel guides. Each is revised annually, to provide the most accurate information available on vacation destinations around the world.

Canada 1990	$13.95
Caribbean, Bermuda, and the Bahamas 1990	$13.95
Europe 1990	$14.95
France 1990	$13.95
Great Britain 1990	$13.95
Hawaii 1990	$13.95
Ireland 1990	$13.95
Italy 1990	$13.95
Mexico 1990	$13.95
South America 1990	$13.95
Spain and Portugal 1990	$13.95
United States 1990	$13.95

Stephen Birnbaum brings you indispensable business travel advice in two unique guides.

USA for Business Travelers 1990	$8.95
Europe for Business Travelers 1990	$8.95

Available in bookstores everywhere. Or, order directly by mail. Send your check or money order for the price listed plus $1.50 for shipping and tax (where applicable). Allow 4 weeks for delivery:

> Travel Guides Department GG
> Houghton Mifflin Company
> 2 Park Street, Boston, MA 02108

Direct inquiries regarding discounts on bulk purchases to:

> Special Sales Manager
> Houghton Mifflin Company
> 2 Park Street, Boston, MA 02108